THE SWISS CIVIL CODE
ENGLISH VERSION

THE SWISS CIVIL CODE

ENGLISH VERSION

by

IVY WILLIAMS, M.A., D.C.L., Oxon; LL.D., Lond.
Barrister-at-Law

published by Oxford University Press, 1925
reprinted by Remak Verlag Zürich, 1976

completely reset, revised and up-dated edition
with Notes, Vocabularies, Index and a Synopsis
of all changes of the law since 1912

by

SIEGFRIED WYLER, Dr. phil. **BARBARA WYLER,** Dr. iur.
Professor of English   Barrister-at-Law

VOLUME I

PRELIMINARY CHAPTER
PART I: LAW OF PERSONS
PART II: FAMILY LAW

ReMaK
Verlag Zürich

Copyright © 1987 by
Siegfried Wyler, Barbara Wyler and Verlag Remak AG, Zürich
All rights reserved
Made and printed in Switzerland by Hans Schellenberg, Winterthur

No part of this publication may be reproduced or transmitted in any form or by any means, electronic or mechanical, including photocopy, recording, or any information storage and retrieval system, without permission in writing from the publisher.
Except in the United States of America, this book is sold subject to the condition that it shall not, by way of trade or otherwise, be sold, re-sold, hired out, or otherwise circulated without the publisher's prior consent in any form of binding or cover other than that in which it is published and without a similar condition being imposed on the subsequent purchaser.

ISBN 3 85856 002 2

From the 1925 edition of the Swiss Civil Code, English Version:

"The author has been given permission by the Swiss Ministry of Justice to mention the appreciation of the Swiss Federal Authorities of this book in the following terms:

'The translation by Miss Ivy Williams, M.A., D.C.L., of the Swiss Civil Code, is considered to have brought within the reach of the British public a most conscientious and correct version of the Code in question. The numerous commentaries are very much to the point and augment the value of a mere translation. Although it lies not within our competence to give an official approval to a work of this kind, we wish nevertheless to express our private and personal appreciation of Miss Williams's work.'"

I. Introduction and Editor's Preface

In 1925, Miss Ivy Williams, M.A., D.C.L., LL.D., Barrister-at-Law, published her English translation of the Swiss Civil Code (Schweizerisches Zivilgesetzbuch), two years after the publication of her doctoral thesis "The Sources of the Law". The translation of the Code was accompanied by numerous annotations. With this outstanding work Miss Ivy Williams has rendered invaluable services to the legal profession. In the original edition the author was given permission by the Swiss Ministry of Justice to mention the appreciation of the Swiss Federal Authorities of her work in the following terms:

"The translation by Miss Ivy Williams, M.A., D.C.L., of the Swiss Civil Code, is considered to have brought within the reach of the English speaking public a most conscientious and correct version of the Code in question. The numerous commentaries are very much to the point and augment the value of a mere translation. Although it lies not within our competence to give an official approval to a work of this kind, we wish nevertheless to express our private and personal appreciation of Miss William's work."

In view of the fact that since the publication of Miss Ivy Williams' translation the English language has gained more and more importance in law, Miss Williams' translation, originally published by Oxford University Press, was out of print, the Remak Verlag Zürich reprinted Miss Williams' work in 1976 in four separate volumes (Volume 1: Preliminary Chapter, Law of Persons, Family Law; Volume 2: Law of Inheritance; Volume 3: Law of Property, Final Title; Volume 4: The Sources of the Law).

The present edition in two volumes is the revised and enlarged version of Miss Ivy Williams' text: Approximately 350 articles have been modified, inserted and in some cases annulled since Miss Williams' translation was published in 1925. A list at the beginning of volume 1 gives a synopsis of the change the Swiss Civil Code has undergone in this period. The present editors and translators have taken care of all newly adopted provisions since the coming into force of the Code on 1st of January 1912. They have endeavoured to retain the mode of diction used by Miss Ivy Williams, both in style and terminology, of her translated version of the Code. The vocabularies in English, French and German have also been revised and enlarged, the Index at the end of volume 2 has been newly compiled, referring to articles and no longer to pages as it was the case in the original edition. We hope the joint work of the lawyer and the linguist has added to the clarity and readability of the text.

In the referendum of 22nd September 1985, the Swiss citizens adopted the Federal Statute of 5th October 1984 with a revised version of the Titles V and VI of the Code regarding the Effects of Marriage in General and the Matrimonial Property Law. Other provisions of the Code which are thematically related to the provisions of Titles V and VI are affected by this change of law, in particular the Law of Inheritance. This important partial revision comes into force on 1st January 1988. As it is our wish to present an edition of the Swiss Civil Code which is up-to-date and will remain so for many years, we have decided to place the revised Titles V and VI at their future place in the Code as per 1st January 1988. Yet since the old law is still in force when this edition appears and, as a number of provisions of the old law will retain their validity for those married couples who choose to be ruled by the provisions of the old law also in the future, we have added the text of the old law in an appendix. Index references are made to both the old and the new law (re. OLD LAW, NEW LAW), the detailed Table of Contents at the beginning of volume 1 refers to the titles of the new law.

Finally we would like to thank lic. iur. Jürg S. Wyler, Barrister-at-Law (Zurich), wo has given us valuable advice in legal matters, and Privat-Docent Dr. A.T.J. Bennett of the Hochschule St. Gallen, who has read the proofs and has made helpful comments on the present version of the text.

St. Gallen/Zurich, September 1986

Siegfried Wyler
Barbara Wyler

VII

II. Revised, inserted or annulled articles of the Swiss Civil Code since 10th December 1907

Article	Statute	In Force/Annulled
20–21	30th June 1972	1st April 1973
25	5th October 1984	1st January 1988
27	16th December 1983	1st July 1985
28–28*l*	16th December 1983	1st July 1985
30	25th June 1976	1st January 1978
	5th October 1984	1st January 1988
47	25th June 1976	1st January 1978
89bis	21st March 1958	1st July 1958
	25th June 1971	1st January 1972 (SR **220**)
	25th June 1982	1st January 1985 (SR **831.40, 831.401**)
100	30th June 1972	1st April 1973
	25th June 1976	1st January 1978
120	30th June 1972	1st April 1973
	29th September 1952	1st January 1953 (SR **141.0**)
121–122	29th September 1952	1st January 1953 (SR **141.0**)
129	30th June 1972	annulled
133	25th June 1976	1st January 1978
134	5th October 1984	1st January 1988
145	5th October 1984	1st January 1988
149	5th October 1984	1st January 1988
154–155	5th October 1984	1st January 1988
156	25th June 1976	1st January 1978
159–251	5th October 1984	1st January 1988
252–264	25th June 1976	1st January 1978
264*a*–266	30th June 1972	1st April 1973
267	25th June 1976	1st January 1978
267*a*–269*c*	30th June 1972	1st April 1973
270	25th June 1976	1st January 1978
	5th October 1984	1st January 1988

VIII

Civil Code

Article	Statute	In Force/Annulled
271–313	25th June 1976	1st January 1978
314	25th June 1976 6th October 1978	1st January 1978 1st January 1981
314a	6th October 1978	1st January 1981
315–329	25th June 1976	1st January 1978
331	30th June 1972 25th June 1971	1st April 1973 1st January 1972 (SR 220)
334–334bis	6th October 1972	15th February 1973
355	30th June 1972	1st April 1973
397a–f	6th October 1978	1st January 1981
405–506	6th October 1978	1st January 1981
421	6th October 1978	cipher 13 annulled
429a	6th October 1978	1st January 1981
457	30th June 1972	1st April 1973
460	5th October 1984	1st January 1988
461	25th June 1976	annulled
462	5th October 1984	1st January 1988
463–464	5th October 1984	annulled (1st January 1988)
465	30th June 1972	annulled
466	5th October 1984	1st January 1988
470–471	5th October 1984	1st January 1988
472	5th October 1984	annulled (1st January 1988)
473	25th June 1976 5th October 1984	1st January 1978 1st January 1988
503	30th June 1972	1st April 1973
561	5th October 1984	annulled (1st January 1988)
603	6th October 1972	15th February 1973
612a	5th October 1984	1st January 1988
618	6th October 1972	paragraph 2 annulled
619–619sexies	19th March 1965	1st July 1965
620	12th December 1940 6th October 1972	1st July 1947 (SR 211.412.12) 15th February 1973

Revised, inserted or annulled articles of the Swiss Civil Code

Article	Statute	In Force/Annulled
620bis–621bis	6th October 1972	15th February 1973
621ter	12th December 1940	1st January 1947 (SR **211.412.12**)
621quater	12th December 1940 6th October 1972	1st January 1947 (SR **211.412.12**) 15th February 1973
625	6th October 1972	15th February 1973
625bis	12th December 1940 12th June 1951	1st January 1947 (SR **211.412.12**) 1st January 1953 (SR **211.412.11**)
631	5th October 1984	1st January 1988
633	6th October 1972	annulled
635	5th October 1984	1st January 1988
647–650	19th December 1963	1st January 1965
655	19th December 1963	1st January 1965
665	5th October 1984	1st January 1988
682	19th December 1963	1st January 1965
703	3rd October 1951	1st January 1954 (SR **910.1**)
712*a–t*	19th December 1963	1st January 1965
747	5th October 1984	annulled (1st January 1988)
779*a–l*	19th March 1965	1st July 1965
848	12th December 1940	1st January 1947 (SR **211.312.12**)
850	12th December 1940	1st January 1947 (SR **211.412.12**)
916–918	25th June 1930	annulled (SR **211.423.4**)
943	19th December 1963	1st January 1965

Final Title

Article	Statute	In Force/Annulled
8–11*a*	5th October 1984	1st January 1988
12	25th June 1976	1st January 1978
12*a–c*	30th June 1972	1st April 1973
12*d*–13*a*	25th June 1976	1st January 1978
14*a*	6th October 1978	1st January 1981
20–20quater	19th December 1963	1st January 1965
45	19th December 1963	1st January 1965

Article	Statute	In Force/Annulled
56	22nd December 1916	1st January 1918 (SR 721.80)
57	8th November 1934	annulled (SR 952.0)
59	5th October 1984	paragraph 2 annulled (1st January 1988)

369 total amount of revised, inserted or annulled articles since the coming into force of the Swiss Civil Code on 1st January 1912

Synopsis

	Article	Page
Volume 1		
I. Introduction and Editors' Preface		V
II. Revised, inserted or annulled articles of the Swiss Civil Code since 10th December 1907		VII
Table of Contents		XVII
Abbreviations		XLVII
Preliminary Chapter	1– 10	1

Part I: Law of Persons

Title I: Natural Persons

		Article	Page
Chapter I:	Legal Personality	11– 38	3
Chapter II:	Registration of Civil Status	39– 51	14

Title II: Corporate Bodies

		Article	Page
Chapter I:	General Provisions	52– 59	18
Chapter II:	Societies	60– 79	21
Chapter III:	Foundations	80– 89bis	26

Part II: Family Law

Section I: Husband and Wife

Title III: Marriage

		Article	Page
Chapter I:	Betrothal	90– 95	30
Chapter II:	Disabilities and Impediments to Marriage	96–104	31
Chapter III:	Publication and Solemnization of Marriage	105–119	34
Chapter IV:	Void and Voidable Marriages	120–136	38

XII   Civil Code

		Article	Page
Title IV:	Divorce	137–158	43
Title V:	The Effects of Marriage in General	159–180	49
Title VI:	Matrimonial Property Law		
Chapter I:	General Provisions	181–195a	56
Chapter II:	The Ordinary Matrimonial Property System of Participation in Acquisitions	196–220	61
Chapter III:	Community of Property	221–246	70
Chapter IV:	Separation of Estates	247–251	77

Section II: The Relatives

		Article	Page
Title VII:	The Origin of the Child-Parent Relationship		
Chapter I:	General Provisions	252–254	78
Chapter II:	The Paternity of the Husband	255–259	79
Chapter III:	Acknowledgement and Judicial Decree of Paternity	260–263	82
Chapter IV:	Adoption	264–269c	85
Title VIII:	The Effects of the Child Relationship		
Chapter I:	The Community of the Parents and the Children	270–275	92
Chapter II:	The Parents' Duty of Maintenance	276–295	94
Chapter III:	Parental Power	296–317	101
Chapter IV:	The Child's Property	318–327	110
Title IX:	The Family		
Chapter I:	Maintenance	328–330	113
Chapter II:	Authority of the Head of the Family	331–334bis	115
Chapter III:	Family Property	335–359	117

Synopsis

		Article	Page

Section III: Guardianship

Title X: General Organization of Guardianship

Chapter I:	The Organs of Guardianship	360–367	124
Chapter II:	Cases of Guardianship	368–375	126
Chapter III:	Competence	376–378	128
Chapter IV:	Appointment of Guardian	379–391	129
Chapter V:	Office of Curator	392–397	133
Chapter VI:	Deprivation of Liberty for Personal Assistance	397a–397f	135

Title XI: Administration of Guardianship

Chapter I:	Duties of Guardian	398–416	138
Chapter II:	Duties of Curator	417–419	143
Chapter III:	Functions of Guardianship Authorities	420–425	144
Chapter IV:	Liabilities of Organs of Guardianship	426–430	146

Title XII: How Guardianship ends

Chapter I:	Termination of Incapacity	431–440	148
Chapter II:	Termination of Guardian's Functions	441–450	150
Chapter III:	Effect of Determination of Guardianship	451–456	152

Part III: Law of Inheritance

Section I: Heirs

Title XIII:	Statutory Heirs	457–466	154

Title XIV: Testamentary Dispositions

Chapter I:	Testamentary Capacity	467–469	157
Chapter II:	Freedom of Disposition	470–480	158
Chapter III:	Kinds of Dispositions	481–497	161

		Article	Page
Chapter IV:	Formalities Required for Testamentary Dispositions	498–516	166
Chapter V:	Executors	517–518	171
Chapter VI:	Voidance and Reduction of Testamentary Dispositions	519–533	172
Chapter VII:	Actions Arising from Testamentary Pacts	534–536	176

Section II: Devolution of the Estate

Title XV:	Opening of the Succession	537–550	178

Title XVI:	Effects of Devolution		
Chapter I:	Provisional Measures	551–559	182
Chapter II:	Vesting of the Inheritance	560–579	185
Chapter III:	Public Inventory	580–592	191
Chapter IV:	Official Liquidation	593–597	194
Chapter V:	Action to Recover Inheritance	598–601	196

Title XVII:	Partition		
Chapter I:	Community before Partition	602–606	197
Chapter II:	Mode of Partition	607–625bis	198
Chapter III:	Hotchpot	626–633	209
Chapter IV:	Completion and Effect of Partition	634–640	211

Synopsis

| | | Article | Page |

Volume 2

Part IV: Law of Property

Section I: Ownership

		Article	Page
Title XVIII:	General Rules	641–654	213
Title XIX:	Ownership of Land		
Chapter I:	Subject-Matter, Acquisition and Loss of Ownership of Land	655–666	222
Chapter II:	Nature and Limits of Ownership of Land	667–712	225
Chapter III:	Condominium Principled Ownership (Storey Ownership)	712a–712t	240
Title XX:	Ownership of Movable Property	713–729	249

Section II: Limited Rights *in rem*

		Article	Page
Title XXI:	Servitudes and Rent-Charges		
Chapter I:	Praedial Servitudes	730–744	254
Chapter II:	Usufruct and Other Servitudes	745–781	258
Chapter III:	Rent-Charges	782–792	271
Title XXII:	Mortgages and Other Securities on Land		
Chapter I:	General Provisions	793–823	274
Chapter II:	Mortgages	824–841	283
Chapter III:	Mortgage Certificates and Land Charge Notes	842–874	289
Chapter IV:	Issues of Securities on Land	875–883	298
Title XXIII:	Law of Pledge		
Chapter I:	Pledges and Liens	884–898	300

		Article	Page
Chapter II:	Pledges of Debts and Other Rights	899–906	304
Chapter III:	Pawn	907–915	306
Chapter IV:	Debentures	916–918	309

Section III: Possession and Land Register

		Article	Page
Title XXIV:	Possession	919–941	309
Title XXV:	Land Register	942–977	315

Final Title:	Provisions for the Application and Introduction of Code		
Chapter I:	Application of Old and New Law	1– 50	325
Chapter II:	Introductory and Transitionary Provisions	51– 61	348

Appendix 1

Title VI:	Matrimonial Property Law	178–193	357
Chapter II:	Marital System	194–214	363
Chapter III:	Community of Property	215–240	370
Chapter IV:	Separation of Estates	241–247	378
Chapter V:	Matrimonial Property Register	248–251	380

Appendix 2	388
Appendix 3	392
Vocabulary	393
Index	411

Table of Contents

		Article	Page
I.	Introduction and Editors' Preface		V
II.	Revised, inserted or annulled articles of the Swiss Civil Code since 10th December 1907		VII

Abbreviations   XLVII

Preliminary Chapter

A. Application of Law 1
B. Limits of civil rights
    I. Misuse of a right 2
    II. *Bona fides* 3
    III. Discretion of judge 3
C. Federal and Cantonal Law
    I. Private Law and local custom 5
    II. Cantonal Public Law 6
D. General rules of Law of Obligations 7
E. Rules of evidence
    I. Burden of proof 8
    II. Proof of public documents 9
    III. Procedure 10

Part I: Law of Persons

Title I: Natural Persons

Chapter I: Legal Personality

A. Personality in general
    I. Subject of rights 11
    II. Capacity to act
        1. Purport 12
        2. Conditions 12
            a. General 13
            b. Majority 14

				Article
			c. Emancipation	15
			d. Discretion	16
	III.	Incapacity to act		
		1.	In general	17
		2.	Absence of discretion	18
		3.	Minors and persons under a committee who have discretion	19
	IV.	Relationship and relationship by marriage		
		1.	Relationship	20
		2.	By marriage	21
	V.	Home and domicile		
		1.	Citizenship	22
		2.	Domicile		
			a. Definition	23
			b. Change of domicile or residence	24
			c. Domicile of dependent persons	25
			d. Residence in an institution	26
B.	Personality, how protected			
	I.	Excessive commitment		27
	II.	Against injury		
		1.	Principle	28
		2.	To bring action	28a
		3.	Place of jurisdiction	28b
		4.	Precautionary measures		
			a. Prerequisites	28c
			b. Procedure	28d
			c. Execution	28e
			d. Indemnity	28f
		5.	The right to make a counter-statement		
			a. Principle	28g
			b. Form and content	28h
			c. Procedure	28i
			d. Publication	28k
			e. To apply to the judge	28l
	III.	Right to name		
		1.	How protected	29
		2.	Change of name	30
C.	When personality begins and ends			
	I.	Birth and death		31
	II.	Proof of life and death		
		1.	Burden of proof	32
		2.	Modes of proof		
			a. In general	33
			b. Presumption of death	34

Table of Contents   XIX

Article

III. Declaration of absence
    1. In general 35
    2. Procedure 36
    3. Failure of application 37
    4. Effect of declaration .38

Chapter II: Registration of Civil Status

A. In general
    I. Registers 39
    II. Organisation 40
    III. Officials 41
    IV. Liabilities 42
    V. Supervision
        1. Complaints 43
        2. Penalties 44
    VI. Rectifications 45

B. Register of births
    I. Notification 46
    II. Entry of modifications .47

C. Register of deaths
    I. Notification 48
    II. Where the body is not found 49
    III. Declaration of absence 50
    IV. Entry of modifications .51

Title II: Corporate Bodies

Chapter I: General Provisions

A. Personality 52
B. Capacity to have rights 53
C. Capacity to act
    I. Conditions 54
    II. Mode 55
D. Domicile 56
E. Dissolution
    I. Application of property 57
    II. Liquidation 58

XX   Civil Code

                                                                                      Article

F.   Public Law and law of companies and co-operative societies 59

Chapter II: Societies

A.   Formation

     I.   Incorporation 60
     II.   Registration 61
     III. Societies not incorporated 62
     IV.   Relation between constitution and law 63

B.   Organisation

     I.   General meeting
           1.   Its function and summons 64
           2.   Powers 65
           3.   Resolutions
                a. Form 66
                b. Right to vote and majority 67
                c. Where vote disallowed 68
     II.   Directors 69

C.   Membership

     I.   Admission and resignation 70
     II.   Subscriptions 71
     III. Grounds for expulsion 72
     IV.   Effect of resignation and expulsion 73
     V.   Maintenance of objëct of society 74
     VI.   Maintenance of members' rights 75

D.   Dissolution

     I.   Modes
           1.   By resolution 76
           2.   By operation of law 77
           3.   By the court 78
     II.   Erasure of entry in register 79

Chapter III: Foundations

A.   Constitution

     I.   In general 80
     II.   Form 81
     III. Opposition 82

B.   Organisation 83

C.   Supervision 84

  Article

D. Modifications
   I.   In the organization 85
   II. In the object 86
E. Family and ecclesiastical foundation 87
F. Dissolution
   I.   By operation of law and by the court 88
   II. On application. Erasure of entry 89
G. Staff welfare foundations 89bis

Part II: Family Law

Section I: Husband and Wife

Title III: Marriage

Chapter I: Betrothal

A. Promise of marriage 90
B. Its effect
   I.   No right of action to enforce marriage 91
   II. Consequences of breach
        1. Damages 92
        2. Moral compensation 93
   III. Return of presents 94
   IV. Period of limitation 95

Chapter II: Disabilities and Impediments to Marriage

A. Disabilities
   I.   Age 96
   II. Discretion 97
   III. Consent
        1. For minors 98
        2. For persons under a committee 99
B. Impediments to marriage
   I.   Relationship 100
   II. Previous marriage
        1. Proof of dissolution

XXII   Civil Code

                                                                                                 Article

              a. In general 101
              b. In case of declaration of absence 102
          2. Period of delay
              a. For a woman 103
              b. For divorced persons 104

Chapter III: Publication and Solemnization of Marriage

A. Publication
    I.   Form of notice 105
    II.   Where application and publication to be made 106
    III. Publication refused 107

B. Opposition
    I.   Right of opposition 108
    II.   Official opposition 109
    III. Procedure
        1. Opposition notified 110
        2. Decision 111
        3. Period of delay 112

C. Solemnization of marriage
    I.   Conditions
        1. Competent official 113
        2. Solemnization refused 114
        3. Solemnization without publication 115
    II.   Formalities
        1. Publicity 116
        2. Form of solemnization 117
    III. Marriage certificate and religious ceremony 118

D. Regulations 119

Chapter IV: Void and Voidable Marriages

A. Void marriages
    I.   Grounds for nullity 120
    II.   Obligation and right of suit 121
    III. Restrictions and exceptions 122

B. Voidable marriages
    I.   At instance of a spouse
        1. Absence of discretion 123
        2. Mistake 124

Table of Contents   XXIII

	Article
3. Fraud	.125
4. Duress	.126
5. Limitation of actions	.127
II. At the instance of parent or guardian	.128
C. Cases where marriage not void	
I. Adoptive relationship	.129 (annulled)
II. Non-observance of period of delay	.130
III. Non-observance of formalities	.131
D. Declaration of nullity	
I. Purport	.132
II. Effect	
1. On the issue	.133
2. For the spouses	.134
E. Transmissibility	.135
F. Competence and procedure	.136

Title IV: Divorce

A. Grounds of divorce
  - I. Adultery 137
  - II. Attempt on life of spouse, ill-usage, affronts 138
  - III. Crime and infamous conduct 139
  - IV. Desertion 140
  - V. Insanity 141
  - VI. Domestic disturbances 142

B. Suit
  - I. Purpose 143
  - II. Competence 144
  - III. Precautionary measures 145

C. Judgement
  - I. Divorce or judicial separation 146
  - II. Duration of separation 147
  - III. Decree at termination of separation 148
  - IV. Status of the divorced wife 149
  - V. Period of delay 150
  - VI. Payments on divorce
      1. Damages and moral compensation 151
      2. Maintenance 152
      3. Annuity 153

			Article
	VII.	Division of matrimonial property system	
		1. In case of divorce	154
		2. In case of separation	155
	VIII.	Rights of parents	
		1. Judicial discretion	156
		2. Change of circumstances	157
D.	Procedure		158

Title V: The Effects of Marriage in General

			Article
A.	Conjugal union; rights and duties of the spouses		159
B.	The family name		160
C.	Citizenship		161
D.	The conjugal home		162
E.	The maintenance of the family		
	I.	In general	163
	II.	Amount for free disposal	164
	III.	Extraordinary contribution of a spouse	165
F.	Representation of the conjugal union		166
G.	Profession and trade of the spouses		167
H.	Legal transactions of the spouses		
	I.	In general	168
	II.	Apartment of the spouses	169
J.	Obligation to give information		170
K.	Protection of the conjugal union		
	I.	Councils to give advice	171
	II.	Measures ordered by the judge	
		1. In general	172
		2. During the existence of the conjugal union	
		a. Payments	173
		b. Revocation of the right of representation	174
		3. Discontinuation of the conjugal home	
		a. Causes	175
		b. Regulation for a separate life	176
		4. Orders to debtors	177
		5. Restriction of right of disposal	178
		6. Change of circumstances	179
		7. Competence	180

Article

Title VI: Matrimonial Property Law

Chapter I: General Provisions

- A. Ordinary system 181
- B. Marriage covenant
  - I. Choice of system 182
  - II. Capacity of parties 183
  - III. Form required 184
- C. Exceptional system
  - I. At instance of a spouse
    1. By order of court 185
    2. Competence 186
    3. Rescission 187
  - II. On bankruptcy and execution on property
    1. On bankruptcy 188
    2. On execution
       - a. Order 189
       - b. Competence 190
    3. Removal 191
  - III. Division of matrimonial property 192
- D. Protection of creditors 193
- E. Competence for suits for division of matrimonial property 194
- F. Administration of a spouse's property by the other spouse 195
- G. Inventory 195a

Chapter II: The Ordinary Matrimonial Property System of Participation in Acquisitions

- A. Ownership
  - I. Composition 196
  - II. The acquisitions 197
  - III. A spouse's own property
    1. By operation of the law 198
    2. By a marriage covenant 199
  - IV. Evidence 200
- B. Administration, use and disposal 201
- C. Liability towards third parties 202
- D. Debts between the spouses 203

  Article

E.   Dissolution of system and division
   I.   Date of determination 204
   II.   Taking back of property and settlement of debts
         1.   In general 205
         2.   The spouse's share of the increased value 206
   III. Calculation of a spouse's matrimonial profit
         1.   Separation of each spouse's own property
              and the acquisitions .207
         2.   Addition. 208
         3.   Claims for compensation between the acquisitions
              and a spouse's own property 209
         4.   Matrimonial profit 210
   IV.   Determination of value
         1.   Selling value. 211
         2.   Value based on annual yield
              a.   In general 212
              b.   Special circumstances 213
         3.   Decisive date 214
   V.   Participation in the matrimonial profit
         1.   By operation of the law 215
         2.   By a marriage covenant
              a.   In general 216
              b.   Upon divorce, judicial separation, annulment
                   of a marriage or system of separate estates by
                   order of court. 217
   VI.   Payment of the claim due to participation
         and increased value
         1.   Delay for payment 218
         2.   Apartment and personal chattels 219
         3.   Actions towards third parties 220

Chapter III: Community of Property

A.   Matrimonial property
   I.   Composition 221
   II.   Common property
         1.   General community of property 222
         2.   Limited community of property
              a.   Community of acquisitions 223
              b.   Other communities of property 224
   III. A spouse's own property 225
   IV.   Evidence. 226

Table of Contents

Article

- B. Administration and disposal
    - I. Common property
        1. Ordinary administration .... .227
        2. Extraordinary administration .... .228
        3. Profession or business of the conjugal union ..... .229
        4. Disclaimer and acceptance of an inheritance ..... .230
        5. Liability and cost of administration .... .231
    - II. The spouses' own property .... .232
- C. Liability towards third parties
    - I. Liability of a spouse's own property and the common property .... .233
    - II. Liability of a spouse's own property .... .234
- D. Debts between the spouses .... .235
- E. Dissolution of the matrimonial property system and division
    - I. Date of the dissolution .... .236
    - II. Allotment to a spouse's own property .... .237
    - III. Claims for compensation between a spouse's own property and the common property .... .238
    - IV. Share in increased value .... .239
    - V. Determination of value .... .240
    - VI. Division
        1. In case of death or agreement on another matrimonial property system .... .241
        2. In the other cases .... .242
    - VII. Execution of the division
        1. A spouse's own property .... .243
        2. Apartment and equipment .... .244
        3. Other items of property .... .245
        4. Other provisions of division .... .246

Chapter IV: Separation of Estates

- A. Administration, use and disposal
    - I. In general .... .247
    - II. Proof .... .248
- B. Liability towards third parties .... .249
- C. Debts between the spouses .... .250
- D. Allotment of items in co-ownership .... .251

XXVIII

Civil Code

Article

Section II: The Relatives

Title VII: The Origin of the Child-Parent Relationship

Chapter I: General Provisions

A. Origin of the relations of children to their parents in general 252
B. Establishing or disavowal of child-parent relationship
   I. Competence 253
   II. Procedure   254

Chapter II: The Paternity of the Husband

A. Presumption
B. Disavowal 255
   I. Right of action 256
   II. Ground of action
      1. Conception during marriage 256a
      2. Conception before or during the marriage or dissolution of common household 256b
   III. Period of limitation of action 256c
C. Concurrence of two presumptions   257
D. Action brought by the parents 258
E. Marriage of the parents 259

Chapter III: Acknowledgement and Judicial Decree of Paternity

A. Acknowledgement
   I. Admissibility and form 260
   II. Disavowal
      1. Right of action 260a
      2. Ground for action 260b
      3. Period of limitation 260c
B. Action to establish paternity
   I. Who can bring it 261
   II. Presumption 262
   III. Period of limitation 263

Table of Contents   XXIX

Article

Chapter IV: Adoption

A. Adoption of minors
- I. General conditions 264
- II. Joint adoption 264a
- III. Adoption by a single person 264b
- IV. Age and consent of the child 265
- V. Consent of the parents
    1. Its form 265a
    2. Time 265b
    3. Waiving of consent
        a. Conditions 265c
        b. Decision 265d

B. Adoption of majors and persons placed under commission 266

C. Its effects
- I. In general 267
- II. Legal home 267a

D. Procedure
- I. General 268
- II. Investigation 268a
- III. Secrecy of adoption 268b

E. Voidability
- I. Grounds
    1. Lack of consent 269
    2. Other deficiencies 269a
- II. Period of limitation 269b

F. Procuring children for adoptions 269c

Title VIII: The Effects of the Child Relationship

Chapter I: The Community of the Parents and the Children

A. Surname 270

B. Legal home 271

C. Mutual duties 272

D. Personal contact
- I. Parents
    1. Principle 273
    2. Limitations 274

			Article
	II.	Third persons	.274a
	III.	Competence	.275

Chapter II: The Parents' Duty of Maintenance

A.	Subject and extent		.276
B.	Duration		.277
C.	Married parents		.278
D.	Complaint		
	I.	Right of complaint and competence	.279
	II.	Procedure	.280
	III.	Precautionary measures	
		1. In general	.281
		2. Before establishing paternity	
		a. Deposit	.282
		b. Provisional payments	.283
		3. Competence	.284
	IV.	How the contribution to maintenance is fixed	.285
	V.	Change of circumstances	.286
E.	The contracts regulating the cost of maintenance		
	I.	Periodical payments	.287
	II.	Compensation	.288
F.	Settlement		
	I.	Creditor	.289
	II.	Execution	
		1. Suitable assistance	.290
		2. Directions to the debtor	.291
	III.	Security	.292
G.	Public Law		.293
H.	Foster parents		.294
J.	Claims of the unmarried mother		.295

Chapter III: Parental Power

A.	Conditions		
	I.	In general	.296
	II.	Married parents	.297
	III.	Unmarried parents	.298

Table of Contents

Article

	IV.	Step parents	299
	V.	Foster parents	300
B.	Extent		
	I.	In general	301
	II.	Education	302
	III.	Religious education	303
	IV.	Representation	
		1. With third party	
		a. In general	304
		b. The child's capacity to act	305
		2. Within the family	306
C.	Protection of the child		
	I.	Suitable measures	307
	II.	Curatorship	
		1. In general	308
		2. Establishment of paternity	309
	III.	Removal of parental custody	310
	IV.	Deprivation of paternal power	
		1. through the guardianship supervisory authorities	311
		2. through the guardianship authorities	312
	V.	Change of the circumstances	313
	VI.	Procedure	
		1. In general	314
		2. Deprivation of liberty through custody	314*a*
	VII.	Competence	
		1. of the guardianship authorities	315
		2. of the judge	315*a*
	VIII.	Supervision of foster children	316
	IX.	Collaboration in youth assistance	317

Chapter IV: The Child's Property

A.	Administration	318
B.	Use of income	319
C.	Part payments made from children's property	320
D.	Child's separate estate	
	I. Donations	321
	II. Compulsory portion	322
	III. Earnings, gift by way of advancement for profession or trade	323

				Article
E.	Protection of the child's property			
	I.	Suitable measures		.324
	II.	Deprivation of administration		.325
F.	End of administration			
	I.	Return of the property		.326
	II.	Liability		.327

Title IX: The Family

Chapter I: Maintenance

		Article
A.	Who is liable to support	.328
B.	Extent of liability and how enforced	.329
C.	Maintenance of foundlings	.330

Chapter II: Authority of the Head of the Family

A.	Conditions				.331
B.	Effect				
	I.	Rules of the house			.332
	II.	Liability			.333
	III.	Claims of children			
		1.	Conditions		.334
		2.	To enforce reimbursement		.334bis

Chapter III: Family Property

A.	Family foundations				.335
B.	Community of property				
	I.	How constituted			
		1.	Conditions		.336
		2.	Form required		.337
	II.	Length of term			.338
	III.	Effect			
		1.	Joint undertaking		.339
		2.	Management and representation		
			a.	In general	.340
			b.	Powers of the head of the community	.341
		3.	Common and separate property		.342

Article

- IV. Dissolution
    1. Grounds .343
    2. Notice, insolvency, marriage .344
    3. Death of one of the parties .345
    4. Division .346
- V. Share in income only
    1. Conditions .347
    2. Ground of dissolution .348

C. Homesteads
- I. Within Cantonal Law .349
- II. Constitution
    1. Conditions as to subject-matter .350
    2. Form and procedure
        a. Official citation .351
        b. Rights of third parties .352
        c. Entry in land register .353
- III. Effect
    1. Restrictions on alienation .354
    2. Admittance of relatives to home .355
    3. Insolvency of owner .356
- IV. Dissolution
    1. On death .357
    2. During owner's life .358
- V. Cantonal regulations .359

Section III: Guardianship

Title X: General Organization of Guardianship

Chapter I: The Organs of Guardianship

A. In general .360
B. Guardianship authorities
- I. Public bodies .361
- II. Family control
    1. Conditions and powers .362
    2. How set up .363
    3. Family council .364
    4. Security .365
    5. Determination .366

C. Guardian and curator .367

XXXIV Civil Code

Article

Chapter II: Cases of Guardianship

A. Minority 368
B. Commission of persons of full age
    I.   Insanity and feeblemindedness 369
    II.   Prodigality, drunkenness, immorality and mismanagement 370
    III. Imprisonment. 371
    IV.   At own request 372
C. Procedure
    I.   In general 373
    II.   Hearing, expert evidence 374
    III. Public announcement 375

Chapter III: Competence

A. Domicile of ward 376
B. Change of domicile 377
C. Powers of home Canton 378

Chapter IV: Appointment of Guardian

A. Conditions
    I.   In general 379
    II.   Preferential right of kindred and spouse 380
    III. Wishes as to choice of guardian 381
    IV. Obligation to accept 382
    V.   Valid excuses 383
    VI. Grounds of exclusion 384
B. Procedure in appointment
    I.   Appointment of guardian 385
    II.   Provisional measures 386
    III. Notification and public advertisement 387
    IV. Refusal to act and opposition
        1. Procedure 388
        2. Temporary duties of person appointed 389
        3. Decision 390
    V.   Investment of office 391

Article

Chapter V: Office of Curator

A. Cases
  I. Representation 392
  II. Administration of property
    1. By operation of law 393
    2. At party's request 394
  III. Restricted capacity 395
B. Competence 396
C. Appointment 397

Chapter VI: Deprivation of Liberty for Personal Assistance

A. Conditions 397*a*
B. Competence 397*b*
C. Obligation to inform 397*c*
D. Appeal to judge 397*d*
E. Procedure in Cantons
  I. In general 397*e*
  II. At court 397*f*

Title XI: Administration of Guardianship

Chapter I: Duties of Guardian

A. On entering upon office
  I. Inventory 398
  II. Custody of deeds and objects of value 399
  III. Sale of movables 400
  IV. Cash
    1. Its investment 401
    2. Conversion 402
  V. Business and industry 403
  VI. Immovable property 404
B. Care of ward and representation
  I. Care of ward's person
    1. Where he is a minor
      a. In general 405
      b. Deprivation of liberty to secure care of ward 405*a*

	2.	Where he is placed under committee	.406
	II.	Representation	
		1. In general	.407
		2. Prohibited acts	.408
		3. Concurrence of ward	.409
		4. Ward's own acts	
		a. Consent of guardian	.410
		b. Consent of withheld	.411
		5. Trade or profession of ward	.412
C.	Administration of property		
	I.	Duties of guardian and accounts	.413
	II.	Ward's separate estate	.414
D.	Duration of office		.415
E.	Honorarium		.416

Chapter II: Duties of Curator

A.	Nature of office		.417
B.	Duties		
	I.	For single transaction	.418
	II.	For administration of an estate	.419

Chapter III: Functions of Guardianship Authorities

A.	Complaints		.420
B.	Consent required		
	I.	Of guardianship board	.421
	II.	Of supervisory authority	.422
C.	Examination of reports and accounts		.423
D.	Where consent withheld		.424
E.	Cantonal regulations		.425

Chapter IV: Liabilities of Organs of Guardianship

A.	In general		
	I.	Guardian and authorities	.426
	II.	Communes, district authorities and Cantons	.427

Table of Contents   XXXVII

                                                                     Article

B.   Conditions of liability
   - I.   Of members of authorities *inter se* 428
   - II. Of the different organs *inter se* 429
C.   Deprivation of liberty to secure care of ward 429*a*
D.   Actions 430

Title XII: How Guardianship Ends

Chapter I: Termination of Incapacity

A.   In the case of minors 431
B.   Where sentenced to imprisonment 432
C.   In the case of other persons
   - I.   Condition of release 433
   - II. Procedure
     1. In general 434
     2. Public advertisement 435
     3. In case of insanity 436
     4. In case of prodigality, drunkenness, immorality, mismanagement 437
     5. Where committed at ward's own request 438
D.   In the case of a curator
   - I.   In general 439
   - II. Public advertisement 440

Chapter II: Termination of Guardian's Functions

A.   Incapacity, death 441
B.   Dismissal, non-reappointment
   - I.   Expiration of term of office 442
   - II. Supervening grounds for exclusion or excuse 443
   - III. Duty to continue in office 444
C.   Dismissal
   - I.   Grounds 445
   - II. Procedure
     1. At request of parties and officially 446
     2. Inquiry and infliction of penalty 447
     3. Provisional measures 448

XXXVIII   Civil Code

                                                                  Article
           4.   Further measures 449
           5.   Appeal 450

Chapter III: Effect of Determination of Guardianship

A.   Final account and surrender of property 451
B.   Examination of final report and accounts 452
C.   Discharge of guardian 453
D.   Action to enforce liability
     I.   Limitation of actions in ordinary cases 454
     II.   Limitation of actions in special cases 455
E.   Priority of ward's claims 456

Part III: Law of Inheritance

Section I: Heirs

Title XIII: Statutory Heirs

A.   Heirs who are relatives
     I.   Descendants 457
     II.   Parents and their descendants 458
     III.   Grandparents and their descendants 459
     IV.   Extent of the right of inheritance 460
     V.   Illegitimate relations . . . . .461 (annulled)
B.   The surviving spouse 462
                                                                  463 (annulled)
                                                                  464 (annulled)
C.   Adopted children . . . . .465 (annulled)
D.   Canton and Commune 466

Article

Title XIV: Testamentary Dispositions

Chapter I: Testamentary Capacity

A.	By will	.467
B.	By testamentary pact	.468
C.	Void dispositions	.469

Chapter II: Freedom of Disposition

A. Devisable portion
- I. What is 470
- II. Compulsory portion 471
- 472 (annulled)
- IV. Gifts to surviving spouse 473
- V. Computation of devisable portion
  - 1. Deduction of debts 474
  - 2. Donations *inter vivos* 475
  - 3. Insurance claims 476

B. Disinheritance
- I. Grounds 477
- II. Effect 478
- III. Burden of proof 479
- IV. Disinheritance of insolvent person 480

Chapter III: Kinds of Dispositions

A. In general 481
B. Burdens and conditions 482
C. Institution of heir 483
D. Legacies
- I. Their subject-matter 484
- II. Duty of person charged .485
- III. Relation between legacies and inheritance 486

E. Substitution 487
F. Reversionary heir
- I. Appointment by testator .488
- II. Time for transfer 489
- III. Safeguards 490

Civil Code

Article

	IV.	Effect of appointment		
		1.	On first heir	.491
		2.	On reversionary heir	.492
G.	Foundations			.493
H.	Testamentary pacts			
	I.	Institution of heir and legacies		.494
	II.	Renunciation		
		1.	Its purport	.495
		2.	Failure of renunciation	.496
		3.	Rights of creditors of estate	.497

Chapter IV: Formalities Required for Testamentary Dispositions

A.	Wills				
	I.	Forms			
		1.	In general		.498
		2.	Public will		
			a.	How made	.499
			b.	Duties of official	.500
			c.	Duties of witnesses	.501
			d.	Where testator neither reads nor signs document	502
			e.	Parties	.503
			f.	Safe custody of document	.504
		3.	Holograph will		.505
		4.	Oral will		
			a.	How made	.506
			b.	Subsequent formalities	.507
			c.	Lapse	.508
	II.	Revocation and destruction			
		1.	Revocation		.509
		2.	Destruction		.510
		3.	Subsequent will		.511
B.	Testamentary pacts				
	I.	How made			.512
	II.	Rescission			
		1.	By the parties		
			a.	By contract or by will	.513
			b.	For non-performance	.514
		2.	Where heir predeceases testator		.515
C.	Reduction of devisable portion				.516

Article

Chapter V: Executors

A. Appointment 517
B. Position 518

Chapter VI: Voidance and Reduction of Testamentary Dispositions

A. Voidance
    I. Incapacity, undue influence, illegality or immorality 519
    II. Want of formality 520
    III. Period of limitation 521
B. Claim for reduction
    I. Conditions
        1. In general 522
        2. Legacies to heirs entitled to compulsory portions ... 523
        3. Rights of heir's creditors 524
    II. Effect
        1. In general 525
        2. Specific legacy 526
        3. Gifts *inter vivos*
            a. Cases 527
            b. Obligation to return them 528
        4. Insurance claims 529
        5. Usufructs and rent-charges 530
        6. In case of reversionary heir 531
    III. Order of reduction 532
    IV. Period of limitation 533

Chapter VII: Actions Arising from Testamentary Pacts

A. Where property has passed *inter vivos* 534
B. Reduction and restitution
    I. Claim for reduction 535
    II. Restitution 536

Civil Code

Article

Section II: Devolution of the Estate

Title XV: Opening of the Succession

- A. Date of opening 537
- B. Place and forum 538
- C. Conditions on part of heir
    - I. Capacity to take
        1. Legal capacity 539
        2. Unworthiness
            - a. Grounds 540
            - b. Effect on descendants 541
    - II. Surviving the deceased
        1. Heirs 542
        2. Legatees 543
        3. Child before birth 544
        4. Reversionary heirs 545
- D. Declaration of absence
    - I. Succession by absentee
        1. Delivery and security 546
        2. Restitution 547
    - II. Right of inheritance of absentee 548
    - III. Relation between the two cases 549
    - IV. Official procedure 550

Title XVI: Effects of Devolution

Chapter I: Provisional Measures

- A. In general 551
- B. Affixing of seal 552
- C. Inventory 553
- D. Official administration
    - I. In general 554
    - II. Where heirs unknown 555
- E. Opening of wills
    - I. Obligation to deliver them up 556
    - II. The opening ceremony 557
    - III. Notice to interested parties 558
    - IV. Delivery of possession 559

Table of Contents

XLIII

Article

Chapter II: Vesting of the Inheritance

A. Vesting
- I. Heirs .... .560
  - 561 (annulled)
- III. Legatees
  1. Vesting of legacies .... .562
  2. Rights of legatees in different cases .... .563
  3. Relative position of creditors and legatees .... .564
  4. Reduction .... .565

B. Disclaimer
- I. Declaration
  1. Right to disclaim .... .566
  2. Period within which allowed
     - a. In general .... .567
     - b. Where an inventory has been made .... .568
  3. Right of disclaimer passes to the heirs .... .569
  4. Form required .... .570
- II. Lapse of right of disclaimer .... .571
- III. Disclaimer by co-heir .... .572
- IV. Disclaimer by all nearest heirs
  1. In general .... .573
  2. Right of surviving spouse .... .574
  3. Disclaimer in favour of more distant heirs .... .575
- V. Extension of time limit .... .576
- VI. Disclaimer of legacy .... .577
- VII. Securing heir's creditors .... .578
- VIII. Liability on disclaimer .... .579

Chapter III: Public Inventory

A. Conditions .... .580
B. Procedure
- I. Inventory .... .581
- II. Public citation .... .582
- III. Claims and debts included officially .... .583
- IV. Result .... .584

C. Position of heirs during inventory
- I. Administration .... .585
- II. Execution for debt, legal proceedings, limitation of actions .... .586

XLIV   Civil Code

                                                                   Article

D. Effect
   I.   Time for deliberation 587
   II. Heir's declaration. 588
   III. Effect of acceptance subject to an inventory
        1. Liability according to inventory 589
        2. Liability outside inventory 590
E. Liability on guarantees 591
F. Devolution on Canton or Commune 592

Chapter IV: Official Liquidation

A. Conditions
   I.   At instance of heir 593
   II. At instance of creditors of deceased 594
B. Procedure
   I.   Administration 595
   II. Ordinary liquidation 596
   III. Liquidation in bankruptcy .597

Chapter V: Action to Recover Inheritance

A. Conditions 598
B. Effect 599
C. Period of limitation 600
D. Action by legatee. 601

Title XVII: Partition

Chapter I: Community before Partition

A. Effect of opening of succession
   I.   Community among heirs 602
   II. Liability of heirs 603
B. Action for partition 604
C. Postponement of partition 605
D. Rights of members of household 606

Table of Contents   XLV

                                                                         Article

Chapter II: Mode of Partition

A. In general 607
B. Rules
    I.   Dispositions of deceased 608
    II. Concurrence of Probate authority 609
C. Effecting the partition
    I.   Equality of heirs' rights 610
    II.   Arrangement of lots 611
    III. Allotment and sale of single articles 612
    IV. Allotment of lodging and chattel to surviving spouse 612a
D. Special cases
    I.   Things which belong together, family papers 613
    II.   Claims of deceased against an heir 614
    III. Property charged with debt 615
    IV. Immovables
        1. Parcelling 616
        2. Allotment
            a. Valuation 617
            b. Procedure of valuation 618
        3. Share of co-heirs in profit
            a. Claim 619
            b. Profit 619bis
            c. Substitute for agricultural land 619ter
            d. Repairs on buildings 619quater
            e. Liability of the new owner 619quinquies
            f. Settlement by contract 619sexies
    V.   Farms
        1. No partition
            a. Conditions 620
            b. Allotment of movables 620bis
            c. Designation of the new owner 621
            d. Testamentary disposition 621bis
            e. Descendants in minority 621ter
        2. Exception 621quater
        3. Community
            a. Claim to postpone partition 622
            b. Dissolution of community 623
        4. Settlement by estate charge 624
        5. Other industries 625
        6. Alienation 625bis

XLVI

Civil Code

Article

Chapter III: Hotchpot

A.	Duty of heirs	.626
B.	Hotchpot in case of incapacity or disclaimer	.627
C.	Conditions	
	I. Hotchpot or diminished share	.628
	II. Gifts in excess of statutory share	.629
	III. Mode of computation	.630
D.	Cost of education	.631
E.	Customary presents	.632
F.	Compensation for assisting the family	.633 (annulled)

Chapter IV: Completion and Effect of Partition

A.	Completion of partition	
	I. Partition agreement	.634
	II. Contracts relating to rights of inheritance	.635
	III. Contracts before the opening of the succession	.636
B.	Mutual liabilities of co-heirs	
	I. Guarantees	.637
	II. Rescission of partition agreement	.638
C.	Liability towards third persons	
	I. Joint and several liability	.639
	II. Indemnities among the heirs themselves	.640

Abbreviations

art., arts.	Article(s)
AS	Official Compendium of the Federal Statutes, quoted according to volume and number of page
BBl	Official Federal Gazette
BS	Verified Compendium of the Federal Statutes and Regulations as from 1848 to 1947, quoted according to volume and number of page
cf.	compare
CO	Code of Obligations of 30th March 1911 (SR 220)
e.g.	for example
etc.	and so on
et seq.	and following
Fr., frz.	French
FN	footnote
G.	German
i.e.	that is
lit.	literally
OG	Federal Statute of 16th December 1943 on Organisation of Federal Judicial Affairs (SR 173.110)
SR	Systematic Compendium of the Federal Law (as from 1970)

Swiss Civil Code

Preliminary Chapter

Art. 1

¹ The Law must be applied in all cases which come within the letter or the spirit of any of its provisions.

² Where no provision is applicable, the judge shall decide according to the existing Customary Law and, in default thereof, according to the rules which he would lay down if he had himself to act as legislator.

³ Herein he must be guided by approved legal doctrine and case-law.

A. Application of Law

Art. 2

¹ Every person is bound to exercise his rights and fulfil his obligations according to the principles of good faith.[1]

² The law does not sanction the evident abuse of a person's rights.

B. Limits of civil rights
I. Misuse of a right

Art. 3

¹ *Bona fides* is presumed whenever the existence of a right has been expressly made to depend on the observance of good faith.

² No person can plead *bona fides* in any case where he has failed to exercise the degree of care required by the circumstances.

II. *Bona fides*

Art. 4

Where the law expressly leaves a point to the discretion of the judge, or directs him to take cir-

III. Discretion of judge

---

[1] The masculine includes both sexes unless it appears from the context that it is applicable to males only.

cumstances into consideration, or to appreciate whether a ground alleged is material, he must base his decision on principles of justice and equity.

Art. 5

C. Federal and Cantonal Law
I. Private Law and local custom

¹ Cantons have the right to set up or annul rules of Private Law where and in so far as their jurisdiction has been reserved by Federal Law.

² References in the Code to usage or local custom are taken to indicate rules contained in Cantonal Law valid at the time, provided no contrary custom can be proved to exist.

Art. 6

II. Cantonal Public Law

¹ Federal Private Law does not affect the competence of the Cantons in the matter of Public Law.

² The Cantons can, within the limits of their jurisdiction, restrict or prohibit the trading in certain things or declare void any transaction relating to them.

Art. 7

D. General rules of Law of Obligations

The general rules laid down in the Law of Obligations regarding the formation, the effect and the determination of contracts apply also to the other parts of Private Law.

Art. 8

E. Rules of evidence
I. Burden of proof

In the absence of a special provision to the contrary, the burden of proving an alleged fact rests on the party who bases his claim on that fact.

Art. 9

II. Proof of public documents

¹ Entries made in public registers and duly authenticated documents[1] are sufficient evidence of

---

[1] Öffentliche Urkunden, *titres authentiques,* are rendered by "duly authenticated documents"; they are documents which are drawn up

the facts which they state, provided that their inaccuracy is not proved.

² The proof of inaccuracy is not required to be in any special form.

Art. 10

Cantonal Law cannot prescribe a special form of evidence for proving any transaction for the validity of which Federal Law does not lay down any such form. III. Procedure

Part I: Law of Persons

Title I: Natural Persons

Chapter I: Legal Personality[1]

Art. 11

¹ Any person can be the subject of rights.

² Accordingly all persons have, within the limits imposed by law, an equal capacity to have rights and duties.²

A. Personality in general
I. Subject of rights

---

by officials empowered by law to do this and executed with the formalities required.
[1] The "Law of Persons" here deals in general outline with the legal position of individuals or bodies of persons and other things invested with personality considered as persons, and not with any modifications in their status due to family relationships or disabilities; these modifications are set out in Part II under Family Law. The term "natural persons", renders **natürliche Personen,** *personnes physiques* to distinguish them from "corporate bodies" or **juristische Personen,** *personnes morales,* dealt with in Title II.
"Legal personality" has been chosen as the nearest equivalent for **das Recht der Persönlichkeit,** *la personnalité.* The term is intended to denote the nature of the legal conception of a person.
[2] **Rechtsfähig,** *qui jouit des droits civils,* is here translated by "subject of rights, **Rechtsfähigkeit,** *jouissance des droits civils,* "capacity to have rights and duties."

Art. 12

II. Capacity to act
1. Purport

Every person who has the capacity to effect a legal transaction is capable of acquiring rights and incurring obligations by such transaction.[1]

Art. 13

2. Conditions
a. General

Every person who is of full age and discretion is held to have the capacity to effect a legal transaction.

Art. 14

b. Majority

[1] Every person who has completed his twentieth year is held to have attained his majority.[2]

[2] Marriage constitutes majority.[3]

Art. 15

c. Emancipation

[1] A minor who has completed his eighteenth year can, with his own consent and that of his parents, be declared to be of full age by the guardianship supervisory authority.[4]

[2] If the minor has a guardian, the guardian must first be consulted about the emancipation.

Art. 16

d. Discretion

Every person is held to have discretion as the term is used in the Code who is not incapacitated from acting rationally through tender age, insanity, feeblemindedness, drunkenness or other similar cause.[5]

---

[1] The term "legal transaction" has been adopted as the shortest and nearest equivalent of **Rechtsgeschäft**, *acte juridique*. It is sometimes translated "juristic act" or "act-in-the-law".

[2] *i.e.* who is 20, not 21 years of age.

[3] Women may marry at the age of 18 or, in exceptional cases, 17. But men may not, as a general rule, marry until they are of age; it is only in exceptional cases that this rule is relaxed (art. 96).

[4] For the meaning of "guardianship supervisory authority" see arts. 361 and 422.

[5] The Code does not fix the age of discretion nor does it attempt to define it, but it leaves the question to be decided by the judge in each case. For the provisions relating to insanity, etc., see arts. 369 *et seq.*

Art. 17

Persons who are devoid of discretion, minors and persons placed under a committee are incapable of effecting a legal transaction.[1]

III. Incapacity to act
1. In general

Art. 18

Where a person who is devoid of discretion purports to effect a legal transaction, the transaction is, with certain statutory exceptions, null and void.[2]

2. Absence of discretion

Art. 19

[1] Where minors and persons placed under a committee have discretion, they can bind themselves by their transactions only with the consent of their guardian or committee.

[2] Without this consent they can validly accept purely gratuitous benefits and exercise purely personal rights.[3]

[3] They are liable to make good all damage caused by their wrongful acts.[4]

3. Minors and persons under a committee who have discretion

Art. 20

[1] The degree of relationship[6] between two persons is determined by the number of generations that separate them.

[2] A person is said to be in a direct line of descent from another where he is descended from that other, and to be a collateral to another, where he is not descended from that other but from the same common ancestor as the other.

IV.[5] Relationship and relationship by marriage
1. Relationship

---

[1] *i.e.* legal incapacity is confined to these three classes of persons.
[2] One exception to this rule is to be found in art. 132, where a marriage, even though contracted by a person devoid of discretion at the time, is held to be valid until it is annulled by the court.
[3] *e.g.* making a will.
[4] *i.e.* just as persons who are under no incapacity.
[5] Wording of the marginal heading according to cipher I 3 of the Federal Statute of 30th June 1972, in force since 1st April 1973 (AS 1972 2819 2829, 1973 92; BBl 1971 I 1200).
[6] This word is used according to cipher I 3 of the Federal Statute of 30th June 1972, in force since 1st April 1973 (AS 1972 2819 2829; BBl 1971 I 1200).

Art. 21

2. By marriage

¹ A person who is related[1] to another is held to be related by marriage to the other's spouse in the same line of descent and in the same degree.

² The dissolution of the marriage does not put an end to this relationship.

Art. 22

V. Home and domicile
1. Citizenship

¹ The legal home of a person is determined by his citizenship.[2]

² His citizenship is determined by Public Law.

³ Where a person has a right to citizenship in several places, his legal home is held to be the place where he is domiciled or was last domiciled, or, if he has no domicile, the place where he or his ancestors last acquired citizenship.

Art. 23

2. Domicile
a. Definition

¹ A person is said to be domiciled in the place where he resides with the intention of settling there.

² No person can be domiciled in several places at the same time.

³ This last clause does not apply to commercial domicile.

Art. 24

b. Change of domicile or residence

¹ Every person retains his old domicile until he has actually acquired a new domicile.

---

[1] This word is used according to cipher I 3 of the Federal Statute of 30th June 1972, in force since 1st April 1973 (AS 1972 2819 2829; BBl 1971 I 1200).

[2] "Home" or "legal home" purports to render **Heimat,** *canton d'origine* or *lieu d'origine, attinenza.* As seen by this article it is not the same thing as either nationality or domicile. "Citizenship" has been chosen rather than the more familiar term "nationality" as the equivalent of **Bürgerrecht,** *droit de cité,* because a Swiss national has rights of citizenship which join him not merely to the Federation but to some Canton, and within that Canton again to some Commune or parish. The commune or parish of which he is a citizen is his legal home.

² His domicile is taken to be the place where he resides in all cases where a previous domicile is not proved, or where he has abandoned a domicile abroad and has not acquired a new domicile in Switzerland.

Art. 25[1]

c. Domicile of dependent persons

¹ The parents' domicile is considered as the domicile of a child under parental power or, where the parents do not have a common domicile, that parent's domicile under whose guardianship the child is; in the other cases the place where the child resides is deemed his domicile.

² Persons under guardianship have their domicile at the seat of the competent guardianship board.

Art. 26

d. Residence in an institution

The mere fact that any person is resident in a place for educational purposes or has been sent to live in a school or college, home, hospital, asylum, reformatory or similar institution does not constitute his domicile there.

Art. 27

B. Personality, how protected
I. Excessive commitment[2]

¹ No person can wholly or partially renounce his capacity to have rights and to effect legal transactions.

² No person can alienate his personal liberty nor impose any restrictions on his own enjoyment thereof which are contrary to law and morality.

Art. 28[2]

II. Against injury
1. Principle

¹ Where anyone is injured in his person by an illegal act, he can apply to the judge for his protection from any person who takes an active part in effecting the injury.

---

[1] Wording according to cipher I 2 of the Federal Statute of 5th October 1984, in force since 1st January 1988 (BBl 1979 II 1191).
[2] Wording according to cipher I of the Federal Statute of 16th December 1983, in force since 1st July 1985 (AS 1984 778 782; BBl 1982 II 636).

² An injury is illegal where it is not justified by the injured person's consent, by a predominantly private or public interest or by the law.

Art. 28a[1]

2. To bring action

¹ The plaintiff can apply to the judge for:

1. an injunction of an imminent injury;
2. the removal of an existing injury;
3. a statement of illegality of an injury where the continuation of the illegal act has a disturbing effect.

² In particular he can demand that the rectification or the judgement is made known to a third party or published.

³ Reservations are made for an action for damages and moral compensation as well as the handing over of a profit in compliance with the provisions made for agency of necessity.

Art. 28b[1]

3. Place of jurisdiction

¹ The judge either at the domicile of the plaintiff or the defendant is competent to judge an action brought in to obtain a person's protection from injury.

² Where at the same time the plaintiff brings in an action for damages, moral compensation or the handing over of a profit caused by the injury, this action can also be filed at the plaintiff's domicile.

Art. 28c[1]

4. Precautionary measures
a. Prerequisites

¹ Where a person can substantiate that he has been injured by an illegal act or that he must fear such an act will injure him and that from this injury a disadvantage will arise which cannot be easily compensated, he can apply for precautionary measures.

---

[1] Inserted by cipher I of the Federal Statute of 16th December 1983, in force since 1st July 1985 (AS 1984 778 782; BBl 1982 II 636).

² In particular the judge can:

1. restrain or remove the injury as a precautionary measure;

2. take the necessary steps to secure the evidence.

³ Where an injury is caused by periodically appearing media, the judge can take steps to restrain or remove the injury by way of precautionary measures only then if it could be the reason for an especially serious disadvantage or if there exists no obvious legal justification or if the precautionary measure is not disproportionate.

Art. 28d[1]

¹ The person opposing the application is given the opportunity to be heard by the judge.   *b.* Procedure

² Where an imminent danger makes it impossible to hear the opponent before the application is made, the judge can take steps to introduce tentative precautionary measures after having received the application, unless the applicant has made an obvious attempt to delay his application.

³ Where a precautionary measure may prove to be harmful for the opponent, the judge can request the applicant to give a guarantee.

Art. 28e[1]

¹ Precautionary measures are executed in the same way as judgements in all Cantons.   *c.* Execution

² Precautionary measures which have been ordered before an action is pending become ineffective if the applicant does not bring action within the delay fixed by the judge, at the latest within thirty days.

---

[1] Inserted by cipher I of the Federal Statute of 16th December 1983, in force since 1st July 1985 (AS **1984** 778 782; BBl **1982 II** 636).

Art. 28f[1]

d. Indemnity

[1] The applicant has to compensate for the damage which has been caused by a precautionary measure if the claim for which it has been permitted did not exist by right; if, however, he is not, or only slightly, responsible for the damage, the judge can reject the application or reduce the compensation.

[2] The judge who has ordered the precautionary measure or the judge at the domicile of the defendant is competent to judge the damages suit.

[3] A given security must be released as soon as there is certainty that no damages suit will be lodged; where there is uncertainty the judge fixes the delay for filing a suit.

Art. 28g[1]

5. The right to make a counter-statement
a. Principle

[1] Where anyone is directly injured in his person by the presentation of facts in periodically appearing media, in particular the press, radio or television, he is entitled to make a counter-statement.

[2] The right to make a counter-statement does not exist where public negotiations of an authority have been truly reported and the person concerned has taken part in the negotiations.

Art. 28h[1]

b. Form and content

[1] The text of the counter-statement must be brief and restricted to the object of the presentation to which exception is taken.

[2] A counter-statement can be prohibited where it is obviously incorrect or against the law or morality.

---

[1] Inserted by cipher I of the Federal Statute of 16th December 1983, in force since 1st July 1985 (AS **1984** 778 782; BBl **1982 II** 636).

Art. 28*i*[1]

¹ The person concerned must send the text of the counter-statement to the media institution or enterprise within twenty days after having cognizance of the presentation of facts to which exception has been taken, in no case, however, later than three months after the presentation has been circulated or broadcast.

² The media institution or enterprise shall inform the person concerned immediately when the counter-statement will be published or why they reject it.

c. Procedure

Art. 28*k*[1]

¹ The counter-statement must be published as soon as possible and in such manner that it reaches the same group of people as the presentation of the facts to which exception has been taken.

² The counter-statement must be marked explicitly so that it can be recognized as such; the media institution or enterprise is only entitled to add a declaration whether they maintain the previously published presentation of the facts or on what sources their presentation is founded.

³ The counter-statement has to be published free of charge.

d. Publication

Art. 28*l*[1]

¹ Where the media institution or enterprise prevents the execution of the right to make a counter-statement or refuses to publish a counter-statement or publishes it incorrectly, the person concerned can apply to the judge.

e. To apply to the judge

---

[1] Inserted by cipher I of the Federal Statute of 16th December 1983, in forces since 1st July 1985 (AS **1984** 778 782; BBl **1982 II** 636).

² The judge at the domicile of the plaintiff or at the domicile of the defendant is competent to judge the action.

³ The judge decides immediately on the basis of the available evidence.

⁴ An appeal to the judge has no suspensory effect.

Art. 29

III. Right to name
1. How protected

¹ Where a person disputes the right of another person to his name, the latter can apply to the judge to have his right established.

² Where a person assumes the name of another to the latter's prejudice, the latter can apply for an injunction to restrain the continuation of this assumption, and can in addition claim damages if the act is proved to be wrongful, and moral compensation if this is justified by the nature of the wrong suffered.

Art. 30

2. Change of name

¹ Persons may be authorized by the government of their home Canton to change their names where there are material grounds for the change.

² Where an engaged couple requests that the wife's surname should be the surname of the family after the wedding, the request is to be granted if there are grounds worthy of consideration.[1]

³ Every person who is prejudiced by the change of name can bring legal proceedings to oppose it within a year from his cognizance thereof.

Art. 31

C. When personality begins and ends
I. Birth and death

¹ Legal personality begins at birth if the child is born alive, and ends at death.

² Between conception and birth the child is held to have legal capacity, conditional on his being born alive.

---

[1] Wording according to cipher I 2 of the Federal Statute of 5th October 1984, in force since 1st January 1988 (BBl 1979 II 1191).

Art. 32

¹ Where a person bases a claim on an allegation that another person is alive or dead or was living at a certain date or survived a third person, he must prove the fact which he alleges.

² Where several persons have died and it is impossible to prove that one survived the others, they are all presumed to have died at the same time.

II. Proof of life and death
1. Burden of proof

Art. 33

¹ Entries in the register of civil status are proof of the birth or death of a person.

² In default of such entry or where the entry is proved to be incorrect, any other evidence is admitted.

2. Modes of proof
a. In general

Art. 34

Where a person has disappeared under such circumstances that his death seems certain, his death is taken as established, though his body has not been found.

b. Presumption of death

Art. 35

¹ Where the death of any person is deemed very probable, in that he disappeared under circumstances of mortal danger, or in that he has not been heard of for a long time, the court can, on the application of an interested party, declare him to be a legal absentee.

² The competent court is the court of the absentee's last domicile if in Switzerland, or, if he has never been resident in Switzerland, the court of his legal home.¹

III. Declaration of absence
1. In general

Art. 36

¹ An application for a declaration of absence can be made at the expiration of one year at least from

2. Procedure

---

¹ *i.e.* a person may have a legal home in Switzerland, though he has never resided there; see art. 22 above.

the date of the mortal danger incurred by the absentee, or at the expiration of five years from the date when news was last heard of him.

² The court shall by means of duly published notices call upon all persons who might give information relative to the absentee to declare themselves within a specified period.

³ This period shall be at least one year from the date of the first notice.

Art. 37

3. Failure of application

Where before the expiration of the official notice the absentee reappears, or news is heard of him, or the date of his death is proved, the application fails.

Art. 38

4. Effect of declaration

¹ Where within the specified period no information is forthcoming relative to the absentee, the court makes a declaration of absence, and the rights arising from his death may be exercised just as if his death had been proved.

² This declaration takes effect as from the time when the mortal danger was incurred by the absentee or when news was last heard of him.

Chapter II: Registration of Civil Status

Art. 39

A. In general
I. Registers

¹ The civil status of a person is established by the registers set up for the purpose.

² The Federal Council shall issue the necessary regulations relative to the keeping of the registers and the notifications required by law.[1]

---

[1] *i.e.* the Code does not go into these detailed rules but leaves them to the Cantons and to the Federal Council, which is the highest administrative body in Switzerland.

Art. 40

¹ The delimitation of areas for the purpose of this registration, the appointment and pay of the registrars and the setting up of supervisory authorities fall within the province of the Cantons.

² The regulations made by the Cantons require for their validity to be approved by the Federal Council.

II. Organisation

Art. 41

¹ The registers of civil status are kept by laymen.¹

² The registrars have to make the entries in the registers and furnish extracts from these entries.

³ The Federal Council can charge the official representatives of Switzerland in foreign countries with the duties of registrars of civil status.

III. Officials

Art. 42

¹ The registrars and the authorities immediately above them are held personally liable for all damage caused by their own wrongful act or omission or by that of their subordinates appointed by them.

² The rules relating to the liability of the supervisory authorities are the same as those governing the liability of guardianship authorities.

³ The Cantons are secondarily liable for all damage not made good by the officials who are primarily liable.

IV. Liabilities

Art. 43

¹ The registries of civil status are under regular supervision.

² Complaints are heard by the Cantonal supervisory authorities, from whom there is a final appeal to the Federal Council.²

V. Supervision
1. Complaints

---

¹ *i.e.* as opposed to clerics.
² Today: the Federal Court (art. 97 *et seq.* OG – SR 173.110).

Art. 44

2. Penalties

¹ The supervisory authority inflicts penalties on a registrar who is guilty of misconduct in his office.

² This provision does not exclude a criminal prosecution.

Art. 45

VI. Rectifications

¹ No entry shall be rectified without an order from the court.

² Where, however, the error is the result of an obvious oversight or mistake, the supervisory authority can order its rectification.

Art. 46

B. Register of births
I. Notification

¹ Every birth and every miscarriage after six months of pregnancy must be notified within three days to the registrar of civil status.

² Where any person finds a child whose parentage is unknown, he must inform the local authority and the latter must notify the registrar.

Art. 47[1]

II. Entry of modifications

Where modifications occur in the status of any person, as in the case of a child by reason of his father's acknowledgement of him or the official declaration of paternity or in the case of adoption of a child or the establishment of the parentage of a foundling, such modifications are entered in the margin of the register on receipt of an official notice or at the instance of interested parties.

---

[1] Wording according to cipher I 2 of the Federal Statute of 25th June 1976, in force since 1st January 1978 (AS 1977 237 264; BBl 1974 II 1).

Art. 48

Every death and every discovery of a dead body must be notified within two days to the registrar of civil status.   C. Register of deaths
I. Notification

Art. 49

¹ Where any person has disappeared under such circumstances that his death seems certain, the entry of his death is made in the register by order of the supervisory authority, even if his body has not been found.   II. Where the body is not found

² However, all interested parties can demand an official declaration by the court of the continued existence or the death of the said person.

Art. 50

Declarations of absence are entered in the register of deaths on receipt of a notice from the court.   III. Declaration of absence

Art. 51

Where it is shown that an entry is incorrect either by reason of a wrong notification or the identification of a person who has been entered as unknown or the revocation of a declaration of absence, the necessary modifications are entered in the margin of the register.   IV. Entry of modifications

Title II: Corporate Bodies[1]

Chapter I: General Provisions

Art. 52

A. Personality

[1] Incorporated associations and those foundations which have a specific object and an independent existence acquire the status of a person by registration in the commercial register.[2]

[2] Those associations and foundations that fall under Public Law,[3] societies that have no industrial object[4] and religious and family foundations are exempt from the necessity of registration.

[3] Those associations and foundations that have an unlawful or immoral object cannot acquire the status of a person.

Art. 53

B. Capacity to have rights

Corporate bodies are legally capable of having rights and incurring obligations save those rights and obligations which are inseparably bound up with human nature, such as with sex, age or family relationship.

---

[1] lit. "Juristic Persons".

[2] *i.e.* the Code personifies not only associations of men or corporations, but also property which has been tied up by the owner and founder for some specific purpose. A "foundation" as here used to render the German **Anstalt** (or, as the same idea is expressed later, **Stiftung**) and the French *établissement* is not a trust, because it is not vested in trustees; but it is taken to have an independent existence of its own, just as if it were not a "thing" but a "person" with rights and duties that are not connected with any specific person or body of persons.

[3] Examples of public corporations in Switzerland are the State itself, the Cantons, municipalities.
Examples of public foundations are the Swiss National and Cantonal Banks, municipal and Cantonal hospitals, universities, etc.

[4] See art. 60 *et seq.*

Art. 54

Corporate bodies are held to have the capacity to effect a legal transaction as soon as their official organs have been appointed in accordance with the requirements of the law and of their own constitution.[1]

C. Capacity to act
I. Conditions

Art. 55

[1] Corporate bodies act through their official organs.[2]

[2] These organs by their legal transactions and their other acts or commissions bind the corporate body which they represent.[3]

[3] They are moreover personally liable for their own wrongful acts or omissions.[4]

II. Mode

Art. 56

Corporate bodies are, in the absence of a contrary clause in their constitution, held to be domiciled at the seat of their administration.

D. Domicile

Art. 57

[1] Where a corporate body is dissolved and it is not otherwise provided by law[5] or by its constitution or its instrument of foundation or its competent organs, its corporate property passes to the administrative body of the Federation, Canton or Commune with which its object was connected.

E. Dissolution
I. Application of property

---

[1] *i.e.* because a corporation can only act through an agent.
[2] lit. "These organs are appointed to give effect to the will of the juristic person." But this translation was rejected on the ground that it seemed unnecessary to attribute a "will" to a "foundation" (cf. FN 2, art. 52).
[3] *i.e.* by transactions, such as contracts, and by other acts or omissions, such as torts. The sense "in their official capacity" is understood.
[4] *i.e.* for a tort or a crime.
[5] Thus art. 667 of the Code of Obligations provides for the division of assets in the case of joint stock companies that have been dissolved.

² This property is to be applied as nearly as possible in accordance with the original object of the corporate body.

³ Where a corporate body is wound up compulsorily, as having an illegal or immoral object, its property shall pass to the said administrative body notwithstanding any contrary provision.[1]

Art. 58

II. Liquidation

The liquidation of the property of a corporate body is carried out according to the rules laid down for co-operative societies.[2]

Art. 59

F. Public Law and law of companies and co-operative societies

[1] Public Federal and Cantonal Law governs both public and ecclesiastical corporations and foundations.[3]

[2] Associations that have an industrial object are governed by the rules of Company Law and that relating to co-operative societies.[4]

[3] Where land is held in common or associations exist for the common cultivation of the land, Cantonal Law shall continue to apply.[5]

---

[1] *i.e.* in this case the property passes beneficially to the public body and may be applied for any public object within the area.

[2] For these see CO art. 711 *et seq.*

[3] For examples of public corporations and foundations see FN 2, art. 52. The terms "ecclesiastical corporations and foundations" are here confined to public bodies, such as churches of different denominations, and to public foundations, such as convents; thus they do not include private foundations, even though these may have a religious object.

[4] The Code of Obligations lays down the rules relating to companies in arts. 524–677, and to co-operative societies in arts. 678–715.

[5] The term "**Allmendgenossenschaft**" (G.), *"société d'allmends"* (Fr.), has been paraphrased in the English version. Prof. Huber in his explanations of the Preliminary Draft of the Code states that this paragraph refers to those associations which have come down from the ancient system of common ownership of land and which therefore, like other old-established customs, have been properly reserved for Cantonal Law (cf. the British institution of "the Commons").

Chapter II: Societies[1]

Art. 60

¹ Associations which have a political, religious, scientific, artistic, charitable, social, or any other than an industrial object, acquire the status of a person as soon as they show by their constitution their intention to have a corporate existence. — A. Formation / I. Incorporation

² The constitution must be drawn up in writing and state the object, the capital and the organisation of the society.

Art. 61

¹ When the constitution of a society has been passed and its directorate appointed, it can be registered in the commercial register.[2] — II. Registration

² If for the better attainment of its object the society carries on an industry on commercial lines, registration is compulsory.[3]

³ The application for registration must be accompanied by the written constitution and the names of the directors.

Art. 62

Societies that cannot acquire or have not yet acquired the status of a person, are governed by the same rules as partnerships.[4] — III. Societies not incorporated

---

[1] The word "association" is here used as a generic term, whereas "society" is confined, except in combination with "co-operative", to associations with non-commercial objects, which form the subject of this chapter.

[2] *i.e.* registration is optional; it is not required by law and does not affect the status of the association.

[3] Here the industry is merely of a subsidiary character, and does not form the principal object of the society; for if this were its principal object, the association would fall under art. 59 paragraph 2, above, and not be included in this Code but be governed by the Code of Obligations.

[4] For the rules governing partnerships see CO arts. 530 *et seq.*

Art. 63

IV. Relation between constitution and law

¹ The following provisions apply in so far as the constitution of a society does not contain regulations about its organisation and the relations between the society and its members.

² No constitution can modify provisions which are laid down by law as binding in all cases.

Art. 64

B. Organisation
I. General meeting
1. Its function and summons

¹ The general meeting of the members is the highest organ of society.

² It is summoned by the directors.

³ The conditions for its summons are laid down by the constitution; in any case the law requires that it be summoned on the demand of one fifth of the members.

Art. 65

2. Powers

¹ The general meeting decides on the admission and expulsion of members, appoints the directors and disposes of all matters not specifically assigned to any other organ of the society.

² The general meeting has the control of the other organs of the society and can at any time revoke the authority conferred upon them, without prejudice, however, to any rights which they may possess by special agreement.

³ The power of revocation on material grounds is an absolute right granted to the general meeting by law.[1]

Art. 66

3. Resolutions
a. Form

¹ Resolutions affecting the society must be passed by the general meeting.

---

[1] *i.e.* it cannot be taken away or restricted by the constitution of the society.

Art. 67

¹ All members have equal votes at the general meeting. *b. Right to vote and majority*

² Resolutions are passed by a majority of the members present.

³ They cannot be passed on motions that are not on the agenda, unless the constitution expressly sanctions it.

Art. 68

No member is by law allowed to vote on motions that relate to any transaction or legal proceedings between the society of the one part and himself, his spouse or any of his ascendants or descendants in a direct line of the other part. *c. Where vote disallowed*

Art. 69

The directors have the right and the duty to manage the affairs of the society and to represent it in accordance with the provisions of its constitution. *II. Directors*

Art. 70

¹ A society can at any time admit new members. *C. Membership
I. Admission and resignation*

² All members are by law entitled to resign their membership, provided they give notice of their intention at least six months before the end of a calendar year or, if a definite period of membership has been fixed, at least six months before the end of that period.

³ Membership is inalienable and does not pass on death.

² Where all members assent in writing to a motion, this is equivalent to a resolution by the general meeting.

Art. 71

II. Subscriptions

¹ Members' subscriptions are fixed by the constitution of the society.

² Where it does not fix them, members must contribute equally to the necessary expenses incurred in carrying out the object of the society and to the payment of its debts.

Art. 72

III. Grounds for expulsion

¹ The constitution can determine the grounds for the expulsion of a member. It can also sanction expulsion with non-disclosure of the grounds.

² In this case no right of action arises in regard to the grounds for the expulsion.[1]

³ Where, however, the constitution contains no provisions on this point, a member can be expelled only by a resolution passed at a general meeting and on material grounds.

Art. 73

IV. Effect of resignation and expulsion

¹ Members who resign or are expelled from a society lose all rights over the common property of the society.

² They continue to be liable to pay a proper proportion of their subscription according to the period of their membership.

Art. 74

V. Maintenance of object of society

No change in the object of the society can be forced upon any of its members.

---

[1] *i.e.* a member cannot sue where he has been expelled either for the grounds sanctioned in the constitution of the society or without being informed of the grounds, if in this latter case the constitution expressly provides that the grounds need not be disclosed.

Art. 75

Every member of a society is absolutely entitled by law to apply to the court to avoid any resolutions passed by the society without this assent, which are contrary to law or the constitution of the society, provided the application is made within one month from the day on which he became cognizant of such resolutions.

VI. Maintenance of members' rights

Art. 76

A society can at any time resolve upon its own dissolution.

D. Dissolution
I. Modes
1. By resolution

Art. 77

A society is dissolved by operation of law, when it has ceased to be solvent or when it has become impossible to appoint a directorate in accordance with its constitution.

2. By operation of law

Art. 78

The court will, on the application of the competent authority or of an interested party, declare a society dissolved, where it has an illegal or immoral object.[1]

3. By the court

Art. 79

Where a society is entered in the commercial register, its dissolution must be notified to the registrar by the directors or by the court for the erasure of the entry.

II. Erasure of entry in register

---

[1] The competence of the authority for this purpose is a matter for Cantonal Law.

Chapter III: Foundations

Art. 80

A. Constitution
I. In general

In order to constitute a foundation it is necessary to set apart a fund for a specific object.

Art. 81

II. Form

¹ A foundation must be constituted by a duly authenticated instrument or by a will.

² The foundation is entered in the commercial register in accordance with the instrument of foundation or, if necessary, according to the instructions of the supervisory authority; the entry must state the names of the directors.[1]

Art. 82

III. Opposition

The heirs or the creditors of the founder can oppose the foundation just as in the case of a gift.

Art. 83

B. Organisation

¹ The instrument of foundation must indicate its organs and the method of its administration.

² Where it does not sufficiently define the organisation, the supervisory authority must make all necessary provisions.

³ Where the foundation cannot be organised in accordance with its object,[2] the supervisory authority must apply the fund to another foundation whose object is most similar to the one in question, provided the founder does not object, or the instrument of foundation contains no contrary provision.

---

[1] *i.e.* if all the necessary particulars are not contained in the instrument of foundation, the entry is made in accordance with the instructions of the authority.

[2] *e.g.* where the fund is clearly not adequate for the carrying out of the object of the foundation.

Art. 84

¹ Foundations are subject to the supervision of the administrative body of the Federation, Canton or Commune with which their object is connected.

² The supervisory authority has to see that the fund is in all cases applied in accordance with the object of the foundation.

C. Supervision

Art. 85

The competent Cantonal authority or, if the foundation is subject to direct Federal supervision, the Federal Council[1] can, at the instance of the supervisory authority and after consultation with the highest organ of the foundation, institute changes in its organization if these changes are urgently required for the preservation of the fund and the maintenance of the object of the foundation.

D. Modifications
I. In the organization

Art. 86

¹ The competent Cantonal authority or, if the foundation is subject to direct Federal supervision, the Federal Council[2] can, at the instance of the supervisory authority and after consultation with the highest organ of the foundation, make modifications in its object, where this object has acquired a totally different significance or effect, so that the foundation has manifestly ceased to carry out the intentions of the founder.

² Similarly charges and conditions imposed on the foundation can be suppressed or modified, where they are prejudicial to the carrying out of its object.

II. In the object

---

[1] Today: the competent Department of the Federal Conseil (art. 61 paragraphs 2 and 3 of the Federal Statute of 19th September 1978 on the Organization of the Federal Administration – SR 172.010). The decisions of the Department and of the Cantonal supervisory authorities are subject to the Administration Court Complaint, to be lodged with the Federal Court (arts. 97 *et seq.* OG – SR 173.110).

[2] Today: the text of this footnote is identical with the footnote of art. 85.

Art. 87

E. Family and ecclesiastical foundation

¹ Subject to the rules of Public Law, family and ecclesiastical foundations are not under the control of the supervisory authority.

² Where disputes arise within the sphere of Private Law, they are heard and settled by the court.

Art. 88

F. Dissolution
I. By operation of law and by the court

¹ Foundations *ipso jure* cease to exist where their object has become unattainable.

² They are dissolved by the court where their object has become illegal or immoral.

Art. 89

II. On application. Erasure of entry

¹ Foundations can be dissolved at the instance of the supervisory authority or of an interested party.[1]

² Notice of the dissolution must be sent to the registrar for the cancellation of the entry.[2]

Art. 89bis [3]

G. Staff welfare foundations[4]

¹ The following additional provisions apply for staff welfare institutions which, in accordance with art. 331 of the Code of Obligations,[5] have been constituted in the form of a foundation.[4]

² The organs of the foundation are obliged to give the donees the required information on the

---

[1] *i.e.* where the object of the foundation has become illegal or immoral. No application to the court is necessary where the object has become impossible, for in that case the foundation comes to an end *ipso jure*.

[2] *i.e.* where the foundation has been entered in the commercial register, which is done *inter alia* where the instrument of foundation requires it.

[3] Inserted by cipher II of the Federal Statute of 21st March 1958, in force since 1st July 1958 (AS **1958** 379 381; BBl **1956 II** 825).

[4] Wording according to cipher II Art. 2 cipher 1 of the Federal Statute of 25th June 1971, in force since 1st January 1972 (SR **220** at the end, Final and Transitional Provisions relating to Title X).

[5] SR **220**.

organization itself, the activities and the financial standing of the foundation.

³ If the employees make contributions to the foundation, they are to be given the right to participate in the administration of the foundation at least in proportion to the size of their contributions; as far as possible the employees have to choose their representatives from the personnel of the employer.¹

⁴ The foundation capital may, as a rule, not consist of a claim to the employer to the extent of the amount paid in by the employees in accordance with the articles 331a and 331b of the Law of Obligations, except in cases where the claim is secured.

⁵ The donees can sue the foundation for payments, if they have made contributions to the foundation or if they have a right to demand payments in accordance with the provisions made in the Act of Foundation.

⁶ For staff welfare foundations whose objects are within the scope of the Old Age Pensioning Scheme, the provisional insurance schemes for members of the family in case of bereavement and for invalids the provisions of the Federal Statute of 25th June 1982 for the Professional Old Age, Widow and Orphans and Invalid Insurance apply: article 52 relating to liability, article 53 relating to control, the articles 61 and 62 relating to supervision as well as articles 73 and 74 relating to the administration of justice.²

---

¹ Wording according to cipher II Art. 2 cipher 1 of the Federal Statute of 25th June 1971, in force since 1st January 1972 (SR 220 at the end, Final and Transitional Provisions relating to Title X).
² Inserted by cipher 1 of the Appendix to the Federal Statute of 25th June 1982 relating to the Professional Old Age, Widow and Orphan and Invalid Insurance, in force since 1st January 1985 (SR 831.40, 831.401 Art. 1 Sect. 1).

Part II: Family Law

Section I: Husband and Wife

Title III: Marriage

Chapter I: Betrothal

Art. 90

A. Promise of marriage

¹ An agreement to marry constitutes betrothal.

² Minors and persons under a committee are not bound by a promise of marriage unless the promise was made with the consent of their guardian or committee.

Art. 91

B. Its effect
I. No right of action to enforce marriage

¹ Betrothal does not give rise to an action for specific performance of the agreement.

² Where a penalty has been fixed by the parties in case of breach, it cannot be recovered by action.

Art. 92

II. Consequences of breach
1. Damages

Where one of the parties without material ground breaks an agreement to marry, or where either party renounces it as the result of the fault of one of them, the party at fault is liable to pay damages to the other party or his parents, or third persons *in loco parentis* to him, to cover the *bona fide* expenses incurred in view of the marriage.

Art. 93

2. Moral compensation

¹ Where one of the parties is seriously injured in his person or reputation by the other's repudiation of his promise of marriage, and he, the plaintiff, was not himself at fault, while the defendant was at fault in repudiating, the court may award the plaintiff a sum of money as moral compensation.

… Marriage

² This claim for moral compensation cannot be assigned to another. But it passes at the plaintiff's death to his heirs, where at the date of the opening of the succession the claim was recognised or the action begun.[1]

Art. 94

¹ Both parties can in case of breach claim the return of their presents to each other.   III. Return of presents

² Where the presents no longer exist in their original form, the same rules apply as in the case of money had and received to the use of the plaintiff.[2]

³ Where the agreement to marry is terminated by the death of a party, the return of the presents cannot be claimed.

Art. 95

The period of limitation in the case of actions for breach of promise of marriage is one year from the date of the breach.   IV. Period of limitation

Chapter II: Disabilities and Impediments to Marriage

Art. 96

¹ A man must have completed his twentieth year and a woman her eighteenth before they can contract a marriage.   A. Disabilities I. Age

² In exceptional cases, however, where there are material grounds for it, the Government of the Can-

---

[1] The word "heirs" is used throughout to include personal representatives. For the meaning of "opening of the succession" see arts. 537 *et seq.* below.
[2] **Ungerechtfertigte Bereicherung,** *l'enrichissement illégitime,* has been translated "money had and received to the use of the plaintiff", as this seems to be the nearest equivalent in terms of English Law. A more literal translation would be "unjustified benefit" or "unjustified acquisition of money or possessions". For the rules here referred to see CO art. 62 *et seq.*

ton of the party's domicile can pronounce as capable of marriage a woman who has completed her seventeenth year or a man who has completed his eighteenth year, provided the parents or guardian give their consent.

Art. 97

II. Discretion

[1] Only those persons who have discretion can contract a marriage.

[2] Persons who are of unsound mind are absolutely incapable of marrying.[1]

Art. 98

III. Consent
1. For minors

[1] Minors can contract a marriage only with the consent of their father or mother or of their guardian.

[2] Where at the date of the publication of the betrothal the parental power is confined to one parent, that parent's consent is sufficient.

Art. 99

2. For persons under a committee

[1] Persons under a committee can contract a marriage only with the consent of their committee.

[2] Where this consent is refused, they can appeal to the guardianship authorities.

[3] They have a further right of appeal to the Federal Court.

---

[1] See art. 16 above for the meaning of the word "discretion". It is for the court to decide whether the parties to an agreement to marry have sufficient discretion to contract the intended marriage. They may be ordered to wait until one or the other is of maturer understanding or has ceased to be a drunkard, etc. The second paragraph absolutely prohibits marriage where one of the parties is insane or feeble-minded.

Art. 100[1]

[1] Marriage is prohibited: B. Impediments to marriage
I. Relationship

1.[2] between relations in the direct ascending or descending line, between brothers and sisters of the whole or half blood and between uncle and niece, nephew and aunt, whether the relationship results from descent or adoption.

2. between parents-in-law and sons-in-law and daughters-in-law and between foster-parents and step-children, even where the marriage that joins them has been annulled or dissolved by death or divorce.

[2] The Government of the Canton of the party's domicile can, where grave considerations justify it, permit relatives by adoption to contract marriage, except between relatives of direct ascending or descending line.

[3] Adoption does not remove the impediment to marriage resulting from relationship or relationship by marriage between the adopted child and this child's descendants on the one side and the family into which the child was born on the other side.

Art. 101

All persons who wish to contract a second marriage must prove that their previous marriage has been declared void or has been dissolved by death or divorce.   II. Previous marriage
1. Proof of dissolution
a. In general

Art. 102

[1] The husband or wife of a person who has been declared absent cannot contract a marriage until the court has annulled the former marriage.   b. In case of declaration of absence

---

[1] Wording according to cipher I 3 of the Federal Statute of 30th June 1972, in force since 1st April 1943 (AS 1972 2819 2829; BBl 1971 I 1200).

[2] Wording according to cipher I 2 of the Federal Statute of 25th June 1976, in force since 1st January 1978 (AS 1977 237 264; BBl 1974 II 1).

² The application for a declaration of nullity can be made either at the same time as that for the declaration of absence or separately.

³ The procedure is the same as for divorce.

Art. 103

2. Period of delay
a. For a woman

¹ Married women whose marriage has been dissolved either by the death of the husband or by a divorce or declaration of nullity cannot contract another marriage before the expiration of three hundred days from the date of the dissolution.

² This period of delay, however, terminates with the birth of a child.

³ The period can further be reduced by the court, where the possibility of the birth of a child from the former marriage is excluded or where the divorced couple re-marry each other.

Art. 104

b. For divorced persons

¹ Divorced persons cannot contract another marriage before the expiration of the statutory period.

² This period can be reduced by the court, where the divorced couple re-marry each other.

Chapter III: Publication and Solemnization of Marriage

Art. 105

A. Publication
I. Form of notice

¹ The first requirement for the publication of the intended marriage is that the parties must give notice of the betrothal to the registrar of civil status.

² This notice must be given either in person or by a writing signed and officially attested.[1]

---

[1] *i.e.* authenticated according to the requirements of Cantonal Law.

³ The application for publication must be accompanied by the birth certificates of the parties, and, where circumstances require it, the written consent of their parents or guardian as also the death certificate of the former spouse or the judgment of the court pronouncing the nullity of the former marriage or the divorce of the parties to it.

Art. 106

¹ The notice of the betrothal must be given to the registrar of civil status at the place of the bridegroom's domicile. *II. Where application and publication to be made*

² Where, however, the bridegroom is a Swiss subject domiciled abroad, the notice must be given to the registrar of civil status of his legal home.

³ The publication must be made at the registries of civil status of the domicile and the legal home of both parties.

Art. 107

The publication of the intended marriage will be refused where the notice is irregular or where there is some disability in either party or some legal impediment to the marriage. *III. Publication refused*

Art. 108

¹ All interested persons may, within the statutory period of delay, oppose the marriage by alleging a disability in either party or the existence of some legal impediment to the marriage. *B. Opposition I. Right of opposition*

² The opposition must be made in writing to one of the registrars who have published the intended marriage.

³ Where the opposition is not based on an alleged incapacity or impediment, it must be rejected by the registrar without further inquiry.

Art. 109

II. Official opposition

Where there appears to be a ground for the nullity of the intended marriage, the competent authority must oppose it officially.

Art. 110

III. Procedure
1. Opposition notified

¹ Where the marriage has been opposed, the registrar to whom notice of the betrothal has been given must inform the parties to it of the opposition raised as soon as the statutory period of delay has expired.

² Where either party to the betrothal wishes to contest the opposition, the person opposing must be notified immediately.

Art. 111

2. Decision

If the person opposing the marriage intends to maintain his allegations, he must apply to the court of the place where the betrothal has been notified so that the solemnization of the marriage may be prohibited.

Art. 112

3. Periods of delay

¹ The period within which the marriage must be opposed, that within which the opposition must be contested and that within which the application for the prohibition of the marriage must be brought is in each case ten days.

² The period runs in the first case from the day of publication; in the second case from the day on which the betrothed parties were officially informed of the opposition; and in the third case from the day on which the person opposing was notified that his opposition was contested.

Art. 113

¹ Where there is no opposition to the marriage or where the opposition raised has not been brought before the court or has been rejected by the court, the registrar of civil status to whom notice of the betrothal has been given must, on the demand of the parties, proceed to solemnize the marriage or give them a certificate of publication.

² The certificate of publication authorises the betrothed parties to marry within six months before any Swiss registrar of civil status.

C. Solemnization of marriage
I. Conditions
1. Competent official

Art. 114

¹ A registrar of civil status must refuse to solemnize the marriage where he discovers a fact which would be a ground for refusing the publication of an intended marriage.

² The publication lapses at the expiration of six months.

2. Solemnization refused

Art. 115

Where, owing to illness of one of the betrothed parties, there is a danger that the marriage could not be solemnized, if the statutory periods of delay were observed, the supervisory authority may allow the registrar to reduce the periods, or even to proceed to solemnize the marriage without having first published the intended marriage.

3. Solemnization without publication

Art. 116

¹ Marriages are solemnized publicly in the marriage room of the registry before two witnesses of full age.

² A marriage can only be solemnized elsewhere on a medical certificate that one of the parties is, owing to illness, unable to attend at the registry.

II. Formalities
1. Publicity

Art. 117

2. Form of solemnization

¹ The registrar of civil status asks both the parties to the marriage whether they desire to be joined in matrimony.

² On their reply in the affirmative, he declares them legally married by virtue of their mutual consent.

Art. 118

III. Marriage certificate and religious ceremony

¹ Immediately after the solemnization the registrar gives the parties a marriage certificate.

² The religious ceremony can take place only upon presentation of this certificate.

³ The provisions of this Code do not otherwise affect the religious ceremony of marriage.

Art. 119

D. Regulations

All other necessary regulations regarding the publication and the solemnization of marriages and the keeping of the registers shall be drawn up by the Federal Council and, within the limits of their competence, by the Cantonal authorities.

Chapter IV: Void and Voidable Marriages

Art. 120

A. Void marriages
I. Grounds for nullity

A marriage is null and void:

1. where at the date of the marriage one of the parties is already married;

2. where at the date of the marriage one of the parties is insane or, from some permanent cause, without discretion;

3.¹ where the parties are within the prohibited degrees of relationship or relationship by marriage;

---

¹ Wording according to cipher I 3 of the Federal Statute of 30th June 1972, in force since 1st April 1973 (AS 1972 2819 2829; BBl 1971 I 1200).

4.[1] where the wife does not intend to found a conjugal community, but tries to circumvent the provisions made for acquiring Swiss citizenship.

Art. 121[2]

[1] The suit for a declaration of the nullity of the marriage shall be instituted officially by the competent authority. II. Obligation and right of suit

[2] In addition it can be instituted by any interested party, in particular by the authorities of a person's legal home or domicile.

Art. 122

[1] Where the marriage has been dissolved, the suit for a declaration of nullity is no longer instituted officially in the cases of article 120 ciphers 1–3, but any interested party may demand the declaration of nullity.[3] III. Restrictions and exceptions

[2] Where one of the spouses was insane or without discretion and has recovered his sanity or discretion, a declaration of nullity can no longer be demanded by any person but the husband or wife.

[3] Where in the case of a marriage with a person already married the other party acted *bona fide* and the former marriage has since been dissolved, there is no ground for a declaration of nullity.

Art. 123

A marriage can be avoided by one of the parties to it, where the party concerned was at the date of the marriage temporarily without discretion. B. Voidable marriages
I. At instance of a spouse
1. Absence of discretion

---

[1] Added by art. 56 paragraph 1 of the Federal Statute of 29th September 1952 relating to the Acquisition and the Loss of Swiss Citizenship, in force since 1st January 1953 (SR **141.0**).
[2] Wording according to art. 56 paragraph 2 of the Federal Statute of 29th September 1952 relating to the Acquisition and the Loss of Swiss Citizenship, in force since 1st January 1953 (SR **141.0**).
[3] Wording according to art. 56 paragraph 3 of the Federal Statute of 29th September 1952 relating to the Acquisition and the Loss of Swiss Citizenship, in force since 1st January 1953 (SR **141.0**).

Art. 124

2. Mistake

A marriage can be avoided by one of the parties to it:

1. where a party entered upon the marriage ceremony through a mistake, in that either he or she did not in reality intend to contract a marriage at all or to marry that person;

2. where a party was induced to contract the marriage by a mistaken impression that the other party possessed certain qualities so indispensable that their absence makes life in common intolerable.

Art. 125

3. Fraud

A marriage can be avoided by one of the parties to it:

1. where a party has been wilfully deceived by the other party or by a third person with the connivance of that party as to the latter's moral integrity and has thereby been induced to contract the marriage;

2. where a disease has been concealed from a party which gravely endangers his or her own health or that of their issue.

Art. 126

4. Duress

A marriage can be avoided by one of the parties to it where a party was induced to contract it only by threats of a grave and imminent danger to his or her own life or health or honour or that of one closely related to that party.

Art. 127

5. Limitation of actions

Actions to avoid the marriage must be brought within six months from the date of the plaintiff's discovery of the existence of a ground for avoidance or from the withdrawal of the threats, and in any case at the latest within five years from the date of the marriage.

Art. 128

¹ Where a marriage has been contracted by a person who is not of marriageable age or is a minor or placed under a committee, and the consent of his or her parents or guardian or committee has not been obtained, these latter can avoid the marriage.

² The marriage can, however, no longer be declared null and void, when the said person has in the meantime reached a marriageable age or attained majority or full capacity, or, if a woman, she has become pregnant.

II. At the instance of parent or guardian

Art. 129[1]

C. Cases where marriage not void
I. Adoptive relationship

Art. 130

Where a marriage has been contracted before the expiration of the period required for a second marriage by statute or by the court, it cannot on this account be declared null and void.

II. Non-observance of period of delay

Art. 131

Where a marriage has been solemnized before the registrar, it cannot be declared null and void merely in consequence of the non-observance of the prescribed formalities.[2]

III. Non-observance of formalities

Art. 132

¹ A marriage does not become legally null and void until it is so declared by the court.

² Until this declaration it has all the effects of a valid marriage even though there is good ground for its nullity.

D. Declaration of nullity
I. Purport

---

[1] Annulled by cipher I 3 of the Federal Statute of 30th June 1972 (AS 1972 2819; BBl 1971 I 1200).

[2] *e.g.* where the notice of betrothal is not in the regular form.

Art. 133

II. Effect
1. On the issue

¹ Where a marriage is declared null and void, the husband is all the same the legal father of the children even where neither he nor the mother acted *bona fide*.¹

² The relative position of the parents and children is governed by the same rules as in the case of divorce.

Art. 134²

2. For the spouses

¹ Where a marriage is declared null and void, the wife who married in good faith retains the citizenship which she acquired by the marriage.

² The spouse who changed his or her surname retains the surname acquired by the marriage, unless this spouse declares before the civil status registrar within six months after the decree became valid that he or she chooses to resume the original surname or the surname he or she bore before the marriage.

³ The division of the matrimonial property system as well as the claims of the spouses for damages, maintenance or moral compensation are governed by the same rules as in the case of divorce.

Art. 135

E. Transmissibility

¹ The right of any person to demand a declaration of nullity is not transmissible to his heirs.

² A plaintiff's heirs can, however, continue an action that has been begun.

Art. 136

F. Competence and procedure

The competence and the procedure in the case of a declaration of nullity are governed by the same rules as in the case of divorce.

---

[1] Wording according to cipher I 2 of the Federal Statute of 25th June 1976, in force since 1st January 1978 (AS 1977 237 264; BBl 1974 II 1).

[2] Wording according to cipher I 2 of the Federal Statute of 5th October 1984, in force since 1st January 1988 (BBl 1979 II 1191).

Title IV: Divorce

Art. 137

A. Grounds of divorce
I. Adultery

¹ Where either the husband or the wife has committed adultery, the other can sue for a divorce.

² This suit must be brought within six months from the time when the injured party has had cognizance of the ground of divorce, and in any case within five years from the date of the adultery.

³ The right of action is lost where the injured party consented to the adultery or has since condoned it.

Art. 138

II. Attempt on life of spouse, ill-usage, affronts

¹ Where either the husband or the wife has made an attempt on the life of the other or seriously ill-used or gravely affronted the other, the latter can sue for a divorce.

² This suit must be brought within six months from the time when the injured party has had cognizance of the ground of divorce, and in any case within five years from the date of the injury or affront.

³ The right of action is lost where the injured party has condoned the offence.

Art. 139

III. Crime and infamous conduct

Where either the husband or the wife has committed an infamous crime or been guilty of such dishonourable conduct that life in common has become intolerable, the other spouse can sue for a divorce.[1]

Art. 140

IV. Desertion

¹ Where either the husband or the wife has wrongfully deserted the other or without material

---

[1] By an infamous crime is meant one which is regarded as socially degrading to the perpetrator and his family. Thus some political crimes might be excluded.

ground refuses to return to the conjugal home, the injured party can sue for a divorce, provided this desertion or absence has continued for at least two years and still continues.

² At the instance of the injured party the court must, if necessary by a public citation, call upon the absent spouse to return to the conjugal home within six months.

³ The suit for divorce cannot be brought before the expiration of this period.

Art. 141

V. Insanity

Either the husband or the wife can at any time sue for a divorce on the ground of the insanity of the other, where the latter's mental condition makes life in common intolerable and is after three years' duration held by experts to be incurable.

Art. 142

VI. Domestic disturbances

¹ Either the husband or the wife can sue for a divorce, where the conjugal relations are so seriously strained that life in common has become intolerable.

² Where the domestic disturbances are principally the fault of one of the parties, the suit can only be instituted by the other.

Art. 143

B. Suit
I. Purpose

The suit is brought either for divorce or for judicial separation.

Art. 144

II. Competence

The proper court is the court of the plaintiff's domicile.

Art. 145[1]

III. Precautionary measures

[1] As soon as the suit has been filed each spouse can refrain from life in common for the time of the proceedings.

[2] The judge takes the necessary precautionary measures, in particular those relating to the lodging and the maintenance of the family, the management of the matrimonial property and the custody of the children.

Art. 146

C. Judgement
I. Divorce or judicial separation

[1] Where a ground for divorce has been proved, the judge must grant either a divorce or judicial separation.

[2] Where only judicial separation is asked for, he cannot grant a divorce.

[3] Where the suit is for a divorce, he can grant judicial separation only if a reconciliation between the husband and wife seems probable.

Art. 147

II. Duration of separation

[1] Judicial separation is granted for a period of one to three years or for an indefinite time.

[2] Where the separation is granted for a definite period, it lapses at the expiration thereof; and either the husband or the wife can demand a divorce if no reconciliation has taken place.

[3] Where the separation is granted for an indefinite time, the husband or the wife can, if the separation has continued for three years, demand either a divorce or the rescission of the decree of separation.[2]

---

[1] Wording according to cipher I 2 of the Federal Statute of 5th October 1984, in force since 1st January 1988 (BBl 1979 II 1191).

[2] lit. "a divorce or the cessation of separation". Thus the Code does not contemplate the indefinite duration of separation as distinct from the absolute dissolution of the marriage by divorce. After the expiration of three years the parties must either be divorced or must resume cohabitation where either the husband or the wife does not wish to continue under the decree of separation.

Art. 148

III. Decree at termination of separation

¹ At the expiration of the period fixed in the decree of separation, or of three years where the decree was for an indefinite time, a divorce must be granted even where it is demanded by only one of the spouses, unless indeed the facts on which the application for the divorce is grounded are exclusively chargeable to the petitioner.

² And even where this is the case the divorce shall be granted, if the respondent refuses to return to the conjugal home.

³ The judgment in this suit shall take into consideration not only the facts proved in the former suit but also any that may have taken place since.

Art. 149[1]

IV. Status of the divorced wife

¹ The divorced wife retains the citizenship which she acquired by the marriage.

² The spouse who changed his or her surname retains the surname acquired by the marriage, unless he or she declares before the civil status registrar within six months after the decree became valid that he or she chooses to resume the original surname or the surname he or she bore before the marriage.

Art. 150

V. Period of delay

¹ The decree of divorce shall contain a clause fixing a period of not less than one year and not more than two within which the guilty party may not contract a second marriage; where the ground of divorce was adultery, the period can be extended to three years.

² The period of a preceding judicial separation is reckoned as part of the delay imposed by this section.

---

[1] Wording according to cipher I 2 of the Federal Statute of 5th October 1984, in force since 1st January 1988 (BBl **1979 II** 1191).

Art. 151

VI. Payments on divorce
1. Damages and moral compensation

[1] Where a divorce prejudices the innocent spouse in his pecuniary rights or expectations, the guilty party must duly indemnify him.[1]

[2] Where the circumstances that led to the divorce have seriously prejudiced the innocent spouse in his person or reputation, the court may award him a sum of money as moral compensation.

Art. 152

2. Maintenance

Where an innocent spouse is reduced by the divorce to a state of destitution, the court may require the other spouse, even if the latter is innocent also, to contribute according to his means to the maintenance of the destitute party.

Art. 153

3. Annuity

[1] Where an annuity has been decreed by the court or agreed upon between the parties by way of indemnity, moral compensation or a maintenance grant, the right to this annuity is forfeited by the remarriage of the party entitled to it.

[2] The party charged with an annuity by way of maintenance can demand its permanent suspension or reduction in amount, where the party entitled is no longer destitute or is in materially improved circumstances; and similarly where the annuity has ceased to be commensurate with the means of the party charged.

Art. 154[2]

VII. Division of matrimonial property system
1. In case of divorce

[1] The division of the matrimonial property is governed by the special provisions made for the matrimonial property system.

---

[1] Thus a divorced husband or wife loses the right of inheritance on the death of the other under art. 462.

[2] Wording according to cipher I 2 of the Federal Statute of 5th October 1984, in force since 1st January 1988 (BBl 1979 II 1191).

² A divorced spouse has no statutory right of inheritance towards the other spouse and cannot claim any benefits from testamentary dispositions which the spouses made before the divorce.

Art. 155[1]

2. In case of separation

Where the parties are judically separated the system of separate estates is to be applied by operation of the law.

Art. 156

VIII. Rights of parents
1. Judicial discretion

¹ In divorce or judicial separation the judge must, after having heard the parents and, if necessary, the guardianship board, make the necessary orders with reference to the exercise of parental power and the personal relations of the parents and children.

² The personal relations of a parent with the children who have been removed from his or her custody and the contribution the parent is to make towards the expenses of their maintenance is governed by the provisions made for the relation of children to their parents.[2]

³ ...[3]

Art. 157

2. Change of circumstances

Where circumstances are changed through the marriage, departure or death of either parent or from any other cause, the court must, at the instance of the guardianship board or of the father or mother, make orders to meet the case.

---

[1] Wording according to cipher I 2 of the Federal Statute of 5th October 1984, in force since 1st January 1988 (BBl 1979 II 1191).
[2] Wording according to cipher I 2 of the Federal Statute of 25th June 1976, in force since 1st January 1978 (AS 1977 237 264; BBl 1974 II 1).
[3] Annulled by cipher I 2 of the Federal Statute of 25th June 1976 (AS 1977 237; BBl 1974 II 1).

Art. 158

The procedure in divorce is governed by Cantonal Law subject to the following provisions: D. Procedure

1. the judge must not take as proved any essential fact on which the claim for divorce or judicial separation is based without being himself convinced that the fact took place as asserted;

2. no oath or affirmation in the place of an oath can be administered to either husband or wife in regard to such essential fact;

3. no statement of any kind made by husband or wife is binding on the judge;

4. the acceptance or rejection of evidence is in the discretion of the judge;

5. agreements relating to the subsidiary effects of the divorce or judicial separation require for their validity to be confirmed by the judge.

Title V: The Effects of Marriage in General[1]

Art. 159[2]

[1] The solemnization of a marriage creates a conjugal union between the parties. A. Conjugal union; rights and duties of the spouses

[2] They thereby mutually bind themselves to co-operate with each other in safeguarding the interests of the union and in caring and providing for the children.

[3] They owe each other fidelity and assistance.

Art. 160[2]

[1] The husband's name is the surname of the husband and the wife. B. The family name

---

[1] For the provisions made for The Effects of Marriage in General existing before 1st January 1988 and still valid after this date for couples who choose to be governed by the Old Law or who have concluded a marriage covenant see Appendix I.

[2] Wording according to cipher I 1 of the Federal Statute of 5th October 1984, in force since 1st January 1988 (BBl **1979 II** 1191).

² The bride is entitled to declare in the presence of the registrar that she wants her former name to be placed in front of the husband's surname.

³ Where the bride has such a double name already, she can place only the first of the two names in front of the husband's surname.

Art. 161¹

C. Citizenship

¹ The wife acquires the husband's citizenship without losing the citizenship she had before the marriage.

Art. 162¹

D. The conjugal home

The spouses determine the conjugal home jointly.

Art. 163¹

E. The maintenance of the family
I. In general

¹ The spouses, each according to his or her capacity, care jointly for the proper maintenance of the family.

² They agree on how much each of them contributes to the maintenance, in particular through payments, keeping the household, looking after the children or through assisting the other spouse in his or her work, profession or trade.

³ In doing so they consider the requirements of the conjugal union and their personal circumstances.

Art. 164¹

II. Amount for free disposal

¹ The spouse who has the management of the household, looks after the children or assists the other spouse in the execution of his or her profession or trade, is entitled to regularly receive from the other spouse a fair amount for her or his free disposal.

---

[1] Wording according to cipher I 1 of the Federal Statute of 5th October 1984, in force since 1st January 1988 (BBl 1979 II 1191).

² In fixing the amount there are to be considered the personal income of that spouse who is entitled to receive this amount and his or her duty to make provisions with adequate care about the future of the family, profession or trade.

Art. 165[1]

¹ Where a spouse has contributed to the execution of the profession or trade of the other spouse considerably more than is required of him or her for the maintenance of the family, this spouse is entitled to receive fair compensation.   III. Extraordinary contribution of a spouse

² This is also the case where a spouse has contributed to the maintenance of the family from his personal income or fortune considerably more than he or she was obliged to do.

³ However, a spouse cannot claim a compensation where he or she has made an extraordinary contribution on account of an employment contract, a loan contract, any kind of contract of partnership or any other legal relationship.

Art. 166[1]

¹ Each spouse represents the conjugal union in matters of the current requirements of the family during their life in common.   F. Representation of the conjugal union

² For the other requirements of the family one spouse can only represent the conjugal union:

1. if he or she is authorized by the other spouse or by the judge;

2. if the interest of the conjugal union does not allow a delay of action and the other spouse is unable to consent on account of illness, absence or similar reasons.

---

[1] Wording according to cipher I 1 of the Federal Statute of 5th October 1984, in force since 1st January 1988 (BBl 1979 II 1191).

³ Each spouse is personally liable for his or her own acts and, where they do not exceed a spouse's authority of representation in a way which is perceptible for third parties, such acts are also binding for the other spouse, jointly and severally.

Art. 167[1]

G. Profession and trade of the spouses

In choosing or executing a profession or trade each of the spouses is obliged to take into account the other spouse and the welfare of the conjugal union.

Art. 168[1]

H. Legal transactions of the spouses
I. In general

Each spouse can enter into any legal transaction with the other spouse or with a third party provided the law makes no exception.

Art. 169[1]

II. Apartment of the spouses

¹ A spouse can only with the express consent of the other spouse terminate a lease, sell the house or the apartment of the family or restrict through other legal transactions the family's right of use of the abode.

² Where a spouse cannot secure the other spouse's agreement or where it is refused without serious cause, he or she can appeal to the judge.

Art. 170[1]

J. Obligation to give information

¹ Each spouse can request information as regards income, fortune and debts from the other spouse.

² On a spouse's request the judge can oblige the other spouse or a third party to give the information required and to produce the necessary documents.

---

[1] Wording according to cipher I 1 of the Federal Statute of 5th October 1984, in force since 1st January 1988 (BBl 1979 II 1191).

³ Provisions are made for the professional secrecy of attorneys, notaries, medical doctors, ministers of the church and their staffs.

Art. 171[1]

The Cantons make provisions for the existence of marriage or family guidance councils to which the spouses can apply jointly or singly in cases of matrimonial difficulties.

K. Protection of the conjugal union
I. Councils to give advice

Art. 172[1]

¹ Where one of the spouses neglects his or her duties to the family or where the spouses disagree in a matter which is important for the conjugal union, they can apply to the judge jointly or singly and ask him to mediate.

² The judge will seek to admonish the spouses to fulfil their duties and try to reconcile them; he can, with their consent, call in experts or order them to see one of the marriage or family guidance councils.

³ Where it is required the judge will, on request of one of the spouses, take the measures provided by the law.

II. Measures ordered by the judge
1. In general

Art. 173[1]

¹ At the instance of one of the spouses the judge determines the amounts to be paid for the maintenance of the family.

² He also determines, at the instance of one of the spouses, the amount to be paid to that spouse who has the management of the household affairs, looks after the children or helps the other spouse in his or her profession or trade.

³ The payments can be claimed for the future and for the year preceding the filing of an application.

2. During the existence of the conjugal union
a. Payments

---

[1] Wording according to cipher I 1 of the Federal Statute of 5th October 1984, in force since 1st January 1988 (BBl 1979 II 1191).

Art. 174[1]

b. Revocation of the right of representation

[1] Where a spouse abuses his or her right to represent the conjugal union or shows himself or herself incapable of exercising it, the judge can, at the instance of the other spouse, revoke the right of representation totally or restrict it within certain limits.

[2] The spouse who files the request may inform third parties only by personal communications.

[3] Such a revocation has no effect on third parties in good faith unless it has been published on the order of the judge.

Art. 175[1]

3. Discontinuation of the conjugal home
a. Causes

A spouse is entitled to discontinue the maintenance of the common home for so long as his or her personality, economic security or the welfare of the family is seriously imperilled by a continuance of life in common.

Art. 176[1]

b. Regulation for a separate life

[1] Where there are serious grounds for the suspension of a common home, the judge must, at the instance of one of the spouses:

1. determine the amounts which one spouse owes to the other;
2. issue rules for the use of the home and the household equipment;
3. give orders for a system of separate estates where the circumstances justify it.

[2] A spouse can also request to live a separate life if life in common has become impossible, particularly because the other spouse refuses to continue life in common without giving reasons.

---

[1] Wording according to cipher I 1 of the Federal Statute of 5th October 1984, in force since 1st January 1988 (BBl 1979 II 1191).

³ Where the spouses have children who are minors, the judge will take the necessary measures in accordance with the provisions made for the effects of the child-relationship.

Art. 177[1]

Where one of the spouses neglects his or her duties to the family, the court can order his or her debtors to make all or part of the payments to the other spouse.

4. Orders to debtors

Art. 178[1]

¹ Where the protection of the material basis of the family or the discharge of a pecuniary obligation stemming from the conjugal union make it necessary, the judge can, at the instance of one of the spouses, make the disposal of certain assets dependent on this spouse's consent.

5. Restriction of right of disposal

² The judge will take adequate protective measures.

³ Where the judge refuses permission to one of the spouses to dispose of a landed property, he will have this refusal notified in the land register *ex officio*.

Art. 179[1]

¹ Where the circumstances change the judge will, at the instance of one of the spouses, adapt the measures taken by the court to the new situation or discontinue them as soon as their grounds have ceased to exist.

6. Change of circumstances

² Where the spouses decide to continue their life in common, all measures taken for a separate life will be discontinued with the exception of those taken for a system of separate estates.

---

[1] Wording according to cipher I 1 of the Federal Statute of 5th October 1984, in force since 1st January 1988 (BBl 1979 II 1191).

Art. 180[1]

7. Competence

[1] The judge at the domicile of one of the spouses is competent for measures for the protection of the conjugal union.

[2] Where the spouses have different domiciles and where both desire protective measures, the judge who is first appealed to is competent.

[3] The judge at the local venue where the measures were originally taken is competent for changes, completion or the discontinuance of these measures or, if neither of the spouses has his or her domicile at that place any longer, the judge at the new domicile of one of the spouses is competent.

Title VI: Matrimonial Property Law

Chapter I: General Provisions

Art. 181[1]

A. Ordinary system

Parties on marriage are placed under the system of participation in acquisitions, unless they have themselves provided otherwise by a marriage covenant, or the provisions for the exceptional system are held to apply.[2]

[1] Wording according to cipher I 1 of the Federal Statute of 5th October 1984, in force since 1st January 1988 (BBl 1979 II 1191).
[2] The Code provides three systems for holding matrimonial property:
  a. The regular system which operates unless otherwise provided by the parties or by law is the "participation in acquisitions" (see arts. 181, 196–220). This system replaces the former "marital system", *union des biens,* see Appendix I. This matrimonial property system is based on the equality of rights and duties of both spouses. Each spouse has his or her own property (see art. 198) which are also administered by each spouse. At the division of the matrimonial property system each spouse keeps his or her own property and is entitled to one half of the other spouse's acquisitions (see art. 215).
  b. The system of "community of property" (see arts. 215–246), by which both spouses' property, with the exception of each spouse's own property, belong to the two parties in common. This matrimonial property system is always adopted by a mar-

… Matrimonial Property Law

Art. 182[1]

B. Marriage covenant
I. Choice of system

[1] The parties can make an ante-nuptial or a post-nuptial marriage covenant.

[2] The betrothed or the spouses can choose, rescind or modify their matrimonial property system only within the legal limits.

Art. 183[1]

II. Capacity of parties

[1] Only those persons who have discretion can make a marriage covenant.

[2] Minors or persons placed under committee need the consent of their guardian or committee.

Art. 184[1]

III. Form required

A marriage covenant is valid only where it is made by a duly authenticated instrument signed by the parties and, if necessary, by their guardian or committee.

    riage covenant. The common property belongs to both spouses undividedly and profits are shared at the division of the matrimonial property system.
  c. The system of "separate estates" (see arts. 185, 247–251), called the exceptional system, by which each spouse retains his or her own property and its management. This applies in certain cases determined by the Code in arts. 185 *et seq.* or where the parties have so provided in the covenant.

The parties can vary the first two systems in certain particulars or adopt the third system by making a covenant.

For greater clearness the following glossary is appended:

Eheliches Vermögen, *biens matrimoniaux,* matrimonial property.
Güterrecht or **Güterstand,** *régime matrimonial,* matrimonial property system.
- **Errungenschaftsbeteiligung,** *participation aux acquêts,* participation in acquisitions
- **Errungenschaft,** *les acquêts,* acquisitions
- **Eigengut,** *les biens propres de chaque époux,* a spouse's own property
- **Gütergemeinschaft,** *communauté des biens,* system of community of property
- **Gesamtgut,** *les biens communs,* common property
- **Gütertrennung,** *séparation de biens,* system of separate estates
- **Ehevertrag,** *contrat de mariage,* marriage covenant
- **Güterverbindung,** *union des biens,* marital system (Old Law).

[1] Wording according to cipher I 1 of the Federal Statute of 5th October 1984, in force since 1st January 1988 (BBl **1979 II** 1191).

Art. 185[1]

C. Exceptional system
I. At instance of a spouse
1. By order of court

[1] Where a material ground exists, the court shall make an order for the separation of estates at the instance of a spouse.

[2] In particular a material ground exists:

1. where the other spouse is excessively indebted or the other spouse's share of the property held in common is distressed;
2. where the other spouse endangers the interests of the petitioner or of the conjugal union;
3. where the other spouse, without material grounds, refuses to give his or her consent which is required for a disposal of the property held in common;
4. where the other spouse refuses to give the petitioner information regarding his or her income, assets and liabilities or the property held in common without having material grounds for his or her refusal;
5. where the other spouse is permanently devoid of discretion.

[3] Where a spouse is permanently devoid of discretion, his or her guardian or committee can, also for this reason, request the separation of estates.

Art. 186[1]

2. Competence

The proper court is the court at the domicile of one of the spouses.

Art. 187[1]

3. Rescission

[1] By way of marriage covenant the spouses may at any time, agree upon their previous or a different matrimonial property system.

[2] Where the ground for the separation of estates has been removed, the court can, at the instance of a spouse, order the resumption of the previous matrimonial property system.

---

[1] Wording according to cipher I 1 of the Federal Statute of 5th October 1984, in force since 1st January 1988 (BBl 1979 II 1191).

Art. 188[1]

Where a spouse living under the system of community of property goes bankrupt, the matrimonial property will, by operation of the law, fall under the system of separate estates.

II. On bankruptcy and execution on property
1. On bankruptcy

Art. 189[1]

Where a spouse living under the system of community of property suffers enforced payment of debts regarding his or her own property and execution on his or her share of the property held in common, the supervising authority for the enforcement of payments can demand that the court makes an order for the separation of estates.

2. On execution
a. Order

Art. 190[1]

[1] The petition is directed against both spouses.

[2] The proper court is the court at the debtor's domicile.

b. Competence

Art. 191[1]

[1] Where the creditors are paid in full, the court at the instance of a spouse shall order the resumption of the system of community of property.

[2] By way of marriage covenant the spouses may place their matrimonial property under the system of participation in acquisitions.

3. Removal

Art. 192[1]

Where the separation of estates takes place, the division of matrimonial property is governed by the provisions of the previous matrimonial property system, unless provided otherwise by the law.

III. Division of matrimonial property

---

[1] Wording according to cipher I 1 of the Federal Statute of 5th October 1984, in force since 1st January 1988 (BBl 1979 II 1191).

Art. 193[1]

D. Protection of creditors

[1] Neither the establishment nor the modification of a matrimonial property system nor the division of matrimonial property shall place beyond the reach of the creditors of a spouse or of the conjugal union any property against which they had a right to proceed for the settlement of their debts.

[2] Where any such property has passed to a spouse, he or she becomes personally liable to pay the said creditors, but can be freed from such liability by proving that the property received is of insufficient value to meet their claims.

Art. 194[1]

E. Competence for suits for division of matrimonial property

The proper court for suits for the division of matrimonial property among the spouses or their heirs is:

1. where the ground for the division of matrimonial property is death the court at the deceased's last domicile;

2. in the case of divorce, separation, declaration of nullity of a marriage or of a court order by which the system of separate estates is introduced between the spouses, the court with the respective jurisdiction;

3. in all other cases at the defendant spouse's domicile.

Art. 195[1]

F. Administration of a spouse's property by the other spouse

[1] Where a spouse has explicitly or implicitly let the other spouse administer his or her property, the provisions regarding the mandate apply unless the spouses have made a different arrangement.

[2] Provisions are made for the redemption of debts between the spouses.

---

[1] Wording according to cipher I 1 of the Federal Statute of 5th October 1984, in force since 1st January 1988 (BBl 1979 II 1191).

Art. 195a[1]

[1] Each spouse can at any time request the other spouse to participate in compiling an inventory of their common property, which is to be duly authenticated.   G. Inventory

[2] Such an inventory is deemed correct if it was compiled within one year after the acquisition of the property.

Chapter II: The Ordinary Matrimonial Property System of Participation in Acquisitions

Art. 196[2]

The matrimonial property system of participation in acquisitions consists of the acquisitions and of each spouse's own property.   A. Ownership
I. Composition

Art. 197[2]

[1] A spouse's acquisitions is that property which a spouse acquires as income during the matrimonial property system.   II. The acquisitions

[2] The acquisitions of a spouse comprise in particular:

1. his or her income from work;

2. payments made by staff welfare institutions, social insurances and social welfare institutions;

3. indemnities for incapacity to work;

4. the revenues from his or her own property;

5. replacements of items which have been part of the acquisitions.

---

[1] Inserted by cipher I 1 of the Federal Statute of 5th October 1984, in force since 1st January 1988 (BBl **1979 II** 1191).

[2] Wording according to cipher I 1 of the Federal Statute of 5th October 1984, in force since 1st January 1988 (BBl **1979 II** 1191).

Art. 198[1]

III. A spouse's own property
1. By operation of the law

The following property is, by operation of the law, each spouse's own property:

1. articles which are intended for the exclusive personal use of a married person;
2. property which belongs to a spouse at the beginning of a matrimonial property system or which comes to the spouse during marriage by succession or other gratuitous title;
3. claims for payment of a sum of money by way of moral compensation;
4. replacements of items which have been part of a spouse's own property.

Art. 199[1]

2. By a marriage covenant

[1] The spouses can provide by a marriage covenant that such property of the acquisitions is declared as a spouse's own property which is required for the execution of a profession or the running of a business.

[2] In addition the spouses can stipulate in a marriage covenant that revenues from a spouse's own property do not belong to the acquisitions.

Art. 200[1]

IV. Evidence

[1] The spouse who asserts that a certain property is his or her property must provide evidence for this assertion.

[2] Where this evidence cannot be provided it is assumed that the property is owned by both spouses jointly.

[3] All property of a spouse is deemed as acquisitions before the contrary can be proved.

---

[1] Wording according to cipher I 1 of the Federal Statute of 5th October 1984, in force since 1st January 1988 (BBl 1979 II 1191).

Art. 201[1]

B. Administration, use and disposal

[1] Within the legal limits each spouse administers and uses his or her own acquisitions and his or her own property and disposes of them in his or her right.

[2] Where a property is co-owned by both spouses, neither of the spouses can dispose of his or her share without the other spouse's consent, unless a different arrangement has been agreed upon.

Art. 202[1]

C. Liability towards third parties

Each spouse is liable for his or her debts with his or her whole property.

Art. 203[1]

D. Debts between the spouses

[1] The matrimonial property system is of no influence for the maturity of debts between the spouses.

[2] However, where the reimbursement of debts or the restitution of things owed presents to the spouse who is liable a serious problem which endangers the conjugal union, he or she can demand to be granted a period of time; where justified by the circumstances, the claim is to be secured.

Art. 204[1]

E. Dissolution of system and division
I. Date of determination

[1] The matrimonial property system is dissolved on the death of a spouse or by an agreement upon a different matrimonial property system.

[2] In the case of divorce, judicial separation, declaration of nullity of a marriage or of a court order by which the system of separate estates is introduced between the spouses, the dissolution of the matrimonial property system is dated back to the day on which the petition was filed.

---

[1] Wording according to cipher I 1 of the Federal Statute of 5th October 1984, in force since 1st January 1988 (BBl 1979 II 1191).

Art. 205[1]

II. Taking back of property and settlement of debts
1. In general

[1] Each spouse takes back his or her property which is in the possession of the other spouse.

[2] Where there is co-ownership of property and a spouse provides evidence of a preponderant interest in this property, he or she can, beside the legal measures, demand that this property is undividedly allotted to him or her against compensation.

[3] The spouses settle their mutual debts.

Art. 206[1]

2. The spouse's share of the increased value

[1] Where one of the spouses has contributed to the acquisition, improvement or maintenance of property belonging to the other spouse without adequate consideration and where at the date of the division an increased value exists, his or her claim is proportionate to his or her contribution and it is calculated on the basis of the present value of the property; however, where at the date of the division the property has decreased in value, the spouse's claim is proportionate to the original contribution.

[2] Where such property has been sold previously, the claim is calculated according to the proceeds which were realized and becomes due immediately.

[3] The spouses can exclude or change the share of the increased value by an arrangement made in writing.

Art. 207[1]

III. Calculation of a spouse's matrimonial profit
1. Separation of each spouse's own property and the acquisitions

[1] Each spouse's acquisitions and each spouse's own property are separated according to their existence and their value at the date of the dissolution of the matrimonial property system.

[2] The payments which a spouse has received from a welfare fund or on the ground of his or her

---

[1] Wording according to cipher I 1 of the Federal Statute of 5th October 1984, in force since 1st January 1988 (BBl 1979 II 1191).

incapacity to work are added to the spouse's own property at the capital value of the annuity to which a spouse would be entitled at the dissolution of the matrimonial property system.

Art. 208[1]

[1] To the acquisitions are added: 2. Addition

1. donations which a spouse has made without the other spouse's consent during the last five years before the matrimonial property system was dissolved, with the exception of ordinary gifts;

2. the divesting of property which a spouse has carried out during the duration of a matrimonial property system in order to encroach upon the participation claim of the other spouse.

[2] Where disputes regarding such donations or divestings arise, the decree can be opposed to the third party who is beneficiary, provided that third-party notice was served on him.

Art. 209[1]

[1] Where debts owed by the acquisitions have been settled by a spouse's own property or where debts owed by a spouse's own property have been settled by a spouse's acquisitions, a claim for compensation is given at the time of the division of matrimonial property.

3. Claims for compensation between the acquisitions and a spouse's own property

[2] A debt encumbers the mass of property with which it is objectively connected, but in cases of doubt the acquisitions.

[3] Where means belonging to a mass of property have contributed to the acquisition, improvement or maintenance of property belonging to another mass of property and an increased value or an undervalue has arisen, the claim for compensation equals the

---

[1] Wording according to cipher I 1 of the Federal Statute of 5th October 1984, in force since 1st January 1988 (BBl 1979 II 1191).

share of contribution and is calculated according to the value of the property at the time of the division or the sale.

Art. 210[1]

4. Matrimonial profit

[1] The difference between the total value of the acquisitions, including the pieces of property and the claims for compensation which have been added hereto, after deduction of the debts by which they are encumbered, is considered the matrimonial profit.

[2] A matrimonial deficit is not taken into account.

Art. 211[1]

IV. Determination of value
1. Selling value

At the division of the matrimonial property system the property is to be assessed at its selling value.

Art. 212[1]

2. Value based on annual yield
a. In general

[1] Where a spouse continues to farm an agricultural enterprise himself or herself as the owner or where the surviving spouse or a descendant raises a well-founded claim for an undivided allotment, the share of the increased value of the agricultural enterprise and the claim for participation are assessed according to the value based on the annual yield.

[2] The owner of the agricultural enterprise or his heirs can claim from the other spouse as their share of the increased value or their claim of participation only that amount which they would receive if the value of the enterprise were assessed on the basis of its selling value.

[3] The provisions made by the operation of the law of inheritance for the valuation and the co-heirs' shares of the profit apply analogously.

---

[1] Wording according to cipher I 1 of the Federal Statute of 5th October 1984, in force since 1st January 1988 (BBl 1979 II 1191).

Art. 213[1]

[1] Where extraordinary circumstances justify it, the value assessed at the allotment of the agricultural enterprise can be increased in fair proportion. *b. Special circumstances*

[2] Extraordinary circumstances are, in particular, the requirements for maintenance of the surviving spouse, the purchasing price of the agricultural enterprise including the investments or the pecuniary circumstances of the spouse who owns the agricultural enterprise.

Art. 214[1]

[1] The decisive date for assessing the value of the acquisitions existing at the time of the dissolution of the matrimonial property system is the date of the division. *3. Decisive date*

[2] The decisive date for assessing the value of property which is added to the acquisitions is the date when it was sold.

Art. 215[1]

[1] Each spouse or his or her heirs are entitled to half of the other spouse's matrimonial profit. *V. Participation in the matrimonial profit*
1. By operation of the law

[2] Claims are compensated.

Art. 216[1]

[1] Another arrangement regarding the participation in the matrimonial profit can be agreed upon in a marriage covenant. *2. By a marriage covenant*
a. In general

[2] Such arrangements must not encroach on the compulsory portions of children who were not born in the spouses' conjugal union and their issue.

---

[1] Wording according to cipher I 1 of the Federal Statute of 5th October 1984, in force since 1st January 1988 (BBl 1979 II 1191).

Art. 217[1]

b. Upon divorce, judicial separation, annulment of a marriage or system of separate estates by order of court

Upon divorce, judicial separation, annulment of a marriage or the introduction of the system of separate estates by order of court, agreements regarding the change of the legal participation in the matrimonial profit only apply where this is explicitly put down in the marriage covenant.

Art. 218[1]

VI. Payment of the claim due to participation and increased value
1. Delay for payment

[1] Where the immediate payment of the claim due to participation in the matrimonial profit and an increased value cause serious difficulties for the spouse liable to honour such claims he or she can request that delays for payment be granted.

[2] Interest is to be paid for the claim due to participation and the share of the increased value from the end of the division of matrimonial property, unless the parties have made a different arrangement, and where the circumstances justify it, they have to be secured.

Art. 219[1]

2. Apartment and personal chattels

[1] To enable the surviving spouse to continue the style of life he or she has been able to enjoy hitherto, he or she is granted at his or her instance, against compensation the usufruct of, or the right of residence in, the house or the apartment in which the spouses have lived and which belonged to the deceased spouse; provisions are made for another arrangement by a marriage covenant.

[2] Under the same circumstances he or she can demand the ownership of the personal chattels.

[3] Where the circumstances justify it, at the instance of the surviving spouse or the other legal heirs of the deceased spouse, the usufruct or the

---

[1] Wording according to cipher I 1 of the Federal Statute of 5th October 1984, in force since 1st January 1988 (BBl **1979 II** 1191).

right of residence can be replaced by the ownership of the house or the apartment.

⁴ The surviving spouse cannot claim these rights to the rooms where the deceased spouse exercised a trade or a profession provided a descendant of the deceased spouse requires these rooms for the continuation of exercising this trade or profession; provisions are made for the operation of the laws of inheritance relating to agricultural estates.

Art. 220[1]

¹ Where the property of the spouse who is liable or of his or her succession does not cover the claim of participation in the matrimonial profit due at the division of the matrimonial property, the spouse who has a legitimate claim or his or her heirs can collect from the favoured third parties allocations, which are to be added to the acquisitions, to the extent of the shortfall.

² The right to bring action expires one year after the spouse or his or her heirs have cognizance of the violation of their rights, but in any case ten years after the dissolution of the matrimonial property system.

³ Furthermore the provisions regarding the successoral action for reduction apply analogously, with the exception of those relating to the place of jurisdiction.

3. Actions towards third parties

---

[1] Wording according to cipher I 1 of the Federal Statute of 5th October 1984, in force since 1st January 1988 (BBl **1979 II** 1191).

Chapter III: Community of Property

Art. 221[1]

A. Matrimonial property
I. Composition

The matrimonial system of community of property comprises the common property and each spouse's own property.

Art. 222[1]

II. Common property
1. General community of property

[1] The general community of property merges the spouses' property and their income to a common property, with the exception of that property which, by operation of the law, is a spouse's own property.

[2] The common property belongs to both spouses undividedly.

[3] No spouse may dispose of his or her share in the common property.

Art. 223[1]

2. Limited community of property
a. Community of acquisitions

[1] The spouses may reduce the community of property to the acquisitions by marriage covenant.

[2] The returns from a spouse's own property belong to the common property.

Art. 224[1]

b. Other communities of property

[1] By way of marriage covenant the spouses may exclude from the community certain specific property, such as immovables, a spouse's income from work or property which serves a spouse for the exercise of a profession or the running of a business.

[2] Where nothing else has been stipulated, the returns from these items of property do not belong to the common property.

---

[1] Wording according to cipher I 1 of the Federal Statute of 5th October 1984, in force since 1st January 1988 (BBl 1979 II 1191).

Art. 225[1]

[1] A spouse's own property arises under a marriage covenant, under allocations from third parties, or by operation of the law.

[2] To a spouse's own property belong, by operation of the law, the items which serve exclusively for his or her personal use, as well as money to be paid as moral compensation.

[3] What a spouse can claim as compulsory portion cannot be allocated to this spouse by his or her relatives as the spouse's own property if the marriage covenant determines that this item belongs to the common property.

III. A spouse's own property

Art. 226[1]

All items of property are considered common property as long as no evidence is given that they belong to a spouse's own property.

IV. Evidence

Art. 227[1]

[1] The spouses administer the common property in the interest of the conjugal union.

[2] Each spouse can, within the limits of the ordinary administration, make the community liable and dispose of the common property.

B. Administration and disposal
I. Common property
1. Ordinary administration

Art. 228[1]

[1] Except for the ordinary administration the spouses can only jointly or one spouse only with the consent of the other spouse make the conjugal union liable and dispose of the common property.

[2] Third parties may presume that this consent was given, unless they know or ought to know that it was not given.

2. Extraordinary administration

---

[1] Wording according to cipher I 1 of the Federal Statute of 5th October 1984, in force since 1st January 1988 (BBl **1979 II** 1191).

^{3} A proviso is made for the provisions relating to the representation of the conjugal union.

Art. 229[1]

3. Profession or business of the conjugal union

Where a spouse with the consent of the other spouse exercises a profession alone or runs a business alone with means which belong to the common property, he or she may carry out all legal transactions which are necessary for these activities.

Art. 230[1]

4. Disclaimer and acceptance of an inheritance

^{1} Without the other spouse's consent a spouse may neither disclaim an inheritance which would become part of the common property nor accept an excessively indebted inheritance.

^{2} Where a spouse cannot obtain this consent or where a spouse refuses to consent without material grounds, he or she can apply to the judge at his or her domicile.

Art. 231[1]

5. Liability and cost of administration

^{1} At the dissolution of the matrimonial property system each spouse is liable for transactions which concern the common property in the same way as a mandatary.

^{2} The cost of the administration is borne out of the common property.

Art. 232[1]

II. The spouses' own property

^{1} Each spouse administers his or her own property within the legal limits and disposes of it.

^{2} Where returns from a spouse's own property become part of this spouse's own property, the cost of administration is borne out of his or her own property.

---

[1] Wording according to cipher I 1 of the Federal Statute of 5th October 1984, in force since 1st January 1988 (BBl 1979 II 1191).

Art. 233[1]

Each spouse is liable with his or her own property and the spouses' common property for: C. Liability towards third parties

1. debts which he or she incurred in exercising his or her competence to represent the conjugal union or in administering the common property; I. Liability of a spouse's own property and the common property

2. debts which he or she incurred in exercising a profession or running a business if for these activities means of the common property have been used or their returns become part of the common property;

3. debts for which also the other spouse is personally liable;

4. debts where the spouses have arranged with a third party that beside the debtor's own property the common property is answerable for the debt.

Art. 234[1]

[1] For all other debts a spouse is only liable with his or her own property and to the extent of half the value of the common property. II. Liability of a spouse's own property

[2] A proviso is made for claims due to enrichment of the community of property.

Art. 235[1]

[1] The matrimonial property system is of no influence for the falling due of the debts between the spouses. D. Debts between the spouses

[2] However, where the payment of debts or the restitution of owed items causes the spouse who is liable serious problems which endanger the marital union, he or she can demand to be allowed time; where the circumstances justify it, the claim is to be secured.

---

[1] Wording according to cipher I 1 of the Federal Statute of 5th October 1984, in force since 1st January 1988 (BBl 1979 II 1191).

Art. 236[1]

E. Dissolution of the matrimonial property system and division
I. Date of the dissolution

[1] The matrimonial property system is dissolved with a spouse's death, the conclusion of another matrimonial property system or with the adjudication of bankruptcy against a spouse.

[2] Where a marriage is divorced, judicially separated or annulled or where the system of separate estates has been instituted on a court's order, the dissolution of the matrimonial property system is backdated to the day on which the petition was filed.

[3] The date of the dissolution of the matrimonial property system is substantial for the composition of the common property and a spouse's own property.

Art. 237[1]

II. Allotment to a spouse's own property

Where a spouse received a capital payment from a pension fund or on the ground of his or her incapacity work and where this payment has become part of the common property, the amount of the capital value of the annuity to which the spouse would be entitled at the dissolution of the matrimonial property system is added to his or her own property.

Art. 238[1]

III. Claims for compensation between a spouse's own property and the common property

[1] Where debts which encumber the property of one spouse have been paid with means belonging to the other spouse, there exists a claim for compensation between the common property and each spouse's own property at the time of the division of the matrimonial property.

[2] A debt encumbers the mass of property with which it is objectively connected, but in cases of doubt the common property.

---

[1] Wording according to cipher I 1 of the Federal Statute of 5th October 1984, in force since 1st January 1988 (BBl 1979 II 1191).

Art. 239[1]

Where a spouse's own property or the common property has contributed to the acquisition, improvement or maintenance of an item of property which belongs to another mass of property, the provisions relating to the participation in the acquisitions apply accordingly for the share in the increased value.

IV. Share in increased value

Art. 240[1]

The date of the division is decisive for the value of the common property which exists at the dissolution of the matrimonial property system.

V. Determination of value

Art. 241[1]

[1] Where the community of property is dissolved by a spouse's death or by agreeing on another matrimonial property system, each spouse or his or her heirs are entitled to half of the common property.

[2] By way of marriage covenant another form of division may be agreed upon.

[3] Such arrangements may not affect the claims of heirs with rights to a compulsory portion.

VI. Division
1. In case of death or agreement on another matrimonial property system

Art. 242[1]

[1] On divorce, judicial separation, annulment of a marriage or institution of the system of separate estates by operation of the law or by a court's order, each spouse takes back from the common property what under the matrimonial property system of the participation in acquisitions would be considered his or her own property.

[2] The rest of the common property falls to each spouse in half-shares.

2. In the other cases

---

[1] Wording according to cipher I 1 of the Federal Statute of 5th October 1984, in force since 1st January 1988 (BBl 1979 II 1191).

³ Agreements wherein the division by operation of the law is modified are only valid where this is foreseen explictly in the marriage covenant.

Art. 243¹

VII. Execution of the division
1. A spouse's own property

Where the community of property is dissolved by a spouse's death, the surviving spouse can demand that those items of property which under the matrimonial property system of the participation in acquisitions would fall into his or her own property are left to him or her against compensation.

Art. 244¹

2. Apartment and equipment

¹ Where the house or the apartment in which the spouses lived or the household equipment belonged to the common property, the surviving spouse can demand that the ownership thereof is allotted to him or her against compensation.

² Where the circumstances justify it, the surviving spouse or the other legal heirs of the deceased can demand that in place of ownership the usufruct of the house or the apartment or a right of residence is granted.

³ Where the community of property is not dissolved by a spouse's death, each spouse can make these petitions, provided this spouse proves that he or she has a preponderant interest.

Art. 245¹

3. Other items of property

Where a spouse proves his or her preponderant interest, he or she can also demand the allotment of other items of property against compensation.

---

¹ Wording according to cipher I 1 of the Federal Statute of 5th October 1984, in force since 1st January 1988 (BBl 1979 II 1191).

Art. 246[1]

The provisions relating to the division of co-ownership and the execution of the partition of the inheritance apply accordingly.

4. Other provisions of division

Chapter IV: Separation of Estates

Art. 247[1]

Within the limits of the law each spouse administers and uses his or her property and disposes of it.

A. Administration, use and disposal
I. In general

Art. 248[1]

[1] The burden of proving that a certain item of property is in a spouse's ownership is on the spouse who alleges it.

[2] Where this proof cannot be given, co-ownership by both spouses is assumed.

II. Proof

Art. 249[1]

Each spouse is liable for his or her debts with the whole of his or her property.

B. Liability towards third parties

Art. 250[1]

[1] The matrimonial property system is of no influence for the falling due of debts between the spouses.

[2] However, where the settlement of debts or the restitution of owed items of property causes the spouse who is liable serious problems which endanger the conjugal union, he or she may demand to be allowed time; the claim is to be secured where the circumstances justify it.

C. Debts between the spouses

---

[1] Wording according to cipher I 1 of the Federal Statute of 5th October 1984, in force since 1st January 1988 (BBl **1979 II 1191**).

Art. 251[1]

D. Allotment of items in co-ownership

Where an item of property is in co-ownership and a spouse proves a preponderant interest, he or she can, in addition to the other legal measures, demand that this item of property be, against compensation, undividedly allotted to the other spouse at the dissolution of the matrimonial property system.

Section II: The Relatives

Title VII: The Origin of the Child-Parent Relationship

Chapter I: General Provisions[2]

Art. 252[2]

A. Origin of the relations of children to their parents in general

[1] Between the child and the mother the child-parent relationship begins to exist with the child's birth.

[2] Between the child and his father the relationship is established by force of the mother's marriage to the father or by acknowledgement or by judicial decree.

[3] Further the child-parent relationship is established by adoption.

Art. 253[2]

B. Establishing or disavowal of child-parent relationship
I. Competence

A declaratory action to establish or to disown relationship with the child is to be filed with the judge at the domicile of one of the parties at the time of the birth or the filing of the action.

---

[1] Wording according to cipher I 1 of the Federal Statute of 5th October 1984, in force since 1st January 1988 (BBl 1979 II 1191).

[2] Wording according to cipher I 1 of the Federal Statute of 25th June 1976, in force since 1st January 1978 (AS 1977 237 264; BBl 1974 II 1).

The Origin of the Child-Parent Relationship

Art. 254[1]

II. Procedure

The procedure to establish or disown relationship with the child is ordered by the Cantonal procedural law provided the following provisions are observed:

1. The judge investigates the facts of the case *ex officio* and appreciates the evidence at his own discretion.

2. The parties and third parties are to take an active part in investigations which are required for the discovery of the child's descent and which must be without danger for the child's health.

Chapter II: The Paternity of the Husband[1]

Art. 255[1]

A. Presumption

[1] Where a child is born during the marriage or within three hundred days after the dissolution of the marriage, the husband is held to be the child's father.

[2] Where a child is born later than this, the husband is only then presumed to be the child's father if the child was begot before the dissolution of the marriage.

[3] Where the husband has been declared missing, the delay of three hundred days begins with the moment of mortal danger or the last news.

Art. 256[1]

B. Disavowal
I. Right of action

[1] Action to contest the presumption of paternity can be brought with the judge:

1. by the husband;

---

[1] Wording according to cipher I 1 of the Federal Statute of 25th June 1976, in force since 1st January 1978 (AS 1977 237 264; BBl 1974 II 1).

2. by the child where the conjugal union of husband and wife has ceased to exist during the child's minority.

²The action filed by the husband is brought against the child and his mother, the action brought by the child is brought against the husband and the mother.

³The husband has no right of action where he has consented to the begetting of the child by a third person.

Art. 256a[1]

II. Ground of action
1. Conception during marriage

¹The plaintiff has to prove that the husband is not the father where a child was begot during the marriage.

²Where a child is born not earlier than one hundred and eighty days after the solemnization and not later than three hundred days after the dissolution of the marriage, it is presumed that the child was begot during the marriage.

Art. 256b[1]

2. Conception before or during marriage or dissolution of common household

¹Where a child is conceived before the solemnization of the marriage or at a time when the conjugal union was disrupted, no further evidence need be brought in support of the contestation.

²A presumption of the paternity of the husband, however, is raised even in this case, where it can be substantiated that the husband cohabited with the child's mother at the date of the child's conception.

Art. 256c[1]

III. Period of limitation of action

¹The husband has to file an action within the delay of one year after he has learned of the birth

---

[1] Inserted by cipher I 1 of the Federal Statute of 25th June 1976, in force since 1st January 1978 (AS 1977 237 264; BBl 1974 II 1).

and the fact that he is not the father or that a third party cohabited with the mother at the time of conception, however, in any case before a period of five years after the birth.

² The action of the child is to be filed not later than one year after the child has come of age.

³ After the periods allowed an action for disavowal can only be filed if there are good grounds to justify the delay.

Art. 257[1]

C. Concurrence of two presumptions

¹ Where a child is born within three hundred days before the dissolution of the marriage of the mother and where in the meantime she has contracted a new marriage, the second husband is held to be the child's father.

² Where this presumption is rebutted by proof of facts, the first husband is held to be the father.

Art. 258[1]

D. Action brought by the parents

¹ Where the husband has died or has become devoid of discretion before the expiration of the period of limitation, an action of disavowal can be filed by either his father or his mother.

² The provisions concerning the disavowal by the husband are applied accordingly.

³ The one-year-period of limitation for an action of disavowal begins with the cognizance of the husband's death or his being devoid of discretion at the earliest.

Art. 259[1]

E. Marriage of the parents

¹ Where the parents contract marriage the child born out of wedlock is subject to the provisions made

---

[1] Wording according to cipher I 1 of the Federal Statute of 25th June 1976, in force since 1st January 1978 (AS 1977 237 264; BBl 1974 II 1).

for the child born in wedlock as soon as the paternity is established either by acknowledgement or by judicial decree.

²The acknowledgement can be opposed:

1. by the mother;

2. by the child, or after his death by his issue, provided that the common househould of his parents was dissolved during his minority or the acknowledgement was not pronounced before the end of his twelfth year of age;

3. by the legal home or domicile of the husband;

4. by the husband.

³The provisions made for the disavowal are applied accordingly.

Chapter III: Acknowledgement and Judicial Decree of Paternity[1]

Art. 260[1]

A. Acknowledgement
I. Admissibility and form

¹Where the relationship exists only between a child and his mother, the father can acknowledge the child.

²Where the acknowledging person is a minor or incapacitated, the consent of his parents or his guardian is required.

³The acknowledgement must be made by a statement in the presence of the registrar of civil status or by a testamentary disposition or, where an action to establish paternity is pending, in the presence of a judge.

---

[1] Wording according to cipher I 1 of the Federal Statute of 25th June 1976, in force since 1st January 1978 (AS 1977 237 264; BBl 1974 II 1).

Art. 260a[1]

II. Disavowal
1. Right of action

[1] Acknowledgement can be opposed by any interested party by bringing an action in the court, in particular by the mother, the child or at the latter's death his issue as well as by the domicile or the legal home of the acknowledging party.

[2] The acknowledging party has this right of action only where he acknowledged the child under the pressure of a threat of an imminent and serious danger for the life, health, honour or fortune of his own self or a closely acquainted person or where he acknowledged paternity erroneously.

[3] The action is brought against the acknowledging party and the child provided these do not bring an action themselves.

Art. 260b[1]

2. Ground for action

[1] The plaintiff has to prove that the acknowledging person is not the father of the child.

[2] However, mother and child are only then obliged to furnish this evidence if the acknowledging person can substantiate his claim to have cohabited with the mother at the time of conception.

Art. 260c[1]

3. Period of limitation

[1] The plaintiff can bring an action within a period of one year from cognizance of acknowledgement and of the fact that the acknowledging party is not the father or that a third party cohabited with the mother at the time of conception, or from the time when the error was discovered or the threat ceased to exist, but in any case before the expiration of a five year period from the date of acknowledgement.

---

[1] Inserted by cipher I 1 of the Federal Statute of 25th June 1976, in force since 1st January 1978 (AS 1977 237 264; BBl 1974 II 1).

² The child can bring an action in any case before the expiration of one year after reaching majority.

³ After the expiration of this period of limitation an action of disavowal is only admitted if there are good grounds to justify the delay.

Art. 261¹

B. Action to establish paternity
I. Who can bring it

¹ The mother as well as the child can file a declaratory action to establish the relationship between the child and the father.

² The action to establish paternity is brought against the father or, where he is dead, successively against his issue, his parents or his brothers or sisters or, where none of these exist, against the competent authorities of his last domicile.

³ Where the father has died the judge informs the wife that an action to establish paternity has been filed to enable her to safeguard her rights.

Art. 262¹

II. Presumption

¹ A presumption is raised by law that the defendant is the father of the child where he cohabited with the child's mother in the period between the three hundredth and the one hundred and eightieth day before the child's birth.

² This presumption is also raised where the child was conceived before the three hundredth or after the one hundred and eightieth day before his birth and the defendant cohabited with the mother of the child at the date of conception.

³ This presumption is rebutted where the defendant can prove that his paternity must be excluded or is less probable than that of a third party.

---

¹ Wording according to cipher I 1 of the Federal Statute of 25th June 1976, in force since 1st January 1978 (AS 1977 237 264; BBl 1974 II 1).

Art. 263[1]

[1] The action can be brought before or after the birth of the child, but it must be brought:

1. by the mother within one year from the date of the child's birth;

2. by the child within one year from the date of reaching majority.

[2] Where there exists a relationship of the child with another man, an action can be brought in any case within one year from the day on which this relationship ceases to exist.

[3] After the period allowed an action can be brought if there are good grounds to justify the delay.

III. Period of limitation

Chapter IV[2] : Adoption

Art. 264[1]

A child may be adopted where the adopting parents have given the child to be adopted care and education for at least two years and where, on the grounds of the general circumstances, it can be expected that the establishment of a child relationship will be for the benefit of the child without unduly impairing the interests of other children of the adopting parents.

A. Adoption of minors
I. General conditions

Art. 264a[3]

[1] A child cannot be adopted by two persons together, unless they are husband and wife; joint adoption is not permitted to any other persons.

II. Joint adoption

---

[1] Wording according to cipher I 1 of the Federal Statute of 25th June 1976, in force since 1st January 1978 (AS 1977 237 264; BBl 1974 II 1).
[2] Originally Chapter III.
[3] Inserted by cipher I 1 of the Federal Statute of 30th June 1972, in force since 1st April 1973 (AS 1972 2819 2829; BBl 1971 I 1200).

² Husband and wife have to be married for at least five years or must have completed their 35th year of age.

³ A married person can, however, adopt the child of his or her spouse, provided he or she has been married for at least two years or has completed his or her 35th year of age.

Art. 264b[1]

III. Adoption by a single person

¹ An unmarried person can adopt singly, provided this person has completed his or her 35th year of age.

² A married person who has completed his or her 35th year of age can adopt singly where a joint adoption has proved to be impossible because the conjugal partner is permanently devoid of discretion or has been absent for at least two years and his place of abode is unknown, or where husband and wife have been judicially separated for more than three years.

Art. 265[2]

IV. Age and consent of the child

¹ The child must be at least 16 years younger than either of his adopting parents.

² Where the child to be adopted has discretion, his consent is required for the adoption.

³ Where the child is placed under commission inspite of the fact that he has discretion, an adoption is only possible with the consent of the supervisory guardianship board.

---

[1] Inserted by cipher I 1 of the Federal Statute of 30th June 1972, in force since 1st April 1973 (AS 1972 2819 2829; BBl 1971 I 1200).

[2] Wording according to cipher I 1 of the Federal Statute of 30th June 1972, in force since 1st April 1973 (AS 1972 2819 2829; BBl 1971 I 1200).

Art. 265a[1]

V. Consent of the parents
1. Its form

[1] The adoption requires the consent of the father and the mother of the child.

[2] A statement of consent has to be made either by word of mouth or in writing before the guardianship board at the domicile or the place of sojourn of the parents or the child and to be entered in the minutes.

[3] The consent is valid even though the parents are not named or are not yet determined.

Art. 265b[1]

2. Time

[1] The consent may not be given earlier than six weeks after the birth of the child.

[2] The consent can be revoked within six weeks after it has been given.

[3] The consent is final if it is given a second time after it has been revoked.

Art. 265c[1]

3. Waiving of consent
a. Conditions

The consent of one parent can be waived:

1. where one of the parents is unknown, has been absent for a considerable period of time and his or her place of abode is unknown, or where he or she is permanently devoid of discretion,

2. where one of the parents has not shown any serious intention to take care of the child.

Art. 265d[1]

b. Decision

[1] Where the child has been given into custody with the purpose of a future adoption and where the consent of one parent is missing, the guardianship board at the child's domicile decides if the consent can be waived on request of a private or public

---

[1] Inserted by cipher I 1 of the Federal Statute of 30th June 1972, in force since 1st April 1973 (AS **1972** 2819 2829; BBl **1971 I** 1200).

institution arranging the adoption or on request of the adopting parents; as a rule this decision is taken before the child is given into custody.

² In all other cases this decision is taken at the time of the adoption.

³ Where the consent of one parent is waived because he or she has shown no serious sign of intention to take care of the child, the decision has to be brought to the notice of this parent in writing.

Art. 266¹

B. Adoption of majors and persons placed under commission

¹ If there are no offspring a major or a person under tutelage can be adopted,

1. where this person requires permanent care on the ground of physical or mental disabilities and the adopting parents have given this person care and assistance for at least five years,

2. where the adopting parents have given the person to be adopted care and provided for his education during his minority for at least five years,

3. where there are other material grounds for the adoption and the person to be adopted has lived with, and shared the home of, the adopting parents for at least five years.

² A married person can only be adopted with the consent of his or her spouse.

³ In all other cases the provisions for the adoption of minors are applied accordingly.

Art. 267²

C. Its effects
I. In general

¹ The adopted child acquires the legal rights and duties of a child of the adopting parents.

---

[1] Wording according to cipher I 1 of the Federal Statute of 30th June 1972, in force since 1st April 1973 (AS 1972 2819 2829; BBl 1971 I 1200).

[2] Wording according to cipher I 1 of the Federal Statute of 25th June 1976, in force since 1st January 1978 (AS 1977 237 264; BBl 1974 II 1).

² The former child relationship is dissolved; it is, however, continued with either the mother or the father where she or he is married to the adopter.

³ The child can be given a new Christian name in the course of the adoption.

Art. 267a[1]

Where the adopted child is a minor he acquires the right of citizenship of the adopter, which replaces his former place of citizenship.

II. Legal home

Art. 268[2]

¹ The adoption is effected by the competent Cantonal authorities at the domicile of the adopter.

D. Procedure
I. General

² Where an application for adoption has been filed, the death or the loss of discretion of the adopter does not prevent the adoption, provided the conditions for adoption are not affected otherwise.

³ Where a child becomes a major after an application for adoption has been filed, the provisions valid for the adoption of minors are to be applied, provided the conditions for the adoption of minors were fulfilled at the time when the application was made.

Art. 268a[1]

¹ The adoption can only be effected after a full investigation into all essential circumstances, where required with the assistance of experts.

II. Investigation

² In particular there are to be investigated the personality and health of the future foster parents and the child to be adopted, their mutual relations, their suitability for education, the financial standing,

---

[1] Inserted by cipher I 1 of the Federal Statute of 30th June 1972, in force since 1st April 1973 (AS **1972** 2819 2829; BBl **1971** I 1200).
[2] Wording according to cipher I 1 of the Federal Statute of 30th June 1972, in force since 1st April 1973 (AS **1972** 2819 2829; BBl **1971** I 1200).

the motives for adoption, and living conditions of the family of the future foster parents, as well as the development of the foster relationship while the child to be adopted was in the custody of his future adopting parents.

³ Where the adopting parents have descendants, their attitude towards adoption is to be considered.

Art. 268b^1

III. Secrecy of adoption

The name of the adopting parents may not be revealed to the parents of the child without the consent of the adopting parents.

Art. 269²

E. Voidability
I. Grounds
1. Lack of consent

¹ Where the consent has not been obtained without legal grounds, the persons entitled to give consent for the adoption can bring an action before the court to avoid the adoption, provided thereby the welfare of the child is not seriously affected.

² The parents of the child can, however, not file such an action to avoid the adoption before the court where they can bring an action to declare the adoption null and void before the Federal Court.

Art. 269a^1

2. Other deficiencies

¹ Where other serious conditions for the adoption have not been fulfilled, anyone who has an interest, in particular the commune of the legal home or domicile, can bring an action of avoidance before the court to declare the adoption null and void.

² Such an action of avoidance can, however, not be brought where the deficiencies have been

---

[1] Inserted by cipher I 1 of the Federal Statute of 30th June 1972, in force since 1st April 1973 (AS **1972** 2819 2829; BBl **1971 I** 1200).

[2] Wording according to cipher I 1 of the Federal Statute of 30th June 1972, in force since 1st April 1973 (AS **1972** 2819 2829; BBl **1971 I** 1200).

remedied in the meantime or concern rules of procedure exclusively.

Art. 269b[1]

Action to avoid adoption must be brought within six months from the date of the plaintiff's discovery of a ground for avoidance and in any case within two years from the date of the adoption.

II. Period of limitation

Art. 269c[2]

[1] The Cantons supervise the procuring of children for later adoption.

F. Procuring children for adoptions

[2] Persons who procure children for later adoption either on account of, or in connection with, their professional activities require permission; the procuration of children for adopting by guardianship boards is not subject to this regulation.

[3] The Federal Council decrees the rules of execution.

---

[1] Inserted by cipher I 1 of the Federal Statute of 30th June 1972, in force since 1st April 1973 (AS **1972** 2819 2829; BBl **1971** I 1200).
[2] Inserted by cipher I 3 of the Federal Statute of 30th June 1972, in force since 1st April 1973 (AS **1972** 2819 2829; BBl **1971** I 1200).

Title VIII: The Effects of the Child Relationship[1]

Chapter I: The Community of the Parents and the Children[2]

Art. 270[1]

A. Surname

[1] Where the parents are a married couple, the child assumes the surname of the family.

[2] Where they are not a married couple the child bears the name of the mother or, where the mother has a compound surname in consequence of an earlier marriage, the child bears the mother's first surname.[3]

Art. 271[1]

B. Legal home

[1] Where the parents are a married couple the child acquires the father's citizenship.

[2] Where the parents are not a married couple the child acquires the mother's citizenship.

[3] Where a child of unmarried parents assumes his father's surname on account of a change of name because the child grows up under his father's parental power, he also acquires his father's citizenship.

Art. 272[1]

C. Mutual duties

Parents and children owe to each other such mutual assistance, consideration and respect as the welfare of the family demands.

---

[1] Wording according to cipher I 1 of the Federal Statute of 25th June 1976, in force since 1st January 1978 (AS 1977 237 264; BBl 1974 II 1).

[2] Inserted by cipher I 1 of the Federal Statute of 25th June 1976, in force since 1st January 1978 (AS 1977 237 264; BBl 1974 II 1).

[3] Wording according to cipher I 2 of the Federal Statute of 5th October 1984, in force since 1st January 1988 (BBl 1979 II 1191).

Art. 273[1]

D. Personal contact
I. Parents
1. Principle

The parents have a legal claim to adequate personal contact with a child in minority who is neither subject to their parental power nor in their custody.

Art. 274[1]

2. Limitations

[1] The father and the mother must refrain from everything which impairs the relation of the child to the other parent or which renders the educator's task more difficult.

[2] Where the well-being of the child is endangered by the personal contact, where the parents fail to practise this personal contact in disregard of their duties, where they have not taken serious care of the child or where there are other serious grounds, the parents can be refused or deprived of the right of personal contact.

[3] Where the parents have consented to the adoption of their child or where their consent can be waived, the right of personal contact expires as soon as the child has been given into custody with the purpose of a future adoption.

Art. 274a[2]

II. Third persons

[1] Where there exist extraordinary circumstances, the right of personal contact can also be given to other persons, in particular to relatives, provided this is for the well-being of the child.

[2] The limitations of the right of personal contact which are valid for the parents apply accordingly.

---

[1] Wording according to cipher I 1 of the Federal Statute of 25th June 1976, in force since 1st January 1978 (AS 1977 237 264; BBl 1974 II 1).

[2] Inserted by cipher I 1 of the Federal Statute of 25th June 1976, in force since 1st January 1978 (AS 1977 237 264; BBl 1974 II 1).

Art. 275[1]

III. Competence

[1] The guardianship board at the domicile of the child is competent for making arrangements ordering personal contact.

[2] Provisions are made for the competence of the judge in accordance with the regulations in regard to divorce and the protection of the paternal community.

[3] Where such arrangements have not yet been made personal contact cannot be undertaken in disregard of the will of the person who was endowed with the paternal power or into whose custody the child was given.

Chapter II: The Parents' Duty of Maintenance[2]

Art. 276[1]

A. Subject and extent

[1] The parents are held responsible for the maintenance of the child, including the cost of upbringing, education and all necessary measures for the protection of the child.

[2] Maintenance comprises care and education or payments in money where a child is not in the custody of his parents.

[3] The parents can be relieved of their duty of maintenance to the amount which can be expected to be paid by the child himself either from his own income or from other sources in the possession of the child.

---

[1] Wording according to cipher I 1 of the Federal Statute of 25th June 1976, in force since 1st January 1978 (AS 1977 237 263; BBl 1974 II 1).

[2] Inserted by cipher I 1 of the Federal Statute of 25th June 1976, in force since 1st January 1978 (AS 1977 237 264; BBl 1974 II 1).

Art. 277[1]

[1] The duty of the parents to provide for the maintenance of the child lasts until his majority.　B. Duration

[2] Where on reaching majority the child has not yet completed his professional training or education, the parents are bound to continue to provide for the maintenance in proportion to their possibilities until this professional training or education is completed within due course.

Art. 278[1]

[1] During their wedded life the parents bear the cost of maintenance in accordance with the regulations of Matrimonial Law.　C. Married parents

[2] Both husband and wife are bound to assist each other appropriately to provide for the maintenance of pre-marital children.

Art. 279[1]

[1] The child can bring an action against the father or the mother or against both to enforce the provision of maintenance in the future as well as the payment of the cost of maintenance for the year prior to the lodging of the action with the judge.　D. Complaint I. Right of complaint and competence

[2] The action must be brought before the court where either the plaintiff or the defendant is domiciled.

[3] The competence of the judge is subject to the reservations made for the rules relating to the recognition of child-parent relationship, divorce and the protection of the conjugal partnership.

---

[1] Wording according to cipher I 1 of the Federal Statute of 25th June 1976, in force since 1st January 1978 (AS 1977 237 264; BBl 1974 II 1).

Art. 280[1]

II. Procedure

[1] The Cantons have to make provisions for a simple and expedient procedure to settle disputes about the duty of child maintenance.

[2] The judge investigates the facts of the case *ex officio* and weighs the evidence according to his own judgment.

[3] The action for cost of maintenance can be combined with the action to establish paternity.

Art. 281[1]

III. Precautionary measures
1. In general

[1] Where the action has been filed, the judge, at the plaintiff's request, takes the necessary precautionary measures for the duration of the trial.

[2] Where the child relationship has been established the defendant can be obliged to make an adequate deposit or to make provisional payments.

[3] A deposit is made by the payment of a sum of money to an institution entrusted with the keeping of deposits named by the judge.

Art. 282[1]

2. Before establishing paternity
a. Deposit

Provided action for the cost of maintenance has been lodged with the judge together with the action to establish paternity and paternity has been plausibly established, the defendant, at the plaintiff's request, has to make a deposit which covers appropriately the cost of the birth itself and the cost of maintenance of the mother and the child before the judgement is delivered.

Art. 283[1]

b. Provisional payments

Where there is a presumption of paternity and this presumption is not destroyed by immediately

---

[1] Wording according to cipher I 1 of the Federal Statute of 25th June 1976, in force since 1st January 1978 (AS 1977 237 264; BBl 1974 II 1).

available evidence, the defendant, at the plaintiff's request, has to contribute adequately to the cost of the child's maintenance even before the judgement is delivered.

Art. 284[1]

The judge who will deliver judgement is competent to decide upon deposits, provisional payments, payment of deposited contributions and the refund of provisional payments.

3. Competence

Art. 285[1]

[1] The amount of the contribution to maintenance is to be fixed in accordance with the child's requirements as well as the social position and the financial capacity of the parents; moreover the child's private property and personal income are to be considered.

IV. How the contribution to maintenance is fixed

[2] Children's allowances, social security annuities and similar payments specified to contribute to the maintenance of the child and to which the person who is liable to bear the cost of maintenance has a claim, are to be paid in addition to the fixed amount of the contribution to maintenance, unless the judge decides otherwise.

[3] The amount of the contribution to the cost of maintenance is payable by instalments in advance at the times stated by the court.

Art. 286[1]

[1] The judge is authorized to order that, without further proceedings, the amount of the contribution to maintenance is either increased or reduced if there occurs a marked change in the requirements of the

V. Change of circumstances

---

[1] Wording according to cipher I 1 of the Federal Statute of 25th June 1976, in force since 1st January 1978 (AS 1977 237 264; BBl 1974 II 1).

child or the financial capacity of the parents or the cost of living.

² Where the circumstances of the parties have undergone material changes, the court will, at one of the parents' or the child's request, settle the amount of the maintenance grant anew, or the grant can be suspended altogether.

Art. 287[1]

E. The contracts regulating the cost of maintenance
I. Periodical payments

¹ Contracts which order the cost of maintenance do not become binding for the child until they are approved by the guardianship board.

² Contributions to the cost of maintenance ordered by contracts can be altered, provided such changes have not been excluded with the approval of the guardianship board.

³ Where the contract has been concluded by legal process, the judge is competent for approval.

Art. 288[1]

II. Compensation

¹ A compensation for the cost of maintenance of the child can be fixed if this is justified by the child's interest.

² This arrangement is not binding for the child:

1. until the supervisory guardianship board or, where legal proceedings have been concluded, the judge has authorized the parties to make such an arrangement for compensation, and

2. until the amount of the compensation payment has been remitted to the institution determined in the arrangement for compensation.

---

[1] Wording according to cipher I 1 of the Federal Statute of 25th June 1976, in force since 1st January 1978 (AS 1977 237 264; BBl 1974 II 1).

Art. 289[1]

[1] The child has a claim to contributions to the cost of maintenance and it is settled through payments to the child's legal representative. F. Settlement
I. Creditor

[2] Where the local authorities bear the cost of maintenance, the claim to contributions with all appertaining rights is transferred to these authorities.

Art. 290[1]

Where the father or the mother fails to fulfil his or her duty of maintenance, the guardianship board or another institution or office, appointed on the basis of Cantonal law, is bound to assist the other parent at this parent's request to execute the claim for maintenance in a suitable manner and without charging any cost. II. Execution
1. Suitable assistance

Art. 291[1]

Where the parents fail to give the child proper care, the judge can order that the payments of their respective debtors are either partly or wholly made to the legal representative of the child. 2. Directions to the debtor

Art. 292[1]

Where the parents consistently fail to fulfil their duties of maintenance or where it can be surmised that they are preparing their escape or are squandering their property or are removing it to hiding, the judge can require them to give fair security for the future cost of maintenance. III. Security

Art. 293[1]

[1] Where neither the parents nor the child himself can bear the cost of maintenance Public Law deter- G. Public Law

---

[1] Wording according to cipher I 1 of the Federal Statute of 25th June 1976, in force since 1st January 1978 (AS 1977 237 264; BBl 1974 II 1).

mines who is to bear the cost, with the proviso of the duty of the child's relations to bear the cost of maintenance.

² Further to this Public Law orders advance payments for the support of the child, if the parents fail fo fulfil their duty of maintenance.

Art. 294¹

H. Foster parents

¹ Foster partents have a claim for a fair maintenance grant, provided no other arrangement has been made or the circumstances unmistakably suggest another procedure.

² Maintenance without any contribution to the cost of maintenance can be surmised where the foster child is the child of a near relation or a child who has been taken into custody with the intention of future adoption.

Art. 295¹

J. Claims of the unmarried mother

¹ An action for indemnification against the father of the child or his heirs can be filed by the mother with the judge who is competent for actions to establish paternity not later than one year after the child's birth:

1. for the cost of confinement;

2. for the cost of maintenance during at least four weeks before and at least eight weeks after birth;

3. for other expenses necessarily incurred as the result of pregnancy or confinement including the first equipment of the child.

² For reasons of fairness the judge can decree partial or total compensation for the cost incurred by the pregnancy where it is prematurely terminated.

---

¹ Wording according to cipher I 1 of the Federal Statute of 25th June 1976, in force since 1st January 1978 (AS 1977 237 264; BBl 1974 II 1).

³ Payments made by third parties to which the mother has a claim either by law or contract are to be deducted as far as the circumstances justify it.

Chapter III: Parental Power[1]

Art. 296[2]

¹ Children are subject during their minority to parental power.

² Minors and persons placed under a committee cannot exercise parental power.

A. Conditions
I. In general

Art. 297[2]

¹ During the marriage the parents exercise the parental power jointly.

² Where the common housekeeping has been dissolved or where the parents are judicially separated, the judge can determine which of the parents is to exercise parental power solely.

³ If one of the parents dies, the parental power belongs to the surviving parent and in case of divorce to the parent in whose custody the children are placed.

II. Married parents

Art. 298[2]

¹ Where the parents are not married, the parental power belongs to the mother.

² Where the mother is a minor, placed under a committee or has died or where she has been deprived of parental power, the board of guardianship appoints a guardian or transfers parental power to the father as the well-being of the child requires.

III. Unmarried parents

---

[1] Wording according to cipher I 1 of the Federal Statute of 25th June 1976, in force since 1st January 1978 (AS 1977 237 264; BBl 1974 II 1).

[2] Inserted by cipher II of the Federal Statute of 6th October 1978, in force since 1st January 1981 (AS 1980 31 35; BBl 1977 III 1).

Art. 299[1]

IV. Step parents

Conjugal partners have to assist each other appropriately in the exercise of parental power in relation to either the husband's or the wife's children; each partner is equally obliged to represent the other partner where the circumstances demand this.

Art. 300[1]

V. Foster parents

[1] Where a child is given into the custody of a third party, the foster parents represent the parents in the exercise of the parental power as far as the appropriate execution of this task requires it, provided that no other arrangements have been made.

[2] Important decisions shall not be made before seeking the foster parents' opinion.

Art. 301[1]

B. Extent
I. In general

[1] The parents, bearing the welfare of the child in mind, are in charge of his care and education and make the necessary decisions, with the proviso of the child's own capacity to act.

[2] The child owes obedience to his parents; they are bound to grant that the child live his own life in accordance with the respective physical or mental maturity of the child and to take the child's opinion into consideration in all important matters as far this is practicable.

[3] The child is not allowed to leave the parental home without the consent of the parents, nor can the child be taken from his parents illegally.

[4] The parents give the child his Christian name.

---

[1] Wording according to cipher I 1 of the Federal Statute of 25th June 1976, in force since 1st January 1978 (AS 1977 237 264; BBl 1974 II 1).

Art. 302[1]

II. Education

[1] The parents are bound to bring up the child according to their means and to further and protect his physical, mental and moral capabilities.

[2] They must provide for the general and professional training, taking into consideration, as far as possible, the child's capacities and personal inclinations; in particular they are bound to provide for a physically or mentally deficient child in a manner that is suitable to the child's condition.

[3] For this purpose they are requested to co-operate with the school or, where the circumstances demand it, with the public or charitable Youth Welfare.

Art. 303[1]

III. Religious education

[1] The parents determine the religious education of their children.

[2] Any agreement which restricts this right is null and void.

[3] If a child has completed his sixteenth year, he determines his adherence to a religious faith himself.

Art. 304[1]

IV. Representation
1. With third party
a. In general

[1] The parents have within the limits of their parental power the statutory right to represent their children in transactions with third parties.

[2] Where the parents are married, any *bona fide* third party may assume that each parent acts in agreement with the other parent.

[3] The provisions governing the representation of a person under commission are applicable by analogy, with the exception of those relating to the co-operation of the guardianship authorities.

---

[1] Wording according to cipher I 1 of the Federal Statute of 25th June 1976, in force since 1st January 1978 (AS 1977 237 264; BBl 1974 II 1).

Art. 305[1]

b. The child's capacity to act

[1] A child under parental power has the same restricted capacity to act like a person under commission.

[2] The child's property is made liable for his obligations, without regard to his parents' rights over it.

Art. 306[1]

2. Within the family

[1] Children under parental power can, where they have discretion and the authority of their parents, represent the family community; they do not, however, incur thereby any personal obligation themselves, but bind their parents.

[2] Where the parents have interests which run contrary to those of the child, the provisions for the representation of the child by a curator will take effect.

Art. 307[1]

C. Protection of the child
I. Suitable measures

[1] Where the child's well-being is endangered and the parents do not make the necessary provisions to remove this danger of their own accord or where they are incapable of taking remedial measures, the guardianship authorities will take all necessary measures for the protection of the child.

[2] The guardianship authorities are equally required to take remedial measures on behalf of children who are given into the custody of foster-parents or live in any other way outside the parental community of the parents.

[3] In particular, the guardianship authorities can admonish the parents, the foster-parents or the child, give them clearly defined directions relating to the

---

[1] Wording according to cipher I 1 of the Federal Statute of 25th June 1976, in force since 1st January 1978 (AS 1977 237 264; BBl 1974 II 1).

care, upbringing or education of the child, and appoint a person or an institution suited to this task and entitle them to have access to the persons concerned and receive the information they may wish to receive.

Art. 308[1]

II. Curatorship
1. In general

[1] Where the circumstances demand it the guardianship authorities appoint a curator who assists the parents in their care for the child by giving advice as well as practical help.

[2] The guardianship authorities can equip the curator with special powers, in particular to act for the child in order to secure the cost of maintenance and other rights and to supervise the child's personal contact.

[3] The parental power can be limited accordingly.

Art. 309[1]

2. Establishment of paternity

[1] In all cases as soon as an unmarried woman during her pregnancy requests the guardianship authorities or as soon as the authorities have been notified of the birth of the child, the board must appoint a curator who is required to take the necessary measures to determine the relation of the child to his father and to advise and take care of the mother as the circumstances may demand.

[2] The guardianship authorities take the same measures where a father-child relationship has been removed as a result of an action for disavowal of paternity.

[3] Where the relationship has been established or no action for paternity has been filed within two years after the child's birth, the guardianship board must,

---

[1] Wording according to cipher I 1 of the Federal Statute of 25th June 1976, in force since 1st January 1978 (AS 1977 237 264; BBl 1974 II 1).

Art. 310[1]

III. Removal of parental custody

[1] Where there are no other ways or means to remove existing dangers for the child's well-being, the guardianship board must take the child from the custody of the parents, or a third party in a case where the child has been placed in its custody, and board him according to the circumstances.

[2] The guardianship board will at the parents' or the child's request take the same measures where the parent-child relationship has deteriorated to a degree which makes the presence of the child in the same home or family unreasonable and where the circumstances do not allow any other solution.

[3] Where a child has been in the custody of foster parents for a fairly long time, the guardianship board can decline a request for the child's return into the custody of his parents if such a return might seriously endanger the child's development.

Art. 311[1]

IV. Deprivation of paternal power
1. through the guardianship supervisory authorities

[1] Where other measures for the protection of the child have failed to be successful or where they appeared to be insufficient from the start, the guardianship authorities may deprive the parents of their parental power:

1. if the parents are incapable of exercising their parental power dutifully owing to inexperience, illness, physical disability, absence from the child's domicile or similar grounds;

---

[1] Wording according to cipher I 1 of the Federal Statute of 25th June 1976, in force since 1st January 1978 (AS 1977 237 264; BBl 1974 II 1).

2. if the parents have not made a serious attempt to take care of the child or are guilty of gross neglect of their duties towards the child.

² If both parents have been deprived of their power, a guardian is appointed for the children.

³ Unless explicit arrangements to the contrary have been made, the deprivation takes effect in regard to all children, even to those who are born at a later date.

Art. 312[1]

The guardianship board may deprive the parents of their parental power: 2. through the guardianship authorities

1. if the parents request it for important reasons;

2. if the parents have given their consent to a later adoption by an unnamed third party.

Art. 313[1]

¹ Where the circumstances change, the measures taken for the protection of the child are to be adapted to the new situation. V. Change of the circumstances

² The restoration of parental power cannot in any case take effect before the expiration of one year from the date of the deprivation.

Art. 314[1]

The procedure is settled by Cantonal Law subject to the following provisions: VI. Procedure 1. In general[2]

1. Where the supervisory board is no judicial authority, reservation must be made for an appeal against the deprivation of parental power to a Cantonal judicial authority.

---

[1] Wording according to cipher I 1 of the Federal Statute of 25th June 1976, in force since 1st January 1978 (AS 1977 237 264; BBl 1974 II 1).

[2] Wording according to cipher II of the Federal Statute of 6th October 1978, in force since 1st January 1981 (AS 1980 31 35; BBl 1977 II 1).

2. If an appeal against the measures for the protection of the child has a suspensory effect, the complaint can be deprived of this effect either by the authority ordering the measures for the protection of the child or by the authority with which the complaint has been lodged.

Art. 314a^1

2. Deprivation of liberty through custody

^{1} Where a child is given into custody to an educational institution, the provisions for judicial decisions and the procedure for deprivation of liberty through custody relating to majors or incapacitated persons apply accordingly.

^{2} A child who is younger than sixteen years old cannot request judicial decisions himself.

^{3} For cases where a delay involves danger or the child is suffering from a mental illness, the Cantons can also entrust another qualified body than the guardianship board with the competence to give the child into custody in an institution.

Art. 315^2

VII. Competence
1. of the guardianship authorities

^{1} The measures for the protection of the child are ordered by the guardianship authorities of the child's domicile.

^{2} If the child is in the custody of foster-parents or is living outside the parental community, or if there exists the danger of a delay in the execution of the order, the authorities of the child's place of sojourn are competent as well.

^{3} If the authorities at the place of sojourn take steps for the protection of the child, the authorities at the child's domicile are to be notified.

---

[1] Inserted by cipher II of the Federal Statute of 6th October 1978, in force since 1st January 1981 (AS 1980 31 35; BBl 1977 III 1).

[2] Wording according to cipher I 1 of the Federal Statute of 25th June 1976, in force since 1st January 1978 (AS 1977 237 264; BBl 1974 II 1).

Art. 315a[1]

[1] Where the judge must order the parental rights and the personal relations of the parents to their children in compliance with the provisions ruling a divorce, he also takes the necessary steps for the protection of the children and entrusts the guardianship authorities with their execution.

2. of the judge

[2] However, the guardianship authorities are competent subject to the following provisions:

1. if the procedure to take steps for the protection of the child was completed or instituted before the divorce case procedures;

2. when it can be assumed that the precautionary measures necessary for the immediate protection of the child cannot be taken by the judge in due course.

[3] If the circumstances change after the judge has delivered judgment, the guardianship authorities can alter the measures for the protection of the child taken by the judge in regard to one parent as long as the position of the other parent is not directly affected by this change.

Art. 316[2]

[1] Any person taking a foster child into custody requires an authorization issued by the guardianship board or any other authority at his domicile named by Cantonal Law, and he is subject to supervision by this authority.

VIII. Supervision of foster children

[2] Provisions governing the execution are issued by the Federal Council.

---

[1] Inserted by cipher I 1 of the Federal Statute of 25th June 1976, in force since 1st January 1978 (AS 1977 237 264; BBl 1974 II 1).

[2] Wording according to cipher I 1 of the Federal Statute of 25th June 1976, in force since 1st January 1978 (AS 1977 237 264; BBl 1974 II 1).

Art. 317[1]

IX. Collaboration in youth assistance

The Cantons make appropriate provisions which guarantee the effective collaboration of the authorities and the institutions with regard to the protection of children as prescribed by civil law, further with regard to juvenile criminal law and all other youth assistance.

Chapter IV: The Child's Property[2]

Art. 318[1]

A. Administration

[1] The parents have the right and are under the duty to administer the property of their children, so long as they retain their parental power.

[2] Where only one parent retains parental power, this one is required to give the guardianship board an inventory of the children's property.

[3] Where on account of the size of the children's property or the parents' personal situation the guardianship board considers it advisable, it requires the parents to account and report on the administration of the children's property periodically.

Art. 319[1]

B. Use of income

[1] The parents are entitled to use the income from the children's property for their maintenance, education and training, and in fair proportion also for the family expenses.

[2] Any excess becomes part of the children's property.

---

[1] Wording according to cipher I 1 of the Federal Statute of 25th June 1976, in force since 1st January 1978 (AS 1977 237 264; BBl 1974 II 1).

[2] Inserted by cipher I 1 of the Federal Statute of 25th June 1976, in force since 1st January 1978 (AS 1977 237 264; BBl 1974 II 1).

Art. 320[1]

[1] Fractional amounts of compensations, indemnifications and similar payments can be used for the maintenance of the child in accordance with the child's personal requirements.

[2] Where the cost of maintenance, education and training demands it, the guardianship board can permit the parents to use the residue of the child's property in clearly defined amounts.

C. Part payments made from children's property

Art. 321[1]

[1] The parents are not entitled to use any income from the child's property if an explicit charge to this effect has been made or if the property has been donated under the proviso of an interest accruing investment or as the child's personal savings.

[2] Administration by the parents is only excluded if this has been expressly provided at the time when the gift was made.

D. Child's separate estate
I. Donations

Art. 322[1]

[1] The parents can be excluded from the administration of the compulsory portion of the child by testamentary disposition.

[2] Where the testator entrusts a third party with the administration, the guardianship board can require this party to submit periodic accounts and reports.

II. Compulsory portion

Art. 323[1]

[1] The child administers and has the user of his personal earnings and of that part of his property

III. Earnings, gift by way of advancement for profession or trade

---

[1] Wording according to cipher I 1 of the Federal Statute of 25th June 1976, in force since 1st January 1978 (AS 1977 237 264; BBl 1974 II 1).

which has been portioned out to him by his parents by way of advancement for profession or trade.

² Where the child lives together with his parents in the parental home, the parents are entitled to require the child to make a fair contribution towards his maintenance.

Art. 324[1]

E. Protection of the child's property
I. Suitable measures

¹ Where the careful administration is not sufficiently safeguarded, the guardianship board is required to take the necessary measures for the protection of the child's property.

² In particular the guardianship board can draw up regulations for the administration and order that security against loss is given or a deposit is made, should the periodic accounts and reports prove to be insufficient.

³ Procedure and competence fall under the provisions made for the protection of the child.

Art. 325[1]

II. Deprivation of administration

¹ Where there is no other way of removing the danger to the child's property, the guardianship board entrusts a curator with the administration.

² The guardianship board takes the same measures if the child's property which is not administrated by the parents is in danger.

³ Where there are serious grounds to fear that the income or fractional amounts from the child's property which are determined for use or set free are not used in accordance with the drawn up regulations, the guardianship board can entrust a curator with the administration also of these sums.

---

[1] Wording according to cipher I 1 of the Federal Statute of 25th June 1976, in force since 1st January 1978 (AS 1977 237 264; BBl 1974 II 1).

Art. 326[1]

When the parental power over a child or the administration of the child's property ceases, the parents have to restore his property, after accounts have been drawn up, to the child himself if he is of full age, or to his guardian or his curator.

F. End of administration
I. Return of the property

Art. 327[1]

[1] The parents are under the same liability to restore the child's property as a consignee.

[2] If they have *bona fide* sold any of the property, they must give the child the sum they have received for it.

[3] They are not liable to restore the amounts which they were authorized to take out of the child's property for the use of the child or for the upkeep of the common household.

II. Liability

Title IX: The Family

Chapter I: Maintenance

Art. 328[1]

[1] All persons are bound to contribute towards the maintenance of their ascendants and descendants in the direct line as well as of their brothers and sisters, where without such assistance they would become destitute.

[2] Sisters and brothers can only be made liable to contribute if they themselves are in easy pecuniary circumstances.

A. Who is liable to support

---

[1] Wording according to cipher I 1 of the Federal Statute of 25th June 1976, in force since 1st January 1978 (AS 1977 237 264; BBl 1974 II 1).

[3] Provisions are made for the support of parents and either the husband or the wife.

Art. 329

B. Extent of liability and how enforced[1]

[1] The order of their liability is the order of their right of succession to the claimant; he can demand a grant which would suffice to maintain him and is at the same time commensurate with the means of the person liable.

[2] Where it appears to be unfair to demand contributions from a person liable by law owing to particular circumstances, the judge can reduce the contributions or even annul the duty to contribute towards the cost of maintenance.[1]

[3] The provisions made for the action for maintenance by the child and the transference of the claim for maintenance to the communal authorities are to be applied accordingly.[1]

Art. 330

C. Maintenance of foundlings

[1] Foundlings are maintained by the Commune that has accepted them as citizens.

[2] If the parentage of the foundling is ascertained, the Commune can demand from his relatives who are liable to maintain him, and in the last resort from the Communal authority which is bound to assist him, the reimbursement of all expenditure incurred for his maintenance.

---

[1] Wording according to cipher I 1 of the Federal Statute of 25th June 1976, in force since 1st January 1978 (AS 1977 237 264; BBl 1974 II 1).

Chapter II: Authority of the Head of the Family

Art. 331

[1] The person who is regarded by law or agreement or tradition as the head of a group of persons living together in one household is held to have a certain authority over them.

A. Conditions

[2] This authority extends over all persons who being related[1] or being related by marriage to relatives or by virtue of an agreement between them as employees or in a similar position live together and form one household.[2]

Art. 332

[1] The rules of the house to which the members of the household have to conform must be framed with due regard to the interests of all of them.

B. Effect
I. Rules of the house

[2] The members of the household must in particular be given all necessary freedom of action for the purpose of their education or the exercise of their trade or business and the practice of their religion.

[3] The head of the family must use the same care with regard to the preservation and security of the property belonging to the members of the household as he does with his own property.

Art. 333

[1] The head of the family is liable for any damage caused by minors and by persons under commission for lunacy or feeblemindedness who have been placed under his authority, unless he can prove that he has given them the customary amount of supervision and the care required by the circumstances of the case.

II. Liability

---

[1] This word is used in accordance with cipher I 3 of the Federal Statute of 30th June 1972, in force since 1st April 1973 (AS 1972 2819 2829; BBl 1971 I 1200).

[2] Wording according to cipher II art. 2 cipher 2 of the Federal Statute of 25th June 1971, in force since 1st January 1972 (SR 220 *in fine*, Final and Transitionary Provisions to Title X).

² He is bound to see that an insane or feeble-minded member of his household does not occasion danger or damage to himself or to any other person.

³ In case of necessity he must apply to the competent authority for the adoption of any measures required by the circumstances.

Art. 334[1]

III. Claims of children
1. Conditions

¹ Children or grandchildren of full age, living in the home of either their parents or their grandparents, who have contributed their labour or their income to the common household can put in a claim for fair reimbursement.

² Where this claim is contested the judge determines the amount of the reimbursement and issues orders as to what kind of security is required to safeguard the reimbursement and the manner in which payment has to be effected.

Art. 334bis[2]

2. To enforce reimbursement

¹ The children or grandchildren who have a right to reimbursement can demand the payment at the time of the debtor's death.

² Reimbursement can already be demanded in the debtor's lifetime where execution for debt is levied against him or in the case of the debtor's bankruptcy, further where the common household is terminated or where the enterprise changes hands.

³ The reimbursement is not subject to limitation of action, however, the claim must be put in not later than at the time of the partition of the debtor's estate.

---

[1] Wording according to cipher I 1 of the Federal Statute of 6th October 1972, in force since 15th February 1973 (AS **1973** 93 102; BBl **1970 I** 805, **1971 I** 737).

[2] Inserted by cipher I 1 of the Federal Statute of 6th October 1972, in force since 15th February 1973 (AS **1973** 93 102; BBl **1970 I** 805, **1971 I** 737).

Chapter III: Family Property

Art. 335

A. Family foundations[1]

[1] Property can be settled on a family for the purpose of providing for the cost of the education, outfitting or maintenance of the members of the family or for similar purposes according to the provisions contained in the Law of Persons or in the Law of Inheritance.

[2] The settlement of property in perpetual trust for the benefit of a family is henceforth prohibited.[2]

Art. 336

B. Community of property
I. How constituted
1. Conditions

Members of a family can constitute a community of property by agreeing to leave the whole or a portion of an inheritance accrued to them as their common undivided property, or by bringing their property into the common stock.

Art. 337

2. Form required

The agreement to constitute a community of property requires for its validity a duly authenticated instrument signed by all the parties to it or their agents.

---

[1] This chapter deals with the different forms of settlement of property for the benefit of a family; they are:
  1. **Familienstiftung,** *fondation de famille,* family foundation, which constitutes a corporate body of its own, a person in the eyes of the law.
  2. **Gemeinderschaft,** *indivision,* community of property: here the property belongs to all the members in common, who are thereby joined together for the purpose of holding it (see arts. 336 *et seq.*).
  3. **Heimstätte,** *asile de famille,* homestead: here the property belongs to the one person named, but his powers of disposing of the property are restricted for his own protection and he is under certain obligations towards the other members of the family (see arts. 349 *et seq.*).

[2] *i.e.* in strict settlement in perpetuity, the effect of which would be to tie up property in one family from generation to generation.

Art. 338

II. Length of term

¹ The parties can agree that the property shall continue to be held in common for a definite or an indefinite time.

² In the latter case any of the parties to the agreement can determine it by giving six months' previous notice.

³ Where the property is farmed land, this notice can be given only on the days which are by the custom of the particular locality the spring and autumn terminal days.

⁴ The parties to the community of property are joined together by their common interests in it.

Art. 339

III. Effect
1. Joint undertaking

¹ Where it is not otherwise provided the parties are held to have equal rights in it.

² While the community is in force, the parties cannot demand a division nor dispose of their undivided shares.

Art. 340

2. Management and representation
a. In general

¹ The business connected with the common property is managed by all the parties jointly.

² Each one can, however, do simple administrative acts without the concurrence of the others.

Art. 341

b. Powers of the head of the community

¹ The parties can appoint one of their number to be the head of the community.

² The head can represent the community in all that concerns the common property and he directs the common undertaking.

³ The fact that the others are thereby excluded from the right of representing the community affects the rights of innocent third parties only where the name of the head is entered in the commercial register.

Art. 342

¹ The property comprised in the community is in the common ownership of all the parties.

² They are jointly and severally liable for the debts incurred in respect of it.

³ The property belonging to any of the parties other than his share in the common property and that which he acquires by succession or other gratuitous title while the community is in force, constitutes in the absence of an agreement to the contrary his separate estate.

3. Common and separate property

Art. 343

The community is dissolved:

1. by mutual agreement or by notice by one of the parties;¹

2. by the expiration of the time for which it was constituted, provided it is not continued by tacit agreement;

3. where the share of one of the parties has been seized in execution for debt and sold;

4. by the bankruptcy of one of the parties;

5. on the demand of one of the parties if it is based on material grounds.

IV. Dissolution
1. Grounds

Art. 344

¹ Where one of the parties has given notice to determine the community or has become bankrupt, or where his share has been seized in execution for debt and is to be sold, the other parties can continue the community among themselves by buying out that party or by satisfying his creditors.

² Where one of the parties marries, he can demand the redemption of his share without giving previous notice.

2. Notice, insolvency, marriage

---

¹ A party can dissolve the community by notice only where it was constituted for an indefinite time (see art. 338).

Art. 345

3. Death of one of the parties

¹ Where one of the parties dies, his heirs, if they are not themselves parties, can only demand the redemption of his share.

² Where these heirs are his issue, they can with the consent of the other parties be admitted in his place and to his share in the community.

Art. 346

4. Division

¹ The division of the common property or the redemption of the share of an outgoing party is in each case effected according to the value of the common property at the date when the cause of the dissolution arose.

² Neither the division nor the redemption can be demanded at an unreasonable time.

Art. 347

V. Share in income only
1. Conditions

¹ The parties can depute the full management of the common property and the power to act on their behalf to one of their number on the understanding that he is to pay annually to each a share of the net profits.

² This share must, in the absence of a contrary agreement, be fixed in an equitable manner according to the average profits over a reasonable number of years derived from the common property and after deducting the amount due to the manager himself.

Art. 348

2. Ground of dissolution

¹ Where the deputed manager does not administer the property held in common in a proper manner, or where he fails in his duties towards the other parties, they can demand the dissolution of the community.

² At the instance of any one of the parties, the court can authorize him to take a part in the management of the property, regard being had to the rules governing the division of an inheritance.

³ In other respects the rules governing this form of community are the same as in the other cases of community of property.

Art. 349

The Cantons have the right to authorize the constitution of homesteads and, subject to the following provisions, to formulate all rules relating to them.

C. Homesteads
I. Within Cantonal Law

Art. 350

¹ A farm or a messuage used for industrial purposes or a dwellinghouse with its appurtenances can be constituted into a homestead under the following conditions.

² The farm or dwellinghouse must not be larger than is necessary to support or house one family, without reckoning either mortgages or charges that may be on it or any source of revenue that the owner may have independently of it.

³ The owner himself or his family must personally manage the farm or carry on the industry or inhabit the dwellinghouse as the case may be, unless on material grounds the competent authority allows a temporary exception to be made.

II. Constitution
1. Conditions as to subject-matter

Art. 351

¹ The constitution of a homestead must be preceded by an official citation summoning creditors or other persons who consider themselves prejudiced by it to come forward and oppose it.

² Creditors secured on the land must be given special notice of this citation.

2. Form and procedure
a. Official citation

Art. 352

¹ The authority will sanction the constitution of the homestead, where it does not prejudice the

b. Rights of third parties

rights of third parties, and the farm or dwellinghouse satisfies the requirements of the law.

² The homestead cannot be constituted where a creditor has opposed it.

³ The debtor can, however, by payment discharge his liability to such creditor without the delays of notice.

Art. 353

c. Entry in land register

The constitution of a homestead requires for its validity to be entered in the land register; the fact of registration must then be officially announced.

Art. 354

III. Effect
1. Restrictions on alienation

¹ A farm or dwellinghouse which has been constituted into a homestead cannot as from that date be further mortgaged or otherwise charged.

² The owner can neither alienate it nor lease it nor let it.

³ The land or house with its appurtenances cannot be seized in execution for debt; this rule does not, however, affect its liability to be placed in the hands of an official receiver.

Art. 355

2. Admittance of relatives[1] to home

The competent authority can compel the owner to admit into the homestead his relatives[1] in the direct ascending or descending line and his brothers and sisters, where their circumstances urgently require it and they are not unworthy of it.

Art. 356

3. Insolvency of owner

¹ Where the owner becomes insolvent, the homestead is placed in the hands of a receiver, whose

---

[1] This word is used in accordance with cipher I 3 of the Federal Statute of 30th June 1972, in force since 1st April 1973 (AS 1972 2819 2829; BBl 1971 I 1200).

duty it is to maintain the object for which the homestead was constituted and at the same time safeguard the interests of the creditors.

² The creditors are paid in the order of date of the certificates which they hold of unsatisfied claims and they have the same priority as in bankruptcy.

Art. 357

¹ Where the owner dies, the homestead is dissolved unless there is a special provision in his will to the effect that it shall be transferred to his heirs. IV. Dissolution 1. On death

² Where there is no such provision, the homestead is crossed off the land register on the owner's death.

Art. 358

¹ The owner can dissolve the homestead in his lifetime. 2. During owner's life

² For this purpose he must apply to the competent authority with a request that it be crossed off the land register, whereupon the application will be officially announced.

³ Where the application is not opposed on material grounds, it must be granted.

Art. 359

Regulations made by the Cantons in regard to homesteads must be submitted to the Federal Council for approval. V. Cantonal regulations

Section III: Guardianship[1]

Title X: General Organization of Guardianship

Chapter I: The Organs of Guardianship

Art. 360

A. In general

The organs of guardianship are the guardianship authorities, the guardian, and the curator.

Art. 361

B. Guardianship authorities
I. Public bodies

[1] The guardianship authorities are the guardianship board and the supervisory authority.

[2] They are appointed by the Cantons and, where the supervisory authority consists of two divisions, one of first instance and the other of appeal, the Cantons determine the competence of each.

Art. 362

II. Family control
1. Conditions and powers

[1] In exceptional cases, where this is in the interest of the ward, such as for the purpose of carrying on a trade or directing a company, the control can be placed in the hands of the family.

[2] In these cases the rights, duties and liabilities of the guardianship board pass to a family council.

Art. 363

2. How set up

The supervisory authority can sanction the setting up of family control on the application of any two of the ward's near relatives[2] who are under

---

[1] **Vormundschaft**, *tutèle*, guardianship are here used as generic terms to include the office of a tutelary controlling authority as well as that of a guardian or curator. Similarly, unless the context shows otherwise, the term "guardian" may include a "committee", and "ward" a person placed under a committee.

[2] According to the French text "parents ou alliés" (relatives or relatives by marriage).

no incapacity or on that of any one of these and the ward's husband or wife.

Art. 364

¹ The family council is appointed by the supervisory authority for four years at a time and consists of at least three of the ward's relatives¹ who are suited to be guardians.   3. Family council

² The ward's husband or wife can be a member of the family council.

Art. 365

¹ The members of the family council must give security for the proper execution of their duties.   4. Security

² Family control can be set up only on that condition.

Art. 366

The family control can be determined at any time by the supervisory authority, where the family council fails in its duties or where the interests of the ward demand it.   5. Determination

Art. 367

¹ A guardian has to look after the person and property of his ward and acts on his behalf.   C. Guardian and curator

² A curator is appointed for the management of a specific piece of business or property.

³ With the exception of certain special provisions contained in this Code, the rules that govern a guardian apply equally also to a curator.

---

¹ According to the French text "parents ou alliés" (relatives or relatives by marriage).

Chapter II: Cases of Guardianship

Art. 368

A. Minority

¹ A guardian shall be appointed for every minor who is not subject to parental power.

² Registrars of civil status, administrative bodies and courts are required without delay to inform the competent guardianship authority of every case requiring the appointment of a guardian which comes to their notice in the exercise of their functions.

Art. 369

B. Commission of persons of full age
I. Insanity and feeblemindedness

¹ A guardian or committee¹ shall be appointed for every person of full age, who by reason of insanity or feeblemindedness is incapable of managing his own affairs, or who for his own protection needs permanent care and supervision, or who is a danger to the community.

² Administrative bodies and courts are required immediately to inform the competent authority of any such case which comes to their notice in the exercise of their functions.

Art. 370

II. Prodigality, drunkenness, immorality and mismanagement

A committee shall be appointed for every person of full age, who by reason of his prodigality, drunkenness, immorality or the mismanagement of his affairs, exposes himself or his family to the risk of being reduced to poverty or want, or needs permanent care and supervision, or is a danger to the community.

Art. 371

III. Imprisonment

¹ A committee shall be appointed for every person of full age who has been sentenced to imprisonment for one year or upwards.

---

¹ A guardian of a person of full age will in the following sections be called a committee.

² The person whose duty it is to execute the sentence is required immediately to inform the competent guardianship authority that the sentenced person has entered upon his term of imprisonment.

Art. 372

A committee can be appointed for every person of full age at his own request, where he can show that he is prevented from managing his affairs properly through old age or physical infirmity or inexperience.

IV. At own request

Art. 373

¹ The Cantons determine which are the competent authorities for the commission of persons of full age and what procedure shall be adopted.

² An appeal lies to the Federal Court.

C. Procedure
I. In general

Art. 374

¹ No person can be placed under a committee for prodigality, drunkenness, immorality or the mismanagement of his affairs, unless he has first been heard.

² No person can be placed under a committee for insanity or feeblemindedness except on the report of an expert, which must also state whether the person in question is in a fit state to be heard, before he is committed.

II. Hearing, expert evidence

Art. 375

¹ Where a committee has been appointed for a person of full age, the appointment must, as soon as it takes effect, be publicly advertised in at least one edition of an official gazette published at the said person's domicile and at his legal home.

² The supervisory authority can in exceptional cases authorize the postponement of the announcement, where and so long as the person placed under a

III. Public announcement

committee for insanity, feeblemindedness, or drunkenness is in an institution.

³ Until the appointment of the committee has been publicly announced, it is not valid as against third parties who are *bona fide* ignorant of it.

Chapter III: Competence

Art. 376

A. Domicile of ward

¹ The place where the appointment of a guardian must be made is that of the ward's domicile.¹

² Cantons are entitled to declare that the guardianship authorities of the ward's legal home shall be competent to appoint guardians for their citizens who are domiciled within their borders, where the Poor-Law authorities of the ward's legal home are wholly or in part charged with the burden of his relief.

Art. 377

B. Change of domicile

¹ A ward cannot change his domicile without the consent of the guardianship board.

² Where the change has been effected, the rights connected with the guardianship pass to the authorities of the ward's new domicile.

³ In this case the appointment of the committee must be announced at the new domicile.

Art. 378

C. Powers of home Canton

¹ Where the citizen of one Canton is domiciled in another Canton, the guardianship board of his legal home can require the board of his domicile to appoint a guardian for him.

---

¹ *i.e.* the authorities competent to appoint are those of the ward's domicile.

² It can further apply to the competent authority for the purpose of safeguarding the interests of one of its citizens who is to be or has been placed under a guardian in another Canton.

³ Where there is occasion to make some regulation in regard to the religious education of a minor, the authority of his domicile must ask for instructions from that of his legal home and carry them out.

Chapter IV: Appointment of Guardian

Art. 379

¹ The guardianship board must appoint as guardian a person of full age who is fitted for the purpose.

A. Conditions
I. In general

² In special cases several persons can be appointed to act either jointly or in accordance with the special powers that have been officially conferred upon each.

³ No joint guardianship can, however, be laid upon any two or more persons without their consent.

Art. 380

In the absence of material grounds to the contrary, the board is required in the choice of a guardian to give the preference either to one of the ward's near relatives[1] who is fitted for the purpose, or to his spouse, while at the same time taking into consideration the personal relations of the parties and the proximity of residence.

II. Preferential right of kindred and spouse

Art. 381

In the absence of material grounds to the contrary, the board shall appoint as guardian the person preferred by the ward or his parents.

III. Wishes as to choice of guardian

---

[1] According to the French text "parents ou alliés" (relatives or relatives by marriage).

Art. 382

IV. Obligation to accept

¹ Neither the male relatives nor the husband of the ward, nor any other man with civic rights resident in the area comprised under any one guardianship board can as a rule refuse to accept the office of guardian, if appointed.

² This obligation to accept office does not exist where the man is chosen by the family council.

Art. 383

V. Valid excuses

The following persons can refuse the office of guardian:

1. anyone who has completed his sixtieth year;

2. anyone who by reason of physical infirmity would find it difficult to hold office;

3. anyone who exercises parental power over more than four children;

4. anyone who is already burdened with two guardianships or with one specially onerous guardianship;

5. members of the Federal Council, the Chancellor of the Federation, and members of the Federal Court;

6. officials and members of Cantonal authorities who have been dispensed from this office by the Cantons.

Art. 384

VI. Grounds of exclusion

The following persons are ineligible as guardians:

1. anyone who is himself a ward;

2. anyone who has been deprived of his civic rights[1] or leads an immoral life;

---

[1] Deprivation of civic rights has been abolished (annulment of arts. 52, 76, 171 and 284 of the Criminal Law – SR 311.0 – as well as art. 28 paragraph 2 sentence 2 in the wording of 13th June 1927 – BS 3 391 –, art. 29 paragraph 2 sentence 2 in the wording of 13th June 1941 – BS 3 391 –, arts. 39 and 57 of the Code of Military Justice, in the wording of 13th June 1941 – SR 321.0). On the other hand the consequences of a deprivation of civic rights as regards eligibility for appointment to authorities or public offices are not waived in cases

3. anyone whose interests are in serious conflict with those of the person to whom he is to be appointed guardian, and any one who is at enmity with that person;

4. members of the guardianship authorities acting in the case, where there are other persons fitted to hold office.

Art. 385

[1] The guardianship board is required to appoint the guardian without delay.

[2] Where necessary, the preliminary steps can be taken with a view to the appointment of a committee for a person, even before he has attained his majority.

[3] If children of full age require a committee, they are as a rule placed under parental power instead of under a committee.

B. Procedure in appointment
I. Appointment of guardian

Art. 386

[1] Where before the appointment of a guardian any business connected with the guardianship has to be transacted, the guardianship board in its official capacity takes the necessary measures.

[2] In particular it can provisionally deprive the person to be placed under a committee of his capacity to effect a legal transaction and appoint an agent to act for him.

[3] Such measures must be publicly announced.

II. Provisional measures

---

where deprivation of civic rights was pronounced in a judgement passed by a criminal court before 1st July 1971 (SR **311.0** *in fine,* Final Provisions, alteration of 18th March 1971, cipher III 3 paragraph 3). Equally the consequences of deprivation of civic rights are not terminated in cases where judgement was passed in accordance with the Code of Military Justice before 1st February 1975 (SR **321.0** *in fine,* Final Provisions, alteration of 4th October 1974, cipher II 2).

Art. 387

III. Notification and public advertisement

¹ The guardian must immediately be notified in writing of his appointment.

² The name of the person appointed as guardian must at the same time as the fact of appointment be advertised in the official gazette of the ward's domicile and in that of his legal home.

Art. 388

IV. Refusal to act and opposition
1. Procedure

¹ The person appointed can within ten days of receiving notice of his appointment refuse to act, if he can support his refusal with a valid excuse.

² Moreover any interested party can within ten days of cognizance of the appointment oppose it as being contrary to law.

³ Where the refusal to accept office or the opposition to the appointment is admitted as justified by the guardianship board, the board makes a fresh appointment; where it is not admitted, the board lays the case together with a report on it before the supervisory authority for decision.

Art. 389

2. Temporary duties of person appointed

The person appointed, who refuses to accept office or whose appointment is opposed, is nevertheless bound to carry out the duties incident to the office until he has been relieved of it.

Art. 390

3. Decision

¹ The supervisory authority notifies the person appointed and the guardianship board of its decision.

² If he is relieved of the office, the board immediately proceeds to make a fresh appointment.

Art. 391

V. Investment of office

On the final appointment of the guardian the guardianship board invests him with his office.

Chapter V: Office of Curator

Art. 392

The guardianship board will at the request of an interested party or officially of its own accord appoint a curator in the cases specially provided by law and further in the following cases:

1. where a person of full age by reason of illness, absence, or other similar cause cannot in some urgent matter act personally or appoint another to act for him;

2. where the legal representative of a minor or person under a committee has interests in some transaction which are in conflict with those of the person for whom he is acting;

3. where the legal representative is prevented from acting.

A. Cases
I. Representation

Art. 393

Where there is no one to administer an estate, the guardianship board is required to make the necessary provisions and more particularly to appoint a curator in the following cases:

1. where a person has been away for a considerable time and his place of residence is unknown;

2. where a person is unable to manage his affairs himself or to appoint an agent to act for him and yet it is not a case for the appointment of a guardian or committee;

3. where rights of succession are not clearly determined or where the interests of a child before birth must be safeguarded;

4. in the case of a corporate body or foundation, where its organisation is not yet completed and no other provision has been made for its administration;

5. in the case of a public collection of moneys for a charitable or other useful public object, where no

II. Administration of property
1. By operation of law

provision has been made for their administration or application.

Art. 394

2. At party's request

A curator can be appointed for any person of full age at his own request, where the circumstances are such that he could have demanded the appointment of a committee.

Art. 395

III. Restricted capacity

[1] Where there is not sufficient ground for placing a person under a committee and yet his own interests demand that his legal capacity be practically restricted, a quasi-guardian can be appointed, whose concurrence will be required in the following cases:[1]

1. to bring or compromise an action;
2. to purchase, sell, mortgage or otherwise charge immovable property;
3. to purchase, sell or pledge securities;[2]
4. to carry out building operations, where these go beyond the limits of ordinary acts of administration;
5. to lend and to borrow money;
6. to receive re-payment of borrowed principal;
7. to make a donation;
8. to become a party to a negotiable instrument;
9. to enter into a contract of suretyship.

---

[1] **Beirat,** *Conseil légal,* lit. "legal adviser", is a kind of curator, but differs from him in that the appointment restricts to a certain extent the legal capacity of the person subject to it.

[2] "Securities" is used to render the German, **Wertpapiere,** and the French, *papiers-valeurs.* The term includes papers which constitute documents of title, and which therefore are of value in themselves as conferring a right upon the person entitled to hold them, *e.g.* certificates of shares in a company, coupons for interest on investments, bills of exchange and other negotiable instruments, etc.

From these "securities", distinguish "securities on land", which are mortgages or similar charges, registered in the land register, and "security" or guarantee, which may take a variety of forms for protecting the interests of the person to be guaranteed against loss.

² Under similar conditions a person can be deprived of the right to manage his property while retaining the right to freely dispose of the income derived therefrom.

Art. 396

¹ A curator is appointed by the guardianship board of the domicile of the person for whom he has to be appointed.   B. Competence

² Where, however, the curator is required for the administration of an estate, he is appointed by the guardianship board of the place where the chief part of the estate has been administered or has come into the possession of the person for whom the curator has to act.

³ The home Commune has, for the safeguarding of the interests of its citizens, the same rights as in the matter of guardianship.

Art. 397

¹ The procedure is the same as in the case of the appointment of a guardian.   C. Appointment

² The appointment is publicly advertised only where the guardianship board deems it advisable.

Chapter VI: Deprivation of Liberty for Personal Assistance[1]

Art. 397a[1]

¹ Any major or a person under committee can be placed or retained in a suitable institution by reason of insanity, feeblemindedness, drunkenness, drug addiction or a serious state of neglect if there is no   A. Conditions

---

[1] Inserted by cipher I of the Federal Statute of 6th October 1978, in force since 1st January 1981 (AS 1980 31 35; BBl 1977 III 1).

other way of providing the necessary care for this person.

² In making this decision it must be taken into account to what extent the person concerned is a burden to his environment.

³ The person concerned must be released from custody as soon as his state permits it.

Art. 397b[1]

B. Competence
¹ A guardianship board at the domicile or, where a delay involves danger, a guardianship board at the place of the person's present sojourn is competent for the decision to be made.

² For all cases where delay involves danger or the person is suffering from a mental illness, the Cantons can also entrust other qualified authorities with this competence.

³ Where a guardianship board has ordered that a person be placed or retained in an institution, the guardianship board also decides upon the person's release; in all other cases the institution decides.

Art. 397c[1]

C. Obligation to inform
The guardianship board at the place of the person's present sojourn and the other bodies determined by Cantonal Law inform the guardianship board at the domicile, if they want to place or retain a person under committee in an institution or if, in the case of a major, they consider further guardianship measures necessary.

Art. 397d[1]

D. Appeal to judge
¹ The person concerned or a person who entertains a close relation to the person concerned can

---

[1] Inserted by cipher I of the Federal Statute of 6th October 1978, in force since 1st January 1981 (AS 1980 31 35; BBl 1977 III 1).

apply to the judge within ten days after receiving notice in writing.

² This right also exists where an application for release is rejected.

Art. 397e[1]

The procedure is determined by Cantonal Law. The following provisions are made:

E. Procedure in Cantons
I. In general

1. The person concerned must be informed about the reasons justifying the decision in every single case and his attention must be drawn in writing to the possibility that he can apply to the judge.

2. Anyone who enters an institution must be informed in writing immediately that in case he is retained in the institution or if his request for a release from the institution is rejected, he can apply to the judge.

3. A request for judgement by the court must be brought to the competent judge's notice without delay.

4. The authority which ordered the person's being placed in an institution or the judge can accord the application for a judicial decision a suspensory effect.

5. Where a mental patient is concerned a decision may only be made on the report of an expert; where this has been done in an earlier proceeding at court, higher courts can renounce the expert's report.

Art. 397f[1]

¹ The judge decides in a simple and rapid procedure.

II. At court

² He appoints, if necessary, judicial assistance for the person concerned.

---

[1] Inserted by cipher I of the Federal Statute of 6th October 1978, in force since 1st January 1981 (AS 1980 31 35; BBl 1977 III 1).

³ The person concerned must be heard, orally, by the judge in the first instance.

Title XI: Administration of Guardianship

Chapter I: Duties of Guardian

Art. 398

A. On entering upon office
I. Inventory

¹ On entering upon his office, a guardian must with the help of a representative of the guardianship board draw up an inventory of the ward's property.

² Where the ward has discretion, he is invited if possible to take part in the drawing up of the inventory.

³ Where circumstances require it and at the instance of the guardian and the guardianship board, the supervisory authority can order a public inventory which has the same effect as the public inventory in the Law of Inheritance.

Art. 399

II. Custody of deeds and objects of value

Deeds, objects of value, important papers and such like must, as far as the management of the property allows, be deposited for safe custody under the supervision of the guardianship board.

Art. 400

III. Sale of movables

¹ The other movable property must, where the ward's interests require it, be sold by public auction or private treaty, according to the directions of the guardianship board.

² Objects that the ward himself or his family specially value should, wherever possible, not be sold.

Art. 401

The cash which the guardian does not require for the use of the ward must immediately be deposited at interest in a bank specified by the guardianship board or some Cantonal regulation, or in an investment approved by the board as safe after examination. *IV. Cash 1. Its investment*

Art. 402

¹ Investments that are not sufficiently secure must be converted into secure investments. *2. Conversion*

² This conversion must, however, be effected at an opportune moment and in such a manner as to safeguard the ward's interests.

Art. 403

If there is a business or industry connected with the property, the guardianship board will give the necessary instructions to wind it up or continue it. *V. Business and industry*

Art. 404

¹ The sale of immovable property can take place only in pursuance of instructions from the guardianship board and it will be permitted only if the ward's interests require it. *VI. Immovable property*

² The sale must take place by public auction, and the adjudication of the property cannot be made without the approval of the guardianship board; this must be signified without delay.

³ In exceptional cases and with the consent of the supervisory authority the sale may take place by private treaty.

Art. 405

B. Care of ward and representation
I. Care of ward's person
1. Where he is a minor
a. In general[1]

[1] Where the ward is a minor, it is the duty of the guardian to look after his maintenance and education.

[2] For this purpose he has the same rights as parents, subject, however, to the necessity for the concurrence of the guardianship authorities in the specified cases.

Art. 405a[2]

b. Deprivation of liberty to secure care of ward

[1] The guardianship board decides on the guardian's proposal about placing a minor in an institution; where delay involves danger the guardian himself decides.

[2] Further the provisions relating to competence, judicial decision and the procedure for the deprivation of liberty apply accordingly where majors or persons under committee are concerned.

[3] Where the child is not yet sixteen years old, he cannot request judgement by the judge himself.

Art. 406[3]

2. Where he is placed under committee

[1] Where the ward is a major, it is the committee's duty to give him protection and assistance in all personal matters.

[2] Where a delay involves danger, the guardian can give orders for placing or retaining the ward in an institution according to the provisions made for the deprivation of liberty in order to secure care.

---

[1] Corrected by the Editorial Committee of the United Federal Assembly (art. 33 of the Course of Business Act – SR 171.11).
[2] Inserted by cipher II of the Federal Statute of 6th October 1978, in force since 1st January 1981 (AS 1980 31 35; BBl 1977 III 1).
[3] Wording according to cipher II of the Federal Statute of 6th October 1978, in force since 1st January 1981 (AS 1980 31 35; BBl 1977 III 1).

Art. 407

The guardian acts on behalf of the ward in all legal transactions, subject, however, to the necessity for the concurrence of the guardianship authorities.

II. Representation
1. In general

Art. 408

No contract of guarantee nor donation of any value can be made, nor foundation created at the expense of the ward.

2. Prohibited acts

Art. 409

[1] Where the ward has discretion and is at least sixteen years old, the guardian must in all important transactions as far as possible consult him before making any decision.

[2] The fact, however, that the ward has given his consent does not exempt the guardian from liability.

3. Concurrence of ward

Art. 410

[1] A ward who has discretion can with the guardian's express or tacit consent beforehand or his subsequent ratification enter into a binding obligation or renounce a right.

[2] The other party to the transaction is discharged from any liability thereunder, if the ratification is delayed beyond a reasonable time, which has been fixed either by that party himself or by the court at his request.

4. Ward's own acts
a. Consent of guardian

Art. 411

[1] Where the ward's act is not ratified, both parties can claim the return of anything which has passed under it; the ward, however, is only liable to restore the amount by which he has benefited under it, or by which he has been enriched and which is still in his possession at the date of the action, or which would

b. Consent withheld

have been in his possession if he had not fraudulently alienated it.

² If the ward has fraudulently induced the other party to believe that he was under no disability, he will be held liable for all damage which the other has thereby suffered.

Art. 412

5. Trade or profession of ward

Where a ward has been expressly or tacitly authorized by the guardianship board to carry on a trade or profession, he can do all acts incident to it and thereby make himself liable to the extent of his whole property.

Art. 413

C. Administration of property
I. Duties of guardian and accounts

¹ The guardian is required to administer the ward's property with care.

² He must keep accounts and submit them for examination to the guardianship board at stated periods according to the board's directions, but at least every two years.

³ Where the ward has discretion and is at least sixteen years old, he must where possible be invited to attend at the rendering of accounts.

Art. 414

II. Ward's separate estate

A ward can deal by himself with everything which is given to him as his separate estate or which he has acquired with his guardian's consent by his own efforts.

Art. 415

D. Duration of office

¹ A guardian is generally appointed for a period of two years.

² At the end of any two years, his office can be continued for another two years by a mere confirmation in office.

Administration of Guardianship

³ At the end of four years the guardian can refuse to continue in office.

Art. 416

A guardian is entitled to a honorarium paid out of the ward's property; its amount will be fixed by the guardianship board for each period of office according to the work involved and the ward's income.

E. Honorarium

Chapter II: Duties of Curator

Art. 417

¹ Subject to the rules relating to the need for the concurrence of a quasi-guardian, the appointment of a curator does not affect the legal capacity of the person in whose interests he is appointed.

A. Nature of office

² The period for which a curator holds office and his honorarium are fixed by the guardianship board.

Art. 418

Where a curator is appointed for a single transaction, he must follow minutely the instructions of the guardianship board.

B. Duties
I. For single transaction

Art. 419

¹ Where a curator is appointed to look after some property or to manage an estate, he must confine himself to acts necessary for its administration or the maintenance of its revenues.

II. For administration of an estate

² He cannot do any acts outside this without the consent of the person for whom he is acting, or if he is incapacitated from giving his consent, without the authorization of the guardianship board.

Chapter III: Functions of Guardianship Authorities

Art. 420

A. Complaints

¹ The ward himself if he has discretion and any interested party can lodge a complaint with the guardianship board about any of the guardian's acts.

² An appeal to the supervisory authority can be brought against the decisions of the guardianship board within ten days from the date when they were made known.

Art. 421

B. Consent required
I. Of guardianship board

The consent of the guardianship board is required for the following acts by or on behalf of the ward:

1. to purchase or sell, mortgage or otherwise charge immovable property;

2. to purchase, sell or pledge other forms of property, where this does not form part of the ordinary administration and management of the ward's affairs;

3. to carry out building operations where these go beyond the limits of ordinary administration;

4. to lend and to borrow money;

5. to become a party to a negotiable instrument;

6. to make an agricultural lease for a term of one year or over, or an occupation lease for a period of three years or over;

7. to authorize the ward to carry on a trade or profession on his own account;

8. to bring, defend or compromise an action, agree to arbitration or to a composition between debtor and creditors, except where in urgent cases the guardian can take provisional measures;

9. to make a marriage covenant and to partition an inheritance;

10. to make a declaration of insolvency;

11. to make a contract of insurance on the ward's life;

12. to make a contract for the ward's apprenticeship to a trade or profession;

13. ...[1]

14. to change the ward's domicile.

Art. 422

The further consent of the supervisory authority in confirmation of the decision of the guardianship board is required for the following cases:

II. Of supervisory authority

1.[2] adoption of a ward or by a ward;

2. acquisition or renunciation of citizenship;

3. taking over or winding up of a business, membership of an association where this involves the personal liability of the ward or the bringing in of considerable capital;

4. making a contract for a life allowance or annuity or for care and maintenance for life;[3]

5. acceptance or renunciation of an inheritance or making a testamentary pact;

6. emancipation of the ward;

7. making valid contracts between the guardian and the ward.

---

[1] Annulled by cipher II of the Federal Statute of 6th October 1978 (AS 1980 31; BBl 1977 III 1).

[2] Wording according to cipher I 3 of the Federal Statute of 30th June 1972, in force since 1st April 1973 (AS 1972 2819 2829; BBl 1971 I 1200).

[3] This is taken to be the nearest equivalent of the German: **Leibgedings-, Leibrenten- und Verpfründungsverträge**, of the French: *contrats dont l'objet est une pension, une rente viagère ou l'entretien viager*, and of the Italian: *i contratti di vitalizio e di rendita vitalizia*. The first two forms, rendered in the Italian by a single term, are much the same, but the third is somewhat different; it is a contract by which one person, A, hands over property or a capital sum to another, B, on condition that B shall engage to maintain and care for A for the rest of his life. The rules are given in CO arts. 516 *et seq.*

Art. 423

C. Examination of reports and accounts

¹ The guardianship board examines the periodical reports and accounts of the guardian and where necessary orders them to be supplemented or rectified.

² It approves or rejects them and where necessary takes the proper measures to safeguard the ward's interests.

³ Cantons can order a revision or confirmation of the reports and accounts by the supervisory authority.

Art. 424

D. Where consent withheld

Acts done on behalf of the ward without the required consent of the competent guardianship authority have for him only the same effect as those done by him without his guardian's consent.

Art. 425

E. Cantonal regulations

¹ The Cantons are required to draw up regulations in greater detail in regard to the concurrence of the guardianship authorities.

² They must in particular make rules for the investment and conservation of the ward's capital, as well as for the method of keeping and of rendering accounts and of drawing up reports.

³ These rules require for their validity to be approved by the Federal Council.

Chapter IV: Liabilities of Organs of Guardianship

Art. 426

A. In general
I. Guardian and authorities

The guardian and the members of the guardianship authorities must in the discharge of their respective duties exercise the degree of care required by good management, and are liable for all damage which they do wilfully or through negligence.

Art. 427

¹ The Canton is liable for all damage which has not been made good by the guardian or the members of the guardianship authorities.

² The Cantons are, however, entitled to require that this liability, which falls on them through the default of the guardian and the guardianship authorities, shall be satisfied in the first place by the Communes and district authorities concerned.

II. Communes, district authorities and Cantons

Art. 428

¹ Each member of the guardianship authority, which has incurred liability as such, shares in this liability, unless he can prove his complete innocence in the matter.

² Each responsible member is liable for his share of the damage caused.

B. Conditions of liability
I. Of members of authorities *inter se*

Art. 429

¹ Where the members of the guardianship board are liable as well as the guardian, they are only secondarily liable after the guardian himself has failed to make good the damage.

² Where the members of the supervisory authority are liable as well as those of the guardianship board, the former are only secondarily liable after the latter have failed to make good the damage.

³ All persons are primarily liable for damage caused by fraud in which they are concerned, and this liability is joint and several.

II. Of the different organs *inter se*

Art. 429a[1]

¹ Where a person is injured by illegal deprivation of liberty, he is entitled to receiving an indemnity and,

C. Deprivation of liberty to secure care of ward

---

[1] Inserted by cipher II of the Federal Statute of 6th October 1978, in force since 1st January 1981 (AS 1980 31 35; BBl 1977 III 1).

where the gravity of the injury justifies it, to being given moral satisfaction.

²The Canton is liable with the proviso of recourse against the persons who have caused the injury wilfully or through serious negligence.

Art. 430

D. Actions[1]

¹The court decides all cases in which the plaintiff seeks to enforce the liability of guardians, members of the guardianship authorities, Communes, district authorities and Cantons.

²These actions cannot be made to depend on a previous inquiry by an administrative body.

Title XII: How Guardianship Ends

Chapter I: Termination of Incapacity

Art. 431

A. In the case of minors

¹The guardianship of a minor comes to an end on his attaining his majority or on his emancipation.

²Where the competent authority pronounces his emancipation, it fixes at the same time the day on which the guardianship shall determine and provides for its public advertisement in an official gazette.

Art. 432

B. Where sentenced to imprisonment

¹The guardianship of a person sentenced to imprisonment comes to an end with his discharge from prison.

²A temporary or conditional release does not determine the guardianship.

---

[1] Originally lit. C.

Art. 433

¹ The guardianship of other persons comes to an end by an order of the competent authority for their discharge.   C. In the case of other persons
I. Condition of release

² The authority is bound to make this order as soon as the reason for their guardianship has ceased to exist.

³ The ward himself or any interested party can demand the discharge.

Art. 434

¹ The procedure for obtaining a discharge is regulated by the Cantons.   II. Procedure
1. In general

² An appeal lies to the Federal Court.

Art. 435

¹ The discharge must be publicly advertised, if the appointment of the guardian was advertised.   2. Public advertisement

² Such advertisement is, however, not essential to the ward's resumption of his full legal capacity.

Art. 436

The discharge of a person placed under a committee for insanity or feeblemindedness can be ordered only on the report of an expert stating that the reason for his commission has ceased to exist.   3. In case of insanity

Art. 437

A person under a committee for prodigality, drunkenness, immorality or the mismanagement of his affairs can demand his discharge only where for one year at least he has given no further grounds of complaint of the kind which led to his commission.   4. In case of prodigality, drunkenness, immorality, mismanagement

Art. 438

5. Where committed at ward's own request

The discharge of a person placed under a committee at his own request can be ordered only where the reason for his commission has ceased to exist.

Art. 439

D. In the case of a curator
I. In general

¹ The representation of a person by a curator comes to an end with the completion of the business for which he was appointed.

² The administration of property by a curator comes to an end as soon as the reason for which he was appointed has ceased to exist and he has been relieved of his office.

³ The legal assistance of a quasi-guardian comes to an end by an order of the competent authority, the same rules being applicable as in the case of a discharge from commission.

Art. 440

II. Public advertisement

The discharge from a curator must be publicly advertised in an official gazette, if his appointment was advertised or if the guardianship board otherwise holds it advisable.

Chapter II: Termination of Guardian's Functions

Art. 441

A. Incapacity, death

The functions of a guardian are determined by his death or loss of capacity.

Art. 442

B. Dismissal, non-reappointment
I. Expiration of term of office

The functions of a guardian are determined by the expiration of the term for which he has been appointed, unless the term is renewed by a confirmation in office.

Art. 443

¹ Where a ground for his exclusion from office supervenes after his appointment, a guardian must resign his office.

² If a ground for his being excused from office supervenes, a guardian cannot generally demand his release before the expiration of his term of office.

II. Supervening grounds for exclusion or excuse

Art. 444

The guardian is bound to continue to perform all necessary acts of administration until his successor has entered upon his duties.

III. Duty to continue in office

Art. 445

¹ Where a guardian is guilty of gross negligence or of a misuse of his official position or of such misconduct that it makes him unworthy of an office of trust, or where he becomes insolvent, he must be dismissed from office by the guardianship board.

² Where a guardian fails in his official duties, the guardianship board can, even if he committed no wrong, relieve him of his office, if the ward's interests are imperilled.

C. Dismissal
I. Grounds

Art. 446

¹ An application for a guardian's dismissal can be made by the ward himself if he has discretion or by any interested party.

² Where a ground for dismissal comes to the notice of the guardianship board in some other way, it will proceed officially to dismiss the guardian.

II. Procedure
1. At request of parties and officially

Art. 447

¹ Before dismissal the guardianship board must inquire into the circumstances of the case and hear the guardian's defence.

2. Inquiry and infliction of penalty

Art. 448

3. Provisional measures

²In the case of minor irregularities the board may simply threaten the guardian with dismissal and inflict a fine, with a maximum of one hundred francs.

Art. 448

3. Provisional measures

Where delay would be dangerous, the guardianship board can temporarily suspend a guardian from office and if necessary institute proceedings for his arrest and the sequestration of his property.

Art. 449

4. Further measures

Besides dismissal and the imposition of penalties the guardianship board must take all necessary measures to safeguard the ward's interests.

Art. 450

5. Appeal

An appeal from the decisions of the guardianship board lies to the supervisory authority.

Chapter III: Effect of Determination of Guardianship

Art. 451

A. Final account and surrender of property

At the determination of his office the guardian must present the final report and the final accounts to the guardianship board and hold the property ready for its surrender to the ward or his heirs or to the guardian appointed to succeed him.

Art. 452

B. Examination of final report and accounts

The final report and accounts will be examined and approved by the guardianship authorities in the same manner as the periodic reports and accounts.

Art. 453

C. Discharge of guardian

¹When the final report and accounts have been approved and the ward's property is ready for its

How Guardianship ends

surrender to him or his heirs or to the new guardian, the guardianship board relieves the guardian of his office.

² The final accounts must be shown to the ward or his heirs or to the new guardian, and the rules relating to the action to enforce liability are also brought to their notice.

³ They are at the same time notified of the board's decision to relieve the guardian of his office or to reject the final accounts.

Art. 454

¹ Actions to enforce the liability of the guardian and the primary liability of the members of the guardianship authorities must be brought within a year from the submission of the final accounts. D. Action to enforce liability
I. Limitation of actions in ordinary cases

² Actions against the members of the guardianship authorities who are only secondarily liable and against the Communes, the district authorities and the Cantons must be brought within one year from the date of accrual of the right of action.

³ The period of limitation of the action against members of the guardianship authorities, the Communes, the district authorities, or Cantons does not in any case commence to run before the determination of the guardianship.

Art. 455

¹ Where there is an error in the accounts or where the fact that constitutes the ground of liability could not have been discovered until after the commencement of the ordinary period of limitation, the period of limitation is extended to one year from the discovery of the error or of the ground of liability, but in any case to not more than ten years from the commencement of the ordinary period of limitation. II. Limitation of actions in special cases

² An action to enforce liability for an act which also constitutes a criminal offence is not subject to

the period of limitation in ordinary cases, but can be brought at any time within the period allowed for criminal proceedings.

Art. 456

E. Priority of ward's claims

In the case of bankruptcy of the guardian or of members of the guardianship authorities or an execution for debt levied against them, the ward's claims against them have the priority conferred by the Federal Statute of 11th April 1889 on Bankruptcy and Execution.[1]

Part III: Law of Inheritance

Section I: Heirs[2]

Title XIII: Statutory Heirs

Art. 457

A. Heirs who are relatives[3]
I. Descendants

[1] The nearest heirs of a deceased person are his descendants.

[2] Children take *per capita*.

[3] Predeceased children are represented by their descendants; these take *per stirpes* in all degrees of descent.

---

[1] SR 281.1.
[2] The term "heir" has been adopted to designate any person who has a right to succeed on the death of another to his estate or to part of it, whether by law or under a will. Where his right is given him by law, he is called a "statutory heir", where by will, an "instituted heir".
[3] This term is used according to cipher I 3 of the Federal Statute of 30th June 1972, in force since 1st April 1973 (AS 1972 2819 2829; BBl 1971 I 1200).

Art. 458

¹ Where the deceased leaves no descendants, the inheritance passes to his parents. II. Parents and their descendants

² They take *per capita.*

³ A predeceased father or mother is represented by his or her descendants; these take *per stirpes* in all degrees of descent.

⁴ In default of descendants on the paternal side, the whole inheritance passes to the heirs on the other side.

Art. 459

¹ Where the deceased leaves no descendants nor parents or their descendants, the right of inheritance passes to the grandparents. III. Grandparents and their descendants

² Where he leaves grandparents on both the paternal and the maternal side, they take *per capita* the half share that falls to each side.

³ A predeceased grandparent is represented by his descendants, and they take *per stirpes* in all degrees of descent.

⁴ Where the grandfather or the grandmother on the paternal or the maternal side predeceases leaving no descendants, the whole of his half share falls to the surviving heirs on the same side.

⁵ In default of heirs on the paternal or the maternal side, the whole inheritance passes to the heirs on the other side.

Art. 460[1]

The right of inheritance based on relationship ceases with the *stirps* of the grandparents. IV. Extent of the right of inheritance

---

[1] Wording according to cipher I 2 of the Federal Statute of 5th October 1984, in force since 1st January 1988 (BBl **1979 II** 1191).

Art. 461[1]

V. Illegitimate relations

annulled

Art. 462[2]

B. The surviving spouse

The surviving spouse takes:

1. the property in one half where he or she has to share the estate with descendants;

2. the property in three quarters where he or she has to share the estate with the heirs of the parental stirps;

3. the whole inheritance where there are not any heirs of the parental stirps either.

Arts. 463 and 464[3]

annulled

Art. 465[4]

C. Adopted children

annulled

Art. 466[2]

D. Canton and Commune

In default of heirs of the deceased, the inheritance devolves to the Canton of the deceased's last domicile or to the Commune entitled under the law of the Canton.

---

[1] Annulled by cipher I 2 of the Federal Statute of 25th June 1976 (AS 1977 237; BBl 1974 II 1).

[2] Wording according to cipher I 2 of the Federal Statute of 5th October 1984, in force since 1st January 1988 (BBl 1979 II 1191).

[3] Annulled by cipher I 2 of the Federal Statute of 5th October 1984, with effect from 1st January 1988 (BBl 1979 II 1191).

[4] Annulled by cipher I 3 of the Federal Statute of 30th June 1972 (AS 1972 2819; BBl 1971 I 1200). However, see art. 12 lit. a of the Final Title hereinafter.

Title XIV: Testamentary Dispositions[1]

Chapter I: Testamentary Capacity

Art. 467

Every person who has discretion and has completed his eighteenth year has testamentary capacity within the limits and forms established by law.

A. By will

Art. 468

To conclude a testamentary pact the testator must have attained his majority.

B. By testamentary pact

Art. 469

[1] All testamentary dispositions are null and void where the testator has made them under the influence of mistake, fraud, threats or violence.

[2] They become operative, however, where the testator fails to revoke them within one year after discovering the mistake or fraud or after ceasing to be under the influence of the threats or violence.

[3] Where the disposition contains an evident misdescription of a person or thing and the true intentions of the testator can be established with certainty, the mistake must be rectified accordingly.

C. Void dispositions

---

[1] lit. "Dispositions to take effect on death". The shorter title has been adopted because the expression occurs very frequently in the body of the text. These dispositions may be either wills or testamentary pacts; therefore, where the meaning is clear, the words "wills and pacts" or "a will or pact" have been substituted for the term "testamentary disposition(s)".

Chapter II: Freedom of Disposition

Art. 470

A. Devisable portion
I. What is

¹Where the testator leaves descendants, parents or a spouse as the closest heirs, he or she is entitled to make testamentary dispositions regarding his or her property after deducting their compulsory portions.¹

²In all other cases he can dispose of the whole of his estate.

Art. 471¹

II. Compulsory portion

The compulsory portion is as follows:

1. for a descendant three quarters of his or her statutory share of inheritance;
2. for each of the parents one half;
3. for the surviving spouse one half.

Art. 472²

annulled

Art. 473

IV. Gifts to surviving spouse

¹A testator can by testamentary disposition leave to his or her surviving spouse the usufruct in the whole of the share of the inheritance devolving on their common descendants, the non-common descendants begotten during the time of their marriage and their descendants.³

²Such usufruct is taken to be in satisfaction of the right of inheritance conferred by law on the surviving spouse where these descendants are co-heirs with the spouse.³

---

[1] Wording according to cipher I 2 of the Federal Statute of 5th October 1984, in force since 1st January 1988 (BBl 1979 II 1191).
[2] Annulled by cipher I 2 of the Federal Statute of 5th October 1984, with effect from 1st January 1988 (BBl 1979 II 1191).
[3] Wording according to cipher I 2 of the Federal Statute of 25th June 1976, in force since 1st January 1978 (AS 1977 237 264; BBl 1974 II 1).

³ If the surviving spouse re-marries, he or she loses the usufruct of that portion of the inheritance which at the time of the devolution of inheritance could not have been encumbered with the usufruct in compliance with the ordinary provisions relating to the compulsory portions of descendants.¹

Art. 474

¹ The devisable portion of the estate is determined by its value at the death of the testator.

² In this computation the debts of the deceased, his funeral expenses, the cost of sealing the inheritance and of making an inventory, and that of maintaining for one month the members of the deceased's household must first be deducted from the gross value of the estate.

V. Computation of devisable portion
1. Deduction of debts

Art. 475

Gifts made by the deceased *inter vivos* are included in the value of the estate in so far as they are subject to reduction.

2. Donations *inter vivos*

Art. 476

Where the life of the deceased is insured and he has undertaken by an agreement *inter vivos* or by will or pact to assign the policy to a third person, or has gratuitously transferred it in his lifetime, the redemption value of the policy at the date of the death of the insured is added to the value of the estate.

3. Insurance claims

Art. 477

A testator has the right by will or pact to deprive an heir of his compulsory portion:

1. where he has committed a serious offence against the testator or one of his near kinsmen;

B. Disinheritance
I. Grounds

---

¹ Wording according to cipher I 2 of the Federal Statute of 5th October 1984, in force since 1st January 1988 (BBl **1979 II** 1191).

2. where he has seriously failed in the duties laid upon him by law towards the testator or the latter's family.

Art. 478

II. Effect

¹ The disinherited person can neither claim a share in the inheritance nor bring the action for reduction.

² His share passes, where the testator has not directed otherwise, to the latter's statutory heirs, as if the disinherited person had not survived the testator.

³ The descendants of the disinherited person have the same right to their compulsory portion, as if he had predeceased them.

Art. 479

III. Burden of proof

¹ A disinheritance is valid only where the testator has stated the ground for it in his will or pact.

² In an action by the disinherited person to contest the validity of the ground given, the burden of proving its validity is on the heir or legatee who benefits by the disinheritance.

³ Where this proof is not established or the ground for the disinheritance is not stated, the disposition will be held valid to the extent to which it does not deprive the disinherited person of his compulsory portion, unless indeed it can be shown that the testator made the disposition under an evident mistake as to the ground for the disinheritance.[1]

Art. 480

IV. Disinheritance of insolvent person

¹ Where the creditors of one of the testator's descendants hold certificates of unsatisfied claims against him, the testator can deprive him of the moiety of his compulsory portion, provided he leaves

---

[1] In which case the disinherited person will get not merely his compulsory portion, but his whole statutory share.

that moiety to the descendant's children then born or not.

² This partial disinheritance, however, will be declared void at the instance of the descendant, where at the opening of the succession there are no longer any certificates of unsatisfied claims against him, or where the total amount specified on them does not exceed one quarter of his statutory share of inheritance.

Chapter III: Kinds of Dispositions

Art. 481

¹ A testator can by will or pact dispose of the whole or a part of the devisable portion of his estate.   A. In general

² The part which has not been devised passes to his statutory heir.

Art. 482

¹ A testator can attach burdens or conditions to his dispositions, which all interested parties can enforce as soon as the disposition itself takes effect.   B. Burdens and conditions

² Where an immoral or illegal charge or condition is attached, it voids the disposition itself.

³ Where a charge or condition is senseless or merely vexatious to other persons, it is held to be non-existent.

Art. 483

¹ A testator can institute one heir or several co-heirs for the whole or for only a part of the inheritance.   C. Institution of heir

² Every disposition which purports to give the whole or a part of the inheritance to a beneficiary is held to be an institution of an heir.

Art. 484

D. Legacies
I. Their subject-matter

¹ A testator can leave a beneficiary a legacy of some of his property without instituting him heir.

² He can leave him a specific thing forming part of the estate or the usufruct either in the whole or in part of the estate, or charge his heirs or other beneficiaries to give him some benefit out of the estate or release him from some liability.

³ Where a testator has left a specific legacy, the person charged with it is not bound by it, if the thing bequeathed does not form part of the estate and no contrary intention on the part of the testator is implied in the legacy.

Art. 485

II. Duty of person charged

¹ The thing bequeathed must be delivered in the state and condition in which it is at the date of the opening of the succession, whether it has deteriorated or increased in value since it was bequeathed and whether it is free from, or burdened with, any charges.

² The person charged with the legacy has the same rights and is under the same obligations as an uncommissioned agent in regard to expenses he has incurred in respect of the thing and deteriorations subsequent to the accrual of the inheritance.

Art. 486

III. Relation between legacies and inheritance

¹ Where the legacies exceed either the total value of the inheritance or the benefit conferred upon the person charged with them or the devisable part of the estate, their proportionate reduction can be demanded.

² Legacies remain operative even where the persons charged with them do not survive the testator, or are unworthy to succeed, or disclaim the inheritance.

³ Where a testator has left a legacy to a statutory or instituted heir, the latter can claim it even where he disclaims the inheritance.

Art. 487

A testator can in his will or pact appoint one or more persons to take the inheritance or legacy, if the heir or legatee predeceases the testator or disclaims the inheritance or legacy.

E. Substitution

Art. 488

¹ A testator can in his will or pact charge the instituted heir to pass on the inheritance to another as reversionary heir.¹

² He cannot lay a similar obligation on the reversionary heir.

³ These provisions apply to legacies.

F. Reversionary heir
I. Appointment by testator

Art. 489

¹ In the absence of a contrary direction by the testator, the time at which the inheritance must be passed on is the death of the first heir.²

² Where another time is fixed and it has not arrived at the death of the first heir, the inheritance passes in the meantime to the latter's heirs, provided they give a guarantee.

³ Where for some reason it becomes impossible for the time fixed to arrive, the inheritance passes absolutely to the heirs of the first heir.

II. Time for transfer

Art. 490

¹ In all cases where reversionary heirs are appointed, the competent Probate authority must order the making of an inventory.

III. Safeguards

---

¹ The term "reversionary heir" has been adopted as an equivalent for the German **Nacherbe** and the French *appelé*. Perhaps "remainder heir" would have been more exact, but it seemed advisable wherever possible to keep the terms already coined rather than try to coin new ones.

² The "first heir" has been taken to translate the German **Vorerbe** and the French *grevé*.

² In the absence of a contrary direction by the testator, the inheritance will not be delivered to the first heir unless he gives a guarantee; where the inheritance comprises immovable property, the guarantee may consist of an entry in the land registry of the charge laid upon the heir.

³ Where he cannot give this guarantee or where he prejudices the interests of the reversionary heir, the official administration of the estate must be ordered.

Art. 491

IV. Effect of appointment
1. On first heir

¹ The inheritance is vested in the first heir in the same way as in any other instituted heir.

² He becomes the owner of the estate subject to the obligation to transfer it.

Art. 492

2. On revisionary heir

¹ The inheritance is vested in the reversionary heir, if he is alive, when the time arrives which was fixed for the transfer.

² If he is not alive at that time and the testator has not otherwise provided, the estate remains the property of the first heir.

³ If the first heir does not survive the testator or if he is unworthy to inherit or disclaims the inheritance, it accrues immediately to the reversionary heir.

Art. 493

G. Foundations

¹ The testator can devote the whole or any part of the devisable portion of the estate for some special purpose by way of a foundation.

² But the foundation is valid only where it satisfies the requirements of the law.

Art. 494

¹ A testator can by making a testamentary pact with another person bind himself to leave the inheritance or a legacy to him or to a third person.

² He still retains the right to deal with the property and dispose of it.

³ Testamentary dispositions and donations, however, which conflict with his obligations can be avoided by the other party.

H. Testamentary pacts
I. Institution of heir and legacies

Art. 495

¹ A testator can conclude a pact with one of his heirs by which the heir voluntarily renounces or sells his right of inheritance.

² The renouncing party thereby loses his rights of inheritance.

³ Where the parties do not expressly provide otherwise, the pact is binding on the descendants of the renouncing party.

II. Renunciation
1. Its purport

Art. 496

¹ The renunciation is without effect where in the pact certain heirs are instituted in place of the renouncing party and for some reason they do not acquire the inheritance.

² Where an heir renounces his right of inheritance for the benefit of co-heirs, the renunciation is held to operate only in favour of those of his co-heirs who are within the same nearest stock of descent as himself, and does not benefit more distant heirs.[2]

2. Failure of renunciation[1]

---

[1] "Failure of renunciation" is intended to render the German **lediger Anfall** and the French *loyale échute;* this refers to cases where the renunciation does not pass the share renounced to other heirs but is void.

[2] *i.e.* if the testator's son renounces the inheritance, his share passes to his brothers and sisters and their descendants, but not to any more distant relatives.

Art. 497

3. Rights of creditors of estate

Where the estate is insolvent at the opening of the succession, and the creditors are not satisfied in full by the heirs, the creditors can sue the renouncing party and his heirs, and they will be liable to the extent of the property, which they have received in virtue of the pact during the last five years preceding the death of the testator, and which they still have in their possession at the date of the opening.

Chapter IV: Formalities Required for Testamentary Dispositions

Art. 498

A. Wills
I. Forms
1. In general

A testator can make his will either by a public document, or by a writing in his own hand, or orally.

Art. 499

2. Public will
a. How made

A public will is made in the presence of two witnesses before a notary or other official qualified for this purpose by Cantonal Law.

Art. 500

b. Duties of official

[1] The testator must make his wishes known to the official, who thereupon himself draws up or gets another person to draw up the document and hands it to the testator to read through.

[2] The document must be signed by the testator.

[3] It must further be dated and signed by the official.

Art. 501

c. Duties of witnesses

[1] Immediately after the dating and signing, the testator must make a declaration to the two witnesses in the presence of the official to the effect that he has

read the document and that it represents his last will and testament.

² The witnesses must both sign an attestation clause appended to the document to the effect that the testator has made this declaration in their presence and that they are of opinion that he had testamentary capacity at the time.

³ It is not necessary that the witnesses should be told the contents of the document.

Art. 502

¹ Where the testator neither reads nor signs the document, the official must read it out to him in the presence of the two witnesses, and the testator must thereupon make the declaration that the document represents his last will and testament. *d. Where testator neither reads nor signs document*

² The witnesses have in this case to certify, by signing an attestation clause, not only that the testator has made the above mentioned declaration to them and appeared to have testamentary capacity, but that the document has been read out to him by the official in their presence.

Art. 503

¹ The following persons cannot be parties to a public will either as officials establishing the legality of the document or as witnesses: persons who are under legal incapacity or who have been deprived of their civic rights and honours by a sentence passed on them by a Criminal Court,[1] or who cannot read or

---

[1] Deprivation of civic rights has been abolished (annulment of arts. 52, 76, 171 and 284 of Criminal Law – SR 311.0 – as well as art. 28 paragraph 2 sentence 2 in the wording of 13th June 1927 – BS 3 391 –, art. 29 paragraph 2 sentence 2 in the wording of 13th June 1941 – BS 3 391 –, arts. 39 and 57 of the Code of Military Justice in the wording of 13th June 1941 – SR 321.0). On the other hand the consequences of a deprivation of civic rights as regards eligibility for appointment to authorities or public offices are not waived in cases where deprivation of civic rights was pronounced in a judgement passed by a criminal court before 1st July 1971 (SR 311.0 *in fine,*

e. Parties

write, as well as the relatives in descending or ascending line[1] and the testator's brothers and sisters and their spouses or the wife or the husband or wife of the testator himself.

[2] Neither the official concerned nor the witnesses, nor yet the descendants or brothers or sisters of any of these can be made beneficiaries under the will.

Art. 504

f. Safe custody of document

The Cantons must see that the officials charged with making public wills themselves preserve the original or a copy of the will they have made, or else deposit it for safe custody at some office destined for the purpose.

Art. 505

3. Holograph will

[1] Where the will is to be a holograph will, the testator must write and sign it himself by hand from beginning to end including the mention of the place, year, month and day it was made.

[2] The Cantons must see that such wills can be deposited for safe custody, either open or sealed, at some office destined for this purpose.

Art. 506

4. Oral will
a. How made

[1] Where a testator by reason of exceptional circumstances, such as imminent danger of death, absence of means of communication, an epidemic or war, is prevented from making his will in any other form, he is entitled to make it orally.

Final Provisions, alteration of 18th March 1971, cipher III 3 paragraph 3). Equally the consequences of deprivation of civic rights are not terminated in cases where judgement was passed in accordance with the Code of Military Justice before 1st February 1975 (SR **321.0** *in fine,* Final Provisions, alteration of 4th October 1974, cipher II 2).

[1] The term is used according to cipher I 3 of the Federal Statute of 30th June 1972, in force since 1st April 1973 (AS 1972 2819 2829; BBl 1971 I 1200).

² For this purpose he must declare his last wishes in the presence of two witnesses and charge them with the business of setting them down with the required formalities.

³ In regard to the incapacity to be a witness, the same rules apply as in the case of a public will.

Art. 507

¹ The oral will must immediately be set down in writing by one of the witnesses with mention of the place, year, month and day in which it was set down. It must be signed by the two witnesses and lodged in court without delay with a statement that the testator having apparently testamentary capacity has declared his last wishes to them under the special circumstances stated.   *b.* Subsequent formalities

² The two witnesses can, instead, appear before the court with a similar declaration and give evidence of the testator's last wishes.

³ Where the testator makes an oral will when on military service, an officer of the rank of captain or a higher rank can take the place of the court for this purpose.

Art. 508

An oral will becomes inoperative at the end of fourteen days after the testator's inability to make his will in another form has ceased to exist.   *c.* Lapse

Art. 509

¹ The testator can at any time revoke his will, provided he makes use of one of the forms prescribed for the making of the will.   II. Revocation and destruction
1. Revocation

² The revocation may be total or partial.

Art. 510

¹ A testator can revoke his will by destroying the document.   2. Destruction

² Where the document is destroyed by accident or through another person's fault, and it cannot be reconstructed accurately or in its entirety, the will becomes void; the remedy is an action for damages.

Art. 511

3. Subsequent will

¹ Where a testator makes a will without expressly revoking an earlier one, it will altogether supersede the earlier one, unless it clearly purports to be only a supplementary disposition.

² Similarly a specific legacy is revoked where the testator subsequently disposes of the thing bequeathed in some manner inconsistent with the legacy.

Art. 512

B. Testamentary pacts
I. How made

¹ A testamentary pact is valid only where the formalities required by a public will have been observed.

² The contracting parties must simultaneously declare their intentions to the official and sign the document in his presence and in the presence of two witnesses.

Art. 513

II. Rescission
1. By the parties
a. By contract or by will

¹ A testamentary pact can at any time be rescinded by the parties by an agreement in writing.

² The testator can for his part revoke the institution of heir or the gift of a legacy under a pact, where after its conclusion the heir or legatee commits an act in relation to the testator which would have constituted a good ground for his disinheritance.

³ Such revocation must be made in one of the forms required for the making of a will.

Art. 514

b. For non-performance

Where a party to a pact can claim some benefit *inter vivos* by virtue of it and he has not received the benefit promised or a guarantee that he will receive it, he can renounce the pact according to the provisions of the Law of Obligations.

Art. 515

¹ Where the heir or legatee dies before the testator, the pact lapses by operation of law.

² Where, however, the testator is at the death of the heir enriched by the pact, the heirs of the deceased can, in the absence of a contrary agreement, claim the return of the amount of such benefit.

2. Where heir predeceases testator

Art. 516

Where a testator has made a will or pact and the devisable portion of his estate is subsequently reduced, the will or pact is not thereby annulled but only becomes subject to the claim for reduction.

C. Reduction of devisable portion

Chapter V: Executors

Art. 517

¹ A testator can in his testamentary disposition appoint one or more persons, who have legal capacity, to execute his last wishes.

² Executors must be notified officially of their appointment, and they must declare within fourteen days from this notice, whether they are willing to accept the appointment; their silence is taken to mean consent.

³ They are entitled to a fair remuneration for their services.

A. Appointment

Art. 518

¹ Where the testator has not provided otherwise, the executor has the rights and is subject to the duties of the official administrator of an inheritance.

B. Position

² He must see that the wishes of the testator are carried out, and in particular must administer the estate, pay the debts of the testator, give effect to the legacies and carry out the division of the inheritance according to the directions of the testator or the provisions of the law.

³ Where several executors are appointed, they are, in the absence of a contrary direction, considered to hold their office jointly.

Chapter VI: Voidance and Reduction of Testamentary Dispositions

Art. 519

A. Voidance
I. Incapacity, undue influence, illegality or immorality

¹ A will or pact is voidable:

1. where it was made at a time when the testator had no testamentary capacity;
2. where it was made under undue influence;
3. where it is illegal or immoral or subject to an illegal or immoral condition.

² The action to void the will or pact can be brought by any heir or beneficiary who is an interested party.

Art. 520

II. Want of formality

¹ A will or pact is voidable if it is not made in the proper form.

² Where the flaw in its form is due to the fact that persons have been made parties to its execution who are themselves beneficiaries or the members of whose families are beneficiaries under it, only the clauses in their favour will be voided.

³ This action is governed by the same rules as that on the ground of testamentary incapacity.[1]

---

[1] *i.e.* as the actions brought for the other grounds of voidance specified in the preceding section. The Code for the sake of brevity merely mentions one of these grounds.

Art. 521

¹ The action to void a will or pact must be brought within one year from the date when the plaintiff had cognizance of the testamentary disposition and of the ground for nullity, and in any case not later than ten years from the date of the opening of the will. *III. Period of limitation*

² It can be brought within thirty years against a beneficiary who has acted fraudulently, where the will or pact is voidable by reason of illegality or immorality or the testamentary incapacity of the testator.

³ The fact that the will or pact is voidable on one of the above mentioned grounds can always be pleaded as a defence to an action to enforce it.

Art. 522

¹ Where a testator has exceeded his rights of disposition, the heirs who have not received the full value of their compulsory portion can demand the reduction of the bequests to their proper limits. *B. Claim for reduction I. Conditions 1. In general*

² In the absence of evidence of a contrary intention on the part of the testator, clauses that specify the shares of the statutory heirs are held to be merely directions as to the method of partition.

Art. 523

Where a testator has by will or pact given to heirs entitled to a compulsory portion, legacies over and above that portion and in excess of the testator's rights of disposition, these legacies will be proportionately reduced to their proper limit. *2. Legacies to heirs entitled to compulsory portions*

Art. 524

¹ Where a testator has exceeded his rights of disposition to the prejudice of an heir who is insolvent, the administrator in his bankruptcy or his creditors, who at the date of the opening of the succession hold *3. Rights of heir's creditors*

certificates of unsatisfied claims against his estate can, if the heir at their request fails to do so, themselves bring the action in reduction of the excess until their claims can be satisfied, provided they do so within the time allowed for the heir himself.

² The same rule applies in the case of a disinheritance where the disinherited person refuses to oppose it.

Art. 525

II. Effect
1. In general

¹ In the absence of evidence of a contrary intention on the part of the testator, the reduction is effected in the same proportion for all instituted heirs and other beneficiaries.

² Subject to the same proviso, where a beneficiary has suffered a reduction of his benefit and he is at the same time charged with a legacy in favour of a third person, he can claim that the amount of his charge be proportionately reduced.

Art. 526

2. Specific legacy

Where a reduction has to be made in a specific legacy and the thing bequeathed cannot be divided up without loss in value, the legatee can either pay the excess and claim the thing, or claim instead of the thing the balance in money due to him after the reduction has been made.

Art. 527

3. Gifts *inter vivos*
a. Cases

The following gifts are subject to the same reduction as testamentary dispositions:

1. gifts *inter vivos* made by the deceased as satisfaction of the donee's right of inheritance or by way of dower, or for the donee's outfitting or as a division of the donor's estate, where they are not liable to be brought into hotchpot;[1]

---

[1] They must be brought into hotchpot, unless the testator directs otherwise (see art. 626).

2. alienations in consideration of a renunciation or sale of rights of inheritance;

3. gifts which the donor had full liberty to revoke and those which he made within the five years preceding his death, with the exception of presents made on occasions where they are customary;

4. alienations made by the deceased with the evident intention of evading the rules restricting his freedom of disposition.

Art. 528

b. Obligation to return them

¹ A donee who has acted *bona fide* is liable to restore only the amount by which he is still enriched by the gift at the date of the opening of the succession.

² Where the benefit received by virtue of a testamentary pact has to be reduced, the beneficiary is entitled to claim the return of a proportionate part of what he gave in consideration for the benefit.

Art. 529

4. Insurance claims

Where the life of the deceased is insured and he has undertaken by an agreement *inter vivos* or by will or pact to assign the policy to a third person or has gratuitously transferred it in his life time, the redemption value of the policy is subject to reduction.

Art. 530

5. Usufructs and rent-charges

Where a testator has burdened the inheritance with usufructs and rent-charges to such an extent, that according to the presumed duration of these rights, their capitalised value would exceed the devisable portion of the estate, the heirs can either demand that they shall be reduced to their proper limit, or redeem them by surrendering the devisable portion of the estate to those entitled.

Art. 531

6. In case of reversionary heir

The appointment of a reversionary heir is not binding on an heir who is entitled to a compulsory portion, in so far as it constitutes a burden on that portion.

Art. 532

III. Order of reduction

Reductions are made in the first place in testamentary dispositions and then in gifts *inter vivos*, beginning with the latest in time and continuing in that order until the compulsory portions are fully restored.

Art. 533

IV. Period of limitation

[1] The action for reduction must be brought within one year from the time when the heirs had cognizance of the infringement of their rights, and in any case not later than ten years from the opening of the will in respect of testamentary dispositions, and from the death of the donor in respect of other gifts.

[2] Where a disposition has been declared void and an earlier one has in consequence revived, the periods run from the date of the declaration of nullity.

[3] The claim for a reduction can always be pleaded as a defence to an action.

Chapter VII: Actions Arising from Testamentary Pacts

Art. 534

A. Where property has passed *inter vivos*

[1] Where a testator transfers his property during his life to his heir under a testamentary pact, the transferee can have a public inventory taken of the property.

[2] Where the testator has not transferred the whole of his property or has acquired property after

the transfer, the pact refers only to the property transferred, unless the parties have agreed otherwise.

³ Where and in so far as the transfer has taken place during the testator's life, the rights and obligations arising from the pact pass in the absence of a contrary provision to the heirs of the instituted heir.

Art. 535

¹ Where under a pact the testator has during his life made transfers to the heir who has renounced his rights, and the property transferred exceeds the devisable portion of the estate, the reduction can be claimed by the other heirs.

² The extent of the reduction is the amount by which the property transferred exceeds the compulsory portion due to the heir who has renounced his rights.

³ The value of the property transferred is estimated according to the rules on hotchpot.

B. Reduction and restitution
I. Claim for reduction

Art. 536

Where the heir who has renounced his rights is compelled by the order for reduction to make some restitution to the estate, he has the right to choose whether he will make this restitution, or bring all that he has received into hotchpot and then claim his share in the distribution of the estate as if he had not renounced his rights.

II. Restitution

Section II: Devolution of the Estate

Title XV: Opening of the Succession[1]

Art. 537

A. Date of opening

[1] The succession opens with the death of the deceased.[2]

[2] Where gifts or divisions of property made by the deceased in his life time are such that they are held to be testamentary, the property passing thereunder will be valued according to the condition of the inheritance at his death.

Art. 538

B. Place and forum

[1] The succession to the whole estate opens at the last domicile of the deceased.

[2] Actions for the avoidance or reduction of testamentary dispositions as well as for the delivery of possession or the distribution of the estate must be brought before the court of this domicile.

Art. 539

C. Conditions on part of heir
I. Capacity to take
1. Legal capacity

[1] Every person can take as heir or otherwise benefit under a will or pact, if he is not under a legal incapacity to inherit.

[2] Where a legacy is left for a definite object to a number of persons together and they do not form a corporate body, it is taken by the legatees individually under a charge to apply it for the prescribed object, or, if this is impossible, the legacy is held to be a foundation.

---

[1] German: **Eröffnung des Erbganges** and French: *Ouverture de la succession*.

[2] The German text always has **Erblasser**, lit. "person leaving the inheritance" for "deceased", Fr. *défunt*.

Art. 540

¹ The following persons are held to be unworthy to take as heirs or otherwise to benefit under a testamentary disposition: 2. Unworthiness
a. Grounds

 1. a person who has intentionally and unlawfully caused or attempted the death of the deceased;

 2. a person who has intentionally and unlawfully made the deceased permanently incapable of making a will or pact;

 3. a person who by fraud, force or threats has induced the deceased to make or revoke a testamentary disposition or prevented him from so doing;

 4. a person who has intentionally and unlawfully suppressed or destroyed a will or pact under circumstances which prevented the testator from re-making it.

² The testator can remove this disability by pardoning the offender.

Art. 541

¹ Unworthiness to inherit affects the offender alone.   *b.* Effect on descendants

² His descendants inherit as if he had died before the deceased.

Art. 542

¹ In order to be able to take an inheritance, the heir must be alive and under no incapacity at the date of the opening of the succession.   II. Surviving the deceased
1. Heirs

² The rights of an heir who died after the opening pass to his heirs.

Art. 543

¹ A legatee has the right to take his legacy, if he is alive and under no incapacity at the date of the opening of the succession.   2. Legatees

² Where he dies before the testator, his legacy devolves, in the absence of evidence of a contrary intention on the part of the testator, to the person who would have been obliged to pay over the legacy.

Art. 544

3. Child before birth

¹ A child is, as from the date of conception, capable of inheriting subject to the condition that it is born alive.

² A still-born child does not inherit.

Art. 545

4. Reversionary heirs

¹ The whole estate or a thing forming part of it can be left to a person who is not born at the date of the opening of the succession, if it is left to him as a reversionary heir or legatee.

² Where no one is appointed as first heir, the statutory heirs are held to be the first heirs.

Art. 546

D. Declaration of absence
I. Succession by absentee
1. Delivery and security

¹ Where a person has been officially declared absent, the heirs or beneficiaries must before the delivery of possession of the estate give security that it shall ultimately be restored to the absentee or to third parties who have a better title.

² This security must be given for five years where the absentee disappeared in circumstances of deadly peril, and for fifteen years where he has been so declared because his place of abode is not known, but in any case at most until the absentee would have attained the age of a hundred years.

³ The period of five years runs from the date of the delivery of possession of the estate, that of fifteen years from the date when the absentee was last heard of.

Art. 547

¹ Where the absentee returns or where persons with a better title make good their claims, the heirs who have entered on the inheritance must restore the estate according to the rules of possession.

² Where they have entered in possession in good faith, they are bound to make restitution to third parties with a better title only during the period allowed for the action to claim an inheritance.

2. Restitution

Art. 548

¹ Where at the date of the opening of the succession no proof exists of the life or death of an heir in consequence of his disappearance, his share must be placed under official administration.

² The persons, to whom the absent heir's share would have devolved if he did not exist, can at the expiration of one year from his disappearance in circumstances of deadly peril, or of five years from the date when he was last heard of, apply to the court for an official declaration of absence, and, when this has been made, for the delivery to them of his share.

³ The delivery takes place according to the rules on the delivery of an absentee's share to his heirs.

II. Right of inheritance of absentee

Art. 549

¹ Where the absentee's heirs have been put in possession of his share, and subsequently another inheritance devolves upon him, his co-heirs can plead this delivery and demand to be put in possession of the property accrued to them without being required to apply for a second declaration of absence.

² Similarly the absentee's heirs can plead a declaration of absence made at the instance of his co-heirs.

III. Relation between the two cases

Art. 550

IV. Official procedure

¹ Where the property of an absent person or his share in an inheritance has been officially administered for ten years, or where he would have attained the age of a hundred years, a declaration of absence will be made officially at the instance of the competent Probate authority.

² If thereupon no claims are made within the period allowed, the property in question passes to the Canton or Commune which would have succeeded in default of heirs, or, if the absentee has never resided in Switzerland, to the Canton where he had his legal home.

³ In regard to the absentee and third parties with a better title, the Canton or Commune is under the same liability to restore the property as heirs who have been put in possession.

Title XVI: Effects of Devolution

Chapter I: Provisional Measures

Art. 551

A. In general

¹ The competent Probate authority of the deceased's last domicile is required to take all necessary measures to secure the devolution of the inheritance.

² In particular it is, in the cases specified by law, required to affix a seal, make an inventory, administer the estate officially and open the will or pact.

³ Where the deceased did not die at his domicile, the Probate authority of the place of his death must notify the Probate authority of his domicile of the fact and take all necessary measures to preserve the property left there by the deceased.

Art. 552

Seals are affixed in the cases provided by Cantonal Law.

B. Affixing of seal

Art. 553

¹ The making of an inventory will be ordered:

C. Inventory

1. where an heir requires the appointment of a guardian or is under guardianship;

2. where an heir is permanently absent and has not appointed an agent to act for him;

3. where one of the heirs demands it.

² The inventory must be made according to the rules laid down by Cantonal Law and be completed as a general rule within two months from the date of the death of the deceased.

³ Cantonal Law may require an inventory in other cases.

Art. 554

¹ The official administration of the estate will be ordered:

D. Official administration
I. In general

1. where an heir is permanently absent and has not appointed an agent to act for him, if such administration is necessary to safeguard his interests;

2. where none of the claimants to the inheritance can supply sufficient proof in support of their claims, or where it is uncertain whether there is an heir;

3. where all the heirs of the deceased are not known;

4. in other special cases specified by law.

² Where the testator has appointed an executor, the administration is placed in his hands.

³ Where a person dies who is under guardianship, the administration is, in the absence of a different provision, placed in the hands of the guardian.

Art. 555

II. Where heirs unknown

¹Where the Probate authority is not certain whether the deceased has left any heirs at all or whether it knows who all the heirs are, claimants are invited by a public citation to notify the authority of their claims within one year.

²Where no claims are notified within this period and the authority does not know of any heirs, the inheritance passes, subject to any action claiming the inheritance, to the Canton or Commune entitled to it.

Art. 556

E. Opening of wills
I. Obligation to deliver up

¹Where a will is found at the death of the deceased, it must be delivered up without delay to the Probate authority, even if it appears to be invalid.

²The official who has drawn up the will or in whose care it was deposited, as well as any person who has taken charge of it or found it among the testator's effects is held personally liable for it and is bound to deliver it up to the Probate authority, as soon as he has cognizance of the testator's death.

³After the delivery up of the will, the Probate authority will either give provisional possession of the estate to the statutory heirs or order official administration of it; where possible the parties interested are first given a hearing.

Art. 557

II. The opening ceremony

¹The will must be opened by the competent Probate authority within a month from its delivery to the authority.

²All the heirs that are known to it are summoned to the opening ceremony.

³Where the deceased left more than one will, they must all be delivered up to the authority and opened by it.

Art. 558

¹ All parties interested in the inheritance receive a copy of the portion of the will that concerns them; the cost of this comes out of the estate. III. Notice to interested parties

² The beneficiaries whose address is not known are informed by public advertisement.

Art. 559

¹ At the expiration of one month after notice to the interested parties, the instituted heirs, whose claims have not been openly contested by the statutory heirs or by beneficiaries under an earlier will, can obtain from the Probate authority a certificate to the effect that they are recognised as heirs subject to an action to void the will or to claim the inheritance. IV. Delivery of possession

² At the same time the official administrator of the estate, if there is one, will be ordered to put these heirs in possession.

Chapter II: Vesting of the Inheritance

Art. 560

¹ The inheritance is vested as a whole in the heir or heirs by operation of law at the death of the deceased. A. Vesting I. Heirs

² Subject to certain statutory exceptions, all rights that belonged to the deceased including debts due to him, choses in action, ownership, rights of possession and other real rights pass *ipso jure* to the heirs, and the latter become personally liable for the debts of the deceased.

³ The vesting of the inheritance in the instituted heir dates back to the time of the opening of the succession, and the statutory heirs are bound to deliver up the estate to them according to the rules on possession.

Art. 561[1]

annulled

Art. 562

III. Legatees
1. Vesting of legacies

[1] Legatees have a personal action against the person charged with the legacy, or if no such person has been specifically appointed, against the statutory or instituted heirs.

[2] Where no other intention appears from the will, the right of action accrues as soon as the person charged has accepted the inheritance or can no longer renounce it.

[3] Where the heirs fail in their obligation towards the legatee, they can be sued either for the delivery of the thing bequeathed or, if the legacy consists in the performance of some act, for damages for non-performance.

Art. 563

2. Rights of legatees in different cases

[1] In the absence of a provision to the contrary, the position of a legatee to whom a usufruct or a rent-charge or the right to some other periodical payment has been bequeathed, is governed by the rules laid down in the Law of Obligations.

[2] Where the bequest is of a policy of insurance on the life of the testator, the legatee can enforce his claim against the insurance office directly.

Art. 564

3. Relative position of creditors and legatees

[1] The rights of the creditors of the deceased take precedence over those of legatees.

[2] The creditors of an heir who has unconditionally accepted the inheritance have the same rights as those of the deceased.

---

[1] Annulled by cipher I 2 of the Federal Statute of 5th October 1984, with effect from 1st January 1988 (BBl **1979 II** 1191).

Art. 565

4. Reduction

¹ Where, after discharging the legacies in full, the heirs pay debts of the estate of which they had no previous knowledge, they are entitled to require that the legatees should pay back the amount by which their legacies would have been reduced if the heirs had enforced their claims to reduction.

² The legatees can, however, be sued only for the amount by which they are still enriched at the date of the action.

Art. 566

B. Disclaimer
I. Declaration
1. Right to disclaim

¹ Statutory and instituted heirs have the right to disclaim the inheritance that has accrued to them.

² A disclaimer is presumed by law, if the deceased was insolvent at his death and this insolvency was common knowledge or officially declared.

Art. 567

2. Period within which allowed
a. In general

¹ The period allowed for a disclaimer is three months.

² It runs for statutory heirs from the day when they had cognizance of the death of the deceased, unless they can prove that they did not know of their rights of succession until later; it runs for instituted heirs from the day on which they were officially notified of the dispositions in their favour.

Art. 568

b. Where an inventory has been made

Where an inventory has been made as a provisional measure, the period allowed for a disclaimer runs for all heirs from the day on which they received official notice of the completion of the inventory.

Art. 569

3. Right of disclaimer passes to the heirs

¹ Where an heir dies before disclaiming or accepting the inheritance, the right of disclaimer passes to his heirs.

² The period runs for the latter heirs from the day on which they had cognizance of the accrual of the inheritance to the deceased heir and does not expire until the expiration of the period allowed for his own disclaimer.

³ Where these heirs disclaim and the inheritance passes to other heirs who had previously no right of inheritance, the period runs for the latter from the date of their cognizance of the disclaimer.

Art. 570

4. Form required

¹ The disclaimer must be made by a written or oral declaration on the part of the heir to the competent Probate authority.

² It must be made unconditionally and without any reservation.

³ The Probate authority must keep a special register for disclaimers.

Art. 571

II. Lapse of right of disclaimer

¹ Where an heir does not make the required declaration of disclaimer within the time limit, the inheritance passes to him unconditionally.

² Where an heir has within the time limit intermeddled with the inheritance or done acts which were not required for the mere management of the estate and the carrying on of the affairs of the deceased, or appropriated or concealed anything forming part of the estate, he thereby loses his right of disclaimer.

Art. 572

III. Disclaimer by co-heir

¹ Where the deceased has died intestate and one of several co-heirs disclaims, his share devolves as if he had not survived the deceased.[1]

---

[1] *i.e.* if he has no issue, his share lapses and falls to his co-heirs; if he has issue, they inherit it.

[2] Where the deceased has died testate, and one of the instituted heirs disclaims, his share passes, in the absence of a contrary intention shown by the testator, to the latter's nearest statutory heir.

Art. 573

[1] Where all the nearest statutory heirs of the deceased disclaim the inheritance, it will be wound up by the official in bankruptcy.[1]

[2] Surplus assets left after payment of all the debts pass to the persons entitled, as if no disclaimers had been made.[2]

IV. Disclaimer by all nearest heirs
1. In general

Art. 574

Where the descendants of the deceased have disclaimed, the surviving husband or wife will be officially notified of this and has one month in which to accept.

2. Right of surviving spouse

Art. 575

[1] In their disclaimer heirs can demand that the winding up be postponed until the heirs entitled immediately after them have been given the opportunity to declare their intentions.

[2] In this case these latter will be officially notified of the disclaimer, and if they do not accept within one month, they also will be held to have disclaimed.

3. Disclaimer in favour of more distant heirs

Art. 576

The competent Probate authority can on material grounds grant an extension or a renewal of the time allowed for statutory and instituted heirs.

V. Extension of time limit

---

[1] *i.e.* there is no *successio graduum,* the reason being that the disclaimer by the nearest heirs would be due to the insolvency of the estate and even if the heirs in the next rank to the first were given the chance of accepting, they would not do so. But see art. 575.

[2] *i.e.* though the nearest heirs have disclaimed, they are allowed to benefit by the surplus, if there is one.

Art. 577

VI. Disclaimer of a legacy

In the absence of evidence in the will of a contrary intention, the disclaimer by a legatee of his legacy operates in favour of the person charged with it.

Art. 578

VII. Securing heir's creditors

[1] Where an insolvent heir has disclaimed for the purpose of depriving his creditors of the estate, they themselves or the official in bankruptcy can within six months oppose the disclaimer, unless their claims are duly secured.

[2] Where the disclaimer is in consequence declared void, the inheritance will be wound up officially.

[3] Surplus assets are assigned in the first place for the satisfaction of the claims of the creditors who have opposed the disclaimer; and in the second place for the payment of the other creditors; the balance, if any, falls to the heirs in whose favour the disclaimer was made.

Art. 579

VIII. Liability on disclaimer

[1] Where heirs disclaim an insolvent inheritance, they are nevertheless held liable to the creditors of the estate to the extent of the property which they have received from the deceased within the five years preceding his death and which they would have had to bring into hotchpot if they had claimed in the partition of the inheritance.

[2] Customary gifts received by the heirs by way of dower on marriage and money laid out on their education and training do not fall under this liability.

[3] Heirs who have acted *bona fide* are liable only to the extent by which they are enriched at the time.

Chapter III: Public Inventory

Art. 580

¹ Every heir who is entitled to disclaim the inheritance can demand a public inventory. A. Conditions

² His demand must be made within a month to the competent Probate authority and with the same formalities as a disclaimer.

³ A demand made by one of several co-heirs is operative for them all.

Art. 581

¹ The inventory is made by the competent Probate authority according to the directions laid down by Cantonal Law, and consists of a statement of the assets and debts of the estate with a valuation of every item of property in it. B. Procedure I. Inventory

² Any person who can give any information on the financial position of the deceased is under a personal obligation to give it to the Probate authority, if required to do so.

³ The heirs in particular are bound to notify the authority of all the debts of the deceased known to them.

Art. 582

¹ The authority charged with making the inventory issues the necessary public citations to the creditors and debtors of the deceased including the creditors under contracts of guarantee, and calls upon them to state their claims and their debts respectively within a certain fixed time. II. Public citation

² The attention of the creditors is at the same time called to the consequences of their failure to comply with the notice.

³ The period fixed must be one month at least from the date of the first notice.

Art. 583

III. Claims and debts included officially

¹ Claims and debts shown from public registers and lists and the papers of the deceased are officially included in the inventory.

² The creditors and debtors must be notified of the inventory.

Art. 584

IV. Result

¹ At the expiration of the time fixed for the notices the inventory is closed and is then free for inspection by the interested parties for a period of one month at least.

² The costs are borne by the estate and, where this is not sufficient, by the heirs who demanded the inventory.

Art. 585

C. Position of heirs during inventory
I. Administration

¹ Pending the making of the inventory, only necessary acts of administration are allowed.

² If the Probate authority permits one of the heirs to carry on the business of the deceased, his co-heirs can demand the giving of security.

Art. 586

II. Execution for debt, legal proceedings, limitation of actions

¹ Pending the making of the inventory, no execution for the debts of the deceased is allowed.

² The period for the limitation of actions does not run.

³ Except in urgent cases legal proceedings that have already been instituted are suspended and no new proceedings can be instituted.

Art. 587

D. Effect
I. Time for deliberation

¹ After the closing of the inventory, each heir is called upon to declare within one month what his intention is in regard to accepting the inheritance.

² Where circumstances require, the competent Probate authority can extend this period for the purpose of new valuations or the settlement of disputes or other similar purposes.

Art. 588

¹ The heir has within the period fixed the right to disclaim the inheritance, to demand its official winding up, or to accept it either subject to an inventory or unconditionally. *II. Heir's declaration*

² Silence on his part is held to be an acceptance subject to an inventory.

Art. 589

¹ Where an heir accepts subject to an inventory, the debts of the deceased as specified in the inventory pass to him together with the assets. *III. Effect of acceptance subject to an inventory 1. Liability according to inventory*

² The vesting of the inheritance with its rights and liabilities dates back to the time of the opening of the succession.

³ The heir is liable for the debts specified in the inventory not only to the extent of the assets, but also to the extent of his own private property.

Art. 590

¹ An heir is not liable either personally or to the extent of the assets to those creditors of the deceased whose claims are not specified in the inventory because they neglected to state them within the time fixed. *2. Liability outside inventory*

² Where, however, the creditors omitted to state their claims through no fault of their own, or where their claims have not been specified in the inventory in spite of their having duly stated them, the heir is liable to the extent to which he is enriched by the inheritance.

Art. 591

[3] In any case the creditors can enforce their claims to the extent to which these are secured by the estate.

E. Liability on guarantees

Contracts of guarantee made by the deceased are entered separately in the inventory: for these an heir, even where he accepts the inheritance unconditionally and without reservation, is liable only to the extent of the dividend which would have been paid in respect of the guarantees if the estate had been administered in bankruptcy.

Art. 592

F. Devolution on Canton or Commune

Wherever an inheritance devolves on the Canton or the Commune, an inventory is officially made according to the rules laid down above, and the Canton or Commune is liable for the debts of the estate only to the extent of the assets received.

Chapter IV: Official Liquidation

Art. 593

A. Conditions
I. At instance of heir

[1] Every heir, instead of disclaiming the inheritance or accepting it subject to an inventory, can demand its official liquidation.

[2] Where, however, one of his co-heirs accepts unconditionally, this request will not be granted.

[3] In the case of an official liquidation, the heirs are not liable for the debts of the estate.

Art. 594

II. At instance of creditors of deceased

[1] Where the creditors of the deceased have reasonable grounds for anxiety lest they might not be paid, and their claims have not been satisfied on demand nor has security been given, they can, within

three months from the death of the deceased or from the opening of the will, demand the official liquidation of the inheritance.

² Legatees can under the same conditions demand provisional measures for the safeguarding of their interests.

Art. 595

¹ The official liquidation is carried out by the competent Probate authority or at its request by one or more administrators. B. Procedure
I. Administration

² It begins with an inventory and the public citations connected with it.

³ The administrator acts under the supervision of the Probate authority and the heirs can appeal to it against any measures which the administrator intended to take or has already taken.

Art. 596

¹ In liquidating an estate the administrator must settle the current affairs of the deceased, perform his obligations, recover the debts due to him, as far as possible discharge the legacies, obtain where necessary a judicial pronouncement on his rights and obligations, and realise his property. II. Ordinary liquidation

² The sale of the immovables of the deceased must take place by public auction, unless all the heirs consent to its taking place by private treaty.

³ The heirs can demand that the effects and moneys forming part of the estate which are not required for the liquidation, shall be handed over to them in whole or in part even before the liquidation is completed.

Art. 597

Where the estate is insolvent, the liquidation is carried out by the official in bankruptcy according to the Law of Bankruptcy. III. Liquidation in bankruptcy

Chapter V: Action to Recover Inheritance

Art. 598

A. Conditions

¹ Where a person considers that he has as statutory or instituted heir a better right to an inheritance or to property forming part of it than the person who has been put in possession of it, he can enforce his rights by an action for the recovery of an inheritance.

² On the application of the plaintiff the court will take all necessary measures to safeguard his rights, such as, *inter alia,* require security to be given or order a provisional note to be made in the land register.

Art. 599

B. Effect

¹ Where the action succeeds, the party in possession must restore the inheritance or the property forming part of it to the plaintiff in accordance with the law relating to possession.

² The defendant cannot in this action plead that he has acquired a title to the property by prescription.

Art. 600

C. Period of limitation

¹ The period of limitation of the action for the recovery of an inheritance from a *bona fide* possessor is one year from the date on which the plaintiff first had cognizance of the defendant's possession and of his own superior title, but in any case not longer than ten years from the date of death of the deceased or of the opening of the will.

² As against a *mala fide* possessor the period of limitation is in all cases thirty years.

Art. 601

D. Action by legatee

The period of limitation of the action brought by a legatee to recover his legacy is ten years from the date on which he received notice of the legacy or from that on which the legacy was vested, whichever is later.

Title XVII: Partition

Chapter I: Community before Partition

Art. 602

¹ Where there are several heirs, all the rights and obligations comprised in the inheritance constitute an undivided community among the heirs until partition.

² The heirs are joint owners of the property forming part of the estate and deal with it jointly, subject to the rights of representation and administration conferred by agreement or by law.

³ On the application of one of the co-heirs, the competent Probate authority can appoint an agent to represent the community until partition.

A. Effect of opening of succession
I. Community among heirs

Art. 603

¹ The heirs are liable jointly and severally for the debts of the deceased.

² Where children or grandchildren lived together with the deceased in a common home, the fair compensation owed by the deceased for contributions they made to this home is to be added to the liabilities attaching to the inheritance, provided this does not effect the insolvency of the estate.[1]

II. Liability of heirs

Art. 604

¹ Each of the co-heirs has at all times the right to demand the partition of the estate, unless he is expressly bound by agreement or by law to continue the community of property.

² At the instance of one of the heirs the court can provisionally order the postponement of the partition of the estate as a whole or of certain property

B. Action for partition

---

[1] Inserted by cipher I of the Federal Statute of 6th October 1972, in force since 15th February 1973 (AS **1973** 93 102; BBl **1970 I** 805, **1971 I** 737).

forming part of it, where an immediate liquidation would considerably lessen the value of the inheritance.

³ Where one of the heirs is insolvent, his co-heirs have the right, immediately on the opening of the succession, to demand that measures be taken to safeguard their rights.

Art. 605

C. Postponement of partition

¹ Where the rights of a child conceived but still unborn have to be taken into consideration, the partition must be postponed until its birth.

² In the meantime the mother of the child has the right to share in the income derived from the estate in so far as she requires it for her maintenance.

Art. 606

D. Rights of members of household

Heirs who were members of the household of the deceased at the date of his death and were kept at his expense can require that the cost of their board and lodging shall be borne by the estate for one month after his death.

Chapter II: Mode of Partition

Art. 607

A. In general

¹ Statutory heirs must share not only among themselves but with the instituted heirs according to the same rules of division.

² In the absence of a contrary provision they can freely agree among themselves as to the mode of partition to be adopted.

³ Co-heirs, who are in possession of property forming part of the inheritance or who are debtors of the deceased, are bound to give precise information on these points at the time of partition.

Art. 608

B. Rules
I. Dispositions of deceased

¹ The testator can by will or pact give directions to his heirs on the mode of partition and the arranging of the lots.

² Subject to the rectification of inequalities in the shares which were not intended by the testator, these directions are binding on the heirs.

³ In the absence of evidence of a contrary intention in the testamentary disposition, the allotment by the testator of a specific thing to an heir is not held to be intended as a specific legacy but as a direction for the purpose of partition.

Art. 609

II. Concurrence of Probate authority

¹ Where a creditor has acquired or seized the share of an inheritance that has accrued to an heir or holds a certificate of an unsatisfied claim against him, that creditor can demand that the Probate authority shall concur in the partition in the place of the heir.

² Cantonal Law can provide for the concurrence of the Probate authority in a partition also in other cases.

Art. 610

C. Effecting the partition
I. Equality of heirs' rights

¹ In the absence of a contrary disposition, heirs have in a partition equal rights to the property forming part of the inheritance.

² They are bound to give one another every information in regard to their relations with the deceased which would tend to the just and equitable distribution of the estate.

³ Every co-heir can require that the debts of the deceased shall all be paid or secured before partition.

Art. 611

II. Arrangement of lots

¹ The heirs divide the estate into as many shares or lots as there are heirs entitled or stocks of descent represented by two or more co-heirs.

² If they cannot agree, any one of them can require the competent Probate authority to settle the lots, which will be carried out by taking into account local custom, the circumstances of the heirs and the wishes of the majority of them.

³ The lots are distributed by agreement among the heirs or by drawing for them.

Art. 612

III. Allotment and sale of single articles

¹ An article which would materially lose in value by being divided must be allotted as a whole to a single heir.

² Where the heirs cannot agree on the division or the allotment of an article, it must be sold and the proceeds must be divided.

³ On the demand of one of the heirs, the sale must take place by auction and if the heirs cannot agree, the competent Probate authority will decide whether the auction is to take place in public or only among the heirs themselves.

Art. 612a[1]

IV. Allotment of lodging and chattel to surviving spouse

¹ Where the house or the apartment in which the spouses lived or household effects are part of the inheritance, the surviving spouse can demand that they become his or her property against compensation.

² Where the circumstances justify it, the ownership can be replaced by the usufruct or a right of residence at the instance of the surviving spouse or the other statutory heirs of the deceased.

---

[1] Inserted by cipher I 2 of the Federal Statute of 5th October 1984, in force since 1st January 1988 (BBl 1979 II 1191).

³ The surviving spouse is not entitled to these rights where rooms are concerned which the testator used for exercising his profession or running a business and which a descendant needs for the continuance of his profession or business; provisions are made for the law of inheritance for agricultural enterprises.

Art. 613

¹ Things which by their nature belong together must not be divided if one of the heirs is opposed to their division. **D. Special cases / I. Things which belong together, family papers**

² Family papers and articles valued for their family associations must not be sold, if one of the heirs is opposed to their sale.

³ Where the heirs cannot agree, the competent Probate authority must decide whether the article shall be sold or allotted to an heir with or without a valuation,¹ and it does so by taking into account local custom and, in default of any, the personal circumstances of the heirs.

Art. 614

Claims which the deceased had against one of the heirs must be charged against the heir at partition. **II. Claims of deceased against an heir**

Art. 615

Where at partition an heir receives property forming part of the inheritance which the deceased had charged for his debts, the heir takes over with the property the liability for these debts.² **III. Property charged with debt**

---

¹ With a valuation, if it has some pecuniary value, so that this is deducted from the total share due to the heir.
² But he will be entitled to compensation for taking over the debt, *e.g.* he may by way of compensation be excused from liability for one of the other debts on the estate.

Art. 616

IV. Immovables
1. Parcelling

The Cantons can direct that land shall not be cut up into smaller areas than a definite minimum fixed according to the requirements of the form of agriculture for which the land is laid out.

Art. 617

2. Allotment
a. Valuation

[1] Immovables are allotted to the heirs according to their value at the date of the partition.

[2] Agricultural land is for this purpose to be assessed according to its value as based on its annual return, other land according to its selling value.

Art. 618

b. Procedure of valuation

[1] Where the heirs cannot agree on the valuation of their shares, these will be fixed finally by official valuers.

[2] ...[1]

Art. 619[2]

3. Share of co-heirs in profit
a. Claim

[1] Where an heir has been allotted agricultural land for which a lower take-over price has been arranged than its proper selling value, the co-heirs are entitled to claim a share of the profit made by the sale or expropriation of the property or part of the property within a period of 25 years after partition.

[2] Any legal transaction by which the value of the property is materialized either wholly or in part is to be considered as equal to the sale of the property, in particular establishing a right to build on the land or to exploit components of the land.

[3] The date of the sale is the time when the contract is signed by which the heir binds himself

---

[1] Annulled by cipher I 1 of the Federal Statute of 6th October 1972 (AS 1973 93; BBl 1970 I 805, 1971 I 737).
[2] Wording according to cipher II of the Federal Statute of 19th March 1965, in force since 1st July 1965 (AS 1965 445 450; BBl 1963 I 1969).

to transfer his property, in case of expropriation it is the time when the proceedings are instituted.

Art. 619$^{\text{bis}\,1}$

^{1} The profit is the amount by which the selling price or the indemnity for expropriation exceeds the take-over price plus an increment value resulting from investments made by the heir himself. *b. Profit*

^{2} Exempt from the co-heirs' claim to a share of the profit are two percent of the profit for each year the heir has been the owner of the property.

Art. 619$^{\text{ter}\,1}$

^{1} Where in order to continue his trade an heir acquires new land to replace land which he sold or which was expropriated, he can deduct from the selling price or the expropriation indemnity the purchasing price of a substitute whose annual return is, at the most, equal to the return of the land sold or expropriated. *c. Substitute for agricultural land*

^{2} The co-heirs have the right to a share of the remainder as well as the profit resulting from the sale or expropriation of the substituting land.

Art. 619$^{\text{quater}\,1}$

^{1} An heir can deduct from the selling price or the expropriation indemnity that amount which he spent on repairs carried out on a building forming part of the farm he is managing and which he received from the same inheritance. *d. Repairs on buildings*

^{2} However, the heir is not entitled to deduct this amount as his personal expense from the proceeds when the building is either sold or expropriated.

---

^{1} Inserted by cipher II of the Federal Statute of 19th March 1965, in force since 1st July 1965 (AS **1965** 445 450; BBl **1963** I 969).

Art. 619 quinquies [1]

e. Liability of the new owner

The purchaser is liable for the payment of the share of profit jointly and severally with the seller, provided the claim to a share of the profit has been pre-notified in the land register by a party entitled to do so.

Art. 619 sexies [1]

f. Settlement by contract

[1] The co-heirs' claim to a share of the profit can only be validly annulled or changed if this is done in writing.

[2] Settlements as regards the modification of the co-heirs' claim to a share of the profit for non-agricultural land can be notified in the land register by any party who is entitled to do so.

Art. 620 [2]

V. Farms
1. No partition
a. Conditions

[1] Where a farm forms part of the inheritance and one of the heirs is prepared to take it over and appears capable of managing it, it must be allotted to him in its entirety, if it forms as such an economic entity; its valuation will be based on its annual return.

[2] In order to judge if the farm yields a sufficient income to a farmer, shares of agricultural land or farms and agricultural land which are farmed together with the farm in question over a longer period can be considered.[3]

[3] In this case the take-over price is to be assessed according to the Federal Statute of 12th December

---

[1] Inserted by cipher II of the Federal Statute of 19th March 1965, in force since 1st July 1965 (AS 1965 445 450; BBl 1963 I 969).
[2] Wording according to art. 94 of the Federal Statute relating to the Disencumbrance of Agricultural Homesteads, in force since 1st January 1947 (SR 211.412.12).
[3] Wording according to cipher I 1 of the Federal Statute of 6th October 1972, in force since 15th February 1973 (AS 1973 93 102; BBl 1970 I 805, 1971 I 737).

1940[1] ordering the disencumbrance of agricultural homesteads.[2]

Art. 620bis[3]

b. Allotment of movables

The new owner can demand the allotment of the farming implements, supplies and livestock serving the farm at their use value.

Art. 621[2]

c. Designation of the new owner

[1] Where the new ownership is disputed, the competent authority decides about the allotment of the farm, taking into account the personal circumstances of the heirs.

[2] An heir who desires to carry on the farm in person and who appears to be suited for such a task has the first right to have it allotted to him in its entirety.

[3] Where an heir's qualification for carrying on the farm as a whole has to be judged, the qualification of the heir's spouse must also be considered.

Art. 621bis[3]

d. Testamentary disposition

[1] An heir who desires to carry on the farm in person and who seems to be qualified for this task can be deprived of this right neither through testamentary disposition nor through a testamentary pact.

[2] Provisions are made for disinheritance and renunciation of inheritance.

---

[1] SR 211.412.12.
[2] Wording according to cipher I 1 of the Federal Statute of 6th October 1972, in force since 15th February 1973 (AS 1973 93 102; BBl 1970 I 805, 1971 I 737).
[3] Inserted by cipher I 1 of the Federal Statute of 6th October 1972, in force since 15th February 1973 (AS 1973 93 102; BBl 1970 I 805, 1971 I 737).

³ Where several heirs are qualified to have the farm allotted to them as a whole, one of them can be designated as the new owner by testamentary disposition.

Art. 621$^{\text{ter}1}$

e.[1] Descendants in minority

Where the deceased leaves descendants in minority the heirs shall, provided the guardianship authority agrees, let the community among heirs remain or they shall form a community of property until that time when the circumstances allow a decision on the allotment to one of the descendants.

Art. 621$^{\text{quater}1}$

2. Exception[2]

¹ If the size and the nature of the farm permit parcelling into several farms yielding a sufficient income, a partition can be executed by allotting parts of the original farm at the value of their annual returns, provided several heirs declare themselves prepared to take over these farms and appear to be qualified for their tasks.

² Where one of the co-heirs is opposed to the settlement the competent authority decides on partition.

Art. 622

3. Community
 a. Claim to postpone partition

¹ An heir to whom a farm has been allotted can claim that the partition be postponed so far as the farm is concerned, where he is so heavily burdened by the rights of his co-heirs in the farm, that in order to secure them against loss, he would be obliged to

---

[1] Inserted by art. 94 of the Federal Statute of 12th December 1940 relating to the Disencumbrance of Agricultural Homesteads, in force since 1st January 1947 (SR **211.412.12**). Numbering according to cipher I 1 of the Federal Statute of 6th October 1972, in force since 15th February 1973 (AS **1973** 93 102; BBl **1970** I 805, **1971** I 737).

[2] Wording according to cipher I 1 of the Federal Statute of 6th October 1972, in force since 15th February 1973 (AS **1973** 93 102; BBl **1970** I 805, **1971** I 737).

charge it to such an extent that the total charges on it, including already existing mortgages, would amount to more than three quarters of its assessed value.

² In this case the heirs are given an undivided interest in the rents and returns of the farm.

Art. 623

b. Dissolution of community

¹ Where the heir in possession of the farm comes to be in a position to redeem the rights of the co-heirs without unduly charging the farm, any of these can demand the dissolution of the community of profits and the liquidation of his claim.

² The heir in possession himself can at any time demand the dissolution of the community, unless it has been agreed otherwise.

Art. 624

4. Settlement by estate charge

¹ Where the heir in possession of the farm has demanded the postponement of the partition, any one of the co-heirs, instead of continuing within the community of profits, can at any time require that his share be assigned to him in the form of a sum of money secured by a charge on the common property.

² Where, however, the common property would in consequence of this arrangement be burdened beyond three quarters of its assessed value, the heir in possession is, as regards the excess, bound to give only an estate charge note terminable at the end of ten years at the earliest and bearing no higher rate of interest than that allowed in the case of other land charges.[1]

---

[1] "Land charge note" or "negotiable land charge", German **Gült**, French *lettre de rente*, is a form of negotiable security peculiar to Swiss Law, see arts. 842 *et seq.* below. The land charge here spoken of is in the German text called **Erbengült**, French *lettre de rente successorale*, "estate charge note"; it differs in certain respects from the ordinary land charge note.

³ The rules in the case of ordinary land charge notes in regard to the limit beyond which property may not be burdened with them and the liabilities of the Canton are not applicable to estate charge notes.

Art. 625[1]

5. Other industries

¹ Where there is another industry closely connected with the farm and accessory to it and both together yield a sufficient income, they must be allotted as an undivided whole to an heir who is prepared to manage it and appears suited for the task.

² The farm is to be assessed at the value of its annual return, the additional industry at its selling value.

³ Where one of the co-heirs is opposed to this, the competent authority decides on the allotment, sale or partition of the accessory industry after taking into consideration whether the farms which have so far been connected yield a sufficient income when farmed individually, as well as the personal circumstances of the heirs.

Art. 625bis [2]

6. Alienation

Where none of the heirs raises a claim to an undivided allotment of the farm or where such a claim is rejected, each of the co-heirs can demand the sale of the farm as a whole.

---

[1] Wording according to cipher I 1 of the Federal Statute of 6th October 1972, in force since 15th February 1973 (AS 1973 93 102; BBl 1970 I 805, 1971 I 737).

[2] Inserted by art. 94 of the Federal Statute of 12th December 1940 on the Disencumbrance of Agricultural Homesteads (SR 211.412.12). Wording according to art. 49 of the Federal Statute of 12th June 1951 relating to the Preservation of Agricultural Property, in force since 1st January 1953 (SR 211.412.11).

Chapter III: Hotchpot

Art. 626

¹ Statutory heirs are mutually obliged to bring into hochpot all that the deceased has given to them in his lifetime by way of advancement on their share in the inheritance.

² In the absence of a contrary intention expressed in the will, gifts made by the deceased to his descendants by way of dower, or as outfitting, or by way of surrender of property, or as the remission of a debt, and other similar gifts must be brought into hotchpot.

A. Duty of heirs

Art. 627

¹ Where an heir loses his right of inheritance either before or after the opening of the succession, the persons who inherit in his stead take over at the same time his liability to hotchpot.

² The descendants of an heir who has received a portion by way of advancement are bound to bring it into hotchpot even where it has not passed into their possession.

B. Hotchpot in case of incapacity or disclaimer

Art. 628

¹ An heir can elect whether he will bring the property he has received into hotchpot, or keep it and forfeit his share or part of it according to the value of the property received; and this is the case even where the property exceeds the amount of his statutory share of inheritance.

² This provision is subject, however, to the right of the testator to leave a different direction in his will and to that of the heirs to bring an action for reduction.

C. Conditions
I. Hotchpot or diminished share

Art. 629

II. Gifts in excess of statutory share

¹ Where the gifts are in excess of the statutory share of inheritance, the excess is, subject always to the action for reduction, not liable to hotchpot, if it can be shown that the deceased intended it as an extra benefit to the donee.

² This intention is presumed in the case of gifts made to descendants in the customary amounts to set them up on their marriage.

Art. 630

III. Mode of computation

¹ The computation for hotchpot is made by taking the value of the gifts at the date of the opening of the succession or, where the donee has already sold what he received before that date, the price at which they were sold.

² In regard to expenses incurred, deteriorations and gathered fruits, heirs have the rights and are subject to the obligations of a possessor.

Art. 631

D. Cost of education

¹ Outlays on the education and training of children, in the absence of evidence of a contrary intention on the part of the deceased, are liable to hotchpot only to the extent by which they exceed the customary limit.

² Children who at the death of the deceased had not yet completed their education or training or are subject to some infirmity must be allowed at partition to receive a fair amount paid in advance.[1]

Art. 632

E. Customary presents

Customary presents need not be brought into hotchpot.

---

[1] Wording according to cipher I 2 of the Federal Statute of 5th October 1984, in force since 1st January 1988 (BBl 1979 II 1191).

Art. 633[1] F. Compensation for assisting the family

Chapter IV: Completion and Effect of Partition

Art. 634

¹ The partition becomes binding on the heirs as soon as either the lots have been formed and distributed or the partition agreement has been concluded.

² A partition agreement is valid only if it is in writing.

A. Completion of partition
I. Partition agreement

Art. 635

¹ Contracts made between the co-heirs for the assignment of their rights of inheritance are valid only if made in writing.[2]

² Where the contract is made by one of the heirs with a third person, it does not give the latter any right to join in the partition, but only a claim to the share allotted at partition to the heir who has assigned it.

II. Contracts relating to rights of inheritance

Art. 636

¹ All contracts are void where made between two or more heirs or between an heir and a third person in regard to a succession which has not yet been opened, unless they were made with the consent and concurrence of the person leaving the inheritance.

² Property passed by virtue of such contract can be claimed back.

III. Contracts before the opening of the succession

---

[1] Annulled by cipher I 1 of the Federal Statute of 6th October 1972 (AS 1973 93; BBl 1970 I 805, 1971 I 737).
[2] Wording according to cipher I 2 of the Federal Statute of 5th October 1984, in force since 1st January 1988 (BBl 1979 II 1191).

Art. 637

B. Mutual liabilities of co-heirs
I. Guarantees

¹ After partition, the heirs are mutually liable *inter se* for the property forming part of the inheritance, as if they were vendors and purchasers.

² They mutually guarantee the existence of the debts and other choses in action allotted to each heir at partition, and are responsible like simple sureties[1] for the ability of the debtors to pay these debts according to their valuation at partition, unless the debts are in the form of negotiable securities.[2]

³ The period of limitation for the action on this guarantee is one year from partition or from the time when the debts are payable, whichever is later.

Art. 638

II. Rescission of partition agreement

The partition agreement can be rescinded under the same conditions as any other contract.

Art. 639

C. Liability towards third persons
I. Joint and several liability

¹ For the debts on the estate heirs are even after partition liable jointly and severally to the extent of the whole of their own property, provided the creditors have not expressly or tacitly assented to the division of the liability among the heirs or to its delegation to one or more of them.

² This liability, however, ceases at the expiration of five years from the partition or from the time when the claims can be enforced, whichever is later.

Art. 640

II. Indemnities among the heirs themselves

¹ Where an heir has paid a debt of the deceased for which he was not made liable at partition, or a greater part of a debt than the amount which he had

---

[1] *i.e.* as laid down in art. 495 of the Code of Obligations. A simple surety is liable only where the principal debtor is insolvent or out of the country.

[2] In this case the heirs are surety for the existence and validity of the debts but not for the solvency of the debtors.

undertaken, he is entitled to be indemnified by his co-heirs.

[2] This right to an indemnity can be claimed in the first place against the heir who undertook the liability for it at the time of partition.

[3] Otherwise, in the absence of a contrary agreement, the heirs are liable for the payment of the debts in proportion to their shares in the inheritance.

THE SWISS CIVIL CODE
ENGLISH VERSION

THE
SWISS CIVIL CODE

ENGLISH VERSION

by

IVY WILLIAMS, M.A., D.C.L., Oxon; LL.D., Lond.
Barrister-at-Law

published by Oxford University Press, 1925
reprinted by Remak Verlag Zürich, 1976

completely reset, revised and up-dated edition
with Notes, Vocabularies, Index and a Synopsis
of all changes of the law since 1912

by

SIEGFRIED WYLER, Dr. phil. **BARBARA WYLER,** Dr. iur.
Professor of English Barrister-at-Law

VOLUME II

PART III: LAW OF INHERITANCE
PART IV: LAW OF PROPERTY
FINAL TITLE
APPENDICES

ReMaK
Verlag Zürich

Table of Contents

Part IV: Law of Property

Section I: Ownership

Title XVIII: General Rules

			Article
A.	Nature of ownership		.641
B.	Extent of right		
	I.	Integral parts of a thing	.642
	II.	Natural fruits	.643
	III.	Accessories	
		1. Definition	.644
		2. Not accessory	.645
C.	United ownership		
	I.	Co-ownership	
		1. Rights of owners *inter se*	.646
		2. Regulations for the use and management	.647
		3. Usual acts of management	.647*a*
		4. More important administrative acts	647*b*
		5. Measures for building and repairs	
		a. Necessary measures	.647*c*
		b. Useful measures	.647*d*
		c. Measures to improve appearance and comfort	.647*e*
		6. Disposing of the property	.648
		7. Distribution of costs and charges	.649
		8. Entrance of a new share owner	.649*a*
		9. Exclusion from the body of co-owners	
		a. Co-owners	.649*b*
		b. Other party entitled	.649*c*
		10. Dissolution	
		a. Right to partition	.650
		b. Method	.651
	II.	Ownership in common	
		1. Conditions	.652
		2. Effect	.653
E.	Determination		.654

VI   Civil Code

                                                                    Article

Title XIX: Ownership of Land

Chapter I: Subject-Matter, Acquisition and Loss of Ownership of Land

A. Subject-matter 655
B. Acquisition
    I.   Registration 656
    II.   Modes of acquisition
        1.   Transfer 657
        2.   Occupation 658
        3.   Formation of new ground 659
        4.   Landslips 660
        5.   Adverse possession
            a. In ordinary cases .661
            b. In exceptional cases 662
            c. Running of years 663
        6.   Ownerless and public property 664
    III. Right to registration 665
C. Loss of ownership 666

Chapter II: Nature and Limits of Ownership of Land

A. Nature of right
    I.   Its extent 667
    II.   Boundaries
        1.   How determined 668
        2.   Obligation to fix them 669
        3.   Boundary lines on common ground 670
    III. Buildings on the land of another
        1.   Materials
            a. Ownership 671
            b. Compensation 672
            c. Adjudication of ownership of the land 673
        2.   Encroachment 674
        3.   Right over a building 675
        4.   Conduits 676
        5.   Movable structures .677
    IV. Plants 678
    V.   Liability of owner of land 679
B. Limits of right
    I.   In general 680

Table of Contents VII

Article

    II. On alienation
        1. Right of pre-emption
            a. By entry in register .... .681
            b. Between co-owners and holders of rights over a building .... .682
        2. Rights of purchase and redemption .... .683
   III. *Jus vicinorum*
        1. Mode of using own land .... .684
        2. Excavations and buildings
            a. General rule .... .685
            b. Cantonal regulations .... .686
        3. Plants
            a. General rule .... .687
            b. Cantonal regulations .... .688
        4. Natural flow of water .... .689
        5. Drainage .... .690
        6. Conduit pipes and wires
            a. Obligation to suffer them .... .691
            b. Safeguarding interests of servient owner ...... .692
            c. Change of circumstances .... .693
        7. Rights of way
            a. Of necessity .... .694
            b. Other rights of way .... .695
            c. Registration .... .696
        8. Enclosures .... .697
        9. Upkeep .... .698
   IV. Right of access to another's property
        1. Forests and fields .... .699
        2. Drifts and strays .... .700
        3. In defence of person or property .... .701
    V. Limitations under Public Law
        1. In general .... .701
        2. Improvements of soil .... .703

C. Springs

     I. Ownership and servitudes .... .704
    II. Confining waters in conduits .... .705
   III. Springs cut off
        1. Damages .... .706
        2. Restoration .... .707
   IV. Common springs .... .708
    V. Use of springs .... .709
   VI. Water supply of necessity .... .710
  VII. Expropriation
        1. Of springs .... .711
        2. Of land .... .712

Civil Code

Article

Chapter III: Condominium Principled Ownership (Storey Ownership)

A. Nature and Object

    I. Content 712a
    II. Object 712b
    III. Right to dispose of object 712c

B. Foundation and destruction

    I. Foundation 712d
    II. Value quotas 712e
    III. Destruction 712f

C. Management and Usage

    I. Applicable provisions 712g
    II. Common costs and liabilities
        1. Inventory and distribution 712h
        2. Liability for contributions
            a. Real security by operation of law 712i
            b. Right of lien 712k
    III. Competence to act 712l

D. Organization

    I. Assembly of the storey owners
        1. Competence and legal position 712m
        2. To call and conduct meetings 712n
        3. Execution of vote 712o
        4. Quorum 712p
    II. The manager
        1. Appointment 712q
        2. Discharge 712r
        3. Duties
            a. Execution of the regulations and resolutions concerning the administration and the use 712s
            b. Representation of opposite third party 712t

Title XX: Ownership of Movable Property

A. Subject-matter 713
B. Modes of acquisition

    I. Transfer
        1. Delivery of possession 714
        2. Pact to reserve ownership
            a. In general 715
            b. Payment by instalments 716

Article

		3.	Transfer of ownership without possession	717
	II.	Occupation		
		1.	Things that have no owner	718
		2.	Stray animals	719
	III.	Lost property found		
		1.	Public advertisement and inquiries	720
		2.	Custody and sale by auction	721
		3.	Acquisition of ownership and restitution	722
		4.	Treasure-trove	723
		5.	Objects of scientific value	724
	IV.	Drifts and strays		725
	V.	Manufactured articles		726
	VI.	Fusion		727
	VII.	Prescription		728
C.	Loss of ownership			729

Section II: Limited Rights *in rem*

Title XXI: Servitudes and Rent-Charges

Chapter I: Praedial Servitudes

A.	Their nature			730
B.	Creation and extinction			
	I.	Creation		
		1.	Registration	731
		2.	Agreement	732
		3.	Servitude over one's own property	733
	II.	Extinction		
		1.	In general	734
		2.	Merger	735
		3.	By order of the court	736
C.	Effect			
	I.	Rights and duties		
		1.	In general	737
		2.	By virtue of registration	738
		3.	Changed requirements	739
		4.	Cantonal Law and local custom	740
	II.	Cost of maintenance		741
	III.	Changes in servitude		
		1.	Transferring place of its exercise	742

Civil Code

Article

    2. Partition
       a. Of dominant property 743
       b. Of servient property 744

Chapter II: Usufruct and Other Servitudes

A. Usufruct
   I. *Res fructuaria* 745
  II. How it arises
     1. In general 746
     2. Statutory usufruct .747 (annulled)
 III. Extinction
     1. Grounds 748
     2. Duration 749
     3. Restoration of *res fructuaria* when destroyed 750
     4. Return of *res fructuaria*
       a. Obligation 751
       b. Liabilities 752
       c. Outlays 753
     5. Limitation of actions for compensation 754
 IV. Effect
     1. Rights of usufructuary
       a. In general 755
       b. Natural fruits 756
       c. Interest 757
       d. When assignable 758
     2. Rights of owner
       a. Control 759
       b. Right to security .760
       c. Security in case of gifts and statutory usufructs . .761
       d. Effect of failure to give security 762
     3. Inventory 763
     4. Duties of usufructuary
       a. Preservation of *res fructuaria* 764
       b. Cost of maintenance, taxes and other charges . . .765
       c. Interest on debts on estate 766
       d. Insurance 767
  V. Special cases
     1. Immovables
       a. Fruits 768
       b. Industrial character of *res fructuaria* 769
       c. Forests 770
       d. Mines 771
     2. Perishable and valued things 772

				Article
		3.	Usufruct in a right	
			a. Purport	.773
			b. Repayment and re-investment	.774
			c. Right to assignment of debt	.775
B.	Right of residence			
	I.	In general		.776
	II.	Extent of right		.777
	III.	Duties of person entitled		.778
C.	Right of building			
	I.	Object and entry in the land register		.779
	II.	The deed of foundation		.779a
	III.	Effect, rights and duties		.779b
	IV.	Consequences of the extinction of the right		
		1.	Reversion	.779c
		2.	Indemnification	.779d
		3.	Arrangements	.779e
	V.	Premature reversion		
		1.	Requirements	.779f
		2.	Execution of right of reversion	.779g
		3.	Other cases of application	.779h
	VI.	Security for the right of building-charges		
		1.	Claim to create a mortgage	.779i
		2.	Registration	.779k
	VII.	Maximal duration		.779l
D.	Right to a spring in another's land			.780
E.	Other servitudes			.781

Chapter III: Rent-Charges

A.	Purport			.782
B.	Creation and extinction			
	I.	Creation		
		1.	Mode of acquisition and registration	.783
		2.	Rent-charges under Public Law	.784
		3.	Charges by way of security	.785
	II.	Extinction		
		1.	In general	.786
		2.	Redemption	
			a. Right of creditor to demand	.787
			b. Right of debtor to redeem	.788
			c. Redemption price	.789

			Article
	3.	Limitation of actions	790
C.	Effect		
	I.	Rights of creditor	791
	II.	Nature of debt	792

Title XXII: Mortgages and Other Securities on Land

Chapter I: General Provisions

- A. Conditions
  - I. Forms of real security 793
  - II. Nature of debt secured
    - 1. Principal 794
    - 2. Interest 795
  - III. The property
    - 1. What can be mortgaged 796
    - 2. Description
      - a. One property only 797
      - b. In the case of several properties 798
- B. Creation and extinction
  - I. Creation
    - 1. Registration 799
    - 2. Where the property is in co-ownership 800
  - II. Extinction 801
  - III. Where plots of land grouped together
    - 1. Transfer of security 802
    - 2. Notice by the debtor 803
    - 3. Indemnities 604
- C. Effect
  - I. Rights of creditor 805
  - II. Rents 806
  - III. No limitation of actions 807
  - IV. Safeguards
    - 1. In case of depreciation of property
      - a. Measures for its preservation 808
      - b. Security, restoration, repayment 809
    - 2. Depreciation without owner's fault 810
    - 3. Alienation of parts of property 811
  - V. Further charge 812
  - VI. Place of the security in register
    - 1. Effect 813
    - 2. Order of priority 814

Table of Contents

XIII

Article

		3. Vacant places	.815
	VII.	Realization of security	
		1. Method	.816
		2. Payment of creditors	.817
		3. Extent of security	.818
		4. Security for necessary outlays	.819
	VIII.	In case of improvements of soil	
		1. Priority	.820
		2. Extinction of debt and security	.821
	IX.	Right to insurance sums	.822
	X.	Representation of creditor	.823

Chapter II: Mortgages

A. Purport of mortgage 824
B. Creation and extinction

    I.   Creation 825
    II.   Extinction
          1. Right to have it erased 826
          2. Position of owner .827
          3. Redemption
              a. Conditions 828
              b. Sale by public auction 829
              c. Official valuation 830
          4. Notice 831

C. Effect

    I.   Ownership and liability
          1. Total alienation 832
          2. Property parcelled 833
          3. Notice to mortgagee .834
    II.   Assignment of mortgage debt 835

D. Statutory mortgages

    I.   No registration 836
    II.   With registration
          1. Cases 837
          2. Vendors, co-heirs and co-owners 838
          3. Workmen and contractors
              a. Registration 839
              b. Degree of priority 840
              c. Preferential claims 841

XIV   Civil Code

                                                                                             Article

Chapter III: Mortgage Certificates and Land Charge Notes

A. Mortgage certificates
   - I. Object and nature 842
   - II. Valuation 843
   - III. Notice to pay off 844
   - IV. Position of owner 845
   - V. Alienation or division 846

B. Land charge notes
   - I. Object and nature 847
   - II. Maximum charge allowed 848
   - III. Responsibility of the Cantons 849
   - IV. Right of redemption 850
   - V. Debt and ownership 851
   - VI. Where the property is parcelled 852
   - VII. Land charges under Cantonal Law and Law of Inheritance 853

C. Provisions common to both mortgage certificates and land charge notes
   - I. Creation
     1. Nature of debt 854
     2. Relation between security and debt secured 855
     3. Registration and instrument
        - a. Necessity of instrument 856
        - b. The drawing of the instrument 857
        - c. Form of instrument 858
     4. Description of creditor
        - a. In instrument 859
        - b. With appointment of agent 860
     5. Place of payment 861
     6. Payment after assignment by creditor 862
   - II. Extinction
     1. In default of a creditor 863
     2. Erasure 864
   - III. Rights of creditor
     1. *Bona fides*
        - a. Entry in register .865
        - b. Wording of instrument 866
        - c. Relation between instrument and entry in register 867
     2. How exercised 868
     3. Delivery of instrument 869
   - IV. When annulled
     1. Loss of instrument 870
     2. Citation of creditor 871

Table of Contents   XV

                                                              Article

	V.	Defences	.872
	VI.	Return of instrument	.873
	VII.	Modifications in position of parties	.874

Chapter IV: Issues of Securities on Land

A. Bonds secured on land .... .875
B. Issues of mortgage certificates and land charge notes in a series

    I. In general .... .876
    II. Form .... .877
    III. Paying off .... .878
    IV. Registration .... .879
    V. Effect
        1. Issuing office .... .880
        2. Repayment
            a. Plan .... .881
            b. Control .... .882
            c. Repayments, how used .... .883

Title XXIII: Law of Pledge

Chapter I: Pledges and Liens

A. Pledges

    I. Creation
        1. Possession of creditor .... .884
        2. Pledge of cattle .... .885
        3. A pledge upon a pledge .... .886
        4. Pledge by pledge .... .887
    II. Extinction
        1. Loss of possession .... .888
        2. Obligation to return chattel .... .889
        3. Liability of pledgee .... .890
    III. Effect
        1. Rights of pledgee .... .891
        2. Extent of pledge .... .892
        3. Rights of priority .... .893
        4. Agreement for forfeiture of chattel .... .894

B. Liens

    I. Conditions .... .895
    II. Exceptions .... .896

			Article
	III.	Insolvency of debtor	897
	IV.	Effect	898

Chapter II: Pledges of Debts and Other Rights

A.	In general		899
B.	Creation		
	I.	In case of ordinary debts	900
	II.	Negotiable and other securities	901
	III.	Goods bills	902
	IV.	A pledge upon a pledge	903
C.	Effect		
	I.	Rights of pledgee	904
	II.	Shares	905
	III.	Administration and payment off	906

Chapter III: Pawn

A.	Pawnbrokers			
	I.	Licences		907
	II.	Duration		908
B.	Pawning			
	I.	How carried out		909
	II.	Effect		
		1.	Sale of things pawned	910
		2.	Right to the balance	911
	III.	Redemption		
		1.	Right to redeem	912
		2.	Rights of pawnbroker	913
C.	Purchase and re-sale			914
D.	Cantonal Law			915

Chapter IV: Debentures

916–918
(annulled)

Article

Section III: Possession and Land Register

Title XXIV: Possession

A. Nature and kinds

    I. Nature .... .919
    II. Original and derivative possession .... .920
    III. Temporary interruption .... .921

B. Transfer

    I. *Inter praesentes* .... .922
    II. *Inter absentes* .... .923
    III. Without delivery .... .924
    IV. In case of goods bills .... .925

C. Effect

    I. Protection of possession
        1. Right of defence .... .926
        2. Action for restitution .... .927
        3. Action for trespass .... .928
        4. Lapse of right of action and period of limitation .... .929
    II. Protection of right to possession
        1. Presumption of ownership .... .930
        2. Presumption in the case of derivative possession .... .931
        3. Action against the person in possession .... .932
        4. Right of alienation and recovery
            a. In case of goods delivered to another .... .933
            b. In case of lost or stolen property .... .934
            c. In case of cash and negotiable instruments to bearer .... .935
            d. In case of bad faith .... .936
        5. Presumption in regard to immovables .... .937
    III. Liabilities
        1. Of *bona fide* possessor
            a. For use .... .938
            b. Indemnity .... .939
        2. *Mala fide* possessor .... .940
    IV. Prescription and adverse possession .... .941

Title XXV: Land Register

A. Organization

    I. Register itself
        1. In general .... .942

XVIII   Civil Code

Article

        2. Entries
            a. Subject 943
            b. Exceptions 944
        3. Registers
            a. The big book 945
            b. A page in the register 946
            c. Several properties on one page 947
            d. Day-book, title deeds 948
        4. Regulations 949
        5. Plans 950
    II. How the land register is kept
        1. Areas
            a. Competence. 951
            b. Properties situated in several areas 952
        2. Registries 953
        3. Fees 954
    III. Officials
        1. Liability 955
        2. Supervision 956
        3. Penalties. 957

B. Registration
    I. What rights are registered
        1. Ownership and other real rights 958
        2. Notes
            a. Personal rights .959
            b. Restrictions on alienation 960
            c. Provisional registration 961
    II. Restrictions of Public Law 962
    III. Conditions
        1. Statements
            a. For entries 963
            b. For erasures 964
        2. Proof
            a. Valid proof 965
            b. Completion of proof 966
    IV. Mode of registration
        1. In general 967
        2. In the case of servitudes 968
    V. Official notices 969

C. Public character of land register 970

D. Effect
    I. Of non-registration 971

			Article
	II.	Of registration	
		1. In general	972
		2. In regard to third persons of good faith	973
		3. In regard to third persons of bad faith	974
E.	Erasures and modifications		
	I.	Wrongful entry	975
	II.	Extinction of real right	976
	III.	Rectifications	977

Final Title: Provisions for the Application and Introduction of Code

Chapter I: Application of Old and New Law

A.	General principles		
	I.	No retrospective effect	1
	II.	Retrospective effect	
		1. Public policy and *boni mores*	2
		2. Relations arising by operation of law	3
		3. Where right not acquired	4
B.	Law of Persons		
	I.	Capacity	5
	II.	Declaration of absence	6
	III.	Corporate bodies	7
C.	Family law		
	I.	Solemnization, divorce and effects of marriage in general	
		1. Principle	8
		2. Surname	8a
		3. Citizenship	8b
	II.	Matrimonial Property Law applicable to marriages contracted before 1st January 1912	9
	IIbis.	Matrimonial Property Law applicable to marriages contracted after 1st January 1912	9a
		2. Change from marital system to participation in acquisitions	
		a. Change of the masses of property	9b
		b. Privilege	9c
		c. Division of matrimonial property under the new law	9d
		3. Maintenance of the marital system	9e
		4. Maintenance of the system of separate estates by operation of the law or by order of the court	9f

				Article

                5. Marriage covenant
                    a. In general 10
                    b. Legal force towards third parties 10*a*
                    c. To be governed by the new law 10*b*
                    d. System of separate estates under the old law
                        by marriage covenant 10*c*
                    e. Marriage covenants made in view of the
                        coming into force of the new law 10*d*
                    f. Marriage property register 10*e*
                6. Settlement of debts at the division of matrimonial
                    property system 11
                7. Protection of creditors .11*a*
        III. The child-parent relationship in general 12
        IIIbis. Adoption
                1. Continuation of the old law 12*a*
                2. Placing under the new law 12*b*
                3. Adoption of majors and persons placed under
                    committee 12*c*
        IIIter. Contestation of legitimation 12*d*
        IV. Action for establishing paternity
                1. Pendent actions 13
                2. New actions 13*a*
        V.   Guardianship 14
        VI. Deprivation of liberty to secure personal assistance 14*a*
D. Law of Inheritance
    I.   Heirs and devolution of estate 15
    II. Testamentary dispositions 16
E. Law of Property
    I.   Real rights in general 17
    II.   Claims to registration 18
    III. Prescription and adverse possession 19
    IV.   Special rights of ownership
          1. Trees planted in another person's ground 20
          2. Storey ownership
              a. original 20bis
              b. changed 20ter
              c. Correction of the land register 20quater
    V.   Praedial servitudes 21
    VI.   Securities on land
          1. Recognition of existing securities 22
          2. Creation of new forms of real security 23
          3. Cancellation of securities 24
          4. Scope of real security .25

Table of Contents   XXI

Article

        5. Rights and duties under a mortgage
- *a.* In general 26
- *b.* Safeguards 27
- *c.* Notice of repayment, transfer 28

        6. Order of priority 29
        7. Place in the register .30
        8. Restrictions on the charge
- *a.* In general 31
- *b.* Continuation of the old law 32

        9. Relation between real securities under old and new law 33

VII. Pledges
    1. Form 34
    2. Effect 35

VIII. Liens 36
IX. Possession 37
X. Land register
    1. Establishment 38
    2. Mensuration
- *a.* Cost 39
- *b.* Relation to land register 40
- *c.* Periods allowed for the work 41
- *d.* How survey made 42

    3. Registration of real rights
- *a.* Procedure 43
- *b.* Consequences of non-registration 44

    4. Rights *in rem* that are abolished 45
    5. Delay in establishment of register 46
    6. Introduction of Property Law before establishment of land register 47
    7. Procedure laid down by Cantonal Law 48

F. Periods of limitation 49
G. Form of contracts 50

Chapter II: Introductory and Transitionary Provisions

A. Cantonal Law repealed 51
B. Supplementary Cantonal regulations
    I. Rights and duties of Cantons 52
    II. Orders in default of Cantonal regulations 53
C. Designation of competent authorities 54
D. Form of authentication of documents 55

		Article
E.	Concession of water rights	56
F.–H.		57 (annulled)
J.	Execution of debts and bankruptcy	58
K.	Application of Swiss and foreign laws	59
L.	Annulment of the Provisions of the Federal Civil Code	60
M.	Final provision	61

Appendix 1

1. Titles V and VI in the wording according to the Federal Statute of 10th December 1907, in force since 1st January 1912 until 31st December 1987 (effective until the coming into force of the Federal Statute of 5th October 1984 on 1st January 1988)

Title V: General Effects of Marriage

A. Rights and duties
  I. Of husband and wife 159
  II. Of husband 160
  III. Of wife 161

B. Representation of conjugal union
  I. By husband 162
  II. By wife
    1. In ordinary cases
      a. Scope 163
      b. Revocation 164
      c. Reinstatement 165
    2. In exceptional cases 166

C. Trade or profession of wife 167

D. Capacity of wife to bring and defend actions 168

E. Protective measures
  I. In general 169
  II. Life in common suspended 170
  III. Orders to debtors 171
  IV. Discontinuance of measures 172
  V. Execution on property of spouses
    1. General rule 173

Table of Contents XXIII

Article

		2.	Exceptions	
			a. Where a married person is a debtor	174
			b. Where a married person is a creditor	175
			c. For the separation of property and recovery of maintenance	176
F.	Legal transactions between husband and wife and for benefit of husband			177

Title VI: Matrimonial Property Law

Chapter I: General Provisions

A. Ordinary system 178
B. Marriage covenants
    I. Choice of system 179
    II. Capacity of parties 180
    III. Form required 181
C. Exceptional system
    I. Separation of estates by operation of law 182
    II. Judicial separation of estates
        1. At instance of wife 183
        2. At instance of husband 184
        3. At instance of creditors 185
    III. Commencement of separation of estates 186
    IV. Determination of system of separate estates 187
D. Modification of system
    I. Rights of creditors secured 188
    II. Division of property on separation of estates 189
E. Separate estates
    I. How they arise
        1. In general 190
        2. By operation of law .191
    II. Effect 192
    III. Burden of proof 193

Chapter II: Marital System

A. Proprietary rights
    I. Matrimonial property 194
    II. Rights of ownership of husband and wife 195

Civil Code

Article

    III.   Burden of proof .... .196
    IV.   Inventory
          1.   Its form and validity .... .197
          2.   Its effect............................ .198
    V.   Ownership of husband in wife's unreserved property ... .199

B.   Administration, user and alienation

    I.   Administration .... .200
    II.   User .... .201
    III. Alienation
          1.   Rights of husband .... .202
          2.   Rights of wife
               a.   In general .... .203
               b.   Disclaimer of an inheritance .... .204

C.   Security for wife's property .... .205
D.   Liability

    I.   Of husband .... .206
    II.   Of wife
          1.   To extent of whole property .... .207
          2.   To extent of her separate estate .... .208

E.   Compensation

    I.   When recoverable .... .209
    II.   Bankruptcy of husband and execution for debt
          1.   Rights of wife .... .210
          2.   Rights of priority .... .211

F.   Determination of system

    I.   Death of wife .... .212
    II.   Death of husband .... .213
    III. Profits and losses .... .214

Chapter III: Community of Property

A.   General community

    I.   Matrimonial property .... .215
    II.   Administration and alienation
          1.   Administration .... .216
          2.   Alienation
               a.   Of common property .... .217
               b.   Disclaimer of an inheritance .... .218
    III. Liability
          1.   Of husband .... .219

Article

		2.	Of wife	
			a. Personally and to extent of common property	.220
			b. To extent of her separate estate	.221
		3.	Execution for debt	.222
	IV.	Compensation		
		1.	In general	.223
		2.	Claims of wife	.224
	V.	Dissolution of community		
		1.	Division of property	
			a. By operation of law	.225
			b. By marriage covenant	.226
		2.	Liability of survivor	.227
		3.	Allocation of unreserved property	.228

B. Continuation of community

- I. Conditions 229
- II. Extent of community 230
- III. Administration and representation 231
- IV. Dissolution
    1. By the parties 232
    2. By operation of law 233
    3. By order of the court 234
    4. By the marriage or death of a child 235
    5. Division 236

C. Limited community

- I. With certain property as separate estate 237
- II. With certain property under marital system ... 238
- III. Community of "voluntarily acquired" property
    1. Its purport 239
    2. Profits and losses 240

Chapter IV: Separation of Estates

A. General effect 241
B. Ownership, administration and use 242
C. Liability for debt
 - I. In general 243
 - II. Bankruptcy of husband or execution against him .244
D. Income and earnings 245
E. Liability for maintenance of household 246
F. Dower 247

XXVI   Civil Code

                                                                 Article

Chapter V: Matrimonial Property Register

A. Effect of registration 248
B. Entry
  I. Its purport 249
  II. Where made 250
C. How register kept 251

2. Other provisions in the wording according to the Federal Statute of 10th December 1907, in force since 1st January 1912 until 31st December 1987 (effective until the coming into force of the Federal Statute of 5th October 1984 on 1st January 1988)

    c. Domicile of dependent persons 25
    Article 30, Paragraph 2 (annulled)
   2. On the husband and wife 134
  III. Provisional orders 145
  IV. Position of divorced wife 149
  VII. Division of matrimonial property
   1. On divorce 154
   2. On judicial separation 155
    Article 413, Paragraph 2
  IV. Great-grandparents 460
B. Surviving husband or wife
  I. Rights of inheritance 462
  II. Conversion and security .463
  III. Security for co-heirs 464
D. Canton and Commune 466
A. Devisable portion
  I. What is 470
  II. Compulsory portion 471
  III. Cantonal Law 472
  II. Usufructuaries 561
   Article 631, Paragraph 2
   Article 635, Paragraph 1
   Article 665, Paragraph 3
   2. Statutory usufruct   747

Article

Final Title

C. Family Law
    I. Solemnization, dissolution and personal effect of marriage
        marginal note and Paragraph 1 8
    II. Matrimonial Property Law
        1. Statutory system 9
        2. Marriage covenants 10
        3. How third persons are secured 11
           Article 59, Paragraph 2

Appendix 2

Changes of other Federal Statutes according to cipher II of the Federal Statute of 5th October 1984, in force since 1st January 1988

1. The Federal Statute of 25th June 1891 relating to the Civil Legal Situation of Holders of Permits for Permanent or Temporary Residents

        Article 20, Paragraph 1
        Article 36 lit. b

2. The Code of Obligations

VII. The family's lodging .... .271*a*
     Article 494, Paragraph 4 (annulled)

3. The Federal Statute on Bankruptcy and Execution

Vbis. To enforce payment from a spouse living under
       a system of community of property
       Article 68*a*
       Article 68*b*
       Article 95*a*
       Article 107, Paragraph 5 (annulled)
       Article 219, Paragraph 4, Forth Class, lit. a (annulled)
       Article 219, Paragraph 4, Fifth Class

4. The Federal Statute of 29th April 1920 relating to Consequences under Public Law of Futile Distraint and Bankruptcy

Article 2*a*

Appendix 3

The coming into force of the Federal Statute of 5th October 1984 according to its cipher III

Vocabulary

I.	English, German, French	393
II.	German, French, English	399
III.	French, German, English	405

Index   411

Part IV: Law of Property

Section I: Ownership

Title XVIII: General Rules

Art. 641

[1] The owner of anything has the right, within the limits of the law, to dispose of it at will.

[2] He has the right to demand it back from anyone who wrongfully detains it and take measures to prevent any unlawful interference with it.

A. Nature of ownership

Art. 642

[1] The owner of a thing is the owner of all the integral parts of which it is composed.

[2] An integral part of a thing is that which according to the local acceptation of the conception constitutes an essential element of that thing and which cannot be separated from it without destroying or damaging it or changing its character.

B. Extent of right
I. Integral parts of a thing

Art. 643

[1] The owner of a thing is held to be the owner of its natural fruits also.

[2] Natural fruits are its periodical products and everything which may be derived from it according to what is customarily held to be the object to which it is to be put.

[3] They are an integral part of the parent thing until they are severed from it.

II. Natural fruits

Art. 644

III. Accessories
1. Definition

¹ Any legal transaction affecting a certain thing affects its accessories also, unless an express reservation has been made.

² Accessories are movable things which according to local usage or to the clear intention of the owner of the principal thing are permanently destined for its use, enjoyment or preservation and which are joined or adapted to it or otherwise connected with it in such a manner that they may serve its purpose.

³ Accessories do not lose their character as such by being temporarily separated from the principal thing.

Art. 645

2. Not accessory

Movable things are not accessories, where they are used by the person in possession of the principal thing merely for his temporary enjoyment or their consumption, or where they are foreign to the nature and object of the principal thing or connected with it only for the purpose of safe custody, sale or hire.

Art. 646

C. United ownership
I. Co-ownership
1. Rights of owners *inter se*

¹ Where a certain thing is in the ownership of several persons, each of whom owns a share of it and yet it is outwardly undivided, they are held to be co-owners.¹

² In the absence of a contrary arrangement all are held to have equal shares.

³ In respect of his share each co-owner has the rights and is under the obligations of an owner; he

---

[1] **Miteigentum** has been translated "co-ownership" in order to leave the term "ownership in common" for **Gesamteigentum**. "Joint ownership" is not known in Swiss Law and therefore the term has been avoided.

can alienate or pledge it and it can be seized by his creditors for debt.

Art. 647[1]

2. Regulations for the use and management

[1] The co-owners can set forth regulations for the use and management which deviate from the legal orders issued by the authorities and have them entered in the land register.

[2] However they cannot repeal or restrict the rights to which each of the co-owners is entitled:

1. to demand that the administrative acts which are required for the preservation of the value and for the use of the object are executed and, if required, are ordered to be executed by the judge;

2. to take on his own the necessary steps which have to be taken without loss of time in order to preserve the object from imminent or increasing damage. The costs for these administrative acts must be borne by all co-owners jointly.

Art. 647a[2]

3. Usual acts of management

[1] Each co-owner is entitled to execute the usual administrative acts, in particular the execution of small repairs, sowing and harvesting, to keep things in custody during a short period of time and to supervise the property, also to conclude contracts which serve these purposes and to execute the rights laid down in these contracts and the occupation lease, the agricultural lease and contracts for building, as well as the payment and acceptance of sums of money on behalf of all co-owners.

---

[1] Wording according to cipher I of the Federal Statute of 19th December 1963, in force since 1st January 1965 (AS **1964** 993 1005; BBl **1962** II 1461).
[2] Inserted by cipher I of the Federal Statute of 19th December 1963, in force since 1st January 1965 (AS **1964** 993, 1005; BBl **1962** II 1461).

² With the consent of the majority of all co-owners the competence for these acts of management can be ordered differently under the proviso of the provisions made by law for necessary and urgent measures.

Art. 647*b*[1]

4. More important administrative acts

¹ The consent of the majority of the co-owners representing the greater part of the object is required for the execution of major acts of management, in particular, a change in the methods of cultivation or the way the property is used, the conclusion and dissolution of an occupation lease or agricultural lease, the participation in land amelioration and the appointment of a manager whose competence is not limited to the usual acts of management.

² Exception is made for the provisions for the necessary measures for building and repairs.

Art. 647*c*[1]

5. Measures for building and repairs
a. Necessary measures

With the consent of all co-owners maintenance work, repairs and renovations which are essential for the preservation of the value and the serviceableness of the object can be executed provided these acts are not usual acts of management to which each co-owner is entitled singly.

Art. 647*d*[1]

b. Useful measures

¹ Renovations and alterations which are undertaken with the intention to increase the value or improve the rentability or serviceableness of the object require the consent of the numerical majority

---

[1] Inserted by cipher I of the Federal Statute of 19th December 1963, in force since 1st January 1965 (AS **1964** 993 1005; BBl **1962 II** 1461).

of all the co-owners who at the same time represent the larger part of the property.

² Alterations which would make the use and the enjoyment of the object considerably and constantly difficult or unprofitable for one of the co-owners cannot be undertaken without the consent of the co-owner concerned.

³ Where the alterations would require a contribution from one of the co-owners which exceeds what can fairly be expected from him, in particular because it is unproportioned as regards the value of the share he owns, they can be carried out without this co-owner's consent only if the other co-owners are prepared to pay his share of the cost to the extent as it exceeds the amount he could be expected to contribute.

Art. 647e[1]

¹ Building investments made for the sole purpose of making the object appear more beautiful or respectable or providing increased comfort in usage require the consent of all co-owners.

c. Measures to improve appearance and comfort

² Where such work is carried out with the consent of the majority of all co-owners who also represent the larger part of the property, it can also be undertaken against the will of a co-owner refusing to consent, provided his right to use and enjoy the object is not encroached upon constantly and the other co-owners are willing to indemnify him, either in money or kind, for the temporary impairment and are prepared to pay his share of the cost.

---

[1] Inserted by cipher I of the Federal Statute of 13th December 1963, in force since 1st January 1965 (AS **1964** 993, 1004; BBl **1962 II** 1461).

Art. 648[1]

6. Disposing of the property

[1] Each co-owner is entitled to represent the property and to use and enjoy it, so far as this is compatible with the rights of the others.

[2] In the absence of a unanimous agreement between them to the contrary, the consent of all is required for alienating or encumbering the property, as well as for changing the object to which it is to be put.

[3] Where a co-owner's share of the property is encumbered with real security on land or rent-charges, the co-owners cannot encumber the property itself with such additional rights.

Art. 649[1]

7. Distribution of costs and charges

[1] In the absence of contrary agreement, costs of administration, taxes and other charges arising from co-ownership or burdening the co-owned property are borne by the co-owners in proportion to their shares.

[2] Where one of the co-owners has paid more than his share, he can claim to be indemnified by the others in the same proportion.

Art. 649a[2]

8. Entrance of a new share owner

The regulations for the use and management of the property agreed upon by the co-owners and the decisions made regarding the administration of the object as well as all judgments passed and orders ruled by a judge are equally binding for the legal successor of a co-owner and the purchaser of a co-owner's share of the rights *in rem.*

---

[1] Wording according to cipher I of the Federal Statute of 19th December 1963, in force since 1st January 1965 (AS **1964** 993 1005; BBl **1962 II** 1461).

[2] Inserted by cipher I of the Federal Statute of 19th December 1963, in force since 1st January 1965 (AS **1964** 933, 1005; BBl **1962 II** 1461).

Art. 649*b*[1]

9. Exclusion from the body of co-owners
a. Co-owners

¹ Where a co-owner, through his own behaviour or the behaviour of the persons to whom he has given the enjoyment and usage of the object or for whom he can be held responsible, has neglected his duties and obligations towards all co-owners or individual co-owners so seriously that his membership of the body of co-owners cannot be expected of these, this co-owner can be excluded from the body of co-owners by the judgment of the court.

² Where the body of co-owners comprises only two co-owners, each of them has the right of action; in all other cases and in the absence of an agreement to the contrary an action to be brought against one of the co-owners requires the authorization of the majority of all co-owners with the exception of the co-owner against whom the action is to be brought.

³ If the judge passes judgment which excludes the defendant from co-ownership, he orders him to sell his share; for the case where this sale is not executed within the officially fixed delay the judge orders a public auction for the sale of this share in compliance with the regulations valid for the execution of the sale of landed property excluding the provisions made for the dissolution of co-ownership.

Art. 649*c*[2]

b. Other party entitled

The provisions made for the exclusion of a co-owner apply accordingly to the party actually enjoying the usufruct of the object or the holder of another right *in rem* or pre-notified personal title to enjoy and use a co-owner's share of the property.

---

[1] Inserted by cipher I of the Federal Statute of 19th December 1963, in force since 1st January 1965 (AS **1964** 993 1005; BBl **1962 II** 1461).

[2] Inserted by cipher I of the Federal Statute of 13th December 1963, in force since 1st January 1965 (AS **1964** 993 1005; BBl **1962 II** 1461).

Art. 650[1]

10. Dissolution
a. Right to partition

[1] Each co-owner is entitled to demand the partition of the property, unless this is made impossible by some legal transaction, by a partition resulting in creating condominium principled ownership or in consequence of the permanent character of the object of the ownership.

[2] The dissolution can be excluded for a period not exceeding thirty years by an agreement which for its validity must be publicly verified as is required for landed property and which can be pre-notified in the land register.

[3] A partition must not be demanded at an unreasonable moment.

Art. 651

b. Method

[1] Co-ownership is dissolved by the distribution of the property among the owners, by sale by private treaty or by auction followed by the division of the price, or by the allotment of the whole property to one or more of the owners who have redeemed the shares of the rest.

[2] Where the owners cannot agree on the method of division, the court will order the distribution of the property among them, or, where this cannot be done without serious loss, its sale by public auction or by private auction confined to the owners themselves.

[3] In the case of the distribution of the property any inequality in the parts can be rectified by means of compensation in money.

---

[1] Wording according to cipher I of the Federal Statute of 19th December 1963, in force since 1st January 1965 (AS 1964 993 1005; BBl 1962 II 1461).

Art. 652

Where several persons, who are joined in a community either by operation of law or by contract, are by virtue of that community owners of the same property, they are held to be owners in common and each of them has the right of ownership in the whole property.

II. Ownership in common
1. Conditions

Art. 653

¹ The rights and duties of the owners in common are determined by the rules of the statutory or contractual community in which they are joined.

² In the absence of a contrary provision, the rights of the owners, the right of alienation in particular, cannot be exercised over the common property except with the consent of all the owners.

³ While the community continues, no owner can demand partition or alienate his share.

2. Effect

Art. 654

¹ Ownership in common ceases with the alienation of the property or the dissolution of the community.

² In the absence of a contrary provision, partition is effected in the same way as in the case of co-ownership.

E. Determination

Title XIX: Ownership of Land

Chapter I: Subject-Matter, Acquisition and Loss of Ownership of Land

Art. 655[1]

A. Subject-matter

[1] Ownership of land means ownership of all immovable property.

[2] Immovable property in the Code includes:

1. land and houses;

2. independent and permanent rights entered in the land register,[2]

3. mines;

4. co-ownership shares of immovables.

Art. 656

B. Acquisition
I. Registration

[1] Registration in the land register is required for the acquisition of ownership of land.

[2] Where a person, however, acquires land by occupation, succession, expropriation, execution for debt, or a judgment of the court, he becomes owner of the land before registration, but he cannot deal with it through the register until after registration has taken place.

Art. 657

II. Modes of acquisition
1. Transfer

[1] A contract for the transfer of ownership of land is void unless made by a duly authenticated instrument.

[2] Testamentary dispositions and marriage covenants must be made in the form required by the Law of Inheritance and the Matrimonial Property Law respectively.

---

[1] Wording according to cipher I of the Federal Statute of 19th December 1963, in force since 1st January 1965 (AS 1964 993 1005; BBl 1962 II 1461).

[2] These are rights *in rem* over another person's land as described in arts. 730 *et seq.*, below.

Art. 658

¹ The ownership of land entered in the land register can only be acquired by occupation where it can be shown by reference to the register to have no owner.

² Where a piece of land is not entered in the register, its acquisition by occupation is governed by the rules in regard to things which have no owner.

2. Occupation

Art. 659

¹ Where by alluvion or deposit or landslips or alterations in the course or the level of public waters or in any other manner serviceable ground is formed from waste places, it belongs to the Canton in the borders of which it is situated.

² The Canton has the right to assign the new ground to the owners of the adjacent land.

³ Where a person can prove that some part of his land has been torn away, he is entitled to retake possession of it within a reasonable time.

3. Formation of new ground

Art. 660

¹ Where land shifts from one property to another, this does not effect a change in the boundaries.

² Soil and other things transported from one property to another are subject to the rules on drifts or fusion.¹

4. Landslips

Art. 661

Where a person has been entered in the land register as owner of a piece of land without having any title to it, his right to the ownership in it cannot be contested after he has been for ten years in continuous *bona fide* peaceable possession of it.

5. Adverse possession
a. In ordinary cases

---

¹ See arts. 725 and 727.

Art. 662

b. In exceptional cases

[1] Where a person has for thirty years been in continuous peaceable possession as owner of a piece of land which is not entered in the register, he can claim to be registered as owner.

[2] The person in possession can under the same conditions claim the same right in regard to a piece of land, the owner of which is not shown in the register, or was dead or officially declared absent at the beginning of the period of thirty years.

[3] This registration can, however, take place only by the order of the court and where no objection has been lodged within a period officially fixed and publicly advertised, or where the objection that was lodged has been rejected.

Art. 663

c. Running of years

The rules laid down in regard to the limitation of actions apply here by analogy for the purpose of calculating the period required for adverse possession and of determining in what cases the running of years is stopped or suspended.[1]

Art. 664

6. Ownerless and public property

[1] Public property and things which have no owner are under the Public Law of the Canton or State[2] in which they are situated.

[2] In the absence of evidence to the contrary no private ownership is possible in public waters or in places unsuitable for cultivation, such as rocks, moraines, névés, or glaciers, or in the springs issuing forth from them.

[3] Cantonal Law lays down the necessary regulations in regard to the acquisition by occupation of land that has no owner, as well as the development

---

[1] These rules are laid down in the Code of Obligations.
[2] *i.e.* the Federation itself, *e.g.* railways.

and the common use of public property, such as roads, open spaces, public waters and river beds.

Art. 665

¹ Where a person has acquired a good title to the ownership of property, he has a right *in personam* against the owner for the registration of his title and, if the latter refuses, is entitled to apply to the court for the establishment of his rights of ownership.

² Acquisition of land by occupation, succession, expropriation, execution for debt or a judgment of the court, confers upon the person who acquires it the right to demand that his title be registered.

³ Changes in the ownership of land which occur by operation of the law in consequence of the system of community of property or its dissolution are entered in the land register at the instance of one of the spouses.[1]

III. Right to registration

Art. 666

¹ The ownership of immovable property is lost by the erasure of the entry in the register or by the complete destruction of the immovable.

² In the case of the expropriation of the property, the point of time at which the ownership is lost is determined by Federal or Cantonal Law on Expropriation.

C. Loss of ownership

Chapter II: Nature and Limits of Ownership of Land

Art. 667

¹ The ownership of the soil implies the ownership of all that is above and below the surface to such

A. Nature of right
I. Its extent

---

[1] Wording according to cipher I 2 of the Federal Statute of 5th October 1984, in force since 1st January 1988 (BBl **1979 II** 1191).

a height and depth respectively as the owner may require.

² It extends, subject to certain legal restrictions, to all buildings on the ground as well as plants and springs in it.

Art. 668

II. Boundaries
1. How determined

¹ Boundaries are determined by the plans in the land register and the boundary lines on the land itself.

² If the boundaries on the plans do not agree with those on the land, the former are presumed to be correct.

Art. 669

2. Obligation to fix them

Where the boundaries are uncertain, every landowner is bound, at his neighbour's request, to join with him in fixing them either by rectifying the plans or setting up boundary lines.

Art. 670

3. Boundary lines on common ground

Erections or other things which purport to fix the boundary between two properties, such as walls, hedges or fences, and stand on the boundary line, are presumed to belong to the two neighbours jointly.

Art. 671

III. Buildings on the land of another
1. Materials
a. Ownership

¹ Where one person builds on his own land with another person's materials or on another person's land with his own materials, the materials become an integral part of the land.

² If, however, the materials have been used without their owner's consent, he can require that they should be removed from the land at the expense of the owner of the land and restored to himself, provided that this can be done without unreasonable damage.

³ Similarly under the same conditions, where the materials have been used without the consent of

the owner of the land, he can require that they shall be removed at the builder's expense.

Art. 672

¹ Where the materials are not removed from the land, the owner of the land is bound to pay reasonable compensation for them.   *b.* Compensation

² If the owner of the land has built in bad faith, the court may condemn him to make full reparation for the damage done.

³ If the owner of the materials has built in bad faith, he can claim only that amount of compensation which represents the minimum value of the building to the owner of the land.

Art. 673

If the value of the building evidently exceeds that of the land, the party who has acted *bona fide* can require that the ownership of the land and building together shall be adjudicated to the owner of the materials in return for reasonable compensation.   *c.* Adjudication of ownership of the land

Art. 674

¹ Where buildings or other erections encroach on a neighbour's land, they remain an integral part of the land from which they issue, provided the owner of this land has a right *in rem* over the part of the construction that encroaches.   2. Encroachment

² The right over the encroaching part can be entered as a servitude in the land register.

³ Where the encroachment is wrongful, and yet the injured party does not after cognizance thereof object within the period allowed, the party encroaching can, if he has acted *bona fide* and the circumstances warrant it, demand that the court adjudicate to him in return for reasonable compensation a right *in rem* in the encroaching part or the

ownership of the piece of land covered by the encroachment.

Art. 675

^{3. Right over a building[1]}

¹ Buildings and other erections set up on or underneath the surface of a certain piece of land in such a manner that they are permanently joined to it, can be the property of a person other than the owner of the land, if this right is entered as a servitude in the land register.

² The different stories of one and the same house cannot be the object of this kind of right.

Art. 676

4. Conduits

¹ Conduits for water, gas, electricity and such like, even where they pass beyond the land for which they have been laid, are, in the absence of a contrary provision, held to be accessory to the works from which they run and to be the property of the owner of these works.

² If the laying of the conduit is not justified by the *jus vicinorum*,[2] it does not create a real charge on the other person's land unless a servitude to this effect has been constituted.

³ Where the conduit is not visible from the outside, the servitude is constituted by entry in the land register, in other cases by the laying of the conduit itself.

Art. 677

5. Movable structures

¹ Light structures such as huts, booths or sheds, erected on another person's ground without being intended as permanent buildings, remain the property of their owner.

---

[1] German **Baurecht,** French *droit de superficie,* is akin to the Roman Law *superficies,* with this difference that here the person having the right is looked upon as the owner of the building.

[2] As under art. 691 below.

² They are not entered in the land register.

Art. 678

¹ Where a person has set in his own ground plants belonging to another person or his own plants in the ground of another, the parties are in the same legal position as in the case of the use of building material or the erection of movable structures.¹ — IV. Plants

² No servitude can be constituted in plants or woods.

Art. 679

Where damage is caused or threatened by an owner of land who exceeds his rights of ownership, the party injured can apply to the court for an order that the damage shall be made good or for an injunction to restrain the continuance of the wrong and for damages for the wrong done. — V. Liability of owner of land

Art. 680

¹ The restrictions imposed by law on the rights of an owner of land do not require to be entered in the land register. — B. Limits of right I. In general

² These restrictions cannot be removed or modified by the parties except by a duly authenticated instrument and an entry in the register.

³ Restrictions imposed in the public interest can neither be removed nor modified.

Art. 681

¹ Where a right of pre-emption over a piece of land has been entered against it in the land register, it is operative as against every successive owner of the property during the period of time stated in the entry and subject to the conditions therein stated if any, — II. On alienation 1. Right of pre-emption a. By entry in register

---

¹ *i.e.* the plants are accessory to the land.

and if not, subject to the conditions contained in the sale to the defendant.

² The person who has the right of pre-emption must be notified of the sale by the vendor.

³ His right of pre-emption is extinguished at the end of one month after his cognizance of the sale and in any case not later than at the end of ten years from the entry of the right in the register.

Art. 682[1]

b. Between co-owners and holders of rights over a building

¹ Co-owners have a right of pre-emption against any third party who acquires one of the shares.

² A right of pre-emption against any acquirer also belongs to the owners of a property which is encumbered with an independent and permanent right over a building with regard to this right and the holder of this right with regard to the encumbered property, as far as it is concerned by the execution of his right.

³ Agreements regarding the removal or alteration of the right of pre-emption need for their validity due authentication and can be annotated in the land register.

Art. 683

2. Rights of purchase and redemption

¹ Where a right of purchase or of redemption of certain land is entered in the land register, it is operative against every successive owner of the land for the period of time stated in the entry.

² Rights of purchase and redemption lapse in every case at the end of ten years from their entry in the register.

---

[1] Wording according to cipher I of the Federal Statute of 19th December 1963, in force since 1st January 1965 (AS 1964 993 1005; BBl 1962 II 1461).

Art. 684

¹ Every owner of land is bound in the exercise of his rights and especially in carrying on an industry on the land to abstain from any unreasonable act which prejudices his neighbour's property.

² He is in particular forbidden to emit smoke, soot or noxious fumes, or cause noise or vibration which would prejudice his neighbours and be held unreasonable in view of the situation and character of the properties or be contrary to local usage.

III. *Jus vicinorum*
1. Mode of using own land

Art. 685

¹ In making exavations or erecting buildings the owner of land must not injure his neighbour's property by shaking or endangering his foundations or prejudicing any existing works or erections.

² Buildings which violate the *jus vicinorum* are governed by the provisions in regard to encroachments on adjacent land.

2. Excavations and buildings
a. General rule

Art. 686

¹ Cantons can fix the distance from the boundaries that must be observed by an owner of land for excavations or buildings.

² They can further lay down other building regulations.

b. Cantonal regulations

Art. 687

¹ Every owner of land has the right to cut and keep branches that overhang his property and roots that spread into it, where they damage it and have not been removed at his request within a reasonable time.

² Where branches spread over neighbouring land that is built on or cultivated, and the owner of the land suffers them to remain, he has the right to the fruits growing on them.

3. Plants
a. General rule

³ These rules do not apply where forests come down to the boundaries of adjacent landowners.

Art. 688

b. Cantonal regulations

Cantons can fix the distance from the boundary line between two properties that must be observed for plantations according to the character of the land and the nature of the plantation; they can, on the other hand, compel an owner to allow the branches and roots of his neighbour's fruit trees to spread to his land and define or suppress his rights to the fruit growing on them.

Art. 689

4. Natural flow of water

¹ Every owner of land is bound to take the water that drains naturally off higher ground on to his own land, such as rain water, water from the melting of snow or from springs that have not been confined within artificial channels.

² No owner can divert this natural flow of water to the prejudice of his neighbour.

³ Water that flows naturally on to lower ground and is necessary to this ground cannot be diverted from it, unless and in so far as it is indispensable to the property above.

Art. 690

5. Drainage

¹ The owner of land is bound to take, without demanding compensation, water coming to his land from the ground above him in consequence of the artificial drainage of that ground, where before the drainage the water flowed naturally on to his land.

² If he suffers damage from such artificial drainage, he can require the owner of the higher ground at the latter's expense to carry the drains right through the lower land.

Art. 691

¹ Every owner of land is bound, subject to full compensation being paid him for all damage caused, to allow the passage across his land of aqueducts, drain pipes, gas pipes and other pipes, as well as of electric overhead or underground wires, where these pipes and wires could not, without making use of the land, be laid at all or at a moderate cost. *6. Conduit pipes and wires a. Obligation to suffer them*

² The right to lay conduits and wires across another person's land cannot be claimed as part of the *jus vicinorum* in the cases where Cantonal or Federal Law provides for the expropriation of the land for this purpose in the public interest.

³ Where such conduits have been laid, the dominant owner can have this fact entered at his expense in the land register.[1]

Art. 692

¹ The servient owner can require that his interests be fairly taken into consideration. *b. Safeguarding interests of servient owner*

² In exceptional cases and where the conduits are to be above ground, he can require that a reasonable portion of his land over which the conduits are to be laid shall be bought of him at a price which fairly compensates him.

Art. 693

¹ Where the circumstances are changed, the servient owner can require that the conduits shall be moved to a different part of his property in accordance with his interests. *c. Change of circumstances*

² The cost of moving them must as a rule be borne by the dominant owner.

---

[1] For the sake of brevity the two parties are called the dominant and the servient owner respectively, though the right here spoken of is not a servitude.

[3] The servient owner can, however, where this is justified by the special circumstances of the case, be made liable to bear a reasonable proportion of the cost.

Art. 694

7. Rights of way
a. Of necessity

[1] Where the owner of land has no sufficient access from his land to a public road, he can require his neighbours to cede to him a right of way of necessity in return for full compensation.

[2] He can exercise his right in the first place as against the neighbour who could most reasonably be expected to grant a right of way by reason of the previous state of the properties and the mode of access to them, and in the second place as against the neighbour who would least be prejudiced by the right of way.

[3] The question of the way must be settled by taking into consideration the interests of both parties.

Art. 695

b. Other rights of way

The Cantons must make further regulations in regard to the rights of an owner of land to go on his neighbour's property for the purpose of effecting improvements or repairs or building operations on his own land, as well as for the purpose of tillage, watering cattle, transit over fallow ground or in the dead season, carting timber and other similar purposes.

Art. 696

c. Registration

[1] Rights of way arising by operation of law do not require registration.

[2] They are, however, noted in the register, if they are permanent.

Art. 697

¹ Subject to the rules in regard to the co-ownership of boundary fences, the cost of enclosure is borne by the owner of the land to be enclosed.

² The obligation to enclose and the nature of the enclosure are regulated by Cantonal Law.

8. Enclosures

Art. 698

The cost of setting up or maintaining an erection in the exercise of the *jus vicinorum* must be borne by the adjacent owners in proportion to their interest in it.

9. Upkeep

Art. 699

¹ Every person has, to the extent allowed by local custom, free access to the forests and fields of another person and can pick wild berries, mushrooms and such like, provided the competent authority has not issued special prohibitory notices in regard to certain lands for the sake of the crops.

² In regard to access on another person's land for the purpose of hunting, shooting and fishing, the Cantons can make special regulations.

IV. Right of access to another's property
1. Forests and fields

Art. 700

¹ Where some person's things have by the action of water, wind, avalanches or other forces of nature or by accident drifted to another person's land, or where animals such as cattle, sheep or pigs, or swarms of bees, fish or fowl have strayed to it, the owner of the land must allow the person entitled to the things or animals to enter and recover them.

² Where the owner of the land has suffered any damage therefrom, he can claim compensation and has a lien on the things or animals to enforce his claim.

2. Drifts and strays

Art. 701

3. In defence of person or property

¹ Where a person can ward off some impending damage or existing danger from himself or from others only by trespassing on the land of another person, the latter is bound to suffer the trespass, provided the infringement of his rights is trifling in comparison with the damage or danger to be warded off.

² Where the owner of the land has suffered damage thereby, he can claim reasonable compensation.

Art. 702

V. Limitations under Public Law
1. In general

The Federation, Cantons and Communes retain the right to impose further limitations on the ownership of land in the public interest, such as in regard to buildings, fires, public health, forests, roads, towpaths, boundary lines and landmarks, improvements of the soil, the parcelling of estates, the grouping together of plots for agricultural and for building purposes respectively, the preservation of antiquities and natural curiosities, of beauty spots and mineral springs.

Art. 703[1]

2. Improvements of soil

¹ Where improvements in the soil, such as correcting watercourses, draining land, afforestation, road making, grouping together of woodland and land for agricultural purposes respectively and such like, can be carried out only by the co-operation of several owners of land, and the majority of these owning more than half the land concerned have agreed to a scheme, the other owners are bound to co-operate with them in carrying it out. The owners who do not participate in passing the resolution are considered as agreeing to it. The co-operation is to be annotated in the land register.

---

[1] Wording according to art. 121 of the Agriculture Act of 3rd October 1951, in force since 1st January 1954 (SR 910.1).

² The procedure is determined by Cantonal Law.

³ The Cantons can still further facilitate the execution of these improvements and extend to building land the rules set out above.

Art. 704

¹ Springs are an integral part of the land from which they issue, and the ownership of them cannot be acquired independently of the ownership of the land itself.

² Where one person is to have a right in the springs issuing from the land of another, it must be constituted as a servitude by being entered as such in the land register.

³ Subterranean water falls under the same rules as springs.

C. Springs
I. Ownership and servitudes

Art. 705

¹ The right of confining and abducting natural waters can be regulated, restricted or prohibited by the Cantons in the public interest.

² If this leads to a dispute between the Cantons, the Federal Council decides it, and this decision is final and conclusive.

II. Confining waters in conduits

Art. 706

¹ Where a considerable use is made of a certain spring or well, or the spring has been confined or collected in order that it may be conserved, and it is cut off, reduced or polluted by building operations, excavations or other work of that kind to the prejudice of the owner or other person entitled, he can claim damages for the loss he has thereby suffered.

² Where the damage was caused neither intentionally nor negligently, or where it was due to the plaintiff's own fault, it is for the judge to decide in his discretion whether damages are due and, if so, to fix their amount.

III. Springs cut off
1. Damages

Art. 707

2. Restoration

¹ Where springs and wells are indispensable to the owner of land for industrial or household purposes, or are required as drinking water, and they are cut off or polluted, their restoration *in statu quo* can be demanded in so far as this can be effected.

² In other cases such restoration cannot be demanded except under special circumstances.

Art. 708

IV. Common springs

¹ Where several adjacent springs belonging to different owners have a common source of supply and thus form a single basin, each owner can require that the springs be confined and collected under one system and distributed to each of the persons entitled in the same proportion as he was supplied before.

² The costs of the installation are borne by the persons entitled in proportion to their interest in the water supply.

³ Where one of them is opposed to the scheme, each can confine and conduct his own spring provided he does it in a proper manner, even if he thereby reduces the volume of water in the other springs, and is only bound to indemnify the others in so far as his own spring has by this means increased in volume.

Art. 709

V. Use of springs

The Cantons can determine to what extent springs, wells and streams which are privately owned may be used by neighbours and other persons for drawing water, watering cattle and similar purposes.

Art. 710

VI. Water supply of necessity

¹ Where the owner of property has not the water necessary for his house and land and cannot without excessive trouble and expense procure it otherwise, he has the right to demand that his neighbour shall in

return for full compensation let him have from his own supply what water he himself does not require.

² The conditions are settled by taking more particularly into consideration the interests of the party bound to accede to this demand.

³ Where the circumstances change, a corresponding change in the conditions fixed can be demanded.

Art. 711

¹ Where springs, wells or streams are of no use to their owner or of little use in comparison with their actual value, he can be compelled in return for full compensation to surrender his rights in them, in order that they may be used for public purposes, such as for the supply of drinking water, or hydrants, or other works of public utility.

² Such compensation may consist of a supply of water from the new installation.

VII. Expropriation
1. Of springs

Art. 712

Owners of drinking water installations can demand the expropriation of land situated round the springs that supply the water, where this is necessary to prevent their pollution.

2. Of land

Chapter III: Condominium Principled Ownership[1] (Storey Ownership)[2]

Art. 712a

A. Nature and Object
I. Content

[1] Condominium principled ownership means a co-owner's share of an immovable property which concedes to the co-owner the special privilege of using clearly defined parts of a building alone and entitles him to carry out structural changes in these parts of the building.

[2] As regards management, usage and architectural changes in his own rooms, the owner of a flat held in storey ownership is free to make his own decisions, yet he must not encroach on the same right of any of the other co-owners, nor must he damage or interfere with the functioning or impair the external appearance of the parts of the building and the installations and equipment which all co-owners own and have a right to use jointly.

[3] He is obliged to keep his rooms in a state of repair which is required to keep the building in perfect condition and preserve its good appearance.

Art. 712b

II. Object

[1] Object of the special privilege can be: individual storeys or parts of storeys which as either dwellings or units of rooms used for business or other purposes must form a closed body of rooms and have a separate entrance. They can, however, comprise separate additional rooms as well.

---

[1] Inserted by cipher II of the Federal Statute of 19th December 1963, in force since 1st January 1965 (AS **1964** 993 1005; BBl **1962 II** 1461).

[2] The terms "storey ownership" and "storey owner" have been adopted in order to designate that this type of ownership does not only refer to flats, but, in a more general way, to rooms, used for any purpose, which are located on a storey. For definition of storey ownership see art. 712a and b.

² The following rights cannot be conceded as special privileges to a co-owner of an object held in condominium principled ownership:

1. the ground of the property and the right of building which may be prerequisites for the erection of the building;

2. the parts of the building which are of importance for the general condition, the architectural structuring and the stability of the building in general or the rooms of other co-owners in particular or which determine the shape and the outer appearance of the building;

3. installations and equipment which also serve the other co-owners in the use of their rooms.

³ Other parts of the building can be declared as being in united ownership in either the original act of agreement or in the same form in a later act of agreement made by the co-owners; where this has not been done it is presumed that they have been separately listed as special privileges.

Art. 712c

¹ The co-owner of a storey or part of a storey has no right of pre-emption against a third party who acquires one of the shares by operation of the law; however, a right of pre-emption can be entered in the act of agreement or it can be established at a later date and entered in the land register.

III. Right to dispose of object

² In the same way it can be agreed that the sale of a storey or the encumbrance with a right of usufruct or a right of residence or the right to let the storey is only legally valid if the other co-owners do not object on the grounds of a decision made by them within 14 days after having been notified thereof.

³ Where there are no serious grounds the objection is without effect; the judge rules on the qualification of the objection in summary proceeding on request of the opponent to the objection.

Art. 712*d*

B. Foundation and destruction
I. Foundation

¹Ownership on condominium principle is established by entry in the land register. The entry can be requested:

1. on account of a contract agreed upon by the co-owners regarding the transformation of their shares into condominium principled shares of ownership;

2. on account of a declaration made by the owner of a property or the holder of an independent and lasting right over a building made for the creation of co-owners' shares and their qualification as condominium principled shares of ownership.

²The legal transaction is only valid if it is publicly verified or where it is a testamentary disposition or a partition agreement; it has to comply with the rules laid down in the Law of Inheritance.

Art. 712*e*

II. Value quotas

¹In the act of agreement not only the rooms have to be attributed and specified, but also the value of the share of each storey has to be given in hundredths and thousandths of the value of the property or the right over the building.

²Changes of the value of the respective quotas require the consent of all persons having a direct interest in the property and an act of agreement pronounced by the assembly of the co-owners; however each has the right to have his quota rectified if any error in fixing the quota has occurred or the quota has become incorrect as the result of constructional changes carried out in the building itself or its environment.

Art. 712*f*

III. Destruction

¹The condominium principled ownership ends with the destruction of the immovable or the extinction of the right of building and its erasure in the land register.

² The erasure can be requested on account of an agreement made for the determination of the condominium principled ownership; it can also be requested without such an act of agreement by a co-owner who is in possession of all shares, however, he requires the consent of all persons who have a right *in rem* to the individual storeys and whose rights cannot be transferred to the property as a whole without incurring a disadvantage for them.

³ The determination of the condominium principled ownership can be requested by each individual co-owner when the building is destroyed in the value of more than half of its full value and the reconstruction cannot be undertaken without incurring a substantial financial burden which this co-owner cannot be expected to bear; yet those co-owners who express the wish to continue the community of co-owners can avoid the determination by paying compensations to the others.

Art. 712*g*

¹ The competence for acts of management and structural measures are subject to the provisions made for co-ownership.

² As far as these provisions do not exclude it *eo ipso*, they can be replaced by another order; however, this can only be done either in the original act of agreement or with the unanimous consent of all owners of storeys.

³ Further to this each owner of a storey is entitled to request that written regulations for the management and the usage of the property are set up and notified in the land register; to be valid they must be accepted by the majority of the co-owners of storeys who must also represent more than half of the shares and these regulations can be changed with this same majority, even if they formed a part of the original act of agreement.

C. Management and Usage
I. Applicable provisions

Art. 712*h*

II. Common costs and liabilities
1. Inventory and distribution

¹ The co-owners of storeys must contribute to the encumbrance of the property held in united ownership and the costs of the joint management of the property as a whole in proportion of the value of their quotas.

² Such encumbrances and costs are:

1. expenses for ordinary maintenance, for repairs and renovation of the parts of the site and building as well as installations and equipment belonging to all co-owners together;

2. the costs of managing the property, inclusive of the costs of a person in charge of the management;

3. the payments caused by operation of public law and taxes to which all co-owners of a property held in condominium principled ownership are subject as a body;

4. interest and amortizations to mortgagers to whom the property serves as a pledge and to whom all owners of storeys of the property are liable jointly and severally.

³ Where jointly owned parts of the building, installations or equipments were intended to serve all co-owners but serve certain individual storey units in fact only in a very small degree or not at all, this has to be considered in the distribution of the costs.

Art. 712*i*

2. Liability for contributions
a. Real security by operation of law

¹ The community of the co-owners has a right to claim the contributions due for the last three years of ownership of the co-owner concerned and they have a right to be given real security as regards his share.

² The entry of the real security in the land register can be requested by the manager or, where a manager has not been appointed, by any one of the storey owners who is authorized by a decision made by the majority of the owners of storeys or by the judge and by the creditor on whose behalf the contributions due are levied.

³ Further to this the provisions made for statutory mortgages to which workmen and contractors are entitled apply analogously.

Art. 712k

The community of co-owners has a right of lien in the same way as a landlord for their claim of contributions for the last three years, for movable chattels which are in a co-owner's room and which are part of their equipment or are required for the use of the rooms.

b. Right of lien

Art. 712*l*

¹ The community of co-owners acquires the capital resulting from the community's managing activities in its own name, which implicitly includes the claim for contributions and the available financial means resulting from these, as well as the fund for renovations.

² The community of storey owners can bring action and enforce payment in its own name and at the place where the property is situated an action can be brought against it or payment can be enforced.

III. Competence to act

Art. 712*m*

¹ Apart from the rights mentioned in other articles the assembly of storey owners has, in particular, the following rights:

1. to decide in all matters of management which are not in the competence of the manager;

2. to appoint a person as manager and to superintend his activities;

3. to choose a board of representatives or appoint a delegate who can be entrusted with matters of administration, in particular the task of giving advice to the manager, to superintend his managing activities and to report to the assembly of storey owners on

D. Organization
I. Assembly of the storey owners
1. Competence and legal position

his managing activities and to put resolutions to the vote;

4. to approve the annual budget, the accounts and the distribution of costs among the storey owners;

5. to decide upon creating a fund for maintenance and renovations;

6. to insure the building against fire and other dangers and to take out the usual liability insurances, further to this to oblige a storey owner who outfits his rooms with additional structural alterations to pay an additional share of the premium, unless he has taken out an additional insurance on his own account.

²Where there are no provisions to the contrary by law, the provisions made for the organs of societies and opposition to resolutions passed by societies apply to the assembly of all storey owners and the board of representatives.

Art. 712*n*

2. To call and conduct meetings

¹The assembly of storey owners is convened and chaired by the manager if no other procedure has been laid down.

²The decisions are to be put on record and the minutes are to be kept in custody by the manager or the storey owner who chairs the meeting.

Art. 712*o*

3. Execution of vote

¹Several persons who own a storey in united ownership have only one vote, which is cast by their representative.

²Further the owner and the persons who have a right to enjoy and use a storey must make an agreement regarding the execution of their right to vote; where this is not the case the person who is given the right to enjoy and use the storey has the right of vote for all administrative concerns, with the exception of structural measures which are merely useful or

serve the embellishment of or the comfort offered by the building.

Art. 712*p*

¹ The assembly of storey owners constitutes a quorum if half of all storey owners who, at the same time, represent half of the shares of the property are present or represented; in no case may there be fewer than two of the owners of storeys.

² In the case of insufficient numbers at an assembly a second assembly has to be convened which may not be held earlier than ten days after the first.

³ The second meeting constitutes a quorum if one third, but in no case less than two, of all storey owners are present or represented.

4. Quorum

Art. 712*q*

¹ Where the assembly of storey owners cannot agree upon appointing a manager, each individual storey owner is entitled to demand the appointment of a manager by the judge.

² Any other person who has a justifiable interest in a manager being appointed by the judge has the same right, in particular the mortgagee or the insurer.

II. The manager
1. Appointment

Art. 712*r*

¹ The manager can be discharged at any time by a resolution passed by the assembly of storey owners with the proviso of a possible indemnification.

² Where the assembly of storey owners declines to discharge the manager, thereby ignoring important reasons, each storey owner has the right to demand the discharge by the judge within a delay of one month.

³ A manager who has been appointed by the judge cannot be discharged before the time for which he has been appointed without the judge's permission.

2. Discharge

Art. 712s

3. Duties
a. Execution of the regulations and resolutions concerning the administration and the use

¹ The manager executes all administrative acts concerning the common administration in compliance with the provisions made by the law and the regulations and the resolutions of the assembly of the storey owners and he, by his own initiative, takes any urgently required measures to avoid or remove damages.

² He attributes the common costs and charges to the individual storey owners, bills them, collects their contributions and is in charge of administering and using the available financial means in compliance with the provisions made for the use of such money.

³ He takes care that the execution of the special rights and the enjoyment and usage of those parts of the site and building which are for the common enjoyment and usage of all storey owners, and the enjoyment and usage of the commonly used equipment and installations complies with the provisions made by the law, the written regulations for the management and the usage and the accepted house regulations.

Art. 712t

b. Representation of opposite third party

¹ The manager represents both the community of storey owners and the individual storey owners opposite any third party in all matters concerning the common administration within the scope of his legal duties.

² Where the manager is required to conduct a civil law suit, be it either to institute it or to defend a law suit instituted by an opposite party, he needs for other than summary proceedings the preceding authorization of the assembly of the storey owners, with the proviso that in urgent cases the authorization can be received after the beginning of legal proceedings.

³ Declarations, requests, judgements and legal orders which are addressed to all storey owners can be delivered with legal effect to the manager at his domicile or at the location of the property.

Title XX: Ownership of Movable Property

Art. 713

Movable property comprises corporeal chattels that by their nature are movable, as well as those forces of nature in which legal rights can be acquired and which are not held to be accessory to immovable property.

A. Subject-matter

Art. 714

¹ Delivery of possession is necessary for the transfer of ownership in movable property.

² Where a person is put in possession of a movable as owner and himself takes it *bona fide,* he is held to acquire the ownership in it as soon as his rights are protected by the Law of Possession, even if the transferor had no right to transfer the ownership of it.

B. Modes of acquisition
I. Transfer
1. Delivery of possession

Art. 715

¹ A pact by which a transferor reserves the property in the movable transferred is operative only when it has been entered in the public register of the transferee's domicile, which is kept for this purpose by the bankruptcy office.

² In sales of cattle pacts to reserve ownership are prohibited.

2. Pact to reserve ownership
a. In general

Art. 716

Where a movable has been sold with a reserve of ownership and under the instalment system, the vendor cannot demand the re-delivery of the thing sold, unless he returns to the purchaser the amounts already received less a reasonable sum for the hire and use of the thing.

b. Payment by instalments

Art. 717

3. Transfer of ownership without possession

[1] Where on the transfer of ownership of a movable the parties agree that it shall remain in the possession of the transferor, such transfer is inoperative as against third parties, where the agreement was made with the object of prejudicing them or of evading the Law of Pledge.

[2] The judge decides the question in his discretion.

Art. 718

II. Occupation
1. Things that have no owner

Any person, who takes possession of a chattel that has no owner with the intention of becoming owner of it, acquires the ownership in it.

Art. 719

2. Stray animals

[1] Wild animals that have been captured cease to have an owner as soon as they recover their liberty, if their owner does not seek to recapture them by immediate and uninterrupted pursuit.

[2] Domesticated animals are held to have no owner when they revert to their natural state and cease to return to their owner.

[3] Swarms of bees do not cease to have an owner merely because they settle on another person's land.

Art. 720

III. Lost property found
1. Public advertisement and inquiries

[1] Any person who has found lost property is bound to inform the owner and, if he does not know him, to notify the police or himself arrange to advertise the find and make due inquiries.

[2] He is required to notify the police if the value of the thing evidently exceeds ten francs.

[3] Where a person finds lost property in an inhabited house or in a building used or frequented by the public, he must deliver it up to the master of the house, to the tenant, or to one of the staff in charge of the building.

Art. 721

¹ The property found must be kept with reasonable care.   2. Custody and sale by auction

² It can be sold by public auction with the consent of the competent authority and after public advertisement, where its upkeep is costly, or it is perishable, or it has been retained by the police or in a public depository for more than one year.

³ The purchase-money takes the place of the property found.¹

Art. 722

¹ Where the finder carries out the requirements of the law, he acquires the ownership in the property found after five years from his notification of the police or his public advertisement, provided the former owner cannot be discovered within that time.   3. Acquisition of ownership and restitution

² Where it is restored to its owner, the finder is entitled to all his expenses connected with it and to a suitable reward.

³ Where the property was found in an inhabited house or in a building used or frequented by the public, the finder is held to be the master of the house or the tenant or the staff in charge, but none of these can claim a reward.

Art. 723

¹ Where a thing of value is discovered under such circumstances that it is reasonable to suppose that it was buried or hidden a long time ago and has ceased to have an owner, it is held to be treasure-trove.   4. Treasure-trove

² Subject to the provisions in regard to objects of scientific value, treasure-trove belongs to the owner of the immovable or movable property in which it was discovered.

---

¹ *i.e.* as from the date of its receipt by the finder.

³ The finder can claim a suitable reward which must not, however, exceed half the value of the treasure-trove itself.

Art. 724

5. Objects of scientific value

¹ Where natural curiosities or antiquities are found which have no owner and are of considerable scientific value, they become the property of the Canton in whose borders they were found.

² The owner of the land in which such objects are found is bound to permit all necessary excavations, but must receive compensation for all damage caused thereby.

³ The finder of the object and, if it is treasure-trove, the owner thereof also have the right to a suitable reward which, however, must not exceed the value of the object found.

Art. 725

IV. Drifts and strays

¹ Where chattels have drifted by the action of water, wind, avalanches, or other forces of nature, or by accident, or animals have strayed to a person's land, that person is in the same legal position as if he had found lost property.

² Where a swarm of bees settles in an occupied hive belonging to another person, it becomes the property of the owner of the hive, and no compensation can be claimed for the loss of it.

Art. 726

V. Manufactured articles

¹ Where a person has used another's material to make or transform some article, the new product becomes the property of the craftsman if the work done is more valuable than the material and that of the owner of the material in the contrary case.

² If the craftsman has not acted in good faith, the court can, even if the work is more valuable than

the material, assign the new product to the owner of the material.

³ This provision, however, does not take away the right to bring an action for damages for loss suffered or for the return of profits made.

Art. 727

¹ Where materials belonging to different owners have been intermixed or joined together in such a way that they cannot be separated without material damage or excessive labour and expense, the parties interested in them become co-owners of the new product, their shares in it being proportionate to the value of the different materials at the time of mixing. VI. Fusion

² Where things are mixed or joined together in such a way that one of them can be held accessory to the other, the whole belongs to the owner of the principal thing.

³ This provision does not, however, take away the right to bring an action for damages for loss suffered or for the return of profits made.

Art. 728

¹ Where a person has been continuously in *bona fide* and peaceable possession of another's chattel for five years as owner, he is held to have acquired the ownership of it by prescription. VII. Prescription

² The running of the years is not interrupted by involuntary loss of possession, provided possession is recovered within one year or an action to recover it has been brought within one year.

³ The rules laid down in regard to the limitation of actions apply here by analogy for the purpose of calculating the period of prescription and of determining in what cases the running of years is stopped or suspended.

Art. 729

C. Loss of ownership

The ownership of a chattel is not destroyed by loss of possession, provided the owner has not abandoned his right to it or the chattel has not been acquired by a third person.

Section II: Limited Rights *in rem*

Title XXI: Servitudes and Rent-Charges

Chapter I: Praedial Servitudes

Art. 730

A. Their nature

¹ A praedial servitude is a burden imposed on immovable property for the benefit of another immovable, which obliges the owner of the servient property to permit certain acts of interference on the part of the owner of the dominant property, or himself to abstain for the benefit of the dominant owner from exercising certain rights of ownership over his own property.

² An obligation to do certain positive acts can be attached to land only as a burden annexed to a servitude.¹

Art. 731

B. Creation and extinction
I. Creation
1. Registration

¹ Entry in the land register is required for the constitution of a servitude.

² In the absence of a contrary provision, the acquisition and registration of a servitude are governed by the rules relating to the ownership of land.

³ Servitudes can be acquired by prescription only over such land as can be acquired by adverse possession.

---

¹ *e.g.* as a rent-charge (see art. 788 below). In this chapter the term "servitude" is confined to "praedial servitude".

Art. 732

An agreement to create a servitude is valid only where it is made in writing.

2. Agreement

Art. 733

The owner of two properties has the right to charge one of them with a servitude for the benefit of the other.

3. Servitude over one's own property

Art. 734

Every servitude is extinguished by the erasure of its entry in the register or by the total destruction of the servient or dominant property.

II. Extinction
1. In general

Art. 735

[1] Where two properties are merged under one owner, the latter can demand the erasure of the servitude.

[2] Until such erasure the servitude continues to exist as a right *in rem.*

2. Merger

Art. 736

[1] Where a servitude has ceased to benefit the dominant property, the servient owner can demand its erasure.

[2] Where the servitude is still of some benefit to the dominant property, but this benefit is of little importance in comparison with the burden imposed on the servient owner, the latter can, by payment of due compensation, obtain a total or partial relief from it.

3. By order of the court

Art. 737

[1] The dominant owner is entitled to do all that is necessary to maintain and make use of the servitude.

[2] He is bound, however, in the exercise of his rights, to do as little damage as possible to the property charged.

C. Effect
I. Rights and duties
1. In general

³ The servient owner must not in any way prevent the dominant owner from exercising his rights or place obstacles in his way.

Art. 738

2\. By virtue of registration

¹ The entry in the register is conclusive on the rights and duties of the parties under the servitude, in so far as these are clearly defined in the entry.

² Subject to this, the rights and duties of the parties under the servitude can be determined either by its mode of creation or by the way in which it has been exercised for some length of time without opposition and in good faith.

Art. 739

3\. Changed requirements

Changes in the requirements of the dominant owner do not entitle him to impose an additional burden on the servient owner.

Art. 740

4\. Cantonal Law and local custom

Rights of way, such as the use of foot-paths or cart-tracks either across open fields or in the dead season or for carting wood, or metalled roads, as well as rights of pasture, of taking wood, of watering cattle or irrigation and other similar rights are, in the absence of a special agreement to the contrary in any given case, defined by Cantonal Law or local custom.

Art. 741

II. Cost of maintenance

¹ Where work has to be done to enable the dominant owner to exercise his rights, he must bear the expense of it.

² Where the work is equally for the benefit of the servient owner, he must bear his share of the expenses in proportion to the benefit which he is receiving.

Art. 742

¹ Where the servitude affects one part only of the servient property, the servient owner can, by showing that the change would be for his benefit and by undertaking to bear the cost of it, require that the servitude be moved so that it may affect a different part of his property, provided this would not be prejudicial to the dominant owner.

² He has this right, even if the particular place affected by the servitude is entered in the register.

³ In regard to the moving of conduits the rules of the *jus vicinorum* are applicable.

III. Changes in servitude
1. Transferring place of its exercise

Art. 743

¹ Where the dominant property is partitioned, the servitude continues, as a general rule, for the benefit of all the parts.

² Where, however, the benefit of the servitude is actually confined to one part of the property, the servient owner can require that it shall be erased in regard to the other parts.

³ The registrar of the land register must notify the dominant owner of this request, and effect the erasure if the latter does not lodge an objection within one month.

2. Partition
a. Of dominant property

Art. 744

¹ Where the servient property is partitioned, the servitude continues, as a general rule, as a burden on all the parts.

² Where, however, the servitude is not, and, from the nature of the case, could not be, exercised over certain parts of the property, the owners of these parts can each demand to be relieved of it.

³ The registrar of the land register must notify the dominant owner of this demand, and effect the erasure if the latter does not lodge an objection within one month.

b. Of servient property

Chapter II: Usufruct and Other Servitudes

Art. 745

A. Usufruct
I. Res fructuaria

¹ A usufruct can be created over a movable, an immovable, a single right or a whole estate.

² In the absence of a contrary provision it confers on the usufructuary the right to the full use and enjoyment of the *res fructuaria*.

Art. 746

II. How it arises
1. In general

¹ A usufruct of movables and of rights is created by their transfer to the usufructuary, that of immovables by registration in the land register.

² In the absence of a contrary provision the acquisition and registration of a usufruct are governed by the rules relating to ownership.

Art. 747[1]

2. Statutory usufruct

annulled

Art. 748

III. Extinction
1. Grounds

¹ A usufruct is extinguished by the total destruction of the *res fructuaria* and, in addition in the case of an immovable, by the erasure of the entry in the register if registration was necessary for its creation.[2]

² Other grounds of extinction, such as lapse of the time for which it was created or the renunciation or death of the usufructuary, only give the owner of the *res fructuaria,* where this is an immovable, the right to demand the erasure of the entry in the register.

³ A usufruct arising by operation of law ceases to exist with the ground which gave rise to it.

---

[1] Annulled by cipher I 2 of the Federal Statute of 5th October 1984, in force since 1st January 1988 (BBl 1979 II 1191).
[2] *i.e.* in all cases of usufruct over land other than a statutory usufruct.

Art. 749

¹ A usufruct is extinguished by the death of the usufructuary and, if the usufructuary is a corporate body, by the dissolution of the corporation.

² Where the usufructuary is a corporate body, however, the usufruct cannot continue longer than for a period of one hundred years.

2. Duration

Art. 750

¹ Where the *res fructuaria* is destroyed, its owner is not bound to restore it.

² But if he does, the usufruct revives with it.

³ Where something is substituted for the thing that is destroyed, such as in the case of its expropriation or insurance, the usufruct continues in the substituted thing.

3. Restoration of *res fructuaria* when destroyed

Art. 751

At the determination of the usufruct, the person in possession of the *res fructuaria* must return it to the owner.

4. Return of *res fructuaria*
a. Obligation

Art. 752

¹ The usufructuary is liable for the destruction or depreciation in value of the *res fructuaria*, unless he can prove that the damage was not caused by his own fault.

² He must replace anything which he has wrongfully consumed.

³ He is not bound to give any compensation for depreciation in value caused by fair usage.

b. Liabilities

Art. 753

¹ Where the usufructuary has, without being under an obligation to do so, laid out money on the *res fructuaria* or made improvements in it, he can,

c. Outlays

on the return of the thing, claim compensation for them in the same way as an uncommissioned agent.

² Where he has made improvements for which the owner refuses to compensate him, he has the right to remove them, but must restore the thing to its original condition.

Art. 754

5. Limitation of actions for compensation

The owner of the *res fructuaria* must bring his action for compensation for alterations or depreciation of the thing within one year from its return, and the time limit is the same for the usufructuary to claim compensation for outlays or to remove improvements he has made.

Art. 755

IV. Effect
1. Rights of usufructuary
a. In general

¹ The usufructuary has the right to the possession, use and enjoyment of the *res fructuaria*.

² He has also the management of it.

³ In the exercise of his rights, he must use the degree of care looked for in a good manager.

Art. 756

b. Natural fruits

¹ Natural fruits, which have matured during the continuance of the usufruct, accrue to the usufructuary.

² Where one party has cultivated the land and the other party gets the matured fruits, the former can claim compensation for what he has expended on it, but the amount is not to exceed the value of the fruits when mature.

³ Integral parts of the *res fructuaria* which are neither fruits nor produce continue to be the property of the owner of the *res*.

Art. 757

Interest on capital forming part of the *res fructuaria* and other periodical returns derived from it are vested in the usufructuary as from the day on which his right commences until the day on which it determines, even where they are not payable until after that day.

c. Interest

Art. 758

¹ A usufruct is assignable to a third person, provided it is not of an essentially personal character.

² The assignment establishes privity between the owner and the assignee.

d. When assignable

Art. 759

The owner can prevent any unlawful or unreasonable use of the *res fructuaria*.

2. Rights of owner
a. Control

Art. 760

¹ Where the owner can prove that his rights are imperilled, he can demand security of the usufructuary.

² He can, even without such proof and before the transfer of the *res fructuaria,* demand security, where the usufruct is in perishable things or in bills or other securities.

³ Where the usufruct is in securities, it is sufficient if the usufructuary gives up possession of the documents of title and puts them on deposit.¹

b. Right to security

Art. 761

¹ Security cannot be demanded from a donor who has reserved to himself the usufruct of the thing given.

² In the case of usufructs arising by operation of law, the obligation to furnish security is subject to special rules.

c. Security in case of gifts and statutory usufructs

---

¹ *i.e.* on deposit with a third person from whom he cannot take them away during the continuance of the usufructuary's rights.

Art. 762

d. Effect of failure to give security

Where a usufructuary does not furnish the security required within a reasonable time fixed for the purpose, or where in spite of the owner's opposition he continues to make an improper use of the *res fructuaria,* the court shall for the time being take the thing out of his possession and place it in charge of a curator.

Art. 763

3. Inventory

The owner and the usufructuary have the right at any time to require a public inventory to be made of the *res fructuaria* at their joint cost.

Art. 764

4. Duties of usufructuary
a. Preservation of *res fructuaria*

[1] The usufructuary is bound to maintain the substance of the *res fructuaria* intact and on his own account to carry out ordinary repairs and restorations incident to its upkeep.

[2] If more important work or measures are necessary for the preservation of the thing, the usufructuary is bound to notify the owner and to permit them to be carried out.

[3] Where the owner fails to take these necessary measures, the usufructuary can carry out the work himself at the owner's cost.

Art. 765

b. Cost of maintenance, taxes and other charges

[1] In regard to the ordinary expenses of maintenance and management of the *res fructuaria,* interest payable on debts charged thereon, as well as rents and taxes, the usufructuary must bear his proper share of them according to the term of his usufruct.

[2] If the rents or taxes are paid by the owner, the usufructuary must indemnify him to a like extent.

[3] All other charges are borne by the owner; he may, however, in order to pay them, realize some

Servitudes and Rent-Charges

part of the *res fructuaria,* if the usufructuary does not gratuitously advance him the necessary funds at his request.

Art. 766

Where the usufruct is of an estate and there are debts charged on it, the usufructuary must as a general rule pay the interest on them; he can, however, under special circumstances be relieved of this duty by requiring that the debts be paid out of the estate and his rights reduced to a usufruct in the remainder of the property.

c. Interest on debts on estate

Art. 767

¹ The usufructuary must insure the *res fructuaria* against fire and other risks in the interests of the owner, in so far as such insurance is by local usage held to be part of the duties of a good manager.

² He must pay the premiums during the continuance of the usufruct, whether the *res* was already insured when he took it or not.

d. Insurance

Art. 768

¹ The usufructuary of land must take care that it is not farmed beyond the limits of good husbandry.

² The fruits which are gathered beyond these limits belong to the owner.

V. Special cases
1. Immovables
a. Fruits

Art. 769

¹ The usufructuary of land must not make any material changes in its industrial character, which would seriously prejudice the owner.

² The *res fructuaria* itself must not be transformed or materially changed.

³ He cannot open new quarries or clay- or turf-pits nor start any other similar works except after previous notice to the owner and except in so far as

b. Industrial character of the *res fructuaria*

the industrial character of the land would not be materially changed thereby.

Art. 770

c. Forests

¹ The usufructuary of a forest can use it within the limits of good forestry.

² The owner as well as the usufructuary can require that a scheme of forestry be adopted which does not prejudice his rights.

³ Where as the result of storms, snowfalls, fire, plagues of insects or any other cause, an excessive amount of wood is gathered in, the cutting must be reduced so that the damage done is gradually repaired, or else a new scheme drawn up to meet the new conditions; the money realised from the excessive yield must be invested and used to supplement smaller yields.

Art. 771

d. Mines

Where the usufruct consists in winning some substance from the land which forms an integral part of the soil such as in the case of the usufruct of a mine, similar rules apply as in the case of the usufruct of a forest.

Art. 772

2. Perishable and valued things

¹ Where the usufruct is in perishable things, the usufructuary in the absence of a contrary provision acquires the ownership in the things, but is liable to restore the value they possessed at the commencement of the usufruct.

² Where any other movables are delivered to the usufructuary under a valuation, he can in the absence of a contrary provision dispose of them freely, but if he does, he thereby becomes liable to restore their value.

³ In the case of usufructs of agricultural stock or produce, flocks or herds or similar things, the

usufructuary can restore to the owner things of the same kind and quality.

Art. 773

¹ Where the usufruct is in a right or other incorporeal property, the usufructuary can take the dividends or other income derived from it.

² The creditor and the usufructuary must both join for the purpose of giving a notice to the debtor or for disposing of the securities, and notices by the debtor must be made to both.

³ Where the existence of the rights is imperilled, the creditor and the usufructuary can each require the other to join in adopting measures which would be taken by a good manager.

3. Usufruct in a right
a. Purport

Art. 774

¹ Where the debtor has not been authorized to repay the debt forming the object of the usufruct to the creditor or the usufructuary singly, he must either make the payment to them jointly or place the money on deposit.

² The usufructuary thereby acquires the use and the enjoyment of the capital sum repaid or other obligation fulfilled by the debtor which forms the object of the usufruct.

³ The creditor and the usufructuary can each require that the capital be put out in a safe and productive investment.

b. Repayment and re-investment

Art. 775

¹ The usufructuary can, within three months from the commencement of the usufruct, require that the debt and securities forming the object of the usufruct should be assigned to him.

² If the assignment takes place, the usufructuary becomes liable to the creditor for the value of the debt and securities as on the day of assignment, and

c. Right to assignment of debt

must give security up to that amount unless the creditor dispenses with it.

³ If the creditor does not dispense with this security, the assignment does not take effect until the security has been given.

Art. 776

B. Right of residence
I. In general

¹ The right of residence is the right to occupy a house or part of a house.

² It is inalienable and is not transmissible to the heirs.

³ With certain exceptions contained in the following provisions, the rules governing usufruct are applicable.

Art. 777

II. Extent of right

¹ The right is in general regulated by the personal requirements of the person entitled to it.

² Where it is not expressly limited to his own person, it entitles him to allow the members of his family and his household to live in the house with him.

³ Where the right is limited to a part only of a house, he can enjoy all conveniences set up for the common use of those living in the house.

Art. 778

III. Duties of person entitled

¹ The person entitled to the exclusive use of a house or apartment is liable for the ordinary upkeep of the premises.

² If he has only a right to inhabit the premises jointly with the owner, the cost of their upkeep is borne by the owner.

Art. 779

C. Right of building
I. Object and entry in the land register[1]

¹ The owner of a piece of land can create a servitude in favour of another by giving him the right to construct or retain a building or other construction on or under the land.

² In the absence of a contrary agreement, this right is alienable and transmissible to the heirs.

³ If this purports to be a permanent and independent right, it can be entered as an immovable in the land register.

Art. 779a[2]

II. The deed of foundation

The deed of foundation of an independent and permanent right of building requires for its validity public authentication.

Art. 779b[2]

III. Effect, rights and duties

The regulations put down in the deed of foundation concerning effect, rights and duties connected with the right of building, in particular concerning the position, shape, dimensions and purpose of the buildings, as well as the use of the pieces of land which, though not built up, are made use of in the execution of the right of building are binding for every person acquiring the right of building and the encumbered site.

Art. 779c[2]

IV. Consequences of the extinction of the right
1. Reversion

Where the right of building is extinguished, the existing edifices lapse to the owner of the land by becoming an integral part of his immovable.

---

[1] Wording of the marginal note according to cipher I of the Federal Statute of 19th March 1965, in force since 1st July 1965 (AS 1965 445 450; BBl 1963 I 969).
[2] Inserted by cipher I of the Federal Statute of 19th March 1965, in force since 1st July 1965 (AS 1965 445 450; BBl 1963 I 969).

Art. 779d^1

2. Indemnification

^{1} The owner of the immovable must pay the former holder of the right of building an adequate sum of indemnification for the reverting edifices; this sum of indemnification, however, is not to be paid to the former holder of the right of building before the creditors to whom the right of building was mortgaged are satisfied and agree to the payment of the indemnification.

^{2} Where the indemnification is neither paid nor secured, the former holder of the right of building or a creditor to whom the right of building was mortgaged, can demand that the right of building which is to be extinguished is replaced by an entry of the real security in the same rank in the land register as the security for the claim for indemnification.

^{3} The entry in the land register must be made within three months after the extinction of the right of building.

Art. 779e^1

3. Arrangements

Arrangements can be made for the amount of the indemnification and the procedure to fix it as well as for the annulment of the duty to indemnify and the restoration of the original state of the immovable; such arrangements have to be made in the form which is prescribed for the establishment of the right of building and must be entered in the land register.

Art. 779f^1

V. Premature reversion
1. Requirements

If the holder of the right of building grossly exceeds his right *in rem* or violates the duties laid down in the deed of foundation, the owner of the immovable can adduce the premature reversion of the right of building by demanding the conveyance

---

[1] Inserted by cipher I of the Federal Statute of 19th March 1965, in force since 1st July 1965 (AS **1965** 445 450; BBl **1963 I** 969).

of the right of building with all its rights and duties to himself.

Art. 779g[1]

¹ The right of reversion can only be executed where an adequate sum of indemnification is paid for the edifices to be reverted; culpable behaviour of the holder of the right of building can be taken into account as a reason for a lower rating of the amount of indemnification.

² The conveyance of the right of building to the owner of the immovable does not take place before the indemnification is either paid or secured.

2. Execution of right of reversion

Art. 779h[1]

Any right the owner of the immovable has reserved to himself with regard to the premature annulment or the re-transfer of the right of building owing to the violation of duties by the holder of the right of building is subject to the provisions made for the execution of the right of reversion.

3. Other cases of application

Art. 779i[1]

¹ To secure the right of building-charges the owner of the immovable is entitled to have the holder of the right of building for the time being create a mortgage in his favour encumbering the right of building which is entered in the land register to an amount not exceeding the total of three annual right of building-charges.

² Where the charges for the right of building are not fixed as annual payments, the claim for creating a mortgage by operation of the law is to the amount which would be payable for three years with equal distribution.

VI. Security for the right of building-charges[2]
1. Claim to create a mort- mortgage

---

[1] Inserted by cipher I of the Federal Statute of 19th March 1965, in force since 1st July 1965 (AS **1965** 445 450; BBl **1963** I 969).
[2] The term "right of building-charge" has been chosen to translate German "Baurechtszins", French *"la rente du droit de superficie"*.

Art. 779k^1

2. Registration

¹ The right of mortgage can be entered in the land register at any time as long as the right of building is in force and is excepted from extinction in the case of legal procedure for the execution of debt.

² Further to this the provisions made for statutory mortgages to which workmen and contractors are entitled apply accordingly.

Art. 779l^1

VII. Maximal duration

¹ As an independent right the right of building cannot exceed 100 years.

² It can, at any time, be extended for another period not exceeding 100 years in the form which is prescribed for establishing the right; however, an obligation to this effect entered into in advance is not binding.

Art. 780

D. Right to a spring in another's land

¹ Where a person has a right to a spring which has its source in another person's land, the owner of that land is obliged to permit him to appropriate it to his own use and to confine it in a conduit.

² In the absence of a contrary agreement, the right is alienable and transmissible to the heirs.

³ If it purports to be a permanent and independent right, it can be entered as an immovable in the land register.

Art. 781

E. Other servitudes

¹ The owner of land can create other servitudes over his land in favour of any individual person or group of persons, wherever the land is capable of being used for some definite purpose, such as for butts or for a right of way.

---

[1] Inserted by cipher I of the Federal Statute of 19th March 1965, in force since 1st July 1965 (AS 1965 445 450; BBl 1963 I 969).

² In the absence of a contrary agreement, these rights are inalienable and their extent is determined by the ordinary requirements of the person who has acquired the right.

³ In other respects the rules on praedial servitudes are applicable.

Chapter III: Rent-Charges[1]

Art. 782

¹ A rent-charge lays the present owner of land under an obligation in favour of another person for the fulfilment of which the land alone is security.   A. Purport

² The charge may be in favour of the owner for the time being of another piece of land.

³ With the exception of negotiable land charges and rent-charges created under Public Law, the nature and extent of the obligation must correspond to the industrial character of the land charged or the economic requirements of the dominant land.

Art. 783

¹ Registration in the land register is required for the valid creation of a rent-charge.   B. Creation and extinction
I. Creation

² The entry must specify the capital value of the charge in terms of Swiss currency; where the charge consists of periodical payments, its capital value is, in the absence of a contrary agreement, to be taken at twenty times the annual payment.   1. Mode of acquisition and registration

---

[1] The term "rent-charge" has been chosen to translate **Grundlast**, *charge foncière*, so as to distinguish the conception from a charge by way of security for a loan which is treated in the next title. A "rent-charge" here does not, however, necessarily imply an obligation to make regularly recurring payments, though this is the more usual.

[3] In the absence of a contrary provision the acquisition and registration of charges are governed by the rules on the ownership of land.

Art. 784

2. Rent-charges under Public Law

[1] Rent-charges created under Public Law do not, unless otherwise provided, require to be registered.

[2] Where the law confers on a creditor the right only to demand the creation of a rent-charge, such charge does not become operative until it is registered in the land register.

Art. 785

3. Charges by way of security

Where a charge is created by way of security for the payment of a debt, it is governed by the rules on negotiable land charges.

Art. 786

II. Extinction
1. In general

[1] A rent-charge is extinguished by the erasure of the entry in the register or by the total destruction of the immovable charged.

[2] Renunciation, redemption or other grounds of extinction give the owner of the land charged the right to demand the consent of the creditor[1] to the erasure of the entry in the register.

Art. 787

2. Redemption
a. Right of creditor to demand

The creditor can demand the redemption of the rent-charge, where the parties have specially agreed that he shall have this right and further:

1. where the land charged has been broken up and the rights of the creditor are thereby materially prejudiced;

---

[1] As in the French version "creditor" is used to denote the person who benefits by the rent-charge. As the charge need not necessarily be attached for the benefit of some piece of land but created for the benefit of some person, the term "dominant owner" cannot well be used in this connection.

2. where the owner of the land has reduced its value without offering security in exchange;

3. where the debtor is three years in arrears with his payments or other dues.

Art. 788

b. Right of debtor to redeem

¹ The debtor can insist on redeeming, where the parties have specially agreed that he shall have this right and further:

1. where the pact creating the rent-charge has been broken by the creditor;

2. after the expiration of thirty years from its creation, even where it was constituted for a longer term or stated to be irredeemable.

² Where the debtor redeems after the expiration of thirty years, he must in every case give one year's previous notice of his intention to redeem.

³ A rent-charge which is annexed to a perpetual servitude is not redeemable.

Art. 789

c. Redemption price

The price at which a charge is redeemable is the sum set down as its capital value in the land register, subject, however, to proof that the charge is in reality of less value.

Art. 790

3. Limitation of actions

¹ A rent-charge is not subject to the limitation of actions.

² The right of enforcing any single due under the charge is subject to the limitation of actions as soon as the debt becomes the personal debt of the servient owner.

Art. 791

C. Effect
I. Rights of creditor

¹ A rent-charge does not give any right of action to the creditor against the debtor personally, but merely a right to be paid out of the land charged.

² Each single due under the charge becomes a personal debt three years after its accrual and is then no longer secured on the land charged.

Art. 792

II. Nature of debt

¹ Where the land charged changes owners, the new owner *ipso facto* takes over with the land the liabilities under the charge.

² Where the land charged is parcelled out, the same consequences follow as in the case of a negotiable land charge.

Title XXII: Mortgages and Other Securities on Land

Chapter I: General Provisions

Art. 793

A. Conditions
I. Forms of real security

¹ Real security on land can take the form of a mortgage, a mortgage certificate, or a negotiable land charge.

² All other forms are prohibited.

Art. 794

II. Nature of debt secured
1. Principal

¹ Real security can only be given to secure a liquidated debt, and the amount must be stated in Swiss currency.

² If the claim to be secured is not for a sum certain, the parties must fix a sum to represent the maximum amount for which the land in question shall be charged.

Art. 795

2. Interest

¹ The rate of interest can be fixed at the will of the parties provided it does not exceed the rate allowed by law.

² The Cantons can determine the maximum rate of interest chargeable on a debt secured on land.

Art. 796

¹ A mortgage or other security can be created only on land which is entered in the land register.

² The Cantons can lay down special rules in regard to mortgages of public land, land in common cultivation, or pasture land belonging to corporations, as well as to charges on usufructs existing over these lands; or these mortgages can be prohibited altogether.¹

III. The property
1. What can be mortgaged

Art. 797

¹ The property charged must be accurately described at the date of the creation of the mortgage or other security.

² Where property has been partitioned but the partition has not been entered in the land register, no individual parts of it can be charged.

2. Description
a. One property only

Art. 798

¹ Several properties can be given in security for the same debt, where they belong to the same owner or to debtors who are jointly and severally liable.

² In all other cases where several properties are given as security for the same debt, each property must be charged with a specified part of the debt.

³ In the absence of a contrary agreement, the liability is apportioned according to the value of the different properties charged.

b. In the case of several properties

Art. 799

¹ Subject to special exceptions provided by law, mortgages or other securities become operative by entry in the land register.

B. Creation and extinction
I. Creation
1. Registration

---

¹ Where the term "mortgage" is used by itself in this chapter, it includes the three forms of security on land.

² An agreement to create a mortgage is valid only when made by a duly authenticated instrument.

Art. 800

2. Where the property is in co-ownership

¹ Where several persons are united owners of certain property, each can charge his own share in it.

² Where they are owners in common, it can only be mortgaged as a whole and in the name of all.

Art. 801

II. Extinction

¹ A mortgage or other security is extinguished by the erasure of the entry in the register or by the total destruction of the immovable charged.

² Extinction in the case of the expropriation of the land in the public interest is governed by the Federal or Cantonal Law on expropriation.

Art. 802

III. Where plots of land grouped together
1. Transfer of security

¹ Where plots of land have been redistributed with the concurrence or under the direction of the public authorities, the mortgages or other securities on the plots to be surrendered must be transferred with their order of priority to the plots substituted for them.

² Where one piece of land is substituted for several others which are charged as security for different debts or which are not all charged, the mortgages are transferred to charge the land substituted, and the rights of priority are retained as far as possible.

Art. 803

2. Notice by the debtor

By giving three months' previous notice the debtor can at the time of the grouping together of the plots redeem the mortgages or other securities then existing on them.

Art. 804

¹ Where a money indemnity is payable for the land charged,¹ it is divided among the creditors in the order of their priorities or, if they are of equal rank, in the order of the value of the debts secured.

² The money cannot be paid to the debtor without the consent of the creditors, where it amounts to more than one twentieth part of the debt secured, or where the land substituted does not constitute a sufficient security.

3. Indemnities

Art. 805

¹ The mortgage or other security is a burden on the property including its integral parts and all its accessories.

² Where in the mortgage certain things are expressly mentioned as accessories and entered as such in the land register, such as machines and hotel furniture, they are held to be accessories, unless it can be shown that they could not legally be included under that heading.

³ Rights of third parties over such accessories are not affected.

C. Effect
I. Rights of creditor

Art. 806

¹ Where there is a lease of the property mortgaged, the security includes the rent which has accrued due under the lease as from the date when the creditor instituted proceedings to realize his security or the debtor has been declared bankrupt up to the time when the security is actually realized.

² This right to the rent cannot be enforced as against the lessees or tenants, unless and until they have had notice of these proceedings or the declaration of the debtor's bankruptcy has been published.

II. Rents

---

¹ *i.e.* to equalize the exchange of the plots on redistribution.

³ Where the owner of the land has purported to deal with the rent that has not yet accrued, or where other creditors have taken it in execution, neither of these transactions are operative as against the secured creditor, if he instituted proceedings to realize his security before the time when the rent accrued.

Art. 807

III. No limitation of actions

There is no period of limitations for an action on a debt secured by a mortgage or other security entered in the register.

Art. 808

IV. Safeguards
1. In case of depreciation of property
a. Measures for its preservation

¹ Where the owner of the property charged reduces its value, the creditor can apply to the court for an injunction restraining him from continuing the damage.

² He can further be authorized by the court to take all necessary measures, and can take them of his own accord where delay would be dangerous.

³ He has the right to lay the cost of these measures to the charge of the owner of the property, and this right is secured by that property and has priority over all the charges entered in the register.

Art. 809

b. Security, restoration, repayment

¹ Where there has been a reduction in the value of the property, the creditor can demand that the debtor should give further security for his debt or restore the property to its former condition.

² He can also demand further security where there is danger of a reduction in value.

³ Where the debtor does not satisfy his demand within the period fixed by the court, the creditor can require the debtor to repay a portion of the debt in order that the security may be sufficient to cover the debt.

Art. 810

¹ Where the property charged depreciates in value through no fault of the owner, the creditor has no right to further security or repayment except in so far as the owner can be re-imbursed for the depreciation.

² The creditor can, however, take measures for removing or warding off the causes of depreciation; the costs of these measures he can charge on the property, and this charge, without being registered, has priority over all charges entered in the register, but the owner is not personally liable for the costs.

2. Depreciation without owner's fault

Art. 811

Where a part of the property charged is alienated from the rest and its value does not amount to one twentieth of the debt secured, the creditor cannot oppose the release of that part from the mortgage, where a proportionate part of the debts is repaid or the rest of the property offers sufficient security for the whole debt.

3. Alienation of parts of property

Art. 812

¹ The owner of the property charged cannot validly deprive himself of the right to create further charges on it.

² Where property has been mortgaged and it is subsequently burdened with a servitude or rent-charge without the consent of the creditor, the mortgage has priority over the subsequent servitude or rent-charge, and the latter will be erased from the register, where its existence prejudices the rights of the creditor on the realization of his security.

³ The dominant owner, however, has on the realization of the prior security a preferential claim on the amount realized for the value of his servitude or rent-charge in priority to creditors subsequently registered.

V. Further charge

Art. 813

VI. Place of the security in register
1. Effect

¹ The security furnished by the mortgage is permanently assigned to the place in the register in which it is entered.¹

² Mortgages or other securities can be created in the second or any other place in the register, provided a fixed amount is expressly reserved for the preceding place or places.

Art. 814

2. Order of priority

¹ Where securities of different degrees of priority have been created over the same property and one of them is paid off, the creditor next in order of priority is not entitled to move up to the vacant place in the register.

² Another mortgage can be created in the place of the one that is paid off.

³ Agreements whereby creditors may move up to higher places that are vacant do not confer upon them rights *in rem*,² unless these agreements have been noted in the register.

Art. 815

3. Vacant places

Where a mortgage or other security occupies the second or a later place in the register and follows upon a vacant one, or the debtor has not made use of a prior security,³ or the prior claim does not

---

¹ Thus if A mortgages his land to B, they can agree that the mortgage shall occupy the first place in the column for charges in the register; B then holds the rank of first mortgagee. If A later charges his land in favour of C and this charge occupies the second place in the register, and if B's mortgage is repaid, C's charge cannot be moved to the first place occupied by the mortgage to B. He will always retain the second rank, for A can mortgage the land for the third time, to D, and give him the first place in the register. D then has priority over C, though he was later in point of time.
² *i.e.* as against creditors who are not parties to it.
³ *i.e.* a mortgage certificate or negotiable land charge note ready drawn in case he wanted to use it, and so that the security would, if used, have priority, because it occupies the prior place in the register.

amount to the sum entered in the register, the total amount obtained at the realization of the securities is assigned to the secured creditors in their order of priority without regard to the vacant places.

Art. 816

[1] Where the debtor fails to fulfil his obligations, the creditor has the right to pay himself out of the proceeds of the property charged.

[2] Any clause providing that the creditor shall become the owner of the property charged if the debt is not paid in full is null and void.

[3] Where several properties are charged as security for the same debt, proceedings for the realization of the security must be instituted on all at once, but only so much will actually be realized as is held to be necessary by the official in bankruptcy.[1]

VII. Realization of security
1. Method

Art. 817

[1] The amount realized on the sale of the property charged is paid to the creditors in their order of priority.

[2] Creditors in the same degree of priority have equal rights to the satisfaction of their claims.

2. Payment of creditors

Art. 818

[1] A mortgage or other security on land secures the creditor to the extent of:

1. the principal debt;
2. the cost of realizing the security and interest due for delay in payment;
3. the interest that has accrued due during the three years preceding the institution of proceedings in bankruptcy or for the realization of the security

3. Extent of security

---

[1] Realization of securities on land is carried out according to the provisions of the Execution and Bankruptcy Act.

and the interest current from the last day of payment.[1]

[2] The original rate of interest agreed upon cannot be increased to the prejudice of later creditors to more than five per cent.

Art. 819

4. Security for necessary outlays

Where the creditor has incurred necessary expenditure for the preservation of the property charged, especially where he has laid out the insurance premiums which were payable by the owner of the property, he can without any entry in the land register include such expenditure with the debt under the same security.

Art. 820

VIII. In case of improvements of soil
1. Priority

[1] Where agricultural land has increased in value through certain improvements in the soil which have been carried out with the concurrence of the public authorities, the owner can charge the land as security for his share of the cost and enter it in the land register, so that it has priority over all other charges on the land entered there.[2]

[2] Where the improvements have been carried out without a public subsidy, the owner cannot register a charge on the land for more than two-thirds of the cost which he has incurred.[3]

Art. 821

2. Extinction of debt and security

[1] Where the improvements in the soil have been carried out without a public subsidy, the debt must be paid off in yearly instalments of at least five per cent of the capital amount entered in the register.

---

[1] *i.e.* from the half-yearly or quarterly day before the proceedings are instituted.
[2] The improvements meant are those specified in art. 703.
[3] Because in this case he is not compelled to make the improvements.

² The security is extinguished both for the whole debt and each annual payment after the lapse of three years from the date when it became enforceable, and subsequent creditors move up according to their degree of priority.

Art. 822

¹ Insurance sums accrued due must not be paid over to the owner of the property charged except with the consent of all the creditors secured by it.

² But where the owner gives sufficient security, they must be paid over to him for the purpose of restoring the property charged.

³ Otherwise, however, the rules apply which are laid down by the Cantons in regard to fire insurance.

IX. Right to insurance sums

Art. 823

¹ Where the law requires the personal concurrence of a creditor and the case is urgent, and yet his name or residence is unknown, the guardianship board can, on the application of the debtor or other interested parties, appoint a curator to represent him.

² The guardianship board competent for this purpose is the board of the place where the property charged is situated.

X. Representation of creditor

Chapter II: Mortgages[1]

Art. 824

¹ A mortgage can be created as security for any kind of debt, present, future or contingent.

² The property mortgaged need not belong to the mortgagor.[2]

A. Purport of mortgage

---

[1] *i.e.* of immovable property.
[2] Therefore "mortgagor" is used to mean the person who owes the debt secured on the property, whether he owns that property or not.

Art. 825

B. Creation and extinction
I. Creation

[1] A mortgage, even where it is created as security for a claim for an unliquidated or variable amount, is entered in a special place in the land register and retains in spite of any variations in the amount secured the degree of priority indicated by the entry.

[2] An official extract of the entry of the mortgage in the register is at the creditor's request handed to him, but it is only evidence of the mortgage that has been created and does not constitute a security in itself.

[3] As evidence in the place of this extract a certificate of registration can be endorsed on the mortgage agreement.

Art. 826

II. Extinction
1. Right to have it erased

Where the debt is extinguished, the owner of the mortgaged property has the right to demand that the mortgagee should consent to the erasure of the mortgage from the register.

Art. 827

2. Position of owner

[1] Where the owner of the property mortgaged is not at the same time the mortgagor, he can redeem the mortgage under the same conditions as the mortgagor can redeem his debt.

[2] Where he pays the debt in full, he acquires all the rights of the mortgagee against the mortgagor.

Art. 828

3. Redemption
a. Conditions

[1] Where property is mortgaged beyond its value and it is acquired by a person who is not personally liable for the debts secured by the mortgages, Cantonal Law can authorize the new owner, before proceedings have been taken to realize the securities, to redeem the mortgages by paying over to the creditors either the purchase-money or, where he acquired the

property gratuitously, the sum of money at which he values it.

² He must give the creditors six months' notice in writing of his intention to redeem.

³ The redemption money is divided among the creditors according to their order of priority.

Art. 829

¹ In this case the creditors have the right, within one month from the owner's notice, to demand a sale by public auction of the mortgaged property on condition that they advance the cost of the sale; it must take place after due advertisement within a further month from their demand. *b.* Sale by public auction

² If a larger sum is realized in this sale, it is held to be the proper redemption price and is divided among the creditors.

³ The cost of the sale must be borne by the owner if the sum realized is larger than the amount he previously offered, but, if not, by the creditor who demanded the sale.

Art. 830

Cantonal Law can substitute for a sale by public auction an official valuation which will determine the price of redemption. *c.* Official valuation

Art. 831

Where the owner of the property is not at the same time the mortgagor, a notice by the creditor to repay the mortgage debt is only then valid if it has been given to the mortgagor as well as to the owner of the property. 4. Notice

Art. 832

C. Effect
I. Ownership and liability
1. Total alienation

¹ The alienation of the property mortgaged does not in the absence of a contrary agreement affect the liability of the land under the mortgage nor the personal liability of the mortgagor.

² If, however, the new owner takes over the liability for the mortgage debt, the former mortgagor is discharged, unless the mortgagee gives him within one year from alienation a notice in writing of his intention to maintain his rights against him.

Art. 833

2. Property parcelled

¹ Where part only of the mortgaged property or one of several mortgaged properties belonging to the same owner is alienated, or where the mortgaged property is parcelled out, the security must, in the absence of a contrary agreement, be divided so that each part of the mortgaged property is burdened proportionately to its value.

² Where the mortgagee does not accept this appointment, he can, within one month from the time when it has become operative, demand that his mortgage be redeemed within one year.

³ Where the new owners have taken over the part of the mortgage debt apportioned to their properties, the former mortgagor is discharged, unless the mortgagee gives him within one year a notice in writing of his intention to maintain his rights against him.

Art. 834

3. Notice to mortgagee

¹ The registrar of the land registry must notify the mortgagee that the new owner has taken over the debt.

² The period of one year allowed for the mortgagee to give his notice runs from such notification.

Art. 835

The assignment of a debt secured by a mortgage is valid without registration in the land register.[1]

II. Assignment of mortgage debt

Art. 836

Mortgages, created by Cantonal Law to secure debts arising under Public Law or obligations imposed on owners of property generally, do not in the absence of a contrary provision require registration.

D. Statutory mortgages
I. No registration

Art. 837

[1] A creditor is entitled by law to the creation of a mortgage by registration in the following cases:

1. to secure the rights of the unpaid vendor of land;[2]

2. to secure the rights of co-heirs and other co-owners arising from the partition of the common property;

3. to secure the rights over property of workmen or contractors who are employed in buildings or other works on the property and have supplied material and labour or labour alone, whether these rights are against the owner of the land or against a contractor.

[2] The party entitled by law to such mortgages cannot renounce his rights in advance.

II. With registration
1. Cases

Art. 838

The statutory mortgage to which are entitled vendors, co-heirs, or co-owners must be registered at the latest within three months from the transfer of the property.

2. Vendors, co-heirs and co-owners

---

[1] *i.e.* not only the personal rights and liabilities arising from the debt, but those under the mortgage itself, because an ordinary debt can be assigned without registration, and the mortgage is attached to, and inseparable from, the debt which it secures.

[2] Cf. the English lien.

Art. 839

3. Workmen and contractors
a. Registration

[1] The statutory mortgage to which workmen and contractors are entitled can be registered in the land register at any time after they have undertaken to carry out the work.

[2] The registration must take place at the latest within three months after the completion of the work.

[3] It can only take place where the claims are acknowledged by the owner or established by an order of the court, and cannot be demanded where the owner offers sufficient security to satisfy the amount stated in the claims.

Art. 840

b. Degree of priority

Where several mortgages are entered in the register to secure the claims of workmen and contractors, they have the same degree of priority among themselves even where they bear a different date.

Art. 841

c. Preferential claims

[1] Where the workmen and contractors suffer any loss at the realization of their security, the creditors prior in order to them must compensate them out of the value of the property other than the ground itself which has been assigned to them, to the extent of the prejudice which they could reasonably know they were causing to the workmen and contractors by the creation of their mortgages.[1]

[2] Where a prior creditor assigns a negotiable security,[2] he must compensate the workmen and contractors for the amount by which he has thereby reduced their security.[3]

---

[1] *e.g.* if they knowingly allowed the land to be overburdened before the buildings were put up.
[2] *i.e.* a mortgage certificate or land charge note issued by the registrar to the creditor and which can be assigned by him free from equities.
[3] *i.e.* by this paragraph a creditor is prevented from evading his liabilities under paragraph 1, by assigning a negotiable security on the property: for even after assigning he still remains liable to compensate the builders, if he has thereby prejudiced their interests.

³ From the time when the building has begun and this fact has on the demand of an interested party been stated in the register to the termination of the period allowed for the registration of the statutory mortgage in favour of the workmen and contractors,[1] no charges other than mortgages can be entered in the register.[2]

Chapter III: Mortgage Certificates and Land Charge Notes

Art. 842

A mortgage certificate creates a personal debt secured by a charge on land.[3]

A. Mortgage certificates
I. Object and nature

Art. 843

¹ Cantonal Law can provide for the valuation of property for the purpose of the creation of mortgage certificates, and it may leave it to the will of the parties or make it compulsory on them.

² It can require that mortgage certificates should be created only up to the estimated value of the property charged or some fraction of this value.

II. Valuation

Art. 844

¹ In the absence of a contrary agreement, notice by the creditor or the debtor to repay the debt on a mortgage certificate must be a six months' notice to terminate on the customary terminal days fixed for the payment of interest.

III. Notice to pay off

---

[1] See art. 839.
[2] For if negotiable charges were allowed, the danger mentioned in paragraph 2 would be greatly increased.
[3] *i.e.* as distinct from a land charge note, this form of security is a charge not only on the debtor's land, but all his personal property is liable also.

² Cantonal Law can restrict the rights of the parties to give notice to repay the debt on a mortgage certificate.

Art. 845

IV. Position of owner

¹ The position of the owner of the property charged, where he is not at the same time the debtor, is determined by the provisions on mortgages.

² He has the same defences in an action by the creditor as the debtor would have.

Art. 846

V. Alienation or division

The effect of the alienation or the division of the property charged is the same in the case of a mortgage certificate as it is in the case of a mortgage.

Art. 847

B. Land charge notes
I. Object and nature

¹ A land charge note creates a real security on land.

² Agricultural land, dwelling-houses and building ground only can be so charged.

³ The charge does not create any personal liability on the debtor, and the instrument does not specify the ground of the liability.

Art. 848[1]

II. Maximum charge allowed

¹ A land charge on agricultural properties can be created up to three quarters of the value of the ground as estimated by its annual yield, which is to be determined according to the Federal Statute of 12th December 1940 relating to the Disencumbrance of Agricultural Homesteads.[2]

---

[1] Wording according to art. 93 of the Federal Statute of 12th December 1940 relating to the Disencumbrance of Agricultural Homesteads, in force since 1st January 1947 (SR **211.412.12**).
[2] SR **211.412.12**.

² A land charge on other rural properties can be created up to two-thirds of the value of the ground as estimated by its annual yield and in addition, if the ground is built on, up to one half of the value of the buildings as such.

³ A land charge on urban property can be created up to three-fifths of the mean between their value as estimated by their annual yield and the selling value of the ground and buildings.

⁴ These values are officially estimated in the manner provided by Cantonal Law.

Art. 849

¹ The Cantons are responsible for the exercise of proper care in the carrying out of the valuation.

² They have a right to be indemnified by the officials at fault.

III. Responsibility of the Cantons

Art. 850

¹ The owner of the land charged has the right to redeem the charge at the termination of any period of six years by giving twelve months' previous notice, even where by the agreement the charge was not to be redeemable for a longer period of time.

² The creditor can foreclose except in the cases provided by law only at the termination of any period of fifteen years by giving twelve months' previous notice.[1]

IV. Right of redemption

Art. 851

¹ The debtor under the charge must be the owner for the time being of the property charged.

V. Debt and ownership

---

[1] Wording according to art. 93 of the Federal Statute of 12th December 1940 relating to the Disencumbrance of Agricultural Homesteads, in force since 1st January 1947 (SR **211.412.12**).

² Where the property is transferred, the new owner *ipso jure* takes over the liability under the charge and the former owner is discharged.

³ Interest due under the charge becomes a personal debt as soon as the property ceases to be liable for it.

Art. 852

VI. Where the property is parcelled

¹ Where the property charged is broken up, the owners of the different parts become the debtors under the charge.

² The rules for the apportionment of the debt are the same as those laid down in the case of a mortgage.

³ Where the creditor can demand the redemption of the charge,¹ he must do so by giving the debtors one year's notice within one month from the time when the apportionment of the debt became operative.

Art. 853

VII. Land charges under Cantonal Law and Law of Inheritance

Land charges arising under Cantonal Law are subject to special rules, in particular in regard to restrictions on the rate of interest and the effect of a place in the register: similarly with those arising under the Law of Inheritance.

Art. 854

C. Provisions common to both mortgage certificates and land charge notes
I. Creation
1. Nature of debt

Neither mortgage certificates nor land charge notes can contain any conditions or obligations on the part of the creditor.²

---

¹ *i.e.* in cases under art. 787. He cannot, as other mortgagees, foreclose merely because he objects to the apportionment of the debt (art. 833 paragraph 2).
² This is because they are both negotiable instruments.

Art. 855

¹ The creation of a mortgage certificate or land charge novates the obligation giving rise to it.

² Any agreement to the contrary binds only the parties to it and third parties if they have not acted *bona fide*.

2. Relation between security and debt secured

Art. 856

¹ Where a mortgage certificate or land charge has been created, it must not only be registered, but a document of title must be issued in each case.

² Both kinds of charges become operative by registration even before the issue of the instrument.

3. Registration and instrument
a. Necessity of instrument

Art. 857

¹ The mortgage certificate and the land charge note are drawn by the registrar of the land registry.

² They must be signed by the registrar and by a magistrate or other public official specified by Cantonal Law.

³ These instruments cannot be delivered to the creditor or to his authorized agent except with the consent of the debtor and the owner of the property charged.

b. The drawing of the instrument

Art. 858

The form required for a mortgage certificate and a land charge note will be laid down by order of the Federal Council.

c. Form of instrument

Art. 859

¹ Mortgage certificates and land charge notes can be drawn to the order of a specified person or to bearer.

4. Description of creditor
a. In instrument

² They can be drawn to the order of the owner of the land himself.¹

Art. 860

b. With appointment of agent

¹ At the drawing up of a mortgage certificate or land charge note an agent can be appointed with full powers to make and receive payments due under it, receive notices, consent to the reduction of the security and in general safeguard with all diligence and impartiality the rights of the creditor as well as those of the debtor and owner.

² The name of the agent must be entered in the land register and on the instruments.

³ Where the agency comes to an end and the interested parties cannot agree, the court takes the necessary measures.

Art. 861

5. Place of payment

¹ Unless the instrument provides otherwise, the debtor must make all payments at the house of the creditor and this even where the instrument is payable to bearer.

² When the creditor's address is not known, or he has moved to another place and the debtor is prejudiced thereby, the latter can discharge his obligations by depositing the money with the competent authority at his own place of residence or at the creditor's old place of residence.

³ Where coupons are attached, payment of the interest must be made only to the bearer of the coupons.

---

¹ *i.e.* in blank as to the debt to be secured. If at some future time he incurs some debt which he wishes to secure by a security of this kind, he can use the ready-drawn negotiable instrument by negotiating it: he can thus retain for this security priority over other charges on the same land.

Art. 862

¹ After an assignment of the debt by the creditor, the debtor can, so long as he has not had notice of it, pay interest and annuities for which there are no coupons to the assignor, even where the instrument is to bearer. *6. Payment after assignment by creditor*

² But the repayment of the whole or any part of the principal cannot be validly made, except to the person who at the date of payment is shown to be the actual creditor.

Art. 863

¹ Where there is no creditor or where the creditor renounces his rights, the debtor can choose whether he will have the entry erased in the register or let it stand. *II. Extinction 1. In default of a creditor*

² He is entitled to make a second use of the instrument which has been returned to him.

Art. 864

The entry in the register of a mortgage certificate or a land charge cannot be erased until the instrument has been cancelled or annulled by the court. *2. Erasure*

Art. 865

Claims under a mortgage certificate or land charge are determined by the entry in the register in so far as the claimant has relied on its terms. *III. Rights of creditor 1. Bona fides a. Entry in register*

Art. 866

Claims under a mortgage certificate or land charge are determined by the wording of a properly drawn instrument in so far as the claimant has *bona fide* relied on this wording. *b. Wording of instrument*

Art. 867

c. Relation between instrument and entry in register

¹ Where the wording of the mortgage certificate or land charge note does not correspond with the entry in the land register, or where there is no entry, the register is conclusive.

² A *bona fide* holder of the instrument has, however, the right to claim damages according to the law on land registration.

Art. 868

2. How exercised

¹ The rights under a mortgage certificate or land charge note, whether to order or to bearer, cannot be assigned absolutely or as security or otherwise exercised apart from the instrument itself.

² The creditor, however, can exercise his rights apart from the instrument, where it has been annulled by the court or where it has not yet been drawn up.

Art. 869

3. Delivery of instrument

¹ The assignment of a debt for which a mortgage certificate or land charge note has been drawn up, in all cases requires for its validity the delivery of the instrument itself.

² Where the instrument is made payable to order, the assignment including the assignee's name must be endorsed on it.

Art. 870

IV. When annulled
1. Loss of instrument

¹ Where an instrument or coupon attached to it is lost or has been destroyed without the intention of extinguishing the debt, the creditor can apply to the court that it shall be annulled and the debtor be made to pay, or, if the debt is not yet payable, a new instrument be drawn up.

² The procedure is the same as for the cancellation of securities to bearer; but the period allowed for contesting the application is one year.

³ The debtor has a similar right to have the instrument annulled by the court, where it cannot be found after the debt has been paid off.

Art. 871

¹ Where the creditor secured by a mortgage certificate or land charge has not been known for ten years and no demand for interest has been made for that length of time, the owner of the property charged can require that the creditor be publicly cited by the court to appear, according to the provisions relating to a declaration of absence. *2. Citation of creditor*

² Where the creditor does not appear and after inquiry it is held highly probable that the debt is extinguished, the instrument will be declared null and void by the court and the place in the register vacant.

Art. 872

The debtor can plead only those defences which are either connected with the entry in the register or the instrument, or which are open to him personally in an action brought against him by the creditor. *V. Defences*

Art. 873

Where the debtor pays off the whole of the debt, he can demand that the instrument be returned to him by the creditor, if it is not annulled. *VI. Return of instrument*

Art. 874

¹ Where modifications have been made in the legal position of the parties, such as by a part payment of the debt or the reduction of the debtor's obligations or of the security, the debtor has the right to have them entered in the land register. *VII. Modifications in position of parties*

² The registrar must endorse them on the instrument.

[3] Unless they are entered in the register, they do not affect the rights of a *bona fide* holder of the instrument, except where the annual payments required by the instrument have been duly made.[1]

Chapter IV: Issues of Securities on Land

Art. 875

A. Bonds secured on land

Bonds drawn to the order of the creditor or to bearer can be secured on land either:

1. by the creation of a mortgage or mortgage certificate as security for the whole loan, and the appointment of an agent who shall represent both creditor and debtor, or

2. by the creation of a charge on land for the whole loan in favour of a body authorized for the purpose and the issue of bonds charged on the debt thus secured in favour of the bondholders.[2]

Art. 876

B. Issues of mortgage certificates and land charge notes in a series
I. In general

Mortgage certificates and land charge notes issued in a series are, subject to the following sections, governed by the general provisions on these securities.

Art. 877

II. Form

[1] These instruments are drawn for one hundred francs or a multiple of one hundred francs.

---

[1] Because where these annual payments are ordered in the instrument, the holder would know that they were due and must be presumed to be aware that they have been duly made.

[2] *i.e.* the money is advanced as a whole loan by a bank or other body: this loan is secured by a mortgage on land. The bank issues bonds to the private individuals who are willing to lend the money necessary to make up the loan. These bonds are secured not on the land direct, but on the claims of the bank against the mortgagor. Thus the bondholders have privity only with the bank and not with the mortgagor.

² All instruments in a series bear consecutive numbers and have the same form.

³ Where they are not issued by the owner himself of the property charged, the body issuing them must be described as the representative of the creditor and debtor.

Art. 878

¹ The debtor can agree to pay in addition to the interest due a sum as part payment of the principal until the whole series is paid off.   III. Paying off

² The amount of the annual part payment must be so fixed that it represents a certain number of securities.

Art. 879

¹ The securities for the whole loan must be entered as one transaction in the land register, and their number specified.   IV. Registration

² In exceptional cases where there are only a small number of securities, each can be entered separately.

Art. 880

The person or body who issues the bonds or other securities cannot, even where appointed to represent the creditor and the debtor, make any alterations in the conditions of the debtor's obligations, unless this right has expressly been reserved at the time of the issue.   V. Effect
1. Issuing office

Art. 881

¹ The redemption of the securities is carried out according to the plan which either was settled at their issue or is settled by the agent who was appointed and empowered for the purpose at their issue.   2. Repayment
a. Plan

² Where a security is redeemed, the amount is paid over to the creditor and the instrument cancelled.

³ In the absence of a contrary agreement, the erasure of the entry in the land register cannot take place before the debtor has completely fulfilled his obligations as specified in the entry and delivered up the instrument with the coupons, or deposited amounts equivalent to the value of the coupons which are not delivered up.

Art. 882

b. Control

¹ The owner or the body charged with the issue of the securities is bound to proceed to the drawing of the lots according to the plan of redemption and cancel the securities that are paid off.

² In the case of land charge notes the drawing of lots and cancellations must be officially controlled by the Cantons.

Art. 883

c. Repayments, how used

The amounts repaid must in all cases be used at the next drawing of lots towards the redemption of the securities.

Title XXIII: Law of Pledge

Chapter I: Pledges and Liens

Art. 884

A. Pledges
I. Creation
1. Possession of creditor

¹ With certain exceptions provided by law,[1] movable chattels can be given in pledge only by delivery of possession of the chattel to the creditor.

² Where the creditor *bona fide* takes possession of the chattel, he acquires the rights of a pledgee over it, even where the pledgor has no right to dispose of it, subject always, however, to the rights of third parties derived from their prior possession.

---

[1] *e.g.* pledges of cattle.

³ No pledge can be constituted so long as the pledgor retains exclusive control over the chattel.

Art. 885

¹ Cattle can be pledged without delivery of possession by means of an entry in a public register and a notice lodged at the office of executions for debt, in order to secure advances made by public institutions for the supply of credit or by co-operative societies which have been authorized for this purpose by the competent authorities of the Canton in whose borders they have their head office.   2. Pledge of cattle

² In regard to the keeping of the register and the dues payable, detailed rules will be laid down by an order of the Federal Council.

³ The Cantons settle the areas for the various registries and appoint the registrars.

Art. 886

A pledge can be created to take effect upon another by a written notice to the pledgee advising him of the subsequent pledge and calling upon him to pass on the chattel to the second pledgee when his own rights in it have been satisfied.   3. A pledge upon a pledge

Art. 887

The pledgee cannot himself pledge the chattel without the consent of the pledgor.   4. Pledge by pledgee

Art. 888

¹ A pledge is extinguished when the pledgee ceases to have possession of the chattel and cannot demand it back from third parties in possession.   II. Extinction 1. Loss of possession

² The pledge is suspended while the chattel is in the exclusive possession of the pledgor with the consent of the pledgee.

Art. 889

2. Obligation to return chattel

[1] Where the pledge is extinguished in consequence of the payment of the debt or for any other reason, the pledgee must give up possession of the chattel to the person entitled.

[2] Until his claim is fully satisfied he is not bound to give up the chattel wholly or in part.

Art. 890

3. Liability of pledgee

[1] The pledgee is liable for the damage suffered by the reduction in value or the destruction of the chattel where he cannot prove that it was caused through no fault of his own.

[2] Where the pledgee has alienated or repledged the chattel without consulting the pledgor, he is liable for all the damage caused thereby.

Art. 891

III. Effect
1. Rights of pledgee

[1] A pledgee whose claims have not been fully satisfied has the right to pay himself out of the proceeds from the sale of the chattel.

[2] The pledge secures him to the extent not only of the principal debt and interest agreed upon, but also of the cost of proceedings in respect of it and arrears of interest.

Art. 892

2. Extent of pledge

[1] The pledge burdens the chattel with its accessories.

[2] In the absence of an agreement to the contrary, the pledgee must surrender the natural fruits of the chattel to the owner, as soon as they cease to form an integral part of it.

[3] Fruits that formed an integral part of the chattel at the date of the realization of the pledge are included in it.

Art. 893

¹ Where the same thing is pledged to several creditors in succession, they will be satisfied out of it in the order of their priority.

² Their priority is determined by the date of the pledge.

3. Rights of priority

Art. 894

Any agreement by which the chattel shall become the property of the pledgee if his claims are not satisfied is null and void.¹

4. Agreement for forfeiture of chattel

Art. 895

¹ Where a creditor is in possession of movable chattels or securities with the debtor's consent, he can retain possession of them until his claim is satisfied, provided it is enforceable and by its nature closely connected with the chattel retained.²

² Such connection is always held to exist where the parties are in trade or business and the possession and the claim arise from their business relations.

³ The lien extends even over chattels which are not the property of the debtor, provided the creditor took possession of them in good faith, and subject always to the rights of third parties derived from a prior possession.

B. Liens
I. Conditions

Art. 896

¹ No lien can be exercised over things which have no selling value.³

² Similarly no lien is possible, if it is not in accordance with the obligations undertaken by the creditor, or with the conditions imposed by the

II. Exceptions

---

¹ Cf. *lex commissoria* in Roman Law.
² *e.g.* where the chattel has caused damage to the person in possession, he has a lien on it for damages.
³ *e.g.* letters, receipts, etc.

debtor at or before the delivery of the chattel, or with public policy.

Art. 897

III. Insolvency of debtor

¹ On the insolvency of the debtor the creditor has a lien even before the debt becomes payable.

² Where the insolvency has supervened or has come to the creditor's notice after the delivery of the chattel, he can exercise his lien, even where it is not in accordance with the obligations which he has previously undertaken or with a special condition imposed by the debtor.

Art. 898

IV. Effect

¹ Where the debtor does not fulfil his obligations, the creditor, if he is not sufficiently secured, can after previous notice to the debtor sell the chattel over which he has a lien, just as if it had been pledged to him.

² Where the lien is over securities payable to order, the official in bankruptcy or in execution for debt must take proceedings for their realization in the place of the debtor.

Chapter II: Pledges of Debts and Other Rights

Art. 899

A. In general

¹ Debts and other rights can be pledged if they can be assigned.

² Except where it is expressly provided otherwise, the ordinary rules on pledge are applicable.

Art. 900

B. Creation
I. In case of ordinary debts

¹ In order to constitute a pledge of a debt for which there is no negotiable security or which is evidenced only by a receipt, the agreement to give

it in pledge must be in writing, and, if there is a receipt, this must be delivered up to the pledgee.

² The pledgee and the pledgor can notify the debtor of the pledge.

³ Where other rights[1] are to be pledged, not only must the agreement be in writing, but the form required for their assignment must be observed.

Art. 901

¹ Securities to bearer are pledged by their mere delivery to the pledgee.

² In the case of other securities, the delivery must be supplemented by an endorsement or written assignment.[2]

II. Negotiable and other securities

Art. 902

¹ Where goods are represented by bills, the goods can be pledged by pledging the bills.

² Where there is a warrant besides the bill, the goods can be pledged by pledging the warrant alone, provided the bill is endorsed with the pledge, the amount of the debt and the day of payment.

III. Goods bills[3]

Art. 903

A subsequent pledge of a debt which is already subject to a prior pledge is valid only where the prior pledgee is notified in writing of the subsequent pledge either by the original creditor or the subsequent pledgee.

IV. A pledge upon a pledge

Art. 904

¹ A pledge of debts for which interest or other periodic payments such as dividends are due does not, in the absence of a contrary agreement, cover

C. Effect
I. Rights of pledgee

---

[1] *e.g.* patents.
[2] The text does not say that the assignment must be in writing, but this is inferred.
[3] Cf. bills of lading in English Law.

any but the current interest or dividends, and the pledgee has no claim over interest or dividends that accrued due before.

² Where, however, special securities or coupons have been given for these subsidiary dues, they are in the absence of a contrary agreement held to be covered by the pledge, where they have been pledged in the proper form.[1]

Art. 905

II. Shares

Shares that have been given in pledge are represented at the general meeting of shareholders by the shareholder who has pledged them and not by the pledgee.

Art. 906

III. Administration and payment off

¹ Where careful management demands it, the creditor can give notice requiring the debt that has been pledged to be paid off, and the pledgee can insist on this being done.

² Where the debtor has been notified of the pledge, he cannot make any payments to either party except with the consent of the other.

³ In the absence of such consent, he must place the payments on deposit.

Chapter III: Pawn

Art. 907

A. Pawnbrokers
I. Licences

¹ Where a person wishes to pursue the occupation of a pawnbroker, he must have a licence from his Cantonal government.

---

[1] *e.g.* coupons payable to order for last year's dividends must be endorsed.

² The Cantons can decide that this licence shall be granted only to public institutions in the Canton or Commune and to public benevolent societies.

³ They can require pawnbrokers to pay a tax for their licence.

Art. 908

¹ A pawnbroker's licence is granted to private establishments only for a definite time, but it can be renewed. *II. Duration*

² It can at any time be revoked, where the pawnbroker does not observe the conditions of his licence.

Art. 909

To place a thing in pawn it must be delivered over in return for a ticket. *B. Pawning* *I. How carried out*

Art. 910

¹ Where the thing pawned is not redeemed by the date fixed, the pawnbroker can, after a previous public notice to the borrower, apply to the competent authority to have the thing sold. *II. Effect* *1. Sale of things pawned*

² The pawnbroker has no personal action against the borrower.

Art. 911

¹ Where on the sale of the thing there is a balance over after the settlement of the debt, it must be paid to the borrower. *2. Right to the balance*

² Where the borrower is liable to the pawnbroker for several debts, they can in calculating this balance be added together and counted as one debt.

³ The period of limitation of the action for the recovery of this balance is five years from the sale of the thing.

Art. 912

III. Redemption
1. Right to redeem

¹ The person entitled can take the thing out of pawn by returning the pawnticket, so long as no sale has taken place.

² If he cannot produce the ticket, he can nevertheless redeem the thing as from the date fixed for the payment of the debt, if he can prove his right to the thing.

³ The person entitled has this right after the lapse of six months from that date, even where the pawnbroker has expressly made it a term in the contract that he would not give up the thing except on the production of the ticket.

Art. 913

2. Rights of pawnbroker

¹ The pawnbroker has in each case the right, on the redemption of the thing, to demand interest for the whole of the current month.

² Where he has expressly agreed to give up the thing to anyone who produces the ticket, he is entitled to do so, provided he did not know or could not be expected to know that the bearer had wrongfully acquired possession of the ticket.

Art. 914

C. Purchase and re-sale

Where a person carries on a systematic business of purchasing things with a view to re-sale, he is held to be in the same position as a pawnbroker.[1]

Art. 915

D. Cantonal Law

¹ The Cantons can lay down further regulations in regard to pawnbrokers.

² Such regulations require for their validity to be confirmed by the Federal Council.

---

[1] The price paid is held to be the money lent and the difference between that and the amount received on the re-sale is held to be the interest.

Chapter IV: Debentures

Art. 916–918[1]

Section III: Possession and Land Register

Title XXIV: Possession

Art. 919

[1] Effective control over something constitutes possession of it.

[2] In the case of servitudes and rent-charges, possession consists of the effective exercise of the right conferred.

A. Nature and kinds
I. Nature

Art. 920

[1] Where the person in possession of something delivers it to another in order to confer upon him a limited real or a personal right in it, they are both held to be in possession of it.

[2] The owner is held to have the original possession, the other the derivative possession.

II. Original and derivative possession

Art. 921

A purely temporary interruption or suspension of the exercise of effective control over the thing does not involve loss of possession.

III. Temporary interruption

Art. 922

[1] Possession is transferred from one person to another by the delivery of the thing itself to the other person or by putting at his disposal the means by which he can acquire control over it.

B. Transfer
I. *Inter praesentes*

---

[1] Annulled by art. 52 paragraph 2 of the Federal Statute of 25th June 1930 relating to the Issue of Debentures (SR **211.423.4**).

²The delivery is complete when the transferee has, by the wish of the former possessor, been placed in the position of exercising effective control over the thing.

Art. 923

II. *Inter absentes*

Delivery *inter absentes* is complete when the thing is actually handed over to the transferee or his authorized agent.

Art. 924

III. Without delivery

¹ Possession of a thing can be acquired without delivery, where a third party or the person himself who is alienating continues in possession of it under a distinct title by virtue of some legal transaction.¹

² Such transfer is not binding on the third party who continues in possession until the transferor has given him notice of the transfer.

³ The third party can refuse to deliver up possession to the transferee for the same reasons for which the transferor could have refused.

Art. 925

IV. In case of goods bills

¹ Where bills have been drawn to represent goods which have been delivered to a carrier or placed in a repository, the delivery of these bills has the same effect as the delivery of the goods themselves.

² Where, however, the bills have come into the *bona fide* possession of one party and the goods into that of another, the latter has the prior right to them.

---

¹ *e.g.* the owner A can agree with his bailee B to hold the goods bailed to him for C to whom he has sold them: C has thereby acquired possession under this article. B, the third party, is only bound by the transfer as from the date of notice given him by A.

Art. 926

C. Effect
I. Protection of possession
1. Right of defence

¹ A person in possession has the right to use all necessary force to prevent any unlawful attack on his rights.

² Where he has been deprived of his possession secretly or by violence, he can, if it is land, resume possession by driving out the trespasser, or, if it is a movable chattel, retake it by force provided he can catch the trespasser in the very act or in immediate pursuit.

³ He must in so doing abstain from all acts of violence that are not justified by the circumstances of the case.

Art. 927

2. Action for restitution

¹ Where any person has wrongfully deprived another of his possession, he is bound to restore it even though he maintains that he has a better right to the property in question.

² Where the defendant can at once prove a better title which would empower him to retake the property from the plaintiff, he can refuse to restore it.

³ The plaintiff can sue for the recovery of the property and damages.

Art. 928

3. Action for trespass

¹ Where anyone has been unlawfully disturbed in his possession, he can sue for trespass even though the defendant pleads that he has a right to the property in question.

² The action is for an injunction to cease the trespass and to abstain from similar acts in the future, and for damages.

Art. 929

4. Lapse of right of action and period of limitation

¹ The injured party can bring the action for trespass only if he demands the restitution of the property in question or the cessation of the trespass

immediately after the commission of the wrong and the identity of the wrongdoer have come to his knowledge.

² The period of limitation for this action is one year from the dispossession or trespass, even though the plaintiff did not know of the wrong or the identity of the wrongdoer until a later date.

Art. 930

II. Protection of right to possession
1. Presumption of ownership

¹ The person in possession of a movable chattel is presumed to be its owner.

² A person who has been, but has ceased to be, in possession is presumed to have been the owner during the period of his possession.

Art. 931

2. Presumption in the case of derivative possession

¹ Where a person is in possession of a movable chattel without any intention to hold it as owner, he can plead the presumption that the person from whom he acquired *bona fide* possession is the owner.

² Where a person is in possession of a movable chattel by virtue of a personal right to it or a real right short of ownership, the existence of the right is presumed, but he cannot validly plead it as against the person from whom he acquired possession.

Art. 932

3. Action against the person in possession

The person in possession of a movable chattel can in every action brought against him plead the presumption that he has the better title; subject nevertheless to the provisions on wrongful dispossession and trespass.

Art. 933

4. Right of alienation and recovery
a. In case of goods delivered to another

Where a movable chattel is transferred with a view to passing ownership or some other real right to the transferee, and he takes possession in good faith, his right over the chattel must be protected, even where the transferor had himself no authority to alienate it.

Art. 934

¹ Where a person in possession of a movable chattel loses it or has it stolen from him or otherwise taken from him against his will, he can demand it back within a period of five years from any person who is detaining it.

² Where the chattel has been bought at a public auction or in market overt or from a dealer in property of the same kind, it cannot be recovered from the first purchaser or any subsequent *bona fide* purchaser, unless he is compensated for the purchase-money paid.

³ The rules in regard to the restoration of the thing are in other respects the same as those governing the rights of a *bona fide* possessor.

b. In case of lost or stolen property

Art. 935

Cash and negotiable instruments to bearer cannot be recovered from the *bona fide* holder, even though the plaintiff was deprived of his possession in them against his will.

c. In case of cash and negotiable instruments to bearer

Art. 936

¹ Where a person has acquired possession of a movable chattel in bad faith, he is always bound to restore it to the former possession.

² If, however, the latter was not a *bona fide* possessor himself, he cannot recover it from any subsequent possessor.

d. In case of bad faith

Art. 937

¹ Where the property is an immovable entered in the land register, only the person whose name is on the register is presumed to have the right to its possession and to the actions for its protection.

5. Presumption in regard to immovables

² The person, however, who has effective control of the immovable can bring an action for dispossession or trespass.

Art. 938

III. Liabilities
1. Of *bona fide* possessor
a. For use

¹ Where any person is in *bona fide* possession of some property, he is not liable to the person entitled to it for any damage caused by his use of it.

² He is not bound to make good any losses or deterioration consequent on such use.

Art. 939

b. Indemnity

¹ Where the person entitled to the property demands its return, the defendant can if he is a *bona fide* possessor claim compensation for any necessary and useful outlay on it and refuse to return it until this has been paid.

² For other expenditure he cannot demand compensation, but, if this is not offered, he can before returning the property remove any improvements or additions that he has made to it, provided this can be done without injury to the property.

³ The value of the fruits that the possessor has gathered must be deducted from the amount of compensation due to him for his expenditure.

Art. 940

2. *Mala fide* possessor

¹ Where any person is in *mala fide* possession of property, he must restore it to the person entitled to it and also give compensation for the damage caused by the wrongful detention and for the fruits which he has gathered or neglected to gather.

² He cannot make any claims for expenditure on the property, unless the person entitled would have been obliged to incur them himself.

³ If the possessor does not know to whom he is to return the property, he is liable only for the damage which has been caused by his own fault.

Art. 941

Where a person claims the property by prescription or adverse possession, he can add to his own period of possession that of his predecessor, provided the latter's possession also was such that a prescriptive title could be based on it.

IV. Prescription and adverse possession

Title XXV: Land Register

Art. 942

¹ A land register is kept of rights over immovable property.

² It consists of the big book, supplementary plans, lists of properties, their title deeds and particulars, and the day-book.

A. Organization
I. Register itself
1. In general

Art. 943[1]

¹ The following are entered in the register as immovables:

1. land and houses;
2. independent and permanent rights in immovables;
3. mines;
4. co-owned shares of immovables.

² The Federal Council will draw up an order to regulate the mode of registration of independent and permanent rights and mines and the co-owned shares of immovables.

2. Entries
a. Subject

Art. 944

¹ Immovables which are not subject to private ownership and those which are used for public purposes are not entered in the register, unless real

b. Exceptions

---

[1] Wording according to cipher III of the Federal Statute of 19th December 1963, in force since 1st January 1965 (AS 1964 993 1005; BBl 1962 II 1461).

rights are attached to them which must be registered or unless Cantonal Law expressly requires it.

² Where registered immovable property is transformed into property which is excluded from the register, it is crossed off.

³ A special register is kept for public railways.

Art. 945

3. Registers
a. The big book

¹ Every immovable property has its own page and number in the big book.

² The Federal Council will make an order regulating the procedure where a property is partitioned or several properties are joined into one.

Art. 946

b. A page in the register

¹ On each page the following are entered in separate columns:

1. the ownership;
2. servitudes and rent-charges created for the benefit of the property or as a charge on it;
3. mortgages and other securities on it.

² At the request of the owner the accessories to the property may also be entered; they cannot then be erased except with the consent of all whose rights are entered in the register.

Art. 947

c. Several properties on one page

¹ Several properties can, with the consent of the owner, be entered on one page, even where they are not naturally connected together.

² The entries on that page with the exception of praedial servitudes are held to apply to all the properties equally.

³ The owner can at any time demand that any one of the properties entered on the page be removed, provided the rights attached to it are not thereby prejudiced.

Art. 948

¹ Applications for registration are entered without delay in the day-book in the order in which they are made, with the name of the person applying and the object of the application. *d.* Day-book, title deeds

² The title-deeds which form the basis of the registration are duly sorted and preserved.

³ In those Cantons where the registrar has power to draw up authenticated documents, the title-deeds can be replaced by an official abstract of title which on forming part of the register constitutes the legal title to the property.

Art. 949

¹ The Federal Council shall prescribe the proper forms to be observed in registration and make all necessary regulations, and can for the better maintenance of the register order the establishment of branch registries. 4. Regulations

² The Cantons are entitled to make special regulations in regard to the entry of the real rights in land which are subject to Cantonal Law: these require for their validity, however, to be confirmed by the Federal Council.

Art. 950

¹ The entry and description of every property in the register is carried out in accordance with a plan based as a general rule on an ordnance survey. 5. Plans

² The Federal Council will lay down the rules in regard to the drawing of the plans.

Art. 951

¹ For the purpose of the land register, the Cantons are divided into areas. II. How the land register is kept
1. Areas
a. Competence

² Properties are entered in the register of the particular area in which they are situated.

Art. 952

b. Properties situated in several areas

¹ Where a property is situated in several areas, it is entered in the register of each area, with a reference to the register of the other areas.

² Applications for registration and the entries which constitute the rights in the property¹ must be made in the register of the area in which the greater part of the property is situated.

³ Notice of the entries in this register must be sent by the registrar to the registries of the other areas.

Art. 953

2. Registries

¹ The organization of the registries, the arrangement of the areas, the appointment and pay of the officials and the ordering of proper supervision are all within the province of the Cantons.

² The Cantonal provisions require for their validity to be confirmed by the Federal Council.

Art. 954

3. Fees

¹ The Cantons can require the payment of fees for registration in the land register and the measurements incident to it.

² No fees can be demanded for entries which are connected with improvements in the soil or redistribution of plots made for the purpose of carrying out an industrial scheme.

Art. 955

III. Officials
1. Liability

¹ The Cantons are liable for all damage arising from the management of the land register.

² They have, however, the right to be indemnified by the registrars or other officials employed in the registries and by the authorities that have the direct

---

[1] *e.g.* entries of praedial servitudes.

supervision of the registries to whose fault the damage is due.

³ They can demand security from the registrars and other officials.

Art. 956

¹ The work of the registrars of the land registries is subject to regular supervision. 2. Supervision

² Complaints against them in the conduct of their office and disputes relating to the title-deeds handed in or to be handed in and declarations made or to be made are decided by the Cantonal supervisory authority, unless the law requires the matter to be settled in court.

³ Appeals to the Federal authorities are regulated by special provisions.

Art. 957

¹ Penalties are imposed by the Cantonal supervisory authority on registrars and other officials in the land registries for breach of any of their official duties. 3. Penalties

² The penalty may be a reprimand, a fine up to one thousand francs or, in serious cases, dismissal.

³ Criminal prosecutions may also be brought.

Art. 958

The following rights in land are entered in the land register: B. Registration
I. What rights are registered
1. Ownership and other real rights

1. ownership;
2. servitudes and rent-charges;
3. mortgages and other real securities.

Art. 959

¹ Personal rights, such as the right of pre-emption, the right of purchase and resale, agricultural and 2. Notes
a. Personal rights

occupation leases can be noted in the register in the cases expressly provided by law.

² These rights thereby become enforceable as against any right subsequently acquired over the land.

Art. 960

b. Restrictions on alienation

¹ Restrictions on the right to alienate a property can be entered in the register where they are the result of:

1. an official decision given in order to secure disputed[1] or executory claims;

2. an execution for debt or a declaration of bankruptcy or a temporary suspension of liquidation proceedings;

3. a legal transaction which can be noted in the register, such as the constitution of a homestead or the charge laid on a reversionary heir.

² By virtue of their entry in the register these restrictions become enforceable as against any right subsequently acquired over the land.

Art. 961

c. Provisional registration

¹ Provisional entries can be made:

1. to secure a person who asserts a real right,[2]

2. where the law permits the applicant to complete the proof of his rights.

² They are made with the consent of all the interested parties or by order of the court: the effect is that if the right in question is established at a later date, it becomes operative as a right *in rem* as from the date of the entry.

---

[1] *e.g.* a vendor of land refuses to allow the purchaser's name to be entered in the register and the latter brings an action for a declaration of ownership in his own favour. In the meantime an entry can in certain cases be made to restrict the vendor's right of alienation to third persons.

[2] *e.g.* where an entry has wrongfully been erased and the party reasserts his rights.

³ The court decides by summary procedure and authorizes the provisional entry, if the applicant can give *prima facie* proof of his rights; it fixes the precise duration and effect of the entry and, where necessary, sets a time limit within which the applicant must establish his rights in court.

Art. 962

¹ The Cantons can provide that restrictions of Public Law, such as building lines and such like, are to be entered in the register. — II. Restrictions of Public Law

² Such provisions require for their validity to be confirmed by the Federal Council.

Art. 963

¹ Entries are made in the register on a written statement by the owner of the property to which the purported transaction refers. — III. Conditions 1. Statements a. For entries

² Such statement is not required where the party acquiring the property can base his application on a statutory provision or a valid judgment of the court or an equally valid title.

³ The Cantons can require the officials authorized to draw up authenticated documents to apply for the registration of the rights resulting from the documents they have drawn.

Art. 964

¹ Erasures or modifications of an entry can be made only on the written statement of the persons on whom rights were conferred by the entry. — b. For erasures

² The signatures of these persons in the day-book can be substituted for the statement.

Art. 965

¹ No disposition of property through the register can take place, whether by way of entry or the modification or erasure of an entry, unless proof is — 2. Proof a. Valid proof

produced of the applicant's right to alienate and the validity of the title on which the disposition is based.

² The right to alienate is established by proof that the applicant is the person who has the right to alienate according to the entries in the register, or has been given the power to represent him as his agent.

³ The validity of the title on which the disposition to be registered is based is established by proof that the required forms have been observed.

Art. 966

b. Completion of proof

¹ Where the necessary proof is not produced the application must be rejected.

² Where, however, the title exists, and it is only a question of completing the proof of the existence of a right to alienate, a temporary entry can be made with the consent of the owner or by the order of the court.

Art. 967

IV. Mode of registration
1. In general

¹ Entries in the big book are made in the order in which applications are lodged, or in which the documents or statements are signed in the presence of the registrar.

² At the request of the interested parties extracts are made for them of all the entries.

³ The form in which entries, erasures and extracts are to be made will be determined by an order of the Federal Council.

Art. 968

2. In the case of servitudes

Praedial servitudes are entered or erased on the pages reserved for the dominant and the servient properties.

Art. 969

¹ The registrar must give notice to the interested parties of the dispositions in the register which have taken place without their previous knowledge.

² Time limits within which such dispositions can be opposed run from the receipt of this notice.

V. Official notices

Art. 970

¹ The register is public.

² Any person who can give *prima facie* proof of being an interested party can demand to inspect specified pages of the register together with the deeds and documents belonging to them in the presence of a registry official, or to have extracts from them prepared for him.

³ No person can allege that he has no knowledge of a particular entry in the register.

C. Public character of land register

Art. 971

¹ Where registration is required by law for the creation of a real right, it has the force of a real right only where it is registered as such.

² The extent of the right can within the limits set by the terms of the entry in the register be determined by title-deeds or in any other manner.

D. Effect
I. Of non-registration

Art. 972

¹ Real rights arise and acquire their order of priority and date from their entry in the big book.

² Their validity relates back to the time of their entry in the day-book, provided that the proof required by law is subjoined to the application or, in the case of a temporary registration, is subsequently produced within the time allowed.

³ Where by Cantonal Law the authenticated instrument is drawn by the registrar in the form of an entry made in the abstract of title-deeds, this takes the place of the entry in the day-book.

II. Of registration
1. In general

Art. 973

2. In regard to third persons of good faith

Where any person has acquired the ownership or other real right in land by *bona fide* relying on an entry in the register, his rights must be protected.

Art. 974

3. In regard to third persons of bad faith

[1] Where a real right has been wrongfully entered in the register, a third person who has or should have cognizance of the defect in the title cannot base his claims on the entry.

[2] The entry is wrongful where it has been made without the existence of a good title or by virtue of a void transaction.

[3] Where any person has thereby been injured in respect of a real right, he can plead the wrongfulness of the entry in an action against a third person who has acted in bad faith.

Art. 975

E. Erasures and modifications
I. Wrongful entry

[1] Where a wrong entry is made of a real right or a right entry is wrongfully erased or modified, any person who has thereby been injured in his real rights can demand the erasure or the modification of the entry.

[2] This provision leaves untouched the rights acquired through the entry by third persons who have acted *bona fide,* as also all claims for damages.

Art. 976

II. Extinction of real right

[1] Where an entry has lost all legal significance in consequence of the extinction of the real right entered, the person burdened with it can demand its erasure.

[2] If the registrar accedes to this demand, any interested party can within ten days appeal to the court against the erasure.

[3] The registrar is authorized officially to apply for a judicial inquiry and decision in regard to such

extinction and then carry out the erasure in accordance with the decision.

Art. 977

¹ The registrar may not, in the absence of the written consent of the interested parties, make any rectifications without a direction of the court.   III. Rectifications

² Instead of rectifying a wrong entry, the registrar can erase it and make a new entry.

³ The rectification of purely clerical errors is officially carried out in accordance with an order of the Federal Council.

Final Title: Provisions for the Application and Introduction of Code

Chapter I: Application of Old and New Law

Art. 1

¹ The legal effect of facts which occurred before the coming into force of this Code continues to be determined by the rules of Federal or Cantonal Law in force at the time of the occurrence of these facts.   A. General principles
I. No retrospective effect

² Accordingly the binding force and effect of transactions which took place before the 1st January 1912 continue to be determined after that date by the rules of the law in force at the time when they took place.

³ On the other hand, facts subsequent to that date are, except in certain cases expressly excluded by law, governed by the present Code.

Art. 2

¹ The provisions of this Code which are due to considerations of public policy and *boni mores* are   II. Retrospective effect
1. Public policy and *boni mores*

applicable, as from the date of its coming into force, to all facts not expressly excluded from its scope.

² Accordingly the rules of the old law, which by the new law are contrary to public policy or *boni mores,* cannot be applied as from the coming into force of the Code.

Art. 3

2. Relations arising by operation of law

Legal relations that arise by operation of law independently of the intention of the parties are made subject to the new law as from its coming into force, even where they arose before this date.

Art. 4

3. Where right not acquired

Where facts have arisen under the old law but no rights have in consequence been acquired by the date of the coming into force of the new law, the legal effect of these facts is governed as from this date by the new law.

Art. 5

B. Law of Persons
I. Capacity

¹ The capacity of parties is in all cases determined by the rules of this Code.

² Where, however, any person had legal capacity under the rules of the old law, but would not have it under those of the new law, he shall not suffer any diminution in his rights.

Art. 6

II. Declaration of absence

¹ A declaration of absence is governed by the new law as from the coming into force of this Code.

² Declarations of death or absence made under the old law have the same effect as those under the new law: the legal consequences, however, that had already set in before by virtue of the old law, such as succession on death or the dissolution of a marriage, continue unchanged.

³ Where proceedings had commenced at the date of the coming into force of the new law, they shall be commenced again and be carried out under the new law, but the time that had already elapsed shall be taken into account in reckoning time limits; at the request, however, of the interested parties, they can be carried out according to the procedure and with the time limits imposed by the old law.

Art. 7

¹ Associations and societies or foundations, which had acquired a corporate personality under the old law, retain it under the new law, even where they would not have acquired it under the new law.

² If, however, associations incorporated under the old law require to be registered under the new law, they must be registered within five years from the coming into force of the Code, even where the old law did not require this formality; if they are not registered within five years, they lose their corporate character.

³ The legal position of a corporation is determined in all cases by the new law, as from the date of its coming into force.

III. Corporate bodies

Art. 8

¹ The solemnization, the divorce and the effects of marriage in general are governed by the new law as from the date the Federal Statute of 5th October 1984 comes into force.[1]

² Celebrations and dissolutions of marriages effected under the old law are recognized as valid by the new law.

³ Marriages which would not be valid under the old law cannot be annulled after the coming into force of the new law except in accordance with the

C. Family law[1]
I. Solemnization, divorce and effects of marriage in general
1. Principle

---

[1] Wording according to cipher I 2 of the Federal Statute of 5th October 1984, in force since 1st January 1988 (BBl **1979 II** 1191).

new provisions, but the time that has in each case elapsed before this date is counted in for the purpose of calculating time limits.

Art. $8a^1$

2. Surname

The wife who married under the old law can declare before the civil status registrar within one year of the coming into force of the new law that she wants to place the surname which she had borne before the marriage in front of the surname she acquired by the present marriage.

Art. $8b^1$

3. Citizenship

A Swiss woman who married under the old law can declare before the competent authority of her original Home Canton within one year of the coming into force of the new law that she wishes to retain the citizenship which she had as an unmarried woman.

Art. 9^2

II. Matrimonial Property Law applicable to marriages contracted before 1st January 1912

The legal effects on matrimonial property of marriages contracted before 1st January 1912 are governed by the rules of the Civil Code for the application of the old and the new law which came into force on that day.

Art. $9a^1$

IIbis. Matrimonial Property Law applicable to marriages contracted after 1st January 1912

^{1} Marriages which exist at the coming into force of the Federal Statute of 5th October 1984 are governed by the new law, unless other provisions have been made.

^{2} The legal effects on the matrimonial property of marriages which were annulled before the coming

---

^{1} Inserted by cipher I 2 of the Federal Statute of 5th October 1984, in force since 1st January 1988 (BBl 1979 II 1191).
^{2} Wording according to cipher I 2 of the Federal Statute of 5th October 1984, in force since 1st January 1988 (BBl 1979 II 1191).

into force of the Federal Statute of 5th October 1984 are governed by the old law.

Art. 9b[1]

2. Change from marital system to participation in acquisitions
a. Change of the masses of property

¹ Spouses who have hitherto been ruled by the marital system are governed in their relations *inter se* and towards third parties by the provisions made for the participation in acquisitions.

² The assets of each spouse become his or her own property or acquisitions in accordance with the provisions made for the participation in acquisitions; separate estate established by a marriage covenant becomes a spouse's own property.

³ The wife takes back into her own property her unreserved property which became her husband's property or lodges a claim for compensation.

Art. 9c[2]

b. Privilege

Where a husband suffers bankruptcy or where his assets are distressed the existing provisions made for claims for compensation for the wife's unreserved and no longer available property remain applicable within ten years after the coming into force of the new law.

Art. 9d[2]

c. Division of matrimonial property under the new law

¹ After the coming into force of the new law the division of the matrimonial property held by the spouses is governed by the provisions made for the participation in acquisitions for the whole duration of the old and the new regular matrimonial property system, unless the spouses have already completed the division of the matrimonial property in accordance with the provisions made for the marital system at the time when the new law comes into force.

---

[1] Inserted by cipher I 2 of the Federal Statute of 5th October 1984, in force since 1st January 1988 (BBl **1979 II** 1191).

[2] Wording according to cipher I 2 of the Federal Statute of 5th October 1984, in force since 1st January 1988 (BBl **1979 II** 1191).

²Before the coming into force of the new law each spouse can inform the other spouse in writing that the former marital system shall be dissolved in accordance with the provisions made in the old law.

³Where the matrimonial property system is dissolved because an action filed before the coming into force of the new law has been sustained, the division of the matrimonial property system is governed by the old law.

Art. $9e^1$

3. Maintenance of the marital system

¹Spouses who are ruled by the regular marital system and who have not changed this matrimonial property system by a marriage covenant can maintain the marital system by making a joint declaration in writing to the marriage property registrar within one year of the coming into force of the new law at the latest; the marriage property registrar keeps a register of the declarations of maintenance, which is open for inspection to everybody.

²The matrimonial property system can only be opposed to third parties if they knew or should have known it.

³The separate estates of the spouses are governed, from now onwards, by the new provisions made for the system of separate estates.

Art. $9f^2$

4. Maintenance of the system of separate estates by operation of the law or by order of the court

Where the system of separate estates has come into existence either by operation of the law or by order of the court, the spouses are governed by the new provisions made for the system of separate estates.

---

[1] Wording according to cipher I 2 of the Federal Statute of 5th October 1984, in force since 1st January 1988 (BBl **1979 II** 1191).

[2] Inserted by cipher I 2 of the Federal Statute of 5th October 1984, in force since 1st January 1988 (BBl **1979 II** 1191).

Art. 10[1]

[1] A marriage covenant made in accordance with the provisions of the Civil Code of 10th December 1907 retains its validity and the whole of the spouses' matrimonial property system remains under the old provisions with the exception of the provisions of this Title in regard to separate estates, the legal force towards third parties and the system of separate estates by covenant.

[2] The separate estates of the spouses are from now onwards ruled by the provisions made for the system of separate estates.

[3] Covenants made for a participation in profits and losses in connection with the marital system must not encroach on the compulsory portions of children who are not the common issue of the spouses and their descendants.

5. Marriage covenant
a. In general

Art. 10a[2]

[1] The matrimonial property system can only be opposed to third parties if they know or should know it.

[2] Where the marriage covenant has no legal force towards third parties, the relations to these third parties are, from now onwards, governed by the provisions made for participation in acquisitions.

b. Legal force towards third parties

Art. 10b[2]

[1] Spouses who are ruled by the marital system but have changed this matrimonial property system by a marriage covenant can declare by making a joint application in writing to the marriage property registrar at their domicile within one year of the coming into force of the new law, at the latest, that

c. To be governed by the new law

---

[1] Wording according to cipher I 2 of the Federal Statute of 5th October 1984, in force since 1st January 1988 (BBl **1979 II** 1191).

[2] Inserted by cipher I 2 of the Federal Statute of 5th October 1984, in force since 1st January 1988 (BBl **1979 II** 1191).

their matrimonial property shall be governed by the new regular matrimonial property system of participation in acquisitions.

[2] In this case the contractual participation in profits extends, from now onwards, to the total amount of the profits made by both spouses, unless provided otherwise by marriage covenant.

Art. $10c^1$

d. System of separate estates under the old law by marriage covenant

Where the spouses agreed upon a system of separate estates under the old law, they are, from now onwards, ruled by the new provisions made for the system of separate estates.

Art. $10d^1$

e. Marriage covenants made in view of the coming into force of the new law

Marriage covenants made before the coming into force of the Federal Statute of 5th October 1984, but which shall become operative only under the new law, are not subject to authorization by the guardianship board.

Art. $10e^1$

f. Marriage property register

[1] With the coming into force of the Federal Statute of 5th October 1984 no new entries will be made in the marriage property register.

[2] The right to inspect the register remains in force.

Art. 11^2

6. Settlement of debts at the division of matrimonial property system

Where, in connection with the coming into force of the new law, the division of the matrimonial property system causes serious difficulties to the spouse who is liable to pay pecuniary debts or to restitute owed items of property, he or she can

---

[1] Inserted by cipher I 2 of the Federal Statute of 5th October 1984, in force since 1st January 1988 (BBl 1979 II 1191).

[2] Wording according to cipher I 2 of the Federal Statute of 5th October 1984, in force since 1st January 1988 (BBl 1979 II 1191).

demand to be allowed time; where the circumstances justify it, the claims are to be secured.

Art. 11a[1]

Where the matrimonial property law changes with the coming into force of the Federal Statute of 5th October 1984, the liability is ruled by the provisions made for the protection of creditors at the change of the matrimonial property system.

7. Protection of creditors

Art. 12[2]

[1] Origin and effect of the child parent relationship are governed by the new law as soon as this law comes into force; the family name and the citizenship which have been acquired by operation of the law in force until hitherto will be retained.

III. The child-parent relationship in general

[2] Where by operation of the law children who would be in parental power according to the new law are under guardianship at the date of the new law coming into force, these children must be placed under parental power not later than one year from this date, unless in accordance with the provisions made for the deprivation of parental power the contrary has been ruled.

[3] Where by operation of the old law parental power was conferred on another person or the parents had been deprived of their parental power through an order issued by an authority these measures remain valid even after the introduction of the new Code.

---

[1] Inserted by cipher I 2 of the Federal Statute of 5th October 1984, in force since 1st January 1988 (BBl 1979 II 1191).
[2] Wording according to cipher I 2 of the Federal Statute of 25th June 1976, in force since 1st January 1978 (AS 1977 237 264; BBl 1974 II 1).

Art. 12a[1]

IIIbis. Adoption
1. Continuation of the old law

An adoption which was effected before the coming into force of the new provisions of the Federal Statute of 30th June 1972 concerning the change of the Civil Code continues to be governed by the law which came into force on 1st January 1912[2]; agreements which were validly made in accordance with the old Code remain valid in any case.

Art. 12b[1]

2. Placing under the new law

[1] An adoption of a minor which was pronounced under the old law can be placed under the new law on the joint request of the adopting parents and the adopted child within five years of the coming into force of the new law.

[2] The adopted child's reaching his majority is no hindrance to this request.

[3] The new regulations for the procedure apply; the consent of the parents is not required.

Art. 12c[1]

3. Adoption of majors and persons placed under committee

[1] A person who is a major or who is placed under committee can be adopted in accordance with the new provisions made for the adoption of minors if the old law did not permit an adoption during minority although the requirements of the new Code would have been fulfilled at that time.

[2] However, the provisions of the old and the new law concerning the consent of the parents for the adoption of minors do not apply.

---

[1] Inserted by cipher I 3 of the Federal Statute of 30th June 1972, in force since 1st April 1973 (AS 1972 2819 2829; BBl 1971 I 1200).
[2] Art. 465 of the Civil Code in the wording of 1st January 1912:
   1. In relation to the adopter the adopted child and his issue have the same right of inheritance as the issue from marriage.
   2. In relation to the adopted the adopter and his blood relations have no right of inheritance.

³ The request must be made within five years of the coming into force of the new provisions.

Art. 12*d*¹

For disputing legitimation in accordance with the old Code the provisions of the new Code for disputing acknowledgement after the marriage of the parents apply analogously.

IIIter. Contestation of legitimation

Art. 13²

¹ An action pending at the date of the coming into force of the new law is to be judged in accordance with the new law.

² The effects until the new law comes into force are governed by the old law.

IV. Action for establishing paternity
1. Pendent actions

Art. 13*a*³

¹ Where a pecuniary obligation of the father has been established either by decree of the court or an agreement made before the new law came into force and where at the time of the new law coming into force the child has not yet completed his 10th year of age, the child is entitled to bring declaratory action in order to have the child-parent relationship established within two years in accordance with the provisions of the new law.

² Where the defendant can prove that his paternity is to be excluded or is less likely than that of a third party, the claim for future maintenance expires.

2. New actions

---

[1] Inserted by cipher I of the Federal Statute of 25th June 1976, in force since 1st January 1978 (AS 1977 237 264; BBl 1974 II 1).
[2] Wording according to cipher I 2 of the Federal Statute of 25th June 1976, in force since 1st January 1978 (AS 1977 237 264; BBl 1974 II 1).
[3] Inserted by cipher I 2 of the Federal Statute of 25th June 1976, in force since 1st January 1978 (AS 1977 237 264; BBl 1974 II 1).

Art. 14

V. Guardianship

¹ Guardianship falls under the rules of the new law as from the date of the introduction of this Code.

² Where the appointment of a guardian is made before this date, the guardianship remains valid, but must be made to conform to the new law by the guardianship authorities.

³ If the appointment is made in accordance with the old law but would not be admissible according to the new law, it must be annulled, but it remains valid until this is done.

Art. 14a[1]

VI. Deprivation of liberty to secure personal assistance

¹ As soon as the change of the Federal Statute of 6th October 1978 is in force, deprivation of liberty to secure personal assistance is under the new law.

² Anyone who happens to be in an institution at that date is to be informed of his right to apply to the judge within one month.

Art. 15

D. Law of Inheritance
I. Heirs and devolution of estate

¹ The rights of inheritance arising on the death of a parent or spouse who died before the introduction of this Code are determined even after this date by the rules of the old law; the same is the case in regard to the effect of such a death on the matrimonial property system where by Cantonal Law such effect is legally inseparable from the rights of inheritance.

² This provision applies both to the heirs and the devolution of the estate.

Art. 16

II. Testamentary dispositions

¹ Where a testamentary disposition is made or revoked before the introduction of this Code, and

---

[1] Inserted by cipher II of the Federal Statute of 6th October 1978, in force since 1st January 1981 (AS **1980** 31 35; BBl **1977** **III** 1).

the disposition or its revocation was made by a testator who had testamentary capacity according to the law in force at the time, it cannot be invalidated on the ground that the testator died after the introduction of the Code and by this law would have had no testamentary capacity.

² A testamentary disposition cannot be invalidated for a defect in form where the requirements as to form have been observed which were in force at the time of the making of the disposition or at the time of the testator's death.

³ An action brought for the reduction of the amount disposed of, or in regard to, the mode of disposition is governed by the rules of this Code in all cases where the testator died after the introduction of the Code.

Art. 17

¹ Real rights in existence at the introduction of this Code are recognized under the new law, subject always to the rules on registration in the land register.

² The scope, however, of the right of ownership and of the real rights short of ownership is, after the introduction of the Code, determined by the new law except in the cases specifically excluded by this law.

³ Real rights which could not be created under the new law continue to be governed by the old law.

E. Law of Property
I. Real rights in general

Art. 18

¹ Where claims to the creation of a real right have been established before the introduction of this Code, they will be recognized as valid, provided they fulfil the requirements as to form either of the old or of the new law.

² The regulations to be issued on the mode of keeping the land register will determine the proofs required for the registration of such claims.

II. Claims to registration

³ If the scope of a real right has been determined by a legal transaction previously to the coming into force of the Code, it is not modified by the mere fact of the introduction of the new law, unless it is contrary to the provisions of this law.

Art. 19

III. Prescription and adverse possession

¹ Prescription and adverse possession are governed by the new law as from the date of the introduction of this Code.

² Where, however, the time has begun to run under the old law and the possession is such that it can be recognized by the new law also, the time that had run before the introduction of the Code is counted in for the calculation of the period required for a prescriptive title.

Art. 20[1]

IV. Special rights of ownership
1. Trees planted in another person's ground

¹ Rights of ownership existing at the date of the introduction of this Code in trees planted in another person's ground continue to be recognized by Cantonal Law.

² Cantons are entitled to limit these rights or annul them.

Art. 20bis[2]

2. Storey ownership
a. original

Storey-ownership which has been governed by the former Cantonal Law is now ruled by the provisions of this Code even if the storeys or parts of the storeys are not divided into separate business or dwelling units.

---

[1] Wording according to cipher IV of the Federal Statute of 19th December 1963, in force since 1st January 1965 (AS **1964** 993 1005; BBl **1962** II 1461).

[2] Inserted by cipher IV of the Federal Statute of 19th December 1963, in force since 1st January 1965 (AS **1964** 993 1005; BBl **1962** II 1461).

Art. 20ter [1]

¹ The Cantons are entitled to place under the new provisions for storey-ownership that storey-ownership which was entered in the land register in accordance with the forms of the law which came into force on 1st January 1912.

² The placement under the new law becomes effective as soon as the change is entered in the land register.

b. changed

Art. 20^quater [1]

The Cantons can order the correction of the land register and they can make special provisions for the procedure to place the changed storey-ownership under the provisions of the new Code and for the entry of the existing original storey-ownership in the land register.

c. Correction of the land register

Art. 21

Praedial servitudes created before the introduction of this Code continue to be valid without registration after the institution of the land register, but until they are registered they cannot be enforced as against third parties who are *bona fide* ignorant of their existence.

V. Praedial servitudes

Art. 22

¹ Mortgage deeds and other documents constituting securities on land which are already in existence at the date of the introduction of this Code continue to be valid without the necessity of being conformed to the requirements of the new law.

² The Cantons are, however, entitled to require that the documents should within a fixed limit of

VI. Securities on land
1. Recognition of existing securities

---

[1] Inserted by cipher IV of the Federal Statute of 19th December 1963, in force since 1st January 1965 (AS **1964** 993 1005; BBl **1962 II** 1461).

time be drawn afresh according to the dispositions of the Code.

Art. 23

2. Creation of new forms of real security

[1] Real security which is given after the introduction of this Code can be constituted only in one of the forms laid down in it.

[2] Until the institution of the land register, however, the forms must be used which are prescribed by the old Cantonal Law.

Art. 24

3. Cancellation of securities

[1] The cancellation or modification of a security and the release from the burden of a mortgage or charge and similar matters are, as from the date of the introduction of the Code, governed by its provisions.

[2] Until the institution of the land register, however, the formalities for these proceedings continue to be regulated by Cantonal Law.

Art. 25

4. Scope of real security

[1] The scope of any form of real security is in all cases determined by the new law.

[2] Where, however, the creditor has under a special agreement received certain definite things with the land charged, and this was a valid security when given, his rights continue in these things, even where they could not have been pledged in that way under the new law.

Art. 26

5. Rights and duties under a mortgage
a. In general

[1] The rights and duties of the creditor and debtor under a mortgage or other security created before the introduction of this Code are determined by the old law, in so far as they result from agreement between the parties.

² On the other hand, the new law applies to the rights of the parties under the mortgage which arise by operation of law and which cannot be modified by agreement.

³ Where the mortgage is created over several properties, the liabilities under it resting on the properties continue unchanged as they were under the old law.

Art. 27

The rights of the creditor during the continuance of the mortgage, in particular the right to take measures to protect his interests, as also the rights of the debtor, are in all cases of mortgages or other securities governed by the new law as from the date of its coming into force.

b. Safeguards

Art. 28

In regard to all mortgages or other securities created before the introduction of the Code, notices of repayment and transfers of securities are governed by the old law, unless the Code expressly provides otherwise.

c. Notice of repayment, transfer

Art. 29

¹ Until the registration of immovables in the land register, the order of priority among mortgages is governed by the old law.

² After the insitution of the register, the order of priority is determined according to the provisions of this Code.

6. Order of priority

Art. 30

¹ The provisions of the Code in regard to a fixed place in the register and the right of a subsequent creditor to profit by the vacant places apply as from the institution of the land register and in any case at the end of five years after the introduction

7. Place in the register

of the Code, subject, however, to any special rights secured to the creditor by agreement.[1]

[2] The Cantons can lay down further transitionary rules, but they require for their validity to be confirmed by the Federal Council.

Art. 31

8. Restrictions on the charge
a. In general

[1] The rules of this Code limiting the amount by which property can be charged according to the value of the property apply only to the charges created subsequently to the introduction of the Code.

[2] Places validly reserved in the register according to the old law can be maintained under the new law until they are erased, and the existing charges entered in these places can be renewed notwithstanding the restrictive provisions of the new law.

Art. 32

b. Continuation of the old law

[1] The provisions of the old law in regard to the maximum amount allowed for mortgage certificates shall remain in force so long as the Cantons do not set up new regulations thereon.

[2] The old law further remains in force until its repeal by the Cantons which fixes a maximum for mortgages created by agreement of the parties on land in rural districts.

Art. 33

9. Relation between real securities under old and new law

[1] The Cantonal laws passed to bring the Code into force can provide that a certain form of real security created under the old law shall either in general or in certain particulars be held equivalent to one of the forms under the new law.

---

[1] By this article a creditor loses some of the rights which he possessed by virtue of the old law, but retains those conferred upon him by special agreement on the creation of the mortgage.

² In so far as this is done the rules of this Code as from its introduction are also applied to these Cantonal forms of real security.

³ The provisions of Cantonal Law in regard to these forms of security require for their validity to be confirmed by the Federal Council.

Art. 34

¹ Pledges of movable property can, as from the date of the introduction of this Code, be made only in the forms provided by the new law. VII. Pledges
1. Form

² Where a pledge has been made before this date and in another form, it is extinguished at the expiration of a period of six months, which begins to run, if the debt is already payable, from the introduction of the Code, and, in other cases, from the time when it becomes payable or when notice of repayment can be given.

Art. 35

¹ The effect of a pledge, the rights and duties of the pledgee, the pledgor and the debtor are governed by the new law as from the date of its coming into force, even where the pledge was made before that date. 2. Effect

² An agreement made before that date, by which the pledgee is given the right to keep the thing pledged in default of payment, loses its validity as from that date.

Art. 36

¹ The right of lien given by the Code extends equally to things which were in the disposition of the creditor before its introduction. VIII. Liens

² It can also be exercised by a creditor in respect of claims which arose before this date.

³ The effect of rights of lien, even where they originated under the old law, is determined by the provisions of the Code.

Art. 37

IX. Possession

Possession is governed by the new law as from the date of the introduction of the Code.

Art. 38

X. Land register
1. Establishment

¹ The Federal Council will after consultation with the Cantons draw up a general scheme for the establishment of the land register and the land survey.

² The registries and measurements already in existence shall as far as possible be utilized as part of the new order of land registration.

Art. 39

2. Mensuration
a. Cost

¹ The cost of the survey is chiefly to be borne by the Federation.

² This provision shall apply to all mensuration work carried out after 1st January 1907.

³ The detailed adjustment of the costs will finally and conclusively be made by the Lower House of the Federal Parliament.

Art. 40

b. Relation to land register

¹ As a rule a survey must precede the establishment of the land register.

² With the consent, however, of the Federal Council, the land register can be established beforehand, where there are already sufficiently accurate descriptions of properties to be entered.

Art. 41

c. Periods allowed for the work

¹ In regard to the time within which the survey must be made, due consideration must be given to the special conditions prevailing in the Cantons and the interests existing in the different areas in them.

² The survey and the establishment of the register can take place successively in the different areas of any one Canton.

Art. 42

¹ The Federal Council must after consultation with the Cantons determine the method of making the survey in the different districts.   *d.* How survey made

² In districts where a detailed survey is not necessary, such as woods and meadow land extending over a considerable area, a simplified plan shall be ordered instead of the survey.

Art. 43

¹ On the establishment of the register the real rights already in existence shall be entered in it.   3. Registration of real rights *a.* Procedure

² For this purpose a public citation shall be made for the notification and registration of these rights.

³ Real rights that are already entered in public registers according to the requirements of the old law shall officially be entered in the land register, provided they could be created under the new law.

Art. 44

¹ Real rights created under the old law which are not entered in the land register retain their validity, but cannot be enforced against third persons who *bona fide* rely on the register.   *b.* Consequences of non-registration

² The Federation or the Cantons, however, can by legislation provide that all real rights not entered in the register shall after a certain date and previous public notice be declared extinct.

Art. 45[1]

4. Rights *in rem* that are abolished

[1] Rights *in rem* which can no longer be created under the new system of land registration, such as ownership in trees planted on another person's ground, mortgages in usufructs and such like are not entered in the land register as rights *in rem,* but are noted in an expedient manner.

[2] Where for some reason these rights have become extinct, they cannot be created anew.

Art. 46

5. Delay in establishment of register

[1] The establishment of the land register ordered by this Code can be deferred by the Cantons with the consent of the Federal Council, if Cantonal Law has provided a procedure to secure publicity and this appears sufficient with or without supplementary regulations to effect the purpose of the land register as intended by the new law.

[2] The procedure laid down by Cantonal Law which is to effect this purpose must at the same time be specified precisely.

Art. 47

6. Introduction of Property Law before establishment of land register

The Law of Property as contained in this Code shall come into force generally, even before the establishment of the land register.

Art. 48

7. Procedure laid down by Cantonal Law

[1] The Cantons can, on the introduction of the Law of Property and before the establishment of the land register, lay down the procedure for carrying out immediately the purpose of the register, such as for the drawing up of the necessary forms and for registration in registers of land, mortgages and servitudes.

---

[1] Wording according to cipher IV of the Federal Statute of 19th December 1963, in force since 1st January 1965 (AS 1964 993 1005; BBl 1962 II 1461).

² The Cantons can provide that these formalities shall even without and before the establishment of the land register have the same effect as registration in that register with respect to the creation, transfer, modification and extinction of real rights.

³ On the other hand such registration has no effect in favour of third persons *bona fide* relying on it, so long as the land register itself has not been established in a Canton or its place is not taken by some other equivalent form of registration.[1]

Art. 49

F. Periods of limitation

¹ Where the Code introduces a period of limitation of actions of five years or more, the time that has already elapsed in any one case before the coming into force of the new law will be counted in, but at least two years longer must elapse as from that date before the period is held to have expired.

² Shorter periods of limitation of actions or of expiration of rights fixed by the Code begin to run only as from its introduction.

³ In other respects the limitation of actions is governed as from that date by the provisions of the new law.

Art. 50

G. Form of contracts

Contratcts which were made before the introduction of the Code continue to be valid even where their form is not in accordance with the provisions of the new law.

---

[1] *i.e.* only the proper land register or its equivalent set up by the Cantons with the consent of the Federal Council is held to protect the rights of third persons who rely on the effectiveness of registration. In other cases a third person even if *bona fide* cannot acquire a good title where the transferor had no title.

Chapter II: Introductory and Transitionary Provisions

Art. 51

A. Cantonal Law repealed

In the absence of some provision of the Federal Law to the contrary, all Private Cantonal Law is repealed as from the introduction of this Code.

Art. 52

B. Supplementary Cantonal regulations
I. Rights and duties of Cantons

¹ The Cantons will make the necessary regulations to supplement this Code, such as in regard to the competence of the authorities and the organization of the registries of civil status, the guardianship authorities and the land registries.

² In so far as these supplementary Cantonal regulations are required for the application of this Code, the Cantons are bound to make them, and they can issue them in the form of orders.

³ Such regulations require for their validity the confirmation of the Federal Council.

Art. 53

II. Orders in default of Cantonal regulations

¹ Where a Canton does not make the necessary regulations in time, the Federal Council in the meantime will issue the required ordinances in the place of the Canton and notify the Lower House of the Federal Parliament of this fact.

² Where a Canton does not avail itself of its power to make supplementary regulations and they are not necessarily required, the provisions of the Code are applied.

Art. 54

C. Designation of competent authorities

¹ Where the Code speaks of a competent authority the Cantons determine whether already existing authorities, and if so which of them, shall be competent, or whether a new authority shall be constituted.

² Where the Code does not expressly state whether the authority is to be the court or an administrative body, the Cantons can determine which

of the two, judicial or administrative, shall be the competent authority for the purpose.

³ The Cantons regulate the procedure to be adopted before the competent authority.

Art. 55

¹ Each Canton determines within its own borders the mode in which a document is to be duly authenticated.   D. Form of authentication of documents

² The Cantons further have to make provisions for the drawing up of authenticated documents in a foreign language.

Art. 56[1]

Until the passing of a Federal Statute in regard to concessions of water rights, the following rule applies: E. Concession of water rights

Concessions of rights in public waters, if made to extend over thirty years at least or an indefinite period and not constituted into servitude for the benefit of a dominant property, can be entered in the land register as independent and permanent rights.

Art. 57[2]   F.–H.

Art. 58[3]

With the introduction of this Code the Federal Statute of 11th April 1189 on Bankruptcy and Execution[4] is changed as follows: J. Execution of debts and bankruptcy

...[5]

---

[1] See today art. 59 of the Federal Statute of 22nd December 1916 relating to the Use of Public Waters (SR **721.80**).
[2] Annulled by art. 53 paragraph 1 lit. b of the Federal Statute of 8th November 1934 relating to Banks and Savings Banks.
[3] The last four articles have been given new numbers as a consequence of the annulment of the original articles 58 and 59, in accordance with cipher I of the Transitory Provisions of the Code of Obligations, in force since 1st January 1912 (SR **220**).
[4] SR 281.1.
[5] See text in the Federal Statute mentioned. For the wording of arts. 132bis, 141 paragraph 3 and 258 paragraph 4 see AS **24** 233 Final Title art. 60.

Art. 59[1]

K. Application of Swiss and foreign laws

[1] The Federal Statute of 25th June 1891 relating to the Civil Legal Situation of Holders of Permits for Permanent or Temporary Residence[2] remains in force and orders the legal situation of Swiss citizens abroad and foreigners in Switzerland; this also applies where deviating Cantonal Law is applicable.

[2] ...[2]

[3] The following insertion is added to the Federal Statute of 25th June 1891[3]:

...[4]

Art. 60[5]

L. Annulment of the Provisions of the Federal Civil Code

[1] With the coming into force of this Code all provisions made by the Federation in regard to Civil Law that are contradictory are annulled.

[2] In particular there are annulled:

the Federal Statute of 24th December 1874 relating to the Evidence and Registration of Civil Status and Marriages;[6]

the Federal Statute of 22nd June 1881 relating to Personal Capacity;[7]

the Federal Statute of 14th June 1881 of the Code of Obligations.[8]

---

[1] The last four articles have been given new numbers as a consequence of the annulment of the original articles 58 and 59, in accordance with cipher I of the Transitory Provisions of the Code of Obligations, in force since 1st January 1912 (SR 220).
[2] Annulled by cipher I 2 of the Federal Statute of 5th October 1984, in force since 1st January 1988 (BBl **1979 II** 1191).
[3] **SR 211.435.1.**
[4] This refers to arts. 7a–7i, inserted in the Federal Statute mentioned.
[5] Wording according to cipher I of the Transitory Provisions of the Code of Obligations, in force since 1st January 1912 (SR 220).
[6] AS 1 506.
[7] AS 5 556.
[8] AS 5 635, 11 490; SR **221.229.1** art. 103 paragraph 1.

³ The following specific Federal Statutes remain in force: those relating to Railways, Steam-boats, Postal, Telegraph and Telephone Services, the Encumbrance and Enforced Liquidation of Railways, those for Work in Factories and the Reliability Stemming from Running Factories and other Enterprises as well as all Federal Statutes relating to objects of the Law of Obligation which were issued apart from the Federal Statute of 14th June 1881 relating to the Law of Obligation.¹

Art. 61²

¹ This Code comes into force on 1st January 1912.
² With the consent of both Houses of the Federal Parliament the Federal Council is entitled to put individual provisions into force before this date.

M. Final provision

---

¹ AS 5 635, 11 490.
² The last four articles have been given new numbers as a consequence of the annulment of the original articles 58 and 59, in accordance with cipher I of the Transitory Provisions of the Code of Obligations, in force since 1st January 1912 (SR 220).

Appendix 1

1. **Titles V and VI in the wording according to the Federal Statute of 10th December 1907, in force since 1st January 1912[1] until 31 December 1987 (effective until the coming into force of the Federal Statute of 5th October 1984 on 1st January 1988)**

Title V: General Effects of Marriage

Art. 159

A. Rights and duties
I. Of husband and wife

[1] The solemnization of a marriage creates a conjugal union between the parties.

[2] They thereby mutually bind themselves to cooperate with each other in safeguarding the interests of the union and in caring and providing for the children.

[3] They owe each other fidelity and assistance.

Art. 160

II. Of husband

[1] The husband is the head of the conjugal union.

[2] He chooses the place of abode and duly provides for the maintenance of wife and children.

Art. 161

III. Of wife

[1] The wife acquires the husband's surname and citizenship.

[2] She must to the extent of her ability assist him by word and deed in his effort to maintain the home.

[3] She has the management of the household affairs.

---

[1] AS 24 233, 27 207 and BS 2 3, BBl **1904** IV 1, **1907** VI 367.

Art. 162

¹ The husband represents the conjugal union.¹

² He is also personally liable for his own acts whatever may be the system under which the matrimonial property is held.

B. Representation of conjugal union
I. By husband

Art. 163

¹ The wife has, for the purpose of providing the current necessaries for the home, the same authority as the husband to represent the conjugal union.

² The husband is personally liable for the contracts of the wife with third parties which they have reason to believe are within the scope of her authority.

II. By wife
1. In ordinary cases
a. Scope

Art. 164

¹ Where the wife has abused her statutory powers of agency in household matters, or where she shows herself incapable of exercising them, the husband can revoke them altogether or restrict them within certain limits.

² Such an act of revocation or limitation of the wife's powers is not binding on innocent third parties until it is published by the competent authority.

b. Revocation

Art. 165

¹ At the instance of the wife the court will reinstate her in her former powers by cancelling the husband's revocation or limitation of them, where she can prove that this was not justified.

² This reinstatement must be published if the husband's act was published.

c. Reinstatement

Art. 166

The wife can exercise more extensive powers only with the express or tacit consent of the husband.

2. In exceptional cases

---

¹ *i.e.* he binds the conjugal union by his acts in the same way as an agent his principal where he is acting for the principal.

Art. 167

C. Trade or profession of wife

¹ With the express or tacit consent of the husband, the wife has the right to engage in a trade or profession whatever may be their matrimonial property system.

² Where the husband refuses his consent, the wife can be authorised by the court to engage in a trade or profession, where she can prove that this is in the interest of the conjugal union or of the family.[1]

Art. 168

D. Capacity of wife to bring and defend actions

¹ The wife can, under any of the matrimonial property systems, bring or defend actions in her own name.

² Where, however, the action is with a third party and regards her unreserved property, the husband alone can bring or defend it.[2]

Art. 169

E. Protective measures
I. In general

¹ Where one of the spouses neglects his duties to the conjugal union or brings danger, dishonour or material injury upon the other, the injured party can apply to the judge for his intervention.

² The judge will seek to recall the offender to his duties and if this has no effect will take the measures that are necessary and provided by law for the protection of the conjugal union.

Art. 170

II. Life in common suspended

¹ Where the health, reputation or material prosperity of either husband or wife is imperilled by

---

[1] *i.e.* in the interest of husband and wife and the matrimonial property, or of the other members of the family not being the husband or wife, *e.g.* their children or the near relations of the husband or wife who are dependent on either of them.

[2] This property is defined in art. 195 below. It belongs to the wife and yet is under the husband's management, and therefore it is the husband and not the wife who must bring and defend actions in regard to it.

a continuance of life in common, the injured party is entitled to live a separate life so long as the danger persists.

² After the presentation of a petition for a divorce or for judicial separation, both the husband and the wife are entitled to live a separate life pending the proceedings.

³ Where there are good grounds for the suspension of life in common, the court must, at the instance of either husband or wife, determine the amount of the contributions to be made by one of the parties for the maintenance of the other.

Art. 171

Where the husband neglects his duties to his family, the court can, under whatever system the matrimonial property may be held, order the debtors of the spouses to make all or part of their payments to the wife alone.

III. Orders to debtors

Art. 172

Measures taken by the court shall, at the instance of either husband or wife, be discontinued as soon as the grounds for them have ceased to exist.

IV. Discontinuance of measures

Art. 173

¹ During the continuance of the marriage no execution is allowed at the instance of husband or wife on the property of the other except in the cases provided by law.[1]

² The deprivation of rights, which may be imposed on a debtor where his property seized in execution has proved insufficient or where he has

V. Execution on property of spouses
1. General rule

---

[1] *i.e.* neither husband nor wife can satisfy any claim he or she may have against the other whether under contract or otherwise out of the property of that other. The exceptions are contained in arts. 175–6.

become bankrupt, cannot be imposed on either husband or wife in respect of any loss suffered by the one at the hands of the other.[1]

Art. 174

2. Exceptions
a. Where a married person is a debtor

Where a third party is prosecuting a married person for debt, the latter's spouse can put in a claim in the execution on his property or in his bankruptcy.

Art. 175

b. Where a married person is a creditor

[1] Where execution has been levied on the property of a married person and it has proved insufficient, his claims against his spouse fall into his assets and can be attached.

[2] Where a married person becomes bankrupt, his claims against his spouse form part of the assets in his bankruptcy.

Art. 176

c. For the separation of property and recovery of maintenance

[1] Execution can always be levied for the purpose of enforcing the separation of matrimonial property required by law or ordered by the court.

[2] Similarly for the purpose of recovering contributions due by a husband or wife for the maintenance of the other under an order of the court.

Art. 177

F. Legal transactions between husband and wife and for benefit of husband

[1] A husband can enter into any legal transaction with his wife and the wife with her husband.

[2] Transactions, however, entered into between them, which relate to the wife's unreserved property or to property held in common by the husband and

---

[1] *i.e.* even in those cases where the law allows execution on the property of husband or wife by the other, this section prevents the legal consequences that may follow under the law of execution and bankruptcy, which is considered to be Public Law and is governed by the Federal Statute of 11th April 1889 relating to Execution and Bankruptcy.

wife, are valid only with the consent of the guardianship board.

³ The same rule applies to obligations which are incurred by the wife with third parties for the benefit of the husband.

Title VI: Matrimonial Property Law

Chapter I: General Provisions

Art. 178

Parties on marriage are placed under the marital system, unless they have themselves provided otherwise by a marriage covenant, or the provisions for the exceptional system are held to apply.¹

A. Ordinary system

---

¹ The Code provides three systems for holding matrimonial property:
  a. The regular system which operates unless otherwise provided by the parties or by law, by which the wife's property with the exception of her separate estate falls into the usufruct of the husband; the wife remains the owner of it, except of her perishable property which falls under the ownership of her husband, but the husband takes all the profits from it. Hence it has been termed the "marital system" (arts. 194–214).
  b. The system of "community of property", by which both the husband's and the wife's property, with the exception of separate estate, belong to the two parties in common. Normally their shares in the total are equal, but they can be fixed otherwise in the marriage covenant. The husband administers it but profits are shared (arts. 215–228).
  c. The system of "separate estates", called the "exceptional" system, by which each party retains his or her own property and its management. This applies in certain cases determined by the Code in arts. 182 *et seq.* or where the parties have so provided in the covenant.
The parties can vary the first two systems in certain particulars, or adopt the third system by making a covenant. Marriage covenants are dealt with in the following sections.
For greater clearness the following glossary is appended:
Eheliches Vermögen, *biens matrimoniaux,* matrimonial property.
Güterrecht or **Güterstand,** *régime matrimonial,* matrimonial property system (or paraphrased as: system of holding matrimonial property).
Eingebrachtes Gut, *apports,* unreserved property. This is the property of the husband or the wife which does not remain the separate

Art. 179

B. Marriage covenants
I. Choice of system

¹ The parties can make an ante-nuptial or a post-nuptial marriage covenant.

² They must in the covenant adopt one of the systems provided by the Code for the holding of matrimonial property.¹

³ Post-nuptial covenants cannot prejudice the existing rights of third parties over the property of the spouses.

Art. 180

II. Capacity of parties

¹ Only those persons who have discretion can make, modify or rescind a marriage covenant.

² Minors and persons under a committee must have the consent of their guardian or committee.

Art. 181

III. Form required

¹ A marriage covenant is valid only where it is made by a duly authenticated instrument signed by the parties and, if necessary, by their guardian or committee; the same rules apply to a modification or the rescission of a covenant.

² Post-nuptial covenants must in addition be submitted for approval to the guardianship board.

³ Marriage covenants are operative as regards third persons when the rules for the registration of matrimonial property have been observed.

---

estate of the owner, but falls under the system of holding matrimonial property obtaining in any given case.
Sondergut, *biens réservés,* separate estate.
Güterverbindung, *union des biens,* marital system.
Gütergemeinschaft, *communauté des biens,* system of community of property.
Gesamtgut, *communauté,* common property.
Gütertrennung, *séparation de biens,* system of separate estates.
Ehevertrag, *contrat de mariage,* marriage covenant.

¹ *i.e.* either one of the systems as they stand or with the variations allowed by the Code.

Art. 182

¹ Where on the bankruptcy of either husband or wife a creditor is not paid in full, the matrimonial property will by operation of law fall under the system of separate estates.

² Where a creditor holds a certificate of unsatisfied claims[1] against a debtor and the latter is about to marry, the debtor himself or his future spouse can set up the system of separate estates by having this system entered in the matrimonial property register before the solemnization of the marriage.[2]

C. Exceptional system
I. Separation of estates by operation of law

Art. 183

The court shall make an order for the separation of estates at the instance of the wife:

1. where the husband fails to provide for the maintenance of his wife and children;

2. where he fails to give the required security for his wife's unreserved property;[3]

3. where the husband is insolvent or the property held in common is overcharged with liabilities.

II. Judicial separation of estates
1. At instance of wife

Art. 184

The court shall make an order for the separation of estates at the instance of the husband:

1. where the wife is insolvent;

2. where the wife without material grounds refuses to give the husband her consent which is required by law or under the marriage covenant for his disposal of the matrimonial property;[4]

2. At instance of husband

---

[1] These certificates are issued under the provisions of the Federal Statute of 11th April 1889 on Bankruptcy and Execution.
[2] These provisions are clearly intended to relieve the party to the marriage who has not incurred the liabilities that have not been discharged; for where the property is held separately, only the debtor himself and his own separate estate is liable for the debt.
[3] See art. 205.
[4] Her consent is required by law in the cases provided by arts. 202 and 217 below.

Art. 185

3. At instance of creditors

The court shall make an order for the separation of estates at the instance of a creditor who has not been satisfied in full by his execution on the goods of either husband or wife.[2]

Art. 186

III. Commencement of separation of estates

[1] The separation of estates resulting from bankruptcy takes effect from the presentation of the certificates of unsatisfied claims; but in respect of any property that may have accrued to the husband or wife by way of succession or otherwise since the declaration of bankruptcy, the separation relates back to the date of such accrual.

[2] The separation of estates by order of the court relates back to the date of application to the court.

[3] The separation of estates resulting from bankruptcy or from an order of the court is notified officially for the purpose of registration to the registrar of the matrimonial property register.

Art. 187

IV. Determination of system of separate estates

[1] The system of separate estates set up as the result of bankruptcy or insufficiency of assets in the case of execution for debt is not determined by the mere fact that the creditors have since been paid in full.

---

[1] And the husband finds it less burdensome to forego his rights over his wife's unreserved property than comply with her demand.

[2] This would generally happen where the creditor has sued the wife under art. 207 and has not been able to recover the debt, and now wishes to realise on the claims which she possesses against her husband for compensation for the perishable part of her unreserved property. See art. 201.

(Note: Item 3 at top reads: "3. where the wife has demanded security for her unreserved property.[1]")

² The court can, however, at the instance of the husband or the wife order the resumption of the previous system which had temporarily been suspended.

³ This decree is notified officially for the purpose of registration to the registrar of the matrimonial property register.

Art. 188

¹ Neither the separation of estates nor any modification of an existing system shall place beyond the reach of the creditors of the husband or wife or conjugal union any property against which they had the right to proceed for the satisfaction of their debts.

D. Modification of system
I. Rights of creditors secured

² Where any such property has passed to the husband or wife, he or she becomes personally liable to pay the said creditors, but can be freed from such liability by proof that the property received is of insufficient value to satisfy their claims.[1]

³ The amount which the wife recovers by claiming in her husband's bankruptcy or joining in an execution on his property cannot be touched by the husband's creditors unless they are also at the same time the wife's creditors.

Art. 189

¹ Where the separation of estates takes place during the marriage, the matrimonial property falls into the separate estate of the husband and of the wife respectively; but this provision shall not prejudice the existing rights of creditors.

II. Division of property on separation of estates

² Increments are divided between the husband and wife according to the rules of the system which existed before; any depreciation is borne by the husband, unless he can prove that it has been caused by the act of the wife.

---

[1] *i.e.* the husband or wife can free himself or herself from any personal liability beyond the value of the property received.

³ Where pending the division the husband retains the control of property belonging to the wife, he must at her request give her security for it.

Art. 190

E. Separate estates
I. How they arise
1. In general

¹ Separate estates arise either under a marriage covenant or under a gift from a third person or by operation of law.

² The compulsory portion which a married person can claim by law on the death of a relative cannot be assigned to him as separate estate.¹

Art. 191

2. By operation of law

The following property is by law separate estate:

1. articles which are exclusively intended for the personal use of a married person;

2. property belonging to a married woman which she uses in her trade or profession;

3. earnings of a married woman outside her domestic sphere.

Art. 192

II. Effect

¹ Property which forms part of the separate estate of a married person is subject to the provisions relating to the system of separate estates, and in particular to the provision on the wife's liability to contribute to the maintenance of the home.²

² The wife must, where necessary, use her earnings to defray household expenses.

Art. 193

III. Burden of proof

The burden of proving that any property is separate estate is on the husband or wife who alleges it.

---

¹ For the meaning of "compulsory portions" see arts. 471 *et seq.*
 The reason for this provision is that the portion must not be fettered in any way.
² See art. 246, below, on the wife's liability to contribute towards household expenses.

Chapter II: Marital System

Art. 194

¹ All property belonging to the parties at the date of their marriage as well as their after-acquired property becomes matrimonial property.

² The wife's separate estate is excepted.[1]

A. Proprietary rights
I. Matrimonial property

Art. 195

¹ That part of the matrimonial property which belonged to the wife at the date of the marriage or which comes to her during marriage by succession or other gratuitous title constitutes her unreserved property and remains in her ownership.

² The husband is owner of his unreserved property and of all the other matrimonial property which does not form part of the wife's property.

³ All the wife's income as from the date of accrual and the natural fruits of her property as from the date of their severance, fall into the ownership of the husband, subject always to the provisions in regard to her separate estate.

II. Rights of ownership of husband and wife

Art. 196

¹ The burden of proving that any property is the unreserved property of the wife is on the husband or wife who asserts this.[2]

² Property acquired during marriage with the proceeds obtained from the sale of property belonging

III. Burden of proof

---

[1] *i.e.* does not become "matrimonial property" at all. As to what is included in her separate estate see arts. 190–192 above.

[2] Under the marital system of holding matrimonial property most of the property of the wife as well as the husband's own property falls under his management. Now third persons dealing with him are rightly entitled to presume that the property which he alone administers is his own. And, therefore, it is for the married person, generally in the wife's interest, to prove that the property in question is not the husband's own, but merely under his management.

to the wife or received in exchange for it is deemed to be her unreserved property.

Art. 197

IV. Inventory
1. Its form and validity

¹ Both the husband and the wife can at any time require that a public inventory be made of their respective unreserved properties.

² Where this inventory is made within six months from the falling in of the property, it is by law presumed to be correct.[1]

Art. 198

2. Its effect

¹ Where a valuation of the property is annexed to the inventory and is thereby duly authenticated, this valuation determines as between the husband and wife the extent of their mutual liabilities of compensation for losses.[2]

² Where property has during the marriage been sold *bona fide* below its estimated value, the price realised shall be taken to be its true value.

Art. 199

V. Ownership of husband in wife's unreserved property

The husband and wife can, subject to the rules on marriage covenants and within six months from the falling in of the wife's unreserved property, append to the valuation of the property a provision, by which the ownership in it shall pass to the husband at the value fixed for it and the husband's

---

[1] *i.e.* from the date at which the property becomes matrimonial property. Thus if it already belonged to the wife at her marriage, it would become matrimonial property at the solemnization of the marriage, unless specially reserved by her as her separate estate.

[2] *i.e.* as between husband and wife the valuation is binding, so that if any of the wife's property depreciates in value under the husband's management, he will have to pay her or her heirs compensation for the loss suffered on the basis of the valuation. But this valuation does not affect the rights of third persons, for if it did it might open the door to fraud on creditors.

liability to the wife in respect of the property be immutably fixed by that valuation.¹

Art. 200

¹ The husband administers all the matrimonial property.

² He bears the cost of administration.

³ The wife can administer it only within the limits of her power to act as the agent of the conjugal union.²

B. Administration, user and alienation
I. Administration

Art. 201

¹ The husband has the user of the wife's unreserved property and incurs in respect thereof the liabilities of a usufructuary.

² This liability is not increased by the valuation in the inventory of the property.

³ The wife's cash, her other fungible property and her negotiable securities that are not specifically marked as her own property are vested in the husband as owner; for these things he becomes liable to pay her their value.³

II. User

---

[1] Under the marital system the husband does not become owner of the whole of his wife's unreserved property, but only of certain parts of it, as laid down in art. 195 above. This article (199) allows the parties under certain safeguards to modify the system by passing the ownership in her unreserved property to the husband, so that he becomes owner of the whole of her property with the exception always of her separate estate. He then becomes liable, on the dissolution of the marriage, to refund to her or her heirs the value of the property transferred to him: this value is based on the valuation agreed upon at the date of the transfer and no subsequent depreciation or increase in value will modify his liabilities.

[2] See arts. 163 and 166 above.

[3] Thus a negotiable security belonging to the wife can remain her property if it is marked with her name or is otherwise earmarked as her own, and retained in her possession.

Art. 202

III. Alienation
1. Rights of husband

¹ The husband cannot, without his wife's consent, dispose of her unreserved property which has not passed into his ownership; but her consent is not required where the act in question is merely incident to the ordinary administration of the property.

² Third persons can, however, presume that her consent has been given, unless they know or ought to have known that it was not given, or unless the fact that the property in question belongs to the wife can reasonably be taken to be a matter of common knowledge.¹

Art. 203

2. Rights of wife
a. In general

The wife has the right to dispose of matrimonial property within the limits of her power to represent the conjugal union.

Art. 204

b. Disclaimer of an inheritance

¹ The wife cannot disclaim an inheritance except with the consent of her husband.

² Where he refuses his consent, she can appeal to the guardianship board.

Art. 205

C. Security for wife's property

¹ The husband must at all times at his wife's request inform her as to the condition of her unreserved property.

² The wife can at any time demand security from her husband.

---

[1] The presumption that her consent was given where required is a *presumptio juris*. It can be rebutted by proof that the third person in favour of whom the presumption is raised was aware, or is taken from the circumstances to have been aware, that the wife as a matter of fact did not give her consent. The question whether the third person should have known this fact is for the judge to decide, as also the question whether the ownership of the property is common knowledge and whether, therefore, the third person was put on inquiry as to the wife's consent.

³ The right of a creditor under the Federal Statute of 11th April 1889 on Bankruptcy and Execution to annul the security is, however, reserved.¹

Art. 206

The husband is liable:² D. Liability
1. for his own ante-nuptial debts; I. Of husband
2. for his own debts incurred during marriage;
3. for the debts incurred by the wife as agent for the conjugal union.

Art. 207

¹ The wife is liable to the extent of her whole property, with no regard to the rights conferred upon the husband by their matrimonial property system: II. Of wife
1. To extent of whole property

1. for her ante-nuptial debts;
2. for the debts which she incurred with her husband's consent, or for his benefit with the sanction of the guardianship board;
3. for the debts which she incurred in the ordinary pursuit of her trade or profession;
4. for the debts which burden an inheritance that has passed to her;
5. for the obligations arising from her unlawful acts.

² The wife is liable for debts incurred either by herself or by her husband for the maintenance of the home only where her husband is insolvent.

---

¹ Under arts. 285 *et seq.* of the Federal Statute of 11th April 1889 on Bankruptcy and Execution, creditors in bankruptcy have the right to void gifts and certain other specified transactions made or entered into by the bankrupt under certain circumstances. This article (205) reserves this right in the case of the husband's bankruptcy.
² *i.e.* to the extent of the whole of his property, whether unreserved or forming part of his separate estate.

Art. 208

2. To extent of her separate estate

¹ The wife is liable during and after the marriage to the extent of her separate estate only:

1. for debts which she incurred while limiting her liability to her separate estate;

2. for debts which she incurred without her husband's consent;

3. for debts which she incurred while exceeding her authority as agent of the conjugal union.

² These provisions shall not prejudice any claims for money had and received for the use of the plaintiff.

Art. 209

E. Compensation
I. When recoverable

¹ The husband and wife can claim compensation the one from the other where debts payable out of the unreserved property of the one have been paid out of that of the other; but subject to the statutory exceptions this compensation is recoverable only after the determination of the marital system.

² Where debts payable out of the wife's separate estate have been paid out of matrimonial property, or where debts payable out of matrimonial property have been paid out of her separate estate, compensation can be recovered during the continuance of the marriage.

Art. 210

II. Bankruptcy of husband and execution for debt
1. Rights of wife

¹ Where the husband has become bankrupt or execution has been levied on his property, the wife can put in a claim for compensation for the loss of any part of her unreserved property.

² Counterclaims of the husband are set off against the wife's claims.

³ The wife can recover possession as owner of that part of her property which is still intact.

Art. 211

¹ Where, by resuming possession of her property or obtaining security against the loss of it, the wife is not guaranteed to the extent of one half of the value of her unreserved property, her claim in respect of the remainder of that half will be given priority according to the Federal Statute of 11th April 1889 on Bankruptcy and Execution.

² This right of priority cannot be ceded or renounced in favour of any creditor.

2. Right of priority

Art. 212

¹ On the death of the wife her unreserved property passes to her heirs, subject, however, to the husband's rights of succession to her.

² The husband is liable to the wife's heirs to make good all losses for which he is responsible; any compensation due to him from his wife is deducted.

F. Determination of system
I. Death of wife

Art. 213

On the death of the husband, the wife's unreserved property is restored to her and she can claim compensation from his heirs for any losses suffered.

II. Death of husband

Art. 214

¹ Where on the division of the unreserved properties of the husband and the wife there is found to be a balance due to profits made on them, this belongs as to one third thereof to the wife or her heirs and as to the remainder to the husband or his heirs.

² If there is a deficit, it is borne by the husband or his heirs, provided there is no evidence that it was caused by the wife.

³ Any other arrangement in regard to profits or deficit can be agreed upon in the marriage covenant.

III. Profits and losses

Chapter III: Community of Property

Art. 215

A. General community
I. Matrimonial property

¹ Under the general system of community of property all the property and income of the husband and the wife are brought into the common property of the two parties; in this both have undivided ownership.

² Neither party can dispose of his share in it.

³ The burden of proof lies on the husband or wife who alleges that a certain property does not form part of the common stock.

Art. 216

II. Administration and alienation
1. Administration

¹ The husband administers the common property.

² The cost of administration is borne out of the common property.

³ The wife has the right of administration only within the limits of her power to represent the conjugal union.

Art. 217

2. Alienation
a. Of common property

¹ Any act which purports to dispose of any part of the common property and which is not merely incident to its ordinary administration requires for its validity the co-operation or consent of both husband and wife.

² Third persons can, however, presume that this consent was given, unless they knew or ought to have known that it was not given, or unless the fact that the property in question is common property can reasonably be taken to be a matter of general knowledge.

Art. 218

b. Disclaimer of an inheritance

¹ Neither husband nor wife can during marriage disclaim an inheritance without the consent of the other.

² Where the consent is refused, an appeal lies to the guardianship board.

Art. 219

The husband is liable personally[1] and to the extent of the common property:

1. for the ante-nuptial debts of himself and his wife;
2. for debts incurred by the wife as agent of the conjugal union;
3. for all other debts incurred during marriage either by the husband or, if in respect of the common property, by the wife.

III. Liability
1. Of husband

Art. 220

¹ Liability rests on the wife personally and on the common property:

1. for her ante-nuptial debts;
2. for the debts which she incurred with her husband's consent, or for his benefit with the sanction of the guardianship board;
3. for the debts which she incurred in the ordinary course of her trade or profession;
4. for the debts which burden an inheritance that has passed to her;
5. for the obligations arising from her unlawful acts.

² The wife is personally liable for the debts incurred by her husband or herself for the maintenance of the home only in so far as the common property is insufficient to meet them.

³ She is not liable personally for the other debts payable out of the common property.[2]

2. Of wife
a. Personally and to extent of common property

---

[1] *i.e.* to the extent of his property not brought into the common stock.
[2] Cf. this section with art. 207 which relates to the wife's liability under the marital system.

Art. 221

b. To extent of her separate estate

¹ The wife is liable during and after marriage to the extent of her separate estate only:

1. for debts which she incurred while limiting her liability to her separate estate;

2. for debts which she incurred without her husband's consent;

3. for debts which she incurred while exceeding her authority as the agent of the conjugal union.

² These provisions shall not prejudice any claims for money had and received for the use of the plaintiff.

Art. 222

3. Execution for debt

During the continuance of the system of community of property all executions for the debts payable out of the common property shall be levied against the husband.

Art. 223

IV. Compensation
1. In general

¹ Where debts payable out of the common property have been paid out of it, there is no claim for compensation as between the husband and wife.

² Where, however, debts payable out of the common property have been paid out of separate estate or debts payable out of separate estate have been paid out of the common property, claims for compensation arise and can be made even during the continuance of the marriage.

Art. 224

2. Claims of wife

¹ In the bankruptcy of the husband or execution levied on the common property the wife can put in a claim for the amount of her unreserved property; her claim up to one half of this amount will have the priority accorded to it by the Bankruptcy and Execution Act.

² This right of priority cannot be ceded or renounced in favour of any creditor.

Art. 225

¹ On the death of the husband or wife, half the common property devolves on the survivor. V. Dissolution of community
1. Division of property
a. By operation of law

² The other half passes to the heirs of the deceased, subject, however, to the statutory right of inheritance of the survivor.

³ Where the survivor has lost his right of inheritance, he has no greater claim to any of the common property than he would have in the case of divorce.¹

Art. 226

¹ The parties can in the marriage covenant provide for a division of the property other than in equal shares. b. By marriage covenant

² The descendants of the deceased husband or wife can claim the fourth part of the common property as at the date of his death and this right cannot be taken away from them.

Art. 227

¹ Where the husband is the survivor, he remains personally liable for all the debts payable out of the common property. 2. Liability of survivor

² Where the wife is the survivor, she can by disclaiming her share of the common property free herself from all liability for those debts for which she is not personally liable.

³ Where she accepts her share, she remains liable, but she can limit her liability by proving that what she has received is insufficient to discharge the debts in full.²

---

¹ For the ways in which the statutory right of inheritance can be lost see art. 540.

² *i.e.* she need only pay the debts covered by the assets: she can pay the creditors in the order of their application and stop payment as soon as the assets are exhausted; or else she can have an inventory made of the assets and pay the creditors at a percentage of what is owed.

Art. 228

3. Allocation of unreserved property

On the division of the matrimonial property, the surviving husband or wife can demand as the whole part of his share the return of his unreserved property.

Art. 229

B. Continuation of community
I. Conditions

[1] The surviving husband or wife can continue the system of community of property with the children of the marriage.[1]

[2] Where the children are under age this continuation must be approved by the guardianship board.

[3] Where this continuation has taken place, rights of inheritance arising from the death of the husband or wife cannot be enforced until the determination of the system.

Art. 230

II. Extent of community

[1] The community of property thus continued extends not only to the property previously held in common, but also to the income and the earnings of the parties to it, with the exception of separate estate.

[2] Any property that comes to the children or their surviving parent by succession or other gratuitous title during the continuation of the community is, in the absence of a contrary provision, held to form part of their separate estate.

[3] Execution for debt is excluded as between the parties to this community in the same way as between the husband and wife.

---

[1] *i.e.* where it seems more beneficial to the surviving parent and his children, the division of the common property is deferred until a later date, and in the meantime the system of community is artificially continued.

Art. 231

¹ Where the children are under age, the surviving parent administers and acts on behalf of the continued community.

² Where the children are of full age, other provisions can be made by agreement between the parties.

III. Administration and representation

Art. 232

¹ The surviving parent can at any time dissolve the community.

² The children who are of full age can at any time either singly or collectively withdraw from the community.

³ Where the children are under age, the guardianship board can withdraw on their behalf.

IV. Dissolution
1. By the parties

Art. 233

¹ The continued community is determined by operation of law:

1. by the death or re-marriage of the surviving parent;
2. by his bankruptcy or that of the children.

² Where only one of the children becomes bankrupt, the other parties can demand his exclusion.

³ Where the father is the survivor and he becomes bankrupt, or execution for debt is levied on the common property, the children step into the place of their deceased mother.

2. By operation of law

Art. 234

¹ A creditor, who has not been satisfied in full in the execution levied for the debt of the parent or of one of the children, can apply to the court for an order to dissolve the continued community.

² Where the application is made by a creditor of one of the children, the other parties to the community can demand the exclusion of the child.

3. By order of the court

Art. 235

4. By the marriage or death of a child

¹ Where one of the children marries, the other parties to the community can demand his exclusion.

² Where one of the children dies leaving issue, the other parties can demand the exclusion of his issue.

³ Where he dies without leaving issue, his share remains in the common stock, without prejudice, nevertheless, to the rights of his heirs who are not parties to the community.

Art. 236

5. Division

¹ On the determination of the continued community or the exclusion of one of the children, the division of the common property or the allocation of the excluded child's share is effected according to the state of the property at the time of the determination or exclusion.

² The surviving parent retains his right of inheritance to the shares that are allocated to the individual children.

³ The division and allocation must not be effected at an unreasonable time.¹

Art. 237

C. Limited community
I. With certain property as separate estate

¹ The husband and wife can modify the general system of community of property by agreeing in the marriage covenant that certain specific items of property or certain kinds of property, such as immovables, shall be excluded from the common stock.

² The property so excluded is governed by the provisions in regard to the system of separate estates.

---

¹ *i.e.* the system can be terminated at any time but the actual division of the property must wait, if necessary, for a date which suits the parties concerned. This date is like other questions of what is fair and reasonable in the discretion of the court.

Art. 238

¹ The husband and wife can agree in the marriage covenant that the property belonging to the wife and excluded from the common property shall fall under the marital system.

² This agreement is presumed by law where the wife in the marriage covenant gives her husband the administration and use of her property.[1]

II. With certain property under marital system

Art. 239

¹ The husband and wife can agree in the marriage covenant that the common property shall consist only of "voluntarily acquired" property.[2]

² "Voluntarily acquired" property here includes income received and property earned by the husband or wife during marriage, excluding property obtained by way of compensation or exchange for unreserved property: it is governed by the rules of the system of community of property.

³ The unreserved property of the husband or wife, whether it belonged to them at the date of marriage or devolved upon them during marriage, is governed by the rules of the marital system.

III. Community of "voluntarily acquired" property
1. Its purport

Art. 240

¹ Where on the dissolution of the community, the property is shown to have increased in value, the

2. Profits and losses

---

[1] Because this act on the part of the wife is held to indicate her intention to submit such property to the marital system.
[2] "Voluntarily acquired property" has been chosen to translate the German *Errungenschaft* and the French *acquets*. Thus under this agreement there are three distinct kinds of property:
  1. The unreserved property of the husband or wife, which stands under the marital system by virtue of paragraph 3 of this article.
  2. Their separate estate, which is always excluded from the very nature of the property.
  3. Their common property which is confined to the voluntarily acquired property as determined by paragraph 2 of this article and which stands under the system of community of property. It includes the income derived from the unreserved property.

increment is divided in equal half shares between the husband and the wife or their heirs.

² A deficit is borne by the husband or his heirs, provided there is no evidence that it was caused by the wife.

³ Some other division of the profits or deficit can be agreed upon in the marriage covenant.

Chapter IV: Separation of Estates

Art. 241

A. General effect

¹ The separation of estates which takes effect by operation of law or by order of the court extends to the whole property of the husband and the wife.

² Where the separation of estates takes effect under the marriage covenant, it extends to the whole property in so far as there are no express reservations in the covenant.

Art. 242

B. Ownership, administration and use

¹ The husband and the wife each retains the ownership, administration and use of his or her own property.

² Where the wife hands over the administration of her property to the husband, the law presumes that she thereby renounces her right to demand accounts of his administration during marriage and that she authorizes him to take the income from the property towards defraying the household expenses.

³ The wife cannot, however, validly deprive herself of her right at any time to take back this administration into her own hands.

Art. 243

C. Liability for debt
I. In general

¹ The husband is personally liable for his antenuptial debts and for those debts which are contracted

during marriage either by himself, or by his wife acting as agent for the conjugal union.

² The wife is personally liable for her own debts, whether ante-nuptial or post-nuptial.

³ Where the husband becomes insolvent the wife is further liable for debts contracted by him or by herself for the maintenance of their household.

Art. 244

¹ Where the husband becomes bankrupt or suffers execution on his property for debt, the wife has no priority over his creditors, not even where she has handed over the administration of her property to him.

² This provision does not affect the rules relating to dower.

II. Bankruptcy of husband or execution against him

Art. 245

The husband and the wife have each a right to all income or earnings, derived from their respective property or labour.

D. Income and earnings

Art. 246

¹ The husband can require his wife to contribute her due share to the expenses of their household.

² Where the parties cannot agree on the amount of this contribution, either of them can apply to the competent authority to have it fixed.

³ The husband is not liable to repay the sums which the wife has contributed.

E. Liability for maintenance of household

Art. 247

¹ The parties can in the marriage covenant agree that a portion of the wife's property shall constitute her dower and be her contribution to her husband towards the maintenance of their household.

F. Dower

²The property thus handed over to the husband shall, unless otherwise agreed, fall under the marital system.

Chapter V: Matrimonial Property Register

Art. 248

A. Effect of registration

¹Marriage covenants, orders of the court relating to matrimonial property systems and legal transactions between a husband and wife relating to the wife's unreserved property or their common property are not binding on third parties, unless and until they have been entered in the matrimonial property register and published.

²The heirs of a deceased husband or wife are not held to be third parties within the meaning of this clause.

Art. 249

B. Entry
I. Its purport

¹The entry in the register must contain the provisions which are intended to affect third parties.

²Where it is not otherwise provided by law or where registration is not specifically disallowed in the marriage covenant, either husband or wife can require registration.

Art. 250

II. Where made

¹The registration must be effected at the place of the husband's domicile.

²Where the husband changes his domicile to an area served by a different registry, the same entry must be made within three months in the register of his new domicile.

³The previous entry becomes null and void at the end of three months from the date of the change of domicile.

Art. 251

¹ The matrimonial property register is kept by the registrar of the commercial register, provided the Cantons do not appoint special registrars and constitute special areas for the purpose. C. How register kept

² The public have the right to inspect the register and to have copies of entries made on application.

³ The publication of a marriage covenant shall mention only the system of holding the matrimonial property adopted by the parties.

2. Other provisions in the wording according to the Federal Statute of 10th December 1907, in force since 1st January 1912 until 31st December 1987 (effective until the coming into force of the Federal Statute of 5th October 1984 on 1st January 1988)

Art. 25

¹ A wife is held to have her husband's domicile, a child under parental power that of his parents, and a ward that of the place where his guardianship board holds its sessions. c. Domicile of dependent persons

² Where the domicile of the husband is unknown or where the wife is entitled to live apart from her husband, she can acquire a domicile of her own.

Art. 30, Paragraph 2

annulled

Art. 134

¹ Where a marriage is declared null and void, the wife who married in good faith retains the status which she acquired by the marriage, but she resumes the name which she bore before the marriage. 2. On the husband and wife

[2] The division of the matrimonial property, and the claims of the parties to damages, maintenance, or moral compensation are governed by the same rules as in the case of divorce.

Art. 145

III. Provisional orders

As soon as proceedings have commenced the court makes all necessary orders pending the proceedings, such as for the lodging and maintenance of the wife, the management of the matrimonial property and the custody of the children.

Art. 149

IV. Position of divorced wife

[1] Where a marriage has been dissolved by divorce, the wife retains the status which she acquired by her marriage, but she resumes the surname which she bore before the marriage.

[2] Where she was a widow before the marriage, permission may be given to her in the decree to resume her maiden name.

Art. 154

VII. Division of matrimonial property
1. On divorce

[1] On divorce both the husband and the wife resume separate control of their own property, under whatever system the matrimonial property was held.

[2] Increments are divided between them according to the rules of their system; a depreciation, however, must be borne by the husband alone, unless indeed he can prove that it was caused by the wife.

[3] A divorced husband or wife has no statutory right of inheritance on the other's death and cannot claim any benefits under the marriage covenant or from testamentary dispositions made before the divorce.

Art. 155

2. On judicial separation

[1] Where the parties are judicially separated, the court decrees either the dissolution or the continuation

of the system under which they have held their matrimonial property, having regard to the probable duration of the separation and the position of the husband and wife.

² Where either husband or wife demands the separation of the matrimonial property, the demand cannot be refused.

Art. 413, Paragraph 2

² Where the parents are not a married couple, the child assumes the mother's surname.

Art. 460

¹ The right of inheritance based on relationship[1] ceases with the grandparents and their descendants.

IV. Great-grandparents

² Great-grandparents have, however, a usufruct for life in the share that would have accrued to their descendants if these had survived the deceased.

³ This usufruct devolves, in the case of the predecease of the great-grandparents, to the great-uncles and -aunts of the deceased.

Art. 462

¹ The surviving husband or wife of the deceased can, if the latter leaves descendants, choose either the usufruct in one half or the property in one quarter of the deceased's estate.

B. Surviving husband or wife
I. Rights of inheritance

² Where there are parents of the deceased or their descendants to take as heirs, the surviving spouse takes the property in one quarter and the usufruct in the other three quarters; where there are grandparents or their descendants, he takes the property in one half and the usufruct in the other half; in default of grandparents and their descendants, he takes the whole inheritance.

---

[1] This term is used according to cipher I 3 of the Federal Statute of 30th June 1972, in force since 1st April 1973 (AS **1972** 2819 2829; BBl **1971** I 1200).

Art. 463

II. Conversion and security

¹ The surviving spouse can, where he has the right to a usufruct, claim in the place of it an annuity of equal value.

² Where a usufruct has thus been converted and the rights of the spouse are imperilled, he can demand security from his co-heirs.

Art. 464

III. Security for co-heirs

On the demand of the co-heirs the spouse must give them security where he re-marries or imperils their rights.

Art. 466

D. Canton and Commune

In default of heirs of the deceased the inheritance devolves, subject to the usufruct in favour of grandparents or granduncles and -aunts, to the Canton of the deceased's last domicile or the Commune entitled under the law of that Canton.

Art. 470

A. Devisable portion
I. What is

¹ Where the testator leaves descendants, parents, brothers or sisters, or a spouse, he is entitled to dispose of the residue of the estate after deducting their compulsory portions.¹

Art. 471

II. Compulsory portion

The compulsory portion is as follows:

1. for a descendant three quarters of his statutory share of inheritance;

2. for the father or mother one half;

3. for a brother or sister one quarter;

4. for the surviving spouse the whole of his statutory share where there are statutory co-heirs with him, and one half of it where he is sole heir.

---

[1] "Compulsory portion" has been adopted for German **Pflichtteil** and French *réserve*.

Art. 472

The Cantons are entitled in the matter of succession to their citizens who had their last domicile within their borders, either to suppress the compulsory portion of brothers and sisters or to extend it to their descendants.

III. Cantonal Law

Art. 473, Paragraph 3

[3] The surviving spouse loses half his usufruct when he remarries.

Art. 561

[1] The statutory usufruct of the surviving husband or wife, the great-grandparents, great-uncles and -aunts is governed by the rules on legacies.[1]

II. Usufructuaries

[2] The usufruct, however, confers a right *in rem* as from the date of the opening of the succession, where and in so far as it is valid as against the creditors of the estate.[2]

Art. 631, Paragraph 2

[2] Children who at the date of the death of the deceased had not yet completed their education or are subject to some infirmity must be allotted at partition a reasonable sum by way of portion.

Art. 635, Paragraph 1

[1] Contracts between two or more heirs for the assignment of their rights of inheritance and contracts between one of the parents and his children relating

---

[1] *i.e.* though they are statutory heirs, they are in the position of legatees rather than heirs, inasmuch as they do not acquire the property but only a usufruct in the estate, and therefore are not liable as heirs.

[2] *i.e.* they differ from legatees in that they have a right *in rem* like other usufructuaries over the *res fructuaria* and not merely a personal right against the heirs. Creditors of the deceased have a prior claim on the estate, at least until the usufruct is registered.

to the children's share in the succession to the other parent are valid only if made in writing.

Art. 665, Paragraph 3

³ Changes in the ownership of land, which are the consequence of a certain system of holding matrimonial property, are officially entered in the land register, as soon as the system has been entered in the matrimonial property register and publicly advertised.

Art. 747

2. Statutory usufruct

¹ A usufruct of immovable property arising by operation of law is binding on third persons who have cognizance of it, even without registration.

² By registration it becomes operative as against all persons alike.

Art. 8

C. Family Law
I. Solemnization, dissolution and personal effect of marriage

¹ The solemnization and dissolution of a marriage and its effect on the persons of the parties to them are all governed by the new law as from the date of its coming into force.

Art. 9

II. Matrimonial Property Law
1. Statutory system

¹ The effect of marriage on the proprietary relations of husband and wife *inter se* is governed even after the coming into force of this Code by the rules of the old Family Law and Law of Inheritance which are applied by Cantonal Law to the system of holding matrimonial property, with the exception of the provisions in regard to the exceptional system, to separate estate and marriage covenants.

² In relation to third persons, husband and wife are subject to the new law where they have not before its coming into force made a joint declaration in writing to keep their former system of holding

property and had this declaration entered in the matrimonial property register.

³ Husband and wife can, by making a joint application in writing to the competent authority, make the new law applicable also for the regulation of their own proprietary relations *inter se.*

Art. 10

¹ A marriage covenant made before the introduction of this Code retains its validity after this date, but after this date it is operative in regard to third persons only under the condition that an application is made before this date to the competent authority for its entry in the matrimonial property register. 2. Marriage covenants

² Where a marriage covenant was entered under the old law in a public register, the entry will officially be transferred to the matrimonial property register.

Art. 11

The changes that have to be made for the securing of the rights of third parties in consequence of the introduction of this Code are governed by the rules laid down for the modification of a system of holding matrimonial property. 3. How third persons are secured

Art. 59, Paragraph 2

² In particular the provisions made by Cantonal Law in regard to the compulsory portions of sisters and brothers and their issue are recognized as the law of the legal home of the citizens of the Canton (art. 22 of the statute mentioned).

Appendix 2

Changes of other Federal Statutes according to cipher II of the Federal Statute of 5th October 1984, in force since 1st January 1988

1. The Federal Statute of 25th June 1891 relating to the Civil Legal Situation of Holders of Permits for Permanent or Temporary Residents is changed as follows:

Art. 20, Paragraph 1

[1] Where the spouses change their domicile, they can declare by making a joint application to the competent authority (art. 36 lit. b) that their legal relations also between themselves shall be governed by the law of the new domicile.

Art. 36 lit. b

The Cantons appoint:

b. the authority which is competent to accept applications made in accordance with article 20.

2. The Code of Obligations is changed as follows:

Art. 271a

VII. The family's lodging

[1] Where a rented object serves the lessee as the family's lodging, the landlord or buyer of the object must send the notice to leave or any other announcement whose purpose it is to terminate the lease separately to the lessee and his or her spouse.

[2] The rights of the lessee to oppose these announcements of the landlord, in particular the right to extend the lease, can also be exercised by the other spouse.

³ The lessee can terminate the lease only with the consent of his or her spouse in accordance with the provisions of the Marriage Law.

Art. 494, Paragraph 4

annulled

3. The Federal Statute on Bankruptcy and Execution is changed as follows:

V^{bis} To enforce payment from a spouse living under a system of community of property

Art. 68*a*

¹ Where from a spouse living under the system of community of property payment is enforced, the order to pay and all other documents in the service of enforced payment must also be submitted to the other spouse; where only in the course of the proceedings the debtor claims that he or she is living under a system of community of property, the authority competent for the enforcement of payment delivers the order to pay and all other documents immediately after having cognizance of this fact.

² Each spouse can oppose the order for the enforcement of payment.

³ Where the debtor or his or her spouse claims that not the common property, but just the debtor's own property and his or her share in the common property are liable, he or she has to give reasons for opposing the order for the enforcement of payment.

Art. 68*b*

¹ Each spouse can assert in the proceedings to oppose enforced payment (articles 106–109) that a

distressed value is part of a debtor's spouse's own property.

² Where the enforced payment is restricted to the debtor's own property and his or her share in the common property, each spouse can, in addition, oppose the distraint of items belonging to the common property in the proceedings to oppose the enforcement of payment (articles 106–109).

³ Where the enforcement of payment is continued with the aim of lying the creditor's claim from a spouse's own property and his or her share in the common property, the attachment and the execution of his or her share in the common property are subject to article 132.

⁴ A spouse's share in the common property cannot be sold by auction.

⁵ The supervisory authority can request that the judge shall order the establishment of a system of separate estates.

Art. 95a

The debtor's claims against his or her spouse can be distrained only where the remainder of the debtor's property is insufficient to satisfy a creditor's claims.

Art. 107, Paragraph 5

annulled

Art. 219, Paragraph 4, Fourth Class, lit. a

annulled

Art. 219, Paragraph 4, Fifth Class

All other claims.

4. The Federal Statute of 29th April 1920 relating to Consequences under Public Law of Futile Distraint and Bankruptcy is changed as follows:

Art. 2*a*

Where a spouse suffers a loss caused by the other spouse, no consequences under public law of the futile distraint or bankruptcy may be ordered.

Appendix 3

The coming into force of the Federal Statute of 5th October 1984[1] according to its cipher III

[1] This law is subject to Facultative Referendum.[2]

[2] The Federal Council determines the coming into force.[3]

[3] As far as the other Federal Statutes than the Civil Code have to be changed in consequence of this law, their transitory provisions are applied.

---

[1] BBl 1979 II 1191.
[2] *i.e.* optional referendum. Adopted in the referendum held on 22nd September 1985.
[3] Fixed to be effective by virtue of a Resolution of the Federal Council as per 1st January 1988.

Vocabulary

I. English, German, French

Accessory: Zugehör: accessoire.
accounts, keeping of: Rechnungsführung: comptabilité.
accounts, rendering of: Rechnungstellung: reddition des comptes.
acknowledgment: Anerkennung: reconnaissance.
acquisitions: Errungenschaft: acquêts.
acquisitions, participation in: Errungenschaftsbeteiligung: participation aux acquêts.
action: Klage: action.
adoption: Kindesannahme: adoption.
affinity: Schwägerschaft: alliance.
age, of full: mündig: majeur.
allocation, allotment (of land): Zuweisung: attribution.
allowance for life: Leibgedinge: pension.
alluvion: Anschwemmung: alluvion.
annuity: Rente: rente.
annuity, life: Leibrente: rente viagère.
appeal: Weiterziehung Rekurs, Appellation: recours.
arbitration agreement: Schiedsvertrag: concordat.
assets (in bankruptcy): Konkursmasse: masse.
association: Personenverbindung: société, association.
auction: Versteigerung: enchères.
authenticated document, duly: öffentliche Urkunde: titre authentique.

bankruptcy: Konkurs: faillite.
bearer, payable to: auf einen Inhaber: au porteur.
benefit: Zuwendung: libéralité.

betrothal: Verlöbnis: fiançailles.
bona fides: Treu und Glauben: bonne foi.
bond: Anleihensobligation: obligation.
burden of proof: Beweislast: fardeau de la preuve.

capacity (legal): Rechtsfähigkeit: jouissance des droits civils.
capacity to bring and defend actions: Prozessfähigkeit: droit d'ester en justice.
capacity to effect a legal transaction: Handlungsfähigkeit: exercice des droits civils.
capita, per: zu gleichen Teilen; pro Kopf: par tête.
carrier: Frachtführer: voiturier.
case: Rechtsfrage; Rechtsfall: matière.
case-law: "Fallrecht", auf Präzedenzfällen beruhend: jurisprudence.
cash: Barschaft: argent comptant.
charge, rent-: Grundlast: charge foncière.
citation: Vorladung: sommation.
citizenship: Bürgerrecht: droit de cité.
Civil Law: Zivilrecht: droit civil.
cohabitation: Beischlaf: cohabitation.
co-heir: Miterbe: cohéritier.
commercial register: Handelsregister: registre de commerce.
common property: Gesamtgut: communauté.
Commune: Gemeinde: commune.
community of property: Gemeinderschaft: indivision.
community of property, system of: Gütergemeinschaft: communauté des biens.

compensation: Ausgleich: récompense.
compensation, against: Anrechnung: en imputation sur sa part.
competence: Zuständigkeit: compétence.
compromise an action: einen Vergleich abschliessen: transiger.
compulsory portion: Pflichtteil: réserve héréditaire.
concession of water rights: Wasserrechtskonzession: concession hydraulique.
conjugal union: eheliche Gemeinschaft: union conjugale.
constitution, articles of: Statuten: statuts.
contract: Vertrag: contrat.
conversion: Umwandlung: conversion.
co-operative society: Genossenschaft: société coopérative.
corporate body: juristische Person: personne morale.
corporation: Körperschaft: corporation.
counterclaim: Gegenforderung: créance.
counter-statement: Gegendarstellung: rectification.
criminal prosecution: strafgerichtliche Verfolgung: poursuite pénale.
curator: Beistand: curateur.
custom: Brauch, Sitte: usage, coutume.
Custom, see Customary Law.
Customary Law: Gewohnheitsrecht: droit coutumier.
custody: Bevormundung, Obhut (der Kinder): garde.

damage: Schaden: dommage.
damages: Schadenersatz: dommages-intérêts.
debenture: Pfandbrief: lettre de gage.
deceased: Erblasser: défunt.
declaration of absence: Verschollenerklärung: déclaration d'absence.
defence: Einrede: exception.
delay, period of: Wartefrist: délai.
delivery: Übergabe: tradition.
delivery up of possession: Auslieferung: délivrance.
deposit (of land): Anschüttung: remblais.
descendant, issue: Nachkomme: descendant.

desertion: Verlassung: abandon.
determination: Aufhebung: extinction.
devisable portion: verfügbarer Teil: quotité disponible.
devolution of estate: Erbgang: dévolution.
directorate: Vorstand: direction.
disavowal: Anfechtung der Ehelichkeit: désaveu.
disclaimer: Ausschlagung: répudiation.
discretion: Urteilsfähigkeit: discernement.
discretion, judicial: Ermessen: pouvoir d'appréciation.
disinheritance: Enterbung: exhérédation.
dismissal: Enthebung: destitution.
disown: die Ehelichkeit anfechten: désavouer.
dissolution: Auflösung: dissolution.
division (of matrimonial property): Auseinandersetzung, güterrechtliche: liquidation des biens des epoux.
divorce: Scheidung: divorce.
doctrine, legal: bewährte Lehre: doctrine.
domicile: Wohnsitz: domicile.
dominant: berechtigt: dominant.
dower: Ehesteuer: dot.
drunkenness: Trunksucht: ivrognerie.

effect: Erfüllung (i.e. of contracts), Wirkung: effets.
emancipation: Mündigerklärung: émancipation.
equity: Billigkeit: équité.
estate charge note: Erbengült: lettre de rente successorale.
evidence: Beweis: preuve.
execution, on property/for debts: Zwangsvollstreckung: execution forcée, poursuite des dettes
executor: Willensvollstrecker: exécuteur testamentaire.
executory: vollziehbar: exécutoire.
expert evidence: Begutachtung: expertise.
expropriation: Enteignung: expropriation.

Family Law: Familienrecht: droit des familles.
farm, farmed land: Gewerbe, landwirtschaftliches: domaine agricole, entreprise a., exploitation a.
Federal Council: Bundesrat: Conseil fédéral.
Federal Court: Bundesgericht: Tribunal fédéral.
Federal Law: Bundesrecht: droit fédéral.
feeblemindedness: Geistesschwäche: faiblesse d'esprit.
fine: Busse: amende.
formation (e.g. of contracts): Entstehung: conclusion.
foundation: Anstalt, Stiftung: établissement, fondation.
foundation, instrument of: Stiftungsurkunde: acte de fondation.
fraud: arglistige Täuschung, Arglist: dol.
freedom of disposition: Verfügungsfreiheit: faculté de disposer.

ground, see material ground.
guarantee: Bürgschaft: cautionnement.
guardian: Vormund: tuteur.
guardianship: Vormundschaft: tutelle.
guardianship board: Vormundschaftsbehörde: autorité tutélaire.

heir: Erbe: héritier.
heir, instituted: eingesetzter Erbe: (héritier) institué.
heir, reversionary: Nacherbe: appelé.
heir, statutory: gesetzlicher Erbe: héritier légal.
home (legal): Heimat: origine, lieu d'origine.
homestead: Heimstätte: asile de famille.
hotchpot: Ausgleichung: rapport.

illegal: rechtswidrig: illicite.
immorality: unsittlicher Lebenswandel: inconduite.
incapable: unfähig: incapable.
incapacity: Unfähigkeit: incapacité.
incorporated: körperschaftlich organisiert: organisé corporativement.

indemnity: Entschädigung: indemnité.
industrial: wirtschaftlich: économique.
inheritance: Erbschaft: succession.
inheritance, right of: Erbanspruch: droit de succession.
insanity: Geisteskrankheit: maladie mentale.
instituted heir: eingesetzter Erbe: héritier institué.
institution of heir: Erbeinsetzung: institution d'héritier.
insurance, contract of: Versicherungsvertrag: contrat d'assurance.
integral part: Bestandteil: partie intégrante.
intentionally: vorsätzlich: à dessein.
interested party: Beteiligter: intéressé.
investment: Anlage: placement.
issue: Kinder, Nachkommen: enfants, descendants.
issue, not the common: nicht gemeinsame Kinder: des enfants non communs.

judicial separation: Trennung: séparation de corps.
jus vicinorum: Nachbarrecht: rapports de voisinage.

land register: Grundbuch: registre foncier.
landslip: Bodenverschiebung, Erdschlipf: glissement de terrain.
lapse: Verwirkung: déchéance.
law: Gesetz, Recht: loi, droit.
law, by operation of: von Gesetzes wegen: de plein droit.
Law of Inheritance: Erbrecht: droit de succession.
Law of Obligations: Obligationenrecht: droit des obligations.
Law of Persons: Personenrecht: droit des personnes.
legacy: Vermächtnis: legs.
(legacy), specific: einer bestimmten Sache: d'une chose déterminée.

legal transaction: Rechtsgeschäft: acte juridique.
legatee: Vermächtnisnehmer: légataire.
legislator: Gesetzgeber: législateur.
legitimacy: Ehelichkeit: légitimité.
legitimation: Ehelicherklärung: légitimation.
liability: Haftbarkeit: responsabilité.
liable: haftbar: responsable.
lien: Retentionsrecht: droit de rétention.
limitation of actions: Verjährung: prescription.
local custom: Ortsüblichkeit: usage local.

maintenance: Unterhalt: pension alimentaire, entretien.
maintenance for life: Verpfründung: entretien viager.
majority: Mündigkeit: majorité.
making (e.g. of contract): Entstehung: conclusion.
marital system: Güterverbindung: union des biens.
marriage: Eheschliessung: mariage.
marriage certificate: Eheschein: certificat de mariage.
material ground: wichtiger Grund: juste motif.
matrimonial property: eheliches Vermögen: biens matrimoniaux.
matrimonial property system: ehelicher Güterstand: régime matrimonial.
meeting, general: Hauptversammlung (jährlich): assemblée générale.
minor: unmündig: mineur.
minority: Unmündigkeit: minorité.
money had and received to use of plaintiff: ungerechtfertigte Bereicherung: enrichissement illégitime.
moral compensation: Genugtuung: réparation morale.
morality: Sittlichkeit: moeurs.
mortgage: Hypothek, Grundpfandverschreibung: hypothèque.
mortgage certificate: Schuldbrief: cédule hypothécaire.
motion: Antrag: proposition.

negligence: Fahrlässigkeit: négligence.
negotiable instrument: wechselrechtliche Verbindlichkeit: engagement de change.
notice: Ankündigung: dénonciation.
nullity: Nichtigkeit: nullité.

occupation: Aneignung: occupation.
opening of the succession: Eröffnung des Erbganges: ouverture de la succession.
order, payable to: auf eine bestimmte Person: nominatif.
ownership: Eigentum: propriété.

parental power: elterliche Gewalt: puissance paternelle.
partition: Teilung: partage.
partnership: einfache Gesellschaft: société simple.
paternity: Vaterschaft: paternité.
pawn: Versatzpfand: prêt sur gage.
payment, enforced: Betreibung: poursuite des dettes, execution forcée.
penalty: Ordnungsstrafe: peine disciplinaire.
person (natural): natürliche Person: personne physique.
plaintiff: Kläger: partie demanderesse.
pledge: Fahrnispfand, Faustpfand: gage mobilier.
portion compulsory: Pflichtteil: réserve héréditaire.
possession: Besitz: possession.
possession, derivative: unselbständiger Besitz: possession dérivée.
possession, original: selbständiger Besitz: possession originaire.
pre-emption, right of: Vorkaufsrecht: droit de préemption.
prescription (positive): Ersitzung: prescription acquisitive.
presumption: Vermutung: présomption.
priority: Vorrecht, Vorrang: privilège.
Private Law, see Civil Law.
procedure: Verfahren: procédure.
prodigality: Verschwendung: prodigalité.

Vocabulary 397

profession or trade, to engage in: ein Gewerbe ausüben: exercer une profession ou une industrie.
profit, matrimonial: Vorschlag: bénéfice.
profit, participation in matrimonial: Vorschlagsbeteiligung: participation légale au bénéfice.
proof: Beweis: preuve.
property: Eigentum: propriété.
property: Vermögenswerte: les biens.
property, common: Gesamtgut: les biens communs.
property, system of holding matrimonial: Güterstand, Güterrecht: régime (matrimoniale).
property, unreserved: Frauengut: apports.
property, a spouse's own: Eigengut: biens propres.
provision: Bestimmung, Vorschrift: disposition.
provisions, to make p. with adequate care: verantwortungsbewusste Vorsorge (treffen): le devoir d'assurer l'avenir de la famille et de pourvoir aux besoins de sa profession ou de son entreprise.
Public Law: öffentliches Recht: droit public.

quasi-guardian: Beirat: conseil légal.

ratification: Genehmigung: ratification.
real: dinglich: réel.
recoverable: fällig: exigible.
rectification: Berichtigung: rectification.
redemption: Ablösung: purge hypothécaire.
redemption, right of: Rückkaufsrecht: droit de réméré.
redemption value: Rückkaufswert: valeur de rachat.
reduction: Herabsetzung: réduction.
register of civil status: Zivilstandsregister: registre de l'état civil.
registry office, matrimonial property: Güterrechtsregisteramt: régistre des régimes matrimonaux.

repeal: Aufhebung: abrogation.
request: Begehren: demande, requête.
rescission: Aufhebung: révocation.
resolution: Beschluss: décision.
reversionary heir: Nacherbe: appelé.
reversionary heir, appointment of: Nacherbeneinsetzung: substitution fidéicommissaire.
revocation: Entziehung, Widerruf: déchéance, révocation.
right: Recht: droit.
right of building-charge: Baurechtzins: rente du droit de superficie.
rule: Bestimmung: disposition.

savings deposit: Spareinlage: dépôt d'épargne.
security on land: Grundpfand: gage immobilier.
securities: Wertpapiere: papiers-valeurs.
(securities,) negotiable: mit Kurswert: cotés à la bourse.
seizure of property for debt: Pfändung: saisie.
separate estate: Sondergut: biens réservés.
sequestration: Beschlagnahme: séquestre.
servient: belastet: servant.
servitude: Dienstbarkeit: servitude.
servitude, praedial: Grunddienstbarkeit: servitude foncière.
set-off: in Abzug bringen: compenser.
severance: Trennung: séparation.
share (in company): Aktie: action.
shareholder: Aktionär: actionnaire.
society: Verein: association, société.
status (civil): Personenstand: état civil.
statute: Gesetz: loi.
stirpes, per: nach Stämmen: par souche.
substitution: Ersatzverfügung: substitution vulgaire.
succession: Erbgang: succession.
succession, opening of, see opening.
suit: Klage: action.
supervisory authority: Aufsichtsbehörde: autorité de surveillance.

testamentary capacity: Verfügungsfähigkeit: capacité de disposer.
testamentary disposition: Verfügung von Todes wegen: disposition pour cause de mort.
testamentary pact: Erbvertrag: pacte successoral.
testator: Erblasser: disposant.
title deed: Rechtstitel: pièce justificative.
transfer: Übertragung: transfert.
treaty, by private: aus freier Hand: de gré à gré.
trust, perpetual: Fideikommiss: fidéicommis.

unreserved property: eingebrachtes Gut: apports.
unsatisfied claims, certificate of: Verlustschein: acte de défaut de biens.
usage: Übung: usage.

user: Nutzung: jouissance.
usufruct: Nutzung, Nutzniessung: usufruit.
usufructuary: Nutzniesser: usufruitier.

value based on annual return: Ertragswert: valeur de rendement.
value, selling: Verkehrswert: valeur vénale.
value, share of increased: Mehrwertanteil: part à la plus-value.
void: nichtig: nul.
voidability: Anfechtbarkeit: nullité relative.
voidable: anfechtbar: qui peut être attaqué.

ward: Bevormundeter: pupille.
warrant: Pfandschein: warrant.
way, right of: Wegrecht: droit de passage.
will: letztwillige Verfügung: testament.
wording: Wortlaut: teneur.

II. German, French, English

Ablösung: purge hypothécaire: redemption.
Abzug: compensation: set-off.
Aktie: action: share in company.
Aktionär: actionnaire: shareholder.
Allmendgenossenschaft: société d'allmends: association for common cultivation of land.
Aneignung: occupation: occupation.
Anerkennung: reconnaissance: acknowledgment.
Anfechtbarkeit: nullité relative: voidability.
Anfechtung der Ehelichkeit: désaveu: disavowal.
Anlage: placement: investment.
Anleihensobligation: obligation: bond.
Anrechnung, als: en imputation sur sa part: against compensation, as the whole or part of his share.
Anschüttung: remblais: deposit (of land).
Anschwemmung: alluvion: alluvion.
Anstalt: établissement: foundation, establishment.
Antrag: proposition: motion, application.
Arglist, arglistige Täuschung: dol: fraud.
Aufhebung: extinction, révocation, abrogation: determination, rescission, repeal.
Auflage: charge: burden, charge.
Auflösung: dissolution: dissolution.
Aufsichtsbehörde: autorité de surveillance: supervisory authority.
Auseinandersetzung, güterrechtliche: liquidation des biens des époux: division of the matrimonial property.
Ausgleichung: rapport, récompense: hotchpot, compensation.
Auskündung: sommation: citation.
Auslieferung: délivrance: delivery up.
Ausschlagung: répudiation: disclaimer.
Ausserehelich: illégitime: illegitimate.

Barschaft: argent comptant: cash.

Baurecht: droit de superficie: right of building, right over a building.
Baurechtszins: rente du droit des superficie: right of building-charge.
Begehren: demande, requête: request.
Begutachtung: expertise: expert evidence.
Beirat: conseil légal; quasi-guardian.
Beistand: curateur: curator.
beitreibbar: exigible: recoverable
Beiwohnung: cohabitation: cohabitation.
Belege: pièces justificatives: title deeds.
Berechtigter: ayant-droit: person entitled, dominant owner.
Berichtigung: rectification: rectification.
Beschlagnahme: séquestre: sequestration.
Beschluss: décision: resolution.
Beschwerter, Belasteter, Schuldner: débiteur, partie aggrevée: aggrieved party, person charged.
Besitz: possession: possession.
Besitz, selbständiger: possession originaire: original possession.
Besitz, unselbständiger: possession dérivée; derivative possession.
Bestandteil: partie intégrante: integral part.
Bestimmung: dispositions: provision, disposition: provision, disposition, rule.
Beteiligter: intéressé: interested party.
Betreibung, Pfändung: execution forcée, poursuite des dettes: enforced payment, execution on property, for debts.
bevormunden: mettre sous tutelle: place under guardianship.
Bevormundeter: pupille: ward.
Beweis: preuve: proof, evidence.
Beweislast: fardeau de la preuve: burden of proof.
Billigkeit: équité: equity.
Bodenverschiebung, Erdschlipf: glissement de terrain: landslip.
Bundesgericht: Tribunal fédéral: Federal Court.

Bundesrat: Conseil fédéral: Federal Council.
Bundesrecht: droit fédéral: Federal Law.
Bundesversammlung: Assemblée fédérale: Joint Assembly of Nationalrat (national representatives) and Ständerat (2 representatives per Canton).
Bürgerrecht: droit de cité: citizenship.
Bürgschaft: cautionnement: guarantee.
Busse: amende: fine.

Dienstbarkeit: servitude: servitude.
dinglich: réel: real, in rem.

ehelich: légitime: legitimate.
eheliche Gemeinschaft: union conjugale: conjugal union.
eheliches Vermögen: biens matrimoniaux: matrimonial property.
Ehelicherklärung: légitimation: legitimation.
Ehelichkeit: légitimité: legitimacy.
Ehelichkeit anfechten: désavouer: disown, dispute legitimacy.
Eheschein: certificat de mariage: marriage certificate.
Eheschliessung: mariage: marriage.
Ehesteuer: dot: dower.
Ehevertrag: contrat de mariage: marriage covenant.
Eigengut: biens propres: a spouse's own property.
Eigentum: propriété: property, ownership.
Eigentumsvorbehalt: pacte de réserve de propriété: pact to reserve ownership.
eingebrachtes Gut: apports: unreserved property.
Einrede: exception: defence.
Enteignung: expropriation: expropriation.
Enterbung: exhérédation: disinheritance.
Enthebung: destitution: dismissal.
entmündigen: interdire: place under committee.
Entschädigung: indemnité, dommages-intérêts: indemnity.
Entstehung: conclusion: formation (of contracts).

Entziehung: déchéance: revocation, deprivation.
Erbe: héritier: heir.
Erbe, eingesetzter: institué: instituted heir.
Erbe, gesetzlicher: héritier légal: statutory heir.
Erbeneinsetzung: institution d'héritier: institution of heir.
Erbengült: lettre de rente successorale: estate charge note.
Erbgang: dévolution: devolution of estate.
Erblasser: défunt, disposant: deceased, testator.
Erbrecht: droit de succession: right of inheritance, Law of Inheritance.
Erbschaft: succession: inheritance, estate, succession.
Erbvertrag: pacte successoral: testamentary pact.
Erbverzicht: renonciation à la succession: renunciation of inheritance.
Erfüllung: effets: effect, fulfilment.
Ermessen: pouvoir d'appréciation: discretion, at a person's.
Eröffnung des Erbganges: ouverture de la succession: opening of the succession.
Ersatzverfügung: substitution vulgaire: substitution.
Ersitzung: prescription, prescription acquisitive: prescription, adverse possession.
Errungenschaft: acquêts: acquisitions.
Errungenschaftsbeteiligung: participation aux acquêts: participation in acquisitions.
Ertragswert: valeur de rendement: value based on annual yield.
Erwerb: acquisition: acquisition.
Erwerb ohne Besitz: constitut possessoire: transfer of ownership without possession.

Fahrlässigkeit: négligence: negligence.
Fahrniseigentum: propriété mobilière: ownership of movable property.

Vocabulary

Fahrnispfand: gage mobilier: pledge.
fällig: exigible: due, payable.
"Fallrecht" (auf Präzedenzfällen basierend): jurisprudence: case-law.
Familienrecht: droit de famille: Family Law.
Faustpfand: gage mobilier: pledge.
Fideikommiss: fidéicommis: perpetual trust.
Frachtführer: voiturier: carrier.
Frauengut: apports: unreserved property.

Gegendarstellung: rectification: counter-statement.
Gegenforderung: créance: counterclaim.
Geisteskrankheit: maladie mentale: insanity.
Geistesschwäche: faiblesse d'esprit: feeblemindedness.
Gemeinde: commune: Commune.
Gemeinder: indivis: party to a community.
Gemeinderschaft: indivision: community of property.
Genehmigung: ratification: ratification.
Genossenschaft: société coopérative: co-operative society.
Genugtuung: réparation morale: moral compensation.
Gesamtgut: communauté: common property.
Gesamtgut: biens communs: common property (of husband and wife).
Gesellschaft (einfache): société simple: partnership.
Gesetz: loi: law, statute; **von Gesetzes wegen:** de plein droit: by operation of law.
Gesetzgeber: législateur: legislator.
Gewalt, elterliche: puissance paternelle: parental power.
Gewerbe: industrie, entreprise: trade or profession.
Gewerbe, ausüben: exercer une profession ou une industrie: to engage in a trade or profession.
Gewerbe, bäuerliches/landwirtschaftliches: exploitation agricole, domaine agricole, entreprise agricole: farm, farmed land.
Gewohnheitsrecht: droit coutumier: Customary Law, Custom.
Grund, wichtiger: juste motif: material ground.
Grundbuch: registre foncier: land register.
Grunddienstbarkeit: servitude foncière: praedial servitude.
Grundeigentum: propriété foncière: ownership of land.
Grundlast: charge foncière: rent-charge.
Grundpfand: gage immobilier: security on land.
Grundpfandverschreibung: hypothèque: mortgage.
Gütergemeinschaft: communauté des biens: system of community of property.
Güterrechtsregisteramt: registre des régimes matrimoniaux: matrimonial property registry office.
Güterstand (ehelicher), Güterrecht: régime matrimonial: matrimonial property system.
Gütertrennung: séparation de biens: system of separate estates.
Güterverbindung: union des biens: marital system.

haftbar: responsable: liable.
Haftbarkeit: responsabilité: liability.
Hand, aus freier: de gré à gré: by private treaty.
Handelsregister: registre de commerce: commercial register.
handlungsfähig: qui a l'exercice des droits civils: capable of effecting a legal transaction.
Handlungsfähigkeit: exercice des droits civils: capacity to effect a legal transaction.
Hauptversammlung, Jahresversammlung: assemblée générale: general meeting.
Heimat: origine, lieu d'origine: legal home.
Heimstätte: asile de famille: homestead.

Herabsetzung: réduction: reduction.

Inhaber, auf einen: au porteur: payable to bearer.

Kinder, nicht gemeinsame: enfants non communs: not the common issue of the spouses.
Kindesaufnahme: adoption: adoption.
Klage: action: action, suit.
Klagender: partie demanderesse: plaintiff.
Konkurs: faillite: bankruptcy.
Konkursmasse: masse (en faillite): bankrupt's estate, assets.
Körperschaft: corporation: corporation.
körperschaftlich organisiert: organisé corporativement: incorporated.
Kündigung: dénonciation: notice.

Lebenswandel, unsittlicher: inconduite: immorality.
lediger Anfall: loyale échute: failure of renunciation.
Lehre (bewährte): doctrine: legal doctrine.
Leibgedingsvertrag: contrat dont l'objet est une pension: agreement for life allowance.
Leibrente: rente viagère: life annuity.
letztwillige Verfügung: testament: will, testament.
Liegenschaft: biens-fonds: land, landed property.

Mehrwertanteil: part à la plus-value: share of increased value.
Mietvertrag: bail à loyer: occupation lease.
Misswirtschaft: mauvaise gestion: mismanagement.
Miteigentum: copropriété: united ownership, co-ownership.
Miterbe: cohéritier: co-heir.
mündig: majeur: of full age, major.
Mündigerklärung: émancipation: emancipation.
Mündigkeit: majorité: majority.

Nachbarrecht: rapports de voisinage: jus vicinorum.
Nacherbe: appelé: reversionary heir.
Nacherbeneinsetzung: substitution fidéicommissaire: appointment of reversionary heir.
Nachkomme: descendant: descendant, issue.
Nachlassstundung: sursis concordataire: suspension of liquidation proceedings.
Nachverpfändung: droit de gage subséquent: pledge upon a pledge.
Nachweis, see Beweis.
Namenpapiere: titres nominatifs: securities payable to order.
nichtig: nul: void.
Nichtigkeit: nullité: nullity.
Nutzniesser: usufruitier: usufructuary.
Nutzniessung: usufruit: usufruct.
Nutzung: jouissance: user.

Obligationenrecht: droit des obligations: Law of Obligations.
Öffentliches Recht: droit public: Public Law.
öffentliche Urkunde: titre authentique: duly authenticated document.
Ordnungsstrafe: peine disciplinaire: penalty.
Ortsgebrauch: usage local: local custom.

Pachtvertrag: bail à ferme: agricultural lease.
Person, juristische: personne morale: corporate body.
Person, natürliche: personne physique: (natural) person.
Personenrecht: droit des personnes: Law of Persons.
Personenstand: état civil: (civil) status.
Personenverbindung: société: association.
Persönlichkeit: personnalité: personality.
Pfandbrief: lettre de gage: debenture.
Pfandschein: warrant: warrant.
Pfandstelle: case hypothécaire: place of security in register.
Pfandtitel: titre: document of title, security.

Vocabulary

Pfändung: saisie: seizure of property in execution.
Pflichtteil: réserve héréditaire: compulsory portion.
Prozessfähigkeit: droit d'ester en justice: capacity to bring and defend actions.

Rechnungsführung: comptabilité: keeping of accounts.
Rechnungsstellung: reddition des comptes: rendering of accounts.
Recht: loi, droit: law, right.
rechtsfähig: qui jouit des droits civils: subject of rights.
Rechtsfähigkeit: jouissance des droits civils: capacity to have rights and duties, legal capacity.
Rechtsfrage: matière: case.
Rechtsgeschäft: acte juridique: legal transaction.
rechtswidrig: illicite: illegal.
Rente: rente: annuity.
Retentionsrecht: droit de rétention: lien.
Rückkaufsrecht: droit de réméré: right of redemption.
Rückkaufswert: valeur de rachat: redemption value.

Schaden: dommage: damage.
Schadenersatz: dommages-intérêts: damages, indemnity.
Scheidung: divorce: divorce.
Schiedsvertrag: concordat: arbitration agreement.
Schlussrechnung: compte définitif: final account.
Schuldbrief: cédule hypothécaire: mortgage certificate.
Schwägerschaft: alliance: relationship by marriage, affinity.
Sittlichkeit: moeurs: morality.
solidarisch: solidairement: jointly and severally.
Sondergut: biens réservés: separate estate.
Spareinlage: dépôt d'épargne: savings deposit.

Stämmen, nach: par souche: per stirpes.
Statuten: statuts: articles of constitution.
Stiftung: fondation: foundation.
Stiftungsurkunde: acte de fondation: instrument of foundation.
Stockwerkeigentum: propriété par étages: storey-ownership.
strafgerichtliche Verfolgung: poursuite pénale: criminal prosecution.

Teilung: partage: partition, division.
Titel: titre: security, document of title.
Trennung: séparation de corps: judicial separation.
Treu und Glauben: bonne foi: bona fides.
Trunksucht: ivrognerie: drunkenness.

Übergabe: tradition: delivery.
Übertragung: transfert: transfer.
Übung, Brauch: usage: usage.
Umwandlung: conversion: conversion.
unfähig: incapable: incapable.
Unfähigkeit (Geschäfts-): incapacité: incapacity.
ungerechtfertigte Bereicherung: enrichissement illégitime: money had and received to use of plaintiff.
unmündig: mineur: minor.
Unmündigkeit: minorité: minority.
Unterhalt: pension alimentaire, entretien: maintenance.
urteilsfähig: capable de discernement: who has discretion.
Urteilsfähigkeit: discernement: discretion.
Urteilsunfähigkeit: incapacité de discernement: absence of discretion.

Vaterschaft: paternité: paternity.
Verarbeitung: spécification: manufacture.
Verein: association: society, association.
Vereinsversammlung: assemblée: meeting.
Verfahren: procédure: procedure.
Verfallvertrag: pacte commissoire: agreement for forfeiture of chattel pledged.
verfügbarer Teil: quotité disponible: devisable portion.

Verfügung: disposition: disposal, disposition.
Verfügung von Todes wegen: disposition pour cause de mort: testamentary disposition.
Verfügungsfähigkeit: capacité de disposer: testamentary capacity.
Verfügungsfreiheit: faculté de disposer: freedom of disposition.
Verfügungsrecht: droit d'aliéner: right of alienation.
Vergleich abschliessen: transiger: compromise an action.
Verjährung: prescription: limitation of actions.
Verkehrswert: valeur vénale: selling value.
Verkündung: publication (d'un mariage): publication (of marriage).
Verlassung: abandon: desertion.
Verlöbnis: fiançailles: betrothal.
Verlustschein: acte de défaut de biens: certificate of unsatisfied claims.
Vermächtnis: legs: legacy.
Vermächtnisnehmer: légataire: legatee.
Vermögenswerte: biens: property.
Vermutung: présomption: presumption.
Verpachtung, see Pachtvertrag.
Verpfründung: entretien viager: maintenance for life.
Versatzpfand: prêt sur gage: pawn.
Verschollenerklärung: déclaration d'absence: declaration of absence.
Verschwendung: prodigalité: prodigality.
Versicherungsvertrag: contrat d'assurance: contract of insurance.
Versorgung: garde: custody.
Versteigerung: enchères: auction.
Vertrag: contrat: contract.
Verwirkung: déchéance: lapse.
vollziehbar: exćutoire: executory.
Vorerbe: grevé: first heir.
Vorkaufsrecht: droit de préemption: right of pre-emption.
Vormund: tuteur: guardian.
Vormundschaft: tutelle: guardianship.
Vormundschaftsbehörde: autorité tutélaire: guardianship board.

Vorrecht: privilège: priority.
vorsätzlich: à dessein: intentionally.
Vorschlag: bénéfice: matrimonial profit.
Vorschlagsbeteiligung: participation légale en bénéfice: participation.
Vorschrift: disposition: provision.
Vorsorge, verantwortungsbewusste: assurer l'avenir de la famille et de pourvoir aux besoins de sa profession ou de son entreprise: (to make) provisions with adequate care about.
Vorstand: direction: directorate.

Warenpapiere: titres représentatifs de marchandises: goods bills.
Wartefrist: délai: period of delay.
Wasserrechtsverleihung: concession hydraulique: concession of water rights.
wechselrechtliche Verbindlichkeit: engagement de change: negotiable instrument.
Wegrecht: droit de passage: right of way.
Weiterziehung, Rekurs, Appellation: recours: appeal.
Wertpapiere: papiers-valeurs: securities.
Wertpapiere, kotierte: papiers-valeurs cotés à la bourse: securities quoted at Exchange.
Widerruf: révocation: revocation.
Willensvollstrecker: exécuteur testamentaire: executor.
wirtschaftlich: économique: industrial.
Wohnsitz: domicile: domicile.
Wortlaut: teneur: wording.

zahlungsunfähig: insolvable: insolvent.
Zivilrecht: droit civil: Civil Law.
Zivilstandsregister: registre de l'état civil: register of civii status.
Zugehör: accessoire: accessory.
Zuständigkeit: compétence: competence.
Zuweisung: attribution: allocation, allotment (of farmland).
Zuwendung: libéralité: benefit.
Zwangsvollstreckung: exécution forcée: execution for debt.

III. French, German, English

Abandon: Verlassung: desertion.
abrogation: Aufhebung: repeal.
accessoire: Zugehör: accessory.
acquêts: Errungenschaftsbeteiligung: participation in acquisitions.
acte de défaut de biens: Verlustschein: certificate of unsatisfied claims.
acte juridique: Rechtsgeschäft: legal transaction.
action: Klage, Aktie: action, suit, share in company.
actionnaire: Aktionär: shareholder.
adoption: Kindesannahme: adoption.
alimentaire, pension: Unterhalt: maintenance.
alliance: Schwägerschaft: affinity, relationship by marriage.
alluvion: Anschwemmung: alluvion.
amende: Busse: fine.
appelé: Nacherbe: reversionary heir.
apports: eingebrachtes Gut, Frauengut: unreserved property.
argent comptant: Barschaft: cash.
asile de famille: Heimstätte: homestead.
Assemblée fédérale: Bundesversammlung: Joint assembly of the two chambres, Conseil nationale and Conseil d'états of the Swiss Parliament.
assemblée générale: Hauptversammlung, Jahresversammlung: general meeting.
association: Verein: society.
assurance, contrat d': Versicherungsvertrag: contract of insurance.
assurer l'avenir de la famille: verantwortungsbewusste Vorsorge: make provisions for the future of one's family.
attribution: Zuweisung: allocation, allotment (of farm land).
autorité de surveillance: Aufsichtsbehörde: supervisory authority.
autorité tutélaire: Vormundschaftsbehörde: guardianship board.
ayant-droit: Berechtigter: person entitled, dominant owner.

bail à ferme: Pachtvertrag: agricultural lease.
bail à loyer: Mietvertrag: occupation lease.
bénéfice: Vorschlag: matrimonial profit.
bénéfice, participation légale au: Vorschlagsbeteiligung: participation in the matrimonial profit.
biens: Vermögenswerte: property.
biens communs: Gesamtgut: common property.
biens-fonds: Liegenschaft: land, landed property.
biens propres: Eigengut: a spouse's own property.
biens réservés: Sondergut: separate estate.
bonne foi: Treu und Glauben: bona fides.

case hypothécaire: Pfandstelle: place of security in register.
cautionnement: Bürgschaft: guarantee.
cédule hypothécaire: Schuldbrief: mortgage certificate.
certificat de mariage: Eheschein: marriage certificate.
charge: Auflage: burden, charge.
charge foncière: Grundlast: rent-charge.
cohabitation: Beischlaf: cohabitation.
cohéritier: Miterbe: co-heir.
commissoire, pacte: Verfallsvertrag: agreement for forfeiture of chattel pledged.
communauté: Gesamtgut: common property.
communauté des biens: Gütergemeinschaft: system of community of property.
commune: Gemeinde: Commune.
compenser: in Abzug bringen: set-off.
compétence: Zuständigkeit: competence.
comptabilité: Rechnungsführung: keeping of accounts.
concession hydraulique: Wasserrechtsverleihung: concession of water rights.

conclusion: Entstehung: formation (e.g. of contract).
concordat: Schiedsvertrag: arbitration agreement.
Conseil fédéral: Bundesrat: Federal Council.
conseil légal: Beistand, Beirat: quasi-guardian.
constitut possessoire: Erwerb ohne Besitz: transfer of ownership without possession.
contrat: Vertrag: contract.
conversion: Umwandlung: conversion.
copropriété: Miteigentum: united ownership, co-ownership.
corporation: Körperschaft: corporation.
curateur: Beistand: curator.

déchéance: Entziehung, Verwirkung: revocation, lapse.
décision: Beschluss: resolution.
déclaration d'absence: Verschollenerklärung: declaration of absence.
défunt: Erblasser: deceased.
délai: Wartefrist: period of delay.
délivrance: Auslieferung: delivery up (of possession).
demande: Begehren: request.
dénonciation: Verkündigung: notice.
dépôt d'épargne: Spareinlage: savings deposit.
désaveu: Anfechtung der Ehelichkeit: disavowal.
désavouer: die Ehelichkeit anfechten: disown.
descendant: Nachkomme: descendant, issue.
dessein, à: vorsätzlich: intentionally.
destitution: Enthebung: dismissal.
dévolution: Erbgang: devolution of estate.
direction: Vorstand: directorate.
discernement: Urteilsfähigkeit: discretion.
discernement, capable de: urteilsfähig: who has discretion.
disposant: Erblasser: testator.

disposition: Vorschrift, Bestimmung: disposal, provision, rule.
disposition pour cause de mort: Verfügung von Todes wegen: testamentary disposition.
dissolution: Auflösung: dissolution.
divorce: Scheidung: divorce.
doctrine: bewährte Lehre: legal doctrine.
dol: arglistige Täuschung, Arglist: fraud.
domaine agricole: landwirtschaftliches Gewerbe: farm, farmed land.
domicile: Wohnsitz: domicile.
dommage: Schaden: damage.
dommages-intérêts: Schadenersatz: damages.
dot: Ehesteuer: dower.
droit: Recht: law, right.
droit, de plein: von Gesetzes wegen: by operation of law.
droit civil: Zivilrecht: Civil Law, Private Law.
droit coutumier: Gewohnheitsrecht: Customary Law.
droit d'ester en justice: Prozessfähigkeit: capacity to bring and defend actions.
droit de famille: Familienrecht: Family Law.
droit des obligations: Obligationenrecht: Law of Obligations.
droit des personnes: Personenrecht: Law of Persons.
droit de succession: Erbrecht, Erbanspruch: Law of Inheritance, right of inheritance.
droit fédéral: Bundesrecht: Federal Law.
droit public: öffentliches Recht: Public Law.

économique: wirtschaftlich: industrial.
effets: Erfüllung, Wirkung: effect.
émancipation: Mündigerklärung: emancipation.
enchères: Versteigerung: auction.
enfants non communs: nicht gemeinsame Kinder: not the common issue.
engagement de change: wechselrechtliche Verbindlichkeit: negotiable instrument.

Vocabulary

enrichissement illégitime: ungerechtfertigte Bereicherung: money had and received to use of plaintiff.
entreprise: Gewerbe: trade or profession.
entretien: Unterhalt: maintenance.
entretien viager: Verpfründung: maintenance for life.
équité: Billigkeit: equity.
établissement: Anstalt, Stiftung, foundation, establishment.
état civil: Personenstand: (civil) status.
exception: Einrede: defence.
exécuteur testamentaire: Willensvollstrecker: executor.
exécution forcée: Zwangsverwertung, Zwangsvollstreckung: execution on property, execution for debt.
exécutoire: vollziehbar: executory.
exercer une profession ou une industrie: ein Gewerbe ausüben: to engage in a trade or profession.
exercice des droits civils: Handlungsfähigkeit: capacity to effect a legal transaction.
exhérédation: Enterbung: disinheritance.
exigible: fällig: due, payable.
expertise: Begutachtung: expert evidence.
exploitation agricole: bäuerliches Gewerbe: farm, farmed land.
expropriation: Enteignung: expropriation.
extinction: Aufhebung: determination, rescission.

faiblesse d'esprit: Geistesschwäche: feeblemindedness.
faillite: Konkurs: bankruptcy.
fardeau de la preuve: Beweislast: burden of proof.
fiançailles: Verlöbnis: betrothal.
fidéicommis: Fideikommiss: perpetual trust.
fondation: Stiftung: foundation.
fondation, acte de: Stiftungsurkunde: instrument of foundation.

gage immobilier: Grundpfand: real security on land.
gage, lettre de: Pfandbrief: debenture.
gage mobilier: Faustpfand, Fahrnispfand: pledge.
gage subséquent, droit de: Nachverpfändung: pledge upon a pledge.
garde: Versorgung: custody.
glissement de terrain: Bodenverschiebung, Erdschlipf: landslip.
gré à gré, de: aus freier Hand: by private treaty.
grevé (d'une substitution): Vorerbe: first heir.

héritier: Erbe: heir.
héritier institué: eingesetzter Erbe: instituted heir.
héritier légal: gesetzlicher Erbe: statutory heir.
hypothèque: Grundpfandverschreibung: mortgage.

illicite: rechtswidrig: illegal.
imputation sur sa part: Anrechnung: against compensation.
incapable: unfähig: incapable.
incapacité: Unfähigkeit: incapacity.
inconduite: unsittlicher Lebenswandel: immorality.
indemnité: Entschädigung: indemnity.
indivis: Gemeinder: party to a community of property.
indivision: Gemeinderschaft: community of property.
industrie: Gewerbe, Industrie: industry.
intégrale, partie: Bestandteil: integral part.
interdire: entmündigen: to place under a committee.
intéressé: Beteiligter: interested party.
ivrognerie: Trunksucht: drunkenness.

jouissance: Nutzung: user.
jouissance des droits civils: Rechtsfähigkeit: capacity to have rights and duties, legal capacity.

jurisprudence: "Fallrecht": case-law.
justificative, pièce: Rechtstitel: title deeds.

légataire: Vermächtnisnehmer: legatee.
législateur: Gesetzgeber: legislator.
légitime: ehelich: legitimate.
légitimité: Ehelichkeit: legitimacy.
legs: Vermächtnis: legacy.
lettre de rente: Gült: land charge note.
lettre de rente successorale: Erbengült: estate charge note.
libéralité: Zuwendung: benefit.
liquidation des biens des epoux: güterrechtliche Auseinandersetzung: division of the matrimonial property.
loi: Gesetz: law, statute.
loyale échute: lediger Anfall: failure of renunciation.

majeur: mündig: of full age.
majorité: Mündigkeit: majority.
maladie mentale: Geisteskrankheit: insanity.
mariage: Eheschliessung: marriage.
masse (en faillite): Konkursmasse: bankrupt's estate, assets.
matière: Rechtsfrage: case.
mineur: unmündig: minor.
minorité: Unmündigkeit: minority.
moeurs: Sittlichkeit: morality.

négligence: Fahrlässigkeit: negligence.
nominatif: auf einen bestimmten Namen: payable to order.
nul: nichtig: void.
nullité: Nichtigkeit: nullity.
nullité relative: Anfechtbarkeit: voidability.

occupation: Aneignung: occupation.
organisé corporativement: körperschaftlich organisiert: incorporated.
origine: Heimat: home.
ouverture de la succession: Eröffnung des Erbganges: opening of the succession.

pacte successoral: Erbvertrag: testamentary pact.
papiers-valeurs: Wertpapiere: securities.
papiers-valeurs cotés à la bourse: kotierte Wertpapiere: securities quoted at the Exchange.
partage: Teilung: partition, division.
partie demanderesse: Klagender: plaintiff.
passage, droit de: Wegrecht: right of way.
paternité: Vaterschaft: paternity.
peine disciplinaire: Ordnungsstrafe: penalty.
pension: Leibgedinge, Rente: allowance for life.
personnalité: Persönlichkeit: personality, status of person.
personne morale: juristische Person: corporate body.
personne physique: natürliche Person: (natural) person.
placement: Anlage: investment.
plus-value, la part à la: Mehrwertanteil: share of increased value.
porteur, au: auf den Inhaber: payable to bearer.
possession: Besitz: possession.
possession dérivée: unselbständiger Besitz: derivative possession.
possession originaire: selbständiger Besitz: original possession.
poursuite des dettes: Betreibung, Zwangsvollstreckung: execution for debts, enforced payment.
poursuite pénale: strafgerichtliche Verfolgung: criminal prosecution.
pourvoir aux besoins de sa profession ou son entreprise: verantwortungsbewusste Vorsorge: make provisions with adequate care about.
pouvoir d'appréciation: Ermessen: at a person's discretion.
prescription: Verjährung: limitation of actions.
prescription acquisitive: Ersitzung: adverse possession, prescription.

Vocabulary

présomption: Vermutung: presumption.
prêt sur gage: Versatzpfand: pawn.
preuve: Beweis: proof, evidence.
privilège: Vorrecht: priority.
procédure: Verfahren: procedure.
prodigalité: Verschwendung: prodigality.
profession ou une industrie, exercer une: Gewerbe ausüben: engage in trade or profession.
proposition: Antrag: motion, proposition.
propriété: Eigentum: property, ownership.
propriété foncière: Grundeigentum: ownership of land.
propriété mobilière: Fahrniseigentum: ownership of movable property.
puissance paternelle: elterliche Gewalt: parental power.
pupille: Bevormundeter: ward.
purge hypothécaire: Ablösung: redemption.

quotité disponible: verfügbarer Teil: devisable portion.

rapport: Ausgleichung: hotchpot.
ratification: Genehmigung: ratification.
récompense: Ausgleich: compensation.
reconnaissance: Anerkennung: acknowledgment.
recours: Weiterziehung, Rekurs, Appellation: appeal.
rectification: Berichtigung: rectification.
reddition des comptes: Rechnungsstellung: rendering of accounts.
réel: dinglich: real, in rem.
régime matrimonial: ehelicher Güterstand: matrimonial property system.
registre de l'état civil: Zivilstandsregister: register of civil status.
registre des régimes matrimoniaux: Güterrechtsregisteramt: matrimonial property registry office.
registre du commerce: Handelsregister: commercial register.
registre foncier: Grundbuch: land register.

remblais: Anschüttung: deposit (of land).
réméré, droit de: Rückkaufsrecht: right of redemption.
rente: Rente: annuity.
rente de droit de superficie: Baurechtzins: right of building-charge.
rente viagère: Leibrente: life annuity.
réparation morale: Genugtuung: moral compensation.
répudiation: Ausschlagung: disclaimer.
requête: Begehren: request; at the instance of.
réserve héréditaire: Pflichtteil: compulsory portion.
réserve de propriété, pacte de: Eigentumsvorbehalt: pact to reserve ownership.
responsabilité: Haftbarkeit: liability.
responsable: haftbar: liable.
rétention, droit de: Retentionsrecht: lien.
révocation: Aufhebung, Widerruf: rescission, revocation.

saisie: Pfändung: seizure of property in execution.
séparation (de fruits): Trennung: severance.
séparation de biens: Gütertrennung: system of separate estates.
séparation de corps: Trennung: judicial separation.
séquestre: Beschlagnahme: sequestration.
servitude: Dienstbarkeit: servitude.
servitude foncière: Grunddienstbarkeit: praedial servitude.
société: Personenverbindung: association, society.
société coopérative: Genossenschaft: co-operative society.
société d'allmends: Allmendgenossenschaft: association for common cultivation of land.
société simple: einfache Gesellschaft: partnership.
sommation: Auskündung: citation.
souche, par: nach Stämmen: per stirpes.
spécification: Verarbeitung: manufacture.

status: Statuten: (articles of) constitution.
substitution fidéicommissaire: Nacherbeneinsetzung: appointment of reversionary heir.
substitution vulgaire: Ersatzverfügung: substitution.
succession: Erbschaft: inheritance, succession.
superficie, droit de: Baurecht: right of building, right over a building.
sursis concordataire: Nachlassstundung: suspension of liquidation proceedings.

teneur: Wortlaut: wording.
testament: letztwillige Verfügung: will, testament.
titre: Titel: security, document of title.
tradition: Übergabe: delivery.
transfert: Übertragung: transfer.
transiger: einen Vergleich abschliessen: compromise an action.
Tribunal fédéral: Bundesgericht: Federal Court.
tutelle: Vormundschaft: guardianship.

tutelle, mettre sous: bevormunden: place under guardianship.
tuteur: Vormund: guardian.

union conjugale: eheliche Gemeinschaft: conjugal union.
union des biens: Güterverbindung: marital system.
usage: Übung: usage.
usage local: Ortsgebrauch, Ortsübung: local custom.
usufruit: Nutzung, Nutzniessung: usufruct.
usufruitier: Nutzniesser: usufructuary.

valeur de rachat: Rückkaufswert: redemption value.
valeur de rendement: Ertragswert: value based on annual return.
valeur vénale: Verkehrswert: selling value.
voisinage, droit de: Nachbarrecht: jus vicinorum.
voiturier: Frachtführer: carrier.

warrant: Pfandschein: warrant.

Index

The numbers refer to articles of the Code. The references "Old Law" and "New Law" refer to the articles of Titles V and VI, General Effects of Marriage and Matrimonial Property Law. F.T. is the abbreviation for Final Title. "Et seq." refers to at least the two following articles.

ABSENCE, declaration of 35 et seq., 50, 102, 546 et seq., F.T. 6

ABUSE, of right 2, representation of wife 164 (Old Law), 174 (New Law), parental power 311, guardianship 445

ACCESSORIES, as part(s) of a thing 644, 645, 805, 892, 946

ACCOUNTS, presented by guardian 413, 451, 452

ACKNOWLEDGMENT, of a child 47, 252 et seq., 256, 260 et seq., 461, F.T. 13

ACQUISITION of land 656 et seq., 665, of chattel 718, of movable property 714 et seq., of servitudes 731, of usufruct 746, of rent-charge 783

ACQUISITIONS IN MARRIAGE, in divorce 154, in Old Law also "voluntarily acquired property" 239, 240, also "profit and losses" 189, 214, 240, in New Law: system of 181 et seq., 197, 198, at dissolution of matrimonial property system 207, also "profit (and losses)" 206, 210

ACT, unlawful (illegal) 28, 52, 57, 78, 88, 482, 519, 521, wrongful 19; 207, 220 (Old Law), 318

ACT, wrongful 19; 207, 220 (Old Law); 318

ACTION, continuation by plaintiff's heirs 93, 135

ADMINISTRATION, in conjugal union 200, 216, 242 (Old Law), 195, 227, 228, 232 (New Law), of child's property 318 et seq., deprivation of 370, by guardian 413, 414, of inheritance 554, 555, 585, 595, co-ownership 647, storey-ownership 712g, 712h

ADOPTION 264 et seq., of minors 264 et seq., of majors and persons without discretion 26, effects of 267, 267a, procedure of 268, voidability of 269, 269b, consequences for right to inherit 465

ADULTERY 137

ALLOTMENT, at dissolution of common property system 237, of immovables to heirs 617

ANIMALS 700, 719, 725

ANTIQUITIES, acquisition of 724, preservation of 702

AREAS, of registration 40, 427, 430, 454, 951 et seq.

ASSEMBLY, Federal F.T. 39, 53, 61

ASSIGNMENT, of debts and securities in usufruct 758, 775, of debts and rights to be pledged 899

AUCTION, public 400, 404, 596, 612, 625bis, 651, 721, 829, 830, 934

AUTHORITIES, local (commune) 57, 330, 376, 377, 378, 386, 427, 430, 454, 466, 550, 555, 592, 702, 907, competent 46, 86, 109, 121; 164, 167, 246 (Old Law), Appendix 2: 20, 36, 68a, 68b (New Law); 253, 260, 279, 311 et seq., 329, 333, 355, 368, 369, 371, 373, 378, 397b, 433, 490, 505, 550, 551, 553 et seq., 559, 570, 580 et seq., 602, 609, 611, 612, 621, 625, 721, 861, 885, 910, 916, F.T. 52, 54

AUTHENTICATION (duly authenticated instrument) 9, 81; 181, 147, 198

AUTHENTICATION (continuation) (Old Law); 184, 195a (New Law); 337, 398, 490, 498, 553, 657, 682, 712d, 731, 763, 779, 779a, 779e, 857, F.T. 55, by witnesses 507, 512

BANKRUPTCY, of husband 188, 210, 224, 244 (Old Law), 188, 236 (New Law); 343, 455
BETROTHAL 90 et seq., 105 et seq.
BIRTH 31, 33, 46, 47, 252 et seq., 267
BOARD, of storey-owners 712m
BODIES, corporate 52 et seq., 393, 796
BONA FIDE(S) 3; 122, 133, 134; 164, 167 (Old Law); 375, 411, 528, 547, 579, 600, 661, 673, 714, 726, 728, 738, 865, 866, 867, 874, 884, 895, 925, 931, 933 et seq., 938, 939, 973, 975
BONDS, secured on land 875 et seq.
BOUNDARIES 668 et seq., 702
BUILDING(S) 671 et seq., 686, 702, 779, 836 et seq., right of 675, 682, 779, 779a et seq.
BROTHERS & SISTERS 100, 328, 329, 355, 458, 470 et seq., 503, Appendix 1: 59
BROTHERS-IN-LAW & SISTERS-IN-LAW 21, 100, 120
BURDEN (encumbrance), on property 899, 900 et seq., co-owner's share 648, 721i

CAPABILITY, of marriage 96
CAPACITY, to have rights 11, 53, to act 12 et seq., 18, 306, 712l, 712t, F.T. 5; of wife 168, to make marriage covenant 180 (Old Law), of spouse 163, 168, 183 (New Law); restricted 305, 395, 421, of ward 398, 409 et seq., 446, of testator 467
CASE-LAW 1
CATTLE, pledge of 885
CERTIFICATE, of unsatisfied claims 182, 186, 480
CHARGES, imposed on foundation 86
CHILD, before birth 31, 393, 544

CHILD-PARENT RELATIONSHIP 252 et seq., 264 et seq., 270 et seq., 296 et seq., 318 et seq., F.T. 12, 13
CITATION, public – to debtors and creditors of deceased 582, 592, 595
CITIZENSHIP 22, 161, 267a, 271, abuse in marriage 120 et seq.
CIVIC RIGHTS, to be a guardian 382, to give evidence 503
CIVIL STATUS REGISTER, entries as proof 33, registration 39 et seq., 119, notification 39, 51, registrars 40 et seq., 110, 113 et seq., 117, 118, 131, 260, 368, modifications 47, nullity of marriage 134
CLAIM, of wife in case of bankruptcy 180 (Old Law), of spouse in case of bankruptcy 188, in case of execution 189 (New Law); of heirs for board and lodging 606, against lessees and tenants 806, secured on land 794, 795, 847, 854, 855, for injury to person where plaintiff dies 93, unsatisfied certificate of 182, 186, 480
CO-HEIRS (also see HEIRS) 602 et seq., 626 et seq., 634 et seq., 837, 838
COMMITTEE, under a: see PERSONS under a committee
COMMUNITY, of property 336 et seq.; system of 215 (Old Law), 188, 189 (New Law)
COMPENSATION, moral 28a, 28b, 29, 93, 134, 151, 153, reduction of inheritance 535, 626 et seq.
COMPETENCE 35, 113, 136, 144; 180, 190 (New Law); 253, 275, 279 et seq., 397c, 538, 952
COMPLAINTS, against civil status registrar 43, against guardian 99, 420, against guardianship board 378, 420, 450, against administrator of official liquidation 595, against registrar of land register 956
CONDITIONS, made by testator 482, illegal or immoral 482, 519, 521, of mortgage certificates and land-charges 854

Index

CONSENT 15, 19, 98, 137; 228 et seq., (New Law), 265, 265a, 266, 269, 269b, 352, 395, 410 et seq., 424

CONSTITUTION, of corporate bodies 54, 56, 57, of societies 60, 61, 63 et seq.

CONTRACTORS & WORKMEN, rights of 837 et seq.

CONTRACTS 7, 422, 635, 636, 657, 732, made under Old Law F.T. 50

CO-OWNERSHIP (also see OWNERSHIP, united/in common) 646 et seq., of storey-ownership 712a et seq., 648, 670, 682, 800

COUNCIL, Federal 39 et seq., 85, 86, 119, 269c, 316, 359, 383, 425, 705, 885, 915, 945, 949, 950, 953, 962, 967, 977, F.T. 30, 33, 38, 40, 42, 46, 52, 53, 57, 61

COUNTER-STATEMENT 28g et seq.

COUPONS 861, 870, 904

COURT, competent 35, 111, 144; 180, 186, 190, 194, 220, 230 (New Law); 253, 275, 279, 284, 315, 315a, 329, 538

CRIME, as cause of divorce 139, of disinheritance 477

CURATOR 282, 306, 308, 309, 325, 367, 392 et seq., 417, 418, 419, 439, 762, 823, 861

CUSTOM (customary) 5, 579, 629, 631, 632, 643

DAMAGES, for damage caused by minors and incapacitated persons 19, 411, for injury to person 28a, 28b, 28f, for assumption of name 29, for damage caused by registrars and authorities 42, in divorce 151, 153, in guardianship 426 et seq., for destruction of will 510, in action against heirs 562, for building in bad faith 672, 726, 727, owner exceeds his rights 679, for drifts and strays 700, 701, with springs 706, damage done to res fructuaria 752, workmen and contractors 841, in land register 867, 955, 975, mala fide possessor 940 (also see COMPENSATION and LIABILITY)

DEATH 31, 32 et seq., 35 et seq., 48 et seq., 100, 101; 233, 235 (Old Law), 194, 204, 241, 243, 244 (New Law); 261, 297, 345, 357, 441, 487, 489, 537, 546

DEBTS (also see LIABILITIES), of spouse 166, 177, 185, 189, 193, 195, 202, 209, 233 et seq., 238, 249 (New Law), of testator 474, 518, 603, 615, 626, 639, 640, liabilities of co-heirs 637, repayment of pledged – 809, taking over mortgage by new owner 834, mortgages and land-charges 842 et seq., with broken up property 852

DECREE, judicia – of paternity 252, 259, 260 et seq.

DEFENCE, of person or property 727, 926

DEPRIVATION, of liberty through custody 314 et seq., for personal assistance 397 et seq., F.T. 14a; of parental power 311 et seq., F.T. 12

DESERTION 140

DISAVOWAL, of paternity 256, 260a

DISCLAIM, of inheritance 486, 492, 566 et seq., by wife 204, 218 (Old Law), by spouse 230 (New Law)

DISCRETION 16

DISINHERITANCE 477 et seq.

DISPOSITIONS, testamentary (wills or pacts) 467 et seq., F.T. 16, restrictions 516, 681 et seq., 702, 920, capacity 467 et seq., 501, 507, F.T. 16, freedom of 470 et seq., disinheritance 477 et seq., F.T. 16

DISPOSSESSION (expropriation, execution for debt, etc.) 656, 665, 666, 691, 750, 801

DISTURBANCES, domestic 142

DIVISION, of matrimonial property: on divorce 154; in marriage 189, 214, 225 et seq., 236, 240 (Old Law), 192, 194, 211, 214, 240, 242, 243 (New Law); of common property 346

DIVORCE 137 et seq., procedure 158, F.T. 8
DOCTRINE, approved legal 1
DOMICILE 23 et seq., 56; 186 (New Law); local venue 28b, 28f, 35, 144, 256, 261, 262, 312, further competences 121, 250, 253, 375, 378, 387, 396, 421, 538
DONATION 395, 408, 527, 761
DUTY/DUTIES, to contribute to maintenance of wife 161, 192 (Old Law), of spouses 156, 170, 176, 246 (Old Law), 159, 163 (New Law), to register births and deaths 46, 47, 48, breach of official – by civil status officials 44, by land registrars 957

EDUCATION 301 et seq., 319, 320, 378, 405, 631
EFFECT, retrospective – of Civil Code F.T. 1
ENRICHMENT 94, 208, 221, 411, 515, 565, 579, 590, 726, 727
ENTRIES, in land register 963, rights of way 696, mortgages in favour of contractors and workmen 841, absence of heir 490
EQUITY, principle of justice and 4, of share in income 347
ERASURES, in land register 964
ERROR, civil status register 45, land register 977, marriage 124, last will 469, 519, disinheritance 479
ESTATE, separate see SEPARATE ESTATE, a person's as a object of testamentary dispositions 481
EXECUTOR 517 et seq., 554
EXPENSES 317, 722, 819, 939, 940
EXPULSION, board member of society 65, manager of community of storey-owners 712r
EXTINCTION, in land register 826, 864, 964 et seq.
EXTRACTS, from matrimonial property register 251 (Old Law), from land register 967, 970

FAMILY 331 et seq., head 331 et seq., property 335 et seq., register 39, 40, foundation 52, 87, 335, guardianship 362 et seq.
FARM 338, 617 et seq.
FORCE, to use – to protect possessions 926 et seq.
FORESTS 678, 687, 699, 770
FOSTER-PARENTS (foster-child) 294, 310, 316
FOUNDATION, status of 52, 59, family 52, 87, 335, in general 80 et seq., F.T. 7, conditions and charges imposed on 86, rights of testator 493
FRAUD, relating to marriage 125
FRUITS, natural 195 (Old Law); 643, 756, 892

GIFT, to surviving spouse 473, to heirs 629, to descendants at marriage 629, customary gifts 579
GOOD FAITH, principle of 2
GOODS, delivered to another 714, 884, 933
GREAT-GRANDPARENTS, inheritance 460
GROUND, material 4, 30, 65, 72, 92, 96, 140; 185 (New Law); 256c, 260c, 263, 343, 348, 350, 380, 381, 576
GUARANTEE, mutual by heirs 637
GUARDIAN, family as 362 et seq., appointment of 379 et seq., excuses to accept office of 383, grounds for exclusion 384, refusal to act 388, duration of office 415, rendering accounts 413, 451, 452, dismissal from office 443, 445 et seq., criminal offence 455; to make marriage covenant 183, 184 (New Law)
GUARDIANSHIP 360 et seq., F.T. 14, 14a, 52
GUARDIANSHIP AUTHORITIES, marriage of persons under committee 99, child represented by parents 279, protection of child 283, 285, competence etc. 376 et seq.

Index

GUARDIANSHIP BOARD 25, 99, 157; 177, 181, 204, 207, 218, 220, 229, 232 (Old Law), 183, 184 (New Law); 275, 287, 288, 307 et seq., 318, 324, 325, 380, 381, 391 et seq., 396 et seq., 401, 403, 404, 412, 413, 416 et seq., 440, 445 et seq., 823

HEAD, of conjugal home 160 (Old Law); of group living together in one household 331 et seq., of community of property 341

HEIR(S), divorced spouse 154, adopted child 267, institution of 483, 494, certificate 559, community of 241, 246 (New Law), 457 et seq., 467 et seq., 537 et seq., 502, F.T. 15, 16, 17, substitution of 487, reversionary 488 et seq.

HOME, conjugal 160 (Old Law), 162 (New Law), legal (also see CITIZENSHIP) 22, 35, 121; 161 (Old Law), 161 (New Law); 259, 260a, 263, 375, 378, 387

HONORARIUM (remuneration, reward), of guardian or curator 416, 417, of executors 517, of finder 722 et seq.

HUSBAND 160 et seq. (Old Law), also see Part I, Section I, 160 (New Law), also see SPOUSE(S)

ILLNESS, effects 16, 115, 120, 122, 125, 126; 170 (Old Law); (266), (268a), 302, 392, 397a et seq.

INCAPABILITY, of exercising right of representation 174 (New Law), for exercising parental power 311, 312, of major to manage his own affairs 369, 372, 393, 395, as witness or to establish legal document 503, to make will or pact 519, 521

INCAPACITATION 368 et seq., 413 et seq., at person's own request owing to old age or infirmity 372, prohibited acts of ward 408

INHERITANCE, unworthiness 225 (Old Law), 486, 492, 540, 541, official administration 490, 548, 554 et seq., renunciation 495 et seq., securities to be given to beneficiaries or creditors 497, 546, 589, 594, vesting 560 et seq., to enforce right by action 598 et seq., selling value of non-agricultural land 617, 618, of additional industry 625, 625bis, great-grandparents 460

INSOLVENCY 77, 356, 421, 445, 497, 566, 604, 897

INSTITUTION(S), to act as pawn-brokers 907

INTENTION, lack of 469, 519

INTEREST, on capital 757, 765, res fructuaria 818, on charged property 862, 891, 904, guardian's duty to lay money out at 401, pawnbroker's right 913

INVENTORY 197 et seq. (Old Law), 195a (New Law); 318, 398, 490, 553, 568, 580 et seq., 620, 763

JUDGE 1, 28b et seq., 35, 45 et seq., 75 et seq., 87, 93, 111, 144 et seq., 155 et seq.; 163, 167, 169 et seq., 183 et seq. (Old Law), 166, 169, 172, 174, 176, 178, 180, Appendix 2: 68b (New Law); 252, 253, 256, 260, 261, 279 et seq., 291 et seq., 430, 598, 604, 651, 662, 665, 712c, 712q, 712r, 717, 762, 809, 870, 871, 961, 966, 976, 977, F.T. 54, at discretion of 4, 145, 334, 717, 796

JUDGMENT, of court in divorce and separation 148, in acquisition of land 656, 665, publication of 28a

LAND-CHARGE 847 et seq., 624, redemption of 850

LAND-CHARGE NOTE, document 856 et seq., 868 et seq., 873, form of certificate 858

LAND-REGISTER 178 (New Law), 353, 367, 368, 490, 598, 619, 655, 658, 661, 662, 665, 666, 674 et seq., 680 et seq., 691, 696, 712d, 712f, 731, 734 et seq., 738, 743, 744, 746 et seq., 776 et seq., 783, 784, 786, 789, 799 et seq., 807, 819, 820, 825, 834,

LAND-REGISTER (continuation) 835, 841, 856, 860, 864, 865, 867, 870, 874, 879, 881, 942 et seq., 944, 959, 963, 964, 977, 959, F.T. 38 et seq.

LAST WILL (also see DISPOSITIONS, testamentary/wills and pacts), forms and procedure 498 et seq.

LAW, application of 1, application of Swiss and Foreign F.T. 59, Case Law 1, Customary Law 1, Federal 5, 702, 918, Federal Private 6, Cantonal 59, 349, 376, 397e, 423, 472, 553, 609, 616, 659, 664, 686, 688, 695, 697, 699, 709, 740, 795, 796, 822, 828, 830, 845, 918, 944, 948, 949, 963, 972, F.T. 9, 15, 20, 22, 24, 30, 32, 44, 46, 48, 52, 57, Cantonal Public 5, 6, 22, 52, 59, 87, 289, 293, 314 et seq., 384, 427, 641, 659, 664, 680, 699, 702, 703, 801, 822, 907, 954, 957, Law of Obligations 7, 514, 563, Private Law 7, Public Law 2a

LEASE 354, 959

LEGACY 484 et seq., 511, 513, 515, 525, 526, 543, 562 et seq., 594, 601

LEGAL DOCTRINE, approved 1

LESSEE, claims against 806

LIABILITIES, joint and several 342, 429, 603, 619quinquies, 639

LIABILITY 55; 188, 206 et seq., 219 et seq., 227, 243, 300 (Old Law), 166, 193, 202, 203, 218, 220, 231, 233 et seq., 260 (New Law); 293, 326, 327, 328 et seq., 333, 412, 579, 589 et seq., 603, 637 et seq., 782, 832, 847

LIBERTY, personal 27

LIEN 700, 712k, 895 et seq., F.T. 63

LIMITATION 95, 127, 137, 138, 256c, 260c, 263, 454 et seq., 521, 533, 600, 601, 637, 639, 754, 790, 807, 911, 929, F.T. 49

LIQUIDATION, property of corporate body 58, bankruptcy 573, 578, official − of inheritance 593 et seq.

MACHINES, as accessories 805

MAINTENANCE, in marriage and divorce 134, 151, 152; 160, 170, 183 (Old Law), 163, 165, 173, 213 (New Law); liability 293, 328 et seq., in parent-child relationship (family) 276 et seq., 319, 320, 323, 328 et seq., 335, in guardianship 308 (curator), 405, 422, in inheritance 474, 605, 606, of foundlings 330

MAJORITY (full age) 13, 14, emancipation of ward 15, 431, incapacity to act 17, 19, 468, parental power 296, 385, continued community of property 232 (Old Law), of votes 67, of heirs (co-heirs) 602 et seq., of storey-owners 712p, 712r

MANAGER, in storey-ownership 712m, 712q et seq.

MARITAL SYSTEM 178 et seq., 194 et seq., 200 et seq., 238 et seq., 235 et seq. (Old Law)

MARKET 934

MARRIAGE 90 et seq., capable of 96, opposition 108 et seq., voidability of 123 et seq., divorce 137 et seq.; effects of 159 et seq. (Old Law), 159 et seq. (New Law); F.T. 8, dower 247, transfer of rights in repudiation of promise 93

MARRIAGE COVENANT 180, 181, 190, 214, 226, 237 et seq., 247, 248 et seq. (Old Law); choice of system 182, capacity 183, form 184, recission 187, participation in acquisitions 191, spouse's profession, revenues, matrimonial profit 216, upon divorce, separation, nullity 217, appartment and personal chattels 219, community of property 223, 224, division 241 (New Law)

MATRIMONIAL PROPERTY SYSTEM 178 et seq. (Old Law), 178 et seq. (New Law)

MEASURES, precautionary for protection of personality 28c et seq., in marriage 145; 169 (Old Law), 172 (New Law); parent-child relationship

Index 417

281 et seq., in guardianship 386, 448, 449
MEDIA, injury to person 28c, 28g, institution 28i, 28k, 281
MILITARY SERVICE, to make oral will 507
MINORS 17, 19, 90, 98, 128; 180, 229, 231 (Old Law), (173), 176, 183, (216) (New Law); 277, 296, 298, 318, 333, 368, 621bis
MODIFICATION, in status of persons 47, 51, in organization of foundation 86, circumstances after divorce 157, requirements of child 286, in ownership of land 665, res fructuaria 769, in legal position of mortgagor and mortgagee 874
MORALITY (IMMORALITY) 27, 52, 57, 78, 482, 519, 521, F.T. 2
MORTGAGE, purpose etc. 842 et seq., as safeguard 808 et seq., extent 805, 892, 904, redemption of 828, right to create 836 et seq., form of certificate 858, document of 856 et seq., 868 et seq., 873, other forms of real security 793, also see REAL SECURITY
MORTGAGED PROPERTY, repayment by portions 809, alienation 811, 832 et seq., 846, 868, 890
MOTHER 252, 255 et seq., 260a et seq., 270 et seq., 276 et seq., 295, 297, 298, 301, 309, 462 et seq., 473

NAME 29, 30, 134, 149; 161 (Old Law), 160 (New Law); 207, 267, 301
NEIGHBOURS, rights 684 et seq.
NOISE AND NOXIOUS AIR 684
NOTICE, to give 338, 344, 623, 773, 831, 844, 850, 906
NULLITY, of marriage 120 et seq.

OATH, divorce 158
OFFENCE, criminal of guardian 455
OPPOSITION, to foundation 83, to acknowledgment of establishment of paternity 259, 260a et seq., to adoption 269, 269a et seq., in partition of inheritance 638, to resolutions by community of storey-owners 712m
ORGANS, official – of corporate bodies 54, 55, of societies 64 et seq., of foundation 83, 85, of guardianship 360 et seq.
OWNERS, united 646 et seq., 800, in common 652 et seq., 800, undivided 215 et seq. (Old Law), 226 et seq. (New Law)
OWNERSHIP 641 et seq., extent 642, 667 et seq., united 646 et seq., in common 652 et seq.; of spouses 215 (Old Law), 226 et seq. (New Law); family 336 et seq., 342, of land 655 et seq., 800, of springs 704, 780, reserve of 715, 716

PARTITION, directions 522, 608, of inheritance 604 et seq., agreement, of property 650, 651, 653, 654
PATERNITY, action to contest (252), 253, 254, 256, 256a, 256c, (257), 259, 260a et seq., (282), (283), 295
PAYMENTS BY INSTALMENTS of movables with reserve of ownership 716
PERSON, status of corporate bodies 52 et seq., 60 et seq., 80 et seq., F.T. 7
PERSONALITY 11, 12 et seq., 20 et seq., F.T. 5, 6, 7, beginning of legal 31
PERSONS UNDER COMMITTEE 19, 90, 99, 180 (Old Law), 183, 184, 185 (New Law), 266, 333
PLEDGE 717, 884 et seq., F.T. 34, 35, 36
PORTION, compulsory 470 et seq., 477, 480, 522, F.T. 59
POSSESSION(S) 919 et seq., F.T. 37, (bona fide) peacable 661 et seq., 728, 941, F.T. 19, original and derivative 920
POWER, parental 296 et seq., F.T. 12
PREGNANCY 103, 128, 295, 309
PRESCRIPTION (ADVERSE POSSESSION) 661 et seq., 728, 941, F.T. 19

PRESENTS 94, 527, 979, 632
PRESS 28g
PROOF 8, 9, 10, 28c, 32, 158; of unreserved property of wife 196 (Old Law), of a spouse's property 200 (New Law); of paternity 254, of disinheritance 479, of existence of heirs 548, 554 et seq., land register 965, 966
PROPERTY, immovable 395, 404, 490, 596, 616 et seq., 655 et seq., 768 et seq., 781, 782 et seq., 793 et seq., 943, 944, 951, 952, unreserved and held in common − transaction of 177, lack of consent for transaction 167 (Old Law), system of community of common 215 et seq. (Old Law), 185, 189 (New Law), a spouse's own 198 et seq. (New Law); continued system of community of 229 et seq. (Old Law), matrimonial − system 178 et seq. (Old and New Law), 145, 154, 235 et seq. (New Law); common F.T. 68a, 68b, child's, right of parents over 318 et seq., deprivation of 324, 325, of family 335 et seq., received and brought into hotchpot 628, defence of 701, movable 713, acquisition 714 et seq., safeguards against where depreciation of real estate 808 et seq., rights over of contractors and workmen 837 et seq., lost or stolen 934
PROTECTION 27, 28 et seq., 74, 75; 169 (Old Law), (172), 180, 193 (New Law), of child 307, 311, 313 et seq., movable property 714, possessions 926 et seq., 930 et seq., 938, 939
PUBLICATION 28a, 28i, 28k, 30, 106; 164, 165, 167, 248, 251 (Old Law), 174 (New Law); 353, 358, 375, 377, 386, 387, 397, 431, 440, 555, 595, 662, 720, 871, F.T. 43
PUBLICITY, of solemnization of marriage 16
PURCHASE, right of − entered in land register 683, 959

RADIO 28g
RECTIFICATIONS, in civil status register 45, in land register 977
REDEMPTION, of rent-charge 787, of mortgage 828, of land-charge 850
REDUCTION, of inheritance 535, claim for 552 et seq.
REGISTER CIVIL STATUS, registration, areas of 40, 427, 430, 454, 951 et seq., error 45, in general 46 et seq.
REGISTER, COMMERCIAL 52, 61, 79, 81, 89, 251, 341, of immovable property 942 et seq.
REGISTER, MATRIMONIAL PROPERTY 181, 182, 186, 187, 248 et seq., F.T. 10, 19, 90 (Old Law)
REGULATIONS, of storey-ownership 712g, 712s
REIMBURSEMENT, a child's right to enforce 334bis
RELATIONSHIP, RELATIVES 20, 21, 100, 120, 252 et seq., 363, 364, 380
RELIEF, from servitude 736
RENT-CHARGE, redemption of 782 et seq., 787
REPAYMENT, of mortgaged property by portions of debt 809, of pledged debts 906
REPRESENTATION, of conjugal union 162 et seq., of wife in bringing or defending action 168, of wife's property 201, of wife's debts incurred in marriage 206, in continued community of property 231 (Old Law), representation of conjugal union 166, 174, 228 (New Law); of children 304 et seq., of family, community of property 340, 341, by curator 392, of ward and his property 405, 407 et seq. in storey-ownership 712t, of creditor and mortgagee 823, 860, of creditor and debtor 877, 880, of shares given in pledge 905
RESCISSION, of matrimonial property system 172 (New Law), of partition of inheritance 638
RESERVE, of ownership 715, 716
RESIGNATION, from membership 70

Index 419

REWARD, finder's 722
RIGHT, to status 47, 259, 270, 271, to administer or use child's property 318 et seq., of building 675, 779, 779a et seq., of purchase 681 et seq., 959, of pre-emption 681, 682, 712c, 959, of redemption 683, 959, to encumber shares of co-owners 648, 712i, to create mortgage 836 et seq., to encumber property 899 et seq., of unpaid vendor to pledge 837, 838, of residence 776 et seq., of vote in societies 67, 68, in storey-ownership 712o, 712p
RIGHTS, civic 382, 503, sale of (inheritance) 495, assignment of 635 et seq., independent and permanent 655, 779, 780, 943, of contractors and workmen 837 et seq., personal, notation in land register 959, real 971 et seq., F.T. 17
RULE, of the house 332 et seq.

SALE, of inherited farm 625bis, of co-owned property 648, of mortgaged property 811, 832 et seq., 846, 868, 890, restrictions 681 et seq., 702, 960
SECURITY, real 793 et seq., 824 et seq., 842 et seq., 875 et seq., F.T. 22, 23, securities to bearer 859, 901, 985, securities payable to order 898
SEPARATE ESTATE 190 et seq., 208, 209, 221, 223, 230 (Old Law); under family continuity 342, of ward 414, also see CHILD'S PROPERTY 318 et seq.
SEPARATE ESTATES, system of 182, 183 et seq., 237, 241 et seq. (Old Law), 179, 185, 187 et seq., 192, 194, 217, 236, 242 (New Law), in case of separation 155
SEPARATION, of husband and wife 143 et seq., 150, 155, 156; (170, Old Law), 176, 179, 194, 204, 217, 236, 242 (Old Law)
SERVITUDE, right over building 675, conduits 676, praedial 730 et seq., relief from 736, extent 737 et seq., right of residence 776 et seq., springs 780, on mortgaged land 812, in land register 946, 958, 968; others 781, 730 et seq., 734 et seq., 737 et seq., 788, 812, (920, 958), F.T. 21
SHARE, a spouse's share of other spouse's common property in case of other spouse's death 241 (New Law); of co-heirs in profit 619 et seq., of co-owners 646
SHARES, given in pledge 905
SOCIETIES 60 et seq., 64 et seq., 70 et seq.
SPOUSE(S) 159 et seq., 174 et seq. (Old Law), 159 et seq. (New Law); preferential right as guardian 380, inheritance of surviving 462 et seq., 471, 473
SPRINGS 667, 704, 705 et seq.
STAFF WELFARE, foundation 89bis
STATUS of person, foundations and associations 52, 59
STEP-PARENTS (step-child) 100, 299
STIRPS (per stirpes) 457 et seq., 496
STOREY-OWNERS, board of community of 712m
STOREY-OWNERSHIP 675, 712a et seq., F.T. 20bis et seq.
SUCCESSION (devolution of estate) 537 et seq., 602 et seq.
SUPERVISORY AUTHORITIES 15, 40, 43 et seq., 84, 265, 361, 363, 364, 366, 375, 388, 390, 404, 422, 423, 426 et seq., 450, 956, 957

TELEVISION 28g
TENANTS, claims against 806
TESTAMENTARY PACT 468, 494 et seq., 512 et seq., 534 et seq.
THINGS, trading of 6; wife's property 201 (Old Law), spouse's property 247, 248, 250 (New Law); parts of 642 et seq., 655, 713, 805, 892, without owners 658, 664, 718, 719, new ground 659, perishable – in usufruct 760, 772
THREATS 126, 469, 540

TRADE OR PROFESSION, of wife 167, 207, 220 (Old Law), of spouses 167, 229, 233 (New Law)

TRANSACTION, legal 6, 7, 55, 68; 177 (Old Law), 168, 169, 229, 231 (New Law), 306, 650, 689, 712d

TRANSFER, of plaintiff's rights in broken promise of marriage 93, of ownership of land 657, of movables 714 et seq., of secured debt 835, 869, of possessions 922 et seq.

USUFRUCT, of surviving spouse 219, 244 (New Law); in inheritance (300), 460, 462, 463, 473, 530, 561, 745 et seq., 758, assignment of debts and securities 712c, 775, of rights and movables 746, restoration 750

VALUATION of property, official 830, 843, 848

VALUE, of share in storey-ownership 712e

VOIDABILITY, of marriage 120 et seq., 133, 134 (New Law), of adoption 269, 269a, 269b

VOIDNESS, of testamentary dispositions 469, 519 et seq., 538

WATER 676, 689 et seq., 740, also see SPRINGS

WIFE 161, 163 et seq., 167, 168, 177, also see Part II, Section I (Old Law), 161, see SPOUSE(S) (New Law)

WITNESSES, at wedding ceremony 116, at the making of testamentary dispositions 499, 501 et seq., 506, 507, 512

WORKMEN AND CONTRACTORS, rights 837 et seq.

WRITING, in 60, 81, 105, 108, 303, 337, 498 et seq., 634, 635, 828, 886, 903 et seq., 907, 963, F.T. 9

D1755200

Alles zu Nützen

L. F. Z. ANHALT

Die Fruchtbringende Gesellschafft

Die deutsche Akademie des 17. Jahrhunderts
Fruchtbringende Gesellschaft

Kritische Ausgabe der Briefe,
Beilagen und Akademiearbeiten (Reihe I),
Dokumente und Darstellungen (Reihe II)

Begründet von
Martin Bircher † und Klaus Conermann

Im Auftrag der Sächsischen Akademie der Wissenschaften zu Leipzig,
in Kooperation mit der Herzog August Bibliothek Wolfenbüttel

herausgegeben von

Klaus Conermann

Reihe I, Abt. A: Köthen
Abt. B: Weimar
Abt. C: Halle

Reihe II, Abt. A: Köthen
Abt. B: Weimar
Abt. C: Halle

In Kommission: De Gruyter

Briefe der Fruchtbringenden Gesellschaft und Beilagen: Die Zeit Fürst Ludwigs von Anhalt-Köthen 1617–1650

Siebter Band 1644–1646
Teil I: Januar 1644 – Juli 1645

Herausgegeben von Klaus Conermann und Andreas Herz
unter Mitarbeit von Gabriele Ball

Reihe I
Abteilung A: Köthen
Band 7, Teilband I

In Kommission: De Gruyter

Das Vorhaben „Die deutsche Akademie des 17. Jahrhunderts: Fruchtbringende Gesellschaft" ist ein Forschungsvorhaben der Sächsischen Akademie der Wissenschaften zu Leipzig und wird im Rahmen des Akademienprogramms von der Bundesrepublik Deutschland und dem Bundesland Niedersachsen gefördert. Das Akademienprogramm wird koordiniert von der Union der deutschen Akademien der Wissenschaften.

ISBN 978-3-11-051976-1

Bibliografische Information der Deutschen Nationalbibliothek

Die Deutsche Nationalbibliothek verzeichnet diese Publikation in der Deutschen Nationalbibliografie; detaillierte bibliografische Daten sind im Internet über http://dnb.dnb.de abrufbar.

© Sächsische Akademie der Wissenschaften zu Leipzig 2016;
in Kommission bei Walter de Gruyter GmbH & Co. KG, Berlin/Boston

Gesamtherstellung: Hubert & Co GmbH & Co. KG, Göttingen
∞ Gedruckt auf säurefreiem Papier
Printed in Germany

www.degruyter.com

Inhalt

Zum vorliegenden Bande	7
Editorische Vorbemerkung	26
Sigeln, Abkürzungen, Zeichen und Monatsnamen	31
Sigeln	31
Abkürzungen des Herausgebers	33
Häufige Abkürzungen in Quellen	36
Sonderzeichen für Wochentage — Deutsche Monatsnamen	41
Verzeichnis der edierten Quellen	42
I. Handschriftenbestände	42
II. Druckschriften	44
Häufiger benutzte Literatur	51
I. Handschriften	51
II. Druckschriften	53
Chronologische Übersicht der Briefe und Beilagen	117
Liste der Briefschreiber und Verfasser von Beilagen	127
Liste der Briefempfänger und Adressaten von Beilagen	129
Zu den Abbildungen	131
BRIEFE UND BEILAGEN 1644–1646	147
1644	149
1645	404
1646	781
Wörterverzeichnis	1075
Glossar der sprachwissenschaftlichen Termini	1093
Sachregister	1106
Personenregister	1147

Zum vorliegenden Bande

Die Fruchtbringende Gesellschaft zwischen Krieg und Frieden 1644–1646

Im Dezember 1641 hatten sich die Gesandten des Kaisers, Schwedens und Frankreichs im Hamburger Präliminarfrieden auf die Einberufung eines allgemeinen Friedenskongresses in Münster und Osnabrück geeinigt. Erste Gesandte trafen dort 1643 ein, auch Vertreter der deutschen Territorialstaaten, deren Teilnahme der Kaiser zunächst verhindern wollte, dann aber im Juni 1645 mit einer förmlichen Einladung bewilligen mußte. Zu diesem Zeitpunkt hatten Vertreter der Reichsstände, darunter auch viele Mitglieder der Fruchtbringenden Gesellschaft (FG), bereits auf eigene Faust mit Unterhandlungen im Fürstenrat begonnen. Die Fürsten von Anhalt hatten nach internen Beratungen und Absprachen mit Sachsen-Weimar und Kurbrandenburg den fürstlichen Rat und Kanzler Martinus Milagius (FG 315) im Mai 1645 als eigenen Unterhändler nach Münster und Osnabrück entsandt. Nach jüngsten Zerwürfnissen zwischen den Fürsten August (FG 46), Ludwig (FG 2), Johann Casimir (FG 10) und Friedrich (FG 62) auf der einen und den Fürsten Christian II. (FG 51) und Johann (FG 398) auf der anderen Seite hatten die vier Erstgenannten neben der offiziellen Instruktion des gesamten Hauses ihrem Abgesandten noch ein „Geheimes Memorial" aufgetragen, das eine enge Anbindung an die schwedische Verhandlungsführung und die Interessen der evangelischen Stände, vorab der reformierten Konfessionsverwandten Kurbrandenburg, Hessen-Kassel und der Stadt Bremen, wie auch Sachsen-Weimars und Braunschweig-Lüneburgs vorschrieb (s. 450220 K 1 und 450721 K 3). Die erste förmliche Sitzung des Kurfürstenrates fand im August 1645 statt. Die Verhandlungen begannen schleppend, bis die kaiserlichen Gesandten im Mai 1646 einen ersten Vertragsentwurf für ein Abkommen mit Schweden vorlegten, der aber wichtige Streitpunkte noch nicht entschärfen konnte. Im September folgte ein Entwurf für einen Friedensvertrag mit Frankreich, der dem Friedensvertrag vom Oktober 1648 schon sehr nahe kam. Die führenden Köpfe der Fruchtbringenden Gesellschaft hatten spätestens seit dem Prager Frieden (Mai 1635) parteiliches Denken insofern überwunden, als sie sich für einen raschen Universalfrieden im Reich und mit den auswärtigen Mächten einsetzten.

Im Bemühen, die Einbettung der Fruchtbringenden Gesellschaft in die allgemeinen Zeitverhältnisse nicht außer Betracht zu lassen, wurden im vorliegenden Band auch die vielen Erwähnungen von Treffen, Belagerungen, Besatzungen, Kontributionen, Ausplünderungen und anderen Kriegsplagen kriegsgeschichtlich zugewiesen und kommentiert. Das Fürstentum Anhalt selbst wurde unmittelbarer

Schauplatz des Hauptkriegsgeschehens, als sich im Herbst 1644 monatelang die kaiserlichen und schwedischen Hauptarmeen in und um Bernburg gegenüberlagen und das Land ruinierten (vgl. 440927 K 1, ferner 440809, 441205, 441231, 450124, 450217, 450505A K 3, 450711 u. 450730). Kriegsavisen durchziehen so manche Briefe, etwa die Korrespondenz Johann Valentin Andreaes (FG 464. 1646) in Stuttgart und Herzog Augusts d. J. von Braunschweig und Lüneburg zu Wolfenbüttel. Die selbstlose Saatgutspende Herzog Wilhelms IV. von Sachsen-Weimar (FG 5) an das ausgeplünderte Fürstentum Anhalt-Köthen bezeugt ein Brief (450220), der mit seinen Hinweisen auf einen Besuch Fürst Ludwigs aus Anlaß des Geburtstags seiner Nichte Eleonora Dorothea von Sachsen-Weimar (TG 4) in geradezu rührender Weise bekundet, wie das Leben der Fruchtbringenden Gesellschaft und unterschiedliche kulturelle Belange selbst in einer von zerstörerischen und erpresserischen schwedischen Truppen geplagten Zeit weitergefördert wurden: Aufnahme von vielen Prinzen und Hofleuten in die Akademie, Pflege der Poesie, „Kinderlehr", Vertonung, Kupferstiche und Architekturzeichnungen.

Ein Streben nach friedensstiftendem Ausgleich tat sich in einer intensiven literarischen Friedensagenda im Umkreis der Gesellschaft kund (z. B. 440100 I, 440616 II u. III, 440715 u. 460825 VI). Da aber weder der Hamburger Präliminarvertrag noch die einsetzenden Westfälischen Friedensverhandlungen einen Waffenstillstand vereinbarten, wütete der Kriegsfuror unvermindert fort. Mit der Schlacht bei Jankau (6. 3. 1645 n. St.) sank das Kriegsglück des Kaisers und mit der Niederlage von Alerheim (3. 8. 1645 n. St.) auch das Bayerns und der Ligisten, wie zuvor mit der Schlacht von Rocroi im Mai 1643 das des Königs von Spanien. Schweden und Franzosen schienen die Morgenluft wenn nicht einer Kriegsentscheidung, so doch eines großen Vorteils bei den Friedensverhandlungen zu wittern.

Arte et Marte: Diederich von dem Werder

Ein Echo aus den Tagen der größten Kriegshitze vernehmen wir in einer Widmungsepistel Diederichs von dem Werder (FG 31) an Conrad von Burgsdorff (FG 404), mit der er dem kurbrandenburgischen Oberkammerherrn, Geheimen Rat, Obristen und Befehlshaber der märkischen Festungen seine Loredano-Übersetzung *DJANEA Oder Rähtselgedicht* (Nürnberg 1644) zuschrieb (440000). Die von uns zusammengestellten Dokumente (Widmungsepistel und Beilagen) versammeln unbekannte Zeugnisse zur „Verschwörung" und Ermordung Wallensteins im Frühjahr 1634. Sie werfen ein helles Licht auf die Epochengestalt Werder in seiner vollendeten Verkörperung der adeligen *arte et marte*-Devise. Der Tasso- und Ariostübersetzer erscheint nicht nur mit einem weiteren Auftritt auf der zeitgenössischen Bühne großer ‚moderner' Literatur, sondern auch als militärischer und politischer Kopf, der als schwedischer Obrist seinerzeit genauestens um die geheimen Verbindungen zwischen Wallenstein und Hans Georg von Arnim (FG 255) bzw. Kursachsen und die damit verbundenen Friedenshoffnungen wußte. Im Hessen-Kasseler Auftrag reist Werder Ende 1645 an den Königsberger Hof des Großen Kurfürsten Friedrich Wilhelm von Brandenburg (FG 401), wird zum kurbrandenburgischen Geheimen Rat, Obristen und Amtshauptmann ernannt und nutzt die Gelegenheit, um sich durch Simon Dach ein Preisgedicht schreiben zu lassen (460204 I). Damit haben wir den einzigen — abgesehen von Martin Opitz (FG 200) — bisher bekannten wichtigen fruchtbringenden Kontakt zu der fernen Dichtergruppe der Königsberger Kürbshütte vor uns (KKH; vgl. 431028A K 2 u. *Opitz: BW* 380817 I). Nach der Aufnahme des Großen Kurfürsten und seines Favoriten Burgsdorff sollten, ähnlich wie vordem Burggraf und Herr Christoph zu Dohna (FG 20), Christoph von Lehndorf (FG 32), Hempo von dem Knesebeck (FG 88) und Gerhard Romilian von Kalcheim gen. Leuchtmar (FG 276), ab 1647 auch viele kurbrandenburgische Lehnsleute und Räte in die Fruchtbringende Gesellschaft eintreten. Dazu hätte auch Achaz, der Bruder Christophs zu Dohna gehören können, der zur Zeit von Werders Reise die Korrespondenz mit Fürst Ludwig von Anhalt-Köthen (FG 2. Der Nährende) über Sprachfragen in toskanischer Sprache aufnimmt — einer Sprache, die er ebenso wie Fürst Ludwig und Christoph bei dem gemeinsamen Aufenthalt in Florenz offenbar von dem Crusca-Sekretär Bastiano de' Rossi gelernt hatte (460120A u. 460217). Dort hatten sie zusammen mit einigen anderen Aristokraten, zu denen auch Markgraf Christian von Brandenburg-Bayreuth (FG 145), Fürst Ludwigs Bruder Rudolph von Anhalt-Zerbst (FG 12) und der erwähnte Hofmeister Lehndorf gehörten, eine kleine Schule oder, wie der Biograph Friedrich von Spanheim sagte, *une Académie de Princes Allemands* gebildet.

Staatsmann und Poet

Die politisch-mondäne Kultur der Epoche findet einen programmatischen Niederschlag in der zwischen Johann Michael Moscherosch (FG 436. Der Träumende) und Georg Philipp Harsdörffer (FG 368. Der Spielende) geführten französischsprachigen Diskussion (450818 und 450901) über die seit dem Humanismus in den Mittelpunkt rückende Frage, ob ein Poet zu den „affaires d'estat & du Monde" tauge, eine Frage von zentralem Stellenwert für Konzept und Selbstverständnis der modernen „Humaniora"-Bildung insgesamt, die von beiden zugunsten einer lebensklugen, weltoffenen, auch die Poesie umfassenden Universalbildung bejaht wird.

Moscherosch empfindet sich selbst als lebenstüchtig, als ein im Staat engagierter, nützlicher Amtsträger, dabei zugleich als Poet der Pariser Gesellschaft voll zugehörig. Harsdörffer stimmt mit Moscherosch grundsätzlich überein, entwickelt seine Antwort jedoch aus der Auseinandersetzung mit Platons Verbannung der Dichter, die in dem von ihnen geschaffenen Schein der Wirklichkeit Lügen über die Götter verbreiteten und das Staatswesen moralisch unterhöhlten. Harsdörffers Widerspruch liefert somit eine ästhetisch-politische Verteidigung der Poesie, welche die in seiner Zeit angestrebte Rolle des Dichters oder Literaten umreißt — die auch in dem Wahlspruch *Arte et Marte* zum Ausdruck kommt —, aber auch in besonderer Weise einer meistens aus Adligen und Amtsträgern bestehenden Fruchtbringenden Gesellschaft und ihrer Sprachpflege diente. Das

Dichtertum ist nicht nur mit Staat und Gesellschaft vereinbar, sondern ihm kommt darin die entscheidende Rolle zu, weil der Poet in letzter, sogar juristischer Instanz über Sprache entscheidet. So sehr dieser Anspruch auch noch die Rolle des humanistischen Poeta als Schöpfer der Fama des politisch Handelnden weiterspielt, so sehr erhebt sie doch Einspruch gegen die zeitgenössische Verachtung des Humanisten als Sprach-Pedanten und Gegner der nützlichen Realien. In der Berührung mit dem rationalistischen Utilitarismus (Devise der Fruchtbringen Gesellschaft „Alles Zu Nutzen") und in der Nähe zum Programm der Ritterakademien und des Ratichianismus ist Harsdörffers und Moscheroschs ästhetische Programmatik des Poeta als eine Art sprachlicher Allzweckfunktionär doch auch ganz im Sinne der Fruchtbringenden Gesellschaft.

Martinus Milagius gibt ebenso wie Diedrich v. dem Werder ein gutes Beispiel für Moscheroschs Vorstellung von einem idealen Poeten ab, der auch in seiner Dichtung nicht auf die Ebene des gelehrten Pedanten oder berufsmäßigen Schreibers zurückfiel und zugleich Literat und Staatsmann sein wollte. Zu einer Zeit, in der die anhaltinischen Fürstentümer schwer unter der Kriegslast zu leiden hatten (440927), und die auch für den fürstlichen Gesamtrat eine Phase erschöpfter Tatenlosigkeit heraufführte, fand Milagius nach eigenem Bekunden endlich die nötige Muße, um ein Werk zu verfassen, das in gleicher Weise dazu geeignet sei, das fruchtbringerische Ziel der Förderung des Deutschen und den irenischen Impetus der Gesellschaft zu befördern.

Durch sein literarisches Hauptwerk, den *Singenden Jesaja*, belegt Milagius, daß in der Fruchtbringenden Gesellschaft weder Literaturschaffen noch Sprachdebatte auf einen kleinen Kreis hauptberuflicher Gelehrter beschränkt gewesen ist. Aus diesem Grund wäre es auch eine nicht zulässige Verkürzung, im *Singenden Jesaja* allein eine jener umfangreichen, poetischen Bibelparaphrasen zu sehen, wie sie in dieser Zeit vielfach gedichtet wurden. Milagius' Werk, dessen Anhang mit Liedern fruchtbringerischer und alter, im 16. Jahrhundert wirkender Verfasser wir schon früher beschreiben konnten (380504), ist vielmehr als Positionsbestimmung in der aktuellen Poetik- und Sprachdiskussion zu lesen. Milagius formulierte sie in der programmatischen Vorrede (460825) in ebenso konzentrierter wie konzilianter Form aus. Da er wegen seiner umfangreichen Amtsgeschäfte nicht die nötige Ruhe und Zeit zu anhaltenden eigenen Forschungen zur Verfügung hatte, richtete er sich, wie er gesteht, bei seiner dichterischen Arbeit vornehmlich nach poetologischen Postulaten und sprachreformerischen Bestimmungen von Mitgesellschaftern wie Justus Georg Schottelius (FG 397), Georg Philipp Harsdörffer (FG 368), Augustus Buchner (FG 362) und vielen anderen mehr. Ungeachtet dieses demonstrativen Bescheidenheitsgestus bezieht der dichtende Staatsmann Milagius dennoch Stellung, beispielsweise in seiner Entscheidung für eine allgemeinverständliche Dichtersprache, die nicht nur Gelehrten, sondern auch ‚gemeinen Leuten' zugänglich ist; aber auch wenn es um die Adaption des prosodischen und metrischen Regelwerks geht, das er an seine eigene, sächsische Mundart anpaßt; oder wenn er die Korrektur der im Anhang des *Jesaja* gedruckten Kirchenlieder damit begründet, daß sie mitunter auf den aktuellen Stand von Sprache, Prosodie und Metrik gehoben werden mußten.

Moscherosch, aus dem vom Krieg besonders betroffenen Südwesten des Reiches, artikuliert in seinen *Epigrammata* und in den *Gesichten Philanders von Sittewalt* negative, teilweise kraß abfällige Stereotype über die Franzosen (440616 u. III). Aus dem intellektuellen Milieu Straßburgs und dem Umkreis der dort gegründeten Aufrichtigen Gesellschaft von der Tannen (AGT) sind ähnlich kulturkritisch-sprachpatriotisch motivierte Gegensätze von ‚Frantzösischen sinnen Und wälschem beginnen' und deutscher Treue und Beständigkeit hervorgegangen (440525 und Beilagen). In seinem erwähnten, von Moscherosch selbst veröffentlichten Brief (450818) lobt er hingegen Frankreichs politische Führungsfiguren Ludwig XIII. und Richelieu, den in Paris exilierten Hugo Grotius und die großen Essayisten, Historiker und Stoizisten von Montaigne über Pasquier und Charles Pascal bis zu Du Vair, und damit auch die Gruppe der unter den Parlementsjuristen bzw. der *Noblesse de robe* vertretenen *Politiques* zur Zeit der Könige Heinrich III. und Heinrich IV. Diese Amtsadeligen forderten, auch noch vorbildlich für Deutschland, den Primat der Politik und des Friedens, um das Land aus den Bürger- und Religionskriegen zu führen. Der politisch brauchbare Poet unterscheide sich, das betonte Moscherosch, vom gelehrten Pedanten und berufsmäßigen Reimeschmied, da seine Kunst auf dem natürlichen Genie und nicht auf versponnener Gelehrsamkeit beruhe. Wenn Moscherosch selbst die poetische Meisterschaft Richelieus herausstellt und einem rednerisch begabten Bauern wie Nikolaus von der Flüe politische Weisheit beimißt, dann feilt er an jenem zeitgenössischen Ideal des von der Natur begabten und zum Mäzenaten taugenden Dilettanten oder Poeta-Princeps, um das es auch Martin Opitz von Boberfeld (FG 200), selbst ein Poeta und Politicus, im Herrscherkatalog seiner Widmung an Fürst Ludwig zu tun gewesen war (250700). Harsdörffer stimmte darin ganz mit Moscherosch und seiner Zeit überein, als er in seinem Antwortbrief Herrschern wie Augustus, Nero, Nerva, Antoninus Pius und Franz I. von Frankreich, die sich mitunter der Poesie widmeten, den Namen eines Herkules Musagetes und den ewigen Ruhm ihres Namens verlieh. In der Ambivalenz der Urteile über Frankreich und die französische Politik begegnen kulturelle Austauschbeziehungen bei Moscherosch, Harsdörffer und anderen somit in einer dynamischen, kreativ bereichernden, aber auch konfliktreichen Zone kulturellen Transfers und kultureller Distanz, abzulesen auch in Harsdörffers Übersetzung des *Catechisme Royal* des Philippe Fortin sieur de la Hoguette von 1645 (451217 K 9), die sich krasser einseitiger Urteile enthält.

Der gelehrte christliche Fürst und sein Hof

Der lutherische Herzog August d. J. von Braunschweig-Wolfenbüttel (FG 227. Der Befreiende), das vielbewunderte Vorbild des gelehrten christlichen Fürsten, nahm gern Lobschriften entgegen und ließ sich oft porträtieren, beides in auffallendem, nicht nur durch seine reicheren Einkünfte bedingten Gegensatz zu dem streng reformierten, noch durch seinen Vater hochverschuldeten anhaltischen Duodezfürsten Ludwig. Jahr für Jahr schrieb Johann Valentin Andreae ein Preisgedicht auf den Befreienden. Er spitzte auch durch den Hinweis auf die Munifizenz des Herzogs den Straßburger Historiker Johann Heinrich Boeckler an, einen Panegyrikus auf August zu verfassen und diesen zusammen mit dem Neudruck einer Preisrede des Pfarrers Martin Nessel und einer eigenen Lobschrift zu einer Art panegyrischem Dreiergespann zu verknüpfen. Besonders aufwendig geriet der große illustrierte Panegyrikus *Porticus (Virtutis)* Harsdörffers, den der Verfasser dem Herzog als Manuskript und mit Entwürfen der Kupfer einreichte und gleich zweifach veröffentlichte, einmal als Teil seines Sprachbuchs *Specimen Philologiae Germanicae* von 1645 (460912, vgl. 450927) und zum anderen in einem revidierten Einzeldruck (1647). Wie sehr der Spielende den Befreienden nicht nur als gelehrten Mäzenaten betrachtete, sondern auch als sprachbeflissenen Fruchtbringer, geht aus den der Schrift eingefügten Gedichten und auch aus dem Titelemblem, der Abbildung Augusts auf dem Pegasus, aus einem „Programma ad Heroes Frvctiferi Sodalitii", aus Erwähnungen der Spracharbeit des Herzogs u.a. hervor. Herzog August von Braunschweig-Wolfenbüttel habe nicht durch Steine, sondern durch Tugend und Bücher eine Halle errichtet, die ewig dauern werde (461204A).

Als Reformer des biblischen Deutsch gehörte er neben seiner komponierenden und schreibenden Gemahlin Sophia Elisabeth (Die Befreiende), seinen bald auch schreibenden Kindern Anton Ulrich (FG 716. 1659), Sibylla Ursula und Ferdinand Albrecht (FG 842. 1673), dem bedeutenden Dichter und Philologen Justus Georg Schottelius, dem ersten Historiker der Akademie, Carl Gustav von Hille (FG 302. Der Unverdrossene), dem lateinisch dichtenden Arzt Martin Gosky, dem Emblematiker und Hofmarschall Franz Julius von dem Knesebeck (FG 396), dem zeitweilig in Wolfenbüttel lehrenden Dichter Sigmund von Birken (FG 681. 1658), damals noch Betulius genannt, und dem geistlichen Poeten Joachim von Glasenapp (FG 451) zu den Glanzlichtern dieses Hofs und der Fruchtbringenden Gesellschaft. Das Albert Freyse zugeschriebene große Gemälde von Herzog Augusts Familie und Hofgesellschaft, führt uns manche der genannten Personen vor Augen (Abb. zu 450126).

Frauen in der Fruchtbringenden Gesellschaft

Auch Frauen sollten nach den Lehren Stefano Guazzos als Gleiche an der *Conversazione civile* teilhaben. In der höfischen Konversationsliteratur, schon in Castigliones *Cortegiano*, sind oft sie es, die selbstbewußt und gewandt die Diskursregie führen. In einer noch vom höfischen Verkehr der Geschlechter und auch von Rechtsvorstellungen des hohen Adels geprägten Kultur, die die Frau zudem als stellvertretende, als mitregierende Teilhaberin (consors) oder sogar (im Allod) als alleinige Herrscherin des Landes kannte, fällt es doch auf, daß Frauen nicht selbständig in die Fruchtbringende Gesellschaft eintreten konnten. Ein- und untergeordnet in zumeist adligen und fürstlichen Häusern wurden sie mit dem feminin abgeleiteten Gesellschaftsnamen ihres Gemahls z.B. als die Nährende oder Befreiende bezeichnet, aber durchaus als Beiträgerinnen zur fruchtbringerischen

Arbeit willkommen geheißen — auch dies offenbar eine Teilhabe an den Aufgaben des aristokratischen Hauses. Als ein bürgerlicher Gelehrter, der hallische Gymnasialrektor Christian Gueintz (FG 361. Der Ordnende), einmal den Unterschied zwischen einem bewußten, geregelten Deutsch und einem Schreiben bloß nach Gutdünken, wie es die Frauen pflegten (440129), hervorhob, verwandte sich Fürst Ludwig entschieden gegen solche Beurteilung des weiblichen Geschlechts: „Der unterscheid zwischen den erfarenen und unerfarenen ist leichte zuerkennen, wan es aber auf des Frauenzimmers schrift, wie etwas hönisch angezogen worden, solte gemeinet und gesetzet sein, so lieffe es wieder die Fruchtbringende geselschaft, die auf die Mannespersonen und nur die weibespersonen, so weit sie mit den Männern verehlichet, und sich nach ihnen im nahmen und der that zurichten haben, gegründet, und möchte der Ordenende mit solchem argwon, die andern geselschafter verschonen." (440209). Frauen, wenn auch nur verehelichte, zählten als Mitglieder und sollten ebenso die deutsche kultivierte Sprache pflegen, wie dies ihren Männern aufgetragen war. Mochte es auch unter männlichen, lateinisch redenden Gelehrten erlaubt sein, die deutsche Sprache der Frauen geringzuschätzen, so entsprach das nicht dem höfischen Komment und auch gar nicht den Zielen der Fruchtbringenden Gesellschaft. Durch eine Art von fiktivem Salon seiner *Frauenzimmer-Gesprächspiele* wollte Georg Philipp Harsdörffer — dem Verhaltensideal der *Conversazione civile* gemäß – das gebildete, nichtgelehrte Gespräch zwischen Teilnehmern beiderlei Geschlechts entwickeln. Dabei verteidigte er seine *Gesprächspiele*, die sich auch explizit an eine weibliche Leserschaft richten, gegen Kritiker, denen die *Gesprächspiele* „mißfallen [...]/ weil das Frauenzimmer darbey eingeführt/ welche dergleichen Kurtzweil nach ihrem Wahn nicht fähig geachtet werden". Ihnen hält Harsdörffer 1644 entgegen, daß die Musen nicht umsonst weiblichen Geschlechts seien und jeder Mensch, unabhängig von seinem Geschlecht, eine „natürliche Begierde zur Wissenschaft" habe. Er schließt die rhetorische Frage an: „Hat dann das Teutsche Frauenzimmer der Tugend- und Sittenlehre nicht von thun *[sic]*/ oder können sie allein nichts aus den Gesprächen erlernen?" Er schließt: „Es beruhet nicht die geringste Ehre der Gesprächspiele darinnen/ daß selbe von etlichen hochgebornen Fürstiñen und Fräulein mit gnädigster Gewogenheit beliebet und geübet werden/ deren gnädiges Gutsprechen aller niderverständigen Boßheit beharrlich entgegen stehet." (Vgl. 460803 K 1, auch 451101).

Die Fruchtbringende Gesellschaft im Kreise deutscher und europäischer Akademien

Schon 1637 trat in unserer Dokumentation (370900) im Zusammenhang mit einem *Lob- und Leich-gedicht* auf den Fruchtbringer Graf Eberhard von Rappoltstein (FG 147) ein anderer Poetenzirkel (‚Sprachgesellschaft') in unseren Gesichtskreis, welchen der Stifter Jesaias Rompler von Löwenhalt (370900) im Sinne der Zeit aufschlußreicher als Akademie bezeichnete und damit in eine Reihe mit der Fruchtbringenden Gesellschaft stellte. Mit der Aufrichtigen Gesellschaft von der Tannen richtet sich der Blick von Königsberg aus in das geographisch entgegengesetzte Straßburg. Nur Johann Matthias Schneuber (FG 498), einem Mitglied dieses kleinen Zirkels, sollte 1648 die Aufnahme in die große Fruchtbringende Gesellschaft gelingen, jedoch eröffneten er, Rompler (450308A) und besonders der den Tannengesellen nahestehende Johann Michael Moscherosch im Zeitraum des vorliegenden Bands den Blick auf einen weiteren Kreis von Straßburgern, zu denen — abgesehen von dem Exilanten Markgraf Friedrich V. von Baden-Durlach (FG 207), dem einflußreichen Straßburger Pastor Johann Schmidt und dem dortigen Mäzen Johann Küffer — besonders die Sprachpatrioten Johann Heinrich Schill, Johann Christian Keck, Christoph Schorer, Johannes Freinsheim (AGT) und Johann Heinrich Boeckler zählten (440525 u. Beil. I–II; 440616). Andreae, Harsdörffer und auch Philipp von Zesen (450308A) unterhielten Beziehungen zu einigen dieser Begeisterten. Stellt man noch den bereits verstorbenen Martin Opitz (FG 200) und seine lange in Straßburg weilenden Freunde Georg Michael Lingelsheim, Matthias Bernegger, Balthasar Venator und Christophorus Colerus (440119) dazu, zeigen sich auch Verbindungen zur pfälzischen und zur schlesischen Literaturszene. Letzterer ist außer Colerus Andreas Tscherning zuzurechnen, der auch mit Briefen im vorliegenden Band zu Wort kommt (440324 u. 450726).

Aus einem anderen Ort im entfernten Südwesten des Reichs meldete sich der Bruder des Winterkönigs, Pfalzgraf Ludwig Philipp von Simmern (FG 97) — kaum daß er aus seinem Exil heimgekehrt und in Kaiserslautern seine Residenz eröffnet hat — mit dem Begehren zurück, selbst eine lange Reihe von Kandidaten in die Fruchtbringende Gesellschaft aufzunehmen (460104, 460321, 460423, 460424, 460424A u. I, 461026 usw.). Nach der Räumung der seit 1627 von einer kaiserlichen Garnison besetzten Residenz und Festung Wolfenbüttel konnte auch der Befreiende, Herzog August von Braunschweig-Wolfenbüttel, 1643 in den Vorort seines ererbten Fürstentums ziehen (s. Abb. zu 440100) und dort das nach Köthen und noch vor Weimar und später Halle a. d. S. sicherlich kulturträchtigste höfische Zentrum der Akademie zur Blüte bringen.

Im Vergleich mit dem Personal des überschaubaren höfischen Kulturzentrums verteilen sich die Mitglieder der wichtigen deutschen Akademien, anders als die zumeist städtischen oder regionalen Akademien Italiens, über fiktive Räume großen Ausmaßes. Das gilt zwar nicht für die Königsberger Kürbshütte oder die Aufrichtige Gesellschaft von der Tannen, aber für die Deutschgesinnete Genossenschaft (DG) und die Fruchtbringende Gesellschaft, selbst den Pegnesischen Blumenorden (PBO) und den Elbschwanenorden (ESO). Zum Vorbild gesellschaftlicher Poesie und Spracharbeit und zum Mittelpunkt derselben wurde die Fruchtbringende Gesellschaft vollends in den vierziger Jahren mit einer zunehmenden Zahl von Gelehrten und Dichtern, darunter Philipp von Zesen (FG 521. Der Wohlsetzende. 1648), den jungen ehrgeizigen Poeten, Übersetzer und Stifter einer eigenen Genossenschaft (DG 1643), und Johann Rist (FG 467. Der Rüstige. 1647), der viel später den Elbschwanenorden gründete. Beide wollten ihre Akademien zu Pflanzgärten der Fruchtbringenden Gesellschaft machen. Georg Philipp Harsdörffer, der mit Johann Klaj um den Jahreswechsel 1644/45 herum eine kleine Schar poetisierender Hirten und einer Hirtin in Nürnberg und ganz Norddeutschland für den Pegnesischen Blumenorden auftrieb, entfaltete in diesen Jahren eine große literarische, philologische und sozietäre Aktivität, besonders durch seine in acht Teilen erscheinenden *Frauenzimmer-Gesprächspiele*, sein *Specimen Philologiae Germanicae* und seine unermüdlichen Empfehlungen vieler Poeten und Übersetzer für die Aufnahme in die Fruchtbringende Gesellschaft, darunter Johann Michael Moscherosch und den Holsteiner Johann Rist. Sehr angetan war er von dem Vorschlag, Prinz Anton Ulrich von Braunschweig-Wolfenbüttel (FG 716. 1659) zum Präses des Pegnesischen Blumenordens zu machen und in Wolfenbüttel eine Art Kolonie der Hirtengesellschaft zu errichten. Die Fruchtbringende Gesellschaft und den gerade entstandenen Pegnesischen Blumenorden verbindend machte er gleich Vorschläge für Schäfernamen und Gewächs des Prinzen, erwog die Zuschreibung des siebenten Teils seiner *Frauenzimmer-Gesprächspiele* an ihn: „Sein Fürstlich Braunschweigischer Schäferstab wird gewißlich von einem Fruchtbringenden Holze seyn" (Schreiben Harsdörffers an S. Betulius vom 4.4.1646, zit. in 460406 K 4). Im Brief 441223 entwirft Harsdörffer auch einen Plan, Deutschgesinnete Genossenschaft und Fruchtbringende Gesellschaft durch Doppelmitgliedschaft zu verbinden. Er verweist in diesem Brief ausdrücklich darauf, daß solche Verknüpfungen in italienischen Akademien gang und gäbe seien. Sogar ein europäisches Akademieprojekt schlägt er Fürst Ludwig vor (450817, 450923C, 451101 u. 460120 u. ö.). Zu diesem Vorhaben und zur Struktur europäischer Akademien im allgemeinen, auch unter Einschluß der Fruchtbringenden Gesellschaft und des PBO, s. jetzt *Conermann: Harsdörffers Plan*. Wenn dieser Plan auch vor allem an der verschiedenen Sprache der Fruchtbringenden Gesellschaft und der italienischen Akademien scheiterte, förderte Harsdörffer doch die Ausbreitung der Fruchtbringenden Gesellschaft unter den Gelehrten über die deutschsprachigen höfischen Zirkel hinaus und betrieb, auch über den Crusca-Nachahmer Fürst Ludwig hinausgehend, in seinem Briefwechsel, den *Frauenzimmer-Gesprächspielen* und seinen Erzählsammlungen den Anschluß an die europäische Akademiebewegung der Frühen Neuzeit. Besonders durch seine *Frauenzimmer-Gesprächspiele* erweiterte sich der thematische Umfang von der Übersetzung historischer und erbaulicher Werke und von der Sprach- und Dichtkunst auch auf Wissenschaften wie Rhetorik, Logik und Recht. Diese waren zwar schon in der Köthener ratichianischen Reform schulisch gepflegt worden, aber nun sollten sie nicht ausbilden und Gelehrsamkeit fördern, sondern höfisch-höfliche und allgemeinverständliche Rede in den höfischen und städtischen Schichten kultivieren. Hiermit knüpfte Harsdörffer, der in der Fruchtbringenden Gesellschaft der Spielende hieß, an die Dialoge und Spiele besonders in italienischen Akademien und Gesellschaften an und folgte Vorbildern wie Sorels *Maison des Ieux* (1642) und Théophraste Renaudots *Conférences des beaux-esprits*. Er tat dies allerdings nur literarisch in Form seiner *Gesprächspiele* und Novellensammlungen, aber noch nicht in Salons, Zeitungen und öffentlichen Vorträgen und Diskussionen, welche Renaudot dank der Unterstützung König Ludwigs XIII. und Kardinal Richelieus eine kleine Weile organisieren konnte.

Dichtungs-, Sprach- und Kulturreform

Ursprünglich eine höfische Gruppierung von anhaltischen und ernestinischen Protestanten hatte sich die Fruchtbringende Gesellschaft der christlich-patriotischen Förderung des ratichianischen Sprach-, Wissens- und Schulprogramms verschrieben. Nach dem (vor allem durch die Inflation) finanziell bedingten Scheitern dieses Programms wandte sie sich zunehmend im allgemein christlichen, irenischen Sinne einer Förderung der Muttersprache zu, über die politischen, konfessionellen und kriegsparteilichen Grenzen hinweg. Damit wurde eine Ausweitung der Gesellschaft über die ostfälisch-westsächsischen Regionen in das übrige Reich und sogar auf europäische Militärs ermöglicht, für die wenigstens innerhalb der Fruchtbringenden Gesellschaft eine Friedenspflicht galt, wie wir diese zivilisatorische Konfliktbändigung auch von Hof- und Ritterorden und Adelsgesellschaften kennen. Als Mäzene und Anhänger einer christlichen und kulturellen Reform sollten darüber hinaus breitere Führungsschichten über die Schranken höfischer Konversation, der Poesie, Übersetzung, Essayistik und religiösen Erbauungsliteratur hinweg auch auf die administrative und wissenschaftliche Sprache Einfluß ausüben.

Von den späten Dreißiger Jahren an flossen solche Bestrebungen wie die Herzog Augusts, Moscheroschs und Harsdörffers in der Fruchtbringenden Gesellschaft demnach in eine breiter ausgerichtete Reform ein, welche alle sprachlichen Anwendungsbereiche, auch die Poetik und Sprachwissenschaft einschloß. Mit der Aufnahme von Gelehrten stadtbürgerlicher und patrizischer Herkunft konnte nun zunehmend die wissenschaftliche Regulierung der Sprache in den Mittelpunkt rücken, die sich vor allem in Schottelius' *Vers- oder Reimkunst* (1645) den Grammatiken von Gueintz (1641) und Schottelius (1641, 1643, 1651), im *Specimen* Harsdörffers (1645), in der Korrektur der Rechtschreibung durch Gueintz und Fürst Ludwig (1645) und in den Wörterbuchplänen und -sammlungen von Harsdörffer, Gueintz, Schottelius und Zesen niederschlug. Schottelius versuchte Herzog August über seine Dichtung, Poetik und Spracharbeit auf dem laufenden zu halten. Der wollte in seiner *Evangelischen Kirchen-Harmonie* offenbar sprachlich sein eigener Herr bleiben, glich daher die Abweichungen seiner eigenen Mundart selbst aus (421206), ließ sich allerdings Andreaes Zusammenstellung von Unterschieden zwischen dem Schwäbischen und seinem niedersächsisch gefärbten Hochdeutsch gefallen (421225 K 5). Einmal verglich Schottelius die Spracharbeit des Herzogs mit der Karls d. Gr. und verstand sie wohl so, wie August selbst seine *Kirchen-Harmonie* empfand. „Vestra Serenitas delicias sanctas et artem linguæ coniunxit et decore et rei amœnitate penetrat" (441231A). Deshalb pries der eifrige Schottelius später einmal Herzog Augusts *Evangelische Kirchen-Harmonie* als Vorbild und Quelle seiner *SprachKunst* von 1651 (510900; NSTA Wolfenbüttel: 2 Alt Nr. 40, Bl. 79v–80v): „Non tantum Illustrissimi Authoris Gustavi Seleni [d.i. Herzog August] authoritate et auxilio in plurimis locis usus, sed analogiam et principia in orthographicis, quae Vestra Serenitas in Harmonia, aliisque opusculis Germanos docuit, maximam partem et ego secutus adductisque multis rationibus, amplexus fui."

Schottelius pflegte seine nichtamtlichen Schreiben an den Herzog nur selten zu datieren, so daß diese oft nur ungefähr zeitlich eingeordnet werden können. Damit erwies sich gelegentlich auch die Identifizierung bestimmter Werke als problematisch. Einmal ließ sich nicht mit Gewißheit entscheiden, ob ein wichtiges Schreiben der ersten oder zweiten Fassung von Schottelius' *SprachKunst* (1641 u. 1646) zuzuweisen ist, zumal die zweite Auflage dieser Grammatik nicht als Manuskript erhalten ist und erst 1651 (wiederum verändert) erscheinen konnte. Diesem Dilemma können wir einmal nur durch eine Doppelveröffentlichung eines Briefs nach verschiedenen Überlieferungen entgehen. S. 410706 I und den Band *DA Köthen I. 9*. Leider gibt es bisher keine kritische Ausgabe des Schottelius-Briefwechsels, so daß die Ermittlung und Sichtung des Bestands erst für unsere Ausgabe erfolgen mußte, um die für unsere Belange aufschlußreichen Briefe zu veröffentlichen oder im Kommentar zu berücksichtigen.

Schottelius scheint durch die Regulierung und das erschöpfende Exerzieren aller Versfüße, Versarten und Gedichtgattungen in seiner Poetik (s. Abb. zu 440100 I: Schottelius' *Pindarische Ode*) zumindest in der Fruchtbringenden Gesellschaft die Führerschaft in der Beurteilung der Kunstdichtung für sich reklamieren zu wollen — ähnlich wie in der Grammatik. Harsdörffer, sein Mitstreiter, konnte rechtzeitig vor dem Erscheinen dieses Werks darin einen langen Freundschaftsbrief an den Suchenden (441020) unterbringen, der Schottelius' Leistung unterstreicht, indem er den Vorrang der neuen deutschen Poeten selbst vor den allernamhaftesten französischen, italienischen und spanischen dadurch zu erweisen sucht, daß deutsche Kritiker nach dem Gehör (gemeint ist der opitzianische Zusammenfall von Vers- und Wortbetonung) Verse so beurteilen können, wie es Nachbarn noch nicht zu tun vermögen und vielleicht niemals vollbringen werden. Daß diese ihre Verse nicht nach den Kriterien der germanischen Sprachen schmiedeten, spielte für den Spielenden keine Rolle.

Die genannten anderen Gesellschaften und manche ihrer wichtigsten Vertreter wie Harsdörffer (PBO, DG), Zesen (DG), Rist (ESO) und Betulius-Birken (PBO) wollten solche gelehrte Spracharbeit unterstützen, traten untereinander und mit der Fruchtbringenden Gesellschaft in Kontakt. Die von Martin Opitz und der Fruchtbringenden Gesellschaft ausgehenden Impulse mündeten in eine sich verbreitende Strömung. Der vorliegende Band enthält daher Zeugnisse der Anteilnahme seitens einiger Sprachreformer und Dichter, die somit teilweise schon lange vor ihrer Aufnahme in die große Akademie an den Debatten und Mitteilungen der hochangesehenen Gesellschafter partizipierten. Die Fruchtbringende Gesellschaft tritt auch außerhalb dieses Kreises in Kontakt mit Außenstehenden, deren Interesse oder Bewerbung jedoch auf kein Echo oder Ablehnung stößt (z. B. Christophorus Colerus 440119; Andreas Tscherning 440324 u. ö.; Johann Heinrich Boeckler 440616; Abraham von Franckenberg 440826; Friedrich Greiff 431123, 450219 u. ö.; Johann Helwig, Georg Conrad Osthof und Georg Friedrich Behaim 451101). An Arbeiten und Bestrebungen der Fruchtbringenden Gesellschaft nehmen auch Außenstehende teil — z. B. Marcus Fridericus Wendelinus (451220) und Daniel Sachse (460103) —, welche als Theologen eigentlich zur Vermeidung des Zeitübels konfessioneller Kontroversen aus der Fruchtbringenden Gesellschaft ausgeschlossen bleiben sollten. Aus dieser Berufsgruppe gelangten der friedfertige Johann Valentin Andreae und der Poet Johann Rist 1646 bzw. 1647 dennoch in die Gesellschaft.

Diese Autoren sind untereinander vernetzt, und in dem so gebildeten Netzwerk steht die Fruchtbringende Gesellschaft im Mittelpunkt einer sprachbezogenen Kulturreform, die selbst wiederum eng mit der Frömmigkeitsreform der Zeit, an deren Spitze u. a. auch Andreae mit seiner Unio Christiana und der Societas Christiana stand, und mit dem Bemühen um eine Beendigung des großen Dreißigjährigen Krieges im Westfälischen Frieden verknüpft ist. So heißt es im Reimgesetz des kurbrandenburgischen Diplomaten im Westfälischen Friedenswerk, Matthaeus (von) Wesenbeck (FG 433), daß er „mit allen sinnen [...] Fruchtbringend möchte sein, beym frieden dieser Zeit | Das unser Vaterland, erlangte ruh' und freud." (450504A K 1). Eine große, Politik, Sprache und die Konfessionen umfassende Reform, eine Erneuerung und Fortführung der Reformation, wie sie Wolfgang Ratke in einem an den Reichstag geschickten Memorial konzipierte, brachte der Friedensschluß von 1648/50 ebensowenig zustande wie die Sprachdebatten der Fruchtbringenden Gesellschaft zu der von Ratke konzipierten Sprach- und Friedensordnung beitrugen. In der fruchtbringerischen Spracharbeit schlugen sich die Unterschiede der Mundarten und das Ungenügen an der inzwischen als veraltet empfundenen Bibelsprache Luthers nieder, gekoppelt mit den im Gemeinen Deutsch bewahrten Differenzen und dem Beharrungswillen der Lutheraner, so daß es im Streit zwischen der Geltung des Sprachusus und dem Vertrauen auf analogisierende Systematik im Aufbau einer Formenlehre und im Ausbau des Sprachschatzes zu keiner Übereinkunft kam.

Sprachdebatten

Im vorliegenden Band und in dem geplanten Materialienband (*DA Köthen I. 9*) lernen wir die Thesen und Debatten von Mitgliedern und Gutachtern — voran Fürst Ludwig, Christian Gueintz, Justus Georg Schottelius, Georg Philipp Harsdörffer, Philipp von Zesen und Marcus Fridericus Wendelinus — über deutsche Rechtschreibung und Grammatik (als Voraussetzungen eines umfassenden deutschen Wörterbuchs) und über sprachliche Einzelfragen wie die Vorbildlichkeit des Meißnischen und die Ableitung der Stammsilben oder über die grundlegenden Kriterien der Gewohnheit (usus) und der Normierung (durch Analogie oder Etymologie) kennen. Da die Fruchtbringende Gesellschaft immer wieder eines besonders im Bannkreis des Allgemeinen Deutschen Sprachvereins entwickelten Fremdwortpurismus' verdächtigt wurde, mag in diesem Zusammenhang darauf hingewiesen werden, daß die Fruchtbringer den eingebürgerten Wortschatz fremden Ursprungs keineswegs ausmerzen wollten. S. schon 240109 und noch besonders 440525. Der Fremdwortpurismus ist nämlich von dem rhetorischen Begriff der Puritas oder grammatischen und stilistischen Reinheit und der in diesem Sinne von der Fruchtbringenden Gesellschaft als erster geforderten ‚Deutschheit' zu unterscheiden (*Conermann: Purismus*). Der Neologismus

Deutschheit ist als Neubildung zu Latinitas keinesfalls, wie besonders im 19. Jahrhundert, vor allem ein patriotischer oder nationalistischer Begriff. Letztlich haben die Versuche Fürst Ludwigs keinen Konsens durch akademiegemäße Korrespondenz unter den wichtigsten Sprachgelehrten bewirkt — ähnlich wie in unserer Zeit die öffentliche Rechtschreibdebatte. In der Antwort des Patriziers Harsdörffer (460131) auf ein leider verlorenes Gutachten des Hallenser Gymnasialrektors Gueintz zeigt sich in der Ermahnung, Gueintz möge in seinem Angriff auf die Schreibweise kk (statt ck) doch pauschale „Unbescheidenheit" vermeiden, nicht eigentlich die Tugend der Modestia, sondern ein Mangel an Distinctio, die nach Harsdörffer durch „die Bescheidenheit der Sache den Verstand" beschäftigen muß (441020, vgl. K 14).

Für Harsdörffer, der zur *Fortpflantzung der Hochlöblichen Fruchtbringenden Geselschaft* (1651) eine *Lobrede deß Geschmackes* halten sollte, ist „Bescheidenheit" auch das Kriterium eines Stils, in dem sich grammatische und inhaltliche Richtigkeit und stilistische Idiomatik besonders in der Poesie mit der „Sinnbeherschenden Süßigkeit der Wörter" verbindet. „Jn dem nemlich tapfere Gedanken aus der Sache selbst geschöpfet/ und nicht bey den haaren/ wie wir zu reden pflegen herbey gezogen/ die Redart rein und scheinlich/ ohne unzeitige Härtligkeit/ selbstfliessend in das Gedicht geleitet werden sollen." Selbst in die orthographische Auseinandersetzung dringt so ein Zwiespalt zwischen bloß gelehrter Rechthaberei und rational distanzierter, ästhetischer Selbstwahrnehmung — ein Zwiespalt, wie er in der Fruchtbringenden Gesellschaft beim Umgang von bürgerlichen Gelehrten und höfisch-weltklugen Adligen nicht überrascht. Im Zusammenhang solcher Diskussionen entwickelt der Sprachreformer Harsdörffer — noch vor dem Import des sozialen und künstlerischen Goût der Franzosen — ein neuartiges Kriterium des Sprachgeschmacks. Vgl. *Conermann: Akademie, Kritik und Geschmack.*

Auch ein schon in der Renaissance aufgeflammter Streit (die später sog. Querelle des anciens et des modernes) wird durch die Sprachdiskussion der Fruchtbringer neuentzündet. Er setzt sich im Grunde mit dem antiken Problemzusammenhang auseinander (z. B. Platons *Kratylos* oder Aristoteles' Lehre vom Satz in *Peri hermeneias*), ob Sprache allein überhaupt Wahres benenne und ob sie das aus der Natur der Sache (*physei*) oder aus Gewohnheit oder Übereinkunft (*thesei*) leiste. Christian Gueintz vertritt hier eindeutiger als Fürst Ludwig die Position der Alten, den im überkommenen Sprachgebrauch begründeten Usus (der auch die Überlieferung älterer Kulturvölker einschließt), während an diesem Punkte selbst Neuerer wie Schottelius und andere Gueintz-Kritiker die Rechtschreibung aus der Sprachnatur und daraus gewonnen Regeln reformieren wollen. Auf die Einwände Fürst Ludwigs und einer Versammlung von Fruchtbringern antwortet Gueintz daher: „Gewiß Deutschen sind nach den andern Völckern kommen, wo nicht will dafür gehalten werden, daß zur Zeit der Babylonier Deutschland schon bewohnet, vnd durch die Sündflut Sie nicht mit untergangen. Zwar ist in andern auch viel geendert, doch helt man von denen am meisten, die es mit den alten halten, wie derer Schrifften, so in händen, außweisen. Der Neuen neues gutachten wird deßwegen für neu gehalten." (440219, vgl. 400528 K II)

Ausgleichsprozeß und Regulierung des Deutschen

Wenn Fürst Ludwig und Diederich von dem Werder sich gegen die Polyflexion und die überreichen Pluralendungen aussprechen, liefern sie Belege für die Teilnahme der Fruchtbringenden Gesellschaft am großen Ausgleichsprozeß des Deutschen im 17. Jahrhundert, in dem mundartliche Besonderheiten und schriftsprachliche Flexions-Hypertrophien bei der Entwicklung des Gemeinen Deutsch zum Neuhochdeutsch eliminiert wurden. Vgl. Harsdörffers mundartlich bedingtes ‚der Starckziehend Magnet' und Schottelius' gelehrte Formen ‚der Nehrender' oder ‚die Mördere' (450124 u. I). Schon Martin Luther galt als Gewährsmann und unbestrittene Autorität in Sachen Sprachausgleich und Normierung des Deutschen. Immer wieder beriefen sich Sprachgelehrte der Fruchtbringenden Gesellschaft auf Luthers Sprachausgleich (vgl. 460131 K 2). Andererseits wurde Luthers im 17. Jh. als veraltet empfundene Sprache und seine offensichtlich hohe Variantentoleranz (die das Frühneuhochdeutsche des 16. Jahrhunderts generell auszeichnet) kritisiert. Viele orthographische Unstimmigkeiten der Luther-Bibel wurden dabei jedoch auf Druckfehler bzw. auf Eigenmächtigkeiten der Drucker geschoben. Vgl. *Gueintz: Rechtschreibung (1645)*, S. 5: „Lutherus ist billich der Deutschen sprache in KirchenSachen Urheber/ die ReichsAbschiede in Weltlichen dingen die Haubtbücher/ Wie wol bey beyden/ weil sie von eintzelen Personen aufgesetzet/ auch zu der Zeit/ so wol als ietzo/ die Schreiber und Drucker oftmals gefehlet/ noch viel erinnerungen/ was die Rechtschreibung betrifft/ zu thun seind." Auch hatte Herzog August von Braunschweig-Wolfenbüttel eine gründliche sprachliche Revision der Luther-Bibel angestrebt. Infolge des Widerstandes der lutherischen Geistlichkeit hatte er sie 1638 aufgegeben, jedoch einstweilen durch eine Modernisierung und Regulierung der Bibelsprache in seinem Passionsbüchlein (1640, 1641) und in seiner *Evangelischen Kirchen-Harmonie* (1646ff.) ersetzt. Vgl. 391217 I, 411214, 430515, 451001, 461204 u. ö. Von der Teilnahme an diesem Ausgleichsprozeß zeugen auch viele Briefe über andere Fragen, z. B. die Ableitung von Substantiven von den auf -ig- endenden Adjektiven und Adverbien, zu der sogar eine eigene Sprachkonferenz in Anhalt tagte und Diederich von dem Werder ein längeres Exposé beisteuerte (450505). Die Diskussionen drehten sich dort und immer wieder um die rechte Bestimmung der Stammwörter als Grundlagen der Wortbildung, sei es im unergiebigen Meinungsaustausch zwischen Harsdörffer und Zesen (450410 u. 450808), sei es in den fruchtlosen Debatten zwischen Harsdörffer und Schottelius einerseits und Fürst Ludwig und Gueintz andererseits. Daran hängt auch die Regelung der Rechtschreibung, um die sich Gueintz und Ludwig in einem eigenen Werk bemühten, das zugleich das erste veröffentlichte Wörterbuch der Fruchtbringenden Gesellschaft darstellt. Zur Reform der Rechtschreibung und zur deutschen Wortbildung versuchte sogar Herzog August faktisch vorentscheidend, jedoch wenig einflußreich in seiner Evangelienharmonie beizutragen.

Fürst Ludwig schlug vor, Sprecher verschiedener Mundarten sollten ihre Mundart selbst regulieren und die Ergebnisse untereinander vergleichen (450919A). Diese Initiative entsprang einer phonographischen Auffassung, der gemäß man schreiben sollte, wie man spricht. Da es weder eine allgemein anerkannte Hochlautung noch eine gesprochene Leitsprache gab, drehte sich der Streit um die Normierungskriterien der Rechtschreibung, d.h. darum, was überhaupt als beste und reinste Aussprache gelten könne, im Kreis. Der Weg eines Ver- und Abgleichs der Mundarten war unter diesen Umständen naheliegend, jedoch mühsam, wohl auch illusionär oder überflüssig angesichts der historisch vorbereiteten Priorität des Ostmitteldeutschen. Die andere, von Schottelius und Harsdörffer vorgezogene Lösung bestand darin, die Rechtschreiblehre aus den morphologisch-grammatischen Gesetzen der Sprache abzuleiten, d.h. im wesentlichen morphematisch zu begründen. Zwischen diesen beiden Polen bewegten sich die fruchtbringerischen Argumentationen teils gegen-, teils miteinander.

Da sich die Fruchtbringende Gesellschaft in ihrer Spracharbeit vor die Aufgabe einer systematischen Entwicklung einer deutschen Grammatik und einer grundlegenden und umfassenden Regulierung des deutschen Wortschatzes gestellt sah, mußte sie sich zunächst ihrer Kriterien versichern. Mit der Diskussion über die ersten eingereichten Teile (431227) von Gueintz' (und Fürst Ludwigs) *Rechtschreibung* (1645) in Fürst Ludwigs (verlorenem) Gutachten (s. 440127) tauchen sogleich grammatische Fragen nach der Etymologie und den Stammwörtern auf, so daß auch der Schriftwechsel der Jahre 1644–1646 (und darüber hinaus) die damals diskutierten Fragen der Orthographie und der Lexikographie mitbestimmt. Justus Georg Schottelius, dessen systematisches Denken besonders ausgeprägt war, kehrte, kaum hatte er seine Poetik *Teutsche Vers- oder Reimkunst* (1645) verfaßt, daher zur Ausweitung seiner grammatischen Arbeit auf das Fundament der Rechtschreibung und die Arbeit am Wörterbuch zurück. In der von Fürst Ludwig und sodann auch von Harsdörffer verlangten Verständigung der Sprachgelehrten der Fruchtbringenden Gesellschaft über solche Fundamente konnte er sich aber nicht mit ihnen über prinzipielle Fragen, besonders über die seit der Antike gestellte Kernfrage nach dem Vorrang des Sprachgebrauchs oder der Sprachnorm einigen und vermied es, wie Fürst Ludwig von ihm verlangt hatte, seinen Entwurf der neuen Sprachkunst 1646 zum Zwecke der Kritik und Vereinbarung einzureichen. Es dauerte bis zum Jahre 1651, nach dem Tode von Fürst Ludwig und Gueintz, bis Schottelius seine *Sprachkunst* publizierte, im wesentlichen nur wenig gegenüber der Erstausgabe von 1641 verändert, jedoch zu einem energischen Analogismus zugespitzt. Inzwischen hatte Schottelius' Herr, Herzog August von Braunschweig-Wolfenbüttel, seit 1646 seine *Evangelische Kirchen-Harmonie* mehrfach veröffentlicht. In deren Rechtschreibung und Wortbildung stellte er sich nur am Rande der Kritik seines theologischen Beraters Johann Valentin Andreae, unterwarf sich aber nicht einer Verbesserung durch Fürst Ludwig, Gueintz oder Harsdörffer. Diese nahezu freihändig entwickelte, auch ursprünglich keineswegs von Schottelius konzipierte Orthographie radikalisierte der Herzog, soweit wir dies im Briefwechsel der bisher vorliegenden Bände verfolgen konnten, geradezu ‚beratungsresistent'.

Harsdörffer erklärte, so als ob er Zesens wechselnde und alle Fruchtbringer empörenden Regelungen vorausgeahnt hätte, schon im Brief 441223, es könne „ein wort, (ohne versehrung seiner grunddeutung) mit unterschiedlichen buchstaben ausgedrukket werden. Solte man dieses nicht belieben und die strittige Schreibung nicht zu reiffern nachgründen stellen, würden viel darvon abgeschrekket und unser Vorhaben merklich gehemmet werden."

Ein gemeinsames Wörterbuch der Fruchtbringenden Gesellschaft?

So wie auf diesem Feld keine Stetigkeit oder gar endgültige Einigung erzielt wurde, so konnte auch trotz Harsdörffers Wörterbuchplan in der Lexikographie kein gemeinsamer Fortschritt erreicht werden. Obgleich Gueintz, Schottelius, Zesen und Harsdörffer Stammwörter sammelten und ihre Wörter in zum Teil abenteuerlich anmutenden Etymologien herleiteten und danach zusammensetzten, konnten sie sich noch nicht einmal auf ein alle verpflichtendes Verständnis des deutschen Stammworts einigen. In seinem *Nathan und Jotham* (1659) kennzeichnete Harsdörffer den Streit um die Rechtschreibung als einen Krieg der Federn zwischen Verstand und Gewohnheit: „[...] verbliebe also ein jeder Theil in seinem Lager/ und hat der Streit kein Ende." Ergebnisse ließen sich offenbar nur im Alleingang erzielen, in kleinem Umfang zum Beispiel in dem deutschen Glossar und den deutschen Übersetzungen, die Augustus Buchner (FG 362) seiner Bearbeitung des lateinischen *Thesaurus Eruditionis Scholasticae* (1662) von Basilius Faber beigab, und vor allem in dem großen, nach Schottelius' grammatischen Regeln konstruierten Wörterbuch Caspar von Stielers (FG 813. 1668). Das konnte jedoch erst 1691 erscheinen, als die Fruchtbringende Gesellschaft keine Leitung und keine sozietäre Debatte mehr kannte. Alles hing mit allem zusammen: Grammatik, Etymologie, Orthographie und Ausbau des Wortschatzes, ohne welchen man auch nicht zu stilistischer Puritas und zum Decorum der Rede gelangen konnte. Obwohl das Gemeine Deutsch des 16. und frühen 17. Jahrhunderts ein großes, auch an Fachwörtern reiches Vokabular anbot, das sich vor allem am Meißnischen der Sächsischen Kanzlei, an den Reichstagbeschlüssen und an Luthers deutscher Bibel orientieren wollte, bot dies kein festes Fundament für die grammatische Regulierung und die stilistischen Aspekte einer *Conversazione civile*, nach deren Entwicklung die Fruchtbringende Gesellschaft seit ihren Satzungen im *Kurtzen Bericht* von 1622 strebte (*DA Köthen II. 1*). Aufschlußreich ist in diesem Zusammenhang die Sammlung des Fachwortschatzes, worum sich Schottelius (s. 450000) von seinen *Sprachkünsten* bis hin zur *Ausführlichen Arbeit* (1663) und dem *Kurtzen Tractat Von Vnterschiedlichen Rechten* (1671 u. ö.) und Moscherosch (440616) schon seit 1644 in seiner *Technologie Allemande & Françoise Das ist/ Kunst-übliche Wort-Lehre Teutsch und Frantzösisch* bemühten (vgl. 440826 K 4). Daran zeigt sich die Verschiedenheit der Sprachentwicklung im Französischen und Deutschen besonders markant. Schon seit Malherbe begann man im Nachbarland auszuscheiden „les mots techniques des sciences, particulièrement ceux des sciences naturelles et medicales, qui avaient le défault d'êtres «sales»" (F. Brunot: Histoire de la langue française III, S. 189). Die Vorrede zum *Dictionnaire de l'Académie Françoise* (1694) vollendete die sich hier anbahnende Entwicklung, indem sie das erste Wörterbuch der Französischen Akademie beschränkte auf „la Langue commune, telle qu'elle est dans le commerce ordinaire des honnestes gens, & telle que les Orateurs & les Poëtes l'employent; Ce qui comprende tout ce qui peut servir à la Noblesse & à l'Elegance du discours." Solche Kriterien finden gemäß der Vorrede Stielers in seinem großen fruchtbringerischem Wörterbuch (*Der Teutschen Sprache Stammbaum und Fortwachs/ Oder Teutscher Sprachschatz*. Nürnberg 1691) keine Anwendung, obgleich er die Fülle der deutschen Fachwörter und mundartlichen „Sprichwörter" sowie die der lateinischen „Küchenwörter" und der modernen fachspezifischen Termini nicht berücksichtigte.

Gueintz: Rechtschreibung (1645) besteht nach einer knappen Einführung allgemeiner und besonderer orthographischer Regeln aus einer die Einführung im Umfang deutlich übertreffenden Homophonenliste. Diese ist also keine Stammwörterliste, sondern eine Liste gleichlautender Wörter unterschiedlicher Wortart und Bedeutung, die durch die Schreibweise unterschieden werden müssen. Bei den Substantiven werden immer das Geschlecht, gelegentlich auch weitere Deklinationsformen angegeben. Diese Liste ist von Harsdörffer in der zweiten Ausgabe seines *Teutschen SECRETARIUS* (Nürnberg 1655) wörtlich übernommen worden und stellt, obwohl orthographisch motiviert, ein wichtiges Zeugnis fruchtbringerischer Lexikographie dar. Sie bettet sich in einen langen Prozeß der gesellschaftlichen Wörterbuchdiskussion und -projektierung ein, an dessen Ende, keineswegs so einzigartig wie meist angenommen, Caspar von Stielers erstes umfassendes deutsches Wörterbuch von 1691 steht. Schon im Dokument 400301 hielt es Gueintz für „gut, daß ein wörterbuch (**Lexicon**) wie auch **phrases** oder Redensartbuch mit ehesten aus den besten Schrifften man verfertigett, ans tageliecht keme." Das Wörterbuchprojekt rückte dann ab etwa 1645 in den Vordergrund der fruchtbringerischen Spracharbeit. Harsdörffer schnitt das Thema in seinem *Specimen Philologiae Germanicae* (Nürnberg 1646, z.B. S.251ff. u. 272f.) an und trug die Diskussion um deutsche Lexikologie und Lexikographie durch eine Stammwörterliste mit, die im zweiten Teil seines *Poetischen Trichters* (Nürnberg 1648; „Anhang: bestehend Jn kurtzer Verfassung/ wo nicht aller/ jedoch der meisten Stamm- und Grund-Wörter unsrer Teutschen Sprach") als Nucleus eines künftigen deutschen Wörterbuchs steht und ergänzt wird durch ein handschriftliches „Bedencken, wie ein Teutsches Dictionarum oder wortbuch zuverabfassen" (s. *DA Köthen I. 9*, aus: HM Köthen: V S 545, Bl. 405r–408v; *KE*, 387–392). Vollends ist auch die alphabetisch gegliederte Wörterliste mit den jeweiligen semantischen Worterklärungen und den poetisch-bildlichen Umschreibungen im dritten Teil des *Poetischen Trichters* ein zeitgenössischer Beitrag zur Lexikographie: *Prob und Lob der Teutschen Wolredenheit* (Nürnberg 1653), S. 112–504 (vgl. 451219 K 8).

Schottelius hatte in seinem Fürst Ludwig gewidmeten Werk *Der Teutschen Sprache Einleitung (1643)* Klage über ein fehlendes „völliges vollkommenes **Lexicon** der Teutschen Sprache" (S.109) geführt. Georg Henischs Wörterbuch *Teutsche Sprach vnd Weißheit* von 1616 war zwar unvollständig geblieben, galt Fürst Ludwig, Schottelius und anderen Fruchtbringern aber als ein trefflicher Versuch, wenngleich „die **positio thematum**, wie auch **derivatio** und **compositio** oftmals übergangen und misgesetzet" worden seien, also die Ansetzung der Stammwörter, ihrer Ableitungen und Kompositionen öfters nicht überzeugte (S. 110). Daß Schottelius mit Henischs Wörterbuch intensiv arbeitete, zeigt auch der Brief 460000. Schottelius' Konzept eines vollkommenen deutschen Wörterbuchs sah in seiner *Einleitung* von 1643 vor: 1. Liste der Stammwörter; 2. zu jedem Stammwort Angabe von genus, casus genitivus und numerus pluralis, 3. Ableitungen (mit ihren „Haubtendungen"); 4. Komposita, geordnet nach ihrem Grundwort; 5. Richtige Kenntnis der Vorwörter (Präfixe); 6. Stammverben (Verba primitiva) mit Angabe, ob gleich- oder ungleichfließend (regular/ regelmäßig, irregular/ unregelmäßig), mit Angabe der 1. und 2. Pers. Präsens, Imperfekt u. Partizip Perfekt: „Brich/ ich breche/ du brichst. ich brach. gebrochen" usw.; 7. Erklärung der Bedeutung, Maßgabe dabei: „der Teutsche rechte Gebrauch". Ein solches Wörterbuch wäre wohl nur als Gemeinschaftsleistung „gelahrter Teutschliebender Männer" zu verfassen (S. 112–114) gewesen. Seine eigene Stammwörterliste in der *Ausführlichen Arbeit (1663)* (S. 1277–1450) gibt indes außer Bedeutungen bei Substantiven nur das Geschlecht und das lateinische Lexem an, bei Verben nur den Imperativ (als Stammform), den Infinitiv und lateinische Entsprechungen. In einem undatierten, wohl ins Jahr 1646 fallenden Schriftstück für Herzog August von Braunschweig-Wolfenbüttel bekräftigte Schottelius den Wunsch nach einem deutschen Wörterbuch: „Radices seu Primitivæ Linguæ Teutonicæ erant colligenda et explicanda, quod non exiguo stetit labore, nemo enim hactenus prævivit, et ob dialectorum varietatem res non adeò plana: Stevini [Simon Stevinus] interim et Henischij manus auxiliatrix subinde erat et per tot intervalla inter alios investiganda quam ductricem etiam sæpissimè sum expertus, moræ ergò huic ultra annuæ veniam precor." (460000)

Die beiden Briefe 450410 und 450808 aus der Harsdörffer-Zesen-Korrespondenz zeigen beispielhaft, wie Mitglieder der Gesellschaft das Kriterium des Stammworts (vgl. 451219) in ihrer Auseinandersetzung über dessen Ableitung aus ein- oder auch mehrsilbigen Quellen (Imperativ Singular? Verben oder auch Nomina?) zu gewinnen strebten (vgl. 450308A). Hierbei übten hebräische Wurzelwörter und die Reduktion auf einsilbige Stämme bei Stevinus für Schottelius und Harsdörffer eine Vorbildfunktion aus, während Zesen, Gueintz und Fürst Ludwig mit der Zulassung zweisilbiger Stammwörter die Geltung dieser Vorbilder abschwächten und in diesem Zusammenhang den Einfluß der Mundart auf die Bestimmung des deutschen Stammworts in das Bewußtsein rückten (oberdeutsch *Denk!* meißnisch *Denke!*). „Es ist nicht zu wundern", schrieb Harsdörffer, „wann man sich wegen kunstrichtiger verfassung der Deutschen Sprache noch der zeit nicht vergleichen kan; maßen in allen andern Haubtsprachen, an welchen von etlich Hundert, ja tausent Jahren gearbeitet worden, unter den Gelehrten und Sprachrichtern (Criticis) noch mancherley zweiffelfrag wegen der Rechtschreibung" (450410) herrsche.

*Das Meriansche Gesellschaftsbuch von 1646 —
Finanzierung, Illustrierung, Druck und Verteilung eines prächtigen Buchs
im Zeitalter des Dreißigjährigen Kriegs*

Obgleich die im siebenten Band veröffentlichten Briefe, wie auch Schreiben der Vorgängerbände, immer wieder auf die Veröffentlichung von Büchern, deren Finanzierung, Einrichtung, Illustrierung, Drucklegung und Distribution zu sprechen kommen, gab es zuvor keinen ausreichenden Anlaß und Quellenvorrat, um so umfangreich und detailliert über eines der herausragenden Bücher des 17. Jahrhunderts zu handeln: das in der Werkstatt Matthäus Merians d. Ä. gestochene und unter seiner Aufsicht gedruckte Gesellschaftsbuch der Fruchtbringenden Gesellschaft von 1646 (440130, 440310, 450126, 450509, 450711 u. ö.) Zwar hatten schon der leider so früh verstorbene Martin Bircher, der Mitbegründer dieser Ausgabe — und nach ihm der verdiente Merian-Forscher Lucas Heinrich Wüthrich in abgekürzter Form —, einen großen Teil der Dokumente veröffentlicht, jedoch konnten die Funde im vorliegenden Band noch ergänzt und vielfach auch genauer erläutert werden, auch in puncto der Finanzierung und Darstellung des Kreises der Beteiligten: allein 75 Schreiben, nicht eingerechnet die ebenfalls veröffentlichte Korrespondenz Fürst Ludwigs, Carl Gustav von Hilles und anderer, die auch von Subskription, Verlagsverhandlungen, Druck und dem Ankauf von Teilauflagen spricht (vgl. 440130, 450308 u. ö.). In diesem Zusammenhang verdient auch der die Bankiers und andere Handelsleute betreffende Briefwechsel Erwähnung, weil er die damaligen Finanz- und Handelstechniken offenlegt und ebenso interessante wie schwerverständliche Belege des Kaufmannsdeutsch liefert (z. B. 451019).

Wie sehr auch Geldknappheit selbst Fürsten der deutschen Akademie einschränkte und zu peinlichen Verschleppungen der eigenen Verpflichtungen zwang, zeigt die Geschichte der Finanzierung dieses illustrierten Gesellschaftsbuchs von 1646 (s. 450126 K 4 u.ö., vgl. in *DA Köthen I.6* besonders 421031A, 430121 K 2 u. 430513). Im 6. und besonders im 7. Band unserer Ausgabe bietet der Briefwechsel einen vielleicht in dieser Zeit einmalig reichhaltigen Schatz der Information zur Planung, Finanzierung, Illustrierung und Vermarktung eines herrlichen Buchs.

Materialienband

Umfangreiche Dichtungen und oft undatierte Entwürfe erweisen sich als zu sperrig oder können als Beilagen oft nicht den vorhandenen Einzelbriefen zugeordnet werden, so daß wir dafür einen eigenen Band I. 9 (Materialien der Spracharbeit und Dichtkunst in der Fruchtbringenden Gesellschaft. Bis 1650) reserviert haben, auf dessen Texte auch im Fall eines thematischen oder zeitlichen Zusammenhangs besonders in dem vorliegenden Band wiederholt hinzuweisen war, da die meisten der dort versammelten sprachkritischen Arbeiten in den Jahren 1644 bis 1646 entstanden.

Dank an Förderer, Gutachter und Mitarbeiter

Unser Dank geht stellvertretend für alle, die das Vorhaben wohlwollend und fördernd begleitet oder den wissenschaftlichen Austausch belebt haben, an die Mitglieder unserer vorhabenbezogenen Kommission mit ihrem langjährigen Vorsitzenden Prof. Dr. Helwig Schmidt-Glintzer, an die Gutachterinnen und Gutachter Prof. Dr. Barbara Bauer-Mahlmann, Prof. Dr. Robert Seidel und Prof. Dr. Barbara Stollberg-Rilinger, an Dr. Dieter Merzbacher, Dr. Carsten Nahrendorf und Dr. phil. habil. Annett Volmer. Dankbar ist auch an die Unterstützung durch unsere jeweils befristet angestellten Hilfskräfte und die PraktikantInnen Anne Dickel, Nico Dorn, Kirsten Anna van Elten, Gordon Herenz (Potsdam), Jürgen May, Jelena Petrovic (Bern), Joanna Raisbeck (Oxford), Julia Steiner (Freiburg) und Dr. Alexander Zirr (Hannover) zu erinnern. Dr. Zirr und ganz besonders Nico Dorn bildeten eine unschätzbare Hilfe bei der Erstellung des vorliegenden Bandes. Schließlich haben wir den Kolleginnen und Kollegen der Sächsischen Akademie der Wissenschaften zu Leipzig und der Herzog August Bibliothek Wolfenbüttel für eine vorzügliche Zusammenarbeit zu danken.

Wolfenbüttel, im Januar 2016

Klaus Conermann   Andreas Herz

Editorische Vorbemerkung

Das *Datum* jedes Briefes und Schriftstücks wird in der Formel einer sechsstelligen Zahl zugleich als Ordnungsnummer des Briefes angegeben. Die ersten beiden Ziffern bedeuten stets das Jahr, es folgen der Monat und der Tag (also z. B. 171224 für 24. Dezember 1617). Wenn mehrere Briefe desselben Datums vorliegen, erhält der zweite den Zusatz A, der dritte den Zusatz B usw. Da die meisten Briefe in den benutzten Quellen nach dem in protestantischen Ländern üblichen Julianischen Kalender datiert sind, erfolgt unsere Datumsangabe grundsätzlich nach dem alten Stil, auch wenn die Vorlage beide Datierungen angibt, oder wenn sie nach dem neuen Stil datiert ist. In diesem Fall müssen im 17. Jahrhundert 10 Tage abgezogen werden, um die Datierung nach dem älteren Kalender zu erreichen. Nicht rekonstruierbare Daten sind durch 00 markiert. Alle das Datum betreffenden Unklarheiten werden im Quellenhinweis (Q) bzw. im Kommentar (K) angezeigt und nach Möglichkeit beseitigt.

Die *Überschrift* gibt den Namen des Ausstellers und Empfängers an. Alle Mitgliedernamen wurden normiert. Das einzige neuere vollständige gedruckte Mitgliederverzeichnis nach Personen- und Gesellschaftsnamen ist im Druck in *Bircher/ Palme* I, S. 129–163, zu finden. Eine verläßlichere Mitglieder-Datenbank ist jedoch über unser Internet-Portal www.die-fruchtbringende-gesellschaft.de abrufbar. Die Namensformen der Mitglieder 1–527 halten sich an die bei *Conermann I–III* festgelegten Vorgaben. Fürst Ludwig von Anhalt-Köthen wird in den Briefbänden der Abt. A: Köthen stets gekürzt genannt (Fürst Ludwig). Dementsprechend meint Herzog Wilhelm das zweite FG-Oberhaupt (Herzog Wilhelm IV. von Sachsen-Weimar) und Herzog August das dritte (Herzog August von Sachsen-Weißenfels).

Inhaltsangaben dienen der schnellen Orientierung, erleichtern das Verständnis fremdsprachiger oder schwieriger deutscher Briefe, entlasten den Sachkommentar und dienen der Auffindung und Identifizierung von Personen und Sachverhalten.

Die *Beschreibung der Quelle* (**Q**) enthält vorab den Standort und die Signatur des Dokuments und Angaben zum Umfang bzw. zur Foliierung/ Paginierung innerhalb eines Bandes oder einer Mappe. Hier wird auch mitgeteilt, ob es sich um einen Druck, eine Ausfertigung, eine Reinschrift, ein Konzept oder eine Abschrift handelt, ob Beilagen dazugehören, die u. U. verloren sind usw., ob der Text eigenhändig, von Schreiberhand oder von verschiedenen Händen geschrieben wurde oder ob der Zustand der Quelle die Edition beeinträchtigt (Wasserschäden, Papierriß usw.). In Q erfolgen auch Hinweise auf den Eingangsvermerk durch den Empfänger, auf das Siegel oder andere Besonderheiten sowie unter der Sigle *D* Angaben zu früheren Veröffentlichungen bzw. Erwähnungen der Quelle in älteren Editionen oder in der Forschungsliteratur. Bei zeitgenössischen Drucken wird nach Möglichkeit die Erstausgabe zitiert, wichtige Varianten späterer Drucke des 17. Jahrhunderts werden aufgeführt (vgl. z.B. 461204). Eine Reihe von im vorliegenden Band edierten Briefen aus dem Köthener Erzschrein ist bereits früher von dem anhaltischen Archivar Gottlieb Krause veröffentlicht worden (*KE* und *KL III*, s. Verzeichnis „Häufiger benutzte Literatur II"). Regelmäßig nahm er stillschweigend Kürzungen und andere Eingriffe in Orthographie und Zeichensetzung vor. Da die Quellenveröffentlichungen in *KL III* von *KE* abhängen, haben wir grundsätzlich darauf verzichtet, Textvarianten in *KL III* in unseren Textapparaten (s. u.) anzuführen. Ebenso hat uns die generelle Unzuverlässigkeit der Überlieferung in *KE* veranlaßt, nur diejenigen Abweichungen und „Lesarten" zu berücksichtigen, die sich auf Inhalt und Sinn des betreffenden Briefes auswirken. Ansonsten belassen wir es in unserem Quellenhinweis bei einem kursorischen Hinweis auf unvollständige Überlieferung in *KE*. Unter der Sigle *BN* wird die Quellenbeschreibung Q durch Hinweise auf bibliographische Nachweise der jeweiligen Quelle abgeschlossen.

Die *Adresse oder Anschrift* (**A**) eines Briefes wird, im Gegensatz zu den meisten Briefausgaben, grundsätzlich mitgeteilt, da sie Aufschluß über die korrekte Titulatur des Adressaten, über dessen Wohnort oder die postalische Übermittlung gibt.

Zur *Textgestalt*. Druckschriften werden, soweit mit den verfügbaren Zeichensätzen generierbar, dokumentarisch genau wiedergegeben, ausgenommen bei sinnvoll abgekürzten Zitationen im Kommentar. Die Grundschrift einer handschriftlichen Quelle hingegen, in der Regel in deutschen Texten Fraktur, in fremdsprachigen Texten Antiqua, wird in der vorliegenden Edition grundsätzlich durch Antiqua (Schrifttyp StempelGaramond) wiedergegeben. Bei Quellen der Fruchtbringenden Gesellschaft, die für ihren Kampf gegen das Fremdwort und das sprachliche Alamode-Wesen berühmt wurde, konnte indessen (außer in den Kommentaren) nicht darauf verzichtet werden, die Differenzierung der Schreibarten zwischen Grundschrift und einer für Fremdwörter gebräuchlichen, davon abweichenden Schrift beizubehalten, d.h. durch einen eigenen serifenlosen Schrifttyp für Fremdwörter anzuzeigen (Schrifttyp **MyriadPro**). Überdies sind des öfteren bei Anreden, bestimmten Namen oder Begriffen, Schlußkurialien u. dgl. kalligraphische Hervorhebungen, wie oft auch in zeitgenössischen Drucken, anzutreffen. Da diesen zierschriftlichen Auszeichnungen ebenfalls eine gewisse inhaltliche Bedeutung zukommen mag, ist auch für ihre Wiedergabe eine eigene Schriftart, die dritte also, verwendet worden: die Kursivschrift *Zapf Chancery Medium Italic*. Graphische Hervorhebungen besonderer Art oder sonstige Auffälligkeiten können im Textapparat (T) erläutert werden. Die Texte halten sich im Zeilenfall eines Prosatextes natürlich nicht an das Original. Bei der Anrede, den Grußformeln und den Angaben von Ort und Datum wird die originale Anordnung sinnvoll vereinfacht wiedergegeben. Den Seitenwechsel bezeichnen Blatt- bzw. Seitenangaben in eckigen Klammern vor der anzuzeigenden neuen Seite, um eine Kontrolle am Originaldokument zu erleichtern. Vorhandene Kustoden werden nur vermerkt, falls sie einmal vom Anfang der folgenden Seite abweichen. Bei Unleserlichkeit und Textverderbnis durch Ausriß, Flecken, Papierschäden etc. werden, falls möglich, die vom Herausgeber vermuteten Buchstaben oder Wörter in eckigen Klammern ergänzt, andernfalls wird das Fehlende durch drei in eckige Klammern gesetzte Punkte angezeigt. In T erfolgen erläuternde Hinweise.

Die Textwiedergabe folgt grundsätzlich der Rechtschreibung des Originals. In orthographischen Zweifelsfällen, vor allem bei gewissen Buchstaben (a, d, g, h, j, k, r, v, w, z), bei denen häufig nicht ausgemacht werden kann, ob der Schreiber orthographische Groß- oder Kleinschreibung intendierte, folgte die Transkription dem heutigen Rechtschreibgebrauch nur im Satz- oder Versanfang, sonst aber der in der Quelle vorherrschenden graphischen Konvention (in der Regel Kleinschreibung außer bei Namen und Titeln). Auch bei der Interpunktion hält sich die Transkription an die Vorlage, ausgenommen bei heute ungebräuchlichen und mißverständlichen Zeichen, die nach ihrer Funktion mit entsprechenden „modernen" Zeichen wiedergegeben wurden (Bindestriche, Abkürzungszeichen, Klammern). Heute mißverständliche Punkte hinter Kardinalzahlen entfallen.

Die Texte bieten drei Kategorien von Abkürzungen, die unterschiedlich behandelt werden: 1. Abkürzungen, die wegen ihres häufigen Auftretens in besonderen Abkürzungsverzeichnissen aufgeführt und aufgelöst werden; 2. Abkürzungen, die heute noch gebräuchlich und verständlich sind und daher beibehalten werden, z.B.: u., N. N., etc.; 3. Ungewöhnliche und heute nicht ohne weiteres verständliche Abbreviaturen, die im Text kursiv aufgelöst werden, z.B. besondere Kürzel oder abgekürzte Ortsnamen. Stillschweigend recte aufgelöst werden Abkürzungen, die den Wortlaut eindeutig bezeichnen, z.B. ds/dz > das/daß, d mit Aufwärtsschleife > der. Ligaturen und römische Ziffern in Monatsnamen wurden dagegen nicht aufgelöst, ebenso werden Planetensymbole für Wochentage wiedergegeben.

Der *Textapparat* (**T**) erfaßt alle Lesarten der Quelle, die nicht in den transkribierten Text aufnehmbaren Textzusätze, Konjekturen, Entschlüsselungsprobleme und graphischen Besonderheiten, Beschreibungen von Überlieferungsschäden usw. Hinweise auf den Textapparat erfolgen durch hochgestellte kleine Buchstaben, während die hochgestellten arabischen Ziffern dem Kommentar (**K**) vorbehalten bleiben.

Bei allen Briefen befindet sich der Apparat am Ende des Textes; nur bei längeren Texten können die T-Anmerkungen am Fuß der Seite aufgeführt sein. Herausgeberzusätze erscheinen *kursiv*, Quellenzitationen recte, <spitze> Klammern bedeuten „in der Quelle gestrichen".

Die *Kommentare* (**K**) liefern sprachliche Erläuterungen und Übersetzungen sowie sachliche Kommentare, auch biographische und bibliographische Hinweise.

Literatur, die nur zur Erhellung einer einzelnen Textstelle oder eines Briefes heranzuziehen war, wird nur im Kommentar und ggf. sinnvoll gekürzt angeführt. Handelt es sich um Literatur, die häufiger verwendet wurde, so ist sie mit einem *Kürzel* zitiert, das im Verzeichnis „Häufiger benutzte Literatur" aufgelöst wird.

Das *Wörterverzeichnis*, das erstmals in *DA Köthen I. 5* eingeführte *Glossar sprachwissenschaftlicher Termini* und das *Sachregister* werden innerhalb der Reihe I, Abt. A: Köthen kumuliert, so daß der Benutzer jeweils nur das Register des letzten Bandes benutzen muß. Aus zwingenden Raumgründen kann jedoch das *Personenregister* nicht alle Verweisungen auf die vorhergehenden Bände mitübernehmen. Das kumulierte Personenregister sowie auch Wörterverzeichnis, Glossar und Sachregister können online im FG-Portal www.die-fruchtbringende-gesellschaft.de (Edition/ Register) eingesehen werden. Auch bieten die Web-Seiten des Projekts über die Homepage der Sächsischen Akademie zu Leipzig www.saw-leipzig.de bzw. die Herzog August Bibliothek http://www.hab.de/de/home/wissenschaft/projekte.html den Zugriff auf diese Register. Die Register verweisen auf das Vorwerk jedes Bandes (z.B. *DA Köthen I. 1*, S. 18) und auf die Datierungsnummern der Briefe, deren Beilagen (römische Ziffern), ggf. auch auf Kommentarstellen. Wenn ein Name nur mit der Briefnummer oder auch zusätzlich mit der Beilagenziffer angeführt wird, kann der Benutzer daran die quellenmäßige Wichtigkeit dieser Angabe erkennen. Auf die allein im Quellenhinweis oder Kommentar genannten Personen oder dort behandelten Sachzusammenhänge weisen die Register hingegen durch die Buchstaben Q bzw. K hin, im Falle nur einmaliger Erwähnung auch durch den Zusatz der Anmerkungsnummer. In erforderlichen Fällen wurde den einzelnen numerierten Stellenkommentaren eine allgemeine Erläuterung vorangestellt. Auf dort genannte Personen oder Sachverhalte wird in den Registern mit K 0 verwiesen. Bei längeren Texten wird das Auffinden von Namen durch den Hinweis auf die Seite (bzw. den Vers) erleichtert. Das alphabetisch geordnete Wörterverzeichnis erfaßt jenen frühneuhochdeutschen, mundartlichen, gelegentlich aber auch fremdsprachigen Wortschatz, der nicht oder heute nicht mehr ohne weiteres verständlich ist und daher einer Kommentierung bedurfte. Sach- und Personenregister erleichtern das Auffinden anderer gewünschter Informationen. Da die Edition fortschreitend wächst, kann das von Band zu Band überarbeitete Sachregister immer nur als ein vorläufiges Orientierungsinstrument dienen.

In den Kommentaren wird bei allen ersten 527 Mitgliedern der FG auf biographische Grunddaten verzichtet, die bequem in *Conermann III* oder gekürzt im bereits erwähnten FG-Portal www.die-fruchtbringende-gesellschaft.de (Mitgliederdatenbank) nachgesehen werden können.

Sigeln, Abkürzungen, Zeichen und deutsche Monatsnamen

Sigeln

Vgl. auch das Verzeichnis „Häufiger benutzte Literatur".

A	Anschrift
AGT	Aufrichtige Gesellschaft von der Tannen
AL	La Noble Académie des Loyales
ALB Dessau	Anhaltische Landesbücherei Dessau
B	Bibliothek
BB Dessau	Behördenbibliothek Dessau
BJ Kraków	Biblioteka Jagiellońska Kraków
BL London	British Library London
BN	Bibliographischer Nachweis
BN Paris	Bibliothèque Nationale Paris
BN Madrid	Biblioteca Nacional Madrid
BU	Biblioteka Uniwersytecka
D	Druckveröffentlichung
DG	Deutschgesinnete Genossenschaft
E	Erzschrein (HM Köthen)
ESO	Elbschwanenorden
FB Gotha	Universitäts- und Forschungsbibliothek Erfurt/ Gotha, Forschungsbibliothek Gotha
FG	Fruchtbringende Gesellschaft
FS	Festschrift
GB/ GBB	Gesellschaftsbuch, Gesellschaftsbücher, vgl. „Häufiger benutzte Literatur I u. II"
GB Kö.	Köthener Gesellschaftsbuch, s. „Häufiger benutzte Literatur I u. II"
GNM Nürnberg	Germanisches Nationalmuseum Nürnberg
GSTA — PK Berlin	Geheimes Staatsarchiv — Preußischer Kulturbesitz Berlin
HAAB Weimar	Herzogin-Anna-Amalia-Bibliothek Weimar
HAB	Herzog August Bibliothek Wolfenbüttel
HB	Hofbibliothek
HM Köthen	Historisches Museum für Mittelanhalt und Bachgedenkstätte Köthen
HSTA	Hauptstaatsarchiv

IP	Instrumentum publicum, s. „Häufiger benutzte Literatur I"
K	Kommentar
KB Den Haag	Koninklijke Bibliotheek Den Haag
KB København	Det Kongelige Bibliotek København
KE	s. Verzeichnis „Häufiger benutzte Literatur"
KKH	Königsberger Kürbshütte
KL	s. Verzeichnis „Häufiger benutzte Literatur"
LA	Landesarchiv
LAO	LA Oranienbaum, siehe jetzt LHA Sa.-Anh./ Dessau
LA Oranienbaum	Landeshauptarchiv Sachsen-Anhalt, Abt. Oranienbaum, s. jetzt LHA Sa.-Anh./ Dessau
LB	Landesbibliothek
LB Schwerin	Landesbibliothek Mecklenburg-Vorpommern
LHA	Landeshauptarchiv
LHA Sa.-Anh.	Landeshauptarchiv Sachsen-Anhalt (Dessau; Magdeburg; Wernigerode)
LP	Leichenpredigt, Funeralschrift
MVAG	Mitteilungen des Vereins für Anhaltische Geschichte und Landeskunde
MVAL	Mitteilungen des Vereins für Anhaltische Landeskunde
NB Prag	Nationalbibliothek der tschechischen Republik, Prag (Národní knihovna České republiky, Praha)
NF	Neue Folge
NSTA	Niedersächsisches Landesarchiv – Staatsarchiv (Aurich; Bückeburg; Oldenburg; Stade; Wolfenbüttel)
PA	L'Académie des Parfaits Amants
PBO	Pegnesischer Blumenorden
Q	Quellenhinweis
RA	Reichsarchiv
RA Stockholm	Riksarkivet Stockholm
RB Zwickau	Ratsschulbibliothek Zwickau
SB	Staatsbibliothek
SLUB Dresden	Sächsische Landesbibliothek — Staats- u. Universitätsbibliothek Dresden
SS	Sommersemester
StA	Stadtarchiv
STA	Staatsarchiv
StB	Stadtbibliothek
STB Berlin — PK	Staatsbibliothek zu Berlin — Preußischer Kulturbesitz
StUB	Stadt- und Universitätsbibliothek

SUB	Staats- und Universitätsbibliothek
SuStB	Staats- und Stadtbibliothek
T	Textapparat
TG	Tugendliche Gesellschaft
ThHSTA	Thüringisches Hauptstaatsarchiv
ThSTA	Thüringisches Staatsarchiv
TULB Jena	Thüringische Universitäts- und Landesbibliothek Jena
UB	Universitätsbibliothek
UB/ LMB Kassel	Universitäts-, Landes- und Murhardsche Bibliothek Kassel
UL	University Library
ULB Halle	Universitäts- und Landesbibliothek Sachsen-Anhalt in Halle (Saale)
UStB	Universitäts- und Stadtbibliothek
VD17	Verzeichnis der im deutschen Sprachraum erschienenen Drucke des 17. Jahrhunderts (http://www.vd17.de)
WBN	Wolfenbütteler Barock-Nachrichten
WDB	Wolfenbütteler digitale Bibliothek
WLB Stuttgart	Württembergische Landesbibliothek Stuttgart
WS	Wintersemester
Yale UL	Yale University Beinecke Rare Book & Manuscript Library

Abkürzungen des Herausgebers

Die in Kurzform genannten drei Oberhäupter der FG:

Fürst Ludwig	Fürst Ludwig I. von Anhalt-Köthen (1579–1650; FG 2. Der Nährende, Oberhaupt der FG von 1617 bis 1650)
Herzog Wilhelm	Herzog Wilhelm IV. von Sachsen-Weimar (1598–1662; FG 5. Der Schmackhafte, Oberhaupt der FG von 1651 bis 1662)
Herzog August	Herzog August von Sachsen-Weißenfels (1614–1680; FG 402. Der Wohlgeratene, Oberhaupt der FG von 1667 bis 1680)
ahd.	althochdeutsch
ao.	außerordentlich
a. St.	alten Stils (Julianischer Kalender)
Bearb./ bearb.	Bearbeiter/ bearbeitet (von)
Bernb.	Bernburg

Bf./ bfl.	Bischof/ bischöflich
Bl./ -bl.	Blatt
Bst.	Bistum
Burggf./ -gfn.	Burggraf/ -gräfin
Christian: Tageb.	Fürst Christian II. von Anhalt-Bernburg: Tagebuch, s. „Häufiger benutzte Literatur I"
C. P. C.	Comes palatinus Caesareus (Ksl. Hofpfalzgraf)
Dess.	Dessau
d. d.	de dato
Dig./ dig.	Digitalisat/ digitalisiert
dto.	dito
Ebf./ ebfl.	Erzbischof/ erzbischöflich
Ebst.	Erzbistum
Ehz./ Ehzn.	Erzherzog/ Erzherzogin
eigenh.	eigenhändig
Ex./ Expl.	Exemplar
F./ f(l).	Fürst/ fürstlich
f.	Gulden
Fn.	Fürstin
fnhd.	frühneuhochdeutsch
Frf.	Freifrau
Frh./ frhl.	Freiherr/ freiherrlich
Fs.	Festschrift
Ft.	Fürstentum
Gese	Katalog der Schloßbibliothek Köthen, s. „Häufiger benutzte Literatur I"
Gf./ gfl.	Graf/ gräflich
Gfn.	Gräfin
Gft.	Grafschaft
Gymn.	Gymnasium
H., -h.	Hand, -händig
H.	Heft
hd.	hochdeutsch
Hft.	Herrschaft
Hg./ hg.	Herausgeber/ herausgegeben (von)
hl.	herzliebe(r), heilig
Hs./ hsl.	Handschrift/ handschriftlich
Hz./ hzl.	Herzog/ herzoglich
Hzn.	Herzogin
Hzt.	Herzogtum
imm.	immatrikuliert
Inc.	Incipit (Anfang eines Textes)
Jh.	Jahrhundert
Kat.	Katalog
Kd.	Kardinal

Kf./ kfl.	Kurfürst/ kurfürstlich
Kfn.	Kurfürstin
Kg./ kgl.	König/ königlich
Kgn.	Königin
Kö.	Köthen
Ks./ ksl.	Kaiser/ kaiserlich
Ksn.	Kaiserin
Lgf./ lgfl.	Landgraf/ landgräflich
Lgfn.	Landgräfin
LL.D.	Doctor of Laws (Legum Doctor)
Mat.	Matrikel
md.	mitteldeutsch
Mgf./ mgfl.	Markgraf/ markgräflich
Mgfn.	Markgräfin
Mgft.	Markgrafschaft
mhd.	mittelhochdeutsch
nd.	niederdeutsch
Ndr.	Nachdruck, Neudruck
n. St.	neuen Stils (Gregorianischer Kalender)
o.	ordentlich
o. D./ J.	ohne Datum/ Jahr
omd.	ostmitteldeutsch
o. O.	ohne Ort
P. L./ P. L. C.	Poeta Laureatus/ Poeta Laureatus Caesareus
Pgf./ pgfl.	Pfalzgraf/ pfalzgräflich
Pgfn.	Pfalzgräfin
Prof.	Professor
Ps./ ps.	Pseudonym
Pz.	Prinz
Pzn.	Prinzessin
r	recto
Rd.	Rand
ref.	reformiert
Rtl.	Reichstaler
Sig.	Sigillum, Siegel; Siegelspuren
s. v.	sub voce
T.	Tafel
Tageb.	Tagebuch
teilw.	teilweise
Tl.	Teil; Taler
U.	Universität
Überl.	Überliefert
Übers./ übers.	Übersetzer/ übersetzt
u. d. T.	unter dem Titel
unbek.	unbekannt

unfol.	unfoliiert
unpag.	unpaginiert
urspr.	ursprünglich
V.	Vers
v	verso
verw.	verwitwet
Wwe.	Witwe
Z.	Zeile
zit.	zitiert
Zs.	Zeitschrift

Häufige Abkürzungen in Quellen

A./ AA.	Altesse/ Altesses
A./ An./ Ao.	Anno
Al$^{t.}$	Altissimo/ Altezza, Altesse
Ampl./ Ampliss.	Amplissimus
A. V.	Altezza Vostra
C.	Candidatus
c. a. d.	c'est à dire
Cand.	Candidatus
Celsiss.	Celsissimus, -a, -o
Chr.	Christi
Churf.	Churfürstlich
citissime	eiligst
cito	eilig
Cl./ CL.	Clarissimus, -a, -o
clementiss./ -o	clementissimus, clementissimo
Colendiss.^{o}	Colendissimo
Col^{mo}	Colendissimo
comp$^{e.}$	compagnie
d.	Heller/ Pfennig
D.	Doctor
D.	Dominus
D./ Dhl./ Dhlt.	Durchlaucht
devotiss.^{a}/ $^{-o}$	devotissima, -o
dienstfr.	dienstfreundlich
dienstw.	dienstwilliger
DL	Dero Liebden
DL	Durchlaucht
Dn.	Dominus
doctiss.	doctissimus, -e
Dt.	Durchlaucht
Du./ Durchl.	Durchlaucht

dw./ d.w.	dienstwilliger
E./ Eu.	Euer, Eure
E. E.	Euer Ehren
E. Ed. L.	Euer Edlen Liebden
EFG/ E. F. G./ E. f. g.	Eure Fürstliche Gnaden
E. F. Gdn./ Gn.	
E. Fl. Gndn.	
e. g.	exempli gratia
EG/ E G/ E. G./ EGn./ E. Gn.	Euer Gnaden
E. G./ E. Gestr.	Euer Gestrengen
E. G. und H.	Euer Gnaden und Herrlichkeit
ehl.	ehemalig
E. H./ Hrl./ Hrlt.	Eure Herrlichkeit
E. H.	Euer Herzliebden [?]
e.l./ EL./ E. L./ E LB/	Euer Liebden
ELd./ Eld.	
Emp$^{r.}$	Empereur
Er./ Ern.	Ehrwürden
Eu./ Ew.	Euer, Eure
Ex$^{ce.}$	Excellence
Excellent.$^{mo.}$	Excellentissimo
f./ F.	Frau
f./ F.	Fürst
FeldM.	Feldmarschall
fl.	freundlich
f./ fl.	fürstlich
f./ fl.	Gulden
F/ Fl. Gnd./ FG/ fg	Fürstliche Gnaden
Ffurt/ ffurt	Frankfurt a. M.
fhl.	freundherzliebste(r)
fortunatiss.^{o}	fortunatissimo
fr./ frdl./ frl.	freundlich
Fr./ Frucht./ Fruchtbr.	Fruchtbringende Gesellschaft
G./ Ges./ Gesellsch.	
Franc.	Franco
frl.	fürstlich
Fruchtbr.	Fruchtbringend
FZ	Fürst zu
fzA	Fürst zu Anhalt
g.	gnädig(st)
g.	groschen
G./ Gd./ Gdn./ Gn.	Gnaden
Geh.	Geheim
Gf./ gfl./ Gfn.	Graf/ gräflich/ Gräfin
G. F. v. H.	Gnädiger Fürst und Herr

g. g./ gg.	gebe Gott/ geliebts Gott
g. g.	großgünstiger
ggl.	gute Groschen
G. Gr.	Gnädiger Graf
gl.	General
g./ gn./ gnäd./ gned.	gnädig(st)
gndt.	genannt
gr.	Groschen
Gr. G.	Gräfliche Gnaden
großg.	großgünstig [?]
H./ h.	Herr
H. H.	Herren
h.	hohen/ hochgeehrt/ heilig
h. e.	hoc est
herzl.	herzliebe(r)
Hft.	Herrschaft
HL/ hl. /hhl.	Herzliebe(r), herzliebe(r)
Hn.	Herrn
Hochgeb.	Hochgeboren
hochg.	hochgünstige(r)
hochg./ HochG./ Hochgert(er)	hochgeehrt(er)
hochl.	hochlöblich
höchstg./ HöchstG./ Höchstgert(er)	höchstgeehrt(er)
Hochw.	Hochwürdig(st)
Hz/ hz	Herzog zu
HZS	Herzog zu Sachsen
JFg./ J. F. Gn.	Ihro Fürstliche Gnaden
Jhr Hoch.	Ihre Hoheit
Jhrl.	Ihro Liebden
I. J./ J. J.	Im Jahr
J. K. M./ J. Kön. M.	Ihre königliche Majestät
IL/ Jl./ JL/ JLd.	Ihro Liebden
Ill$^{mo.}$/ Ill$^{ma.}$/ Ill$^{mi.}$/ Ill$^{mj.}$	Illustrissimo/ -a/ -i
Jlld./ Jltn.	Ihro Liebd(t)en
Illust.^{mo} / Jllustriss.^{o}	Illustrissimo
JM/ J. M.	Ihre(r) Majestät
I. U. D./ J. U. D./ J. V. D.	Juris Utriusque Doctor
J. V. L.	Juris Utriusque Licentiatus
Kay./ Kays./ Kaiserl./Key.	Kaiserlich
-l.	-lich
l.	liebe(r)
l.	löblich
L./ Ld./ Ldn.	Liebden

löbl.	löblich
m	mille/ tausend
m.	Meile(n)
M.	Monat
M./ Mag.	Magister
Maij.	Majestät
mapp.	manu propria
Mat(h)./ May./ Mayst.	Majestät
Med.	Medicinae
m. g. f.	meinem gnädigen Fürsten
M$^{gr.}$/ Monseig$^{n.}$/ Monseig$^{r.}$/ Monsr	Monseigneur
Msier.	
mp/ m. p./ mpp/ mppria/ mpria	manu propria
M.^{r}	Monseigneur
m$^{re.}$/ m$^{te.}$	maître/ maistre
Mstt.	Majestät
N. S.	Nostro Signore
Obr.	Obrist
P.	pinxit, Pictor
Phil.	Philosophiae
pl.	plurimus, -e
P. P.	Professor publicus
p. p.	prae(ter)missis prae(ter)mittendis
pp.	perge perge
pr./ p$^{r.}$	pour
Pr.	Prince (Fürst)/ Prinz, Prinzen/ Principus (lat.)
Praes./ Praesent.	Praesentatum
Pres.	Praesentatum
Pri.	Princesse (Fürstin)
P. S./ PS	Postscriptum
PS./ ps.	Praesentatum
R./ rd./ Rdl./ rt./ Rth./ Rthl./ Rthr./	Reichstaler
Recom.	Recommendatur/ Recommendatio
Röm.	Römisch
Röm. Kay. Mays./ Röm. Keyß. Mst.	Römische Kaiserliche Majestät
S	selig
S. A.	Son Altesse (frz.); Sua Altezza (ital.)
Sac. Rom. Imp.	Sacrum Romanum Imperium
schll.	Scheffel
SE/ S. E.	Seine Exzellenz/ Son Excellence/ Sua Eccellenza
Secr.	Secretarius

Seel./ sehl.	Seelig
Seig.ʳ	Seigneur
Ser.ᵐᵃ/ ⁻ᵐᵒ/ Seren.ˢˢᵒ	Serenissima/ -mo
S. F. G./ Sr. F. G.	Seine(r) Fürstliche(n) Gnaden
Sig.ᵒʳ/ Sig.ʳ/ ʳᵉ	Signor(e)
SL/ Sl./ S. L. / S. Ld.	Seine(r) Liebden
Sn./ Sr	Sein, -en/ -er
soggiettiss.ᵃ/ ⁻ᵒ	soggiettissima, -o
S. P.	Salutem Plurimam
S. P. C.	Serenissimi Principis Celsitudini/ Serenitati Principis Celsissimi
S. P. D.	Salutem Plurimam Dicit
Sr./ Sʳ·	Seigneur
Sr. G./ Sr. Gdn.	Seiner Gnaden
ß	Schilling
S. T./ Sᵉʳ· T.	Serenitas Tua
St. N./ St. n./ St. no.	Styli Novi (Gregorianischer Kalender)
St. vet.	Styli Veteris (Julianischer Kalender)
Subscr.	Subscriptum
T.	Tuus
T. E.	Tua Excellentia
th/ thl./ Thll./ Thllr.	Taler
Tit./ Tt./ tt./ t.	Titulatur, Titel
tresaffné.	tresaffectionné
tresh.	treshonoré
tresh./ treshumblem.ᵗ	treshumblement
tresob.	tresobéissant
T. T.	Totus Tuus; *s. auch unter* Tit.
Uberg./ Ubergeb., Überg./ Übergeb.	übergeben
Und./ Vnd.	untertänig(st)
unterdienstl.	unterdienstlich
unterth.	unterthänig(st)
v. (lat.)	vide (siehe)
v.	vnd/ von
VA/ V. A./ V. Alt.	Vostre Altesse (frz.); Vostra Altezza (ital.)
VE/ V. E.	Vostre Excellence (frz.)
vielg.	vielgeliebte(r)
Vnd.	s. Und.
V.ʳᵃ	Vestra, Vostra
V. S.	Vostra Serenissima
weyl.	weyland
wolgb.	wohlgeboren

Sonderzeichen für Wochentage

☽	Montag
♂	Dienstag
☿	Mittwoch
♃	Donnerstag
♀	Freitag
♄	Samstag
☉	Sonntag

Deutsche Monatsnamen

Eismonat	Januar
Hornung	Februar
Lenzmonat	März
Ostermonat	April
Wonnemonat	Mai
Brachmonat	Juni
Heumonat	Juli (auch August)
August/ Ost	August
Herbstmonat	September
Weinmonat	Oktober
Wintermonat	November
Christmonat	Dezember

Verzeichnis der edierten Quellen

I. Handschriftenbestände

Geheimes Staatsarchiv – Preußischer Kulturbesitz BERLIN
I. HA GR Rep. 9, A 3 Fasz. 5: 460125 u. II
BPH Rep. 34 Nr. 114: 460204

Staatsbibliothek zu BERLIN — Preußischer Kulturbesitz
Dep. Breslau 9: 440119
Dep. Breslau 17: 440324 I, 440826, 460610
141/11: 460103, 461006

Landeshauptarchiv Sachsen-Anhalt, Abt. DESSAU
(ehemals ORANIENBAUM)
Z 18 Abteilung Bernburg A 10 Nr. 5^{a-2}: 460714
Z 18 Abteilung Bernburg A 10 Nr. 6: 460613
Z 18 Abteilung Bernburg A 10 Nr. 46^d: 450326
Z 44 Abteilung Dessau A 10 Nr. 44: 460424, 461124
Z 70 Abteilung Köthen A 9a Nr. 25: 450408, 450508A
Z 70 Abteilung Köthen A 9a Nr. 26^d: 450507A, 450526
Z 70 Abteilung Köthen A 9a Nr. 33^{III}: 460120A, 460217
Z 70 Abteilung Köthen A 9a Nr. 49: 450220 II, 450301
Z 70 Abteilung Köthen C 18 Nr. 53: 450224

Thüringisches Staatsarchiv GOTHA
Geh. Archiv F A☉ IIIa Nr. 4^1: 450217

Staats- und Universitätsbibliothek HAMBURG
Sup. ep. 24: 440616, 440616 II, 461104
Sup. ep. 28: 440724, 441223

Historisches Museum für Mittelanhalt KÖTHEN
V S 544: 440204, 440310A, 440310B, 440723, 440723A, 450325, 450420, 450500, 450504A, 450505, 450505A, 450613, 450730, 450900, 450919, 450921, 450921A, 450923, 450923B, 451001, 460104, 460218, 460301, 460309, 460321, 460403, 460422, 460423 u. I, 460424A u. I, 460705 III, 460721, 460726, 460816 u. I, 460825 IV, 461026, 461031A u. IB, 461206
V S 545: 440127, 440129, 440130, 440209, 440209A, 440219, 440310, 440313, 440317, 440323 u. I, 440426 u. I, 440504, 440809, 440809A, 440824, 441226, 441226A, 441231, 450124 u. I, 450126, 450221, 450305, 450308, 450317,

450317A, 450400, 450504, 450506, 450506A, 450507 u. I, 450508, 450529, 450611, 450817 u. I u. II u. III u. IV u. V, 450919A, 450923C, 451007, 451008, 451028, 451028A, 451101, 451209, 451217, 451219, 451220, 460119, 460120, 460131, 460200, 460406, 460426, 460609, 460620, 460620A u. I, 460705 u. II, 460718, 460720, 460902, 460915, 460915A u. I, 460916, 461029, 461031, 461106 u. I u. II, 461213, 461216 I

V S 546: 440310A I u. II, 440816 u. I u. II, 450127, 450220 I, 450305 I, 450417, 450419, 450503, 450509, 450510, 450614, 450711, 450800 u. I, 450905, 450922, 450930, 451015, 451019, 451028B, 451119, 460206 u. I u. II, 460303, 460315, 460324, 460519, 460620B, 460703, 460708, 460810, 461023, 461031A IA.

Biblioteka Jagiellońska Kraków

acc. ms. 1913.21/9: 460410

Germanisches Nationalmuseum Nürnberg

Historisches Archiv K. 24: 441205

Wissenschaftliche Bibliothek der Universität Tartu

Mscr. 47: 450410

Herzogin Anna Amalia Bibliothek Weimar

Stammbuch 375: 450817 VI

Thüringisches Hauptstaatsarchiv Weimar

Fürstenhaus A 205: 440927, 450220
Kunst und Wissenschaft – Hofwesen A 11817[1]: 441010

Herzog August Bibliothek Wolfenbüttel

166.11 Eth. (eingebunden in Druck): 450927 u. I
BA (Bibliotheks-Archiv) II, 3 Nr. 265: 460808
BA (Bibliotheks-Archiv) II, 4 Nr. 313: 460912
BA (Bibliotheks-Archiv) II, 11 Nr. 5: 460908 III
Cod. Guelf. 11.12 Aug. 2°: 440429, 440900, 460317 I, 460414
Cod. Guelf. 56 Extrav.: 450100 I
Cod. Guelf. 65.1 Extrav.: 450219, 450319, 450806, 460715, 460819 u. I, 460908 I u. II, 460909 u. I, 461216
Cod. Guelf. 236.2 Extrav.: 450722
Cod. Guelf. 236.3 Extrav.: 460127, 460317, 460804, 460908, 461117, 461204
Cod. Guelf. 97 Novi 2°: 460715 II
Cod. Guelf. 376 Novi 2°: 440731, 460112
Cod. Guelf. 406 Novi 2°: 440731 II (440824)
Cod. Guelf. 3 Noviss. 2°: 450923A
Cod. Guelf. 74/75 Noviss. 2°: 460715 I
Cod. Guelf. 170 Noviss. 2°: 451030

Niedersächsisches Staatsarchiv WOLFENBÜTTEL

1 Alt 22 Nr. 134: 450331 u. I
2 Alt Nr. 40: 441000, 441011, 441200, 441231A, 450000, 450100, 450202, 460000 I, 460700
2 Alt Nr. 3520: 440100, 440400, 450200, 451000, 451100, 460000, 460000 II, 460200A

Biblioteka Uniwersytecka WROCLAW

R 3108: 440324, 450726

II. Druckschriften

Andreae: Autobiographie (2012)
Johann Valentin Andreae: Autobiographie. Bücher 6 bis 8. ... Bearbeitet von Frank Böhling. Übersetzt von Beate Hintzen. Stuttgart-Bad Cannstatt 2012.

461216 II

Bellin: Sendeschreiben (1647)
Johann Bellin (Hg.): Etlicher | der hoch-löblichen | Deutsch-gesinneten | Genossenschaft | Mitglieder/ | Wie auch | anderer hoch-gelehrten | Männer | Sendeschreiben | Ehrster teil; | Darinnen von vielen zur aus- | arbeitung der hoch-deutschen sprache | höchst-nötigen stükken und andern nüz- | lichen sachen gehandelt | würd: | Auff erheischen und ansuchen der | ganzen hoch-löbl. Deutsch-Zunft | zusammen geläsen/ und mit einem | Blat-weiser gezieret | durch | Johan Bellinen der freien Künste | Meistern/ und der höchst-löbl. Deutsch- | gesinneten Genossenschaft | Mitglied. | [Linie] | Hamburg | Bei Heinrich Wärnern/ | 1647. HAB: 437.16 Quod.

450308A, 450808, 460812

Bodemann: Justus Georg Schottelius an Herzog August d. J. von Braunschweig-Wolfenbüttel (1899)
Eduard Bodemann: Zwei Briefe von Leibniz betr. eine „Teutsche Gesellschaft" zu Wolfenbüttel nebst zwei Briefen von J. G. Schottelius an Herzog August von Braunschweig-Wolfenbüttel. In: Zs. des Histor. Vereins f. Niedersachsen (1899), 299–307, hier 306 f.

450929

Colerus: Raht des Heils (1658)
Gottfried Colerus: Der | Vom Vater gegebene/ | Vom Sohne ausgeführte/ | Und vom H. Geiste versiegelte | Raht des Heils | Bey Hochansehnlicher Leichbestattung | ... Dieterichs von dem Wer- | der ... Welcher am 18. Decembris des 1657sten Jahres ... entschlaffen/ | Und im jahre 1658 den 13. maj/ ... daselbst ... beygesetzet worden (Cöthen: Jacob Brand in der Fürstlichen Druckerei, 1658).

HAB: Xa 1: 47 [10].

460125 I

Dach: Lob-Spruch Dem HochEdlen Gestrengen und MannVesten Herrn Dietrich von dem Werder (1646)
Simon Dach: Lob-Spruch | Dem | HochEdlen Gestrengen und MannVesten | **Herrn Dietrich von dem Werder/** | **Obristen/ etc.** | **Fürstl: Anhaltischen geheimbten Rahte/** *etc.* | vnd Vnter Directori *etc.* Erbsassen vff Reinsdorff/ | Werders Hausen etc. | Jetzo | Seiner Fürstlichen Durchl. | **Hn. Wilhelmen Landgrafen zu Hessen/** *etc. etc.* | **Abgesandten** | An dem Churfl. Brandenb. Hofe zu Königsberg/ | Vnterdienstlichst | geschrieben | Von | Simon Dachen/ | 1646. 26. Jenner. | [Linie] | Königsberg/ gedruckt durch Johann Reusnern.
STB Berlin — PK: Yi 851-1.

460204 I

Gosky: Arbustum (1650)
Martin Gosky (Hg.): [Titelblatt mit Titelkupfer] ARBUSTUM vel ARBORETUM | AUGUSTÆUM, | Æternitati ac domui Augustæ Selenianæ | sacrum, | Satum autem & educatum | à | MARTINO GOSKY, L. Silesio, Med. D. | & Archiatro, C. Pal. Caes. [Titelkupfer:] Typis Johan et Henr. Stern. Anno 1650 EX OFFICINA DUCALI WOLPHERBYTTANI.
HAB: T 904.2° Helmst. (1).

450726 I

Greiff: Evangelienharmonie in Versen (1647)
Friedrich Greiff: Der vier Evangelisten | ubereinstimmende | Geschicht Beschreibung CHristi | Von seiner Heylsamen Geburt/ biß zu seiner | Siegreichen Himmelfahrt. | Jn vier Theil oder Bücher/ nach den | Osterfesten/ unnd deren jedes gewisse Ge | schichten abgetheilt/ deren jeder Jnhalt kurtz in zwey baar | Versen verfaßt/ die Son- vnnd Feyrtägliche Evangelien | aber in Gesang/ oder Lieder gebracht/ vnd | mit einem kurtzen Gebettlin | beschlossen. | Alles in Reimen verfasset | durch Friderich Greiffen. | Sampt zweyen Vorreden | Eine von ... D. Melchior Nicolai Fürstl. Würt. | Rhat/ der heyligen Schrifft Doctorn vnd Profes- | sorn, wie auch ProCancellario bey hiesigen | Vniversität Tübingen. | Die ander von ... D. Valentin Andreæ | F. W. Rath/ vnd Hoffprediger zu Stutgarten. | Getruckt zu Tübingen/ | Bey Philibert Brunnen. | [Linie] | Jm Jahr 1647.
HAB: 501.7 Theol.

460819 II

Harsdörffer: Frauenzimmer-Gesprächspiele I (²1644)
[Georg Philipp Harsdörffer:] FRAVENZJMMER GESPRECHSPJELE/ | so bey | Ehr- und Tugendliebenden Gesellschaften/ | mit nutzlicher Ergetzlichkeit/ beliebet und geübet werden mögen/ | Erster Theil. | Aus Jtaliänischen/ Frantzösischen und Spanischen Scribenten | angewiesen/ | und jetzund ausführlicher auf

sechs Personen gerichtet/ | und mit einer neuen Zugabe gemehret/ | Durch | Einen Mitgenossen der Hochlöblichen | FRVCHTBRJNGENDEN GESELLSCAFT *[sic]*. | Nürnberg/ | Gedruckt und verlegt bey Wolffgang Endtern. | Jm Jahre 1644.
HAB: Lo 2622: 1.

440715, 440715A

Harsdörffer: Frauenzimmer-Gesprächspiele IV (1644)
[Georg Philipp Harsdörffer:] GESPRACHSPIELE/ | So | Bey Teutschliebenden Geselschaften an- und außzuführen/ | Vierter Theil: | Samt einer Rede von dem Worte | SPIEL. | Gefertiget | Durch einen Mitgenossen der hochlöblichen | FRVCHTBRJNGENDEN GESELSCHAFT. | Nürnberg/ | Gedruckt und verlegt bey Wolffgang Endtern. | Jm Jahre 1644.
HAB: Lo 2622: 4.

440204 I, 440616 I (431201), 440616 III (440112), 440731 I

Harsdörffer: Frauenzimmer-Gesprächspiele V (1645)
[Georg Philipp Harsdörffer:] GESPRECHSPJELE/ | Fünfter Theil: | Jn welchem | Vnterschiedliche/ in Teutscher Sprache niebekante | Erfindungen/ | Tugendliebenden Gesellschaften aus zuüben/ | Vorgestellet worden: | Benebens einer Zugabe/ überschrieben | Die Reutkunst/ Durch | Einen | Mitgenossen der hochlöblichen | FRVCHTBRJNGENDEN GESELSCHAFT. | Nürnberg/ | Gedrukkt und verlegt bey Wolffgang Endter. | Jm Jahre 1645.
HAB: Lo 2622: 5.

450808 I, 450927 II

Harsdörffer: Frauenzimmer-Gesprächspiele VI (1646)
[Georg Philipp Harsdörffer:] GESPRECHSPJELE/ | Sechster Theil; | in welchem | Vielerley seltene Fragen/ Gedichte/ und Geschichte/ | zu nutzlicher Belustigung allen | Tugend- und Sprachliebenden Gesellschaften/ | behandelt werden: | Samt Beylage XII. Andachtsgemählen. | Durch | Einen Mitgenossen der hochlöblichen | FRUCHTBRJNGENDEN GESELLSCHAFT. | Nürnberg/ | Gedrukkt und verlegt bey Wolfgang Endtern. | Jm Jahre 1646.
HAB: Lo 2622: 6.

460705 I, 460803

Harsdörffer: Specimen (1646)
GEORGI PHILIPPI | HARSDORFFERI | SPECIMEN | PHILOLOGIÆ, | GERMANICÆ | Continens | Disquisitiones XII. | De Linguæ nostræ vernaculæ | Historia, Methodo, & Dignitate. | Præmissa est | PORTICVS VIRTUTIS, | Serenißimo atque Celsißimo Principi, | ac Domino, Domino | AUGUSTO, | Brunsvvicensium atq Lü- | næburgensium Duci | potentissimo &c. | SACRA. | Norimbergæ | Impensis Wolfgangi Endteri. | M. DC. XLVI. — [Kupfertitel]: G. P. HARSDÖRFFERI Specimen

Philologiæ Germanicæ. M D CXLVI. Sic labor assiduus linguæ fundamina nostræ firmabit junctis solicitè manibus.
HAB: QuN 1090 (1).

460912 I u. II

Harsdörffer: PORTICUS (1646)
[Georg Philipp Harsdörffer:] PORTICUS | Serenissimo atque Celsissimo Principi, | ac Domino, Domino | AUGUSTO, | Brunsvvicensium atque Luneburgensium | Duci potentissimo, | Principum eruditissimo, Do- | mino Clementissimo &c. | SACRA: | Cultu | GeorgI Philippi Harsdörfferi, Patricii Noric. & ejusdem | Dicasterii Adsessoris. | M. DC. XXXXVI.
HAB: 10.6 Pol.

461204A

Loredano: Lettere (1653)
Giovanni Francesco Loredano: LETTERE | DEL SIG. | GIO: FRANCESCO | LOREDANO: | Nobile Veneto. | Diuise in cinquantadue Capi, | e Raccolte. | DA | HENRICO GIBLET | CAVALIER: | [10 Zierstücke] | VENETIA; M. D. C. LIII. | Appresso li Guerigli. | Con Licenza de' Superiori, e Priuilegio.
HAB: Lk 477:6.

460000A

Milagius: Singender Jesaia (1646)
[Martinus Milagius]: Der Singende | Jesaia / | Oder | Der Prophete Jesaia/ | Jn reine deutsche Reime | gebracht/ | Vnd | Jn ein hundert und vierzehen Gesänge | eingetheilt/ | Die | Nach den bekandten Frantzösischen | melodeyen der Psalme D. Ambrosii | Lobwassers gesungen werden | können: | Gefertiget | Durch den Mindernden. | Samt | Einem anhange etlicher neuen und verbes-| serten Lieder. | [Zierstück] | Gedruckt zu Bremen/ bey Berthold de | Villiers/ im Jahre 1646. (Anhang Etlicher Geistlichen/ theils gar neuen/ theils alten/ doch verbesserten Lieder Mit jhren melodeyen/ So Täglich und auf gewisse zeiten können gebrauchet werden.)
HAB: Lo 5456.

460825 u. I u. II u. III u. V u. VI

Moscherosch: Centuria Epigrammatum (1648)
Centuria | Epigrammatum | IOHANNIS-MICHAELIS | MOSCHEROSCH | Germani. | [Linie] | Levant & Carmina curas. | Olymp. Nomes. Eclog. 4. | [Signet: PMS] | ARGENTINÆ | Typis & Sumptibus | JOH. PHILIPPI MüLBII | ET JOSIÆ STÆDELII. | [Linie] | M. DC. XXXXVIIII.
HAB: 230.8 Poet.

450818 u. I, 450901

Moscherosch: Gesichte II (1650)
Johann Michael Moscherosch: Gesichte | Philanders von Sittewald/ | Das ist | Straff-Schrifften | Hanß-Michael Moscheroschen | von Wilstädt. | Ander Theil. | [Vignette] | Straßburg/ | Bey Johan-Philipp. Mülben. | und Josias Städeln. | [Linie] | M. DC. L.
HAB: Lo 5511: 2.

460829, 461020

Rist: Schauplatz (1646)
Johann Risten | [Zierleiste] | POetischer Schauplatz/ | Auff welchem allerhand Waaren | Gute und Böse | Kleine und Grosse | Freude und Leid-zeugende | zu finden. | [Linie] | Hamburg/ Bey und JnVerlegung[!] | Heinrich Werner/ 1646.
HAB: Lo 6467.

441216 I, 460829 I

Rist: Allerunterthänigste Lobrede (1647)
Johann: Risten | Allerunterthänigste Lobrede | An die | Allerdurchläuchtigste Unüberwindlichste Römische | Kaiserliche Maiestätt/ | [Zierleiste] | Herren Ferdinand den Dritten | Als Allerhöchstgedachte Kaiserl. Maiest. | Jhn Durch den Hochwolgebohrnen Grafen und | Herren | Herren Herman Tschernin/ | Des Heiligen Römischen Reiches Graffen von | Chudenitz/ Herren auff Petersburg/ Gissibel/ Neüdek/ | Kost/ Mildschowes/ Sedschitz/ Schmidberg/ Römischer Kaiser- | licher Maiestätt Raht/ würklichen Kämmerer/ Landrechts Beisitzer | im Königreich Böheim/ Obristen und **Oratorem** an die Otto- | mannische Porten & cæt. | Mit Adelichen Freiheiten/ Schild/ Helm und Wapen | auch der Poetischen Lorberkrohn von dero Kaiserlichen | Hofe aus allergnädigst hatte verehren | lassen/ | Nebenst beigefügten nützlichen Anmerkungen und wolgemein- | ten Glük-wünschungen vornemer Herren und vertrauter | Freünde. | [Linie] | Hamburg/ | Gedruckt bey Jacob Rebenlein [1647].
HAB: 43.6 Pol. (7).

461104 I u. II u. III

Rist: Neüer Teütscher Parnass (1652)
Johann Rist: Neüer Teütscher | [Zierleiste] | Parnass/ | Auff welchem befindlich | Ehr' und Lehr | Schertz und Schmertz | Leid- und Freüden- | Gewächse/ | Welche zu unterschiedlichen | Zeiten gepflantzet/ nunmehr aber Allen/ | der Teütschen Helden-Sprache und dero- | selben edlen Dichtkunst vernünfftigen Liebhabern/ | zu sonderbarem Gefallen zu hauffe gesamlet und | in die offenbahre Welt außgestreüet/ | Von | Johann Risten. | [Signet] | Lüneburg/ | Gedrukt und verlegt durch Johann und Heinrich/ | denen Sternen/ Gebrüdern. | [Linie] | M DC LII.
HAB: Xb 3246.

461104 IV

[Schill:] Der Teutschen Sprach Ehren-Krantz (1644)
[Johann Heinrich Schill]: Der | Teutschen Sprach | Ehren-Krantz. | Neben einem | Namenbuch. | Dariñen der bißhero getragene Bet- | telRock der Teutschen Sprach auß: vnd | hergegen sie mit jhren eygnen Kleidern | vnd Zierde angezogen | wird. | [Signet] | Straßburg/ | Jn Verlegung Johañ Philipp Mülben. | 1644.
HAB: 74.15 Gram. (2), Ko 184 u. 387.4 Quod. (2).

440525 u. I u. II

Schottelius: Fruchtbringender Lustgarte (1647)
Justus Georg Schottelius: [Kupfertitel] Frucht- | bringender | Lustgar- | te, | voller | Geistliche. | und Weltliche. | Neuen erfin- | dungen | Zu | Ergetzlichen | Nutz | Zubereitet | von | Iusto-Georgio | Schottelio | I. U. D. | ... | Gedruckt in der Fürstl: Residenz Wolffenbüttel. 1647. [Drucktitel]: Fruchtbringender Lustgarte | Jn sich haltend | Die ersten funf | Abtheilungen/ | Zu ergetzlichem Nutze | Ausgefertiget/ | Und gedrukt | Jn der Fürstlichen Haupt-Vestung | Wulffenbüttel/ | Durch Johañ Bißmark/ Jn verlegung | Michael Cubachs/ Buchhändlers in | Lüneburg. | [Linie] | Jm Jahr/ 1647.
HAB: Lo 6993.

451100 I

Schottelius: Pindarische Ode (1643)
Justus Georg Schottelius: ODE Auff neue Pindarische Art/ Dem ... Herrn Augusto/ Hertzogen zu Braunschweig und | Lüneburg/ &c. Als Seine Fürstl. Gn. in dero Haubt-Vestung | und ResidentzStat Wolfenbüttel glücklichen und mit Freuden eingezogen/ | unterthänig überreichet/. Von J. G. S. (Braunschweig: Balthasar Gruber 1643). Einblattdruck.
HAB: G3:A36.

440100 I

Schottelius: Teutsche Vers- oder ReimKunst (1645)
[Kupfertitel:] Iusti-Georgii | Schottelii | Teutsche Vers- oder | ReimKunst | darin | Vnsere Teutsche | MutterSprache, So viel | dero süßeste Po- | esis | betrift, in eine | richtige Form der | Kunst zum ersten | mahle gebracht | worden. | getruckt zu | Wolfenbüttel | in verlegung | des Autoris | im jahre | M DC XL V. *Kolophon (S. 319):* Gedruckt zu Wulffenbüttel/ | durch Johann Bißmarck/ | Jm Jahr 1645.
HAB: 172.1 Poet.

440100 II, 440400 I, 441020, 441200 I u. II, 441216

Werder: DJANEA (1644)
[Diederich v. dem Werder:] DJANEA | Oder | Rähtselgedicht/ | in welchem/ | Vnter vielen anmuhtigen Fügnussen/ | Hochwichtige Staatsachen/ | Denklöbliche Geschichte/ und | klugsinnige Rahtschläge/ | vermittelst | Der Majestätischen Deutschen Sprache/ | Kunstzierlich | verborgen. | [Vignette: Purpurmuschel mit

Schriftband, „Voll Königlicher Farb"] | Nürnberg/ | Jn Verlegung Wolfgang Endters/ | [Linie] | M. DC. XXXXIV. 8°.

440000 u. I

Zesen: Jbrahim (1645)
[Madeleine de Scudéry: *Ibrahim ou l'illustre Bassa*, zuerst 4 Bde. Paris: Antoine de Sommaville 1641. Dt. Übers. von Philipp v. Zesen u. d. T. (Kartusche in Kupfertitel):] Jbrahims | oder | Des Durchleuchtigen Bassa | Und | Der Beständigen Jsabellen | Wunder-Geschichte: | Durch | Fil. Zaesien von | Fürstenau. [Verlegerzeile unter dem Kupferstich:] Amsteldam bey Ludwig Elzevieren. 1645.
HAB: Lm 3375; *Zesen SW* V. 1.

441201

Zesen: Gebundene Lust-Rede (1645)
Philipp v. Zesen: Filip Zesiens von | Fürstenau | Lustinne/ | Das ist/ | Gebundene Lust-Rede | von Kraft und Würkung | der Liebe. | [Linie] | Hamburg/ Bey Heinrich Wernern/ | Jm Jahr/ 1645.
SUB Göttingen: 8 P GERM II; *Zesen SW* I.1.

450000A

Häufiger benutzte Literatur

Dieses Verzeichnis enthält nur Schriften, die häufiger konsultiert oder zitiert wurden. Für das ältere Schrifttum über die FG ist allgemein auf die Bibliographie in *Conermann II*, 317–374 zu verweisen, außerdem auf *Bulling* und *DDL III* B I, 217–226.

I. Handschriften

Akten Weimar
Thüringisches Hauptstaatsarchiv Weimar
Kunst und Wissenschaft – Hofwesen A 11817[1]: Zehen-Jährige | Acten | Der Hochlöblichen Fruchtbringenden | Gesellschaft. | Vorgangen | Bey der Regierung und Oberverwal- | tung des Hochgeehrten | Schmackhaften | Des Durchleuchtigen, Hochgebohrnen Fürsten und Herrns/ | Herrn Wilhelms, Herzogs zu Sachsen, | Jülich, Cleve und Bergen, Landgrafens in Thüringen, | Markgrafens zu Meissen, Grafens zu der Mark | und Ravensberg, Herrns zu Ravenstein. | Von dem Jahre an | 1651 bis 61.
Erster Band des Weimarer Erzschreins der FG.

Catalogus primus
Anhaltische Landesbücherei Dessau
BB 9562: Handschriftlicher Katalog der Bibliothek F. Christians I. v. Anhalt-Bernburg. Undatiert, erstellt nach 1662; 1300 Nummern.
„CATALOGUS PRIMUS BIBLIOTHECÆ BERNBURGENSIS."

Catalogus secundus
Anhaltische Landesbücherei Dessau
BB 9562: Handschriftlicher Katalog der Bibliothek F. Christians II. v. Anhalt-Bernburg. Undatiert, erstellt nach 1662; 657 Nummern.
„CATALOGUS Secundus Bibliothecæ Berenburgensis."

Christian: Tageb.
Landeshauptarchiv Sachsen-Anhalt/ Dessau
Abt. Bernburg A 9b Nr. 14: Fürst Christian II. v. Anhalt-Bernburg: Tagebuch, Bd. I–XXIII; Bd. XXIV: Sigismund Ladisla: Auszug aus Fürst Christians II. von Anhalt-Bernburg Tagebuch.
Abt. Bernburg A 9b Nr. 14a: Fürst Christian II. von Anhalt-Bernburg: Tagebuch. Abschrift (25.2.1621 – 4./14.9.1624).

GB Kö.
Historisches Museum KÖTHEN
V S 677c, 677a u. 677b
Köthener Gesellschaftsbuch der FG, 3 Bde. I (V S 677c): Druck des *GB 1629/30* mit unikalen Wappen- und Schrifteinträgen der Mitglieder 1–200; II (V S 677a) u. III (V S 677b): Handschriften: Reimgesetze und Wappen, tw. mit eigenh. Einträgen der Mitglieder 201–400 und 401–527. S. „Häufiger benutzte Literatur: II. Druckschriften".
Dig. (WDB): Bd. I: http://diglib.hab.de/mss/ed000035-3b/start.htm
Bd. II: http://diglib.hab.de/mss/ed000035-1b/start.htm
Bd. III: http://diglib.hab.de/mss/ed000035-2b/start.htm
Vgl. Faksimile von *GB Kö.* I in *Conermann I.*

IP
Landeshauptarchiv Sachsen-Anhalt/ DESSAU
Abt. Köthen A 7a Nr. 3: Inventar des Nachlasses Fürst Ludwigs v. Anhalt-Köthen (1650).
Jeremias Walburger [Notar]: „Instrumentum Publicum Über die geschehene Obsignation, apertur testamentj, undt der darauff angestaltenn inventirung der gantzlichen verlaßenschafft. Des weylandt durchlauchtigen Hochgebohrnen Fürsten undt Herren, Herren Ludwigs Fürsten zu Anhalt Graffen zu Ascanien Herren zu Bernburgk und Zerbst. &c."

Köthener Erzschrein
Historisches Museum KÖTHEN
V S 544, 545 u. 546
Archiv der FG, 3 Bde. Briefe, Handschriften, gedruckte Beilagen. S. auch „Verzeichnis der edierten Quellen, I: Handschriftenbestände".

WB Weimar
Herzogin Anna Amalia Bibliothek WEIMAR
Ms. Fol. 219b: Wapen-Buch | Derer/ | Unter dem Durchleuchtigen | Schmakkhaften | als erwehltem Oberhaupte des | Palmenordens | Eingetretenen Fruchtbringenden | Gesellschafter | vom Jahr 1651 an.

Weimarer Impresen
Thüringisches Hauptstaatsarchiv WEIMAR
Fl. Hausarchiv A 11816: Der zweyte Theil | Fruchtbringender Kräuter | Der Jenigen | Mittglieder, | so unter | Dem Nehrenden | Dem Durchleuchtigen, Hochgebohrnen Fürsten und Herrn | Herrn Ludwigen, | Fürsten zu Anhalt/ Grafen zu Askanien, Herrn zu | Zerbst und Berenburg, | als dem Ersten | Oberhaupte und Regenten | Der hochlöblichen Fruchtbringenden Gesellschaft | Nach und nach auf- und angenommen | worden | Von dem 1643sten, biss | zu dem 1650sten | Jahre.

Dieser Band enthält 90 farbige Impresen-Gemälde der zwischen 1643 und 1649 eingetretenen FG-Mitglieder von Christoph Steger. (Vollständig schwarz-weiß abgebildet in *Conermann II*, S. [223 ff.])

II. Druckschriften

ABEPI I–III
Archivo biogràfico de España, Portugal e Iberoamérica. Ed. Victor Herrero Mediavilla, L. Rosa Aguayo Nayle. München [u. a.] 1986. Mikrofiche-Ausg. (ABEPI I). Archivo biogràfico de España, Portugal e Iberoamérica. Dirección y Redacción Victor Herrero Mediavilla. München [u. a.] 1991–1994. Mikrofiche-Ausg. (ABEPI II). Archivo biogràfico de España, Portugal e Iberoamérica 1960–1995. Ed. Victor Herrero Mediavilla. München [u. a.] 1996. Mikrofiche-Ausg. (ABEPI III).

ABF I–III
Archives biographiques françaises. Rédactrice: Susan Bradley (u. a.). 3 séries. Mikrofiches. London u. a. 1991–.

ABI I–IV
Archivo biografico italiano. A cura di Tommaso Nappo. Serie I – IV. Mikrofiches. München u. a. 1990–.

Acta Pacis Westphalicae
Acta Pacis Westphalicae. Im Auftrage der Vereinigung zur Erforschung der Neueren Geschichte hg. Max Braubach u. Konrad Repgen. 3 Serien. Münster 1962–2012. Seit 1979 hg. v. der Rheinisch-Westfälischen Akademie der Wissenschaften in Verbindung mit der Vereinigung zur Erforschung der Neueren Geschichte e. V. durch Konrad Repgen.

AD
L'Allemagne dynastique. Bearb. Michel Huberty, Alain Giraud, François u. Bruno Magdelaine. 7 Bde. Le Perreux 1976–1994.

AdC1–4
Vocabolario degli Accademici della Crusca; 1: Prima edizione, Venezia 1612; 2: Seconda edizione, Venezia 1623; 3: Terza edizione, Venezia 1691; 4: Quarta edizione, Venezia 1729–1738.
Online unter http://www.lessicografia.it

Adam
Adam, Wolfgang: Bibliotheksgeschichte und Frühneuzeit-Forschung. Bilanz und Perspektiven am Beispiel des Nachlaßverzeichnisses von Fürst Ludwig von Anhalt-Köthen. In: Euphorion 102 (2008), 1–38.

ADB
Allgemeine deutsche Biographie. Hg. Historische Commission bei der Königl. Akademie der Wissenschaften. 56 Bde. Leipzig 1875–1912. Ndr. Berlin 1967–1971.

Adelslexikon
Adelslexikon. Hauptbearbeiter Walther v. Hueck. 18 Bde. Limburg a. d. Lahn 1972–2012.

Adelung
Adelung, Johann Christoph (u. a.): Fortsetzung und Ergänzung zu Christian Gottlieb Jöchers allgemeinem Gelehrten-Lexicon. 7 Bde. Ab Bd. 3, bearb. v. Heinrich Wilhelm Rotermund. Bd. 7. Hg. Otto Günther. Leipzig 1784–1787, Delmenhorst 1810, Bremen 1813–1819, Leipzig 1897. Ndr. Hildesheim 1960/61.

Adelung Wb.
Adelung, Johann Christoph: Grammatisch-kritisches Wörterbuch der Hochdeutschen Mundart, mit beständiger Vergleichung der übrigen Mundarten, besonders aber der Oberdeutschen. 5 Tle. 2., verm. u. verb. Ausgabe. Leipzig 1793–1801.
Als CD-Rom-Edition Berlin: Directmedia 2004.

Adelung Wb. (1811)
Adelung, Johann Christoph: Grammatisch-kritisches Wörterbuch der hochdeutschen Mundart, mit besonderer Vergleichung der übrigen Mundarten, besonders aber der oberdeutschen. 4 Bde. Wien 1811.
http://lexika.digitale-sammlungen.de/adelung/angebot/adelung

Aler
DICTIONARIUM GERMANICO-LATINUM, IN QUO GERMANICA VOCABULA, … ità redduntur, Ut quodvis Scholasticum Pensum Germanicum facile, & emendatè in latinum verti ac sæpius eleganter variari possit. … VERBA OMNIA LATINA CUM EORUM PRÆteritis, ac Supinis accuratè examinata: Ac præcipuè explicatur, quænam Verba Deponentia Activi, quænam Verbi Neutri, & in quibus temporibus Passivi significationem habeant; … hucusque exponi neglectum fuit. … à R. P. PAULO ALER S. J. SS. Theol. Doctore, Studiorum viginti quinque annis Præfecto. 2 Bde. (Coloniæ: Servatius Noethen 1727).

Andreae: Schriften
Andreae, Johann Valentin: Gesammelte Schriften. In Zus.arb. mit Fachgelehrten hg. Wilhelm Schmidt-Biggemann. Bd. 1–, Stuttgart-Bad Cannstatt 1994–.

AOSB
Rikskansleren Axel Oxenstiernas Skrifter och Brefvexling. Utgifna af Kongl. Vitterhets- Historie- och Antiqvitets-Akademien. Förra Afdelningen [FA], Bd. 1–

16. Stockholm 1888–2009; Senare Afdelningen [SA], Bd. 1–14. Stockholm 1888–2012.

BA
Briefe und Acten zur Geschichte des Dreißigjährigen Krieges in den Zeiten des vorwaltenden Einflusses der Wittelsbacher. Hg. Histor. Commission bei der Königl. Academie der Wissenschaften. Bd. 1–3 Bearb. Moriz Ritter. Bd. 4–6 Bearb. Felix Stieve. Bd. 7 u. 8 Bearb. Karl Mayr. Bd. 9–11 Bearb. Anton Chroust. München 1870–1909. Bd. 12 Bearb. Hugo Altmann. München u. Wien 1978.
N. F.: Die Politik Maximilians I. von Bayern und seiner Verbündeten 1618–1651. Hg. Histor. Kommission bei der bayerischen Akademie der Wissenschaften. Tl. 1, Bd. 1 Bearb. Georg Franz; Bd. 2 Bearb. Arno Duch. München u. Wien 1966 u. 1970. Tl. 2, Bd. 1–3 Bearb. Walter Goetz. Leipzig 1907–1942; Bd. 4 Bearb. Walter Goetz. München 1948; Bd. 5 Bearb. Dieter Albrecht. München u. Wien 1964; Bd. 8 u. 9 Bearb. Kathrin Bierther. München u. Wien 1982–1986. Bd. 10: Der Prager Frieden von 1635. Tlbde. 1–4. Bearb. Kathrin Bierther. München u. Wien 1997.

BAA
Biographisches Archiv der Antike. Bearb. Hilmar Schmuck. München: Saur, Mikrofiche-Edition 1996–1999.

BACh
Biographisches Archiv des Christentums. Bearb. Axel Frey. München: Saur, Mikrofiche-Edition 2009.

Ball: Altmark-FG
Ball, Gabriele: Spuren der Fruchtbringenden Gesellschaft in der Altmark unter Berücksichtigung des „Ausjagenden" Gebhard von Alvensleben (1619–1681). In: 81. Jahresbericht des Altmärkischen Vereins für vaterländische Geschichte zu Salzwedel e. V. Hg. Ulrich Kalmbach u. Frank Riedel. Salzwedel 2011, 87–107.

Ball: Anna Sophia-Inventar
Ball, Gabriele: Das Inventar der Gräfin Anna Sophia von Schwarzburg-Rudolstadt als Spiegel eines fürstlichen Netzwerks im 17. Jahrhundert. In: Frühneuzeitliche Bibliotheken als Zentren des europäischen Kulturtransfers. Hg. Claudia Brinker-von der Heyde, Annekatrin Inder, Marie Isabelle Vogel und Jürgen Wolf. Stuttgart 2014, 77–94.

Ball: Anna Sophia-Schulstifterin
Ball, Gabriele: Die Schulstifterin Gräfin Anna Sophia von Schwarzburg-Rudolstadt (1684–1652). In: Schule und Bildung in Frauenhand. Anna Vorwerk und ihre Vorläuferinnen. Hg. G. B. und Juliane Jacobi. Wiesbaden 2015 (Wolfenbütteler Forschungen, 141), 93–139.

Ball: Anna Sophia-TG
Ball, Gabriele: Fürstinnen in Korrespondenz: Die Gräfin Anna Sophia von Schwarzburg-Rudolstadt und die Tugendliche Gesellschaft. In: WERKSTATT-GESCHICHTE 60 (2012), 7–22.

Ball: Diederich von dem Werder
Ball, Gabriele: Der Dichter und *Criticus* Diederich von dem Werder (1584–1657) in der Fruchtbringenden Gesellschaft. In: Unsere Sprache. Beiträge zur Geschichte und Gegenwart der deutschen Sprache. Schriftenreihe der Neuen Fruchtbringenden Gesellschaft zu Köthen/ Anhalt 2 (2009), 7–28.

Ball: FG-Alles zu Nutzen
Ball, Gabriele: *Alles zu Nutzen* — The Fruchtbringende Gesellschaft (1617–1680) as a German Renaissance Academy. In: The Reach of the Republic of Letters. Literary and Learned Societies in Late Medieval and Early Modern Europe. Ed. by Arjan van Dixhoorn and Susie Speakman Sutch. Leiden 2008, Vol. II, 389–422.

Ball: Johannes Kromayer
Ball, Gabriele: *Terenz in Weimar*. Johannes Kromayers Bearbeitung der *Sechs FrewdenSpiel* und die Ratichianische Schulreform. In: WBN 36 (2009), 39–54.

Ball: Sophia Elisabeth
Ball, Gabriele: Das sozietäre Netzwerk der Herzogin Sophia Elisabeth von Braunschweig-Wolfenbüttel. „Die Fortbringende" — „Die Gutwillige" — „Die Befreiende". In: Schütz-Jahrbuch 34 (2012), 29–48.

Ball: Tugendliche Gesellschaft
Ball, Gabriele: Die Tugendliche Gesellschaft. Programmatik eines adeligen Frauennetzwerkes in der Frühen Neuzeit. In: Sammeln, Lesen, Übersetzen. Die böhmische Bibliothek der Fürsten Eggenberg im Kontext der Fürsten- und Fürstinnenbibliotheken ihrer Zeit. Hg. Jill Bepler u. Helga Meise. Wiesbaden 2010 (Wolfenbütteler Arbeiten zur Barockforschung, 126), 337–361.

Ball, s. auch Herz/ Ball

Banneck
Banneck, Catharina: Georg Philipp Harsdörffers „Specimen Philologiae Germanicae": Strategien zur Profilierung des Deutschen im 17. Jahrhundert. Berlin 2012.

Barbarić
Barbarić, Stjepan: Zur grammatischen Terminologie von Justus Georg Schottelius und Kaspar Stieler. Mit Ausblick auf die Ergebnisse bei ihren Vorgängern. 2 Bde. Bern, Frankfurt a. M., Las Vegas 1981.

Barthold
Barthold, Friedrich Wilhelm: Geschichte der Fruchtbringenden Gesellschaft. Sitten, Geschmacksbildung und schöne Redekünste deutscher Vornehmen vom Ende des XVI. bis über die Mitte des XVII. Jahrhunderts. Berlin 1848. Ndr. Hildesheim 1969.

BBA I–II
British Biographical Archive [Series 1]–3. Microfiche-Edition. Managing Editor: Laureen Baillie. Editor: Paul Sieveking bzw. Managing Editor: David Bank. Editor: Anthony Esposito bzw. Tommaso Nappo. London, München, New York, Paris 1984–.

Bechtold: Schriften Moscheroschs
Bechtold, Arthur: Kritisches Verzeichnis der Schriften Johann Michael Moscheroschs. Nebst einem Verzeichnis der über ihn erschienenen Schriften. München 1922.

Beckmann
Beckmann, Johann Christoff: Historie des Fürstenthums Anhalt In Sieben Theilen verfasset. Zerbst 1710. HAB: Wa 2° 50:1 (weiteres Expl.). — S. auch *Lentz*.

Beckmann: Accessiones
Beckmann, Johann Christoff: ACCESSIONES HISTORIAE ANHALTINAE Von unterschiedenen Das Hoch-Fürstl. Hauß Und Fürstenthum Anhalt belangenden Materien sampt dazu gehörigen Documenten: Wobei zugleich Eine CONTINUATION der Hoch-Fürstl. Anhaltischen Geschichte von A. 1709. biß 1716. Jngleichen Eine Beschreibung Etlicher Adelicher zu dem Fürstenthum Anhalt gehörigen Geschlechter/ Auch einiger andern daselbst vorgegangenen Veränderungen. Zerbst 1716. HAB: Wa 2° 50:2 (weiteres Expl.).

Begemann: FG und Andreae
Begemann, Wilhelm: Die Fruchtbringende Gesellschaft und Johann Valentin Andreä. Entgegnung auf Ludwig Kellers Ausführungen im Maiheft der Comenius-Gesellschaft. Berlin 1911 (Sonderabdruck aus: Zirkelkorrespondenz für die BBr. Johannis-Meister, N. F. IV, 1, Okt. 1911).

Bei der Wieden: Schottelius
Bei der Wieden, Brage u. a.: Archivalien zu Schottelius in den Beständen des Niedersächsischen Landesarchivs – Staatsarchiv Wolfenbüttel. In: WBN 39 (2012): Die vielen Gesichter des Justus Georg Schottelius, 135–156.

Bellin: Sendeschreiben (1647)
Bellin, Johann (Hg.): Etlicher | der hoch-löblichen | Deutsch-gesinneten | Genossenschaft | Mitglieder/ | Wie auch | anderer hoch-gelehrten | Männer | Sendeschreiben | Ehrster teil; | Darinnen von vielen zur aus- | arbeitung der hoch-deut-

schen sprache | höchst-nötigen stükken und andern nüz- | lichen sachen gehandelt | würd: | Auff erheischen und ansuchen der | ganzen hoch-löbl. Deutsch-Zunft | zusammen geläsen/ und mit einem | Blat-weiser gezieret | durch | Johan Bellinen der freien Künste | Meistern/ und der höchst-löbl. Deutsch- | gesinneten Genossenschaft | Mitglied. | [Linie] | Hamburg | Bei Heinrich Wärnern/ | 1647. HAB: 437.16 Quod.

Benecke/ Müller/ Zarncke
Mittelhochdeutsches Wörterbuch mit Benutzung des Nachlasses von Georg Friedrich Benecke. Ausgearb. v. Wilhelm Müller (Bde. 1–3) und Friedrich Zarncke (Bd. 2 f.). 3 Bde. Leipzig 1854–1861. Ndr. Hildesheim [u. a.] 1986.

Benzing: Buchdrucker
Benzing, Josef: Die Buchdrucker des 16. und 17. Jahrhunderts im deutschen Sprachgebiet. 2. verb. u. erg. Aufl. Wiesbaden 1982.

Benzing: Verleger
Benzing, Josef: Die deutschen Verleger des 16. und 17. Jahrhunderts. Eine Neubearbeitung. In: Archiv für Geschichte des Buchwesens 18 (1977), 1078–1322.

Bepler: Hille
Bepler, Jill: Karl Gustav von Hille (ca. 1590–1647): Zu seiner Biographie und zu seinen Beziehungen nach England. In: Chloe 6 (1987), 253–290.

Biblia (Cramer 1634)
BIBLIA. | Das ist: | Die gantze heilige Schrifft | Deutsch/ | D. Mart. Luth. | Mit außgehenden Versiculn/ Marginalien vnd Vorreden Lutheri/ | Concordantzien/ Chronologien/ vnd vnterschiedlichen Registern der Historien vnd Hauptleren/ sampt | den Summarien D. Danielis Crameri/ auch den vbrigen Büchern Esra vnd Maccabeorum/ Auff | solche Art noch nie gesehen. | Mit Churfürstl. Sächs. Privilegio. | ... Lüneburg bey den Sternen/ | Jm tausend hundert sechs/ vier vnd dreyssigstem Jahr/ | Da stoltzer Fried lieblich blüht/ ich gedrucket war. HAB: 519.4.1 Theol. 2°.
Von Hz. August d. J. v. Braunschweig-Wolfenbüttel handschriftlich revidiertes Ex.

Biblia (Luther 1545)
D. Martin Luther: Biblia. Das ist die gantze Heilige Schrifft Deudsch auffs new zugericht. Wittenberg 1545. Hg. Hans Volz unter Mitarb. v. Heinz Blanke. Textred. Friedrich Kur. München 1974.

Biblia (Piscator), AT bzw. NT
BIBLIA, Das ist: Alle bücher der H. Schrift des alten vnd newen Testaments: Aus Hebreischer vnd Griechischer spraach ... ietzund aufs new vertheutscht: Auch eines ieden buchs vnd capitels inhalt/ samt beygefügten concordantzen/ vnd angehengter erklärung der tunckeln geschichten/ worten/ reden vnd sachen/

aufs kürtzest vnd einfeltigst verfasset: Darneben sind auch bey einem ieden capitel hinzugesetzt allerhand nutzliche notwendige lehren: Ferner die Apocrypha ... an das alte Testament angehengt ... Durch Johan Piscator/ Professor der H. Schrift zu Herborn/ mit raht vnd hülf Christliebender gelehrter männer/ derselben dolmetschungen vnd erklärungen/ verfertiget. (Herborn: Christoff Rabe 1602–1604). [Altes Testament 1602–1603, 4 Tle. u. Anhang; Neues Testament 1604, 2 Tle.].

Biographisch-Bibliographisches Kirchenlexikon
Biographisch-bibliographisches Kirchenlexikon. Begr. u. hg. v. Friedrich Wilhelm Bautz. Fortgef. v. Traugott Bautz. Bd. 1. Hamm (Westf.) 1975. Bd. 2–19 Herzberg 1992–2001. Bd. 20–33 Nordhausen 2002–2012.

Bircher: Kraków
Bircher, Martin: Autographen barocker Autoren. Quellen zur Fruchtbringenden Gesellschaft in der Biblioteka Jagiellońska Kraków, aus dem Besitz der ehem. Preußischen Staatsbibliothek Berlin. In: Respublica Guelpherbytana. Wolfenbütteler Beiträge zur Renaissance- und Barockforschung. FS f. Paul Raabe. Hg. August Buck u. M. B. Amsterdam 1987 (Chloe, 6), 291–356.

Bircher: Merian
Bircher, Martin: Matthäus Merian d. Ä. und die Fruchtbringende Gesellschaft. Der Briefwechsel über Entstehung und Drucklegung des Gesellschaftbuchs von 1646. In: Archiv für Geschichte des Buchwesens 18 (1977), 667–730.

Bircher: Palme
Bircher, Martin: Im Garten der Palme. Kleinodien aus dem unbekannten Barock: die Fruchtbringende Gesellschaft und ihre Zeit. Bd. 1. Berlin 1992 (Ausstellungskataloge der Herzog August Bibliothek, 68). Bd. 2: Katalog einer Sammlung von Dokumenten zur Wirksamkeit der Fruchtbringenden Gesellschaft. Wiesbaden 1998 (Wolfenbütteler Arbeiten zur Barockforschung, 32).

Bircher: Stubenberg
Bircher, Martin: Johann Wilhelm von Stubenberg (1619–1663) und sein Freundeskreis. Studien zur österreichischen Barockliteratur protestantischer Edelleute. Berlin 1968 (Quellen und Forschungen zur Sprach- und Kulturgeschichte der germanischen Völker, N. F. 25).

Bircher/ van Ingen
Sprachgesellschaften, Societäten, Dichtergruppen. Hg. Martin Bircher u. Ferdinand van Ingen. Hamburg 1978 (Wolfenbütteler Arbeiten zur Barockforschung, 7).

Birken: Werke u. Korrespondenz
Birken, Sigmund von: Werke und Korrespondenz. Hg. v. Klaus Garber, Dietrich

Jöns, Hartmut Laufhütte, Ralf Schuster u. Johann Anselm Steiger. Bd. 1–. Tübingen: Niemeyer (jetzt Berlin: De Gruyter) 1988– (Neudrucke deutscher Literaturwerke, N. F.).

Bischoff
Bischoff, Theodor: Georg Philipp Harsdörffer. Ein Zeitbild aus dem 17. Jahrhundert. Nürnberg 1894.

Blume: Porticus
Blume, Herbert: Harsdörffers „Porticus" für Herzog August d. J. (zu bisher unbekannten bzw. unbeachteten Briefen Harsdörffers). In: Wolfenbütteler Beiträge 1 (1972), 88–101.

Bock (1577)
Bock, Hieronymus: Kreutterbuch, Darin vnderscheidt, Nammen, vnd Würckung der Kreutter … Item von den vier Elementen/ zamen vnd wilden Thieren … Jetz- und auffs new mit allem fleiß vbersehen … Auch wie man die Kreutter zu rechter Zeit samlen vnd Distillieren soll. Durch den Hochgelehrten Melchiorem Sebizivm (Straßburg: Josias Rihel, 1577). HAB: Microfiche 1518:B865-B873. Ndr. Grünwald b. München 1964.

Bopp: Tannengesellschaft
Bopp, Monika: Die ‚Tannengesellschaft': Studien zu einer Straßburger Sprachgesellschaft von 1633 bis um 1670. Johann Matthias Schneuber und Jesaias Rompler von Löwenhalt in ihrem literarischen Umfeld. Frankfurt a. M. u. a. 1998 (Mikrokosmos, 49).

Borcherdt
Borcherdt, Hans Heinrich: Augustus Buchner und seine Bedeutung für die deutsche Literatur des siebzehnten Jahrhunderts. München 1919.

Borcherdt: Tscherning
Borcherdt, Hans Heinrich: Andreas Tscherning. Ein Beitrag zur Literatur- und Kulturgeschichte des 17. Jahrhunderts. München u. Leipzig 1912.

Braunschweig. Biograph. Lexikon (Jarck)
Braunschweigisches Biographisches Lexikon. 8. bis 18. Jahrhundert. Hg. Horst-Rüdiger Jarck. Braunschweig 2006.

Brecht: Andreae u. Hz. August
Brecht, Martin: J. V. Andreae und Herzog August zu Braunschweig-Lüneburg: ihr Briefwechsel und ihr Umfeld. Stuttgart-Bad Cannstatt 2002 (Clavis pansophiae, 8).

Brecht: Andreae Biographie
Brecht, Martin: Johann Valentin Andreae 1586–1654: eine Biographie. Göttingen 2008.

Buchner: Poemata (1720)
AVGVSTI BVCHNERI | POETÆ ET ORATORIS CELEBERRIMI | POEMATA | ELEGANTIS- | SIMA, | NVNC ALTERA VICE MVLTO | CORRECTIORA QVAM ANTEA. | SINGVLARI STVDIO ADIECTVS EST, | A | M. A. S. | INDEX | RERVM ET OBSERVATIONVM | ACCVRATVS, MAXIME NECESSARIVS, | COPIOSVS, ET THESAVRI INSTAR | POETICI VTILISSIMVS. | CVM PRIVILEGIO REGIS POLONIÆ ET | ELECTORIS SAXONIÆ. | [Linie] | LIPSIÆ & FRANCOFVRTI, | Apud GODOFREDVM LESCHIVM, | ANNO M DCC XX. HAB: P 1612b.8° Helmst.

Buchner: Poeterey (1665)
Buchner, Augustus: Anleitung zur deutschen Poeterey [1665]. Poet [1665]. Hg. Marian Szyrocki. Tübingen 1966.

Buchner (1720)
AUGUSTI BUCHNERI EPISTOLARUM PARTES TRES. OPERA M. JOH. JACOBI STÜBELII. Francofurti et Lipsiæ: Godofredus Leschius 1720. HAB: Li 1023.

W. Buchner
Buchner, Wilhelm: August Buchner, Professor der Poesie und Beredsamkeit zu Wittenberg, sein Leben und Wirken. Hannover 1863.

Bulling
Bulling, Klaus: Bibliographie zur Fruchtbringenden Gesellschaft. In: Marginalien. Blätter der Pirckheimer-Gesellschaft, Heft 20 (1965).

Burckhard: Bibliotheca Augusta
HISTORIA BIBLIOTHECAE AVGVSTAE QVAE WOLFFENBVTTELI EST. DVOBVS LIBRIS COMPREHENSA: QVORVM PRIOR SERENISSIMI BRVNSVIC. LVNEBVRG. DVCIS AVGVSTI, MVNIFICENTISSIMI BIBLIOTHECAE CONDITORIS, IMMORTALIA ... MERITA, POSTERIOR IPSIVS BIBLIOTHECAE ... COMPLECTITVR, A IACOBO BVRCKHARD ... BIBLIOTHECAE PRAEFECTO, ADVMBRATA ANNO MDCCXLIV ... ACCEDVNT FIGVRAE ATQVE INDICES.
Lipsiae Typis Breitkopfianis, SVMPTIBVS IO. CHISTOPHORI MEISNERI, BIBLOPOLAE WOLFFENBVTTEL. (Teil 1–2. 1744–1746). HAB: Wa 4° 337 (weitere Expl.).

Bürger
Verzeichnis der gedruckten Briefe deutscher Autoren des 17. Jahrhunderts. Teil 2. Drucke zwischen 1751 und 1980. Bearb. Thomas Bürger. 4 Tl.bde. Wiesbaden 2002 (Repertorien zur Erforschung der Frühen Neuzeit, 12.2). — Vgl. *Estermann*.

Calepinus
AMBROSII CALEPINI DICTIONARIVM, QVANTA MAXIMA FIDE AC DILIGENTIA ACCVRATE emendatum, & tot recèns factis accessionibus ita locupletatum, vt iam THESAVRVM LINGVÆ LATINÆ quilibet polliceri sibi audeat. Adiectæ sunt Latinis dictionibus Hebrææ, Græcæ, Gallicæ, Jtalicæ, Germanicæ, Hispaniæ, atque Anglicæ ... Adornatum à R. P. IOANNE LVDOVICO DE LA CERDA, Societatis IESV. EDITIO NOVISSIMA. Lugduni: Haered. Petri Prost, Philippi Borde & Laurentii Arnaud 1647. 2 Tle. (Tl. 2 1667 [recte 1647]). HAB: Kb 2° 40:1 u. 2.

Campe Fremdwb.
Campe, Joachim Heinrich: Wörterbuch zur Erklärung und Verdeutschung der unserer Sprache aufgedrungenen fremden Ausdrücke. Ein Ergänzungsband zu Adelung's und Campe's Wörterbüchern. Neue starkvermehrte und durchgängig verbesserte Ausgabe. Braunschweig 1813.

Campe Wb.
Campe, Joachim Heinrich: Wörterbuch der deutschen Sprache. 5 Teile. Braunschweig 1807–1811.

Castan
Castan, Joachim: Hochschulwesen und reformierte Konfessionalisierung. Das Gymnasium Illustre des Fürstentums Anhalt in Zerbst, 1582–1652. Halle a. d. S. 1999 (Studien zur Landesgeschichte, 2).

Chemnitz
Chemnitz, Bogislaff Philipp v.: Königlichen Schwedischen In Teutschland geführten Kriegs Erster Theil. Alten Stettin 1648. ... Ander Theil. Stockholm 1653. ... Dritter Theil. Stockholm 1855. ... Vierter Theil. Stockholm 1856–1859. Das Manuskript des 3. u. 4. Teils war 1668 fertiggestellt, wurde aber damals nicht veröffentlicht. Der 3. Teil verbrannte 1696. Eine überarb. Abschrift des 1. Buchs des 3. Teils aus der kfl. Bibliothek Hannover war mit einer 1848 im Nachlaß Greve Axel Oxenstiernas aufgefundenen älteren Handschrift desselben Bruchstücks Grundlage der hier angezeigten Veröffentlichung. Teil I und II erfassen die Zeit vom Kriegseintritt Schwedens in Deutschland im Sommer 1630 bis zu Oxenstiernas Abreise Juni 1636. Der nur fragmentarische dritte Teil behandelt den Zeitraum Juli bis Dezember 1636, der vierte Teil Juli 1641 bis Juli 1646.

Codex Anhaltinus minor
Codex Anhaltinus minor oder die vornehmsten Landtags-, Deputations- und Landrechnungs-Tags-Abschiede, auch Theilungs-, Seniorats und andere Recesse des Fürstenthums Anhalt de Anno 1547 bis 1727 sambt deren nöthigsten Beylagen. Leipzig 1864.

Conermann, Klaus, s. *DA*; *Opitz: BW*

Conermann I–III
Fruchtbringende Gesellschaft. Der Fruchtbringenden Gesellschaft geöffneter Erzschrein. Das Köthener Gesellschaftsbuch Fürst Ludwigs I. von Anhalt-Köthen 1617–1650. Hg. Klaus Conermann. 3 Bde. Leipzig [zugleich: Weinheim] 1985.
– Bd. 1: Der Fruchtbringenden Gesellschaft Vorhaben, Namen, Gemälde und Wörter. Faksimile des ersten Bandes des im Historischen Museum Köthen aufbewahrten Gesellschaftsbuches Fürst Ludwigs I. von Anhalt-Köthen. Hg. K. C. = *Conermann I*. — GB Kö., Bd. 1.
– Bd. 2: K. C.: Die Fruchtbringende Gesellschaft und ihr Köthener Gesellschaftsbuch. Eine Einleitung. Günther Hoppe: Fürst Ludwig I. von Anhalt-Köthen. Bilddokumentation: Das Köthener Gesellschaftsbuch. Wappen des zweiten und dritten Bandes. Die Weimarer Gemälde der Fruchtbringenden Kräuter. = *Conermann II*.
– Bd. 3: K. C.: Die Mitglieder der Fruchtbringenden Gesellschaft 1617–1650. 527 Biographien. Transkription aller handschriftlichen Eintragungen und Kommentare zu den Abbildungen und Texten im Köthener Gesellschaftsbuch. = *Conermann III*.

Conermann: Adami
Conermann, Klaus: Art. „Adami, Tobias". In: Frühe Neuzeit in Deutschland 1520–1620. Literaturwissenschaftliches Verfasserlexikon. Hg. v. W. Kühlmann u. a. Berlin usw. Bd. 1 (2011), 32–38.

Conermann: Akademie
Conermann, Klaus: War die Fruchtbringende Gesellschaft eine Akademie? Über das Verhältnis der Fruchtbringenden Gesellschaft zu den italienischen Akademien. In: *Bircher/ van Ingen*, 103–130.

Conermann: Akademie, Kritik und Geschmack
Conermann, Klaus: Akademie, Kritik und Geschmack. Zur Spracharbeit der Fruchtbringenden Gesellschaft des 17. Jahrhunderts. In: Unsere Sprache. Beiträge zur Geschichte und Gegenwart der deutschen Sprache. Schriftenreihe der Neuen Fruchtbringenden Gesellschaft zu Köthen/ Anhalt 1 (2008), 17–52.
Gekürzt nachgedruckt in: Braunschweigische Wissenschaftliche Gesellschaft. Jahrbuch 2008 (Braunschweig 2009), 91–99.

Conermann: Anhalt
Conermann, Klaus: Die Fruchtbringende Gesellschaft und das Fürstentum Anhalt. In: MVAL XVI (2007), 11–39.

Conermann: Aufnahmeurkunden
Conermann, Klaus: „Einnehmungs-Brieff" Caspar Stielers entdeckt – oder über den merkwürdigen Umgang mit Aufnahmeurkunden und Vollmachten in der Fruchtbringenden Gesellschaft. In: WBN 33 (2006), 97–119.

Conermann: Fürstl. Offizin
Conermann, Klaus: Die fürstliche Offizin zu Köthen. Druckerei, Verlagswesen und Buchhandel im Dienste des Ratichianismus und der Fruchtbringenden Gesellschaft (1618–1644/50). In: WBN 24 (1997), 122–178.

Conermann: Harsdörffers Plan
Conermann, Klaus: Harsdörffers Plan einer Vernetzung europäischer Akademien. In: „Erfreuliche Nützlichkeit – Keim göttlicher Ehre". Beiträge zum Harsdörffer-Birken-Colloquium des Pegnesischen Blumenordens im Oktober 2014. Hg. Werner Kügel. Passau 2015, 1–65.

Conermann: Hochsprache und Umgangssprache
Conermann, Klaus: Hochsprache und Umgangssprache in der Fruchtbringenden Gesellschaft. Beobachtungen anläßlich der Neuentdeckung einer handschriftlichen Köthener *Sprach-lehr* als Grundlage für Christian Gueintz' *Deutscher Sprachlehre Entwurf*. In: Germanistische Linguistik als Lebensaufgabe. Gotthard Lerchner zum 75. Geburtstag. Hg. Klaus Bochmann. Leipzig 2013 (Abhandlungen der Sächsischen Akademie der Wissenschaften zu Leipzig, Philologisch-historische Klasse, Bd. 82, H. 4), 14–31.

Conermann: Hofmann
Conermann, Klaus: Der Stil des Hofmanns. Zur Genese sprachlicher und literarischer Formen aus der höfisch-politischen Verhaltenskunst. In: Europäische Hofkultur im 16. und 17. Jahrhundert. Vorträge und Referate ... des Kongresses des Wolfenbütteler Arbeitskreises für Renaissanceforschung und des Internationalen Arbeitskreises für Barockliteratur in der Herzog August Bibliothek Wolfenbüttel, 4.–8. 9. 1979. Hg. August Buck (u. a.). 3 Bde. Hamburg 1981, I, 45–56.

Conermann: Impresa
Conermann, Klaus: Impresa und Akademie. Entstehungsgeschichtliche Überlegungen zur Sinnbildkunst europäischer Akademien. In: Res Publica Litteraria. Die Institutionen der Gelehrsamkeit in der frühen Neuzeit. Hg. Sebastian Neumeister und Conrad Wiedemann. 2 Tle. Wiesbaden 1987 (Wolfenbütteler Arbeiten zur Barockforschung, 14), I, 45–70.

Conermann: Köthen
Conermann, Klaus: „Köthen". In: Handbuch kultureller Zentren der Frühen Neuzeit. Hg. Wolfgang Adam u. Siegrid Westphal in Verbindg. mit Claudius Sittig. 3 Bde. Berlin 2012, II, 1211–1252.

Conermann: Lope de Vega
Conermann, Klaus: Der Fremde in seinem Vaterland. Zur Rezeption eines Romans Lope de Vegas in Frankreich, England und Deutschland. In: Helmut Koopmann/ Klaus Dieter Post (Hg.): Exil. Transhistorische und transnationale Perspektiven. Exile. Transhistorical and Transnational Perspectives. Paderborn 2001, 65–99.

Conermann: Ludwig Fürst v. Anhalt
Conermann, Klaus: Art. „Ludwig Fürst von Anhalt-Köthen". — In: *Literatur-Lexikon*², Bd. 7 (2010), 538–542.

Conermann: Ludwig-FG
Conermann, Klaus: Fürst Ludwig von Anhalt-Köthen (1579–1650). — Die Fruchtbringende Gesellschaft. Zwei Aufsätze. Köthen 2002 (Veröffentlichungen des Historischen Museums für Mittelanhalt, 25).

Conermann: Ludwig und Christian II. von Anhalt
Conermann, Klaus: Editionsdesiderate: Die Werke der Fürsten Ludwig und Christian II. von Anhalt im Kontext der Akademiearbeiten der Fruchtbringenden Gesellschaft. In: Editionsdesiderate zur Frühen Neuzeit. Beiträge zur Tagung der Kommission für die Edition von Texten der Frühen Neuzeit. Hg. Hans-Gert Roloff unter redaktioneller Mitarb. v. Renate Meincke. 1. Tl. Amsterdam, Atlanta/GA 1997 (Chloe, 24), 391–490.

Conermann: Nachlaßinventar
Conermann, Klaus: Die Sammlungen Fürst Ludwigs von Anhalt im Köthener Schloß. Ein Nachlaßinventar als Quelle für das Studium der Fruchtbringenden Gesellschaft. In: WBN 16 (1989), 73–91.

Conermann: Nutzen
Conermann, Klaus: Vom Nutzen der Sprache. Die Fruchtbringende Gesellschaft in Anhalt 1617–1650. In: 800 Jahre Anhalt. Geschichte, Kultur, Perspektiven. Hg. Anhaltischer Heimatbund. Wettin-Löbejün 2012, 226–241.

Conermann: Opitz auf der Dresdner Fürstenhochzeit
Conermann, Klaus: Opitz auf der Dresdner Fürstenhochzeit von 1630. Drei satirische Sonette des Boberschwans. In: Daphnis 27 (1998), 587–630.

Conermann: Opitz' Druckkorrekturen
Conermann, Klaus: Ein Widmungsband der Sammlung Deutscher Drucke in der Herzog August Bibliothek. Opitz' Druckkorrekturen seiner *Acht Bücher Deutscher Poematum* (1625) als biographisches Zeugnis. In: WBN 36 1/2 (2009), 21–30.

Conermann: Opitz — Patria
Conermann, Klaus: Martin Opitz: Patria — Nation — Europäische Renaissance. Neue biographische Forschungen zur Stellung des ‚Gekrönten' in der Literaturgeschichte. In: Abhandlungen der Braunschweigischen Wissenschaftlichen Gesellschaft, Bd. 64 (Braunschweig 2012), 37–62.

Conermann: Ort der Akademie
Conermann, Klaus: Der Ort der Akademie. Netzwerke in der Fruchtbringenden Gesellschaft und anderen deutschen und europäischen Akademien des 17. Jahrhunderts. In: Kieler Symposium „Residenzstädte der Vormoderne. Umrisse eines europäischen Phänomens". Residenzenkommission, Akademie der Wissenschaften zu Göttingen. *In Vorbereitung.*

Conermann: Purismus
Conermann, Klaus: Purismus in der Spracharbeit der Fruchtbringenden Gesellschaft? Zur Bedeutung von Richtigkeit und Reinheit in der Puritas- und Decorum-Rhetorik der deutschen Sprachreform im 17. Jahrhundert. In: Muttersprache. Vierteljahresschrift für deutsche Sprache 123 (2013), H. 3, 181–205.

Conermann: Rist
Conermann, Klaus: Johann Rist (1607–1667). „Der Rüstige" in der Fruchtbringenden Gesellschaft. In: Zeitschrift für Schleswig-Holsteinische Kirchengeschichte 1 (2013), 21–88.

Conermann: Sinnbildkunst
Conermann, Klaus: Sinnbildkunst in Büchern der Frühen Neuzeit. In: Von der Augsburger Bibelhandschrift zu Bertolt Brecht. Zeugnisse der deutschen Literatur aus der Staats- und Stadtbibliothek Augsburg und der Universitätsbibliothek Augsburg. Ausstellung der Staats- und Stadtbibliothek Augsburg in Zusammenarbeit mit der Universität Augsburg anläßlich des Deutschen Germanistentags 1991 Augsburg 4. Oktober bis 10. November 1991. Katalog hg. v. Helmut Gier u. Johannes Janota. Weißenhorn 1991, 281–318.

Conermann: Sprachkultur
Conermann, Klaus: Über Literatur und Sprachkultur im 17. Jahrhundert. A. a. O., 319–361.
Gekürzt nachgedruckt in: Augsburg – Pittsburgh. Zusammenarbeit im Bereich der Deutschen Literaturwissenschaft. Klaus D. Post (Hg.) Augsburg 1997, 37–52.

Conermann: Stieler
Conermann, Klaus: Aufnahmeurkunden der Fruchtbringenden Gesellschaft am Beispiel Caspar Stielers. In: Palmbaum. Literarisches Journal aus Thüringen. Heft 44 = Jg. 15 (2007), 136–152.

Conermann TG
Conermann, Klaus: Die Tugendliche Gesellschaft und ihr Verhältnis zur Fruchtbringenden Gesellschaft. Sittenzucht, Gesellschaftsidee und Akademiegedanke zwischen Renaissance und Aufklärung. In: Daphnis 17 (1988), 513–626. (= Sprachgesellschaften — galante Poetinnen [Literary societies/ Literary women] Zusammengestellt v. Erika A. Metzger u. Richard Schade. Amsterdam 1989, 95–208).

Conermann: Tiersatiren
Conermann, Klaus: Rosenkreuzerischer *Eselkönig* und bäurische *Legation oder Abschickung der Esell in Parnassum*. Zwei Tiersatiren des frühen 17. Jahrhunderts. Auflösung einer Stofftradition und Entstehung eines politischen komischen Romans. In: Daphnis 14 (1985), 721–757. (= Satire in der Frühen Neuzeit. Hg. Bärbel Becker-Cantarino. Amsterdam 1984).

Conermann: Vielsprachigkeit in der Frühzeit der FG
Conermann, Klaus: Das Deutsche und die Vielsprachigkeit in der Frühzeit der Fruchtbringenden Gesellschaft. Der Köthener Hof als Laboratorium der Sprach- und Versarbeit. In: Höfe als Laboratorien der Volkssprachigkeit zur Zeit der Renaissance (1480–1620) / Les Cours: lieux d'élaboration des langues vernaculaires à la Renaissance (1480–1620). Hgg. Jean Balsamo, Anna Kathrin Bleuler. Genève: Librairie Droz, 2015, 335–380 u. 444–445.

Conermann: Zwischen Literatur- und Nationalsprache
Conermann, Klaus: Die Fruchtbringende Gesellschaft zwischen Literatur- und Nationalsprache. Vom Minnesänger Heinrich von Anhalt bis zu Hoffmann von Fallersleben. In: Unsere Sprache 5 (2014), 5–46.

Conermann/ Herz/ Schmidt-Glintzer
Conermann, Klaus, Andreas Herz u. Helwig Schmidt-Glintzer: Die Fruchtbringende Gesellschaft. Gesellschaftsgedanke und Akademiebewegung. In: Gelehrte Gesellschaften im mitteldeutschen Raum (1650–1820). Teil I. Hg. Detlef Döring u. Kurt Nowak. Stuttgart u. Leipzig 2000, 19–38.

Croxton/ Tischer
Croxton, Derek u. Anuschka Tischer: The Peace of Westphalia. A. Historical Dictionary. Westport/ CT u. London 2002.

Crusca, s. *Vocabolario della Crusca 1623*

Cunrad: Silesia togata
JOH. HENRICI, CASP. FIL. CUNRADI SILESIA TOGATA, Sive Silesiorum doctrina & virtutibus clarissimorum ELOGIA ... edidit CASPAR THEOPHIL. SCHINDLERVS. Liegnitz 1706. HAB: Da 97.

DA
Die deutsche Akademie des 17. Jahrhunderts. Fruchtbringende Gesellschaft. Kritische Ausgabe der Briefe, Beilagen und Akademiearbeiten (Reihe I), Dokumente und Darstellungen (Reihe II). Begr. v. Martin Bircher † und Klaus Conermann. Im Auftrag der Sächsischen Akademie der Wissenschaften zu Leipzig, in Kooperation mit der Herzog August Bibliothek Wolfenbüttel hg. v. Klaus Conermann. Reihe I, Abt. A: Köthen, Abt. B: Weimar, Abt. C: Halle. Reihe II, Abt. A: Köthen, Abt. B: Weimar, Abt. C: Halle. Wolfenbüttel bzw. Leipzig 1991–.

Halle I
Briefe der Fruchtbringenden Gesellschaft und Beilagen: Die Zeit Herzog Augusts von Sachsen-Weißenfels 1667–1680. Mit dem Breslauer Schuldrama „Actus Von der Hochlöbl. Fruchtbringenden Gesellschaft" (1670) und mit den Registern der Mitglieder. Unter Mitarbeit von Gabriele Henkel und Andreas Herz hg. v. Martin Bircher. Wolfenbüttel 1991 (*DA*, Reihe I, Abt. C: Halle).

Halle II. 1
Die Fruchtbringende Gesellschaft unter Herzog August von Sachsen-Weißenfels. Die preußischen Mitglieder Martin Kempe (der Erkorne) und Gottfried Zamehl (der Ronde). Mit Kempes Versgedicht *Neugrünender Palm-Zweig Der Teutschen Helden-Sprache und Poeterey* (1664) und seinem Dichterlexikon *Unvorgreiffliches Bedencken/ Uber die Schriften derer bekantesten Poeten hochdeutscher Sprache* (1681). Hg. Martin Bircher und Andreas Herz. Wolfenbüttel 1997 (*DA*, Reihe II, Abt. C: Halle, Bd. 1).

Halle II. 2
Die Fruchtbringende Gesellschaft unter Herzog August von Sachsen-Weißenfels. Süddeutsche und österreichische Mitglieder. Johann Christoph Arnschwanger (der Unschuldige), Michael Frankenberger (der Erscheinende), Hieronymus Ambrosius Langenmantel (der Wenigste), Michael Praun d. J. (der Vorstellende), Joachim von Sandrart d. Ä. (der Gemeinnützige). Mit Sigmund von Birkens und Martin Limburgers Prosa-Ekloge *Ehren-Preiß Des Durchleuchtigst-Fruchtbringenden Teutschen Palmen-Hains* in Joachim von Sandrarts *Iconologia Deorum* (1680). Hg. Martin Bircher und Andreas Herz. Wolfenbüttel 1997 (*DA*, Reihe II, Abt. C: Halle, Bd. 2).

Köthen I. 1
Briefe der Fruchtbringenden Gesellschaft und Beilagen: Die Zeit Fürst Ludwigs von Anhalt-Köthen 1617–1650. Erster Band: 1617–1626. Unter Mitarbeit

von Dieter Merzbacher hg. v. Klaus Conermann. Wolfenbüttel 1992 (*DA*, Reihe I, Abt. A: Köthen, Bd. 1).

Köthen I. 2
Briefe der Fruchtbringenden Gesellschaft und Beilagen: Die Zeit Fürst Ludwigs von Anhalt-Köthen 1617–1650. Zweiter Band: 1627–1629. Unter Mitarbeit von Andreas Herz und Dieter Merzbacher hg. v. Klaus Conermann. Wolfenbüttel 1998 (*DA*, Reihe I, Abt. A: Köthen, Bd. 2).

Köthen I. 3
Briefe der Fruchtbringenden Gesellschaft und Beilagen: Die Zeit Fürst Ludwigs von Anhalt-Köthen 1617–1650. Dritter Band: 1630–1636. Unter Mitarbeit von Gabriele Ball und Andreas Herz hg. v. Klaus Conermann. Leipzig 2003 (*DA*, Reihe I, Abt. A: Köthen, Bd. 3).

Köthen I. 4
Briefe der Fruchtbringenden Gesellschaft und Beilagen: Die Zeit Fürst Ludwigs von Anhalt-Köthen 1617–1650. Vierter Band: 1637–1638. Unter Mitarbeit von Gabriele Ball und Andreas Herz hg. v. Klaus Conermann. Leipzig 2006 (*DA*, Reihe I, Abt. A: Köthen, Bd. 4).

Köthen I. 5
Briefe der Fruchtbringenden Gesellschaft und Beilagen: Die Zeit Fürst Ludwigs von Anhalt-Köthen 1617–1650. Fünfter Band: 1639–1640. Unter Mitarbeit von Gabriele Ball und Andreas Herz hg. v. Klaus Conermann. Leipzig 2010 (*DA*, Reihe I, Abt. A: Köthen, Bd. 5).

Köthen I. 6
Briefe der Fruchtbringenden Gesellschaft und Beilagen: Die Zeit Fürst Ludwigs von Anhalt-Köthen 1617–1650. Sechster Band: 1641–1643. Unter Mitarbeit von Gabriele Ball und Andreas Herz hg. v. Klaus Conermann. Leipzig 2013 (*DA*, Reihe I, Abt. A: Köthen, Bd. 6).

Köthen I. 8
Briefe der Fruchtbringenden Gesellschaft und Beilagen: Die Zeit Fürst Ludwigs von Anhalt-Köthen 1617–1650. Achter Band: 1647–1650. *In Vorbereitung* (*DA*, Reihe I, Abt. A: Köthen, Bd. 8).

Köthen I. 9
Briefe der Fruchtbringenden Gesellschaft und Beilagen: Die Zeit Fürst Ludwigs von Anhalt-Köthen 1617–1650. Neunter Band: Beilagen und Materialien. *In Vorbereitung* (*DA*, Reihe I, Abt. A: Köthen, Bd. 9).

Köthen II. 1
Fürst Ludwig von Anhalt-Köthen. Werke. Bd. I. Die ersten Gesellschaftsbücher der Fruchtbringenden Gesellschaft (1622, 1624 und 1628). — Johannis Baptistae Gelli Vornehmen Florentinischen Academici Anmutige Gespräch Capricci del Bottaio genandt (1619). Hg. Klaus Conermann. Wolfenbüttel 1992 (*DA*, Reihe II, Abt. A: Köthen, Bd. 1).

DAF1, DAF4
Dictionnaire de l'Académie Françoise; 1: Paris: Coignard 1694; 4: Quatrième édition, Paris: Brunet 1762.

Das Haus Württemberg
Das Haus Württemberg. Ein biographisches Lexikon. Hg. Sönke Lorenz, Dieter Mertens, Volker Press (†). Stuttgart, Berlin, Köln 1997.

Dasypodius
Dasypodius, Petrus: Dictionarium latinogermanicum. [1536]. Mit e. Einf. v. Gilbert de Smet. Hildesheim, Zürich, New York 1995 (Documenta Linguistica. Quellen zur Geschichte der deutschen Sprache des 15. bis 20. Jahrhunderts. Reihe I: Wörterbücher des 15. und 16. Jahrhunderts).

DBA I–III
Deutsches Biographisches Archiv [I]–III. Microfiche-Edition. Hg. Bernhard Fabian, ab Tl. 3 Victor Herrero Mediavilla; bearb. unter d. Leitung v. Willy Gorzny. München u. a. 1982–.
Vgl. Deutscher Biographischer Index. 2. kumulierte und erw. Ausg. German Biographical Index. 2nd cumulated and enlarged edition. 8 Bde. München 1998.

DBE
Deutsche Biographische Enzyklopädie. Hg. Walther Killy. 13 (Teil-)Bde. München 1995–2003.

DBE²
Deutsche Biographische Enzyklopädie. Hg. Rudolf Vierhaus unter Mitarb. v. Dietrich v. Engelhardt. 2., überarb. u. erw. Ausg. 12 Bde. München 2005–2008.

DBF
Dictionnaire de biographie française. Sous la direction de J. Balteau, M. Barroux et M. Prevost [e. a.]. Bd. 1–. Paris 1933–.

DBI
Dizionario biografico degli Italiani. Istituto Della Enciclopedia Italiana. Fondata da Giovanni Treccani. Bd. 1–. Roma 1960–.

DBL
Dansk Biografisk Leksikon. Grundlagt af C. F. Bricka. Redigerat af Povl Engelstoft under medvirkning af Svend Dahl. 26 Bde. København 1933–1944.

De Gruyter Allgemeines Künstlerlexikon (vormals Saur Allgemeines Künstlerlexikon)
De Gruyter Allgemeines Künstlerlexikon. Hg. v. Andreas Beyer, begründet u. mithg. v. Günter Meißner. Die Bildenden Künstler aller Zeiten und Völker. Bd. 1 ff. München, Leipzig 1992–; dazu: *Bio-bibliographischer Index* A – Z. 10 Bde. München, Leipzig 1999–2000; außerdem Bio-bibliographischer Index nach *Berufen*, Bd. 1 ff. München, Leipzig 2002–; [Nachtrag].

Dickmann
Dickmann, Fritz: Der Westfälische Frieden. Münster 1965.

Diefenbach
Diefenbach, Lorenz u. Ernst Wülcker: Hoch- und nieder-deutsches Wörterbuch der mittleren und neueren Zeit. Zur Ergänzung der vorhandenen Wörterbücher insbesondere des der Brüder Grimm. Basel 1885.

Diefenbach: Glossarium
Diefenbach, Lorenz: Glossarium latino-germanicum mediae et infimae aetatis e codicibus manuscriptis et libris impressis. Francofurti ad Moenum 1857. Unveränd. Ndr. Darmstadt 1997.

Diepenbroick-Grueter
Diepenbroick-Grueter, Hans Dietrich v. (Hg.): Allgemeiner Porträt-Katalog. Verzeichnis einer Sammlung von 30.000 Porträts des 16. bis 19. Jahrhunderts in Holzschnitt, Kupferstich, Schabkunst und Lithographie. Mit biographischen Notizen. Nebst Nachträgen 1–5. Hamburg 1931–1939. 2 Bde. Ndr. Hildesheim 1967; wiederum ebd. 2000.

Digitaler Porträtindex
http://www.portraitindex.de

Dissel
Dissel, Karl: Philipp von Zesen und die Deutschgesinnte Genossenschaft. Hamburg 1890 (Wissenschaftliche Beilage zum Osterprogramm des Wilhelm-Gymnasiums in Hamburg 1890).

DNB
(The) Dictionary of National Biography. Ed. by Leslie Stephen/ Sidney Lee (u. a.). 63 Bde. London, Berlin 1885–1900, mit Fortsetzungen.

Documenta Bohemica
Documenta Bohemica bellum tricennale illustrantia. Hg. Miroslav Toegel u. a. 7 Bde. Praha, Wien u. a. 1971–1981.

Dreyhaupt
Dreyhaupt, Johann Christoph v.: Pagvs Nelectici et Nvdzici, Oder Ausführliche diplomatisch-historische Beschreibung des zum ehem. ... ertz-Stifft ... Magdeburg gehörigen Saalkreyses ... Jnsonderheit der Städte Halle, Neumarckt, Glaucha. 2 Tle. Halle 1749–1750. HAB: Gm 2° 136:1 u. 2.

Drugulin
Drugulin, Wilhelm Eduard: Allgemeiner Portrait-Katalog. Verzeichnis einer Sammlung von Portraits berühmter Personen aller Länder und Zeiten (mit biographischen und chalkographischen Notizen). 2 Bde. Leipzig 1859–1860.

DSB
Dictionary of Scientific Biography. Ed. Charles Coulston Gillispie. 16 Bde. New York 1970–1981.

Dt. Fremdwb. (1913)
Schulz, Hans: Deutsches Fremdwörterbuch. 7 Bde. [Ab Bd. 2] Fortgeführt v. Otto Basler. [Ab Bd. 3] bearb. v. Alan Kirkness. Straßburg (Berlin u. New York) 1913–1988.

Dt. Fremdwb. (1995)
Schulz, Hans u. a.: Deutsches Fremdwörterbuch. 2. Aufl. völlig neu bearb. im Institut für Deutsche Sprache v. Gerhard Strauß. Bd. 1 ff. Berlin 1995–.

Du Cange
Du Cange, Charles du Fresne: Glossarium Mediae et Infimae Latinitatis ... cum supplementis integris Monachorum Ordinis S. Benedicti D. P. Carpenterii, Adelungii, aliorum, suisque digessit G. A. L. Henschel. 7 Bde. Paris 1840–1850.

van Dülmen: Utopie
Dülmen, Richard van: Die Utopie einer christlichen Gesellschaft: Johann Valentin Andreae (1586–1654). Tl. 1. Stuttgart-Bad Cannstatt 1978.

Dünnhaupt: Druckerei
Dünnhaupt, Gerhard: Die Fürstliche Druckerei zu Köthen. Ein Beitrag zum 400. Geburtstage des Fürsten Ludwig von Anhalt-Köthen (1579–1650). In: Archiv für Geschichte des Buchwesens 20 (1979), 895–950.

Dünnhaupt: Handbuch
Dünnhaupt, Gerhard: Personalbibliographien zu den Drucken des Barock. 2. verb. u. wesentl. verm. Auflage des Bibliographischen Handbuchs der Barocklite-

ratur: Tl. 1–6. Stuttgart 1990–1993 (Hiersemanns Bibliographische Handbücher IX, 1–6).

Dumrese: Sterne
Dumrese, Hans: Der Sternverlag im 17. und 18. Jahrhundert. In: Lüneburg und die Offizin der Sterne. Lüneburg 1956, 3–132.

D. v. dem Werder, s. unter Werder

DW
Grimm, Jacob u. Wilhelm: Deutsches Wörterbuch. Hg. Preußische Akademie der Wissenschaften [Deutsche Akademie der Wissenschaften zu Berlin in Zusammenarbeit mit der Akademie der Wissenschaften zu Göttingen]. 16 Bde. u. Quellenverzeichnis. Leipzig 1854–1971. Ndr. München 1984.
Zit. nach der Bandzählung der Erstausgabe.

DW (Neubearb.)
Deutsches Wörterbuch. Von Jacob Grimm u. Wilhelm Grimm. Hg. Deutsche Akademie der Wissenschaften zu Berlin [Akademie der Wissenschaften der DDR, Bd. 7: Berlin-Brandenburgische Akademie der Wissenschaften] in Zusammenarbeit mit der Akademie der Wissenschaften zu Göttingen. Bd. 1 ff., Leipzig 1983 ff. Verlags-Änderung Bd. 7: Stuttgart u. Leipzig (1993).

Emblemata
Emblemata. Handbuch zur Sinnbildkunst des XVI. und XVII. Jahrhunderts. Hg. Arthur Henkel u. Albrecht Schöne. Stuttgart 1967 (Taschenausg. Stuttgart u. Weimar 1996).

Englund
Englund, Peter: Die Verwüstung Deutschlands. Eine Geschichte des Dreißigjährigen Krieges. Aus d. Schwedischen v. Wolfgang Butt. Stuttgart ²1998.

EST
Europäische Stammtafeln. Stammtafeln zur Geschichte der europäischen Staaten. Begründet von Wilhelm Karl Prinz zu Isenburg, fortgeführt von Frank Baron Freytag von Loringhoven. Neue Folge. Hg. v. Detlev Schwennicke. Bd. I ff. Marburg, Berlin 1980–. Mit Band XVII erscheinen diese unter folgendem Titel: Europäische Stammtafeln. Neue Folge. Hg. Detlev Schwennicke. Frankfurt 1998 ff. Eine Bearbeitung erscheint mit neuer Gliederung seit 1998 unter der Bandzählung I.1 ff.

Estermann
Verzeichnis der gedruckten Briefe deutscher Autoren des 17. Jahrhunderts. Teil 1. Drucke zwischen 1600 und 1750. Bearb. Monika Estermann. 4 Tl.bde. Wiesba-

den 1992/93 (Repertorien zur Erforschung der Frühen Neuzeit, 12.1). — Vgl. *Bürger*.

Etymolog. Wb. (Pfeifer)
Etymologisches Wörterbuch des Deutschen. Erarbeitet im Zentralinstitut für Sprachwissenschaft, Berlin, unter der Leitung von Wolfgang Pfeiffer. 2. Aufl., durchgesehen u. ergänzt v. Wolfgang Pfeiffer. Berlin 1993 (Taschenbuchausg. München 1995).

Faber/ Buchner
BASILII FABRI SORANI THESAURUS ERUDITIONIS SCHOLASTICÆ: SIVE Suppellex Instructissima vocum, verborum, ac locutionum; tum rerum, sententiarum, ac exemplorum ..., Cum adjunctâ plerisqve in locis interpretatione Germanicâ; Dictionum item præcipuarum appellationibus græcis diligenter apposita qvantitate; vocum & Phrasium germanicarum Indice luculento: JAM OLIM POST ALIORUM OPERAS PER AUGUSTUM BUCHNERUM, RECENSITUS, EMENDATUS AC SUPPLETUS, PLURIMISQVE ACCESSIONIBUS INSIGNITER AUCTUS: NUNC VERÒ Clarissimorum qvorundam Virorum novâ curâ ... castigatus, Ordini suo pleniùs ... restitutus ... locupletatus. Lipsiae: Haeredes Schürerio-Gözianorum et Johannes Fritzschius 1672. HAB: Kb 4° 34 u. P 436c.2° Helmst.

Faber/ Buchner (1664)
BASILII FABRI SORANI THESAURUS ERUDITIONIS SCHOLASTICÆ: SIVE SUPPELLEX INSTRUCTISSIMA VOCUM, VERBORUM, AC LOcutionum; tum rerum, sententiarum, ac exemplorum ..., Cum adjuncta in locis plerisque interpretatione Germanicâ: jam olim per AUGUSTUM BUCHNERUM, Recensitus atque emendatus. nunc verò Nova cura denuo revisus, atque quam plurimis accessionibus auctus & suppletus. Accedunt PLERARUMQUE DICTIONUM APpellationes Græcæ, itemq. syllabarum quantitates diligenter annotatæ: vocum denique & phrasium Germanicarum luculentus Index. Francofurti, Lipsiae: Schürerio-Gözianorum Heredes 1664. VD17 1:042631P.

Faber du Faur
Faber du Faur, Curt v.: German Baroque Literature. A Catalogue of the Collection in the Yale University Library. 2 Bde. Bd. 2 Hg. Heinrich Henel. Bd. 1: New Haven 1958, Bd. 2: New Haven u. London 1969.

Findebuch mhd.
Gärtner, Kurt, Christoph Gerhardt, Jürgen Jaehrling, Ralf Plate, Walter Röll, Erika Timm. Datenverarbeitung: Gerhard Hannieder: Findebuch zum mittelhochdeutschen Wortschatz. Mit einem rückläufigen Index. Stuttgart 1992.

Findeisen
Findeisen, Jörg-Peter: Der Dreißigjährige Krieg. Eine Epoche in Lebensbildern. Darmstadt 1998.

Fischer/ Tümpel
Fischer, Albert u. Wilhelm Tümpel: Das deutsche evangelische Kirchenlied des siebzehnten Jahrhunderts. 6 Bde. Gütersloh 1904–1916.

Flood
Flood, John L.: Poets Laureate in the Holy Roman Empire. A Bio-bibliographical Handbook. 4 vol.s. Berlin u. New York 2006.

Fnhd. Wb.
Frühneuhochdeutsches Wörterbuch. Hg. Robert R. Anderson, Ulrich Goebel u. Oskar Reichmann. Bd. 1 ff. Berlin u. New York 1989–.

Frank
Frank, Karl Friedrich v.: Standeserhebungen und Gnadenakte für das Deutsche Reich und die Österreichischen Erblande bis 1806 sowie kaiserlich österreichische bis 1823 mit einigen Nachträgen zum „Alt-Österreichischen Adels-Lexikon" 1823–1918. 5 Bde. Schloß Senftenegg 1967–1974.

Friedenssäle
‚...zu einem stets währenden Gedächtnis'. Die Friedenssäle in Münster und Osnabrück und ihre Gesandtenporträts. Hg. Karl Georg Kaster u. Gerda Steinwascher mit heraldischen Beiträgen von Ulf-Dietrich Korn. Bramsche 1998.

Frisch dt.-lat.
Frisch, Johann Leonhard: Teutsch-Lateinisches Wörter-Buch, Darinnen ... auch die bey den meisten Künsten und Handwerken ... gewöhnliche Teutsche Benennungen befindlich, Vor allem ... Denen Einheimischen und Ausländern, so die in den mittlern Zeiten geschriebenen Historien ... verstehen wollen, möglichst zu dienen, ... Samt angehängter ... Etymologie ... . Nebst einem Register der lateinischen Wörter. 2 Tle. Berlin 1741. HAB: Kb 4° 33 (nur Tl. 1).
Ndr. Teutsch-lateinisches Wörter-Buch. 2 Bde. in 1 Bd. Mit einer Einf. und Bibliogr. von Gerhardt Powitz. Hildesheim [u. a.] 1977.

Frisius
[Frisius, Johannes:] DICTIONARIVM Latinogermanicum, Ioanne Frisio Tigurino interprete. HVIVS VERO PRAECIVVS EST VSVS AD LATINI sermonis fœlicitatem, & cum Germanico idiomate consensionem demonstrandam. ... ijs qui meliores authores ... imitari, suamq̨. eorum, quæ uel iam exciderunt, uel hoc tempore probata sunt, uocabulorum memoriam ... reficere desyderant. Editio noua. Tiguri: Christophorus Froschouer 1556. HAB: P 438.2° Helmst.

Fuchs (1543)
Fuchs, Leonhart: NEW Kreuterbuch/ in welchem nit allein die gantz histori/ das ist/ namen/ gestalt/ statt vnnd zeit der wachsung/ natur/ krafft vnd würckung/ des meysten theyls der Kreuter beschriben/ sonder auch ... abgebildet vnd contrafayt ist (Basel: Michael Isengrin 1543). HAB: 2.1.6 Med. 2° u. Mf 2° 4. Ndr. München 1964.

Fuchs/ Raab
Wörterbuch Geschichte. Von Konrad Fuchs u. Heribert Raab. München [13]2002.

Fürst Christian II.: Vnterweisung Eines Christlichen Fürsten (1639)
[Antonio de Guevara: *Libro llamado relox de príncipes* (1529 u. ö.), ins Ital. übers. u. bearb. v. Mambrino Roseo da Fabriano (d. i. Collenuccio Costo): *L'institutione del prencipe christiano* (1543 u. ö.), dt. Übers. von F. Christian II. v. Anhalt-Bernburg u. d. T.:] Die Vnterweisung | Eines Christlichen Fürsten/ | Aus dem Spanischen ins Jtaliänische | erstlich übergesetzt/ | Durch | MAMBRINUM ROSEUM | von Fabriano, | Vor Jahren verdeutschet durch ein Mitglied | der Fruchtbringenden Geselschaft/ | Vnd anetzo im Druck | gegeben. | [Ziervignette] | Cöthen im Fürstenthumb Anhalt/ | [Linie] | Jm Jahr 1639. HAB: 218.4 Quod. (1) (weitere Expl.)

Fürst Christian II.: Von der Beharligkeit der Außerwehlten (1641)
[Charles Drelincourt d. Ä. (1595–1669): *De la Persévérance des Saincts, ou de la fermeté de l'amour de Dieu* (Charenton 1625), dt. Übersetzung von F. Christian II. v. Anhalt-Bernburg u. d. T.:] Von der Beharligkeit der | Außerwehlten. | Oder | Von Besten- | digkeit der Liebe Gottes. | Anfangs im Jahre | 1625. | Durch Carlen Drelincourt, Pre- | diger und diener am worte Gottes/ in | der Reformirten Kirche zu Pariß Fran- | tzösisch geschrieben: | Nachgehendes aber ihme selbst/ und den | Seinigen/ auch andern frommen Chri- | sten zu nützlicher erbauligkeit/ | Zusamt den letzten Stunden des Herren von | Plessis Mornay, verdeutschet | Durch ein Mitglied der Frucht- | bringenden Gesellschaft. | [Linie] | Gedruckt zu Cöthen im Fürstenthume | Anhalt/ | Jm Jahre unsers HErren/ 1641. | Wer beharret biß ans ende/ der wird selig. HAB: 1293.11 Theol. (1); Lm 1133.

Fürst Ludwig: Das Buch Hiob (1638)
[F. Ludwig v. Anhalt-Köthen:] Das Buch Hiob/ | Nach der Hebreischen Grund- | sprache Gottsfürchtiger vnd gelehrter | Lehrer Auslegung: | Jn zwölf vnd dreyzehen silbige deutsche | Reime gesetzet/ | Sampt den Jnhalt des gantzen Buchs/ | Vnd | Einer kurtzen erzehlung/ wer dieser | heilige Mann gewesen/ vnd zu welcher | zeit er gelebet. | Die Jnhalte seind bey jedem Capittel anfangs | in ein vierzeiliches gesetzt/ | Die Lehren aber zu ende deßelben in sechs zeilige | gesetze verfaßet. | [Zierleiste] | Wittenberg/ | Gedruckt bey Johann Röhnern/ der Vniversität | Buchdrucker/ im Jahr 1638. HAB: 235.9 Theol. (1).

Fürst Ludwig: Heilige Weltbeschreibung (1643)
[Paul Geslin de La Piltière: *La saincte chorographie* (Amsterdam 1641), dt. Übers. v. F. Ludwig u. d. T.:] Die heilige | Weltbeschreibung/ | Der Völcker und

örter/ wo die Christliche Kirche/ durch den | gantzen umbkreis der Welt/ von Morgen bis gen Abend/ von | Mittage bis in Mitternacht/ jhren sitz und woh- | nung hat. | Verfertigt | Jn Frantzösischer Sprache | Durch P. Geslin/ | Und | Jns Deütsche übergesetzt. | [Holzschnitt-Vignette] | Gedruckt zu Cöthen im Fürstenthume Anhalt/ | Jm Jahre 1643. HAB: 23.3 Eth. (3).

Fürst Ludwig: Kurtze Anleitung zur Deutschen Poesi (1640)
[F. Ludwig v. Anhalt-Köthen:] Kurtze Anleitung | Zur Deutschen Poesi oder Reim-Kunst | mit ihren unterschiedenen Arten und | Mustern Reimweise verfertiget | und vorgestellet. | [*Radierung der FG-Imprese „Die fruchtbringende Geselschafft" — Uferlandschaft mit Kokospalmen — und Wort „Alles zu Nutzen"*] | Gedruckt zu Cöthen Jm Fürstenthume Anhalt/ | [Linie] | Im Jahre 1640. HAB: Um 40 (weitere Expl.).

Fürst Ludwig: Romulus und Tarquinius (1647)
[Virgilio Malvezzi Marchese di Castel Guelfo: *IL ROMULO* (Bologna 1629) und *IL TARQUINIO SVPERBO* (Bologna 1632), ins Deutsche übers. v. F. Ludwig u. d. T.:] Der Romulus, | und | Tarquinius der | Hoffertige. | Das ist: | Das Leben | Des Ersten/ | und | Letzten Königs der Römer. | Beschrieben | Von dem Jtalianischen | Herren Marggrafen Virgilio | Malvezzi. | und | Jns Deütsche übergesetzet | Auch | Auf gut befinden der Fruchtbringenden Geselschaft/ mit | angehencketer erklerung etlicher Nahmen/ örter/ | und wörter auf dem Rande/ an den | tag gegeben. | Gedruckt zu Zerbst im Fürstentume | Anhalt. | [Linie] | Jm Jahre 1647. HAB: 180.7 Quod. (2) (weitere Expl.).

Fürst Ludwig: Sechs Triumphi oder Siegesprachten (1643)
[Francesco Petrarca: *I Trionfi*, dt. Übers. v. F. Ludwig u. d. T.:] FRANCISCI PETRARCHÆ, | Des vornemen alten Florentinischen | Poeten/ | Sechs Triumphi oder | Siegesprachten/ | I. Der Liebe/ II. Der Keüschheit/ III. Des Todes/ IV. Des Gerüchtes/ V. Der Zeit/ und VI. Der Ewigkeit/ | Aus den Jtalianischen Eilfsylbigen | Jn | Deütsche zwölf und dreytzehensylbige Reime der Hel- | den art vor jahren übergesetzet: | Samt der erzelung seiner Krönung zum Poeten/ | seines lebens/ und sonderbaren erklerungen vieler | Nahmen und Geschichte: | Mit angehefteter eigentlicher Reimweise gefertigter kurtzer | Beschreibung des erdichteten Gottes der Liebe Cupidinis/ | und einem nützlichen verzeichnüs der vornemesten sachen in | diesem Wercklein begrieffen. | Von neüem übersehen/ mit beliebung und gutheissen der Frucht- | bringenden Geselschaft/ ietzo erst an den tag gegeben | und gedruckt | Zu Cöthen im Fürstenthume Anhalt/ | [Linie] | Jm Jahre 1643. HAB: 23.3 Eth. (4) u. QuN 268 (2).

Fürst Ludwig: Tamerlan (1639)
[Jean Du Bec-Crespin: *Histoire du grand Empéreur Tamerlanes* (erstmals Rouen 1595); ins Deutsche übers. von Johann Joachim v. Wartensleben, vollendet u. veröffentlicht von F. Ludwig u. d. T.:] Denckwürdige Geschichte/ | Des grossen Tamerlanis/ | der Parthen vnd Tartern Käysers | Der gelebt im Jahre nach der geburt

Christi: | Ein tausent dreyhundert fünf vnd funfzig | Biß | Ein tausent vierhundert vnd viere/ | Darinnen beschrieben seindt alle begegnungen/ Scharmützel/ | Schlachten/ Belagerungen/ Anfälle/ Stürme/ Besteigung- vnd erobe- | rung fester Städte vnd Plätze/ die mit vielen Kriegesrencken verthädigt/ | vnd angegriffen worden/ wie er dieselben bey wehrender seiner Regierung | in die vierzig vnd funfzig Jahr wohl geführet vnd glücklich geen- | det/ Benebenst andern vnterweisungen/ in Krieges- vnd | Regierungs sachen/ die denen nicht vnbekant sein | sollen/ die zur wissenschaft der Krieges- vnd | Regierkunst gelangen wollen. | Für etzlichen Jahren ins Französische aus den alten ge- | dechtnus Briefen der Araber zusammen gebracht/ | vnd nun verdeütscht. | [Zierleiste] | Gedruckt zu Cöthen im Fürstenthumb Anhalt/ | Jm Jahr 1639. HAB: QuN 199 (4) u. 295.1 Hist.

Fürst Ludwig: Der weise Alte (1643)
[Simon Goulart de Senlis: *LE SAGE VIEILLARD* (zuerst Lyon 1605), dt. Übers. von F. Ludwig u. d. T.:] Der weise Alte/ | Welcher | Durch geistreiche betrachtungen eines langen und | kurtzen Lebens/ | Dessen beschaffenheiten/ art und ursprungs der Bäume/ | des lebens/ und der wissenschaft/ darauf die leibs | und seelen beschwerungen | folgen/ | Den Nutzen/ | So die weisen Alten/ aus Philosophischen und tröstlichem Rahte | götlicher Schrift wider alle schwachheiten leibes und der seelen/ | ja den tod selbst/ den man fürchten und nicht fürchten sol/ | nemen können/ | Wie auch | Eine rechtschaffene verfassung gegen den tod für iederman/ | wes Standes und Würden er sey: von der leiber auferstehung/ | und der seelen unsterbligkeit. | Und schlieslich | Eine ernste vermanung an alle | Alte und Junge/ | Jn zwantzig Capitteln vorgestellet. | Aus dem Frantzösischen ins Deutsche vor Jahren versetzet/ | und anietzo | Gedruckt zu Cöthen im Fürstentume Anhalt/ | [Linie] | Jm Jahre 1643. HAB: 23.3 Eth. (1) u. QuN 199 (3).

Garber: Das alte Buch (2006)
Garber, Klaus: Das alte Buch im alten Europa. Auf Spurensuche in den Schatzhäusern des alten Kontinents. München 2006.

Garber, s. *Hb. Gelegenheitsschrifttum*

Garber: Opitz/ Fleming/ Dach (2012)
Garber, Klaus: Drei Dichter des 17. Jahrhunderts in Bibliotheken Mittel- und Osteuropas. Köln, Weimar, Wien 2012 (Aus Bibliotheken und Archiven Mittel- und Osteuropas, 4).

Gardt: Sprachreflexion
Gardt, Andreas: Sprachreflexion in Barock und Frühaufklärung. Entwürfe von Böhme bis Leibniz. Berlin, New York 1994.

Gauhe
Gauhe, Johann Friedrich (Hg.): Des Heil. Röm. Reichs Genealogisch-Historisches Adels-Lexicon. 2 Tle. Leipzig 1740–1747. HAB: Ff 59.

GB 1622
[Anhalt-Köthen, Fürst Ludwig v. (u. a.)]: Kurtzer Bericht der Fruchtbringenden Gesellschafft Zweck und Vorhaben. Cöthen 1622. [Angebunden]: DER FRVCHT-bringenden Gesellschafft Nahmen/ Gemählde/ und Wörter. [Köthen] 1622. — Vgl. *DA Köthen II. 1.*

GB 1624
[Anhalt-Köthen, Fürst Ludwig v. (u. a.)]: Kurtze Vnd Jn Reim verfaste Erklärung der Fruchtbringenden Gesellschafft Nahmen/ Wort und Gemählde. [Köthen] 1624. — Vgl. *DA Köthen II. 1.*

GB 1628
[Anhalt-Köthen, Fürst Ludwig v. (u. a.)]: Kurtzer Bericht Von der Fruchtbringenden Gesellschafft Vorhaben/ auch dero Nahmen/ Gemählde und Wörter Jn Reimen verfast. [Köthen] 1628. HAB: Wa 6098 — Vgl. *DA Köthen II. 1.*

GB 1629
[Anhalt-Köthen, Fürst Ludwig v. (u. a.)]: Der Fruchtbringenden Gesellschafft Vorhaben/ Nahmen/ Gemählde Vnd Wörter. Nach jedweders einnahme ordentlich Jn kupffer gestochen mit Vndergesetzten teutschen Reimen. [Frankfurt a. M.] 1629. HAB: XFilm 115.

GB 1629/30
[Anhalt-Köthen, Fürst Ludwig v. (u. a.)]: Der Fruchtbringenden Gesellschafft Vorhaben/ Nahmen/ Gemählde Vnd Wörter. Nach jedweders einnahme ordentlich Jn kupffer gestochen mit Vndergesetzten teutschen Reimen. [Frankfurt a. M.] 1629 [–1630]. HAB: Wa 5864 — Vgl. *Conermann I.*

GB 1641
[Anhalt-Köthen, Fürst Ludwig v. (u. a.)]: Kurtzer Bericht Von der Fruchtbringenden Geselschaft Vorhaben/ auch dero Namen/ Gemählde Und Wörter Jn Achtzeilige Reimgesetze verfasset. Cöthen 1641. VD17 3:603400E.

GB 1641/44
[Anhalt-Köthen, Fürst Ludwig v. (u. a.)]: Kurtzer Bericht Von der Fruchtbringenden Geselschaft Vorhaben/ auch dero Namen/ Gemählde Und Wörter Jn Achtzeilige Reimgesetze verfasset. Cöthen 1641 [–1644]. ULB Halle: 64550a.

GB 1646
[Anhalt-Köthen, Fürst Ludwig v. (u. a.)]: Der Fruchtbringenden Geselschaft Nahmen/ Vorhaben/ Gemählde und Wörter. Frankfurt a. M. 1646. HAB: 17.4.1 Eth. (weitere Expl.). Ndr. München 1971 (Die Fruchtbringende Gesellschaft. Quellen und Dokumente in vier Bänden. Hg. Martin Bircher. Bd. 1).

GB Kö.
s. *Conermann I*

GB Kö. I-III
s. „Häufiger benutzte Literatur, I. Handschriften".

Geck
Geck, Karl Wilhelm: Sophie Elisabeth Herzogin zu Braunschweig und Lüneburg (1613–1676) als Musikerin. Saarbrücken 1992 (Saarbrücker Studien zur Musikwissenschaft, N. F. 6).

GHdA
Genealogisches Handbuch des Adels. Bd. 1– (Gesamtreihe). Glücksburg 1951–1958, Limburg 1959–.

Giermann
Die neueren Handschriften der Gruppe Novissimi. 1 Noviss. 2° – 100 Noviss. 2°, 1 Noviss. 4° – 78 Noviss. 4°, 1 Noviss. 8° – 235 Noviss. 8°, 1 Noviss. 12° – 19 Noviss. 12°. Beschrieben von Renate Giermann. Frankfurt a. M. 1992 (Kataloge der Herzog August Bibliothek Wolfenbüttel, 20).

Gobiet
Der Briefwechsel zwischen Philipp Hainhofer und Herzog August d. J. von Braunschweig-Lüneburg. Bearb. v. Roland Gobiet. München 1984.

Gobiet: Auszüge
Auszüge aus der Korrespondenz Herzog August [sic] des Jüngeren von Braunschweig-Lüneburg mit dem Augsburger Patrizier Philipp Hainhofer aus den Jahren 1613–1647, exzerpiert und kommentiert von Dr. Ronald Gobiet. (7 Tle.). München: Deutscher Kunstverlag 1979 (masch.; HAB: 38.4° 641).

Goedeke
Goedeke, Karl: Grundriß zur Geschichte der deutschen Dichtung. Aus den Quellen. Bd. II. 2. Auflage, Dresden 1886. Bd. III. 2. Aufl. Dresden 1887.

Gosky: Arbustum (1650)
Gosky, Martin (Hg.): [Titelblatt mit Titelkupfer] ARBUSTUM vel ARBORETUM | AUGUSTÆUM, | Æternitati ac domui Augustæ Selenianæ | sacrum, | Satum autem & educatum | à | MARTINO GOSKY, L. Silesio, Med. D. | & Archiatro, C. Pal. Caes. [Titelkupfer:] Typis Johan et Henr. Stern. Anno 1650 EX OFFICINA DUCALI WOLPHERBYTTANI. HAB: T 904.2° Helmst. (1).

Gottfried II
Gottfried, Johann Ludwig: Fortgesetzte Historische Chronick Oder Beschreibung Der Merckwürdigsten Geschichte, So sich von Anfang der Welt bis auf den heutigen Tag zugetragen. Zweyter Theil: So sich von Anno 1618. bis zu Ende des Jahrs Christi 1659. zugetragen Mit vielen Merianischen Kupferstichen und Einem vollständigen Register versehen. Frankfurt a. M.: Hutter 1745. HAB: Gb 2° 8:2.

Götze
Götze, Alfred: Frühneuhochdeutsches Glossar. 7. Aufl. Berlin 1967.

Graesse
Graesse, Johann Georg Theodor: Trésor de livres rares et precieux ou nouveau dictionnaire bibliographique. 7 Bde. (7: Supplemente). Dresden, Genf, London, Paris 1859–1869.

Graf: Anh. Pfarrerbuch
Graf, Herrmann: Anhaltisches Pfarrerbuch. Die evangelischen Pfarrer seit der Reformation. Hg. Landeskirchenrat der Evangelischen Landeskirche Anhalts. Dessau 1996.

Grotefend
Grotefend, Hermann: Zeitrechnung des deutschen Mittelalters und der Neuzeit. In 2 Bänden. 2. Ndr. der Ausg. Hannover 1892–1998, Aalen 1984.

Grotius: Briefwisseling
Briefwisseling van Hugo Grotius. Uitgegev. door Philipp Christian Molhuysen (u. a.). Bd. 1–27, 1 Supplement- u. Ergänzungsbd. 's-Gravenhage 1928–2001.

Grove^2
The New Grove Dictionary of Music and Musicians. Second edition ed. by Stanley Sadie. 29 Bde. London [u. a.] 2001.

Gueintz: Rechtschreibung (1645)
[Gueintz, Christian u.a.:] Die | Deutsche | Rechtschreibung | Auf sonderbares gut befinden | Durch den | Ordnenden | verfasset/| Von der Fruchtbringenden Geselschaft | übersehen/ und zur nachricht an den | tag gegeben. | [Zierstück] | Gedruckt zu Halle in Sachsen bey | Christof Salfelden/ | [Linie] | Jm Jahre 1645. HAB: Ko 209 (2). Ndr. Hg. Claudine Moulin. Hildesheim, Zürich, New York 2008 (Documenta Orthographica, Abt. A, Bd. 3).

Gueintz: Rechtschreibung (1666)
[Rot-Schwarz-Druck] [Gueintz, Christian u.a.:] Die | Deutsche | Rechtschreibung | Auf sonderbares gut befinden | Durch | Christianum Gueintz/ Philosoph. | und des Gymnasii zu Hall Rectorn, | sonst | den | Ordnenden/ | verfasset: | Von der Fruchtbringenden Geselschaft ü- | bersehen/ und zur nachricht/ auff anhalten

und | begehren/ ietzo zum andern mal an den tag | gegeben von des Autoris | Sohne | Johann Christiano Gueintz/ | J.U.D des Fürstl. Magdeb. Schöppenstuels da- | selbst Assessorn &c. | [Zierleiste] | Hall in Sachsen/ | Jn Verlegung Christoph. Milii. | Gedruckt bey Matthaeus Henckeln. | Jm Jahr 1666. HAB: Xb 3764 (1).

Gueintz: Sprachlehre (1641)
Christian Gueintzen/ | Deutscher | Sprachlehre | Entwurf. | [Holzschnitt-Vignette] | Gedruckt zu Cöthen im Fürsten- | thume Anhalt/ | [Linie] | Jm Jahre CHRisti 1641. HAB: Ko 209 (1). Ndr. Hildesheim, New York 1978. (Documenta Linguistica. Reihe V).

Guthrie II
Guthrie, William P.: The later Thirty Years War. From the Battle of Wittstock to the Treaty of Westphalia. Westport/ Conn. [u. a.] 2003.

Haag
Haag, Eugène u. Émile: La France protestante. 2. éd. pub. sous les auspices de la Société de l'Histoire du Protestantisme Française. 6 Bde. in 12. Paris 1877–1888. Ndr. Genève 1966.

Haberkern/ Wallach
Haberkern, Eugen u. Joseph Friedrich Wallach: Hilfswörterbuch für Historiker. Mittelalter und Neuzeit. 6. Aufl. 2 Tle. München 1980.

Habichthorst
Habichthorst, Andreas Daniel: Wohlgegründete | Bedenkschrift | über die | Zesische | Sonderbahre Ahrt Hoch- | deutsch zu Schreiben und zu | Reden/ | den Sprachliebenden zum diensamen Nachrichte | zusammen und zu tage getragen | durch | L. Andreas Daniel Habichthorsten/ | der Hohen Schuhle zu Rostok öffentlichen Lehrern/ u. a. m. wie auch der hochpreiswürdigen | Deutschgesinten Genossenschaft/ | unter dem | Zunftnahmen des Blühsamen/ | Mit-Ertzschreinhaltern. (Hamburg: Fleischer, Lichtenstein 1678). HAB: Ko 211 u. Xb 3768 (5).

Halle I, Halle II. 1 bzw. Halle II. 2
s. unter *DA*

Harsdörffer: Fortpflantzung der FG
Harsdörffer, Georg Philipp: Fortpflantzung der Hochlöblichen Fruchtbringenden Geselschaft: Das ist/ Kurtze Erzehlung alles dessen/ Was sich bey Erwehlung und Antrettung hochbesagter Geselschaft Oberhauptes/ Deß Höchteuersten und Wehrtesten SCHMACKHAFTEN/ begeben und zugetragen. Samt Etlichen Glückwünschungen/ und Einer Lobrede deß Geschmackes. Gedruckt zu Nürnberg/ bey Michael Endter/ Jm Jahre 1651. — In: *GB 1646* (Die Fruchtbrin-

gende Gesellschaft. Quellen und Dokumente in vier Bänden. Hg. Martin Bircher. Bd. 1).

Harsdörffer: Frauenzimmer-Gesprächspiele
Harsdörffer, Georg Philipp: FRAUENZJMMER GESPRECHSPJELE/ | so bey | Ehr- und Tugendliebenden Gesellschaften/ | mit nutzlicher Ergetzlichkeit/ beliebet und geübet werden mögen/ | Erster [bis Achter und Letzter] Theil. | Aus Jtaliänischen/ Frantzösischen und Spanischen Scribenten | angewiesen/ | und jetzund ausführlicher auf sechs Personen gerichtet/ | und mit einer neuen Zugabe gemehret/ | Durch | Einen Mitgenossen der Hochlöblichen | FRUCHTBRJNGENDEN GESELLSCHAFT. | Nürnberg/ Gedruckt und verlegt bey Wolffgang Endtern. | Jm Jahre 1644 [–1657]. HAB: Lo 2622:1 bis 8.
(Ndr.) Die endgültige Neufassung der *Frauenzimmer Gesprächspiele* in 8 Queroktavbänden, Nürnberg 1643–1657. Hg. Irmgard Böttcher, Tübingen 1968–1969 (Deutsche Neudrucke, Reihe Barock, Bd. 13–20).

Harsdörffer: Frauenzimmer-Gesprächspiele I (1641)
Harsdörffer, Georg Philipp: Frawen-Zimmer Gespräch-Spiel. So bey Ehrliebenden Gesellschafften zu nützlicher Ergetzlichkeit beliebet werden mögen. Erster Theil. Auß Spanischen/ Frantzösischen vnd Jtaliänischen Scribenten angewiesen Durch Georg Philipp Harsdörffern. Nürnberg/ Jn Verlegung Wolffgang Endters. M. DC. XXXXI. HAB: Lo 2621 (1).

Harsdörffer: Poetischer Trichter
Harsdörffer, Georg Philipp: Poetischer Trichter. Die Teutsche Dicht- und Reimkunst/ ohne Behuf der Lateinischen Sprache/ in VI. Stunden einzugiessen. 3 Tle. in 1 Bd. (Nürnberg 1648–1653). HAB: 182.4 Poet. Ndr. Hildesheim [u. a.] 1971.

Harsdörffer: Porticus Virtutis (1646), s. Harsdörffer: Specimen (1646)

Harsdörffer: Porticus Virtutis (1647)
Harsdörffer, Georg Philipp: Porticus Serenissimo atque Celsissimo Principi, ac Domino, Domino Augusto, Brunswicensium atque Luneburgensium Duci potentissimo, Principum eruditissimo, Domino Clementissimo &c. Sacra:/ Cultu Georgi[i] Philippi Harsdörfferi, Patricii Noric. & eiusdem Dicasterii Adsessoris. (Norimbergae: officina Endteriana, 1646 [erschienen 1647]). HAB: Gn 4460 u. 10.6 Pol.

Harsdörffer: Schutzschrift (1644)
Harsdörffer, Georg Philipp: Schutzschrift/ für Die Teutsche Spracharbeit/ und Derselben Beflissene: zu Einer Zugabe/ den Gesprächspielen angefüget. Durch den SPJELENDEN. In: *Harsdörffer: Frauenzimmer-Gesprächspiele* I (^{2}1644), eig. Pag., Ndr. S. 339–396.

Harsdörffer: Specimen (1646)
GEORGI PHILIPPI | HARSDORFFERI | SPECIMEN | PHILOLOGIÆ, | GERMANICÆ | Continens | Disquisitiones XII. | De Linguæ nostræ vernaculæ | Historia, Methodo, & Dignitate. | Præmissa est | PORTICVS VIRTUTIS, | Serenißimo atque Celsißimo Principi, | ac Domino, Domino | AUGUSTO, | Brunsvvicensium atq Lü- | næburgensium Duci | potentissimo &c. | SACRA. | Norimbergæ| Impensis Wolfgangi Endteri. | M. DC. XLVI. — [Kupfertitel]: G. P. HARSDÖRFFERI Specimen Philologiæ Germanicæ. M D CXLVI. Sic labor assiduus linguæ fundamina nostræ firmabit junctis solicitè manibus. HAB: QuN 1090 (1). — Mit *Harsdörffer: Porticus Virtutis (1646)*.

Hartweg/ Wegera
Hartweg, Frédéric u. Klaus-Peter Wegera: Frühneuhochdeutsch. Eine Einführung in die deutsche Sprache des Spätmittelalters und der frühen Neuzeit. 2., neu bearb. Aufl. Tübingen 2005.

Haßler/ Neis
Haßler, Gerda und Cordula Neis: Lexikon sprachtheoretischer Grundbegriffe des 17. und 18. Jahrhunderts. 2 Bde. (durchgeh. pag.). Berlin, New York 2009.

Hb. Gelegenheitsschrifttum
Handbuch des personalen Gelegenheitsschrifttums in europäischen Bibliotheken und Archiven. Im Zusammenwirken mit der Forschungsstelle zur Literatur der Frühen Neuzeit der Universität Osnabrück hg. v. Klaus Garber. Hildesheim 1997–.

Hederich
Hederich, Benjamin: Gründliches mythologisches Lexicon … sorgfältigst durchgesehen, ansehnlich vermehret und verbessert von Johann Joachim Schwaben. Leipzig 1770. Ndr. Darmstadt 1996.

Henisch
Henisch, Georg: Teutsche Sprach vnd Weißheit. Thesaurus linguae et sapientiae Germanicae. Augustae Vind.: Francus 1616. HAB: 16 Gram. 2°. Ndr. Hildesheim u. New York 1973 (Documenta Linguistica. Reihe II).

Henke: Calixtus
Henke, Ernst Ludwig Theodor: Georg Calixtus und seine Zeit. 2 Bde. Halle 1853 u. 1856.

Herdegen
Amarantes [Johann Herdegen]: Historische Nachricht von deß löblichen Hirten- und Blumen-Ordens an der Pegnitz Anfang und Fortgang/ biß auf das durch Göttl. Güte erreichte Hunderste Jahr, mit Kupfern geziert, und verfasset von ei-

nem Mitglied dieser Gesellschafft Amarantes (Nürnberg: Christoph Riegel 1744). HAB: Hm 57.

Herz: Aufrichtigkeit, Vertrauen, Frieden
Herz, Andreas: Aufrichtigkeit, Vertrauen, Frieden. Eine historische Spurensuche im Umkreis der *Fruchtbringenden Gesellschaft*. In: Euphorion 105 (2011), 317–359.

Herz: Edle Ritter dieser Zunft
Herz, Andreas: „Edle Ritter dieser Zunft". Beobachtungen zur sozietären Performanz der *Fruchtbringenden Gesellschaft*. In: Die Kunst des Adels in der Frühen Neuzeit. Hg. Claudius Sittig u. Christian Wieland. *In Vorbereitung*.

Herz: Gewohnheit
Herz, Andreas: Die Macht der Gewohnheit. Die Regulierung der deutschen Sprache in der Fruchtbringenden Gesellschaft und ihre Hintergründe. In: Unsere Sprache. Beiträge zur Geschichte und Gegenwart der deutschen Sprache. Schriftenreihe der Neuen Fruchtbringenden Gesellschaft zu Köthen/ Anhalt 3 (2010), 7–30.

Herz: Harsdörffers Teutscher Secretarius
Herz, Andreas: „Die Ursach nicht der Wahn". Georg Philipp Harsdörffers *Teutscher Secretarius* und die damalige deutsche Sprachdebatte. In: WBN 36 (2009), 55–63.

Herz: Harsdörffer und Sandrart
Herz, Andreas: „Es dichten ja zugleich/ der Mahler und Poet". Georg Philipp Harsdörffer und Joachim von Sandrart. In: Aus aller Herren Länder. Die Künstler der *Teutschen Academie* von Joachim von Sandrart. Hg. Susanne Meurer, Anna Schreurs-Morét u. Lucia Simonato. Turnhout 2016, 414–431.

Herz: Die Namen der Pflanzen
Herz, Andreas: Die Namen der Pflanzen. In: Zeitschrift f. Ideengeschichte, H. VII.1 (2013), 48–55.

Herz: Palmenbaum und Mühle
Herz, Andreas: Der edle Palmenbaum und die kritische Mühle. Die Fruchtbringende Gesellschaft als Netzwerk höfisch-adeliger Wissenskultur der frühen Neuzeit. In: Denkströme. Journal der Sächsischen Akademie der Wissenschaften, Heft 2 (2009), 152–191.
Online abrufbar unter http://www.denkstroeme.de

Herz: Ratio und consuetudo
Herz, Andreas: *Ratio* und *consuetudo*. Sprachnorm und Sprachvarianz in der grammatikologischen Kontroverse der Fruchtbringenden Gesellschaft. In: Wis-

sen in Bewegung. Institution — Iteration — Transfer. Hg. Eva Cancik-Kirschbaum u. Anita Traninger. Wiesbaden 2015 (Episteme in Bewegung, Bd. 1), 255–287.

Herz: Rechtschreibdebatte
Herz, Andreas: Die Rechtschreibdebatte in der *Fruchtbringenden Gesellschaft*. Probleme und Parameter der Normierung. In: „Erfreuliche Nützlichkeit — Keim göttlicher Ehre". Beiträge zum Harsdörffer-Birken-Colloquium des Pegnesischen Blumenordens im Oktober 2014. Hg. Werner Kügel. Passau 2015, 67–137.

Herz/ Tölkki: Stålhandske
Herz, Andreas u. Esa Tölkki: Torsten Stålhandske (1594–1644) — ein berühmter *homme de guerre* und unbekannter Fruchtbringer. In: WBN 42 (2015), 63–78.

Herz: Tagebücher F. Christians II.
Herz, Andreas: „... ma fatale destinèe ...". Krisen- und Leidenserfahrungen Fürst Christians II. von Anhalt-Bernburg (1599–1656) in seinen Tagebüchern und anderen Zeit- und Lebensdokumenten. In: Passion, Affekt und Leidenschaft in der Frühen Neuzeit. Hg. Johann Anselm Steiger in Verb. mit Ralf Georg Bogner, Ulrich Heinen, Renate Steiger u.a. Wiesbaden 2005 (Wolfenbütteler Arbeiten zur Barockforschung, 43), 981–1035.

Herz: Vier Funde
Herz, Andreas: Vier Funde zur Fruchtbringenden Gesellschaft. Philipp von Zesen, Johann Wilhelm von Stubenberg/ Graf Friedrich Casimir von Ortenburg, Fürst Ludwig von Anhalt-Köthen, Johann Ludwig Prasch. In: WBN 38 (2011), 51–65.

Herz: Wältz recht
Herz, Andreas: „Wältz recht". Fruchtbringerisches Zeremoniell und sein ‚Hintergrund' in einem Stich Peter Isselburgs. In: Ars et Amicitia. Beiträge zum Thema Freundschaft in Geschichte, Kunst und Literatur. FS f. Martin Bircher zum 60. Geb. Hg. Ferdinand van Ingen u. Christian Juranek. Amsterdam, Atlanta/ GA 1998 (Chloe, 28), 353–408.

Herz: Zesen
Herz, Andreas: Philipp von Zesen und die Fruchtbringende Gesellschaft. In: Philipp von Zesen. Wissen — Sprache — Literatur. Hg. Maximilian Bergengruen u. Dieter Martin. Tübingen 2008 (Frühe Neuzeit, 130), 181–208.

Herz/ Ball (2004)
Herz, Andreas u. Gabriele Ball: Eine deutsche Akademie im Spannungsfeld von Sprache, Kultur und Politik: Die Fruchtbringende Gesellschaft. In: neu entdeckt. Thüringen — Land der Residenzen. 2. Thüringer Landesausstellung Schloß Son-

dershausen. 15. Mai – 3. Oktober 2004. 2 Katalogbde. und ein Essay-Bd. Hg. Konrad Scheurmann u. Jördis Frank. Mainz 2004, Katalogbd. 1, 132–146.

Herz/ Ball (2008)
Herz, Andreas u. Gabriele Ball: Friedenssehnsucht und Spracharbeit. Die Fruchtbringende Gesellschaft 1637–1638. In: MVAL 17 (2008), 47–84.

Herzog August v. Braunschweig-Lüneburg, s. Sammler Fürst Gelehrter.

Herzog August: Evangelische Kirchen-Harmonie

(1644/45)
Der Evangelischen | Kirchen-Harmonien/ | Erster Teihl. | Wolffenbüttel. 1.6.44. – Ander Teihl/ | Der | Evangelischen | Kirchen-Harmonien. | Wolfenbüttel/ 1.6.45. HAB: 508.16 Th.

(1646. 8°)
Evangelische | [Zierleiste] | KIrchen-Harmonie/ | Das ist: | Der hoch-heiligen göttlichen Skrift | unterschiedene Texte/ und Worte: | Welche | Von unsern gottseligen Vorfahren/ | aus deñ Geschicht-Büchern der Evan-| gelisten/ und deñ Briefen der Aposteln: | So wol auch deñ Skriften des alten/ und ersten Bun|des/ oder Testamentes/ vor vielen hundert Jahren/ heraus- | gezogen/ und an gewissen Tagen des HErren/ und der | Festen/ in öffentlichen Zusammen-Künften/ und Versamme- | lungen/ deñ Gemeinen der Christen/ jährlich vorzulesen/ | und zu erklären/ aus besonderer Andacht wolmeinend- | lich verordnet: Und | von Einem Liebhaber seines liebsten HErren | Jesu/ und dessen heiligen Wortes/ neulich übersehen/ | zusammen getragen/ und mit skriftmässiger Erklärung/ | ausgeführet seynd. | In der Fürstlichen Hof-Stadt zu Wolfen|Büttel/ drükketen/ und verlegeten diesel- | bige: Hans/ und Heinrich/ die Sterne. | [Zierstück] | ANNO | En LIbro harMónIas VVLgat tIbI BrVnsVIgIVs DVX. [1646].
Evangelischer | [Zierleiste] | KIrchen-Harmonien/ | Ander Teihl. | In welchem/ | Das Leben Jesu Christi/ | von dem Anfange seiner Empfäng | nüs an/ bis zu seiner Himmelfahrt/ ordent | lich beskrieben ist; so viele mañ dessen/ in deñ Texten der | jährlichen Christ-FeierTagen/ und etlicher des HErren Tagen/ befindet: Dañ auch/ die Sendung des heiligen Geis- | tes: Das Fest der hochheiligen Drei-Einigkeit: und das En- | gel-Fest. Darauf folgen dañ die Worte und Texte/ welche aus | deñ heiligen Skriften des lezten/ und ersten Bundes/ heraus gesu- | chet seynd/ und in deñ versammelten Gemeinen der Christen/ | auf deñ Fest- und Gedächtnüs-Tagen/ von dem Leben/ | Wandel und Absterben/ der heiligen Jünger/ und Aposteln | des HErren Jesu/ und etlicher Martyrer/ öffentlich | vorgelesen/ und ausgeleget | werden. | [Zierleiste] | ANNO. | VItæ ConCorDans qVæ AVgVsto à prInCIpe IVnCta. | DIVIna ChrIstI nasCItVr hIstoria. | D. J. V. A. [1646]. HAB: 548.8 Theol.

(1646. 4°)
Evangelische | [Zierleiste] | Kirchen Harmonie/ | Das ist: | Der hoch-heiligen Skrift unterschiedene Texte und | Worte: | Welche von unseren gottseligen | Vorfahren/ aus deñ Geschicht-Büchern der Evangelisten/ | und aus deñ Briefen der Apostelen/ so wol auch aus deñ Skriften | des alten/ und ersten Bundes/ oder Testamentes/ vor vielen hundert Jahren her- | ausgezogen/ und an gewissen Tagen des Herren/ und der Festen/ in öffentlichen Zu- | sammen-Künften/ und Versamlungen/ deñ Gemeinen der Christen/ jährlich vor- | zulesen/ und zu erklären/ aus besonderer Andacht wolmeinendt- | lich verordnet: Und | von | Einem Liebhaber seines liebesten Herren Jesu/ und dessen heiligen | Wortes/ neulich übersehen/ zusammen getragen/ und mit skriftmässiger Erklärung ausge- | führt seynd. | [Vignette] | In der Fürstlichen Hof-Stadt zu Wolfen-Büttel/ drükke- | ten/ und verlegten dieselbige: | Hans/ und Heinrich/ die Sterne. | [Linie] | ANNO | En LIbro harMónIas VVLgat tIbI BrVnsVIgIVs DVX. [1646].
Evangelischer | [Zierleiste] | Kirchen Harmonien | Ander Teihl. | In welchem zu finden | Die Worte/ und Texte/ welche | aus deñ Skriften | des lezten/ und ersten Bundes/ in deñ | versamleten Gemeinen der Christen/ auf deñ Gedächtnis-Tagen/ | von dem Leben/ Wandel/ und Absterben/ der heiligen Jünger/ und | Apostel des HErren Jesu/ und etlicher Martyrer/ So wol auch auf deñ Fest-Tagen/ von der reinen Jungfrauen Marien/ von | dem Taufer Johanne/ von deñ Englen/ von der Erhöhung des | Kreuzzes Jesu/ und dañ bey Einsegnung einer neu-erbaueten | Kirchen/ öffentlich vorgelesen/ und ausge- | leget werden | [Vignette] | ANNO, [Linie] | Es habens so gestaLt naCh ChrIstLICheñ geVVerben/ | zV DrVCken hIer VerLegt In VVoLVerbIt/ DIe Sternen. | M. G. D. & A. HAB: 51.4 Theol.

(1646. 12°)
Hand-Büchlein: | aus | Der Evangelischen Kir- | chenHarmonie: Von des HEr- | ren Jesu Ewigen Geburt: Menschwerdung: | Empfängnüs zu Nazareth: Geburt zu Beth- | lehem: Besneidung: Darstellung in dem | Tempel zu JeruSalem: Beschenkung von | deñ Morgen-Ländischē: Flucht in Aegypten: | Zwelften Jahre: Taufe in dem Jordan: Ver- | suchung in der Wüsten: | Einzuge in Jeru- | Salem: Leiden/ Sterben/ und Begräbnüs: | Wieder-Erstehen: Hinauf-Fahrt: und | Sendung des H. Geistes. | [Vignette] | WulfenBüttel/ Im Jahre | 1646. | In Verlegung der Gebrüder/ | Hans und Heinrichen/ der Sternen. HAB: 1218.3 Theol.

(1647)
Evangelische Kirchen- | Harmonie/ | Das ist: | Der Hoch-hei- | ligen Skrift unterschiede- | ne Worte/ und Texte: | Welche von unseren gottseligen | Vorfahren/ aus deñ Geschicht-Büchern | der Evangelisten/ und aus deñ Briefen der | Apostlen/ so wol auch aus deñ Skriften des alten/ | und ersten Bundes/ oder Testamentes/ vor | vielen hundert Jahren heraus gezogen/ und an ge- | wissen Tagen des HErren/ und der Festen/ in | öffentlichen Zusammen-Kunften und Versamlungen/ | deñ Gemeinen der Christen/ jährlich vorzule- | sen/ und zu erklären/ aus besonderer Andacht | wolmeinentlich verordnet: Und | Von ei-

nem Liebhaber seines liebes- | ten HErren JEsu/ und dessen heiligen Wortes/ zusam- | men getragen/ mit skriftmässiger Erklärung ausgeführet/ | und mit besonderm Fleisse/ auch in diesem klei- | nen Format/ nochmahl überse- | hen seynd. | In der Fürstl. Hof-Stadt zu Wolfen-Büttel/ | drükketen/ vnd verlegten die selbige: | Hans/ und Heinrich/ die Sternen. | [Linie] | Den 10. April. | Anno M. DC. XLVII. HAB: Th 2966.

HbS
Handbuch der historischen Stätten Deutschlands, Bd. I–. Stuttgart 1958–.

Hille: Teutscher Palmbaum
Hille, Carl Gustav v.: Der teutsche Palmbaum: Das ist/ Lobschrift Von der Hochlöblichen/ Fruchtbringenden Gesellschaft Anfang/ Satzungen/ Vorhaben/ Namen/ Sprüchen/ Gemählen/ Schriften und unverwelklichem Tugendruhm. Allen Liebhabern der Teutschen Sprache zu dienlicher Nachrichtung verfasset/ durch den Unverdrossenen Diener derselben. Nürnberg 1647. Ndr. München 1970 (Die Fruchtbringende Gesellschaft. Quellen u. Dokumente in vier Bänden. Hg. Martin Bircher, Bd. 2).

Hirsch
Hirsch, August: Biographisches Lexikon der hervorragenden Ärzte aller Zeiten und Völker. 2. Aufl. durchges. u. erg. v. Wilhelm Haberling, Franz Hübotter u. Hermann Vierordt. 5 Bde. u. Erg.bd. Berlin u. Wien 1929–1935.

Hoppe
Hoppe, Günther: Traditions- und Spannungsfelder um die Fruchtbringende Gesellschaft im Spiegel ihres Alltags (1617–1629). In: *Europäische Sozietätsbewegung*, 1230–1260.

Hübner: Andere Woche (1622)
[Guillaume de Saluste sieur Du Bartas: *La Sepmaine ou Création du Monde* (erstmals Paris 1578; zahlreiche weitere Ausgaben), hg. u. übers. v. Tobias Hübner u. d. T.:] LA SECONDE | SEPMAINE | DE GUILLAUME DE SA-| luste Seigneur du | BARTAS. | Die Andere Woche | Wilhelms von Saluste Herrn zu | Bartas/ | Aus dem Frantzösischen gegen übergesatzten in Teut-| sche Reime/ mit ebenmässigen und gleichlautenden endungen/ auch | nicht mehr/ oder weniger Sylben/ gebracht/ und so viel jmmer müglich/ und | nach art Teutscher Sprach zuläßlich/ fast von wort zu worten | rein Teutsch gegeben: M DC | [Holzschnitt-Vignette] | XXII. | Gedruckt zu Cöthen/ im Fürsten-| thumb Anhalt. HAB: 10 Poet.

Hübner: Erste Woche (1631)
[Guillaume de Saluste sieur Du Bartas: *La Sepmaine ou Création du Monde* (erstmals Paris 1578; zahlreiche weitere Ausgaben), hg. u. übers. v. Tobias Hübner u. d. T.:] Wilhelms von Sa- | luste/ Herren zu | B A R T A S | Des vornemsten sinn:

und geistreichst: auch | unsträfflichsten Frantzösischen Poeten/ vor/ | zu und nach seiner zeit | Erste Woche/ | Von Erschaffung der Welt und aller/ | Geschöpffe. | Jn sieben Tage ausgetheilet/ | Vnd | Aus den Frantzösischen/ gegen über gesatzten Ver- | sen/ in teutsche gemessene Reime mit ebenmässigen/ und gleich ausgehen- | den endungen/ auch nicht minder oder mehr Sylben/ gebracht/ und so | viel immer müglich/ auch nach art und eigenschafft teutscher Sprache/ | und der materi beschaffenheit/ zuläßlich gewesen/ fast von wort zu | wort/ rein teutsch gegeben und übersetzet/ | Sampt einer Vorrede an die Hochlöbliche | Fruchtbringende Gesellschafft. | Allen denen/ die/ jhre/ von andern/ jhres beruffs/ | geschäfften/ noch übrige zeit/ lieber/ in der betrachtung/ der hohen | wunderthaten unsers grossen Gottes/ und seiner herrlichen Geschöpffe/ | als sonsten/ mit ichtwas anderes/ zubringen wollen/ sehr anmu- | tig und erbawlich/ der Frantzösischen/ und reinen teutschen | Sprache begierigen aber auch sehr nutzbarlich | zu lesen. | [Linie] | Gedruckt zu Cöthen bey Johann Röhnern/ | Jn vorlegung Matthiæ Götzen/ Buchhändler in Leipzig, | im Jahr Christi M. DC. XXXI. HAB: 295.25 Quod. (1).

Hübner, Fürst Ludwig, Werder: Die Erste und Andere Woche (1640)
[Guillaume de Saluste sieur Du Bartas: *Les Semaines*; ins Deutsche übersetzt u. verbessert von Tobias Hübner; bearb. u. hrsg. v. Fürst Ludwig u. Diederich v. dem Werder:] Die Erste und An- | dere Woche | Wilhelms von Saluste | Herren zu Bartas. | Darinnen enthalten/ sampt der Welt erschaffung/ die vor= | nehmesten Geschichte in der heiligen Schrifft | zu finden. | Von der Welt anfang an/ bis an die zerstörung Jerusa= | salems [!]/ und die Babylonische Gefengnüs/ zu zeiten | des Jüdischen Königs Zedekiæ geschehen. | Vor Jahren | Aus dem Frantzösischen in wolgemessene deutsche Reime/ mit | ebenmessigen endungen/ auch nicht mehr oder weniger Silben/ | durch ein Mittglied der fruchtbringenden Gesellschafft | gebracht und ausgangen. | An ietzo aber | Eines theils durch den Ubersetzer selbsten bey seinem | leben/ als nach seinem tödlichen abgange durch andere | beyder Sprachen kündige/ übersehen/ verbessert | und mit den Jnhalten iedes Stückes/ auch | sonderbahren anmerckungen und erklä= | rungen auf dem Rande gezieret/ ver= | mehret und von Neuen an den | Tag gegeben. | [Zierleiste] | Gedruckt zu Cöthen Jm Fürstenthume Anhalt/ | [Linie] | Jm Jahre 1640. HAB: P 491.4° Helmst. (1) (weitere Expl.).

Hueck: Gelegenheitsgedichte
Hueck, Monika (Bearb.): Gelegenheitsgedichte auf Herzog August von Braunschweig-Lüneburg und seine Familie (1579–1666). Ein bibliographisches Verzeichnis der Drucke und Handschriften in der Herzog August Bibliothek Wolfenbüttel. Wolfenbüttel 1982 (Repertorien zur Erforschung der frühen Neuzeit, 4).

Huguet
Huguet, Edmond: Dictionnaire de la langue françoise du seizième siècle. 7 Bde. Paris 1925–1967.

Hundt
Hundt, Markus: „Spracharbeit" im 17. Jahrhundert. Studien zu Georg Philipp Harsdörffer, Justus Georg Schottelius und Christian Gueintz. Berlin, New York 2000 (Studia Linguistica Germanica, 57).

HWDA
Handwörterbuch des deutschen Aberglaubens. Hg. unter besonderer Mitwirkung v. Eduard Hoffmann-Krayer u. Mitarb. zahlreicher Fachgenossen v. Hanns Bächtold-Stäubli. 10 Bde. Berlin u. Leipzig 1927–1942. 3. unveränd. Aufl. mit e. neuen Vorwort v. Christoph Daxelmüller. Berlin, New York 2000.

HWPh
Historisches Wörterbuch der Philosophie. In Verbindung mit Günther Bien ... hg. v. Joachim Ritter u. Karlfried Gründer. 12 Bde. u. 1 Reg.bd. Basel [u.a.] 1971–2007.

HWRh
Historisches Wörterbuch der Rhetorik. Hg. Gert Ueding. 10 Bde. Darmstadt 1992–2012.

Ingen
Ingen, Ferdinand van: Philipp von Zesen in seiner Zeit und seiner Umwelt. Berlin, Boston 2013.

Ingen: Zesen
Ingen, Ferdinand van: Philipp von Zesen. Stuttgart 1970.

Ising
Ising, Erika: Wolfgang Ratkes Schriften zur deutschen Grammatik (1612–1630). Teil I: Abhandlung, Teil II: Textausgabe. Berlin 1959.

Jaumann: Repertorium
Jaumann, Herbert: Handbuch Gelehrtenkultur der Frühen Neuzeit. Bd. 1: Bio-bibliographisches Repertorium. Berlin, New York 2004.

JBA
Lapide, Pinchas (Hg.): Jüdisches biographisches Archiv (Jewish biographical archive). München: Saur, Mikrofiche-Edition 1998.

Jellinek: Nhd. Grammatik
Jellinek, Max Hermann: Geschichte der neuhochdeutschen Grammatik von den Anfängen bis auf Adelung. Erster Halbbd. Heidelberg 1913. Zweiter Halbbd. Heidelberg 1914.

Jöcher
Jöcher, Christian Gottlieb: Allgemeines Gelehrten-Lexicon, Darinne die Gelehrten aller Stände ... vom Anfange der Welt bis auf ietzige Zeit ... Nach ihrer Geburt, Leben ... und Schrifften ... in alphabetischer Ordnung beschrieben. 4 Tle. Leipzig 1750–1751. Ndr. Hildesheim 1960–1961.

Jones
Jones, William Jervis: A Lexicon of French Borrowings in the German Vocabulary (1575–1648). Berlin u. New York 1976 (Studia Linguistica Germanica, 12).

Jones: Lexicography
Jones, William Jervis: German Lexicography in the European Context. A descriptive bibliography of printed dictionaries and word lists containing German language (1600–1700). Berlin, New York 2000.

Jones: Sprachverderber
Sprachhelden und Sprachverderber. Dokumente zur Erforschung des Fremdwortpurismus im Deutschen (1478–1750). Ausgewählt u. kommentiert v. William Jervis Jones. Berlin u. New York 1995 (Studia Linguistica Germanica, 38).

Jürgensen: Repertorium
Jürgensen, Renate: Melos conspirant singuli in unum. Repertorium bio-bibliographicum zur Geschichte des Pegnesischen Blumenordens in Nürnberg (1644–1744). Wiesbaden 2006 (Beiträge zum Buch- und Bibliothekswesen, 50).

Jürgensen: Utile
Jürgensen, Renate: Utile cum dulci. Mit Nutzen erfreulich. Die Blütezeit des Pegnesischen Blumenordens in Nürnberg 1644 bis 1744. Wiesbaden 1994.

Kalcheim: David (1638)
[Virgilio Malvezzi Marchese di Castel Guelfo: *Davide perseguitato*, dt. Übersetzung von Wilhelm v. Kalcheim gen. Lohausen u. d. T.:] [Holzschnittrahmen] Der | Verfolgte | David/ | Auß | Jtalianischem/ Herrn | Marggraffen Virgilio | Malvezzi, | Teutsch vbergesetzt | Durch | Wilhelm von Kalcheim/ ge- | nant Lohausen/ Obristen- Feld- | Wachtmeister/ vnd zur Zeit Ober- | gebietigern, in | Rostock. | Gedruckt daselbst/ Durch Michael | Meder/ Jn verlegung Johann | Hallervorts. | [Linie] | 1638. HAB: 1164.93 Theol.; H: C 77.8° Helmst.

Kalcheim, Fürst Ludwig, Diederich v. dem Werder u. a.: David (1643)
[Virgilio Malvezzi Marchese di Castel Guelfo: *Davide perseguitato*, dt. Übersetzung von Wilhelm v. Kalcheim gen. Lohausen, Fürst Ludwig, Diederich v. dem Werder u.a.:] Der verfolgte David/ | Des | Jtalianischen Herren Marggraffen/ | VIRGILIO MALVEZZI. | Deütsch übergesetzet | Durch | Weiland | Wilhelm von Kalckheim genant Lohausen/ | Obristen Feld-Wachtmeistern/ | und | Obristen Kriegsbefehlichten | zu Rostock. | Aufs neüe übersehen und verbessert/ | Mit

angehefter erklerung etzlicher | gebraucheten neüen | Wörter/ | Auch mit vorwissen und einwilligung der Frucht- | bringenden Geselschaft an den Tag | gegeben. | [Holzschn.-Vignette] | Gedruckt zu Cöthen im Fürstentume Anhalt/ | [Linie] | Jm Jahre 1643. HAB: 23.3 Eth. (2).

Kalender Herlitz 1646
[Herlitz, David:] Alter vnd Newer Schreib-Calender auff das Jahr Jesu Christi M. DC. XXXXVI. ... Durch D. Dav. Herlicium. Nürnberg: Wolff Endter. HAB: Xb 6222.

Kalender Zerbst 1654
Geistlicher Calender. Alle Jahr vnd Tage zu gebrauchen/ durch dessen tägliche beschawung/ ein jeder Mensch lernen kan ... Angefangen Anno 1654. Zerbst/ Durch Andream Betzeln Gedruckt. HAB: Ti 254.

Kampmann
Kampmann, Christoph: Europa und das Reich im Dreißigjährigen Krieg. Geschichte eines europäischen Konflikts. Stuttgart 2008.

Kat. Dessau BB
[Gröpler, Wilhelm]: Katalog der Herzoglich Anhaltischen Behörden-Bibliothek zu Dessau. Katalogband. 2 Zugangsverzeichnisse u. Register v. Wilhelm Kulpe. Dessau 1896–1910.

KE
Der Fruchtbringenden Gesellschaft ältester Ertzschrein. Briefe, Devisen und anderweitige Schriftstücke. Urkundlicher Beitrag zur Geschichte der deutschen Sprachgesellschaften im XVII. Jahrhunderte. Hg. Gottlieb Krause. Leipzig 1855. Ndr. Hildesheim u. New York 1973.

Keller: Akademien der Renaissance
Keller, Ludwig: Die Akademien der Renaissance und ihre Nachfolger. Neue Beiträge zu ihrer Charakteristik. In: Monatshefte der Comenius-Gesellschaft für Kultur u. Geistesleben, N. F. Bd. 3, H. 3 (Mai 1911), 97–115.

Kiel: Briefe des J. Rompler v. Löwenhalt
Kiel, Anna Hendrika: Unveröffentlichte Briefe des Jesaias Rompler zu Löwenhalt an Johann Heinrich Boecler (1647–1648). In: Zeitschrift für die Geschichte des Oberrheins, N. F. 56 (1943), 232–255.

KL
Ludwig Fürst zu Anhalt-Cöthen, und sein Land vor und während des dreißigjährigen Krieges. Hg. Gottlieb Krause. 3 Bde. Cöthen u. Neusalz 1877–1879.

Kl. Pauly
Der Kleine Pauly. Lexikon der Antike. Auf der Grundlage von Pauly's Realencyclopädie der classischen Altertumswissenschaft unter Mitwirkung zahlreicher Fachgelehrter hg. Konrat Ziegler u. Walther Sontheimer. 5 Bde. München 1979. — Vgl. *N. Pauly* und *RE*.

Kluge/ Mitzka
Kluge, Friedrich: Etymologisches Wörterbuch der deutschen Sprache. 20. Aufl. Bearb. Walther Mitzka. Berlin 1967.

Kneschke
Kneschke, Ernst Heinrich (Hg.): Neues allgemeines Deutsches Adels-Lexicon. 9 Bde. Ndr. der Ausgabe Leipzig 1859–1870, Hildesheim u. New York 1973.

Knesebeck: Dreiständige Sinnbilder
[Knesebeck, Franz Julius v. dem:] [Kupfertitel:] | Dreiständige | Sinnbilder. | Zu Fruchtbringen-| dem Nutze, und belieben-| der ergetzlichkeit, | ausgefertiget | durch den | Geheimen. | Braunschweig | bei | Conrad Buno | Kunst und Kupfer | stechern | im Jahr | 1643. HAB: 90.19 Eth.

Köbler
Köbler, Gerhard: Historisches Lexikon der deutschen Länder. Die deutschen Territorien vom Mittelalter bis zur Gegenwart. 5., vollst. überarb. Aufl. München 1995.

Köbler (2007)
Köbler, Gerhard: Historisches Lexikon der deutschen Länder. Die deutschen Territorien vom Mittelalter bis zur Gegenwart. 7., vollst. überarb. Aufl. München 2007.

Köthen I. 1–5 bzw. Köthen II. 1
s. unter *DA*

Kramer dt.-it.
Das herrlich Grosse Teutsch-Jtaliänische DICTIONARIUM, Oder Wort- und Red-Arten-Schatz Der unvergleichlichen Hoch-teutschen Grund- und Haupt-Sprache … Erster [– Anderer] Theil … von Matthia Kramer/ Sprachmeistern. Nürnberg 1700–1702. (= IL GRAN DITTIONARIO REALE TEDESCO-ITALIANO cioè TESORO Della Lingua Originale ed Imperiale TEUTONICA-GERMANICA … PARTE PRIMA [– SECONDA] … Da MATTIA CRAMERO). HAB: Kb 48. Desgl. I–II (1724).

Krause: Werder
Krause, Gottlieb: Diederich von dem Werder. In: Mittheilungen des Vereins für Anhaltische Geschichte und Altertumskunde 4 (1886), 30–54.

Krieg und Frieden I–III
1648. Krieg und Frieden in Europa. 26. Europaratsausstellung. Münster/ Osnabrück 24.10.1998 – 17.1.1999. Ausstellungskatalog und 2 Textbde. Hg. Klaus Bußmann u. Heinz Schilling. O. O. [1998].

Kromayer: Deutsche Grammatica (1618)
Kromayer, Johannes: Deutsche Grammatica. Zum newen Methodo der Jugend zum besten zugerichtet. Weimar 1618. Ndr. Hildesheim u. a. 1986 (Documenta Linguistica, Reihe IV: Deutsche Grammatiken des 16. bis 18. Jahrhunderts).

Krüger
Supellex epistolica Uffenbachii et Wolfiorum. Katalog der Uffenbach-Wolfschen Briefsammlung. Hg. Nilüfer Krüger. 2 Tl.bde. Hamburg 1978 (Katalog der Handschriften der Staats- und Universitätsbibliothek Hamburg, 8).

Krünitz
Krünitz, Johann Georg: Oekonomische Enzyklopädie, oder allgemeines System ..., 242 Bde. 1773–1858.
Online unter http://www.kruenitz1.uni-trier.de

KU
Urkunden, Aktenstücke und Briefe zur Geschichte der Anhaltischen Lande und ihrer Fürsten unter dem Drucke des dreißigjährigen Krieges. Hg. Gottlieb Krause. 7 Tle. in 5 Bdn. Leipzig 1861–1866.

Kühlmann: Korrespondenz Moscheroschs
Kühlmann, Wilhelm: Johann Michael Moscherosch in den Jahren 1648–1651: Die Briefe an Johann Valentin Andreae (Mit einer Aufstellung der bisher bekannten Korrespondenz Moscheroschs). In: Daphnis. Zeitschrift für Mittlere Deutsche Literatur XIV, H. 2 (1985), 244–276.

Kühlmann/ Schäfer: Oberrhein
Kühlmann, Wilhelm u. Walter E. Schäfer: Frühbarocke Stadtkultur am Oberrhein. Studien zum literarischen Werdegang J. M. Moscheroschs (1601–1669). Berlin 1983 (Philologische Studien und Quellen, 109).

Laufhütte (Hg.): PBO
Der Pegnesische Blumenorden unter der Präsidentschaft Sigmund von Birkens. Gesammelte Studien der Forschungsstelle Frühe Neuzeit an der Universität Passau (2007–2013). Hrsg. von Hartmut Laufhütte. Passau 2013.

Lausberg
Lausberg, Heinrich: Handbuch der literarischen Rhetorik. Eine Grundlegung der Literaturwissenschaft. Zweite, durch einen Nachtrag vermehrte Auflage. München 1973.

Lentz
Lentz, Samuel: Becmanvs envcleatvs, svppletvs et continvatus. Oder Historisch-Genealogische Fürstellung des Hochfürstlichen Hauses Anhalt. Köthen u. Dessau 1757. — S. auch *Beckmann*.

Lexer: Handwb.
Lexer, Matthias: Mittelhochdeutsches Handwörterbuch. 3 Bde. Leipzig 1872–1878. Ndr. mit e. Einleitung v. K. Gärtner. Stuttgart 1992.

Lexer: Taschenwb.
Lexer, Matthias: Mittelhochdeutsches Taschenwörterbuch. Mit den Nachträgen von Ulrich Pretzel. 38., unveränd. Aufl. Stuttgart 1992.

Lexikon Geographie
Vollständiges Lexicon Der Alten Mittlern und Neuen Geographie. Leipzig 1730.

Lexicon Grammaticorum
Lexicon Grammaticorum. A Bio-Bibliographical Companion to the History of Linguistics. Second Edition, revised and enlarged. Vol. I–II. Tübingen 2009.

Literatur-Lexikon²
Killy Literaturlexikon. Autoren und Werke des deutschsprachigen Kulturraumes. 2., vollst. überarb. Aufl. hg. v. Wilhelm Kühlmann in Verbindung mit Achim Aurnhammer, Jürgen Egyptien, Karina Kellermann u.a. 13 Bde. Berlin, New York 2008–2012.

Littré
Littré, Émile: Dictionnaire de la langue française. 4 Bde. Paris, London 1874, 1 Suppl.bd. ebd. 1892.

Londorp
Londorp, Michael Caspar: Der Römischen Kayserlichen Majestät Und desz Heiligen Römischen Reichs Geist- und Weltlicher Stände/ Chur- und Fürsten/ Grafen/ Herren und Städte ACTA PUBLICA Und Schrifftliche Handlungen/ Außschreiben/ Sendbrieff/ Bericht/ Vnterricht/ Klagten und Supplicationes ... von Anno 1629. biß Anno 1641. ... Vierdter Theil. Frankfurt am Mayn: Johannes Baptista Schönwetter 1668; Fünffter Theil (1641–1646; ebd., 1668).

LP Roth
Roth, Fritz: Restlose Auswertungen von Leichenpredigten und Personalschriften für genealogische Zwecke. 10 Bde. Boppard a. Rh. 1959–1980.

LP Stolberg
Katalog der fürstlich Stolberg-Stolberg'schen Leichenpredigten-Sammlung. Hg. Friedrich Wecken u. Werner Konstantin v. Arnswald. 4 Bde. in 5. Leipzig 1928–1935 (Bibliothek familiengeschichtlicher Quellen II).
Seit 1977 befindet sich die Stolbergsche Leichenpredigten-Sammlung als Dauerleihgabe in der HAB.

LThK (1993)
Lexikon für Theologie und Kirche. Begr. v. Michael Buchberger. 3., völlig neubearb. Aufl. Hg. Walter Kasper. 11 Bde. nebst Abkürzungsverzeichnis. Freiburg [u. a.] 1993–2001.

Luther: Werke
D. Martin Luthers Werke. Kritische Gesamtausgabe (Weimarer Ausgabe). Abt. 1–4 (Abt. 1: Werke; Abt. 2: Die Deutsche Bibel; Abt. 3: Tischreden; Abt. 4: Briefwechsel). Weimar 1883–. Abt. 1: Bd. 1 (1883) – 66 (1995). Abt. 2: Bd. 1 (1906) – 12 (1961). Abt. 3: Bd. 1 (1912) – 6 (1921). Abt. 4: Bd. 1 (1940) – 18 (1985). (Eingeschlossen: Nachtrags-, Berichtigungs- und Registerbände). Auch als CD-Rom-Ausg.

Manecke
Manecke, Urban Friedrich Christoph: Biographische Skizzen von den Kanzlern der Herzöge von Braunschweig-Lüneburg, die Rechtsgelehrte gewesen sind; insbesondere Biographie des Kanzlers Klammer. Lüneburg 1823.

Manger: Teutschherzige Gesellschaft
Die Fruchtbringer — eine Teutschhertzige Gesellschaft. Hg. Klaus Manger. Heidelberg 2001.

Marzell
Marzell, Heinrich: Wörterbuch der deutschen Pflanzennamen. Unter Mitwirkung von Wilhelm Wissmann. 5 Bde. Leipzig u. Stuttgart usw. 1943–1979.

Mat. Altdorf
Die Matrikel der Universtiät Altdorf. Hg. Elias von Steinmeyer. 2 Bde. Würzburg 1912 (Veröffentlichungen der Gesellschaft für Fränkische Geschichte. Vierte Reihe: Matrikeln Fränkischer Schulen, 1–2). Ndr. Nendeln/ Liechtenstein 1980.

Mat. Helmstedt
Die Matrikel der Universtät Helmstedt 1636–1685. Bd. 2. Hildesheim 1981 (Veröffentlichungen der Historischen Kommission für Niedersachsen und Bremen, 9 Abt. 1).
http://diglib.hab.de/drucke/f4f-211-2b/start.htm

Maurer-Stroh: Dt. Wortgeschichte II (1959)
Deutsche Wortgeschichte. Hg. Friedrich Maurer u. Fritz Stroh. 2. Bd.: Humanistische Strömungen — Luther und die nhd. Schriftsprache — Barock ... 2. neubearb. Ausgabe. Berlin 1959.

Maylender
Maylender, Michele: Storia delle Accademie d'Italia. 5 Bde. Bologna 1926–1930.

McLelland: Ausführliche Arbeit
McLelland, Nicola: J. G. Schottelius's *Ausführliche Arbeit von der Teutschen HaubtSprache* (1663) and its place in early modern European vernacular language study. Chichester 2011.

Merian s. Theatrum europaeum

Merian: Topographia
Zeiller, Martin (u. a.): Matthæus Merians d. Ä. „Topographia Germaniae". Faksimileausgabe. Mit einem Nachwort. Hg. Lucas Heinrich Wüthrich (u. a.). 16 Bde. Kassel 1959–1964. „Topographia Hassiæ" 2. verb. Ausg. Kassel 1966.

Merzbacher: Schottelius
Merzbacher, Dieter: Handschriftliche Zeugnisse zu Justus Georg Schottelius in der Herzog August Bibliothek Wolfenbüttel. In: WBN 39 (2012): Die vielen Gesichter des Justus Georg Schottelius, 157–167.

Merzbacher: Werder
Merzbacher, Dieter: „O seltner Held/ Dem Mars und Febus frönt" — Diederich v. dem Werder, der hochrangige „Reimmeister" der Fruchtbringenden Gesellschaft. In: MVAL 3 (1994), 47–77.

Merzbacher: Werder und Hübner
Merzbacher, Dieter: Lambendo demum ursus conformatur. Die Edition der Werke Diederichs v. dem Werder und Tobias Hübners. In: Editionsdesiderate zur Frühen Neuzeit. Beiträge zur Tagung der Kommission für die Edition v. Texten der Frühen Neuzeit. Hg. Hans-Gert Roloff unter redaktioneller Mitarb. v. Renate Meincke. 1. Tl. Amsterdam, Atlanta/ GA 1997 (Chloe, 24), 491–510.

Meßkataloge Leipzig
Die Messkataloge des 16., 17. und 18. Jahrhunderts. Kataloge der Frankfurter und Leipziger Buchmesse. Michaelismesse 1594 – Michaelismesse 1699. Reproduktion auf 211 Mikrofiches. Besorgt v. Bernhard Fabian. Hildesheim u. New York 1986.

Meßkataloge Leipzig online
http://www.olmsonline.de/kollektionen/messkataloge/

MGG
Die Musik in Geschichte und Gegenwart. Allgemeine Enzyklopädie der Musik. Hg. Friedrich Blume. 17 Bde. (Bd. 15 u. 16: Supplemente; Bd. 17: Register). Kassel u. Basel 1949–1986. — 2., neubearb. Ausg. Hg. Ludwig Finscher. 21 Bde. in 2 Teilen. Sachteil in 9 Bdn., Personenteil in 12 Bdn. Kassel [u. a.] 1994–.
Wenn nicht anders angegeben wird die 1. Ausgabe zitiert.

Milagius: Singender Jesaia (1646)
[Milagius, Martinus]: Der Singende | Jesaia / | Oder | Der Prophete Jesaia/ | Jn reine deutsche Reime | gebracht/ | Vnd | Jn ein hundert und vierzehen Gesänge | eingetheilt/ | Die | Nach den bekandten Frantzösischen | melodeyen der Psalme D. Ambrosii | Lobwassers gesungen werden | können: | Gefertiget | Durch den Mindernden. | Samt | Einem anhange etlicher neuen und verbes-| serten Lieder. | [Zierstück] | Gedruckt zu Bremen/ bey Berthold de | Villiers/ im Jahre 1646. (Anhang Etlicher Geistlichen/ theils gar neuen/ theils alten/ doch verbesserten Lieder Mit jhren melodeyen/ So Täglich und auf gewisse zeiten können gebrauchet werden.)

Mittelelb. Wb.
Mittelelbisches Wörterbuch. [Hg. v. der Martin-Luther-Universität Halle-Wittenberg (Germanistisches Institut) und der Sächsischen Akademie der Wissenschaften zu Leipzig]. Begr. v. Karl Bischoff. Weitergeführt u. hg. v. Gerhard Kettmann. Bd. 1: A–G. Unter der Ltg. des Hgs. bearb. v. Hans-Jürgen Bader u. Ulrich Wenner. Berlin 2008. Bd. 2: H–O. Unter der Leitung des Herausgebers bearb. v. Hans-Jürgen Bader, Jörg Möhring, Ulrich Wenner. Berlin 2002.

Mitzka
Mitzka, Walther: Schlesisches Wörterbuch. 3 Bde. Berlin 1963–1965.

Mnd. Handwb.
Lübben, August: Mittelniederdeutsches Handwörterbuch. Nach dem Tode des Verfassers vollendet von Christoph Walther. Norden u. Leipzig 1888. Ndr. Darmstadt 1990.

Mnd. Wb.
Mittelniederdeutsches Wörterbuch. Hg. Karl Schiller u. August Lübben. 5 Bde. und 1 Nachtragsbd. Bremen 1875–1881.

Mortzfeld
Katalog der Graphischen Porträts in der Herzog August Bibliothek Wolfenbüttel 1500–1850. Reihe A: Die Porträtsammlung der Herzog August Bibliothek Wolfenbüttel. Hg. Herzog August Bibliothek Wolfenbüttel. Bearb. Peter Mortzfeld. Bd. 1–28: Abbildungen. München [u. a.] 1986–1995. Bd. 29–50 Biographische und bibliographische Beschreibungen mit Künstlerregister. München usw. 1996–2008.

Moscherosch: Gesichte I/ II (1650)
Moscherosch, Johann Michael: Wunderliche und wahrhafftige | Gesichte | Philanders von Sittewald/ | Das ist | Straff-Schrifften | Hanß-Michael Moscherosch | von Wilstädt. | Jn welchen | Aller Weltwesen/ Aller Mänschen | Händel/ mit jhren Natürlichen Farben der | Eitelkeit/ Gewalts/ Heucheley/ Thorheit bekleidet/ of- | fentlich auff die Schau geführet/ als in einem | Spiegel dargestellet und gesehen | werden | Erster Theil. | Von Jhme zum letztern mahl auffgelegt/ ver- | mehret/ gebessert/ mit Bildnüssen gezieret/ und | Männiglichen unvergreifflich zulesen | in Truck gegeben. | [Druckersignet] | Straßburg/ | Bey Johan-Philipp. Mülben | und Josias Städeln. | [Linie] | M DC L.
Gesichte | Philanders von Sittewald/ | Das ist | Straff-Schrifften | Hanß-Michael Moscheroschen | von Wilstädt. | Ander Theil. | [Druckersignet] | Straßburg/ | Bey Johan-Philipp. Mülben. | und Josias Städeln. | [Linie] | M. DC. L
HAB: Lo 5511:1-2.

Moser: Frühnhd. Grammatik
Moser, Virgil: Frühneuhochdeutsche Grammatik. 1. Bd.: Lautlehre. 1. Hälfte: Orthographie, Betonung, Stammsilbenvokale. Heidelberg 1929 (Germanische Bibliothek 1. Sammlung germanischer Elementar- und Handbücher. 1. Reihe, Grammatiken, Bd. 17).
Lautlehre. 3. Teil: Konsonanten, 2. Hälfte (Schluß). Heidelberg 1951 (Germanische Bibliothek 1. Sprachwissenschaftliche Elementar- und Handbücher, Bd. 6).

Moser/ Stopp: Grammatik des Frühnhd.
Grammatik des Frühneuhochdeutschen. Beiträge zur Laut- und Formenlehre. Hg. Hugo Moser u. Hugo Stopp. Heidelberg 1970–. (Germanische Bibliothek 1. Sprachwissenschaftliche Elementar- und Handbücher).
1. Bd., 1. Tl.: Vokalismus der Nebensilben I. Bearb. v. Karl Otto Sauerbeck. 1970.
1. Bd., 2. u. 3. Tl.: Vokalismus der Nebensilben II–III. Bearb. v. Hugo Stopp. 1973–1978.
3. Bd.: Flexion der Substantive. Bearb. v. Klaus-Peter Wegera. 1987.
4. Bd.: Flexion der starken und schwachen Verben. Bearb. v. Ulf Dammers, Walter Hoffmann, Hans-Joachim Solms. 1988.
6. Bd.: Flexion der Adjektive. Bearb. v. Hans-Joachim Solms u. Klaus-Peter Wegera. 1991.
7. Bd.: Flexion der Pronomina und Numeralia. Bearb. v. Maria Walch u. Susanne Häckel. 1988.

Moulin: Katalog
Deutsche Grammatiken vom Humanismus bis zur Aufklärung. Ausstellung der Forschungsstelle für deutsche Sprachgeschichte der Universität Bamberg in Zusammenarbeit mit der Staatsbibliothek Bamberg. Ausstellung und Katalog: Claudine Moulin. Bamberg 1988.

Moulin-Fankhänel: Bibliographie
Moulin-Fankhänel, Claudine: Bibliographie der deutschen Grammatiken und Orthographielehren. Bd. 1: Von den Anfängen der Überlieferung bis zum Ende des 16. Jahrhunderts. Bd. 2: Das 17. Jahrhundert. Heidelberg 1994 u. 1997.

Narciss
Narciss, Georg Adolf: Studien zu den Frauenzimmergesprächspielen Georg Philipp Harsdörffers (1607–1658). Ein Beitrag zur deutschen Literaturgeschichte des 17. Jahrhunderts. Leipzig 1928.

NDB
Neue Deutsche Biographie. Hg. Hist. Kommission bei der bayerischen Akademie der Wissenschaften. Bd. 1 ff. Berlin 1953–.

Neumark: Palmbaum
Neumark, Georg: Der Neu-Sprossende Teutsche Palmbaum. Oder Ausführlicher Bericht Von der Hochlöblichen Fruchtbringenden Gesellschaft Anfang/ Absehn/ Satzungen/ Eigenschaft/ und deroselben Fortpflantzung ... Von dem Sprossenden. Nürnberg u. Weimar 1668. HAB: Ln 341; Ln 342. Ndr. München 1970 (Die Fruchtbringende Gesellschaft. Quellen u. Dokumente in vier Bänden. Hg. Martin Bircher, Bd. 3).

Nicot
Nicot, Jean: Thresor de la langve françoise, tant ancienne que Moderne. Paris 1621.
Ndr. Paris 1960.

Niedersächs. Wb.
Niedersächsisches Wörterbuch. Hg. Abteilung f. nieders. Mundartforschung des Seminars für Deutsche Philologie der Universität Göttingen durch Wolfgang Jungandreas u. a. Bd. 1–. Neumünster 1965–.

NNBW
Nieuw Nederlandsch Biografisch Woordenboek onder redactie van Philipp Christiaan Molhuysen (u. a.). 10 Bde. Leiden 1911–1937. Registerbd. Amsterdam 1974.

N. Pauly
Der Neue Pauly. Enzyklopädie der Antike. Hg. Hubert Cancik u. Helmuth Schneider. Bd. 1–12: Altertum. Stuttgart u. Weimar 1996–2003. Bd. 13–15: Rezeptions- u. Wissenschaftsgeschichte. Stuttgart u. Weimar 1999–2003. Bd. 16: Register. Stuttgart u. Weimar 2003. 5 Supplementbde. 2004–2008. — Vgl. *Kl. Pauly* und *RE*.

Nübling
Nübling, Damaris, in Zusammenarbeit mit Antje Dammel, Janet Duke, Renata Szczepaniak: Historische Sprachwissenschaft des Deutschen. Eine Einführung in die Prinzipien des Sprachwandels. 2. überarb. Aufl. Tübingen 2008.

Obersächs. Wb.
Wörterbuch der obersächsischen Mundarten. Begründet von Theodor Frings und Rudolf Große. 4 Bde. Bd. 1 (A–F) u. d. Leitung v. Dagmar Helm, Bd. 2–4 (G–K, L–R, S–Z) u. d. Leitung v. Gunter Bergmann. Berlin 1994–2003 (Sächsische Akademie der Wissenschaften. Sprachwissenschaftliche Kommission).

Ökumenisches Heiligenlexikon
Online unter http://www.heiligenlexikon.de

Opitius latinus
Opitz, Martin: Lateinische Werke. In Zusammenarbeit mit Wilhelm Kühlmann, Hans-Gert Roloff und zahlreichen Gelehrten hg., übers. u. komm. v. Veronika Marschall u. Robert Seidel. 3 Bde. Berlin 2009–2015 (Ausgaben deutscher Literatur des XV. bis XVIII. Jahrhunderts).

Opitz
Opitz, Martin: Gesammelte Werke. Kritische Ausgabe. Hg. George Schulz-Behrend. Bd. 1 ff., Stuttgart 1968–. (Bibliothek des Literarischen Vereins in Stuttgart, 295 [Bd. I], 300/301 [Bd. II. 1/2], 296/297 [Bd. III. 1/2], 312/313 [Bd. IV. 1/2]).

Opitz: Anno (1639)
Opitz, Martin: INCERTI | POETÆ TEVTONICI | RHYTHMVS | DE SANCTO ANNONE | COLON. ARCHIEPISCOPO | *ANTE D. AVT CICITER* [!] | *annos conscriptus.* | MARTINVS OPITIVS | primus ex membrana | veteri edidit. | & *Animadversionibus* | *illustravit.* | [Signet] | DANTISCI. | Ex Officina Andr. Hünefeldii, | M DC XXXIX. | *CVM PRIVILEGIO REGIS.*

Opitz: Buch von der Deutschen Poeterey (1624)
Opitz, Martin: Buch von der Deutschen Poeterey. In welchem alle ihre eigenschafft und zugehör gründtlich erzehlet/ und mit exempeln außgeführt wird. Gedruckt in der Fürstlichen Stadt Brieg/ bey Augustino Gründern. In Verlegung David Müllers Buchhändlers in Breßlaw 1624. (als Studienausg. mit dem *Aristarch* [1617] und den Opitzschen Vorreden zu seinen *Poemata* [1624 u. 1625] sowie der Vorrede zu seiner Übers. der *Trojanerinnen* [1625] hg. Herbert Jaumann. Stuttgart 2002).

Opitz: BW
Opitz, Martin: Briefwechsel und Lebenszeugnisse. Kritische Edition mit Übersetzung. Drei Bände. An der Herzog August Bibliothek zu Wolfenbüttel heraus-

gegeben von Klaus Conermann. Unter Mitarbeit von Harald Bollbuck. Berlin 2009.

Opitz: Florilegium I (1639)
Opitz, Martin: FLORILEGII | VARIORVM | EPIGRAMMATVM | LIBER VNVS. | *MART. OPITIVS* | *ex vetustis ac recentioribus Poëtis* | congessit, | & versibus Germanicis reddidit. | [Emblem] | CVM GRATIA & PRIVILEGIO | *S. R. M.* | GEDANI, | *Typis ac sumptibus Andreæ Hünefeldii.* | Anno M D C XXXIX.

Opitz: Florilegium II (1639)
Opitz, Martin: FLORILEGII | VARIORVM | EPIGRAMMATVM | LIBER ALTER. | *MART. OPITIVS* | *ex vetustis ac recentioribus Poëtis* | congessit, | *& versibus Germanicis reddidit.* | [Emblem] | CVM GRATIA & PRIVILEGIO | *S. R. M.* | GEDANI, | *Typis ac sumptibus Andreæ Hünefeldii.* | Anno M D C XXXIX.

Opitius latinus
Opitz, Martin: Lateinische Werke. In Zusammenarbeit mit Wilhelm Kühlmann, Hans-Gert Roloff und zahlreichen Gelehrten hg., übers. u. komm. v. Veronika Marschall u. Robert Seidel. Bd. 1–. Berlin 2009– (Ausgaben deutscher Literatur des XV. bis XVIII. Jahrhunderts).

Opitz: Poemata (1624)
MARTINI OPICII. Teutsche Poëmata vnd ARISTARCHVS Wieder die verachtung Teutscher Sprach, Item Verteutschung Danielis Heinsij Lobgesangs Iesu Christi, vnd Hymni in Bachum Sampt einem anhang Mehr auserleßener geticht anderer Teutscher Poëten. Der gleichen in dieser Sprach Hiebeuor nicht auß kommen. Straßburg: Eberhard Zetzner 1624.

Opitz: Poemata (1625)
MARTINI OPITII Acht Bücher, Deutscher Poematum durch Jhn selber heraus gegeben/ auch also vermehret vnnd vbersehen/ das die vorigen darmitte nicht zu uergleichen sindt. Breßlaw: David Müller 1625.

Opitz: Poemata (1629) I–II
I: MARTINI OPITII Deütscher Poëmatum Erster Theil; Zum andern mal vermehrt vnd vbersehen herauß gegeben. Breßlau: David Müller 1629.
II: MARTINI OPITII Deütscher Poëmatum Anderer Theil; Zuevor nie beÿsammen, theils auch noch nie herauß gegeben. Breßlau: David Müller 1629.

Opitz: Geistl. Poemata (1638)
MARTINI OPITII Geistliche Poëmata, Von jhm selbst anjetzo zusammen gelesen/ verbessert vnd absonderlich herauß gegeben. [Breslau]: David Müllers Erben 1638. Ndr. hg. Erich Trunz. 2., überarb. Aufl. Tübingen 1975 (Deutsche Neudrucke. Reihe: Barock, 1).

Opitz: Poemata (1641)
MARTINI OPITII Deütsche POEMATA Auffs Newe übersehen vnd vermehret. Danzig: Andreas Hünefeldt (1641).
I: [Ohne Titelblatt: Deutsche Poemata, erster Teil.]
II: MARTINI OPITII Deutscher POEMATUM Ander Theil; Darinnen noch viel des Seel. Autoris Gedichten hinzu gesetzt/ welche in vorher außgegangenen Editionen nicht zu finden. Danzig: Andreas Hünefeldt 1641. — *Beide Teile sind durchgehend paginiert.*

Opitz: Weltl. Poemata (1644) I–II
Martini Opitij Weltliche Poemata Zum Viertēmal vermehret vnd vbersehen herraus geben. Frankfurt a. M.: Thomas Matthias Götze 1644.
I: [Ohne Titelblatt: Weltliche Poemata, erster Teil.] Ndr. unter Mitwirkung v. Christine Eisner hg. Erich Trunz. Tübingen 1967 (Deutsche Neudrucke. Reihe: Barock, 2).
II: MARTINI OPITII Weltliche Poëmata. Der Ander Theil. Zum vierdten mal vermehret vnd vbersehen herauß gegeben. Franckfurt: Thomas Matthias Götze 1644. Ndr. Mit einem Anhang: Florilegium variorum epigrammatum. Unter Mitwirkung v. Irmgard Böttcher u. Marian Szyrocki hg. Erich Trunz. Tübingen 1975 (Deutsche Neudrucke. Reihe: Barock, 3).

Opitz: Poemata (1645–1646) I–III
MART. OPITII OPERA POETICA. Das ist Geistliche vnd Weltliche Poemata Vom Autore selbst zum letzten vbersehen vnd verbessert. Amsterdam: Iohan Ianßon 1646.
I: [Ohne Titelblatt: Weltliche Poemata, erster Teil. Amsterdam 1645.]
II: MARTINI OPITII Weltliche POËMATA. Der Ander Theil. Letzte Truck auffs fleissigst vbersehen vnd verbessert. Amsterdam 1645.
III: MARTINI OPITII Geistliche Poëmata. Von jhm selbst anjetzo zusammen gelesen/ verbessert vnd absonderlich herauß gegeben. Amsterdam 1645.

Opitz: Poemata (1689) I–III
Des berühmten Schlesiers MARTINI OPITII von Boberfeld/ Bolesl. OPERA Geist- und Weltlicher Gedichte/ Nebst beygefügten vielen andern Tractaten so wohl Deutsch als Lateinisch/ Mit Fleiß zusammen gebracht/ und von vielen Druckfehlern befreyet/ Jetzo zum siebenden mahl gedruckt. Breßlau: Jesaias Fellgibel [1689].
I: [Ohne Titelblatt: Weltliche Poemata, erster Teil. Breslau 1689.]
II: MARTINI OPITII Weltliche POEMATA Der Ander Theil. Letzte Truck auffs fleißigste übersehen und verbessert. Breßlau: Jesaias Fellgibel [1689].
III: MARTINI OPITII Geistliche POEMATA. Der Dritte Theil. Von ihm selbst zusammen gelesen/ verbessert und absonderlich herauß gegeben. Breßlau: Jesaias Fellgibel [1689].

Opitz: Psalmen (1637)
Die | Psalmen Davids | Nach den Frantzösi- | schen Weisen gesetzt. | Durch | Martin Opitzen. | Cum gratia & privilegio S. R. M. | [Holzschnitt-Vignette mit Umschrift: SIC FLORET HOMO + SICVT FLOS AGRI.] | Dantzigk/ | Gedruckt und verlegt durch | Andream Hünefeldt/ | Buchhändler/ 1637.
Ndr. Hg. Eckhard Grunewald und Henning P. Jürgens. Hildesheim u. a. 2004.

Opitz: Psalmen (1639)
Die | Psalmen Davids | vnd | Episteln | Der Sontage vnd Fürnemb- | sten Feste deß gantzen | Jahres/ | Beydes auff vnd nach den | Frantzösischen Psalmen-weisen | gesetzt vnd verfast | Durch | Martin Opitzen. | Jetzo alles aufs New vbersehen | verbessert/ vnd Erstmals in die- | sem Format herauß gegeben/ | theiles anfangs | Gedruckt zu Dantzigk | ANNO | [Linie] | M. DC. XXXIX.

Opitz: Silvae
MART. OPITII SILVARVM LIBRI III. EPIGRAMMATVM LIBER VNVS. E Museo BERNHARDI GVILIELMI NÜSSLERI. Francofurti: David Müllerus 1631.

Pacificatores (1697)
PACIFICATORES ORBIS CHRISTIANI, SIVE ICONES PRINCIPUM, DUCUM, ET LEGATORUM, QVI MONASTERII atque OSNABRUGÆ PACEM EUROPÆ RECONCILIARUNT, Quosque singulos ad nativam imaginem expressit A. van Hulle, celsissimi Principis Auriaci dum viveret Pictor. Optimorum artificum dexteritate CXXXI tabulis aeneis incisae, nunc demum post viri illustris mortem in lucem editae, & descriptione recens auctae. ROTERODAMI, Typis PETRI vander SLAART, Bibliopolæ ad insigne Ciceronis. MDCXCVII. — HAB: Xb FM 1

Padley
Padley, George Arthur: Grammatical Theory in Western Europe 1500–1700. Trends in Vernacular Grammar. 2 Vols. Cambridge etc. 1985–1988.

Paul
Paul, Hermann: Mittelhochdeutsche Grammatik. 20. Aufl. v. Hugo Moser u. Ingeborg Schröbler. Tübingen 1969.
Dass., 23. Aufl. Neu bearb. v. Peter Wiehl u. Siegfried Grosse. Tübingen 1989. (*Paul 1989*).

Paul: Dt. Grammatik
Paul, Hermann: Deutsche Grammatik. 5 Tle. Halle a. S. 1916–1920.

Paul Wb.
Paul, Hermann: Deutsches Wörterbuch. Bedeutungsgeschichte und Aufbau un-

seres Wortschatzes. 10., überarbeitete und erweiterte Aufl. v. Helmut Henne, Heidrun Kämper und Georg Objartel. Tübingen 2002.

Pauly, s. Kl. Pauly und N. Pauly

Pfeilsticker
Pfeilsticker, Walther: Neues Württembergisches Dienerbuch. 3 Bde. Stuttgart 1957–1974.

Polenz
Polenz, Peter v.: Deutsche Sprachgeschichte vom Spätmittelalter bis zur Gegenwart. Bd. II: 17. u. 18. Jahrhundert. 2. Aufl. bearb. v. Claudine Moulin unter Mitarb. v. Dominic Harion. Berlin, Boston 2013.

Pufendorf: Kriegs-Geschichte
Pufendorf, Samuel v.: Herrn Samuel von Pufendorf Sechs und Zwantzig Bücher Der Schwedisch- und Deutschen Kriegs-Geschichte Von König Gustav Adolfs Feldzuge in Deutschland an/ Biß zur Abdanckung Der Königin Christina. ... Aus dem Lateinischen in die hochdeutsche Sprache übersetzet Von J. J. M. v. S. Frankfurt a. M. und Leipzig: Johann Friedrich Gleditsch 1688. [Tl. I: Buch 1–13; Tl. II: Buch 14–26]. HAB: Gs 2° 10.

Pusch
Pusch, Oskar: Die Breslauer Rats- und Stadtgeschlechter in der Zeit von 1241 bis 1741. 5 Bde. Dortmund 1986–1991.

Quintilian: Institutio oratoria
Quintilianus, Marcus Fabius: Ausbildung des Redners. Zwölf Bücher. Lateinisch und deutsch. Hg. u. übers. v. Helmut Rahn. Darmstadt ^{5}2011.

RE
Paulys Real-Encyclopädie der classischen Altertumswissenschaft. Neue Bearb., begonnen v. Georg Wissowa, unter Mitwirkung zahlreicher Fachgenossen. Hg. Wilhelm Kroll. 66 Halbbde., 15 Erg.bde., 1 Suppl.bd. Stuttgart (u. a.) 1894–1980.

Rebitsch
Rebitsch, Robert: Matthias Gallas (1588–1647). Generalleutnant des Kaisers zur Zeit des Dreißigjährigen Krieges. Eine militärische Biographie. Münster 2006.

Rehtmeier: Braunschweig Kirchen-Historie
Rehtmeier, Philipp Julius: ANTIQUITATES ECCLESIASTICÆ INCLYTÆ URBIS BRUNSVIGÆ Oder: Der berühmten Stadt Braunschweig Kirchen-Historie ... Von PHILIPPO JULIO Rehtmeyer. 7 Tl.e (Braunschweig: Christoph-Friedrich Zilliger, ab Tl. 4 Ludolph Schröder 1707–1720). HAB: Gn 9848 (u. weitere Expl.).

Rehtmeier: Braunschweig-Lüneburgische Chronica
Bünting, Heinrich, Johannes Letzner u. Philipp Julius Rehtmeyer: Braunschweig-Lüneburgische Chronica, Oder: Historische Beschreibung der Herzogen zu Braunschweig und Lüneburg wie dieselben anfänglich aus den Fürstlichen Häusern Este und Sachsen ihren Ursprung genommen, was sie in diesen Landen für Helden-Thaten verrichtet, ... / Henricus Bünting, Joh. Letzner. Nunmehr ... vermehrt und nach von Leibnitz Script. Brunso. verbessert, mit notis, documentis, sigillis ... bestärkt und biß auf die jetzige Zeit continuiret von Phil. Julius Rehtmeier. 3 Bde. Braunschweig 1722. Darin Teil III: In sich haltend Das Neue Haus Braunschweig-Lüneburg samt dem Anhang oder Nachlese, und Register (Braunschweig: Detleffsen 1722). HAB: Gn 4° 328.

Reichmann/ Wegera: Frühnhd. Grammatik
Reichmann, Oskar u. Klaus-Peter Wegera (Hg.): Frühneuhochdeutsche Grammatik. Von Robert Peter Ebert, Oskar Reichmann, Hans-Joachim Solms u. Klaus-Peter Wegera. Tübingen 1993 (Sammlung kurzer Grammatiken germanischer Dialekte. A. Hauptreihe Nr. 12).

Reifferscheid
Reifferscheid, Alexander: Briefe G. M. Lingelsheims, M. Berneggers und ihrer Freunde. Nach Handschriften der Kgl. Bibliothek in Kopenhagen, der Reichsbibliothek in Stockholm, der Stadtbibliotheken in Bremen, Breslau, Hamburg und Lübeck, der Universitätsbibliothek in Leiden, Der Bibliothek der Kgl. Ritterakademie in Liegnitz, der Ständ. Landesbibliothek in Kassel, des Kgl. Staatsarchivs in Breslau, des Stadtarchivs in Danzig und des Reichsarchivs in Stockholm hg. u. erl. v. A. R. Heilbronn 1889 (Quellen zur Geschichte des geistigen Lebens in Deutschland während des siebzehnten Jahrhunderts, 1).

Reinitzer: Biblia
Reinitzer, Heimo: Biblia deutsch. Luthers Bibelübersetzung und ihre Tradition. Wolfenbüttel 1983 (Ausstellungskataloge der HAB, 40).

Reske
Reske, Christoph: Die Buchdrucker des 16. und 17. Jahrhunderts im deutschen Sprachgebiet. Auf der Grundlage des gleichnamigen Werkes von Josef Benzing. Wiesbaden 2007.

REThK (1896)
Realencyklopädie für protestantische Theologie und Kirche. Begr. v. J. J. Herzog. In 3., verb. u. verm. Aufl. unter Mitwirkung vieler Theologen und Gelehrten hg. Albert Hauck. 21 Bde., 1 Reg.bd. u. 2 Nachtragsbde. Leipzig 1896–1913.

RGG[4]
Religion in Geschichte und Gegenwart. Handwörterbuch für Theologie u. Reli-

gionswissenschaft. 4., völlig neu bearb. Aufl. Hg. Hans Dieter Betz, Don S. Browning, Bernd Janowski, Eberhard Jüngel. 8 Bde. Tübingen 1998–2005.

Richelet
Richelet, Pierre: Dictionnaire françois, Contenant Les Mots Et Les Choses, Plusieurs Nouvelles Remarques Sur La Langue Françoise. Tom. 1–2. Genève 1679/1680. Ndr. Genève 1970.

RISM
Répertoire international des sources musicales. Internationales Quellenlexikon der Musik. Hg. Intern. Gesellschaft f. Musikwissenschaft u. Intern. Vereinigung d. Musikbibliotheken. Reihen A, B, C und Sonderbd. Duisburg 1960 ff. u. Kassel 1960 (Sonderbd.).

Rist: Schauplatz (1646)
Johann Risten | [Zierleiste] | POetischer Schauplatz/ | Auff welchem allerhand Waaren | Gute und Böse | Kleine und Grosse | Freude und Leid-zeugende | zu finden. | [Linie] | Hamburg/ Bey und Jnverlegung [!] | Heinrich Werner/ 1646. HAB: Lo 6467.

Ritter: Deutsche Geschichte
Ritter, Moriz: Deutsche Geschichte im Zeitalter der Gegenreformation und des Dreißigjährigen Krieges (1555–1648). Bd. 3: Geschichte des Dreißigjährigen Krieges. Stuttgart u. Berlin 1908 (Bibliothek deutscher Geschichte, 7).

Ritter: Lexicon[9]
Ritters geographisch-statistisches Lexikon über die Erdteile, Länder, Meere, Häfen, Seen, Flüsse, Inseln, Gebirge, Staaten, Städte, Flecken, Dörfer, Bäder, Kanäle, Eisenbahnen, Post- und Telegraphenämter u. s. w. 9., vollst. umgearb., sehr stark verm. u. verb. Aufl. Unter der Redaktion von Johannes Penzler. 2 Bde. Leipzig 1905–1906.

Roelcke
Roelcke, Thorsten: Latein, Griechisch, Hebräisch. Studien und Dokumentationen zur deutschen Sprachreflexion in Barock und Aufklärung. Berlin, Boston 2014.

Roth, s. LP Roth

Roth Fremdwb.
Simon Roths Fremdwörterbuch. Hg. Emil Öhmann. In: Mémoires de la Société Néo-Philologiques de Helsingfors XI (Helsinki 1936), 226–370.

Sachse: Einhelligkeit I–III
Sachse, Daniel: Einhelligkeit Der Vier Evangelisten Vber Vnsers HErren und Heylandes JESV CHRJSTJ Geburt und Leben/ Leiden und Sterben/ Auferstehung und Himmelfahrt/ Aus Jhren Vier Büchern in richtige Ordnung zusammen getragen/ und der Gemeine Gottes zu Cöthen erkleret: Von Daniel Sachsen/ Pfarrern und Superintendenten daselbst/ Erster [Ander/ Dritter und Letzter] Theil/ Jn Hundert Predigten verfasset/ samt zweyen [II dreyen/ III Zusamt Einer Zugabe aus den Apostolischen Geschichten/ von Der Sendung des heiligen Geistes. Mit beygefügten] notwendigen Registern. Cöthen 1641 [1643 / 1644]. HAB: 317.2 Theol. 2°; 317.3 Theol. 2°; 317.4 Theol. 2°.

Sammler Fürst Gelehrter
Sammler Fürst Gelehrter. Herzog August v. Braunschweig-Lüneburg 1579–1666. Braunschweig 1979 (Ausstellungskataloge der Herzog August Bibliothek, 27).

Saur Allgemeines Künstlerlexikon, s. *De Gruyter Allgemeines Künstlerlexikon*

SBL
Svenskt Biografiskt Lexikon. Red.komm.: J. A. Almquist [u. a.]. Redaktör: Bertil Boëthius. Bd. 1–. Stockholm 1918 [1917]–.

Schäfer: Moscherosch
Schäfer, Walter Ernst: Johann Michael Moscherosch. Staatsmann, Satiriker und Pädagoge im Barockzeitalter. München 1982.

Schäfer: Moscherosch und Harsdörffer
Schäfer, Walter Ernst: Eine Freundschaft im Zeichen ‚Deutscher Spacharbeit': Moscherosch und Harsdörffer. In: Daphnis 34 (2005), 137–183.

Schielein
Schielein, Chrystèle: Philipp von Zesen: Orthographiereformer mit niederländischen Vorbildern? Inaug.Diss. an der Philosoph. Fak. II (Sprach- und Literaturwissenschaften) der Friedrich-Alexander-Universität Erlangen-Nürnberg. 2002. Online unter http://www.opus.ub.uni-erlangen.de/opus/volltexte/2004/79/pdf/Zesen.pdf

Schmeller
Schmeller, Johann Andreas: Bayerisches Wörterbuch. 2., verm. Ausg. Bearb. G. K. Frommann. 2 Bde. München 1872–1877.

Schnabel: Stbb.
Die Stammbücher und Stammbuchfragmente der Stadtbibliothek Nürnberg. Bearb. v. Werner Wilhelm Schnabel. 3 Tle. Wiesbaden 1995 (Die Handschriften der StB Nürnberg, Sonderbd.).

Schottelius
Justus Georg Schottelius 1612–1676. Ein Teutscher Gelehrter am Wolfenbütteler Hof. Ausst. der Herzog August Bibliothek Wolfenbüttel, 23.10.1976 – 2.1.1977. Ausst. u. Katalog: Jörg Jochen Berns unter Mitarb. v. Wolfgang Borm. Wolfenbüttel, Braunschweig 1976 (Ausstellungskataloge der Herzog August Bibliothek, 18).

Schottelius: Ausführliche Arbeit (1663)
Schottelius, Justus Georg: Ausführliche Arbeit | Von der | Teutschen | Haubt-Sprache/ | Worin enthalten | Gemelter dieser HaubtSprache Uhrankunft/ | Uhralterthum/ Reinlichkeit/ Eigenschaft/ Vermögen/ Unvergleichlich- | keit/ Grundrichtigkeit/ zumahl die SprachKunst und VersKunst Teutsch und guten | theils Lateinisch völlig mit eingebracht/ wie nicht weniger die Verdoppelung/ Ableitung/ die | Einleitung/ Nahmwörter/ Authores vom Teutschen Wesen und Teutscher Spra- | che/ von der verteutschung/ Jtem die Stammwörter der Teutschen | Sprache samt der Erklärung und derogleichen | viel merkwürdige Sachen. | Abgetheilet | Jn | Fünf Bücher. | Ausgefertiget | Von | JUSTO-GEORGIO SCHOTTELIO D. | Fürstl. Braunschweig: Lüneburg. Hof- und Consi- | storial-Rahte und Hofgerichts Assessore. | Nicht allein mit Röm: Käyserl. Maj. Privilegio, sondern auch | mit sonderbarer Käyserl. Approbation und genehmhaltung/ als einer gemeinnutzigen | und der Teutschen Nation zum besten angesehenen Arbeit/ laut des | folgenden Käyserl. Privilegii. | [Zierstück] | Braunschweig/ | Gedrukt und verlegt durch Christoff Friederich Zilligern/ | Buchhändlern. | [Linie] | Anno M. DC. LXIII. HAB: 37.5 Gram. u. Ko 306. Ndr. hg. Wolfgang Hecht. 2 Tle. Tübingen 1967 (Deutsche Neudrucke, Reihe: Barock, 11).

Schottelius: Der Teutschen Sprache Einleitung (1643)
Schottelius, Justus Georg: Der Teutschen | Sprache | Einleitung/ | Zu richtiger gewisheit und | grundmeßigem vermügen der | Teutschen Haubtsprache/ samt | beygefügten Erklär- | ungen. | Ausgefertiget | Von | JUSTO GEORGIO | SCHOTTELIO, Dicasterij Guel- | phici Assessore. | [Zierstück] | Lübeck/ | Gedruckt durch Johan Meyer/ | Jn Verlegung | Matthæi Düncklers Buchh. in Lüneburg. | [Linie] | Anno 1643. HAB: 96.7 Gram.

Schottelius: FriedensSieg (1642/48)
[Schottelius, Justus Georg:] [Kupfertitel:] Neu | erfundenes | FreudenSpiel | genandt | FriedensSieg. | Jn gegenwart vieler Chur- und | Fürstlicher auch anderer Vornehmen | Personen, in dem Fürstl. BurgSaal | zu Braunschweig im Jahr 1642. | von lauter kleinen Knaben | vorgestellet. | Auf vielfältiges begehren mit kupfer | Stücken gezieret und verlegt | durch Conrad Buno | Jn Wolfenbüttel | Jm Jahr | 1648. HAB: 166.1 Eth. (1) u. Lo 6992.

Schottelius: Fruchtbringender Lustgarte (1647)
Schottelius, Justus Georg: [Kupfertitel] Frucht- | bringender | Lustgar- | te, | voller | Geistliche. | und Weltliche. | Neuen erfin- | dungen | Zu | Ergetzlichen | Nutz

| Zubereitet | von | Iusto-Georgio | Schottelio | I. U. D. | ... | Gedruckt in der Fürstl: Residentz Wolffenbüttel. 1647. [Drucktitel]: Fruchtbringender Lustgarte | Jn sich haltend | Die ersten funf | Abtheilungen/ | Zu ergetzlichem Nutze | Ausgefertiget/ | Und gedrukt | Jn der Fürstlichen Haupt-Vestung | Wulffenbüttel/ | Durch Johañ Bißmark/ Jn verlegung | Michael Cubachs/ Buchhändlers in | Lüneburg. | [Linie] | Jm Jahr/ 1647. HAB: Lo 6993.
(Ndr.) Justus Georg Schottelius: Fruchtbringender Lustgarte. Hg. Marianne Burkhard. Mit e. Nachwort v. Max Wehrli. München 1967.

Schottelius: Sprachkunst (1641)
JUSTI-GEORGII SCHOTTELII | Einbeccensis, | Teutsche | Sprachkunst/ | Darinn die | Allerwortreichste/ | Prächtigste/ reinlichste/ voll- | kommene/ Uhralte Hauptsprache | der Teutschen auß jhren Gründen erhoben/ | dero Eigenschafften und Kunststücke völliglich ent- | deckt/ und also in eine richtige Form der Kunst | zum ersten mahle gebracht | worden. | Abgetheilet in Drey Bücher. | [Zierstück] | Braunschweig/ | Gedruckt bey Balthasar Grubern/ | Jm Jahr 1641. HAB: 51.3 Gram.

Schottelius: Sprachkunst (1651)
Justi-Georgii Schottelii J. V. D. | Teutsche | SprachKunst/ | Vielfaltig vermehret und ver- | bessert/ darin von allen Eigenschaften | der so wortreichen und prächtigen | Teutschen Haubtsprache aus- | führlich und gründlich gehan- | delt wird. | Zum anderen mahle heraus gegeben | im Jahr 1651. | [Linie] | Braunschweig | Jn verlegung Christof-Friederich Zilligern. HAB: 75.3 Gram.

Schottelius: Teutsche Vers- oder ReimKunst (1645)
[Kupfertitel:] Iusti-Georgii | Schottelii | Teutsche Vers- oder | ReimKunst | darin | Vnsere Teutsche | MutterSprache, So viel | dero süßeste Po- | esis | betrift, in eine | richtige Form der | Kunst zum ersten | mahle gebracht | worden. | getruckt zu | Wolfenbüttel | in verlegung | des Autoris | im jahre | M DC XL V. *Kolophon (S. 319):* Gedruckt zu Wulffenbüttel/ | durch Johann Bißmarck/ | Jm Jahr 1645. HAB: 172.1 Poet.

Schottelius: Teutsche Vers- oder ReimKunst (1656)
[Kupfertitel:] Iusti-Georgii | Schottelii | Teutsche Vers- oder | ReimKunst | darin | Vnsere Teutsche | MutterSprache, So viel | dero süßeste Po- | esis | betrift, in eine | richtige Form der | Kunst zum ersten | mahle gebracht | worden. | Franckfurtt | am Mayn | in Verlegung | Michael Cubachs | Auch | in Lüneburg | im jahre | 1656. HAB: Um 180 (1). Ndr. Hildesheim, New York 1976.

Siebmacher
Johann Siebmacher's großes und allgemeines Wappenbuch in einer neuen, vollständig geordneten und reich vermehrten Auflage mit heraldischen und historisch-genealogischen Erläuterungen. Grund-Saeze der Wappenkunst. Einleitungsbde. A u. B; 7 Bde. in 98. Nürnberg [u. a.] 1854–1961.

Singer ABK
Singer, Hans Wolfgang: Allgemeiner Bildniskatalog. 14 Bde. Leipzig 1930–1936. Ndr. Stuttgart u. Nendeln/ Liechtenstein 1967.

Singer NBK
Singer, Hans Wolfgang: Neuer Bildniskatalog. Leipzig 1937–1938. Ndr. Stuttgart u. Nendeln/ Liechtenstein 1967.

Sprachgeschichte. Handbuch²
Sprachgeschichte. Ein Handbuch zur Geschichte der deutschen Sprache u. ihrer Erforschung. 2., vollst. neu bearb. u. erw. Aufl. Hg. Werner Besch, Anne Betten, Oskar Reichmann, Stefan Sonderegger. 4 Teilbde. Berlin u. New York 1998–2004.

Steinbach
Steinbach, Christoph Ernst: Vollständiges Deutsches Wörter-Buch vel Lexicon Germanico-Latinum. 2 Teile. Breslau 1734. Ndr. Hildesheim, New York 1973.

Stieler
Stieler, Caspar (v.) (Der Spate): Der Teutschen Sprache Stammbaum und Fortwachs, oder Teutscher Sprachschatz. Nürnberg 1691. VD17 12:130745W; unvollst. Expl. HAB: 22.2 Gram. Ndr. Mit e. Nachw. v. Stefan Sonderegger. München 1968.

Stoll
Stoll, Christoph: Sprachgesellschaften im Deutschland des 17. Jahrhunderts. Fruchtbringende Gesellschaft. Aufrichtige Gesellschaft von der Tannen. Deutschgesinnte Genossenschaft. Hirten- und Blumenorden an der Pegnitz. Elbschwanenorden. München 1973.

Szyrocki: Opitz (1956)
Szyrocki, Marian: Martin Opitz. Berlin 1956 (Neue Beiträge zur Literaturwissenschaft, 4).

Szyrocki: Opitz (1974)
Szyrocki, Marian: Martin Opitz. 2. Aufl. München 1974.

Tacitus: Germania (Conring 1652)
Tacitus, Publius (oder Gaius) Cornelius: C. CORNELII TACITI | DE MORIBVS GER- | MANORVM | LIBER. | Accedunt præter alia, de rebus Germaniæ antiquæ, ex priscis monu- | mentis EXCERPTA. | Ex recensione H. CONRINGII. | Cum ejusdem de usu historiæ & reipubl. Germanicæ | notitia præfatione, hujusque à ca- | lumnia vindiciis. | [Zierstück] | HELMSTADI, | Typis & sumtibus HENNINGI MVLLERI, | ACADEM. TYPOGR. | [Linie] | M D C LII. HAB: 979 Helmst. Dr. (1).

Takada
Takada, Hiroyuki: Grammatik und Sprachwirklichkeit von 1640–1700. Zur Rolle deutscher Grammatiker im schriftsprachlichen Ausgleichsprozeß. Tübingen 1998 (Reihe Germanistische Linguistik, 203).

TdLF
Trésor de la langue française. Dictionnaire de la langue du XIXe et du XXe siècle (1789–1960). Paris 1971–1994.

Theatrum europaeum
THEATRVM EUROPÆVM, oder/ Außführliche vnd Warhafftige Beschreibung aller vnd jeder denckwürdiger Geschichten/ so sich hin vnd wider in der Welt ... vom Jahr Christi 1617. biß auff das Jahr 1629 [–1651] ... zugetragen haben/ &. Beschrieben durch M. Joannem Philippum Abelinum. 6 Thle. (Tl. 3: Vf. Henricus Oraeus; Tl. 5: Vf. J. P. Lotichius; Tl. 6: Vf. Joannes Georgius Schlederus). Frankfurt a. M. 1643–1652. 3. Aufl. (Tl. 1–5) bzw. Forts., 21. Thle. (1617–1718). Frankfurt a. M. 1662–1738.
Dig. (WDB): Bd. 2 (1633): http://diglib.hab.de/periodica/70-b-hist-2f/start.htm
Bd. 3 (1639): http://diglib.hab.de/periodica/70-c-hist-2f/start.htm
Bd. 4 (1643): http://diglib.hab.de/periodica/70-d-hist-2f/start.htm
Bd. 5 (1647): http://diglib.hab.de/periodica/70-1-hist-2f/start.htm

Thieme/ Becker
Allgemeines Lexikon der bildenden Künstler von der Antike bis zur Gegenwart. Hg. Ulrich Thieme u. Felix Becker. 37 Bde. Leipzig 1907–1950.

Thüringisches Wb.
Sächsische Akademie der Wissenschaften zu Leipzig, sprachwiss. Kommission: Thüringisches Wörterbuch. Auf Grund der von V. Michels begonnenen und H. Hucke fortgeführten Sammlungen bearb. unter Leitung v. K. Spangenberg. 6 Bde. u. Beibd. Berlin 1966–1999.

TRE
Theologische Realenzyklopädie. Hg. Gerhard Krause u. Gerhard Müller. 36 Bde. u. 2 Gesamtreg.bde. Berlin u. New York 1976–2007.

Tscherning: Früling (1642)
[Kupfertitel:] Andreas Tschernings | Deutscher Getichte | Früling. | Breßlaw, | Jn Verlegung | Georg Baumanns | Buchdruckers. | 1642. VD17 3:612815V; unvollst. Ex. HAB: Xb 1835 (1).

Tscherning: Früling (1646)
Andreas Tschernings | Deutscher Getichte | Früling | Auffs | neue übersehen verbessert | und | nachgedruckt | Jn Rostock durch Johann Richeln | Jn verlegung Joachim Wilten [1646]. VD17 39:119918T.

Tscherning: Früling (1649)
Andreas Tschernings | Deutscher Getichte | Früling | Auffs neue übersehen und verbessert. | Nachgedruckt | Jn Rostock durch Johann Richeln/ | Jn verlegung Joachim Wilten [1649]. HAB: 122.11 Poet. (3).

Verfasserlexikon Fr. Nz
Frühe Neuzeit in Deutschland 1520–1620. Literaturwissenschaftliches Verfasserlexikon. Hg. Wilhelm Kühlmann, Jan-Dirk Müller, Michael Schilling u. a. Bd. 1–, Berlin, Boston 2011–.

VL (2. Aufl.)
Die deutsche Literatur des Mittelalters. Verfasserlexikon. Begr. v. Wolfgang Stammler, fortgef. v. Karl Langosch. 2., völlig neu bearb. Aufl. Hg. Kurt Ruh zus. mit Gundolf Keil, Werner Schröder, Burghart Wachinger, Franz Josef Worstbrock. 11 Bde. Berlin, New York 1978–2004 (Veröffentlichungen der Kommission für Deutsche Literatur des Mittelalters der Bayerischen Akademie der Wissenschaften).

Vocabolario della Crusca 1623
VOCABOLARIO DEGLI ACCADEMICI DELLA CRVSCA, IN QVESTA SECONDA IMPRESSIONE da' medesimi rieduto, e ampliato, con aggiunta di molte voci degli autor del buon secolo, e buona quantità di quelle dell'vso. CON TRE INDICI DELLE VOCI, LOCVZIONI, e prouerbi Latini, e Greci, posti per entro l'Opera. Venezia 1623.

Wachter
Wachter, Johannes Georg: Glossarium germanicum, continens origines & antiquitates totius linguæ germanicæ, et omnium pene vocabulorum, vigentium et desitorum. Opus bipartitum et quinque indicibus instructum. Leipzig 1737. HAB: Kb 2° 44. Ndr. Hildesheim, New York 1975.

WB Weimar
s. „Häufiger benutzte Literatur, I. Handschriften".

Weimarer Impresen
s. „Häufiger benutzte Literatur, I. Handschriften".

D. v. dem Werder: Friedensrede (1639)
[Werder, Diederich v. dem]: Friedensrede | in gegenwart | vieler Fürsten/ Fürstin- | nen und Freulein/ | Auch | Grosser anzahl HochAdelicher/ Gelehrter und an- | derer vornehmen Mannes- Frauen und Jung- | fräulichen Personen/ | Sehr behertzt/ fertig/ mit zierlicher geschick- | ligkeit und wohlbequemeten tapfferen ge- | berden fürgebracht und abge- | leget/ | Durch | Einen funftzehen Jährigen Edelen Knaben. | Wo diese werden schweigen/ so werden die Steine schreyen. | Luc. 19. | [Vignette] | Jm Jahre | 1639. HAB: 171.42 Quod. (9).

D. v. dem Werder: Krieg vnd Sieg
[Werder, Diederich v. dem]: Krieg vnd Sieg | Christi | Gesungen | Jn 100. Sonneten | Da in jedem vnd jeglichem Verse die bey- | den wörter/ KRJEG vnd SJEG auffs | wenigste einmahl/ befindlich seyn. | Gedruckt bey Johann Röhnern/ | [Linie] | Jm Jahr 1631. VD17 39:121069C.

D. v. dem Werder: Jerusalem (1626)
[Torquato Tasso: *Il Goffredo. overo Gerusalemme liberata*, dt. übers. v.] Werder, Diederich v. dem: Gottfried von Bulljon, Oder Das Erlösete Jerusalem. Franckfurt am Mayn 1626. HAB: 9 Poet. Ndr. Hg. Gerhard Dünnhaupt. Tübingen 1974 (Deutsche Neudrucke. Reihe: Barock, 14).

D. v. dem Werder: Jerusalem (1651)
[Torquato Tasso: *Il Goffredo. overo Gerusalemme liberata*, dt. übers. v. Diederich v. dem Werder] [Kupfertitel]: Gottfried. Oder Erlösetes Jerusalem. Deutsch. Verbessert. Zum zweyten mahl gedruckt. Franckfurt am Mayn/ Gedruckt bey Caspar Röteln/ Jn Verlegung Johann Pressen. ANNO M. DC. LI. HAB: 14.3 Poet.

D. v. dem Werder (LP 1658)
Colerus, Gottfried: Der | Vom Vater gegebene/ | Vom Sohne ausgeführete/ | Und vom H. Geiste versiegelte | Raht des Heils | Bey Hochansehnlicher Leichbestattung | ... Dieterichs von dem Wer- | der ... Welcher am 18. Decembris des 1657sten Jahres ... entschlaffen/ | Und im Jahre 1658 den 13. Maj/ ... beygesetzet worden (Cöthen: Jacob Brand in der Fürstlichen Druckerei, 1658). HAB: Xa 1: 47 [10].

D. v. dem Werder: Roland
Ariosto, Ludovico: Die Historia vom Rasenden Roland übers. v. Diederich v. dem Werder. (Leipzig 1632 bis 1636). Hg. u. kommentiert v. Achim Aurnhammer u. Dieter Martin. 3 Teile. Stuttgart 2002 (Bibliothek des Literarischen Vereins in Stuttgart, 329–331).

D. v. dem Werder, Fürst Ludwig: Seelen Ancker (1641)
[Ellardus van Mehen: *Den ancker der ziele* (Harderwijk 1611); dt. Übers. von Diederich v. dem Werder, bearb. von F. Ludwig v. Anhalt-Köthen u. d. T.:] Der Seelen | Ancker/ | Das ist/ | Von der Beharligkeit oder Besten- | digkeit der Heiligen/ | Gegründet | Auf die unverenderliche erwehlung | Gottes/ | Als auch | Auf die kräfftige beruffung der Heili- | gen zu der seligen gemeinschaft | Gottes in Christo Jesu. | Vor etzlichen Jahren in Niederländischer | Sprache beschrieben/ | An ietzo aber | Jn Hoch-Deutsch allen frommen glau- | bigen Christen zu troste | übergesetzet. | [Linie] | Gedrucket zu Cöthen im Fürstenthume | Anhalt/ Jm Jahre 1641. HAB: 1293.11 Theol. (2).

Will
Will, Georg Andreas: Nürnbergisches Gelehrten-Lexicon oder Beschreibung aller Nürnbergischen Gelehrten. 8 Tle. Erg. und fortges. v. Christian Conrad Nopitsch. Nürnberg 1755–1758, Altdorf 1802–1808. Ndr. Neustadt a. d. Aisch 1997–1998.

Wilson
Wilson, Peter H.: Europe's Tragedy. A New History of the Thirty Years War. London 2010.

Witkowski
Witkowski, Georg: Diederich von dem Werder. Leipzig 1887.

Woeste
Woeste, Friedrich: Wörterbuch der westfälischen Mundart. Neu bearb. u. hg. v. Erich Noerrenberg. Norden u. Leipzig 1930. Ndr. Wiesbaden 1964.

Wüthrich: Druckgraph. Werk v. Merian
Wüthrich, Lucas Heinrich: Das druckgraphische Werk von Matthaeus Merian d. Ä. 4 Bde. Basel (ab Bd. 3 Hamburg) 1966–1996.

Wüthrich: Merian Biographie
Wüthrich, Lucas Heinrich: Matthaeus Merian d. Ä. Eine Biographie. Hamburg 2007.

Wüthrich: Merian Briefe
Matthaeus Merian d. Ä. Briefe und Widmungen. Hg. Lucas Heinrich Wüthrich. Hamburg 2009.

Zedler
Grosses vollständiges Universal Lexicon Aller Wissenschaften und Künste. Hg. Johann Heinrich Zedler. 64 Bde. u. 4 Bde. Nötige Supplemente. Leipzig 1732–1754. HAB: H 2° 2. Ndr. Graz 1961–1964.
Online unter http://www.zedler-lexikon.de/

Zesen SW
Philipp von Zesen: Sämtliche Werke. Unter Mitwirkung von Ulrich Maché u. Volker Meid hg. Ferdinand van Ingen. 18 Bde. (in mehreren Tl.bden.). Berlin [u. a.] 1970–2011.

Zöllner
Zöllner, Friedrich: Einrichtung und Verfassung der Fruchtbringenden Gesellschaft vornehmlich unter dem Fürsten Ludwig zu Anhalt-Cöthen. Berlin 1899.

Chronologische Übersicht der Briefe und Beilagen

440000	Diederich von dem Werder an Conrad von Burgsdorff
	I. Diederich von dem Werder nach Loredano über die Ermordung Wallensteins
	II. Fürst Christians II. von Anhalt-Bernburg Nachrichten über die Ermordung Wallensteins
	III. Valeriano Castiglione über Loredanos *Dianea* und dessen Darstellung der Ermordung Wallensteins
440100	Justus Georg Schottelius an Herzog August d. J. von Braunschweig-Wolfenbüttel
	I. Schottelius' *Pindarische Ode* (1643)
	II. Schottelius' *Ringelgedicht*
440119	Christian Beckmann an Christophorus Colerus
440127	Fürst Ludwig an Christian Gueintz
440129	Christian Gueintz an Fürst Ludwig
440130	Fürst Ludwig an Carl Gustav von Hille
440204	Diederich von dem Werder an Fürst Ludwig
	I. Gedicht Diederichs von dem Werder zu Georg Philipp Harsdörffers viertem Teil der *Frauenzimmer-Gesprächspiele*
440209	Fürst Ludwig sendet ein Gutachten von Mitgliedern der Fruchtbringenden Gesellschaft an Christian Gueintz
440209A	Carl Gustav von Hille an Fürst Ludwig
440219	Christian Gueintz an Fürst Ludwig
440310	Fürst Ludwig an Carl Gustav von Hille
440310A	Diederich von dem Werder an Fürst Ludwig
	I. *Art dreyfach geschrenckter Reime* von Fürst Ludwigs Hand
	II. *Art dreyfach geschrenckter Reime* verbessert von Diederich von dem Werder und eingetragen von Fürst Ludwig
440310B	Diederich von dem Werder an Peter Knaudt
440313	Fürst Ludwig an Christian Gueintz
440317	Christian Gueintz an Fürst Ludwig
440323	Carl Gustav von Hille an Fürst Ludwig
	I. (440323) Carl Gustav von Hille an Herzog August d. J. von Braunschweig-Wolfenbüttel
440324	Andreas Tscherning an Matthaeus Apelles von Löwenstern
	I. Johann Rist knüpft Kontakte zu Andreas Tscherning

440400   Justus Georg Schottelius an Herzog August d. J. von Braunschweig-Wolfenbüttel
          I. Schottelius' Gratulationssextine zum 10. April 1644
440426   Georg Philipp Harsdörffer an die Fruchtbringende Gesellschaft
          I. Georg Philipp Harsdörffers Entwurf der Figurentableaus zu zwei Freudenspielen über die „Vernunftkunst" und die „Wolredkunst"
440429   Justus Georg Schottelius an Johann Valentin Andreae
440504   Christian Gueintz an Fürst Ludwig
440525   Johann Michael Moscheroschs Briefgedicht in Johann Heinrich Schills *Der Teutschen Sprach Ehren-Krantz*
          I. Johann Matthias Schneubers Freundschaftsgedicht in Schills *Ehren-Krantz*
          II. Aus Schills *Ehren-Krantz*
440616   Johann Michael Moscherosch an Johann Heinrich Boeckler
          I. (431201) Moscherosch gratuliert Georg Philipp Harsdörffer zum vierten Teil der *Frauenzimmer-Gesprächspiele*
          II. (431229) Johann Michael Moscherosch an Johann Heinrich Boeckler
          III. (440112) Boeckler preist Harsdörffer und das fruchtbringerische Sprachspiel
440715   Georg Philipp Harsdörffers Widmungsgedicht an Fürst Ludwig
440715A   Georg Philipp Harsdörffers Widmungsbrief an Herzog Christian Ludwig von Braunschweig-Calenberg
440723   Fürst Ludwig an Herzog Christian Ludwig von Braunschweig-Calenberg
440723A   Fürst Ludwig an Carl Gustav von Hille
440724   Johann Rist an Philipp von Zesen
440731   Georg Philipp Harsdörffer an Herzog August d. J. von Braunschweig-Wolfenbüttel
          I. Georg Philipp Harsdörffers Widmungsgedicht für Herzog August d. J. von Braunschweig-Wolfenbüttel
          II. (440824) Georg Philipp Harsdörffer an Herzogin Sophia Elisabeth von Braunschweig-Wolfenbüttel
440809   Christian Gueintz an Fürst Ludwig
440809A   Winand von Polhelm an Fürst Ludwig
440816   Diederich von dem Werder an Fürst Ludwig
          I. Fürst Ludwigs Reimgesetze auf die Neumitglieder 407–415 in einer frühen Fassung
          II. Eine verbesserte spätere Abschrift der Reimgesetze FG 407–415 als Vorlage der Verbesserungen Werders
440824   Georg Philipp Harsdörffer an die Fruchtbringende Gesellschaft
440826   Abraham von Franckenberg an Gottfried Sturm
440900   Justus Georg Schottelius an Herzog August d. J. von Braunschweig-Wolfenbüttel

440927	Fürst August von Anhalt-Plötzkau an Herzog Wilhelm IV. von Sachsen-Weimar
441000	Justus Georg Schottelius an Herzog August d. J. von Braunschweig-Wolfenbüttel
441010	Zacharias Prüschenk von Lindenhofen über seine Aufnahme in die Fruchtbringende Gesellschaft
441011	Justus Georg Schottelius an Herzog August d. J. von Braunschweig-Wolfenbüttel
441020	Georg Philipp Harsdörffer an Justus Georg Schottelius
441200	Justus Georg Schottelius an Herzog August d. J. von Braunschweig-Wolfenbüttel
	I. Schottelius' Widmungsgedicht auf Herzogin Sophia Elisabeth von Braunschweig-Wolfenbüttel
	II. Georg Philipp Harsdörffers Madrigal auf das Porträt der Herzogin
441201	Philipp von Zesen an die Fruchtbringende Gesellschaft
441205	Landgraf Hermann IV. von Hessen-Rotenburg an Fürst Ludwig
441216	Johann Rist an Justus Georg Schottelius
	I. Schäferliches Freundschaftsgedicht Rists für Schottelius
441223	Georg Philipp Harsdörffer an Philipp von Zesen
441226	Fürst Ludwig an Curt von Einsiedel
441226A	Fürst Ludwig an Christian Gueintz
441231	Christian Gueintz an Fürst Ludwig
441231A	Justus Georg Schottelius an Herzog August d. J. von Braunschweig-Wolfenbüttel
450000	Justus Georg Schottelius an Herzog August d. J. von Braunschweig-Wolfenbüttel
450000A	Philipp von Zesen an Justus Georg Schottelius
450100	Justus Georg Schottelius an Herzog August d. J. von Braunschweig-Wolfenbüttel
	I. Schottelius preist Herzog Augusts *Evangelische Kirchen-Harmonie*
450124	Fürst Ludwig an Georg Philipp Harsdörffer
	I. Diederichs von dem Werder Kommentar zum vorliegenden Brief
450126	Carl Gustav von Hille an Fürst Ludwig
450127	Fürst Ludwig an Peter Knaudt
450200	Justus Georg Schottelius an Herzog August d. J. von Braunschweig-Wolfenbüttel
450202	Justus Georg Schottelius an Herzog August d. J. von Braunschweig-Wolfenbüttel
450204	Justus Georg Schottelius an Fürst Ludwig
450217	Herzog Ernst I. von Sachsen-Gotha an Fürst Ludwig
450219	Johann Valentin Andreae an Herzog August d. J. von Braunschweig-Wolfenbüttel

450220	Fürst Ludwig an Herzog Wilhelm IV. von Sachsen-Weimar
	I. Fürst Ludwigs Geburtstagssonett auf seine Nichte Eleonora Dorothea
	II. Lied einer selig abgeschiedenen Seele
450221	Fürst Ludwig an Carl Gustav von Hille
450224	Fürst Ludwig an Herzog Ernst I. von Sachsen-Gotha
450301	Herzogin Eleonora Dorothea von Sachsen-Weimar an Fürst Ludwig
450304	Herzogin Eleonora Maria von Mecklenburg-Güstrow an Fürst Christian II. von Anhalt-Bernburg
450305	Winand von Polhelm an Fürst Ludwig
	I. (450228) Der von Polhelm an Fürst Ludwig überschickte Brief des Adolph Fabritius
450308	Carl Gustav von Hille an Fürst Ludwig
450308A	Philipp von Zesen an Jesaias Rompler von Löwenhalt
450317	Fürst Ludwig an Landgraf Hermann IV. von Hessen-Rotenburg
450317A	Fürst Ludwig an Winand von Polhelm
450319	Johann Valentin Andreae an Herzog August d. J. von Braunschweig-Wolfenbüttel
450325	Diederich von dem Werder an Fürst Ludwig
450326	Fürst Ludwig an Fürst Christian II. von Anhalt-Bernburg
450331	Fürst Ludwig an Herzog August d. J. von Braunschweig-Wolfenbüttel
	I. Lieferungsverpflichtung Fürst Ludwigs über 48 Exemplare des Gesellschaftsbuchs von 1646
450400	Georg Philipp Harsdörffer an Fürst Ludwig
450408	Fürst Johann Casimir von Anhalt-Dessau an Fürst Ludwig
450410	Georg Philipp Harsdörffer an Philipp von Zesen
450417	Matthäus Merian d. Ä. an Peter Knaudt
450419	Johann Hammer an Peter Knaudt
450420	Diederich von dem Werder an Fürst Ludwig
450500	Diederich von dem Werder an Fürst Ludwig
450503	Hans Beyer an Johann Hammer
450504	Fürst Ludwig an Christian Gueintz
450504A	Diederich von dem Werder an Fürst Ludwig
450505	Fürst Ludwig an Diederich von dem Werder
450505A	Diederich von dem Werder an Fürst Ludwig
450506	Fürst Ludwig an Winand von Polhelm
450506A	Christian Gueintz an Fürst Ludwig
450507	Fürst Ludwig an Hans von Dieskau
	I. (450507) Fürst Ludwig an Christian Gueintz
450507A	Landgraf Hermann IV. von Hessen-Rotenburg an Fürst Ludwig
450508	Christian Gueintz an Fürst Ludwig
450508A	Fürst Johann Casimir von Anhalt-Dessau an Fürst Ludwig
450509	Matthias Götze an Johann Hammer
450510	Johann Hammer an Peter Knaudt

450526	Winand von Polhelm an Fürst Ludwig
450529	Fürst Ludwig an Georg Philipp Harsdörffer
450611	Fürst Ludwig an Georg Philipp Harsdörffer
450613	Diederich von dem Werder an Fürst Ludwig
450614	Matthias Götze an Peter Knaudt
450711	Matthäus Merian d. Ä. an Peter Knaudt
450721	Fürst Ludwig an Herzog August d. J. von Braunschweig-Wolfenbüttel
450722	Herzog August d. J. von Braunschweig-Wolfenbüttel an Johann Valentin Andreae
450725	Diederich von dem Werder an Fürst Ludwig I. Ein Gedicht und sechs Reimgesetze Fürst Ludwigs von 1645
450726	Andreas Tscherning über Herzog August d. J. von Braunschweig-Wolfenbüttel in einem Brief an Matthaeus Apelles von Löwenstern I. Tschernings Gedicht auf Herzog August d. J. von Braunschweig-Wolfenbüttel
450730	Diederich von dem Werder an Christian Ernst von Knoch
450800	Peter Knaudt an Matthäus Merian d. Ä. I. Streichung im Dokument 450800
450806	Johann Valentin Andreae an Herzog August d. J. von Braunschweig-Wolfenbüttel
450808	Philipp von Zesen an Georg Philipp Harsdörffer I. Zesens Widmungsgedicht für Harsdörffers fünften Teil der *Gesprächspiele* (1645)
450817	Georg Philipp Harsdörffer an Fürst Ludwig I. Ein Andachtsgemälde Harsdörffers II. (450801) Marco Aurelio Severino an Georg Philipp Harsdörffer III. Durch Severino an Harsdörffer und Fürst Ludwig gelangte Mondansichten Francesco Fontanas IV. Marco Aurelio Severinos Gesellschaftsschrift *La Querela della & accorciata* (1644) V. Das Verzeichnis der Werke Severinos VI. Eintragung Marco Aurelio Severinos in Volckamers Stammbuch
450818	Johann Michael Moscherosch an Georg Philipp Harsdörffer I. Moscheroschs Epigramme zum Lobe Venedigs
450900	Fürst Ludwigs Verzeichnis fruchtbringerischer Drucke bis 1645
450901	Georg Philipp Harsdörffer an Johann Michael Moscherosch
450905	Matthäus Merian d. Ä. an Peter Knaudt
450919	Diederich von dem Werder an Fürst Ludwig
450919A	Fürst Ludwig an Georg Philipp Harsdörffer
450921	Fürst Ludwig an Diederich von dem Werder
450921A	Diederich von dem Werder an Fürst Ludwig
450922	Matthäus Merian d. Ä. an Peter Knaudt
450923	Fürst Ludwig an Herzog Christian Ludwig von Braunschweig-Calenberg

450923A	Fürst Ludwig an Herzog August d. J. von Braunschweig-Wolfenbüttel
450923B	Fürst Ludwig an Justus Georg Schottelius
450923C	Georg Philipp Harsdörffer an Fürst Ludwig
450927	Georg Philipp Harsdörffer an Herzog August d. J. von Braunschweig-Wolfenbüttel
	I. Aus Harsdörffers *Porticus Virtutis* zum Ruhme Herzog Augusts
	II. Zuschriften Georg Philipp Harsdörffers an Herzogin Sophia Elisabeth von Braunschweig-Wolfenbüttel
450929	Justus Georg Schottelius an Herzog August d. J. von Braunschweig-Wolfenbüttel
450930	Matthäus Merian d. Ä. an Peter Knaudt
451000	Justus Georg Schottelius an Herzog August d. J. von Braunschweig-Wolfenbüttel
451001	Herzog August d. J. von Braunschweig-Wolfenbüttel an Fürst Ludwig
451007	Justus Georg Schottelius an Fürst Ludwig
451008	Carl Gustav von Hille an Fürst Ludwig
451015	Matthäus Merian d. Ä. an Peter Knaudt
451019	Georg Winckler an Peter Knaudt
451028	Fürst Ludwig an Carl Gustav von Hille
451028A	Fürst Ludwig an Justus Georg Schottelius
451028B	Matthäus Merian d. Ä. an Peter Knaudt
451030	Gaspar Corneille de Mortaigne dit de Potteles an Fürst Ludwig
451100	Justus Georg Schottelius an Herzog August d. J. von Braunschweig-Wolfenbüttel
	I. Schottelius' Widmung und Sonett an Herzog Anton Ulrich von Braunschweig-Wolfenbüttel
451101	Georg Philipp Harsdörffer an Fürst Ludwig
451119	Matthäus Merian d. Ä. an Peter Knaudt
451209	Fürst Ludwig an Georg Philipp Harsdörffer
451217	Georg Philipp Harsdörffer an Fürst Ludwig
451219	Fürst Ludwig an Christian Gueintz
451220	Marcus Fridericus Wendelinus an Fürst Ludwig
460000	Justus Georg Schottelius an Herzog August d. J. von Braunschweig-Wolfenbüttel
	I. Justus Georg Schottelius an Herzog August d. J. von Braunschweig-Wolfenbüttel
	II. (630000) Justus Georg Schottelius an Herzog August d. J. von Braunschweig-Wolfenbüttel
460000A	Giovanni Francesco Loredano an Georg Philipp Harsdörffer
460103	Wilhelm Heinrich von Freyberg an einen Fürsten [F. Ludwig?]
460104	Extrakt eines Briefs Pfalzgraf Ludwig Philipps von Simmern an Fürst Johann Casimir von Anhalt-Dessau

460112	Georg Philipp Harsdörffer an Herzog August d. J. von Braunschweig-Wolfenbüttel
460119	Fürst Ludwig an Carl Gustav von Hille
460120	Fürst Ludwig an Georg Philipp Harsdörffer
460120A	Burggraf und Herr Achaz zu Dohna an Fürst Ludwig
460125	Kurfürst Friedrich Wilhelm von Brandenburg an die Fürsten von Anhalt
	I. Gesandtschaftsreisen Diederichs von dem Werder
	II. (460100) Bestallung Diederichs von dem Werder in kurbrandenburgische Dienste
460127	Herzog August d. J. von Braunschweig-Wolfenbüttel an Johann Valentin Andreae
460131	Georg Philipp Harsdörffer an Christian Gueintz
460200	Fürst Ludwig an Christian Gueintz
460200A	Justus Georg Schottelius an Herzog August d. J. von Braunschweig-Wolfenbüttel
460204	Diederich von dem Werder an Conrad von Burgsdorff
	I. Simon Dachs *Lob-Spruch dem HochEdlen Gestrengen und MannVesten Herrn Dietrich von dem Werder*
460206	Matthäus Merian d. Ä. an Peter Knaudt
	I. (460222) Fürst Ludwigs Anweisung für Knaudts Antwort an Merian
	II. Peter Knaudts Nachricht an Fürst Ludwig
460217	Fürst Ludwig an den Burggrafen und Herrn Achaz zu Dohna
460218	Fürst Ludwig an Herzog Christian Ludwig von Braunschweig-Calenberg
460301	Herzog Christian Ludwig von Braunschweig-Calenberg an Fürst Ludwig
460303	Matthäus Merian d. Ä. an Peter Knaudt
460309	Fürst Ludwig an Herzog Christian Ludwig von Braunschweig-Calenberg
460315	Christoph Steger an Christian Clepius
460317	Herzog August d. J. von Braunschweig-Wolfenbüttel an Johann Valentin Andreae
	I. Justus Georg Schottelius an Herzog August d. J. von Braunschweig-Wolfenbüttel
460321	Pfalzgraf Ludwig Philipp von Simmern an Fürst Ludwig
460324	Matthäus Merian d. Ä. an Peter Knaudt
460403	Herzog Christian Ludwig von Braunschweig-Calenberg an Fürst Ludwig
460406	Georg Philipp Harsdörffer an Fürst Ludwig
460410	Georg Philipp Harsdörffer an Georg Sigmund Fürer von Haimendorf
460414	Justus Georg Schottelius an Johann Valentin Andreae
460422	Fürst Johann Casimir von Anhalt-Dessau an Fürst Ludwig

460423	Fürst Ludwig an Pfalzgraf Ludwig Philipp von Simmern
	I. Fürst Ludwigs Vorschlag für die Impresen für 14 durch Pfalzgraf Ludwig Philipp von Simmern neu aufzunehmende FG-Mitglieder
460424	Fürst Ludwig an Fürst Johann Casimir von Anhalt-Dessau
460424A	Fürst Ludwig an Pfalzgraf Ludwig Philipp von Simmern
	I. Liste der von Fürst Ludwig notierten, von Pfalzgraf Ludwig Philipp von Simmern zur Aufnahme vorgesehenen FG-Mitglieder
460426	Fürst Ludwig an Georg Philipp Harsdörffer
460519	Matthäus Merian d. Ä. an Peter Knaudt
460609	Fürst Ludwig an Georg Philipp Harsdörffer
460610	Andreas Tscherning an Matthaeus Apelles von Löwenstern
460613	Herzog Rudolf August von Braunschweig-Wolfenbüttel an Fürst Christian II. von Anhalt-Bernburg
460620	Georg Philipp Harsdörffer an Fürst Ludwig
460620A	Joachim von Glasenapp an Fürst Ludwig
	I. Impresenzettel des Erwachsenden mit Reimgesetz
460620B	Matthäus Merian d. Ä. an Peter Knaudt
460700	Justus Georg Schottelius an Herzog August d. J. von Braunschweig-Wolfenbüttel
460703	Matthäus Merian d. Ä. an Peter Knaudt
460705	Fürst Ludwig an Georg Philipp Harsdörffer
	I. Lobverse Fürst Ludwigs für den sechsten Teil der *Frauenzimmer-Gesprächspiele* (1646) von Georg Philipp Harsdörffer (Der Spielende)
	II. Konzept der Lobverse Fürst Ludwigs
	III. Korrekturen Diederichs von dem Werder zu Fürst Ludwigs Lobversen
460708	Fürst Ludwig an Peter Knaudt
460714	Fürst Ludwig an Fürst Christian II. von Anhalt-Bernburg
460715	Johann Valentin Andreae an Herzog August d. J. von Braunschweig-Wolfenbüttel
	I. (460715) Andreae an Philipp Hainhofer
	II. (460723) Philipp Hainhofers Zitat aus einem Brief Andreaes und seine eigenen Bemerkungen darüber. An Herzog August
460718	Carl Gustav von Hille an Fürst Ludwig
460720	Christian Gueintz an Fürst Ludwig
460721	Herzog Georg Rudolph in Schlesien zu Liegnitz und Wohlau an Fürst Ludwig
460726	Johann Michael Moscherosch an Fürst Ludwig
460803	Justus Georg Schottelius an Georg Philipp Harsdörffer
460804	Herzog August d. J. von Braunschweig-Wolfenbüttel an Johann Valentin Andreae
460808	Herzog Franz Carl von Sachsen-Lauenburg an Herzog August d. J. von Braunschweig-Wolfenbüttel
460810	Matthias Götze an Peter Knaudt
460812	Augustus Buchner an Fürst Ludwig

460816 Fürst Ludwig an Georg Philipp Harsdörffer
        I. Anmerkungen zu Christian Gueintz' Gutachten über Harsdörffers *Specimen Philologiae Germanicae* (1646)
460819 Johann Valentin Andreae an Herzog August d. J. von Braunschweig-Wolfenbüttel
        I. Andreae sendet Herzog August einen von ihm kompilierten Index über das Gesellschaftsbuch von 1646
        II. (460725) Andreaes Vorrede auf Friedrich Greiffs Evangelienharmonie in Versen
460825 Martinus Milagius an die Leser seines *Singenden Jesaia*
        I. Erinnerungen Martinus Milagius' zur Orthographie
        II. Milagius' Vorrede zum Anhang seines *Singenden Jesaia*
        III. Widmung Martinus Milagius' an die Landgräfin Amalia Elisabeth von Hessen-Kassel
        IV. Fürst Ludwig an Martinus Milagius
        V. (460421) Fürst Ludwig an Martinus Milagius
        VI. Widmung Georg Philipp Harsdörffers an Martinus Milagius
460829 Johann Michael Moscherosch an Johann Rist
        I. Johann Rists Urteil über Moscheroschs *Gesichte Philanders von Sittewald*
460902 Fürst Ludwig an Georg Philipp Harsdörffer
460908 Herzog August d. J. von Braunschweig-Wolfenbüttel an Johann Valentin Andreae
        I. Beigelegte Notiz Andreaes über den Katalog seiner zu verkaufenden Bücher
        II. (461103) Andreae sendet Herzog August d. J. von Braunschweig-Wolfenbüttel einen Überschlag über seine zu verkaufende Büchersammlung
        III. Anderer Überschlag der Herzog August angebotenen Bücher Andreaes
460909 Johann Valentin Andreae an Herzog August d. J. von Braunschweig-Wolfenbüttel
        I. (460805) Andreae plant seine *Seleniana Augustalia* (1649)
460912 Georg Philipp Harsdörffer an Herzog August d. J. von Braunschweig-Wolfenbüttel
        I. Harsdörffers Gedicht auf die Helden der Fruchtbringenden Gesellschaft
        II. Übersicht der Texte und Kupferstiche in den Fassungen von Harsdörffers *Porticus Virtutis*
460915 Georg Philipp Harsdörffer an Christian Gueintz
460915A Carl Gustav von Hille an Fürst Ludwig
        I. Hille sendet Fürst Ludwig Abschriften Herzog Augusts d. J. von Braunschweig-Wolfenbüttel aus zwei Briefen Johann Valentin Andreaes
460916 Georg Philipp Harsdörffer an Fürst Ludwig

461006	Johann Dietrich von Brincken an Christian Ernst von Knoch
461020	Johann Rist an Johann Michael Moscherosch
461023	Matthäus Merian d. Ä. an Peter Knaudt
461026	Pfalzgraf Ludwig Philipp von Simmern an Fürst Ludwig
461029	Carl Gustav von Hille an Fürst Ludwig
461031	Fürst Ludwig an Georg Philipp Harsdörffer
461031A	Pfalzgraf Ludwig Philipp von Simmern an Fürst Ludwig
	I. A. Liste der von Pfalzgraf Ludwig Philipp von Simmern bis Ende Oktober 1646 aufgenommenen FG-Mitglieder
	B. Liste aller von Pfalzgraf Ludwig Philipp von Simmern aufgenommenen FG-Mitglieder (frühestens 28. Februar 1647)
461104	Johann Rist an Johann Heinrich Boeckler
	I. Johann Heinrich Boeckler auf Rists kaiserliche Dichterkrönung und Adelsverleihung
	II. Johann Michael Moscherosch auf Rists kaiserliche Dichterkrönung und Adelsverleihung
	III. Georg Philipp Harsdörffer auf Rists kaiserliche Dichterkrönung und Adelsverleihung
	IV. Johann Matthias Schneuber auf Rists kaiserliche Dichterkrönung und Adelsverleihung
461106	Fürst Ludwig an Carl Gustav von Hille
	I. Fürst Ludwigs Erklärung über die Aufnahme Johann Valentin Andreaes in die Fruchtbringende Gesellschaft
	II. Fürst Ludwig informiert Carl Gustav von Hille über den Ausführenden, Hans Ernst von Freyberg
461117	Herzog August d. J. von Braunschweig-Wolfenbüttel schickt Johann Valentin Andreae Fürst Ludwigs Aufnahmebrief
461124	Fürst Ludwig an Fürst Johann Casimir von Anhalt-Dessau
461204	Herzog August d. J. von Braunschweig-Wolfenbüttel schickt Johann Valentin Andreae einen Auszug aus Jacob Wellers Kritik an seiner *Evangelischen Kirchen-Harmonie*
461204A	Georg Philipp Harsdörffer an Herzog August d. J. von Braunschweig-Wolfenbüttel
461206	Fürst Johann Casimir von Anhalt-Dessau an Fürst Ludwig
461213	Fürst Ludwig an Georg Philipp Harsdörffer
461216	Johann Valentin Andreae an Herzog August d. J. von Braunschweig-Wolfenbüttel
	I. (461217) Andreaes lateinische Selbstverpflichtung gegenüber der Fruchtbringenden Gesellschaft
	II. Andreae über seine Aufnahme in die Fruchtbringende Gesellschaft

Liste der Briefschreiber und Verfasser von Beilagen

Andreae, Johann Valentin: 450219, 450319, 450806, 460715, 460715 I, 460819, 460819 I, 460819 II, 460908 I, 460908 II, 460908 III, 460909, 460909 I, 460915A I, 461216, 461216 I, 461216 II
Anhalt-Bernburg, Fürst Christian II. von: 440000 II
Anhalt-Dessau, Fürst Johann Casimir von: 450408, 450508A, 460422, 461206
Anhalt-Köthen, Fürst Ludwig von: 440127, 440130, 440209, 440310, 440310A I, 440313, 440723, 440723A, 440816 I, 440816 II, 441226, 441226A, 450124, 450127, 450220, 450220 I, 450221, 450224, 450317, 450317A, 450326, 450331, 450331 I, 450504, 450505, 450506, 450507, 450507 I, 450529, 450611, 450721, 450725 I, 450900, 450919A, 450921, 450923, 450923A, 450923B, 451028, 451028A, 451209, 451219, 460119, 460120, 460200, 460206 I, 460217, 460218, 460309, 460423, 460423 I, 460424, 460424A, 460424A I, 460426, 460609, 460705, 460705 I, 460705 II, 460708, 460714, 460816, 460816 I, 460825 IV, 460825 V, 460902, 461031, 461106, 461106 I, 461106 II, 461124, 461213
Anhalt-Plötzkau, Fürst August von: 440927
Beckmann, Christian: 440119
Beyer, Hans: 450503
Boeckler, Johann Heinrich: 440616 III, 461104 I
Brandenburg, Kurfürst Friedrich Wilhelm von: 460125, 460125 II
Braunschweig-Calenberg, Herzog Christian Ludwig von: 460301, 460403
Braunschweig-Wolfenbüttel, Herzog August d. J. von: 450722, 451001, 460127, 460317, 460804, 460908, 460915A I, 461117, 461204
Braunschweig-Wolfenbüttel, Herzog Rudolf August: 460613
Brincken, Johann Dietrich von: 461006
Buchner, Augustus: 460812
Castiglione, Valeriano: 440000 III
Dach, Simon: 460204 I
Dohna, Burggraf und Herr Achaz zu: 460120A
Fabritius, Adolph: 450305 I
Fontana, Francesco: 450817 III
Franckenberg, Abraham von: 440826
Freyberg, Wilhelm Heinrich von: 460103
Glasenapp, Joachim von: 460620A
Götze, Matthias: 450509, 450614, 460810
Gueintz, Christian: 440129, 440219, 440317, 440504, 440809, 441231, 450506A, 450508, 460720
Hainhofer, Philipp: 460715 II

Hammer, Johann: 450419, 450510
Harsdörffer, Georg Philipp: 440426, 440426 I, 440715, 440715A, 440731, 440731 I, 440731 II, 440824, 441020, 441200 II, 441223, 450400, 450410, 450817, 450817 I, 450817 V, 450901, 450923C, 450927, 450927 I, 450927 II, 451101, 451217, 460112, 460131, 460406, 460410, 460620, 460825 VI, 460912, 460912 I, 460915, 460916, 461104 III, 461204A
Hessen-Rotenburg, Landgraf Hermann IV. von: 441205, 450507A
Hille, Carl Gustav von: 440209A, 440323, 440323 I, 450126, 450308, 451008, 460718, 460915A, 460915A I, 461029
Knaudt, Peter: 450800, 460206 II
Loredano, Giovanni Francesco: 460000A
Mecklenburg-Güstrow, Herzogin Eleonora Maria: 450304
Merian, Matthäus d. Ä.: 450417, 450711, 450905, 450922, 450930, 451015, 451028B, 451119, 460206, 460303, 460324, 460519, 460620B, 460703, 461023
Milagius, Martinus: 460825, 460825 I, 460825 II, 460825 III
Mortaigne dit de Pottelles, Gaspard Corneille: 451030
Moscherosch, Johann Michael: 440525, 440616, 440616 I, 440616 II, 450818, 450818 I, 460726, 460829, 461104 II
Polhelm, Winand von: 440809A, 450305, 450526
Prüschenk von Lindenhofen, Zacharias: 441010
Rist, Johann: 440724, 441216, 441216 I, 460829 I, 461020, 461104
Sachsen-Gotha, Herzog Ernst I. von: 450217
Sachsen-Lauenburg, Herzog Franz Carl von: 460808
Sachsen-Weimar, Herzogin Eleonora Dorothea von: 450301
Schill, Johann Heinrich: 440525 II
Schlesien zu Liegnitz und Wohlau, Herzog Georg Rudolph in: 460721
Schneuber, Johann Matthias: 440525 I, 461104 IV
Schottelius, Justus Georg: 440100, 440100 I, 440100 II, 440400, 440400 I, 440429, 440900, 441000, 441011, 441200, 441200 I, 441231A, 450000, 450100, 450100 I, 450200, 450202, 450204, 450929, 451000, 451007, 451100, 451100 I, 460000, 460000 I, 460000 II, 460100, 460200A, 460414, 460700, 460803
Severino, Marco Aurelio: 450817 II, 450817 IV, 450817 VI
Simmern, Pfalzgraf Ludwig Philipp von: 460104, 460321, 461026, 461031A
Steger, Christoph: 460315
Tscherning, Andreas: 440324, 440324 I, 450726, 450726 I, 460610
Weller, Jacob: 461204
Wendelin, Marcus Friedrich: 451220
Werder, Diederich von dem: 440000, 440000 I, 440204, 440204 I, 440310A, 440310A II, 440310B, 440816, 450124 I, 450325, 450420, 450500, 450504A, 450505A, 450613, 450725, 450730, 450919, 450921A, 460204, 460705 III
Winckler, Georg: 451019
Zesen, Philipp von: 441201, 450000A, 450308A, 450808, 450808 I

Liste der Briefempfänger und Adressaten von Beilagen

Andreae, Johann Valentin: 440429, 450722, 460127, 460317, 460414, 460804, 460908, 460915A I, 461117, 461204
Anhalt-Bernburg, Fürst Christian II. von: 450304, 450326, 460125, 460613, 460714
Anhalt-Dessau, Fürst Johann Casimir von: 460104, 460424, 461124
Anhalt-Köthen, Fürst Ludwig von: 440129, 440204, 440209A, 440219, 440310A, 440317, 440323, 440504, 440715, 440809, 440809A, 440816, 441205, 441231, 450124 I, 450126, 450204, 450217, 450301, 450305, 450308, 450325, 450400, 450408, 450420, 450500, 450504A, 450505A, 450506A, 450507A, 450508, 450508A, 450526, 450613, 450725, 450817, 450919, 450921A, 450923C, 451001, 451007, 451008, 451030, 451101, 451217, 451220, 460103, 460120A, 460125, 460206 II, 460301, 460321, 460403, 460406, 460422, 460620, 460620A, 460705 III, 460718, 460720, 460721, 460726, 460812, 460915A, 460915A I, 460916, 461026, 461029, 461031A, 461206
Anhalt-Plötzkau, Fürst August von: 460125
Apelles von Löwenstern, Matthaeus: 440324, 450726, 460610
Boeckler, Johann Heinrich: 440616, 440616 II, 461104
Braunschweig-Calenberg, Herzog Christian Ludwig von: 440715A, 440723, 450923, 460218, 460309
Braunschweig-Wolfenbüttel, Herzog Anton Ulrich von: 451100 I
Braunschweig-Wolfenbüttel, Herzog August d. J. von: 440100, 440100 I, 440323 I, 440400, 440400 I, 440731, 440731 I, 440900, 441000, 441011, 441200, 441231A, 450000, 450100, 450100 I, 450200, 450202, 450219, 450319, 450331, 450721, 450726 I, 450806, 450923A, 450927, 450927 I, 450929, 451000, 451100, 460000, 460000 I, 460000 II, 460100, 460112, 460200A, 460700, 460715, 460715 II, 460808, 460819, 460819 I, 460908 I, 460908 II, 460908 III, 460909, 460909 I, 460912, 461204A, 461216
Braunschweig-Wolfenbüttel, Herzogin Sophia Elisabeth von: 440731 II, 441200 I, 450927 II
Burgsdorff, Conrad von: 440000, 460204
Clepius, Christian: 460315
Colerus, Christophorus: 440119
Dieskau, Hans von: 450507
Dohna, Burggraf und Herr Achaz zu: 460217
Einsiedel, Curt von: 441226
Fruchtbringende Gesellschaft: 440426, 440824, 441201, 460912 I, 461216 I
Fürer von Haimendorf, Georg Sigmund: 460410

Gueintz, Christian: 440127, 440209, 440313, 441226A, 450504, 450507 I, 451219, 460131, 460200, 460915
Hainhofer, Philipp: 460715 I
Hammer, Johann: 450503, 450509
Harsdörffer, Georg Philipp: 440204 I, 440616 I, 440616 III, 450124, 450529, 450611, 450808, 450808 I, 450817 II, 450817 III, 450818, 450919A, 451209, 460000A, 460120, 460426, 460609, 460705, 460705 I, 460803, 460816, 460902, 461031, 461213
Hessen-Kassel, Landgräfin Amalia Elisabeth: 460825 III
Hessen-Rotenburg, Landgraf Hermann IV. von: 440317
Hille, Carl Gustav von: 440130, 440310, 440723A, 450221, 451028, 460119, 461106, 461106 II
Knaudt, Peter: 440310B, 450127, 450417, 450419, 450510, 450614, 450711, 450905, 450922, 450930, 451015, 451019, 451028B, 451119, 460206, 460206 I, 460303, 460324, 460519, 460620B, 460703, 460708, 460810, 461023
Knoch, Christian Ernst von: 450730, 461006
Machner, Matthias: 440324 I
Merian, Matthäus d. Ä.: 450800
Milagius, Martinus: 460825 IV, 460825 V, 460825 VI
Moscherosch, Johann Michael: 450901, 461020
Polhelm, Winand von: 450305 I, 450317A, 450506
Rist, Johann: 460829, 461104 I, 461104 II, 461104 III, 461104 IV
Rompler von Löwenhalt, Jesaias: 450308A
Sachsen-Gotha, Herzog Ernst I. von: 450224
Sachsen-Weimar, Herzog Wilhelm IV. von: 440927, 450220
Sachsen-Weimar, Herzogin Eleonora Dorothea von: 450220 I
Schill, Johann Heinrich: 440525, 440525 I
Schottelius, Justus Georg: 441020, 441216, 441216 I, 450000A, 450923B, 451028A
Simmern, Pfalzgraf Ludwig Philipp von: 460423, 460423 I, 460424A
Sturm, Gottfried: 440826
Volckamer, Johann Georg: 450817 VI
Werder, Diederich von dem: 450505, 450921, 460125 II, 460204 I
Zesen, Philipp von: 440724, 441223, 450410

Zu den Abbildungen

Vor dem Titel: *Vorderseite des Schilds der Fruchtbringenden Gesellschaft* (um 1650). HAAB Weimar: Ge 644/1980.

Beschreibung in *DA Köthen I. 1*, S. 77–80, vgl. *DA Köthen I. 2*, S. 85; Gabi Schwitalla: Die Gemälde des 16. und der ersten Hälfte des 17. Jahrhunderts in der Herzogin Anna Amalia Bibliothek zu Weimar. Halle 1994 (Dipl.arb. masch.schr.), 159 ff.

S. 163. *Feierlicher Einzug Hz. Augusts d. J. v. Braunschweig-Wolfenbüttel* (FG 227) *in Wolfenbüttel, 17. 9. 1643, vor der Kirche Beatae Mariae Virginis.* Zu 440100.

Die Festungs- und Residenzstadt Wolfenbüttel blieb nach ihrer Eroberung durch den ksl. General Gf. Gottfried Heinrich v. Pappenheim im Dezember 1627 fast 16 Jahre besetzt, so daß Hz. August erst nach dem Frieden von Goslar (1642) im September 1643 in die Festung einziehen konnte. Erst im Folgejahr verließ er jedoch seine zeitweilige Residenz in Braunschweig. S. unten, zu 440100 I.
Triumphengel schwebend über der Kirche (Nordansicht der am Kornmarkt gelegenen prächtigen Renaissancekirche, einem der ersten protestantischen Kirchenbauten Deutschlands). Posaune (mit seitenverkehrtem Schriftzug „VICTORIA") und Friedenswedel. Der Engel hält ein Medaillon mit dem Brustbild Hz. Augusts. 1. Stich in einer Serie von 4 Stichen mit Ansichten der Kirche. S. unten zu 461204.
Unter dem Bild lat. Verse des hzl. Leibarztes Martin Gosky (M. G.), darunter Datum.

Zeichner Albert Freyse (Adresse an der Nordwestecke der Kirche; teilweise nach Elias Holweins Holzschnitt von 1625), Kupferstich von Sebastian Furck (um 1600–1655).

In: Heinrich Wideburg: Denkwürdige Danksagungs-Predigt. Wolfenbüttel: Sterne 1646, Bl. nach S. 91. Freundliche Auskunft von Eelco Nagelsmit.
HAB: Gn 13488 (dig.); 168.1 Quod. (9) (dig.); T 904. 2° Helmst. (1). Auch Nachstich in *Gosky: Arbustum (1650)*, Bl. zw. 283v u. 284r (dig.).

Lit.: *Schottelius*, 45; *Sammler Fürst Gelehrter*, Nr. 150 (Abb.); *Brecht: Andreae u. Hz. August*, 260 (Abb.).

S. 169. *Justus Georg Schottelius: Ode Auff neue Pindarische Art* (1643). Zu 440100 I.

Die im Deutschen als neuartig geltende Pindarische Ode könnte Justus Georg Schottelius (FG 397) aus Anlaß des Einzugs Hz. Augusts in Wolfenbüttel im September 1643 oder mit Blick auf dessen bevorstehende tatsächliche Übersiedlung in das Residenzschloß (26. 2. 1644) geschrieben haben. Das angegebene Druckjahr 1643 ist hier nicht entscheidend.

Schottelius: Pindarische Ode (1643). Einblattdruck.
HAB: Sign.: G3: A36. Zum Wiederabdruck des Gedichts s. 440100 I Q.

S. 187. *Fürst Ludwig: Der weise Alte (1643), Titelblatt mit Besitzvermerk Carl Gustav v. Hilles* (FG 302. Der Unverdrossene) *von 1644*. Zu 440130.

Mit dem Brief 440130 sandte F. Ludwig dem Wolfenbütteler Frauenhofmeister Hille, der im Auftrag Hz. Augusts d. J. v. Braunschweig-Wolfenbüttel (FG 227) den fruchtbringerischen Schriftwechsel mit dem Köthener Erzschrein führte, seine Übersetzung von Simon de Goularts (de Senlis) Erbauungsbuch Le Sage Vieillard. Das hier gezeigte Titelblatt dürfte nach Ausweis der Besitzeintragung Hilles zu dem ihm geschenkten Exemplar gehören. Nachdem die Übersetzung spätestens schon im Juli 1643 in Köthen gedruckt worden war, erhielt F. Ludwig von einem unbekannten Sender ein Sonett, das wir in 431206 II veröffentlicht haben. Wie im vorliegenden Schreiben F. Ludwigs an Carl Gustav v. Hille hatte der Fürst dieses Sonett in seinen Briefen 431206 und 431211 schon an Georg Philipp Harsdörffer (FG 368) bzw. an F. Christian II. v. Anhalt-Bernburg (FG 51) geschickt.

Fürst Ludwig: Der weise Alte (1643). Titelblatt.
HAB: 23.3 Eth. 1 (dig.).
Lit.: *DA Köthen I.6*, S. 779 u. 781 (Sonett); *Bepler: Hille*, 289 f.

S. 286. *Georg Philipp Harsdörffers* (FG 368) „*Vbereigungsgedicht AN den NEHRENDEN*". Zu 440715.

In seinem Widmungsgedicht (Bl. [A iv] v – [A vi] r) an F. Ludwig (FG 2. Der Nährende) verwendet Harsdörffer 2 emblematische Holzschnitt-Initialen:
1. Zierinitiale A mit der Kokospalme, die die Nutzbarkeit der Fruchtbringenden Gesellschaft ausdrückt. Vgl. z. B. den Schild der Akademie (mit der Devise „Alles Zu Nutzen") vor jedem Band unserer Ausgabe.
2. Zierinitiale N im Namen des „NEHRENDEN" mit einer Weizengarbe. Der Fürst kritisierte diese Garbe, da seine Imprese keine Garbe, sondern ein ausgebackenes Weizenbrot zeigt. S. 440715 K 2.
3. Zierinitiale E mit Brustbild Fürst Ludwigs.

S. 287. *Georg Philipp Harsdörffers* (FG 368) *Doppelimprese "Es Nützet vnd behagt Auff manche art" mit einem auslegenden Gedicht: "Erklärung."* Zu 440715.

Nach den letzten beiden, hier nicht abgebildeten Seiten des Widmungsgedichts (Text s. 440715) erscheint die Pictura einer Doppelimprese Harsdörffers, die in der Mitte von der Kokospalme der Fruchtbringenden Gesellschaft gespalten wird. Die Schriftrolle (LINKS: „Es Nützet vnd behagt", RECHTS: „Auff manche art") über der rechten Abbildung ahmt die Imprese des Spielenden in seiner Fruchtbringer-Imprese nach. Auch der Gesellschaftsname wird angegeben (Bl. [A vi] v).

Rechts und links 2 halbe von Kletterpflanzen (Efeu) umwundene Obstbäume, die zusammen mit dem Erdreich und den Laubkronen den Durchblick auf den Hintergrund mit Garten und Gebäuden umrahmen. RECHTS: Schloßanlage mit Laubengängen vor der Gesellschaftspflanze Harsdörffers (*GB 1646* Nr. 368. „Bunte Bönelein"), die von einem Rondell von Beeten umrundet ist, das selbst von der Umschrift „DER SPIELENDE" umringt wird. Die schloßartige Anlage im Hintergrund ahmt auch in seinen Laubengängen das Gebäude in der Imprese des Spielenden im Gesellschaftsbuch von 1646 nach. Es besteht wohl keine Ähnlichkeit mit einem Besitz Harsdörffers, da die Bilder („Gemälde") nach den Entwürfen der Gesellschaftsmaler F. Ludwigs gestochen wurden.

LINKS: Die Devise „Es Nützet vnd behagt." wird durch das ‚Wort' in der rechten Impresenhälfte zu einem Satz ergänzt. Eine Art Gartenhaus mit Laubengängen und einem Brunnen vor einer großen Sonnenuhr, bestehend aus einem Rondell von Beeten um eine Weinrebe, umringt von den römischen Ziffern der 12 Stunden.

Neben der Doppelimprese das Gedicht (Subscriptio) zur „Erklärung" der voranstehenden Pictura (Bl. [A vii] r). Es enthält:
4. Zierinitiale N mit einer Sonnenuhr (welche auch im Gartenbild der Pictura erscheint).

Harsdörffer: Frauenzimmer-Gesprächspiele, 1. Teil (Nürnberg ²1644). Auf der Rückseite des Titelblatts und Bl. A v der Anfang des durch den „Spielenden" (Harsdörffer) d. d. Nürnberg 15. 9. 1644 gezeichneten „Vbereigungsgedicht[s]", gefolgt auf Bl. [vj]v u. Bl. [vij]r von der Pictura und Subscriptio („Erklärung.") einer Imprese Georg Philipp Harsdörffers.
Text u. Erläuterungen dazu in 440715 K 1–3.
HAB: Lo 2622:1 (dig.).

S. 290. *Die FG-Imprese Georg Philipp Harsdörffers* (FG 368) *aus dem GB 1646*. Zu 440715.

Als Harsdörffer in die Fruchtbringende Gesellschaft aufgenommen wurde, erhielt er als Imprese neben dem Gesellschaftsnamen *Der Spielende* „die kleinen bunten Englischen **Bönlein**/ unterschiedener Farben/ und zum Worte/ **auff**

manche Art" (410909). Stattdessen schlug er vor die „welschen *Böhnlein* (massen er noch Zur Zeit von den Englischen Bohnen keine nachricht in den Kräuterbüchern befinden können) in welchen die Natur *auf manche art* zu spielen pfleget" (411126). Phaseolus vulgaris L., die Gartenbohne. Leonhart Fuchs schreibt in seinem *New Kreuterbuch* (Basel: Michael Jsengrin 1543), Cap. 269: „Ein yede schott hat inn jhr frucht vnd körner/ deren seind ettlich rot/ ettlich leibfarb/ mit schwartzen flecken besprengt/ ettlich leberfarb/ auch besprengt/ ettlich schneeweiß/ ettlich weißgraw/ ettlich geel." *Conermann III*, 428. Vgl. oben in Harsdörffers Doppelimprese (zu 440715) Pflanze, Schloßgarten, Schloß.

Kupferstich aus der Werkstatt Matthäus Merians d. Ä. in *GB 1646*, Bl. Bbbbb ij r.
HAB: 17.4.1 Eth.

S. 345. *Die gegenseitige Blockade der kaiserlichen und der schwedischen Armee vor Bernburg 1644*. Zu 440927.

Kupferstich. Stadt und Schloß Bernburg beiderseits der Saale, umgebende Orte im Fürstentum Anhalt, die befestigten Lager der kaiserlichen und schwedischen Truppen. Legende A–K zu den beiden Hauptquartieren mit Bezeichnung der Flügel und Batterien. Zur militärischen Lage s. 440927 K.

DELINEATIO CASTRORUM TAM CÆSAREANORUM QUAM SVECORUM, EORUNDEMQ. CIRCUM VALACIONIS, APUD BERNBURGUM M. DC. XLIV. Kaÿßrisch vnd Schwedisch lager beÿ Bernburg.

Aus *Theatrum europaeum*, 5. Teil: 1643–1647. Frankfurt a. M. 1647.
HAB: 70.1 Hist. 2°, nach S. 146.

S. 368. *Bildnis der Herzogin Sophia Elisabeth von Braunschweig-Wolfenbüttel* (AL 1629. TG 42b) *mit Versen von Justus Georg Schottelius* (FG 397). Zu 441200 I.

Hüftbild der noch jungen Hzn. Sophia Elisabeth, geb. Hzn. v. Mecklenburg-Güstrow (1613–1676), die 1635 die 3. Gemahlin Hz. Augusts d. J. v. Braunschweig-Wolfenbüttel (FG 227) geworden war. Dasselbe Porträt wurde 1645 inmitten eines Kokospalmenhains als Brustbild auf einer Säule nochmals in *Harsdörffer: Frauenzimmer-Gesprächspiele* V, 9 (Ndr.) veröffentlicht. Vgl. 450927 K II 0.
Kupferstich von Conrad Buno und Verse von Justus Georg Schottelius (FG 397), gez.: „J. G. Schottelius. Subiectissima observantia ergò ad vivum exsculpsit et dedicat Conr. Buno." Dieses Porträt wurde nicht mehr in *Schottelius: Teutsche Vers- oder ReimKunst (1656)* veröffentlicht.

Schottelius: Teutsche Vers- oder ReimKunst (1645). Bl. [Aiij]r.
HAB: 172.1 Poet.; SUB Göttingen: 8 P GERM I, 1290 (dig.).

S. 369. *Georg Philipp Harsdörffers (FG 368) Madrigal auf das Porträt der Herzogin.* Zu 441200 II.

Französisches Madrigal auf das vorhergehende Bildnis, gez. G. P. Harsdorf.
Schottelius: Teutsche Vers- oder ReimKunst (1645), Bl. [Aiij]v. Fehlt in *Schottelius: Teutsche Vers- oder ReimKunst (1656)*.

S. 381. *Johann Rist (FG 467. 1647) auf Justus Georg Schottelius (FG 397) als Perlenfischer.* Zu 441216.

Emblematisches „Sinne Bild" Johann Rists mit Inscriptio an den Widmungsempfänger Schottelius, mit einer Subscriptio, von der wir nur den Anfang des Gedichts abbilden. S. Text in 441216.
Schottelius, dem Meer entsteigend und unter seinem rechten Arm ein Netz, zeigt zwei Muschelhälften, deren eine eine Perle enthält. Über sein Haupt hält eine aus Wolken hervorragende Hand einen Lorbeerkranz. Im Vordergrund etliche andere Muscheln. Vgl. die Beschreibung in 441216 T b.
Kupferstich von Conrad Buno höchstwahrscheinlich nach einer Zeichnung von Johann Rist.

Schottelius: Teutsche Vers- oder ReimKunst (1645), Bl. b v. HAB: 172.1 Poet.
Auch in *Schottelius: Teutsche Vers- oder ReimKunst (1656)*, Bl. b v.
HAB: Um 180 (1).
Lit: *Conermann: Rist*, S. 85 f.

S. 428 f. *Hofgesellschaft Herzog Augusts d. J. v. Braunschweig-Wolfenbüttel (FG 227) in Wolfenbüttel.* Zu 450126.

Die Braunschweiger Hofgesellschaft um die hzl. Familie. Etwa 1645. In der Mitte Hz. August d. J. (FG 227) mit Jacobus Lampadius beim Schachspiel, worüber der Herzog unter dem Kryptonym Gustavus Selenus ein Buch geschrieben hatte (Das Schach- oder König-Spiel. 1616). Der bisher nicht identifizierte Lampadius (1593–1649), ein bedeutender Staatsrechtler, hatte an der Universität Helmstedt gelehrt, wurde 1623 Hofrat Hz. Friedrich Ulrichs v. Braunschweig-Wolfenbüttel (FG 38), dann Rat und Vizekanzler (1641) Hz. Georgs v. Braunschweig-Calenberg (FG 231) bzw. Christian Ludwigs (FG 372). Er vertrat diesen und die welf. Lande auf dem Westfälischen Friedenskongreß. Nicht nachgewiesen wurden bisher auch 2 Personen hinten in der rechten Ecke des Saals: 1. der jugendlich wirkende Präzeptor Pz. Anton Ulrichs (FG 716. 1659), Pz. Ferdinand Albrechts (FG 842. 1673) und einiger Prinzessinnen v. Braunschweig-Wolfenbüttel, der Philologe und Dichter Justus Georg Schottelius (FG 397. Der Suchende), blond, roter Wams; vgl. Bildnis zu 421110 u. *DA Köthen I. 6*, S. 118. Schottelius schickte dieses Kupferstichporträt im Dokument 460414 an Johann Valentin Andreae (s. unten); 2. Carl Gustav v. Hille (FG 302. Der Unverdrossene), olivbrauner Wams u. Degengehenk, braune Locken; vgl. Porträt in *Hille: Teutscher Palmbaum* (1647), dem ersten Buch über die Fruchtbringende Gesellschaft.

Links die hzl. Kinder beim Gambenkonzert um eine Cembalo-Spielerin, die in der Literatur oft als Hzn. Sophia Elisabeth v. Braunschweig-Wolfenbüttel (geb. 1613) identifiziert wird, wogegen Geck das jugendliche Alter der Cembalistin ins Feld führt. Dieser Einwand muß nicht stimmen, vergleicht man das jugendliche Aussehen der Fürstin auf dem Porträt zu 441200 mit dem Gemälde. Ist es die älteste Pzn. Sibylla Ursula (geb. 1629) oder eine unbekannte Dame? Sie sitzt zwischen links Pz. Rudolf August (FG 754. 1660; geb. 1627) und rechts Pz. Anton Ulrich (geb. 1633). Der kleine Prinz ist Ferdinand Albrecht v. Braunschweig-Bevern (geb. 1636). Von den übrigen jungen Damen und Mädchen kommt unter den Töchtern Hz. Augusts außer Pzn. Sibylla Ursula altersmäßig noch Pzn. Clara Augusta (geb. 1632) in Frage, kaum junge Verwandte (*Geck*, 53). Hz. Augusts braunschweig-dannenberg. Nichte, Hzn. Maria Catharina v. Mecklenburg-Schwerin [geb. 1616, seit 1635 Gemahlin Hz. Adolph Friedrichs I. FG 175], aus der calenberg. Linie auch wohl nicht Hzn. Sophia Amalia (geb. 1628), die schon 1643 Friedrich III. v. Dänemark geheiratet hatte. 2 Güstrower Schwestern der Herzogin sind ihrem Alter nach noch in Erwägung zu ziehen: Hzn. Christina Margaretha v. Sachsen-Lauenburg (geb. 1615; Wwe. v. Hz. Franz Albrecht FG 194) und Pzn. Anna Sophia v. Mecklenburg-Güstrow (geb. 1628). Am wahrscheinlichsten handelt es sich bei den übrigen Streicherinnen aber einfach um Mitglieder des hzl. Frauenzimmers — ausgenommen Pzn. Sibylla Ursula und Pzn. Clara Augusta. Die komponierende und musizierende Herzogin muß mangels eines professionellen Orchesters solche Frauen ebenso wie ihre Söhne und Töchter zum Spielen herangezogen haben. Dann wäre die Cellistin aber doch Hzn. Sophia Elisabeth selbst. Geck, a. a. O., spekuliert: „Sie dürfte [...] die Dame zur Linken des Regenten sein, die mit verklärtem Blick dem Spiel der Gruppe lauscht."

Öl auf Leinwand von Albert Freyse (?). Höhe 1344 mm, Breite 1827 mm. Landesmuseum Braunschweig: Inv.-Nr.: VMB 3278.

Häufig stark verkleinert oder ausschnittsweise abgebildet, z.B. *Sammler Fürst Gelehrter*, Nr. 592. Zu Lampadius s. Kupferstich in: *Pacificatores* (1697), Nr. 89; *Sammler Fürst Gelehrter*, Nr. 154 (mit Lit.) — Lit.: *Geck*, 53; Linda M. Koldau: Frauen, Musik, Kultur. Köln 2005, 198; Susanne Rode-Breymann: Lexikon Musik und Gender. Hg. Annette Kreutziger-Herr, Melanie Unseld, Kassel 2010, 75; Meike Buck: Albert Freyse: Gambenkonzert. In: Tatort Geschichte. 120 Jahre Spurensuche im Braunschweigischen Landesmuseum. Petersberg 2011, 128f.; zu Lampadius s. jüngst die Dissertation von Tina Braun: Der welfische Gesandte Jakob Lampadius auf dem Westfälischen Friedenskongress (1644–1649). U. Bonn 2015. http://hss.ulb.uni-bonn.de/2015/4104/4104.htm

S. 458. *Schriftproben der Köthener Druckerei.* Zu 450224.

Druckschriftproben mit handschriftlichen Anmerkungen. Deutsche, lateinische, griechische, hebräische und syrische Schriftgattungen und -grade der Köthener Presse F. Ludwigs. Lettern waren nach 1631 schon nach Weimar (2872 Pfd.) geliefert worden, so daß die hebräischen und griechischen Lettern aus den übrigen,

in Köthen verbliebenen Schriften (2068 Pfd.) Hz. Ernst v. Sachsen-Gotha (FG 19) zum Tausch gegen Wein zur Verfügung standen. Vgl. 450224.
LHA Sa.-Anh./ Dessau: Z 18, Abt. Köthen C 18 Nr. 53, Bl. 85r.

Lit.: Abb. u. Erklärung in *Conermann: Fürstl. Offizin*, 164f. (einschl. Anm. 114).

S. 574f. *Fürst Ludwigs Entwürfe* (2 Seiten) *eines Titelblatts* (Gesellschaftsbuch 1646) *für Merian*. Zu 450711.

Abschrift der Entwürfe für die Drucktitel des 1. und 2. Hunderts der Impresen des *GB 1646*. Das 1. Titelblatt sollte vor die Beschreibung des Zwecks und Vorhabens („Kurtzer Bericht Von der Fruchtbringenden Geselschaft Zwecke und Vorhaben") gesetzt werden, so daß das Vorhaben nicht mehr im 2. Titelblatt genannt wurde. Darauf folgen im Druck vor jedem Hundert der 400 Mitgliederimpresen das „Kling-Gedicht" auf die Akademie und der von Matthäus Merian d. Ä. schon für das *GB 1629/30* geschaffene und signierte Kupferstich der Gesellschaftsimprese (in *Conermann I* u. Abb. zu 310000 I [Beschreibung *DA Köthen I. 3*, S. 104f.]).
HM Köthen: V S 546, Bl. 163rv.

S. 604. *Merians Yucca gloriosa L. Vorbild für die Imprese Jobst Heimarts von Lenthe* (FG 384). Zu 450800. Abb. I.

Kupferstich. Der Titel des Blatts lautet: „HYIVCCA sive Yucca Canadana, nostris nunc Iucca gloriosa Indorum, ad vivum delineata." Vgl. auch *Conermann II*, 101. Auf dem Blatt mit der Yucca-Pflanze, Nr. 142, heißt es zur Herkunft der Pflanze und in sämtlichen von uns konsultierten Exemplaren: „Floruit Basileae A. C. M. DCXLIV. Mense Septembri, in hortulo Remigii Feschii I. C. flore tam copioso et hactenus inaudito, ut flores, numeratis etiam calicibus clausis, ramis 26. distinctis, protulerit 281." Das offenbar 1644 dem *Florilegium* (1641) seines Schwiegervaters Johann Theodor de Bry hinzugefügte Kupfer ist sehr selten, es fehlt auch im Exemplar HAB: 21.5 Phys. 2°. Über die Schwierigkeiten der Beschaffung einer Visierung und über die damals in Europa noch sehr seltene nordamerikanische Pflanze (Yucca gloriosa L.) s. *Conermann II*, 100f. und III, 450f., vgl. auch 450800 K 4. Vgl. 450930, 451015 u. 451119.

In: Johann Theodor de Bry: Florilegium Renovatum Et Auctum: Das ist: Vernewertes und vermehrtes Blumenbuch (Frankfurt: Merian 1641), [Nr.] 142 (doppelseitige gefaltete Tafel, die dem Band nachträglich eingeklebt wurde).
SB München: RES/ 2 Oecon. 40. (Exlibris: Biblioth. Bosian. Hortens. i. e. Garten des Leipziger Rats- und Handelsherrn Georg Bose [1650–1700])

Auch UB Heidelberg: O 3040 Folio RES (u. Dig.); Hunt Institute for Botanical Documentation, Carnegie-Mellon University, Pittsburgh/PA, USA (danach beschrieben in *Conermann III*, 100, Anm. 121).

Einem in der Widmung des dritten Teils von *Harsdörffer: Poetischer Trichter*, Bl. a ij r – a v v als FG-Mitglied apostrophierten, jedoch nie in die Gesellschaft aufgenommenen Kandidaten, nämlich dem Hamburger Ratsherrn u. schwed. Residenten Vincent Moller (1610–1668), Nachfolger von Johan Adler Salvius, hatte Harsdörffer die Gesellschaftspflanze Yucca gloriosa L. (hier: Juca gloriosa, Bl. a v r) zugeschrieben. Vgl. zur Nichtaufnahme Vincent Mollers und seines entfernten Verwandten Eberhart Moller ausführlich mit Literaturangaben *Conermann: Rist*, 72–75 u. demnächst *DA Köthen I. 8:* 470927.

Ein Mitglied der Leopoldina, der Gießener Physik- und Medizinprofessor Michael Bernhard Valentini (1657–1729), verwendete 233 Kupferplatten des *GB 1646* für Abbildungen von Pflanzen in seinem Werk: Viridarium Reformatum, Seu Regnum Vegetabile, Das ist: Neu-eingerichtetes und Vollständiges Kräuter-Buch, Worinnen auff noch nicht geschehene Weise Derer Vegetabilien/ als Kräutern/ Sträuchen/ Bäumen, Bluhmen und anderer Erd-Gewachsen Art, Krafft und Würckung dergestalt beschrieben werden, daß man dieses Werck statt einer Botanischen Bibliothec haben/ jedes Kraut zu seiner rechten Haupt-Art bringen, auch dessen Nutzen in der Artzney deutlich und umständlich finden ... Und endlich denen Liebhabern Göttlicher Wunder in der Natur ein Opus Mago-Cabalisticum eines wahrhafften Adepti beygefüget ... Von D. Mich. Bernh. Valentini (Frankfurt a. M. 1719). HAB: Ng 2° 16. Valentini besprach das Gewächs S. 355 zusammen mit vielen von ihm Aloe genannten Arten, obgleich er die Yucca gloriosa nicht zur selben Gattung stellte. Für die Abbildung benutzte er in diesem Fall nicht den Kupferstich des *GB 1646*, sondern einen blaß wirkenden Abzug des Merian-Stichs mit dem vollen ursprünglichen Text. Die Platte war also offenbar schon stark für Abzüge gebraucht worden (Tab. CCXIX). Auf der im Anhang folgenden Tab. CCXX ließ er (neben anderen Blumen) eine vergrößerte Teilansicht des Blütenstengels der Yucca folgen. Hierzu vermerkte er auf der Teilansicht: „Iuca Nova gloriosa. Ab Anglis ex India advecta & primò flores in omnibus ramis suis octaginta supra centum tulit. folium ejus americano aloe simile est, non tamen adeò crassum. Quotannis ferè floret, frigusque non timet."

S. 605. *Die Yucca-Imprese Jobst Heimarts von Lenthe* (FG 384). Zu 450800. Abb. II.

Die Imprese des *GB 1646* (FG 384 Jobst Heimart v. Lenthe. Der Schönblühende) wurde nach einem Kupferstich Matthäus Merians d. Ä. in dessen Werkstatt vereinfacht und verkleinert nachgestochen. Die 25 Stengel der Rispe wurden auf 16 verringert, auf einige nach unten weisende Blätter und auf den Pflanzenkübel in der Vorlage verzichtete man ganz. Statt dreier abgefallener Blüten zeigt das ‚Gemälde' des Gesellschaftsbuchs nur zwei.

Der Hintergrund der Pictura ist seitenverkehrt nach dem der Imprese FG 75 (Ernst v. Freyberg) gezeichnet. Vgl. schon *GB 1629/30* (*Conermann I*).

Eine unbekannte Hand schrieb den Taufnamen Lenthes unter die Initialen des Drucks.

Kupferstich aus der Werkstatt Matthäus Merians d. Ä. in *GB 1646*, Bl. Fffff ij r.
HAB: 17.4.1 Eth.

S. 627. *Zwei Mondansichten für F. Ludwig* (FG 2) *aus den Händen Marco Aurelio Severinos.* Zu 450817 III. Abb. I u. II.

Der Arzt Marco Aurelio Severino, ein Mitglied der Neapolitaner Accademia degli Oziosi, schickte Georg Philipp Harsdörffer (FG 368) neben medizinischen und sprachkritischen Materialien auch 2 Ansichten des Monds, die der Neapolitaner Francesco Fontana nach eigenen Beobachtungen gezeichnet hatte. Diese aus den Jahren 1629 und 1630 datierten und sehr genauen astronomischen Entdeckungen von Sonnenflecken nach dem Vorbild Galileo Galileis erreichten F. Ludwig noch vor ihrer Veröffentlichung. S. 450817 K III.
HM Köthen: V S 545, Bl. 317v–318r.
Lit.: *Conermann: Harsdörffers Plan.*

S. 629. *Titelblatt* La Querela della & accorciata (1644) *u. Imprese Severinos.* Zu 450817 IV. Abb. I u. II.

LA QVERELA | Della (&) accorciata | SCHERZO | DI MARC'AVRELIO | SEVERINO, | Philosopho, & Medico Napoletano, Academico Otioso, | Detto L'Assettato. | ALL' ILLVSTRISSIMO SIGNORE | CASSIANO DAL POZZO, | Commendatore dell'Ordine di S. Stephano. | [Kupferstich: im breitovalen Rahmen eine &-förmig gewundene gekrönte Schlange; Subscriptio: „Hor chi fia mai, che scioglia", Stellenangabe: (Giovanni della) „Casa Canz. 2"] | IN NAPOLI, Per Camillo Cauallo. MDCXLIV.
Auf der Titelrückseite in einem Lorbeerkranz die Imprese Marco Aurelio Severinos (1589–1656): ein geometrischer Würfel (Pictura) mit der Inscriptio „VNDIQVE COMPAR." Sein Gesellschaftsname in der Accademia degli Oziosi L'Assettato (Der Geordnete) läßt sich unmittelbar auf seine Pictura beziehen. Vgl. 450817 Q u. K IV 2.
HM Köthen: V S 545, Bl. 319rv.

S. 682 f. *Schlacht von Alerheim am 3. August 1645.* Zu 450905.

Unter dem Kommando des bayer. Generals Frh. Franz v. Mercy (FG 364), unterstützt von Johann v. Werth und dem kurköln. General Gf. Gottfried Huyn Frh. v. Geleen, verloren die Ligisten am 3. 8. 1645 (n. St.) die Schlacht von Alerheim (Lkr. Nördlingen) gegen die Franzosen unter Henri II de Bourbon prince de Condé duc d'Enghien und die hessen-kasselschen Truppen unter Johann v. Geyso. Im Rücken von der Wörnitz und auf den Flügeln von ihrer befestigten Stellung auf dem Winnenberg und von der Schloßruine von Alerheim gedeckt, trafen die Bayern in Alerheim (wo Mercy durch einen Kopfschuß getötet wurde) mit der Infanterie Condés zusammen, während Werth auf dem bayer. linken Flügel die Infanterie und Kavallerie des Duc Antoine III de Gramont schlagen konnte. Anstatt Condés Mitte einzukesseln und auf dem französ. linken Flügel Henri de La Tour d'Auvergne vicomte de Turenne und die Hessen Geysos zu attackieren, zog Werth — von Pulverqualm und einsetzender Dunkelheit behindert — seine Reiter zusammen, so daß Turennes Truppen den Winnenberg erobern und die frischen Hessen die bayer. Artillerie erkämpfen und und Alerheim angreifen konnten. Werth sammelte die verbliebenen Ligisten auf dem Schloßberg und führte sie zum Schellenberg bei Donauwörth ab. Nach dem Verlust der böhm. Schlacht von Jankau im März und der Niederlage von Alerheim konnten Schweden, Franzosen und Hessen neue Hoffnung schöpfen und ihre Position in den Westfälischen Friedensverhandlungen stärken, zumal die Schweden nach Jankau auch das prokaiserl. Kursachsen am 6. 9. 1645 durch den Waffenstillstand von Kötzschenbroda zur Neutralität brachten.

Kupferstich, Werkstatt Matthäus Merians d. Ä., Frankfurt a. M. Merian schickte mit seinem Brief 450905 F. Ludwigs Kammermeister Peter Knaudt seinen Stich.

PRÆCIPUÆ CRVENTÆQ; ILLIVS PVGNÆ inter Elect. Baūari, et Galliarū Regis Año 1645., d. 3. Augusti, apud Allerheimum commißæ delineatio. Abbildung des Haupt Treffens zwischē den Chur Bayrischen, vnd Frantzösischen Armeen, bey Allersheim geschehen den 3 Augusti A°. 1645.
In: *Theatrum Europaeum* V (1647), zwischen S. 822 und 823.
HAB: 70.1 Hist. 2°. Dig.

Lit.: *Guthrie II*, 221–230; *Wilson*, 701–705; Günter Barudio: Der Teutsche Krieg 1618–1648. Frankfurt a. M. 1988, 547–549; vgl. 450905 K 3.

S. 703. *Georg Philipp Harsdörffers* (FG 368) Porticus Virtutis (1645) *zum Ruhme Herzog Augusts d. J. von Braunschweig-Wolfenbüttel* (FG 227). Zu 450927. Vgl. 460700 K 4, 460912 u. 461204A.

Die Überlieferung des Baus einer Säulenhalle und Bibliothek durch den römischen Kaiser Augustus regte Georg Philipp Harsdörffer (FG 368. Der Spielende) dazu an, einen reichillustrierten Panegyricus auf Hz. August d. J. v. Braunschweig-Wolfenbüttel (FG 227. Der Befreiende) zu verfassen, weil dieser nicht durch Steine, sondern durch Tugend und Bücher eine Bibliothek errichtet habe, die durch die Frömmigkeit und Bildung ihres Stifters ewig dauern werde. Harsdörffers Widmungsgedicht „PROGRAMMA ad HEROES FRVCTIFERI SODALITII" und von uns zitierte Texte beweisen, daß der Spielende dabei auch in besonderem Maße an die Spracharbeit des Befreienden und dessen Mitgliedschaft in der Fruchtbringenden Gesellschaft dachte.

Kupferstich: Blick in die von Reliefs und Wappen geschmückte Porticus Virtutis. Auf einem Sockel Hz. August mit Lorbeerkranz auf dem steigenden Pegasus, in der Rechten der Stab Merkurs als Götterbote und als Gott der Künste und Wissenschaften. Inschrift des Sockels: AUGUSTO, PIO *FORTI FELICI*. Im 2., separat erschienenen Druck der Preisschrift (s. 460912) neuer Stich des Wolfenbütteler Hofmalers Albert Freyse mit einer neuen Inschrift auf dem Denkmalsockel. Vgl. 450927 K I 1.

1. Druck
[Kupfertitel]: Porticus Augusti AugustÆ Virtutis Imago, PrÆbuit exemplum Posteritas stupeat.
In: *Harsdörffer: Specimen (1646)*, Bl.)(r –)( )( )(9v. Hier Bl.)( )(7r.
HAB: QuN 1090 (1).

S. 721. *Titelblattentwurf von 1645 für den Oktavdruck der Evangelischen Kirchen-Harmonie (1646) Herzog Augusts d. J. von Braunschweig-Wolfenbüttel* (FG 227). Zu 451001.

Den abgebildeten Titel umrahmen 4 Engelköpfe mit Flügeln und Medaillons von 8 Evangelisten und Aposteln: Oben Mitte Paulus (2 Schwerter), oben links Matthäus (1 Engel), oben rechts Markus (geflügelter Löwe), links Mitte Petrus (Schlüssel), rechts Mitte Johannes d. Evangelist (Bücher), links unten Lukas (geflügelter Stier), rechts unten der Johannes der Offenbarung (Adler), unten Mitte Lukas als Autor der Apostelgeschichte und Begleiter des Paulus (? Wanderstab).

Bruns- | wikischer | Evangeli | scher | Kirchen | Harmoneyen | Erster Theil | 1645.
HAB: Cod. Guelf. 236.2. Extrav., Bl. 1r Eingeklebtes Titelkupfer.

Auf der Rückseite (Bl. 1v, nicht abgebildet) eingeklebtes Titelkupfer mit 8 biblischen Szenen in Medaillons und mit den Attributen der 4 Evangelisten (Engel, Löwe, Stier und Adler), umrahmt:

Bruns- | wikischer | Evangeli | scher | Kirchen | Harmoneyen | Ander Theil | 1645.

Die beiden Titelkupfer kamen in der ersten vollständigen Ausgabe der *Evangelischen Kirchen-Harmonie*, der Oktavausgabe von 1646 (s. 411214 II A), zur Verwendung. Im Exemplar HAB: 548. 8 Theol. ist die 5 in der Jahresangabe jeweils mit Tinte zu einer 6 korrigiert. Die Bezeichnung des Stechers wurde erst für den Buchdruck hinzugesetzt: Tl. 1 „Ioh. P. S.", Tl. 2 „I. P. S.", d. i. Iohann Pfann Sculpsit.

Lit.: Lexikon der christlichen Ikonographie. Hg. Engelbert Kirschbaum SJ u. (ab Bd. 4) Wolfgang Braunfels in Zusammenarbeit mit G. Bandmann u. a. 8 Bde. Rom u. a. 1968–1976.

S. 797. *Porträt Johann Michael Moscheroschs* (FG 436. Der Träumende). Zu 460120.

Brustbild mit Schulterbandelier in einem perspektivisch schrägen Medaillon, von einem Pflanzenband oval umkränzt. Um den Hals ein Gesellschaftspfennig am

Bande (Avers: Gesellschaftssinnbild der Kokospalme). Angabe des Gesellschaftsnamens Moscheroschs: „Der Traumende." Taufname in Zierschrift: „Johann Michael Moscherosch." Handschriftlicher Zusatz: „in die Gesellschafft komen 1645." Während Mortzfeld die umrankende Pflanze Efeu mutmaßt, interpretiert Schäfer sie als Stechpalmblätter. Tatsächlich handelt es sich bei den abgebildeten, mehrfach geschwungen gezähnten Blättern mit angedeuteten Fruchtständen wohl um jene des (Schwarzen) Nachtschattens (Solanum nigrum), der Gesellschaftspflanze Moscheroschs. S. *Conermann III*, S. 525.

Kupferstich 89 x 70 mm (Blatt). GNM Nürnberg, Graph. Samml., Inv.-Nr. MP 16511, Kapsel 286. Die Nürnberger Provenienz könnte darauf verweisen, daß Georg Philipp Harsdörffer, der Moscheroschs Aufnahme in die Fruchtbringende Gesellschaft empfohlen hatte, diese Unterschrift auf das Blatt setzte.

Von diesem Porträt existiert ein Nachstich des Straßburger Verlegers Peter Aubry II. (1596–1666) mit dessen lateinischer Widmung aus dem Jahre 1652.

Aubrys Nachstich: 130 x 92 mm (Platte; Blatt 320 x 198 mm), HAB Inv.-Nr. 14460 (*Mortzfeld* A 14460), mit 2 Impresen mit lateinischer Umschrift.

Die 2. Imprese beruht auf Moscheroschs Wappen und zeigt ein mit einem achtstrahligen facettierten Stern belegtes Tatzenkreuz („PER CRUCEM AD LUCEM"). Das Wappen Moscheroschs zeigt im Schild das von vier (heraldischen) Rosen begleitete Tatzenkreuz/Stern und führt als Helmzier ebenfalls die Rose. Die 2. Imprese in Aubrys Stich zeigt eine solche Rose mit der Umschrift „ARMATA. TRIUMFAT. SPINIS". Unmittelbar unter dem Medaillon stehen Verse des zeitgenössischen Breslauer städt. Sekretärs und Opitz-Sammlers Matthias Machner:

Hic ille, Lector exhibetur MOSCHEROSCH
Politioris literaturæ Stater:
Quem seculi in mores Philander invehens
Commendat Orbi: sed Fides & Crux DEO.
*   Amico Veteri faciebat Wratislaviæ*
*   Matthias Machnerus.*

Ein anderes Exemplar des Aubry-Stichs in der Kunstsammlung Coburg, mit einer darunter geklebten Unterschrift „Moscherosch". S. *Digitaler Porträtindex*.

Es existieren 2 formal gleiche Abbildungen für 2 weitere Mitglieder der Fruchtbringenden Gesellschaft, beides nur mit den Gesellschaftsnamen unterschriebene Brustbilder im ovalen Pflanzenband: Georg Philipp Harsdörffer (FG 368. Der Spielende) und Justus Georg Schottelius (FG 397. Der Suchende). Der Abgebildete zeigt jeweils seinen Gesellschaftspfennig auf dem Avers. S. *DA Köthen I.6*, S. 522 u. 647. Vgl. *Mortzfeld* A 8894 bzw. A 19576. Harsdörffers Bildnis trägt auf dem ovalen Rahmen die Bohnenranken, die auf seine Gesellschaftspflanze, die „Welschen Bohnen" (Phaseolus vulgaris), verweisen. S. dazu *Conermann III*,

426–429. Die in Schottelius' Stich den ovalen Rahmen umfassende Pflanze, die Mortzfeld als Lorbeer identifiziert und die wir in *DA Köthen I.6*, S. 118 als „Lorbeer- und Zypressenrahmen" bezeichneten, erinnert mit den grundständig am Stengel sitzenden, eiförmig-lanzettartigen Blättern durchaus auch von fern an die Blattform von Schottelius' Gesellschaftspflanze „Gemsenwurtzel/ oder Schwindelkraut", d. i. Kriechende Gämswurz (Doronicum pardalianches). S. dazu *Conermann III*, 466–468. Die Ungenauigkeit der Abbildung der bodenwachsenden krautigen Pflanze, die keine längeren Ranken ausbildet, kann sich aus der Unkenntnis des Zeichners der Stichvorlage über das exakte Aussehen der Pflanze erklären. Die Abbildung im Gesellschaftsbuch, in welchem Schottelius' Imprese auftaucht, erschien erst 1646. Zum *GB 1646* s. 440130 K 3. Sein Bildnis schickte Schottelius in seinem Brief 460414 an Johann Valentin Andreae (FG 464).

Die formal identische Ausführung aller drei Stiche weist auf einen gemeinsamen Zeichner bzw. Stecher hin. Als Urheber dieser Kurzserie ist der erwähnte Peter (II.) Aubry nicht vorstellbar. Während der Kupferstich für Harsdörffer keinerlei Adresse besitzt und auch jener für Moscherosch nur in der Version Aubrys dessen Namen nennt, trägt der Stich für Schottelius in der allein bekannten Version (in der HAB: Inv.-Nr. A 19576) den Stechervermerk „Troschel. Scul." direkt im Pflanzenoval. Dabei handelt es sich um den in Nürnberg geborenen Kupferstecher Peter Troschel (Droschel, 1615–1680), der zwischen 1635 und mindestens 1667 in seiner Heimatstadt und zeitweise wohl auch in Breslau tätig war. In Nürnberg arbeitete Troschel für die großen druckgraphischen Verlage (Endter, Fürst etc.). Gemeinsam mit dem Weimarer Hofmaler Christian Richter, der viele von Troschels Vorlagen entwarf, arbeitete er u. a. als Illustrator an der reich bebilderten sog. „Weimarer Bibel", die im Auftrag Hz. Ernsts des Frommen von Sachsen-Weimar ab 1641 in mehreren Auflagen bei Wolfgang Endter in Nürnberg herausgegeben wurde. S. *DA Köthen I.5*, 101. Es ist daher zu vermuten, daß Troschel alle 3 Porträts auf Anregung Harsdörffers 1645 aus Anlaß der Aufnahme Moscheroschs stach. Die Vorlagen dürfte er über Harsdörffer von Zeichnern in Wolfenbüttel (Albert Freyse?), Straßburg und Nürnberg erhalten haben. Das Freundschaftsepigramm Machners unter Aubrys Nachstich wird — wie dieser Stich selbst — wohl von Moscherosch in Straßburg angeregt und auf seine Bitte oder unter Vermittlung des auch in Breslau bekannten Troschel zustande gekommen sein. Im Zusammenhang mit Aubrys Nachstich sei angemerkt, daß das Titelkupfer für den 2. Teil von Moscheroschs *Gesichte Philanders von Sittewald* (Straßburg 1650) von Jesaias Rompler v. Löwenhalt entworfen („Rumpler fecit") und von Peter Aubry nur gestochen wurde („P. Aubry scu[lpsit]"). Derselbe Stich zierte bereits Teil 1 der Ausg. von 1643 (VD17 3:308245Y), dort jedoch noch mit dem Stechervermerk „J. K. sc[ulpsit]".

Lit.: *Conermann III*, 523–527; *Mortzfeld* A 14460; *Digitaler Porträtindex*. Schäfer: *Moscherosch und Harsdörffer* S. 180 f., Anm. 94. Zu Machner s. Opitz: *BW* I, 64 f. u. ö.; zu Aubry s. *De Gruyter Allgemeines Künstlerlexikon* V, 585, vgl. *Thieme/ Becker* II, 232 f.; zu Troschel s. *Thieme/ Becker* XXXIII, 431 f.; Hermann Oertel: Die Frankfurter Feyerabend-Bibeln und die Nürnberger Endter-Bibeln. In: Mitteilungen des Vereins für Geschichte der Stadt Nürnberg 70 (1983), 75–116; Rolf-Dieter Jahn: Die Weimarer Ernestinische Kurfürstenbibel und Dilherr-Bibel des Endter-Verlags in Nürnberg 1641–1788. Versuch einer vollständigen Chronologie und Bibliographie. Köln 1986.

S. 803. *Die Imprese Kurfürst Friedrich Wilhelms von Brandenburg* (FG 401. Der Untadeliche. 1641). Zu 460125.

Kf. Friedrich Wilhelm v. Brandenburg (FG 401. Der Untadeliche). Aquarellierte kolorierte Federzeichnung des Gesellschaftsmalers Christoph Steger als Vorlage für einen nicht ausgeführten Kupferstich in Matthäus Merians d. Ä. Werkstatt für die geplante Fortsetzung des Gesellschaftsbuchs (s. 460703 K 5) der Fruchtbringenden Gesellschaft. Vgl. *GB 1646*. Steger berichtete in seinem Brief 460315, daß die Visierungen der ersten 68 Impresen (FG 401–468) fertig seien.
In einer Phantasielandschaft mit weitem Tal, Felsen, Gebirge und Gebäuden auf einem Repoussoir ein Mirabolanenbaum mit Früchten (Terminalia chebula Retz). Steger malte ihn seitengetreu nach der Vorlage im Kräuterbuch von Tabernaemontanus. S. *Conermann III*, 475. Der Baum erschien im fruchtbringerischen Kontext 1647 inmitten eines vor das Wolfenbütteler Schloß gepflanzten (imaginären) Gartens in *Hille*, S. 180. Dessen 8 Beete zeigen jeweils eine Impresenpflanze. Abb. schon in *Conermann: Anhalt*, S. 39.

In: *Weimarer Impresen*, Bl. 2.
ThHSTA Weimar: A 11816
Auch schwarz-weiß abgebildet in *Conermann II*, S. [225].

S. 863. *Brief von Justus Georg Schottelius* (FG 397) *an Johann Valentin Andreae* (FG 464). Zu 460414.

Lateinische und deutsche Handschriftenprobe.

HAB: Cod. Guelf. 11.12 Aug. 2°; Bl. 227r, eigenhändig.

S. 879. *Christoph Stegers Visierung der Imprese Johann Michael Moscheroschs* (FG 436). Zu 460426.

Johann Michael Moscherosch (FG 436. Der Träumende). Aquarellierte kolorierte Federzeichnung des Gesellschaftsmalers Christoph Steger als Vorlage (1645) für einen nicht ausgeführten Kupferstich in Matthäus Merians d. Ä. Werkstatt für die geplante Fortsetzung des Gesellschaftsbuchs (s. 460703 K 5) der Fruchtbringenden Gesellschaft. Vgl. *GB 1646*. Steger berichtete in seinem Brief 460315, daß die Visierungen der ersten 68 Impresen des 5. Hunderts (FG 401–468) fertig seien.
In einer Phantasielandschaft auf einem Repoussoir der Schwarze Nachtschatten (Solanum nigrum L.). Die Vorlage der Pflanzenzeichnung bildete die Abbildung 392 in Leonhart Fuchs' Kräuterbuch (1543). S. *Conermann III*, 525.

Moscherosch hatte sich in Anlehnung an sein später erweitertes und häufig nachgedrucktes Werk LES VISIONES DE DON FRANCESCO DE QVEVEDO VILLEGAS. Oder Wunderbahre Satyrische gesichte Verteutscht durch Philander von Sittewalt &c. (Strasburg: Johann Philipp Mülbe [1640]) den Gesellschaftsnamen, ein ‚Wort' und die Pflanze wohl mit Hilfe seines unmittelbaren Korrespondenzpartners Georg Philipp Harsdörffer (FG 368) ausgesucht (vgl. 450500 K 1, 3 u. ö.) und durch ihn aus Köthen auch eine Visierung seiner Imprese für einen Gesellschaftspfennig empfangen. Die vorgeschlagene Devise „mit offenen Augen" ersetzte F. Ludwig durch „Hohe sachen", was Diederich v. dem Werder (FG 31) Moscherosch durch Harsdörffer wissen ließ (450504A K 2). F. Ludwig stellte die Wahl des ‚Worts' jedoch ins Belieben Moscheroschs; er regte auch an, Werder möge das Reimgesetz des Träumenden entwerfen (450505). Werder wies es ihm dann in 450505A selbst zu, und in 450613 konnte er wohl infolge eines Briefs Harsdörffers das Reimgesetz mit einigen eigenen Änderungen F. Ludwig schicken, welcher diese Änderungen aber nicht übernahm. Andere Änderungen Werders finden sich aber im Köthener Gesellschaftsbuch (*GB Kö.*).

In: *Weimarer Impresen*, unpag.
ThHSTA Weimar: A 11816
Auch schwarz-weiß abgebildet in *Conermann II*, S. [260].

S. 907. *F. Ludwigs eigenhändiges Konzept seines Widmungsgedichts zum 6. Teil von Georg Philipp Harsdörffers* (FG 368) *Frauenzimmer Gesprächspiele (1646).* Zu 460705 II.

Handschriftprobe.
HM Köthen: V S 545, Bl. 418r.

S. 1059. *Innenansicht der Wolfenbütteler Kirche Beatae Mariae Virginis nach Westen.* Zu 461204.

Sicht auf die Gemeinde, die Taufe und den Orgelprospekt. Auf der Kanzel ein Prediger. Abbildung aus einer Serie von vier Stichen. Einer zeigt die Ansicht der Kirche von außen (vgl. zu 440100), ein anderer eine Innenansicht nach Osten. Der Prediger sollte den Perikopentext aus Hz. Augusts sprachlich modernisierter *Evangelischer Kirchen-Harmonie* (1646 u. ö.) vor dem Altar vortragen, während der entsprechende Text der Lutherbibel auf der Kanzel gelesen werden sollte. S. 411214 I A (*DA Köthen I. 6*) u. 451001. S. auch 440100.

Zeichner Albert Freyse, Kupferstich von Sebastian Furck. Beide Adressen rechts unten.
In: Heinrich Wideburg: Denkwürdige Danksagungs-Predigt. Wolfenbüttel: Sterne 1646, Bl. nach S. 91.
HAB: Gn 13488 (dig.); 168.1 Quod. (9), dig. Auch in *Gosky: Arbustum (1650)*, Bl. zw. 283v u. 284r. HAB: T 904.2° Helmst. (1) (dig.). — Danach [Hz. August d.

J. v. Braunschweig-Wolfenbüttel]: Evangelische Kirchen-Harmonie 1646 (8°), Tl. 2, S. 556. HAB: 548.8 Theol. 8°, vgl. 411214, S. 340 u. 374. — Ders.: Evangelische Kirchen Harmonie 1646 (4°), 2. Tl., S. 692 (Inc. „An diesem lezten Tage des Jahres ... aus dem 21. Capitel des H. Matthäi [...]."). HAB: 51.4 Theol., vgl. 411214, S. 355 f. u. 374.

S. 1063. *Bildnis Georg Philipp Harsdörffers* (FG 368). Zu 461204 A.

Brustbild Georg Philipp Harsdörffers (FG 368), um den Hals sein Gesellschaftspfennig (Avers mit Kokospalmen-Hain aus der Imprese der Fruchtbringenden Gesellschaft). In den Ecken: links oben Helm des Harsdörffer-Wappens; rechts oben Schild des Harsdörffer-Wappens; links unten Taschenuhr mit aufgeklapptem Deckel, auf einem Buch; rechts unten Zirkel auf einem Blatt mit geometrischer Zeichnung. Im Köthener Gesellschaftsbuch (*GB Kö.*) fehlt das Wappen. Vgl. *Conermann III*, 428.

Zeichnung (Feder u. getuscht) von Georg Strauch (Adresse, 1651); 178 x 143 mm (Blatt). Diese Zeichnung bildet die Vorlage für einen Kupferstich (in HAB: PS A 8893).

GNM Nürnberg: Graphische Sammlung (Paul Wolfgang Merkel'sche Familienstiftung), Inventar-Nr. MP 9968a, Kapsel-Nr. 164.

S. 1071. *Johann Valentin Andreaes* (FG 464. 1646) lateinische Selbstverpflichtung gegenüber der Fruchtbringenden Gesellschaft. Zu 461216 I.

Dem Brief 461216 beiliegendes Blatt mit Andreaes rotem Wachssiegel (Rosenwappen). Handschriftprobe.
HM Köthen: V S 545, Bl. 468r, ungez. Rücks. leer, eigenh. in Zierschrift.

Das Blatt wurde Hz. August d. J. zusammen mit dem erwähnten Brief geschickt, dann von Carl Gustav v. Hille (FG 302) zusammen mit seinem Brief *DA Köthen I. 8:* 470112 an F. Ludwig weitergesandt. — Bl. 468v (Vorders. ungez.) mit Hz. Augusts eigenh. Anweisung an Hille: „S.ʳ L. Furst Ludwigen zu Anhalt zuzuschikken nebst dem Extract."

Briefe und Beilagen
1644–1646

440000

Diederich von dem Werder an Conrad von Burgsdorff

Diederich v. dem Werder (FG 31), bereits seit 1620 Mitglied der FG, widmet sein Buch Conrad v. Burgsdorff (FG 404) unter dem Anagramm „Ich rede dir von Treue". Burgsdorff möge das Fürstenkind Dianea mehrfach beschauen — auf ihre Geschichte, Redekunst, Beschreibung und immer wieder auf den Sinn hin, damit sich die Weisheit, Ratschläge und Staatsgeheimnisse nicht ohne heimliche Lust erschlössen.

Q Giovanni Francesco Loredano: *La Dianea*, zuerst Venedig 1635, verdeutscht von Diederich v. dem Werder (FG 31): DJANEA | Oder | Rähtselgedicht/ | in welchem/ | Vnter vielen anmuhtigen Fügnussen/ | Hochwichtige Staatsachen/ | Denklöbliche Geschichte/ und | klugsinnige Rahtschläge/ | vermittelst | Der Majestätischen Deutschen Sprache/ | Kunstzierlich | verborgen. | [Vignette: Purpurmuschel mit Schriftband, „Voll Königlicher Farb"] | Nürnberg/ | Jn Verlegung Wolfgang Endters/ | [Linie] | M. DC. XXXXIV. 8°. Bl.[Avj]r. Zit. nach dem Faksimiledr. der Ausgabe A von 1644 (Expl. der LB Coburg: Cas A 2045). Hg. u. eingel. v. Gerhard Dünnhaupt. Bern usw. 1984. (Nachdrucke deutscher Literatur des 17. Jahrhunderts, 22); Dig. SB München; zur Ausg. B (Nürnberg: Christoph Endter 1671) s. Ausg. Dünnhaupt, 75*.

Der HAB-Band 101.5 Eth., der nach dem Frontispiz keinen Drucktitel aufweist, könnte ein Vorausexemplar sein, das Werder an Hz. August d. J. v. Braunschweig-Wolfenbüttel (FG 227. Der Befreiende) schickte, denn dieser Pergamentband trägt als Supralibros in goldenen Lettern die Inschrift „DEM BEFREYENDEN." Der Widmungsbrief an Burgsdorff (s. u.) steht auf dem nach dem Frontispiz (HAB) bzw. dem Drucktitel folgenden nichtfoliierten oder -paginierten Blatt. Auf der jeweiligen Rückseite ein dt. Sonett Werders, über dem im HAB-Expl. unter dem Titel „Sinnbild" die Pictura u. Inscriptio eines Emblems (Purpurschnecke; „Voll Königlicher Farb!") erscheinen. Das Emblem kommt im Coburger Expl. nur auf dem Drucktitel selbst vor. In diesem Band steht über dem Sonett: „Klingreimen/ erklärende Des Titels Sinnbild/ mit der Purpurmuschel." Zum HAB-Exemplar s. schon Dünnhaupt: Neue Funde zur Werder-Bibliographie. In: WBN 3 (1976), 190f. Der Romantext stimmt in den genannten Exemplaren von 1644 überein, es ergeben sich auch nur wenige kleine Unregelmäßigkeiten im Satz, die den Eindruck eines sorgfältig durchgesehenen u. korrigierten Buches nicht stören: Coburg, S. 9 Blattsignatur „B iij"; HAB, S. 9 ohne Blattsignatur; Coburg, S. 279 u. HAB, S. 279 übereinstimmend falscher Seitentitel „Zweytes Buch" (recte: Drittes Buch); Coburg, S. 408 u. HAB, S. 408 fälschlich übereinstimmend S. „308". Coburg, S. 411 u. HAB, S. 411 übereinkommend falsche Bogensignatur „D iiij" statt Dd iiij. — Vgl. Loredanos Brief an Georg Philipp Harsdörffer (FG 368), in dem er diesen irrtümlich als Übersetzer der *Dianea* vermutet. S. 460000A. Harsdörffer mag das Erscheinen des Romans in dem Nürnberger Verlag Wolfgang Endters allerdings vermittelt haben. Vgl. z. B. sein Angebot in 451101: „[J]ch hoffe zu des *Vielgekörnten* [R]asenden Roland einen Verlag [Z]ufinden; [...]."

A *Ohne Anschrift.*

Herrn
Herrn Curt von Burgsdorff[1]

NJm/ O Edler Held/ diese Königliche Dianea von der treuen Hand deines aufrichtigen Dieners/ zum unausleschlichen Zeugnus/ seiner allerbeständigsten Freundschaft. Schaue und beschaue dieses schönste Fürstenkind zum öftern. Das erstemal kan nur auf den Lauf der Geschichte; Das zweyt- und drittemal auf der Rede Fertikeit/ und der Sachē artige Beschreibung/ genaue Acht gegeben werden. Das viert- und mermal aber müssen die Gedancken auf tieffere Verständnüsse gerichtet seyn. Dann diese und dergleichen fröliche Erfindungē halten oft Geistreiche Weisheit/ fürtrefliche Rahtschläge/ samt hohē Geheimnüssen wichtiger Stadsachen/ in sich verborgen/ und pflegen mit/ nicht gemeiner/ lieblichen Belustigung/ unter der Schale der Fabeln/ viel warhafte Geschichte/ verdeckter Weise/ mit eingewickelt zu füren. Gehab dich allhier lange lange/ dort aber ewiglich wohl.

Jch rede dir von Trewe.[2]

I

Diederich von dem Werder nach Loredano über die Ermordung Wallensteins

Q DJANEA Oder Rähtselgedicht *usw.*, 133–141 (2. Buch, Abschnitt 17–27). Abschn. 27 wird fälschlich als 127 bezeichnet. — Die Erstauflage des ital. Romans erschien nach Dünnhaupt, 31* Anm. 75 in Venedig bei Sarzina. Werder hätte für seine Übersetzung auch eine der folgenden Ausgaben benutzen können: LA DIANEA DI GIO: FRANCESCO LOREDANO Nobile Veneto. LIBRI QVATTRO. VENETIA, Appresso Giacomo Sarzina. M DC XXXVI. CON LICENZA DE' SVPERIORI, E PRIVILEGI. SB München, dig. — LA | DIANEA | DI | GIO: FRANCESCO | LOREDANO | Nobile Veneto. | LIBRI QVATTRO. | All'Illust.^{mo} & Excellent.^{mo} | SIG. BENEDETTO QVERINI | Cavalier, & Ambasciatore del Regno di Candia. | [Signet] | IN VENETIA, | Presso Giacomo Sarcina. | [Linie] | M DC XXXVIII. | CON LICENZA DE' SVPERIORI, E PRIVILEGI. Gr. 8°, S. 67–71, HAB: Lk 481, zit. *Dianea 1638*, mit Eintragung des Vorbesitzers Carl Gustav v. Hille (FG 302). Auch Digitalisat der SB München. In F. Ludwigs Bibliothek fand sich „*Dianea* Nürnberg 1644" (*IP*, 330v), jedoch nicht die ital. Vorlage. — LA | DIANEA | DI | GIO. FRANCESCO | LOREDANO. | Nobile Veneto. LIBRI QVATTRO. | [Adler-Signet] | IN VENETIA, M. DC. XLIII. | [Linie] | Ad Istanza dell'Academia. | Con licenza de' Superiori, e Priuilegi. S. 100–106. HAB: 551.4 Quod. (2), zit. *Dianea 1643*. Die Widmungsbriefe Loredanos u. die darauf folgende Dichtung übersetzte Werder nicht: EPISTOLA DI HIDRASPE A DIANEA DI PIETRO MICHIELE Gentilhuomo Venetiano. In Venetia, Per il Sarzina, MDCXXXVIII. Con Licenza de' Superiori. (Im Anhang zur Ausgabe von 1638 bzw. vor dem Roman in der Fassung von 1643). Der kurze „Argomento" Loredanos blieb unübersetzt. Werder ergänzte seinen Text durch ein hilfreiches „Register über die Vier Bücher DJANEA: Jn welchen ordentlich/ benebens der Geschichte und Lehren Jnhalt/ die eigenen Namen/ und viel sonderliche den

Teutschen Lippen noch der Zeit unbenamte Wörter bemerket zu finden." Z.B. Angelstern/ Polus; Begängnus/ solennitas, ein Favor/ zu Teutsch ein Gunstzeichen, Meerbusen/ sinus maris, Neurikeit/ novitas, eine Schaubühne/ eschauffo, der Umfang/ Circuitus, Verselbsten/ transsubstantiare, ein Wink/ nutus.

Erzählung Florideas, Tochter des Königs Dinanderfo von Negroponte, über Herzog Lastevins Ende:

17. Der Hertzog[1] verwaltete sein Amt noch eine Zeitlang mit grossem Lobe: Als er aber vernam/ daß ihm seine Feinde ferner an den Hals/ und ihn solcher Sachen/ die ihm nimmermehr in die Gedanken kamen/ beschuldigen wolten: Daß man ohne ihn von Friedensartickeln handelte; Und daß der Aspiner König/ eben zu dem Ende/ den Hertzog von Riafe Gesandtenweise abschickte. Auch die Fürsten von Catanosa/ als freiwillige/ aber übel befriedigte/ dem Lager folgeten: So fieng er an auf seiner Wohlfahrt Sicherheit bedacht zu seyn/ lies etzliche Gefangene los/ begehrte nichts als ein Zeugnus der Ehren darvon zu erlangen: Stiftete Freundschaft mit dem Haubt der Belgen/ der Aquitanen/ und Celten. Endlich machte er/ daß des Kriegsheers vornemste Obersten und Haubtleute eine gewisse Schrift/ mit Hand und Siegel/ unterzeichneten/ in welcher sie sich ihm in allen Begegnussen zu dienen/ und von ihm/ [134] bis in den Tod/ nicht auszusetzen/ verbündlich machten.

18. Meinem Vatter[2] ward von diesem allen Theil gegeben/ er aber solchem Anbringen (wiewohl es durch manchen wahrhaften Mund geschahe) nicht glaubende, wolte sich der Wahrheit/ durch noch grössere Gewisheit/ erkundigen/ lies den Graven von Assalimino/ des Hertzogs Lastevin BrudersSohn[3]/ für sich erfordern/ demselben that er eine Erzehlung vom Verdienst/ Tugend/ und Siegen seines Vettern des Feldherrn: Und wie er willens were/ ihn hinzuschicken/ ihm ein Hertz einzusprechen/ und ihn zu versichern/ daß die ungleichen Berichte sein Hertz von einem solchẽ Manne/ den er so hoch als sich selber liebte/ nicht abwendig machen könten. Er erkennete der grossen Höfe übels Wesen/ als an welchem die allerwürdigsten der Schmach alles Neides und aller Boßheit/ am allerersten/ unterworffen weren.

19. Bey dieser Gelegenheit gab er ihm einen von seinen Rähten mit zu/ trug demselbẽ/ in höchster geheim/ absonderlich auf/ auf alles des Hertzoges von Lastevin Thun vnd [135] Lassen genaue Acht zu haben/ seine Gedanken/ Werke/ und seinen vorhabenden Zweck zu durchgründen. Als der abgeschickte Raht ins Lager kam/ ward er genugsam von des Feldherrn Veränderung/ von seinen/ mit den Feinden/ gepflogenen Wechselschriften und von tausend andern/ ihn schuldig machenden Händeln/ unterrichtet.[4] Dieser machte J. M. alles wissend/ denn es kamen etzliche von den fürnemsten/ die sich mit unterschrieben hatten/ und entdeckten ihm das gantze Werk in Person.

20. Mein Vater entsatzte sich über diesem erschrecklichen Beginnen/ und weil er sahe/ daß die Summa dieser Sache auf der Geschwindikeit bestünde/ so erkläret er den Hertzog des Generalats verlustig/ der Crone Aufrührer und seines Für-

sten Feind: Befahl allen Provintzen/ ihm nicht mehr zu gehorsamen/ und machte denen grosse Hoffnung/ die ihn ihm in die Hände liefern würden. Er trug dem Milocopini/ einem Sicilianischen Fürsten/ und dem Graven von Lagasso/[5] beiden in Dapfrikeit und Krieges Weisheit wohlerfahrnen/ des Feldes Aufsicht auf. Diesem befal er die Feinde [136] aufzuhalten/ und jenem/ den Hertzog zu fahen/ eh er Zeit gewönne/ sich zu schützen oder zu entrinnen.[6]

21. Der von Lastevin war dazumal, als er J. M. Schlus vernommen/ an den Grenzen Beotia/ in einem wohlvermaurtem Orte. Ob er sich nun alda/ weil er Volk/ auch Kraut und Lot genug/ wohl hätte wehren und beschützen können/ so flohe er doch/ weil er den Graven von Lagasso (der ihn/ unter dem Schein der Freundschaft/ zu überfallen vorhabens) mit viel Fähnlein ankommen sahe/ samt zween Regimentern zu Ros/ und vier Obersten/ auch andern Herren/ so ihm mit Freundschaft zugethan waren/ in höchster Eile darvon; Begab sich in eines der vestesten Schlösser in Boetia/ in Hoffnung/ alda für aller Welt Macht sicher zu seyn. Der Ort[7] war von Natur und Kunst unüberwindlich/ die Soldaten von probirter Treue; Vnd der Haubtmann[8] daselbst seine Creatur/ denn er hatte ihn/ als einen fremden/ wegen seiner Dapfrikeit und Treue/ zu diesem Befehl befördert/ und diesen vesten Platz anvertrauet. [137]

22. Des von Lagasso Nachricht und Warnung war des Hertzogs Ankunft zuvorkommen/ dahero nam ihm[a] gedachter Haubtmann für (als er ihn erstlich mit freundlicher Demut/ wie einem untern/ und zwar einem mit so viel Gutthatē verpflicht gemachten/ gebüret/ empfangen hätte) sich seiner/ auf was Weise es auch geschehen könte/ zu bemächtigen.

23. Der Hertzog verblieb/ von Gedanken oder Unpäslikeit beladen/ in einem Gemach alleine; Verordnete/ daß man ihn ungessen ruhen lassen solte. Die andern/ vom Haubtmann eingeladen/ giengen mit demselben zur Abendmahlzeit. Nachdem nun schier alle/ dieses Werks Wissenschaft tragende/ mit hierbey waren/ und eben am frölichsten zu seyn vermeinten/ wurden sie/ nach gegebenem Zeichen/ mit weniger oder schier keiner Gegenwehre/ darnieder gemacht/ und ermordet.

24. Kurtz darauf giengen sie/ von dar/ nach des Hertzogs Gemach/ warffen die Pforte zur Erden/ unnd fielen/ mit gewaltiger üngestümme/ hinein. Er sprang auf/ lief/ sich darvonzubringen/ oder Hülf-[138]fe zu ruffen/ zum Fenster. Als er aber die Höhe tödlich/ das Ausreissen unmüglich/ und seine Wacht zu weit/ sahe/ machte er sich herfür/ einen Soldaten die Helleparte aus den Händen zu reissen; Dieser aber/ auf sein Gewehr wohl Acht habende/ machte/ daß sich der Hertzog selber spisset/ uñ tödlich verwundete. Nachdem er sich hinauf aufs Bette geworffen/ redte er viel Worte/ seine Unschuld bezeugende. Er hätte J. M. Zorn entweichen/ und keine andere/ als seiner Sicherheit/ Gedanken haben wollen: Wann er etwas gegen J. M. Leben/ oder dero Reich/ im Siñe gehabt/ so solte es ihm an gewissen und erschrecklicheren Mitteln nicht ermangelt haben. Berief sich auf J. M. selbsten/ wann sie nur seiner boshaften Widerwärtigen beygebrachte Einbildungen auf ein Seite gesetzet/ und hergegen seine Dienste und

Thaten erwogē hätten. Beklagete das Elend derjenigen sehr hoch/ die da gezwungen seyn/ grossen Herren/ so stets können/ was sie wollē/ ohne Ende zu dienen.
25. Die herumstehende liessen ihn reden/ bis ihm die Seele ausgieng/ entweder aus Ehrerbietung gegen einen solchen Mann/ [139] der oftermals dem Könige selber Gebot fürgeschrieben/ oder daß sie an einem/ mit dem Tode ringenden/ keine Grausamkeit verüben wolten. Auf diese Zeitung konte mein Vatter die Threnen nicht verhalten. Befahl viel Opfer den Göttern/ für seine Seele/ zu halten/ ob nun wohl ihrer viel an dieser Zusammenverschwerung mit schuldig waren/ so lies er doch nicht mehr/ als zween/ in Verhaftung nemen: Dafür haltende/ es were eine grosse Rache/ wann er den andern zeigte/ daß er sie/ wann er wolte/ züchtigen könte.
26. Diese übermässige Gütikeit gab etzlichen übeln Gemütern Anlas/ des Hertzogs von Lastevin Unschuld hoch herauszustreichen/ und zwar mit solcher Freiheit/ die meinen Vatter in grosse Furcht seiner eigenen Person setzten. Sie sagten: daß die Dienste/ die er der Krone geleistet/ hätten einen solchen erbärmlichen und schmählichen Tod nicht verdienet: Man solte das Recht/ so man auch einem geringsten gestattet/ dem grösten der Welt nicht versagen: Dinanderfo lernete die Undankbarkeit von andern Fürsten; dieses Laster were in allen [140] verhasset/ aber in J. M. ein Greuel/ dieweil sie wolten/ daß Güte und Barmhertzikeit die höchste Zierde ihres Throns seyn solten. Numehr empfünde das Reich/ was ein solcher Verlust für Schaden brächte; Es hätten auch die Feinde keinen grössern Sieg/ als den Tod eines so grossen Kriegeshaubts/ erlangen können.
27. Der Hertzog von Gobra/ ein Verwandter des von Lastevins[9]/ ergrösserte allein des Vettern Verbrechen aufs allerhöchste/ klagte über meines Vatters alzugrossen Mildikeit/ daß er nun einen eintzigen zu seiner Versicherung hätte aufopfern lassen: Wann auch nichts anders schon verhanden/ als daß er mit dem Feinde Verständnus gehabt/ so were doch solches allein aller Todesmarter würdig: Dieses hohe Herausstreichē nam meines Vatters Gütikeit so ein/ daß er (unbetrachtet der Beleidigungen/ so dem Hertzog ehmals wiederfahren/ und daß solche/ als unausleschlich in Hertzen angeschrieben/ nicht eh als mit dem Hertzen sterben) mit aller der Ehre/ so müglich/ ihn begnadigte/ und ihm letzlichen die Beschützung seiner eigenen Person auf-[141]tragen lies. J. M. befelstigten *[sic]* sich in der Gunst gegen diesen Menschen/ in dem/ daß er etwas begieng/ dardurch er sich für den getreuesten halten machte.

II

Fürst Christians II. von Anhalt-Bernburg Nachrichten über die Ermordung Wallensteins

Q *Christian: Tageb.* XIV, Bl. 189v–191v (27. 8. 1636) u. ö.

Vormittags vmb zehen vhr, habe ich das haus besehen[1], darinnen die stube, in welcher der Friedlandt oder Wallensteiner ist durchstochen word*en*. Sein bette ist nahe am ofen gestanden, wegen Kälte (die er so gar nicht erdulden können,) vndt alß er erst den tumult gehöret ist er zum fenster zu gelauffen im hembde. Jndeßen wirdt sein Kammerdiener, welcher verwehren wollen, daß man zu seinem herren nicht also hinein lauffen sollen, mitt einem stich verwundet, (soll aber nicht dran gestorben sein,) vndt die thür mitt gewalt aufgestoßen, in dem läuft der hertzog, vom fenster an tisch nahe darbey, so fragt ihn der capitain Ebrox[2] ein Jrrländer, Bistu der Rebell, der die armada von vnserm Kayser will abfällig machen, vndt vber zum feindt führen. Jn dem Sperrt der Friedländer das Maul auff, sagt aber [190r] nichts, so gibt ihm der Ebrox einen starcken stoß mitt dem spieß oder hellebarte, oder partisane, in die brust hinein, daß der von Fridlandt, ob er schon mitt der handt die wunde zudecken wollen, dennoch baldt darnach zur erden gesuncken, vndt die ziegel mitt blut besprützett, So haben sie ihn hernacher mitt einem schlechten Leilach[3] zugedeckt, vndt die stiege hinundter geschlept, daß sein haüpt die staffeln fast alle gezehlt, vndt haben ihn also aufs schloß zu den andern Offizirern gebrachtt, welche schon zuvor niedergemacht gewesen. Die stube ist lenglicht ein feines zimmer, hat nur einerley licht nach der gaßen vndt Marckt zu, vndt vber die Kammerthür, noch zween andere thüren. Zu der einen ist der Ebrox gar allein hinein gegangen, zu der andern ein ander capitain[4], welcher den Friedländer vmbbringen sollen, wo ferrne Ebrox manquirt hette. Die andern Leutte vndt wachten seindt schon weggeschaft gewesen, vndt Cordon[5], Pudler[6], Leßle[7], bey dem Volck auf dem Marckte, in der Stadt vndt sonsten gewesen, anzuordnen, damitt kein auflauff endtstünde weder im Schloß noch in der Stadt, haben auch diesen anschlag vor sich selbsten gemacht, ehe ihnen der Kayß. [190v] befehlich, sich seiner zu bemächtigen, zukommen, dann Sie besorgt, weil er ein großen anhang, es möchte ihnen (wo er lebendig bliebe) ihre hälse kosten, sonderlich weil sie den Jlo[8], Trtzschka[9], Kinsky[10] vndt Naẇmann[11] albereitt im Schloß erwürget. Dieses alles, haben mir zween Jesuiter, so in selbigem hause wohnen, erzehlet, vndt wusten nicht was partisane oder hellebarte war [...] Das schreckliche ende dieses herren, gemahnt mich nicht allein an das dictum: Tolluntur in altum; ut lapsu graviore ruant, welches er selber ao. 1626 im munde geführt, vom Könige in Dennemarck, weil derselbe nicht nach seinem kopf zu Braunschweig in friedenstractaten sich einlaßen wollen, nicht aber vermeint, daß es ihm selber begegnen köndte. Wiewol damals Mein herr vatter Sehl.[12] als Sie mitt mir eben hiervon geredet, præsagiente spiritu vndt lächelnde gedachtt: der general sehe zu, daß es ihn nicht selber treffe [191r] oder das er sich nicht selber treffe. NB. NB.: Sondern es gemahnt mich noch mehr an Gottes wortt, Sie gehen vndter, vndt nehmen ein ende mitt schrecken. Jtem: Jch sahe einen Gottlosen, der breittet sich aus, wie ein Lorbeerbawm, da ich nach ihm fragte, wardt er nirgendt funden etc. Jtem: Bleibe from vndt halte dich recht, denn solchem wirdts zu letzt wolgehen. Jtem: Menge dich nicht vndter die aufrührer, damitt du nicht mitt ihnen, aufgerieben werdest. Jtem: die Obrigkeitt träget das schwert nicht vmbsonst. Sie ist eine rächerinn zur strafe vber den so böses thut. Vndt an[a] viel andere sprüche mehr so in der bibel stehen. [...] Sie sagten auch des hertzogs von Fridlandt sein **Astrologus**[13] wehre eine stunde zuvor bey ihm gewesen, hette ihn gewarnet, sich innerhalb 15 tagen, vor gift wol zu hüten vndt vorzusehen! Er Fridlandt selber hette sich auch nichts gutes schwahnen laßen, zwar nicht vor gifft, aber vor **mutination** der Regimenter sich geförchtett, offt zum fenster hinauß gesehen, den angsten Schweiß [191v] von der Stirn, offt abgewischtt, daß viel Leutte auf den gaßen vndt sonsten, es sollen sein gewahr worden. **Fata interdum possunt præviderj, non tamen**ᵃ **evitarj**. Ach wie gar nichts seindt doch alle Menschen, die so sicher leben. *[Ps. 39, 6]* Hela! Quj stat, videat, ne cadat!

F. Christian besichtigte auch den Ort im Schloß, wo Trčka,⁹ Kinsky,¹⁰ Ilow⁸ u. Niemann¹¹ erschlagen wurden, indem Sie mitt dem Obersten **Cordon**[5], **Budler**[6], vndt Leßle[7] gegeßen, vndt habe die **circumstantien** wie es zugegangen, vom proviandtschreiber erzehlen hören.

Am 26.11.1636 machte Christian in Regensburg am ksl. Hof kurz Bekanntschaft mit Leslie⁷:
bin ich darnach gen hof geritten, **la ou il m'a estè impossible d'aborder les grands, que je cerchois**. Bin aber mitt dem Obersten Leßle[7] bekandt wor*den*, welcher außdrücklich sagt: der Kayser hette ihnen nit befohlen, den Fridtländer zu Eger vmbzubringen, sondern Sie hetten sich vndtereinander selber also verglichen, dieweil es wieder ihre pflicht lieffe, ihrem herren, sein Landt zu nehmen, dann Fridl. hette dem Kayser nicht allein, das Königreich Böhmen nehmen wollen, sondern auch das Kayserthumb. Darnach abrumpirt er, diese matery, vndt eilete weg. *(A. a. O., Bl. 258r).* Dieser Oberste Leßle[7] [...] hat nebenst dem Obersten Buttler[6] vndt Obersten Cordon[5], nach vollbrachter depeschirung des generals Fridländers, stadtliche recompenßen beko*mmen*. Jst auch Päbstisch worden, wie auch Buttler[6]. Cordon[5] aber nichtt. *(Bl. 259r).*

III

Valeriano Castiglione über Loredanos *Dianea* und dessen Darstellung der Ermordung Wallensteins

Q LETTERE DELL' ABBATE D. VALERIANO CASTIGLIONE. SV L'OPERE DELL'Illustrissimo Signor GIO. FRANCESCO LOREDANO Nobile Veneto. IN TORINO ET IN VENETIA, M. DC. XLVI. per il Valuasense. Con licenza de' Superiori. S. 33. — HAB: 117.13 Eth.(3).

La Caduta del Valdestain.

FV' il Valdestain vittima di ribellione caduta sotto le securi di Cesare. Non cadrà però dalla memoria de' Posteri la tragica relatione, che ne ha scritto V. S. Illustriss. Poiche dalle auliche, e politiche consideratione in essa contenute acquista egli merito d'immortalità. Grandezza infelice, che lasciò precipitar da i colpi dell'Inuidia chi fra tante battaglie gl'assalti non ha temuto della Morte. Con tal'essempio si mortalmente discorre V. S. Illustriss. intorno le vicende della Fortuna inconstante, e della caducità dell'humano fauore, che degna si rende dell'amore de i ben fortunati, e de fauoriti di Corte. Passo a gli Scherzi Geniali[1] promessimi da V. S. Illustriss. Offerta c'ha stimolato il mio Genio all'impatienza di leggerli. Io la prego a non ritardamene il dono per felicitarmi l'Ingegno. Mi prefiguro valor di Penna, e merito di sapere di sapere ambidue persuadenti la marauiglia. Su questo pensiero mi fermo dallo scriuere per baciar a V. S. Illustriss. come fò, caramente le mani.

T I a *Lies:* sich

T II a *Eingefügt.*

K 1 Conrad v. Burgsdorff (FG 404) trug sich 1644 in das *GB Kö.* III ein. *Conermann III*, 481. Im Köthener Erzschrein hat sich die Niederschrift von Burgsdorffs FG-Imprese u. Reimgesetz von der Hand Diederichs v. dem Werder (FG 31) erhalten. HM Köthen: V S 546, Bl. 69r. Der kurbrandenburg. Oberkammerherr, Geheime Rat, Obrist u. Befehlshaber der märk. Festungen war nach dem Regierungsantritt des Großen Kurfürsten Friedrich Wilhelm (FG 401) zu dessen einflußreichem Berater aufgestiegen. Er hatte unter dem Vater Friedrich Wilhelms, Kf. Georg Wilhelm (FG 307), zeitweilig gegen Gf. Adam v. Schwarzenberg eine Anlehnung an Hans Georg v. Arnim (FG 255) u. Wallenstein empfohlen. Diederich v. dem Werder wurde erst 1646 zu einem Kollegen Burgsdorffs. Er leistete am 25.1.1646 zu Königsberg in Gegenwart Kf. Friedrich Wilhelms u. Burgsdorffs den Diensteid auf seine Bestallung zum Geheimen Rat u. Kriegsobristen. S. 460125 u. Otto Meinardus: Protokolle und Relationen des brandenburgischen Geheimen Rathes aus der Zeit des Kurfürsten Friedrich Wilhelm. Bd. III: Vom Januar 1645 bis Ende August 1647. Osnabrück 1965, 225 u. 357.

2 Anagramm des Briefschreibers: Dietrich von dem Werder. Werder benutzte das Anagramm auch als Unterschrift eines Epicediums in der Funeralschrift auf seinen Mitgesellschafter in der FG, Freund, Nachbarn u. Kollegen in der anhaltischen Ständevertretung, Cuno Ordomar v. Bodenhausen (FG 69): Martin Beutnitz: **Mors piorum, finis omnium malorum** ... **Bey Wohlansehnlicher Leichbestattung** ... **Herren Cuno Ordemars von Bodenhausen** ... **Welcher den 2. Octobris** ... **1654.** ... **selig entschlaffen; Wie auch bey Leichbestattung seines hertzgeliebten Jüngsten Sohnes/** ... **Ernst Lebrecht von Bodenhausen** (o. O. 1655), Bl. K[iv] r – M[i] r. *LP Stolberg* 6356/ 6357. S. *DA Köthen I. 4*, 405 f. — Zu Werders Autorschaft der *Dianea*-Übersetzung s. Dünnhaupts Einleitung zu seiner Ausgabe, S. 37*; ders.: Diederich von dem Werder oder Georg Philipp Harsdörffer? Zur Klärung der umstrittenen Autorschaft der *Dianea* von 1644. In: Germanisch-Romanische Monatsschrift 23 (1973), 115–118. — Zu Loredano s. 450817 (bes. K 8) u. 460000A. — Sigmund v. Birken (FG 681. Der Erwachsene. 1658) erwähnt in der „Vor-Ansprache zum edlen Leser" in der *Aramena* (1669) Hz. Anton Ulrichs v. Braunschweig-Wolfenbüttel (FG 716. 1659) nach der Aufzählung europäischer Epen u. Romane („Geschichtgedichte"): „Aber zu zeigen/ daß auch Teutschland grosse geister habe/ die etwas aus eigenem gehirn herfür bringen können/ haben die zween teure Palmgenossen/ der Vielgekörnte (besagter Obrister von Werder) die Dianea/ und der Sinnreiche (Herr von Hohberg/) die Proserpina und den Ottbert/ ihre eigene Sinnbruten/ so preisbar an das tagliecht gestellet/ daß sie nicht allein denen ausländischen die wage halten/ sondern auch vielen derselben fürwägen können." Hz. Anton Ulrich v. Braunschweig-Wolfenbüttel: Die durchleuchtige Aramena. Der erste Teil. Hg. u. mit e. Nachw. vers. v. Blake Lee

Spahr. Bern u. a. 1975, Bl.)(5r. Birken lebte wie Harsdörffer in Nürnberg u. müßte von diesem die Vorlage für Werders Übertragung erfahren haben. Er besaß dieses Buch auch bereits 1646/47 u. bezeichnete Werder als alleinigen Autor eines der ersten neueren höfischen Romane der dt. Literatur. Zu Birkens Besitz eines Exemplars s. *Birken: Werke u. Korrespondenz* IX.1, 50 u. 2, 670f.

K I 1 Albrecht Wenzel Eusebius v. Wallenstein, der bekannte ksl. Generalissimus u. Herzog v. Friedland, wurde aufgrund Verratsvorwürfen seiner Ämter enthoben u. am Abend des 25.2.1634 n. St. in Eger ermordet. In der dt. Romanübersetzung heißt der Herzog Lastevin (ital. Lovastine). Diederich v. dem Werder (FG 31) erfand oft neue Pseudonyme für die Schlüsselfiguren des Romans. Vor diesem Werk veröffentlichte Loredano eine historische Arbeit über den Generalissimus unter dem Pseudonym Gneo Falcidio Donaloro: Ribellione, e morte del Volestain, generale della maestà cesarea (Milano: per Filippo Ghisolfi: ad instan. di Gio. Battista Cerri 1634), 8°, 52 Bll.; Biblioteca Nazionale Centrale, Florenz; Biblioteca Nazionale Braidense, Mailand; Ribellione e morte del Volestain, generale della Maestà Cesarea. All'illustre sig. mio osseruandissimo il sig. Gualtier Vanderuort. (Venetia: presso il Sarzina, 1634); Biblioteca Universitaria, Bologna u. a. ital. Nachweise. Von uns benutzt die Ausgabe *La Morte de Volestain.* In: Opere di Gio. Francesco Loredano nobile veneto. Diuise in sei volumi. All'illustriss. sig. sig. mia osseruand. la signora, Maria Cristina Malaspina (Venetia: li Guerigli 1653ff.), Vol. 3 (1653), 91–118 (zit. *Morte*); HAB: Lk 477. — Übers.: Lebens Außgang Deß Wallensteiners/ Hertzogen zu Friedland und Sagan/ Käyserlichen Majestät General Feldmarschalln. Geschrieben Von dem Edlen Venetianer Franciscus Loredanus. Gedeutschet Von Samuel Sturm. Jm Jahr 1664. HAB: 572.15 Qu. (3). Zit. *Wallersteiner.* — Loredanos Beschreibung *La Morte de Volestain* ist in der Form eines Briefs an einen unbekannten Auftraggeber geschrieben. Es ist eine zeithistorische, keine literarische oder rednerische Darstellung. — Der Fruchtbringer Carl Gustav v. Hille (FG 302), der auch eine ital. Ausgabe von Loredanos Roman besaß (s. o.), erwähnte in 440209A (K 4) ein englisches Wallenstein-Drama Henry Glapthornes, das Harsdörffer (FG 368) ihm senden wolle. Ob Diederich v. dem Werder, der 1644 in Nürnberg in seiner Übersetzung der *Dianea* Giovanni Francesco Loredanos den Sturz u. die Ermordung Wallensteins behandelte, durch F. Ludwig oder Harsdörffer auch von diesem Drama erfahren u. dessen Druck empfangen hat, konnte nicht festgestellt werden. — Werder war über die geheimen Verhandlungen zw. Kursachsen u. Wallenstein sowie das schwed. Interesse genau unterrichtet, war er doch im Frühjahr 1634 als außerordentlicher Gesandter Schwedens in Dresden tätig, wo er auch mit Generallt. Hans Georg v. Arnim (FG 255) zusammentraf. Berichte an Axel Oxenstierna bezeugen sein Insider-Wissen. Vgl. Georg Irmer: Die Verhandlungen Schwedens und seiner Verbündeten mit Wallenstein und dem Kaiser von 1631 bis 1634. 3 Tle. Leipzig 1888–1891, III, 305f. sowie S. 251 Anm. 1 u. S. 255 Anm. 1; vgl. auch I, 150–157. Werders Trauersonett auf Arnim (410500) bezeugt i. Ü. die nahe Verbindung, die zwischen beiden bestanden hatte.

2 Florideas Vater Dinanderfo, König der von Böotien (Böhmen) durch einen Fluß getrennten Insel Negroponte, erinnert in Loredanos Roman u. dessen Übersetzung an Ks. Ferdinand II. Loredanos *Dianea* ist, wie Dünnhaupt in der Einleitung seiner Ausgabe betont, trotz mancher Bezüge auf historische Ereignisse u. Personen jedoch kein Schlüsselroman im strengen Sinn, so daß viele Gestalten im Bereich der Fiktion bleiben.

3 Gf. Maximilian v. Waldstein (Wallenstein) († 1654), ital. Duca di Lassimano, ksl. Kämmerer u. kgl. ungar. Oberstallmeister, war Vetter u. Haupterbe des Ermordeten. Vgl. *Morte*, 93: „Risolse finalmente S M. di far vn' atto veramente da Cesare. Mandò a chiamare il Conte Massimiliano Nipote del Volestain, alquale con encomij non ordinarij esaltò i

meriti, le virtù, e la fede del Zio: ch'egli nō si conosceua più obligato ad altri: e che la sicurezza, e la difesa dell'imperio era riposta nelle sue mani [...]." Der Graf v. Assalino des Romans ist lt. *Wallersteiner*, 10 f. der Neffe des Feldherren: „Sie [Majestät, Ks. Ferdinand II.] befahl den Grafen Maximilian von Wallenstein seinen Vettern vor sich zuberuffen/ dem er mit absonderlich hohen Lobreden des Generals/ Tugenden und Treue rühmete: daß er sich keinem andern so hoch verpflichtet befünde: daß die Sicherheit und Beschützung des Reichs in seine Hände und Gewalt übergeben were: sandte ihn nach Pilsen/ damit er solche Worte mündlich dem Wallenstein berichten sollte. Versicherten jhn/ daß anderer Personen Zungen und Reden jhn sein Hertze zu bewegen keine solche Krafft hätten/ weil sein eigendliches Begehren/ daß seine Dienste/ Mühe und Arbeit vor das Reich in aller Menschen Augen das Ansehen haben möchten/ vornehmlich mehr wegen der empfindlichen Meinung/ die er wegen der Gewalt und Hochheit des Generalats gefast/ als des Zweiffels/ so bey jhm entstehen [11] können/ daß er seine Dienste und Bestallung nicht wol sollte versehen und verwaltet haben." Der Kaiser sandte einen Rat mit, der den General Wallenstein beobachten sollte: „schickten auch einen Käyserlichen Cammer-Raht mit/ dem dieser Vnterricht ertheilet/ des General Wallensteins Worte/ Beginnen/ und Geberden wol zu beobachten/ und sein Vornehmen fleissig zuerforschen." In der *Morte* bzw. im *Wallersteiner* werden viel mehr Umstände berichtet. So sagt Loredano, daß der Generalissimus von den Absichten der Gesandtschaft erfahren habe, bevor der Rat in Pilsen eingetroffen sei: „Mit solchem allen können die großwichtigen Anschläge nimmer bemäntelt und verlarfet werden/ dann in dergleichen Begebenheiten reden die Bäume und Felsen." (S. 12). Solche Lehren kommen im Roman selten vor. Loredano räsoniert in seiner historischen Darstellung auch darüber, woran sich die Untreue des Generals zeigte, der Gelegenheiten zum Schlagen des Feindes ausgelassen, neue Kapitulationen geschlossen u. die gegnerischen Gefangenen Duval u. Thurn losgelassen habe. *Wallersteiner*, 14: „Daß er aber heimliche Berahtschlagungen mit den Churfürsten von Sachsen und Brandenburg gepflogen: Da sie nahe auff den Schluß der Vergleichung und Friedens gestanden/ weßwegen man seine Schreiben gesehen/ die jhn dessen schuldig gemacht/ war keine Forwendung mehr zu finden/ damit er seinem Thun und Vorhaben eine Farbe anstreichen können." Der Roman faßt die Berichte des Rats u. der treuen Offiziere auf S. 135 (Abs. 19) dagegen kurz zusammen. Das Werben Wallensteins um Piccolomini läßt der Roman aus. Wallenstein wird vor Piccolomini gewarnt, entgegnet aber: „Er antwortete/ Er dürffte sich vor keinem Verraht fürchten/ weil Er auß des Picolomini Natiuität ersehen/ daß sie eine gleichheit des Gebuhrt Geistes und Gemühtes/ eine gleiche zusammenkunfft der Planeten hätten [...]. Der Wallenstein verrahtet seinen Fürsten seinen eigenen Ehrsüchtigen Begührden nach zu hangen; hingegen hindergehet der Piccolomini seinem Freundt/ damit Er seinem Fürsten schuldigen Dienste nicht vergessen mögte." (S. 18/19).

4 Vgl. dagegen die differenzierten Mitteilungen des Historikers u. die Beurteilung Wallensteins durch den Politicus in *Morte*, 94 f.: „Non era il Consigliere gionto in Pilzen, che il Volestain fù preauertito della ispeditione di questo soggetto, e delle commissioni, che teneua. Si sforzò di preuenirlo con incontrar in molte cose i comandi, e i desideri di S. M. Con tutto ciò le grand'intraprese non possono mascherarsi giamai. Gli sterpi, e le pietre parlano in simili occasioni. Fù di subito auuertito dell'alienatione del suo animo, e dell'infedeltà del suo cuore. Che i suoi pensieri erano assai maggiori del suo debito, e che le sue speranze trapassauano di grā lunga l'honore di Generale dell'Imperio.
Gli argomenti principali, che lo conuiceuano di perfidia era l'operare lentamente nell'opportunità dell'occasione, che poteuano renderlo vittorioso. L'obligo particolare di chi comanda è il non trascurare le congionture. Si sdegna la fortuna non abbracciata a suo tempo. Si finge con l'ali, perche fugge da coloro, che non sanno prenderla per lo crine.

Rinouò la tregua, pratticò le capitulationi, quando per li progressi dell'armi, per l'ardire dei soldati, per l'essortationi de i Capitani, e per le stragi della peste nello stato di Sassonia si credeua inopportuna ogn'altra cosa, che'l proseguire la guerra. Permetteua rincorarsi gli animi, e rinuigorirsi le forze de i Protestanti in tempo, che con sicurezza de' suoi poteua accelerare il loro precipitio."

5 Die ksl. Generäle Octavio Piccolomini d'Aragona Duca d'Amalfi (FG 356) u. Gf. Matthias Gallas v. Campo (1588–1647), Hz. v. Lucera. *Morte*, 95 f. u. 98. In den ital. Ausgaben des Romans heißen die beiden Collateral Picomeni bzw. Conte di Lagasso.

6 In *Morte* wirbt Wallenstein, obwohl vor dem Italiener gewarnt, um die alte Freundschaft Piccolominis, dessen Horoskop ihm ihre geistige Verwandtschaft bestätigt. Dazu sendet er ihm Gallas u. Johann v. Aldringen (1588–1634) entgegen, um sie zu seinem, Wallensteins Heer, zurückzuführen. Vgl. oben Anm. 3. Piccolomini tat aber das Gegenteil: „Parti con tal carico il Piccolomini, e ritrouati l'Aldringher, e Galasso, gli auuertì allontanarsi da Pilzen, perche senza dubbio v'hauerebbono lasciato, o la vita, o la fede, onde vniti si ritirorono, mandando l'Aldringher a Cesare con gli auuisi." (S. 96).

7 Eger in Böhmen. Vgl. *Morte*, 106: „Stimò il Volestain ottimo ispediente di ritirarsi in Egra: non solo perche il sito era auantaggioso, la fortezza inespugnabile, il popolo ben'affetto; ma perche il Gouernatore era Protestante posto da lui alla difesa di quella Piazza. L'haueua di pouero soldato solleuato al comando d'vna Cittá, ch'egli credeua la sicurezza della sua salute, e il ricouero delle sue speranze."

8 *Dianea 1638*, 70: „Disse di molte parole protestando la sua innocenza: ch'egli fuggiua da gli sdegni di Sua Maestà, senz'hauer' altro pensiero, che quello della propria sicurezza: che se hauesse hauuto opinione sopra la vita del Rè, ò del Regno non gli sarebbero mancati mezi più sicuri, e più esecrabili: che s'appelaua a Sua Maestà, quando deposta la mala impressione de i maleuoli, hauesse seueramente ponderate le sue operationi. Essagerò le miserie di coloro, che sono necessitati a seruire a i Grandi, che possono ciò, che vogliono." Wortgleich *Dianea 1643*, 103 f. — Vgl. dagegen die Letzten Worte Wallensteins in *Morte*, 110 f.: „Questi venuti alla Camera del Volestain gittata la porta in terra se le auuentarono contro. Egli perduto dal sonno, e dal timore corse ad vna finestra per saluarsi. Considerando in vn subito la caduta mortale, e lo scampo impossibile s'auento con le braccia aperte ad vn Soldato per leuargli vn'Alabarda. Il Soldato ritirandosi vn passo indietro lo fece infilzare da se medesimo, e darsi la morte. Esalando lo spirito mandò fuori alcune parole, che ò mal dette, ò male intese hanno hauuto mille interpretationi. Disse però, che raccomandaua alla giustitia di Cesare le sue ragioni, e la sua innocenza. Che hauerebbe felicitati gli horrori della sua morte, quando sapesse che l'Imperatore l'hauesse comandata, e che non hauendo tenuto della vita negli Esserciti, molto meno ne temeua tra i soldati, anchorche traditori."

9 *Dianea 1643*, 105 „il Duca di Lassimano Nepote di Louastine".

K II Diederich v. dem Werder (FG 31) waren die Ereignisse um den Fall Wallensteins allgegenwärtig, wie aus seinem Schreiben 380509A an F. Ludwig hervorgeht, welches er „am tage des friedtländischen Mörders den 9. Maij. 1638" (Gordon) datierte. Vgl. auch K I 1. Die Erwartung, daß F. Ludwig Werders *Dianea* erhielt, bestätigt das Nachlaßverzeichnis mit 3 Exemplaren *IP* 330v u. 335r. Italienische Ausgaben fehlen, wie oben bemerkt, darin. Daß die Anhaltiner u. ihr Umkreis über nähere Einzelheiten des Wallenstein-Mordes unterrichtet waren, zeigt der von uns entdeckte u. hier veröffentlichte Eintrag im Tagebuch F. Christians II. v. Anhalt-Bernburg (FG 51). Während eines Eger-Aufenthaltes hatte F. Christian sogar die Orte des Geschehens besichtigt. — Hauptakteure jener Mordnacht waren der kathol. Ire Walter Butler († 1634), Obrist eines ksl. Dragonerregiments, sowie die calvinist. Schotten Walter Leslie (1607–1667), Obristwachtmeister u. stellvertretender Befehlshaber in Eger, u. John Gordon († 1649), Obristleutnant u. Festungskommandant, der sich in das Komplott hineinziehen ließ. Die eigentliche Exekution übertrug Butler drei Offizieren seines Regimentes: MacDaniel, Geraldin u. Butlers Adjutanten, dem Hauptmann Walter Deveroux (Devereux), der den tödlichen Hellebardenstoß gegen Wallenstein führte. Vgl. *Theatrum europaeum* III (1644), 182 f.; *Krieg und Frieden I*, 377; Friedemann Bedürftig: Taschenlexikon Dreißigjähriger Krieg. München, Zürich ²1999, 238; Heinrich Bücheler: Von Pappenheim zu Piccolomini. Sechs Gestalten aus Wallensteins Lager. Sigmaringen 1994, 66 ff.; Golo Mann: Wallenstein. Frankfurt a. M. 1971, 1114 ff.; Josef Polisenský u. Josef Kollmann: Wallenstein. Feldherr des 30j. Krieges. Köln usw. 1997, 248 ff. — Im März 1637 erneut in Regensburg, erfuhr Christian die abenteuerlichsten Gerüchte u. Räuberpistolen über das Ausmaß der Wallensteinschen Verschwörung aus dem Munde des ksl. Hofkriegsratspräsidenten, Gf. Heinrich Schlick zu Bassano u. Weißkirchen (1580–1650). Vgl. a. a. O., Bl. 372v–373r: „Piccolominj hette befehl gehabt, auf Wien zu gehen, den Kayser vndt König vmbzubringen, wie auch den Ertzhertzogk, ingleichen die Königinn wo ferne sie Schwanger wehre, sonst nicht, die Kayserinn allein sollte man Leben Lassen, aber alles waß Männlich, vom hauß Oesterreich in Deutschlandt, (darundter auch Erzh. Leopold söhne zu Inspruk) hinrichten wie Phocas mitt Kayser **Mauritio** vmbgegangen. Man hette auch sollen dem Kayser den paß nach der Neẅstadt oder dem gebirge zu, zu endtweichen, abschneiden, Jhne Graf Schlicken, vndt Obristen Löbl, weil sie sich in Wien doch wehren würden, sollte man Laßen am Marckt aufhencken [373r] vndt hat sie beyde schelme genennet. Den *Grafen* von Megkaw, vndt *Grafen* von Schlawata, die er beyde vor alte Narren gescholten, sollte man auch also tractiren. Die vbrigen rähte wollte er wol auf seine seitte bekom̄en, außer den *Grafen* v. Trauttmanßdorf, welchem man eben wie den andern mittspielen sollte. Er Graf Schligk beklagte es, daß man diese sachen, wie vnchristlich vndt vngühtlich dem guten Kayser beschehen, nicht recht Ließ in druck außgehen. Er hette es oft erinnert, aber etzlich wenig sezten sich auß allzugroßem bedencken darwieder. Fridlandt hette auch gesagt: Er wollte daß hauß Oesterreich in Deutschlandt außrotten, daß in Spannien, wollte er dem König in F*rankreich* zu vertilgen, vberlaßen."

1 Es handelt sich um das sog. Pachelbelhaus (heute: Museum der Stadt Cheb) am Markt, d. h. das Haus des damaligen Bürgermeisters von Eger, Alexander Pachelbel, in dem Wallenstein ermordet wurde.

2 Hauptmann Walter Deveroux (Devereux). S. Anm. 0.

3 Einfaches Leintuch. S. *Götze*, 149.

4 Robert Geraldin. Erwähnt in Anm. 0.

5 John Gordon, Obristleutnant u. Festungskommandant. S. Anm 0.

6 Walter Butler, ein Ire, Obrist eines ksl. Dragonerregiments. S. Anm. 0.

7 Walter Leslie, calvinistischer Schotte, Obristwachtmeister u. stellvertretender Befehlshaber in Eger. S. Anm. 0.

8 Wallensteins Feldmarschall u. Vertrauter Frh. Christian v. Ilow, ein Brandenburger.

9 Der junge böhm. Gf. Adam Erdmann Trčka v. Lipa.

10 Der böhm. Emigrant Gf. Wilhelm Kinsky v. Wchinitz u. Tettau.

11 Gf. Trčkas (s. Anm. 9) Kanzleichef u. Rittmeister Heinrich Niemann.

12 F. Christian I. v. Anhalt-Bernburg (FG 26).

13 Giovanni Battista Senno († 1656), Astrologe u. Leibarzt Wallensteins. Schiller setzte Senno im Drama „Wallensteins Tod" (1799) mit der Figur des „Seni" ein Denkmal.

K III Valeriano Castiglione, * 3.1.1593, Sohn des Francesco Castiglione, „letteratissimo Protofisico degli Esserciti della Maestà Cattolica", aus dem Geschlecht des Gf. Baldassare Castiglione, des Autors des *Cortigiano*. Vgl. LE GLORIE DE GLI INCOGNITI O vero GLI HVOMINI ILLVSTRI DELL'ACCADEMIA DE' SIGNORI INCOGNITI DI VENETIA (Venetia: Francesco Valuasense 1647), 420–423. HAB: 58.20 Hist. — Castiglione wurde Mönch zu Monte Cassino u. dann Abt. Das Mitglied der Incogniti wurde auch unter die Erranti von Brescia aufgenommen u. von Carlo Emanuele Duca di Savoia eingeladen, die Geschichte seiner Taten zu schreiben. Auch Vittorio Amadeo u. dessen Mutter, die Madama Reale, beauftragten ihn mit historischen Arbeiten. Auch für Kd. Richelieu beschrieb er dessen Leben. Kg. Ludwig XIII. v. Frankreich verschaffte ihm eine Pension u. die Ernennung zum Historico Italiano des Königs. Castiglione schrieb: Lo Statista Regnante; Il Prencipe Bambino; Lettere di Ringratiamento; Panegirico à Luigi XIII. Rè di Francia; Lettere sopra l'Opere del Loredano. Druckfertig hatte er: L'Historie de' suoi tempi. — In seinem Brief über Loredanos *La Dianea* (S. 30 f.) beginnt Castiglione: „STauo scriuendo di Madama di Sauoia, quando mi fù recata la principessa Dianea. Vedutala glorificata in fronte del nome di V. S. Illustrissima la baciai, e ribaciai". C. preist das Werk Loredanos in allgemeinen Worten.

1 In seinem Brief vom 8.7.1634 schreibt Loredano „Mando gli Scherzi, perche li chiede."(S. 35).

440100

Justus Georg Schottelius an Herzog August d. J. von Braunschweig-Wolfenbüttel

Justus Georg Schottelius (FG 397) schickt eine nach griechischer Manier in einem freien Stündchen verfaßte neuartige (Pindarische) Ode, außerdem noch Ringelreime an Hz. August d.J. v. Braunschweig-Wolfenbüttel (FG 227). Solche in der deutschen Poesie bisher unbekannten Gedichte dienen zusammen mit vielen anderen Texten zur Erklärung und als Beispiele einer neuen deutschen Poetik (*Schottelius: Teutsche Vers- oder Reimkunst*). — Da er, Schottelius, bisher kein eigenes Studierzimmer und nicht einmal einen Tisch zum Lesen eines Buchs habe, bittet er den Herzog um einen kleinen eigenen Raum. Der andere Präzeptor (Abraham Marconnet), der sehr gern für sich alleine arbeite und unbehelligt bleibe, besetze das vorhandene Studierzimmer für seinen Morgenunterricht und das morgendliche und abendliche Gebet mit den Prinzen. Schottelius verbringe am Morgen einige Stunden mit den drei Prinzessinnen, am Nachmittag mit den Prinzen. An manchen Tagen kämpfe er, besonders in der Frühe und am Abend, mit der Kälte und sehne sich danach, in den Morgenstunden, nachts oder sonst zwischendurch den Raum verlassen zu dürfen, um zu studieren oder nachzudenken und um den anderen Präzeptor oder gar die Prinzen nicht zu stören. Hinzu kommt, daß er oft Akten aus dem Kirchenrat zu bearbeiten habe, auch möchte er seinen eigenen, gar nicht so kleinen Büchervorrat benutzen. Er werde aber keinen Augenblick seine Pflicht versäumen. Auch der andere Lehrer bitte darum, wenigstens morgens und nachmittags teilweise in seinem Zimmer allein gelassen zu werden. Beide hätten sich den Tag über zu wechselndem Unterricht verabredet. Schottelius bittet vor allem wegen des nahenden Winters auch im Namen seines Kollegen darum, entweder in Braunschweig oder in der Nähe einen eigenen Raum zu bekommen oder in Wolfenbüttel ein eigenes bequemeres Studierzimmer nutzen zu dürfen.

Q NSTA Wolfenbüttel: 2 Alt 3520, Bl. 46r–47v [A: 47v]; eigenh.

A Serenissim° Jllustrissimo ad manus Clementissimas

Serenissime Illustrissimque Princeps, Domine Clementissime

Oden quandam, Pindarico more et stylo Græcissantem, apud nos autem, generis novj,[1] per vacantis horulæ veniam composuj: uti et aliam quandam, circulo-recurrentem oden:[2] Utramque literis hisce adiunctam Vestræ Serenitati exhibere humillimus debuj. Non modò enim hisce duabus, sed et aliis multis, pio et devoto affectu, pro nova occasione materiis (vestigia enim aut exempla Germanis Poetæ, non ita hactenus exstant) compositis, exempli et declarationum loco in Poetica linguæ Germanicæ, non raró venient.[3] Quod qvidem, insciâ omninò Vestra Serenitate, ut fieri non debvit, ita confidam, sicut ad aliqualem, subiectissimæ meæ fidelitatis memoriam fortasse durabunt, et ex mente gnarâ profecta sunt, non inclementi affectu eiusmodj Musarum contestationes haberj, aut dissensu eas his vocibus audirj.

Porrò Serenissime Princeps, Domine clementissime, molestiâ quadam, vel tantum non summâ, urgeor et divexor, quæ et has preces meas expressit ad Vestræ Serenitatis aures afferendas, quas toties clementissimè mihi adapertas recorder, quare et in hac re tam facilj mihi non occlusas fore, confidenter spero. Commorati fuimus hactenus Ego et alter Præceptor[4] simul, commoratus autem ego et adhuc commoror, non modò sine musæolo, sed et sine mensâ et exiguo aliquo loco, ubi solus cum libello vivere possem: Musæolum enim ipsum cum Illustrissimis Principibus alter Præceptor sibi servat: ille enim horis antemeridianis Eosdem informat, et manè et vespere precibus eorum solus iam interest: Nam et Principes [46v] eo modo bene iam tractare novit, et lubenter id solus agit et agere vult: Equidem autem, qui horis aliquot antemeridianis Illustrissimas Vestræ Serenitatis Filias tres informandas habeo, pomeridianis autem horis totis Illustrissimis Principibus Vestræ Serentatis Filiis charissimis, adsum,[5] singulis diebus imprimis manè et vesperj, frigore conflictor, et omni oportunitate loci exulo, nec horas matutinas aut[a] noctis partem aut[b] alia veniæ intervalla ut saepè anxiè desidero. studiis aut meditationj dare possum, misi aut alterum Præceptorem, qui omnino solus esse gaudet, turbem, aut etiam ipsis Principibus impedimento sim: Quod sanè quantis molestiis et impatientiae vicibus subiectum sit, Vestra Serenitas clementissime et facillimé animadvertit: Accedit quod ex Dicasterio Acta subinde habeam, quibus Relatio extrahenda et scripta concipienda est: Librorum etiam meorum supellex non adeò parva est, cuius liberum et impeditum usum vehementissimé desidero. Quapropter Vestram Serenitatem sollicitatione humillimâ adire cogor, tandem omni prece rogans, vetit hac tam diu sperata mihi commoditate per gratiosum adnutum me beare, ut Musis et meditationibus meis proprium aliquod exiguum Musaeolum habere queam: Nec horula, imò nec momentum debitis officij, dedecet, nec vel in minimo ullo Jllustrissimis Principibus aliquid ullâ in re, volente DEo, aberit: Et alter etiam Præceptor eò alacrior sua trac-

440100 Justus Georg Schottelius 163

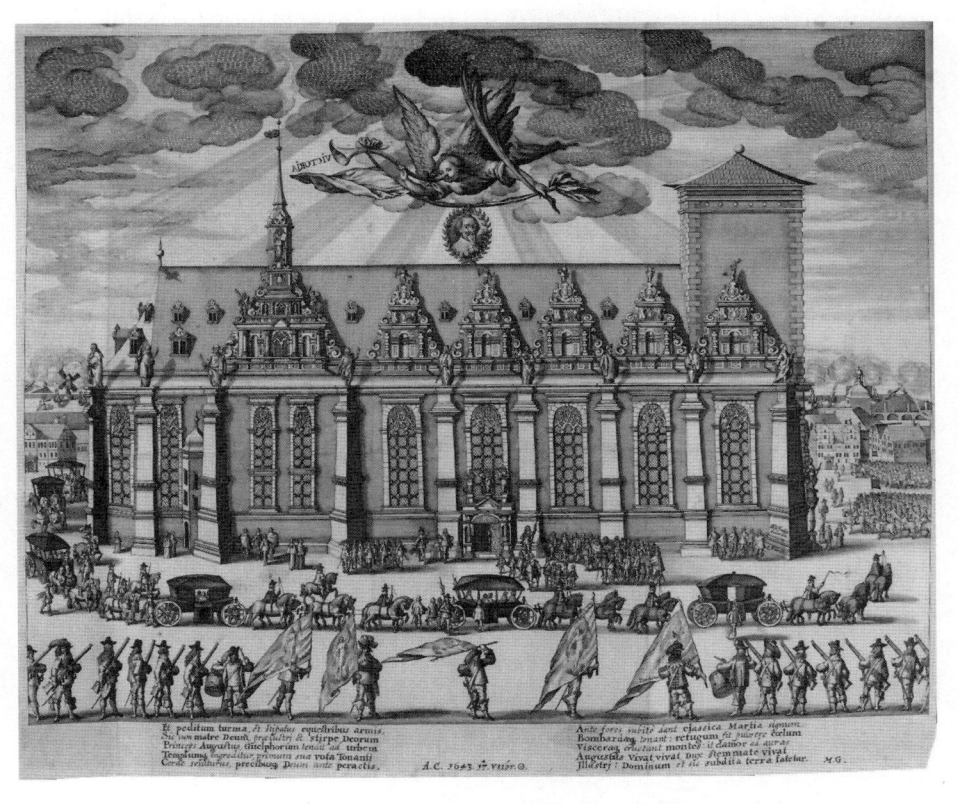

Feierlicher Einzug Herzog Augusts d.J. v. Braunschweig-Wolfenbüttel (FG 227) in Wolfenbüttel, 17.9.1643, vor der Kirche Beatae Mariae Virginis. Zu 440100.

tabit, qui^c id à me expetit, se solum^d matutinis et vespertinis horis cum suo studio relinqui, quod ibidem ego mihi summè expeto. Totum autem diem ita dividimus, ut continue per vices informationi adsimus. V*est*ra Serenitas ergo [47r] consensu clementj nobis succurrere, mihiq*ue* concedere velit, ut, si per asperiora venientis hyemis adhuc nobis hîc^6 manendum, vel in propinquo Musaeolum possidere cum meis rebus aut Wolferbutelj proprio et commodiore loco frui queam: Si enim frigus iterum invalescat, sanè sine incommodo meæ valetudinis, ut hactenus sustinere, sustinere amplius non potero, nec, à Vestra Serenitate eiusmodj mej detrimentj incommodentis liberationem, clementissimè non faveri, non etiam sperare debeo. Responsione clementissimâ dignare valet Vestra Serenitas

Eiusdem Fidelissimum Obedientissimumq*ue* Servum
Justum-Georgium Schottelium

I

Schottelius' *Pindarische Ode* (1643)

Q Justus Georg Schottelius: ODE Auff neue Pindarische Art/ Dem … Herrn Augusto/ Hertzogen zu Braunschweig und Lüneburg/ &c. Als Seine Fürstl. Gn. in dero Haubt-Vestung und ResidentzStat Wolfenbüttel glücklichen und mit Freuden eingezogen/ unterthänig überreichet. Von J. G. S. (Braunschweig: Balthasar Gruber 1643) VD17 23:668341Z; Dig. der HAB: G3:A36 (zit. als A); Nachdr. in *Schottelius: Teutsche Vers- oder ReimKunst (1645)*, 298–301 (zit. als B) bzw. *Schottelius: Teutsche Vers- oder ReimKunst (1656)*, 251–253; *Gosky: Arbustum (1650)*, Bl. 228v–229v (zit. als C); *Schottelius: Ausführliche Arbeit (1663)*, 978–980, jeweils mit leichten Abweichungen gegenüber dem Erstdruck. S. Abb. S. 169.

ODE
Auff neue Pindarische Art/[1]

Dem
Durchleuchtigen/ Hochgebornen Fürsten und Herrn/

Herrn Augusto/ Hertzogen zu Braunschweig und
Lüneburg/ *etc.* Als Seine Fürstl. Gn. In dero Haubt-Vestung und ResidentzStat Wolfenbüttel[2] glücklichen und mit Freuden eingezogen/ unterthänig überreichet.

Von J. G. S.

Στροφὴ oder Satz I.
EDle Burg/ berühmtes Büttel/[a2]
Hochbelobtes^b Welpen-Haus/^{c}
Heb dein freyes^d Haupt heraus/
Lös^e jetzt ab/ und von dir schüttel
Deinen eingelegten Zügel/
Stahl- und Eisenstarcken Riegel:

Zeig dein blanck-beschmutztes Maul/[f]
Deine grüne Erden-Mauren[g]
Laß[h] zum Trotz' eins sicher lauren/
Sey[i] auß Stoltz und Hoffart faul.
Schau nun üm dich weit und lang/
Du bist Alt/ Neu/ Frey und Franck.

Ἀντίστροφ oder Gegensatz I.
HOhe Vestung/ wolgelegen/
Unsers Landes Trotzensteyn:
Wer hat müssen dann der seyn
Unter Welpen/ unter Degen/[j]
Der dich zwingend hat gebogen?
Und in dich mit Sieg[k] gezogen?
Paustestu mit vollem Rachen
Donner/ Blitz und Hagel auß/
Den besteht ein TodesGraus[l]/
Der sich nur an dich wil machen:
Tapffer-Körisch bleibstu stehn/[m]
Lest es/ wie es gehet/ gehn.

Ἐπῳδός oder Nachklang I.[n]
NJcht blitzen der Büchsen/ nicht Spitzen der Degen
Kunten dich legen:
Das sausen und brausen der Donner-Canonen
Musten dein schonen:
Das thönen und drönen des[o] Krieges-Getümmel
Stiege gen Himmel:
Das Gewässer dich vmbfloß/[p]
Wall und Häuser übergoß[2]/
Jederman doch bey dir saß
Jn[q] dem Wasser ohne naß.
Nichtes von diesen zerstürmenden Sachen[r]
Kunt dich zur freudigen WelpenStat machen.

Στροφὴ oder Satz II.
ENdlich auff jhr Baceninnen/[s]
Wo jhr in den Grüfften klagt/
Wo jhr von viel Jammer sagt/
Wo jhr ruhet auff den Zinnen:
Schöne Nympfen komt zum Reyhen/
Welpenburg wir wolln einweyhen/
Bringet mit euch Ehrenpreis/
Friedelar[3] und frische Rosen/

Liljen/ Tulpen und Zeitlosen^s4/
Menget alles Handvollweis/
Flechtet einen EhrenKrantz/
Stellet euch zum GötterTantz.

Ἀντίστροφος oder Gegensatz II.
Fürst Augustus kömt gefahren⁴/
Frewd' und Glück begleitet jhn/
GötterVölcklein eilet hin/
Und ümringt jhn mit viel paren/
(Blasser Neydhart laß dich quicken/
Neydes Pein muß dich ersticken.)
Fürst Augustus/ Friedens-Held⁵/
Der den Krieg^t mit seinen Schaaren/
Und den Neyd mit SchlangenHaaren
Unter sich durch Krafft gestellt/
Krafft/ die jhm der Himmel bringt/
Und auß TugendQuellen^u springt.

Ἐπωδος oder Nachklang II.
DRum menget Zeitlosen und Rosen zusammen/
TulipenFlammen/
Die Nägelein/ Liljen und Friedelar^v schneidet/
Eisenkraut meidet:
Bestreuet das Land und erfrewet die Leute
Jmmer und heute.
Kriegsgewölcke^w soll verwehn/
FriedensRöthin^x eins auffgehn/
Wachsthum/ Recht/ Gerechtigkeit/
Bey uns blühn mit Lust und Frewd:
**Dieses uns Hertzog Augustus wird^y geben/
Welcher Hochfürstlich und glücklich sol leben.**
Gedruckt zu Braunschweig bey Balthasar Gruber/ im Jahr 1643.

II

Schottelius' *Ringelgedicht*

Q [Kupfertitel:] Iusti-Georgii | Schottelii | Teutsche Vers- oder | ReimKunst | darin | Vnsere Teutsche | MutterSprache, So viel | dero süßeste Po- | esis | betrifft, in eine | richtige Form der | Kunst zum ersten | mahle gebracht | worden. | getruckt zu | Wolfenbüttel | in verlegung | des Autoris | im jahre | M DC XL V. S. 253 f.; *Kolophon S. [319]:* Gedruckt zu Wulffenbüttel/ | durch Johann Bißmarck/ | Jm Jahr 1645; *Schottelius: Teutsche Vers- oder ReimKunst (1656),* 211–213 [zit. 1656]; *Schottelius: Fruchtbringender Lustgarte (1647),* 315 f. („Nachtlust-Nachtunlust. (umgehende Ringelreime.)").

440100 Justus Georg Schottelius

Umgehende Ringelreime[1]

1.

WAs ist doch besser als die Nacht/
Die Nacht die alles sicher macht?
Die uns begräbt bis auf den Tag
Macht sterben alles Ungemach:
Der müden Arbeit Enderinn
Und aller Sorgen Medicin:
Was ist doch besser als die Nacht/
Die Nacht/ die alles sicher macht?

2.

Was ist doch lieber als die Nacht
Die Nacht die alles süsser macht?
Die Nacht die kühne Buhlerinn
Verräht der Jungfern keuschen Sinn;
Wer Diebstahl in der Liebe sucht
Dem gibt die sichre Nacht zuflucht. [254]
Was ist wol lieber als die Nacht/
Die sicher/ süsser alles macht?

3.

Was ist wol böser als die Nacht/
Die Nacht/ die alles ärger macht?
Die Nacht die voller Lügen ist/
Voll mörderischer Hinderlist/
Voll Diebstahl/ Ehbruch/ Hurerey/
Die Nacht/ die sich nennt Lasterfrey.
Drüm was ist böser als die Nacht/
Die Nacht die alles ärger macht.

4.

Was ist so traurig als die Nacht/
Die Nacht die alles traurig macht?
Misgönnt den Himmel und das Licht/
Und nimt der Welt jhr Angesicht/
Macht alle dinge Nahmenlos[a]/
Und macht den Menschen Siñebloß/
Was ist so traurig als die Nacht/
Die ärger/ traurig alles macht? *,[b]

T **a** *Statt* <nec> — **b** *Eingefügt bis* intervalla — **c** *Folgt ein unlesbares gestrichenes Wort.* — **d** *Folgt* <cum>

T I a *In A als Anmerkung zum Versmaß* — ⏑ — ⏑ — ⏑ — ⏑ *am Rand.* — **b** *C* Hochgelobtes — **c** *A* Wolffenbüttel *am Rand.* — **d** *C* stoltzes — **e** *B C* Reis *bzw.* Reiß — **f** *A* Geschütz *am Rand.* — **g** *A* Wall *am Rand.* — **h** *B C* Laß sein trotzig-sicher lauren — **i** *B C* einmahl aus Hofart faul — **j** *A als Anmerkung* (Degen/ das ist Held.) *am Rand.* — **k** *B C* sich — **l** *B* TodesStraus *bzw.* C Todes-Strauß — **m** *A Anmerkung am Rand:* Tapffer-Körisch/ das ist/ tapffer vnd unerschrocken/ wie die alten Körischen oder Cerusci/ gewesene Einwohnere dieses Landes — **n** *A als Anmerkung* — ⏑⏑ — ⏑⏑ — ⏑⏑ — ⏑⏑ — ⏑⏑ — *am Rand.* — **o** *B C* von — **p** *A als Anmerkung* — ⏑ — ⏑ — ⏑ *am Rand.* — **q** *B* Fast im Wasser *C* Fast in Wasser — **r** *A als Anmerkung* — ⏑⏑ — ⏑⏑ — ⏑⏑ — ⏑ *am Rand.* — **s** *A als Anmerkung am Rand* (Bacenis ist der Hartzwald.) — **t** *B C* Mars — **u** *B C* Friedensquellen — **v** Lilien/ Friedelar *Anmerkung am Rand:* (Durch diese KräuterNamen Friedelar und Eisenkraut/ wird auff Fried und Krieg gedeutet.) — **w** *B* Kriegeswölke *C* Krieges-Wolcke — **x** *A Anmerkung am Rand* (FriedensRöthin *pulcra lux vel ipsa aurora pacis.* — **y** *B* sol *C* soll

T II a *1656* Nahmenloß — **b** *Das Sternchen zeigt Schottelius' Autorschaft an.*

K 1 S. Beil. I K 1.
   2 S. Beil. II K 1.
   3 Der Erstdruck der Pindarischen Ode (1643) u. des Ringelgedichts (*Schottelius: Teutsche Vers- oder ReimKunst [1645]*) u. die Überreichung dieser Poetik an Hz. August d. J. v. Braunschweig-Wolfenbüttel (FG 227) am 2.2.1645 (450202) können nur wenig zur ungefähren Datierung des vorliegenden Briefs beitragen. Die Ode könnte Justus Georg Schottelius (FG 397) aus Anlaß des Einzugs des Herzogs in Wolfenbüttel im September 1643 oder im Blick auf dessen bevorstehende Übersiedlung (26.2.1644) geschrieben haben. Das angegebene Druckjahr 1643 ist hier nicht entscheidend. Der im Brief erwähnte bevorstehende Wintereinbruch könnte auch noch auf den Dezember 1643 oder die Jahreswende verweisen. Der Goslarer Frieden zw. dem Welfenhaus u. Ks. Ferdinand III. war im April 1642 in Braunschweig geschlossen worden. Der vereinbarte Abzug der ksl. Truppen aus Wolfenbüttel verzögerte sich jedoch bis zum September 1643, die Übersiedlung Hz. Augusts, die für Mitte Dezember 1643 geplant war, konnte erst im Frühjahr 1644 erfolgen (s. Anm. 6 u. die Anmerkungen in K I). Vgl. 410621 K 6 u. 431209 K 5. S. Abb. S. 163.
   4 Der aus dem württemberg. Mömpelgart (Montbéliard) stammende Abraham Marconnet (1617 – nach 1683), der in der Forschung als der eigentliche Präzeptor Pz. Rudolf Augusts v. Braunschweig-Wolfenbüttel (FG 754. 1660) gilt, unterrichtete also auch morgens die jüngeren Prinzen Anton Ulrich (FG 716. 1659) u. Ferdinand Albrecht (FG 842. 1673) u. betete morgens u. abends mit ihnen allen. Am 9.1.1644 erinnerte ihr Vater, Hz. August d. J., Johann Valentin Andreae (FG 464. 1646) daran, ihm einen neuen Präzeptor zu empfehlen, da Marconnet in seine Heimat gerufen worden sei. HAB: Cod. Guelf. 236.2 Extrav., Bl. 3rv (PS. v. 20.1.1644). Zu Marconnet vgl. schon 431028A K 3. Marconnet hatte in Helmstedt unter Johann Lotichius am 21.9.1643 disputiert: Disputatio Inauguralis Iuridica De Iure Primogeniturae, seu de De Primogeniis Illustrium Imperii (Helmaestadii: Henning Mullerus 1643). Er übersetzte den Hofmannsspiegel von Eustache de Refuge (Traicté de la Cour. 1616 u. ö.) ins Lateinische: AULICUS INCULPATUS, Duabus Partibus è Gallico in Latinum sermonem versus. Edente, ABRAHAMO MARCONNET Montisbelgaidensi [sic], J. U. D. (Halae: Christoph. Mylius 1664; Neuaufl. ebd. 1684); gewidmet Hz. Johann Adolf v. Sachsen-Weißenfels (FG 719. 1659), d. d. „Barbie, d. 16. Aprilis 1664". Dieses Werk hatte Georg Philipp Harsdörffer (FG 368) bereits zuvor verdeutscht: Mr. Du Refuge Kluger Hofmann (Franckfurt u. Hamburg: Naumann 1655). Marconnet wurde gfl. barbyscher Rat u. Amtmann zu Rosenburg. Neben Gelegenheitsge-

J G S

Auff neue Pindarische Art,
Dem
Durchleuchtigen/ Hochgebornen Fürsten und Herrn/

Herrn Augusto / Hertzogen zu Braunschweig und Lüneburg/ ꝛc. Als Seine Fürstl. Gn. in dero Haubt-Vestung
und ResidentzStat Wolfenbüttel glücklichen und mit Freuden eingezogen/
unterthänig überreichet.

Von J. G. S.

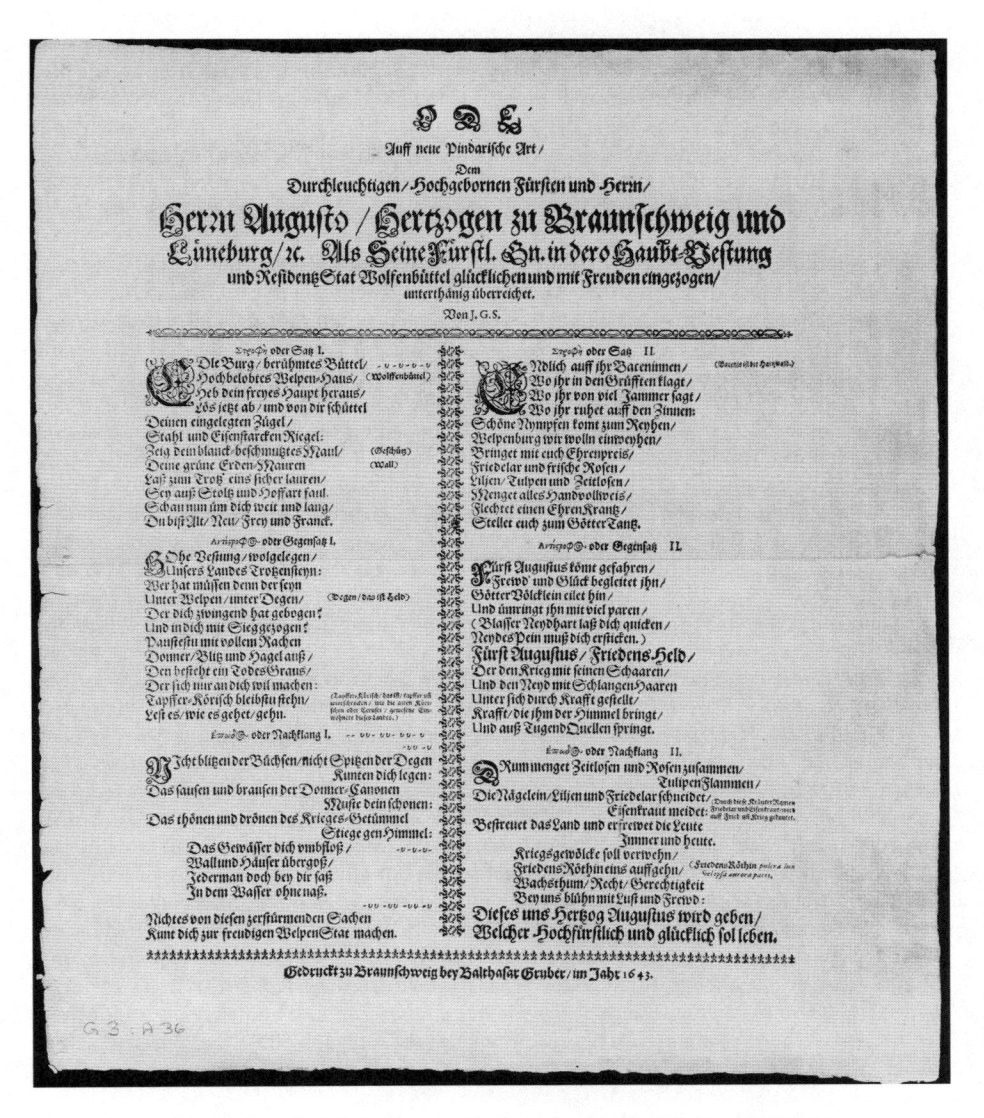

Στροφή oder Satz I.

Die Burg/ berühmtes Büttel   (Wolffenbüttel)
Hochbelobtes Welpen-Hauß/
Heb dein freyes Haupt heraus/
Lös jetzt ab/ und von dir schüttel
Deinen eingelegten Zügel/
Stahl und Eisenstarcken Riegel: (Geschütz)
Zeig dein blanck-beschmutztes Maul/
Deine grüne Erden-Mauren   (Wall)
Laß zum Trotz eins sicher lauren/
Sey auß Stoltz und Hoffart faul.
Schau nun üm dich weit und lang/
Du bist Alt/ Neu/ Frey und Franck.

Ἀντιστροφή oder Gegensatz I.

Hohe Vestung/ wolgelegen/
Unsers Landes Trotzensteyn:
Wer hat müssen denn der seyn
Unter Welpen/ unter Degen   (Degen/ das ist Held)
Der dich zwingend hat gebogen?
Und in dich mit Sieg gezogen?
Paustestu mit vollem Rachen
Donner/ Blitz und Hagel auß/
Den bestehet ein TodesGraus/
Der sich nur an dich wil machen:
Tapffer-Hörisch bleibstu stehn/
Lest es/ wie es gehet/ gehn.

Ἐπῳδή oder Nachklang I.

Jtzt blitzen der Büchsen/ nicht Spitzen der Degen
Kunten dich legen:
Das sausen und brausen der Donner-Canonen
Muste dein schonen:
Das thönen und drönen des Krieges-Getümmel
Stiege gen Himmel:
Das Gewässer dich umbfloß/
Wall und Häuser übergoß/
Jederman doch bey dir saß
In dem Wasser ohne naß.
Nichtes von diesen zerstürmenden Sachen
Kunte dich zur freudigen WelpenStat machen.

Στροφή oder Satz II.

Endlich auff ihr Bacenninnen/   (Bacenis der Hartzwald.)
Wo ihr in den Grüfften klagt/
Wo ihr von viel Jammer sagt/
Wo ihr ruhet auff den Zinnen:
Schöne Nymphen komt zum Reyhen/
Welpenburg wir wolln einweyhen/
Bringet mit euch Ehrenpreis/
Friedelar und frische Rosen/
Lilien/ Tulpen und Zeitlosen/
Menget alles Handvollweiß/
Flechtet einen Ehren-Krantz/
Stellet euch zum Götter Tantz.

Ἀντιστροφή oder Gegensatz II.

Fürst Augustus kömt gefahren/
Freud' und Glück begleitet ihn/
Götter Völcklein eilet hin/
Und inmringt ihn mit viel paren/
(Blasser Neydhart laß dich quicken/
Neydes Pein muß dich ersticken.)
Fürst Augustus/ Friedens-Held/
Der den Krieg mit seinen Schaaren
Und den Neyd mit Schlangenhaaren
Unter sich durch Krafft gestellt:
Krafft/ die ihm der Himmel bringt/
Und auß TugendQuellen springet.

Ἐπῳδή oder Nachklang II.

Nun menget Zeitlosen und Rosen zusammen/
Tulipen Flammen/
Die Nägelein/ Lilien und Friedelar schneidet/   (Durch diese Kräuter Namen
Eisenkraut meidet: Friedeliar und Eisenkraut wird
Bestreuet das Land und erfrewet die Leute   auff Fried und Krieg gedeutet.)
Immer und heute.
Kriegsgewölcke soll verwehn/   (Friedens Röthin palores ac
Friedens Röthin eins auffgehn/   bellicosa amoris partes.)
Wachsthum/ Recht/ Gerechtigkeit
Bey uns blühn mit Lust und Freud:
Dieses uns Hertzog Augustus wird geben/
Welcher Hochfürstlich und glücklich sol leben.

Gedruckt zu Braunschweig bey Balthasar Gruber/ im Jahr 1643.

Justus Georg Schottelius: ODE Auff neue Pindarische Art (1643). Zu 440100 I.

dichten verfaßte Marconnet auch ein längeres heroisches Gedicht (Albis Salae Nympharum ... In ... obitum ... Augusti Ludovici, Comitis Barbyensis & Muhlingensis ... Qui Wolferbyti, in arce Guelphica, 17. Octobr. A. C. M.DC.LIX. aetatis vigesimo primo ineunte ... ad Coelestem quietem translatus est ... Gvelpherbyti Typis Sterniis) auf den letzten Grafen von Barby, August Ludwig, der 1659 gerade 20-jährig in Wolfenbüttel starb, u. hinterließ eine Genealogie der Grafen von Barby. Er bezeichnete sich noch 1675 im Dienste von Hz. August (v. Sachsen-Weißenfels), dem ein Teil der Gft. Barby zugefallen war, als barbyscher Rat (LP f. Balthasar Hartranfft), trug aber auch den Titel eines hzl. sächs. Rats (1679). Vgl. 1679 LP f. Wilhelm v. Kospoth (1628–1678, FG 728. 1659); *Jöcher* III, 152.

5 Schottelius gilt hauptsächlich als Präzeptor der jüngeren Prinzen Anton Ulrich u. Ferdinand Albrecht sowie von Hz. Augusts ältester Tochter Sibylla Ursula (1629–1671, seit 1663 Gattin Hz. Christians v. Schleswig-Holstein-Sonderburg-Glücksburg). Er war jedoch, wie es der Brief zeigt, auch an der Bildung Rudolf Augusts u. der drei Prinzessinnen beteiligt, außer an der Sibylla Ursulas auch an der Erziehung der jüngeren Mädchen Clara Augusta (1632–1700; heiratete 1653 Hz. Friedrich v. Württemberg in Neuenstadt) u. Maria Elisabeth (1638–1677; heiratete 1663 Hz. Adolf Wilhelm v. Sachsen-Eisenach [FG 423. 1645] u. nach dessen Tod 1668 im Jahre 1676 Hz. Albrecht v. Sachsen-Coburg). Schottelius' Bestallungsbrief „In dem achte tage der H. Ostern Anno 1638" ist veröffentlicht in: Jörg Jochen Müller: Fürstenerziehung im 17. Jahrhundert. Am Beispiel Herzog Anton Ulrichs von Braunschweig und Lüneburg. In: Stadt – Schule – Universität – Buchwesen und die deutsche Literatur im 17. Jahrhundert. Hg. v. Albrecht Schöne. München 1976, 243–260, hier S. 257 f. 1641 wurde Schottelius auch die Erziehung Pz. Ferdinand Albrechts aufgetragen. Von Weihnachten 1645 an wurde er in seiner Tätigkeit durch Sigmund Betulius, geadelt als Sigmund v. Birken (FG 681. 1658), unterstützt, der am 9. 10. 1646 seinen Abschied erhielt. S. 451100A K 9. Nach dem Abschlußexamen der beiden Prinzen am 3. 2. 1646 folgte Schottelius' juristische Promotion an der U. Helmstedt (26. 2. 1646) u. am 24. 5. 1645 seine Beförderung zum Hof- u. Konsistorialrat, bes. für Dannenbergische Sachen. NSTA Wolfenbüttel: 2 Alt 2985, Bl. 42 f.; vgl. *Bei der Wieden: Schottelius.*

6 Da Hz. August erst am 26. 2. 1644 das Wolfenbüttler Schloß bezog, war auch noch eine (vorläufige) Zuteilung eines Studierzimmers im Braunschweiger Schloß oder in dessen Nähe denkbar. Ein undatierter Dankbrief von Schottelius an den Herzog bezeugt, daß dieser dem Lehrer seiner Kinder tatsächlich einen Raum in Wolfenbüttel zuwies u. zwar noch vor seinem eigenen Umzug dorthin. Deshalb bedurfte es zur Inbesitznahme des Raums durch Schottelius einer Reise nach Wolfenbüttel. Schottelius informierte Hz. August, daß er gleich mit (dem Generalsuperintendenten u. Konsistorialrat) Heinrich Wideburg aufbreche u. den Raum abteile, bequem einrichte u. schmücke. Bis zum Mittag des nächsten Tages wolle er (in Braunschweig) zurück sein. NSTA Wolfenbüttel: 2 Alt Nr. 40, Bl. 19r. Zu Heinrich Wideburg (1587–1648) vgl. auch 461204 K 1.

K I 1 In *Schottelius: Teutsche Vers- oder ReimKunst (1645)*, 298, definiert der Autor in einer dem Abdruck vorangestellten Erklärung diese Gedichtform: Um eine Pindarische Ode handelt es sich „wan der ersten Strophe[n], oder dem ersten Reimschlusse (welchen man ordnen, längen und kürtzen kan nach belieben) folgen muß eine andere gantz gleiche Strofe oder Reimschluß: Die dritte Strophe, oder der dritte Reimschluß aber ist den beiden ersten, weder nach den Versen, noch Reimungen gleich, sonderen bleibet frey, und nach des Dichters gefallen einzurichten: Diese drey Reimschlüsse heissen sonst Strophe, Antistrophe und Epodos, bey uns, Satz, Gegensatz und Nachklang. Es können aber diese

Strofen ein, zwey oder mehr mahl wiederholet werden, müssen alsdan aber die wiederholeten mit den ersten, an Zeilen und Reimarten gleich werden."

2 Aufgrund der militärischen Unterstützung, welche Hz. Friedrich Ulrich v. Braunschweig-Wolfenbüttel (FG 38) seinem Oheim, Kg. Christian IV. v. Dänemark (1577–1648), in seiner Opposition gegen Ks. Ferdinand II. geleistet hatte, wurde die hzl. Hauptresidenz Wolfenbüttel nach der verlorenen Schlacht bei Lutter am Barenberge (August 1626) durch ksl. Truppen unter General Gf. Gottfried Heinrich v. Pappenheim belagert. Da der stark befestigten Welfen- oder „Welpen"-Stadt nicht anders beizukommen war, ließ der General mittels eines Dammes die Oker stauen u. damit die sog. Heinrichstadt zu Wolfenbüttel fluten. Schließlich mußte sich die Festungsbesatzung im Dezember 1627 ergeben. Wolfenbüttel wurde darauf für nahezu 16 Jahre von einer ksl. Garnison besetzt gehalten, nicht zuletzt deswegen, weil die welf. Herzöge von Braunschweig u. Lüneburg aus den Linien Lüneburg (Celle), Calenberg-Göttingen u. Wolfenbüttel weiterhin die Opposition gegen den Kaiser unterstützten, die seit 1630/31 jahrelang durch die Krone Schweden angeführt wurde. Seit 1641 wurde Wolfenbüttel abermals belagert u. durch Anstauen der Oker geflutet, diesmal durch Truppen unter schwed. Oberbefehl. S. 410621 K 6, 421011 K 7; *Rehtmeier: Braunschweig-Lüneburgische Chronica* II, 1271.

3 Bei der Blume „Friedelar" handelt es sich vermutlich um die in mehreren Arten vorkommende Schachblume (lat. frittilaria). Sie ist ein beliebtes Motiv in der barocken Dichtung, da sie aufgrund ihres Namens auch als Hinweis auf den Frieden oder das Kaisertum (Aar) gedeutet wurde. Unter der Bezeichnung „Königes Krone" bzw. „Keysers-kronen" kommen Fritillaria imperialis L. sowie „Persianische Lilge" (Fritillaria persica L.) in den Gesellschaftsbüchern der FG vor. S. FG 152 (Bodo v. Bodenhausen) bzw. 277 (Tönnies Wulf v. Haxthausen). Vgl. *Conermann II*, 94 u. 119; *III*, 152 u. 309. Im PBO wurde die Blume Friedelar oder Frittelar 1679 an den Dichter u. späteren Altdorfer Professor Christoph Wegleiter (1659–1706) verliehen, weil „dessen friedsamer und stiller Wandel genugsam bekannt war" und er deshalb Irenian im Orden genannt wurde. *Herdegen*, 472f. Vgl. *Jürgensen: Repertorium*, 472–480.

4 Obwohl ihm bereits 1635 die Erbfolge in dem durch Aussterben der älteren (mittleren) Linie Braunschweig-Wolfenbüttel zugefallenen Fürstentum zugesprochen worden war, konnte Hz. August d. J. (FG 227) — nachdem im Januar u. April 1642 der Ausgleich mit den Kaiserlichen getroffen worden war (s. o. K 3) — erst im September 1643 feierlich seinen Einzug in seiner neuen Residenz halten u. dorthin am 26.2.1644 endgültig übersiedeln. S. auch 440130 K 6; *Conermann III*, 243–245.

5 Hz. August d. J. war maßgeblich beteiligt an den Verhandlungen zw. den Welfen u. dem Kaiser, die 1642 zum Abschluß des Goslarer Friedens führten, mit dem die Welfen aus dem Dreißigjährigen Krieg ausschieden. S. Michael Reimann: Der Goslarer Frieden von 1642. Hildesheim 1979. S. dazu auch K 3.

K II 1 Vgl. *Schottelius: Teutsche Vers- oder ReimKunst (1645)*, 251 bzw. 253: „DJe RingelReime seind/ welche gleichen anfang und gleichen ausgang haben/ also daß sich der Reimschluß mit eben den Worten/ mit welchen er sich anhebet/ schliessen muß: Und gleich wie in einem Umgange eines runden Kreisses oder Ringes/ man eben zu dem anfange wiederkoṁet/ also wandert das Reimgedichtlein/ bis es zu ende gleichsam hinwieder seinen anfang antrift. [...] 3. Es ist auch dieses noch eine neue Art Ringelreime/ die sich also ringsüm schliessen müssen/ daß die beiden ersten Verse in jedem Reimschlusse sich zuende wiederfinden/ und also das Gedicht einringen und bezirken. Zur anzeige folgen Umgebende Ringelreime".

440119

Christian Beckmann an Christophorus Colerus

Glückwünsche zum neuen Jahr und Antwort auf zwei Briefe von Christophorus Colerus, die beinahe desselben Inhalts gewesen seien. Johann Weitz sei gestorben und schon vor einigen Jahren Tobias Hübner (FG 25), der das Deutsche verfeinert habe. Es lebe aber noch Diederich v. dem Werder (FG 31), der viele elegante Dichtungen über Geschichtliches (darunter den Tasso) und Geistliches geschrieben habe und dies auch weiterhin tue. F. Ludwig habe vordem in einer Gesellschaft zur Verbesserung der Sprache reiche Frucht gebracht. Martin Opitz v. Boberfeld (FG 200) stehe dabei aber an der ersten Stelle. Er habe vorgeführt, wie wir die Gemüter zur deutschen Dichtung anreizen sollen. Leider habe der Krieg alles gestört und auch die FG erheblich geschwächt. Mit der Wiederkehr des Friedens werde auch sie sich gewiß erheben, jedoch stehe alles bei Gott. — Sicher seien Gerardus Joannes Vossius und Claudius Salmasius gelehrte Autoren, jedoch seien gerade die Humaniora oft durch die Schuld weniger Menschen der Unbeständigkeit ausgesetzt, wie einst im Falle des Justus Lipsius. Zwischen Daniel Heinsius und Salmasius solle es in aller Öffentlichkeit Rechtsstreit geben, jedoch wisse er, Beckmann, nicht genug darüber und habe auch nichts Gedrucktes gesehen. Colerus werde ihm gewiß auf schnellstem Wege Veröffentlichungen zum Tode von Opitz und Bernhard Wilhelm Nüßler schicken. Beckmann wolle Colerus dagegen mit den gewünschten Nachrichten über die FG versorgen, sobald seine Bekannten Näheres erfuhren.

Q STB Berlin — PK: Dep. Breslau 9, Nr. 62. 1 Bl. [A: Rücks.]; eigenh.; Sig.

A VIRO clariss. & excellentissimo D. Christophoro Colero Histor. prof. &c. Domino & amico plurimè observando.

Præfatus salutem & ineuntis annj decursum felicissimum, respondeo binis tuis ejusdem fermè argumenti: Vir clariss. & præstantiß. Dn. & amjce plurimum observande. Jta est: Iohannes Weitzius[1] noster abijt hinc in communem locum: & ante aliquot annos Tobias Hübnerus[2] etiam, ille quj nostram linguam multâ operâ & quidem cum laude excoluit. Sed superstes etiamnunc floret Dieterich à Werder[3], quj versibus Germanjcjs multa historica (& inter hæc Tassum Jtalum) nec non sacra satis eleganter complexus est: & quantum scio, adhuc pergit. Collegium[4] à Pr. Ludovico ante[a] hoc instauratum est, quo fructus fundantur uberes, ad meliorem linguæ nostræ culturam. Ubi institutum laudabile: ita non carujt suo fructu optabili. Et Martinus Opitius[5] noster primatum hic videtur tenere & alijs monstrasse modum, quo anjmos ad poësin Germanjcam nostrj appellant. Verum vti bellum njmjs pertinax hactenus omnia turbavit aut potius dejecit: Jta etiam illud collegium hac culpâ non parum defecisse iudicatur. Haud dubiè resurget, vbi denuò surrexerit pax dudum expetita. An verò hæc ipsa in Westphaliâ[6] nobis restituenda sit: multi dubitunt: nos optamus: immò pacem te poscimus omnes. Ταῦτα γὰρ ἐν γούνασι τοῦ θεοῦ κεῖται.[7] Vossius[8] & Claudius Salmasius[9], ambo sunt eruditi scriptores: sed nescio quæ varj[e]tas literis humanjorjbus sæpè adhærescit, non tamen proprià, sed hominum nonnullorum culpa. Sicuti toties etiam

conqueritur jam olim Justus Lipsius[10]. Salmasio cum Heinsio[11], etiam cum JCtis dicitur esse litigium & quidem in luce publicâ. Quale autem sit & quomodo habeat: necdum satis scio, nec litus eo nomjne scriptos vidj. Ea quæ in objtum Opitij & Nüßlerj evulgata[12] sunt, proximâ viâ mecum communicabis. Rescribam etiam illud, quod de collegio frugifero inprimjs nosse cupis, cum paulo meliusculè nostris fuerjt. Jta vale & salue, à Tuo
Christiano Becmano

1644. 19. Jan.

T a *Gebessert aus* <antea>

K Christian Beckmann (Becman[us], 1580–1648) stammte aus dem sächs. Steinbach (b. Bad Lausick), wo sein Vater Pfarrer war. Nach dem Besuch der Fürstenschule zu Grimma nahm er 1599 sein Studium an der U. Leipzig auf, wo er, nach kurzem Aufenthalt an den Universitäten Wittenberg u. Jena, 1604 den Magistergrad erwarb. 1608 wurde er vom Wittenberger Prof. Friedrich Taubmann, C. P. C., zum (lat.) Poeten gekrönt. 1616–1625 Rektor u. Prof. am Gymn. in Amberg (Residenz des Statthalters der Oberpfalz F. Christian I. v. Anhalt-Bernburg. FG 26), ref. Exulant, 1625 Rektor der Stadtschule in Bernburg. Noch im selben Jahr wurde er als Superintendent u. Pastor an St. Nicolai nach Zerbst berufen, wo er zugleich am dortigen Gymnasium illustre Theologie lehrte. S. 291028 K 1 (S. 380), 300509 K 5 (S. 246), 330603 K 2 (S. 475 ff.; 1633 in die anhalt. Verhandlungen mit dem Ireniker John Durie um eine gesamtprotestant. europ. Synode involviert) u. K 6, 410102 K 4, 410106 K 5 u. 440525 K II. Beckmann fand auch durch sprachgeschichtliche Abhandlungen zum Lateinischen Beachtung, in denen er Becanus' These von der Einsilbigkeit der Stammwörter zurückwies. S. 400528 K II 7, vgl. 410106 K 5 und zum strittigen Theorem der Einsilbigkeit der dt. Stammwörter 450410 K 3. Vgl. *ADB* II, 240; *Beckmann* VII, 325–328 (Johann Christoph Beckmann, der Autor des letzteren Werks, war der Sohn des Briefschreibers u. seit 1667 Prof. an der U. Frankfurt a. d. Oder); *Jöcher* I, 904; *Zedler* III, 877 f. — Christophorus Colerus (1602–1658), Freund von Bernhard Wilhelm Nüßler (s. Anm. 12) u. Martin Opitz v. Boberfeld (FG 200). Er wurde dessen poet. Nachfolger, Prof. Historiarum et Eloquentiae, auch Konrektor am Breslauer Elisabeth-Gymn. sowie seit 1639 Bibliothekar der dortigen berühmten Maria-Magdalenen-Bibliothek. In seiner Laudatio auf den verstorbenen Freund lieferte er die erste Opitz-Biographie. S. *Opitz: BW* passim, bes. I (250510A K 16) u. III (391111 Gedenkrede). S. auch *Opitius latinus* passim, zur Bibliothek u. Colers Bibliotheksamt bes. III, 599 f. u. Klaus Garber: Bücherhochburg des Ostens. Die alte Breslauer Bibliothekslandschaft (…). In: *Garber: Das alte Buch (2006)*, 313–438, bes. S. 331–345. Grundlegend Max Hippe: Christoph Köler, ein schlesischer Dichter des siebzehnten Jahrhunderts. Sein Leben und eine Auswahl seiner deutschen Gedichte. Breslau 1902; s. auch David G. Halsted: Poetry and Politics in the Silesian Baroque. Neo-stoicism in the work of Christophorus Colerus and his circle. Wiesbaden 1996; *NDB* XII (1979), 316. — Die erwähnte Lobschrift auf Opitz konnte der Breslauer Gymnasiallehrer Melchior Weise erst nach Colerus' Tod herausbringen: Laudatio Honori & Memoriæ V. CL MARTINI OPITII paulò post obitum ejus A. M DC. XXXIX. in Actu apud Uratislavienses publico solemniter dicta à Christophoro Colero … Publici juris fecit Melchior Weise Vratislav. (Lipsiae: Philippus Fuhrmann/ Dr. Johannes Wittigau 1665), in *Opitz: BW* III, 1684 ff. Colerus wollte das Buch zusammen mit Ehrengedichten veröffentlichen u. sprach darauf Johann Weitz (s. Anm. 1), Augustus Buchner (FG 362) u. Christian Beckmann an. Hippe, a. a. O., 226f. zit. seinen Brief vom 10.12.1639 an Beckmann: „Cum etiam brevi Panegyricus Manibus Cl. Opitii publice in Gymnasio nostro dictus publicandus sit, rogo, nisi itidem molestum sit, aliorum summorum Virorum exemplo Epicedium aliquid addas."

1 Johann Weitz (Sept. 1576 – 24. 4. 1642), P. L., Philologe, Lehrer u. 1631–1640 (?) Rektor des Gymn. Gotha, wo Opitz ihn im Herbst 1630 auf seiner Reise von Paris nach Breslau traf. Veit Ludwig v. Seckendorff (FG 615. 1654) trat 1641 in die oberste Klasse des nun von Andreas Reyher (s. 450217 K 1 u. 3) geleiteten Gymn.s ein. S. *Opitz: BW* 301103 K 1, 301108, 310117 K 6, 310119 K 1, 390401 K 1, 390822 K u. 391111 (S.47). *Flood* IV, 2220–2223 (mit Werkeverzeichnis); Gotha macht Schule. Bildung von Luther bis Francke. Katalog zur Ausstellung ... Gotha 2013, 43 u. 146–149; *Estermann*; *Bürger*.

2 Tobias Hübner (FG 25), der anhalt-dessauische Kanzler u. Dichter, berühmt durch seine kunstvolle Übersetzung der *Sepmaines* des Guillaume de Saluste sieur du Bartas (1619/22 u. 1631), starb schon am 5.5.1636. *Conermann III*, 27–29 u. *Dünnhaupt: Handbuch* III.

3 Diederich v. dem Werder (FG 31), ehemals Kasseler Hofmarschall, seit 1646 kurbrandenburg. Obrist u. Gesandter sowie kfl. Geheimer Rat, lebte von 1584–1657. Er wurde gerühmt wegen seiner Übersetzung von Torquato Tassos *La Gerusalemme liberata* (1626, ²1652). Er übersetzte auch Ariosto u. schrieb viele geistl. Gedichte. S. *Conermann III*, 34–36 u. *Dünnhaupt: Handbuch* VI.

4 Die Fruchtbringende Gesellschaft, deren Stiftung Beckmann hier allein F. Ludwig zuschreibt.

5 Martin Opitz v. Boberfeld (1597–1639; FG 200), der schles. Dichter u. Freund v. Christophorus Colerus (Anm. 0) u. Bernhard Wilhelm Nüßler (Anm. 12). Vgl. den Briefwechsel in *Opitz: BW*, s. auch *Opitius latinus* u. *Dünnhaupt: Handbuch* IV. Opitz gilt als der Vater der neuen deutschen Kunstdichtung des 17. Jahrhunderts u. als Erfinder des dt. akzentuierenden Verses. K. Garber in: *Literatur-Lexikon*² VIII, 715–722. Zu Opitz' Versreform im Verhältnis zu jener der FG jetzt *Conermann: Vielsprachigkeit in der Frühzeit der FG*. — Am 13.4.1643 hatte Beckmann an Colerus geschrieben: „[...] submitto breve epicedium communj nostro amico Opitio destinatum [...]. Virgilio Latium, sed Græcja plaudit Homero: At Teutho Opitius cedit utrique nihil."

6 Der in den Verhandlungen zum Westfäl. Frieden in Münster u. Osnabrück zu erreichende Friedensschluß.

7 So liegt es denn in Gottes Schoß, d. h. in dessen Entscheidung.

8 Gerardus Joannes Vossius (1577–1649), Philologe u. Theologe, geboren als Sohn eines ref. Glaubensflüchtlings (Joannes Vossius) in Heidelberg, aus der Kurpfalz von den Lutheranern vertrieben. Er war Student in Dordrecht u. Leiden, wurde Rektor in Dordrecht u. Rektor der theolog. Fakultät der U. Leiden, resignierte jedoch wegen seiner kirchengeschichtlich-dogmatischen *Historia Pelagiana* (1618) u. infolge seiner Verdächtigungen als Arminianer 1619. 1622 zum Prof. der Redekunst u. Geschichte berufen, wurde er 1630 LL.D. in Oxford u. schließlich 1632 Prof. historiae am neugegründeten Athenaeum zu Amsterdam. Zu seinen historischen, rhetorischen, philologischen u. poetologischen Werken zählen: *Commentariorum Rhetoricorum, sive oratoriarum institutionum libri VI* (1606 u.ö.); *De historicis Graecis libri IV* (²1601 u.ö.); *Rhetorices contractae, sive partitionum oratoriarum libri V* (1621 u.ö.); *De historicis Latinis libri III* (1627 u.ö.); *Aristarchus, sive de arte grammatica libri septem* (1635 u. 1695); *Poeticarum institutionum. Libri III* (1647 u.ö.); *De artis poeticae natura ac constitutione liber* (1647 u.ö.); *De imitatione cum Oratoria, tum praecipue Poetica; Deque Recitatione veterum liber* (1647 u.ö.); *Etymologi-*

cum linguae Latinae (1662). — Die wechselhaften Lebensumstände von Vossius, Salmasius u. Lipsius führte Beckmann als Beispiele für die gerade von Vertretern der Humaniora erlittene varietas an. Cornelis S. M. Rademaker: Life and Works of Gerardus Joannes Vossius (1577–1649). Hilversum 1999; *Jaumann: Repertorium,* 691 f.

9 Claudius Salmasius (Claude de Saumaise) (1588–1653), ref. französ. Philologe, Jurist, Kirchenhistoriker. Nach Studien in Paris u. Heidelberg qualifizierte er sich als Parlamentsadvokat, wurde jedoch Privatgelehrter in Dijon. 1632 wurde er Nachfolger auf dem Lehrstuhl Josephus Justus Scaligers an der U. Leiden. Vor allem wegen des Streits mit Daniel Heinsius (s. Anm. 12) kehrte er 1636 nach Dijon zurück. Salmasius kritisierte Heinsius auch in seinem Werk *De modo usurarum liber* (1639), in dem er die Verzinsung des Kapitals rechtfertigte. Er entzog sich dem Dienst Richelieus u. kehrte 1645 nach Leiden zurück. 1650/51 ging er auf Einladung Kgn. Christinas v. Schweden nach Stockholm. 1653 erfolgte die Rückkehr nach Leiden. Salmasius trat 1608/1612 mit einer Ausgabe des Ebf.s Nilus v. Thessaloniki (*De primatu Papae*; 1645 zus. mit Salmasius' gleichnamigem Buch) hervor, veröffentlichte weitere Editionen (Florus; des Isaac Casaubonus' Anmerkungen zu den Autoren der *Historia Augusta* 1620; des Solinus *Polyhistor* bzw. dessen Quelle C. Plinius Secundus 1629) u. erregte Aufsehen durch seine Verteidigung Kg. Karls I. v. England (*Defensio regia, pro Carolo I.* [1649], benutzt von Andreas Gryphius [FG 788. 1662] in seinem Drama *Carolus Stuardus*), die den Widerspruch John Miltons erregte (1651), welchen Salmasius wiederum zu widerlegen suchte (Salmasii ad Miltonum responsio, postum 1660). Salmasius korrespondierte auch mit Opitz. S. *Opitz: BW* 390121 K 2. *Biographisch-Bibliographisches Kirchenlexikon* VIII (1994), 1232 f.; *Jaumann: Repertorium,* 579 (Lit.). Vgl. Anm. 11.

10 Justus Lipsius (1547–1606), auf dem Kölner Jesuitengymn. (bis 1559) u. seit 1563 an der U. Löwen erzogen, konnte ab 1568 als lat. Sekretär Kd. Granvellas zwei Jahre u. a. mit Studien in Rom verbringen, wo er seine Methode der philolog. Textkritik entwickelte. 1570 wanderte er über Wien bis an die U. Jena, wo er als Prof. der Geschichte u. Redekunst (1572–1573) mit dem Luthertum konform ging. Auf der Rückreise über Köln (1574) nach Löwen (1576/77) fand er dort zur kathol. Kirche zurück. Der Religionskrieg trieb ihn als Prof. der Geschichte u. der Rechtswissenschaft an die neue U. Leiden (seit 1578), wo er sich dem Calvinismus anpaßte. Dort arbeitete er seine Seneca- u. Tacitus-Editionen aus, schrieb eine *Satyra menippea. Somnium* (1581), die wichtigste neustoizist. Abhandlung im taciteischen Stil (*De constantia libri duo.* 1584) u. die *Politicorum sive civilis doctrinae libri sex* (1589), in denen er dem Staat die gewaltsame Durchsetzung der konfessionellen Einheit zuwies. 1590 schloß er sich im Einklang mit dieser Lehre in Mainz wieder dem kathol. Bekenntnis an u. ließ sich — mittlerweile wie Salmasius ein berühmt gewordener Gelehrter — als vom Unterricht befreiter Prof. für Latein wieder nach Löwen berufen. Er verfaßte dort u. a. *De militia romana libri V., commentarius ad Polybium* (1595), *Diva virgo Hallensis* (1604), *Manuductio ad Stoicam philosophiam, libri III* (1604) u. eine Einführung in die Geschichte Brabants (Lovanium. 1605). *Jaumann: Repertorium* (Lit.); Justus Lipsius: Von der Bestendigkeit [De Constantia]. Faks.dr. d. dt. Übers. v. Andreas Viritius ... ca. 1601 ... Hg. Leonard Forster. Stuttgart 1965; Gerhard Oestreich: Geist und Gestalt des frühmodernen Staates. Ausgewählte Aufsätze. Berlin 1969. Vgl. *NDB* XIV, 676 ff.

11 Daniel Heinsius (1580–1655), lat., griech. u. nl. Dichter, Philologe u. Theologe, Prof. Politices et Historiarum u. Bibliothekar an der U. Leiden, verfeindet mit Claudius Salmasius, befreundet mit seinem Briefpartner u. Besucher Opitz, der Heinsius' Lobgesänge auf Bacchus u. Christus übersetzte. S. Dan. Heinsii Lof-Sanck van Iesvs Christvs. den eenigen ende eeuvvigen Sone Godes: Met noodelicke Vytleggingen ... (Amsterdam: Willem Ians-

zoon 1616); Hymnus oft Lof-Sanck van Bacchus. In: Dan: Heinsii Nederduytsche Poemata. By een vergadert en uytgegeven door P[ieter] S[chrijver] (Amsterdam: Willem Janßen 1618), 95 ff. Zur Korrespondenz mit Opitz s. *Opitz: BW* 201000 I–II u. 380720A. Jean-Louis Guez sieur de Balzac u. Claudius Salmasius gerieten über die Mischung antikheidnischer Mythologie u. biblischer Themen in *Danielis Heinsii Herodes Infanticida, Tragoedia* (Lugd. Batavorum: Elzeviriana 1632) in einen Streit mit dem Verfasser. Vgl. *Opitz: BW* 380720A K I 1. Zu Heinsius' exeget. Schriften gehört das umfangreiche Werk *Sacrarum Exercitationum ad Novum Testamentum libri XX* (1639), das auch zusammen mit dem folgenden Werk erschien (1667 auch separat): *Aristarchus sacer sive ad Nonni in Johannem metaphrasin exercitationes.* Vgl. Baerbel Becker-Cantarino: Daniel Heinsius. Boston 1978.

12 Bernhard Wilhelm Nüßler (1598–1643), Opitz' Freund seit der Bunzlauer Schulzeit (1610). Studierte Jura in Frankfurt a. d. Oder, wo er Hz. Georg Rudolf in Schlesien (FG 58) seinen *Princeps literatus* (1616) widmete, u. ab 1617 an der U. Marburg. Nüßler, der auch selbst lat. u. dt. dichtete, gab *Opitz: Silvae* heraus (1631). 1630 ließ ihn Opitz in seiner Prosaschäferei *Hercinie* auftreten. Nüßler wurde hzl. liegnitz. (und seit 1624) auch brieg. Sekretär bzw. Rat. S. *Opitz: BW* 181008 I K 2 u. passim; *Opitius latinus* I, 298 f. u. ö.; *Adelung* V, 859 f. — Zeugnisse des Gedenkens an Opitz' Tod in *Opitz: BW* III, Tl. 2. Am 13.4.1643 hatte Beckmann an Colerus geschrieben: „[...] submitto breve epicedium communj nostro amico Opitio destinatum [...].

Virgilio Latium, sed Græcja plaudit Homero:
   At Teutho Opitius cedit utrique nihil.
Ampliss. nostrum, Dn. Nusslerum, virum à Musis et gratiis quasi concinnatum, meo nomjne salutem velim, qui etiam fasciculum Lipsiâ ocjus accipiat: si nondum acceperit." STB Berlin — PK: Dep. Breslau 9, Nr.63. Am 14.5.1644 bestärkte Beckmann Colerus in dieser Absicht: „Quod Nüslerj manes oratione & versibus condecorare velis: sanè pro amico facis & ex voto amicorum, quos reliqujt ille. Equjdem applaudo: & insignjs virj memorjam per literas conservarj opto, vtpote quj de literis optimè meritus fuerat. Quod etiam de Martino Opitio (heu) olim nostro dictum sit quj immortale nomen adeptus est, dum pöesin Germanicam solerte ingenjo insigniter excolujt. Vos, Colere, & amjci superstites, videbitis." A. a. O. Nr. 64. Diese Arbeiten des Colerus sind unbekannt. — Über Nüßler vgl. Beckmanns Brief an Colerus vom 13.8.1643: „Mortem amplissimj Nusleri prænunciabat nuncius, quj hac transierat & ejus nomjne ultimùm VALE mihi dixerat. Equidem, doleo mortem amjcj singularjs, cuj etiam calido affectu adijcio, sed breve & extemporale.

   Ad Viatorem.
Nuslerjné vjdes tumulum? Nuslerum ubj dico:
Nomina virtutum dixi, pietatis & artis.
Heu vjrtus, pjetas ars nescit vjncere mortem!" STB Berlin — PK: Dep. Breslau 9, Nr.65. — Eine Arbeit des Colerus über den verstorbenen Nüßler ist auch Hippe (s. Anm.0) u. im *Hb. Gelegenheitsschrifttum* unbekannt.

440127 Fürst Ludwig

Fürst Ludwig an Christian Gueintz

Antwort auf 431227. Beantwortet durch 440129. — F. Ludwig bestätigt dankend, von Christian Gueintz (FG 361. Der Ordnende) den Anfang eines Entwurfes zur deutschen Rechtschreibung empfangen zu haben. Den Entwurf hat der Fürst im Kreise von Mitgliedern der FG beraten und sendet jetzt Anmerkungen dazu an Gueintz. Wenn dieser seine Arbeit unter Berücksichtigung der kritischen Hinweise beendet hat und die Korrekturvorgänge abgeschlossen sind, werden die Möglichkeiten, das Werk zum Druck zu bringen, zu erwägen sein.

Q HM Köthen: V S 545, Bl. 170rv, 170v leer (Bl. 170 ist vor das Bl. 169 eingebunden worden); eigenh. — D: *KE*, 262; *KL* III, 237. — BN: *Bürger*, 949 Nr. 42.

A *Fehlt.*

Vom Ordnenden hat vor weniger Zeit der Nehrende einen anfang des entwurfes zur[a] Rechtschreibung[b] deutscher[c] wörter empfangen[1], darin[d] er noch mit zuziehung etzlicher anwesender[c] geselschafter etwas übersehen, und die notwendige erinnerungen zu pappier gebracht, welche hiermit ubersendet werden,[2] daraus zusehen, wohin man zu zielen hat, und wird der Ordnende[e] anderweit ersuchet, mit fernerer einschickung des abgeschriebenen fortzufarn, wan das gantze wercklein verfertiget, wird man auf mittel gedencken, wie nach einheliger übersehung und genommenen[f] schlusse der Sprache Kundigen solches fuglich könne an den tag gegeben[c], und diese erinnerungen darzu mit gebrauchet werden. Welches dem Ordnenden vermeldet werden sollen.
Cöthen den 27. des Jenners 1644.

T **a** *Folgt* <deutschen> — **b** *Folgt* <der> — **c** *Eingefügt.* — **d** *Folgt* <von> *KE* darinnen — **e** *Folgt* <f> — **f** *Am Rand ergänzt.*

K 1 Christian Gueintz' (FG 361. Der Ordnende) Arbeit an einer deutschen Orthographie hatte sich vielleicht schon mit 430329 angekündigt. In 431016 bat F. Ludwig (Der Nährende), Gueintz möge seine Anstrengungen beschleunigen, damit man alsbald über „eine richtige, deutsche Wortschreibung" verfüge. In 431020 bestätigte Gueintz, auftragsgemäß „wegen der wortschreibung alles verfertiget" zu haben; jedoch bedürfe es noch einer sauberen Abschrift. Diese, zumindest deren ersten Teil (den „anfang des entwurfes zur Rechtschreibung deutscher wörter") empfing F. Ludwig wohl zum Jahresanfang 1644, mit Gueintz' Brief 431227 (dort leider kein Empfangsvermerk). Darin räumte Gueintz seinen Verzug ein und übersandte eine Beilage, „mit versprechen, daß übrige, so unter der feder, vnd nur noch nicht wieder überlesen", schleunigst nachzuliefern. Die Arbeiten an der deutschen Rechtschreibung seitens der FG zogen sich noch das ganze Jahr 1644 und bis mindestens Mai 1645 hin. Vgl. 430419 K 5 u. 431206 K 2; im vorliegenden Band 440129, 440209, 440219, 440313 — ein Brief, dem eine „vollige ubersehung" der Gueintzschen *Rechtschreibung* durch die FG beilag —, 440317, 440504, 440525 K II 13, 440809, 441201 K 0, 441223 K 23, 441226 K 2, 441226A, 441231, 450124, 450326, 450410 K 3, 450420 K, 450504, 450505, 450506A, 450507 u. I, 450508, 450529, 450900, 450919A (die *Rechtschrei-*

bung ist erschienen), 450923B, 451007, 451028, 451028A K 6, 451101, 451219, 460120A K 3, 460131 K, 460217, 460406, 460718, 460720 K 3, 460825 K I 2 u. 4, 460915 K 9 u. 16, 461031 u. 461106. Eine Übersicht über die Briefe und Dokumente zur Rechtschreibdebatte sowie die gewechselten Gutachten und Stellungnahmen dazu in vollem Wortlaut in *DA Köthen I. 9*. Im Druck erschien Gueintz' *Deutsche Rechtschreibung* wohl im September 1645: Die | Deutsche | Rechtschreibung | Auf sonderbares gut befinden | Durch | Den Ordnenden/ | verfasset/ | Von der Fruchtbringenden Geselschaft übersehen/ und zur nachricht an den | tag | gegeben. | [Zierstück] | Gedruckt zu Halle in Sachsen bey | Christof Salfelden/ | [Linie] | Jm Jahre 1645. HAB: Ko 209 (2). Im Historischen Museum Köthen hat sich ein Manuskript erhalten: „Die Deutsche Rechtschreib<ordn>ung angeordnet und der fruchtbringenden hochlöblichen Geselschafft übergeben von Dem Ordnenden" (V S 670; Dig. http://diglib.hab.de/mss/ed000005/start.htm). Es handelt sich dabei nicht um das Druckmanuskript, sondern um eine Vorstufe, die angesichts der vielen Korrekturen und Ergänzungen die damalige intensive und komplexe Diskussion in der FG dokumentiert und sehr wohl aus den Jahren 1643/44 stammen könnte. Zwar sind in der Handschrift auch schon das Widmungsgedicht David Schirmers (im Druck Bl. [)(viij]rv) und Gueintz' Widmungsvorrede [an Hz. Wilhelm IV. v. Sachsen-Weimar FG 5 u. Hz. Ernst I. v. Sachsen-Gotha FG 19, im Druck Bl. [)(ij]r – [)(vi]r] enthalten, sie dürften aber nachträglich beigelegt worden sein, da der Haupttext von F. Ludwig eigenhändig paginiert wurde, jedenfalls von S. 1 [!] – 18. Für Claudine Moulin stellt das Manuskript „wohl eine Zwischenstufe" dar, „die nicht als unmittelbare Druckvorlage gedient hat, dessen Korrekturen und Zusätze jedoch Eingang in die gedruckte Fassung gefunden haben." Claudine Moulin in der Einleitung zu dem von ihr 2008 herausgegebenen Reprint von *Gueintz: Rechtschreibung (1645)*, S. X; vgl. S. VIII–X. S. Conermann: *Ludwig und Christian II. von Anhalt*, 403 f.: „Die handschriftliche Überlieferung der begleitenden Texte (Briefe, Kritiken, Entwürfe usw.) ist dichter als im Falle der Sprachlehre. Das Manuskript des Werkes ist genau von den Fruchtbringern untersucht und von Fürst Ludwig in der Wortbildung und Orthographie beinahe zu jedem Lemma eigenhändig verbessert worden, so daß das Buch eher als eine Hervorbringung der Gesellschaft als seines ursprünglichen Autors angesehen werden muß."

2 Diese Beilage scheint sich nicht erhalten zu haben. Damit fehlt das erste und vielleicht grundlegende Stück der fruchtbringerischen Diskussion um Gueintz' deutsche *Rechtschreibung* ebenso wie jenes Manuskript, das Gueintz zum Jahreswechsel 1643/44 eingereicht hatte und das den Diskussionsprozeß in der FG eröffnete. Im Köthener Erzschrein der FG haben sich einige Akten zur *Rechtschreibung* von Gueintz erhalten:

1.) HM Köthen: V S 545, Bl. 209r–210r: „Erinnerungen wegen der Rechtschreibung, außer was im schreiben schon geendert"; Schreiberh. mit Zusätzen u. Verbesserungen von F. Ludwig, ungez., undat. Der Titel zeigt bereits an, daß diese Stellungnahme nicht die dem vorliegenden Brief beigegebene erste Kritik F. Ludwigs und anderer anwesender Fruchtbringer sein kann. Der erste Korrekturhinweis lautet: „p. 1. l. 7. Also ist derowegen beydes aller grund, wird nicht verstanden." In der Köthener Handschrift V S 670 (s. Anm. 1) ist auf S. 1, Z. 7 der zitierte, Unverständnis auslösende Satz nicht zu finden. Das gilt auch für das folgende Beispiel. Diese Handschrift kann also nicht die Vorlage gewesen sein, an der F. Ludwig und andere ihre Korrekturen vornahmen.
Dasselbe, Konzept von F. Ludwigs H. auf Bl. 219r–220v. Demnächst in *DA Köthen I. 9* (440200).

2.) Bl. 211r–212v, 212v leer (auch HM Köthen: V S 546, Bl. 203rv): „Weiter ist am buchstaben Z hinzuzusetzen"; andere, saubere Schreiberh., ungez., undat. Korrekturen

und Zusätze von F. Ludwig. Es handelt sich um eine Liste von Wörtern, die mit *-z*-beginnen und erläutert werden: zwagen, zwacken, usw. Sie endet mit „zwölffe" (die Wörter sind in *Gueintz: Rechtschreibung (1645),* 172ff. aufgenommen). Danach ergehen Vorschläge zum Satz: Die Wortergänzungen könnten den letzten Druckbogen der ‚Rechtschreibung' vervollständigen. Falls der Ergänzungen aber zu viele seien, sollten die besten Beispiele ausgewählt werden, um auf jeden Fall noch Platz für das abschließende Druckfehlerverzeichnis zu lassen. Dabei ergeht auch der Hinweis auf zu suchende taugliche „Exempel aus der Bibel". Diese Hinweise bezeugen, dass dieses Stück unmittelbar vor oder, wahrscheinlicher, gegen Ende der schon laufenden Drucklegung aufgesetzt worden sein muß. Abschließend folgende eigenh. Vorschläge F. Ludwigs zur Anordnung der Widmungsgedichte für *Gueintz: Rechtschreibung (1645)*:
Die Reime können folgender maßen gedruckt werden
1. Nach dem tittel das Erste <Auf> die <Recht> deutsche Rechtschreibung in [...]. [S. *Gueintz: Rechtschreibung (1645),* Bl. [)(i]v.]
2. Das andere klinggedichte Christian Kieselings mit der bloßen uberschrift Ein anders. [S. ebd.]
3. Des Ordnenden sechtzehen Zeilen. [S. ebd., Bl. [)(vi]v.]
4. An die hochlobliche fruchtbringende geselschaft <Christof> Andreas Hartmans <Weisens>. [S. ebd., Bl. [)(vi]v f., hier schließt sich ein Gedicht David Krügers an, das in F. Ludwigs Aufzählung fehlt.]
5. Die Reime in sechtzehen Zeilen Christof Weisens. [S. Bl. [)(viii]r.]
Die dactylische Reime weil sie so bald nicht verbessert werden können, <auch> die ha[...?] beßer der deutsche sprache folget auch bey dem ersten bogen kein platz mehr sein wird, bleiben zurücke. [Hier ist das im Druck, Bl. [)(viii]r f., sehr wohl veröffentlichte letzte Widmungsgedicht David Schirmers „Langekürtzte (*sic*) Reime" gemeint.]
Auch dieser Zusatz F. Ludwigs ist ein klares Indiz, daß dieses Stück bei laufender Drucklegung aufgesetzt und übermittelt worden sein muß. Demnächst in *DA Köthen I. 9* (450800A).

3.) Bl. 213r, v leer: Gueintz' eigenes Widmungsgedicht „Und so [*sic*]" betitelt, das seiner Zueignungsschrift auf Bl. [)(vi]v folgt. Schreiberh. mit Eingriffen F. Ludwigs und einem am Ende von Gueintz eigenh. hinzugesetzten Vermerk: „Nach der ubereignungs schriften". Auch dieses Stück kann aufgrund des Satzvermerks nur am Ende der Drucklegung, nämlich beim Druck des Vorwerks (= 1. Bogen), niedergeschrieben worden sein. Weitere Textzeugen in HM Köthen: V S 546, Bl. 50r, 199v u. 201r.

4.) Brief 450504, s. dort.

5.) Bl. 217r–218r: Korrekturen und Anmerkungen F. Ludwigs zu Gueintz' *Rechtschreibung*, eigenh., beginnend mit Hinweisen zu „S. 76. Z. 3" bis S. 83. Es handelt sich um die Fortsetzung von Bl. 227r–236v (s. dort). Da sich auf Bl. 218v F. Ludwigs Briefkonzept 440313 befindet, in welchem von einer beiliegenden „völligen" Übersehung der *Rechtschreibung* die Rede ist, dürfte dieses Gutachten die genannte Beilage gewesen sein. Das Gutachten selbst ist nicht datiert.

6.) Bl. 219r–220v: „Erinnerungen von der Rechtschreibung außer was im schreiben geendert". Wie Bl. 209r–210r (s. dort), aber von F. Ludwigs H. Demnächst in *DA Köthen I. 9*.

7.) Bl. 221r u. 222r, 222v leer, Zettel: Bestimmungen der Präpositionen/ Präfixe „vor" und „für", Schreiberh. (?) mit Korrekturen von F. Ludwig. Demnächst in *DA Köthen I. 9*.

8.) Bl. 223r–224v: „Druckfehler" — Liste zu Gueintz' *Rechtschreibung* von F. Ludwigs H. Auch bei diesem Stück dürfte der Druck bereits angelaufen gewesen sein. Demnächst in *DA Köthen I. 9.*
9.) Bl. 227r–236v: „Erinnerungen bey der aufgesetzten deutschen Wort oder Rechtschreibung." F. Ludwigs H., Korrekturen beginnend mit Verweis auf S. 1 bis S. 75 (Fortsetzung und Abschluß mit Bl. 217r-218v). Demnächst in *DA Köthen I. 9* (Zu 440313).
10.) Bl. 237r, 237v leer. Einige orthograph. u. inhaltl. Worterklärungen zu [S. 75?] „Z. 24", 26 u. 28; Schreiberh.: Sau/ Saw; sichel, Siegel; ungez., undat.
238rv: leer.
11.) Bl. 154r–157v: Wörterverzeichnis (Synonyme); Schreiberh. (?). Inc.: „Ballieren | [b]olieren. | [b]lätten. glat machen. | [b]läncken. blanck machen. ..." Demnächst in *DA Köthen I. 9* (400000 „Wörterverz., Synonyme").
Vielleicht in den Zusammenhang der dt. Rechtschreibung oder der Wörterbucharbeit gehörend.
12.) Bl. 225rv: Grammatische lateinische Termini und ihre Verdeutschung nebst Flexionsregeln; F. Ludwigs H. Inc.: „Nominativo Singulari Wo das er in der Nennendung der eintzigen Zahl wen man das geschlecht ...". Demnächst in *DA Köthen I. 9.* 226rv: leer.
13.) HM Köthen: V S 546, Bl. 166r–168v, 171rv, 174r–176v, 199r–201v u. 204rv Gedichte und Texte aus dem Vorwerk der *Deutschen Rechtschreibung (1645)* in versch. Bearbeitungsstufen.

440129

Christian Gueintz an Fürst Ludwig

Antwort auf 440127. Beantwortet durch 440209. — Auf die (verlorene) Stellungnahme Fürst Ludwigs (Der Nährende) und einiger Mitglieder der FG, besonders auf die darin vorgebrachte orthographische Richtlinie, man solle nur die Buchstaben schreiben, die man spricht, antwortet Christian Gueintz (FG 361. Der Ordnende) mit vier Einwänden: 1. Reden und Schreiben seien unterschiedliche Sprachmodi. Beim Sprechen seien der Wohllaut und die jeweilige Mundart bestimmend, beim Schreiben komme es aber auch auf die Etymologie („Vrsprung") der Wörter an, wie es die anderen Sprachen übereinstimmend beweisen. 2. Hielte man sich an jene Richtlinie, weiche man von den anderen Sprachen ab, die im Gegensatz zum Deutschen ihre (auch für die korrekte Rechtschreibung notwendige) sprachtheoretische Fundierung bereits durch Gelehrte gewonnen haben. 3. Im Rahmen eines Fremdspracherwerbs des Deutschen seien Hilfestellungen beim Erkennen der Stammbuchstaben nötig. 4. Der Unterschied zwischen einem bewußten, regelhaft angeleiteten Schreiben und einem Schreiben bloß nach Gutdünken, wie es die Frauen zu tun pflegten, müsse beachtet werden. Schließlich könnte man sonst auch etliche Buchstaben fallen lassen, etwa das -V-, das die gleiche Lautqualität wie das -F- habe, wie dies auch für -J- und -G- gelte, oder für das -Y-, das wie -J- klingt. Auch das -X- sei dann überflüssig, weil es lautlich als -gs- wiedergegeben werden könnte. — Gueintz überläßt die Fragen weiterem Nachdenken und kündigt eine ausführlichere Stellungnahme zu F. Ludwigs Gutachten an. Die Silbentrennung („abtheilung") wie etwa „ge-rin-glich" stamme von Gelehrten, wie auch im Falle anderer Sprachen, eine andere Silbentrennung wäre ungelehrt. — Am Beispiel von „novus" weist Gueintz die Auffassung, das Lateinische hänge vom Deutschen ab und nicht umgekehrt, zurück. Das Lateinische sei weit früher reguliert gewesen als das Deutsche, und schwerlich dürften die Römer in Chaldea oder Rom Deutsch gelernt haben oder nach Deutschland gereist sein, um dort ihre Sprache richtig zu erlernen. Lateinische Worte (wie „novus") gingen aufs Griechische, dieses aufs Hebräische zurück (der adamitischen Ursprache), und ähnlich wie die Abfolge der Weltmonarchie, die auf die Griechen, von denen auf die Römer und von diesen auf die Deutschen übergegangen sei, verhalte es sich mit den Sprachen. Doch stehe es jedem frei, seine eigene Meinung dazu zu haben. — In einer Randglosse distanziert sich F. Ludwig von zänkischen Gelehrten-Disputen. Gelehrte könnten wohl auch eine falsche Schreibung gebrauchen, gar schön sei diese nur selten. Den Kopf in den Wolken, verfehlten sie das Naheliegende, das der Natur doch am nächsten komme.

Q HM Köthen: V S 545, Bl. 169rv u. 171rv [A: 171v], 171r leer; Schreiberh. mit eigenh. Notiz (169v) u. eigenh. Empfangsvermerk von F. Ludwig. Bl. 170rv eingelegt: 440127. — *D:* Jeweils gekürzt in *Barthold*, 311 f.; *KE*, 263 f.; *KL* III, 237 f. — *BN: Bürger*, 634 Nr. 8.

A [*Postalisches Zeichen?*] *Dem Nährenden* [*Zierornament*] Hall Cöthen *etc. Empfangsvermerk F. Ludwigs:* 31. Jenners 1644.

Es hat deß *Nährende* [sic] vernünfftige Erinnerung¹ mit bedacht erwogen der *Ordenende*, vnd befindet ins gemein notwendig zu gedencken, daß zu beobachten, ob dieße meinung könte mit grund vnd fug der gelarten welt erhärtet werden, man solte nur die buchstaben schreiben, so im außreden gebrauchet werden, weill 1. Ein anders daß reden, ein anders daß schreiben, in Jenem siehet man auff den wohllaut, vnd auff iedes Landes Mundart, in dießem auff den Vrsprung, wie einhelliglich auß den andern Sprachen zu schließen.² 2. würde man in dießem von den andern abschreiten, da doch bekant, daß die andern Sprachen durch die Gelahrten in richtigkeit gebracht, die Deütsche noch zubringen.³ 3. würde es den frembden schwehr fallen, wann Sie ohne nachricht solten die Stambuchstaben errathen.⁴ 4. Muß ein unterscheid, wie bißanhero gehalten werden, unter dem Schreiben der Erfahrnen, vnd unter denen, so nach ihrem Düncken vnd redarten, wie daß FrawenZimmer pflegt, etwas sagen. Endlich könte man auff sothane weise etlicher Buchstaben entbehren, Denn warumb wolte man nicht alles mit einem **F** schreiben, nach der außrede, daß man kein zugeschloßen **V**, deßen laut gleich Jenem, bedürffte, dergleichen würde es auch mit dem **J** vnd **G** eine beschaffenheit haben, worzu wehre **Y** weill es wie ein **J** klinget? Daß **x** ist unnötig nach der Sprache, weil es lautet wie ein **gs**.⁵

Sonsten bleibt daß meiste zu mehrem nachdencken, [169v] waß erinnert worden, soll auch mit nächstem gründliche nachricht folgen, die abtheilung der wörter alß ge-rin-g[lich]ᵃ ist der gelährten, wie auß den andern sprachen zu ersehen, die andere ist derer, so sich dessen nicht rühmen können.⁶

Ob **Novus** vnd dergleichen Nahmen von den Deütschen oder hingegen die Deütschen von denen herrühren, mögen die zweife[ln,]ᵇ dieᶜ dafür halten daß man Deütsch in Chaldæa oder zu Rom geredet habe, gewiß, die Lateinische Sprache ist eher in richtigkeit gewesen, vnd wird man nicht[d] beweisen können, daß die Lateiner in Deütschland gereiset, Sie zuerlernen[e]. Der gelährte weiß daß **novus** vom griechischen νεός herrühre, vnd dießes vom hebraischen **nave**[f], weil der erste Mensch Hebraisch geredt, die erste Monarchy hernacher gedien [sic] auf die Griechen, von Grie[chen][b] auff die Römer, von Römern auff die Deütschen, vnd so fo[l]gen[b] auch billich die Sprachen.[7] Doch läßet man einem ieden w[ie][b] seinen Hut, also auch seine meinung. Der *Nährende* wirds in gnaden vermercken, wie denn darumb bittend der verbleibet

    Zeit Lebens
    Schuldigst gehorsamer
    der[g] Ordenende *mp.*

Hall den 29 Jenner 1644.

Dis[h] ist ein lateinischer deutscher, nicht ein deutscher lateiner[.] mit disputiren und zäncken kömmet man aus dem handel nicht und können die gelehrten wol verkehrt schreiben, man findet auch selten einen gelehrten der eine gute schrift hat, und weil sie mit gar hohen sinreichen sachen wollen zu thun haben, so können sie in den niedrigen, die der natur am nähesten kommen gar leicht irre gehen.

T a *Textverlust im Falz. Barthold und KE* ge=rin=glich — **b** *Textverlust im Falz. Konjektur in eckigen Klammern.* — **c** *Anstreichung am Rand (von F. Ludwig?) bis* Lateinische Sprache ist — **d** *KE liest falsch* auch nicht — **e** *KE fälschlich* Sie zu lernen — **f** *Anstreichung (von F. Ludwig?) am Rand bis* Griechen, von Grie[chen] — **g** *Eigenh. von Gueintz* Der Ordenende mp. — **h** *Der nachstehende Absatz ist eine eigenh. Notiz F. Ludwigs am Rand, beginnend neben der Anstreichung T f. Fehlt in KE.*

K 1 Christian Gueintz (FG 361. Der Ordnende) reagiert mit diesem Schreiben auf den Brief 440127 F. Ludwigs (Der Nährende), mit dem dieser seine Stellungnahme zur ersten hsl. Lieferung einer deutschen Orthographie von Gueintz (mit 431227) übersandt hatte. Diese Stellungnahme des Fürsten scheint sich nicht erhalten zu haben. Die in Frage kommenden Schriftstücke im Köthener Erzschrein dürften allesamt etwas jünger sein, s. 440127 K 2. Gueintz geht im vorliegenden Brief kritisch auf drei Themenbereiche ein, die in F. Ludwigs Stellungnahme angesprochen worden sein müssen: 1.) F. Ludwigs Richtlinie, nur die Buchstaben zu schreiben, die auch ausgesprochen werden. Vgl. hier Anm. 2–5. 2.) Die Silbentrennung („abtheilung"), die der Fürst offenbar kritisch kommentierte. S. hier Anm. 6. 3.) Das Abhängigkeitsverhältnis der Sprachen, insbesondere des Lateinischen u. Deutschen.

2 Die einfache Äquivalenzrelation von Aussprache u. Schriftsprache, d.h. der phonetische Normierungsparameter für die Rechtschreibung wird von Christian Gueintz in Frage gestellt, zumindest ergänzt durch das etymologische Prinzip, das nach der Wortherkunft fragt. Das etymologische Argument war übrigens schon in der jüngst zurückliegenden fruchtbringerischen Debatte um die deutsche Grammatik u. in *Gueintz: Sprachlehre (1641)* angeführt worden: vgl. etwa 400112 I, 400528 II; *Gueintz: Sprachlehre (1641)*, 2 f., 18, 24 sowie die einschlägigen Dokumente in *DA Köthen I. 9*. Zum etymologischen Argument trat das morphematische hinzu, das etwa die Schreibung eines Substantivs nach den

Casus obliqui oder einer infiniten Verbform nach den finiten Verbformen regulierte (Schwerter, daher Schwert usw.). Vgl. Etwa 400214 I, 410208 I; *Gueintz: Sprachlehre (1641),* 18; *Schottelius: Der Teutschen Sprache Einleitung (1643),* 91 ff. u. die einschlägigen Dokumente in *DA Köthen I.* 9. Zur Frage der orthograph. Normierungsparameter vgl. *Herz: Rechtschreibdebatte.*

3 Gueintz weist zu Recht darauf hin, daß eine unregulierte Aussprache, d. h. ein fehlender phonematischer Standard, nicht als einziger Regulationsmaßstab der noch ungeregelten, dialektal zerklüfteten Rechtschreibung taugen kann.

4 Gueintz meint hier: Es muß jenen, die die deutsche Sprache als Fremdsprache lernen, geholfen werden, das Stammwort u. die enthaltenen Stammlettern zu erkennen, um die richtige Wortmorphologie u. folgends die richtige Schreibweise zu beherrschen.

5 Vor allem Philipp (v.) Zesen (FG 521. 1648) wird solche Fragen stellen. In seiner *Hooch-Deutschen Spraach-übung* von 1643 will er das -C- u. -Q- als idiomfremde Buchstaben aus dem Deutschen ganz verbannen, das -h- sei außer in der Kombination mit -c- „nichts nütze", insbesondere -th- u. -ph- werden verworfen. Zesen *SW* IX, 44 ff. Vgl. Zesen an Adolph Rosel. In *Bellin: Sendeschreiben (1647),* Bl. E ii v. Auch Harsdörffer meinte: „Für das ph kann durch und durch ein f geschrieben werden/ wie bey den Jtaliänern". *Harsdörffer: Frauenzimmer-Gesprächspiele* III (1643, Ndr. 1968), 315/ Ndr. 335. Harsdörffer ging später von dieser Meinung ab, vgl. 460131 K 10. — Ferner: „das c hat keinen Gebrauch ausser im ch/ sch/ und in fremden Wörtern/ soll dem k nicht beygesetzt werden". A. a. O., 315/ 335 f.

6 In der Frage der Silbentrennung schieden sich die Geister: den Befürwortern einer Trennung nach Sprechsilben (etwa *Gueintz: Rechtschreibung [1645],* 19: nicht sing-en, schreib-en, sondern sin-gen, schrei-ben usw.) standen die Verteidiger einer Trennung von Stammwort u. möglichen Prä- u. Suffixen gegenüber: „Un-auff-bring-lich und nicht bringlich [...] Denn es werden die Stammbuchstaben/ wie gesagt/ nicht zertrennt noch verwirret durch die Hauptendungen der abgeleiteten/ verdoppelungen und andere zufälle". *Schottelius: Sprachkunst (1641),* 192. Vgl. 451028A K 6.

7 Dem wird F. Ludwig in 440313 deutlich widersprechen. In seiner *Rechtschreibung* von 1645 scheint Gueintz ein wenig den Kompromiss zu suchen u. diesen Streit um genealogischen Vorrang der Sprachen vermeiden zu wollen: „Man mus aber dabeneben gestehen/ sintemal die Deutschen von andern Völckern viel erlernet/ als wie die Römer von den Griechen/ und die Deutschen von beyden/ das man auch solcher Völcker Nahmen und wörter/ weil die Deutschen selbst keine dergleichen gehabt/ von ihnen genom*m*en/ und in ihrer sprache behalten/ und das durch solchen gebrauch gleichsam das Bürgerrecht bey uns Deutschen erlanget: Wie hingegen was sie aus Deutschland geborget/ und in Jhrer Sprache mit angeführet/ von ihnen behalten/ und als ihr eigen aufgenommen und gebrauchet: Daraus dan folget/ und man in keiner abrede sein kan/ das fast gleiche wörter bey diesen sprachen untergemenget worden. Doch ist daraus nicht zu schliessen/ das eine sprache alles von der andern entlehnet/ ob schon eine der andern/ und die Deutsche so wol der Griechischen und Lateinischen/ als diese der Deutschen/ die hand gebotten." *Gueintz: Rechtschreibung (1645),* 5 f.

440130

Fürst Ludwig an Carl Gustav von Hille

Antwort auf 431209. — F. Ludwig (Der Nährende) nimmt an, daß Carl Gustav v. Hille (FG 302. Der Unverdrossene) etliche Drucke (Neuerscheinungen der Köthener Presse) durch Vermittlung von Justus Georg Schottelius (FG 397. Der Suchende) erhalten habe. Der Köthener Bote (Ernst Stellbogen) habe so viele Bücher überbracht wie er tragen konnte; ebenso geschehe es bei dem vorliegenden Brief. Der Rest werde bei Gelegenheit folgen. — Man warte beim Bankier in Leipzig noch immer auf Überweisung des finanziellen Zuschusses von jeweils 200 Rth. durch Hz. August d. J. v. Braunschweig-Wolfenbüttel (FG 227. Der Befreiende) und Hz. Christian Ludwig v. Braunschweig-Calenberg (FG 372. Der Reinherzige). Ohne diese Gelder könne nicht mit dem Druck des *GB 1646* begonnen werden. Der Anteil Hz. Friedrichs III. v. Schleswig-Holstein-Gottorf (FG 388. Der Hochgeachte) liege bereits vor, und Hille solle seinem Gesellschaftsnamen gemäß „unverdrossen" an die fehlenden 400 Rth. erinnern. Falls die Zahlung demnächst erfolge, könnten die Zeichnungen der Impresen bereits bis Ostern zum Stechen (zu Matthäus Merian d. Ä.) nach Frankfurt a. M. gesandt werden. Sonst könnte solche Verzögerung den Gesellschaftern unangenehm auffallen, welche ihre Zahlung schon geleistet haben. — Dem Brief beigelegt wurde ein dem *Weisen Alten* gewidmetes Sonett, das F. Ludwig nach dem Druck des Buches (etwa Mitte Juli 1643) erreichte. — Hille möge Hz. August, Franz Julius v. dem Knesebeck (FG 396. Der Geheime), Schottelius und — die Anwesenheit bei Hofe vorausgesetzt — auch Friedrich Wilhelm v. Gans (FG 229. Der Verhaltende) einen fröhlichen Einzug in Wolfenbüttel wünschen.

Q HM Köthen: V S 545, Bl. 22rv, 22v leer; Konzept, eingelegt in 431209. — *D: KE*, 200f. — *BN: Bürger*, 951 Nr. 73.

A *Fehlt.*

Von dem Unverdroßenen hat verwichener Zeit der Nehrende ein schreiben den neunten Christmonats abgewichenes Jhar gegeben wol eingehendiget empfangen, indeßen wird er vom Suchenden auch seinestheils etzliche der gedruckten bucher uberkommen haben, so viel der bote dermalen[a] zu seinem theile mit tragen konnen, und dergleichen ietzunder[1] kriegen, die ubrigen können[b] mit gelegenheit folgen.[2] Zur verlegung des geselschaftsbuchs ist in Leipzig vom Befreyenden nichts erfolget,[3] Und kan zum anfange desselben nicht geschritten[c], oder deswegen verordnung gethan werden[d], es sey dan das verheißene[e] geld[f] beysammen, so vom Befreyenden auf zweyhundert thaler, als auch vom Reinhertzigen versprochen worden: Aus Holstein ist[g] es richtig erleget mangelt nur an diesen, deswegen der Unverdrossene unbeschwert unverdroßene erinnerung dieser[h] vier[h]undert Thaler [h]alben thun wird, geschicht die erlegung in kurtzem so[i] können[d] noch gegen oder[j] auf Ostern die Gemählde abgerissen hienaus auf[k] Franckfurt geschicket werden, sonsten wird es so lange mugen anstehen, und wird den andern geselschaftern, so albereit eingeleget, vorfalen[4] das man mit diesen so lange zurücke gehalten.

Hierbey ein Klinggedicht uber den weisen Alten, [s]o[l] nach den ge[d]ruckten ankommen.^{5} und des Nehrenden grus an den Befreyenden, Geheimen, Suchenden, auch den Verhaltenden wan er zur stelle in Braunschweig oder Wulffenbuttel ist.

Es wunschet der Nehrende dem Befreyenden zufoderst,^{m} wie^n auch allen andern bey ihme anwesenden geselschaftern einen frölichen einzug in Wulfenbuttel,^{o6} — wo derselbe [ni]cht schon geschehn, und verbleibet des Unverdroßenen
    gantzwilliger geselschafter
    der Nehrende

Cöthen den 30. des Jenners 1644.

T **a** *Eingefügt.* — **b** *Folgt gestrichenes Wort.* — **c** *Folgt* <werden> — **d** *Eingefügt.* — **e** *Folgt gestrichenes Wort.* — **f** *Folgt* <alle> — **g** *Folgt unleserliche Streichung.* — **h** *Am Rande eingefügt bis* halber — **i** *Folgt* <kan> — **j** *Eingefügt bis* auf — **k** *Am Rand eingefügt bis* Franckfurt — **l** *Am Rand eingefügt bis* kommen. — **m** *Folgt* <als> — **n** *Eingefügt bis* auch — **o** *Eingefügt bis* geschehn

K **1** *Stieler*, 886, kennt gleichbedeutend „Jetz/ Jetzt/ Jetzo/ Jetzund/ & Jetzunder".
2 Folgende Köthener Drucke aus dem Besitz Carl Gustav v. Hilles (FG 302. Der Unverdrossene) aus dem Jahre 1643 haben sich in der Herzog August Bibliothek als Sammelband (HAB: 23.3 Eth. 1–4) erhalten: **1.** *Fürst Ludwig: Der weise Alte (1643)* mit hsl. Besitzvermerk Hilles; vgl. Anm. 5. S. 187. **2.** *Kalcheim, Fürst Ludwig, Diederich v. dem Werder u. a.: David (1643).* Vgl. 450900 K 9. **3.** *Fürst Ludwig: Heilige Weltbeschreibung (1643).* Vgl. 450900 K 11. **4.** *Fürst Ludwig: Sechs Triumphi oder Siegesprachten (1643).* S. 450900 K 12. Vgl. die Liste der in der Herzog August Bibliothek erhaltenen Bücher aus dem Besitz Hilles in *Bepler: Hille*, 280–290, hier 289f. — Der Bote war Ernst Stellbogen, der in einer Köthener Bestallungsliste vom 14.3.1650 als Amtmann zu Köthen u. Nienburg begegnet. LHA Sa.-Anh./ Dessau: Abt. Dessau A 18b Nr. 13, Bl. 37r–38v.
3 Bereits ein Jahr zuvor übermittelte Hille F. Ludwig (Der Nährende) die konkret formulierte Absichtserklärung Hz. Augusts d. J. v. Braunschweig-Wolfenbüttel (FG 227. Der Befreiende), den Druck des *GB 1646* mit 200 Rtl. zu unterstützen, eine Absicht, auf die sich der Herzog auch schriftlich festgelegt hatte. S. 430121 (K 2) u. schon 421031A K 14 mit Hinweisen auf das mit Hille häufig verhandelte Thema des Verlags u. der Finanzierung des *GB 1646* (Briefe 1639–1643). — Im vorliegenden Band intensiviert sich die Korrespondenz, die sich um das im Jahre 1646 publizierte Gesellschaftsbuch rankt u. die in *DA Köthen I.* 5 ihren Anfang nahm. In 460206 verheißt Matthäus Merian d. Ä. (als Kommissionsverleger): „Das werkh geht zu Endt, werde in 14 tagen alles fertig haben". Gelistet ist das *GB 1646* bereits im Katalog der Ostermesse 1646: Catalogus universalis, hoc est designatio omnium librorum, qui hisce nundinis ... Francofurtensibus & Lipsiensibus anno ... vel novi vel emendatiores & auctiores prodierunt (Leipzig 1646), Bl. D 2r. — Die ersten 400 Impresen der Gesellschaftsmitglieder erschienen einschließlich Reimgesetz, Eintrittsjahr u. Initialen im Quartformat gedruckt u. unter Verwendung der ersten 200 Kupferplatten des *GB 1629/30*. Die Reimgesetze (in Stanzenform) wie auch die übrigen Textteile des *GB 1646* unterscheiden sich im Wortlaut nur geringfügig vom *GB 1641* u. *GB 1641/44*. Zu eingesehenen Exemplaren, Buchgeschichtlichem u. sonstigen Besonderheiten s. *Conermann II*, 52f. Der Kreis der mit der unmittelbaren Genese des *GB 1646* befaßten Personen, die an mehreren Orten aktiv beteiligt waren u. das Projekt vorantrieben, erweiterte sich beträchtlich. In Köthen waren dies F. Ludwig selbst u. Peter Knaudt (1593–1652), seit 1623 Kammermeister u. seit

1634 Oberaufseher über die gesamte Köthener Hofökonomie, der die arbeitsintensiven Vermittlungsaufgaben zwischen Köthen u. Frankfurt übernahm. In Frankfurt a. M. spielt naturgemäß der Verleger Matthäus Merian d. Ä. (1593–1650) die wichtigste Rolle. In Leipzig sind die folgenden Personen beteiligt: der Buchhändler Andreas Kühne (1599–1648) mit besten Beziehungen zum Frankfurter Buchhandel (vgl. 450124 K 8), der Verleger Matthias Götze (1585–1662) — der in die berühmte Buchhändlerfamilie Schürer eingeheiratet hatte (s. *Bircher: Merian*, 698) —, als Händler u. Ratsmitglied Johann Hammer (1600–1650) u. der einflußreiche Handelsherr Georg Winckler (1582–1654), der 1650 von Ks. Ferdinand III. geadelt wurde. Zu Winckler s. 451019 K 0. Am Wolfenbütteler Hof vertrat Carl Gustav v. Hille, der Frauenhofmeister, die hzl. Interessen. Hille nimmt als Vermittler zwischen Wolfenbüttel u. Köthen eine Sonderstellung ein, was bereits die stattliche Anzahl von 15 erhaltenen Briefen beweist, die zwischen F. Ludwig u. ihm zwischen 1642 u. 1643 gewechselt wurden (s. *DA Köthen I. 6*). Die mit der Entstehung des *GB 1646* befaßte Gesamtkorrespondenz von insgesamt 75 Briefen — u. hier ist die fl. Korrespondenz, die um die Verlagsbeiträge kreist, nicht eingeschlossen — wurde in *DA Köthen I. 6* u. wird im vorliegenden Band u. in den folgenden Briefbänden erstmals vollständig erfaßt. In *DA Köthen I. 6* hatte sie sich bereits mit sechs Briefen, die zwischen Merian u. Knaudt im Jahre 1643 gewechselt wurden, niedergeschlagen (s. 430106, 430214, 430306, 430418A, 430513, 430905 u. I). Auch im nächsten Band unserer Briefedition, *DA Köthen I. 8*, werden sich diese beiden Korrespondenten in drei Briefen äußern. Im letzten Schreiben Merians an F. Ludwig lassen sich Merians gewachsene Nähe zur FG u. sein Einbezug in die Belange der Gesellschaft besonders deutlich erkennen. Hier wirkt der Frankfurter Verleger als Vermittler in Sachen FG, wenn er sich nach dem Aufnahmeprozedere der Sozietät erkundigt, um einigen Schweizer Bürgern „weltlichen und geistlichen Standes" Auskunft geben zu können. Er schreibt am 6.10.1648: „Gelangt deshalben mein dinstliche bitte an meinen gg. herrn mich mit nechsten zu verständigen, was es für eine beschaffenheit habe, mit der Auffnehmung in dise so lobliche Geselschafft, damit ich disen redlichen leuthen zu Zürich, wider auff ihr schreiben antworten möchte". S. zur Entstehung des *GB 1646* besonders den dritten Teil des Köthener Erzschreins (HM Köthen: V S 546). Hier soll besonders auf den Korrekturprozeß betreffs *GB 1646* aufmerksam gemacht werden (ebd., Bl. 180r–182v passim), der sich beispielsweise auf einem Zettel von unbekannter H. wie folgt niederschlägt: „Der bedeutende [FG 296. Ernst v. Berg] mangelt die Ziefer 296" (ebd. Bl. 180r) oder „Der Einfache [FG 279. Ernst v. Wietersheim] ist dem Gemah[l]de in der Landschaft nicht gleich" (ebd.). S. auch 450800 u. I. — Die Kosten für die Auslieferung an die im Brief genannten Verlagsteilhaber Hz. Christian Ludwig v. Braunschweig-Calenberg (FG 372. Der Reinherzige), Hz. Friedrich III. v. Schleswig-Holstein-Gottorf (FG 388. Der Hochgeachte) u. (den nicht erwähnten) Anthon v. Wietersheim (FG 273. Der Umfahende) werden ebenso im Erzschrein auf einem undatierten Zettel (v. unbekannter H.) festgehalten (HM Köthen: V S 546, Bl. 178r). S. dazu das Zitat in 460721 K 4. Die Verteilung des *GB 1646* an Hz. August u. die erwähnten Verlagsteilhaber resp. der Verkauf während dreier verschiedener Leipziger Messen wird in *DA Köthen I. 8*: 470223 thematisiert. S. auch 450126 K 4. — Zu bisher veröffentlichten Merian-Briefen vgl. *Bircher: Merian*. Zu Merians Vita s. *Wüthrich: Merian Biographie*. Zu den GBB s. hauptsächlich die von Klaus Conermann veröffentlichten u. kommentierten Bücher in *Conermann I–III* u. *DA Köthen II. 1*. S. zum *GB 1646* auch 421031A K 14 u. im vorliegenden Band 440209A, 440310, 440323 u. I, 440723, 440723A, 441226A K 5, 441231 K 8, 450126, 450127, 450220, 450221, 450301, 450308, 450317, 450319 K, 450331 u. I, 450417, 450419, 450503, 450509, 450510, 450529 K 10, 450611 K 1, 450614 K 2, 450711, 450721, 450722, 450800 u. I, 450806, 450817 K 11, 450905, 450919A, 450922, 450923, 450923A, 450930, 451001, 451008, 451015, 451019, 451028, 451028B, 451119, 460119, 460206 u. I u.

Der weise Alte/

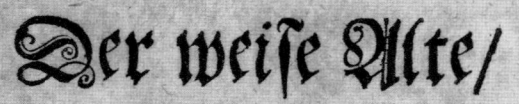

Welcher

Durch geistreiche betrachtungen eines langen und kurtzen Lebens/

Dessen beschaffenheiten/ art und ursprungs der Bäume/ des lebens/ und der wissenschaft/ darauf die leibs und seelen beschwerungen folgen/

Den Nutzen/

So die weisen Alten/ aus Philosophischen und tröstlichem Rahte götlicher Schrift wider alle schwachheiten leibes und der seelen/ ja den tod selbst/ den man fürchten und nicht fürchten sol/ nemen können/

Wie auch

Eine rechtschaffene verfassung gegen den tod für iederman/ wes Standes und Würden er sey: von der leiber auferstehung/ und der seelen unsterbligkeit.

Und schlieslich

Eine ernste vermanung an alle Alte und Junge/

In zwantzig Capitteln vorgestellet.

Aus dem Frantzösischen ins Deutsche vor Jahren versetzet/ und anietzo

Gedruckt zu Cöthen im Fürstentume Anhalt/

Im Jahre 1643.

Fürst Ludwig: Der weise Alte (1643), Titelblatt mit Besitzvermerk Carl Gustav v. Hilles (FG 302. Der Unverdrossene) von 1644. Zu 440130.

II, 460218, 460301, 460303, 460309, 460317, 460324, 460403, 460519, 460613, 460620B, 460703, 460708, 460714, 460715 u. I u. II, 460718, 460721 K 4, 460804, 460808 K 1, 460819 I, 460915A u. I, 460916, 461023, 461029, 461031, 461106, 461213; ferner *DA Köthen I. 8*: 470223.

4 D. h. auffallen, s. *DW* XII.2, 1021 2) a): „innerlich in die Erscheinung treten, der aufmerksamkeit sich darbieten".

5 Der Druck der Simon-Goulart-Übersetzung *Der weise Alte* lag bereits (spätestens) im Juli 1643 vor. Es handelt sich hier um ein nach der Veröffentlichung zugesandtes u. ungezeichnetes Sonett auf den *weisen Alten*. Vgl. 431206 u. II. S. auch 431211. Diesem Brief vom 11. Dezember 1643 an den Neffen F. Christian II. v. Anhalt-Bernburg (FG 51) wurde, genau wie 5 Tage zuvor Georg Philipp Harsdörffer (FG 368, s. 431206 u. II), das korrigierte Sonett beigelegt. Ob das Sonett von F. Ludwig selbst stammen könnte, bleibt bloße Vermutung (vgl. 460705 K II 1). — Zu *Fürst Ludwig: Der weise Alte* s. 440824 K 8.

6 Der Umzug des Hofes von Braunschweig in die alte Wolfenbütteler Dammveste war für Mitte Dezember 1643 vorgesehen. Von dort war im September desselben Jahres die ksl. Besatzung nach 16 Jahren abgezogen. Tatsächlich fand der Umzug nach Abschluß der Renovierungsarbeiten jedoch erst am 26.2.1644 statt. S. 440100 K 3 u. K I.

440204

Diederich von dem Werder an Fürst Ludwig

Diederich v. dem Werder (FG 31. Der Vielgekörnte) bittet F. Ludwig (Der Nährende), ihm für einen Tag die beiden ersten Teile von *Harsdörffer: Frauenzimmer-Gesprächspiele* (1641 u. 1642) leihweise herüberzuschicken. Morgen oder übermorgen werde er sie mitsamt dem 3. Teil (1643) wieder zurücksenden. Georg Philipp Harsdörffer (FG 368. Der Spielende) habe ihm nämlich zugesetzt, er möge zu dem anstehenden 4. Teil (1644) ein Lobgedicht beisteuern. Nach Fertigstellung werde Werder sein Gedicht F. Ludwig zur kritischen Durchsicht vorlegen.

Q   HM Köthen: V S 544, Bl. 469r–470v [A: 460v], 469v u. 470r leer; eigenh.; rotes Lacksiegel. — *D: KE*, 172. — *BN: Bürger*, 1440 Nr. 50.

A   Dem Nehrenden   Cöthen   zu handen
Dabei F. Ludwigs eigenh. Empfangsvermerk: 5. Hornungs 1644.

Neben dienstlichster begrüßung, wird der Nehrende gebeten, die ersten zwey theile der Gesprächspiele nur auf 1 tag zuübersenden, sollen morgen oder übermorgen beneben dem dritten theil mit danck wieder eingeschickt werden. Dieweil mich der Spielende so anstrenget etwas auf sein viertes theil zum lob zu machen,[1] so wolte ich mich gerne in[a] den zeigern[2] ersehen. Gott mit uns
    Des Nehrenden
    Dienstwilligster Der Vielgekörnte.

Reinsdorff 4. Hornung 1644.

Wan etwas aufgesetzt sein wird, so soll dem Nehrenden es erstlich, zur verbesserung, mitgetheilet werden.

I

Gedicht Diederichs von dem Werder zu Georg Philipp Harsdörffers viertem Teil der *Frauenzimmer-Gesprächspiele*

Q *Harsdörffer: Frauenzimmer-Gesprächspiele* IV (1644), 433–437.

          Beglorwürdigung der Gesprächspiele

ES ist ja leider wahr/ daß Kunst und Wissenschafft
   (drauf doch der Menschē Heil und Länder Wolfahrt hafft/
drauff alle Weisheit ruht/ drauf sich auch Tugend gründet.)
Jetzt gar verachtet steht: So daß man wenig findet
     die dieser edlen Gab'/ aus Eifer/ jagen nach/
   als ihrem Eigenthum; Nein: diese wehrte Sach'
und unermessnes Gut ist ihnen gantz zu wieder/
der Geist der hasset sie/ des Leibes faule Glieder
     empfinden Eckel dran/ und scheuen sich für ihr.
   Wie? wunderst du dich drob? die Vrsach ist ja hier:
Dieweil der Lehrer Zunft (so unsrer Jugend pflegen/)
vermeinen/ daß sie gantz nicht können/ als mit Schlägen/
     mit steter Rutenzucht/ mit Schelten und Geschrey/
   die süsse Wissenschafft der Jugend bringen bey. [434]
Daher geschihet diß; daß meistlich alle Kinder
viel lieber müssig gehn/ ja hüten Schwein und Rinder/
     Seynd dienstbar/ lauffen eh' dem grimmen Kriege nach/
   erdulten Hunger/ Durst/ Frost/ Hitz' und Vngemach;
Nur daß sie dieser Plag' und steten Marterwehen
einst mügen kommen ab; Seynd frölich zu entgehen
     des scharffen Meisters Hand: verändern alle Gunst
   (da sie der Musen Schaar und deren freyen Kunst
mit waren zugethan) im Groll/ Verdruß und Hassen.
Der *Spielend'* aber weiß viel besser diß zu fassen;
     Er bringet alles/ das man wissen soll und kan/
   mit Lust und Lieblichkeit/ durch *Spielen* auf die Bahn.
Hier hört man kein Geschrey/ kein Schelten/ Zörnen/ Weinen/
noch so verdrüßlichs was: Nein/ nein/ wer hier erscheinen
     bey diesen Spielen wird/ der findet lautre Lust/
   auch Wonn' und Frölichkeit. Allhier wird jede Brust [435]
gelehrt und unterricht/ durch Lieb' in süssen *Spielen*:
Jn *Spielen*; die dahin gantz unvermerket zielen/
     wie doch/ durch *Spielen*/ uns das werde beygebracht/
   so sonsten in gemein/ bey Morgen/ Tag und Nacht/
durch Müh' und grossen Fleiß/ gar sauer wird erlernet.

Komt/ komt deswegen her! Jhr Lehrer/ und entfernet
　　Euch mit der Jugend nicht von dieser schönen Art:
　　Schaut wie so Freudenreich/ wie doch so süß und zart
durch *Spiel* der *Spielend'* euch schier alle Weißheit zeiget.
Steht einem sein Gemüht zur Gottesfurcht geneiget/
　　hier find er sie im *Spiel*. Die Rechte haben hier
　　ihr Vbung eben wol. Allhier wird mit Manier
auch von Artzney ge*spielt*. Krieg/ Friede/ Tod und Leben/
Kunst/ Tugend/ Warheit/ Glück/ Natur und Weißheit schweben
　　bey diesen *Spielen* rümb. Der hohe Königs Stand/
　　Fürst/ Adel/ Bauersmann/ das trachtbar' Ackerland/ [436]
Druck- Mahl- und Kupferwerk/ scharf schnitzen/ Bilder hauen/
Schach- Damen- Ritterspiel/ Musicke/ Schlösser bauen/
　　Lieb'/ Ehe/ Lachen/ Trost/ Gold/ Eitelkeit der Welt/
　　Wein/ Dantzen/ Springen/ Lust/ wird alles dargestellt
in diesem *Spiel*-Gespräch: Hier *spielt* man von Soldaten/
von Sprachen/ von Wolthun/ wol reden und wol rahten/
　　von Keuschheit/ Redligkeit/ Furcht/ Hoffnung/ Reichthum/ Zahl
　　von Rossen/ Schiffen/ Wind/ von Armut/ von der Wahl/
und von dem Element. Der Sternen schöne Gänge
sicht man ingleichen auch bey diesem *Spiel*-Gepränge:
　　Die Engel kommen selbst auf diesen *Spiele*-Plan;
　　Der Jäger/ durch dis *Spiel*/ auch viel erlernen kan.
Die Länder/ die man sonst durch Waffen nicht kan zwingen/
die weiß der *Spielend'* her in diß sein *Spiel* zu bringen.
　　Der Hofmann lernet hier/ hier lernet der Poet/
　　und zwar bey Spielen nur/ was ihnen wol ansteht. [437]
Jn Summa nichtes ist im Himmel/ auf der Erden/
im Meer und in der Luft/ so nicht soll können werden
　　vom *Spielenden* durch *Spiel*/ mit Frölichkeit gelehrt/
　　und nützlich fürgebracht. Darüm bleibt unverfährt[1]
Herr *Spielender*/ mein Freund; Euch muß nicht irre machen
des Momi schlimme Schaar; last sie hin immer lachen
　　nach ihres Abgotts Art. *Spielt* ihr nur freudig fort/
　　es geht ja ewer *Spiel* schon rüm von Ort zu Ort.
Also daß ewer Nam' und *Spiele* werden bleiben
so lang/ als unsre Welt wird *spielen*/ reden/ schreiben/
　　ja biß wir alle sehn/ in jener schönen Zeit/
　　Wie für dem HERREN *spielt*/ der HERR der Herrligkeit. Sprichw.8/ 30.31[2]

　　Der Vielgekörnte

T a in den *eingefügt für* <im[?]>

K 1 Zum unsicheren Erscheinungstermin des vierten Teils der *Gesprächspiele* (1644) von Georg Philipp Harsdörffer (FG 368. Der Spielende) im April 1644 s. 440426 K 2. Ein Antwortschreiben F. Ludwigs oder eine Dokumentation seiner möglichen Verbesserungen des ursprünglichen Gedichttextes Diederichs v. dem Werder (FG 31. Der Vielgekörnte) fehlen. Bis hin zu 450505 fehlen uns sogar jedwede Gegenschreiben F. Ludwigs in seiner Werderkorrespondenz. Werders Gedicht in Beil. I.

2 „Zeiger" hier im Sinne von Index (*Stieler*, 2609). „Ordnungs-" u. „Inhaltsregister" hatte Harsdörffer in der Tat seinen *Gesprächspielen* nachgesetzt. S. etwa *Harsdörffer: Frauenzimmer-Gesprächspiele* III (1643, Ndr. 1968), Anhang (Ndr. S. 493 ff.) u. IV (1644), Anhang (Ndr. S. 669 ff.). Werder wollte sich demnach einen Überblick über die vielseitigen Themen u. Inhalte der *Gesprächspiele* verschaffen, wie er sie in seinem Gedicht rühmend würdigt.

K I Im Vorwerk von *Harsdörffer: Frauenzimmer-Gesprächspiele* IV (1644; Ndr. 1968), finden sich zahlreiche Bezüge auf die FG, darunter etliche Widmungsgedichte (tw. mit druckgraphischen Illustrationen u. Schmuckinitialen im Holzstich) von Fruchtbringern, zunächst ein Sonett der FG insgesamt, d. d. 24.7.1643 (Ndr. S. 11, s. 430801 I); sodann von Franz Julius v. dem Knesebeck (FG 396. Der Geheime) ein „Dreyständiges Sinnbild" (undatiert, Ndr. S. 11); von Carl Gustav v. Hille (FG 302. Der Unverdrossene) ein „Lobgesang" (mit Noten), ein von Hille selbst entworfenes „Gemälde" (Kupferstich) u. ein „Reimgedicht" (alles undatiert; Ndr. S. 12–19); von Justus Georg Schottelius (FG 397. Der Suchende) ein „Sinnbild", d. d. Braunschweig 22.8.1643 (Ndr. S. 21 f.) u. ein weiteres Gedicht „Letterwechsel Auf vorhergehendes Sinnbild" (Ndr. S. 23); von Johann Rist (FG 467. 1647) ein Gedicht „An den SPIELENDEN", d. d. Wedel 10.8.1643 (Ndr. S. 24–28) sowie ein undatiertes Gedicht von Adam Staden: „Zeitung aus dem Parnassus" (Ndr. S. 29–31). Am Ende der *Gesprächspiele* u. vor den Zugaben weitere Gedichte: Diederichs v. dem Werder (FG 31. Der Vielgekörnte) undatierte „Beglorwürdigung" (s. o. I Q) sowie Gedichte von Johann Michael Moscherosch (FG 436. 1645), inc. „DEine Spiele voller Lust", d. d. Benfeld/ Elsass 1.12.1643 (Ndr. S. 483), Clara Maria Domwald, d. d. Braunschweig 6.2.1644 (Ndr. S. 482), Johann Heinrich Boeckler, d. d. Straßburg 12.1.1644 (Ndr. S. 484–487), u. Adrian von Wettgerstein, d. d. „Cöllen" 25.1.1644 (Ndr. S. 488–490). Vgl. 440426 K 2.

1 D. i. unbesorgt, nicht bange. *Stieler*, 402: „Verfären/ pertimescere, cohorrescere."

2 Spr. 8, 29–31: „[…] Da er den grund der Erden legt/ da war ich der Werckmeister bey jm/ vnd hatte meine lust teglich/ vnd spielet fur jm allezeit. Vnd spielet auff seinem Erdboden/ Vnd meine lust ist bey den Menschenkindern." *Biblia (Luther 1545)*.

440209

Fürst Ludwig sendet ein Gutachten von Mitgliedern der Fruchtbringenden Gesellschaft an Christian Gueintz

Antwort auf 440129. Beantwortet durch 440219. — F. Ludwig bestätigt, Christian Gueintz' (FG 361. Der Ordnende) Antwort auf die (verschollene) Kritik an der von ihm im Umfang mehrerer Bögen eingereichten deutschen Rechtschreibung sowie deren Fortsetzung erhalten zu haben. Dazu geben benachbarte FG-Mitglieder, auch Gelehrte, das Folgende zu bedenken: 1. Die Schreibung müsse sich nach der Aussprache richten und zwar nach der besten und wohlklingendsten. Der Ursprung der Wörter könne zwar sinn-

voll angezeigt werden, da in Verbindung mit der Deklination (casus obliqui) die richtige
Schreibung insbesondere hinsichtlich verdoppelter Konsonanten (fälschlich: Vokale) am
Wortauslaut deutlich werde. In der Wortmitte sei derartiges nicht nötig, da sich der
Ursprung aus der Bedeutung des Wortes von selbst ergebe. Die (unaussprechliche) Konsonantenhäufung aber sei unnütz und jedem Sprachlernen hinderlich. Auch deshalb sei –
wie bei anderen Sprachen: Italienisch, Französisch, Lateinisch – der Grundsatz zu schreiben, wie man spricht, so notwendig. Warum sollte ausgerechnet das Deutsche, ausgezeichnet durch eine enge Kongruenz von Laut, Schrift, Sinn und Bedeutung, darin eine Ausnahme machen? Eine vernünftige Regulierung der Sprache schließe solcherart ungeschickte Regeln wie die Gueintzische aus. Auch in der lateinischen Sprache hätten deren
Sprecher veraltete Schreibweisen zugunsten neuer und eleganterer aufgegeben. — 2. Zugegebenermaßen seien die griechische und die lateinische Sprache durch Gelehrte reguliert
worden, aber nach der jeweils eigenen Sprachart, nicht nach fremdem Sprachmuster. Und
so müsse der Sprachausbau auch durchgeführt werden: auf der Grundlage der jeweiligen
eigenen Sprache. — 3. Der Fremde könne leicht die Stammwörter aus den bleibenden
Stammlettern erkennen; überflüssige Verdoppelungen führten nur zu Unsicherheiten. —
4. Die Schreibweisen der sprachlich Gebildeten und Ungebildeten seien leicht zu unterscheiden. Der etwas höhnische Hinweis auf die Schreibweise der Frauen widerspreche
dem Wirken der FG, das auf Männern und verehelichten Frauen beruhe, welche sich in
ihren Gesellschaftsnamen und auch sonst nach dem Tun ihrer Männer richteten. Gueintz
möge die Gesellschafter mit derlei Argwohn verschonen. — 5. Haltlos sei Gueintz' Einwand, man könne einige Buchstaben abschaffen (V, J, y, x zugunsten des F, G, i und gs),
wenn man sich im Schreiben nur nach der Aussprache richtete. Die Gelehrten müßten nur
Fehler in der Aussprache korrigieren und das Richtige deutlich vermitteln. Wo die Rede
aber der Natur und dem allgemeinen Gebrauch folge, da erübrigten sich Korrekturen
anhand fremder oder abgestorbener Sprachen. Auch leuchte nicht ein, warum Aussprache
und Silbentrennung „ge-rin-glich" der Aussprache und Syllabierung „ge-ring-lich" vorzuziehen sei: Das Wurzelwort sei „gering", die Endung „-lich" und nicht „-glich". Abermals
wird „Novus" nicht als Ursprung von „neu" anerkannt, wie es Gueintz behauptet. Vielmehr sei es vom hebr. „Nave" abgeleitet, da das Deutsche ebenso wie das Griechische älter
als das Lateinische sei, indem jene anders als dieses bereits bei der babylonischen Sprachverwirrung entstanden seien. Wie der Einfall des Brennus mit seinen Galliern bzw. Deutschen belege, hätten die alten Deutschen ihre Sprache sehr wohl nach Rom mitgeführt und
das Lateinische bereichert. Die Römer könnten Deutsch aber auch an der Grenze zu bzw.
in Germanien gelernt haben. Auch das Französische und Italienische wiesen viele Wörter
deutschen Ursprungs auf. Die Theorie eines historischen Kulturtransfers von den
Hebräern oder Chaldäern oder sogar den Ägyptern über die Griechen und Römer zu den
Deutschen läßt F. Ludwig auf sich beruhen, allerdings sei in alten Quellen belegbar, daß
die alten Deutschen besonders in Glaubenssachen den Griechen näher als den Römern
ständen. Gelehrtes Wissen beruhe immer auf Sachen und Taten, nicht auf der sprachlichen
Überlieferung, die im großen und offenen Deutschland oft in Kriegszeiten verlorengegangen und vergessen worden sei, so daß man Nachrichten der älteren Geschichte nur bei den
Nachbarvölkern finden könne. Dennoch hätten sich das Volk und seine Sprache erhalten.
Wie die alten Römer mit der Ausweitung ihres Imperiums auch ihre Sprache verbreiteten,
so sollten auch die Deutschen, da das Kaisertum auf sie übergegangen sei, ihre Hoheit
wahren. An Macht, Land und Leuten bestehe kein Mangel, Gott gebe ihnen nur Einigkeit.
— Gehe man mit Vernunft auf den Grund einer Sprache, folge man auf diesem Weg billigerweise. Latein und Deutsch seien jedoch schon wegen der Zeit und der Herkunft der
Völker zu unterschiedlich, als daß man nicht den Deutschen den Vorzug vor den Römern

und Italienern geben müsse. Das Lateinische sei keineswegs so alt und ursprünglich wie etwa das Etruskische, ja ob es direkt aus der babylonischen Sprachverwirrung hervorgegangen sei, wie das Deutsche mit Ascenas, sei fraglich. — Die Anmerkungen zu den überschickten weiteren Teilen der Gueintzschen *Rechtschreibung* lägen diesem Brief bei. Künftige Textlieferungen von Gueintz würden desgleichen durchgesehen. — Gueintz möge diese Hinweise fruchtbringerisch (konstruktiv) annehmen, zum Nutzen der Gesellschaft und des ganzen deutschen Vaterlands.

Q HM Köthen: V S 545, Bl. 172r–174v, 174v leer; Abschrift von Schreiberh. mit eigenh. Korrekturen F. Ludwigs.
Dazu hat sich im Erzschrein auch das Konzept erhalten: A.a.O., Bl. 175r–176v; F. Ludwigs H. Seitenverkehrte Einbindung: Der Text beginnt auf Bl. 175v (>175r, 176r, 176v). — Zit. als *K*.
D: *KE*, 264–267; *KL* III, 239–242 (beide datieren falsch auf den 14.2.1644). — *BN*: *Bürger*, 949 Nr. 43 (falsch datiert 14.2.1644).

A *Fehlt.*

Was von dem *Ordenenden*[a] unterm 29. abgewichenes Monats auf die erinnerungen, so bey etzlichen bogen seiner Wortschreibung gethan worden, eingewendet, das ist mit einem weitern verfolge derselben wol einkommen.

Darüber von den in der nähe befindlichen geselschaftern, darunter auch gelährte[b], fernere erwegung geschehen, und anderweite[c] erklerung darbey zu thun gutgefunden[d], inmaßen folgender gestalt[e] geschicht.[1]

1. Jst es unvereinlich[f], wie[g] sich das stellen und schreiben, nach dem steller und schreiber der es zu pappier bringet, und nach der rede aufschreibet, richten mus, sonsten were es unverstendlich, sol es nun nach dem reden, so mus es auch nach der besten und anmutigsten ausspreche geschehen, und was anders geschrieben wird,[h] unrecht, oder ein überflus, und also unnütze sein.[2]

Den ursprung der wörter mit etwas einem gemercke der buchstaben anzuzeigen, ist zwar gut, sonderlich da es eine abmerckung, der verenderungen ist, als zu[i] ende etlicher Nennwörter die verduplirung der selblautenden [*recte:* mitlautenden] buchstaben darmit in den andern fällen oder endungen anzudeuten, in der mitte aber ist es nicht von nöten, da der ursprung aus dem verstand doch ohne das leichte kan genommen werden.[3] Es dienet[j] die zusammensetzung so vieler Mitlautenden[k], die nicht gelesen werden, zu anders nichts, als den anfahenden auch frembden leser irre zumachen, und das pappier unnötig zufüllen. Ja alle frembde völcker bemühen sich dahin, also zuschreiben, wie sie[l] reden und aussprechen. Bey den Frantzosen und Jtalianern ist es am tage, Bey den Lateinern findet man es nicht anders: Warumb wolten dan die Deutschen, die sonsten den Ruhm haben, das Rede, wort, aussprache[m], verstand, wie[n] auch das schreiben eines wie das andere gleich[o] sein sol[4], deswegen einen nachklang ietzunder erst an sich nehmen, und[p] solche ungeschickte regeln machen, da sie in vernünftiger ausarbeitung ihrer sprache bemühet. [172v] Ja man wird in der Lateinischen sprache die wortschreibun[g][q] vieler alten wörter ausgemustert finden, die nach dem ursprunge^r erstlich gerichtet gewesen, hernach aber verbeßert und lieblicher gesetzet worden. Dergestalt kan man aus den andern sprachen, wie^s wol nach deutsc[her]^q und nicht Lateinischer art, weil die Lateinische sprache kürtzer, als die deutsche, schließen.

2. Die Griechische und Lateinische sprache seind durch die gelehrten in richtigkeit gebracht, dieses wird gestande[n]^q, die sie aber zurechte in gewiße ordnung und Regeln gebracht, haben es^t nach der Griechischen und Lateinischen art, nicht aber nach^u einer frembden sprache, die mit ihr keine gemeinschaft gehabt, eingerichtet. Also mu[s]^q der grund aus der sprache herkommen, die man orden[t]lich^q erkleren und ausarbeiten sol, und darin^v auf fremb[de]^q sprachen^w und wie sie ihren ursprung herziehen, nicht sehen.

3. Dem frembden kan es nicht schwer fallen die Stamw[ör]ter^q zuerkennen, weil doch die Stambuchstaben bleiben[,] ob sie schon nicht allezeit verdupliret werden, das übrige oder überflüßige machet sie viel mehr irre.

4. Der unterscheid zwischen den erfarenen und unerfar[e]nen^q ist leichte zuerkennen, wan es aber auf des Fraue[n]zimmers^q schrift, wie etwas hönisch^x angezogen^y worden, so[l]te^q gemeinet^z und gesetzet sein, so lieffe es wieder die Fruchtbringende geselschaft, die auf die Mannesperson[en]^q und nur^aa die weibespersonen^ab, so weit^ac sie mit den Männ[ern]^q verehlichet^ad, und sich nach ihnen im nahmen^ae und der that zur[ich]ten^q haben[,] gegründet, und^af möchte der *Ordenende*^ag mit solch[em]^q argwon, die andern geselschafter verschonen.^5

Die fünfte einwendung das man der^ah gestalt etzlicher buchstaben als das **V** an stat des **F**, das **J** an stat des **G**, das **y** an stat des **i**, auch^ai das **x** einer^aj eingebildeten folgerey nach entbehren könte^6, schicket sich^ak hieh[er]^q gar nicht. Wo fehler im^al aussprechen seind, sollen sie die gelehrten weisen^am und beßern, auch nicht verhelen, sonste[n]^q behielten sie die kunst alleine im kopfe, und würde and[ern]^q [173r] nicht mittgetheilet, wo^ao man aber der natur, und dem^an gemeinen gebrauche nachgehet, da können sie es^ap aus frembden und theils abgestorbenen sprachen, die nicht mehr von der Amme, sondern aus büchern gelernet werden, nicht thun. Und mag^ar man noch nicht ergründen oder absehen, worumb^as ge-rin-glich^at solte beßer ausgesprochen, **Sillabiret**^au und geschrieben sein als ge-ring-lich^av, den^aw der ursprung^ax von^ay geringe^az ist, der anhang lich, und nicht glich. Was endlich wegen **Novus** abermals^ba angezogen wird^7, so solte man eher und mit beßerer gründlicher vermutung glauben, das neu vom hebräischen **Nave** herkommet, weil die deutsche sprache mit der Griechischen als^bb einer haubtsprache bey der verwirrung zu **Babel** zugleich aufkommen, die Lateinische aber lange darnach; das man zu Rom niemals^bc deutsch geredet haben^bd sol, ist ein seltzamer einwurf, seind die völcker^be dar gewesen, so werden sie auch ihre sprache geredet haben, also wie **Brennus** der Brenner^8 dar war^bf, und die Stadt eingenommen, werden^bg seine **Gallier** oder Deutschen nicht alle Lateinisch gekant^bh haben, oder die sprache zulernen hienein gezogen sein, also^bi reden die Schweitzer, des Pabstes Leibwache, noch heutiges tages, deutsch drinne^bj. So wenig ist auch zuschließen, das die Römer und Lateiner gar nicht solten etwas^bk deutsch gelernet und gekunt haben, da^bl sie so ofte in Deutschland kommen, und es guten theils beseßen, sondern das wiederspiel daher abzunemen, das sie auch die Deutsche Nahmen der vornemen herren, Lateinisch gemacht, also^bm wird sonder zweiffel mit vielen andern wörtern auch^bk geschehen sein, wie solches im Frantzösischen und Jtalianischen, welche^bn sprachen auch viel vom deutschen überkommen, gar klar zuweisen.

Das die künste^bo von den Hebreern oder Chaldeern ja^bp Egyptern auf die Griechen, von den Griechen auf die Lateiner^bq und von den Lateinern oder Römern auf die deutschen gekommen sein, das leßet man dahin gestellet sein, es^br wird sich aber in alten geschichten finden, das meistentheils die Deutschen den Griechen sonderlich in geist- [173v] lichen glaubens sachen näher als den Lateinern^bs gekommen. Wie^bt nun die gelehrtheit^bu nicht^bv allezeit in der sprache stehet, sondern in^bw den sachen und^bx geschichten, darin die sprache ausgearbeitet wi[rd]^q und die man verstehen und lernen sol^by. [also haben]^bz Die unruhigen alten u[nd]^q kriegerischen^ca Zeiten aber^cb, in einem offenen lande, wie gros Deutschland ist,^cc sonder zweiffel viel geschriebene sachen und die alten geschichte [sic] abhanden^cd und in^ce ein vergeßen gebracht, d[as]^q man sich deren^cf nur bey den frembden erholen müßen, So ist doch drumb^cg die Sprache und das volck nicht unterga[n]gen^q, ob es sich^ch schon bey ihnen vielmals^ci geändert.

Die Römer haben wegen der beherschung ihre sprache erweitert, und das sie die alten einwoner vertilgen, ihr[e]^q Landsleute^cj hocherheben und ausbreiten wollen, da nun d[as]^q Keyserthum auf die Deutschen kommen, solten sie eben^ck d[a]rinnen^q auf ihre hoheit in^cl dem ihrigen auch sehen, und haben darzu^cm Landes und leute genug, als^cn auch vermögen, wan ihnen Gott g[na]de^q zur einigkeit giebet, das sie es fürs vaterland rech[t]^q anstellen.

Guter ordnung die auf den grund der sprache mit vern[ünf]tigen^q ursachen gehet, folget man billich, Latein aber und Deutsch ist alzu weit von einander, wie auch die Zeit, beyd[er]^q völcker ursprung, das ein^co Deutscher ehren[-] und^cp der gebü[hr]^q halber nicht anders kan als den Deutschen den Vorzug für den Römern^cq oder Jtalianern zugeben und zugönne[n]^cr.⁹ Solte auch Janus oder Noah schon^cs in Jtalien gekommen se[in,]^q¹⁰ wie noch^ct nicht gewiß^cu ist, so wird er doch nicht^cv Late[in]^q geredet haben. So ist auch die Hetrurische oder aber Tuscische oder Toscanische^cw sprache älter und^cx anders als die Lateinische gewesen^cy, und kan nicht bewiesen werd[en,]^q das die^cz Lateinische, mit der^da verwirrung der sprachen zu^db Babel, angefangen, welches von der Deutschen ehe[r]^q kan gesaget werden, als^cm von Ascenas, so deutsch hei[s]set, herrührende.

Die andern überschickte und überschriebene bogen seind vollend übersehen, und werden die erinnerungen darübe[r]^q¹¹ ietzo^dc auch überschicket, kommet was weiter ein, sol ferner^cm hand mit dran geleget werden. [174r]

Der *Ordenende*^dd wird diese erklerung geselschaftmeßig zu unserer Muttersprache notturft also erwogen^de vermercken, und^df die sachen also einrichten, wie es der fruchtbringenden geselschaft, auch^dg dem gantzen deutschen Vaterlande, rühmlich und anstendig,^{dh} So ihme^{di} hiermit vermeldet werden sollen, Geben an den^{dj} ietzigen orte des Ertzschreines, und auf gutbefinden anwesender geselschafter, unterm Geselschaft Jnsiegel ausgefertiget, So geschehen^{dk} den IX^{dl}. des Hornungs im Jhare 1644 etc.

T **a** *In der Abschrift und in K von F. Ludwig (?) gebessert aus Ordenden.—* **b** *K* gelehrte — **c** *Von F. Ludwig gebessert aus* andererweite — **d** *K folgt* <worden> — **e** *In der Abschrift und in K von F. Ludwig eingefügt für* <maßen> — **f** *Gebessert aus* unverneinlich *K* unverneinlich — **g** *K* wie das schreiben <oder> und stellen sich — **h** *Folgt in der Abschrift und in K* <ist> — **i** *In K zu ende eingefügt für* <in den endungen> — **j** *Folgt in K* <zu anders> — **k** *Mitlautenden, die nicht gelesen werden in K eingefügt für* <buchstaben> — **l** sie reden und aussprechen *in K gebessert aus* man redet und ausspricht — **m** *In K folgt* <und> — **n** *In K eingefügt für* <also> — **o** *In K eingefügt.* — **p** *Bis* regeln machen *in K am Rand ergänzt.* — **q** *Buchstabenverlust im Falz. Konjektur in eckigen Klammern.* — **r** *Von F. Ludwig gebessert aus* ursprung *K* ursprung — **s** *K* wiewol *eingefügt für* <doch> — **t** *In K gebessert aus* sie — **u** *In K eingefügt.* — **v** *K* darbey *gebessert aus* darauf — **w** *In K eingefügt für* <und ihren ursprung> — **x** *In K eingefügt für* <spärlich> *[?]* — **y** an- *eingefügt.* — **z** gemeinet und *in K eingefügt.* — **aa** *Eingefügt von F. Ludwig für* <auf> *K* und nur *eingefügt.* — **ab** *In K folgt* <nur bei denen die> — **ac** *Eingefügt von F. Ludwig für* <wie> *K* so wie sie *eingefügt.* — **ad** ehlichet *am Rand ergänzt für* ver<gleichet> ver<ehlichet> — **ae** *Gebessert aus* namen *K* nahmen — **af** *Der folgende Satz in K am Rand ergänzt.* — **ag** *Von F. Ludwig (?) gebessert aus* Ordende *K* Ordende — **ah** dergestalt *in K eingefügt.* — **ai** *In K eingefügt.* — **aj** *Bis* folgerey nach *in K am Rand ergänzt.* — **ak** *In K folgt* <daher> — **al** *Von F. Ludwig (?) gebessert aus* in — **am** *In K Reihenfolge der Wörter durch Exponentialziffern gebessert aus* beßern und weisen — **an** *Von F. Ludwig gebessert aus* den — **ao** *In K bis* nicht thun *am Rand ergänzt.* — **ap** *In K eingefügt.* — **ar** *In K eingefügt für* <kann> — **as** *Lies* warum — **at** *Am Rand ergänzt für* <geringlich> *In K gebessert aus* gering-lich *für* <geringlich> — **au** *In K eingefügt.* — **av** *Von F. Ludwig gebessert aus* gering-lich — **aw** *Von F. Ludwig gebessert aus* d[...?] — **ax** *In K für* <anfang> — **ay** *Gebessert aus* vom *[?].* — **az** *Von F. Ludwig (?) gebessert aus* geringen *[?] In K* gering an *gebessert aus* gering<en> — **ba** *In K eingefügt für* <von neuem> — **bb** *Folgt* <ha> — **bc** *In K eingefügt für* <habe Celtisch oder> — **bd** haben sol *von F. Ludwig eingefügt, fehlt in K.* — **be** *In K eingefügt für* <nation> *[?]* — **bf** *In K eingefügt für* <gewesen> — **bg** *Von F. Ludwig gebessert aus* wurden *oder* würden — **bh** *Oder* gekont *wie in KE. Von F. Ludwig gebessert aus* ge<lernet> — **bi** *In K bis* deutsch darinne *am Rand ergänzt.* — **bj** *Unsichere Lesung. In K* darinne *[?]* — **bk** *In K eingefügt.* — **bl** *In K bis* beseßen *am Rand ergänzt.* — **bm** *In K gebessert aus* so — **bn** *In K bis* überkommen *am Rand ergänzt.* — **bo** *In K folgt* <auch> *[?]* — **bp** ja Egyptern *in K eingefügt.* — **bq** *In K eingefügt für* <Römer> — **br** *In K bis* gekommen *am Rand ergänzt.* — **bs** *Von F. Ludwig gebessert aus* Lateiner — **bt** Wie nun *in K eingefügt.* — **bu** *In K folgt* <aber> — **bv** *In K Reihenfolge der Wörter durch Exponentialziffern umgestellt aus* stehet nicht allezeit in der sprache — **bw** *In K eingefügt.* — **bx** und geschichten *von F. Ludwig eingefügt, fehlt in K.* — **by** *In K gebessert aus* mus *anschließend Komma.* — **bz** also haben *eingefügt nur in K, fehlt in der Abschrift.* — **ca** *Von F. Ludwig eingefügt für* <verderblichen> *in K* verderblichen *(eingefügt).* — **cb** *Eingefügt von F. Ludwig, nicht in K.* — **cc** *In K folgt* <haben> — **cd** *Von F. Ludwig eingefügt für* <verderbet> *K* verderbet — **ce** *In K bis* gebracht *eingefügt für* <ver[...]et[?]> ein *fehlt in KE.* — **cf** *Von F. Ludwig gebessert aus* der *K* der *KE* darin — **cg** *Darüber ein Zeichen, das sich als* er *lesen, jedoch nicht als sinnvolle Korrektur erkennen läßt. Der Satz bis dahin* *in K:* Später *[?] für* <Es> ist aber drumb *In KE fehlt* doch — **ch** *K* schon sich <auch> — **ci** *In K gebessert aus* viel — **cj** *In K folgt* <aber> — **ck** *In K veränderte Wörterfolge durch Exponentialziffern aus* auf ihre hoheit eben darinnen auch sehen — **cl** in dem ihrigen *von F. Ludwig am Rand ergänzt. Fehlt in K.* — **cm** *In K eingefügt.* — **cn** als auch *in K eingefügt für* <darzu auch> — **co** *In K eingefügt für* <man auch> *KE hat* was *anstatt* das — **cp** und der gebühr <halber> *in K am Rand ergänzt. KE hat* geburt *statt* gebühr — **cq** *In K Reihenfolge der Wörter durch Exponentialziffern umgestellt aus* Jtalianern oder Römern — **cr** *In K zu* gönnen *am Rand ergänzt.* — **cs** *In K* schon in Jtalien *eingefügt für* <gen Rom> — **ct** *Von F. Ludwig eingefügt.* — **cu** gewiß ist *von F. Ludwig eingefügt für* <geglaubet wird> *K* wie nicht geglaubet wird — **cv** *In K folgt* <alsob[ald?]> — **cw** *Von F. Ludwig gebessert. In K* oder Toscanische *eingefügt, unsichere Lesung auch in K (*Toscarische?*).* — **cx** und ve[...?] *in K eingefügt.* — **cy** *In K eingefügt.* — **cz** *In K* die lateinische *am Rand ergänzt für* <sie> — **da** *In K folgt* <Babe> — **db** zu Babel *in K am Rand ergänzt.* — **dc** ietzo auch *in K am Rand ergänzt.* — **dd** *Gebessert aus* Ordende *K* Ordenende — **de** *Fehlt in K.* — **df** *Bis* einrichten *in K am Rand ergänzt.* — **dg** *Bis* Vaterlande *in K am Rand ergänzt.* — **dh** *In K folgt* <noch> — **di** *In K folgt* <die frucht> — **dj** *K* dem — **dk** *Von F. Ludwig gebessert aus* gescheen *[?]* — **dl** *Von F. Ludwig eingefügt für* <7> *K* 9 *(gebessert aus* 7 *[?]). KE hat* 14

K 1 Christian Gueintz (FG 361. Der Ordnende) hatte mit seiner Stellungnahme 440129 auf jene kritischen Anmerkungen F. Ludwigs u. weiterer FG-Genossen reagiert, die ihm zu einem mit 431227 übersandten ersten Entwurf seiner *Deutschen Rechtschreibung* (1645 publiziert) zugegangen waren. Diese kritischen Anmerkungen, die F. Ludwig mit 440127 an Gueintz überschickte, scheinen sich nicht erhalten zu haben. Vgl. aber in *DA Köthen I.* 9 die Dokumente zur Rechtschreibdiskussion, darin v. a. 440200. Gueintz hatte in 440129 eine Antwort auf die „erinnerungen" wegen seiner „Wortschreibung" eingereicht — „mit einem weitern verfolge derselben". Zu den Verfassern der ursprünglichen, am 27.1.1644 übersandten Kritik könnten viele anhaltische Mitglieder der FG gehört haben — vgl. 440127 „mit zuziehung etzlicher anwesender geselschafter". Bei der erneuten, vorliegenden Erwiderung (auf 440129) erwähnt F. Ludwig Gelehrte, wobei wohl nicht insbesondere gelehrte FG-Mitglieder wie Martinus Milagius (FG 315) oder Gottfried Müller (FG 353) gemeint waren, sondern hinzugezogene Gelehrte wie Marcus Fridericus Wendelinus (1584–1652), Rektor am Zerbster Gymn. illustre, Joachim Mechovius (FG 483. 1647) u. Johann Köppen (FG 485. 1647), vielleicht auch Geistliche wie der Köthener Superintendent u. Hofprediger Daniel Sachse (1596–1669).

2 Kern der kontroversen Diskussion ist F. Ludwigs hier verteidigte Position, nur die Buchstaben zu schreiben, die man ausspricht. Dieser Grundsatz dürfte sich vorrangig auf die v. a. in den herkömmlichen Druckschriften zur Gewohnheit gewordene Konsonantenhäufung bezogen haben. Gueintz hatte diesen Parameter allein als nicht ausreichend für eine Rechtschreibnormierung angesehen. S. 440129. Schon in seiner Stellungnahme zu Augustus Buchners (FG 362) u. F. Ludwigs Gutachten zu seinem Entwurf einer deutschen Grammatik hatte Gueintz zu bedenken gegeben: „wenn mann aber alle zeit solle so schreiben wie man redet, so were kein vnterscheidt vnter gelahrten vndt vngelahrten". *DA Köthen I. 5*: 400301 I, S. 467. In 451219 wird F. Ludwig die Grundregel bestätigen, „das man schreibe wie man redet", um normative Willkür auszuschließen. Übrigens begründete Philipp v. Zesen (FG 521. 1648) sogar seine heftig beanstandeten Neuerungen in der Schreibung des Deutschen, die keinen Rückhalt in der gewöhnlichen Schreibpraxis hatten, damit, die Uneinheitlichkeit in der schriftlichen Markierung von Vokallängen u. -kürzen widerspreche der Aussprache u. mache den Fremdspracherwerb des Deutschen

„überaus mühsam/ ja unmüglich". S. sein undat. „Sendeschreiben" an Christian Gueintz in *Habichthorst*, 14–22, hier S. 15 (da dieses „Sendeschreiben" frühestens 1651 verfaßt worden sein kann, bleiben Zweifel am Adressaten Gueintz, der am 3.4.1650 verstorben war).

3 Wie sehr hier grammatische, lexikographische u. orthographische Bestimmungen zusammenfließen, zeigt Justus Georg Schottelius' (FG 397) Konzept eines vollkommenen deutschen Wörterbuches in seiner *Der Teutschen Sprache Einleitung (1643)*, 112–114: Basis sollte eine Liste aller deutschen Stammwörter sein. Jedes Substantiv sei mit der Angabe von genus, casus genitivus u. numerus pluralis zu kennzeichnen u. um seine Derivata mit ihren „Haubtendungen" sowie seine Komposita zu ergänzen. Die Stammverben (verba primitiva) seien mit dem Hinweis, ob sie zu den regelmäßigen („gleichfließenden") oder unregelmäßigen („ungleichfließenden") Verben gehören, u. mit Angabe der 1. u. 2. Person Sg. Präsens Aktiv, des Imperfekts u. des Partizips Perfekt zu versehen, etwa: „Brich [Imperativ Sg. als Stammform des Verbs]/ ich breche/ du brichst. ich brach. gebrochen". Sodann habe eine Erklärung der Bedeutung zu folgen, wobei „der Teutsche rechte Gebrauch" maßgeblich sei. Mit diesen Angaben sei das jeweilige Stammwort u. seine Wortmorphologie erfaßt u. könne leicht gelernt werden. Dies scheint ähnlich auch der Sinn der obigen Passage F. Ludwigs zu sein. Allerdings spricht er hier irrtümlich von „selblautenden buchstaben" (Vokalen). Sinnvoll können hier nur Konsonanten (Mitlauter) gemeint sein. Deren Verdoppelung in der Wortmitte lehnt Ludwig aus phonematischen Gründen ab, das Stammwort sei auch so zu erkennen, etwa im Falle von Herr/ herlich. Vgl. 451219 u. 460915.

4 Die enge Korrelation von Laut, Schrift, Bedeutung — letzteres etwa in der vergleichsweise geringen Anzahl doppeldeutiger Wörter im Deutschen — galt als Ausweis der Würde u. „Redlichkeit" der deutschen Sprache. So hatte F. Ludwig 1640 als Anmerkung zu einem Gutachten Augusts Buchners auf das Manuskript zu *Gueintz: Sprachlehre (1641)* notiert: „Man soll reden wie man schreibett, sonderlich auff Deutsch, ist es alzeit gleich zuthun, der redligkeit zufolge, im brauche gewesen." (*DA Köthen I. 5*: 400122 I, S. 426). Seinem Brief 460720 an F. Ludwig hatte Gueintz kritische „Erinnerungen Bey des Spielenden [Georg Philipp Harsdörffer, FG 368] Wercklein die deutsche Sprache betreffend" beigelegt. Darin erklärte er anläßlich einer von Harsdörffer verfolgten stammwortorientierten Silbentrennung, daß „man so schreiben sol, wie man Redet. [...] Anders schreiben vnd anders Reden, geziemet der Deutschen Aufrichtigkeit schwehrlich: Altes ändern vnd neues suchen ist derselben Standthaftigkeit zu wieder". S. *DA Köthen I. 9* (Zu 460720). Die enge Verbindung von Laut, Schrift u. Sinn zeigte sich Schottelius zufolge auch in der vergleichsweise geringen Anzahl doppeldeutiger Wörter, in der Kürze u. Prägnanz der dt. Stammwörter u. der „natürlichen Verwantschafft unter den Wörteren und der Natur selbst", der „innerlichen Gleichheit des gleichsam natürlichen Wesens des Dinges in denselbigen [den Wörtern]". *Schottelius: Der Teutschen Sprache Einleitung (1643)*, 83; vgl. *Schottelius: Sprachkunst (1641)*, 16 f., 29 f. u. ö. *Harsdörffer: Frauenzimmer-Gesprächspiele* II (1642, ²1657, Ndr. 1968), S. 229/ Ndr. 247: „Unsere Teutsche Muttersprach ist so redlich/ daß man in derselben wenig zweydutige Wörter findet."

5 Frauen konnten nicht förmlich Mitglieder der FG werden, sie wurden aber bisweilen in der feminisierten Form des Gesellschaftsnamens ihres Mannes wie solche behandelt, wie etwa die Nährende (Fn. Sophia v. Anhalt-Köthen), die Befreiende (Hzn. Sophia Elisabeth v. Braunschweig-Wolfenbüttel), die Vielgekörnte (Juliana Ursula v. dem Werder) u. a. m. Vgl. zuletzt 410101 K 2. Diese Stelle verdient große Beachtung, weil der Fürst hier die Frauen in die Fruchtbringende Gesellschaft einbezieht u. sie besonders an deren sprachlichen Bestrebungen u. Ansprüchen beteiligt. Vgl. die Einleitung „Zum vorliegen-

440209 Fürst Ludwig

den Bande". Vgl. ferner 450921, 450927 II, 451028, 460718 K 1 u. 460803 K 1; *Neumark: Palmbaum*, 180.

6 Gegen F. Ludwigs Auffassung, man solle nur die Buchstaben schreiben, die man spricht, hatte Gueintz in 440129 eingewendet, dann könne man auch gleich etliche Buchstaben als überflüßig ganz aus dem Alphabet verbannen: das V, da es den Lautwert F habe, das J, das lautlich an das G reiche, das Y, das durch I zu ersetzen wäre, sowie das X, das mit einem GS wiedergegeben werden könnte.

7 Gueintz muß das deutsche Wort „neu" bereits in seinem eingereichten hsl. Entwurf zur deutschen Rechtschreibung vom lat. „novus" hergeleitet haben, um diese Etymologie in 440219 zu verteidigen. In einem Gutachten F. Ludwigs zu Gueintz' Rechtschreibungsentwurf heißt es: „Das Neu von Novus sol herkommen und darumb new geschrieben werden sol, ist so eine vermutung, die gar un[er]weislich, dan die deutsche sprache für älter als die lateinische, ja wo nicht älter doch mit der Griechischen gleich, und eine aus den Haubtsprach[en] in Babel entsprungen zu achten: Als sonderlich Av[en]tinus aus alten geschichtschreibern angezogen. Kan also Novus eher vom deutschen, als New von Novus herkommen sein." S. *DA Köthen I. 9* (Zu 440313). In *Gueintz: Rechtschreibung (1645)*, 106, ist die Ableitung von „neu" aus dem Lateinischen aufgegeben.

8 Brennus, gallischer Heerführer, der im Jahre 387 v. Chr. Rom angegriffen u. geplündert hatte; nur die Burg auf dem Kapitol hatte sich gegen die Angreifer halten können. Vgl. *Kl. Pauly* I, 942. Wie die alte deutsche Sprache mit der alten keltischen in eins gesetzt wurde, so auch die Germanen mit den Kelten in ihrem gemeinsamen Ursprung vom biblischen Ascenas. Vgl. etwa *Schottelius: Sprachkunst (1641)*, 63 f.: „Denn alle Völcker/ welche die Griechen und Lateiner Celtas nennen/ haben Teutsch geredet/ [...] Jst also diese uhralte Sprache bey den freyen Teutschen vornemlich geblieben/ auch ihren Nahmen von den Teutschen/ als den Vornehmsten Hauptgeschlechte der Celten/ hernachmals behalten." Vgl. auch a. a. O., 271; *Schottelius: Der Teutschen Sprache Einleitung (1643)*, 27, 31, 42 u. 70. Zur „Keltomanie" bei Schottelius' Gewährsmann Adriaan van Schrieck (Adrianus Schrieckius Rodornius) vgl. Arno Borst: Der Turmbau zu Babel. Geschichte der Meinungen über Ursprung und Vielfalt der Sprachen und Völker. 4 Teile in 6 Bd.en, Bd. III.1, Stuttgart 1960, 1224 f.

9 Diese u. viele andere Stellen der fruchtbringerischen Sprachdebatte ordnen sich in den wahrhaften „Paragone" ein, der in der frühen Neuzeit um Alter, Würde u. Vorrang der europäischen Einzelsprachen entbrannte. Vgl. Harald Haarmann: Die Entwicklung des Sprachbewußtseins am Beginn der europäischen Neuzeit. In: Sprachkultur und Sprachgeschichte. Herausbildung und Förderung von Sprachbewußtsein und wissenschaftlicher Sprachpflege in Europa. Hg. Jürgen Scharnhorst. Frankfurt a. M. 1999, 89–110, hier S. 104 ff.; Ferdinand van Ingen: Sprachpatriotismus im Europa des Dreißigjährigen Krieges. In: Frieden und Krieg in der Frühen Neuzeit. Erfahrung und Deutung von Krieg und Frieden: Religion – Geschlechter – Natur und Kultur. Hg. v. Klaus Garber u. a. München 2001 (Der Frieden. Rekonstruktion einer europäischen Vision, Bd. 1), 943–956.

10 IO. AVENTINI ANNALIVM BOIORVM LIBRI VII (Basel 1580; zuerst 1554 in Ingolstadt erschienen) [UB Göttingen: 4 H BAV I, 622], 12: Sabatius, König der Armenier, war vor dem Eroberer Ninus zu Tuisco geflohen, der selbst aus Armenien kam (a. a. O., 10) u. den F. Ludwig mit Ascenas gleichsetzt, „so deutsch hei[s]set". „Vnde in Italiam ad Ianum, qui & Noas, post aliquot annos profiscitur. Nam anno regni Tuisconis centesimo, tricesimo septimo Noas perlustrata Asia, Aphrica, in Europam transitum facit, in Italiaque in agro Viterbensi consedit. Etruscos Italiæ indigenas condidit, dictus Ianus, id est Vini repertor: Iain Hebræi vinum vocare solent. Intelligens denique atque considerans ipse pater Germanorum, Sarmatarumque Tuisco sine iustitia, & absque religionis metu,

neque Rempublica coalescere, neque licentiam hominum contineri posse, iura dedit, leges tulit, carminibusque complexus est, quæ publicè & priuatim cantarentur: ne aut obliuio obliteraret, aut ignorantia excusaret. [...] Tradunt quidam ipsum quoque literas inuenisse." Für F. Ludwigs Argumentation, die das Deutsche für älter als das Lateinische hält, bildete auch Aventinus die Anregung. Der betont (a. a. O., 13) die enge Gemeinschaft mit dem *sermo Saxonum*, um dann fortzufahren: „plurimum retinet commercij cum Græcorum lingua, rectiusque literis Græcis scribitur. Infinita sunt vocabula, quæ nobis & Græcis idem valent." S. auch die deutsche Fassung in Johannes Turmair's genannt Aventinus Sämtliche Werke. Hg. Kgl.-Bayer. Akademie der Wissenschaften. 4. Bd.: Bayerische Chronik. Hg. Matthias Lexer. 1. Tl.bd., München 1882, 75. Vgl. auch S. 92, ferner 51–53 u. 63 f. Aventinus zufolge hatte sich Noah nach der Sintflut in Armenien niedergelassen, zahllose Nachkommen gezeugt, bis er die Erde unter seine Söhne aufteilte u. sie in ihre Reiche einwies. Sein Sohn „Tuitschen oder Teutschen" (griech./ lat. Tuischon oder Tuiscon) machte sich mit 30 Helden nach Europa auf u. besiedelte „Großgermanien", das Land vom Rhein bis an den Don. Auch der Noah-Enkel Gomer war nach Europa gezogen, nach Italien, wo auch sein Großvater Noah in „Viterb" wohnte. Die alten „Etrusci" sollten auf diese Einwanderung zurückgehen. „Den Noah von dem wein, den er erfunden hat, der in der jüdischen und altwälschen sprach ‚jain' haist, nennen die alten und noch die Lateiner Janum, wir Jener [Lies: wie Jenen], davon das neu jar und erst mânat noch den namen behelt." — Schon Giovanni Nanni alias Annius von Viterbo hatte mit den *Antiquitates Italiae ac totius orbis* (1498) eine antike Quellensammlung veröffentlicht, die angeblich auf den babylon. Priester, Astronom u. Geschichtsschreiber Berosus (Berossos, spätes 4./ frühes 3. Jh. v. Chr.) zurückging u. als „Pseudo-Berosus" im Humanismus eine beachtliche Wirkung entfaltete. Sein Geschichtswerk der sog. „Babyloniaka" hat sich zwar nur in dürftigen, allerdings als zuverlässig geltenden Fragmenten erhalten, doch boten Nannis erfundene Quellen den lange gesuchten Stoff, Genaueres über die Vorgeschichte der Völker einschließlich der Deutschen zu erfahren u. letzteren jene *vetustas*-Autorität zu vermitteln, deren sie bislang schmerzlich entbehrten. Zudem erlaubten sie eine Synchronisation der biblischen Geschichtserzählungen mit den antiken Quellen Griechenlands u. Roms. Demnach sollte die Erde nach der Sintflut unter den vier Söhnen Noahs aufgeteilt worden sein. Noah selbst ließ sich in Italien nieder, sein Sohn Tuisco — bei Tacitus (Germ. 2.2) Tuisto als erdentsprossener Gott u. Stammvater der Germanen — bevölkerte Germanien. Diese Genealogie griffen viele deutsche Humanisten auf, zuerst Johannes Nauclerus (1425–1510) in seiner Chronik *Res memorabiles seculorum omnium ac gentium* (1490/1510), dann u. a. Johannes Aventinus' *Bayerischer Chronicon* (1522). — Auch der Florentiner Giovanni Villani (1280–1348) hatte in seiner *Cronica* der Stadt bereits Noah u. Janus verknüpft u. zu Stammvätern Italiens gemacht. Vgl. Herfried Münkler, Hans Grünberger, Kathrin Mayer: Nationenbildung. Die Nationalisierung Europas im Diskurs humanistischer Intellektueller. Italien und Deutschland. Berlin 1998, 84; Annette Helmchen: Die Entstehung der Nationen im Europa der Frühen Neuzeit. Ein integraler Ansatz aus humanistischer Sicht. Berlin [u. a.] 2005, 223 ff.; Ludwig Krapf: Germanenmythus und Reichsideologie. Frühhumanistische Rezeptionsweisen der taciteischen *Germania*. Tübingen 1979, 61 ff.

11 Liegt dem Briefkonzept nicht (abschriftlich) bei; nicht ermittelt.

440209A

Carl Gustav von Hille an Fürst Ludwig

Antwort auf 440130. Beantwortet durch 440310. — Carl Gustav v. Hille (FG 302. Der Unverdrossene) bestätigt, daß Hz. August d. J. v. Braunschweig-Wolfenbüttel (FG 227. Der Befreiende) die Veröffentlichung des *GB 1646* finanziell unterstützen werde. Da Hille der Name des Leipziger Kaufmanns entfallen sei, bittet er F. Ludwig, ihm nach Gutdünken einen Frankfurter oder Leipziger Kaufmann zum Zwecke der Geldüberweisung zu nennen. — Hille dankt F. Ludwig (Der Nährende) für die ihm mit der letzten Briefsendung geschickten Bücher. — Falls F. Ludwig den Wunsch hege, Hille zur Übersetzung eines italienischen oder französischen Werkes zu veranlassen, würde dies für Hille aus Gründen der FG-Mitgliedschaft Ehre und Verpflichtung bedeuten. Daneben habe Georg Philipp Harsdörffer (FG 362) Hille vorgeschlagen, ein englisches Büchlein, (Glapthornes) *The tragedy of Albertus Wallenstein*, zu verdeutschen. Dieses Werk habe Hille jedoch noch nicht erreicht.

Q HM Köthen: V S 545, Bl. 24r–25v [A: 25v], 24v leer; eigenh. mit Empfangsvermerk von F. Ludwigs H.; rotes Lacksiegel. — Auf Bl. 25r undat. Konzept F. Ludwigs an Hille; s. 440310 Q.

A Dem durchleuchtigen hochgebornen Fürsten und Herrn Herrn Ludwig Fursten zu Anhalt, Grafen zu Aßcanien Herrn zu Bernburg und Zerbsten *etc.* meinen H. Fursten und Herrn underthenigk *etc.*
Empfangsvermerk F. Ludwigs: Pres. 22. Febr. 1644

Höchstgehrter H. Nehrender,

demselben gebe ich hiemit gehorsambst zuvernemen, daß der Befreyende, wie angedeutet seinem Versprechen in Allem nachzukommen;[1] Wenn aber ich meine sachen Naher Wolfenbuttel ohnlängsten uberbracht,[2] und also deß Kaufmanß Namen in Leipzigk mir entfallen, alß wird der höchstgeEhrte h. Nehrende gehorsambst ersucht, sich belieben zu lassen, einen Kauffmann, entweder zu Leipzigk oder Franckfurt am Mayn (wie eß dan an bequemsten fallen wird) zubenennen, so wil ich mich eussers angelegen sein lassen, daß werck zubefordern. Jnmittelst thue ich mich wegen der uberschicketen bucher gehorsamst bedancken. Da der höchstgeEhrte h. Nehrende dem Unverdrossen*en*, ein kleineß Jtalienischeß oder Frantzöscheß buchlein, so den würde in unsere Mutter Sprache zu ubersetzen uberschickete[a], were derselbe entschlossen seine Geselschaftß-Schuldigkeit zuerweisen und abzulegen.[3] Eß hatt sonsten der Spilende dem Unverdrossenen ein Englischeß buchlein, genandt die Wallensteinische Tragedie[4], vorgeschlagen, ist aber noch zur zeit nicht uberschicket, womit, nebenst gehorsamer anbefhelung deß höchsten Schutzeß, verbleibet

       deß höchstgeEhrten h. Nehrenden
           gehorsambster Geselschafter *etc.*
             der Unverdrossene *etc.*

[Br]aunßwich den [9][b5] hornungß 1644.

T a *Am Rand eingefügt.* — **b** *Tagesangabe durch Falz verdeckt; vgl. Antwortbrief F. Ludwigs 440310.*

K 1 Carl Gustav v. Hille (FG 302. Der Unverdrossene) bestätigt die finanzielle Unterstützung Hz. Augusts d. J. v. Braunschweig-Wolfenbüttel (FG 227. Der Befreiende) für das *GB 1646*. S. das Versprechen des Herzogs in 430121 (K 2). S. zum *GB 1646* 440130 K 3; zu den Verlagsbeiträgen 450126 K 4 u. zum Zahlungsverkehr s. 450127 K 1.

  2 Hille hielt sich zwischen 1638 u. 1639 neun Monate in England auf u. bemühte sich, da sein Vater aus England stammte, während dieser Zeit intensiv um die englische Sprache u. Kultur. Selbst in Pommern geboren, hatte es ihn bereits in den 1620er Jahren nach London verschlagen. Im Januar 1629 schrieb er auch in englischer Sprache an Lgf. Moritz v. Hessen-Kassel (FG 80), der zu diesem Zeitpunkt ein Exil in England erwog. Vgl. *Bepler: Hille*, 253–290. Vgl. auch Gilbert Waterhouse: The Literary Relations of England and Germany in the Seventeenth Century, Cambridge 1914, 118 f.

  3 Deutlich läßt sich an den Hille durch F. Ludwig geschenkten Büchern (s. 440130 K 2) der Gesellschaftsanspruch ablesen, zur Beförderung der deutschen Muttersprache Übersetzungen zu verfassen. Um welches Büchlein es sich hier handelt, läßt sich dem Briefwechsel nicht entnehmen. Vgl. 440310 zu diesem Zusammenhang u. zu F. Ludwigs Idee.

  4 Erwähnt in *Bepler: Hille*, 256 u. 265. Diesem Beitrag ist ein Verzeichnis beigegeben (S. 280–290), das die in der Herzog August Bibliothek erhaltenen Bücher aus dem Besitz Hilles aufführt. Das u. g. Werk fehlt jedoch in der Bücherliste. — Bei dem Drama handelt es sich um *The tragedy of Albertus Wallenstein late Duke of Fridland, and generall to the Emperor Ferdinand the second. Written by Henry Glapthorne. The scene, Egers. And acted with good allowance at the Globe on the Banke-side, by his Majesties Servants. Imprinted at London: By Tho. Paine, for George Hutton dwelling at the Turn-stile in Holborne* (London 1639). Henry Glapthorne (1610–1643) war ein von Sidneys *Arcadia* beeinflußter Dramenautor u. Dichter aus Cambridgeshire. Diese Ausgabe sowie eine aus dem Jahre 1640 finden sich im Early English Books Online, http://eebo.chadwyck.com/home. Vgl. auch *Bepler: Hille*, 275. Ob Diederich v. dem Werder (FG 31), der sich 1644 in Nürnberg in seiner Übersetzung der *Dianea* Loredanos mit dem Sturz u. der Ermordung Wallensteins beschäftigte, auch von diesem Drama erfahren oder gar dessen Druck empfangen hat, bleibt offen. S. 440000 K I 1.

  5 Die Tagesangabe im Falz. Ludwigs Antwort in 440310 erwähnt als Datum des Vorläuferbriefes den 9. des vorigen Monats, i. e. 440209.

440219

Christian Gueintz an Fürst Ludwig

Antwort auf 440209. Beantwortet durch 440313. — Christian Gueintz (FG 361. Der Ordnende) beantwortet die Erwiderungen Fürst Ludwigs (Der Nährende), die dieser ihm nach Beratung mit weiteren FG-Mitgliedern zu Gueintz' erneuter Verteidigung seiner Arbeit über die deutsche Rechtschreibung (440129) geschickt hatte. Das meiste empfehle eine mündliche Beratung, jedoch wolle Gueintz eine einstweilige Stellungnahme übermitteln: Man könne den überkommenen Schreibusus nicht so stark hintansetzen und eine völlig neue Rechtschreibung einführen. Man könne den Altvordern ja schwerlich Vorhaltungen machen, wie sie hätten sprechen und schreiben sollen, jenen, von denen man die Sprache doch schließlich gelernt habe. Die Deutschen seien gewiß jünger als andere Völker, es sei denn, man nehme an, daß Deutschland schon vor dem Turmbau zu Babel bevölkert gewesen, aber in der Sündflut nicht untergegangen sei. Zwar seien auch andere Sprachen in vielem der Veränderung unterworfen, jedoch fahre man am besten, wenn man sich an die Parteigänger der Alten und ihre Schriften halte. Das neue Gutachten der Fruchtbringer sei deshalb leider „neu". Da man sich aber über die Rechtschreibung einigen müsse, sei das Gutachten gleichwohl zu loben, wenn man die eingeführten Neuerungen auch überzeugend darlege und begründe. — Die Gesellschafter mögen seine Freizügigkeit gestatten, doch „Herz, Wort und Taten" der Deutschen, wie auch der Zweck und der gesellschaftliche Verkehr („anmuth vnd ergetzligkeit") der FG erforderten die Wahrheit.

Q HM Köthen: V S 545, Bl. 177r–178v [A: 178v], 177v u. 178r leer; Schreiberh., Unterschrift fehlt; kein Eingangs- oder Empfangsvermerk; Sig. – *D: KE*, 267 f. – *BN: Bürger*, 634 Nr. 10.

A *Dem Nährenden*, [Ornament] Halle Cöthen

Waß der *Nährende*, sambt denen[a] anwesenden vornehmen Geselschafftern dem *Ordenenden* wieder eingeschicket[1], ist willigst gelesen, vnd in eyl so viel vermercket, daß das meiste in Zusammenkunfft vnd unterredung bestehe. Soll aber doch aufs eilfertigste nachgesonnen, beobachtet vnd wieder hinterbracht werden. Unterdeß, daß mich fast zurückhelt, vnd behutsam zuverfahren anmahnet ist: Wan fast alles im schreiben solte geendert werden, würde man den alten Vorschreiben müßen, wie sie hetten schreiben vnd reden sollen, da wir doch schreiben, reden und anders von ihnen erlernet.[2] Gewiß[b] Deutschen sind nach den andern Völckern kommen, wo nicht will dafür gehalten werden, daß zur Zeit der Babylonier[c] Deutschland schon bewohnet, vnd durch die Sündflut Sie nicht mit untergangen.[3]

Zwar ist in andern[d] auch viel geendert, doch helt man von denen am meisten, die es mit den alten halten, wie derer Schrifften, so in händen, außweisen.

Der[e] Neuen neues gutachten wird deßwegen für neu gehalten.[4] Dennoch aber da man einen algemeinen Schluß machen, vnd von den meisten einmahl beliebet werden könte, zumahl wann die ursachen der enderung gründlich außgeführet würden, wehre es nicht zu tadeln, sondern zu adeln;

Unterdeß bittet der Ordenende es wolten die Geselschaffter die freyheit, deren Er sich erkühnet, Jhnen nicht mißfallen laßen,

Der Deutschen[f] hertz, wort vnd thaten erfodern die warheit, der Geselschaffter Zweck, anmuth vnd ergetzligkeit wird es auch belieben, wie sothanes wüntschet

Deß Nährenden gehorsamer untterthaniger[g]

Hall den 19 Hornungs 1644.

T a *Folgt* <bey> — **b** *Ergänze:* die — **c** *Anstreichung am Rand bis* doch helt — **d** *Ergänze:* Sprachen — **e** *Anstreichung am Rand bis* den meisten — **f** *Anstreichung am Rand bis* wie sothanes — **g** *Die zu erwartende eigenh. Unterschrift von Gueintz fehlt, wurde vielleicht*

vergessen oder abgeschnitten. Das Stück ist wegen der Adresse auf Bl. 178v nebst erkennbaren Siegelresten jedenfalls keine Abschrift.

K 1 F. Ludwig (Der Nährende) hatte Christian Gueintz (FG 361. Der Ordnende) mit 440127 seine unter Hinzuziehung „etzlicher anwesender geselschafter" aufgesetzten „erinnerungen" zur von Gueintz aufgesetzten dt. Rechtschreibung übersendet. Dazu hatte sich Gueintz bereits in 440129 geäußert. Die dort vorgebrachten Einwände wurden erneut im Kreise der FG diskutiert u. führten zu der Stellungnahme F. Ludwigs in 440209, auf die Gueintz im vorliegenden Brief kurz reagiert. Vgl. zur Erzschrein-Überlieferung der Diskussionspapiere zur Rechtschreibung 440127 K 2.

2 Gueintz verteidigt hier den diachronen Zusammenhang der Sprachgemeinschaft zumindest im Rückblick auf die letzten hundert Jahre. In seiner *Rechtschreibung* von 1645 jedenfalls lobt er dieses Jahrhundert, weil darin „die Deutsche sprache hochgestiegen" sei, der normierende Rückgang auf ältere Sprachstufen wird ebenso abgelehnt wie eigenmächtige Regulierungen einzelner Sprachkritiker. Vgl. *Gueintz: Rechtschreibung (1645), 7.* In der Tat hatte F. Ludwig, vielleicht unter dem Einfluß von Justus Georg Schottelius' *Der Teutschen Sprache Einleitung (1643)*, stärker als zuvor die Notwendigkeit vernunftgeleiteter sprachkritischer Korrektur eingeschlichener, unnützer und vom analogistischen Standpunkt irrtümlicher u. fehlerhafter Usancen im Sprachgebrauch betont, dabei aber die Regeln *fremder,* teilw. schon abgestorbener Sprachen, die mit der eigenen nicht verwandt seien („keine gemeinschaft" haben, s. 440209), für eine untaugliche Richtlinie erklärt. Basis der Sprachnormierung könne allein „der grund", die „natur" u. der „gemeine gebrauch" der jeweiligen Sprache selbst sein (440209). Letzteres betont Gueintz stärker als F. Ludwig, u. zwar auch in Abwehr willkürlicher Neuerungen: „Was bis anhero bey den Deutschen gelobet und vernünftig beliebet worden/ das sol man behalten." *Gueintz: Rechtschreibung (1645), 4.* Scharf formuliert er seinen Gegensatz zum sprachtheoretischen Ansatz eines Justus Georg Schottelius (FG 397), dem sich F. Ludwig offensichtlich angenähert hatte, nämlich, daß „keine sprache von Natur/ sondern alle nach der übung/ und durch die gewonheit/ aufkommen/ geredet/ und geschrieben wird." A. a. O., 3. Folglich beruft sich Gueintz auf Luther als vorbildlich für die deutsche geistliche Sprache, auf die Reichsabschiede für weltliche Sachen, wobei beide durch Entstellungen der Schreiber u. Drucker die Glättung u. Vereinheitlichung durch eine normierende, einheitliche Orthographie durchaus nötig haben. Noch ältere Sprachstufen, wie etwa das Mnd. im Sachsenrecht, seien als sprachliche Muster allerdings untauglich: „es ist alt/ nicht mehr üblich/ nicht verständlich […] viel Wörter gantz unbekant und undeutsch" wirkend. „Wer wollte nun solches veraltete/ ausser wo es noht ist/ und mit verstande geschehen kann/ gebrauchen? Der Deutsche würde von dem Deutschen selbst nicht verstanden werden." Und weiter: „Warlich uns ist nicht frey/ wie wir reden wollen/ sondern wir müssen reden wie andere/ so wir wollen von Jhnen verstanden werden; […] Und wan wir so reden wölten und schreiben wie die alten Sachsen [*auch dies eine Invektive an die Adresse Schottelius', d. Hg.*]/ so weren wir nicht die ietzigen zierliche hochDeutschen." Vgl. a. a. O., 4f., Zitate S. 5. Da wir hier Gueintz' ursprüngliche Argumentation, die sich offenbar auf die klassischen Sprachen der Antike berief, nicht kennen, bleibt diese Kontroverse schwer greifbar. Vgl. auch Anm. 3 u. 4 sowie schon 440129, wo Gueintz mit der „Etymologie", d. h. nicht im engeren Sinne einer Wortgeschichte, sondern der „Wortforschung" überhaupt, argumentiert u. also durchaus eine metasprachliche Kategorie für die Regulierung der Schriftsprache einführt. Nicht nur der Gebrauch u. die Aussprache, heißt es in 440129, auch die Wortherkunft seien für die Rechtschreibung wesentlich. In diesem Sinne hatte schon Wolfgang Ratke in seiner Universalgrammatik *Allgemeine Sprachlehr Nach der Lehrart*

Ratichii (Köthen 1619) Aussagen zur „Wortschreibung", zur „Wortsprechung" u. zur „Wortforschung" getroffen, bevor er zu den flektierenden u. unflektierenden Wortarten überging. Die „Wortforschung" handelte nach Ratkes Definition „von eines jeden Worts Natur insonderheit". Zit. n. *Ising* II, 28. Gueintz folgte in seiner *Deutschen Sprachlehre* (1641) exakt diesem Schema u. bestimmte analog: „DJe Wortforschung ist ein theil der sprachlehre von eines ieglichen wortes natur." *Gueintz: Sprachlehre (1641)*, 24, vgl. 123. Das *Dictionnaire de l'Académie francaise* (1694) hatte der Etymologie ebenfalls nicht nur den Gegenstand „Origine d'un mot" zugesprochen, sondern desgleichen seine Morphologie „La maniere dont un mot a esté formé". Zit. n. Gerda Haßler: Art. „Etymologie". In: *Haßler/ Neis* I, 625–658.

3 Replik auf F. Ludwigs Ansicht in 440209, die deutsche Sprache sei älter als die lateinische u. wie die griechische direkt aus der babylonischen Sprachverwirrung hervorgegangen. Auch hatte der Fürst die fehlende schriftliche Überlieferung der frühen Deutschen nicht als Beweis gegen das Altertum der Deutschen u. ihrer Sprache anerkennen wollen. In 440313 wird F. Ludwig die Argumentation von Gueintz unter Hinweis auf die biblische Chronologie nachdrücklich zurückweisen. Georg Philipp Harsdörffer (FG 368) sollte übrigens genau die von Gueintz inkriminierte Theorie aufwerfen: Die dt. Sprache sei mit Japhets Stamm schon vor der *confusio linguarum* ins mittlere u. nördliche Europa gelangt. Dies sei bibelkonform, da die biblische Chronologie zwischen der Sintflut u. dem babylon. Turmbau mehrere Generationen nach Noah einschaltete. Vgl. 460915 K 11.

4 Innovation als Schimpfwort in legitimistischen Gesellschaften, aber auch in der Philologie wie im Begriff „Criticus hodiernus" usw. Vgl. 400528 K II 2. Vielleicht eine ironisch-überspitzte Anspielung auf die fortgesetzte Kontroverse um die Herleitung des Wortes „Neu"/ novus. S. 440129 u. 440209. Zu Kritik u. Geschmack im Zusammenhang mit dem Streit der Alten u. Neuen in der Renaissance u. in der FG vgl. *Conermann: Akademie, Kritik u. Geschmack*.

440310

Fürst Ludwig an Carl Gustav von Hille

Antwort auf 440209A. Beantwortet durch 440323. — F. Ludwig bestätigt den Empfang von Carl Gustav v. Hilles (FG 302. Der Unverdrossene) Schreiben 440209A. Der Leipziger Kaufmann, an den die Gelder für das *GB 1646* zu überweisen sind, heiße Georg Winckler. Der (Köthener) Bote, der den vorliegenden Brief überbringt, könnte (auf der Rückreise) den Wolfenbütteler Wechsel (für Winckler) mitbringen. Sollte eine nachrichtliche Abschrift davon (nach Köthen) mitgeschickt werden, könnte dann die Anweisung (über Winckler) nach Frankfurt a. M. (Matthäus Merian d. Ä.) erfolgen. Umso besser wäre es, wenn die (zugesagte) Zahlung Hz. Christian Ludwigs v. Braunschweig-Calenberg (FG 372) für das *GB 1646* aus Hannover gleich mit veranlaßt würde. — F. Ludwig (Der Nährende) erwartet einige italienische und französische Bücher, die kürzlich erschienen sind. Aus diesen werde er ein Werk an Hille senden. Außerdem ist eine lesenswürdige Biographie des Admirals Châtillon in frz. Sprache erschienen. Falls Hille das Buch noch nicht kenne, bietet F. Ludwig an, es ihm leihweise zukommen zu lassen. Ein Mitgesellschafter (Paris v. dem Werder. FG 339) hat sich mit dem Werk bereits beschäftigt, jedoch kennt F. Ludwig den Stand (der Übersetzung) nicht. — Grüße übermittelt F. Ludwig an Hz. August d.J. v. Braunschweig-Wolfenbüttel (FG 227. Der Befreiende) und an Franz Julius v. dem Knesebeck (FG 396. Der Geheime).

Q HM Köthen: V S 545, Bl. 25r (vgl. 440209A Q); eigenh. Konzept o. O. u. D.; Datierung geschätzt. Nicht in *KE*.

A *Fehlt.*

Des Unverdroßenen antwort vom 9 abgewichnes Monats ist dem Nehrenden bey wieder gekommenen boten wol eingehandiget worden. Der kaufman zu leipzig an deme die gelder zu dem gesellschaft-buche zu übermachen heißet George Winckler[1], und kan dieser abermals abgefertigte bote den wechselbrieff an denselben wol mitbringen, wan aber abschrift darvon zur nachricht mitgeschicket wird; darauf sol dan verordnung auf frankfurt geschehn, wen dan[a] zugleich von Hannover und dem Reinhertzigen[2] auch etwas kommen möchte, were es desto[b] beföderlicher.

Es erwartet der Nehrende etzlicher Jtalianischen und frantzösischen büchlein, so in neuligkeit ausgegangen, daraus er dann eines von ferne kommen laßen, und dem Unverdroßenen zu schicken wil;[3] Es ist sonsten des **Admirals Chastillon** sein leben[4] auch kurtz[5] frantzösisch ausgegangen, so wol wurdig zu lesen, solte es der Unverdroßene nicht gesehn haben, so kan es ihme auf widersendung zugefertiget werden. ein geselschafter hat es unterhanden gehabt,[c][6] man weis aber nicht was darbey gethan worden.

Dem Befreyenden werde des Nehrenden dienste als auch dem geheimen[d][7] entboten, und verbleibet des Unverdrossenen
                      gantzwilliger

T a *Eingefügt bis* zugleich *für zwei gestrichene Wörter.* — **b** *Folgt* <mehr> — **c** *Satz beginnt mit* <Es>, *fährt fort mit* hat es ein geselschafter. *Diese Wörter sind durch übergeschriebene Ziffern umgestellt.* — **d** *Folgt im Konzept ungestrichenes* zu

K 1 Der Leipziger Handelsherr Georg Winckler (1582–1654). Zu Person u. Funktion im Kontext *GB 1646* s. 451019 K 0.
    2 F. Ludwig (Der Nährende) wartete auf Zuschüsse zweier Welfenherzöge, um die Finanzierung des *GB 1646* zu sichern: 1. Hz. August d. J. v. Braunschweig-Wolfenbüttel (FG 227. Der Befreiende), in dessen Dienst Carl Gustav v. Hille (FG 302. Der Unverdrossene) den die FG betreffenden Briefwechsel führte; 2. Hz. Christian Ludwig v. Braunschweig-Calenberg zu Hannover (FG 372. Der Reinherzige). Daß das Geld der Herzöge zusammen nach Frankfurt a. M. überwiesen werde, schlägt F. Ludwig vor, weil die Summe dann gleich zur Bezahlung Merians verwandt werden könnte. S. auch 430905 I u. ö. Zum *GB 1646* s. 440130 K 3 u. ö. Vgl. den 1645 erneut einsetzenden Briefwechsel zum *GB 1646* zwischen Matthäus Merian d. Ä. mit dem anhalt. Kammermeister Peter Knaudt. Der anhalt. Bote hieß Ernst Stellbogen, s. 440130 K 2.
    3 Hier geht F. Ludwig auf das Angebot Hilles in 440209A ein, ein frz. oder ital. Buch zu übersetzen oder übersetzen zu helfen. In 451008 wird Hille davon Abstand nehmen u. stattdessen sein Werk *Teutscher Palmbaum* (1647) ankündigen.
    4 Es handelt sich um das folgende Werk des Jean de Serres (1540–1598): *La Vie de Messire Gaspar de Colligny Seigneur de Chastillon, Admiral de France. Laqvelle sont Adiovsté*

ses memoires sur ce qui se passa au siege de S. Qventin (Leiden: Elzevier 1643). HAB: 576.1 Quod. (3). Diesem bei Bonaventure u. Abraham Elzevier in Leiden erschienenen Nachdruck ging das im gleichen Jahr veröffentlichte Amsterdamer Buch voraus. — Gaspard de Coligny, Comte de Châtilon (1519–1572) wirkte als politischer u. vor allem militärischer Hugenottenführer (Admiral). Er war 1560 zum Calvinismus übergetreten und eines der ersten Opfer der Bartholomäusnacht. Im *RGG* findet man unter dem Stichwort *Coligny* mehrere relevante Hinweise: *RGG*⁴ II, 420 *(Coligny)*, I, 1142 *(Bartholomäusnacht)*, III, 230 *(Frankreich)*, III, 1926 *(Hugenotten)*.

5 Vor kurzem.

6 Diederich v. dem Werder (FG 31) schreibt an F. Ludwig am gleichen Tag (440310A), daß sich sein Sohn Paris (FG 339) mit dem „leben des Admirals" (s. Anm. 4) zwar auseinandersetze, sich jedoch mit einer Übertragung überfordert sehe u. das Buch deshalb einem versierteren Gesellschafter zur Übersetzung gegeben werden möge.

7 Franz Julius v. dem Knesebeck (FG 396. Der Geheime), Hofmarschall in Wolfenbüttel.

440310A

Diederich von dem Werder an Fürst Ludwig

Diederich v. dem Werder (FG 31. Der Vielgekörnte) übersendet F. Ludwig (Der Nährende) Korrekturen zu dessen Gedicht und merkt dazu an, daß dieses Poem (eine Strambotto-Nachahmung) nicht streng einem (alternierenden) Metrum folge. Das treffe auch für seine eigenen nachstehenden Probeverse zu. Hier sei nicht so genau auf die Silbenlängen zu achten, sondern auf den jambisch-daktylischen Mischvers. An der Wortwahl findet Werder nichts zu verbessern, wobei er relativiert, die überschickten Sachen seien ihm ansonsten „zu hoch". Allemal stellten die (Misch-)Verse Beispiele dar, welche in einer vollständigen deutschen Verslehre nicht fehlen dürften, wenn sie auch in der Praxis kaum genutzt würden. — Sein Sohn Paris v. dem Werder (FG 339. Der Friedfertige) habe sich an dem ‚Leben des Admirals' [Jean de Serres: La Vie de Messire Gaspar de Colligny Seigneur de Chastillon, Admiral de France] versucht, fürchte aber, der Übersetzungsaufgabe nicht gewachsen zu sein. Deshalb befürwortet Werder, F. Ludwig möge einen geübteren Übersetzer beauftragen.

Q   HM Köthen: V S 544, Bl. 472rv [A: 472v]; eigenh. mit einer Randnote von Schreiberh., s. T j. — HM Köthen: V S 546, Bl. 197v, gekürzte Abschrift F. Ludwigs unter gleichem Datum (zit. als *L*). Sie beginnt mit „Die abgewechselte Reime […] " u. endet mit „nötig" sowie der anschließenden Datierung, s. T o. Die Überschrift in F. Ludwigs Teilabschrift: „Des Vielgekörnten bedencken über die dactylischen Wechselreime".

A   Dem Nehrenden zuhanden Cöthen

Vnvorgreiffliche Errinnerungen
über die dreyfache geschrenckte Reimen.

3. — — — — — umb haabeª gutt vnd geld

4. da die gottlosen frey ihr mütleinᵇ inne laben

5. Es ist in warheit gantz unchristlich angestellt.
NB.ᶜ recht unchristlich scheint einander zuwieder sein

8. Vnd bringt im Geize zu das kurtz' elende leben

9. Ein blosses hembd; du kanst dem tode nicht entlauffen

13. Vnd folg' im übelthun nicht dem gottlosen hauffen.

21. Hab' acht, das du ihm nicht vnsinnig — — —

22. Vnd das kein' vngedult im kreutze hersche mit.

23. das rechte ziel du sonst gewislich überschnellest

26. Ruff embsiglich ihn an

30. Vergreiffe dich ja nicht an deinem Gott mit hass

34. So achte keine quaal verfolgung — — —

35. Dan er kan alles das bey dir gar leichtlich stillen

Die abgewechselte Reimen kommen meines ermessensᵈ auch nicht wohl wie die nachfolgende, so ich heute zurᵉ probe aufgesetzt auch ausweisen

Der Wein macht lustig; Er macht auch schwere gedanckenᶠ.
Wie sich ein' iede Natur ihm vnterschiedlich erweiset
Michᵍ setzet er in die lieb', vnd dich in eiteles Zanckenʰ.
Diese macht er gar verhastⁱ, jehn' über alle gepreist.ʲ

Man hatt in diesen reimen nicht eben hoch auf die länge vnd kürtze der syllaben zusehen, ausgenommen, das die **Dactyli**[1] ihren lauff recht haben.

Dieᵏ überschickte sachen seind meinem verstande sonsten zu hoch, halte doch darfür, das die wörter nicht zuverbessern seind, vnd zur beschreibungˡ einerᵐ volkommenen deutschenⁿ Reimekunst nötig.ᵒ Sonst aber ohne grossen nutz. Der Friedfertige hatt zwar etwas am leben des Admirals[2] gearbeitet er befahret[3] sich aber, er würde, als ein ungeübter dem wercke, nicht genug gewachsen sein. Dannenhero erfordert das tractätlein einen geschickteren. Hiermit göttlicher gnaden empfholen. Reinsdorff 10. Mertz 1644.
    Des Nehrenden dienstwilligster
    Der Vielgekörnte

I

Art dreyfach geschrenckter Reime von Fürst Ludwigs Hand

Q HM Köthen: V S 546, Bl. 198r, eigenh.

Art dreyfach geschrenckter Reime
welche erst in Sicilien sol erfunden sein.
Doch im Jtalianischen ist[a] sie weiblicher endung. hier abgewechselt[1]

[1] Was sol ich sagen viel vom übeln stand der welt,
[2] da man auf nichtes denckt, als preßen, schinden, schaben,
[3] das arm' elende volck umb ihr haab gut und geld,
[4] Und die gotlose rott drin mus ihr mütlein laben[.]
[5] Es ist gewislich recht[b] unChristlich angestelt,
[6] Ja nichts als unglück kan der Mensch darvon doch haben:
[7] Wo komt es aber her das man ist so verblend,
[8] Und nichts als geitzen wil in unserm kurtzen leben
[9] Das zweiffelhaftig geht zu seinem schnellen end
[10] Da diesem laster man solt höchlich wieder streben,
[11] das von dem guten uns[c] alleine sonst abwend,
[12] Und der begierde sich im minsten nicht ergeben.
[13] Was meinst du lieber Mensch zu tragen mit dir weg,
[14] Nur auf ein bloßes hembd' es bey dir wil auslauffen,
[15] Sieh das zum himmel du gleich gehst den schmalen steg,
[16] für unrecht hute dich, fur freßen, schlemmen, sauffen
[17] Jn deinen gottes dienst erzeige dich nit treg
[18] Nicht folg' in mißethat dem großen losen hauffen.

[19] Wan dan aus schwachheit du in sunden etwa fellest,
[20] den Herren deinen Gott bald umb verzeihung bitt,
[21] Dich wahre, das du ihm' unsinnig wiederbellest
[22] Aus ungeduld und zorn im kreutze nimmer nit,
[23] Sonst du des rechten wegs gewislich leicht verfehlest,
[24] Drumb nötig ist, das er dir leite deine tritt'[,]
[25] Auf das durch seinen geist er dir dein hertze rüre
[26] Jhn ruff' an embsiglich, zu beten ab nicht laß',
[27] Und das er deinen ernst im wercke richtig spüre
[28] Gehorsam im gemüt dich durch und durch so faß'
[29] Erbaulich in geduld, das solche dich regiere,
[30] Und wieder Gott du nicht vergreiffest dich mit haß:
[31] Es ist dir demut not zu folgen seinem willen,
[32] Jn welchem deiner sol geschloßen gentzlich sein,
[33] Und das du sein gebot getreulich mögst erfüllen,
[34] Nicht achte trubsal, angst, verfolgung, marter, pein
[35] Dan er gar leichtlich wird sie bey dir können stillen
[36] wan nur[d] sein reicher[e] trost in dir gegangen ein.

II

Art dreyfach geschrenckter Reime verbessert von Diederich von dem Werder und eingetragen von Fürst Ludwig

Q HM Köthen: V S 546, Bl. 197r; Abschrift v. Schreiberh. F. Ludwig trug dann eigenh. die Datierung („dreizehend*en*") nach u. die Verbesserungen Werders (s. o. 440310A) sowie einige eigene neue Verbesserungen ein. Alle Zusätze u. Verbesserungen stammen von F. Ludwigs H.

Art dreyfach geschrenckter Reime
welche erst in Sicilien sol erfunden sein
Doch im[a] Jtalianischen ist sie weiblicher endung; hier abgewechselt.[1]

[1] Was sol ich sagen viel vom übeln stand der welt,
[2] da man auf nichtes[b] denckt, als preßen, schinden, schaben,
[3] das arm' elende volck umb[c] haabe gut und geld,
[4] Da[d] die Gottlosen frey ihr mütlein inne laben
[5] Es ist in[e] warheit gantz unChristlich angestelt,
[6] Ja nichts als unglück kan der Mensch darvon doch haben:
[7] Wo komt es aber her das man ist so verblend
[8] Und[f] bringt im geitze zu das kurtz' elende leben
[9] Das zweiffelhaftig geht zu seinen [sic] schnellen end?
[10] Da diesem[g] laster man solt höchlich wieder streben,
[11] Das von dem guten uns alleine sonst[h] abwend,
[12] Und der begierde sich im minsten nicht ergeben.
[13] Was meinst du lieber Mensch zu tragen mit dir weg,
[14] Ein[i] bloßes hembd, du kanst dem tode nicht entlauffen,
[15] Sieh das zum himmel du gleich gehst den schmalen steg,
[16] Für unrecht hüte dich, für freßen, schlemmen, sauffen,
[17] Jn deinem Gottes dienst erzeige dich nit treg'
[18] Und[j] folg' in ubelthun[k] nicht[l] dem Gottlosen[m] hauffen.

[19] Wan dan aus schwachheit du in Sünden etwa fellest,
[20] Den Herren deinen Gott bald umb verzeihung bitt,
[21] Hab[n] acht, das du Jhm nicht[l] unsinnig wiederbellest.
[22] Und[o] das kein ungeduld im kreutze hersche mit,
[23] das[p] rechte ziel du sonst gewislich uberschnellest,
[24] Drümb nötig ist, das er dir leite deine tritt,
[25] Auf das durch seinen geist er dir dein hertze rüre,
[26] Ruff[q] embsiglich Jhn an, zu beten ab nicht laß',
[27] Und das er deinen ernst im wercke richtig spüre
[28] Gehorsam im gemüt dich durch und durch so faß'

[29] Erbaulich in geduld, das solche dich regiere,
[30] Vergreiffe^r dich ja nicht an deinem Gott mit haß',
[31] Es ist dir demut not zu folgen seinem willen,
[32] Jn welchem^s deiner sol geschloßen gentzlich sein,
[33] Und das du sein gebot getreulich mögst erfüllen,
[34] So^t achte keine^u qual, verfolgung, Marter, pein
[35] Dan^v er kan alles das bey dir gar leichtlich stillen
[36] wan nun sein rechter trost in dir gegangen ein.

Cöthen den dreizehenden^{w 2} des Mertzens, im jahre 1644 *etc.*

das blat umb.

T a haabe gutt *eingefügt für* <ihre haab'> — **b** *Gebessert aus* mühtlein — **c** *Zeile am rechten Rand mit geschweifter Klammer hinzugefügt.* — **d** *L* sens *im Falz.* — **e** *L Endbuchstabe* r *im Falz.* — **f** *L* gedank[en] *Endung* en *im Falz.* — **g** *In L darüber* <Mich setz> — **h** *L* Zank[en] *Endung* en *im Falz.* — **i** *L* verhaßt — **j** *L Endbuchstabe* t. *im Falz. Hierzu eine Marginalnote von Schreiberh. zur Abschrift (s. Q), welche zweifellos eine Bemerkung F. Ludwigs wiedergibt:* Es ist aber kein richtig maß darinnen so<ll> billich sein solte. — **k** *Der nachstehende Gliedsatz in L:* Bey den uberschickten sachen halte ich dafür, das die reime nicht zu verbeßern seind — **l** *Eingefügt.* — **m** *L* der — **n** *Fehlt in L.* — **o** *Folgt in L:* Reinsdorf den 10. Mertzens 1644. *Damit endet F. Ludwigs Abschrift.*

T I a ist sie *eingefügt.* — **b** *Gebessert aus* dies [?] — **c** *Eingefügt für* <sonst> — **d** *Eingefügt für* <ist> — **e** *Eingefügt für* <rechter> *S. Beilage II Abschrift [36]* rechter. *Vgl. auch K II 1.*

T II a *Gebessert aus* in — **b** *Gebessert aus* nichts — **c** umb haabe *gebessert aus* umb ihr haab — **d** *Zeile gebessert aus:* Und die Gottlose Rott drin mus ihr mütlein laben — **e** in warheit gantz *eingefügt für* <gewislich recht> — **f** *Zeile gebessert aus:* Und <nichts als geitzen wil in unserm> kurtz<en> leben, — **g** *Gebessert aus* dieser [?] — **h** *Gebessert für* <fast> — **i** *Zeile gebessert aus:* <Nur auf> ein bloßes hembd <es bey dir wil aus>lauffen, *Dieser Vers bezieht sich in 440310A Vnvorgreiffliche Erinnerungen nicht auf Vers 14, sondern auf Vers 9.* — **j** *Eingefügt für* <Nicht> *Dieser Vers bezieht sich in 440310A Vnvorgreiffliche Erinnerungen nicht auf Vers 18, sondern auf Vers 13.* — **k** *Eingefügt für* <mißethat> — **l** *Eingefügt.* — **m** *Gebessert aus* <großen> losen — **n** Hab' acht *eingefügt für* <Dich wahre> — **o** *Zeile gebessert aus:* Aus ungeduld und zorn im kreutze nimmer nit, — **p** *Zeile gebessert aus:* Sonst du den rechten weg gewislich leicht verfehlest, — **q** *Wörterreihenfolge* Ruff embsiglich Jhn an *durch Bezifferung umgestellt aus ursprünglich:* Jhn ruff an embsiglich — **r** *Zeile gebessert aus:* <Und wieder> Gott <du nicht vergreiffest dich> mit haß', — **s** *Gebessert aus* welcher [?] — **t** *Eingefügt für* <Nicht> — **u** keine qual *eingefügt für* <trübsal, angst> — **v** *Zeile gebessert aus:* Dan er gar leichtlich <wird sie> bey dir <können> stillen — **w** *Vom Schreiber freigelassenes Spatium von F. Ludwig mit dem Tagesdatum* dreizehenden *ergänzt.*

K 1 Diederich v. dem Werder (FG 31. Der Vielgekörnte) schreibt hier daktylisch ausgehende, sonst wie im deutschen Alexandriner eher jambische Verse mit Mittelzäsur, nachdem er die Verse in dem Gedicht F. Ludwigs (s. Beil. I) zu durchgehend alternierenden

Jamben verbessert hatte. Er dispensiert sich in seinen Probeversen sozusagen unter Weingenuß vom quantifizierenden Schema des Lateinischen und der Betonung des alternierenden Jambus. Der Vielgekörnte unternimmt also wohl nur im Scherz einen (nicht gelungenen) Ausflug in eine bewegtere (daktylische) Form, die F. Ludwig (Der Nährende) in den jambischen Alexandrinern seines ernsten Gedichts (s. Beil. I) keinesfalls zulassen wollte. Solche Mischverse gehörten aber, so Werder, aus Gründen der Vollständigkeit in eine deutsche Verskunst mit hinein.

2 F. Ludwig scheint diese Biographie (Jean de Serres: La Vie de Messire Gaspar de Colligny Seigneur de Chastillon, Admiral de France [Leiden: Elzevier 1643]) tatsächlich für sehr wichtig zu halten, da er diese nach dem gescheiterten Versuch des jungen Paris v. dem Werder (FG 339. Der Friedfertige) Carl Gustav v. Hille (FG 302) zur Übersetzung andient. S. 440310 (K 4).

3 Von befahren, d.i. befürchten, (sich) sorgen. *DW* I, 1246. Vgl. 370422 K II 3, auch 451028A K 7.

K I 1 Die von F. Ludwig als „sizilianisch" bezeichneten Verse werden in der Forschung später Toskanische Verse genannt. Es handelt sich um 36 Wechselreime mit jeweils sechs zusammengehörenden kreuzgereimten Versen (ababab – cdcdcd usw.) mit männlich-weiblich alternierender Kadenz. Der Abschnitt nach der Hälfte, dem 18. Vers, wird im Manuskript mit einem Abstand und durch den Verzicht auf den alternierenden Versabschluss verdeutlicht. Der 19. Vers fährt mit einer weiblichen Kadenz fort. Diese Sonderform des sechsversigen Strambotto der Toskana behandelt S. Tullio Ortolani: Studio rassuntivo sullo strambotto: parte I. Lo strambotto popolare. Feltre 1898. Auf welche ital. Vorbilder sich F. Ludwig bezieht, ist nicht auszumachen. Es könnte sich bei dem vorliegenden Poem um eine eigene Dichtung F. Ludwigs handeln, möglicherweise übersetzte F. Ludwig aber auch ein ital. Gedicht (mit Endecasillabi und der vorherrschenden, von F. Ludwig so benannten weiblichen Kadenz), das er auf deutsche Verhältnisse (Alexandriner) übertrug. Diese Gedichtform kommt in *Fürst Ludwig: Kurtze Anleitung zur deutschen Poesi (1640)* nicht vor.

K II 1 Diederich v. dem Werder (FG 31. Der Vielgekörnte) lag mit großer Wahrscheinlichkeit eine von der vorliegenden Abschrift leicht unterschiedene Fassung vor. Darauf weisen die von ihm unter Nr. 9 u. 13 korrigierten Verse hin, die sich in der hier abgedruckten Version 440310A II auf andere Versnummern (14 u. 18) beziehen. Sämtliche Korrekturvorschläge Werders wurden von F. Ludwig akzeptiert u. eingetragen. Seine wohl erst später in 440310A I vermerkte Verbesserung im letzten Vers „rechter" zu „reicher" ist die einzige zusätzliche u. deutliche Differenz zwischen F. Ludwigs Text u. der Abschrift. Vernachlässigbare Unterschiede betreffen Umlautkennzeichnungen sowie Klein- u. Großschreibung.

2 Daß F. Ludwig das Datum der Abschrift von eigener H. nachgetragen hat, weist zurück auf den vorliegenden Brief Werders an F. Ludwig, der auf den 10.3.1644 datiert ist. Vermutlich ist unter dem Datum des 13.3. eine saubere Abschrift des korrigierten Gedichts an Werder gesandt worden.

440310B

Diederich von dem Werder an Peter Knaudt

Diederich v. dem Werder (FG 31) läßt durch Peter Knaudt einen Brief an F. Ludwig (440310A) übermitteln. Werder erklärt, Antwort aus Frankfurt a. M. (von seinem Verleger Johann Press) zu erwarten. Er habe außerdem ein Exemplar der drei bei Johann Press gedruckten und zu Leipzig gehaltenen Predigten des Dessauer Superintendenten (Johannes Hofmeister) vom Autor selbst per Post erhalten.

Q HM Köthen: V S 544, Bl. 471rv [A: 471v]; eigenh.; rotes Lacksiegel.

A Dem Ehrenvesten vnd Grosachtbaren Herren Peter Knautt Fürstlichem Anhaltischem Cammermeister zu Cöthen, meinem insonders geehrtem Herren vnd werthem Freunde. Cöthen.

Ehrenvester Grosachtbarer Herr Cammermeister.
Die überschickte sachen findet er hierbey gefügt wieder, neben etzlichen wenigen errinnerungen, an vnsern gnedigen Fürsten vnd Herren haltende.[1]
Mich verlanget, das ich einmahl von[a] Franckfurt andwort bekomme auf meine beyde schreiben.[2] Wan ich in 3 wochen nichts verneme, so wil ich noch einmahl schreiben, vnd mich seines nichtandwortens beschwehren. Es hatt sonsten johan presse[3] des herren Superintendentens von Dessaw[4] drey, zu leibtzig gehaltene, predigten gedruckt, davon mir wohlgedachter herr **superintendens** ein **exemplar** zugeschickt. Gott mit vns.
Reinsdorf 10. Mertz 1644.
Des Herren dienstwill.

DvdWerder *mp.*

T a von Franckfurt *eingefügt.*

K 1 Wahrscheinlich hatte Diederich v. dem Werder (FG 31) Peter Knaudt seinen Brief 440310A an F. Ludwig beigelegt, der Werders Korrekturen eines Gedichts des Fürsten enthält.
2 Es handelt sich wahrscheinlich um Schreiben an den weiter unten im Brief genannten Frankfurter Verleger Johann Press. Seit 1642 trieb Werder die Revision seiner schließlich erst 1651 bei Press erschienenen Tasso-Nachdichtung *D. v. dem Werder: Jerusalem (1651)* unter Verwendung der Merianschen Kupfer der Erstauflage (1626) voran. Vgl. 420506 K 3. S. auch die Unterstützung dieses Vorhabens durch den Leipziger Verleger Andreas Kühne in 430121A u. 430527. Vgl. zu Kühne auch 440824 K 8 u. zur Tasso-Nachdichtung *Ball: Diederich von dem Werder*, 16–21.
3 Johann Press(e), Hanauer und Frankfurter Verleger. S. 450417.
4 Johannes Hofmeister (1596–1646), Hofprediger u. Superintendent in Dessau zwischen 1635 u. 1646 (s. auch 330603 u. 360600 Q u. II). Vgl. *Beckmann* VII, 343 f. u. *Graf: Anh. Pfarrerbuch*, 46 u. 292 f. S. zu den Leipziger Predigten: Waß der Reformirten Kirchen Lehre und Cerimonien seyn sampt Gründtlicher Bescheidentlicher Ableinung Der

Vornemsten Unziemlichen Bezüchtig- und Beymessungen/ Mit welchen Dieselbige von vielen Jahren her in der gantzen Christenheit verhasset und verdächtig gemachet worden: In Christlicher Versamlung vieler Hoher und Vornehmer Reformirten der Königl. Mayestet und Krohn Schweden Krieges Officirer/ in Vier unterschiedlichen Predigten/ Zu Leipzig im außgang des 1642- Jahres ... Ausgeführet und Erkläret/ Und jetzo ... zum Druck außgefertiget Von Johanne Hoffmeistero, Pfarrern und Superintendenten zu Dessaw im Fürstenthumb Anhalt (Franckfurt am Meyn: Press 1644). VD17 14:681937X. Vgl. auch den nach *Beckmann* VII, 343 zitierten, unvollständigen Titel ohne Angabe des Druckkers Press in 330603 K 9. In dieser Anmerkung wird bereits auf die Finanzierung des Drucks durch den schwed. Oberstleutnant u. späteren General u. Feldmarschall (Greve) Robert Douglas (FG 420. 1644) hingewiesen. Vgl. zu dieser Angelegenheit u. ihren Hintergründen sowie zur Förderung des reformierten Gottesdienstes im schwed. Heer durch einen anderen schwed. General, Gaspard Corneille de Mortaigne dit de Potteles (FG 419), 451030.

440313

Fürst Ludwig an Christian Gueintz

Antwort auf 440219. Beantwortet durch 440317. — F. Ludwig schickt Christian Gueintz (FG 361. Der Ordnende) eine vollständige kritische Durchsicht des von Gueintz (in mehreren Tranchen) eingereichten Entwurfs zu seiner *Rechtschreibung (1645)*. Gueintz' in 440219 vorgebrachte Auffassung, die Deutschen (und ihre Sprache) seien historisch erst nach den Römern (und dem Lateinischen) aufgetreten, weist der Fürst gestützt auf die biblische Chronologie zurück. Die Deutschen und ihre Hauptsprache gingen mit dem Stammvater Ascenas unmittelbar auf die babylonische Sprachverwirrung zurück, was für die Römer und das Lateinische zumindest fraglich sei. Johannes Turmair gen. Aventinus nenne in seiner *Bayerischen Chronik* zwei unterschiedliche Personen „Janus", eine, die mit Noah identifiziert, und eine, die in der Bibel als Bruder Gomers und Thubals genannt werde. Es dürfte doch wohl der Letztere gewesen sein, der in der (klassischen lateinischen) Poesie erscheine, und es sei kaum anzunehmen, daß er, gerade erst in Italien angekommen, sofort Lateinisch gesprochen habe. Das sei erst viel später entstanden, zumal das Etruskische eine ältere und andersgeartete Sprache war und das Griechische und Lateinische erst allmählich ausgebildet und erweitert worden seien. Im übrigen hätten viele Deutsche, Männer und Frauen, am Trojanischen Krieg teilgenommen, also müßten die Deutschen älter als die Römer sein. — Vernünftige und begründete (orthographische) Neuerungen seien nicht zu verwerfen. Selbst in der Luther-Bibel fänden sich viele Entstellungen durch Druckfehler, aber auch Verstöße gegen die deutsche Grammatik. F. Ludwig exemplifiziert dies an den Zehn Geboten, wo die Morphologie nicht beachtet werde („du Solt" statt „du Solst"). Man habe sich an derlei Fehler zwar gewöhnt, jedoch blieben es Verstöße gegen die Sprach- und Schreibrichtigkeit. Gueintz möge diese Hinweise bedenken und verarbeiten. — F. Ludwig übersendet beiliegend auch Bemerkungen über die „deutsche Reimkunst" (von Gueintz). — Gueintz möge zwei Bücher von Justus Georg Schottelius (FG 397), die ihm F. Ludwig geliehen hatte, bald zurücksenden.

Q HM Köthen: V S 545, Bl. 218v, eigenh. Konzept F. Ludwigs. Unsere Konjekturen in eckigen Klammern. — D: *KE*, 268f. — BN: *Bürger*, 949 Nr. 44.
Als Beilage Bl. 227r–236v: „Erinnerungen bey der aufgesetzten deutschen Wort oder

Rechtschreibung", eigenh. Konzept F. Ludwigs, beginnend mit Verweis auf die S. 1 bis S. 75 einer unbekannten Vorlage von Gueintz. Der Text bricht mit Bl. 236v ab. Seine Fortsetzung a. a. O., Bl. 217r–218r, mit Verweisen F. Ludwigs auf „S. 76. Z. 3" bis S. 83. Es liegt also eine fehlerhafte, das Stück auseinanderreißende Einbindung dieser zweiten Tranche der „Erinnerungen" im 2. Band des Köthener Erzschreins vor, die auf den früheren hzl. anhaltischen Archivar Gottlieb Krause zurückgehen dürfte.

Bl. 237r–238v: Der ersten Tranche eingebunden ein Doppelbl. mit der Reinschrift einiger Verbesserungen F. Ludwigs (zu „Sau", „Sichel" und „Siegel") von Schreiberh.; 237v u. 238rv leer.

Diese Beilagen werden im Materialienband *DA Köthen I. 9* veröffentlicht.

A *Fehlt.*

Dem Ordenden wird auf sein anderweites schreiben vom 19. abgewichenes monats die vollige[a] ubersehung seiner wortschreibung zugeschicket.[1] Jn diesem seinem schreiben wird gemeldet, das die Deutschen nach den andern völckern, und also folgig nach den Lateinern gewiß[b] gekommen seyen[b], sonsten würde[c] man[b] dafür halten[d] müßen, das zu zeit der Babilonier Deutschland bewonet[e], und[f] durch die Sündflut sie nicht mi[t][g] untergangen.[2] Dieses einwenden mag nicht begriffen werd[en,][g] dan das die Sündflut lange für[h] erbauung des Babilonischen Thurns[i] hergangen, und nach[j] verenderung und verwirrung d[er][g] sprachen die völcker sich erst zertheilet und fortgewandert[,] ist unleugbar. Und von der zeit an müßen sich so die **nation**en nach den unterschiedenen[b] sprachen angefangen haben, wie solches in[b] den alten geschichtschreibern[k] sonderlich[l] der[m] **Aventi**no[n] in seinen Beyerischen Deutschen[o] **Cronicae**[3] klerlich zu[p] finden, und ja[b] vermutlich das die völcker auf[q] dem festen lande in Deutschland eher, als über das Meer in Jtalien mit schiffen gekommen[.] Jm **Aventino** finden sich zweyerley **Jani**, einer der fü[r][g] **Noah** gehalten wird, und ein ander der ein bruder Gomer[s][g] und[r] Thubals[s] gewesen.[4] Solte der letzte nicht eher de[r]jenige[g] gewesen sein, von deme so viel die poeten geschrieb[en][g][5] und wird doch solcher auch nicht stracks Latein geredet hab[en,][g] weil dieselbe sprache lange hernach aufkommen, die Hetrurische älter und die[t] lateinische und[u] Griechische sehr erweiter[t][g] worden. Ja zu zeiten des Trojanischen krieges seind viel deutschen darbey gewesen, so wol kriegsmannen, als kriegsmetzen, die alle älter als die Lateiner seind, von welchen[v] im **Homero** nichts zu finden.[6] So viel von der[w] älte beyder völcker[x].

Was vernunftig ursachen und[y] beweise hat auch[z] gut ist, deme hat man bill[ich][g] zu folgen, ob es[aa] schon[ab] manchem[ac] solte neu vorko[m]men[g]. Das auch[ad] in der deutschen Lutheri Bibel[ae] vie[le][g] druckfehler und[af] wieder die deutsche gründliche[b] sprachlehre b[e]funden[g] seind, kan gar leichtlich vorgezeiget werden, dan[ag] die [sic] Endungen[ah] bey den Nenwörtern und vorne[n]wörtern[g] anietzo zu geschweigen, nehme man nur die ze[hen][g] gebotte für, da wird man stracks im ersten den feh[ler][g] finden: Als da stehet du Solt kein' ander[e][g] götter haben, das den heißen sol, du Solst kei[ne][g] andere götter haben, den es ist die andere person, u[nd][g] nicht die erste[ai] und dritte, ich[aj] solte, oder der solte oder solt. Man ist es ab[er]ᵍ so gewohnet worden, obᵃᵏ es schon nicht recht geredetᵃˡ und geschriebenᵃᵐ ist, das [die]ᵃⁿ ersteᵃᵒ und drit[te]ᵍ person des Zeitworts für die andere in allen nachfol[gen]denᵍ gebotten also misbrauchet wird. Wen man ein Capittel nach dem andern vornimmet, wird sich hie[r]ᵍ und dar ein mehreres finden. Wolle also der Ordende alles erinnerte wol bedencken und danᵃᵖ sein vernu[nfti]gesᵍ ferner herbey tragen. Wegen der deutschen Rei[m]kunstᵍ⁷ seind die gedancken auchᵃᑫ hierbey.

Geben den 13 des Martijᵃʳ im Jhare 1644.

Desᵃˢ Schottelij zwey deutscheᵇ bücher werden auch hiermit wieder anhero zuschicken begeret⁸

T a *KE* willige — b *Eingefügt.* — c *Eingefügt für* <müste> *KE* sonsten man dafür halten müsse — d *Gebessert aus* gehalten — e *Gebessert aus* <bey>wonet — f *Folgt* <sie> — g *Buchstabenverlust im Falz.* — h *Lies:* vor — i *KE* Thurmes — j *nach* verenderung *und eingefügt für* <als bey>; *KE* und nach verwirrung der sprachen — k *KE* geschichtschriften — l *Bis* Cronicae *am Rand ergänzt.* — m *Vergessene Kasuskorrektur. Lies:* dem *KE* dem — n *Gebessert aus* Aventinus Das Folgende *in seinen* Beyerischen Deutschen Cronicae *fehlt in KE.* — o *Unklares Wort verbessert zu* Deutschen — p zu finden *eingefügt für* <finden> [?] — q auf dem festen *eingefügt für* <in Deutschland> *KE* nach *statt* auf — r *Eingefügt. Fehlt in KE.* — s *Folgt* <und dis> *KE* Thubal — t die lateinische *eingefügt für* <sie> — u *Folgt* <die> — v *Eingefügt für* <denen> — w *KE* dem alter — x *Folgt* <auf dis mal> — y und beweise *eingefügt.* — z *Eingefügt für* <und> *In KE fehlt* auch gut ist — aa *Folgt* <uns> — ab *Folgt* <solte> — ac *KE* manchen — ad *Eingefügt. KE* sich — ae *Folgt* <auch> — af *Folgt* <nach der> — ag *Eingefügt für* <und> — ah *Marginalie am Rand:* Casus — ai erste und *eingefügt.* — aj ich solte, oder *eingefügt.* — ak ob es schon *eingefügt für* <also drumb> — al *Bis* geschrieben ist *am Rand ergänzt.* — am *Das Nachfolgende bis* mit benutzet wird *fehlt in KE.* — an *Zu ergänzen.* — ao erste und *am Rand ergänzt.* — ap *Eingefügt für* <dan> — aq *KE* noch — ar *KE* Mertzen — as *Dieser Satz ohne Einschaltzeichen am Rand ergänzt.*

K 1 „Erinnerungen bey der aufgesetzten deutschen Wort oder Rechtschreibung", s. Q; demnächst in *DA Köthen I. 9*. Betrifft Christian Gueintz' (FG 361. Der Ordnende) Manuskript zur *Rechtschreibung (1645)*. Vgl. dazu 440127 K 1.

2 In 440219 hatte Gueintz den Deutschen ein unter den postdiluvialen Völkern relativ junges Alter zugesprochen. F. Ludwig behauptete unter Verweis auf die biblische Chronologie den Altersvorzug der Deutschen gegenüber den Römern, der deutschen gegenüber der lateinischen Sprache. S. 440209. Gueintz hielt in 440317 an seiner Meinung fest.

3 Für seine Auffassung vom Alter der deutschen Sprache, das jenes des Lateinischen übertreffe u. mit dem der griechischen Sprache zumindest gleichziehe, hatte sich F. Ludwig schon in 401109 auf Johannes Turmair gen. Aventinus (1477–1534) berufen. IO. AVENTINI ANNALIVM BOIORVM LIBRI VII (Basel 1580), s. 440209 K 10; Johannis Aventini Des Weitberümbten Hochgelehrten Beyerischen Geschichtschreibers Chronica/ Darinn ... auch der vralten Teutschen Vrsprung/ Herkommen/ Sitten/ Gebräuch/ Religion/ Mannliche vnd treffliche Thaten ... zusammen getragen/ vnd in acht Bücher getheilet ... Anfenglich durch den Authorem in Latein verfertiget/ nachmals aber ... von ihm selber in gut gemein Hochteutsch gebracht ... Vnd ... durch ... Niclaus Cisner ... in

Druck gegeben ... An jetzo aber von newem durchsehen (Frankfurt a. M. 1622). HAB: Gm 4° 68. Die deutsche Erstausgabe war erstmals 1556 in Frankfurt a. M. erschienen. Vgl. *ADB* I, 700–704; *NDB* I, 469f. Aventinus sieht in der Tat die Deutschen (und ihre Sprache) um rund 1000 Jahre älter als die Römer u. ihr Latein an. S. Anm. 6 u. 440129.

4 Zu Noah, Janus, Tuisco, den Etruskern, ihrer Sprache u. der der Griechen vgl. schon 440209 (K 10 Aventinus) u. nochmals 440317 (K 4). Ein Hinweis auf „Janus oder Noah" ist weder in *Gueintz: Rechtschreibung (1645)* zu finden noch in der älteren Hs. „Deutsche Rechtschreib<Orden>ung angeordnet und der fruchtbringenden hochlöblichen Geselschafft übergeben von Dem Ordnenden" (HM Köthen: V S 670). Diese Hs. weist eine Janus/Noah-Passage nicht (mehr) auf (vgl. die Quellenbeschreibung in *DA Köthen I. 9*). Auch in den anderen von uns gesichteten u. zusammengetragenen Quellen (Briefe im vorliegenden Band; Gutachten in *DA Köthen I. 9*) taucht ein solcher Passus bei Gueintz nicht auf. Vgl. *Conermann: Hochsprache und Umgangssprache,* 19ff. Nach der Völkertafel in 1 Mo 10 waren Gomer u. Thubal Söhne Japhets, des dritten u. jüngsten Sohnes Noahs. Vgl. Art. „Völkertafel" in *REThK (1896)* XX, 708–717, hier S. 711ff.

5 Humanisten hatten sich darum bemüht, die Übereinstimmung von biblischer u. antiker Überlieferung zu erweisen, also auch von Noah/ Jain u. Janus. Vgl. 440209 K 10 u. 440317 K 4. Das schillernde Porträt des Gottes Janus hatten vor allem Ovid (*Fasti* I, 89–288) u. Macrobius (*Saturnalia* I, 7, 19–24 u. I, 9) zusammengefaßt, während es Cicero in *De Natura Deorum* (II, 67) bei einem knappen Hinweis auf Ianus als Gott der Tore u. Durchgänge belassen hatte. Ovid, der seine Darstellung in die Form eines Dialogs des Poeten mit dem Gott gekleidet hatte, u. Macrobius führen die verschiedenen Facetten zusammen: Ianus als Gott der Götter, des Anfangs, des Friedens, des Universums, der Luft, als zweigesichtiger Türhüter oder Mittler zwischen Himmel u. Erde, Göttern u. Menschen, als Gott der Türen, Tore u. Torbögen usw. Zugleich erscheint Ianus als erster vorzeitlicher Herrscher Latiums, der den exilierten Saturn gastfreundlich aufnahm u. von ihm die Kunst des Ackerbaus u. die Zivilisation empfangen habe (Ovid: *Fasti,* I, 227–254). Vergils *Aeneis* (VIII, 314ff.) hatte diese Legende erstmals gestaltet, hier kam Saturn aber vom Himmel (vom Sohn Jupiter vertrieben), bei Ovid wird Saturns Strafe übergangen, u. er kommt per Schiff nach Latium. Vgl. Steven J. Green: Ovid *Fasti* I. A Commentary. Leiden, Boston 2004, 112ff. Ianus als Vater von Feldbau, Religion u. Kultur bei Macrobius, Sat. I, 7, 19–25: „Regionem istam quae nunc vocatur Italia regno Ianus optinuit, qui — ut Hyginus Protarcham Trallianum secutus tradit — cum Camese aeque indigena terram hanc ita participata potentia possidebant, ut regio Camesene, oppidum Ianiculum vocitaretur. Post ad Ianum solum regnum redactum est, qui creditur geminam faciem praetulisse, ut quae ante quaeque post tergum essent intueretur [...]. hic igitur Ianus, cum Saturnum classe pervectum excepisset hospitio et ab eo edoctus peritiam ruris ferum illum et rudem ante fruges cognitas victum in melius redegisset, regni eum societate muneravit [...]. hos una concordesque regnasse vicinaque oppida communi opera condidisse [...]. cum inter haec subito Saturnus non cpmparuisset, excogitavit Ianus honorum eius augmenta [...]."
Ianus habe dann den Saturn-Kultus eingeführt zu Ehren des Gottes, „quasi vitae melioris autorem", denn mit ihm erwarben die Menschen das Wissen um Feld- u. Landbau, mithin Zivilisation u. Kultur: „et omnium cuiuscemodi fertilium tribuunt disciplinas". In Sat. I.9 werden dann alle möglichen Attribute u. Zuweisungen von bzw. an Ianus aufgezählt, wie sie auch bei Ovid begegnen. S. Macrobius: Saturnalia. Books I–II. Ed. and transl. by Robert A. Kaster. Cambridge/ Mass. & London 2011. Vgl. *RE*, Suppl.bd. III (1918), 1174–1191, hier v.a. 1185; *N. Pauly* V, 858–862, hier 859f. u. W. H. Roscher: Ausführliches Lexikon der griechischen und römischen Mythologie. Bd. II.1, Leipzig 1890–94, 15–55.

6 F. Ludwig lanciert hier ein weiteres Argument zum historischen Vorsprung der Deutschen u. ihrer Sprache vor den Römern, den nicht nur Schottelius unablässig vertreten hat, sondern bereits ältere deutsche Humanisten wie Franciscus Irenicus (1494–1553), während sich andere Humanisten wie der Elsässer Jakob Wimpfeling (1450–1528) — u. übrigens auch Gueintz (s. 440317) — noch mit einer Ebenbürtigkeit zufriedengaben. Gewährsmann ist wieder der Chronist Aventinus (s. Anm.3). Deutsche Kriegsmänner nebst energischen, harten Kriegsfrauen seien schon 100 Jahre vor der Zerstörung Trojas nach Asien gezogen u. hätten auch Troja mit Krieg überzogen, aber auch auf seiten Trojas gekämpft. Bei der Belagerung u. Zerstörung Trojas unter dessen Kg. Priamos seien wiederum Deutsche beteiligt gewesen. Es sei bezeugt u. jedenfalls glaubwürdig, „die Teutschen sollen auch in disem krieg und ir kriegsfrauen […] gewesen und davon wieder haim kommen sein", während Rom mit dem Auszug des Aeneas erst aus den Trümmern Trojas hervorgegangen sei. „Darumb ist es eine grosse torhait, auch schand, das etlich unser teutsch herren und fürsten ie von Troia herkommen wellen [lies: wollen], so lauter verräter darvon nit in diese land [Teutschland] sunder nur in Italiam kummen sein, gleich sam [lies: so als ob] niemant vor Troia in Teutschland gewesen wär, so doch vor dem künigreich Troia wol sibenhundert jar das teutsch erzkünigreich gestanden ist und Troia nit lenger under obgenanten sex künigen gewert hat dan zweihundert und sibenundneunzig jar. Und do Troia zerstört wart, zalt [lies: zählt] man von anfang an des teutschen erzkünigreichs bis tausend jaren […], von anfang der welt zweitausend achthundert, zwelf jar minder." Johannes Turmair's genannt Aventinus Bayerische Chronik (wie Anm.4), 192 u. 191, vgl. 158, 160 f., 185 f. u. 190 ff.

7 Daß Gueintz auch an eigenen Entwürfen zur deutschen „Reimkunst" arbeitete, zeigen einige ältere Briefe, vgl. bes. 400314 (K 3), 431016, 431020. Vgl. auch 441231.

8 Ein Exemplar von *Schottelius: Der Teutschen Sprache Einleitung (1643)* hatte F. Ludwig Gueintz mit 430403 zugesandt, eines von *Schottelius: Sprachkunst (1641)* bereits mit 430328. Die Rückgabe beider Bücher hatte F. Ludwig bereits in 431016 angemahnt. In 441226A wird F. Ludwig seine Bitte um Rückgabe wiederholen.

440317

Christian Gueintz an Fürst Ludwig

Antwort auf 440313. — Christian Gueintz (FG 361. Der Ordnende) erklärt, er werde die von F. Ludwig (Der Nährende) mitgeteilten Hinweise sorgsam berücksichtigen, so rasch es seine Amtsgeschäfte zuließen. Auch schlägt er einen Besuch bei F. Ludwig vor, um im direkten Gespräch die fraglichen Positionen gründlicher erörtern zu können. Zwar solle die deutsche Sprache erhoben werden, doch nicht auf Kosten anderer, schon besser regulierter Sprachen. Von den Ureinwohnern Deutschlands fehlten eigene Zeugnisse, daher sei man hinsichtlich ihrer Sprache auf Nachrichten in fremden Sprachen angewiesen. Alle Historiographen bezeugten, daß Janus und Noah identisch seien, daß aber der von den (antiken) Dichtern besungene Janus ein Bruder Gomers (Sohn des Japhet, Enkel Noahs) gewesen sein solle, bleibe Spekulation. Aventinus habe Javan vielleicht mit Janus verwechselt. Eine Verständigung unter den Fruchtbringern sei das Mittel der Wahl, und dies sollte in der Vorrede (zu *Gueintz: Rechtschreibung [1645]*) ausgeführt werden.

440317 Christian Gueintz

Q HM Köthen: V S 545, Bl. 181r–182v [A: 182v], 181v u. 182r leer; Schreiberh. mit eigenh. Unterschrift; kein Empfangsvermerk. — *D: KE*, 269f.; *KL* III, 242. — BN: Bürger, 634 Nr. 11.

A *Dem Nährenden*
Jn Cöthen   zuhanden.

Dem Nährenden zugehorsamen soll alles nach möglichkeit aufs schleunigste, als die Ambtsgeschäffte zulaßen, in satsame obacht genommen werden, auch, da gelegenheit, wird der *Ordenende* aufzuwarten sich willig finden: Weill gegenwart beßere nachricht vnd gründlicher antwortt zuschließen geben kan.¹ Sonsten bleibet dießer noch in der meinung, man hette die teutsche Sprache hochzuheben zwar ursache, aber andern, so schoneᵃ außgeübet vnd in richtigkeit gebracht, fürzuziehen nicht beliebten grund.² Daß vielleicht Leuthe in Deutschland gewohnet, kan man zugeben, aber wie vnd waß Sie geredet, ist keine andere nachrichtung alß waß die anderen Sprachen hinterlaßen.³ Janus ist **Noah**, auß aller Geschichtschreiber bewährung, vnd der ümbstände gezeugnus, aber daß deß Gomers bruder der sey, davon die gedichte, ist eine dünckele mutmaßung, **Javan**ᵇ hat einer geheißen, der vielleicht von **Aventino** für **Janum** gehalten.⁴ im übrigen wird daß beste seyn, daß die gesellschaffter sich vergleichen, vnd deßwegen solches in der vorrede mit mehrerm ein- und außgeführet werde.⁵ Welches in unterthänigkeit hinterbringen sollen

Deß *Nährenden*
Ordenender

Hall 17ᶜ Merzens 1644.

T **a** *KE* schon — **b** *Gebessert aus* Jaschan [?] — **c** *Datum gebessert aus unleserlicher Ziffer.*

K 1 Auch aufgrund der Unsicherheit der Verkehrswege verzögerte sich Christian Gueintz' (FG 361. Der Ordnende) Besuch F. Ludwigs (Der Nährende) in Köthen, s. 440504. Eine mündliche Beratung zog Gueintz auch schon in 440219 in Betracht.
 2 Gueintz nimmt Stellung zu F. Ludwigs Einwand in 440313, die Deutschen und ihre Sprache seien älter als die Römer und das Lateinische. Vgl. Gueintz' Aussage schon in 440219. S. auch 440209.
 3 Das Fehlen eigener frühgeschichtlicher schriftlicher Zeugnisse belastete den Stolz auf die „vetustas" Deutschlands im Wettstreit mit den anderen europäischen Nationen. Zwar wurde für das uralte Deutsche stets die Nähe zum Griechischen und das einstige Verwenden der griechischen Buchstaben reklamiert (vgl. Aventinus in 440209 K 10), bis man in den Runen eine eigene uralte deutsche Schrift entdecken zu können glaubte. Ole Worm (1588–1654) hatte in seinen *Danicorum monumentorum libri sex* (Hafniae: Moltke, 1643) die wissenschaftliche Erforschung der Runenschrift begründet. Vgl. 460915 K 7; Klaus von See: Barbar, Germane, Arier. Die Suche nach der Identität der Deutschen. Heidelberg 1994, 68 ff.; ferner *Herz: Aufrichtigkeit, Vertrauen, Frieden*, 350f.
 4 Zu Janus und Noah s. 440209 u. 440313. Zur Völkertafel in *Biblia (Luther 1545)*

1 Mo 10 s. *REThK (1896)* XX, 708–717. Als Söhne Japhets werden neben Gomer und Thubal genannt: Magog, Madai, Jauan, Mesech und Thiras. Von Gomer wiederum stammte u. a. Ascenas, der vermeintliche Stammvater der Deutschen, ab. Der Völkername „Javan" bezeichnet im AT und im ganzen Orient „die Griechen im allgemeinen". Ebd., 712; vgl. Art. „Javan", a. a. O. VIII, 611. Basierend auf Pseudo-Berosus wollte die späthumanistische Altertumsspekulation den antiken Mythos mit der biblischen Genealogie synchronisieren und führte deshalb Janus, den römischen Gott des Durchgangs (s. 440313 K 5), auf das Hebräische zurück: „und wie Jain daselbst so viel, als der Wein heißt; so soll er solchen [Namen] daher bekommen haben, weil er und Noah, der den Wein zuerst gepflanzet, einerley seyn sollen." *Hederich,* 1317. Vgl. schon Aventinus in 440209 K 10.

5 In der Widmungszuschrift in *Gueintz: Rechtschreibung (1645),* Bl.)(iv]v f. heißt es: „Weil dan die Hochlöbliche **Fruchtbringende Geselschaft** einmal diesen fürsatz und zweck hat/ die Deutsche/ als unsere Muttersprache/ so viel müglich aus zuüben und zuverbessern/ habe ich als ein unwürdiges mitglied derselben/ einen entwurf der Rechtschreibung/ so von den ältesten/ und fürnemsten/ obgedachter Geselschaft/ durchsehen und beliebet/ darstellen wollen/ wornach man sich/ doch ohne masgeben/ zurichten. Nicht als wan sie allen andern mundarten/ an orten und enden/ da man deren verhandenen und wolgefasseten grund/ noch nicht allerdings innen ist/ solte und müste eine Richtschnure sein/ sondern männiglich dahin zuveranlassen und zuérinnern/ das man sich billich einerley art recht zuschreiben vergleichen solte". Zur Gueintzschen Rechtschreibung s. allgemein 440127 K 1.

440323

Carl Gustav von Hille an Fürst Ludwig

Antwort auf 440310. — Carl Gustav v. Hille (FG 302. Der Unverdrossene) fühlt sich durch den Antwortbrief F. Ludwigs (Der Nährende) geehrt, bedankt sich und versichert, er werde F. Ludwigs Briefsendungen sämtlich seinen Nachkommen zur Verwahrung anvertrauen. Hz. Augusts d. J. v. Braunschweig-Wolfenbüttel (FG 227. Der Befreiende) Antwort auf Hilles Nachfrage finde F. Ludwig beiliegend (s. Beil. I). Hille schlägt vor, F. Ludwig möge den Befreienden vor Ostern noch einmal (an die ausstehende Zahlung) erinnern. Wenn der Fürst diesem Erinnerungsschreiben auch noch ein entsprechendes Schreiben an Hz. Christian Ludwig v. Braunschweig-Calenberg (FG 372. Der Reinherzige) beifüge, werde es recht und richtig weiterbefördert werden. — Wenn sich unter den italienischen oder französischen Büchern eines befinde, zu dem F. Ludwig ihm, Hille, eine Übersetzung auftragen wolle, werde er dies gerne übernehmen und das Originalwerk anschließend unbeschadet zurückgeben. — Die (Impresen-)Zeichnungen seien gebührend beachtet worden und gingen hiermit wieder an F. Ludwig zurück. — *Nachschrift:* Sollten neue Köthener Drucke erschienen sein, wünscht Hille deren Übersendung mit Angabe des Kaufpreises, der sogleich beglichen werden solle.

Q HM Köthen: V S 545, Bl. 26rv u. 28rv [A: 28v], 26v u. 28r leer; eigenh. mit eigenh. Empfangsvermerk von F. Ludwig; schwarzes Lacksiegel. Bl. 27rv (eingelegter Zettel): Beilage I. — Fehlt in *KE.*

A Dem durchleuchtigen hochgebornen Fürsten und herrn, herrn Ludewigen Fürsten zu

Anhalt, Graven zu Aschcanien, herrn zu Bernburgk und Zerbst, meinem gnedig*en* Fürsten und herrn vnderthenigk *etc.* Cöthen *etc.*

Empfangsvermerk F. Ludwigs: Pst. den 27. Martii 1644 *etc.*

HöchstgeEhrter herr Nehrender,

daß derselbe seinen gehorsambsten Geselschafter, mit einer erfreulichen antwort würdigen wollen; solcheß neme ich zu einem ewigen ruhm auf und an[.] Werde auch mit höchstem fleiß selbige großachtbare schreiben, meinen Nachkommen[1] verwahrlichen beilegen, Und die Zeit meineß lebenß deß Nehrenden vnverdrossener[2] diener verbleiben. Waß deß Befreyenden erklerung ist, hatt der höchstgeEhrte Nehrende, auß einliegendem mit mehrem zuersehen.[3] Ermesse doch unvorgreiflich, daß eß nicht vndienlichen sein würde, Wann mein Höchstg. Nehrender Noch vor die bevorstehende Ostern, ein klein Ehrinnerungßschreiben an den Befreyenden abgehen liesse. Da auch zu gleich an den Reinhertzigen[4] da bey eins gefüget würde, solte eß zu recht uberschicket werden. Da unter den Jtalienschen, oder Frantzößschen Büchleinß, einß sein möchte; daß mir zu Ubersetzen von dem Nehrenden anbefholen würde, hette ich demselbigen willig zu gehorsamen, vnd solcheß sauber wieder zuUbersenden grosse Uhrsache.[5] Die Abrüsse seind gehorsambst beobachtet, und werden hiemit Wieder geburend zu rucke geschicket. Und verbleibet allewege deß h. Nehrenden

Gehorsambster Knecht, der
Unverdrossene.

[W]olfenbuttel[a] [den][a] 23th. Martij Ao. 1644.

Da etwaß Neueß zu[b] Cöthen gedrucket[6] bitte gehorsambst, solcheß mir nebenst dem Kauf dessen zu uberschicken, so wil ich mich damit gehorsambst einstellen. Gott mit Unß *etc.*

I

440323

Carl Gustav von Hille an Herzog August d. J. von Braunschweig-Wolfenbüttel

Nicht in Gesellschaftsmanier geschriebener Brief. — Carl Gustav v. Hille (FG 302) fragt Hz. August d. J. v. Braunschweig-Wolfenbüttel (FG 227), was er dem ansonsten abgefertigten Boten F. Ludwigs auf dessen an Hille adressiertes Schreiben hinsichtlich der Begleichung des von Hz. August zugesagten Beitrages von 100 Reichstalern für das Gesellschaftsbuch (*GB 1646*) antworten solle. — In einer Antwortnotiz bestätigt Hz. August seine Absicht, die Zahlung über seinen Kammermeister noch vor der kommenden Ostermesse zu veranlassen. (Hille legt dieses Schriftstück seinem Brief an F. Ludwig bei.)

Q HM Köthen: V S 545, Bl. 27rv [A: 27v]; eigenh. mit einer Antwortnotiz Hz. Augusts. — Fehlt in *KE*.

A Ad manus III[mi] mei Principis, Dni. Clementissimi *etc.*

IIIme Princeps

Demnach der Anhaltische botte¹ seine **Expedition** hierselbsten erlanget, und bei mir anhelt J. f. gn. Furst Ludewigen die **resolution** wegen der 100 Rth.², zum verlage deß Geselschaftß buchß zuhinterbringen, Alß neme ich hiemit in Underthenigkeit glegenheit *[sic]* bei[a] E. f. gn. mich zu erkündigen[b], waß ich hochgedachte J. F. Gn. auf dero an mich gethaneß schreiben, hinwieder antworten solle. erwarte itzo gn. **resolution** und verbleibe

[W]olf.[c] den [2]3th.[c] Martij 1644

    E. f. Gn.
    undertheniger und Gehorsamer Diener *etc.*
    Carl Gustav von Hille *mp.*

Eigenh. Antwortnotiz von Hz. August d. J. von Braunschweig-Wolfenbüttel:
Gegen die OsterMeß wollen wir befehlen daß es ubermachet werde; so wird[d] unser Cammermeister[a3] darzu gerahten konnen.
Aug[e]

T a *Textverlust im Falz. Konjektur in eckigen Klammern.* — **b** *Gebessert aus* <von>

T I a *Folgt* <bei> — **b** *Präfix* er *aus* <vnt> — **c** *Textverlust im Falz. Konjektur in eckigen Klammern.* — **d** *Folgt* <etwan> [?] — **e** *Abzeichnungskürzel Hz. Augusts, vielleicht als* Aug *zu lesen.*

K 1 Der im September 1647 verstorbene Carl Gustav v. Hille (FG 302. Der Unverdrossene), über den uns keine Leichenpredigt mit Personalien vorliegt, hinterließ mindestens einen Sohn, folgt man seinem Werk *Hille: Teutscher Palmbaum*, Bl. 71*, d. i. Bl. [)()()()(iii] *[sic]* r. Dort ist ein kleines emblematisches Gedicht aus drei mit unterschiedlichen Landschaften verzierten Herzen bestehend mit den Motti „Hochentsprossen. Stillgeflossen. Rechtgenossen." u. einer jeweils vierzeiligen Auslegung veröffentlicht. Signiert wurde es mit einem sprechenden Attribut, das sich aus der Emblemform „Herz" u. der verwandtschaftlichen Bindung zum Unverdrossenen zusammensetzt: „Aus hertzsöhnlichem Gehorsam *etc.* Philip Carl von Hille". Hille war mit Helena Catharina v. Oeynhausen vermählt. Man findet einen Stammbucheintrag der Witwe aus dem Jahre 1650 mit einer erklärenden Anmerkung, daß ihr Mann „der Wolfenbüttelsche Hofmeister Carl Gustav v. Hillen" war, in Adolf Matthias Hildebrandt: Stammbuch-Blätter des norddeutschen Adels, Berlin 1874, 155, u. erfährt, daß Hille Lgf. Wilhelm V. v. Hessen-Kassel (FG 65) zu seiner Hochzeit in Allersheim (bei Holzminden) am 12.6.1634 einlud. S. Julius von Oeynhausen (Bearb.): Geschichte des Geschlechts von Oeynhausen. Aus gedruckten und ungedruckten Quellen. T. II Regesten und Urkunden von 1606 bis 1832 nebst Nachträgen zum ersten Theile. Mit zwei Siegeltafeln. Frankfurt a. M. 1887, 142. S. auch *Conermann III*, 339 u. *Bepler: Hille*.

 2 Hille spielt hier auf seinen Gesellschaftsnamen „Der Unverdrossene" an.

 3 S. die eigenhändige Antwortnotiz Hz. Augusts d. J. v. Braunschweig-Wolfenbüttel (FG 227. Der Befreiende) in Beil. I, in der der Herzog zusagt, den angegebenen Betrag kurz vor der Leipziger Ostermesse über seinen Kammermeister (Andreas Reiche, s. K I 3)

440323 Carl Gustav von Hille 223

anweisen zu lassen. Es geht hier um eine seit längerem geplante, auf den aktuellen Mitgliederstand gebrachte Neuausgabe des mit Impresenstichen Matthäus Merians d. Ä. illustrierten *GB 1629/30*. Diese Pläne führten schließlich zum Gesellschaftsbuch von 1646 (*GB 1646*), das die Nameninitialen, Impresen, Impresenstiche, Reimgesetze u. Aufnahmejahre der ersten 400 FG-Mitglieder umfassen wird. Während Merian erneut als für die Produktion des Werkes zuständiger Kommissionsverlag fungierte, wollte sich F. Ludwig für den kostspieligen Verlag auf verschiedene FG-Mitglieder u. deren finanzielle Beteiligung stützen, eine Art Konsortium, zu dem sich Hz. August, Hz. Christian Ludwig v. Braunschweig-Calenberg (s. Anm. 4) — bei Ihnen nahm F. Ludwig immer wieder die Vermittlungsdienste Hilles in Anspruch —, Hz. Friedrich III. v. Schleswig-Holstein-Gottorf (FG 388), Anthon v. Wietersheim (FG 273), Gf. Christian IX. v. Oldenburg-Delmenhorst (FG 375) u. a. bereit erklärt hatten. Pläne zu diesem neuen, aktualisierten Gesellschaftsbuch, Kalkulationen, Anfragen bei potentiellen Beiträgern/ Teilhabern usw. kursierten seit 1639. Vgl. 391203 u. I (s. dort K I). Allerdings kostete es F. Ludwig erhebliche, tw. vergebliche Mühe u. langwierige Schriftwechsel, um die jeweils zugesagten Gelder auch einzutreiben. Zu den Beteiligungen am Verlag des *GB 1646* s. 421031A (K 14) u. 430121 (K 2) u. im vorliegenden Band 450126 K 4. Seine beabsichtigte finanzielle Beteiligung am Verlag des *GB 1646* hatte Hz. August ursprünglich auf 200 Rtl. beziffert, zwischenzeitlich aber anscheinend auf 100 reduziert. S. K I 2, 440723A u. 450721. Erstmals thematisiert wird ein (zunächst) verminderter Verlagsbeitrag Hz. Augusts in 430706 u. 430724A. Am Ende wird der Herzog seine 200 Rtl. beisteuern. Vgl. etwa 440130 K 3 u. 450923A. Zu den Dokumenten den Zahlungsverkehr das *GB 1646* anlangend s. 450127 K 1.
4 Hz. Christian Ludwig v. Braunschweig-Calenberg (FG 372. Der Reinherzige). Vgl. F. Ludwigs „anmanungs"-Schreiben 440723, in dem er erneut nach dem Zuschuß des Herzogs in Höhe von 200 Reichstalern fragt, den dieser wohl aus Anlaß seiner Aufnahme in die FG im Juli 1642 in Aussicht gestellt hatte. Am Ende wird Christian Ludwig seinen Beitrag um die Hälfte schuldig bleiben. S. 440723 K 2 u. zu den Verlagsbeteiligungen 450126 K 4.
5 In 440209A erbot sich Hille, ein von F. Ludwig empfohlenes oder ausgewähltes Werk aus dem Italienischen oder Französischen zu übersetzen. In seinem Schreiben 440310 kündigte F. Ludwig (Der Nährende) daraufhin an, Hille ein Werk aus einer erwarteten Sendung ital. u. frz. Bücher zum Übersetzen zukommen zu lassen. Dies ist aber anscheinend nicht geschehen. Hille wendete sich (stattdessen) der Fertigstellung seiner FG-Geschichte zu, seinem *Teutschen Palmbaum* von 1647. Vgl. 451008.
6 Aus 440130 erfahren wir von einer umfangreichen Sendung von Köthener Neuerscheinungen, die per Boten kürzlich nach Wolfenbüttel geschafft worden waren. Weitere, noch ausstehende Bücher könnten bei Gelegenheit herübergeschafft werden, so F. Ludwig im genannten Brief. Entweder artikuliert Hille hier sein Interesse an dem noch ausstehenden Teil, oder er bekundet grundsätzlich seinen Wunsch, Neuerscheinungen aus der Köthener Druckerpresse zu erwerben. Dafür spricht die Wiederholung seines Anliegens in 460718. Dort spricht er allgemein von „deß Ortß außgegangenen herrlichen" Büchern. Im Jahre 1644 wurde ein Köthener Druck veröffentlicht: *Sachse: Einhelligkeit* III (vgl. 441205 K 3). Von Sachses 3. Teil erhielt Hille ein Exemplar. S. 460119 u. 460718 K 3.

K I 1 Vermutlich Ernst Stellbogen, s. 440130 K 2.
2 Carl Gustav v. Hille (FG 302. Der Unverdrossene) bezieht sich auf einen Teil des ursprünglich angekündigten Verlagsbeitrags Hz. Augusts d. J. v. Braunschweig-Wolfenbüttel (FG 227. Der Befreiende) für das *GB 1646*: 100 Reichstaler. S. die reduzierte Summe schon in 430801A u. die Bestätigung des Teilbetrages von 100 Reichstalern auch in

440723A. Zugesagt hatte Hz. August in 430121 einen Betrag von 200 Reichstalern. In *DA Köthen I. 8*: 470223 bestätigt Matthäus d. Ä. Merian dem Köthener Kammermeister Peter Knaudt, daß Hz. August die ihm zustehenden 48 Exemplare (buchmaterieller Gegenwert für 200 Reichstaler) erhalten habe. S. 440130 K 3 u. besonders 450126 K 4.

3 Andreas Reiche († 1655), anfangs Kanzlist u. Kammerschreiber, dann ab 1629 Hofkämmerer Hz. Friedrich Ulrichs v. Braunschweig-Wolfenbüttel (FG 38), seit 1636 Kammermeister unter dessen Nachfolger, Hz. August. Er blieb wahrscheinlich bis zu seinem Tod in diesem Amt. S. Helmut Samse: Die Zentralverwaltung in den südwelfischen Landen vom 15. bis zum 17. Jahrhundert. Hildesheim, Leipzig 1940 (Quellen u. Darstellungen zur Geschichte Niedersachsens 49), 197; Hermann Kleinau: Geschichte des Niedersächsischen Staatsarchivs in Wolfenbüttel. Göttingen 1953, 41, 43, 49 u. 111.

440324

Andreas Tscherning an Matthaeus Apelles von Löwenstern

Andreas Tscherning dankt seinem Förderer und „Vater" Matthaeus Apelles v. Löwenstern für dessen Brief vom 1. März. Die gute Aufnahme, Ergänzung und „Edition" seines Gedichts, das er nur zum Spaß und zur privaten Verwendung vorgesehen hatte, habe ihn freudig überrascht, auch in der Hoffnung, daran etwas zu verdienen. Er wüßte nicht, welcher (angesehene) Breslauer in seinem Gedicht vergessen worden sei, höchstens der junge (Hans Georg) Zang. Verse und Stil seien doch gut, kaum sonst von seiner eigenen Kunst zu unterscheiden, den viele verdächtigten, der Verfasser des (Liedes vom) *Soldatenlob* zu sein. — Tscherning bittet Apelles, sich für sein Stipendium einzusetzen. Vor 8 Tagen habe er deswegen auch an Franz Langer über den Danziger Postweg geschrieben. Apelles' Zusage lasse ihn jedoch hoffen, daß er ein Stipendium erhalte, so daß er Apelles dafür und für dessen eigenes Geschenk schon dankt. — Tscherning entschuldigt sich, daß sein Gedicht „Ara gratitudinis" so lange ausbleibe. Ein guter Anfang sei gemacht, es solle nun künftig unter hoffentlich besseren Lebensumständen fertiggestellt werden. Was er einst für Paul Neander und Apelles im häuslichen Kreise vorgebracht habe, liege fertiggestellt bei. Besonders dankt er für die Glückwünsche zu neuen Ehren, den Wunsch nach einer glücklichen Ehe möge Gott wahrmachen. Was dies betreffe, so wolle er sich nach seiner akademischen Promotion und Einführung (in das Amt des Professors der Dichtkunst) mit Gottes Hilfe um eine Heirat bemühen. Sein Gastgeber (Heinrich Rahne/ Rahnius) rate ihm zur Ehe mit einer hiesigen Professorenwitwe, einer noch jungen, schönen und kinderlosen Frau. Innerhalb der nächsten 14 Tage wolle sich Tscherning dem Magisterexamen stellen, da er vorher seine Professur nicht antreten könne. Er befürchtet für den üblichen anschließenden Magisterschmaus aber hohe Kosten, da mit ihm nur drei weitere Kandidaten zur Promotion angemeldet seien. — Er möchte gern seine Bücher bei sich haben, aber nicht nur die im Kasten („die Pudel"), die mittlerweile bei (Johannes) Mochinger eingetroffen sein sollen, sondern auch die, die er bei (Petrus) Czimmermann (in Thorn) zurückgelassen habe. Dank für die gute Beförderung der Bücher im Kasten. Dem Verleger Georg Baumann sendet er dessen Unterschrift und Siegel des Vertrags zurück. Sein Kolleg über die Prosodie trage ihm 40 Reichstaler ein, die er für die Promotion und angemessene Kleidung anzulegen gedenke. Die Promotion solle noch vor Ostern unter Johann(es) Huswedel(ius) vonstatten gehen. — Es gebe genug Avisen (verkäufliche Zeitungsberichte) zu schreiben, doch wage er das nicht in Rostock. Das Manifest Kg. Christians IV. v. Dänemark werde vielleicht schon in Schlesien erhältlich sein, ebenso das Schreiben Kgn. Christinas v. Schweden an ihre Reichsstände, in dem sie den Feldzug nach Dänemark rechtfertigte. Mehr lieber mündlich. — Johann Rist (FG 467. 1647) habe ihm kürzlich erneut geschrieben und dränge ihn zur Abfassung eines Gratulationsgedichts auf seine Schrift *Starker Schild Gottes* (1644). Wegen des vermuteten nur satirischen Charakters der Arbeit vermied Tscherning darauf zu antworten. Er zitiert aus diesem Brief: Rist hätte Tschernings Musen-Epigramme (*Schediasmatum liber unus*, 1644) gern erhalten, mit großer Freude gelesen und schließlich mit derselben Sorgfalt wie andere berühmte Männer gelobt. Wenn noch ein oder zwei Exemplare für ihn übrig wären, möchte er, Rist, schon in aller Welt bekannte Leute wie Georg Philipp Harsdörffer (FG 368), welcher ihm seine Abhandlungen *Aulaea Romana* (1642) und *Gallia deplorata* (1641) zusammen mit anderen Lobschriften und Gedichten geschickt habe, oder auch Justus Georg Schottelius (FG 397), dessen *Verskunst* (1645) hoffentlich bald erscheine, mit diesen Gedichten beglücken. Rist schickt Tscherning Philipp v. Zesens (FG 521. 1648) *Scala Heliconis Teutonici* (1643), obgleich sie seinen, Rists, guten Ruf dreifach stehle. Harsdörffer habe ihm, Rist, in seinem jüngsten Brief geschrieben, daß Apelles v. Löwenstern und Tscherning Zesen noch für unfähig hielten, einen *Deutschen Helicon* zu schreiben. Er machte die Sachen schwerer und undeutlicher als sie eigentlich wären. Schottelius würde die Sache besser zu behandeln wissen. Nach Rists Meinung hätte Harsdörffer die Sache richtig beurteilt und Zesen durchschaut, welcher weder durch seinen Geist noch durch seine Wissenschaft andere überträfe. Er, Rist, kenne Zesen und wisse um dessen geringe Bildung in den Künsten und Sprachen. Über dieses Urteil möge Tscherning jedoch Stillschweigen bewahren. — Tscherning drückt seine Verwunderung über diese Worte aus. — Grüße an Apelles' Gattin, Herrn Tarnau und die Braut Rosina.

Q BU Wrocław: R 3108, Bl. 17r–18v [A: 18v]; eigenh.; rotes Lacksiegel. — *D: Borcherdt: Tscherning*, 129f., 154 u. 309 Anm. 21 (Auszüge). — *BN: Bürger*, 1365 Nr. 7; *Borcherdt: Tscherning*, 334 Nr. 73.

A A Monsieur
Mons. MATTHIEU APELLES de Lovenstern in Langenhof, Conseillier de sa Majesté Imperiale, & de son Altesse Duc de Monsterberg.
à Breslau

Salutem à Dno. JESU!

Edler, Gestrenger und hochbenambter, insonders hochgeehrter lieber herr Vater,[1]

Jn was für freude deß hn. Vaters Schreiben, **sub dato** den 1. Martii, mein gemüte gesetzet habe, weiß ich warlich mit worten nicht an tag zu geben. Auff solche **invention** habe ich bey verfertigung deß **carminis**[2] nicht dencken können, weil es meistentheils **ludicrum** und nur **intra privatos parietes** zu behalten geschrieben war. Jndeßen kan ich desselben **edition** wol leiden, und nehme den zusatz zu hohem danck an, bevor[a] wofern mir dadurch, als mich die hoffnung nähret, mit etwas mitteln kan geholffen werden. Wer von Breßlauern darinnen vergessen sey, sehe ich nicht, ohne daß der kleinere Zang[3], vielleicht der statur halben, durchgefallen. Die Verse sind sehr gut, der **stylus** wird hierinn auch nicht zu unterscheiden sein, heisset es doch bey vielen dieses ortes, Tsche*rn*ing habe das Soldatenlob geschmiedet. Wegen deß Stipendii[4] bitte ich ja hochdinstlich omnem lapidem zu moviren. Vor acht tagen habe ich uber Dantzig an hn. Frantz Langer[5] geschrieben, und darum gleichfalls gebeten. Getröste mich indeßen E. Gestr. deß hn. Vatern tröstlichen Zusage, und laße mir träumen, es würde der herr Vater davon noch nichts meldung gethan haben, wann nicht allbereit gute sperantz dazu, oder ja schon etwas ausgerichtet were. Für solche väterliche und unverhoffte Vorsorge, wie auch[b] selbsteigene verehrung sage ich schuldigen hohen danck, und werde solches die zeit meines lebens, nach bestem vermögen, zu rhümen und vor aller welt zu preisen wissen. Daß Ara gratitudinis solange aussenbleibet, schaffet mir freylich keinen nutzen, muß es wol bekennen. Ein guter anfang war gemacht, hat aber bißher nicht können zu ende gebracht werden, soll aber inkünfftig gewiß und in besserer ferne folgen, wann mich Gott anders leben läßt.[6] Was E. Gestr. und hn. Neandro ich allbereit längst fertig intra Vestæ penetraliæ gehalten, ist hierbey zu finden.[7] Pro gratulatione de novis honoribus ago itidem gratias singulares, das votum aber pro felici matrimonio wolle Gott wahrmachen. Nach der promotion und introduction wil ich Deo iuvante, im letzteren mein heil versuchen. Mein herr Hospes rathet mir zu eines vorm jahr verstorbenen Profeßoris hinterlaßenen wittib, einer noch jungen und unbekinderten Frauen, von zimlicher schönheit, wie mir referiret worden, denn ich bin noch zur zeit nicht bauschauen[8] [sic] gewesen.[9] Jnnerhalb 14 tagen wil ich mich examiniren laßen, noch zur zeit sind aber promovendorum nur vier, nemlich 2 Priester, ein Schwedischer Studiosus und ich. Wofern sich nicht mehr angeben, soll unß das convivium pro parte zimlich anlauffen. Was soll ich aber machen. Neceßitas non habet legem.[10] Jch kan zur profeßion nicht eher introduciret werden, biß ich gradiret bin. Meine bücher wünsch ich mir, nicht allein aber die Pudel[11], so bey hn. Mochingern[12] schon sein sol, darinn vielleicht nur die nachgeschickten bücher werden behalten sein, sondern auch die wagenlade[13], so ich bey hn. Czimmermann verlaßen, und darum ich neulich erst geschrieben. Bedancke mich für jener bücher in der Pudel gute beföderung. Hn. Baumann sende ich hierbey seinen Namen und Pitschafft von der obligation.[14] Mit meiner[c] prosodie prosperire ich anietzt auß meinem collegio 40 Reichstaler.[15] welche ich auff die promotion und ein kleid dabey destiniret habe. Die promotion wird noch vor Ostern[16] ihren fortgang haben, unter Huswedelio[17]. Auisen hette ich genung zu schreiben, aber auß erheblichen ursachen dörffen wir es nicht wagen, an diesen orten. Das Manifestum deß Königes in Dennemarck[18] wird vielleicht bei ihnen schon zukauffe [sic] sein,[d] werden sie auch allbereit das Schreiben Königl. Majestet in Schweden an Jhre Reichsstände[19] darinnen die ursachen deß dänischen Krieges, erhalten haben. Was sonst paßiret, mochte ich gerne in aurem sagen, aber p. Herr Rist hat mir neulich[e] abermal geschrieben, plaget mich hefftig um ein gratulatorium auff ein Tractätlein so er herauß zu geben gedencket, welches heissen soll Schild Gottes wider den Neid.[20] Weil ich dann verspüre, daß es ein blosses Satyricum sein wil, habe ich keine antwort geschrieben. Inter alia scribet: Schediasmata seu potius aurea tua Epigrammatia Thespiadum[21] in ode locanda, vix credibile est, quanta aviditate acceperim; quanta jucunditate pellegerim, quanta denique diligentia viris quibusdam summis meritò laudaverim; utinam mihi unum aut alterum eorum adhuc supereßet exemplar, quo viros clarißimos & orbi fere notos, magnificum videlicet & nobilißimum Dominum HARSDORFERUM, qui mihi medius tertius aulæa sua Romana, Galliam itidem deploratam[22] cum aliis quibusdam Scriptis panegyricis & elegantißimis suis poëmatiis transmisit, ut et eruditißimum dominum SCHOTTELIUM, cujus Ars poëtica brevi, ut spero, prodibit,[23] doctißimis hisce carminibus beare possim. P. Cæsii Scalam Heliconis Teutonicam nomini meo dicatam,[24] nuperrimè verò a prædonibus quibusdam[a] famulo[a] meo neque ter ereptam denuo lubens transmitto, de quo libellulo judiciosißimus modò dictus Harstorfferus in novißimis suis litteris se-[17v]quentia memorat: Herr Löwenstern und herr Tscherning sollen von dem Cæsio geurtheilet haben: Er sey noch nicht der Mann, einen Teutschen Helicon[25] zu schreiben, & addit doctißimus ille vir: Fürwar er machet die sachen undeutlicher und schwerer, als es an sich selbsten ist: Herr Schottel wird deutscher herauß gehen,[26] daß die unberichteten auch hernach kommen können. Hæc ille. Fateor autem, si apertè & simpliciter mihi loquendum, ingeniosißimum hunc Phoebum Noricum rem totam ex veritate æstimaße, & fortaßis adhuc multo felicius secerneret & internosceret simulatum à veris, si P. Cæsius neque ingenio neque doctrina præter cæteros præstans ipsi satis cognitus aut perspectus eßet: Ego quidem, qui penitius novi hominem, nullam aut sané exiguam artium & linguarum peritiam in ipso deprehendere unq. potui. verum hæc omnia silentio relinquam etc. Hæc Ristius.

Jch wundere mich uber die worte, & quid tu judices, avidè expello, Conjugi suavißimæ, Dn. Tarnovio, ut & ROSINÆ sponsæ[d 27] salutem plurimam dico.

Rostock in eyl den 24 Martii 1644.[28]

I

Johann Rist knüpft Kontakte zu Andreas Tscherning

Aus einem Brief Andreas Tschernings an Matthias Machner vom 11.12.1642.

Q STB Berlin — PK: Dep. Breslau 17 (ehem. StB Breslau: Ms. Rehd. 402), 862–865 [A: 865] (Nr. 359), hier S. 863, eigenh.; Sig.
Abschrift in BU Wrocław: Akc. 1949/ 713 (ehem. StB Breslau: Abschrift Klose 175, d.i. Abschrift der Hs. Ms. Rhed. 402), Bl. 239v–241r, hier 240v. Zur Abschrift Klose 175 vgl. 440826 K 2.
D: Auszug gedruckt in *Borcherdt: Tscherning*, 153; Zitat in Peter Epstein: Matthäus Apelles von Löwenstern, ein schlesischer Dichter, Musiker und Gelehrter (1594–1648). In: Zeitschrift d. Vereins f. Geschichte Schlesiens 62 (1928), 1–30, hier S. 4 Anm. 3. — BN: *Bürger*, 1366 Nr. 36; *Borcherdt: Tscherning*, 333 Nr. 44.

A A Monsieur Monsieur Matthias Machner mon tres-cher amy. a Breslau. — *Empfangsvermerk:* Praes. 2 Febr. 1643.

[...] Ristius[1] hat neulich an meiner commensalen einen, gedachten R. Schwager, von mir mit denen worten geschrieben, wie ich sie folgender weise abcopiret: Ferner vernehm ich auß seinem Schreiben, daß er zum tischgesellen einen hat nahmens Tscherning, ich möchte sehr gerne wißen, ob es der herr Andreas Tscherning sey, welcher sonst ein berümbter Poet vnd sehr feine sachen hat heraußgegeben. Es ist vor seinem buch ein Kupferstück mit hn. Opitzen seel. bildnüs.[2] Dofern nun er derselbe ist, wie ich schier nicht zweifele, so bitte ich höchlich, er wolle ihm meinen freundlichen gruß und stets gefließene dinste vermelden, vnd dabenebenst andeuten, daß mir nichts liebers sein solte, als rechtschaffene gute vertreulichkeit mit ihme zu halten. Wolt er auch meine himmlische Lieder[3] mit etlichen Versen vorehren [sic], welches aber bald und zum allerlängsten innerhalb 3 wochen geschehen müste, würde er mich ihme dadurch hoch verbündlich machen, als der ich ohne das bereit bin ihm alle mögliche dinste zu erweisen etc. Mit einem **gratulatorio** habe ich ihm allbereit gratificiret,[4] erwarte darauff noch antwort.[5] [...]

T a *Lies:* vorab, zumal, insbesondere — **b** *Folgt unleserlich gestrichenes Wort.* — **c** *Folgt* <ietzt> — **d** *Folgt* <ges> — **e** *Folgt* <pl>

K Obgleich Andreas Tscherning (1611–1659) u. die von ihm wiedergegebenen Worte Johann Rists (FG 467. 1647) u. Georg Philipp Harsdörffers (FG 368) die FG oder deren zentrale Projekte nicht ausdrücklich erwähnen, findet dieser Brief im vorliegenden Bande Berücksichtigung, da er neben den Beziehungen des in die FG drängenden Andreas Tscherning (s. auch 450726), des Schülers Martin Opitzens (FG 200), Tschernings Einbindung in das Netzwerk einiger der damals oder bald darauf tonangebenden Mitglieder der Gesellschafft enthüllt: Johann Rist, Georg Philipp Harsdörffer, Justus Georg Schottelius (FG 397) u. Philipp v. Zesen (FG 521. 1648). Mit 400113 hatte Augustus Buchner (FG 362) Gedichte aus Breslau an F. Ludwig gesandt, von denen diesem die Gedichte Tschernings am besten gefallen hatten, s. 400214. Zu Tschernings Rolle als präsumtiver Opitz-Nachfolger s. auch *Opitz: BW* I, 191 u. 390715 I, 390730 I u. 401122 K 3. Zu einer Aufnahme Tschernings in die FG hat dies offenbar nicht gereicht. Zu Tscherning vgl. grundlegend *Borcherdt: Tscherning*; ferner Ralf Georg Bogner: Andreas Tscherning. Konstruktionen von Autorschaft zwischen universitärem Amt, urbaner Öffentlichkeit und nationaler Literaturreform. In: Theorie und Praxis der Kasualdichtung in der Frühen Neuzeit. Hg. Andreas Keller u. a. Amsterdam, New York 2010 (Chloe 43), 185–196; Jörg-Ulrich Fechner: Ein poetischer Nachrichtenbrief von Andreas Tscherning nach Breslau. Zu einer vergessenen Gattung des deutschen Barock. In: Memoriae Silesiae. Leben und Tod, Kriegserlebnis und Friedenssehnsucht in der literarischen Kultur des Barock. Zum Gedenken an Marian Szyrocki (1928–1992). Hg. Mirosława Czarnecka, Andreas Solbach u. a. Wrocław 2003, 271–280; David G. Halsted: Andreas Tscherning. In: German Baroque Writers 1580–1660. Hg. James Hardin. Detroit u. a. 1996, 344–349; Hans Heckel: Geschichte der deutschen Literatur in Schlesien. Bd. 1: Von den Anfängen bis zum Ausgange des Barock. Breslau 1929, 210–214; Arno Lubos: Geschichte der Literatur Schlesiens. Bd. I.1: Von den Anfängen bis ca. 1800. Würzburg 1995, 144f.; Lesław Spychała: Wegweiser durch die Handschriftenbestände der Universitätsbibliothek Wrocław/ Breslau. In: Kulturgeschichte Schlesiens in der Frühen Neuzeit. Hg. Klaus Garber. 2 Bde., Tübingen 2005, 744;

440324 Andreas Tscherning

Oskar Friedrich Tscherning: Tscherningsches Vergißmeinnicht. Altes und Neues über die Familie Tscherning aus Bunzlau in Schlesien. Heilbronn (Selbstverlag) 1905. Eine Epicediensammlung erschien aus Anlaß von Tschernings Tod: MAUSOLEUM sive ARA EXEQVIALIS MEMORIÆ ÆTERNÆ Super Luctuosissimo Obitu ... DN. ANDREÆ TSCHERNINGII, Philologi elegantissimi & Poet. Prof. Publ. celeberrimi, Ampliss. Facult. Philos. p. t. DECANI spectabilis, publicè erecta à Professoribus & Amicis (Rostock 1659). HAB: Db 4757 (13).

1 Der mit Martin Opitz entfernt verwandte Bunzlauer Andreas Tscherning, seit dem 16.5.1644 als Nachfolger Peter Laurembergs (1585–1639) Prof. der Poesie an der U. Rostock, war 1642 durch seinen Mäzen („Vater") Matthaeus Apelles v. Löwenstern (1594–1648) zur Wiederaufnahme u. zum Abschluß seiner Studien in Rostock befähigt worden. Der als Matthias Apel/ Appelt aus einfachen Verhältnissen in Neustadt/ Oberschlesien stammende Apelles war nach dem Besuch des Brieger Gymnasiums (1610–1613) Lehrer u. Kantor in Leobschütz, das er kriegsbedingt 1625 verließ. Zunächst Sekretär Hz. Heinrich Wenzels v. Münsterberg-Oels in Bernstadt (1592–1639, aus dem böhm. Haus Podiebrad), stieg er zum Leiter der Hofkapelle, zum Aufseher über das Schulwesen, dann der Kanzlei, des Steueramtes u. der fl. Kammer auf. 1631 wurde er zum hzl. Rat ernannt, 1634 vom Kaiser geadelt. Noch in Leobschütz hatte er sich mit Martha Adam vermählt († 1636). 1637 ging er die Ehe mit der verwitweten Barbara v. Tarnau u. Kühschmalz (s. Anm.2) ein, die das Gut Langenhof b. Bernstadt mit in die Ehe brachte. Wenzel Scherffer v. Scherfferstein hat diese Hochzeit in einem Liederkranz besungen. S. Epstein (1929, s. u.), 5. Als nach dem Tode Hz. Heinrich Wenzels die hzl. Oelser Regierung unter dem Bruder Hz. Karl Friedrich (1593–1647) nach Breslau ins dortige „Oelser Haus" verlegt wurde, ging Apelles mit u. wurde zum Mittelpunkt eines großen, vielseitig interessierten Freundeskreises. Tscherning gehörte zu den von ihm nachhaltig geförderten Talenten. Vgl. Tschernings Geburtstagsgratulation *Ode an den woledlen, gestrengen vnd hochbenambten Herren Matheus Apelles von Löwenstern auf Lanngehoff* (Breslau: Baumann 1641). In: *Faber du Faur,* Nr.262. HAB: MF 1:59. Tscherning dürfte Apelles nicht vor dem Sommer 1639 kennengelernt haben, nachdem er 1636 sein Studium in Rostock aus Geldmangel hatte abbrechen müssen u. sich in Breslau als Hauslehrer durchschlug. Trotz Apelles' Förderung blieben Tschernings Lebensverhältnisse bis 1645 gedrückt, woran seine Bestallung zum Prof. der Poesie an der U. Rostock aufgrund ausbleibender Gehaltszahlungen nicht viel änderte. Von Apelles' dichterischem u. kompositor. Schaffen ist u.a. die Sammlung geistlicher Oden zu nennen, nämlich das Gesangbuch: Früelings-Mayen. Von dreyssig/ in einem Haußgärtlein auffgewachsenen/ doch etwas zu früe abgebrochenen Blumen/ Zusammen gebunden/ und in einem Heliconischen Geväß/ auff begehren dargestellt/ durch Einen Liebhaber der Geistlichen Garten-gesellschafft ([o. O.] 1644). TULB Jena: 8 Art. lib. XIV,22 (1); auch Dig. Vgl. Epstein (1929, s.u.), 12. Erstmals in der Geschichte des dt. Kirchenlieds wurden hier antike Metren in die Liedtexte eingeführt. Johann Sebastian Bach hat später sieben dieser Melodien vierstimmig bearbeitet. Apelles schuf ferner 11 drei- bis vierstimmige Chöre mit Generalbaß zu Opitz' Drama *Judith* (Breslau 1635), das Tscherning bearbeitet u. von drei auf fünf Akte erweitert hatte: Martin Opitzen | Judith/ | auffs neu außgefertiget; | worzu das vördere Theil der Historie | sampt den Melodeyen auff iedwedes | Chor | beygefüget | von | Andreas Tscherningen. | [Zierleiste] | Rostock/ | Gedruckt durch Johann Richeln/ Rahts Buchdr. | in vorlegung Joachim Wildens/ Buchhändlers/ | im Jahr 1646. HAB: Lo 5835 (Text u. Noten; auch Dig.). Vgl. dazu 450726 u. *Opitz: BW* 350323 *ep* u. K 5. Apelles verfaßte auch ein 3-stimmiges Hochzeitlied auf den Herren Hans Georg v. Wartenberg (FG 143) u. Sabina, geb. Pgfn. bei Rhein, im Jahre 1625. FB Gotha: Theol. 4° 933 (24), Ndr. in Ratte (s.u.), 380–387. Hans

Heckel beurteilte die *Judith* als Werk der Zusammenarbeit von Tscherning u. Apelles kritisch. Tschernings Judith-Bearbeitung habe den „Libretto-Charakter" der opitzischen Dichtung verkannt u. sie auf die „Manier des Schuldramas" zurückgeholt; Apelles wiederum habe ganz im Sinne Tschernings die Chöre nicht im neuartigen Opernstil, sondern als „musikalische Einlagen eines gesprochenen Schauspiels" komponiert. Ratte hingegen bescheinigte Apelles ein kompositorisches Schaffen auf der Höhe der zeitgenössischen Musik-Rhetorik u. Deklamationsrhythmik. H. H.: Geschichte der deutschen Literatur in Schlesien (s. Anm. 0), 213; Ratte (s. u.), 375. Vgl. *Borcherdt: Tscherning*, v. a. 71 ff. Zu Apelles vgl. *ADB* XIX, 318; *DBA* III 20/ 390–395; *Literatur-Lexikon*², 181; *Cunrad: Silesia togata*, 6; Konrad Ameln: Art. „Löwenstern". In: *MGG* VIII (1960), 1117–1121; Peter Epstein: Matthaeus Apelles von Löwensterns weltliche Lieder. In: Zs. f. Musikwissenschaft 10 (1928), 263–273; ders.: Apelles von Löwenstern. Mit einer Neuausgabe der Chöre zu Martin Opitz' „Judith". Breslau 1929; Das Evangelische Schlesien. Hg. Gerhard Hultsch. Bd. IV.2: Die schlesische Kirchenmusik im Wandel der Zeiten. Bearb. v. Fritz Feldmann. Lübeck 1975, 80–82; Michael Fischer: Art. „Löwenstern" in *MGG*², Personenteil XI, 529–531; Lothar Hoffman-Erbrecht: Musikgeschichte Schlesiens. Dülmen 1986, 74; ders. (Hg.): Schlesisches Musiklexikon. Augsburg 2001, 12; Remigiusz Pośpiech: Breslau als Zentrum der Musikkultur Schlesiens im 17. Jahrhundert. In: Schütz-Jahrbuch 32 (2010), 7–15, hier S. 11; Franz Josef Ratte: Die musikalischen Werke des Matthäus Apelles von Löwenstern. In: Die oberschlesische Literaturlandschaft im 17. Jahrhundert. Hg. Gerhard Kosellek. Bielefeld 2001, 357–387; Hugo Steinitz: Über das Leben und die Compositionen des Matthaeus Apelles von Löwenstern. Breslau 1892.

 2 Tschernings Neujahrsgedicht 1644, inc.: „O hätt' ich vom Mercur die schnelle Krafft der Flügel!" *Borcherdt: Tscherning*, 73 f.; gibt es nach der Breslauer Hs. R 3109 wieder (Kriegsverlust). Das Gedicht führt in das gesellige Treiben im Hause Apelles' ein u. nennt viele Gäste dieses gebildeten Zirkels, die ein- u. ausgingen: Daniel von Tarnau (s. u.), Paulus Neander (s. Anm. 7), Christophorus Colerus (1602–1658, Opitz-Freund u. Konrektor des Breslauer Elisabeth-Gymnasiums seit 1637, seit 1639 Bibliothekar der berühmten Gymnasialbibliothek zu Maria Magdalena), Matthias Machner (s. K I 1), vielleicht auch Abraham v. Franckenberg (s. 440826). Ein Daniel v. Tarnau (u. Kühschmalz, 1603–1656) erscheint in Tschernings *Semicenturia SCHEDIASMATUM* (Rostock 1643; HAB: Li 9222, auch dig.) in einem Gedicht in der Zugabe („Mantissa") als „Patr[icius] Vratisl[aviensis]" u. war vermutlich mit Apelles' zweiter Frau, der Witwe des hzl. münsterberg-oelsnischen Staatsrates Ernst Lange († 1632), verwandt. Tarnau, aus schles. Uradel, 1623 U. Leipzig, 1627 U. Wittenberg, war seit 1647 Schöffe im Breslauer Stadtrat, dann Ratsherr u. Schulinspektor in Breslau. Vgl. *Borcherdt: Tscherning*, 71 f.; *Cunrad: Silesia togata*, 302; *Pusch* IV, 283. Das Neujahrsgedicht wurde mit einigen Varianten, jedoch ohne Apelles' Zusätze in *Vortrab Des Sommers Deutscher Gedichte* (Rostock 1655. STB Berlin — PK: an Yi 1503; auch dig.), Bl. Bij v – Biiij v, aufgenommen. Der Erstdruck, der ohne Wissen Tschernings von Apelles veranlaßt wurde, zeigt in der Abweichung von der Handschrift die von Tscherning im vorliegenden Brief freudig begrüßten Zusätze Apelles': NewJahrs-Postilion An Den WolEdlen/ Gestrengen vnd Hochbenambten Herren Matthäus Apelles Von Löwenstern/ auff Langenhoff ... Vbersendet von Andreas Tscherningen Poes: Profess: Publ: in Rostock. Anno 1644. STB Berlin — PK: Yi 1461:7. Vgl. *Dünnhaupt: Handbuch*, 4120 (Art. Tscherning, Nr. 83). Nach diesem Erstdruck veröffentlicht in Fechner (s. Anm. 0), 278–280. Hier finden sich in Einschüben Apelles' weitere, auch auswärtige Wohltäter u. Bekannte Tschernings: ein Diener des Apelles namens „Moser"; „Langer, mein Patron" — vermutlich der im Brief genannte Franz Langer (s. Anm. 5); ein (fl. münsterberg-oelsn. Regierungsrat u. Sekretär) „Herr Hubrig" (Johann Hubrig [1604–

1663], hzl. münsterberg.-oelsn. Regierungs-, 1638 Konsistorial- u. Kammerrat, 1646 Vizekanzler, später Kanzler; *Cunrad: Silesia togata*, 135f.; *Pusch* II, 290), ein „Herr Albert" (Arzt), „Herr Seidel" (Georg Seidel [1596–1667], Pastor in Oels; *Cunrad: Silesia togata*, 285), „Herr Böhm"' (David Behme/ Böhm/ Bohemus [1605–1657], Pfarrer u. Hofprediger in Bernstadt u. als neulat. u. Lieder-Dichter lebenslang mit Apelles befreundet; s. *Cunrad: Silesia togata*, 25; Epstein [1929, s. Anm. 1], 7, 15 u. 20f.; Schlesisches Musiklexikon [wie Anm. 1], 12; vgl. auch 450726 K 0), „Titz" (Christoph Titz, Pastor in Paskerwitz), Christoph Freitag (evang. Pfarrer in Lossen/ Hzt. Oels), sowie ein „Bittner" u. „Franke", sodann auch der Nürnberger Theologe Johann „Saubert" (d. Ä. [1592–1646], s. auch 450726 K 0), Johannes „Mochinger" (s. Anm. 12), der Fruchtbringer u. Wittenberger Poesie-Prof. Augustus „Buchner", dem Tscherning sein *Lob der Buchdruckerey* (Breßlaw: Baumann 1640) gewidmet hatte u. der Tscherning nach Wittenberg holen wollte (vgl. 460610 K 10), Petrus „Zimmermann" (Czimmermann, Rektor des Thorner Gymnasiums), Sebastian „Alscher" (Alischer, 1602–1674, Prediger an St. Peter u. Paul in Liegnitz; stammte wie Opitz, Colerus u. Tscherning aus Bunzlau; *Cunrad: Silesia togata*, 4), Heinrich „Rhan" (Rahne/ Rahnius, s. Anm. 9) u.a.m. Zu Apelles' Zusätzen u. einer Änderung Tschernings in der *Vortrab*-Fassung vgl. *Borcherdt: Tscherning*, 282f. Anm. 51ff. Eine Liste seiner Freunde u. Gönner auch im Brief vom 27.2.1643 (s. Anm. 3). Petrus Zimmermann hatte die einzige bekannte öffentliche Aufführung von Tschernings u. Apelles' *Judith* in Thorn „cum maximo applausu" besorgt. Brief Tschernings an Apelles vom 27.2.1643 (s. Anm. 3), Bl. 9r. Viele dieser Gönner u. Freunde tauchen in der Gratulationsschrift auf, die Tscherning zur Magisterpromotion u. zum Antritt seiner Rostocker Professur zuteil wurde: Viro Clarissimo Praestantissimo Dn. Andreae Tscherningio, P. L. C. De capessenda Laureâ Magistrali, itemque Poëseos Professione Publicâ, in Inclutâ Rosarum Academiâ, gratulantur Fautores et Amici jam-jam agonizantis Silesiae Anno 1644 (Oels [1644]). (Georg Seidel, Johannes Hubrig, Chr. Albert, David Bohemus, Matthias Machner, Sebastian Alischer, Christoph Freitag u.a.m.). *Borcherdt: Tscherning*, 128 u. 296 Anm. 14. Die Gratulationsschrift fehlt bei *Dünnhaupt: Handbuch* u. im VD17. Sein persönliches Beziehungsgeflecht tritt uns auch in Tschernings lat. u. dt. Gedichtsammlungen entgegen, im *Deutscher Getichte Früling* (1642 u.ö.), im *Vortrab Des Sommers Deutscher Gedichte* (1655; s. Anm. 1), in der *Semicenturia SCHEDIASMATUM* (1643; s.o.) usw.

3 Ein Hans Zang wird in Tschernings Brief an Matthaeus Apelles v. Löwenstern, d. d. Rostock 27.2.1643, genannt. BU Wrocław: R 3108, Bl. 8r–9v. Dort handelt es sich um Johann Zang(e) (1594–1658), Bürger u. Handelsmann in Breslau, Vorsteher der Kirche u. des Hospitals zu St. Bernhardin. Aus der 1626 geschlossenen Ehe mit Ursula Germersheim (1605–1658) ging Hans Georg (1634–1684) hervor, wie sein Vater Kaufmann, 1669 Schöffe im Rat der Stadt bis 1677, danach Bürgermeister; 1674 nobilitiert zu „von Zangen und Oberlahnstein". Als zum Zeitpunkt der Abfassung des vorliegenden Briefes Zehnjähriger könnte er der „kleinere Zang" gewesen sein. S. *Pusch* V, 131–133. — Im folgenden Satz protzt Tscherning nicht schamlos mit den eigenen Versen in dem bewußten Carmen, sondern stellt diese scherzhaft auf dieselbe Stufe mit einem damals kursierenden satirischen anonymen „Soldatenlob", das dem aus Ohrdruf in Thüringen stammenden lat. Epigrammatiker Georg Nicolaus Erasmi (fl. 1636–1678) zugeschrieben wurde: Soldaten-Lob. | Jm Jahr/ Anno 1644 ([o.O.] ca.1644). STB Berlin — PK: Ye 7091: R; UB Augsburg, beide Expll. dig. Eine Bekanntschaft des in Rostock weilenden Tscherning mit dem 1645 in Güstrow (und später in Rostock) tätigen Erasmi ist denkbar. *Adelung* II, 907. Den Verfassernamen entnahmen Michael Holzmann u. Hans Bohatta (Deutsches Anonymen-Lexikon 1501–1850. 4 Bde. Weimar 1907, IV, 94: „Soldaten-Lob. O. O. [1645?]") aus den vorangestellten Versen:

Laus ea tàm doctè depicta est militis, ut vel
Mutari à Cöo possit Apelle nihil.
        Georg Nicolaus Erasmus, P. L.

Der mit einem Titan (Coeus) verglichene (Ov. met. 6, 186. 366) Maler Apelles erinnert nur im Namen an Tschernings Mäzen. Allerdings enthält das uns vorliegende Exemplar auch die Notenschrift für „Tenor solus" u. Basso continuo für ein 36 Strophen zählendes Gedicht, so daß Apelles bzw. sein Schützling Tscherning mit dem Werk in Verbindung gebracht worden sein mögen. Vor dem Lied 3 Strophen „An den Ehrliebenden Soldaten", inc.:

LAndsknecht frage dein Gewissen/
    Obs von solcher Voppigkeit/
    Wie allhier steht/ ist befreyt:
Dann so laß dichs nicht verdriessen/
    Das die Laster in gemein/
    Welche der Soldat jetzt übet/
Vnd dadurch das Land betrübet/
    Etwas scharff gestraffet seyn.

Die Verse werden im eigentlichen Lied regelmäßiger, z.B. in der viele Strophen langen Aufzählung der Kriegsplagen, inc.:

DOnner/ Plitz vnd Hagelsteine/
Alle Wetter groß vnd kleine/
Wolckenbrüche/ Wasserfluth/
Erderbeben/ Fewergluth/ [...].

Dennoch sind sie nicht Tscherning zuzutrauen, der, wie angedeutet, sich mit seinem Korrespondenzpartner einig wußte, daß der Verfasser kein guter Poet war.

4 Im Frühjahr 1639 hatte sich Tscherning mit der Bitte um ein Stipendium an den Rat der Stadt Breslau gewandt, um sein Universitätsstudium fortsetzen zu können. Der Rat verhielt sich ablehnend. *Borcherdt: Tscherning*, 64. Für den Abschluß seiner Studien in Rostock ab 1642 hatte Apelles dann unter Gönnern u. Freunden gesammelt. Voraussetzung dieses Stipendiums war nach *Borcherdt: Tscherning*, 122, „daß Tscherning ihre Namen durch Widmung von Gelegenheitsdichtungen unsterblich mache." In seinem Brief vom 15.2.1644 hatte Apelles in dieser Hinsicht die „Nachlässigkeit" Tschernings getadelt (s. Tschernings Antwort vom 27.2.1643, wie Anm.3) u. wiederholt „Dankbarkeit" angemahnt. Diese abhängige u. dennoch notorisch angespannte finanzielle Lage belastete Tscherning. Infolgedessen scheint er um ein Bunzlauer u. erneut ein Breslauer Stipendium eingekommen zu sein, offenbar vergeblich. *Borcherdt: Tscherning*, 122 u. 127.

5 Franz/ Franciscus Langer (1599–1650), hzl.-münsterberg-oelsn. Rat zu Bernstadt, gehörte zu den Gönnern u. Förderern Tschernings. S. Anm.2. Vgl. *Cunrad: Silesia togata*, 164; Tschernings Gedicht in *Tscherning: Früling (1642)*, 353f., u. *Tscherning: Früling (1649)*, 392f.: „Auff das Glaß Der Vertreulig und Auffrichtigkeit An Hn. Frantz Langer Jhr Fürstl. Gn. Heinrich Wentzels/ Hertzogs zu Münsterberg/ zur Oelß und Bernstadt etc. weyland Procancellarium anietzo der Fürstlichen Wittiben RegierungsRath". Von Langer ist eine Trauerrede auf die erste Gemahlin Hz. Heinrich Wenzels v. Münsterberg u. Oels zu Bernstadt (s. Anm.1), Anna Magdalena, geb. Pgfn. bei Rhein-Veldenz (1602 – 20.8.1630), überliefert, die am 22.10.1630 gehalten wurde. In: Schatz-Kammer Unterschiedener Glückseelig-erfundener/ hertzdringender Trauer-Reden und Abdanckungen ... zusammen getragen ... und zum Druck befördet von Esaias Fellgiebeln/ Buchh. in Breßlau (Breslau 1665), [2. Teil] 24–30 (HAB: Xa 7). Die von Hz. Heinrich Wenzel hinterlassene Witwe war dessen Gemahlin in seiner 1636 geschlossenen 2. Ehe, Anna Ursula, geb.

v. Reibnitz, die 1648 starb. Die aus dieser Ehe hervorgegangenen Kinder, Anna Elisabeth (1637–1642) u. zwei Söhne, starben im Kindes- bzw. Säuglingsalter.

6 In seinem Brief an Apelles vom 27.2.1643 (s. Anm.3) hatte Tscherning auf den Vorwurf der „Nachlässigkeit" seinen Gönnern gegenüber u. a. angeführt, er habe neulich Paulus Neander (s. Anm.7) versprochen, seinen Gönnern u. Wohltätern ein „Aram gratitudinis" aufzusetzen, u. eine Liste seiner Wohltäter angefügt. Er beabsichtige, hinter seine Danksagung die Propemptica drucken zu lassen, die ihm von Freunden u. Gönnern zu seiner Abreise nach Rostock (zwecks Abschluß seiner Studien) gewidmet worden waren. Anscheinend ist es dazu nicht gekommen. Das deutsch verfaßte Alexandrinergedicht „Ex Ara grat.", das sich dem vorliegenden Brief anschließt, bezieht sich allein auf Apelles, dem überschwenglich gedankt wird. Es ist mit geringfügigen Änderungen im *Vortrab des Sommers Deutscher Gedichte* (1655, s. Anm.1), Bl. Fiij v – Fv v, aufgenommen worden.

7 Paulus Neander (Namslau 1592 – Breslau 18.10.1653), langjähriger u. in den Bildungs- u. Honoratiorenzirkeln der Stadt verankerter Breslauer Stadtvogt. Vgl. *Borcherdt: Tscherning*, S.282 Anm.54; *Cunrad: Silesia togata*, 198. In Tschernings *Semicenturia SCHEDIASMATUM* (1643; s. Anm.2) erscheint er als „J. C. Praetorem Reip. Vratisl." (Bl. B 5v f.). Die im vorliegenden Brief genannte Beilage ist uns unbekannt, könnte sich aber in der Breslauer Akte erhalten haben. Vgl. die Epicediensammlung: Benevola atq; Officiosa Pietas, Viro ... DN. PAULO NEANDRO J.C. In Inclutissimâ VRATISLAVIENSIUM Repub. Spectatissimo Advocatiæ Præfecti Munere ... A. D. XV. Calend. Novembr. Ann. Chr. M D CLIII. Anno autem ætatis LXII. currente, piè placideq̨; obito ... ab Amicis declarata (Breslau [1653]). STB Berlin — PK: 25 in: Xc 577; auch dig.: BU Wrocław (5 Ex.): 444269 (u.a.). Eine weitere Funeralschrift stammte von dem Rektor des Breslauer Elisabeth-Gymn.s, Elias Major d. Ä. (1588–1669). S. Richard Mende: Katalog der Leichenpredigten-Sammlung der Peter-Paul-Kirchenbibliothek und anderer Bibliotheken in Liegnitz. Marktschellenberg 1938, 342. Neander verschied ein Jahr, nachdem sein gleichnamiger einziger Sohn am 4.11. des Vorjahres als Student der Rechte in Helmstedt gestorben war. S. *LP Stolberg* 17061.

8 Wohl Verballhornung für „auf Brautschau gehen".

9 Angesichts des kargen Salärs wollte sich Tscherning reich verheiraten, wozu ihm Matthaeus Apelles v. Löwenstern u. andere geraten hatten, da selbst die Rostocker Universitätsdozentur keinen ausreichenden Lebensunterhalt versprach. Sein Gastgeber („hospes"), der Prof. beider Rechte Heinrich Rahne/ Rahnius (1601–1662), bei dem er in Rostock wohnte, wurde mit einem gezielten Vorschlag offenbar noch konkreter. Jedoch entschied sich Tscherning für die wohlhabende Katharina Marsilius aus Lübeck, Witwe eines Advokaten am dortigen Obergericht u. Tochter des lübischen Domherren Johann Marsilius. Die Hochzeit fand um Ostern 1645 in Lübeck statt, bevor der Hausstand in Rostock gegründet wurde. *Borcherdt: Tscherning*, 123, 125 ff. u. 130 ff.

10 *Borcherdt: Tscherning*, 128, zit. angeblich aus dem vorliegenden Brief: „Bey der Promotion muß jedweder zum Convivio eine Frau, als Mutter, u. dann eine Schwester mit sich bringen die Tische zu berathen. Wann des Hrn. Vaters Hertzliebste, als meine hochgeehrte Frau Mutter samt Jungfrau Rosinen hier wären, wolten wir die Rostockischen Frauen mit beyder ihren Tractamenten und Complimenten unsäglich beschämen." Andreas Tschernings Magisterpromotion erfolgte am 2.4.1644 mit fünf weiteren Kandidaten. Sie war Bedingung für den Antritt der Poesie-Professur an der U. Rostock (s. Anm.1). Im Anschluß wurde das übliche Festmahl gehalten, über dessen Usancen *Borcherdt: Tscherning*, S.295 f. Anm.13, interessante Quellen sprechen läßt. So sollten „vber jtzerwehnte zahl vnd Persohnen einem jglichen der Promovendorum, nach altem gebrauch, eine Ehrliebende matron zu füglicher außrichtung dieses convivij notturft zu erbitten, vnbenommen sein." (Aus der Rektoratsordnung von 1619, unverändert in derselben von 1625). Von einer „Schwester" erfahren wir nichts. Am 16.5. fand dann Tschernings feierliche Amtseinführung in sein Lehramt statt. „Jungfrau Rosinen" war Apelles' Tochter Rosina aus erster Ehe, die Tscherning wohl vergeblich zu heiraten gehofft hatte. Vgl. Anm. 27 u. *Borcherdt: Tscherning*, 127 ff.

11 *DW* VII, 2204: Die Pudel, „bair.-östr. [...] die lange tafel oder der kasten in einem kaufmannsgewölbe, worauf die waaren vorgelegt usw. werden", Ladentisch, Tresen. Hier wohl Kasten. S. auch Johann Andreas Schmeller: Bayerisches Wörterbuch. 2 Bde. (München 1872/77). Ndr. München 1996, I, 382, dito, im Österr. auch großer Kasten.

12 Johannes Mochinger (1603–1652), aus Danzig gebürtig u. nach seiner Studienreise dorthin zurückgekehrt, seit 1630 Professor für Beredsamkeit am Danziger Gymnasium, seit 1638 auch Pastor an St. Katharinen, befreundet mit Martin Opitz, zu dessen Tod er eine Trauerschrift herausgab. Vgl. *Opitz: BW*, 692. Tscherning hatte, als er 1642 von Thorn an die U. Rostock ging, eine Bücherkiste dort zurückgelassen, weitere Bücher lagerten bei Mochinger in Danzig u. der Rest, den er durch Matthias Machner (s. K I 1) verkaufen ließ, war in Breslau zurückgeblieben. Der Mangel an Büchern zwang Tscherning, den Beginn seiner Rostocker Vorlesungstätigkeit bis nach Pfingsten 1644 aufzuschieben. Vgl. *Borcherdt: Tscherning*, 138.

13 Wohl Wagenladung, übertragen: eine große Menge. Vgl. *DW* XIII, 458. *Fnhd. Wb.* IX.1, 29 f.: die „läde", Ladung, bestimmte Menge an geladenen Waren.

14 Der Breslauer Drucker Georg Baumann (1592–1650), bei dem bereits Tschernings *Lob der Buchdruckerey* (1640; s. Anm. 2), seine *Ode an ... Matheus Apelles von Löwenstern* (1641; s. Anm. 1) u. seine Gedichtsammlung *Deutscher Getichte Früling* (1642) gedruckt worden waren. Gedichte auf Baumann finden sich in *Tscherning: Früling (1642)*, 239–241, u. *Tscherning: Früling (1649)*, 155–158 u. 262–265. Vgl. zu Baumann auch K I 1; *Benzing: Buchdrucker*, 66; *Reske*, 130 f.; *LP Stolberg* 4322 u. die Trauerpredigt von Caspar Wohlfart: Leich-Sermon/ über den plötzlichen doch seeligen Hintritt Herrn Georg Baumanns/ Buchdruckers in Breßlau/ den 5. Jan. 1650. gehalten von M. CASPARE Wolfarth. In: Schatz-Kammer Unterschiedener Glückseelig-erfundener/ hertzdringender Trauer-Reden und Abdanckungen (s. Anm. 5), [1. Teil] 1084–1090. Vgl. ferner Klaus Garber: Das alte Breslau. Kulturgeschichte einer geistigen Metropole. Köln u. a. 2014, 188 ff. Tscherning beabsichtigte, eine eigene Poetik oder eine überarbeitete Neufassung von *Opitz: Buch von der Deutschen Poeterey (1624)* aufzusetzen. S. Anm. 23. Er gewann den Breslauer Drucker Georg Baumann für dieses Vorhaben, löste aber den Vertrag unter Rückzahlung der vorgeschossenen 20 Rtl., da ihm ein Lübecker Verleger, vielleicht Heinrich Schernwebel (s. 450726 K 6), ein besseres Angebot unterbreitet haben mochte. Vgl. ferner Tschernings Brief an Apelles vom 27.2.1643 (s. Anm. 3): Die „Teutsche Prosodia" stocke in Danzig. Der „Autor" (d. i. Johann Peter Titz, dessen Poetik *Zwey Bücher von der Kunst Hochdeutsche Verse und Lieder zu machen* 1642 in Danzig bei Andreas Hünefeld erschienen war) habe schon öfter bei ihm nachgefragt, wann denn wohl seine, Tschernings, Arbeit herauskomme. Vermutlich halte er die seine so lange zurück. So solle nun Tschernings Arbeit in Gottes Namen „heraußwischen", sobald er Nachricht von Augustus Buchner habe. Der ganze Plan zerschlug sich im unablässigen Hin u. Her. Erst 1658 erschien Tschernings Poetik. Vgl. Anm. 23 u. 450726 K 6; *Borcherdt: Tscherning*, 172 ff.

15 Die philosoph. Fakultät der U. Rostock hatte Tscherning erlaubt — der Lehrstuhl für Poesie war damals noch vakant — ein „Collegium Germanicum poeticum" abzuhalten, zu dem sich 18 Studenten einfanden u. das ihm ansehnliche 40 Reichstaler eintrug. *Borcherdt: Tscherning*, 124.

16 Ostern fiel 1644 auf den 21. April a. St. Andreas Tschernings Magisterpromotion erfolgte am 2.4.1644, s. Anm. 10.

17 Johann(es) Huswedel(ius) (1575–1651), aus Hamburg stammend, Besuch des Johanneums u. der U. Rostock, der U. Wittenberg u. der U. Leiden. 1605 Konrektor am Hamburger Johanneum, 1615 Konrektor des Gymnasiums in Rostock, zugleich Prof. f. praktische Philosophie u. seit 1623 des Griechischen an der U. Rostock, 1627/28 Intermezzo als Rektor des Johanneums in Hamburg, resignierte erneut nach Streitigkeiten mit der Geistlichkeit u. kehrte an die U. Rostock zurück. *ADB* XIII, 458 f.; *Borcherdt: Tscherning*, 295 Anm. 10; *DBA* I 583/ 302–311; *Zedler* XIII, 1295; Universität Rostock: Catalogus Professorum Rostochiensium, http://cpr.uni-rostock.de/metadata/cpr_person_00001377.

18 Ende September 1643 hatte sich der schwed. Generalfeldmarschall Lennart Torstensson mit der schwed. Hauptarmee aus dem nördlichen Mähren in Bewegung gesetzt, um eine streng geheimgehaltene militär. Operation durchzuführen: den kriegerischen Überfall auf Dänemark, den der schwed. Reichsrat im Mai 1643 beschlossen hatte. In einem beispiellosen Gewaltmarsch überschritten die schwed. Truppen am 12.12.1643 bei Trittau mit 16.000 Mann die Grenze zu Holstein. Ende des Jahres waren die Hzt.er Schleswig u. Holstein, mit Ausnahme der Festungen Glückstadt u. Krempe, in schwed. Hand; im Januar 1644 erfolgte der Einmarsch in Jütland, das gegen Ende des Monats unter schwed. Kontrolle war. Vgl. 440616 II, 440927 K 8; *Englund*, 330 ff. Um diesen Einfall u. Krieg gegen Dänemark zu legitimieren, „hat die designirte Königin in Schweden/ damit solches Zugs/ und gegen die Cron Dännemarck angefangenen Kriegs/ so wol außländische Nationes, als zuförderst deß Schwedischen Reichs Ständen und Unterthanen/ sattsame Nachricht hätten/ auß was unumbgänglichen Bewegnuß und Ursachen ein solcher Ernst diesmals gebraucht werden müssen/ beydes ein Eröffnungs/ und Berichtschreiben/ als auch Erinnerung an dero Reichsstände und Unterthanen abgehen lassen". *Londorp* V, 838. Das Dokument war auf Stockholm, den 16.1.1644 datiert. Text ebd., 838–840; *Theatrum europaeum* V: 1642–1647 (Frankfurt a. M. 1647), 222–224. Daraufhin erging die dän. Gegendarstellung: Auf diese „publicirte Königliche Schwedische Schrifft/ hat die Kön. M. in Dännemarck hingegen ein Manifest oder Summarischen Bericht edirt: Worab unter andern zu ersehen/ wie dero Fürstenthümer Schleßwig/ Holstein/ und Provintz Jütland/ von der Schwedischen Armee gantz unvermutlich/ ohn einige Noth/ Recht und Ursach/ ja wider auffgerichtete Pacta und Erbverträge überfallen/ und gantz feindlich tractirt worden". *Londorp* V, 840. Text des Manifests, d. d. Odense 30.1.1644, u. seiner Beilagen in ebd., 840–846, u. im *Theatrum europaeum* V: 1642–1647 (Frankfurt a. M. 1647), 224–233. Vgl. zum Schwedisch-Dänischen Krieg auch 440616 II u. 440927 K 8; ferner Klaus-Richard Böhme: Lennart Torstensson und Helmut Wrangel in Schleswig-Holstein und Jütland 1643–1645. In: Zeitschrift der Gesellschaft für Schleswig-Holsteinische Geschichte 90 (1965), 41–82; Leon Jespersen: Dänisch-schwedische Rivalität und das Scheitern der nordischen Zusammenarbeit. In: Der Westfälische Frieden von 1648 — Wende in der Geschichte des Ostseeraums. Für Prof. Dr. Dr. h. c. Herbert Ewe zum 80. Geb. Hamburg 2001, 47–64, hier S. 55; Ulrich Lange: Konflikte und Kriege im 17. Jahrhundert. In: Ders. (Hg.): Geschichte Schleswig-Holsteins. Von den Anfängen bis zur Gegenwart. Neumünster 2003, 225–266, hier S. 236–240; Paul Douglas Lockhart: Denmark in the Tirty Years' War, 1618–1648. King Christian IV. and the Decline of the Oldenburg State. Selinsgrove, London 1996, 259 ff.; Stefanie Robl Matzen: Der Schwedisch-Dänische Krieg 1643–1645. In: Handbuch zur nordelbischen Militärgeschichte. Heere und Kriege in Schleswig, Holstein, Lauenburg, Eutin und Lübeck, 1623–1863/67. Hg. Eva Susanne Fiebig u. Jan Schlürmann. Husum 2010, 309–326.

19 Zum Schreiben Kgn. Christinas v. Schweden s. Anm. 18

20 Johann Risten | Starker Schild | GOTTES | Wider die gifftige Mordpfeile falscher | und verleumderischer Zungen | Das ist/ | Kräfftiger Hertzentrost | vor alle fromme Christen/ | Welche | Unschüldiger weise von bößhafften | Lügnern geschmähet und von mißgün- | stigen Neidern verlästert | werden. | Hamburg/ | Bey und in Verlegung Heinrich Wernern/ | [Linie] | Jm Jahre Christi/ m. dc. xljv. SUB Göttingen: 8 P GERM II, 7370 (auch Dig.), ohne ein Lobgedicht Tschernings. Vgl. auch 440724. In seinem Brief an Apelles vom 27.2.1643 (s. Anm. 3) hatte sich Tscherning sehr ablehnend über Rist geäußert: „und ubersende hingegen E. G. [Euer Gestrengen] ein Satyricum deß Hn. Ristii das er auf etliche so ihm einen Spiritum Familiarem und Zauberey zugetrauet, im höchsten eyfer geschrieben, da ich doch auß seinen Schrifften nicht sehen kan, wo er sitzen musse. Den Mag. Wise seinen Antagonistam in der Rettung der Teutschen Sprache kenne ich numehr auch, als bey dem ich neulich in einem convivio gesessen bin. Ristius sucht treffliche freundschafft zu mir, schrieb neulich an einen freund, er hette mich mit einem Schreiben ersucht[,] weil ich aber darauff keine antwort gebe, besorgte er es müße intercipirt sein. Jch rieche den braten wol. Auf ein theil seiner himmlischen lieder habe ich neulich ein carmen geschrieben, ist auch schon mitgedruckt, darinnen ich einen guten stich auf ihn gesetzet. Es sind uns von Jhm bißhero etliche carmina zuhanden kommen, welche so garstig und unzüchtig gewesen, daß es für einen Priester schande ist." A. a. O., Bl. 8v; vgl. K I 3 u. 440724.

21 ANDREÆ TSCHERNINGII | SCHEDI- | ASMATUM | LIBER UNUS | [Zierleiste] | RostochI. | ANNO M. DC. XLIV. In: *Faber du Faur*, Nr. 264 (HAB: MF 1:59).

22 [Georg Philipp Harsdörffer]: AULÆA ROMANA, | CONTRA | PERISTROMATA TVRCICA | SIVE | DISSERTATIO EMBLEMATICA, | CONCORDIÆ CHRISTIANÆ | OMEN | REPRÆSENTANS. | I. ad Corinth. XIV. v. XXX. | EXVrget protInVs IehoVa, qVIa non est DeVs | DIssensIonIs, seD PaCIs. (1642). HAB: 34.6 Pol. (4); auch Dig. — Darin bezog Harsdörffer einen reichspatriotisch-irenischen Standpunkt gegenüber seiner Übersetzung der profranzösischen *Peristromata Turcica* (1641), überboten noch von der Richelieu-feindlichen *Gallia deplorata* (1641), vermutlich ebenfalls einer Übersetzung Harsdörffers, die die Schärfe des Originals aber herunterstufte u. den Text überaus stark kürzte. S. den ausführlichen Kommentar nebst Literaturangaben zu diesem Komplex in 411126 K 6 u. jüngst Max Reinhart: Georg Philipp Harsdörffer and the emblematic pamphlets of 1641: „Peristromata Turcica" and „Aulaea Romana". Ed., trans. and with an introd. and commentary by Max Reinhart. In: Emblematica 20 (2013), 277–375; dass. Part 2: Aulaea Romana. In: Emblematica 21 (2014), 233–357. Die beiden Folgen enthalten Editionen der latein. Texte der *Peristromata Turcica* u. *Aulaea Romana* mit engl. Übers., Anmerkungen u. Kommentar. Auch hier, wie in seinen früheren Arbeiten, schreibt Reinhart die *Aulaea Romana* Martin Milagius (FG 315) zu mit Harsdörffer als eine Art Schattenmann des Projekts. Harsdörffers Brief 411126 u. einige textuelle Auffälligkeiten (s. 411126 K 6) geben dieser Zuschreibung aber wenig Spielraum. Zu Harsdörffers Übersetzung der frankophilen, Richelieu feiernden „Comédie Héroique" *Japeta* (1643, aus dem Frz. des Jean Desmaret de Saint-Sorlin) vgl. 430920 K 8, 450818 K 12 u. Sylvie Taussig/ Claus Zittel: „La vérité si dangereuse de l'histoire réelle". Art de la traduction et jeu de cryptage dans la Comédie Héroique *Japeta* de Harsdörffer. In: Georg Philipp Harsdörffer: Japeta. Édition, traduction, introduction et notes, par Sylvie Taussig et Claus Zittel. Turnhout 2009, 7–67. Zur frankreichfreundlichen Haltung Harsdörffers vgl. auch den Briefwechsel mit Johann Michael Moscherosch (FG 436. 1645): 450818 u. 450901.

23 *Schottelius: Teutsche Vers- oder ReimKunst (1645).* In seinem Brief an Apelles vom 7.1.1646 ging Tscherning auf Schottelius' Poetik genauer ein: „Schottelius hat auch eine Prosodie oder Verß Kunst herauß gegeben, habe selbige noch nicht gelesen nur durchblättert und gesehen, daß er meine Verse sehr offt anzeucht, ist sonst hierinnen (in Praeceptis) ein durchübter Mann und in der Fruchtbringenden Gesellschafft genannt der Suchende, in welche Gesellschafft Caesius auch eingeflickt und heist der Färtige. Wo der Hr. Vater [d. i. Apelles] seine neulich herauß gegebene Lustinne [Zesens *Lustinne/ Das ist/ Gebundene Lust-Rede von Kraft und Würkung der Liebe* (Hamburg 1645), s. 450000A] nicht gesehen hat, So kauffe er sie doch wundershalben und urtheile hernach von seiner Ortographie. Wo wollen wir Deutschen doch endlich hin! Ristius berichtet mich, daß sich Caesius auch schreibe den blauen Ritter, woher, weiß ich noch nicht." Ehem. StB Breslau: Ms. Rhed. R 3109 (Kriegsverlust), Bl. 74, zit. n. *Borcherdt: Tscherning*, 310 Anm. 28 bzw. 331 Anm. 32. Zum Verlust des Originals s. Klaus Garber: Bücherhochburg des Ostens — Die alte Breslauer Bibliothekslandschaft, ihre Zerstörung im Zweiten Weltkrieg u. ihre Rekonstruktion im polnischen Wrocław. In: Kulturgeschichte Schlesiens in der Frühen Neuzeit. 2 Bde. Hg. Klaus Garber. Tübingen 2005, II, 539–654, hier S. 631. — Philipp v. Zesen (s. K 0) kam als der „Wohlsetzende" erst 1648 in die FG (FG 521). Den „Färtigen"/ „Fertigen" nannte er sich in der von ihm gegründeten Deutschgesinneten Genossenschaft. In 440724 fragte schon Johann Rist (FG 467. 1647), ob Zesen unter dem Namen des „Färtigen" in die FG aufgenommen worden sei u. wunderte sich darüber, daß Schottelius ihm dies nicht mitgeteilt habe. In der FG hieß Carl Milchling v. Schönstadt (FG 282) schon seit 1636 „Der Fertige". Zesen nannte sich auch „Ritterhold von Blauen", s. den Titel seines Romans: Ritterholds von Blauen. | Adriatische Rosemund | Last hägt Lust. | Amsteldam, | Bei Ludwich Elzevihren. 1645. In: *Zesen SW IV/ 2*. Das Pseudonym übersetzt seinen Vor- u. Nachnamen: griech. „phil-hippos", der Pferdefreund/ Reiter/ Ritter; lat. „caesius", blau (blaugrau). S. auch 460610 (K 11). Eine weitere interessante Stelle zu Schottelius entnehmen wir Tschernings Brief an Matthias Machner (s. in Beil. I K 1) vom 20.8.1642 (STB Berlin — PK: Dep. Breslau 17 [ehem. StB Breslau: R 402], 874; BU Wrocław Akc. 1949/ 713 [Abschrift Klose 175], 874. — Teilzitate in *Borcherdt: Tscherning*, 317 Anm. 5 u. 311 Anm. 31). In diesem Brief kommt Tscherning auf seinen Plan zu sprechen, eine eigene Poetik zu schreiben, die jedoch erst 1658 erschien: Unvorgreiffliches Bedencken über etliche mißbräuche in der deutschen Schreib- und Sprach-kunst/ insonderheit/ der edlen Poeterey (Lübeck: Volck 1658). Außerdem plante er 1642 u. noch 1645, *Opitz: Buch von der Deutschen Poeterey (1624)* zu kommentieren u. neu herauszugeben. Enoch Hanmann veröffentlichte jedoch 1645 ein eigenes Werk dieses Zuschnitts. Vgl. Anm. 14; *Borcherdt: Tscherning*, 173 f., 316 Anm. 5 u. 318 Anm. 5. In diesem Zusammenhang schrieb Tscherning: „Prosodiaca præcepta brevi submittam, quibus locupletandis non parum mihi inservire poterit Schottelii deutsche Sprachkunst, elegans libellus, cuius heri demum particeps factus sum." Gemeint ist *Schottelius: Sprachkunst (1641)*.

24 [Philipp v. Zesen:] PHIL. CÆSII | SCALA | HELICONIS | TEVTONICI: | seu | Compendiosa omnium Carmi- | num Germanicorum simplicium, tum | hactenus usitatorum, tum recens ad Græcorum & Latinorum formas effi- | ctorum. DELINEATIO. | cum brevibus Additamentis. | [Vignette] | AMSTELODAMI, | APUD IOANNEM IANSSONIVM. | ANNO M DC XLIII. HAB: 128.8 Poet. (4). Dig. in der SB München. Auf der Rückseite des Titelblatts steht eine lat. Inscriptio, die Rist als dreifache Schmähung aus der Feder Zesens empfand: „IOHANNI RISTIO. THEOLOGO. MATHEMATICO. PHILOLOGO. AD PERENNITATEM. POESEOS. TEUTONICÆ. ERUENDAM. FOVENDAM. CONSERVANDAM. NATO. MUSARUM. IMPRIMIS. DIVÆ. VRANIÆ. DELECTAMENTO. ET. HOLSATIÆ. ORNAMENTO. AMICO SUO. INTIMO. AC. SUMMO SCALAM HANC HELICONIS. SACRAM. ESSE. VULT. ET IUBET. M. PHILIPPVS CÆSIVS."

25 Philipp v. Zesen hatte schon zwei Fassungen dieses Werks herausgebracht: PHIL-

IPPI CÆSII Deütscher Helicon/ Oder Kurtze verfassung aller Arten der Deütschen jetzt üblichen Verse (Wittenberg: Johann Röhner 1640), mit einem Gedicht Augustus Buchners; PHILIPPI CÆSII Deütsches Helicons Erster und Ander Theil (Wittenberg: Johann Röhner 1641) = *Zesen SW* IX. Zwei weitere Ausgaben folgten 1649 u. 1656.

26 Verweis auf *Schottelius: Teutsche Vers- oder ReimKunst (1645)*, s. Anm. 23.

27 Rosina war Apelles' Tochter aus erster Ehe. Tscherning scheint ein Auge auf sie geworfen u. sich mit Heiratsabsichten getragen zu haben, die aber scheiterten. Als „Chrysis" taucht Rosina mehrfach in Tschernings Gedichten auf. Ihr Verlöbnis traf ihn hart, obwohl er sich schon mit anderen Heiratsplänen trug. S. Anm. 9. *Borcherdt: Tscherning*, 83 f. u. 129.

28 Es folgt ein langes dt. Dank- u. Lobgedicht auf Apelles: „Ex Ara grat." (Bl. 17v–18r), s. Anm. 6.

K I 1 In seinem langen Brief an den breslauischen städt. Sekretär, Kirchen- u. Waisenhausnotar u. Korrespondenzsammler Matthias Machner (1598–1662) bedauert Andreas Tscherning (Rostock) anfangs, Machners Brief ebensowenig wie ein Schreiben Augustus Buchners (FG 362) empfangen zu haben. Er trauert um Martin Opitz' (FG 200) verstorbenen Freund Michael Bartsch (1592 – 4.6.1642), ksl. gekrönten Poeten u. hzl. liegnitz. Rat. Vgl. *Opitz: BW*, 190704 *ep* u. ö. Tscherning erkennt in Buchner seinen eigenen „Patronus et defensor eximius" (vgl. auch 460610 K 10). Vom Breslauer Georg Baumann (s. K 14) als Drucker u. Verleger der geplanten neuen Ausgabe seiner Gedichtsammlung *Tscherning: Früling* (zuerst Breslau: Baumann 1642; Nachdrucke Rostock 1646 u. 1649) würde sich Tscherning gern lossagen. „Jngenii mei foetus omnes impensè flagitat bibliopola Lubecensis. Proverbia Arabica planè sedet mihi nativis suis litteris & notis illustrioribus heic loci vulgare, sumtibus ejusdem bibliopolæ. An Baumann*us* consentiat, perscribe." A. a. O., S. 862. Ähnlich in Tschernings Brief an Matthaeus Apelles v. Löwenstern (s. K 1) vom 27.2.1643 (s. K 3): „Gedachter Baumann wil inkünfftig die Arabischen Proverbia zu den deutschen nicht beydrucken laßen, Jch aber wolte dieselben hertzlich gern mit den typis nativis alhier, durch verlegung deß Lübeckischen Buchführers sampt den Teutschen, wie er zu beyden sich verstehet, zusammen mit Oeßers notis drucken laßen, wenn ich nur deß contracts von dem druckfilsel könte loß sein. J. G. wollen helffen einrathen." Tschernings lat.-dt. annotierte Übersetzung der arab. Sprüche des Kalifen ʿAlī ibn Abī Tālib (CENTURIA PROVERBIORUM ALIS Imperatoris Muslimici distichis), die Baumann zuerst 1641 separat veröffentlicht hatte, fand Aufnahme in den Ausgaben des *Früling (1642)*, *(1646)* u. *(1649)*. Ohne Vorwerk u. Kommentare wurden sie 1654 erneut separat veröffentlicht: PROVERBIA ARABICA Germanicè expressa ab Andrea Tscherningio Prof. Poëtices. Rostochi Ex Officinâ Typographicâ Iohannis Richelii, Senatus Typographi, Anno M DC LIV. HAB: Xb 42. Zu der von Baumann gedruckten u. verlegten Erstauflage des *Früling* s. Anm. 2. Nach einer Erwähnung von Machners Verwandtem Gottfried Scultetus, der den Briefen aus Danzig zufolge „ad nos" (Rostock oder doch Breslau?) reise, u. einer unbekannten „Conditio [...] Thorunensis" kommt der Schreiber ziemlich unvermittelt auf den wiedergegebenen Brief Johann Rists (FG 467. 1647) zu sprechen. Danach äußert sich Tscherning über unterschiedliche private Bekanntschaften u. Dinge, u. a. fragt er Machner, wo sich der Kupferstecher (David) Tscherning, sein Vetter, aufhalte. Dieser hatte in Straßburg bei Jacob van der Heyden gelernt, in der Schweiz u. in Krakau, Breslau u. Graz gewirkt, war 1644 wieder in Breslau u. 1658–1673 in Brieg tätig, wo er 1690 gestorben sein soll. Vgl. *Borcherdt: Tscherning*, 8 f.; *Thieme/ Becker* XXXIII, 461; *Opitz: BW*, 350606 *ep* K 8 u. 360923 *ep*. Über Opitz' Freund, den Dichter Christophorus Colerus (s. K 2), setzt Tscherning kryptisch hinzu: „h. Colerus ist in seinem Ehrengetichte, so er hn. Apelli geschrieben ein zu schläffriger Politicus, und gar zu treuer Historicus. Plura vellem coram." David Tschernig stach auch Colers Porträt. S. 450726 K 10 u. *Opitz: BW*, zu 391111 (1644), S. 1678. Zu Machner, Sekretär u. Inhaber weiterer Ämter beim Breslauer Stadtrat, vgl. *Cunrad: Silesia togata*, 180; *Borcherdt: Tscherning*, 276 Anm. 21 u. ö. Von der engen Verbindung Tschernings u. Machners zeugt Tschernings Trauerrede auf Machners Frau Maria: Abdanckung/ Bey Fr. Maria Jæckoschin/ Hr. Matthiæ Machners etc. Eheliebsten/ Gehalten den 12. Maji 1641. Der Rede schließt sich ein deutsches Trauergedicht an. In: Schatz-Kammer Unterschiedener Glückseelig-erfundener/ hertzdringender Trauer-Reden und Abdanckungen (s. K 5), 848–859.

2 David Tschernings Kupferstich des Titelblatts von Andreas Tschernings Gedichtsammlung *Früling (1642)*. Auf dem Blatt erscheinen unterhalb einer Szene, die die Vertreibung der Dichter durch Plato darstellt, u. oberhalb der Abbildung eines Gartens am Flusse Bober Apollo u. Opitz als Halter eines Schildes, auf dem der Buchtitel steht: „Andreas Tschernings Deutscher Getichte Früling. Breßlaw, Jn Verlegung Georg Baumans Buchdruckers. 1. 6 42." Abb. in VD17 3:612815V.

3 Johann: Risten | H. P. | Himlischer Lieder/ | Mit sehr anmuthigen/ von dem weit- | berühmten/ Herrn Johann: Schopen | gesetzten Melodeyen. | Das Fünffte und letzte | Zehn. | [Zierband] | Lüneburg/ | Bey Johann vnd Heinrich Sternen. | [Linie] | ANNO M. DC. XLII. HAB: 1067.2 Theol. Neuerdings liegen die *Himlischen Lieder* in allen fünf „Zehn" der Ausgabe 1641/42 in einer von Johann Anselm Steiger besorgten kritischen u. kommentierten Edition vor: Berlin: Akademie-Verlag 2012. Tschernings Widmungsgedicht auf Bl. B: „Auff Herrn Johann Ristens/ berühmten Poeten Himlische Lieder." (Neuedition S. 374–376).
In seinem Brief an Apelles vom 27.2.1643 (s. oben K 3) schrieb Tscherning, wie oben zitiert (K 20): „Auf ein theil seiner himmlischen lieder habe ich neulich ein **carmen** geschrieben, darinnen ich […] einen guten stich auf ihn gesetzet." Die angesprochene Spitze gegen Rist, die Ralf Georg Bogner (s. K 0), 189, entgangen ist, dürfte in der strikten Distanz zu suchen sein, die Tscherning zur „Venus Raserey" der antiken Dichtung u. ihrer modernen Nachahmer einnahm. Opitz habe zwar in seiner Jugend auch „von Liebeswerck" geschrieben, jedoch habe er später, zu reiferem Verstand gekommen, „die junge Hand Von Venus wieder ab"-gezogen. Gegen den „Tant" weltlicher „Eitelkeit" wird Rists geistliche Poesie dann ausdrücklich gelobt u. in Beziehung zu Tschernings großem Meister Opitz gesetzt:

> […] Mein Landesmann/ der die Bahn
> Zur deutschen Poesie am ersten auffgethan/
> Hat zwar von Liebeswerck im Anfang auch geschrieben/
> Jst aber nicht dabey ein steter Jüngling blieben. […]
> Wenn mich der Psalter hat/ so bin ich kaum mein eigen:
> Des grossen Davids Werck/ der Außzug aller Schrifft/
> Den noch kein Deutscher nicht/ was Kunst und Geist betrifft/
> So rühmlich umbgesetzt. Du führest gleiche Sinnen/
> **Du hochbegabter Rist**/ diß zeiget dein Beginnen.
> Wie billich schaffstu dir mit HimmelsLiedern Ruhm/
> Weil du auch Priester baust des Himmels Heiligthumb/
> Und er selbst in dir ruht. […]

Tschernings Widmungsgedicht auch in den späteren Ausgaben der *Himlischen Lieder*, Lüneburg 1652 (HAB: Lo 6456 [2]) bzw. 1658 (HAB: Xb 3296) sowie in Tschernings *Vortrab Des Sommers Deutscher Gedichte* (1655; STB Berlin — PK: an Yi 1503; auch dig.; s. K 2), Bl. [C vj]v – [C viij]r. Zum Verhältnis Rists zu Tscherning s. auch *Conermann: Rist*,

27 f., 33, 51, 54 u. 83. Den 5. Teil der *Himlischen Lieder* (1642) begleitet auch ein Ehrengedicht von Justus Georg Schottelius (FG 397), d. d. 20.10.1642, das Rist lobt: „Jhr sendet Seelentrost / jhr tapffrer Cimber/ jhr | **Setzt unsre Teutsche Sprach in rechte Himmels Zier.**" (Bl. [A viii]v; Neuedition S.371 f.). Auch Philipp v. Zesen (FG 521. 1648), „Aus Amsteldam M. Phil. Cæsius von Fürstenau", gehörte zu den Beiträgern (Bl. B v f., Neuedition S.377) des 5. Zehnts der *Himlischen Lieder* — so wie er auch das 2., 3. u. 4. „Zehn" mit seinen Freundschaftsgedichten bereichert hatte (Neuedition S.104 f., 190 f. u. 279). — Eine weitere „Spitze" gegen Rist ist zu erwähnen. In seinem *Poetischen Schauplatz* (Hamburg 1646; HAB: Lo 6467) hatte Rist ein Gedicht plaziert, das er zuvor an Tscherning gesandt haben muß: „Auf den Hochgelahrten Herren M. Andreas Tscherning/ der Poesi berühmten Professorn bey der weitbenahmten hohen Schuel zu Rostok/ seinen grossen Freund/ Als er in einer geraumen zeit kein schreiben von ihm empfangen" (S.296–299). Dort orakelte Rist über mögliche Gründe für das Ausbleiben von Tschernings Briefen: „Solten auch wol deine Sinnen | mit der neu-verdienten Ehr [*die im Mai 1644 angetretene Poesie-Professur an der U. Rostock*] | sich erheben etwas mehr | und zu wachsen fast beginnen?" Diese Frage wehrte Rist dann selbst durch die rhetorische Hintertür mit Hinweis auf Tschernings Redlichkeit usw. ab. Tschernings 2. Widmungsgedicht im *Poetischen Schauplatz* — „Antwohrt An eben denselben auff seine mier neulich übergeschikte Ode" (Bl. aiij v – a5 r) — nimmt genau darauf Bezug: Wankelmut, Ruhmsucht, „Ehrgeitz", „Hoffart" seien ihm, Tscherning, in der Tat fremd, und er ermahnt Rist:

> [...] Zeuch mich nicht als du gethan/
> Mehr so hoch vor Leuten ann/
> dann ich kan mich selber messen.
> Es gehört sich nicht Bekanten.
> Wo du meinen Raht verlachst/
> denn so sag Jch daß du machst
> Aus den Mücken Elefanten.

Dieses Gedicht muß im Mai 1645 geschrieben worden sein; es ist gekürzt auch in *Borcherdt: Tscherning*, 155, zitiert. Tscherning druckte es selbst in seinem *Vortrab Des Sommers Deutscher Gedichte* ab (Rostock 1655; s.o.), Bl. E ij r – E iij v. Dort folgt ein Achtzeiler auf Rists (Schwan-)Wappen, Bl. E iij v. Vgl. *Conermann: Rist*, 52 (Abb. mit Wappen u. Gedicht). Dieses hatte Rist mit dem Gedicht Tschernings bereits abgebildet u. veröffentlicht in seiner *Allerunterthänigste[n] Lobrede An die Allerdurchlaüchtigste [...] Römische Kaiserliche Maiestätt/ Herren Ferdinand den Dritten* (Hamburg [1647], Rückseite des Titelblatts), aus Anlaß der Verleihung des Adelsdiploms u. des Poetenlorbeers. HAB: 43.6 Pol. (7), auch dig. in der WDB. Das Gedicht im Wortlaut in *DA Köthen I. 8*: 470206 I. In der *Lobrede* auf S.103 f. noch ein lat. Glückwunschgedicht Tschernings. Vgl. dazu 460610 (K 5). Ein weiteres Gelegenheitsgedicht auf Rist ist Tschernings „Sonett Auff den Schauplatz der Freud- und Traurgedichte/ Des WollEhrwürdigen/ Ehrenfesten/ Großachtbahren und hochgelahrten Herrn Johann Risten/ ... Seines grossen Freundes" in Rists *Poetischem Schauplatz* (1646), Bl. aiij r f. Inc.: „UNd kanst du noch/ mein Rist/ bey diesem Wetter tichten?" Erneut abgedruckt in Tschernings *Vortrab Des Sommers*, Bl. H iiij rv. Tscherning bedankte sich wiederum für ein ihm von Rist geschicktes Gedicht. „Antwohrt An eben denselben/ auff seine mier neulich überschickte Ode." A.a.O., Bl. a iij v – a 5r, inc.: „SOlt' Jch deiner ie vergessen." Zu Tschernings Abwehr übertriebenen Lobs vgl. auch Bogner (s. K 0), 190. Auch an Harsdörffer ergeht im *Vortrab* eine Entschuldigung für langes Schweigen, Bl. J iiij v – J v v: „An den HochEdlen/ Gestrengen und Vesten Herrn. Georg Philipp Harstörffer/ Zu Nürnberg/ den Fruchtbringenden weitberühmten Spielenden. Geschrieben in Lübeck." Es heißt darin (Bl. J v r): „[...] Ein Mann/ der vor der Stirne | Den deutschen Glauben trägt/ der Klugheit und Gehirne | Als jhr/ in Schrifften pflantzt: der alle Welt gelehrt/ | Sich selbst unsterblich macht [...]". Auszug auch zit. in *Borcherdt: Tscherning*, 159.

4 Ein Gratulationsgedicht Rists findet sich weder in Tschernings *Früling*-Ausgaben von 1642, 1646 u. 1649 noch andernorts; Martin Opitz u. Augustus Buchner erscheinen hier unter den Beiträgern von Widmungsgedichten als einzige Fruchtbringer.

5 *Borcherdt: Tscherning*, 153 f., verfolgt den Brief- u. Gedichtwechsel mit Rist weiter genau. Von Tschernings Interesse an der FG zeugt erst wieder sein oben veröffentlichter Brief 440324.

440400

Justus Georg Schottelius an Herzog August d. J. von Braunschweig-Wolfenbüttel

Justus Georg Schottelius (FG 397) möchte ein deutsches Anagramm mit den angehängten Zeilen nicht zu dem folgenden Gedicht hinzufügen, weil dieses zu einer neuen Gattung gehöre und nach Sinn und Absicht eigenständig sei. Hz. August d.J. v. Braunschweig-Wolfenbüttel (FG 227) solle bestimmen, ob das Anagramm an dem bestimmten Ort entfernt oder vielleicht dem dreiständigen Emblem angehängt werde. — Schottelius hat dem folgenden Gratulationsgedicht eine kleine Erklärung angefügt, die z. Tl. die deutsche Sprache betrifft. Nach der vollständigen Lektüre werde der Herzog leicht entscheiden können, ob sie beibehalten oder ausgelassen werden soll. Sie sei in einem ungepflegten Stil ohne sachliche und sprachliche Eleganz geschrieben, zeuge jedoch von seiner, Schottelius', Hingabe an den Herzog.

Q   NSTA Wolfenbüttel: 2 Alt 3520, Bl. 6r; eigenh.

A   *Nicht vorhanden.*

Serenissime Princeps, Domine Clementissime,

Anagramma germanicum, cum adjunctis versiculis,[1] non videtur commodo loco et apto sensu inserendum carmini posteriori, quod novi est generis, et sensu intentioneq*ue* suâ constans. In Serenitatis V*est*ræ clementissimo arbitrio erit, aut illud destinato loco removere, aut Emblemati trimembrj subiungere, cui non nihil forsan concordare poterit. Cæterum̀ explicatiunculam quandam, quæ aliqua in parte, Teutiscam Linguam contiget, gratulatorio posteriori[2] subiunxi: Eâ totâ perlecta, facilè, an apponenda an omittenda, apparebit: Rudi stylo est conscripta, et si non V*est*ra Serenitas in ea verborum, rerumvé nitorem, / qvi deest / at tamen animum addictissimum devotumq*ue* inveniet
     servi obedientissimi fidelissimiq*ue*
      Just-Georgij Schottelij,

I

Schottelius' Gratulationssextine zum 10. April 1644

Q [Kupfertitel:] Iusti-Georgii | Schottelii | Teutsche Vers- oder | ReimKunst | darin | Vnsere Teutsche | MutterSprache, So viel | dero süßeste Po- | esis | betrifft, in eine | richtige Form der | Kunst zum ersten | mahle gebracht | worden. | getruckt zu | Wolfenbüttel | in verlegung | des Autoris | im jahre | M DC XL V, 294–297. HAB: 172.1 Poet. Mit einzelnen unbedeutenden orthographischen Abweichungen erneut abgedruckt in: *Schottelius: Teutsche Vers- oder ReimKunst (1656)*, 247–250; auch abgedruckt mit leichten orthographischen und etlichen anderen Abweichungen bei *Gosky: Arbustum (1650)*, 454v–456r [zit. als *A*]. — BN: Hueck: Gelegenheitsgedichte, Nr. 182.

Glükwünschende
Sechstine

So auf den hochfeyerlichen GeburtsTag Des Durchleuchtigen Hochgebornen Fürsten und Herrn/ Herrn Augusti/ Heertzogen zu Braunschweig[a] und Lüneburg &c. als S. F. Gn. denselben mit guter gewünschter LeibesGesundheit eben zum 66. mahle hinter sich gelegt/ zum ersten mahle aber in dero HaubtFestung Wolfenbüttel denselben[b] in gnaden begehen lassen/ S. F. Gn. unterthenig überreichet worden. Dabey aber zuwissen daß aus dem Nahmen [295]

Fürst Augustus Heertzog zu Braunschweig unnd Lüneburgk. etce.
Durch Letterwechsel sich finde

Gewünscht Glük wird Er nach Verzug groß bawen/ fest besitzen.[c]

(Aus diesem Letterwechsel[d] sind die Sechstinischen Wörter genommen/ nemlich Verzug/ Glük/ bawen/ besitzen/ fest/ gewünscht/ wie zusehē) in folgender

Sechstine

1.

1. Es wikkelt sich gar oft und spielet mit verzug
2. Eh sich zu eigē gibt ein hochgewünschtes[e] glük:
3. Man muß mit Meisterhand/ und mühsamlich aufbauen
4. Eh mā sein eigen Haus versichert kā besitzen:
5. Nur wā mā wol geharrt/ gebaut/ getrauet fest/
6. Dan folgt die Nießung recht gantz eigen und gewünscht.

2.

6. Die OsterSonne kom̄t und strahlet uns gewünscht/
1. Blikt lieblich-klar/ und scheinet viel schöner nach verzug/
2. Bringt den GeburtsTag her und drin ein hohes Glük/
3. Ein[f] langes hohes Glük/ so wil d*er* Him̄el bauē/ [296]
4. Und unser Fürst und Herr ruhmwürdigst soll besitzen/
5. Und die Stam̄reiche Seul Hochfürstlich gründen fest.

3.

5. Hochweiser Fürsten-Held/ jhr habt so wol und fest/
6. Jhr habt klugmutiglich^g/ jhr habt so hoch gewünscht/
1. Durch ungebahnten Weg/ durch eil uñ durch verzug
2. Gegründet uñ erbaut des Vaterlandes glük:
3. Wir wollen Land und Hertz mit treu und lieb ümbauen/
4. Und lassen d*as* mit lust uñ nach geboht besitzen.

4.

4. Gott schenkt zu diesem Jahr das Stam̃hauß zubesitzen
5. Uñ Stam̃et unsren Wunsch/ jhn pflantzend wol^h und fest/
6. Weil den GebuhrtsTag einsⁱ/ mit freudē/ so gewünscht/
1. Jn dieser Welpenstat/ nach langem hinverzug/
2. Des LandesVaters Sehn/ uñ in jhm unser Glük/
3. Gott wird jhn und sein Hauß/ und uns durch jhn aufbauen.

5.

3. Fried/ Treu/ Gerechtigkeit soll bey uns Wohnung bauen/
4. Die Tugend jhren Trohn/ so sehr verwüst/ besitzen [297]
5. Die wahre Gottesfurcht sich Stam̃en tief und fest/
6. Die from̃en jhren Stand auch^j finden wolgewünscht/
1. Die Bösheit nach verdienst gestraffet ohn verzug/
2. Auf^k Gott/ auf Fried/ auf Recht/ soll stehen unser Glük.

6.

2. Nun/ Gott schik Unglük weg! Send gnädig rechtes Glük!
3. Strek aus die Gnadenhand noch lange zeit zubauen
4. Das Jahr voll Glük uñ Lust/ das unser Fürst besitzen
5. Uñ stets geniessē soll: Gott/ bau die Festung fest
6. Und schleus den Himmel auf/ streu Segen aus gewünscht/
1. Send^l Gnadenblikke her zu uns/ Herr ohn verzug

Nachklang der Sechstine.^m

Nun es sey kein Verzug/ der Tag ist hie gewünscht;
Augustus stehetⁿ fest: Er soll die Ruh besitzen
Die wir mit wünschen baun/ und GOtt beschert mit Glük.

T I a *A* Bruns-Wieg — **b** *In A folgt:* mit Fröligkeit und Lust in Gnaden — **c** *A* Glük wird er nach Verzug groß bauen/ fest besitzen/ gewünscht. — **d** *A* Anagrammate — **e** *A* hochverhoftes — **f** *A* Ja langes hohes Glük — **g** *A* klugmächtiglich — **h** *A* tief und fest — **i** *A* wir — **j** *A* hie finden hoch gewünscht — **k** *A* Auf Gott/ auf Recht/ auf Fried — **l** *A* Send Gnadenblikke her/ wan wir flehn/ ohn Verzug — **m** *Zwischentitel fehlt in A.* — **n** *A* steht doch

K 1 Ein deutsches Anagramm mit nachfolgenden kurzgefaßten Zeilen, die einem neuartigen Gedicht vorhergehen, schrieb Justus Georg Schottelius (FG 397) zum 65. Geburtstag Hz. Augusts d. J. v. Braunschweig-Wolfenbüttel (FG 227). Aus den in *Schottelius: Teutsche Vers- oder ReimKunst (1645)* veröffentlichten neuartigen u. auch für einen fürstlichen Empfänger geeigneten Gedichten kommt das Anagramm mit Sextine auf S. 247–250 in Betracht, da andere innovative Gedichte wie die Pindarische Ode (s. 440100) schon in anderen Briefen des Dichters an den Herzog erwähnt werden. Die von Schottelius festgestellte Selbständigkeit des Gedichts nach Absicht u. Bedeutung könnte darauf verweisen, daß er im Nachhinein doch noch Namens- u. Anagrammzeilen mit der Sextine verzahnte. S. Beil. I. Anagramm oder Gedicht wären demnach im Anschluß an den vorliegenden Brief umgeschrieben worden. Das erwähnte dreiständige Emblem ist unbekannt. Derartige Embleme hatte Schottelius schon in *Knesebeck: Dreiständige Sinnbilder* (1643) beigetragen.

2 Der vorliegende undatierte Brief wurde zeitig vor Hz. Augusts 65. Geburtstag am 10.4.1644 geschrieben. Die Überschrift „Glükwünschende Sechstine" usw. bezeichnet diesen Geburtstag als den 66., weil man damals den eigentlichen Tag der Geburt (10.4.1579) mitzählte. Außerdem weist dieser Titel auch darauf hin, daß es der Geburtstag sei, den August „zum ersten mahle aber in dero HaubtFestung Wolfenbüttel" begangen habe. Der Herzog war zwar nach dem Abzug der ksl. Besatzung schon im September 1643 in der Stadt eingezogen, residierte darin aber erst vom 26.2.1644 an. S. 440100 K I 4.

K I *Schottelius: Teutsche Vers- oder ReimKunst (1645)*, 293 f.: „Von Der Sechstine. 1. DJE Sechstine nennet man/ wan die Verse nach jhren Reimmaassen und Abschnitten zwar völlig und untadelhaft gemacht/ aber gantz ungereimet gesetzet/ und zwar also geordnet sein/ daß der erste Reimschluß [Strophe, d. Hg.] in sechs Zeilen oder Versen bestehe/ welche sich aber nicht reimen/ sonderen das letzte Wort in dem letzten Verse/ muß in dem folgenden Reimschlusse das erste bleiben/ und das letzte Wort der ersten Versen in dem ersten Reimschlusse/ muß in des anderen Reimschlusses anderem Verse das letzte werden/ und also ördentlich jmmerfort: Dan allemahl muß das letzte Wort in jedem Reimschlusse/ in dem ersten Verse des folgenden Reimschlusses sich finden/ bis die sechs Wörter/ so zur Sechstine gebrauchet werden/ durch abgewechselte Sechs Reimschlüsse jhren umlauff vollendet haben. Der Siebende Reimschluß/ als ein Nachklang/ wird halbiert/ weil in jedem Verse zwey Sechstinische Wörter ördentlich gesetzet werden. H. Opitz hat ein Exempel in der Hercinia/ wie auch Herr Cæsius."

440426

Georg Philipp Harsdörffer an die Fruchtbringende Gesellschaft

Antwort auf 431007. Beantwortet durch 450124. — Georg Philipp Harsdörffer (FG 368. Der Spielende) übersendet der FG den vierten Teil seiner *Gesprächspiele* (1644). Er teilt sein Vorhaben mit, weitere Teile folgen zu lassen, wofür bereits ein Anfang bei dem dritten Hundert der Gesprächspiele gemacht sei. Auch beabsichtige er alle Wissenschaften in Form von Freudenspielen darzustellen. Für die beiden ersten (über die „Vernunftkunst"/ Logik und die „Wolredkunst"/ Rhetorik) legt er kurze Entwürfe bei. Da es aber noch an einer allgemeinverbindlichen und wissenschaftlich begründeten Orthographie mangele, die Veröffentlichung der angekündigten Rechtschreibungslehre wie auch (der neuen Ausgabe) des Gesellschaftsbuches (*GB 1641/44* bzw. *1646*) noch auf sich warten lasse, sei er vorerst bei seiner Schreibweise geblieben. — Der Mgf. Virgilio Malvezzi habe vor 5 oder 6 Jahren Bologna verlassen und sich in span. Dienste begeben. In der Zwischenzeit habe er aufgrund seiner politisch-diplomatischen Inanspruchnahme (keine weiteren Biographien der römischen Könige, sondern) nur zwei Traktate veröffentlicht: *Il Rittrato Del Privato Politico Christiano* (1636) und *Svccessi Principali della Monarchia Di Spagna nell'anno M. DC. XXXIX.* (1639). Jetzt werde dieser in den (span.) Niederlanden erwartet. Harsdörffer berichtet, einen guten Freund dort gebeten zu haben, Erkundigungen über Malvezzis Schriften einzuholen.

Q HM Köthen: V S 545, Bl. 300r–301v [A: 301v], 300v u. 301r leer; eigenh.; rotes Lacksiegel mit Bandresten. Beigelegt ist das jeweilige Figurentableau zu zwei Freudenspielen (s. Beilage I). — *D: KE*, 329f. — *BN: Bürger*, 674 Nr. 29.

A *Der Hochlöblichen Fruchtbringenden Geselschaft zu gnädigen Handen* Zu Leipzig bey H. Gottfried Stahlen[1] abzugeben. Cöthen.
Eigenh. Empfangsvermerk F. Ludwigs: Eingeben 19. des Jenners 1645.
Portoangabe mit Tinte: XII groschen

Der hochlöblichen Fruchtbringenden Geselschaft, wird, hier mit kommend, in unterthänigkeit übergeben der vierte Theil von des Spielenden Gesprächspielen,[2] als die heurige[3] Frucht seiner geringen Handarbeit. Er ist gewillet dieses Spielgewächs ferners fortzupflantzen [a]lle[a] Wissenschaften in unt[ersc]hiedlichen[b] Freudenspielen [v]orzustellen[b] (wie von d*en* [b]eiden[b] ersten ein kurtzer [e]ntwurf[b] beygelegend[c] zu [Ver]stehen[b] geben wird)[4], und nechst verleihung Göttlicher gnade, Gesundheit und des Lebens, solches nach und nach höher anzuführen; massen bereit zu ersetzung des dritten hunderts ein anfang gemachet worden.[5] Weilen er aber wegen kunstgründiger Rechtschreibung noch in vielen stücken anstehet,[6] und derselben endliche Richtigkeit, wie auch des Geselschaftbuches, vertröster massen, erwartet: Hat er in zwischen sich nicht unterfangen wollen, einer unbekanten Mundarte nachzuahmen, oder selbe mit der seinen zu vermischen.

Der Marggraf **Virgilio Malvezzi** hat sich bereit vor fünf, oder sechs Jahren, von **Bolognia** hienweg, und in Spanische Dienste begeben; mittlerzeit aber nicht mehr geschrieben, als **il Politico Privato**, und **lo Successo della Monarchia di Spagna**,[7] weil er beharrlich mit schweren Gesandschaften und hohen angelegenheiten bemühet seyn müssen. Wolbesagter Marggraf wird ietzund wiederum in Niederland erwartet, dar ich bereit einen guhten freund ersucht, weg*en* seiner Schriften mehreren bericht einzuzihen. Hiermit befihlet die hochlöbliche Fruchtbringende Gesellschaft zu des Hochsten obschutze, und sich zu dero beharrliche Gnad*en*

[G]eben[b] Nürnberg d*en* 26t*en* Ostermonats, im Jahre 1644.[8]

Der Spielende.

I

Georg Philipp Harsdörffers Entwurf der Figurentableaus zu zwei Freudenspielen über die „Vernunftkunst" und die „Wolredkunst"

Q HM Köthen: V S 545, Bl. 304rv; eigenh.; auf Bl. 304v eine Verbesserung von F. Ludwigs H.; der 440426 beigelegte Zettel ist, mit Ausnahme der Überschrift, zweispaltig beschrieben. — D: KE, 330–332.

LOGICA
oder
Die Vernunftkunst in einem Freudenspiele vorgestellet, durch folgende
Personen.

Redrich (Discursus) der König.
Wahrmund (Demonstratio) sein Sohn.
Denkraht (Topicus) der andere Sohn.
Trügewicht oder *Trüglach* (Fallacia) des Redrichs Bastart.
Alart quasi *Aalart* (Ambiguitas) und
Umbricht (Jgnoratio Elenchi) Fallaciæ Diener.
Sinnewalt (Intellectus) Seelewigs (Animæ) junger Printz.
Finnigund (Jnventio) des Printzen Hofmeisterin und Topici Bulschaft.
Rechthold (Judicium) des Printzen Hofmeister.
Wisstraut (Scientia) Wahrmundes Vertraute.
Wahngart (Opinio) Topici Bulschaft
Wesemar (Definitio)
Widermann (Opositio)
Sagolf (Propositio) } *Reichsstände.*
Trennheim (Divisio)
Gegling (Contradictio)
Federwitz (Descriptio)
Bleichhelm (Æqui[po]llentia)
Schlimram (Confusio) } Jhre Diener.
Sonderwig (Distinctio)ᵃ
Schiedlob (Analysis) der Artzt.
Schlüsshart (Conclusio) Kerkermeister.
*Bringbold*ᵇ (Reductio) sein Diener

Der Schauplatz (Theatrum) ist Freyredreich (παρρησία) in welchem folgende Hertzogthum:

Stoffland.		Substantiæ.
Land zur Maaß	} Prædicam. {	Quantitatis.
Wieland.		Qualitatis.
Sipland.		Relationis.

Anmerkung.

Jn diesem Freudenspiele müssen die Namen, wegen besseren Verstandes, lateinisch behalten werden: Die Deutschen aber so[c] beyzusetzen sind theils bekant, u*nd* theils nach des[d] Goldasts Register, Tom. 2. Alem*m*anic. Rer.[1] verdoppelt[2]; wie Friedrich, Sigmund, Silberraht, Böswicht, Aslach, Folart, Gotabrecht, Sebald, Hildigund, Frechhold, Gertraut, Hildegart, Ottomar, Hermann, Adalwolf, Artwig, Eheling, Reginwitz, Friedhelm, Alfram, Filelob, Eberhart, Adalbold, Udelheim, u. d. g.

Auf verbesserung.
N. S.
Der Vorredner ist Prometheus, oder Hermes nach gutbefind*en*.

[304v]

Rhetorica.[3]
Die wolredkunst in einem Freudenspiele ausgebildet, durch folgende *Personen.*

Der Vorredner ist Terminus.
INVENTJO die Königin.

Genus { Deliberativum. ihre Tochter.
         Demonstrativum } Jhre[e] Söhne.
         Judiciale. }

Elocutio Der Cantzler.
Dispositio Der Marschalk.
Actio Der Hofmeister.
Tropi[,][f] Metaphora, Metonymia, Sy[n]echdoche[g], Antomasia Zügeinerin, des Cantzlers entführte Töchter.
Figuræ dictionis Hofjungfrauen.
Figuræ sententiarum die Hofjunkeren.
Prosopopœia Ein Mahler.
Hypotyposis sein jung.
Exclamatio Ein Musicus.
Jnterrogatio. sein Diener.

Exordium.
Propositio.
Narratio. } Edelknaben.
Confutatio.
Confirma*t*io.
Epilogus.

Hyperbole Ein Markschrey oder Zahnbrech*er*. Chymi*cu*s.
Frequentatio sein Diener
Correctio. Momus.[4]

Dactylus.
Jambus. } Zech- oder Bierbrüder.
Trochæus. } Spielleute.[h]
Spondæus.
Jronia } Schergen
Extenua*tio*.
Amplificatio der Wirth beym Sprichwörten [sic]
Ellipsis ein armer[i] Fischer.
Pleonasmus ein Reicher Edelmann.
Theatrum ist Philologia.

Domicilia Theatri sunt Loci Jnventionum: Historia, Apologi, Fabulæ, Adagia, Hieroglyphica, Emblematæ, Sententiæ, Leges
                    Ænigmata *etc.*
                    N. S.

Die Hochlöbliche Fruchtbringende Geselschaft geruhe ihr hochvernünftiges Bedenken geselschaftmessig hierüber zu ertheilen: Des Spielenden absehen ist seinen Namen auf so manche art zu bewähren.

T a *Textverlust im Falz, Konjektur in eckigen Klammern nach KE. Bis geben wird am Rand ergänzt.* — **b** *Textverlust im Falz, Konjektur in eckigen Klammern nach KE.* — **c** *Gebessert aus* beygeligend

T I a *Am Ende der Seite ergänzt, durch Asterisk (*) eingefügt.* — **b** *Gebessert aus* Bringold — **c** so beyzusetzen *eingefügt.* — **d** *Gebessert aus* de<nen alten> — **e** *Folgt* <Töchter> — **f** *Folgt* <sind> — **g** *Wohl Verschreibung:* Syechdoche — **h** *Eingefügter Verbesserungsvorschlag von F. Ludwigs Hand.* — **i** *Folgt* <Schäfer>

K Der Briefverkehr zwischen Georg Philipp Harsdörffer (FG 368. Der Spielende) u. F. Ludwig/ der FG war auch in der Vergangenheit teilw. sehr stockend verlaufen, was nicht zuletzt seine Aufnahme in die FG verdunkelte. Vgl. 411200 K 0, auch 411126 u. den dortigen Empfangsvermerk. Die nach dem Empfangsvermerk F. Ludwigs — der durch das Antwortschreiben 450124 bestätigt wird — lange Beförderungsdauer des vorliegenden Briefes u. somit die späte Beantwortung erscheinen allerdings ungewöhnlich.
    1 Gottfried Stahl (1600–1670), Leipziger Bürger u. Handelsmann mit langjährigen Nürnberger Verbindungen u. lt. der Anschrift in 430624 „Fürstl. Anhaltischer Factor" in Leipzig. Stahl stammte aus dem unterfränk. Rüdenhausen u. wuchs nach dem Tod des Vaters (1611) in Nürnberg u. Leipzig auf, wo er sich ab 1621 dauerhaft niederließ. Anfangs bei dem Bürger u. Tuchhändler Johann Beer in Diensten, eröffnete Stahl nach der 1631 erfolgten Eheschließung mit Martha Finsinger (†1646), verw. Schamberger, mit seinem Schwiegervater Zacharias Finsinger eine Handelskompanie. Seit 1648 war Stahl in zweiter Ehe mit Rosina, Tochter des Leipziger Bürgers u. Handelsmanns Sebastian Otten verheiratet. S. *LP Stolberg,* Nr. 21320; *LP Roth,* R 1874. — Sein gleichnamiger Sohn (1640–1700) kommt hier nicht in Frage. Über Gottfried Stahl d. Ä. liefen nicht nur der Briefverkehr zwischen Harsdörffer u. F. Ludwig, sondern auch der Austausch von Informationen u.

verschiedene finanzielle u. sonstige Transaktionen. Vgl. 430920 K 1 u. im vorliegenden Band 440824, 450400, 450817 A, 451101, 451217, 460120 K 4, 460406, 460620, 460726 u. 460916.

2 *Harsdörffer: Frauenzimmer-Gesprächspiele* IV (1644; Ndr. 1968). Seine eigene „Erinnerung" an den Leser ist nicht datiert. Hingegen trägt eine Gruppe von Widmungsgedichten (vgl. 440204 K I 0), darunter das erste („N. I") von Diederich v. dem Werder (FG 31) „Beglorwürdigung der Gesprächspiele", Erstellungsdaten zwischen dem 10.8.1643 u. dem 6.2.1644. Das undatierte Gedicht Werders hatte dieser F. Ludwig gegenüber erst in 440204 angekündigt u. ihm noch zur kritischen Durchsicht vorzulegen versprochen. Da ein Gegenbrief oder eine Stellungnahme F. Ludwigs dazu fehlt, kann nur vermutet werden, daß es frühestens Mitte Februar Harsdörffer zuging (das Gedicht im vorliegenden Band als 440204 Beil. I). Diese Gedichte erreichten Harsdörffer vielleicht zu spät, um neben einer ganzen Reihe anderer Widmungsgedichte (datiert zwischen dem 24.7. u. dem 22.8.1643) noch im (schon gesetzten/ gedruckten) Vorwerk des 4. Teils berücksichtigt werden zu können. Sie wurden am Ende der *Gesprächspiele* hinzugedruckt (S.433/ Ndr. S.477 – 446/ 490; vgl. auch 440616 I u. III), vor der „Zugabe/ bestehend in einer Rede von dem Worte SPIEL" (S.499/ Ndr. S.493 – 482/ 526) u. weiteren Anhängen. Da auch die Zugaben durchgehend paginiert sind, der vorliegende Brief aber anzuzeigen scheint, daß der 4. Teil der *Gesprächspiele* im April 1644 erschienen sein muß, wäre die Zeit von Zusendung u. Druck des Werder-Gedichtes denkbar knapp gewesen. Der Antwortbrief F. Ludwigs 450124 läßt tatsächlich Zweifel an einem Erscheinungstermin im April zu, weil er dort nicht ausdrücklich den Empfang eines Druckexemplars des 4. Teils der *Gesprächspiele* bestätigt, sondern den Erhalt von „zweyen stücken des vierdten theils seiner gesprechspiele" angibt, die mit dem Schreiben 440426 eingekommen seien. Das könnten zwei Druckexemplare gewesen sein, jedoch auch nur die dem vorliegenden Brief beiliegenden Figurentableaus zu Harsdörffers zwei Freudenspielen über die „Vernunftkunst" u. die „Wolredkunst" (s. Beil. I). Da Harsdörffer in 440824 aber die frühere Übersendung von vier Exemplaren der *Gesprächspiele*, vierter Teil, über den Leipziger Kaufmann Gottfried Stahl bestätigt u. nach dem Erhalt fragt, da F. Ludwig in 450124 den verspäteten Erhalt der Sendung 440426 mitteilt u. dabei auch zwei dieser Sendung beigelegene „verschloßene schreiben und beylagen" an Diederich v. dem Werder (FG 31) u. F. Christian II. v. Anhalt-Bernburg (FG 51) erwähnt, wäre F. Ludwigs Empfang zweier Druckexemplare sowie auch der Verbleib des 3. u. 4. Druckexemplars geklärt. Mit 450220 wird F. Ludwig dann ein Exemplar an Hz. Wilhelm IV. v. Sachsen-Weimar (FG 5) senden. Der vierte Teil der *Gesprächspiele* (1644) wurde im Katalog der Leipziger u. Frankfurter Buchmessen zu Ostern u. Michaelis 1644 in der Rubrik „Teutsche Historische/ Politische/ Geographische/ Poetische und Kunstbücher" angezeigt: „Der Gesprächspiele vierter Theil/ ib. [d.i. Nünberg: Wolfgang Endter] in 8 oblongo." CATALOGUS UNIVERSALIS, Hoc est: DESIGNATIO omnium Librorum, qvi Nundinis Vernalibus & Autumnalibus ... 1644 ... prodierunt (Leipzig [1644]), Bl. [E4]r. Vgl. zum 4. Teil der Gesprächspiele auch 440204 u. I, 440616 u. I u. III, 440715 K 5 u. 9, 440731 I, 440824, 441216 K I 0, 441223 K 23, 450124 u. I, 450220, 450317A, 450400, 450808 K 3, 460803 K 0 usw.

3 Mhd. *hiure*, das auf das ahd. *hiuru*, ein Kompositum aus *hiu jāru*, ‚in diesem Jahr', zurückgehe. *Stieler*, 836: „Heurig/ *adj.* hornus. Heuriger Wein/ vinum hornum. Heurige Früchte/ fruges hornae." Zuweilen auch jetzig, in der Jetztzeit. Heute nur noch im Süddt.-Österreichischen. *DW* IV.2, 1292; *Paul Wb.*, 471. Vgl. auch 450923C u. 460916 K 5.

4 Zu Harsdörffers beiden Freudenspielen „Die Vernunftkunst" (*Harsdörffer: Frauenzimmer-Gesprächspiele* V (1645; Ndr. 1969), S.85/ Ndr. S.200 – 280/ 397). u. „Die Redkunst" (ebd., S.326/ Ndr. S. 451 – 443/ 575) s. Beil. I.

5 *Harsdörffer: Frauenzimmer-Gesprächspiele* V (1645; Ndr. 1969) enthält die Gesprächspiele Nr. 201–225 nebst Zugaben.

6 Schon in 430419 hatte Harsdörffer den Umstand angesprochen, daß die „Wortschreibung […] noch derzeit nicht zu grundrichtichem Stande gelanget" sei, u. auch seine „Kurtze Entschuldigung" anläßlich der zahlreichen Korrekturen F. Ludwigs zu Harsdörffers Rechtschreibung im 3. Teil der *Frauenzimmer-Gesprächspiele* (1643, Ndr. 1968), die er seinem Brief 430920 beigelegt hatte, bediente sich dieses Arguments. Die entsprechenden Dokumente werden in den Materialienband *DA Köthen I. 9* aufgenommen. Sein Bedauern über die Uneinheitlichkeit der „Schreibarten" wird Harsdörffer auch in der Folgezeit bekunden. Vgl. z. B. 450817 Nachschrift. — Um die Fortsetzung der Gesellschaftsbücher (durch *GB 1641/44* bzw. *GB 1646*) hatte Harsdörffer schon in 430920 gebeten.

7 F. Ludwig trug sich vielleicht schon seit 1639 mit dem Gedanken einer Übersetzung der zwei römischen Königsviten des Virgilio Malvezzi marchese di Castel Guelfo (1595–1653): IL ROMULO/ DEL MARCHESE VIRGILIO/ MALVEZZI. [Kolophon:] IN BOLOGNA/ Presso Clemente Ferroni M.DC.XXIX./ Con licenza de' Superiori. — IL TARQUINIO SVPERBO/ DEL MARCHESE VIRGILIO MALVEZZI/ DEDICATO/ ALL'ILL.MO ET ECC.MO SIG./ D. GOMEZ SVAREZ DE FIGHERROA/ DVCA DI FERIA, GOVERNATORE, E CAPITAN/ GENERALE. DELLO STATO DI MILANO,/ SVO PRON COL.MO. [Kolophon:] In Bologna, presso Clemente Ferroni./ M.DC.XXXII./ Con licenza de' Superiori. Nachdem sich F. Ludwig im Sommer 1643 venezian. Ausgaben des italien. Originals beschaffen konnte u. die Übersetzung anfertigte (vgl. 430505 u. 430724), hielt er mit der Drucklegung noch inne, da Malvezzi weitere Königsviten angekündigt hatte. Ludwigs Bitte um Nachforschung nach solchen (431007) kam Harsdörffer nach, jedoch blieben seine Erkundigungen in Bologna u. Venedig (s. 431124) nach Ausweis des vorliegenden Briefes ergebnislos. So blieb es bei F. Ludwigs Übersetzung der beiden genannten, wiederholt gedruckten u. in verschiedene europ. Sprachen übersetzten polit.-histor. Biographien: Der **Romulus,** | und | **Tarquinius** der | Hoffertige. | Das ist: | Das Leben | Des Ersten/ | und | Letzten Königs der Römer. | Beschrieben | Von dem Jtalianischen | Herren Marggrafen **Virgilio** | **Malvezzi.** | und | Jns Deütsche übergesetzet | Auch | Auf gut befinden der Fruchtbringenden Gesellschaft/ mit | angehencketer erklerung etlicher Nahmen/ örter/ | und wörter auf dem Rande/ an den | tag gegeben. | Gedruckt zu Zerbst im Fürstentume | Anhalt. | [Linie] | Jm Jahre 1647. HAB (3 Expll.): 180.7 Quod. (2); QuN 199 (5) u. T 645.4° Helmst. (11), dig. Vgl. 390921 K 4; 430505 K 2, 431007 K 3 u. 431124 K 10; 440130 K 2, 440525 K II 9, 440826 K 3, 441226, 450326 K 4 u. 450900 K 9. In 441226 wird F. Ludwig Curt v. Einsiedel (FG 417. 1644) wegen dessen guter Italienischkenntnisse um kritische Durchsicht seiner Malvezzi-Übersetzungen bitten. — Der aus Bologna stammende Malvezzi war früh in span. Dienste getreten u. 1643 zum Rat des Kardinalinfanten Fernando d'Austria, Statthalter der Niederlande, ernannt worden. Zwischen seinem *Davide perseguitato* (1634) u. den *Considerationi con occasione d'alcuni luoghi delle vite d'Alcibiade et di Coriolano* (1648) waren tatsächlich nur die beiden von Harsdörffer genannten Schriften veröffentlicht worden: die politische Olivares-Biographie *Il Rittrato Del Privato Politico Christiano, Estratto dall'originale d'alcune attioni Del Conte Dvca di S. Lvcar/ Escritto alla Cattolica Maestà di Filippo IIII.* (Milano 1636; HAB: 557.2 Quod. [4]. Etliche weitere Ausgaben seit 1635) u. die Verherrlichung Kg. Philipps IV., *Svccessi Principali della Monarchia Di Spagna nell'anno M. DC. XXXIX.* (o. O. [1639]; TULB Jena. Weitere Ausgaben seit 1639). Vgl. 431124 K 10.

8 Im Jahre 1644 fiel Ostern (Ostersonntag) auf den 21. April (alten Stils).

K I Die beiden Freudenspiele erschienen im fünften Teil der *Frauenzimmer Gesprächspiele* (1645; Ndr. 1969) unter dem Titel „Die Vernunftkunst" (S. 85/ Ndr. 200 – 280/ 397) u. „Die Redkunst" (S. 326/ Ndr. 451 – 458/ 591). Personenlisten sind den Freudenspielen in den *Gesprächspielen* V vorangestellt: *Die Vernunftkunst*, 89–92 (hier ein Großteil des Personals mit Brustbildern in Zierinitialen) u. „Die Redekunst", 329 f. Die Namen des dramatischen Personals weisen einige Abweichungen zu den beiden handschriftlichen Tableaus auf, v. a. in der „Redkunst" wurde das Personal auch deutlich reduziert. Die „Vernunftkunst" basiert, wie Harsdörffer a. a. O., 85 selbst mitteilt, auf einem englischen Freudenspiel *The Sophister*, dessen Autor Harsdörffer unbekannt geblieben war u. das er „mit Hülff eines vertrauten Freundes" übersetzt hatte. Es handelte sich um das anonym erschienene Stück: The | Sophister. | A Comedy. | [Linie] | [Motti von Horaz und Martial] | [Linie] | [Zierstück] | London: | Printed by J. O. for Humphrey Mosley, and are to be sold at | his shop at the Signe of the Princes Armes | in Pauls Church-yard, 1639. Exemplare in der SUB Göttingen, der UB Braunschweig u. a. m., dig. University of Illinois (Urbana-Champaign). — Als Verfasser des Stückes gilt aufgrund eines Eintrages im Exemplar der Bodleian Library Richard Zouch(e) (1589–1661) aus einer Familie des höheren Adels in der Gft. Wiltshire, den eine juristische Karriere in verschiedene hohe u. höchste Lehr- u. Richterämter u. bis in den High Court of Admiralty geführt hatte. Zwischen 1621 u. 1624 war er Mitglied im House of Commons, zeitweilig auch Kanzler der Diözese Oxford; unter Cromwells Protektorat verlor er seine Richterämter, verhielt sich aber neutral u. konnte seine Lehrämter aufrechterhalten, bis er unter der Restoration rehabilitiert wurde, jedoch starb er schon am 1. März 1661. Seine Fachpublikationen brachten ihm den Ruf eines international bedeutenden frühen Vertreters des entstehenden modernen Völkerrechts ein. Sein wichtigstes Ziel waren die Erreichung tragfähiger Friedensregelungen. Eine poetische Jugendarbeit stellt seine Beschreibung Europas, Asiens u. Afrikas dar, *The Dove, or certain passages of Cosmography* (London 1613); als seine wichtigsten juristischen Werke gelten die *Elementa Jurisprudentiae, definitionibus, regulis et sententiis selectioribus Juris Civilis illustrata* (Oxord 1629 u. ö.) u. die *Juris et Judicii fecialis, sive Juris inter gentes, et quaestionum de eodem explicatio* (Oxford 1650 u. ö.). Es wäre sinnvoll, dem *Sophista* einen Seitenblick auf das Zouch attestierte (anonym erschienene) Büchlein logischer, rhetorischer u. ethischer Maximen zu gönnen, das *Eruditionis ingenuae specimen, scilicet Artium Logicae, Dialecticae et Rhetoricae, necnon moralis Philosophiae, M. T. Ciceronis definitionibus, praeceptis et sententiis illustratae* (Oxford 1657). — In der Komödie *The Sophister* wird das Königreich „Hermenia" von König „Discourse" regiert, dessen dritter Sohn „Fallacy" (Betrug, Täuschung) „of base birth" die Macht an sich reißen will. Er verabreicht „Discourse" einen Gifttrank, der diesen in Wahnsinn verfallen u. das Königreich in eine Krise stürzen läßt. „Fallacies" Handlanger, „Ambiguity", stößt wiederum „Intellect" unter dem tückischen Vorwand, ihn in eine prachtvolle Bibliothek zu führen, in den Kerker; „Intellects" Anhänger „Invention" u. „Iudicium" werden aus dem Königreich vertrieben. Es folgt eine Debatte unter den drei Söhnen „Discourses" — „Demonstration", „Topicus" u. „Fallacy" — um die Thronfolge, ohne daß eine Entscheidung getroffen werden kann. „Contradiction", der die Kandidatur „Fallacies" unterstützt, reizt „Topicus" u. „Demonstration" zum Zorn, bis sie sich gegenseitig in einem Duell schwer verletzen. Daraufhin erklärt sich „Fallacy" selbst zum Nachfolger des Königs u. läßt sich in „Sophime" (veraltete Form von ‚Sophist') umbenennen, um seine Machtergreifung legitimatorisch zu verschleiern. Doch dann werden seine Machenschaften entlarvt: „Distinction" entdeckt den Giftanschlag auf „Discourse", „Analysis" heilt „Discourse" von dem Wahnsinnsanfall. Es wird dringend nach „Fallacy" gefahndet, er ist aber schon geflohen. Anstatt des Königsmörders wird „Ambiguity" in Haft genommen. „Iudicium"

u. „Invention" haben den letzten Auftritt. Am Ende macht der Epilog klar, daß das Stück nicht die Logik an sich auf den Prüfstand stellt, sondern eine mit Fallstricken, Ehrgeiz, Blendung u. Betrug operierende Sophistik. Damit wird die humanistische Zeit- u. Wissenschaftskritik des Stückes deutlich: „Invention" u. „Iudicium" werden, wie etwa bei Juan Luis Vives, gegen das scholastische Trivium u. seine Dominanz des *verbum rationale* u. des Syllogismus aufgewertet. Nutzloses Wissen u. Pedanterie, Blauäugigkeit u. schematischer Doktrinalismus ersetzen bei den meisten Figuren wahres Weltwissen u. Urteilskraft. „Description" oder „Division" etwa verstricken sich im eigenen Netz starrer Formalismen u. scheitern an der Klärung der rechtmäßigen Thronfolge. — Vgl. *BBA I* 1213, 205–231; *III* 492, 417; *DNB* LXIII, 417–420; Dieter Janssen: Richard Zouch und die Entstehung des klassischen Völkerrechts. In: Macht und Moral — Politisches Denken im 17. und 18. Jahrhundert. Hg. Markus Kremer u. Hans-Richard Reuter. Stuttgart 2007, 216–237. — Über Zouchs satirisches Stück teilte Harsdörffer, den seine lange Bildungsreise 1627 auch nach England geführt hatte, a. a. O., 87/ Ndr. 202, mit: „Des Verfassers Namen ist nicht beygesetzet/ scheinet aber/ als ob viel kluge Geister zugleich darunter bemühet gewesen weren/ und ist gewiß dieses Freudenspiel/ in Engeland/ hoch und geheim gehalten/ massen es nur einmal von den Studenten zu Oxenfurt/ für dem König gespielet worden. Jch kan mit Wahrheit sagen/ daß ich viel hundert/ ja tausent Freudenspiele in allerley Sprachen gelesen/ dergleichen aber ist mir noch nie zu Handen kommen/ das so witzig erfunden/ und so spitzig alle Wort gesetzet; daß man wol sagen möchte/ der Verfasser habe sie mit einem Cirkel geschrieben/ dessen Knopf beyderseits Augen gehabt: Dieses bedeutet die kunstsinnige Erfindung; jenes die abgemessene Wort."
Harsdörffers Übersetzung „Die Vernunftkunst" wird in den Konversationsrahmen der *Frauenzimmer-Gesprächspiele* eingebettet, erlaubt sich Freiheiten in der Übersetzung (s. S. 93/ Ndr. 208), folgt aber dem (nicht unbedingt stringenten) Plot des engl. Originals. Noch bevor der Erzähler Reymund Discretin, „ein gereist und belesener Student" (Ndr. S. 112), mit dem Vortrag „seiner" Übersetzung beginnt, bittet er die Gesprächsrunde um Mithilfe. Die Aufgaben, die er der Reihe nach verteilt, kommen einer diskursiven Kommentierung gleich u. werden auch für das Stück über die *Redkunst* (s. hier Anm. 3) beibehalten: Nach jedem Aufzug gibt Julia von Freudenstein, „eine kluge Matron" (Ndr. S. 112), eine kurze inhaltliche Zusammenfassung des Gehörten, worauf Vespasian von Lustgau, „ein alter Hofmann" (ebd.), die vorkommenden schweren lateinischen Wörter übersetzt u. erklärt. Angelica von Keuschewitz, „eine Adeliche Jungfrau" (ebd.), soll den tieferen Sinn des jeweiligen Aufzugs entdecken u. Auffälliges wie seltene Wörter erwähnen, während Degenwert von Ruhmekk, „ein verständiger und gelehrter Soldat" (ebd.), für Verbesserungsvorschläge u. kritische Nachfragen zuständig ist. Zuletzt unterbreitet Cassandra Schönlebin, auch sie „eine Adeliche Jungfrau" (ebd.), ihre Ideen, wie das Stück konkret aufgeführt werden soll, d. h. zu Kostümen, Kulissen etc. In diesen Kommentierungen wird auch die ratichianische „Cöthische Verstandlehre" erwähnt, um den Begriff des „Elenchus" u. seiner Spielarten zu erklären (S. 227/ Ndr. 344). D. i. Kurtzer Begriff Der Verstandt-Lehr/ Zu der Lehrart (Köthen 1621), eine Übersetzung des *Compendium logicae* von Jacob Martini (Köthen 1621) durch Ludwig Lucius.
Der eigentlichen Erzählung vorgelagert ist eine Erläuterung des Wortes Sophist bzw. Sophista, in der Vespasian kurz die Herkunft des Wortes u. die bedenkliche Verschiebung seiner ursprünglich positiven zur negativen Bedeutung eines Verfechters leerer Scheinwahrheit umreißt (S. 88/ Ndr. 203). Sobald Mercurius seine Vorrede geendet hat, soll der Vorhang fallen, so das szenische Konzept, die bis dahin reglos postierten steinernen Bildnisse der Grundbegriffe der Logik sollen von ihren Podesten steigen u. als lebendige Personifikationen mit dem Stück beginnen: Im Land Freyredstatt (Παρρησία) herrscht

König Redrich (Discursus), der drei Söhne hat: Wahrmund (Demonstratio), Denkraht (Topicus) u. den unehelichen Sohn Trügewicht (Fallacia). Letzterer, wohl aufgewachsen am Hofe, aber im stetigen Schatten seiner nachteiligen Erzeugung, ersinnt im Groll gegen seinen Vater einen Plan, wie er als nicht erbberechtigt doch an die Krone gelangen kann. Er gibt dem König einen Gifttrunk, der ihn unsinnig macht u. Ungnade gegen seinen Sohn Trügewicht in höchste Gnade verkehrt, u. räumt mithilfe seiner immer geschmeidig zweideutigen Diener oder vielmehr Hofschranzen Alart (Ambiguitas) u. Umbricht (Ignoratio Elenchi) alle Gegner aus dem Weg. Es kommt zum Streit der Brüder um die Königskrone, den die Reichsstände bestehend aus den Herren Wesemar (Definitio), Widermann (Oppositio), Sonderwig (Divisio) u. Sagolf (Propositio) entscheiden sollen, dies aber vertagen. Daraufhin fallen die Brüder Wahrmund u. Denkraht über einander her u. schlagen sich, angestachelt durch Gegling (Contradictio), einem Handlanger Trügewichts, fast zu Tode. Trügewicht erklärt sich zum König u. will künftig mit dem Namen „großer Sophist" angeredet werden. Durch Zufälle kommen die Königstreuen an den Giftkrug, u. allmählich finden sich alle vom Hof Entfernten wieder ein, wodurch es gelingt, das Komplott Trügewichts aufzudecken, u. schließlich kann sogar Redrich von dem Arzt Schiedlob (Analysis) geheilt werden. Trügewicht flieht in die Verbannung, Redrich kann seinen Thron wieder einnehmen, dankt seinen Dienern für ihre Treue u. übergibt Alart, den hinterlistigen Diener seines unehelichen Sohnes, der Strafe. Zum Schluß steht ein Gedicht der Findigund (Inventio), gelesen von Rechthold (Judicium), das die Zuschauer zum Applaus auffordert u. die Schlußpointe liefert: „Es reisset der Sophist von diesem Schauplatz aus; | Ein jeder findet ihn/ vielleicht/ in seinem Haus." (S. 276/ Ndr. 393). Hofkritik u. Kritik am Mißbrauch der Logik verbinden sich in diesem Freudenspiel in seiner Funktion, „vermittelst der Belustigung/ die böse Gewohnheiten/ und derselben jederzeit unglükklichen Ausschlag/ lehrartig/ vorzustellen" (278f.). — 1647 publizierte Harsdörffer seine „Vernunftkunst" separat u. in lateinischer Sprache unter dem Titel *Sophista, sive Logica et Pseudo-Politica* (Norimbergae 1647), s. 450817 K II 6. Hierzu *Conermann: Harsdörffers Plan*. Die latein. Version verzichtet auf die zwischengeschalteten Gesprächspartien (Kommentierungen) der dt. Fassung. Vgl. zu Harsdörffers beiden Freudenspielen auch 450124, 450400 K 2, 450529 u. *DA Köthen I. 8:* 470401.

1 Melchior Goldast v. Haiminsfeld: Alamannicarvm Rervm Scriptores Aliqvot Veteres, ... Tomus alter in duas partes tributus. Cvm Annotationibvs Et Indice ... (Frankfurt am Main 1606), 122–133 (Index der alten deutschen Eigennamen). HAB: 215 Hist. 2° (2). Exemplar der SB München dig.

2 „Verdoppelung" ist bei Justus Georg Schottelius (FG 397) u. Harsdörffer, aber auch bei Christian Gueintz (FG 361) der dt. grammatische Terminus für die Zusammensetzung/ Komposition von Wörtern. S. im vorliegenden Band das „Glossar der sprachwissenschaftlichen Terminologie", s. v. „Verdoppelung(e)".

3 Die „Redkunst" (*Harsdörffer: Frauenzimmer-Gesprächspiele* V [1645; Ndr. 1969], S. 326/ Ndr. S. 451 – 443/ 575), wenngleich räumlich durch drei andere Gesprächspiele („Die Tugendsterne", „Der Liebe Stammbaum" u. „Das Schäfergedichte") von der „Vernunftkunst" (s. Anm. 0) getrennt, knüpft direkt an diese an: Reymund bekennt die Schwierigkeit von der Vernunft- zur Redkunst zu kommen u. verweist auf die *Teutsche Rhetorica oder Redekunst* (Coburg 1634, Ndr. Tübingen 1977) von Johann Matthäus Meyfart (1590–1642). Doch ist der Gesellschaft nicht mit Büchern gedient, „die man zu Hause lesen kan"; sie erwartet das Spiel (S. 326/ Ndr. 451). Bevor Reymund seine Erzählung beginnt, betont er, dass er sich jetzt keineswegs für einen Redner halte, „dann gantz eine andere Sache ist die Abtheilung/ Zu- und Angehör dieser Kunst wissen/ und ein Redner seyn. Jenes lernet man in den Schulen/ dieses in Regiments-Geschäfften. Der weiß/ wie

man reden sol/ ist darum kein Redner zu nennen" (331/ 456). Der Verweis auf die Regimentsgeschäfte dient gleichfalls als Bindeglied zum vorherigen Spiel, das – wie Reymund offen bekennt – „vielmehr politische Händel/ als die Vernunftkunst/ welche man in den Schulen lehret" (326/ 451), ab- u. ausbildet. Beiden Stücken geht es also um kurzweilige Kritik einer Praxis in ihren Verfehlungen, sie wollen keineswegs die theoretische Ausbildung von Logik u. Rhetorik dem Spott des Zuhörers preisgeben. Stattdessen folgt der Aufbau des Stücks bemerkenswerteweise dem rhetorischen Aufbau einer wirkungsvollen, regelgeleiteten Rede (Prologus, Exordium, Propositio u. Conclusio). Wie in der „Vernunftkunst" treten diese Elemente u. allerhand rhetorische Begriffe als Personen auf. Prinzessin Wortigund (Elocutio), Tochter der Königin Findegard (auch Findegund/ Inventio) von Wortdodland (Lehrland, Redinen) u. ihres Gemahls Denkraht [das war in der „Vernunftkunst" Topicus], gesteht auf einer Jagd dem Grafen Wahltemar (auch Wahlmar/ Genus Deliberativum) ihre Liebe u. lädt ihn, der ihre Liebe erwidert, des Nachts in ihre Gemächer zur näheren Unterredung. Unbemerkt wird Graf Kargkram (Genus Judiciale) Zeuge dieser Verabredung u. bringt die Königin dazu, Wahlmar über Nacht einzusperren, um statt seiner Wortigund aufzusuchen, sie zur Ehe zu bereden u. die Verlobung zu begehen. Am nächsten Tag reist er vom Hof ab u. hinterläßt einen verwirrten Wahlmar, der auf die vertraulichen Liebesbekundungen der Prinzessin mit Verständnislosigkeit reagiert: er sei nicht nachts bei ihr gewesen. Angesichts solcher vermeintlichen Treulosigkeit betrübt sich die Prinzessin so sehr, daß sie aberwitzig wird, indes auch Wahlmar den Hof verläßt. Jahre später kehrt er mit seiner Frau Sittraut (Actio) u. den zwei Söhnen Siegstab (Vox) u. Handnod (Gestus) zurück u. erst jetzt erfährt die Königin von ihrer Tochter, daß sich dieser angeblich mit ihr verlobt hatte. Durch Bitte um Rat in einer verklausulierten Treuebruchsaffäre bringt sie Wahlmar dazu, das Todesurteil über die Frau des anonymen Treuebrechers, also seine eigene Frau Sittraut zu sprechen. Der ausersehene Vollstrecker Graf Zeigraht (Genus Demonstrativum) zeigt jedoch Erbarmen u. schickt sie unter Vortäuschung der vollbrachten Hinrichtung verkleidet über das Meer, ihre Söhne zum Großvater nach Ubland (Übungsland). Wahlmar wird über den Verlust seiner Familie unsinnig, u. so verzögert sich die angeordnete Vermählung mit Wortigund. Als Sittraut in Seenot gerät, errettet sie Kargkram, der ihr sein einstiges Komplott entdeckt u. sie zurück ins Wortdodland bringt. Dort stehen zu der Zeit die inzwischen zu Jünglingen herangewachsenen Söhne Sittrauts u. Wahlmars kampfbereit mit Heerscharen gegen die vorgeblichen Mörder ihrer Mutter: Findigund u. Wortigund. Kargkram rückt selbst mit seinem Betrug heraus, doch weil er durch seine Offenbarung den Krieg abwenden konnte, darf er sich mit Wortigund vermählen. Auch Wahlmar u. Sittraut sind mit ihren Söhnen wiedervereint, u. so findet alles ein glückliches Ende. Der Epilogus verteidigt das Freudenspiel, „da man alles/ was man sonst aus den Bücheren mit Verdruß erhalten und lernen muß/ durch so würkliche Ausbildungen dem Gedächtniß mit Belusten einspielen kann." (S.438/ 570). Ein Nachspiel über die „Reimkunst" mit ihren drei Hauptversen Jambus, Trochäus u. Daktylus, verkörpert durch „Herhink", „Hinkher" u. „Springeschalk", ergänzt um die Auftretenden „Zierwalt" (Epitheta) u. „Vielbacht" (Synonyma) als deren Dienern, beschließt das Stück (443/ 575 – 458/ 591). Harsdörffer griff für seine „Redkunst" auf Lope de Vegas *La fuerza lastimosa* zurück. *Conermann: Lope de Vega*, 71 Anm. 15.

4 Momus, griech. mytholog. Figur, Gott der Tadelsucht u. des Spotts, auch Personifikation der Satire: „Er war zwar ein Gott, that aber nichts, als daß er nur der andern Götter, wie auch der Menschen Thun und Verrichtungen tadelte" u. an allem etwas auszusetzen fand. *Hederich*, 1660 f.

440429

Justus Georg Schottelius an Johann Valentin Andreae

Lange habe Justus Georg Schottelius (FG 397) vorgehabt, an Johann Valentin Andreae (FG 464. 1646) als ein ihm Unbekannter zu schreiben und eine, wenn auch ungleiche Beziehung aufzunehmen. Die öffentlichen Zufluchtsorte aller Gerechtigkeit und Ehre erblicken wir größtenteils abgestumpft und ohne Schmerzempfinden, da ja der gottlose Mars uns auch von allen hohen und ehrenvollen Gedanken ablenkt. Der Furor des Kriegs verbreitet sich täglich mehr und mehr. Die Neigung zum Fremden und damit alle Bosheit nehmen täglich zu, nachdem Frömmigkeit und die Liebe zum Frieden selbst in die Fremde getrieben wurden. Das vom Feuer rauchende Vaterland gerät sterbend immer tiefer ins Elend, unentrinnbar. Der durch eitle Namen verdorbene Glanz wahrer Wissenschaft und der Stern bewährter Gelehrsamkeit strahlen kaum noch in Deutschland. Die stolze Burg der Christenheit, durch so viele Jahrhunderte unbesiegt, wankt und droht einzustürzen. Die Laster haben schon gesiegt, die Barbarei ist eingedrungen und selbst der Türke, Gott bewahre, dräut mit dem Ende der Christenheit, während unser kranker Leib nur noch in seinem Stamm lebt und wächst. Aber wozu sage er dies Andreae?! Noch lebten Menschen, die ihr Christentum bewahrt und das Gemeinwesen im Sinne haben, die das Vaterland, den Frieden und die vaterländische Sprache lieben und inmitten des Kriegslärms sich für ein vollkommenes und kunstvolles deutsches Wörterbuch mit Rat und Tat einsetzen. Die Menge der Wörter und Inhalte mache diese Arbeit sehr groß und schwierig, erfordere viele Hände. Auch ergäben sich bei der Aufstellung der Grundsätze und bei der Konstruktion der Wurzeln, Gliederungen und Fachbegriffe viele Meinungsverschiedenheiten. Daher erbitte er von Andreae, diesem Muster der Gelehrsamkeit und Wissenschaft, sein Urteil, seine Zustimmung und seine Hilfe.

Q HAB: Cod. Guelf. 11.12 Aug. 2°; Bl.224rv [A: 224v]; eigenh.; Sig. — Unvollständig erhaltene Datierung v. Andreaes H. „[…] Aug. 44."

A Viro admodum Reverendo Excellentissimo, Dño Joh. Val. Andreæ SS. Theol. Doct. Duci Wurtenbergiæ Ecclesiasti Aulico et reverendi Eiusdem consistorij Consiliario Jntimo &c. Fautori et Mico meo pl*urimè* reverendo &c. Stutgard

Vir admodum Reverende Excellentissime,
Fautor et Amice pl*urimè* venerande.

Jam diu est cùm animo feci, quod re nunc præstare audeo: Verba destinabam et iis iam adsum; nimis fortasse impetui indulgens, (quia solito maius est, scripto ignoto adirj) qvi fœdus quoddam Societatis, quamvis inæquale coire percupit, ubi Ego quidem cultum, amorem et cupidos discendi sensus afferam, Tu verò et Favorem et docendj, monitionumq*ue* placita conferre ne dedigneris.

   Publica omnis ferè iusti et honesti exsilia adspicimus, et adspicimus maximam partem hebetes, et sine doloris sensu, ut quos Jmpius Mars ab omni alta et honsta cogitatione avertit. Spargitur indies magis et magis bellicus furor, amor alieni, et simul cum eo, omnis iniquitas increscit, omni Pietate et ipsius Pacis amore in orbem alienum acto: Fumante autem morienteq*ue* Patriâ miseriæ ineluctabili ut involutâ, sic magis se involvente.

Splendor veræ Virtutis (nam quot Vanitatem Nominibus ea est hodie corrupta) et solidæ eruditionis sidus aliquod ubinam, et quam rarissimum in fumanti hac Germaniâ emicat! Suprema hæc maiestatis Christianæ arx, tanta seculorum serie, et invicto suæ ipsius robore potentiæ[a] fulta, miserè nutat, vacillat, ruinam et rudera minatur! Vitia iam vicere, babaries ingruit, et ipse Turca, supplementum demum miseriarum, minitabundus se se armat (avertat Deus!) in exitium eius, quod forsan solidum vigens et vegetans in trunco n*ost*ro et ægro corpore restat. Sed, quid Tibj ego hæc? aut quid opus his verbis? An quod aliquis, qvi Christianum nondum exuit, et boni publici cupidine tenetur, sublevamen doloris arbitratur querelas liberas! Concedas, quæso. Aut, potius admittas, quod primo statim loco volui dicere, esse et futuros procul dubio plures, vivos Patriæ, Pacis et linguæ Patriæ amantes, communi consilio et auxilio, inter strepitus etiam et tempestates Bellonæ, promoturos structuram aliquam perfectam et artificialem linguæ n*ost*ræ matricis, Lexicon inquam Germanicum. Quandoquidem autem congeries rerum et tenorum laborum erit extensissimus et difficilis, nec tenius sine dubio aut pauciorum hominum; sicuti et in ponendis fundamentis et adstruendis radicum etc ordinibus, nominib*us* etc non una et eadem opinio, scriberem non nulla plura, et iudicium, consensum et auxilium tuum, qvi (loquor ex vero) nobis eminentissimæ Eruditionis et Virtutis imago in terris adhuc existis, expeterem, modò hæc talia molestiæ loco non ventura, scire possem.

Affectum (quo sum indignus) quem toties in literis mihi affers, cum omnj ubi quo possum, cultûs et observantiæ fœnore refero; mej veraci calamo consigno
    Tuæ Reverentiæ et Virtutjs cultorem ut observatissimum ita fidelissimum
    Justum Georgium Schottelius mp

xxix April. ex arce Guelphica Ao. 1644

T a *Eingefügt.* — **b** *Nach 3 gestrichenen Buchstaben.*

K Dies ist der erste Brief, den Justus Georg Schottelius (FG 397. Der Suchende) an den schwäbischen Theologen Johann Valentin Andreae (FG 464. 1646), den geistlichen Rat Hz. Augusts d. J. v. Braunschweig-Wolfenbüttel (FG 227) u. Berater des Herzogs bei dessen sprachlich innovativer *Evangelischer Kirchen-Harmonie* (s. 411214 u. ö.), zu schreiben wagte. Hz. August hatte schon 1642 Schottelius' Rechtfertigung wegen des Schicksalsbegriffs in einem der Gedichte des Suchenden an Andreae geschickt. Vgl. 421101. Vgl. auch Hz. Augusts Brief 430425 (K 12) mit einer Erwähnung von Schottelius. Nun erhoffte sich Schottelius durch Andreae offenbar bei seinem Vorhaben Unterstützung, ein umfassendes, grammatisch fundiertes deutsches Wörterbuch (in der Fruchtbringenden Gesellschaft) in Angriff zu nehmen. Eine Antwort Andreaes auf den Brief 440429 ist nicht bekannt, wahrscheinlich auch nicht erfolgt. Daher unternahm Schottelius zwei Jahre später einen erneuten Anlauf u. sandte einen neuen Brief (460414) an Andreae, nachdem der Herzog Andreae kurz zuvor ein kleines Schreiben seines Präzeptors seinem Brief an seinen Rat beigelegt hatte. S. 460317 I.

440504

Christian Gueintz an Fürst Ludwig

(Kriegsbedingte) Unsicherheit verhindert, daß Christian Gueintz (FG 361. Der Ordnende) seinen angekündigten Besuch bei F. Ludwig (Der Nährende) in Köthen antreten kann, ein Zusammentreffen, das zur Verständigung über die deutsche Rechtschreibung dienen sollte. Sobald sich die Reiseumstände sicherer gestalten, werde Gueintz dieses Vorhaben bereitwillig in die Tat umsetzen.

Q HM Köthen: V S 545, Bl. 179r–180v [A: 180v], 179v u. 180r leer; Schreiberh. mit eigenh. Unterschrift; Sig.; kein Empfangsvermerk. — *D: Nicht in KE und KL.*

A Dem Nährenden   Hall   Cöthen *etc.*

Die gegenwertige Troubeln vnnd unsicherheit verhindern daß dem *Nährenden* der verheißung vnd notturfft nach wegen vergleichung in der wortschreibung der *Ordenender* Sich nicht stellen vnd aufwartten kann,[1] wünschet aber nur sichere gelegenheit in beiden die Schuldigkeit zu erweisen vnd darzuthun daß unter den zeitlichen glücksstücken vor daß höchste achtet, dem *Nährenden* seine Trewe vnd Pflicht zubezeigen, verbleibet unterdeß, nebenst empfehlung Gottes obacht

Deß *Nährenden*
unterthaniger Ordenender *mp*.

Hall am 4 Meyens 1644.

K 1 In 440317 hatte Christian Gueintz (FG 361. Der Ordnende) ein baldiges Erscheinen bei F. Ludwig (Der Nährende) in Köthen vorgeschlagen, um strittige Fragen zu seinem Entwurf einer deutschen Rechtschreibung (s. 440127 K 1) ausführlicher u. gründlicher als im Schriftverkehr möglich zu erörtern u. zu klären. In 440809 wird sich Gueintz erneut u. mit der gleichen Begründung für die Reise-Verzögerung entschuldigen. Erst am 13. oder 14.5.1645 scheint es zur angesetzten Zusammenkunft in Köthen gekommen zu sein. Vgl. 450507 I u. 450508. — Die Jahre 1643, 1644 u. 1645 brachten, so der spätere Chronist Carl Renatus Hausen, zwar „keine besonderen Begebenheiten" des Krieges, die das Erzstift Magdeburg u. die Stadt Halle betroffen hätten (C. R. H.: Geschichte des Herzogthums Magdeburg, der Stadt Halle und des Saalkreises, Halle 1772, 92f.), jedoch waren Halle u. der Saalkreis im März bis Mai 1644 von Einquartierungen u. Unterhaltsforderungen des schwed. Korps unter Generalmajor Hans Christoph v. Königsmarck (FG 515. 1648) betroffen, dem im Frühjahr der militär. Oberbefehl im schwed. Kriegsestat in Meißen u. Thüringen übertragen worden war u. der sein Hauptquartier zeitweise in Halle nahm. Einquartierungen u. Unterhaltsforderungen wiederholten sich im September u. Dezember sowie von Januar bis März 1645; ständige Truppendurchzüge u. Proviantforderungen kamen hinzu. 1642 hatte F. Ludwig seinen Hofjunker Bernd Heinrich v. Warnstedt (FG 370) zum Legaten an die schwed. Generäle Lennart Torstensson u. Hans Christoph v. Königsmarck (FG 515. 1648) ernannt. In einem Brief vom 15.3.1644 aus Warmsdorf (heute OT von Güsten; damals eine Exklave F. Ludwigs im Teilft. Anhalt-Bernburg) berichtete Warnstedt, diesen Abend aus Halberstadt zurückgekehrt zu sein. Er habe vom

Generalmajor (d.i. Königsmarck, seit März 1640 kgl.-schwed. Generalmajor) die Auskunft erhalten, der für den nächsten oder übernächsten Tag angesetzte Marsch nach Aschersleben oder „Mörseburg" (Merseburg?) werde Köthen wohl nicht berühren. Für den Fall, Köthen beim Rückmarsch in Mitleidenschaft zu ziehen, verspreche Königsmarck größtmögliche Schonung. Königsmarck sei vor einigen Tagen in Halberstadt eingetroffen. Seine mitgeführten drei Reiterkompanien habe er in Wernigerode (2) u. Ballenstedt (1) einquartiert. Weitere Regimenter seien bereits über den Harz nach Osterode gezogen. Warnstedt fragt, ob er in Warmsdorf verharren oder nach Köthen zurückkehren solle. BJ Kraków (ehem. STB Berlin): Acc. ms. 1913. 21/27. — Im September 1644 bezog Generalleutnant Matthias Gallas mit der ksl. Hauptarmee zum Entsetzen des vergeblich intervenierenden F.en Christian II. v. Anhalt-Bernburg (FG 51) Stellung in u. vor Bernburg, um auf ksl. bzw. kursächs. Unterstützung für seine vom Feldzug nach Holstein (s. 440324 K 18) geschwächten Truppen zu warten. Die ihn verfolgende schwed. Hauptarmee unter Lennart Torstensson setzte mit überlegener Kavallerie u. Artillerie nach, so daß sich die beiden verfeindeten Hauptarmeen seit September verschanzt gegenüberlagen, sich unentwegt mit Kanonaden u. Scharmützeln zusetzten u. das umliegende Land schwer mitnahmen. Erst Mitte November wurde die sog. „Bernburger Blockade" aufgelöst. Vgl. 440927 K 1. — Eine verheerende Feuersbrunst äscherte im März 1645 große Teile Halles ein, nur mit Mühe konnte das Gymnasium gerettet werden. Der Konrektor desselben, Friedrich Cahlenus (1613–1663) setzte ein gedrucktes *Denck- und Danck-mal der grimmigen Feuersbrunst* auf, zu dem Gueintz eine Rede beisteuerte (o. O. 1645. NLB Hannover: T-A 994). Dies dürften jene „inwendige vnd außwendige troubeln" (440809) gewesen sein, mit denen Gueintz sein Ausbleiben in Köthen bis hin zum Mai 1645 entschuldigte. Aber auch die Drucklegung der *Deutschen Rechtschreibung* verzögerte sich, da sie „wegen kundbarer gefeh[r]ligkeit des in diesem lande in neuligkeit sich gesetzten Stules des Krieges noch nicht können gedrucket werden, welches aber vermutlich noch in diesem Jhare erfolgen s[ol]." (450124) Vgl. *Dreyhaupt* I, 438 f.; *KU* V.1, 306–351; *Rebitsch*, 281 ff.; *Theatrum europaeum*, Teil V: 1643–1647 (Frankfurt a. M. 1647), 557, 576, 581 f., 586, 598 u. 624; *Chemnitz* IV.4, 63 f., 67 f., 108–110 u. 111–114; Gottfried Olearius: I. N. J. HALYGRAPHIA Topo-Chronologica, Das ist: Ort- und Zeit-Beschreibung der Stadt Hall in Sachsen (Leipzig 1667. HAB: Gm 1846[2]), 424 ff.; Gustav Frd. Herzberg: Geschichte der Stadt Halle während des 16. und 17. Jahrhunderts (1513–1717). Halle a. S. 1891, 466 ff.; Jan Brademann: Gewalt, Not und Krisen — das frühneuzeitliche Halle und seine Bürger im Krieg. In: Geschichte der Stadt Halle. Bd. 1: Halle im Mittelalter und in der Frühen Neuzeit. Hg. Werner Freitag u. Andreas Ranft. Halle a. d. S. 2006, 314–332, hier 318, 321, 322 u. 324.

440525

Johann Michael Moscheroschs Briefgedicht in Johann Heinrich Schills *Der Teutschen Sprach Ehren-Krantz*

Johann Michael Moscherosch (FG 436. 1645) schickt Johann Heinrich Schill (Chorion) einen poetischen Lorbeerkranz für dessen Sprachbuch *Der Teutschen Sprach Ehren-Krantz* (1644).

Q [Johann Heinrich Schill]: Der | Teutschen Sprach | Ehren-Krantz. | Neben einem | Namenbuch. | Dariñen der bißhero getragene Bet- | telRock der Teutschen Sprach auß: vnd | hergegen sie mit jhren eygnen Kleidern | vnd Zierde angezogen | wird. | [Signet] | Straßburg/ | Jn Verlegung Johañ Philipp Mülben. | 1644. Bl. [):(7rv]. — HAB: 74.15 Gram. (2), Ko 184 u. 387.4 Quod. (2); *Faber du Faur* Nr. 441. — BN: *Bulling*, 33; *Neumark: Palmbaum*, 104.

WAnn ich deß Apollo Gunst
    Seiner stimme Sinnen-zwinger/
    Seine Sayten-feste Finger/
Seine Weißheit/ seine Kunst
    Was zuschreiben köndt erlangen/
    Wolt ich mich deß vnderfangen.
Einen Reyen wolt ich dir[a]/
    Chorion[1], entgegen bringen/
    Jn den Reyen dises singen:
Dir/ deß Teutschen Pindus zier/
    Der die Feder also führet/
    Diß vnd daß vnd mehr gebühret.
Einen Reyen/ dessen sich
    Clio solte seelig preisen/
    Vnd sich danckbar zuerweisen/
Wie man köndte loben dich/
    Vns mit dehn fünff Worten lehren:
    Chorion, dich soll man Ehren.
Einen Krantz wolt dir hernach
    Mit vnsterbligkeit zu binden
    Jch mich ernstlich vnderwinden:
Dir/ der du vns vnsre Sprach
    hast mit Teutscher zierde kleidet/
    Wälsche huddeley verleydet.
[):(7v] Einen Krantz/ Ein Loberkrantz
    Den sich Phœbus anzunehmen/
    Solt bey keiner Hochzeit schämen/
Dessen Arbeit/ Fleiß vnd Glantz
    Solt von Tugend-Edelsteinen
    Heller als Carfunckel scheinen.
Einen Krantz/ daß alle Welt
    Dich in solcher Ehr zu sehen
    Solt von Wunder bleiben stehen.
Einen Reyen so gestellt/
    Daß man Phœbus ohne nennen
    Vor dir schwerlich solte kennen.
Mein Freund/ warumb wiltu dann
    Daß dein Nahm verschwigen bleibe?
    Jch/ so schlecht als ich waß schreibe/

Laß es wissen jederman;
  Solst dann du verschwigen bleiben?
  Der so trefflich weiß zu schreiben.
Nun/ Jch will zwar schweigen still/
  Dann du hast mir so befohlen/
  Doch sag ich diß vnverholen:
Mann wird doch dich wer nur will/
  Vnd wer Chorion gewesen
  Mit deim Ruhm vnd Ehre lesen.
Chorion ist doch bekant!
  Schweige wen gelust zu schweigen/
  Schweigend will ich doch bezeugen/
Daß/ zu hülff dein Vatterland/
  Deine Feder vns mehr schutzet
  Als offt manches Kriegsheer nutzet.

  Seinem hochgeehrten Freund schreibts auß
  Bennfelden/ den 25. Mayen 1644.[1]
  Hanß-Michel Moscherosch.

I

Johann Matthias Schneubers Freundschaftsgedicht in Schills *Ehren-Krantz*

Q Johann Heinrich Schill: Der Teutschen Sprach Ehren-Krantz. A. a. O. (s. o., Q), Bl. [):(8rv].

Nochmals in: Johann Matthias Schneübers | Gedichte. | Gedruckt Zu Strasburg bey Joh: Philipp | Mülben. | M.dc.vl.jv, 355–357: „An den Chorion/ als derselbe der Deütschen sprach Ehrenkrantz ausgehen liesse" (HAB: 136.5 Poet. [2]). Mit leichten orthographischen und seltenen sonstigen Abwandlungen.

Nach dem Erstdruck in *Jones: Sprachverderber*, 376–378; nach dem zweiten Druck in: Deutscher Sprache Ehrenkranz. Dichterische Zeugnisse zum Werden und Wesen unserer Muttersprache gesammelt und erläutert von Paul Pietsch. Berlin 1915, 45–47 u. 603–605 (zur Rezeption des Lieds).

EDele Teutschen jhr habet empfangen
  Träffliche gaben und himmlischen Preiß
Meyster zu bleiben und herrlich zu prangen
  Uber die Völker/ auff mancherley weiß:
    Euch müsten gerahten
    Die mannliche Thaten
      Jn mächtigem Krieg
    Die Feinde zu schlagen
    Zu tödten und jagen

Daß alles im Lande sich frewet' im Sieg
Dapffere Tugend und Sitten zu üben
    Waret jhr rühmlich von alters gewohnt;
Redliches Leben/ und träuliches lieben
    Wurde vom Himmel so gnädig belohnt
        Mit Künsten und Sprachen
        Und heyligen Sachen
            Biß euwere Zier
        Die Ehre gewonnen/
        Daß unter der Sonnen
Sich seeliger niemand könt preisen/ als ihr.
Hätten sich euere Kinder gehalten
    Dankbarlich gegen dem Göttlichen schatz
Nimmermehr lägen sie solcher gestalten
    Schräklich-gefället auff blutigem platz.
        Weil aber die Sünden
        Die straffen anzünden
            So brännet das Fewr?
        Frantzösische sinnen
        Und wälsches beginnen
Die machen die alte beständigkeit theur. [):(8v]
Dannoch befinden sich wakere Geyster/
    Welche von ädelem teutschen geschlecht
Kommen/ und zeygen sie seien noch Meyster/
    Straffen die schanden/ und lehren was recht;
        Sie mahnen die Jugend
        Daß redliche Tugend
            Keynn fleken nicht hab'/
        Und ziehen der Sprache
        Mit billicher Rache
Den häßlich-gestükelten Bättelrok ab.
Solcherley Geyster seind höchlich zu preisen/
    (Deren du/ Chorion/[1] eyner auch bist)
Welche die Teutschheyt[2] der alten recht weisen
    Lauter/ und wo sie mit fremdem vermischt/
        Dasselbe fein scheyden.
        Und weil sie bekleyden
            Jhr' herrliche Sprach
        Mit kräntzen der Ehren
        Jhr' hoheyt zu mehren
So folget jhr wirdiges Lob gewiß nach.
Werden die Teutschen schon kräfftig getruket
    Tringen sie dannoch wie Palmen empor/[3]

Mitten im Feüer die Zunge sich schmuket/
   Thut es auch andern Sprachen weit vor.
      Und solte der Brande
      Verlöschen im Lande/
         So würde man sehn/
      Die Sprache verjünget
      Mit zieraht umringet
Auß eygener Aschen/ wie Fönix/ erstehn.

     J. M. S.[4]

II

Aus Schills *Ehren-Krantz*

Q Johann Heinrich Schill: Der Teutschen Sprach Ehren-Krantz. A. a. O. (s. o., Q), Bl.):(
ij r –):(iiij v (die Vorrede endet ohne Unterschrift), von uns veröffentlicht Bl.):(ij r –
):(iij r; S. 311 f., 312 f., 320–325 u. 342 f.
Ndr. in *Jones: Sprachverderber*, 356, 367 f., 369 f. u. 373 f.

           Vorrede.
    An den wolwollenden vnd günstigen Leser.
             […]

[):(ij v] Jch/ der gesehen/ wie eifferig vnd rühmlich sich etliche Jahr hero fürtreffliche vnd edele Geister bemühet/ jhrer teutschen MutterSprach hoheit/ fürtrefflig: vñ zierlichkeit an tag zu geben/ derselben reinligkeit zuerhalten/ sie von außländischẽ bastard vñ eingeschlichenen findlingen zubefreyẽ/ hab ebenermassen nit vnterlassen wollẽ/ so viel an meinem wenigen orth sein köñen/ auch meine Geschäfften solches zulassen wollẽ/ von vnterschiedlichen gelährten Männern/ was zu nutz/ froñen/ Ehr/ Würde/ vnd Herrligkeit vnserer teutschen Sprach dienet/ etwas zusañen zuziehen/ vnd dem gemeinen Leser mittheilen wollen.[1] Folge aber hierinnen nicht den Spinnen/ welche von sich selbsten ein Gewebe machen; sondern den Bienen/ welche auß unterschiedlichen wolriechenden Blümlein ein süsen Honig zusañen tragen/ vnd melde [):(iij r] demnach ohne schew/ wer zu diesem Wercklein ist gebraucht worden.

    [311] Teutsche Bastard Wörter.[a]
Es seynd in der Teutschen Sprach viel frembde Lateinische/ Frantzösische/ Jtaliänische/ Grichische vnnd Spannische Wörter eingeschlichen/ die man gar wol vnd füglich teutsch geben kan/ als da seynd **Alluvio**, Anflüsung[2]/ **apophtegma**[3], ein kluge vnd Sinnreiche Hoff-Rede. **Comœdia** Schaw-Spiel[4]/ **Conversatio** Gespräch/ **Disputatio** Streit-Frage/ **Emblema** Sinnebild/ **Exemplum** Beyspiel/ **Ius Canonicum**[5] das geistlich Recht/ **Methodus** Lehr-Ordnung/ **Notæ** Merckzeichen[6]/ **Artilleri**[3]

Geschütz/ Fewerwerck/ **Armada**³ Krigs-Heer/ **Brave**³ tapffer/ wacker/ stoltz/ schön/ **Camerade**⁷ Spieß-Gesell/ **Campiren** zu Feld ligen/ **proportion**³ ebenmaß/ **Paronomasia**³ wortgleichheit/ **Gratiæ**³ Huld-Göttin. **Homonyma**⁸ gleichbenahmte Wörter. **Termini artis**³ Kunst-Wörter. **Transferiren**³ vberbringen/ **Interregnum**³ Schaltreich/ **Heredes ab Intestato**³ Noth-Erben/ **Philosophia**⁹ Vernunfft-Lehre/ **Logica**⁹ Redgebkunst/ [312] **Metaphysica**⁹ Wesenkündigung/ **Ballet**¹⁰ Dantz-Spiel/ **Durampet**¹¹ verdeckter Weg/ **Gage** ordentliche Bezahlung/ **vivres** Proviand/ **Colonel** Oberster¹²/ **Bataille** Schlacht-Ordnung. Vnd noch viel andere mehr/ die bey Herrn Zeilern in 3 cent. Epist. 35. zusehen. [...]

Es seynd aber beneben auch viel andere Kunst-Wörter/ die die Teutschen noch zur Zeit nicht in jhrer Sprach recht artlich geben können/ biß zuvor daß jenige Unkraut so in dem edlen Garten der saubern teutschen Sprach eingewurtzelt/ mit Butzen vnd Stiel außgereutet vnd ver-[313]stossen ist. Dann dieses zu mercken/ daß welchen das teutsche Burger-Recht ertheilt vnd vergonnt/ dieselbe also in der teutschen Sprach geduldet vnd gelitten werden; sie müssen aber diese folgende Eigenschafften haben. Erstlich daßselbe in vnserer teutschen Sprach nicht können anderst gegeben werden/ oder ohne Umbschweiffung nicht füglich außzureden seyn. Zum andern/ daß solche Wort bereits bey Jederman bekannt/ auch von denen/ welche anderer Sprachen nicht kündig/ verstanden werden/ vnd dañ für das dritte/ daß selbige sich Bürgerlich halten/ das ist teutsch geschrieben/ vnd teutsch geendet werden. Harßdörff. in 2. Theil deß Fraw-Zimmer Gespräch-Spiel. f. 152.¹³ Zeil. in seinen ewiges Preyses würdigen Episteln vnnd Büchern/ welche nunmehr vnser Teutsch-Land gleich vielen hellglänzenden Sternen vberstrahlen/ wie Ristius sagt 3. cent. Epist. 34. in f.¹⁴ [...]

[320] Der Sprach-Verderber ziehet neben andern auch die Prediger durch¹⁵/ in dem sie allerhand Lateinische Wörter in die Predig mit einwerffen. Es ist nicht ohn/ man findet Prediger/ daß sie zu zweyen oder dreyen Worten gleich ein Lateinisches gleichbedeutendes (synonymum würde es in der Schul genañt) mit einwürffen/ nur daß sie es lang machen/ oder sich eines andern besinnen/ ob aber je ein Predigt könte gehalten werden/ daß nicht nothwendig Lateinisch oder Grichisch darbey eingebracht werde/ würd mich niemand vberreden. Dann lieber was ist Capittel/ was ist das alte vnd newe Testament/ was seynd Sacramen-[321]ta/ was ist Catechismus? was Catholisch? was ist Doctor? was Exempel? was Altar? was Epistel? was Evangelium? was Apostel? was Christus? was Jesus? was Verß oder Versicul? wer will den Herrn D. Lutherum straffen/ daß er gesetzt hat Legion? Jtem das Band Orion? &c. Welche Wörter alle/ wie auch besser oben mehr zu finden/ eintweder von dem Grichischen oder Lateinischen herkommen/ vnd nunmehr das teutsche Bürger-Recht erlangt haben/ auch mit grossem Schaden nicht mehr können außgemustert werden. Dahero ich/ spricht Herr Harßdörffer in andern Theil deß Fraw-Zimmer Gespräch-Spiel/ f. 148. in dem vnvergreifflichen Wahn stehe/ man solle die Bastard-Wörter/ welche durch beeder Sprachen Verehligung/ vnnd Vermischung von vnerdencklichen Zeiten/ (gleichsamb geehelicht) legitimirt worden/ nicht mit Schand vnnd Schmach Auß-

zurotten vnd Außzumustern be-[322]gehren/ sondern selbige als Einkömbling erdulden.[16] Jn sonderlichem Bedencken/ daß man vielmahls die vermeinte teutsche Wort weniger/ als das langgewohnte halb Lateinische verstehen kan/ vnnd die allzulang eingewurtzte Art zu reden nicht wol außzureuten thunlich seyn würd.

Von dẽ Predigern kom̃t der Sprach-Verderber auff die Cantzley vnnd zu den Rechts-Gelehrten/ zeucht dieselbe tapffer durch die Hechel.[17] Herr Zeiler in seiner Reiß-Beschreibung durch Teutsch-Land c. I. n. 39 schreibet/[18] daß zu den zeiten Keysers Rudolphi deß ersten/ als man alle Schrifften/ Mündliche Fürträg vnnd entscheide in teutscher Sprach zustellen vnnd fürzubringen angefangen/ so seye nit zu sagen gewesen/ was für Ehr vnd Nutz hierdurch unserm Vatter-Land zugewachsen/ vnd wie solche Sprach an Zierligkeit nach vnnd nach dermassen zugenommen/ daß sie jetzt an Vollkommenheit keiner andern Sprach etwas gibt: wie dann solche [323] noch täglich an Schön vnd Liebligkeit zunimmet auch gemeine Leut der Zier vnd Höffligkeit in reden sich befleissen/ vnd die Liebhaber jhres Vatter-Landts nützliche Bücher in jhrer Mutter-Sprach/ anderer Nationen löblichem Exempel nach/ in den Druck gegeben/ vnd würde derselben noch ein grössers Ansehen gemacht werden/ [(Randnotiz): Wie die teutsche Sprach in das Auffnehmen köndte gebracht werden.] wann man/ sonderlich an Fürsten-Höfen/ dieselbe etwas bessers in acht nehme: auch man die Außländer darzu anhielte/ daß sie ihre Sachen in dieser vnserer Mutter-Sprach müsten fürbringen/ als wie sie es in ihren Ländern/ bey welchen doch die Hoheit deß Keyserthumbs nicht ist/ in ihrer Sprach von vns begehren: oder/ auffs wenigste/ daß wir solche vnsere Sprach mit außländischen Sprachen-Wörtern nicht beschmitzten/ vnd verderbeten/ vnd alles auff Welsch/ Frantzösisch vnnd Hispanisch haben wolten. Welches alles daß es in acht genommen werde/ wol zu wünschen aber besorglich [324] nimmermehr geschehen würd. Dann solang jedem Schreiber vergunnt zu schreiben/ wie es jhm beliebt/ vnd allerhand Wörter einzuführen macht hat/ ist dieses in ewigkeit nimmer zu hoffen.

Fürstliche Cantzeleyen.[a]

Bevorab/ da/ wie Phylander in seinem Alamode Kehrauß fol. 124. sagt/[19] die Herrschaften nicht meinen daß ein Diener was wisse oder gelernet habe/ wann er seine Schrifften nicht dergestalt mit Welschen vnd Lateinischen Wörtern ziere vnd schmücke. Vnd geschicht offt/ daß ein gut Gesell/ der sich deß puren Teutschen gebraucht/ vnd solcher vnteutschen Reden sich mit allem Fleiß müssiget vnd enthaltet/ für einen vnverständigen Esel gescholten/ oder wol gar abgeschafft/ vnd an seinem Glück würd verkürzet. Will dann ein gut Kerl jrgend ein Dienstlein haben/ so muß er sich nach der Herrschafft vnd deren Herren Räthen Weise richten: vnd jhnen antworten/ wie sie fragen: singen wie sie geigen: tantzen wie sie [325] pfeiffen: schreiben wie sie es haben wollen.

[342] Jch stehe hiermit still/ vnd wil dieses Ehren-Kräntzlein mit Herrn Opitij in seinem Aristarcho wolrichenden Blumen vmwinden/ da er sagt;

Es kan vnd soll ja niemand mehr verborgen sein/ daß keine Verhindernuß/

sondern die höchste Zeit da seye/ auch vnsere Sprache auß dē Staub zu heben/ vnnd anß Tage-Liecht zu bringen die uhralte Sprache/ die zierliche Sprache/ die prächtige Sprache/ die allein würdig gewesen die teutsche Welt/ daß Wohn-Hauß so vieler halb Göttlichen Helden zu bewohnen: die Sprache/ die vollständig vnnd vnvermengt durch die grimme Fluth so langer Jahren gedrungen/ vnd sich bey vns [343] erhalten hat.

Diese ist die Sprach/ O ihr Teutsche/ die euch einzig zu lieben/ diese ist es/ wo jhr euch nicht wolt dero vnwürdig machen/ die jhr müsset in ehren vnd würde halten/ die jhr müsset zieren vnd außschmücken/ vnnd so jhr etwas könnet/ hierinnen ein Meister-Stück thun. Ermahnet euch doch/ jhr Teutschen/ mißgönnet doch ewren Nachkommen nicht dasselbe/ was von Gott durch ewre Vorfahren auff euch gebracht worden: Bemühet euch/ daß diese ewre Sprach bey ewer Trew vnd Tapffrigkeit/ womit jhr alle Welt vbertrefft/ die rühmliche Neben-Stelle dermahl eins vberkommen möget.[20]

T a *Druckfehler* der

T II a *Marginalnote*.

K Johann Heinrich Schill (etwa 1615 – Herbst 1645) aus Durlach; Imm. 20.7.1632 jur. U. Straßburg; 1.9.1638 Dr. jur. U. Straßburg; 23.4.1641 Hofrat Mgf. Friedrichs V. v. Baden-Durlach (FG 205); 1641 Heirat der Straßburgerin Salome Dürr. Schill, wohl ein Bruder des Johann Georg Schill (440616 K I 0), siedelte nicht an den Exil-Hof des Markgrafen in Basel über, sondern blieb in Straßburg, wo er dem Kreis der AGT zuzurechnen ist. *Bopp: Tannengesellschaft*, 518 u.ö.; Walter E. Schäfer: Johann Heinrich Schill (ca. 1615–1645). Zwei kleine Funde. In: WBN 17 (1990), 12–13; Alexander Weber: Johann Matthias Schneuber: der Ich-Erzähler in Günter Grass' „Das Treffen in Telgte." Entschlüsselungsversuch eines poetisch-emblematischen Rätsels. In: Daphnis 15 (1986), 95–122, hier 119.

1 Es dürfte sich um eine Ableitung von chorus, Chortanz, Schar, handeln u. Schill als Mitglied der Gesellschaft ‚freier Geister' (AGT; vgl. unten Beil. II, Zitatanfang „edele Geister") ehren. (Das Namenswort ist natürlich nicht abzuleiten von „Chorion, [Χοριόν] Membrana foetus, cui is inuolutus est. [...] Videtur etiam Architectorum vox esse Chorium." Matthias Gesnerus: Novus Lingvae et Ervditionis Romanae Thesavrvs. Lipsiae 1749, 887.) Johann Michael Moscherosch (FG 436. 1645) u. Johann Matthias Schneuber (FG 498. 1648, s. Beil. I) gebrauchen Chorion wie ein Pseudonym, da Schill seinen bürgerlichen Namen geheimhält. Obwohl sie den Verfasser unter dem Namen Chorion kennen, ist es zweifelhaft, ob dies Schills Gesellschaftsname in der AGT war, wie Schäfer (s. oben Anm.0) vermutet. Dagegen Guenter Voigt: Die Dichter der Aufrichtigen Tannengesellschaft zu Strassburg, Gross-Lichterfelde 1899, 9 Anm.2. *Bopp: Tannengesellschaft*, 23 konnte als Mitglieder dieser kleinen Akademie nur Jesaias Rompler v. Löwenhalt (s. 370900, 440724 K 4 u.ö.), Johann Freinsheim, Johann Matthias Schneuber, Andreas Hecht u. Peter (Samuel) Thiederich nachweisen. Vgl. Johann Heinrich Boecklers lat. Gedicht in: Des Jesaias Romplers von Löwenhalt erstes gebüsch seiner Reim-getichte. Getruckt zu Strasburg/ bei Joh. Phil. Mülben/ in dem 1647.ten jar Chri.[er] z. (Hg. v. Wilhelm Kühlmann u. Walter E. Schäfer. Tübingen 1988), 230. Rompler berichtet in seiner Vorrede zu diesem Buch nur: „Es wäre zuwünschen/ daß man in löblichen wissenschaften/ und künsten/ da und dort verträulich miteinander anlege/ wie in Jtalien gebräuchlich ist/ vornemlich unter dem adel; alwa beinahe in allen stätten academien (wie sie es heysen) gefunden werden/ deren iede etwas sonders handelt/ darvon man ehr und nutzen erlangen kan. Solcher gestalt haben unser etliche im verschienenen 1633.ten iar den anfang der ‚Aufrichtigen gesellschaft von der Tannen' gemacht/ derer vorsatz und absehen ist: alter Teütscher aufrichtigkeit/ und rainer erbauung unserer währten Mutter-sprach sich zu befleisen. Jn welcherlej academien oder samlungen gute anstalten zumachen/ daß man allen mißbräuchen vorbiege/ damit die einreissung derselben dem vorgesätzten zweck nicht verhinderlich im weg steh; welches am füglichsten kan verhütet werden/ wan man genaue aufsicht hat/ kein untüchtige gesellen einzunemmen: warfür dan auch das bäste mittel ist/ so man nur eine wenige zahl bestimt/ und beständig darbej bleibt […]." A. a. O., Bl. ☉ ☉ ☉ 4v f.

K I 1 S. K 1.
2 Vgl. den Neologismus „Deutschheit" im sprachlich-rhetorischen Sinne (entsprechend zu latinitas) in der nur hsl. überlieferten Köthener Grammatik (um 1620). *Conermann: Hochsprache und Umgangssprache*, 18. Auffällig ist die Metamorphose dieses Begriffs in der genannten Handschrift über den Pleonasmus in einer Reinschrift der ersten zwei Kapitel von Gueintz' *Deutscher Sprachlehre*: „Die Deutschheit ist eine kunstmäßige Vbereinstimmung der rede nach der kunst, mit den bewehrten Deutschen Scribenten" (HM Köthen: V S 544, Bl. 36r–39v; undatierte u. nur verstümmelt überlieferte Reinschrift von Schreiberh. mit Korrekturen u. Marginalien von F. Ludwig u. Christian Gueintz, hier Bl. 36r) bis hin zum Druck der Gueintzschen *Deutschen Sprachlehre (1641)*, S. 1: „Die Deutschheit ist eine kunstmeßige übereinstimmung der rede nach der art der bewehrten Deutschen." Vgl. *Conermann: Purismus*; *Conermann: Zwischen Literatur- und Nationalsprache*, 38 f. u. *Herz: Ratio und consuetudo*, 276 ff.
3 Wohl auf die FG gemünzt, deren Imprese die Kokospalme zeigt. Zum Widerstreben der Palme gegen Unterdrücken vgl. die Imprese F. Johann Casimirs v. Anhalt-Dessau (FG 10). S. *Conermann I*, Bl. C ij r, u. *Conermann III*, 14. Johann Matthias Schneuber (FG 498) wurde erst 1648 in die FG aufgenommen. In der Sammlung seiner *Gedichte* von 1644 (s. I Q) finden sich einige weitere Gedichte Schneubers auf Schill: „Ehrengedicht Auf Herrn Hans Henrich Schillen Doktorat" (S. 211–216); auf Schills Vermählung mit Salome Dürr (216–227) u. „Eben an denselben/ über sein Stambuch" (357 f.). Im Anhang lateinischer Gedichte *LIBELLUS POEMATUM LATINORUM* (Zwischentitelbl., aber durchgehend paginiert) das Gedicht „Amicissimo meo JOH. HENRICO SCHILLIO, de Crimine Laesae Majest. disputanti, cum paucis ante diebus disputationem de Metatis habuisset" (429 f.). Alle Gedichte ohne Datumsangaben. Die Fortsetzung der Schneuberschen Sammlung *Teütscher gedichten Anderer Theil* (Straßburg 1656. TULB Jena: 8 Art. lib. XIV, 28 [1], auch dig.) enthält keine Gelegenheitsgedichte auf Schill, wohl aber im Anhang *Fasciculus POEMATUM LATINORVM* (Zwischentitelbl., eig. Paginierung), S. 118 das Epicedium „In Obitum JOH: HENRICI SCHILLII. U. J. D." (Inc.: „DVm cunctatur adhuc …"). TULB Jena: 8 Art. lib. XIV, 28 (2), auch dig.
4 D. i. Johann Matthias Schneuber.

K II Die folgenden Auszüge aus Schills Buch wollen die Spracharbeit im Straßburger Umfeld vergegenwärtigen, in dem Johann Michael Moscheroschs *Gesichte Philanders von Sittewald* (erstmals Straßburg 1640; viele Fortsetzungen u. Ausgaben, s. *Dünnhaupt: Handbuch*, S. 2851 ff. Nr. 1–7) u. Johann Matthias Schneubers *Gedichte* (1. Teil Straßburg 1644, 2. Teil Straßburg 1656, s. *Dünnhaupt: Handbuch*, S. 3696 f. Nr. 1) entstanden, vor allem jedoch die Verknüpfung der FG mit dem in Straßburg konzentriert auftretenden sprachpatriotischen Schrifttum (*Sprachverderber*, s. Anm. 15) dokumentieren. Moscherosch (FG 436. 1645) u. Schneuber (FG 498. 1648) gehörten zur FG, jedoch nicht Schill, Boeckler (s. 440616 u.ö.), dessen Schüler Johann Christian Keck (s. *DA Köthen I. 8*: 480218 I), der Opitz-Freund Matthias Bernegger, der Straßburger Arzt Johann Küffer (welcher Georg Rodolf Weckherlins u. Schneubers Gedichte mit fremdwortpuristischen Aufrufen unterstützte) oder der Student Christoph Schorer (s. unten Anm. 15), der Verfasser der *Sprachverderber* (s. *Jones: Sprachverderber*, 77 ff., 131 ff. bzw. 286 ff.). Unter diesen gehörte nur Schneuber auch zur AGT. S. *Bopp: Tannengesellschaft*, 23. Da Schill sich auch auf Sprachkritiker der FG (s. Anm. 1) stützt, mit Moscherosch u. Schneuber befreundet u. mit den Straßburger Professoren Bernegger u. Boeckler verbunden war (s. 440616 K I 0), zeichnet sich ein Netzwerk ab, das zwar sprachpatriotische, aber nicht radikalpuristische Tendenzen offenbart. Es vertritt z. B., wie auch schon die frühe FG (s. 240109) oder Moscheroschs Briefpartner Georg Philipp Harsdörffer (FG 368), das ‚Bürgerrecht' gebräuchlicher Fremdwörter u. übernimmt schwer entbehrliche Fachwörter fremder Herkunft. Vgl. zu fachsprachl. Wortschatz 440616 K I 0 u. 440826 K 4 u. zur Behandlung von Fremdwörtern 450000A K, 450500 K 5, 460131 K 10, 460720 K 3. Es herrscht hier kein Sprachbellizismus, noch nicht einmal die radikaltechnische Kombinatorik der Wortbildung mit Wurzel- oder Stammwörtern. Schills *Ehren-Krantz* enthält auf Bl.):(5r–6v ein „Verzeichnuß der Bücher/ deren man sich in disem Wercklin gebraucht hat/ vnd darin angezogen werden." Von wichtigen neuzeitlichen Poeten, Philologen, Historikern u. Juristen u. unter den mittelalterlichen Quellen werden erwähnt: Johannes Turmair gen. Aventinus, Ioannes Goropius Becanus, Christian Beckmann, Matthias Bernegger, Christoph Besold, Andreas Heinrich Bucholtz, Philipp v. Zesen (FG 521), Iohannes Freinsheim (AGT), Konrad Gesner, Melchior Goldast v. Haiminsfeld, Georg Philipp Harsdörffer (FG 368), „Heldenbuch", Georg Henisch, „Hunibaldus", Matthias Flacius Illyricus (s. Otfrid), Hadrianus Junius, Martin Luther, Olaus Magnus, Otfrid von Weißenburg, Martin Opitz (FG 200), Johann Rist (FG 467. 1647), Johann Georg Schottelius (FG 397), Johann Balthasar Schupp, Valentin Schindler (vgl. 280122 I), Johannes Trithemius, Georg Rodolf Weckherlin, Markus Welser, Eberhard v. Weyhe („Wahremund ab Erenberg"; FG 79), Jakob Wimpfeling, Martin Zeiller, Julius Wilhelm Zincgref. Schill beruft sich in der folgenden Textauswahl auch auf die Fruchtbringer Opitz u. Harsdörffer, denen bald auch die erwähnten Moscherosch u. Rist zur Seite traten.

1 Die folgende Auswahl von Fremdwörtern u. deren Verdeutschungen bezog Schill zum Teil aus: Das Dritte Hundert Episteln/ oder Sendschreiben/ Von vnterschiedlichen Politischen/ Historischen/ vnnd andern Materien/ vnd Sachen. Gestellet / vnd verfertigt/ Durch Martin Zeillern. VLM/ Jn Verlegung Johann Görlins/ 1643, 293 ff. SB München: Epist. 957-3, auch dig. — Zeiller bietet in seinem 35. Brief viele Verdeutschungen zum Beweis dafür an, „wie ein Zeit hero die Gelehrte in Teutschland sich bemühet hetten/ die Kunst- vnnd andere der frembden Spraachen Wörter Teutsch zu geben". „Kunstwörter" ist auch bei Zeiller (wie in der FG) die Bezeichnung für Fachbegriffe. Wir führen im folgenden nur inhaltliche u. lautliche Abweichungen in Schills Wiedergabe der Liste Zeillers an.

2 Zeiller, 294 „Anflössung". *Stieler*, 514: „Anfluß/ der/ **alluvio**. Anfluß des Meers".
3 Nicht bei Zeiller.
4 Zeiller, 295 „Schaw- oder Frewdenspiel".
5 Zeiller, 297 „Geistliche Recht-Satzung".
6 Zeiller, 298 „Merckzeichen/ Anmerckungen".
7 Zeiller, 301 „**Camarada**, ein Spießgesell/ Stuben- oder Bettgesell".
8 Zeiller, 297 „gleichbenamte".

9 Nicht bei Zeiller. Um die Verdeutschung von Fachbegriffen bemühten sich auch die deutschen ratichianischen, in Köthen gedruckten Lehrbücher, z.B. *Metaphysica Pro Didactica Ratichii* (1619)/ *Wesenkündigung Nach der Lehrart Ratichii* (1619) oder das *Compendium Logicae: Ad Didacticam* (1621)/ *Kurtzer Begriff Der Verstandt-Lehr/ zu der Lehrart* (1621). Vgl. *Dünnhaupt: Druckerei*, Nr. 13/14 u. 44/45. S. *Dünnhaupt: Handbuch*, s. v. Ratke. „Redgebigkunst" bzw. „Redengebkunst" schlug 1638 Wilhelm v. Kalcheim gen. Lohausen (FG 172) für Dialectica (Logica) in seiner Übertragung von Virgilio Malvezzis *Il Davide perseguitato* vor. S. 381028 K IV 32, 34 u. 63. Vgl. hier Anm. 13 u. 440826 (K 4).

10 Zeiller, 301 „Ballets, Dantzspiel".

11 Zeiller, 302 „**Durampet, durampert**, der verdeckte Weg".

12 Zeiller, 302 „Obrister."

13 Vgl. *Harsdörffer: Frauenzimmer-Gesprächspiele* II (^{2}1644; Ndr. 1968), das 70. Gesprächspiel „Die Fremden Wörter" („vom Teutschen Burgerrecht frembder Wörter"), 175 ff.: „Die fremden Wörter/ welchen das Teutsche Burgerrecht ertheilet werden solle/ müssen dreyerley folgende Eigenschafften haben: I. Das selbe in unserer Sprach ermanglen/ oder ohn Umschreibung nicht füglich auszureden sein. II. Das solche Wort bereit bey jederman bekand/ und auch von denen/ welche anderer Sprachen nicht kundig/ verstanden werden. III. Daß selbe sich Burgerlich halten/ ich will sagen/ Teutsch geschrieben/ und Teutsch geendet [d. h. flektiert] werden." (S. 178 f.). Vgl. hierzu schon 240109; ferner 460131 K 10 u. 460720 K 3. Auch schon in der Erstausgabe des 2. Teils: [Georg Philipp Harsdörffer]: Frauen-Zimmer Gespräch-Spiel/ So bey Rühmlichen Geselschaften mit erfreulichen Nutzen beliebet und geübet werden mögen/ Andern Theil. Auß Spanischen/ Frantzösischen/ Jtalianischen- Scribentē in Teutscher Sprach verfasset/ Zusambt einer Zugab überschrieben Das Schau-Spiele Teutscher Sprichwörter. Durch Einen Mitgenossen der Hochlöblichen Fruchtbringenden Geselschaft (Nürnberg 1642: Wolffgang Endter), 150. HAB: Lo 2621 (2). Vgl. auch das 144. Gesprächspiel „Von den fremden Wörtern in Teutscher Sprache" in *Harsdörffer: Frauenzimmer-Gesprächspiele*, 3. Teil (1643, Ndr. 1968), 323–330. — Die Flexion griechischer oder lateinischer Personennamen im Deutschen bildete einen Sonderfall. In der von Christian Gueintz (FG 361. Der Ordnende) stammenden u. von F. Ludwig mit vielen Anmerkungen versehenen Handschrift „Die Deutsche Rechtschreibung angeordnet und der fruchtbringenden hochlöblichen Geselschaft übergeben von Dem Ordnenden" (HM Köthen: V S 670), heißt es auf S. 9/ Bl. 11r nur knapp: „Denn die frembden wörter aus einer andern sprache entlehnet, auch ihrer ankunfft gemäß müßen gestellet werden." F. Ludwig hatte am Rande ergänzt: „insonderheit in den Griechischen und lateinischen Menschennamen, das man sie nicht immerdar in der Nennendung [Nominativ] stehen laße, sondern nach ihrer grundsprache in ihre verwandelung [Deklination] setze, als der Plato, des Platonis, dem Platoni, den Platonem a [<PPlatone>] vom Platone, also der Augustus, des Augusti, dem Augusto, den Augustum, ab von dem Augusto und dergleichen." Diese Ergänzung übernommen in *Gueintz: Rechtschreibung (1645)*, 11 f. Für die sonstigen, allgemein bekannten u. verwendeten eingedeutschten Fremdwörter sprach sich auch F. Ludwig für eine grammatisch-orthographische Angleichung aus: Zettel statt Zettul (mlat. cedula), Titel statt Titul (lat. titulus), Testamente statt Testamenta u. a. m. S. seine kritischen Anmerkungen zum 3. Teil der Harsdörfferschen *Frauenzimmer-Gesprächspiele*: „Etzliche erinnerungen, bey dem dritten theile der gesprächspiele am meisten die wortschreibung betreffende". HM Köthen: V S 545, Bl. 419r–424v u. 426r (demnächst in *DA Köthen I. 9*), hier Bl. 419r, 421v, 420v u. ö. Zu Philipp v. Zesens (FG 521. 1648) Übers. antiker mytholog. Namen s. 450000A K 1. — Zu Moscheroschs u. Hans Caspar Hermanns *Technologie Allemande & Françoise Das ist/*

Kunst-übliche Wort-Lehre Teutsch und Frantzösisch (1656) s. 450500 K 5. Vgl. auch das Fremdwörterlexikon: [Michael Heubel:] Der ungelährte Staats-Mann/ Durch Erklärung etlicher fremd ... Wörter ... unterrichtet. Jena 1669. HAB: Xb 3764 (2); *Stieler* (3. Teil): „Nachschuß etlicher fremden und zurückgebliebenen Wörter. Supplementum peregrinorum quorundam & in opere superiori praetermissorum vocabulorum", eigene Pagination, S. 1–40; Christian Juncker: Christian Weisens Curieuse Gedancken von den NOUVELLEN oder Zeitungen. Frankfurt a. M., Leipzig 1703 (S. 608–876: mit dem Anhang eines Fremdwörter-Lexikons: „Curieuses Nouvellen-LEXICON, Oder Kurtze und deutliche Erklärung/ wo nicht aller/ jedoch der meisten und vornehmsten ... Deutscher/ Frantzösischer und Jtaliänischer/ auch zum Theil verstümmelter Lateinischer Wörter und Redensarten", beginnend mit „Abandoniren/ verlassen", schließend mit „Zeugwärter/ der das Gewehr und Rüstung in einem Zeughause wol in acht nimmt. super armamentarium positus"), HAB: Ge 846, auch dig. Vgl. ferner Andreas Gardt: Das Fremdwort aus der Sicht der Grammatiker und Sprachtheoretiker des 17. und 18. Jahrhunderts. Eine lexikographische Darstellung. In: Zeitschrift f. dt. Philologie 116 (1997), 388–412; Hugo Harbrecht: Verzeichnis der von Zesen verdeutschten Lehn- oder Fremdwörter. In: Zeitschrift f. deutsche Wortforschung 14 (Berlin 1912), S. 71–81; Anette Kremer: Die Anfänge der deutschen Fremdwortlexikographie. Metalexikographische Untersuchungen zu Simon Roths „Ein Teutscher Dictionarius" (1571). Heidelberg 2013. S. *Roth Fremdwb*. Begriffsgeschichtlich ist der Fremdwortpurismus von dem rhetorischen Begriff der Puritas oder stilistisch-grammatischen Reinheit u. der in diesem Sinne von der FG geforderten Deutschheit zu unterscheiden. S. *Conermann: Purismus*.

14 Zeiller, a. a. O. (s. Anm. 1), 34. Brief, S. 292 f.: „Also sollen auch wir Teutschen vnsere Spraach höher/ als eine Zeit hero beschehen/ halten/ dieselbe im Reden vnd Schreiben/ nicht mit andern Zungen vnklar vnd vnvollkommen machen; sondern vns der frembden Spraachen vernünfftig vñ mässig/ vnd so viel möglich/ allein auff den Nothfall; sonderlich aber/ wann man nicht in Teutscher spraach etwas zu verhandlen hat/ gebrauchen; vnd auff diese drey Lehrsätze oder Reglen achtung geben/ daß nemblich Wörter/ welchen das Teutsch Burgerrecht ertheilt werden solle/ dreyerley folgende Eigenschafften haben/ 1. daß selbe in vnserer Spraach/ ermanglen/ oder ohn Vmbschreibung nicht füglich außzureden seyn. 2. Das solch Wort bereit bey jederman bekannt/ vnd auch von denen/ welche anderer Spraachen nicht kundig/ verstanden werden. 3. Daß selbe sich burgerlich halten/ das ist/ Teutsch geschrieben/ vnnd Teutsch geendet werden." Zeiller berufft sich explizit für diese drei Lehrsätze auf die in Anm. 13 wiedergegebene Passage aus dem 2. Teil von Harsdörffers *Frauenzimmer-Gesprächspielen*.

15 [Christoph Schorer]: C. S. Teutscher vnartiger Sprach- Sitten vnd Tugend verderber. Gemehret vnd verbessert/ vnd zum andern mal in Truck gegeben. Getruckt im Jahr/ Da Sprach/ Sitten vnd Tugend verderbet war. 1644. TULB Jena: Art lib. XIV, 27 (6) (auch dig.), Bl. D iiij r ff.; *Jones: Sprachverderber*, Auswahl S. 304–342. Zu dem Kreis der Straßburger Sprachreformer um die Aufrichtige Tannengesellschaft (s. o., Anm. 0) gehörte auch der Straßburger Student Christoph Schorer mit seiner mehrfach gedruckten fremdwortpuristischen Schrift. Vgl. bes. *Jones: Sprachverderber*, a. a. O., 286 ff. Wichtige Vorläufer dieser sprachpatriotischen Veröffentlichungen sind nach Martin Opitz' (FG 200) *Aristarchus* (s. u.) vor allem zwei 1638 erschienene Gedichte, der in verschiedenen Fassungen kursierende volkstümliche *Teutsche Michel* mit seinen Fremdwortlisten in bierzeitungshaften Strophen (*Jones: Sprachverderber*, 138–160) u. die anonyme, wiederholt gedruckte *Deutsche Satyra wieder alle Verterber der deutschen Sprache* (Breszlaw: Bey Christof Johischen, so wol vndter dem Sandthor daselbst zu finden, o. J.), in auffällig guten Versen u. regulierter Sprache. Die u. a. von August Heinrich Hoffmann v. Fallersleben (Weimarisches Jb. f. dt. Sprache, Litt. u. Kunst I, 1854, S. 296–298; vgl. *Goedeke*, 232), von Pietsch (s. I Q), 51–55 u. von *Jones: Sprachverderber*, 160–163 veröffentlichte Fassung, die *Faber du Faur*, Nr. 442 ohne zureichenden Grund Johann Heinrich Schill zuschreibt, weist sprachliche Nachlässigkeiten u. Druckfehler auf u. stellt einen Nachdruck eines jetzt aufgetauchten Zeitungstexts dar, der unter dem Titel erschienen war: Num. 42. Anno 1638. 1638. | Der Wöchentlichen Zeitungen. | Deutsche Satyra | Wieder alle Verderber der Deutschen | Sprache. | Spanische Victori wieder die Frantzosen/ so vor S. Omer | geschehen/ allda das gantze Läger ruiniret worden. 3 Bl., 4°. Diese Schlachtmeldung fehlt in dem Exemplar der UB Erlangen-Nürnberg (in H00/DISS.A.S 1124). Zu dieser Zeitung vgl. Else Bogel/ Elger Blühm: Die Zeitungen des 17. Jahrhunderts. 3 Bde. Bremen 1971–1985, I, 117 u. II, 126: keine Orts- oder Verlagsangaben; wöchentl. Publikation von 4 Bl. (das 4. Bl. der zit. Ausgabe wird die Nachricht vom span. Sieg enthalten haben). — Christoph Schorer aus Memmingen hatte sich 1639 an der medizin. Fakultät in Straßburg eingeschrieben. Er scheint von Johann Matthias Schneuber u. Jesaias Rompler v. Löwenhalt zum Sprachpatriotismus ermuntert worden zu sein, so daß er 1643 den *Sprachverderber* veröffentlichte: Der | Vnartig | Teutscher | Sprach- | Verderber. | Beschrieben | Durch | Einen Liebhaber der redlichen | alten teutschen Sprach. | [Vignette] | Gedruckt/ im Jahr vnserer | Erlösung/ | [Linie] | M DC XLIII. (1 Bl., 45 S.), HAB: 74.15 Gram. (1). Das Werk wurde nochmals 1644 stark erweitert publiziert (s. o.). Schorer setzte seine Studien in Basel, Montpellier u. Padua fort, wo er 1654 promoviert wurde. In die Heimatstadt zurückgekehrt, wurde er Stadtarzt u. veröffentlichte neben einer Reihe anderer „Verderber" („Mann-Verderber", Einfluß auf Grimmelshausen) u. astrologischer Ratgeber auch medizinische Handbücher in deutscher Sprache für den Hausgebrauch. *ADB* XXXII, 378; Otto Hartig: Christoph Schorer von Memmingen und sein „Sprachverderber". München 1922 (Sb. Bayer. Akademie d. Wiss. Philos.-philol. u. hist. Kl. 1921: 2); Friedrich Braun: Christoph Schorer von Memmingen. Nürnberg 1926.

16 Harsdörffer: Frauen-Zimmer Gespräch-Spiele, 2. Teil (Nürnberg: Endter 1642), a. a. O. (s. Anm. 13), Bl. 147 f.: „Nachmals aber/ als die Römer theils durch die Waffen/ theils durch Kauffmannschafft sich mit den Teutschen bekand zu machen/ und sich unter sie zu vermischen angefangen/* [(Fußnote): Sidon. Apoll. 4.17) haben zugleich die Sprachen miteinander vermenget werden müssen: sonderlich aber in solchen Sachen/ welche den Teutschen bevor gantz unbekand und notwendig mit frembden Worten außzureden gewesen. Biß endlich Carolus genant der Grosse/ mit dem Reich auch die Sprach zu erheben angefangen. *† [(Fußnote): C. Gueintz. in Entwurff Teutscher Sprach-lehre 5. u. 6. Bl.] Jedoch hat man dazumal noch nicht Teutsch schreiben können/ sondern in Befehln/ Befreyungsbriefen und öffentlichen Schrifften hat man sich deß Lateins/ bedient/ *†* [(Fußnote): Heigius in der 11. Frage/ an der 8. Zahl.] biß auff das jahr 1243. und hernach erst das Teutsche mit Lateinischen Buchstaben zu schreiben begunt/ daher ich dann in den unvergreifflichen Wahn stehe/ man solle die Bastard-wörter/ welche durch beeder Sprachen Verehelichung und Vermischung von unerdencklichen Zeiten legitimiret worden/ nicht [148] mit Schand und Schmach außzurotten und außzumustern begehren/ sondern selbe als Einkömbling erdulten." Vgl. *Harsdörffer: Frauenzimmer-Gesprächspiele*, 2. Teil (²1644, Ndr. 1968, s. Anm. 13), 175 f. Die Randglosse *† berufft sich auf *Gueintz: Sprachlehre (1641)*, 5 f., obwohl es da S. 3 f. nur heißt: „Johannes Stumpfius in der Schweitzer Chronic berichtet/ das Carolus der grosse ins gemein das Deutsche Schreiben erst aufgebracht. Wiewol/ wie er gedencket/ man dazumal meistlich die Lateinische sprache gebrauchet/ bis im Jahre Christi 1200. da man Deutsch mit Griechischen buchstaben geschrieben. Gesner." Vgl. unten Anm. 18.

17 Schorer: Sprach- Sitten vnd Tugend verderber, a. a. O. (s. Anm. 15), Bl. D 8r ff.

18 ITINERARIUM GERMANIÆ NOV-ANTIQUÆ Teutsches Reyßbuch Hoch vnd Nider Teutschland ... Durch MARTINUM ZEILLERUM (Straßburg: Lazari Zetzners Seligen Erben 1640), S. 35–38, hier: S. 36. HAB: 257.3 Hist. 2°. Vgl. oben Anm. 16. Zu der verbreiteten, aber mit Abweichungen überlieferten Nachricht über den Übergang zum Deutschen in öffentlichen u. rechtlichen Schriftstücken u. allgemein in Büchern vgl. einen Brief Gfn. Anna Sophias v. Schwarzburg-Rudolstadt (TG 1) vom 7.1.1648 u. dessen mittelalterliche u. humanistische Quellen u.a. in *Conermann: TG*, 596–606; ders.: *Purismus*, 183 u. Anm. 5 (mit Hinweisen auf das Vorkommen dieser Nachricht bei den Fruchtbringern Zesen, Schottelius u. Harsdörffer).

19 [Johann Michael Moscherosch:] VISIONES DE DON QUEVEDO. Wunderliche vnd Wahrhafftige Gesichte Philanders von Sittewalt. ... Zum andern mahl auffgelegt. von Philander selbsten/ vbersehen/ vermehret vnd gebessert. Straßburg/ Gedruckt bey Johan-Philipp Mülben. M DC XXXXJJ. — Anderer Theil der Gesichte Philanders von Sittewalt. Straßburg/ Bey Johan-Philipp Mülben. M. DC. XXXXJJJ, S. 124. HAB: 403.38 Quod.

20 ARISTARCHUS sive De Contempto Linguæ Teutonicæ. Auctore Martino Opitio. BETHANIÆ, EXCUDEBAT JOHANNES DÖRFER. [1617], Bl. D rv. Faksimile in: Martin Opitz: Jugendschriften vor 1619 ... Hg. Jörg-Ulrich Fechner. Stuttgart 1970, veröffentl. auch in *Opitz* I, 75: „Nemo igitur ignorare diutius potest, nihil obstare quo minus nostra etiam lingua emergat imposterum ac in lucem protrahatur: lingua venusta, lingua [Dv] decens, lingua gravis ac patriæ suæ, tot ingentium heroum nutrici, dignissima, lingua quæ integra & incommista
  **tot jam labentibus annis*
ad nos pervenit. Hanc, si qui cœlo vostro, hoc est, vobis ipsis non invidetis, amate, hanc expolite, hic viros vos præstate. Hic Rhodus, hic saltus. Quod si precibus dandum aliquid & obsecrationi censetis: per ego vos dilectissimam matrem vestram Germaniam, per majores vestros prægloriosissimos oro & obtestor, ut nobilitate vestra gentisque dignosque spiritus capiatis; ut eadem constantia animorum, qua illi fines suos olim tutati sunt, sermonem vestrum non deseratis." Zu dem abgesetzten Zitat gehört die Randglosse „sesquimille, ut quidem computat Goldastus." Vgl. PARÆNETICORVM VETERVM Pars I. ... Cum Notis MELCHIORIS HAIMINSFELDI[I] GOLDASTI. EX BIBLIOTHECA & SVMTIBVS BARTHOLOMÆI SCHOBINGERI IC. (Insulae 1604: Ioannes Ludovicus Brem), 261: „ast Germanis integra [lingua] incommistaque perennat, nec alio nunc sermone, quàm maiores nostri ante annos sesquimille, vtimur. qua in re soli Germani habemus gloriari."

Johann Michael Moscherosch an Johann Heinrich Boeckler

Da die Truppen Turennes abzögen, komme er, Johann Michael Moscherosch (FG 436. 1645), hiermit zu Johann Heinrich Boeckler. Moscherosch erklärt, er habe die ihm von anderen auferlegten Pflichten erfüllen müssen und keine Zeit für sich und die ersehnte Muße gehabt, so daß er wohl Boecklers Vergebung für sein etwas langes Schweigen erlangen werde. — Moscherosch teilt mit, den 4. Teil von Harsdörffers *Frauenzimmer-Gesprächspielen* (1644) erhalten zu haben. Er müsse aber seine Reaktion darauf um wenige Tage hinausschieben. — Moscherosch freut sich über Exemplare von Boecklers Herodian- und Cornelius Nepos-Editionen und fragt, wie er sich für dessen Wohlwollen revanchieren könne. — Er lobt, wie verständig Boeckler über deutsche Daktylen denke. Viele ergötzten sich daran, die ernste Würde der deutschen Sprache mutwillig durch französische Unbeständigkeit und Leichtfertigkeit in Rede und Schrift zu besudeln. — Obgleich wir närrisch tun, warnen wir dadurch doch die Narren! Wenn es sie danach jucke, sei das nicht Sprachpflege zu nennen, sondern eine große und verhängnisvolle modische Krankheit. Moscherosch erklärt, er sage das nicht allein Boeckler, sondern stimme bei Gott darin und in anderen jüngst erörterten Themen allein seinem Urteil bei. Boecklers Meinung sei ihm Gesetz und gelte für ihn als Regel und Norm aller gehobenen Literatur.

Q SUB Hamburg: Sup. ep. 24 Ad J. H. Boeclerum. VI. Varii, 271. 1 Blatt, Rücks. A; eigenh., Sig. — *D*: *Reifferscheid*, 605 f. — *BN*: *Bürger*, 1025 Nr. 1; *Krüger* I, 716; *Kühlmann: Korrespondenz Moscheroschs*, 267.

A Excellentissimo Viro, Domino Johanni Henrico Boeclero Eloquentiæ & Historiarum Professori publico in Universitate Argentoratensi, Magno fautori suo. Argentinam.[1]

Excellentissime Domine.

Abeuntibus tandem Turiannis[1] ad Te venio. magna pars mei mea non est, quumque maxime de otio meditari volo, ad alia vocor; vincior, quum liber esse laboro. Ideoque istam à Te Veniæ gratiam longiori silentio meo facile impetraturum confido. Harsdörfferi nostri Colloq. part. IV.[2] accepi: Responsionem paucis diebus[a] differe cogor.

   Sed Herodianum[3] etiam et Nepotem[4] Tuos: Munus, quo me Christe nihil mihi acceptius in tota mortalitate. Quid quæso officij de me expectare potes, quem nullis meis meritis adeo fauenter habes! Omne id Tuæ in me Benevolentiæ adscribo, quam egregie admodum testari soles semper. Utinam; & sic spero, dabunt propitia aliquando Numina hanc purioris adfectus Tui constantiam, si[b] non demereri, certe deprædicare. De Dactylicis Germanicis,[5] quam Cordate sentis! indignum facinus, vernaculam nostram ista scribendi lascivia pollui, qua adeo delectantur non pauci, qui, quum[c] Germanam sonent gravitatem unicé, ipsissimam gallicam mobilitatem[d] an levitatem loquendo prodent, & scribendo, sed serio quandoque insanire videmus de Jnsania alios monentes. pruritum istum non ego cultum linguæ dixero, sed novum aliquem morbum, & magnum & ominosum. Non Tuis ego auribus hoc do; sed DEUM sancté testor, Te Unum eum mihi esse cuius sententiæ in his & similibus, quorum nuper apud Te Facta mentio fuerant, soli subscribo: Tu Unus mihi & lex es, et norma & regula in omni Nobilioris literaturæ studio tractando. Vale vero, & me imparem non voto sed Fato voluisse in his talibus porro ama et fove. Spem facit opimam Cæres, Bellonæ quam maximus semper metus comitatur. iterum vale. dab. Benfeldæ[e] 16. Junii 1644.

   T. E. devinctissimus Jo. Mich. Moscherosch.

I

431201

Moscherosch gratuliert Georg Philipp Harsdörffer zum vierten Teil der *Frauenzimmer-Gesprächspiele*

Q   *Harsdörffer: Frauenzimmer-Gesprächspiele* IV (1644; Ndr. 1968), 439 (Ndr. 483). — *BN: Bechtold: Schriften Moscheroschs,* 59; *Schäfer: Moscherosch,* 145; *Dünnhaupt: Handbuch,* 2868f.; *Schäfer: Moscherosch u. Harsdörffer,* 149f.

DEine Spiele[1] voller Lust/
Ohne Zanksucht und Verlust
mich in mir so gar ergetzen:
 daß ich/ sonder Klügel-scheu/
 wolt all meine Zeit dabey
mitzuspielen bahr aufsetzen.
 Weißleich heisset das gespielt/
 wer so/ wie der Spielend ziehlt:
Ob er auch an Zeit verliehret,
 doch/ verliehrend er gewint/
 (als der **Suchend** sucht und findt)
was **Frucht bringet**/ freuet/ zieret.

> schreibts seinem hochgeehrten Freunde zu Bezeugung Alt-Teutscher beständiger Treue
> Hans Michel Moschrosch [sic]
> von Wilstädt.

Geschrieben in Benfeld/ den 1. Christmonats 1643.

II

431229

Johann Michael Moscherosch an Johann Heinrich Boeckler

Q   SUB Hamburg: Sup. ep. 24, Bl. 270rv [A: v]; eigenh.; 1 Blatt; Sig.— D: *Reifferscheid,* 602f. — *BN: Bürger,* 148 u. 1025 (falsch gelesenes Datum: 29. Okt. 1643); *Krüger* I, 716; *Kühlmann: Korrespondenz Moscheroschs,* 267.

A   Excellentissimo Viro, Johanni-Henrico Boeclero, Historiarum & Eloquentiæ Professori Celebratissimo Fautori & Amico summe colendo *etc.* Straßburg.

Vir Excellentissime *etc.*

Nunc vero in salvo est ill*ustrissimus* D*omi*n*us* Legatus noster[1]: non sine nullo rerum publicarum periculo, quæ nova subinde tempestate exoriente magis magisq*ue* exorbitare videntur. Ego quod super obitu ei*us* nunc scribam, nihil habeo, nec propter occupationes crebriores adhuc quidquam officij licuit, ne in versu quidem: Adde, quod autographo interdixerit laudationes post mortem, vir summas ob virtutes laudandus merito: totus animus suspirium est, si has considero; Et Jllustria plura habemus Ex*em*pla fuisse Hominem: Neq*ue enim* dantur in natura ullæ præter naturam perfectiones. Tu, vir Ex*cellentissi*me non tamen veterem tuam erga me Benevolentiam unà interire patieris. Dabit alium Legatum, dabit Patronum etiam Legati largitor & Patroni DEVS. Vale. De Danico Bello[2] quæ nova habes? Nos hic mira. proh hominum fidem! an Judicium credant vniversale machinatores fraudis potentes, ambigo; Non id Genti dant facinus nostrates, sed nocturnis consilijs un*ius* Vlyssis. Num inscité cordatiores nuper?

    An has ruinas orbis in cinerem datas
        hic excitabit? hæ man*us* Germaniam erigent?
    Nullas habet Spes Germania si tales habet.

En tibi quæ per Ph*i*landr*um*[3] super eo metu ante mensem.

    Te Mediatorem Pacis Germania credit?
        quam male! Nam Dano est par Danaisq*ue* fides.
    Dimidiatorem Pacis te Patria cernet:
        De medio Pacem tollis enim mediam.
    Jn Pacis medijs meditans sua commoda, Pacis
        Dimidiator erit, non Mediator erit.

Benf*eldae* 29. Xbris 1643.

    Ex*cellentiam* T*uam* Omni officio Colens
        Joh. Mich. Moscherosch.

Proxime Ampl. Styrzelio[4] & Harsdörffero[5], nostris, Respondebo.

III

440112

Boeckler preist Harsdörffer und das fruchtbringerische Sprachspiel

Q *Harsdörffer: Frauenzimmer-Gesprächspiele* IV (1644; Ndr. 1968), 440–443; Ndr. 484–487.

    NVn hat das Spiel ein End/ so Teutschland lang verwirret/
so vor und mit dem Krieg spielt üm die Teutsche Sprach/[1]
daß aus derselben wurd ein solche Wunder-Sach/

in der sich niemand mehr/ als Teutsche selbst/ verirret.
    Die edle Teutsche Sprach/ die zu den ersten Zeiten/
da viel aus einer Sprach sind worden/ hat allein
erhalten/ daß sie möcht' ein **Helden-Sprache** seyn/
    die reiche Teutsche Sprach/ mit ihren Zierligkeiten:
    Die reine Teutsche Sprach/ mit ihren satten Worten/
ward dergestalt vermischt/ verwelscht/ vermumt/ verstellt/
mit fremder Art und Farb/ das in der gantzen Welt
    kein solches Muster war/ wie in den Teutschen Orten.
    Man redete nicht mehr von Sachen und Geschichten/
nur von *affai*ren gieng es *discurir*lich her/
kein Schrift wurd mehr verfast/ kein Brief verschicket mehr/
Incaminirt, spedirt, darnach must man sich richten [441]
    Darnach[a] must unser Sprach sich *faconi*ren[b] lassen/
O pfui dich der *facon*![c] Habt ihr sie mit gebracht/
ihr wolgereiste Leut/ die ihr an nichts gedacht
    in euren Reisen/ als/ was eitel ist/ zu fassen?
    Könt ihr die Welsche Sprach/ so lasset sie Welsch bleiben:
Last Spanisch/ Spanisch seyn/ das Teutsch hab Teutsche Wort:
Warumb behellfft ihr euch des Stimplens[2] immer fort/
    aus vielen eine Sprach/ Stück- und Flickweiß zu schreiben?
    Wann ein gemeiner Mann sein unvergreifflichs Denken
nach Hof erstrecken darff/ so frag ich/ ob sich wol
zu grosser Herren Ehr verwelscht-Teutsch reimen soll?
    Dann nach des Herren Sprach die Knechte müssen lenken.
    Wer aber selbst von Gott mit höchster Macht geehret/
wie soll der fremde Sprach mehr lieben als sein Reich?
Wie bald bedeutet es nichts gutes/ wann zugleich
    die Zung und das Gemüht/ nur fremdes Ding begehret? [442]
    Man[a] frag die Römer drum/ wie sie ihr Reich geführet;
Gantz Römisch must es seyn; zuvorderst Hertz und Sinn/
dann aber auch der Mund/ man schrieb dort und da hin
    nichts als was Römisch war/ nichts fremdes wurd gespüret.
    So soll es billich seyn. Gott Lob/ daß nunmehr scheinet/
Es hab das Welsche Spiel mit Teutscher Sprach ein End/
das Teutsch wird widerüm für **Hof-gemeß** erkent/
    Teutsch wird noch blühen mehr und schneller als man meinet.
    Das ist ein **Frucht**/ die uns Eur grosser Fleisse bringet/
Jhr **Edle Teutsche Frucht**/ die Jhr mit Förderung/
mit Gunst und Kunst bißher in reiner Teutscher Zung/
    was **nutzet und behagt**[3]/ erfindet und erringet.
    Vnd Jhr/ **Herr Harsdorff**/ seit üm so viel mehr zu preisen/
weil Jhr durch **Spielen** zeigt/ wie sehr das Spiel verderbt/

und schier verderbet war/ was Jhr im Spiel erwerbt/
   das wird **der Teutsch Gewinn**/ von Teutschem Spielen heissen. [443]
   Nunª spielet immer fort/ die Weißheit selber liebet
die Spielenden/ und spielt mit ihren Kinderlein
ein manches nutzlichs Spiel. O möchte Friede seyn/
   nach langem Kriege-Spiel/ so unser Spiel betrübet!
   Wir wolten immerzu auf einen Spielplatz zielen/
da kein Gefahr im Spiel/ da kein Verlust im Satz/
da man gewinnen wirdᵈ den unerschöpfften Schatz!
   Das ist das Spiel/ Gewinn; Gewinn ein ewigs Spielen.

Straßburg den 12.   Seinem sehrwehrtem Freunde
   Jenner 1644.   überschicket dieses

                         Joh. Heinrich Böckler.

T a *Verschrieben* dibus — **b** si non *eingefügt.* — **c** *Reifferscheid falsch* quam — **d** *Reifferscheid falsch* nobilitatem — **e** *Reifferscheid* Benfeldi

T III a *Auch Kustode.* — **b** u. **c** *Lies* façoniren *bzw.* façon — **d** *Satzfehler* wied

K Johann Heinrich Boeckler (1611–1672). Stud. 1631 U. Altdorf u. Tübingen, schon seit Mai 1631 U. Straßburg, 1636 Lehrer am dortigen Gymnasium. Seit 1637 Prof. der Redekunst an der U. Straßburg, wohin er nach seiner Tätigkeit an der U. Uppsala (seit 1649, Eloquenz u. Politik) u. in Stockholm (1650, kgl. schwed. Historiker) 1652 auch zurückkehrte (seit 1654 als Historiarum Prof.). 1662 kurmainz. Rat, 1663 ksl. Rat u. Comes palatinus; erhielt von Kg. Ludwig XIV. v. Frankreich ein Ehrengehalt, Lehrer Johann Benedikt Carpzovs d. J., Gottfried Wilhelm Leibniz', Johann Ludwig Praschs, Veit Ludwigs v. Seckendorff (FG 615. 1654; vgl. B.s Beitrag in Seckendorffs *Außzug Der Kirchen-Historien ... Durch Ein Mitglied der Fruchtbringenden Gesellschafft.* Gotha 1661: Reyher), Philipp Jakob Speners u.a. Als Schüler des Straßburger Theologen Johannes Schmidt, des Historikers u. Mathematikers Matthias Bernegger, dem er 1640 auf dem Straßburger Geschichtslehrstuhl folgte, u. als Tacitist bezog er sich zwar auf die Bibel u. die antiken Historiker (Oratio Prima. De C. Cornelii Taciti Historia, 1636; Caivs Svetonivs Tranqillvs Cum Isaaci Casavboni Animadversionibus Et Dissertationibus Politicis Io. Henr. Boecleri. 1647; In C. Corn. Taciti qvinqve libros Histor. svperstites, 1648; Herodian u. Velleius Paterculus, s. K I 1), deren Werke er herausgab u. erläuterte, schrieb aber auch *In Hvgonis Grotii Jus Belli et Pacis Ad ... Baronem Boineburgium Commentatio* (1663/64 u.ö.) u. richtete sich, ohne die Grenze zur Ethik zu verwischen, nach Machiavellis Vorbild am Nutzen der Fürsten aus, deren Interessen er im Streit des Mainzer Kurfürsten mit der Stadt Erfurt (Assertio Juris Mogvntini Contra Affectatam Justitiam Protectionis Saxonicæ in Civitate Erffurtensi, 1663) u. in anderen Angelegenheiten vertrat. Diesen Streit erwähnt *Neumark: Palmbaum,* 419 neben dem Türkenkrieg als eine der beiden Ursachen für die Verzögerung bei der Bestallung des neuen Oberhaupts der FG nach dem Tode Hz. Wilhelms IV. v. Sachsen-Weimar (FG 5; starb am 17.5.1662). 1649 war Boeckler von Kgn. Christina v. Schweden als Prof. der Rhetorik nach Uppsala berufen u. 1650 zum Reichshofhistoriographen ernannt worden. Moscherosch verfolgte diese Karriere sehr genau, s.

Kühlmann: Korrespondenz Moscheroschs, 253 ff. — Boeckler versuchte, göttliches Recht u. Naturrecht weiterhin zu vereinbaren, eine Position, die auch Seckendorff in der Tradition der lutherischen Rechtstheologie gegen Samuel Pufendorfs Begründung der Rechtssätze aus dem Naturrecht beibehielt. Obgleich Boeckler als Protestant die Hegemonie des Kaisers befürchtete u. zeitweise in schwed. Diensten wirkte, bekämpfte er als Reichspatriot doch Bogislaw Philipp v. Chemnnitz' Kritik an der Reichsverfassung (Hippolithus a Lapide, pseud.: Dissertatio de ratione status in imperio nostro Romano-Germanico. 1640 u. ö.). — B. sollte später auch die Straßburger Dissertation von Johann Christian Keck (De Lingua Celtica Sive Germanica. 1647; s. *DA Köthen I. 8:* 480218 I) u. von Moscheroschs zweitem Sohn Quirinus betreuen [Votum Imperatorivm. Ad Tac. 4. A. 38. (1658)]. — Wilhelm Kühlmann: Boeckler, Johann Heinrich. In: Geschichte der Altertumswissenschaften. Biographisches Lexikon. Hgg. P. Kuhlmann u. H. Schneider. Stuttgart u. a. 2012, 122 f. (Der Neue Pauly, Suppl. VI); *NDB* II, 372 f.; *ADB* II, 792 f.; Ernst Jirgal: Johann Heinrich Bökler. In: Mitt. d. österreich. Inst. f. Geschichtsforschung XLV (1931), 322–384; Michael Stolleis: Veit Ludwig v. Seckendorff. In: Staatsdenker im 17. und 18. Jahrhundert. Reichspublizistik, Politik, Naturrecht. Hg. Michael Stolleis. 2. erw. Aufl. Frankfurt a. M. 1987, bes. 150, 157, 166 ff. u. ö.; *Bopp: Tannengesellschaft*, 119–123.

1 Die Truppen des franz. Generals Henri de La Tour d'Auvergne Vicomte de Turenne (1611–1675), seit 1643 Maréchal de France u. General der franz. Truppen in Deutschland unter Louis II. de Bourbon duc d'Enghien (seit 1646 prince de Condé). Aus dem Elsaß kommend führte er im Mai 1644 seine Armee über den Rhein u. entsetzte zusammen mit Enghien das von den Kaiserlichen belagerte Freiburg. S. K II.

2 *Harsdörffer: Frauenzimmer-Gesprächspiele* IV (1644). Georg Philipp Harsdörffer (FG 368).

3 ΗΡΩΔΙΑΝΟΥ ΙΣΤΟΡΙΩΝ ΒΙΒΛΙΑ Η HERODIANI Hist. Lib. VIII. Editi CVRA IO. BOECLERI (Argentorati: Io. Phil. Mülbius 1644). HAB: 383.15 Hist. (2) u. a.

4 Corn. Nepotis vulgo Aemili Probi, De Excellentibus Viris, Quae extant. Editio Secunda e Cura, Jo. Henri. Boecleri (Argentorati: F. Sporus 1644). STB Berlin – PK: Wl 3578.

5 Boeckler scheint Johann Michael Moscheroschs (FG 436. 1645) moralische u. antifranzösische Vorbehalte gegen tänzerische, daher Unbeständigkeit u. Leichfertigkeit suggerierende Daktylen geteilt zu haben. Der Bezug auf den Gebrauch von frz. Daktylen bleibt vage, während der Hinweis in *Reifferscheid*, 946 auf Philipp v. Zesens (FG 521. 1648) *Deutschen Helicon* (1640/41) u. auf Zesens Vorbild Augustus Buchner (FG 362) die Auslöser dieser literarischen Mode u. deren Kritik richtig bezeichnen. Vgl. in *Zesen SW* IX, 13 f. Zesens „Dactylisch Sonnet an den Edlen und Weltberühmten Herrn August Buchnern/ über die Erfindung der Dactylischen und Anapästischen Verse". In seiner Poetik empfiehlt Zesen die daktylischen (u. anapästischen) Verse im Gegensatz zu Moscherosch gerade deshalb, „weil sie nicht weniger Anmuth mit ihrer so flüchtigen lieblikeit den Ohren erwecken als etwan andere […]." (A. a. O., 35). Im soeben ihm übersandten vierten Teil der *Frauenzimmer-Gesprächspiele* hätte Moscherosch schon im Register Harsdörffers Hinweise auf „Dactylische Liedlein […] wie sie in Music zu setzen […] werden vermischet mit anderen Reimen/ hin und wieder in Seelewig" finden können. Zur Diskussion F. Ludwigs mit Augustus Buchner über daktylische Verse s. 391028, 391119 u. I–III sowie 391216 u. zum Streit des Fürsten mit Martin Opitz (FG 200) über die daktylische Betonung deutscher Wörter s. 381116 u. 381218, vgl. 380828 u. I. Vgl. insgesamt zur Streitfrage um den Daktylus auch 420503 K 7 u. im vorliegenden Band 450124 K 6.

K I *Schäfer: Moscherosch* (1982), 145 vermutete, daß Johann Michael Moscherosch (FG 436. 1645) schon in seiner Benfelder Dienstzeit in einen lebhaften literarischen Austausch mit Georg Philipp Harsdörffer (FG 368. Der Spielende) in Nürnberg eintrat, wofür das vorliegende Gedicht in Beil. I die einzige „faßbare Spur" darstelle. Vgl. jedoch 421018 (= 430103 I) u. unten Beil. II; *Schäfer: Moscherosch u. Harsdörffer*. Daß Moscherosch, der erst 1645 unter dem Gesellschaftsnamen ‚Der Träumende' in der FG rezipiert wurde, auch schon früh Verbindung zum Wolfenbütteler Hof u. hier namentlich zu Justus Georg Schottelius (FG 397. Der Suchende) aufgenommen hatte (*Schäfer: Moscherosch*, a. a. O.), belegen ein lat. Gedicht Moscheroschs in *Schottelius: Sprachkunst (1641)* u. Schottelius' Brief 430103 an Moscherosch. Vgl. Centuria | Epigrammatum | IOHANNIS-MICHAELIS | MOSCHEROSCH | Germani. | [Linie] | Levant & Carmina curas. | Olymp. Nomes. Eclog. 4. | [Signet] | ARGENTINÆ | Typis & Sumptibus | JOH. PHILIPPI MÜLBII | ET JOSIÆ STÆDELII. | [Linie] | M. DC. XXXXVIIII. (HAB: 230.8 Poet.) S. 32 (Nr. 40 f.) Epigramm auf Schottelius (inc.: „Nos tua scripta […]") bzw. auf das auch von diesem geplante Wörterbuch („Super Lexico Germanico edendo", inc.: „Omnis habet sua dona […]"). Vgl. 450929. Die Sammlung enthält Moscheroschs lat. Widmungsvorrede (Bl. A r ff.) an Hz. August d. J. v. Braunschweig-Wolfenbüttel (FG 227) u. dessen Sohn Pz. Anton Ulrich (FG 716. 1659), ebenso die Centuria II der Ausgabe von 1665 (S. 57 ff., vgl. 450818 Q). Vgl. in Centuria 1649, S. 25 f. Nr. 97 ein anderes Epigramm auf Hz. August. — Zu Moscheroschs Spracharbeit vgl. auch *Schäfer: Moscherosch u. Harsdörffer*, 151 f. Zu der seit 1644 in Meßkatalogen angezeigten, aber erst später (namentlich von Hans Caspar Hermann) vervollständigten u. publizierten Schrift Moscheroschs, *Technologie Allemande & Françoise Das ist/ Kunst-übliche Wort-Lehre Teutsch und Frantzösisch. Vortgesetzt Durch H. C. H.* [Hans Caspar Hermann] (Straßburg: Josias Stähel 1656), HAB: 394.77 Quod., s. auch 440826 K 4, 450500 K 5, 450526 K 4; ferner *Bechtold: Schriften Moscheroschs*, 54 f.; Walter E. Schäfer: Johann Michael Moscheroschs Technologie Allemande & Françoise. Ein Beitrag zur Spracharbeit der „Fruchtbringenden Gesellschaft". In: Simpliciana 30 (2008), 219–233 (S. 223: Anzeige auch in den Meßkatalogen 1648–1651, 1653 u. 1655). Zur frz. Fachwortsprache vgl. z. B. Hans-Josef Niederehe: Les vocabulaires techniques dans la lexicographie française du 16e au 18e siècle. In: La lexicographie française du XVIe au XVIIIe siècle. Actes … publiés par Manfred Höfler. Wolfenbüttel 1982, 65–79. Harsdörffer selbst hatte in seiner „Schutzschrift für die Teutsche Spracharbeit/ und Derselben Beflissene" (Anhang in *Frauenzimmer-Gesprächspiele* I, ²1644), 362 die Forderung erhoben, daß „man alle Kunstwörter von Bergwerken/ Jagrechten/ Schiffarten/ Handwerkeren/ u. d. g. ordentlich zusammentrage." Vgl. dazu 440826 K 4 u. Schottelius in 450000 K 3. — Der Herbstmeßkatalog 1642 u. der Ostermeßkatalog 1643 kündigten an: Hans Michel Moscherosch Teutsche Heldensprach/ das ist/ Rettung der vhralten Teutschen Hauptsprach. Straßburg/ bey Johan Philipp Mülben. *Bechtold*, 60; vgl. *Dünnhaupt: Handbuch*, 2885. Die Verschiedenheit dieses Titels von dem des terminologischen Wörterbuchs erlaubt keine Gleichsetzung, schließt aber einen entstehungsgeschichtlichen Zusammenhang der beiden Vorhaben auch nicht aus. — Der Pflege des Deutschen diente auch die Herausgabe eines guten Dialogbuchs, das in seiner französischen Fassung auf den Genfer Sprachmeister Samuel Bernard zurückgeht: Tableav Des Actions Dv Ievne Gentilhomme: Diuisé en forme de Dialogues: Povr L'Vsage De Cevx Qvi Apprennent la langue Françoise; Parseme De Discovrs, Histoires, sentences & prouerbes, non moins vtiles que facetieux (Straßburg: Ledertz, 1607); 2 Digitalisate (HAB u. Google). Das Werk erschien wiederholt: Straßburg 1613 (2 Tle., [6], 201 u. 104 S.) u. 1615, Leiden 1624, Genf 1625, Straßburg 1637 u. Genf 1638; auch als Köthener Nachdruck, der den Zwecken des dortigen ratichianischen Schulversuchs diente: DIALOGUES, | POUR L'USAGE DE | CEUX

440616 Johann Michael Moscherosch

QUI APPREN- | NENT LA LANGUE | Françoise, | *PARSEMES DE DISCOURS,* | *HISTOIRES, SENTENCES ET PRO-* | *verbes, non moins utiles que* | *facetieux.* | [Vignette] | A Cothen | [Linie] | L'an M. DC. XX. 1 Bl., 215 gez. S., 15 S. TABLE DES PROVERBES, Sentences, & autres choses [...], 1 S. Druckfehlerberichtigung, letzte S. vacat. HAB: 295.25 Quod. (2), auch dig., u. 289.1 Quod. (10); ULB Halle: AB 127614 u. AB 44 3/i,6; SLUB Dresden: Ling. var. 385m. S. *Conermann: Fürstl. Offizin,* Anm. 28; *Dünnhaupt: Druckerei,* Nr. 37. Vorlage Moscheroschs dürfte die dreisprachige Ausgabe mit der Verdeutschung eines unbekannten Übersetzers u. der ital. Übertragung durch Johann Georg Schill (G. G. Schillio) gewesen sein: Tableau des actions d'un jeune gentilhomme divisé en forme de dialogues parsemé de discours histoires, sentences & proverbes non moins utiles que facetieux (Strasbourg 1637), mit den ital. bzw. dt. Titeln: Ritratto delle attioni d'un Giouane Gentiluomo, divisa in forma di dialoghi; Abbildung dess Lebens und Handlungen eines jungen von Adel gesprächsweiss verfasst, von ... Samuel Bernhard frantzösisch beschrieben, ... ins Teutsche uebersetzt ... tradotti in Toscano da G. G. Schillio. (http://www.sudoc.fr./117315508). Digitalisat nach dem unvollständigen Expl. ohne Titelbl. in der SLUB Dresden: Ling. Gall. 457g. Vgl. *Conermann: Harsdörffers Plan,* bes. Anm. 53–57. Das Buch widmete der Moscherosch wohl bekannte Blasius Eggen P. L., Mitglied des Straßburger Großen Rats u. zeitweiliger Amtmeister, dem Übersetzer Schill mit einem Gedicht. Blasius Eggen war ein gebildeter Verwandter des Moscherosch-Freunds Carolus Eggen. *Kühlmann/ Schäfer: Oberrhein,* 22 Anm. 38. Der Straßburger Blasius Eggen ist 1613–1641/42 durch Straßburger Disputationen u. durch seine lat. Gelegenheitsgedichte bezeugt: *Flood,* 478 f. Über den aus Durlach stammenden Schill wissen wir noch weniger. Walter E. Schäfer: Johann Heinrich Schill (ca. 1615–1645). Zwei kleine Funde. In: WBN 27 (1990), 12 f. entdeckt J. G. Schill als Studenten in Bourges u. vermutet, daß er ein Bruder Johann Heinrich Schills war, welcher dem Kreis um die AGT zuzurechnen ist (s. 440525 II). Im *VD17* werden 1620, 1622 u. 1623 drei juristische Straßburger Disputationen J. G. Schills verzeichnet, außerdem eine Diatribe zu Sueton (1623 unter dem Vorsitz von Matthias Bernegger, VD17 23:247821U), die auch ein lat. Gedicht von Blasius Eggen enthält. HAB: 241.1 Hist. (10). *Schäfer: Moscheroschs Technologie* (s. o.), 222 kannte diese Ausgabe nicht (vgl. ders., Freundschaft, 152 Anm. 41), behauptete aber, daß diese von Moscherosch unter dem Titel einer *Anleitung* herausgegebene Fassung von Moscherosch übersetzt u. erweitert worden sei: „Agil, wie er war, nutzte er die Nebenarbeit zur Übersetzung und Erweiterung eines Lehrbuchs des Französischen für junge Adlige." — Bei der von Moscherosch besorgten Auflage des erstmals 1637 gedruckten Werks handelt es sich um eine Titelauflage, die im Wesentlichen mit der Erstausgabe identisch ist. Auch wenn das Titelblatt dieses älteren, in der SLUB Dresden erhaltenen Drucks fehlt (daneben fehlen die Bogen X u. Y, das Inhaltsverzeichnis auf Bl. [Zz viij] v – Aaa 3 r u. der Abschiedsgruß an den ‚geliebten Leser' auf Bl. Aaa 3 v — [Aaa 4] r), dürfte er mit ziemlicher Gewißheit ebenfalls in der Offizin Johann Philipp Mülbes hergestellt worden sein, zumal die Drucke ab Bl. A ij den exakt identischen Satz haben, was nicht nur der Augenschein nahelegt, sondern auch aus einem Stichprobenvergleich kleinerer Setzfehler resultiert (s. u.). Dem Druck von 1645 wurde ein neuer, vollständiger (da es sich um ein Oktavbändchen handelt, heißt das: achtblättriger) Bogen vorangestellt, der mit dem Titelblatt beginnt u. der u. a. die Widmung Moscheroschs umfaßt. Entfernt wurde dafür Bl. A [i] (in der Erstausgabe paginiert als S. 1 u. 2), wodurch es zu einem Bruch bei der Bogenzählung kam: Auf Bl. [):(viij], dem letzten Blatt des neu hinzugefügten ersten Bogens, folgt in der Titelauflage Bl. A ij. Von dem in beiden Auflagen auf S. 2 beginnenden Haupttext (S. 1 ist in der Titelauflage nicht paginiert) wurde allein diese Seite, auf der sich der Anfang der zweispaltig gesetzten frz. u. ital. Version befindet, für die Titelauflage neu

gesetzt. Der Neusatz ist augenfällig (die beide Spalten überspannende, in großen Typen gesetzte ital. Überschrift der Erstauflage wurde in die rechte Spalte verlagert, in der linken Spalte findet man nun eine frz. Übersetzung), läßt sich aber auch durch einen kleinen Fehler am Seitenende belegen: Anstatt des in der Originalausgabe korrekten „Arr." schließt sie nun mit dem Kustos „Art.". Einige Belege dafür, daß der Druck vom selben Satz herrührt:
- Bl. A ij v, S. 4: Im Kolumnentitel „DIALOGVE PREMIER." ist das D in beiden Auflagen leicht nach rechts gekippt;
- Bl. B [1] v, S. 18: Im Kolumnentitel „DIALOGVE PREMIER." sind beide I deutlich unter die Grundlinie gerutscht;
- Bl. C ij v, S. 36: Die Paginierung lautet in beiden Auflagen fälschlicherweise „63";
- Bl. G ij v, S. 102: Die Paginierung lautet in beiden Auflagen fälschlicherweise „192";
- Bl. [O vij] v, S. 222: Die Paginierung ist in beiden Auflagen so schräg gedruckt, daß die letzte 2 nicht mehr auf der Grundlinie, sondern der unteren Begrenzung für Unterlängen zu stehen scheint;
- Bl. [Q viij] r, S. 253: In beiden Auflagen lautet der Kolumnentitel fälschlicherweise „Das Vierdtr Gerspräch." (sonst „Vierdte");
- Bl. Ee iij r, S. 435: In den ersten beiden Zeilen ist das jeweils letzte Zeichen (eine Virgel bzw. ein E) in beiden Auflagen in derselben Weise stark in die Oberlänge gerutscht;
- Bl. Ss v v, S. 648: Die Paginierung lautet in beiden Auflagen fälschlicherweise „684".

Der Befund ergibt, daß man für die Auflage, die unter Moscheroschs Namen läuft, Restbestände der Auflage von 1637 verwendete, wobei man vorn u. hinten jeweils einen neuen Bogen hinzufügte. Außerdem wurde auf der letzten freien Seite des Bogens Zz, auf dem der Haupttext endet, nachträglich die erste Seite des Inhaltsverzeichnisses gedruckt (d. h. Bl. [Zz viiJ] v).

1 Die beiden Gedichte Moscheroschs u. Boecklers (Beil. I u. III) zum vierten Teil von Harsdörffers *Frauenzimmer-Gesprächspielen* (1644) beziehen dessen Gesellschaftsnamen (Der Spielende) auf seine Arbeit zum Nutzen der deutschen Sprache (Stichwörter: Spiel/ Gewinn, Fruchtbringen, Nutzen, bezogen auf die deutsche Sprache). Beide Poeme folgen in der Quelle aufeinander. In seiner Zugabe zum vierten Teil („MANTISSA") verfaßte Harsdörffer lat. Emblembeschreibungen u. Anagrammata u. a. auf Boecklers Herodian- u. Velleius-Paterculus-Ausgaben (S. 727 f. „EMBLEMA in emaculatissimam editionem *Herodiani*" u. S. 729–731 „EMBLEMA ad eundem *Vellejum Paterculum* accurantem"). Vgl. oben K 3 (Herodian) u. C. VELLEII PATERCVLI Hist. Rom. Ad M. VINICIUM COS: Libri duo. Cum annotatis JOANNIS HENRICI BŒCLERI (Argentorati 1642: Joan. Philippus Mülbius). HAB: Ln 2464 (1). Mit Gedicht Harsdörffers u. a.; JOANNIS HENRICI BŒCLERI CHARACTERES POLITICI Velleiani (Argentorati 1642: Joan. Philippus Mülbius). 72 Bl.; HAB: Ln 2464 (2) u. a. Vgl. auch Moscheroschs undat. Brief an Boeckler mit Versen auf die vollendete Velleius Paterculus-Ausgabe in SUB Hamburg: Sup ep. 24, Bl. 336.

K II 1 Friedrich Reichard Mockel († Dez. 1643), schwed. Resident in Benfeld. In dessen Dienst war Johann Michael Moscherosch (FG 436. 1645) etwa im Mai 1643 als Sekretär getreten, nachdem er ihm proschwed. Verse gesandt hatte. Vgl. J. B. Ellerbach: Der Dreißigjährige Krieg im Elsaß 1618–1648. 3 Bde. Mühlhausen (Ober-Elsaß) 1912–1928, III (1633–1648), hg. August Scherlen, 443 u. ö.; E. Trittin: Johann Michael Moscherosch. Zu Leben und Werk und einer wieder aufgefundenen Schrift auf Gustav Adolf. In: Schicksalswege am Oberrhein. Heidelberg 1952, 136–164; *Schäfer: Moscherosch*, 127–133. Schäfer setzt ohne Grund Mockels Tod erst im Dezember 1644 an. Hugo Grotius schrieb jedoch

440616 Johann Michael Moscherosch

am 23.12.1643 an Friherre Axel Oxenstierna (FG 232): „Mockelium mortuum hic intelligo et doleo, fuit enim publico utilis." *AOSB* SA IV, 375. Auch der Inhalt u. die Jahresangabe des vorliegenden Briefs weisen deutlich nach, daß Moscherosch noch über ein Jahr nach Mockels Tod weiter in Benfeld amtierte, ehe er sich am 30.3.1645 an Oxenstierna mit dem Gesuch um eine Neuverpflichtung (als „Amtman, Agenten oder Secretaire d'Estat" oder als Vogt zu Ehrstein) wandte, das aber zu keiner weiteren Anstellung führte. *Reifferscheid*, 607–610. Moscherosch trug Oxenstierna sogar ein seltenes Manuskript aus seinem Besitz an, das Axel Lewenhaupt (Löwenhaupt) Graf v. Raspurg u. Falckenstein „von König Carle in Schweden [Karl IX.] hochseeligster Gedechtnus Gnaden mit eigen handen auf seinem haüslein zu Rossheim im Elsas geschrieben" habe. Vgl. *Reifferscheid*, 607–610.

2 Der dänisch-schwedische Krieg (1643–1645) hatte soeben (12.12. n. St.) mit dem überraschenden Einfall des schwed. Feldherrn Lennart Torstensson in Holstein begonnen. Vgl. 440324 K 18 u. 440927 K 8.

3 Unter dem Schein Philanders oder Philanders halber, d.h. wohl nur in satirischer Manier, in der Rolle Philanders. Die Epigramme stehen verständlicherweise nicht in Moscheroschs *Wunderliche Satyrische vnd Warhafftige Gesichte Philanders von Sittewalt* oder in den Ausgaben seiner *EPIGRAMMATA* (1643, 1649 u. 1665; s. zu diesen oben K I, 450818 Q u. 450901 Q).

4 Johann Georg Styrzel (1591–1668), Bürgermeister in Rothenburg ob der Tauber u. Gelehrter. Der Briefwechsel zwischen Styrzel u. Moscherosch ist Ende 1643 oder Anfang 1644 ebensowenig überliefert wie die Korrespondenz zwischen Georg Philipp Harsdörffer (FG 368) u. Moscherosch. Hier können Gelegenheitsgedichte Aufschluß bieten. Vgl. Styrzels lat. Epigramm in *Harsdörffer: Frauenzimmer Gesprächspiele* IV (1644), 725f. (Styrzels undat., aber wohl vor dem April 1644 an Harsdörffer gesandtes „Carmen Gratulatorium Ad Colloquia Dramatica", s. 440426).

5 Der Briefwechsel zwischen Moscherosch u. Harsdörffer ist für Ende 1643 u. Anfang 1644 nicht überliefert. S. Anm. 4.

K III Johann Heinrich Boeckler wurde weder ein Mitglied der FG noch der AGT, die er schon 1634 erwähnte u. deren Gründungsmitglieder er in einem Ehrengedicht nennt: Des Jesaias Romplers von Löwenhalt erstes gebüsch seiner Reim-getichte. Getruckt zu Strasburg/ bej Joh. Phil. Mülben/ in dem 1647.ten jar Chrl.er z. (Nachdr. hg. v. Wilhelm Kühlmann u. Walter E. Schäfer. Tübingen 1988), 230. Auch in Johann Matthias Schneubers (FG 498. 1648) Gedichtsammlungen erschienen Boecklers Zuschriften (Johann-Matthias Schneübers Gedichte, Gedruckt zu Strasburg bey Joh: Philipp Mülben. M.DC.XL.IV., S. 16; Fasciculus POEMATUM LATINORVM M. JOH. MATTHIÆ SCHNEUBERI P. L. Gymnasiarchæ Argentoratensis. ARGENTORATI. Ex Officina JOSIÆ STÆDELI, ACADEMIÆ TYPOGRAPHI. ANNO M. DC. LVI., S. 138. *Bopp: Tannengesellschaft*, 122f., 389, 396 u. 430. Betreffs der FG scheint Boeckler Vorbehalte gegenüber Jesaias Rompler v. Löwenhalt geäußert zu haben. Sie betrafen auch Carl Gustav v. Hilles (FG 302) Buch über die FG, *Hille: Teutscher Palmbaum* von 1647 (s. zu diesem Werk 451008), u. die Werke des Carl Melchior Grotnitz v. Grodnau (FG 601. 1653). S. *Kiel: Briefe des J. Rompler v. Löwenhalt*, 241f. u. *DA Köthen I. 8:* 470824.

1 Vgl. dazu die Ablehnung des Sprachbellizismus in 440525 II.

2 ‚Stimplen' verweist auf zwei verschiedene Verben, die in diesem Fall beide semantisch präsent zu sein scheinen: *stümpeln*, im Sinne von ‚stümpern, unsachgemäß handeln oder pfuschen', u. *stümmeln*, im Sinne eines körperlichen Verstümmelns, das in der nicht allein durch diesen Fall belegten Bedeutung „form und gestalt von worten ungehörig kürzen

und verunstalten" (*DW* X.4, 408) deutlich sichtbar ist. S. *DW* X.4, 403–409, s.v. stümmeln u. *DW* X.4, 418–419, s.v. stümpeln. Vgl. Art. „Stümper" u. „Stümpler, Pfuscher", in: Ernst Martin/ Hans Lienhart: Wörterbuch der elsässischen Mundarten. Straßburg 1899–1907, II, 597a. Bei *Stieler*, 2226 werden die beiden Wortformen noch nicht semantisch, sondern allein dialektal voneinander geschieden: „Stümpelen/ & *aliâ dialecto* Stümmeln". Neben der Hauptbedeutung ‚verstümmeln' („mutilare, truncare, membrorum parte mulctare", d.i. mulcare) führt Stieler allerdings auch eine figurative Bedeutungsebene im Sinne von ‚ein Werk oder eine Arbeit schlecht machen' auf: „*ac* hebetare opus aliqvod, depravare labores". Der *Stümper*, der „urspr. wohl der Handwerker [ist], der mit stumpfem, also unzulänglichem Werkzeug am Werkstoff herumpfuscht, vielleicht auch der Schneider, der aus Reststückchen ein Kleidungsstück zus.-flickt" (*Kluge/ Mitzka*, 761), wird in der Formulierung Boecklers sichtbar, ohne daß die etymologische Herkunft aus dem Handwerk schon ganz verblaßt wäre – definiert er ‚Stimplen' doch im folgenden Vers als „Stück- und Flickweiß zu schreiben".

3 *Harsdörffer: Frauenzimmer-Gesprächspiele* IV (1644; Ndr. 1968), 191 (Ndr. 235) führt als Beispiel für emblematische Figuren das „Obersinnbild der Gesprächspiele" an: „eine Sonnenuhr von Blumwerke/ mit der Schrift: **Es nutzet und behagt.**" Dieses für die *Gesprächspiele* programmatische Sinnbild („Es Nützet vnd behagt Auff manche art") war mit einer poetischen „Erklärung" erstmals im 1. Teil der *Gesprächspiele* (²1644; Ndr. 1968), Bl. [Avj]v (Kupferstich) u. [Avij]r (Gedicht) veröffentlicht worden (Ndr. S.10 u. 11), sodann im 3. Teil (1643; Ndr. 1968) mit einer anderen Erklärung, Ndr. S.10 u. 11; wie in einer Variante des Stichs auch im 2. Teil (1642 u. ²1657/ Ndr. 1968), Rückseite des Titelblatts mit einer dialogisierten Auslegung des Emblems S.1–3. S. im vorliegenden Band die Abb. S.287 (zu 440715) u. 440715 nebst Erläuterungen dort in K 9.

440715

Georg Philipp Harsdörffers Widmungsgedicht an Fürst Ludwig

Q *Harsdörffer: Frauenzimmer-Gesprächspiele* I (²1644; Ndr. 1968), Bl. [A iv] v – [A vj] r (Ndr. S.6–9). D. i. [Georg Philipp Harsdörffer:] FRAVENZJMMER GESPRECH-SPJELE/ | so bey | Ehr- und Tugendliebenden Gesellschaften/ | mit nutzlicher Ergetzlichkeit/ beliebet und geübet werden mögen/ | Erster Theil. | Aus Jtaliänischen/ Frantzösischen und Spanischen Scribenten | angewiesen/ | und jetzund ausführlicher auf sechs Personen gerichtet/ | und mit einer neuen Zugabe gemehret/ | Durch | Einen Mitgenossen der Hochlöblichen | FRVCHTBRJNGENDEN GESELLSCAFT *[sic]*. | Nürnberg/ | Gedruckt und verlegt bey Wolffgang Endtern. | Jm Jahre 1644. HAB: Lo 2622: 1 (auch dig.). Dieses Ex. stammt aus dem Besitz von Lgf. Hermann IV. v. Hessen-Rotenburg (FG 374). Sein Besitzvermerk auf dem Titelblatt: „HermanLzHeßen 1647". Das Ex. ging nach Ausweis eigenh. Schenkungs- und Besitzeinträge auf den Vorsatzblättern 1692 von den Händen seiner Schwägerin, Lgn. Eleonora v. Hessen-Eschwege (1626–1692), in die ihrer Tochter über: Hzn. Christina v. Braunschweig-Bevern (1649–1702), Gattin Hz. Ferdinand Albrechts I. (FG 842. 1673). Christina schenkte das Ex. dann ihrer ältesten Tochter Sophia Eleonora (1674–1711) zu ihrem Namenstag am 21.2.1695. Weiteres HAB-Expl.: 166.7 Eth. — Das Widmungsgedicht „An den Nehrenden", das auf den 15.7.1644 datiert ist, fehlt in der Erstausgabe des ersten Teils der *Frauenzimmer Gesprächspiele* von 1641, s. 410300 Q. Dem Übereignungsgedicht folgt ein emblematischer Kupferstich mit der Inscriptio „Es Nützet vnd behagt Auff manche art", der auf Harsdörffers FG-Imprese („Der Spielende" — „Auf manche art", *GB 1646*) und im Bild der Kokospalme und der daneben gesetzten „Erklärung" in Gedichtform auf die FG und den Nährenden (F. Ludwig) anspielt (s. u., Abbildung S. 287 und Gedichttext). Die Widmungszuschrift der Erstausgabe (410300) folgt in der 2. Ausgabe als „Alte Vorrede An die Hochlöbliche FRVCHTBRJNGENDE GESELLSCHAFT" auf Bl. [Aiij] v – Bij r. Das Vorwerk beschließen ein „Vorbericht An den Lesenden" und des Verlegers („Buchführers", d. i. Wolfgang Endter, Nürnberg) „Bericht an den Leser" (Bl. Bij v – Bv r). — *BN: Bischoff*, 407; *Dünnhaupt: Handbuch*, 1981 (Art. Harsdörffer, Nr. 9.I).

Vbereig[n]ungsgedicht
An[a1] den
Nehrenden[b2]
der Hochlöblichen
FRVCHTBRJNGENDEN GESELLSCHAFT
Höchstansehlichen und Ruhmwürdigsten
Stiffter und Vrheber.

Advertida la Naturaleza distinguiò las Provincias, y las cerco con altos montes, rios y olas del mar, para dificultar sus intentos à la ambition humana: con este fin constituyo la diversidad de climas, de naturales y de lenguas. Saavedra en los Empres. Polit. f. 323.[4]	[Av r] ES[c3] ist Betrachtens wehrt/ wie richtig die Natur besondert jedes Volk/ und als mit einer Schnur
	    ümzogen jedes Land. Das Meer diß Reich beschliesset/
	    und jener tiefe Strom sein Grentzgebiet ümgiesset:
	die hohen Pyreneen/ der Schweitzer Berg und Thal/
	der Alpen Wolkenspitz ist solcher Markung Mahl.
	    Es muß der Berge Gurt* die weite Welt ümgeben/
	    und jedes Volk vernügt *[sic]* und friedlich lehren leben;
	wie gleich zu solchen End' ein sondre Sittenart/
	nach Leitung der Natur/ in jedem Land gebahrt.
	    Doch darf der Menschen Geitz/ und Blutesdurst zu streiten/
	    so grentzbefeste Stein' aus Frevel überschreiten/
	und durch der Waffen Trotz den Lastren machen Raum/
	ja selbest der Natur entreissen ihren Zaum.

*CLXXI, 12.[5]	Jst nicht auch jede Sprach' in allen unterschieden?
	    und dannoch sind damit die Teutschen nicht zu frieden; [Av v]
	So gar/ daß oftermals der grobe Pövelmann
	zerstümmelt Teutschlatein/ daß er noch weiß noch kan.
	    Er wil Frantzösisch/ Welsch/ und fremde Wörter führen;
	    das/ was er nie versteht/ sol seine Rede zieren.
	Hierüber eifert recht ein Fürst von hohem Stand/

☞ Spielrede 20.[6]	der wider solchen Gifft/ **in altem Allmanns Land**/
	    als seinem Stammgebiet/ bepflantzet einen Garten/
	    daraus nun nach und nach viel Früchte zu gewarten/
	die steuren dieser Pest/ und heilen ohn Beschwert/

was aus der fremden Luft' uns insgesamt gefehrt[7].
 Er hat mit Müh' und Fleiß besämet und gemehret/
gepfropfet und benetzt/ (in dem der Krieg verstöret/
und alles schlägt zu Grund/) so manche Frucht und Kraut/
und manches Kunstgewächs mit eigner Hand gebaut.
 Er hat die **Bonenerbs**[8]/ die sonst zur Erden lieget/
und in dem Felde sich auf schlanke weise bieget/ [Avi r]
aus sonder hoher Gnad' an einen Stab gehenkt/
erhaben Erden aus/ und dergestalt beschenkt/
 daß/ bald die bunte Blüh' an Blätlein zu erkennen/
er selbst davon beginnt den **Spielenden** zu nennen:
deswegen bringt er ihm die Erstlinge der Frucht/
die vor der Klügelhitz so wehrten Schatten sucht.
 Der anfangs das Gewächs/ so ring es ist/ **genehret**/
mit solchem Gnadenschein erhaben vnd gemehret/
der frische diese Frucht mit Hulde ferner an/
daß dieser **Bonenzucht** grun' auf der Musen Bahn.
Krön ihn/ O höchster Gott/ mit Glückbereiften Jahren/
daß Kunst und Fried/ durch ihn/ je mehr und mehr sich
bahrē.

   Dem höchstgeehrten
   NEHRENDEN
Nürnberg den 15. des Heumo- Zu unterthäniger Ehrbezeugung
nats/ im Jahre 1644.   übersendet durch
             Den Spielenden.

[Avii r]   **Erklärung.**[9]

NVtzlich[d] behagend' ausbildende Schrift/
 Bist du bedachtsam hiehero gestifft?
 Die nehrende Kertze der **Sonnen** erfreut:
Der fröhliche **Rebensaft** frommet dem Magen/
die lieblichen **Blümelein** pflegen zu tragen
 viel niedliche Labung/ die Kranken gedeit!
 Die Sonne die **Sinne** so Rähtselweis deut/
die **fröhlichen Geister**/ der Reben behagen/
die mancherley Blumen/ ergetzliche **Fragen**
 verblümen die Schwelle/ darauf sie gestreut.
Dieses dreyschichtig zusammengeschifft/
Leser/ dein **Nutz** und **Belusten** betrifft.

Erklärung zum „Vberreichungsgedicht" im „Ordnungsregister", hier Bl. Cc v/
Ndr. S.398:

440715 Georg Philipp Harsdörffer

> Das Vberreichungsgedicht.
> AN[a] den
> *NEHRENDEN*.[b]

☞ LII/5.[10]
Weiset in dem **A** der Hochlöblichen **Fruchtbringenden Gesellschaft Jndianischen Palmbaum**: Das **N** eine Weitzengarbe des höchstgeehrten *NEHRENDEN* Gesellschafts Gemähl. Der Anfangsbuchstab zeiget erstermeldten **Stiffters der Fruchtbringenden Gesellschaft** Bildnis.

T **a** *Initiale A in Schmuckvignette mit Zierstück: Palmenbaum, s. Abb. S. 286.* — **b** *Initiale N mit Zierstück: Weizengarbe, s. Abb. S. 286.* — **c** *Initiale E in Zierstück mit dem Porträt F. Ludwigs, s. Abb. S. 286.* — **d** *Initiale N mit Zierstück: Sonnenuhr, s. Abb. S. 287.*

K 1 Vgl. die Erklärung Georg Philipp Harsdörffers (FG 368. Der Spielende) zu seinem „Vberreichungsgedicht" im ‚Ordnungsregister' der *Gesprächspiele*, I (²1644, Ndr. 1968, 398). Das Gedicht zeige in der Initiale A die Gesellschaftspflanze des Palmbaums.
  2 Erklärung Harsdörffers, a. a. O. (wie Anm. 1): Die Initiale N zeige des Nährenden Imprese, die Weizengarbe. F. Ludwig sollte diese Initiale später kritisieren, da seine FG-Imprese nicht eine Weizengarbe, sondern ein weißes Weizenbrot zeigt. S. 440616 K III 3, 450400 K 4, 450529 K 1, 450611 K 1, 450817 K 11 u. 450919A.
  3 Erklärung Harsdörffers, a. a. O. (wie Anm. 1): „Der Anfangsbuchstab [E] zeiget erstermeldten **Stiffters der Fruchtbringenden Gesellschaft** Bildnis."
  4 Diego de Saavedra Fajardo (1584–1648): IDEA DE VN Principe politico Christiano, Representada en cien Empresas (München 1640), mit den Emblemstichen von Johann Sadeler (1588–1665). HAB: Sf 211; auch dig. S. 323 zeigt das 48. der 101 ausgiebig erläuterten Embleme, „COL SENNO E CON LA MANO" (Mit Verstand u. mit der Hand) mit gepanzerter Hand, die ein Stachelschwein erfaßt u. niederdrückt. Die Erläuterung S. 323–340. Eine vom Autor ergänzte u. völlig neu bearbeitete Fassung erschien 1642 in Mailand, hier erscheint die besagte Imprese als Nr. 59 in der Rubrik „Cómo se ha de haber el Príncipe en el gobierno de sus estados": Wie der Fürst sich in der Regierung seiner Staaten verhalten soll (Ausg. Madrid 1999, s. u., S. 182). Die Erklärung zum 59. Emblem (S. 685–704) beginnt mit den Worten: „Advertida la Naturaleza, distinguió las provincias y las cercó ya con murallas de montes, ya con fosos de ríos y ya con las soberbias olas del mar, para dificultar sus intentos a la ambición humana. Con este fin constituyó la diversidad de climas, de naturales, de lenguas y estilos. Con lo cual, diferenciada esta nación de aquélla, se uniese cada una para su conservación, sin rendirse fácilmente al poder y tiranía de los estranjeros. Pero no bastaron los reparos de estos límites y términos naturales para que no los violase el apetito insaciable de dominar, porque la ambición es tan poderosa en el corazón humano, que juzga por estrechas las cinco zonas de la tierra." (S. 685 f.) Die Mailänder Ausgabe wurde bis ins 19. Jh. immer wieder aufgelegt u. in mehrere Sprachen, auch ins Deutsche (1655) übersetzt. Verschiedene Neuausgaben sind greifbar, darunter Diego Saavedra Fajardo: Empresas políticas. Ed. de Sagrario López Poza. Madrid 1999 (mit Bibliographie der Ausgaben der *Idea* S. 145 ff.), obige Zitate nach dieser Ausgabe. Vgl. Christine Kielmann: Diego de Saavedra Fajardo: „Empresas Políticas". In: Sinnbild — Bildsinn: Emblembücher der Stadtbibliothek Trier. Red. Michael Schunck. Trier 1991, 69–78; Christian Romanoski: Tacitus Emblematicus: Diego de Saavedra

> **Vbereigungsgedicht**
> **AN den NEHRENDEN**
> der hochlöblichen
> **FRVCHTBRINGENDEN GESELLSCHAFT**
> Höchstansehlichen und Ruhmwürdigsten
> Stiffter und Vrheber.

Georg Philipp Harsdörffers (FG 368) „Vbereigungsgedicht An den NEHRENDEN". Zu 440715.
1. Zierinitiale A mit der Kokospalme, die die Nutzbarkeit der Fruchtbringenden Gesellschaft ausdrückt.
2. Zierinitiale N im Namen des „NEHRENDEN" mit einer Weizengarbe.

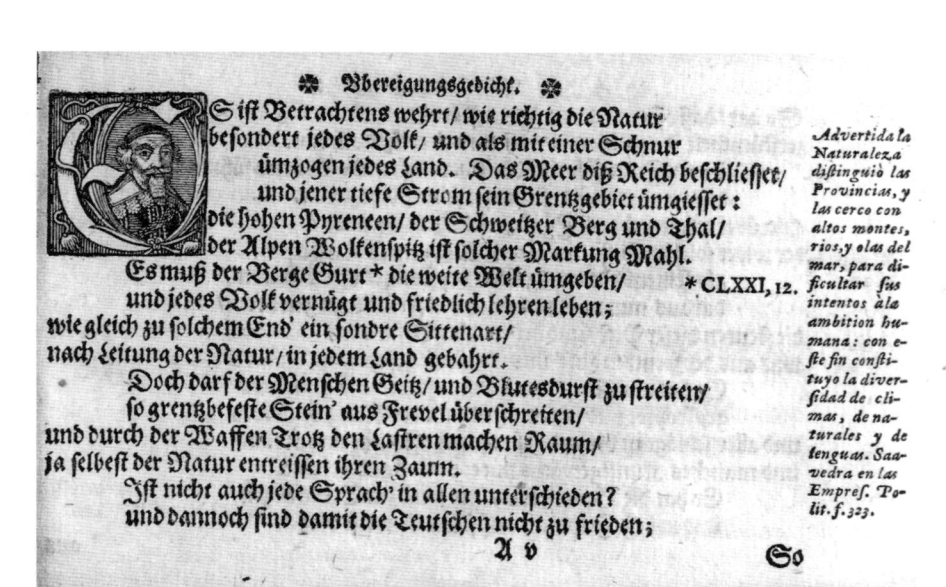

> ❋ **Vbereigungsgedicht.** ❋
> ES ist Betrachtens wehrt/ wie richtig die Natur
> besondert jedes Volk/ und als mit einer Schnur
> ümzogen jedes Land. Das Meer diß Reich beschliesset/
> und jener tiefe Strom sein Grentzgebiet ümgiesset:
> die hohen Pyreneen/ der Schweitzer Berg und Thal/
> der Alpen Wolkenspitz ist solcher Markung Mahl.
> Es muß der Berge Gurt * die weite Welt ümgeben/   * CLXXI, 12.
> und jedes Volk vernügt und friedlich lehren leben;
> wie gleich zu solchem End' ein sondre Sittenart/
> nach Leitung der Natur/ in jedem Land gebahrt.
> Doch darf der Menschen Geitz/ und Blutesdurst zu streiten/
> so grentzbefeste Stein' aus Frevel überschreiten/
> und durch der Waffen Trotz den Lastren machen Raum/
> ja selbst der Natur entreissen ihren Zaum.
> Ist nicht auch jede Sprach' in allen unterschieden?
> und dannoch sind damit die Teutschen nicht zu frieden;
>   A v   So

Advertida la Naturaleza distinguió las Provincias, y las cerco con altos montes, rios, y olas del mar, para dificultar sus intentos àla ambition humana: con este fin constituyo la diversidad de climas, de naturales y de lenguas. Saavedra en las Empres. Polit. f. 323.

3. Zierinitiale E mit Brustbild Fürst Ludwigs.

Erklärung.

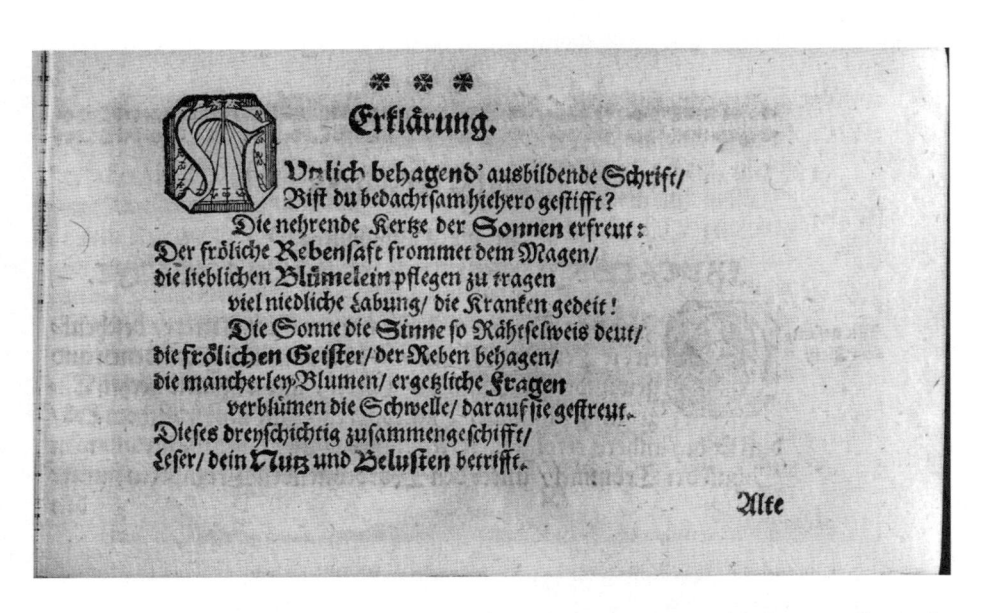

Vnlich behagend' ausbildende Schrift/
Bist du bedachtsam hiehero gestifft?
Die nehrende Kertze der Sonnen erfreut:
Der fröliche Rebensaft frommet dem Magen/
die lieblichen Blümelein pflegen zu tragen
viel niedliche Labung/ die Kranken gedeit!
Die Sonne die Sinne so Rähtselweis deut/
die frölichen Geister/ der Reben behagen/
die mancherley Blumen/ ergetzliche Fragen
verblümen die Schwelle/ darauf sie gestreut.
Dieses dreyschichtig zusammengeschifft/
Leser/ dein Nutz und Belusten betrifft.

Alte

Georg Philipp Harsdörffers (FG 368) Doppelimprese „Es Nützet vnd behagt. Auff manche art" mit einem auslegenden Gedicht: „Erklärung." Zu 440715.

Fajardo und seine „Empresas Políticas". Berlin 2006, insbes. S. 513–516. Harsdörffer verwendete die Aussage aus Saavedra Fajardo auch in seiner „Rede von dem Worte SPIEL", einer „Zugabe" im 4. Teil der *Frauenzimmer-Gesprächspiele* (1644, Ndr. 1968), 461/ Ndr. 505: „Es hat die Natur selbsten jedes Landes Bezirk mit hohen Gebürgen befestiget/ mit der Völker Sitten unterschieden/ durch die mancherley Sprachen abgesondert: Wir Teutsche überfahren diese Marksteine/ wir unterbrechen das Wolständige/ und zerrütten die im Sprichwort berühmte Teutsche Treue/ in dem wir/ durch einen neuen Babelbau/ uns groß zu machen bemühet sind." — Auch hier dient die gleichsam topographisch-natürlich vorgegebene Unterscheidung der Sprachen u. Kulturen der Argumentation gegen das Überhandnehmen von Fremdwörtern im Deutschen.

5 *Harsdörffer: Frauenzimmer-Gesprächspiele* IV (1644; Ndr. 1968), 171. Gesprächspiel („Der Sinnbilder Obschrift"), Absatz 12 (S. 224 f./ Ndr. S. 268 f.). Dort heißt es unter Verweis auf Athanasius Kirchers *Magnes siue De arte magnetica opvs tripartitvm* (Rom 1641. Ex. in der LB Eutin. In der HAB ein Ex. der 2. Ausg., Köln 1643: 218.25 Quod. [1]): „Der Magnet dienet in den Feldmessen/ Schiffarten/ Sonnenuhren/ Artzneyen/ u. d. g. daß also der hochlöblichen Fruchtbringenden Geselschaft Gemählwort/ **alles zu Nutzen**/ zur Figur eines Sinnbildes haben kann/ eine **Magnetketten**/ deren Glieder durch besagte **Anhaltende Tugend** aneinander hangen. Der Meinung/ daß nunmehr ungezweiffelt der Teutschen Sprache TugendVermögen nach und nach ergründet und durchforschet werde/ weilen auch die natürlichen Vrsachen des Magnetes/ welche bishero unbewust gewesen/ und an das Liecht herfürkommen: Jn dem nemlich aus der Erfahrung erhellet/ daß der starckziehend Magnet aus den tieffsten/ und der Erden Mittelpuncte nähesten Gründen erhaben [*Lies:* erhoben] wird; daß die Erden mit hohen Gebürgen (aus welchen allen man das nöhtigste Metall das Eisen und den Magnet gräbet/) von Mittag gegen Mitternacht zu gleichsam umgürdet/ wie sie anderseits die Sonne von Morgen gegen Abend mit ihrem Laufe umwindet; daraus zu schliessen/ der Magnet wende sich nicht nach dem Nord- oder Leitsterne/ (wie man ins gemein wähnet) sondern nach den Mitternächtischen Erden [...]." Harsdörffers dazu ersonnenes Sinnbild (S. 226/ Ndr. 270; auch in *Harsdörffer: Frauenzimmer-Gesprächspiele* II [²1657; Ndr. 1968], S. 8/ Ndr. S. 26) zeigt eine senkrechte Eisenkette mit einem Magnetstein in der Mitte, die Himmel u. Erde verbindet, mit der Inscriptio: „Allen zu Nutzen". Sein mit Längen- oder Betonungszeichen versehenes Gedicht gibt dieses als in zwölfsilbigen Mischversen (Verszeile bestehend aus Spondeus, Daktylus, Trochäus, Daktylus, Trochäus; Zäsur nach der 5. Silbe) verfaßtes zu erkennen u. legt das Emblem aus (S. 227/ Ndr. S. 271): „Nun der Kunstverstand alle Nutzbarkeit findet | die der Eisenhold/ oder Wunderstein führet: | Wie Magnetische Kräften werden gespüret | Von dem Mittelpunct/ der den Erdenkreiß gründet; | Wie der Bergegurd dieses Weltgebeu bindet/ | der von Süden an gegen Norden zu rühret; | Wie sich Eisenwerk aller Orten gebühret/ | und nach solcher Spur der Magnete sich windet. | Sol dann unsere Sprache niemand ergründen? | Von Anhaltischer Tugend löblichem Stammen/ | Die Fruchtbringenden ihre Wurtzelkraft finden! | unsre herrliche Teutsche Zunge beschutzen | und mit Fürstlichen Gnaden halten zusammen/ | bringt vielfältige Frücht' uns allen zu Nutzen." Vgl. zu Harsdörffers kunstvollen Mischversen auch 431124 u. 431206 u. I. Mischverse probierte auch Diederich v. dem Werder (FG 31) in 440310A aus.

6 *Harsdörffer: Frauenzimmer-Gesprächspiele* IV (1644; Ndr. 1968), bemerkt in der 20. Spielrede der angehängten „Zugabe/ bestehend in einer Rede von dem Worte SPJELE: Verfasset Durch den Spielenden.": „So viel ist gewiß/ daß **Ascenes** [dazu 3 Randnoten: „des Gomers Sohn und Japets Enkel."; „de hoc nomine Gorop. Becan. I. 5. Indoscythico p. 459. ☞ CLXXVIII."] der Teutschen Stammvatter/ das Fürstenthum **Anhalt** zu seinem Ansitze erkieset/ und desselbē **Christlöblichen Fürsten das Schutzrecht unserer edlen**

Sprache gleichsam erblich hinterlassen: Gestalt dann eben in berührten Ankunft-Gebiete der Teutschen Völker/ hochernante Fürsten den **Fruchtbringenden Sprachgarten** angepflanzet/ auch noch fort und fort desselben Wachsthum pflegen/ darüber halten und handhaben." A. a. O., S. 465/ Ndr. S. 509.

7 Gefährdet oder auch gefährlich zukommt. Im Mhd. stv. „gevarn" noch neutral als „geschehen". *Lexer: Taschenwb.*, 69; vgl. *DW* IV.1.1, 2079; *Stieler*, 402 (s. v. „Fahren/ gefären/ & Gefärden").

8 Harsdörffers Gesellschaftspflanze waren „Die kleinen bunten Englischen oder Welschen Böhnlein" (*GB 1641/44*) bzw. die „Bunte[n] Bönelein von farben mancher art" (*GB Kö.* II u. *GB 1646*). Vgl. 410909 u. 411126 (K 4) u. die Abb. seiner Imprese aus dem *GB 1646* S. 290.

9 Die Doppelimprese und die dichterische „Erklärung". S. Abb. S. 287. Derselbe Stich war schon im 3. Teil der *Gesprächspiele* (1643; Ndr. 1968, S. 10) erschienen, jedoch mit einer anderen „Erklärung" (Sonett). Das Emblem zeigt in der Mitte eine Kokospalme mit dem Spruch „Es Nützet vnd behagt — Auff manche art", die Ränder links u. rechts markieren zwei früchtetragende Pomeranzenbäume. Innerhalb eines Gartens vor einer Schloßkulisse sind vorn zwei Sonnenuhren angelegt: die rechte mit an Stangen gezogenen Bohnen, der Gesellschaftspflanze Harsdörffers in der FG (s. Anm. 8), die linke mit einem Rebstock. Der Schatten fällt den Tagesstunden entsprechend auf 12 geometrisch abgeteilte Beete, die rechts mit den Großbuchstaben „DER SPIELENDE" u. links mit römischen Zahlbuchstaben gekennzeichnet sind. (Zum Thema „Sonnenuhren" vgl. auch Harsdörffers *Speculum Solis*, zuerst Nürnberg 1652). Im 3. Teil der *Gesprächspiele* liefert ein das Sinnbild auslegendes Sonett die „Erklärung" (im Ndr. ebenfalls auf S. 11). Es thematisiert den Wettstreit der Kunst mit der Natur, die in ihren mannigfaltigen Früchten, wie der Weinrebe oder den Bohnen, ebenso spielt wie die künstlichen Erfindungen des Menschen. Den Früchten gleichen die Worte, sie nutzen u. behagen, womit Harsdörffer zugleich die Absicht seiner Gesprächspiele benennt. Unter freier Zitation zweier Stellen aus den Sprüchen Salomonis — „Viel guts kompt einem durch die frucht des mundes" (Spr 12, 14, nach *Biblia [Luther 1545]*) u. „EJn wort geredt zu seiner zeit/ Jst wie gülden Epffel in silbern Schalen" (Spr 25, 11, nach *Biblia [Luther 1545]*) — schließt das Sonett: „Ein Wort zu seiner Zeit ist oft nicht zu bezahlen/ | den Pomerantzen gleich in schönen Silberschalen. | Oft nutzt es und behagt/ auf manche Weiß und Art!" Eine Variante dieses Kupfers auch im 1. Teil (1641 u. ²1644/ Ndr. 1968, S. 10), eine weitere im 2. Teil der *Gesprächspiele* (1642 u. ²1657/ Ndr. 1968), auf der Rückseite des Titelblatts. Sie zeigt in einem anderen u. prächtiger ausgestalteten Rahmenwerk nur die linke Hälfte des Emblems, den Weinstock als Sonnenuhr mit der Überschrift „Es nutzet vnd behagt". Die gesprächsweise Auslegung dieses Stichs folgt in der Erst- u. Zweitausgabe auf S. 1–3. Im 4. Teil der *Gesprächspiele* (1644; Ndr. 1968), S. 191 (Ndr. 235), kommt Harsdörffer erneut auf dieses „Obersinnbild" der *Gesprächspiele* zu sprechen, „welches ist eine Sonnenuhr von Blumwerke/ mit der Schrift: **Es nutzet und behagt**. Hier ist das Blumenfeld/ die umgesetzte Zahlen desselben/ der Zeigerreben/ nur für eine Figur zu halten; die Sonnen für die andere/ der Schatten für die dritte. Daß aber der Zeiger ein Reben [d. i. eine Weinranke]/ und der Schatten auf die siebende Zahl triffet/ sind Nebendeutungen." Vgl. dazu das 168. Gesprächspiel, ebd. 189/234 – 201/245: „Der Sinnbilder Figuren".

10 Das 52. Gesprächspiel (in *Harsdörffer: Frauenzimmer-Gesprächspiele* II [1642]. HAB: Lo 2621 [2]) behandelt die Sinnbilder (Embleme). Auf S. 9 ist die Palmenvignette abgebildet (s. die Vorderseite der Schutzumschläge dieser Edition) u. danach folgt das aus dem *GB 1629/30* bekannte Sonett auf die Palmenimprese der FG: „KOmpt/ lernt vom Palmenbaum [...]" (S. 9f.). Vgl. die 2. Ausg. des ersten Teils der *Gesprächspiele* (Nürnberg

290   Georg Philipp Harsdörffer 440715

Auf manche art.

Der Spielende.   368.

Die Bunte Bönelein von farben mancher art
    Ergetzen in sich / auch mit wolluſt gleichſam ſpielen:
  Der Nahme Spielend drumb mir nun gegeben ward/
Weil im gemüte man ergetzligkeit kan fülen/
Wan im geſpreche wird gantz tugendlich gebahrt/
  Zu theilen mit was man begriffen hat in vielen
Und frembden Ländern wol: Das nutzt dem Vaterland
Und bringet früchte vor Spielweiſ' in iedem ſtand'.
    G.P.H.   1642.

Georg Philip Harsdörffer

Die FG-Imprese Georg Philipp Harsdörffers (FG 368) aus dem GB 1646. Zu 440715.

1657, Ndr. 1968), S. 11–13 (mit Vignette u. Sonett). Vgl. insgesamt dazu *DA Köthen I. 1*, S. 76 u. 78–80.

440715A

Georg Philipp Harsdörffers Widmungsbrief an Herzog Christian Ludwig von Braunschweig-Calenberg

In der zweiten Auflage des Erstbands der *Frauenzimmer-Gesprächspiele* widmet Georg Philipp Harsdörffer (FG 368. Der Spielende) Hz. Christian Ludwig v. Braunschweig-Calenberg (FG 372. Der Reinherzige) seine „Schutzschrifft für die Teütsche Spracharbeit" als deren Protektor. Er wendet sich gegen die Bewahrer der eingefahrenen Sprachgewohnheit, die Sprachreformer wie Martin Opitz (FG 200) verfolgten und deren Werke unterdrücken. Schon die Alten haben geistige Erfindungen den Göttern zugeschrieben, so daß moderne Arbeiten wie Justus Georg Schottelius' (FG 397) ‚kunstgründige' Werke über die deutsche Sprache auch ruhmwürdig seien. Das gelte auch für erneute Erfindungen, wie die seit Platon (Sokrates) und Lukian bekannten Dialoge, z. B. Erasmus, Vives und Majoli, weil diese es auch im Deutschen erlauben, Streitfragen, Rätsel, Sprichworte, Lehren und Gedichte frei zu behandeln. Der Reinherzige, dem der Unverdrossene (Carl Gustav v. Hille. FG 302) die *Frauenzimmer-Gesprächspiele* gegeben hatte, zeigte sich dieser Arbeit so gewogen, daß Harsdörffer ihm nun die Schutzschrift widme.

Q Undatierter Widmungsbrief in [Zwischentitelblatt:] Schutzschrift/ | für | Die Teutsche Spracharbeit/ | und | Derselben Beflissene: | zu Einer Zugabe/ | den | Gesprächspielen | angefüget. durch den | SPJELENDEN. In: *Harsdörffer: Frauenzimmer-Gesprächspiele* I (^{2}1644, Ndr. 1968), Bl. [Yvj] r – Z v, jedoch mit eigener Paginierung S. 1–7 (Ndr. S. 343–350). HAB: Lo 2622 (1). Vgl. auch HAB: 166.7. Eth.

Das Zuschreiben
an der Hochfürstlichen
FRVCHTBRJNGENDEN GESELLSC[H]AFT
Tugend eiferiges/ und Christlöbliches
Mitgliede/
DEN REJNHERTZIGEN
der Teutschen Heldensprache
Vielmögenden Schutzherrn/ preiswürdigen
und Höchstgeehrten Handhaberen.   [S. 1]

Demosth. in Orat. contra Timocrat. edit. Basil. part. 3. f. 216.[2]

DJe[a] Locrenser[1] haben über ihren alten Gesetzen mit solcher Blindheit geeifert/ daß/ wer bey ihnen von einer Neurung reden wollen/ den Strang am Halse tragen/ und/ wann seine Meinung nicht gut befunden worden/ dardurch das Leben verlieren müssen. Mit so unfugsamer Strengigkeit wolten viel gerne über den ungeschriebenē Gesetze der langbeliebtē Gewonheit halte/ daß die Vrheber wolbedachter Neurungē unserer Mutterzunge als Freveler ernstlich abgestraffet werdē würden/ wann es in ihren

Vermögen stünde/ darüber zu erkennen/ und auszusprechen: Jndem sie aber solches nicht unterfangen dörffen/ bemühen sie sich die Teutsche Sprache und ihre Beflissene mündlich und schriftlich zu be- [S. 2] schmützen/ lästerlich zu verachten/ und bey jederman verächtlich und unwürdig zu machen.

Dieses hat der nunmehr selig *GEKROENTE*[3] und fast alle/ die ihm den Fus nachgesetzet/ schmertzlichst erfahren/ und ist offenbar/ daß auch der Allmächtige selbsten/ der alles in höchster Vollkommenheit wolgemacht/ den bößlichen Menschenkindern nicht recht thun kan. Etliche lassen sich abschrecken/ daß sie ihre Arbeit/ bis nach ihrem Tod/ nicht an das[b] Tagesliecht bringen wollen/ da sie ihr wolverdientes Lob noch hören/ noch die begangenen Fehler vermitteln können. Etliche halten ihre Schriften zu rucke/ weil sie eine gelehrtere Zeit/ als die unsere ist/ bevorsehen/ und beförchten ihren Namen bey der Nachwelt zu beschimpfen/ nicht betrachtend/ daß eine jede Jahrzeit seine gewiese Erdgewächse bringet/ ob wol selbe alle mit den reifen Herbst- [S. 3] früchten nit zu vergleichen sind. Etliche achten ihre Werk viel zu hoch/ als daß sie es durch die Gemeinmachung vernachtheilen und gleichsam in Vnwürden setzen solten/ da uns doch obliegt dem Nechsten auch mit unseren Schaden zu dienen.

Die Gewonheit ist ein Tyrannisches Gesetz/ welches nicht deswegen gut/ weil es uns von langen Jahren her aufgedrungen/ sondern dieweil es fälschlich für gut gehalten worden. Das Althum des Fehlers läst sich durch die Verjährung nicht rechtfertigen. Eine böse Gewonheit kan kein gutes Gesetz seyn/ dessen Seele ist die rechtmessige Vrsach/ ohne welche alle Satzung tod und Kraftlos/ in ihrer Nichtigkeit beruhet.

Die neuen Erfindungen sind gleichsam neue Geschöpfe unseres Verstandes/ und von den Heiden so hoch gehalten worden/ daß sie sel- [S. 4] be nicht den Menschen/ sondern überirdischen Geistern und Götteren zugeschrieben haben/ und obwol solche den alten Gewonheiten entgegen zu setzen sehr bedenklich/ so können sie doch/ sowol als jene/[c] nach und nach schetz- und achtbar gemachet werden: Ja es erhellen in der Menschen Gedanken sonderliche Schickungen Gottes/ wie aus der Erfindung der neuen Welt/ der Stücke/ Buchdrückens/ und vieler Chimischen Probstücklein zu schliessen. Es ist keine Kunst eine gemeine Landstrassen zu treffen/ aber einen niebetrettenen/ lieblichen und nähren Abweg angehen/ klugmütig ausbahnen/ und durch der folgenden Samthülffe gangbar machē/ ist eine solche Sache/ in welcher der Wille auch seines Ruhms nicht ermanglen kan.

Jn unserer geehrten/ Adelichen Muttersprache ist viel neues

Iniquum est negligentiā imperitorū inveteratorumque errorum diligentiæ ac Virtuti præscribere. Avent. lit. V. in Nomenclat.[4] Antiquitas nō est erroris Patrocinium Veritatis. Causab. [*sic*] in Præf. Exerc. contra Barō.[5]

☞ Die Dichtkunst im V. Theil der Gesprächspiele.[6]

unerhörtes zu finden/ gestalt sie von kurtzen Jahren her von fremden [S.5] Vermischungen durch die Poeterey abgesondert/ jüngsthin aber von dem *SVCHENDEN* Kunstgründig verfasset/ und sol bey so beharrter Bemühung höher/ als keine andere erhaben/ in den Thron aller Geschicklichkeiten und Wissenschaften majestätisch eingesetzet werden.

Die Gesprächspiele sind nicht unter die neuen/ sondern erneuten Erfindungen zu zehlen/ massen solche in Welschland üblich/ und Plato/ Lucian/ Vives/ Erasmus Majolus[8]/ und andere sich dergleichen in ihren Schriften bedienet: werdē aber zu Ausübung unserer Sprache/ deswegē für schicklich gehalten/ weil solche eine freye Art allerhand Fragen/ Aufgaben/ Erzehlungen/ aus demselben entstandene Zweiffel/ Antwort/ Rähtsel/ Sprichwörter/ Lehren/ Gedicht und im Ende alles das/ was jungen Leuten zu wissen geziemet/ zu behandeln: [S.6] wie solches verständige Spielgenossen besser nacheignen/ wol vermögen aus- als der Verfasser anzuführen wissen.

Diese Arbeit ist durch des *VNVERDROSSENEN* grosgünstige Vermittelung zu des *REINHERTZIGEN* gnädigen Handen gelanget/ und mit so hoher Gewogenheit an- und aufgenommen worden/ daß der *SPIELENDE* sich erkühnet/ dieses aufgelegten und vermehrten ersten Theils geringe Zugabe zu des hochbesagten *REINHERTZIGEN* Gnadenschutze gebührend zu befehlen: des ungezweiffelten Versehens/ selber werde nicht die Vnwürdigkeit der Gabe/ sondern die schuldige Dankbarkeit des Vbergebers/ mit Fürstlichen Gnaden ansehen; und geschehen lassen/ daß sein so wahrrühmlicher *REINHERTZIGER* GesellschaftsName allen unartigen und falschhertzigen Verächtern der Teutschen [S.7] Spracharbeit entgegen stehe/ und sie doch einmal von dem Jrrwege zu rechte führe/ damit sie erkennen mögen/ daß hierdurch die Ehre ihrer beliebten Vorfahren/ der Ruhm ihrer belobten Landsleute/ und der Nutzen den verhofften Nachkommen/ mit Teutschtreuem Gemühte abgesehen und gesuchet werde.

Hiermit verbleibet/ nechst Empfehlung des Allwalten Obschutzes/

>des höchstgeehrten
> *REINHERTZIGEN*
> die Zeit seines Lebens
> in Vnterthänigkeit
> Gehorsamster Knecht
> Der Spielende.

T a *Zierinitiale D mit dem vierfeldrigen Wappen des Hzts. Braunschweig u. Lüneburg, vereinfacht und seitenverkehrt, vermutlich nach einem Holzstich von Hans Burgkmaier d. Ä. (1473–1531) von 1523 (in Öffentliche Kunstsammlung Basel). Alle Angaben nach* http://commons.wikimedia.org/wiki/File:Wappen_des_Herzogtums_Braunschweig_Burgk mair.png — **b** *Druckfehler:* des — **c** *Druckfehler:* [...] als je/ nenach und nach [...]

K Datierung nach der Widmungszuschrift Georg Philipp Harsdörffers (FG 368. Der Spielende) an F. Ludwig (Der Nährende) 440715. — Die „Schutzschrift" steht noch nicht in der Erstausgabe des 1. Teils der *Frauenzimmer-Gesprächspiele* von 1641 (HAB: Lo 2621 [1]), sondern erschien erst als Anhang in der 2. Ausgabe des 1. Teils (1644; Ndr. 1968). Sie entstand auch erst für diese Ausgabe. Die in der Neuauflage dem Hauptteil angehängten „Ehrengedichte [...] von Vertrauten Herren und Freunden" sind z. Tl. datiert: Johann Michael Moscherosch (FG 436. 1645), Benfeld 1.10.1644 (Bl. Y ij v), u. Wenzel Scherffer v. Scherffenstein, Brieg 19.12.1644 (Bl. Y iij v). Da sich die „Schutzschrift" mit eigener Paginierung, aber durchgehender Foliierung diesen anschließt (Ndr. S.339ff.), dürfte sie mitsamt der Widmungszuschrift auch erst Anfang 1645 gedruckt worden sein. Vgl. dazu auch 440824 K 4. Es folgen dahinter (Bl. Cc r ff./ Ndr. S.397ff.) Erklärungen zu dem Übereignungsgedicht an F. Ludwig (440715) u. den Gesprächspielen, ein Inhaltsregister zum 4. u. eine Übersicht über den 5. Teil der *Gesprächspiele* (erscheint 1645/ Ndr. 1969) sowie ein „Lustgedicht" Harsdörffers über den Regen.

1 Einwohner der Stadt Locros/ Locri(s), griechische Kolonie in Süditalien, dem einstigen Graecia magna. Ihre Verfassung, die sie von Zaleukos empfangen haben sollen, ging bis ins 7. Jh. v.Chr. zurück u. galt den Griechen als die älteste schriftlich fixierte. Sie soll über Jahrhunderte unverändert geblieben sein u. wurde schon von Pindar u. Platon wegen ihrer strengen Gerechtigkeit u. guten Gesetzesordnung gerühmt. *N. Pauly* VII, 421–425, hier 422; *Zedler* XVIII, 127f.

2 Aus der Rede des Demosthenes gegen Timokrates, der zur Zeit des Bundesgenossenkrieges (358–356 v.Chr.) in Athen ein nach Demosthenes' Meinung eigennütziges, parteiisches, ungerechtes u. gemeinschädliches Gesetz einbrachte, das er bei der Verhandlung (353 v.Chr.) scharf zurückwies, v.a. weil es gegen die bestehende Verfassung u. das geltende Recht verstoße. Dabei führte er als ein bemerkenswertes Beispiel für die Bewahrung des hergebrachten Rechts die Lokrenser (s. Anm.1) an: „Narrabo autem vobis, Iudices, quo pacto Locris leges ferre soleant. nihil enim uobis nocuerit exemplum aliquod audivisse, tale præsertim, quo laudata republica vtitur. Nam illi usque adeo censent veteribus legibus vtendum, & instituta patria ornanda eße: non ad cuiusvis libidinem & iniuriarum impunitatem leges ferendas: vt si quis legem nouam rogare velit, collo in laqueum inserto id facere cogatur. Quæ lex si honesta & vtilis videtur, autor eius vivit, & abit. Sin minus: perijt, constricto laqueo. Proinde nouas rogare leges non audent: sed veteribus religiosè vtuntur." DEMOSTHENES ET AESCHINIS Principum Græciæ Oratorum OPERA ... ex Quarta, eaque postrema recognitione, GRAECOLATINA ... Per HIERONYMVM VVOLFIVM (Basel 1572), 480. HAB: Lg 25 2°.

3 D. i. Martin Opitz v. Boberfeld (FG 200), in der FG „der Gekrönte". Sein früher Tod 1639 verhinderte, daß er sich an der Sprachdebatte der FG in den 1640ern beteiligen konnte. Seine Versreform legte den Grund für die deutsche Kunstdichtung des 17. Jahrhunderts.

4 Ein Zitat aus der „NOMENCLATVRA QVORVNDAM PROPRIORVM GERMANORVM NOMINVM", einem Verzeichnis deutscher Eigennamen mit Erklärungen der Bedeutung, in Johannes Turmairs gen. Aventinus (1477–1534) *Annales ducum Boiariae* (ausgearbeitet zw. 1519 u. 1521, dann ins Deutsche übersetzt u. bearbeitet, 1533 als

Bairische Chronik abgeschlossen). Unter dem Buchstaben V, Bl.)()(4v heißt es dort (grammatisch leicht von dem bei Harsdörffer gegebenen Zitat abweichend): „Iniquum est negligentiam imperitorum inueteratumque errôrem diligentiæ ac virtuti præscribere." Hier zit. nach der Ausgabe: IOANNIS AVENTINI *Viri CL:* ANNALIVM BOIORVM, SIVE VETERIS GERMANIÆ. LIBRI VII. (Frankfurt 1627); Zitat identisch in der Ausg. Basel 1615, hier jedoch der Ausgabe voranstehend. Vgl. 440313 K 3, 4 u. 6, 440525 K II 0.

5 Isaac Casaubonus (1559–1614), hochgelehrter Humanist, in Genf als Sohn französ. Reformierter geboren u. an der dortigen Universität Professor für Griechisch (1581–1596), dann für drei Jahre an der U. Montpellier, anschließend in Lyon, bis ihn Kg. Heinrich IV. nach Paris holte. Die letzten Lebensjahre verbrachte er unter der Förderung Kg. Jakobs I. in London, wo ihn die anglikanische Kirche auf ihrem Mittelweg zwischen Puritanismus u. Altkirchlichkeit aufgrund seines Irenismus als einen der ihren begrüßte. — Das von Harsdörffer angeführte Zitat findet sich so nicht. Er verweist auf die Widmungszuschrift an Kg. Jakob I. in Casaubonus' Werk DE REBVS SACRIS ET ECCLESIASTICIS EXERCITATIONES XVI. Ad Cardinalis BARONII Prolegomena in Annales, & primam eorum partem, de DOMINI NOSTRI IESV CHRISTI Natiuitate, Vita, Paßione, Assumtione. AD IACOBVM, Dei gratia, Magnæ Britanniæ, Hiberniæ, &c. Regem Serenissimum (London 1614. HAB: 499 Theol. 2°), Widmungszuschrift Bl. *2r – ******4v. In diesem großangelegten Werk setzte sich Casaubonus kritisch mit der populären Kirchengeschichte des Katholiken Cesare Baronio, den *Annales Ecclesiastici* (Rom 1588/89), auseinander, die ihrerseits die Magdeburger Centurien (13 Bde., 1559–1574) zurückgewiesen hatten. In seiner Klage über den Verlust der christlichen Einheit spart Casaubonus in dieser Vorrede nicht mit strengster Kritik an der Papstkirche, teilt aber auch energisch nach der Seite protestantischer u. anderer Sekten aus (Täufer, Schwenckfelder, Neu-Arianer, Socinianer usw.). Seine Vorstellung einer Reformation der entstellten u. gespaltenen christlichen Religion ist die einer Restitution auf der Grundlage der Hl. Schrift, der Lehren Jesu u. der Apostel, der Kirchenväter mit ihren Konzilen u. Synoden. Die Verteidiger einer solchen wahren Reformation in ihrem Streben nach Wiedergewinnung kirchlicher Einheit aber werden verunglimpft u. unterdrückt: „auctores veræ reformationis, aut Ecclesias ab illis institutas, quarum extant Confessiones, in vnius corporis harmoniam redactæ, in invidiam vocant, ij parum Christiano animo (ne dicam aliquid grauius) artes veterum paganorum imitantur, & ipsorum calumnias aduersus doctrinam Christi, non sine offensione Dei maxima, reuocant ex Orco." (Bl. ***2v). Über die Jahrhunderte wurden vielerlei „Neuerungen" („nouitates") in der christlichen Kirche eingeführt, die sich Casaubonus nur scheinbar als althergebracht, in Wirklichkeit aber als korrupt u. depraviert darstellen. Daher ist sein Anliegen, die „veram Antiquitatem contra Nouitatem" in Schutz zu nehmen u. der letzteren „falso creditæ antiquitati larua" (Bl. ******3r) herabzureißen. Ganz zurück muß der Weg gehen ad „veram Antiquitatem", „quod fuit a principio" (Bl. ****r u. v), „ad primitivæ Ecclesiæ tempora, quæ est demum vera antiquitas" (Bl. ******3v). Die Neuerungen der späteren Papstkirche in Lehren u. Gebräuchen u. die Machtusurpation des Papstes müssen abgelegt werden, zum Vorteil des einfachen Schriftsinns, der Konzile u. der christlichen Fürsten u. Völker. Immer geht es Casaubonus um die „veram antiquitatem", mit der allein man „ad concordiam inter Principes & populos Christianos" gelangen u. die wahre Antiquitas „in lucem & vsum Ecclesiæ" zurückrufen könne (Bl. ******r). Die Neuerer u. die Verteidiger des falschen Alten kommen, obwohl scheinbar im Widerstreit, durchaus überein: „Nam quid est antiquitas non vera, nisi latens sub larua nouitas? aut quæ vetustas contra Veritatem stare potest: quum sit extra omne dubium, id verius esse, quod prius: id prius, quod à principio?" (Bl. *3r). Deshalb muß u. wird die „falsa antiquitas" dem wahren Altertum weichen (Bl. *4r). Die Argumentation Casaubons

weicht damit doch von jener Harsdörffers ab, wenn dieser aus der grammatischen Sprachratio systemisch abgeleitete Korrekturen an der hergebrachten Sprachgewohnheit, Neuerungen also, verteidigt u. keineswegs „ad principium" der dt. Sprache zurückgehen kann u. will. In der Ablehnung eines über Jahre u. Jahrhunderte eingeschlichenen u. verwurzelten falschen „Usus" sind sich aber beide einig. — Vgl. *Opitz: BW* I, 353 f.; Christian Thorsten Callisen: Georg Calixtus, Isaak Casaubon, and the consensus of Antiquity. In: Journal of the history of ideas 73 (2012), 1–23; Irene Dingel: Art. „Casaubonus, Isaac", in: Religion Past & Present. Encyclopedia of Theology and Religion. Ed. Hans Dieter Betz e. a., Vol. 2, Leiden, Boston 2007, 408; dies.: Art. „Casaubonus (Casaubon), Isaac", in: *RGG*[4] II, 76 f.; Anthony Grafton: Defenders of the Text. The Traditions of Scholarship in an age of Science (1450–1800). Cambridge 1991, 145–177; William McCraig: Art. „Casaubon, Isaac". In: Encyclopedia of the Renaissance. Ed. Paul F. Grendler. Vol. 1, New York 1999, 357; Hanns-Peter Neumann: Hermes oder Pythagoras: Die Diskreditierung des Hermetismus durch Isaac Casaubon und der Versuch seiner Rehabilitation bei Ralph Cudworth. In: Welche Antike? Konkurrierende Rezeptionen des Altertums im Barock. Hg. Ulrich Heinen. Tl. 1, Wiesbaden 2011 (Wolfenbütteler Arbeiten zur Barockforschung, 47), 627–640.

6 Das 204. Gesprächspiel „Die Dichtkunst" in *Harsdörffer: Frauenzimmer-Gesprächspiele*, 5. Teil (1645, Ndr. 1969), S. 16/ Ndr. 128 - 59/ 171, trifft keine solche Aussage, betont aber, daß alle Künste „in gewiesser Lehrverfassung können vorgetragen werden" u. daß die Dichtkunst keineswegs nur auf dem unergründlichen poetischen Talent oder der unkontrollierten poetischen Einbildungskraft beruht. Ja diese „Lehrverfassung" u. ihr systematisches Regelwerk erheben für Harsdörffer u. Justus Georg Schottelius (FG 397) eine natürliche Fähigkeit (facultas) — etwa zur Sprache — erst zur Kunst (ars). Dies war schon Quintilian zu entnehmen u. ein Grundaxiom humanistischer Wissenschaftslehre: Die „Kunst" — etwa die Grammatik — bildet das natürlich Gegebene — etwa den Sprachgebrauch — durch Sammlung, Ordnung u. Erklärung zu einer theoretisch begründeten u. methodisch vorgehenden wissenschaftlichen Lehre aus. Als solche leitet sie dann zu einem fehlerlosen Sprechen an. Deshalb stellte Schottelius seiner *Sprachkunst* (1641) schon im Titel das Prädikat aus, sie habe die „Uhralte Hauptsprache der Teutschen auß jhren Gründen erhoben/ dero Eigenschafften und Kunststücke völliglich entdeckt/ und also in eine richtige Form der Kunst zum ersten mahle gebracht". Strittig war in der Sprachdebatte der FG allerdings, inwieweit die Kunst die Natur, also etwa die Grammatik den praktischen Sprachgebrauch übermeistern darf. Vgl. *Quintilian: Institutio oratoria*, 11, 83, 89 u. 93; Volkhard Wels: Triviale Künste. Die humanistische Reform der grammatischen, dialektischen und rhetorischen Ausbildung an der Wende zum 16. Jahrhundert. Berlin 2000, 91 ff.

7 D. i. Justus Georg Schottelius (FG 397. Der Suchende). Seine Grammatik *Teutsche Sprachkunst* (erstmals 1641) u. seine *Der Teutschen Sprache Einleitung* (1643) erhoben genau diesen von Harsdörffer markierten Anspruch. Vgl. Anm. 6.

8 In Frage kommen hier Platons sokratische Dialoge einschließlich des *Symposion* u. von Lukian von Samosata (um 120–180 n. Chr.) wohl vornehmlich dessen satirische Dialoge mit den Götter-, Meergötter-, Hetären- u. Totengesprächen (*Dialogi Deorum, Dialogi Marini, Dialogi Meretricii, Dialogi Mortuorum*). Zur Lukian-Philologie u. -Rezeption im europäischen u. dt. Humanismus (Willibald Pirckheimer, Erasmus von Rotterdam, Philipp Melanchthon, Ulrich von Hutten usw.) vgl. Manuel Baumbach: Lukian in Deutschland. Eine forschungs- und rezeptionsgeschichtliche Analyse vom Humanismus bis zur Gegenwart. München 2002, 28 ff. Erasmus von Rotterdam ließ sich von Lukian, dessen *Opuscula* er gemeinsam mit Thomas Morus 1506 herausgab, zu seinen eigenen, oft aufgelegten *Colloquia familiaria* (1518, von Beatus Rhenanus erweitert) inspirieren: in 57 Dialogen werden alle möglichen Themen aufgegriffen (vgl. Baumbach, s. o., 38 ff.; Elsbeth Gutmann: Die *Colloquia familiaria* des Erasmus von Rotterdam. Basel, Stuttgart 1968). Die erasmischen *Colloquia familiaria* dürfte Harsdörffer hier ebenfalls im Blick gehabt haben. Dem in Gesprächsform gehaltenen Schulbuch von Juan Luis Vives (1493–1540), den *Colloquia sive exercitatio linguae latinae* (editio princeps Basel 1539) war mit 601 Ausgaben u. Übersetzungen in 80 Verlagsorten ein beispielloser Erfolg durch ganz Europa u. ein Einsatz in ungezählten Lateinschulen beschieden. In dem dem künftigen span. König Philipp II. gewidmeten Werk treten Lehrer, Aufseher u. Schüler auf, ein „ludimagister", Knaben, Mädchen, Väter u. Mütter, ein Bauer, aber auch Plinius, Epiktet, Aristipp, Demokrit u. v. a. In der Vermittlung von lat. Sprach- u. sozialer Verhaltenskompetenz – in den Übersetzungen (im Paralleldruck) tritt die Unterweisung in der Muttersprache hinzu – werden spielerisch alle möglichen Lebensbereiche behandelt, vom morgendlichen Aufstehen über Körperpflege, dem menschlichen Körper überhaupt, Mahlzeiten, Kleidung, Spiele, Reisen, der Stadt Valencia (Vives' Geburtsort), Erziehungsregeln bis zum Umgang mit Dienern, Verhalten gegenüber Vornehmen u. v. m. Die früheste im Besitz der HAB befindliche Ausgabe ist die Baseler vom März 1539 (s. o.): LINGVAE LATINAE EXERCITATIO. IOAN. LODO. VIVIS VALENTINI. Libellus ualde doctus & elegans, nuncq̃; primum in lucem editus. Vna cum rerum & uerborum memorabilium diligentißimo Indice. Cum gratia & priuilegio ad triennium. BASILEAE. (Kolophon:) BASILEAE, IN OFFICINA ROBERTI VVINTER, MENSE Martio. Anno M.D. XXXIX. HAB: 331 Quod. (2). Der Hinweis am Ende des Textes: „Bredae in Brabantia, de Visitationis Diuae Virginis. 1538" stellt kein Druck-Kolophon dar, sondern gibt den Termin des Abschlusses des Werkes durch Vives an. Er hat mißverständlicherweise wohl zur Annahme geführt, das Werk sei 1538 in Breda erschienen. Eine höchst interessante, aber unvollständige Übersicht über die Vives-Bestände in der HAB in: Maria v. Katte: Vives' Schriften in der Herzog August Bibliothek und ihre Bedeutung für die Prinzenerziehung im 16. u. 17. Jahrhundert. In: Juan Luis Vives. Arbeitsgespräch in der Herzog August Bibliothek Wolfenbüttel vom 6. – 8. November 1980. Vorträge hg. v. August Buck. Hamburg 1981, 193–210. Möglicherweise kannte Harsdörffer auch Nürnberger Ausgaben in der Bearbeitung durch Johannes Thomas Freig(ius) (1543–1583): 1571, 1582 (HAB: P. 2131.8° Helmst.), 1585 (HAB: 356 Quod. [2]), 1622, oder die mehrfach aufgelegte, von Ulrich Koch (Huldrichus Coccius, 1525–1585) herausgegebene erste lat. Werkausgabe *Opera, In Dvos Distincta Tomos* (Basel 1555. HAB: 34 Quod. 2°). Vgl. ferner Dietrich Briesemeister: Die gedruckten deutschen Übersetzungen von Vives' Werken im 16. Jahrhundert. In: ebd., 177–191, hier 178 f., 180 u. 187 f.; A Companion to Juan Luis Vives. Ed. Charles Fantazzi. Leiden, Boston 2008, 12, 13, 178, 190, 203, 278 u. 312; Enrique González González u. Víctor Gutiérrez Rodríguez: Los diálogos de Vives y la imprenta. Fortuna de un manual escolar renacentista (1538–1994). Valencia 1999. Die erste dt. Übersetzung stammt aus dem Jahre 1587. Eine moderne kritische Edition besorgte M. P. García Ruiz: Luis Vives. Los dialógos (Linguae Latinae exercitatio). Estudio introductorio, edición crítica, y commentario. Pamplona 2005. — Der erwähnte Majolus ist nicht der langjährige Abt Maiolus von Cluny (910–994), der Führer der Cluniazensischen Reform, sondern Simone Majoli (1520–1597), ein ital. Bischof u. Verfasser eines wiederholt (seit 1597) gedruckten Werks von großem Umfang u. enzyklopädischem, bes. naturgeschichtlichem u. dämonologischem Interesse: Dn. SIMONIS MAJOLI EPISCOPI VULTURARIENSIS Dierum Canicularium TOMI SEPTEM COLLOQVIIS QVADRAGINTA sex; Physicis novis ac penitus admirandis, nec non lectu jucundis ... Opus hac ultima editione revisum & planè novum, ... adauctum (Francofurti: Ioannes Godefredus Schönwetterus

1647), HAB: Li 2° 110.1, dig. (SUB Göttingen). Z. B. VII, 1 ff. Gespräch von Eques, Philosophus und Theologus „DE ANGELIS ET SPIRITIBVS".

9 D. i. Carl Gustav v. Hille (FG 302. Der Unverdrossene), der Hauptansprechpartner F. Ludwigs in Sachen FG am Wolfenbütteler Hof. Vgl. etwa 440130, 440209A, 440723A u. ö. Auch zu Harsdörffer unterhielt Hille gute Kontakte. Hilles Widmungsgedichte in der 2. Auflage des 1. Teils der *Frauenzimmer-Gesprächspiele* (1644/ Ndr. 1968), Bl. [Xv]r–[Xvj]v, im 4. Teil (1643/ Ndr. 1968), Bl. [Avj]r–Biiij r, u. im 5. Teil (1645/ Ndr. 1969), Bl. [)()(6]r – [)()(8]r vergalt Harsdörffer mit einem längeren „Lobgedicht" in *Hille: Teutscher Palmbaum* (1647/ Ndr. 1970), Bl.)()()(v – [)()()(vij]v. Zu diesem Werk s. 451008 K 2. Hille beabsichtigte, bis Ostern 1645 Wolfenbüttel zu verlassen u. Hz. Christian Ludwig v. Braunschweig-Calenberg (FG 372. Der Reinherzige) als Drost zu dienen. Dieses (nie realisierte) Vorhaben bestätigt die gute Verbindung Hilles zum Celler Herzog u. seine hier angedeutete Vermittlerrolle zugunsten des Reinherzigen. Vgl. 450126.

440723

Fürst Ludwig an Herzog Christian Ludwig von Braunschweig-Calenberg

F. Ludwig (Der Nährende) erklärt, in guter Erinnerung zu haben, daß zwei Jahre zuvor bei einer Zusammenkunft in Hannover die gemeinschaftliche Finanzierung des *GB 1646* beschlossen worden sei und Hz. Christian Ludwig v. Braunschweig-Calenberg (FG 372. Der Reinherzige) bei diesem Treffen einen Zuschuß von 200 Reichstalern zugesagt habe. Die Einlagen sollten durch Exemplare der gedruckten und in Kupfer gestochenen Bücher entgolten werden. Da von anderer Seite ein ebensolcher Betrag bereits eingegangen sei, jedoch Hz. Christian Ludwigs Anteil noch immer ausstehe, sei der Unverdrossene (Carl Gustav v. Hille. FG 302) beauftragt worden, die 200 Reichstaler einzutreiben und weiterzuleiten, damit mit der Herstellung des Buchs begonnen werden könne. Darauf warte u. a. besonders auch Hz. Friedrich III. v. Schleswig-Holstein-Gottorf (FG 388. Der Hochgeachte), der als einziger seinen Anteil bereits zugeschossen habe. Die Impresen(-visierungen) lägen bereits vor.

Q HM Köthen: V S 544, Bl. 57rv [A: 57r], 57v leer; eigenh. Konzept. 57r untere Hälfte F. Ludwigs Konzept 440723A an Carl Gustav v. Hille. — D: KE, 46f. — BN: Bürger, 948 Nr. 23.

A An den Rein hertzigen[a]

Dem Reinhertzigen
Entbeut der Nehrende seine freundliche dienste, und verlanget ihme[b] von dessen gutem und gesunden zustande nachricht zu haben.

Vermeldet darneben, wie das er Nehrende noch in[c] gutem andencken hat, als fur zwey Jharen in der Hannoverischen anwesenheit wegen wieder auflegung der Fruchtbringenden geselschaft gemählde von einer zusammen lage geredet worden, sich der Reinhertzige auf ein[1] zwey hundert Reichsthaler seinerseits erkleret:[2] Nun dan von[c] anderen örter dergleichen verlag, so hernach mit so vielen in Kupfer gestochenen büchern wieder gezahlet wird, einkommen, es aber an diesen noch erwindet, als ist dem Unverdrossenen aufgetragen solche zweyhundert Reichsthaler einzufodern und zu ubermachen damit ein anfang in dem werke gemacht werde, wie dan andere vorneme geselschaftere und unter andern der Hochgeachte mit verlangen darauf auch^c wartet, man aber bisher ausser diesem Zuschuße ^d zu dem^e anfange noch nicht gelangen konnen, da sonsten alle gemählde³ darzu fertig.

Der Reinhertzige wolle diese anmanung im besten vermercken, sich hierunter gewierig⁴ erzeigen, und durch^c den Unverdrossenen dem^f Nehrenden gute schleunige antwort wiederfaren laßen.^g Es verbleibet
des Reinhertzigen allezeit dienstwilliger
der Nehrende
Geben den 23 Heumonats 1644

T a *Adressatennennung am Rande.* — b *Lies:* ihn *(F. Ludwig).* — c *Eingefügt.* — d <dar> — e *Am Rande eingefügt bis* noch — f dem Nehrenden *eingefügt.* — g *Folgt* <Sonsten>

K 1 D. h. ungefähr. S. 401214 K 6.
2 Der junge Hz. Christian Ludwig v. Braunschweig-Calenberg (FG 372. Der Reinherzige) war 1641 seinem Vater Hz. Georg (FG 231) als Regent des calenberg. Besitzes mit der Hauptresidenz Hannover gefolgt, den er 1648 mit dem Ft. Lüneburg u. der Residenz Celle vertauschte. Eine große norddt. Reise hatte F. Ludwig (Der Nährende) im Juli 1642 zweimal nach Hannover geführt, wo Hz. Christian Ludwig als 372. Mitglied in die FG aufgenommen wurde. Vgl. 421129 K 1. Da Christian Ludwig am 20.7.1642 der FG beitrat u. er wohl dann auch die finanzielle Zusage zu seiner Subskription machte, stellte F. Ludwigs Schreiben eine zeitgemäße Mahnung dar. *Conermann III*, 434. Vgl. auch 421031A u. 421129, wo die konkrete Summe von 200 Rth. genannt wird. Der im vorliegenden Brief ergehende Hinweis auf Carl Gustav v. Hilles (FG 302. Der Unverdrossene) Vermittlung bei Hz. Christian Ludwig erklärt sich daraus, daß auch der vorliegende Brief dem Adressaten über Hille zugestellt wurde. S. 440723A, vgl. auch 440323. Die Zahlung steht auch mehr als ein Jahr später noch aus, s. 450126, 450221, 450923, 451028 u. 460218. Christian Ludwig beglich seine Schuld am Ende nur zur Hälfte u. ließ die ihm versprochenen Exemplare des *GB 1646* in Frankfurt a. M. offenbar nicht einmal abholen. S. 460301, 460309 u. 460403; vgl. *KE*, 43, 46, 51, 203 u. 213; *Conermann III*, 435 Anm. 2. Zu den Verlagsbeiträgern allgem. s. 450126 K 4. Zum *GB 1646* 440130 K 3.
3 Nicht die Stiche der für das erweiterte *GB 1646* benötigten Impresen (FG 201–400) aus der Werkstatt Matthäus Merians d. Ä. seien fertig, sondern deren Köthener Visierungen. Vgl. zur Einrichtung des *GB 1646* 450711 K 4.
4 Im Sinne von ‚willfährig'; ‚gewährig' von ‚gewähren' = ‚praestare'. *DW* IV. 3, 4865 u. 5797.

440723A

Fürst Ludwig an Carl Gustav von Hille

F. Ludwig (Der Nährende) teilt mit, sich erkundigt zu haben, ob der zugesagte Zuschuß Hz. Augusts d. J. v. Braunschweig-Wolfenbüttel (FG 227. Der Befreiende) zum (vorbereiteten) *GB 1646* inzwischen bei Georg Winckler in Leipzig eingegangen wäre. Da dies nicht der Fall sei, möchte er diesen Umstand Carl Gustav v. Hille (FG 302. Der Unverdrossene) zur Kenntnis geben; er bittet um Begleichung durch Hz. August, zumal eine (weitere) Verzögerung für das Buchprojekt nicht gut sei. — Hilles Vorschlag aufgreifend (440323) sei (mit dem vorliegenden Schreiben) auch ein nichtverschlossener Brief (440723) an Hz. Christian Ludwig v. Braunschweig-Calenberg (FG 372. Der Reinherzige) vorbereitet und Hille zur freundlichen Übermittlung anvertraut worden. Sobald nun Hz. Christian Ludwigs 200 Reichstaler und die 100 Reichstaler Hz. Augusts eingegangen sein würden, solle Hille ihm dies mitteilen. Er, F. Ludwig, werde sich sodann um die zweckmäßige Überweisung des Geldes (an den Stecher Matthäus Merian d. Ä.) kümmern.

Q HM Köthen: V S 544, Bl. 57rv; [A: 57r], 57v leer; eigenh. Konzept. Der Brief folgt (auf der unteren Blatthälfte von Bl. 57r) dem Brief 440723, einem Konzept F. Ludwigs an Hz. Christian Ludwig v. Braunschweig-Calenberg (FG 372). Nicht in *KE*.

A An den Unverdroßenen[a]

Es hat der Nehrende bishero erwartet auch erkundigung eingezogen, ob von wegen des Befreyenden die versprochene hundert Rthaler zum ersten[b] verlage des geselschaftbuches in Kupfer an Georg Wincklern in Leipzig möchten übermacht seyn,[1] weil aber noch nichts erfolgt, hat es hiemit berichtet werden sollen, und erwartet man ihrer mit verlangen, ist auch nicht gut das dieses werk daher solange mus verzögert werden.

An den Reinhertzigen ist beyliegend auch ein brieflein, seinem vorschlage nach, ausgefertiget,[2] und offen gelaßen, das er zu rechte zu bringen, ihme[c] und zu guter beförderung wolle angelegen sein laßen;[d] Wan diese 200, und des Befreyenden 100 *Rth* beysammen, wolle es der Unverdroßene nur wißen laßen, wird man auf mittel sie an ort und ende, wohin sie gehören, zu bringen bedacht sein. Welches erheischender noturft nach vermeldet werden sollen und verbleibet

    des Unverdroßenen gantzwilliger
        Der Nehrende

Cöthen den 23. Heumonats 1644.

T a *Adresse am Rand der ersten Briefzeile vermerkt.* — b *Eingefügt.* — c *Lies: sich (d. h. Hille).* — d *Folgt* <Jst d>

K 1 Der einflußreiche Leipziger Handelsherr Georg Winckler wurde von den Anhaltinern F. Ludwig (Der Nährende) u. F. Christian II. v. Anhalt-Bernburg (FG 51) besonders als Bankier eingesetzt. Vgl. 451019 K 0.
2 S. F. Ludwigs Erinnerungsbrief 440723 für Hz. Christian Ludwig v. Braunschweig-Calenberg (FG 232. Der Reinherzige), der ebenfalls als eigenh. Konzept im Erzschrein

überliefert u. dort dem vorliegenden Brief vorangestellt ist (s. Q). F. Ludwig greift damit Carl Gustav (v.) Hilles (FG 302. Der Unverdrossene) Vorschlag in 440323 auf, sich beim Befreienden (Hz. August d.J. v. Braunschweig-Wolfenbüttel, FG 227) u. beim Reinherzigen für die Bereitstellung der zugesagten Gelder einzusetzen. Bemerkenswerterweise ist auch in 440323 I von einem Betrag von 100 Reichstalern, der Hälfte des am Ende von Hz. August tatsächlich gezahlten Betrags, die Rede. S. dazu den Brief vom Juli 1645 (450721). Noch immer scheint der von Hz. August beizusteuernde Betrag zu schwanken, u. F. Ludwig spricht von 100 oder 200 Reichstalern. Zu fl. Verlagsbeiträgen s. 450126 K 4. Zum Zahlungsverkehr s. 450127 K 1. Zum *GB 1646* allgemein 440130 K 3.

440724

Johann Rist an Philipp von Zesen

Johann Rist (FG 467. 1647) erklärt, er habe vor diesem Brief bereits dreimal an Philipp v. Zesen (FG 521. 1648; DG 1) geschrieben, jedoch habe dieser, wie Rist aus dessen Brief vom 24.6.1644 und aus dem Fehlen jedweder Empfangsbestätigung schließe (Rist bekam diesen Brief erst am 23.7.), anscheinend keinen jener Briefe erhalten. Rist habe Zesens frühere Briefe und deren beigefügte Schriften hingegen richtig empfangen und sie, wie gesagt, nicht nur zügig beantwortet, sondern auch eigene Arbeiten, darunter zweimal seinen *Starken Schild Gottes* mitgesandt. Rist hofft, Zesen werde diese Sendung mittlerweile zugegangen sein. Zesen möge den Erhalt des vorliegenden Briefes rasch bestätigen und seine Schreiben künftig und ausnahmslos an den Hamburger Weinhändler Johann Hagedorn richten. — Rist teilt mit, er habe durch Zesen den Brief des Jesaias Rompler v. Löwenhalt (AGT, DG 16) erhalten: „ein hurtiger Geist", wie sich aus seinem Brief an Justus Georg Schottelius (FG 397) erweise. Er bittet für eine Antwort um Romplers Anschrift. Rist schickt Grüße an Gottfried Hegenitz (DG 4) und Nikolaus Witte v. Lilienau (DG 5), einen „Fortsetzer unserer teutschen Reim- und Ticht-Künste". Rist sendet Zesen seinen *Starken Schild Gottes* zum dritten Mal und wünscht sich Zesens *Ibrahim*-Übersetzung. Zesens *Lobrede von der Druckerei* habe er, Rist, nur zum Teil gesehen. Der Verleger Jakob Rebenlein, ein ‚Kauz', habe Rists *Galathee* wiederveröffentlicht und dies in hoher Auflage. Rist verspricht, Zesen sein Poem *Holsteins erbärmliches Klag- und Jammerlied* (1644) zu senden, sobald es fertig gedruckt sei. Es folgt angesichts von Zesens Gesellschaftsnamen „Der Färtige" (in der DG) die erstaunte Frage, ob Zesen tatsächlich in die FG aufgenommen worden sei, worüber ihn Schottelius nicht informiert habe.

Q SUB Hamburg: Sup. ep. 28, Bl.272r–273v [A: 273v], eigenh.; Sig. — D: In modernisierter Orthographie in *Dissel*, 54f. — BN: *Bürger*, 1220 Nr.22; *Krüger* II, 850.

A Dem WolEhrenvesten, Grosachtbaren und hochgelahrten herren Filip Zæsius von Fürstenau, weitberühmten Poeten, meinem sonders vielgeliebten herren und hochvertrauten wehrten Freunde. **Amsteldamm**

WolEhrenvester, Grosachtbahr und hochgelahrter, sonders grosgünstiger hochgeehrter herr und sehr wehrter vertrauter freund,
    Dieses ist nun das vierte Briefelein, welches Jch von anfange des Mayen an Jhn habe abgehen lassen, Jch kan es nicht genugsahm klagen, mit waß grosser unge-

dult Jch verneme, daß Jhm derselben keines zu handen kommen, dan Jch aus meines vielgeliebten herren letstem Schreiben am 24. des Rosenmonahts gegeben (welches mir aber erstlich heute am 23. des heumonahts und also in der vierten woche seines alters ist eingehändiget)[1] gahr nicht vernemen können, das Er auch nur einzige antwohrt, mit welcher Jch doch gahr nicht saümig gewesen, empfangen. Unterdessen habe Jch nicht wollen ablassen bei dieser guhten begebenheit Jhme mit weinigem zu verständigen, das mier seine vormahls übergeschikte Briefe mit beigefügten Sachen (wofür Jch mich nochmahls höchlich bedanke, auch solche freundschafft tähtlich zu erwidern mich billig erbiete) richtig sind eingeliefert, Jch habe auch solche Schreiben nicht allein beantwohrtet, sondern auch von meinen geringfügigen Sachen, und unter denselben meinen starken Schild Gottes[2] zum zweiten mahl dem herren übersendet, wil hoffen, sie werden Jhm nunmehr endlich sein eingereichet. Dieweil es [272v] mir aber sehr verdrieslich[a] ist, deswegen lenger im zweifel zu stehen; Als wolle Er Jhme[b] belieben lassen mir ehist zu antwohrten, und sein Brieflein auß[c] Hamburg an herren Johann Hagedorn[3], weinhändlern am Fischmarkte, (bei welchem alle an mich geschriebene Briefe, sie kommen auch von was ohrten der welt sie wollen, abgegeben werden) senden, werde Jhn alsden mit begehrter antwohrt bald begrüssen. Des redlichen Teutschen Edelmans des Josias Rümplern von Leuenhalt[4] sehr angenehmes Brieflein ist mier zu recht worden, es mus gahr ein hurtiger Geist sein, wie solches insonderheit aus dem Schreiben an herren Schottel*ius*[5] erhellet, mein liebwehrter freund, lasse mich doch wissen, an was ohrten Jch Jhme meine antwohrt, die schon längst färtig gewesen, könne beibringen lassen. Der hochberühmter Herr Hegenitz[6], der mier seiner weltbekanten geschiklichkeit halber vorlängst schon bekant gewesen, doch mehr dem nahmen nach als der person, wird von mier negst anerbietung meiner stets gefliessenen willigsten Dienste zu tausend mahl[d] freundlich gegrüsset, vieleicht werde Jch einmahl die Ehre haben denselben persönlich zu begrüssen. Den herren Nicolaus Weissen[7], einen eiferigen fohrtsetzer[e] unserer Teutschen Reim und Ticht-künste habe Jch in meiner behausung einsmahl gesehen, mein herr wolle Jhm gleichfals meinen Dienst und grus vermelden und das Jch mich Jhme als einem freunde in seine guhte gedechtnisse befehle. [273r] Meinen Starken Schild Gottes[2] übersende Jch dem herren zum dritten mahl, verhoffe das Er Jhn endlich einmahl[f] richtig empfangen werde. Kan Jch seines Jbrahims[8] vor dankbahre doppelte bezahlung mächtig werden, so unterlasse Er nicht mich ehist damit zu beseligen. Des herren lobrede von der Drukkerei[9] habe Jch niemahls vollenkömlich gesehen, vieleicht komt sie mier noch einst zu handen, doch Rebenlein ist ein wunderbahrer kautz[10], Er hat meine Galatheen (die[g] zum ersten mahl wieder meinen willen gedrukket worden) zum anderen mahl auffgeleget und sehr viel 100[h] Exemplar gedruket,[11] dieses aber soll sich woll finden. So bald mein Erstes Klagelied holsteins inn *[sic]* 100 Sätzen abgetheilet (welches der verlogene Wärner unter der press hat) färtig ist,[12] will Jch Jhm selbiges[i] treulichst übersenden. Aber was mein herr? Jst er vieleicht in die Fruchtbringende Geselschafft auffgenommen? Der Zunahme, der Färtige solte mich solches schier glauben machen, mich wundert aber das mir herr Schottelius nicht das geringste davon geschrieben.¹³ Mein herr antworhte mier ia bald und berichte mier von diesem und vielem anderen alle beschaffenheit, unterdessen Gott befohlen und Jch sterbe

Mein herr Sein treuergebener bestendiger freund.
Johannes Rist.

Geschrieben zu Wedel am 24. des heumonahts Jm Jahr 1644.

T a *Folgt* <d> — b *Lies:* sich — c *Verschreibung für* auf *(im Sinne von nach)?* — d *Folgt* <von mir> — e *Folgt* <und teu> — f *Folgt* <b[?]> — g *Folgt* <Jch> — h *Dissel:* 200 — i *Folgt* <so bal>

K 1 Nicht ermittelt.
2 Johann Rist: *Starker Schild GOTTES* (1644), verlegt von Heinrich Werner (s. Anm. 12). Zu Rists genanntem Erbauungswerk s. 440324 K 20.
3 Johann Rist (FG 467. 1647) verfaßte 1643 anläßlich der Hochzeit des Weinhändlers Johann Hagedorn mit Ilse Schärtling, Tochter des Hamburger Bürgers u. Weinhändlers Peter Schärtling, ein Gelegenheitsgedicht. Erschienen als Einzeldruck unter dem Titel: Hochzeitlicher Schimpf und Ernst/ | Dem | Ehrenvesten/ Vorachtbahren und wollbenahmten | H. Johann Hagedorn/ | vornemen Weinhändlern/ als | Bräutigam (Hamburg: Heinrich Werner 1643). SUB Göttingen: 8 P Germ. I, 6463 (6), sodann in *Rist: Schauplatz (1646)*, 293–296. Es könnte sich um einen Verwandten von Rists Freund Philipp Hagedorn (s. *Opitz: BW*, 390922 K 2) handeln, der im Gegensatz zu Philipp kein direkter Vorfahre des Dichters Friedrich v. Hagedorn (1708–1754) gewesen zu sein scheint. Vgl. Hubert Stierling: Leben und Bildnis Friedrichs von Hagedorn. Hamburg 1911, 12, Anm. 3 (linke Sp.).
4 Jesaias Rompler v. Löwenhalt (auch Rumpler, 1605–1676. AGT, DG), 1626 Studium in Altdorf, 1628 Magister in Tübingen, im selben Jahr Aufnahme eines Jurastudiums in Straßburg, das er 1630 abbrach. Seine Arbeit als Erzieher führte Rompler in den Jahren 1642 bis 1644 mehrfach nach Frankreich, wo er 1643 in Paris Philipp v. Zesen (FG 521. 1648; DG 1) kennenlernte, den er zur Gründung der DG ermunterte. Rompler selbst wurde 1645 als Mitglied Nr. 16 („der Freie") aufgenommen (*Dissel*, 59; *Zesen SW* XII, 244, 317, 424 u. 454; in 450308A teilt Zesen Rompler seine Aufnahme mit). Mit Martin Opitz (FG 200) war Rompler persönlich bekannt, würdigte neben diesem aber besonders Georg Rodolf Weckherlin als Verkündiger einer verbesserten deutschen Poesie (vgl. *Reimgebüsch* [s.u.], Bl. ☉☉☉ ii v – ☉☉☉ iii r). Rompler stand darüber hinaus mit weiteren Fruchtbringern in engem Kontakt: Auf Gf. Eberhard v. Rappoltstein (FG 147) ließ er ein umfangreiches Epicedium ausgehen (s. 370900). Anläßlich von Rists Erhebung zum poeta laureatus steuerte er ein Glückwunschgedicht zu dessen *Allerunterthängisten Lobrede* von 1647 bei (S. 106–109, s. dazu 461104 K 2). Ferner stammt eines der Widmungsgedichte im fünften Teil von Georg Philipp Harsdörffers (FG 368) *Frauenzimmer-Gesprächspielen* (1645) von Rompler. Harsdörffer verfaßte im Gegenzug eines der Widmungsgedichte in Romplers einziger Gedichtsammlung Des | Jesaias Romplers von | Löwenhalt | erstes gebüsch | seiner | Reim-getichte. | [Zierleiste] | Getruckt zu Strasburg/ bej Joh. Phil. Mülben/ in dem 1647.ᵗᵉⁿ jar Chrl.ᵉʳ z. [Christlicher Zeitrechnung], 234f. ULB Halle: AB 120481. Ein zweiter Bd. ist nie erschienen. Matthias Schneuber (FG 498. 1648; s. auch

461104 K 4) war Mitglied der Aufrichtigen Tannengesellschaft, u. Johann Michael Moscherosch (FG 436. 1645) stand der von Rompler mitbegründeten AGT zumindest nahe. Im Gegensatz zur FG wurde in der AGT, auf die Romplers Pseudonym „Wahrmund von der Tannen" Bezug nimmt, die zunftbürgerliche Literatur in der Tradition des Meistersangs durchaus geschätzt. Ziele u. Prinzipien der 1633 in Straßburg gegründeten Akademie sind allein in Romplers knapper „Vorred" zu seinem *Reimgebüsch* überliefert. Dort heißt es, der Tannengesellschaft „vorsatz und absehen" bestehe darin, „alter Teütscher aufrichtigkeit/ und rainer erbauung unserer währten Muter-sprach sich zubefleisen." (*Reimgebüsch*, Bl. ☉☉☉ iiii v). Spracharbeit u. ethisch-moralische Ansprüche sollten mithin ineinandergreifen. Die Unterschiede zu Gesellschaften wie der FG betreffen laut Kühlmann 1981, 171 „sowohl Organisationsform (Beschränkung auf einen kleinen Kreis mit strengen Auswahlkriterien) als auch Einzelheiten des literarischen Programms (Berufung auf Weckherlin statt auf Opitz; Einbezug oberdeutscher Traditionen; Widerstand gegen strenge Normierung in Wortwahl und Stil zugunsten ‚altdeutscher' Offenheit und Freiheit)." Romplers Beschäftigung mit der deutschen Literatursprache u. besonders seine Überlegungen zu Lexik u. Orthographie übten einen erheblichen Einfluß auf Zesen aus. Vgl. hierzu 370900, bes. K 1 u. Romplers Anmerkungen im *Reimgebüsch*, Bl. ☉☉☉ ii v – ☉☉☉ iiii r. Vgl. ferner: 440525 K 1, 440616 K III 0, 441223, 450308A, 450400 K 8, 450410, 450806, 461104 K 2 u. 3 u. später. Zur Biographie: *ADB* XXIX, 673f.; *DBA* III 759/ 305–311; *NDB* XXII, 25f. Zur Tannengesellschaft: *Bopp: Tannengesellschaft*; Wilhelm Kühlmann: Rompler, Hecht und Thiederich. Neues zu den Mitbegründern der Straßburger Tannengesellschaft. In: Jahrbuch der dt. Schillergesellschaft 25 (1981), 171–195; Karl F. Otto: Die Sprachgesellschaften des 17. Jahrhunderts. Frankfurt a. M. 1972, 57–59. Das im vorliegenden Brief erwähnte Schreiben Romplers an Rist konnte nicht ermittelt werden.

5 Ein zeitlich passendes Schreiben von Rompler an Justus Georg Schottelius (FG 397) wurde nicht gefunden.

6 Gottfried Hegenitz (auch Hegenitius, 1598 – nach 1646 u. vor 1669), schon 1611 an der U. Frankfurt a. d. O. eingeschrieben, zwischen 1616 u. 1627 an zahlreichen Universitäten immatrikuliert (Jena, Marburg, Altdorf, Tübingen, Straßburg, Leiden); 1619 jur. Promotion an der U. Marburg. 1627 trug er sich in Hamburg in das (verschollene) Stammbuch des Joachim Morsius (vgl. 430826) ein. Seine Reisen in die Niederlande 1627 u. 1628 schlugen sich in seinem *Itinerarium Frisio-Hollandicum* (Leiden: Elzevier 1630) nieder. Hegenitz stand immer nur kurzfristig in diplomatischen Diensten, u.a. 1629 für Hz. August d.J. v. Braunschweig-Wolfenbüttel (FG 227), damals noch in Hitzacker residierend, weswegen er in der DG auch als „Braunschweigischer Rat" firmiert (*Zesen SW* XII, 423; *Dissel*, 58). Danach verliert sich seine Spur; erst 1643 ist er wieder in Deventer bezeugt, bis er 1644 als 4. u. ranghohes Mitglied („Untererzschreinhalter") unter dem Namen des Ernstsittigen in die DG aufgenommen wurde. Nach 1646 versiegen die Nachrichten über ihn. Hegenitz verdingte sich als Übersetzer für den Verleger Ludwig Elzevier. So begann er die von Zesen vollendete Übersetzung von Matthias Dögens *Architectura Militaris Moderna* (Amsterdam 1647): *Matthiae Dögens Heutiges tages Übliche Krieges Bau-Kunst* (Amsterdam 1648). Zusammen mit Zesen arbeitete er an der Übersetzung von Vital d'Audiguiers Roman *Histoire des amours de Lysandre et de Caliste* (*Liebesbeschreibung Lysanders und Kalisten*, Amsterdam: Ludwig Elezevier 1644; vgl. 460217 [K 4]). Zesens *Scala Heliconis Teutonici* (Amsterdam 1643) steuerte Hegenitz ein Freundschaftsgedicht bei. Durch Hegenitz trat Zesen wohl überhaupt erst in Verbindung mit Ludwig Elzevier, der zwischen 1645 u. 1660 mehrere Werke Zesens verlegte. Vgl. *DBA* I 494/ 365; *DBA* III 365/ 387f.; Herbert Blume: Søren Terkelsen, Philipp von Zesen, Gottfried Hegenitz und Konrad von Höfeln. In: Daphnis 2 (1973), 54–70, hier 57–63; Jan Hendrik Scholte: Zesens „Adriatische Rosemund". In: Dt. Vierteljahresschrift f. Literaturwissenschaft u. Geistesgeschichte 23 (1949), 288–305, hier 297 ff.

7 Nikolaus Witte v. Lilienau (1618–1688. DG 5. „Der Selbliche"), aus Riga stammender Leibarzt des schwed. Königshauses, 1640 Immatrikulation an der U. Rostock, 1642 an der U. Leiden, wo er sich noch oder wieder 1648 aufgehalten haben muß, wie der Eintrag im Stammbuch des Philologen Hiob Ludolf (1624–1704) belegt (HAAB Weimar: Stb 285, Bl. 248r, ora-web.swkk.de/digimo_online/digimo.entry?source=digimo.Digitalisat_anzei gen&a_id=17122). Im Mitgliederverzeichnis der DG in *Dissel*, 58 wird er — analog zum vorliegenden Brief — als „Niclas Weisse von Lilienau, [...] der *Selbliche*" bezeichnet, ebenso im Verzeichnis von Johann Peisker (1631–1711. DG 158): „Niklaß Weisse von Liljenau" (*Zesen SW* XII, 423). Zesens Bericht über die „Rosen- und Liljen-Zunft" von 1676 weist ihn — anders als sein Namenszusatz es vermuten läßt — als Mitglied der Rosen- u. nicht der Lilienzunft aus: „Niklaß Weisse von Rosenau / [...] ein blühender weisser Rosenstok / mit weissen Liljen ümgeben". (Der Hoch-preis-würdigen Deutschgesinneten Genossenschaft ... Rosen- und Liljen-Zunft/ sämtlicher Zunftgenossen Zunft- Tauf- und Geschlächts-Nahmen/ ... Hamburg 1676. In: *Zesen SW* XII, 311–332, hier 315.) Die Namensform *Weisse* scheint direkt auf Wittes „Zunftzeichen" (ebd., 315) zurückzugehen (*weiße* Rosen u. Lilien), deren Farbe man wiederum als Anlehnung an die Wortbedeutung seines nd. Nachnamens verstehen darf: hd. weiß, mnd. wit, as. huit (vgl. *Mnd. Wb.* V, 746 f.). Geadelt wurde Witte 1666 durch den noch unter Vormundschaft stehenden schwed. Kg. Karl XI. als Dank für seine leibärztliche Tätigkeit. Die Wahl des Namenszusatzes *von Lilienau* erklärt sich aus seiner DG-Mitgliedschaft, orientiert sich aber nicht an der Zunftzugehörigkeit oder symbolischen Blume der Gesellschaft selbst (i. e. die Rose), sondern an der individuellen Pflanze seines Zunftzeichens, der Lilie. Witte war seinen Zeitgenossen nicht nur als Mediziner, sondern auch als (lat., griech., dt.) Dichter bekannt. Erhalten sind einige Drucke, die zum Feld des Gelegenheitsschrifttums zu zählen sind (Leichenpredigten, Glückwunschgedichte). *DBA* I 408/ 281–286, 765/ 285 f. Witte war eine der zahlreichen Personen aus dem Umfeld des schwed. Hofes, zu denen Zesen Kontakt hatte. Vgl. *Ingen*, 28 f.

8 Zesens Roman-Übersetzung *Ibrahim Bassa* (1645), s. 441201 Q.

9 Phil. Caes. von Fürstenau | Gebundene Lob-Rede | Von der | Hochnütz- und Löblichen zweyhundert- | Jährigen | Buchdrückerey-Kunst/ | Wenn/ wo/ wie und durch wen sie erfun- | den worden; | Bey Volckreicher Versamlung und Einführung | eines neuen Drücker-Gesel- | lens | Michael Pfeiffers/ | öffentlich gehalten | Jn Hamburg den XX. Tag des Hornungs | im M. DC. XLJJ. Jahre nach der | Christ-Geburt/ | Nach Erfindung aber der Drücker-Kunst im ccjj. Jahre. | [Linie] | Hamburg/ | Gedruckt und verlegt durch Jacob Rebenlein. SUB Hamburg: Scrin AQ/87. Auch in: *Zesen SW* I.1, 201–234. Zesens Text ist nur eines von zahlreichen Gedichten, die 1640 den zweihundertsten Jahrestag der Erfindung des Buchdrucks feierten. Vgl. etwa Christian Gueintz (FG 361): Lob der Edlen vnd nützlichen Druckerey-Kunst, Auff das ander hundert Jährige Jubel-Fest (Halle a. d. S.: Peter Schmidt 1640). Marienbibliothek Halle a. d. S.: Oelh 381 (41) Q. Vgl. auch Andreas Tschernings *Lob der Buchdruckerey* (Breslau 1640, s. 440324 K 14). Zesen hat seinen Text zwar erst am 20. 2. 1642 anläßlich der Einführung eines Hamburger Druckergesellen vorgetragen, er muß aber zumindest im Kern früher entstanden sein, nämlich pünktlich zum Jubiläum, worauf die ersten Verse hindeuten: „JCH der ich flügen ließ vor zweyen Jahres-Zeiten | Die Feder in dein Lob und rühmte dich von weiten/ | Du edle Drucker-Kunst" (ebd. S. III). Auch Rist hat eine Dichtung der Buchdruckerei gewidmet, allerdings kein Jubiläumsgedicht, sondern eines, das die (rohe) Gesellenmacherei bei Buchdruckern

beschreibt: Depositio cornuti typographici, Das ist: Lust- oder Freuden-Spiel/ Welches bey Annehmung und Bestetigung eines Jungen Gesellen/ der die Edle Kunst der Buchdruckerey redlich hat außgelernet ... kann fürgestellet ... werden ... Anjetzo ... vermehret (Frankfurt a. M. 1677). HAB: Xb 9934. Ndr. Darmstadt 1983. Vgl. auch Wolfgang Adam: Urbanität und poetische Form. Überlegungen zum Gattungsspektrum städtischer Literatur in der Frühen Neuzeit. In: Stadt und Literatur im deutschen Sprachraum der frühen Neuzeit. Hg. v. Klaus Garber. Bd. 1. Tübingen 1998, 90–111, hier 104f; *Dissel*, 10.

10 Der aus Nürnberg stammende Hamburger Buchdrucker Jakob Rebenlein († 1662). Er wirkte ab 1651 offenbar auch als Ratsbuchdrucker. *Reske*, 339f.; *DBA* I 1004/ 153; *DBA* III 731/ 172f. „Wunderbar" hier im Sinne von „wunderlich, sonderbar". Vgl. *Paul Wb.*, 1186.

11 Johann Rist: Des DAPHNJS | aus Cimbrien | GALATHEE. Hamburg: Rebenlein 1642. Im Jahr der Erstausgabe produzierte Rebenlein mehrere leicht voneinander abweichende Drucke (s. VD17). Ebenfalls 1642 erschien ein (Raub-?)Druck mit Druckort Lüneburg (VD17 15:728871L). 1643 (VD17 23:279623S) resp. 1644 (VD17 1:635187N) folgten zwei weitere Ausgaben, auf denen weder Verlag noch Ort vermerkt sind. *Dünnhaupt: Handbuch*, S. 3390 Nr. 19.2 notiert die Ausgabe von 1644 als ersten vermehrten Neudruck der *Galathea*. Rists Bemerkung zur Neuauflage wird sich auf diesen Druck beziehen, dessen Verleger Rebenlein hiermit erstmals belegt ist. — Wenn Rist konstatiert, die Erstausgabe der *Galathee* sei „wieder meinen willen gedrukket worden", spielt er auf die Herausgeberfiktion in der „Vorrede an die guthertzigen Leser" (*Galathee*, 2–15) an: „des redlichen Daphnis [i. e. Rist] Hirten-Lieder" habe man „durch getreue Hand" erhalten u. auf eigene Faust veröffentlicht; „ob wol solches alles ihme [Daphnis] unwissend geschehē", hätte der Autor dagegen gewiß nichts einzuwenden, „weil anders nichts als die fortsetzung unser edlen Teutschen Haupt-Sprache/ und derselben hochfliegenden Poesy dadurch gesuchet wird." Ebd., 11f. In einem Brief (d. d. Wedel 4. April 1642) an Zesen, der sich damals in Hamburg aufhielt, hatte sich Rist nach dem Fortgang des Drucks der *Galathee* erkundigt. „Zu diesem mahl habe ich lenger nicht wahrten, besondern mich erkündigen wollen, ob meine Galatheen an das helle tages liecht zu führen der anfang sei gemachet worden, bitte freundlich, da deme also, mier eine kleine probe deswegen zu schicken. [...] und wolle er sich meiner Galatheen ehiste ausfertigung bester mahssen anbefohlen sein lassen". Und in einer Nachschrift: „Ob das kupfer gestochen und die Galathee in Octavo, (welches ich den gern wolte) gedrucket werde, lasse mich mein herr unfehlbahr wissen." (SUB Hamburg: Sup. ep. 28, Bl. 270r–271v; veröffentlicht auch in *Dissel*, 53).

12 Johann Rist: HOLSTEJNS | Erbärmliches | Klag- und Jammer-Lied/ | Das Erste/ | Jn hundert Sätzen außge- | färtiget und gesungen | Durch | Friedelieb von Sanfteleben. Hamburg: Heinrich Werner 1644. SUB Göttingen: 8 P Germ. II, 7245. Ungeachtet seiner Beschuldigung hat Rist in den folgenden Jahren neben diesem auch weitere Werke von dem aus Braunschweig stammenden Buchdrucker Heinrich Werner (1601–1648) herstellen lassen. Auch für Zesen besorgte Werner zwischen 1642 u. 1646 mehrere Drucke. Vgl. *Bellin: Sendeschreiben (1647)*, Bl. [A viij r] wo sich Zesen darüber beschwert, daß seine bei Werner erschienene *Hooch-Deutsche Spraach-übung* (1643) zu dessen Nachteil (von Andreas Hünefeld) in Danzig nachgedruckt worden sei. Zu Heinrich Werner s. *Reske*, 340. — Das Attribut „verlogene" ist abgeleitet von dem nicht mehr gebräuchlichen Verb *verlügen*, hat hier mithin die noch heute gebräuchliche Bedeutung. S. *DW* XII.1, 826f.; *Stieler*, 1149.

13 Tatsächlich wurde Zesen erst nach mehreren Anläufen u. nicht ohne Vorbehalte im Dezember 1648 unter dem Gesellschaftsnamen „Der Wohlsetzende" aufgenommen (FG 521). Augustus Buchner (FG 362) u. Harsdörffer hatten sich zuvor vorsichtig für seine

Mitgliedschaft eingesetzt, Zesen persönlich F. Ludwig zweimal in Köthen besucht (im Jan. 1647 u. Okt. 1648). „Der Färtige" war Zesens Gesellschaftsname in der DG: „Filip von Zesen, Der *Färtige*" (*Dissel*, 58; *Zesen SW* XII, 225 ff., 315, 423 u. 457), abgeleitet von fahren im Sinne von zur Fahrt gerüstet, abfahrbereit „promtus, paratus ad vectionem aut profectionem", auch „strenuus, agilis, pernix", also reise-, eil- u. dienstfertig, geschäftig usw., daneben im heutigen Sinne von fertiggestellt: „peractus, expletus, perfectus, absolutus, finitus, elucubratus, elaboratus" (*Stieler*, 405; vgl. *Nübling*, 110 f.). Zesen muß einen oder mehrere Briefe an Rist mit diesem Gesellschaftsnamen unterzeichnet haben. In Anspielung auf seinen DG-Namen unterschrieb Zesen 441201 die „Auf-traags-schrift An die Höchst-löbliche Frucht-bringende GESELSCHAFT" zu seiner Übersetzung *Ibrahim Bassa* (1645) darum auch als „untertähnigster alzeit-färtiger Knächt Filip Zesius von Fürstenau", ein Sprachspiel, das er in dem an die DG gerichteten, mit seinem Gesellschaftsnamen gezeichneten Widmungsgedicht, das dem dritten Teil vorangeht, wiederholt. Dort beteuert er, er wolle sich „färtig zeugen / | so lange Seel' und Geist die Lunge räge macht" (*Zesen SW* V.2, 636). Wie die genannte „Auf-traags-schrift" dürfte auch die dieser folgende „Schuz-räde An die unüberwündlichste Deutschinne" u. das angeschlossene Widmungsgedicht der DG-„Bey-sizzer" Ende 1644 (oder Anfang 1645) entstanden sein. Jenes ist gezeichnet von „F. Zesius von Fürstenau", jenes aber „Dem ädlen/ fästen und hoochgelährten Hern/ unserer Deutsch-gesünneten Genossenschaft zur zeit Erz-schrein-haltern/ Dem Färtigen" zugeschrieben (*Zesen SW* V.1, 21 u. 23). Lt. Aussage in Zesens *Hochdeutschem Helikonischen Rosentahl* (Amsterdam 1669) wurde die DG am 1.5.1643 in Hamburg gegründet. (*Zesen SW* XII, 192 f.). In der FG trug Carl Milchling v. Schönstadt seit 1636 den Gesellschaftsnamen „Der Fertige" (FG 282). In einem Brief an Matthaeus Apelles vom 17.1.1646 (vermutlich n. St.) teilt Andreas Tscherning das Gerücht von der Aufnahme Zesens in die FG noch als Tatsache mit. (StB Breslau: R 3109, Bl. 74 [Abschrift von Christian Ezechiel], verloren; zit. in Hans Heinrich Borcherdt: Andreas Tscherning. Ein Beitrag zur Literatur- und Kulturgeschichte des 17. Jahrhunderts. München, Leipzig 1912, S. 310 Anm. 28.) Die schnippische Frage Rists deutet bereits den sich allmählich zwischen ihm u. Zesen entspinnenden Konflikt an, während Rist Zesen 1643 noch hoch gelobt hatte. S. sein Widmungsgedicht „Auff des hochgelahrten Herren Philipp Caesiens Spraachübung/ An alle redliche Teütschen", in Zesens *Hooch-Deutsche Spraach-Übung Oder unvorgreiffliches Bedenken Über die Hooch-deutsche Haupt-Spraache und derselben Schreibrichtigkeit* (Hamburg: Heinrich Werner 1643). S. *Zesen SW* XI, 1–77, hier 9 f. Das Gedicht in unwesentlich überarbeiteter u. orthographisch leicht abgewandelter Fassung (z. B. „Spraache" statt „Sprach"; „Zesius" statt „Caesius") unter dem zurückhaltenderen Titel „Auff Herren Philip Zesiens Spraach-übung Oder Bedenken von der Schreibrichtigkeit", abgedruckt auch in *Rist: Schauplatz (1646)*, 47 f. Im Gedicht wird der Tod Martin Opitz' beklagt, doch sei sein verwaister Platz nunmehr durch neue „Helden" eingenommen: Schottelius, Harsdörffer, Zesen, Tscherning, Andreas Heinrich Bucholtz u. was sonst noch „gründlich schreiben kann". Das Gedicht schließt mit einer Verpflichtung auf die Tugend: „Wier dienen und sie bleibt die Königinn allein/ | Doch soll Herr Caesius ihr Kammer-Juncker seyn." Vgl. 441201; *Conermann: Rist,* 33 f.; *Herz: Zesen,* 181–187; Claudius Sittig: Zesens Exaltationen. Ästhetische Selbstnobilitierung als soziales Skandalon. In: Philipp von Zesen. Wissen — Sprache — Literatur. Hg. Maximilian Bergengruen und Dieter Martin. Tübingen 2008, 95–118, hier 102; Rosmarie Zeller: Grimmelshausen und die Sprachtheorie seiner Zeit. In: Simpliciana 35 (2013), 63–81, hier S. 65.

440731

Georg Philipp Harsdörffer an Herzog August d. J. von Braunschweig-Wolfenbüttel

Hz. August d. J. v. Braunschweig-Wolfenbüttel (FG 227), schreibt Georg Philipp Harsdörffer (FG 368), ahme das wohltätige Zusammenwirken der vier Elemente im Weltall nach, indem er nicht nur die unterdrückten Musen schütze und ihr Fortleben sichere, sondern auch Verfolgte wie den Überbringer des vorliegenden Schreibens, Harsdörffers Verwandten Sigismund Harsdörffer (der neulich Österreich habe verlassen müssen), unter seine Pagen aufnehme. Der werde sich durch Frömmigkeit, Rechtschaffenheit, Fleiß und Dienste dieses Glücks würdig erweisen. Harsdörffer bittet Gott, er möge den Herzog für sein Volk bewahren.

Q HAB: Cod. Guelf. 376 Novi 2°, Bl. 154r–155v [A: 155v], 154v u. 155r leer; eigenh.; Sig. — *D: Narciss*, 178f. (sehr fehlerhaft transkribiert. Narciss erklärt das Datum als 15.8.1644). — BN: *Bürger*, 673 Nr. 8.

A Serenissimo atque Celsissimo Principi Dom. DOMINO AUGUSTO DUCI Brunswicens. et Lüneburgens, &c. Domino meo clementissimo.   Ad arcem Guelphicam

Serenissime atque Celsissime Princeps, Domine clementissime.

Elementa ad complexum huius vniversi subalternis studiis concurrere videmus: quæ aqua respuit, excipit terra: quæ Terra exhalat, haurit äer: quæ äer subducit, sufflaminat Ignis. Serenitas atque Celsit. V.ª haud absimili beneficentiâ Naturam rerum imitatur, dum non modò Musas, hinc inde profligatas, suo præsidio munire, et ad seram vsque Posteritatem transmittere satagit; sed etiam afflictos, et inter hos Latorem præsentium Sigismundum Harsdörfferum[1], gentilem meum, Austriam nuper linquentem, in famulitium suum recipere dignatur. Hoc gratioso imperio ad sublimem erectus felicitatem sibi videbitur, dabitque operam vt calido Pietatis et Probitatis affectu, industriâ et officiis, quæ quidem in ipsius tenuitatem cadere possunt, sese hâc fortunâ condignum præstare valeat[a]. Jta Sponsor sum, Deumque veneror ut Seren.ⁱˢ atque Celsit.ⁱˢ V.æ incolumitatem ad populi sui emolumenta[b] perennare faciat propitius. Scribeb. Norimb. prid. Kal. Aug. 1644

Serenit. atque Celsit. V.ræ
    æterno cultu addictus
    Georg-Philippus Harsdörffer *mp.ia*

I

Georg Philipp Harsdörffers Widmungsgedicht für Herzog August d. J. von Braunschweig-Wolfenbüttel

Q *Harsdörffer: Frauenzimmer-Gesprächspiele* IV (1644, Ndr. 1968), Bl. [A iv] r – A v r (Ndr. S. 7–9).

440731 Georg Philipp Harsdörffer

Der
Hochlöblichen Fruchtbringenden
GESELSCHAFT
Hochansehnlichem und Lobwürdigstem
Mitgeliede
dem
Befreyenden[1]
übereiget in Vnterthänigkeit
diesen
Vierten Theil der Gesprächspiele
DER SPJELENDE/
Durch
folgendes Sinnbild.[2]

[A v r] **Klingreimen.**

ES[a] ließ der Majen Sohn[3] (als ich im Traum' ersehen)
   den schwanken Bottenstab entfallen auß der Hand'/
üm den die Bonen sich beginnten aufzudrehen/
dieweil die Schlangen beid' im fallen abgewand/
und sich mit blauem Gifft darwider wolten blehen;
   Doch schwebt sein Flügelhut[4] hoch ob dem grünē Band'
und ließ dem Spielgewächs[5] von jhnen nichts geschehen/
   Erwachend auß dem Traum' ich diese Deutung fand':
Hier der BEFREYENDE die bunte Bonenfrucht
   wird mit der Oberhuht'[6] erfreuen und befreyen.
Bey den sie nidere so hohen Schutz gesucht/
   und süsse Sicherheit vor Spott und Klügelschaum[7].
Wird dieser Gnadenschein dem Spielenden gedeyen/
   so ist sein grōstes Glück der wahrerfolgte[8] Traum![9]

II

440824

Georg Philipp Harsdörffer an Herzogin Sophia Elisabeth von Braunschweig-Wolfenbüttel

Q   HAB: Cod. Guelf. 406 Novi 2°, Bl. 411r–412v [A: 412v], 411v u. 412r leer; eigenh. — *D: Narciss*, 179f. (sehr fehlerhaft; unvollständig). — *BN: Bürger*, 676 Nr. 97.

A   A son Altesse   Madame Sophie Elisabeth Düchesse de Brünschweig et Lüneburg *etc.* Wolfenbüttel.

Madame
Si j'estois capable d'Ambition, celle de vostre Altesse m'en pourroit donner, me comblant des Loüanges, que je ne puis cognoistre, sans me mescognoistre moy mesme. Je reüssys avec le proverbe, Bonne mine [à] mauvais jeuez et L'autre, c'est bien joüé, quand l'on gaigne[1]: ayant obtenü par les imperfections de ma plume, La grace d'icelle, qu'est maniée par La plus accomplie Princesse de nostre temps. Cette particuliere et tres-chere faveur, me tiendra lieu d'vne Idee Informante, pour me rendre digne d'vne si haute approbation, et d'y conformer La suitte de mes essais, par[a] vne industrie plus exacte.[2]

Madame, J'offre à Vost. Altes. l'Embleme adjoint, environné des armes de Vostre tres-ancienne et Royale maison, avec brieve deduction d'iceluy.[3] Il plaise à vostre Altesse d'agreer La sterilité de moy esprit, et de commender celuy, qui est, et sera à jamais

    Madame
    à Vostre Altesse,
    Le tres-humble, tres-obeissant et tres-fidelle Serviteur
    George Philippe Harsdorf.

De Norimberg le 24 d'Aoust, l'an. 1644.

T a *Eingefügt für* <possit> — **b** *Eingefügt für* <perennitatem>

T I a *E-Schmuckinitiale mit Porträt Hz. Augusts d.J. von Braunschweig-Wolfenbüttel (FG 227); Holzschnitt.*

T II a *Folgt* <la suitte d'>

K 1 *Narciss*, 178, vermutet einen Neffen Georg Philipp Harsdörffers (FG 368). Harsdörffers eigener Sohn Hans Siegemund (1639–1699) kommt schon wegen der Formulierung im vorliegenden Brief, sodann wegen seines Alters nicht in Betracht: er war zu dieser Zeit gerade 5 Jahre alt. Keine Anhaltspunkte in: Johann Gottfried Biedermann: Geschlechtsregister des Hochadelichen Patriciats zu Nürnberg, welches aus denen bewährtesten Urkunden … zusammen getragen worden. Bayreuth 1748. Ndr. Neustadt a. d. Aisch [1988], Tab. CXLV–CLXV; Korb'sches Sippenarchiv: Personenregister zu den 624 Stammtafeln aus dem 1748 erschienenen Werk von Johann Gottfried Biedermann. Regensburg 1983 (Die Fundgrube, H. 43); Peter Fleischmann: Rat und Patriziat in Nürnberg. Die Herrschaft der Ratsgeschlechter vom 13. bis zum 18. Jahrhundert. Bd. 2: Ratsherren und Ratsgeschlechter. Nürnberg [2008], 545–566; Gunther Friedrich: Bibliographie zum Patriziat der Reichsstadt Nürnberg. Neustadt a. d. Aisch 1994, 62–67 (Harsdorf/ Harsdörffer).

K I 1 Durch die Zierbuchstaben des Namenszuges „*BEFREYENDEN*" zieht sich eine Gliederkette mit zwei geöffneten Handschellen am linken u. rechten Ende. In der Mitte des Wortes ist die Kette zerrissen.

2 Mit 430526 hatte Georg Philipp Harsdörffer (FG 368. Der Spielende) Hz. August d. J. v. Braunschweig-Wolfenbüttel (FG 227. Der Befreiende) den dritten Teil seiner *Frauenzimmer-Gesprächspiele* (1643) zugesandt. Mit dem vorliegenden Gedicht widmete Harsdörffer „dem 𝓑𝓔𝓕𝓡𝓔𝓨𝓔𝓝𝓓𝓔𝓝" den 4. Teil seiner *Frauenzimmer-Gesprächspiele* (1644). Der Zueignung folgend u. dem Widmungssonett vorausgehend (Bl. [A iv] v/ Ndr. S. 8) ein Sinnbild, das vom Widmungssonett (Bl. A v r/ Ndr. S. 9) erklärt wird: Umrahmt von einer Kartusche, die mit den Einzelschilden des augusteischen Gesamtschilds in Kranzform belegt ist, erheben sich im Vordergrund ein geflügelter Hut u. ein Merkurstab, der von Harsdörffers Gesellschaftspflanze, den bunten Böhnlein, umrankt ist. Zwei Schlangen am Boden vermögen der Pflanze keinen Schaden zu tun. Über diesem Sinnbild ein Spruchband: „Mit Freuden Befreyet." (Vgl. dazu 430526: „*Augustus hat mich Befreÿet!*"). Im Bildmittelgrund eine Ansicht der Festung Wolfenbüttel mit Schloß u. Marienkirche. Im Hintergrund eine gebirgige Phantasielandschaft mit Burg.

3 Hermes/ Merkur, Sohn des Zeus/ Jupiter u. der Gebirgsnymphe Maia. *Hederich*, 1591ff.

4 Geflügelter Reisehut, vgl. *DW* III, 1842: Petasus. Vgl. Anm. 6.

5 Die FG hatte Harsdörffer in 410909 die im Farbenspiel bunten Böhnlein als Gesellschaftspflanze nebst dem Gesellschaftsnamen „Der Spielende" vorgeschlagen: „daß er könne heissen der **Spielende**/ zum Gemälde haben die kleinen bunten Englischen **Bönlein**/ unterschiedener Farben/ und zum Worte/ **auff manche Art**". Harsdörffer selbst variierte seine Gesellschaftspflanze in 411126 leicht zugunsten der „welschen *Böhnlein* [...] in welchen die Natur *auf manche art* zu spielen pfleget". Vgl. dazu 411126 K 4.

6 Wortspiel: der Hut (Kopfbedeckung, hier Merkurs Flügelhut) u. die Hut (Schutz, Aufsicht, Obhut). Vgl. Anm. 4.

7 Kein lexikalischer Nachweis in *Stieler* u. *DW*. Wahrscheinlich Harsdörffers Neubildung, im Sinne von pedantischer Rechthaberei, Besserwisserei.

8 Kein lexikalischer Nachweis in *Stieler* u. *DW*. Wahrscheinlich Harsdörffers Neubildung, im Sinne von wahrgeworden, erfüllt.

9 Es folgt auf Bl. A v v/ Ndr. S. 10 das Widmungsgedicht F. Ludwigs, gez. „Von der Fruchtbringenden Geselschaft": „Auf des Spielenden Gesprächspiele", d. d. „Cöthen dē 24. Tag deß Heumonats im Jahre 1643." S. 430801 u. I. Die Initiale D (inc. DEr Spielend' alzeit wol mit seiner Leire spielt) mit einer Kokospalme, dem Sinnbild der FG.

K II 1 Seit François Villon (1431 – nach 1463) bekanntes frz. Sprichwort: faire bonne mine à mauvais jeu, ins Deutsche übernommen: gute Miene zum bösen Spiel machen. Vgl. Sabine Kowallik: Zur Typologie französischer Lehnübersetzungen im Deutschen. In: Das Französische in den deutschsprachigen Ländern. Romanistisches Kolloquium VII. Hg. Wolfgang Dahmen, Günter Holtus, Johannes Kramer (u.a.). Tübingen 1993, 18–24, hier S. 20, u. die Erläuterungen zu den „Proverbes Francoys" in *Nicot* (Anhang), hier S. 18. Das 2. Sprichwort: Es heißt gut gespielt, wenn man gewinnt. Ein historischer Nachweis ist uns dafür nicht gelungen. Vgl. die figürlichen Redewendungen von „jouer" in Dictionnaire de L'Académie Française. Siexième Edition. Tome 2, Paris 1835, 74f.

2 Georg Philipp Harsdörffer (FG 368) kann aus zeitlichen Gründen mit diesem Brief Hzn. Sophia Elisabeth v. Braunschweig-Wolfenbüttel (FG Die Befreiende. AL 1629. TG 42b) nicht den 5. Teil seiner „essais", seiner *Gesprächspiele*, überreicht haben, den er ihr aber im Folgejahr (1645), wie angekündigt, als einer „Mitgenossinn" der FG in einer prächtigen Zuschrift widmen wird. Die Gelegenheitsgedichte sind dort, soweit datiert, zwischen dem 10.12.1644 u. dem 16.5.1645 entstanden. Der Band wird im September 1645 erscheinen (vgl. 450817 u. 450923C). Der vierte Teil der *Gesprächspiele* (1644) ist dem Befreienden, Hz. August d.J. v. Braunschweig-Wolfenbüttel (FG 227) gewidmet u. vermutlich im April 1644 erschienen. Die Gedichte tragen darin Datierungen zwischen dem 10.8.1643 u. dem 6.2.1644. S. 440426 u. dort K 2.

3 Unbekannt, vielleicht ähnlich dem Sinnbild Harsdörffers mit den Schilden des braunschweigisch-lüneburgischen Wappens, das Sophia Elisabeths Gatten, dem Befreienden, gewidmet ist. S. Beil. I.

440809

Christian Gueintz an Fürst Ludwig

Christian Gueintz (FG 461. Der Ordnende) erklärt, seinen (in 440317) angekündigten Besuch bei F. Ludwig (Der Nährende) in Köthen zwecks Besprechung offener Fragen zur deutschen Rechtschreibung längst angetreten zu haben, wenn ihn nicht innere und äußere Hemmnisse daran gehindert hätten. Bei ehester Gelegenheit werde er sich einstellen. Er schlägt vor, seine eingeschickten Anmerkungen zu drucken, damit sie anderen Fruchtbringern zur Kenntnis bzw. Verbesserung vorgelegt werden könnten.

Q HM Köthen: V S 545, Bl. 183rv [A: 183v]; Schreiberh. mit eigenh. Kurialien u. Unterschrift u. eigenh. Empfangsvermerk F. Ludwigs; Sig. — D: Nicht in KE und KL.

A Dem Nährenden,   Hall   Cöthen
Empfangsvermerk F. Ludwigs: [?][a] Jenners 1645[1]

Dem *Nährenden* hette der gebühr vnd Schuldigkeit nach der *Ordenende* längst auffwarten sollen, vnd wegen der wortschreibung seine schlüssige gedancken entdecken, Aber die inwendige vnd außwendige troubeln[2] verhindern alles. So bald gelegenheit sich ereignen wird, ist Er bereit, sich zustellen. Unter deß bittet Er demütigst[b] nachricht, ob nicht möchten die abgeschickten Anmerckungen in Druck verfertiget werden, daß seine bemühungen der Fruchtbringenden Gesellschafft dargestellet werden, und die andern dadurch veranlaßet, es zuverbessern.[3]

Erwartet unterdeß nebens getreuer Empfehlung Gottes Schutzes vnd Obacht, Genädiges Schlusses vnd Meinung

Des *Nährenden*
gehorsamer[c] Ordenender *mp.*

Halle den 9 AugstMonats 1644.

T a *Unleserliche Verbesserung des Tagesdatums.* — b *Ergänze:* um — c gehorsamer Ordenender *mp. von Gueintz' H.*

K 1 Angesichts der geringen Entfernung von Halle a. d. S. nach Köthen eine erstaunlich lange Zustellungsfrist. Sie spricht für die von Christian Gueintz (FG 361. Der Ordnende) angesprochenen, auch kriegsbedingten Unsicherheiten u. Schwierigkeiten inner- u. außerhalb der Stadt Halle. Vgl. dazu 440504 K 1.

2 S. Anm. 1.

3 Wir wissen nicht, ob oder wie F. Ludwig sich zu diesem Vorschlag geäußert hat. Zum Druck dieser „abgeschickten Anmerckungen" ist es jedenfalls nicht gekommen. In 441231 meldet Gueintz schon den Abschluß seiner orthographischen Arbeit. In 450504

steht bereits der endgültige Druck des Buches an. *Gueintz: Rechtschreibung (1645).* Zur Gueintzschen Rechtschreibung s. 440127 K 1.

440809A

Winand von Polhelm an Fürst Ludwig

Winand v. Polhelm (FG 405. Der Entnehmende) dankt F. Ludwig (Der Nährende) auch im Namen Conrad Rötgers v. Diepenbroick (FG 406. Der Süßliche) für die auf ihre FG-Impresen verfaßten Verse (Reimgesetze). Polhelm erklärt, er habe einen verdeutschten Traktat (Teil der Vulson-Übersetzung *Von des Pabstes gewalt*) gleich dem Kasseler Verleger zugestellt, der ihn bereits der Druckerei geliefert habe. Der Verleger habe zugesichert, auch einen weiteren Teil nach seiner möglichst baldigen Übersendung auf gleiche Bedingung wie den ersten drucken zu lassen, damit beide Stücke gleichzeitig fertig würden.

Q HM Köthen: V S 545, Bl. 461r–462v, 462rv leer; eigenh. — *D: KE,* 47. — BN: Bürger, 1157 Nr. 1.

A *Fehlt.* — *Empfangsvermerk F. Ludwigs:* Eingeben 18. Aug. 1644.

Dem Nehrenden sagen der Sußliche vnd Entnehmende[1] vor die gnaden gedechtnuß der ihrentwegen abgefasten vnd vnlengst vberschickten Reymen[2] nachmahls vnderthenigen danck, vnd hatt der Entnehmende daß bewuste verdeutschte Tractätlein[3] woll empfangen vnd dem hiesigen buchführer[4] zugestellet, welcher es alsobaldt in die Druckerey[5] gegeben, mit dem erbieten, daß wen daß ander ge*nan*te Tractätlein von des Pabst gewaldt[6], baldt kondte hervber geschicket werden, er es auch mit vorigem bedingh wolte drucken laßen, damit beide zugeleich fertigh werden mogten *etc.*

Welches dem [461v] Nehrenden der Entnehmende in vnderthe[nig]keit[a] nicht verhalten sollen, alß der sich iederzeit bedregt, alß

Des Nehrenden

      Undertheniger
      Entnehmender
      W v Polh[elm]

Caßell den 9 Aug. 1644.

T a *Buchstaben im Falz verdeckt. Konjektur in eckigen Klammern.*

K 1 Zum Zeitpunkt ihrer vermutlich gemeinsamen Aufnahme in die FG standen Winand v. Polhelm (FG 405. Der Entnehmende) u. Conrad Rötger v. Diepenbroick (FG 406. Der Süßliche, mit der Pflanze Zuckerwurzel) beide in Diensten der hessen-kasselischen Paragiatslinie Hessen-Rotenburg, dem sog. „Rotenburger Quart" — ersterer als Gesamtrat, letzterer als Hofmeister Lgf. Hermanns IV. (FG 374). Zuvor war Polhelm der Hofmeister von dessen jüngeren Brüdern Friedrich (v. Hessen-Eschwege. FG 566. 1651), Christian (1622–1640) u. Ernst (v. Hessen-Rheinfels-Rotenburg, 1623–1693) gewesen. Zugleich übernahm Polhelm wiederholt Gesandtschaften für die vormundschaftlich regierende

Lgfn. Amalia Elisabeth v. Hessen-Kassel, Witwe Lgf. Wilhelms V. (FG 65). Vgl. 450305 K 1. Die beiden Mitglieder sind die letzten, die noch 1643 aufgenommen wurden; ihr Eintritt in die FG dürfte daher gegen Ende des Jahres erfolgt sein. Ihre Reimgesetze haben sich handschriftlich im *GB Kö.* III u. gedruckt im *GB 1641/44* erhalten (s. Anm. 2). Ihre Impresen fehlen im *GB 1646*, da dies nur die Mitglieder 1–400 erfaßt. Sie sind jedoch unter den *Weimarer Impresen* eingemalt. S. *Conermann II*. Beide trugen sich noch 1643 eigenh. bei ihren Wappenabbildungen im *GB Kö.* III ein, entweder bei einem gemeinsamen Besuch in Köthen oder bei einer Besuchsreise F. Ludwigs (Der Nährende) nach Kassel, wo dieser ihnen bei ihrer Aufnahme das *GB Kö.* vorgelegt haben könnte. S. *Conermann III*, 482–484.

2 Die Reimgesetze in *GB Kö.* III, Bl. [6]r u. [7]r u. im *GB 1641/44*, Bl. S 2v f.

3 Wohl kein verschollenes oder unbekanntes Werk, sondern Teil der in Anm. 6 identifizierten Übersetzung. Vgl. die Übersichten über verschollene Werke u. über Werkmanuskripte in *Conermann: Fl. Offizin*, 139 Anm. 58; *Conermann: Nachlaßinventar*, 82 ff.; *Conermann: Ludwig und Christian II. von Anhalt*, 432 ff.

4 In 450317 weist F. Ludwig auf den Buchdrucker Hans Schütz hin. Dessen Saumseligkeit u. Unentschlossenheit vereitele die Drucklegung der beiden ‚Traktate'. Allerdings ist Johann Schütz nicht als Drucker in Kassel bezeugt, sondern als Buchbinder, der auch verlegerisch tätig war. Von ihm sind Verlagswerke aus den Jahren zwischen 1634 u. 1669 belegt. *Benzing: Verleger*, 1264. In Kassel ließ Schütz nachweislich bei Johann Saur († 1636) u. Jakob Gentsch (um 1613–1661; Nachf. Wesselsche Offizin) drucken. Vgl. *Theophili Newbergers Soliloquia Vom Göttlichen leben eines wahren Christen in dieser Welt* (Getruckt zu Cassel/ bey Johan Saurn/ in verlegung Johann Schützens, 1633), HAB: 860. 8 Theol. Gentsch druckte für Johannes Crocius (1590–1659), seit 1612 Hofprediger Lgf. Moritz' v. Hessen-Kassel (FG 80) u. seit 1633 Rektor der neugegründeten Universität Kassel, den *Commentarius In epistolam S. Pauli apostoli ad Ephesios* in Schütz' Verlag (CASSELLIS, Typis JACOBI GENTSCHII, Impensis Johannis Schützen. M.DC.XLII. HAB: 817.61 Theol.) Von Crocius findet sich auch das Werk *De Ecclesi unitate et schismate* (CASSELLIS, Impensis Johannis Schützen. Anno M DC L. HAB: 815.14 Theol. [1]). — Auswärtige Druckereien scheinen ebenso für Schütz gearbeitet zu haben, etwa Salomon Schadewitz in Hofgeismar (seit 1639 in Hofgeismar nachgewiesen, seit 1650 in Kassel; † 1682) mit dem *Verteutschten Justinus Oder Viertzig vier Bücher Derer Geschicht-Beschreibungen des Justinus* von Johann Friedrich Sveser: Hoff Geißmar, Gedruckt bey Salomon Schadewitz, In verlegung Johann Schützen, in Cassel, 1649 (HAB: Lh 1110). Ebenfalls bei Schadewitz hatte Schütz einige Jahre zuvor Theophilus Neubergers (1593–1656) *Newes, lang gewünschtes Trost-Büchlein* (Hofgeismar 1646. HAB: 739.4 Theol.) in den Druck gegeben. Vgl. *Benzing: Buchdrucker*, 227 (Gentsch); *Reske*, 381 (Schadewitz) u. 411 f. (Saur, Gentsch, Schadewitz). Zu Schütz s. auch 450228 (= 450305 I), 450305, 450317, 450506, 450507A, 450526.

5 Auch in 450317 erwähnt F. Ludwig den Drucker Johann Schütz, gemeint ist der Kasseler Verleger, s. Anm. 4.

6 Das „bewuste verdeutschte Tractätlein" u. das „ander genante Tractätlein" weisen auf die ersten beiden Bücher des folgenden, insgesamt sechs Teile (Bücher) umfassenden Werkes hin *Von des Pabstes gewalt*, d. i. Von des Pabstes gewalt | und | Der alten Gallicanischen ietzo | Frantzosischen Kirchen | Freyheiten. | Durch Marcum de Vulson Königli- | chen Raht in dem Parlamentsge- | richte des Delphinats verfaßet | und | Im jahre 1635. ausgegangen, | anietzo verdeutschet | und | Gedrucket im jahre [*Jahreszahl fehlt*]. HM Köthen: V S 676 (alte Signatur: Xq 239), Hs., 215 Bl.; Schreiberh.; Marginalnoten einer anderen Hand; Korrekturen dieser Hand u. F. Ludwigs; Bl. 2r, 4r u. ö. Einen 3. Teil der

Übersetzung sandte F. Ludwig in 450317. Dessen Titel u. damit der Beweis für unsere Identifikation geht aus 450317A hervor. — Das romkritische Originalwerk wurde von dem Reformierten Marc de Vulson sieur de La Collet († 1640) verfaßt. Er stammte aus protestant. Amtsadel der Dauphiné u. war Rat im Parlament dieser Provinz in Grenoble. Das Buch erschien u. d. T. *De la puissance du pape et des libertés de l'Église Gallicane*, Genève 1635 (SUB Göttingen u. ULB Halle; Dig. SB München). Vgl. *ABF I*, 1038/ 286ff. Der Verfasser der Übersetzung ist nicht bekannt, jedoch könnte F. Ludwig die treibende Kraft, vielleicht sogar der Hauptübersetzer sein. Winand v. Polhelm (FG 405) war vielleicht in die Übersetzung, auf jeden Fall in die Drucklegung einbezogen. Es liegt auch nahe, an Ludwigs Hofprediger Daniel Sachse oder an die Zerbster Theologen Christian Beckmann oder Marcus Fridericus Wendelinus als Übersetzer zu denken. Das Nachlaßverzeichnis des Fürsten führt die Handschrift auf: „Ein geschriebener Tractat cum titul. Von deß Papst gewalt undt der altten Gallicanischen Kirchen Freiheit", mit dem Zusatz „in ein grauen bogen Pappier geleget so ich mit num 1 bezeichnet" (*IP*, Bl. 342r Nr. 2). Es handelt sich um ein Druckmanuskript. — Polhelm erbot sich im vorliegenden Brief, das Übersetzungswerk in Kassel verlegen u. drucken zu lassen (vgl. Anm. 5). Da der Verleger zu lange säumte, forderte Ludwig am 6.5.1645 die Handschrift von Polhelm zurück. S. 450305, 450317 u. 450506. Ein Druck der Übersetzung ist nicht mehr erfolgt. Vgl. *Conermann: Nachlaßinventar*, 88; *Conermann: Ludwig und Christian II. von Anhalt*, 433 f. S. dazu auch 450305 u. I, 450317, 450317A, 450506, 450526 u. 450818 K 4.

440816

Diederich von dem Werder an Fürst Ludwig

Diederich v. dem Werder (FG 31. Der Vielgekörnte) sendet F. Ludwig seine Verbesserungen der Reimgesetze auf die 1644 neu aufgenommenen Mitglieder Christian Heinrich v. Börstel (FG 407. Der Erlängernde), Albrecht v. Zerbst (FG 408. Der Ballernde), Otto Wilhelm v. Berlepsch (FG 409. Der Nangehende), Niclas Henrich (v.) Lüninck (FG 410. Der Befestende), Caspar Pfau (FG 412. Der Anhaltende) und Frh. Detloff v. Kappell (FG 414. Der Eingezogene). — Er entschuldigt sich dafür, daß er F. Ludwigs Verse nicht persönlich entgegennehmen konnte, und verspricht, sich künftig zuhause verfügbar zu halten, wenn er zuvor benachrichtigt werde.

Q HM Köthen: V S 546, Bl. 70rv, 70v leer; eigenh. Schreiben oder Beilage (ohne Anrede an F. Ludwig).

A *Fehlt.*

407.

[Ver]s[a]
[5][a] . Die sich dan zeiget schön klar hell' vnd offenbar (weil[b] |klar| sich in dem abschnitte mit der endung reimet, so habe ich dasselbe wort nur versetzet.[1])
[7][a] . Also wird lange frucht *Erlangernd'* auch gebracht.[2]

408.

[3][a] . den namen ballernd' hab' ich drümb genommen an[3]

                        409.
[2]ᵃ . das sie nimt weg die Gicht⁴

                        410
8. So zeigt mit nutzen sich ein rechter Biederman.⁵

                        412.
2. Sein Sahme kan gar wohl den starcken flus anhalten⁶
3. Garᵇ leichtlich stillen auch⁷

                        414.
7. Er triege sich dan selbst — — — — —⁸

Es ist dem Vielgekörndten leid, das er nicht hatt die ehre haben sollen, diese Reimgesetze eigenhändig zuᵈ empfangen, wan er auf ein andermal ein wenig nachricht darvon hatt, wird der sich einheimisch zuhalten wissen, vnd seine gebür leisten. Reinsdorff den 16. AugustMonats 1644.

I

Fürst Ludwigs Reimgesetze auf die Neumitglieder 407–415 in einer frühen Fassung

Q HM Köthen: V S 546, Bl. 72rv (falsch eingeheftet, der Text beginnt auf Bl. 72v); eigenh.

                        407.
Der Erlängernde   Des Haarstrangs waßer fein erlängert unser Haar,
                       Die wurtzel mit dem kraut hierzu ist gleich und eben
                   Drumb ich Erlängernd heiß, und bin begierig gar
Haarstrang   Die tage meiner Zeit der Tugend nach zustreben
                   Die sich dan zeiget vor klar, hell, und offenbar
                       Wen man aufrichtig geht ohn' heucheley im leben
Die Haare   Erlängernd' also wird auch lange frucht gebracht,
                   Wen man der laster schar abthut mit gantzer macht.
        C.H.V.B.   1644.

                        408.
Der Ballernde   Ein blaues Blumeleinᵃ hat der kleine Baldrian
                       Der Birckhan ballern sol, wan er es hat genoßen:
                   Den Nahmen Ballernd ich drumb hab genommen an
Der kleine blaue   Wiewol man sonsten mich nit findet von so großen
Baldrian   Und worten voller lauts: Die inre kraft mehr kan,
                   Den man mit pralen doch nur pfleget zuverstoßen

Bluhend genossen	Man nicht mit Ballern leicht die Laster treibet aus
	Furnemlich wan dahin man immer lebt im Saus'.
	A.V.Z. 1644.

409.

Der Nangehende	Gichtwurtzel ist gantz weis viel wirckung hat in sich
	Die Gicht zu nehmen weg, nan die geländer gehet
	Jhr kraut fast unvermerckt und windet festiglich
	Sich an dieselbe rumb: Nangehend' ihr nun sehet
Die gichtwurtzel	Auch meinen Nahmen hier. Wer dan bescheidenlich
	Jn wort und wercken ist, derselbe wol bestehet.
Fast unvermerckt	Er wird der tugend pfad nangehen unvermerckt,
	Und doch in seinem thun fruchtbringend sein gesterckt.
	O.W.V.B. 1644.

410.

Der Befestende	Die weiße Weidewind' auf Erden kreuchet her
	Und in die höhe leuft, befestet was versehret
	Von Adern ist im leib', als wen man blutes mehr
weise Weidewind	Auswirft als ist gesund, daher ich werd geehret
	Mit diesem Nahmen gern: Hieraus nemt diese Lehr'
	Jn uns werd das geblut so tugendhaft gemehret,
	Und was ihm schaden mag Fruchtbringend abgethan,
	So sich mit nutzen zeigt ein rechter Biederman.
	N.H.L. 1644.

411.

Der Steigende	Schön in die höhe steigt das glocken blümelein
	Von himmelblauer farb', Und ich drumb Steigend hei[ße]ᵇ
	Wer bey dem kriege wil bald Steigen hoch und sein
Das blaue glocken	Der aller tapferkeit und tugend sich befleiße
blumelein	Von unten fang' er an, Seh' auf die Ehr' allein,
	Und wans gebotten wird nein mit den fäusten schmei[ße]ᵇ
	Dan wird fort Steigend' er vorbringen solche frucht
Jn die höhe	Die hoch erfodert wird bey rechter kriegeszucht.
	M.V.D.L. 1644.

[72r]

412.

Der Anhaltende	Der Fenich wechst im Feld' ist fast der hirse gleich
	Der Sahme wan der flus zustarck ist, ihn anhalten

Fenich Sahmen und kraut	Und stillen leichtlich kan, das nicht der leib sey weich.
	    Anhaltend heiß^c ich nun. Man laß' es Gotte walten
	Wan starcker Kriegeslauf uns druckt und bringet seuch'
	    Auch sol man im gebett darinnen stille halten

Den starcken ausflus	Umb linderung der straff' anhalten im gebett, Das er durch seine güt' uns gnediglichen rett. C.Pf. 1644.

413.

Der Berühmete	Von wegen ihrer Kraft die Krebsblum' ist berühmt Dieweil sie treflich heilt die schäden welche fressen Mit ihrer schärff' umb sich: Berühmt drumb mir bestimt
Die Krebsblume	Der Nahm mit willen ward: die höfligkeit vergeßen Nit werden kan, wan^d vor ein edel hertz sie nimt Und leßet ohne not zu eßen nichts raus preßen. Man allem uberfluß' im freßen steur und wehr
[H]eilt^b freßende schäden	Und so mit guter frucht zu nutzen alles kehr'. J.H.K. 1644.

414.

Der Eingezogene	Der Roshuf aufgedreugt gepulvert ist sehr gut Furs keuchen wan er wird vom Athem eingezogen, Jm rauche durch die Nas', Ein eingezogner mut
Roshuf	Jst meinem Nahmen gleich weil sitsam er bewogen Durch lautre gütigkeit kein böses iemals thut. Von frommen keiner wird mit fürsatz nie betrogen Er sich betriege dan: drumb eingezogen leb'
Furs keuchen	Ein frommer Mensch, und stets dem ubel wiederstreb. D.V.C. 1644.

415.

Der Dienende	Der Heidrichsahmen dient der^e Kranckheit in der br[ust]^f Wan die mit vielem schleim' ist gantz hindurch erfüllet Jch dienend bin genant zu helffen diesem wust
Heiderichsahmen	Jnmaßen den ein hertz vol güte böses stillet Und dienet wie es mag.^{g} Zu aller freuden lust, Weil es zu tugend ist auch^h immerdar gewillet
Jn brustkranck- heiten	Zu bringen gute frucht' es mercklich dienen kan, Und sich des Nechsten nimt mit nutzen gleichsfals an. C.G.V.A.G.F. 1644

II

Eine verbesserte spätere Abschrift der Reimgesetze FG 407–415 als Vorlage der Verbesserungen Werders

Q HM Köthen: V S 546, Bl.71rv u. 73rv, 73v leer; Schreiberh. mit Korrekturen von F. Ludwig.

407.

Der Erlängernde	Wer[a] Haarstrangs waßer braucht erlängert ihm[b] die haar,
	Hierzu[c] ist mit dem kraut Die wurtzel gleich und eben
	Drumb ich *Erlängernd*' heiß', und bin begierig gar
Haarstrang	Die tage meiner Zeit der Tugend nach zustreben,
	Die sich dan zeiget[d] klar, schön,[e] hell und offenbar,
	Wen man aufrichtig geht ohn' heucheley im leben:
	Erlängernd' also wird auch lange frucht gebracht,
Die Haare	Wen man der laster schar abthut mit gantzer macht.
	C.H.V.B. 1644.

408.

Der Ballernde	Ein blaues Blumlein hat der kleine Baldrian
	Der Birckhan ballern sol, wan er es hat genoßen:
	Den Nahmen *Ballernd*' ich drumb hab genommen an
[De]r[f] kleine blaue	Wiewol man sonsten mich nit findet von so großen
Baldrian	Pral[g] worten voller ruhms[h]: die inre kraft mehr kan
	Den man mit Pralen doch nur pfleget zu verstoßen:
	Mit[i] Ballern Man nicht leicht die laster treibet aus,
[Bl]ühend[f] genoßen	Fürnemlich wen dabey[j] man immer lebt im Saus.
	A.V.Z. 1644.

409.

[D]er[f] *Nangehende*	Gichtwurtzel die[k] ist[l] weis[m] hat diese[n] kraft in sich
	Das[o] sie Die Gicht nimt[p] weg, nan die[k] geländer gehet
	Jhr kraut fast unvermerckt [sic] und windet festiglich
Die Gichtwurtzel	Sich an dieselbe rumb: *Nangehend*' ihr nun sehet
	Auch meinen Nahmen hier. Wer nun[q] bescheidenlich
	Jn wort und wercken ist, derselbe wolbestehet
	Er wird der Tugend pfad fast[k] unvermerckt[r] nangehn
[Fa]st[f] *unvermerckt*	Jn[s] seinem thun auch sich Fruchtbringend laßen sehn.
	O.W.V.B. 1644.

410.

[D]er꜠ Befestende	Die weiße weidewind' auf Erden kreuchet her,
	Und in die höhe leuft, befestet was versehret
	Von Adern ist im leib', als wen man blutes mehr
[W]eise꜠ weidewind	Auswirft dan᳷ ist gesund, daher ich ward᳑ geehret
	Mit diesem Nahmen gern: Hieraus nemt diese Lehr'
	Jn uns werd das geblüt so tugendhaft vermehret᳎,
	Und was da᳏ schädlich ist fruchtbringend abgethan,
[Ve]rsehrte꜠ Adern	So sich mit nutzen zeigt ein rechter Biedermann.
	N.H.L. 1644.

[71v]

411.

Der Steigende	Schön in die höhe steigt˟ das glocken blümelein
	Von himmel blauer farb',ʸ ich darumbᶻ *Steigend* heiß[e]꜠
	Wer bey dem Kriege wil bald Steigen hoch und sein,
Das blaue glocken blümelein	Der aller tapferkeit und tugend sich befleiße,
	Von unten fang' er an, Seh' auf die Ehr' allein,
	Und wansᵃᵃ gebotten wird, frischᵃᵇ unverzagt nein schmei[ße]꜠
	Dan wird fort *Steigend* er vorbringen solche frucht,
In die höhe	Die hocherfodert wird bey rechter Kriegeszucht.
	M.V.D.L. 1644.

412.

Der Anhaltende	Der Fenich wechst im feld' ist fast der hirse gleich,
	Seinᵃᶜ Sahme, wan einᵃᵈ flus zu starck ist, ihn anhalten
	Und stillen leichtlich kan, desᵃᵉ Leibesᵃᶠ böseᵃᵍ seuch'
Fenich Sahmen und kraut	*Anhaltend* heiß ich nun: Man laßeᵃʰ Gott nur walten,
	Wan starckeᵃⁱ Krieges lastᵃʲ uns druckt und machetᵃᵏ weich,
	Soᵃˡ sollen in gedultᵃᵐ wir ihme stille halten,
	Umb linderung der straff' anhalten im gebett,
Den starcken ausflus	Das er durch seine güt' uns gnediglichen rett'.
	C.P.ᵃⁿ 1644.

413.

Der Berühmete	Dieᵃᵒ krebesblume wird von ihrer kraft berühmt
	Dieweil sie treflich heilt die schäden welche freßen
	Mit ihrer schärff' umb sich: Deshalbenᵃᵖ mir bestimt
Die krebs blume	*Berühmt*ᵃᵠ mein Nahme ward: Ein edel hertz verge[ssen]꜠
	Allᵃʳ üppigkeiten sol, hergegen an es nimt,
	Wasᵃˢ tapfer, tugendhaft, ist nicht darbey vermessen,
Heilt freßende schäden	Dieᵃᵗ tugend frisset auf die laster in gemein
	Mitᵃᵘ der ein tapfer hertz stets sol gezieret sein.
	J.H.K. 1644.

414.

Der Eingezogene Der Roshuf aufgedreugt gepulvert ist sehr gut
　　　　　　　　　Fürs keuchen, wan sein[av] rauch vom Athem eingezogen
　　　　　　　　Starck[aw] durch die Nase[ax] wird[k]: Ein eingezogner Mut
Roshuf　　　　　　Jst meinem Nahmen gleich, weil sitsam er bewogen
　　　　　　　　Durch lautre gütigkeit kein böses iemals thut.
　　　　　　　　　Von frommen keiner wird mit fürsatz nie betrogen
　　　　　　　　Er sich betriege dan: Drümb eingezogen leb'
Fürs Keuchen　　Ein frommer Mensch, und stets dem übel wiederstreb'.
　　　　　　　　　D.V.C.　　　　　　　　1644.

[73r]

415.

Der Dienende　　Der Heidrich sahmen dient der kranckheit in der brust
　　　　　　　　　Wan die mit vielem schleim' ist gantz und[ay] gar erfüllet,
　　　　　　　　Drum[az] Dienend heiß'[ba] ich hier zu helffen diesem wust'
Heiderichsahmen　Ein[bb] hertze voller güt das böse leichtlich stillet,
　　　　　　　　Und dienet wie es mag, zu aller freuden lust,
　　　　　　　　　Weil[bc] tugend immerdar und lieb' aus solchem quillet,
Jn brust kranck-　Ein[bd] Solcher edler muht fruchtbringend dienen kan,
heiten.　　　　　Weil[be] seines Nechsten sich er nimmet treulich an.
　　　　　　　　　C.G.V.A.G.F.　　　　　　1644.

T a *Textverlust im Falz. Konjektur in eckigen Klammern.* — b *Der Zusatz* bis versetzet *wird von Werder mit einer geschweiften Klammer auf die erste Zeile bezogen.* — c *Darüber* <jhn> — d *Eingefügt.*

T I a *Von F. Ludwig wider das Metrum gebessert aus* Blumlein — b *Textverlust im Falz. Konjektur in eckigen Klammern nach GB 1641/44.* — c *Wörterreihenfolge durch Bezifferung umgestellt aus:* Anhaltend ich nun heiß — d *Wörterreihenfolge durch Bezifferung umgestellt aus* wan sie ein edel hertz vornimt — e *der* Kranckheit *gebessert aus den* Kranckheiten — f *Textverlust durch Papierausriß am Rand. Ergänzung in eckigen Klammern nach GB 1641/44.* — g *Eingefügt für* <kan> — h *Gebessert aus* <geneiget> immerdar gewillet

T II a *Eingefügt für* <Des> — b ihm die *eingefügt für* <unser> Für ihm lies sich — c *Wörterreihenfolge durch Bezifferung umgestellt aus:* Die wurtzel mit dem kraut hierzu ist gleich und eben — d *Folgt* <vor> — e schön, *eingefügt.* — f *Buchstabenverlust im Falz. Konjektur in eckigen Klammern nach GB 1641/44.* — g *Eingefügt für* <Und> — h *Eingefügt für* <lauts> — i *Wörterreihenfolge bis* nicht *durch Bezifferung umgestellt aus:* Man nicht mit Ballern — j *Gebessert aus* dahin — k *Eingefügt.* — l *Folgt* <gantz> — m *Folgt* <viel wirckung> — n diese kraft *eingefügt.* — o Das sie *eingefügt.* — p *Eingefügt für* <zu nehmen> — q *Eingefügt für* <dan> — r *Wörterreihenfolge durch Bezifferung umgestellt und gebessert aus:* nangehen unvermerckt — s *Zeile mit Einfügungen und Streichungen gebessert aus:* <Und doch> in <allen> seinem thun Fruchtbringend <sein gesterckt> <wol bestehn> — t *Eingefügt für* <als> — u *Gebessert aus* werd — v *Gebessert aus* <ge>mehret

w da schädlich ist *eingefügt für* <ihm schaden mag> — **x** *Gebessert aus* steiget — **y** *Folgt* <und> — **z** *Gebessert aus* drumb — **aa** *Gebessert aus* wens — **ab** Bis nein *eingefügt für* <nein mit den fäusten> — **ac** *Eingefügt für* <Der> — **ad** *Eingefügt für* <der> — **ae** *Gebessert aus* das *folgt* <nicht der> — **af** *Gebessert aus* Leib — **ag** böse seuch *eingefügt für* <sey weich> — **ah** Bis nur *gebessert und eingefügt für* Laß' <es> Gotte — **ai** *Gebessert aus* starcker — **aj** *Gebessert aus* lauff — **ak** machet weich *eingefügt für* <bringet seuch> — **al** So sollen *eingefügt für und gebessert aus* <Auch> sol <man> — **am** geduld wir ihme *gebessert aus* ge<bett darinnen> — **an** *Folgt* <F.> — **ao** *Zeile gebessert aus* Von <wegen> ihrer kraft die krebsblum ist berühmt — **ap** *Eingefügt für* <*Berühmt* drumb> — **aq** *Zeile gebessert aus* <Der> Nahm <mit willen> ward: <Die hofligkeit> verge[ssen] — **ar** *Zeile gebessert aus* Nit werden kan, wan vor ein edel hertz sie nimt, — **as** *Zeile gebessert aus* <Und leßet ohne not, zu eßen> nicht<s raus preßen> — **at** *Zeile eingefügt für* <Man allem überflus im freßen steur und wehr> — **au** *Zeile gebessert aus* <Und so> mit <guter frucht zu nutzen alles kehr>. — **av** sein rauch *eingefügt für* <er wird> — **aw** *Eingefügt für* <Jm rauche> — **ax** *Gebessert aus* Nas — **ay** und gar *eingefügt für* <hindurch> — **az** *Eingefügt für* <Jch> — **ba** Bis hier *eingefügt für* <bin genant> — **bb** *Zeile gebessert aus* <Jnmaßen den> ein hertz vol güte böses stillet — **bc** *Zeile gebessert aus* Weil <es zu> tugend <ist auch> immerdar gewillet — **bd** *Zeile gebessert aus* <Zu bringen gute frucht es mercklich> dienen kan — **be** *Zeile gebessert aus* <Und sich des> Nechsten <nimt mit nutzen gleichsfals> an.

K Ein vorhergehendes Schreiben F. Ludwigs an Diederich v. dem Werder (FG 31) fehlt. Insgesamt muß die Korrespondenz Diederichs v. dem Werder (FG 31. Der Vielgekörnte) mit dem Fürsten in der Überlieferung Einbußen erlitten haben. Der erhaltene Briefwechsel erreicht 1644 jedenfalls bei weitem nicht mehr den Umfang früherer Korrespondenzjahrgänge.

1 Die Zeile in F. Ludwigs Originaltext (Beil. I): „Die sich dan zeiget vor klar, hell, und offenbar". Weder hier noch in Werders Korrektur treffen wir auf einen Binnenreim in der alexandrinischen Langzeile vor der Verszäsur (Abschnitt): klar / -bar. Nur in der korrigierten Abschrift (Beil. II) haben wir, vielleicht aufgrund einer Einfügung von „schön" an der falschen Stelle, den von Werder anscheinend vermiedenen Binnenreim: „Die sich dan zeiget klar schön hell' vnd offenbar". Das *GB Kö.* III, Bl. 8r u. das *GB 1641/44*, Bl. S 3r, haben die Zeile im Wortlaut der Werder-Korrektur: „Die sich dan zeiget schön/ klar/ hell' und offenbar". Christian Heinrichs v. Börstel (FG 407) Impresenvisierung in *Weimarer Impresen*, Nr. 407, abgebildet in *Conermann II*, Abbildungsteil (nicht pag.).

2 In der korrigierten Abschrift (Beil. II) ist F. Ludwig bei seiner ursprünglichen Fassung (Beil. I) geblieben. Das *GB Kö.* III, Bl. 8r u. das *GB 1641/44*, Bl. S 3r haben Werders Korrektur übernommen.

3 Albrecht v. Zerbst (FG 408. Der Ballernde). Zu seiner Imprese u. Reimgesetz vgl. auch 460424 K 14. In der korrigierten Abschrift (Beil. II) ist F. Ludwig bei seiner ursprünglichen Fassung (Beil. I) dieser Zeile geblieben. Das *GB Kö.* III, Bl. 9r u. das *GB 1641/44*, Bl. S 3r haben Werders Korrektur übernommen. Impresenvisierung in *Weimarer Impresen*, Nr. 408, abgebildet in *Conermann II*, Abbildungsteil (nicht pag.).

4 Otto Wilhelm v. Berlepsch (FG 409. Der Nangehende). In der korrigierten Abschrift (Beil. II) hat F. Ludwig Werders Korrektur nicht vollständig übernommen, dies geschieht erst im *GB Kö.* III, Bl. 10r u. im *GB 1641/44*, Bl. S 3v. Impresenvisierung in *Weimarer Impresen*, Nr. 409, abgebildet in *Conermann II*, Abbildungsteil (nicht pag.).

5 Niclas Henrich (v.) Lüninck (FG 410. Der Befestende). In der korrigierten Abschrift (Beil. II) ist F. Ludwig bei seiner ursprünglichen Fassung (Beil. I) dieser Zeile geblieben.

Das *GB Kö.* III, Bl. 11r u. das *GB 1641/44*, Bl. S 3r haben Werders Korrektur übernommen. Impresenvisierung in *Weimarer Impresen,* Nr. 410, abgebildet in *Conermann II,* Abbildungsteil (nicht pag.).

6 Caspar Pfau (FG 412. Der Anhaltende). In der korrigierten Abschrift (Beil. II) hat F. Ludwig seine ursprüngliche Fassung (Beil. I) dieser Zeile nur leicht abgewandelt. Das *GB Kö.* III, Bl. 13r u. das *GB 1641/44*, Bl. S[4]r haben Werders Korrektur übernommen. Impresenvisierung in *Weimarer Impresen,* Nr. 412, abgebildet in *Conermann II,* Abbildungsteil (nicht pag.).

7 In der korrigierten Abschrift (Beil. II) ist F. Ludwig bei seiner ursprünglichen Fassung (Beil. I) dieser Zeile geblieben. Das *GB Kö.* III, Bl. 13r u. das *GB 1641/44*, Bl. S [4]r haben Werders Korrektur übernommen.

8 Frh. Detloff v. Kappell (FG 414. Der Eingezogene). In der korrigierten Abschrift (Beil. II) ist F. Ludwig bei seiner ursprünglichen Fassung (Beil. I) dieser Zeile geblieben. Das *GB Kö.* III, Bl. 15r u. das *GB 1641/44*, Bl. S [4]r haben Werders Korrektur übernommen.

K I Diese eigenhändig von F. Ludwig niedergeschriebenen Reimgesetze der FG-Mitglieder 407–415 (s. K) bildeten die Grundlage für die von F. Ludwig dann korrigierte Abschrift eines Schreibers (Beilage II). F. Ludwigs Korrektureinträge in dieser Abschrift haben noch nicht Diederichs v. dem Werder (FG 31) Korrekturen (s. obigen Brief) aufgegriffen u. übernommen, die uns aber sämtlich in der identischen Endfassung der Reimgesetze in *GB Kö.* III u. *GB 1641/44* begegnen. Es war vermutlich eine saubere Kopie dieser korrigierten Abschrift oder doch eine ähnliche Fassung, die die Grundlage für Werders Korrekturen bildete. Gleich sein erster Korrekturvorschlag kann sich sinnvoll nicht auf die Textfassung in Beil. I, sondern auf den Text in Beilage II beziehen. S. K 1, vgl. K II.

K II Es handelt sich hier um eine Abschrift der als Beilage I gebotenen Niederschrift F. Ludwigs. Diese Abschrift von Schreiberh. wurde dann von F. Ludwig durchgesehen u. korrigiert. Seine Verbesserungen kommen der Endfassung der Reimgesetze in *GB Kö.* III u. im *GB 1641/44* schon näher, weisen aber noch nicht die Korrekturen Diederichs v. dem Werder (FG 31) im obigen Brief auf. Diese Abschrift stellt also eine Zwischenstufe dar.

440824

Georg Philipp Harsdörffer an die Fruchtbringende Gesellschaft

Beantwortet durch 450124. — Georg Philipp Harsdörffer (FG 368. Der Spielende) teilt mit, der FG mit seiner Sendung vom 20. (recte 26.) April vier Exemplare des druckfrischen vierten Teils seiner *Frauenzimmer-Gesprächspiele* (1644) über Gottfried Stahl in Leipzig zugeschickt zu haben. Da er keine Empfangsbestätigung erhalten und von Diederich v. dem Werder (FG 31. Der Vielgekörnte) erfahren habe, daß die zugedachte Sendung nicht im Erzschrein eingetroffen sei, bittet er, in Leipzig nach dem Verbleib zu forschen. — Nunmehr sei auch die 2. Auflage des ersten Teils der *Frauenzimmer-Gesprächspiele* im Druck und die Arbeit an deren fünftem Teil nahezu abgeschlossen. — In Nürnberg sei das Interesse an der deutschen Sprache rege, auch die *Teutsche Sprachkunst* (1641) von Justus Georg Schottelius (FG 397. Der Suchende) an den Schulen eingeführt worden. Der Theologe Johann Klaj sei mit zwei Gedichten in jambischen, trochäischen, anapästischen, daktylischen, sapphischen, anakreontischen, alkäischen und anderen Formen öffentlich hervorgetreten. All dies führe zur Nachfrage nach den Druckwerken der FG, speziell werde (F. Ludwigs) *Der weise Alte* (1643) in Regensburg und Augsburg begehrt. Harsdörffer hofft daher, daß diese Werke auf der künftigen Leipziger Buchmesse käuflich oder im Tausch gegen Papier oder Bücher zu erwerben sein würden. — Harsdörffer bittet erneut um ein Verzeichnis der jüngsthin aufgenommenen FG-Mitglieder. — In der Nachschrift wiederholt Harsdörffer seine bereits dreimal vorgebrachte, jedoch nicht beantwortete Bitte um Instruktion, wie er in Angelegenheiten Werders verfahren solle.

Q HM Köthen: V S 545, Bl. 302r–303v [A: 303v], 302v u. 303r leer; eigenh. mit eigenh. Empfangsvermerk F. Ludwigs; Portovermerk mit rotem Kreidestrich auf der Anschriftseite. — D: KE, 333. — BN: Bürger, 674 Nr. 30.

A t. 54[a] *Der Hochlöblichen Fruchtbringenden Geselschaft zu gn. Handen.* Franco bis Leipzig[a] Zu Leipzig bey H. Gottfried Stahlen abzugeben. *Cöthen. Empfangsvermerk F. Ludwigs:* Eingegeben den 9. Herbstmonats 1644.[b]

t.

Der hochlöblichen Fruchtbringenden Geselschaft, hat der Spielend[e][c] iüngstverwichenen 20. April[1], den Vierten Theil seiner Gesprechspiele in unterthänig*keit* übersendet, und solcher, vier Exemplar, an H. Gottfried Stahlen[2] nach Leipzig abgegeben: Wann er aber inzwischen keine nachrichtung erhalten, auch von dem Vielgekörnten, *ver*standen daß selbe[d], in dem Ertzschrein, nicht eingelanget worden, hat ihm[e] oblie*gen* wollen solches nochmals anzufügen, und üm nachfrage zu Leipzig gebührender[f] massen zu bitten.[3]

Der erste Theil der Gesprechspiele ist nun zum zweitenmal der Druckarbeit untergeben,[4] und ist der fünfte Theil fast auch zu ende gebracht.[5] Weilen nun dieses ortes, die Teutsche Sprache in gang und schwang gelanget, die Sprachkunst des Suchenden[6] in den Schulen eingeführet, und Johann Clajus, ein beflissener der H. Schrift, zwey herrliche Gedichte, von jam[bi]s[c]hen[g], troschäischen [sic], Anpästischen [sic], Sapphisch[en,][c] Dactylischen, Anaceontischen [sic], [A]lcasch[en] [sic][g] und anderen mehr Reimarten öffentlich hören lassen[7]; werden der hochlöblichen Fruchtbringenden Geselschaft Bücher befraget, und *ver*langet; sonderlich aber ist der Weise Alte[8] zu Rengßpurg[9], und Augßpurg begehret worden. Diesemnach möchte die unmassgebliche *ver*ordnung zu thun seyn, daß bey *ver*hoffentlicher leipziger messe, berührte Bücher erkauffet, oder gegen papyr und andere, eingetauschet wer*den* könten. Sonsten bitte[t][c] der Spielende nochmals üm die *ver*zeichnus der lezt eingenom*m*ene[n][c] GeselschaftsGenossen[10], und verbleibet, nechst empfehlung in des Allerhöchsten obschutze,

Der hochlöblichen Fruchtbringenden Geselschaft
in unterthänig*keit* dienstergebener,

Der Spielende.

Geben Nürnberg den 24 Augustmonats im Jahre 1644.

N. S.

[Jn]^h des Vielgekörnten Geschefften wird alhier schleunigste verordnung erwartet, massen solche zum dritten mal begehret worden, und keine antwort erfolget.¹¹

T **a** *Postalischer Vermerk von unbekannter H.* — **b** *Darunter unleserlicher Schriftzug von F. Ludwigs H.* — **c** *Am Blattrand eingeschränkte Lesbarkeit, Konjektur in eckigen Klammern.* — **d** *Gebessert aus* solche — **e** ihm obliegen wollen *eingefügt für* <er nicht ümgehen sollen> — **f** gebührender massen *eingefügt.* — **g** *Ein Tintenfleck verdeckt das Wort teilweise, Konjektur in eckigen Klammern.* — **h** *Textverlust im Falz, Konjektur in eckigen Klammern.*

K 1 Recte 26. April, s. 440426.
2 Der Leipziger Kaufmann Gottfried Stahl d. Ä. (1600–1670). Vgl. 440426 K 1.
3 *Harsdörffer: Frauenzimmer-Gesprächspiele* IV (1644, Ndr. 1968) war vermutlich im April 1644 erschienen. Im vorliegenden Brief fragt Georg Philipp Harsdörffer (FG 368. Der Spielende) nach dem Verbleib seiner früheren Sendung vom 20. (recte: 26.) April 1644 mit vier Exemplaren des 4. Teils seiner *Gesprächspiele*, die er über den Leipziger Kaufmann Gottfried Stahl gesandt hatte. Erst in 450124 kann F. Ludwig endlich den verspäteten Erhalt der Sendung 440426 melden einschließlich zweier Druckexemplare besagten Teils. Er erwähnt dabei auch zwei in dieser Sendung enthaltene „verschloßene schreiben und beylagen" an Diederich v. dem Werder (FG 31. Der Vielgekörnte) u. F. Christian II. v. Anhalt-Bernburg (FG 51), die das 3. u. 4. Druckexemplar enthalten haben dürften. Vgl. 440426 K 2.
4 Die veränderte u. erweiterte, F. Ludwig (Der Nährende) zugeeignete 2. Auflage des 1. Teils der *Frauenzimmer-Gesprächspiele* ist erst im Frühjahr 1645 erschienen, obwohl das Impressum das Erscheinungsjahr 1644 angibt. S. 450400, 450410 u. 440715A K 0. F. Ludwig ging anscheinend mit 450400 ein Exemplar zu, er dankte für den Erhalt in 450529. Auch Harsdörffers Übereignungsgedicht an den Nährenden ist früh auf den 15.7.1644 datiert. S. 440715, vgl. 440715A. Wegen des aufwendigen Bildschmucks u. des kunstvollen Satzes könnte die Drucklegung dieser *Frauenzimmer-Gesprächspiele* durchaus mehrere Monate in Anspruch genommen haben, s. Anm. 5.
5 Der fünfte Teil der *Frauenzimmer-Gesprächspiele* wird im September 1645 erscheinen. In 450400 teilt Harsdörffer mit, der 5. Teil sei bereits unter der Druckerpresse, die Fertigstellung werde jedoch gewiß noch ein halbes Jahr in Anspruch nehmen. Im August 1645 ist der Druck noch nicht abgeschlossen (s. 450817). Mit 450923C kann Harsdörffer F. Ludwig ein Druckexemplar schicken. Vgl. 451101.
6 *Schottelius: Teutsche Sprachkunst (1641).* Auf diese deutsche Grammatik (und sprachwissenschaftliche Programmschrift) von Justus Georg Schottelius (FG 397. Der Suchende) bezog sich Harsdörffer immer wieder, während er zu *Gueintz: Deutsche Sprachlehre (1641)* auf Distanz ging. Vgl. etwa 450817, zu Gueintz' *Sprachlehre* 450504 K 9.
7 In enger Verbindung zu Johann Michael Dilherr (1604–1669), der seinen Lehrstuhl der Rhetorik, Historie u. Poesie an der U. Jena 1642 aufgegeben hatte, um die Aufsicht über das nürnberg. Schulwesen u. andere Ämter, 1646 auch das Pfarramt von St. Sebald zu übernehmen, hatte Johann Klaj (1616–1656) zu Ostern 1644 unter Dilherrs Patronage sein Auferstehungsoratorium in Dilherrs neuer Lehranstalt, dem Auditorium bei S. Egidien, vorgetragen: Aufferstehung JESV CHRJSTJ Jn ietzo neuübliche hochteutsche Reimarten verfasset/ und in Nürnberg Bey hochansehnlicher Volkreicher Versamlung abgehandelt

(Nürnberg 1644). Ndr. in J. K.: Redeoratorien und „Lobrede der teutschen Poeterey". Hg. Conrad Wiedemann. Tübingen 1965, [1]–[55]. Zu den Aufführungsdaten u. -orten dieses Redeoratoriums u. der folgenden vergleichbaren Stücke s. die von Wiedemann zitierte Chronik in J. K.: Friedensdichtungen und kleinere poetische Schriften. Hg. v. C. W. Tübingen 1968, 17*. In seinem ersten Redeoratorium hatte Klaj alle möglichen Metren, Versarten u. Strophenformen erprobt — „Dactylische Verse auff Sapphische Manier" (S. 1), „Trocheische Ode" (3), jambische Alexandriner (4), „Anapestische Verse" (6), jambische Vers communs (9), „Anacreontische Ode" (11) usw. — u. in gelehrten Anmerkungen annotiert, vgl. S. 25, 28, 30 u. 35. Harsdörffer hatte in dem Druck dieses Werkes ein „Lobgedichte. Wiederkehr/ Entgegengesetzt den Verächteren der Teutschen Sprache" beigesteuert (S. [52]). Dem Auferstehungsoratorium ließ Klaj im großen Saal des Augustinerklosters zum Sonntag Trinitatis 1644 einen weiteren Redeactus folgen: Höllen- und Hiṁelfahrt JESV CHRJSTJ/ nebenst darauf erfolgter Sichtbarer Außgiessung GOTTES deß Heiligen Geistes. Jn jetzo Kunstübliche Hochteutsche Reimarten verfasset/ und in Nürnberg Bey Hochansehnlichster Volkreichster Versamlung abgehandelt (Nürnberg 1644). Ndr. a. a. O., [57]–[127]. Auch hier begegnen Jamben, Trochäen, Anapeste u. Daktylen in unterschiedlichen Versarten. Unter den Verfassern der „Lobgedichte" erscheinen Harsdörffer [121 f.] u. Justus Georg Schottelius [122 f.], der später als Fontano I. Mitglied des PBO wurde. Noch im Herbst desselben Jahres (18. 10. 1644), aber zu spät, um hier von Harsdörffer gemeint zu sein, traten Klaj u. Harsdörffer mit ihrem *Pegnesischen Schäfergedicht* auf, das 1644 im Druck erschien: PEGNESJSCHES SCHAEFERGEDJCHT/ in den BERJNORGJSCHEN GEFJLDEN/ angestimmet von STREFON und CLAJVS (Nürnberg 1644). Ndr. in Georg Philipp Harsdörffer, Sigmund von Birken, Johann Klaj: Pegnesisches Schäfergedicht 1644–1645. Hg. Klaus Garber. Tübingen 1966. Vgl. auch 441223 K 15 u. 450504 K 4. Zur gleichen Zeit, zu St. Simon u. Juda (18./28. 10. 1644), rezitierte Klaj in Prosa wohl im Augustinerkloster eine Rede von Herodes' Kindermord (vgl. auch 441223) u. seine *Lobrede der Teutschen Poeterey/ Abgefasset und in Nürnberg Einer Hochansehnlich-Volkreichen Versamlung vorgetragen* (Nürnberg 1645). Ndr. in J. K.: Redeoratorien (s. o.), [377]–[416]. Vgl. zur *Lobrede* auch 441223 K 13, 450504 K 4 u. 450927 K II 11; zu Klaj ebd. u. 450504. In der Fastenzeit 1645 folgte *Der Leidende CHRJSTVS/ Jn einem Trauerspiele vorgestellet Durch Johann Klaj/ Der H. Schrifft Beflissenen/ und gekrönten Poeten* (Nürnberg 1645) [Ndr. a. a. O., 201–280] u. am Sonntag nach Ostern HERODES der Kindermörder/ Nach Art eines Trauerspiels ausgebildet und Jn Nürnberg Einer Teutschliebenden Gemeine vorgestellet durch Johan Klaj (Nürnberg 1645) [Ndr. a. a. O., 129–200].

8 *Fürst Ludwig: Der weise Alte (1643)*. F. Ludwig hatte Harsdörffer mit 430724 ein Druckexemplar zugesandt. Zu diesem Erbauungswerk, einer Übersetzung aus dem Französischen des Simon Goulart de Senlis: LE SAGE VIEILLARD (zuerst Lyon 1605), vgl. 310411 u. I, 401214 K 12, 430505 K I 12 u. im vorliegenden Band 440130, 450124 K 2, 450900 u. 460705 K II 1. In 450124 versicherte F. Ludwig Harsdörffer, daß die nachgefragten Fruchtbringer-Werke „in nechstfolgenden Leiptziger Jharmarck, der auf Lichtmeße angesetzet, bey dem Buchführer Andreas Kühnen, im Franckfurter buchladen" zu erhalten sein würden. Der Leipziger Buchhändler Andreas Kühne (1599–1648) arbeitete in verschiedenen fruchtbringerischen Verlagsprojekten mit. Vgl. 450124 (K 2).

9 „Reng/ reng" als (gesprochene) fränk. Form für Regen/ regnen. Die Ansetzung „rengspurg" für Regensburg in Ulrich Füetrers (vor 1450 – zw. 1493/1502) aufgesetzter *Bairischer Chronik* (zw. 1478 u. 1481; vgl. Reinhold Spiller [Hg.]: Bayerische Chronik. München 1909), nach *DW* XI. 1. 1, 1532 (s. v. „Traunis"). Im Ostfränkischen erscheinen die vier Konsonanten l, m, n sowie der Nasal ng als Silbenträger, wenn ihnen ein unbetontes e vorangeht, wie dies im Falle Regen > gesprochen: Reng oder Reing der Fall ist, entsprechend regnen > gespr. reng, Regenschirm > gespr. rengschärm. Vgl. Georg Schübel: Die Ostfränkisch-Bambergische Mundart von Stadtsteinach im ehemaligen Fürstbistum Bamberg. Lautlehre und Beugungslehre. Gießen 1955, 11 f., 31, 115, 145, 196 u. 250. Zur Verschmelzung von n und g zu *einem* Laut (stimmhafter velarer Nasal -ng) s. auch *Jellinek: Nhd. Grammatik* I, 12 u. 31. Eine ganze Reihe von Wörtern haben im Ostfr. den mhd. Anlaut b- für das spätere p- behalten, diese Lenisierung der Verschlußlaute ist ein typ. Kennzeichen für das Fränkische, etwa gespr. brygl für Prügel, budsn für putzen usw. Die Schreibweise „-purg" dürfte daher eher mittelbairischen oder anderweit obd. Ursprungs sein, zumal das Ostfr. einen Übergangsraum zw. Md. u. Obd. darstellte.

10 Wie im Falle von Christian Gueintz (FG 361) in 441231 erhielt auch Harsdörffer mit 450124 eine auf den letzten Stand gebrachte Mitgliederliste, wie sie F. Ludwig für die Ergänzung des *GB 1641* — es endete mit FG 353: Gottfried Müller — zum *GB 1641/44* nachdrucken ließ. Da er die Initialen der Mitglieder nicht aufzulösen vermochte, erbat Harsdörffer von F. Ludwig in 450400 ein Verzeichnis der Personennamen. Mit 450529 wird er sie unter den üblichen Hinweisen auf diskreten u. rein privaten Gebrauch erhalten. Vgl. zu Harsdörffers regelmäßigen Anfragen nach Mitgliederlisten 450529 K 10 u. insgesamt auch 450126, 450220, 450221, 450400 K 12 u. 15, 450500 K 2, 450505A K 3, 451001/460000, 460104 K 1, 460916, 461031A K 11 u. 461106.

11 Von der unzweifelhaft bezeugten Korrespondenz zwischen Harsdörffer u. Diederich v. dem Werder — vgl. außer dem Hinweis eingangs des vorliegenden Briefes etwa 440204, 450500, 450504A, 450505, 450505A, 450919 u. ö. — hat sich nichts erhalten. Da aus dem Sommer 1644 mit Ausnahme von 440816 auch keine Korrespondenzen zw. F. Ludwig u. Werder vorliegen, die Aufschluß über die Werderschen „Gescheffte" versprechen könnten, u. F. Ludwig in seiner Antwort 450124 auf den vorliegenden Brief nicht auf die Bitte Harsdörffers um Anweisung in dieser Sache eingeht, bleibt die Angelegenheit für uns im Dunkeln.

440826

Abraham von Franckenberg an Gottfried Sturm

Abraham v. Franckenberg teilt (dem anhalt-köthnischen Prinzenpräzeptor) Gottfried Sturm seine Beobachtungen und Auffassungen zur deutschen Sprache mit. Die Sprache weiter zu ergründen sei ein lohnendes Unterfangen, nicht nur was den Spezialwortschatz der mechanischen (Handwerke) und freien Künste betreffe, der in den Büchern kaum (in zusammengetragener Form) aufgefunden werde. Mehr noch lohne es, der ursprünglichen Natursprache, den inneren, natürlichen Eigenschaften der Wörter und Redensarten nachzuforschen. So könnten nach dem Vorbild der Kabbalisten die deutschen Buchstaben in fünf Klassen eingeteilt werden: die Pectorales, die Gutturales oder Palatinales, die Linguales, die Dentales und Sibilantes und schließlich die Labiales und Flantes. Damit könnte die Eigenschaft eines jeden Wortes von Grund auf analysiert und die Entstehung des „lebendigen" Wortes im Gedanken, Herzen und Mund sowie ihre Bedeutung und Verwendung wie auf einer Goldwaage geprüft werden. Ebenso, führt Abraham v. Franckenberg weiter aus, verspreche die sprachwissenschaftliche Fundierung von Rede und Schrift im Zusammenhang einer pansophischen Weltlehre Ertrag. Desgleichen könne die Sprachforschung die Wörter systematisch (wie anhand eines Katalogs topischer Argumente) nach Ursprung, Ordnung, Veränderung, Erneuerung, Kultus, Macht, Gewohnheit, Ähnlichkeit usw. durchgehen. Freilich, welcher Mensch sei zu einer so hohen Spracherfassung imstande? Wer komme an das lebendige Wort Gottes heran, welches doch alle Kreaturen auszudrücken sich nach Kräften bemühten? Dies täten 1. die Vögel und ihre je eigene Stimme, 2. die vierfüßigen Tiere mit ihren jeweiligen Lauten, 3. sogar das Gewürm, das sich auf seine Weise äußere, 4. das je besondere Geräusch menschlicher Tätigkeiten und Werkzeuge und schließlich 5. sogar die vier Elemente. Sie alle gäben Laute von sich je nach ihrer Art und Eigenschaft und die menschliche, ja besonders die deutsche Sprache bilde sie alle wunderbar treffend nach. Auch die gemeinen Gassen- und grobianischen Spottwörter gäben laut- und klangmalerisch das wieder, was sie bezeichneten. Die deutsche Sprache drücke alles gründlich und verständlich, lebendig, kräftig und schöpferisch aus und übertreffe darin alle anderen Sprachen, wie dies auch Justus Georg Schottelius (FG 397. Der Suchende) in seinen Lobreden (über die deutsche Sprache) und Georg Philipp Harsdörffer (FG 368. Der Spielende) in seinen *Frauenzimmer-Gesprächspielen* gezeigt hätten. Dies lasse hoffen, daß man immer näher an das „große Geheimnis des eingefleischten Wortes Jesu Christi" gelangen werde.

Q STB Berlin — PK: Dep. Breslau 17 (ehem. StB Breslau: Ms. Rehd. 402): Farrago | Epistolarum et Carminum | Diuersorum ad Diuersos, | à | Nicolao Henelio ab Hennenfeld | et | Matthia Machnero | congesta | et | Bibliothecæ Rhedigerianæ | destinata, 636–640 (Brief Nr. 297); unvollst. Abschrift des 17. Jhs. nach dem unbekannten Original.[1] Zit als *A*.

Spätere Abschrift: BU Wrocław: Ms. Akc. 1949/ 713 (ehem. StB Breslau: Hs. Klose 175), Bl. 170r–172r (Brief Nr. 297), vollständige Abschrift von *A* durch den Breslauer Schulrektor Samuel Benjamin Klose (1730–1798) in zeitgemäß modernisierter Schreibweise.[2] Zit. mit der Sigle *B*. Offenbar nicht von Telle (s. *D*) herangezogen.

D: Abraham von Franckenberg: Briefwechsel. Eingel. u. hg. v. Joachim Telle. Stuttgart-Bad Cannstatt 1995, 185–189 (nach *A* mit gelegentlichen Normalisierungen in Schreibung und Zeichensetzung). Zit. als *Telle*. — Modernisiert und ungenau veröffentl. in Will-Erich Peuckert: Die Rosenkreutzer. Zur Geschichte einer Reformation. Jena 1928, 353–357; ders.: Das Rosenkreuz. 2., neugefaßte Aufl. mit e. Einl. hg. v. Rolf Christian Zimmermann. Berlin 1973, 296–298; Wolfgang Kayser: Die Klangmalerei bei Harsdörffer. Ein Beitrag zur Geschichte der Literatur, Poetik und Sprachtheorie der Barockzeit. 2. unveränd. Aufl. Göttingen 1962, 147–149 (Auszüge und Zusammenfassungen).

BN: János Bruckner: Abraham von Franckenberg. A bibliographical catalogue with a shortlist of his library. Wiesbaden 1988, 69 Nr. B 25; Wilhelm Frels: Deutsche Dichterhandschriften von 1400 bis 1900. Gesamtkatalog der eigenhändigen Handschriften deutscher Dichter in den Bibliotheken und Archiven Deutschlands, Österreichs, der Schweiz und der ČSR. Leipzig 1934, 74.

A *Fehlt.*

Von der deutschen Sprache Natur und Eigenschafft. An Gotfried Sturm.[3]

Was noch ferner in <u>deutscher Sprache zuverbeßern</u> und außzupoliren seyn möchte, laße ich den jenigen, welche beßern trieb und licht hierzu empfangen.

Erinnere nur dieses, daß es an sehr vielen singularitäten noch ermangelt, denen nicht unbillich nachzudencken.

Dann daß ich der jenigen unbekandten wörter, welche sowohl in Mechanicis als liberalioribus Termini technologici oder Kunstwörter, handwerckszeug und gewonheit genennet⁴, und gar selten oder gar nicht in den büchern gefunden werden, geschweige, were es keine so schlechte und vergebliche arbeit, die alte ursprüngliche Natursprache widerumb hervohr, und die natürlich eingepflanzten oder eingeschaffene eigenschafften der Geister, Stimmen und außgebehrungen solcher wörter und redensarten zudurchsuchen.⁵ Als zum exempel könten nach art der Kabalisten die deutsche buchstaben in fünferley arten (als 1. Pectorales, JEHOVA. 2. Gutturales seu Palatinas, G. R. Z. X. J-C $\frac{a}{m}$-Oᵃ. 3. Lingvales, D.T.L.N.R. 4. Dentales, V.C.Z. Sibilantes S.X. 5. Labiales, B.P.M.F. Flantes F.V.phᵇ. Wehen, Wind, Weben.) unterschieden, und die eigenschafft eines ieglichen worts dadurch gleichsfalls anatomiret werden.⁶ Weil es gleichwol mercklich angelegen, die Geburtsart deß lebendigen worts in den gedancken, im herzen, im Geist und in dem munde oder auf der Zungen recht zuprüfen, und mit den weisen auf der Goldwage abzuwegen, was und wie, und wann und [637] wo zureden oder zugeschweigen.

Jtem ob Gott, Engel, Mensch, viehe, Teuffel in und aus oder durch den redenden hall schalle oder würcke.

Unde in Pansophicisᶜ ⁷ 1. VERBUM, Vox, Spiritus. 2. Lingva, Ignis, aqva. 3. Babel, Natio, clima. 4. Litera, Numerus, Figura: atq̃; adeò Καλλι-Poly-ortho-crypto-Tachy-Stegano-graphia. Item A urergo [sic]ᵈ, Ordo, Mutatio, Renovatio, Cultus, Potestas, Usus, Encyclopædia, Affinitas, Syzygia, Differentia, Opposita, jure merito exacte ponderanda, atq̃; applicanda esse doctoribusᵉ videntur.⁸ Aber wer kan unter den Sterblichen solch scharff und hochgraduirtes wagerecht außstehen, weil auch der große Belhazarᶠ gewogen und zu leichte gefunden worden?⁹ und der Mensch auf tausend nicht kan eins antworten? Ja wer wil deß ewigen wortes, welches Gott ist, anfang, ort oder ende erforschen? über welchem sich alle Creaturen bemühen, nach allen ihren kräften und vermögen daßelbige außzudrucken, als wir hören

1. an den <u>Vögeln</u>, da der Rabe grap grap;ᵍ der Sperling tschirp tschirp; die fincke pinck, pinck; die Wachtel buit wuckowiet; die Ganß ga, ga, ga, Ziganʰ; der Kiewiz, Kiewiz; der Kuckuck kukuk tönet; Die Mauerschwalb zwizert; die Ente schnadert; der Storch klappert; die Turteltaube girret; die haußschwalbe wütschert; die Jmmen brummen summen.

2. an den <u>vierfüßigen Thieren</u>: Das Pferd wihert, oder wie beim Hiob 39.38. spricht Huy; der Hund billet oder maffetⁱ; die Kaze schrayet Mie mau; die Kuhe mu.

3. an dem <u>Gewürm</u>, wann der drach kröchzet, die Schlange wispelt, die Nater zischet, die Kröte pipet, der frosch qvacket.

4. Ja auch <u>der widerhall in der lufft</u> von denen unterschiedenen werckzeugen der Menschen und deren arbeiten gibet das schalbare wort in unsrerʲ deutschen Muttersprache [638] zu vernehmen. Dann es klinget die Glocke bumbaum; der Mörser pimpamp; der Amboß Pinckepanck; die Drommel bumbumbum, bidi-

bum, (hütt dich Pauer, ich kom.)[;] der Münzscheid Kippedewipp; der Waßerfall Plumps; der Harnisch raßelt, der Wald praßelt, die Cymbaln klingen, das Thor karret[k], die thür knarret, der Stein klitschet, das holz klippert, der hecht schnappet, der blinde tappet.

Und 5. die <u>Elementa</u> selber lauten nach ihrer aigenschaft: Das feuer brüßelt, die lufft sauset, das wasser brauset, die Erde rißelt *etc.*

Wie solte dann nu das Redeliche thür[l], der Mensch[,], nicht lernen alles nach- und außsprechen? Jch wil mich weiter hierinnen nicht aufhalten; aber es fallen mir etliche <u>gemeine Gaßenwörter</u> mit ihrer verdoppelung ein, als wisch wasch; misch masch; Klips Klaps; Knips Knaps; Kneutel, Knobloch; ripps, rapps; schnips, schnaps; schrips, schraps; mix max; pliz plaz; praz präz[m]; schmiz schmaz; grämmeln, bämmeln; stümmeln, grümmeln; lißbeln, wißbeln *etc.*

Dazu dann auch die Spottwörter der Grobianer[n], als Maz laz; Schlüffel, püffel; Pfingstlimmel, Osterflegel, bun-Jgel, Grund-Jgel, Lauß-Jgel, Knörzel, Zudel, Schmudel, Zuzel, Schmuzel, SaugeZippel, Faulheinze, Pauerkunze, Zumpe, Klunte, Schlumpe, Schluchze, Schnappe, Müze, Muz, Schudelpuz, Kurzmuz, Küchenmuz, OfenLorz, Maußkopff, Dockmauser, Rüntschel, Tüntschel, Schlimgsschieß, Lumpslecks, Lurz sez den Leim warm, Entemaz, Lotschadam, Kuhbertel[o], Wursthanß, Jockel sihestu auch die Pfüze, [639] Lulllapp, Tilltapp, Monsieur Fettlapp, Lorzleckelöffel, Momo Schelmo[p], Lerbaum, Knustock[q], Rungestock, Pumpsack, Knollfinck, Lambsgritte,[r] Mistfincke; Ochsegebratens, wirst den Limmel[s] verschütten; Rinderne gebärde, Laschman trauft[t] dir auch der Kober, Rolcke, Kichelgrolms[u], Mufs hastu eine halb Hocke, SchäfferJockel, Mollepappaus, Hanß Tappinsmuß, Jockelrühr[d]enbrey, Scharrhanß, Schlimschlem[v], Rülpel, Tripstrill auf der Gickrille, Schlegel, Flegel, Lumpslambs, Timpstamps, Klitschklatsch, Titschtatsch, Pitschpatsch; Schmitsch schmatsch, leihe mir die geißel; Aschewedel, Starrest wie prizel, Starrest wie ein Südesack, du Seusack[w], Lodesack, Schlapsack[x], Triefsack, Quetschsack, Laasche; Jch gehe knip und knap, was mich druckt das schneid ich ab; Knolle molle, Lülle, Plaze, schmaze, Mantsche, prantschke, Flantsch, plantsch, Grindnatsche, Pfundsche, Pfnächze, Hacke gemacke, Maulaffe, Brodtraffe, Gänaffe, Dorfringel, Hudler, Sudler, Schuf dich, Puf dich; Du bist ein kaler schuft, der T*eufel* führe dich in die lufft, und werf dich herunter, daß pufft, bleibst dennoch ein Kaler Schufft; Säumagen, Säurüßel, Saunase[y], Lumprecht, Gumprecht, Stümpler, Hümpler, Schlingel, pengel, Rülz, Filz, Pülz, Schwa*m*mdrücker, Schmuzbart, Schlauder, Hinckepinck, Schlumpergirle, Läppisch laß nicht schnappen, Gix gax, Schlaloß, Durchloß[q], Hanglig, Thu nicht gutt, Verdürblig[z], Schadenfro, Streubel kenstu auch pömseln, Kaze, Mucketauben[aa], Meztappe, Plimppanck, Schlingschlang, Kühkamp, Johannes, Hänsel, Hanß, Hampe, Hantsche, Großmuntsche, Plizblo, Kizgro, Tillem, Tallem, Schlampamper, Schwülstel, Knebel, Esell, und viel andere dergleichen eigenschafftliche nahmen[10] gehören, daß sich billich zu verwundern, [640] wie sich unsere deutsche Zunge so meisterlich und musterlich wenden, verändern, und alles gleichsam mit Adam natürlich und weit über andere Sprachen gründ- und verständlich[,] klar und außtrücklich andeuten, also fast selber lebendig, thätig und kräftig schaffen und darstellen kan.

Davon auch der *VielSuchende* und *findende* in seinen Lobreden[11] und andern deutschen Schriften, wie ingleichen der *Spielende* in seinem FrauenZimmer GesprächSpiel[12] sehr lieb- und löblich handeln, daß zuhoffen, man auch immer weiter auf den grund und ewigen heiligen wortverstand, als in das große geheimnis deß eingefleischten worts *Jesu Christi* wird gelangen.

Dann Gott[,] das einige und ewige Gutt[,] ist ja geoffenbaret im Fleisch, und ist CHRISTUS, in welchem die ganze völle der Gottheit wohnet, und welcher auch alles in Allem mit seiner gnadenkraft in uns und in allen creaturen erfüllet. Dem sey lob von allen Zungen izt und ewig nachgesungen *etc.*

Abraham Von Franckenberg

Da*tum* 26. Augusti A*nno* 1644.

T a *Telle* οὐ *als unsichere Lesung.* — b *Telle* sch *[!].* — c *Über* sophicis *eingefügt* glottia — d *Verschreibung für* origo? *Schreibweise* urergo *auch in B und Telle.* — e *Telle* doctioribus — f *B* Belsazar — g *Die Handschrift A setzt bei dieser Aufzählung der Vogelstimmen Kommata, Doppelpunkte und gelegentlich Punkte. Des besseren Textverständnisses halber setzen wir nach der Wiedergabe des Vogellauts ein Semikolon. So auch bedarfsweise im Nachstehenden.* — h *B* Zigag — i *B* waffet — j *Telle* unser — k *Gebessert aus* knarret — l *B* Thier — m *Telle* praz, praz *mit der Vermutung einer Textverderbnis als* priz praz — n *Ganz am Ende der folgenden pantagruelischen Wörterliste folgt das Prädikat gehören* — o *Telle* Kuhbartel — p *Telle* Schelma — q *Unsichere Lesung. Auch in B und Telle.* — r *Folgt* <Mistf> — s *B* Lümmel — t *B* treuft — u *B* Kachelgrolms — v *B* Schlimschelm — w *Telle* Sausack — x *Unsichere Lesung. B* Schlepsack — y *Unsichere Lesung. B* Seunase — z *B* Verdürblich — aa *B* Stucketauben

K In der älteren Literatur wurde Franckenberg gelegentlich als Mitglied der FG mit dem Gesellschaftsnamen „Der Auffgerichtete" gehandelt, so in *Zedler* I, 1703 (vgl. *Telle*, 30), was sich allerdings nicht halten läßt. 1651 teilte er Ehrenfried Hegenich mit: „Man hat mir die Fruchtbringende Gesellschaft offeriret; weil ich aber alt, kranck, magis seria vor der Hand, habe ich H*errn* Dan*ielem* Cepkonem [Daniel Czepko v. Reigersfeld (1605–1660)], als einen überaus hochgradirten sinnreichen Kopff substituiret: der unter andern deutsche SchlußReime von solchen hoch Taulerianischen *etc.* materien gefertiget, welche ein grosses Licht in Theologia mystica et vita abstracta anzünden werden; ob sie in publica kommen: wie er Willens Sie dem Schmackhafften (Itzigem Oberhaupt der fruchtbr. Gesellschafft Fürst Wilh*elm* zu Weinmar), zu dediciren." Zit. n. *Telle*, 291, vgl. auch 292 f. Tatsächlich legt ein Brief Georg Philipp Harsdörffers (FG 368) an Heinrich v. Schwechhausen (FG 532. 1651) vom 30.10.1651 nahe, daß sich Franckenberg 1651 um die Mitgliedschaft in der FG bewarb: „Es hat sich inzwisch*en* H. Freyherr Geitzkofler, H. Abrah. von Franckenberg, ein Schleßischer sehr gelehrter Edelmann, H. Graf Bianchi del Pla[no] [FG 579. 1652], H. Freyherr von Hohenberg [Frh. Wolf Helmhard v. Hohberg, FG 580. 1652], H. von Greiffenberg [Johann Rudolf Frh. v. Greiffenberg] und noch etliche andre angemeldet, und als liebhaber unsrer Sprache eingeno*mm*en zu werden gebetten, desweg*en* der Spielende, auff ferners eingelangte Nachrichtung, an den höchstgeehrt*en* Schmackhaft*en* [d.i. Hz. Wilhelm IV. v. Sachsen-Weimar, FG 5, das damalige Oberhaupt der FG] zu schreiben nicht unterlass*en* wird, v*er*hoffend daß solches vorbringen zu S. F. G. unterthänigen Ehren reichend, mit gn. willfahrung beliebet werden möchte: weiß aber nicht ob zugleich die [Gesellschaft-]Namen und Früchte fürgeschlag*en* werd*en* müssen; mass*en* zu zeit*en* manch[er] einen GesellschaftsNamen, oder Gemähl wehlet, das zuvor v*er*handen. Bitte deßweg*en* umb dienliche Nachrichtung." Erzschrein Weimar, 1. Bd.: ThHSTA Weimar: Kunst und Wissenschaft – Hofwesen A 11817[1], Bl. 53r–54v, hier 54r [*Buchstabenverlust im Falz, Konjekturen in eckigen Klammern*]; vgl. *Telle*, 62 u. 313. In einem Brief Gf. Georg Adams v. Kuefstein (FG 540. 1651) an Harsdörffer, d. d. Wien 2.11.1651, den dieser einem eigenen Brief an Schwechhausen oder Hz. Wilhelm beilegte, werden ebenfalls Gf. Bianchi sowie Frh. Hohberg zur Aufnahme in die FG empfohlen. A. a. O., Bl. 55rv. Ein daruntergesetzter Zusatz Harsdörffers unterstützt das Gesuch, hält poetische Verdienste u. Talente der beiden fest u. entwirft Gesellschaftsnamen. Von Franckenberg ist hier u. in Harsdörffers Folgebriefen an Schwechhausen, vom (Dezember?) 1651 u. 23.2.1652 sowie an Hz. Wilhelm IV. v. Sachsen-Weimar (der Schmackhafte) vom 24.2.1652 nicht mehr die Rede; auch Czepko wird nicht genannt. A. a. O., 64r–65v, 71r–72v u. 73r–74v. Alle genannten Briefe veröff. in Carl August Hugo Burckhardt: Aus dem Briefwechsel Georg Philipp Harsdörffers zur Geschichte der Fruchtbringenden Gesellschaft 1647–1658. In: Altes und Neues aus dem Pegnesischen Blumenorden III (1897), 23–140, 77–92. Aus der Korrespondenz Harsdörffer—Franckenberg hat sich nur ein Brief Harsdörffers vom 30.5.1652 im Marburger Herder-Institut (Provenienz: ehem. StB Breslau) erhalten, der aber Franckenberg vielleicht nicht mehr erreicht hat: Er starb am 25.6.1652. Von der FG oder von Sprachfragen wird in diesem Brief nicht gehandelt. Vgl. Konrad Gajek: Georg Philipp Harsdörffers Brief vom 30. Mai 1652 an Abraham von Franckenberg. In: Studien zur Literatur des 17. Jahrhunderts. Gedenkschrift f. Gerhard Spellerberg. Amsterdam 1997 (Chloe, 27), 403–412. Am 28.9.1652 unterrichtete Harsdörffer Johann Valentin Andreae (FG 464. 1646) vom Tode Franckenbergs u. übersandte „pie defuncti nostri Frankenbergii Epitaphium". Weiter heißt es: „Martyrio proximum est propter flagrantissimum studium pietatis publico laborare odio, id quod Dn. Frankenbergio eiusq; Fratri germano accidit. Quam cupide aliam Christianae Ecclesiae faciens optaverit et quantum scriptis promoverit eius passim opuscula testantur." HAB: Cod. Guelf. 10.5 Aug. 2°, Bl. 97rv, Zitate 97r. Der Brief hat keine Adresse, das Lagenumfeld aber sind Harsdörffer-Briefe an Andreae. Das Epitaphium liegt dem Brief nicht mehr bei. Der Einblattdruck hat sich in der Hs. Dep. Breslau 14 (ehem. Ms. Rhed. 402 der StB Brelau) in der STB — PK Berlin, Bl. 712 erhalten — gefolgt von einem hsl. Trauergedicht („EPITAPHION") von Johann Peter Titz (Bl. 713) — u. wurde abgedruckt in Peuckert (1973, s. Q), 320. Vgl. zu diesem Brief Richard van Dülmen: Sozietätsbildungen in Nürnberg im 17. Jahrhundert. In: Gesellschaft und Herrschaft. Forschungen zu sozial- und landesgeschichtlichen Problemen vornehmlich in Bayern. Festg. Karl Bosl zum 60. Geb. München 1969, 153–190, hier 188f. Weder Franckenberg noch Czepko wurden Mitglied der FG. Seine Ablehnung der „collegii Carpophororum fructus Venusinos" mit der Empfehlung, seinen Fleiß lieber an „labores in melioribus" zu verwenden, hatte Franckenberg im August 1649 artikuliert (zit. n. *Telle*, 360). *Telle* sah Franckenbergs Rolle als späthumanistisch gelehrter, in mystisch-spiritualistischen u. pan- u. theosophischen Traditionen verwurzelter, zum heterodoxen Flügel des dt. Protestantismus zählender „Laientheologe, Gelehrter, Philologe und Naturkundiger" am „Schnittpunkt von Wissen und Glauben, Gelehrsamkeit und Frömmigkeit, Wissenschaft und Religion" und beseelt von einer Generalreformation des Lebens, die ihn mit dem Rosenkreuz, einem Joachim Morsius, Heinrich Hein (s. 430509 K 1 u. 430826) u. a. verband (*Telle*, 31 u. 37, vgl. 20ff., 34ff. u. 49).

1 Eintrag auf dem Vorsatzblatt des Bandes: Hunc Librum, | Vratislaviensium | Bibliothecæ Publicæ | REHDIGERIANÆ, | à | Beato | MATTHIA MACHNERO, | Reip. Vrat. ab Expeditionibus | Latinis, | In Ecclesiastico et Orphanorum Indiciis | NOTARIO | destinatum consecravit | IOHANNES GEBHARDUS, | Gymn. Vrat. Elisabetani | PRORECTOR et PROFESSOR. | M. DC. LXXXI. | XXI. Martii. Es handelt sich bei diesem Konvolut von 1055 S. (407 Nummern) überwiegend um Abschriften von Gelehrtenbriefen des 17. Jhs., die von dem Breslauer Syndicus Nicolaus Henel v. Hennenfeld (1582–1656) u. dem Breslauer Ratssekretär Matthias Machner (1598–1662) angefertigt wurden. Eine genauere Quellenbeschreibung des Konvoluts in *Opitz: BW* I, 64f.

2 Die Hs. Klose 175 ist eine z. T. stark gekürzte Abschrift der Breslauer Sammlung Hs. Rehd. 402 (s. Q u. Anm. 1) u. war Teil der jahrelangen Arbeit des Breslauer Schulrektors Samuel Benjamin Klose (1730–1798) an der Abschrift der wichtigsten Urkunden u. Handschriften der Bibliotheca Rehdigerana, die den Grundstock der einstigen Breslauer Stadtbibliothek gebildet hatte. Kloses Abschriften umfaßten insgesamt 248 Bände. Eine genauere Quellenbeschreibung des Konvoluts in *Opitz: BW* I, 79f.

3 Der Empfänger des vorliegenden Briefs von dem Jakob-Böhme-Biographen Abraham v. Franckenberg (1593–1652), Gottfried Sturm, war wohl schon damals Präzeptor Pz. Wilhelm Ludwigs v. Anhalt-Köthen (FG 358), des Sohnes F. Ludwigs. S. die Akte LHA Sa.-Anh./ Dessau: Abt. Köthen A 9a Nr. 22: Zur Erziehung Pz. Wilhelm Ludwigs nebst Korrespondenzen zwischen F. Ludwig, seinem Sohn u. Gottfried Sturm 1646/49. Dieser Zusammenhang war bisher unbekannt; *Telle* verzichtete auf Angaben zu Sturm u. auch auf eine Sachkommentierung des vorliegenden Briefes. Gottfried Sturm, Sohn des ehemaligen Anhalt-Zerbster Kanzlers Johann Sturm (1587–1636), war lt. Empfehlungsschreibens F. Ludwigs an den Bürgermeister Ernst [Friedrich v.] Brinck in Harderwijk vom 20.5.1648 (vgl. 260619 K 21) „in die vier Jar" Präzeptor Pz. Wilhelm Ludwigs u. wünschte, nachdem sich offenbar die Anstellung als Präzeptor/ Hofmeister des Sohns der Anna Catharina, geb. v. Eckart, Wwe. von Gerhard Romilian v. Kalcheim gen. Leuchtmar (FG 276) zerschlagen hatte, eine Empfehlung für eine Tätigkeit, die ihm eine Peregrination in Holland u. sodann in Frankreich ermöglichte. A.a.O., Bl. 8r. In derselben Dessauer Akte finden sich ein Tätigkeitsbericht Sturms aus seiner Zeit als Prinzenlehrer (23.2.1648; Bl. 5r), ein F. Ludwig gewidmetes dt. Neujahrsgedicht v. 1.1.1647 (Bl. 21r) u. ein Schreiben Sturms an F. Ludwig vom 7.5.1648, in dem sich Sturm über Malvezzis Werke u. dessen Übersetzer Leon Cambier ausließ, den er in Danzig angetroffen habe (a. a. O., Bl. 19r–20v, d. i. *DA Köthen I. 8:* 480428A). Vgl. 440426 K 7. Dort, in Danzig, lebte Franckenberg unter ärmlichen Bedingungen von 1642 bis 1649 in kriegsbedingtem Exil. Gottfried Sturm muß ihn dort kennengelernt haben, denn am 18.9.1643 schenkte er Franckenberg ein Werk des religiös toleranten franzöz. Humanisten u. (lat. u. frz.) Bibelübersetzers Sebastian Castellio (Sébastien Châteillon, 1515–1563), vielleicht das Calvin-kritische *De Haereticis, an sint persequendi & omnino quomodo sit cum eis agendum* (Basel 1554 u.ö.), seine lat. Übersetzung der *Theologia Deutsch: Theologia Germanica* (Basel 1557) oder seinen *Anti Inquisitor* (o. O. 1592). Vgl. *Telle,* 61. Castellio gehörte zu jenen Gewährsmännern, auf die sich Franckenberg in seiner *Via Veterum Sapientum. Das ist: WEG der Alten Weisen* (Amsterdam 1675; entstanden wohl in den 30er Jahren) berief als Zeugen wider die „verführische *Aristotelische Philosophy*, unnütze Schwätz- und subtile Spitzkunst" (ebd., 86f.; zit. n. Siegfried Wollgast: Philosophie in Deutschland zwischen Reformation und Aufklärung 1550–1650. Berlin 1988, 794f.). Franckenberg nennt u. zitiert Castellios „De Calumnia" aus dessen *Dialogi quatuor* (postum Basel 1578) auch in seiner *Trias mystica* (Amsterdam 1650), 96ff. S. Hans R. Guggisberg: Sebastian Castellio 1515–1563. Humanist und Verteidiger der religiösen Toleranz im konfessionellen Zeitalter. Göttingen 1997, 291.

Später sollte Philipp v. Zesen (FG 521. 1648) die Toleranzlinie eines Castellio in seiner Anthologie *Handlungen und Urteile wider den Gewissenszwang in Glaubenssachen* (Amsterdam 1665) aufgreifen (vgl. *Ingen*, 294ff.). Zu Castello vgl. auch Anthony Grafton: Defenders of the Text. The Traditions of Scholarship in an Age of Science, 1450–1800. Cambridge/ Mass.u. London 1991, 173f. sowie v.a. Stefania Salvadori: Sebastiano Castellione e la ragione della tolleranza. L'*ars dubitandi* fra conoscenza umana e *veritas* divina. Milano, Udine 2009. Aus Sturms Zeit als Prinzenpräzeptor stammt auch sein Eintrag im Stammbuch des Johannes Merckel, Bl.59r, d. d. Köthen 28.9.1646 (HAAB Weimar). Später wurde Sturm kurbrandenburg. Erster Geheimer Estats-Secretarius u. Hofrat. Er starb im 77. Jahre seines Lebens. *Beckmann* VII, 193. Vgl. allg. Milada Blekastad: Comenius. Versuch eines Umrisses von Leben, Werk und Schicksal des Jan Amos Komenský. Oslo u. Prag 1969, 422 (kurzer Briefauszug); Karl Viëtor: Probleme der deutschen Barockliteratur. Leipzig 1928, 70 (kurz zum vorliegenden Brief). Nicht eingesehen werden konnte: Hubert Schrade: Beiträge zu den deutschen Mystikern des 17. Jahrhunderts. II. Abraham von Franckenberg. Diss. Phil. Heidelberg 1923, 144–146.

4 Ein Wörterbuch des Fachwortschatzes im Deutschen wurde in Kreisen der FG gewünscht. Vgl. etwa *Gueintz: Sprachlehre (1641)*, 10f., oder *Schottelius: Der Teutschen Sprache Einleitung (1643)*, 99, zum Fachwortschatz des Deutschen. Vgl. auch ebd., 143; *Schottelius: Ausführliche Arbeit (1663)*, 1247–1261, u. *Harsdörffer: Specimen (1646)*, 225ff. Auch ein Wörterbuch der Nomina propria wurde empfohlen, da diese zwar unter die Gemeinsprache, nicht aber unter die deutschen Stammwörter u. in deren Wörterbuch fielen (*Schottelius: Ausführliche Arbeit [1663]*, 1273). In seiner „Schutzschrift/ für Die Teutsche Spracharbeit/ und Derselben Beflissene" (in: *Harsdörffer: Frauenzimmer-Gesprächspiele* I ²1644/ Ndr. 1968, S.19/ Ndr. 362) rechnete Georg Philipp Harsdörffer (FG 368. Der Spielende) unter die Aufgaben der dt. Spracharbeit: „V. Daß man alle Kunstwörter von Bergwerkē/ Jag[d]rechten/ Schiffarten/ Handwerkeren/ u. d. g. ordentlich zusammentrage". Denselben Anspruch an ein wirklich umfassendes Wörterbuch brachte Harsdörffer auch 1648 in seinem „Unvergreifflichen wolgemeinten Bedencken, Wie ein Teutsches Dictionarium oder wortbuch Zuverabfassen" vor. Demnach müßten auch „die kunstwort **termini technici** von allen handwercken, handlungen und Arbeiten, als jagen, schiffen, mahlen, schmieden etc. mit eingebracht werden" (*KE*, 389f., vgl. 387ff.). Eine Zusammenstellung ökonomischer Fachbegriffe findet sich in Harsdörffers *Der Teutsche SECRETARIUS: Das ist: Allen Cantzley- Studir- und Schreibstuben nützliches und fast nohtwendiges Formular- und Titularbuch* (1. Ausg. Nürnberg 1655. HAB: 104.3 Rhet.), 551–553. Philipp v. Zesen (FG 512) hat in seiner *Hochdeutschen Helikonischen Hechel* (1668) allerhand Fachwortschätze behandelt (Militär, Jagd, Falknerei, Bergbau) u. viele Beispiele aus dem Fachwortschatz des Bergbaus erläutert. S. *Zesen SW* XI, 275–402, hier S.351–359. Johann Michael Moscherosch (FG 436. 1645) hatte mit seiner *Technologie Allemande & Françoise Das ist/ Kunst-übliche Wort-Lehre Teutsch und Frantzösisch* (Straßburg 1656) einen umfassenderen fachwortlexikalischen Versuch gemacht (vgl. dazu 440616 K I 0), u. auch Schottelius sammelte deutschen Fachwortschatz, s. 450000 u. 460000 K 3. Vgl. ferner 440525 K II 9 u. 13–15, 450124 u. I, 451220 K 2, 460000 K 3 u. 460902. — Wolf Peter Klein: Gab es eine Fachsprachenforschung im 17. Jahrhundert? Versuch einer Antwort mit besonderer Berücksichtigung von Johann Heinrich Alsted. In: Historiographia Linguistica 31 (2004), 297–327; Peter O. Müller: Deutsche Lexikographie des 16. Jahrhunderts. Konzeptionen und Funktionen frühneuzeitlicher Vokabulare u. Wörterbücher. Tübingen 2001, 467ff.

5 Jakob Böhmes (1575–1624) Konzept der Natursprache, das Franckenberg aufgriff, trug seine Abkehr vom „toten" oder äußeren Buchstaben, der nur zu Auslegungskämpfen,

Zank, Streit u. Krieg, zum Verlust des wahren, geistigen Gotteswortes geführt habe, aus. Alles sinnlich Wahrnehmbare ist dieser Lehre ein Zeichen der inneren, gottgeschaffenen Wahrheit. In den Dingen besteht das göttliche Schöpfungswort, der göttliche Hauch, der sie in die Existenz rief, fort. Die menschliche Sprache hat am göttlichen Schöpfungswort teil, doch sie schafft die Dinge nicht, sondern benennt sie nur. Dabei sind die Worte nicht beliebige, konventionell verwendete Laut- oder Buchstabenfolgen; sie lassen schon in ihrem „Hall" u. „Schall", in ihren hörbaren Qualitäten, das Wesen oder die göttlich eingeschriebene „Signatur" des jeweiligen Dinges an- u. durchklingen. „Durch die Worte des Göttlichen, die ausgesprochen werden, werden die Formen in Fülle in den Raum ausgegossen, der durch den Schall entstand." Gottes Wort erfüllt als „Schall" die Welt (Schmidt-Biggemann, s. u., II, 223). Sprache ist für Böhme markanterweise v. a. Laut; sie ist performativ. Und nicht die Bibel, sondern die lebendige Natur ist ihm „Repräsentant der göttlichen primordialen Schöpfungssprache", die der Mensch mit dem Sündenfall verloren habe, die aber als Sprache der Natur in ihrer sinnlichen Erfahrung u. göttlichen Weisheit begegne (ebd., 225 u. 229). Die metaphysischen Botschaften in den Dingen werden im menschlichen Sprechen nachvollzogen, u. die eigene Muttersprache „recht" zu verstehen, heißt, die Natursprache in ihr zu vernehmen u. einen Zugang zur in Babel verlorenen adamitischen Ursprache zu finden. Auch für Franckenberg ist die Schöpfung „Entäußerungsprozess Gottes sowie [...] Offenbarung und Fleischwerdung des Wortes" (ebd., 245). Damit kommt den Worten ein pneumatischer Kern von Geheimnis u. Offenbarung zu, der den Zeichencharakter von Sprache transzendiert u. eine unmittelbare, utopische Identität von Zeichen u. Bezeichnetem gewährleisten will. Hat die Natur jedem Ding seine „Sprache" nach dessen Eigenschaften gegeben, so redet u. offenbart sich jedes Ding natürlich aus denselben, adäquat aufgefangen in der Sprachgebung des prälapsarischen Adam, welche zwar verdorben u. verschüttet, jedoch residual immer noch enthalten ist in den postbabylonischen Einzelsprachen. In der Natursprache redet „iedes Ding aus seiner Eigenschaft" (Jakob Böhme: De signatura rerum, oder Von der Geburt und Bezeichnung aller Wesen [1622], hier zit. nach Gardt: Das Konzept der Eigentlichkeit [s. u.], S. 146). Solcherlei Natursprache liegt als metasprachliche Universalie den Einzelsprachen noch verborgen zugrunde. Sie verbürgt eine Spracheinheit am Grunde der seit der babylonischen Sprachverwirrung irreversiblen Sprachenvielfalt; ihr Verstehen als inverser Schöpfungsprozeß leitet zur Erkenntnis Gottes. Diese Natursprache aber kennt keine Zweideutigkeiten u. Unklarheiten der Denomination. Ihre „semantische Substanz" ist *„selbstverständlich"*. Wolf Peter Klein: Am Anfang war das Wort. Theorie- und wissenschaftsgeschichtliche Elemente frühneuzeitlichen Sprachbewußtseins. Berlin 1992, 215, vgl. 203 ff. Vgl. auch 450200, 450410 K 3, 450901 K 9 u. 460915 K 20; ferner *Gardt: Sprachreflexion*, 89 ff.; *Padley* I, 87 ff.; Andreas Gardt: Das Konzept der *Eigentlichkeit* im Zentrum barocker Sprachtheorie. In: Sprachgeschichte des Neuhochdeutschen. Gegenstände, Methoden, Theorien. Hg. A. G., Klaus J. Mattheier, Oskar Reichmann. Tübingen 1995, 145–167; Paul Hankamer: Die Sprache. Ihr Begriff und ihre Deutung im 16. u. 17. Jahrhundert. Bonn 1927, 118 ff.; Wolfgang Kayser: Böhmes Natursprachenlehre und ihre Grundlagen. In: Euphorion XXXI (1930), 521–562; Richard Nate: Natursprachenmodelle des 17. Jahrhunderts. Münster 1993, 74 ff.; ders.: Natursprachtheorien des 16. und 17. Jahrhunderts. In: Sprachtheorien der Neuzeit I. Der epistemologische Kontext neuzeitlicher Sprach- und Grammatiktheorien. Hg. Peter Schmitter. Tübingen 1999 (Geschichte der Sprachtheorie, 4), 93–115; Walter Pape: Heiliges Wort und weltlicher Rechenpfennig. Zur Entwicklung der Sprachauffassung im 17. Jdt. (Jacob Böhme, Athanasius Kircher, Leibniz). In: Religion und Religiosität im Zeitalter des Barock. In Verbindung mit Barbara Becker-Cantarino ... hg. v. Dieter Breuer. 2 Bde. Wiesbaden 1995, II, 817–843, hier 821 f.; Wilhelm Schmidt-

Biggemann: Geschichte der christlichen Kabbala. 3 Bde., Stuttgart-Bad Cannstatt 2012/13, Bd. 2: 1600–1660 (2013), 223 ff. (Jakob Böhme) u. 235–257 (Franckenberg-Kapitel, geht nicht auf den vorliegenden Brief ein); ders: Abraham von Franckenberg als christlicher Kabbalist. In: Realität als Herausforderung. Literatur in ihren konkreten historischen Kontexten. FS Wilhelm Kühlmann zum 65. Geb. Hg. Ralf Bogner u.a. Berlin 2011, 233–248 (dito).

6 Der „magische Materialismus" der spezifisch jüdischen Sprach- u. Schriftreflexion zeigt sich auch in ihrer „Lehre von der magischen Wirkungskraft der Buchstaben", die nach Assmann (s.u.), 24, der christlich-griech. Pneumatologie eigentlich fremd war u. eine ganz eigene, jedenfalls unbildliche „magische Zeichenbindung" entwickelte. Das Zentrum der jüdischen Kabbala bildeten Sprachspekulation (Harold Bloom: Kabbala. Poesie und Kritik. Aus d. Amerikan. v. Angelika Schweikhart. Basel, Frankfurt a. M. 1997, 20f., 43 u. 48) u. Sprachmetaphysik (Kilcher, s.u., 4), denn „die geheime Welt der Gottheit ist eine Welt der Sprache, eine Welt göttlicher Namen" (Scholem [1960, s.u.], 54). Der Name bildet den nächsten Zugang zum Wesen der Dinge. Die Laute u. Buchstaben sind nicht leerer Schall oder tote Lettern, sondern schaffen als energetische, sinnerfüllte „präkonzipierte symbolische Welt-Zeichen" (Schmidt-Biggemann: Geschichte [s. Anm. 5] I, 13) Wirklichkeit, machen deren Geheimnis kommunizierbar u. bilden „eine Brücke zwischen dem Schöpfer und seiner Welt": „Während Gott im Christentum Fleisch und Geist wird, wird er im Judentum Sprache und Schrift" (Assmann, 27 u. 28). Dabei entwickelte die Kabbala bestimmte Techniken auf der Ebene der Wortgestalt, um die verborgene Bedeutung zu ermitteln u. immer neu artistisch aufzuschließen. Dazu gehörte die „Gematria", wonach die 22 Buchstaben (Konsonanten) des hebr. Alphabets auch Zahlen bedeuten. Harsdörffer (s. Anm. 12) kannte das Geheimnis der „Zahlbuchstaben", vgl. sein 147. Gesprächspiel (*Frauenzimmer-Gesprächspiele* III [1643/ Ndr. 1968], 332/ Ndr. 352 – 335/ 355) u. die mystischen Buchstaben-Zahlen-Korrelationen bzw. die Zahlensymbolik in seiner Fortsetzung von Daniel Schwenters *Deliciae Physico-Mathematicae* (Nürnberg 1636; in 2 weiteren Teilen fortgef. v. Harsdörffer, Nürnberg 1651 u. 1653, alle 3 Teile Ndr. Frankfurt a. M. 1990), III, 39ff., 61, 85ff. u.ö. — dazu *Gardt: Sprachreflexion*, 111ff. Kabbalistische Wortsemantik begegnet auch in Harsdörffers *Ars Apophthegmatica* (2 Bde., Nürnberg 1655 u. 1656, Ndr. Frankfurt a. M. 1990), I, 7–10 — dazu Zeller: Adamitische Sprache, s. u., 151f. Die Renaissance nahm die jüdische Weisheit auf u. formte in Vertretern wie Pico della Mirandola, Agrippa von Nettesheim, Johannes Reuchlin (*De Verbo Mirifico* [1494], *De Arte Cabbalistica* [1517]), Guillaume Postel, Johannes Buxtorf d. Ä., Robert Fludd, dem jüdischen Konvertiten Paolo Riccio (Paul Ritz/ Paulus Ric[c]ius, auch Paulus Israelita genannt), Jakob Böhme, später Johann Angelus Werdenhagen, den Sulzbacher Kabbalisten Franciscus Mercurius van Helmont sowie Christian Knorr v. Rosenroth (*Kabbala denudata*, 1677–1684) eine eigentümliche christliche Hebraistik bzw. christliche Kabbala. Auch Leone Ebreos *Dialoghi d'amore* (vgl. 371027 u. dort Beil. IV) wurden zur christlichen Kabbala gezählt. Wenn die Kabbala in der Grammatik der 22 hebr. Buchstaben (sowie der Urzahlen 1–10) die Bausteine der Welt u. „das metaphysische Muster aller Dinge" (Kilcher, s.u., 33), eine Art Matrix der Schöpfung also, erkannte, so konnten Böhme u. Franckenberg aus der Artikulationsweise der deutschen Buchstaben u. Wörter Heilsbotschaften u. Gotteserkenntnis ziehen. Schon im Laut der Buchstaben u. Silben offenbarte sich ihnen Bedeutung in der mimetisch-symbolischen Manifestation der göttlichen Sprache der Natur. Denn es ist „die Grundtrope" der Kabbala, „daß Gott, um die Welt zu bilden, gesprochen habe" (Bloom, s.o., 68). Auf solcher Grundlage kann sich Franckenberg, wie vor ihm Böhme, im vorliegenden Brief von der lautlichen Analyse („Anatomie") der Buchstaben eine Aufschließung des semantischen Grundcodes der Welt

versprechen. Dazu *Gardt: Sprachreflexion*, 91 ff.; vgl. auch Kayser: Böhmes Natursprachenlehre (s. Anm. 5), 527. Die folgenden Zitate belegen die Nähe der Rosenkreuzer-Schriften zur Wort- u. Buchstabenmystik der Kabbala: Derjenige, „welchem es zugelassen, daß er die grosse Buchstaben und Characteres [Schriftzeichen], so Gott der Herr dem Gebäw Himmels und der Erden eingeschrieben und durch die Verenderung der Regimente für und für ernewert hat, anschawen lassen und zu seinem Unterricht gebrauchen kan, derselbe ist schon allbereit", der Fraternität des Rosenkreuzes anzugehören. Die „heimliche verborgene Schrifften" helfen, „das grosse Buch der Natur" zu lesen, das zwar allen Menschen offenstehe, jedoch nur von wenigen verstanden werde. „Solche Characteres und Buchstaben, wie Gott hin und wider der heiligen Bibel einverleibet, also hat er sie auch dem wunderbahren Geschöpff Himmels und der Erden, ja aller Thiere gantz deutlich eingedruckt [...], von welchen Buchstaben wir denn unsere Magische Schrifften entlehnet und uns eine newe Sprache erfunden und zuwege gebracht haben, in welcher zugleich die Natur aller dinge außgedrucket und erkläret wird". Johann Valentin Andreae (FG 464. 1646): Confessio Fraternitatis. Oder Bekanntnuß der löblichen Bruderschafft deß hochgeehrten Rosen Creutzes an die Gelehrten Europae geschrieben (1615). In: Joh. Valentin Andreae: Fama Fraternitatis (1614), Confessio Fraternitatis (1615), Chymische Hochzeit Christiani Rosencreutz Anno 1459 (1616). Eingel. u. hg. v. Richard van Dülmen. Stuttgart 1973, 31–42, hier 37, 38f. u. 39. Vgl. dazu Johann Valentin Andreae: Gesammelte Schriften, Bd. 3: Rosenkreuzerschriften. Bearb., übers., komm. u. eingel. v. Roland Edighoffer. Stuttgart-Bad Cannstatt 2010, 214 ff. u. 245 f. Auch Schottelius (s. Anm. 11) zeigt Nähe zu natursprachlicher Buchstabendeutung: „Denn/ ein jedes ding/ wie seine Eigenschafft und Wirckung ist/ also muß es vermittelst unserer Letteren/ und krafft derer/ also zusammengefügten Teutschen Wörter/ auß eines wolredenden Munde daher fliessen/ und nicht anders/ als ob es gegenwertig da were/ durch deß Zuhörers Sinn und Hertze dringen." *Schottelius: Sprachkunst (1641)*, 4. Lobrede, 85. — Franckenbergs gründliche Vertrautheit mit kabbalistischen Sprachreflexionen u. -techniken steht schon nach Ausweis seiner *Notae mysticae et mnemonicae ad Bechinas Olam sive Examen Mundi* (1650 entstanden, postum 1673 ohne Ortsangabe erschienen) außer Frage (vgl. Rusterholz, s. u.). Sein „kabbalistisches" Klassifizierungsschema gehorcht freilich nicht der heute gängigen Klassifizierung der Laute/ Buchstaben nach ihrer Artikulationsweise im Mund, sondern trägt spiritualistische Sprachauffassungen hinein. Christoph Helwig etwa hatte in seiner *HEBRÆÆ LINGUÆ COMPENDIOSA Institutio* (Wittenberg 1608. HAB: P 257 Helmst. 4°), Bl. A3r, die 22 hebräischen Buchstaben in Labiales, Gutturales, Palatinales, Linguales u. Dentales eingeteilt, was der Phonetik der heutigen Sprachwissenschaft in etwa entspricht. Auch Harsdörffer, der in Disquisitio VII seines *Specimen* (1646) die bes. enge Verwandtschaft des Deutschen mit dem Hebräischen nachweisen wollte, unterschied im Hebr. „Gutturales, die Gurgelbuchstaben", „Labiales, die Leffzen oder Lippenbuchstaben", „Palatinae, die Gaumenbuchstaben", „Linguales, Zungenbuchstaben" u. „Dentales, Zähnbuchstaben". A. a. O., 134 f. Auch neuere hebr. Grammatiken folgten dieser Einteilung (Wilhelm Gesenius: Hebräische Grammatik. Völlig umgearb. v. Emil Kautzsch. 26., vielfach verb. u. verm. Auflage. Leipzig 1896, 22 ff. u. 30) oder ergänzten sie um Sibilantes/ Zischlaute, Liquidae u. a. (Oskar Grether: Hebräische Grammatik f. den akademischen Unterricht. München 1951, 27 f.). Die Frage nach der möglichen Quelle für Franckenbergs Klassifizierung muß hier somit offenbleiben. Der im Brief folgende Vergleich mit der Goldwaage erscheint bereits in einem Grundtext der hebr. Kabbala, dem spätantiken *Sefer Jezirah* (zw. 2. u. 6. Jh. n. Chr.), als Wiegen der Buchstaben durch den Schöpfergott. Der Text war bereits Johannes Reuchlin bekannt, denn das „Buch der Schöpfung"/ *Sefer Jezirah* taucht im Katalog der kabbalist. Schriften in seiner *De arte cabalistica* (1517) auf. S.

Andreas B. Kilcher: Die Sprachtheorie der Kabbala als ästhetisches Paradigma. Die Konstruktion einer ästhetischen Kabbala seit der Frühen Neuzeit. Stuttgart, Weimar 1998, 33, 54 u. 83. Vgl. Aleida Assmann: Schriftspekulationen und Sprachutopien in Antike und früher Neuzeit. In: Kabbala und Romantik. Hrsg. v. Eveline Goodman-Thau u. a. Tübingen 1994, 23–41; Susanne Edel: Ideenmetaphysik und Buchstabenmystik: Leibniz, Böhme und die prophetische Kabbala. In: The Language of Adam. Die Sprache Adams. Ed. Allison P. Coudert. Wiesbaden 1999, 171–191, hier v. a. 188 f.; *Gardt: Sprachreflexion*, 62 ff.; Nate, op. cit. (s. Anm. 5), 85 ff.; Sibylle Rusterholz: Elemente christlicher Kabbala bei Abraham von Franckenberg. In: Christliche Kabbala. Hg. Wilhelm Schmidt-Biggemann. Ostfildern 2003, 183–197 (ohne Bezug zum vorliegenden Brief); Gershom Scholem: Art. „Kabbalah" in: Encyclopaedia Judaica X (Jerusalem 1971), 489–654 u. in Encyclopaedia Judaica, 2nd. Ed. XI (Detroit usw. 2007), 586–677; ders.: Zur Kabbala und ihrer Symbolik. Zürich 1960, 54, 87 ff., 219 ff. u. ö.; ders.: Ursprung und Anfänge der Kabbala. 2. Aufl. Berlin, New York 2001, 22, 24 ff., 245 ff., 278 f. u. 292 ff.; Wollgast, op. cit. (s. Anm. 3), 799 ff.; Rosmarie Zeller: Adamitische Sprache, Natursprache und Kabbala. Überlegungen zu Sprachtheorie und Poesie im 17. Jh. In: Morgen-Glantz 6 (1996), 133–154; dies.: Natursprache, Kabbala und die Friedensbemühungen in der Frühen Neuzeit. In: Der Frieden — Rekonstruktion einer europ. Vision. Bd. 1, München 2001, 907–922. Zum Philosemitismus u. der Rezeption jüd. Mystik bei Franckenberg vgl. auch *Telle*, 48.

7 Zur „natürlichen Pansophie" u. Physikotheologie Franckenbergs s. *Telle*, 50. Angesichts der Verbreitung pansophischer Konzepte in der frühen Neuzeit, die sich von der Theosophie durch die Fokussierung auf den *liber naturae* unterschied u. durch alle möglichen Spielarten reformerisch-unorthodoxen Denkens wanderte, ließ sich für uns hier keine konkrete Quelle ausmachen.

8 Die Aufzählung unter Punkt 4 betont das inhärente Bedeutungspotential der Buchstaben u. der Schrift („Καλλι-Poly-ortho-crypto-Tachy-Stegano-graphia"), die sich mit einer an die förmlichen Kategorien- oder Argumentenlisten der Topik (Topoi/ Loci communes) erinnernden Begriffsreihe — „Ordo, Mutatio, Renovatio, Cultus, Potestas, Usus, Encyclopædia, **Affinitas, Syzygia, Differentia, Opposita**", also Ordnung, Veränderung, Verwandtschaft, Differenz usw. — klassifizieren u. auslegen lassen. Darin mag diese Brief-Passage wiederum an die Kabbala anschließen, sofern diese der „Vorstellung einer verborgenen, aber in allen Dingen wirksamen theosophischen Topik" nachging, die sich symbolisch in der Sprache wiederfinden bzw. aus dieser herauslesen läßt (Kilcher, s. Anm. 6, 44 f.). In den 10 Sephiroth oder Schöpfungskategorien der Kabbala taucht zudem die Syzygie als Unterschied u. Vereinigung der beiden Geschlechter u. Prinzipien des Männlichen/ Aktiven bzw. Weiblichen/ Passiven auf. Vgl. Scholem: Ursprung (s. Anm. 6), 125 f. u. 134 ff. Zu den verschiedenen Topoi-Katalogen seit der Antike vgl. etwa Lothar Bornscheuer: Topik. Zur Struktur der gesellschaftlichen Einbildungskraft. Frankfurt a. M. 1976, 34, 67 u. ö.; Joachim Dyck: Ticht-Kunst. Deutsche Barockpoetik und rhetorische Tradition. Bad Homburg v. d. H. [u. a.] 1966, 43 ff. u. 57 ff.; Peter Hess: Zum Toposbegriff in der Barockzeit. In: Rhetorik X (1991), 71–88; K. Ostheeren, G. Kalivoda, F. Ranieri u. a.: Art. „Topos", in: Historisches Wörterbuch der Rhetorik. Hg. Gert Ueding. Bd. IX (Darmstadt 2009), 630–724; T. Wagner: Art. „Topik" in: ebd., 605–626; Volkhard Wels: Triviale Künste. Die humanistische Reform der grammatischen, dialektischen und rhetorischen Ausbildung an der Wende zum 16. Jahrhundert. Berlin 2000, 104–118.

9 Das Buch Daniel berichtet vom babylonischen Herrscher Belsazar, wie ihm bei einem Trinkgelage, das die aus dem Tempel zu Jerusalem geraubten Trinkgefäße entweihte, eine Hand erschienen sei, die mit dem Finger geheimnisvolle Zeichen an die Wand schrieb. Niemand konnte sie dem beunruhigten König deuten u. so wurde nach Daniel geschickt,

der sie las u. erklärte: „Mene/ Mene/ Tekel/ Vpharsin. Vnd sie bedeutet dis/ Mene/ das ist/ Gott hat dein Königreich gezelet vnd volendet, Tekel/ das ist/ Man hat dich in einer wage gewogen/ vnd zu leicht funden. Peres/ das ist/ dein Königreich ist zuteilet/ vnd den Mede[r]n und Perse[r]n gegeben" — ein Orakel, das zutreffend den baldigen Untergang des neubabylon. Reiches voraussagte. Dan. 5.25–28 nach *Biblia (Luther 1545)*.

10 Diese wahrhaft pantagruelische Liste erinnert stark an Johann Fischarts *Geschichtklitterung* (erstmals 1575) mit ihren ausufernden, grotesken Wort- u. Sprachspielen, einschließlich eines unermeßlichen Kanons von Scherz-, Spott- u. Schimpfnamen, wie sie schon in der Vorrede „Ein und VorRitt, oder das Parat unnd Bereytschlag, inn die Chronick vom Grandgoschier, Gurgellantual und Pantadurstlingern" u. sonst verstreut im Werk begegnen, tw. in förmlichen Aufzählungen, Reihungen u. Listen. S. Johann Fischart: Geschichtklitterung (Gargantua). Text der Ausg. letzter Hand von 1590. Mit e. Glossar hg. Ute Nyssen. Nachw. v. Hugo Sommerhalder. 2 Bde., Düsseldorf 1963/64, I, 19 ff., auch 85 ff., 117, 124 ff., 198, 239 ff., 289, 342, 415 ff. u. ö. (das Glossar von Ute Nyssen ist allerdings als Stellenkommentar u. nicht alphabetisch angelegt, was seine Nutzbarkeit als „Glossar" erheblich einschränkt). „Tilltapp", „Säutrüssel", „mistheintz", „schelmio", „Hudler" (289 f., 340) u. v. m. erscheinen hier u. könnten bei näherer Untersuchung die Quelle Franckenbergs abgegeben haben. Franckenbergs Studien-Aufenthalt in Basel u. Straßburg 1617 legt eine Bekanntschaft mit Fischarts Werk nahe. Vgl. Schmidt-Biggemann: Abraham von Franckenberg (s. Anm. 5), 233. In der Erzählung, wie Gargantua zu seinem Namen „Gorgellantua oder Gurgelstrozza" kam, heißt es, sie sei nach seiner offenkundigen Eigenart als unerhört durstiger „Schreiling" erfolgt. „Dann also auff die weiß haben die alten Hebreer ihren Kindern Namen angeeignet, und dieselbige nach gestalt der sach auff ihre Sprach gegeben" (152). Folgerichtig erscheint exempelweise eine Liste geeigneter abbildlicher Namen (152 f.). Dabei wird gegen entlehnte hebräische, griechische oder lateinische Namen für sprechende deutsche Namen plädiert, denn „unser sprach ist auch ein sprach, unnd kan so wol ein Sack nennen, als die Lateiner saccus"; einem jeden soll der passende „Helm" aufgesetzt werden, „so kent man die Mummer undereinander" (154 u. 157). Nebenbei: F. Ludwig hatte in einem Gutachten zu einem Entwurf der Rechtschreibung von Gueintz vom März 1644 angemerkt: „Der Sack wird sich in allen sprachen also ausgeredet und geschrieben finden, darumb man der lateinischen sprache die ehre des ursprungs nicht alleine, sondern vielmehr der Hebraischen zu geben." (HM Köthen: VS 545, Bl. 234r. Demnächst in *DA Köthen I. 9*: „Zu 440313") Fischart erbaut mit seinen unablässigen Paronomasien, Verballhornungen, Alliterationen, Buchstabenvertauschungen, Wortverdrehungen, Wort- u. Reimspielen eine ‚kabbalistische' Sprachwelt, in der die Namen eine kaum überschaubare Sachwelt menschlicher Erfahrungen u. Verhältnisse wiedergeben, nicht als zufällige, arbiträre Zeichen, sondern als Träger einer Bedeutung, die vom Namen nicht geschieden ist. Dies könnte Fischarts Sprach- u. Namenkosmos für Franckenberg attraktiv gemacht haben. Auch diese Verbindung scheint der bisherigen Franckenberg-Forschung verborgen geblieben zu sein. Peuckert (1973, s. Q), 299, wies darauf hin, daß auch Johan Amos Comenius „eine besondere Vorliebe für deutsche Sprichwörter und Kraftausdrücke" gehabt habe. Zuletzt sei nicht unerwähnt, daß sich Fischart auch mit der hermetischen Sprache des Paracelsismus u. Fachsprachen beschäftigte. Er unterstützte Michael Toxites (1514–1581) im 2. Teil von dessen Lexikon *ONOMASTICA II. I. PHILOSOPHICVM, MEDICVM, SYNONYMVM ex varijs vulgaribusque linguis. II. THEOPHRASTI PARACELSI hoc est, earum vocum, quarum scriptis eius solet usus esse, explicatio* (Straßburg 1574). Vgl. Corpus Paracelsisticum. Bd. II: Dokumente frühneuzeitlicher Naturphilosophie in Deutschland. Der Frühparacelsismus. 2. Teil. Hg. u. erl. v. Wilhelm Kühlmann u. Joachim Telle. Tübingen 2004, 25 f., 57 u. 330; Wilhelm Kühlmann: Rätsel der Wörter. Zur Diskussion von „Fachsprache" u. Lexikographie im Umkreis der Paracelsisten des 16. Jahrhunderts. In: Das Wort. Seine strukturelle u. kulturelle Dimension. Festschr. f. Oskar Reichmann zum 65. Geb. Hg. Vilmos Ágel, Andreas Gardt u. a. Tübingen 2002, 245–262, bes. 259; Peter O. Müller: Deutsche Lexikographie des 16. Jahrhunderts (s. Anm. 4), 472 ff. u. 492 ff.

11 Der Vater der deutschen Sprache sei Gott, die Mutter die Natur, der Geburtsort Babylon, so Justus Georg Schottelius (FG 397. Der Suchende) in *Der Teutschen Sprache Einleitung (1643),* 3. Das faßt die sprachtheologische Axiomatik in Schottelius' Sprachdenken bündig zusammen. Die biblischen Erzählungen von der Sprache Adams, der die Dinge so bezeichnete, wie sie eigentlich waren, bildeten ebenso den Hintergrund wie etwa Platons Dialog *Kratylos*, in dem die „Wahrheit" der Rede von der Wahrheit des Namens (Noma) abhängig gemacht wurde, bis sie im Laufe des Dialogs in die Richtung einer allein möglichen Wahrheit der Aussage (Rhema) verschoben wurde. Gleichwohl blieb die enge Kopplung u. Äquivalenzrelation von Laut- bzw. Schriftgebilde des Wortes u. der bezeichneten Sache auch bei Schottelius u. vielen seiner Zeitgenossen ein zentrales Kriterium für die „Sinn- und Wahrhaftigkeit der Wörter" (Wolf-Peter Klein: Fachsprachenforschung [s. Anm. 4], 308), so wie die Wortforschung überhaupt Dreh- u. Angelpunkt der zeitgenössischen Grammatiken war, die relativ wenig (Satz/ Syntax) oder gar nichts (Text) zu höheren sprachlichen Ebenen aussagten. „Es ist eine alte Streitfrage", läßt Schottelius seine Kenntnis des platonischen physei-thesei-Streits durchblicken, „ob die [Wörter von] Natur oder Chur [*d. h.: Wahl*]/ oder/ ob sie wilkührlich [oder] natürlich waren ihrem Uhrsprunge nach" (*Der Teutschen Sprache Einleitung (1643),* S. 73. *Dieser Satz wurde augenscheinlich schwer verdruckt. Konjekturen in eckigen Klammern*).

Besonders in der 4. „Lobrede" in seiner *Sprachkunst (1641)* machte Schottelius die starke Naturmotiviertheit zu einer besonderen Auszeichnung der deutschen Sprache. So pries er die „innere Schicklichkeit" der deutschen Sprache, durch die das Wort „das lebhafte Bild eines dinges" perfekt u. „als ob es gegenwertig da were" vorzustellen vermöge, so daß sich „die Natur […] völlig und aller dinges" darin „außgearbeitet" habe (84 f.) — nicht nur in den onomatopoetisch-lautmalerischen Wörtern, für die auch Franckenberg im vorliegenden Brief einige Tierlaute u. -namen anführt, sondern auch in einer fast durchgängigen sinnlichen Klangqualität u. Lautsymbolik der deutschen Wörter, die die Eigenschaften des Dinges „lebhafftiglich" wiedergeben (86). Dieses Privileg habe „die mildreiche allgemeine Mutter/ die gütige Natur" der dt. Sprache verliehen (88), die „auß den Kräfften der Natur reinlich und reichlich die klingende Stimme gehen lesset" (93) u. der Natur „am nechsten" komme (6. Lobrede, a. a. O., 121). Die „gewissesten Gründe/ welche Gott und die Natur" in der dt. Sprache „ausgewircket haben" (5. Lobrede, a. a. O., 98; vgl. 1. Lobrede, 4), zu analysieren u. in einer systematischen Grammatik darzustellen, sieht Schottelius als Aufgabe u. Verdienst seiner *Sprachkunst.* Auch andernorts spricht Schottelius der deutschen Sprache den Vorzug zu, „die dinge und dero Eigenschafften/ auch sonsten das/ was GOtt und die Natur dem Verstande offenbart hat […] auffs eygentlichste/ deutlichste und reinlichste außdrücken/ außsprechen/ außbilden" u. „alles was die Natur wircket/ in unseren Verstand legen" zu können (1. Lobrede, 17): „was die Natur uns wil verstehen lassen/ daß können wir der Natur/ in teutscher Sprache nachreden" (19). In der dritten Lobrede (a. a. O., 58) prägt Schottelius für diese, eine unmittelbare Adäquation von res u. vox leistende Ausdrucksfähigkeit der dt. Sprache den Begriff oder das Prädikat „Welträumig"; ihre Vollkommenheit verdanke sie dem Umstand, daß sie „in rerum natura" gründe (ebd., 73). Und in der 9. Lobrede schließlich hat die Natur in der dt. Sprache „ihr Meisterstück gethan" (a. a. O., 171). Ein letztes Zitat, in dem Schottelius die Sprache nicht in den Sprachsubjekten u. ihrem Sprachgebrauch, sondern in höheren Ordnungen wurzeln läßt, wodurch sich der göttliche, kreative Logos der Welt u. die innere Vernunft, der „Geist" der Sprache, wechselseitig reflektieren, entnehmen wir *Schottelius: Der Teutschen Sprache Einleitung (1643)*, 83 f., wonach „eine natürliche Verwantschafft unter den Wörteren und der Natur selbst", eine „innerliche Gleichheit des gleichsam natürlichen Wesens des Dinges in denselbigen [den dt. Stammwörtern]" bestehe. Vgl. *Banneck*, 107 f. Zum Begriff Sprach-„Geist" s. ebd., 98 u. 127, auch 19 u. 71. Zu Schottelius' Aufnahme kabbalist. Argumentationstraditionen s. Zeller: Natursprache (s. Anm. 6), 914. Zu seiner Vorstellung einer geheimen Kraft in den Buchstaben u. Wörtern vgl. auch 450200. Kein Titel von Schottelius in der Kurzliste von Franckenbergs Bibliothek (Bruckner [s. Q], 94ff.).

12 Wie sein grammatisch-analogistischer Gewährsmann Schottelius war auch Georg Philipp Harsdörffer (FG 368. Der Spielende) von der herausgehobenen Naturmotiviertheit der deutschen Sprache überzeugt: Die deutsche Sprache „redet mit der Zungen der Natur/ in dem sie alles Gethön und was nur einen Laut/ Hall und Schall von sich giebet/ wol vernemlich ausdrucket [...]. Die Natur redet in allen Dingen/ welche ein Getön von sich geben/ unsere Teutsche Sprache/ und daher haben etliche wähnen wollen/ der erste Mensch Adam habe das Geflügel und alle Thier auf Erden nicht anderst als mit unseren Worten nennen können/ weil er jedes eingeborne selbstlautende Eigenschafft Naturmässig ausgedrucket". G. P. H.: „Schutzschrift/ für Die Teutsche Spracharbeit/ und Derselben Beflissene", als Anhang in *Harsdörffer: Frauenzimmer-Gesprächspiele* I ²1644, Ndr. 1968, S. 12 u. 14/ Ndr. 355 u. 357. Für Adams „deutsche" Sprachgebung ist auf Ioannes Goropius Becanus' „cimbrische" (d.h. nl.) Sprachursprungstheorie zu verweisen, s. dazu *Harsdörffer: Specimen (1646)*, 50 f. u. *Schottelius: Sprachkunst (1641)*, 58. Im 139. Gesprächspiel unterhält sich die Gesprächsrunde mit der Nennung solcher Wörter, „welche die Natur gleichsam selbsten außspricht: als es donnert" usw. Auch hier zeigen die dt. Wörter eine sonst unerreichte Fähigkeit, die schiere Präsenz oder „den Nachdruck deß Dings selbsten/ so gar eigentlich auß[zu]bilden". *Harsdörffer: Frauenzimmer-Gesprächspiele* III (1643, Ndr. 1968), S. 290/ Ndr. 310. In seiner den Fruchtbringern Carl Gustav v. Hille (FG 302) u. Franz Julius v. dem Knesebeck (FG 396) gewidmeten „Spielrede" „von dem Worte Spiel" als Zugabe im 4. Teil der *Frauenzimmer-Gersprächspiele* (1644, Ndr. 1968), 461/ Ndr. 505, heißt es: „Wir Teutsche führen in unserem Munde/ eine Krafft- Verstand- und Wortreiche Zunge". Vgl. dort S. 467/ Ndr. 511 u. 476 ff./ 520 ff. (Harsdörffer legt seine FG-Imprese aus). Kein Titel von Harsdörffer in der Kurzliste von Franckenbergs Bibliothek (Bruckner [s. Q], 94 ff.). Vgl. 450901 K 8; *Banneck*, 142 ff.; *Gardt: Sprachreflexion*, 53 ff.; *Hundt*, 61 u. 190 ff.; Ferdinand van Ingen: Georg Philipp Harsdörffer und seine Experimente mit „der Natur Sprache". In: Georg Philipp Harsdörffer und die Künste. Hg. Doris Gerstl. Nürnberg 2005, 77–88; Christopher J. Wells: Deutsch: eine Sprachgeschichte bis 1945. Tübingen 1990, 309.

440900

Justus Georg Schottelius an Herzog August d. J. von Braunschweig-Wolfenbüttel

Justus Georg Schottelius (FG 397) erinnert daran, daß von ihm verlangt worden sei, ein kleines Werk (*Schottelius: Teutsche Vers- oder ReimKunst [1645]*) zum Druck nach Nürnberg oder Hamburg zu senden. Da Drucker dergleichen bisher noch nicht in deutscher Sprache gedruckt hätten, habe er das Buch jedoch lieber selbst in den Druck gegeben, damit er sich darum kümmern und sein eigener Korrektor sein könne. Nun seien noch drei Figuren und Embleme in Kupfer zu stechen, zwei in Hamburg, eins in Nürnberg. Die neuen Apostrophe und die Schrift Cicero würden in Helmstedt gegossen werden. Damit das Werk bis zum Jahresende ausgedruckt werden könne und die Buchhändler alle Exemplare erhielten, bittet Schottelius Hz. August d.J. v. Braunschweig-Wolfenbüttel (FG 227) darum, ihm den Rest seines Halbjahresgehalts (75 Rth.) auszahlen zu lassen. — Er habe sich nun einmal auf die Herausgabe des Buchs in Wolfenbüttel eingelassen, obgleich dem Drucker dort Notwendiges fehle. Auch habe er dort derzeit drei Bücher zur Hand, die er dem Herzog zur Billigung einreichen müsse. Vor ein, zwei Jahren habe er manches aus seiner Kunstform und aus seinen Erfindungen Freunden mitgeteilt, die ihm dann zuvorgekommen seien und die Kunst heimlich, aber gutgemeint hier und da entwendet und das Werk öffentlich erwähnt hätten, ein wenig auch seiner eigenen Absicht entsprechend. Die Freunde drängten nun, da mit dem Werk schon mehr als ein Jahr nichts passiert sei, auf die Veröffentlichung.

Q HAB: Cod. Guelf. 11.12 Aug. 2°, Bl.225rv; o. O., undat., eigenh. — Von Hz. August an Johann Valentin Andreae (FG 464. 1646) mitgeschickt, der sein Empfangsdatum („31. Oct. 44.") auf der Vorderseite oben links vermerkte.[1] — BN: Merzbacher: *Schottelius*, 160.

A *Nicht vorhanden.*

Serenissime Jllustrissimeque Princeps Domine Clementissime

Potuissem quidem opusculum[2], cuius non semel mentionem feci, vel Noribergam vel Hamburgum typis exscribendum mittere, expetebatur enim: Sed quoniam ob rei novitatem, nam Typographi in Teutisca n*os*tra lingua hæc talia non tentarunt, ipse ego corrector exigebar, prælo submisi, et necessaria maximam partem procuravj.[3] Restant autem ex figuris et emblematibus cupro incidendis tres, duæ Hamburgi, altera Noribergæ sculpitur: Notæ apostrophes novæ, et literarum formæ, Cicero vocant, Helmstatj funduntur, in hisce et in aliis (nam promissum e*st*, si ante novi annj tempus opusculum perficietur, ab vno atq*ue* altero Bibliopola o*mn*ia exemplaria simul receptum irj) ne mora nociva mihi porrò injiciatur, humillimè peto, salarii semestris (75 Vallensibus constat) subsidio, quod tantum restat, clementissimè subvenire:

Si rem non incepissem, non inceptarem hic locj, quia necessaria variè Typographo defecerunt. Interim tamen edere cogebar, quia tres libelli ad manum mihi sunt (ostentandi ad nutum Serenitatis Vestræ) ubi Amici[4], quibus iam ante annum et biennium non nulla de hac artis forma et novis inventis communicarem, honesto furto in aliquibus anteverterunt, in aliquibus, publicâ huius operis mentione factâ, à mente meâ ex vero non[a] nihil aberrant; [225v] Quicquid autem sit, editionem opusculj maturandam amici subinde admonent: quievit enim iam ultra annum. Vestra Serenitas in hac re neccesaria, et suum Fatum expecta, petito adminiculo clementissimè ut adsit, iterum prece humilima sollicito, qvi
Seren*itati* V*es*træ obedientis*simè* interero
Justus-Georg*ius* Schottelj*us*.

T a *Eingefügt* non nihil

K 1 Hz. August d. J. v. Braunschweig-Wolfenbüttel (227) weckte durch den mitgeschickten Brief Johann Valentin Andreaes (FG 464. 1646) Interesse an Justus Georg Schottelius (FG 397) u. dessen Poetik *Schottelius: Teutsche Vers- oder ReimKunst (1645).* Andreae schrieb am 6.11.1644 an den Herzog. „CL. Schottelius vir elegantissimi ingenij. quid molietur, nondum capio. Me sitiscum quid fore. facile conjicio. Opitij fortassis æmulatione, nisi quod nova plane, et numquam prius tentata, minatur. acclamo feliciter." HAB: Cod. Guelf. 65.1 Extrav., Bl. 191r. Er setzte am 22.1.1645 hinzu: „In h. Schottelii Poetischem werkh hat man ex ungue leonem zuerkennen. Verhoffe, das ganze buch ein mahl zu sehen, Vnd werden die Teutschen Poeten Einmahl a licentia ad regulam gebracht werden. Salveat ex me Vir industrius." A. a. O., Bl. 206v. Zu Andreaes Einstellung zu Martin Opitz (FG 200) vgl. 270429.

2 *Schottelius: Teutsche Vers- oder ReimKunst (1645).* Sie erschien im Selbstverlag Anfang 1645 in Wolfenbüttel, da Schottelius Exemplare mit 450202 u. 450204 an Hz. August d. J. u. F. Ludwig übersandte. Der Stoff dieser auf die Verskunst beschränkten Poetik wird in drei Büchern über „Maasforschung", „Abmessung" u. die zweite „Abtheilung und Ordnung der Reimarten [...] nach den Reimschlüssen und Reimen" abgehandelt. Vgl. zur *Vers- oder ReimKunst* 431028A K 3; 440100 K 3 u. I u. II, 440324 K 23, 440400 K 1 u. I, 441000, 441011, 441020, 441200 K 1 u. I u. II, 441216, 441231 K 9, 441231A K 1, 450000 K 0, 450000A K 0, 450100, 450126, 450202, 450204, 450219, 450221, 450308, 450317A, 450410 K 3, 451100 K 1, 451217 K 7, 451219, 451220 u. 460825 K. Da die datierten Freundschaftsbriefe u. -gedichte in diesem Buch von Georg Philipp Harsdörffer (FG 368), Johann Michael Moscherosch (FG 436. 1645), Henricus Becker (aus Einbeck) u. Johann Rist (FG 467. 1647) vom 20.10.1644, 1.10.1644, 18.11.1644 bzw. 16.12.1644 stammen, Justus Georg Schottelius die Vorrede am 26.1.1645 unterzeichnete u. er das Buch Hz. August d. J. v. Braunschweig-Wolfenbüttel (FG 227) am 2.2.1645 überreichte (s. 450202), scheint uns eine Datierung des vorliegenden Schreibens um 440900 plausibel. Zur zeitlichen Einordnung dieses Briefs vgl. auch 441000 u. 441011.

3 Wie der Buchtitel mitteilt, wurde die Poetik „getruckt zu | Wolfenbüttel | in verlegung | des Autoris | im Jahre | M DC XL V."

4 Zu diesen Freunden gehörten sicher auch die in Anm. 2 genannten Beiträger.

440927

Fürst August von Anhalt-Plötzkau an Herzog Wilhelm IV. von Sachsen-Weimar

F. August v. Anhalt-Plötzkau (FG 46) schildert seinem Neffen Hz. Wilhelm IV. v. Sachsen-Weimar (FG 5) die für Anhalt verheerende Kriegslage angesichts des Zusammentreffens der feindlichen Hauptheere der Kaiserlichen unter Generalleutnant Matthias Gallas und der Schweden unter dem Generalfeldmarschall Lennart Torstensson bei Bernburg: Weder Protest noch diplomatische Intervention hülfen. Die Armeen ruinierten sich selbst; völliger Untergang des Landes sei das Resultat. Die Heere versuchten einander auszuhungern oder zum Abzug zu zwingen. Sie hätten sich früher in ihren Forderungen einschränken sollen, da jetzt die Untertanen bereits hungern müßten und nichts anbauen könnten. F. Christian II. v. Anhalt-Bernburg (FG 51) habe mit seiner Familie Zuflucht in Köthen suchen müssen, da die von den Schweden aus dem Bernburger Schloß vertriebenen Kaiserlichen dieses aus der Stadt Bernburg unter Artilleriebeschuß genommen und großen Schaden angerichtet hätten. Auch wenn solche unerhörte, nie gesehene Landesverderbnis eigenen Sünden und Gottes gerechtem Zorn zuzuschreiben sei, so wisse man doch um die Rolle einiger hochgestellter Personen, die zum Magdeburger Beschluß beigetragen hätten. Näheres könne Hz. Wilhelm anderweitig mitgeteilt werden. Er, F. August, schreibe dies im Wissen um das wohlbegründete eigene Interesse Hz. Wilhelms an der Situation im Ft. Anhalt. F. August erklärt, Neutralität anzustreben, jedoch bislang nicht mit dem gewünschten Erfolg. Er bekräftigt seinen Friedenswunsch. Der Kaiser habe neue Vollmachten für die Friedensverhandlungen in Osnabrück und Münster ausgestellt. F. August empfiehlt seine Familie im Falle seines Ablebens dem Schutz Hz. Wilhelms.

Q ThHSTA Weimar: Fürstenhaus A 205, Bl. 224r–225v [A: 225v], eigenh.; Sig.

A Dem Hochgebornen Fürsten, Herrn Wilhelmen, Hertzogen zu Sachsen, Jülich, Cleve vnd Berg, Landgraffen in Thüringen, Marckgrafen zu Meißen, Grafen zu der Marck vnd Ravensburg, Herrn zu Ravenstein *etc.*, vnserm freundlichen geliebten Herrn Vetter, Sohn, Vnd Gevattern handen.   Weimar

Hochgeborner fürst freundlicher hochgeehrter herr Vetter und gefatter, El hab ich hirmitt berichten wollen, wie wir alhier im lande Numehr in die 3 wochen vom herrn Gn. Leut. Gallas und in die 12 tage vom herrn Feld M. TorstenSohn auß **fouragiret**[a] word*en* und gar wenig mehr ubrig[,] auch fast verlautten will, daß es noch so lange möcht werden¹, wan aber alles **remonstrirens** entrahtet, die Armeen verderben, alhier nichtes als unsern Unttergang **Lucriren**² können, So stecket doch die **reputation** so sehr, daß einer das ander vermeinet auszuhungern oder zu Nötigen daß er aufbrechen muß, daß also lautter **extrema** vorgehen, man fenget itzo auch ahn, zu **menassiren**³, welches wohl eher Nötig gewesen, dieweil Jnmittelst auch das brott den armen Untterthanen nicht Ubrig gelaßen worden noch daß sie ein korn säen könnten, Des Vettern f. Christian L. sind mit derer **Famili** auf Cöth*en* gezogen, Nachdem die Kais*erlichen* zwar die **Garnison** vor Torstensohn fruhe[b] fur [den ber]gk⁴ ge[rück]et, ausgenommen, von selb*en* aber wieder besezet word*en*, welches verursachet, daß aus dem wohl untractirten[a] ⁵ Ks. lager, die Scheunen und der Bergk durch die Sprengkugeln Jn die Aschen geleget, ins haus⁶ aber mit so um[a] 80 **Pfund** Steine eingeworffen werden, die **Schw**e*dischen* haben sehr [224v] ins Ks. lager **Canoniret**, daß solches auch sich retiren[c] müßen, es hat aber den **Effect** nicht erreiche[t][d] als man verhoffet, iezo stehets darauff daß sie wieder Neher rucken, alles dißeiz der Saalen, und die forathe[e] vollend einander abstricken, Uns und uns[ern][d] Armen[f] Unterthanen, welche alle bis auf diesen sch[lechten][g] orth ausgeplündert theils verbrand, und gar ins lager [ab]getragen,)[h] gestehets abreit[a] ⁷ uber 40.000 Scheffel [in/ von][d] warmsdorff so mit gewalt **occupirt**, noch einst [so][d] viel, dem Vetter von Bernburgk und Dessau 3 [mahl][d] so viel, ohne was im Cötnisch*en* und deßausch*en* e[hist][d] und ins kunftige zu **liqui**diren sein wird, wir k[önnen][d] zwar alleine unsern und des landes Sünd*en* diese g[roße][d] verderbung, dergleich*en* bei wehrend*em* kriege nicht vor[handen,][d] zumeßen und daher Gottes gerechten verheng-

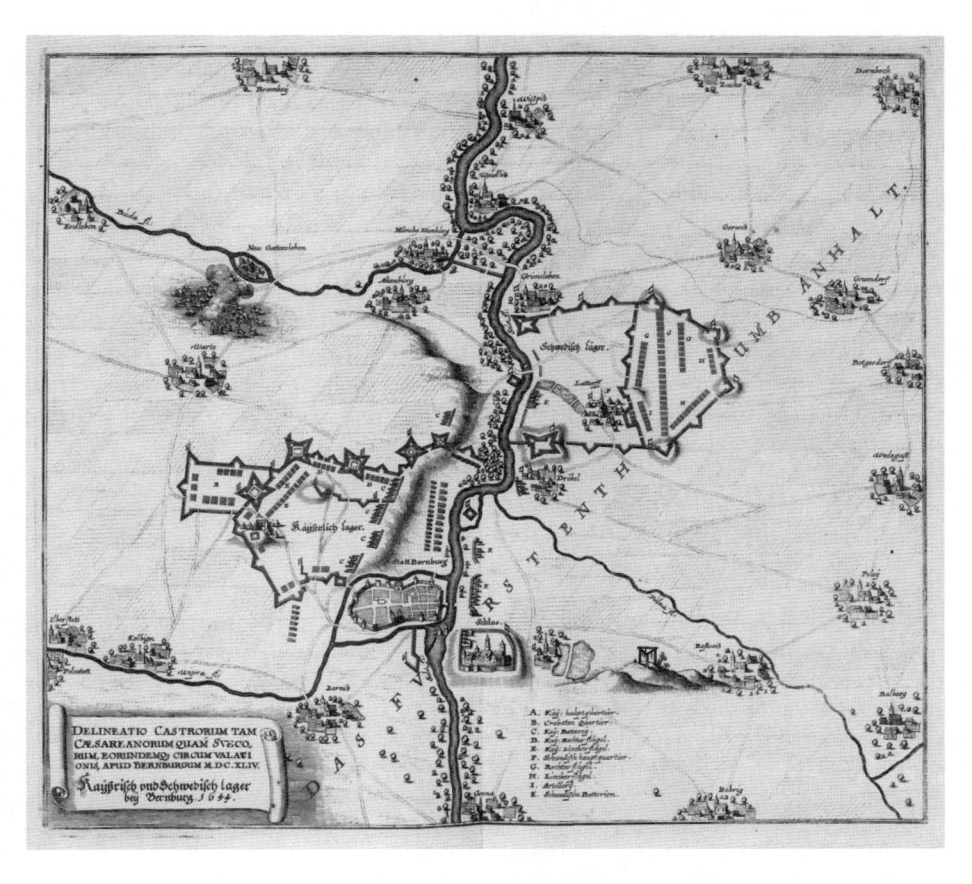

Die gegenseitige Blockade der kaiserlichen und der schwedischen Armee vor Bernburg 1644. Zu 440927.

nus, haben aber^i auch etzliche grandes darzu geholff[en]^d, die uns wohl bewust, und den Schluß zu Mag[de]burg^d ^8 machen helffen, anderer Accidentien [zu] geschwe[igen,]^d welche EL wollts gott können enddecket werden, welche[s EL]^d kürzlich vermelden wollen[,] da ich weis daß sie große vr[sach]^d haben unsern zustand zuwißen, damitt sie darvon nachricht haben möchten, diesen schlechten orth wil[l man]^d neutral machen, die Sachen aber sind noch nicht zu[r]^d [225r] perfection gerichtet, und wird helffen was es kan, Got der Allmechtige wolle EL und dero herrn bruder lande vor dergleichen landverderben gn. behütten, uns von dieser trangsal Erretten, und dermaleinst den lieben Frieden gn. wieder geben, Die Ks. Mt. sollen mehr Neue volmachten, nach Osnabruck und Münster zur reassumption^9 der Tractaten ausgefertiget haben, Auf allen fall [daß] gott der Almechtige uber mich in diesen trubbeln gebitten^j und uns [aus] dieser Mühseligkeit abfodern würde, wollen EL. die meinigen sich f. laßen anbefohlen sein, Herr Bierschenk^10 ist meines wißens noch zu Deßa, welchem die zeitt wohl lang werden mag, werden auch^a Numehr die tractaten^11 desto^k schwerer fallen, weil Capital und gefelle nit einander endsprechen und nichts mehr angebauet werden kan, El nebest unsrer dienstlichen begrußung des Almechtigen beobachtung damit treuligst ergebend und verbleibe

    EL. dienstwilliger getreuer Vetter und Diener
    Augustus FzAnh.
    27 Sept. 1644.

T a *Unsichere Lesung.* — b *Am Rand ergänzt bis gerücket (Buchstabenverlust im Falz, unsichere Konjekturen in eckigen Klammern).* — c *Lies:* retirieren — d *Buchstabenverlust im Falz, unsichere Konjektur in eckigen Klammern.* — e *Lies:* Vorräte — f *Eingefügt für* <andern> — g *Buchstabenverlust im Falz. Lies:* einschließlich dieses schlichten Orts (Plötzkau). — h *Anfang der Einklammerung nicht erkennbar.* — i aber auch *durch hochgestellte Ziffern in der Reihenfolge geändert aus* auch aber — j *Lies:* gebieten — k *Folgt* <mehr>

K F. Augusts v. Anhalt-Plötzkau (FG 46) Brief an seinen Neffen Hz. Wilhelm IV. v. Sachsen-Weimar (FG 5) fällt durch eine vergleichsweise irreguläre Schreibweise, aber auch durch mangelhafte morphologische u. syntaktische Fügungen auf, die das Sprachbewußtsein seines Bruders Ludwig v. Anhalt-Köthen vermissen lassen. Der Brief ist zwar kein genuin fruchtbringerisches Schreiben, dient uns aber dazu, in die für Anhalt desaströse Kriegslage des Jahres 1644 einzuführen.
    1 Im Juni 1644 war das schwed. Korps unter Generalmajor (Greve) Hans Christoph v. Königsmarck (FG 515. 1648) aus Niedersachsen ins Halberstädtische zurückgekehrt, um die unter dem ksl. Generalleutnant Matthias Gallas nach Holstein ziehende Reichsarmee im Auge zu behalten, doch kehrte er nach dessen Vorbeimarsch an die untere Weser zurück. Nachdem sich Königsmarck des größten Teils des Erzstiftes Bremen bemächtigt hatte, wandte er sich Ende Juli 1644 wieder gen Obersachsen, um die dort durch Kursachsen bedrängten schwed. Einheiten zu unterstützen. *Chemnitz* IV.4, 108–110 u. 111–114. Anfang August wurde das erzstift. magdeburg. Egeln besetzt, u. es ergingen die ersten Unterhaltsforderungen an das benachbarte Ft. Anhalt. Caspar Pfau (FG 412. 1644)

berichtete am 4.9. aus Bernburg, daß „uns die arméen wohl über den hals kommen möchten […] Die sachen stehen gantz desperat […] Jch bin alhier des bestellens gantz müde vnd überdrüßig, dann alles in einer solchen confusion, daß es nicht zu beschreiben." (*KU* V.1, 311). Am 6.9.1644 hatte die ksl. Armee unter Generalleutnant Gallas nach einer erfolglosen Diversion nach Holstein (s. Anm. 6) über Stendal, Tangermünde, Magdeburg (Ende August) u. Staßfurt (4.9.) kommend Stadt u. Schloß Bernburg eingenommen u. ein befestigtes Feldlager in der westlichen Saale-Aue aufgeschlagen. Während die schwed. Hauptarmee unter Torstensson in gewissem Abstand folgte, Alsleben am 16.9. passierte u. am 17.9. auf dem östlichen Saaleufer in Latdorf vor der Bernburger Bergstadt (s. Anm. 4) Stellung bezog, besetzte Königsmarcks Korps F. Ludwigs Städtchen u. Schloß Nienburg westlich der Saale am 20.9. Schon am 18.9. konnten Torstenssons Truppen dank überlegener Artillerie die ksl. Musketiere aus dem Bernburger Schloß vertreiben u. ans westliche Saaleufer zurückdrängen. Am 21.9. bezogen die Schweden ihr Hauptquartier im Nienburger Schloß. Zwar kam es zu keiner Entscheidungsschlacht, aber ein wochenlanges Beobachten, Belagern, Scharmutzieren u. der Artilleriebeschuß der feindlichen Lager führten zu immensen Zerstörungen. Dabei gestaltete sich die Lage der allmählich von allen Seiten eingeschlossenen Kaiserlichen immer schwieriger, ja geradezu desaströs. Zwei ksl. Angriffe auf Nienburg (am 22.9. u. am 3.10.) wurden abgeschlagen, das Plünderungen, Kontributionen, Angriffe u. Gegenangriffe der feindlichen Parteien zu erleiden hatte, bis „kein Mensch einiges Körnleins oder bißen brodts weder aufm Fürstl. Hause noch im Städtlein mächtig gewesen". Viele Häuser u. Scheunen wurden abgerissen oder niedergebrannt u. der Ort samt Vorwerk u. Grimsleben von Grund auf zerstört. Auch das übrige Land wurde von den Schweden „dem Raube unterworffen […] und stehet iederman wegen totalausplünderung in leibes- und lebensgefahr. […] Jch habe", so klagte Diederich v. dem Werder (FG 31) aus Reinsdorff bei Köthen am 22.9.1644, „nicht eine Hand voll mehl und nicht eine tonne bier mehr im Vorrath, Weiß auch keinen Rath und leide dießfals große noth" (*KU* V.1, 315f. u. 321). Bernburg wurde zwischen den Schweden, die das Ostufer mit Schloß u. Bergstadt beherrschten, u. den Kaiserlichen, die im westlichen Teil der Stadt („im Tal", s. Anm. 4) standen, zerrieben. Erneut, wie schon 1636, mußte F. Christian II. seine Residenz räumen; er fand Zuflucht bei seinem Onkel Ludwig in Köthen. Auch die Residenz Köthen wie die übrigen anhalt. Landesteile waren mit unablässigen schwed. Unterhaltsforderungen völlig überfordert, wobei F. August v. Anhalt-Plötzkau vor allem unter den Kaiserlichen litt, da „alle meine Vorwerge, Adeliche Heuser, Dörffer und Kirchen bis auf den Grund niedergerissen, auch dieser mein Residentzort abgetragen, und die Unterthanen gantz ausgezogen und verjagd worden". Er selbst habe „nicht einen bißen brodt behalten können […] Jch glaube nicht, daß ein Fürst im Reich, so lange dieser Krieg gewehret, solcher maßen, wie ich nunmehr in meinen hohen Jahren tractiret und zugerichtet sey". Er wäre verschmachtet, hätte ihm nicht Gallas rühmlicherweise mit Geld u. Getreide ausgeholfen (Brief an den Kaiser, Plötzkau 27.11.1644; *KU* V.1, 342). Der Schaden war im ganzen Lande Anhalt enorm; das Schloß Bernburg etwa „samt allen vnentbehrlichen gebeuden vnd getreyde neben dem Bergk daselbsten verwüstet, auch respective abgebrandt, keiner Stadt noch Residentzort mehr ähnlich" usw. Zugleich mußten sich die Fürsten von Anhalt gegen die Unterstellung wehren, den Schweden bereitwillig gegeben zu haben, was sie den Kaiserlichen angeblich verweigert hätten. Stattdessen sei es mit ihnen wie den Untertanen dahin gekommen, daß alle Lebensmittel herausgepresst u. fortgenommen seien u. sie daher, „wan es Christlich, den Tod vor das Leben wünschen möchten" (Brief der Fürsten an den Kaiser, 4.12.1644. *KU* V.1, 348–351, Zitate S. 348 u. 349). Die Stadt Bernburg u. ihre Umgebung waren „nach den Kämpfen ein ödes und zerstörtes Land" u. hatten am Ende des Krieges einen

Bevölkerungsverlust von zwei Dritteln zu beklagen. Der „Gallassische Ruin" blieb lange im kollektiven Gedächtnis von Stadt u. Land verankert. *Rebitsch*, 284. Noch Martin Milagius (FG 315) erinnert in der Vorrede seines *Singenden Jesaja* (1646) daran (s. 460825). Im Dezember 1644 konnten die anhalt. Abgesandten Christian Ernst (v.) Knoch (FG 268) u. Caspar Pfau (FG 412. 1644) bei Torstensson erreichen, daß „Dero sämbtlichen Fürstenthümer von dato an, ein Jahr lang der Contribution enthoben sein sollen". (Torstensson an die Fürsten von Anhalt, d. d. in seinem Hauptquartier Zeitz, 21.12.1644. *KU* V.1, 334f.; vgl. *Krause: Werder*, 42). Leider fehlen für das Jahr 1644 die Tagebuchaufzeichnungen F. Christians II. — Eine katastrophale Versorgungssituation im eingeschlossenen u. unter schwed. Artilleriefeuer gelegenen ksl. Feldlager zwang Gallas, dem von den schwed. Truppen nahezu jegliche Möglichkeit zum Proviantieren u. Furagieren genommen worden war, zu einer Verzweiflungstat. In einer militärischen Finte, bei der er seine sämtliche Reiterei nach Westen aussandte, der die schwed. Kavallerie nachsetzte, gelang es dem ksl. Generalleutnant Mitte November 1644 auszubrechen. Unter Zurücklassung der Verletzten u. Kranken sowie des Großteils von Artillerie u. Tross erreichten die Reste der ksl. Infanterie die Vorstädte Magdeburgs, wo sich kurz danach auch die Kavallerie einfand. Torstensson sandte Königsmarck Gallas nach, der vor Magdeburg abermals eingeschlossen wurde. Die schwed. Hauptarmee zog unterdessen weiter nach Kursachsen, wo sie überwintern sollte. Der Abzug beider Hauptheere wurde in Anhalt wie eine Erlösung gefeiert. Ende November 1644 gelang der ksl. Kavallerie der Ausbruch aus der Magdeburger Blockade, auch wenn sie, von schwed. Truppen verfolgt, bei Jüterbog schwere Verluste hinnehmen mußte. Um den Jahreswechsel 1644/45 glückte auch der ksl. Infanterie die Flucht über die teils vereiste Elbe. Über Wittenberg u. die Lausitz zog sie nach Böhmen. Nur einem Bruchteil der wenige Monate zuvor ausgesandten Reichsarmee gelang damit die Rückkehr in die ksl. Erblande. Das Fazit im Kriegsmemorial des William Forbes (FG 527. 1649), des letzten von F. Ludwig aufgenommenen FG-Mitglieds: „Wir folgeten [den Kaiserlichen] und kahmen beederseits heraus nach Bährenburgk [Bernburg], da die Kayserliche unterschietliche Mahll geschlagen, gantz ruiniret wurden und sich zertrewet nach Praag reterirten." Zit. n. Detlev Pleiss: Das Kriegsfahrtenbuch des schwedischen Offiziers William Forbes. Von seiner Landung an der Unterelbe im Sommer 1634 bis zu seiner Rückkehr nach Stade im Winter 1649/50. In: Stader Jahrbuch 85 (1995), 133–153, hier 143. Aufgrund des katastrophalen Verlaufs des Feldzuges nach Dänemark wurde Gallas sein Oberbefehl entzogen, der an Gf. Melchior v. Hatzfeld (1593–1658) übertragen wurde. Torstensson brachte ihm jedoch in der Schlacht von Jankau (Jankov, 60 km südöstl. von Prag) am 6.3.1645 eine vernichtende Niederlage bei. Zum weiteren Kriegsverlauf vgl. 441205 (K 2), 441231, 450124, 450217, 450219, 450419 K 3, 450505A K 3, 450711, 450721, 450730, 451030 K 0 u. K 2 (Schlacht bei Jankau), 460321 K 2, 460422, 460424 u. 460825; ferner auch 440504 K 1 u. 440809. Vgl. auch die Flugschrift: Bericht Außm Schwedischen Feldläger bey Bernburg, vom 6. und 13. Novembr. dieses 1644. Jahrs: darinn von dem Gallasischen Abmarsch und wie solcher abgangen, vermeldet wird. O. O. 1644. (4 S.), UB Augsburg (Slg. Oettingen-Wallerstein): 02/IV.13.4.187angeb.04; vgl. auch 441205 u. *Documenta Bohemica* VII, 130–161; *Englund*, 411ff.; *Theatrum europaeum* V: 1642–1647 (Frankfurt a. M. 1647), 555ff., 576, 581ff. u. 598 (HAB: Ge 4° 54); *Chemnitz* IV.4, 163f.; Volker Ebersbach: Geschichte der Stadt Bernburg in zwei Bänden. Bd. 1, Dessau 1998, 105–107; Mark Hengerer: Kaiser Ferdinand III. (1608–1657). Eine Biographie. Wien, Köln, Weimar 2012, 208–211; Cornelia Müller: Schrecken des Krieges in Stadt und Land. Der Dreißigjährige Krieg in und um Latdorf. In: Susanne Friederich, Judith Blödorn, Hans-Jürgen Döhle (u.a.): Archäologie am Kalkteich 22 bei Latdorf Halle a. d. S. 2008 (Archäologie in Sachsen-Anhalt, Sdbd. 9), 95–104; Jochen Fahr u. Peter

Pacak: Das schwedische Feldlager Latdorf. In: ebd., 105–114; Hans-Jürgen Döhle: Pferde im Graben des schwedischen Feldlagers Latdorf, in: ebd., 115–117; Jochen Fahr, Cornelia Müller, Peter Pacak: Das schwedische Feldlager von Latdorf bei Bernburg von 1644 (Salzlandkreis, Sachsen-Anhalt). Ergebnisse der Ausgrabungen am Kalkteich 22 und an der L 73. In: Schlachtfeldarchäologie. Battlefield Archaeology. 1. Mitteldeutscher Archäologentag vom 09. bis 11. Oktober 2008 in Halle (Saale). Hg. Harald Meller. Halle a. d. S. 2009 (Tagungen des Landesmuseums f. Vorgeschichte Halle, Bd. 2), 151–162; H. Suhle: Die Stadt Bernburg im dreißigjährigen Kriege. In: MVAG 11 (1908), 105–221 (Bd. nicht im Bestand der HAB, konnte nicht eingesehen werden). — S. die Abb. „Kaÿßrisch vnd Schwedisch lager bey Bernburg. 1644." auf S. 345.

2 Aus dem lat. u. mlat. lucrari, lucrificare, d. h. gewinnen, erlangen, profitieren, Nutzen haben, s. heute noch „lukrativ". Vgl. *Diefenbach: Glossarium*, 338; Klara Hechtenberg: Fremdwörterbuch des siebzehnten Jahrhunderts. Berlin 1904, 81; [Michael Heubel:] Der ungelährte Staats-Mann/ Durch Erklärung etlicher fremd ... Wörter ... unterrichtet. Jena 1669, 494: „Lucriren/ gewinnen/ Gewinst haben oder bekommen". HAB: Kg 346.

3 Vielleicht abgeleitet von frz. „menacer", d. h. jemanden (mit einer Waffe o. ä.) bedrohen. — Eher denkbar ist aber eine Ableitung von „menagiren", von frz. „mesnage/ ménage" (Haushalt), „ménager", haushalten, sparen, sich mit etwas versehen, sich schonen oder mäßigen. Vgl. Christian Juncker: Christian Weisens Curieuse Gedancken von den NOUVELLEN oder Zeitungen. Frankfurt a. M., Leipzig 1703 (S. 608–876: mit dem Anhang eines Fremdwörter-Lexikons: „Curieuses Nouvellen-LEXICON, Oder Kurtze und deutliche Erklärung/ wo nicht aller/ jedoch der meisten und vornehmsten ... Deutscher/ Frantzösischer und Jtaliänischer/ auch zum Theil verstümmelter Lateinischer Wörter und Redensarten"), hier 774 f. (HAB: Ge 846; dig.); Hechtenberg (Anm. 2), 85; *Nicot*, 406; *Littré* III, 506 f.

4 Bernburg bestand eigentlich aus drei zunächst selbständigen Städten: der Alt- u. der Neustadt am westlichen Saaleufer („im Tal") u. der Bergstadt, die um die am östlichen Saale-Ufer auf steilem Sandsteinfelsen erbaute Burg entstanden u. jünger als jene war: Die zwei Talstädte besaßen schon 1278 getrennte Stadtrechte, bis sie sich 1561 zusammenschlossen, die Bergstadt erhielt sie erst um 1450. Die topographische Bezeichnung „vor dem Berge" umfaßte also das Schloßareal, das fl. Vorwerk (aus der weiträumigen ehemal. Vorburg entstanden) u. die Stadtsiedlung „vor dem Berge". Vgl. Volker Ebersbach: Geschichte der Stadt Bernburg in zwei Bänden. Bd. 1, Dessau 1998, 19 u. 43–54; *Merian: Topographia Superioris Saxoniae* (1650), 29 f.

5 Von Tractament, tractieren, d. h. hier bewirten, versorgen, besolden. *DW* XI.1.1, 1012 f. u. 1018 ff.

6 D. h. ins Bernburger Schloß. Nachdem sich die Schweden des fl. Schlosses bemächtigt u. die ksl. Besatzung daraus vertrieben hatten (18.9.1644, s. Anm.1), haben die Kaiserlichen „auß der [am jenseitigen westl. Saale-Ufer gelegenen] Statt Bernburg mit Fewer vber die Saal gegen dz Schloß geworffen/ vnd dasselbe in Brand bracht/ daß ein grosser Vorrath an Getraidig/ wie auch alle Schewern vnd Ställ/ verbrant/ das Schloßgebäw stunde noch/ welches die Schweden damals dannoch inbehielten." *Theatrum europaeum* V (1647. HAB: Ge 4° 54), 174, irrtümlich ins Jahr 1643 vorverlegte Schilderung. Vgl. aber S. 557 zu diesen Vorfällen im September 1644. „Sprengkugeln", mit Pulver gefüllte Granaten, s. *DW* X.2, 143.

7 Allbereit, schon. *Stieler*, 1502.

8 Unklar, was damit konkret gemeint ist. Möglicherweise betraf dies eine Übereinkunft bzw. einen Beschluß hinsichtlich der ksl.-kursächs. Garnison in der Stadt Magdeburg, zu deren Unterhalt die Anhalter Fürsten mitverpflichtet worden waren. Vgl. *KU* V.1, 202–

214. Möglicherweise handelte es sich auch um einen in Magdeburg getroffenen Beschluß einer Ständeversammlung. Zwischen 1639 u. 1649 hat es keine nds. Kreistage gegeben, der Kreis war politisch „fast vollständig lahmgelegt" (Gittel, s.u., S.171). Im Gegensatz zum Erzstift Magdeburg gehörte das Ft. Anhalt dem obersächs. Reichskreis an, jedoch traten auch die obs. Kreisstände zwischen 1638 u. 1649 nicht zusammen. Im Juli 1644 sollen sich Kg. Christian IV. v. Dänemark u. die Herzöge von Braunschweig u. Lüneburg mit der Absicht getragen haben, einen nds. Kreistag einzuberufen. Der nds. Kreis war damals vom schwed.-dän. Krieg betroffen. Es kam im Juni 1644 aber zu einer „Präliminarkonferenz" der Kreisausschreibenden Fürsten des nds. Kreises, die von der Abhaltung eines Kreistages Abstand nahmen, um sich nicht schwed. Feindseligkeiten zuzuziehen. Udo Gittel (Die Aktivitäten des Niedersächsischen Reichskreises in den Sektoren „Friedenssicherung" und „Policey" [1555–1682]. Hannover 1996, 171 Anm.463.) verweist auf verschiedene Korrespondenzen in diesem Zusammenhang, nennt aber nicht den Ort dieser Konferenz u. deren Beschlüsse im einzelnen. Magdeburg käme in Frage. Am 9.8.1644 befahl Ks. Ferdinand III. Gallas, von den nds. Ständen allseitige Hilfe u. Unterstützung der ksl. Armee gegen die Schweden zu verlangen. *Documenta Bohemica* VII, 126. Vgl. Winfried Dotzauer: Die deutschen Reichskreise (1383–1806). Stuttgart 1998, 348f., 373, 608 u. 610. — Nach einem beispiellosen Gewaltmarsch von Böhmen nach Jütland war es Torstenssons Schweden bis Mitte Januar 1644 zwar gelungen, Holstein, Schleswig u. Jütland zu erobern, die dän. Seevorherrschaft konnten sie aber zunächst nicht brechen u. daher Fünen u. Seeland nicht erobern. Vgl. 440324 K 18. — Bereits im Frühjahr 1644 hatte der Frankfurter Deputationstag die Hilfe der Reichsarmee für das bedrängte Dänemark beschlossen, wobei insbesondere Kf. Johann Georg I. v. Sachsen u. der nds. Kreis militär. Hilfe leisten sollten. Eine offizielle Unterstützungserklärung für Christian IV. übersandte Ks. Ferdinand III. am 23.6.1644 (n. St.). Im Juli 1644 traf die rund 12.000 Mann starke ksl. Armee unter Gallas in Holstein ein u. vereinigte sich mit den dän. Truppen. Zwar konnte u.a. Anfang August Kiel besetzt werden, jedoch blieben größere Erfolge aus, nicht zuletzt, weil Gallas eine Entscheidungsschlacht gegen das schwed. Heer vermied. Dennoch hinderten die Ankunft des ksl. Heeres u. die Dominanz der dän. Flotte Torstensson daran, nach Fünen überzusetzen. Massive Versorgungsprobleme, die durch Mangel u. Desertionen das ksl. Heer zusammenschmelzen ließen, sowie Unstimmigkeiten mit den dän. Truppen, denen Gallas' zurückhaltende Kriegsführung mißfiel, zwangen noch im Sommer 1644 den ksl. Generalleutnant zur Aufgabe des Feldzugs. Um dem geschwächten Reichsheer ein erneutes Kräftesammeln in Nieder- u. Obersachsen zu verwehren, entschied der schwed. Generalfeldmarschall Torstensson mit seiner Hauptstreitmacht Gallas zu folgen. Den Kampf gegen Dänemark überließ er einem starken Armeekorps unter Oberst Helm Wrangel (1599–1647). Wie oben geschildert (Anm.1) bezogen die Kaiserlichen an der Saale bei Bernburg ein befestigtes Lager, um dort auf Unterstützung durch kursächs. u. ksl. Truppen zu warten, wurden jedoch von den nachfolgenden Schweden blockiert. — Der Frieden von Brömsebro vom 13. August 1645 beendete den schwed.-dän. Krieg zum Nachteil Dänemarks, das die norweg. Gebiete Härjedalen u. Jämtland sowie die Ostseeinseln Gotland u. Ösel abtreten mußte. Vgl. *Englund*, 379ff., 402ff. u. 411ff.; *Theatrum europaeum* V (1647), 540ff.; Hengerer (s. Anm.1), 210f.; Leon Jespersen: Dänisch-schwedische Rivalität und das Scheitern der nordischen Zusammenarbeit. In: Der Westfälische Frieden von 1648 — Wende in der Geschichte des Ostseeraums. (FS Herbert Ewe). Hamburg 2001, 47–64; Paul Douglas Lockhart: Denmark in the Thirty Years' War, 1618–1648. King Christian IV. and the Decline of the Oldenburg State. Selinsgrove, London 1996, 259ff.; Stefanie Robl Matzen: Der Schwedisch-Dänische Krieg 1643–1645. In: Handbuch zur nordelbischen Militärgeschichte. Heere und Kriege in Schleswig, Holstein, Lauen-

burg, Eutin und Lübeck, 1623 – 1863/67. Hg. Eva Susanne Fiebig u. Jan Schlürmann. Husum 2010, 309–326; *Wilson*, 684 ff. Auch Ks. Ferdinand III. forderte im Juli 1644 die rasche Abhaltung eines nds. Kreistages, um die ksl. u. Reichsinteressen bei der Abwehr der schwed. Kriegsvölker zu wahren. Die Kreisstände sollten die ksl. Truppen unterstützen, den Feind zu Friedensverhandlungen zwingen helfen u. eine Reichssteuer in Höhe von 240 Römermonaten entrichten. Vgl. die ksl. Instruktion an die Emissäre Gf. Wilhelm Leopold v. Tattenbach u. den ksl. Kriegskommissar Dr. Jordan, d. d. Wien 11.7.1644, wiedergegeben in *Documenta Bohemica* VII, 115.

9 Reassumierung, d. h. Wiederaufnahme; „reassumiren", eine Sache wieder aufgreifen, „wieder anfangen/ wo man es zuruckgelassen. **denuo rem aggredi**", auch erneuern. Juncker (s. Anm. 3), 826. Vgl. Hechtenberg (Anm. 2), 112; Heubel (Anm. 2), 121 („Assumtio", An- oder Aufnehmung) u. 649 („Reassumtio Litis", d. i. „die Erneuerung und Bekräftigung des Verstorbenen Streits oder Handels"). HAB: Xb 3764 (2). — Der Beginn der Westfälischen Friedensverhandlungen in Münster u. Osnabrück war im Hamburger Präliminarfrieden vom 25.12.1641 auf den 25.3.1642 festgesetzt, dann auf den 11.7.1643 verschoben worden, nachdem der Kaiser u. Kg. Philipp IV. v. Spanien das Abkommen erst im Juli 1642 bzw. im April 1643 ratifiziert hatten. Es dauerte jedoch noch bis zum 23.11. bzw. 4.12.1644, bis die ksl. Gesandten mit den ersten Propositionen an die Schweden bzw. die Franzosen die eigentlichen Verhandlungen eröffneten. Die entscheidende Streitfrage zwischen dem Kaiser u. den beiden auswärtigen Mächten, die Beteiligung der Reichsstände an den Friedensverhandlungen, war förmlich erst mit der ksl. Einladung der Stände zum Kongress vom 29.8.1645 beigelegt, als sich freilich viele Stände bereits längst in Osnabrück u. Münster eingefunden hatten. Vgl. *Croxton/ Tischer*, 120 f.; *Ritter: Deutsche Geschichte*, 617 ff.; *Wilson*, 617 ff.; Maria-Elisabeth Brunert: Friedenssicherung als Beratungsthema der protestantischen Reichsstände in der Anfangsphase des Westfälischen Friedenskongresses. In: Frieden und Friedenssicherung in der Frühen Neuzeit. Das Hl. Römische Reich und Europa. (FS Maximilian Lanzinner). Hg. Guido Braun u. Arno Strohmeyer. Münster 2013, 229–258, hier 242. — Das *Theatrum europaeum* V (1647. HAB: Ge 4° 54), 566, berichtet, daß „vmb den 2. Septembris [1644] die Kays. Herrn Gesandten zu Oßnabruck zu Producirung der Praeliminarien vnd Vollmachten sich erklärt hatten/ welches dann von den Königlichen Schwedischen H. **Legatis** acceptiert/ die Vmbstände/ **ratione temporis, loci ac personarum**, verglichen/ vnd solchem nach **primo huius**, Nachmittags daselbsten/ **in loco tertio**, durch beyderseits **Legation-Secreta**rios, die Originalia der Vollmachten fürgewiesen/ und collationirte Copien gegeneinander außgewechselt worden [...] vnd giengen die Tractaten zu Münster ziemblich jetzo für sich".

10 Eine Anspielung auf den Trinker Matthias Gallas, der sein Hauptquartier damals aber noch in Bernburg hatte? Der „Bierjörg" genannte Kf. Johann Georg I. v. Sachsen hielt sich zu dieser Zeit nur in Sachsen auf. Vgl. *Theatrum europaeum* V (1647), 542 u. 564 f.

11 Verhandlungen. *DW* XI.1.1, 1015. Dem Sinn nach könnte sich F. August auf die Kontributionen des Ft.s Anhalt bezogen haben, die sich an diesem Punkt des Krieges nur noch schwer in militärische Erfolge ummünzen ließen.

441000

Justus Georg Schottelius an Herzog August d. J. von Braunschweig-Wolfenbüttel

Justus Georg Schottelius (FG 397) bittet Hz. August d. J. v. Braunschweig-Wolfenbüttel (FG 227), die aus dessen Bibliothek entliehenen Bücher (Philipp Clüvers *Germania antiqua* 1616, einen Teil von Johann Heinrich Alsteds *Encyclopaedia* 1630 und Iulius Caesar Scaligers *Poetices libri septem* 1561) noch auf zwei volle Monate behalten zu dürfen, um herangezogene Stellen in seinem Buch (*Schottelius: Teutsche Vers- oder ReimKunst* 1645) berichtigen zu können. Der Typograph (der Verleger Balthasar Gruber), der den Druck immer wieder verzögert habe, werde damit übermorgen beginnen. — Wegen der Lehre von der Silbenlänge, die er am Anfang seines Buchs behandeln wolle, und wegen der eigens dafür gegossenen Zeichen bittet Schottelius den Herzog, ihm einen halben Tag Urlaub zu gewähren, damit er sich in Braunschweig um diese Dinge kümmern könne, welche sich schlecht brieflich erledigen ließen. Schottelius wolle mit dem Wolfenbütteler Amtmann (Caspar Wulff) mitfahren und sofort zurückkommen.

Q NSTA Wolfenbüttel: 2 Alt Nr. 40, Bl. 11rv, 11v leer; undat., eigenh.

A *Nicht vorhanden.*

Serenissime Princeps Domine clementissime

Germaniam Cluveri,[1] Partem Encyclopediæ Alstedij[2] et Poeticam Scaligeri[3] ex concesso â Vra. Serenitate usu adhuc possideo, quorum quidem librorum ad unum atque alterum mensem actum[a] concedendam[b] clementissimè copiam, humillimè peto: Restabunt enim allegatorum locorum explicationes in correctione necessariæ:[4] Typographus (qui usque et usque moras peperit)[5] initium imprimendj perendie faciet eius libri, quem de Poesi Germanicâ, formæ artis inclusâ, conscripsi. Quandoquidem autem ob doctrinam quantitatum, quæ [ad][c] primum libri primj locum occupabit, et cuius aptiùs indicandæ gr*ati*â, novæ zifrarum formæ sunt fusæ, monstravj, quod per literas commodè fieri non potest, precor humillimè dimidium diej clementissimè mihi concedj; ut Brunsvigæ corām et pluribus, quæ res poscat, informatio fieri possit.[6]

Cum AmtManno Wolferbytano commodè iturus, et reditum statim maturaturus sum.[7] Expectat humillimè brevis temporis veniam.

Vestræ Serenitate subiectissimè obediens
Justus-Georgius Schottel*ius* mppa.

T a *Eingefügt.* — **b** cede *eingefügt über gestrichenen Buchstaben des Worts.* — **c** *Der folgende Tintenklecks verdeckt etwa 2 Buchstaben.*

K Unsere Datierung des vorliegenden Briefs auf Ende September oder Anfang Oktober 1644 stützt sich auf die von Justus Georg Schottelius (FG 397) in 441011 berichtete Absage an den Braunschweiger Drucker u. Verleger Gruber. S. Anm. 5.

1 In der riesigen Büchersammlung Hz. Augusts d. J. v. Braunschweig-Wolfenbüttel (FG 227) fand Schottelius dieses u. viele weitere für seine Arbeiten benötigte Werke, darunter die Erstauflage: Philippi CluverI Germaniæ Antiqvæ Libri tres (Lugduni Batavorum: Ludovicus Elzevirius 1616), HAB: 190 Hist. 2°. S. 450000.

2 Johannes Henricus Alstedius: Enciclopædia septem tomis distincta (Herbornae Nassoviorum 1630); HAB: 39.1-2 Quod. 2°. Schottelius meint wohl den in den ersten 2 Bänden vorhandenen Teil oder nur den 2. Band, der *Lexica. Grammatica. Rhetorica. Logica. Oratoria. Poetica* behandelt.

3 Ivlii Cæsaris Scaligeri, Viri Clarissimi, Poetices libri septem ([Lyon]: Vincentius; [Genf]: Crespin 1561), HAB: 12.3 Poet. 2°.

4 Korrekturen in *Schottelius: Teutsche Vers- oder ReimKunst (1645)*.

5 Balthasar Gruber, braunschweigischer Verleger u. Drucker (1629–1645), über den sich Schottelius beim Herzog beklagte u. von dem er sich bald trennte. Vgl. 441011. Seit Schottelius' Werk „Die hertzliche Anschawunge Vnsers gecreutzigten Heylandes/ … Gedancken Von seynem Leyden" (Braunschweig: B. Gruber 1640), [HAB 608.3 Quod. (1); 1336.10 Theol.] waren seine dt. Schriften bei Gruber erschienen. Zu den Gründen, warum Schottelius für seine *Vers- oder ReimKunst* den Verlag selbst übernahm, s. 440900. Carl Ludwig Grotefend: Geschichte der Buchdruckereien in den Hannoverschen und Braunschweigischen Landen. Hannover 1840, o. Pag. (etwa Bl. 99), gibt nur an, daß Grubers Witwe 1646 das Geschäft weiterführte, es aber bald an Christoph Friedrich Zilliger übergab.

6 Sicherlich wollte Schottelius mit Gruber über Einzelheiten des Satzes seiner Poetik sprechen. Im ersten Buch der *Teutschen Vers- oder ReimKunst* behandelt Schottelius die von ihm so bezeichnete Maßforschung („Maasforschung") bzw. die „Wortzeit", die er in die längere, kürzere u. mittlere unterteilt. „Die kürtzere Wortzeit ist der Laut des Wortes/ welcher in geschwinder kurtzer Zeit wird außgesprochen und daher felt; als gerichtet/ erweisen/ liebliche." (S. 6 f.). (Schottelius hatte F. Ludwig schon 1643 einen lat. Entwurf geschickt, der Anlaß zu einem Meinungsstreit lieferte. „Doctrina quantitatum omnium vocabulorum Germanicorum, summatim tantum ex lingua fundamentis delineata", s. *KE*, 282 ff. u. demnächst in *Köthen I.9*.) Zu den Einzelheiten, die Schottelius schlecht brieflich mit Gruber besprechen konnte, gehören wohl die Bögen u. Linien, die am Anfang der Poetik kurze u. lange Silben bezeichnen. Zum Guß von Typen in Helmstedt, auch für die Längenbezeichnungen, s. 441011.

7 Unbekanntes Geschäft, zu dem der hzl. Wolfenbütteler Amtmann mit Schottelius nach Braunschweig reisen wollte. Hierbei handelte es sich um Caspar Wulff, von 1639 bis 1660 Amtmann in Wolfenbüttel. Christoph Woltereck: Chronicon Der Stadt und Vestung Wolffenbüttel … Blankenburg/ Helmstedt 1747, 742. S. auch Ulrich Brohm: Die Handwerkspolitik Herzog Augusts des Jüngeren von Braunschweig-Wolfenbüttel. Zur Rolle von Fürstenstaat und Zünften im Wiederaufbau nach dem Dreißigjährigen Krieg. Stuttgart 1999, S. 93 (Zitat einer Interzession von 1649) u. passim.

441010

Zacharias Prüschenk von Lindenhofen über seine Aufnahme in die Fruchtbringende Gesellschaft

Zeugnis Zacharias Prüschenks v. Lindenhofen (FG 418. Der Fördernde) über seine Aufnahme in die FG in Köthen am 10.10.1644 mit Angabe seiner Gesellschaftsimprese, Abschrift des Reimgesetzes und Nennung der bei dem Aufnahmeactus anwesenden Mitglieder.

Q ThHSTA Weimar: Kunst und Wissenschaft – Hofwesen A 11817[1], Bl. 16rv, v leer; Schreiberh. mit eigenh. Unterschrift. — Das Reimgesetz auch im 3. Band des Köthener Erzschreins: HM Köthen: V S 546, Bl. 51rv, v leer; Reinschrift von Schreiberh., zit. als *E*. Dieses Gedicht steht auch und damit genau übereinstimmend im *GB Kö*. III (HM Köthen: V S 677b), Bl. 19r.

A *Nicht vorhanden.*

Den 10. Octobr. anno 1644. bin von dem Durchläuchtigen Hochgebornen Fürsten vnnd Herrn, Herrn *Ludwigen* Fürsten zue Anhaldt *etc.* meinem gnädigen Fürsten vnd Herrn, Ich endesbenandter in Seiner Fürstl. Gn. Hofflager zu Cöthen, in die hochansehenliche Fruchtbringende Gesellschafft an- vnd auffgenommen worden, in der Ordnung der 418. Vnd hab den Nahmen des *Förderenden*, zur frucht den *Indianischen Pfeffer*, zum Wortt aber die *Dauung* empfangen, worüber hochermeldt Seine Fürstl. Gn. nachfolgende achtzeilige Reimgesetze verfertiget:

Die *Dauung* fördert recht der *Pfeffer* so gebracht
    Wird auß[a] dem *InderLand*, den nahmen hat genommen
Der *Fördernd* auch darümb[b]: Es ist gar wol bedacht
    zu fördern was zuvor in stecken[c] etwa kommen,
Doch das die billigkeit genommen werd' in acht,
    Vnd man befördre mit gemeinen Nutz vnd[d] frommen.
Fruchtbringend wird ein Mensch hier fördern alles wol,
    Wann Er in seinem Geist[e] ist *Christi* Liebe woll[f],[1]

    Gegenwertig seind gewesen, alß Mit-gesellschaffter Seiner Fürstl. Gn. Iunger Printz Fürst *Wilhelm Ludwig* zu Anhalt *etc.*[2], Christian Ernst Knoche[3], Obrister Lieutenant, Wolff Schlegel[4] vnd Bernhardt Henrich von Warnsted[5],

    Zacharias Prüeschenck mp

T a *E* aus — b *E* darumb — c *Lies:* ins Stocken — d *E* und — e *E* geist' — f *E* vol *In E abschließend die Initiale und die Jahreszahl: Z. P. 1644.*

K Der Jurist Zacharias Prüschenk v. Lindenhofen (FG 418. Der Fördernde) war nach dem Tode seines Schwiegervaters Friedrich Hortleder (FG 343) 1640 von Hz. Wilhelm IV. v. Sachsen-Weimar (FG 5) am 31.1.1641 zum weimar. Hofrat berufen worden u. setzte Hortleders jurist. u. (landes)geschichtl. Arbeiten fort. S. *Conermann III,* 392f. u. 499. 1645 wurde er zum Landesdirektor des Ft.s Eisenach u. zum weimar. Geheimen Rat befördert. Neben seinen zahlreichen jurist. Schriften trat er publizistisch mit seiner Parteinahme im Synkretismus-Streit für Georg Calixt u. für eine Verständigung der christl. Konfessionen hervor. Dahin gehören u. a. die unter seinem FG-Gesellschaftsnamen veröffentlichten Schriften: Gottes zweyfache Bundes-Lade/ Durch Weiland Herrn D. Georgium Calixtum, Unter dem Titul eins Tractatus de Pactis Dei *etc.* verfertiget/ Nunmehr aber durch ein vortreffliches Glied der Fruchtbringenden Gesellschafft den Fördernden Männiglich zu durchgehenden Nutzen u. Unterricht aus dem Lateinischen in die Teutsche Sprache übersetzt. [Helmstädt: Friederich Lüderwaldt, Braunschweig: Johann Heinrich Duncker 1678] (HAB: 240.5 Theol. u. Li 1176; Vorrede d. d. 25.6.1667); ferner eine Übersetzung von Calixts *De Pactis quae Deus cum hominibus iniit,* sowie die Übersetzungen von Caspar v. Barths (1587–1658) *Soliloquia* (Zehn Auserlesene Geistreiche Andachten und Betrachtungen, Leipzig u. Jena 1675. HAB: Li 258) u. dessen Ausgabe des Dialogs *Theophrastos* von Aineias v. Gaza (Vortreffliches Gespräch/ genandt Theophrast Von Unsterblichkeit der Seelen, Frankfurt a. M. 1671. HAB: Lg 23.2) aus dem Lateinischen ins Deutsche. *Conermann III,* 498–500. Was der Anlaß für Prüschenks Besuch in Köthen war, ist unbekannt. Auch verschiedene, im zeitlichen Umfeld des vorliegenden Briefes ermittelte Schreiben geben keinerlei Auskunft. So bat F. Christian II. v. Anhalt-Bernburg (FG 51) Hz. Wilhelm IV. in einem Brief vom 17.2.1645 um Saatgetreide; F. Ludwig bedankte sich in einem Brief an denselben vom 25.2.1645 für 50 Taler u. eine erste Lieferung von Saatgerste u. -hafer. ThHSTA Weimar: Fl. Haus A 205, Bl. 228 f. u. 23; vgl. auch 450220 K II 0.

1 Im Köthener Erzschrein, Bd. 3 (s. Q), Bl. 74rv haben sich Prüschenks Imprese u. Reimgesetz zusätzlich u. in identischem Text in einer Impresenliste mit Reimgesetzen erhalten. Diese Liste beginnt mit Prüschenks Imprese u. Reimgesetz u. endet mit FG 427: Hz. Bernhard v. Sachsen-Jena (Der Nachfolgende. 1645). Im *GB Kö.* III, neben dem Reimgesetz (Bl. 19r) auf Bl. 18v die farbige Wappenzeichnung mit eigenh. Eintrag Prüschenks: „1644. | Gott, brich meinen willen! | Zacharias Prüschenck". Vgl. *Conermann III,* 499 f. u. *II* (Abb.teil, Wappen Nr. 418).

2 F. Wilhelm Ludwig v. Anhalt-Köthen (FG 358), der damals sechsjährige Sohn F. Ludwigs. *Conermann III,* 411 f.

3 Christian Ernst (v.) Knoch (FG 268), 1643 anhalt. Gesamtrat. In seinem Kriegsdienst (1631–1639) war er zum Obristl. der Kavallerie aufgestiegen. Knoch wurde anscheinend in Angelegenheiten der FG wie der Verbesserung von Reimgesetzen einbezogen u. bereitete 1651 die Übertragung der FG-Leitung auf Hz. Wilhelm IV. v. Sachsen-Weimar vor. *Conermann III,* 297 f.

4 Wolf (v.) Schlegel (FG 72), anhalt. Landedelmann u. ehemaliger (?) Hofmeister. *Conermann III,* 78.

5 Bernd Heinrich v. Warnstedt (1610–1682; FG 370), Hofjunker F. Ludwigs. *Conermann III,* 431.

441011

Justus Georg Schottelius an Herzog August d. J. von Braunschweig-Wolfenbüttel

Justus Georg Schottelius (FG 397) klagt bei Hz. August d. J. v. Braunschweig-Wolfenbüttel (FG 227) über den Braunschweiger Drucker Gruber, der ungeachtet des mit ihm geschlossenen Vertrags und des von Schottelius getragenen Anteils der Kosten nun schon ein Jahr lang den Druck von Schottelius' *Teutscher Vers- oder ReimKunst* (1645) mit Lug und Trug hinausgezögert habe. Schottelius habe mit ihm gebrochen und daran gedacht, dem Drängen der Freunde und der Drucker zu folgen und sein Buch in Nürnberg oder Lübeck auflegen zu lassen. Er habe jedoch aus zwingenden Gründen seine Absicht geändert und einen Drucker in Wolfenbüttel gewählt, dem er zwar wegen Unerfahrenheit nach Möglichkeit beim Satz helfen müsse, mit dem er aber das Werk in zwei Monaten zu vollbringen hoffe. — Der Herzog möge die Erlaubnis erteilen, das Buch in seiner Wolfenbütteler Druckerei (der Brüder Stern) erscheinen zu lassen. Eine schlechte Aufnahme des Buchs bei den Gelehrten fürchte er nicht. Da Schottelius doch die Druckkosten trage und die Schrift noch in Helmstedt geschnitten und zum Teil gegossen werden müsse, möge der Herzog ihm zur Beschleunigung der Veröffentlichung sein halbjähriges Gehalt von 75 Talern und auch die von Ostern bis Michaelis noch fehlende Summe auszahlen lassen.

Q NSTA Wolfenbüttel: 2 Alt Nr. 40, Bl. 23, 23v leer; eigenh.

A *Nicht vorhanden.*

Serenissime Illustrissimeq́ue Princeps Domine clementissime Typographus in Vr*æ*. Serenitatis Urbe Brunswico, nomine Grüber,[1] prorsus Punicæ[2] et pessimæ fidei homo, iam annuum tempus in me decipiendo consumpsit; Contraximus enim, sumptus etiam ego in apparandis necessariis feci, ille quotidie mentiendo inceptavit, donec ego tandem, hominis pertæsus, renunciavi. Licet autem opusculum, Poesin Germanicam intelligo, ad petita Typographorum et Amicorum aut Noribergam aut Lubecam mittere potuissem,[3] fuit tamen prorsus ex necessitate, me ipsum, ob varia nova, ordinare ponenda, et posita corrigere.

Curavj igitur hîc Wolferbytj initium exscribendj[4] fieri, et quia Typographus malè instructus, juvj ipsum, in quibus potuj, et speramus post menses duos nos opusculum hîc absoluturos.

Concedat **Serenitas Vestra** libellum hunc, super quo Eruditorum iudicia non reformidabo, ex illustrj Vrā. Guelphica provenire, et, quia res meâ impensâ agit*ur*, ut quæ sculpenda et fundenda restant, (forma enim literarum Helmstetj funditur, alia autem forma et quantitat*is* notæ fusæ iam sunt) eò celerius[a] fiant, humillimè peto semestre Salarium 75 Vallensibus constans et quod à Paschate ad Michaelem restat:

    Fidelitatem et obedientiam cum animo porrò offert

              Vestræ Serenitatj subiectis[s]imè
              Justus-Georgius Schottelius.

11 Octobr. Ao. 1644.

441020   Georg Philipp Harsdörffer

T a *Über einem gestrichenen unlesbaren Wort.*

K 1 Der Braunschweiger Verleger u. Drucker Balthasar Gruber (fl. 1629–1645). S. 441000 K 5.
2 *Fides punica*, Treulosigkeit, von den Römern den Karthagern zugeschrieben. Liv. 22.6: „Quae Punica religione servata est fides ab Hannibale, atque in vincula omnes coniecti." Vgl. 21.4 u. Sal. Iug. 108.
3 *Schottelius: Teutsche Vers- oder ReimKunst (1645)*, erschien dem Kupfertitel zufolge in „Wolfenbüttel in verlegung des Autoris". Zum vorliegenden Brief vgl. 440900.
4 Justus Georg Schottelius (FG 397) bittet Hz. August d.J. v. Braunschweig-Wolfenbüttel (FG 227) um Erlaubnis, seine Poetik in Wolfenbüttel drucken zu lassen. Der Drukker der damals dort schon länger stilliegenden hzl. Druckerei hieß Johann (Hans) Bismarck. Vgl. 450100 K 11. S. oben den Hinweis auf *illustris Vestra Guelphica*. Lange vor der datierten Vorrede vom 26.1.1645 muß das Buch in den Druck gegangen sein, denn Schottelius konnte es schon in 450202 seinem Herzog überreichen u. mit 450204 an F. Ludwig schicken. Vgl. auch 440900, 441000 u. 441200. Erst zu Weihnachten 1645 beauftragte der Herzog — unter Schonung Bismarcks — Johann u. Heinrich Stern mit der Aufsicht u. Neuausstattung der Druckerei. Vgl. *Dumrese: Sterne*, 59. Schottelius empfahl schon in 451100 dem Herzog einen Drucker namens Johann Ritmar.

441020

Georg Philipp Harsdörffer an Justus Georg Schottelius

In seinem Freundschaftsbrief beurteilt Georg Philipp Harsdörffer (FG 368. Der Spielende) Justus Georg Schottelius' (FG 397. Der Suchende) *Teutsche Vers- oder ReimKunst (1645)*. Im ersten Buch derselben begegne eine so gründliche Ausarbeitung der deutschen Silbenmaße, daß Kritiker nach dem Gehör deutsche Verse beurteilen könnten, wie es die französischen, italienischen und spanischen Nachbarn in ihren Landessprachen noch nicht zu tun vermochten und vielleicht niemals könnten. Selbst Ronsard und andere berühmte französ. Dichter wie Saint-Amant, Malherbe und Colletet verstießen in ihren Versen — wie schon Belleforest bemerkt habe — gegen die natürlichen Längen und Kürzen des Französischen, und nicht anders begingen die Italiener, sogar Dante und Petrarca, solche metrischen Fehler. Die Spanier achteten zwar genauer auf das natürliche Silbenmaß ihrer Sprache, verstießen aber doch auch gelegentlich dagegen in ihren Metren, z.B. Lope de Vega, Perez de Montalvan und andere. Alle diese betrachteten das gar nicht als Fehler, da sie — wie die deutschen Meistersänger — glaubten, im Vers nur auf die Silbenzahl achten zu müssen. Es komme vielmehr auf die Länge der Silben an. Schottelius habe dazu im ersten Buch seiner Poetik eine systematische Quantitätenlehre der deutschen Silben als Grundlage der Verskunst vorgelegt. — Im 2. Buch stelle Schottelius in mustergültiger Weise über 40 verschiedene deutsche Versarten vor und biete sie für die freie Kombination von Metren und Versarten an. Auf einer solchen herausragenden Grundlage könne wohl niemand der deutschen Poesie ihre Spitzenstellung streitig machen. — Die Kunst des Reimens und der Reimordnung, die Schottelius im 3. Buch behandelt, biete jedem Einfall in deutscher Sprache und Poesie reiche Möglichkeiten zur schmückenden und zierenden Einkleidung, während die anderen Sprachen Mangel litten. Die Franzosen täten sich z.B.

in Nachahmung der leicht dahinfließenden deutschen daktylischen Versarten schwer. Die dt. Poesie sei zu einer wahren Kunst geworden und habe die fremde Dichtung übertroffen, obgleich Könige, Kardinäle, Fürsten und Herren diese unterstützt hätten. — Die vielfältige Zusammensetzung und die Abwechslung der Verse vermöge in besonderer Weise die menschlichen Gemüter zu bewegen, wie dies von Aristoteles und Jules de La Mesnadière bewiesen und von Euripides, Sophokles, Seneca, Francisco de Rojas, Manzini und La Mesnadière in die Tat umgesetzt worden sei. — Der liebliche Verston vergnüge das Ohr, die behandelte Sache fordere die lustvolle Unterscheidung des Verstands. Scaliger fordere vom Poeten kluge überraschende Einfälle wie auch den Nachdruck und die sinnliche, süße Wirkung der Wörter. Die Stimmigkeit der Einfälle, die Reinheit des Stils und der Fluß der Rede sollten sich mit der Wahrscheinlichkeit verbinden und im Gedicht wie von selbst ergeben. Im Horaz und bei Petrarca fänden sich dagegen unstimmige, widersprüchliche Metaphern. Dies und anderes noch zur Poetik Gehörende werde zu Ende des 3. Buches angeschnitten. Auf Schottelius' Verskunst aufbauend würden dt. Poeten und Poetiker auch auf diesem Felde den Alten, Spaniern und Franzosen nicht das Ruhmesfeld überlassen.

Q [Kupfertitel:] Iusti-Georgii | Schottelii | Teutsche Vers- oder | ReimKunst | darin | Vnsere Teutsche | MutterSprache, So viel | dero süßeste Po- | esis | betrifft, in eine | richtige Form der | Kunst zum ersten | mahle gebracht | worden. | getruckt zu | Wolfenbüttel | in verlegung | des Autoris | im jahre | M DC XL V.
Kolophon (S. 319): Gedruckt zu Wulffenbüttel/ | durch Johann Bißmarck/ | Jm Jahr 1645. Bl. [A vii]r – B 2r. HAB: 172. 1 Poet. — zit. *A*; SUB Göttingen: 8 P GERM I, 1290; dig.
Schottelius übernahm Harsdörffers Brief in der 2. Auflage seiner *Teutsche[n] Vers- oder ReimKunst (1656):* [Kupfertitel:] Iusti-Georgii | Schottelii | Teutsche Vers- oder | ReimKunst | darin | Vnsere Teutsche | MutterSprache, So viel | dero süßeste Po- | esis | betrifft, in eine | richtige Form der | Kunst zum ersten | mahle gebracht | worden. | Franckfurtt | am Mayn | in Verlegung | Michael Cubachs | Auch | in Lüneburg | im jahre | 1656, Bl. [a vi]r – [a viij]v. HAB: Um 180 (1) — zit. *B*. — Auch in *Schottelius: Ausführliche Arbeit (1663),* 794–798, zit. *C.*

Geehrter Suchender.^a

DEn Entwurff der Teutschen Poesie/¹ welchen er so wol anderen/ als auch mir zubetrachten überschikket hat/ achte ich von hoch-nützlicher Wichtigkeit: Und wan ich Kraft unserer Gesellschaft bündlichen Vertrauens/² und zwischen uns absonderlich geschlossenen Freundschaft/ meine meinung davon frey heraus sagen sol/ so bedünckt mich **der Suchende**ᵇ habe im Teutschen numehr erfunden/ wornach man vieleicht in anderen Sprachen vergeblich arbeiten wird. Jch wil erstlich sagen/ **Die gründliche und ungezweiffelte Maasforschung der Silben**/ durch welche unsere Ohren erst recht Poetisch/ und solche/ bishero unrichtige Richtere der Verse/ Kunstverständig unterrichtet werden.³

Die Frantzösischen/ Jtaliänischen und Spanischen Poeten haben hierin noch zur zeit keine gewißheit/ wie man auch aus jhren vornemsten Schriften zubeobachten hat. Ronsart führet seinen verliebten Riesen *(le Cyclope amoureux)* also redend ein:

Tom. 4.
fol. 100.

    Cŏntre (für: *contre*) *lĕ māl̆ᶜ d'ămōur,*

    quĕ tōus lĕs māux ĕxcĕdĕ

L'ārtĭfĭce (für: *L' ărtĭfĭce*) *n'ĭnvēntĕ*

    ŭn plūs prĕsēnt rĕmēdĕ etc. &c.⁴

[A vii v] Dergleichen ist fast in allen der berühmten Frantzosen Gedichten zufinden. So schreibet auch *Saint Amant* an *Damon: f.* 129

Dămōn, ĭe lănguīssŏĭs (für: *lănguīssŏĭs*) *dăns ēn sŏmbrĕ* (für: *sōmbrĕ*) *sĭlēncĕ etc.*⁵

Malherbe und *Colletet* achten solche wieder ihre Aussprache lauffende misstimmung nicht als gefehlet/ und sagt hiervon *Belleforest, Tom. VI. f.* 77 *on voit un nombre infiny en France, lesquels sans avoir iamais gousté le mesure de vers, poetisant en leur langue, guidé du naturel.* &c.⁶

Die Jtaliäner sind hierinnen nicht achtsamer. *Petracha* setzet in dem 29. *Sonetto*ᵈ*, f.* 32.

S'ĭo crĕdēssĕ pēr (*credēssĕ pēr*) *mōrtĕ ēssĕrĕ scārco* (*essere scarco*)⁷
    Dante in seinem dritten Gesange von der Hölle f. 10

Pēr mĕ sĭ vā nēl ĕtērno dŏlōrĕ (*etērno*) *etc.*⁸
Die Spanier beobachten den Lang- und Kurtzlaut jhrer Wörter zwar genauer/ vermissen⁹ aber doch mannichmahl die rechte [A viii r] Reimmaas/ als *Lope de Vega Carpio* führet *Anfriso f.* 448 solcher gestalt singend ein:

Ăltōs dēssĕōs dĕ căntār &c. (für: *ăltōs*)¹⁰
Perez de Montalvan in seinem Buche/ welches er *Los Prodigios de amour* [sic] nennet/ setzet also f. 75.

No os lastime & amor que he de teneros

    Pōrque dĕspŭēs &c. | für : *Pōrqŭe* |¹¹
Dergleichen ist bey *Monte Major, Boscan, Polo, Garcilasso de la Vega,*¹² und fast in allen Spanischen Poeten zu finden.

    Jch wil nicht sagen/ daß so berühmte Leute gefehlet haben/ sonderenᵉ vielmehr glauben/ Sie haben nur die anzahl der Silben (wie auch bey uns Teutschen die alten MeisterSänger) und nicht die rechte Wortzeit/ oder den langen und kurzen Thon in acht genommen: Daß aber solches gar nicht gnug/ noch der Kunst/ eigenschaft und gründen der wahren Poesis gemäß/ bedarf gar keines andeutens. Der Suchender hat sein Gesuch alhie wol und mit Glück in Teutscher Sprache gethan/ und die richtige Anweisung der Wortzeit/ das ist/ die Kunstmessige Erkennung und Abmessung aller Silben (derer viel 100 000 seyn können) [A viii v] durch gewisse Kunstregulen in dem ersten Buche dieser Verskunst uns vorgestellet.

Jn dem anderen Buche hat ein Teutscher fast mit Verwunderung wahrzunehmen/ daß nicht allein über viertzig/ gantz reine unterschiedene Reimarten in unserer Muttersprache zufinden/ sonderen auch durch richtige Anführung deroselben können wir nach aller Lust/ so wol die Reimarten als die Reimmaaßen wechseln/ mengen/ verschwesteren und verbrüderen/ und also/ so wol an menge als Lieblichkeit allerhand Reimarten/ nicht sage ich keiner anderen Sprache etwas zuvorgeben/ sonderen behalten hierin offenbarlich/ und durch Ausspruch der Sonnenklaren Warheit den Vortrit und die Oberstell: Wie dan auch hierzu nicht wenig hilft das jenige/ was der Suchender in dem dritten Buche von der vielfältigen/ und bißhero unbewusten lustigen lieblichen Enderungen der Versen nach derer Reimschlüssen/ Reimungen und Sätzen/ hervorgebracht hat. Wohin nur ein Sinnreicher Geist seine Gedancken und Einfälle lenket/ begegnet jhm alhie mit gnüglichkeit unsere Teutsche Sprache/ beut das Geschmükke und Gezierde da/ aufs mannigfaltigste unsere Erfindungen einzukleiden. Ein Sprachverständiger uhrteile recht/ wie weit die anderen [B r] Sprachen hierin unserer hochgelobtē MutterSprache gleichen werden. Jch setze zum Exempel/ daß die Frantzosen zwar einen Versuch gethan haben/ unseren lieblich fliessenden Dactilischen arten nachzuahmen/ aber unglüklich/ wie zu sehen aus ihrem gemeinen Liedlein

Bergere voyezcy la saison, &c.

Da sie doch sonsten sagen *Bergere la saison*.

Erhellet demnach aus dieser **des Suchenden neuergründeter Anführung**/ daß unsere Poesis viel weiter gerathen und zu gewisserem Stande gekommen/ als vorerwehnter Sprachen befliessene/ noch zur zeit in dem jhrigen es vermöcht haben: Ungeachtet jhnen von hochverstendigen Königen/ Cardinälen/ Fürsten und Herren/ jederzeit die hülfliche Gnadenhand geboten worden; Welchen nemlich nicht unwissend/ daß sie sterben müssen wie andere Menschen/ Gott aber jhnen vor anderen Menschen die Mittel gegeben/ Sich durch Guhttätigkeit gegen die Poeten unsterblich zumachen.

Denen mancherley Abwechselungen/ Bindungen/ von- und zusammen-setzungen der Reimarten ist nicht ein geringes Meisterstük [B v] zuzueignen/ eine sondere Bewegung in unser Gemüthe zu spielen/ wie davon *Aristoteles* und *Jules de la Mesnardiere f. 415*. ein mehrers beweislich anführen/ und also vom *Euripide, Sophocle, Seneca, Francesco de Rojas, Manzini* vorbesagtem *Mesnardiere*[f 13] und anderen verstendig gebrauchet worden.

Der liebliche **Versthon** belüstiget unsere Ohren; die Bescheidenheit der Sache (von *Aristotele Poet. cap. 25 Eukrinea* genant) den Verstand: Daher *Scaliger* von seinem Poeten erfodert/ benebenst der Klugheit unerwarteter einfälle/ **die nachdrükliche/ eingrifige und Sinnbeherschende Süßigkeit der Wörter**: Jn dem nemlich tapfere Gedanken aus der Sache selbst geschöpfet/ und nicht bey den haaren/ wie wir zu reden pflegē herbey gezogen/ die Redart rein und scheinlich/ ohne unzeitige Härtligkeit/ selbstfliessend in das Gedicht geleitet werden sollen.[14]

Dieser Fehler ist sonderlich zu bemerken/ wan die Vernennung (*Metaphora*) nicht fortgesetzet wird/ wie beim *Horatio*:

Et malè tornatos incudi reddere versûs.[15]

Wan auf der Trexelbank der Vers ist gantz zergliedet
Hört mā dē Ambosschall daß mā jhn wieder schmiedet [B 2 r]

Und Petracha spricht vom *Virgilio* uñ *Circerone*:
    Questi sono gli occhi della lingua nostra.[16]
Die Augen unserer Zungen/ bedünket mich sei wider den natürlichen Verstand geredt/ denn die Augen so wenig auf der Zungen/ als auf den Versen nützen. So ist auch fast lächerlich/ wan man eine betrübte und bestürtzte Person Kunstzierlich redend einführet/ da doch die wahl der Wort bey solcher Person so wenig seyn kan/ als der Gegenschein eines Bildniß/ in einem trüben Wasser. Dieses aber und derogleichen Gehörte[g] zu der **Dichtkunst**/ davon zu ende des dritten Buches der Suchende[b] alhier etwas vermeld;[17] die Hofnung aber uns dennoch übrig bleibet/ Teutschliebende gelahrte Gemüther werden auch hierin den Griechen/ Lateinern/ Spaniern und Franzosen/ den Vortheil und Ruhm nicht lassen; sonderen[e]/ weil die Form der Verskunst/ als der Grund dieses Gebeues/ numehr wol angewiesen/ mit rechter Meisterhand und Kunstgründiger Wolständlichkeit das volle Kunstgebeu zu fernerem ende setzen. Uns hiermit beiderseits Göttlicher Obhut befehlend verbleibt

Nürnberg den 20.   **Des Suchenden**
des Weinmonats /   treuverbundener Freund
im Jahre[h] 1644.   **Der Spielende.**

T a C *Statt der Anrede* Des Hochgelahrten/ berühmten und nunmehr seeligen Mannes Herrn Harsdorfers Meinung und Uhrteihl über die invention Dieses Buches. — **b** *Statt der vorherrschenden Polyflektion in der* Suchender *hier A, B, C* der Suchende — **c** *C* über le mal Druckfehler ˜ ˜ — **d** *A, B, C* Senetto — **e** *C* sondern — **f** *A, B, C* Mesnediere — **g** *Wie B. Dagegen C* gehörte — **h** *C Druckfehler* Jahr Jahre

K 1 Der Stoff dieser Poetik (Schottelius: *Teutsche Vers- oder ReimKunst* [1645], s. 440900 K 2) wird in drei Büchern über „Maasforschung", den Versbau („Reimfügung") u. „Abtheilung und Ordnung der Reimarten [...] nach den Reimschlüssen und Reimen" abgehandelt. Vgl. 431028A K 3 u. *DA Köthen I. 9:* 450126. — Zum Vorwerk der Ausgabe von 1645 (vgl. 450100 K 13): Dem Kupfertitel folgen auf Bl. [A]v ein Motto von Tacitus, sodann
1.)   eine „ZueignungsSchrift" von Justus Georg Schottelius (FG 397. Der Suchende) in Gedichtform an Hzn. Sophia Elisabeth v. Braunschweig-Wolfenbüttel (AL 1629;

TG 42b), Gemahlin Hz. Augusts d.J. (FG 227) (Bl. [Aij]rv). S. 441200 I. Die Zierinitiale mit ihrem Porträt (s. dazu 450219 K 8) fehlt in der Ausg. von 1656.
2.) Ein Kupferporträt der Herzogin mit daruntergesetzten dt. Versen von Schottelius (Bl. [Aiij]r). Abbildung u. Verse fehlen in der Ausg. von 1656. S. 441200 I u. 450100 K 13.
3.) Georg Philipp Harsdörffer (FG 368. Der Spielende): „Madrigal Sur le Portrait de son Altesse" (frz.). (Bl. [Aiij]v). S. 441200 II, Bl. [Aiij]v. Fehlt in der Ausg. von 1656.
4.) Emblem Carl Gustav v. Hilles (FG 302), des Unverdrossenen, mit Inscriptio (Widmung) u. Gedicht (Subscriptio) „Dem Suchenden" (Bl. [Aiv]r – [Av]r).
5.) Rauchfaß-Sinnbild Georg Philipp Harsdörffers mit Inscriptio u. Subscriptio-Gedicht (Bl. [Av]v–[Avi]v).
6.) Der vorliegende Brief Harsdörffers an Schottelius, d. d. Nürnberg 20.10.1644 (Bl. [Avij]r – B2 r), dieses Dokument 441020.
7.) Lat. Epigramm Abraham Marconnets (Präzeptor Pz. Rudolf Augusts v. Braunschweig-Wolfenbüttel, FG 754. 1660) (Bl. B2 v).
8.) Johann Rist (FG 467. 1647): „Sinne Bild"-Porträt des Perlenfischers Schottelius mit auslegendem Gedicht, d. d. Wedel 16.12. o. J. (1644) (Bl. Biij r – Biiij v). S. 441216.
9.) Dt. Gedicht Johann Michael Moscheroschs (FG 436. 1645), d. d. Benfelden 1.10.1644 (Bl. Biiij v – Bv r).
10.) Henricus Becker, dt. Gedicht, d. d. Einbeck 18.11.1644 (Bl. Bv rv).
11.) Samuel Hund (PBO): Dreiständiges Sinnbild mit Inscriptio und auslegendem Gedicht, undat. (Bl. [Bvi]r – [Bvij]r).
12.) Schottelius lat. Vorrede an den Leser, d.d. 26.1.1645. S. *DA Köthen I. 9:* 450126.
13.) „INDEX RERUM Oder kurtzer Jnhalts-Register" (Bl. Ciij r – [Cvi]v).
14.) Druckfehler (Bl. [Cvij]rv).
15.) Hinweis von Schottelius auf Sternchen-Markierung selbstverfaßter Beispielgedichte (Bl. [Cvij]v).
16.) Eine weitere „Erinnerung" (Bl. [Cviij]rv).
Schottelius schickte seine *Teutsche Vers- oder ReimKunst (1645)* an Hz. August mit einem Schreiben (450202), das dieser zusammen mit dem vorliegenden Brief an Andreae weitersandte. Er verlangte den Brief von Andreae zurück, schenkte ihm aber das Buchexemplar. S. 450202 K 1. An F. Ludwig sandte Schottelius das Werk mit 450204.

2 Fruchtbringende Gesellschaft.

3 Trotz der Anwendung des antiken Quantitätenschemas spielt in Georg Philipp Harsdörffers (FG 368. Der Spielende) deutscher Prosodie u. Metrik Martin Opitz' (FG 200) Kriterium des Zusammenfalls von natürlichem Wortakzent u. metrischer Betonung (*Opitz: Buch von der Deutschen Poeterey [1624]*) die entscheidende Rolle, so daß der Spielende die romanische Verskunst nach deutschen Maßstäben beurteilen kann. Deshalb vermeint er, Fehler der romanischen Dichter feststellen u. die deutsche Verskunst herausstellen zu können. Die Redensart der Ohren (oder des Gehörs) als Kunstrichter geht auf antike Vorbilder zurück. Vgl. Hor. ars v. 386ff.: „id tibi iudicium est, ea mens. siquid tamen olim scripseris, in Maeci descendat iudicis auris et patris et nostras"; Mart. ep. 6, 1 „Tergere libellum aure diligenti". Obgleich an sich nicht ungewöhnlich, verdient diese Redensart doch bei Harsdörffer auch in anderer Hinsicht Aufmerksamkeit, da er wenige Jahre später in seiner *Lobrede des Geschmackes* (1651) als erster Deutscher eine Auffassung vom Sprachgeschmack entwickelt. Vgl. *GB 1646* (s. Ausg. Bircher 1971) u. *Conermann: Akademie, Kritik und Geschmack.* — Harsdörffer war ursprünglich in seiner eigenen Poetik ausgegangen von den in seinen *Frauenzimmer-Gesprächspielen* II (¹1642), 201–204 geäußerten Meinungen. Degenwert ließ er dort im 85. Gesprächspiel erklären:

„Unsere Sprach ist noch ungeübt in der Poeterey/ uñ ich wolte gern sagē solcher fast unfähig/ wann die Reimen sollen nach den Reguln der Griechen und Lateiner gerichtet werden. Man kan zwar wol die Wort zusammennöhten/ es hat aber doch keine rechte Art/ weil die Stuffen (pedes) unserer Wort meistentheils bestehen/ in doppel-langen (— — spondæis), und Lang-kurtzen (— ◡ trochæis) in wenig kurtz-langen (◡ — Jambis,) in noch weniger lang-gekürtzten (— ◡ ◡ dactylis,) da in diesen Letzten die gröste Lieblichkeit ist." Raymund unterscheidet nach hebräischem Muster „dreyerley Reimwort": lange oder männliche Silben (wie „Kunst/ Gunst"), zweisilbige oder weibliche „Reimenworten" mit lang-kurzer Silbenfolge (wie „loben/ toben"). Die dritte Art hebr. Reimsilben, nämlich dreisilbige, sei im Deutschen „nicht gebräuchlich". „Die Stuffē (pedes) sind bey den Ebreern nur zweyerley/ die erste bestehet in einer langen Sylbē/ [...] die andere in zweyen/ als nemlich in einer langen und kurtzen Sylben [...] Bey uns Teutschen aber ist auch unlangst/ von den Welt-berühmten Herrn August Buchner/ die dritte Stuffen erfunden worden/ nemlich die lang-gekürtzte/ oder der Dactylus, als
gŭldēnē/ lŏblĭchē/ &c. Bey den Gespräch-Spielen aber muß man nicht alles nach der Kunst außmessen/ sondern was jedem beyfält gerne anhören/ wolmeinend verbessern/ und mehr vernünfftiger Beurth[ei]lung untergeben." Die zit. Passagen übereinstimmend auch in der 2. Ausgabe des 2. Teils der *Frauenzimmer-Gesprächspiele* (1657, Ndr. 1968), 239 f./ Ndr. 257 f.

4 Pierre de Ronsard (1524–1585): LES ECLOGVES ET MASCARADES, DE P. DE RONSARD, GENTILhomme Vandomois. ... PLVS, LES ELEGIES ET LES HYMNES du mesme Auteur. TOME IIII (Lyon: Thomas Soubron 1592), 100 (LE CYCLOPE AMOVREVX, v. 1 f.):
COntre le mal d'amour qui tous les maux excede,
L'artifice n'inuente vn plus present remede
Soit pillule ou breuuage, emplastres ou liqueurs,
Que la science apprinse à l'eschole des sœurs.
SB München: 71499774 P.o.gall; dig. Harsdörffer benutzte vielleicht die Ausgabe „Pierre de Ronsard: Poësies. 8. Paris 1587". S. *Harsdörffer: Frauenzimmer-Gesprächspiele* I (1641), Bl. Dd 6r.

5 Marc Antoine de Gérard de Saint-Amant (1594–1661): LES OEUVRES DV SIEVR DE SAINT-AMANT (Paris: François Pomeray et Toussainct Quinet 1629: Rob. Estienne), 129 (ELEGIE A DAMON), v. 1:
DAMON, ie languissoit dans vn sombre silence,
ÖNB Wien: *38.D.15; dig.; diese Ausgabe erwähnt in *Harsdörffer: Frauenzimmer-Gesprächspiele* IV (1644, Ndr. 1968), 714.

6 François de Malherbe (1555–1628); Guillaume Colletet (1598–1659). Zitat François de Belleforest (1530–1583): Le 6 Tome Des Histoires Tragiques (Lyon: Farine 1583), 154–156 (SB München: 6035407 P. o.it. 104; dig.): "Ce Gentil-homme quoy qu'il ne fust des plus riches, estoit neantmoins orné, & doüé de plusieurs graces, & dons requis en vn homme de sa qualité, veu que outre les armes qui luy sembloyent estres nees au poing, il sçauoit quelque peu aux lettres, & s'adonnoit à faire quelques vers, plus guidé du naturel, que de la doctrine, comme on en voit vn nombre infiny en France, lesquels sans auoir iamais gousté la mesure des vers latins, poetisent en leur lãgue, auec assez d'heur, & suyuans la grauité de ceux qui s'en font dire maistres, de sorte que ce Gentil-homme accompagnant les rithmes auec la Musique, gaignoit la grace de chacun, & se rendoit amye celle qu'il souhaitoit pour sa maistresse, toutesfoys l'humeur farouche du Capitaine le destournoit de poursuivre sa poincte & luy glaçoit ses desseins, tout aussi tost qu'il leur donnoit quelque ouuerture, & noisoit œillarder celle qui le regardoit de bon cœur, estimant qu'elle vsait de tels apasts, pour

se moquer, ou bien pour voir s'il serait si mal apris, que de, s'enhardir de descouvrir son affectiō, pour puis apres en faire ses cōptes, ou s'en plaindre au general son frere; dequoy vn iour estant fort calme, & eux hors de la peine de voguer, se mit à chanter ces vers sur vn luth, qu'il auoit porté pour accongner son harquebuze, & pour s'en dōner plaisir, apres le son effroyable des canons qui estoient dans le navire pour leur deffence.
Chanson de l'Amant.
Helas ô filles Athlantides,
Riches & belles Hesperides
Qui autour de voz bleues eaux
Entendez flotter noz vaissaux. [...]"
Harsdörffer verkehrt Belleforests Lob einer natürlichen, der antiken Verskunst enthobenen französischen Poesie geradezu in einen Mangel an docta poesis, die er in der von Schottelius wiederentdeckten *Teutsche[n] Vers- oder ReimKunst (1645)* rühmt. Er benutzte wohl die Ausgabe: „Fran. de BELLE-FOREST: Histoires Tragiques. 12. Rouen. 1602." S. *Harsdörffer: Frauenzimmer-Gesprächspiele* I (1641), Bl. Cc 7v.

7 Petrarca, Sonetto 29: „S'io credesse per morte essere scarco". Francesco Petrarca: Canzoniere. Introd. R. Antonelli, Testo critico e saggio di G. Contini, Note al testo di D. Ponchiroli. Torino 1964, 50 (Son. 36); ders.: Rime, trionfi e poesie latine. A cura di F. Neri et al. Milano, Napoli o. J., 52 (Son. 36). Postume Ausgaben des 16. u. 17. Jh.s haben meistens wie heute normalisiertes „credessi" (1. Pers. Sg. Imperf. Konj.). Vgl. PETRARCA COLLA SPOSITIONE DI MISSER GIOVANNI ANDREA GESVALDO (o. O. 1541), Bl. LIIII „S'IO credessi per morte scarco"; IL PETRARCHA CON L'ESPOSITIONE D'ALESSANDRO VELLVTELLO (Venetia: Al Segno della Speranza 1550), Bl. 14v „S'IO credessi per morte essere scarco"; IL PETRARCA CON DICHIARATIONI NON PIV STAMPATE. Insieme con alcune belle Annotationi, tratte dalle dottißime Prose di Monsignor Bembo (Venetia: Nicolò Bevilacqua 1568), 50: „S'io credeßi per morte scarco"; IL PETRARCA RIVEDVTO, ET CORRETTO (Vinegiae: Gio. Griphio 1573), Bl. 15r „S'io credeßi per morte essere scarco"; IL PETRARCA CON NVOVE SPOSITIONI Et alcune ... Annotationi d'intorno alle regole della lingua Toscana (Venetia: Giorgo Angelieri 1586), 65 (Sonetto XXIX): „s'io credessi per morte essere scarco"; IL PETRARCA NVOVAMENTE Ridotto alla vera Lettione. Con vn Nuouo Discorso sopra la qualità del suo amore (Venetia: Mattio Zanetti u. Comino Presegni 1595), 28: „S'io credessi per morte essere scarco". Vgl. dagegen LE RIME DEL PETRARCA breuemente sposte PER LODOVICO CASTELVETRO (Basilea: Pietro de Sedabonis 1582), 82: „S'io credesse per morte scarco". Harsdörffer benutzte vielleicht die Ausgabe „Fr. PETRARCA: opere 12. Lione. 1547." S. *Harsdörffer: Frauenzimmer-Gesprächspiele* I (1641), Bl. Dd 5r.

8 Dante Alighieri: La Divina Commedia. A cura di Natalino Sapegno. Vol. I Inferno. Firenze 1955, 28; canto 3 (v. 1–3): „Per me si va nella città dolente, per me si va nell'eterno dolore, per me si va tra la perduta gente [...]".

9 D. i. verfehlen, versäumen. *Stieler*, 1281 „Jch habe ihn underwegens vermißt/ perdidi eum in viâ, aberravi ab ejus vestigiis." *DW* XII.1, 877 (mit Harsdörffers Satz).

10 Félix Lope de Vega Carpio (1562–1635): Arcadia con una esposicion de los nombres Historicos y Poeticos — a Don Pedro Tellez Giron, Duque de Ossuna, &c. (Anvers: Bellero 1617), 443 (HAB: 154.2.1 Eth.; SB München: 1135326 P.o.hisp., dig.: „Condenó la vida ociosa, el loco amor, y los desseos solecitos, y desseoso de mostrar lo que de passo en tã famosas escuelas auia visto, dandole primero la sabia del agua versifera de la Cabalina corriente, escogiendo por sujeto las alabanças del famoso Duque de Alua don Fernando, y el nacimiento de su heroyco nieto, como en vaticinio, y arrebatado de vn furor poetico

(como Platon dixo que no por arte, sino mouidos de vn diuino aliento, cantauā los poetas estos preclaros versos, llenos de deydad, y agenos de si mismos, que Aristoteles y Ciceron llamauan furia) escuchandole Frondoso canto assi:
    ANFRISO.
 ALtos desseos de cantar me encienden
    El nacimiento del heroyco Albano:
    Tan alta empresa, y no menor emprenden."
Harsdörffer benutzte wahrscheinlich die Ausgabe „Lope de VEGA Carpio [...] Arcadia 12. Anvers. 1611." S. *Harsdörffer: Frauenzimmer-Gesprächspiele* I (1641), Bl. Dd 7v.

11 Juan Perez de Montalvan (1602–1638): SVCESSOS Y PRODIGIOS DE AMOR EN OCHO NOVELAS Exemplares. POR. EL LICENCIADO IVAN Perez de Montalvan, natural de Madrid. Dirigidas à diuersas personas. (Brusselas 1626: Huberto Antonio), 75 (La fuerça del desengaño):
    No os lastime el amor que he de teneros,
    Aunque con ella mueren todo el año:
SB München: 129 980892 P.o.hisp.; dig.

12 Jorge de Montemayor (1520–1561) [u. Gaspar Gil Polo (1535–1591)]. Vgl. die dt. Übersetzung: DIANA Von H. J. De Monte-Major, in zweyen Theilen Spanisch beschrieben/ und aus denselben geteutschet Durch ... Johann Ludwigen Freyherrn von Kueffstein/ etc. An jetzo aber Mit deß Herrn C. G. Polo zuvor nie gedolmetschten dritten Theil vermehret/ und Mit reinteutschen Red- wie auch neu-üblichen Reim-arten ausgezieret. Durch G. P. H. [Georg Philipp Harsdörffer, Mitübersetzer Johann Klaj] (Nürnberg: Michael Endter 1646). Vgl. 451217 K 7. — Die beiden Freunde Juan Boscán Almogávar (um 1490–1542) u. Garcilasso de la Vega (1503–1536) gehören zu den frühen Renaissance-Poeten Spaniens. Vgl. Las obras de Boscan, Y Algvnas de Garcilasso dela Vega, Repartidas en quatro Libros (Barcelona 1554: Viuda Carles Amorosa); auch schon Lisboa: Rodriguez 1543.

13 Hippolyte Jules Pilet de La Mesnardière (1610–1663): LA POETIQVE DE IVLES DE LA MESNARDIERE. TOME PREMIER (Paris: Antoine de Sommaville 1639), 414 [Randnote: „Horreur nécessaire aux Prisons de Théatre, & pour quelle raison."] „La noirceur & l'obscurité éclairées d'vn rayon de feu, & d'vne lumiere sombre, rendront la Prison effroyable; pource que l'intention du Poëte dans la pluspart des Tragédies est d'émouuoir la Compassion pour la Personne captiue; & que plus ces lieux sont horribles, plus ils touchent le Spectateur par vn sentiment de Pitié. Ce que ie dis pour les Prisons, pourra estre appliqué aux Grottes. [...] Mais si ces Antres solitaires tiennēt lieu d'vne Prison, comme par exemple la grotte creusée dans le Mont Cytheron, où le Roy confine Antigone dans la Tragédie de Sophocle; il faut [415] que ce lieu ténébreux n'ait point d'ouuerture [...]." La Mesnardière spricht angelehnt an Aristoteles' Poetik von der Kunst des Poeten, den Zuschauer durch Gefängnisse, Grotten u. andere Orte effektiv u. der Wahrscheinlichkeit nach emotional zu bewegen.

14 Harsdörffer übersetzt εὐκρίνεια (zu κρίνω scheide, wähle aus, (be)urteile, entscheide) mit *Bescheidenheit*, etwa im Sinne von discretio. *Diefenbach/ Wülcker*, 199. Das Wort oder eines seiner Verwandten kommt aber nicht in der Poetik des Aristoteles vor, nur als Adjektiv in Problemata XI.33, wo der Philosoph von der Frage handelt, warum die Nacht hellhöriger als der Tag ist. Eine der angebotenen Erklärungen ist, daß das Gehör am Tage schlechter als in der Nacht unterscheiden kann, weil tagsüber die Körper den Geist zerstreuen oder ablenken: „διὸ οὐκ εὐκρινές ἐστι πρὸς τὴν ἀκοήν". Aristotelis Opera ex recensione Immanuelis Bekkeri edidit Academia Regia Borussica. Editio altera quam curavit Olof Gigon. 5 vol.a, I, 903 a 17. Harsdörffer bezog seine Information wohl nicht aus Herm. Id. 202.2 (Hermogenis Opera. Ed. Hugo Rabe. Lipsiae 1913, 226, 14 ff.), sondern aus Scaligers Kritik an Hermogenes' mangelnder Einteilung der Klarheit/ Deutlichkeit (σαφήνεια claritas) in Reinheit (καταρόντητα puritas) u. Wohlgeordnetheit (εὐκρίνεια). Hermogenes fasse εὐκρίνεια als elegantia (Erlesenheit) auf, während die bei den alten Grammatikern eher als facilitas zu übersetzen sei. Hermogenes bezeichne mit dem Wort zwar auch die umsichtige Anordnung, was Scaliger auf die Erklärung von εὐκρίνεια als distinctio bringt. Scaliger will sie deutlich von dem Verständnis dieser Stilnorm als elegantia trennen, welche erlesene Wörter gebrauche, also die Deutlichkeit vermindere. Harsdörffer scheint also mit Bescheidenheit Scaligers Verständnis von εὐκρίνεια zu folgen. Auch im folgenden bezeichnet Scaligers 4. Buch die Quelle für Harsdörffers Stilkriterien. Vgl. Iulius Caesar Scaliger: Poetices libri septem. Sieben Bücher über die Dichtkunst. U. Mitwirkung v. M. Fuhrmann hg. v. L. Deitz u. G. Vogt-Spira. 6 Bde. Stuttgart-Bad Cannstatt 1994–2011, III, 289–293 (Scaliger IV.1, 180a). Vgl. 460131 K 19.

15 Hor. ars, v. 441: Quintilius ermahnt den Poeten, schlecht gedrechselte Verse von neuem auf dem Amboß zu schmieden. Das paßt nach Harsdörffer nicht zur Metapher der gedrechselten Verse. Gegen den nachfolgend zitierten Petrarca-Vers erhebt er daher auch Einwände.

16 Petrarca: Trionfi (Triumphus Fame), c. 3, v. 16–21 (Rime, trionfi e poesie latine. A cura di F. Neri et al. Milano, Napoli o. J., 543 f.) über Vergil u. Cicero:
    A man a man con lui cantando giva
il Mantoan, che di' par seco giostra:
ed uno, al cui passar l'erba fioriva;
    quest' è quel Marco Tullio, in cui si mostra
chiaro quanti 'ha eloquenzia à frutti e fiori;
questi son gli occhi de la lingua nostra.
Vgl. dagegen die Übersetzung in *Fürst Ludwig: Sechs Triumphi oder Siegesprachten* (1643), 126: „Ja das sie bringet vor dar reicher früchte lohn/ Der reinen Muttersprach' her tregt die edle kron".

17 *Schottelius: Teutsche Vers- oder ReimKunst (1645)*, 315–317: „Jn vörigen Bücheren ist gnugsamlich von den Teutschen Reimarten/ so wol wie sie nach den Reimschlüssen/ als nach den Reimmaassen zuerkennen/ zubetrachten und zumachen sein gesagt: Nun aber were nach aller lenge übrig/ wie die Reimarten nach der **Materi** selbst/ davon sie handelen/ unter sich zu theilen/ nach rechter Eigenschaft zubetrachten und zuverfertigen sein. […] daran es noch zur zeit in unserem Teutschen oft mangelen/ und man dieselbe mit verlohrner Mühe suchen würde. Sonsten hat der hochberühmter Held *Iulius Scaliger* aufs aller subtileste/ weitleuftigste und gründlichste Bericht gethan/ wie in diesen erwehnten uñ allen anderen Stükken der Poetischen Kunst/ man sich recht verhalten und anweisen lassen künne: […] Wiewol wir doch in einem und anderen/ sonderlich in Freuden- und Traurspielen/ nicht eben nach der Griechen und Lateiner Gesetzen/ sonderen vielmehr nach unseren und jtzigen Arten und Weisen solche Spiele zuverfertigen/ uns einzurichten haben möchten […]."

441200

Justus Georg Schottelius an Herzog August d. J. von Braunschweig-Wolfenbüttel

Justus Georg Schottelius (FG 397) schickt Herzog August d. J. v. Braunschweig-Wolfenbüttel (FG 227) ein Gedicht der Heldenart (auf dessen Gemahlin Hzn. Sophia Elisabeth, geb. Pzn. v. Mecklenburg-Güstrow [AL 1629, TG 42b]). Er wisse nicht, ob er dies tun müsse, doch haben ihn der Eifer um die Dichtkunst und der Anlaß dazu bestimmt. Zwar fragt sich Schottelius, ob das Gedicht überhaupt lesenswürdig sei, doch wolle er dem Herzog so seine Verehrung bekunden.

Q NSTA Wolfenbüttel: 2 Alt Nr. 40, Bl. 25rv; A (Absender) 25v; eigenh.

A *Nicht vorhanden.* — *Absender:* Schöttelius

Serenissime, Illustrissime Princeps Domine clementissime

Cecini hosce Jambos heroici generis,[1] pro exiguo Teutisces Musæ favore: porrigendos, dubitavj: vicit tamen amor Et in rem eam ipsam propensio, cuius causâ enatj erant.

An perlectu quodammodo digni, nescio: Unum fuit, Vestræ Serenitati quod exiguum devotissime mentis attestationem humillimè relinquere voluit

Eidem obedientis*simè* inserviens
Justus-Georgius Schottel*ius*

I

Schottelius' Widmungsgedicht auf Herzogin Sophia Elisabeth von Braunschweig-Wolfenbüttel

Q [Kupfertitel] Iusti-Georgii | Schottelii | Teutsche Vers- oder | ReimKunst | darin | Vnsere Teutsche | MutterSprache/ So viel | dero süßeste Po- | esis betrifft/ in eine | richtige Form der | Kunst Zum ersten | mahle gebracht | worden. | getruckt Zu | Wolfenbüttel | in Verlegung | deß Authoris | im jahre M DC XL V. Kolophon: „Gedruckt zu Wulffenbüttel/ durch Johann Bißmarck/ | Jm Jahr 1645, nicht signiert. Bl. [Aij]rv. HAB: 172. 1 Poet.; SUB Göttingen: 8 P GERM I, 1290; dig. Gedicht auch in der 2. Ausg. von 1656 (zit. als *B*), s. 441020 K 1.

ZueignungsSchrift an die
Durchleuchtige und Hochgeborne
Fürstinn und Frau/ Frau
Sophien Elisabeth/
Vermählte Hertzogiñ zu Braunschweig und
Lüneburg/ &c. Geborne von Meckelburg/ Fürstinn zu
Wenden/ Gräffin zu Schwerin/ Der Landen
Stargard und Rostock Frauen.

> Die Durchl. Hochgeborne Fürstinn und Fraü, Fraü
> Sophia Elisabeth, hertzogin Zu Braunschweig und Luneburg etc.
> geborne von Meckelburg, Fürstin der Wenden, Gräffin Zü Schwerin,
> der Landen Stargard und Rostock Fraü

> Weil die tugend wesentlich, und der wahren liebe blitz
> Nur im himmel hat den sitz;
> Fleucht sie unsren erdenklumpf, wird von uns nicht angebl.
> Nur ein ebenbild uns schickt.
> Wiltü denn das Tügendbild, hoher liebe schönsten plan
> Schaü! Schaü diese Fürstinn an.
>
> J. G. Schottelius.
>
> Subiectissimæ observantiæ ergò ad vivum exsculpsit et dedicat Conr. Buno.

Bildnis der Herzogin Sophia Elisabeth von Braunschweig-Wolfenbüttel (AL 1629. TG 42b) mit Versen von Justus Georg Schottelius (FG 397). Zu 441200 I.

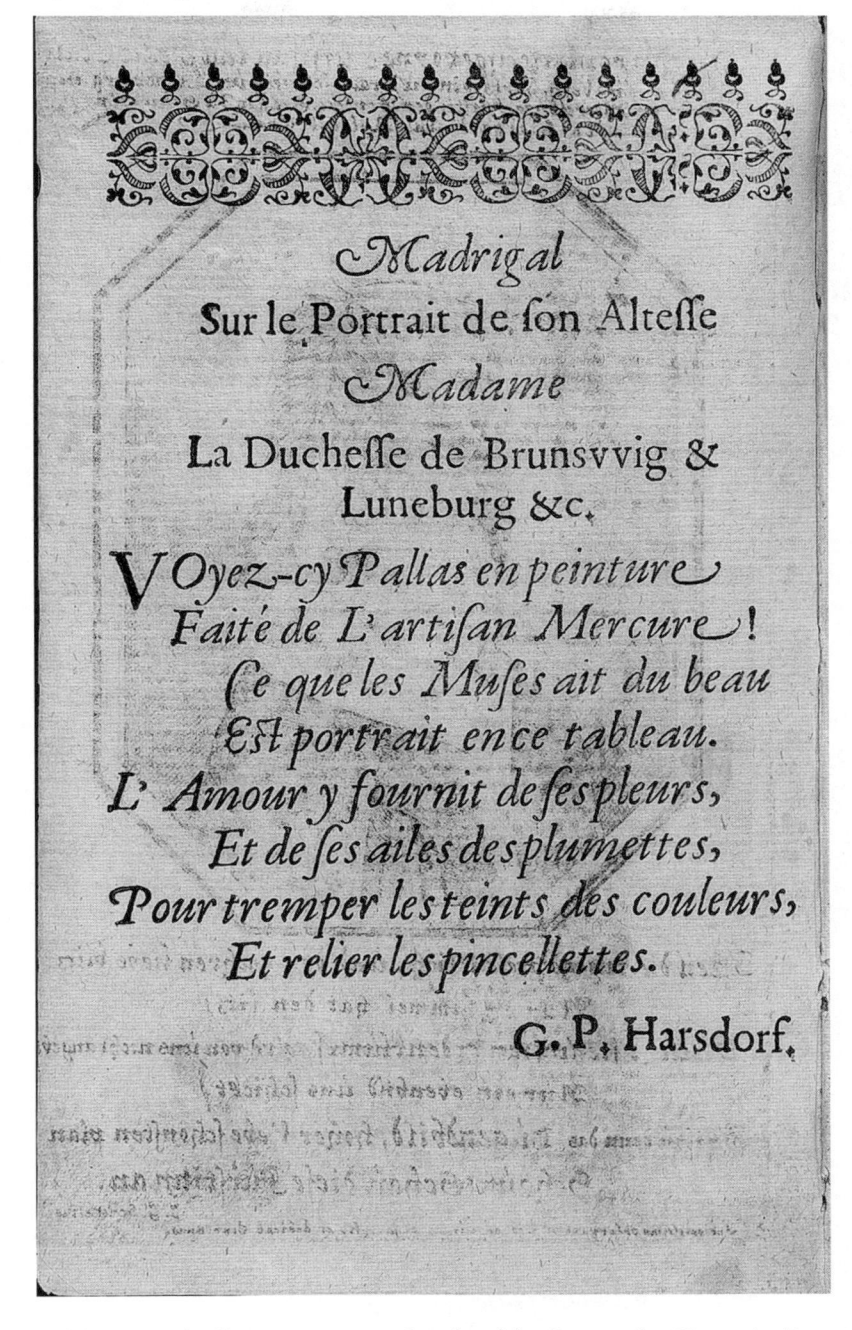

Madrigal
Sur le Portrait de son Altesse
Madame
La Duchesse de Brunsvvig & Luneburg &c.

VOyez-cy Pallas en peinture
Faite de L'artisan Mercure!
Ce que les Muses ait du beau
Est portrait en ce tableau.
L' Amour y fournit de ses pleurs,
Et de ses ailes des plumettes,
Pour tremper les teints des couleurs,
Et relier les pincellettes.

G. P. Harsdorf.

Georg Philipp Harsdörffers (FG 368) Madrigal auf das Porträt der Herzogin. Zu 441200 II.

JHr Edle Princessin/ deß Himmels Hertz und Wonne
Der Menschen Lust und Zier/ der Tugend schöne Sonne/
    Nemt gnadenwillig an/ mit hochbegabter Hand
    Von Teutscher MusenZunfft ein schüldig-treues[a] Pfand.
Es wil durchaus nicht mehr nur auff Parnassi Spitzen
Das süsse MusenVolk in schöner Reihe sitzen:
    Wir lokken sie zu uns durch Teutscher Sprache macht/
    Vnd schmücken sie durch Glück mit höher WörterPracht[b]. [Aij v]
Es fodert das Geschick auch unser neu beginnen/
Wir baun ein Ehrenschloß[1] hier bey den Welfenzinnen/
    Dort wo die Pegnitz kreucht/ wo unser Asch[2] gehaußt/
    Und wo der Bober fleußt/ und wo die Elbe saußt.[3]
Reumt euren Helicon jhr schönen Castelinnen/
Besucht des Mannen-Land/[4] und unsre Semaninnen:
    Apollo richte recht/ ob hie sey oder dort/
    Ein besser Tugendplatz und schöner Ehrenort.
Verweilt Calliope? geneigt den frömden Landen
Eilt nur selb-Achte her/ Eur Haubt ist schon verhanden
    Die höchste Pieris/ und schönste Charitiñ
    Und Phebi liebstes Hertz ist diese Princessiñ.

II

Georg Philipp Harsdörffers Madrigal auf das Porträt der Herzogin

Q *Schottelius: Teutsche Vers- oder ReimKunst (1645)*, Bl. [Aiij]v. Vgl. Beil. I. Das Madrigal fehlt ebenso wie das Porträt der Herzogin in *Schottelius: Teutsche Vers- oder ReimKunst (1656)*.

Madrigal
Sur le Portraict de son Altesse
Madame
La Duchesse de Brunsvvig & Luneburg &c.

VOyez-cy Pallas en peinture
Faite de L'artisan Mercure!
    Ce que les Muses ait du beau
    Est portrait en ce tableau.
L'Amour y fournit de ses pleurs,
    Et de ses ailes des plumettes,
Pour tremper les teints des couleurs,
    Et relier les pincelettes.
        G. P. Harsdorf.

T I a *B* schuldig-treues — b *B* Wörter Pracht

K 1 Heldenart, d.h. paargereimte Alexandriner. S.391119 I S.328 u. zur hier benutzten Variante S.329–335 („Die rechte Helden artt anfahende mitt weiblicher endung von Dreyzehen und zwelff Sylben"). S. auch *Schottelius: Teutsche Vers- oder ReimKunst (1645)*, 220–222 („Heldenart/ sich anfahend mit Fallender Reimung"). Vgl. *Schottelius: Teutsche Vers- oder ReimKunst (1656)*, 179–181.

K I Vgl. 441020 K 1 u. *DA Köthen I. 9*: 450126. Holzschnitt-Initiale J mit dem Hüftbild Hzn. Sophia Elisabeths v. Braunschweig-Wolfenbüttel, geb. Hzn. v. Mecklenburg-Güstrow (AL 1629. TG 42b), 3. Gemahlin Hz. Augusts d.J. v. Braunschweig-Wolfenbüttel (FG 227). S. Abb. (Porträt) S.368 u. Abb. (Madrigal) S.369.
1 Eine Säulenhalle sollte bald darauf Georg Philipp Harsdörffer (FG 368) in seiner Dichtung *Porticus Virtutis* Hzn. Sophia Elisabeths Gemahl Hz. August d.J. errichten. S. 450927, 460112, 460406, 460912, 461204A, *DA Köthen I. 8*: 470114 u. 470215.
2 Asch bzw. Ascenas, Nachfahr Noahs u. Stammvater der Celten u. der celtischen (d.i. deutschen) Sprache. Vgl. *Schottelius: Sprachkunst (1641)*, 60f.; *Schottelius: Ausführliche Arbeit (1663)*, 34f. Vgl. 400528 K II 4.
3 Die Anspielung auf die Welfenzinnen (Festung Wolfenbüttel), Pegnitz, Bober u. Elbe weist auf die Sitze vieler als Sprachreformer u. Dichter maßgeblichen Mitglieder der FG u. der mit ihnen u. besonders Justus Georg Schottelius (FG 397) vernetzten Zeitgenossen hin: Wolfenbüttel (Hz. August, Schottelius), Pegnitz (Nürnberg: Georg Philipp Harsdörffer, FG 368; Johann Klaj, Johann Michael Dilherr), Bober (Martin Opitz v. Boberfeld, FG 200), Elbe (Anhalt: F. Ludwig; Diederich v. dem Werder, FG 31; Wedel/ Holstein: Johann Rist, FG 467. 1647).
4 Zu Mannus, dem Sohn des Erdgotts Tuisco (Tuisto) u. seiner Gattin Sonna s. neben Tac. germ. c. 2 auch Christian Gueintz u. Augustus Buchner in 400122 S.422. Vgl. Jan de Vries: Altgermanische Religionsgeschichte. 2 Bde. Berlin 1970. *Schottelius: Ausführliche Arbeit (1663)*, 36 u. 70. Eine Ableitung Semannin konnten wir nicht nachweisen. Wahrscheinlich Druckfehler für *Germanninen*, der allerdings auch in der 2. Ausgabe der Poetik unverbessert blieb.

441201

Philipp von Zesen an die Fruchtbringende Gesellschaft

Philipp v. Zesen (FG 521. 1648) widmet seinen *Ibrahim Bassa* (1645), eine Übersetzung des Romans *Ibrahim ou l'Illustre Bassa* (1641) von Madeleine de Scudéry, der FG und bittet um günstige Aufnahme.

Q [Madeleine de Scudéry: *Ibrahim ou l'illustre Bassa*, zuerst 4 Bde. Paris: Antoine de Sommaville 1641. Dt. Übers. unter dem Titel (Kartusche in Kupfertitel:)] Jbrahims | oder | Des Durchleuchtigen Bassa | Und | Der Beständigen Jsabellen | Wunder-Geschichte: | Durch | Fil. Zaesien von | Fürstenau. [Verlegerzeile unter dem Kupferstich:] Amsteldam bey Ludwig Elzevieren. 1645. — Ndr. in: *Zesen SW* V.1, S.5f.

Auf-traags-schrift[1]
An die Höchst-löbliche
Frucht-bringende
GESELSCHAFT.

(Palmen-Vignette)

Höchst- und Hooch-geehrte Herren / von
Frucht und Zucht Aedele Helden;

WAn ein unwürdiger Reichs-sasse der Groos-mächtigsten Deutschinnen[2] Gnade führ ihren augen gefunden/ und sich erkühnen darf/ Ihrer Hooch-ansähnlichen viel-früchtenden Gesel-schaft seine unermüdete Dienste in untertähnigkeit auf zu tragen; so würd sich meine Wenigkeit nicht schäuen dürfen/ den Wält-wallenden Ibrahim/ dehr nuhn-mehr aus einem Franzosen ein Deutscher worden/ zu Ihren füßen zu lägen; mit bey-gefügter Bitte/ daß Sie Ihm die Gnaden-hand zu büten und günstig auf zu nähmen geruhen wollen. Daführ ich mich dan/ wie schohn vohrlängst in geheim / also auch hinführ öffendlich erweisen wärde/ wie daß ich sey und zu verbleiben wündsche

Der hooch-preis-würdigen Frucht-bringenden Geselschaft

Utrecht[4] / den 1. taag
des Christ-mandes
1644.

untertähnigster alzeit-färtiger[3]
Knächt Filip Zesius
von Fürstenau.

K Madeleine de Scudéry (1607–1701) hatte ihren in Zusammenarbeit mit ihrem Bruder Georges (1601–1667) erstellten Roman *IBRAHIM OV L'ILLVSTRE BASSA. DEDIÉ A MADEMOISELLE DE ROHAN* erstmals 1641 in einer vierbändigen Ausgabe in Paris bei Antoine de Sommaville veröffentlicht (SUB Göttingen: 8 FAB IV, 956: 1–4). Weitere Auflagen folgten 1643, 1644 u. ö. Philipp v. Zesens (FG 521. 1648. DG 1: Der Färtige) Übersetzung erschien 1645 in Amsterdam bei Ludwig Elzevier. Etliche von *Bellin: Sendeschreiben (1647)* veröffentlichte Stücke aus dem Zesen-Briefwechsel bezeugen, daß Zesen andere, insbesondere das DG-Mitglied Adolph Rosel(ius) (*um 1620. DG 6: Der Bemühete) mit der Durchsicht des Druckmanuskripts u. der Drucküberwachung beauftragt hatte. Vgl. *Bellin: Sendeschreiben (1647)*, Nr. 6, Bl. C[i]v – Cijr, undatiert, in dem sich Zesen bei Rosel für dessen Bereitschaft, seinen *Ibrahim* zu korrigieren, bedankt. Dieser fand ausreichend Grund zur Klage über die anstrengende Korrekturarbeit aufgrund der vielen Fehler u. orthographischen Inkonsequenzen Zesens, der besser daran getan hätte, sein Werk zunächst selbst kritisch durchzugehen. S. *Bellin: Sendeschreiben (1647)*, Nr. 9, Bl. Dv v – [Dviij]v, undatiert); vgl. Zesens rechtfertigende Antwort ebd., Nr. 10, Bl. [Dviij] v – G[i] v, undatiert, gez. „Der Färtige"). Vermutlich ins zeitige Frühjahr 1645 ist Zesens undat. Brief an Rosel (*Bellin: Sendeschreiben [1647]*, Nr. 5, Bl. [B6]v – C[i]v) zu datieren, in dem es noch einmal um Rosels Korrekturarbeit am *Ibrahim* u. die daraus entstandenen Fragen geht. Ungefähr zur gleichen Zeit oder etwas später, nämlich am 8.2.1645 sandte

Zesen den ersten Druckbogen des *Ibrahim* an das neue DG-Mitglied Gf. Rüdiger Günther v. Starhemberg (DG 10: Der Fäste). S. *Bellin: Sendeschreiben (1647)*, Nr. 3, Bl. B[i]v – B3r. Zesen selbst am Ende des 4. Buches seines *Ibrahim* („Dem Läser"): „Nachdähm man mit der Ausfärtigung dises Wärkes so sehr geeilet hat/ daß Ich auch nicht so vihl zeit haben können/ dasjenige/ was ich in der Hast übersäzzen müssen/ noch einmahl durch zu sähen: und über das auch bei der Truk-sauberung selbsten nicht gewäsen bin: so hat man meine meinung/ die Schreibe-rüchtigkeit beträffend/ in etlichen nicht erreichen/ noch ihr folgen können: ist auch hihr und dahr etwas in solcher über-eilung von dem bemüheten Truk-verbässerer [d. i. Rosel] über-sähen worden/ dehr sonst im meisten/ so vihl in der eile mühglich gewäsen/ gewachchet. Würd däs-wegen ein ihder Deutsch-libender/ wan er ohn-gefähr etwas versähenes ersihet/ solches der Eilfärtigkeit bei zu mässen/ und im bässten/ seiner Kluhg- und Bescheidenheit zur Folge/ zu deuten wüssen" (*Zesen SW* V.2, 1288).

Zwei unautorisierte, stark veränderte Nachdrucke der Zesenschen Übersetzung wurden zu seinem Ärger 1665 u. 1667 durch Johann Frantz in Zweibrücken herausgebracht. Vgl. *Zesen SW* V.2, 1307 ff.

Die vorliegende Widmungszuschrift ist als der erste Versuch Zesens zu werten, sich der FG zu nähern. Die der „Auf-traags-schrift" folgende „Schuz-räde" (*Zesen SW* V.1, 7–21) rechtfertigt die von ihm angewandte Orthographie, welche in der FG aufgrund ihrer als willkürlich empfundenen Eigenwilligkeit auf heftigen Widerspruch stieß. Zwar verzichtet die „Schuz-räde" auf eine Begründung für Zesens höchst ungewöhnlichen Vokalismus u. Konsonantismus sowie für seine Stammwort-Herleitung u. deren orthographische Konsequenzen, führt aber in Zesens Übersetzung verschiedener, sogar längst eingebürgerter Fremd- u. Lehnwörter („Bast-ahrt-wörter") ein u. in seine Ablehnung bestimmter „fremder Buhchstaben": ph, c, q, wodurch auch das ch u. sch in Mitleidenschaft geraten u. besser mit gh bzw. ßh oder nur s wiederzugeben seien: „aght" statt acht, „toghter" statt Tochter, „staghelight" für stachelicht (stachlig), „bußh" statt Busch, „mänßh" statt Mensch, „slagen", „smäkken", „swahn", „sreiben" usw. *Bellin: Sendeschreiben (1647)*, Nr. 10, Bl. [Dviij]v – G[i]v u. Nr. 12, Bl. Gijr – [Gvj]v, hier Giijr. Vgl. auch 460812. Grundlage der Orthographie im *Ibrahim* waren die entsprechenden Erörterungen in der *Hooch-Deutschen-Spraach-übung* (1643), in der sich Zesen aber mit orthographischen Neuerungen noch zurückgehalten hatte (*Zesen SW*, XI, 1–77). Schon im vorgerückten Jahr 1644 oder Anfang 1645 war Zesen übrigens von der Markierung der Vokaldehnung durch Doppelvokale, wie er sie im *Ibrahim* praktiziert hatte, abgerückt u. hatte Akzente (Zirkonflex) bzw. Dehnungs-h vorgeschlagen. S. seine Briefe an Rosel in *Bellin: Sendeschreiben (1647)*, Nr. 5 (s. o.) u. an Gf. Rüdiger Günther v. Starhemberg, d. d. Utrecht 8.2.1645, ebd., Nr. 3 (s. o.). Zur auffälligen Umlautschreibung v. a. der Verben, die aus seiner Stammwort-Ableitung aus den Präteritumsformen resultiert, vgl. 450308A u. 450808.

In 450504 spornt F. Ludwig Christian Gueintz (FG 361) zur eiligen Druckfertigstellung der *Deutschen Rechtschreibung (1645)* an (s. 440127 K 1), weil „nicht alleine vom Spielenden [Georg Philipp Harsdörffer. FG 368. Der Spielende] und Clajo [Johann Klaj] in Nürnberg und dan von dem Suchenden [Justus Georg Schottelius. FG 397. Der Suchende] im lande zu Braunschweig unterschiedene Neue und sich ubel schickende schreibarten wollen aufgebracht, sondern auch vornemlich noch eine fremdere und ungewöhnlichere von Zäsio [Zesen] eingeführet werden, wie aus seiner verdeutschung des Jbrahims Baßa und der Bestendigen Isabellen wundergeschichte in diesem Jhare zu Amsterdam gedruckt, zu ersehen: Dan ob schon sonsten die redensart [der Stil] darinnen fein läuffig und rein, so wil doch solche von ihme genante schreiberichtigkeit nit verantwortlich sein, in deme es scheinet, das sie auf keinem rechten grund, sondern nur auf sonderbaren einbildungen und anleitungen aus fremden sprachen genommen". In 450529 moniert F. Ludwig gegenüber Harsdörffer, Zesen führe im *Ibrahim* unglückliche Neuerungen in der Rechtschreibung u. unpassende Neologismen ein. Darum sei zunächst auf die Mittel „zugedencken, Wie vorgedachter Cæsius [...] vollend zur rechtmeßigen gleichförmigkeit möge bracht werden", ehe eine Aufnahme in die FG in Betracht zu ziehen sei. Gegenüber Harsdörffer freut sich Zesen in 450808 gleichwohl, daß die Mitglieder seiner DG die von ihm vorgeschlagene, auf Vernunftprinzipien gegründete Rechtschreibung akzeptieren u. für ihre eigenen Werke verwenden. Gleichwohl hörte er nicht auf zu beteuern, daß niemand in der DG gezwungen würde, Zesens Schreibweisen zu übernehmen. Auch die DG-Genossen stellten Zesen das Zeugnis aus, er habe nie beabsichtigt, sich mit der in der *Hooch-Deutschen Spraach-übung* u. im *Ibrahim* verbreiteten Schreibart zu begnügen oder diese anderen aufzudrängen, sondern wolle seine Mitgenossen nur anregen, über die richtige Schreibart nachzudenken. Nicht die Behauptung eigener Positionen zur „schreib-richtigkeit", sondern Debatte u. Vergleich aller Sprachbeflissenen seien das Ziel der DG. Falls dies nicht gelinge, wäre eine Rückkehr zur alten Schreibart beabsichtigt. Wenn jeder seine eigenen Regeln mache u. aus Hoffart oder Hartnäckigkeit nicht nachgebe, was solle dann aus der Rechtschreibung werden? Vorrede („Die Deutsch-gesiñete Genossenschaft allen Deutschliebenden Herzen einhälligkeit/ gedeihen und segen!"), d. d. Amsterdam 20.10.1646 in *Bellin: Sendeschreiben (1647),* Bl. [Avj]v–B[i]r, hier Aviijr u. [Aviij]r f. Noch in seinem *Helikonischen Rosentahl* (1669) versicherte Zesen, „daß kein Mitglied unserer Genossenschaft gehalten ist/ sich an eine gewisse dieses oder jenes Schreibahrt/ [...] zu binden". Zugleich stellt er die Sprachpraxis der DG in eine von der FG ausgehende Traditionslinie, wenn er es zur Aufgabe der Gesellschaft erklärt, das Deutsche „ohne einmischung fremder ausheimischer wörter/ aufs müglichste und tuhnlichste/ den Fruchtbringenden zur löblichen folge/ zu erhalten" (*Zesen SW* XII, 205). Auch wenn Zesen durch seine Widmung u. die dem dritten Teil vorangestellte Zuschrift an die DG seinen *Ibrahim* als einen Beitrag zu den Bestrebungen beider Sprachgesellschaften empfiehlt, treten die Ziele der Akademien in einem kritischen Punkt, der Rechtschreibnormierung, empfindlich auseinander. Das wird die Aufnahme Zesens in die FG letztlich um Jahre verzögern. S. zur Aufnahme Zesens 440724 K 13; vgl. außerdem *Herz: Zesen*, 181–193, zum *Ibrahim* 184f.; zu Zesens Übersetzungsarbeit: Florian Gelzer: Der Einfluss der französischen Romanpraxis des 17. Jahrhunderts auf die Romane Philipp von Zesens. In: Philipp von Zesen. Wissen — Sprache — Literatur. Hg. v. Maximilian Bergengruen u. Dieter Martin. Tübingen 2008, 119–139; *Ingen*, 76–87, zum *Ibrahim* 83–86. Vgl. zum *Ibrahim* ferner 440724, 441223 K 1, 450308A K 1, 450400, 450504, 450506A K 1, 450529, 450808 K 6, 450921, 460217 (K 4) u. 460812 K 1.

1 *Auftrag* wird hier im Sinne von Darreichung oder Aufopferung verwendet, einen Auftrag zur Übersetzung durch die FG gab es nicht. Zesen greift somit auf eine schon im 17. Jahrhundert kaum noch gebräuchliche Bedeutungsschicht des Wortes zurück, die in mhd. *ûf tragen* mit ,darbringen, opfern' noch deutlicher greifbar ist (*Lexer: Handwb.* II, 1705). *Stieler*, 2311 beschreibt das Verbum *auftragen* zwar zunächst in den Grenzen des heute noch gebräuchlichen Bedeutungsspektrums, verwendet es jedoch auch im Artikel „Opfer/ opfern/ geopfert" (*Stieler*, 1392), dessen Stamm er von lat. *offerre* ableitet: „Opfern *nimirum iis est ab* offerre, *qvasi* offerre *non sit nomen generale & qvamlibet præbitionem seu dationem significet.*" *Opfern* im Sinne einer Darreichung oder Gabe (praebitio, datio) sei eine Ableitung von „Beren/ & Ob/ aufberen/ *sive* auftragen", welches wiederum im semantischen Feld von „ferre, portare, elevare, tollere, erigere" verortet wird (*Stieler*, 133). *Paul Wb.*, 110 u. *DW* I, 761 f. führen darüber hinaus an, daß *auftragen* im Fnhd. auch als Rechtsbegriff im Sinne von ,übertragen, überantworten, zum Lehen geben' geläufig

441205 Landgraf Hermann IV. von Hessen-Rotenburg

war. Spricht Zesen von einer „Auf-traags-schrift" u. davon, daß er als „unwürdiger Reichs-sasse [...] seine unermüdete Dienste in untertähnigkeit auf zu tragen" gedenke, markiert er sein Werk als (Weihe-)Gabe, die er an die FG heranträgt, u. nicht als Aufgabe, die ihm übertragen wurde. Vgl. auch 450000A K 5.

2 Zesens Ausdruck für deutsche Musen. In seiner „Schuz-räde" spricht er „die unüberwündlichste Deutschinne" im Singular u. als „Heldin" an, die wohl als eine Art Schutzgöttin u. Personifizierung Deutschlands (Germania) aufzufassen ist. Grundsätzlich plädierte Zesen dafür, heidnische Götternamen u. allegorische Personifikationen ins Deutsche zu übertragen, um den Geschmack u. Verdacht des Götzentums abzulegen: „Wier können ja die Liebe/ den Frühling und dergleichen/ in eben solcher gestalt als die Heiden/ doch etwas kristlicher fohrstellen" (Brief Zesens an B. Knipping vom 6.2.1647, in *Bellin: Sendeschreiben [1647]*, Nr. 20, Bl. Jiiij v – [Jvj]v). Entsprechend seine Übersetzungen „Lustinne" für Venus, „Holdinnen" für Grazien, „Kluginne" für Pallas/ Minerva usw. Vgl. etwa seine „Schuz-räde" in der *Ibrahim*-Übersetzung (*Zesen SW* V.1, 8) u. die „Frage. Ob man die Eignen Nahmen der Götter und Göttinnen/ als Jupiter/ Venus etc. könne deutsch geben?" in Zesens *Deutschem Helicon* (²1641), hier *Zesen SW* IX, 250–252; vgl. dazu 450000A K 1, 450308A K 1 u. 450808 K I 3 u. 4; zur Fremdwörter-Übersetzung auch 440525 II, 450410 (Hz. August), 460720 K 3 (Gueintz) u. 460915 (Harsdörffer).

3 Eine Anspielung Zesens auf seinen Gesellschaftsnamen in der DG („Der Färtige"). S. hierzu 440724 (K 13).

4 Nach seinem Studium in Wittenberg, das er mit dem Magistertitel abschloß, wandte sich Zesen 1642 nach Hamburg. Aus dieser Zeit stammt seine Verbindung zu Johann Rist (FG 467. 1647), der später sein erbittertster Gegner werden sollte. Hier gründete er die DG, nach eigener Aussage im *Helikonischen Rosentahl* (1669) im Mai 1643 als dreiköpfigen Freundschaftsbund, der 1644 dann weiter anwuchs (vgl. *Zesen SW* XII, 190f.). Danach u. bis 1648 hielt sich Zesen überwiegend in den Niederlanden, v.a. in Amsterdam, Leiden u. Utrecht auf, immer wieder unterbrochen von Reisen nach Deutschland, England u. Frankreich. Der erste sichere Nachweis seines Aufenthalts in den Niederlanden ist der 8.10.1642, denn auf diesen Tag mit der Ortsangabe Leiden ist die Zuschrift in seiner *Hooch-Deutschen Spraach-übung* (1643) datiert (*Zesen SW* XI, 6). Vgl. *Ingen*, 8–24; *Ingen: Zesen*, 3–5.

441205

Landgraf Hermann IV. von Hessen-Rotenburg an Fürst Ludwig

Lgf. Hermann IV. v. Hessen-Rotenburg (FG 374) bezieht sich auf seinen zwei Wochen zuvor an F. Ludwig gerichteten Brief, in dem er über seinen Zustand berichtet, sich nach der Kriegssituation in Anhalt erkundigt und gefragt hatte, ob die Anhaltiner die gegenseitige Blockierung der schwed. und ksl. Heere überstanden hätten. Da er vergeblich auf eine Antwort gewartet habe, habe er die sich bietende Gelegenheit genutzt, um dem aus Westfalen über Rotenburg reisenden Dessauer Boten den vorliegenden Brief mitzugeben und darin seine versuchte Erkundigung zu wiederholen. — Da gemäß Lgf. Hermanns Meinung nun auch der dritte Teil des Werks *Sachse: Einhelligkeit* erschienen sein müßte, bittet er um Zusendung, weil er die beiden ersten Teile schon besitze. — Außerdem habe er schon lange sein versprochenes Büchlein zuschicken wollen, woran ihn jedoch ständige

Reisetätigkeit und Überfälle gehindert hätten. — Winand v. Polhelm (FG 405. Der Entnehmende) arbeite gerade an einem Buch und werde zu rechter Zeit damit herausrücken. — Grüße von Gattin zu Gattin.

Q GNM Nürnberg: Historisches Archiv K. 24, Bl. 1v–2v [A: 2v], 2r leer; eigenh.; Sig.

A Dem Hochgebornen Fursten Herren Ludwigenn Fursten zu Annhalt Graven zue Ascanien Herrn zu Zerbst vndt Bernburg vnserm freundlichen vielgeliebtenn Vettern, Schwagern, vnd herrn Vattern Coetenn
Eigenh. Empfangsvermerk F. Ludwigs: Ps. 24. December 1644.

Hochgeborner Fürst, fr. vielgeliebter H. Vetter, Schwager vnd H. Vatter *etc.*

Nachdeme ELn ich vor 14 Tagen bey damahliger Leipziger Post geschrieben,[1] vnsern Zustand berichtet, vnd darneben mitt sonderbahrem Verlangen ELn vnd der ihrigen wie auch der vbrigen H. vettern vndt Fürsten zu Anhalt G. vnd Ld. Zustands; vnd wie sie sich bey so gewehleten Kriegsstillager beider KriegsHerren vf ihren heusern erhalten vnd durchbracht,[2] ohnbeschwehrt zu berichten gebehten, annoch aber keine antwort eingelanget, habe ich diese gelegenheit des aus Westfalen zurückkomenden dessauer botens, nicht vorüber gehen laßen wollen, El nochmals mitt diesem vorigen aufzuwarten vnd vorige geringe bitte zu erwiedern.

Darbeneben weil ich vermeine, daß nuhmehr das dritte theil der Einhelligkeitt der Vier Evangelisten fertig gedrucket sein werden,[3] ob El. mir die gnade thun möchten, ein abtruck darvon (weil ich die Erste Zwey theile schon habe) bey der Post oder erster gelegenheit zuzuschicken.

El. wolte ich mein versprochenes büchlein vorlengst auch zugeschickt haben,[4] weil ich aber diese zeitt her viel verreisen müßen auch fast stetigen vberfall gehabt, darzu nicht gelang*en* können.

Der Entnehmende hatt zwar etwas vnter der feder,[5] wird zweifelsohne zu gelegener zeitt damitt hervorwischen, da El ich sonst einigerley weise gedient sein kan, wollen sie mich kühnlich mitt dero befehl belegen, vnd erwarte dero g. antwort nechst Göttlicher befehlung verpleibende

El. treudienstwilliger vetter vnd sohn
Hermanlzheßen[a]
Rotenbergk der 5te Christmonats 1644.

Meine[b] gemahlin[6] ergiebt vnd erbeutt sich El. vnd dero hl. gemahlin[7] neben mir gantz dienstfreundlich.

T a *Darunter von späterer H. eines Archivars* 1644 — **b** *Am Rand hinzugefügt bis* dienstfreundlich.

K 1 Der Brief findet sich nicht im Köthener Erzschrein u. wurde von uns auch sonst nicht ermittelt.
2 Seit dem August 1644 waren Anhalt u. speziell Bernburg zum Hauptkriegsschauplatz

geworden, als sich die beiden feindlichen Hauptheere der Schweden u. der Kaiserlichen bis in den November bei Bernburg gegenüberlagen u. das umliegende Land ruinierten. Vgl. 440927 K 1.

3 *Sachse: Einhelligkeit* I–III. Der dritte Teil erschien tatsächlich 1644, wurde aber von F. Ludwig offenbar deutlich später an die Interessenten versandt. Obwohl der Versand schon im Januar 1645 erwartet worden war (s. 450126), schrieb der Fürst erst in 450721 an Hz. August d.J. v. Braunschweig-Wolfenbüttel (FG 227), dem Brief liege ein Exemplar bei. F. Ludwig entschuldigte in 450721 den Verzug mit der durch die Kriegsläufte eingefallenen Landesverderbnis u. der Ermangelung eines Buchbinders. In 460103 berichtete Wilhelm Heinrich v. Freyberg (FG 439) von seinen Versuchen, bei Gelegenheit einer Kavallierstour Pz. Johann Georgs II. v. Anhalt-Dessau (FG 322) im Haag und wohl auch in Paris die Finanzierung bzw. den Absatz des großen Werks zu sichern. Im Haag hatte Ludwig schon früher versucht, eine Subskription durch Johann v. Mario (FG 100) anzustoßen. S. 420120 u. 420219. F. Ludwig konnte wegen derselben Umstände mit 460119 ein zweites gebundenes Buch auch nicht schicken, jedoch legte er diesmal ein (wohl ungebundenes) Stück an Carl Gustav v. Hille (FG 302) bei, verbunden mit der Ankündigung, ein weiteres Exemplar für Hz. August folgen zu lassen, sobald man es habe einbinden lassen können, was durch die stetige „unruhe" bislang nicht erfolgen konnte. Zu *Sachse: Einhelligkeit* s. 420712 K 1; ferner (v.a. zu deren 3. Teil) s. 440323 K 6, 450126 (K 3), 450221 (K 4), 450308, 450509 K 3, 450721, 460103 (K 1), 460119 (K 3) u. 460718 K 3.

4 Aus inhaltlichen u. zeitlichen Gründen kann es sich nicht, soweit bekannt, um eigene Schriften Lgf. Hermanns IV. v. Hessen-Rotenburg (FG 374. Der Fütternde) gehandelt haben: 1. PROTESTATION: vnd WahrungsSchreiben/ An Herrn Landgraf GEORGENS zu Hessen Fr. Gn. Von Herrn Landgraf HERMANS zu Hessen Fr. Gn. Wegen deren/ im OberFürstenthumb Hessen jetzo vorgehender gewaltsamer und Landfriedbrüchiger **proceduren** vnd Thathandlungen/ **sub dato** den 20. Februarii, dieses 1646. Jahrs abgelassen. HAB: 31.8 Pol. (e). — 2. Historia Meteorologica. Das ist: Vier vnd zwantzig Jährige eigentliche vnd trewfleissige **Observation** vnd tägliche verzeichnuß des Gewitters, vom 1. Januarii 1623 an, biß zum letzten Decembris 1646 in dreyen **membris** verfasset ... Durch Uranophilum Cyriandrum, der Meteorolog. Cultorem. (Kassel 1651). HAB: 42.4 Astron. — 3. Hexamereon Oder Sechs-Tägiges Gespräch vber etzliche schwere Puncten in verschiedenen Wissenschaften ... Durch Einen der höchlöblichen Fruchtbringenden Gesellschafft Mitgenossenen gnandt der Fütternde (Kassel 1652), s. Titel u. Vorrede, Bl. [)(viii r]). Dieses Werk enthält eine Widmung an Hz. August d.J. v. Braunschweig-Wolfenbüttel (FG 227) u. F. August v. Anhalt-Plötzkau (FG 46). HAB: 403.49 Quod. u. 416. 3 Hist. (2). S. *Conermann III*, 437f. — Lgf. Hermann spricht nicht von einem Werk seiner Feder. Er könnte F. Ludwig jedoch folgendes Buch geschickt haben, das damals gerade in Hermanns verwandtschaftlichem Umkreise kursierte u. gut zu einem die FG interessierenden Werk (*Harsdörffer: Frauenzimmer-Gesprächspiele*) u. Thema paßt: Johann Peter Lotichius (1598–1669): Gynaicologia: id est: De nobilitate et perfectione sexus faeminei <dt.>: GYNAICOLOGIA. Das ist: Grund- unnd Außfuhrlicher Discurs/ Von PERFECTION, vnd Fürtrefflikeiten/ deß löblichen Frawenzimmers: So Allen und jeden/ jhren Feinden entgegen gesetzet/ Durch IO. P. LOTICHIVM, D. Medicum, der Zeit der Vniversität Rinteln Professorem, Nun aber Jns hoch Teutsch vbersetzt Durch IOAN. TACKIVM, Medic. Licentiatum. Getruckt zu Franckfurt am Mayn Bey Johann Friederich Weissen/ Jn Verlegung Philipps Jacobs Fischers. ANNO M. DC. XXXXV. (Kupfertitel: Von der Perfection des löblichen Frawen-Zimmers.) HAB: 328.2 Quod. (2), dig. Gewidmet vom Verfasser d.d. Butzbach 6.8.1644 an Gfn. Hedwig v. Holstein-Schaumburg, geb. Lgfn v. Hessen u. an Gfn. Elisabeth v. Holstein-Schaumburg, geb. Gfn. zur Lippe, u. Gfn.

Maria Magdalena zur Lippe, geb. Gfn. v. Waldeck. Mit einer früheren Widmung von Lotichius d. d. 11.2.1633 an Gfn. Hedwig, an deren Hof in Bückeburg er als Leibarzt Gf. Jobst Hermanns tätig gewesen war. Lat. Ehrengedichte an Lotichius von den Rintelner Professoren Johannes Gisenius, D. theol.; Hermann Goehausen, D.; M. Reinhardus König, Polit. & Histor. Profess., auch von Johannes Theodorus Sprenger. Lotichius kommt in dem wie eine akademische Disputation aufgebauten Werk zu dem Schluß: „Vnter dessen erlangen durch jhre Zucht die Weiber so viel Lobs/ daß wann sie schon zu Hause ohne Lehrmeister vnd Vnterricht gelassen werden/ sie dennoch (a) durch jhre natürliche Geschickligkeit so viel erlangen vnd besitzen/ daß sie bißweilen/ vielen hin vnd hergereiseten auch in Kriegen/ vnd auff Academien/ Herrenhöffen/ vnd Schlössern/ aufferzogenen Mannes personen fürgehen können. Bevorab aber dann zumal/ wann sie in den studiis aufferzogen werden (b) vbertreffen sie dieselbe weit/ vnd setzen sie zurücke." (S. 178). 1630 war Lotichius' Buch bereits u. d. T. erschienen: GYNAICOLOGIA: ID EST: De NOBILITATE & perfectione sexus Feminei: CONTRA MASTIGES: Διάσκεπσισ Physica: Publici exercitii igitur in Academia Rintelana, Proposita à JO. PETRO LOTICHIO, Medicin. D. ejusdemq; ibidem Prof. P. P. (Rinthelij ad Visurgim 1630: Petrus Lucius). HAB: N 50.8° Helmst. (4), nur Gfn. Hedwig gewidmet, mit Gedichten von Gisenius, König u. Goehausen. In seiner ersten dt. Widmung sagt Lotichius, daß er „auß Antrieb discreter, vnd fürnehmer Cavalieri, als bey der löblichen Vniversität Rintelen die Medicinalische Profession bedienet/ vnd bey der Soldatesca bekand gewesen" (ohne Bogensignatur), die lat. Disputation vorgestellt habe und verteidigen ließ. D. i. GYNAICOLOGIA ... Sub Præsidio JO. PETRI LOTICHII ... Publico agone ... sistit ad diem XXX. Ianuar. ... M: LAURENTIUS ECKARDI (Rintelii ad Visurgum 1630: Petrus Lucius), STB Berlin—PK: No 3391 (unvollst.?). Lotichius gibt in seiner Widmung an die drei Damen an, er habe seine Schrift von Johann Tackius Lic. med. (1617–1676) verdeutschen lassen. Zu dem lat. Poeten (P. L. C.), Leibarzt (Hanau, Bückeburg), Rintelner, Herborner u. Marburger Professor sowie Stadtarzt in Frankfurt a. M. (seit 1646) Lotichius s. *Flood*, 1197 f.; August Heimpel: Johann Peter Lotichius, ein Hanauer Arzt und Gelehrter im 30jährigen Krieg. In: Hanauisches Magazin XII (1933), 25–30; Karl Siebert: Johann Peter Lotichius. In: Hanauer Geschichtsblätter 1919, H. 3/ 4, 125–127; *ADB* XIX (1884), 268 f.; *Jöcher* II, 2540.

5 Der Entnehmende ist Winand v. Polhelm (FG 405), der in Diensten Lgf. Hermanns IV. v. Hessen-Rotenburg u. seiner Brüder, der Lgf.en Friedrich v. Hessen-Eschwege (FG 566. 1651) u. Ernst v. Hessen-Rheinfels-Rotenburg (1623–1693) stand u. zugleich für Lgfn. Amalia Elisabeth v. Hessen-Kassel als Gesandter wirkte. Vielleicht handelt es sich um eine Übertragung der berühmten und weitverbreiteten orientalischen *Kalila und Dimna*-Fabel, die auch unter dem Namen *Fabeln des Bidpai* bekannt geworden ist. S. 450305 (K 5). Zu Polhelm vgl. 440809A, 450506, 450526 u. 450818 K 4.

6 Lgfn. Kunigunde Juliane, geb. Fn. v. Anhalt-Dessau (PA. TG 26), 2. Gattin Lgf. Hermanns.

7 Fn. Sophia v. Anhalt-Köthen, geb. Gfn. zur Lippe (AL. TG 38), 2. Gattin F. Ludwigs.

441216

Johann Rist an Justus Georg Schottelius

Johann Rist (FG 467. 1647) vergleicht in seinem „Sinne Bild" Justus-Georg Schottelius' (FG 397. Der Suchende) Poetik *Teutsche Vers- oder ReimKunst (1645)* mit einer Perle und Schottelius demnach mit einem Perlenfischer.

Q [Kupfertitel] Iusti-Georgii | Schottelii | Teutsche Vers- oder | ReimKunst | darin | Vnsere Teutsche | MutterSprache/ so viel | dero süßeste Po- | esis betrifft/ in eine | richtige Form der | Kunst zum ersten | mahle gebracht | worden. | getruckt Zu | Wolfenbüttel | Jnverlegung *[sic]* | deß Authoris | im jahre M DC XLV. Kolophon: „Getruckt zu Wulffenbüttel/ durch Johann Bißmarck/ Jm Jahr 1645." Bl. B iij r – B iiij v. HAB: 172.1 Poet.; SUB Göttingen: 8 P GERM I, 1290 (dig.). — Auch: *Schottelius: Teutsche Vers- oder ReimKunst (1656)*, Bl. b v – b ij v. Zit. *B*. Auch in *Rist: Schauplatz (1646)*, 306–308. HAB: Lo 6467. Zit. *C*. — *Interpunktionsdifferenzen und orthographische Varianten zwischen den Drucken werden von uns nicht vermerkt.*

                    Sinne Bild
        Über des Edlen, Vesten und Hoch
        gelahrten Herren Justus-Georg[a]
        Schottelien, Beider Rechten Licen-
        tiaten[b] teütsche poetische Kunst.

SEht diesen/der das Meer **Durchsuchend**[1] unverdrossen/
Der allerschönsten **Perl** nun endlich hat genossen; [B iij v]
    Kunstgründig suchet' er/ verlies das sichre Land/
    Und trat hin in die See/ bis Er die **Muschel** fand.
Dem **PerlenFischer** war das Wasser nicht zuwider/
Ob jhm vom Kälte gleich erstarretē die Glieder:
    Itz kom̃t Er aus der See/ trägt seiner Arbeit Lohn/
    Die wunderschöne **Perl** zusamt der Ehrenkrõ'.
Was nütz- uñ lieblich ist hat dieser hie ergriffen[c]/
Dieweil der Himmel selbst jhm den Verstand geschliffen/
    So daß Er numehr[d] hat die Muschel aufgebracht/
    Die unser Vaterlād[e] so hoch berühmet macht.
Die werthe Teutsche Sprach[f] (O könt[g] ichs jhm verdanken!)
Hat Er zu allererst in wolgebaute Schranken
    Der Lehr[h] und Kunst gesetzt; so/ daß ein Teutscher Mann
    Durch jhn/die Muttersprach[i] grundrichtig schauet[j] an.
Nun trit Er her aufs neu/ als der aus diesen dingen
Noch einen schönen Schatz bedacht war herzubringen: [B iiij r]
    Die **Muschel** thut[k] Er auf und zeiget uns den Glantz
    Der auserlesnen **Perl**/ die Kugelrund und gantz/

Ja vollenkommen ist. Das Herz muß einem lachen
Weñ man nun sehen mag die lengst-erwünschte[l] Sachen
　　Der edlen Poesie/ der grossen[m] Hiñelskunst/
　　Die gleich den **Perlen** gibt **Kraft/ Ehre/ Schonheit**[n]/ Gunst/
Sie lies zwar vor der zeit jhr Antlitz etwas blikkē/
Durch des **Gekröhnten***[2] fleis/ doch wolt' es sich nicht schikken
　　Zur vollenkommenheit/ aus mangel ebner Bahn/
　　Auch war die Muschel nur ein wenig[o] aufgethan:
Nun hat der **Suchender**[1] durch Arbeit überwunden/
Und den begehrten Schatz/ die theure **Perl**/ gefunden/
　　Die zeigt er uns mit Lust/ wie man im Teutschen wol
　　Jn allem/ nach der Zier und Kunst verfahren sol.
Glük zu Herr **Suchender**; jhr habt das Eis gebrochen/
Und numehr[d] durch die **Perl** ein solches Loch gestochen/
　　Daß man sie fassen kan. Da kriegt jhr nun zu Lohn/
　　Der Menschen Preis und Dank/ des Hiñels Ehr' und Krohn.[p]

　　　　Aus hertzlicher Liebe und Zuneigung ist
　　　　dieses seinem hochgeliebten vertrautem
　　　　　　Freunde zu ehren gesungen am 16.
　　　　　　　Tage des Christmonats zu
　　　　　　　　　Wedel an der Elbe
　　　　　　　　　　　Von
　　　　　　　　　Johan Risten.

I

Schäferliches Freundschaftsgedicht Rists für Schottelius

Q　Johann Risten | [Zierleiste] | POetischer Schauplatz/ | Auff welchem allerhand Waaren | Gute und Böse | Kleine und Grosse | Freude und Leid-zeugende | zu finden. | [Linie] | Hamburg/ Bey und Jn Verlegung | Heinrich Werner/ 1646, S. 127 f. HAB: Lo 6467.

　　　　　An den Edlen und Hochgelahrten/
　　　　　　　　　　Herren
　　　　　　　Justum Georg Schottelien/
　　　　　　　　der Rechte Licentiaten/
　　　　　　　Seinen großwehrten besonderen
　　　　　　　　　　Freund/
　　　　　Warum Er etliche seiner vor dieser Zeit geschrie-
　　　　　　benen Schäffer-Getichte diesem Büchlein
　　　　　　　　habe inverleibet.

Sinne Bild

Uber des Edlen, Vesten und hoch
gelahrten herren Justus Georg
Schottelien, Beider Rechten Licentiaten teütsche poetische Kunst.

SEht diesen/ der das Meer Durchsuchend
unverdrossen/
Der allerschönsten Perl nun endlich hat
genossen;
Kunstgründig suchet er/verlies das sichre Land/
Und trat hin in die See/bis er die Muschel fand.
Dem

Johann Rist (FG 467. 1647) auf Justus Georg Schottelius (FG 397) als Perlenfischer. Zu 441216.

DAß Jch von Hirten und von schönen Schäfferinnen/[1]
von ihrer keüschen Brunst und fest-verliebten Siñen/
von Lämmern/ von der Leyr/ von Wiesen/ vom Gesang/
vom Hirtenstab' und von der grünen Pfeiffen klang' [128]
Herr **Schottel** ein Gedicht vor diesem auffgeschrieben/
das machet/ daß Jch nie von Hertzen konte lieben
    der grossen Stätte Pracht. Jch binn den Feldern hold/
    Ein dikbegrünter Wald ist mier für rohtes Gold/
Der Thäler Lieblichkeit kann besser mich erfreüen
als alle Haüser/ da mann Bluhmen muß inn streüen/
    Was die Natur gemacht/ das gehet vor die Kunst/
    Drum trag' Jch zu dem Feld' ein' übergrosse Gunst.
Die Schäffer seh' Jch offt die krausen Lämmer weiden/
Jch selbst samt Koridon spatzier' inn grüner Heiden/
    und wahrlich diese Lust im Feld' ist nicht gering/
    was wunder/ daß Jch offt von Schäffereien[a] sing'?

T a C Justus Georg — **b** C Licentiaten/ Teutsche Verß- oder Reim-Kunst. *Ohne Abbildung. Es folgt eine Beschreibung*: (Merke: Das Sinnebild ist ein Perlen-Fischer/ der gleichsahm aus dem Meer steigend in der einen Hand eine auffgethane runde Muschel/ hiedurch verstehe ich seine teutsche Spraachkunst) hält/ in welches Mittel eine grosse runde Perl (verstehe die edle teutsche Verskunst liget. Es wird aber dem Perlen-fischer von einer anderen auß den Wolken ragenden Hand ein Lorbeerkrantz auffgesetzet/ wie solches alles im Kupferstükke besser und deutlicher zu sehen.) *Die Versanfänge in C werden im Gedicht nur am Satzbeginn groß geschrieben.* — **c** C begrieffen *reimt mit* C geschlieffen — **d** C nunmehr — **e** C Vatterland — **f** C Sprach' — **g** C könt' — **h** C Lehr' — **i** C Mutterspraach — **j** C schauen kan. — **k** C thuet — **l** C längst erwünschte — **m** C wehrten — **n** B Schönheit — **o** C weinig — **p** *Folgende Zeilen fehlen in C.* — * *Randnote:* *M. Opitz.

T I <Schäferinnen> *von Rist als Druckfehler verbessert, S. [321].*

K Johann Rist (FG 467. Der Rüstige. 1647), noch längst nicht selbst in die FG aufgenommen, preist den 1642 aufgenommenen Justus Georg Schottelius (FG 397. Der Suchende) für die Abfassung einer gelungenen Poetik: *Teutsche Vers- oder ReimKunst (1645).* Vgl. 441020. Der Stoff dieser auf die Verskunst beschränkten Poetik wird in drei Büchern über „Maasforschung", „Abmessung" u. die zweite „Abtheilung und Ordnung der Reimarten … nach den Reimschlüssen und Reimen" abgehandelt. S. 431028A K 3. Viele Ehrengedichte u. andere Freundschaftsgaben begleiten das Buch. Vgl. 440900 K 2. S. Abb. Schottelius als Perlenfischer S. 381.
    1 Wie unten „Suchender" Anspielung auf Justus Georg Schottelius' Gesellschaftsnamen in der FG: Der Suchende.
    2 Martin Opitz (FG 200. Der Gekrönte). Rist gab sich oft als Opitz-Bewunderer zu erkennen. S. z. B. Johannis Ristii, Lob- Trawr- vnd Klag-Gedicht/ Vber gar zu frühzeitiges/ jedoch seliges Absterben/ Des … MARTINO OPITZEN (Hamburg: Zacharias Hertel 1640); s. *Opitz: BW* III 390922 rel; vgl. *Conermann: Rist,* 87f.

K I Wie sich Johann Rist FG 467. Der Rüstige. 1647) anfangs nicht nur mit Justus Georg Schottelius (FG 397. Der Suchende), sondern auch mit Georg Philipp Harsdörffer (FG 368. Der Spielende), Tscherning (s. 440324 I) u.a. sowie selbst mit dem jungen Philipp v. Zesen (FG 521. 1648, vgl. 440724) zu einem Netzwerk der die deutsche Sprache u. Poesie kultivierenden Dichter zu verbinden suchte, auch wenn diese z. Tl. noch nicht die Aufnahme in die FG erreicht hatten, zeigt folgendes Beispiel (s. *Conermann: Rist*, 31–33): Die Gedichte, mit denen Rist die einzelnen Bände der *Frauenzimmer-Gesprächspiele* Harsdörffers versah, sind an sich nicht immer der FG zuzuordnen, spielen aber auf Vorhaben u. Eigenschaften an, welche Autor u. Widmungsempfänger mit ihren Rollen auch in dieser oder anderen Gesellschaften verbanden. So dichtete Rist in Anspielung auf Harsdörffers fruchtbringerischen Gesellschaftsnamen über das Ziel, das dieser auch im vierten Teil seiner *Frauenzimmer-Gesprächspiele* (1644) verfolgte:

Jhr **spielet** zwahr mit Lust/ und schreibet solche Sachen
die unsre Teutschen Teutsch/ geschikt und witzig machen/
    (denn dahin zielet jhr) iedoch bekenn' ich frey/
    daß ein so grosses Werk kein blosses Spielen sey.

(*Harsdörffer: Frauenzimmer-Gesprächspiele* IV. 1644/ Ndr. 1968, 24–28; auch *Rist: Schauplatz*, 132–134). Es fällt auf, daß Rist hier auf Harsdörffers Gesellschaftsnamen „Der Spielende" hinwies, obgleich er, Rist, noch nicht Mitglied der Fruchtbringer war u. als Daphnis aus Cimbrien im PBO den Nürnberger höchstens mit dessen bukolischen Namen Strephon angeredet haben könnte. Vgl. Rists Gedichttitel in seinem *Schauplatz*, 262f. „Spielen ist suchen/ Suchen ist spielen/ An die beyde vortreffliche/ durch wahre Freundschafft treuverbundene Geister und edle Mittglieder der höchst-löblichen Fruchtbringenden Gesellschafft Nemlich Den Herrn Spielenden und den Herrn Suchenden/ Seine beiderseits hochgeehrte Herren und sehr liebwehrten Freunde." Rist hatte auch Philipp v. Zesen, den wegen seiner grammatischen u. poetischen Neuerungssucht erst 1648 u. unter Vorbehalt in die Fruchtbringende Gesellschaft aufgenommenen Dichterkollegen, beim Erscheinen von dessen *Hooch-Deutscher Spraach-übung* (1643) als „Kammer-Juncker" bei „der Spraachen Trohn" geehrt, der von der auf Opitz folgenden Generation deutscher Dichter einmütig weitergebaut werde:

Der Bau geht redlich fohrt. **Herr Schottel** wird Jhn heben
Harßdorffer folgt Jhm nach und **Zesius** daneben
    Herr Tscherning/ Buchholtz und was gründlich schreiben kann/
    Das legt itz nebenst mier die Hand mit Freüden ann.

Ph. Caesiens Hooch-Deutsche Spraach-übung Oder unvorgreiffliches Bedenken Über die Hooch-deutsche Haupt-Spraache und derselben Schreibrichtigkeit; Jn unter-redung gestellet/ und auff begehren und guhtbefinden der Hoochlöblichen Deutsch-Zunfft herfür-gegeben. (Hamburg: Heinrich Werner 1643), in: *Zesen SW* XI, 9f. Auch in Rists *Schauplatz*, 48. — Auch auf den 5. Teil der *Frauenzimmer-Gesprächspiele* (1645; Ndr. 1969) Harsdörffers verfaßte Rist Verse (S.41f.), die aber in *Rist: Schauplatz*, 234f. fehlen. Im 5. Teil stehen auf S.234f. Verse Rists mit dem Titel „Sinne-Bild Uber das fünfte Theil der nie genug-gepriesenen Gespräch-spiele/ Des WolEdlen/ Vesten und hochberümten Herrn Spielenden zu Nürnberg […]." Ohne Pictura. Im 6. Teil (1646; Ndr. 1969), 26f. pries Rist nochmals den Spielenden in einer „Kling-Rede An das Teutsche Reich"; verbessert u. ergänzt auch in Rist: Neüer Teutscher Parnass/ Auff welchem befindlich Ehr' und Lehr Schertz und Schmertz Leid- und Freüden-Gewächse/ … Allen/ der Teütschen Helden-Sprache und deroselben edlen Dichtkunst vernünfftigen Liebhaberen … außgestreüet (Lüneburg: Johann u. Heinrich Stern 1652), 513f. (Ndr. Hildesheim u.a. 1978). Auch entspann sich ein Austausch von Gedichten u. Geschenken, so im *Schauplatz* Rists

„Antwohrt Auff das schöne Klaag-Sonnett" Harsdörffers „Betreffend den jämmerlichen Untergang deß Edlen Teütschen Landes." (Bl. 10f.), bzw. in einem Dankgedicht Rists für Harsdörffers „schönes/ mit zweyen nachdenklichen Sinnenbildern geziertes und sehr künstlich geschlieffnes Trink-Glaß aus Nürenberg" (S. 124–126). S. 430000.

441223

Georg Philipp Harsdörffer an Philipp von Zesen

Auf die Nachricht Georg Conrad Osthofs (DG. Der Sammlende. 1644) hin, Georg Philipp Harsdörffer (FG 368. Der Spielende; DG 12. Der Kunstspielende. 1644; PBO. Strephon. 1644/45) sei in die Deutschgesinnete Genossenschaft aufgenommen worden, nimmt dieser die Mitgliedschaft an und dankt dafür dem Oberhaupt dieser Akademie, Philipp v. Zesen (FG 521. 1648. DG 1. Der Färtige). Er kenne zwar noch nicht die zentralen Statuten der DG, wisse aber um das Genossenschaftsziel der Erhebung und Ableitung des Deutschen aus seinen Gründen. Dabei unterbreitet er Vorschläge für das Sinnbild der Genossenschaft und seine eigene Imprese. Als Anleitung für die Gestaltung der Rosensymbolik der DG sendet Harsdörffer eine Abbildung des Indianischen Palmbaums auf dem Siegel der Fruchtbringenden Gesellschaft. Die DG könne einen von Rosen umkränzten Brunnen nach dem Vorbild der römischen Fontanalia wählen und somit sich gewissermaßen mit den Rosen ihrer Spracharbeit für das Geschenk der Muttersprache bedanken. Er schlägt Zesen die Verbindung der DG mit der FG vor und regt ihn zur Aufnahme weiterer Poeten in die Genossenschaft an (auch in den ital. Akademien sei die Mitgliedschaft in mehreren Akademien unter versch. Gesellschaftsnamen üblich): Wenzel Scherffer v. Scherffenstein (DG 22. 1645), Jesaias Rompler v. Löwenhalt (AGT; DG 16. 1645), Johann Klaj (PBO 1644/45; DG 23. 1645), Johann Michael Moscherosch (DG 24. 1645; FG 436. 1645), Samuel Hund (PBO 1645; DG 25. 1645) und Sigmund Betulius (geadelt S. v. Birken; PBO 1645; DG 26. 1645; FG 681. 1658). Der Kunstspielende entwirft auch nach dem Vorbild des FG-Gesellschaftspfennigs einen Plan für Medaillons der Deutschgesinneten Genossen. Ebenfalls regt Harsdörffer Zesen an, das Vorhaben seiner Gesellschaft im Druck vorzustellen, um die Spracharbeit auf weitere Mitstreiter auszudehnen und auch durch Gelehrte des Deutschen an den Hochschulen zu befördern. Einer allein müsse — wie F. Ludwig im Gesellschaftsbuch der Fruchtbringenden Gesellschaft — die formal gleichgestalteten Verse zu den Sinnbildern für die DG verfassen. Im „Stiftungsbriefe" der DG sei auch festzulegen, daß die Rechtschreibung „kein wesentliches Stück der Sprache sei", damit strittige Orthographie nicht die gutwilligen Förderer der Sprachreform abschrecke. Maßgeblich seien die Stammwörter und deren Zusammensetzung mit Vor- und Nachsilben, so wie sie Justus Georg Schottelius (FG 397) in seiner *Sprachkunst* ausbreite, welche mittlerweile von den Gelehrten und auch bei den Münsteraner Friedensverhandlungen beachtet würde. Der Kunstspielende erklärt, sich gern mit dem Färtigen einmal eine Weile darüber unterhalten zu möchten. Er erkundigt sich nach dem eigenwilligen Vokalismus Zesens und verspricht, sich von der DG belehren zu lassen. Zesen möge ihn auch über die bisherigen Mitglieder der DG und ihre laufenden Projekte unterrichten. — *Nachschrift:* Harsdörffer regt nach französischem und niederländischem Vorbild an, in der Genossenschaft die Anrede „mein Herr" ohne Titulatur zu benutzen. Er hofft, daß seine früheren Sendungen einschließlich eines beigelegten Sinnbildes eingetroffen seien und wünscht sich Widmungsgedichte der Deutschgesinneten zu seinen *Frauenzimmer-Gesprächspielen*.

Q SUB Hamburg: Sup. ep. 28, Bl. 370r–373v [A: 373v], eigenh.; Sig.; ältere Paginierung teilweise verblasst, beginnend bei 709 (?), fortgesetzt mit 712 bis 718. — *D:* In modernisierter Orthographie in *Dissel*, 55–57, vgl. S. 22 f.; danach in *Stoll*, 48–51. — *BN: Bürger*, 677 Nr. 107; *Krüger*, 1. Teilbd., 375 f.

A A Monsieur Monsieur Philippe Cæsius, Gentilhomme Allemand, demeurant à present à Utrecht. Zu Amsterdam bey H. Elzevieren[1] abzugeben.

Hochgeehrter Herr Färtiger.

Demnach mir der *Samlende*[2] bedeutet, welcher gestalt der hochlöblichen *Deutschgesinnten*[a] *Genosschaft* gefalen mich mit der dritten Stelle des zweyten Sizzes in derselben großg. zu Ehren; hab ich meiner Schuldigkeit zu seyn erachtet, solche hiermit, benebens möglichster Danksagung anzu nehmen, und[b] verpflichte mich so hohe Gewogenheit auf alle Fügnissen treueiferigen fleisses zu bedienen.

Ob mir[c] nun von dero Grund-Satzungen noch der zeit nichts ümständiges wissend ist, halte ich doch[d] für ungezweiffelt, es werde das freydeutsche und offenhertzige guhtachten eines jeden stat finden, und mit Bescheidenheit nach befinden verbessert werden: massen ich den zweck dieser Genoßschaft dahin verstanden, das die deutsche HaubtSprache durch vertreuliche zusammensetzung mit starker hand aus ihren Gründen in ihren Majestet-[370v]ischen Ehrenthron erhaben werden sol.[3] Diesem nach will ich[e] meine geringe Gedanken meh[r][f] verständigerem erachten folgender gestalt wolmeinend hiermit untergeben haben, und forderlichste nachrichtliche Belerung erwarten.

I. Jst vernünftig ausgedacht daß diese Genoßschaft die Blumen, und unter denselben die Rose, wie d[ie][f] Fruchtbringenden allerley Gartenfrüchte erkies[en][f] Jhr allgemeines (**general**) Sinnbild ist der Jndianische Palmbaum, als mitkommend auf ihrem **Sigill**[4] zu ersehen: Die *Deutschgesinnten* könten gleicherweis führe[n][f] einen Brunen, dessen röhren ein Adler; oder Adlerskopf, bekrönet ümzieret[g], oder behegt mit vielen Rosenkräntzen[5]: absehend auf der Römer **Fontinalia** von welchen zu lesen **Varro l. 5. de lingua Latin. si aquam hauris; puteum corona.**[6] Dieser Meinung, daß wie uns die deutsche Sprache gleichsam mit der Muttermilche guhtthätig eingetreiffelt worden, daß wier sie[d] zu gebuhrender d[ank]barkeit[h] mit den wolrüchenden Rosen unserer Sp[rach]arbeit[h] wiederum beschenken usw. [371r]

II. Sol man bemühet seyn die Genosschaft zu erstrekken, und die[i] Fruchtbringenden, mit ihrem belieben, darzuzihen[j]; gestalt auch in Jtalien gewohnlich, daß sich[d] ein **Academicus** in drey, vier, und mehr **Academien**, jedoch mit geänderten Namen, begiebet[7]: Also möchte ich heissen der *Kunstspielende* oder[k] der *Gewinnende*, unter den Fruchtbringenden der Spielende. Zu meinem Sinnbild wird dieses vorgeschlagen: **Mercurius** schneidet die dörner von einem Rosenholtz, an welchem oben eine Zukkerrosen zusehen, um einen Spielstab zu machen.[8]

III. Die Fruchtbringenden tragen ihre GesellschaftsPfenning an einem Sittiggrünem Band, auf Gold geschmeltzt (meiner hat bey 20 Rthl. gekostet.) Wier könten sie auf einer Seiten mit dem vorbesagten Haubt Sinnbilde den Brunnen, auf der anderen mit iedes absonderlichen Schrift, Namen und Gemähl bemercket, an einem Rosenfarben band von^l Silber und verguldt tragen.⁹

IV. Solte nicht ausser dem wege seyn einen Entwurff von dem Vorhaben der Deutschgesinnten, mit dem Haubt Sinnbild, und etwan denen drey oder vier ersten Sizzen in offentlichen drukk zugeben, benebens vermelden was noch in unserer Sprach zu thun; und angehängter Einladung [371v] aller deutschliebenden Gemühter, daß also mit gesamter hand dieses werk angegangen und sonderlich auf den hohen Schulen durch die deutschgelehrte beförderet werden möchte.¹⁰

V. Mier sind, ohne ruhm zu schreiben, viel tapfere Poëten mit Freundschaft zugethan, welche alle mit eintretten solten, wann sie, wie ich hoffe, von^d der Genosschaft unter^d folgenden oder dergleichen Namen möchten aufgenommen werden.

1. *Wenzel Scherffer von Scherffenstein* Ein Schlesischer von Adel[,]^h hat die **Pia Desideria H. Hermani** gedeutschet, verlanget zu wissen, ob der Färtige nicht desgleichen gethan und^m im fall es nicht geschehen, ob es Elzevier verlegen wolte. Er kann heissen *der Verlangende*: Zum Sinnbild haben einen Engel auf einem Anker stehend, dessen ring ein rosenkrantz ist, und ihm das Haubt bekrönet.¹¹

2. *Jesaias Rumpler von Löwenhalt*, Ein Elsasser. Wird seine Gedichte von mancherley Erfindung ehester tagen dem drukk untergeben: kan heißen *der Freye*: sein Gemähl sol seyn weisse rosen deren Blätlein der Wind verwähet, und von einem liebskind aufgelesen werden. jhden^n stäht es frei¹²

3. *Joh. Clajus*. Ein wolgeborner Poët hat hier öffentlich Geistliche Lieder auf die hohen feste, und jüngsthin eine Rede freye von der deutschen Poëterey hören lassen: kan [372r] heissen der *Fremde*, und zum Gemähl haben eine hand mit einem Rosenbusch, und unter den Rosen die Jerusalems Blume. Jetz arbeitet er an dem kindermord Herodes.¹³

4. *Joh. Michael Moscherosch*, sonsten Philander von S[itte]walt° kan heissen der *Traumende*, und zum Sinnbild habe[n]° , Ein liebskind auf den Blumen, die Nachtschatten, oder **flores Noctis** benammet, schlaffend, dem Venus a[...]^p die Freye (daher freyen und Freytag dies ♀^q den Namen bey den alten Deutschen gehabt) einen Rosenkrantz^r aufsetzet.¹⁴

5. *Samuel Hund* kan heissen der *Erneurende*, und zum Sinnbild haben die Monatrosen, welche von einem wassergefäß begossen werden. hat etliche Gedichte drukkfertig.¹⁵

6. *Samuel Betulius*. hat unterschiedliche^s feine Gedicht gemachet, und sol dieser samlen alle zweydeutige wörter in unserer Sprache, wie **de La Noue** in dem Frantzösischen gethan. Wann ich hierinnen vollmacht zu werben, sol die Gesellschaft bald vermehret werden: Erstbesagter Betulius kan heissen der rüchende, und zum Sinnbild haben ein Glas mit Rosenwasser, in einem von rohten und weissen rosen gebundenen Krantze stehend.¹⁶

VI. Die *Reimen* oder *Verse* der Sinnbilder müssen gleichartig und von einem allein aufgesetzet werden, wie bey [372v] den *Fruchtbringenden* der *Neherende* thut.[17]

VII. Daß man unter anderen Gesetzen in den Stifftung[s]brief[h] gedenke, wie die rechtschreibung kein wesentliches[t] Stuck der Sprache sey[18]: massen die Gedanken, durch die wort, die wort durch die Schrift ausgebildet werd[en,][h] wie nun eine Sache durch unterschiedliche wort, so kan auch ein wort, (ohne versehrung seiner grunddeutung) mit unterschiedlichen buchstaben ausgedrukket werden. Solte man dieses nicht belieben und die strittige[u] Schreibung nicht[d] zu reifferm nachgründen stellen, würden viel darvon abgeschrekket und unser Vorhaben merklich gehemmet werden. Einmahl sind[v] die Stammwörter, Vor- und nachsylben kuns[t]gewiß[h] zu[d] beobachten[w], welche nach des Suchenden Sprachkunst[19] insgemein von den Gelehrten, (sonderlich bey der Reichshandlung zu Münster) für richtig angenommen und[x] gebrauchet worden, wie ich in etlichen Schriften selbst gelesen.[20] Jch wolte wünschen mit meinem hochgeehrten Herrn ein Stündlein hiervon zureden: dan ich nicht begreiffen kan, warüm man schreiben solte Sü[nn,][o] fünden, wüllen für Sinn, sinnen, willen finden usw.[21] [373r] Dieses, wie auch alles andere, will ich zu der höchlöblichen Gesellschaft verständigen Erachtung gestellet, und mich deroselben wolgewogenen belehrung dienstl. untergeben haben. Bitte mier die Namen der bisher eingetrettenen Genossen, und ihren unter handen habenden werken, ehest zu meiner und anderer Nachrichtung zu übersenden. Ein mehrers mit nechstem. Meinen hochgeehrten Herrn hiermit des Höchsten obschutz und mich zu seinen beharrlichen Gunsten befehlend. Geben Nürnb[erg][o] den 23 Christmonats 1644. durch

  des Färtigen Getreuen Knecht
  den Spielenden

N. S.
Unter anderen könten wier auch aufbringen das man ohne Titel schriebe Mein Herr, wie die Frantzosen und Niederländer. Mier zweiffelt nicht meine jüngste[y] werden zurechtkommen seyn, mit eingelegtem Sinnbilde.[22] Wolte wünschen daß etliche von den Deutschgesinnten den[z] Gesprächspielen ihre guhte Gedanken möchten beyschicken.

T *Im Wort* Teutsch-/ Deutsch- *scheint der T-Anlaut regelmäßig durch D ersetzt worden zu sein. Üblicherweise bevorzugte Harsdörffer die Schreibung Teutsch.*[23] *Sind die Verbesserungen eine Konzession an die Schreibweise Zesens oder gar von diesem ausgeführt?* — **a** *Verschreibung:* Deutschgeschgesinnten — **b** *Korrigiert aus* vnd — **c** *Korrigiert aus* mier — **d** *Eingefügt.* — **e** *Folgt* <dem> — **f** *Unsichere Lesung, da in den Falz übergehend; Konjektur in eckigen Klammern.* — **g** *Bis* behegt *am Rand ergänzt.* — **h** *Buchstabenverlust im Falz; Konjektur in eckigen Klammern.* — **i** *Folgt* <aus der> — **j** *Lies:* dazuzuziehen (*i. S. v.* hinzuzuziehen). — **k** *Bis* Gewinnende *am Rand ergänzt.* — **l** *Bis* vergulth *am Rand ergänzt.* — **m** *Bis* wolte. Er *am Rand ergänzt.* — **n** *Bis frei von Zesen (?) eingefügt.* — **o**

Buchstabenverlust durch Papierabrieb; Konjektur in eckigen Klammern. — **p** *Buchstabenverlust durch Papierabrieb.* — **q** dies ♀ *eingefügt.* — **r** *Von Zesen (?) unterstrichen.* — **s** *Eingefügt für* <etliche> — **t** *Korrigiert aus* <wissentliches> — **u** *Eingefügt für* <einzige> — **v** *Eingefügt für* <müssen> — **w** *Korrigiert aus* beobachtet <werden> — **x** *Eingefügt für* <word> — **y** *Ergänze:* Briefe/ Sendungen — **z** *Gebessert aus* würden

K Georg Philipp Harsdörffer (FG 368. Der Spielende; DG 12. 1644) verwendet im vorliegenden Brief durchweg die Schreibung „Genosschaft"/ „Genoßschaft". Im Sinne seines grammatischen Analogismus forderte er einheitliche Wortansetzungen, womit es entsprechend der „Kauffmannschaft" dann auch „Genoßschaft" anstatt „genossenschaft" heißen müsse. Diese „Gleichstimmung der Sprache" nannte er „Analogia", das Hauptinstrument der sprachlichen „Ratio". Harsdörffer: Der Teutsche SECRETARIUS: Das ist: Allen Cantzley- Studir- und Schreibstuben nützliches und fast nohtwendiges Formular- und Titularbuch. [2. Ausg.] Nürnberg 1655, 727f. Folgerichtig erscheint auf dem Siegel des PBO die Wortansetzung „Blumgenosschafft". Das Siegel abgebildet in *Bircher: Palme* I, 16.

1 Ludwig Elzevier (1604–1670) aus der berühmten holländ. Buchdrucker- u. Verlegerfamilie, selbständiger Drucker u. Buchhändler in der von ihm 1638 gegründeten Amsterdamer Offizin, die er 1665 seinem Cousin Daniel (1626–1680) überließ. Vgl. Rudolf Schmidt: Deutsche Buchhändler. Deutsche Buchdrucker. Beiträge zu einer Firmengeschichte des deutschen Buchgewerbes. 6 Bde., Berlin, Eberswalde 1902–1908, II (1903), 209 u. 211 (genealog. Tafel); Alphonse Willems: Les Elzevier. Histoire et Annales Typographiques. Bruxelles (u. a.) 1880, S. LXIf. Zwischen 1645 u. 1660 kam es zu einer engen Zusammenarbeit Zesens mit Ludwig Elzevier, der ihn mit Übersetzungen beauftragte u. bei dem er sich vielleicht auch als Korrektor verdingte. In Elzeviers Amsterdamer Verlag erschienen jedenfalls Zesens *Adriatische Rosemund* (1645), seine Roman-Übersetzungen *Liebesbeschreibung Lysanders und Kalisten* (1644), *Ibrahim Bassa* (1645, vgl. 441201), die *Afrikanische Sofonisbe* (1647) u. die Übersetzung eines Standardwerks zum Festungsbau, Matthias Dögens *Heutiges tages übliche Krieges Bau-kunst* (1648). Vgl. *Ingen*, 23; ferner 440724 K 6 u. 450410 K 2.

2 Von seiner Aufnahme in die DG (am 4.12.1644) erfuhr Harsdörffer demnach durch Georg Conrad Osthof aus Celle, in der DG „Der Sammlende" (DG 8; 8.10.1644) u. im PBO 1648 Amyntas. Harsdörffer schlug ihn auch (erfolglos) zur Aufnahme in die FG vor. S. 451101 u. 451209. Osthof hatte Anfang der 40er Jahre in Helmstedt u. Altdorf studiert u. war Ende 1644 von Nürnberg nach Norddeutschland (Celle) zurückgekehrt. Ein Brief an Harsdörffer vom 31.1.1648 hat sich im PBO-Archiv im GNM Nürnberg erhalten. S. *Jürgensen: Repertorium*, 181f. Harsdörffer sollte lt. 450400 in der DG „Der Durchbrechende" heißen mit dem Sinnbild: „ein Bohtsmann, mit einem brechschifflein, damit man in Niederlanden den anderen Schiffen den Weg durch das Eis zu bahnen, und fürfahrt durchzubrechen pfleget [...] Diesen Bohtsmann beschenket eine KunstGöttin (musa) am Ufer mit einem Rosenkrantz". In seiner Antwort 450529 gab F. Ludwig zu bedenken, es sei „der vorgeschlagene Nahme des Durchbrechenden Bohtsmannes, der durch das eis nach dem RosenKrantze schiffet, etwas weitleuftig, und wie der *Spielende* weis, sich ein uberflüßiges gemälde in den Emblematibus oder Sinnebildern nicht wol schicken wil". Harsdörffer hatte sich schon im vorliegenden Brief selbst eine andere DG-Imprese mit dem Gesellschaftsnamen „der *Kunstspielende* oder der *Gewinnende*" entworfen. Die Gesellschaftsschriften der DG führen ihn unter dem Gesellschaftsnamen „der Kunstspielende" auf, allerdings mit einem anderen Bild als dem von Harsdörffer selbst vorgeschlagenen: „eine Kunstgöttin/ welche in einem lieblichen Tahle/ unten am Helikon/ unter den

Rosen/ auf einer Laute/ von Rosenholtze gemacht/ ein kunstliedlein spielet; mit beigefügtem Zunftworte: Es ist lieblich/ und löblich." Philipp v. Zesen (FG 521. 1648; DG 1. 1643. Der Färtige): Das Hochdeutsche Helikonische Rosentahl/ das ist/ Der höchstpreiswürdigen Deutschgesinneten Genossenschaft Erster Oder Neunstämmiger Rosen-Zunft Ertzschrein (Amsterdam 1669). In: *Zesen SW* XII, 178–310, hier 240 f.; vgl. auch S. 316, 424 u. 448.

3 Ein Bericht über die (in Wirklichkeit zweifelhafte) Gründung am 1.5.1643 in Hamburg, dazu über Mitglieder, Impresen, Organisation, Ehrenämter, Ziele u. Gepflogenheiten der DG erschien erst 1669 im Druck, Zesens *Hochdeutsches Helikonisches Rosentahl* (s. Anm. 2). Darin, nämlich im „Vorbericht an den Deutschgesinten Leser", erscheint u. a. das Gesellschaftsziel, die deutsche Sprache „in ihrem wesen und stande/ ohne einmischung fremder ausheimischer wörter/ aufs müglichste und tuhnlichste/ den Fruchtbringenden zur löblichen folge/ zu erhalten/ und sich der besten und reinesten Meisnischen oder Obersächsischen mundahrt/ so wohl im reden/ als schreiben/ es sei gereimt/ oder ungereimt/ zu befleissigen." A. a. O., 205. Anders als die FG hat die DG auch ein ausgearbeitetes Statut, die „algemeine Zunftsatzungen", veröffentlicht, die sich dem „Vorbericht" anschließen u. das Ziel des Sprachausbaus gleich eingangs bekräftigen: „1. ALle [sic] diejenigen/ welche der löblichen Deutschgesinneten Genossenschaft einverleibet zu werden begehren/ sollen der Edelen Hochdeutschen Sprache mächtig sein/ und derselben zuwachs und aufnehmen/ entweder durch schriften/ oder andere mittel/ zu befördern angeloben. — 2. Vor allen dingen sollen alle und jede Zunftgenossen verpfichtet sein/ ihren euersten fleis an zu wenden/ daß gemelter Sprache eigene angebohrne grundzierde nicht allein erhalten/ und vor allem fremden unwesen und gemische bewahret; sondern auch je länger je treflicher vermehret/ ja alles eingeschlichene unreine/ ungesetzmäßige/ und ausheimische abgeschaffet/ und in ein besseres/ wo immer tuhnlich/ verändert werde." A. a. O., 206. Ebd., 210 wird noch einmal verdeutlicht, daß „unser fürnehmstes absehen auf die erhaltung/ fortpflanzung/ und volkomnere auswürkung der reinligkeit unserer edlen Hochdeutschen Sprache gerichtet: einer solchen Sprache/ die von den Haupt- stam- und grund-sprachen der welt die einigste [lies: einzige] ist/ welche/ nach aller der andern untergange/ nur allein/ in ihrem gantzen grundwesen/ noch rein und unverfälscht geblieben" usw.

4 Wie bei auswärtigen Aufnahmen üblich, war Harsdörffer von dem bevollmächtigten, in der Nähe Nürnbergs lebenden Hans Philipp (v.) Geuder (FG 310) rezipiert worden (vgl. 411200 K 0), jedoch war ihm mit 410909 ein gesiegeltes Einladungsschreiben der FG zugegangen. — In F. Ludwigs Nachlaß fanden sich 1650 „Zwey Sigel in Meßing der Fruchtbringenden gesellschaft eines mit einem höltzernen Stiehl, daß ander gantz Meßing" (*IP*, 394r). *Conermann: Nachlaßinventar,* 74. Erwähnt ist ein „Jnsiegel" der FG auch in 461026 (F. Ludwigs Aufnahmevollmacht an Pgf. Ludwig Philipp v. Simmern. FG 97) u. *DA Köthen I. 8*: 480703 (Vollmacht für Christian Ernst v. Knoch. FG 268; s. *KE*, 60). In Knochs erster Vollmacht (401107) zeigt das Abbild im ovalen Rahmen mit der Devise u. dem Namen der FG („ALLES ZV NVTZEN FRVCHTBRINGENDE GESELSCHAFFT") eine Kokospalme vor einem Palmenhain. Abb. des Papiersiegels in *DA Köthen I. 5*, 581. Eine maßstabsgetreue Abb. des FG-Hauptsiegels in *Neumark: Palmbaum,* Tafel zu S. 219; in *Conermann: Stieler,* passim, mit Abb. eines Siegelabdrucks der FG von 1668. In seiner *Fortpflanzung der Hochlöblichen Fruchtbringenden Geselschaft,* 1651 aus Anlaß der Übernahme der Oberhauptschaft der FG durch Hz. Wilhelm IV. v. Sachsen-Weimar (FG 5) veröffentlicht, berichtet Harsdörffer auf S. 3, wie jenem die „volle Gewalt und das gewönliche Geselschaft-Siegel/ samt allen im vorigen [Köthener] Ertzschreine befundenen nötigen Urkunden übergeben" wurden. Harsdörffer dürfte das

FG-Siegel auf seinem Einladungsschreiben abgezeichnet oder kalkiert (abgepaust) an Zesen gesandt haben. Das Originalschreiben konnte nicht ermittelt werden u. ist offenbar verloren. Das Bildelement des Köthener Siegels ist nicht identisch mit der Palmen-Vignette, die Harsdörffer erstmals im 2. Teil der *Frauenzimmer-Gesprächspiele* (2. Aufl. 1644, Ndr. 1968), auf S. 12 (Ndr. S. 30) verwendete u. die den vorderen Umschlag unserer Editionsbände ziert. In den *Frauenzimmer-Gesprächspielen* findet sich darüber hinaus keine Abbildung eines FG-Siegels. Vgl. zum FG-Siegel 271201 K 4, 371110 K 11; *DA Köthen I*. 5, 106; 450410, 450817, 450919A, 460000A K, 460816 u. 461006 K 0.

5 Die DG führte „zum algemeinen Wahrzeichen oder Sinbilde/ einen Rosenstok/ mit drei großen weissen Zibeth- oder Bisem-rosen/ davon zwar die eine schon völlig ausgeblühet/ doch die andere nur halb geöfnet/ und die dritte/ in ihrer knubbe [d.i. Knospe]/ noch gantz geschlossen/ wiewohl sie allerseits durch die strahlen der Sonne angeblikket werden/ in einem sterbeblauen felde; mit dieser algemeinen Zunftlosung: Unter den Rosen/ | ist liebliches Losen". Philipp v. Zesen: *Hochdeutsches Helikonisches Rosentahl* (s. Anm. 2), 218. Im Anschluß folgen ein Kupferstich dieses Sinnbildes u. ein Gedicht Zesens zu seiner Erklärung (S. 219f.). Harsdörffers Vorschlag für die Imprese der DG fand also keine Aufnahme. Zur Bedeutung der Farbe „sterbeblau"/ bleu mourant bei Zesen vgl. 450808 K I 4.

6 M. TERENTII VARRONIS DE LINGVA LATINA NOVA EDITIO. GASP: SCIOPPIVS RECENSVIT (Ingolstadt 1605), darin LIBER QVINTVS. Ad M. Tullium Ciceronem, 73–107, S. 82: „Fontanalia à fonte, quòd is dies feriæ eius: ab eo autem tum, & in fontes coronas iaciunt, & puteos coronant." HAB: Xb 8387; dig. Die Stelle bezieht sich auf das altröm. Brunnenfest („Fontanalia") zu Ehren des Quellengottes Fons/ Fontus, das alljährlich am 13. Oktober gefeiert wurde, wenn nach der Sommertrockenheit die Quellen wieder strömten.

7 Harsdörffer war mit den Usancen italien. Akademien vertraut. In 450817 umreißt er einen Plan, ein Netz von Beziehungen zwischen der FG u. einer Reihe von italien. Akademien, insbes. der Accademia degli Oziosi (Neapel) aufzubauen. S. *Conermann: Harsdörffers Plan.* Vgl. auch 450919A, 450923C, 451101, 451217 u. 460120, ferner *Harsdörffer: Frauenzimmer-Gesprächspiele*, 2. Teil (²1657, Ndr. 1968), 4/ Ndr. 22 – 11/ 39 („Von Fremden Sinnbildern" mit den Impresen der Intronati [Siena] u. der Umoristi [Rom]).

8 Zu Harsdörffers Gesellschaftsnamen u. Imprese in der DG vgl. Anm. 2.

9 Das allgemeine „Zunftzeichen" der DG (s. Anm. 5) oder der „Zunftschmuk", den „alle und jede Zunftglieder üm den hals/ und auf der brust/ zu einem sonderlichen kenzeichen/ bei ihren zusammenkünften/ nach belieben tragen sollen: der ist ein zukker-rosenfärbiges seidenes Band; welches vom halse herab bis auf die brust gehet: da es/ unten am buge/ mit einem güldenen oder silbern-vergüldetem Brust- oder Prunk-pfennige; über dem buge aber/ zur rechten mit dem Nahmen Rosenzunft/ zur linken mit des Zunftgliedes eigenem Zunftnahmen/ mit himmelblauer seide gestükt [lies: gestickt]/ gezieret wird. Auch stehet auf des Brustpfenniges einer seite des Zunftgliedes eigenes Zunftzeichen; auf der andern aber der gantzen Rosenzunft algemeines […] entweder geprägt/ oder eingeschmolzen." Philipp v. Zesen: *Hochdeutsches Helikonisches Rosentahl* (s. Anm. 2), 196, vgl. auch 203 f. — Das auf Gold farbig emaillierte Gesellschaftsmedaillon der FG zeigte auf der Vorderseite die Palmenimprese der Gesellschaft, auf der Rückseite die jeweilige Mitgliedsimprese. Jedes Mitglied sollte einen solchen Gesellschaftspfennig anfertigen lassen, jedoch scheinen keine Originalpfennige in öffentlichen Münzsammlungen mehr erhalten zu sein. Vgl. die Abb. des Gesellschaftspfennigs F. Augusts v. Anhalt-Plötzkau (FG 46) in *DA Köthen I*. 3, 138. Zu den Gesellschaftspfennigen der FG vgl. auch den *Kurtzen Bericht* in den Gesellschaftsbüchern der FG, z. B. *DA Köthen II*. 1, S. [10] (*Kur-*

tzer Bericht im *GB Kö. 1622* u. *1628), Conermann I (Kurtzer Bericht* im *GB Kö. [1629/ 30]), GB 1641, GB 1641/44, GB 1646*. Auf Fruchtbringer-Porträts ist der Gesellschaftspfennig häufig, aber selten genau abgebildet, s. z. B. Harsdörffers Porträt auf S. 1063 u. *DA Köthen I*. 6, 522 u. 647. Der Gesellschaftspfennig spielt im vorliegenden Band v. a. in der Korrespondenz zwischen F. Ludwig, Harsdörffer u. Johann Michael Moscherosch (FG 436. 1645) eine Rolle. Vgl. 410914 K 4; 450100 K I 4, 450500 K 1, 450504A K 5, 460120, 460406, 460426, 460609 u. 460726, ferner das Lemma „Gesellschaftspfennig FG" im kumulierten Sachregister dieses Bandes.

10 Ein solches Dokument erschien erst 1669 mit Zesens *Hochdeutschem Helikonischen Rosentahl* (s. Anm. 2) im Druck. Vgl. Anm. 18.

11 Wenzel Scherffer v. Scherffenstein (1603–1674), wurde am 3.4.1645 als 22. Mitglied unter dem Namen des „Verlangenden" in die DG aufgenommen. Sein Zunftzeichen folgte Harsdörffers Vorschlag: „einen Engel/ der auf einem in die höhe gerichtetem Anker stehet/ dessen ring ein Rosenkrantz ist/ und dem Engel das heupt bekräntzet." Philipp v. Zesen: *Hochdeutsches Helikonisches Rosentahl* (s. Anm. 2), 250, s. auch 424 u. 454. Dem ersten Teil der *Frauenzimmer-Gesprächspiele* (^{2}1644, Ndr. 1968) hatte Scherffer ein Widmungs-Sonett beigesteuert, d. d. Brieg 19.12.1644, inc.: „OB ihr gleich meine Schaar, ihr edle Pierinnen" (Ndr., 337 f.). Scherffers Übersetzung von Hermann Hugos (1588–1629) *Pia desideria* (zuerst 1624) erschien erst 1662: HERMANNIS HUGONIS S. J. Gottsäliger Verlangen Drey Bücher/ nehmlich: 1. Wehklagen der Büssenden Seelen. 2. Wünsche der Heiligen Seelen. 3. Seufftzen der Liebenden Seelen (o. O.: Selbstverlag 1662; Ndr. Tübingen 1995). *Dünnhaupt: Handbuch*, S. 3605 Nr. 39. In die Gefilde der FG wurde Scherffer nicht eingeladen. Er schrieb allerdings zur Aufnahme Hz. Christians in Schlesien zu Brieg, Wohlau u. Liegnitz (FG 505. Der Beliebige) in die FG am 15.6.1648 eine „Trochaische Reis- und Glückwünschungs Ode", die ebenso wie ein Libretto zur Heimführung von Christians Braut Fn. Louise v. Anhalt-Dessau (19.1.1649) Kenntnis über die Einnahmegepflogenheiten der FG verrät. S. *DA Köthen I. 8:* 480615 u. I, *Conermann III*, 636–639 u. 460718 K 8.

12 Jesaias Rompler v. Löwenhalt (1605–1676). Das aus Dinkelsbühl stammende Gründungsmitglied der 1633 ins Leben gerufenen Aufrichtigen Gesellschaft von der Tannen in Straßburg war als „Der Freie" Mitglied in der DG (Nr. 16; 4.2.1645) mit dem Sinnbild: „einen im freien offenen felde gepflantzten Rosenstok/ dessen abgewehete Rosenblätter ein Liebeskind [Putto] auflieset; mit diesem Zunftspruche: Jedem steht es frei". Philipp v. Zesen: *Hochdeutsches Helikonisches Rosentahl* (s. Anm. 2), 244; vgl. auch 424 u. 454. In 450308A wird Zesen Rompler den Beschluß der DG zu seiner Aufnahme sowie Harsdörffers Erfindung seines Gesellschaftsnamens u. Sinnbilds in der DG mitteilen. Damit wurden die von Harsdörffer vorgeschlagenen DG-Kandidaten alle, mit Ausnahme Romplers, am 3.4.1645 aufgenommen. S. Anm. 11, 13, 14, 15 u. 16. Zu Rompler vgl. ferner 370900 u. 440724 K 4, auch zu seiner Kritik an der FG, in die er nicht aufgenommen wurde, u. zu seiner Bekanntschaft mit Zesen bzw. seiner Aufnahme in die DG. — Seine Gedichte erschienen u. d. T. [Holzschnitt]: Des | Jesaias Romplers von | Löwenhalt | [Zierstück] | erstes gebüsch | seiner | Reim_getichte. | [Zierleiste] | Getruckt zu Strasburg/ bej Joh. Phil. Mülben/ | in dem 1647.ten jar Chrl.^{er} z. [Christlicher Zeitrechnung]. Weitere Teile der „Reimgebüsche" sind nicht erschienen.

13 Johann Klaj (1616–1656), aus Meißen stammender u. in Nürnberg eingewanderter großer Dichter, der trotz Harsdörffers Empfehlung (450505) nicht in die FG eintreten konnte. Er gründete mit Harsdörffer Anfang 1645 in Nürnberg den PBO als Orden; sein Gesellschaftsname war „Clajus". Zur Gründung des PBO s. jüngst *Conermann: Harsdörffers Plan* (mit Lit.). In der DG, in der er als „Der Fremde" u. Nr. 23 am 3.4.1645 verzeichnet wurde, führte er als Zunftzeichen „eine hand mit einem busche von Rosen/ darunter die Jerusalemsblume herfür blikket". Philipp v. Zesen: *Hochdeutsches Helikonisches Rosentahl* (s. Anm.2), 251; vgl. auch 425 u. 450. Zu seinen frühen, öffentlich vorgetragenen Redeoratorien vgl. 440824 K 7. Am 18./ 28.10.1644 deklamierte er seine Anfang 1645 bei Endter in Nürnberg erschienene *Lobrede der Teutschen Poeterey/ Abgefasset und in Nürnberg Einer Hochansehnlich-Volkreichen Versammlung vorgetragen* (HAB: Xb 90 [1]), Ndr. J. K.: Redeoratorien und „Lobrede der teutschen Poeterey". Hg. Conrad Wiedemann. Tübingen 1965. Vgl. 440824 K 7. Im Verlag Endter erschien 1645 auch Klajs Bearbeitung von Calderóns *El mayor monstro del mundo* (Madrid 1637): *Herodes der Kinder-Mörder*. Vgl. *Dünnhaupt: Handbuch*, 2355f.; *Jürgensen: Repertorium*, 50–63.

14 Johann Michael Moscherosch (FG 436. 1645. Der Träumende), in der DG als 24. Mitglied (3.4.1645) u. „Der Treumende", mit dem Zunftzeichen: „ein Liebeskind/ welches auf dem Nachtschatten/ und Schlafrosen oder schlafkuntzen ruhet und schläfet/ und von der Liebe mit Rosen bekräntzet wird". Philipp v. Zesen: *Hochdeutsches Helikonisches Rosentahl* (s. Anm.2), 252; vgl. auch 425 u. 452. Zu Moscherosch, den Harsdörffer für die Aufnahme in die FG empfohlen hatte s. 450500 K, 450818 K 1, 460726 u.ö.

15 Samuel Hund (um 1620 – nach 1680), 1644–1646 in Nürnberg, wo er die Bekanntschaft mit Harsdörffer machte u. zum Freundeskreis um Johann Klaj gehörte; im PBO „Myrtillus I.". Er gehörte Anfang 1645 zu den eigentlichen Gründern des PBO, die nach der Anregung durch Harsdörffers u. Klajs *Pegnesischem Schäfergedicht* (Sept. 1644) als Orden u. d. T. „Der Pegnitz-Schäfer Lobgetichte" im 5. Teil von *Harsdörffer: Frauenzimmer-Gesprächspiele* auftraten. *Conermann: Harsdörffers Plan*, 43. In der DG hieß Hund „Der Erneuernde" (Nr.25; 3.4.1645) mit dem Zunftzeichen „die Mahnrosen/ welche mit einem gartenkruge begossen werden". Philipp v. Zesen: *Hochdeutsches Helikonisches Rosentahl* (s. Anm.2), 252f.; vgl. auch 425 u. 451. Widmungsgedichte zum 5. Teil der Harsdörfferschen *Gesprächspiele* (1645, Ndr. 1969, S.46–52) u. in anderen Werken aus dem Umkreis des PBO. 1651 veröffentlichte er in Leiden eine Sammlung geistlicher Lieder, die sich nicht erhalten hat. Vgl. *Jürgensen: Repertorium*, 102–104; *Conermann: Harsdörffers Plan*, zu Anm.76 u. 77.

16 „Samuel" Betulius, d.i. der Dichter Sigismund(us) Betulius, der nach seiner ksl. Nobilitierung (1654) Sigmund v. Birken (FG 681. 1658) hieß. Seit 1645 war er als „Floridan" Mitglied, nach dem Tod Harsdörffers (1658) wurde er 1662 zum Neugründer u. Oberhaupt des PBO. Hartmut Laufhütte: Gründung, Neugründung und Neuorientierung des Pegnesischen Blumenordens durch die beiden ersten Präsidenten. In: *Laufhütte (Hg.): PBO*, 173–186. Im Dezember 1645 begab sich Birken mit einem Empfehlungsschreiben Harsdörffers nach Wolfenbüttel, wo er als Hilfslehrer bei der Erziehung der Prinzen deren Präzeptor Justus-Georg Schottelius (FG 397) beigegeben wurde. Der hzl. Leibarzt Martin Gosky krönte Betulius zum Dichter. Im Oktober 1646 wurde Betulius entlassen. Er begab sich auf eine Reise durch Norddeutschland, wo er u.a. Johann Rist (FG 467. 1647) besuchte. In die DG wurde Birken als 26. Mitglied am 3.4.1645 als der „Riechende" aufgenommen. Sein Zunftzeichen war „ein glas mit Rosenessige/ welches in einem von roht- und weissen Rosen gewundenem Krantze stehet". Philipp v. Zesen: *Hochdeutsches Helikonisches Rosentahl* (s. Anm.2), 253; vgl. auch 425 u. 446; *Jürgensen: Repertorium*, 64–101. — Der Reformierte François de La Noue (1531–1591), berühmt als Heerführer der Hugenotten u. Provinzgouverneur, verschaffte sich mit den beiden in span. Gefangenschaft von 1580 bis 1585 verfaßten Werken, den 25 *Discours politiques et militaires* (mit vielen Referenzen auf den von ihm hochgeschätzten Plutarch — von Napoleon die „Bible du soldat" genannt) u. den *Observations sur plusieurs choses advenues aux trois premiers troubles* das Renommé eines der bemerkenswertesten historischen u. moralistischen

Schriftsteller seiner Zeit. Beide Werke erschienen, versehen mit einem Widmungs-Vorwort an Kg. Heinrich v. Navarra (1553–1610; seit 1589 als Heinrich IV. König von Frankreich) von Philippe Canaye, Seigneur de Fresnes (d. d. Lausanne, 1.4.1587), unter dem Titel: DISCOVRS POLITIQVES ET Militaires du Seigneur de la Nouë. NOVVELLEMENT REcueillis & mis en lumiere. A Basle, De l'Imprimerie de François Forest. HAB: O 142. 4° Helmst. Die „OBSERVATIONS SVR PLVSIEVRS CHOSES ADVENVES AVX trois premiers Troubles, auecques la vraye declaration de la plusport d'icelles" über die ersten drei Hugenottenkriege (1562–1570) erschienen darin als 26. Discours. Als seine „Mémoires" wurde dieser Text mehrfach separat veröffentlicht, u. a. in Jean-Antoine Roucher (Ed.): Collection universelle des mémoires particulières à l'histoire de France. Tome 47, Paris 1807; Joseph Michaud (Ed.): Nouvelle collection des mémoires pour servir à l'histoire de France, Serie I, Tome 9, Paris 1838. Eine dt. Übersetzung der *Discours* erschien 1592: Discours Oder Beschreibung vnd vßführliches rähtliches bedencken/ von allerhand so wol Politischen/ als Kriegssachen. Erstlich durch den Edlen/ hocherfahrnen ... Frantzösischen KriegsObristen/ den Herren De la Nove Jn Frantzösischer sprach beschriben/ hernach durch den Herren de Fresnes zu samen gefaßt/ vnd an Tag geben. Jetzundt aber auß dem Frantzösischen in vnser geliebte Teutsche sprach auffs trewlichst vnd fleissigst vertirt. Durch: Jacob Rahtgeben/ Fürstlichen Würtembergischen Secretarium zu Mümpelgarten &c. (Frankfurt a. M. 1591). HAB: 13 Pol. La Noue hinterließ eine interessante *Correspondance* (Hg. Ph. Kervyn de Volkaersbeke, Paris, de la Haye 1854; Reprint Genève 1971). Eine von ihm veranstaltete Sammlung frz. zweideutiger Wörter, wie sie Harsdörffer hier nennt, ist uns nicht bekannt — auch Bachmann (s. u.) teilt nichts dazu mit —, wohl aber, daß er sich für eine Bildungsreform v. a. für die adelige Jugend in Frankreich einsetzte, abgesichert durch bis ins Detail von La Noue entworfene, moderne kgl. (Ritter-)Akademien (*Discours* 5). Sein Konzept für eine moderne Bildungsreform für den jungen frz. Adel sah „plusieurs sortes d'exercices, tant pour le corps que pour l'esprit" (op. cit., 127) vor, darunter Studien der antiken Klassiker „en nostre langue", da diese „traitent des vertus morales, de la police, & de la guerre". Ebenso sollten gelesen werden „les histoires, tant anciennes que modernes. On enseigneroit aussi les Mathematiques, la Geographie, la Fortification, & quelques langues vulgaires: ce qui est fort vtile à vn gentilhomme (i'entens d'en sauoir autant qu'il en peut mettre en vsage)" (127f.), also weniger nach Art eines formalen Grammatikerwerbs, als vielmehr nach dem Sprachgebrauch u. der Sprachpraxis. Der Praxisbezug bestimmt das gesamte Bildungsprogramm La Noues u. sein Ziel, die Adligen zu „Professeurs de vertu" (200) u. geschickt zu „toutes choses honnestes" (110) zu machen, zu allen Tugenden u. allen öffentlichen Geschäften, „sur la vocation generale, qui est bien viure" (200). Dies ging mit ausführlichen Behandlungen der Sprachstilistik u. -ästhetik einher. So bevorzugte er einen kurzen, klaren, einfachen Stil mit kompakter, realistischer u. nützlicher Darstellung, gegen jede Form von „superflu". Vgl. Husemann (s.u.), 120–122. Sutcliffe lobte an Noues Stil „la précision du vocabulaire, la souplesse de la phrase et l'économie des moyens d'expression sont animés par un souffle humain, par toute la passion et la conviction d'un homme qui a, à la fois, l'amour de l'action et une grande bonté d'âme." (Introduction, in op. cit. [s.u.], S. XXXII). Dies käme mit einer Vermeidung zweideutiger Wörter durchaus überein. Eine lat. Übersetzung des 5. „Discours" über die Verbesserung der Erziehung u. Bildung des jungen Adels des Herren Radslav Kinsky v. Wchynicz u. Tettau (1582–1660) war 1601 in Nürnberg erschienen: DOMINI DE LA NOVE DISCVRSVS De MELIORI IVVENVM NOBIL. GAL. INSTITVTIONE, LATINÈ È GALLIC. INTERPRETATVS à RADISLAO IVNIORI WCHYNSKIO LIB. BARO. DE WCHYNICZ ET TETTAV. NORIBERGÆ Excudebat Paulus Kauffmann. M DC I. HAB: 28. Rhet. (17). Auch diese Übersetzung muß, wie das Original, eine Liste der zweideutigen frz. Wörter natürlich schuldig bleiben. In seinem 82. Gesprächspiel über „Die zweydeutigen Wörter" weist Harsdörffer nicht auf La Noue hin (*Harsdörffer: Frauenzimmer-Gespräspiele* II [²1657/ Ndr. 1968], 225/ Ndr. 243 – 230/ 248). Vgl. (ohne Hinweise auf eine Homonymen-Liste) François de la Noue: Discours politiques et militaires. Publiés avec une introduction et des notes par F. E. Sutcliffe. Genève, Paris 1967; Moyse Amyrault: La Vie de François Seignevr De La Nouë, dit Bras-De-Fer (Leyden 1661. HAB: 150. 8 Hist.); Alfred Bachmann: Die Sprache des François de la Noue. Inaug.-Diss. U. Leipzig. Borna-Leipzig 1914; Reinhard v. Dalwigk: Das Leben und die Schriften des François de la Noue. In: Einladungsschrift des Gymnasium Casimirianum zu der öffentlichen Prüfung und Schlußfeier am 22., 23. u. 24. März 1875. Coburg (1875), 3–24; Art. „La Noue (François de)". In: Emile et Eugène Haag (Hg.): La France Protestante. Tome VI (Paris, Genève 1856), 280–304; Henri Hauser: François de la Noue (1531–1591). Genève 1970, 170 ff. u. 200; William H. Huseman: La Personnalité littéraire de François de la Noue 1531–1591. Paris 1986, 91 ff. u. 118 ff.

17 Nach dem Vorbild der FG, in der F. Ludwig (Der Nährende) — häufig unterstützt von Diederich v. dem Werder (FG 31) — die Reimgesetze (Strophen) zu den Impresen der Mitglieder aufsetzte, war es Zesen, in der DG „der Färtige", der die Gedichte zur Auslegung der Impresen („Zunftzeichen"/ „Sinnbilder") der DG-Genossen verfertigte, allerdings in unterschiedlichen Längen u. Metren, während bei F. Ludwig die Reimgesetze durchgehend als jambische Alexandriner in der Ottava-rime-Strophe gestaltet wurden. S. *GB 1641, GB 1641/44* u. *GB 1646*; Philipp v. Zesen: *Hochdeutsches Helikonisches Rosentahl* (s. Anm. 2).

18 Während die FG ihr Gesellschaftsmanifest — den „Kurtzen Bericht" des Gesellschaftsbuchs — fünf Jahre nach ihrer Gründung, nämlich erstmals 1622 im Druck vorlegte (*GB 1622*, s. *DA Köthen II. 1*), ließ sich die DG nach ihrem eigenen Bekunden 26 Jahre damit Zeit, bis 1669 Zesens *Hochdeutsches Helikonisches Rosentahl* (s. Anm. 2) erschien — mit der Begründung, nun erst sei die Rosenzunft mit 9 x 9 (81) Mitgliedern zur „glüklichen volendung gediehen" (S. 214). Zesen betont, daß die Schreibart einem jeden DG-Mitglied freigestellt sei, „jedoch also/ daß es mit der rechtmässigen vernunft/ oder zum wenigsten mit dem erleidlichsten üblichem gebrauche/ ob er schon zu weilen jener schnuhrstracks zugegen leuft/ übereinkomme" (S. 205). In *DA Köthen I. 8*: 490509 (*KE*, 416 f.) wird Zesen Harsdörffers Argument fast wörtlich gegen F. Ludwigs kritische Bedenken ins Feld führen, nämlich daß die Rechtschreibung „kein wesendliches, sondern nuhr ein zufälliges stükke unserer sprache bleibet, und sie doch wohl kann verstanden werden, man schreibe wie man wolle; im fall sie (die sprache) an sich selbst rein behalten wird." In der „Schutzschrift/ für Die Teutsche Spracharbeit" (in *Frauenzimmer-Gespräspiele* I, ²1644, Ndr. 1968, S. 339–396), 372 hatte Harsdörffer dieselbe Formulierung gebraucht: „Noch zur Zeit ist für kein wesentliches Stuk der Spracharbeit die Rechtschreibung zu halten/ verstehe/ daß man sich deswegen etwas zu dolmetschen/ oder ein Gedichte abzufassen/ hindern lassen solte". Im Anhang „Unvergreifliches Bedencken von der Rechtschreibung/ und Schriftscheidung unserer Teutschen HELDENSPRACHE" im ersten Teil des *Poetischen Trichters* (Nürnberg ²1644; Ndr. Darmstadt 1969), S. 131, schränkte Harsdörffer ebenfalls ein: „Doch muß man hierinnen [in der Rechtschreibung] einem jeden seine Meinung lassen; weil solches alles keine Glaubenssachen belanget/ und ein jeder nur eine Stimme in dem Capitel hat." Ähnlich im 2. Teil des *Poetischen Trichters* (Nürnberg 1648, Ndr. Darmstadt 1969), S. 118: „weil aber ein jeder nach seiner angebornen Landsart redet/ pfleget er auch nach derselben zu schreiben/ und scheinet fast schwer/ sich hierinnen zuvergleichen." Und schließlich im 3. Teil des *Poetischen Trichters* (Nürnberg 1653, Ndr. Darmstadt 1969), 7 f.: „Welche ausrede und also nachgehends welche

Schreibart die reinste und richtigste seye/ wollen wir nicht entscheiden", daher sei geboten, „Daß man wegen der unverglichnen Schreib-Art kein gutes Buch verwerffen oder verachten/ und mehr auf den Jnhalt/ als die Verabfassung sehen sol." Vgl. auch *Harsdörffer: Specimen (1646)*, 221 ff., wo aufgrund der mundartlichen Uneinheitlichkeit der Aussprache an einer allgemein verbindlichen deutschen Rechtschreibung gezweifelt wird. In seinem *Nathan und Jotham* (Nürnberg 1659), Bd. II, S. 320, Nr. 80 kennzeichnete Harsdörffer den Streit um die Rechtschreibung als einen Krieg der Federn zwischen Verstand u. Gewohnheit: „[...] verbliebe also ein jeder Theil in seinem Lager/ und hat der Streit kein Ende."

19 *Schottelius: Sprachkunst (1641).*

20 Hatte der Hamburger Präliminarvertrag zwischen dem Kaiser, Schweden u. Frankreich vom 25.12.1641 allgemeine Grundlagen für den auf die Städte Münster u. Osnabrück aufgeteilten Friedenskongreß gelegt, so trafen ab September 1643 die ersten Gesandten ein. Es dauerte jedoch bis Juni 1645, bis die ersten Friedens-„Propositionen" vorgelegt u. die Verhandlungen konkret aufgenommen wurden, die am 24.10.1648 mit dem Instrumentum Pacis Osnabrugensis, ausgehandelt von kaiserlichen, schwedischen u. reichsständischen Abgesandten, u. dem Instrumentum Pacis Monasteriensis zwischen dem Kaiser, Frankreich u. reichsständischen Deputierten, abgeschlossen wurden. Zwar bewilligte der Kaiser den Reichsständen erst im August 1645 die Teilnahme am Friedenskongreß, doch waren viele den Einladungen Schwedens u. Frankreichs schon vorher gefolgt, so im Mai oder Anfang Juni 1645 der gesamtanhaltinische Gesandte Martin Milagius (FG 315) u. ebenfalls im Mai 1645 die erzstift-magdeburg. Delegation in Osnabrück, die die ranghöchsten fl. Deputierten stellte u. daher das Direktorium im Fürstenrat übernahm. Zu dieser Delegation, aber bereits 1644 nach Osnabrück entsandt, gehörte der erzstift-magdeburg. u. niedersächs. Kreis-Sekretär Christian Werner (1610–1663). Er war mit Christian Gueintz (FG 361. Der Ordnende) bekannt u. hatte zu dessen *Sprachlehre (1641)* zwei Widmungsgedichte beigesteuert. Er gehörte zu den vereidigten Protokollanten der Fürstenratssitzungen u. fand seiner sorgfältigen, verständlichen u. orthographisch sauberen Protokollführung wegen hohe Anerkennung. Auf welche Informationen sich Harsdörffer im vorliegenden Brief hatte stützen können, bleibt unklar, jedoch bekräftigte er in 451101: „Zu Münster und Ossnabruck haben etliche angefangen Rein Deutsch und fast nach des Ordnenden Anweisung zu schreiben". Vgl. *Acta Pacis Westphalicae* III A, Bd. 3.1, S. LVI ff.; zu Werner 410324 I u. jüngst Maria-Elisabeth Brunert: Vom Rapular zum Dictatum. Entstehungsstufen der reichsständischen Protokolle. In: Verständigung und Diplomatie auf dem Westfälischen Friedenskongress. Historische und sprachwissenschaftliche Zugänge. Hg. Annette Gerstenberg. Wien [u.a.] 2014, 201–223, hier 209 u. 219.

21 Ein Antwortschreiben Zesens hat sich anscheinend nicht erhalten. In Zesens *Hooch-Deutscher Spraach-übung (1643)* findet sich keine Erklärung für die Verkehrung der „Stammletter" i in ü. Vgl. aber seine Stammwort-Etymologien in 450308A, 450410 K 3 u. K 16 u. 450808. In einem nach seiner Aufnahme in die DG (8.10.1646. Der Willige) verfaßten Brief hatte Johann Bellin Zesen gefragt, warum dieser seine Orthographie so oft ändere u. so oft ä, ö oder ü statt herkömmlichem e bzw. i setze, z. B. ämsig, ärde, ässen, föchten (für fechten), verwürrung usw. Möge dies auch der meißnischen Aussprache u. dem Stammwortprinzip entsprechen [!], so unterschieden die Niedersachsen diese Laute viel genauer als die Hochdeutschen, u. es käme ihnen äußerst befremdlich vor. S. *Bellin: Sendeschreiben (1647)*, Nr. 7, Bl. Cijv – Ciijv. In seiner (undatierten) Antwort darauf begründet Zesen, die Wörter müßten sich auch in ihren Ableitungen, Flexionen usw. nach ihren Stämmen richten. Sei der Stammvokal a, o oder u, müßte dementsprechend ä, ö bzw. ü gebildet werden. Vgl. 450808 K 11. Dabei wendet sich Zesen gegen Schottelius' auf einsilbige Stammwörter gestützte Theorie u. gegen die Bildung der Stammwörter nach dem Imperativ Singular. In der Ablehnung dieser Lehre zeigt sich indes Zesens Unsicherheit: Zunächst erkennt er die Stammform des Verbs im Imperfekt: er galt, daher richtig gälten, nicht gelten; er barg, daher richtig bärgen, nicht bergen; er fuhr, daher führen. Wenn man das Stammwort im Imperfekt nicht finden könne, müsse es im Perfekt oder im Substantiv gesucht werden: fisch, daher fischen; „sak", daher „sakken"; man, daher „übermannen/ mänlich/ männisch/ mänsch" usw. Man könne das Stammwort des Verbs aber auch im Präsens suchen oder bei den Nachbarsprachen: nl., schwed., dän., isl., engl., vor allem aber im Nd. (Niedersächsischen), z.B. nl. „nuchten", daher nüchtern; nds. „lucht", daher leuchten; nl. „swaert", daher schwärt; nl. „bas", daher bässer; nl. „paert", daher Pfärd; nl. „swaer", daher schwär; entsprechend adelär, nadelär, Predigär; nds. „lucht", daher lücht statt Licht; engl. „heart", folglich härz; engl. „learn", daher lärnen; weiterhin hd. er „vergahs", daher vergässen; er las, also läsen; bund, daher bünden; fund, daher fünden; schwund, daher schwünden, gewust, daher weusheit; gefochten, daher föchten (Bl. [Cvij] v). Zwar solle man sich erst, so Zesen, im Hd. umsehen, bevor man in anderen Sprachen suche, doch entbehren seine wilden, einfallsabhängigen Etymologien einer Systematik, wie sie Schottelius am Sprachmaterial durchexerzierte. S. *Bellin: Sendeschreiben (1647),* Nr. 8, Bl. [Ciiij] r – [D v] v.

22 Frühere Schreiben Harsdörffers an Zesen liegen uns nicht vor; das erwähnte Sinnbild kann daher nicht identifiziert werden.

23 In seinem die erste Auflage des ersten Teils der *Frauenzimmer-Gesprächspiele* (1641) abschließenden Nachwort „An den Sprach- vnd Gesprächliebenden Leser" (Bl. [Oviij r] — P[j] v) rechtfertigt sich Harsdörffer noch dafür, daß er in dem vorliegenden Werk durchgängig „teutsch" u. nicht „deutsch" schreibe, „weil die Teutschen Teutones, vor fast vnerdencklichen Jahren benambst worden." Im 178. Gesprächspiel „Teut oder Deut" in *Harsdörffer: Frauenzimmer-Gesprächspiele* IV (1644, Ndr. 1968), 298/ Ndr. 342 – 304/ 348, wird die Frage diskutiert, „ob Deutsch oder Teutsch recht geschrieben werde". „Die Lateiner", so Harsdörffer, „alle und jede schreiben Teut/ Teuto, oder Theut." Da die Deutschen zwar das latein. „T" in ein „D" verwandlet, dieses aber nicht durchgängig, sondern nur „bisweilen" getan haben, so könne daraus „keine Regel gemacht werden". Nach Austausch von allerhand etymologischen Thesen lautet das Fazit: „Kan also beide Meinung behaubtet/ und Teutsch/ nach der Alten Schrift/ Deutsch nach der gemeinen Aussprache geschrieben werden." A. a. O., 303 f./ Ndr. 348 f. Ebenso *Harsdörffer: Specimen (1646),* 28 f.: „utraq; scriptio, ut dixi, defendi potest." Vgl. dazu auch 460816 K I 1 u. 460915 sowie 450400 T f (!); ferner Harsdörffers „Kurtze Entschuldigung Die begangene Fehler in den Hundert Spielreimen betreffend" (demnächst in *DA Köthen I. 9*). Vgl. dazu 430920 u. *Banneck*, 296 ff. — Zesen hingegen verteidigte die Schreibweise „Deutsch" mit „einem weichklingenden d.", weil die alten Deutschen „ie und allwege" diese Schreibung angewendet hätten, weil abgeleitete Wörter noch heute mit dem d-Anlaut geschrieben würden (wie z.B. deutlich, andeuten, deutung, verdeutschen usw.) u. weil auch Luther, „welcher die Hochdeutsche Spraache zu erst wieder ausgearbeitet und zu ihrem glantze gebracht […] das wort Deutsch selbst allezeit mit einem D. geschrieben" habe. Die Schreibung „Teutsch" wird als eine unnötige u. „ungegründete Neurung" verworfen. Philipp (v.) Zesen: Hooch-Deutsche Spraach-übung (1643). In: *Zesen SW* XI, 1–77, hier S. 24 f. Ähnlich Gueintz in seiner *Rechtschreibung (1645),* 21 f., wo er dezidiert für eine Schreibung mit D plädiert.

441226 Fürst Ludwig

Fürst Ludwig an Curt von Einsiedel

F. Ludwig (Der Nährende) sendet Curt v. Einsiedel (FG 417. Der Ersprießliche) über Hans v. Dieskau (FG 212. Der Tilgende) seine Verdeutschung zweier Bücher des Virgilio Malvezzi marchese di Castel Guelfo: *Il Romulo* und *Il Tarquinio Svperbo* nebst den italienischen Originalwerken. Als einen des Italienischen Kundigen bittet er Einsiedel um kritische, vergleichende Lektüre der Übersetzung und um Aufzeichnung etwa vorzunehmender Korrekturen. F. Ludwig beklagt, er habe bislang leider keine weiteren Lebensbeschreibungen der römischen Könige zwischen dem ersten, Romulus, und dem letzten, Tarquinius, ermitteln können. Er verweist (für weitere Informationen) auf den Zusteller Hans v. Dieskau (FG 212. Der Tilgende).

Q HM Köthen: V S 545, Bl. 186rv, 186v leer; eigenh. Konzept, auf einem Papierbogen zusammen mit konzipierten Schreiben F. Ludwigs an Hz. August v. Sachsen-Weißenfels (FG 402) vom 26.12.1644 und Christian Gueintz (FG 361), d.i. 441226A. — D: KE, 47. — BN: Bürger, 948 Nr. 28.

A *Fehlt.*

Dem Erspriesichen entbeut der Nehrende seinen willigen grus, und überschicket ihme bey dem Tilgenden zwey ins Deutsche aus dem Jtalianischen gesetzte büchlein,[1] neben deme in seiner grundsprache, mit ersuchen, weil er der Jtalianischen sprache wol mächtig, er solche gegen einander halten, und der verdolmetschung wegen seine gedancken, wen er darzu müßig gelangen kan, mit verbeßerung absonderlich aufzeichnen wolle.[2] Es wird ihme sonder zweiffel die materi wol gefallen, und were zu wüntschen, das die Römischen Könige so zwischen diesen[a] ersten und letzten gewesen, auch also möchten erwogen, und ihre geschichte ausgearbeitet sein, so aber der Nehrende noch nicht erfaren können.[3] Jm ubrigen berufet sich der Nehrende auf den Tilgenden, und verbleibet

Des Erspriesichen gantz williger[b]

T a *Eingefügt über* den — b *Unterschrift und Datum fehlen.*

K Unsere Datierung stützt sich auf den Briefentwurf F. Ludwigs an Hz. August v. Sachsen-Weißenfels (FG 402. Der Wohlgeratene), der auf demselben Blatt Papier wie der vorliegende Brief u. das Schreiben 441226A notiert u. auf den 26.12.1644 datiert wurde. Das Schreiben an Hz. August enthält aber nur Neujahrswünsche u. wurde daher nicht in diesen Editionsband aufgenommen, seine Datierung für die beiden Briefe 441226 u. 441226A aber übernommen. S. Q.
1 *Fürst Ludwig: Romulus und Tarquinius (1647)*, d.i.: Der Romulus, | und | Tarquinius der | Hoffertige. | Das ist: | Das Leben | Des Ersten/ | und | Letzten Königs der Römer. | Beschrieben | Von dem Jtalianischen | Herren Marggrafen Virgilio | Malvezzi. | und | Jns Deütsche übergesetzet | Auch | Auf gut befinden der Fruchtbringenden Geselschaft/ mit | angehencketer erklerung etlicher Nahmen/ örter/ | und wörter auf dem Rande/ an den | tag gegeben. | Gedruckt zu Zerbst im Fürstentume | Anhalt. | [Linie] | Jm Jahre 1647.

HAB: QuN 199 (5), auch dig. Es handelt sich um die Übersetzung der wiederholt gedruckten und in verschiedene europ. Sprachen übersetzten polit.-histor. Biographien des Virgilio Malvezzi marchese di Castel Guelfo: IL ROMULO/ DEL MARCHESE VIRGILIO/ MALVEZZI. [Kolophon:] IN BOLOGNA/ Presso Clemente Ferroni M. DC.XXIX./ Con licenza de' Superiori. — IL TARQUINIO SVPERBO/ DEL MARCHESE VIRGILIO MALVEZZI/ DEDICATO/ ALL'ILL.MO ET ECC.MO SIG./ D. GOMEZ SVAREZ DE FIGHERROA/ DVCA DI FERIA, GOVERNATORE, E CAPITAN/ GENERALE. DELLO STATO DI MILANO,/ SVO PRON COL.MO. [Kolophon:] In Bologna, presso Clemente Ferroni./ M.DC.XXXII./ Con licenza de' Superiori. Vgl. *Conermann: Ludwig und Christian II. von Anhalt*, 454f. Vgl. unten Anm. 3 u. 440426 K 7.

2 F. Ludwig bezog Curt v. Einsiedel (FG 417. 1644), der sehr gebildet u. des Französischen, Italienischen u. Spanischen kundig war, offenbar öfter in Arbeiten der FG ein. Über die Umstände seiner Aufnahme in die FG ist nichts bekannt, jedoch trug er sich 1645 eigenhändig in den 3. Band des *GB Kö.* ein. Vgl. *Conermann III*, 497f. Von 1638 bis 1668 stand Einsiedel als Geheimer Rat u. Amtshauptmann in Diensten des Wohlgeratenen u. 3. Oberhaupts der FG, Hz. Augusts v. Sachsen-Weißenfels (FG 402), der in Halle a. d. S. residierte. Diesem war zwar schon 1638 als Administrator des Erzstifts Magdeburg in Halle von den Landständen, dem Rat der Stadt u. dem Domkapitel gehuldigt worden, aber seine Residenz Halle konnte er erst am 31.12.1642 endgültig beziehen. Vgl. 391026A K 1, 400203 K 8 u. 410324 K I; *Conermann III*, 497f. F. Ludwig empfahl Christian Gueintz, dessen *Deutsche Rechtschreibung (1645)* auch Einsiedel zur Durchsicht vorzulegen. S. 441231 u. 450504.

3 In 431007 hatte F. Ludwig Georg Philipp Harsdörffer (FG 368) um Auskunft gebeten, ob er von weiteren Viten altrömischer Könige wisse, die Malvezzi im Vorwort des *Romulo* angekündigt hatte. In 431124 hatte Harsdörffer seine Unkenntnis eingeräumt, aber mitgeteilt, er habe nach Venedig u. Bologna geschrieben, um Erkundigungen einzuholen. Diese blieben ergebnislos: in 440426 mußte Harsdörffer bescheinigen, solche seien dort unbekannt. F. Ludwigs Suche nach weiteren Königsviten Malvezzis könnte dazu beigetragen haben, das Erscheinen seiner Übertragungen bis zum Jahre 1647 zu verschieben.

441226A

Fürst Ludwig an Christian Gueintz

Beantwortet durch 441231. — F. Ludwig (Der Nährende) mahnt Christian Gueintz (FG 361. Der Ordnende) zur Veröffentlichung seiner *Deutschen Rechtschreibung* und bittet um Rücksendung zweier Bücher von Justus Georg Schottelius (FG 397) vermittels des (bei Halle ansässigen) Hans v. Dieskau (FG 212. Der Tilgende). Da ihm Schottelius diese beiden Bücher persönlich verehrt habe, möchte der Fürst sie weiter gern zu seiner Verwendung zurückbekommen. — Gueintz empfängt ferner die Druckbögen des um die neuen Mitglieder erweiterten *GB 1641/44*.

Q HM Köthen: V S 545, Bl. 186rv, 186v leer; eigenh. Konzept, auf einer Seite zus. mit Konzepten F. Ludwigs an Hz. August v. Sachsen-Weißenfels (FG 402), dat. 26.12.1644, u. Curt v. Einsiedel (FG 417), undat. (441226). — Nicht in *KE*.

A *Fehlt.*

441226A Fürst Ludwig

Der Ordende wird nechst gebuhrender zuentbietung[a] hiemit guter wolmeinung erinnert, an seine[b] Rechtschreibung[1], ob die nicht einsten könte an den tag kommen, wie den auch der Nehrende seine zwey buchlein des Schotelij,[2] die er ihme fur diesem zugefertiget, durch[c] den Tilgenden[3] wieder[d] zuzuschicken begeret, weil sie der verfaßer selbsten[e] dem Nehrenden verehret,[4] und er sie deswegen da[e] in[f] seiner verwendung gerne aufheben wolte, so hat er auch die nachgedrucketen geselschafter[5] hierbey zu entpfahen, und verbleibet der Nehrende

des Ordenden[g]

T **a** *Unsichere Lesung, vielleicht auch als* zuertheilung *zu lesen.* — **b** *Folgt ein unleserliches eingefügtes Wort, vielleicht* aufgetragene [?] — **c** *Davor* <ihme> — **d** *Folgt eingefügt* her *Durch die fehlende Streichung eines der beiden folgenden Präfixe* zu- *grammatisch unstimmig.* — **e** *Eingefügt.* — **f** *Wohl zu* in *gebessert.* — **g** *Schlußgruß fehlt im Konzept. Ergänze etwa:* gantz williger Geselschafter

K Die Datierung erfolgte nach dem Konzept Fürst Ludwigs (Der Nährende) an Hz. August v. Sachsen-Weißenfels (FG 402), das auf derselben Seite wie 441226 u. der vorliegende Brief steht u. auf den 26.12.1644 datiert ist. Das Schreiben an Hz. August v. Sachsen-Weißenfels enthält nur Neujahrswünsche. S. Q.

1 Zur Gueintzschen Rechtschreibung s. 440127 K 1.

2 Die beiden Bücher des Justus Georg Schottelius (FG 397): *Schottelius: Sprachkunst (1641)* u. *Schottelius: Der Teutschen Sprache Einleitung (1643).* Erstere hatte F. Ludwig Christian Gueintz (FG 361. Der Ordnende) mit 430328 zugesandt, letztere mit 430307. Auch dabei war schon der Tilgende (s. Anm. 3) als Bote aufgetreten. Frühere Mahnungen um Rückgabe schon in 431016 u. 440313.

3 Der auf Dieskau bei Halle lebende Hans v. Dieskau (FG 212. Der Tilgende), dessen sich F. Ludwig immer wieder als Mittelsmann in Halle bediente, wo Gueintz als Rektor des Gymnasiums wirkte. Zu Dieskau vgl. 390110 (K 2), 390112, 390114 u.ö., im vorliegenden Band v. a. 441226, 450504, 450507 u. I, 460718 K 8 u. 461106 K 6.

4 F. Ludwig hatte *Der Teutschen Sprache Einleitung (1643),* die Schottelius F. Ludwig gewidmet hatte, von diesem mit 430307 zugesandt bekommen. Vgl. auch 421110 (Widmungsepistel Schottelius' an F. Ludwig) sowie 430318. *Schottelius: Sprachkunst (1641)* hingegen war Hz. August d.J. v. Braunschweig-Wolfenbüttel (FG 227) zugeschrieben worden. S. 410706 u. I. F. Ludwigs Besitz u. Kenntnis der *Sprachkunst* ergibt sich bereits aus 421031A.

5 1641 war das nichtillustrierte *GB 1641,* das die Mitglieder Nr. 1–353 mit ihren Impresen u. Reimgesetzen aufführt, im Druck erschienen. Die Reimgesetze waren dafür in Stanzenform umgeschrieben worden. 1644 wurde eine Ergänzung um die Mitglieder bis zu Nr. 417 (d.i. Curt v. Einsiedel) gedruckt u. dem *GB 1641* beigefügt: *GB 1641/44.* Das genaue Aufnahmedatum Einsiedels ist uns unbekannt; da aber das Mitglied Nr. 418, Zacharias Prüschenk v. Lindenhofen, am 10.10.1644 in Köthen in die FG aufgenommen worden war (s. 441010), Einsiedel also spätestens kurz vorher aufgenommen worden sein muß, ist der Versand des im Druck erweiterten *GB 1641/44* am 26.12.1644 gut möglich. Vgl. zuletzt 430724A. In einigen Exemplaren ist dem GB eine gedruckte zweispaltige chronologische Mitgliederliste mit den Personennamen der Mitglieder Nr. 1–353 beigefügt. Im Expl. *Faber du Faur,* Nr. 165a wurde diese Liste bis Nr. 417 handschriftlich ergänzt. In seiner Antwort auf den vorliegenden Brief erwartet Gueintz noch das *GB*

1641/44 u. das Verzeichnis der Taufnamen der Mitglieder, dazu auch schon das illustrierte *GB 1646.* S. 441231. Zum *GB 1641/44* vgl. 440809A K 1, 440824 K 10, 441231 K 8, 450124 K 3, 450126 K 11, 450220 K 7, 450301, 450317 K 9, 450319 K 3, 450400 K, 450529 K 10, 450611 K 1, 450721, 451015 K 2 u. 460916 K 7; *Conermann II*, 51 f. (zum *GB 1641 u. 1641/44*). Zum *GB 1646* s. 440130 K 3.

441231

Christian Gueintz an Fürst Ludwig

Antwort auf 441226A. Beantwortet durch 450504 (?). — Christian Gueintz (FG 361. Der Ordnende) drückt F. Ludwig (Der Nährende) sein Mitgefühl über die Drangsale aus, die dieser und seine Lande erlitten. Gueintz habe persönlich und mit seinen Schülern Gott um Rettung angefleht. Möge Gott mit dem Ausgang dieses bedrückenden Jahres F. Ludwig und der ganzen Christenheit eine bessere und friedliche Zukunft schenken. — Mit Bewunderung erkennt Gueintz die unverdrossene Mühe und Arbeit, mit der der Nährende danach strebe, die FG emporzubringen. Der Beilage könne F. Ludwig entnehmen, daß Gueintz die deutsche Rechtschreibung längst abgeschlossen haben mochte, jedoch fehle es in Halle an geeigneten Verlagen und Druckereien. Er bittet den Fürsten, das Buch in seiner Köthener Offizin drucken zu lassen. Da er über keine Abschrift mehr verfüge, könne er das Werk nicht Curt v. Einsiedel (FG 417. Der Erspießliche) zukommen lassen. Doch werde er es nicht unterlassen, ihn über mögliche Bedenken zu befragen. — Gueintz dankt für eingeschickte Bücher und die Fortsetzung des *GB 1641*; er erwarte nun das Register und das vollständige Namensverzeichnis der Mitglieder sowie ihre gestochenen Impresen. Hinsichtlich Gueintz' Verskunst sollte auf einer Zusammenkunft der Mitglieder darüber beraten werden, damit er sie schnellstmöglich fertigstellen könne, zumal inkompetente, angemaßte neue Dichter die ganze Poetik verunstalteten.

Q HM Köthen: V S 545, Bl. 184r–185v [A: 185v], 184v u. 185r leer; Schreiberh. mit eigenh. Empfangsvermerk F. Ludwigs. — *D: KE*, 270 f.; *KL* III, 242 f. — *BN: Bürger*, 634 Nr. 7.

A *Dem Nährenden* etc.   Hall   Cöthen
Empfangsvermerk F. Ludwigs: 3. Jenners 1645.

Waß für Elend, Jammer vnd Hertzleid vor vielen andern der *Nährende* sambt[a] dessen von Gott untergebener Zirck[1] bißanhero empfunden[2], kan nicht mit gedancken vielweniger mit wortten angedeutet werden: Der *Ordenende* hat darüber wie öffentlich mit seinen Lernern, also auch absonderlich umb Errettung hertzlich geflehet. Anietzo mit ausgang deß Alten schwehren vnd hartdrückenden[b] wünschet[c] daß der allein Barmhertzige vnd Ewiggütige Gott dem *Nährenden* sambt der gantzen Christenheit neben Gedult ein frölichers, friedlichers, vnd der Deutschen Auffrichtigkeit ersprießlichers, auch deme vielfolgende Jahre väterlich verleihen vnd schencken wolle; Daß dermahleins Güte und Treue einander begegnen, Gerechtigkeit und friede sich küssen![3]

Sonsten verwundert sich mit bestürtzung[4] über deß *Nährenden* Standthafftigkeit der *Ordenende*, Jndeme[d] Er annoch der Fruchtbringenden Gesellschafft auffnehmen zubefördern und dießelbe auffzumuntern sich befleißet. Es hat zwar der *Ordenende* wie auß beyliegendem⁵ zuschließen längst sich bemühet, daß mit der Wortschreibung möchte ein Schluß gemachet werden: Wann aber alhier keine gute Druckergesellen auch kein tauglicher verlag, Alß bittet Er unterthänigst es wolle der *Nährende* sich belieben laßen, es an seinem ort zubefördern.⁶ Keine abschrift ist hier mehr verhanden, sonsten solte auch dem Erspießlichen⁷ es fürgetragen werden. Eß will aber doch der *Ordenende* nicht unterlaßen eines oder daß andere zuerinnern, ob waß zu bedencken.

Vor eingeschickte büchlein⁸ wie auch der Gesellschaffter Fortstellung wird man verpflicht sich danckbarlich zuerzeigen, mit verlangen erwartend das Register vnd völlige Nahmen, wie auch ein abdruck der Gemählde und Küpfferstück.⁸ Wegen der Reimenkunst⁹ einen ausschlag zugeben, weil alles von denen übel unterrichteten selbstgewachßenen Dichtern verwogen[e10] wird, ist die zusammenkunfft der fruchtbringenden Gesellschafft das beste Mittel, und giebt die schleunigste außfertigung, welche auf begehren ins werck stellen wird

Deß *Nährenden* unterthäniger
Ordenender

Hall abends 9 Vhr am Ende des 1644.

T a *Bis Zirck in KE und KL III ausgelassen.* — b *Ergänze:* Jahres — c *Ergänze: er (der Ordnende).* — d *KE, KL III* Zudeme — e *KL III* erwogen

K 1 Zirk, *m.*, „circus, circulus, *infreqvens est.* Bezirk *autem,* & Umzirk *freqventiora sunt, notantq.* orbem, districtum, circumferentiam, regionemqve, *vel* terram certis limitibus circumscriptam. Bezirk *etiam est* ditio, territorium, dioecesis, *alias* LandsBezirk/ finitio provinciae." *Stieler,* 2648.
2 Zur verheerenden Verfassung Anhalts aufgrund des „Gallassischen ruins" (Sept. bis Nov. 1644) u. zur Lage der Anhaltiner s. **440927 K 1.**
3 Frei nach Ps. 85: „Das Güte vnd Trewe einander begegnen/ Gerechtigkeit vnd Friede sich küssen. Das Trewe auff der Erden wachse/ Vnd Gerechtigkeit vom Himel schawe." *Biblia (Luther 1545).* Eine Anlehnung an diesen Friedens-Psalm auch in *Hille,* Bl.)( )(iijr. Christian Gueintz hatte 1640 in Halle die stark überarbeitete, gekürzte u. auch politisch entschärfte zweite Ausgabe seiner Friedensdichtung, *Krieges-Discours Zweyer Schäffer Damon vnd Corydon,* veröffentlicht (Württ. LB Stuttgart: HBK 502. 4°). Ihr ist ein „Friedens-Seufftzer" nach Ps. 85 angehängt, der in der Erstausgabe fehlt. Auch dort heißt es,
  „Das reiche Gütigkeit entgegen geh der Trew;
  Daß Fried vnd rechtes Recht sich immer freundlich küssen/
  Das Wahrheit/ Lieb und Huld auff Erden blühen müssen/
  Auff das Gerechtigkeit schaw von des Himmels Thron." — Vgl. 400314 K 4; *Herz: Aufrichtigkeit, Vertrauen, Frieden,* 331f. u. 341.
4 *Stieler,* 2231 „Bestürtzung/ stupor/ exanimatio/ *vulgò* perculsio animi, mentis deliqvium, consternatio"; Fassungslosigkeit, starke Betroffenheit, bis ins 19. Jh. aber auch in einer neutraleren Bedeutung „überrascht sein", in Verlegenheit gebracht sein. *DW* I, 1687; *Paul Wb.,* 164.
5 Keine Beilage im Brief bzw. seinem Lagenumfeld erhalten. Hatte Gueintz ein von

ihm fertiggestelltes Stück des Manuskripts der *Deutschen Rechtschreibung* beigelegt? Möglicherweise war diese Beilage die Korrekturvorlage für die in 450504 angesprochene Durchsicht durch weitere FG-Mitglieder. Zur Gueintzschen Rechtschreibung s. 440127 K 1.

6 F. Ludwig sah sich in 450504 nicht imstande, das Werk in Köthen drucken zu lassen. *Gueintz: Deutsche Rechtschreibung* erschien 1645 in Halle a. d. S., gedruckt von Christoph Salfeld d. Ä. (1599–1670). Salfeld war erster Geselle in der Druckerei von Christoph Bißmarck. Als dieser 1624 starb, heiratete Salfeld 1625 seine Witwe Ursula (geb. Felsecker, verw. Hynitzsch) u. übernahm die Bißmarcksche Offizin. Salfeld verfügte in Halle über zwei Druckwerkstätten. Vgl. *Reske*, 328.

7 Curt v. Einsiedel (FG 417. 1644), Geh. Rat Hz. Augusts v. Sachsen-Weißenfels (FG 402) in Halle a. d. S. S. 441226 K 2.

8 F. Ludwig hatte Gueintz in 441226A zum wiederholten Male um Rücksendung zweier Bücher gebeten: *Schottelius: Sprachkunst (1641)* u. *Schottelius: Der Teutschen Sprache Einleitung (1643)*. Demselben Brief hatte F. Ludwig auch die Ergänzung (Druckbögen) des *GB 1641* zum *GB 1641/44* beigelegt. Vgl. dazu 450529 K 10. Gueintz erhoffte ferner ein Register der Personennamen der FG-Mitglieder. S. dazu 441226A K 5. Da das letzte illustrierte *GB 1629/30* nur Impresenstiche der Mitglieder Nr. 1–200 enthielt, erwartete Gueintz auch schon das noch nicht erschienene Gesellschaftsbuch *GB 1646*, das die Kupferstiche der Impresen u. die Reimgesetze der Mitglieder 1–400 umfaßt. Zum *GB 1641*, *GB 1641/44* u. *GB 1646* vgl. *Conermann II*, 51–53. Zum *GB 1646* im vorliegenden Band s. 440130 K 3.

9 Aus dem vorliegenden Brief ergibt sich, was sich schon in den Briefen 400314 (K 3), 431016 u. 440313 andeutete: Gueintz war offensichtlich mit einem Werk zur deutschen Verslehre oder ganzen Poetik beschäftigt, die er abzuschließen u. der FG vorzulegen versprach. Da Justus Georg Schottelius (FG 397) seine ähnlich betitelte Poetik *Teutsche Vers- oder ReimKunst* (1645) erst mit 450204 F. Ludwig zusandte, kann es sich nicht darum handeln. Genaue Beschreibungen oder Belege für eine eigene, selbständige Arbeit von Gueintz zur deutschen Verskunst fehlen jedoch. Immerhin sprach F. Ludwig in einem Gutachten, wohl vom Dezember 1642, eine solche (tatsächlich nie erschienene) Arbeit an: „Sonsten wil dafür gehalten werden, das man in allerley art versen wie sie bey den Lateinern gebreuchlich auch in Deutsch doch auf Reimen art schreiben könne, wie solches unterschiedene die von der deutsch[en] Poesi geschrieben, ausweisen, Als Opitz, Buchner, und Guein[zi]us, die beyden letzen aber dürfen noch nicht volkommen heraus sein" (HM Köthen: V S 545, Bl. 261r–262v; *KE*, 301–305; demnächst in *DA Köthen I. 9*). Nach Lage der Dinge könnte es sich auch um ein Gutachten, eine poetologische Erweiterung von F. Ludwigs Verslehre (*Kurtze Anleitung zur Deutschen Poesi* [Köthen 1640], s. 391119 I) oder Hinweise zu einer anderen Arbeit im Umkreis der Prosodie- u. Verskunst-Diskussion in der FG gehandelt haben. Vgl. die dazu versammelten Quellen in *DA Köthen I. 9*. Bei seinem Ausfall gegen die „übel unterrichteten selbstgewachßenen Dichter" mochte Gueintz wohl auch an Philipp (v.) Zesen (FG 521. 1648) gedacht haben, übrigens einen seiner eigenen Schüler, dessen Aufnahme in die FG er später zu verhindern strebte.

10 *Stieler*, 2409: „Verwegen/ verwogen/ temerè audere. Sich worauf verwegen/ impetu ferri in rem aliqvam, coecum in certamina & pericula ruere. *Verùm hoc verbum non adeò freqvens est, descendit tamen ab eo:* Verwegen/ *adj. & adv.* Temerarius, improvidus, incogitatus, inconsultus, desperatus, &: desperanter, temerè, incautè, audacter."

441231A

Justus Georg Schottelius an Herzog August d.J. von Braunschweig-Wolfenbüttel

Justus Georg Schottelius (FG 397) schickt Hz. August d.J. v. Braunschweig-Wolfenbüttel (FG 227) ein (nicht beiliegendes) Neujahrsgedicht. Wie Karl d. Gr., der die Sachsen bezwang, Heiliges in die vaterländische Sprache zu übertragen unternahm, so habe der Herzog heilige Wonne und Sprachkunst verbunden und mit Zier und Schönheit durchdrungen. — Er überreiche ein ungewöhnliches, erklärungsbedürftiges Gedicht, welches in den ersten vier Versen jeder Strophe ein fünfzehnsilbiges trochäisches Maß aufweise, in griechischer Poesie Tetrameter acatalepticus genannt. Die nachfolgenden abnehmend kürzeren Verse, deren Schema er beilege, seien anapästisch. Sie büßten ihre Anmut ein, würden sie nicht nach diesem Metrum gehört und gelesen.

Q NSTA Wolfenbüttel: 2 Alt Nr. 40, Bl. 18r, eigenh.

A *Nicht vorhanden.*

Serenissime Princeps,
Domine clementissime

Affero humillimè annuj voti et strenuæ loco affectum syncerum et qualecunque animj indicium, festinato et rudj carmine declaratum. Quid autem versiculj intendant non facilè, nisi totis perlectis, lectori innotescet. Carolus M. primus sacra in linguam Patriam transferre incepit, et ferro duros Saxones ursit: Vestra Serenitas delicias sanctas et artem linguæ coniunxit et decore et rei amœnitate penetrat: Statuendum monumentum rei inceptæ, quod Carolo; et alterum rei perfectæ, quod VESTRÆ Serenitati debetur.

Carmen quædam continet, quæ non ita vulgaria et cuilibet cognita sunt, si tantj, ut et aliorum oculos subeat, explicanda quædam, et qvid velim, apponendum non nullibj erit. Versus quatuor priores in qualibet stropha sunt eius generis, qvi Tetrameter acatalecticus Græcis, in Germanicâ Poesi funfzehnSilbig-Langkurtze vocatur; Sequentes, qvi semper se abbreviant sunt omnes, ex genere Anapæstico, Schema adiunctum:[1] Gratia enim, si quæ verborum Germanicorum esse potest, abit, nisi verba cum cursu metrj audiuntur et leguntur. Vestra Serenitas impetui meo, quem dulcem et non intermorientem erga Eandem nutrio, clementissimè ignoscere, et principali gratiâ porro latebit
   obedientissimum Servum
   JGSchotteli[um]

K 1 **Unbekanntes Neujahrsgedicht.** Wir datieren den vorliegenden Brief daher auf den Jahreswechsel 1644/45. Nur in zeitlicher Nähe zu *Schottelius: Teutsche Vers- oder Reim-Kunst (1645)* wird Justus Georg Schottelius (FG 397) dieses experimentelle Gedicht als neuartig genug empfunden haben, um es Hz. August d.J. v. Braunschweig-Wolfenbüttel (FG 227) mit Stolz zu schicken. In seiner Poetik stellt Schottelius S. 147–150 15silbige

langkurze (trochäische) Verse unterschiedlicher Art vor: a) auf kurzer bzw. unbetonter Silbe endend, b) mit Zäsur nach der 7. Silbe u. auf langer/ betonter Silbe endend:
   a) Wer der Tugend sich ergiebet und auf Gottes Hülfe traut/
   Hat auf Diamanten Gründen und auf Felsen fest gebaut.
   b) Und hergegen wer sich nur | wil auff Eitelkeiten gründen/
   Deßen Hofnung muß dahin | wie ein Dampf und Rauch verschwinden.
Neben diesen eigenen Versen zitiert Schottelius auch derartige Verse von Johann Klaj. In *Gosky: Arbustum (1650)*, Bl. 6v lesen wir solche Verse in Abwechslung mit kürzeren:
   AUs der alten Guelfen Stam/ und aus hohem Fürsten Stande
      Schutz und Vater in dem Lande/
   Aus der grossen Helden-Zunfft/ hocherleuchter Herz und Sinn
      Stahl und Eisen geht dahin:
   Dieses Herren Tugend-Lust/ Friedens-Liebe/ heiligs Wesen
      Wird die Nach-Welt immer lesen.
Diese Verse sind auch als Subscriptio eines Porträtstichs Conrad Bunos verwandt worden. S. Katalog *Sammler Fürst Gelehrter* (Nr. 10 August, Nr. 10) u. unter einem Ganzfigurporträt Conrad Bunos (a. a. O., Nr. 496).
In seiner *Teutsche[n] Vers- oder ReimKunst (1645)*, 217, führt Schottelius auch 15zehn- bzw. 14zehnsilbige langgekürzte (daktylische) Verse vor:
   Wiltu mit ruhe/ wiltu mit ehren/ deine zeit leben/
   Soltu nach Demuht/ soltu nach Tugend allezeit streben &c.
S. 167 behandelt er auch „die Gekurtzlangen oder Anapestischen in Fünfzehnsilbigen Versen", z. B.
   Sich selbsten mit klugem bedachtem Verstande regieren/
   Das lehret dich andere Leute sehr löblich an[zu]führen
In *Schottelius: Fruchtbringender Lustgarte (1647)* kommen 14- u. 15silbige Verse wiederholt vor (S. 93, 127, 212 u. 341).

450000

Justus Georg Schottelius an Herzog August d. J. von Braunschweig-Wolfenbüttel

Justus Georg Schottelius (FG 397) entschuldigt sich, daß er schon wieder ein Buch aus der Bibliothek Hz. Augusts d. J. v. Braunschweig-Wolfenbüttel (FG 227) zu entleihen begehre, diesmal Cluverus' *Germania antiqua*, das er dann in ein, zwei Wochen zusammen mit dem Stevinus zurückgeben wolle. Auch möchte er gern kurz die Verdeutschung von (Georg Agricolas) *De re metallica*, ein Werk über die Jagd und die sog. *Meistergesänge* lesen. Die Namen der Verfasser der beiden letztgenannten Werke habe er vergessen, auch wisse er nicht, wessen Arbeit vorzuziehen sei. Er brauche Cluverus und *De re metallica* wegen der in den bisher vorliegenden Lexika und Wörterbüchern fehlenden Fachbegriffe. Deren Termini seien nämlich nach der Art und Weise und dem Sinn der lateinischen Begriffe gebildet.

Q   NSTA Wolfenbüttel: 2 Alt Nr. 40, Bl. 10rv, 10v leer; eigenh.

A   *Nicht vorhanden.*

450000 Justus Georg Schottelius

Serenissime Illustrissimeq̀ue Princeps Domine clementissime,

Vereor sanè nec immeritò, ne nimius aut importunus sim, dum bis & iterum rem eandem prece subiectissimâ efflagitare audeam. Vehementer cuperem Cluverium in suâ Germaniâ antiquâ¹ aliquot locis denuò consulere; post unum atque alteram septimanam unà cum Stevino², cuius usum adhuc habeo, sine maculâ remittendum.

Vetustius aliquod scriptum Germanicum de re metallica³ et re venatoriâ⁴, ubi et illum librum quem vocamus **Meistergesänge**,⁵ libenter perlegerem, si sperare auderem, humillimam meam petitionem importunitate carere, nec molestiis propiorem esse.

Esset autem ad breve tempus inspectio et usus horum lib. certas ob causas mihi et gratissimus et in re unâ atque alterâ pernecessarius. Vestra autem Serenitas ne inclementi adnutu illud fiduciæ habeat, subiectissimè petit
         eiusdem Servus obedientissimus
         Justus Georgius Schottelius.

Nomen authoris in re metallicâ³ et Venatoriâ⁴ mihi non occurrit, nec, quis forte præferendus, novi; percuperem tamen talem, unde Termini possent peti, quia in lexicis et vocabulariis quæ hactenus habemus, hæc non ita existant, sunt enim ea facta ad numerum et sensum vocabulorum latinorum.

K Justus Georg Schottelius (FG 397) datierte besonders seine nichtamtlichen Schreiben an seinen Dienstherren Hz. August d. J. v. Braunschweig-Wolfenbüttel (FG 227) nur selten. Den vorliegenden Brief vermögen wir ebenso wie die Schreiben in 460000 wegen ihres Inhalts auch nicht wenigstens auf den Monat oder die Jahreszeit genau zu datieren. Die aufgeführten Hilfsmittel können für alle Werke von Schottelius über die deutsche Sprache eingesehen worden sein: *Schottelius: Sprachkunst (1641), Der Teutschen Sprache Einleitung (1643), Sprachkunst (1651), Ausführliche Arbeit (1663)*. Der Begriff „opusculum" in 460000 I könnte jedoch offenbar auf *Der Teutschen Sprache Einleitung (1643)*, die kleinste dieser Arbeiten, verweisen, obgleich ‚Opusculum' oder deutsch ‚Büchlein' im Sprachgebrauch der Zeit häufig auch ein Werk von großem Umfang u. Format bezeichnen kann, weil der Schreiber aus Gründen der Bescheidenheit diesen Ausdruck wählte. Uns kommt bei unserer Datierung zu Hilfe, daß Schottelius schon 1642 die *Einleitung* nicht nur als „Libellus iste" bezeichnete, sondern das dünne Bändchen auch inhaltlich kennzeichnete. S. 421110 I. Dort konnten wir den Begleitbrief, mit dem Schottelius das Werk Hz. August überreichte, nur nach einer alten Abschrift veröffentlichen, haben aber inzwischen Schottelius' Originalschreiben entdeckt im NSTA Wolfenbüttel: 2 Alt Nr. 40, Bl. 12r. — Da Schottelius sich kurz vor der Publikation seiner *Teutschen Vers- oder ReimKunst (1645)* (s. 440900 K 2, *DA Köthen I. 9:* 450126A u. 450202) der Arbeit an einem neuen Sprachbuch zuwandte — das jedoch nicht erschien u. in die *Sprachkunst* von 1651 einging —, halten wir es zumindest für denkbar u. auf dem Höhepunkt der fruchtbringerischen Sprachdiskussion (vgl. z. B. 450923B u. 451007) für vorstellbar, daß die Entleihung u. Rückgabe der erwähnten Bücher 1645 bzw. 1646 erfolgte. S. 460000. Ein weiterer Grund für unsere zeitliche Einordnung des vorliegenden Briefs liegt darin, daß Schottelius von einer erneuten Ausleihe von Clüvers Werk redet. Deshalb könnte diese nach der in 441000 erwähnten Entleihung erfolgt sein. Entscheidend ist in diesem Zusammenhang jedoch, daß der vorliegende Brief wegen des fehlenden Doktortitels des Schreibers vor Schottelius' Promotion (Februar 1646) verfaßt worden sein dürfte.

1 Philippi CluverI Germaniæ Antiqvæ Libri tres (Lugduni Batavorum: Ludovicus Elzevirius 1616), HAB: 190 Hist. 2°. Von einer Entleihung dieses Werks berichtet schon 441000. Vgl. auch 450927 II (K II 5).

2 Simon Stevin (1548–1620). Über die benutzten Schriften dieses niederländischen Mathematikers u. Ingenieurs geben detailliert *Schottelius: Sprachkunst (1641)*, 40 f., *Schottelius: Sprachkunst (1651)*, Bl. [C 6] u. S. 33–35 u. *Schottelius: Ausführliche Arbeit (1663)*, 20 u. 1167 Auskunft. Danach läßt sich aus den alten Beständen Hz. Augusts (sog. Augusteer) in der HAB als das vermutlich entliehene Exemplar in nl. Sprache ein Quartband mit drei Schriften Stevins ermitteln: DE WEEGHDAET BESCHREVEN DVER SIMON STEVIN van Brugghe. TOT LEYDEN, Inde Druckerye van Christoffel Plantijn, By François van Raphelingen. M. D. LXXXVI.; DE BEGHINSELEN DER WEEGHCONST BESCHREVEN DVER SIMON STEVIN van Brugghe. TOT LEYDEN, Inde Druckerye van Christoffel Plantijn, By François van Raphelingen. M. D. LXXXVI.; DE BEGHINSELEN DES WATERWICHTS BESCHREVEN DVER SIMON STEVIN van Brugghe. TOT LEYDEN, Inde Druckerye van Christoffel Plantijn, By François van Raphelingen. M. D. LXXXVI. HAB: 8 Geom. (1)–(3). Aus *De Weeghdaet* (Bl. bBr – dD 4v) hob *Schottelius: Ausführliche Arbeit*, 20, die Rede VYTSPRAECK VANDE WEERDICHEYT DER DVYTSCHE TAEL hervor: „Er hat auch eine eigene Uitsprake/ Lobrede/ von der Teutschen Sprache geschrieben/ daraus ich diese seine Worte/ doch in Hochteutscher Mundart/ anziehen wil [...]: denn es eine jämmerliche Blindheit ist/ durch die Schikkung GOttes bißhero gleichsam verordnet [...]" usw. Als besonders hilfreich erwiesen sich für Schottelius besonders die Listen einsilbiger niederländischer, lateinischer u. griechischer Wörter, Namen u. Teilwörter: „DVYTSCHE EENSILBIGHE VVOORDEN"; Listen lat. u. griech. einsilbiger Wörter; „D'ANDER DVYTSCHE YNCKEL GHELVYDEN, ALS DER NAMEN; BYNAMEN; VOOSETtinghen, &c. siin in ghetale tot 1428 de Latijnsche Tot de tsaevouging onbequaem) alleenlick 158 de Griesche 220 Als volght." Die Einsilbigkeit war ein Grundaxiom Schottelius' in seiner Konzeption der dt. Stammwörter. Vgl. etwa 450410 K 3. Stevin übersetzte das Niederländische auch ins Französische u. Italienische, das Lateinische ins Französische u. Niederländische, die griech. Namen ins Niederländische. Zu Stevin s. 430403 K 3–5. Vgl. auch Flip G. Droste: Simon Stevin en de Uytspraeck van de weerdicheyt der duytsche tael (1586). In: Leuvense Bijdragen 96 (2007–2010), 1–8.

3 In den Beständen der augusteischen Büchersammlung (HAB) s. die deutschsprachigen Ausgaben: Georg Agricola: Vom Bergwerck 12 Bücher: darinn alle Empter, Instrument, Gezeuge unnd alles zu disem handel gehörig, mitt schönen figuren vorbildet und klärlich beschriben seindt/ erstlich in lat. sprach durch Georgium Agricolam, jetzundt aber verteütscht durch Philippum Bechium (Basel: Froben & Bischoff 1557). 4°; CCCCXCI S. HAB: 20.5 Phys. 2° — BerckwerckBuch: Darinn nicht Allain alle Empter Instrument Gezeug/ vnd alles/ so zu disem Handel gehörig/ mit figuren vorgebildet/ vnd klärlich beschriben. Sondern auch/ wie ein rechtverstendiger Berckman seyn sol/ vnd die Gäng außzurichten seyen ... Durch ... Georgium Agricolam ... in Latein beschriben/ vnd ... durch ... Philippum Bechium ... verteutscht (Franckfort am Main: Feyrabend 1580: Schmidt). 2°, 4 Bl., CCCXCI S., 3 Bl., 1 Faltbl. HAB: 21.3 Phys. 2° (2). — Ausg. Basel: Ludwig König 1621. 2°; HAB: 15.2 Phys. 2°. — Zur Sammlung deutscher Fachwörter vgl. auch bes. 440826 K 4 (Franckenberg) u. Moscheroschs Arbeit in 440616 K I.

4 Schottelius wußte keinen Autor oder Titel zu nennen. Beispiele für deutschsprachige

Jagdbücher in den Sammlungen Herzog Augusts: Andreas Angelus: Jägerhörnlein (Franckfurt am Main: Joh. Kollitz 1597). 4°, 4 Bl., 85 S., 1 S., 123.2 Quod. (19) u. 160.11 Quod (3); Ausgabe Hamburg 1598, 515 Quod. (3). — Jaques Du Fouilloux: Neuw Jag unnd Weydwerck Buch. 2 Tle. (Franckfurt am Mayn: Sigmund Feyerabend 1582). 4°, 4 Bl., 103 u. 1 Bl.; 73 Bl.; 19.1 Phys. 2°. — Jägerkunst und Waldgeschrey (Nürnberg: Georg Leopold Fuhrmann 1610). 8°, 16 Bl., 498 Quod. (2); Ausgabe Nürnberg: Fuhrmann 1611. 8°, 47 Bl., 515 Quod. (4).

5 Außer einer kleinen Handschrift mit 19 Liedern des Wiedertäufers Peter Walbot (Cod. Guelf. 87.3 Aug. 12°) gibt es heute nur wenige geschriebene Lieder u. Fragmente in der HAB, so daß an gedruckte Ausgaben von Hans Sachs u. anderen Dichtern zu denken ist. S. Repertorium der Sangsprüche und Meisterlieder des 12. bis 18. Jahrhunderts. Hgg. Horst Brunner u. Burghart Wachinger unter Mitarb. v. Eva Klesatschke u. a. Bd. 1. Tübingen 1994, 302 u. 325 ff. (Druckbibliographie). Vgl. auch Klaus Zimmermann: Die Hans-Sachs-Drucke des 16. Jahrhunderts. Ein Beitrag zur Bestandsgeschichte der Herzog August Bibliothek. In: 500 Jahre Hans Sachs. Handwerker, Dichter, Stadtbürger. Wiesbaden 1994, 56–62 (Ausstellungskataloge der Herzog August Bibliothek 72). In Fruchtbringerkreisen bekannt war Adam Puschmans (1532–1600) *Gründlicher Bericht des deutschen Meistergesangs,* der seit 1571 in verschiedenen Fassungen u. Auflagen erschienen war. Vgl. A. P.: „Gründlicher Bericht des deutschen Meistergesangs" (die drei Fassungen von 1571, 1584 u. 1596). Texte in Abbildung mit Anhang u. einleitendem Kommentar. Hg. Brian Taylor. 2 Bde. Göppingen 1984. Christian Gueintz (FG 361) hatte eine Ausgabe vordem F. Ludwig zugeschickt, s. 400301. Falls Schottelius diesen Titel im Kopf gehabt haben sollte, so wäre die Nachfrage vergeblich gewesen. Heute jedenfalls findet sich keine alte Ausgabe dieses Werkes im HAB-Bestand. In den Zusammenhang des Meistersangs gehört nicht: Die Vier Geistreiche freudenreiche Meistergeseng vnd güldene Kleinod des Newen Testaments. Als/ das 1. Magnificat Mariæ. 2. Benedictus Zachariæ. 3. Der Lobgesang der heiligen Engel, bey der Geburt des Herrn Christi. 4. Nunc dimittis Simeonis. Auffs newe ausgelegt vnd in druck verfertiget/. durch Christofferum Vischer den eltern/ Fürstlichen Lüneburgischen Superintendenten vnd Pastorn zu Zell (Ulssen: Michael Kröner 1588). 8°; 351 Bl., HAB: Td 352. Es handelt sich um umfangreiche Prosaauslegungen Vischers über jeweils wenige biblische Verse in bekannten liturgischen Gesängen.

450000A

Philipp von Zesen an Justus Georg Schottelius

Philipp v. Zesen (FG 521. 1648) widmet in Amsterdam seine Venus-Dichtung *Lustinne* Justus Georg Schottelius (FG 397. Der Suchende).

Q Widmungszuschrift Philipp v. Zesens: Filip Zesiens von | Fürstenau | Lustinne/ | Das ist/ | Gebundene Lust-Rede | von Kraft und Würkung | der Liebe. | [Linie] | Hamburg/ Bey Heinrich Wernern/ | Jm Jahr/ 1645. Bl. Aij rv. SUB Göttingen: 8 P GERM II, 9180. Ndr. in: *Zesen SW I.1,* 235–258, hier S. 239 f.
Die Widmungsvorrede fehlt im *Lustinne*-Anhang in der Ausgabe [Kupfertitel] Ritterholds | von | Blauen | Adriatische | Rosemund | Last hägt Lust. | Amstelam, | Bei Ludwich Elzevihrn. 1645. | gemacht durch den wachenden. HAB: 135.5 Eth. (2). Auch Dig. Darin S. 299–368: Filip Zesens von Fürstenau | Lustinne/ | der un-vergleichlichen | ROSEMUND | zu ehren und gefallen verfasset/ | und | DEM SUCHENDEN | über-

eignet. | mit noch etlichen lustigen äben selbiges | verfassers getichten. Ndr. in: *Zesen SW IV.*2, 283–337. In der Titelauflage der *Adriatischen Rosemund* von 1664 fehlt die Widmungsvorrede an Schottelius demzufolge ebenfalls: [Kupfertitel] Ritterholds | von | Blauen | Adriatische | Rosemund | Last hägt Lust. | Amsteltam, | Bei Heinrich von Aken. 1664. | gemacht durch den wachenden. HAB: Xb 2533. SUB Göttingen: 8 FAB VI, 1848 (auch Dig.); dementsprechend auch in der Edition der ersten *Rosemund*-Ausgabe von 1645 durch Max Hermann Jellinek, Halle a. d. S.1899 (Neudrucke deutscher Litteraturwerke des XVI. u. XVII. Jahrhunderts, Nr. 160–163). Jellinek geht nirgendwo auf Zesens ursprüngliche Widmungsepistel in der *Lustinne* ein.

Dem ädlen/ fästen und hooch-
gelehrtem
Hern Just-Georg Schotteln
Fürstl. Lühneburgischem Rahte/ uam. der
Hooch-deutschen Grund-Sprache/ und
derselben Zier und Lob zu vermehren
Suchenden;
Der Höchst-löblichen Frucht-bringenden Ge-
selschaft ahnsähnlichem Mitgliede;

Seinem Hooch-geehrtem Hern/und groos-
günstigem/ lieben Freunde
übereignet der Verfasser diese seine Lustinne aus
wohl-meinendem/ träu-deutschen Gemühte.

Az!

Mein Her/

NAachdehm ich gesähen/ daß die Deutsche Venus (oder wie ich sie lieber benännen wil) Lustinne[1] in unserer Mutter-sprache noch niemahls recht besungen worden/ so hab' ich mich neulicher zeit/ doch mehr auf Ahnhalten unserer träugeliebten Mitgenossen[2]/ als aus eitelem Vohr-wiz/ Selbige naach meiner wenigen Geschiklichkeit unserer Hooch- und groos-mächtigsten Deutschinnen[3] vohr zu stållen/ gelüsten laßen. Weil sie nuhn [Aijv] aber auch eines Schuzzes in Hoochdeutschland/ davon ich nuhn leider! entfernet läbe/ bedürftig ist/ und sich so bloos/ als eine noch gleichsam Fremde/ bey unserer höchst-berührten Deutschinnen nicht ahngäben darf/ so hab' ich vohr guht ahngesähen/ meinem hooch-geehrtem Hern Schotteln (dehr sonst bey unserer Heldin/ weil er sich ihre Ehre/ durch aus-übung seiner Muttersprache/ so eifrig zu suchen[4] bemühet/ in großen gnaden ist) den Auftraag[5] zu tuhn/ daß er Jhm[a] groosgünstig wolle belieben laßen/ diese von mier gleichsam Verstoßene (dan sie würd ohne zweyfäl aus Freundes Hand den Klauen des schmaachsüchtigen Neides[6] übergäben) vohr allem ungewitter zu schirmen/ sie eines freundlichen Ahnblikkes würdigen und bey unserer Heldin ihr wort zu reden. Welches ich bey aller Gelägenheit mit dankbarem Gemühte bäster maßen wärde zu erwiedern wüssen. Mitler zeit verbleib' ich dehr jenige/ dehr ich schohn längst gewäsen/ und halte mich hooch/ wan ich mit recht heissen maag

> Gegäben in dem Ertz-schreine der
> Amstelinnen/ 1645.
>
>> Mein Her
>> Sein träu- und dienstfärtiger
>> F. Z. v. F.⁷

T a *Lies:* sich

K Philipp v. Zesen (FG 521. 1648) widmete dieses Werk Justus Georg Schottelius (FG 397. Der Suchende) mit seiner Zuschrift aus Amsterdam. Eine unmittelbare Reaktion von Schottelius ist uns nicht bekannt. Seine grundsätzliche Haltung gegenüber Zesen in *Schottelius: Ausführliche Arbeit (1663)*, S. 1201: „*Philippus Caesius* hat in Trukk kommen lassen viele und mancherley Poetische Tractätlein/ auch sonst ein und anderst aus Frantzösischen und Holländischen ins Hochteutsche übergesetzt/ woraus wol abzunehmen/ daß er der Teutschen Sprache mechtig/ und sonderlich in Poesi eine fertige nicht unliebliche Art habe: Alles aber so vorhin entweder Teutsches Herkommens ist/ oder Teutsches Verstandes seyn kann/ in anderweitiges Unteutsches Teutsch zusetzen; oder auch die Teutschen Worte/ der Schreibung und offenem Ansehen nach/ in eine andere Gestalt kleiden/ oder jhnen das Kleid/ worin sie überall kennlich und hergestammt/ ohn gründliche Uhrsach ausziehen/ ist ein Werk eigener Einbildung/ so sich verständigen Beyfals wenig versicheren kan." Schottelius vertrat mit diesem Urteil die opinio communis innerhalb der FG, die Zesens literarische Arbeiten, seine flüssige Stilistik u. seine Poetik anerkannte, seine selbstgefällige Eitelkeit u. seine Eingriffe in Rechtschreibung u. Lexik sowie seine etymologischen Spekulationen aber größtenteils als angemaßte u. haltlose Neuerungen ablehnte. Schottelius wurde kein Mitglied in Zesens DG (s. Anm. 2). Vgl. *Herz: Zesen*, 189ff. u. 197ff. In seinem Brief an Matthaeus Apelles von Löwenstern vom 7.1.1646 kam Andreas Tscherning auf Schottelius' *Teutsche Vers- oder ReimKunst (1645)* u. auf Zesens „neulich herauß gegebene Lustinne" zu sprechen: Apelles möge sich letztere „wundershalben" beschaffen „und urtheile hernach von seiner Orthographie. Wo wollen wir Deutschen doch endlich hin!" S. 440324 K 23.

1 Zesens Übersetzung für Venus. Dem Gedicht folgt S. 12–19 ein Anhang „Oedipus oder Entwikkelung etlicher fremden Nahmen und Ahrten zu reden" (*Zesen SW* I.1, S. 252–257). Darin wird als dt. Übersetzung für Venus/ Aphrodite als Göttin der Liebe „Lustinne/ Liebinne oder (wie er uns von den alten Deutschen hinterlassen ist) Freije" angegeben. Analog „Bluhminne" für Flora/ Chloris, „Holdinnen" für die Grazien/ Charites usw. Ein Glossar seiner fremden Namen- und Wortübersetzungen im Anhang „An den Läser" in der *Adriatischen Rosemund* (1645). *Zesen SW* IV.2, 336f. mit „Pallas, Kluginne/ Blauinne", „Diana, Weidinne/ Jagtinne", „Venus, Lustinne/ Libinne", „Juno, Himmelinne", aber auch „pistohl/ reit=puffer", „fänster/ tage=leuchter", „nonnen=kloster/ Jungfer=zwünger" u.a.m. Vgl. hier auch Anm. 3; 441201 K 2 u. 450808 K I 3. In der 2. Ausgabe seines *Deutschen Helikons* (Wittenberg 1641), Bl. T2r–T3v hatte Zesen die

Frage „Ob man die Eignen Nahmen der Götter und Göttinnen/ als Jupiter/ Venus etc. könne deutsch geben?" verneint. Die mythologischen Namen der Griechen u. Römer seien so allgemein gebräuchlich u. verständlich, „daß es fast nicht geändert werden kann/ müssen wier also auch dem gemeinen Gebrauch nachhängen." In den Gedichten jedoch, in denen „mann etwa seiner Eignen Buhlschafft zugedencken pfleget", sollte man „rechte Deutsche Nahmen" verwenden bzw. erfinden. Zesen verzichtete hier auf Beispiele. *Zesen SW* IX, 252.

2 Nach Zesens eigenen Angaben im *Hochdeutschen Helikonischen Rosentahl* (Amsterdam 1669) wurde seine Deutschgesinnete Genossenschaft (DG) am 1. Mai 1643 in Hamburg gegründet, jedoch sind auch andere Gründungsangaben überliefert oder wahrscheinlich. Vgl. die Literaturangaben zu Ort u. Datum demnächst in *Conermann: Ort der Akademie*, zu Anm. 53–55. In: Mitteilungen der Residenzen-Kommission der Akademie der Wissenschaften zu Göttingen. N. F. Stadt u. Hof, Jg. 4. — Weitere Gründungsmitglieder sollen Theodor Peterson (1609–1652; DG 2. Der Verharrende) u. Hans Christoph v. Liebenau (DG 3. Der Aemsige) gewesen sein. *Zesen SW* XI, 192f. u. 225ff., vgl. 451 u. 453. Seit dem Mai 1644 wurde die DG erweitert u. wuchs bis zum Ende des Jahres auf 14 Mitglieder an, im Laufe des Jahres 1645 traten 21 weitere Mitglieder ein. Ebd., 232–263.

3 „Deutschinne" als Zesens Personifizierung für Germania/ Deutschland, dessen Schutzgöttin, wohl auch mit der Konnotation „deutsche Musen". Kein Hinweis im Anhang „Oedipus oder Entwickelung etlicher fremden Nahmen und Ahrten zu reden" u. im Anhang „An den Läser" (s. Anm. 1). Vgl. 441201 K 2.

4 Anspielung auf Schottelius' FG-Gesellschaftsname Der Suchende.

5 „Auftraag" hier nicht im Sinne einer strengen Anordnung, sondern im Sinne von etwas an- oder auftragen, wie bei der Bedienung einer Speisetafel oder einem sakralen Opfer. Vgl. 441201 K 1.

6 Zesens eigene Immunisierung gegen Kritik (durch deren Verächtlichmachung als Neid u. Mißgunst) ist als geradezu notorisch aufgefallen. „Tugend hat leider! allzuviel neider" hieß es in seinem Eintrag von 1648 im *GB Kö.* III, Bl. 121v, den er, obgleich noch nicht geadelt, sogar als „Filip von [!] Zesen" unterschrieb. Vgl. Anm. 7 u. Claudius Sittig: Zesens Exaltationen. Ästhetische Selbstnobilitierung als soziales Skandalon. In: Philipp von Zesen. Wissen — Sprache — Literatur. Hgg. Maximilian Bergengruen u. Dieter Martin. Tübingen 2008, 95–118, hier 105 u. 117.

7 Obwohl Zesen erst 1653 nobilitiert wurde u. aus Priorau bei Dessau stammte, unterschrieb er Briefe oder veröffentlichte Werke häufiger mit Filip Caesius/ Zesen/ Zesien/ Zesius von Fürstenau, etwa 441201 u. 450808 I, seine *FrühlingsLust oder Lob- und LiebesLieder* (1642, *Zesen SW* I.1, 35–200) oder seine Lobrede auf die Buchdruckerkunst: *Phil. Caes. von Fürstenau Gebundene Lob-Rede Von der Hochnütz- und Löblichen zweyhundert-Jährigen Buchdrückerey-Kunst* (Hamburg 1642, *Zesen SW* I.1, 201–234). Vgl. auch 440724 K 9 bzw. Sittig (Anm. 6), 99 u. 101 ff.

450100

Justus Georg Schottelius an Herzog August d. J. von Braunschweig-Wolfenbüttel

Auf Befehl habe Justus Georg Schottelius (FG 397) (wenige) Seiten (der *Evangelischen Kirchen-Harmonie*) Hz. Augusts d. J. v. Braunschweig-Wolfenbüttel (FG 227) auf Druckfehler durchgesehen und keine gefunden, da das leuchtende Gestirn des Fürsten alle Dunkelheit durchdringe und mit strengerer Genauigkeit mit der Zier unserer Sprache verfahre, als er es könne. — Übrigens sei Schottelius im Lesen die Bedeutung einer scheinbar nicht so wichtigen Einzelheit aufgefallen, die zu erwähnen er als seine Pflicht erachte. Sie betreffe die Grundlage der deutschen Rechtschreibung. Gerade werde schon in Wolfenbüttel ein Büchlein (*Schottelius: Teutsche Vers- oder ReimKunst [1645]*) gedruckt, das die neue Form der poetischen Kunst behandele und bei der Rechtschreibung die Grundlagen der Wurzelbuchstaben, der eigentlichen und der zugehörigen, berühre. Davon handle er in wenigem in der Beilage A. Ausführlicheres stehe bereit. Unter Gelehrten würde über die Grundlegung der Orthographie schon eine Entscheidung getroffen werden. In der Beachtung der Grundbuchstaben stimmten sie überein, darunter seine Förderer und Freunde Vogel, Dilherr, Harsdörffer, Moscherosch, Hager und Rist. Nicht aus Neuerungssucht habe er in dem erwähnten Buch schon die neue Schreibweise befolgt und auf ihre Grundlagen hingewiesen, sondern vor allem auch wegen der Auswärtigen, die die Hinweise begierig erwarteten, besonders die neuen, welche durch Hz. August aus dem alten Wolfenbüttel hervorkämen. Zwar gäbe es Kritiker, die darüber schimpften, wonach sie doch suchten, doch würden die Hinweise im allgemeinen von Mitgliedern der Fruchtbringenden Gesellschaft gutgeheißen. Nicht zu Unrecht schienen von Gelehrten die Grundlagen erforscht zu werden, denn sie irrten dabei wohl angesichts durchgehend mangelnder Gewißheit gleichsam hin und her. — Der Setzer habe sich an einigen Stellen, die Schottelius auf dem Zettel B notiert habe, nicht an seine Anweisungen gehalten. In der Schreibweise von Grundwörtern habe er, wie Zettel C zeige, sich nach der alten Orthographie gerichtet. — Es fehle an Geld für den Druck seiner feinen Poetik. Von den sechs Kupfern habe er eines erlangt, während die übrigen fünf noch in Nürnberg und Hamburg lägen. Die Erklärung der Gedichtarten behindere der Mangel der Typen, von denen der Schriftgießer in dem beigefügten Brief berichtet habe, denn die Verse und Laute müssten durch Linien unterschieden werden und dem hiesigen Drucker fehlten dazu die Typen. — Schottelius bittet den Herzog wegen seines Buchs und seiner anderen Bedürfnisse nochmals um Auszahlung des restlichen halbjährlichen Gehalts. Er könne dann den Engpaß beim Druck überwinden und sich durch den Absatz aller Exemplare von seinen Schulden befreien.

Q NSTA Wolfenbüttel: 2 Alt Nr. 40, Bl. 3rv [A: nach Bl. 5], eigenh. — Zur Beilage A (Bl. 4r–5v) s. *DA Köthen I. 9.* — Die zwei weiteren ursprünglichen Beilagen (bezeichnet B u. C) fehlen.

A Serenissimo Illustrissimoque ad manus Clementissimas humillimè

Serenissime Princeps, Domine clementissime

Jussus ego pagellas inclusas perlegere, et an aliquid sphalmatis typographicj insit innuere;[1] equidem perlustravj: monere autem pro tenuitate mea nihil potui; et quis in hisce poterit? tenebras suas objiciendo splendescenti amabiliqùe Vestræ Serenitatis Sideri, profluentiqùe, cum accuratiore gravitate, quam toties cum[a] penetrabili linguæ nostræ decore audimus.

Cæterum subiit memoriam perlegentis alia res, non adeò exiguj forsan momentj, cuius aliqualem[b] rationem Vestræ Serenitati à me reddi, ex debito subiectissimæ obedientiæ, tum etiam ex alia gravi causâ fieri, existimabam. Concernit autem ea res fundamenta orthographiæ Germanicæ. Jmprimitur hîc iam libellus, in Vestræ Serenitatis sede et Arce illustrj, cuius non unam mentionem feci, et quod novam artis Poeticæ formam continet;[2] in eo ipso quo ad Orthographia*m* observata sunt fundamenta <u>literarum radicalium</u>, <u>essentialium</u> et <u>accidentalium</u>, de qvibus in literis inclusis, .A. notatis,[3] pauca dicta sunt: plures, nec minus relevanter rationes, si tantj est, facilè dici porrò prosunt, in promptu enim sunt: Disceptatum inter doctos viros fuit de ponendo et suscipiendo certo Orthographiæ fundamento, et in eo consentitur [3v] observanda fundamenta dictarum[b] literarum, ex iis qui taliter sentiunt, nomine Fautores et amicos Dn. Vogelium,[4] Dilherum,[5] Harsdorferum,[6] Mosheroshrum,[7] Hagerum,[8] Ristium.[9] Cum ergo in dicto libello ubiqùe hæc circa scriptionem observata sint, ne novitatis improbandæ amans[10] viderer, indicium fundaminis ad hoc ducentis facere debuj. Tum ob exterorum et longinqùe remotorum indicia, à quibus multis ea, quæ per Vestram Serenitatem ex vetusto celebrj hoc loco noviter prodibunt, avidè expectan*tur*: inter quos credo non nullos qvi sine causa quærunt, quod sugillant. Exprobatur in genere iis qvi ad Fructiferam Societatem pertinent. Non immeritò ijs vide*n*tur investigari ab Eruditis fundamenta, qvibus usq*ue* fluctuanti certitudini quodammodo oberare[c] possit:

Typotheta[11] videtur in paucis quibusdam immemor, quod jnter perlegendum breviter in schedula .B. notata, signavj. Novam non esse, sed dudum visam illam juxta literarum fundamentalium ductûs, scriptionem, etiam ex iniecta pagella .C. notatâ, non nihil apparere potest.[12]

Jn opere Poetico exscribendo perscit*um* quidem, sed ægrè et vix, quia sumptus, q*ui* adhuc restant faciendi, desunt. Cupreæ imagines sunt sex, una*m* ex iis intuli, reliquæ sunt adhuc Norimb. et Hamb.[13] In enarrendis variis Carmin*um* generibus omninò necessariæ et illæ literæ, de q*uibus* ille, qui fusit eas, in literis adjectis[14] mentione*m* facit; non *enim* per lineas erunt vers*us* soniq*ue* dividendi, congruentes a*utem* literæ[d] Typographo hîc desunt. Vestram Serenitatem humillimâ prece denuò solicito, ne velit diutius mej, tum ob alias, tum ob hanc mihi p*er* necessariam (si enim opusculum constituto tempore absolvi poterit, cu*m* emolumento omnib*us* exemplaribus me liberare possum) et p*er* se favorabilem causam, oblivisci, sed clementissimè concedere, ut adiutamentum à restante semestrj Salario mihi fieri[e] possit, hæreo aliàs et occasiones omittere cogor. Clementissime adiutum à Vestrâ Serenitate exspecto

eiusdem fidelis*simè* obediens
JGSchotteli*us*.

I

Schottelius preist Herzog Augusts *Evangelische Kirchen-Harmonie*

Q HAB: Cod. Guelf. 56 Extrav., Bl. 244rv; o. D., eigenh.

A *Fehlt.*

Serenissime Princeps, Domine clementissime

Harmoniam Evangelicam in Arbore illâ (Jerem. 17. v. 8) super aquas plantatâ, suasq*ue* radices ad rivos extendente,[1] optimè comparamus. Cælestis aquæ Rivus est, quæ eflorescens Manuum Vestrarum opus irrigavit. Non timebit lignum illud Prophetæ, cum venerit æstus;[2] Nec Arbor illa Selenica ob fervidos invidiæ Soles et uredines unquam marcescet.

Folium arboris propheticæ erit semper-viride, nec solicitum in Tempore siccitatis;[3] Augustæ Arboris fructus non acescent, ob acerbas decerpentis manus, nec dulcedo eius exsiccabitur, ob siccum et frigidum maligni alicujus oris saporem.

Non desinet facere fructum Arbor illa apud Prophetam; Fructifera Gustavi Olea, et semper-virescens Seleni Palma,[4] fœcundi fructum amoris, et pacificam dulcemq*ue* animæ requiem spirat, ingerit, plantat, novis usq*ue* pulcritudinis christianæ gemmulis protuberando, quæ Lecturis in multam utilitatis varietatem crescunt, maturescunt, dulcescunt.

Fructus fert Arbor illa Davidica (ψ 1 v. 3)[5] suo tam Tempore; Fructifera sancti laboris Vestri proles habet, habebitq*ue* etiam suum Tempus, et fœcundum et gloriosum; licet non desit alicubi et invidiosum et inimicæ sicei-[244v]tatis sine tamen timore Jerem. el. I.[6] Quoties Harmoniæ allegata in textu aliquo diligenter evolvo et adiungo, **exsatians cor vestrum** (Esaj. 58 v. 10)[7] simulq*ue* tranquillum fructum largiter invenio: Nec aliter hinc esse poterit, Gloriosum hunc Præmonstratorem etiam largiter et intimiùs à nobis amarj.

Attestor hîc, in lingua Patriâ, aliquem mei cordis sensum, quo feror et ducor, quoties ab Harmoniâ doceor, et me ineunda cum attentione in eâ exerceo.

Amando non peccamus. Ignosces SERENISSIME Princeps, amantissime Domine, nostro in Te amore, qvi tamen usq*ue* et pro viribus in tuam Laudem conspirabit.

Serenitati Vestræ
devotione fidelissima addictus
Justus-Georgius Schottel*ius*.

T a *Eingefügt.* — **b** *Folgt ein gestrichenes, unlesbares Wort.* — **c** *Lies* oberrari — **d** *Vor 2 gestrichenen, unlesbaren Buchstaben.* — **e** *Folgt* <possunt>

K 1 Justus Georg Schottelius (FG 397. Der Suchende) liest wahrscheinlich die *Evangelische Kirchen-Harmonie* Hz. Augusts d.J. v. Braunschweig-Wolfenbüttel (FG 227. Der Befreiende) Korrektur. Denkbar wäre auch die Durchsicht eines anderen, etwa eines administrativen Texts, jedoch ist nur im Zusammenhang mit der Spracharbeit der FG der Hinweis des Suchenden auf die Rechtschreibung bei diesem theologisch-sprachlichen Vorhaben des Befreienden wichtig. Schottelius las demnach nur wenige Blätter („pagellas"), anfängliche Probedrucke der *Kirchen-Harmonie*, die noch vor dem ersten im Juni 1645 vollendeten Probedruck des Werks angefertigt worden sein müssen. S. 411214, bes. S. 386. Vgl. 451001 u. ö. Wie Anm. 2 zu Schottelius' Poetik zeigt, kann Schottelius nur nichterhaltene Anfänge des Probedrucks durchgesehen haben, da der vorliegende Brief vor dem 26.1.1645 geschrieben worden sein muß. Danach paßt Schottelius' Durchsicht in die Zeit, als Julius Willershausens Abschrift bereits gelesen worden war; sie weist nämlich eigenh. Korrekturen des Herzogs u. seine Datierungen des Kirchenjahrs auf (ausgeführt v. 29.11. – 21.12.), dazu die Bogensignaturen des Drucks (HAB: Cod. Guelf. 36 Noviss. 8°). Der Herzog arbeitete an Autographen der Kirchen-Harmonie bis zum Januar 1645 (HAB: Cod. Guelf. 35 Noviss. 8° u. Cod. Guelf. 37 Noviss. 8°). Vgl. *Giermann*, 95 f. — Schottelius sah schon einen Teil der *Passionsharmonie* Hz. Augusts (s. 411214, S. 352 f.) aus dem Zeitraum 1639–1641 durch. S. Eduard Bodemann: Zwei Briefe von Leibniz betr. eine „Teutsche Gesellschaft" zu Wolfenbüttel nebst zwei Briefen von J. G. Schottelius an Herzog August von Braunschweig-Wolfenbüttel. In: Zeitschr. d. Histor. Vereins f. Niedersachsen 1899, 299–307, hier S. 304–306, von uns für die Veröffentlichung in DA Köthen I. 9 vorgesehen. Zu einer späteren Korrektur der *Evangelischen Kirchen-Harmonie* s. auch das Schreiben vom 28.3.1646 (von Schottelius?): NSTA Wolfenbüttel: 2 Alt Nr. 3520, Bl. 212 (Druck mit eigenh. Korrekturen des Herzogs).

2 Schottelius: *Teutsche Vers- oder ReimKunst (1645)*, die auf Kosten des Autors in der neueingerichteten Wolfenbütteler Druckerei der Brüder Stern mit Erlaubnis des Herzogs (s. 441011) hergestellt wurde u. die den Herzog selbst nicht erwähnt. Dieser Brief u. die dortige Vorrede an den Leser (d. d. 26.1.1645) bezeichnen den Zeitraum, in dem der vorliegende undatierte Brief abgefaßt worden sein muß. Das Schreiben 441011 betont die Neuartigkeit der Behandlung der Poesie in besagter *Teutsche[n] Vers- oder ReimKunst*.

3 Vgl. Schottelius' Exposé mit der Aufschrift „A." in DA Köthen I. 9: „Zu 441200 Schottelius über die Grundlagen des Deutschen u. dessen Wortbildung".

4 Da dieser Name im Zusammenhang mit Johann Michael Dilherr (s. Anm. 5) u. Georg Philipp Harsdörffer (s. Anm. 6) genannt wird, dürfte Schottelius Johan Vogel(ius) (1589–1663), den Rektor der Schule zu St. Sebald in Nürnberg, Psalmdichter u. gekrönten Poeten, gemeint haben. Dessen Sammlung *Die Psalmen, geistlicher Lieder und Hausgesänge* (Nürnberg 1653) hat Dilherr mit einer Vorrede versehen. Vgl. *Flood*, 2172–2174; *Jöcher* IV, 1690; Dieter Wölfel: *Geistliche Erquickstunden*. Beobachtungen zur Interdependenz von lutherischer Frömmigkeitsbewegung und Nürnberger Sprachgesellschaft am Beispiel populärer Gesangbücher der Pegnitzschäfer. In: *der Franken Rom. Nürnbergs Blütezeit in der zweiten Hälfte des 17. Jahrhunderts*. Hg. John Roger Paas. Wiesbaden 1995, 364–382, hier 366 u. 375.

5 Johann Michael Dilherr, Theologe u. Leiter des Schulwesens in Nürnberg. S. 440824 K 7, 441200 K 3, 450400 K 6 u. 11, 450504A K 4, 460317 K I 0, 460700 u. ö.

6 Georg Philipp Harsdörffer (FG 368; DG 1644; PBO Strephon), Dichter, Literat u. Patrizier in Nürnberg.

7 Johann Michael Moscherosch (FG 436. 1645; DG 1645), Schriftsteller, Verwaltungsbeamter im Elsaß.

8 Christoph Achaz Hager (1584–1657), aus Frankenberg in Meißen gebürtig, seit etwa 1614 in Hamburg als Rechenmeister, Buch- u. Schulhalter sowie Deutschlehrer. Unter seinen oft wiedergedruckten Werken zur Buchhaltung, Briefstellerei, Orthographie u. Grammatik die *Orthographia Oder Teütscher Sprache Wegweiser. Das ist: Naturgemäßer und*

wolbegründter Vnterricht: Wie die Hochlöb- und liebliche Teütsche Sprache/ recht zu läsen und zu schreiben (Hamburg: Andreas Venus 1634), StB Braunschweig: C 432/3. Unklare Überlieferungshinweise suggerieren (nicht nachweisbare) frühere Ausgaben von 1616, 1619, 1624 u. 1630. Zwei weitere nachgewiesene Drucke Hamburg 1639 (BN Paris) u. Hamburg 1640 (SUB Hamburg; Kriegsverlust). Bei letzterem ist das Erscheinungsjahr 1640 bereits von Jellinek bezweifelt worden. Er zitiert nämlich aus Hagers Vorrede dessen Urteil: „Zwar inn Fortpflanzung der Zierligkeit, Reinigkeit etc. und anderen zubehören teutscher Sprache ist von den F r u c h t b r i n g e n d e n so viel g e s u c h e t und g e s p i e l e t worden [...]". Dies konnte sich schon für Jellinek sinnvoll nur auf Schottelius (FG 397. Der Suchende) u. Georg Philipp Harsdörffer (FG 368. Der Spielende) beziehen, die allerdings erst 1642 in die FG aufgenommen wurden. S. *Jellinek: Nhd. Grammatik* I, 110. Das Hager-Zitat dürfte kritisch gemeint gewesen sein, zumindest faßt es Pape (s. u.), 803 so auf: „Er [Hager] steht damit wohl den Tendenzen der altdeutschen Opposition und der protestantischen Stilreinigung im Barock nahe, wenn auch Zweckliteratur und späthumanistische Wissenschaftstradition sich oft von den neuen Stilidealen fernhielten." Tatsächlich könnte die bürgerlich-kaufmännische Motivation Hagers, die auf eine orthographische Elementarbildung zielte, zu einer Kritik an Harsdörffer oder Schottelius geführt haben. Ein Nachdruck der Hamburger Ausgabe von 1639 in: Heino Lambeck: Düedsche Orthographia (1633). Christoph Achatius Hager: Teütsche Orthographia (1639). Hgg. Rolf Bergmann u. Ursula Götz. Hildesheim [u. a.] 2007. Erwartungsgemäß fehlt hier in der Vorrede Jellineks Zitat. — Weite Verbreitung fand Hagers Formular- oder Musterbriefe-Buch: FORMULAR Teütscher Missiven/ Oder Sände-Schreiben/ Darinn enthalten I. Vonn der Teütschen Orthographien, Zubehör/ Natur/ und Eigenschafft. II. Vonn den Nohtwändigen Stücken und Teihlen einer Teütschen Missiv- oder Brieffs. III. Von mehrerley Briefen/ unter Bürgerlichen Stands-Persohnen üblich. IV. Vonn mehrerley Kauff- und Handels-Briefen. V. Vonn den Titulen/ der Geist- Welt- und Häußlichen Standes Persohnen. Anjetzo zum Fünfftenmahl übersähen/ vermehrt/ und wiederum in Druck gegäben (Hamburg 1644: Jacob Rebenlein). SUB Göttingen: 8 Ling. VII, 8909. Frühere Ausgaben o. O. 1630 (LB Wiesbaden), o. O. 1634 (nicht nachgewiesen), Hamburg 1637 (HAB: 579.3 Quod. [1]), Nürnberg 1640 (UB Leipzig), Hamburg 1642 (SUB Hamburg: Scrin. A/1935; auch Dig.), Hamburg 1649 u. 1654 (beide nicht nachgewiesen). Der vorangestellte (erste) Teil zur „Teütschen Orthographie", eine deutlich überarbeitete, inhaltlich aber weitgehend mit Hagers *Teütscher Orthographia* von 1639 übereinstimmende Fassung, findet sich nur in den Ausgaben von 1642 u. 1644. Weder in diesem Teil noch in der „Hamburg/ ex meo Musæo, ANNO CHRISTI 1642" datierten Vorrede an den Leser aus der Ausgabe von 1644 findet sich das von Jellinek gebrachte Zitat. Interessant ist hier aber, wie schon ähnlich in Hagers *Teütscher Orthographia* von 1639, das Bekenntnis zur meißnischen Sprachnorm: Er habe sich bemüht, so Hager in der Vorrede an den „Läser", sein Formular-Buch „nach rechtem Gebrauch der reinen teütsch Meischnischen [sic] Sprache" aufzusetzen (Bl. A ij r). Vgl. auch das Bekenntnis zur „Meißnisch-teütschen Sprache" im ersten oder Orthographie-Teil, S. 4. Zu erwähnen bleibt noch Hagers *Läse: Gebät: Vnd Schreib-büchlein für die Teütsche Jugend* (Hamburg 1640: Heinrich Werner). Vgl. *Moulin-Fankhänel: Bibliographie* II, 96–103; *Takada*, 16, 49, 55, 155 u. 205f.; Ursula Götz: Einleitung im oben genannten Ndr. der *Teütschen Orthographia* von 2007, S. XLVII–LXXXI; Dirk Josten: Sprachvorbild und Sprachnorm im Urteil des 16. und 17. Jahrhunderts. Sprachlandschaftliche Prioritäten. Sprachautoritäten, sprachimmanente Argumentation. Frankfurt a. M. 1976, 33, 186 u. 202; Walter Pape: Buchhaltung und Orthographie, christliche Erziehung und frühbürgerlicher Roman: Christoph Achatius Hagers Lehr- und Gebrauchsschriften. In: Literatur und Volk im 17. Jahrhundert. Probleme populärer

Kultur in Deutschland. Hg. Wolfgang Brückner u. a. Tl. 2. Wiesbaden 1985, 797–815, bes. 802 f. Im Zusammenhang von Hagers Verweis auf Schottelius u. Harsdörffer führt Papes Hinweis (s. dort Anm. 42 u. 43) auf Manfred Windfuhr: Die barocke Bildlichkeit und ihre Kritiker. Stuttgart 1966, 343, in die Irre.

9 Johann Rist (FG 467. 1647; PBO Daphnis aus Cimbrien; ESO Palatin), Dichter u. Pfarrer in Wedel (Holstein).

10 Hierbei dachte Schottelius wohl auch an die wechselhafte Orthographie Philipp v. Zesens (FG 521. 1648; DG 1 Der Färtige).

11 Lt. Kolophon Johann Bismarck. Schottelius selbst hatte ihn offenbar nicht so erfolgreich eingewiesen. S. 441011 K 4.

12 Die beiden Listen fehlen im Bestand.

13 *Schottelius: Teutsche Vers- oder ReimKunst (1645)*, HAB: 172.1 Poet. Das schön gebundene Exemplar mit Goldschnitt könnte das Widmungsex. Hzn. Sophia Elisabeths v. Braunschweig-Wolfenbüttel (AL 1629. TG 42b) gewesen sein, der Schottelius sein Werk zugeschrieben hatte. Das Ex. zeigt aber keine Besitzspuren der Herzogin. Neben der Holzschnitt-Initiale mit einem Porträt Sophia Elisabeths zu Schottelius' Zueignungsgedicht auf seine Gönnerin (Bl. [Aij]r) weist das Buch 6 Kupferstiche auf: 1.) das Titelkupfer („D. Dirick: H. Fecit"), d. i. Dirk Diricks (auch Dierksen, Dietrichsen), Kupferstecher, in Hamburg 1613 geboren u. dort 1653 gestorben. S. *Thieme/ Becker* IX, 326; *De Gruyter Allgemeines Künstlerlexikon* XXVII, 542; 2.) Bl. [Aiij]r: Porträtstich Sophia Elisabeths von Conrad Buno, zu diesem s. *DA Köthen I.* 6, S. 115 u. 421200 K 1 S. 546 f. Dieser Stich fehlt in der Ausg. von 1656 (Ndr. 1976); 3.) Bl. [Aiv]r: ein emblematischer Stich zu Carl Gustav v. Hilles (FG 302) Widmungsgedicht, „C.G.V.H. Inv.", die zeichnerische Vorlage stammte also von Hille selbst, eine Stecheradresse fehlt; 4.) Bl. [Av]v: ein emblematischer Stich zu Harsdörffers Widmungsgedicht, Stecheradresse fehlt; 5.) Bl. Biij r: Schottelius als Perlenfischer, zu einem Gedicht Johann Rists, gez. „C. Buno"; 6.) Bl. [Bvi]r: Dreiständiges Sinnbild zum Widmungsgedicht von Samuel Hund, Stecheradresse fehlt. Vgl. 441020 K 1.

14 Ein uns heute fehlender Brief Bismarcks, der die fehlenden Typen für die Bezeichnung der Silbenquantitäten über dem dt. Gedichttext erwähnte bzw. nachzeichnete.

K I 1 Biblia sacra iuxta Vulgatam Versionem, rec. Robertus Weber OSB. Editio tertia emendata. Stuttgart 1983: Jerem. 17, 8: „et erit quasi lignum quod transplantatur super aquas quod ad humorem mittit radices suas".

2 Jerem. 17, 8: „et non timebit cum venerit aestus".

3 Jerem. 17, 8: „et erit folium eius viride et in tempore siccitatis non erit sollicitum".

4 Namentliche Anspielungen auf den Ölzweig bzw. die Palme des Lüneburgers (Selenus) Hz. August d. J. von Braunschweig (und Lüneburg) zu Wolfenbüttel, vielleicht zugleich Anspielungen auf dessen Mitgliedschaft in der FG. Der offenbar nicht überlieferte Gesellschaftspfennig des Herzogs (FG 227) müßte allerdings eine spezifische Kokospalme u. einen Edelgamander gezeigt haben, also nicht die hier nach der biblischen Vorlage allgemein bezeichneten Pflanzen der Bibel. Vgl. *Conermann III*, 244.

5 Ps. 1, 1.3: „Beatus vir qui [...] erit tanquam lignum [...] quod fructum suum dabit in tempore suo".

6 Jerem. 1, 8: „ne timeas a facie eorum quia tecum ego sum ut eruam te dicit Dominus".

7 Die Vulgata oder eine andere konsultierte protestantische lat. Bibel bieten diese Formulierung nicht. Wir fanden sie auch nicht bei Castellio und Tremellius/ Junius. Die Ausgabe Lucas Osianders d. Ä. behält an dieser Stelle die Vulgata-Übersetzung u. kommentiert sie nicht: BIBLIA SACRA VETERIS ET NOVI TESTAMENTI, SECVNDVM VVLGATAM VERSIONEM, AD EBRAEAM VERITATEM IN VEteri; ad Graecam verò in Novo Testamento, à D. LVCA OSIANDRO perpurgata: & ad D. D. LVTHERI versionem Germanicam collata; praefationibus denique eiusdem, in latinum sermonem transfusis, nec non argumentis ornata, & versibus singillatim distincta. IENAE excudebat Tobias Steinman, Sumtibus Henningi Grosij Bibliopolae Lipsensis. Anno M.D.IC. SB München, dig. Eine andere Ausgabe mit gekürzter Wiedergabe des Kommentars Osianders behält auch „anima" aus der Vulgata: „Cum effuderis esurienti animam tuam, & animam afflictam repleneris: [...]." Biblia Sacra. QVÆ PRÆTER ANTIQVÆ LATINÆ VERSIONIS NECESSARIAM EMENdationem, & difficiliorum locorum succinctam explicationem (ex Commentarijs Biblicis ... D. LUCÆ OSIANDRI ... depromptam) ... Studio & operâ ANDREÆ OSIANDRI ... TVBINGÆ Typis & expensis Georgij Gruppenbachij. ANNO MDC. HAB: A 79 Helmst 2°. Die Osiander-Übersetzung David Förters, die 1650 in die Lüneburger Bibel der Sterne übernommen wird, ersetzt jedoch Seele durch Herz. Biblia Das ist: Die gantze heilige Schrifft/ Mit einer kurtzen/ aber doch Gründtlichen Erklerung des Texts ... Also das der Text auß des Hocherleuchten Mannes/ Doctor Martini Luthers Dolmetschung unverendert/ mit etwas gröbrer Schrifft besonders getruckt: Die Erklerung aber desselben mit kleinern Buchstaben darneben gesetzt: Erstlich in Latein/ durch ... Lucam Osiandrum ... An jetzo aber ... in die Teutsche Sprach/ auff das trewlichst gebracht/ vnd an tag geben. Durch M. Dauid Förter ... Sampt den Summarien ... Getruckt zu Stutgarten/ durch Marx Fürstern/ Jm Jahr Christi/ M. DC. [– M. DC. X.]. 9 Tle. HAB: 202.3–9 Theol. 2°. Tl. 6: „Vnd wirst den Hungerigen lassen finden dein Hertz/[d] vnnd die elende Seele sättigen/ [...]." Die Anmerkung [d] zu „Dein Hertz/ Wenn du die Hungerigen vnnd elende Leut aus hertzlichem Mitleiden erquickest/ Daß wo es möglich were/ du jhnen möchtest das Hertz im Leibe mittheilen." Die Verdeutschung Herz steht auch in der von Hz. August benutzten Cramerbibel: BIBLIA. Das ist: Die gantze heilige Schrifft Deutsch/ D. Mart. Luth. Mit außgehenden Versiculn/ Marginalien vnd Vorreden Lutheri/ Concordantzien/ Chronologien/ vnd vnterschiedlichen Registern der Historien vnd Hauptleren/ sampt den Summarien D. Danielis Crameri/ auch den vbrigen Büchern Esra vnd Maccabeorum/ Auff solche Art noch nie gesehen. ... Lüneburg bey den Sternen/ Jm tausend hundert sechs/ vier vnd dreysigstem Jahr/ ... [1634, erschienen 1635]. HAB: 519.4.1 Theol. 2°. „Vnd wirst den Hungerigen lassen finden dein Hertz/ vnd die elende Seele sättigen/ [...]." Schottelius könnte also die Bibel Förters oder Cramers an dieser Stelle (ungenau) ins Lateinische zurückübersetzt haben, wobei es ihm auf das Herz (im Unterschied zu Seele) angekommen sein dürfte. Das entspricht an dieser Stelle in etwa der Unterscheidung der recht wörtlich übersetzten hebräischen Bibel: Und du spendest dem Hungrigen dein eigenes Begehren und sättigst eine niedergebeugte Seele.

450124

Fürst Ludwig an Georg Philipp Harsdörffer

Antwort auf 440426 u. 440824. Beantwortet durch 450400. — F. Ludwig bestätigt dankend den Empfang zweier Schreiben Georg Philipp Harsdörffers (FG 368. Der Spielende): eines vom 24. August 1644, das am 9. September empfangen wurde, ein anderer österlicher Brief vom 26. April 1644, dem zwei Exemplare des vierten Teils von *Harsdörffer: Frauenzimmer-Gesprächspiele* (1644) nebst zwei Sendungen an Diederich v. dem Werder (FG 31. Der Vielgekörnte) u. F. Christian II. v. Anhalt-Bernburg (FG 51. Der Unveränderliche) beigelegen hatten. Dieses Paket u. seine Anlagen waren erst am 19. Januar 1645 eingegangen. Harsdörffers Frage (in 440824) nach Büchern der FG wird positiv beschieden: Es sei dafür gesorgt worden, daß diese Werke bei der anstehenden Leipziger Buchmesse im Frankfurter Buchladen beim (Leipziger) Buchhändler Andreas Kühne zu erhalten seien. — Als Anlage übersendet F. Ludwig als Fortsetzung des *GB 1641* (FG Nr. 1–353) zusätzliche gedruckte Impresen (*GB 1641/44*; Mitglieder 354–417). — F. Ludwig bedankt sich für die (mit 440426) übersandten Entwürfe zweier Freudenspiele Harsdörffers über die Logik u. die Rhetorik. Er kündigt an, andere in den freien Künsten u. Wissenschaften kompetente FG-Mitglieder um ihr Urteil zu bitten u. es Harsdörffer mitzuteilen. Zugleich sendet er ihm die ratichianischen Köthener Lehrwerke *Compendium Logicae* (1621) u. dessen dt. Übersetzung *Kurtzer Begriff Der Verstandt-Lehr* (1621) als Anlage zu, damit sich Harsdörffer der darin verwendeten deutschen Fachtermini bedienen könne. — F. Ludwig kritisiert die Einmischung daktylischer Verse in der jambischen Versart, wie sie vielfältig im vierten Teil der *Gesprächspiele* begegne. Die Formen „der Nehrender, Spielender und dergleichen" verstießen auch gegen die dt. Grammatik u. den richtigen Sprachusus. Der Fürst formuliert eine Regel für deren Deklination sowie die schwache u. starke Flexion attribuierender Adjektive im Nominalgefüge. Einen weiteren Verstoß gegen die dt. Grammatik moniert F. Ludwig in der Pluralmarkierung männlicher Substantive auf -er durch das Pluralsuffix -e (der Meister, die Meistere). Diese Pluralbildung komme im Sprachgebrauch nirgendwo vor. Schottelius u. die ihm nachfolgen irrten sich u. sollten diese falsche Korrektur aufgeben. — Die Kriegsläufte, die Anhalt jüngst zum direkten Kriegsschauplatz gemacht hätten, verhinderten bislang die Drucklegung der deutschen Rechtschreibung (von Christian Gueintz). Damit würde aber noch im Verlaufe des Jahres zu rechnen sein. — F. Ludwig dankt Harsdörffer für seinen Fleiß u. bittet ihn, mit seinen erfreulichen literarischen Arbeiten fortzufahren.

Q HM Köthen: V S 545, Bl. 305rv; Abschrift von Schreiberh. mit eigenh. Korrekturen u. Ergänzungen. Originalkonzept F. Ludwigs a. a. O., Bl. 415rv, zit. als *K*. Bl. 306r: P. S. von Diederich v. dem Werder, s. Beilage I. — *D: KE*, 333–335; *KL* III, 258–260. — *BN: Bürger*, 950 Nr. 54.

A *Fehlt.*

Es seind von dem Spielenden abgewichener Zeit an die Fruchtbringende[a] geselschaft zwey schreiben kommen[b]: Das erste vom 24. Augustmonants[c] [sic] abgefloßenes Jhares und eingereicht den neunden Herbstmonats alleine, das zweyte aber vom[d] 26. Ostermonats den man für den April des 1644 Jhares helt, ob schon die Ostern zuweilen auch in den Mertzen zu fallen pflegen, ist neben zwey stükken des vierten[e] theils seiner gesprechspiele, und zweyen verschloßenen schreiben und beylagen an den Vielgekörnten und Unverenderlichen[f], welche nach der ordnung ihrer eintretung hier gesetzet werden, den 19. des Jenners in diesem angefangenen Jhare wol eingehendiget worden, Für[g] beyderley bezeigung wird dem Spielenden hochfleißiger danck gesaget;[1] Und ist wegen erlangung etzlicher aus der geselschaft ausgegangenen und alhier gedruckten bücher verordnung geschehen, das man solche in nechstfolgenden Leiptziger Jharmarck, der auf Lichtmeße angesetzet,[h] bey dem Buchführer Andreas Kühnen[i], im Franckfurter buchladen[j] wird erlangen können.[2]

[k]Beygefügt wird überschicket was von neuen Geselschaftern an die vorige in

ordnung mit den achtzeiligen reimgesetzen nachgedruckt, so zu den erstgedruckten mag angeheftet werden.³

ᵏDer eingeschickte entwurf zweyer Freudenspiele^l über die Logica oder VerstandLehre^m, wie man sie dieses orts für jahren genennet, und über^n die Rhetorica die° Rednerlehre,⁴ sol andern der freyen künste und wißenschaften verstendigen^p geselschaftern mitgetheilet, und ihr bedencken eingeholet^q auch solches ferner dem^r Spielenden kundgethan werden:⁵ Jn deßen kömmet^s ihme angeleget zu, was für Jahren an diesem orte für eine Logica oder VerstandLehre in Deutsch und Lateinisch gedruckt worden, [305v] ob er sich etwa der^t Deutschen Kunstwörter die^u darinnen enthalten^v, gebrauchen könte.

ᵏDarnebe[n]^w wird guter wolmeinung abermal der geselschaft wegen, und sonderlich bey den Deutschen Reimen erinnert, weil vielfältig in dem Vierten^e überschickten theile zufinden, da[s]^w die Dactyli in der Cæsur, oder abschnitte, als der Nehrender, Spielender und dergleichen gar übel stehen, und so wol wieder die deutsche Sprachlehre und rechte art zu reden, da es sol heißen der Nehrende, de[r]^w Spielende, als wieder die Jambische Reimart lauffet^x⁶ darbey^y mögen folgende beyde regeln in acht genomen werden[.] Erstlich wird gesagt ein Nehrender, ein Spielender, bey dem Artickel aber gemercke^z oder geschlechtsworte (der)^aa mus das r^ab hinden ausbleiben, furs^ac andere Wo das r in der Nennendung der eintzelen Zahl Nominativo^ad singulari wan man° das geschlechtswort oder° gemerck, Articulum (der) fur das wort setzet, so mus notwendig das r in der nennendung der mehreren Zahl Nominativo plurali, auch bleiben Als, der denker, die denker, der Mörder, die Mörder, der leinweber, die leinweber, der freßer, die freßer, der Säuffer, die Sauffer *etc.* und wird man kein beyspiel dargegen finden. Ja man sol auch nicht das e^ae zu dem r in mehrerer Zahl setzen, das man sagen wolte, die denkere, Mördere, und so fort, welches sich nicht schicket. Weiter saget oder schreibet man nicht, der^af Durchleuchtiger, der^af hochgeborner, in der eintzigen^ag Zahl numero singulare^ah, sondern der^ai Durchleuchtige, der^ai hochgeborne, derowegen dieses die regel das alle Se[l]bstendige nenwörter mänliches geschlechtes, substantive masculin[i]^w generis, so in dergleichen endung fallen das r im ende behalten s[o]^w wol in der Nennendung der mehreren, als der einzelen Zahl. Hingegen enden sich die beystendige Nenwörter adjectiva, alle auf ein e so wol in der Nenendung^aj der eintzeln als mehrern Zahl, wan sie dieser art sein[d]^w und das geschlechtwort oder der Artickel (der)^aa darvor gesetzt wird.^ac worinnen Schottelius und die ihm nachfolgen, auch andere^ak, irren u[nd]^w sich verhoffentlich beßern werden^al[.]⁷ Bela[n]gende^w die Rechtschreibung ist solche zwar vorlengsten wieder Jhrem Verfaßer zug[e]schicket^w, hat aber wegen kundbarer gefeh[r]ligkeit^w des in diesem lande in neuligkeit sich gesetzten Stules des Krieges⁸ noch nicht können gedrucket werden, welches aber vermutlich noch in diesem Jhare erfolgen s[ol]^w[.]⁹ Jm übrigen wird des Spielenden hoch angewanter fleis in seinen schriften auch hochgehalten und gerühmet, und dersel[be]^w zu fernerer fortsetzung solcher seiner ergetzlichen^am arbeit nochmals gebürlich anve[r]manet^w. Welches dem^an Spielenden zu gehöriger geselschaftmeßiger antwort nechst wüntschung aller gedeylichen wolfahrt vermelde[t]^w werden sollen.

Geben an dem^an bewusten orte des ertzschreines den Vierundzwantzigsten^ao des Jenners im Jhare 1645[.]

I

Diederichs von dem Werder Kommentar zum vorliegenden Brief

Diederich v. dem Werder (FG 31) gibt (vermutlich auf Bitten F. Ludwigs) eine Stellungnahme zu dessen Antwortschreiben (450124) an Georg Philipp Harsdörffer (FG 368. Der Spielende) ab. Er stimmt F. Ludwigs Ablehnung der starken (Poly-)Flexion der (substantivierten) Adjektive nach bestimmtem Artikel zu und formuliert dazu eine Regel. Er stellt es ins Belieben der FG, ob sie diese in ihre Antwort an Harsdörffer aufnehmen wolle. Auf jeden Fall möge das Urteil Martin Milagius' (FG 315. Der Mindernde) dazu eingeholt werden. Werder entschuldigt sich, daß er die grammatische Fachterminologie entgegen dem Anspruch der FG nicht durchweg deutsch gegeben habe.

Q HM Köthen: V S 545, Bl. 306rv, 306v leer; eigenh.; abweichendes Papierformat. — *D: KE*, 335 Anm.

P. S.

Die andwort an den Spielenden habe ich belesen, finde dieselbe also beschaffen, das sie nicht zuverbessern. Jch habe heute an einem orte, da ich bessere gedancken hette haben sollen[1], nachgedacht warumb vnd^a aus was vrsachen man nicht sagt oder schreibt der durchleuchtiger, sondern der durchleuchtige. Jch gebe diese vrsache.

Wo das r. in **nominatiuo singulari** am ende gebraucht wird, wan man den **articul** (der) erst für das wort setzet, So mus nottwendig das r. in **nominatiuo plurali** auch bleiben. Als zum exempel. der decker die decker, der mörder die mörder, der leinweber die leinweber, der fresser die fresser[,] der Ehbrecher die Ehbrecher etc. vnd wird man kein exempel dargegen finden. Nun sagt oder schreibt man aber nicht die durchläuchtiger die hochgeborner in **plurali numero**, Sondern die durchläuchtige die hochgeborne. Derowegen setze ich (**saluo saniorum judicio**) dieses zur regel. Das alle **substantiua masculini generis** so in dergleichen **termination** fallen, das r. **in fine** behalten, so wohl in **nominatiuo plurali** als **singulari**: hergegen die **adiectiua** enden sich alle auf ein e, [so]wohl^b in [sin]gulari^c als [pl]urali^c nomi[n]atiuo^c[,] Wan sie dieser art sein, vnd der **articul** (der) darvor gesetzet wird.

Es Stehet dahin ob die Fruchtbringende geselschaft gut befindet, das diese **ratio** mit eingeflickt werde.[2]

Des Mindernden **judicium** ist hierüber zuvernemen.[3] Man verzeihe mir das ich in diesem P. S. auf der Fruchtbringenden art rein deutsch zuschreiben wegen eilfertikeit vnd ümb mehrer deutlikeit willen, geschrieben bin.

450124 Fürst Ludwig   421

[D]er^c Spielende setzt folio 225 der Starckziehend Magnet: Er hatt wohl gesehn [d]as^c der Starckziehender Magnet nicht klappen würde^d, vnd der starckziehende hatt er nicht set[z]en^e wollen, elidirt derowegen das e. sed pessimé.⁴

T *Die Verbesserungen und Ergänzungen stammen grundsätzlich von F. Ludwig. Sind sie vom Schreiber eingetragen worden, wird dies im Folgenden explizit angemerkt. Die Verbesserungen innerhalb des Konzeptes K werden nicht angemerkt, wenn sie mit der Abschrift übereinstimmen.* — a *Gebessert aus* fruchtbringende — b *Gebessert aus* <ein>kommen — c *K* Augstmonats — d *Gebessert aus* von — e *Gebessert aus* vier<d>ten *K* vierten — f *Gebessert aus* unvrenderlichen *K* Unverenderlichen — g *Gebessert aus* für *K* Für — h *Folgt* <und> *K und bey dem mit nachfolgender Leerstelle bis* wird erlangen können — i *Bis* Franckfurter *von Schreiberh. ergänzt.* — j *Gebessert aus* laden — k *Davor eine Absatzmarkierung von Schreiberh. durch ein Paragraphzeichen:* § — l *Gebessert aus* zweyen freudenspiele *K* zweyer — m *Gebessert aus* verstandLehre *K* verstandlehre — n *über die eingefügt.* — o *Eingefügt.* — p *Gebessert aus* verstendigern *K* verstendigen — q *Unleserliche Besserung am Wortende.* — r *Gebessert aus* den *K* dem — s *K* kommet — t *Gebessert aus* die *K* dieser — u *Eingefügt. Fehlt in K.* — v *Gebessert aus* enthaben *K* enthaben *undeutlich zu lesen, vermutlich* enthalten *gemeint.* — w *Textverlust im Falz. Konjektur in eckigen Klammern.* — x *Folgt* <(Es> *K ergänzt hier am Rand nur:* Es wird gesagt ein Nehrender, ein Spielender, bey dem articket aber oder gemercke der mus das r hinden aus bleiben, worinnen Schottelius und die ihme nachfolgen irren, und sich verhoffentlich beßern werden. — y *Bis* Erstlich *am Rand ergänzt.* darbey mögen *gebessert aus* und mögen darbey — z *Reihenfolge der Wörter geändert aus* oder gemercke *durch darübergestellte Ziffern 1 u. 2,* geschlechtsworte *mit Ziffer 3 am Rand ergänzt.* — aa *Nachträglich zur Markierung des bestimmten Artikels „der" eingeklammert.* — ab *Ergänze: beim folgenden Nominalpartizip ([der] Spielende)/ Substantiv.* — ac *Am Rand als lange Passage ergänzt bis* darvor gesetzet wird. — ad *Folgt* <plurali> — ae *Folgt* <dem> — af *Gebessert aus* die — ag *Eingefügt für* <mehreren> — ah *Eingefügt für* <plurale> — ai *Gebessert aus* des — aj *der Nenendung eingefügt.* — ak auch andere *eingefügt für* <wan sie es hinzusetzen> andere *unsichere Lesung.* — al *Folgt das gestrichene Zeichen für die schließende Klammer* <:|> — am *Gebessert aus* ergätzlichen — an *Gebessert aus* den — ao *Folgt in K eingefügt* tag

T I a *Eingefügt bis* vrsachen — b *Eingefügt bis* nomi[n]atiuo *Textverlust im Falz, Konjektur in eckigen Klammern.* — c *Textverlust im Falz, Konjektur in eckigen Klammern.* — d *Gebessert aus* würde<n> — e *Vermutlich Verschreibung.*

K Zur langen Zustellungsdauer von Georg Philipp Harsdörffers (FG 368. Der Spielende) Brief 440426 s. dort K 0. Zur Datierung auf April s. dort K 8.

1 Von Harsdörffers Schreiben an Diederich v. dem Werder (FG 31. Der Vielgekörnte) u. F. Christian II. v. Anhalt-Bernburg (FG 51. Der Unveränderliche) sind keine Abschriften im Köthener Erzschrein der FG erhalten. Über das Tagebuch F. Christians läßt sich nicht ermitteln, welchen Inhalt der Brief von Harsdörffer an ihn hatte, weil der Tagebuchband von 1644 verloren ist. Bei den Beilagen, die Werder u. F. Christian erhalten haben, dürfte es sich um je ein Exemplar des 4. Teils der *Frauenzimmer-Gesprächspiele* (1644) gehandelt haben. Aus Brief 440824 geht hervor, daß Harsdörffer insgesamt vier Exemplare versandte; zwei waren offenbar für F. Ludwig u. den Erzschrein vorgesehen. S. 440824 K 3.

2 Harsdörffer hatte F. Ludwig in 440824 für ein mit 430724 zugesandtes Exemplar von dessen übersetztem Erbauungsbuch *Der weise Alte (1643)* gedankt u. um zwei weitere Exemplare gebeten, nach denen sich Interessenten in Augsburg u. Regensburg erkundigt hatten. Dabei hatte Harsdörffer ein allgemeines Interesse an Büchern der FG vermeldet. — Andreas Kühne (1599–1648) war Bürger u. Buchhändler zu Leipzig. Er wurde zu verschiedenen fruchtbringerischen Buchprojekten herangezogen. S. 410313. Kühne stammte aus Deesdorf b. Halberstadt. Nach seiner Schulausbildung in Egeln u. Halberstadt kam er 1617 nach Leipzig, wo er in die Dienste des Bürgers u. Buchhändlers Henning Große d. Ä. (1553–1621) trat. Nach der Teilung der Buchhandlung diente er bei dessen Sohn Gottfried Große (1591–1637), dem Buchhändler, Verleger u. Ratsherrn. Ab 1630/31 war er in Leipzig der Vertreter des Frankfurter Verlegers Clemens Schleich († 1638) bzw. von dessen Partner u. Nachfolger Johann Press. Nachdem dieser die aufgrund des Kriegsgeschehens ins Stocken geratene Buchhandlung in Leipzig aufgegeben hatte, machte sich Kühne selbständig. Zu Kühne s. *LP Stolberg*, Nr. 2312 u. 13935; 430121A, 430527 u. im vorliegenden Band 440130 K 3, 440824 K 8, 450507A K 3 u. 450930. — Im 17. Jahrhundert gab es in Leipzig drei Meßtermine (Neujahrsmarkt, Ostermarkt, Michaelismarkt), die auch während des Dreißigjährigen Krieges recht regelmäßig abgehalten wurden (s. detailliert dazu 461031 K 6). Lichtmeß, der 2. Februar, ist kein regulärer Meßtermin. Für das Jahr 1644 liegt nur ein Meßkatalog der Leipziger Büchermesse vor, der laut Titelblatt sowohl für den Oster- als auch für den Michaelismarkt galt. S. Catalogus universalis, hoc est designatio omnium librorum, qui hisce nundinis ... Francofurtensibus & Lipsiensibus anno ... vel novi vel emendatiores & auctiores prodierunt (Leipzig 1644); Catalogus universalis, hoc est designatio omnium librorum, qui hisce nundinis ... Francofurtensibus & Lipsiensibus anno ... vel novi vel emendatiores & auctiores prodierunt (Leipzig 1645). Für den Neujahrsmarkt wurden nie Kataloge mit den erhältlichen Büchern gedruckt. — Aufgrund des Kriegsverlaufs u. der um den Jahreswechsel 1644/45 in Kursachsen in den Winterquartieren liegenden schwed. Hauptarmee wurde auf Befehl der schwed. Generalität durch Patent des schwed. Oberkommandanten in Leipzig, Oberst Otto Schulmann (1601–1653), der Neujahrsmarkt 1645 auf Mariae Lichtmeß (2. Februar) verschoben. HSTA Dresden: Geh. Rat, loc. 9260/1, Bl. 111 (gedruckter Erlaß Schulmanns, d.d. Leipzig 13.12.1644). Vgl. Johann Jacob Vogel: Leipzigisches Geschicht-Buch Oder Annales, Das ist: Jahr- und Tage-Bücher Der Weltberühmten Königl. und Churfürstlichen Sächsischen Kauff- und Handels-Stadt Leipzig (Leipzig 1714), 607. Zu den Leipziger Messen der Zeit s. allgemein Manfred Straube: Die Leipziger Messen im Dreißigjährigen Krieg. In: Uwe John, Josef Matzerath (Hgg.): Landesgeschichte als Herausforderung und Programm. FS f. Karlheinz Blaschke. Stuttgart 1997, 421–441; Ernst Hasse: Geschichte der Leipziger Messen. Leipzig 1963 [Ndr. der Ausg. Leipzig 1885].

3 F. Ludwig übersendet Harsdörffer drei ergänzende Druckbögen, mit denen das *GB 1641* zum *GB 1641/44* anwuchs: Mitglieder FG 354–417. S. dazu 441226A K 5 u. 450529 K 10.

4 F. Ludwig denkt im folgenden an ein Lehrbuch zur Logik von Jacob Martini (1570–1649), Prof. f. Logik u. Metaphysik in Wittenberg, das in der ratichianischen Schulreform in Köthen u. Weimar in den Jahren 1618–1622/24 u. darüber hinaus eingesetzt worden war: COMPENDIUM | LOGICÆ | AD | DIDACTICAM | [Vignette] | COTHENIS | ANHALTINORUM. | [Linie] | M. DC. XXI.; HAB: 293.1 Quod. (1). Noch im selben Jahr war diese Logik als „Verstandt-Lehr" von Ludwig Lucius (1577–1642), Theologe u. Prof. der aristotelischen Logik in Basel, vollständig übersetzt u. in Köthen gedruckt worden: Kurtzer Begriff | Der | Verstandt-Lehr/ | Zu der Lehrart. | [Vignette] | Cöthen/ | Jm Fürstenthumb Anhaldt/ | Jm Jahr/ | [Linie] | M. DC. XXI. HAB: 293.1 Quod. (2). S. zu

Martini 190424 K 1; zu Lucius 190220 K 12. Harsdörffer wird das Angebot, sich der übersetzten Fachtermini der Köthener Übersetzung zu bedienen, nicht annehmen. Der Titel von Harsdörffers „Freudenspiel" lautet im fertigen Druck ebenso wie in dem ursprünglichen Personaltableau „Vernunftkunst" (s. Anm. 5) u. nicht ‚Verstandlehre'. In *Harsdörffer: Frauenzimmer-Gesprächspiele* V (1645, Ndr. 1969), 202 findet sich die Übersetzung: „Logica oder Vernunftlehre" für die akademische Disziplin. Über die englische Quelle der „Vernunftkunst" Harsdörffers u. seine lat. Übersetzung s. 440426 K I 0 u. 450817 K II 6. Zum Druck von Harsdörffers *Sophista* s. *DA Köthen I. 8*: 470426.

5 Harsdörffer hatte seinem Brief 440426 mit Bitte um gesellschaftliche Kritik die Personenverzeichnisse von zwei Freudenspielen beigelegt, die er im 5. Teil der *Frauenzimmer-Gesprächspiele* (1645) zu veröffentlichen beabsichtige: „Logica oder *Die Vernunftkunst*" u. „Rhetorica *Die wolredkunst*". Dieses Vorhaben wurde ausgeführt, erfuhr aber im dramatischen Personal Abänderungen. Ausführlich zu den beiden Freudenspielen 440426 K I 0 u. K I 3 (zur *Rhetorica*). In 450529 teilt F. Ludwig einige wenige Bedenken zu den Figurentableaus seitens „etlicher Geselschafter" mit, weiß aber (aus Harsdörffers Brief 450400), daß sie wegen der bereits stattfindenden Drucklegung des 5. Teils der *Gesprächspiele* zu spät kommen werden, um noch berücksichtigt zu werden.

6 Die Widmungsgedichte des 4. Teils der *Frauenzimmer-Gesprächspiele* folgen oft nicht dem von F. Ludwig bevorzugten, strikt alternierenden Versschema. Seine Forderung, im Umfeld der (Mittel-)Zäsur des Verses als natürliche Daktylen empfundene Wörter wie Nährender oder Spielender nicht zu verwenden, wird sehr wahrscheinlich auf das Widmungsgedicht Harsdörffers für Hz. August d.J. v. Braunschweig-Wolfenbüttel (FG 227. Der Befreiende) zurückgehen. *Harsdörffer: Frauenzimmer-Gesprächspiele* IV (1644, Ndr. 1968), Ndr. S. 9. In dem Sonett finden sich die Verse: „Hier der BEFREYENDE die bunte Bonenfrucht", und: „Wird dieser Gnadenschein dem Spielenden gedeyen". Harsdörffer mag die beiden Verse als regulär alternierende Jamben betrachtet haben, indem er die Betonung an sich unbetonter Endsilben wie im Falle von „BEFREYENDE" u. „Spielenden" nach Maßgabe des Versmaßes als variabel begriff u. mit leichter Tonhebung versah. F. Ludwig hingegen sah hier drei Senkungen in Folge, wodurch sich die Versmitte nicht mehr erkennen ließe. Die von Harsdörffer genutzte prosodische Variabilität hatte Augustus Buchner (FG 362) in seiner 1665 postum veröffentlichten Poetik gefordert, denn mit dem Ausschluß der natürlich-daktylischen dreisilbigen Wörter würde man viel zu viele gute u. schwerlich ersetzbare deutsche Wörter für die Verskunst verlieren: „Wenn wir den Opitius ansehen/ und denen Exempeln/ die er uns hinterlassen/ werden wir befinden/ daß dergleichen Dactylische Wörter in allerhand Arten der Reime/ nicht allein vor oder mit dem Abschnitte/ in den Alexandrinischen und gemeinen [Vers communs]/ sondern auch nach demselben und in der Endung des Verses stat haben." Buchner sah keinen Grund, die dreisilbigen natürlichen Daktylen nicht auch im jambischen Vers zu verwenden, da dies auch nicht „übel und wiederwärtig klingt. Denn ja noch allezeit die letzte Sylbe etwas schärfer und höher/ als die vorhergehende […] fället" u. der jambische Versfuß so gewahrt bleibt. Dasselbe gilt für einsilbige Wörter, die je nach Stellung im Vers „lang und kurtz gesetzet werden" können. Augustus Buchner: Anleitung zur deutschen Poeterey. Poet. Hg. Marian Szyrocki. Tübingen 1966, 115, 141 u. 144. Harsdörffer schloß sich dieser Meinung an: Bei konsequenter Beachtung des Wortakzents u. bei Verzicht auf leichte Versetzungen des Worttones, etwa durch Akzentuierung an sich unbetonter Neben- oder Ableitungssilben bzw. durch variable Betonung von Einsilbern, wären ganze Wortgruppen aus dem Vers zu verbannen. Vgl. seine „Kurtze Entschuldigung, Die begangene Fehler in den Hundert Spielreimen betreffend" (HM Köthen: V S 545, Bl. 290rv u. 289rv; demnächst in *DA Köthen I. 9*). Nur durch Berücksichtigung der Akzente im Verssatz waren solche

Unbequemlichkeiten zu vermeiden. *Schottelius: Der Teutschen Sprache Einleitung (1643)*, 66: „Weñ die Abgeleiteten mehr als zweisilbig sein/ können unterweilen die Haubtendungen lang gesetzet werden/ als: Běgŏnstǐgūng [...] Běfŏrděrnīß [...] Trāwrǐgkēit. Būhlīsch [...] Wūndĕrbār. etc." Ebd., 67: Alle zufälligen Endungen/ Letteren seien „kurtz", es sei denn, ein kurze Silbe ginge voran, dann liege auf der unbetonten Silbe ein „Mittelthon": „běschūldǐgēst", „Chrīstlǐchēr" usw. In besonders negativer Weise dürfte F. Ludwig die komplizierte Metrik im Sonett „Nun der Kunstverstand alle Nutzbarkeit findet" (*Harsdörffer: Frauenzimmer-Gesprächspiele* IV [1644, Ndr. 1968], 227/ Ndr. 271) aufgestoßen sein, zumal es sich auf die FG bezieht. Die Terzette lauten:
   Sol dann unsere Sprache niemand ergründen?
      Von Anhaltischer Tugend löblichem Stammen/
   Die Fruchtbringenden ihre Wurtzelkraft finden!
   unsre herrliche Teutsche Zunge beschutzen/
      und mit Fürstlichen Gnaden halten zusammen/
   bringt vielfältige Frücht' uns allen zu Nutzen.
Das Sonett stellt die Auslegung (Subscriptio) eines Emblems dar, dessen Pictura auf der gegenüberliegenden Seite abgebildet ist: Sie zeigt in einem von zwei Greifen gekrönten Zierrahmen eine am oberen Rand des Bildes befestigte, bis auf den Boden reichende, eiserne Gliederkette mit einem „Magnetstein" in der Mitte. Darum ein Spruchband mit dem Wort (Inscriptio) „Allen zu Nutzen". Der erste Vers des Sonetts ist mit einem Betonungsschema versehen:

‒ ‒ ‒ ‒ ‿ ‿ ‒ ‿ ‒ ‿ ‿ ‒

Der Mischvers (Spondäus, Daktylus, Trochäus, Daktylus, Trochäus) erinnert an Harsdörffers Phaleuci/ Hendecasyllabi (s. 431124), nur daß wir es hier mit 12 Silben pro Verszeile zu tun haben, wobei der vorletzte Trochäus des Phaleucus durch einen (zweiten) Daktylus ersetzt ist. Die abwechselnd aufeinanderfolgenden Versfüße lassen eine Mittelzäsur allenfalls nach der 5. Silbe erkennen. — F. Ludwig hatte Harsdörffer im Juli/ August 1643 zwei ausführliche Gutachten vornehmlich zur Schreibung im 3. Teil der *Gesprächspiele* u. in deren Anhang der *Hundert Spielreime* (demnächst in *DA Köthen I. 9*) zugesandt. Dort kritisierte er den ersten der insgesamt 100 Spielreime, die i. d. R. aus je zwei Alexandrinern bestehen. Er lautet (*Harsdörffer: Frauenzimmer-Gesprächspiele* III [1643, Ndr. 1968], 437/ Ndr. 457):
   Wie sich für Josefs Garb' die andern musten neigen/
   So soll dem NEHRENDEN ein jeder Ehr' erzeigen.
F. Ludwig monierte in seinem Gutachten (zu den *Hundert Spielreimen*): „Dem Nehrenden ist ein Dactilus, und kurtz in dem abschnit, also sollen in den Jambischen reimen die Dactyli nicht gebraucht werden." Harsdörffer verwahrt sich in seiner Replik auf das Gutachten gegen diese Kritik („Kurtze Entschuldigung, Die begangene Fehler in den Hundert Spielreimen betreffend", demnächst in *DA Köthen I. 9*. Für sich stehend sei das Wort *Nährender* wohl ein Daktylus, im Kontext des Verses bilde die erste Silbe zusammen mit dem Artikel gleichwohl einen Jambus, dem ein Pyrrhichius (antikes Versmaß, das aus zwei Kürzen besteht) folge. Die wiederholt demonstrierte Reserve F. Ludwigs gegenüber der Verwendung von Daktylen wird von Johann Michael Moscherosch (FG 436. 1645) in 440616 geteilt u. als Verstoß gegen die ‚Würde' der deutschen Sprache begriffen. Vgl. zur jahrelangen Streitfrage des Daktylus 391028 K 3, 420503 K 7 u. im vorliegenden Band 440310A, 440616, 440715 K 5, 440824, 441020, 441231A K 1, 450400 K 3, 450529 K 2, 450808 I, 460705 K II 1 u. 460825.

7 Wenn F. Ludwig sich gegen die Polyflexion wie auch gegen die überreichen Pluralendungen ausspricht, liefert er Belege für die Teilnahme der FG am großen Ausgleichprozeß

des Deutschen im 17. Jahrhundert, in dem mundartliche Sonderungen u. schriftsprachliche Flexions-Hypertrophien bei der Entwicklung des Gemeinen Deutsch zum Neuhochdeutsch eliminiert wurden. S. *Conermann: Hochsprache und Umgangssprache*, bes. 28–31. An der Briefstelle kommen zwei Hyperkorrekturen von Justus Georg Schottelius (FG 397) zusammen, die im Sprachgebrauch keine Stütze fanden: 1. Seine Forderung, den männlichen Substantiven auf *-er* oder *-el* (z. B. der Meister, der Bürger, der Engel), durch das Suffix *-e* die fehlende Pluralmarkierung zu geben, denn die Meister, Bürger, Engel seien, „wan man wil eigentlich und **grammaticè** reden, […] gar nicht recht". Der endungslose Plural stelle einen „algemeinen misbrauch" dar. In alten Schriften tauche zuweilen die korrekte Form auf – damit gebe es so kräftige „authoritates", daß sie „seine misbräuchere [!] selbst" überzeugen müßten. Da „auch der Natürliche verstand unserer Sprache es also erfodert, ists ia unbillig, das man dem misbrauche so viel einräume, das er auch uber die warheit hersche." *DA Köthen I*. 5, 400528 I, S. 509. Konsequent heißt es in der *Sprachkunst* von 1651, alle Substantive, „welche auf er und el außgehen/ müssen in der Mehreren Zahl das E an sich nehmen/ als Bürger/ Bürgere; Thäter/ Thätere/ Schwester/ Schwestere; Himmel/ himmele/ Engel/ Engele." Denn wenn man „nach dem Hauptgrunde und dem natürlichen Verstande der Teutschen Sprache schliessen wird/ befindet sich solches [der endungslose Plural] jrrig/ und durch den Mißbrauch eingeschlichen". *Schottelius: Sprachkunst [1651]*, 290 u. 409ff. — 2. In *Schottelius: Sprachkunst (1641)*, 226 verteidigt er die ungebräuchliche starke Flexion der Adjektive in der Substantivgruppe nach bestimmten Artikeln u. Pronomen (Polyflexion): statt der gute Mann, die gute Frau, das gute Kind u. dgl. könne es heißen: der guter Mann, der „trefflicher Plutarchus", dieses gutes Kind usw. — „ob es aber also überall von jedem zu gebrauchen und auffzubringen sey/ müchte man billich zweiffeln". Dieser Zusatz u. damit die Konzession an den Sprachgebrauch fehlen in der 2. Auflage *Schottelius: Sprachkunst [1651]*, 290. Harsdörffer folgte ihm (nicht konsequent) in dieser Vorgabe, F. Ludwig u. Christian Gueintz, auch Diederich v. dem Werder widersprachen, wie der vorliegende Brief u. seine Beilage zeigen. Sie beugten das attributive Adjektiv nach bestimmten Artikeln u. Pronomen — wie wir heute auch — schwach, weil ja bereits das Pronomen stark flektiert wird. Nachdem im 15. u. 16. Jahrhundert endungslose Adjektivformen häufig waren, sollte sich im Nhd. der Sprachgebrauch in der starken oder „pronominalen" Adjektivflexion bei fehlenden oder unbestimmten Artikeln, der schwachen oder „attribuierenden" Deklination nach bestimmten Artikeln, Pronomen gegen die grammatische Hyperkorrektur durchsetzen. Vgl. *Conermann: Purismus*, 192 f.; *Jellinek: Nhd. Grammatik* II, 246 ff.; Rolf Bergmann, Peter Pauly: Neuhochdeutsch. Arbeitsbuch zur Grammatik der deutschen Gegenwartssprache. Göttingen 1983, 48 ff.; Elena Trojanskaja: Einige Besonderheiten in der Deklination der deutschen Adjektive im 16. und 17. Jahrhundert. In: Studien zur Geschichte der deutschen Sprache. Berlin 1972, 43–78, hier S. 69; Klaus Peter Wegera, Hans-Joachim Solms: Morphologie des Frühneuhochdeutschen. In: *Sprachgeschichte. Handbuch*[2] II, 1542–1554, hier S. 1551.

8 Wörtliche Übersetzung der latein. „sedes belli". Heute „Kriegsschauplatz".

9 *Gueintz: Rechtschreibung (1645)* erschien im August oder Anfang September 1645 in Halle a. d. S. Vgl. 450919A.

K I 1 Vielleicht in der Kirche oder beim Gottesdienst? Im Jahre 1645 fiel der 24. Januar (F. Ludwigs vorliegender Brief 450124) auf einen Donnerstag. S. *Grotefend*. Da Diederich v. dem Werder (FG 31) F. Ludwigs Anfragen i. d. R. rasch beantwortete, zumal sein Gut Reinsdorff in unmittelbarer Nähe Köthens lag, könnte er sein Postscriptum am Samstag, den 26. oder Sonntag, den 27. 1. aufgesetzt haben.

2 Wir haben hier ein illustratives Beispiel für den Kooperations- u. Werkstattcharakter der fruchtbringerischen sprachlich-philologischen u. prosodisch-metrischen Kritik vor uns. F. Ludwigs Entwurf eines Antwortschreibens an Harsdörffer (FG 368. Der Spielende) dürfte Werder mit einer Vorlage der uns vorliegenden Abschrift oder sogar mit dieser selbst zugegangen sein. Dieser Text entsprach i. W. dem eigenhändigen Konzept des Fürsten (s. o. Q u. die Korrektur- u. Variantennachweise in T). Die lange, nachträgliche Ergänzung Ludwigs am Rande der Abschrift griff die „ratio" (Regel) Werders auf u. arbeitete sie in seinen eigenen ursprünglichen Brieftext ein. Daß es sich so verhalten haben muß u. Werders Nachschrift nicht der Endausfertigung des Antwortbriefes des Fürsten an Harsdörffer einfach als Postscriptum angehängt wurde, bestätigt Harsdörffers Reaktion in seiner Antwort 450400, in der der Name Werders nicht fällt. Als Unterschlagung des Fürsten darf dies nicht gewertet werden, da Ludwig seine Briefe an Harsdörffer meist namens der FG (oder metonymisch „Ertzschrein") zeichnete, vgl. etwa 430802 oder 431206.

3 Urteil Martin Milagius' (FG 315. Der Mindernde). Nicht überliefert.

4 Werders Hinweis ist korrekt. In *Harsdörffer: Frauenzimmer-Gesprächspiele* IV (1644, Ndr. 1968), 225 (Ndr., 269), findet sich eine Emblembeschreibung in Prosa, in der die wohl mundartliche Form „der starkziehend Magnet" vorkommt, eine Apokope, die also nicht auf metrischen Zwängen beruht. Vgl. oben K 6 zu dem Harsdörfferschen Magnet-Emblem auf „die Erheber und Handhaber der hochlöblichen Fruchtbringenden Geselschaft" (S. 221 ff./ Ndr. 265 ff.).

450126

Carl Gustav von Hille an Fürst Ludwig

Beantwortet durch 450221. — Carl Gustav v. Hille (FG 302. Der Unverdrossene) bedankt sich für F. Ludwigs Brief und dessen Beilagen und wünscht zum neuen Jahr Gesundheit und Gottes Segen und Schutz vor weiteren Durchzügen. — Hz. August d. J. v. Braunschweig-Wolfenbüttel (FG 227. Der Befreiende) habe er F. Ludwigs Gruß und Entschuldigung übermittelt. Man erwarte nun den dritten und letzten Teil von *Sachse: Einhelligkeit*. Was die Bezahlung des Verlagsanteils (am *GB 1646*) anbelange, seien sowohl Hz. August als auch Hz. Christian Ludwig v. Braunschweig-Calenberg (FG 372. Der Reinherzige) auf gutem Wege, jedoch hätten Durchzug und Geldforderungen Hans Christoph v. Königsmarcks (FG 515. 1648) dieses Vorhaben zunichte gemacht. Hille schlägt F. Ludwig vor, an beide Partner zu schreiben, die Briefe aber an seine Adresse zu schicken, damit er besonders den Reinherzigen daran effektiv erinnern könne. Er wolle nämlich zu Ostern als Drost in dessen Dienste treten. Der Abschied von Wolfenbüttel und besonders von Hzn. Sophia Elisabeth v. Braunschweig-Wolfenbüttel (AL 1629. TG 42b) falle ihm schwer, jedoch habe er das Angebot des Reinherzigen angenommen, da er in Wolfenbüttel keine Beförderung mehr zu erwarten habe, seine Kräfte nachließen und er nun insgesamt vier mal sechs Jahre an (verschiedenen) Höfen gedient habe. F. Ludwigs Briefe an ihn möchten künftig über die Befreiende, Hzn. Sophia Elisabeth, gesandt werden. — Des weiteren übermittelt Hille Grüße von Franz Julius v. dem Knesebeck (FG 396. Der Geheime) und Justus Georg Schottelius (FG 397. Der Suchende). Dieser, der bald seine „Deutsche Reimkunst" veröffentliche, denke wohl auch an einen Ortswechsel. Da er, Hille, sein Exemplar der FG-Mitgliederliste an Hz. Christian Ludwig habe geben müssen und keine Kopie davon behalten habe, bittet er um baldige Zusendung der Namen von dem letzten Mitglied im gedruckten GB an sowie um ein Verzeichnis der ins Französische übersetzten

450126 Carl Gustav von Hille

Gesellschaftsnamen. Zweifellos seien zwischenzeitlich von F. Ludwig viele Gesellschafter aufgenommen worden, auf deren Namen man am Hofe gespannt sei. — Daß Wolfenbüttel elend daniederliege, müsse F. Ludwig aufgrund eigener unglücklicher Erfahrungen nicht näher erläutert werden.

Q HM Köthen: V S 545, Bl. 29r–30v [A: 30v]; eigenh., rotes Lacksiegel; 30r Antwortkonzept F. Ludwigs 450221. — *D: KE*, 201 f. (gekürzt); *KL* III, 222 (unvollst.); Bircher: *Merian*, 696 (Inhaltsangabe). — *BN: Bürger*, 722 Nr. 7.

A Dem Durchläuchtigen und hochgebornen Fürsten und Herrn Herrrn Ludwigen Fürsten zu Anhalt, Grafen zu Ascanien, Herrn zu Bernburg und Zerbst meinem gnädigen Fürsten und Herrn unterthänig. Cöthen *etc.*
Darunter eigenh. Empfangsvermerk F. Ludwigs: Pres. 3. Febr. 1645.

HöchstgeEhrter H. Nehrender *etc.*
deroselben gnädigeß schreiben, nebenst den beylagen habe ich gehorsambst erhalten. Thue mich der erzeigten höchschätzenden würde demutigst bedancken, wünsche und bitte von dem allerhöchsten er wolle in diesem Neuen Jhar seine gnaden hand Ueber deroselben[a] alß auch dero höchstverdorbene Land und leüte gnädig ausstrecken, und dieselbige fur dero *[sic]* gleichen verderbliche ein- und durchzüge g. behutten und bewahren, damit dieselbe noch viele folgende Jhaar, im anfang mittel und Ende, bey fl. wolstande, gewunscheten leibeßaufnemung[1] und aller selbstbeliebenden wolfhärigkeit[2] vollenden und zubringen mügen.
  Dem Befreyenden habe ich gehorsambst die fl. begrüssung auch zuentbottene endschüldigung hinterbracht, und erwarten mit verlangen den letzten theil der vier Evangelischen Einhelligkeiten.[3]
  Waß den versprochenen verlag anbelanget, Jst der Befreyende alß auch der Reinhertzige[4] auf gutem Wege geweßen, dießelbige zu uberliefern, deß Königßmarckß beschwerlicher Durchzug und forderung einß grossen stücke geldeß hatt daß gantze Werck wieder umbgestossen;[5] Also daß ich vor Rathsamb, doch unvorgreiflichen darvor halte, eß wolle der Nehrende Sich g. belieben lassen, an beyde nachmalen forderlichst zu schreiben, und an meine Wenigkeit die lieferung zu richten, so soll eß durchauß an fleisiger und getreuwer anregung nicht ermangeln; insonderheit bey dem Reinhertzigen, in dessen Dienste ich mich bey Verwaltung einß Drosten Diensteß, auf dem Lande[b] diese Ostern vermittelst beystand deß höchsten begeben werde.[6] Jch verlasse ungern diesen ort, insonderheit meine gnedige hertzogin. Weilen ich aber hier keine befor-[29v]derung zugewarten; zu dem Alt und unvermügen werde, auch uber dieß bey die viermal 6 Jhar dem Hoffle[ben] nachgewallet, Alß habe ich diese von dem Reinhertz[igen] mir angebottene und demselbigen von Gott eingeb[ene] gnade nicht abhänden gehen lassen mussen, sondern mich e[r]kläret daß Elend auf dem Lande zu bauen he[lfen].[7] Gott gebe gesundheit und Friede; Da eß meinen höchstgeEhrten Nehren*den* gnädig beliebet hinkünftiche an me[i]ne Wenigkeit zu schreiben, alß bitte ich gehorsambst selbige der Befreyendin zuUberschicken so we[rde] mir schon gnade wiederfharen.

Carl Gustav von Hille 450126

Hofgesellschaft Herzog Augusts d. J. v. Braunschweig-

Wolfenbüttel (FG 227) in Wolfenbüttel. Zu 450126.

Der Geheime und Suchende[8] entbietten dem h. Nehrenden ih[re] gehorsambste dienste und wird der Suchende in kürtz[e] seine deutsche Reimkunst hervorkommen lassen, u[nd] dem h. Nährenden gehorsambsten zu schicken.[9] Eß schei-[net] daß derselbe diesen Ort auch endern dürffte,[10] und weilen daß auß großen gnaden erhalteneß Verzeichn[iß] der Geselschaftß Namen ich dem Reinhertzig[en] geben müssen, und dessen keine abschrift behalten, alß bittet der unverdrossene gehorsambsten solche noc[h]malen mir auß g. von dem ienigen an, so der letzte in dem gedrücketen[c] Gesellschaftß buch zu finden abzuschr[eiben] lassen, und selbige mir nebenst denen Frantzoschen namen mir gnädig bei der ersten glegenheit *[sic]* zu uberschicken.[11] Es zweifelt mir nicht eß wer[den] unter dessen noch viele liebe MitGeselschafte[r] von unserm höchstgeEhrten Nehrenden eingenommen worden seyn; deren namen wir dan allerseitß zu wissen höchst begierig. Den Elenden Zustand, dieseß orteß kan der h. Nehrende, nach außgestandem ihrem grossen unglück, dieseß ortes auch leichtlichen ermessen.

Thue den h. Nehren*den* nebenst dero f. liebe angehörige Gottlichen gnaden schützeß gehorsambst befehlen, und verbleibet biß in seine grube
  Deß höchstgeEhrten h. Nehrenden
    gehorsambster und demütigster Knecht.
      Der Unverdrossene *etc.*
[W]olfenbüttel den
[2]6 th. Jennerß[12]
1645 *etc.*

T *In eckige Klammern gesetzte Ergänzungen im Falz verdeckt.* — **a** *Gebessert aus unleserlichem Wort.* — **b** *Folgt gestrichenes Wort.* — **c** *Am Rand eingefügt.*

K 1 Aufnehmung, d. h. Aufnahme im Sinne von incrementum u. Aufnehmen als prosperitas, Gedeihen. *DW* I, 595 u. 697.

2 Im Sinne von Glück, Heil, Wohlfahrt. S. *DW* XIV.2, 1112.

3 Der Hof Hz. Augusts d. J. v. Braunschweig-Wolfenbüttel (FG 227. Der Befreiende) u. seiner ref. Gemahlin, Hzn. Sophia Elisabeth (Die Befreiende; AL 1629. TG 42b), erwartete den dritten u. letzten Teil der Predigtsammlung des ref. Köthener Hofpredigers Daniel Sachse (*Sachse: Einhelligkeit* III). Vgl. 441205 K 3. F. Ludwig versprach in 450221, den 3. Teil nach Wolfenbüttel zu senden, jedoch scheint sich die Überschickung eines Exemplars für Hz. August bis zum Brief 450721 verzogen zu haben. Damals war es jedoch nicht präsentabel gebunden, so daß F. Ludwig noch ein in Köthen gebundenes Exemplar versprach. Vgl. 460119. Lt. 450308 könnte Hzn. Sophia Elisabeth bereits Anfang März ein Exemplar erhalten haben, denn dort freut sich Carl Gustav v. Hille (FG 302), „„daß die Befreyende mit dem g. dancksagungß schreiben wegen des ubersendeten Buchß eingekommen", d. h. an F. Ludwig geschrieben habe. S. Abb. der Hofgesellschaft S. 428 f. u. „Zu den Abbildungen", S. 135 f.

4 Der Verlag des *GB 1646* bereitete F. Ludwig (Der Nährende) bereits seit mehreren Jahren einige Mühe. Dieses letzte gedruckte, illustrierte Gesellschaftsbuch der FG erschien schließlich im Frühling 1646 unter hohem organisatorischen Aufwand von seiten F. Lud-

450126 Carl Gustav von Hille

wigs, des Frankfurter Verlegers Matthäus Merian d. Ä., des fl. Köthener Kammerherrn Peter Knaudt u. eines (in 440130 K 3 u. 450127 K 1 ausgebreiteten) Netzwerks aus Kaufleuten u. Mittelsmännern. Im Verlauf der mehrjährigen Vorbereitung wurden zehn potentielle Beiträger gewonnen, vier sprangen aber wieder ab, manche erwiesen sich als finanziell unzuverlässig oder zumindest sehr zögerlich in puncto Begleichung des zugesagten Beitrags. Dagegen stand F. Ludwigs eigener Verlagsanteil in Höhe von 400 Rth. nie in Frage u. wurde bereits im Zusammenhang mit der nicht ausgeführten, illustrierten Erweiterung des *GB 1629/30* erstmals genannt (400605 I). Dieser Betrag entsprach einem Viertel des Kostenvoranschlags. 75 Prozent sollten, so F. Ludwig, Freunde u. Verwandte stemmen (401228A). Als mögliche Beiträger sind im Verlauf der fünf bis sechs Jahre andauernden Vorbereitung des *GB 1646* quellenmäßig belegt: Hz. Wilhelm IV. v. Sachsen-Weimar (FG 5. Der Schmackhafte), Hz. Ernst I. v. Sachsen-Gotha (FG 19. Der Bittersüße), Hz. Joachim Ernst v. Schleswig-Holstein-Sonderburg-Plön (FG 101. Der Sichere), Anthon v. Wietersheim (FG 273. Der Umfahende), Friedrich Schenk v. Winterstedt (FG 325. Der Treibende), Hz. Christian Ludwig v. Braunschweig-Calenberg (FG 372. Der Reinherzige), Bodo v. Hodenberg (FG 373. Der Enthärtende), Lgf. Hermann IV. v. Hessen-Rotenburg (FG 374. Der Fütternde), Gf. Christian IX. v. Oldenburg-Delmenhorst (FG 375. Der Vergüldete) u. Hz. Friedrich III. v. Schleswig-Holstein-Gottorf (FG 388. Der Hochgeachte). Seit Juli 1643 fielen die Namen des Enthärtenden (B. v. Hodenberg) u. des Vergüldeten (Gf. Christian IX.), den der Befreiende (Hz. August, s. 421031A) gewinnen sollte, nicht mehr (430706). Auch die später ins Spiel gebrachten beiden Neffen F. Ludwigs, der Schmackhafte (Hz. Wilhelm IV.) u. der Bittersüße (Hz. Ernst I.), zogen sich anscheinend aus dem Verlagsgeschäft zurück, denn uns liegen keine Reaktionen auf die in 450220 von F. Ludwig geäußerte Bitte um Beteiligung vor. Dem Fütternden (Lgf. Hermann IV., s. 450317) wiederum, der sich überraschend als Interessent meldete, war — im übrigen wie dem Sicheren (Hz. Joachim Ernst, s. 401228A) — nur ein kurzes Gastspiel ohne tatsächliche finanzielle Beteiligung beschieden. Als „Verlagskonsortium" festigte sich die folgende, bereits in 421031A (F. Ludwig an Hille) präsentierte Mitgliedergruppe, die im Brief mit den jeweils vorgesehenen Verlagsbeiträgen vermerkt sind: Der Nährende (400 Rth.), Der Reinherzige (200 Rth.), Der Hochgeachte (200 Rth.), Der Umfahende (100 Rth.). Pro 100 Rth. wurden als Gegenleistung 24 Exemplare des *GB 1646* zugesagt. S. auch 450127 K 3 u. 460721 K 4. Der Befreiende sollte laut F. Ludwigs Ausführungen „dergleichen oder ein mehreres als die ersten drey thun", sprich 200 oder mehr Rth. zahlen (421031A). Sowohl der Hochgeachte (s. 450721 K 5) als auch der Umfahende hielten ihre Zusagen termingerecht ein u. spielen im vorliegenden Band deshalb eine untergeordnete Rolle. Es war der Befreiende, Hz. August, der das Projekt über den Frauenhofmeister Hille (und anfangs den weiteren Vermittler Franz Julius v. dem Knesebeck [FG 396. Der Geheime]) oder im persönlichen Briefwechsel (s. bereits 391203 u. I, 391217) mit dem Nährenden nicht nur am längsten begleitete, sondern auch die intensivste u. durchaus von Konflikten getragene Korrespondenz aufweist. S. 440130, 440209A, 440310, 450221, 450331, 451008 u. ö. Im Oktober 1645 konnte F. Ludwig endlich den Eingang der 200 Rth. Hz. Augusts im Brief an Hille bestätigen (451028). Im selben Brief wurde Hz. Christian Ludwigs schlechte Zahlungsmoral offengelegt: Noch immer fehlten die von ihm versprochenen 200 Rth. Hz. Christian Ludwig reduzierte im März 1646 (460301) aufgrund großer finanzieller Belastungen den Betrag (kurzerhand) um die Hälfte u. verärgerte damit F. Ludwig, der daraufhin auf einer sofortigen Begleichung der nunmehr 100 Rth. bestand (460309). Die Liste der Verlagsbeiträger wurde am 23.2.1647 präsentiert: F. Ludwig erhielt 156 Exemplare, Hz. August d. J. 48, Hz. Friedrich III. 48, Hz. Christian Ludwig 24, Wietersheim ebenfalls 24, d. h. insgesamt 252 Stück. Folgt man dem Briefwechsel, so dürfte Merian für den eigenen Handel kaum mehr als 50 gedruckt haben, u. es dürfte bei der im September 1643 (430905 I) vorgeschlagenen Auflage von 300 Stück geblieben sein. Vgl. dagegen 400605 I, ein Dokument, in dem noch von 500 Exemplaren die Rede ist. Zu Verlagsbeiträgen s. 421031A, 430121 (K 2), 440130, 440209A, 440310, 440323 u. I, 440723, 440723A, 450220, 450221, 450301 (K 3), 450308, 450317, 450331 u. I, 450503, 450510 (K 3), 450711 (K 2), 450721, 450722, 450919A, 450923, 450923A, 451001, 451019, 451028, 451028B (K 3), 460119, 460206 I u. II, 460218, 460301, 460303, 460309, 460317, 460324, 460403, 460620B, 460703, 460718, 460721 K 4. Zum *GB 1646* s. 440130 K 3. Zu den Dokumenten, die den Zahlungsverkehr betreffen s. 450127 K 1.

5 Im Januar 1645 wurde Greve Hans Christoph v. Königsmarck (FG 515. 1648) zum schwed. Generalleutnant ernannt. Folgt man seinem Brief vom 18.1.1645 an das Bremer Domkapitel, hielt er sich zu diesem Zeitpunkt in Osterwieck bei Wolfenbüttel auf u. war im Anzug auf Bremen begriffen. S. *Theatrum europaeum* V 1643–1647 (Frankfurt a. M. 1647), 639. Die Eroberung von Bremen u. Verden geschah im Februar u. März 1645. Vgl. auch *Conermann III*, 63. Zu den schwed. Durchzügen allgemein s. 450219 u. 450711 K 6.

6 Diese Stelle trat Carl Gustav v. Hille (FG 302. Der Unverdrossene) nie an. Er kaufte kurz darauf (1646) das mecklenburg. Gut Lalendorf (b. Güstrow). Vgl. *Conermann III*, 339f. Vgl. auch 451028 u. 460718 K 1. Zu Hilles Biographie s. auch 440323 K 1. Seine Verbindung mit Hz. Christian Ludwig bezeugt Hilles Vermittlung eines Widmungsbriefs Georg Philipp Harsdörffers (FG 362) an den Herzog in Harsdörffers *Frauenzimmer-Gesprächspielen* I (²1644, Ndr. 1968), 343–350. S. 440715A.

7 *DW* III, 406f. (Abschnitt I.a): „das elend bauen", *mhd.* „daz ellende bûwen" in der Bedeutung von „in der Fremde wohnen".

8 Franz Julius v. dem Knesebeck (FG 396. Der Geheime) u. Justus Georg Schottelius (FG 397. Der Suchende).

9 Schottelius übersandte seine *Teutsche Vers- oder ReimKunst (1645)* F. Ludwig zusammen mit seinem Schreiben 450204. Vgl. 440900 (K 2) u. ö. Vgl. auch 431028A K 3.

10 Schottelius hat den Wolfenbütteler Dienst des Befreienden seit seiner Bestallung als Präzeptor Hz. Anton Ulrichs v. Braunschweig-Wolfenbüttel (FG 716. 1659) im Jahre 1638 nie verlassen. S. *Schottelius*, 6. Dachte Hille an ein Ausscheiden von Schottelius nach dem Ende der Präzeptorentätigkeit? Nach seiner Promotion (460414 K 3) u. der Schlußprüfung seiner hzl. Schüler im Februar/ März 1646 wurde Schottelius jedoch nicht entlassen, sondern von Hz. August am 24.5.1646 zum Hof- u. Konsistorialrat befördert. NSTA Wolfenbüttel: 2 Alt 2985, Bl. 42f.

11 Offensichtlich wünscht Hille hier eine aktuelle Liste der Mitglieder, die nach Gottfried Müller (FG 353), dem letzten Namen im *GB 1641* (ohne Gemälde), aufgenommen wurden. Vielleicht bezieht er sich dabei aber auf die kursierende, bis FG 417 reichende Mitgliederliste zum *GB 1641/44*. Vgl. 441226A (K 5). Etwa zur gleichen Zeit, mit 450220, übersendet F. Ludwig seinem Neffen Hz. Wilhelm IV. v. Sachsen-Weimar (FG 5) schon ein bis zu FG 432 reichendes Verzeichnis. Das ist Hz. Friedrich v. Sachsen-Weimar, der offenbar erst bei dem kurz zuvor stattgefundenen Besuch F. Ludwigs in Weimar in die Akademie aufgenommen worden war. Hille bittet F. Ludwig zugleich mit der erwünschten Liste um eine Übersetzung der betreffenden Gesellschaftsnamen ins Französische. S. auch *Hille: Teutscher Palmbaum*, 145–175. Dort lassen sich, neben it. u. lat., frz. Übersetzungen der Gesellschaftsnamen für mehr als 450 Mitglieder finden. S. dazu auch das demnächst in *DA Köthen I. 9* erscheinende Dokument 451001/ 460000, welches eine synoptische Liste der Mitgliedernamen mit französischen, italienischen und lateinischen Übersetzungen aus den Jahren 1645 und 1646 enthält. Vgl. zur Kommunikation von Mitgliederlisten z. B. Christian Gueintz' Brief 441231 an F. Ludwig, in dem der Briefschreiber um eine

450127 Fürst Ludwig

Liste bittet, die auch die aufgelösten Gesellschaftsnamen enthält: „mit verlangen erwartend das Register vnd völlige Nahmen".
12 Erschlossen aus der Antwort F. Ludwigs 450221.

450127

Fürst Ludwig an Peter Knaudt

Fürst Ludwig bittet seinen Kammermeister (Peter Knaudt), ihm die ausgehandelten Konditionen Matthäus Merians d. Ä. betreffs der Kupferstiche des *GB 1646* zu übermitteln und fragt nach, wie viele Freiexemplare die Verlagsteilhaber pro eingelegter 100 Taler erhalten würden. — Zugleich bittet F. Ludwig um Nachricht darüber, ob der Amtsschreiber Stefan Ungar die Kammer- und Kellerrechnungen beglichen habe.

Q HM Köthen: V S 546, Bl. 27rv, 27v leer; eigenh. Konzept. — D: *Bircher: Merian*, 696 (fehlerhaft u. unvollst.).

A *Nicht vorhanden.*

27 Jenners 1645.
Der Kammermeister[1] wolle unversiegelt den anschlag herauf schicken wie mit Merian[2] wegen des Kupferstechens des geselschaftbuches gehandelt worden, und wie viel[a] einer der hundert thaler anleget exemplar dargegen krieget:[3]

Jngleichen wolle er berichten, ob der Ambtschreiber Stefan Unger[4] diesen abend den Sachen, so er in die kammer, und Kellern eingegeben, ein genügen gethan.

T a *Am Rand eingefügt.*

K 1 Der fl.-köthenische Kammermeister Peter Knaudt. S. 410510 K 2 u. 440130 K 3. Das zwischen F. Ludwig (Der Nährende), Matthäus Merian, Peter Knaudt, Johann Hammer, Hans Beyer, Matthias Götze, Georg Winckler u. Andreas Kühne intensiv verhandelte Thema der Kosten u. Zahlungsmodalitäten des *GB 1646* wird in den folgenden Briefen dokumentiert: 440130, 440209A, 440310, 440723A, 450331, 450417, 450419, 450503, 450509, 450510, 450614, 450711, 450721, 450800, 450905, 450922, 450923, 450930, 451015, 451019, 451028, 451028B, 451119, 460206 u. I u. II, 460303, 460309, 460317, 460324, 460403, 460519, 460620B, 460703, 460708, 460715 u. 461023. Zur Genese des *GB 1646* s. Anm. 3 u. 440130 K 3.
    2 Der bekannte Maler, Zeichner, Kupferstecher u. Kunstunternehmer Matthäus Merian d. Ä. Zu der Übereinkunft zwischen Merian u. F. Ludwig s. 430513, 430905, 450417, 450503, 450510 u. ö.
    3 Der Entstehungsprozeß des *GB 1646* zeigt, daß 24 Exemplare pro eingelegter 100 Rth. in der umfangreichen Korrespondenz zum Thema *GB 1646* als Konsens gilt. S. zum Thema 24 (resp. 48) Ex. bei einer Einlage von 100 (resp. 200) Rth. 400218 K 4, 450923A, 460218 u. ö. Das Dokument 450317, ein Brief F. Ludwigs an Lgf. Hermann IV. v. Hessen-Rotenburg (FG 372), dagegen bildet hier eine Ausnahme: Dort ist erst- u. einmalig von 12 Exemplaren pro 100 Rth. die Rede. — Am Ende erhielt Hz. August d. J. v. Braunschweig-

Wolfenbüttel (FG 227) für seinen Verlagszuschuß von 200 Rth. die von ihm erwarteten 48 Druckexemplare des *GB 1646* (460303), Hz. Christian Ludwig v. Braunschweig-Calenberg (FG 372) für 100 Rth. 24 Bücher. S. 450923 K 4. Zu den Verlagsgeldern u. Beiträgern insgesamt s. 450126 K 4.

4 Der Köthener Amtsschreiber Stephan Ungar (auch Unger) begegnet uns gelegentlich in Archivalien der Zeit, so am 14.7.1641 (LHA Sa.-Anh./ Dessau: Abt. Bernburg A 10 Nr. 5a², Bl. 23rv) u. 24.9.1643 als amtlicher Korrespondent aus Köthen (ebd.: Abt. Dessau A 10 Nr. 77, Bl. 172r–173v). In einer kurz nach F. Ludwigs Tod erstellten Köthener Bestallungsliste vom 14.3.1650 wird er weiterhin als Amtsschreiber geführt. Ebd.: Abt. Dessau A 18b Nr. 13, Bl. 37r–38v. Auf seine Frau Elisabeth (1600–1639) verfaßte Daniel Sachse eine Leichenpredigt: Christliche LeichPredigt Bey dem Begräbnüß Der … Frawen Elisabeth/ Deß … Herren Stephan Vngars/ Fürstlichen Anhaltischen Ambtschreibers zu Cöthen/ Weilandt Ehelichen Haußfrawen (Zerbst 1639). HAB: Yv 418. 8° Helmst. (6).

450200

Justus Georg Schottelius an Herzog August d. J. von Braunschweig-Wolfenbüttel

Justus Georg Schottelius (FG 397) sei auf den eleganten Titel eines gewiß erscheinenden Buchs (Hz. Augusts d. J. v. Braunschweig-Wolgenbüttel *Evangelische Kirchen-Harmonie*) gestoßen, nach dessen Lektüre er sich sehne. Er wisse nicht, ob den Konsonanten und den Wörtern zuweilen nicht auch etwas Geheimes innewohne und was denn die Wörter in dem vom Herzog gebrauchten Titel ausdrückten. Den Sinn habe er, Schottelius, in einem kurzen Trochaicum erhellt. Er bittet Herzog August (FG 227), das Gedicht eines Blicks zu würdigen und seine Zudringlichkeit zu übersehen.

Q   NSTA Wolfenbüttel: 2 Alt 3520, Bl. 4rv; eigenh., undat.

A   Serenissimo &c. ad munus clementissimum^a humillimè

SERENISSIME ILLUSTRISSIMEq*ue* PRINCEPS Domine clementissime

Jncidi in titulum quendam perelegantem libelli procul dubio proditurj,¹ vix eundem aspeueram^b, cum statim ardens votum libellum ipsum perlegendi succederet:
    Nescio, annon interdum aliquid occulte consonantis literis, vocabulisq*ue* invicem inhabitet; verba dicti à V*es*trâ SERENITATE positi Titulj quemnam sensum per anagramma exactum proferant,² quemq*ue* brevi Trochaico humillimè illustrauj clementissimo aspectu Eadem^c dignarj, meoq*ue* impetuj, quem erga V*es*tram Serenitatem et devotissimum et omni obedienti amore calidum gero, itidem clementissimè ignoscere velit.

VESTRÆ SERENITATI
humillimè obediens
Justus-Georgius Schottelius

T a *Schreibfehler* clementissimus — b *Aus* asperaveram — c *Eingefügt.*

K 1 Bezieht sich auf die *Evangelische Kirchen-Harmonie* Hz. Augusts d.J. v. Braunschweig-Wolfenbüttel (FG 227). S.411214, bes. S.374 u. 386ff. Vgl. 450410 K 19 u.ö. Da der Titel Schottelius geradezu begeistert u. in ihm das Verlangen nach Lektüre des Werks weckt, dürfte er für Justus Georg Schottelius (FG 397) neu sein u. auf eine handschriftliche, dem ersten Teildruck (Der Evangelischen Kirchen-Harmonien/ Erster Teihl. Wolfenbüttel. 1.6.44.) vorausgehende Fassung verweisen. Der Text wurde im Juni 1645 vollendet u. sodann probeweise gedruckt (a. a. O., S.355). Die erste vollständige Edition von 1646 (Oktavausgabe, a. a. O., S. 354 u. 340) u. die folgenden Ausgaben behielten in unterschiedlicher Schreibweise u. ungeachtet der Titelzusätze den Grundtitel *Evangelische Kirchen-Harmonie* bei.

2 Gemeint ist wohl die kürzere handschriftliche Fassung von Schottelius' Gedicht „EIn irrdisch-wüster Mensch/ dem Himmel abgeneiget/", das unter einem Anagramm im Folgejahr in der Oktavausgabe von Herzog Augusts *Evangelischer Kirchen-Harmonie* (1646) veröffentlicht wurde. Das Metrum ist sechshebig-trochäisch mit Auftakt. S.411214, S.344f. (längere Druckfassung) u. S.374 mit Angaben zu zwei abweichenden Abschriften (eine mit Schottelius' Unterschrift), auch zu orthographischen Varianten u. zu anderen Hinweisen Hz. Augusts. Ein Autograph des Dichters ist unbekannt. Das Gedicht erschien auch in *Gosky: Arbustum (1650)*, Bl.177v–178r, u. in der Ausgabe der *Evangelischen Kirchen-Harmonie* von 1656.

450202

Justus Georg Schottelius an Herzog August d.J. von Braunschweig-Wolfenbüttel

Justus Georg Schottelius (FG 397) überreicht Hz. August d.J. v. Braunschweig-Wolfenbüttel (FG 227) seine *Teutsche Vers- oder ReimKunst (1645)*. Sie sei völlig unanstößig und den deutschen Musen geweiht, welche seit dem Altertum meistens geruht und sich nicht durch Kunst weiterentwickelt hätten. Dieses wilden Gärtleins habe er sich in ehrenhafter Muße angenommen, sie sei vielleicht aber auch eines Tadels nicht einmal wert. Mit dem Buch betreibe er beispielhaft, jedoch nur ein kleines Stück weit, das Studium und die Förderung der Sprache. — Der Herzog möge den unzureichenden Ausdruck seiner Verehrung in dem Buch nicht übelnehmen, immerhin dichte man darin deutsch in völlig neuer Weise. Was Schottelius' eigene Beispiele betreffe, so habe es die Schuldigkeit erfordert, auf seine Verfasserschaft aufmerksam zu machen. Habe er Fehler begangen, so hoffe er auf baldige Vergebung.

Q NSTA Wolfenbüttel: 2 Alt Nr.40, Bl. 24rv [A: 24v]; eigenh.; Sig.

A Serenissimo Illustrissimoq*ue* Principi ac Domino Dno. AUGUSTO Duci Bruns. et Luneb. *&c.* Domino meo clementissimo humillimè.

Serenissime Illustrissimeque Princeps Domine clementissime

Libellum in hac perillustri et avitâ V*estræ* Serenitatis Sede has[tata ...] impressum,[1] ad Eiusdem clementissimas manus humillimè affero: Cuiq[ue] sit, quod contineat, illud manifestum est, nemini noxius, nemini scand[alosus] aut asper erit. Dicatus Castissimis Musis Teutiscis,[2] quæ ab omni hactenus antiquitate, artis et decoris, maximam partem q[ui]evere, nec certum per artem iter ingredj potuere. Hortulus interdum & labori & studiis exemptus, honesto huic otio mihj insumptus, vituperio forsan dignum non erit. Studium et promotio lingu[æ] pro modulo et in particula aliqua intenditur.

Serenitas Vra. clementissimè affectui devoto ignoscat, quod alicubj eiusdem et Do[min]i illust^imi mentio fiat; Res in poesi Germanicâ nova, nec alib[j] vestigium inveniens, exempla sua, quibus innotuit primum [inno]tare non debuit:³ Et si debuisset, tempus et otium defuit: Si peccatum, innocenti devotione peccatum^a, eòque spei, indulgenti[m] adepturæ, proximior erit

Welferbyti 2 Febr. ao. 1645.

Serenissimæ Celsitudinj Vestræ
subiectissimè obediens
Justus-Georgius Schottelius

T *[Eckige Klammern] bezeichnen durch Wasserschäden am rechten Blattrand verblaßten Text.* — **a** *Aus* <peccavi>

K 1 Justus Georg Schottelius (FG 397) überreicht seine *Teutsche Vers- oder ReimKunst (1645)* Hz. August d. J. v. Braunschweig-Wolfenbüttel (FG 227). Vgl. 440900 K 2. Im Folgenden vergleicht Schottelius den Inhalt des Buchs mit einem kleinen Garten, jedoch kann schon aus Zeitgründen noch nicht sein *Fruchtbringender Lustgarte (1647)* gemeint sein. Zum Druck in Wolfenbüttel s. 441000 u. 441011. — Schottelius schickte sein Werk auch an F. Ludwig zusammen mit 450204. Am 4. 2. 1645 sandte Hz. August das Buch an Johann Valentin Andreae (FG 464. 1646): „Hiebei des Schöttelii Teutsche Poesis: Es ist das Exemplar, so Er mir offerieret: Die Epistolā wolle er mir wiederschikken: das Buch aber p*er*lustrieren und behalten." HAB: Cod. Guelf. 236.2 Extrav., Bl. 62r. Andreae teilte dem Herzog sein Urteil über Schottelius' Arbeit in 450219 mit.
2 Schottelius widmete dieses Buch den deutschen Musen. Er bezeichnete in 441200 I Hzn. Sophia Elisabeth v. Braunschweig-Wolfenbüttel (AL 1629. TG 42b), die dritte Gemahlin Hz. Augusts, selbst als „höchste Pieris/ und schönste Charitiñ Und Phebi liebstes Hertz".
3 Diese Mitteilung erhellt aus der Anmerkung in Schottelius' Buch (Bl. [b viij]r): „Die *Authores* und Poeten/ welche in diesem Werklein angezogen/ seind allemahl aus beygesetzten Namen zusehen und zu erkennen: Weil aber diese neue Form der Verskunst/ und so viel bißhero unbekante neue Reimarten/ des Authoris Erklärung und behülfliche Hand oftmahls erfodert haben/ als sind die *exempla*, so der Author aus den seinigen hinbey gefüget/ allemahl mit diesem * unterzeichnet." Dieser Hinweis u. die Kennzeichnungspraxis auch in *Schottelius: Teutsche Vers- oder ReimKunst (1656)*, Bl. [b viij]r usw.

450204

Justus Georg Schottelius an Fürst Ludwig

Justus Georg Schottelius (FG 397) überreicht F. Ludwig seine *Teutsche Vers- oder ReimKunst (1645)*. Sie enthalte eine Form der dt. Dichtkunst, die die Erforschung der dt. sprachlichen Grundlagen verlange. Ohne ein festes Fundament könne man kein vollkommenes Gebäude erhoffen. F. Ludwig möge nach Lust urteilen, verbessern, auslassen oder hinzufügen. — Schottelius entschuldigt sich, daß er in seinem Werk nicht die anhaltische Verskunst (*Fürst Ludwig: Kurtze Anleitung zur Deutschen Poesi* 1640) erwähnt habe.

Q HM Köthen: V S 545, Bl. 253rv [A: 253v]; eigenh.; Sig. — *D: KE,* 295; *Barthold,* 312. — *BN: Bürger,* 1262 Nr. 14.

A Jllustrissimo, Celsissimoq̀ue Principi ac Domino Dño. Ludovico, Principi Anhaltino, Comitj Ascaniæ Dñi. in Zervesta et Berenburgo etc. — Domino et Principi meo clementissimo. — *Eigenh. Empfangsvermerk von F. Ludwig:* Pres. 12. Febr. 1645.

Serenissime Illustrissime Princeps Domine clementissime

Libellus¹, formam quandam Artis Poeticæ continens, ad clementissimas Celsitudinis Vestræ manus affertur: Pro modulo et in particula aliqua fundamen linguæ inexhaustæ quæritur et investiga*tur.* Nisi positis firmiter fundamentis perfectio sperati ædificij sperari non potest.

Illust*rissima* Celsitudo V*est*ra iudicet, corrigat, demat, addat pro lubitu, modò firma fundaminis regula nobis tandem struj possit. Invento addi potest, lapis erutus facilius adaptarj potest.

Clementissimè ut ignoreatur^a devoto meo affectuj, quod non una Luminis Anhaltinj² mentio^b facta est, humillimus peto: si peccavi, innocentj amore peccavj, eoq*ue* sum spei, indulgentiam adepturæ, proximior.

                    Illust*rissimæ* Celsitudinis V*est*ræ
                          humillimè obediens
                                Justus-Georgius Schottelius

Welfenbyti 4 Febr. ann. 1645.

T a *KE falsch* ignoveatur — b *KE falsch* montis

K 1 Justus Georg Schottelius (FG 397) schickt F. Ludwig seine *Vers- oder ReimKunst* (1645). Vgl. zur *Vers- oder ReimKunst* 440900 K 2 u. zuletzt 450202. — Ob der vorliegende Brief oder ein anderer von Schottelius' synoptischem lat. Schema „PROSODIA Verß- oder ReimenKunst" (mit deren dt. Fachbegriffen und den entsprechenden lat. Termini) begleitet war, scheint nicht auszumachen. HM Köthen: V S 545, Bl. 214r–215v, fehlt in *KE.* Hierauf beziehen sich F. Ludwigs „Gutachten Über den Lateinischen denckzettel, so der Suchende die Deütsche Poesi betreffende eingeschicket" (a. a. O., Bl. 261r–262v, *KE,* 301–305; vgl. F. Ludwigs Konzept Bl. 263r–264v; Abschrift Bl. 265r–266v) und ein dichotomisches Schema der Verskunst, Bl. 267rv (*KE,* Faltblatt zw. S. 292 u. 293). Alle genannten Schriften demnächst in *DA Köthen I.9.*

2 *Fürst Ludwig: Kurtze Anleitung zur Deutschen Poesi (1640).* Vgl. 391119 K 1 u. 420503.

450217

Herzog Ernst I. von Sachsen-Gotha an Fürst Ludwig

Beantwortet durch 450224. — Hz. Ernst I. v. Sachsen-Gotha (FG 19) wiederholt die bereits vor einiger Zeit u. mehrmals F. Ludwig (Der Nährende) vorgetragene Bitte nach Schriftmatrizen für seine hzl. Druckerei. Da dieser wegen der Kriegsläufte dem Wunsch bisher nicht habe entsprechen können, zudem der dortige Schriftgießer Weimar verlassen habe, jedoch Hz. Ernst für die Schulbücher der Gothaischen Landschule hebräische und kleine griechische Schrifttypen noch immer dringend benötige, bittet er seinen Onkel F. Ludwig nachdrücklich, das Gothaische Schulwesen mit der vorübergehenden Ausleihe dieser Schriften zu befördern. Wenn F. Ludwig die Matrizen in seiner Offizin entbehren könne, würde Hz. Ernst sie auch käuflich erwerben.

Q ThSTA Gotha: Geh. Archiv F ☉ IIIa Nr. 4[1], Bl. 3r; [A: 3r am oberen linken Rand]; Konzept v. Schreiberh.

A An f. Ludwig zu Anhallt fg.

p p. ELd. erinnern sich[a] freundtlich, was maßen wir vorweniger Zeit an EGnd. geschrieben, vnd sie gebetten, vnß etlicher schrifften, so wir in vnserer buchtrukerey[1] bedörfftig, **matrices** zu leihen, daß wir dieselben gießen laßen mögen. Wann dann EGnd. vnß damalen wegen der bekandten[b] Krieges Vnruhe[2] damit nicht willfharen mögen; in deßen aber der Schrifftgieser sich von[c] weinmar hinweg[d] begeben, wir aber gleichwol zu etlichen[e] vor vnser Landschul[3] allhier gemachte bücher die hebreische, auch kleine Griechische Schrifft, **corpus Græcum**[4] genandt,[c] sehr notdurfftig sein, Als ersuchen wir EGnd. mit freundtlicher bitte sie wollen zubeförderung[f] besagten vnsers schulwesens entwed*er* solche beiderley schrifften ein Zeitlang leihen, oder da sies auch [in] Jhrer trukerey endtberen könten[,] dieselb*en* gar keuflich vberlassen. An deme geschicht vnß zu frevndvetterlichen gefall*en*, vnd wir verbleib*en etc.*

Gotha am 17. Febr. 1645.

T a *Folgt* <guter maßen> — **b** *Folgt gestrichenes Wort* <d> — **c** *Folgt gestrichener Buchstabe.* — **d** *Folgt* <ge> — **e** *Folgt* <schu> — **f** *Eingefügt bis* schulwesens

K Dem Brief geht ein seit März 1644 bestehender Briefwechsel zwischen F. Ludwig (Der Nährende) u. Hz. Ernst I. v. Sachsen-Gotha (FG 19) voraus, der mit drei Briefen Hz. Ernsts belegt ist, dokumentiert in *Conermann: Fürstl. Offizin*, 162–165. Die Antwortbriefe F. Ludwigs sind nicht erhalten. Bereits am 28.3.1644 hatte sich Hz. Ernst mit der Bitte an F. Ludwig gewandt, ihm Matrizen griech., hebr., syr. u. arab. Schrift für seine hzl. Druckerei, die zum „beßeren aufnehmen" des Gymnasiums eingerichtet worden war, zu überlassen, um die Drucktypen gießen lassen zu können. LHA Sa.-Anh./ Dessau: Abt. Köthen C 18 Nr. 53, Bl. 80rv; Bl. 81r mit Aufzählung der gewünschten Schriften. Am 3.6.1644 antwortete Hz. Ernst auf zwei nicht erhaltene Briefe F. Ludwigs, die zwar die Erinnerung an eine schon 1630 gestellte Schuldforderung F. Ludwigs enthielten (betr. weimar. Anteil an den ursprünglichen Kosten der Schriften im Rahmen des gemeinsamen ratichianischen Schulprojekts), aber auch bereits F. Ludwigs grundsätzliche Zusage beinhalteten, die gewünschten Matrizen bereitzustellen (a. a. O., Bl. 83r u. 84r). Am 3.6.1644 dankte Hz. Ernst für diese Zusage u. mahnte F. Ludwig, auch ein „verzeichnus" der Schriften nicht zu vergessen. A.a.O., Bl. 84r. Hz. Ernst erhielt jedoch erst nach weiteren Bittbriefen, einem vom 16.9.1644 u. dem vorliegenden, die endgültige positive Rückmeldung in 450224. Am 16.9.1644 entschuldigte sich Hz. Ernst dafür, auf das letzte (unbekannte) Schreiben F. Ludwigs verspätet zu antworten. Er bat nochmals darum, ihm „die newlich begerten matrices" auszuleihen, damit ein „abguß davon möge gemacht wer*den*." Die Matrizen sollten nach Leipzig gebracht werden, wo sie dann von Gotha aus abgeholt werden könnten. ThSTA Gotha: Geh. Archiv F ☉ IIIa Nr. 4[1], Bl. 1r–2r. Der Antwort F. Ludwigs 450224 war das am 3.6.1644 von Hz. Ernst begehrte Verzeichnis beigelegt, wohl ähnlich der Schriftprobe der Köthener Druckerei mit handschriftlichen Notizen, die im anhaltin. Aktenbestand erhalten u. in *Conermann: Fürstl. Offizin*, 164, abgebildet u. kommentiert ist (vgl. die Abb. im vorl. Band, S. 458). Unter den dort aufgeführten Schriftarten findet sich zwar nicht die Wittenberger Hebraeum, aber die kleine Corpus Graecum, die Hz. Ernst im vorliegenden Brief erbittet. Vgl. Anm. 4 u. 450224 K 1.

1 Die Gothaer Druckerei wurde zwischen 1641 u. 1644 von Peter Schmidt (Schmid, Schmied; Petrus Faber; Schmidius) geführt. Ursprünglich kam der Schleusinger Drucker Peter Schmidt auf Empfehlung des Gymnasialdirektors Andreas Reyher (1601–1673) als Erstdrucker nach Gotha u. schloß bereits am 31.12.1640 mit Hz. Ernst einen Vertrag ab. Dieser besagte, daß er für Hz. Ernst alle Patente, Bußzettel, Mandate nebst Büchern u. Schulsachen gegen Lieferung des Papiers u. Zahlung von 1 Pfg. für den Bogen drucken sollte; dafür erhalte er Steuerfreiheit, Braugerechtigkeit für die Familie u. eine jährliche Besoldung von 50 fl., wobei 20 fl. für die Wohnung im Augustinerkloster einbehalten würden. Im Vorfeld, nämlich am 4.10.1633, hatte er eine Druckerei in Frankfurt a. M. mit hebr., griech., lat. u. dt. Typen sowie Musiknoten erstanden. Diese wollte er in seinem Grauen Haus in Schleusingen aufstellen, wo er nach einigem Widerstreben der Meininger Regierung 1634 auch die offizielle Genehmigung zur Verwendung der griech. Drucktypen erhielt. In Schleusingen unterhielt er eine Presse, in der er täglich lediglich anderthalb Bogen herstellen konnte, u. er verfügte über Gesellen u. einen Diener. Gotha stellte somit für ihn einen deutlichen „Aufstieg" dar. Anfang 1644 wurde Schmidt jedoch wegen ungebührlichen Verhaltens entlassen, u. der Gymnasialrektor Andreas Reyher (1601–1673) übernahm die Offizin. Faktor wurde Schmidts Schwiegersohn Johann Michael Schall, da Andreas Reyher keine einschlägige Ausbildung besaß. Dennoch erhielt Reyher 1647 das herzogliche Druckprivileg. S. *Reske*, 304f. u. 824f. Vgl. auch Christoph Köhler: Andreas Wilke und Gottfried Vockerodt — zwei namhafte Rektoren des Gothaer Gymnasiums. Ihre schulreformerischen Berstrebungen im Spiegel deklamatorischer Reden. In: Gotha macht Schule. Bildung von Luther bis Francke. Katalog zur Ausstellung der Universitäts- und Forschugsbibliothek Erfurt/ Gotha in Zusammenarbeit mit der Stiftung Schloss Friedenstein Gotha. Hg. Sascha Salatowsky. Gotha 2013, 24f.; Detlef Ignasiak: Einleitung. In: Magister Andreas Reyher (1601–1673). Handschriften und Drucke. Bestandsverzeichnis bearb. v. Annette Gerlach, Cornelia Hopf, Susanne Werner. Mit e. Einl. v. D. I. Gotha 1992, 9–32, hier S. 28f.

Allein zwischen 1644 u. 1645 lassen sich im VD17 an die 30 Werke nachweisen, die unter der Drucker-Autor-Kooperation Schall o. Reyher/ Reyher erschienen, darunter viele Schulbücher wie das berühmte „Arithmetica Oder Rechenbüchlein" von 1644 (HAB: N 42.8° Helmst.) Unberücksichtigt blieben bei dieser Aufstellung die Werke anderer Autoren, wie z.B. Salomon Glaß', in denen Reyher als Drucker genannt wird. („Typis Reyherianis" als alleinige Angabe führt für 1644/45 zu 45 Treffern im VD17). Wenn auch die hebr. Schrifttype unter all diesen Drucken keine erkennbare Rolle spielt, s Werke, die griech. Schriften benötigten, darunter zu finden, etwa A VOCABULARIUM GRAMMATICUM GRÆCO-LATINUM ... Pro GOTHANO. Gotha: Typis Autoris, Exscripsit Johannes Michael Schalliu 1645 (HAB: Xb 3818 [2]. VD17 23:244259D) u. ders.: SYNOPSEΩS GRAMMATICÆ GRÆCÆ COMPLEMENTUM ... Pro Gymnasio & Scholis Gothanis. Gotha: Typis Reyherianis Excudebat Johannes Michael Schallius 1644 (UB Erfurt: Phil 8° 01444/09. VD17 39:146718D).

2 Hz. Ernst bezieht sich hier auf F. Ludwigs nicht erhaltene Antworten, denn am 3.6.1644 schrieb er an den Fürsten: „heute brechen die keiserlichen in franken auch auff werden sich mit gallas coniungiren". Zu den Kriegsbelastungen im Fürstentum Anhalt im Zuge des „Gallassischen ruins" Ende 1644 s. besonders 440504 K 1 u. 440927 K 1.

3 Gemeint ist das Gothaer Gymnasium, das 1641 zu einer landesherrlichen Lehranstalt erhoben wurde u. „Fürstliche Land-Schul" genannt werden konnte. Die Zugehörigkeit des Gymnasiums zum Stadtrat wurde aufgehoben u. die Schule verwaltungsorganisatorisch der neu gegründeten Landesbehörde, dem Konsistorium mit dem Kanzler als Konsistorialpräsidenten an der Spitze, unterstellt. Als Rektor stellte Hz. Ernst im Januar 1641 Andreas Reyher (s. Anm.1) ein, der die Schule im Sinne Wolfgang Ratkes u. Jan Amos Comenius' reformierte. Dazu erging von Reyher u.a. sein *Special- vnd sonderbahrer Bericht/ Wie nechst Göttlicher verleyhung/ die Knaben vnd Mägdlein auff den Dorffschafften/ vnd in den Städten die vnter dem vntersten Hauffen der Schule Jugend begriffene Kinder im Fürstenthumb Gotha/ Kurtz-vnd nützlich vnterrichtet werden können vnd sollen* (Gotha 1642). Diese pädag. Programmschrift wurde als sog. *Schulmethodus* bis 1672 mehrfach erweitert u. neu aufgelegt (1648, 1658, 1662, 1672). Vgl. Christine Freytag: Der *Schulmethodus*: Einflüsse, Entwicklungen und Auswirkungen der Gothaer Verordnung von 1642 bis 1672. In: Gotha macht Schule (wie Anm.1), 40–54, sowie Katja Vogel: Die Elitenbildung in der *„Fürstlichen Land-Schul"* unter Herzog Ernst I. von Sachsen-Gotha-Altenburg, ebd., 80–88; Juliane Brandsch: Der Gothaer Schulmethodus. In: Ernst der Fromme (1601–1675). Staatsmann und Reformer. Wissenschaftliche Beiträge und Katalog zur Ausstellung. Hg. Roswitha Jacobsen, Hans-Jörg Ruge. Bucha bei Jena 2002, 369–373. Zum Einfluß Gfn. Anna Sophias v. Schwarzburg-Rudolstadt (TG 1) auf die pädagogischen Bestrebungen ihres Neffen Ernst s. auch *Ball: Anna Sophia-Schulstifterin*.

4 Hieronymus Hornschuch führte 1608 unter den allg. gebräuchlichen Typographien auch eine „Wittenberger Hebræum" u. vier griechische Schrift(größ)en in jeweiligem Beispielsatz auf: „Grobe Græcum", „Mittel Græcum", „Cicero Græcum" u. als kleinsten Schriftgrad „Corpus Græcum". H. H.: Ὀρθοτυπογραφία, Hoc est: INSTRVCTIO, operas typographicas correcturis; et ADMONITIO, scripta sua in lucem edituris Utilis & necessaria. ADIECTA SUNT SUB FINEM VARIA TYPORUM SIVE SCRIpturarum typographis usitatarum genera & appellationes (Leipzig 1608), 35f. In: H. H. ORTHOTYPOGRAPHIA lateinisch/ deutsch. 1608 Leipzig 1634. Ndr. hg. Martin Boghardt, Frans A. Janssen u. Walter Wilkes. Darmstadt 1983. In F. Ludwigs Offizin waren bis 1631 an hebr. Schriften „Mittel Hebræum" u. „Cicero Hebræum" — keine Wittenberger Type — u. an griechischen Schriften „Parangon Græcum", „Mittel Græcum", „Cicero Græcum" u. „Corpus Græcum" vorhanden. S. das Schriftprobenblatt in LHA Sa.-Anh./ Dessau: Abt. Köthen C 18 Nr.53, Bl.81r. Vgl. die näheren Einzelheiten (und die Abb. des Schriftprobenblatts) in *Conermann: Fürstl. Offizin*, 163f., vgl. auch oben Anm.0.

450219 Johann Valentin Andreae

450219

Johann Valentin Andreae an Herzog August d. J. von Braunschweig-Wolfenbüttel

Johann Valentin Andreae (FG 464. 1646) bestätigt, den Brief Hz. Augusts d.J. v. Braunschweig-Wolfenbüttel (FG 227) vom 4.2.1645 am 15.2.1645 empfangen und darin von der Bedrohung durch die Schweden erfahren zu haben. — Er freue sich über Hz. Augusts Arbeit an der für die Kirche vielversprechenden *Evangelischen Kirchen-Harmonie* und schließe aus einem Bogen in Quarto, daß August in seinem Werk auch das Leiden Jesu beschreiben wolle. — Andreae erbittet zusätzliche Abzüge der Bibelillustrationen (Conrad Bunos), eines Porträtstichs der drei Söhne Hz. Augusts, der Abdrucke der „Genealogien" (der Lüneburger Druck von Andreaes *Speculum* auf Hz. August. 1644) und des Bildnisses von Hz. Augusts Gemahlin Sophia Elisabeth aus Justus Georg Schottelius' (FG 397) Werk *Teutsche Vers- oder ReimKunst (1645).* — Andreae lobt an dieser Poetik Schottelius' Fleiß und eine zuvor nicht bekannte Regulierung der deutschen Sprache und Poesie, die er fortgesetzt zu werden wünscht. Friedrich Greiff werde davon profitieren. Johann Matthias Schneuber (FG 498. 1648) sei kürzlich in Stuttgart gewesen und habe ein großes Interesse an dieser Poetik bekundet. Schottelius muntere andere deutsche Dichter zum Wettbewerb mit anderen Literaturen und Sprachen auf. — Andreae erklärt, daß sich seine körperliche Verfassung gebessert habe. Er müsse jedoch auf seine Diät achtgeben. — Christoph Zeller habe sein Amt (als Stuttgarter Hofkaplan) wegen seines kriegsbedingt ärmlichen Gehalts noch nicht angetreten. — Andreae teilt mit, daß sein Bankier Simon Beham dank Hz. August das zu Ostern fällige Gehalt schon jetzt auszahlen könne. Das ordentliche württemberg. Salär sei von den staatlichen Kriegsausgaben geschluckt worden. — Die durch den (Kemptner) Prediger Johann Rudolf Schalter verursachte Unruhe, die auch die württemberg. Stände involviere, setze sich noch immer fort.

Q HAB: Cod. Guelf. 65.1 Extrav., Bl. 210rv, eigenh. [A: 210v]; Sig. 8. Brief des Jahres, Antwort auf Hz. Augusts 6. Schreiben v. 4.2.1645 (vgl. 450202 K 1). — D: Begemann: *FG und Andreae,* 30 (Auszug, unzuverlässig).

A Dem Durchleuchtig. Hochgebohrnen Fursten vnd herren. herren **Augusto**, herzogen zu Brunschwig vnd Lüneb. *etc.* Meinem g. Fursten vnd herren. *Wolfenbüttel* (8.) 19. Feb.

Durchleüchtig. Hochgebohrner, Gnediger Fürst vnd Herr.
E. F. G. 6. auf mein 3. den 4. Feb. ist den 15.ten eiusdem zu recht einkomen, woraußen ich mitleidenlich vernommen, daß die **Septentrionales**[1] in E. f. g. Landen ebenso wilkomm vnd hospitales. Aber vnsere laidige gest, von denen wir besorglich das **Exitium finale** zu gewarten haben, wo nicht der höchste Gott nach seiner Almacht solches verwendet, deßen barmherzigkeit wir vnß zu befehlen.

Daß hingegen das **Harmonische Edle werkh**[2] **invito Satana** aufgehet erfrewet mich herzlich. Gott helfe glucklich an das Liecht **in illustrum vsum Ecclesiæ.** weilen ich auch einen bogen **in forma quarta**[3] gesehen. mache ich mir die gedankhen daß etwa der Paßion zu dem Kirchengebrauch auf solche weis muchte absonderlich geteutschet werden.[4]

Die kleine Contrafetlin sein gar artig sambt dem titulum zu dem werkhlin.[5] vnd pite vmb etliche Exemplaria. Auch wo es sein könte. Eines der herrn Prinzen mit farben illuminirt. vndter*t*hänig gebeten haben.[6] maßen ich auch noch etlicher wenigen Exemplaren der Genealogien[7] bedörftig. Der F. Gemahlin. Meiner g. Fürstin vnd Frawen &c. Contrafete (so in H. Schottelij buch)[8] etliche Abtrukh. wolte ich vnd. erbetten haben.[a]

Herren Schottelij schönes buch[9] (darumben ich mich vnd. bedankhe.) habe ich durchblättert. vnd befunde nach meiner wenigkeit. daß Er nicht allein singularem industriam darinnen erwiesen. sondern auch zu Aufbringung der Teutschen Sprach vnd Poesie. eine richtige Regul, (derogleichen noch nie beschehen,) gefunden. vnd ohne Zweifel noch weiter außführen wurt. Vnser Gryphius[10] wirt sich deren wol bedienen. Vnd noch vil zu Lernen finden. Jo: Matth. Schneuberus Argentinæ[b] Poeta. so Newlich seine Teutsche Poemata außgehen laßen. Vnd alhier gewesen,[11] hat großes Verlangen solches werkh zu sehen. Werden Also die Teütsche Poeten einander Aufmuntern. Vnd Mit denen Anderen Sprachen Contendiren. Da zu ich gluck vnd heil wunsche.

Meine leibs indisposition hat sich Gott lob vmb etwas weniges gebeßert. Muos aber mit der Diæta gar behutsam sein. Zellerus[12] ist noch nicht vorhanden. weil Er sich mit den Salarijs abermahl sehr wehrt. Dan die Martis filij, et insatiabiles voragines alles deuorieren. Vnd ordinarie es an vnß zerrinnet. wan schon Alle andere noch ihren part davon bringen. Mein Kaufman Simon Beham[13] hat mir schon das g. deputat auf Ostern. fast eingegeben. dan ich sonsten kein mittel zu Leben hette. Weil das ordinarium salarium. so in parato gewesen. mußen eilends auf die Einquartierung. Durchzug. vnd opposition den Franzosen. verwendet. vnd Angegriffen werden.

Die Schalterische Vnruw. so sich der dissociation der Schwäbischen Stende bedinet Continuieret. vnd sein alle admonitiones verlohrn.[14]

Befehle hiemit E. F. g. dem Schuz des Almechtigen, wunschendt von herzen bald bei deroselben zu sein. vnd meine Vnd. affection in dem werkh zu bezeugen, Dero zu bestandigen großen gnaden ich mich vndergebe. verbleibend biß in den Todt
    E. F. G. Vndertänig. gehorsams Verpflichter Rhat vnd diener
        Jo. Valentin. Andreæ D.
M. Flemmig[15] laßet noch nichts von ihme vernemmen. quem salvere iubeo.

19. Feb. ☿ 1645.

T a *Diesen Satz fügte Andreae als Marginalie hinzu.* — **b** Argentinæ Poeta *eingefügt.*

K 1 Johann Valentin Andreae (FG 464. 1646) sagt ironisch, die schwedischen Truppen seien im Lande Hz. Augusts d.J. v. Braunschweig-Wolfenbüttel (FG 227) ebenso willkommen wie im Hzt. Württemberg. Am 12.2.1645 (HAB: Cod. Guelf. 65.1 Extrav., Bl. 209rv) gab sich Andreae auf eine Nachricht Augusts über den Schwedeneinfall hin „sehr betrübt. daß zu Helmstett vnd E. f. g. Landen, die Laidige Bellona abermahlen angesezet." Über die eigene Lage fügte er hinzu: „Da die Französische armee, in fronte. Die Baierische aber a tergo. Vnd wir zwischen innen. in pressura, atque omnium iniurijs expositis sein. Vnd haben vns die Franzosen. (quibus nulla fides est, et disciplina.) schon zum gruß aller Pferd vnd Viher. damit das Land hette gebawet werden sollen. bej etlich 100 Stukh beraubet." Der Herzog antwortete Andreae Ende Februar 1645: „Konigsm. komt dem Ohrte auch sehr nahe: und wird der bishero, unangefochtene Ohrt, cessante beneficio Ordinis, auch endlich, andern örtern, gleich gemachet werden." HAB: Cod. Guelf. 236.2 Extrav., Bl. 64r. Der erwähnte schwed. Kommandeur ist der gefürchtete Generallt. Greve Hans Christoph v. Königsmarck (FG 515. 1648), der damals auch die Stifte Bremen u. Verden eroberte. S. 450126 K 5.

2 Die Arbeit zu *Herzog August: Evangelischer Kirchen-Harmonie (1644/45)*. S. 411214 III F, vgl. 451001 u. ö.

3 Daraus entsteht die zweite vollständige Ausgabe *Herzog August: Evangelischer Kirchen-Harmonie (1646. 4°)*. S. 411214 III H. Am 11.3.1645 erklärte der Herzog Andreae den Gebrauch solcher Bögen u. den Plan der Veröffentlichung: „Die Bogen so ich etliche mahl umbgeschlagen überschikket, seynd nuhr den Lectoribus vorm Altar zum besten gedrukket; und helffen mir sehr zum kunfftigen drukke: dan man dergestalt noch was findet, das sonsten mit untergeschloffen: Es ist sonsten der Trukker nicht abgeneigt, in 8va et quarta formâ zugleich die Harmoniam heraus zu geben; die in 8va wird mit den figuren, die in qvarta aber zum ablesen, für dunkele augen und Kirchen noch mit groberen typis, als das übersandte in 4t. ohne Figuren: und die allegaten in fine cujuslibet textus: die izzo in fine cujuslibet §.¹ geordenet seynd und im 8.^{v} trukke verbleiben werden." HAB: Cod. Guelf. 236.2 Extrav., Bl. 67r. Tatsächlich erschienen die Oktav- u. die Quartausgabe nacheinander im selben Jahre (1646), jene ohne biblische Illustrationen, diese mit solchen Bildern. Vgl. Anm. 5 u. 411214 III G u. H.

4 Andreae spricht hier nicht von den bereits erschienenen Ausgaben der Passionsharmonie des Herzogs von 1640 u. 1641 (s. 411214 III C u. E), sondern von der Überarbeitung der Passionshistorie für die Gesamtausgaben der *Evangelischen Kirchen-Harmonie*, die zuerst in der ersten oder Oktavausgabe von 1646 erschien. Vgl. Anm. 3. Am 25.2.1645 kündigte der Herzog Andreae an: „Uber 8 Tage schikke ich den anfang von der Passion, si Deo placuerit." HAB: Cod. Guelf. 236.2 Extrav., Bl. 65r.

5 Neben Porträts zeichnete u. stach Conrad Buno (1613–1671) auch biblische Szenen für die Evangelischen Kirchenharmonien Hz. Augusts. S. *DA Köthen I. 6*, S. 115 f. u. 2 Abbildungen zu 411214, S. 353 u. 356. Der Herzog pflegte kleinformatige Kupferstiche der Bibelszenen auf die Adreßseite seiner Briefe an Andreae zu kleben, so auch in seinem Schreiben vom 4.2.1645. Am 1.3.1645 gab Andreae an, bereits 120 solche „figürlin" empfangen zu haben. HAB: Cod. Guelf. 65.1 Extrav., Bl. 212r. Vgl. im Brief v. 12.2.1645 (a. a. O., Bl. 209rv) Andreaes positives Urteil über den Künstler Buno im Vergleich mit einem anderen, auch nicht untalentierten (ungenannten) Illustrator.

6 Hz. August antwortete im erwähnten Brief vom 11.3.1645: „An die Sterne will ich umb das kleine buchlein und Kupferblättlein schreiben, das illuminieren sol auch verrichtet werden." Andreae hatte den Herzog am 12.2.1645 (HAB: Cod. Guelf. 65.1 Extrav., Bl. 209rv) gebeten: „Könte ich der Genealogien, wie sie zu dem Speculo klein getruckht. noch etwa 3 Exemplar haben. wolte ich darumb Vnd. bitten. damit sie denen. so ich noch hab. beigebunden werden muchten." Dieser kleinformatige, zweite Druck von Andreaes Werk zum Geburtstag Hz. Augusts am 10.4.1644 enthält vorgebunden ein Kupferstichporträt Hz. Augusts u. eines seiner damals lebenden drei Söhne: Rudolf August (*1627; FG 754. 1660), Anton Ulrich (*1633; FG 716. 1659) u. Ferdinand Albrecht (*1636; FG 842. 1673). Vor dem Drucktitel gleichfalls vorgebunden ein Frontispiz mit zwei Löwen als

Titelhalter: „AUGUSTUM PRINCIPIS VIRTUTIS SPECULUM." Der Titel ist oben von einem Emblem (springendes Niedersachsenroß, von einer Hand aus der Wolke gezügelt, darüber „FRENA") u. unten von einem Schild (gesp., vorn 1 Löwe, hinten 2 Löwen) mit Hz. Augusts Wahlspruch („EXPENDE") begleitet. Drucktitel: AUGUSTUS | PRINCIPIS | EXEMPLUM. | In Plausum natalis se- | xagesimi sexti feli- | cissimi | EXPOSITVS | per | JOHANNEM VALEN- | TINUM ANDREÆ, | S. T. D. | [Holzschnitt-Zierstück] | LUNEBURGI, | Typis STELLARUM, 1644. HAB: Gn 212; 12°, auch dig.; StB Nürnberg; 3 Bl., 43 S. Die Widmungsvorrede Andreaes an die drei Prinzen stammt d. d. „Stutgardiæ IV. Eid. Apr." — Ein früherer Druck mit Drucktitelvariante „... | sexagesimi | sexti felicissimi | EXPOSITUS | ... STUTGARDIÆ, Typis Rudolphi Kautti. | [Linie] | MDC XLIV." findet sich im Exemplar HAB: 602.17 Hist. (12°, 4 Bl., 60 S., 4 Bl., 1 gefaltetes Bl.; prächtiger seidenbezogener Pappbd.). Es enthält einen kolorierten Kupfertitel u. einen größeren Stich der drei Prinzen (gez. Wolff. Kilian f., vor der Widmungsvorrede). Hinten eingeklebt auch ein gestochenes Bildnis Andreaes von W. Kilian. Hinter der Widmung ein aufgeklebter, ausgeschnittener u. von einer getuschten Kartusche umrankter kolorierter Porträtstich Hz. Augusts, gefolgt von einer farbigen Zeichnung auf Pergament (von ‚Welpen' getragener, von Blumen umwundener Pylon auf einem Postament mit der Inschrift „HÆC ERIGIT. ISTUD AMBIT". Auf dem Pylon Sichel des zunehmenden Monds, darüber eine Sonne mit der Inschrift „CRESCAT". Ein Adler mit der Unterschrift „MAIORIBUS ALIS" fliegt zur Sonne empor.) Dieses Sinnbild dürfte von dem talentierten Zeichner Andreae stammen. Vgl. *DA Köthen I*. 6, 155. Hsl. Anmerkungen Hz. Augusts hinter S. [69] u. auf dem letzten Vorsatzblatt hinten („Errata corrigenda"). Das Porträt der drei Prinzen ist nach dem Exemplar 602.17 Hist. abgebildet in *Sammler Fürst Gelehrter*, 254 (Kat. Nr. 464). — Ein anderes Exemplar des Stuttgarter Drucks im rotseidenen Pappband (HAB: Li 88) weist auch einen farbig bemalten Kupfertitel, ein ausgeschnittenes u. aufgeklebtes, koloriertes Bildnis Hz. Augusts (in tuschgezeichneter Kartusche) u. im hinteren Spiegel ein Porträt Andreaes auf (beide Bildnisse von Wolfgang Kilian), es fehlt jedoch das Porträt der drei Prinzen. Weitere Exemplare: SUB Göttingen: H BRUNSV 1175 (1) rara; SLUB Dresden: Hist. Sax. inf. 482; dig. — Zu Andreaes Plan, sein in Lüneburg erscheinendes Buch zusammen mit einem Panegyricus von Johann Heinrich Boeckler drucken zu lassen, s. 450319 K 3, 9 u. 10.

7 Das in Anm. 6 zit. Büchlein enthält auch die hier erwähnte beschreibende Genealogie Hz. Augusts bis auf dessen Söhne, S. 34–39 „BREVIARIUM VITÆ AUGUSTÆ.", S. 40 ein Stammbaum Augusts u. seiner Frauen u. Kinder, S. 41–44 einen lat. Brief Pz. Rudolf Augusts v. 29.4.1644.

8 Das Porträt Hzn. Sophia Elisabeths in *Schottelius: Teutsche Vers- oder ReimKunst (1645)*, Bl. [Aiij]r. S. 441200 I, vgl. 441020 K 1.

9 *Schottelius: Teutsche Vers- oder ReimKunst (1645)*. Das Werk hatte Hz. August Andreae zusammen mit seinem erwähnten Brief v. 2.2.1645 überreicht (450202).

10 Der Tübinger Poet Friedrich Greiff. S. 431123 mit I u. II; 460317 I.

11 Johann Matthias Schneuber (FG 498. 1648; AGT). Georg Philipp Harsdörffer (FG 368) setzte sich um die Jahreswende 1646/47 für die Aufnahme dieses Straßburger Poetikprofessors u. dt. u. lat. Dichters in die FG ein. *KE*, 377 u. *Conermann III*, 623. S. *DA Köthen I*. 8: 470100.

12 Christoph Zeller (1605–1669), Pfarrer, Nachfolger Andreaes in Calw (Spezialsuperintendent) u. 1645 sein Kollege in Stuttgart. Andreae schreibt hier offenbar über Zellers Gehaltsverhandlungen. Der sollte Andreae als Hofkaplan entlasten. Zeller nahm Andreae auf dessen Sterbebett 1654 das Bekenntnis der Gläubigkeit ab u. hielt ihm auch die Leichenpredigt. *Brecht: Andreae u. Hz. August*, 56, 194 u. 274.

13 Simon Beham (Behem, Behaim), Stuttgarter Kaufmann. *Brecht: Andreae u. Hz. August*, 10.

14 Ein in Kempten Unruhe stiftender, demagogischer Pfarrer namens Johann Rudolf Schalter (*1605) beschäftigte als württemberg. Landeskind auch das hzl. Konsistorium (und damit Andreae) wie auch die theol. Fakultäten zu Tübingen u. Straßburg. Er wurde 1646 vertrieben. *Brecht: Andreae u. Hz. August*, 52 f.

15 Andreae hatte den Amberger Dietrich Flemming († 1664) als Poeta u. Kenner des Hebräischen am 20.11.1644 empfohlen u. nach Wolfenbüttel als Theologen vermittelt (HAB: Cod. Guelf. 65.1 Extrav., Bl. 193r), jedoch mußte dieser 1649 nach Württemberg zurückgeschickt werden, wo er Lehrer der Prinzessinnen u. schließlich Pfarrer wurde. *Brecht: Andreae u. Hz. August*, 169. Vgl. 450319 K 7 u. 460131 (K 13).

450220

Fürst Ludwig an Herzog Wilhelm IV. von Sachsen-Weimar

F. Ludwig dankt Hz. Wilhelm IV. v. Sachsen-Weimar (FG 5) für die ehrenvolle und freundliche Aufnahme bei seinem jüngsten Besuch in Weimar. Der Überbringer dieses Briefes sei sein Amtsschreiber Stephan Ungar, der die nötigen Absprachen mit Hz. Wilhelms Leuten treffen solle, nachdem dieser ihm, F. Ludwig, freundlicherweise Saathafer und -gerste versprochen habe. Die Zeit der Aussaat nahe heran, und Wege und Wetter seien für einen Transport z. Zt. günstig. Hz. Wilhelm möge ihm über Ungar das Nötige über Termin und Organisation des Transportes mitteilen. Dasselbe gelte für die in Aussicht gestellte Hilfe für F. Ludwigs verarmte Untertanen, die des Saatgetreides sehr bedürftig seien. — Wie versprochen übersendet F. Ludwig ein Exemplar des vierten Teils der *Gesprächspiele* (1644) von Georg Philipp Harsdörffer (FG 368). Sprache und Verse seien nicht immer die besten, jedoch würden Hz. Wilhelm die Vertonungen darin gefallen, die sich vielleicht für die von Hz. Wilhelm beabsichtigte Dichtung eigneten, bei welcher F. Ludwig hinsichtlich der Sprache und Verse seine Hilfe anbiete. Das „Seelen liedelein" habe er, Ludwig, noch einmal durchgesehen. Es sollte nun gut eingerichtet sein. — Anbei sendet F. Ludwig ein Verzeichnis der (neuen) FG-Mitglieder bis auf Hz. Friedrich v. Sachsen-Weimar (FG 432. Der Friedenreiche. 1645), Hz. Wilhelms Sohn. Die Reimgesetze würden folgen. Einer ebenfalls beiliegenden Liste könne Hz. Wilhelm jene Buchtitel entnehmen, die F. Ludwig aus Köthen liefern könne. Hz. Wilhelm möge ggf. diesbezügliche Wünsche äußern. Der Köthener Buchbinder sei allerdings weniger zu empfehlen, und so fragt Ludwig, ob Wilhelm die Bücher ungebunden erhalten wolle. — Dem schließt sich die Frage an, ob Wilhelm und sein Bruder Hz. Ernst I. v. Sachsen-Gotha (FG 19) mit einer Verlagseinlage die Publikation des illustrierten *GB 1646* unterstützen und wieviel sie ggf. beitragen möchten. Ein (darüber unterrichtender) Zettel sei in das Kästchen auf dem Schreibtisch Hzn. Eleonora Dorotheas, geb. Fn. v. Anhalt-Dessau (PA. TG 4) und Gemahlin Hz. Wilhelms, gelegt worden. Dieser Dame übersendet F. Ludwig auch Kinderlehren für ihre jüngsten Prinzen bzw. FG-Gesellschafter. Pz. Johann Ernst v. Sachsen-Weimar (FG 342. Der Richtigste. 1639), Hz. Wilhelms (schon herangewachsenem) Sohn, habe er sie seinerzeit selbst geschenkt. — Grüße von F. Ludwigs Gemahlin Sophia (AL 1629. FG 38) und Dank von Pz. Wilhelm Ludwig v. Anhalt-Köthen (FG 358), der sich sehr über die Kupferstiche, Zeichnungen und kolorierten Aufzüge gefreut habe.

Q ThHSTA Weimar: Fürstenhaus A 205, Bl. 232rv u. 235rv [A: 235v], 235r leer; eigenh., A von Schreiberh. mit Kanzleivermerk; fünf Sig. — Ein größtenteils wörtlich übereinstimmendes, leicht verkürztes Konzept F. Ludwigs an Hz. Wilhelm IV. v. Sachsen-Weimar (FG 5) im LHA Sa.-Anh./ Dessau: Abt. Köthen A 9a Nr. 49, Bl. 24rv. Zit. als *K*.

A Dem Hochgebohrnen Fürsten, Herren *Wilhelmen* Hertzogen zu Sachsen, Jülich, Cleve und Berg, Landgrafen v. Thüringen, Marggrafen zu Meißen, Grafen zu der Marck und Ravensberg, herren zum Rabenstein, Unserm freündlichen geliebten herren Sohne, Vetter und Gevattern *etc.*
Zu S. Ld. handen.
Kanzleivermerk: Allerhandt Fürstl. Anhaltische Schreiben *etc.*

Hochgeborner fürst, freundlicher vielgeliebter herr Vetter und gevatter,

Gegen E. L. bedancke ich mich freundvetterlich wegen der vielen mir erzeigeten ehre und gutthat bey jüngster meiner anwesenheit zu Weymar¹, und bin solches hinwieder freundlichen zuverschulden soᵃ erbötig als bereitwillig.

Jch habe nicht unterlaßen sollen an E. L. hiermit meinen hiesigen ambtschreiber Stefan Ungern² abzufertigen, weil EL. mir die hohe freundschaft erwiesen, das sie mir mit Sahmhaffern und Sahmgersten aushelffen wollen, da die sahmzeit heran nahet, undᵇ das wetter mit dem wege zur anfure noch gut ist, zu vernemen wan E. L. die lieferung für mich thun laßen wolten, Daᶜ er mit E. L. leuten, wohin ihn E. L. anweisen werden, allerhand notwendige abrede halten sol: Ersucheᵈ demnach E. L. freundlich sie wollen ihnᵉ desto eher wieder abfertigen, und anweisung thun laßen, auff das er mir in allem gewiße nachricht bringen, oder solche voran schicken möge.

So wird auch zu E. L. freundlichemᵍ gefallen gestellet, ob sie mir wegen der hülffeʰ, so für die verderbeteʰ vnd verarmte unterthaneniˊ, die sehr drum anhalten, geschehen sol, auch gewisheit zukommenʲ laßen wollen.³

Sonsten uberschicke ich E. L. hiermit das jüngst zugesagte büchleinᵏ, als den vierten theil der gesprächspiele⁴: die Sprache und Reime seind nicht uberal die bestenˡ, die weisen⁵ aber hoffeᵐ ich sollen E. L. gefallen, und vielleicht darauf etwas können gemacht werden, zu deme was E. L. vorhaben, darbeyⁿ ich gerne das meinige in der sprache und den reimen thun wil, wan mir E. L. solches wollen zusenden.

Es ist auch der Seelen liedelein⁶ noch einmal übersehen, welchesᵒ verhoffentlich nun wol wird eingerichtet sein.

Also haben E. L.ᵖ das verzeichnus der geselschafter,⁷ so sie bisᵠ hieher noch nicht gehabt, bis auf den Friedenreichen⁸ einschlieslich zu empfahenʳ: die Reimgesetze sollen ins kunftige folgen.⁹

Mit was für Büchern ich E. L. vonˢ hier aus versorgen kan, wan solche E. L. nochᵍ nicht haben, giebet inliegendesᵗ verzeichnus,¹⁰ und wollen nur E. L. mir wißen laßen, was sie darvon begeren. Der buchbinder¹¹ ist alhier nicht der beste, stehet also zu E. L. belieben, ob sie dan solcheᵘ wollen ungebunden nehmen. Soᵛ mögen E. L. auch mit ihrem herren brudern hertzog Ernsten[12] sich bereden, ob sie beiderseits zu dem geselschaftbuche in kupferstucken[13] verlagsweise auch etwas[w] thun möchten, und was, [232v] das Zetlein darvon ist in E. L. Kästlein auf [dem][x] schreibtische von E. L. gemahlin[14] geleget.

Deros[elben][y] uberschicke[z] ich die kinderlehren[15] für die jung[sten][x] gesellschafter[aa][16], der[ab] Richtigste[17] hat die seinige [da]mals[x] von mir selbsten bekommen. Mein [ge]mahl[ac][18] entbeut sich gegen El. zu allen freund[lichen][x] ehrendiensten: Es hat sich mein kleiner[19] u[ber][x] die schönen kupferstucke, und eigenhendige[n][x] [von][x] E.L., wie auch die in farben gemahlte aufz[üge][x][20] höchlich erfreuet, und ist E. L. deswegen hoch [ver]bunden[x]: Jch befehle E. L. und alle die ihrig[en in][x] den sicheren schutz götlicher Almacht, und verb[leibe][x] E. L.

       Dienstwilliger getreuer V[etter][x]
       Ludwig fzu A[nhalt][x]

Cöthen[ad] 20. des Hartmonats[21] 1645.

I

Fürst Ludwigs Geburtstagssonett auf seine Nichte Eleonora Dorothea

Q HM Köthen : V S 546, Bl. 195rv, v leer; eigenh. A. a. O. zwei Versionen des alexandrinischen Sonetts. Die verbesserte und datierte Zweitversion bildet die Textgrundlage. Die Varianten der ersten Fassung im Textapparat unter der Sigle *A*.

       Auf[a] den[b] geburts- und freudentag[c]

Jhr[d] allerliebste[e] Muhm'[1]: Es seind nun viertzig Jhar
   Und drey verflossen gantz, als euch Gott hat gegeben
   Zu[f] sehn des tages licht, und auf der welt zu leben
Für allen[g] freunden es ein tag der freuden war
Der[h] Segen Gottes ist bey euch auch offenbar
   Jn dem'[i] er euch begabt mit sieben[i] schönen reben
   Die an und umb den tisch bey euch herummer schweben.
Und[j] eures hauses Zierd ist diese fürsten schar.[2]
   Mein wuntsch[k] ist drumb das euch in[l] vielen langen Jharen
   Viel[m] heiles liebs und guts noch möge wiederfaren
Vom allerhöchsten Gott, der segen'[n] euch noch mehr
   Am leib und an der sehl, euch laße wol gedeyen
   Was ihr nur nemet für, auch[o] ferner woll' erfreuen
Mit aller gnad' und trost zu seines nahmens Ehr'.

Weymar[p] am sechsten tage
des Hartmonats im Jhare 1645.

II
Lied einer selig abgeschiedenen Seele

Q LHA Sa.-Anh./ Dessau: Z 70 Abt. Köthen A 9a Nr. 49, Bl. 33r; unbekannte H. mit eigenh. Verbesserungen F. Ludwigs.

Lied
Einer Vom Leibe selig abgeschiedenen seele, von derselben
himmlischen zustand im Ewigen Leben,

1

Es[a] ist Nun
Alles thun
Und[b] meinen[c] lauf vollendet
Jn dem mir
Gott alhier
seinen Engel sendet
mich, die seele holen liß
Und[b] der leib starb sanft Und süß

2

Ob er zwar
gantz Und gar
diese welt verließe
was sie hoch
liebet doch
Hinder sich abwiese
Sprach es ist ein bloßer schein
Es muß doch geschieden sein

3

Ohne fehl
Jch die seel'
leb' in großen freuden
Jtzt hab' ich
Völliglich
Ein rechtselig' scheiden
Hinfort ist mir beygelegt
Eine Crone Unbewegt[d]

4

Taußent Welt
alles gelt

mag Ja nicht zureichen
Alle Macht
Großer Pracht[1]
Jst nicht zu vergleichen
Einer solchen Seeligkeit
da ich bleib' in Ewigkeit

5

Stellet ein
kan es sein
Alles trauren klagen
tragt ihr leid
Dieße Zeit
Gottes Wort[e] wird sagen
Jhr solt trauren nicht zu sehr
gebt die[f] Ehre Gott vielmehr

6

Segn' euch Gott
Die in Not
ihr noch[g] müßet leben
Jch die seel
hab' die stell'
Und[b] den thron zu schweben
Gottes heilges Angesicht
schau' ich itzt im hellen licht

7

Aldar ich
wart bis sich
hören lest mit schalle
Gott: der ruffte
zu der gruffte
Komt[h] Jhr toden alle
Alsdan wird mit hellen schein
der leib mir Vor Ein bett sein

8

Es wird Gott
Creutz Und Not
Wie auch alle threnen
wischen rein,
Jnsgemein

Da^i bey allen denen
Volle freude findet sich
Lieblichs weßen Ewiglich

T a *K* so gefließen als erbötig — **b** *K und das wetter zur fuhre noch gut ist* — **c** *Gebessert aus* Dabey *K* darbey er allerhand abrede mit El. leuten halten sol — **d** *K* bitte El. demnach freundlich, — **e** *Gebessert aus* ihme — **f** *Statt* auf das hat *K* damit — **g** *Fehlt in K.* — **h** verderbete *und fehlt in K.* — **i** *K* unterthanen geschehen sol, die sehr drumb anhalten — **j** *K* können laßen zukommen — **k** *K* büchlein vierten theils der — **l** *K* allerbesten — **m** *K* verhoffe — **n** *Dieser Nebensatz fehlt in K.* — **o** *K* verhoffe es sol so wol eingerichtet sein. — **p** *In K folgt* auch — **q** *K* bis hernach — **r** *K* empfangen — **s** *Statt* von hier aus hat *K* alhier — **t** *K* inliegend — **u** *K* dieselbe — **v** *Der ganze Satz fehlt in K.* — **w** *Eingefügt.* — **x** *Textverlust im Falz. Konjektur in eckigen Klammern.* — **y** *Textverlust im Falz. Konjektur in eckigen Klammern. K* El gemahlin — **z** *K* sende — **aa** *In K folgt* zu — **ab** *Der Satz fehlt in K.* — **ac** *Textverlust im Falz. Konjektur in eckigen Klammern. Satz in K* meine gemahlin entbeut El ihre fr. ehrendienste und ich verbleibe El. etc. — **ad** *K* Cöthen 20. Febru. 1645.

T I a *Überschrift in A:* Auf den geburtstag einer hohen fürstlichen person — **b** *Folgt eingefügt* <heutigen> — **c** *Folgt* <Einer nahe anverwandten Fürstin> — **d** *In A eingefügt für* <Seht> — **e** allerliebste Muhm' *gebessert aus* liebes Muhmelein *A* liebes Muhmelein — **f** *Zeile in A eingefügt für* <das helle licht der welt, drin als ein Mensch zu leben> — **g** allen freunden *eingefügt für* <euren Eltern> *A* euren Eltern — **h** *Zeile in A eingefügt für* <Wie auch fur große gnad euch Gott bezeigt> — **i** *In A eingefügt für* <fünff gar> — **j** *Zeile gebessert aus* Und komt dem hause wol doch [?] *Zeile in A* Und kömt dem hause wol doch diese fürsten schar *für* <Dem hause kömmet wol doch diese fürst> — **k** *In A eingefügt für* <hertz> — **l** *A* zu — **m** *Zeile in A gebessert aus* Viel heiles guts und trost stets möge wiederfaren — **n** *Lies:* segne — **o** *Halbsatz in A unleserlich gebessert.* — **p** *Datierung fehlt in A.*

T II a Es ist *von F. Ludwig eingefügt für* <u>Jch hab</u> — **b** *Von F. Ludwig gebessert aus* Vnd — **c** *Von F. Ludwig eingefügt für* <u>den</u> *Der Akkusativ ist eine korrupte Form, die fälschlich nach der Verbesserung von* <Jch hab> *zu* Es ist *stehen geblieben ist.* — **d** *Von F. Ludwig gebessert aus* Vnbewegt — **e** *Von F. Ludwig gebessert aus* Wortt *oder* Worth — **f** *Wörterreihenfolge durch Bezifferung von F. Ludwig geändert aus:* Vielmehr Gott die Ehre — **g** noch müßet *von F. Ludwig gebessert aus* annoch müst — **h** *Von F. Ludwig gebessert aus* Kombt — **i** Da bey *von F. Ludwig gebessert aus* Dabey

K 1 Über diese jüngst erfolgte Reise F. Ludwigs zu seinem Neffen Hz. Wilhelm IV. v. Sachsen-Weimar (FG 5) liegen uns keine direkten Nachrichten vor. Jedoch hat sich im Köthener Erzschrein ein aufschlußreiches Gedicht „Auf den geburtstag einer hohen fürstlichen person" erhalten, das in zwei eigenh. Versionen von F. Ludwig vorliegt. Eine davon ist von ihm unterzeichnet „Weymar am sechsten tage des Hartmonats im Jhare 1645." Die Gefeierte ist die am 6.2.1602 geborene Pzn. Eleonora Dorothea v. Anhalt-Dessau (PA. TG 4), die seit 1625 mit Hz. Wilhelm vermählt war. S. Beil. I u. 450301. Damit ist möglicherweise der Anlaß, ganz sicher aber der Zeitpunkt des Weimar-Besuches ermittelt, in dessen Verlauf auch die jungen Weimarer Prinzen in die FG aufgenommen wurden. S. Anm. 16. Daß es bei diesem Besuch auch um politische Sondierungen ging, ist anzunehmen. Zu dieser Zeit, am 1.2.1645, war es zu einem Zusammentreffen in Weimar gekommen, zu dem Martin Milagius (FG 315) von den Fürsten August (FG 46), Ludwig, Johann Casimir (FG 10) u. Friedrich (FG 62) entsandt worden war. Gegenstand dieser Gespräche, die ein Protokoll von der Hand Milagius' dokumentiert, war die Beschickung des Westfälischen Friedenskongresses u. die Verständigung über eine gemeinsam getragene Position. Das Protokoll im Wortlaut in R. Köhler: Ergänzungen zu G. Krause, Urkunden, Aktenstücke und Briefe zur Geschichte der Anhaltischen Lande und ihrer Fürsten etc. Leipzig 1866. In: Mitteilungen des Vereins f. Anhaltische Geschichte u. Altertumskunde 5 (1890), 98–114, hier S. 104–107. Eine ähnliche Mission Milagius' an den kurbrandenburg. Hof erfolgte kurz darauf, s. seine Instruktion vom 23. 2. 1645 (*KU* V.1, 383–385) u. seinen Bericht über die Beratungen in Berlin vom 9. 3. 1645 (ebd., 386–393). Vgl. Anm. 21 u. 450721 K 3, eine Notiz F. Ludwigs wiedergegeben in 450529 Anm. T bw; ferner die Milagius-Biographie in *Beckmann* VII, 184–186.

2 Stephan Ungar (Unger), fl.-köthn. Amtsschreiber. S. 450127.

3 Vgl. dazu F. Ludwigs in Anm. 21 zit. Brief vom 25. 2. 1645.

4 *Harsdörffer: Frauenzimmer-Gesprächspiele* IV (1644, Ndr. 1968). In 450124 hatte F. Ludwig gegenüber Georg Philipp Harsdörffer (FG 368) den (verspäteten) Erhalt zweier Druckexemplare des 4. Teils der *Gesprächspiele* bestätigt. Vgl. 440426 K 2.

5 Vertonungen finden sich in *Harsdörffer: Frauenzimmer-Gesprächspiele* IV (1644, Ndr. 1968) in verschiedenen Rhythmen zu „Das Geistliche Waldgedicht/ oder Freudenspiel/ genant SEELEWJG/ Gesangsweis auf Jtalianische Art gesetzet", 489–622 (Ndr. 533–666); im Vorwerk zum „Lobgesang" auf Harsdörffer von Carl Gustav v. Hille (FG 302) (Ndr., 13 f.) sowie zum 151. Gesprächspiel „Die Poeterey", 1–15 (Ndr. 45–59). Die in *Conermann III*, 10 f. Hz. Wilhelm IV. attestierten „gelegentlichen poetischen Stimmungen" werden greifbar in zwei schlichten Kirchenliedern, in Trauergedichten zum Tod Diederichs v. dem Werder (FG 31), seines Bruders Hz. Bernhard (FG 30. S. 390800 I) u. F. Christians II. v. Anhalt-Bernburg (FG 51), letzteres in der Leichenpredigt von Johannes Mencelius: Die Schwere Last und sanffte Ruh Davids, Köthen 1656, Bl. N ii r (HAAB Weimar: 30,4:42). Vgl. Ernst Böhme: Die weimarischen Dichter von Gesangsbuchliedern und ihre Lieder: litterargeschichtlich dargestellt und beurteilt. In: Zeitschrift des Vereins f. Thüringische Geschichte und Altertumskunde N. F. 8 (1892/93), 311–390, bes. 328–333. Diese literarischen Etüden unterstützen den Hinweis auf ein beabsichtigtes (dichterisches) Werk des Herzogs. Möglicherweise ist (auch) das „Lied Einer Vom Leibe selig abgeschiedenen seele" (Beil. II) hierzu zu rechnen. S. Anm. 6.

6 Dieses Gedicht könnte von Hz. Wilhelm IV. stammen, dürfte zumindest aus dem Kreis seiner Verwandten bzw. seines Hofes hervorgegangen sein. Trotz der Verbesserungen F. Ludwigs u. der wechselnden Rhythmik bleibt es in seiner topischen Anlage eher schlicht u. nicht frei von metrischen Inkonsequenzen u. Unzulänglichkeiten. S. Beil. II, v. a. Strophe 7, Zeile 8.

7 Hz. Wilhelm muß in einem früheren Schreiben oder mündlich bei einem Besuch — vielleicht bei F. Ludwigs im Brief erwähnten Aufenthalt in Weimar — um eine aktuelle Mitgliederliste der FG gebeten haben. Vgl. 450126 (betrifft wohl Liste bis zu FG 417, vgl. *GB 1641/44*). Die dem Brief beigelegte Mitgliederliste ist nicht überliefert. Es ist jedoch zu vermuten, daß es sich dabei um die Mitglieder ab Zacharias Prüschenk v. Lindenhofen (FG 418) bis zu Hz. Friedrich v. Sachsen-Weimar (FG 432. Der Friedenreiche. 1645) handelte, da im *GB 1641/44* alle Mitglieder bis zu Curt v. Einsiedel (FG 417) erfaßt sind. Von den im 3. Band des Köthener Erzschreins (HM Köthen: V S 546) erhaltenen Listen kommt keine für diese Beilage in Frage. Hz. Friedrich/ Der Friedenreiche erscheint aber in einer Impresenliste von FG 423 (Hz. Adolf Wilhelm v. Sachsen-Eisenach. Der Edele. 1645) bis FG 432 (Hz. Friedrich. Der Friedenreiche), a. a. O., Bl. 75rv (Impresen u. Reimgesetze);

ferner Bl. 79rv Liste der Impresen u. Reimgesetze von FG 428 (Georg Frantzke. Der Gleichende) bis FG 437 (Matthias v. Biedersehe. Der Niederlegende). Es gibt dort auch eine Liste der Mitglieder FG 423 (Hz. Adolf Wilhelm v. Sachsen-Eisenach) bis 512 (Friedrich Asche v. Hardenberg. 1648) nach Tauf- u. Geschlechtsnamen u. mit den Impresen, s. Bl. 143r–144v.
8 Hz. Friedrich v. Sachsen-Weimar (FG 432. 1645), der damals knapp fünfjährige Sohn Hz. Wilhelms. *Conermann III,* 518f.
9 Die Reimgesetze zur Mitgliederliste (vermutlich von FG 418 bis FG 432, s. Anm. 8) sind in den hsl. Listen u. Zusammenstellungen zu finden, die in Anm. 7 genannt sind sowie im *GB Kö.* III, Bl. 18v–33r.
10 F. Ludwig war bestrebt, Köthener Drucke zu verkaufen u. versandte zu diesem Zweck eine Bücherliste u. a. auch an Lgf. Hermann IV. v. Hessen-Rotenburg (FG 372), vgl. 450317 u. 450507A; auch Carl Gustav v. Hille (FG 302) fragte Köthener Drucke nach, vgl. 440323 u. 460718. S. auch die Bücherliste in 430505 I, vgl. schon 410313 K 3.
11 Der Name des Köthener Buchbinders wurde nicht ermittelt.
12 Hz. Ernst I. („der Fromme") v. Sachsen-Gotha (FG 19), jüngerer Bruder Hz. Wilhelms.
13 F. Ludwig bittet hier um finanzielle Unterstützung durch Hz. Wilhelm u. seinen Bruder Ernst für das geplante *GB 1646*. Die Finanzierung des Verlags spielt im Berichtszeitraum des vorliegenden Bandes u. schon in *DA Köthen I*. 6 eine wichtige Rolle. Vgl. 421031A K 14 u. 440130 K 3. Zu den Verlagsbeteiligten der FG am *GB 1646* s. 450126 K 4; zum Zahlungsprocedere s. 450127 K 1.
14 Hzn. Eleonora Dorothea v. Sachsen-Weimar, geb. Fn. v. Anhalt-Dessau (PA. TG 4). Vgl. Anm. 1 u. K I 1; 450301.
15 Eine von F. Ludwig autorisierte „Kinderlehre" ist uns nicht bekannt. Es handelt sich dabei sehr wahrscheinlich nicht um die folgenden luther. Kinderlehren: Die von Weischner 1626 neu aufgelegte *Ordnung der Kinderlehr* von Johannes Kromayer ursprünglich aus dem Jahre 1598 (HAAB Weimar: Cat XVI: 189; VD17 32:666493U) u. die in F. Ludwigs Bibliothek verzeichnete *Kinderlehr* von Aegidius Hunnius: Catechismus oder Kinderlehr von den fürnemmen Häuptpuncten Christlicher Religion (Frankfurt 1596). HAB: J 420.8° Helmst.; *IP,* Bl. 319r. Könnte es sich trotz der konfessionellen Unterschiede um die in den beiden Ausgaben der ref. *Gebete und anderen Kirchendienste* (Köthen 1629 bzw. 1643), S. 17–19 u. 97–112 bzw. 18–20 u. 104–127, genannte „Kinderlehr" handeln? Vgl. 380504 K 14, 430505 K I 16 u. 430802 K 1. Auch der luth. „Catechismus der Kinderlehr" von Lgf. Georg II. v. Hessen-Darmstadt aus dem Jahr 1634 käme in Frage, zumal F. Ludwigs Mutter Eleonora in 2. Ehe mit Lgf. Georg I., dem Großvater des gleichnamigen Landgrafen, verheiratet war: VNsere/ Georgen von GOTtes gnaden/ Landgrafen zu Hessen/ Grafen zu Catzenelnbogen/ Dietz/ Ziegenhain vnd Nidda/ &c. Ordnung/ Von fleissiger übung deß Catechismi/ der Kinderlehr/ mehrer Kirchen-disciplin, vnd anderer/ zu erbawung deß wahren Christenthumbs nötiger Stücke (Marburg 1634). HAB: 243.7.5 Quod. u. 235.26 Theol. (3). Wahrscheinlicher ist wohl, daß F. Ludwig in scherzhafter Verbrämung das *GB 1641/44* meint, denn die vier Weimarer Prinzen danken über ihre Mutter in 450301 artig für deren Erhalt. Dies ist vielleicht auch deshalb anzunehmen, weil sich die FG u. a. auch als eine Akademie zur Erziehung der Jugend verstand u. daher auch Kinder u. Jugendliche aufnahm. Vgl. 300718. Beispiele für die Rolle der Jugend in Akademien (außerhalb der Ritterakademien) jetzt auch *Conermann: Harsdörffers Plan,* passim.
16 Die jüngeren Söhne Hz. Wilhelms u. seiner Gattin Eleonora Dorothea (Anm. 14), die F. Ludwig bei seinem Besuch in Weimar zusammen mit einigen Weimarer Hofleuten am 3.2.1645 (s. FG 425 u. FG 426, *Conermann III,* 510f.) in die FG aufgenommen hatte:

Adolf Wilhelm (1632–1668), später Hz. v. Sachsen-Eisenach (FG 423), Johann Georg (1634–1686), seit 1672 als Johann Georg I. Hz. v. Sachsen-Eisenach (FG 424), Bernhard (1638–1678), seit 1672 regierender Herzog des kleinen Hzts. Sachsen-Jena (FG 427), u. der in jugendlichem Alter verstorbene Friedrich (1640–1656. FG 432), vgl. Anm. 7. Mit den Prinzen wurden bei F. Ludwigs Besuch in Weimar nach Ausweis des *GB Kö.* (mit einigen Eintragungen d. d. 3.2.1645) u. des vorliegenden Briefes, der besagt, daß auch Pz. Friedrich (Der Friedenreiche) damals schon aufgenommen worden sein muß, folgende Hofleute in die FG aufgenommen: Samuel v. Goechhausen (FG 425), Kanzler Hz. Wilhelms IV.; Christian Legell (FG 426), weimar. Hofmann; Georg Frantzke (FG 428), langjähriger hzl. Rat in Weimar, ehe er 1641 als Geh. Rat, Kanzler u. Konsistorialpräsident in den Dienst Hz. Ernsts (s. Anm. 12) nach Gotha wechselte; Georg Friedrich v. Witzleben (FG 429), über dessen Beziehungen zu den Ernestinern uns nichts bekannt ist; Dietrich v. Werthern (FG 430), kursächs. Appellationsrat; Ernst Friedemann v. Selmnitz (FG 431), der ebenfalls in Beziehungen zum sächs. Kurhaus stand. Nach diesem Schwung neuer Mitglieder erfolgte die nächste Aufnahme im Jahr 1645 mit Matthaeus (v.) Wesenbeck (FG 433) erst am 19. Mai. Vgl. *Conermann III*, 507–520.

17 Hz. Johann Ernst d.J. v. Sachsen-Weimar (*1627. FG 342. Der Richtigste). Er war durch Diederich v. dem Werder (FG 31) etwa Mitte August 1639 an der Spitze einer Gruppe weimar. u. altenburg. Hofleute in die FG aufgenommen worden. Vgl. 390807A I (K 3).

18 Fn. Sophia v. Anhalt-Köthen, geb. Gfn. zur Lippe (AL 1629. TG 38).

19 Der damals sechsjährige Pz. Wilhelm Ludwig v. Anhalt-Köthen (FG 358).

20 Gemeint sind kolorierte Stiche, Zeichnungen u. dgl., vermutlich von Maskeraden, öffentlichen Festzügen, möglicherweise aber auch architekton. Ansichten: „aufzug, in der baukunst ein aufrisz des gebäudes von der seite her." S. *DW* I, 50. Das Interesse Hz. Wilhelms IV. an Architektur ist nachgewiesen. S. *Conermann III,* 10; Frank Boblenz: Zum Einfluß Wilhelms IV. von Sachsen-Weimar (1598–1662) auf die Entwicklung der Architektur in Thüringen. In: Residenzkultur in Thüringen vom 16. bis zum 19. Jahrhundert. Hg. Roswitha Jacobsen. Bucha bei Jena 1999, 114–137.

21 Das Konzept *K* dieses Briefes ist gut lesbar auf den 20. Februar 1645 datiert. Die eigenh. Ausfertigung F. Ludwigs läßt im Datum den „Hartmonat" erkennen. Diese alte dt. Monatsbezeichnung benannte meist den Januar, konnte aber auch auf den Februar verweisen. Vgl. Anm. 1, 380221 K 8 u. 450221 K 1. Die Aussaat des Sommergertreides, wozu auch Hafer u. Sommergerste gehörten, geschah i. d. R. gegen Ende März. Da im Februar 1645 noch relative Frostsicherheit herrschte, könnte dies den Hinweis auf günstige Transportwege erklären. Vgl. Bernhard Michels: Der immerwährende ganzheitliche Natur- und Wetterkalender. München [u. a.] 1998, 120 u. 166. In der Akte ThHSTA Weimar: Fl. Haus A 205 findet sich auf Bl. 230r ein Brief F. Ludwigs an Hz. Wilhelm IV. vom 25.2.1645 mit einer Nachschrift vom 26.2. Darin dankt F. Ludwig für einen Brief Hz. Wilhelms vom 20.2., der ihm durch einen Boten des Herzogs samt für Berlin bestimmten Beilagen u. 50 Talern am folgenden Sonntag ausgehändigt worden war. Noch am selben Tag seien die Beilagen u. das Geld durch einen eig. Boten zu Kanzler Martinus Milagius (FG 315) nach Dessau geschickt worden. Von dort werde der Bote schleunigst weiterreisen; man sei benachrichtigt, daß der Aufbruch von Dessau bereits erfolgt sei. Das Reiseziel Milagius' war Berlin, wo es sich mit dem Kurfürsten über die Beschickung des Westfälischen Friedenskongresses zu verständigen galt. S. Anm. 1. F. Ludwig dankt weiterhin Hz. Wilhelm, daß er sich beim Kommandanten von Erfurt dafür eingesetzt habe, daß er von diesem Saatgetreide erhalte. Je 25 Erfurtische Malter Gerste u. Hafer habe Ludwig so bereits erhalten. Nun möge Hz. Wilhelm den ausstehenden Rest, der dringend für den Wiederanbau in den verwüsteten Ämtern gebraucht werde, auch noch aufbringen u. selbst „darzu schießen". Gern u. wie es Wilhelm u. seinen Leuten am bequemsten sei, könne der Transport auch auf mehrere Fuhren aufgeteilt werden, wie es Wilhelm von Ludwigs abgesandten Amtsschreiber Stephan Ungar sicher vernommen haben werde, der sich ganz nach Wilhelms Dispositionen richte. Ludwig bittet um rasche („aufs eheste") erste Lieferung. Diese Guttat werde man nach Kräften zu entgelten suchen. In der eigenh. Nachschrift erinnert F. Ludwig nochmals an Saatgetreide für seine ruinierten Untertanen. — Auch F. Christian II. v. Anhalt-Bernburg (FG 51) bat im Februar 1645 Hz. Wilhelm um Kornlieferungen. S. die angegebene Akte, Bl. 228 f.

K I 1 Hzn. Eleonora Dorothea v. Sachsen-Weimar, geb. Fn. v. Anhalt-Dessau (PA. TG 4). Sie war am 6.2.1602 als Tochter F. Johann Georgs I. v. Anhalt-Dessau (FG 9) u. seiner 2. Gemahlin Dorothea, geb. Pgfn. bei Rhein-Simmern (1581–1631. TG 24) geboren worden, hatte sich am 23.5.1625 mit Hz. Wilhelm IV. v. Sachsen-Weimar (FG 5) vermählt u. starb am 26.12.1664. In 450301 wird sie sich für das Sonett in dt. Alexandrinern bedanken.

2 Ihre Kinder waren damals neben Johann Ernst d.J. (s. K 17), Adolf Wilhelm, Johann Georg, Bernhard u. Friedrich (s. K 16) noch Wilhelmine Eleonora (1636–1653) u. Dorothea Maria (1641–1675), seit dem 3.7.1656 vermählt mit Hz. Moritz v. Sachsen-Zeitz (FG 450).

K II Das Gedicht könnte sich auf den im Alter von 45 Jahren am 20.12.1644 verstorbenen Hz. Albrecht v. Sachsen-Eisenach (FG 17) beziehen, den um ein Jahr jüngeren Bruder Hz. Wilhelms IV. v. Sachsen-Weimar (FG 5). Strophe zwei spricht auf jeden Fall explizit von einem männlichen Toten. Ob F. Ludwigs „Kling und Klagegedicht über den plötzlichen abgang Einer hohen nahe anverwandten Fürstlichen person" (450725 I) ebenfalls damit zusammenhängt? Ein eigentliches Funeralwerk auf den Tod Hz. Albrechts ließ sich nicht ermitteln. Drei ephemere Trauerschriften weisen das „Lied einer seelig abgeschiedenen Seele" jedenfalls ebensowenig auf wie das eben genannte Klagesonett. Es handelt sich bei diesen Trauerschriften um 1.) das latein. Gedicht des Professors für Moral an der U. Leipzig, Friedrich Leibnüz: Cupressus in arâ *MEMORIÆ* … DOMINI ALBERTI III. SAXONIÆ, Juliæ, Cliviæ ac Montium DUCIS, &c. … Die *XX. Decembris ANNI* M DC XLIV. *PIE ET PLACIDISSIME DENATI* erecta (Leipzig [1645]), 2 Bl. SLUB Dresden: Hist. Sax. B 34,6 (auch Dig.); weiteres Ex. in UB Leipzig, s. Katalog der Leichenpredigten und sonstiger Trauerschriften in der Universitätsbibliothek Leipzig. Katalogteil, Bd. 3. Bearb. v. Rudolf Lenz, Gabriele Bosch, Daniel Geißler u.a. Stuttgart 2010, S. 1285. — 2.) Klag-Schrifft Vff den **Velocem obitum: sed felicem abitum** Geschwinden Abschied: aber gelinden Hintritt Weyland Deß … Herrn ALBRECHTEN/ Hertzogen zu Sachssen … Welcher den 20. *Decembr.* in dero Fürstlichen **Residentz** Eisenach … von dieser Welt abgeschieden Jm Jahr 1644 (Coburg 1645). 4°, 4 Bl. FB Gotha: Theol. 4° 00939-940 (6), auch Dig. Enthält je ein dt. Epicedium von Felix Rauschard, hzl. Amtmann in Eißfeld, Felix Hannibal Rauschard u. Felix Ludwig Rauschard; ein lat. von Christian(us) Goeldel(ius) u. ein lat.-dt. von Johann Leib. — 3.) Klagens An- und Abmahnung Vber dem unverhofften … Ableiben Des Weyland … Herrn ALBRECHTS/ Hertzogen zu Sachsen … Als Seiner Fürstl. Gnaden abgeseelter Leichnam in das Fürstl. Begräbnis zu Eysenach den XIV. Tag des Mertzen dieses lauffenden **MDCXLV**. Jahres … beygesetzet worden. O. O. [1645]. 4°, 2 Bl. FB Gotha: Th 8° 02725/01 (58), auch Dig. D. i. ein dt. Epicedium von Johann Heinrich Kolhans, Jurist u. Advokat in Weimar u. Gotha (Wirkungsjahre 1610–1645). Das ‚Seelen-Lied' findet sich, wie gesagt, auch in diesen Quellen nicht. — Ein Kondolenzschreiben F. Christians II. v. Anhalt-Bernburg (FG 51) an Hz. Wilhelm vom Februar

1645 zum Tode des Bruders hat sich im ThHSTA Weimar: Fl. Haus A 205, Bl. 228 f. erhalten (s. K 21). Da F. Ludwig im vorliegenden Brief mitteilt, daß er das Gedicht übersehen (und hier u. da verbessert) hat, dürfte Hz. Wilhelm wohl am ehesten als Verfasser in Frage kommen, der 1639 auch schon seinen verstorbenen Bruder Bernhard (FG 30) bedichtet hatte (s. 390800 I). Vgl. K 5 u. 6. — Das Gedicht läßt sich nur aufgrund seiner Thematik mit Georg Philipp Harsdörffers (FG 368) Singspiel *Seelewig*, das über seine „Weisen" (Vertonungen) im vorliegenden Brief genannt wird (s. K 5), in Verbindung bringen. Das „Seelen liedelein" liegt in der angegebenen Dessauer Akte im unmittelbaren Lagenumfeld unseres Briefkonzepts *K*. Es befindet sich nicht in Harsdörffers „Das Geistliche Waldgedicht/ oder Freudenspiel/ genant SEELEWJG/ Gesangsweis auf Jtalianische Art gesetzet" in *Harsdörffer: Frauenzimmer-Gesprächspiele*, 4. Teil (1644, Ndr. 1968), 489 ff. Vgl. den Text ohne Noten a. a. O., 41 ff. „Ein Geistliches Waldgedicht". F. Ludwig kann somit u. aus verschiedenen Gründen nur die Korrekturdurchsicht dieses „Seelen liedeleins" gemeint haben.

1 Das Substantiv „Pracht" kannte bis ins 18. Jh. neben dem weiblichen (wie heute) auch noch das männliche Genus. *Stieler*, 1474; *Paul Wb.*, 759 f.

450221

Fürst Ludwig an Carl Gustav von Hille

Antwort auf 450126. Beantwortet durch 450308. — F. Ludwig erwähnt gleich zu Beginn zwei dem Brief beigefügte Anlagen: ein Schreiben F. Ludwigs (Der Nährende) an Hz. Christian Ludwig v. Braunschweig-Calenberg (FG 372. Der Reinherzige) und ein Brief des Fürsten an Hz. August d. J. v. Braunschweig-Wolfenbüttel (FG 227. Der Befreiende) mitsamt dem Versprechen, ihm die noch fehlenden Predigten Daniel Sachses zu schicken. In beiden (nicht nachgewiesenen) Schreiben mahnt der Fürst die Empfänger, ihren Zuschuß zum Verlag des *GB 1646* zu entrichten. Wenn hier weiterhin nichts geschähe, müsse Hz. Friedrich III. von Schleswig-Holstein-Gottorf (FG 288. Der Hochgeachte) sein Beitrag zurückgegeben werden. F. Ludwig bittet Carl Gustav v. Hille (FG 302. Der Unverdrossene) deshalb um seine Unterstützung, um die beiden säumigen Gesellschaftsmitglieder zur Zahlung zu bewegen. Das käme sowohl der Gesellschaft als auch der Allgemeinheit zugute. — Der Fürst schickt Hille ein Verzeichnis der Tauf- und Gesellschaftsnamen der neueren FG-Mitglieder und regt an, davon Abschriften anzufertigen, falls auch Hz. August und Hz. Christian Ludwig ein Verzeichnis dieser Namen begehren sollten. — F. Ludwig bestätigt, *Schottelius: Teutsche Vers- oder ReimKunst (1645)* erhalten zu haben. Er werde das Buch, welches er gerade einbinden lasse, genau lesen und sodann nur genau begründete und auf dem sprachlichen Usus beruhende Kritik üben. Die Grüße in Hilles Schreiben (450126) verspricht F. Ludwig weiterzugeben.

Q HM Köthen: V S 545, Bl. 30r (vgl. 450126); eigenh. Konzept. — D: *KE*, 202 f. (unvollst.); *KL*, 223 (unvollst.); *Bircher: Merian*, 696 (Auszug). — BN: *Bürger*, 951 Nr. 74; *KE*, *KL* und *Bürger* datieren falsch auf den 21. 1. 1645.

A *Fehlt*.

Des Unverdroßenen schreiben vom 26. abgewichenes monats ist dem Nehrenden den 3. dieses wol zu kommen:[1] Beigefuget ist an den Befreyenden[2] und Reinhertzigen³ geschrieben: dem ersten werden die noch hinderstellige predigten⁴ zugeschicket, und bey beyden umb richtigmachung des verheißenen Zuschußes zum geselschaftbuche angehalten; Solte hierauf abermals nichts erfolgen, so wirdᵃ manᵇ das aus Holsteinᶜ⁵ und sonsten entpfa[n]gene geldᵈ wiederᵉ geben mußen.ᶠ [Wir]ᵈᵍ demnach gebetenʰ es wolle derⁱ Unverdroßene seinen [Einfluß]ʲ die geselschaft und de*n* [gemei]nenʲ nutzen zu befodern [dest]oʲ fleissiger an[wen]denᵏ, und bey disen [mit?]ˡ gewisheitᵐ uber[sen]denⁿ

Werden vom Befreyenden und Reinhertzigen die Tauf und geselschaft nahmen⁶ begeret, kan sie der Unverdroßene abschriftlich alle mittheilen.

Des Suchenden deutsche Vers oder Reimkunst⁷ hat der Nehrende auch wol entpfa[n]gen, und wird sie mit fleiße belesen, leßet sie vor ietzo einbinden, er wird aber darbey nichts erinnern, was nicht seinen rechten grund hat, und im guten wol hergebrachten gebrauche bestehet, welches man dan nicht übel aufnemen kan.

Jm ubrig*en* wird er die gruße im besten verrichten, und sich des Nehrenden freundschaft iederzeit versichert halten, der dan verbleibet
    Cothen 21 Hartmonats¹ 1645

T a wird *ist am Rand wiederholt und wie das folgende* man *eingefügt.* — **b** *Folgt* <mich> — **c** *Folgt gestrichenes Wort.* — **d** *Tintenklecks.* — **e** *Am Rand eingefügt.* — **f** *Folgt* <oder sonsten auf andere mittel gedencken, wie doch die arbeit fortzusetzen, weil sich auf dergleichen vertrostung nicht mehr zu verlaßen> — **g** *Am Rand eingefügt bis* uber[sen]den — **h** *Folgt* <andernf?> — **i** *Folgt* <[…]ende hierinnen seinen> — **j** *Ein Wort(teil) im Falz; ergänzt nach KE.* — **k** *Gebessert aus* anzuwenden — **l** *Unleserliches Wort im Falz.* — **m** *Folgt* <zu> — **n** *Lies den letzten Satzteil etwa* und bei diesen beiden Gesellschaftern Gewißheit erlangen und das Geld in der Folge überschicken.

K 1 Carl Gustav v. Hille (FG 302. Der Unverdrossene) versandte einen Brief im vergangenen („verwichenen") Monat (450126), der F. Ludwig (Der Nährende) am 3. Februar erreichte. In der Regel bezeichnet der am Briefende so bezeichnete Hartmonat entweder den Monat November, Dezember oder Januar, seltener jedoch auch – wie im vorliegenden Fall – den Februar. S. *DW* IV/2, 517.

2 Hz. August d. J. v. Braunschweig-Wolfenbüttel (FG 227. Der Befreiende). Es handelt sich um (von Hille angeregte) Mahnschreiben F. Ludwigs an den Herzog, endlich den zugesagten Beitrag zum Verlag des *GB 1646* zu entrichten. Diese Anlage ist (weder ausgefertigt noch als Konzept) nachweisbar. Vgl. Anm. 3. Zu den Verlagsbeiträgen s. 450126 K 4. Zum *GB 1646* allgemein s. 440130 K 3.

3 Hz. Christian Ludwig v. Braunschweig-Calenberg (FG 372. Der Reinherzige) sollte zur Zahlung des zugesagten Beitrages von 200 Reichstalern zum Verlag des *GB 1646* veranlaßt werden. Auch diese Beilage ist nicht erhalten. Vgl. Anm. 2. Zu den Verlagsbeiträgen s. 450126 K 4. Zum *GB 1646* allgemein s. 440130 K 3.

4 Der dritte u. letzte Teil der Predigtsammlung Daniel Sachses (*Sachse: Einhelligkeit* III) wurde mit 450721 geschickt. Vgl. 441205 K 3 u. 460119 K 3.

5 Bereits knapp zwei Jahre zuvor waren die von Hz. Friedrich III. v. Schleswig-Holstein-Gottorf (FG 388. Der Hochgeachte) beigesteuerten 200 Rth. angewiesen worden.

S. 430724A. S. auch 450126 K 4 zu den Verlagsbeiträgen. Zum *GB 1646* allgemein s. 440130 K 3.

6 Hilles Bitte um eine Liste der Tauf- u. Gesellschaftsnamen der FG-Mitglieder erfüllte F. Ludwig demnach u. fügte zuvorkommend hinzu, Hille möge davon eine Abschrift machen, falls Hz. August u. Hz. Christian Ludwig solche Verzeichnisse begehrten. Letzterer hatte von Hille schon ein Verzeichnis erhalten. S. 450126.

7 Es handelt sich dabei um ein Werk Justus Georg Schottelius' (FG 397. Der Suchende): *Teutsche Vers- oder ReimKunst (1645)*. Dieser hatte es dem Fürsten zusammen mit seinem Brief 450204 gesandt.

450224

Fürst Ludwig an Herzog Ernst I. von Sachsen-Gotha

Antwort auf 450217. — F. Ludwig (Der Nährende) bestätigt den Eingang des Briefes 450217, in dem Hz. Ernst I. v. Sachsen-Gotha (FG 19) seine Bitte wiederholt hatte, ihm hebr. u. griech. Schriften aus der Köthener Offizin zu überlassen. Er habe zwischenzeitlich in der Druckerei diesbezüglich nachgeforscht. F. Ludwig teilt auf einem beiliegenden Verzeichnis mit, welche der gewünschten Schriften neben einer auch noch vorhandenen syrischen Schrift mit den jeweiligen Gewichten (als Anhaltspunkt der jew. Mengen) derselben verfügbar seien. F. Ludwig erklärt sich bereit, dem Wunsch Hz. Ernsts zu entsprechen, besteht jedoch darauf, daß die Schriften in Köthen abgeholt werden müßten, und erkundigt sich, wann und durch welche Person sie vor Ort (zur Kontrolle) nachgewogen und abtransportiert werden könnten. Als Gegenleistung schlägt er vor, daß ihm Hz. Ernst einen Vorrat an gutem Wein zur Verfügung stelle, da die Getreide- und Weinvorräte der umliegenden Ämter aufgrund der kriegsbedingten Landesverderbnis völlig aufgebraucht seien.

Q LHA Sa.-Anh./ Dessau: Z 70 Abt. Köthen C 18 Nr. 53, Bl. 87r [A: 87r], Konzept v. Schreiberh. mit Anmerkungen F. Ludwigs.

A An Herren Ernsten Herzogen zu Sachsen *etc.*

Hochgeborner Fürst, freundlicher lieber herr Vetter und Sohn.
E Ld. schreiben vom 17. dieses, darinnen Sie uns umb etzliche Hebræische[a] und Griechische schriften dieselben ihr aus unserer Druckerey zuüberlaßen fr. ersuchen, ist uns gestriges tages wol eingehändiget worden.

Nun haben Wir bey Unserer Druckerey nachsuchen laßen und was von denselben und noch einer Syrischen schrift am gewichte ohngefehr verhanden, nach inliegendem verzeichnüs gefunden.[1]

Wollen auf E. Ld. mit deren abfolge in gebürendem wehrt Jhrem begeren nach, gerne freundlichen wilfahren, stellen aber E Ld. freundlichen anheim wan[b]? und durch wen? Sie dieselben dieses ortes möchten abfordern[c] auswiegen und abführen laßen, und weil wir bey jüngstem[d] Landverderben[2] in Unsern Ämbtern umb allen unsern Vorrath an[e] getreide[f] und Wein[f] dieses Jhares gekommen, ob Sie uns nicht dargegen etwas an[g] gutem Wein zur ersetzung und[h] desto ehe- wie-

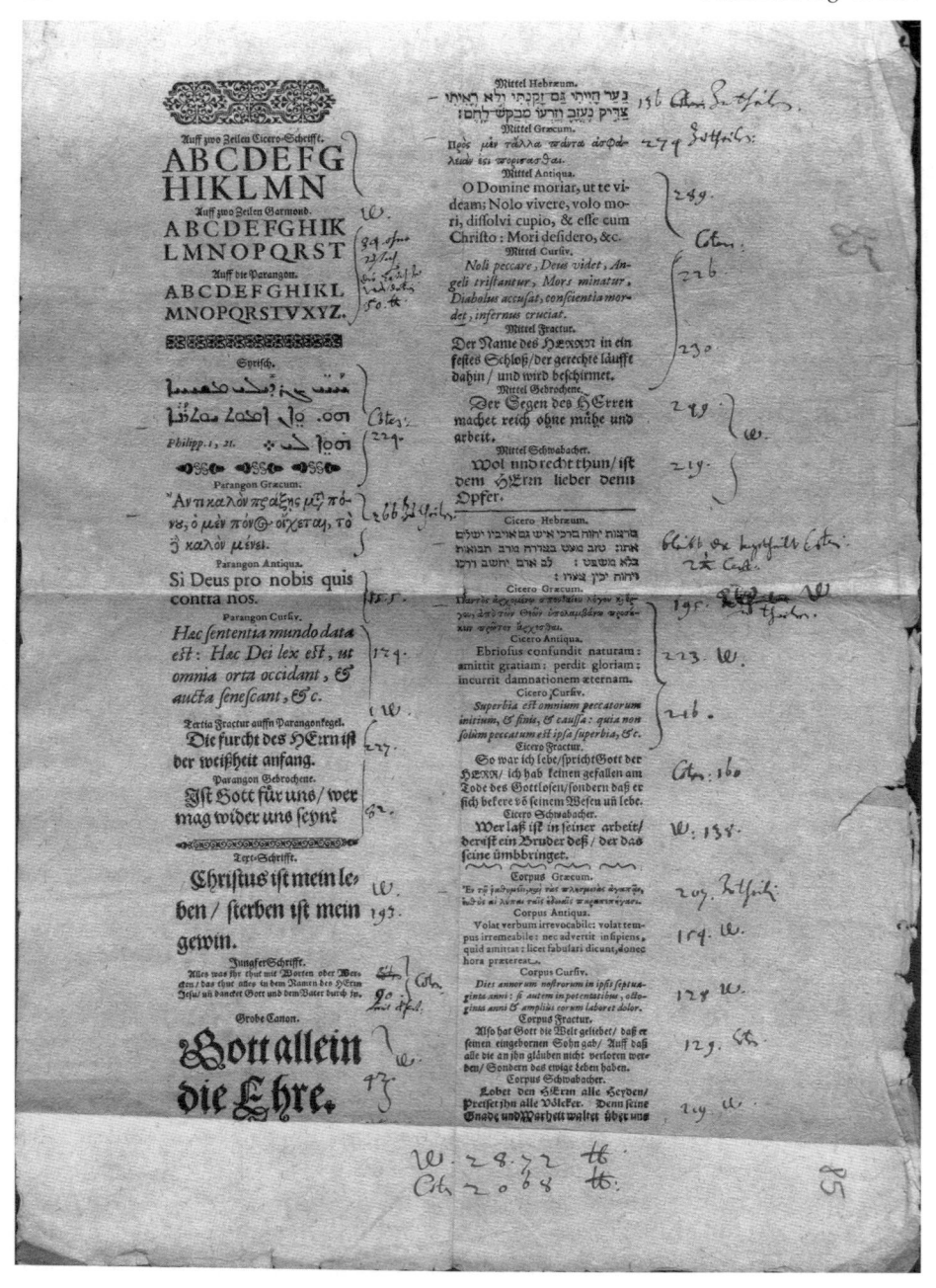

Schriftproben der Köthener Druckerei. Zu 450224.

der wolten liefern laßen.ᶜ Daran uns dan ein sonderbarer gefallen geschehen würde[,]ᶜ wir auchⁱ E. Ld. hinwieder in dergleichen[,] worinnenʲ wir es vermögen[,] fr. zu dienen veranlaßen werden.

Habens E. Ld. in fr. antwort nicht verhalten wollen, dero Wir,
Geben Cöthen den 24 des Hornungs im jahre 1645,
  Ludwig *etc.*

Auszfᵏ
f.ˡ

T **a** *Am Rand eingefügt bis* Griechische — **b** *Folgt* <Sie> — **c** *Folgt* <und> — **d** *Folgt* <Unserm> — **e** *Eingefügt bis* ge, *Präfix von* gekommen — **f** *Folgt* <s>, *Genitiv wird zu Akkusativ verbessert.* — **g** *Ab hier eine schwer lesbare Überschreibung F. Ludwigs:* einen … … [?] — **h** *Am Rand ergänzt bis* ehe-<dem wir selbsten> — **i** *Eingefügt.* — **j** *Am Rand eingefügt bis* vermögen — **k** *D. h.:* Auszufertigen — **l** *Wohl Ausfertigungsvermerk:* fecit *(ausgeführt). Vgl. auch* 460218 *T n.*

K 1 S. *Conermann: Fürstl. Offizin,* S.164f. u. Anm.114. Ein Konzept oder eine Abschrift dieses Verzeichnisses, sollte es nur die von Hz. Ernst I. v. Sachsen-Gotha (FG 19) gewünschten Partien aufgelistet haben, liegt dem Briefkonzept nicht mehr bei. Ein erhaltenes Schriftprobenblatt in derselben Akte dokumentiert aber die bis 1631 in der Köthener Offizin verfügbaren dt., lat., griech., hebr. u. syr. Schriftgattungen u. -grade. Abgebildet in ebd. S.164; Quelle: LHA Sa.-Anh./ Dessau: Abt. Köthen C 18 Nr 53, Bl.85r. S. Abb. S.458. Handschriftlich hat dann F. Ludwig die noch in Köthen vorhandenen Mengen an Lettern (nach Gewicht) wie auch die vordem nach Weimar bereits gelieferten nachgetragen. Demnach waren vordem mehr Schriftgattungen u. -grade bereits nach Weimar gelangt als F. Ludwig noch in Besitz hatte. Allerdings nannte der Fürst wohl noch Stempel u. die einst in Wittenberg gekauften syr. Matrizen sein eigen, außerdem hebr. Schriften u. griech. Schriftgrade, was seinem Neffen, Hz. Ernst — folgt man dem Briefwechsel — wahrscheinlich durch seinen Bruder Wilhelm IV. v. Sachsen-Weimar (FG 5), bekannt war. Das Schriftprobenblatt käme somit als Konzept oder Kopie der (auf jeden Fall ähnlichen) Anlage zum vorliegenden Brief in Frage.

2 Hier sind wohl die Auswirkungen der bereits in 450217 angedeuteten Durchzüge schwed. u. ksl. Truppen gemeint. S. dort K 2.

450301

Herzogin Eleonora Dorothea von Sachsen-Weimar an Fürst Ludwig

Hzn. Eleonora Dorothea v. Sachsen-Weimar (PA. TG 4) dankt F. Ludwig für sein ihr gewidmetes Andenken (ein Geburtstagsgedicht) und hofft, seine (kürzlich bei einem Besuch erfahrene) Aufnahme in Weimar sei geeignet, ihn bald zu einem erneuten Besuch zu veranlassen und dabei seine Gattin (Sophia) und sein Söhnchen (Wilhelm Ludwig. FG 358) mitzubringen. — Sie bedauert seine gesundheitlichen Beschwerden und übermittelt Genesungswünsche. — Ihr Gatte, Hz. Wilhelm IV. v. Sachsen-Weimar (FG 5), werde wegen der Gesellschaftsbücher, die noch in Kupfer gestochen werden sollen (*GB 1646*), selber (auf 450220) antworten. — Die Weimarer Prinzen Adolf Wilhelm (FG 423. Der Edle), Johann Georg (FG 424. Der Trachtende), Bernhard (FG 427. Der Nachfolgende) und Friedrich (FG 432. Der Friedenreiche) bedanken sich für den Erhalt der Gesellschaftsbücher (*GB 1641/44*), die mittlerweile schon eingebunden seien, und erklären, fleißig darin lesen zu wollen. — F. Ludwig möge seine Frau (Sophia. AL 1629. TG 38) und sein Söhnchen grüßen. Sobald Hzn. Eleonora Dorothea ein Schreiben von (der verwitweten) Gfn. Anna Sophia v. Schwarzburg-Rudolstadt (TG 1) in Kranichfeld erhalte, wolle sie es F. Ludwigs Amtsschreiber (Stephan Ungar) zustellen.

Q LHA Sa.-Anh./ Dessau: Z 70 Abt. Köthen A 9a Nr. 49, Bl. 25r–26v [A: 26v], 26r leer; eigenh. mit Eingangsvermerk F. Ludwigs; Sig.

A A Monseigneur mon treshonore Onckle [sic] Monseigneur le Prince Louys d'Anhalt, Cöthen — *Eigenh. Eingangsvermerk F. Ludwigs:* 8 Martij 1645.

Hochgeborner Fürst,

Gnediger vndt Hochgeehrter, Hertzvielgeliebter Herr Vatter, vndt herr vetter,
EG sage ich demütigen danck, das mir EG die große gnadt angethan, vndt mit deroselben gnedigen andencken gewürdigt, wolt Gott wir hetten es hiesiges orts so mit EG gemacht, das EG belieben möcht, baldt wieder zu uns zu kommen[1] vndt die liebe Fraw Muhm vndt das liebste vettergen[2] müste auch mit kommen, es solt mich recht von hertzen[a] freuen. Es ist mir auch von herzten leidt, das EG ihr beschwerung im leibe wieder finden, der Allerhöchste helf EG gnedig hindurch, vndt stercke vndt erhalt EG gnedig, vndt behüt EG für allem unfahl, mein hl. herr, wirdt EG wegen der gesellschafts bücher, selbst beantworten, so[b] in kupfer sollen gestochen werden,[3] der Edle, Trachtende, Nachfolgende, vndt Friedenreiche[4], bedancken sich untertenig, wegen der geselschaft bücher, sie seindt schon eingebunden[5], sie wollen fleißig darin lesen, EG bemühen sich doch auch so viell, vndt grüßen deroselben hl. gemahlin gantz dienstlich, vndt das liebst vettergen, so baldt als ich ein Schreiben [25v] von der Fraw Muhm von Kranichfeldt[6] bekome, wihl ich sie EG Ambdtschreiber[7] wieder zustellen. Jch befehle EG hiermit neben uns allen in den Schutz vndt Schirm des Allerhöchsten, vndt mich in EG beharliche gnadt. bleib bis in meinen todt

EG demütige[8] gehorsahme Tochter und dienerin
Eleonora Dorothea

Weimar den 1 Martii

T a *Folgt* <freüen> — b *Eingefügt bis* werden

K 1 Anfang Februar 1645 hielt sich F. Ludwig besuchsweise am Hof seines Neffen, Hz. Wilhelms IV. v. Sachsen-Weimar (FG 5), auf. Bei dieser Gelegenheit wurden nicht nur dessen jüngere Prinzen (s. Anm. 4) nebst einigen Hofleuten in die FG aufgenommen, sondern F. Ludwig präsentierte seiner Nichte, Hzn. Eleonora Dorothea v. Sachsen-Weimar,

450304 Herzogin Eleonora Maria von Mecklenburg-Güstrow

geb. Fn. v. Anhalt-Dessau (PA. TG 4), aus Anlaß ihres Geburtstages am 6. Februar auch ein Glückwunschgedicht. S. 450220 I.

2 Fn. Sophia v. Anhalt-Köthen, geb. Gfn. zur Lippe (AL 1629. TG 38), Gemahlin F. Ludwigs, u. ihr damals sechsjähriger Sohn Wilhelm Ludwig (FG 358).

3 Gemeint ist das seit längerem vorbereitete *GB 1646*, das Matthäus Merian d. Ä. u. seine Werkstatt mit den Texten u. den in Kupfer gestochenen Impresen der ersten 400 FG-Mitglieder veröffentlichte. F. Ludwig hatte in seinem Schreiben 450220 Hz. Wilhelm u. dessen Bruder Ernst (I. v. Sachsen-Gotha. FG 19) nach einem Beitrag zur Verlagsfinanzierung gefragt.

4 Die vier jüngsten Söhne Hz. Wilhelms IV. u. Hzn. Eleonora Dorotheas, die am 3.2.1645 in Weimar FG-Mitglieder geworden waren: Adolf Wilhelm (1632–1668), später Hz. v. Sachsen-Eisenach (FG 423), Johann Georg (1634–1686), seit 1672 als Johann Georg I. Hz. v. Sachsen-Eisenach (FG 424), Bernhard (1638–1678), seit 1672 regierender Herzog des kleinen Hzts. Sachsen-Jena (FG 427), u. der in jugendlichem Alter verstorbene Friedrich (1640–1656. FG 432). Hz. Johann Ernst v. Sachsen-Weimar (FG 342) war bereits 1639 in die FG aufgenommen worden. Vgl. 450220 K 16 u. 17.

5 Möglicherweise hatte F. Ludwig die vier Exemplare des *GB 1641/44* mit 450220 überschickt u. dabei mit deren Bezeichnung als „Kinderlehre" tiefgestapelt. Vgl. 450220 K 15. Daß die in den GBB zusammengetragene Impresistik als Erziehungslehre oder Tugend-Ethik fungierte, steht allerdings außer Frage. Aufgrund des wenig überzeugenden Leistungsvermögens seines Köthener Buchbinders versandte F. Ludwig damals die Köthener Drucke (wie das *GB 1641/44*) ungebunden. Vgl. 450220. Demnach hätte man sich in Weimar sehr bemüht, die vier Exemplare schnellstmöglich einbinden zu lassen.

6 F. Ludwigs Schwester u. Gründerin der TG, die verwitwete Gfn. Anna Sophia v. Schwarzburg-Rudolstadt (TG 1), deren Witwensitz Kranichfeld zwischen Erfurt u. Rudolstadt gelegen ist.

7 Der Köthener Amtsschreiber Stephan Ungar/ Unger, der F. Ludwigs Schreiben 450220 nach Weimar gebracht hatte. S. zur Person Stephan Ungars 450127 K 4.

8 Hzn. Eleonora Dorothea (s. Anm. 1) führte in der TG den Gesellschaftsnamen „Die Demütige". Vielleicht läßt sich in der Grußformel eine Anspielung darauf erkennen.

450304

Herzogin Eleonora Maria von Mecklenburg-Güstrow an Fürst Christian II. von Anhalt-Bernburg

Antwort auf einen (nicht erhaltenen) Brief vom 15.12.1644. — Hzn. Eleonora Maria v. Mecklenburg-Güstrow (AL 1617. TG 17) beklagt in dem Schreiben an ihren Bruder F. Christian II. v. Anhalt-Bernburg (FG 51) die Sterbewelle unter der Bernburger Bevölkerung, welche ihre Ursache in den drei Landplagen, dem Krieg, der Inflation und der Pest, habe. Aus der Plage ‚Krieg' ergäben sich die anderen beiden und auch der Bevölkerungsrückgang. Die das Ungemach überlebenden Menschen blieben aufgrund des Lehrer- und Pastorenmangels ungebildet und erführen weder von Gott noch der Bibel das Geringste. Es sei nicht selten, daß in Mecklenburg und auch in ihren eigenen Ämtern fünfjährige Kinder mangels Predigern noch immer nicht getauft seien und die meisten Pfarrstellen wegen geringer Bezahlung unbesetzt blieben. Deutschland sei von Barbarei bedroht, da man es verschmäht habe, die Gnade Gottes zu erkennen. Gott könne dies alles ändern, er möge Gnade vor Recht ergehen lassen und seinem Volk gnädig sein. — Hzn. Eleonora Maria hofft, ihr Bruder habe ihre Schreiben empfangen und erfahren, daß das von ihm nach Schöningen und Braunschweig gesandte Paket sie erreicht habe. Der Kanzler lasse ihn grüßen und fragen, ob er, Christian, die Korallentinktur erhalten habe, die Eleonora Marias Schreiben beilag. — Weiterhin bittet Hzn. Eleonora Maria um eines oder drei Exemplare der *Hohelied*-Dichtung Christophs zu Dohna (FG 20). Sie habe das Buch einst mit großer Freude gelesen, konnte es jedoch nicht erlangen. Ob ihr Christian dazu verhelfen könne? — Im Postskriptum wünscht Eleonora Maria ihrer Schwägerin (Eleonora Sophia) eine glückliche Entbindung.

Q LHA Sa.-Anh./ Dessau: Z 18, Abt. Bernburg A 10 Nr. 46d, Bl. 393v–395r [A: 393v]; eigenh.; Sig.

A A Monsieur et treshonoré frere, Monsieur le Prince Chrestien à Anhalt *etc.* à Ballenstet.

Hochgeborner Fürst, Freuntlicher HochgeEhrter Mein HerzVielgeliebter herr Bruder,

eL. schreiben vom 15. Dec. verwichenen Jahres, Jst Mir was langsam aber doch zurecht vberkommen, vernehme darauß sehr vngerne das das sterben zu Bernburg so vberhandt genohmen[.] Aber die 3 Landtplagen seindt Gemeiniglich beisammen, Kriege, theurungen, Pestilenz, dann auß dem Ersten Entspringen die anderen beide, welches wir Jn diesen Landen, für Etlichen Jahren genugsam Erfahren vndt Noch mehr als zuviel Entpfinden, Dann der Mangel an Leuten vber alles gehet, Vndt Jst wol hoch zubeklagen, weil sonderlich die Vbrigen noch Lebende, zu Nichtes Erzogen werden, vndt auß mangel der Prediger vndt Schuldiener, weder Von Gott Noch seinem wort, was wißen, Es hat sich an vielen Orthen hie Jm Lande, alß auch Jn Meinen Eigenen ämptern befunden, das Vnterschiedtliche Kinder, schon 5 Jahr alt gewesen, vndt auß mangel der Prediger Nie getaufet worden, Es stehen auch Noch die meiste [394v] Pfarrstellen Leer,[1] Vndt wollen auß Mangel des vnterhalts sich keine wiederumb finden, die solche dienste begehren anzunehmen,

Ach wie wirdt Deutschlandt Endtlich Eine Barbarei werden, weil Man die Gnade nicht Erkandt, die vns der Liebe Gott biß daher Erwiesen, Nun die Rechte des Herren kan alles ändern, der wolle Gnadt für Recht ziehen, vndt seinem Volck wiederumb Genedig sein,

E. L. werden verhoffentlich Meine Schreiben Entpfangen vndt Daraus Ersehen haben das das Packet so EL. auf Schöningen vndt Braunschweig Addressirt,[2] Mir wol zukommen, dabei hat sich auch Corall Tinctur befunden[3], die Mein H. Cantzler[4] E. L. vberschicket, welcher El. gantz Dienst freundt Schwesterlich *[sic]* grüßet, vnd verlangendt Erwartet, Ob Es EL. zukommen Jst.

E. L. habe Jch auch hiemit fr. Dienstlich bitten wollen, vmb Ein Exemplar oder Drei, der Auslegung vber das hoheliedt Salomon, so H. Christoph von Dona Seeliger aufgesezet,[5] habe Es für diesem mit großen [395r] contentament *[sic]* gelesen Aber kein Exemplar davon bekommen können, hoffe EL. werden Noch welche

haben Vndt Mir darzu verhelffen. Jch bleibe hingegen Vndt so lange Jch Lebe, E. L.
treue von herzen dienstwillige Schwester,
Eleonora maria hzM *etc.*
Streliz d. 4. Merz. 1645
[394v] E.ᵃ L. herzlie*ben* Gemahlin **Recommandire** Jch Mich hochdienst freundt Schwesterlich, Vndt wünsche JL. Eine Glückliche Entbindung,⁶

T a *Am Seitenrand quer eingefügt bis* Entbindung,

K 1 In Strelitz, dem Witwensitz Hzn. Eleonora Marias, wurde beispielsweise der Güstrower Nicolaus Leppin am 3.2.1639 zum Pastor berufen u. am 10.3. in sein Amt eingeführt. 1643 starb er, die Stelle wurde erst etwa ein Jahr später wieder besetzt, durch Hermann Klumpaeus, einen kath. Konvertiten, was der reformierten Hzn. Maria Eleonora durchaus ein Dorn im Auge gewesen sein dürfte. S. Georg Krüger: Die Pastoren im Lande Stargard seit der Reformation. In: Jahrbücher des Vereins für Mecklenburgische Geschichte und Altertumskunde 69 (1904), 1–270, hier S. 193. Ihre langjährige Verbindung mit dem aus Anhalt stammenden u. von F. Ludwig empfohlenen Güstrower Hofprediger Johannes Appelius, welcher der Reformierten Gemeinde Bückeburg bis 1671 vorstand, scheint an dieser Stelle deutlich auf. Eleonora Marias luther. Schwager Hz. Adolph Friedrich I. v. Mecklenburg-Schwerin (FG 175) verbot Appelius nach dem Tod ihres Mannes, Hz. Johann Albrechts II. v. Mecklenburg-Güstrow (FG 158), im Jahre 1636 das Predigen. Auch entzog er ihr die Vormundschaft für ihren Sohn Gustav Adolph (FG 511. 1648) u. die Regentschaft im Teilhzt. Güstrow. Nach einem langen u. vor den höchsten Reichsinstanzen ausgefochtenen Streit mußte sie sich in das ihr zugewiesene Wittum Strelitz zurückziehen. S. 371009 K 0, 390908 K 1, 410221 K 2, ferner 370902 K 7. Eleonora Marias nach ihrer Eheschließung bewiesenes Engagement für die „Kirchen und Schulen" des Landes wird im vorliegenden Brief bestätigt. So existierte von 1632 an bis zur Schließung 1636 durch Hz. Adolph Friedrich in Güstrow eine reformierte Knabenschule. Zur Person Hzn. Eleonora Marias u. ihrer aktiven Mitgliedschaft in AL u. TG s. *Ball: Tugendliche Gesellschaft*, 350–361.

2 Wahrscheinlich wurde ihr das Paket über Schöningen, von der Witwe Hz. Friedrich Ulrichs v. Braunschweig-Wolfenbüttel (FG 38), Hzn. Anna Sophia (TG 2b), geb. Pzn. v. Brandenburg, zugeleitet.

3 Die Korallentinktur, besonders das corallium rubrum bzw. das corallium album, galt bereits in der Antike u. in Persien als vielseitig anwendbare Arznei gegen Geschwüre, Augenleiden, Harn- u. Milzbeschwerden u. diente auch als herzstärkendes Mittel. Vgl. Susanne Grosser: Ärztekorrespondenz in der Frühen Neuzeit. Der Briefwechsel zwischen Peter Christian Wagner und Christoph Jacob Trew. Analyse und kommentierte Edition. Berlin 2015, 343f. (Kommentarstelle mit Literaturhinweisen). S. auch Eugen Dieterich: Neues Pharmaceutisches Manual. 2. Auflage. Berlin 1888, 363. — Bereits eine Woche später, am 10.3.1645, bedankte sich Hzn. Eleonora Marias Schwester Sibylla Elisabeth v. Anhalt-Bernburg (AL 1617. TG 18), die bei ihrer Schwester in Güstrow bzw. Strelitz lebte, für mehrere Schreiben ihres Bruders, F. Christians II. v. Anhalt-Bernburg (FG 51), die u.a. die Nachricht von der glücklichen Entbindung ihrer Schwägerin Fn. Eleonora Sophia v. Anhalt-Bernburg (TG 39) u. die Bestätigung des Empfangs der Tinktur enthielten. Hzn. Sibylla Elisabeth riet ihrem Bruder in ihrem Schreiben, die Korallentinktur zunächst „einen guten Menschen" ausprobieren zu lassen, bevor er diese selbst „einnehme", um sein Mißtrauen zu zerstreuen. Ein (der vorliegende?) Brief Eleonora Marias, so die Schwester weiter, habe F. Christian wohl „troubliret" u. ihn an deren schwesterlicher Loyalität zweifeln lassen. Hier spielt Sibylla Elisabeth offensichtlich auf geschwisterliche Mißverständnisse an, die möglicherweise die Korallentinktur betrafen u. die sie als Vermittlerin aufzulösen sucht (LHA Sa.-Anh./ Dessau: Z 18, Abt. Bernburg, A 10 Nr. 46d, Bl. 396rv).

4 Schwerlich handelt es sich um den Güstrower Kanzler Johann Cothmann (FG 168), der sich nach dem Tod seines reformierten Landesherrn, Hz. Johann Albrechts II. (s. Anm. 1), im Regent- u. Vormundschaftsstreit unrühmlich auf die Seite des vor Gewalttätigkeiten nicht zurückschreckenden Schwagers der verwitweten Herzogin, des luther. Hz.s Adolph Friedrich I. v. Mecklenburg-Schwerin (FG 178) geschlagen hatte. Hzn. Eleonora Maria mußte in Folge der Niederlage im jahrelangen Rechtsstreit die Güstrower Residenz räumen u. ihr Wittum Strelitz beziehen. Wer ihr dort als Kanzler diente, ist uns nicht bekannt. S. 371009 K 0, 390908 K 1, 410221 K 2 u. *Conermann III*, 168f.

5 Der bereits 1637 verstorbene Burggf. u. Herr Christoph zu Dohna (FG 20) veröffentlichte seine *Hohelied*-Bearbeitung 1635: Kurtze und einfältige Betrachtungen vnd Außlegungen Vber das Hohe Lied Salomonis (Basel: Johann Jacob Genath 1635). Eine 2. Aufl. gab F. Christian II. in Zerbst in Auftrag. Diese wurde vom Rektor der Bernburger Lateinschule, Franciscus Gericcius, besorgt. Es ist wahrscheinlich, daß sich die Herzogin im Brief auf die zweite, von ihrem Bruder veranlaßte Ausgabe bezieht: [Holzschnittrahmen] Kurtze vnd Einfältige | Betrachtungen vnd Auß- | legungen | Vber das Hohe | Lied Salomonis. | [Vignette] | Gedruckt zu Zerbst/ | [Linie] | Durch Andream Betzeln/ | Jm Jahr CHristi/ | 1638. S. 380122 K 7.

6 Fn. Eleonora Sophia v. Anhalt-Bernburg (TG 39) brachte am 25.1.1645 die Tochter Maria († 1655) zur Welt. Die Herzogin hatte offensichtlich von der Geburt ihrer Nichte bis zum Zeitpunkt des vorliegenden Schreibens keine Kenntnis. Eine Woche später, am 10.3.1645, sprach Hzn. Eleonora Maria in einem ausführlichen Dankesschreiben ihren Glückwunsch an ihre neugeborene Nichte u. deren Eltern aus, eine Neuigkeit, die ihr mit der ‚notification' F. Christians, datiert 25.1.1645, dem Geburtstag Marias, zuging. Offensichtlich erreichte sie die Nachricht erst sechs Wochen nach der Geburt, am 9.3.1645 (LHA Sa.-Anh./ Dessau: Z 18, Abt. Bernburg A 10 Nr. 46d, Bl. 390r).

450305

Winand von Polhelm an Fürst Ludwig

Beantwortet durch 450317A. — Winand v. Polhelm (FG 405. Der Entnehmende) bestätigt, einen Brief F. Ludwigs und einen verdeutschten Traktat erhalten zu haben. Er habe letzteren sogleich nach Kassel zur Druckerei überschickt. Die vom Buchdrucker geäußerten Bedenken und dessen vorgegebene Gründe, den Druck eines anderen Traktats aufzuschieben, möge F. Ludwig dem beiliegenden Schreiben (Beil. I) entnehmen. Polhelm entschuldigt sich für den Zeitverzug und sein Stillschweigen. Gründe dafür seien die Reiseverpflichtungen und Polhelms Bedenken, F. Ludwig mit Briefen zur Last zu fallen. Er versuche jedoch vor Ort, die Möglichkeiten zu nutzen und das Werk zu befördern, auch möchte er F. Ludwigs Wunsch unbedingt entsprechen. — Weil Polhelm mittlerweile die Ehre zuteil wurde, Mitglied der angesehenen FG zu werden, habe er die Früchte seiner derzeitigen Arbeit überreichen wollen, um seinen guten Willen und pflichtschuldigen Gehorsam zu zeigen. Und da dieses poetische „Kräutlein" noch nie in deutscher Sprache erschienen sei und zugleich einen so guten Duft verbreite, verdiene es, in deutsche Erde eingepflanzt zu werden, zumal es weder Papisterei noch Mönchswesen befördere, sondern vielmehr die wohlriechenden „Lehren und Gesetze der Weisen" verkörpere. Polhelm liege es zwar an einer Verwirklichung seiner Absicht, jedoch unterwerfe er sich wegen seines noch unvollkommenen Stils und Decorum der Kritik erfahrenerer Gesellschafter.

Q   HM Köthen: V S 545, Bl. 459r–460v, 460v leer; eigenh. mit Empfangsvermerk F. Ludwigs auf Bl. 460r; Beilage fehlt. — D: KE, 48; KL III, 212f. — BN: Bürger, 1157 Nr. 2.

A   Fehlt.

Durchleuchtigh Hochgeborner, Gnediger Furst vnd Herr

Ewfg. ahn den Entnemenden[1] gnedigh abgelaßenes schreiben, hatt Er sambt dem dabey vbersendeten verdeutschen Tractätlein[2] in vnderthenigkeit woll empfangen, vnd es alsobaldt nacher Caßell in die Druckerey[3] fortgeschicket, waß nun der buchdrucker bey dießem buchlein noch vor bedencken, vnd bey vorigem vor[a] aufenthalt vorschutzet, Solches haben Ewfg. auß beygehendem schreiben[4] gnedig zuersehen; Vnd gleich wie der Entnemende ahn seinem ort Jhme nach moglichkeit, daß werck zubefordren, ahngelegen sein läßet, vnd Ewfg. gnedigem verlangen ie eher ie lieber, vnderthenigh gern nachgelebt sehen wolte; Alß wollen Ewfg. wegen des verzughs vnd seinem [459v] langen stilschweigen keine vngnadt auf Jhn we[rfen,][b] sondren es vielmehr seinem viellen verreis[en][b] eine zeithero, vnd daß Ewfg. etwan auch mi[t][b] seinem vergeblichen schreiben nicht hatt verdrieß[lich][b] fallen sollen, zuschreiben. Vnderdeßen gele[ich][b] woll, weillen der Entnemende die hohe gna[de][b] empfangen, daß Er in die hochahnsehende vn[d][b] wehrte deutsche Geselschafft, mit aufgenohm[en][b] worden; So hatt Er ein versuch stucklein seiner ie[zt][b] dragenden, wiewoll noch vnzeitiger frucht, nur zu bezeigungh seines gutten Willens vnd pflich[t]schuldigen[b] gehorsambs herbeybringen wollen, v[nd][b] dafern etwan daß kreutlein im deutschen noch n[icht][b] gesehen sein, vnd etwan einen solchen gutten ger[uch][b] von sich geben solte, daß es der muhe werth w[ere,] in ein deutsch[c] erdtreich versetzt zu werden, m[aßen][d] es ihm[e] geringsten nichts nach Papisterey oder a[ber]glaubischem[b] Munchsweßen, sondren nur nach w[oll]richenden[b] Lehren vnd gesetzen der Weißen schmeck[et.][b5] So wolte Er die arbeit, daß es zu seiner zeitig[keit][b] gelangen mogte, darzu ahnwenden; Jedoch mi[t][b] dießem bedingh, daß Er, alß noch vnvolkom[en][b] [460r] in der deutschen reinigkeit vnd zierlichkeit, sich dem vrtheill der alten hocherleuchteten vnd volkomenen Geselschafftren vnderwurffig mach*en* will. Ewfg. wollen Jhme seine freyheit im schreiben gnedigh zu gutt halten, vnd versichert glauben, daß Er, in deme deroselben vnderthenigh die hände kußet, vnd Sie der starcken obhutt Gottes zu allem hochfurstlichem langem wolergehen empfillet, sich iederzeit bedrägt alß,

   Ewfg.
      Vnderthenigh gehorsamer Knecht
         Der Entnemender

Rotenbergh den 5 des Mertzens 1645

Über der Ort- und Datumzeile der eigenh. Präsentationsvermerk F. Ludwigs: Pres. 14. Mertzen 1645

I

450228

Der von Polhelm an Fürst Ludwig überschickte Brief des Adolph Fabritius

Q HM Köthen: V S 546, Bl. 22r–23v [A: 23v], 22v–23r leer; eigenh.; Sig.; kein Empfangsvermerk.

A Dem Wohledlen, Gestrengen, Vndt Vesten, Herrn Winandt von Polhelm, Fürst. Hess. Præsidenten vndt geheimbden Rath zue Rotenberg, meinem hochgeehrten vndt großg. Herrn vndt Freundt, Rotenberg.

WohlEdler Gestrenger vndt Vester, Jnsonders großg. vndt hochgeehrter Herr vnd freundt,

Auf desselben schreyben, hab Jch vnserm Hans Schützen[1], wegen des vorigen Tractats[2] abermahl zuegeredet, welcher aber immer drauf bleibet, es sey kein druckpapier furhanden. Wie es nun stehet; oder ob er sonst vieleicht keine grosse lust mehr hat, dasselbe drucken zue lassen, kan Jch nicht wissen. Jch hab Jhm auch den letzt vberschickten Tractat[2] gezeiget; den er dan so fern angenommen, daß er Jhn durch andere verstendige, wolle durchsehen, vndt Jhr judicium geben lassen, ob er dasselbe auch loß werden könen? Jtzt eben, da Jch in seinem Hause gewesen, vndt umb anwort angehalten, wardt Jhm derselbe von einem Manne alhier, der Jhn vbersehen gehabt, wiedergeschickt mit Vermelden, das buch sey zwar gut: Er zweifele aber dran, obs Jhm hier abgehen werde.

Nichts destoweniger, hat ers bey sich behalten, vndt will es andere mehr sehen lassen. Was nun zueletzt draus werde, vndt ob ers annehmen wirdt, stehet zue erwarten, Vndt will Jch solches dem Herren alßdan mit erster gelegenheit zue wissen thun. Vns vnterdesen allesampt der Göttlichen obacht befehlende, verbleibe Jch

Meines hochgeehrten Herrn
Alzeit dinstwilliger
Adolphus Fabritius*mp.*[3]

Cassel, den 28. Febr. 1645.

T a *Verschreibung, hätte gestrichen gehört. Sinngemäß: was der Drucker an Verzögerungsgründen vorschützt.* — **b** *Buchstabenverlust im Falz, Konjektur in eckigen Klammern.* — **c** *Im Original* deutscherdtreich — **d** *Textverlust im Falz. Konjektur nach KE.* — **e** *Lies:* im

450305 Winand von Polhelm

K 1 Winand v. Polhelm (FG 405. Der Entnehmende), lgfl. hessen-kasselscher Rat u. Hofmeister, vertrat Lgf. Wilhelm V. v. Hessen-Kassel (FG 65) u. später dessen Witwe, die vormundschaftl. Regentin Lgfn. Amalia Elisabeth, auf vielfältigen Gesandtschaften. S. *Conermann III*, 482f. So reiste er u.a. in deren Auftrag im April 1643 nach Schweden. *AOSB* SA VII, 674. Dies erklärt auch seine Inanspruchnahme durch Reisetätigkeit. Vgl. 440809A, 450317, 450317A, 450506, 450507A K 1, 450526 u. 450818 K 4. 1643/44 erhielt Winand v. P. als Gesamtrat der teilsouveränen Lgft. Hessen-Rotenburg u. Hofmeister der lgfl. Brüder Hermann IV. (v. Hessen-Rotenburg. FG 374), Friedrich (v. Hessen-Eschwege. FG 566. 1651) u. Ernst (v. Hessen-Rheinfels-Rotenburg, 1623–1693) für seine langjährigen Dienste die Kalbsburg (b. Fritzlar) zu Lehen. Er starb 1657 kinderlos als Geheimer Rat u. Präsident der Kanzlei u. Rentkammer, welche Ämter er seit 18.9.1644 bekleidete (s. STA Marburg: Urk. 51, Nr. 62), zu Rotenburg a. d. Fulda, wo er seit 1651 das Haus Steinweg 11 in der Neustadt bewohnt hatte. Über seinen Bruder, Tilmann v. P. († 1646), seit mindestens 1636 ständiger Resident der Lgft. Hessen-Kassel in Paris (s. 450818 K 4), hatte er engste Verbindungen zum frz. Hof. S. Familienbriefe der Landgräfin Amalie Elisabeth von Hessen-Kassel. Hg. Erwin Bettenhäuser. Marburg 1994, 90 u. 94f.; Christoph v. Rommel: Geschichte von Hessen, 4. Tl., 4. Abt., 8. Bd. Kassel 1843, S. 434, Anm. 530, S. 641, Anm. 139, u. S. 677, Anm. 165; [Georg] Landau: Beiträge zur hessischen Ortsgeschichte. Die Kalbsburg. In: Zeitschrift des Vereins für hessische Geschichte und Landeskunde 8 (1860), 392–395, hier S. 394; Friedrich Lucae: Das edle Kleinod an der hessischen Landeskrone [Geschichte der Stadt und des Amtes Rotenburg. Rotenburger Chronik Bd. 1: von den Anfängen bis 1700]. Bearb. Hans-Günter Kittelmann. Kassel 1996, 140.

2 Wahrscheinlich das Manuskript *Von des Pabstes gewalt*, eine Verdeutschung des romkritischen Werks des Hugenotten Marc de Vulson sieur de La Collet († 1640): *Traité de la puissance du pape et des libertés de l'Église Gallicane* (Genève 1635). Polhelm hatte dem Kasseler Verleger schon ein anderes Manuskript zugestellt u. angeboten, ein zweites nach der Übersendung ebenfalls dem Verleger zu geben. S. 440809A K 6. Vgl. 450317, 450506 u. 450526. Zu einem Übersetzungsvorhaben Polhelms aus dem Frz. s. 450317A.

3 Da das Buch nicht gedruckt wurde, können wir nur auf den potentiellen Kasseler Verleger (u. Buchbinder) Johann (Hans) Schütz hinweisen. Der Kasseler Drucker Jakob Gentsch, mit dem Schütz damals zusammenarbeitete, wird im vorliegenden Briefwechsel nicht benannt. Vgl. auch 440809A K 4, 450317 K 1, 450317A K 4, 450506 K 1 u. ö. Schütz hatte schon zuvor einen Mangel an Papier behauptet u. war auch auf die unsichere Absatzmöglichkeit aufmerksam gemacht worden. Vgl. Beil. I, 440809A u. 450317A.

4 S. Beil. I. Adolph(us) Fabritius teilte in diesem Brief Winand v. Polhelm mit, daß er aufgrund von Polhelms letztem Schreiben Johann Schütz wegen der Publikation eines zuvor erwähnten Traktats erneut zugeredet habe. Schütz verzögere den Druck jedoch weiter mit dem Argument, es fehle an Papier. Ob dies den Tatsachen entspricht oder ob der Verleger nicht vielmehr das Interesse daran verloren hat, entziehe sich Fabritius' Kenntnis. Er habe Schütz auch den zuletzt überschickten Traktat gezeigt, den dieser unter der Bedingung angenommen habe, daß die Prüfung durch „Verständige" einen guten Absatz des Buchs verheiße. Gerade als Fabritius Schütz aufsuchte u. um Rückmeldung bat, schickte ein Prüfer das Buch dem Verleger mit der Auskunft zurück, der Traktat sei zwar gut, der Absatz in Kassel jedoch unsicher. Dennoch behalte Schütz noch den Traktat, um weitere Meinungen einzuholen. Es stehe in den Sternen, ob Schütz sich zur Publikation entschließen wird. Fabritius werde Polhelm in dieser Sache auf dem laufenden halten. — Zum vorigen Traktat s. 440809A K 3 u. 6.

5 Diese erste Andeutung einer „unzeitigen frucht" Polhelms, welche „nach Lehren vnd gesetzen der Weißen schmeck[et]" — in 450317A folgt der Hinweis auf einen „verdeutsch-

ten Weisen" —, könnte auf die berühmten u. weitverbreiteten orientalischen Fabeln des Bidpai (auch Pilpay) oder arab. Kalīla wa-Dimna (i.e. Kalila u. Dimna) hindeuten, welche in sprachlich-stilistischer Hinsicht als Vorbild besonders für Beamte u. Schreiber am Kalifenhof galten. Der Sammlung liegt eine in Sanskrit abgefaßte, meist aus Tierfabeln bestehende Verhaltenslehre zugrunde, die in der Sekundärliteratur häufig etwas verkürzt als Fürstenspiegel bezeichnet wird. Wahrscheinlich zwischen 200–300 n.Chr. entstanden, ging daraus u.a. der bekannte u. in der Folge häufig rezipierte Text der Weltliteratur „Panchatantra" hervor. Im 6. Jahrhundert wurden die fünf Bücher von Borzōy, einem Leibarzt des sassanidischen Perserkönigs Khusrōy I. Anōshagruwan (571–579) ins Mittelpersische übersetzt u. um weitere Fabeln erweitert (Pahlawi-Version). Dieses heute verschollene Werk war die Grundlage für die um 570 entstandene syr. Übersetzung Qlīlag w-Damnag (so nach den beiden Protagonisten, den Schakalen Karataka u. Damanakah genannt) durch einen Perihodeuten (kirchlichen Visitator) namens Būḏ. Wiederum etwa 150 Jahre später entstand daraus die arab. Übersetzung Kalīla wa-Dimna von Abdallah Ibn Al-Muqaffaʿ (720–756?). Diese arabische Version fand in Orient u. Okzident sowohl in poetischer als auch in prosaischer Form größten Anklang u. entsprechende Verbreitung in fast allen frühneuzeitlichen Literaturen Europas u. des Nahen Ostens: Die bekannteste dt. Übersetzung ist jene Antons v. Pforr: „Das Buch der Beispiele der alten Weisen", entstanden am Anfang der 1470er Jahre, deren lat. Vorlage Johanns v. Capua (1263–1278) „Directorium vitae humanae" bildet. S. das buch der weißhait/ der alten weisen (Ulm 1483). HAB: 19.2 Eth 2°; vgl. auch vier spätere Ausgaben von 1539, 1548, 1565 u. 1583. — F. Ludwigs Interesse läßt sich bereits zu einem früheren Zeitpunkt nachweisen. Er veranstaltete eine ital. Ausgabe des Buchs aus dem 16. Jahrhundert, Agnolo Firenzuolas (d.i. Michelangelo Girolamo Giovannini) Bearbeitung der anon. span. Version „Exemplario contra los engaños y peligros del mundo", die, deutlich als Fürstenspiegel u. politisches Lehrbuch verfaßt, für ein höfisches Publikum bestimmt war u. das erste Buch der Fabelsammlung enthält: DISCORSI | DE GLI | ANIMALI DI AGNOLO | FIRENZUOLA | FIRENTINO | [Holzschn.-Vign.] | M DC XX. 8°, 111 S. (HAB: 30 Eth). S. *IP*, Bl.323v 124 „Discorsi de gl' Animalj. 2 delle bellezze delle donne 3. varij regonamentj. 4. Novelle il tutto di Agnolo Firenzuola 1562" u. *Conermann: Ludwig und Christian II. von Anhalt*, 393f. u. Anm.5. Zeitgleich wird Firenzuolas Version verarbeitet in Pierre de la Rivey: La Philosophie Fabuleuse. Par lequel sous le sens allegoric de plusieurs belles Fables, est monstrée l'envie, malice, & trahison d'aucuns Courtisans. Traictant sous pareilles allegories de l'amitié & choses semblables [Rouen 1620]. HAB: 128.1 Eth. Vgl. auch die im *Kat. Dessau BB* genannten Titel, die aus dem Besitz der Fürsten Christian I. u. Christian II. v. Anhalt-Bernburg (FG 26 bzw. 51) stammen könnten: Nr.11565. Bidpai, - Lokman, - Ali Tschelebi, - Ben Saleh, - Gallard, trad. Les contes et fables Indiennes. II tomes. Mit Kupfern. G. Cavalier. 1 Bd.8°. Ppbd.; Nr.11566. Firenzuola, Agnolo, Consigli degli animali cioè ragionamenti civili (proverbi, istorie etc.). Venetia, 1604, Barezzo Barezzi. 1 Bd.12°. Sammelbd. Wie wir außerdem aus dem Katalog zur Herbstmesse 1641 wissen, wird dort unter den Büchern, „welche in Leipzigscher HerbstMesse 1641. außgangen/ und nicht nach Franckfurt am Meyn kommen seyn", u.a. die Firenzuola-Ausgabe von 1620 aufgeführt: „[Michelangelo Girolamo Giovannini:] Discorsi de Gli Animali di Agnolo Firenzuola Firentino, ibid. [1620] in 8." S.410313 K 3. — Ob die o.g. dt. Übersetzung Anton v. Pforrs in den 1640er Jahren bereits in Vergessenheit geraten war, ist schwer auszumachen. In F. Ludwigs Bibliothek fehlte sie jedenfalls. Da wir voraussetzen, daß diese Arbeit Polhelm nicht bekannt war — er spricht im Brief davon, daß „daß kreutlein im deutschen noch n[icht] gesehen" worden sei — u. da Polhelms Vorlage ein frz. Buch war (s. 450317A) u. nicht der ebenfalls auf den Fabeln des Bidpai beruhende italienische Köthener

Firenzuola-Druck von 1620 — der 1641 offensichtlich noch einmal angeboten wurde —, müßte Polhelm entweder das Buch von Pierre de la Rivey oder das zeitnähere des Gilbert Gaulmin benutzt haben: Livre des Lumières ou la conduite de Roys. Composé Par Le Sage Pilpay (Paris: Piget 1644). — Ergänzend mag hinzugefügt werden, daß es eine weitere ital. Übersetzung von Francesco Doni aus dem 16. Jahrhundert gibt: La Moral Filosofia del Doni 1552 (HAB: 22 Eth.). Deutlich volksnäher in Sprache u. Stil, wurde sie 1570 von Sir Thomas North ins Englische übersetzt. — Eine gute Einführung bietet der Artikel „Kalila und Dimna" in *Kindlers Neues Literatur Lexikon* VIII (2009), 587–594. S. auch Beispiele der alten Weisen Des Johann von Capua. Übersetzung der hebräischen Bearbeitung des indischen Pañcatantra ins Lateinische. Hg. u. übers. v. Friedmar Geissler. Berlin 1960; Frank Piontek: Ein Fürst und sein Buch. Beiträge zur Interpretation des Buchs der Beispiele. Göppingen 1997; Johannes Niehoff-Panagiotidis: Übersetzung und Rezeption. Die byzantinisch-neugriechischen und spanischen Adaptionen von Kalīla wa-Dimna. Wiesbaden 2003; Sir Thomas North: The Moral Philosophy of Doni popularly known as the Fables of Bidpai. (A Collection of Sanskrit, Persian, and Arabic Fables) 1570. Ed. Donald Beecher et al. Ottawa, Canada 2003; Sabine Obermaier: Das Fabelbuch als Rahmenerzählung. Intertextualität und Intratextualität als Wege zur Interpretation des *Buchs der Beispiele der alten Weisen* Antons von Pforr. Heidelberg 2004 (Beih. zum Euphorion; 48); Tierisch moralisch. Die Welt der Fabel in Orient und Okzident. Begleitschrift zur Sonderausstellung des Landesmuseums Oldenburg Natur und Mensch Oldenburg. Oldenburg 2009; Gerald Jasbar: Faszination Holzschnitt. Illustrierte Wiegendrucke aus dem Tresor der Stadtbibliothek Ulm. Ulm 2013. S. auch 441205 K 5 u. 450317A.

K I 1 S. K 3.
2 Wahrscheinlich die aus sechs Büchern bestehende Übersetzung eines frz. Werks des Marc de Vulson sieur de La Collet: *Von des Pabstes gewalt* oder ein Teil desselben. S. 440809A K 6.
3 Adolph Fabritius (1604–1676), ref. Hofprediger der Lgfn. Juliana v. Hessen-Kassel (PA, † 1643), 2. Gattin Lgf. Moritz' v. Hessen-Kassel (FG 80), sowie u. a. Hofmeister des u. g. Sohnes Ernst. *ADB* VI, 284–286. S. auch 370421 K 1. Er verfaßte auch die LP auf Lgfn. Juliana: „Christliche Leich- und Trostpredigt" (Kassel 1643), in der Fabritius auf dem Titelblatt als „Fraw Wittiben/ gewesenen Hoffprediger" genannt wird. HAB: Gm 2238; Da 587 (4). S. Margret Lemberg: Juliane Landgräfin zu Hessen (1581–1643). Eine Kasseler und Rotenburger Fürstin aus dem Hause Nassau-Dillenburg in ihrer Zeit. Darmstadt u. Marburg 1994; Susan C. Karant-Nunn: The Reformation of Feeling. Shaping the Religious Emotions in Early Modern Germany. Oxford 2010, 105. Fabritius ist auch Verfasser der Schrift *Zwölf Predigten wieder die böse Welt* (Cassel 1646, wieder aufgelegt 1672; VD17 39:135062V), die dem 1650 zum Katholizismus konvertierten Sohn Moritz', Lgf. Ernst v. Hessen-Rheinfels-Rotenburg (1623–1693), gewidmet war. Alexander Ritter: Landgraf Ernst von Hessen-Rheinfels (1623–1693). Konversion und Irenik als politische Faktoren. In: Irenik und Antikonfessionalismus im 17. und 18. Jahrhundert. Hg. Harm Klueting. Hildesheim u. a. 2003, 117–140.

450308

Carl Gustav von Hille an Fürst Ludwig

Antwort auf 450221. — Carl Gustav v. Hille (FG 302. Der Unverdrossene) erklärt, F. Ludwigs (Der Nährende) Brief einschließlich der Beilagen erhalten und sowohl den Brief an Hz. Christian Ludwig v. Braunschweig-Calenberg (FG 372. Der Reinherzige) über Bodo v. Hodenberg (FG 373. Der Enthärtende) als auch das Schreiben an Hz. August d. J. v. Braunschweig-Wolfenbüttel (FG 227. Der Befreiende) mit der Bitte um Überweisung des versprochenen Verlagsbeitrags (zum *GB 1646*) zugestellt zu haben. Vom Reinherzigen sei noch keine Rückmeldung gekommen, vom Befreienden jedoch eine gnädige Zusage. Hille drückt seine Hoffnung aus, daß sich diese Mitglieder am Ende ihrem Versprechen gemäß verhalten würden. An seinem, Hilles, Bemühen solle es nicht liegen, doch stellten sich die widrigen Zeiten der Abwicklung dieser Angelegenheit entgegen. Er vernehme mit Freude, daß der Dankesbrief der Befreienden (Hzn. Sophia Elisabeth v. Braunschweig-Wolfenbüttel. AL 1629. TG 42b) für das ihr zugegangene Buch F. Ludwig erreicht habe, welches er ihr pflichtschuldig und umgehend zugestellt hätte. — Eigentlich hätte Justus Georg Schottelius (FG 397. Der Suchende) seine *Teutsche Vers- oder ReimKunst* dem Nehrenden (vor Drucklegung) zur Durchsicht zusenden sollen, doch habe er solche Kühnheit nicht aufgebracht. Nun seien nur noch wenige Exemplare übrig, doch werde Schottelius bei der (geplanten) Neuauflage sicher auf das Anerbieten F. Ludwigs zurückkommen.

Q   HM Köthen: V S 545, Bl. 31r–32v [A: 32v], 31v u. 32r leer; eigenh.; rotes Lacksiegel. — *D: KE*, 203; *KL* III, 223 f.; *Bircher: Merian*, 696 (unvollst.). — *BN: Bürger*, 722 Nr. 7.

A   Dem Durchleuchtigen hochgebornen Fürsten und herrn, Herrn Ludwig Fürsten zu Anhalt Grafen zu Ascanien, Herrn zu Bernburg und Zerbst, meinen gnedigen Fürsten und herrn underthenig. Cöten *etc*.
Darunter eigenh. Empfangsvermerk F. Ludwigs: ps. 15. Martij, 1645

HöchstgeEhrter H. Nehrender

deroselben gnedigeß schreiben habe[a] neben den beilagen auch Hand.[1] erhalten, auch so bald nicht allein daß schreiben an den Reinhertzigen[2] durch deß Enthärtenden[3] händen uberliefern lassen, sondern auch dem h. befreyenden dem fl. versprechen nach umb die uberschickung gehorsambst ersuchet. Von dem H. Reinhertzigen habe ich noch keine gn. antwort erhalten; Von dem H. Befreyenden[4] die gn. Vertröstung[5], wil hoffen es werden solche hohe Gelieder sich endlichen dem vilfältigen versprechen gemäß verhalten. An meiner schüldigen und hochstbeflissen anregung soll eß nicht ermangeln. Nur allein die gegenwertige unzeitten, verrucken daß gutte vorhaben. Verneme gerne daß die Befreyende mit dem g. dancksagungß schreiben wegen des ubersendeten Buchß eingekommen.[6] Dan ich eß an meinem ort an fleisiger und schuldiger bestellung nicht ermangeln lassen.

[b]Deß suchenden deutsche Reimekunst[7] hette billig dem höchstgeEhrten Nehrenden zum ubersehen, in Gehorsamb sollen zugesand werden. Ich vermercke

aber, daß Er sich einer solchen Kühnheit nicht unternemen dürfen. Weil aber Wenige stuck mehr ubrig und solcheß buch wol möchte werden aufgeleget werden⁸, alß wird er die gnedige anbiettung woll wissen in achtzunemen. und verbleibet nebenst emfehlung Gottlicher obhutt
 Meines hochstgeEhrten Nerender gehorsamer Knecht der
  Unverdrossene. *etc.*

Wolfenbüttel d. 8th. MertzMonatß 1645

T a *Folgt* <ich> — **b** *Davor* <Waß>

K 1 Abgekürzt für Handlung/ Handhabung. S. *DW* IV.2, 404. Carl Gustav v. Hille (FG 302. Der Unverdrossene) akzeptiert damit wohl F. Ludwigs (Der Nährende) in 450221 formulierte u. dringliche Bitte, ihn bei der Eintreibung der ausstehenden Gelder für das *GB 1646* zu unterstützen u. unterrichtet ihn sogleich über den derzeitigen Stand.
 2 Hz. Christian Ludwig v. Braunschweig-Calenberg (FG 372. Der Reinherzige). S. 450221. Dort bittet F. Ludwig Hille, dem Herzog einen beigelegten Mahnbrief (wie auch einen weiteren an Hz. August d. J. v. Braunschweig-Wolfenbüttel [FG 227. Der Befreiende]) wegen des Verlagsbeitrags zum *GB 1646* zuzusenden. Zu den fl. Verlagsbeiträgen s. Anm. 4 u. 450126 K 4. Zum Verlag des *GB 1646* s. 440130 K 3.
 3 Bodo v. Hodenberg (FG 373. Der Enthärtende), Hofmarschall u. Geheimer Rat in Diensten Hz. Christian Ludwigs.
 4 Hz. Augusts vorlängst zugesagter Beitrag über 200 Reichstaler zum *GB 1646* stand damals, genau wie jener Hz. Christian Ludwigs, noch aus. Zu den Verlagsbeiträgen s. Anm. 2 u. 450126 K 4.
 5 Hier im heute ungebräuchlichen Sinne von Versprechen. *DW* XII.1, 2008f. Vgl. 450721, wo sich F. Ludwig auf die Jahre zuvor gegebene u. durch Hille übermittelte „vertröstung" Hz. Augusts bezieht, das *GB 1646* zu unterstützen. S. auch zur Zahlungsverzögerung Hz. Christian Ludwigs in gleicher Sache 450923 K 1.
 6 Es handelt sich vermutlich um den letzten Band der Predigten *Sachse: Einhelligkeit* III, der wohl besonders von Hzn. Sophia Elisabeth v. Braunschweig-Wolfenbüttel (AL 1629. TG 42b) erwartet worden war. Vgl. auch bereits 450126 K 3. Zu *Sachse: Einhelligkeit* III u. dem Lieferungsverzug s. 441205 K 3.
 7 *Schottelius: Teutsche Vers- oder ReimKunst (1645)*, zu Jahresbeginn 1645 erschienen. Vgl. 440900 K 2.
 8 Die textlich verbesserte Neuauflage *Schottelius: Teutsche Vers- oder ReimKunst (1656)* erscheint erst elf Jahre später.

450308A

Philipp von Zesen an Jesaias Rompler von Löwenhalt

Philipp v. Zesen (FG 521. 1648; DG 1. Der Färtige) erinnert daran, Jesaias Rompler v. Löwenhalt (AGT; DG 16. 1645) getroffen und seine deutsche Gesinnung dabei kennengelernt zu haben. Er habe Romplers Aufnahme in die DG deren Mitgliedern mit Erfolg vorgeschlagen. Georg Philipp Harsdörffer (FG 368. Der Spielende) habe für Rompler einen DG-Namen und ein DG-Sinnbild vorgeschlagen, welches die DG akzeptiert habe. Über die DG werde er wohl von Harsdörffer schon hinreichend unterrichtet worden sein. — Zesen bittet Rompler, er möge ihm sein Urteil über die von ihnen diskutierte Frage schikken, ob die Stammwörter grundsätzlich und ausnahmslos in den einsilbigen Wörtern zu finden seien. Zesen glaubt, daß nur ¼ aller Einsilber Stammwörter seien und daß man die Stammwörter vielmehr in den Formen des Imperfekts („unfolkommen-vergangene zeit") und Perfekts („folkommen-vergangene" Zeit) wie bei den Hebräern zu suchen habe. Man habe mit der Beschränkung auf eingliedrige Wörter die dt. Sprache hart und spröde gemacht, anstatt lieblich klingend. Zesen erklärt schließlich seine Absicht, ein „Stam- und Wurzel-buch" (Wörterbuch nach Stammwörtern) herauszubringen.

Q *Bellin: Sendeschreiben (1647)*, Nr. 13, Bl. [G vj]v – [G viij]v. HAB: 437.16 Quod. — *D:* Max Gebhardt: Untersuchungen zur Biographie Philipp Zesens. Berlin 1888, 36 (Auszug); Jan Hendrik Scholte: Wahrmund von der Tannen. In: Neophilologus 21 (1936), 265–287, hier 285 (Auszug); ders.: Philipp von Zesen in Frankrijk. In: Neophilologus 28 (1943), 197–203, hier 202 (Auszug). — *BN*: Bürger, 1469 Nr. 34 u. 35; Estermann, 1294 Nr. 9.

A *Fehlt.*

Mein Her/
NAchdem ich die ehre gehabt habe/ denselben nicht alein zusähen/ sondern auch seiner deutsch-gesinneten-träu-eifrigen gunst-gewogenheit zu genüßen/ so bin ich veruhrsachet ([Gvij]r) worden/ seine beliebte selbschaft[1] unserer hochlöblichen deutsch-gesinneten Genossenschaft fohrzu schlagen/ damit sie ihn/ als einen zu ihrem zwekk' und fohrhaben sehr erbaulichen man/ in ihre zunft mit ein zu nähmen geruhen wolle. Welches dan den mitgenossen alsobald und insgesamt beliebet hat; Und ist uns auch derselbe/ kurz nach solchem schlusse/ von dem Spielenden nicht allein aufgetragen/ sondern auch zugleich mit einem nahmen und Sin-bilde (bei welchem es die löbl. deutschgesinnete Genossenschaft verbleiben lässet/ und meines Hern guhtbefünden darüber erwartet) bemärket worden.[2] Wie es aber mit unserer Deutschges. Genossenschaft bewant sey/ solches würd er ohne zweifel von dem Spielenden schohn verstanden haben.

Sonsten/ weil unter uns die frage waltet/ ob die eingliedrigen wörter der deutschen sprache fohr stam- und wurzel-wörter ie und alwege zu halten sein? So wolt' ich wol wündschen/ daß ich meines Hern uhrteil von solcher frage hören möchte. Jch/ nach meinem wenigen verstande/ bin der gäntzlichen meinung/ daß kaum der eingliedrigen wörter vierdes theil unter ob gemälte wurzeln der deutschen sprache zu rechnen sei/ und daß man nicht zuehrst in den eingliedrigen/ sondern entweder in den wörtern/ welche die unfolkommen-vergangene zeit/ oder in denen/ so die folkommen-vergan-([Gvij]v)gene/ bedeuten/ und aus-trükken (nach ahrt der Ebreer) den uhrsprung suchen sol.[3] Dan nimmermehr können **gäld** und **gold**/ wie auch **bärg** und **burg** (ob sie gleich eingliederich) stam- und wurzel-wörter sein/ in dem ich nicht weis/ was sie eigendlich und in ihrer ehrsten uhrsprünglichen bedeutung heissen/ wan ich sie nicht aus dem zeitworte und der wurzel **galt**/ d. **gälten**/ und **barg** d. **bärgen** erforsche. Man sihet alhier/ wie die grosse Zeuge-mutter aller dinge spielet und wie das un- oder halb-folkommene ärz-werk/ **gäld**/ (dadurch man eigendlich das silber/ welches beides auch die Franzosen argent, d. i. argentum, nännen/ verstehet) aus dem worte der folkommen-vergangenen zeit **gegolten**/ (wie **burg** von **verborgen**/ **sün** von **gesonnen**/ **hülfe** von **geholfen**/ **hübsch** von **erhoben**) entsprungen sei. Wie will man/ ferner/ **bärg**/ **gäld**/ **wält**/ **rächt**/ **wüz**/ **schrük**/ **säch** oder **sägh**/ dens aratri, von **sagen** oder **sägen** fohr einfältige und stam-wörter halten/ da ihr selb-lauter nicht einfältig/ noch ein stam-buchstab ist? Dieser irthum/ daß man nämlich bisher vermeinet hat/ es müste die gantze deutsche sprache aus eingliedrigen wörtern herstammen/ und ie mehr eingliedrige wörter (wie ([Gviij]r) Bekanus[4] fohrgegäben hat) eine sprache hätte/ ie älter sie wäre/ hat veruhrsachet/ daß ein ieder die armen wörter am ende so verstümmelt/ vermuzt/ und die sprache dadurch/ wider den gemeinen gebrauch und aus-spruch/ so hart-knallend gemacht hat/ daß einem die ohren darüber weh-tuhn/ wan man es nuhr läsen höret; Da man sich doch vielmehr befleissigen solte/ selbige so lieblich und wohl-klüngend zu machen/ als es sich immer leiden wil/ nachdem sie schon fohrhin und an sich selbst so hart und knallend lauten/ daß man sie nicht noch mehr verhärten darf.[5] Mehr will ich hiervon nicht schreiben/ weil es vernunftmäßig/ und meinem Hern ohne dis bekannt ist/ daß die unfolkommene zeit eher als die folkommene/ und alle beide widerüm eher sein/ als die gegen-wärtige/ und zu-künftige; ja daß die sachen und dinge aller ehrst in und nicht fohr der zeit/ viel weniger die wörter/ welche die sachen bedeuten/ entsprungen sein. Wan mier der Her sein guht-dünken hierüber zuschreiben wollte[6]/ so würd' er mich in wahrheit sehr verpflichten/ und er traue mier/ daß ich diesen knoten fast keinem mänschen so deutlich gelöset hab' als ihm; dan hierauf beruhet der ganze grund meiner Schreib-richtigkeit/ meines Stam- und Wurzel-buches[7]/ welches ich künftig/ so nuhr Got gesund- und gelägenheit darzu verleihen würd/ heraus gäben wärde. — — — —

([Gviij]v) Hiermit befähl ich ihn der götlichen obacht/ mich aber in seine fernere gunst/ und verbleibe/

mein Her/
sein alzeit-träu-und-geflissener knecht
so lang' ich läb' und heisse
Der Färtige

Utrecht den 8. Tag des merzens/ im 1645. Jahre.

K Jesaias Rompler v. Löwenhalt (auch Rumpler, 1605–1676. AGT; DG 16), 1626 Studium in Altdorf, 1628 Magister in Tübingen, im selben Jahr Aufnahme eines Jurastudiums in Straßburg, das er 1630 abbrach. 1633 Gründungsmitglied der AGT. Seine Bestallung als Erzieher führte Rompler in den Jahren 1642 bis 1644 mehrfach nach Frankreich, wo er 1643 in Paris Philipp v. Zesen (FG 521. 1648; DG 1. Der Färtige) kennenlernte, den er zur Gründung der DG ermunterte. Zu Rompler s. 440724 K 4; vgl. Jan Hendrik Scholte:

Zesens „Adriatische Rosemund". In: Dt. Vierteljahresschrift f. Literaturwissenschaft u. Geistesgeschichte 23 (1949), 288–305, hier S. 300.

1 In seinem *Ibrahim Bassa* (1645, s. 441201) hatte Philipp v. Zesen erstmals „Person" mit „Selbstand" übersetzt. Das hier verwendete „selbschaft" ist als Variante dieser Eindeutschung zu verstehen. Vgl. Hugo Harbrecht: Philipp von Zesen als Sprachreiniger. Karlsruhe 1912, 17 u. 22; ders.: Verzeichnis der von Zesen verdeutschten Lehn- oder Fremdwörter. In: Zeitschrift. f. deutsche Wortforschung 14 (1912), 71–78, hier 78.

2 Rompler wurde von Georg Philipp Harsdörffer (FG 368) in 441223 zur Aufnahme in die DG vorgeschlagen u. nach Zesens eigenem Mitgliederverzeichnis am 4. 2. 1645 als Mitglied Nr. 16 („der Freie") aufgenommen, wie ihm im vorliegenden Brief bestätigt wird. S. Zesen: Hochdeutsches Helikonisches Rosentahl (1669), in *Zesen SW* XII, 178–310, hier 244 u. die Anhänge S. 317, 424 u. 454; *Dissel*, 59. Trotz seiner jüngsthin erfolgten Aufnahme spricht ihn Zesen noch nicht mit seinem Gesellschaftsnamen „Der Freie" an, da Rompler diesem u. seiner Imprese erst noch zustimmen sollte.

3 Zesen widersprach der Auffassung Justus Georg Schottelius' (FG 397) u. Harsdörffers, wonach die dt. Stammwörter stets einsilbig seien, der Verben nach dem einsilbigen Imperativ Singular, der Nomen nach den einsilbigen Primitiva. Harsdörffer, der den vorliegenden Brief u. Zesens Argumentation kannte u. in 450410 darauf Bezug nahm, bekräftigte seine Auffassung sehr bestimmt im genannten Brief. Er widersprach dort auch Zesens bevorzugter Stammwort-Ermittlung nach den Vergangenheitsstufen der Verben, worin Zesen den hebr. Stammformen zu folgen beanspruchte. S. 450410 u. dort die Kommentare K 3, 4 u. 11. Vgl. zur Stammworttheorie auch 451219 K 4.

4 Jan Gorp van der Beken (Ioannes Goropius Becanus, 1519–1572), Arzt u. Linguist in Löwen, Antwerpen u. Lüttich, umstritten wegen seiner gewagten Etymologien u. seiner Theorie einer „cimbrischen" Ursprungssprache. Seiner Theorie nach war Nl. die unmittelbar auf die adamit. Ursprungssprache zurückgehende älteste u. einfachste Sprache, aus kurzen Wörtern bestehend, die sich in komplexeren Lexemen anderer Sprachen wiederfinden ließen. Scharfe Gegner fand Gorp in Justus Lipsius u. Joseph Justus Scaliger. Seine unsystematische Methode sollte Gottfried Wilhelm Leibniz in seinen *Nouveaux Essais* (1765) als „goropiser" verspotten. Vgl. *Lexicon Grammaticorum* I, 553 f.; 400528 K II 7 u. 450410 K 3 u. 16. Positive Bezüge auf Gorp in *Schottelius: Sprachkunst (1641)*, 178, 204 u. ö.

5 Zesen tritt damit wohl auch der Kritik auswärtiger Humanisten an der groben, barbarischen Lautung des Deutschen entgegen. Tatsächlich betont dieses etwa die Wortgrenzen viel stärker als die verschleifenden romanischen Sprachen, etwa durch den sog. Knacklaut (Glottiseinatz) vor vokalischem Silben- u. Wortanlaut. Auch der germanische bzw. deutsche „Stammsilbendruckakzent" ist als Faktor solcher ungefälligen Sprachklang-Wahrnehmung zu nennen. Vgl. *Herz: Rechtschreibdebatte*, S. 99 Anm. 94. Vgl. auch Zesens Brief an Hans Christoph von Liebenau (DG 3. Der Ämsige, aufgenommen am 3. 5. 1643): Wegen des Wohlklangs bzw. des Übellauts sei auf Polyflexion der attributiven Adjektive zu verzichten: „der treflicher man", „das schönes glaß" usw. sollten zwar „billich also heissen", denn das Adjektiv habe dem Substantiv zu folgen, aber des Wohlklangs wegen, „damit die rede nicht alzu knarricht und hart klünge", lasse man es sein. Dasselbe gelte für den Nom. Plural der Substantive auf –er oder der Dimunitive auf –ein: die meister, nicht die meistere; die mägdlein, nicht die mägdleine usw. *Bellin: Sendeschriben (1647)*, Nr. 12, Bl. Gijr – [Gvj]v, hier Bl. Giiij r f.

6 Ein Antwortschreiben Romplers an Zesen ist nicht bekannt.

7 Zesen trug sich in dieser Zeit mit der Absicht, ein nach Stammwörtern geordnetes dt. Wörterbuch oder Buch der Wortstämme zu veröffentlichen, u. kündigte dieses am Ende

nicht verwirklichte Vorhaben mehrfach an. So verwies er in einem undatierten, vielleicht ins Jahr 1644 zu datierenden Schreiben an Adolph Rosel (DG 6. Der Bemühete, aufgenommen am 6.7.1644) auf sein „Stam-buch", das „wohl eines mänschen ganzes leben" erfordere. *Bellin: Sendeschreiben (1647)*, Nr. 10, Bl. [Dviij] v – G[i] v, hier Bl. E [i] r. Johann Bellin (DG 38. Der Willige, aufgenommen am 8.10.1646) wiederum verlangte es in einem Brief frühestens vom Oktober 1646, Zesens für nächstkünftig angekündigtes „Stambuch" zu sehen zu bekommen. *Bellin: Sendeschreiben (1647)*, Nr. 7, C ij v – C iij v. Dieses Vorhaben bekräftigte Zesen in seinem Antwortbrief an Bellin. *Bellin: Sendschreiben (1647)*, Nr. 8, Bl. [Ciiij] r – [D v] v, hier Bl. D[i] r. Zur beginnenden Wörterbucharbeit der FG vgl. 451219 K 8.

450317

Fürst Ludwig an Landgraf Hermann IV. von Hessen-Rotenburg

F. Ludwig (Der Nährende) bedankt sich für den Antwortbrief Lgf. Hermanns IV. v. Hessen-Rotenburg (FG 372) vom 3. März auf sein aus Weimar versandtes Schreiben. Er habe den Brief des Landgrafen inzwischen erwidert und ihm den Rest eines ins Deutsche übersetzten Büchleins (*Von des Pabstes gewalt*) beigefügt. — Vom *GB 1646* werde jedes Mitglied, das 100 Rth. zum Verlag beitrage, zwölf Exemplare mit 400 Kupferstichen erhalten; dementsprechend erhalte es bei einem Betrag von 50 Rth. sechs Stück. Sobald sich der Landgraf zu einer bestimmten Summe entschlossen habe, solle ihm mitgeteilt werden, wohin das Geld übermittelt werden müsse. Teurer würde es allemal, wenn die Wappen in das *GB 1646* groß hineingemalt werden würden – im Kleinformat paßten sie nicht zu den Impresen. — F. Ludwig beantwortet die vom Landgrafen (im letzten Brief) gestellte Frage nach seinen Wünschen mit einer Bitte um (Theophilus) Neubergers Predigten und dessen Gebetbuch. Er schlägt dem Landgrafen auch einen Tausch von Köthener Werken gegen Kasseler Bücher vor. Beigelegt habe er, Ludwig, ein Köthener Verzeichnis samt Angabe des Preises. Wenn nun der Kasseler Drucker eine gleichartige Liste seiner Werke nach Köthen sende, so könnte man auf der Grundlage der Berechnung den Austausch vornehmen. F. Ludwig regt bei Lgf. Hermann IV. an, diese Aufgabe dem Entnehmenden (Winand v. Polhelm; FG 405) zu übertragen. Ansonsten habe sich der Drucker als sehr unzuverlässig erwiesen; er werde, falls er sich nicht bessere, keine Druckaufträge aus Köthen mehr erhalten. — F. Ludwig sendet Lgf. Hermann eine gedruckte Liste der ersten 417 Mitglieder der FG, die handschriftlich mit den Namen der Neuaufgenommenen ergänzt wurde.

Q HM Köthen: V S 545, Bl. 464rv, 464v leer (*Foliierung irrig gebessert aus richtig* 454); eigenh. Konzept. — Dort auch F. Ludwigs Konzept 450506.

A *Fehlt.*

Hochg. f. fr vielg. h. vetter und schwager, El antwort vom 3. dieses auf mein schreiben von Weimar ist mir wol uberbracht worden, in dessen habe ich EL. andtwort von hinnen auch geschrieben, und das uberige von dem verdeutschten buchlein nachgeschickt.[1]

Anlangende das geselschaftbuch ist der anschlag so gemacht, das wer hundert Reichsthaler einleget der krieget zwölf geselschaftbucher von vierhundert kupfergemählden iedes wieder, also von funtzig Rth. sechs stucker,² stehet also zu El. gefallen wie viel sie wollen einlegen, und wan sie die summa benennet, muß El. zugeschrieben werden, wohin sie das geld ubermachen konnen. Mit den wappen wolte es kostbarer werden, sollen sie gros sein, und klein schicken sie sich in die gemählde nicht.³

Es^a haben El. auch in ihrem schreiben gedacht, sie möchten gerne wissen worin sie mir etwa wieder konnen zu willen sein, so habe ich El. wollen vorschlagen, ob sie mir herren Neubergers predigten und^b gebetbuch⁴ konten zu wege bringen, und^c ob man etwa gedruckte^d bucher gegen andere^e von hinnen aus vertauschen könte, das verzeichnus der hießigen mit ihrem taxe habe El. hierbey zu empfahen, wan nun der drucker zu Caßel auch der^d seinigen gedrucktes verzeichnus mit dem taxe herschickete, so konte man der gegeneinander auslosen und austauschen nach dem taxe was ieder haben wolte,⁵ Es^f stehet zu El. [ge]fallen^g ob sie die[s]es^g mit dem Ent[n]emenden^g auch re[den]^h und ihm darinnen [vo]lmachten^g [geben] wollen[.]⁶ Sonsten hat sich ietzunder^i der drucker^j⁷ dismals^d zu verenderlich bezeiget, das wan er sich nicht darinnen seinem ersten^d versprechen nach bessert⁸, er von hinnen wie sonst wol geschehen were, nichts mehr zu drukken uberschicket^d bekommen wird.

Die Taufnamen aller geselschafter bis^k auf diese zeit finden sie theils gedruckt, theils abgeschrieben hiebey,⁹ die El. wol rähtlich werden wißen in acht zu nehmen, Meine gemahl und ich entbieten El. und dero gemahlin unsern dienst und grus, und ich verbleibe

EL.

Cöthen den 17 Mertzen 1645.

T a *Eingefügt bis* bekommen wird — **b** *Eingefügt bis* und gebetbuch — **c** *Folgt* <etwa> — **d** *Eingefügt.* — **e** *Eingefügt für* <bucher> — **f** *Am Rand ergänzt bis* hat sich — **g** *Buchstabenverlust im Falz. Konjektur in eckigen Klammern.* — **h** *Buchstabenverlust im Falz. Konjektur in eckigen Klammern. Lies* bereden — **i** *Folgt* <aber hat> — **j** *Folgt* <sich> — **k** bis auf diese zeit *am Rand ergänzt.*

K 1 Es handelte sich höchstwahrscheinlich um eine von F. Ludwig (Der Nährende) an Lgf. Hermann IV. v. Hessen-Rotenburg (FG 372) zwischen dem 3.3. u. 17.3.1645 abgeschickte Briefsendung. Ihr lag der Rest des Manuskripts *Von des Pabstes gewalt* bei, einer Verdeutschung eines Werks von Marc de Vulson sieur de La Collet: *De la puissance du pape et des libertés de l'Église Gallicane* (Genève 1635). S. 440809A K 6 u. 450305. Weder der Brief vom 3.3. noch die erwähnte Briefsendung sind auf uns gekommen.

2 Hier wird nicht nur erstmals die Anzahl der dem jeweiligen Verlagsteilhaber am *GB 1646* zustehenden Stückzahl thematisiert, die je 100 Reichstaler bei zwölf Exemplaren liegen soll, sondern auch das im Zusammenhang mit der Finanzierung des *GB 1646* bisher unbekannte u. hier zutage tretende Interesse Lgf. Hermanns IV. v. Hessen-Rotenburg. Dieser zog offensichtlich die finanzielle Unterstützung des Drucks des *GB 1646* in Betracht. Die Briefe greifen dieses Begehren im Berichtszeitraum jedoch nicht mehr auf.

Bereits in 400605 I wurde ein detaillierter Kostenvoranschlag von F. Ludwig aufgesetzt, der sich auf insgesamt 1600 Reichstaler bei einer Auflage von 500 Exemplaren belief. In 470223 schließlich wird die Liste mit den Verlagsbeiträgern u. der Anzahl der übermittelten Exemplare offengelegt. Lgf. Hermann IV. findet auch hier keine Erwähnung, scheint sich also aus diesem Verlagsgeschäft zurückgezogen zu haben. Es sind die bisher in Rede stehenden Gesellschaftsmitglieder: F. Ludwig mit 156 Exemplaren, Hz. August d.J. v. Braunschweig-Wolfenbüttel (FG 227) mit 48, Hz. Friedrich III. v. Schleswig-Holstein-Gottorf (FG 388) mit 48, Hz. Christian Ludwig v. Braunschweig-Calenberg (FG 372) mit 24, Anthon v. Wietersheim (FG 273) mit ebenfalls 24 Stück. Peter Knaudt erhält fünf Exemplare als Geschenk. Zu fl. Verlagsbeiträgen s. 450126 K 4. Zum *GB 1646* allgem. s. 440130 K 3.

3 Wappenvorlagen wurden von F. Ludwig benötigt u. eingezogen, um sie detailgenau in das *GB Kö.* einzumalen u. sie – wie die Impresen – auf einen Gobelin (im Schloßsaal zu Köthen) zu sticken. S. *Conermann: Nachlaßinventar* u. 410323 K 8. Ein Plan, die Wappen für das *GB 1646* stechen oder darin einmalen zu lassen, ist sonst unbekannt. In den Verhandlungen mit Merian spielen Kupferstiche der Wappen keine Rolle. F. Ludwig scheint hier einen Vorschlag Lgf. Hermanns IV., den er vielleicht in seinem verlorenen Brief vom 3.3.1645 vorgebracht hatte, abzuwehren.

4 Theophilus Neuberger (1593–1656), reformierter Hofprediger in Heidelberg, Güstrow u. Kassel u. schließlich Superintendent am Hof Lgf. Wilhelms V. v. Hessen-Kassel (FG 65). Wahrscheinlich handelt es sich um die folgenden Werke des Predigers: Erbäwliche Außlegung der Sontäglichen Evangelien durchs Jahr. T. I–II. Kassel: Johann Schütz 1636; Newes BettBuch ... Nun zum fünfften mahl mit fleiß corrigirt und verbessert. Kassel: Johann Schütz u. Jacob Gentzsch (Gentsch) 1644. S. zur Zusammenarbeit der beiden auch 440809A K 4. Beide Werke fehlten in F. Ludwigs nachgelassener Bibliothek, was möglicherweise darauf hinweist, daß der Briefempfänger Lgf. Hermann IV. die Werke nicht besorgen mochte oder konnte. Im Bibliotheksbestand läßt sich jedoch ein älteres Werk Neubergers nachweisen. *IP*, Bl. 283v: „Nr. 207 Trostbüchlein *Theophili* Neubergers. Hannov 1624". Eine Liste der tauschbaren Köthener Drucke liegt dem Brief nicht mehr bei.

5 Dieser Versuch F. Ludwigs, Köthener Drucke gegen andere (Kasseler) Bücher zu tauschen, schlug fehl. S. 450507A.

6 Hier schlägt F. Ludwig vor, daß der Bücheraustausch von Winand v. Polhelm (FG 405. Der Entnehmende) verantwortet u. durchgeführt werden könnte. Folgt man dem (in Anm. 5 genannten) Brief 450507A verzichtete Lgf. Hermann darauf, Polhelm mit dieser Aufgabe zu betrauen, sondern kümmerte sich selbst, wenn auch erfolglos, darum.

7 Es handelt sich sehr wahrscheinlich um den in 440809A (s. Anm. 4) u.ö. genannten Johann (Hans) Schütz, Kasseler Buchbinder u. Verleger, der den Druck der Hs. *Von des Pabstes gewalt* hinauszögerte u. am Ende vereitelte. S. Anm. 1.

8 Der unzuverlässige u. saumselige Schütz (s. Anm. 7) ist auch Thema in 440809A, 450305, 450317A u. 450506.

9 Wahrscheinlich eine gedruckte, bis FG Nr. 417 reichende Mitgliederliste, die dem *GB 1641/44* (in etlichen Exemplaren) beigegeben wurde. Dazu kamen in hsl. Ergänzung die Taufnamen der jüngst Neuaufgenommenen. Eine solche auf den aktuellsten Stand gebrachte Liste erhielt z. B. Hz. Wilhelm IV. v. Sachsen-Weimar (FG 5) mit 450220 (vgl. dort K 7). Vgl. auch 441231, 450126 u.ö.

450317A

Fürst Ludwig an Winand von Polhelm

Antwort auf 450305. — F. Ludwig (Der Nährende) bedankt sich für den Brief Winand v. Polhelms (FG 405. Der Entnehmende) und dessen Beilagen und zeigt sich hinsichtlich des Drucks zweier Werke (oder zweier Teile eines Werks) verwundert über die Ausflüchte des Buchdruckers (und Verlegers) Johann Schütz. Hätte Schütz das zweite Buch nicht angefordert und das erste gar zu drucken versprochen, hätte man sich die Mühe sparen können, ihm dieselben zuzuschicken. Man hätte die Bücher längst an einem anderen Ort drucken lassen können. Ein aufrichtiger Mann solle sein Wort halten. Der Entnehmende möge Schütz noch einmal an sein Versprechen erinnern. Wenn dies keine Früchte trage, solle er die zwei Büchlein wieder zurückfordern und sie so lange verwahren, bis sie wieder (nach Köthen) zurückgebracht werden könnten. Unterdessen werde ihn der letzte Teil der Schrift *Von deß Papstes gewalt* auch erreicht haben. Er könne ihn gern lesen und auch dem Fütternden (Lgf. Hermann IV. v. Hessen-Rotenburg; FG 374) zum Lesen weitergeben. Das Werk werde diesem gefallen. Man finde sicherlich Mittel und Wege, es zu drukken, für den Fall, daß dieser unzuverlässige Mensch (Johann Schütz) das Interesse verloren habe. Der übersandte Anfang des aus dem Französischen ins Deutsche übersetzten „Weisen" sei gelesen und der Stoff für gut befunden worden. F. Ludwig stellt es dem Entnehmenden anheim, ob er die Übersetzung weiterführen und nach Abschluß mit der Vorlage zurückschicken wolle. Das Werk würde dann korrigiert und nach den Regeln der Rechtschreibung und Stilistik eingerichtet werden. Der Entnehmende werde sich damit einen guten Ruf erwerben und zugleich ein gutes Werk tun. — Daß vier Teile der *Frauenzimmer-Gesprächspiele* Georg Philipp Harsdörffers (FG 368. Der Spielende) in den letzten Jahren erschienen seien, werde Polhelm gesehen haben. Inhaltlich zwar unterhaltsam geschrieben, seien sie dennoch sprachlich durchaus problematisch. Auch der Suchende habe kürzlich eine deutsche (*Vers- oder*) *Reimkunst* (1645) herausgegeben, die viel Gutes, aber auch Mängel enthalte. Man werde wohl immer sprachliche Korrekturen zu machen und aus diesen (neue) Regeln zu entwickeln haben, was jedoch überlegt und zurückhaltend geschehen solle.

Q HM Köthen: V S 545, Bl. 463rv, v leer; eigenh. Konzept. — *D: KE,* 49 (mit Auslassungen).

A *Fehlt.*

Edler vnd Vehster lieber besonder des Entnemenden vom 5. dieses ist abgewichene tage dem Nehrenden mit den beylagen wol eingehendigt worden, der bedanket sich der begrußung und nachricht: das[a] der Buchdrucker Hans Schutz[1] seinem[b] versprechen zu wieder nun mit auflegung der zweyen gewilligten bucher[2] einen aufschub oder ausflucht suchen wil deßen verwundert man sich nicht wenig, hette er das letzt uberschickte nicht begeret, noch wegen des ersten sich[c] nicht es zu drucken erkleret, hette man die muhe sie[d] ihme zuzuschicken nicht haben dorffen und[e] sollen sie andern orten wol schon gedruckt sein. ein Aufrichtiger Mann sol sein wort halten: Es wolle der Entnemende nochmals bey ihme anhalten und ihn seines versprechens erinnern laßen: Will er etwan nicht fort, wolle er nur die zwey buchlein von ihme doch volkommen wieder[c] abfodern, und sie bei sich behalten, bis sie fuglich können wieder ubergebracht werden. Jn deßen wird er das ubrige von dem letzten der Gallicanischen oder frantzösischen Kirchen freiheit[c2] auch empfangen haben: Er kan, wan es ihme gefällig, sie belesen, auch den Futternden[3] lesen laßen, sie werden ihme wol gefallen, und wird man schon andre und beßere gelegenheit sie zu druken finden, wan dieser[f] verenderliche[g] mensch nicht fort wil.

Der Uberschickte[h] anfang des verdeutschten Weisen[4] aus dem frantzösischen ist durchlesen und die materi sehr gut befunden worden; Es[i] wird zu des Entnemenden gefallen gestellet, ob er wil in der verdolmetschung fortfaren, und wan er damit fertig, dieselbe[j] mit dem französischen überschicken, sol sie[k] mit allem fleiße übersehen und nach der recht und reinschreibung muglichst eingerichtet werden. Der Entnemende wird sich[l] hiedurch einen guten nahmen erwerben, und ein gut werck darbey verrichten.

Des Spielenden vier theile seiner[m] gesprächspiele zu Nurnberg etzliche Jhar nach einander ausgangen[5], wird er auch sonder zweiffel gesehen haben, die sachen seind lustig, aber die Sprache[n] ist[c] nicht allezeit gar reine und wol geschrieben[o], so hat auch der Suchende neulich eine deutsche Reimkunst lassen ausgehen[6], da zwar viel gutes dinges[p] doch[c] auch noch etwas mangel drinnen, Man wird allezeit[q] in der sprache zu anleiten und zu verbeßern, [un]d[r] aus den abgemerckten [fäl]len[s] regeln zu machen haben, doch[t] mus[c] es mit guter bescheidenheit geschehen. Es hat ihme dieses zur antwort geselschaftmeßig werden sollen, und verbleibet

Des Entnemenden gantzwilliger
    Der Nehrende

Cöthen den 17 Mertzens 1645

T a *Folgt* <sich> — b *Folgt* <ersten> — c *Eingefügt.* — d sie *über unleserlichem Wort.* — e *Mit Einschaltzeichen (tw. im Falz) am Rand eingefügt bis* sein. — f *Folgt* <wendehut> — g *Bis* mensch *am Rand eingefügt.* — h *Folgt* <entwurf oder> — i *Ersetzt* <Und>? — j *Eingefügt für* <es> — k *Für* <es> — l *Folgt* <auch> — m *Ersetzt* <der> — n *Folgt* <wil> — o *Folgt* <sein> — p *Folgt* <dabei> — q *Folgt* <noch>? — r *Am Rand eingefügt bis* machen. *Buchstabenverlust im Falz. Konjektur in eckigen Klammern.* — s *Buchstabenverlust im Falz. Unsichere Konjektur in eckigen Klammern.* — t *Folgt* <wol>

K 1 Johann (Hans) Schütz, Kasseler Buchbinder u. Verleger. S. 440809A K 4 u. ö. Von Winand v. Polhelm (FG 405. Der Entnehmende) wird der Kasseler Drucker Jakob Gentsch, mit dem Schütz damals zusammenarbeitete, nie selbst benannt. S. 450305.

2 *Von des Pabstes gewalt*, die Verdeutschung eines Werks von Marc de Vulson sieur de La Collet: *De la puissance du pape et des libertés de l'Église Gallicane* (Genève 1635). Da F. Ludwig Polhelm mit dem vorliegenden Brief den Rest der Übersetzung (Bl. 36v–70v) schickt, könnte es sich bei den „zweyen gewilligten bucher[n]" um vorhergehende Teile des übersetzten Werks handeln. Ein Zweifel an dieser Deutung bleibt allerdings bestehen. Das (gesamte) Buch blieb unveröffentlicht. S. 440809A K 6, vgl. 450305 K 2.

3 Lgf. Hermann IV. v. Hessen-Rotenburg (FG 374. Der Fütternde).

4 Winands v. Polhelm ungedruckt gebliebene Übertragung der sog. Fabeln des Bidpai oder (arab.) Kalīla wa-Dimna wohl nach dem Frz. des Pierre de la Rivey (1620) oder des Robert Gaulmin (1641). S. 450305 K 5. Zu Polhelm s. 450305 K 1 u. 450818 K 4.

5 Die bis zu diesem Zeitpunkt publizierten vier Teile von *Harsdörffer: Frauenzimmer-Gesprächspiele*. Teil 4 war aller Wahrscheinlichkeit nach im April 1644 erschienen. S. 440426 K 2.

6 *Schottelius: Teutsche Vers- oder ReimKunst (1645)*. Vgl. 450221.

450319

Johann Valentin Andreae an Herzog August d.J. von Braunschweig-Wolfenbüttel

Johann Valentin Andreae (FG 464. 1646) bedankt sich für das Schreiben Hz. Augusts d.J. v. Braunschweig-Wolfenbüttel (FG 227. Der Befreiende) vom 11.3.1645 und für Exemplare seines *Speculum* (Lüneburg 1644) mit den von Hz. August beigesteuerten Genealogien der Welfen. — Andreae erklärt, auf eine Reihe von Gesellschaftsnamen der FG gestoßen zu sein und sich bei diesem Anlaß an seine eigenen Pläne zur Bildung christlicher Sozietäten erinnert zu haben, die sich aber nie hätten verwirklichen lassen. In diesem Zusammenhang erwähnt er die von seinem Freund Wilhelm v. der Wense nach Tobias Adamis (FG 181) Vorlage „Civitas Solis" genannte Gesellschaft und die spätere nürnberg. „Antilia". Andreae wünscht sich die Aufnahme in die FG und knüpft daran die Hoffnung, daß der Befreiende ihn aus seiner beschwerlichen Dienststellung in Württemberg befreie. — Dietrich Flemming beklage sich über seinen Mangel an gelehrten Büchern. Andreae äußert sich allgemein über den Erwerb und die Transportkosten von Büchern. — Andreae äußert seine Vermutung, daß Johann Heinrich Boecklers Ausgabe des griechischen Neuen Testaments Hz. August erreicht habe, und zeigt sich erfreut über die Aussicht, daß Boecklers Panegyrikus auf den Fürsten seinem *Speculum* auf Hz. August angehängt werde. — Der Anfall seiner Krankheit, der Andreae am 9.3.1645 auf der Kanzel getroffen habe, setze sich wohl bis in die arbeitsreiche Passionszeit fort, halte ihn aber vormittags nicht von seinen Geschäften ab.

Q HAB: Cod. Guelf. 65.1 Extrav., Bl. 214rv [A: 214v]; eigenh. 12. Brief (Bl. 214r irrtümlich „13.") des Jahres. — Brief erwähnt in 420601 K 2; *Begemann: FG und Andreae*, 32; *Keller: Akademien der Renaissance*, 104; *van Dülmen: Utopie*, 247; *Conermann: Adami*, 32–38.

A Dem Durchleuchtig Hochgebohrnen Fürsten vnd Herren. Herren Augusto, Herzogen zu Brunschw. vnd Lüneb. &c. Meinem gnedigsten Fürsten vnd herren &c. *Wolfenbutel.* (12.) 19. Martij.

Durchleuchtig Hochgebohrner Gnedigster Fürst vnd herr. E. F. G. 11t. auf mein 7t. ist zu recht eingekommen.[1] Vnd habe wegen g. vberschikhter genealogien[2] ich mich vnd. zu bedankhen.

Außer beigelegtem Sinnbild, habe ich nu mehr abermahlen einen Nahmen der Fruchtbringenden gesellschaft vermerkhet,[3] Nemblich den *Befreienden*. Finde also neben diesem. den *Nehrenden*. den geheimen. den Suchenden. den Spilenden. Reinherzigen.ᵃ Vnverdroßenen.ᵃ &c. Vnd erinnere mich Meines geliebten Wensen Sehl. Vorschlags. so er aber Ciuitatem solis genennet. Vnd von Tobia Adamj gestellet worden. Wie auch einer anderen geselschaft zu Nürnberg. Antilia genandt, dahin ich hiebevor Meine Vnionem Christianam gerichtet.⁴ Aber niemahlen zu einer rechtschaffenen verfaßung gelangen mögen. Weilen nu dise Hochlob. Fruchtbringende gesellschaft Jhren Nahmen nicht vergebens. noch in Idea verbleibet. Sondern Rumbliche Frucht bringet. Alß habe ich hierzu Gottes fernere gnad vnd gedeien herzlich zu mahlen auch für mich zu wunschen.⁵ Daß der Befreiende mich dermahl eines außer beschwerlichen dienstbarkeit befreien möge.⁶

M. Flemmich⁷ beklaget sich sehr. daß Er Mangel an Buchern habe, dadurch seine Studia gehindert werden. Ob es nu dahin sihet daß seine Bucher. so noch vorhanden. solten mit großem Vncosten. dorthin transferieret werden. welches kaum rathsam. oder. ob ihme die Noturft zu erkauffen Schwer falle. auch vileichten nicht zu bekommen. kan ich nicht errathen, Es sein gleichwolen Alte bucher bei vnß wolfailer aber guth. Die Neue aber wegen des Tewren fuerlohns. in gar hohem währt. habe ihne also vertröstet es werde E. f. g. ihme wege zu seinen studien gehörig. in g. nicht ermanglen laßen. Vnd erwarte ich nur. daß Er seine schuldigkeit vnclagbar thuge.

Böcklerj, viri egregie eruditj Newes Testament⁸ wurt sich verhoffentlich nu mehr auch Eingestelt haben. Vnd erfrewet mich sehr daß sein panegiricus⁹ meinem finsteren Spiegel. ut Lucem inferat. solle adiungieret werden.¹⁰

Mein Morbus helt seidt dem 9. huius. da er mich auf der Canzel angriffen. Continuirlich hart an. kan gleichwolen den Vormittag noch immer fortkommen. Besorge aber ich werde eine beschwerliche Passion wochen. ubi Labores concurrunt. haben. sed fiat uoluntas Dominj.

Befehle E. f. g. sambt dero hochlob. stato dem Schuz des Algewaltigen Gottes. auch deroselben mich beharrlichen großer gnaden verbleibendt biß an Mein End

E. F. G. Vndertönig. gehorsams verpflichter Rhat vnd diener
       Jo. Valent. Andreæ D.
19. Martij ☿ 1645.

T a *Ohne Einschaltzeichen eingefügt.*

K 1 Das 7. Schreiben Johann Valentin Andreaes (FG 464. 1646) vom 19.2.1645 (HAB: Cod. Guelf. 65.1 Extrav., Bl. 209rv) war durch Hz. August d.J. v. Braunschweig-Wolfenbüttel (FG 227. Der Befreiende) am 11.3.1645 beantwortet worden (HAB: Cod. Guelf. 236.2 Extrav., Bl. 67rv).

2 In 450219 bat Andreae den Herzog um Exemplare seiner Gratulationsschrift zu Augusts Geburtstag 1644, die auch dessen Stammbaum u. beschreibende Genealogie enthält. Sie war u. a. in Lüneburg gedruckt worden. S. dort K 6.

3 Andreae könnte, aus den folgenden Gesellschaftsnamen zu schließen, ein Exemplar des *GB 1641/44* gelesen haben (wohl ohne dessen Liste der Taufnamen), da damals nur dieses auch nach dem Jahre 1641 aufgenommene Mitglieder erwähnt: F. Ludwig (FG 2.

Der Nährende. 1617), Hz. August (FG 227. Der Befreiende. 1634), Carl Gustav v. Hille (FG 302. Der Unverdrossene. 1636), Georg Philipp Harsdörffer (FG 368. Der Spielende. 1642), Hz. Christian Ludwig v. Braunschweig-Celle (FG 372. Der Reinherzige. 1642), Franz Julius v. dem Knesebeck (FG 396. Der Geheime. 1642), Justus Georg Schottelius (FG 397. Der Suchende. 1642). — Am 20.5.1645 versprach der Herzog, Andreae beizeiten das illustrierte *GB 1646* zu senden: „Wann das Anhaltische KreuterGesellschaft Buch fertig; sol es sich einstellen." HAB: Cod. Guelf. 236.2 Extrav., Bl.76r. *Begemann: FG und Andreae*, 30. Am 1.6.1645 antwortete Andreae: „Des Anhaltischen Kreuterbuchs will ich verlanglich erwarten […]" (HAB: Cod. Guelf. 65.1 Extrav., Bl.226r; *Begemann: FG und Andreae*, 34). Hz. August vertröstete ihn am 24.6.1645: „Ascanium Herbarium et […] werden bald kommen." HAB: Cod. Guelf. 236.2 Extrav., Bl.81r; *Begemann: FG und Andreae*, 34. Andreae schrieb seinem Herrn am 2.7.1645: „Jch erwarte mit Vnd. verlangen der Kreuter geselschaft buch. Wie nicht weniger **panegyricj Boecklerianj in minuta forma.**" (Zu Boeckler s. Anm.9 u. 450219 K 6.) HAB: Cod. Guelf. 65.1 Extrav., Bl.231r; *Begemann: FG und Andreae*, 34. Er wiederholte ungeduldig am 9.7.1645: „Nach dem **Ascanico herbario** trage ich großes Verlangen." HAB: Cod. Guelf. 65.1 Extrav., Bl.232r; *Begemann: FG und Andreae*, 34. Der Herzog konnte ihm in 450722 nur antworten: „So bald das augierte Kreuter und Geselschaft Buch mir wird von dem Ernehrenden, Fürst Ludewigen von Anhalt, zugesand werden, wil ich alsbald ein Exemplar übersenden." Andreae schien sich darauf in Geduld zu fassen: „Der Kreuter gesellschaft [*ergänze:* Buch] will ich underthenig erwarten." S. 450806. Das bestätigte er dem Herzog am 10.12.1645: „Ich erwarte noch der Kreuter gesellschaft Buch mit Vnd. Verlangen". HAB: Cod. Guelf. 65.1 Extrav., Bl.259r; *Begemann: FG und Andreae*, 34. Der Fürst konnte Andreaes Ungeduld am 30.12.1645 ein Ziel nennen: „Das KreuterBuch wird gegen das PassahFest fertig werden." HAB: Cod. Guelf. 236.2 Extrav., Bl.108r; *Begemann: FG und Andreae*, 34.

4 Zu Andreaes früheren christlichen Sozietätsplänen, für die er auch Hz. August begeistern wollte, u. zu den Rollen Tommaso Campanellas, Wilhelms v. der Wense u. Tobias Adamis (FG 181) s. 420601, 420627 u. 430826 K 4. Zur Antilia vgl. bes. 430826 K 7.

5 Dieser Wunsch Andreaes fand durch Vermittlung Hz. Augusts Ende 1646 Erfüllung. S. 461117 u. 461216. In seiner Antwort vom 15.4.1645 ging der Herzog einstweilen nur mit folgenden Worten auf Andreaes Fragen ein: „In unser Geselschafft ist unser Patronus, der Nehrende, F. Ludwig zu Anhalt zu Cöthen residirend: Selenus, ist der Befreiende, das Kraut darzu ist Gamanderley: Ein jeder Geselschafter hat ein besonders Kraut: Es ist ein eigenes Buch darvon ediret: So bald die lezte Edition heraus kommet: Sol ein Exemplar communiciret werden." HAB: Cod. Guelf. 236.2 Extrav., Bl.71rv. Zit. auch in *Begemann: FG und Andreae*, 33 u. 37; *Keller: Akademien der Renaissance*, 104f.

6 Andreae hegte noch immer die Hoffnung, Hz. August in Wolfenbüttel aufsuchen zu können u. seiner als beschwerlich empfundenen Situation am Stuttgarter Hofe u. der drückenden Lage der württemberg. Kirche enthoben zu werden.

7 Dietrich Flemming. S. 450219 K 15.

8 Zu dem Straßburger Professor Johann Heinrich Boeckler (1611–1672) s. 440616 K 0. Johann Heinrich Boecklers Hz. August gewidmete Ausgabe des griech. Neuen Testaments: Η ΚΑΙΝΗ ΔΙΑΘΗΚΗ. Novum Testamentum. Accessit PROLOGVS in Epistolas S. Apostoli Pauli, ex antiquissimo MSC. (Argentorati Jo. Phil. Mülbius: 1645), HAB: Bibel-S.702; SUB Göttingen: 8 BIBL I, 1812. Andreae schrieb wohl über die Widmung am 7.3.1645 an Boeckler. S. Anm.9. Am 25.3.1645 erwähnte Hz. August, diese Edition u. einen Panegyrikus Boecklers (s. Anm.9) empfangen zu haben: „sein Schreiben vom 5t. Martii, habe ich wohl empfangen. Auch das N. T. Boeckleri: Jst ein sauberer Truk: Ich werde mich dankbahrlich bald gegen ihm erzeigen; wegen der Dedic. und Paneg.:" HAB:

450319 Johann Valentin Andreae

Cod. Guelf. 236.2 Extrav., Bl.69r. Am 15.4.1645 schrieb der Herzog an Andreae: „Des Boechleri [sic] N. T. Gr. hat sich eingestellet. Ich werde bedacht seyn, die Præfation zu remunerieren. Ich möchte seine Latinam versionem novam, auch wol sehen: dan mir neulich daruon gesagt worden; daß eine herausgegeben seye." A.a.O., Bl.71r. Andreae fragte darauf bei Boeckler am 29.5.1645 sicherheitshalber nach: „Nescio tamen, quis ipsius Celsitudinj persuaserit, te novam versionem latinam Novi Testamenti iam confectam sub prælo habere, quod quia abs te non habeo, nondum crediderim." SUB Hamburg: Sup. ep. 24, Bl.38r. Am 3.11.1645 mußte Andreae Boeckler, der ihm eine Erklärung schuldig geblieben war, daran erinnern, weil Hz. August ihn danach gefragt habe. SUB Hamburg: Sup. ep. 24, Bl.41r. Boeckler lieferte keine lat. Ausgabe.

9 AUGUSTI | DUCIS BRUNOVICENSIS | & Luneburgensis | FAMA | non moritura, | revocata | Calamo | JOANNIS HENRICI BOCLERI [!]: | [Zierstück] | Typis STELLARUM. | [Linie] | M. DC. XLV. Kl. 8° (Satzspiegel 5,6 x 3,6 cm; Blattgröße wechselnd 8,2 x 5cm bis etwa 7,2 x 5,3 cm); HAB: Gn 1328 u. Gn 1329; SLUB Dresden: Hist. Sax. inf. 483, auch dig. Kollation: Titelbl., Rücks. frei, Bl. (A2r)/ S.1 – D 4 v/ S.54 Text Boecklers, inc.: ILlustres virtutum titulos, ac dignas (genealogische u. biographische Lobrede auf Hz. August u. dessen Stammbaum auf 6 S. [Falttafeln nach S.40, separat gezählt S.1–6]). Die Lobrede betont auch Augusts Gelehrsamkeit, Weisheit u. großen Bücherschatz. Bl. D 5rv/ S.55f. lat. Ged. Martin Nessels, inc.: DVX Sapiens, nostri prælustris adorea secli; [I 7r]/ S.57–139 Nessels Panegyrikus. (PANEGYRICUS. Illustrissimo ac Celsissimo Principi ac Domino, | DN. AUGUSTO, Duci Brunovicensi, & Luneburgensi, Domino suo clementissimo. TESTANDÆ DEVOTIONI D. D. D. MARTINUS NESSELIUS, MORAVUS.) Über Boecklers u. Nessels Druck vgl. 450722 K 2 u. 450806 K 2. Nessels Lobrede war schon 1639 erschienen: PANEGYRICUS | ILLUSTRISSIMO AC CELSISSI- | MO PRINCIPI AC DOMINO. | DN. AUGUSTO | DUCI BRUNOVICENSI | ET LUNÆBURGENSI: | Scriptus. | à | MARTINO NESSELIO MORAVO | Poëta Coronato, Con-Rect: | Ultzensi. ANNO. | M.DC.XXXIX. | [Vignette] | HAMBURGI, Typis JACOBI REBENLINI. HAB: Gn 13 (12). Sein Panegyrikus wurde mit dem Gedicht wiederabgedruckt in MARTINI NESSELII MORAVI POEMATA Nunc primùm edita (Rintelij ad Visurgin: Petrus Lucius 1642), 346–387; das Gedicht veröffentlichte Gosky: Arbustum (1650), Bl.558r. Zu Nessel s. 450806 K 2. Von Boecklers u. Andreaes Lobreden wird auch Johann Matthias Schneuber (FG 498. 1648) erfahren haben, denn Andreae schrieb an Boeckler am 17.1.1645: „Schneuberus vester herj mecum fuit, et abs te salutem tulit, quem refero his tumultuariis literis." SUB Hamburg: Sup. ep. 24, Bl.40r. Am 25.2.1645 äußerte sich Andreae über Boecklers Panegyrikus u. dessen Ausgabe des Neuen Testaments (s. Anm.8) an Hz. August d.J.: „Boecklerj Augustus alter. wurt nu mehr sich eingestelt vnd seinen Meister erwiesen haben. Hoc voluj. ne quis alius quam apelles Augustum pingeret. quem vnum hodie novi et exactæ eruditionis. et moribus concinnis, et instituendi peritissimum ac patientissimum. minimi omnium pædagogico ingenio. Der hat nu entzwischen auf Mein gutachten. elegantissimæ editionis græcæ Novi Testamenti. in forma 12. E. F. g. Nahmen præfigieret. Non esse alius quam Augusti nomen dignius. quod. in frontispicio nobilis operis luceat, nec opus hoc elegantissimum alterj convenientius quam Augusto, magisque dubitum. Daß Exemplar wil ich furderlichst an h. Forstenheusern nacher Nurnberg versenden. hierbej aber habe ich Copien der inscription vnd dedication beilegen wullen. Er wurt auch selber. wo es E. f. g. nicht zuwider. sich mit einem Vnd. schreiben einstellen. vnd hoch Erfrewen wan sein werkhlein auch in dem kleinen Formatlin. vnd schönen Strenischen [d.i. Sternischen] typis. dem Meinigen wurt Coniungieret werden." HAB: Cod. Guelf. 65.1 Extrav., Bl.211r. Am 1.3.1645 wünschte Andreae Hz. August: „Des Boecklerj panegyricus wurt verhoffentlich quoad materiam et formam E. f.

g. Contentieren. Mich aber erfrewen daß Er meinem dunkhlen speculo solle adiungieret werden [...]." A. a. O., Bl. 212r. Ein beigedruckter Panegyrikus Andreaes aus dem Jahre 1645 ist nicht auffindbar, obgleich das Schriftenverzeichnis Andreaes vom Januar 1654 unter den „MEMORALIA" mitteilt: „1644. Augustum virtutis speculum. Studtgard, 12. | 1644. *Recusum* cum | August: Fama Beocleri *[sic]*, Luneb. 24. | 2. Panegyricus Nesselii. Lunæb. 24." In: Sereniss. Domus AUGUSTÆ SELENIANÆ PRINCIP. JUVENTUTIS UTRIUSQUE SEXUS ... expositum, à Johanne Valentino Andreæ, Th. D. Abbate Bebenhusano (Ulmae: Balthasar Kühnius 1654), 351. Die Angabe „24" bezeichnet ungenau nur ein kleines Format, die eigentliche Bogenzählung der folgenden Exemplare ergibt 12°. Andreae hatte also seinen früheren Panegyricus von 1644 nochmals drucken u. mit Boecklers u. Nessels Lobreden in einen Band zusammenfassen lassen. S. Anm. 10.

Erhalten sind zwei voneinander verschiedene Ausgaben des Panegyrikus Andreaes. Von der 1. Ausgabe besitzt die HAB zwei verschieden ausgestattete Exemplare:

1a. AUGUSTUS | PRINCIPIS | EXEMPLUM. | In Plausum natalis sexagesimi | sexti felicissimi | Expositus | per | JOHANNEM VALEN- | TINUM ANDREÆ, | S. T. D. | [Zierst.] | Stutgardiæ, | Typis Rudolphi Kautti. | MDC XLIV. 12°; Satzspiegel 10,3 x 6,3 cm. Das Bl. ist auf 12,4 x 7,4 cm beschnitten. HAB: 602.17 Hist. — 6 Bll. leer; Kupfertitel koloriert: AUGUSTUM Principis VIRTUTIS SPECULUM; Rücks. leer; Titelbl., Rücks. mit Inscriptiones an Hz. August u. seine drei Söhne; Kupferstich der drei Prinzen, im Lorbeerkranz „Wolff. Kilian f.", Rücks. leer (Format des Stichs: Bl. 10,6 x 7,5 cm, Platte 8,7 x 7,1 cm); A 2r – A 3r Widmung, inc.: MORTVOS LAVDARE solemne olim fuit, gez. Stutgardiae IV. Eid. Apr. natali Serenissimi D. Patris LXVI. A. C. 1644. JOHAN. VALENTINO ANDREAE, T. D.; Rücks. aufgeklebtes Kupferstichportr. Hz. Augusts, wie in der 2. (Lüneburger) Ausg. HAB: Gn 212, aber koloriert. Auf dem Blatt rundherum mit Kartuschen gezeichnete Umrahmung; ungez. 2. Bl.: eingefügtes Blatt mit Zeichnung (wohl Andreaes): Auf Fliesenboden zwei goldene Löwen vor einem Postament (Inschrift: „HAEC. ERIGIT. ISTU[D.]AMBIT") eine mit Rosen garnierte Pyramide mit wachsender goldener Mondsichel auf g. Knauf, darüber ein von Sonnenlicht umstrahltes „CRESCAT"; heranfliegender Adler mit Beischrift „MAIORIBUS ALIS"; Rücks. leer; Bl. A 4r /S. 1 – [C 9v]/ 60 lat. Text der Lobrede, inc.: EXcelsior est mentis magnitudo; [C10r – 12r] BREVIARIUM VITÆ AUGUSTÆ.; C 12v – [D v] lat. Brief v. Pz. Rudolf August, d. d. Guelpherbyti 29. Aprilis. Anno 1644.; Bl. ***r AUGUSTI DUCIS BRUNOVIC ET LUNEB. Illustris. soboles. (Familienstammbaum Hz. Augusts, seiner Frauen u. Kinder); Bl. ***v – [B ****r] Stammbaum der Welfen von Otto puer bis zu Hz. August 2. Gemahlin Hzn. Dorothea, T. v. F. Rudolf v. Anhalt(-Zerbst) (FG 12), daneben rechts Liste von älteren, meist legendären Welfen von Nr. 1. C. Actius 390 bis Nr. 25. Otto puer, mit eigenh. Berichtigungen Hz. Augusts. Auf Bl. [B ****v] zwei eigenh. Notizen Hz. Augusts; 5 leere Bll., 6. Bl. hinten eigenh. Verzeichnis Hz. Augusts: Errata corrigenda. Auf dem hinteren Spiegel eingeklebt Kupferstich-Porträt Andreaes, Wolff. Kilian sculp. — Pappbd. goldgepunzt, mit Pflanzenmotiven bunt bestickt, abgefallene Schließen, Goldschnitt.

1b. HAB: Li 88. Titel, Blattgröße, Satzspiegel u. Kollation wie 1a. Vor dem kolorierten Kupfertitel 1 leeres Blatt; nach dem Kupfertitel Rücks. mit den Inscriptiones an Hz. August u. seine Söhne, gefolgt von der Widmung; Bl. A 3v aufgeklebtes, koloriertes u. eingerahmtes Kupferstich-Porträt Hz. Augusts wie in 1a; kein Blatt mit Pyramidenmalerei. Weiter wie in 1a. Keine Eintragungen Hz. Augusts. Auf dem hinteren Spiegel eingeklebt Kupferstich-Porträt Andreaes v. Wolff. Kilian sculp. — Roter Pappbd., abgefallene Schließen, Goldschnitt.

2. AUGUSTUS | PRINCIPIS | EXEMPLUM. | In Plausum natalis sexa- | gesimi sexti feli- | cissimi | EXPOSITVS | per | JOHANNEM VALEN- | TINUM ANDREÆ, | S. T. D. | [Zierstück] | LUNEBURGI, | Typis STELLARUM, 1644. 12° (Bl.größe 7,1 x 4,7 cm; Satzspiegel: 5,6 x 3, 6 cm). HAB: Gn 212 (auch dig.), vor dem Titelbl. (Kupferstiche, Rückseiten leer): a. Bildnis Hz. Augusts mit Wahlspruch „Expende"; b. Bildnis der drei Prinzen Anton Ulrich (FG 716. 1659), Rudolf August (FG 754. 1660) u. Ferdinand Albrecht (FG 842. 1673); c. Kupfertitel im Wortlaut der *Selenianae*: AUGUSTUM PRINCIPIS VIRTUTIS SPECULUM; Inhalt: Rücks. des Drucktitels mit Inscriptio an Hz. August u. seine drei Söhne; Bl. A 2rv lat. Widmungsrede, inc.: MORTVOS LAVDARE solemne olim fuit, gez. Stutgardiae IV. Eid. Apr. natali Serenissimi D. Patris LXVI. A. C. 1644. JOHAN. VALENTINO ANDREAE, T. D.; Bl. A 3r/ S.1 – [B 7r]/ 33 lat. Text der Lobrede, inc.: EXcelsior est mentis magnitudo; S. 34–39 BREVIARIUM VITÆ AUGUSTÆ (Stationen des Lebenslaufs bis „1641. 14. Sept. Traditio VVolffenbuttelensis"); S. (40) Stammtafel (nur Hz. August, seine drei Frauen u. die Kinder; S.41–43 lat. Brief Pz. Rudolf Augusts, 29.4.1644 an Andreae, Rücks. vacat.
Der Stuttgarter Druck konnte aus Formatgründen (s. Satzspiegel u. Blattgröße) nicht Teil des Lüneburger, von Andreae in den *Selenianae* (1654) aufgeführten Buchs sein, das die Lobschriften Andreaes, Boecklers u. Nessels vereinigte, aber in dieser Form nicht erhalten zu sein scheint. Der erste, in Stuttgart veranstaltete Druck (602.17 Hist.), der nur Andreaes Panegyrikus mit seinen Beigaben enthält, erschien wie der Lüneburger Einzeldruck von Andreaes Lobrede (Gn 212) mit der Jahresangabe 1644, aber nicht rechtzeitig zur Feier des Geburtstags Hz. Augusts am 10.4.1644. In beiden Drucken findet sich nämlich ein gedruckter Brief Pz. Rudolf Augusts vom 29.4.1644. Der 2. Andreae-Druck (Gn 212) weist jedoch dasselbe Bogenformat (einschließlich Satzspiegel u. Blattgröße) wie der Druck der Lobreden Boecklers u. Nessels auf u. stellte gewissermaßen eine Einladung zum Zusammendruck mit diesen Reden dar. — Andreae hatte in einem Schreiben an Boeckler vom 24.7.1644 diesen selbst zu dem Panegyrikus angeregt, wobei er Boecklers Stil pries u. über seinen eigenen stellte: „En quæ arido stilo in explicanda Augusti. Principis et herj mej Virtute, fuerim ausus. quod ipse quidem. quum est indulgentia siue probavit, siue tolerat. Ego vero, ut ipse mihi minime satisfeci, ita optarim, ab ex exactiore et floridiore stilo, id est tuo. idem fieri. atque quod res poscit, melius. Concede mihi quæso elegantem et omnibus facilem calamum. in hac nobili materia. cuius precium me conciliatore ipsum Principem propitium sine dubio feres." SUB Hamburg: Sup. ep. 24, Bl.35rv. Die vom französ. Heer verursachten Unruhen hätten ihn der Möglichkeit beraubt, Boecklers am 1.9.1644 erklärte Bereitschaft zum Panegyrikus zu beantworten, schrieb Andreae am 23.10.1644 an den Straßburger. Der möge keine weiteren Angaben zur Amplificatio der Lobrede von ihm erwarten: „[…] ne si forte plures ut scribis ad argumenti amplitudinem suppetias a me expectares, intercapedinis culpam artificiosè mihi imputares. Nescio autem an non hæc iam ante tecum communicaverim, quæ denuo mittere non piget, ut nullam elabendj rimam invenias. De animo magni Principis in te propitio, noli dubitare. quod magis experieris, ubi officium tuum. in provehenda Fama summæ Virtutis, explicaveris." A.a.O., Bl.37rv. Am 5.12.1644 konnte Andreae sich für ein „specimen diserti encomij Augustæj" bedanken u. Boeckler die sicher willkommene Mitteilung machen: „De impressione, forma, titulo, et huiusmodj nolo te esse solicitum, quæ omnia ipse curabo. Tuum hoc unicum erit, ut in charta descripta. et probè correcta Tua ad me mittas, quæ prius cum Augusto, non sine nominis tui, et meritorum commendatione, prius communicanda mihi erunt, quam de editione in lucem, quicquam statuamus." A.a.O., Bl.36rv. — Andreae wird dem Herzog die Lobrede Boecklers zuerst im Manuskript zugesandt haben. Am 25.2.1645 hatte der Herzog sie noch nicht ganz durchgelesen. HAB: Cod. Guelf. 236.2 Extrav.,

Bl. 65r. Um den 26.2.1645 (der Brief des Herzogs dürfte um diesen Tag herum geschrieben worden sein. Das Tagesdatum ist überklebt. Andreae notierte auf der Adreßseite Bl. 64v als Empfangstag „Præs. 1. Martij. 45.") teilte der Herzog Andreae im Zusammenhang mit dessen Gratulationsschrift (zu Augusts Geburtstag 10.4.1644; s. 450219 K 6) mit: „Als ich nuhn den panegyricum ergänzet habe; So wil ich mich abmüssigen, und ihn mit fleis perlustrieren: Was ich albereit darinnen gelesen, ist also beschaffen, daß es seinem Speculo wol zu adnectieren seyn wird." Das bezog sich auf Andreaes Panegyrikus, die Ergänzung betraf wohl die Stammtafel sowie genealogische u. biographische Angaben, vielleicht auch Nessels Lobrede. Schließlich wurde das erweiterte Buch in der Druckerei Stern in Lüneburg hergestellt. Das Erscheinen kündigte August Andreae verfrüht am 4.3.1645 an: „der Böcklerus wird sich, von denen Sternen repræsentieret, auch bald einstellen:" HAB: Cod. Guelf. 236.2 Extrav., Bl. 66r. Andreae bedankte sich am 7.3.1645 bei Boeckler: „Elegantissimi tuj libelli exempla duo Sthalinus rectè mihi tradidit, quorum unum ad Principem Augustum, herum meum, primo quoque tempore transmittam, gratiam tibi inde incluti Herois, et libertate munus haud dubio reportaturus. Ac iam quidem inscriptionem descriptam literis meis per veredarios transferendis, inclusi, ut citius Princeps, quanti ipsum faceres, ex te, quis vero esses, ex me intelligeret." SUB Hamburg: Sup. ep. 24, Bl. 45r. Erwähnt ist vielleicht der geistl. Verwalter Konrad Stä(h)lin in Bottwar, später Untervogt in Backnang, angeblich 1646 tot. Er war ein Sohn des Christoph St. Vgl. *Pfeilsticker* § 2151, 2155 u. 3480. Ein Johann Christoph St. Lic. (†1670) war 1650–1657 Hofgerichtssekretär, wurde 1650 Kreissekretär, war 1661–1667 Regierungsrat, 1666/67 Tutelarrat u. danach Syndikus zu Lindau. A. a. O., § 1231, 1253, 1385 u. 1393. Da es sich bei beiden Stä(h)lins um württemberg. Landes- u. Hofbedienstete handelte, könnte Andreae durch einen von ihnen direkt vom Drucker eine erste, separate Ausgabe von Boecklers Panegyrikus erhalten haben. Wie erwähnt, hatte er Boeckler am 5.12.1644 versprochen, sich um den Druck des Werks zu kümmern. Oder hatte Boeckler sein Werk in Straßburg selbst drucken lassen u. es Andreae zugesandt? Das ist aber nicht zwingend der Sinn des Satzes. Wenn Andreae das Büchlein separat in Stuttgart in den Druck gegeben hatte — ebenso wie seinen eigenen ersten Panegyrikus von 1644 —, so wird er es schnellstmöglich an den Herzog geschickt, aber das zweite Exemplar wegen der von ihm erhofften Wiederveröffentlichung seines Panegyrikus (zusammen mit dem Boecklers) bei sich behalten haben. Das schließt nicht aus, daß er baldmöglichst selbst oder durch den Drucker ein weiteres Exemplar an den Autor schickte. Der Einzeldruck Boecklers ist allerdings nicht erhalten. Hz. August ließ Boecklers Text zusammen mit dem Nessels in Lüneburg durch die Gebr. Stern veröffentlichen. — Am 25.3.1645 bestätigte Hz. August Andreae den Empfang der gedruckten *Fama* Boecklers. Andreae vertröstete am 23.4.1645 Boeckler, daß dessen Panegyrikus vom Herzog wohl empfangen u. belohnt werde. SUB Hamburg: Sup. ep. 24, Bl. 47. S. Anm. 8. Der Lüneburger Sammeldruck der Panegyrika auf den Herzog erschien erst im Sommer 1645. S. 450722 K 2.

10 Andreaes in 450219 zit. *Speculum* auf Hz. August wurde in der Lüneburger Ausgabe nachträglich mit der Lüneburger Edition von Boecklers Panegyricus (und Nessels Lobrede) zusammengedruckt. S. 450806.

450325

Diederich von dem Werder an Fürst Ludwig

Diederich v. dem Werder (FG 31. Der Vielgekörnte) schickt F. Ludwig (Der Nährende) die Abschrift eines Lobs auf den Hund „Page". Er habe es an fünf oder sechs Stellen um spontane Einfälle erweitert, denen weitere hinzugefügt werden könnten. — Gute Wünsche für den Nährenden und die Nährende (Fn. Sophia v. Anhalt-Köthen. AL 1629. TG 38) und vielleicht für deren Sohn Wilhelm Ludwig (FG 358. Der Erlangende) oder für Hans Adam v. Hammerstein (FG 111. Der Erhaltende).

Q HM Köthen: V S 544, Bl. 473rv [A: 473v]; eigenh.; Sig. — Nicht in *KE* u. *KL* III.

A Dem Nehrenden Cöthen Zu handen.
Eigenh. Empfangsvermerk F. Ludwigs: 26. Merzens 1645

Auff geschehenes begehren wird dem Nehrenden eine abschrift von des hundes, *Page* genant, lobes[1] zugeschickt, vnd zwar ist solches an fünf oder sechs orten in etwas vermehret, wie es irgend vnter dessen die einfälle mitgebracht haben, vnd wan man Zeit vnd mühe daran wenden wolte, dergleichen sehr[a] viel mit eingerückt werden könten. Der Nehrende wolle es zum besten vermercken, Sich samt der Nehrenden vnd dem Erhaltenden[2] wohlgehaben, darbey auch in dem festen wahn sein, Es sey vnd verbleibe Sein

des Nehrenden
allerwilligster gesellschaftsknecht
Der Vielgekörnte.

Reinsdorff 25. Merzens 1645.

T a *Eingefügt.*

K 1 Bisher konnte kein weiterer Hinweis auf dieses Stück gefunden werden. Ob es als Prosa-Enkomium oder als Gedicht verfaßt wurde, ob es von Diederich v. dem Werder (FG 31. Der Vielgekörnte) stammte oder dieser nur Verbesserungen an einer fremden, möglicherweise von F. Ludwig (Der Nährende) stammenden Vorlage ausführte, bleibt offen. Werders Neigung zum spielerisch-literarischen Capriccio — vgl. etwa 371031 I — legt seine Verfasserschaft nahe.
  2 Ist hier tatsächlich Hans Adam v. Hammerstein (FG 111. Der Erhaltende. 1579–1653) gemeint? Er war lippischer Rat u. der Fn. Sophia v. Anhalt-Köthen, geb. Gfn. zur Lippe (AL 1629. TG 38) wohl aus Kindertagen bekannt. Bis 1646 ist er auch als cellischer Landdrost der Ober- u. Niedergft. Hoya bezeugt. Verwechselt Werder hier vielleicht Gesellschaftsnamen u. bezieht sich auf den gemeinsamen Sohn F. Ludwigs u. Fn. Sophias, F. Wilhelm Ludwig v. Anhalt-Köthen (FG 358)? Dieser war 1641 als Dreijähriger in die FG aufgenommen worden und trug seitdem den Gesellschaftsnamen „Der Erlangende".

450326

Fürst Ludwig an Fürst Christian II. von Anhalt-Bernburg

F. Ludwig bestätigt den Empfang eines Schreibens F. Christians II. v. Anhalt-Bernburg (FG 51) vom 24. März und weist ihn darauf hin, daß er und seine Gemahlin (Fn. Sophia. AL 1629. TG 38) auf die durch einen Boten am 19.3. überbrachte Nachricht vom Ableben Pz. Ferdinand Christians v. Anhalt-Bernburg durch ihre Beileidsschreiben am selben Tag beantwortet und durch denselben Boten abgeschickt hätten. — Er bedankt sich für die Rücksendung des an Christian ausgeliehenen Buches *Le parfaict Ambassadeur*. — Den Brief des Herzogs (Ernst Bogislaw) von Croy (und Aerschott) habe er samt den Beilagen gelesen und sendet diese wieder zurück; einzig von den lat. Anlagen habe er eine Abschrift behalten und möchte den anhaltin. Stamm bis zu Fürst Heinrich aufzeichnen lassen und demnächst übersenden. Genealogische Ausführungen zum Hause Anhalt schließen mit dem Hinweis, Nachrichten über die Grafenhäuser Schwarzburg u. Hohnstein seien am besten von der Gfn. (Anna Sophia) v. Schwarzburg (TG 1, F. Ludwigs Schwester) zu beziehen. Ludwig selbst sei bis zu Sigismund I. im Besitz der Wappen. Falls Christian die erhalten wolle, möge er sie durch Doktor Engelharts Sohn abmalen lassen. — Keineswegs zufrieden ist Ludwig mit einem Schreiben Georg Philipp Harsdörffers (FG 386. Der Spielende), das er nicht mitteilen will, bevor er es Diederich v. dem Werder (FG 31. Der Vielgekörnte) zur Begutachtung vorgelegt hat. Die hoffentlich noch in diesem Jahr erscheinende *Deutsche Rechtschreibung* von Christian Gueintz (FG 361. Der Ordnende) werde hier ein Maß vorgeben. Harsdörffer und Justus Georg Schottelius (FG 397. Der Suchende) werden vermutlich mit vernünftigen und grundlegenden Erklärungen widerlegt werden. — Grüße von Ehepaar zu Ehepaar. — *Nachschrift:* Ein gestern eingekommener Brief Hz. Wilhelms IV. v. Sachsen-Weimar (FG 5) liegt bei.

Q LHA Sa.-Anh./ Dessau: Z 18 Abt. Bernburg A 10 Nr. 46[d], Bl. 407r–408v [A: 408v], 408r leer, Bl. 408 an den Ecken eingeknickt bzw. abgerissen; eigenh.; Sig., Wasserzeichen erkennbar.

A   A Monsieur
    Monsieur mon tresaymé nepveu, Le prince Cristian d'Anhalt. etc
    A Ballested
    <u>En mains propres</u>

Hochgeborner Fürst, freundlicher vielgeliebter herr Vetter und gevatter, auf El. gestern alhier eingekommenes handschreiben vom 24. dieses verhalte ich ihr hertzlich nicht[,] das 1. El. zuwißen fugung[1] des ableibens ihres jüngsten jungen herleins mir den 19. dieses durch einen bernburgischen boten, so von deßau kommen eingeliefert worden, ich El.[a] auch mit demselben noch solches tages geantwortet, und mein freundvetterliches mitleiden zuerkennen gegeben, wie den auch meine gemahl an El. gemahlin dergleichen handschriftlich damals[b] gethan, vnd das brieflein in dem meinigen an El. eingeschloßen gewesen, hat es also an unserer gebühr nicht ermangelt.[2] 2. Fur wieder einschickung des Frantzösischen büchleins, genennet **Le parfaict Ambassadeur**[3] bedancke ich mich auch freundvetterlich. 3.[c] Des Hertzogs von Croye[4] brieflein habe ich mit den beylagen durchle-

450326 Fürst Ludwig 489

sen, thue sie auch hiermit wieder ubersenden,⁵ von den lateinischen habe ich abschrift behalten, vnd wil aus vnserm^d Stammbaume bis auf Fürst Heinrichen⁶ aufwärts die Anhaltischen Ahnen laßen auszeichnen und El. mit nechstem zuschicken: Churfurst Johannes zu Sachsen witwe,⁷ die hernach den hertzog von Pommern⁸ genommen, ist Fürst Wolffens zu Anhalt, schwester gewesen, ihre Frau Mutter die von Schwartzburg⁹ lieget alhier in der Stadtkirche begraben.¹⁰ Die Lini aber ist mit Fürst Wolffgangen, so man damals die Bernburgische lini genant, ausgangen.¹¹ Von furst Georgen dem ältern¹² aber, ist furst Waldemars¹³ herr vatter gewesen, kommen wir her, und ist^e sein sohn Furst Ernst¹⁴ meins elter herr vater gewesen. Diesen bericht habe ich El. voran wollen gehen laßen; Von dem Schwartzburgischen und Honsteinischen stamme aber können El. am besten von der schwester von Schwartzburg¹⁵ bericht einholen. Die wappen habe ich bis auf Furst Sigismunden¹⁶ und weiter nicht. Wen El. solche haben wollen, können sie es etwan durch D. Engelhards Sohn¹⁷ bestellen laßen, der soll sie wol abmahlen. 4. Des Spielenden schreiben¹⁸ habe ich in etwas bey mir behalten, solches dem Vielgekörnten vorzuzeigen, ich hoffe es sol noch in diesem Jhare vom Ordnenden eine rechtschreibung¹⁹ herauskommen, die den sachen zimliche maße geben wird, wil dan der Spielende auf seiner weise bleiben, die einem ieden wolgefelt, aber doch nicht allezeit die beste ist, so ist das^f nicht zuverwundern, weil die welt^g solcher leute gantz voll ist. Der Spielende und Suchende übereilen sich darinnen, und werden vernünftige und grundliche wiederlegung finden.²⁰

Schlieslichen entbeut E.L. und dero gemahlin meine gemahl und ich unseren [407v] willigen^h gruß und dienst mit nochmaliger wiederholung unsres Christlichen treuhertzigen mitleidens, der liebe gott wolle Ell. alles leides wieder ergetzen und ersetzen, in deßen schutz ich Ell. allerseits treulich befehle, und verbleibe

E. L. getreuer Vetter
Ludwig fzu Anhalt

Cöthen den 26. des Mertzen 1645.

Ein schreiben ist gestern an El. von Weimar²¹ aus gekommen ist auch alhier beygeleget.

T **a** *Gebessert aus* <oh> [?]. — **b** *Eingefügt.* — **c** *Zwei längere vertikale Wellenlinien am linken Rand verweisen wohl auf die veränderte Reihenfolge der Punkte 3 und 4.* — **d** *Gebessert aus* <die>sem — **e** *Eingefügt für* <hat> — **f** *Eingefügt für* <es> — **g** *Eingefügt für* <leute> — **h** *Kustode:* willigen gruß und — willigen *fehlt auf Bl. 407v.*

K 1 Lehnübersetzung von Notifikation.
2 Pz. Ferdinand Christian (23.8.1643 – 14.3.1645), der jüngste Sohn F. Christians II. v. Anhalt-Bernburg (FG 51) u. seiner Frau Eleonora Sophia (TG 39). Er war am 18.10.1643 getauft worden; die beiden vornehmsten der 28 Taufpaten waren Kgn. Christina v. Schweden u. Ks. Ferdinand III. S. 431021, 431022 K 9, 431208 K 4 u. 431211 K I 22. F. Christians

Kammerrat Joachim Mechovius (FG 483. 1647; vgl. 400809 u. I u. II) hinterließ ein lat. Trauergedicht zum Tode des Prinzen: „In præmaturum obitum Illustrißimi Celsissimi*que* Principis ac Domini Dn. FERDINANDI CHRISTIANI". LHA Sa.-Anh./ Dessau: Abt. Bernburg A 10 Nr. 46^d, Bl. 270r. Vgl. *Beckmann* V, 372. Ton und Formulierung des Briefanfangs lassen vermuten, daß F. Ludwig Klagen F. Christians hinsichtlich mangelnder Kondolenz richtigstellen wollte. Anscheinend hatte der erwähnte Kondolenzbrief F. Ludwigs und seiner Gemahlin Sophia (AL 1629. TG 38) vom 19. 3. seinen Bernburger Neffen Christian und dessen Gattin Eleonora Sophia nicht erreicht.

3 Autor des Werks *El Enbaxador (Embajador)* (Sevilla 1620) war Juan Antonio de Vera Zuñiga y Figueroa (1581–1659) aus Kastilien, seit 1628 Conde de Roca, Diplomat, Offizier, Verfasser u. Übersetzer histor., polit. und dramat. Schriften. Das Buch wurde von Nicolas Lancelot (ca. 1587 – ca. 1640) ins Frz. übersetzt: Le parfait ambassadeur ... oeuvre très-utile et nécessaire à tous ministres d'estat, gouverneurs de provinces, secrétaires de princes ... composé en espagnol par Antonio de Vera et de Cuñiga ... et trad. en françois par le Sieur de Lancelot (Paris: de Sommaville 1635). HAB: Rq 194. Nach *IP*, Bl. 273v besaß F. Ludwig den 1642 fingiert in Paris, tatsächlich in Leiden erschienenen Raubdruck. HAB: Sf 251. Wann F. Ludwig das Werk an F. Christian II. verlieh, ist nicht bekannt. Vgl. 290129 K I 17.

4 Wahrscheinlich Hz. Ernst Bogislaw v. Croy u. Aerschot (Vinstingen, 26. 8. 1620 – Königsberg, 7. 2. 1684). Sein Vater war Hz. Ernst (um 1578–1620) aus einem katholischen, urspr. in der Picardie begüterten Adelsgeschlecht. Er hatte sich im August 1619 mit Hzn. Anna v. Pommern (1590–1660), Schwester des letzten pommerschen Herzogs aus dem Greifengeschlecht, Bogislaw XIV. (1580–1637), vermählt und so den pommerschen Zweig der Familie begründet. Anna war die letzte Überlebende der Greifendynastie. In ihrem Ehevertrag hatte Hz. Ernst der ev.-luth. Erziehung ihrer Kinder zugestimmt. Als er als ksl. General am 7. 10. 1620 im Feldlager vor Oppenheim a. Rhein starb (ohne wohl je seinen gerade geborenen Sohn Ernst Bogislaw gesehen zu haben), brachen erbitterte Streitigkeiten mit den kathol. Verwandten aus, die die junge Witwe 1622 veranlaßten, unter Zurücklassung ihres Vermögens die ihr als Leibgeding zugesagte lothring. Hft. Vinstingen/ Fénétrange am Oberlauf der Saar zu verlassen und sich über Straßburg nach Pommern in die Obhut ihres Bruders zu begeben. Sie blieb zuerst in Stettin, nach dessen Tod überwiegend in Stolp. Da Hzn. Anna aufgrund der Nachstellungen der Croys davon ausgehen mußte, daß ihr Sohn das väterl. Erbe niemals würde antreten können, stattete ihn Hz. Bogislaw XIV. standesgemäß mit dem Eventualerbe des pommerschen Bst.s Kammin aus, das ihm nach Bogislaws Tod zufallen sollte. Ernst Bogislaws Designation zum Bischof 1633 durch das Domkapitel schloß sich zwei Monate nach dem Tod Hz. Bogislaws XIV. die Wahl zum Kamminer Bischof an. Sie blieb aber folgenlos, da seine Inbesitznahme zunächst von den Schweden, dann von Kurbrandenburg verhindert wurde. 1634 besuchte er die U. Greifswald und ging dann auf eine mehrjährige Reise durch Westeuropa u. Polen. Nachdem Hinterpommern im Westfäl. Frieden Kf. Friedrich Wilhelm v. Brandenburg (FG 401) zugesprochen wurde, der aber das Bst. Kammin nicht an Ernst Bogislaw abtreten wollte, fand er ihn 1650 mit Geld und zwei anderen Herrschaften ab. Zudem hatte das *Instrumentum Pacis Osnabrugensis* im Art. 4 (versch. Restitutionsregelungen), § 28 die Restitution der Hft. Vinstingen, d. h. die Wiedereinsetzung Hzn. Annas u. Hz. Ernst Bogislaws verfügt, und zwar „in eo status, quo fuerunt ante hos motus, salvis permanentibus". Diese Restitution wurde auch im § 35 des *I.P. Monasteriensis* übernommen. *APW* III B, Bd. I.1, 105 f.; vgl. Bd. I.3, 24 u. 45. Johann Michael Moscherosch (FG 436. 1645) wirkte zeitweilig unter schwierigsten Bedingungen als Amtmann in Vinstingen/ Fénétrange (1635–1642), wo Anna und Ernst Bogislaw durchaus auch nach 1622 noch lan-

desherrlich wirkten, bis letzterer seine Anteile an der Herrschaft 1665 verkaufte. Vgl. *Conermann III*, 524; Porada (s.u.), 529f. u. 533f.; Kenneth Graham Knight: Johann Michael Moscherosch. Satiriker und Moralist des 17. Jahrhunderts. Stuttgart 2000, 21ff.; *Schäfer: Moscherosch und Harsdörffer*, 140; *Schäfer: Moscherosch*, 99–119. Von dort aus — „è Fenestrangia tua S.R.I. Mareschallatu" — widmete er am 10.12.1639 die 3. Centuria seiner Epigramm-Sammlung „Domino meo Clementissimo" Hz. Ernst Bogislaw, der zu dieser Zeit in England weilte. (Kupfertitel:) Epigrammata IOH. MICH. MOSCHEROSCH. (Titelbl.:) Centuria Prima [–Sexta] Epigrammatum JOHAN-MICHAELIS MOSCHEROSCH. Frankfurt 1665, Zitate S.121 u. 123. *Faber du Faur*, Nr.436 (Mikrofilm). Nach dem Tod der Mutter Anna erbte Ernst Bogislaw deren Leibgeding Stolp nebst zahlreichen wertvollen Stücken aus dem Nachlaß des Greifengeschlechts, darunter den sog. Croy-Teppich aus dem Stettiner Schloß (s.u.). 1665 wurde er zum kurbrandenburg. Statthalter in Hinterpommern und Kammin mit Amtssitz in Kolberg bestellt. 1670 löste er den verstorbenen F. Bogislaw v. Radziwill als kurbrandenb. Statthalter des Hzts. Preußen ab und zog nach Königsberg. In dieser Funktion verband ihn ein freundschaftlich-kollegiales Verhältnis mit seinem pommerschen Landsmann Frh. Otto v. Schwerin (FG 493. 1648). Ernst Bogislaw v. Croy blieb das einzige ev.-luther. Mitglied des Hauses Croy. Sein mit der Rostocker Bürgerstochter Dorothea Levius gezeugter Sohn Ernst wurde zwar 1670 von Kf. Friedrich Wilhelm legitimiert und zu „von Croyengreiff" geadelt, doch trat er in die S. J. ein und starb enterbt 1700 in Rom. In seinem Testament stiftete Ernst Bogislaw vieles aus dem Greifenerbe, darunter seine Bibliothek mitsamt den Kunstschätzen Kurbrandenburg, den sog. „Croy-Teppich" der U. Greifswald. Möglicherweise sollte dieser berühmte Teppich, der aus Anlaß der 1536 von Martin Luther persönlich in Torgau geschlossenen Vermählung Hz. Philipps I. v. Pommern-Wolgast (1515–1560) mit der ernestin. Hzn. Maria v. Sachsen (1515–1583) im Auftrag Philipps gewirkt wurde und die großen Reformatoren Luther, Melanchthon und Bugenhagen sowie sächs. und pommer. Fürsten darstellte, F. Ludwig als Anregung oder Vorbild für die intendierte anhaltin. Genealogie dienen. Hz. Ernst Bogislaw war für seine heraldischen Kenntnisse und genealog. Interessen bekannt; Kurbrandenburg hatte sich ihrer bedient, und sie dürften auch Gegenstand des brieflichen Austausches zw. dem Herzog und F. Christian II. bzw. F. Ludwig gewesen sein. Ernst Bogislaw besaß ein Exemplar der lat. Ausg. *Princeps, eiusque arcana: in vita Romuli rerpraesentate* (1636. HAB: 151.10 Pol. [2]). Das ital. Original von Virgilio Malvezzi, *IL ROMULO* (Bologna 1629) wurde später von F. Ludwig ins Deutsche übersetzt, s. *F. Ludwig: Romulus und Tarquinius (1647)*. Vgl. *EST* NF XVIII, T. 107; *GHdA* II, 375f.; *Kneschke* II, 370f.; *Köbler*, 114, außerdem 441226. — Zu Hz. Ernst Bogislaw vgl. 321201 K 11 (S. 461); *NDB*, 426f.; Thomas Porada: Zur Bedeutung von Konfession und Dynastie im Leben des letzten Bischofs von Cammin, Ernst Bogislaw von Croy. In: Christi Ehr vnd gemeinen Nutzen Willig zu fodern vnd zu schützen. Beiträge zur Kirchen-, Kunst- und Landesgeschichte Pommerns und des Ostseeraums. FS Norbert Buske. Hg. Michael Lissok u. Haik Thomas Porada. Schwerin 2014, 511–572; Matthias Bollmeyer: Ein neu entdecktes Buch aus dem Besitz des Herzogs Ernst Bogislaw von Croy. In: Der Herold 54 (2011) H. 1–2 (NF, 18), 153–161 (es geht um ein vom Herzog reich annotiertes Exemplar des lat. Romans *Argenis* von John Barclay, Ausg. Leiden 1630); Ludwig Biewer: Ernst Bogislaw Herzog von Croy (1620–1684). Statthalter in Pommern und in Preußen. In: Das Preußenland als Forschungsaufgabe. Hg. Bernhart Jähnig u. Georg Michels. Lüneburg 2000, 133–149; ders.: Ernst Bogislaw von Croy (1620–1684). In: Varziner Hefte 4 (Kiel 2004), 4–36. Vgl. zur Greifenbibliothek 460715 K II 4. Zum „Croy-Teppich" vgl. Der Greifswalder Croy-Teppich. 27. Croy-Fest, 16. Oktober 1992. Greifswalder Universitätsreden N. F. 64. Ernst-Moritz-Arndt-Universität Greifswald WS

1992/93; Birgit Dahlenburg, Rita Sauer: Der Croy-Teppich der Ernst-Moritz-Arndt-Universität Greifswald — national wertvolles Kulturgut Deutschlands. In: Pommern. Zs. f. Kultur u. Geschichte 3 (2014), 42–47; Heimo Reinitzer: *Tapetum Concordiae*. Peter Heymans Bildteppich für Philipp I. von Pommern und die Tradition der von Mose getragenen Kanzeln. Berlin 2012 (zu Croy S. 67f.). Stellt der „Croy-Teppich" ein reformator. Bekenntnisbild dar, so gehörte der Rückbezug auf die Reformation auch zum dynast. Selbstverständnis der Anhaltiner. S. Michael Hecht: Hofordnungen, Wappen und Geschichtsschreibung. In: Die Fürsten von Anhalt. Herrschaftssymbolik, dynastische Vernunft u. politische Konzepte in Spätmittelalter u. Früher Neuzeit. Hg. Werner Freitag u. M. H. Halle a. d. S. 2003, 98–122, hier 113. Dafür spricht bereits die von Philipp Melanchthon verfaßte Vorrede in der fl. Auftragsarbeit Ernst Brotuffs (ca. 1497–1565): GENEALOGIA Vnd Chronica/ des Durchlauchten Hochgebornen/ Königlichen vnd Fürstlichen Hauses/ der Fürsten zu Anhalt/ Graffen zu Ballenstedt vnd Ascanie/ Herrn zu Bernburgk vnd Zerbst/ auff 1055. Jar/ in sechs Büchern/ mit viel schönen alten Historien/ Geschichten/ Königlichen vnd Fürstlichen Wopen [Wappen] gezieret/ vnd beschrieben. Mit einer Vorrede Herrn Philippi Melanthon [*sic*]. [Leipzig 1556]. HAB: 157 Hist. 2° (2). (Ex. Gm 4° 60 auch dig.). Dieses genealogisch-historische Werk erschien in 2. Aufl. 1602 in Amberg und blieb bis zum Ende des 17. Jh.s das „Standardwerk" anhalt. Geschichte und dynast. Legitimation des Fürstenhauses. Hecht, op. cit., 107; ders.: Die Erfindung der Askanier. Dynastische Erinnerungsstiftung der Fürsten von Anhalt an der Wende vom Mittelalter zur Neuzeit. In: Zeitschrift für historische Forschung 22 (2006), 1–33, hier S. 12f.; ders.: Ernst Brotuff — Chronist des anhaltischen Fürstenhauses im 16. Jahrhundert. In: MVAL 15 (2006), 67–78. Ein auf die anhaltin. Genealogie konzentrierter, in 32 Ahnenproben mit 126 Wappenschilden verzierter Wappenteppich war schon 1585 im Auftrag der zweiten Gattin F. Joachim Ernsts (1536–1586), Fn. Eleonoras, geb. Hzn. v. Württemberg (1552–1618), für die Dessauer Kirche angefertigt worden (heute Kunstsammlungen der Veste Coburg). Vgl. dazu Hecht: Hofordnungen (s.o.), 108f.; zur anhaltin. Heraldik vgl. schon 371116 K 4. — Der vorliegende Brief zeigt zweifellos das wache Interesse F. Ludwigs und seines Neffen Christian II. an genealogischen Fragen des Hauses Anhalt, das seine Legitimationsargumente, wie damals üblich, theologisch aus seiner konfessionellen Rolle einer Verteidigerin des wahren Bekenntnisses (hier Reformation und reformierte Konfessionalisierung), und historisch aus seiner Ancienität schöpfte, die in der dynastischen Imagologie bis auf die biblischen Noachiden zurückverfolgt wurde (Ascenas, Askaniermythos), auch wenn *Beckmann* I, 12f. diese biblisch begründete Herkunftslegende bereits aus dem Fundus historisch verbürgter Nachrichten ausschließt und im Reich der Sage beläßt. Ob F. Ludwig mit seinen genealogischen Studien und Arbeiten Brotuffs Werk aktualisieren, dieses durch ein aktuelles gar ersetzen wollte oder ob er andere Absichten damit verfolgte, muß spekulativ bleiben. Daß dynastische Genealogie aber auch für die Anhaltiner ein Hebel war, politische Herrschaftsansprüche zu begründen, zeigt sich an ihren Anstrengungen zum Rückerhalt der 1315 an das Stift Halberstadt verlorenen alten Gft. Ascanien (Aschersleben). In den *Vindiciae Anhaltinae* mit ihrem *Manifestum Ascaniense* ging Martin Milagius (FG 315) zur Begründung dieses Anspruchs bis in die älteste frühmittelalterliche Geschichte zurück und legte dabei auch fünf genealogische Tafeln vor: VINDICIÆ ANHALTINÆ. SEU CELSISSIMORUM ET ILLUSTRISSIMORUM PRINCIPUM ANHALTINORUM, COMITUM ASCANIÆ, DYNASTARUM SERVESTANORUM & BERNBURGENSIUM, etc. Jura liquidissima in & circa Antiquißimum Comitum ASCANIÆ: Repræsentata in MANIFESTO ASCANIENSI (o. O. 1648.) HAB: 106.3 Jur. (2). Es war dies im Rahmen der Westfäl. Friedensverhandlungen der letzte, publizistisch befeuerte, aber vergebliche Versuch der Anhaltiner, sich des verlorenen askan. Erbes wieder zu versichern. Hinsichtlich des historisch-politischen Rückbezuges des anhaltin. Fürstenhauses auf die Reformation ist auch die bewußt gezogene Verbindung der FG-Gründung im 100. Jubiläumsjahr der Reformation 1617 signifikant — bei aller Betonung konfessioneller Neutralität. Vgl. dazu 411200 (Harsdörffer), *Harsdörffer: Schutzschrift (1644)*, Ndr. 358f.; *Hille: Teutscher Palmbaum (1647)*, 9.

5 Liegen dem Brief nicht mehr bei.

6 F. Heinrich I. v. Anhalt u. Ascharien (um 1170? – 1251/52); Enkel Mgf. Albrechts des Bären und Sohn Bernhards III., Hz.s v. Sachsen-Wittenberg. F. Heinrich trat als Minnesänger auf und nahm am „Sängerkrieg" auf der Wartburg teil. S. *EST* NF I.2, T. 186; Andreas Thiele: Erzählende genealogische Stammtafeln zur europäischen Geschichte. Bd. I.2. Frankfurt a. M. ²1994, T. 332; *VL (2. Aufl.)*, 685–687; *Conermann: Zwischen Literatur- und Nationalsprache*, 14ff.; Lutz Partenheimer: Die frühen Askanier und die Entstehung Anhalts. In: 800 Jahre Anhalt. Geschichte, Kultur, Perspektiven. Hg. Anhaltischer Heimatbund. Wettin-Löbejün 2012, 153–173, hier 153f. u. 168f.

7 Kf. Johann v. Sachsen, „der Beständige" (1468–1532, Kf. seit 1525) heiratete in zweiter Ehe am 31.11.1513 Pzn. Margaretha v. Anhalt (1494–1521), die Tochter F. Waldemars VI. v. Anhalt in Köthen (1450–1508) und Schwester F. Wolfgangs (1492–1566). Margarethe starb vor Kf. Johann, demnach täuscht sich F. Ludwig in der Annahme, sie sei als Witwe vom Hz. v. Pommern geehelicht worden. *EST* NF I.2, T. 188; Thiele, Bd. I.2 (s. Anm. 6), T. 336.

8 Ludwigs Irrtum beruht möglicherweise auf einer Verwechslung: F. Georg (II.) (1456–1509), ein Bruder Waldemars VI. (1454–1509), ehelichte 1478/79 Hzn. Agnes v. Pommern (†1512), Witwe Mgf. Friedrichs v. Brandenburg in der Altmark und der Priegnitz (†1463). *EST* NF I.2, T. 188; Thiele, Bd. I.2 (s. Anm. 6), T. 336.

9 Gfn. Margaretha v. Schwarzburg (1464–1539), 1485 Gemahlin v. F. Waldemar VI. v. Anhalt in Köthen (s. Anm. 8), Tochter von Gf. Günther XX., Herr zu Arnstadt u. Sondershausen. *EST* NF I.2, T. 188; Thiele, Bd. I.2 (s. Anm. 6), T. 336.

10 *Beckmann* III, 415: „Vor dem Tische des Herrn/ da die H. Communion gehalten wird/ ist der Fürstin Margariten/ gebohrene Gräfin von Schwartzburg/ GrabStein/ auf welchem oben ein Brust=Bild von einer verhüllten Frauens=Person zu sehen/ und weiter herunter diese Worte: Am Donnerstage den 1. Julij Anno 1539. ist verschieden die Hochgeborne Fürstin Frau Margarita/ Fürstin zu Anhalt/ geborne von Schwartzburg Witwe/ der Gott genade. Darunter stehet das Fürstl. Anhaltische und Schwartzburgische Wapen. Unter dem Tische ist Fürst Ludwigs und dessen Fürstl. Kinder und Zugehörigen begräbnüß." Gegen Ende des 19. Jhs. befand sich der Grabstein mit 23 weiteren im Westteil der Köthener Stadtkirche St. Jakob an den Wänden. Er zeigte die Fürstin als Halbfigur, betend und mit einem Engel über ihr sowie dem anhalt. u. schwarzburg. Wappen zu ihren Füßen. S. Franz Büttner Pfänner zu Thal: Anhalts Bau- u. Kunstdenkmäler. Dessau 1892, 243 u. 245. Keine Angabe in Ernst Haetge u. Marie-Luise Harksen: Die Kunstdenkmale des Landes Anhalt. Bd. 2.1: Die Stadt Köthen und der Landkreis außer Wörlitz. Burg b. Magdeburg 1943 (vgl. S. 142–167 zur Jakobskirche). Der „Dehio" nennt nur kursorisch „zahlreiche Figurengrabsteine 15.–17. Jh." ohne genauere Standortangaben. Georg Dehio: Handbuch der Deutschen Kunstdenkmäler. Sachsen-Anhalt II. Regierungsbezirke Dessau und Halle. Bearb. v. Ute Bednarz u.a. München 1999, 382.

11 F. Wolfgang (s. Anm. 7) starb unvermählt und ohne Nachkommen. Er hatte in enger Anlehnung an Kursachsen die Reformation in Anhalt eingeführt, 1530 die *Confessio Augustana* unterzeichnet und war dem Schmalkaldischen Bund beigetreten. Er war einer der gebildetsten und angesehensten Reichsfürsten seiner Zeit. *EST* NF I.2, T. 188; Thiele, Bd. I.2 (s. Anm. 6), T. 336.

12 F. Georg I. v. Anhalt (1390–1474). *EST* NF I.2, T. 188; Thiele, Bd. I.2 (s. Anm. 6), T. 336.

13 F. Waldemar VI. v. Anhalt in Köthen (s. Anm. 8).

14 F. Ernst v. Anhalt in Zerbst und Dessau (*um 1453 — 1516), Vater F. Georgs III. (1507–1553), der die Reformation im letzten anhalt. Landesteil, im Ft. Anhalt-Dessau einführte und mit Luther und Melanchthon befreundet war. Vgl. *Conermann TG*, 596–609 (mit interessanten sprachgeschichtlichen und reformator. Quellen im Zusammenhang mit Gfn. Anna Sophia v. Schwarzburg-Rudolstadt, s. Anm. 15). F. Ernst war der Großvater F. Joachim Ernsts v. Anhalt (1536–1586) und Urgroßvater F. Ludwigs. Von Joachim Ernst, der das ges. Ft. in seiner Hand vereinigte, stammten alle späteren anhaltin. Linien ab. *EST* NF I.2, T. 188; Thiele, Bd. I.2 (s. Anm. 6), T. 336.

15 Gfn. Anna Sophia v. Schwarzburg-Rudolstadt (TG 1), Tochter F. Joachim Ernsts (s. Anm. 14) und Schwester F. Ludwigs, Gründerin der TG.

16 F. Sigismund I. v. Anhalt in Zerbst und Dessau (†1405), Großvater der Fürsten Waldemar VI. (s. Anm. 8) u. Ernst (s. Anm. 14). Zur Veränderung des fl.-anhaltin. Wappens bis hin zum 9-feldigen Stammwappen seit etwa 1540 vgl. Michael Hecht: Hofordnungen, Wappen und Geschichtsschreibung (s. Anm. 4), 109 ff.; ders.: Landesherrschaft im Spiegel der Heraldik: Das große Wappen des Fürstentums Anhalt in der frühen Neuzeit. In: Sachsen und Anhalt. Jahrbuch der Histor. Kommission f. Sachsen-Anhalt 22 (1999/ 2000), 267–288. *EST* NF I.2, T. 187 u. 188; Thiele, Bd. I.2 (s. Anm. 6), T. 335.

17 Dr. Matthias Engelhardt (Engelhart), 1630–1649 in Köthen nachgewiesen, Leib- und Hofarzt F. Ludwigs und Stadtarzt in Köthen. Sein Sohn Christoph, der hier wohl am ehesten in Frage kommt, legte vielen FG-Mitgliedern sein Stammbuch zur Eintragung vor. Weiterführende Nachrichten liegen uns über Christoph nicht vor. Weitere Söhne waren Andreas und Matthias. S. 270115 K 4 u. 410708 K 3, vgl. auch 450408. Zu Michael Engelhardt, FG 335, vgl. *Conermann III*, 383; *Opitz: BW* 350000A *insc* K 3.

18 Vielleicht Georg Philipp Harsdörffers (FG 368. Der Spielende) Brief 440824, den F. Ludwig erst am 19.1.1645 erhielt, s. 450124. In diesem Antwortbrief hatte F. Ludwig bereits etliche Punkte in Harsdörffers Sprachauffassungen, der sich auch in 440824 als Parteigänger Justus Georg Schottelius' (FG 397. Der Suchende) zu erkennen gab, kritisiert. Schon damals war Diederich v. dem Werder (FG 31. Der Vielgekörnte) einbezogen worden und hatte sich F. Ludwigs Kritik an der von Harsdörffer befürworteten Polyflexion der attributiven Adjektive angeschlossen, s. 450124 I. Hinsichtlich der Meinungsunterschiede in der Rechtschreibung ist auf die zwei Gutachten F. Ludwigs über Harsdörffers Rechtschreibung (im 3. Teil der *Frauenzimmer-Gesprächspiele* 1643) zu verweisen: „Etzliche Erinnerungen, bey dem dritten theile der gesprächspiele" (HM Köthen: VS 545, Bl. 419r–424v u. 426r) u. „Erinnerungen bey dem anhange der hundert Spielreime" (ebd., Bl. 426v–428v u. 425rv). Harsdörffer beantwortete letzteres mir einer „Kurtzen Entschuldigung" (ebd., Bl. 290rv u. 289rv), auf die F. Ludwig wiederum mit einer „Kurtzen Antwort, und erklerung" antwortete. Alle Dokumente demnächst in *DA Köthen I. 9*. Daß es zwischen 440824 und 450400 einen oder mehrere Briefe Harsdörffers an F. Ludwig gab, erscheint unwahrscheinlich. Da der Eingang von 450400 bei F. Ludwig erst am 9.5.1645 bestätigt wurde und dieser Brief zudem kaum auf die kontroverse Sprachdiskussion zw. Harsdörffer und F. Ludwig eingeht, kann dieses Schreiben auch bei möglicher früherer Datierung nicht der gemeinte Harsdörffer-Brief gewesen sein.

19 *Gueintz* (FG 361. Der Ordnende): *Rechtschreibung (1645)*. Sie erschien wohl im September 1645. Vgl. 440127 K 1.

20 Eine Verstimmung F. Ludwigs über Harsdörffers und Schottelius' Festhalten an ihren Sprachauffassungen ist z.B. dem Brief Werders 450420 zu entnehmen, da er Vorschläge macht, wie „denen jenigen so itzo bemühet sein auf ihre eigene hand eine algemeine verfaßung [zur Rechtschreibung] aufzusetzen, oder doch nach ihrem Kopfe verenderlich [d.h. unterschiedlich oder abweichend vom Usus] zuschreiben, als da sein der Suchende vnd der Spielende", durch eine allgemeine Prüfung und Verabschiedung des Richtigen durch die FG eine verbindliche Grundlage zu schaffen. Diese verpflichte die Genannten, „sich in den Schrancken zuhalten, vnd nicht so nach ihrem blossen wahn oben hin regeln vnd neue arten, ohne erhebliche vrsachen, zusetzen vnd einzufüren." S. dort, vgl. auch 450504A u. F. Ludwigs Briefe 450504, 450505 u.ö.

21 Brief von Hz. Wilhelm IV. v. Sachsen-Weimar (FG 5). Liegt nicht mehr bei; vgl. aber 450220.

450331

Fürst Ludwig an Herzog August d. J. von Braunschweig-Wolfenbüttel

F. Ludwig (Der Nährende) bestätigt, auf Hz. Augusts d.J. v. Braunschweig-Wolfenbüttel (FG 227) Erklärung zur Beteiligung am Verlag des *GB 1646* hin dem Braunschweiger Handelsmann Hans Beyer eine Quittung über 200 Rth. geschickt zu haben. Der Herzog möge nun das Geld einzahlen.

Q NSTA Wolfenbüttel: 1 Alt 22 Nr. 134, Bl. 56rv u. 58rv [A: 58v], 58r leer; Schreiberh. mit eigenh. Schlußkurialien u. Unterschrift; Sig. Bl. 56v mit Vermerk v. Schreiberh.: „Von höeff allererst empfangen, den 7ten Julij A° *etc.* 645". Bl. 57rv s. Beil. I.

A *Dem Hochgebornen Fürsten, Herren Augusten*, Hertzogen zu Braunschweig und Lüneburg *etc.* Unserm freundlichen lieben Oheim und Schwager *etc.* — *Eintrag v. H. eines Kanzlisten*: Sr f. gnd. schreiben wegen des geselschafft buchs, sub dato den 31ten Martij 645

Vnsere freundliche dienste, und was Wir mehr liebes und gutes vermögen zuvor:
Hochgeborner Fürst, freundlicher lieber Oheim und Schwager.
Wir haben auf die von E. Ld. gegen uns beschehene freundliche erklerung, wegen des Geselschaftbuches[1], so in Kupfer sol gestochen werden, Johan Beiern[2] Handelsmanne in Braunschweig, die begehrte quittung, auf die zweyhundert thaler, so E. Ld. mit zu deßen verlage darreichen wollen, zugeschicket: Ersuchen sie demnach freundlich, ihme dieselbigen auszahlen zu laßen, und sol unsers theils derselben, also nachgegangen und das werck so viel an uns, möglichst befördert werden, Habens E. Ld. nicht verhalten mögen, und verbleiben deroselben zu angenemen diensten willig.
Geben Cöthen den 31.ten tag des Mertzens im jahre 1645.
Von Gottes gnaden Ludwig Fürst zu Anhalt, Graf zu Ascanien, Herr zu Bernburg und Zerbst *etc.*

E. L dienstwilliger^a Oheim und Schwager
Ludwig fzu Anhalt

I

Lieferungsverpflichtung Fürst Ludwigs über 48 Exemplare des Gesellschaftsbuchs von 1646

Q NSTA Wolfenbüttel: 1 Alt 22 Nr. 134, Bl. 57rv (Doppelbl. mit Siegelwachs zusammengeklebt); 57r Schreiberh. mit eigenh. Unterschrift F. Ludwigs; Bl. 57v Quittungsvermerk eines braunschweig. Beamten: „Ludwieg furstens zu Anhalt *etc.* schein wegen eins Buchs der fruchtbringenden Gesellschafft gämehlde vff – [längerer waagrechter Strich unterhalb der Siegelspur] 200 Rth. Ist durch Hansen Beyern zu Br[aunschweig] *etc.* zahlt [Abstand] Den 31.ten Martij A° 645 [am unteren Seitenrand] Nro. 1"

A *Fehlt.*

Von Gottes gnaden, Wir Ludwig Fürst zu Anhalt Graf zu Ascanien, Herr zu Bernburg und Zerbst *etc.* Hiermit bekennen, das Uns der Hochgeborne Fürst, Herr **Augustus** hertzog zu Braunschweig und Lüneburg, Unser freundlicher lieber Oheim und Schwager, mit zum verlage eines buches, darinnen der Fruchtbringenden Geselschaft gemählde, in die Vierhundert in Kupfer gestochen werden, zweyhundert Reichsthaler erlegen laßen, die Wir auch durch Johan Beiern, Handelsman zu Braunschweig erheben laßen, und an gebürenden ort übermachen wollen, und sollen nach verfertigung deßelben werckes S^r. Ld. achtundvierzig Exemplar dafür ausgefolget werden;[1]

Uhrkundlich haben Wir diesen schein mit Unserm Fürstl. Jnsiegel bekräftiget und eigenen handen unterschrieben.

So geschehen zu Cöthen den 31.ten tag des Mertzens im jahre 1645 *etc.*

Ludwig fzu Anhalt

T a *Von hier an F. Ludwigs H.*

K 1 S. 440130 K 3 (dort auch zum *GB 1646* allgemein). Bereits in 430121 erklärte Carl Gustav v. Hille (FG 302) im Auftrag Hz. Augusts d. J. v. Braunschweig-Wolfenbüttel (FG 227), daß die hzl. Einlage zum Verlag des *GB 1646* 200 Reichstaler betrage. Zu den Verlagsbeiträgen s. Beil. I u. 450126 K 4.
2 Hans Beyer, Handelsmann in Braunschweig u. finanzieller Verbindungsmann zwischen Köthen (F. Ludwig), Wolfenbüttel (Hz. August d. J.) u. Frankfurt a. M. (Matthäus Merian d. Ä.). S. 450503. Vgl. auch 450419 K 2. Zum Zahlungsverkehr das *GB 1646* betreffend s. 450127 K 1.

K I 1 Ein knappes Jahr später findet sich im Brief 460303 u. 460324 die Nachricht, daß Matthäus Merian d. Ä. 48 Exemplare für Hz. August d. J. v. Braunschweig-Wolfenbüttel

(FG 227) auf den Weg brachte. Vgl. 460206 II. An die Zahlung der Verlagseinlage hatte F. Ludwig den Herzog u. andere Teilhaber häufig erinnern müssen. S. K 1 u. 450126 K 4.

450400

Georg Philipp Harsdörffer an Fürst Ludwig

Antwort auf 450124. Beantwortet durch 450529 u. 450611. — Georg Philipp Harsdörffer (FG 368. Der Spielende) bestätigt den Empfang des Briefes 450124 nach 5 Wochen, bedankt sich bei F. Ludwig (Der Nährende) für die *Verstandt-Lehr* (von Jacob Martini/ Ludwig Lucius) und versichert, die (grammatischen und prosodischen) Korrekturvorschläge F. Ludwigs (zu *Frauenzimmer-Gesprächspiele* IV) künftig beherzigen zu wollen. Die vermehrte 2. Auflage des ersten Teils seiner *Gesprächspiele* (1644) habe er F. Ludwig gewidmet (und überschickt ihm hiermit ein Exemplar) in der Hoffnung auf des Fürsten Genehmhaltung. Der 5. Teil der *Gesprächspiele* (1645) befinde sich im Druck, das Vorwerk der Ehrengedichte noch ausgenommen. Die Fertigstellung werde aber gewiß noch ein halbes Jahr in Anspruch nehmen, da dieser Teil anspruchsvoller und wegen der (in Fragen der Sprachrichtigkeit) ungeschulten Setzer mühsamer ausfalle. — Harsdörffer übersendet einige Texte eines anonymen Liebhabers der deutschen Sprache. Philipp v. Zesen (FG 521. 1648) werde wohl auch nicht unterlassen, F. Ludwig ein Exemplar seines neuesten, der FG gewidmeten Werkes *Ibrahim Bassa* (1645) zukommen zu lassen. — Zesen habe in den Niederlanden eine „Deutschgesinnte" Gesellschaft (DG) gegründet. Ihre Impresen seien sämtlich von den Rosen abgeleitet und ersetzten die Überschrift durch kurze Verse. Niemand solle Mitglied werden können, der nicht ein fremdsprachiges Buch in Vers oder Prosa zu übersetzen verspreche. Zesen schreibe, daß sich etliche Adlige, Gelehrte und Berühmte in der Gesellschaft verbunden hätten, um die deutsche Sprache auszuarbeiten und emporzubringen. Auch ihm, Harsdörffer, habe er die Mitgliedschaft angetragen, zumal es auch in Italien üblich sei, daß einer in mehreren Akademien Mitglied sein könne. Harsdörffers Gesellschaftsname solle der Durchbrechende sein, sein „Sinnbild" ein Bootsmann auf einem niederländ. Eisbrecher, der von einer Muse mit einem Rosenkranz beschenkt wird. Das Wort der Überschrift laute ‚Fleiß bricht Eis und erhält den Preis'. Harsdörffer wäre einer Mitgliedschaft nicht abgeneigt, sofern F. Ludwig keine Einwände habe. Auch beabsichtige er, hundert Andachtsgemälde oder geistliche Embleme und vier weitere Teile der *Gesprächspiele* herauszubringen. — Harsdörffer erklärt, die drei übersandten, das *GB 1641* ergänzenden (Druck-)Bögen (mit Gesellschaftsnamen, Reimgesetzen und Initialen der Taufnamen) erhalten zu haben. Da er aber die Initialen nicht auflösen und daher etwa durchreisende FG-Genossen nicht gebührlich empfangen könne, bittet er F. Ludwig, ihm wie auch Hans Philipp (v.) Geuder (FG 310. Der Ergänzende) ein Namensverzeichnis der Mitglieder 317 bis zum „Deuenden" (gemeint ist Zacharias Prüschenk v. Lindenhofen. FG 418) zu übersenden.

Q HM Köthen: V S 545, Bl. 308r–309v [A: 309v], undat.; eigenh.; zwei rote Lacksiegel. — D: *KE*, 336f.; *KL* III, 260f. (gekürzt). — *BN*: Bürger, 674 Nr. 31.

A *Dem Durchleuchtigen, Hochgebornen Fürsten und Herrn, Herrn LUDWIGEN Fürsten zu Anhalt, Grafen zu Ascanien und Ballenstat* und so weiter[a] seinem gnädigen Fürsten und Herrn. Zu Leipzig bey Gottfried Stahlen[1] abzulegen.   Cöthen.
Empfangsvermerk von F. Ludwigs Hand: 9. Maymonats 1645.

Hochgeehrter NEHRENDER.

Der hochlöblichen *fruchtbringenden Gesellschaft* jüngst an den *Spielenden* gegebenes vom 24 des Jenners, ist ihm fünf wochen hernach zu recht eingehändiget worden, bedanket sich so wol wegen der übersandten Verstandlehre,[2] als der treugemeinten Erinnerung,[3] welche er[b] künftiges zu beobachten unvergessen seyn wird. Weil aber inzwischen der erste Theil der Gesprächspiele vermehlet [sic][c], zum zweiten mal aufgelegt worden; hat sich der *Spielende* erkühnet solchen des hochgeehrten *NEHRENDEN* Gnaden schutze in unterthänigkeit anzubefehlen, und die schwelle seines geringen Werkleins mit so hohen ansehen auszuschmucken: der ungezweiffelten Hoffnung Hochbesagter *NEHRENDE* werde ihm[d] solches unternemen gefallen lassen, und wie bis anhero also auch künftig dem *Spielenden* mit gnädiger Gewogenheit beygethan verbleiben.[4]

Der fünfte Theil ermeldter Gesprächspiele ist nun mehr auch der presse untergeben, und sind die ersten bögen, zu unterschiedlichen Ehrgedichten, welche vorneme Herren und freunde theils übersendet, theils zu senden versprochen, liegen verblieben: doch kan das haubtwerk unter sechs monaten, (weil es verhoffentlich sinnreicher[,] wegen[e] der unberichten drucksetzer mühsamer und von mehrerer Wichtigkeit, als die ersten) nicht gefertiget werden.[5] Ein liebhaber der Deutschen[f] Sprache, der nicht wil benamet seyn, schicket benebens etliche Stücke seiner arbeit;[6] wie auch *Cæsius*, der sein letztes werk, überschrieben *Ibraim* der *etc. Fruchtbringenden Gesellschaft* zugeeignet[g] [308v] förderlichst thun wird.[7] Dieser Cæsius, der sich jetzt Zesiens [sic] schreibet, hat in Niederland eine neue Gesellschaft an- und aufgerichtet, und benamet die *Deutschgesinnte,*[8] Jhre Sinnbilder sind alle von den Rosen erfunden, benebens einen kurtzen Reimen anstat der obschrift,[9] und sol niemand mit eingenommen werden, der nicht ein Buch in gebundener[h] oder ungebundener Rede zu dolmetschen verspricht. Er schreibt[,] das Grafen, Freyherren und etliche Gelehrte und berühmte Männer sich solcher gestalt, zu ausarbeitung und hochbringung der Deutschen Sprache verbunden: und weilen auch in Welschland unterschiedliche dergleichen Academien und vielmals einer, zweyen oder auch dreyen, mit absonderlichen Namen zu gethan ist, hat er des *Spielenden*[i] Person darzu eingeladen, und genennet den *Durchbrechenden*. Das Sinnbild ist ein Bohtsmann, mit einem brechschifflein, damit man in Niederlanden den anderen Schiffen den Weg durch das Eis zu bahnen, und fürfahrt durchzubrechen pfleget: absehend auf die anweisung der Gesprächsspiele. Diesen Bohtsmann beschenket eine KunstGöttin (musa)[j] am Ufer mit einem Rosenkrantz. Die obschrift ist: *Fleiß bricht eis, und erhält den Preis.*[10] Wann es mit des hochgeehrten *NEHRENDEN* einwilligung und guhtbefindung geschehen könte, were der *Spielende* nicht abgeneigt, sich ermelder massen auch unter die *Deutschgesinnten* zubegeben, und etwa mit der[k] Zeit hunder[t] *Andachtsgemählen,* oder Geistlichen Sinnbildern, benebens noch vier Theilen der Gesprächspiele, an[l] das liecht zu bringen;[11] welch[es][m] er sonder vorwissen und Einwilligung des *NEHRENDEN* [309r] nicht thun sollen, noch wollen.

Wegen der drey überschickten Bögen zu den [sic] Gesellschaft Buch bedanket sich der *Spielende* dienstlich:¹² weilen er aber die Namensbuchstaben nicht verstehet, ist ihm solches fast wenig dienlich; gestalt er solchen HH. Gesellschaftern, wann selbe zu zeiten hierdurch reisen, nicht aufwarten kan wie seine Schuldigkeit erfordert. Bittet demnach, benebens den [sic] *Ergentzenden*¹³ ihm die Verzeichniß¹⁴ aller der Namen, von 317 den *Beliebten* (*Hanns von Rochau,*) bis auf den *Deuenden*¹⁵ wiederfahren zulassen.

Hiermit verbleibet, nechst empfehlung Gottlichen obschutzes,
des
Hochgeehrten NEHRENDEN
   Unterthäniger *Diener*
   Der Spielende.

T **a** *Gebräuliches Abkürzungszeichen für* „und", *gemeint sein kann aber nur* „und so weiter" *oder* „etc.". — **b** *Eingefügt für* <ihm> — **c** *Lies:* vermehret — **d** *Lies:* sich — **e** *Bis* drucksetzer *am Rand ergänzt.* — **f** *Gebessert aus* Teutschen — **g** *Gebessert aus* zuge-<schrieben> — **h** *Folgt* <und> — **i** *des Spielenden eingefügt für* <auch meine wenige> — **j** *Eingefügt.* — **k** der Zeit *eingefügt.* — **l** *Bis* bringen *eingefügt für* <heraus zu geben> — **m** *Buchstabenverlust im Falz. Konjektur in eckigen Klammern.*

K F. Ludwigs Empfangsvermerk u. Harsdörffers einleitende Bemerkung, der vorhergehende Brief von F. Ludwig (450124) habe eine Laufzeit von 5 Wochen gehabt, läßt vermuten, daß auch der vorliegende, undatierte Brief lang brauchte u. im März oder April 1645 abgeschickt wurde.

1 Gottfried Stahl (1600–1670), Leipziger Kaufmann mit langjährigen Nürnberger Verbindungen u. lt. der Anschrift in 430624 „Fürstl. Anhaltischer Factor" in Leipzig. S. 440426 Anschrift u. K 1.

2 Georg Philipp Harsdörffer (FG 368. Der Spielende) hatte F. Ludwig (Der Nährende) mit 440426 Entwürfe zu zwei Freudenspielen über die Logik („Die Vernunftkunst") u. die Rhetorik („Die Redkunst") überschickt, die dann ausgearbeitet im fünften Teil der *Frauenzimmer-Gesprächspiele* (1645) erschienen. S. dazu 440426 u. I, ferner 450529 K 2. Da eines der Freudenspiele die Logik als Gegenstand hat, ließ F. Ludwig ihm mit 450124 je ein Exemplar von Jacob Martinis *COMPENDIUM LOGICÆ AD DIDACTICAM* u. der dt. Übersetzung von Ludwig Lucius, *Kurtzer Begriff Der Verstandt-Lehr/ Zu der Lehrart*, beide Köthen 1621, zukommen, da sie ihm bei der Verdeutschung philosophischer Grundbegriffe dienlich sein könnten. S. 450124 K 4 u. 5.

3 F. Ludwig hatte in 450124 einige prosodische u. grammatische Probleme im vierten Teil der *Frauenzimmer-Gesprächspiele* angemerkt, die die fehlerhafte Verwendung der Daktylen vor der Mittelzäsur der Verse (Alexandriner u. Vers communs) u. die fehlerhafte Polyflexion einschließlich der überreichen Pluralbildung von männlichen Substantiven mit Auslaut auf -er betreffen. Diese Korrekturhinweise schließen sich an zwei Gutachten des Fürsten zum 3. Teil der *Gesprächspiele* an, welche er im Juli/ August 1643 an Harsdörffer gesandt hatte. Vgl. 450124 K 6 u. 7.

4 Der 2. Auflage des ersten Bandes seiner *Frauenzimmer-Gesprächspiele* (1644, 1. Aufl. 1641) setzte Harsdörffer ein neues „Vbereigungsgedicht [sic] An den NEHRENDEN" voran, s. 440616 K III 3, 440715 K 2 u. 3, 450529 K 1, 450611 K 1, 450817 K 11, 450919A u. 460803 K 0. Die Widmungsvorrede an die FG aus der ersten Auflage wurde beibehalten,

s. 410300. F. Ludwig beschwert sich in 450611 über einen ikonographischen Fehler in der N-Schmuckinitiale des Wortes „NEHRENDEN". In 440824 hatte Harsdörffer F. Ludwig mitgeteilt, daß die Neuausgabe des Bandes (im Queroktavformat) gerade dem Druck übergeben wurde. In 450529 bestätigte F. Ludwig dankend den Erhalt eines Exemplars.

5 In 440824 kündigte Harsdörffer bereits an, daß seine Arbeit am fünften Teil seiner *Frauenzimmer-Gesprächspiele* fast abgeschlossen sei. Im August 1645 ist der Druck noch nicht abgeschlossen (s. 450817), mit 450923C kann er F. Ludwig ein Exemplar des druckfrischen Werkes schicken. Zu den Verfassern der „Ehrengedichte" in *Harsdörffer: Frauenzimmer-Gesprächspiele* V (1645, Ndr. 1969), Ndr. S. 21–86, s. 450808 K I.

6 Die überschickten Texte befinden sich nicht im Erzschrein, zwischen Harsdörffer u. F. Ludwig ist von diesem „liebhaber der Teutschen Sprache" später nicht mehr die Rede. Man kann vielleicht erwägen, ob jene ominöse Person ein früher Pegnitzschäfer oder der Nürnberger Theologe, Schulmann u. Dichter Johann Michael Dilherr ist, der sich von Gesellschaften wie FG oder PBO fernhielt. Harsdörffer selbst sendet erst rund acht Monate später (mit 451217) F. Ludwig die ersten Seiten seiner damals im Druck noch unvollendeten Übersetzung des *Catechisme Royal* (1645) von Philippe Fortin sieur de la Hoguette, auf deren Titel er sich auch als Liebhaber des Deutschen bezeichnet. Mit der Verfasserangabe „Durch Einen Liebhaber der Teutschen Sprache" traten Harsdörffer u. Johann Klaj bald darauf auch noch mit einem weiteren Werk hervor: Der schönen | DIANA | DRITTER THEIL. | Jn fünff Büchern be- | griffen. | Durch | H. C. G. POLO in | Spanischer Sprache | beschrieben. | Anjetzo | Das erstemal gedolmetscht | und mit neuüblichen Reim- | arten außgezieret. | Durch | Einen Liebhaber der Teut- | schen Sprache. | [Zierstück] | Nürnberg/ | Gedruckt/ in Verlegung | Michael Endters. | [Linie] | Jm Jahre 1646. VD17 23:286749W. (Dieses Titelblatt nicht im HAB-Exemplar 137.19 Eth. des folgenden Titels). Es handelt sich um den 3. Teil der *Diana* von Jorge de Montemayor, Alonso Pérez u. Gaspar Gil Polo. Ein fertiges Druckexemplar seiner *Diana*-Übersetzung wird Harsdörffer mit 451217 an F. Ludwig senden. In 460120 bestätigt F. Ludwig dankend den Erhalt des *Diana*-Exemplars. Vgl. 451217 K 7. — Die Bezeichnung ‚Liebhaber der dt. Sprache' zeichnete Harsdörffer freilich nicht vor anderen Zeitgenossen aus. Vgl. den Titel eines von dem Nürnberger Arzt Johann Helwig (PBO Montano. 1645) verfaßten satirischen *ORMVND Das ist: Lieb- und Helden-Gedicht* (1648). S. 451101 K 13. Eher in Betracht kommt eine Übersetzung von Boethius' *De consolatione philosophiae*, an der Helwig schon damals arbeitete, obwohl sie erst 1660 erschien. S. 451101 K 13. Helwig gehörte auch zu den Beiträgern von Ehrengedichten in Harsdörffers *Frauenzimmer-Gesprächspielen* V (1645), S. 46–52 (Ndr.). Das gilt auch für Georg Conrad Osthof (DG 8; PBO Amyntas) aus Celle, den Verfasser einer wohl nie erschienenen Übersetzung der frauenfreundlichen Schrift des Johan van Beverwijk. Vgl. *Frauenzimmer-Gesprächspiele* V (1645, Ndr. 1969), 38–40 (Ndr.). Im Brief 451101 empfahl Harsdörffer neben Helwig u. Osthof auch den Nürnberger Patrizier Georg Friedrich Behaim, den Übersetzer von John Howells satirischen Büchern über den engl. Bürgerkrieg. Harsdörffer dürfte unveröffentlichte Proben aus Übersetzungen eines dieser Bekannten zur Vorbereitung seiner späteren Werbung nach Köthen geschickt haben. S. 451101 K 7, 12 u. 13 u. 451209 K 7.

7 Philipp v. Zesen (FG 521. 1648) hat den ersten Teil des von ihm aus dem Französischen der beiden Scudéry übersetzten *Ibrahim Bassa* (1645) der FG gewidmet. Vgl. die Widmungszuschrift im vorliegenden Band unter 441201. F. Ludwig muß bis spätestens Anfang Mai ein Exemplar bekommen haben: Anfang Februar war der Druck offenbar noch in vollem Gange; bereits in 450504 äußert sich Ludwig gegenüber Gueintz, in 450529 gegenüber Harsdörffer kritisch zu Zesens Rechtschreibung im *Ibrahim Bassa*. Vgl. 441201 K 0.

8 Die Deutschgesinnete Genossenschaft (DG) wurde vielleicht schon im Jahr 1642, nach eigenem Bekunden Zesens aber 1643 in Hamburg gegründet. Vgl. 441223 K 3. Auch wenn die DG Adelige wie Gf. Rüdiger Günther v. Starhemberg unter ihre Mitglieder rechnen konnte — worauf Harsdörffer im folgenden ausdrücklich hinweist —, setzte sie sich doch im Gegensatz zur FG mehrheitlich aus Bürgerlichen zusammen. Die von Harsdörffer erwähnte Verpflichtung zur Übersetzung eines Buches findet in den veröffentlichten Statuten — s. Zesens *Hochdeutsches Helikonisches Rosentahl* (1669) in *Zesen SW* XII, 178–310 — keinen Rückhalt (s. dort bes. 206–210). Notwendige Voraussetzung für eine Aufnahme in die DG war zwar die Beherrschung der deutschen Sprache, zum Schreiben eigener oder Übersetzen fremdländischer Werke waren laut Satzung aber nur Mitglieder angehalten, „die sich fähig darzu erkennen" (ebd., 207). Vgl. zur DG *Ingen*, 18–23, bes. Karl F. Otto: Die Sprachgesellschaften des 17. Jahrhunderts. Stuttgart 1972, 33–42 u. ders.: Soziologisches zu den Sprachgesellschaften. Die Deutschgesinnete Genossenschaft. In: *Bircher/ van Ingen*, 151–161.

9 Die DG war in vier nacheinander errichtete Zünfte unterteilt: die Rosenzunft mit 9 x 9 Mitgliedern, die Liljenzunft (7 x 7), Nägleinzunft (5 x 5) u. Rautenzunft (12 x 12). Die Rose war ihre symbolische Blume, das „algemeine Zunftzeichen der gantzen Genossenschaft" (*Hochdeutsches Helikonisches Rosentahl* [1669] in *Zesen SW* XII, 178–310, hier S. 197). Die Abb. dieses DG-Zunftzeichens mit einem Auslegungsgedicht von Zesen ebd. 219f. Auch als Teil des Zunftzeichens ihrer Mitglieder unabhängig von ihrer Zunftzugehörigkeit tauchen Rosen regelmäßig auf (so z.B. bei Nikolaus Witte von Lilienau, s. 440724 K 7). S. zur DG auch Anm. 8. — Harsdörffers „obschrift" bedeutet soviel wie Aufschrift oder Überschrift (*DW* VII, 1116, s. v. obschrift). *Stieler*, 1925 übersetzt Aufschrift mit „inscriptio". Anstelle der sehr kurzen Inscriptio oder Devise der fruchtbringerischen Imprese bekamen die Gesellschafter der DG einen knappen Reim (z.B. „Alzeit feste/ | bleibt das beste." A.a.O., 238), ‚Zunftwort' oder ‚Zunftspruch' genannt, der von mindestens einem Gedicht gefolgt wird.

10 Zu erwarten wäre, daß Harsdörffer in einem Paratext der ersten vier Teile seiner *Frauenzimmer-Gesprächspiele* bereits auf ein ähnliches Bild oder Konzept zurückgegriffen hätte. Zu finden ist in seinem „Vorbericht An den Lesenden" im ersten Band gleichwohl nur ein sehr allgemeiner Verweis, er habe mit den *Gesprächspielen* „allein Anleitung geben wollen/ und den Weg weisen/ wie bey Ehr- und Tugendliebenden Gesellschaften freund- und fruchtbarliche Gespreche aufzubringen" seien (*Harsdörffer: Frauenzimmer-Gesprächspiele* I [²1644], Ndr. 1969, S. 17). Die „anweisung der Gesprächspiele" wird hier also nicht ersichtlich. In seinem *Hochdeutschen Helikonischen Rosentahl* (1669), a. a. O., 240f. verzeichnet Zesen Harsdörffer als 12. DG-Mitglied (3. Mitglied im 2. Zunftsitz der Rosenzunft), das am 4.12.1644 aufgenommen worden sei. Sein DG-Gesellschaftsname aber war nicht „Der Durchbrechende", sondern „Der Kunstspielende", sein Zunftspruch „Es ist lieblich/ und löblich" u. sein Zunftzeichen „eine Kunstgöttin/ welche in einem lieblichen Tahle/ unten am Helikon/ unter den Rosen/ auf einer Laute/ von Rosenholtze gemacht/ ein kunstliedlein spielet". „Der Durchbrechende" erscheint auch nicht unter den anderen Gesellschaftsnamen der DG. Den Gesellschaftsnamen des Kunstspielenden hatte Harsdörffer in 441223 (K 2) selbst für sich vorgeschlagen, jedoch weder die Bootsmann-Imprese, noch die der lautenspielenden Muse, sondern als Sinnbild einen Rosenholz schneidenden Merkur.

11 Die ersten 12 „Andachts-Gemähle" Harsdörffers erschienen als Beilage zum 6. Teil der *Frauenzimmer-Gesprächspiele* (1646, Ndr. 1969, S. 497–622). Sie sind den *Emblemata sacra* (1634) des Antwerpener Jesuiten Willem van Hees/ Hesius entnommen. Vorangestellt ist ihnen Harsdörffers Übersetzung der Ode *L'Uranie ou muse celeste* (1574) des

Guillaume Saluste sieur du Bartas, die das Programm einer „Dichtung im Dienste der Religion" entwirft. Jean-Daniel Krebs: Georg Philipp Harsdörffer liest die französischen Dichter. In: *der Franken Rom*. Nürnbergs Blütezeit in der zweiten Hälfte des 17. Jahrhunderts. Hg. John Roger Paas. Wiesbaden 1995, 224–242, hier S. 230. Später veröffentlicht Harsdörffer mit seinen *Hertzbeweglichen Sonntagsandachten: Das ist/ Bild- Lieder- und Bet-Büchlein/ aus den Sprüchen der H. Schrifft/ nach den Evangeli- und Festtexten verfasset* (2 Bde., Nürnberg 1649 u. 1652; Ndr. hg. u. m. e. Nachwort vers. v. Stefan Keppler. Hildesheim [u. a.] 2007), eine umfangreiche Sammlung von insgesamt 152 Andachtsgemälden meist jesuitischer Provenienz. Vgl. dazu Krebs, op. cit., 232. Dabei handelt es sich um geistliche Embleme oder „Sinngemähle", die im Unterschied zur anderen von Harsdörffer genannten Emblemgattung, nämlich den „Sinnbildern", den Primat des Bildes zugunsten des Textes aufgeben. Das Sinn-Bild „erklärt" die Sache; im Sinngemähl vertieft das Bild eher rein illustrativ das Verständnis des Textworts, vorab der Sprüche aus den Perikopentexten, die als Inscriptio oder Überschrift fungieren, ergänzt um kurze Erklärungen, Lieder, Gebete, auch Lehrgedichte, homiletische „Betrachtungen" (im 2. Teil). Vgl. Harsdörffers Vorrede im 1. Teil u. Jörg-Jochen Berns: Harsdörffers Technikandacht. Zum Zusammenhang von Naturwissenschaft, Erbauung und Poesie in den „Sonntagsandachten" und „Erquickstunden". In: Doris Gerstl (Hg.): Georg Philipp Harsdörffer und die Künste. Nürnberg 2005, 22–38, hier S. 33 f. Den ersten Teil widmete Harsdörffer Johann Michael Dilherr, der die „unbefleckte Reinigkeit [der dt. Sprache] in unsren Gemeinen eingeführt" habe. (Zuschrift des 1. Teils, Bl. A v v). Zu den *Andachtsgemählen* Harsdörffers vgl. auch Guillaume van Gemert: Andächtige Liebesglut und kurioses Welttheater. Zu Harsdörffers geistlichem Schrifttum als überkonfessioneller Anleitung zur christlichen Lebenspraxis. In: Georg Philipp Harsdörffers Universalität. Beiträge zu einem uomo universale des Barock. Hg. Stefan Keppler-Tasaki u. Ursula Kocher. Berlin, New York 2011, 279–297; Stefan Keppler-Tasaki: Himmlische Rhetorik. Harsdörffers Poetik des Gebets zwischen lutherischer Orthodoxie und europäischem Manierismus. In: ebd., 299–325; Jean-Daniel Krebs: Tradition und Wandel der Allegorese bei Georg Philipp Harsdörffer: Die „zufällige Andacht". In: Mittelalterliche Denk- und Schreibmodelle in der deutschen Literatur der Frühen Neuzeit. Hg. Wolfgang Harms u. Jean-Marie Valentin. Amsterdam, Atlanta/ GA 1993 (Chloe, 16), 219–238, hier bes. 225–230; ders.: Von der Schelde zur Pegnitz oder von den *Emblemata sacra* zum „Lehr-Gedicht". In: Simpliciana 6/7 (1985), 185–203; ders.: G. Ph. Harsdörffers geistliche Embleme zwischen katholisch-jesuitischen Einflüssen und protestantischen Reformbestrebungen. In: Religion und Religiosität im Zeitalter des Barock. Hg. Dieter Breuer in Vbdg. mit Barbara Becker-Cantarino u. a. Wiesbaden 1995, 539–552; Rüdiger Zymner: „Sinnbild", „Lehrgedicht" und „Andachtsgemähl". Zum systematischen Zusammenhang von Parabel und Emblem in der Literatur der Frühen Neuzeit. In: Ästhetische Digressionen. FS f. Ulrich Ernst zum 60. Geb. Hg. Michael Scheffel u. a. Trier 2006, 101–121, hier S. 105–115. Vgl. auch 450529 u. 450817 I. — Von den *Gesprächspielen* werden bis 1657 insgesamt acht Teile erscheinen: *Harsdörffer: Frauenzimmer-Gesprächspiele*.

12 Harsdörffer erhielt von F. Ludwig mit 450124 die letzten drei Druckbögen des *GB 1641/44*, das die Mitglieder bis Nr. 417: Curt v. Einsiedel (Der Erspießliche) umfaßt. Mit 450529 wird F. Ludwig der Bitte um Auflösung der Mitgliederinitialen nachkommen. Vgl. zum *GB 1641/44* s. 441226A K 5. Seit 1642 hatte Harsdörffer den Fürsten wiederholt um die Ergänzung des ihm vorliegenden Mitgliederverzeichnisses u. die Auflösung der Initialen gebeten. S. dazu ausführlich 450529 K 10.

13 Hans Philipp (v.) Geuder (FG 310. Der Ergänzende), Mitglied u. hoher Funktionär der fränk. Reichsritterschaft, der als Vermittler bei der Aufnahme Harsdörffers gewirkt hatte. Auf seinen Gütern Heroldsberg u. Neunhof bei Nürnberg bot er reformierten Glaubensverwandten Gottesdienst u. Abendmahl. Den Anhaltinern diente er, auch in fruchtbringerischen Angelegenheiten, als eine Art Nürnberger Agent. Vgl. 370517 K 6. Zu seiner Vermittlerrolle bei Harsdörffers Aufnahme in die FG s. 411200 K 0.

14 „Verzeichnis" wird im 16. u. 17. Jh. in aller Regel feminin gebraucht. Das Genus neutrum setzt sich erst im Laufe des 18. Jhs. durch. *DW* XII.1, 2505–2508. Bei *Stieler*, 2613 ist „Verzeichnis" bereits Neutrum, in Abgrenzung zum femininen Verbalsubstantiv mit dem Ableitungssuffix -ung: „Verzeichnung/ die/ & Verzeichnüß/ das".

15 Gemeint ist Zacharias Prüschenk v. Lindenhofen (FG 418. Der Fördernde), der am 10. 10. 1644 in die Gesellschaft aufgenommen wurde. Harsdörffer bezeichnet Prüschenk irrigerweise nach dessen Gesellschaftswort: „Die Dauung" (vgl. Prüschenks Imprese in 441010). Dau- und deu- sind bedeutungsäquivalente Realisationen desselben Wortstamms, weswegen *deuen/ dauen* — mhd. *dewen/ döuwen* — sowohl bei *Stieler*, 306, als auch bei *Diefenbach*, 337, völlig gleichbedeutend mit ‚verdauen' wiedergegeben werden. Wegen seines frühen Aufnahmedatums kommt allerdings „Der Verdauende", d.i. Georg v. der Goltz (FG 289. 1636!), nicht in Betracht, zumal Harsdörffer bereits nach eigener Aussage eine Liste der Taufnamen bis FG 317 (Hans v. Rochow) vorgelegen hat. Aus der Bemerkung Harsdörffers kann demnach geschlossen werden, daß F. Ludwig seinem Brief 450124 zusätzlich zu den drei Druckbögen des *GB 1641/44* eine kurze Mitgliederliste beilegte, auf der die nach der Drucklegung des jüngsten GB eingenommenen Mitglieder (das sind FG 418, Zacharias Prüschenk, bis FG 422, Jean Delaporte) — eventuell zusammen mit ihren Taufnamen — notiert waren. Vgl. zum *GB 1641/44* 441226A K 5 u. zu der weitläufigen Geschichte von Harsdörffers Bitten nach Mitgliedernamen u. -verzeichnissen 450529 K 10.

450408

Fürst Johann Casimir von Anhalt-Dessau an Fürst Ludwig

F. Johann Casimir v. Anhalt-Dessau (FG 10) erwidert dankend die Osterwünsche F. Ludwigs. Dessen Nachfrage wird bejaht: Die Mistelpflanze existiere noch und die Blüte ihres Wirtsbaumes stehe kurz bevor. Wenn dies so weit sei, solle die ganze Mistel mit ihren Blättern nach der brieflichen Anweisung Dr. (Matthias) Engelhardts abgenommen und F. Ludwig zugesandt werden. Dabei bittet F. Johann Casimir, das Rezept bzw. eine Dosis des aus der Mistel gewonnenen Steinpulvers zuzuschicken.

Q LHA Sa.-Anh./ Dessau: Z 70 Abt. Köthen A 9a Nr. 25, Bl. 159r–160v [A: 160v], Bl. 159v u. 160r leer; eigenh.; Empfangsvermerk von F. Ludwigs H.; Sig.

A A Monsieur mon trésher Oncle Monsieur le Prince Louis d'Anhalt a Cöten. *Empfangsvermerk F. Ludwigs:* Pres. 8. April. 1645.

Hochgeborner Fürst freundlicher vielgeliebter herr vetter vndt gefatter, gegen EL bedancke Jch mich zum dienstlichsten wegen des beschehenen guten oster wunsches, vndt wünsche von treuem hertzen Jhr vndt allen Jhren lieben zugehörigen dergleichen, hiernechst berichte EL Jch[a] hiemitt das der bewuste Mispel noch vorhanden,[1] soll auch begehreter massen wann der baum blühet, so vermuthlich zum längsten inner 14 tagen geschehen wirdt, abgenommen, vndt gantz, nebenst den blettern, wie h doctor Engelhart² durch ein eygen schreiben errinnert, EL vberschicket werden, mitt bitt, mihr das recept als auch etzliche dosis von solchem steinpulver³ derer^b ort zuzuschicken, empfele sie hiemitt Göttlichem schutz vndt verbleibe

    EL
    treuer vetter
    Johann Casimir fzu Anhalt *mp*.

Dessaw den 8 Ap. 1645

T a *Eingefügt.* — **b** derer ort *eingefügt.*

K F. Ludwigs botanische u. phytopharmakologisch-medizinische Kenntnisse waren eine Quelle für die Impresistik der FG u. bes. für die ‚Gemälde' u. deren Auslegung in den Reimgesetzen der Gesellschaftsbücher. Das Interesse an u. die Kenntnis über Pflanzen sind demnach auch für den ethischen Utilitarismus der FG („Alles zu Nutzen") von Bedeutung. S. zu den Pflanzen der FG, ihrem medizin. u. a. Nutzen u. zur Pflanzensymbolik grundlegend *Conermann II*, 89–127 u. in *Conermann III* (FG 1–527) alle Impresenkommentare (jeweils Absatz I); vgl. *Bircher/ Palme* I, 39ff. u. *Herz: Die Namen der Pflanzen.* — Zwischen F. Ludwig u. F. Johann Casimir v. Anhalt-Dessau (FG 10) ist der Austausch von Pflanzen belegt. So dankte F. Ludwig in 210626 seinem Neffen für ein Exemplar der Gladiolenart Allermannsharnisch, die zur Gesellschaftspflanze F. Augusts v. Anhalt-Plötzkau (FG 46) wurde.
    1 Am 11. April dankte F. Ludwig für die Zusage seines Neffen Johann Casimir, die auf der Eberesche wachsende Mistel („Kinster") demnächst abzunehmen, u. bittet darum, sie mit einem Stück ihres Wirtsastes abzuschneiden u. ihm zu liefern. „Mit der bereitung und wie viel auf einmal zu gebrauchen, sol El. auch gewilfaret werden." LHA Sa.-Anh./ Dessau: Abt. Dessau A 10 Nr. 44, Bl. 86r. In der Akte Abt. Köthen A 9a Nr. 25, Bl. 161r–162v hat sich noch ein Kreditiv F. Johann Casimirs für seinen Rat u. Hofmeister Christian Heinrich v. Börstel (FG 407) ohne weitere inhaltliche Mitteilungen erhalten, d. d. Dessau 21.4.1645. Es trägt F. Ludwigs Empfangsvermerk „22. April. 1645". An diesem Tag traf offenbar der Abgesandte Börstel mit der abgeschnittenen Mistel in Köthen ein, denn noch am selben Tag bedankte sich F. Ludwig brieflich für die wohlerhaltene Sendung. Ihr Wirtsholz erweise sich aber leider als sehr jung, somit auch die Mistel, die bei höherem Alter besser u. stärker sei. Hätte er das gewußt, hätte er mit der Bitte sie abzuschneiden, noch ein Jahr oder länger gewartet. Johann Casimir solle das noch Vorhandene stehen lassen u. achtsam sein, daß es nicht aus Versehen „von handen komme". Das reimt sich allerdings nicht mit der Anweisung zusammen, daß die Mistel „gantz" abgenommen werden solle. Abt. Dessau A 10 Nr. 44, Bl. 88r. Vgl. auch 450508A.
    2 Dr. Matthias Engelhardt (Engelhart), 1630–1649 in Köthen nachgewiesen, Leib- u. Hofarzt F. Ludwigs u. Stadtarzt in Köthen. S. 270115 K 4, 410708 K 3 u. 450326 K 17.
    3 Der Mispelbaum (Mespilus germanica L., aus der Familie der Rosengewächse, auch Mespel oder Nespel genannt) u. die schmarotzende Mistel (Viscum album, auch Kinster, Kemster oder Kenster) wurden namentlich oft miteinander verwechselt. „DIe Mispeln" waren die Gesellschaftspflanze Cunos v. Alvensleben (FG 98). Seine Imprese (Gesellschaftsname: Der Reifende; Gesellschaftswort: Mit Zeit und stro) u. das Reimgesetz im *GB Kö.* (I, Bl. Bb ij r) spielen in Anlehnung an ein ital. Sprichwort (Col tempo e colla

paglia si maturan le nespole) darauf an, daß die kleinen runden, in der Form den Hagebutten u. Äpfeln ähnelnden Mispelfrüchte, wegen ihrer vielen harten Stützfasern auch Steinapfel genannt, erst nach den ersten Frösten geerntet werden sollten u. nur nach längerer Lagerzeit genießbar wurden. *Conermann III*, 101. Vgl. auch 240717 I. Zu Cuno v. Alvensleben (und der Abb. seiner Imprese) s. *Ball: Altmark-FG*, 95–97. „Der Leim von Mißpelholz vnd Beeren" (*GB Kö.* I, Bl. F ij r) hingegen, der das Bildmotiv der Imprese des Leimenden, Jost Andreas v. Randow (FG 22), spendete, wurde tatsächlich nicht aus der Mispel, sondern v. a. aus dem zähen, klebrigen Saft der Mistelbeeren gewonnen. S. dazu 200125 K 2, 210401 u. 450900 K 13; *Conermann II*, 85 ff.; *Marzell* IV, 1197–1209, hier 1203. Daß es im vorliegenden Brief u. seinem Korrespondenzzusammenhang tatsächlich um die Mistel ging, zeigt F. Ludwigs Nennung des „Kinsters" in seinem Brief vom 11. April (s. Anm. 1), aber auch schon die Anweisung, daß die Pflanze „gantz" abgenommen werden solle. Nach Plinius' *Historia naturalis* VI, 249 ff. galt die Mistel bei den gallischen Kelten u. den Germanen als Universalheilmittel, diente der Zauberabwehr u. wurde als Glücksbringer angesehen (bis ins Mittelalter: „Heil alle Welt"). In der Arzneikunst galt sie v. a. als Mittel gegen Epilepsie („Fallsucht"), was ihr auch den Namen „Fallkraut" eintrug. Innerlich u. äußerlich wurde sie zudem gegen Entzündungen, Geschwüre, Krämpfe, gegen Bauchschmerzen, als Geburtshilfe u. bei Menstruationsbeschwerden angewendet. Seltener wurden ihr Heilkräfte bei Lungenleiden wie Asthma zugeschrieben. Schließlich wurden ihr Harn u. feste Stoffe austreibende Wirkungen attestiert. Als Indiz für die Verwechslung von Mispel u. Mistel könnte auch gelten, daß solche Indikation nicht bei Bock vorkommt: Kräutterbuch Weylandt … Hieronymi Tragi genant Bock … gemheret vnd gebessert Durch Melchiorem Sebizium (Straßburg 1630; HAB: Mf 2° 2), 744–746. Als harnsteinaustreibendes oder als auflösendes Heilmittel begegnet dort S. 795 jedoch die Mispel, deren medizinische Wirkung in der Imprese Alvenslebens u. im vorliegenden Brief intendiert ist: „Der Stein [Samenkörner] auß der Nespeln zu Pulver gestossen/ und eines quintlein schwer in einem trunck weissen Wein/ darinnen zuvor Petersilgen Wurtzel gesotten seye/ eingenommen/ bricht vnd treibet den Stein gewaltig." Vgl. *HWDA* VI, 381–393; *Marzell* IV, 1197–1209; Georg Dragendorff: Die Heilpflanzen der verschiedenen Völker und Zeiten. München 1967, 182; Brigitte Hoppe: Das Kräuterbuch des Hieronymus Bock. Stuttgart 1969, 340 f.; Heinrich Marzell: Geschichte und Volkskunde der deutschen Heilpflanzen. Darmstadt 1967, 82–84; Johann Christoph Sommerhoff: Lexicon pharmaceutico-chymicum latino-germanicum et germanico-latinum. Ndr. d. Ausg. Nürnberg 1713 mit e. Nachw. v. Rudolf Schmitz. Hildesheim, New York 1977, 398; Wolfgang Schneider: Lexikon zur Arzneimittelgeschichte. 7 Bde., Frankfurt a. M. 1968–1975, Bd. V.3, 404–406; Karl Frh. v. Tubeuf: Monographie der Mistel. München, Berlin 1923, 37 ff.

450410

Georg Philipp Harsdörffer an Philipp von Zesen

Beantwortet durch 450808. — Es sei nicht verwunderlich, schreibt Georg Philipp Harsdörffer (FG 368. Der Spielende; DG 12. Der Kunstspielende) an Philipp v. Zesen (FG 521. 1648; DG 1. Der Färtige), daß man sich bislang in den strittigen Fragen der deutschen Sprache noch nicht einig geworden sei. Selbst in den anderen Hauptsprachen, die bis zu tausend Jahre Sprachausbau hinter sich hätten, könne die Rechtschreibung noch nicht völlig vereinheitlicht werden. Harsdörffer verweist auf seine Behandlung dieses Problems in der Zugabe zum ersten Teil der *Gesprächspiele* (2. Aufl. 1644: „Schutzschrift/ für die Teutsche Spracharbeit/ und Derselben Beflissene"). Ein Exemplar derselben habe Zesen sicherlich mit einer Frankfurter Büchersendung an den (Amsterdamer) Verleger Elzevier erhalten. — Zesens Frage, ob die deutschen Stammwörter immer einsilbig sein müßten, wird von Harsdörffer im Prinzip bejaht: Als deutsche Stammwörter könnten nur die Primitiva gelten, nicht die Derivativa und Komposita, auch keine nichtflektierenden Wörter (Artikel, Präpositionen und Konjunktionen), welche wie im Hebräischen als Partikel von den Stammwörtern (radices) zu unterscheiden seien. Da im Hebräischen Infinitiv und Imperativ gleich seien, würden sie als Stammform oder Wortwurzel angesetzt, wie dies bei Johannes Buxtorf, Wilhelm Schickard und Balthasar Walther nachzulesen sei. (Der Amsterdamer Jude) Menasseh ben Israel könne Zesen gewiß darüber Aufschluß verschaffen. Auch im Deutschen sei der Imperativ (Gebietungsweise) die Stammform, weil er die kürzeste Verbform und der natürliche Beginn der Sprachartikulation beim Kind sei. Diese Stammform wachse in der Konjugation („Zeitwandlung") durch die verschiedenen Vor- und Endungssilben. — Bei den Verben seien die regelmäßigen (regulären/ „gleichfließenden"), deren Stammbuchstaben immer gleich blieben, und die unregelmäßigen (irregulären/ „ungleichfließenden") voneinander zu trennen. Bei diesen unterscheidet Harsdörffer wie im Hebräischen die begrenzte Zahl derer, die einen zweisilbigen Imperativ bildeten, vergleichbar den hebr. „verbis quadratis", und diejenigen, die gar kein Verb (Zeitwort) bildeten [!] (theoretisch aber im Falle der Verbalisierung die Verbstammform analog imperativisch ableiten könnten, z.B. von „hunden, katzen") bzw. keinen Imperativ kennten („müß, sol"), schließlich jene 190 unregelmäßigen Verben, die Ablaute bildeten. Beispiele für dieselben habe Zesen in seinem Brief an Jesaias Rompler v. Löwenhalt gegeben. Die Flexion dieser unregelmäßigen Verben könne Zesen Justus Georg Schottelius' (FG 397) *Sprachkunst* (1641) entnehmen. Über diese Klassifizierung herrsche Konsens unter allen Sprachgelehrten der FG. — Da Zesen das Deutsche nach dem Muster des Hebräischen regulieren wolle — das auch in Nürnberg allgemein bekannt sei und öffentlich unterrichtet werde —, sei davon auszugehen, daß die Beugung der Verben im Hebräischen wie im Deutschen v.a. auf der Veränderung der Vokale beruhe. Über die Regeln bei der Verwandlung der Vokale a, o, u zu den Umlauten ä, ö, ü unterrichte ebenfalls Schottelius' *Sprachkunst*. Ganz verworren aber sei Zesens Frage, ob man das verbale Stammwort aus Perfekt oder Imperfekt ableite. Unverantwortlich sei auch Zesens Ansinnen, das unbetonte -e- (schwa = hebr. Scheva, pl. Schevaim) und das -v- (vav) aus dem dt. Alphabet zu verbannen. Harsdörffers Hinweise kämen mit dem Urteil vieler Sprachgelehrter überein, sowohl in Nürnberg als auch in Köthen, (Zesens Lehrer) Augustus Buchner (FG 362) eingeschlossen, deren Briefe und Gutachten Harsdörffer bei Bedarf Zesen vorlegen könne. — Bei so eindeutiger Sachlage werde Zesen auch seinen Purismus hoffentlich aufgeben, denn Hz. August d.J. v. Braunschweig-Wolfenbüttel (FG 227. Der Befreiende) habe nach der Kritik von Theologen sein Vorhaben einer neuen Bibelübersetzung mit durchgehend verdeutschten Fremdwörtern aufgegeben, da diese den Text, den jeder Deutsche schon ohnedem verstehe, nur verdunkelt und schwerverständlich gemacht hätten. Im Falle, daß Zesen sich nicht der Kritik zu beugen gedenke, werde sein Ruf Schaden erleiden und die von ihm initiierte Deutschgesinnete Genossenschaft (DG) eingehen; auch er, Harsdörffer, wolle dann mit der DG nicht mehr in Verbindung gebracht werden. Im entgegengesetzten Falle aber werde Zesen Ruhm erlangen und von Harsdörffer jede gewünschte Unterstützung erwarten dürfen. Zudem rät Harsdörffer, sich bei künftigen Veröffentlichungen des Schutzes eines fürstlichen Mäzens zu versichern. Hz. Christian Ludwig v. Braunschweig-Celle (FG 372), in der FG „der Reinherzige", werde sich mit diesem Gesellschaftsnamen wohl kaum dazu verstehen. Einen förmlichen „Erzschreinhalter" gebe es in der FG nicht. Unter „Erzschrein" werde dort viererlei verstanden: 1. Die Geschäftsstelle (Kanzlei/ Registratur), 2. das Archiv der Schriften und Bücher, 3. der mit den Impresen der Mitglieder geschmückte Schloßsaal zu Köthen, 4. das Gesellschaftssiegel, andere Gerätschaften und die Druckerei. F. Ludwig (Der Nährende) werde „der Stiffter und Erheber" der FG genannt.

Q Wiss. Bibl. der Univ. Tartu: Mscr. 47, Bl. 88r–91v [A: 91v], 91r leer; eigenh.; rotes Lacksiegel; auf Bl. 88r zeitgenöss. Eintrag mit roter Tinte: „No. 46." — *D:* Herbert Blume: Beiträge zur Biographie Zesens. In: Daphnis 3 (1974), 196–202, hier 197ff. Stark gekürzt in *Bellin: Sendeschreiben (1647),* Nr. 14, Bl. [G viij]v – H iij r (HAB: 437.16 Quod.). Zit. als *BS* (es werden nur stärkere Texteingriffe vermerkt und keine Veränderungen nach Zesens Orthographie, wie etwa lesen > läsen, wird > würd usw.). — Auszug in Max Gebhardt: Untersuchungen zur Biographie Zesens. Phil. Diss. Straßburg 1888, 45 f. — *BN: Estermann,* 596 Nr. 3; *Bürger,* 677 Nr. 108 u. 109.

A Meinem[a] Herrn Herrn Philip Zesien von Fürstenau *etc.* zu Handen.
  Utrecht.

Mein Herr,
Es ist[b] nicht zu wundern, wann man sich wegen kunstrichtiger verfassung der Deutschen Sprache noch der zeit nicht vergleichen kan; maßen in allen andern Haubtsprachen, an welchen von etlich Hundert, ja tausent Jahren gearbeitet worden, unter den Gelehrten und Sprachrichtern (**Criticis**) noch mancherley zweiffelfrag wegen der Rechtschreibung walten, wie ausführlich zu lesen, in der zugabe des ersten theils der Gesprächspiele[1], so mein Herr mit der *[sic]* Frankfurter Bücheren H. Elzeviers[2], sonder zweiffel empfangen haben wird.

Mein Herr geruhe von seiner aufgegebenen frage: Ob die Stammwörter in unserer Sprache alle einsylbig[c] seyn müssen?[3] meine wenige meinung zu vernemen, und schlüße daraus mein offenes, Deutschgeartes Gemüht, welches niemand zu schmeicheln gelernet hat, sondern seine fehler für glükkselig schetzet, wann dardurch die Gelegenheit eines verständigen unterrichts, von lieber hand erfolget.

Unter den Stamm- oder Wurtzelwörteren werden nicht alle und jede Wörter der Teutschen Sprache verstanden, sondern nur diese, welche durch ihre vor und nachsylben (**pro præfixa et suffixa**) reiflich auswachen: [88v] als da sind die Zeitwörter (**verba**) und etliche Nennwörter (**Nomina**) wie folgen wird, die anderen Geschlecht- vor- und fügwortlein sind unwandelbar, wie bey den Ebreern die[d] **Particulæ** niemals **Radices** können genennet werden. Dieses ist gantz richtig.[4]

Bey den Ebreeren wird die weise zu endigen, welche mit der weise zu gebieten gleich ist, für ein Stammwort gesetzet, viel unrichtigkeiten[e] zu verhüten, wie hiervon zu lesen Buxtorfius[5], Schickhartus[6], Walterus[7], und mein Herr bey Manasse Ben-Israël[8], im fall zweiffels erkundigen kan. Bey uns ist es gleichsowol die weise zu gebieten 1. weil kein wort in der gantzen Zeitwandlung kürtz[er][f] ist, 2. weil es der anfang aller natürlichen Rede ist, wie von[g] den kinderen zuhören die zu sagen beginnen: thu, iß, hör, komm, sih, schlag, lieb, lauff, steh usw.[h][9] Diese Stammwurtzlen wachsen auf mancherley art in der Zeitwandelung durch die vor und nachsylben.[i] Dieser Satz ist auch so beweißlich, daß nichts mit grund darwider aufzubringen seyn wird.

Der ZeitWörter sind zweyerley: Gleichfließende (Regularia) und ungleichfließende (irregularia.)

Die Gleichfließenden sind, wann die Stammbuchstaben niemals verändert werden, als: Hör, Sag, wall[j] schau *etc.* Die ungleichfließende sind wiederum zweyerley art, wie [89r] bey den Ebreeren, 1. diese welche zweysylbige Stammwörter haben, als: eiffer, zweiffel, wechsel, dieser[k] ist eine gewisse Anzahl, und vergleichen sich mit den verbis quadratis[10]. 2. die jenigen, welche entweder gar kein zeitwort haben, als: hund, katz, Haan *etc.* Hiervon ist zu wissen, daß wann sie[l] Zeitwörter hetten, solche nicht anderst als nach der ähnlichkeit der Sprache (ex analogia Linguæ)[m] gestaltet werden müssten, und von hunden, katzen, Haanen, die weise zu gebieten[n] fließen[o] würde; Hund, katz, haan *etc.* oder es sind solche wörter deren Weise zu gebieten nicht im Gebrauch ist, als: müß, sol, mag *etc.* oder es sind ungleich fließende Zeitwörter deren Stimmer und Mitstimmer gewandelt werden, und sind derselben 190[11], und unter diesen ist auch gilt, gelten, birg, bergen, rech[p], rechen und die anderen exempel die der Herr in seinem brief an H. Rumpler anführet[12], ihre Zeitwandlung ist zu lesen, in des hochbelobten und üm[d] gantz Teutschland wolverdienten H. Schottels Sprachkunst, am 456, und 452, 460[d] blat.[13] Dieses wird[q] von allen Teutschgelehrten der Hochlöblichen Fruchtbringenden Gesellschaft für grundrichtig gehalten.

Weil aber[r] mein Herr die Ebreische Sprache (welche in unserer Statt offentlich gelehret[s] wird und sehr gemein ist,) verständig betrachtet, und unsere Deutsche darnach etlicher massen zu richten gedenket, so [89v] betrachte er doch, daß ihre Zeitwandlung meinstentheils in veränderung der Stimmer bestehet,[14] wie auch im Deutschen, als Sprich; die Sprache, Sprechen, gesprochen, der Spruch, Kreuch[t], Kriechen, gekrochen, miß, messen, ich maß *etc.*

Wann aber das, a, o, u in ä, ö, ü gewandelt wird, sind darvon gewisse Reglen in vorbelobter Sprachkunst zu lesen.[15]

Wolte[u] man nun die vollkommene, oder unvollkommene Zeit zu einem Stammwort setzen[16] so were [es] gleich, als wann ich behaubten wolte die früch-[te][v] oder das Laub, were nicht von den Baumen, sondern die Baumen von den früchten erwachsen: oder die mehrer Zahlen von 10 an, weren nicht von der minderen sondern die minderen von den mehreren[w] entstanden. Composita fiunt ex simplicibus, et non contra. Solcher gestalt wird auch für eine unverantwortliche neurung gehalten, wann mein Herr die Schevaim[x] und vav aus dem von so viel Jahren her üblichen a, b, c absondern[y] wil,[17] welches gewisslich so wenig in unserer als [der] Ebreischen Sprache kan erdultet werden.

Dieses ist nicht allein meine meinung, sondern viele[r][f] Gelehrter und in allen Spachen wolerfarnen Männer reifbedachtes Erachten, so wol dieser orten, als zu Cöthen, [90r] wie ich hier von unterschiedliche Briefe aufzuweisen, und ehest H. Buchners gleichstimmiges bedenken[18], diese und andere Strittigkeiten betreffend auf begehren zu[d] übersenden erbietig bin.[z]

Bey so Sonnenklarer bewantniß der Sachen, zweiffelt mir nicht mein Herr werde seinen gefasten wahn fahren lassen: allermassen[aa] der *Befreyende* (H. Augustus zu Braunschweig fürstl. G.) bereit die hand angelegt die Heilig Schrift gantz deusch herauszugeben, und alle fremde wörter, als: Profet, Apostel, Testament, Evangelium, Sacrament *etc.* mit deutschen namen auszudrükken; demnach er aber der H. Schrift Gelehrte hier, und anderer orten darüber befragt, ist ihm solches einmündig widerrahten worden, deswegen er es wolbedächtig verbleiben lassen, und hat[d] das, so bereit[ab] alle und jede Deutsche verstehen, nicht schwer, dunkel und[ac] unbegreifflich machen wollen.[19]

Wolte aber mein Herr dieser wolgemeinten erinnerung nicht stat geben, so wird er gewisslich[ad] mit seines berühmten Namens höchstem nachtheil erfahren, daß seine angefangene Gesellschaft ihre endschaft bald[d] erreichen, und niemand darvon wissen, hören, oder lesen wird: Auf welchen fall ich auch mich nicht mit einzuflechten bitte, oder darzu verstehen kan noch will.[20]

[90v] Wolte aber mein Herr seine Schriften, nach beliebter kunstgründiger richtigkeit,[ae] beqwemen, und die gantze verfassung derselben[af] nicht ümstossen, und zerrütten, ist nicht zuzweiffeln, daß er einen unsterblichen Namen darvon erlangen und bey allen verständigen in höhes[ag] Ansehen gelangen wirdt: auf welchen fall ich alle möglichste beförderung zu leisten schuldig und erbietig bin, Wolte aber rahten man solte nichts in drukk kommen lassen, man habe dann eine fürstl. Person zum Schutz- und Pflegherrn bekommen. Hertzog Christian Ludwig wird [sich] darzu schwerlich verstehen, weil er mit dem Namen des Reinhertzigen in der usw.[ah] Fruchtbringenden Gesellschaft ist,[21] in welcher sich niemand einen Ertzschreinhalter nennet, sondern der Ertzschrein bestehet 1. in Jhrer **Cantz[lei]**[f] und **Registratur.** 2. in den [*sic*] Bücher- und Schriftenschrein. 3. bey dem schönen Saal zu Cöthen, darinnen alle der Gesellschafter Gemähl in Tapeten mit den Namen und Sprüchen aufgehenket sind.[22] 4. in dem **Sigil,** Stiftungsbriefen, der Drukkerey und etlichen sonderlichen Gerätschaften.[23] Fürst Ludwig, der *Nehrende*[,] wird der Stiffter und Erheber benamet. Dieses hab ich meinem Herrn zu dienstlicher nachrichtung unverhalten nicht lassen wollen, und erwarte förderlichste Antwort. Gott mit uns.

    Meines Herrn
    Dienstergebener Knecht
    Georg Philip Harsdörff[er][f] mp.[24]

Nürnberg den 10. Ostermonats im Jahre 1645.

T a *BS* An den Färtigen. — **b** *Folgt* <sich> — **c** *BS* eingliederich — **d** *Eingefügt.* — **e** *Marginalie:* Anomalias — **f** *Buchstabenverlust im Falz. Konjektur in eckigen Klammern.* — **g** *Eingefügt für* <bey> — **h** *Ein bei Harsdörffer häufiger erscheinendes Abkürzungszeichen für usw./ etc., s.* 450400 T a. — **i** *Folgt* <wie> — **j** *Eingefügt. Fehlt in BS.* — **k** *Bis* Anzahl, *am Rand ergänzt.* — **l** *Folgt* <Stam> — **m** *Marginalie:* man lese hiervon Schickarti Horologium Ebr. Regul 47. — **n** *Eingefügt für* <endigen> — **o** *BS verkürzt die folgende Passage:*

[...] die weise zu gebieten nicht im gebrauch ist/ als **müß/ sol/ mag/** udg. Oder es sind ungleich-fließende zeit-wörter [...] — **p** rech, rechen *eingefügt*. — **q** wird von *eingefügt für* <so bey> — **r** *Gebessert aus* also — **s** *Folgt* <ist> — **t** *Wort mit blasserer Tinte von zeitgenöss. (Zesens?) H. unterstrichen mit Marginalie:* NB. — **u** *Folgender Satzteil bis zu gebessert aus* Wen man nun von der vollkommenen, oder unvollkommenen Zeit wolte zu — **v** *Buchstabenverlust im Falz. Konjektur nach BS.* — **w** *Folgt* <erwachsen> — **x** *Wort mit blasserer Tinte von zeitgenöss. (Zesens?) H. unterstrichen mit Marginalie:* ich laß' ihn — **y** *BS* abschaffen — **z** *In BS folgen zwei Zeilen, die mehrfache kurze Striche aufweisen, vermutlich zur Anzeige einer Auslassung, die hier aber noch nicht vorgenommen wurde.* — **aa** *BS läßt im Folgenden längere Passagen aus und verkürzt sie zu:* [...] wahn fahren laßen/ und seine schriften nach beliebter kunst-gründiger richtigkeit beqwemen/ und die ganze verfassung derselbigen nicht ümstoßen/ und zerrütten; dadurch Er dan gewis einen unsterblichen nahmen erlangen/ und mit seiner angefangenen Genossenschaft bei allen verständigen in hohes ansehen gelangen würd; auf welchen fal ich auch alle möglichste beförterung zu leisten schuldig und erbietig bin. Wollte aber rahten/ man solte nichts in truk kommen laßen/ man habe dan eine fürstliche persohn zum Schuzherren bekommen. - - - - - - Dieses hab' ich [...]. — **ab** *Lies:* bereits — **ac** *Gebessert aus* unnd — **ad** *Folgt* <mehr> — **ae** *Folgt* <wie anhero vor etlichen Jahren>, *das Komma nach* richtigkeit *blieb aus diesem Grund versehentlich stehen.* — **af** *Eingefügt für* <alle mundarten> — **ag** *Wohl Flüchtigkeitsfehler. Lies:* höheres — **ah** *Folgt* <Fürst>; *ergänze wohl:* Hochlöblichen

K Ein Bezugsschreiben Philipp v. Zesens (FG 521. 1648), auf das Georg Philipp Harsdörffer (FG 368. Der Spielende) hier offensichtlich antwortet, ist nicht bekannt. Harsdörffer hat aber einen Brief Zesens an Jesaias Rompler v. Löwenhalt (DG 16; aufgenommen am 4.2.1645) gekannt, auf den er im vorliegenden Schreiben explizit eingeht. Dafür kommt wegen der angesprochenen Thematik eigentlich nur 450308A in Frage. Zu Romplers DG-Mitgliedschaft s. hier Anm. 12; Philipp v. Zesen: Das Hochdeutsche Helikonische Rosentahl (Amsterdam 1669) in *Zesen SW* XII, 178–310, hier S. 244 u. die Anhänge S. 424 u. 454.

1 *Harsdörffer: Schutzschrift (1644)*, Ndr. S. 343–396. Zur Schwierigkeit, sich über eine vereinheitlichte Rechtschreibung zu verständigen s. etwa Ndr., 372f. Vgl. zu strittigen Fragen in der Orthographiediskussion der FG *Herz: Rechtschreibdebatte*.

2 Die Elzevirs/ Elzeviers waren eine holländische Verleger-/ Druckerfamilie mit Stammsitz in Leiden, wo Lodewijk/ Ludwig Elzevier (1542–1617) 1580 seinen Fachverlag für gelehrte Schriften gründete. Niederlassungen in Amsterdam, Utrecht u. a. folgten. Zesen soll sich während seiner Aufenthalte in Holland zeitweise als Korrektor im Elzevier-Verlag oder in anderen Amsterdamer Verlagshäusern verdingt haben. Vgl. 441223 K 1; *Ingen*, 23; *Ingen: Zesen*, 15.

3 Harsdörffer folgte in seinen Sprachauffassungen Justus Georg Schottelius, nachdrücklich bezeugt in 460406. In seinem Schreiben an Jesaias Rompler v. Löwenhalt 450308A (vgl. unten Anm. 12) hatte Philipp v. Zesen bestritten, daß alle dt. Stammwörter einsilbig seien u. indirekt in Frage gestellt, daß die Stammform der Verben aus deren (vermeintlich stets einsilbigem) Imperativ abzuleiten sei. Sein Vorschlag, das Stammwort der Verben in den Tempi des Perfekts oder Imperfekts zu suchen, führte dann zu orthographischen Konsequenzen, die in ihrem Verstoß gegen Schreibgewohnheiten u. andere grammatische Auffassungen auf starken Widerstand stießen. So setzte er für das Verb „gelten" die Stammform „galt", oder für „bergen" „barg", so daß er als richtige Schreibung „gälten" (auch das Substantiv „gäld"/ Geld) bzw. „bärgen" verfocht. Hier liegt auch die Ursache für den ausufernden Gebrauch der Umlaute in seiner damaligen Schreibweise.

Vgl. auch Zesens undatiert überlieferten Brief an Johann Bellin (*Bellin: Sendeschreiben [1647]*, Nr. 8, Bl. [Ciiij] r – [D v] v), in dem er ebenfalls gegen die Einsilbigkeit der dt. Stammwörter antrat u. eine durch u. durch heterogene Theorie der Stammwortableitung entwickelte. S. dazu Anm. 16 u. schon 441223 K 21; vgl. *Takada*, 202 f. In seinem Antwortschreiben 450808 an Harsdörffer wies Zesen die Ableitung der Stammwörter der Verben aus dem (einsilbigen) Imperativ Singular erneut zurück u. zeigte darin Nähe zu den Positionen F. Ludwigs u. Christian Gueintz' (FG 361), aber auch etwa zu Christian Beckmann (s. 440119 K 0). In seiner *Hooch-Deutschen Spraach-übung* (1643) hatte sich Zesen zu dieser Frage noch nicht geäußert. Er widmete ihr im *Rosen-mând* (1651) aber einen längeren Abschnitt u. wiederholte seine Argumente: „der gantze grund und stam der Hochdeutschen sprache" beruhe mitnichten auf „eingliedrigen nenn-wörtern" (Nomen), wie dies Georg Henisch, Jan Gorp van der Beken (Goropius Becanus), Beatus Rhenanus oder Simon Stevin behauptet hätten, da viele derselben von anderen Stammwörtern abgeleitet seien. Die hier genannten Autoren hatte bereits *Schottelius: Sprachkunst (1641)*, 87 f. als Gewährsmänner seines Einsilbigkeitslehrsatzes angeführt. Zu Stevins Theorie einsilbiger „grondwoorden", zu Beatus Rhenanus' „vocis primogeniis monosyllabis" oder schon zu Franciscus Irenicus' Auffassung, „omnis imperatiuus, ac omnia pene germanica uocabula monosyllaba sunt", schließlich zu Laurentius Albertus' hebraisierendem Konzept der einsilbigen radices oder Wortwurzeln als Quellen für Schottelius' Konzeption einsilbiger Sprachkonstituenten u. deren Kritik in der FG vgl. *Barbarič*, 1184 ff.; *McLelland: Ausführliche Arbeit*, 107–114; auch *Padley* I, 141. Zudem, so Zesen weiter, sei das Dogma der durchgehenden Eingliedrigkeit der dt. Stammwörter falsch, wie das Beispiel Sonne, Friede, Sprache zeige, u. verhängnisvoll, weil es die Sprache „gliedloß/ knarrend/ hart und unlieblich" mache. *Zesen SW* XI, 208 u. 209. Schließlich sei die Ableitung der Verb-Stammwörter aus (angeblich stets) einsilbigen Imperativen zu verwerfen, weil dies „nichts mehr nützet/ als daß es den ungereimten Reim-schmieden und pranklern unserer Dichterei wohl zu statten kommet/ und die liebligkeit/ ja den gantzen flus der sprache hämmet." Ebd., 210. Für Zesens Stammworttheorie ist zentral, daß er nach dem Vorbild der „Ebreischen Sprach-lehrer" die Stammwörter auch der Nomen von den Verben, u. zwar aus deren Zeitstufe des Imperfekts (oder Perfekts) ableiten wollte. Der singulare Imperativ wie auch der Indikativ Präsens Aktiv werden damit als Verb-Stammform verworfen. Zur Begründung wendet Zesen sich immer wieder natursprachlichen Spekulationen zu, etwa wenn er seine vier Urvokale a, e, o, u mit den vier Elementen analogisiert u. diese Deutung in die Wortbedeutung hineinträgt. Zesen synchronisiert damit zwei zu unterscheidende Verfahren der Stammwort-Ermittlung u. der Stammwort-Erklärung, das semantisch-etymologische der Bedeutung u. das morphologische der Wortgestalt. Ebd., 212 ff. Zesen kritisiert hier auch Justus Georg Schottelius, s. a. a. O., S. 211 Anm. b. Dieser hat in der Tat den Grundsatz einer durchgehenden Einsilbigkeit der dt. Stammwörter verfochten. In seinem Gutachten zu Gueintz' Sprachlehre hatte er zwar noch relativierend formuliert, „die Teutsche Sprache ruhet fest und unbeweglich in ihren, von Gott eingepflantzten haubtgründen, welche <u>lautere, reine, deutliche, meist-einsilbige Stam̃wörter</u> sind". 400528 I, S. 508. In *Schottelius: Sprachkunst (1641)*, 87 f., heißt es dann, es seien „die ersten Würtzelen oder die Stam̃wörter der Teutschen Sprache gleichfalls einsilbig/ [...] Also nun hat die mildreiche allgemeine Mutter/ die gütige Natur/ auch dieses allein den Teutschen verliehen/ daß sie [...] unendlich-viele einsilbige Wörter können außreden/ darunter auch alle Stammwörter". Ebd., 413: Der Imperativ sei „bey den Teutschen die erste und das rechte Stam̃wort/ welches alleine die Stam̃letteren in sich begreifft [...]. Es ist wunderlich/ daß die Zeitstammwörter oder Gebietungsweisen einsilbig sind/ anzuzeigen ihre natürliche/ lautere/ reinliche ankunfft/ ihre schöneste Stammwürtzelen/ die so schön/ kürtz/ safftig und rein sind". Hier liege der „Anfang der natürlichen Rede", wie in der ersten Kindersprache; aus diesen einfachen „wesentlichen Lauten" erwachse das ganze Sprachgebäude u. „solches ist kein zufälliges barbarisches Wesen/ sonderen eine von den höchsten Künsten der Sprachnatur". Auf diese Stelle wird sich Harsdörffer in seinem *Specimen (1646)*, 142, wörtlich beziehen. In *Schottelius: Der Teutschen Sprache Einleitung (1643)*, 68f., u. *Schottelius: Sprachkunst (1651)*, 122ff., 140 u. 708f., wird der Grundsatz der Einsilbigkeit zugespitzt: Die einsilbigen Wörter erscheinen als „der unzerruttelende Grund" wie „ein harter Fels der festeste und unbeweglichste Grund" der dt. Sprache (*Einleitung*, 68). Ausnahmen werden sprachhistorisch erklärt u. delegitimiert, sie ändern an der „uhrankünftlichen einsilbigkeit nichts". *Schottelius: Ausführliche Arbeit (1663)*, 62; vgl. *Schottelius: Sprachkunst (1651)*, 124. Sodann gab Schottelius in seiner *Teutschen Vers- oder ReimKunst (1645)* als „eine untriegliche Anleitung und Richtschnur/ die grundfeste/ richtige/ durchgehende/ Einsilbige Theilung aller Teutschen Wörter und Silben" aus, weil „das gantze Kunstgebeu der Teutschen Sprache auf Einsilbigen Stammen/ Seulen und Stützen beruhet". *Schottelius: Teutsche Vers- oder ReimKunst (1645)*, Bl. [c viij]r; s. auch *Schottelius: Teutsche Vers- oder ReimKunst (1656)*, Bl. [b viij]v. Vgl. ferner zur Stammwortdiskussion 440119 K 0, 441201 K 0, 441223, 450000 K 2, 450420, 450808, 451007 K 2, 451219 (K 4), 451220 K 2, 460000 u. II, 460131, 460200 K, 460406 K 4, 460720 K 3, 460902 (K 3) u. 460915. Gueintz widersprach solcher Auffassung in seiner Entgegnung auf Schottelius' Kritik an seiner Sprachlehre: „Daß alle stamwörter müßen einsylbig sein, ist so vi[el] nach dieses meinung gesagt, daß sie nicht alle Deu[tsch] sein, denn daß wortt **Adam** selber nicht einsyl[big] ist, vnnd derer viel tausendt." Und weiter: „Daß ist noch zu erinnern, daß gesezt wirdt der Imperativus sey das stamwort, aber ich kann e[s] nicht gleuben, weil darvon auch keine vrsache" usw. 400528 II, S. 513 u. 517; ablehnend auch *Gueintz: Rechtschreibung (1645)*, 20f. Vgl. 440127 K 1. Im Abschnitt 9 seines Gutachtens zu Harsdörffers *Specimen Philologiae Germanicae* (1646), s. 460720 K 3 (das Gutachten demnächst in *DA Köthen I. 9*, „Zu 460720"), plädierte Gueintz bei Verben für „die unendige Weise", den Infinitiv, zur Ermittlung des Wortstamms, u.a. auch schon deshalb, weil nicht alle Verben Imperative aufweisen (bes. Hilfsverben wie z.B. müssen, sollen, dürfen), während Harsdörffer auch in 460131 u. 460915 gegenüber Gueintz auf seiner mit Schottelius übereinstimmenden Meinung beharrte. In 451219 wird sich F. Ludwig hinter Gueintz stellen: „Es zeiget gleichwol die erfarung, das alle deutsche Stamwörter nicht einsilbig sein können. Als neben vielen andern, Vater, mutter, bruder, schwester, meßer, waßer, feder, apfel, [...] und dergleichen. Ob dan auch der radix oder Stamm der Zeitwörter in der g[e]bietungsweise ist, solches ist auch sehr zweiffelhaftig, ja das die andere person drinnen allezeit einsilbig sein solte, als man saget weise mir deine wege, und nicht weis mir, reiche mir deine hand, und nicht reich mir, trachte darnach, und nicht tracht". F. Ludwig sekundierte Gueintz auch in 460902, indem sowohl in der 1. Person Sg. Indikativ Präsens Aktiv etwa „ich liebe" u. keineswegs „ich lieb" zu setzen sei, desgleichen sei auch im Imperativ Sg. „liebe du" der Vorzug vor „lieb du" zu geben, welches verzwickter u. „abgebißen" sei. Vgl. auch 460200 u. dort K 1 sowie 460902. Im Falle der zweisilbigen Indikativform kamen Schottelius u. Harsdörffer mit F. Ludwig überein, nur daß sie die Indikativform für zusammengesetzt hielten: Stammform lieb (=Imperativ) u. Endungs-e. Vgl. *Schottelius: Sprachkunst (1641)*, 413, 444 u. 548f.; *Harsdörffer: Specimen (1646)*, 146f., s. dazu 460902 K 3. In 460915 bekräftigte Harsdörffer seine Auffassung: „Das Stamwort wird sein welches alle Stambuchstaben hat, und keine vor oder nachsylb[en.] Dergleichen wird keines außer der gebietungsweise [Imperativ] gefunden werden. Das <u>e</u> welches etzliche derselben anfügen ist eine nachsylbe, und nicht gebreuchlich nach vielen Mundarten. D. Luther schreibet, <u>laß</u>, <u>komm</u>, <u>iß</u>, <u>sitz</u>, <u>gr[eif]</u>, <u>nim</u> etc. Sirach. 31. und hin und wieder an anderen orten meh[r.]" Wie Zesen (s.o.) räumten übrigens auch Schottelius u. Harsdörffer den Verben Priorität bei der Stammwortbildung ein, da „Nomina formantur à verbis [...] æque in Hebræa ac Germanica Lingua". *Harsdörffer: Specimen (1646)*, 138, u. ebd., 292: „Verba esse fundamenta Orationis, ex quib*us* nomina, secundum rectam rationem progignuntur". Vgl. zur Konzeption der Stammwörter u. ihrer Einsilbigkeit bei Schottelius u. Harsdörffer *Banneck*, 105–118 u. 122f.; *Barbarić*, 1190ff.; Kathrin Gützlaff: Von der Fügung Teutscher Stammwörter. Die Wortbildung in J. G. Schottelius' „Ausführlicher Arbeit von der Teutschen HaubtSprache". Hildesheim [u.a.] 1989, 33ff. u. 42ff.; *Hundt*, 78, 153, 248–254; *Takada*, 11f., 25f., 137f., 168 u.ö.; Gisela M. Neuhaus: Justus Georg Schottelius: Die Stammwörter der Teutschen Sprache. Eine Untersuchung zur frühneuhochdeutschen Lexikologie. Göppingen 1991, 78, 80, 85, 88 u.ö.; *Roelcke*, 289, 297 u. 338. Festzuhalten bleibt, daß zum Mhd. u. dann zum Nhd. die mehrsilbigen Stämme v.a. durch Vokaltilgung gekürzt werden, daß Stamm- u. Derivationssysteme zur Einsilbigkeit tendieren, so daß die große Mehrheit der dt. Substantive im Sg. ein-, im Plural zweisilbig werden (in trochäischer Prosodie, 1. Silbe betont mit Vollvokal, 2. Silbe unbetont, oft mit nicht mehr phonetisch realisiertem Nebenvokal), „die ideale Größe und Form des phonologischen Wortes" seit dem Mhd. *Nübling*, 32f.

4 Stammwörter gab es für Harsdörffer hier also nur bei den flektierten Wortarten Nomen, als Primitivum im Nominativ Singular, u. Verbum, in Gestalt des Imperativs Singular. Zesen stimmte darin Harsdörffer in seiner Antwort 450808 zu. Schottelius hatte als ein Kennzeichen der Stammwörter festgehalten, „Daß sie von sich reichlich außwachsen und herleiten lassen" u. „allerley bindungen/ doppelungen und artige Zusammenfuegungen" eingehen, was z.B. auch für Präpositionen galt. *Schottelius: Sprachkunst (1641)*, 75; vgl. *Schottelius: Ausführliche Arbeit (1663)*, 193 (Stammwörter als „Radices, primitiva"). Aus diesen *Radices* entspringt durch Kombination mit anderen Stammwörtern (Komposita), Prä- u. Suffixen einschließlich der Flexionsendungen, Ableitungsmorpheme u. ergänzt durch andere unflektierte Wortklassen wie Präpositionen, Adverbien, Konjunktionen, Interjektionen u. Partikeln der dt. Wortschatz. „Sic in Lingua nostra teneamus. I. Radices, II. Præfixa & suffixa, III. Particulas & palam erit verborum multitudinem nihil esse aliud, quam variam similium iterationem." *Harsdörffer: Specimen (1646)*, Bl.)( )( )( )(3 v (Praefatio), vgl. auch 460131, 460200 u. 460406 K 4. — Der Begriff der „radix"/ der Wortwurzel oder des Stammworts wurde seit Johannes Reuchlins *De rudimentis hebraicis* (1506) im 16. u. 17. Jh. aus der hebräischen Grammatik übernommen (vgl. auch Anm.3). Elias Hutter hatte 1611 die Differenzierung von „Literis Radicalibus & Servilibus" der hebr. Sprache „in allen anderen Sprachen [...] mutatis mutandis" erkannt u. für beweisbar gehalten. Zit. n. Gerda Haßler: Art. „Wortbildung". In: *Haßler/ Neis*, 1470–1491, hier 1470. In einer hsl. Aufstellung unterschied Schottelius bei den Buchstaben zwischen „Literarum radicalium, essentialium et accidentalium. Radicales literæ sunt, quæ radices comprehendunt: Essentiales sunt, quæ Derivandi, modos continent. Accidentales sunt, quæ casuum, numerorum, generum, comparationum et temporum formationes complectuntur." (NSTA Wolfenbüttel: 2 Alt Nr.40, Bl. 4r–5v. Demnächst in *DA Köthen I. 9*: „Zu 441200"). Vgl. auch Schottelius in 441200. Die meisten hebr. Verben, bei denen man davon ausging, daß die Nomen von ihnen abgeleitet sind, bestehen aus drei Konsonanten, eben jenen literae radicales. Aus ihnen gehen die Wortstämme hervor, in deren jedem die Grundbedeutung der Wurzel modifiziert wird. Die häufigsten sieben Verbalstämme im Hebr. sind Kal, Nífal, Píel, Púal, Hítpael, Hífil u. Hófal, s. Oskar Grether: Hebräische Grammatik für den akademischen Unterricht. München 1951, 96ff., vgl. auch *Barbarić*, 1184. Da in fast allen Stämmen die einfachste Form *nicht* etwa der Imperativ Sg., sondern die 3. Pers. mask. Sg. Perfekt ist, sind die Lemmata der hebr. Wörterbücher meist nach dieser jeweiligen Form aufgebaut, so auch in Wilhelm Schickards *Horologium Hebraeum* (1623), in dessen Wörterbuch-Anhang des *Lexicon Compendium*. Vgl. Anm. 6; Grether, 81 ff. u. Walter W. Müller: Hebräische und chaldäische Studien (s. Anm. 6), 92. Harsdörffer u. Zesen (schon in seiner *Spraach-übung* von 1643, s. *Zesen SW* XI, hier 14, 21 u. ö.) unternahmen den angesichts der strukturellen Unterschiede unangemessenen Versuch einer engen Parallelisierung des Deutschen mit dem Hebräischen. Das Hebr. hat nämlich nur zwei Genera, aber drei Numeri, keine Kasus u. Deklinationen, andere Tempora-Auffassungen usw. Demnach lag Zesen mit seiner Ableitung der dt. verbalen Stammwörter aus dem Partizip Perfekt also gar nicht so falsch. Die Stammlettern oder -buchstaben („literae radicales") wurden von den Affixa („literae serviles" oder „accidentales") unterschieden. Vgl. *Barbarić*, 1184; *Takada*, S. 25 Anm. 98. Die hebr. Grammatik etwa Johannes Buxtorfs (s. Anm. 5) zählt zu den „Partikeln" die Wortklassen der Adverbien, der Präpositionen, Konjunktionen u. Interjektionen. Zu Einschränkungen u. Besonderheiten s. Grether, 180 ff.; Walter W. Müller: Hebräische und chaldäische Studien (s. Anm. 6), 92 ff. Dreiteilungen der Wortarten (Nomen, Verben, Partikeln) begegnen auch in lateinbasierten Sprachwerken wie in Franciscus Sanctius' *Minerva* (1587). Vgl. *Padley* I, 128–140; Stephen G. Burnett: From Christian Hebraism to Jewish Studies. Johannes Buxtorf (1564–1629) and Hebrew Learning in the Seventeenth Century. Leiden [u.a.] 1996, 111. Zu den unflektierten „Particulas" heißt es im *Specimen (1646)*, 145: „Reliquas Orationis partes Hebræi vocant *particulas*, sive Syncategoremata, & sunt vel Pronomina & adverbia separata, vel præfixa et suffixa." Unter den „Pronomina" sind hier, Schottelius folgend, Präpositionen u. „unabsonderliche Vorwörter" (Vorsilben; „praepositiones inseparabiles") gemeint, d. h. bedeutungsmodifizierende, aber nicht selbständig bedeutende Vorsilben wie Ge- (Gemüt, Geschrey) oder ant-, be-, ent-, er-, ver- usw. „Absönderliche Vorwörter" sind Präpositionen wie ab-, an-, auf-, die sowohl als Ableitungssilben wie auch für sich allein stehen können. Vgl. *Schottelius: Sprachkunst (1641)*, 483 ff. u. 400528 K I 17. Die Prä- u. Suffixe im *Specimen* zu den „particulas" zu rechnen, ist nach der obigen eigenen Definition Harsdörffers eigentlich unsinnig. Vgl. *Banneck*, 62 f., 113 ff. u. 125 f.; *Padley* I, 128; *Takada*, 25 f.; *Hundt*, 78.

5 Johannes Buxtorf d. Ä. (1564–1629), aus Westfalen gebürtiger reformierter Theologe u. nach Studien an den Universitäten Marburg, Herborn (Johannes Piscator), Heidelberg u. Basel seit 1591 Prof. des Hebräischen an der U. Basel, vertraut mit der ramistischen Methode u. mit Wolfgang Ratke bekannt. Er gilt als bedeutendster Hebraist im deutschen Protestantismus nach Johannes Reuchlin u. tat sich als erster christl. Hebraist mit eingehenden Studien zum Talmud u. überhaupt zur rabbinischen Überlieferung hervor, wie u. a. die *Epitome radicum Hebraicarum* (Basel 1600) oder das *Lexicon chaldaicum talmudicum et rabbinicum* (erst von seinem Sohn, s. u., 1639/40 veröffentlicht) bezeugen. Es führte die hebr. Wörter alphabetisch nach Wurzeln u. unter diesen die Ableitungen auf. Neben seinen bibelkritischen Werken zum AT, für die er auch die jüd. Textüberlieferung (Masorah) heranzog, verfaßte er zahlreiche Arbeiten zur Grammatik u. Lexikographie des Hebräischen u. Aramäischen, wie den *Thesaurus Grammaticus Linguae Sanctae Hebraeae* (zuerst Basel 1609, erneut 1615 u. 1620 u. ö. Die Ausg. von 1651 als Ndr. Hildesheim 1981), die *Praeceptiones Grammaticae de Lingua Hebraea* (1605 u. ö.), das *Lexicon Hebraicum et Chaldaicum* (1607), die *Grammaticae chaldaicae et syriacae Libri III* (1618/19). Sein gleichnamiger Sohn (1599–1664, s. auch *ADB* III, 673–676; *NDB* III, 84 f.), der seinem Vater 1630 in der Baseler Professur nachfolgte, gab postum verschiedene Schriften des Vaters heraus, darunter die *Concordantiae bibliorum hebraicae* (1632), das *Lexicon Chaldaicum, Talmudicum et Rabbinicum* (1639/40), oder den *Thesaurus grammaticus linguae sanctae hebraeae* (1609, erw. 6. Aufl. 1663), der in seiner Behandlung der hebr.

Grammatik ebenfalls auf der rabbin. Tradition beruht. Harsdörffer zitiert Buxtorf (und Schickard, s. Anm. 6) in seinem *Specimen (1646)*, etwa S. 135, 136 u. ö. Vgl. *ADB* III, 668–673; Dieter Cherubim: Art. „Buxtorf" in: *Lexicon Grammaticorum* I, 239; Encyclopaedia Judaica. 2nd. Edition. Vol. 4 (Detroit, New York u. a. 2007), 321; *RGG⁴* I, 1927; Jean-Pierre Rothschild: Quelles notions le „grand public" des lettrés chrétiens dans la France du XVIe siècle eut-il de l'hébreu? Enquête parmi les inventaires de bibliothèques. In: L'Hébreu au temps de la Renaissance, recueillie et édité par Ilana Zinguer. Leiden [u. a.] 1992, 172–196, hier S. 186 u. 189; Stephen G. Burnett: From Christian Hebraism to Jewish Studies (1996, s. Anm. 4), bes. 103–133; Ders.: Christian Hebraism in the Reformation Era (1500–1660). Authors, Books, and the Transmission of Jewish Learning. Leiden, Boston 2012, 46, 86f., 109–111 u. ö.; Emil F. Kautzsch: Johannes Buxtorf d. Ä. Rektoratsrede am 4.11.1879. Basel 1879; Rudolf Smend: Der ältere Buxtorf. In: Theologische Zeitschrift 53 (Basel 1997), 109–117; Thomas Willi: Hebraica Veritas in Basel. Christliche Hebraistik aus jüdischen Quellen. In: A. Lemaire (Hg.): Congress of the Intern. Organization for the Study of Old Testament 17 (Leiden [u. a.] 2002), 375–397, hier 386–394. Vgl. auch 190220 K 12, 191231 K 8 u. 280128.

6 Wilhelm Schickard (1592–1635), württemberg. Hebraist, Orientalist, Mathematiker u. Astronom. Vgl. schon 420627 K I 16. Seit 1619 Professor f. Hebräisch an der U. Tübingen. Obwohl bekennender Lutheraner, gehörte Schickard dem nonkonformen, kryptoheterodoxen Tübinger Kreis um Christoph Besold (1577–1638), Daniel Mögling (1596–1635), Johann Valentin Andreae (FG 464. 1646) u.a. an, argwöhnisch beobachtet von Lukas Osiander d. J. (1571–1638). 1631 folgte er seinem früheren Lehrer Michael Mästlin (1550–1631, s. 401111 u.ö.) in dessen Tübinger Mathematik-Professur u. tat sich in den Fachgebieten der Optik, Meteorologie, Sternenkunde sowie Kartographie hervor. Von seinen hebraist. Schriften ist hier das prägnante grammatische Lehrwerk *Horologium Hebraeum* (1623, 43 Auflagen) mit seinem Wörterbuchanhang zu nennen. Das Hebräische erscheint als Ursprache, aus der alle anderen Sprachen hervorgegangen sind. Herleitungen griech., lat. u. dt. Wörter aus dem Hebr. sollen das unterstreichen. Gefälliger u. umfassender *Der Hebräische Trächter* (schwäb. f. Trichter, 1627). Die Anregung für seinen „Fünffachen Denckring der teutschen Sprache" (in den *Philosophischen und Mathematischen Erquickstunden*, 1651) könnte Harsdörffer einem ähnlichen Drehscheibenmodell der hebräischen Verb-Wurzeln, Stämme u. Affixe entnommen haben, Schickards *Rota hebraea* (1621). Sie ist abgebildet in Wilhelm Schickard: Briefwechsel. Hg. Friedrich Seck. 2 Bde., Stuttgart-Bad Cannstatt 2002. Vgl. ferner *ADB* XXXI, 174f.; Encyclopaedia Judaica. 2nd Edition, Vol. 18 (Detroit, New York u. a. 2007), 128; François Secret: Les Kabbalistes Chrétiens de la Renaissance. Nouvelle édition. Ouvrage orné de XV planches hors texte. Nouv. éd. Milano [u. a.] 1985, 330; Walter W. Müller: Hebräische und chaldäische Studien. In: Friedrich Seck (Hg.): Wilhelm Schickard 1592–1635: Astronom, Geograph, Orientalist, Erfinder der Rechenmaschine. Tübingen 1978; 49–108; F. Seck (Hg.): Wissenschaftsgeschichte um Wilhelm Schickard. Tübingen 1981; Ders. (Hg.): Zum 400. Geburtstag von Wilhelm Schickard. 2. Tübinger Schickard-Symposion 1992. Sigmaringen 1995; ders.: Wilhelm Schickard — Herkunft und Werdegang. In: Die Universität Tübingen zwischen Reformation und Dreißigjährigem Krieg. FS Dieter Mertens. Hg. Ulrich Köpf [u. a.]. Ostfildern 2010, 347–386.

7 Balthasar Walther (Gualtherus, 1586–1640), 1610 Prof. der griech., 1612 zusätzlich der hebr. Sprache an der U. Jena, zuletzt Superintendent der Stadt Braunschweig. 1619 war er Mitarbeiter der Köthen-Weimarer ratichianischen Schulreform, als welcher er eine lat. Genesis Übersetzung *Genesis: sive Liber primus Moysis ad Didacticam* (Köthen 1620) u. eine Ausg. der Genesis im hebr. Urtext erstellt hatte, die aber ungedruckt blieb:

קוטן [...] ספד בדאשית d.i. Biblia Sacra, T. V., Genesis, hebr. Vgl. 190424 u. 391217 K 4, ferner 181023 K 8 u. zuletzt 430509 K 4; *Conermann: Fürstl. Offizin*, 131 u. 170 Anm. 128.

8 Menasseh ben Israel (1604–1657), aus einer portugies. Marranen-Familie stammend, die unter dem Druck inquisitorischer Verdächtigungen geheimen Judaisierens 1613/14 nach Amsterdam geflohen u. zum Judentum rekonvertiert war. Menasseh wurde zum Rabbi u. Prediger in der portugies. jüd. Gemeinde von Amsterdam berufen u. wurde aufgrund seiner nicht nur rabbin., sondern insgesamt theologischen Gelehrsamkeit, seiner vielseitigen Sprachen-Kompetenz, der Fähigkeit, Sympathien für die jüd. Glaubensgemeinschaften zu wecken, u. aufgrund seiner weitgespannten intellektuellen Korrespondenznetze über Landes- u. Bekenntnisgrenzen hinweg — Hugo Grotius, Isaak Vossius, Claudius Salmasius, auch Rembrandt u. v. a. gehörten zu seinem Bekanntenkreis — zum berühmtesten rabbin. Gelehrten Westeuropas. Neben seiner Rolle als führende Epochengestalt hebr. Gelehrsamkeit war er als Gründer der ersten hebr. Presse in Amsterdam (1626) bedeutend. Neben seiner Herausgabe rabbin. Schriften wie des *Mishnah* (1631/32) sprach er auch ausdrücklich nicht-jüdische Leser an: in seiner Verteidigung der Juden in den *Vindiciae Judaeorum* (1656), in *De Creatione* (lat. 1635), *De Resurrectione Mortuorum* (1636), *De Fragilitate Humana* (1642) oder in seinem vierbändigen Werk *El Conciliador* (1631–1651), in welchem er versuchte, widersprüchliche Bibeltexte zu klären u. zu harmonisieren, was auch unter christlichen Theologen auf großes Interesse u. Anerkennung stieß. Sein Ausgleich zwischen Kabbala u. (Neu)Platonismus u. sein Interesse an der *prisca theologia* als Einheits- oder Universalreligion brachte ihn auch in Kontakt mit christlichen Millenaristen wie John Durie oder Henry Jessey, am Ende sogar Oliver Cromwell, mit dem er über die Erlaubnis zur Rückkehr der Juden nach England verhandelte. Vgl. Encyclopaedia Judaica. 2nd Edition. Vol. 13 (Detroit, New York u. a. 2007), 454f.; Encyclopedia of the Renaissance. (Ed.) Paul F. Grendler, Vol. 4 (New York 1999), 113f.; Stephen G. Burnett: Christian Hebraism in the Reformation Era (s. Anm. 5), 152, 216, 219 u. ö.; Jacob H. Coppenhagen: Menasseh ben Israel — Manuel Dias Soeiro, 1604–1657. A Bibliography. Jerusalem 1990; Gerold Necker: Kabbala als Kulturgut: Abraham Cohen de Herreras „spanische" Mystik und ihre christliche Rezeption. In: Gottes Sprache in der philologischen Werkstatt. Hebraistik vom 15. bis zum 19. Jahrhundert. Hg. Giuseppe Veltri u. Gerold Necker. Leiden, Boston 2004, 113–134, hier S. 114, 117 u. 123; Menasseh ben Israel and his World. Ed. by Yosef Kaplan, Henry Méchoulan and Richard H. Popkin. Leiden [u. a.] 1989. — Zesen hielt sich oft in den Niederlanden u. Amsterdam auf u. konnte auch damals, wie von Harsdörffer vorgeschlagen, persönlichen Kontakt zu Menasseh aufnehmen.

9 Zum singulären Imperativ als (einsilbiger) Stammform der Verben s. Anm. 3.

10 Verba quadrata, im Hebräischen Wörter aus vier oder fünf Buchstaben, während die hebr. Verb-Wurzeln oder Radices i. d. R. nur aus drei Konsonanten bestehen sollten. Diese würden Schottelius' u. Harsdörffers Theorie nach den einsilbigen Verbstammwörtern (Imperativ Sg.) des Deutschen entsprechen, jene den von Harsdörffer genannten an sich irregulären zweisilbigen. Vgl. hier Anm. 11; *Barbarić*, 1191 u. 1194 f.; *Takada*, S. 25 Anm. 98; *Zedler* XLVII, 125. V. a. Harsdörffer u. Zesen hatten angestrengt versucht, das Hochdeutsche an das Hebräische anzubinden, Harsdörffer v. a. in der 7. Disquisitio in seinem *Specimen (1646)*: „De Conformitate Hebrææ & Germanicæ Linguæ". — Die Nomina werden im Hebr. wie im Dt. von den Verben abgeleitet, so wollte es Harsdörffer im *Specimen (1646)*, 138 (vgl. schon Anm. 3). Zum nachstehenden Problem der Nomina, die nicht aus einem Verb abgeleitet werden können (Hund, Katze, Hahn) heißt es dort 138 f.: „Licet autem quædam Nomina verba non habeant, ut apud Hebræos ... (Koseth) *veritas*, nihilominus tamen format radicem inusitatam, ... (Kashcaht) ad reliquorum Analogiam; siquidem irregularia illa ad exceptiones & observationes pertinent: quod si verò ejusmodi nomina haberent verba-radicalia, aliter radix formari non posset quàm ad normam reliquorum E. G. der Hund/ die Katz/ das Brod/ carent verbis, non enim dicimus Hunden/ Katzen/ Broden; Sed si hujusmodi verba in usu essent, illorum imperativus alius esse non posset, quàm Hund/ Katz/ Brod/ ideoque dicuntur Radices Nominales, Nenn-Stamwörter. Sed hæc singula usu rectius, quàm præceptis discuntur, particularium enim non est regula, vel scientia." Vgl. auch 460902 K 3 u. *Banneck*, S. 110 Anm. 253.

11 Harsdörffer unterscheidet wie Schottelius hinsichtlich der Konjugation die zwei großen Verbklassen der regelmäßigen („gleichfließenden") u. der unregelmäßigen („ungleichfließenden") Verben („Zeitwörter"). Erstere behalten ihre Stammlettern, wie sie der Imperativ Sg. als Stammwort des Verbums vorgibt, durch alle Tempora, Modi, Numeri u. Personen hindurch bei, deren Formen mit „zufälligen Lettern" (Literae accidentales), den Konjugationsendungen, gebildet werden. Etwa: hör! hören, hörte, gehört. Das Dentalsuffix -t-, mit dessen Hilfe bei den schwachen Verben das Part. Perf. u. das Imperf. gebildet werden, erscheint jedoch noch nicht explizit als Klassifikationskriterium. Die unregelmäßigen Verben, verändern die Stammbuchstaben (v. a. den Stammvokal), worin Harsdörffer erneut eine Nähe zum Hebräischen erkennen wollte. Etwa: brich!, brechen, brach, gebrochen (u. Bruch). Diese Zweiteilung der Verben erschien Schottelius als ausreichend (*Schottelius: Sprachkunst [1641]*, 414 ff. u. 425 ff.; ders.: *Sprachkunst [1651]*, 720 ff.), während Gueintz eine genauere Differenzierung der unregelmäßigen Verben nach ihren Ablauten forderte u. drei Ablautreihen unterschied. Auch ihm fehlte freilich der Begriff des „Ablauts". *Gueintz: Sprachlehre (1641)*, 68 ff. Die heutige deutsche Grammatik kennt nur noch rund 170 ablautende Verben. Diese Wortklasse ist heute nicht mehr produktiv u. im Schwinden begriffen. Vgl. 400528 K I 23 u. 410900 K 8. Schottelius beanspruchte in seiner *Teutschen Sprachkunst (1641)*, 451–469, eine vollständige Liste der unregelmäßigen dt. Verben zu bieten, die er auf „ohngefehr hundert und neuntzig" veranschlagte (425). Vgl. auch *Schottelius: Sprachkunst (1651)*, 747 ff. Harsdörffer unterschied hier u. im *Specimen (1646)*, 140 ff., „Inter verba regularia referuntur radices dissyllabicæ, cum verbis quadratis Ebræorum comparandæ [...] ut Zweiffel/ Eifer/ Marter/ quanquam veteres scripserint Zweiffl/ Eifr/ Martr/ ommissis Schevaim. In verbis irregularibus radicales litteræ vel omittuntur vel mutantur." Zur Verteidigung der Einsilbigkeit der Stammwörter, die schon hier zu gezwungenen, dem Sprachgebrauch widerstrebenden Formen führt, gibt Harsdörffer in Anlehnung an Schottelius (s. Anm. 3) die philosoph. Faustregel an: „Ratio evidens est, composita enim fieri debent ex simplicibus, ut truncus à radice, numerus ex unitatibus, germen ex semine, & non, inverso & propostero naturæ ordine, contrà: & verum etiam hoc sensu Philosophorum dogma: *quò quid simplicius, eò etiam est prius*." Dieses Axiom formuliert Harsdörffer auch weiter unten im vorliegenden Brief. Ähnlich hatten Buxtorf (Anm. 5) u. Schickard (Anm. 6) im Hebräischen die vierbuchstabigen Stammformen als an sich unerhebliche Zusätze oder Ableitungen aufgefasst, „whose fourth root letter could be ignored for purposes of classification". Stephen G. Burnett: From Christian Hebraism to Jewish Studies ... (1996, s. Anm. 4), 125; vgl. Walter W. Müller: Hebräische und chaldäische Studien (s. Anm. 6), 54. Vgl. Anm. 3; *Banneck*, 113 ff.; *Barbarić*, 829 u. 921 ff.; *Hundt*, 78 u. 247 ff.; *Takada*, 201 ff.; Leonard Forster: Zu Harsdörffers *Specimen philologiae germanicae*. In: Georg Philipp Harsdörffer. Ein deutscher Dichter und europäischer Gelehrter. Hg. Italo Michele Battafarano. Bern [u. a.] 1991, 9–21, hier S. 11.

12 Zesens Brief an Jesaias Rompler v. Löwenhalt (DG 16; aufgenommen am 4.2.1645) 450308A, den Zesen oder wahrscheinlicher Rompler abschriftlich Harsdörffer zugesandt haben muß. Harsdörffer stand mit Rompler in gutem Kontakt, hatte er ihn doch in

441223 Zesen zur Aufnahme in die DG vorgeschlagen. Auch Johann Rist (FG 467. 1647) machte — über Zesen, der Rompler 1643 in Paris kennengelernt hatte — Bekanntschaft mit diesem Mitgründer der AGT. Vgl. Rists Brief an Zesen 440724 u. dort zu Rompler K 4. Zesen hatte im besagten Brief an Rompler Substantive wie „gäld" (Geld) u. „burg" aus den Verben „gälten" u. „bärgen" u. zwar aus der (Präteritums-)Wurzel „galt" bzw. „barg" ableiten wollen. Ein Verb „rechen" (rächen) erscheint im Brief nicht, jedenfalls nicht in seiner einzigen, in *Bellin: Sendeschreiben (1647)* überlieferten, möglicherweise gekürzten Form.

13 Die Konjugation („Zeitwandlung") der unregelmäßigen Verben „gelten", „bergen" u. „rechen" (rächen) in *Schottelius: Teutsche Sprachkunst (1641)*, 456: „Gilt/ Gelten. Jch gelte/ du giltest/ er gilt/ wir gelten. Jch galt/ du goltest/ er golt/ wir galten. Gegolten." Ebd., 452: „Birg/ Bergen. Jch berge/ du birgst/ er birgt/ wir bergen. Jch barg/ du bargest/ er barg. Geborgen." Ebd., 460: „Rech/ Rechen. Jch reche/ du rechest/ er rechet. gerochen."

14 Bei den starken Verben des Hebräischen ändern sich in der Konjugation nur die Vokale („Stimmer"), die drei konsonantischen Radicale bleiben in allen Formen bestehen. Vgl. Grether (s. Anm. 4), 82ff. Ähnlich ändert sich im Deutschen bei den unregelmäßigen Verben oft nur der Stammvokal. Die besonders enge Verwandtschaft des Deutschen mit dem Hebräischen hatte Zesen z. B. in einem undatiert überlieferten Brief an Adolph Rosel (keine Lebensdaten bezeugt. DG 6. Aufnahme im Juli 1644) herausgestellt. S. *Bellin: Sendeschreiben (1647)*, Nr. 10, Bl. [Dviij]v – G[i]v. In einem weiteren, ins vorgerückte Jahr 1644 oder 1645 zu datierenden Schreiben an Rosel betont Zesen erneut, das Deutsche sei mit dem Hebräischen verschwistert, „sonderlich in der herstammung der wörter/ da die grosse zeuge-mutter sonderlich spielet/ und die wörter nach dem eigentlichen wäsen der dinge zu bilden weis". *Bellin: Sendeschreiben (1647)*, Nr. 5, [B6]v – C[i]v, hier Bl. C[i]r.

15 Zwar erfolgen weder in der vierten Lobrede (über die dt. Buchstaben etc.), noch im Abschnitt über die Umlaute („Kleinlaute"), noch bei der Flexion der Verben regelhafte Hinweise oder Bestimmungen zur Umlautung von Stammvokalen in *Schottelius: Teutsche Sprachkunst (1641)*. Im Kap. 9 von der „Abwandelung" (Deklination) aber heißt es beispielsweise: „Welche [Nomen] in der eintzelen Zahl haben a/ o/ u/ die veränderen in der mehreren Zahl/ diese selblautende in jhren verwanten Kleinlaut/ nemlich das a in ä/ das o in ö/ und das u in ü/ als: Ein Mann/ die Männer [...]. Der Zoll/ die Zölle [...]. Der Wurm/ die Würme [...]." Ebd., 289. Allgemein zu den Umlauten („Kleinlauten") s. S. 202. Vgl. auch Anm. 16.

16 Wie schon in Anm. 3 u. 12 gezeigt, hatte Zesen in 450308A die Nomen „gäld" (Geld) u. „burg" aus den Verben „gälten" u. „bärgen", u. diese aus den imperfektischen Wurzeln „galt" u. „barg" abgeleitet. Er zeigte sich dann selbst beeindruckt, wie das Nomen („gäld") aus der Stammform des Partizips Perfekt herrühre, nämlich „wie das un- oder halb-folkommene ärz-werk/ **gäld**/ (dadurch man eigendlich das silber/ [...] verstehet) aus dem worte der folkommen-vergangenen zeit **gegolten**/ (wie **burg** von **verborgen**/ **sün** von **gesonnen**/ **hülfe** von **geholfen**/ **hübsch** von **erhoben**) entsprungen sei." Dazu gibt es interessante Wechselschreiben zwischen Johann Bellin (1618–1660. DG 38. Aufnahme als der Willige am 8.10.1646) u. Zesen. In seinem Brief von frühestens Oktober 1646 (*Bellin: Sendeschreiben (1647)*, Nr. 7, Bl. C ij v – C iij v) fragte Bellin Zesen, warum er so oft die Umlaute ä, ö, ü statt der herkömmlichen Vokale e bzw. i setze, z. B. ämsig, ärde, ässen, föchten (für fechten), verwürrung usw. Da die Niedersachsen diese Laute viel genauer als die Hochdeutschen unterschieden, komme ihnen Zesens Schreibweise äußerst befremdlich vor. Zesen antwortete darauf (*Bellin: Sendeschreiben [1647]*, Nr. 8, Bl. [Ciiij] r – [D v] v; vgl. *Habichthorst*, 42–43 u. 45–54): weil sich alle abgeleiteten u. flektierten Formen nach ihren Stammwörtern zu richten hätten. Nach Goropius Becanus meine man meist, daß, angeblich wie im Hebräischen, nur einsilbige Wörter Stämme im Deutschen seien. Viele Substantive wie Sonne, Lehre, Friede, Hölle, Hitze würden so „mit gewalt" zu Einsilbern gemacht u. ihres lieblichen –e beraubt. Entsprechend ergehe es den dt. Verben, wenn deren Stammwort aus dem angeblich immer einsilbigen Imperativ Sg. abgeleitet werde (a. a. O., Bl. [Ciiij]v). Es gebe aber zweisilbige Imperative: liebe, lobe. Diese ganze Lehre stimme weder für das Hebräische noch das Deutsche (Bl. [Cv]r). Zesen sieht die Stammform des Verbs (wie im Hebr.) im Imperfekt: er galt, daher „gälten", nicht gelten; barg, daher „bärgen", nicht bergen (Bl. [Cv]r f.). Wenn man das Stammwort im Imperfekt nicht finden könne, müsse man es im Perfekt suchen oder im Substantiv, schließlich auch im Präsens oder bei den Nachbarsprachen (nl., schwed., dän., isl., engl., v. a. aber niedersächsisch/ nd.). S. schon 441223 K 21. Zesens etymolog. Streifzüge u. die daraus abgeleitete Schreibweise sind äußerst heterogen, tw. bizarr. Zu F. Ludwigs Ablehnung s. 450504. Zur nachstehenden Regel Harsdörffers: „Composita fiunt ex simplicibus, et non contra" s. oben Anm. 11.

17 Zum hebr. Schwa „sive **e** raptissimum, nobis in præfixis & suffixis be/ ge/ er/ en & similibus usitatus, ut cum scribimus beliebe*n*/ & pronunciamus bliebe*n*/ geschriebe*n* & dicimus gschrieben: gehn/ stehn/ pro gehen/ stehen/ etc.", s. *Harsdörffer: Specimen (1646)*, 137 f. Zesen hatte schon in seiner *Hooch-Deutschen Spraach-übung* (1643) einige Buchstaben als von nicht-deutscher Herkunft aus dem dt. Alphabet entfernen wollen: c, q, ph, th, während das -v- noch auf Nachsicht stieß u. nur in geeigneten Fällen durch -f- ersetzt werden sollte. S. *Zesen SW* XI, 26 f., 44–47, 62 f., 66 f. Im *Rosen-mând* (1651) reduzierte Zesen das dt. Alphabet auf 21 Buchstaben (*Zesen SW* XI, 186 f.); „c, q, y" wurden als Buchstaben lat. Herkunft im Deutschen als deplaciert qualifiziert, weil sie „zu ihrer sprache sich gantz nichts schikken und nuhr überflüßig" seien (ebd., 127, vgl. 146 ff.). Das -vwurde als nd. angesehen u. sollte als „fremdling" im Hd. in der Regel durch -f- ersetzt werden (149 u. 159 f.). Das latein. -q- sollte „billich gantz ausgesondert und verworfen werden" (156). Zum Schwa oder unbetonten -e- findet sich keine Aussage, auch nicht im Brief an Rompler 450308A, wie er bei *Bellin: Sendeschreiben (1647)* überliefert ist. Vgl. auch Zesens Brief an Rosel in *Bellin: Sendeschreiben (1647)*, Nr. 10, Bl. [Dviij]v – G[i]v, hier v. a. Bl. E ii v ff. In diesem Brief will Zesen sogar das -ch- durch -gh- („toghter", „aght" usw.) ersetzen. In 450808 stellt Zesen aber klar, daß er nicht gesonnen sei, die „**vav** ganz ab zu schaffen […] sondern ich schaff' es nuhr ab in denen wörtern/ da das f stehen sol/ als **fortern/ fohr/ führ/ führen/ fohraus/ fohrteil/ forschen** (q. d. herfohr suchen) **fol/ füllen/ föllig; folk**", s. dort. Ebenso will er nach Aussage besagten Briefes das unbetonte Schluß-e nur im Falle eines folgenden Vokals elidieren: „es mus ein ieder/ so der Meisnischen und Ober-sächsischen mund-ahrt gewohnet ist/ bekännen/ daß sie [die Meißner/ Obersachsen., d. Hg.] niemahls/ **lieb/ denk/ schlag/ red/ leid/ (du)** und so fort/ **fohr liebe/ denke/ schlage/ rede/ leide/ (du)** aus-sprächen oder schreiben/ es sei dan/ wän ein selb-lauter darauf folget/ da das **e** weg-geworfen werden mus; als **drüm lob' und lieb' und preise deinen Got; drüm schlag' ihn;** (hiermit ist auch das seinige von den **Schevaim** beantwortet)". Zu Zesens überflüssigen Buchstaben vgl. *Schielein*, 27 ff. u. 62 f., 66 u. 80.

18 Ein Gutachten Augustus Buchners (FG 362) zu Fragen der Stammwortansetzung konnte nicht ermittelt werden. Vgl. aber sein Gutachten zu Christian Gueintz' (FG 361) Sprachlehre: 400122 I.

19 Zu Hz. Augusts d. J. v. Braunschweig-Wolfenbüttel (FG 227. Der Befreiende) spätestens seit 1635 vorbereitetem Projekt einer Revision der Bibelübersetzung Martin Luthers s. 411214, 451001 u. ö.

20 Zesens Antwortbrief 450808 wird seine Sprachauffassungen u. Schreibweise sowohl verteidigen, als auch in ihrem Geltungsanspruch relativieren.

21 Ein nicht ganz unmißverständlicher Satz, der sinngemäß wohl bedeuten könnte: Hz. Christian Ludwig v. Braunschweig-Calenberg (FG 372), in der FG „der Reinherzige", werde sich mit diesem Gesellschaftsnamen wohl kaum zu einer Förderung Zesens bereitfinden, wenn dieser bei seinen Sprachansichten bleibe. Dem Herzog hatte Harsdörffer seine „Schutzschrift für Die Teutsche Spracharbeit" gewidmet, s. 440715A.

22 Einen eigens bestellten Erzschreinhalter hat es unter F. Ludwig in der FG tatsächlich nicht gegeben, auch wenn Friedrich v. Schilling (FG 21) bis zum Tode (9.9.1637) fruchtbringerische Korrespondenzaufgaben übernommen hatte. Die „Geschäftsstelle" der FG wurde sodann von F. Ludwig persönlich in Köthen geführt, in den letzten Jahren — er starb am 7.1.1650 — unterstützt von Christian Ernst (v.) Knoch (FG 268), s. 450730. Sie bestand aus dem Gesellschaftsarchiv („Ertzschrein"), das nach der Ordnung durch den Köthener Bibliothekar Gottlieb Krause im 19. Jh. den fruchtbringerischen Schriftverkehr erst ab dem Jahr 1637 versammelt (bis auf wenige frühere Stücke), aber auch das *GB Kö.*, Köthener Druckwerke u. eingesandte Bücher, Siegel u.a.m. umfaßt hatte. Einen Teil der dazu gehörigen handschriftlichen Überlieferung überließ Krause als hzl. Archivar dem Vorläufer des Landeshauptarchivs Sachsen-Anhalt, Abt. Dessau. Anderes, z.B. Impresenvisierungen (*Weimarer Impresen*), war schon nach F. Ludwigs Tod dessen Nachfolger Hz. Wilhelm IV. v. Sachsen-Weimar (FG 5) überbracht worden. Zu den Archivalien des Erzschreins s. *Conermann: Nachlaßinventar*. Vgl. auch *Bulling*. — In der FG wurden die Wappen u. Impresen der Mitglieder auf Atlas gestickt, in prächtigen Wandgobelins zusammengenäht u. im Köthener Schloßsaal aufgehängt. So wurde der „Erzschrein" zum Inbegriff der schriftlichen u. bildlichen FG-Dokumente. S. *Conermann: Nachlaßinventar*. Vgl. 271201 I, 340716, 371110 K 11, 371220 K 12, 390807 K 8, 410323 K 8 u. 440209, 440824, 450124 K I 2, 450505, 450730 (K 2), 451028, 460120, 460423, 460424, 460424A, 460620, 460705, 460718 K 8, 460915, 460916 K 2, 461031 u. 461106. Zum „Erzschrein" vgl. das Lemma im Sachregister des vorliegenden Bandes.

23 Zum Gesellschaftssiegel der FG s. 441223 K 4. Über F. Ludwigs Köthener Druckerei, die er im Dienste der ratichian. Schulreform gegründet u. im Dienste der FG viele Jahre unterhalten hatte, s. *Conermann: Fl. Offizin*. Die Drucke der fl. Köthener Offizin galten unter Zeitgenossen als vorbildlich in ihrer relativ geregelten Orthographie. — Als der FG „Stiffter und Vrheber" wird F. Ludwig auch in Harsdörffers „Vbereigungsgedicht" *[sic]* in der 2. Ausg. des ersten Teils der *Frauenzimmer-Gesprächspiele* (1644) angesprochen.

24 Auffällig ist, daß Harsdörffer (DG 12. Der Kunstspielende. Aufnahme angeblich am 4.12.1644) nicht mit seinem DG-Namen unterschreibt. Wenn nicht Unkenntnis über seinen Mitgliedsstatus dafür verantwortlich ist (vgl. 450400), könnte die zunehmende Distanz zu Zesen der Grund dafür gewesen sein. In 450308A sprach Zesen selbst Harsdörffer mit dessen FG-Gesellschaftsnamen als den „Spielenden" an. Vgl. auch 450529 K 7 u. 450808 K I 2.

450417 Matthäus Merian d. Ä.

450417

Matthäus Merian d. Ä. an Peter Knaudt

Antwort auf einen verloren gegangenen Brief vom 20. März 1645. — Matthäus Merian d. Ä. bittet Peter Knaudt, ihm 200 Reichstaler, die Kupfer des *GB 1629/30* und die Abrisse der Impresen FG 201–400 zu senden. Er teilt Knaudt mit, daß die getroffene Vereinbarung Gültigkeit behalte, und bittet um die Übermittlung des genauen Wortlauts. Sobald er sowohl das Geld als auch die „alten Kupfer" erhalten habe, werde er mit der Arbeit beginnen und es an Fleiß nichts ermangeln lassen, vorausgesetzt die Zeichnungen (Visierungen) der neuen (noch nicht gestochenen) Impresen (ab FG 201) seien dann ebenfalls übersandt worden. Er habe das *GB 1641* von dem inzwischen verstorbenen Hans Ludwig (v.) Knoch (FG 252) erhalten. Somit sei es nicht notwendig, dasselbe an ihn zu schicken. Sämtliche genannte Schriften und Gelder sollen nicht über Johann Press, sondern über Matthias Götze in Leipzig an ihn, Merian, übermittelt werden.

Q HM Köthen: V S 546, Bl. 21rv, v leer, eigenh. Die Hand Merians weist in den Wörterendungen Verschleifungen auf, die stillschweigend ausgeschrieben wurden. — *D: Bircher: Merian*, 696f.; *Wüthrich: Merian Briefe*, 86–89. — *BN: Bürger*, 987 Nr. 7.

A Tt. Dem Edlen vnd vesten Herren Petter Knaud meinem Großg. hochgeehrten Herrn *etc.* Cöthen

Edler vnd vester Großgunstig hochgeehrter Herr *etc.* deme sei mein willige dienst vnd was Jch vermag Jeder Zeit Anvor[1] *etc.*

   Meines gg. Herrn geliebtes vom 20. Martij[2] habe ich wol empfangen vnd verstanden. Betreffendt die Fruchtbringende Gesellschafft, und das der herr nun mehr selbige ins werkh zu setzen Resolviert, darzu die Rthl. 200 sampt den alten 200 Kupfern dise Leipziger Ostermeß herauß zu verschaffen willens, welches mir lieb, vnd begehre bei dem vorigen **Accordt** zu verbleiben. Allein bitte ich mein gg. herr wolle mir eine Copey derer wort des **Accordts** zu ruckh senden, Jch habe es zwar sumariter angeschrieben, weiß aber die Conditionen nicht mehr so eben. Jch will nach erhaltung der alten Kupfer vnd des gelts, also bald dem werkh einen Anfang machen lassen, vnd an meinem ohrt nicht verwinden lassen. Allein müssen die Ne[we]n[a] abriß auch mit gesendet werden. Die zu Cot[he]n[a] in 4° A° 1641 getrukte schrifften[3], habe ich von hrn von Knochen S.[a4] empfangen und dürffen selbige nit mit gesendet werden. Die Rthl. 200 vnd alten Kupfer vnd was mir der herr senden will, kan der herr nicht h. Pressen[5] sondern h. Matthias Götzen[6] Buchhändlern in Leipzig ein hendigen der wirts alßdann mir solches wol zu verschaffen wissen *etc.* Welches meinem gg. Herrn in Antwort habe vermelden wollen. Dem Allmechtigen hier mit wohl befohlen.

Ffurt den 17. Aprill 1645.

   D. Herrn
      Dienstwilligster
      Mattheus Merian.

T a *Beschädigte Stelle im Dokument.*

K Die im vorliegenden Band abgedruckte, etwa 30 Briefe umfassende Korrespondenz des aus Basel stammenden u. in Frankfurt a. M. wirkenden Malers, Kupferstechers u. Verlegers Matthäus Merian d. Ä. (1593–1650) mit Peter Knaudt befindet sich, wie der o. g. Quelle (Q) zu entnehmen, im FG-Archiv, dem Köthener Erzschrein (dritter Band). Sie behandelt hauptsächlich die intensive Arbeit an Druck, Verlag u. Kostenabwicklung des *GB 1646* u. an dem Großunternehmen *Merian: Topographia.* Zum *GB 1646* allgemein s. 440130 K 3; zur Briefdokumente-Übersicht den Zahlungsverkehr das *GB 1646* betreffend s. 450127 K 1; zum fl. Verlag s. 450126 K 4. — Zu *Merian: Topographia* s. 450905 K 4.

1 In der briefüblichen Sprache *bevor, vorab.* S. *Stieler,* 584: *adv.,* anvor *praemittendo, praecipuè, imprimis,* vgl. *DW* I, 512 *praecipue,* „unüblich, wäre aber gleichviel mit voraus, vorab, voran". S. 451015, 460206, 460303, 460519, 460620B, 460703 u. 461023.

2 *Bircher: Merian,* 696 schreibt dazu: „Es ist seltsam, daß kurz nach Empfang dieses nicht allzu hoffnungsvollen Briefes (i. e. 450308 Carl Gustav v. Hille [FG 302] an den FG-Leiter) F. Ludwig den Auftrag an Merian erteilte, das Gesellschaftsbuch auszuführen. Möglicherweise erhielt er gleichzeitig einen (nicht erhaltenen) Brief Hz. Augusts d. J. v. Braunschweig-Wolfenbüttel (FG 227) mit der Zusage des versprochenen Geldes. Peter Knaudt ersuchte Merian mit seinem Brief vom 20. März um den Arbeitsbeginn, u. binnen eines Jahres sollte das Werk vollendet sein". Lt. *Bircher: Merian,* 669f., ist dieses Dokument nicht nachweisbar. Bircher scheint den eben zitierten Inhalt des Schreibens aus dem vorliegenden Brief erschlossen zu haben. Wie der Korrespondenzverlauf zeigt, erhält Merian die 200 resp. 199 Reichstaler (vom Braunschweiger Hans Beyer) per 11. Juli (450711), u. erst zehn Monate später (460519) bestätigt Merian den Eingang des Verlagsbeitrags Hz. Augusts in Höhe von 200 Reichstalern. S. 450509 K 1.

3 *GB 1641* (4°).

4 Wahrscheinlich handelt es sich um den Fruchtbringer Hans Ludwig (v.) Knoch (FG 252), dessen unbekanntes Sterbedatum durch diese Nachricht auf den Zeitraum zwischen 1641/43 u. 1645 eingegrenzt werden kann. Vgl. auch 410909, 430410 u. 430905. Knoch wirkte seit 1642 im Dienst Gf. Friedrich Casimirs v. Hanau-Lichtenberg (FG 695. 1659) in Hanau als Hofmeister u. Geh. Rat; vgl. auch 430905.

5 Johann Press, Frankfurter u. Hanauer Verleger u. Drucker, s. *Benzing: Verleger,* 1236.

6 Matthias Götze (1585–1662), Leipziger Buchhändler u. Verleger; maßgeblicher Mittelsmann in Leipzig den Zahlungsverkehr des *GB 1646* betreffend. Zu ihm s. 450509 K 3.

450419

Johann Hammer an Peter Knaudt

Johann Hammer bedankt sich für einen Brief Peter Knaudts vom 16.4. Mit Verweis auf ein Schreiben Hans Beyers aus Braunschweig, welches er anbei übersende, verspricht Hammer, Knaudt über alles zu unterrichten, was (betreffs des *GB 1646*) anstehe oder folge. Auch empfange Knaudt beiliegend die erwünschten Antworten, die hoffentlich korrekt ausgefallen seien. Gäbe es etwas richtigzustellen, möge es Knaudt mitteilen. — Hammer teilt mit, über eine große Menge alten und jungen Weins von guter, mittlerer und „gemeiner" Qualität zu verfügen, den Eimer zu 10 bis 22 Talern. Gerne wäre er bereit, Knaudt damit zu versorgen. — Aus Mähren und Österreich gebe es keine besonderen Nachrichten.

450419 Johann Hammer

Q HM Köthen: V S 546, Bl. 24rv [A: 24v]; eigenh., A von Schreiberh.; rotes Lacksiegel. — *D: Bircher: Merian*, 698f. — *BN: Bürger*, 670 Nr. 1.

A Titul Herrn Peter Knaudten, Fürstl. Anhält. Wohlbestalten Cammermeistern *etc.* Zue großg. handen. Jn Cöthen.

Insonders Großg. Herr Cam*m*ermeister, hochgeehrter werther Freündt, deßen geliebtes vom 16. diß erhalten[1], hierbey waß mir H Hanß Beyer[2] aus Braunschweig schreibt, waß ferner erfolgt, soll alßbalt gemelt werden. Die begehrten Antworten hatt der herr hierbey zuempf*angen*. Vermeine werden sich recht befinden, da[a] wider verhoffen [in] einem oder anderm theil geirret wehre, kann es d*er Herr* melden.

Mitt allerhandt wein, guth, mittel, vndt gemeine sort, binn ich Gott lob versehen, Neü vndt alt, von 10 biß 22 thr. den Eimer. Bedarff der herr etwas, soll darmit wohl versorgt werden.

Auß Mehren vndt Östereich haben hiesige Schr*iften*[3] nichts sonderliches, alß das es Jnen dorten noch wohl gehet.

Gott gebe friden. Jn deßen schuz den herrn befehl.

Leip*z*ig d*en* 19 Aprill 1645.
D*es* h*errn* d*i*enstwilliger h*i*lfreicher
Hanß Hammer*mp*

T a *Lies:* sofern

K 1 Nicht erhaltener Brief vom 16.4.1645.
2 Der einzige uns vorliegende Brief des Braunschweiger Kaufmanns Hans Beyer stammt aus dem Folgemonat Mai 1645 (450503), in dem er den Empfang der Quittung F. Ludwigs über Hz. Augusts d. J. v. Braunschweig-Wolfenbüttel (FG 227) Zahlungsverpflichtung über 200 Reichstaler, s. 450331, bestätigt. Es ist zu vermuten, daß der von Beyer stammende (und an Knaudt weitergeleitete) Brief an Johann Hammer die (Voraus-)Zahlung der o. g. 200 Reichstaler bestätigt. S. 450509 K 1. Zu fl. Verlagsbeiträgen s. 450126 K 4. Zur Übersicht über die Briefdokumente den Zahlungsverkehr des *GB 1646* anlangend s. 450127 K 1. Zum *GB 1646* allgemein s. 440130 K 3.
3 Vermutlich handelte es sich dabei um Schreiben (Meßrelationen o. dgl.) oder Druckschriften, die an das von den schwed. Besatzungstruppen kontrollierte Posthaus in Leipzig gesandt worden waren u. von den militär. Verhältnissen der zu dieser Zeit in Mähren u. Österreich operierenden schwed. Hauptarmee unter Lennart Torstensson berichteten. Die schwed. Streitmacht war im Frühjahr 1645 in Böhmen einmarschiert u. hatte dem ksl. Heer unter dem neuen Generalleutnant Gf. Melchior v. Hatzfeld — Gallas war dieser Position enthoben worden (s. 440927 K 1) — in der Schlacht bei Jankau/ Jankov (60 km südöstlich von Prag) am 24.2.1645 eine vernichtende Niederlage beigebracht. Danach in Niederösterreich bis an die Nähe Wiens operierend, scheiterten die Schweden mit ihrer Belagerung Brünns in Mähren (Juni – August 1645). Vgl. 451030 K 2.
4 Der Leipziger Wein- u. Spezereyenhändler Johann Hammer (1600–1650), seit 1641 Mitglied des Leipziger Rats. S. seine LP: Christian Lange: Frommer Christen Anfechtung und Drauff folgende Belohnung ... (Leipzig: Köler, 1650). VD17 3:641262C.

450420

Diederich von dem Werder an Fürst Ludwig

Beantwortet durch 450505. — Diederich v. dem Werder (FG 31. Der Vielgekörnte) ruft in Erinnerung, daß bei einem jüngst abgehaltenen Gesellschaftertreffen beschlossen worden sei, in den von Adjektiven/ Adverbien auf -g- abgeleiteten Substantiven das -g- beizubehalten, etwa im Falle von „barmhertzig" „barmhertzigkeit". Werder plädiert im Gegensatz zur Mehrheit der Versammelten dafür, das -g- im Hauptwort auszulassen. Er tritt dafür ein, daß Fruchtbringer ihre abweichenden Ansichten schriftlich begründen und diese den Vornehmsten und besten Kennern vorlegen sollten, sich jedoch einem allgemeinen Beschluß fügen müßten, nicht wie Justus Georg Schottelius (FG 397. Der Suchende) und Georg Philipp Harsdörffer (FG 368. Der Spielende), die im Alleingang eine neue Regelung durchzusetzen versuchen. Ihre Arbeiten sollten verbessert und von F. Ludwig freundlich kritisiert werden. — Werder listet darauf seine Argumente und Gründe für das Auslassen des -g- bei Substantiven des genannten Wortbildungsmusters auf, zumal 1. stichhaltig begründeten Sprachreformen der Vorzug vor der hergebrachten Sprachgewohnheit zu geben sei, analog zu Verbesserungen im Gottesdienst. 2. sollten überflüssige Buchstaben grundsätzlich vermieden werden, nicht unbedingt jedoch Harsdörffers -c- in vielen ck-Verbindungen wie „gedanken" (statt Gedancken). 3. Da das Substantiv nicht vom Adjektiv/ Adverb, sondern von seinem Stammwort abgeleitet werde (z.B. schuld-ig von Schuld), laute das Suffix -keit und das entsprechende Hauptwort Schuldikeit. 4. Selbst wenn das Substantiv vom Adjektiv/ Adverb mal abgeleitet würde, wäre das -g- dennoch zu tilgen. Auch im Lateinischen, Italienischen und Französischen behalte das Substantiv nicht den letzten Buchstaben des Adjektivs, z.B. fragilis > fragilitas. 5. Erscheine das adjektivische -g- als Endbuchstabe auch im Substantiv als unabdingbar, falle doch der Widerspruch auf, wenn dies gar nicht konsequent geschehe. Adjektive, die keineswegs auf -g- ausgingen, zeigten dieses dennoch im Substantiv, etwa im Falle von sterblich > Sterbligkeit. Begründen ließe sich das höchstens mit der Aussprache. 6. Das -g- in der Aussprache dennoch unbedingt hören zu lassen, sei überflüssig und führe nur zu einem üblen Klang. 7. Obwohl das Deutsche nicht unendliche Möglichkeiten zur Eliminierung von Konsonanten biete, gelte, daß deren Reduzierung die Sprache reiner und gefälliger mache. — Werder beteuert, in dieser Frage nicht unbelehrbar zu sein, bittet aber um gründliche und vorbehaltlose Prüfung seiner Auffassung. Er verspricht, sich dem Urteil F. Christians II. v. Anhalt-Bernburg (FG 51. Der Unveränderliche), Martin Milagius' (FG 315. Der Mindernde), Christian Ernsts (v.) Knoch (FG 268. Der Weichende) und Cuno Ordomars v. Bodenhausen (FG 69. Der Bequeme) zu unterwerfen. — In einer Nachschrift bringt Werder noch zwei weitere Argumente vor: 8. Wenn das -g- im Substantiv unbedingt beibehalten werden solle, dann müsse es auch im Stammwort stehen. 9. Werde das Substantiv -g- bewahrt, sollte besser die Ableitungssilbe -heit- folgen: etwa „schuldigheit". Der Wohlklang habe aber dazu geführt, dieses -gh- in ein -k- zu verwandeln: „schuldikeit".

Q HM Köthen: V S 544, Bl. 474r–476v [A: 476v], 475rv eingelegter Zettel (r Nachschrift, v leer); eigenh.; rote Lacksiegelreste. — *D: KE*, 173–176; *KL* III, 262–265 (ohne die Nachschrift); *Krause: Werder,* 50–52 (dito). — *BN: Bürger,* 1440 Nr. 51 u. 52.

A Dem Nehrenden. Cöthen zu handen.
Eigenh. Empfangsvermerk F. Ludwigs: 21 April. 1645.

Höchstgeehrter vnd nimmer genugsam gepriesener Herr Nehrender.

Es errinnert sich derselbe, was bey nähester geschehenen Zusamenkunft vieler hohen vnd anderen geselschaftern¹ für eine erwegung vnd ungleiche meinung über dem buchstaben g. sich erhoben, in dem mehrertheils in denen gedancken verblieben, es müste das g. in denen wörtern da sich die adjectiua oder adverbia auf ein g. enden notwendig auch in den substantiuis verbleiben, Als barmhertzig barmhertzigkeit gottselig gottseligkeit embsig embsigkeit; jch aber in denen gegengedancken gestanden, wie auch noch, das solches .g. ausgelassen werden müste: Dieweil dan bey itziger bemühung vieler vornemen vnd geistreichen geselschaftern, wegen ordentlicher art zu reden vnd zu schreiben vielerley vnvereinte gedancken vnd meinungen vorgehen, Meines erachtens auch nicht wohl thunlich, das in eines^a zweener oder etzlicher wenigen mehr, ansehen, nachsinnen, vnd gutbefinden dieses weitläuftige werck bestehen könne^b, noch ihnen allein^b anzuvertrauen sey, So hielt ich vnmasgebig darfür, das ein ieder liebhaber vnserer werthen Muttersprache, insonderheit aber die von der löblichen Fruchtbringenden geselschaft, vnd vnter denen wiedrumb insonderheit diejenigen welche hierzu einige neigung vnd belieben, neben der erfahrung, tragen, schuldig seyen, dasjenige, so^c einem oder andern in dieser art zu reden oder zuschreiben beyfallen möchte, bevorab wan es etwas sonderlichs vnd verenderlichs ist, nicht alleine aufsetzen, sondern auch grund vnd regeln darbey anfüren, vnd solches hernach den vornemsten vnd geübtesten der Fruchtbringenden geselschaft einschicken vnd deren hochvernünftigen urtheil unterwerffen solten; Nach dem aber ein algemeiner Schlus² von hochwohlgedachten vielen Geselschaftern hierunter genommen, das dan hernach^b dergleichen behaubtete meinung denen [474v] jenigen so itzo bemühet sein auf ihre eigene hand eine algemeine verfaßung aufzusetzen^d, oder doch nach ihrem Kopfe verenderlich zuschreiben, als da sein der Suchende vnd der Spielende, zugeschicket, vnd do sie nichts nachdrücklichs dargegen einzuwenden hetten[,] dardurch verbunden würden, sich in den Schrancken zuhalten, vnd nicht so nach ihrem blossen wahn oben hin regeln vnd neue arten, ohne erhebliche vrsachen, zusetzen vnd einzufüren. Dieses aber nicht allein: Sondern es were wohl hoch nötig, das des Spielenden vnd Suchenden ausgegangene sachen, wegen etzlicher neuer arten zuschreiben, so keinen grund haben, durchgesehen, alle neue erdichtete fehler aufgesetzt, vnd ihnen, zur verbesserung derselben, freundliche vnd wohlgemeinte ermahnung, vnd solche mit wohlgegründetem beweis, zugeschicket würden.

Dieses aber were keinem besser als dem *Nehrenden* anzuvertrauen.³ Ob mein urtheil zwar geringe, So achte ich es doch in diesem pass⁴ hoch, das ich dem geschicktesten hier zu meine Stimme gegeben^b.

Damit ich aber dem^e zufolge, wie auch wieder zu dem, da ich mein schreiben von angefangen komme, So bin ich nochmals der meinung, das das .g. in obgedachten vnd dergleichen wörtern ausgelaßen werden müsse,

   Aus nachfolgenden ursachen vnd regeln.

1. Wan man vermeint etwas neues im schreiben[b] eines vnd andern wortes einzuführen,[f] im fall man dessen nur guten grund hatt, so mus die alte gewohnheit, vnd das es so hehrkommens sey, gantz nicht beobachtet werden, dieweil man in dieser sache auf wohlgegründete verbesserung, vnd nicht auf das alte hehrkommen vnd gewohnheiten allein zusehen hatt: Gleich wie bey verenderung des Gottesdienstes auch geschehen mus.[5]

2. Sollen alle überflüssige buchstaben ausgelassen, vnd vermiden bleiben. Dahehr lässet der Spielende das c. in vielen wörtern aus als gedanken, wanken, der wankelbare der Schlanke. So ich doch dahin [stelle.][g] [6]

3. So wird das **Substantiuum** nicht eben von dem **adiectiuo** oder **aduerbio** sondern vielmehr vom Stamwort, hehrgezogen, als zum exempel: Schuld ist ein Stamwort für sich. Solches macht im **adjectivo** die endung auf .ig. ausgehen, als schuldig, jm **Substantiuo** aber auf keit[h], als schuldikeit. Flucht, Flüchtig, Flüchtikeit. Muht muhtig muhtikeit.[7] [476r] Wolte man mir aber diesen dritten Satz nicht gelten lassen, vnd vorgeben das die substantiua ihren ursprung von dem **adjectiuo** oder **adverbio** hehrnemen (welches doch gantz nichtig, dan es kömt vom Stamwort hehr) So andworte ich zum

4. das alsdan nottwendig der letzte buchstabe .g. dennoch[b] getilgt oder ausgelassen, oder[i] verendert werden müsse, vnd diese **authoritet** neme ich aus der lateinischen Sprache, jn derselben wird man kein einiges **Substantiuum** finden das den[j] letzten buchstaben vom **nominatiuo adiectiui** behalte: Als zum exempel. **Fragilis fragilitas debilis debilitas Bonus bene bonitas, probus probe probitas, sanctus sancte sanctitas** etc. jm welschen vnd frantzösischen ist eben dergleichen.

5. Wan auch das g. im **Substantiuo** nottwendig deswegen stehen solte, weil es im **adjectiuo** der **final** buchstabe sey, wohehr schreiben dan diejenigen, die dieser meinung sein, etzliche andere wörter im **Substantiuo** mit dem .g., welche im **aduerbio** keines[k] in fine haben. Als verweslich verwesligkeit Sterblich Sterbligkeit, [go]ttlos[l] [go]ttlosigkeit [mü]de [mü]digkeit. Dieses kan nirgend grund haben, Man wolte es dan in der ausrede oder **pronuntiation** suchen:

6. So halte ich Sechstens darfür, das diejenigen welche sich bemühen, solches g.[m] in der ausrede hören zu lassen, sich sehr bemühen dem worte einen übelen vnd überflüßigen klang zugeben, mit welchem sie es mehr verstellen als zieren. Dan ie weniger **consonanten**

7. Siebendens in der ausrede gehört werden, ie klingender vnd reiner lauten die wörter,[8] jedoch mus man hierbey zusehen, wie viel vnsere Sprache solches zulassen kan. Jch wil in dieser meiner meinung nicht hartnäckig sein, bitte aber, das man diese meine angeführte ursachen auch nicht, aus vorgesetztem wahn, sondern freymütig erwege, vnd dan nach befinden, dieselbe anneme oder gründlich wiederlege. Verbleibe Meines hochgeehrten Herren *Nehrenden*

Dienstwilligster geselschafter
Der Vielgekörnte

Reinsdorff 20. Aprill 1645.

450420 Diederich von dem Werder

Der hoheit des *Unuerenderlichen* wie auch des Mindernden vnd Erweichenden, auch[n] Bequehmen[9] vnd anderer vernünftigen urtheil vnter werffe ich billich dieses hochwichtige werck.

[475r]   P.S.
Es ist fürs achte nötig noch zuerrinnern befunden worden, das wo das g. im[o] nomine substaniuo mit gewalt stehen bleiben mus, das dasselbige g. alsdan[p] im Stamwort auch befindlich[q]; Dannenhero erscheinet klar, das sich das Substantiuum nicht nach dem adiectiuo, sondern nach dem Stamwort richtet vnd hehrzeucht, Als zum Exempel karg kargheit, träg trägheit, klug klugheit.

Hieraus wolte fürs neunde auch[b] folgen, das wan ie das .g. auch in den andern Substantiuis stehen bleiben müße, das sie[b] alsdan ihre endung auf -heit nemen solten, Als Gottseligheit, schuldigheit, Flüchtigheit, mutigheit. Die Euphonia aber hatt solch .gh. in ein k. verwandelt[.] Gottselikeit schuldikeit Flüchtikeit[r] muhtikeit.

Bleibet endlich darbey das das g.[b] in diesem falle ein überflüssiger buchstabe ist, vnd also billich nach obengesetzter zweiten[s] algemeiner vnd angenommenen regel, bey höchster Straffe, zu vermeiden ist.

T **a** *Folgt* <oder> — **b** *Eingefügt.* — **c** *Folgt* <ihm> — **d** *Folgt* <als da sein der Sp[ielende?]> — **e** *Bis* wie auch *eingefügt.* — **f** *Folgt* <man> — **g** *Textverlust im Falz. Konjektur in eckigen Klammern.* — **h** *Davor* <ein> — **i** oder verendert *eingefügt.* — **j** *Eingefügt für* <der> — **k** *Folgt* <im g. ehe> — **l** *Bis* [mü]digkeit *am Rand ergänzt. Buchstabenverlust im Falz.* — **m** *Folgt unleserlich gestrichenes Wort.* — **n** auch Bequehmen *eingefügt.* — **o** *Eingefügt für* <in fine> — **p** als *eingefügt.* — **q** *Eingefügt für* <stehen> — **r** *Folgt* <mutick> — **s** *Folgt* <regel>

K 1 Einen möglichen Hinweis auf ein Treffen der in u. um Köthen anwesenden Gesellschafter im April 1645 liefert F. Ludwig (Der Nährende) in seinem Brief 450504. Demnach hat kürzlich eine Zusammenkunft von FG-Mitgliedern Christian Gueintz' (FG 361) Entwurf einer deutschen Rechtschreibung kritisch durchgesehen. Die Rechtschreibung könne nun rasch in den Druck gegeben werden. Es ist gut möglich, daß es bei dieser Zusammenkunft zu einer Kontroverse über die Substantivierung der Adjektiv-Ableitungen auf -ig gekommen ist. Zur Gueintzschen Rechtschreibung s. 440127 K 1.

2 Mit diesem Verweis auf ein gültiges Mehrheitsvotum der FG-Mitglieder wendet Diederich v. dem Werder (FG 31. Der Vielgekörnte), hochrangiger Vertreter der Landstände im Ft. Anhalt u. Unterdirektor des Landschaftswesens (vgl. dazu 400320 K 7 u. 410117 K 6), hierbei politisch-administrative Verfahrensmodi des frühneuzeitlichen Ständestaats, wie sie vielfach auf Land- u. Reichstagen erprobt u. zur Entscheidungsfindung erfolgreich angewendet wurden, auf die damalige, intensiv geführte Sprachdebatte der FG an.

3 In seiner Antwort 450505 geht F. Ludwig auf Werders Verfahrensvorschlag nicht näher ein, bekräftigt aber seine Kritik an den neuen Schreibweisen Georg Philipp Harsdörffers (FG 368. Der Spielende) u. Justus Georg Schottelius' (FG 397. Der Suchende). Auch Philipp (v.) Zesens (FG. 521. 1648) sprachliche Eigenmächtigkeiten werden in 450505 kritisiert, wobei F. Ludwig hofft, dieser werde noch eines Besseren zu belehren

sein. „Für wiedrigkeiten und uneinigkeit hat man sich in der geselschaft zu hüten, sonderlich wan die Köpfe auf ihrem eigenen sinnen beharren solten."

4 Schritt, hier: Fall, Vorgang. S. *Stieler*, 1415 f.; *DW* VII, 1496.

5 Eine auffällige Parallelisierung von Sprachreform (als Teil der Kulturreform) u. der Kirchen-Reformation. Vom ref. Bekenntnis Werders her ist etwa an die Abschaffung des Taufexorzismus, des Altars (statt eines Tisches), der Meßgewänder, Bilder, Leuchter u. Hostien (stattdessen Brotbrechen) im späten 16. Jahrhundert in Anhalt zu erinnern. Vgl. z. B. *Conermann: Köthen*, 1217–1223.

6 Als überflüssige Buchstaben galten solche, die beim Sprechen nicht artikuliert bzw. nicht gehört werden. In der grundsätzlichen, aber nicht alleinigen Geltung des phonographischen Arguments bei der Normierung der Schreibung waren sich die Fruchtbringer im Prinzip einig. Strittig war, wie weit etymologisch oder grammatisch bedingte Eingriffe zu akzeptieren waren. Zur Konsonantenverbindung -ck- heißt es in *Gueintz: Rechtschreibung (1645)*, 18: „K wird niemals am ende ohne C gebrauchet/ auch niemals gedoppelt." Demzufolge schrieb Gueintz „Ancker [...] mit dem ck" (29), „Balcke [...] mit dem ck" (34), „Banck [...] mit dem ck" (34), „Bock" (43) usf. F. Ludwig vertrat auch diese Auffassung u. begründete sie phonetisch: „Schmuck, und sol das c am k an solchen orten nie au[sge]laßen werden, den man saget im aussprechen des Schmu[ckes] und nicht Schmukes, dem Schmucke, und nicht Schmuke". F. Ludwig: „Etzliche erinnerungen, bey dem dritten theile der gesprächspiele". HM Köthen: V S 545, Bl. 419r–424v u. 426r, hier 419v. Das Dokument demnächst in *DA Köthen I. 9* (als „Zu 430724"). Das Ausspracheargument kann sich dabei nicht auf den Verschlußlaut k/ck beziehen, da es eine phonetische Konsonantengemination als *gesprochene Quantität* im Deutschen seit dem Spätmittelalter nicht mehr gab, sondern auf den vorangehenden Vokal: Die Konsonantenhäufung dürfte bei F. Ludwig dessen Kürze oder „Schärfe" anzeigen, wie dies auch heute noch in der dt. Grammatik geregelt ist. In dieser Funktion läßt sich die Verwendung des -ck- als Doppelkonsonant -kk- im Fnhd. vielfach belegen. Schon Johann Werner hatte die Verbindung -ck- als korrekten Ersatz des -kk- gefordert: „Wenn das k zwiefach soll gesetzt werden: so bleibet das c an statt des ersten k. stehen. e.g. Ackerman: nicht Akkerman" usw. J. W.: Manuductio Orthographica (1629). Hg. Claudine Moulin. Hildesheim, Zürich, New York 2007, 54. Vgl. Gerhard August: Die linguistischen Grundlagen der Rechtschreibung. In: Deutsche Rechtschreibung mangelhaft? Materialien und Meinungen zur Rechtschreibreform. Hg. v. G. A. Heidelberg 1974, 9–47, hier S. 17–21; Franz Simmler: Probleme frühneuhochdeutscher Orthographie. Die Rolle von Doppelkonsonanten. In: Sprachwissenschaft 29 (2004), 207–255, hier S. 240–242; Utz Maas: Grundzüge der deutschen Orthographie. Tübingen 1992, 276, 285 u. 287 ff. In den „Etzlichen erinnerungen" finden sich zahlreiche Verbesserungen an Harsdörffers Ersetzung des -ck- durch einfaches -k-, s. etwa „Erweckung und nicht Erwekung" (Bl. 420r), „versincken, und nicht versinken" (420v), „Eine Brücke und nicht Bruken" (ebd.), „Zanck und nicht Zank" (ebd.), „Glück mit **ck** und nicht **k** alleine" u. v. m. Harsdörffer hielt in seiner „Kurtzen Entschuldigung" (HM Köthen: VS 545, Bl. 290rv u. 289rv, demnächst in *DA Köthen I. 9*, als „Zu 430920") dagegen: „[...] man sol das **ck** nicht durch und durch für das **k** brauchen. sonderlich aber, wann noch ein anderer Mitlautender darzukom*m*[t] als in danken, denken, sinken, wolken, trunken *etc.* ist aber recht gebraucht in backen, hecken, schicken, Glocken, drucken *etc.*" F. Ludwig wies ihn in seiner „Kurtzen Antwort" (HM Köthen: V S 545, Bl. 291r–292v, hier 291r. Demnächst in *DA Köthen I. 9*, als „Zu 431014") abermals zurecht. Harsdörffer blieb aber bei seiner Meinung u. schränkte die Verwendung des C — wie es auch Zesen tat — als nicht genuin deutschen Buchstaben stark ein. *Harsdörffer: Poetischer Trichter* II (1648, Ndr. 1969), 127: „**C.** Jst eigentlich kein teutscher Buchstab/ und von den Lateinern/ welche kein **K**

habē/ in unsrer Sprache miteingeflochtē worden. Daher nicht ein teutsches Wort/ dem Grund nach zu finden/ das von einē **C** anfängt". Dies treffe nur für „fremde Wörter" zu. Vgl. auch *Poetischer Trichter* I (²1650, Ndr. 1969), 126. Zur Frage der Verwendung von **ck/ k** in medialer u. finaler Wortposition vgl. auch *Harsdörffer: Specimen (1646)*, 213–217; Herz: Rechtschreibdebatte, 91.

7 In einer Stellungnahme zu einem Entwurf der Deutschen Rechtschreibung von Christian Gueintz (s. 440127 K 1) hatte sich F. Ludwig im Frühjahr 1644 im Falle abgeleiteter Adjektive auf -lich gegen die Übernahme dieses Ableitungsmorphems in den substantivierten Formen ausgesprochen u. der Aussprache wegen die Verwendung des -lig- vorgeschlagen: „billich, billigkeit, zeitlich, zeit[lig]keit, verdrieslich, verdriesligkeit". Fand also Billichkeit keine Billigung bei F. Ludwig, so „viel minder wan mans schreiben wolte liebikeit billikeit, zeitlike[it], verdrieslikeit und das **g** ausgelaßen were". HM Köthen: V S 545, Bl. 219r–220v, hier 219v. Demnächst in *DA Köthen I. 9* als Dokument 440200. Auch Harsdörffer gegenüber korrigierte F. Ludwig dessen „beharlichkeit" in „Beharligkeit", „Lieblichkeit" zu „liebligkeit", „Zierlichkeit" zu „Zierligkeit", „Höflichkeit" zu „Höfligkeit" u. „Treflichkeit" zu „treftigkeit". F. Ludwig: „Erinnerungen bey dem anhange der hundert Spielreime" (betr. *Harsdörffer: Frauenzimmer-Gesprächspiele* III 1643). F. Ludwigs „Erinnerungen" in HM Köthen: V S 545, Bl. 426v–428v u. 425rv. Demnächst in *DA Köthen I. 9* als Dokument „Zu 430802". Desgleichen F. Ludwig in 451219. Johann Werner war übrigens ebenso verfahren: „Geschicklich", aber „Geschicklichkeit". J. W.: Manuductio Orthographica (1629. s. Anm. 6), 29. Damit verstießen F. Ludwig u. tw. auch Werder gegen zwei Grundsätze grammatischer Sprachnormierung, den der möglichst durchgängigen Schemakonstanz in einem Wortparadigma u. den der sauberen Differenzierung zwischen den adjektivischen Ableitungsmorphemen -lich u. -ig. Den ersten Grundsatz hatte *Schottelius: Sprachkunst (1641)*, 192 als unbedingt zu wahrende Konstanz der Stammwörter u. ihrer Stammlettern formuliert: „es werden die Stammbuchstaben/ wie gesagt/ nicht zertrennt noch verwirret durch die Hauptendungen der abgeleiteten/ verdoppelungen und andere zufälle". Eine Ausnahme bildete nur die Veränderung des Stammvokals bei der Konjugation der starken Verben (brechen, brich, brach, gebrochen). Im 11. Kapitel seiner *Sprachkunst (1641)* „Von der Ableitung" listete er 21 „Hauptendungen" oder Ableitungsmorpheme auf, darunter -ig, -lich u. -keit — erstere beiden als adjektivische, letztere als feminin substantivische (S. 307 ff., insbes. 318 ff., 329 ff. u. 325 ff.). In der *Ausführlichen Arbeit (1663)*, 43 u. 317–398, werden es 23 „Hauptendungen" sein. Zur korrekten Wortbildung gehört, daß auch die Wortbestandteile, hier also etwa das Stammwort Schuld, die adjektiv. Ableitungssilbe -ig, schließlich die substantivierende Ableitungssilbe -keit nicht beliebig „zertrennt noch verwirret" werden. (Schottelius hat wohl als erster „eine systematisch aufgebaute und grundlegende Lehre von den wortbildenden Elementen der deutschen Sprache" vorgelegt, wie zuvor Wolfgang Ratke als erster „eine eigenständige Wortbildungstheorie" u. „die Wortbildung als eigenständigen sprachwissenschaftlichen Objektbereich" entwickelt hatte; *Barbarić*, 1186; Gerda Haßler: Art. „Wortbildung". In: *Haßler/ Neis*, 1470–1491, hier 1483). Die heute obligatorische Kombination von -keit nach -ig/ -lich hat sich erst im 16./ 17. Jh. durchgesetzt. Werder vertrat mit seinen -g-losen Formen „schuldikeit", „muhtikeit" usw. den älteren Standard des 14. u. 15. Jhs., den er argumentativ nur sehr widersprüchlich u. wortmorphologisch nicht überzeugend stützen konnte. Dieser ältere Standard fußte auf der starken phonematischen Ausrichtung der mhd. Schreibungen, die z. B. „billicheit" oder „diemüeticheit, diemüetekeit" usf. setzte. *Lexer: Taschenwb.*, 21 u. 30. Vgl. *Barbarić*, 1242 ff.; *Hartweg/ Wegera*, 198 f.; *Takada*, 153 ff.; Deutsche Orthographie. 4., neu bearb. Aufl. Unter Ltg. v. Dieter Nerius bearb. v. Renate Baudusch, Rolf Bergmann, Petra Ewald u. a. Hildesheim 2007, 297.

8 Diesen Anstoß, Konsonantenhäufungen zugunsten eines „lieblicheren" oder „zierlicheren" Sprachklanges zu vermeiden, teilten im Grundsatz alle Grammatiker u. Sprachbeflissenen in der u. um die FG. Vgl. *Herz: Rechtschreibdebatte*, 87f.

9 In der Reihenfolge der Nennung: F. Christian II. v. Anhalt-Bernburg (FG 51. Der Unveränderliche), Martin Milagius (FG 315. Der Mindernde), Christian Ernst (v.) Knoch (FG 268. Der Weichende) u. Cuno Ordomar v. Bodenhausen (FG 69. Der Bequeme). Der im Brief tatsächlich genannte „Erweichende", d. i. Otto Heinrich v. Callenberg (FG 132), kann hier nicht gemeint gewesen u. wird nur versehentlich genannt worden sein. Er war Deutschordensherr in Lucklum bei Wolfenbüttel u. bereits am 23.11.1644 gestorben. Zu Werders Verbindung zu Christian Ernst (v.) Knoch s. etwa 450613.

450500

Diederich von dem Werder an Fürst Ludwig

Beantwortet durch 450505 (?). — Diederich v. dem Werder (FG 31. Der Vielgekörnte) sendet F. Ludwig (Der Nährende) ein Schreiben Georg Philipp Harsdörffers (FG 368. Der Spielende), in dem dieser die Aufnahme Johann Michael Moscheroschs (FG 436. 1645) in die FG zu vermitteln sucht. Obgleich Moscherosch noch nichts „Würdiges" bei der Spracharbeit verrichtet habe, billigt Werder Moscheroschs ehrenvolle Aufnahme in die FG mit der gewählten Imprese (Gesellschaftsname, -bild und -wort). Werder erbittet eine rasche und vernünftig-diskrete Antwort des Fürsten. Werde Moscheroschs Aufnahme in die FG befürwortet, dürften weitere (literarisch) hochbegabte Personen um eine Mitgliedschaft anhalten. Schade sei nur, daß ihnen das Aufnahmeritual vor Ort mit dem Einsatz des Ölbergers entgehen werde.

Q HM Köthen: V S 544, Bl. 477r–478v [A: 478v], 477v u. 478r leer; eigenh.; 478v F. Ludwigs Eintrag; rotes Lacksiegel. — *D: KE*, 172; *Schäfer: Moscherosch und Harsdörffer*, S. 153 Anm. 43 (nach *KE*). — *BN: Bürger*, 1439 Nr. 4.

A Dem Nehrenden   Cöthen   zuhanden.
Eintrag von F. Ludwigs H.: 433.[a1] Johan Michael Moscherosch. Der Träumende. Le Songeant.[b2] Eine art Nachtschatten [der] die schläfer[c] schlafen macht. Hohe sachen[.] Mit offen augen[3]

Der Höchstgeehrte herr Nehrende hatt aus inliegendem zusehen, was der Spielende für ansuchung, wegen einnahme herren Moscheroschs in die Fruchtbringende Geselschaft, an mich gebracht hatt.[4]

Mein bedencken, so billich das letzte sey, zielet dahin, das wan gleich herr Moscherosch sonst nichts würdiges bey der deutschen Sprache bishehr gethan,[5] das er doch den Geselschafters Namen, wegen seines vorgeschlagenen Namens wortes vnd Gemäldes auf seine persohn,[d] mit ehren verdienet[e] hette. Jch erwarte ehestes hierauf bescheidentliche[6] erklärung, damit denen ansuchenden richtige und gewüntschte andwort ertheilt, ie eh ie lieber, werden möge. Wan dieses geschiehet dürften sich derselben hochbegabte persohnen mehr angeben. Hierbey

450500 Diederich von dem Werder   531

wird aber grosser schade sein, das sie des wohl^f gehegten Öhlbergers⁷ nicht teilhaftig werden.
Verbleibe hiermit
  Meines höchstgeehrten herren Nehrenden
    dienstwilligster
    Der Vielgekörnte

T a *Gebessert aus 434.* — b *Über dem deutschen Gesellschaftsnamen ist der französische mit blasser Tinte (später?) vermerkt.* — c *Unsichere Lesung.* — d *Folgt <solches>* — e *Eingefügt für <erlanget>* — f *Eingefügt.*

K 1 Johann Michael Moscherosch wurde 1645 unter Vermittlung Georg Philipp Harsdörffers (FG 368. Der Spielende) als 436. Mitglied mit der Imprese „Der Träumende — Nachtschatten — Hohe Sachen" in die FG aufgenommen. Zuvor hatte ihn Harsdörffer schon in die DG vermittelt, in die er am 3.4.1645 als 24. Mitglied u. „der Treumende" aufgenommen worden sein soll. S. 441223 (K 14). Wann genau seine Aufnahme in die FG erfolgte, ist nicht mehr sicher rekonstruierbar. In 450505 versicherte F. Ludwig (Der Nährende) Diederich v. dem Werder (FG 31. Der Vielgekörnte), Moscherosch sei „zu erweiterung der fruchtbringen[den] geselschaft mit allem willen angenommen". Sein Wappen sei bereits für den Erzschrein eingefordert worden. Dann aber zog sich die Diskussion um Moscheroschs Gesellschaftswort u. Reimgesetz monatelang hin; noch in 451217 ist von der Klärung des Beiworts die Rede. Hinzu kam die Gesandtschaftsreise Moscheroschs im Auftrag des Straßburger Rates nach Paris (August 1645 bis in den Sommer 1646), die neben der großen Entfernung zwischen Köthen u. Straßburg eine zügige Kommunikation zusätzlich erschwerte. S. 451101. Harsdörffer teilte dort mit, er wisse nicht, ob Moscherosch bereits wieder zurückgekehrt sei, wohl aber, daß dieser seine Imprese akzeptieren u. sich brieflich bei F. Ludwig für die Aufnahme bedanken u. die geplante Neuausgabe seiner *Gesichte* dem Fürsten widmen werde. Diese vollständige u. mit Stichen u. Holzschnitten illustrierte Ausgabe der *Gesichte* erschien freilich erst 1650, nach F. Ludwigs Tod. Sie ist dem designierten schwed. König, Pgf. Karl Gustav (FG 513. 1648) gewidmet. Vgl. 430103 II Q. Die briefliche Danksagung an F. Ludwig erfolgte mit 460726. Den Erhalt dieses Schreibens bestätigte F. Ludwig in 461031. In seinem Dankschreiben vom 26.7.1646 vermerkte Moscherosch, schon vor einem Jahr durch Harsdörffer von seiner Aufnahme in die FG erfahren zu haben; nun habe ihm ein Brief Harsdörffers vom 19.6. die Visierung seiner Imprese für die Abbildung auf seinem Gesellschaftspfennig übermittelt. Schon in 450817 nannte Harsdörffer Moscherosch ganz selbstverständlich mit seinem Gesellschaftsnamen der Träumende. F. Ludwigs Bestätigung, Moscherosch sei in das Köthener Gesellschaftsbuch eingetragen worden, erfolgte aber erst in 461031. Dies muß mit der Einnahme schon früher geschehen sein, irgendwann nach dem 19. Mai 1645, unter welchem Datum sich Matthaeus (v.) Wesenbeck (FG 433) ins *GB Kö.* eingeschrieben hatte. Vgl. 450504A K 1. Moscherosch folgten im Jahr 1645 lt. den Einträgen im *GB Kö.* noch 14 weitere Neumitglieder, über deren genaue Eintrittsdaten aber Hinweise im *GB Kö.* fehlen. Vgl. zum Verlauf der Aufnahme Moscheroschs in die FG 450504A, 450505, 450505A, 450613, 450725, 450730, 450817, 450919A, 451101, 451217, 460120, 460426, 460609, 460620, 460705, 460726, 460916 u. 461031; ferner *Schäfer: Moscherosch und Harsdörffer,* 151 ff. Zur Diskussion um Moscheroschs FG-Imprese s. Anm. 3.

2 Moscheroschs Gesellschaftsname beggnet in verschiedenen Mitgliederregistern u. -listen einheitlich u. wie das heutige Participe Présent als „Le Songeant" ins Französische

übersetzt. Vgl. 451001/ 460000 (eine synoptische Präsentation verschiedener Mitgliederlisten mit Übersetzungen der Mitgliedernamen ins Französische, Italienische und Lateinische aus den Jahren 1645 und 1646), demnächst in *DA Köthen I. 9*. Auf einen Zettel im Köthener Erzschrein, III, 83v (HM Köthen: V S 546), hatte F. Ludwig notiert: „436. Der Traumende Le Songeant | 437. Der Niederlegende [d.i. Matthias v. Biedersehe] L'accouchant | 438. Der Wiederfindende [d.i. Curt Christoph v. Börstel] Le Rabbattant Le Retrouvant | 439. Der Gleichgefärbte [d.i. Wilhelm Heinrich v. Freyberg] Le Teint de mesme. | Der Wackere [d.i. F. Georg Ludwig v. Nassau-Dillenburg. FG 319. 1638] Le Galant." Die Übersetzungen weichen teilw. von jenen in anderen Listen ab, s. das Dokument 451001/ 460000 in *DA Köthen I. 9*.

3 Harsdörffer muß in seinem von Werder genannten vorangehenden Schreiben einen wohl von Moscherosch selbst aufgesetzten Vorschlag für dessen FG-Imprese mitgeteilt haben. In der Notiz F. Ludwigs auf der Anschriftseite des vorliegenden Briefes erscheint zum ersten Mal die Beiwort-Alternative „Mit offenen augen" oder „Hohe sachen". Vgl. dazu 450504A K 2.

4 Leider hat sich von Harsdörffers Briefen an Werder u. dessen Gegenbriefen nichts erhalten. Bislang hatte F. Ludwig die fruchtbringerische Korrespondenz mit Harsdörffer selbst geführt, jetzt wird Werder zunehmend am Briefverkehr beteiligt, s. schon 440824 u. 450124 u. I.

5 Werder wußte wohl von Moscheroschs Quevedo-Bearbeitung bzw. -Nachahmung, wollte diese Satire aber vor dem Fürsten als nichts „Würdiges" u. wohl auch nicht als herausragende sprachreformerische Leistung im Sinne der FG rühmen. Moscheroschs u. Hans Caspar Hermanns *Technologie Allemande & Françoise Das ist/ Kunst-übliche Wort-Lehre Teutsch und Frantzösisch* erschien erst 1656 (s. 440616 K I 0). Zu Moscheroschs vorliegenden u. weithin bekannten Werken (s. 430103 u. I u. II) gehörten damals als größere selbständige Werke schon die ersten Ausgaben (des ersten Teils) von Moscheroschs *Gesichte Philanders von Sittewalt* (Straßburg Herbst 1640, 1642 u. 1643), einer Bearbeitung der *Sueños y Discursos de Verdades* des Don Francisco de Quevedo y Santibañez Villegas (1580–1645; die *Sueños* erstmals 1628) nach der frz. Übersetzung des Sieur de la Geneste (Paris 1632; Rouen 1634). Ein zweiter Teil folgte Straßburg 1643 u. 1644, dazu allerhand Raubdrucke. 1643 waren erstmals Moscheroschs Sammlung der *Epigrammatum* (Centuria Prima [–Secunda]) u. das Hausvaterbuch *Insomnis cura parentum. Christliches Vermächnuß oder/ Schuldige Vorsorg Eines Trewen Vatters* in Straßburg erschienen (sieht man von der seltenen Straßburger Erstausgabe 1630 ab, vgl. 450818 Q). Auffällig bleibt, daß Werder nicht zu den sieben Fruchtbringern gehört, die die repräsentative Straßburger Neuausg. der *Gesichte* von 1650 mit einem Widmungsgedicht würdigten. Vgl. 430103 K 1 u. K II 0; *Dünnhaupt: Handbuch*, S. 2851 ff.; *Schäfer: Moscherosch und Harsdörffer*, insbes. S. 154 u. 174; Alfred R. Wedel: La nota germanófila y luterana de H. M. Moscherosch en la adaptación alemana de *Los Sueños* de Quevedo. In: Revista de literatura 50 (1988), 141–148.

6 Bedenkt man die alte Bedeutung von bescheidentlich im Sinne von Bescheidenheit, discretio (s. 441020 K 14), so erscheint Werders Bitte schon als recht kühne Ermahnung, die erst angesichts von F. Ludwigs Reserve gegenüber Moscheroschs menippeischer Satire verständlich wird.

7 Der „Ölberger", das zeremonielle Trinkgefäß bei Handlungen der FG, insbesondere beim Aufnahmeactus für neue Mitglieder, der Hänselung, aber auch bei den scherzhaften Gesellschaftsstrafen oder -bußen. Vgl. *DA Köthen I. 5*, S. 480 (Abb.), 400312 K I 1; 410621 K 1 u. K 5; insgesamt das Lemma „Ölberger" im kumulierten Sachregister des vorliegenden Bandes. Zum Aufnahmeritual der FG, der „Hänselung", vgl. 460718 K 8.

450503

Hans Beyer an Johann Hammer

Hans Beyer in Braunschweig bezieht sich auf einen nicht erhalten gebliebenen, vor acht Tagen an Johann Hammer gesandten Brief, in dem er mitgeteilt habe und hier wiederholt, F. Ludwigs Quittung über die von Hz. August d.J. v. Braunschweig-Wolfenbüttel (FG 227) versprochenen 200 Reichstaler Verlagseinlagen empfangen und die Summe abzüglich 1 Reichstaler Provision (für ihn selbst) an das Leipziger Ratsmitglied Johann Hammer über Christof Albrecht angewiesen zu haben.

Q HM Köthen: V S 546, Bl. 26rv [A: 26v]; eigenh. — *D: Bircher: Merian,* 699. — *BN: Bürger,* 128 Nr. 1.

A Tit*u*li Herrn hanß hammer grosg. zu hand*en*   Jn Leipzigk.   1/2 franco
Kanzlistenvermerk: 242
Empfangsvermerk: A*n*no do*m*ini d. 8. May Von Hanß Beyer auß Braunschweig.

Laus Deo Ao. 1645 A[nno]d[omin]j 3 Maij Jn Braunschweigk[1]

Ehrnuester großAchtbar vnd wohlfürnehmer Jnsonders gg. herr ham*m*er, nach an erbietung williger dienste, vnd frl. grus, wardt vor 8 tagen an den herrn, Mein Jungstes, worbey gemelt, das J. H. Gnd. hertzog Augustus, die thl. 200 mir bezalt, dargegen Remittire ich den herrn in meinem eigenen Briefe, vor solche 200 thl. von Herrn Christof Albrecht negsthin[2] er zuempfangen, lauth zwei **solo** wexels thl. 199 und 1 Th. vor meine Provißion abgezogen. Hoffe es werde dem Herrn wohl zukom*m*en, und die **acceptation** geuolget, auch die bezahlung nu wehre zu erwarthen sein, darauf ich gelobter Kürtze halber referire, wan also die bezahlung geuolget, würden wir vor dießes mahl **saldo** sein, kan ich dem Herrn dißes orts was dienen, hat er mir zu **Commandiren**, schließlich was den Herrn dienstl. lieb, Nochmahls gegrüst. Gott in Gnaden befohlen

   *Des h*err*n dienst*williger *freund*
   Hans Beyer *mpria*

K Hans Beyer war Handelsmann in Braunschweig, wo er, wie auch der vorliegende Brief zeigt, u.a. Finanzgeschäfte für Hz. August d.J. v. Braunschweig-Wolfenbüttel (FG 227) abwickelte, ähnlich wie dies der Leipziger Handelsmann u. Ratsherr Johann Hammer für F. Ludwig tat. *Bircher: Merian,* 697. Genauere Informationen über den Briefverfasser ließen sich jedoch nicht gewinnen. Ein Zusammenhang mit dem ursprünglich aus Homburg v. d. Höhe stammenden Verleger Johann Beyer († 1666) in Frankfurt am Main (vgl. 290129 K I 1 u. 371009 K 3) läßt sich ausschließen, da dieser keinerlei Verbindungen nach Braunschweig unterhielt. *Benzing: Verleger,* 1098. Zum Zahlungsverkehr das *GB 1646* betreffend s. auch 450127 K 1. Zum *GB 1646* allgem. s. 440130 K 3.

1 Bei *Bircher: Merian,* 699, fehlt die Tagesangabe; er gibt ohne Quellennachweis April 1645 an. Ein Brief Johann Hammers an Peter Knaudt (450510) berichtet bereits eine Woche später davon, daß Hammer 199 Reichstaler (200 Rth. minus 1 Rth. Provision für

Beyer) erhalten hat. Der Braunschweiger Kaufmann Beyer hatte in Wirklichkeit nur F. Ludwigs Quittung über die von Hz. August versprochenen 200 Rth. Verlagseinlage (vgl. 450331) empfangen, jedoch war der Geldwert dieser Summe noch gar nicht von Hz. August eingezahlt worden, wie F. Ludwigs Mahnung 450721 an den Herzog belegt. S. auch 450509 K 1. Beyer hatte also Hz. Augusts Beitrag vorgestreckt.

2 *Bircher: Merian,* 699, erwähnt hier einen nicht nachweisbaren „Herrn Christof Albrecht Maßhauen". Wir lesen „Herrn Christof Albrechts negsthin". Um welche Person es sich dabei handelt, konnten wir nicht ermitteln.

450504

Fürst Ludwig an Christian Gueintz

Antwort auf 441231 (?). Beantwortet durch 450506A. — Die von Christian Gueintz (FG 361. Der Ordnende) der FG eingeschickte Deutsche Rechtschreibung wird zurückgeschickt und dazu dreierlei angemerkt. 1. Da Gueintz' Deutsche Rechtschreibung mittlerweile von den anwesenden Gesellschaftern kritisch durchgesehen und eingerichtet worden sei, könne das Werk nun guten Gewissens und rasch zum Druck gebracht werden. Für eine eilige Veröffentlichung spreche die gespannte Erwartung, die die Ankündigung des Erscheinens ausgelöst habe. Zur nochmaligen Durchsicht, besonders des Anfangs, sendet der Fürst das Manuskript an Gueintz zurück mit der Bitte, es auch durch Hans v. Dieskau (FG 212. Der Tilgende) und Curt v. Einsiedel (FG 417. 1644. Der Erspießliche) überfliegen zu lassen. — 2. Zur Eile bei der Drucklegung der Rechtschreibung mahnten aber auch und besonders die unangemessenen Schreibarten, die Georg Philipp Harsdörffer (FG 368. Der Spielende) und Johann Klaj aus Nürnberg, Justus Georg Schottelius (FG 397. Der Suchende) aus dem Braunschweiger Land und vor allem Philipp v. Zesen (FG 521. 1648) aufgebracht hätten. Die Schreibweise Zesens, die er in seiner Romanübersetzung des *Ibrahim Bassa* an den Tag gelegt habe, sei am befremdlichsten und ungewöhnlichsten. Zwar sei der Stil flüssig, die Rede rein, doch die Schreibweise unverantwortlich. Sie beruhe auf unbegründeten Vorstellungen und gewagten fremdsprachigen Etymologien. Zesens eigenhändiger Brief, mit dem er F. Ludwig ein Exemplar dieser Übersetzung zugesandt habe, mache dies deutlich und empfehle eine bündige Antwort darauf. F. Ludwig schlägt Gueintz eine mündliche Aussprache darüber noch vor Pfingsten in Köthen vor. Dann könne er ihm auch Zesens *Ibrahim Bassa* vorlegen, falls er ihn nicht schon zu Gesicht bekommen habe. Zesens Begleitbrief dazu möge Gueintz, der sich das Nötige daraus notieren könne, dann gleich wieder mitbringen. — 3. Da die fl. Offizin in Köthen derzeit außer Betrieb sei, möge Gueintz seine Rechtschreibung in Halle drucken lassen, in gleichem Format und gleicher Schrift wie seinerzeit seine *Deutsche Sprachlehre* (1641). Die Widmung sollte an Hz. August v. Sachsen-Weißenfels, den Erzbischof/ Administrator des Ebst.s Magdeburg, gerichtet werden, der auch ein Mitglied der FG sei (FG 402). F. Ludwig bietet an, wöchentlich überschickte Druckbögen der Rechtschreibung Korrektur zu lesen. Die Nachweise der Bibelzitate bedürften noch der Überprüfung, die um Christi Himmelfahrt geschehen solle. Die Angabe der Bibelbücher erfolge auf deutsch, was zu einem Werk über die Deutsche Rechtschreibung passe. An den Druckkosten werde er sich beteiligen, jedoch dürften sie so hoch nicht ausfallen. Abschließend bittet F. Ludwig, Gueintz möge den Termin seines Besuches in Köthen — am besten im Laufe der nächsten Woche — angeben.

Q HM Köthen: V S 545, Bl. 216rv; eigenh. Konzept; 216v Notiz v. F. Ludwigs H. — *D: unzuverlässig KE*, 271 f.; *KL* III, 243 f. — *BN: Bürger*, 949 Nr. 45.

A *Fehlt.*

Auf die vom Ordnenden der fruchtbringenden geselschaft eingeschickete, und wieder beykommende deutsche Rechtschreibung wird folgendes anderweit erinnert.

1.

Das dieselbe verhoffentlich nunmehr so ferne, durch die anwesende geselschafter mit fleiße ubersehen, und zu rechte gebracht,[1] das sie gar wol und mit dem ehesten könne gedrucket, und mit[a] nutzen ans tagelicht gegeben werden, auch[b] aus ursachen, das man darauf schon unterschiedene vertröstungen gethan,[2] und sie mit verlangen bey andern erwartet wird. Jedoch wird sie dem Ordnenden noch einmal zu seiner erwegung zugeschicket, mit dem[c] andeuten, das er sie durch den Tilgenden dem Erspriesslichen, wo er noch bey handen insonderheit[d] den eingang, nur zu durchlauffen wolte uberreichen laßen.[3]

2.

Noch eine andere erhelligkeit, das sie bald möge herauskommen ist diese, das nicht[e] alleine vom Spielenden und[f] Clajo in Nürnberg[4] und[g] dan von dem Suchenden im lande zu Braunschweig[5] unterschiedene Neue und sich ubel schickende schreibarten wollen aufgebracht, sondern auch[h] vornemlich[i] noch eine fremdere und ungewöhnlichere von Zäsio eingefüret[j] werden, wie aus seiner[k] verdeutschung des Jbrahims Baßa und[l] der Bestendigen Isabellen wundergeschichte in diesem Jhare zu Amsterdam gedruckt,[6] zu ersehen: Dan ob schon sonsten die redensart darinnen fein läuffig und rein, so wil doch solche von ihme genante schreiberichtigkeit nit verantwortlich sein,[m] in deme es[n] scheinet, das sie auf keinem rechten grund, sondern nur auf sonderbaren einbildungen und anleitungen aus fremden sprachen genommen bestehet[o]: Jnmaßen aus seinem eigenhändigen schreiben[7] zu sehen, darauf[p] diese rechtschreibung ausgegangen,[q] desto leichter wird können ohne weitleufigkeit geantwortet werden:[r] [A]lso[s] man dan mit dem Ordnenden eine[t] mundliche unterrede hieruber[u] alhier aufs eheste zu pflegen ein sonderes[t] verlangen treget[v], als wolle er einen weg heruber noch fur Pfingsten machen[w]: da[x] ihme[y] solcher druck sol vorgezeiget[z] werden, woferne er ihn sonst nicht gesehen. Das[aa] mitkommende[ab] brieflein aber[t8], wan er daraus gezogen, was ihme zu mercken nötig, kan[ac] bey dieser gelegenheit[ad] mit zurücke[ae] kommen.

3.

Weil alhier zu Cöthen die druckerey[af] nun kalt liegen[ag] mus[t], so könte dieses büchlein am fuglichsten zu Halle gedrucket werden, in der größe wie die Sprachlehre[9] auch[ah] mit der schrift und die ubereignung an den herren Ertzbischof der auch ein hohes[ai] glied der fruchtbringenden Gesellschaft[aj] ist[,] gestellet werden.[10]

Ja man könnte alle wochen ein oder zwey bögen zu ubersehen heruberschicken, damit der druck desto richtiger fiele, die angezogene örter aber aus der heiligen schrift werden so viel die bücher und zahl der Capittel betrift noch einst wol [ge-]gen[ak] Himmelfarts tag müssen[t] durchsehen werden, damit sie richtig seind; Und hat man derowegen[al] die Nahmen der bücher deutsch gesetzet,[11] weil es sich[t] bey dieser deutschen rechtschreibung am besten also fuget. Zu den unkosten wird man von hinnen gerne etwas zuschießen, man vermeinet auch nicht das sie so gar hoch sich belauffen[am], wie solches der umtruck ferner geben wird. Und[an] wolle sich der Ordnende [der] zeit halber seiner [her]uberkunft, die am [fu]glichsten nechstkunftige woche geschehen könte[,] erkleren.[12]

Cöthen den 4. Meymonats 1645.

[216v] Als man nach der Geburt des Herren hat geschrieben
        Ein tausend und darzu fünfhundert Sechtzig Sieben
        Ward Grimmenstein mit Grimm' aus Martis macht verheeret,[13]

T *Die uneinheitliche Textgliederung aufgrund der Abschnittsziffern 1 bis 3 wurde vereinheitlicht.* — **a** mit nutzen *am Rand ergänzt.* — **b** *Durch Tintenklecks überdeckt. Unsichere Lesung.* — **c** *Gebessert aus* deme — **d** *Bis* eingang *am Rand ergänzt.* — **e** *nicht alleine eingefügt für* <so wol> — **f** *Eingefügt für* <als> — **g** *Bis* zu Braunschweig *am Rand ergänzt.* — **h** *Folgt* <also> — **i** *Folgt* <dergleichen> — **j** eingefüret werden *am Rand ergänzt für gestrichene interlineare Einfügung* <vorgenommen werden [?]> — **k** *Eingefügt für* <der seinigen so er in der> *Darüber gestrichene Einfügung* <stets [?]> — **l** *Bis* Isabellen *am Rand ergänzt.* — **m** *Folgt* <zu> — **n** es scheinet, das sie *eingefügt für* <sie scheinet> — **o** *Eingefügt für* <zu [?] beruhet> — **p** *Folgt* <dan wan> — **q** *Folgt* <mit l> — **r** *Folgt* <Wie daraus> — **s** [A]lso man dan *am Rand ergänzt. Folgt* <daraus> *Buchstabenverlust im Falz. Konjektur in eckigen Klammern.* — **t** *Eingefügt.* — **u** *Eingefügt.* — **v** treget, als wolle *eingefügt für* <getragen wird, wan> — **w** *Folgt* <könte> — **x** *Folgt* <sol> — **y** *Folgt* <sol [sol eingefügt] gezeiget werden> — **z** vor *eingefügt.* — **aa** *Gebessert aus* Dieses — **ab** *Am Rand ergänzt.* — **ac** *Folgt* <er> — **ad** *Folgt* <wieder> — **ae** *Folgt* <schicken> — **af** *Folgt* <zu Cöthen die> — **ag** *Gebessert aus* lieget — **ah** *Bis* schrift *am Rand ergänzt.* — **ai** *Unsichere Lesung, da schwer leserlich gebessert aus* <gleiches> — **aj** *Folgt* <und [?]> — **ak** [ge]gen Himmelfarts tag *am Rand ergänzt. Vielleicht Textverlust im Falz, Konjektur in eckigen Klammern.* — **al** *Unsichere Lesung. Eingefügt für* <dadurch> — **am** *Folgt* <solten> — **an** *Bis* erkleren *am Rand ergänzt. Folgt* <wolle> *Textverluste im Falz. Konjekturen in eckigen Klammern.*

K 1 Zum Diskussionsprozeß, den die FG über Christian Gueintz' (FG 361. Der Ordnende) Entwurf einer deutschen Rechtschreibung führte, vgl. 440127 K 1. Eine Übersicht über die Briefe u. Dokumente zur Rechtschreibdebatte in vollem Wortlaut in *DA Köthen I. 9*. Ein Gesellschaftertreffen zu offenen Sprachfragen bezeugt Diederichs v. dem Werder (FG 31) Brief 450420.

2 So etwa gegenüber Georg Philipp Harsdörffer (FG 368. Der Spielende) in 431206 oder F. Christian II. v. Anhalt-Bernburg (FG 51) in 450326.

3 Hans v. Dieskau (FG 212. Der Tilgende), auf Dieskau bei Halle, F. Ludwigs enge Bezugsperson in allen das Erzstift Magdeburg u. die Stadt Halle betreffenden Angelegenheiten. Vgl. 390110 K 2; 441226A (K 3). Sein Einbezug in die Rechtschreibdebatte der FG ergibt sich auch aus 450507. — Curt v. Einsiedel (FG 417. 1644. Der Ersprießliche), sehr gebildet u. des Französischen, Italienischen u. Spanischen kundig. Seit 1638 stand er in Diensten Hz. Augusts v. Sachsen-Weißenfels (FG 402). Vgl. 441226, 441231 K 7, 450506A K 5 u. 450507 K 1 u. 2.

4 Kritik an Harsdörffers Orthographie u. ihre mundartlich (fränkisch) motivierten Verstöße gegen Grammatik u. Rechtschreibung hatten F. Ludwig u. die FG in verschiedenen Stellungnahmen zusammengetragen u. Harsdörffer zugeleitet. Diese Stellungnahmen bezogen sich auf die Rechtschreibung im 3. Teil der *Frauenzimmer-Gesprächspiele* (1643) u. dort auf den „ANHANG HUNDERT SPJELREJMEN", s. 430724 u. 430802. Harsdörffer seinerseits antwortete brieflich u. mit einer „Kurtzen Entschuldigung, Die begangene Fehler in den Hundert Spielreimen betreffend" (s. 430920). F. Ludwig wiederum reagierte darauf mit einer „Kurtzen Antwort, und erklerung Auf das vom Spielenden zugefertigte einwenden über die errinnerungen, so der Druckfehler wegen bey seinem dritten theile der gesprächspiele gethan worden" (s. 431014). Die genannten Stellungnahmen u. Gegenargumentationen in vollem Wortlaut in *DA Köthen I. 9*. — Johann Klaj hatte 1644 mit Harsdörffer den PBO gegründet u. gehörte seit dem April 1645 auch Zesens DG an. In 440824 hatte Harsdörffer F. Ludwig auf Klaj aufmerksam gemacht, vgl. auch 450505. Vermutlich kannte F. Ludwig (über Harsdörffer) die seit 1642 von Klaj veröffentlichten geistlichen u. weltlichen (Gelegenheits-)Dichtungen, die selb- oder unselbständig erschienen waren. Auch vom *PEGNESJSCHEN SCHAEFERGEDJCHT*, das Klaj 1644 zusammen mit Harsdörffer publizierte, hatte der Fürst Kenntnis. Vgl. 440824 K 7. Anfang 1645 erschien bei Endter in Nürnberg Klajs *Lobrede der Teutschen Poeterey/ Abgefasset und in Nürnberg Einer Hochansehnlich-Volkreichen Versammlung vorgetragen*. HAB: Xb 90 (1), Ndr. J. K.: Redeoratorien und „Lobrede der teutschen Poeterey". Hg. Conrad Wiedemann. Tübingen 1965. Vgl. 440824 K 7; *Dünnhaupt: Handbuch*, 2352 ff.

5 Obwohl sich F. Ludwig der strengeren normativen Sprachauffassung Justus Georg Schottelius' (FG 397. Der Suchende) angenähert zu haben scheint (vgl. etwa 440219 K 2 u. 3 oder 440313), blieben hinsichtlich des Analogismus des Suchenden u. seiner Rechtschreibung mit ihren Rückgriffen auf das Niederdeutsche offensichtlich Vorbehalte bestehen, weil F. Ludwig den damaligen Sprachgebrauch immer noch als erste Normierungsinstanz in den Vordergrund rückte.

6 Philipp (v.) Zesen (FG 521. 1648) hatte Madeleine de Scudérys Roman *Ibrahim ou l'illustre Bassa* (Paris 1641) ins Deutsche übersetzt — Jbrahims oder Des Durchleuchtigen Bassa Und Der Beständigen Jsabellen Wunder-Geschichte: Durch Fil. Zaesien von Fürstenau (Amsterdam 1645; Ndr. in: *Zesen SW* V.1) — u. seine Übertragung d. d. Utrecht 1.12.1644 der FG gewidmet. S. 441201. F. Ludwig u. die FG werden auch weiterhin zu differenzieren wissen zwischen der Anerkennung von Zesens stilistischer Kompetenz u. der Ablehnung seiner exzentrischen u. wenig beständigen Orthographie (s. 441201 K 0). Vgl. etwa 450529 oder Diederichs v. dem Werder Urteil über Zesens *Deutschen Helicon* (3. Ausg. 1649) in *DA Köthen I. 8*: 490428 (*KE*, 184 f.). Zesen druckte Werders Brief u. sein Widmungsgedicht dann auch im Vorwerk der dritten u. vierten Ausgabe des *Helicon* (1649 u. 1656) ab. Vgl. *Herz: Zesen*, 188 f. – Zur Kritik F. Ludwigs an der Rechtschreibung von Zesen, Klaj, Harsdörffer u. Schottelius s. wiederum 450505.

7 Der vorliegende Brief bezeugt, daß Zesen ein Exemplar (oder vielleicht mehrere) seines *Jbrahim Bassa* mit einem eigenhändigen Begleitschreiben an F. Ludwig gesendet hatte. Dieser Brief scheint verloren zu sein. Er muß Ausführungen zu Zesens Schreibweise enthalten haben, da ihn F. Ludwig Gueintz zusandte, damit dieser das für ihn u. eine Wider-

legung Aufschlußreiche exzerpiere. Zudem empfiehlt F. Ludwig eine bündige kritische Antwort, die u. a. Gegenstand der vorgeschlagenen mündlichen Unterredung sein sollte.

8 Es kann nur Zesens Begleitbrief gemeint sein, den er seiner Sendung des *Jbrahim Bassa* an F. Ludwig beilegte. Da der Brief im heutigen Köthener Erzschrein fehlt, hat F. Ludwig wohl keine Abschrift davon nehmen lassen, Gueintz aber das Original anscheinend nicht zurückgegeben. S. Anm. 7.

9 *Gueintz: Sprachlehre (1641).* Sie war in Köthen im Oktavformat gedruckt u. verlegt worden und folgte in der typographischen Textgestaltung abgesprochenen formalen Differenzierungen (z. B. in den Schriftgraden). Vgl. 390114 K 13 u. 410324, im vorliegenden Band 440525 K I 2 u. K II 16, 440824 K 6, 441223 K 20, 450410 K 11, 450507 K 2, 450900, 450923B K 2, 460131 K 4, 460406 K 7 u. 460825 K 29. *Gueintz: Rechtschreibung (1645)* erschien bei Christoph Salfeld d. Ä. in Halle a. d. S. (vgl. 441231 K 6) u. entsprach in Format u. typographischer Gestaltung der früheren *Sprachlehre.*

10 Dagegen wurde *Gueintz: Rechtschreibung (1645)* den Brüdern Hz. Wilhelm IV. (FG 5) u. Hz. Ernst I. (FG 19) v. Sachsen-Weimar bzw. Sachsen-Gotha, d. d. Halle 12. 8. 1645, gewidmet. In seinem ganz dem dafür geläufigen Standard folgenden Neujahrsglückwunsch an Hz. August v. Sachsen-Weißenfels (FG 402), den Ebf. bzw. Administrator des Erzstifts Magdeburg, seit 1667 drittes u. letztes Oberhaupt der FG, erwähnt F. Ludwig nichts von einer geplanten Widmung und auch keine anderen Gegenstände fruchtbringerischer Relevanz, weshalb wir den Brief trotz seiner Überlieferung im FG-Erzschrein nicht in unsere Edition aufgenommen haben (26. 12. 1644; HM Köthen: V S 545, Bl. 186r; eigenh. Konzept F. Ludwigs). Auch die Köthener Hs. der Rechtschreibung (HM Köthen: V S 670) weist nur das nachträglich hinzugefügte hsl. Widmungsschreiben an die beiden Ernestiner auf. Vgl. 440127 K 1. Gueintz' Widmungszuschrift wird in *DA Köthen I.* 9 publiziert werden.

11 Die biblischen Bücher, die in *Gueintz: Rechtschreibung (1645)* durchgehend für Beispielsätze herangezogen werden, sind dort tatsächlich mit deutschen Übersetzungen, u. nicht etwa nach der Vulgata, angegeben. Auch die Namen der bibl. Bücher folgen der Lutherbibel, z. B. 1. u. 2. Buch der Könige (Vulgata: Liber Malachim id est regum).

12 Die Zusammenkunft in Köthen hat vermutlich am 13. oder 14. Mai stattgefunden. S. 450508. Vgl. auch 450506A, 450507 u. I.

13 Diese hier notierten Zeilen zitieren drei Verse aus Diederichs v. dem Werder Gedicht auf das Gothaer Schloß (Friedenstein). S. 430000A. Ein inhaltlicher Zusammenhang mit dem voranstehenden Brief ist nicht ersichtlich.

450504A

Diederich von dem Werder an Fürst Ludwig

Beantwortet durch 450505. — Diederich v. dem Werder (FG 31. Der Vielgekörnte) erklärt, durch Martin Milagius (FG 315. Der Mindernde) erfahren zu haben, daß F. Ludwig (Der Nährende) als Sinnspruch in der Imprese Johann Michael Moscheroschs (FG 436. Der Träumende. 1645) „hohe Sachen" den Vorzug vor „mit offenen Augen" gebe. Werder beteuert, es liege ihm fern, diese Wahl zu kritisieren, nur sei Moscherosch seine eigene Wahl des Beiwortes vielleicht doch besser zuzugestehen, zumal das Träumen mit geöffneten Augen auch nicht so verbreitet sei. Nach scherzhaften Vergleichen Moscheroschs und der Fruchtbringer mit Hasen erbittet Werder Maßgaben, was er Georg Philipp Harsdörffer (FG 368. Der Spielende) als Übermittler des Moscherosch-Briefs antworten

450504A Diederich von dem Werder

solle, insbesondere, ob er auch den anderen von Harsdörffer vorgeschlagenen FG-Kandidaten Hoffnung auf eine Mitgliedschaft machen und sie auffordern dürfe, sich mit Impresenvorschlägen zu bewerben. Ferner fragt Werder, ob er Harsdörffer Hinweise zum Stikken der Wappen und Impresen (für die FG-Wandgobelins im Köthener Schloßsaal) geben dürfe. Dieser würde sie sicherlich gern befolgen und auch andere Mitglieder zur Nachahmung anregen.

Q HM Köthen: V S 544, Bl. 482r–483v [A: 483v], 482v leer; eigenh. mit eigenh. Empfangsvermerk u. einer Impresennotiz F. Ludwigs; rotes Lacksiegel. — Bl. 483r: Antwortschreiben 450505 (Konzept F. Ludwigs). — D: KE, 176; *Schäfer: Moscherosch und Harsdörffer*, 155 (Auszug). — BN: Bürger, 1440 Nr. 53.

A Dem Nehrenden.   Cöthen   Zu handen — *Empfangsvermerk F. Ludwigs:* 5. Maymonats 1645. — *Zusatz von F. Ludwigs Hand:* Der Fähige Mastixbaum und sein hartz Zur flusstillung[1]

Meines höchstgeehrten herren Nehrenden meinung, über des Träumenden beywort, habe ich von dem Mindernden wohleingenommen, wie[a] das nemlich das wort | hohe sachen | besser wehre, als | Mit offenen augen | jch meines orts habe nichts darbey zu errinnern, Als ob man dem Träumenden lieber sein eigen erfundenes beywort zugefallen lassen wolte, Sintemahl es auch etwas, nicht so gar[a] gemeines, ist mit offenen augen träumen.[2] Ob nun zwar die hasen vielleicht auch wohl mit offenen augen träumen, weil sie darmit schlaffen, So kan man es doch nicht eben gewis[a] wissen: Über das ist viel an vns Menschen, auch wohl unter uns geselschaftern selbsten, darin die hasen gemeinschaft mit uns haben, vnd wer kan wissen, was der Träumende vielleicht noch für sonderliche gleicheit für andern mit den[b] Hasen haben mag.[3] Stelle es aber nochmals zu des herren Nehrenden endlichen erklärung was ich dem Spielenden zuantworten habe. Hierbey wolte ich auch unvorgreiflich diese beyde puncten vorschlagen. 1. Ob ich dem Spielenden schreiben dörfte, jmfall seine angezogene Neue deutsche Poeten[4] auch[c], sich in die geselschaft zubegeben, lust hetten, das sie sich dan neben den vorschlägen ihres Namens Wort vnd Frucht anzugeben hetten. 2. Ob ich dem Spielenden wegen Stickung seines gemäldes vnd Wapens, etwas andeutung thun solte, dan mich bedünckt, er würde,[d] ihm solches zu ehren anziehen, vnd gerne thun, auch seine Mitgenossen daherumb bey ihme mit darzu anfrischen.[5] Erwarte bey diesen wohl vnd treugemeinten vorschlägen, wo müglich, eilige antwort vnd verbleibe
   des Nehrenden
      dienstwilligster
         Der Vielgekörn[te][e]

Reinsdorff am SingeSontag[6] war der 4. May. 1645.

T a *Eingefügt.* — b *Eingefügt für* <dem> — c *Folgt* <Lust> — d *Folgt* <ümb> — e *Papierausriß. Konjektur in eckigen Klammern.*

K 1 Das Reimgesetz des Matthaeus (v.) Wesenbeck (FG 433) erklärt seine Mitgliedsimprese in der FG: Der Fähige „Zur gliederstärckung" mit dem Bild des aus dem Harz des Terpentinbaumes gewonnenen Terpentinöls. Das Reimgesetz im *GB Kö.* läßt den Fähigen selbst seinen Wunsch bekennen, daß er „mit allen sinnen [...] Fruchtbringend möchte sein, beym frieden dieser Zeit | Das unser Vaterland, erlangte ruh' und freud." Wesenbeck trug sich am 19.5.1645, dem mutmaßlichen Tag seiner Aufnahme in die FG, in das *GB Kö.* ein. *GB Kö.* III, Bl. 33vf. Der Fähige war kurbrandenburg. Kriegs-, Hof- u. Kammerrat, der Kf. Friedrich Wilhelm (FG 401) als Gesandter vom Mai 1643 bis Mai 1645 auf dem Reichsdeputationstag in Frankfurt a. M. sowie als Unterhändler seit September 1645 auf dem Westfälischen Friedenskongreß vertrat. Vgl. *Conermann III*, 519f.; *Friedenssäle*, 250f.; GSTA - PK Berlin: I. HA GR, Rep. 12, Nr. 313–325, 334 u. 353 (Akten, darunter Instruktionen an Wesenbeck, zum Reichsdeputationstag); zahlreiche Akten zu den Westfälischen Friedensverhandlungen ebenfalls in I. HA GR, Rep. 12. — In den überlieferten nachfolgenden Stücken der Korrespondenz Werders u. F. Ludwigs ist nicht mehr persönlich von Wesenbeck die Rede.

2 Die Aufnahme Johann Michael Moscheroschs (FG 436. Der Träumende) erfolgte unter Vermittlung Georg Philipp Harsdörffers (FG 368. Der Spielende). Vgl. 450500 K 1. Diederich v. dem Werder (FG 31. Der Vielgekörnte) nennt in diesem Schreiben nicht explizit den Impresenvorschlag, der nach Aussage des vorliegenden Briefes auf Moscherosch selbst zurückging, F. Ludwig aber notierte die Beiwort-Alternative (Der Träumende) „Hohe sachen" oder „Mit offenen augen". Die erste Devise war, das hatte Werder von Martin Milagius (FG 315. Der Mindernde) erfahren, ein Vorschlag des Fürsten, dem gegenüber Werder Moscherosch u. dem von ihm erfundenen Beiwort „Mit offenen augen" noch eine Chance geben wollte. In 450505 stellte F. Ludwig die Wahl dann ins Belieben Moscheroschs, trug jedoch Werder auf, ein Reimgesetz unter Einbezug beider Beiworte zu entwerfen. Dies wird Werder in seiner Antwort 450505A Moscherosch selbst zuweisen. So scheint auch verfahren worden zu sein, denn mit 450613 leitete Werder einen Brief Harsdörffers (vermutlich an Werder) an F. Ludwig weiter, der auch „den reimsatz des Träumenden" enthielt. In seiner Antwort an Harsdörffer habe er nun das Beiwort „hohe Sachen" u. einige Versänderungen vorgeschlagen, die er auflistet. Im Reimgesetz des *GB Kö.* finden sich diese Verbesserungen nicht wieder (s. *Conermann III*, 525). Danach muß ihm, Werder, F. Ludwig die Reimgesetze für fünf neue Mitglieder zugesandt u. um deren Durchsicht gebeten haben (Briefkonzept nicht erhalten). Das sagt Werder in 450725 zu, ebenso, daß er Harsdörffer das (nochmals verbesserte) Reimgesetz für Moscherosch schikken werde. Wenige Tage später unterrichtet Werder Christian Ernst (v.) Knoch (FG 268. Der Weichende), wie er das Reimgesetz für Moscherosch, bevor er es abgeschickt habe, tatsächlich in der ersten u. fünften Zeile einer Korrektur unterzogen habe, die F. Ludwig hoffentlich billigen werde (450730). Beide Verbesserungen finden sich in der Fassung des *GB Kö.* wieder, die in Zeile 5 allerdings als nachträgliche, interlineare Verbesserung (s. u.). Eine im 3. Bd. des Erzschreins erhaltene Liste der Impresen u. Reimgesetze von FG 428 (Georg Frantzke) bis FG 437 (Matthias v. Biedersehe) weist die beiden Verbesserungen von Werder unter der Imprese „Der Träumende Nachtschatten Hohe sachen" bereits in Reinschrift auf. S. HM Köthen: V S 546, Bl. 79v. In einer eigenhändigen Namenliste der „Jm Jhare 1645" aufgenommenen Mitglieder (mit Mitgliedsnummer u. -imprese) von F. Ludwig lautet der Eintrag zu Moscherosch: „436. Johan Michael Moscherosch Der Traumende Nachtschatten Hohe sachen." Ebd., Bl. 143r. Eine andere Liste, ebenfalls von F. Ludwig, verzeichnet hingegen „Le Songeant Der Täumende Nachtschatten Mit offenen augen" (ebd., Bl. 148v). Für den in Geschäften nach Paris verreisten Moscherosch (vgl. 450818) versichert Harsdörffer im November 1645, daß der Träumende seine ihm zugedachte Imprese samt dem Reimgesetz annehmen werde (s. 451101). Danach muß Harsdörffer Werder geschrieben haben, denn in 451217 teilt er dem Fürsten mit, daß Werder „Wegen des Traumenden Gesellschafts Gemähl" sicher schon Bericht erstattet habe. Damit scheint eine endgültige Verständigung über die Imprese Moscheroschs nebst Reimgesetz erreicht. Das *GB Kö.* III, Bl. 37r führt das Reimgesetz in einer Fassung auf, die beide Sinnspruch-Varianten eingearbeitet hat: „Nachtschatten pfleget sanft den schlaf zu flößen ein, | Und zeigt träume drauf, daher ich mir erwehlet | Den Nahmen mit dem Kraut: Jch wil befließen sein | Als ich vorhin auch war, als ich die träum' erzehlet | Zu träumen mehr und mehr, bey nacht und tagesschein [*Eingefügt für* was lieblich ist und fein] | Und zwar mit ofnem aug': Es sol sein unverhehlet | Was von geschickligkeit, wird träumen meinem fleiß' | Auf das der Träumend ich viel Hohe sachen heiß. | J. M. M. 1645." Vgl. *Conermann III,* 525 f.; *Schäfer: Moscherosch und Harsdörffer,* 154 f.; ferner *Hille: Teutscher Palmbaum,* 205 zum Träumenden: „Jn dem sanften SchattenThron jener hohen Palmenbäume/ | Hat er in bemühtem Schlaf von viel hohen Sachen Träume. | Obwol/ der die Warheit saget/ aller Orten ist verhasst/ | Wird von jedem doch geliebet/ so sie Traumend hat verfasst."

3 *Schäfer: Moscherosch und Harsdörffer,* 155 f., sah in dieser Passage adelsstolz-überhebliche „Bosheiten" auf seiten Werders am Werke. *Merzbacher: Werder,* 59, erkannte darin einen gewissen Überdruß gegen Harsdörffers zahlreiche Vorschläge neuer FG-Mitgliedschaften — Werder vergleicht sie in 450505A mit Truppen-„Werbungen" — u. daraus folgend eine „aristokratisch elitär und sarkastisch unwillig" auftretende Einstellung Werders. Zu derartigem Hinterfragen eines offenkundig harmlosen Scherzes Werders besteht kein Anlaß, zumal ihm zum Verständnis der Devise bzw. des legendären Verhaltens der Hasen noch die Erklärung des ‚Wortes' in Moscheroschs Reimgesetz fehlte. Vgl. 450613. Weder der Volksglaube, noch die christliche Symbolik liefern jenseits der von der Emblematik tradierten humanistischen Hieroglyphik des mit offenen Augen schlafenden Hasen andere als moralische Bedeutung: Wachsamkeit u. ruheloses, schlechtes Gewissen. S. *Emblemata* (1978), 481 f. Die Abbildung der Art Solanum nigrum L., Schwarzer Nachtschatten, im *GB 1646,* deren Beeren nach der Kräuterbuchmedizin den Menschen „doll/ vnd schier unsinnig [machen] oder bringen jn in einen tieffen Schlaff" (Tabernaemontanus: Solanum bacca nigra cerasi), passen auf einen Satiriker, der seine Träume, d.h. Visionen offenen Auges schaut. Moscherosch könnte, um nicht unsinnig zu wirken, seine Träume nach Diosk. mat. med. IV, 72 jedoch aus der Einnahme der milderen Art „Schlaffbeeren. Solanum somniferum" abgeleitet haben. *Conermann III,* 525 f. Wir kennen in diesem Punkt die Textgeschichte des Reimgesetzes nicht, vermuten allerdings, daß F. Ludwigs ‚Wort' „Hohe sachen" den satirischen Träumen Moscheroschs den erwünschten Anstand u. im Sinne der Allegorese verlangten ideellen Sinn verlieh. Die „offnen Augen" Moscheroschs blieben dagegen im Sensus historicus befangen, erfüllten also nicht den literarischen Anspruch.

4 Im uns vorliegenden Briefwechsel mit F. Ludwig stoßen wir auf keine Vorschlagsliste Harsdörffers für Neumitglieder der FG, wie er sie uns für die DG in seinem Brief 441223 an Philipp (v.) Zesen (FG 521. 1648) überliefert hat. Sicher in der Korrespondenz belegt sind Harsdörffers Vorschläge, Johann Michael Dilherr (420608), Johann Klaj (s. 450505) u. Georg Conrad Osthof (s. 451209 u. 451217) einer Aufnahme in die FG zu würdigen. Aus 450505 geht aber hervor, daß wohl neben Johann Klaj auch „andere angegebene deutsche Poeten" zum Kreis jener Kandidaten gehört haben, die Harsdörffer zur Aufnahme in die FG empfahl, darunter die Nürnberger Johann Helwig u. wohl auch Georg Friedrich Behaim (s. 450400 K 6 u. 451101) u. die Hamburger Vincent u. Eberhard Moller (450800 K 4). Später setzte Harsdörffer seine „Werbungen" neuer FG-Mitglieder fort. Vgl. *DA*

Köthen I. 8: 470100 (Ernst Christoph Homburg), 470122A (Johann Rist, Johann Matthias Schneuber), 470206 u. ö.

5 In 450505 antwortet F. Ludwig, bislang habe man nur die (farbigen Zeichnungen) der Wappen von Harsdörffer u. Moscherosch für den Erzschrein erbeten. Die Wappen der Mitglieder wurden in das *GB Kö.* eingemalt. Falls sich Harsdörffer auch zum Sticken (seines Wappens u. seiner Imprese für die FG-Wandgobelins im Saal des Köthener Schlosses) verstehen wolle, könne er dies gegen ein Entgelt von 10 Talern durch einen Sticker in Leipzig ausführen lassen. Vgl. dazu F. Ludwigs Instruktion zum Sticken der Wappen 421123 u. I. Zu den einst im Köthener Festsaal aufgehängten, nicht mehr erhaltenen Gobelins s. *Conermann: Nachlaßinventar,* 74 f. Diese Anweisung sah eine Stickgebühr von 10 Reichstalern bei Stellung des silberfarbigen Atlas-Stoffes mit Vorzeichnung der Impresen-Pictura vor. Werder schlägt in 450505A daraufhin, u. um nicht die Gebühr anmahnen zu müssen, vor, Harsdörffer u. Moscherosch ihre „wapen vnd gemälde" lieber in Nürnberg sticken zu lassen, sobald ihnen der Atlas mit der Vorzeichnung der Imprese zugestellt worden ist. Mit 450613 übersandte Werder F. Ludwig ein Schreiben Harsdörffers, das sich nicht erhalten hat u. in dem er Fragen zum Sticken der „Tapezerey" vorbringt, die F. Ludwig bitte beantworten möchte. Moscherosch, so Werder in 450725, werde er „von dem Atlas vnd gemälde" unterrichten; im September dürfte ein Posten Atlasstoff an Harsdörffer versandt worden sein. S. 450919, 450919A u. 451101. Weil der Nürnberger Sticker aber verstorben war, entschied sich Harsdörffer dafür, sein Wappen u. seine Imprese in Leipzig sticken zu lassen, reichte F. Ludwig Visierungen seines Wappens u. seiner Imprese ein u. entrichtete die für das Sticken vorgesehene Gebühr in Höhe von 10 Reichstalern. S. 451217. F. Ludwig sagte die Erledigung dieses Vorhabens in 460120 zu. Zu diesem Zeitpunkt erwartete F. Ludwig noch immer das Wappen Moscheroschs u. fragte, ob dieser eine eigene FG-Medaille mit seiner Imprese wünsche u. wie er es hinsichtlich des Stickens seines Wappens u. seiner Imprese zu halten gedenke. S. ebd. Daß Moscheroschs Wappen nach Köthen gelangte, wissen wir aus 460620 u. 460705. Es ist farbig eingemalt in *GB Kö.* III, Bl. 36v. Umgekehrt wurde Moscherosch über Harsdörffer mit 460609 auch ein Bild seiner FG-Imprese zugesandt, als Vorlage für die Bemalung seiner Gesellschaftsmedaille. Vgl. 460406, 460426 u. 460726. Damit enden einstweilen die Nachrichten über Harsdörffers u. Moscheroschs Wappen u. Impresen. Zum Gesellschaftspfennig der FG s. 441223 K 9. Zu Wappen in der FG s. 440809A K 1, 450317, 450500 K 1, 450505, 450505A, 450613, 450725, 450919 (K 2), 451101, 451217, 460120, 460406, 460423, 460426, 460609, 460613, 460620, 460705, 460714, 461031A u. 461106.

6 *KE,* 176, liest hier „Rüge Sontag". Ostersonntag fiel 1645 auf den 6. April. *Grotefend* I, 64. Der vierte Sonntag nach Ostern war 1645 demnach der 4. Mai. Er wird nach Ps 98, 1 (Cantate domino canticum novum) im Kreis des Kirchenjahres Sonntag Kantate genannt. *Grotefend* I, 20.

450505

Fürst Ludwig an Diederich von dem Werder

Antwort auf 450420, 450500 (?) u. 450504A. Beantwortet durch 450505A. — F. Ludwig (der Nährende) erklärt sich mit der Devise in der FG-Imprese des jüngst vorgeschlagenen Gesellschafters (Johann Michael Moscherosch. FG 436. Der Träumende. 1645) einverstanden, wie sie der Kandidat selbst für sich gewählt habe. Die vom Fürsten vorgeschlagene Alternative „hohe sachen" möge Diederich v. dem Werder (FG 31. Der Vielgekörnte) aber

450505 Fürst Ludwig 543

Georg Philipp Harsdörffer (FG 368. Der Spielende) mitteilen, damit Moscherosch seine Entscheidung treffen könne. Ansonsten sei Moscherosch mit dem Gesellschaftsnamen und der vorgeschlagenen Pflanze in der FG willkommen. Werder möge nun das Reimgesetz auf Moscheroschs FG-Imprese aufsetzen und darin das Beiwort „mit offenen augen" wie auch F. Ludwigs „hohe sachen" verarbeiten. Er möge sich dabei an das erinnern, was Martin Milagius (FG 315. Der Mindernde) zu Plötzkau gegeben worden sei. F. Ludwig erwartet Werders Entwurf dazu. — Bislang, so meint F. Ludwig, habe man Harsdörffer und Moscherosch nur um Einlieferung ihrer Wappen für den Erzschrein gebeten. Harsdörffer könne gern auch sein Wappen und die Imprese sticken lassen, doch möge ihm Werder irgendwie beibringen, daß er dafür 10 Taler dem Sticker in Leipzig überweisen müsse. — Die Dichtungen Johann Klajs seien kunstvoll, nur seine neue Schreibweise sei wie die von Harsdörffer und Justus Georg Schottelius (FG 397. Der Suchende) außergewöhnlich. Die deutsche Rechtschreibung (von Christian Gueintz. FG 361), deren Rücksendung nach Halle a. d. S. F. Ludwig noch für den selben Tag zusicherte, verspreche hier Aufklärung. — Harsdörffers Vorschläge weiterer deutscher Poeten zur Aufnahme in die FG, erklärt der Fürst, wolle er bedenken, jedoch zuvor etwas von ihren Arbeiten sehen; auch solle sichergestellt sein, daß sie nicht allzuweit (von den hergebrachten Prinzipien der dt. Sprache) abschweiften, wie dies Philipp v. Zesen (FG 521. 1648) tue, der aber hoffentlich noch auf die rechte Bahn zu bringen sei. Abschließend ermahnt F. Ludwig, daß in der FG Streit und Uneinigkeit vermieden werden sollten, die besonders dann drohten, wenn jeder auf seiner eigenen Meinung beharrte.

Q HM Köthen: V S 544, Bl. 483r; eigenh. Konzept auf einer zuvor leergelassenen Seite in Werders Brief 450504A. — D: KE, 177 (gekürzt). Zit. in Schäfer: Moscherosch und Harsdörffer, 155. — BN: Bürger, 955 Nr. 125.

A Fehlt.

Dem[a] Vielgekörneten wird wegen des neuen angegebenen geselschafters dieses zu fernern[b] erklerung, das wan derselbe das wort mit offenen augen selber erwehlet er solches wol behalten mag, doch könte man dem Spielenden also zuschreiben, das ihme dieses andere hohe sachen auch furgeschlagen würde, es aber alleine auf seiner wahl und erklerung beruhete, Der Nahme, der Treumende, auch das kraut die nachtschatten were mit der person zu erweiterung der fruchtbringen[c] geselschaft mit allem willen angenommen.[1] Es wolle aber der Vielgekörnte auf beyde worte unbeschwert das Achtzeilige gesetze [au]ch[d] dem jenigen was sonst ent[lich]en dem Min[dern]den damals uf Plötzkau gegeben worden aufsetzen,[2] das ihme die antwort desto volkömlicher [u]nd[e] vergnugeter [in] der ausfertigung könte zukommen. Welchen aufsatz[3] der Nehrende erwarten wird. Fur dismal helt der Nehrende dafür man hette nur von dem Spielenden und Treumenden ihre wappen zum Ertzschreine gefodert, doch in weinigem zu vernemen, ob Der[f] Spielende für sich zum Sticken verstehen wolte, könte nechst kunftig dem Sticker das geld dafür[g] als[h] zehen thaler dem sticker auf Leiptzig ubermacht werden.[4] Es wird aber dieses letzte auf des Vielgekörneten verbeßerung gestellet, Klaij seine sachen seind sonsten auch fein gesetzet, nur das die neue[i] Schreibeart nebst des Spielenden und Suchenden seine sich nicht[j] fügen wil,⁵ davon aber die deutsche Rechtschreibung, so heute wieder auf Halle geschicket worden[k 6], mehreres licht geben wird. Die vorschlage von den andern angegebenen deutschen Poeten⁷ hette man zwar auch zuerwarten, doch das man darbey versichert were[,] das sie nicht alzuweit ausschweiffen möchten[l], und man etwas von ihren sachen zuvor sehen könte. Jnmaßen Zæsius⁸ aus dem Niederlande sich alzu gleich angeben, und zimlich aus den schrancken der deutschen sprache nach einer fremden weise geschritten, der aber verhoffentlich noch auch[m] zu rechte zubringen. Für wiedrigkeiten und[n] uneinigkeit hat man sich in der geselschaft zu hüten, sonderlich wan die Köpfe auf ihrem eigenen sinnen beharren solten. Jns kunftige[o] dieses dem Vielgekörnten auf sein schreiben hiermit geantwortet werden wollen und verbleibet[p] Des Vielgekornten

    gantz williger

Cöthen 5. May 1645

T **a** *Verbessert aus* vom — **b** *Folgt* <antwort, und> — **c** *Lies:* fruchtbringenden. — **d** *Bis* gegeben worden *in einer Marginalie ergänzt. Textverlust im Falz, tw. unleserlich. Konjekturen in eckigen Klammern. Nicht in KE.* — **e** *Am Rand eingefügt bis* ausfertigung *Textverlust im Falz. Konjekturen in eckigen Klammern.* — **f** *Verbessert aus unleserlichem Wort.* — **g** *Folgt* <uber> — **h** *Eingefügt bis* auf — **i** *Folgt* <art zu> — **j** *Folgt* <wol> — **k** *Folgt* <ein> — **l** *Eingefügt für* <wolten> — **m** *Gebessert aus* zu[recht] — **n** und uneinigkeit *am Rand ergänzt.* — **o** *Folgt* <kan eins mit mehrerm da> *Wohl irrtümlich stehen geblieben:* Jns kunftige — **p** *Verschreibung:* verbleiben

K 1 Der Nürnberger Patrizier Georg Philipp Harsdörffer (FG 368. Der Spielende) u. der anhalt. Adlige Diederich v. dem Werder (FG 31. Der Vielgekörnte) waren als Vermittler bei der Aufnahme Johann Michael Moscheroschs (FG 436. Der Träumende. 1645) in die FG tätig geworden. In einem (verlorenen) Brief Harsdörffers (s. 450500) hatte dieser Moscheroschs Aufnahme empfohlen u. als Imprese gebilligt: Der Träumende — Nachtschatten — Mit offenen Augen. Werder wollte Moscherosch nämlich gern die Wahl seiner Imprese zugestehen (s. 450500). F. Ludwig hatte jedoch „hohe Sachen" als ‚Wort' im Sinn (s. 450504A), akzeptierte u. modifizierte aber im vorliegenden Brief Moscheroschs Impresenvorschlag. Am Ende setzte sich F. Ludwigs Vorschlag „hohe Sachen" als Beiwort durch, jedoch greift das Reimgesetz Moscheroschs Devise „mit offenen Augen" auf. Vgl. dazu 450504A K 2 u. 3; zum Prozeß der Aufnahme Moscheroschs in die FG vgl. 450500 K 1.

2 Aus 450504A ergibt sich, daß Martin Milagius (FG 315. Der Mindernde) in Moscheroschs Aufnahmeprozeß einbezogen war. Der Einschub könnte bekräftigen, daß Werder ein Reimgesetz aufsetzen sollte, das beide Beiwortvorschläge verarbeitete, d.h. auch F. Ludwigs Vorschlag („hohe sachen"), von dem Werder durch Milagius in Kenntnis gesetzt worden war. Eine andere Lesart des verdeckten Texts — s. Anm.d: ([glei]ch statt [au]ch) — könnte daran erinnern, daß möglicherweise auch bei Milagius' Einnahme im Jahre 1637 zwei Vorschläge zur Diskussion gestanden hatten u. beide berücksichtigt worden waren. Obwohl Werder in 450505A von einem gedoppelten Reimgesetz sprach, wird dies nicht zwei Reimgesetze meinen, sondern eine beide Beiworte im Text verbindende Strophe.

3 Entwurf, Niederschrift. *DW* I, 718; *Paul Wb.*, 108.

4 In 450504A hatte Werder bei F. Ludwig nachgefragt, ob er Harsdörffer Hinweise zum Sticken der Wappen u. Impresen (für die FG-Wandgobelins im Köthener Schloßsaal) geben dürfe. Vgl. 421123 u. I und zu dieser Angelegenheit im Hinblick auf Harsdörffer u. Moscherosch 450504A K 5 u. 450505A.

5 Johann Klaj (ca. 1616–1656), mit Harsdörffer Begründer des Nürnberger PBO, seit April 1645 Mitglied der DG, sieht sich hier ähnlicher Kritik an seiner Orthographie ausgesetzt wie Harsdörffer u. Justus Georg Schottelius (FG 397. Der Suchende). Ähnlich wie im Falle Philipp v. Zesens (FG 521. 1648) ergeht diese Kritik bei gleichzeitiger Würdigung seiner literarisch-stilistischen Fähigkeiten. Vermutlich war Klaj einer derjenigen „deutschen Poeten", die Harsdörffer zur Aufnahme in die FG vorgeschlagen hatte, vgl. schon 440824. Dazu ist es im Falle Klajs nicht gekommen. Vgl. Anm. 7 u. 450504 K 4.

6 *Gueintz: Rechtschreibung (1645).* F. Ludwig schickte Christian Gueintz' (FG 361) deutsche Rechtschreiblehre nach kritischer Durchsicht durch einige FG-Mitglieder mit 450504 an Gueintz zurück u. mahnte zu schleuniger Drucklegung. Etwa im September 1645 war der Druck abgeschlossen u. wurde von F. Ludwig an Harsdörffer (s. 450919A), Schottelius (s. 450923B) u. a. m. (vgl. etwa 451028, 460217) versandt. Zur *Deutschen Rechtschreibung* von Gueintz vgl. 440127 K 1.

7 Ein entsprechender Brief oder eine Vorschlagsliste Harsdörffers hat sich nicht erhalten. Vgl. aber 450504A K 4.

8 Zur damaligen Kritik an Philipp v. Zesen vgl. 440324, 450410, 450504, 450506A, 450529, 460217, 460610, 460812 u. *DA Köthen I. 8*: 470206 K II.

450505A

Diederich von dem Werder an Fürst Ludwig

Antwort auf 450505. — Diederich v. dem Werder (FG 31. Der Vielgekörnte) erklärt, das Schreiben F. Ludwigs (Der Nährende) vom selben Tage erhalten zu haben, und verspricht, den erteilten Aufträgen nachzukommen. Allerdings lehnt er das Verfassen des Reimgesetzes für Johann Michael Moscherosch (FG 436. Der Träumende. 1645) ab: Dies überlasse er „dem grossen neuen Poeten selbsten". Ebenso sähe er es lieber, wenn er von Georg Philipp Harsdörffer (FG 368. Der Spielende) und Moscherosch für das Sticken ihrer Wappen und Impresen kein Geld fordern müßte und sie stattdessen diese Arbeit selbst in Nürnberg bestellten, sobald ihnen der Atlasstoff und eine Impresenzeichnung (als Stickvorlage) zugestellt worden sei. Ansonsten werde er Harsdörffer das Nötige und Gewünschte mitzuteilen wissen. — In der Nachschrift vergleicht Werder das Anwachsen der FG mit der Musterung eines ganzen Regiments, nur daß dies ohne Musterungsplatz, Anwerbegelder und Belastung des armen Mannes erfolge.

Q HM Köthen: V S 544, Bl. 479r–481v [A: 481v], 479v u. 481r leer; Bl. 480rv: Zettel mit Nachschrift, v leer; eigenh.; rotes Lacksiegel. — *D: KE*, 177f. — *BN: Bürger*, 1440 Nr. 54.

A Dem Nehrenden   zuhanden.   Cöthen

Auf des Nehrenden heutiges andwortschreiben, verhalte ich nicht, wie das ich in einem vnd andern aufgetragenem mich der^a gebür nach gemäs verhalten wil; Ausser das ich, das gedoppelte achtzeilige gesetze aufzusetzen, mir nicht getraue, sondern wird billich dem grossen Neuen Poeten selbsten anheimbgegeben, wie mir dan auch nicht gebüren wil, demselben vorzugreiffen.[1]

Neben dem wolte ich auch dem Spielenden, vnd durch ihn dem Träumenden, lieber[b] vorschlagen, das sie ihre wapen vnd gemälde selbsten zu Nürnberg sticken liessen, wan ihnen der altlas vnd abris zugeschickt würde, Als das ich ihnen ümb geld schreiben solte.[2] Jm übrigen wil ich eines vnd anders dem Spielenden, zugeschriebener massen, zuhinterbringen wissen. Bitte mich in ansehung meiner täglich zunemenden Faulheit, vnd geschäften, welche beyde übel zusammen kommen, aufs beste [für] endschüldiget zuhalten. Verbleibe meines höchstgeehrten Nehrenden

dienstwilligster
Der Vielgekörnte

Reinsdorff 5. May. 1645

[480r] P. S. Wan die vermehrung vnserer Fruchtbringenden Geselschaft dergestalt fortfähret, So wird in kurtzem ein gantz Regiment ohne Werbegeld vnd Musterplatz aufgebracht, vnd darzu ohne kosten vnd sonder beschwerung des armen Mannes vnterhalten.[3]

T a *Bis* nach *eingefügt.* — b *Eingefügt.*

K 1 Da das Empfehlungsschreiben Georg Philipp Harsdörffers (FG 368. Der Spielende) für die Aufnahme Johann Michael Moscheroschs (FG 436. Der Träumende. 1645) in die FG nicht bekannt ist, wissen wir nicht, mit welchen Worten Harsdörffer Moscherosch angepriesen hatte. In der Bezeichnung als „grossen Neuen Poeten" läßt Diederich v. dem Werder (FG 31. Der Vielgekörnte) aber unüberhörbar Ironie anklingen. Da es für Moscheroschs Mitgliedsimprese zwei Devisenvorschläge gab — (Der Träumende) „mit offenen Augen" oder „hohe Sachen" — hatte F. Ludwig (Der Nährende) Werder in 450505 wohl nur gebeten, statt zweier Strophen ein ‚gedoppeltes' Reimgesetz zu entwerfen, das beide ‚Worte' benutzte — so wie es uns vorliegt. Die Abfassung eines Reimgesetzes für den Träumenden lehnte Werder aber hier auch deshalb ab, damit Moscherosch in seinem Reimgesetz auch seine eigene Devise benutzen konnte. Mit 450613 leitete Werder dann einen Brief Harsdörffers an F. Ludwig weiter, der auch „den reimsatz des Träumenden" enthielt. Vgl. dazu 450504A K 2.

2 Das Sticken der Wappen u. FG-Impresen der Mitglieder für die Gobelins im Köthener Schloßsaal regelte eine eigene Verordnung F. Ludwigs (421123 u. I). Demnach konnten die Mitglieder das Sticken selbst veranlassen, wobei ihnen der silberfarbige Atlasstoff u. die Vorzeichnung der Imprese zugestellt wurden, oder sie konnten das Sticken gegen eine Gebühr von 10 Talern in Leipzig vornehmen lassen. Harsdörffer scheint Letzteres veranlaßt zu haben, von Moscheroschs Entscheidung ist uns nichts bekannt. Vgl. 450504A K 5.

3 Harsdörffer hatte neben Moscherosch eine ganze Reihe neuer Mitgliedskandidaten vorgeschlagen. Vgl. 450504A K 4. Werders Nachschrift ist eine deutlich ironische Replik darauf, zumal damals die Stärke eines Regiments bis zu 3.000 Mann betragen konnte. (Werder war 1631–1635 selbst schwed. Obrist, also Regimentskommandeur gewesen.)

450506 Fürst Ludwig

Der Unterhalt der Truppen erfolgte durch Kriegssteuern, die von den Reichsständen aufzubringen waren, u. durch außerordentliche Kontributionen, die durch die von Durchzügen oder Einquartierungen betroffenen Regionen u. deren Nachbarn gestellt werden mußten. Es traf immer den „armen Mann". Vgl. J. Heilmann: Das Kriegswesen der Kaiserlichen und Schweden zur Zeit des dreißigjährigen Krieges. Leipzig u. Meißen 1850, 1 ff. u. 154 ff.; Peter Engerisser: Von Kronach nach Nördlingen. Der Dreißigjährige Krieg in Franken, Schwaben und der Oberpfalz 1631–1635. Weißenstadt 2004, 26, 447 ff. u. 493 ff.

450506

Fürst Ludwig an Winand von Polhelm

Beantwortet durch 450526. — Unter Bezug auf sein Schreiben 450317A bittet F. Ludwig (Der Nährende) Winand v. Polhelm (FG 405. Der Entnehmende) um Rücksendung zweier verdeutschter Handschriften, sofern der Kasseler Drucker — seinem Versprechen zuwider — mit dem Druck noch nicht begonnen habe oder dies wenigstens beabsichtige. Sonst solle Polhelm F. Ludwig die Bücher bei der sich nun bietenden Gelegenheit sicher zurückschicken. Der Druck, besonders des zweiten übersandten Teils, hätte nicht so verzögert werden dürfen.

Q HM Köthen: V S 545, Bl. 464rv, v leer; eigenh. Konzept F. Ludwigs; unterhalb des Konzepts v. F. Ludwigs Brief an Lgf. Hermann IV. v. Hessen-Rotenburg (450317).

A *Fehlt.*

Der Entnehmende wird sonder zweiffel des Nehrenden antwort vom 17. des Mertzen wol empfangen haben, bey dieser guten gelegenheit hat[a] dieses brieflein an ihme abgehen sollen, vnd wird er ersuchet, wo ferne der drucker in Caßel[1] seinem gethanen versprechen zu wieder, die uberschickete verdeutschete bucher[2] noch nicht angefangen zu drucken, oder zu drucken gewillet, das sie mit dieser bequemigkeit[3] dem Nehrenden wieder wol verwahret uberbracht werden,

Es solte so lange sonderlich mit dem letzt uberschickten[4] nicht zu drucken gewehret haben. Die bemuhung wolle der Entnehmende nicht ubel vermercken und verbleibendt des Entnemenden
   gantz williger
     Der Nehrende
Cöthen den 6. Maij 1645.

T a *Gebessert aus* thut

K 1 Der federführende Buchbinder u. Verleger Johann (Hans) Schütz arbeitete damals in Kassel mit dem Drucker Jakob Gentzsch (Gentsch) zusammen. S. 450305 K 3 u. 450317 K 7, vgl. Anm. 4 u. 440809A K 4 u. ö.

2 Die zwei vordem übersandten Teile des unveröffentlichten Druckmanuskripts *Von des Pabstes gewalt*. S. 440809A K 6.

3 Es gab damals einen vorbeireisenden Boten oder eine Kaufmannsfuhre, der F. Ludwig die Manuskripte anvertraut wissen wollte. In 450317A hatte der Fürst Winand v. Polhelm (FG 405. Der Entnehmende) beauftragt, die Handschriften von Schütz zurückzufordern u. einstweilen bei sich zu verwahren, bis sich ein sicherer Transport ergebe.

4 Der als dritte Tranche übersandte Teil der Übersetzung *Von des Pabstes gewalt*. Die Einteilung des Übersetzungs-Manuskripts in 6 Bücher mit jeweils mehreren Kapiteln (das 2. Buch dabei in 2 Teilen) gibt keinen Hinweis auf die sukzessive übersandten drei Teile. S. 450317A, vgl. auch 450317 K 1. Da F. Ludwig die dritte Tranche des Werks Polhelm u. Lgf. Hermann IV. v. Hessen-Rotenburg (FG 374) erst in 450317A zu lesen gab, forderte er deren Rücksendung wohl noch nicht.

450506A

Christian Gueintz an Fürst Ludwig

Antwort auf 450504. Beantwortet durch 450507 I. — Christian Gueintz (FG 361. Der Ordnende) teilt mit, die Erinnerungen F. Ludwigs (Der Nährende) zur *Deutschen Rechtschreibung* erhalten zu haben. Er verspricht, sie durchzusehen und die Veröffentlichung zu beschleunigen, auch dadurch, daß er sich zu einer sicherlich nötigen Zusammenkunft in der nächsten Woche in Köthen bereitwillig einfinden werde. — Philipp (v.) Zesen (FG 521. 1648) sei sein Schüler gewesen, doch habe er kein besonderes Talent zu erkennen gegeben, außer dem Hang, ständig Neues im Deutschen ohne Grund und Bewährung durch den Sprachgebrauch herbeizusuchen. Seine Schreibweise sei genügender Nachweis dieser Haltung. — Vor seiner Abreise am Tag zuvor habe Curt v. Einsiedel (FG 417. Der Ersprießliche) noch Gelegenheit gehabt, die betreffenden Texte (der Rechtschreibung) durchzulesen. Er habe sie gutgeheißen, wovon Gueintz mündlich genaueren Bericht zu erstatten verspricht.

Q   HM Köthen: V S 545, Bl. 187r–188v [A: 188v], 188r leer; eigenh., A von Schreiberh.; 187v Konzepte F. Ludwigs 450507 u. 450507 I. — *D: Barthold*, 312 (Auszug); *KE*, 272. — *BN: Bürger*, 634 Nr. 12.

A   *Dem Nährenden*

Waß^a Der Nährende wegen der Rechtschreibung gnädig eingeschickt,[1] das hat der Ordnende unterthänig empfangen, will noch solches mit gebürenden fleiß durchsehen[,] daß es desto eher beschleuniget werde, und zu dessen befoderung sich, so bald er abgefodert wird, willig einstellen. Welches doch ohne maaßgeben könnte künfftige wochen, etwan geschehen.[2] Gewiß ist die mündliche unterredung höchst nötig, da man eine gleicheit und gewißheit haben will. Was Zesium anbelanget ist es mein lerner gewesen[3], und hat sein witz niemalß sich so erwiesen, daß man was sonderliches bey ihme verspühret, ausser daß er allezeit was neues in dem Deutschen ohne grund und beliebte Gewohnheit^b, ihme^c eingebildet. Wie den auch die schreibart genugsam es beweiset. Der Ersprießliche ist gestriges Tages verreiset, hat aber vorhin[4] alles, wie dan der Ordnende selbsten es

450506A Christian Gueintz

Ihme zugestellt, durchlesen, es auch gelobet und beliebet[,]⁵ davon in gegenwart⁶ mit mehrern nachrichten und anzeig geben wird

Des Nährenden
untergebener und gehorsamer Ordnender *mp.*

Hall den 6 Meymonats 1645

T a *Am oberen Seitenrand spätere Bleistifteintragungen (von Gottlieb Krause?):* K. 10 66 — **b** *KE* Wahrheit — **c** *Lies:* sich

K 1 Mit 450504 hatte F. Ludwig (Der Nährende) Christian Gueintz (FG 361. Der Ordnende) *Die Deutsche Rechtschreibung* zu einer abschließenden Durchsicht zurückgesandt. F. Ludwig legte seinem Brief auch ein Begleitschreiben Philipp (v.) Zesens (FG 521. 1648) bei, mit dem Zesen ein Exemplar seiner Romanübersetzung *Ibrahim Bassa* (1645) dem Fürsten zugesandt hatte u. aus dem sich Gueintz Notizen machen sollte, da der Fürst Zesens Orthographie nachdrücklich kritisierte.
2 F. Ludwig hatte zur Klärung abschließender Fragen zur Orthographie u. zur Drucklegung in 450504 eine Zusammenkunft „nechstkunftige woche" in Köthen vorgeschlagen. Vgl. auch 450507 u. I.
3 Zesen hatte das von Gueintz geleitete Gymnasium in Halle a. d. S. wohl von 1631 bis (höchstens) 1639 besucht. Ferdinand van Ingen warf Gueintz wegen der Abwertung Zesens im vorliegenden Brief „eine klägliche Rolle" u. einen „deutlichen Mangel an Zivilcourage" vor. *Ingen*, 20; *Ingen: Zesen*, 4. Das Verhältnis zwischen Lehrer u. Schüler trübte sich wohl erst mit den orthographischen Neuerungen Zesens ein. Dieser hatte zuvor Gueintz eine „Dactylische Ode. Als Herr Christian Gueintzius/ des berühmten Gymnasiums zu Hall wohlverordneter Rector etc. seinen Nahmens-tag beging" gewidmet. Sie erschien 1641 in der 2. Ausg. von Zesens *Deutschem Helicon* (*Zesen SW* IX, 342f., vgl. 37) u. danach überarbeitet in dessen 3. u. 4. Ausg., 1649 u. 1656) sowie 1642 in Zesens *Frühlings-Lust* (*Zesen SW* I.1, 93) u. als „Palmenlied" in Zesens *Dichterischem Rosen- und Liljen-tahl* (Hamburg 1670, *Zesen SW* II.1, 284f.). Vgl. auch Ferdinand van Ingen: Philipp von Zesen — Dichter und Poetiker. Poetologische Strategien in der Sammelausgabe *Dichterisches Rosen- und Liljen-tahl* (1670). In: Philipp von Zesen. Wissen — Sprache — Literatur. Hg. Maximilian Bergengruen u. Dieter Martin. Tübingen 2008, 7–23, hier S. 16f.
4 Hier im Sinne von vorher, zuvor. *Götze*, 88; *DW* XII.2, 1202ff.
5 Curt v. Einsiedel (FG 417. 1644. Der Ersprießliche), Rat Hz. Augusts v. Sachsen-Weißenfels (FG 402), des in Halle residierenden Adminstrators des Erzstifts Magdeburg. Vgl. 450504 K 3. Gueintz war in 450504 von F. Ludwig aufgefordert worden, Texte zu der vor der Drucklegung stehenden Deutschen Rechtschreibung Einsiedel zur Prüfung vorzulegen. Vgl. 441226, 441231 K 7 u. 450507 K 1 u. 2.
6 Eine Unterredung zwischen F. Ludwig u. Gueintz in Köthen sollte am 12. Mai stattfinden, wurde aber auf den 13. oder 14. verschoben. Vgl. 450504 K 12, 450507 I u. 450508. Unter Hinweis auf den vorliegenden Brief hatte *Barthold*, 312, übertreibend von einer „Germanisten Versammlung in Köthen" gesprochen, die F. Ludwig für den 12.5.1645 einberufen habe. Vgl. auch *Witkowski*, 52. Fußend auf Barthold meinte *Schäfer: Moscherosch und Harsdörffer*, 170, Harsdörffer habe sich von der Rechtschreibdebatte ausgeschlossen gefühlt u. daher in 450504 (!) Gueintz zur baldigen Publikation der *Rechtschreibung* gedrängt. — Die genannte Zusammenkunft in Köthen dürften F. Ludwig u. Gueintz allein bestritten haben. Vgl. außer den o. g. Briefen auch 450507.

450507

Fürst Ludwig an Hans von Dieskau

F. Ludwig (Der Nährende) bittet Hans v. Dieskau (FG 212. Der Tilgende), Christian Gueintz (FG 361. Der Ordnende) den beiliegenden Zettel F. Ludwigs auszuhändigen. Wenn Dieskau die aufgesetzte *Deutsche Rechtschreibung* empfangen habe, möge er sie durchlesen, schriftlich begutachten und sodann Johann Georg Bohse in F. Ludwigs Namen ebenfalls um kritische Durchsicht und Kommentierung der *Rechtschreibung* bitten. Bohse könne seine Stellungnahme dann versiegelt nach Köthen schicken. Bis zum 12. Mai solle Dieskau das Werk Gueintz zurückgeben, auf daß dieser sie mit den beiden Gutachten (Dieskaus und Bohses) persönlich am kommenden Montag nach Köthen mitbringen könne.

Q HM Köthen: V S 545, Bl. 187v, eigenh. Konzept auf der Rückseite von 450506A. — D: KE, 273. — BN: Fehlt in Bürger.

A Fehlt.

Der Tilgende wird hiermit ersuchet, dem Ordnenden inligendes zetlein[1] einzuhandigen, und wan er[a] die aufgesetzte deu[tsche][b] Rechtschreibung empfangen, solche fur sich erstlich zu durchlesen[c] und zu sehen, ob er noch etwas darbey zuerinnern, darnach dieselbe h. Johan George[d] Bosen[2] zu zu stellen, und[e] ihn des Nehrenden wegen zu ersuchen, das er sie auch durchlauffe und seine gedancken druber[f] eröffnen und[g] anhero versiegelt uberschicken wolle,[h] wolle er die Rechtschreibung dem[i] Ordnenden[j] gegen nechstkunftigen Montags absonderlich[a] wieder uberreichen[k], das[l] er solche mit beyder[m] verschlossenen gutachten heruber bringe.

Cöthen 7. May 1645.

I

450507

Fürst Ludwig an Christian Gueintz

Q HM Köthen: V S 545, Bl. 187v; eigenh. Konzept auf der Rückseite von 450506A. — D: KE, 273. — BN: Bürger, 949 Nr. 46.

A Fehlt.

Des Ordnenden[a] erklerung wegen seiner heruberkunft ist dem Nehrenden wol worden, darauf die verordnung geschehen sol, da[ß][b] er nechstkunftigen Montags den 12. dieses wird[c] abgeholet werden,[1] in deßen wolle er dem Tilgenden die uberschickete Rechtschreibung zustellen, das er sie auch durchsehe, sein[d] gutachten darüber eröffne[e] und ihme gegen die zeit wieder uberliefere.[2]

Cöthen 7. Maymonats 1645.

450507 Fürst Ludwig

T a *Eingefügt.* — b *Buchstabenverlust im Falz. Konjektur in eckigen Klammern.* — c *KE durchlaufen* — d *Am Rand ergänzt.* — e *Bis* durchlauffe und *am Rand ergänzt für einige unleserliche Streichungen.* — f *Folgt* <zuvernemen> — g *Bis* uberschicken *am Rand ergänzt.* — h *1 unlesbares Wort. KE setzt gestrichenes* darnach *Bis* Rechtschreibung *eingefügt für* <darnach solche mit derselben [?] ihme Tilgenden wieder uberreichen, darmit sie> — i *Gebessert aus* der — j *Gebessert aus* Ordnende — k *Eingefügt für* <haben könne> *In KE fehlt* wieder — l das er solche *eingefügt für* <und> — m *Bis* gutachten *eingefügt. Verschreibung:* verschossenen

T I a *Von F. Ludwig selbst gebessert aus* Ordenden — b *Buchstabenverlust im Falz. Konjektur in eckigen Klammern.* — c *Eingefügt für* <sol> — d *Bis* eröffne *am Rand ergänzt.* — e *Verschreibung:* eröstnen *KE* geben

K 1 D. i. 450507 I. Der auf Dieskau bei Halle lebende Hans v. Dieskau (FG 212. Der Tilgende) war F. Ludwigs Verbindungsmann in Halle u. in Verbindung mit Curt v. Einsiedel (FG 417) auch zum Hof des dort residierenden Erzbischofs/ Administrators des Ebsts. Magdeburg, Hz. Augusts v. Sachsen-Weißenfels (FG 402). Vgl. 450504 K 3. Der Fürst hatte Gueintz schon in 450504 gebeten, den Tilgenden in die Durchsicht der Handschrift der *Deutschen Rechtschreibung* einzubeziehen.
2 Johann Georg Bohse (1578–1669), von 1629 bis mindestens 1666 Syndikus der Stadt Halle. Zwar bleibt nur zu vermuten, daß er bereits in den Diskussions- u. Verbesserungsprozeß um *Gueintz: Deutsche Sprachlehre (1641)* einbezogen worden war, mit dem vorliegenden Brief ist seine Heranziehung in Fragen der deutschen Rechtschreibung aber belegt, auch wenn sich im Erzschrein der FG kein Dokument von der Hand Bohses erhalten hat. Vgl. 400301 K 6. Auch Justus Georg Schottelius (FG 397), Friedrich Hortleder (FG 343) oder auch Melchior Goldast v. Haiminsfeld oder Marquard Freher waren Juristen, die sich dem Studium der deutschen Sprache u. der alten deutschen Sprachdenkmäler widmeten. Während der Debatte um Gueintz' deutsche Grammatik scheint sich der Kreis der an dieser Diskussion Beteiligten vergrößert zu haben. War die Spracharbeit ursprünglich auf F. Ludwig, Gueintz, Augustus Buchner (FG 362), Schottelius, Hz. August v. Braunschweig-Wolfenbüttel (FG 224), Jacob Martini, Balthasar Gualtherus u. den zu früh verstorbenen Martin Opitz (FG 200) beschränkt (vgl. *DA Köthen I. 5*, Falttafel nach S. 432), so erweiterte sich der Kreis im Falle der Rechtschreibung auch um Nichtmitglieder wie Bohse u. Philipp v. Zesen (FG 521. 1648) und Fruchtbringer wie Georg Philipp Harsdörffer (FG 368), Diederich v. dem Werder (FG 31), Hans v. Dieskau, Curt v. Einsiedel u. andere namentlich nicht genannte „anwesende", d. h. in u. um Köthen greifbare Gesellschafter. S. 450504. Vgl. etwa 440127 K 1, 440209, 440317 K 5 u. 450506A sowie die Korrekturen F. Ludwigs 440200 (im Materialienband *DA Köthen I. 9*).

K I Antwort auf 450506A. Beantwortet durch 450508. — Die Bereitschaft Christian Gueintz' (FG 361. Der Ordnende) zu einem Besuch F. Ludwigs in Köthen hat der Fürst vernommen. Er kündigt an, ihn am kommenden Montag, den 12.5., in Halle abholen zu lassen. In der Zwischenzeit möge Gueintz die überschickte Rechtschreibung auch Hans v. Dieskau (FG 212. Der Tilgende) vorlegen, damit er sie kritisch durchsehe u. sein Urteil darüber rechtzeitig unterbreite.
1 Die Zusammenkunft in Köthen, um mit Christian Gueintz (FG 361. Der Ordnende) strittige Fragen der deutschen Rechtschreibung zu klären u. den Druck der *Deutschen Rechtschreibung* zu beschleunigen, hatte F. Ludwig in 450504 vorgeschlagen. Der danach vereinbarte Termin des 12.5. wurde anscheinend auf den 13. oder 14.5. verschoben. S.

450508. Vgl. auch 450506A u. 450507. Da aus der Zeit bis 451219 keine weiteren Stücke aus der Korrespondenz zwischen F. Ludwig u. Gueintz überliefert sind, bleiben Termin, Verlauf u. Ergebnis der Köthener Unterredung unbestimmt.

2 Vgl. dazu das zeitgleiche Schreiben 450507 an Hans v. Dieskau (FG 212. Der Tilgende), dem der vorliegende Brief beilag. Ein Gutachten Dieskaus zu Fragen der dt. Rechtschreibung konnte nicht nachgewiesen werden. Dieskau könnte, wie Curt v. Einsiedel (FG 417), sein Urteil Gueintz mündlich mitgeteilt haben. Vgl. 450506A.

450507A

Landgraf Hermann IV. von Hessen-Rotenburg an Fürst Ludwig

Lgf. Hermann IV. v. Hessen-Rotenburg (FG 374) bedankt sich für F. Ludwigs Brief vom 5.3.1645 (recte 17.3.1645) und das darin beigelegte Bücherverzeichnis. Wie gewünscht, aber vergeblich, habe er bei Druckern und Buchhändlern in Kassel nachgefragt, ob sie Köthener Drucke gegen andere F. Ludwig gemäße Bücher tauschen oder auf andere Weise erwerben wollten. Vielmehr habe er erfahren, daß in der Hauptsache Schulbücher das Kasseler Angebot bestimmten und daß der Verleger (Johann Schütz) Bedenken trage, sich mit den Köthener Drucken Ladenhüter einzuhandeln. Nach Meinung Lgf. Hermanns wäre es besser, selbst einen Verantwortlichen während der kommenden Frankfurter Messe abzustellen, der dort wohl größere Aussichten auf Erfolg hätte.

Q LHA Sa.-Anh./ Dessau: Z 70 Abt. Köthen A 9a Nr. 26ᵈ, Bl. 8rv [A: 8v]; Schreiberh.; Sig.

A *Dem hochgebornen Fursten, Herrn* Ludwigen, Fursten zue Anhalt, Graven zu Aßcanien, Herren zu Zerbst vndt Bernburg, Vnsern freundtlichen Lieben H. Vettern vnd Schwagern. Cöthen
Eigenh. Empfangsvermerk F. Ludwigs: Pres. 25. Maij 1645.

Vnsern freundlichen dienst, auch was wihr mehr liebs undt guts vermögen iederzeit zuvor, Hochgeborner Fürst, freundlicher Lieber Vetter vndt Schwager

E. Lbd. ahngenehmes handtbrieflein vom 5*ten* verwichenen Monats Martij¹, neben dem mit vberschikten verzeichnus derer bey E. Lbd. vorhandener bucher, ist vnß wohl zu kommen Vndt haben nicht vnderlassen vnß zu Caßell bey denjenigen so mit der truckerey vnd dem Buchhandel umbgehen, mit fleis zubemuhen, ob denen nicht etwa theilß gegen andere so E. L. ahnstendig, außgetauscht o*der* sonstet abgenommen werden könten, wihr haben aber darinnen nichts zu erhalten vermocht, sondern ist vns die antwortt zuruck kommen, daß deß ortß izo sonderlich nichts alß mehrentheils schuelbucher vorhanden wehren, zu deme dem Buchfuhrer² auch bedenklich solche bucher außzutausch*en*, die ihme demnach leichtlich liegen pleiben vnd er dadurch in schad*en* gerath*en* möchte,³

Hielten derowe*gen* vnuorgreifflich darfur, wan E. L. gegen kunfftige *Frankfurter* messe jemanden daselbst hin abgefertigt hetten,⁴ daß Sie denn wohl loß werden durfften, Vnd habens E. Lbd. zu nachrichtlicher wieder antwort nechst göttlicher entpfelung nicht verhalten wollen, dero wihr zu ahngenehmen freundvetterlichen diensten iederzeit willig vnd geflißen verpleiben, **Datum** Rottenburgk am 7ten May Anno. 1645

Von Gottes gnaden Herman Landgrave zu Heßen, Grave zu Catzenelnbogen
El. dienstwilliger Vetter vnd sohn Herman Lzh.

K 1 Ein solcher Brief ist unbekannt. Der Inhalt des vorliegenden Briefs paßt zu F. Ludwigs Schreiben 450317 an Lgf. Hermann IV. v. Hessen-Rotenburg (FG 374). Dieser könnte das Datum mit dem des Schreibens Winands v. Polhelm an F. Ludwig (450305) verwechselt haben, da Polhelm (FG 405) den Landgrafen davon informiert haben dürfte.

2 Es handelt sich sehr wahrscheinlich um den in 440809A K 4 u. ö. genannten Johann (Hans) Schütz, Kasseler Buchbinder u. Verleger.

3 Vier Jahre zuvor bat F. Ludwigs Kammermeister Peter Knaudt den Leipziger Verleger Andreas Kühne (s. 450124 K 2) um Mithilfe beim Verkauf schwer absetzbarer Drucke aus der Ratichianischen Schulreform u. der Frühzeit der FG, die auch im Katalog zur Herbstmesse 1641 aufgeführt wurden. S. die Bücherliste in 410313 K 3.

4 So wie F. Ludwig einst Johann Le Clerq als Buchhändler abgeschickt hatte. S. 210421 K 6.

450508

Christian Gueintz an Fürst Ludwig

Antwort auf 450507 I. — Christian Gueintz (FG 361. Der Ordnende) bittet F. Ludwig (Der Nährende) um Verschiebung seiner (für den 12. Mai geplanten) Reise nach Köthen auf den 13. oder 14. Mai, da er am 12. Mai eine Rechnung abzulegen habe.

Q HM Köthen: V S 545, Bl. 189rv [A: 189v]; eigenh., A von Schreiberhand; Sig. — *D:* Nicht in *KE* u. *KL* III.

A *Dem Nährenden* etc.

Es wird der Nährende es gnädig vermercken daß, weil des Montags alhier eine rechnung abzulegen, möchte biß Dienstag oder Mittwoch die reise verschoben werden. Alßdan wil sich willig einstellen und gehorsam aufwarten

Des Nährenden
unterthäniger Ordnender *mp.*

Hall den 8 Meyens 1645[a]

T a *Die Jahresziffer* 1645 *sieht aufgrund einer starken Verschnörkelung am Ende wie* 1642 *oder* 1647 *aus, ist jedoch als* 1645 *zu erkennen. Zudem deutet die Absage des Montagstermins im Mai klar auf* 450507 I *als Bezugsschreiben.*

K Zum Zwecke einer Klärung strittiger Rechtschreibfragen u. zur Beschleunigung der Drucklegung der *Deutschen Rechtschreibung* hatte F. Ludwig (Der Nährende) Christian

Gueintz (FG 361. Der Ordnende) zu einer persönlichen Unterredung nach Köthen gebeten u. dafür den 12. Mai vorgeschlagen. Vgl. 450507 I. Aufgrund des Mangels an nachfolgenden Stücken der F. Ludwig-Gueintz-Korrespondenz liegen uns keine Zeugnisse über das Treffen vor.

450508A

Fürst Johann Casimir von Anhalt-Dessau an Fürst Ludwig

F. Johann Casimir v. Anhalt-Dessau (FG 10) teilt mit, am folgenden Tage, nur von seinem Hofmeister (Christian Heinrich v.) Börstel (FG 407) und zwei Dienern begleitet und ohne Wissen seiner Gemahlin Fn. Agnes (TG 25), F. Ludwig auf dessen Wunsch zu besuchen. Er bittet, daß dazu der Ölberger zur Verfügung stehe.

Q LHA Sa.-Anh./ Dessau: Z 70 Abt. Köthen A 9a Nr. 25, Bl. 165r–166v [A: 166v], 165v u. 166r leer; eigenh.; Sig.

A A Monsieur mon treshonore oncle Monsieur Le Prince Louis Prince d'Anhalt. à Cöten
Eigenh. Empfangsvermerk F. Ludwigs: Pres: 8. Mey. 1645.

Hochgebohrner Fürst, freundtlicher hochgeehrter Herr Vetter vndt gefatter

Auff dero freundtliches ersuchen will Jch mich morgen Mittage incontuite¹ meiner hl Gemahlin^a bei E Lbd. einstellen bitte aber vor den Ohlberger², Jch bringe niemandes mehr mitt als hoffmeister Börstel³ vnd 2 diener empfehle hiemitt E. Lbd Gottes schutz mich aber zu dero beharlichen affection als

E Lbd treuer Vetter Johann Casimir Fzu Anhalt Mpp

Dessau den 8 Maji 1645

T a *Folgt* <mich>

K Über den Anlaß der Reise ist uns nichts bekannt. Ob sich F. Johann Casimir v. Anhalt-Dessau (FG 10) bei dieser Gelegenheit das gewünschte medizin. Mistelpräparat abgeholt hat, um das er einen Monat zuvor gebeten hatte? S. 450408.
1 Französ. abgeleitet von lat. „contueri", erblicken, gewahr werden, betrachten, Part. Perf. „contuitus"; mlat. auch beschirmen; die Vorsilbe in- als Verneinungspartikel. *Diefenbach: Glossarium*, 148; vgl. auch Johann Matthias Gesner: Novus Linguae et Eruditionis Romanae Thesaurus. Tom. 1–4. Leipzig 1749, 1223; Adam Friedrich Kirsch: Abundantissimum Cornu Copiae Linguae Latinae et Germanicae Selectum. Leipzig 1774, 705 f. In der Lexikographie des älteren u. heutigen Französisch (und Italienisch) von uns nicht nachgewiesen. Im Zusammenhang des vorliegenden Briefes kann es wohl nur heißen, daß F. Johann Casimir den Besuch ohne Wissen seiner Frau antritt u. nicht etwa unbeschützt, also ohne bewaffnete Salvaguardia, mit seiner Frau.
2 Der „Ölberger", das zeremonielle Trinkgefäß bei Handlungen der FG, insbesondere beim Aufnahmeactus für neue Mitglieder, der Hänselung. Vgl. hier 460718 K 8; ferner *DA*

Köthen I. 5, S. 480 (Abb.) sowie 400312 K I 1; 410621 K 1 u. K 5; insgesamt das Lemma „Ölberger" im kumulierten Sachregister des vorliegenden Bandes.

3 Christian Heinrich v. Börstel (FG 407), Sohn des langjährigen Bernburger Regierungspräsidenten Heinrich v. Börstel (FG 78). Christian Heinrich diente seit 1642 als fl.-dessauischer Rat u. Hofmeister. In die FG wurde er 1644, vor dem 23. Juni, aufgenommen. S. *Conermann III*, 485 f. Vgl. auch 450408 K 1.

450509

Matthias Götze an Johann Hammer

(Der Leipziger Verleger) Matthias Götze bestätigt und quittiert, vom (Leipziger) Ratsmitglied Johann Hammer die im Auftrag F. Ludwigs (von Hans Beyer) übermittelten 200 Rth. und ein Kästlein mit Kupfern (für das *GB 1646*) erhalten zu haben. Beides, Geld- und Sachmittel, seien für Matthäus Merian d. Ä. in Frankfurt a. M. bestimmt.

Q HM Köthen: V S 546, Bl. 29rv, v leer; eigenh. — *D: Bircher: Merian*, 699 (datiert April 1645). — *BN: Bürger*, 468 Nr. 1 (dto.).

A *Fehlt.*

Das mir endesbenandtem der wohl Ehrenvheste, hochAchtbare vndt wohlweise Herr Johann Hammer des Raths alhier wegen Jhr. Fürstlichen Gnaden zu Anhaltt vndt Cöthen, zweyhundert thaler, wie auch ein Kästlein mit Kupfer[1], welche Herr Merian in Frankfurdt am Mayn haben soll, außgezalt vnd gelieferth, thue ich hiermit bekennen, vnd gebürlichen darüber quittiren.

Geschehen im ostermarckt 1645.[2]

Matthias Götze[3] *mppa*

K 1 Das kleine „Kästlein" wird in mehreren Briefen angesprochen. Es enthielt die (alten) Kupferplatten des *GB 1629/30* u. wurde zusammen mit den 200 Rth. versandt, die für Hz. August d. J. v. Braunschweig-Wolfenbüttel (FG 227) zur Verlagsfinanzierung des *GB 1646* durch den Braunschweiger Kaufmann Hans Beyer vorgestreckt wurden. S. 450503, 450510, 450614, 450711, 450800. Zu den Verlagsbeiträgen s. allgemein 450126 K 4. Eine Übersicht über die den Zahlungsverkehr betreffenden Briefdokumente in 450127 K 1. Zum *GB 1646* s. 440130 K 3. Beyer hatte lt. 450503 F. Ludwigs Quittung (bereits im April) über die von Hz. August versprochenen 200 Rth. Verlagsbeitrag (vgl. 450331) empfangen u. die von ihm vorgestreckte Summe an das Leipziger Ratsmitglied Johann Hammer über Christof Albrecht angewiesen, wobei er 1 Rth. Provision für sich abzog (450503). Hammer berichtete in 450510 F. Ludwigs Kammermeister Peter Knaudt, er habe die ursprüngliche Summe (200 Rth.) komplettiert u. dem Leipziger Verleger u. Handelsmann Matthias Götze voll ausgezahlt, ihm auch die (auf Sendung F. Ludwigs bzw. Knaudts) bei ihm eingetroffenen Kupferplatten (zu den ersten 200 Impresenstichen, die das *GB 1629/30* versammelte, s. o.) übergeben. In 450419 hatte Hammer Knaudt einen Brief Beyers an ihn, Hammer, mitgesandt, in dem Beyer möglicherweise das Zahlungsprozedere, Höhe der Provision etc. bestätigte. Merian designierte Peter Knaudt Götze statt Johann Press als Empfänger der 200 Rth. u. der Kupfer. Götze quittierte Hammer mit dem vorliegenden Schriftstück den Empfang von Geld u. Kupferplatten spätestens am 9. oder

10.5.1645. Götze berichtete Knaudt am 14.6.1645, daß er das Kästlein mit den Platten sofort durch den Schmalkaldener Fuhrmann Caspar Frevol an den Stecher, Drucker u. Kunstverleger Matthäus Merian d. Ä. in Frankfurt a. M. geschickt habe. S. 450614. F. Ludwig mußte den Wolfenbütteler Herzog in 450721 nochmals zur Begleichung seiner Schuld mahnen. Da hatte Merian schon 200 Rth. u. die Kupferplatten erhalten, wie er in 450711 Knaudt mitteilte. Vgl. Knaudts Antwort in 450800.

2 Die Ostermesse begann in Leipzig gewöhnlich mit Jubilate, dem dritten Sonntag nach Ostern, u. dauerte zwei Wochen bis Rogate, was bedeutet, daß der Markt im Jahre 1645 am 27.4. seinen Anfang nahm u. mit dem 11.5.1645 endete. Vgl. Wolfgang Borm: Catalogi Nundinales 1571–1852. Die Frankfurter und Leipziger Meßkataloge der Herzog August Bibliothek Wolfenbüttel. Wolfenbüttel 1982, S.14 Anm.3 u. Taschenbuch der Zeitrechnung des deutschen Mittelalters und der Neuzeit. Hg. Theodor Ulrich, entworfen v. Hermann Grotefend. Hannover 1971, 174. Die zweite Woche war traditionell die Zahlwoche. *Zedler* XXV, Sp.2315; *Krünitz* LXXVII, 8. Bereits in 450510 wird die im vorliegenden Brief verhandelte Transaktion als abgeschlossene bezeichnet: „Darmit nun 200 th. Per F[rank]fordt gemacht werden, habe ich Herrn Mathes Götzen solche 200 th. vor voll bezalt". Folgt man dem an Leipziger Ereignissen orientierten Werk von Johann Jacob Vogel: Leipzigisches Geschicht-Buch oder Annales, Das ist: Jahr und Tage-Bücher Der Weltberühmten … Kauff- und Handels-Stadt Leipzig: In welchen die meisten merckwürdigsten Geschichte und geschehene Veränderungen, die … von Anno 661. nach Christi Geburth an, biß in das 1714. Jahr … enthalten sind. Leipzig 1714, passim (s. Register Lemma ‚Ostermesse' [HAB: Gm 2° 97]), dann gab es aufgrund der Kriegsläufte in den Jahren vor 1645 erstmals seit 250 Jahren Verschiebungen, mithin sogar Ausfälle der Leipziger Märkte. So heißt es mit Bezug auf den Ostermarkt 1639, ebd. S.566: „Nach geendigten Oster-Feyertagen/ hat E. E. Rath unterm Rahthause ein Patent anhengen lassen/ Des Inhalts: Daß der Ostermarckt/ der sonst Jubilate gefällig/ wegen des Feindes vielfältigen Streiffen/ biß auf Trinitatis/ war der 9 Junii/ solte prorogiret und auffgeschoben werden/ welches in 252 Jahren nicht geschehen"; ein Jahr später wurde die Verschiebung von Jubilate auf Trinitatis „wegen abermals eingebrochener Kriegs-Gefahr" wiederholt. Ebd., 572. 1642 wurde der Ostermarkt immerhin noch „acht Tage lang prorogiret". Ebd., 581. Der Neujahrsmarkt 1643 fiel aufgrund der kurz zuvor stattgefundenen Schlacht bei Breitenfeld (November 1642) sowie der Anwesenheit der schwed. Hauptarmee unter Torstensson, der bis kurz vor Jahresende über die Übergabe der Stadt Leipzig verhandelte, schlicht ganz aus; es heißt ohne genauere Angaben: Er „wird nicht gehalten", ebd., 604. Sowohl die Oster- als auch die Michaelismesse 1644 wurden zwar wie gewöhnlich eingeläutet, wegen Unsicherheit der Straßen aufgrund der umherziehenden ksl., kursächs. u. schwed. Truppen aber nicht wirklich gehalten. Ebd., 612 u. 616. Der Neujahrsmarkt 1645 wurde auf Anweisung der schwed. Besatzer Leipzigs aufgrund der Einquartierung der schwed. Hauptarmee in Kursachsen verschoben bis Lichtmeß (2. Februar). Ebd., 617. Vgl. 450124 K 2. Erst der Ostermarkt 1645 erfolgte wieder in gewohnter Weise. S. allgemein Manfred Straube: Die Leipziger Messen im Dreißigjährigen Krieg. In: Uwe John, Josef Matzerath (Hg.): Landesgeschichte als Herausforderung und Programm. FS für Karlheinz Blaschke zum 70. Geburtstag. Stuttgart 1997, 421–441.

3 Matthias Götze (1585–1662), Buchhändler u. Bürger zu Leipzig. Aus Lobstädt bei Borna stammend war er 1602 in den Dienst des Leipziger Buchhändlers Thomas Schürer (1563–1615) getreten, dessen älteste Tochter Catharina (†1631) er 1619 ehelichte. Aus dieser Verbindung erwuchsen zwei Kinder (Sohn u. Tochter) u. 12 Enkel. Besonders erwähnenswert erscheint hier der Sohn, Thomas Matthias Götze (1623–1672), der 1644 wiederum Merians Tochter Margaretha heiratete. 1624 übernahm Matthias Götze zusammen mit seinem Schwager Zacharias Schürer (1597–1629) das Verlagsunternehmen seines verstorbenen Schwiegervaters, welches er nach dessen Tod im Namen der Schürerischen Erben weiterführte. S. Leichenpredigt auf ihn: Martin Geier: Lebens-Buch ... Des Weyland EhrenVesten und Wohlfürnehmen Hn. Matthiæ Götzens (Leipzig: Köhler 1662), Bl. F v – [F iv] r (Lebenslauf). HAB: J 49 Helmst. 4°. S. auch *Wüthrich: Merian Briefe*, 89 Anm. 6. Der Sohn Thomas Matthias wird in 420712 K 1 als Verleger der zweiten Gesamtausgabe *Sachse: Einhelligkeit* von 1662 erwähnt u. avancierte in dieser Zeit, den 1660er Jahren, zum wohlhabendsten Buchhändler in Deutschland.

450510

Johann Hammer an Peter Knaudt

Der Leipziger Handelsmann und Ratsangehörige Johann Hammer bestätigt, den (nicht mehr nachweisbaren) Brief Peter Knaudts vom 6.5.1645 erhalten zu haben. Die 199 Rth. seien zwischenzeitlich vom Braunschweiger Kaufmann Hans Beyer an Hammer übermittelt worden, was Knaudt aus der Anlage ersehen könne. Damit wiederum der Gesamtbetrag von 200 Rth. nach Frankfurt gesandt werden könne, habe Hammer an Matthias Götze die volle Summe bezahlt und 1 Rth. als Schuld notiert. Das Kistlein sei auch übergeben worden. Hammer teilt mit, Knaudts Brief Götze gezeigt zu haben. — Die gewünschten Waren standen bereit, ein Fuhrmann sei schon bestellt gewesen, der habe dieselben jedoch stehenlassen. Hammer versichert jedoch, diese am selben oder am folgenden Tag abtransportieren zu lassen.

Q HM Köthen: V S 546, Bl. 25rv [A: 25v]; eigenh., A von Schreiberh.; keine Siegelspuren erkennbar. — *D: Bircher: Merian*, 700. — *BN: Bürger*, 670 Nr. 2.

A *Titul.* Herrn Peter Knaudten, fürstl. Anhält. Wohlbestalten Cammermeistern *etc.* Zue großg. Handen. Jn Cöthen

Ehrenvester Großachtbar wohlgelarter wohlfürnehmer Jnsonders Großg. Herr Cammermeister, hochgeehrter werther freündt, demselben seindt meine willige dinst vnd frl. gruß, bestes vermögens stets beuorn, deß Herrn geliebtes schreiben vom 6 dieß, wohl erhalten, Herr hanß Beyer[1] hatt mir 199 th. zahlen laßen, wie der Herr auß seinem beygehenden zusehen:[2] Darmit nun 200 th. Per F[rank]fordt gemacht werden, habe ich Herrn Mathes Götzen solche 200 th. vor voll bezalt. Den andern einen thaler Nottirt. Das kistle ist auch vbergeben,[3] deß herren brieff wegen deß Meistern[a] vetters[4] H Gözen[5] auch gewißen[6], wirdt also von mir seine richtigkeit haben.

Die begehrten wahren stehen gepackht, hatte ein Fuhrmann darzu, der leichte[7] vogel ließ mir solche stehn, vermein doch solchs datto oder morgen fortzubringen. Jn eill, Gott mit vnß allen. Leip*z*ig *d*en 10 May 1645.

Des herrn dienstwilliger hilfreicher
H. Hammer *mpa.*

T a *Lies:* Cammermeistern

K 1 Hans Beyer, Braunschweiger Handelsmann, in Finanzsachen wegen des *GB 1646* für Hz. August d.J. v. Braunschweig-Wolfenbüttel (FG 227) tätig. S. 450503 K 0. S. auch Anm. 3.

2 Nicht erhaltene Anlage des vorliegenden Schreibens. Vgl. 450503.

3 Vgl. zum mehrfach erwähnten „Kästlein" 450509 K 1. Es enthielt die (alten) Kupferplatten des *GB 1629/30* u. erreichte zusammen mit den (von Hz. August zu zahlenden u. vom Braunschweiger Handelsmann Beyer, s. Anm. 1, vorgestreckten) 200 Reichstalern (s. 450503, 450509) zur Finanzierung des *GB 1646* im Juli den Stecher Matthäus Merian d. Ä. Zum Zahlungsverkehr das *GB 1646* betreffend s. Anm. 5 u. 450127 K 1; zu den Verlagsbeiträgen s. 450126 K 4 u. zum *GB 1646* allgem. s. 440130 K 3.

4 Hier der Gebrauch des Begriffs „Vetter" als Anrede, die die Verbindung Peter Knaudts mit Matthias Götze durch das Projekt *GB 1646* betont. S. *DW* XII.2, 31 (3 c). S. auch Anm. 3.

5 Matthias Götze, Leipziger Verleger u. wichtige Kontaktperson in Sachen *GB 1646*. Im vorliegenden Band sind drei Briefe von ihm abgedruckt: 450509, 450614 u. 460810. S. auch Anm. 4 u. 450509 K 3.

6 *DW* IV.I.3, 5792 gewiesen, ostensus/ monstratus zu weisen.

7 Mit diesem Attribut wird auf das leichtfertige, unzuverlässige Verhalten des Fuhrmanns angespielt. S. *DW* VI, 638, Nr. 21: „leicht, locker, lose, unbeständig".

450526

Winand von Polhelm an Fürst Ludwig

Antwort auf 450506. — Winand (Weinand) v. Polhelm (FG 405) sendet die beiden Bücher (der Vulson-Übersetzung *Von des Pabstes gewalt*) wieder an F. Ludwig zurück und drückt sein Bedauern darüber aus, daß der Buchhändler in Kassel (Johann Schütz) die Werke so lange behalten und sie am Ende doch nicht in den Druck gegeben habe. Er hoffe, daß F. Ludwig ihm, Polhelm, weiterhin gnädig gesinnt bleibe und es ihm nicht übelnehme, daß er ihm — wegen eines so unzuverlässigen Mannes — seine Gewogenheit nicht habe unter Beweis stellen können. — Weder den zweiten Teil der „Ehescheidung" (Pallavicino: *Divortio Celeste*) in dt. oder in ital. Sprache noch die Abhandlung zur dt. Sprache des (Philander v.) Sittewald (Pseud. Johann Michael Moscheroschs, FG 436) habe er unter den Kasseler Drucken entdecken können. Sofern er dieser Werke habhaft werden könne, werde er sie F. Ludwig zusenden.

Q LHA Sa.-Anh./ Dessau: Z 70 Abt. Köthen A 9a Nr. 26ᵈ, Bl. 9rv [A: 9v]; eigenh. Mit eigenh. Empfangsvermerk F. Ludwigs.

A A Son Altesse Monsseigneur le Prince Louys d'Anhalt *etc.* Cothen
Empfangsvermerk F. Ludwigs: Eingeben den 10. Brachmonats 1645.

Durchleuchtigh Hochgeborner Gnediger Furst vnd Herr,
Ewfg. hab Jch bey dießer gelegenheit die beyde bewuste bucher[1] in vnderthenigkeit wieder zu ruckschicken sollen, Es ist mir leid daß der Buchhendtler in Caßell[2] daß werck so langh aufgehalten vnd sich doch endtlich zu nichts verstehen wollen; Lebe der vnderthenighen zuversicht, Ewfg. werden dero hohen bescheidenheit nach mir in keinen vngnaden aufnemen, daß eines solchen losen

450526 Winand von Polhelm

Mans halben Ewfg. meine vnderthenige diensten, wie gern gewolt hette, nicht habe erzeigen konnen,

Von dem andren theill der^a Ehescheidungh³ deutsch^b oder Jtälianisch^b, wie auch waß der Sittenwaldt wegen der deutschen sprach laßen außgehen⁴ davon hab zu Caßell nichts konnen zusehen bekomen, So fern aber ins kunftig etwaß davon solte habhafft werden, sols Ewfg. alsbaldt vnderthenigh zuschicken, Alß der Jch negst empfellungh Ewfg. der starcken obhutt Gottes, vnd ergebungh meiner in deroselben beharlichen gnadt, bin vnd verbleibe,

Ewfg.

Vndertheniger
Knecht
WeinandtVonPolhe[lm]^c

Caßell den 26 May 1645

T a *Durch hochgestellte Ziffern umgestellt aus* der deutschen oder Jtälianischen Ehescheidungh — b *Folgt* <en> — c *Textverlust im Falz.*

K 1 Die ersten beiden Bücher des unveröffentlicht gebliebenen Manuskripts *Von des Pabstes gewalt*, einer Übersetzung von Marc de Vulson sieur de La Collet: *De la puissance du pape et des libertés de l'Église Gallicane* (Genève 1635). S. 440809A K 6 u. 450317A.
    2 Johann Schütz, Buchbinder u. Verleger in Kassel. S. 440809A (K 4) u. ö.
    3 Diese Bemerkung bezieht sich auf Ferrante Pallavicinos (1615–1644) Satire gegen die Papstkirche unter Urban VIII.: IL | DIVORTIO | CELESTE, | CAGIONATO DALLE | dissolutezze della Sposa | Romana. | & | Consecrato alla simplicità de' | Scropolosi Christiani. | [Holzschnitt] | IN VILLAFRANCA [fingiert], | [Linie] | M.DC.XLIII. (HAB: Tm 486) sowie die Übersetzung ins Deutsche, wahrscheinlich von Georg Hans v. Peblis (FG 102): Himmlische Ehescheidung/ | Durch der Römischen | Braut leichtfertiges Leben verursacht. | An | Einfältige/ gar zugewissenhaffte Christen/ (newli- | cher Zeit von einem Bäpstischen Welschen Edelmann in | seiner Muttersprach) außgelassen/ | An jetzo aber | Auffs new in die Hochteutsche fleissig | vbergesetzet/ | Sampt zweyen von der Herrschafft Vene- | dig/ (einem vnterm 25. May jüngsthin an dero Abge- | sandte vnd Residenten an der Potentaten Höfen; vnd dem an- | dern vnterm 7. Höwmonat nechsthin/ an die Regenten jhrer Städt | auff dem Land/ abgegangnen/ vnd die Vrsachen/ wie auch | den Zweck der newen Welschen Liga in sich hal- | tende Schreiben. | [Rundes Signet: Landkarte, von Tierkreiszeichen eingerahmt] | Jm Jahr M. DC. XLIII. HAB: 57.10 Pol. (6) [auch dig.] u. 185.1 Theol (7). S. *DA Köthen I. 6*, S.15f., 431021 (K 1 u. 2) u. 431022 (K 2). Johann Valentin Andreae spricht bereits im Mai 1643 Hz. August d.J. v. Braunschweig-Wolfenbüttel (FG 227) gegenüber, daß ein 2. u. 3. Teil des ital. Originals „auf der bahn" seien, u. im Oktober des gleichen Jahres meldet Hz. August, daß er das „Italianische Divortium" von seinem Agenten Philipp Hainhofer erhalten habe. S. 431021 K 2. F. Ludwig suchte die Fortsetzung vielleicht noch 1646 in Paris bei Gabriel Naudé zu ermitteln. S. 460103 K 6. Daß sich mehrere Personen dieser Übersetzung der *Divortio celeste* widme(te)n, kommt noch einige Jahre später im Briefwechsel Georg Philipp Harsdörffers (FG 368) mit Heinrich v. Schwechhausen (FG 532. 1651) zur Sprache. Harsdörffer wünscht dem Gleichgefärbeten (Wilhelm Heinrich v. Freyberg. FG 439) am 30.10.1651 Glück u. Erfolg bei der Verdolmetschung der „Englischen Andachten. Wann es von Joseph Halls Arbeit ist, so

hat, wie ich vernommen, ein Geistlicher zu Hanau eben die selbigen auch unterhanden: ist es aber ein andrer Autor, so stehet es dahin, und könte es gehen, wie mit dem Divortio Celeste, die drey zugleich geteutschet, weil keiner von dem andern gewust; deßwegen die Freundschaft derer die Bücher schreiben, nicht nur löblich sondern auch nohtwendig ist." Erzschrein Weimar, 1. Bd.: ThHSTA Weimar: Kunst und Wissenschaft — Hofwesen A 11817[1], Bl. 53r–54v, hier 53v.

4 Könnte es sich um die folgende, seit 1644 in Meßkatalogen angezeigte, aber erst später (namentlich von Hans Caspar Hermann) vervollständigte u. publizierte Schrift Moscheroschs handeln? Technologie Allemande & Françoise Das ist/ Kunst-übliche Wort-Lehre Teutsch und Frantzösisch. Vortgesetzt Durch H. C. H. [Hans Caspar Hermann] (Straßburg: Josias Stähel 1656). HAB: 394.77 Quod. S. 440616 K I 0. Wahrscheinlicher erscheint jedoch unter Einbeziehung der Formulierung „was der Sittenwaldt wegen der deutschen sprach laßen außgehen" die von Moscherosch unter seinem Pseudonym veröffentlichte menippeische Satire *Moscherosch: Gesichte Philanders von Sittewald*. Moscherosch traf Polhelm in Paris, s. 450818 (n. St.?). F. Ludwig bat Moscherosch durch Harsdörffer in 450919A um eine authentische Ausgabe der Satire, um sie von den zahlreichen Nachdrukken unterscheiden zu können. In 460406 teilte Harsdörffer F. Ludwig mit, daß Johann Michael Moscheroschs *Gesichte Philanders von Sittewald* in Straßburg noch einmal gedruckt werden sollen. Da die von Moscherosch durchgesehene Neuauflage erst 1650 erschien, konnte Polhelm sie nicht unter den Kasseler Büchern finden. F. Ludwig hatte Lgf. Hermann IV. v. Hessen-Rotenburg (FG 374) in 450317 einen Tausch von Köthener u. Kasseler Büchern vorgeschlagen. Er kam nicht zustande. Auch Ludwigs Wunsch nach der Pallavicino-Übersetzung (s. Anm. 3) konnte nicht erfüllt werden.

450529

Fürst Ludwig an Georg Philipp Harsdörffer

Antwort auf 450400. Beantwortet durch 450817. — F. Ludwig (Der Nährende) bedankt sich für den Brief Georg Philipp Harsdörffers (FG 368. Der Spielende) und die mitgeschickten Beilagen, die er am 9.5. empfangen habe. Besonderen Dank spricht er für die ihm erteilte Widmung der zweiten Auflage des ersten Teils der *Frauenzimmer-Gesprächspiele* (1644) aus, was bei erster Gelegenheit zu entgelten er nicht vergessen werde. Hinsichtlich der übersandten Personentableaus zu den zwei Freudenspielen über die Logik und die Rhetorik halte man im Kreise einiger FG-Mitglieder dafür, die im Rhetorik-Stück eingeführten Zech- oder Bierbrüder besser „Spielleute" zu nennen, die ja nach Maßgabe des Kapellmeisters den jeweiligen Takt zu halten hätten. Schließlich schütte die Hippokrene nicht Bier oder Wein aus, sondern schenke im Schlafe gute Einfälle. Diese Hinweise könnten, da sich der fünfte Teil der *Gesprächspiele* schon in der Drucklegung befinde, vielleicht noch berücksichtigt werden, bevor der Fürst den 5. Teil nach seinem Erscheinen mit Vergnügen und Wohlwollen lesen werde. — Die Frage Harsdörffers, ob Einwände gegen eine Mitgliedschaft in Philipp v. Zesens (FG 521. 1648) durch Rosen versinnbildlichte DG bestünden, wird von F. Ludwig verneint. Grundsätzlich erlaube die FG jedermann, anderen Gesellschaften beizutreten, sofern deren Ziele den fruchtbringerischen nicht widersprächen. Die Entscheidung liege also ganz bei Harsdörffer. — Über Zesens neuerungssüchtige Rechtschreibung und die Vielzahl unpassender Neologismen lege seine jüngst in Amsterdam erschienene Übersetzung des *Ibrahim Bassa* (1645) hinreichend Zeugnis ab. Hinsichtlich der für Harsdörffer vorgesehenen DG-Imprese — auf einem Eisbrecher ein Bootsmann, der auf einen Rosenkranz zuhält — erinnert der Fürst daran, daß sich eine derartige Weitläufigkeit für Embleme oder Sinnbilder nicht recht eigne. Auch über diesen Hinweis möge Harsdörffer nachdenken. — Allerdings sei zu überlegen, wie Zesen von seinen Eigenwilligkeiten abzubringen und einem vernünftigen Konsens zuzuführen sei, zumal seine Übersetzung als gewandt und stilistisch flüssig zu bewerten sei. Vielleicht helfe bei einer Mäßigung Zesens die (von Christian Gueintz [FG 361] aufgesetzte) kurze *Deutsche Rechtschreibung* (1645), die nach kritischer Durchsicht in Kreisen der FG zum Druck gebracht worden sei und demnächst erscheinen werde. — Im Zusammenhang mit den von Harsdörffer projektierten „Andachts-Gemähle[n]" sei Vorsicht geboten: (Bildliche) Äußerlichkeiten dürften keinesfalls vom inneren Gottesdienst ablenken. Die Arbeit Harsdörffers werde gleichwohl für wertvoll und löblich befunden. — F. Ludwig läßt ihm die gewünschte aktuelle Liste der FG-Mitglieder nach Klar- und Gesellschaftsnamen zukommen. Diese Liste dürfe nur diskret von Harsdörffer und Hans Philipp (v.) Geuder (FG 310. Der Ergänzende) verwendet werden.

Q HM Köthen: V S 545, Bl. 311r–312v [A: 311v], 312r leer, 312v Notizen von FLs Hand, die politische Beratungen betreffen, kein fruchtbring. Kontext; Abschrift von Schreiberh. mit Korrekturen F. Ludwigs. — Bl. 310rv, eigenh. Konzept F. Ludwigs, undat. Zit. mit der Sigle K. — D: *KE*, 337–339; *KL* III, 261 f. (Auszug). — BN: Bürger, 950 Nr. 55.

A *In Kurzform am Ende des Briefes, s. dort.*

Vom Spielenden

Jst dem Nehrenden ein brieflein mit etlichen überschickten gedruckten Büchern den 9. dieses Monats wol überreichet worden.[a]

Es bedancket sich der *Nehrende* gegen dem *Spielenden* solcher übersendung[b], insonderheit aber wegen der übereignung des neu aufgelegten ersten theils seiner gesprächspiele,[1] wird es auch gegen Jhme, bey erster begebenheit, zu erkennen unvergeßen sein.

Über[c] den[d] entwurf der Personen zu[e] den[f] Freudenspielen[g] von der Verstand- und RednerLehre ist[h] etlicher[i] Geselschafter[j] meinung[k] vernommen worden, die darfür gehalten, das bey der RednerLehre die also genante Zech oder Bierbrüder füglicher die Spielleute könten genennet werden, weil solche doch das maß, auf unterschiedene arten, müßen in acht nehmen, darzu[l] sie ihr Musicus[e], Cappel-[,][e] Singe- oder Spielmeister mit dem stabe anweiset.[2]

Man findet auch nicht das[m] der Heliconische Musenbrunne[3] bier oder Wein[n], und[o] also zu zechen oder[p] zu bieren[4] ursache[q], wol aber sonsten[r] im schlaffe[s], gute einfälle gegeben, Wird demnach[t] das fünfte theil der Gesprächspiele, weil es schon im vollen[u] Drucke[v], wan es fertig, mit[w] dieser erinnerung, gerne[x] gesehen und gelesen werden.

Betreffende[y] des Cæsii ansinnen an den *Spielenden*, ihn in seine so genante[z] Deutschgesinte genoßenschaft, die[aa] nur auf Rosen sol gewidmet sein,[5] zu nehmen,[ab] darüber des *Nehrenden* gut befinden begeret wird. So erinnert sich zwar der *Nehrende*, das die Fruchtbringende Geselschaft[ac] niemande, was würden und standes er auch sey,[ad] verbeut und wehret anderer[ae] Geselschaft sich zu enteußern und zuentschlagen, wan sie nur ihrem[af] Zwecke nicht entgegen seind, also auch diese einwilligung bloß in des Spielenden Zuneigung und freyem willen beruhet. Weil es aber fast scheinet, als wan **Cæsius** gar etwas[ag] neues in der Deutschen **Orthographi**, oder Wortschreibung[ah] für hat, so zimlich weit gesuchet,[ai] auch[aj] in etzlichen neu aufgebrachten und nicht alzu wol erfundenen wörtern bestehet, inmaßen sein verdeutschter Jbrahim, in diesem Jhare zu Amsterdam gedruckt,[6] mit mehrern ausweiset: Zu deme der[ak] vorgeschlagene Nahme des Durchbrechenden Bohtsmannes, der durch das eis nach dem RosenKrantze schiffet, etwas weitleuftig, und wie [311v] der *Spielende* weis, sich[al] ein uberflüßiges[am] gemälde[an] in den **Emblematibus** oder Sinnebildern[ap] nicht wol[aq] schicken wil[ar], so wird auch dieses zu des *Spielenden* fernerem nachsinnen gestellet;[as] [7]

auf die mittel ist aber[at] zugedencken, Wie[au] vorgedachter **Cæsius** der sonsten in seiner Verdeutschung läuffig, und in[av] der feder flußig, zuvor[aw] vollend zur rechtmeßigen[ax] gleichförmigkeit[ay] möge[az] gebracht werden. Worzu vielleicht das jenige[ba] dienen sol, so auf gut befinden und nach[bb] behöriger Durchsehung der Fruchtbringenden Geselschaft an ietzo dem[bc] Drucke, wiewol kurtz verfaßet,[bd] als eine deutsche Rechtschreibung, untergeben[be], und bald[bf] herauskommen sol.[8]

Bey den vorgeschlagenen andachts gemählden[9] wird ingleichen gute Vorsichtigkeit zugebrauchen sein, damit solche[bg] selbst erfundene Vorbildungen den[bh] Menschen von dem innerlichen rechten[bi] Gottesdienste[bj], durch das eußerliche, wie meistentheils zugeschehen pfleget, nicht verleiten und abführen; Sonsten des *Spielenden* guter fürsatz in fernerer fortstellung seiner wol Spielenden[bk] arbeit wehrt[bl] gehalten und gerühmet wird[e], auch demselben die begehrten Tauf- und Geselschaft[bm] Nahmen hiermit[bn] volkömlich bis auf diese[bo] Zeit zugesendet werden,[10] die er aber, wie man nicht zweifelt, für sich und den Ergäntzenden[bp], der[bq] auch hiermit vom Nehrenden gegrüßet[br] wird, ohne weitleuftigkeit, geselschaft weise zugebrauchen, wormit verbleibet[bs] des *Spielenden*

gantz[bt] williger

[bu]Cöthen den 29. May monat 1645.

[bv]Georg Philips Harsderfern
in Nurnberg
zu handen.[bw]

T a *Die Zierschrift endet im Original mit dem ersten Zeilenwechsel.* — **b** *K folgt* <wegen> — **c** *Davor in K ein § zur Markierung des neuen Absatzes.* — **d** *K gebessert aus* der — **e** *In K eingefügt.* — **f** *Gebessert aus* dem *(unsichere Lesung). K gebessert aus* des — **g** *Gebessert aus* Freudenspiele *K gebessert aus* Freudenspiels — **h** *In K eingefügt für unleserlich gestrichenes Wort.* — **i** *In K gebessert aus* etlichen — **j** *Gebessert aus* Geselschaftern *(geselschaftern in K stehen geblieben).* — **k** meinung vernommen worden *in K am Rand ergänzt für* <uberschicket worden> — **l** *In K gebessert aus* darbey — **m** *In K folgt* <bey> — **n** *In K folgt* <gegeben> — **o** und also *in K eingefügt für* <oder> — **p** *In K eingefügt für* <und> —

q *In K folgt* <gegeben> — r *In K folgt unleserlich gestrichenes Wort.* — s *In K gebessert aus* schlaffen — t *In K eingefügt für* <also> — u *Gebessert aus* Vollem *In K eingefügt.* — v *Gebessert aus* Drucke<n> *Dieselbe Besserung in K.* — w mit dieser erinnerung *in K eingefügt.* — x *In K folgt* <auch> — y *In K geht ein § voraus, um den neuen Absatz zu markieren.* — z so genante *in K eingefügt.* — aa Bis sol gewidmet sein *in K eingefügt.* — ab *In K folgt* <wird> — ac *In K folgt ein Tintenfleck, der ein Wort verdeckt.* — ad *Folgt* <nicht> *(in K nicht gestrichen).* — ae *In K gebessert aus* ander — af *In K eingefügt für* <diesem> — ag *In K gebessert aus* was — ah *Gebessert aus* Rechtschreibung *(diese Besserung schon in K).* — ai *In K folgt* und — aj *Eingefügt von F. Ludwig für* <und nur> *In K bis* bestehet, am Rand *ergänzt für* <alzu neuerlich> *In der Randergänzung wurde dabei das eröffnende* auch *durch* und *ersetzt.* — ak *Gebessert aus* des *(diese Besserung schon in K).* — al sich ein <ein> uberflüssiges *eingefügt für* <so viel> — sich *fehlt hier in K.* — am *In K ein uberflüßiges eingefügt für* <so viel> — an *Gebessert aus* gemälde<s sich> — sich *in K eingefügt.* — ap *Folgt* <so gar> *In K folgt* <sich gar> — aq *Wörterreihenfolge durch Bezifferung geändert aus* wol nicht *Ebenso in K.* — ar *In K eingefügt für* <wollen> — as *Absatz nachträglich eingefügt durch F. Ludwig, markiert durch ein § am Rand und an dieser Stelle des Textes. In K folgt eingefügt* es ist aber *(unsichere Lesung).* — at ist aber *am Rand ergänzt von F. Ludwig.* — au *Gebessert aus unleserlich gewordenem Ausgangswort. Folgt* <etwa> *K* wie etwa — av in der feder flußig *eingefügt für* <ihme die feder sehr wol fleußet> *K* ihme die feder fleußet *dabei* fleußet *eingefügt für* <sehr wol fleußet> — aw *In der Abschrift u. in K eingefügt.* — ax *Von F. Ludwig eingefügt für das zuvor von ihm eingefügte* <förmigkeit> *Fehlt in K.* — ay *Gebessert aus* gleichsinnigkeit *(so auch in K). In K folgt* <in recht vollend> — az *Folgt* <zurechte> *(auch in K diese Streichung).* — ba *Gebessert aus* ienige — bb *In K das* n *von* nach *gebessert aus* d — bc *Von F. Ludwig eingefügt für* <zum> *K* zum — bd *In K folgt* <na[ch] nunmehr dem drucke [?]> — be *In K geht eine unleserliche Streichung voraus.* — bf *Eingefügt von F. Ludwig für* <kurtz> *K* bald *eingefügt für* <in kurtzen> — bg *In K Anfangsbuchstabe gebessert aus* d — bh den menschen *in K eingefügt.* — bi *K eingefügt für* <Got besten [?]> — bj *K* Gottesdiensten — bk *In K* wolspielenden *als Kompositum, dabei* wol *eingefügt für* <schön> — bl *In K eingefügt für* <hoch> — bm *In K eingefügt für* andere — bn *K* Hiemit — bo *Gebessert aus* die, *K* diese *(Tinte stark verwischt).* — bp *Gebessert aus* Ergetzenden *K* Ergentzenden — bq *In K bis* begrüßet wird *am Rand ergänzt.* — br *Gebessert aus* begrüßet — bs *Gebessert aus* verbleiben — bt *Ab hier eigenh. von F. Ludwig. Unterschrift fehlt.* — bu *Ab hier fehlt der Text in K.* — bv *Davor* <An> — bw *Text auf Bl. 412v:*

Zu berahtschlagen
Antwort an F. Christian [*F. Christian II. v. Anhalt-Bernburg. FG 51*] in der abschickung zum friedenstage.
    an F. Johansen [*F. Johann v. Anhalt-Zerbst. FG 398*]
Ob wegen F. Friedrichs [*von Anhalt-Harzgerode. FG 62*] und der angezogenen oder beschuldigten neuerung etwas zu warten. [*oder* endern *unsichere Lesung*]
Ob die contribution nach Ballenstedt ausgeschrieben und was darinnen ferner zuthun.
Vetter F. Chr. suchen wegen des kirchen baues zu Bernburg.

Weimarischer punct
Winningische sache
Pres[...?]
Schwedische

K F. Ludwig (Der Nährende) ergänzte die Abschrift seines vorliegenden Schreibens (das eigenh. Konzept ist undatiert) durch die Angabe des Datums, wobei der Tag durch einen heruntergezogenen Strich durch ihn wohl aus „20" in „29" verändert wurde. Da Georg Philipp Harsdörffer (FG 368. Der Spielende) in 450817 den Empfang zweier Briefe des Fürsten — vom 20. Mai u. 11. Juni — bestätigt, müßte diese Korrektur in der Ausfertigung übersehen oder erst nach der Ausfertigung nachgetragen worden sein.

1 Harsdörffer hatte F. Ludwig die 2. Auflage des ersten Teiles seiner *Frauenzimmer-Gesprächspiele* (1644, erste Ausg. 1641) mit einem „Vbereigungsgedicht [sic] AN den NEHRENDEN" gewidmet. S. 440616 K III 3, 440715 (K 10), 450400 K 4, 450611 (K 1), 450817 (K 11) u. 450919A.

2 Mit 440426 hatte Harsdörffer F. Ludwig die Personentableaus zu Freudenspielen über die Logik u. die Rhetorik gesandt u. um kritische Anmerkungen gebeten. Die Spiele erschienen ausgearbeitet im 5. Teil der *Frauenzimmer-Gesprächspiele* (1645, Ndr. 1969) unter den Titeln „Die Vernunftkunst" (Ndr., 200–397) u. „Die Redkunst" (Ndr., 451–591). Harsdörffer hatte im ursprünglichen Tableau der „Rhetorica" noch geplant, die Versfüße Daktylus, Jambus, Trochäus u. Spondäus personifiziert als „Zech- od*er* Bierbrü*der*" auftreten zu lassen, diese Rollen in der Druckversion dann jedoch kurzerhand gestrichen. Die Verbesserung „Spielleute" trug F. Ludwig auch eigenh. in das ihm vorab zugesandte Tableau ein. Vgl. 440426 I u. 450124.

3 Die mythische, vom Pegasushuf aufgeschlagene Quelle Hippokrene am Helikon, Apoll u. den Musen geweiht. Das Quellwasser sollte den Dichtern Begeisterung u. Imaginationskraft schenken. Vgl. *Hederich*, 1275.

4 Neologismus. Ein Verb „bieren" ist in der historischen u. gegenwärtigen Lexik des Deutschen u. auch in der mittelelb. Mundart nicht belegt. Vgl. 440426 I.

5 Die Rose war das „algemeine Zunftzeichen der gantzen Genossenschaft". Philipp v. Zesen: Hochdeutsches Helikonisches Rosentahl (1669), in: *Zesen SW* XII, 178–310, hier S. 197. Die Abbildung dieses DG-Zunftzeichens ebd., 219, mit einem Auslegungsgedicht von Zesen (FG 521. 1648; in der DG Der Färtige) (219f.). S. dazu 450400 K 9, zur DG allgemein ebd. K 8.

6 Zesen hatte seinen *Jbrahim Bassa* (1645), die Übersetzung des Romans *Ibrahim ou l'illustre Bassa* von Madeleine de Scudéry (erstmals 1641), der FG gewidmet, s. 441201. Die von F. Ludwig kritisierten orthographischen Neuerungen verzögerten Zesens Aufnahme in die FG erheblich. Vgl. 441201 K 0.

7 In 450400 hatte Harsdörffer F. Ludwig von Zesens Vorschlag berichtet, ihn als „den 𝔇urchbrechenden" in die DG aufzunehmen u. ihm als Imprese einen durch das Eis brechenden Bootsmann zu erteilen, der mit seinem Schiff nach einem Rosenkranz steuert. Das nach Zesens eigener späterer Auskunft auf bereits den 4.12.1644 festgelegte Aufnahmedatum Harsdörffers als 12. DG-Mitglied (Philipp [v.] Zesen: Hochdeutsches Helikonisches Rosentahl (1669) in *Zesen SW* XII, 178–310, hier S. 240f.), verschleiert die Unstimmigkeiten seiner Mitgliedschaft, sowohl was Harsdörffers inhaltliche Reserven (450410, vgl. dort K 24) als auch die Ende Mai noch offenen Fragen hinsichtlich seines DG-Namens u. seines DG-Sinnbilds angeht. Fest steht, daß Harsdörffer auch im *Helikonischen Rosentahl*, a. a. O., mit dem (neuen) Namen Der Kunstspielende u. einer neuen, einfacheren Imprese (lautenspielende Muse mit dem Wort: „Es ist lieblich / und löblich") aufgeführt wird. Ob F. Ludwigs Einwand mangelnder Einfachheit des ursprünglichen Sinnbilds zu einer Änderung der Imprese durch Harsdörffer beigetragen hat, bleibt spekulativ.

8 *Gueintz: Rechtschreibung (1645).* Dieses wichtige Referenzwerk der fruchtbringerischen Orthographiedebatte erschien im Spätsommer 1645. S. allgemein dazu 440127 K 1.

Die Vorrede ist auf den 12.8.1645 datiert. Mit 450919A schickte F. Ludwig Harsdörffer ein Druckexemplar zu. — Die zuvor ausgesprochene Anerkennung der Geläufigkeit der Zesenschen Übersetzung u. ihres Stils auch schon ähnlich in 450504.

9 Harsdörffer plante nach seiner Ankündigung in 450400, einhundert Andachtsgemälde, eine bestimmte, stärker textlastige Art geistlicher Embleme, zu verfassen. Die ersten zwölf erschienen als Beilage zum 6. Teil der *Frauenzimmer-Gesprächspiele* (1646, Ndr. 1969, 495–622). Später veröffentlichte er eine umfangreiche Sammlung von insgesamt 152 Andachtsgemälden meist jesuitischer Provenienz in seinen *Hertzbeweglichen Sonntagsandachten: Das ist/ Bild- Lieder- und Bet-Büchlein/ aus den Sprüchen der H. Schrifft/ nach den Evangeli- und Festtexten verfasset* (2 Bde., Nürnberg 1649 u. 1652; Ndr. hg. u. m. e. Nachwort vers. v. Stefan Keppler. Hildesheim [u.a.] 2007). Vgl. dazu 450400 K 11 u. 450817 u. I (ein hsl. Andachtsgemälde aus dem Köthener Erzschrein).

10 Die Mitgliederliste, die F. Ludwig seinem Brief beilegte, ist nicht erhalten. Sie umfaßte die Gesellschafts- u. Klarnamen der FG-Mitglieder „bis auf diese Zeit". Mit 450124 hatte F. Ludwig Harsdörffer bereits ergänzende Druckbögen zum *GB 1641* (und eine kurze hsl. Liste später aufgenommener Mitglieder) zugesandt. Das erweiterte *GB 1641/44* umfaßte damit die Impresen u. Initialen der FG-Mitglieder bis zu Curt v. Einsiedel (FG 417. 1644). Damit scheint Harsdörffer im Besitz eines Exemplars des *GB 1641/44* gewesen zu sein. Da Harsdörffer jedoch „die Namensbuchstaben nicht *v*erstehet", d.h. die Initialen offenbar nicht auflösen konnte, erbat er in 450400 eine aktuelle Liste der Gesellschafts- u. der Taufnamen, die mit dem ihm namentlich bekannten FG-Mitglied, Hans v. Rochow (FG 317. 1637) beginnt u. bis zum ihm offenbar ebenfalls bekannten Zacharias Prüschenk v. Lindenhofen (FG 418. 1644) reicht. Die jetzt überschickte Liste der Klarnamen der FG-Genossen müßte folglich mit Moritz Adolph v. Dehn-Rotfelser (FG 318. 1638) begonnen u. mit Hz. Friedrich v. Sachsen-Weimar (FG 432. 1645) geendet haben. Schon in 460916 wird Harsdörffer nämlich erneut um eine Fortsetzung „der Fruchtbringen*den* Gesellschafter von 433 an" bitten. Diese Mitgliedsnummer hatte Matthaeus (v.) Wesenbeck inne, u. F. Ludwig wird diese neuerliche Aktualisierung seinem Brief 461031 beilegen. Da sich als erstes Neumitglied 1646 Joachim v. Glasenapp (FG 451) ins *GB Kö.* eintrug u. sich die Aufnahme von Hz. Franz Erdmann v. Sachsen-Lauenburg (FG 459) auf November 1646 datieren läßt, wird diese neuerliche Ergänzungsliste maximal bis FG 458 (Bastian v. Wallwitz) gereicht haben. Vgl. 450400 K 12 u. 15. — Um ein Verzeichnis der jüngst aufgenommenen FG-Mitglieder hatte Harsdörffer in der Vergangenheit wiederholt nachgesucht: Erstmals ersuchte er F. Ludwig in 420311 — kurz nach seiner Aufnahme in die FG (s. dazu 411200 K 0) —, ihm u. seinem Nürnberger Freund Hans Philipp (v.) Geuder (FG 310. Der Ergänzende) eine Liste „deren vom Jahre 1638 eingetrettenen Geselschafter Namen" zukommen zu lassen, woraufhin F. Ludwig ihm mit 420503 einige Reimgesetze, aber wohl kein vollständiges Mitgliederverzeichnis übersandte. Darum fragte Harsdörffer in 430920 erneut um eine „fortsetzung des GeselschaftsBuches" an, aus welcher er u. Geuder „die rechten Namen" der Mitglieder ersehen könnten, worauf F. Ludwig ihn in seiner Antwort (431014) um Geduld bat, denn ein neues Gesellschaftsbuch, das alle Mitglieder bis Nr. 400 umfasse, sei in Vorbereitung (die Rede ist vom *GB 1646*). Harsdörffer gab sich mit dieser Antwort allerdings nicht zufrieden, sprach die Causa in 440824 erneut an u. bat um ein „*v*erzeichnus der lezt eingeno*mm*ene[n] GeselschaftsGenossen", das F. Ludwig ihm mit 450124 tatsächlich schickte (s.o.). Nach Auskunft der vorliegenden Quellen ergibt sich somit folgendes Bild: Im Zuge seiner Aufnahme in die FG erhielt Harsdörffer zwischen September u. November 1641 einige Köthener Drucke aus der jüngeren Zeit (s. 411126 K 2), zu denen das spätestens seit März 1641 vorliegende *GB 1641* gehört haben dürfte (s. 410323 [K 6] zum *GB 1641*; vgl. auch die Liste Köthener Drucke der Jahre 1638–1643 in 430505 I). Es umfaßt die Impresen aller Mitglieder bis zum 1641 aufgenommenen Gottfried Müller (FG 353) mit Gesellschaftsname, -pflanze, -wort sowie Reimgesetz u. Namensinitialen. Das *GB 1641* wurde durch drei weitere Druckbögen zum *GB 1641/44* erweitert, die Harsdörffer mit 450124 erhielt. Signifikant nämlich ist, daß die Blätter des *GB 1641* noch römisch beziffert sind, die drei zusätzlichen Druckbögen Q, R u. S des *GB 1641/44* aber arabische Bogenzahlen aufweisen. Das *GB 1641* wurde also nachträglich zum *GB 1641/44* erweitert, ein eigens neugesetztes *GB 1644* hat es nicht gegeben. Endete *GB 1641* noch mit FG 353, so *GB 1641/44* auf Bl. [S 4]v mit FG 417. Darüber hinaus scheint Harsdörffer in den Besitz einer handschriftlichen Mitgliederliste gelangt zu sein, mit deren Hilfe er bis inklusive FG 317 (Hans v. Rochow, s. o.) die Initialen unter den Impresen auflösen konnte. Wie von uns schon in 420311 K 7 vermutet u. durch eine Bemerkung Harsdörffers in 430920 bekräftigt, hatte er diese Liste von Geuder bekommen, der sie wiederum von F. Christian II. v. Anhalt-Bernburg (FG 51) erhalten hatte, der sich Geuders regelmäßig als eines Nürnberger Agenten bediente. S. zu dieser Liste 371220 I. Diese reicht zwar bis FG 324, ab der in diesem Zusammenhang entscheidenden Nummer 318 war sie jedoch von abweichender Hand nachträglich ergänzt worden. Eine Liste, mit deren Hilfe Harsdörffer die Initialen über FG 317 hinaus auflösen konnte, bekam er offenbar mit dem vorliegenden Brief 450529. Zwar ist am Ende einiger Drucke des *GB 1641* eine zweispaltig gedruckte, siebenseitige Liste der Taufnamen aller Gesellschaftsmitglieder in der Reihenfolge ihrer Aufnahme bis inklusive FG 353 angehängt; im Besitz von Harsdörffer dürfte dieses mit dem 1641 aufgenommenen Gottfried Müller endende Verzeichnis aber nicht gewesen sein, hatte er doch von seiner ersten Bitte in 420311 an nach einem Verzeichnis der neu aufgenommenen Mitglieder seit 1638 gefragt u. noch in 450400 ausdrücklich das letzte 1637 hinzugetretene FG-Mitglied, Hans v. Rochow (FG 317), als ihm namentlich bekannt genannt. Die Personennamen jener Liste aus dem *GB 1641* hätten ihn darüber hinaus nicht zufriedenstellen können, weil die auf den gerade überschickten Ergänzungsbögen seines Gesellschaftsbuchs befindlichen Mitglieder (FG 354–417) dort ungenannt bleiben. Noch komplizierter wird diese Angelegenheit durch eine Bemerkung in 430920: Harsdörffer schreibt dort, er habe „großes V*er*langen" nach den „rechten Namen bis auf den 317*ten* die seithero angenom*m*en aber nur bis auf d*en* 268. von dem Ergentzenden [d. i. Geuder], […] empfangen." Klar ist, daß Harsdörffer an dieser Stelle nicht etwa auf ein Verzeichnis der Gesellschaftsnamen, sondern eine Auflösung der Personeninitialen abzielt. Da die Lesung der Ziffer „268" nicht eindeutig ist — die „2" könnte auch als eine gebesserte „3" gelesen werden —, könnte Harsdörffer tatsächlich schon Ende 1643 im Besitz einer über Geuder empfangenen Liste gewesen sein, die bis FG 368 — das ist er selbst! — reicht. Unklar bleibt bei dieser Lesart freilich, warum er in 450400 immer noch ein Verzeichnis ab FG 317 verlangt, das bis zu dem von ihm irrig als „*Deuenden*" bezeichneten Zacharias Prüschenk v. Lindenhofen (FG 418) reicht (vgl. hierzu 450400 K 15). — Zu von versch. Mitgliedern nachgefragten FG-Mitgliederlisten vgl. auch 410621 K II 0; 441231 (Gueintz, FG 361), 450126 (Carl Gustav v. Hille, FG 302), 450220 (Hz. Wilhelm IV. v. Sachsen-Weimar, FG 5), 450221 (Hille), 450317 (F. Christian II. v. Anhalt-Bernburg, FG 51), 450500 K 2, 450721 (Hz. August d. J. v. Braunschweig-Wolfenbüttel, FG 227; Hille), 460104 (Pgf. Ludwig Philipp v. Simmern, FG 97), 460424 (dito), 460424A I (dito), 461031A u. I (dito), 461106 (Hille) usw.

450611

Fürst Ludwig an Georg Philipp Harsdörffer

Antwort auf 450400. Beantwortet durch 450817. — F. Ludwig (Der Nährende) tadelt einen Fehler, der Georg Philipp Harsdörffer (FG 368. Der Spielende) in der 2. Aufl. des ersten Teils seiner *Frauenzimmer-Gesprächspiele* (1644) unterlaufen sei: In einer Zierinitiale habe er den Namen des Nährenden irrtümlich mit einer Weizengarbe illustriert. Die Mitgliedsimprese F. Ludwigs zeige aber ein wohlausgebackenes Weizenbrot mit dem Wort „nichts Besseres" zur Nahrung. Denn das Weizenbrot sei im Vergleich zum Dinkel-, Roggen- und anderen Broten das nahrhafteste. Nach dieser Richtigstellung könne der Irrtum gewiß leicht verbessert werden.

Q HM Köthen: V S 545, Bl. 313rv, v leer; Konzept von Schreiberh. mit eigenh. Korrekturen F. Ludwigs. — *D: KE,* 339. — *BN: Bürger,* 950 Nr. 56.

A *Fehlt.*

Zur nachricht hat dem *Spielenden* von wegen der Fruchtbringenden Geselschaft dieses vermeldet werden sollen, das bey dem wiederaufgelegten ersten theile der Gesprächspiele bey[a] dem Sinbilde des Buchstabens N ein irthum begangen, in[b] deme eine weitzengarbe hinein gesetztet worden, als wan sie des *Nehrenden* gemählde were, da doch in allen gedruckten Geselschaftbüchern, ein wol ausgebacken weitzenbrot gedrucket, und in Kupfer gestochen, zu finden ist, mit dem worte, nichts Beßers, wird verstanden, zur nahrung.[1]

Jnmaßen[c] auch das weitzenbrot, oder die[d] Wecke[2], wie es am Rheinstrom genennet wird, beßer als kein Spelt[3] oder Dünckel, ja Rocken- und ander brot nehret; die garbe mus zuvor[e] ausgedroschen, das Korn gemahlen, hernach gebacken, und dan wird[f] es erst zur besten nahrung, gegeßen[g]. Dieser irthum kan aber,[h] leichtlich, nach dem hiermit wieder[i] angezeigten, und[j] beschriebenen gemählde[k] veränderungen[l] zu verhuten verbeßert werden.

Geben an dem[m] bekanten orte der Fruchtbringenden Geselschaft Ertzschreins, den[m] 11 des Brachmonats im jahre 1645.

T *Alle Korrekturen von F. Ludwigs Hand.* — a *Eingefügt für* <in> — b *Bis* hinein *gebessert aus* da hinein eine weitzengarbe *Die Ziffern zur Veränderung der Reihenfolge wurden wieder gestrichen.* — c *Eingefügt für* <Wie dan> — d *Gebessert aus* der — e *Eingefügt für* <erst> — f *Eingefügt für* <kan> — g *Folgt* <werden> *Danach eingefügt* <und gedeyen> *Weitere gestrichene Ergänzungen am Rand:* <veränderungen (-un- überschrieben mit lich) hierunter> — h *Folgt* <ins künftige> *Darüber eingefügt* <wie den nötig auch> — i *Eingefügt.* — j *Folgt eingefügt* <wieder> — k *Folgt eingefügt* <und> *Am Rand ergänzt:* <unterschiedene widrige meinungen und gedancken zu verhüten> — l *Randergänzung bis* verhuten — m *Bis* Ertzschreins, den *eingefügt, dabei nochmals* <dem bekanten orte>

K 1 Georg Philipp Harsdörffer (FG 368. Der Spielende) hatte F. Ludwig (der Nährende) mit 450400 ein Exemplar der 2. Ausg. des 1. Teils seiner *Frauenzimmer-Gesprächspiele* (1644/ Ndr. 1968; 1. Aufl. 1641) geschickt, dem — zusätzlich zu der schon in der 1. Aufl.

enthaltenen Vorrede an die FG — ein „Vbereigungsgedicht [sic] AN den NEHRENDEN" vorangestellt ist. (Ndr., 6–9) Auf der Rückseite des Drucktitelblatts, auf dem das „Vbereigungsgedicht" beginnt, erscheint in dem verzierten Großbuchstaben N („NEHRENDEN") eine Getreidegarbe, die vom Fürsten hier als falsche Wiedergabe der Pictura seiner Imprese moniert wird. Das *GB 1629/30*, Bl. A ij r, zeigt ein „weisses Weytzenbrot" mit dem Wort „Nichts Bessers". Im *GB 1641/44* heißt es etwas genauer „Ein wolausgebacken Weitzenbrot" (A iij v), im *GB 1646* wieder ein „weisses Weitzenbrot" (A ij r). Die Abbildung der Zierinitiale in 440715. Vgl. 440715 K 2 u. 3, 450400 K 4, 450529 K 1, 450817 K 11 u. 450919A. In seiner Antwort 450817 erkennt Harsdörffer seine Erfindung der Getreidegarbe nicht als Fehler an, was F. Ludwig in 450919A wiederum mit Unverständnis aufnimmt. Zu *GB 1641/44* s. 441226A K 5 u. *GB 1646* s. 440130 K 3. — Am Schluß der *Frauenzimmer-Gesprächspiele* I (²1644) finden sich emblematische Erläuterungen zum Vorwerk u. zu den einzelnen Gesprächspielen. Hier begegnet zum 26. Gesprächspiel über „Die verborgene[n] Sendschreiben" eine andere N-Zierinitiale mit dem Bild einer Getreidemühle u. der moralischen Auslegung: „NJcht anderst sondert das Mühlrad die Kleyen von dem Meel/ als unser Verstand das Gute von dem Bösen unterscheiden sol." Ndr., 407. Diese Initiale findet sich mit einer anderen Auslegung auch in *Frauenzimmer-Gesprächspiele* IV (1644), Ndr. 252: „NJcht anderst als wie eine Mühle alles wieder gibt was man aufgeschüttet/ ohne eignen Nutzen und Nachtheil." Eine unmittelbare Anspielung auf die FG-Imprese Caspars v. Teutleben (FG 1. 1617. Der Mehlreiche), die zur Huldigung auf die Accademia della Crusca einen Schüttelkasten zur Trennung der Kleie (Crusca) vom Mehl zeigt, ist in beiden Fällen nicht zu erblicken.

2 Das *DW* geht noch davon aus, daß sich das Femininum *die Wecke* (im Ggs. zu *der Weck*) vor dem 18. Jh. nicht nachweisen lasse (Sp. 2785) — eine Annahme, die hiermit widerlegt ist. Vgl. *DW* XIII, 2784–2793, bes. die Punkte I. 3 u. II. 3. b). *Stieler*, 2530 kennt für das Weizenbrot tatsächlich nur die maskuline Form „Weck/ der", führt daneben allerdings die Nebenform „Wegge" auf, die vermutlich auch ein Maskulinum sein soll.

3 Spelt od. Spelz(e), auch als Zweikorn, Emmer u. Dinkel bekannt, eine alte, weizenähnliche Getreideart. Abgeleitet von lat. „spelta" (wie es auch noch im modernen Italienisch heißt). Vgl. *DW* X.1, 2139 f.; *Kluge/ Mitzka*, 133; *Paul Wb.*, 224.

450613

Diederich von dem Werder an Fürst Ludwig

Diederich v. dem Werder (FG 31. Der Vielgekörnte) schickt F. Ludwig (Der Nährende) ein Schreiben Georg Philipp Harsdörffers (FG 368. Der Spielende), das auch ein Reimgesetz auf die FG-Imprese Johann Michael Moscheroschs (FG 436. Der Träumende. 1645) enthält. Dazu erklärt Werder, er habe in seiner Antwort an Harsdörffer einige Verskorrekturen dafür vorgebracht, die er F. Ludwig mitteilt. Was Harsdörffer in der Frage des Stickens seines Wappens und seiner Imprese angemerkt habe, möge der Fürst beantworten. — Da Werder noch am selben Tag zu einer Reise aufbrechen und bis zum folgenden Tag auf (dem Familiengut) Werdershausen bleiben werde, könne er bis dahin noch bequem Anweisungen empfangen, falls F. Ludwig bei Lgfn. Amalia Elisabeth v. Hessen-Kassel und ihren Räten etwas zu bestellen oder zu erledigen habe. — Grüße an den FG-Genossen Christian Ernst (v.) Knoch (FG 268. Der Weichende).

450613 Diederich von dem Werder

Q HM Köthen: V S 544, Bl. 484r–485v [A: 485v], 484v u. 485r leer; eigenh.; rotes Lacksiegel. — *D: KE*, 178. — *BN: Nicht bei Bürger*.

A Dem Nehrenden   Cöthen   zuhanden.

Vnser höchstgeehrter herr Nehrender empfängt jnligend des Spielenden schreiben,[1] aus welchem er den reimsatz des Träumenden[2] zubelesen hatt. Meine errinnerungen an den Spielenden habe ich also aufgesetzt.
 1. Das wort sol heissen / hohe Sachen /

Beym ersten verse / eröffnet vns die nacht
 Anderer / da sonst bey tage nur
 Dritter / mit fuge zugedacht
 Vierder / vnd zwar von hohen sachen.

Was sonsten der Spielende errinnert wegen seiner Stücke zur Tapezerey,[3] solches kan vom Nehrenden beandtwortet werden.

Dieweil ich auch heute meiner reise einen kleinen anfang mache, vnd morgen gg. bis in Mittag zu Werdershausen[4] verbleiben werde, als könte mir daselbsten noch hin zugeschickt werden, jm fall ich eines oder andern [*sic*] bey der Fraw landgrävin F. G.[5] vnd dero Rähten[a] in den Angelegenheiten vnserer gnädigen Fürstl. herrschaft vnd dieses landes ich errinnern solte. Vnter dessen bitte ich den Allerhöchsten er wolle vnsern höchstgeehrten herren Nehrenden samt allen liebsten angehörigen gnädig bewahren, vnd mich sein Andlitz bald in gesundheit wieder sehen lassen, als
Des Nehrenden.

 dienstwilligster geselschafter
 Der Vielgekörnte

Der Weichende[6] findet alhier auch seines getreuen Geselschafters getreue begrüssung.

Reinsdorff 13. BrachMonat.

T a *Folgt* <ich>

K 1 Diederich v. dem Werder (FG 31. Der Vielgekörnte) führte im Falle Georg Philipp Harsdörffers (FG 368. Der Spielende), der Johann Michael Moscherosch (FG 436. Der Träumende. 1645) zur Aufnahme in die FG vorgeschlagen hatte, für u. mit F. Ludwig einen Teil der fruchtbringerischen Korrespondenz. Der Austausch von Impresenvorschlägen u. Reimgesetz-Korrekturen zum Neumitglied Moscherosch lief über Harsdörffer u. Werder. Vgl. 450500 (K 1).
 2 D. i. das Reimgesetz auf die FG-Imprese Moscheroschs (FG 436. Der Träumende. 1645). Harsdörffer hatte dazu in seinem Brief, den Werder dem vorliegenden Brief beigelegt hatte, einen Entwurf (wohl von Moscherosch verfaßt) geschickt, den D. v. dem Werder in seiner Antwort an den Nürnberger, wie nachstehend angezeigt, verbesserte u. zugunsten des Beiworts „hohe Sachen" entschied. Vgl. 450504A K 2. Das im *GB Kö*. III,

Bl. 37r aufgeführte Reimgesetz hat die Verbesserungen Werders nicht aufgenommen. S. dessen Text in *Conermann III*, 525. Der Korrekturprozeß setzte sich noch fort. S. 450730.

3 Wappen u. Imprese Harsdörffers, die auf Atlas zu sticken waren. S. 450504A K 5.

4 Heute Ortsteil von Gröbzig, südwestlich von Köthen. Es wurde 1566/67 durch Diederichs Großvater Hartwig v. dem Werder (†1567) auf den Resten des ehemaligen Gröbziger Vorwerks Sorge u. dem wüsten Dorf Gerbißdorff als ein Familienstammsitz gegründet u. ausgebaut. *Beckmann* VII, 286.

5 Die Reise, die Werder zur Lgfn. Amalia Elisabeth v. Hessen-Kassel führte (1602–1651), könnte auch schon im Zusammenhang mit den Heiratsplänen gestanden haben, die 1646 zur Vermählung Lgf. Wilhelms VI. v. Hessen-Kassel (FG 694. 1659) u. Mgfn. Hedwig Sophias (1623–1683), Schwester Kf. Friedrich Wilhelms v. Brandenburg (FG 401), führen sollten. Lgfn. Amalia Elisabeth war es, die die Teilnahme Werders an der hessenkasselschen Gesandtschaft bei den Heiratsverhandlungen wünschte. Vgl. 460125 K 1–3 u. Beil. I. Am 25. Juli ist Werder bereits wieder im heimischen Reinsdorf (s. 450725).

6 Christian Ernst (v.) Knoch (FG 268. Der Weichende), Geh. Rat in Köthen.

450614

Matthias Götze an Peter Knaudt

(Der Leipziger Verleger) Matthias Götze hat das Schreiben Peter Knaudts vom 11.6.1645 bereits erhalten und berichtet, daß Johann Hammer ihm ein für Matthäus Merian d. Ä. in Frankfurt a. M. bestimmtes Kästlein überreicht habe, das er sogleich in ein Bücherfaß verladen und dem Schmalkaldener Fuhrmann Caspar Frevol überantwortet habe. Götze hofft, daß die Fracht mittlerweile gut in Frankfurt angekommen ist, obwohl eine Bestätigung bisher ausblieb.

Q HM Köthen: V S 546, Bl. 28rv; v leer; Schreiberh. — *D: Bircher: Merian*, 700. — *BN: Bürger*, 469 Nr. 2.

A *Fehlt.*

WohlEhrenvhester Hochachtbar vndt Wohlgelarter insonders großgünstiger Herr, hochgeehrter werther freundt, nebenst wüntschung meines freundlichen grußes, ist mir E. W. E. H. A.[1] schreiben den 11. Junij in Cöthen **datirt**, zu recht vberantwortet, thue sie hierauf berichten, das mir H **Johann** hammer ein Kästlein[2], so H **Merian** zu Frankfurdt am Mayn haben soll, zu recht vberantworttet, welches ich als baldt in ein Buch faß[3] gepacket, vndt mit Caspar Frevol bey Schmalkalden Fuhrman fortgeschicket, verhoffe es nunmehr glücklich zu Frankfurdt, wiewohl ich noch keine nachricht, ankommen sein soll, vnterdeßen thue ich E. W. E. H. A.[1] in Gottes gnädigen schutz zum treulichsten befhelen, **Actum** Leipzigk den 14. **Junij** 1645.

      E. W. E. H. A.[1]
      Dienstwilligst
      Matthias Götze*mp*

450711 Matthäus Merian d. Ä.

K 1 Abkürzung für die am Briefanfang gebrauchte Anrede „Euer *WohlEhrenvhester Hochachtbar*" (wahrscheinlich attributive Verwendung).
2 S. zum „Kästlein" die zusammenfassende Darstellung in 450509 K 1. In 450711 erwähnt Merian d. Ä. ausdrücklich die sich in der kleinen Kiste befindlichen Kupferplatten des *GB 1629/30* und den (Hz. August d.J. v. Braunschweig-Wolfenbüttel [FG 227]) vorgestreckten Betrag von 200 Reichstalern (zur Finanzierung des *GB 1646*). Auf Anweisung F. Ludwigs (450331) gelangte der für die Weiterarbeit am *GB 1646* unverzichtbare Kästcheninhalt über Braunschweig und Leipzig nach Frankfurt, wo er im Juli 1645 Merian erreichte. S. 450711. Zum Verlag des *GB 1646* s. 450126 K 4; zum Zahlungsverkehr im Kontext desselben s. 450127 K 1 u. zum *GB 1646* allgemein s. 440130 K 3.
3 Mit dem Bücherfaß bezieht sich Matthias Götze auf das bis ins 19. Jahrhundert übliche Transportmittel, das Holzfaß, in dem sich beim Bücherversand, also nicht im vorliegenden Fall, die rohen ungefalzten (Druck-)Bogen (lat. *in albis*), befanden, die in dieser Form auf der Messe angeboten wurden. Vgl. auch Helmut Hiller: Wörterbuch des Buches. Dritte, durchgesehene u. erweiterte Auflage. Frankfurt 1967, 61.

450711

Matthäus Merian d. Ä. an Peter Knaudt

Antwort auf einen (nicht überlieferten) Brief vom 7. Mai 1645. Beantwortet durch 450800. — Matthäus Merian d. Ä. bestätigt den Erhalt eines Kästchens aus Leipzig mit den Kupferplatten des *GB 1629/30* und den mitgesandten 200 Reichstalern zur Finanzierung des *GB 1646*. Er kann jetzt mit dem Stechen des (dritten) Hunderts der neuen Impresen beginnen und fragt nach, ob jeweils hundert oder zweihundert Impresen mit besonderen Titelseiten herausgegeben werden sollen. Dies wäre auch im Hinblick auf künftige Fortsetzungen des *GB 1646* empfehlenswert. Die Käufer könnten die Separatdrucke dann nach eigenem Dafürhalten binden lassen. Falls alle 400 Impresen nur mit einem Titelblatt erscheinen sollen, würden sie mit der hinzugefügten Fortsetzung einen allzu dicken Band ergeben. Merian schlägt deshalb eigene Titelblätter für jeweils 100 Impresen vor. Ein Generalkupfertitel könne nur den ersten hundert Impresen vorausgehen. Knaudt möge ihm die Entscheidung (F. Ludwigs) mitteilen. Merian erkundigt sich zugleich nach der Lieferung des (vierten) Hunderts Impresen-Visierungen, da er das *GB 1646* sobald als möglich fertigstellen und der Öffentlichkeit vorlegen möchte. Merian schlägt zusätzlich zu den einzelnen Drucktiteln mit großer Schrift einen Kupfertitel für jedes Hundert Impresen vor. In der Nachschrift merkt Merian an, daß er erst jetzt brieflich reagiere, da die Lieferung aufgrund der Kriegsgefahr lange in Gotha gelegen hätte und erst vor vier Tagen bei ihm eingetroffen sei.

Q HM Köthen: V S 546, Bl. 20rv [A: 20v]; eigenh.; Sig. — *D: Bircher: Merian*, 701 f.; Wüthrich: Merian Briefe, 88 f. — BN: Bürger, 987 Nr. 8.

A Tt. Dem Ehrenvesten vnd Großachtparen Herrn Petter Knaudt fürst. Anhaltischen CammerMeistern meinem Großg. hochgeehrten herrn *etc.* Cöthen

Ehrenvester vnd GroßAchtparer Jnsonders Großg. Herr *etc.*

Berichte hiemit das Jch des h. geliebtes vom 7 Maj[1], vnd nunmehr Entlichen das bewuste kistlin mit kupfer durch die Leipziger fuhr, wie auch die Rth 200 wol empfangen.[2] Vndt laße mit verfertigung der 100 Neuen Emblema Jetzo den Anfang machen:

Allein dises möchte ich gern verstendiget sein, ob Jch im trucken dises werks dörffte ein Jedes 100, oder 200 vnter besonderen Tittuln[a] herauß geben, dan wen hernach mehr[b] hinzugethan würden, es auch unter besonderm Tittul füglicher geschehen könte[3]: vnd so ichs also herauß geben dörffte, wehre es dem kauffer vil bequemlicher, es binden zu laßen seines gefallens, sonsten aber[c] da alle 400 unter einem Einigen Tittul begriffen wehren, mußten die vbrigen so hernach volgen würden, auch ohne Tittul hinden angehenckt werden so sich im Bundt nicht wol schicken[d], es auch vil zu dicken Bundt geben würde. Darumb ist mein einfeltige meinung, Es am aller formlichsten vnd bequemsten wehre, wenn Jedes 100 vnter einem besondern Anfang vnd Tittul begriffen, vnd der General Kupfer Tittul vorhero [d]es[e] ersten 100 gesetzt würde,[4] bin hierauff einer Antwort gewertig, auch wie baldt die andern 100 vißirungen Jch empfangen werde, Auff das Jch alles wol anstellen und keine Zeit verlohren würde, damit das werkh so baldt möglich, herauß komen moge. so man will kan wol vber ein Jedes 100 auch ein kupfer Tittul gemacht, oder nur mit großen Buchstaben, den Ersten Tittul gleich, vnd nur bei jedem, das zweite hundert, das drite, virte hundert oder theile gesetzt werden *etc.* welches meinem gg. herrn Jch gutte meinung habe vermelden sollen, vnd bitte vmb Antwort, dem Allm[f] hiemit zu vätterlichen Gnaden wol befohlen

Ffurt den 11. Julij 1645

D. Hrn

Dienstwilligster

Mattheus Merian

Die Vrsach meines langsamen[5] schreibens ist das die fuhr wegen der großen gefahr und vnsicherheit zu Gotha[6] still gelegen, vnd erst vor 4 tagen Allhir angelangt ist.

T a *Folgt* <solle> — **b** *Folgt* <zu> — **c** *Gebessert aus* Aber — **d** *Folgt* <werde> — **e** *Mit Einschaltzeichen im Fließtext am Rande eingefügt bis* 100 — **f** *Lies:* Allmächtigen

K 1 Der Brief vom 7. Mai 1645 ist nicht nachweisbar. Vgl. auch *Bircher: Merian*, 669f. Von Peter Knaudt stammt im Berichtszeitraum nur 450800 an Matthäus Merian d. Ä. Als Empfänger von Merian-Briefen ist Knaudt jedoch sehr präsent, weil er im Auftrag F. Ludwigs (Der Nährende) für den Zahlungsverkehr im Zusammenhang mit dem *GB 1646* verantwortlich war. S. 450417, 450711 u.ö. Vgl. auch 450127 K 1 und zu seiner Person 410510 K 2.

2 Jenes Kistlein war bereits im Mai an Matthias Götze in Leipzig gelangt, der es umgehend an Merian zustellen ließ. S. 450509 u. 450614, vgl. 450800. Es enthielt die Kupferplatten des *GB 1629/30* und erreichte den Stecher Merian zusammen mit 200 Reichstalern (den für Hz. August d.J. v. Braunschweig-Wolfenbüttel [FG 227] vorgeschossenen Beitrag zum *GB 1646*). Merian konnte nun die über den Umfang des alten *GB 1629/30* hinausgehenden Impresen FG 201–300 in Angriff nehmen, deren Visierungen ihm bereits vorlagen.

3 Merian schlägt mit den Einzeltitelblättern vor jedem Hundert oder Zweihundert eine bequem fortsetzungsfähige Reihenpublikation vor. Tatsächlich wurde das 400 Impresen umfassende *GB 1646* jedoch nicht mehr fortgesetzt. Es enthielt aber die vorgeschlagenen Zwischentitelblätter für jedes Impresen-Hundert, s. Anm. 4. Zum *GB 1646* allgemein bereits 421031A K 14 u. 440130 K 3.

4 F. Ludwig schloß sich dem Vorschlag Merians insofern an, als jedes Hundert der Gesellschafter-Impresen tatsächlich mit einem eigenen Titelblatt versehen wurde. Dafür erstellte er selbst einen hsl. Entwurf, den er mit 450800 Merian zusenden ließ. Nicht verwirklicht wurde Merians Vorschlag, einen „**General** Kupfer Tittul" den ersten hundert Gesellschafterimpresen voranzustellen. S. die beiden Entwürfe auf S. 574f. Unter jenem „General Kupfer Tittul" dürfte die Palmenimprese der FG selbst gemeint gewesen sein, die schon im *GB 1629/30* dem Titelblatt und der kurzen Einführung in Gründung und Zweck der FG folgt, also bereits verfertigt vorlag. Da ihr konkrete Titelelemente des Druckes ermangeln, sie aber auch kein Titelkupfer oder Frontispiz ist — sofern dieses gewöhnlich dem gedruckten Titelblatt vorangeht —, spricht für die Wahl der Palmenimprese, daß in 450800 vom „**General** Kupfferstucke mit dem Palmenbaume" (!) die Rede ist und sie selbst bereits eine Art Generaltitel aufweist („Alles zu Nutzen. Die Fruchtbringende Gesellschafft."). An sich ist die Palmenimprese freilich eine eigene, sinnbildliche Druckgraphik, Imprese und definitiv kein „Kupfertitel". Den Teilen des 2., 3. u. 4. Hunderts der Gesellschafter-Impresen sollte nichts, so wollte es 450800 I, als nur das gedruckte jeweilige Zwischentitelblatt, wie es F. Ludwig entworfen hatte, vorgesetzt wer*den*. Statt eines General-Kupferstücks aber wurden im *GB 1646* vor jedem Hundert der Impresen nach dem Drucktitel zunächst das Auslegungs-Sonett und dann die Palmenimprese selbst vorausgeschickt. Die Kollationierung der drei an der HAB vorhandenen Exemplare des *GB 1646* (HAB: Ln 302, HAB: 17.4.1 Eth. u. 18.1 Eth.) zeigt das folgende einheitliche Bild: Drucktitel: Der Fruchtbringenden Geselschaft ... Das Erste Hundert (Bl. [¶] r, Rücks. leer); Kurtzer Bericht (Bl. ¶ ij r – ¶ iij r); „Kling-Gedichte Auf die Fruchtbringende Gesellschaft" [d.i. das Reimgesetz auf die Palmen-Imprese der FG] (Bl. ¶ iij v); Kupferstich: Palmen-Imprese der FG (Bl. [¶ iiij] r, Rücks. leer); Impresen 1–100 (Bl. A r, Rücks. leer – [Bb iiij] r, Rücks. leer); Zwischendrucktitel: Der Fruchtbringenden Gesellschaft ... Das Zweyte Hundert (Bl. [Cc] r); Klinggedicht (Bl. [Cc] v); Kupferstich: Palmen-Imprese der FG (Bl. [Cc ij] r, Rücks. leer); Impresen 101–200 (Bl. [Cc iij] r, Rücks. leer – Bl. Eee ij] r, Rücks. leer); Zwischendrucktitel: Der Fruchtbringenden Gesellschaft ... Das Dritte Hundert (Bl. [Eee iij] r); Klinggedicht (Bl. [Eee iij] v); Kupferstich: Palmen-Imprese der FG (Bl. [Eee iiij] r, Rücks. leer); Impresen 201–300 (Bl. [Fff] r, Rücks. leer – Bl. [Gggg iiij] r, Rücks. leer); Zwischendrucktitel: Der Fruchtbringenden Gesellschaft ... Das Vierdte Hundert (Bl. [Hhhh] r); Klinggedicht (Bl. [Hhhh] v); Kupferstich: Palmen-Imprese der FG (Bl. [Hhhh ij] r, Rücks. leer); Impresen 301–400 (Bl. Hhhh iij r, Rücks. leer – Kkkk ij r, Rücks. leer). In buchgestalterischer wie drucktechnischer Hinsicht werden demnach die jeweils hundert Impresen identisch präsentiert und eignen sich grundsätzlich als separat gebundene und eigenständige Teildrucke einer (möglicherweise weiter fortzusetzenden) Gesamtreihe. Das erste Hundert unterscheidet sich einzig durch den Zusatz des „Kurtzen Berichts" von den folgenden drei Zenturien. Der dem Werk vorausgehende erste Drucktitel (zum ersten Hundert) lautet vollständig: „Der Fruchtbringenden Geselschaft Nahmen/ Vorhaben/ Gemählde und Wörter: Nach jedes Einnahme ordentlich in Kupfer gestochen/ und Jn achtzeilige Reimgesetze verfasset/ Das Erste Hundert.

Der
Fruchtbringenden Gesellschaft
Vorhaben
Nahmen
Gemählde
und
Wörter

Nach jedes Einnahme ordentlich
In Kupffer gestochen
und
In achtzeilige Reimgesetze verfaßet
das erste Hundert
bedruckt

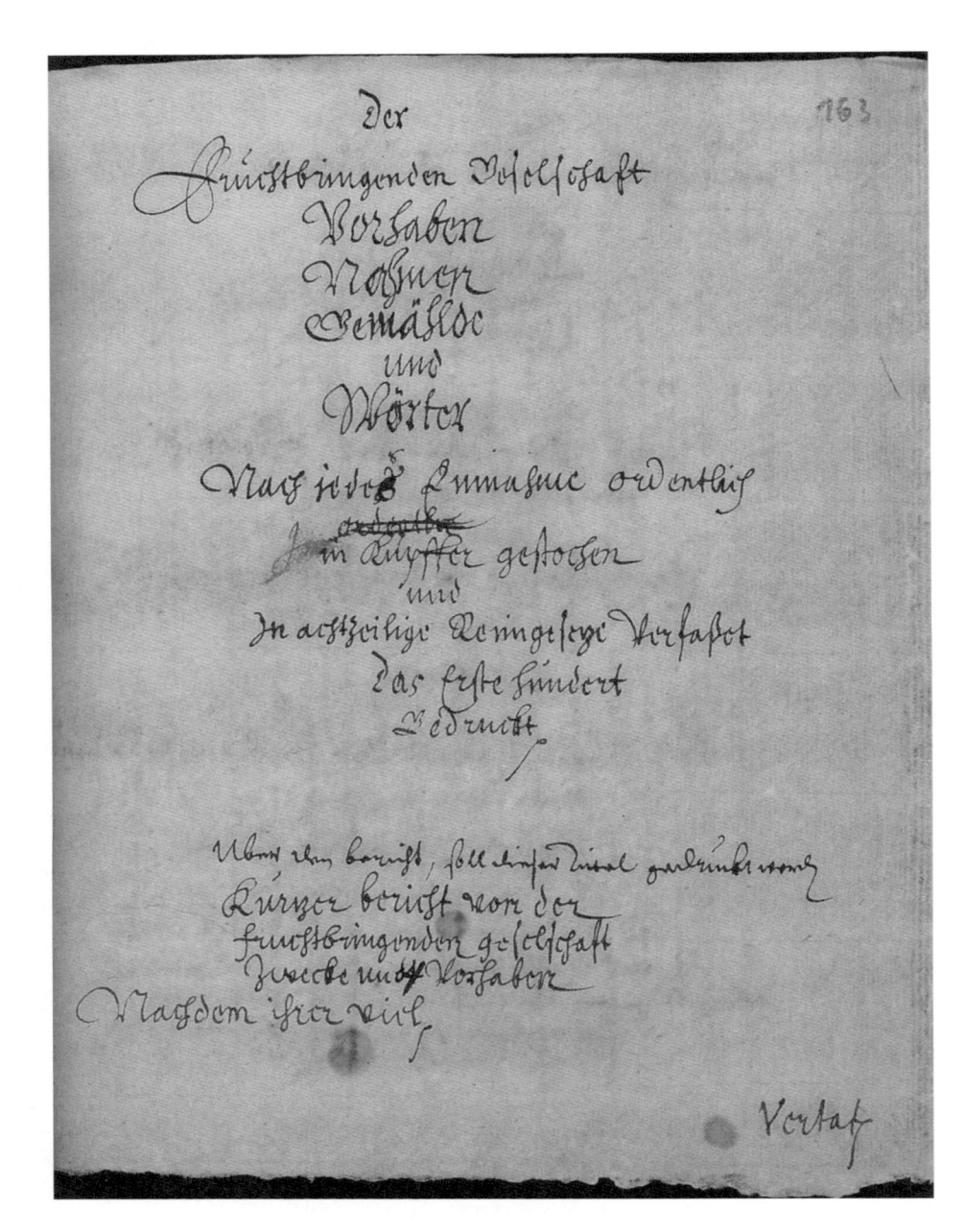

Ubrig ein bericht, soll einsten[?] diesel gedrückt werd[?]
Kurzer bericht von der
fruchtbringenden geselschaft
Zwecke und Vorhaben
Nachdem ihrer viel

Verfaß

Fürst Ludwigs Entwurf eines Titelblatts (Gesellschaftsbuch 1646) *für Merian. Zu 450711.*

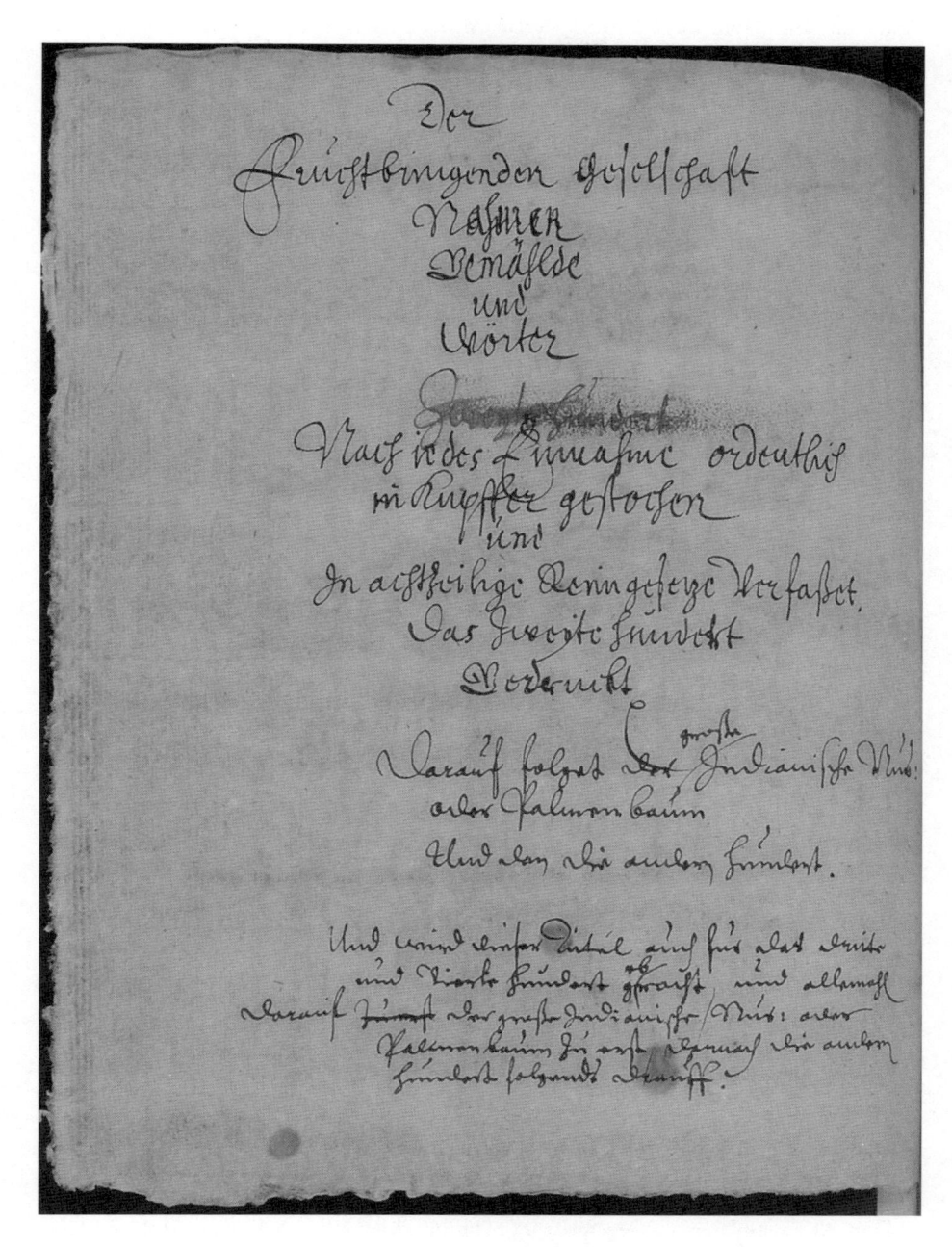

Der
Fruchtbringenden Gesellschaft
Nahmen
Gemählde
und
Wörter

Nach jedes Einnahme ordentlich
in Kupffer gestochen
und
In achtzeilige Reimgesetze Verfaßet.
Das zweyte hundert
Vordruck

Darauf folget der große Indianische Nuß:
oder Palmen baum
Und an die andern hundert.

Und wann einer Artikel auch sein alas dritte
und Vierte hundert gebracht, und allemahl
Darauf zuerst der große Indianisch/Nuß: oder
Palmen baum, zu erst, algemach die andern
hundert folgends drauff.

Fürst Ludwigs zweiter Entwurf eines Titelblatts (Gesellschaftsbuch 1646) *für Merian. Zu* 450711.

Franckfurt am Mayn/ Bey Mattheo Merian. M. DC. XXXXVI". Zur Einrichtung (Visierungen, Stechen, Einband) des *GB 1646* s. Anm. 3, 440723, 450417, 450800 u. I, 450905, 450923A, 450930, 451015, 451028B, 451119, 460206 u. 460303.

5 Dies bezieht sich nicht auf den Schreibprozeß selbst, sondern deutet auf den Zeitraum von etwa zwei Monaten hin, der seit dem Eingang des Briefes Knaudts vom 17. Mai vergangen ist. Vgl. *DW* VI, 179 Nr. 2 u. 3. Hier wird die frühere Bedeutung des Adjektivs *langsam* im Sinne von *zeitlich lange* bzw. *spät* verwendet.

6 Über die Abschickung des Transports durch einen Fuhrmann aus Schmalkalden s. 450614. Die Ernestinischen Fürstentümer waren von den im Frühjahr und Sommer 1645 im sächs.-thüring. Raum zwischen schwed. und ksl.-kursächs. Truppen durchgeführten Militäraktionen betroffen. Nachdem die schwed. Hauptarmee in Kursachsen zu Beginn des Jahres 1645 in den Winterquartieren gelegen hatte, war sie Mitte Januar abermals nach Böhmen aufgebrochen. In Obersachsen versuchte unterdessen der schwed. Gouverneur in Leipzig, Generalmajor Axel Lillie (1603–1662), den sächs. Kf.en Johann Georg I. militärisch zu einem Waffenstillstand zu zwingen. Die von Lillie geführte Militäroffensive war jedoch zu schwach, um den gewünschten Effekt zu erreichen. Stattdessen gelang es Kf. Johann Georg, die Abwesenheit der Hauptarmee zu nutzen, um schwed. besetzte Festungen zurückzuerobern. Daher mußte die Rückkehr des Korps unter Generalleutnant (Greve) Hans Christoph v. Königsmarck (FG 515. 1648) erwartet werden. Dieser war, nachdem er zu Jahresbeginn 1645 in Niedersachsen operiert hatte, im Frühjahr nach Hessen gezogen, um der bedrängten frz. Armee beizustehen. Im Juli 1645 kehrte Königsmarck über Franken nach Kursachsen zurück, wo er Ende des Monats eintraf. Mit seiner Unterstützung gelang es den schwed. Kräften in der Region, Kursachsen zum Waffenstillstand zu bewegen, der am 27. 8. 1645 in Kötzschenbroda geschlossen wurde. S. zur Kriegslage bis Anfang 1645 440927 K 1. Vgl. *Theatrum europaeum* V (1647. HAB: Ge 4° 54), 790; *Chemnitz* IV. 5, 112–116 u. 180–185; Johann Ludwig Gottfried: Fortgesetzte Historische Chronik Oder Beschreibung Der Merckwürdigsten Geschichte, so sich von Anno 1618. bis zu Ende des Jahrs Christi 1659. zugetragen. Teil II. Frankfurt 1745, S. 896.

450721

Fürst Ludwig an Herzog August d. J. von Braunschweig-Wolfenbüttel

F. Ludwig überschickt Hz. August d. J. v. Braunschweig-Wolfenbüttel (FG 227) den versprochenen 3. Teil von *Sachse: Einhelligkeit*. Wegen der Not im Lande und in Ermangelung eines Buchbinders habe er Hz. August nicht schon früher ein Exemplar zukommen lassen können. Nun löst F. Ludwig sein Versprechen ein, die Predigten zu senden und bittet um Verständnis für den Verzug. — Erinnern möchte F. Ludwig Hz. August an seine bereits vor einigen Jahren persönlich als auch durch Carl Gustav v. Hille (FG 302. Der Unverdrossene) erklärte Bereitschaft, einen Beitrag zum Verlag des in Kupfer gestochenen *GB 1646* zu leisten. Hz. August habe doch vorgehabt, 100 oder 200 Rth. beizutragen, mit 24 bzw. 48 Exemplaren als Gegenleistung. Hz. Friedrich III. v. Schleswig-Holstein-Gottorf (FG 388) entrichtete seinen Beitrag von 200 Rth. bereits vor zwei Jahren. Die Zahlung dränge auch deswegen, weil der Stecher Matthäus Merian d. Ä. in Frankfurt mit seiner Arbeit erst fortfahren will, wenn er sein Geld erhalten hat. Darum möge Hz. August sei-

450721 Fürst Ludwig

nen Beitrag alsbald Georg Winckler in Leipzig anweisen und ihn, F. Ludwig, durch seinen an ihn, Hz. August, gesandten Boten davon unterrichten, so daß mit dem Druck (des *GB 1646*) begonnen werden könne. F. Ludwig könne sonst von seiten anderer (Beiträger) der Vorwurf gemacht werden, er habe das Geld zu lange bei sich behalten und es nicht dem Verleger Merian geschickt. — In das frisch gebundene Buch (*Sachse: Einhelligkeit* III) habe F. Ludwig außerdem die ergänzenden Druckbögen des *GB 1641/44* mit den Reimgesetzen gelegt. Die später eingenommenen FG-Mitglieder und ihre Tauf- und Gesellschaftsnamen könne er aus Carl Gustav von Hilles Liste abschreiben lassen.

Q NSTA Wolfenbüttel: 1 Alt 22 Nr. 228, Bl. 38rv; eigenh.

A *Fehlt.*

Hochgeborner Fürst
   Freündlicher vielgeliebter Herr Ohem und Schwager. E. L habe ich fur diesem vertröstung gegeben, das wan das dritte theil der Evangelisten einhelligkeit[1] ausgedrucket, ihm solches, wie die vorigen zwey ersten auch zu überschicken. Nun hette ich es zwar ehe thun sollen, es ist aber das verderben alle des meinigen, sieder[2] vollendung des druckes, auf dem lande eingefallen, so hat es auch an dem buchbinder ermangelt, das ich darzu eher nicht gelangen können:[3] Gegenwertig aber thue ich meiner zusage, mit überschickung solcher predigten ein genüge, und lebe der freundlichen zuversicht, E. L. werden den verzug im besten entschuldigen.
   Nechst deme erinnere ich mich der vertröstung die mir E. L. für etzlichen Jahren so fur sich als durch Carl Gustafen von Hille thun lassen, das sie zu dem geselschaft buche, das in kupfer wieder sol aufgeleget werden, ein oder zwey hundert Reichsthaler verlagsweise mit zuschießen wolten, und dargegen vierundzwantzig oder acht und viertzig stücke, so bald sie verfertiget, gewertig sein.[4] Weil aber bisher sonder zweiffel aus andern eingefallenen verhinderungen, noch nichts erfolget, gleich wol von andern hohen orten sonderlich hertzog friederich zu Holstein, Gottorf Ld ein zimliches schon vor zwey Jharen, nemlich von zweyhundert Reichsthalern, auch einkommen,[5] und der kupferstecher Merian in franckfurt nicht eher mit der arbeit fort wil, bis das geld alle pahr verhanden.
   Als ersuche ich El. freundlichen, sie wollen ihrer vertröstung zufolge, die eheste verordnung thun, damit George Wincklern[6] in leipzig dasjenige, was sie noch einlegen wollen, hundert oder zweihundert Reichsthaler mögen übermachet werden, und wollen E L. es mir bey zeigern zuwissen fugen, auf das mit dem wercke ein anfang könne gemacht, und es mir bey andern das ich das empfangene geld so lange bey mir gehabt, und nichts darzu thun lassen, nicht verarget werde, oder ubel aufgenommen.
   [38v] EL.[a] uberschicke ich auch sonsten in das gebunden buch mit eingeleget, die nachgedruckten gesellschaft Reime, und können sie die ubrigen tauf und gesellschaft Nahmen bey dem Unverdrossenen, deme ich sie mitgetheilet, abschriftlich sich erholen.[7]

Jch erwarte El. freundlichen antwort, und bin deroselben zu aller freundlichen diensten iederzeit bereitwillig.
Cöthen den 21. des HewMonats im Jhare 1645.
E.L.

dienstwilliger Ohem vnd Schwager
Ludwig f zu Anhalt

T a Bis ich *auch Kustode.*

K 1 Ein Exemplar des dritten Teils der Predigtensammlung *Sachse: Einhelligkeit*, der noch 1644 erschienen war, hatte Carl Gustav v. Hille (FG 302. Der Unverdrossene) bereits im Januar von F. Ludwig erwartet. S. 450126. Hz. August d. J. v. Braunschweig-Wolfenbüttel (FG 227) scheint mit 450721 ein einfach gebundenes Druckexemplar empfangen zu haben, denn in 460119 wiederholt F. Ludwig die im vorliegenden Brief vorgebrachten Entschuldigungsgründe für den Verzug bei der Übersendung eines zweiten, in Köthen (offenbar aufwendiger) gebundenen Werks. Er schickt dort Hille ein Exemplar und verspricht ein weiteres für Hz. August, sobald es eingebunden werden könne. Hzn. Sophia Elisabeth v. Braunschweig-Wolfenbüttel (AL 1629. TG 42b) könnte sogar schon im März 1645 ein Exemplar erhalten haben, s. 450308. Zu *Sachse: Einhelligkeit* s. 420712 K 1 u. 441205 K 3.
2 In *DW* X.1, 882 in der Bedeutung von „seit". Vgl. schon 280220 K 2.
3 F. Ludwig bezieht sich hier auf die Verheerungen Anhalts im Herbst 1644 (s. 440927 K 1) und die Kriegssituation im Juli 1645, als die Truppen aus Franken unter Generalleutnant Hans Christoph v. Königsmarck (FG 515. 1648) die Schweden unter dem Kommando des Generalmajors Axel Lillie (1603–1662) in Kursachsen unterstützten. Da Königsmarck als Gouverneur des Erzstifts Bremen u. des Hochstifts Verden, seinem Hauptwirkungsfeld, jederzeit von Obersachsen nach Niedersachsen zurückkehren konnte, wäre auch das Ft. Anhalt vom Marsch der königsmärckischen Truppen betroffen. Wie angespannt die Situation in Anhalt war, bestätigt auch ein Brief der Anhaltiner an ihren Gesamtrat Martinus Milagius (FG 315) vom 29.7.1645: „Dan etzliche Schwedische Regimenter nunmehr fast ein vierzehn tage vor Magdeburg gelegen, daselbst die Erndte verderbet, Unsern unterhanen aber dieselbe sehr unsicher gemacht und verhindert, Liegen auch anitzo in und um Kalbe, und machen es über alle maßen sehr unsicher, welches ihr gleichwol den Schwedischen Herrn Legaten vermelden, Sie Zu mitleiden bewegen, und unsers wegen ersuchen wollet, damit die unserm Fürstenthume auf ein Jahrlang verwilligte **exemption** weiters **prolongiret**, auch Zu etwas samen und viehe wieder gelangen mögen". Die Briefschreiber fahren fort und betonen, daß (vor einer Verbesserung der Lage) Kontributionszahlungen undenkbar seien. *KU* V.2, 6f. Auf Drängen der Anhaltiner hatte das Land von den Schweden auf ein Jahr Befreiung von allen Kontributionen und Kriegsbeschwerden erlangt. S. das Patent Lennart Torstenssons an die Fürsten aus seinem Hauptquartier Zeitz am 21.12.1644 in *KU* V.1, 334f.: Befreiung auf ein Jahr. Diese Zusage sollte den Fürsten auch jene finanzielle Entlastung einbringen, die sie überhaupt in die Lage versetzte, einen eigenen Gesandten zu den Friedensverhandlungen nach Münster und Osnabrück abzuordnen. Dieser Gesandte war Milagius, der im Mai oder Anfang Juni zum Westfälischen Friedenskongreß abreiste, ausgestattet mit einer Generalinstruktion aller Fürsten Anhalts (s. *KU* V.1, 413ff.) und einem Geheimmemorial (Frühjahr 1645, nicht genau datiert; nach Köhler [s. u.], 110–114), das ohne die Fürsten Christian II. v. Anhalt-Bernburg (FG 51) und Johann v. Anhalt-Zerbst (FG 398) Milagius aufgetragen worden

450722 Herzog August d. J. von Braunschweig-Wolfenbüttel

war, und eine enge Bindung an die Vertreter Schwedens, Kurbrandenburgs, Hessen-Kassels, der Stadt Bremen und Sachsen-Weimars und Braunschweig-Lüneburgs sowie auch eine stärkere Ausrichtung auf die (religions-)politischen Interessen der Reformierten vorsah. Spätestens ab 7.7.1645 befand sich Milagius in Münster, danach spätestens ab 20.7. in Osnabrück. Vgl. 450220 K 1, *KU* V.1, 351 ff. u. V.2, 1 ff.; R. Köhler: Ergänzungen zu G. Krause, Urkunden, Aktenstücke und Briefe zur Geschichte der Anhaltischen Lande und ihrer Fürsten etc. Leipzig 1866. In: Mitt.en d. Vereins f. Anhalt. Geschichte u. Altertumskunde 5 (1890), 98–114. Vgl. auch 450730 u. ö.

4 Folgt man dem Briefwechsel, so hatte Matthäus Merian d. Ä. einen Beitrag in Höhe von 200 Rth. zum Verlag des *GB 1646* bereits am 11.7.1645 (450711) empfangen. Diesen auch von Hz. August d.J. v. Braunschweig-Wolfenbüttel versprochenen Beitrag zum Verlag des Buchs, den er in 2 Raten bezahlen wollte (430724A), hatte der Braunschweiger Kaufmann Johann Beyer F. Ludwig vorgestreckt (450331 u. 450503). F. Ludwig bittet im vorliegenden Brief nur um die erste Rate der Verlagsbeteiligung von 200 Rth. (s. zuletzt 440323 I), da die zweite erst vor dem Arbeitsbeginn Merians an den letzten hundert Impresen (FG 301–400) fällig wurde. S. 430724A. Da Hz. August bisher trotz der Erinnerungen F. Ludwigs bzw. Hilles seinen Verpflichtungen nicht nachgekommen war, scheint der Anhaltiner dem Welfen jedoch psychologisch geschickt eine Reduzierung der Gesamtsumme anzubieten, auf die dieser aber verständlicherweise nicht eingehen mochte. Der Herzog versprach also die gesamte Summe von 200 Rth. und zwar schon vor dem 23.9.1645 (450923A). F. Ludwig konnte ihm den Gegenwert von 48 *GB 1646*-Exemplaren also in diesem Brief zusagen. Zu Verlagsbeiträgen s. 450126 K 4. Zum *GB 1646* allgemein s. 440130 K 3.

5 Hz. Friedrich III. v. Schleswig-Holstein-Gottorf (FG 388. Der Hochgeachtete) war im Verlagskonsortium von Anfang an dabei (vgl. 421031A) und erwies sich als zuverlässiger Verlagsbeiträger. S. 440130. Dort berichtet F. Ludwig Carl Gustav (v.) Hille (FG 302. Der Unverdrossene): „Aus Holstein ist es richtig erleget".

6 Auf diese Weise wollte F. Ludwig die von Beyer vorgeschossene und diesem quittierte Summe zurückzahlen. Ob Winckler nur als Bankier die hzl. Zahlung verbuchte und an Beyer überwies, ob Beyer die Summe Winckler abgetreten hatte oder ob Winckler sie gegen Schulden Ludwigs verrechnete, gibt der Briefwechsel nicht zu erkennen. Winckler wartete mit 451019 aber noch auf den Eingang der Zahlung. Zu dem Leipziger Handelsherrn Georg Winckler s. 451019 K 0. Zum Zahlungsverkehr betr. das. *GB 1646* s. 450127 K 1.

7 Carl Gustav (v.) Hille (FG 302) hatte F. Ludwig in 450126 um eine die neu aufgenommenen Mitglieder betreffende Liste ersucht, da er die seine an Hz. Christian Ludwig v. Braunschweig-Calenberg (FG 372) weitergegeben habe. Diese Liste ging Hille mit dem Brief 450221 F. Ludwigs zu, der Hille bat, diese Liste zu kopieren und bei Bedarf Hz. August zukommen zu lassen. Vgl. auch 441231.

450722

Herzog August d. J. von Braunschweig-Wolfenbüttel an Johann Valentin Andreae

Beantwortet durch 450806. — Hz. August d.J. v. Braunschweig-Wolfenbüttel (FG 227) entnimmt Johann Valentin Andreaes (FG 463. 1646) Brief vom 2.7. (1645), daß dieser an Fieber leidet und wünscht ihm Genesung. — Er sendet eine Beilage, die Auskunft über den Druck von (Johann Heinrich Boecklers und Martin Nessels) Panegyrika (auf ihn selbst) gebe. Es mangele noch an Drucktypen. — August läßt die letzte, von ihm verbesserte Fassung seiner *Evangelischen Kirchen-Harmonie* abschreiben. Er habe bereits 36 Bogen bis auf den 2. Sonntag nach Trinitatis im ersten Teil abschreiben lassen. Daher habe die (in das Buch zu integrierende) Passionsharmonie etwas warten müssen, damit Notwendigeres vorgehen konnte. — Sobald er, Hz. August, das vermehrte Gesellschaftsbuch der FG (*GB 1646*) von F. Ludwig (Der Nährende) erhält, werde er Andreae ein Exemplar senden.

Q HAB: Cod. Guelf. 236.2 Extrav., Bl. 85rv, eigenh.; Briefzählung Andreaes in roter Tinte: 30. u. 87, am Rande übereinander 45. 27. — Kurzes Zitat daraus in *Begemann: FG und Andreae*, 34.

A *Fehlt.*

30. L.¹
Ehrwürdiger Hochgelahrter Lieber besonder und getreuer, aus seinem schreiben, vom 2. Julii: vernehme ich mitleidenlich, daß es sich noch zu keiner besserung will anlassen; sondern auch eine Febris continua, sichᵃ anfindet. Gott ändere alles nach seinem väterlichen willen, und verleihe bessere Zeitungen: welches ich von herzen wunsche: Wie es mit den Panegyricis² aufgehet, gibt der beischlus: Es hat an etlichen typis gemangelt, die albereit von der gattung alhie stehen: Ich laß noch fleissig die Harmonica³ abschreiben, nachdem ich sie, nach der lezten Censur, vorher durchgelesen, und verbessert. Habe albereit bei die 36 Bogen bis auf die ii. Dominic. p. F. Trin. im Ersten teihle lassen abschreiben: dannenhero es sich mit der H*armon*iâ Passionis,⁴ in etwas verweilet. Dan Magis necessaria praecedant, heisset es. So bald das augierte Kreuter und Geselschaft Buch⁵ mir wird von d*em* Ernehrenden, Fürst Ludewigen von Anhalt, zugesand werden: wil ich alsbald ein Exemplar übersenden. valescens, verbleibe ich sein und der Seinen,
   stets woll affectionierter Freund,
   Augustus hZBuL *ms.*
Wb. den 22. Jul. Mar. Magd.

T a *Folgt* <auch> *oder* <noch>

K 1 30. Schreiben (L = Litterae) (des Jahres 1645) Hz. Augusts d.J. v. Braunschweig-Wolfenbüttel (FG 227) an Johann Valentin Andreae (FG 463. 1646).
2 Der Lüneburger Neudruck v. Johann Heinrich Boeckler: Augusti ducis Brunovicensis et Luneburgensis fama non moritura (1645), daran angehängt der Neudruck v. Martin Nessel: Panegyricus Illustrissimo ac Celsissimo Principi ac Domini, DN. Augusto, Duci Brunovicensi & Luneburgensi, Domino suo clementissimo, 54–139. S. 450319 K 9 u. 450806 K 2. Der „beyschlus" könnte ein Probedruck, Titelblatt oder eine Probe der gebrauchten Schriftgattungen gewesen sein. Davon fehlten eine ausreichende Zahl von Lettern oder Typen. In 450806 spricht Andreae von dem „Muster famæ non morituræ, vnd panegyricj Nesselianj". Am 28.8.1645 dankte Andreae Boeckler für dessen Brief „cum gemino auspicij regii exemplo", d.h. für 2 Exemplare von Boecklers und Nessels

Panegyrika, von denen er gleich wieder eines an den Herzog zurückgesandt habe. Das andere wundervolle und gelehrte Buch habe er erfreut gelesen und sich belehrt („eruditus") gefühlt. Er fügte offenbar auf eine Frage Boecklers nach seiner beabsichtigten Reise zu Hz. August hinzu: „Iam diu est, cum me invitavit pleno amorj", wolle aber mit Rücksicht auf seine alte Frau, Kinder und Enkel, seinen Herzog (Eberhard III. v. Württemberg), sein geistliches Amt und den bevorstehenden Tod nicht mehr den Ort wechseln. Dafür bot er Boeckler an, ihm die Stelle bei dem so großen Musenführer oder Apollon („tantum Musagetam", d.i. Hz. August) zu verschaffen: „Bibliothecæ ei*us*, inter alia honesta munia præficj posses, quanto rei literariæ proventus!" SUB Hamburg: Sup. ep. 24, Bl. 42rv. Zu Musagetes s. 450901 K 16.

3 Zu Hz. Augusts Revision der Bibelübersetzung Luthers in Form einer *Evangelischen Kirchen-Harmonie* (1646 u.ö.) der gottesdienstlichen Perikopentexte s. 411214, 451101 u.ö.

4 Hz. Augusts Passionsharmonie *Die Historie und Geschichte Von DEs HErrn Jesu/ des *Gesalbten/ Leyden/ Sterben und Begräbniß* war 1641 in der 2. Auflage erschienen. Ob der Herzog zur Zeit des vorliegenden Briefs schon an einer neuen Version arbeiten wollte oder ob er hier nur von der bevorstehenden Darstellung der Passion in seiner *Evangelischen Kirchen-Harmonie* spricht, kann an dieser Stelle unentschieden bleiben. Vgl. 401111 u. I, 411214 III E. Da der Vorausdruck der *Kirchen Harmonie* (1644/45) die Passion aussparte, mag August von der Inkorporation der Leidensgeschichte in der vervollständigten Kirchenharmonie sprechen. S. 411214 III F–G u. 460127. 1650 ließ der Herzog die Passionsharmonie allerdings erneut abschreiben und drucken. S. 411214 III L.

5 *GB 1646.* S. 440130 K 3 u. 450126 K 4 zum Beitrag Hz. Augusts u. anderer Verlagsbeteiligter. Der korrekte Gesellschaftsname F. Ludwigs ist Der Nährende.

450725

Diederich von dem Werder an Fürst Ludwig

Diederich v. dem Werder (FG 31. Der Vielgekörnte) sagt F. Ludwig (Der Nährende) die Durchsicht von fünf Reimgesetzen zu Impresen zu. Dasjenige auf Johann Michael Moscherosch (FG 436. Der Träumende) wird Werder Georg Philipp Harsdörffer (FG 368. Der Spielende) schicken, ebenso wird er Harsdörffer über die Usancen des Stickens der Wappen und Impresen auf Atlas unterrichten. Er hofft, von Harsdörffer eine Ariost-Ausgabe und ein Exemplar von Luigi Alamannis *Girone il Cortese* zu erlangen. — Ein (von F. Ludwig zugestellter) Bogen mit Versen ist von Werder zwar ebenfalls durchgesehen, aber von seinem Diener in Dessau vergessen worden. Er habe bereits veranlaßt, den Bogen herbeizuschaffen, was spätestens am kommenden Tag in der Frühe geschehen müßte. Er macht sich auf die Gesellschaftsstrafe des Weintrinkens aus dem Ölberger gefaßt, wenn nur sein (säumiger) Diener zur Strafe einen Becher Sauerbier oder Wasser zu leeren hat.

Q HM Köthen: V S 544, Bl. 486r–487v [A: 487v], 486v u. 487r leer; rotes Lacksiegel. — *D: KE,* 178f. (vgl. 171). — *BN: Bürger,* 1440 Nr. 55.

A *Dem Nehrenden zu handen. Cöthen*
Von anderer H. eine kurze Zahlenkolonne (Rechnung).

Des Höchstgeehrten Herren Nehrenden schreiben ist samt den beylagen alhier wohl eingehändigt worden¹, vnd wird kürtzlich drauf geantwortet:
1. Die 5 achtzeilige reimen sollen noch heute übersehen werden.²
2. Dem Spielenden sollen, des Träumenden seine, vonᵃ mir auch zukommen.³
3. Demselben sol auch von dem Atlas vnd gemälde vonᵃ mir geschrieben werden.⁴
4. Bey eben demselben hoffe ich den Ariost⁵ vnd Cortese⁶ zuerlangen.
5. O Weh, der mir zugestellte vordreᵇ bogen ist von mir zwar zu dessaw übersehen worden, beneben den reimen, darbey dan auch etzliche errinnerungen geschehen. Es hatt denselben aber mein diener nicht wieder eingepackt, vnd ist zu dessaw in meiner Mutter⁷ haus ligen blieben, jch habe aber eilends einen abgefertigt, solchen hehrzubringen, hoffe er soll noch heute wieder hier sein, oder doch morgen mit dem frühesten. Jch wil mich gerne der Straffe einenᶜ öhlberger⁸ mit gutem Wein auszutrincken unterwerffenᵇ, wan mein diener mitᵇ einem becherᵈ Sauersbiers oder wassers auch angesehen wird. Der Gerechtikeit⁹ alles empfehlende verbleibet

Des Nehrenden
Dienstwilligster
Der Vielgekörnte.

Reinsdorff den 25. Heumonats 1645.

I

Ein Gedicht und sechs Reimgesetze Fürst Ludwigs von 1645

Q HM Köthen: V S 546, Bl. 76rv, eigenh. mit Verbesserungen einer unbekannten H. — Zum Vergleich der Impresen- und Reimgesetztexte wurde die Impresen- und Reimgesetze-Liste FG 423–432, a. a. O., Bl. 77rv herangezogen. Auch sie stammt, tw. in sauberer Abschrift, von F. Ludwig. Zit. mit der Sigle *L2*. Beide Fassungen stimmen nicht bzw. im Falle von *L2* nur partiell mit der Fassung im *GB Kö.* III, Bl. 24r–29r, überein und sind als Vorstufen anzusehen. Die im Textapparat dokumentierten Textvarianten des *GB Kö.* geben vielleicht die im Brief angesprochenen Verbesserungen Diederichs v. dem Werder wieder.

<blockquote>
Kling und Klagegedicht
über den plötzlichen abgang
Einer hohen nahe anverwandten
Fürstlichen person¹

Ach Vetter edler freund, wie seit ihr doch verblichen
   Jn so geschwinder eil'? Es war bestimt die Zeit
   Jhrᵃ soltet eilen fort hin in die Herligkeit,
Drumb ist der leibes tod bey euch bald eingeschlichen
</blockquote>

450725 Diederich von dem Werder

    Und[b] ewres lebens zeit sehr schnell artig gestrichen,
       Das eurer Seelen nicht schad die zergengligkeit
       Dan sie vol freud' und wonn' erlangt die ewigkeit
    Dahin ihr von uns seit gar sanftiglich gewichen[c]
    Der Tod uns[d] plötzlich schreckt[e] ihr aber selig bleibt
       Das[f] ewre Seele möcht' entkommen allem leid,
    Dan[g] sie vor angst und noth erlangt die höchste freud'
       Geordnet ist von Gott' in seine wachsam' hand
       O wie so selig ist darinnen euer stand
    Den kein Mensch in der welt mit wercken kan vergelten.

42..²

Der Edele	Die kleine Schelwurtz wird genant auch Gottes gnad
	Es ist ein edles kraut, das manche kranckheit heilet
Das kraut gottes	Den[h] wunden mercklich hilfft, wan noch so groß der schad'
Gnad, oder die kleine	Drumb Edel mir der Nahm' ist worden zugetheilet
Schelwurtz	Aus[i] obrer kraft von Gott zugehet fein gerad'
	Ein[j] edel[k] tapfer hertz wird[l] doch nicht übereilet
Aus Oberer kraft	[m]Und bringet frucht die ihm zu hohen ehren komt[n]
	[o]Draus guten nutzen es mit hohem Ruhme nimt
A.W.H.Z.S.J.C.u.B.	

42..³

Der Trachtende	Es ist ein wunderding umb diesen Wurtzelbaum
	Er[p] mit den ästen sich rabwarts zur erden beuget
	Und wurtzelt immer[q] fort, nimt einen großen raum
Der Wurtzelbaum	Mit[r] neuen beumen ein und immer weiter steiget,
	Wer trachtet[s] tugend nach der kan ausruhen kaum
	Jhr[t] gehet fleißig nach, und fleißig sich erzeiget
Nach erweiterung	Drumb Trachtend ich genant fruchtbringen gerne wil,
	Und[u] zu erweiterung der[v] tugend steht mein Ziel.
J.G.H.Z.S.J.C.u.B.[w]	

4...⁴

Der Behägliche[x]	Des Mastixbaumes hartz behäglich dem gehirn
	Und unserm Magen ist Es[y] beyden stercke giebet
	So guten [kraft][z] nun wirckt in ihme das gestirn[aa]
Der Mastixbaum und	Behäglich'[ab] ich darumb den Nahmen auch[ac] beliebet
sein hartz	Ein erbar Biederman aufrichtig an der Stirn
	Und in dem hertzen ist, mit willen nie betrübet
Dem Magen und	den[ad] nechsten Sondern sich fruchtbringend so bezeigt
gehirn	Das ihm mit nutzen ist ein iederman geneigt.
S. G.[ae]	
[76v]	

426.⁵

Der Bemühete

Die Springkörner

Zum austreiben
Ch. L.

Springkörner seind bemüht zu treiben weidlich aus
Den unraht in dem leib, Bemühet ich geheißen
Daher geworden bin, das nun des landmans haus
Erhalten werd', als sol man sich dahin befleißen
Zu treiben^af ab was sonst geb' einen harten straus
Doch mus bescheidenheit darbey sein, wen man reißen
Sich^ag aus der kriegsnot wil, dan bringt es solche frucht
Drin der gemeine nutz aufs beste wird gesucht.

1645

427.⁶

Der Nachfolgende

Ein schön jung^ak aufgeschoßenes birnenreis

Seinem stamme
B.H.Z.S.G.C.u.B.

Ein junges birnen reis schmackhafter guter art
Folgt seinem stamme nach, an^ah schmacke^ai größ' und güte,
Nachfolgend drumb^aj der Nahm' auch mir gegeben ward
Dem^al guten nachfolgt^am gern ein tugendhaft gemüte,
Verfüren^an nicht leicht leßt wil man es trücken hart.
Für^ao allen lastern es vornemlich sich auch hüte,
So wird es wahre frucht vorbringen ieder zeit
Sich^ap Mit Nutzen gleichesfals erweitern weit und breit.

1645

428.⁷

Der Gleichende

Der Sevenbaum

Dem Weirauche
G. F.

Des^aq [sic] Sevenbaum vergleicht^ar wol im geruche sich
Dem weirauch' angezünd' am nächsten wol^as vergleichet
Der Gleichend' auch genant darumb^at bin worden ich
Da seht^au wie die Natur die hand freygebig^av reichet
Jn allem unserm^aw leib. Es wil auch williglich
Ein^ax fromm-andechtigs hertz durch gutthat sein erweichet
Zu^ay bringen edle frucht, die uns gar wol gedeyt,
Wan^az wir [durch das?] gebet seind aller angst befreyt

1645

T a *von mir eingefügt*. — **b** *Eingefügt*. — **c** einen öhlberger *gebessert aus* eines öhlbergers — **d** *Folgt* <mit>

T I a *Bis* fort *von der unbek. H. eingefügt für* <Drin ihr abgehen solt'> — **b** *Bis* schnell *von der unbek. H. eingefügt für* <Von unsern augen auch seit ...[?]> Nachfolgendes *artig unsichere Lesung*. — **c** *Von F. Ludwig gebessert aus* geschlichen — **d** *Von F. Ludwig eingefügt für* <zwar> — **e** *Von F. Ludwig eingefügt über und neben unleserlichen Streichungen*. — **f** *Zeile von der unbek. H. eingefügt für* <Und in welt ängsten nicht> nun eure zeit vertreibt — **g** *Zeile von der unbek. H. eingefügt für*: Die Ruh' ist euch bewahret [? *Verbessert aus* bestimmt] die allen auserwehlten *Vermutlich alternativ zu* Dan sie vor angst und noth *hat die unbek. H. auch ergänzt*: Und frey von aller quaal — **h** *GB Kö.* Den wunden hilft es wol *usw.* — **i** *Bis* zugehet *von F. Ludwig eingefügt bzw. verbessert für* <Es sol ein Edel hertz> zugehen — **j** *Zeile von F. Ludwig gebessert aus* <Jedoch sich sehen für, das doch es> nicht werd' übereilet — **k** *Folgt* <hertz> — **l** *GB Kö.* weil sichs *statt* wird doch — **m**

Zeile von F. Ludwig eingefügt für <Aus obrer kraft [*darüber:* <Aufrichtigkeit>] von Gott aufrichtigkeit zukommt> komt her — **n** *Von F. Ludwig eingefügt für* <reicht> *L2 und GB Kö.* reicht — **o** *Zeile eingefügt von F. Ludwig für* <Und macht und bringen frucht> *Zeile in GB Kö.:* Daraus es nutzen auch mit großem ruhme zeucht. *L2 hat ebenfalls bereits* zeucht *für* nimt *L2 u. GB Kö. vermerken das Aufnahmejahr* 1645. *Der Titelzusatz G. [Gülich/ Jülich] C. [Cleve]* u. *B. [Berg] wurde in L2 durchgestrichen u. fehlt auch im GB Kö. (vgl. hier Anm. 2).* — **p** *Zeile in L2 u. GB Kö.:* Der mit den ästen sich rabwarts zur erden beuget *GB Kö. verbessert* rabwarts *zu* abwarts — **q** *L2 u. GB Kö.* drinnen — **r** *Von F. Ludwig eingefügt für* <Von> — **s** *Von F. Ludwig eingefügt für* <nach der> *Zeile in GB Kö.:* Wer an der tugend helt, der kan ja ruhen kaum, — **t** *Von F. Ludwig verbesserte Zeile in L2:* Er geht ihr embsig nach, und eifrig sich erzeiget *Zeile im GB Kö.:* Er trachtet ihr stets nach, und sich behertzt erzeiget, — **u** *Zeile in L2 von F. Ludwig verbessert, hat am Versbeginn* Dan nach *statt* Und zu *GB Kö.* Dan nach — **v** *Von F. Ludwig nach unleserlicher Ergänzung eingefügt für* <sol se [?]> — **w** *L2 u. GB Kö. vermerken das Aufnahmejahr* 1645. *Der Titelzusatz G. [Gülich/ Jülich] C. [Cleve]* u. *B. [Berg] wurde in L2 durchgestrichen u. fehlt auch im GB Kö. (vgl. hier Anm. 2). L2 hat für* J. *[Johann]* H. *[Hans].* — **x** *Mühsam entzifferbar von F. Ludwig gebessert aus* <Ma...> — **y** *GB Kö.* und ihnen stärcke giebet — **z** *Bis* ihme *von F. Ludwig eingefügt für* <einfluß [?] drumb und kraft [...?]> *Fälschlich stehen gebliebene Kasusform* guten *Lies:* gute — **aa** *Zeile in L2 u. GB Kö.:* Wan gute kraft nur wirckt in ihme das gestirn — **ab** *Die von F. Ludwig gebesserte Zeile in L2, übernommen im GB Kö.:* Behäglich auch darumb der Nahme mir beliebet: — **ac** *Von F. Ludwig eingefügt für* <gern [?]> — **ad** *Wörterreihenfolge durch Bezifferung von F. Ludwig geändert aus:* Sondern sich dem Nächsten *L2 u. GB Kö. setzen hinter* nechsten *ein syntaktisch notwendiges Komma.* — **ae** *L2 u. GB Kö. vermerken das Aufnahmejahr* 1645. — **af** *In L2 von F. Ludwig gebessert zu:* wenden *GB Kö.* wenden — **ag** *F. Ludwig verbessert in L2, übernommen in GB Kö.:* Sich wil aus kriegesnot — **ah** *L2 am* — **ai** *L2 u. GB Kö.* schmacke, größe, güte, — **aj** *GB Kö.* hier — **ak** *L2* junges *statt* jung aufgeschoßenes — **al** *Zeile in GB Kö.:* Drumb folg' ich gutem nach: Ein Tugendhaft gemüte — **am** *L2 bessert zu:* folgt nach — **an** *Zeile von F. Ludwig eingefügt und verbessert für:* Verfürt nicht leichtlich wird zum bösen abgekart *Zeile in L2 von F. Ludwig gebessert zu:* sich nit verfüren leßt wan man es drucket hart *Aus:* Verfüren sich nit leßt zum bösen abgekahrt *GB Kö.* Lest sich verführen nicht, und drückt mans noch so hart — **ao** *Zeile von F. Ludwig eingefügt und verbessert für:* Für allen lastern <sich> es <am meisten> sich auch hüte *Zeile in L2 von F. Ludwig gebessert zu*: Für allen lastern doch vornemlich es sich hüte *Aus:* Für lastern allen vornemlich sich auch hüte *GB Kö.* Vornemlich es sich doch für allen lastern hüte — **ap** *Zeile von F. Ludwig eingefügt und verbessert für:* Mit nutzen sich <zugleich> erweitern weit und breit. *Zeile in L2 von F. Ludwig gebessert zu:* Mit Nutzen gleichsfals sich erweitern weit und breit *Übernommen in GB Kö.* — **aq** *Zeile in L2 u. GB Kö.:* Des Sevenbaumes holtz fast im geruche sich *Eine zusätzliche Reinschrift der Imprese und des Reimgesetzes FG 428 von Schreiberh. liegt a. a. O., Bl. 79rv (FG 428–437) vor. Ihre Textfassung entspricht jener im GB Kö.* — **ar** vergleicht wol *als zu streichen markiert.* — **as** Hier *und in L2 von F. Ludwig eingefügt für* <sich> — **at** *L2* daher — **au** *GB Kö. Verschreibung* saht — **av** *Von F. Ludwig eingefügt für* <einander> — **aw** *GB Kö.* uns zu gutt' *statt* unserm leib — **ax** *Zeile bis* hertz *von F. Ludwig gebessert aus:* Ein <unferdecht> fromm<es> hertz — **ay** *Zeile bis* frucht *von F. Ludwig gebessert aus:* Das es bring edle [edle *unsichere Lesung*]. *Zeile in L2 von F. Ludwig gebessert zu:* Zu bringen wahre frucht, die reichlich uns gedyt, *Aus:* Zu bringen gute frucht, die uns gar wol gedyt, *Die Verbesserung in GB Kö. übernommen.* — **az** *Durch mehrfache Streichungen und Einfügungen schwer lesbare Zeile, von F. Ludwig gebessert aus:* Und ... gebete es uns von aller angst befreyt. *L2:* Wan durch gebete wir seind aller angst befreyt. *GB Kö.* Wan wir auf das gebet seind aller angst befreyt.

K 1 Diese Sendung hat sich nicht im Konzept oder in Abschriften im Köthener Erzschrein erhalten und konnte auch andernorts nicht von uns ermittelt werden. Ein Textzeugnis im Köthener Erzschrein der FG dürfte aber der Sendung F. Ludwigs nahegekommen sein, s. Beil. I.

2 Vgl. Beil. I.

3 Mit 450613 hatte Werder einen Brief Georg Philipp Harsdörffers (FG 368. Der Spielende), der als Vermittler zwischen der FG und Johann Michael Moscherosch (FG 436. Der Träumende) fungierte, an F. Ludwig weitergeleitet. Dieser Brief enthielt auch „den reimsatz des Träumenden", den Werder offenbar im Auftrag des Fürsten Korrektur las und dann Harsdörffer zurücksandte. Vgl. 450504A K 2 u. 450730 K.

4 Die Neumitglieder hatten die Möglichkeit, ihr Wappen und ihre FG-Imprese für die FG-Gobelins (im Köthener Schloß) unter Vermittlung F. Ludwigs und gegen ein Entgeld in Leipzig sticken zu lassen oder sich den Atlasstoff und eine Zeichnung der Imprese zusenden und die Stickerei selbst anfertigen zu lassen. Am Ende entschied sich Harsdörffer für die erste Variante. Vgl. 450504A K 5.

5 Das Interesse an Ariost und „Cortese" (s. Anm. 6) steht vermutlich mit dem Wunsch in Zusammenhang, Werders Übersetzung des *Orlando furioso* neu auflegen zu lassen. Harsdörffer versuchte damals, einen Verleger für eine Neuauflage des Werderschen *Rasenden Roland* (Leipzig 1632–1636) zu finden. Er hatte darin Matteo Boiardos älteres Epos *Orlando Innamorato* mitverarbeitet. Vor allem war die dt. Bearbeitung unvollständig geblieben und in mehreren Schüben erschienen. Die Veröffentlichung umfaßte nur die ersten 30 Gesänge, die anschließenden 15 fehlen. Harsdörffer schrieb in 451101 an F. Ludwig, er hoffe, zu Frankfurt in Johann David Zunner einen Verleger ausgemacht zu haben, jedoch sei dessen Bereitschaft nicht gesichert. Weder bei Zunner (1610–1653) noch bei einem anderen Verleger ist es zu einer Neuaufl. gekommen. Der Bericht in *Hille: Palmbaum,* 196 scheint auf einer Fehlinformation zu beruhen: „Des Ludovico Ariosto **rasenden Roland**/ durch gnädige Beförderung des **Untadelichen** [Kf. Friedrich Wilhelm v. Brandenburg. FG 401] zum andern mal gedruckt zu Königsberg in Preussen". Vgl. 450900 K 13 u. 451101; Einleitung der Hgg. in *D. v. dem Werder: Roland* I, S. IX–LXXI, hier S. XXII ff.; *Dünnhaupt: Handbuch,* 4255 f.

6 Vermutlich Luigi Alamanni: GIRONE IL CORTESE (1549), eine Nachdichtung des frz. Artusromans *Guiron le courtois,* die Werder wohl ebenfalls in Versform übersetzt hatte. S. 230819 K 8 u. Beil. I. Unwahrscheinlicher ist, daß sich Werder für den folgenden Titel interessiert hat: Cortesi Cortese: Orestilla. Tragedia boschereccia di Cortese Cortesi Padouano. Novamente Stampata. Con licenza de' Superiori. In Vicenza 1610. HAB: 145.4 Eth. (2).

7 Katharina v. dem Werder, geb. v. Hahn aus dem Hause Basedow (mecklenburg. Adel). Ihre Lebensdaten sind nicht bekannt. Diederichs Vater Gebhard starb bereits 1612. Diederich selbst wurde 1584 geboren. Hätte sie damals noch ihr Haus zu Dessau bewohnt, wäre seine Mutter schätzungsweise 80 Jahre alt gewesen. Vielleicht meint Werder aber nur ein ehemaliges Haus seiner Mutter. S. auch *Merzbacher: Werder* und *Ball: Diederich von dem Werder.*

8 Der sog. Ölberger, das rituelle Trinkgefäß der FG, das v. a. bei der Aufnahme neuer Mitglieder und bei (scherzhaften) Gesellschaftsstrafen eingesetzt wurde. S. zuerst 171224 K 5, vgl. 450500A K 7. Zur scherzhaften Gesellschaftsstrafe vgl. 371110 K 14, zuletzt 421129A K 5; demnächst: *Herz: Edle Ritter dieser Zunft.*

9 Bei substantiv. Ableitungen des Wortbildungsmusters Adjektiv/Adverb auf -ig mit dem Ableitungssuffix -keit wie Barmherzig-keit oder im vorliegenden Falle Gerecht-igkeit hatte Werder in 450420 ausgiebig für den Wegfall des -g- plädiert. Seine Schreibweise „Gerechtikeit" erfolgt also nicht willkürlich, sondern gehorcht morphologischen und phonologischen Argumenten, wenngleich diese gegen den Grundsatz der Morphemkonstanz verstießen.

K I 1 Es ist dies die einzige von uns ermittelte Textüberlieferung dieses Gedichts. Da Diederich v. dem Werder (FG 31. Der Vielgekörnte) im vorliegenden Brief von einem in Dessau vergessenen Bogen spricht, der „beneben den reimen" (den zuvor angesprochenen fünf Reimgesetzen), ebenfalls „etzliche errinnerungen", also Korrekturen Werders an einem anderen Text aufweist, könnte dieses Gedicht in der Tat Gegenstand dieser brieflichen Hinweise gewesen sein. Vgl. K 1. In 450220 K II 0 war bereits die Vermutung geäußert worden, das Gedicht könne von F. Ludwig auf den im Dezember 1644 verstorbenen Hz. Albrecht v. Sachsen-Eisenach (FG 17) verfaßt worden sein.
2 D. i. FG-Nr. 423: Hz. Adolph Wilhelm v. Sachsen-Weimar (Der Edele), der mit seinen jüngeren Brüdern und einer Reihe von Weimarer Hofleuten (insgesamt FG 423–432) am 3.2.1645 in Weimar in die FG aufgenommen worden war. Vgl. 450220 K 1 u. 16. Die Initiale am Schluß des Reimgesetzes kürzt seinen erweiterten Titel ab: „Adolph Wilhelm Herzog zu Sachsen, Jülich, Cleve und Berg". Vgl. *Conermann III*, 507 f.
3 D. i. FG-Nr. 424: Hz. Johann Georg I. v. Sachsen-Eisenach (Der Trachtende). Vgl. Anm. 2 u. *Conermann III*, 508–510.
4 D. i. FG-Nr. 425: Samuel (v.) Goechhausen (Der Behägliche), hzl. sachs.-weimar. Kanzler. Vgl. Anm. 2 u. *Conermann III*, 510 f.
5 D. i. FG-Nr. 426: Christian Legell (Der Bemühete), hzl. sachs.-weimar. Hofmann. Vgl. Anm. 2 u. *Conermann III*, 511 f.
6 D. i. FG-Nr. 427: Hz. Bernhard v. Sachsen-Jena (Der Nachfolgende). Vgl. Anm. 2 u. *Conermann III*, 512 f.
7 D. i. FG-Nr. 428: Georg Frantzke (Der Gleichende), langjähriger hzl. Rat in Weimar, ehe er 1641 als Geh. Rat, Kanzler und Konsistorialpräsident in den Dienst Hz. Ernsts I. (FG 19) nach Gotha wechselte. Vgl. Anm. 2 u. *Conermann III*, 513 f.

450726

Andreas Tscherning über Herzog August d. J. von Braunschweig-Wolfenbüttel in einem Brief an Matthaeus Apelles von Löwenstern

Da sein Brief vom 17.5.1645 unbeantwortet blieb, vermutet Andreas Tscherning, sein väterlicher Förderer Matthaeus Apelles v. Löwenstern könnte noch krank darniederliegen. Besserungswünsche. — Matthias Machners Schreiben mit den Aphorismen Matthias Berneggers hat er erhalten, kann es jedoch wegen einer theologischen Doktorpromotion derzeit nicht beantworten und beläßt es bei der Bitte, Grüße auszurichten. Herr Queisser lasse Matthias Machner bitten, beim Kirchendiener der (Breslauer) Maria-Magdalenenkirche, Balthasar Helle(n), wegen der Petschaft seines Vaters nachzufragen. — Der Lübecker Verleger, der Tschernings Neubearbeitung der Oper *Judith* (von Martin Opitz, FG 200) längst hätte herausbringen sollen, hat die Widmungszuschrift (an drei Danziger Herren und Freunde) und einen Teil der von Apelles komponierten Stimmen verloren. Tscherning liege mittlerweile sein überarbeiteter Text in Rostock fertig gedruckt vor, jedoch benötige er zur Veröffentlichung von Apelles noch eine neue Abschrift der Noten. Tscherning teilt Apelles die Titel der noch vorhandenen Stimmen mit. Ob er Apelles' Namen bei den Chören nennen soll? Wegen der Postgebühren verzichtet Tscherning darauf, Apelles ein Exemplar des Librettos zu senden. — Tscherning erkundigt sich, ob (der Breslauer Drukker) Georg Baumann Tschernings Gedichtsammlung (*Früling, 1642*) erneut aufgelegt habe. — Tscherning plant, sich mit einem Gedicht an Hz. August d.J. v. Braunschweig-Wolfenbüttel (FG 227) auf Anregung von dessen schlesischem Leibarzt (Martin Gosky) zu wenden. Der Herzog gebe viel in deutscher Sprache heraus und gehöre derselben (Fruchtbringenden) Gesellschaft wie der seelige Martin Opitz an. — Demnächst, scherzt Tscherning, werde er mit einem Gedicht alle Schlesier unter seinem Vorsitz zum Erwerb des Magistertitels einladen. — Apelles möge sich dafür auf Drängen einer (Rostocker) Vermieterin dafür einsetzen, daß Schrevinius bei ihr seine Logis-Schulden begleicht. Apelles möge sich auch für den wegen eines Tötungsdelikts einsitzenden Herrn Heß verwenden. Dieser habe vor 3 oder 4 Wochen von allen Kanzeln in Rostock um Versöhnung mit den Gemeinden bitten lassen. Der Sohn des Ratsherrn (Nikolaus) Herbst hält sich noch in einem Gasthaus in Lübeck auf und wartet auf einen Wechsel. — Den Grüßen seiner Frau (Katharina) an Apelles und dessen Ehefrau (Barbara) schließt Tscherning seine eigenen an. *Nachschrift:* Tscherning wünscht sich von Apelles ein vielleicht noch greifbares Exemplar der Gratulationsschrift, die ihm, Tscherning, schlesische Freunde zur Magisterpromotion und zur Bestallung als Professor (der Poesie an der Universität Rostock) gewidmet hatten. — Zwei Rostocker Studenten, Johann Quistorp d.J. und einer namens Schröter, halten sich in Thorn auf, um das anstehende Religionsgespräch zu besuchen. Über (Petrus) Zimmermann können sie für den Fall kontaktiert werden, daß ihnen Sendungen auf ihre Rückreise nach Rostock mitgegeben werden sollen. — Dr. Josephus Adjutus, den die Breslauer mit 150 Rth. unterstützt haben sollen und der zur Zeit in Rostock weilt, mußte Tscherning die Einladung an seinen Tisch abschlagen. — Tscherning wünscht zu erfahren, wie der zur Zeit in Hamburg lebende Student Daniel Hermann von seiner Mutter und von Magister Michael Hermann beurteilt wird. Sein früherer Vermieter und Lehrer in Rostock, Dr. Enzmer, wartet noch immer auf das schuldige Kostgeld und wird deshalb demnächst erneut nach Breslau schreiben.

Q BU Wrocław: R 3108, Bl. 23r–24v [A: 24v]; eigenh.; 2 rote Lacksiegel. — *D:* Borcherdt: *Tscherning*, 158f. u. 311 Anm. 32 (Auszüge). — *BN:* Borcherdt: *Tscherning*, S. 335 Nr. 91; *Bürge*r, 1365 Nr. 18.

A A Monsieur Mons. MATTHIEU APELLES de Lovenstern in Langenhof, Conseillier de sa Majesté Imperiale, & de son Altesse Duc de Monsterberg   à Breslau.
Empfangsvermerk: Præs. d. 28 Augusti 1645.

S. Magnifice, Strenue ac Nobilissi Dn. PARENS.

Heute vor 10 wochen, nemlich den 17 Maj habe an den hn. Vater ich geschrieben, weil ich aber noch zur zeit keine antwort darauff erhalten, muthmasse ich, es müße der h. Vater noch krank zu bette liegen, davon ihm der barmhertzige Gott zu beständiger gesundheit gnädig auffhelffen wolle.[1] hn. **Machners**[2] (den ich dinstlich zu grüßen bitte) liebes an mich sampt deß **Berneggeri aphorismis**[3] *etc.*[a]

habe ich zu recht erhalten, kan aber für diesesmal wegen bevorstehender Doctorpromotion in Facult. Theolog. nicht antworten. Jndeßen bittet Mons. Queisser[4] von ihm, nebenst fr. Salutation, er mochte sich doch unbeschwert bey dem Kirchknechte zu Mar*ia* Magd*alena*[5][,] Balthassar[a] Hellen genannt[,] erkundigen, ob nicht der abdruck oder nachricht wegen seines (deß Queissen) Seel. Vaters pitschafft fürhanden sey. Hæc ad Machnerum nostrum.

Die grösseste ursach an E. G. den hn. Vater zuschreiben ist diese, daß der Buchführer zu Lübeck der Esel, so meine Judith zu drucken auf sich nam, und uber 3 vierteljahr bey sich behilt, nicht allein mitler zeit[b] die Dedication davon, sondern auch etliche stimmen von den noten wegverlohren.[6] Weil dann nun die Judith an ihr selbst, und also der gantze text allbereit allhier zu Rostock, nachdem ich selbigen vielfeltig gebeßert vnd verändert, abgedruckt und fertig liegt, ietzt aber weiter nicht kan fortgefahren werden, biß der herr Vater mir die liebe erzeiget hat, und noch einmal[c] abgeschrieben zuschicket, alß gelanget an denselben, mein gehorsames ersuchen, er wolle mir aufs schleunigste hiermit gratificiren, damit beydes der Verleger und Drucker darüber nicht allzu ungedultig werden. Es ist aber noch fürhanden und übrig dieses, laut[d] den uberschrifften

Hebreer Chor Tenor 2.	
Hebr. Chor Bassus.	
der Könige Chor Ten. 1.	iedes sind 2 blätter, wie der h. vater sich wird zu erinnern wissen, was noch darzu gehört, ist leider hinweg, sonst solte das tractätlin allbereit fertig sein.
Chor der wache.	
Chor der wache 1 Ten.	
Chor der wache 2 Ten.	
Könige Chor 2 Ten. Royes	
Bassus a. 3 Könige	

[23v] Bitte abermal aufs ehiste mich zu födern, und solche grobheit zu verzeihen. Ob E. G. wegen der Chore ich nahmhafftig gedencken solle, bitte ich in gleichen zu berichten.[7] Von dem texte wolte ich ein exemplar mitgesendet haben, wann nicht zu viel auf die post ginge.

Ob Bauman gewiß meine poemata wider aufgelegt, wie der Catalogus berichtet, mochte ich gerne wißen.[8]

An den Fürsten von Braunschweig, der soviel in deutscher Sprache heraußgiebet und die vertraute gesellschaft helt, worinnen auch der Seel. Opitius war,[9] werde ich auf anreitzen seines Archiatri eines Schlesiers, mit gelegenheit schreiben, und zwar carminè. Jst außer schaden, und desto sicherer, weil der Archiater Doctor Gosky es selbst zu insinuiren versprochen.[10]

Auf künfftige wochen wil ich durch ein carmen die jenigen invitiren, so etwan gedächten unter mir Magistri zu werden. Jst iemand in Schlesien, so komme er herauß er soll ohne gradu nicht nach hause kehren.[11]

Die witwe, welcher Schrevinius[12] noch tischgeld schuldig, uberlaufft mich noch wochentlich, mochte gern ein ende sehen. Was aber in diesem negocio außgerichtet, wolle der herr Vater doch unbeschwert avisiren.

Wegen Heßen ist vor 3 oder 4 wochen von allen Cantzeln alhier, auf sein begehren, versöhnung mit der gemeine, als welche er durch verübten todschlag geärgert vorhin hette[,] gebeten worden. War sehr kläglich anzuhören.[13]

hn. Herbstes Senat*oris* filius[14] liegt annoch zu Lübeck stille im wirthshauß, bey dem vor 3 wochen die mutter einen boten herauß gehabt. Erwartet einen wechsel. Plura alias. Von meiner Caja[15] werden E. Gestr., dero Liebste, fr. Tarnau ehrendinstlich gegrüßt, wie auch von mir insonderheit. valete.

Jn Rostock den 26 Hewmon. im 1645sten Jahre.

AT^e.

[24r] P. S. wofern noch ein exemplar der gratulatorien fürhanden, so die Silesii auf meine promotion und officium mir^a zuschickten, bitte ich eines zu ubersenden.[16]

Zu^f Thoren [*Lies:* Thorn] sind anietzo 2 Rostocker Studenten, einer Doct. Quistorpii Sohn, der ander mit nahmens Schröter, welche den Synodum abwarten wollen.[17] Ob mit denselben hernach etwas könne hieher gesendet werden, relinquo tuo gravissimo judicio. Bey hn. Czimmermann[18] können sie erfraget werden, an den ich sie recommendiret.

D. Josephus Adjutus, welchem die Breßlauer sollen anderthalb hundert Ducaten verehret haben, denen er zur danckbarkeit eine orationem de certitudine salutis dediciret,[19] ist ietz und hier, begehrte an meinen tisch, dem ichs aber, auß vielen ursachen abgeschlagen.

Was hn. Mag. Danielis Herrmanni p. m. frau mutter oder Mag. Michael Herrm. von dem Studioso Daniele,[20] so anietzt zu Hamburg ist, für gedancken führen, und für aviso von ihm glauben, mochte ich gern sehen, daß es weitläufftig erkundiget und mir berichtet würde.

Der Doct. Enzmer,[21] dem er noch alhier das tischgeld schuldig, welches doch beydes die Mutter und Mag. Michael Herrman^g versprochen schon für einem jahr zu zahlen, ist sehr ungedultig, und wird ehistes wider hin nach Breßlau schreiben.

I

Tschernings Gedicht auf Herzog August d. J. von Braunschweig-Wolfenbüttel

Q [Titelblatt mit Titelkupfer] ARBUSTUM vel ARBORETUM | AUGUSTÆUM, | Æternitati ac domui Augustæ Selenianæ | sacrum, | Satum autem & educatum | à | MARTINO GOSKY, L. Silesio, Med. D. | & Archiatro, C. Pal. Caes. [Titelkupfer:] Typis Johan et Henr. Stern. Anno 1650 EX OFFICINA DUCALI WOLPHERBYTTANI. Bl. 554rv. — HAB (2 Ex.): T 904.2° Helmst. (1), auch dig.; Gn 4° 766 (Kupfertitel fehlt). — *BN: Hueck: Gelegenheitsgedichte,* Nr. 265.

450726 Andreas Tscherning

21. Martii
An. 1649.   Ad eundem Principem & Ducem.

NObile depositum cæli, stirps Guelphica, Linguæ
    Teutoniæ vindex maxime, & orbis Amor.
Quo primum vitæ generosum limen inisti
    Luciferum[a] fas est lactea gemma notet
Auspiciis sacer ortus erat, domus ignea cæli.
    Sidere conspicuo, vere nitebat humus.
Raros ausa vocant ingentia, quælibet ætas
    Alciden pariat fertilis illa sat est
Quamvis nos bellis afflixerit hactenus æther,
    Cum terris idem te daret, æquus erat.
[554v]   O Auguste tibi debet Germania cultum,
    Dum patrio didicit tersius ore loqui.
Magnarum sit dives opum te principe Teuto
    Redditur ingeno doctior ille tuo.
Tu decus armorum, decus immortale Minervæ:
    Tu benè das populis debita jura tuis.
Te patrem atq́; Ducem veneratur subdita tellus
    Nec tam Dux dici, quam pater esse velis.
Et quis sat digno te prædicet ore Poeta:
    Non si fortè suam tangat Apollo chelyn.
Augebunt reliquas invita silentia laudes,
    Venit & â tacito sæpius ore decus.
Orbis obæratus tibi: quamvis solvere nomen
    Ex animo cupiat, non tamen ille potest.
Nam tantis meritis non sufficit. Optime Princeps
    Solius arca Dei, quod tibi solvat, habet.

                    devotissimo cultu
                        mancipatus
        Andreas Tscherningius, P.P.
        in Academia Rostochiensi.

T a *Eingefügt.* — b *Lies:* inzwischen — c *Folgt* <laßen> — d *Eingefügt für* <nach> — e *Ligatur AT für Tschernings Initiale.* — f *Folgt* <Dantzig> — g Herrman *eingefügt, folgt* <mit ihme>

T I a *Druckfehler* Lnciferum

K Johann Rist (FG 467. 1647) versuchte, Tscherning die Bekanntschaft mit Johann Balthasar Schupp (1610–1661) und mit Justus Georg Schottelius (FG 397) zu vermitteln. Das gelang nicht. Vgl. *Borcherdt: Tscherning*, Kap. 15, Anm. 31 die Stellen, an denen Tscherning von Schottelius mit Hochachtung spricht. Zu Georg Philipp Harsdörffers (FG 368.

Der Spielende) Versuch, im Winter 1643 durch Rist und Matthaeus Apelles von Löwenstern (1594–1662), dem väterlichen Breslauer Freund und Förderer Tschernings, Verbindung zu diesem aufzunehmen, s. *Borcherdt: Tscherning*, 159f., auch 460610. Durch Apelles erhielt Tscherning, wie Borcherdt mitteilt, sogar einen Band von Harsdörffers *Frauenzimmer-Gesprächspiele*. Harsdörffer konnte aber auch auf einem anderen Weg zu Apelles und sicher auch zu Tscherning in Kontakt treten. Als der bekannte Nürnberger Pastor Johann Saubert d. Ä. Apelles am 17.1.1644 für ein Schreiben dankte, übermittelte er auch Grüße Harsdörffers, von denen Apelles Tscherning berichtet haben dürfte: „Dn. Harsdorfferus, Patricius apud nos literatissimus adscribi ex se salutem uoluit, qui ex mea fide T. A. aestimat, ut par est, cui etiam feci de tuis. Ecquid uero de Bohemo nostro? qui tam eleganti carmine immortalem me fecit." BU Wrocław: Akc. 1949/ 713 (Abschrift Klose 175), S.686. Aus Gründen des Standes und der bernstädt. Herkunft läßt sich der Erwähnte als David Behme (Böhm/ Bohemus, vgl. 440324 K 2) bestimmen, der ein Gedicht mit „David Bohemus Past. Eccl. Patriæ Bernst. Presbyt. Ducat. Ölsn. Senior" unterzeichnete, welches zu Ehren Tschernings in dessen Epigrammsammlung erschien: ANDREÆ TSCHERNINGII | SCHEDI- | ASMATUM | LIBER UNUS | [Zierleiste] | RostochI. | ANNO M. DC. XLIV. *Faber du Faur* Nr.264 = HAB: MF 1:59. Übrigens hatte Apelles nicht nur Tscherning, sondern auch Daniel Czepko (1605–1660) ein Exemplar der *Frauenzimmer-Gesprächspiele* von Harsdörffer, vermutlich deren vierten Teil (1644), zukommen lassen. In einem Brief aus Schweidnitz vom 4.10.1644 bedankte sich Czepko dafür und urteilte in interessanter Weise über Harsdörffer: „[…] so habe ich gutte vergnügung aus diesen spielen geschöpfft und gefallet mir die nachsinnliche Arbeit darinnen über die maßen wol. Und wer ist so ein fremdling in der aussauberung unser muttersprache, der nicht gestehen müsse, daß sie die große Hilffe in bedachtsamer umbsetzung ausländischer schrifften, überkomme. […] dannenher ist an dem Nutz nicht zu zweiffeln, den wir nach kurtzer Zeit je mehr und mehr aus solcher umbschreibung empfinden werden; zu geschweigen daß der spielende so artig seine erfindungen aus allerhand sprachen aufzuführen und anzustreichen weiß, vornehmlich auf den sprachgrund sein genawes absehn nimbt. […] Ich meines wenigen bedünckens bleibe noch auf meiner alten meinung: daß nehmlich die gesetze vnd maaßlehren, nirgend als von der Tichtkunst vor unsere sprache zunehmen und zu endlehnen sein. Den wo wird der fall und die steigung der worthe, so wol die ausführung, reinlichkeit und Deutung derselbigen, nachsinnlicher in das Urteil getzogen, als aldar. Reime leiden keine fehler, oder sind nicht reime. Dannenher acht ich es höher einen gutten deutschen Reim abzufassen als einen lateinischen Vers. Weil ich mehr freiheit bei den Lateinern als deutschen habe." Daniel Czepko: Sämtliche Werke. Unter Mitarb. v. Ulrich Seelbach hg. v. Hans-Gert Roloff u. Marian Szyrocki. Bd. 6: Briefwechsel und Dokumente zu Leben und Werk. Bearb. Lothar Mundt u. Ulrich Seelbach. Berlin 1995, 56–58, hier 57f. (Quelle: StB Breslau: R 3100, Kriegsverlust. Überliefert in Peter Epstein: Apelles von Löwenstern. Mit einer Neuausgabe der Chöre zu Martin Opitz' „Judith". Breslau 1929, 25f.).

1 Matthaeus Apelles v. Löwenstern litt schwer an der Gicht, an der er auch verstarb. Vgl. zu Apelles 440324 K 1.

2 Zu Matthias Machner (1598–1662), Sekretär, Kirchen- und Waisenhausnotar des Breslauer Stadtrates und Korrespondenzsammler, vgl. 440324 K u. K I 1.

3 Im Sommer 1645 hielt Tscherning eine Privatvorlesung über die Aphorismen des Justus Lipsius und Berneggers. Privatvorlesungen spülten mit 2 Rtl. pro Teilnehmer Einkünfte direkt in die Taschen des Lehrenden und waren daher für das akademische Auskommen unverzichtbar. Vgl. *Borcherdt: Tscherning*, 142. In Lipsius' Fall dürften dessen *Politicorvm Sive Civilis Doctrinæ Libri Sex* (zuerst Leiden 1589, 2. Ausg. Leiden 1590. HAB: 103 Pol. [1]; Ndr. der Ausg. Frankfurt a. M. 1704 hg. Wolfgang Weber, Hildesheim

[u. a.] 1998) herangezogen worden sein, ein immens erfolgreiches Werk über die politische Kunst, zum Großteil aus kompilierten Denksprüchen, Sentenzen und Aphorismen antiker Klassiker wie v. a. Seneca und Tacitus, aber auch Moderner wie Jean Bodin oder Niccolò Machiavelli bestehend. Ungeachtet der Cento-Manier ist das Werk systematisch aufgebaut und theoretisch strukturiert. Lipsius selbst dazu: „Cùm enim Inuentio tota est Ordo à nobis sint, verba tamen et sententias variè conquisiuimus à scriptoribus priscis. idque maximè ab Historicis: hoc est, vt ego censeo, à fonte ipso Prudentiæ Ciuilis." Lipsius, a. a. O. (Ausg. Leiden 1590), Bl. [† 7]r. Vgl. Lipsius en Leuven. Catalogus van de tentoonstelling in de Centrale Bibliotheek te Leuven, 18 september – 17 oktober 1997 onder de redactie van G. Tournoy, J. Papy en J. de Landtsheer. Leuven 1997, 206–211; George Hugo Tucker: Justus Lipsius and the Cento Form. In: (Un)masking the Realities of Power: Justus Lipsius and the Dynamics of Political Writing in Early Modern Europe. Ed. by Erik De Bom (a. o.). Leiden, Boston 2011, 163–192 (dort auch die Aufsätze von Harald E. Braun, Harro Höpfl); David Martin Jones: Aphorism and the Counsel of Prudence in Early Modern Statecraft. The Curious Case of Justus Lipsius. In: Parergon 28 (2011), H. 2, 55–86; Florian Neumann: Geschichtsschreibung als Kunst. Famiano Strada S. I. (1572–1649) und die ars historica in Italien. Berlin [u. a.] 2013, 102; Wolfgang E. J. Weber: Justus Lipsius und das Politikverständnis seiner Zeit. In: Justus Lipsius und der europäische Späthumanismus in Oberdeutschland. Hg. Alois Schmid. München 2008, 23–36, hier S. 30. Der nicht zuletzt im Interesse an Tacitus mit Lipsius verbundene Matthias Bernegger (1582–1640) hatte eine kommentierte Ausgabe dieses Werkes veranstaltet, die postum erstmals 1641 in Straßburg erschien: IVSTI. LIPSI. POLITICORVM. LIBRI. SEX. CVM. INDICE. ADCVRATO. Ex Instituto MATTHIÆ BERNEGGERI. Edebat IO. FREINSHEMIVS. HAB: Sf 441 (durchschossenes Ex.); vgl. *Dünnhaupt: Handbuch*, S. 504 Nr. 45. Johannes Freinsheim (1608–1660), in Straßburg ein Bernegger-Schüler und Schwiegersohn und Mitbegründer der „Auffrichtigen Gesellschaft von der Tannen", wurde 1642 in Uppsala Prof. der Politik und Rhetorik, sodann 1648–1650 schwed. Hofbibliothekar und -historicus. Er starb als kurpfälz. Rat und Professor zu Heidelberg. Vgl. 400319 K 3. Bernegger hatte zudem als Präses einer akadem. Disputation in Straßburg 200 Denksprüche oder Sentenzen aus Sallust veröffentlicht: Anthologicum Sallustianum, Hoc est Insigniores Sententiae ex Historiâ Catilinariâ C. Sallusti Crispi … dictis Johannis Caroli & Johannis Ludovici Miegiorum Patruelium, darin Florilegii Selectissimarum Sententiarum, Ex. C. Sallustii Crispi Conjuratione Catilinariâ … Centuria prior [Centuria posterior] (Straßburg 1628). HAB: Xb 6379; *Dünnhaupt: Handbuch*, 525 f. (Art. Bernegger Nr. 105). Zum politischen Aphorismus vgl. allgemein *Conermann: Hofmann* u. ders.: Hippolytus a Collibus. Zur Ars politica et aulica im Heidelberger Gelehrtenkreis. In: Europäische Hofkultur im 16. und 17. Jahrhundert. Hg. August Buck u. a. Hamburg 1981, 693–700 (Wolfenbütteler Arbeiten zur Barockforschung, 10).

4 Ein wie Tscherning aus Bunzlau gebürtiger Theologiestudent namens Zacharias Queisser hatte 1619 an der U. Leipzig unter Thomas Weinrich (1587–1629) disputiert: Εξετασεως Theologicae Disputatio VI. opposita Abominationi Pontificæ, in Loco, De BONIS OPERIBUS … Ad examinandum proposita In Academiâ Lipsiensi Die 21. Aprilis. Anno 1619 … ZACHARIA QVEISSERO, Boleslaviâ. Sil. SS. Theologiæ Studioso (Leipzig [1619]). Slg. Alvensleben T 162 (13) (ULB Halle; ehem. Depositum in der HAB). Der Notar Z. Q. wird 1632 zum Stadtschreiber in Bunzlau bestellt und noch 1637 und 1640 in diesem Amt der städt. Kanzlei erwähnt. Ewald Wernicke: Chronik der Stadt Bunzlau von den ältesten Zeiten bis zur Gegenwart. Bunzlau 1884, 339 f. u. 348. Eher in Frage kommt vielleicht der Bunzlauer Marcus Queisser, ein Verwandter Martha Queissers, der Frau des Opitz-Freundes Caspar Kirchner. Vgl. *Opitz: BW* 391111; *Opitius lati-*

nus I, 158. Marcus hatte Tscherning aus Lübeck, wo Tscherning um seine spätere Ehefrau Katharina Marsilius (s. 440324 K 9) warb, ein Gratulationspoem zugesandt: An | H. Andreas Tscherningen/ | Als er in | Rostock | Der Poesie Professor worden war. | Vberschicket | Aus | Lübeck | Von | Marcus Queissern. | [Linie] | [Lübeck] Gedruckt durch Valentin Schmalhertz/ 1644. 6 Bl. 4°. STB Berlin — PK: Yi 1461 (9).

5 Neben St. Elisabeth die andere städtische Hauptkirche Breslaus, spätgotisch, in ihrer heutigen Gestalt von 1342–1362 erbaut. Verbunden mit einem Gymnasium, dessen berühmte Bibliothek der Opitz- und Tscherning-Freund Christophorus Colerus seit 1639 verwaltete. S. 440324 K 2.

6 Martin Opitzen | Judith/ | auffs neu außgefertiget; | worzu das vördere Theil der Historie | sampt den Melodeyen auff iedwedes | Chor | beygefüget | von | Andreas Tscherningen. | [Zierleiste] | Rostock/ | Gedruckt durch Johann Richeln/ Rahts Buchdr. | in vorlegung Joachim Wildens/ Buchhändlers/ | im Jahr 1646. HAB: Lo 5835. S. 440324 K 1. Zu seiner Erweiterung des Stücks hielt Tscherning in der Widmungszuschrift (d. d. Rostock, „am anfange" des Jahres 1646) fest: „Jch habe so viel es möglich gewesen/ und beydes zu den Sachen als Personen sich schicken wollē/ Opitzianischer Redensarten/ ja bißweilen gantzer Verse/ mit allem fleisse mich gebrauchet/ damit ja der Zusatz dem anderen Cörper nicht etwan so ähnlich/ als die Eule der Nachtigal außsehen möchte." A. a. O., Bl. [Aij]v. Vgl. auch 440324 K 1. In Rostock fehlte es an einem finanzkräftigen Verleger und so mußte sich Tscherning für seine 1642 fertiggestellte Neubearbeitung und Erweiterung der Früh oper *Judith* von Martin Opitz (FG 200), 1635 in Breslau bei Georg Baumann erschienen, auswärts nach einem geeigneten Verlag umsehen. Im Dezember scheint es mit dem ungenannten Lübecker Verleger zu einer vertraglichen Vereinbarung gekommen zu sein, jedoch hatte dieser noch im Mai 1645 nicht mit dem Druck begonnen. Noch ärgerlicher war, daß er einen Teil des Notenmanuskripts von Apelles verkramt und verloren hatte, was den Druck, den nun der Rostocker Verleger Joachim Wilde d. Ä. (1601–1670) übernahm, verzögerte. Wilde führte das Geschäft seines Schwiegervaters Johann Hallervord (1581–1645) in Rostock fort und verlegte nachweislich in den Jahren 1645–1670. *Benzing: Verleger*, 1156 u. 1299. Die von Tscherning gewünschte neue Abschrift der verlorenen Stimmen lieferte Apelles erst am 11. 10. 1645. Am 20. 12. 1645 konnte Tscherning dann die Exemplare des Werkes versenden, mit vollständiger Vertonung von 11 Chören à 3–4 Stimmen (2 Tenöre, 1 Bassus) und Basso Continuo. Vgl. *Borcherdt: Tscherning*, 161 f. Das Werk war den Danziger Herren und Freunden Peter Hendreich, Daniel Ernst Czierenberg (Zierenberg) und Christoph Hendreich zugeschrieben. Die Brüder Christoph (1628–1702) und Peter Hendreich (Lebensjahre unbekannt) entstammten einer Danziger Kaufmannsfamilie und hatten um 1648 in Frankfurt a. d. O. studiert, wo Christoph 1664 die Professur f. Jurisprudenz und Geschichte erhielt. Kurz darauf machten sich beide um die Neuordnung der kfl. Bibliothek zu Berlin verdient; Christoph wurde kfl. Rat und Bibliothekar. *ADB* L, 183 ff.; *DBA* I 511/ 207 f., II 558/ 377–379 u. III 377/ 325. Daniel Ernst Zierenberg konnte in den einschlägigen Nachschlagewerken nicht ermittelt werden, er muß der ref. Danziger Patrizierfamilie Zierenberg/ Czi(e)renberg angehört haben, in deren Kreis Martin Opitz verkehrte. Vgl. *Opitz: BW*, 1259, 1569 u. 1622; Joachim Zdrenka: Rats- und Gerichtspatriziat der Altstadt (1377–1792) und der Jungstadt (1387–1454/1455) Danzig. Hamburg 1991. Tscherning in seiner Widmungszuschrift: „Daß aber meinen Hochgeehrten Herren ich diese Arbeit zugeschrieben/ vermeyne ich gnungsame Ursach darzu zu haben. Und beweget mich in gemein/ weil deroselben fürtreffliche Gemüter den Gelarten sonderlich gewogen/ sich selber auch freyer Künsten und Sprachen befliessen/ auch mit meinem Opitz/ dem edlen und unsterblichen Uhrheber der Hochteutschen Poesie/ jederzeit vertraute Freundschafft gepflogen." Auch verdanke er, Tscherning,

diesen drei Gönnern manche „gutthaten". A. a. O., Bl. [Aij]v. Tscherning schrieb 1643 ein Gedicht auf Zierenbergs Hochzeit, in dem er an den gemeinsamen Freund erinnerte:
Solte nun mein Opitz leben/
(Opitz der ja gar zu früh
Seinen Geist hat auffgegeben!)
Wie mit leichter Lust und Müh
Würd er jetzt ein Braut-Lied schreiben
Welches ewig könte bleiben.
(Ehren-Gedichte auff das Hochzeitliche Frewden-Fest des ... Daniel Ernest Czierenberges mit Juditha ... des Peter Hendreichs ... Tochter in Dantzig [Rostock: Johann Richel 1643]). Titel zit. nach *Dünnhaupt: Handbuch*, 4119, Lied zit. nach Herbert Hertel: Die Danziger Gelegenheitsdichtung der Barockzeit. In: Danziger Barockdichtung. Hg. Heinz Kindermann. Leipzig 1939, 178. Erstveröffentlichung verändert wiederabgedruckt in: Vortrab | Des | Sommers | Deutscher Ge- | tichte | von | Andreas Tscher- | ningen/ ausgesen- | det und verlegt | in Rostock. | [Vignette] | Gedruckt/ durch sehl. Nicolaus | Keyln/ Acad. Buchd. Erb. 1655. Bl. B v v – B vi v. STB Berlin — PK: an Yi 1503 (auch dig.). Auch Andreas Gryphius (FG 788. 1662) schrieb kurz darauf ein Widmungsgedicht auf Zierenberg und zwei andere in Georg Andreas Richters Übersetzung des Romans *Ariana* (1644) von Jean Desmarets de Saint-Sorlin. — Welcher Lübecker Verleger hat die oben gerügte Unzuverlässigkeit an den Tag gelegt? In einem Brief an Matthias Machner (s. 440324 K I 1) vom 20. 8. 1642 fällt der Name „Scherenwebelus", d.i. der in Lübeck 1636–1651 tätige Verleger Heinrich Schernwebel, der hier gemeint sein könnte. Der Brief in: STB Berlin — PK: Dep. Breslau 17 (ehem. StB Breslau: R 402), S. 874; BU Wrocław: Akc. 1949/ 713 (Abschrift Klose 175), S. 874. Schernwebel wird in Tschernings Brief an Machner vom 18. 10. 1642 auch distanziert erwähnt: Der Verleger zeige starkes Interesse an Tschernings geplanter Poetik. Nach *Borcherdt: Tscherning*, S. 317 Anm. 5; vgl. 440324 K 14.

7 Auf den Zwischentitelblättern der „Chöre" in Tschernings *Judith* (s. Anm. 6) erscheint Apelles als Komponist unter dem Namen „Matthæo Leonastro d. Longueville Neapolitano" nach seiner Geburtsstadt Neustadt im Ft. Oppeln.

8 Die Neuauflage der Gedichtsammlung *Tscherning: Früling* (1642) erschien 1646 nicht wieder bei Georg Baumann in Breslau, sondern wurde im Verlag Joachim Wilde d. Ä. (s. Anm. 6) in Rostock durch Johann Richel d. J., der 1639 die Rostocker Offizin von den Erben seines gleichnamigen Vaters übernommen hatte und als Ratsbuchdrucker fungierte (s. *Reske*, 799), nachgedruckt: *Tscherning: Früling* (1646). 1649 erschien im selben Verlag und ebenfalls von Johann Richel d. J. gedruckt die 3. Ausgabe: *Tscherning: Früling* (1649). In den gedruckten Büchermeßkatalogen 1645 taucht dieser Titel nicht auf, er erscheint erst im Ostermeßkatalog 1646 mit der Rostocker Verlagsadresse: „Andreas Tschernings Teutscher Gedichte Früling. Rostock/ bey Joachim Wilden: in 8." CATALOGUS UNIVERSALIS, Hoc est: DESIGNATIO omnium Librorum, qvi Nundinis Vernalibus Francofurtensibus & Lipsiensibus Anno 1646 ... prodierunt. Das ist: Verzeichnüß aller Bücher/ so zu Franckfurt in der FastenMeß/ auch Leipzigischen OsterMarckte/ dieses jetzigen 1646. Jahrs ... zu befinden. Leipzig [1646], Bl. D2r. http://www.olmsonline.de/purl?PPN525616772_1646_Oster

9 Hz. August d. J. v. Braunschweig-Wolfenbüttel (FG 227) arbeitete damals an seiner Revision der Luther-Übersetzung der Bibel, von der er bisher aber nur zwei Ausgaben einer Passionsharmonie (1640 u. 1641) und einen Probedruck der gottesdienstlichen Lesungen seiner *Evangelischen Kirchen-Harmonie* (1644/ 45) in den Druck gebracht hatte. S. 401111 u. I, 411214, 450410 K 8 u. 19, 451001 u. ö. Hervorzuheben ist, daß Martin Gosky als Leibarzt Hz. Augusts seinen Landsmann Tscherning (s. Anm. 10) nicht nur von

den frommen landesväterlichen Absichten seines Fürsten unterrichtet haben wird, sondern die Erneuerung der Bibelübersetzung auch als sprachliche Unternehmung im Zusammenhang mit der Zugehörigkeit Augusts zur FG gesehen hat. Vgl. in *Borcherdt: Tscherning*, 158 u. S. 311 Anm. 32 auch die Stelle eines Tscherningbriefs an Apelles v. Löwenstern vom 18.10.1642: „Dux Brunsvicensis cogitat novam editionem Bibliorum, sed Theologis Witenbergens. minime probatur. Emendavit passim versionem B. Lutheri iuxta lapidem Lydium linguae vernaculae". S. das Briefeverzeichnis in *Borcherdt: Tscherning*, S. 333 Nr. 41. Vgl. 380320 u. I. Zum angekündigten Gedicht Tschernings an Hz. August s. Beil. I.

10 Martin Gosky (um 1586 – bestattet 17.6.1656), Arzt u. (lat.) Dichter. Studium in Frankfurt a. d. O. unter Henning Arnisäus (1575–1636) u. Helmstedt, spätestens 1634 Dr. der Medizin; Stadtarzt in Gardeleben/ Altmark (heute Gardelegen, s. *Lexikon Geographie*, 534), seit 1620 auch Leibarzt der Herzöge v. Braunschweig-Lüneburg bzw. Hz. Augusts d. J., seit 1628 in Hitzacker dessen Leibarzt, später in Wolfenbüttel ansässig geworden, seit 1653 Hof- und Leibarzt im Range eines Hofrats. Ksl. Hofpfalzgrafenpatent, d. d. Wien 17.6.1643 n. St. S. *Flood*, 692–696. Gosky veröffentlichte 1650 die monumentale Sammlung von über 700 Gelegenheitsdichtungen auf Hz. August in seinem *ARBUSTUM vel ARBORETUM AUGUSTÆUM* (s. Beil. I Q), eine Neuauflage erschien 1693. Vgl. zu Gosky ferner *DBA* I, 409/ 39f.; Wolfgang Lent: Art. „Gosky, Martin". In: *Braunschweig. Biograph. Lexikon (Jarck)*, 269f.; Joseph Leighton: Deutschsprachige Geburtstagsdichtungen für Herzog August d. J. von Braunschweig-Lüneburg. In: Höfische Festkultur in Braunschweig-Wolfenbüttel 1590–1666. Hg. Jörg Jochen Berns. Amsterdam 1982, 139ff. – Tscherning dürfte Gosky persönlich gekannt und auch von Christophorus Colerus' Glückwunschschrift für Gosky gewußt haben: ARA PERENNITATIS Divæ Memoriæ ac Bonæ Recordationi Eminentium Silesiæ Ingeniorum aliô traductorum, inprimis præcipuorum Medicorum; tùm Beatorum tum Superstitum; nominatim verò Virtuti, Honori & Saluti … DN. MARTINI GOSCI Lubenâ Silesii, Phil. & Med. D. Comitis Palatini Cæsarei, ac Illustriss. … Ducum Brunsvicensium & Lüneburgensium Archiatri … erecta à CHRISTOPHORO COLERO (Breslau: Georg Baumann 1644, „Mense Decemb."). HAB: Db 1714. Unter dem Porträtstich, der Colerus zeigt, ein lat. Vierzeiler von Augustus Buchner (FG 362). Angebunden eine weitere Gratulationsschrift schlesischer Verwandter (Vater Esaias, Bruder Gedeon), Gönner und Freunde: EUPHEMIÆ ET VOTIVÆ PRECES, Pro Virtute, Honore, & Salute … DN. MARTINI GOSCII … devoto ore enunciatæ, à Fratre, Patruelibus, Cognatis, Affinibus & Amicis Silesiis (Breslau: Georg Baumann 1644). HAB: Db 1714 (2). Die Gratulationsschriften entstanden aus Anlaß der ksl. Verleihung der Hofpfalzgrafenwürde an Gosky (s. o.). Tscherning ist in den genannten Schriften nicht vertreten.

11 Der selbstironische Unterton dieser Passage läßt erkennen, warum Tscherning so erpicht auf möglichst zahlreiche Magisterpromotionen war: Sie versprachen angesichts des kargen und zudem äußerst zurückhaltend ausgezahlten Professorensalärs eine willkommene Geldeinnahme, zumal er im Sommersemester 1645 Dekan der philosophischen Fakultät der U. Rostock wurde und ihm ein beträchtlicher Teil der Einnahmen zuflossen. Zu seinem Nachteil fand jedoch keine einzige Promotion in diesem Semester statt. Übrigens kündigte Tscherning auch seine Vorlesungen mit lat. Scherzgedichten an, um mehr Zuhörer anzulocken. S. *Borcherdt: Tscherning*, 142f.

12 Personen und angesprochene Schuldsache nicht ermittelt. Vgl. auch 460610.

13 In seinem Brief an Apelles vom 27.2.1643 (BU Wrocław: R 3108, Bl. 8r–9v, s. 440324 K 3) hatte Tscherning von einem Tötungsdelikt berichtet: Apelles möge „an dienlichen orten" ein gutes Wort für „den guten gefangenen Mr. Heß" einlegen, um „dem guten cavalier" aus der Haft zu helfen. Die Akten habe dieser mit einem eigenen Boten eingesendet, wie auch die Informationen von zwei Universitäten, die ihn von der „**poena ordinaria**

homicidii" freigesprochen und nur zu einem zehnjährigen Aufenthaltsverbot bzw. zu einer Geldstrafe verurteilt hätten (a. a. O., Bl. 8v). Möglicherweise Heinrich Adolf von Hess und Stein (1610–1647). Er hatte 1641 die U. Rostock und dann bis 1643 die U. Königsberg bezogen. 1646 vermählte er sich mit Ursula v. Frankenberg-Ludwigsdorf, starb aber bereits ein halbes Jahr später. S. *Pusch* II, 186.

14 Nikolaus Herbst (1591–1663) aus einer im 16. Jh. vermutlich aus Nürnberg eingewanderten, 1602 geadelten Ratsfamilie. Er gehörte von 1622–1655 als Schöffe und Ratsherr, auch Stadtkämmerer dem Breslauer Rat an. Von seinem Sohn Anton ist nichts bekannt; sein Sohn Georg starb 1686 als Advokat in Breslau. Mit ihm erlosch das Geschlecht in Breslau. S. *Pusch* II, 148; F. G. Adolf Weiß: Chronik der Stadt Breslau von der ältesten bis zur neuesten Zeit. Breslau 1888, 956.

15 Caja, weiblicher Vorname, v. a. im (Alt-)Schwedischen, Dänischen, auch Baltischen und Polnischen, Koseform f. Karin/ Katharina. S. Wilfried Seibicke: Historisches Deutsches Vornamenbuch. Bd. 1 (Berlin, New York 1996), 358; Bd. 2 (ebd. 1998), 636 f. Gemeint ist Tschernings Ehefrau Katharina, die er um Ostern 1645 in Lübeck geheiratet hatte. S. 440324 K 9. Sie ließ Apelles' Frau (in dessen 2. Ehe), Barbara, geb. v. Tarnau u. Kühschmalz, grüßen, s. ebd. K 1.

16 Viro Clarissimo Praestantissimo Dn. Andreae Tscherningio, P. L. C. De capessenda Laureâ Magistrali, itemque Poëseos Professione Publicâ, in Inclutâ Rosarum Academiâ, gratulantur Fautores et Amici jam-jam agonizantis Silesiae Anno 1644 (Oels [1644]). (Georg Seidel, Johann Hubrig, Chr. Albert, David Bohemus, Matthias Machner, Sebastian Alischer, Christoph Freytag u. a. m.). Nach *Borcherdt: Tscherning*, 128 u. 296 Anm. 14. Die Gratulationsschrift scheint in keiner deutschen Bibliothek greifbar; das VD17 verzeichnet sie auch nicht. Vgl. 440324 K 2.

17 Johann Quistorp d. Ä. (1587–1648), Begründer einer einflußreichen Rostocker Theologen-Dynastie. Seit 1615 Prof. der Theologie an der U. Rostock, 1616 Archidiakon an St. Marien zu Rostock, 1646 Superintendent der Stadt; irenisch gesinnt, leistete dem auf der Rückreise von Schweden nach Holland in Rostock erkrankten Hugo Grotius bis zu seinem baldigen Tod geistlichen Beistand, verfaßte dazu eine *Epistola de obitu Grotii*. S. *ADB* XXVII, 51–53; *DBA* I, 991/ 21–38; III, 722/ 449–451 u. 456; Die Rektoren der Universität Rostock 1419–2000. Hg. Angela Hartwig u. Tilmann Schmidt. Rostock 2000 (Beiträge zur Geschichte der Universität Rostock, 23), 96 f. Sein gleichnamiger ältester Sohn (1624–1669) studierte in Greifswald und Rostock Philosophie und Theologie, reiste nach Danzig und von dort mit dem orthodox-luth. Königsberger Theologen Abraham Calovius (1612–1686) zum Religionsgespräch in Thorn 1645. Danach Fortsetzung der Studien in Königsberg, von dort 1646 Reise nach Kopenhagen und 1648 in die Niederlande, u. a. nach Leiden. Der Tod des Vaters im Mai 1648 und ein Ruf als ao. Prof. der Theologie ließen ihn 1649 nach Rostock zurückkehren; 1651 wurde er o. Prof. der Theologie und bekleidete an der Universität und in der Stadt wie sein Vater hohe geistliche Ämter. S. *ADB* XXVII, 53 f.; *DBA* I, 991/39–50; III, 722/ 457 u. 1045/ 99 f.; *RGG*^{4} VI, 1872 f. Das Thorner Religionsgespräch fand auf Einladung des poln. Königs Wladislaus IV. Wasa zwischen 26 kath., 28 luth. und 20 ref. Theologen vom 28. 8. bis 21. 11. 1645 statt. Auch Comenius nahm für die Böhmischen Brüder zwischenzeitlich daran teil, ebenso Georg Calixt (1586–1656), der ref. Berliner Hofprediger Johann Bergius und der wichtige Jesuit Georg Schönhof. Vgl. Anm. 18. Ein Ausgleich oder eine Verständigung über die strittigen Lehrfragen kam nicht zustande. Vgl. *TRE* XXVII, 663; Franz Jacobi: Das liebreiche Religionsgespräch zu Thorn 1645. Gotha 1895; Hans-Joachim Müller: Irenik als Kommunikationsreform. Das *Colloquium Charitativum* von Thorn 1645. Göttingen 2004, 327 ff.; Janusz Małłek: Die Sehnsucht nach Einheit. Das Colloquium Charitativum in Thorn im Jahre

1645. In: Kulturgeschichte Preußens königlich polnischen Anteils in der Frühen Neuzeit. Hg. Sabine Beckmann u. Klaus Garber. Tübingen 2005, 213–225; Manfred Richter: Johan Amos Comenius und das Colloquium Charitativum von Thorn 1645. Ein Beitrag zum Ökumenismus. Siedlce 2013, 308 ff.

18 Petrus Zimmermann († 8.9.1656), Lic. theol., wurde in Thorn Senior des ev. Ministeriums und Rektor des Gymnasiums. *Jöcher* IV, 2210. Vgl. Theses theologicae de Scriptvra Sacra, quas ... sub praesidio Dn. Petri Czimmermanni, ecclesiae Thoruniensis senioris et Gymnasij rectoris ... proponit Abrahamus Schultz, Cotb. Lusat. respondens (Thorunii: Mich. Camall [1647]). SB München (Film). Zimmermann gehörte 1645 auf luth. Seite zu den Teilnehmern am Thorner Colloquium (s. Anm. 17). Joseph Lukaszewicz: Von den Kirchen der Böhmischen Brüder im ehemaligen Großpolen. Grätz 1877, 166.

19 Josephus Adjutus (Mossul 1602 – Wittenberg 1668): ORATIO De Certitudine GRATIÆ ... In Auditorio Majori celeberrimæ atq; inclytæ Wittenbergensis Academiæ solenniter habita Cal. Septemb. ANNO 1644 (Wittenberg 1645). ULB Halle: 94A 7378 (6). VD17 3:011766N. Adjutus, gebürtig aus Ninive/ Mossul (im heutigen Irak), wurde verwaist von Verwandten 1606 nach Jerusalem geschickt und bis 1613 in einem Minoritenkloster in Palästina erzogen. Danach in Neapel in den Franziskaner-Orden als „Hugo Maria" aufgenommen, 1632 Diakon, 1637 in Bologna Promotion zum Dr. der Theologie. Er überwarf sich mit der röm.-kathol. Kirche und ging über Wien, Prag u. Dresden nach Wittenberg, wo er am 23. Oktober 1643 eine *Oratoria revocatoria* hielt, in der er seine Abkehr von der röm. Kirche erklärte. Am 9.6.1643 war er an der Universität Wittenberg eingeschrieben worden; im Dezember 1646 erhielt er eine außerordentliche Professur für italien. Sprache; kurz darauf, im März 1647 vermählte er sich mit der Pfarrerswitwe Blandina Cotten, die ihn um 12 Jahre überlebte. Neben seiner Lehrtätigkeit betrieb er in großem Maßstab das Brauergewerbe und den Weinhandel. Ein Kupferporträt aus dem Jahre 1647 zeigt ihn im luther. Theologenhabit mit der subscriptio von Johann Michael Dilherr: „Diß ist der Mann, den hat die lieb zu Gottes wort, | Von Ninive gen Rom getrieben; und dann fort | (Weil Er es nicht traf ahn:) gen Wittenberg geführet | Alda man nichts von Ihm, dann Lehr und Tugēd spüret. | Seinem sehr werthen Herrn, und lieben freunde, setzte es | Zu stetswehrendem gedächtnis etc. | Johann Michael Dilherr." Graphische Sammlung der HAB: A 71 (auch Digitaler Portrait Index). Abgebildet auch in Burchard Brentjes: Josephus Adjutus, der Chaldäer zu Wittenberg. In: Wissenschaftliche Zeitschrift der Martin-Luther-Universität Halle-Wittenberg, gesellschafts- und sprachwissenschaftliche Reihe 26 (1977), 131–138, 131. Vgl. DNB-Katalog der Deutschen Nationalbibliothek (http://d-nb.info/gnd/125827725); Burchard Brentjes: Reformation und Pietismus in Wittenberg und Halle und die Nationalsprachen des Ostens. In: Reformation und Nationalsprachen. Zusammengestellt und hg. ... v. Burchard Brentjes u. Burchard Thaler. Halle a. d. S. 1983, 3-15, hier S. 8 f.; Heinrich Kühne: Wittenbergisches bei Josephus Adjutus. Neue Forschungsergebnisse aus Wittenberger Archiven. In: Wissenschaftliche Zeitschrift der Martin-Luther-Universität Halle-Wittenberg, gesellschafts- und sprachwissenschaftliche Reihe 28 (1979), 133 f. Das Repertorium Album Amicorum verzeichnet einen Stammbucheintrag des Josephus Adjutus in syr. Schrift aus dem Jahre 1659. www.raa.phil.uni-erlangen.de/recherche.

20 Michael Hermann (1593–1669) gehörte einer sproßreichen Familie von Geistlichen und Schulmännern in Breslau an, hatte in Wittenberg, Tübingen und Straßburg ev. Theologie studiert, wurde 1618 Diakon an St. Maria-Magdalena, stieg dann über verschiedene weitere geistliche Ämter 1644 zum Pastor an St. Maria-Magdalena auf, ab 1665 als Nachfolger seines Vaters Zacharias d. Ä. (1563–1638) Pfarrer an St. Elisabeth und Inspektor der luther. Kirchen und Schulen in Breslau. Vgl. *Cunrad: Silesia togata*, 112; Leichenpredigt von Johannes Gebhard (1611–1681, damals Konrektor am Elisabethanum zu Breslau) in BU Wrocław: 419227 (konnte nicht eingesehen werden); vgl. Richard Mende: Katalog der Leichenpredigten-Sammlungen der Peter-Paul-Kirchenbibliothek in Liegnitz. Marktschellenberg 1938, 201. Der ältere Breslauer Kirchenmann Magister Daniel Hermann (1590–1636), der 1633 als Korrespondenzpartner von Martin Opitz (FG 200) begegnet, scheidet aus; hingegen dürfte sein Sohn Daniel d. J. (1619–1662) hier gemeint sein. Er disputierte zum Lizenziat 1646 in Greifswald *De Possessione* und promovierte im selben Jahr in Rostock zum J.U.D. In der Gratulationsschrift *Honoribus Danielis Hermanni Vratislav. Silesii; Cum Gryphiswaldiae solemni ritu renunciatus esset, Ex Athenis Varniacis Feliciter acclamat Par Amicorum* (Rostock 1646) findet sich auch ein Glückwunschgedicht Tschernings: „Sic tandem fortuna fidem mutata novavit?" S. *Borcherdt: Tscherning*, S. 356, Bibliogr.-Nr. 88. Später wurde Daniel Hermann Hofrat und Hofgerichts- und Konsistorialrat in Holstein. Vgl. *Cunrad: Silesia togata*, 121–123; *Opitz: BW*, 938, 962f. u. 1179ff.; *Pusch* II, 152f.; *Zedler* XII, 1707.

21 Nicht ermittelt.

K I Ein Gedicht Andreas Tschernings auf Hz. August d. J. v. Braunschweig-Wolfenbüttel (FG 227) steht nach *Borcherdt: Tscherning*, S. 311 Anm. 32, auch in: Andreae Tscherningii Poet. Prof. Schediasmatum Pars altera. Impensis Autoris Expressit Rostochi Johannes Richelius, Senat. Typogr. 1650. Nur in der KB Kopenhagen: 173.II 186 lt.: The Royal Library, Foreign Dept. Author Catalogue (1454–1949), Hildesheim o. J., Mfiche 588. Dieses Exemplar konnte weder eingesehen, noch über ein Digitalisat verfügbar gemacht werden.

450730

Diederich von dem Werder an Christian Ernst von Knoch

Diederich v. dem Werder (FG 31. Der Vielgekörnte) übersendet Christian Ernst (v.) Knoch (FG 268. Der Weichende) zwei weitere Änderungen zum Reimgesetz für Johann Michael Moscherosch (FG 436. Der Träumende), wie er solche (an den Mittelsmann Georg Philipp Harsdörffer. FG 368) gesandt habe. Er hofft auf Zustimmung F. Ludwigs (Der Nährende). — Am Ende erkundigt Werder sich nach Truppenbewegungen.

Q HM Köthen: V S 544, Bl. 488rv [A: 488v]; eigenh.; rote Lacksiegel. — Fehlt in *KE*.

A A Monsieur Monsieur Crestien Ernest Knoche Lieutenant Colonell Conseillier d'Estát de son Alt.   a Cöthen
  Abwesend Herren Hoffraht Schumachern[1] zuerbrechen.

Hochgeehrter Herr Weichender[2]

jch habe, bey abfertigung des Träumenden achtzeiligem reimgesetzes, solches nochmals absonderlich zuvor[a] übersehen, vnd nachfolgende Zwo veränderungen hinnein gesetzt, der Hoffnung, es werde vnser höchstgeehrter Herr Nehrender ihm[b] dieselbe gefallen lassen.[3]
Beym 1. verse. — — — — — den schlaff zu flössen ein
  dan der schlaff fleust ein, der Nachtschatten aber flösset denselben ein.[4]

Beym 5. vers. — — — — — bey nacht vnd tagesschein
dan die worte (was lieblich ist vnd fein)⁵ stehen nicht so gar wohl, vnd kommen einem pfeiffer⁶ zimlich nahe.

Auf diese weise seind sothane achtzeilige fortgeschickt worden, habe es eine notturft zusein erachtet[,] solches dem Ertzschreinsverwahrern zu wissen zufügen.

Verbleibe Meines hochgeehrten Herren Weichenden
    williger
    Der Vielgekörnte

Reinsdorff 30. HeuMonats 1645

[W]an er etwas nachricht wegen der Völcker Zuges⁷ hatt [bi]tte ich mit ein paar Zeilen mich dessen zuverständigen.

T *Im Falz verdeckte Buchstaben in eckigen Klammern.* — **a** *Eingefügt.* — **b** *Lies:* sich

K 1 Heinrich Schumacher (FG 359), Hofrat F. Ludwigs (Der Nährende) in Köthen.

2 Christian Ernst (v.) Knoch (FG 268. Der Weichende), aus anhalt. Adel stammend, Sohn Caspar Ernsts (v.) Knoch (FG 33), war in Kriegsdiensten (1631–1639) zum Obristltn. zu Roß aufgestiegen; seit 1643 fl.-anhalt. Gesamtrat, seit 1645 Geh. Rat F. Ludwigs in Köthen. Er war an Geschäften der FG und nach Aussage des vorliegenden Briefes an der Führung des Erzschreins aktiv beteiligt. Vgl. *Conermann III*, 297f.

3 Zunächst hatte Johann Michael Moscherosch (FG 436. Der Träumende) seine FG-Imprese und dann auch das Reimgesetz dazu selbst entworfen. Diederich v. dem Werder (FG 31. Der Vielgekörnte) hatte es mittlerweile schon übersehen und verbessert. S. 450613. In 450725 sagte Werder dem Fürsten zu, das nochmals durchgesehene Reimgesetz Moscheroschs an dessen Mittelsmann Georg Philipp Harsdörffer (FG 368) zu senden. Die beiden letzten Änderungen im vorliegenden Brief finden sich in der Endfassung des Reimgesetzes im *GB Kö.* III, Bl. 37r wieder. Vgl. Anm. 5 u. 450504A K 2.

4 Werder macht hier korrekt auf den Unterschied des intransitiven starken Verbs „einfließen" und des transitiven schwachen Verbs „einflößen" aufmerksam.

5 Im *GB Kö.* III, Bl. 37r, ist die 2. Halbzeile „was lieblich ist und fein" gestrichen und überschrieben mit Werders Verbesserung „bey nacht und tagesschein". Das endgültige Reimgesetz wurde in *Conermann III*, 525 veröffentlicht. Die Impresen- und Mitgliederliste im 3. Bd. des Köthener Erzschreins (HM Köthen: V S 546), Bl. 79rv (FG 428–437) hat im Reimgesetz auf Moscheroschs FG-Imprese in der 5. Zeile die neue Fassung „[…] bey nacht und tages schein". Die erste Zeile hat in beiden Quellen bereits die Werdersche Verbesserung.

6 „Pfeifer" wurde auch der Furz (flatus/ crepitus ventris) genannt. *Stieler*, 1438; *DW* VII, 1644 (s. v. Pfeife), 1649 (s. v. „pfeifen"), 1653 (s. v. „pfeifer").

7 Bei den erwähnten Truppenbewegungen handelt es sich möglicherweise um den Anhalt bedrohenden Durchzug des schwed. Korps unter Generalleutnant Hans Christoph v. Königsmarck (FG 515. 1648). S. 450721. Werders Nachfrage bezieht sich vermutlich auf seine anstehenden Reisen im Zusammenhang seiner Heranziehung zu den Heiratsverhandlungen zwischen Hessen-Kassel und Kurbrandenburg. Vgl. dazu 450919 u. insgesamt 460125 K 1–3 u. Beil. I.

Alles zu Nutzen.

F. Z. ANHALT

Die Fruchtbringende Gesellschafft

Die deutsche Akademie des 17. Jahrhunderts Fruchtbringende Gesellschaft

Kritische Ausgabe der Briefe,
Beilagen und Akademiearbeiten (Reihe I),
Dokumente und Darstellungen (Reihe II)

Begründet von
Martin Bircher † und Klaus Conermann

Im Auftrag der Sächsischen Akademie der Wissenschaften zu Leipzig,
in Kooperation mit der Herzog August Bibliothek Wolfenbüttel

herausgegeben von

Klaus Conermann

Reihe I, Abt. A: Köthen
Abt. B: Weimar
Abt. C: Halle

Reihe II, Abt. A: Köthen
Abt. B: Weimar
Abt. C: Halle

In Kommission: De Gruyter

Briefe der Fruchtbringenden Gesellschaft und Beilagen: Die Zeit Fürst Ludwigs von Anhalt-Köthen 1617–1650

Siebter Band 1644–1646
Teil II: August 1645 – Dezember 1646

Herausgegeben von Klaus Conermann und Andreas Herz
unter Mitarbeit von Gabriele Ball

Reihe I
Abteilung A: Köthen
Band 7, Teilband II

In Kommission: De Gruyter

Das Vorhaben „Die deutsche Akademie des 17. Jahrhunderts: Fruchtbringende Gesellschaft"
ist ein Forschungsvorhaben der Sächsischen Akademie der Wissenschaften zu Leipzig und wird
im Rahmen des Akademienprogramms von der Bundesrepublik Deutschland und dem Bundesland Niedersachsen gefördert. Das Akademienprogramm wird koordiniert von der Union der
deutschen Akademien der Wissenschaften.

ISBN 978-3-11-051976-1

Bibliografische Information der Deutschen Nationalbibliothek

Die Deutsche Nationalbibliothek verzeichnet diese Publikation in der Deutschen
Nationalbibliografie; detaillierte bibliografische Daten sind im Internet
über http://dnb.dnb.de abrufbar.

© Sächsische Akademie der Wissenschaften zu Leipzig 2016;
in Kommission bei Walter de Gruyter GmbH & Co. KG, Berlin/Boston

Gesamtherstellung: Hubert & Co GmbH & Co. KG, Göttingen
∞ Gedruckt auf säurefreiem Papier
Printed in Germany

www.degruyter.com

Peter Knaudt an Matthäus Merian d. Ä.

Antwort auf 450711. Beantwortet durch 450905. — Peter Knaudt berichtet über die am 2. August von F. Ludwig gerne vernommene Nachricht, daß Matthäus Merian d. Ä. das Kästlein ebenso wie das Geld empfangen hat und das *GB 1646* nun ins Werk gesetzt werden kann. F. Ludwig (Der Nährende) regt an, die Arbeit fleißig fortzusetzen, da er schon von verschiedenen Mitgesellschaftern gemahnt worden sei. — Mit dem Einfügen eines Titels vor jedem Hundert (der Gesellschafterimpresen 1–400) ist F. Ludwig einverstanden. Seinen Vorschlag für die Gestaltung der Zwischentitelblätter finde Merian beiliegend. — F. Ludwig bittet darum, das *GB 1646* nicht vorzeitig auf dem Markt zum Verkauf anzubieten, da zuerst und bevorzugt die Gesellschaftsmitglieder das abgeschlossene Werk erhalten sollen. — Die letzten hundert Visierungen folgen in acht Tagen, einzig die Nr. 384 fehle, da die Yucca dieses Orts nicht ausfindig zu machen sei. Hz. Franz Albrecht v. Sachsen-Lauenburg (FG 194) habe sie besorgen wollen, sei aber zwischenzeitlich gestorben. Vielleicht gelingt es Merian, die Pflanze in Frankfurt, Nürnberg oder Augsburg zu beschaffen. Er würde F. Ludwig damit einen großen Dienst erweisen, und Knaudt bittet hier dringend um seine Unterstützung. — Weiterhin äußert der Fürst den Wunsch, Merian möchte doch beim Stechen und auch beim Druck darauf achten, ein V nicht für ein U zu setzen, und andere ähnliche Besonderheiten zu bedenken.

Q HM Köthen: V S 546, Bl. 181rv, v leer; eigenh., Konzept. — *D: Conermann II*, 100 (Zitat); fehlt in *Bircher: Merian* (s. auch *Conermann II*, 100 Anm. 120).

A *Fehlt.*

Ehrenvester und hochgeachter insonders großgünstig*er* Herr und wehrter Freundt,

Deßelben schreiben vom 11 Julij habe Jch den 2 Augusti wol empfangen und[a] daßelbe[b] alsobald[c] meinem gnedigen Fursten und herrn unterthenig[d] zuverlesen geben, Daraus dan SFG.[e] gern vernommen, das das Kestlein mit dem gelde wohl zurecht kommen und das der herr nunmehr[f] zur verfertigung selben werckes den anfang gemachet.[g][1] [G]esinnen[h] auch gnedig der [h]err[i] fleißig damit fort[f]ahren[j] wolle, weil die [J]intereßenten[i] albereits Unterschiedliche[j] erinnerung gethan

Sonsten seind S. F. G. mit des herrn vorschlage, das vor iedes hundert[k] ein[l] titel[m][2] vorgedruckt werde[n] inmaßen SFG solchen aufsetzen laßen, so Er hierbey zuempfahen,

Es wollen aber S. F. G. das der herr dis buch nicht ehe andern verkauffe, bis das ganze werck verfertigt, damit es nicht[o] den herren interessenten von[p] andern ehe[q] zukomme,[r] sie es selbsten empfangen haben.[s]

Die lezten hundert Visirungen, sollen über acht tage folgen, darinnen aber das 384. stuck[3] mangelt, dieweil man das Zwiebelgewechse Giuoca hier nicht haben kan,[4] es ist zwart Sfg von hertzog Franz Albrechten zu[t] Sachsen[5] zuüberschicken[u] zugesagt, weil er aber in der schlacht geblieben hatt man es nicht haben können, ob der herr nun etwa solches zu Franckfurth Nürnberg oder Augsburg zu wege bringen könte, würde Er SFG einen großen dienst thuen, wie^v dan der herr^w sich doch deswegen fleißig zu bemühen gebeten^x wird. sonsten laßen SFG ihn erinnern^y [, d]as^i er doch in den [K]upffern^{iz} [w]ie^i auch in den drücken [fl]eißig^i achtgeben laßen wolle damit nicht ein [V]^i vor ein U gesezet werde und [w]as^i sie etwa vor diesem mehr erinnern laßen

So Jch meinem großg. hern Unverhalten sein laßen wollen, den Jch hiermit Gottes schuz ergebe.

I
Streichung im Dokument 450800

Q A. a. O., Bl. 181r; eigenh.

^aDas darauf das^b General Kupfferstuck^c folge, Als^d erstlich wird der Titel, und^e also auch im 2 3 und 4t*en* hundert, Es mus aber bey die lezten drey theille, der erste titel und die darauf folgende vorrede nicht mit gedruckt werden, sondern vor dieselben lezten drey hundert vor iedes hundert nur dieser beyliegende Tittel und mehr nicht vorangesezt, darnach die Vorrede, dan^f dieser hierbey liegende Titel, und darauf das General Kupfferstucke mit dem Palmenbaume und dan folgends das erste hundert. Wan selbes erste 100 fertig, Soll dan nicht mehr als dieser titel wieder vorgesezt werd*en*, Nemlich
    Der Fruchtbringenden Geselschaft
        Zweites^g Hundert.
Und so fort^h das dritte, und das Vierte hundert, die lezten 100 Visirung*en*

T **a** *Folgt* <nach verlesung> — **b** *Gebessert aus* deßelben — **c** *Eingefügt*. — **d** *Bis* geben *eingefügt für* <solches zugestellet> — **e** *Folgt* <gnedig und> — **f** *Folgt* <den anfang> — **g** *Folgt Einfügung am Rand bis* gethan — **h** *Buchstabenverlust im Falz. Konjektur in eckigen Klammern. Bis* erinnerung gethan *am Rand ergänzt.* — **i** *Buchstabenverlust im Falz. Konjektur in eckigen Klammern.* — **j** *Folgt darunter* <gewiße> — **k** *Folgt* <und> — **l** *Eingefügt für* <dieser> — **m** *Folgt* <wie beyliegend zuersehen> — **n** *Folgt umfangreicher gestrichener Text, s. Beil. I. Fortgesetzt mit* inmaßen — **o** *Folgt* <etwa> — **p** *von andern eingefügt.* — **q** *Gebessert aus* eher. *Folgt* <als sie es selbsten bekommen>. *Am Rand ohne Einschaltzeichen ergänzt* <von den kupffern> — **r** *Folgt* <ehe> — **s** *Aufgrund der Streichungen grammatisch verunglückter Satz.* — **t** zu Sachsen *am Rand ergänzt.* — **u** über *eingefügt.* — **v** wie dan *eingefügt.* — **w** *Folgt* <wolle> — **x** gebeten wird *am Rand ergänzt.* — **y** *Folgt Einfügung am Rand bis* erinnern laßen — **z** *Folgt* <fleißig wolle>

T I **a** *Folgt* <Und> — **b** *Folgt Einschaltzeichen, aber ohne Texteinschaltung am Rand.* — **c** *Folgt unleserlich gestrichenes Wort.* — **d** *Eingefügt bis* Titel — **e** *Das Folgende bis* mehr nicht vorangesezt *muß als Parenthese gelesen und allein auf das 2., 3. und 4. Hundert bezogen werden.* — **f** *Folgt* <auf eine seite> — **g** *Eingefügt für* <Andere> — **h** *Folgt* <die ubrigen>

K 1 Vgl. zum „Kestlein" mit den Kupferplatten des *GB 1629/30* zur Wiederverwendung für das *GB 1646* und dem Verlagsbeitrag von 200 Reichstalern 450509 K 1. Zum Zahlungsverkehr das *GB 1646* betreffend s. 450127 K 1, zu Verlagsbeiträgen 450126 K 4 u. zum *GB 1646* allgem. 440130 K 3.

2 Dieser von F. Ludwig gebilligte Vorschlag Merians wurde im *GB 1646* umgesetzt: Vor jedem Hundert findet man ein Titelblatt, das das jeweilige Segment ankündigt. S. auch K I. S. zur Einrichtung des *GB 1646* Beil. I u. 450711 K 4.

3 Hinter der FG-Nr. 384 verbirgt sich Jobst Heimart v. Lenthe (Der Schönblühende), der bereits Ende August 1642, wohl zusammen mit Johann Rauch (FG 385), in die FG aufgenommen wurde. Lenthe diente seit 1645 Hz. August d. J. v. Braunschweig-Wolfenbüttel (FG 227) als Stallmeister. Vorher war er in Stuttgart angestellt. S. *DA Köthen I.6*: Personenregister; *Conermann III*, 450 f. S. die Yucca-Imprese Lenthes S. 605. Im Erzschrein (HM Köthen: V S 546, Bl. 146r) hat sich ein (damit wohl vor August 1645 einzuordnender) undatierter Zettel von F. Ludwigs H. erhalten, auf dem noch von vier fehlenden Pflanzen-Abbildungen die Rede ist: Neben der Yucca („Giuoca") Lenthes ist dies „im vierten hundert" die „Cardinalblume" des Maximilian v. Sigershoven (FG 354. Der Abstechende); „Jm fünften hundert" der Mirabolanenbaum Kf. Friedrich Wilhelms v. Brandenburg (FG 401. Der Untadeliche) u. „der kleine Baldrian" Albrechts v. Zerbst (FG 408. Der Ballernde).

4 F. Ludwig tritt hier, durchaus nicht ungewöhnlich, als Pflanzensammler und -beschaffer selbst hervor u. bittet Matthäus Merian d. Ä. um Mithilfe bei der Suche nach der Yucca. Über die Ergebnisse hält Merian den Fürsten auf dem laufenden. S. 450930 u. 451015. Schließlich greift der Frankfurter Verleger auf eine Visierung zurück, deren Vorbild aus dem Garten des Juristen, Universitätsrektors und Kunstsammlers Remigius Faesch (1595–1667) stammte. — Die Suche nach der Pflanze hatte wohl schon einige Jahre angedauert, und Hz. Franz Albrecht v. Sachsen-Lauenburg (FG 194) hatte sich anscheinend selbst bereit erklärt, die Yucca oder eine Abbildung derselben zu beschaffen. Da der ksl. Feldmarschall jedoch bereits im Juni 1642 in schwed. Gefangenschaft gestorben war (s. Anm. 5), bat F. Ludwig (über Peter Knaudt) Merian um Unterstützung und um Anfragen bei Bekannten in Frankfurt, Nürnberg und Augsburg. Auch Hz. Ernst I. v. Sachsen-Gotha (FG 19) wurde in die Suche nach der Yucca eingebunden und von F. Ludwig Mitte November um Mithilfe gebeten, was ein Postskriptum in einem Brief Hz. Ernsts an seinen Onkel vom 1.12.1645 belegt: „Auch *etc.* haben E. G. Schreiben vom 15 verwichnen Monats recht empfangen, vnd darauß was sie wegen deß richtigen **contrefaits** der Jndianischen blumen **Juca gloriosa** genandt begeren verstanden. Bitten EG daß in der eyl [...] wir dieselben nicht eigenhendig deßwegen bey dieser gelegenheit beantworten mögen; haben aber bereit darumben geschrieben, vnd hoffen, daselbe ehist zur hand zu bekommen, was denn EG vbersendet werden solle." ThStA Gotha: Geh. Archiv F ☉ IIIa Nr. 8, Bl. 1rv. Der Briefwechsel kommt auf die Ergebnisse der Bemühungen Hz. Ernsts nicht zurück. — Die Formulierung in Merians Brief 451119 (Postscriptum) deutet auf Zuarbeit von außen hin: „Dan dises Kupfer [der Yucca-Pflanze] ist mein und habe es vorm Jahr Machen laßen, von einem Abriß so mir auß Basel zu komen ist". Die Anfragen betreffs der Yucca-Pflanze richtete Merian auch nach Augsburg, Frankfurt, Nürnberg und Berlin. Was nachgewiesen werden konnte, ist die Vorlage, die in einigen Exemplaren des *Florilegium* von 1641 seines Schwiegervaters Johann Theodor de Bry nachträglich eingeklebt wurde. Wir finden die Abbildung der Pflanze als Zusatz und Nr. 142 (in der Regel 141 Nummern) im genannten *Florilegium Renovatum Et Auctum: Das ist: Vernewertes und vermehrtes Blumenbuch* (Frankfurt: Merian 1641). S. Abb. S. 604. — F. Ludwig könnte einen Abzug erhalten haben, nach dem er dann eine neue vereinfachte Visierung für das *GB 1646* erstellen lassen

Merians Yucca gloriosa L. Vorbild für die Imprese Jobst Heimarts von Lenthe (FG 384).
Zu 450800. Abb. I.

Jede drey Jahr.

Der Schönblühende.

MAn find ein schön Gewächs der Zwiebelblumen art/
Das Giuoca wird genant: Schönblühend man ge-
Mich/iede drey Jahr hat/wie dis gewächse spart/   cheissen
So lange seine blüt: Also man den hoch preisen
Sol/der sein hertz allein zur tugend hat gekart/
Und die vor innerlich und eüsserlich wil weisen/
Er hat zu sparen doch damit gar keine zeit/
Das frucht zu bringen er sey immerdar bereit.

J. H. V. L.

1642.

Jobst Heinrich von Lenthe.

Die Yucca-Imprese Jobst Heimarts von Lenthe (FG 384). Zu 450800. Abb. II.

konnte. Die 25 Stengel der Rispe wurden auf 16 verringert, auf einige nach unten weisende Blätter verzichtete man ganz. In *Conermann II*, 101 wird auch die Seltenheit der Yucca in Europa erwähnt. Sie stammt aus dem Südosten Nordamerikas und war wegen ihrer Schönheit und Exotik sehr begehrt. Der englische Botaniker John Gerarde habe bereits 1597 in *The Herball or Generall Historie of Plants*, 1359, berichtet, daß ein Exemplar zwar in seinem Garten gedeihe, jedoch keine Blüten hervorbringe. S. zur Yucca auch *Conermann: Rist*, 74 f. S. *Conermann II*, 100–102, u. zur Yucca- bzw. Giuoca-Pflanze auch 450930, 451015 u. 451119.

5 Hz. Franz Albrecht v. Sachsen-Lauenburg (FG 194) wurde 1629, wahrscheinlich bei einem Besuch in Köthen, in die FG aufgenommen. Er unterlag in der Schlacht bei Schweidnitz dem schwed. Generalfeldmarschall Lennart Torstensson und starb am 10.6.1642 als ksl. Feldmarschall in schwed. Gefangenschaft. S. *Conermann III*, 196 f. Der Zeitpunkt seines Ablebens lag somit bereits über drei Jahre zurück.

K I Matthäus Merian d. Ä. hatte in 450711 zu erwägen gegeben, im *GB 1646* den vier Teilen oder „Hundert" der Gesellschafterimpresen nicht nur je ein eigenes Titelblatt, sondern auch einen je eigenen „kupfer Tittul" voranzustellen. Die hier als Beilage gebrachte Streichung stellt eine allerdings schwer verklausulierte Reaktion darauf dar und muß wohl wie folgt gelesen werden: Das gesamte Werk soll eingeleitet werden mit einem Gesamttitelblatt, der folgenden Vorrede, dann einem Titelblatt für das erste Hundert, dann dem „General Kupfferstucke mit dem Palmenbaume", gefolgt von den Impresen der Mitglieder 1–100. Die folgenden Teile des 2., 3. und 4. Hunderts sollten allein ein je eigenes Titelblatt aufweisen, aber weder den Gesamttitel, noch die Vorrede und die Palmenimprese wiederholen. Für die Titelblätter der vier Teile („Hundert") hatte F. Ludwig zwei Vorschläge entworfen und mit dem vorliegenden Brief Merian zusenden lassen. S. 450711 u. die Abbildungen S. 574 f. Das *GB 1646* wich in seiner endgültigen Gestaltung von dem hier vorgebrachten Konzept ab: Ein Gesamttitelblatt fehlt, und jeder der vier Teile wird nicht nur mit einem eigenen Titelblatt, sondern auch mit der Palmenimprese der FG und dem dazugehörigen Reimgesetz („Kling-Gedichte"), der erste Teil darüber hinaus mit besagter „Vorrede" eingeleitet. S. 450711 K 4. Möglicherweise lagen dieser Gestaltung kaufmännische Interessen Merians zugrunde, um die einzelnen Folgen auch separat besser verkaufen zu können.

450806

Johann Valentin Andreae an Herzog August d. J. von Braunschweig-Wolfenbüttel

Antwort auf 450722. — Johann Valentin Andreae (FG 464. 1646) empfing den Brief Hz. Augusts d. J. v. Braunschweig-Wolfenbüttel (FG 227) am 2. Tage des Monats (2.8.1645), welcher ihm zu seiner Hochzeit im Jahre 1614 einst sehr viel Glück verheißen hatte. Er freut sich über den Probedruck von Panegyrika Johann Heinrich Boecklers und Martin Nessels auf Hz. August und bedauert nur, daß die Commentarii anderer Autoren seine eigene Lobschrift zu kurz erscheinen lassen. Andreae wundert sich, ob das Wort revocata im Titel von Johann Heinrich Boecklers *Fama*-Schrift auf Hz. August (in der Nessels Panegyrikus enthalten ist) nicht mißverständlich ist, da der Ruhm Hz. Augusts in dem Werk zurecht erklärt oder herausposaunt werden müsse (*Fama revocanda*). Andreae will Boeckler informieren, sobald es gedruckt ist. — Die neue Hochzeitordnung des Herzogs sei vorbildlich, so daß man in Württemberg daraus lernen könne. Dort aber liebe man das Durcheinander und mache alles nur noch schlimmer, anstatt durch gute Ordnungen ehrenhaftes Leben und dadurch das Christentum zu befördern. — Andreae wünscht Hz. Augusts *Evangelischer Kirchen-Harmonie*, welche von vielen ersehnt werde, guten Fortschritt. — Das Erscheinen des *GB 1646* wolle er untertänig erwarten. — In Straßburg gibt es den opitzianischen Dichter Jesaias Rompler v. Löwenhalt (AGT, DG), der eine Gesamtausgabe seiner Dichtungen veranstalten wolle. So schreite die neue Dichtkunst voran. Allerdings verirren sich etliche in poetischen Fabeln und hochtrabenden Reden und entziehen — entgegen ihrem Vorbild Opitz — der geistlichen Dichtung Ernst und Andacht.

Q HAB: Cod. Guelf. 65.1 Extrav., Bl. 237rv [A: 237v], eigenh. Ein undat. Zettel (Bl. 238rv), dessen Inhalt von uns in 460317 K 6 wiedergegeben wird. — Zählung von Andreaes H.: sein 32. Brief, als Antwort auf Hz. Augusts 30. Brief. — Kurze Zitate in *Begemann: FG und Andreä*, 34 u. *Brecht: Andreae u. Hz. August*, 237.

A Dem durchleuchtig. Hochgebohrnen Fursten vnd herren, Herren Augusto, hertzogen zu Brunschw. vnd Lüneb. &c. Meinem g*nädigs*ten Fursten vnd herren &c Wolfenbüttel, (.32.) 6. Aug.

Durchleuchtig Hochgebohrner, Gnedigster Fürst vnd Herr,
E. F. G. 30 L. de dato 22. passato. ist den 2. huius qui mihi olim Ao. 1614 nuptialis auspicatissimus fuit.¹ zu recht einkommen, wobej mich das Muster famæ non morituræ. vnd panegyricj Nesselianj² sehr erfrewet. Weil ich sehe daß andere. die es beßer können. schöne Commentarios vber meinen alzukurzen text machen, vnd E. F. g. famam ex merito ebuccinieren³. Jch stehe aber an. ob in dem titulo Bockleriano. das wort reuocata, genugsam oder propriæ gesezet, fama enim non moritura, reuocanda non est, quo nihil habet opus. sed explicanda, vel dilatanda, aut ebuccinanda. Stehet iedoch ad arbitrium literatorum. vnd will ich des Trukh furderlich Mit H. Bökhlern Communiciren. der gewis mit großem verlangen darauf wartet. Nesselij stilus elegantissimus est. Wil verhoffen das ganze werkhlein furderlich zu sehen.

Außer der wolgestelten Commis Ordnung,⁴ hetten wir hie lands Vil gutes zu erlernen vnd nachzuthun. Sed nobis placet confusio. Vnd wer dawider Redet. camarinam⁵ movet. Es were aber hoch zu wunschen. daß wie in diesem. Also auch anderen Mehrern stukhen ad honestatem vitæ pertinentibus. die Abusus vnd Vnordnungen abgestelt. vnd gute Ordnungen anstatt gesezt würden, welches Verum Christianismum mächtig Beforderen könte. sed surdis fabulam.

Gott gebe dem Harmonischen werkh⁶ guten progress. Welches von Vilen frommen herzen hoch desierieret wurt.

Der Kreuter gesellschaft will ich vnd. erwarten.⁷ Es ist einer zu Straßb*ur*g Jsac Rumpler v. Lewenhalt. der Opitianischen geselschaft.⁸ des Vorhabens. seine gedicht sametlich in Trukh zu geben,⁹ Wirt also das werkh immer weiter vnd höher getriben. Wiewol mich bedunkhen will. daß Etliche sich zu weit in den

Poetischen fabeln Vnd^a **cothurnatas phrases** verlauffen. vnd den geistlichen gedichten Allen ernst, andacht. vnd eufer entziehen. welches doch **Opitius** selber nicht gethan. **Sed judicent poetæ.**

Befehle hiemit E. F. G. dem schuz des Almechtigen. Auch deroselben mich zu beharrenden großen g*naden* verbleibendt biß in den Todt,

      E. F. G. Vndertänig-gehorsamer verpflichter Rhat vnd Diener
            Jo. Val. Andreæ D.

6. Aug. ☿ 1645

T a *Eingefügt bis* phrases

K 1 Johann Valentin Andreae (FG 464. 1646) empfing den 30. Brief (des Jahres) Hz. Augusts d.J. v. Braunschweig-Wolfenbüttel (FG 227) am 2.8.1645. S. 450722. — Andreae hatte am 2.8.1614 Agnes Elisabeth Grüninger (1592–1659) geheiratet. Vgl. *DA Köthen I.* 5, S.107.

2 PANEGYRICUS. Illustrissimo ac Celsissimo Principi ac Domino, | DN. AUGUSTO, Duci Brunovicensi, & Luneburgensi, Domino suo clementissimo. TESTANDÆ DEVOTIONI D. D. D. MARTINUS NESSELIUS, MORAVUS. In: AUGUSTI DUCIS BRUNOVICENSIS & Luneburgensis FAMA non moritura, revocata; Calamo JOANNIS HENRICI BOCLERI. Typis STELLARUM. M. DC. XLV., 55–139. 16°. HAB: Gn 1328 u. Gn 1329; SLUB Dresden: Hist. Sax. inf. 483 (= auch dig.). Zwei Lobschriften auf Hz. August, S.1–54 u. 55–139 u. 6 Faltbll. Stammtafeln. S. 450319 K 9 u. 450722 K 2. Zu dem Straßburger Professor Johann Heinrich Boeckler (1611–1672) s. 440616 K 0, 450319 K 9 u.ö. Zum Erscheinungsdatum der Panegyrika s. 450722 K 2. Der luther. Mährer Martin Nessel (Weißkirchen [Hranice] 1607 – Wien oder Brünn 1673) war ein gelehrter lat. Autor, der sich auch um Opitz' Gunst bemühte: MARTINI OPITII v:c: EPIGRAMMATA, Et alia qvædam Latinitate donatæ; cum Mantissâ & M. CHRISTOPHORI STEPHANI CREMNICIO-HUNGARI, Decade Elegiarum: Authore Et Editore MARTINO NESSELIO Moravo P. L. C. (Rostochii 1635: Vidua Joachimus Pedanus), HAB: Li Sammelbd. 62 (10), auch dig., mit Ehrengedicht Andreas Tschernings. *Opitz: BW* 350606 K 12. Stationen seiner schwierigen Laufbahn: Luther. Gymn. Leutschau (Slowakei), stud. jur. Wittenberg 1629–1631 (1643 Mag.), drei Jahre Konrektor am Gymnasium in Schemnitz (Zips), 1634 weiteres Studium in Rostock (ohne Abschluß), 1635 von Peter Lauremberg (1585–1639) zum Poeta laureatus gekrönt, Kontakte zu Andreas Tscherning und Andreas Heinrich Buchholtz. Seit 1636 Konrektor Gymn. Uelzen, 1640–1644 Gymn. Minden. In einem Bittbrief v. 19.8.1646 [mit Lebenslauf, in: Rudolph August Nolte: Commercium litterarium clarorum virorum. 2 Tle., I (Brunsvigae 1737), 125 ff., vgl. dort auch Schreiben an Martin Gosky] wandte sich N. erkrankt an Hz. August. Er erhoffte vergeblich eine Stellung an dessen Hof bzw. eine Professur für Poesie in Helmstedt. 1646–1655 Gymn. Aurich, 1655–1666 Rektor der luth. Domschule Bremen. Nachdem er schon seit 1662 Literatur zu Luther und dem Protestantismus exzerpiert hatte, schied er zu Ostern 1666 aus dem Amt, wandte sich an die Jesuiten in Brünn, konvertierte, schrieb Epigramme auf das Kaiserpaar und wurde zum Leiter der ksl. Bibliothek ernannt. S. Heinrich Janssens biograph. Abriß in: Ostfriesische Landschaft, http://www.ostfriesischelandschaft.de

3 Ebuccinieren, zu lat. bucca, Backe, hier also soviel wie herausposaunen.
4 Hochzeitsordnung Hz. Augusts v. Braunschweig-Wolfenbüttel (FG 227), d. d. Wolfenbüttel 10.4.1645: Fürstliche Brunswigische COMMIS-Ordnung in Wolfenbüttel. Einblattdruck HAB: R 1:19 bzw. Fürstliche Brunswigische COMMIS-Ordnung in Wolfenbüttel ANNO M. DC. XLV, Quartdruck 1 Bl. u. 14 S. HAB: R 4:18. Beide dig.
5 Eine schon im Griech. gebrauchte Redensart nimmt Verg. Aen. 3, 700f. auf: „[...] et fatis numquam concessa moveri apparet Camerina [...]." Servius erklärte dazu, daß die Einwohner der sizilianischen griech. Stadt Kamarine ein Orakel Apolls mißachteten und den gleichnamigen Sumpf trockenlegten, weil er Seuchen verursachte. So ermöglichten die Bürger dem Feinde jedoch die Eroberung der Stadt. Sil. 14, 198, Claud. rapt. Pros. 2, 59.
6 Hz. Augusts *Evangelische Kirchen-Harmonie*. S.411214 u. zuletzt 450722.
7 Ungeduldig erwartet Andreae das Erscheinen des *GB 1646*, das Hz. August ihm zu senden versprach. S. 440130 K 3 zum *GB 1646* allgemein, zuletzt 450722. Zum Empfang des Buchs s. 460715.
8 Die Schar der opitzierenden deutschen Dichter, d.h. der Nachahmer von Martin Opitz v. Boberfeld (FG 200).
9 Jesaias Rompler v. Löwenhalt: Des | Jesaias Romplers von | Löwenhalt | erstes gebüsch | seiner | Reim-getichte. | [Zierleiste] | Getruckt zu Strasburg/ bej Joh. Phil. Mülben/ in dem 1647.ten jar Chrl.er z. [Christlicher Zeitrechnung], 234f. ULB Halle: AB 120481 (VD17 3:608145Z). Nachdr. hg. v. Wilhelm Kühlmann u. Walter E. Schäfer. Tübingen 1988. Vgl. 440724. Johann Rist (FG 467. 1647) empfing durch Philipp v. Zesen (FG 521. 1648) einen Brief des Jesaias Rompler v. Löwenhalt (AGT, DG 16). S. 440724, vgl. auch 450308A. Rompler korrespondierte auch mit Andreae. Am 1.9.1646 dankte er Andreae z.B. für einen Brief, aus dem er von A.s Gesundheitszustand erfahren hatte. Er habe (dem mömpelgard. Kanzler Christoph) Forstner von A.s Liebe zu F. berichtet, als er durch Straßburg reiste. R. erwarte eine kurze Antwort von F. Wenn der doch schneller zu den (Friedens-)Verhandlungen in Westfalen gesandt worden wäre, hätte er den Herzögen von Württemberg und der Respublica nutzen können. Am. 15.8. hat R. von dem klugen Hz. Georg v. Württemberg, der von Stuttgart nach Ansbach gereist war, einen Brief v. 30.6.1646 empfangen (R. hatte ihm gesagt, er solle Andreae besuchen). R. habe an Georg am 1./11.8. geschrieben. R. legte seinem Brief Boeckleriana bei. HAB: Cod. Guelf. 11.12 Aug. 2°, 281rv, lat. eigenh. In die FG wurde Rompler nicht aufgenommen, seine spätere Kritik an der FG war wohl auch durch diese herbe Enttäuschung verursacht worden. S. demnächst *DA Köthen I. 9:* 470604. Vgl. schon 370900.

450808

Philipp von Zesen an Georg Philipp Harsdörffer

Antwort auf 450410. — Philipp v. Zesen (DG 1. Der Färtige; FG 521. 1648) bestätigt, daß Ludwig v. Hitzfeld (DG 27. Der Deutschmeinende) ihm vor vier Wochen zwei Briefe Georg Philipp Harsdörffers (FG 368. Der Spielende; DG 12. Der Kunstspielende) aushändigte. Zesen habe wegen einer anstehenden Reise nicht sofort geantwortet, entschuldigt sich für den Verzug und dankt für Harsdörffers Geschenk (dessen *Frauenzimmer-Gesprächspiele* I [²1644] mit der „Schutzschrift/ für die Teutsche Spracharbeit"). Zesen bedankt sich mit seinem Roman *Adriatische Rosemund* (1645), den (Wolfgang) Endters Diener überbringen werde. Was Harsdörffers erstes (nicht überliefertes) Schreiben anbetrifft, so habe dies Hitzfeld bereits ausführlich beantwortet. Daher gehe Zesen hier auf das zweite Schreiben Harsdörffers (450410) ein. — Zesen stimmt Harsdörffer zu, daß Stammwort nur ein solches Wort heißt, das mit einem Präfix oder Suffix verknüpft werden kann. Daß es jedoch stets aus einem einsilbigen Imperativ gebildet wird, treffe zumindest für die meißnische und obersächsische Mundart nicht zu. Als man alle verbalen Stammformen auf einen einsilbigen Imperativ verkürzte, habe man die deutsche Sprache verstümmelt und den Klang verhärtet. Die meisten hochdeutschen Stammwörter seien verschwunden und müßten in Neben- oder Untersprachen gesucht werden. Wo das Stammwort unbekannt ist, müsse das Imperfekt oder das Perfekt herangezogen werden. So kann aus dem Imperfekt „galt" der richtige Infinitiv „gälten" („ich gälte/ das gäld") abgeleitet werden. Hier sei der Vernunft und der Durchschaubarkeit der Vorzug vor dem falschen Gebrauch zu geben. Er selbst, Zesen, sei keineswegs halsstarrig und beuge sich vernünftiger Erkenntnis. — Die DG, deren Einigkeit ihm wichtiger sei als Rechthaberei, habe im letzten Vierteljahr stark zugenommen und richte sich meistenteils nach Zesens Schreibart. Auch das /v/ wolle er keineswegs ganz abschaffen, sondern nur aus jenen Wörtern verdrängen, die mit /f/ zu schreiben sind. Auch Vater könne nach Ausweis der deutschen Vorfahren und „unter-sprachen" (norw. u. dän. „Fader", schwed. „Fadher", engl. „Father") Fater geschrieben werden.

Q *Bellin: Sendeschreiben (1647)*, Nr. 15, Bl. H iij r – [H vi]r.

A *Fehlt.*

An Hern Georg Filip Harsdörfern.

Mein Her/
DEsselben zwei beliebte schreiben sein mier von Dem von Hizfeld[1] zwar fohr 4. wochen überschikt worden/ weil es aber die geschäfte meiner damahls fohrhabenden reise[2] nicht zulaßen wolten/ daß ich meinem Herrn nuhr mit etlichen zeilen geantwortet hätte/ so hab' ich billich uhrsache gnug mich meines so langen stilschweigens wegen zu entschuldigen. Jch bedanke [Hiij v] mich zum höchsten fohr das geschänke[3]/ damit er seinen unwürdigen/ doch aller träu-färtigsten Diener hat verehren wollen; und überschikk' ihm widerüm/ zu bezeugung meines geringen gegendanks/ meine Adriatische Rosemund[4]/ die ihm durch H. Entners[5] diener würd über-reichet werden. Er gönn' ihr einen kleinen raum in den untersten fächern seines buch-zimmers/ und laß ihm[a] dadurch das gedächtnüs seines Geträuen lieb und anbefohlen sein. Was sein ehrstes schreiben betrifft/ so hab' ich von dem Deutsch-meinenden verstanden/ daß er selbiges aus-führlich beantwortet hätte[6]/ daher ich dan nuhr das andere bei dieser gelegenheit kürzlich beantworten.

Es ist ie und alwege meine meinung auch gewesen/ **daß unter den stam- und wurzel-wörtern nicht alle und iede der deutschen sprache wörter/ sondern nuhr die jenigen/ welche durch ihre fohr- und nach-glieder (præfixa und suffixa) reiflich auswachsen/ verstanden würden.**[7] Daß man aber die weise zu gebieten darunter rechnen solle/ solches würd kein Meisner oder anderer Landsman/ der sie nicht alwege eingliederich schreibet/ und aus-spricht/ zugäben wollen/ und ich hab' es denen jenigen/ die nicht-gebohrne hoch-deutschen sein/ und die weise zugebieten allezeit mit eingliedrigen wörtern schreiben wollen/ gar [Hiiij r] leichtlich abmärken können/ daß sie selbige fohr wurzeln ansähen. Aber es mus ein ieder/ so der Meisnischen und Ober-sächsischen mund-ahrt gewohnet ist/ bekännen/ daß sie niemahls **lieb/ denk/ schlag/ red/ leid/ (du)** und so fort/ **fohr liebe/ denke/ schlage/ rede/ leide/ (du)** aus-sprächen oder schreiben/ es sei dan/ wän ein selb-lauter darauf folget/ da das **e** weg-geworfen werden mus; als **drüm lob' und lieb' und preise deinen Got; drüm schlag' ihn;** (hiermit ist auch das seinige von den **Schevaim** beantwortet) Aber nicht/ **drüm lieb Got/ schlag den man.** Ja unsere sprache ist eine zeitlang durch die jenigen/ welche die eingliedrigen wörter nuhr alein fohr wurzeln gehalten haben/ und daher auch die zwei-gliedrigen eingliederich haben machen wollen/ so sehr verderbet und verhärtet worden/ daß man sie kaum mehr lesen/ oder aus-sprächen kan. Den Meisnischen ohren/ welche die sprache gern lieblich haben/ ist solches ganz zu wider. Drüm solte man billich einen unterscheid machen/ und die jenigen wörter/ der weise zu gebieten/ die nuhr alein eingliederich sein/ als **nein/ kom/ is** udg. von den andern/ welche zwei-gliederich/ als **liebe/ lebe/ zweifle/ handle (du)** oder aber beides sein/ d. i. ein- und zweigliederich können gebraucht werden/ als **trünk** und **trünke/ sih** und **sihe/ steh** und **stehe** [Hiiij v] **(du)** unterscheiden/ und einem ieden worte seine gewöhn- und gebräuchliche selbliche eigenschaft laßen/ wo man die sprache nicht gar unangenähm machen wil. Mein Her kan hieraus leichtlich abnähmen/ was meine fernere meinung ist.[8] Jm übrigen würd ihm auch bekant sein/ daß fast die meisten der hoch-deutschen sprache stamwörter entweder vergangen/ oder in andern ihren neben- und unter-sprachen müssen aufgesuchet wärden/ und daß man an der jenigen stat/ welche vergangen/ oder wohl gar noch nie im gebrauche gewäsen sein/ die unfolkomne/ oder/ wo man die wurzel aus dieser nicht erkundigen kan/ doch die folkomne zeit betrachten mus/ weil man darinnen den uhrsprung der zweifachlauter/ die in der gebietenden weise/ so wohl als in andern fohrkommen/ fünden kan[9]: Als/ ich kan nicht wissen/ warüm ich aus-spreche und nach der aus-sprache schreiben sol/ **gälten/ ich gälte/ das gäld/** wan ich nicht die unfol-komne zeit/ **galt/** darinnen das einfache **a** stehet/ betrachte. Weiter kan ich auch nicht wissen/ warüm ich **gült/ schült/** schreiben sol/ wan ich nicht **gegolten/ gescholten/** usf. betrachte. Man mus auch/ damit ich noch eines erinnere/ fremden fölkern unsere sprache nicht alzu verwürret und als zu [sic] schwer machen/ wan man die lauter so vielmahls/ da es doch nicht nöhtig ist/ und durchaus nicht zugelassen [Hv r] wärden kan/ verändern wil[10]; Ja wan man die ab- und zu-leitung der zeit-wörter recht hand-haben sol/ so mus man in dem einen nicht das **o** oder **u/** in dem andern aber das **i** (da doch **o** und **u** allezeit in **ü** oder **ö** verwandelt werden) gebrauchen[11]/ wie die unachtsamkeit unserer fohr-fahren solches schohn eingeführet hat.[12] Hier mus man nicht auf den irrigen gebrauch achten/ sondern vielmehr der klug-sinnigen vernunft/ die uns in diese richtigkeit leitet/ nachgehen. Dannenher pfleg' ich meine angenommene gewohnheit/ wan ich was richtigers fünde/ wie billich/ zu ändern/ und es würd es mier auch kein verständiger übel aus-deuten/ daß ich so halsstarrig nicht bin/ wie andere/ die auf ihrer einmal gefassten meinung/ da sie doch wohl wissen/ und heimlich bekännen müssen/ daß sie irren/ nichts däs zu weniger so standfäst verharren/ daß sie keinem nach-gäben wollen. Jch wil mich gerne weisen laßen/ so es nuhr mit vernunft und richtigem verstande geschihet. Wan ich aber im widrigen sähe/ daß man mich zu einem dinge bereden wil/ welches ganz wider die richtigkeit und vernunft läuft/ so kan ich mich zu keiner änderung verstehen/ und solt' ich auch das schreiben in unserer deutschen sprache gahr bleiben laßen. Welches ich auch gerne tuhn wil/ damit ich nuhr die mit-glieder unserer Genossenschaft/ die in diesem vierteil-jahre sehr zugenommen hat/ in [H v v] einigkeit erhalte; wan ichs ja auf eine andere weise nicht zu werke richten könte. Aber meine Schreib-ahrt ist unter vielen schohn so eingerissen/ daß sie nicht darvon abstehen wärden/ ob ich gleich darzu stimmen wolte. Mein Her würd künftig viel bücher sähen/ darinnen mier/ wo nicht in allen/ doch meistenteils nachgefolget würd. Man wil mier viel schuld gäben/ davon ich ganz im geringsten nichts weus: Die **vav**[b] ganz ab zu schaffen bin ich nicht gesonnen/ wiewohl es etliche aus unserer Genossenschaft/ aber nicht ohne sonderliche gründe/ tuhn wollen/ sondern ich schaff' es nuhr ab in denen wörtern/ da das **f** stehen sol/ als **fortern/ fohr/ führ/ führen/ fohraus/ fohrteil/ forschen** (q. d. herfohr suchen) **fol/ füllen/ föllig; folk/** welches so viel gesagt ist/ als das Französische **suite,** (à suivre, d.i. folgen) train de gens, **geschläppe/** comitatus: das seinem Herrn oder Heerzoge nachfolget. **Vater** schreiben etliche auch mit einem **F**; weil es in den deutschen unter-sprachen meistenteils also geschrieben würd/ und auch selbst von unserer fohr-fahren also ist geschrieben worden. Die Norweger schreiben **Fader/** die Dähnen auch **Fader/** die Schweden **Fadher/** die Englischen **Father**; es würd auch also aus-gesprochen.[13]

Was nuhn unsere gedachte Genossenschaft [(Hvj) r] anbelanget/ so würd darinnen einem ieden seine meinung und schreib-ahrt frei gelaßen/ weil doch immer einer anders gesiñet ist/ als der andere/ und es nimmermehr geschähen kan/ daß man eine solche geselschaft aufrichten würd/ derer mit-glieder einerlei meinungen führen wärden.[14] —[c] — — — — — — — — — — — Hiermit schlüß ich meine schrift/ aber meine gedanken gahr nicht/ welche allezeit zu meines hochgeehrten Herren träuen diensten sollen gerichtet sein/ damit ich mit recht heissen möge

Der Färtige.

Utrecht den 8. August m.[d] 1645.

I

Zesens Widmungsgedicht für Harsdörffers fünften Teil der *Gesprächspiele* (1645)

Q *Harsdörffer: Frauenzimmer-Gesprächspiele V (1645, Ndr. 1969), Ndr. S.44f.; Bellin: Sendeschreiben (1647), Nr.15, Bl. H[vj]r f., zit. als BS.*

Nach der Palmenart.[a][1]

DEr Spielende[2] spielet und zielet zur Tugend:
sein Spielen ergetzet/ und letzet die Jugend;

Pallas unde.[b]
    dann unsre Kluginne[3] das sichere[c] Bild/
Palladium Trojan.[e]
    die spielet mitunter/ und führet den[d] Schild.
Die[f] sterbe-blau-spielenden Aeugelein blitzen[g]/
und[h] machen Kunstmütige Spieler erhitzen/
    die ihren lieb-spielenden[i] strahlenden Blikk
    nicht[j] können erreichen/ und weichen zu rükk.
[k]Der Spielende findet die tunkelen Künste/

Cæsia Virgo.[4] Ab Ebraico Velatus, absconditus: quia artes ingenuæ obscuræ sunt, arduæ & mirabiles.
Bürginne bezeuget ihm allerley Günste/ [45]
    verbirget ihm nichtes/ eröffnet ihr Spiel/
    und lehret ihn spielen/ und treffen zum[l] Ziel/

Venus.[m]
Lustinne verzukkert die Reden im Spiele/
Cupido.
das[n] muntere Liebeskind spielet zum Ziele:
Gratiæ.
    die trauten[o] Holdinnen verlieblichen auch/
    und lieben solch Spielen nach ihrem Gebrauch.
Ey[p]/ spielet mit solchen Gespielen noch weiter
auf mancherley Weise/ Jhr[r] Tugend Anleiter:
    so[s] werden sie wieder auf mancherley Art
    Euch[t] alle bekräntzen.

    auf flüchtiger Fahrt gesetzet/
    durch
    Filip Zesien von Fürstenau.

Utrecht den 20 des Christmonats 1644.

T a *Lies:* sich — b *Lies:* vau *(Pl. Buchstabe v).* — c *Strichesetzung als Auslassungsmarkierung Bellins?* — d monat

T I a *Überschrift in BS:* Eben desselben [Zesens] Auf des Spielenden fünftes teil seiner Gespräch-spiele. Palmen-reime. — b *In BS folgt Virgel. Randmarginalie:* Pallas seu Minervæ, sapientiæ dea. — c *BS* spielende — d *BS* das — e *Randmarginalie fehlt in BS.* — f *Randmarginalie in BS:* Bleu-mourant. — g *BS* plützen — h *Zeile in BS:* fohr denen viel tapfere Spieler ersitzen/ — **i** *Statt* lieb-spielenden strahlenden *hat BS* Kunst-zielenden spielenden — **j** *BS* nie — **k** *Randmarginalie in BS* Pallas, quidam deducunt ex fonte ebraico אבָּלָה seu בָּלָה, i.e. velatus, absconditus, fuit; arduus & excellens, extra captum nostrum. Quia artes obscuræ sunt arduæ & mirabiles. — **l** *BS* das — **m** *Randmarginalie auch in BS.* — **n** *Statt* das muntere Liebeskind *hat BS* der muntere Liebe-reitz *Dazu die Randmarginalie:* Cupido der Liebe-reizer — **o** *Randmarginalie in BS* Charites seu Gratiæ. — **p** *BS* Wohl! — **r** *Statt* Jhr Tugend Anleiter *hat BS* wohl-spielender Streiter — **s** *Zeile in BS* Sie werden Euch izund auf mancherley Art *Dazu Randmarginalie* Des H. Spielenden sinnen-spruch. *[Harsdörffers Name und Wort in der FG: Der Spielende Auf mancherley Art.]* — **t** *Beim Satz ging der Reimzusammenhang etwas verloren. Die beiden Schlußzeilen in BS:* Sie werden Euch izund auf mancherley Art | Mit ehren bekräntzen. Auf flüchtiger fahrt | schrieb es Der Färtige. *Die Datumszeile fehlt.*

K Antwort Philipp v. Zesens (DG 1. Der Färtige. FG 521. 1648) aus Utrecht auf die beiden durch Ludwig v. Hitzfeld (DG 27. Der Deutschmeinende) etwa Anfang Juli überschickten Briefe Georg Philipp Harsdörffers (FG 368. Der Spielende. DG 12. Der Kunstspielende. Angebl. Dez. 1644): 450410 und einen verschollenen Harsdörffer-Brief, den Hitzfeld in seinem in Anm. 6 zit. Brief an Harsdörffer beantwortet hatte.

1 Ludwig v. Hitzfeld (bezeugt zw. 1645 u. 1679), aus Kleve, am 1.6.1645 als 27. Mitglied u. „der Deutschmeinende" in die DG aufgenommen. S. Philipp v. Zesen: Das Hochdeutsche Helikonische Rosentahl (Amsterdam 1669). In *Zesen SW* XII, 178–310, hier 254f. u. im genannten Band die Anhänge S. 425 u. 449. Zesen kannte Hitzfeld aus Utrechter Studentenkreisen. S. Jan Hendrik Scholte: Zesens „Adriatische Rosemund". In: Dt. Vierteljahresschrift f. Literaturwissenschaft u. Geistesgeschichte 23 (1949), 288–305, hier S. 302. Hitzfeld, der vor 1686 gestorben sein muß, da er damals als Erzschreinhalter des Westfäl. Kreises der DG von Theodor Kornfeld (1636–1698. DG 178) abgelöst wurde, stand auch persönlich in Kontakt mit Harsdörffer. S. Anm. 6; Zesen: Das Hochdeutsche Helikonische Rosentahl, a. a. O., 195; *Ingen: Zesen*, 95; Karl F. Otto Jr.: Sub-groups of the Deutschgesinnte Genossenschaft. In: Daphnis 17 (1988), 627–632, hier S. 629 u. 631f.

2 Zesens geplante Reise führte ihn vermutlich innerhalb der Niederlande umher, in denen er sich zwischen 1642 und 1648 vorzugsweise aufhielt. Der vorliegende Brief ist aus Utrecht datiert. Vgl. Anm. 4; *Ingen: Zesen*, 3; *Ingen*, 23.

3 In 450410 gibt Harsdörffer einen Hinweis auf seine „zugabe des ersten theils der Gesprächspiele, so mein Herr mit der *[sic]* Frankfurter Büch*er*en H. Elzeviers, sonder zweiffel empfang*en* haben wird." Vgl. 450410 K 1 u. 2. In Frage käme aber auch *Harsdörffer: Frauenzimmer-Gesprächspiele* IV (1644).

4 [Philipp v. Zesen; Kupfertitel:] Ritterholds von Blauen Adriatische Rosemund. Last hägt Lust. Amsteltam, Bei Ludwich Elzevihrn. 1645. HAB: 135.5 Eth. (2). *Zesen SW*, IV.2. Der Roman muß gerade erschienen sein, denn Zesens Dedikation ist datiert „Rein=wurf" (Utrecht, lat. Trajectum ad Rhenum) 30.7.1645, wobei aber, abgesehen von den ohnehin notorischen chronologischen Unstimmigkeiten bei Zesen, der Heumonat bei ihm auch den Juni meinte, was hier stimmiger wäre. Vgl. Max Hermann Jellinek in der Einleitung zu seiner Ausg. von Philipp von Zesen: Adriatische Rosemund 1645. Hg. M. H. J. Halle a. d. S. 1899, S. XLVI; Scholte: Zesens „Adriatische Rosemund" (s. Anm. 1), 299; Gustav Schönle: Deutsch-niederländische Beziehungen in der Literatur des 17. Jahrhunderts. Leiden 1968, 128; Karl F. Otto Jr.: Philipp von Zesen. A Bibliographical Catalogue. Bern, München 1972, 53 (Nr. 29).

5 Wolfgang Endter d. Ä. (1593–1659), der Nürnberger Verleger, Buchhändler und Drucker, der das Geschäft seines Vaters Georg (1562–1630) übernommen hatte, zu einer

beherrschenden Stellung in Nürnberg ausbaute und durch Niederlassungen in Frankfurt a. M. und Leipzig erweiterte. Er verlegte auch Harsdörffers *Frauenzimmer-Gesprächspiele, Specimen* (1646) u. andere Werke. Er publizierte die sog. Weimarische, Gothaische oder Kurfürstenbibel (erstmals 1641) im Auftrag Hz. Ernsts v. Sachsen-Gotha (FG 19). 1651 von Ks. Ferdinand III. geadelt, übergab er im gleichen Jahr Druckerei und Verlag seinen Söhnen Wolfgang d.J. (1622–1655) und Johann Andreas (1625–1670). Harsdörffer fand Grund zur Klage über Endters Geiz und filzigen Krämergeist. S. 460620 u. 460916. *ADB* VI, 110f.; 795; *DBA* I 282, 264–266, II 328, 342 u. III 214, 323f. u. 328–331; *Reske*, 718–721.

6 In *Bellin: Sendeschreiben (1647)*, Nr. 17, Bl. [H viij] r – J ij r, findet sich ein undatierter Brief Hitzfelds an Harsdörffer. Darin legitimiert Hitzfeld sein Schreiben an Harsdörffer damit, daß ihn Zesen vor ca. 6 Wochen, als dieser nach Brabant abgereist sei, ermächtigt habe, seine Post zu erbrechen, zu lesen und zu beantworten. Hitzfeld wurde lt. *Helikonischem Rosental* am 1.5.1645 in die DG aufgenommen (a. a. O. [s. Anm. 1], 254). Wenn ihn Zesen kurz danach für die Zeit seiner Abwesenheit zu seinem Korrespondenzverwalter ernannte, müßte Hitzfelds Brief an Harsdörffer etwa Mitte/ Ende Juni 1645 geschrieben worden sein. In diesem Antwortschreiben teilt Hitzfeld Harsdörffer mit, er habe am Vortage Harsdörffers Brief und ein Buchgeschenk an Zesen erhalten. Dieser verschollene Harsdörffer-Brief an Zesen dürfte somit wohl jünger gewesen sein als 450410, d.h. erst im Mai oder sogar Anfang Juni abgefaßt sein. Anfang Juli sandte Hitzfeld dann nach Auskunft Zesens im vorliegenden Schreiben die beiden Harsdörffer-Briefe an Zesen, vermutlich mit einer Abschrift seines eigenen Antwortschreibens an Harsdörffer. Themen dieses Briefes sind u. a.: Harsdörffers Erkundigung nach „des Zidi-buassons Gesellschaften", die Hitzfeld nicht beantworten konnte. Die Schreibweise Zesens hätten viele Deutschgesinnete, ohne dazu genötigt oder verpflichtet zu sein, aus Überzeugung angenommen, und sie gedächten auch, bei ihr zu bleiben, wie künftig zahlreiche Druckschriften bezeugen würden. Harsdörffer möge das respektieren, zumal ihm doch Zesen „fohr etlichen wochen" für die Zeit seiner Reise „die Ertz-schreinhalterschaft", also die Geschäftsführung der DG übertragen habe (!). Auch in der FG herrsche über Fragen der Schreibung keine Einigkeit, so könne dies auch nicht von der DG erwartet werden. Zesens *Ibrahim* (1645) sei dem Hause Anhalt zugesandt worden. Zesen werde nicht versäumen, Harsdörffer bei einem geplanten Besuch in Nürnberg dafür zu danken, daß er sich für die Aufnahme Zesens in die FG einsetzen wolle.

7 Harsdörffer in 450410: „Unter den Stamm- oder Wurtzelwörtern werden nicht alle und jede Wörter der Teutschen Sprache ver*stand*en, sondern nur diese, welche durch ihre vor und nachsylben (pro præfixa et suffixa) reiflich auswachen […]". Zesen schließt sich dieser Bestimmung des Stammwortes an und grenzt Ableitungen und Komposita davon ab. Vgl. 450410 K 4. Hier liegt übrigens auch ein Beweis, daß Zesen mit dem vorliegenden Schreiben diesen Harsdörffer-Brief beantwortete.

8 Zesen bekräftigt seinen schon in 450308A geäußerten und im *Rosen-mând* (1651) wiederholten Widerstand gegen Harsdörffers und Justus Georg Schottelius' (FG 397) Auffassung, wonach die deutschen Stammwörter wie auch die hebräischen Radices oder Wurzeln immer einsilbig und die Stammwörter der Verben in den stets einsilbigen Imperativen („Gebietungsweise") zu finden seien. Beides wird von Zesen, ebenso wie von F. Ludwig und Christian Gueintz (FG 361) bestritten. Damit weist Zesen auch den von Harsdörffer in 450410 erhobenen Vorwurf zurück, er wolle unverantwortlicher Weise „die Sch*e*vaim und vav aus dem von so viel Jahren her üblich*en* a, b, c absondern […] welches gewisslich so wenig in unserer als [der] Ebreisch*en* Sprache kan erdultet werd*en*." Vgl. 441223 K 21, 450308A u. 450410 K 3.

9 Zu Zesens wilden etymologischen Wortmorphologien und zu seiner Ableitung des Verbstamms aus den Vergangenheitsstufen des Perfekts („die folkomne zeit") oder Imperfekts („die unfolkomne") vgl. 441223 K 21, 450308A u. 450410 K 16. Vgl. ferner Zesens undatierten Brief an Adolph Rosel(ius) (DG 6), der wohl in den Januar 1645 fallen dürfte (in: *Bellin: Sendeschreiben (1647)*, Nr. 5, Bl. [B6]v – C[i]v). Dort schlägt Zesen beispielsweise auch vor, „Geschöpf" durch „Geschäft" zu ersetzen, weil Geschöpf vom nd. schaep/ schaepen herstamme. Zesens Begriff „Zweifachlauter" steht für Diphthong, vgl. Anm. 11. Vgl. zur Stammworttheorie auch 450410 K 3.

10 Der Wortstamm und die Stammverwandtschaft der Wörter sollte für Zesen hier durch die Wahrung des Stammvokals ausgewiesen werden (Zesens „Lauter" = Vokale). Er plädiert also im Grunde für die Beachtung des Stammprinzips, verstanden als Morphem- oder Schemakonstanz im Wortparadigma, die sich zum Nhd. hin tatsächlich in einem vielfältigen Ausgleichsprozeß, etwa bei der Pluralbildung (z. B. mhd. hant/ hende > nhd. Hand/ Hände), vollzogen hat. Vgl. Anm. 11 u. *Herz: Rechtschreibdebatte*, S. 97 Anm. 92.

11 Vgl. schon 441223 und dort K 21. In einem Brief an Johann Bellin, etwa vom November 1646, beantwortete Zesen dessen Frage, warum er das übliche i und e durch die Umlaute ä, ö und ü ersetze. Weil sich die Wörter, hier die Verben, so Zesen, auch in ihren Ableitungen, Flexionen usw. nach ihren Stämmen richten müßten. Lautet der Stammvokal auf a, o oder u, so müssen gebeugte oder abgeleitete Formen deren Umlaute annehmen: ä, ö, ü bzw. den Diphthong eu. Da Zesen die Stammform des Verbs vorab im Imperfekt oder Perfekt sieht, müsse es statt „gelten" „gälten" heißen, von galt; „bärgen" von barg, „hälfen" von half, „föchten" von focht usw. „Gleich wie alle wörter/ welche mit einem von den drei Als-zwelautern ä ö ü/ oder mit dem zwelauter eu geschrieben wärden/ allezeit aus andern/ darinnen die einfachen a o oder u stehen/ herstammen müssen; also müssen auch ebner gestalt alle Wörter sich nach ihren grund-stämmen richten/ und wan darinnen das a/ o/ oder u zu fünden ist/ in den davon aus-sprüssenden nicht das e oder i/ sondern allezeit das ä/ ö oder ü haben." *Bellin: Sendeschreiben (1647)*, Nr. 8, Bl. [C iiij] r – [D v] v. In der *Adriatischen Rosemund* (1645) hat Zesen dieses Konzept weitgehend umgesetzt. Dies widersprach der damaligen und heutigen Schreibgewohnheit, fand aber eine Stütze in der phonetischen Entrundung im damaligen Obersächsischen, das in der Aussprache keine Unterschiede zwischen gerundeten (ä, ö, ü) und ungerundeten (e, i) Vokalen machte. Reimbeispiele (z. B. führt/ ziert) auch bei Zesen selbst belegen diese Lautentwicklung. Ausführlich dazu Jellinek in der Einleitung zu seiner Ausg. von Zesens *Adriatischer Rosemund*, Halle a. d. S. 1899 (s. Anm. 4), S. XXIVff.; Klaus Kaczerowsky: Bürgerliche Romankunst im Zeitalter des Barock. Philipp von Zesens „Adriatische Rosemund". München 1969, 147 ff.; *Schielein*, 19, 31 ff. u. 83.

12 Schottelius erschien die deutsche Sprachgeschichte allerdings auch als ein Abfall von der Reinheit des Ursprungs. Erst der Sprachausbau seiner Gegenwart konnte die eingerissenen Mißstände abstellen. Diese Auffassung von sprachlicher Dekadenz trägt bes. seinen *Horrendum Bellum grammaticale* (1673). Vgl. *Herz: Aufrichtigkeit, Vertrauen, Frieden*, 346 ff. Zesen betrachtete jedoch nicht nur die jüngere Sprachvergangenheit, sondern schon die germanische Frühzeit sprach- und kulturgeschichtlich durchaus skeptisch: Bedenkenlos hätten unsere „fohr-ältern [...]/ welche fast keinem einigen dinge/ das wissenschaften betrüft/ nachgedacht haben", das -k- aus dem Griechischen und das latein. Alphabet einschließlich des -c- und -q- „wider ihrer sprache eigenschaft" ins Deutsche eingeführt. (Bl. Eii v). „Die lateinischen lehr-sätze gälten bei uns nicht/ Weil es mit unserer sprache viel ein' andere beschaffenheit und ahrt hat. Töhricht haben wier getahn/ daß wier uns an sie so fäst gebunden haben." Zesen an Adolph Rosel(ius) (DG 6), undat., in: *Bellin: Sendeschreiben (1647)*, Nr. 10, Bl. [Dviij] v – G[i] v, hier Bl. Eii v u. [Evij] v.

13 Das -v- ordnete Zesen der nd. Mundart zu und wollte es aus dem Hd. weitgehend entfernen. Vgl. dazu 450410 K 17 u. *Schielein*, 45f.

14 „Hierbei müssen wir auch nohtwendig erinnern/ daß kein Mitglied unserer Genossenschaft gehalten ist/ sich an eine gewisse dieses oder jenes Schreibahrt/ wie etliche naseweise Neidhämmel uns fälschlich bezüchtiget/ zu binden; sondern ein jedes seine volkommene freiheit habe/ nach seiner eigenen wilkühr damit zu verfahren; jedoch also/ daß es mit der rechtmässigen vernunft/ oder zum wenigsten mit dem erleidlichstem üblichem gebrauche/ ob er schon zu weilen jener schnuhrstraks zugegen leuft/ übereinkomme. Dan es ist einmahl gewis/ daß hierinnen nimmermehr einige gleichstimmigkeit/ ob man schon gern wolte/ auch nicht einmahl unter zween/ zu treffen". Philipp v. Zesen: Das Hochdeutsche Helikonische Rosentahl (Amsterdam 1669). In: *Zesen SW* XII, 178–310, hier S. 205 (Sperrungen weggelassen).

K I *Harsdörffer: Frauenzimmer-Gesprächspiele* V (1645, Ndr. 1969) werden eingeleitet durch „Ehrengedichte dem SPIELENDEN" (Ndr. S. 21–92). Zunächst tritt eine Reihe von Fruchtbringern unter ihren Gesellschaftsnamen auf: Der Geheime (Franz Julius v. dem Knesebeck. FG 396), der Unverdrossene (Carl Gustav v. Hille. FG 302), der Suchende (Justus Georg Schottelius. FG 397; d.d. Wolfenbüttel, 10.12.1644), Der Friedfertige (Paris v. dem Werder. FG 339; d.d. Reinsdorf, 16.5.1645); sodann Christian Brehme (d.d. Dresden, 5.5.1645), gefolgt von DG-Genossen: Conrad Hildebrand (DG 20/ 19.2.1645. Der Beständige), Johann Michael Moscherosch (DG 24/ 3.4.1645. Der Träumende. FG 436. 1645), Georg Conrad Osthof (DG 8/ 8.10.1644. Der Samlende), Johann Rist (FG 467. 1647; d.d. Hamburg, 8.2.1645; PBO, ESO), Jesaias Rompler v. Löwenhalt (DG 16/ 4.2.1645. Der Freie), Philipp v. Zesen (DG 1. Der Färtige. FG 521. 1648): „Nach der Palmenart" (s.o.); danach Mitglieder des PBO: Johann Helwig (1609–1674), Samuel Hund (um 1620 – nach 1680. DG 25), Johann Klaj (1616–1656. DG 23), Sigmund Betulius (v. Birken) (FG 681. 1658. DG 26), Johann Sechst (gest. 1677) und Christoph Arnold (1627–1685). Vgl. zu den PBO-Mitgliedern in der Reihenfolge der Nennung: *Jürgensen: Repertorium*, 146–156, 102–104, 50–63, 64–101, 129–138 u. 105–128. Zum Beschluß dankt Georg Philipp Harsdörffer (FG 368. Der Spielende) diesen Beiträgern und der FG mit zwei Gedichten. Zur Gründung des PBO im Zusammenhang mit der FG s. jetzt *Conermann: Harsdörffers Plan*, 42–45.

1 „Palmenart", d.h. im daktylischen Versmaß mit Katalexe bzw. Kadenz. In der Aufzählung der verschiedenen Versfüße in seinem *Deutschen Helicon* (2. Ausg. 1649) nennt Zesen als dritten den „rollenden" Versfuß oder „reim-tritt" (Bl. F v): „Der rollende wird von den Griechen und Lateinern **Dactylus** [*Fußnote:* in Scalâ Helic. p. 50] d.i. Finger/ weil er drei gelenke und glieder/ ein langes und zwei kurtze hat/ wie ein finger; Von uns kann er 1/ der Färtige/ wie ihn der Schmäkkende/ der hochlöblichen Deutschgesinneten Genoßenschaft mitglied [*d.i. Frh. Johann Adolf v. Alewein. DG 35*]/ benahmet/ weil er so färtig und hurtig von der zungen gehet; 2/ der dattel-schrit/ oder auch palmen-schrit/ von dem Jndischen Palm-baume/ und dessen frucht/ den datteln [*Fußnote:* ib.] genennet werden. Wir nennen ihn alhier lieber den rollenden/ weil die ehrste ahrt [*d.i.* „Der steigende [...] **jambus**] berg-an steiget; die andere [*d.i.* „Der fallende [...] **Trochæus"**] berg-unter stuffen-weise fället/ oder läuffet/ die dritte aber/ nämlich die rollende/ gleich-sam gar berg-ab rollet/ und kullert." (Bl. F ij v). Ähnlich in: Filip Zesens deutsch-lateinische Leiter zum hoch=deutschen HELIKON: das ist Kurtzer entwurf aller hoch=deutschen ... reimbände/ mit kurtzen an=märkungen. h.e. SCALA germanico-latina HELICONIS TEUTONICI (Jena 1656). In: *Zesen SW* XII, 1–175, 104ff.: „De genere Dactylo" oder „Von der [...] Dattel=art": „Dan die dattel ist eine frucht der Palmen/ welche von ihrer ähnligkeit mit den fingern also genennet wird. [...] Dan die stuffen dieser dattel-art haben von den dreien gliedern der finger/ deren das erste lang/ die andern zwei kurtz seind [...] den nahmen bekommen. Zu dem/ nennen wier sie billich die Palmen-art/ weil sie nicht allein unter allen lieder=reimen/ wegen der hurtigkeit und lieblichkeit der stuffen/ den Palmen d. i. die oberstelle verdienet; sondern auch zu der Helden-tahten besser/ als keine andere lieder=art/ kan gebrauchet werden." Vgl. auch Reiner Schmidt: Deutsche Ars Poetica. Zur Konstituierung einer deutschen Poetik aus humanistischem Geist im 17. Jahrhundert. Meisenheim a. Glan 1980, 154f.

2 Obwohl Harsdörffer am 4.12.1644 als 12. Mitglied mit dem Gesellschaftsnamen „Der Kunstpielende" in die DG aufgenommen wurde (vgl. 441223), erscheint er hier mit seinem FG-Namen „Der Spielende" und seinem FG-Wort „Auf manche Art" (hier: „auf mancherley Weise"). Harsdörffer selbst scheint seine DG-Mitgliedschaft schon bald verschleiert, seinen DG-Namen „Der Kunstspielende" jedenfalls nicht benutzt zu haben (aufgrund der unüberbrückbaren grammatischen und orthographischen Strittigkeiten). Vgl. Harsdörffers Brief an Zesen 450410 (bes. K 24).

3 Diese Verdeutschung Zesens für Pallas/ Minerva schon in: Filip Zesiens von | Fürstenau | Lustinne/ | Das ist/ | Gebundene Lust-Rede | von Kraft und Würkung | der Liebe. | [Linie] | Hamburg/ Bey Heinrich Wernern/ | Jm Jahr/ 1645. In: *Zesen SW* I.1, 235–258. Zesen widmete dieses Werk Schottelius mit einer Zuschrift aus Amsterdam. S. 450000A. — Die *Lustinne* auch als Anhang zur *Adriatischen Rosemund* (Amsterdam 1645) in *Zesen SW* IV.2, 283–302. Hierzu und zu den nachstehenden Verdeutschungen Zesens (Lustinne/ Venus, Holdinnen/ Grazien) vgl. 441201 K 2 u. 450000A K 1; auch *Ingen*, 375.

4 „Blauinne" („Caesia Virgo") als weitere Übersetzung für Pallas im Anhang zur *Lustinne. Zesen SW* IV.2, 336. S. Anm.3. Zesens „Spiel mit dem ‚Stärbe-blau'" (Scholte, a. a. O. [s. K 1], 294) — bleu-mourant — und überhaupt der blauen Farbe, etwa in der Schilderung von Rosemunds Schäferei in der *Adriatischen Rosemund* (1645), in der alles in blauen Farben gehalten ist, bezieht sich auf einer ersten, biographischen Ebene auf Zesens Namen: caesius, d.i. (grau-)blau. Entsprechend der fingierte Verfassername der *Adriatischen Rosemund*: Ritterhold von Blauen/ Philipp von Zesen. Vgl. *Dt. Fremdwb. (1995)* III, 384f. (s.v. „blümerant"); Kaczerowsky: Bürgerliche Romankunst im Zeitalter des Barock. Philipp von Zesens „Adriatische Rosemund" (s. K 11), 15f. u. 33; Vgl. Philipp v. Zesen: Die Adriatische Rosemund. Mit Kupfern der Erstausg. von 1645. Hg. Klaus Kaczerowsky. Bremen 1970, 267.

450817

Georg Philipp Harsdörffer an Fürst Ludwig

Antwort auf 450529 u. 450611. Beantwortet durch 450919A. — Eigentlich wollte Georg Philipp Harsdörffer (FG 368. Der Spielende) F. Ludwig (Der Nährende) erst nach dem Abschluß des 5. Teils seiner *Frauenzimmer-Gesprächspiele* diese Schreiben beantworten, jedoch traf ein Brief des Marco Aurelio Severino ein, der die FG zum Teil betreffe und den er F. Ludwig übersenden wolle. — Harsdörffer hatte ein Emblem für Severinos *Zootomia* verfaßt, das er aber vor dem Druck Severino schicken sollte, wie dessen Nürnberger Sachwalter (Johann Georg Volckamer) verlangte. Der Spielende schrieb demnach an Severino und bat ihn auch, der FG die Satzungen und Schriften der Accademia degli Oziosi zu verschaffen. Harsdörffer legt seinem Brief an F. Ludwig die Antwort mit der Bitte um Rücksendung bei. Er schlägt vor, an das Oberhaupt der Oziosi, Giovanni Battista Manso

450817 Georg Philipp Harsdörffer

marchese di Villa Lago, italienisch unter dem Siegel der FG zu schreiben und Harsdörffer mit der Übersendung zu beauftragen, um die Bekanntschaft mit den Oziosi zu suchen und um deren Bücher zu erlangen. Auch könne man sich wegen der Unisoni an Dandolo und wegen der Incogniti an Loredano wenden. Wenn F. Ludwig das tue, bitte Harsdörffer um Mitteilung des Inhalts der Schreiben bzw. um Inhaltsangaben. — Was dem Spielenden in F. Ludwigs Briefen vom 29.5. und 11.6.1645 über die Andachtsgemälde mitgeteilt wurde, beachtete Harsdörffer, indem er das Bild aus der Bibel ableitete. — In der Initiale eines Spruchs habe sich Harsdörffer (in der 2. Aufl. des ersten Teils seiner *Frauenzimmer-Gesprächspiele*) nicht auf F. Ludwigs FG-Imprese, sondern auf die Getreidegarbe des hl. Joseph bezogen. Die Lehrer der Impresistik hielten es für falsch, daß die Pictura durch die Subscriptio erklärt werden müsse. — In der Nachschrift weist Harsdörffer auf ein Angebot von Justus Georg Schottelius (FG 397. Der Suchende) hin, strittige Punkte in seiner schon damals überarbeiteten *Sprachkunst (1651)* vor deren Veröffentlichung mit Christian Gueintz (FG 361. Der Ordnende) oder anderen Kennern schriftlich zu beraten und sich gegebenenfalls dem besseren Argument zu fügen. Das (fränkische) Mitglied Hans Philipp (v.) Geuder (FG 310. Der Ergänzende) sowie alle Nürnberger und Ulmer Gelehrten stimmten den Hauptlehren des Suchenden, nicht aber des Ordnenden zu, auch finde Schottelius' *Sprachkunst (1641)* schon in etlichen Schulen Verwendung. Über die zwischen Gueintz und Schottelius strittigen Punkte könne ein aus Diederich v. dem Werder (FG 31. Der Vielgekörnte), Augustus Buchner (FG 362. Der Genossene) und Hans Michael Moscherosch (FG 436. Der Träumende. 1645) bestehender Ausschuß befinden, und der Nährende (F. Ludwig) seine Entscheidung treffen. — Harsdörffer will zum nächsten Markt mit dem Transport ein Akademiebuch der Intronati und Severinos *La Querela della & accorciata* (1644) überschicken.

Q HM Köthen: V S 545, Bl.314r–316v [A: 315v]; eigenh.; rotes Lacksiegel. Zur Gedichtbeilage auf Bl.315rv s. Anhang I. — D: *KE*, 339–341 (unvollständig); *Schäfer: Moscherosch und Harsdörffer*, 171 (nur die Nachschrift). — BN: *Bürger*, 674 Nr.32. — Lit.: *Schäfer: Moscherosch und Harsdörffer*, 171 (mit Lit.); Jean-Daniel Krebs: Georg Philipp Harsdörffer (1607–1658). Poétique et poésie. 2 Bde. Bern u.a. 1983, I, 31; *Conermann: Harsdörffers Plan*.

A *Dem Durchleuchtigen Hochgebornen Fürsten und Herrn Herrn LUDWIGEN Fürsten zu Anhalt, Grafen zu Ascanien und Ballestat, Herrn zu Zerbst und Bernburg* etc. Meinem gnädigen Herrn. *Cöthen* Zu Leipzig bey H. G. Stahlen abzugeben.
Eigenh. Empfangsvermerk F. Ludwigs: 10 Herbstmonats 1645. — Unbekannte H.: 31

Höchstgeehrter Nehrender.
Obzwar der *Spielende* die Beantwortung beeder Schreiben, (von 20 May und 11t. Brachmonats[1])[a] zu verzögern vermeinet, bis der Fünfte Theil seiner Gesprächspiele[2] gefertiget worden were; So hat sich doch in Zwischen begeben, daß er von Neapoli inliegendes Schreiben,[3] die Hochlöbliche Fruchtbringende Gesellschaft, zum Theil, betreffend, erhalten; und solches derselben mitzutheilen, und dann förderlichst zu beantworten nicht umgehen sollen, und wollen. Die Sache erfolgte also: Als der Spielende vor etlichen Monden ein Sinnbild zu *Marc-Aurelii Severini* Buch von der Thier-Zergliederung (*Zootomia*)[4] aufgesetzet, hat es desselben Sachwalter[5] alhier beyzufügen bedenken getragen, es werde ihm dan

solches zuvor von besagten Spielenden, dem[b] Autori, übersendet, welches auch geschehen; benebens vermelden, der Hochlöbl. *Fruchtbringenden Gesellschaft* sollte sehr lieb seyn, wann sie Satzung und Schriften Academia[c] degl'Ociosi, durch seine Vermittelung, erhalten möchte vnd hierauf erfolgt die Antwort, wie hierbey geschlossen, u. ich wieder zurucke zu schicken bitte.

Bey so geglückter Sachen, solte jedoch ohne maasgebung, nicht ausser Wege seyn, an H. Marggrafen Villa, und seine Gesellschaft,[6] unter des Ertzschreins Jnsigel, Jtalianisch zuschreiben, und dieser subtilen Geister Kundschaft zu suchen; der ungezweiffelten Hoffnung, es werde solcher Brief-wechsel zu der Gesellschaft hohen Ruhm zu überbringen allerhand neuer Bücher dienlich, und beförderlich kommen. [314v]

Solcher gestalt könnte man auch, von hieraus, mit den Unisoni und Jncognitis, durch Dandolo,[7] und Loredano[8] zu Venedig in Kundschaft kommen, die überbringung der[d] Briefe dem Spielenden anbefehlen, und auch von daraus neue Bücher erlangen. Dieses lässet[e] der Spielende zu fernerm nachdenken dem Hochstgeehrten Nehrenden und der gantzen Vielfruchtenden Gesellschaft gebührlich heimgestellet: bittend ihm gut befundenen Schluß förderlichst, zu seiner nachrichtung, zu eröffnen,[9] und im fall solcher unvorgreiffliche vorschlag beliebet werden sollte, ihm den Jnhalt dahin ablauffender Briefe, oder derselben Abschrift bey zu schliessen.

Was in Eingangs berührten Schreiben, von den Andachts-gemählen erinnert worden, ist solcher gestalt beobachtet, daß das Bild niemals aus eigener Erfindung, sondern aus Sprüchen der H. Schrift hergenommen ist; wie aus nachgesetztem Muster zuersehen.[10]

Bey dem Sinnbild des Buchstabens N[11] ist nicht eigentlich auf [das][f] Gesellschafts Gemähl des[g] Nehrenden abgesehen, sondern auf die verslein, welche im dritten Theile der Gesprechsspiele[h] am 437 blat zulesen, dieses Jnhalts.
Wie für Josephs Garbe sich[i] all' andre mußten neigen:
Dem der Der Nehrend' heisst sol jeder Ehr' erzeigen.
Aus dem Gemähl lässt sich das Weizenbrot nicht erkennen; die Meister der Sinnbildkunst halten für einen Fehler, wann das Bild, durch die Schrift, muß erkläret werden. Hiermit verbleibt, nechst empfehlung [in den][j] Obschutz Gottes
    Des Höchstgeehrten Nehrenden
    in Underthänigkeit dienstverbundener Knecht
    Der Spielende.
Nürnberg den 17 Augustmonaths 1645.

[316r]   N. S.[12]
Es erinnert der Spielende, aus gesellschaftmässigem vertrauen, daß sich viel an der Fruchtbringenden unterschiedlichen Schreibarten ärgern: Solchem unheil Zu steuren, u. die Sprache in eine[k] grundfeste, unwidersprechliche richtigkeit zu setzen, ist der Suchende[13] des erbietens, vor wiederauflegung seiner Sprachkunst, welche er an etlich hundert orten geändert, u. vermehret, mit dem Ordneten[l] [14]

oder anderen der Sachen verständigen, die strittigen puncten schriftlich abzuhandeln, und nach eingenommenen bessern bericht, willig zu weichen. Der Ergentzende[15], und alle Gelehrte hier, und zu Ulm[16] achten des Suchenden seine Sprachkunst, in ihren haubtstucken für richtig, massen sie auch in etlichen Schulen eingeführt worden: hingegen will dem Ordneten niemand beypflichten. Diese Streittschriften könten, alsdan, wann beede theile[m] gnugsam gehöret worden, dem Vielgekörnten[17], dem Genossenen[18], u. Traumenden[19] zugeschicket[n], und von dem Höchstgeehrten Nehrenden endlich verschieden werden.

Auf verbesserung schreibet dieses
der Spielende [316v]

Mit künftigem [sic] Jahrmarkswaaren, will ich der Jntronaten Gesellschaftbuch[20] an den *Vielgekörnten* abschicken, samt des **Severini** Werk, von dem Wörtlein &.[21] und wann ich sonsten der hochlöblichen Fruchtbringenden Gesellschaft bedient werde seyn können, bitte ich mir zu befehlen. Gott mit uns.

I

Ein Andachtsgemälde Harsdörffers

Q HM Köthen: V S 545, Bl. 315rv; eigenh.; Ausriß am Rand.

Trostgedicht aus Jacob. 5, 11.
Jhr habt gehört die Gedult
HIOBS etc.[1]
Prosopopœiâ putatæ Litis proprietas Patientiæ declaratur

Der Reben[2] redet.

Der du in deinem Leid hast keinen Trost gefunden,
kom,[a] schau was strömet hier, aus meines Schmertzens wunden.
   Der Lust-erfreute Lentz hat meinen Stamm bedeckt,
   mit grünlich frechem Laub, daß sich bey mir versteckt
das leichte feder-Volk,* des Schattens zu geniessen: *die Glücksfreunde.
Jch liesse meine zweig* in vollem Safte schiessen,   *die Kinder.
   so daß das lentzen kleid mich blossen hatt' ümhüllt,
   und das Zerkerbte Blat* mit[b] füttigen angefüllt.   *zeitliche Güter.
Bald komt der Wintzer her, und trägt in seinen Handen,
das messer Sichelart, samt vielen Weiden-banden.
   Jch zitterte vor Furcht, daß auch das kleinste Blat,
   (mehr als von keinem Wind') an[c] mir, gebebet hatt':
Er steckt' in seinen Bund, nechst seiner rechten seiten,
das schlanke Fesselband, beginnend zu bereiten
   den Werkzeug meiner Zucht. Nicht nur das grüne Laub',[d]
   war seines Eisens grimm bald hingeworffner Raub:

Es stimmelt'³ hin und her mein Haubt, und alle Glieder,*
ergreifft das weiden Band,* lässt sich zur Erden nieder   *Krankeit u. Güter des Leibs.
  und strängt mich an den Pfal. Für meine grüne Zier,
  für meine Frülings Freud' hat er gelassen hier
so manchen falben⁴ Strang, der mich hält^e hart ümfangen
und, daß ich nicht entflieh', an einem Pfal gefangen.
  Die Wunden^f schmertzen mich, ich traure sonder Klag';
  Ach! treuffet, treuffet fort, ihr Zeugen meiner plag'[;]
ihr^g meiner Augen* wort! des^h Sommers Sonnen Kertzen,   *so sagt man daß der
wischt alle^i Zehren ab, und heilte^j meine Schmertzen: reben Aug' gewinne.
  Das grüne Schatten Laub',^d das mir zuvor befacht^k,
  hat mir das Himmels liecht gedoppelt wiederbracht [315v]
Zu lohnen der Gedult. Darbey ists nicht verblieben;
Dann meiner wunden kraft, hat blüt u. Frucht getrieben:
  so hold-erhaltner last⁵ reisst mich von meinem Band,
  und, meiner threnen Bach, ist meines Glückes pfand.

Jn H. Schrift wird die Christliche Kirche einem Weinberg, und die Christen den Fessern verglichen, Jsaiæ. 7. und 24. Enoch. 15. Oseæ. [2].¹⁶

II

450801

Marco Aurelio Severino an Georg Philipp Harsdörffer

Marco Aurelio Severino dankt dem ihm zuvor nicht bekannten Georg Philipp Harsdörffer (FG 368. Der Spielende) für sein Geschenk (eines Emblems) und eine Bitte. Er preist Harsdörffers Herkunft und Geistesgaben und seine gegenüber ihm und den Mitgliedern der Oziosi geäußerte Demut. Er habe die nun zwischen ihm und Harsdörffer gestiftete Freundschaft auch (Johann Georg) Volckamer zu verdanken. Die Accademia (degli Oziosi) fühle sich durch die Bitte so ferner Fürsten, die Beziehung zu ihr aufzunehmen, sehr geehrt und stimme ihr geschlossen zu. Ihr Principe, Giovanni Battista Manso marchese di Villa, der durch seine italienischen Dialoge bekannt sei, habe auf Anfrage Severinos und nachdem er von anderen Mitgliedern von den Vorzügen Harsdörffers erfahren habe, sofort an denselben und seine ‚Helden' (FG) die gedruckten Satzungen der eigenen Akademie geschickt, deren Ergänzungen beizeiten nachgereicht werden sollen. Manso habe auch eine Urkunde über Harsdörffers Aufnahme in die Akademie erstellt, welche ihm reisende Kaufleute pfeilschnell überbrächten. Severino bittet Harsdörffer auch, dem Fürsten (F. Ludwig) gebührend zu danken und die Oziosi durch die Fruchtbringer zu eigenen Werken anzuspornen. Severinus fragt, ob er Harsdörffer eine eigene gedruckte Schachkunde in toskanischer Sprache schicken solle, die auch in seinem mitgesandten Schriftenverzeichnis aufgeführt sei und von vielen Deutschen wie auch vom polnischen Gesandten und seinem Gefolge begehrt werde. Er werde das gewiß tun und auch sein Porträt schicken, obgleich es sein Gesicht nicht richtig darstelle. Er verspricht, später seinen Freunden ein getreueres, in Rom gestochenes Bildnis zu senden. — Severino bittet Harsdörffer, den überlasteten Volckamer bei der Arbeit an seinen, Severinos, Arbeiten über den Magen durch Rat oder Tat oder durch gelehrte Helfer zu unterstützen. Severino wisse auch nicht, wie es um seine in der Hand Michael Rupert Beslers befindliche *TRIMEMBRIS CHIRURGIA* steht, auch nicht, welches der Stand der bei allen möglichen Physiologen kursierenden Abhandlung *De Lapide fungifero* ist. Harsdörffer möge Besler, der schon seit einem halben Jahr nichts von sich hören lasse, zur Edition drängen oder das Geschäft selbst übernehmen. Er, Severino, sei zwar noch rüstig, aber mit seinen 65 Jahren doch daran interessiert, noch vor seinem Ende die Veröffentlichung dieser und anderer Arbeiten zu erleben.

Q HM Köthen: V S 545, Bl. 321r–322v; 322v leer. Abschrift, mit einem am Schluß (Bl. 322r) hinzugefügten lat. Emblem Harsdörffers (Beschreibung ohne Bild, mit Inscriptio und poet. Subscriptio).

Amplissimo D. D. Georgio Philippo Harsdörffer, Viro Patricio Noribergensi,
Genere, Virtutibus, literis, æqui justiùque dicendi muneribus Clarissimo *etc.*
Marcus Aurelius Severinus Tharsiensis
bene beateque vivere.

Satis quidem muneri tuo, subjectoque petitionis operæ fecisti, Georgi Philippe Harsdorfer, Noricorum dignissime, qui cum nulla mihi parte cognitus antea fueris, scribens ad me (sic de tuo tibi fastigio in imum descendendo jucundum fuit) inter hæc amplas animi tui dotes incogitatus aperuisti, quæ etiam videlicet ἡ εὐφυΐα, qualis ab Hippocrate[1] vocata fuit ingenii felicitas, in optimas disciplinas studium et industria, proficiendi ardor in arctius; rerum adjuncta novitate pulcherrimarum indago, assiduus cum eruditissimis quibusque viris convictus, delata tuum in caput æqui justique decernendi facultas, idiomatum peregrinorum interpretandorum adjectum munus, posthæc morum facilitas, lenitas, humilitatis exaltandæ nedum honorandæ nostræ magnanimitas, in Ociosos[2] meos Sodales submissio, in omnibus vitæ actionibus ac deliberationibus prudentia et Catonianum judicium; et quæ non denique viro natalibus claro digna virtus: Te mi Philippe spectatum, conspicuumque tum popularibus tuis felicibus, tum etiam attendentibus exteris abunde faciunt. Quibus ego perspectis eximiis tuis ornamentis in me meosque ausus ingenua voluntate ac propensione; quas non (&) meæ Clientulæ [sic] quas non bonæ fortunæ, quas non autori Volchamero[3] vigilantissimo, quas non humanitati tuæ summæ gratias et agere debeam et immortaliter habeam? Enimverò de tantis sic auspicato, sic inopinato a me compertis thesauris deque nostra præsertim amicitia, credo equidem coelitus à Mercurio Joveque compactâ, tanta meum animum lætitia, tanta voluptas inceßit, ut lautitias, acpetias, delicias, hyblea mella, thasia vina, nectar, ambrosiam, veneris lac, Jovis cerebrum, qui Persis dicendi mos fuit, exhauserim. Nec hercle minus exultavit honorifica tua petitione conventus noster Academicus universus, qui decori sibi maximo, columini suorum incomparabili duxit à Principibus Arcto propinquis, coelo nostro tam longinquis, atque iisdem excultissimæ doctrinæ viris nostram expeti consuetudinem; atque adeo vestris votis honestis lubentissimè acquiescens Princeps noster Joannes Baptista Mansus Marchio Villæ[4] vir omni virtutum genere Clarissimus, atque ædilis de Erocalla dialogis Jtalico meliore sermone conspicuus, rogatusque à me atque ab aliis Academicis auditis de Excellentia vestra præconiis exardescentibus, nulla mora legavit ad vos omni officio ac [321v] pietate colendos Heroas[5], institutorum nostrorum rudimenta, quota et tamem ad hanc horam excusa, nam cætera, quæ supersunt imprimenda, suo maturè tempore supplebuntur: Excellentiam verò tuam, quæ nostros in honores tam efusè gestivit, de nobis tam magnificè sensit, otia nostra tam amicè complexa fuit, in nostrum cooptavit diplomate[6] declaravit suo, quod Mercatoribus intercedentibus concreditum ad te veniet missili sagitta pernici[ter]. Tuum erit Jllo. Principi[7] debitas primum agere gratias, mox egregiis Carpophorum[5] fructibus profeßam, à nobis utinam non exercitam ignaviam inertiamque redimere, excitare, locupletare: Quoniam autem et mea sic unicè suffragatus es, institui eadem lingua conditum et phiolosophia [sic] del givoco de gli schacchi vocatum[8] opusculum xx. capitibus distinctum ad Te mittere, librum antequam vulgatum pro vulgato quæsitum ab eruditis vestratibus plerisque et à Serenissi. Poloni nuncio[9], ejusque familiaribus, qui lingua nostrate seriò delectantur. Hujus Hetrusci[10] voluminis Ideam ubi expetas, in catalogo leges Commentationum mearum, quem ad te mitt[o] verum cum Jcone faciei[11], quam perperam repræsentat, fideliorem imagin[em] vises postmodum, quam Romæ cusam ad vos observantissos. amicos meos spectandam dabo delectationis vestræ gratia. Jnterim quia per summam tuam humanitatem plurimum mihi fiduciæ præbuisti, securus hinc abdita mea vota tuum in sinum exponam? Nil genio meo fuit op[ta]tius, quam partus, quos edidi de cerebro veluti Palladem Jupiter, per omnium manus divagantes, per cunctorum ora celebrati, στομ[α]χωμενα.[12] Huic gloriolæ meam omnem vitam, meosque conatus devovi, mancipavique. Cui quidem operæ, cuique officio studiosissimus. Volchamerus animæ dimidium meæ sedulam suam navat operam: verùm eq[ui]dem vereor, ne immodica distentus sarcina degravetur, vel absolutionis improbo labore par non sit solus, eò magis, qui et familiaribus curis et re medica factitanda distingitur: Anxietudinu[m] igitur eius amici sollicite satagentis huic studio cum agnoveris, rogo te, mi Philippe, bonum virum aut opera aut consilio subleves, vel ipse per te, vel per alios doctos adjutores, qui tabulas aut hoc genus alia elaborent, ubi tamen optimus Volchamerus boni consoluerit atque ex animo voluerit. Præterea est apud Excelm. Michaelem Rupertum Beslerum[13] nostra Chirurgia Trimembris ac de Lapide fungifero disquisitio inter observatores [322r] omnes physiologos sera ac feria, quid autem exitus utrumque horum expectet, ignoro: porro D. Rupertus ab hinc ni fallor sesqui anno non rescripsit, nec quidquam alius ad me rescribendum legavi[t:] Tuum igitur est, officiosisse. Harsdörfere amicum amicè urgere, qui vel edenda hæc procuret, vel in Te provinciam reponat, qui autoritate tua, quicunque nostrum apud vos extet, benignè promoveas sic, ut in lucem perducantur. Est ætatis meæ jam annus LXV. à qua deinceps vitæ parte labatur oportet proclivius nativus virium vigor, etiamsi sit cruda mihi viridisque senectus, qua sus ante fatum æstimarem equidem permagni, lucis usura fruerentur maxima pars lucubrationum mearum. Quare nihil gratius mihi vel ipse vel amici fecerint, quam in hos mihi usus præsto eße, ex adverso ego, si qua in re valeam Ex. T.ᵘᵃᵉ gratificari, nulli [t]uam ob *cau*sam aut diligentiæ aut labori parcam. Optimè vale, Severinumque Tuum, quod gratuitò cœpisti, fervidius amare, perge, qui te [c]olò suspicioque, Neapoli Urbe Cumana Kal. Augusti A M D C XLV.

Emblema[14] Anagrammaticum
in
Zootomiam
Quam miro Labores et exquisita Jndustria exploravit
Marc-Aurelius Severinus
Λέγεισ ἀναγραμματισμὼς
Lumen aurei veris cursans[15]
Pictura est

☉ in ♍ [Tierkreissymbol Jungfrau] totum Zodiacum desuper irradians cum flosculis sucrescentibus
Nempe SEVERINUS Zephyri nova nomina gestat
    ut vox, ingenium et Florida scripta probant
Quid dixi? imo velut Phoebus circumrotat Orbem
    Signiferum, lustrans singula VERE novo
Sic tua te virtus, et circum Animalia terræ
    Cursantem versat lumine perpetuo
Aurea sic veris, Medicis, Tu tempora pandis
    Te vernos flores explicuisse juvat
Certe etiam pia thura Tibi Coralia spargunt
    Gratiferis foliis. Sic jubet Officium!
        S. GPHarsdörfer, N.ᵃ

III

Durch Severino an Harsdörffer und Fürst Ludwig gelangte Mondansichten Francesco Fontanas

Q HM Köthen: V S 545, Bl. 317r–318v, letzte S. leer; unbek. H. 2 Radierungen. — Die in Details korrigierten Radierungen auch in: NOVÆ | CŒLESTIVM, TERRESTRIVMQ. | RERVM OBSERVATIONES, | Et fortasse hactenus non uulgatæ | À FRANCISCO FONTANA, | SPECILLIS À SE INVENTIS, | Et ad summam perfectionem perductis, | editæ. | NEAPOLI | Superiorum Permissu, apud Gaffarum Mense Februarii MDCXLVI. S. 81 u. 83. HAB: 44.13 Astron.; 22.3 Geom. (2).[1]

Lunæ facies macroscopio nobis obseruata, a. D. Francisco Fontana descripta. Marcus Aurelius Seuerinus Cl. D. Harsdörffer obseruavitᵃ ergo mittebat.

[317v erste Abb. Zeichnung der Mondoberfläche mit vielen Flecken (Maculae); Umschrift auf dem Rand des Mondbilds:]

a di 31 Ottb. 1629 a hore 3 mancante Font osser:[b]

[318r zweite Abb. Zeichnung, Ansicht derselben Mondseite, jedoch rechts überschattet; Umschrift auf dem Rand des Mondbilds:]
a di 20 di Giugno 1630 a hore 3 crescente. Fontana osseruabat. (s. Abb. S. 627)

IV

Marco Aurelio Severinos Gesellschaftsschrift *La Querela della & accorciata* (1644)

Severino lobt in seiner Widmungsvorrede die Tugend und Wissenschaft des Cassiano dal Pozzo, besonders seine wohl alle übrigen Zeitgenossen übertreffende Kenntnis der toskanischen Sprache, die er von Jugend auf mit den Wassern des Arno getrunken und die er mit dem Verständnis der Mundarten von Florenz und Siena verfeinert habe. So habe Pozzo — nach dem Motto der Crusca — das feinste Mehl daraus gesammelt. Unter der Anleitung seines Oheims, des Erzbischofs von Pisa — wahrlich ein Herkules des toskanischen Atlas! — förderte solch Verständnis die kunstvolle Beredsamkeit und die übrigen Studien. Wie schon andere Leute Schätze und Instrumente des Toskanischen vor allem Pozzo widmeten, so wolle auch Severino dies mit seinem neuartigen, unterhaltsamen, jedoch gelehrten Streit über die abgekürzte Konjunktion *ed* halten.

Q LA QVERELA | Della (&) accorciata | SCHERZO | DI MARC'AVRELIO | SEVERINO, | Philosopho, & Medico Napoletano, Academico Otioso, | Detto L'Assettato. | ALL'ILLVSTRISSIMO SIGNORE | CASSIANO DAL POZZO, | Commendatore dell'Ordine di S. Stephano. | [Kupferstich: im breitovalen Rahmen eine &-förmig gewundene gekrönte Schlange; Subscriptio: „Hor chi fia mai, che scioglia", Stellenangabe: (Giovanni della) „Casa[1] Canz. 2"] | IN NAPOLI, Per Camillo Cauallo. MDCXLIV. HM Köthen: V S 545, Bl. 319r–320v, insgesamt 8, z. Tl. nichtfol. Bll.; Druck. Auf der Titelrückseite in einem Lorbeerkranz eine Imprese (Severinos): ein geometrischer Würfel mit der Inscriptio „VNDIQVE COMPAR."[2] Es folgen Severinos Widmungsbrief an Cassiano dal Pozzo[5] (Bl. a 2r – a 3v), ein lat. Brief des Thomas Bartholinus[3] an Severino mit lat. Gedicht (Bl. a 4r) und ein ital. Gedicht eines ungenannten Verfassers „Sopra la'impresa dell'annodato Serpente, D'Autore Innominato" (Bl. a 4v), das die Konjunktion *ed* mit einer Schlange vergleicht, die den Menschen davor warnt, ihren verschlungen Körper wie einen gordischen Knoten mit Gewalt aufzulösen: „Romper mio nodo più, saggio huom non tente". Diesem Rat steht entgegen „ARGOMENTO Della giudicial contesa della (&) accorciata, Et la sommaria di lei ragione. Sposte à chi legger dourà. Dal Dott. Onofrio Riccio,[4] & Academico Napoletano." (Bl. a 5r–6v; Bl. 6v mit Imprimatur). Nach einer leeren Seite (Bl. 7r) folgt sodann ein ital. Gedicht Pozzos mit dem ital. Antwortgedicht Severinos (Bl. a 7v – a 8r) sowie eine leere Seite (Bl. a 8v). Im folgenden wird neben der Titelseite und der Imprese (s. die beiden Abbildungen auf S. 629) nur Severinos Widmungsbrief an Cassiano dal Pozzo, das Gedicht auf die verknotete Schlange der Titelseite und der Gedichtwechsel zwischen Pozzo und Severino wiedergegeben. Der im Köthener Erzschrein erhaltene Druck stellt nur den ersten Teil und den Schluß des Gesamtwerks dar, da der Rest offenbar an Harsdörffer zurückging. S. 450919A. Im OPAC SBN Istituto centrale per

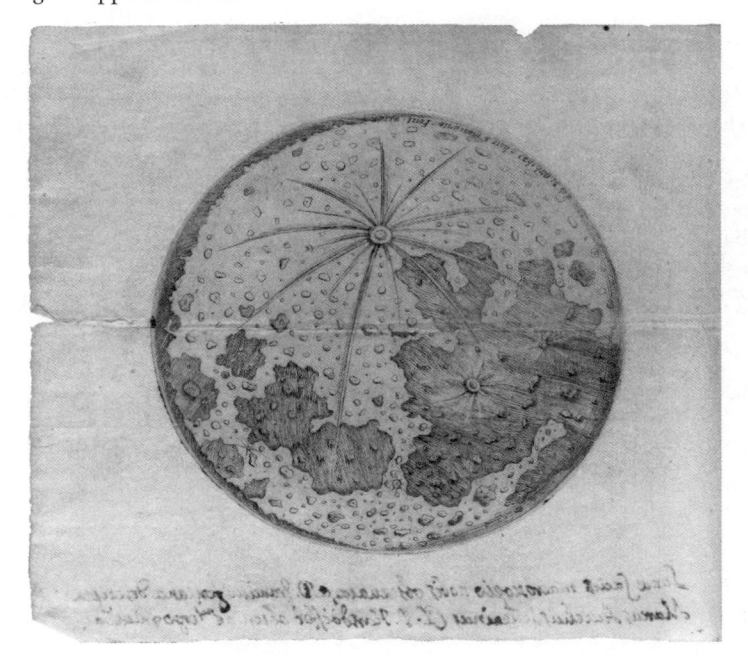

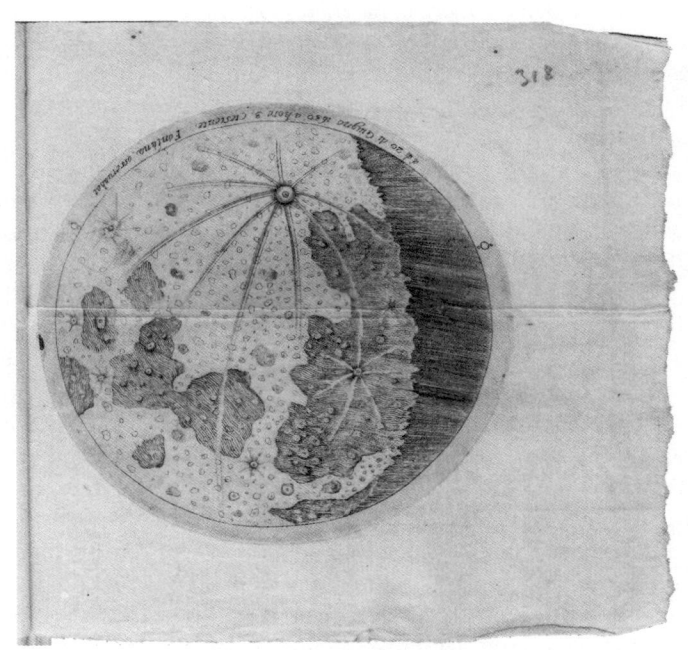

Zwei Mondansichten für F. Ludwig (FG 2) aus den Händen Marco Aurelio Severinos. Zu 450817 III. Abb. I u. II.

il catalogo unico Nachweisungen von (z. Tl.) vollständigen Exemplaren in acht italienischen Bibliotheken, die zurzeit nicht im Karlsruher Virtuellen Katalog erscheinen. Google bietet ein Digitalisat eines solchen Exemplars im Datennetz an. Über das Köthener Exemplar hinaus enthält das erweiterte Buch nach Bl. 6v auf nun paginierten Seiten (1–56; Bl. A r ff.) Severinos Akademierede „Accusa, & difesa della Congiuntione (&) contra gli Accorciatori Volgari. Diceria non piu scherzeuole, che severa, Di Marc'Aurelio Seuerino Philosopho, & Medico Napolitano Academico Otioso."[8] (Überschrift „L'Accusatrice (&) ragiona") u. nach einer leeren Seite ein nichtgez. Bl. mit dem schon oben erwähnten ital. Gedichten Pozzos an Severino und Severinos an Pozzo. Im *IP* auf F. Ludwigs Hinterlassenschaft wird der Titel nicht genannt.

Allo Illustrissimo Signore
CASSIANO
DAL POZZO[5],
Commendatore dell'Ordine di
S. Stephano,
Marco Aurelio Seuerino.

FASSI la virtù comunemente da tutti, etiandio da piu lontani, & da piu ignoti huomini ammirare. Laōde io gia grā tempo dal chiarissimo vostro splendore fortemente infiammato, muouo hoggimai per dedicarmi, & per cōsacrarmi, si come io fo, tutto, al culto della Illustrissima vostra dignità. [...; a 2v] Ma ciò tralasciato, io so ben quāta, & quale sia la vostra scienza di tutto l'affar naturale, della Politica, della Mathematica, dell'Antichità, delle lingue piu belle, in spetieltà della Toscana fauella; della quale hoggi dì nelle Italiane Contrade, io scorger non so veramente, se alcun'altro ingegno sia piu del vostro approueduto. Impercioche le natie bellezze, & le incomparabili vaghezze di questa lingua, l'apprēditrice facoltà uostra, gia da prim'anni le beuue ne'gorghi dell'Arno; ma [3r] quindi piu finemente aguzzato lo'ntendimento; & del Fiorentino; & del Sanese idioma, IL PIV BEL FIOR NE COLSE;[6] Cui poscia seguirono, & oltre modo inuigorirono l'artificiale eloquenza, & gli altri studi quiui forniti, sotto la scorta dell'Illustrissimo Mōsignor l'Arciuescouo di Pisa uostro Zio,[7] che quanto l'ultimo suo uiuer trasse, d'Hercole seruì all'ATLANTE TOSCANO.[8] Per la qual uostra del polito parlar cōtezza[9], assai cōueneuol cosa stimarono far coloro, che Thesori, & gli Arredi della lingua Toscana alla prima & sola vostra Autorità contenti furono di dedicare; si come à me hoggi parimente far conuiene, che essendomi à questi dì per l'otio della State, vscita di mano La querela della (&) accorciata, componimento per la curiosità, che seco mena, & per la di lei nouità sola pregiato: questo di piaceuole phantasia, ma studioso scherzo, testè pur sorto, & in ordine posto, io lo vi'nuio; non senza però pregare, sicome io hora prego la vostra Magnanimità, che di mercè, & di perdono mi faccia degno, se questi fra tanti affari, nati, & [a 3v] vergati miei pensieri, men acconci, & men forbiti, che alla vostra sagacità si conuenga, s'appresenteranno: douendo d'altra parte la bontà vostra perfetta, & la igual vostra perspicacità, ciascuna lor imperfettione compiete[10], & qualūque lor

Titelblatt La Querela della & accorciata (1644) *und Imprese Severinos.* Zu 450817 IV. Abb. I u. II.

disagguagliāza adeguare. senza che per cosa ragguardeuole non già, ma per cagione d'honesto trastullo, & per deceuole delle cure vostre piu graui compenso, vi si porge. Ma quì la sollecita Accusatrice[11], alle sue querele apprestatasi, le piegheuoli orecchie, e'l legitimo suffragio della vostra Equità fra gli altri tutti singolarmēte richiama; a cui pur io la comune di lei, di me protettione & difesa, quanto posso il piu, raccomando; sì l'Illustrissima vostra persona serbi Iddio lungamente felice. Di Napoli al primo d'Ottobre de'MDCXLIV.

[a7v] Dell'Illustrissimo Commendatore Signor
Cassiano del [sic] Pozzo,
All'Eccellentiss. Sig. Marc'Aurelio Seuerino,
Ristoratore della (&) accorciata.

L'Alma tua penna, & l'immortal dottrina,
  SEVERIN SAGGIO, la contraria Schiera
  Che'n lungo error vissa, et sopita s'era,
  Hor desta ammira, et riuerente inchina.
Ma chi non scorge tua virtù diuina?
  Che può bassezza vil render altera?
  Debiltà forte, infermitate intera?
  Ricchezza trar da pouertà tapina?
Che qual da lieue suon folgor disegna
  Trar questa? O se congiugne, ò se diuide,
  O forza altr'hà, di sensi onusta, et pregna.
Si gode inuitta, et vincitrice insegna,
  Ch'ogni spirto sommeßo in Dio si fide,
  Ch'abbaßata humiltà tanto più degna. [a8r]

All'Illustrissimo Commendatore Signor Cassiano dal Pozzo sopra la (&) ristorato.
Che egli con la sua autorità, & commendatione, la sostiene in vita.

RISPOSTA.
LA storpia à torto, errante Peregrina,
  Che chiamando mercè già languid'era;
  Pietoso accolsi, & sol perche non pera,
  Trassile da Chiron sua medicina.
Come à Pelope già virtù diuina
  L'homero aggiunse, & sua sembianza intera;
  Io così à lei la tolta forma vera
  Rendei, non già consimile, & vicina.

450817 Georg Philipp Harsdörffer

> *Poi fieuol pur da lunga offesa indegna*
> *Suo spirto, che trà man di morte stride,*
> *Volsi al tuo SOL, che viuer morti insegna.*
> *Si tua fauilla auuien, che la sostegna,*
> *PROMETHEO nouo, à cui solo s'asside,*
> *Chi viuer spento, & viuer ben s'ingegna.*

V
Das Verzeichnis der Werke Severinos

Q HM Köthen: V S 545, Bl. 323rv, Abschrift von Harsdörffers H. (?). Der vorausgehende Text *Idea Chirurgiae* war schon in dem in Anmerkung K II 3 genannten, von Johann Georg Volckamer herausgegebenen Druck einer Übersetzung Severinos, *Chocolata Inda*, veröffentlicht worden (Norimbergae 1644: Wolfgang Enderus), S. 65–68: „IDEA Chirurgiæ universæ restauratæ feliciter per MARCUM AURELIUM SEVERINUM." Severino hatte ihn und das folgende Verzeichnis seiner Werke Volckamer zusammen mit seinem Brief vom 1.3.1644 zugesandt. S. Briefsammlung Trew (s. K 4), 568.

HM Köthen: V S 545, Bl. 324r–325v, Abschrift von Harsdörffers H.(?) Auch das Verzeichnis „MARCI AURELII SEVERINI OPERA" war Volckamer schon zuvor übersandt und von diesem in dem vorgenannten Druck (Bl. 69–71: MARCI AVRELII SEVERINI Thurii Tarsiensis, Philosophi, Medici, Regio in Auditorio Neapolitano Anatomes & Chirurgiæ Professoris OPERA.) publiziert worden. Ein Verzeichnis handschriftlich überlieferter Werke und Korrespondenzen Severinos in: Pietro de Angelis: Giovanni Maria Lancisi. La Biblioteca Lancisiana. L'Accademia Lancisiana (Nel 250° anno di fondazione). Roma 1965 (Collana di Studi Storici sull'Ospedale di Santo Spirito in Saxia e sugli Ospedali Romani, 26), 152ff., 156, 157f. u. 162. Über den Umfang schreibt De Angelis, 150: „I più copiosi sono gli scritti di M. A. Severini del secolo XVII: cinque volumi di lettere e più di sessanta opere di Medicina, di letteratura e varie." Dort auch Lancisiana „LXXIV 2-28 Volckomero [sic] Io. Georgius: Vita di M. A. Severini Cart. Sec, XVII C. 111." — In unserem Zusammenhang können wir daher zum Teil auf die Transkription der beiden Beilagen Harsdörffers verzichten: „JDEA CHIRURGIAE Et Catalogus varii Generis operum M. Aurelii Severini Profeßorii Neapolit." Nur die in Severinos Brief 450801 (s.o. Beilage II) an Harsdörffer genannten *Opera* und die damit verknüpften Arbeiten des Italieners werden in unseren Erläuterungen erwähnt. Im Folgenden geben wir die von F. Ludwig mit einem Tüpflein gekennzeichneten Titel wieder, nach denen sich der Nährende (F. Ludwig) in 450919A erkundigte:

[324r]
6 De inermi Chirurgia opus,[1] quod est prope incredibile, quam multis novis, pulchris, arcanis, certis ad feliciter medendum experimentis observationibus, historiis, exquisitis agendj rationibus, Varia [324v] deniqùe, doctrina, eruditione, methodo incomparabili, sit undeqùe refertum atqùe contextum. Jn hac autem & spiritalis Chirurgia est ab Autore primum excogitata.
8. Authentica Chirurgia, id est, per locos discreta communes.[2]

10. De Adjumentis chirurgiæ libri tres quorum
   1. Diateticochirurgicum
   2. Pharmacochirurgicum
   3. Chymicochirurgicum inscriptum est.[3]
13. Consultationum Medicarum Centuriæ 2.[4]
16. De Respiratione Piscium.[5]
21. De Natura Lithargyrii. Jtem de stibii pulvere medicato.[6]
22. Veni mecum Medici Curatoris h. e. Praxis curandorum Jnternorum morborum Neapolitana.[7]
30. Pansophia,[8] id est, de Naturali ductu ad omnes scientias ad omnesque Artes via ratioque demonstrata in omni natura & Sapientium monumentis, non ad huc absolutum opus.
31 Paraphrasis lib. de Mixtis perfectis, qui Quartus Meteorologus vulgò vocatur.[9]
32. Vaticinator seu de divinatione Naturali, quæ ex coelo, terris, mari, ventis, ex vario genere animantium captatur.[10]
33. Problematologus Physicus, Anatomicus, Medicus, Philologus.[11]
34. Centuriæ Epistolarum Latinè Scriptarum: Jtemque præfationes variæ.[12]
35. Juvenilia tum carmina, tum prosæ, prolusionesque Academicæ.[13]
36. Græco fonte deducta vocabula nostra corrupta.[14]

Tusco meliore sermone.[15]

37. La Philosofia de gli Scacchi h. e. Ludus Scacchiorum *etc*.[16]
38. Topica di Giulio Camillo Accorciata.[17]
39. Della Comedia antica
41 Declarationi contra megliori antichi Philosofi, Oratori et altri Savi.[18]
42 Jl lamento dello & accorciato.[19]

Thomas Bartholinus[20] Gasp. Filius Danus Χιλίατρος vigilantissimus suis è pluteis discussa & sub hac forma disposita, in Amicorum & longinquorum gratiam edi curavit.

VI

Eintragung Marco Aurelio Severinos in Volckamers Stammbuch

Q HAAB Weimar: Stammbuch 375 (Johann Georg Volckamer), Eintrag 5. Vgl. oben Beil. K II 3.

Mihi non indictus abibis
Suauissime pariter atque eruditissime Volckamere:
Qui quantum trimestri tua consuetudine dignatus
Affatim me beasti,
Tantùmdem nunc abscendens et grauibus et multis
Vsus tui iucundissimi fructibus orbatu semel relinquis.

I Decus I nostrum, melioribus vtere fatis:
Non ullo ipsius habetur pectore vultus.
Sic oculos, sic illius manus, sic ora ferebat.
Marcus Aurelius Seuerinus ex vltimo Crathi
Te sequitur animo, qui me identidem animas.
VII Februarij A. MDCCXLII.

T a *Klammer fehlt im Original.* — **b** dem Autori, *eingefügt.* — **c** *Versehentlich hinter* degl' *eingefügt.* — **d** der Briefe *eingefügt.* — **e** *Eingefügt für* <hatt> — **f** *Von uns ergänzt für* <desselben> *Durch Nachstellung des Genitivobjekts* des Nehrenden *wurde die Satzkonstruktion fehlerhaft (s. Anm. g).* — **g** des Nehrenden *eingefügt.* — **h** *Abgekürzt als* GespSp — **i** *Aus* sich *für* Josephs Garbe *durch Bezifferung der Wörter umgestellt.* — **j** *Von uns ergänzt für* <des Höchsten> *zur Wahrung der Satzkonstruktion.* — **k** *Folgt wegradiertes Wort (?).* — **l** *Folgt* <schriftlich> — **m** *Folgt* <nach> *oder* <noch> — **n** *Folgt* <werden>

T I *Die mit Sternchen markierten Marginalien im Original linksbündig am Rand.* — **a** *Folgt* <her> *das folgende* schau *gebessert aus* schaum [?] — **b** mit füttigen *(d. i.* Fittichen) *eingefügt für* <mich völlig> — **c** an mir *eingefügt für* <erstaunt> — **d** *Folgt ein hochgestelltes, als* c *lesbares Zeichen (Einschaltzeichen?), ohne Marginalie.* — **e** hält hart *eingefügt für zwei gestrichene Wörter. Nach* hält *folgt* <fest> — **f** *Folgt Einschaltzeichen ohne Marginalie.* — **g** *Gebessert aus* und — **h** *Des Sommers eingefügt für* <Bald kommt der> — **i** *Eingefügt für* <meine> — **j** *Gebessert aus* heilet — **k** *Im Sinne von* bedeckt o. dgl. *Unsichere Lesung dieses verbesserten Wortes. Möglich auch* belacht — **l** *Stellenangabe im Falz verdeckt.*

T II a *Unsichere Lesung (Nürnberg).*

T III a *Aus* obseruat — **b** *Lies* Fontana osservabat *[sic].*

K 1 S. 450529 u. 450611. F. Ludwig (Der Nährende) scheint den ursprünglich vom 20.5.1645 stammenden Brief an Georg Philipp Harsdörffer (FG 368. Der Spielende) selbst nachträglich im Konzept, jedoch nicht in der Ausfertigung umdatiert zu haben: „Cöthen den 29. May monat 1645." S. 450529.
    2 *Harsdörffer: Frauenzimmer-Gesprächspiele* V (Nürnberg 1645, Ndr. 1969). Vgl. 440824 u. 450923C.
    3 S. Beil. II.
    4 Marco Aurelio Severino (Tarsa 1589 – Neapel 1656), seit 1610 Chirurg im Spital Nosocomico der Incurabili, 1622–1645 Prof. für Anatomie u. Chirurgie im Studio di Napoli. Er hielt schon 1612 drei von Giambattista Della Porta beeinflußte Reden über die Physiognomie in der Accademia degli Oziosi und wurde auch Viceprincipe der neapolitanischen Kolonie der Lincei als Nachfolger Fabio Colonnas. Drei alte Biographien in Lorenzo Crasso: Elogii d'huomini letterati. 2 Tle. Venetia: Combi u. La Noù 1666, I, 369–377. HAB: Uo 4° 2. Severino stand mit vielen europäischen Ärzten und anderen Gelehrten im Briefverkehr, u.a. mit Harsdörffer, William Harvey, Hermann Conring und den im vorliegenden Brief genannten Nürnberger Ärzten. Johann Georg Volckamer I (s. Anm. 5) wohnte und lernte bei ihm in Neapel 1641/42. Severino schloß sich der Meinung William Harveys über den Blutkreislauf an. Als Wissenschaftler erntete er u.a. Ruhm durch die im vorliegenden Brief genannte große Arbeit zur Anatomie: ZOOTOMIA DEMOCRI-

TÆA: Id est, Anatome Generalis totius animantium Opificii, libris quinque distincta, quorum seriem sequens facies delineabit. Opus, quod omnes omnium bonarum artium Studiosos, nedum Professores anatomicos decet. MARCI AURELII SEVERINI, THURII THARSIENSIS, PHILOSOPHI MEDICI. Primarii Regio in Auditorio Neapolitano Anatomes & Chirurgiæ Professoris. Venite & videte opera Domini, quæ posuit (ex animantibus) prodigia super terram, Psalm. 46. v. 9. Literis Endterianis, Noribergæ Anno M DC XLV. HAB: 180.17; Quod. (1); Nh 199. Das Werk entdeckt Analogien zwischen den Körpern von Pflanzen, Tieren und Menschen und gilt daher als das erste Buch vergleichender Anatomie. Wie der Titel schon andeutet, wendet sich Severino vom vorherrschenden Aristotelismus ab und wieder den Vorsokratikern zu. In den Hippokrates zugeschriebenen Briefen wird die Weisheit Demokrits gepriesen. S. Oreste Trabucci: Tra Napoli e l'Europa: Le relazioni scientifiche di Marco Aurelio Severino (con un'appendici di lettere inedite). In: Giornale critico della filosofia italiana XV (1995), 309–340, hier S. 314 ff. Severinos Buch erschien nur einmal und nur in Nürnberg. Gewidmet ist es Caspar Hofmann, Prof. in Altdorf u. Senior der medizin. Fakultät; Wilhelm Ernst Scheffer, Philosophus u. Medicus, u. Johann Wilhelm Hochstad, Arzt der Stadt Frankfurt a. M. Severino widmete Scheffer auch seine Schrift: SEILO-PHLEBOTOME CASTIGATA Sive De Venæ salvatellæ usu & abusu. Ad præclariβimum Virum GVILIELMVM ERNESTVM SCHEFFERVM Philosophum & Medicum Francofurtensem (Hanoviae: Christophorus Le Bon 1654: Ioannes Aubry), HAB: QuH 48.2 (2). S. unten K II 3 zu der durch Johann Georg Volckamer vermittelten Bekanntschaft Harsdörffers mit Severinos Werken und über zwei Gedichte Harsdörffers. — Zu Severino s. *ABI I/* 901, *II/* 575 u. *III/* 391; *Hirsch* V, 242f.; *Dict. of Scient. Biogr.* XII, 332–334; Luigi Amabili: Marco Aurelio Severino. A cura e studio di Domenico Zangari. Napoli 1922; C. B. Schmitt/ C. Webster: Harvey and M. A. Severino. A Neglected Medical Relationship. In: Bulletin of the History of Medicine XLV (1971), 49–75. Der riesige Briefwechsel Severinos ist vor allem erhalten in der Biblioteca Lancisi (Rom) und der Biblioteca Nazionale di Napoli (Abschriften v. Luigi Amabili: XI. A A. 35–37). S. Virgilio Duccheschi: L'Epistolario di Marco Aurelio Severino (1580–1656). Un fondo per la storia della medicina nella prima metà del sec. XVII. In: Rivista di storia delle scienze mediche e naturali: organo ufficiale della Società Italiana di Storia delle Scienze Mediche e Naturali XIV (1923), 213–223; Pietro de Angelis: Giovanni Maria Lancisi, La Biblioteca Lancisiana, L'Accademia Lancisiana (Nel 250° anno di fondazione). Roma 1965 (Collana di Studi Storici sull'Ospedale di Santo Spirito in Saxia e sugli ospedali Romani, 26). Vgl. auch: Die Briefsammlung des Nürnberger Arztes Christoph Jacob Trew (1695–1769) in der Universitätsbibliothek Erlangen. Bearb. v. El. Schmidt-Herrling. Erlangen 1940 (Katalog der Handschriften der Universitätsbibliothek Erlangen, 5); auch *Bürger*, 1285 u. *Krüger*, 960. Einzelne Briefe u. a. veröffentlicht v. Josiah Trent: Five Letters of Marcus Aurelius Severinus To „The Very Honourable English Physician, John Houghton". In: Bulletin of the History of Medicine XV (1944), 306–323; Maurizio Torrini: Lettere inedite di Tommaso Cornelio a Marco Aurelio Severino. In: Atti e memorie dell'Accademia Toscana di Scienze e Lettere „La Colombaria" (Firenze) XX (1970), 138–155; s. o. C. B. Schmitt/ C. Webster, 73–75 (Appendix C); Francesco Trevisani: Medizinisch-wissenschaftliche Beziehungen zwischen Italien und Deutschland im 17. Jahrhundert. Eine unbekannte Korrespondenz zwischen H. Conring und M. A. Severino. In: Hermann Conring (1606–1681). Beiträge zu Leben und Werk. Symposion der HAB Wolfenbüttel. Hg. Michael Stolleis. Berlin 1983, 121–131.

5 Severinos Nürnberger Herausgeber Johann Georg Volckamer, s. K II 3.

6 Zur Accademia degli Oziosi s. Beil. II. Ein Schreiben der FG an Giovanni Battista Manso Marchese di Villa Lago, das Oberhaupt (Principe) der Accademia degli Oziosi, erfolgte nicht, weil die FG es ablehnte, von sich aus Beziehungen zu den Oziosi aufzunehmen (450919A) und in italienischer Sprache mit ihr zu korrespondieren. Es gibt aber Zeugnisse von Harsdörffers Briefwechsel mit den Oziosi (vgl. Beil. II–V), wenngleich kein offizielles, an den Principe gerichtetes Dokument mit dem Siegel der FG. Dennoch wurde Harsdörffer unter die Oziosi aufgenommen (vgl. *Conermann: Harsdörffers Plan*, 57–65), auch richtete er eigenständig im Namen der FG Grüße aus. S. Beil. II, 450919A, 450923C, 451101, 451217; *DA Köthen I. 8:* 470401 u. 470426. Zu einem doppelgleisigen lat.-dt. Übersetzungsprojekt Harsdörffers, das den Oziosi wie auch der FG zugedacht war, vgl. K II 6.

7 Harsdörffer meint wahrscheinlich Matteo Dandolo (*1611), einen Sohn des Antonio, Patriziers in Venedig. *Adelung* II, 616 (s.v. Matthäus Dandoli). Zusammen mit Matteo Dandolo, Giovanni Francesco Loredano (s. Anm. 8), Vincenzo Moro und vielen Incogniti gründete Giulio Strozzi in Venedig 1637 die offenbar kurzlebige (oder wenig bekannte) Accademia degli Unisoni: Francesco Belli, Francesco Carmeni, Tommaso Cocco, Clemente Molli, Ferrante Pallavicino, Antonio Rocco, Francesco Paolo Speranza, Giambattista Torretti und Paolo Vendramin. Loredano erwähnt in seinen *Bizzarie Accademiche* (Cremona 1630), 324, daß M. Dandolo in der Accademia degli Unisoni 1638 eine Rede *In lode delle lagrime* vortrug, worauf Loredano mit seiner Rede *In lode del Canto* antwortete. *Maylender* V, 396f. Matteo verfaßte auch: Elogio alla Serenissima Repubblica di Venezia di Matteo Dandolo ... sopra la vittoria navale conseguita dalle armi venete li 26 giugno 1656 ai Dardanelli contro l'armata ottomana essendo capitano generale di mare Lorenzo Marcello (Venezia: Giuseppe Antonelli 1656), Biblioteca Nazionale, Venedig. Ihm ist gewidmet: Maiolini Bisaccionis *Demetrio* (Nenezia: Sarzina 1632); Lo Scherzo Di Fortvna Di Girolamo Brvsoni. Cō altri Componimenti del medesimo (Venezia: Corradici 1641). Brusoni gehörte auch zu den Incogniti und zu den Beiträgern der *Novelle amorose de' Signori Academici Incogniti* (Venetia: Sarzina 1641–1643), Hg. Francesco Carmeni (Tl. 2 auch Giovanni B. Fusconi), HAB: 8.4 Eth. — Harsdörffer hatte wohl nicht einen anderen Sohn des Antonio im Sinne, Giovanni Dandolo, obgleich dieser Accademico Ignoto war. Bis 1656 Senator, Inquisitore auf Korfu, 1661 Inquisitore der venezian. Armee, starb an der Pest in diesem Amt. Giovanni Dandolo trug auch selbst zu den *Novelle amorose* bei. *ABI* I. Am 7.3.1639 zog die Accademia degli Incogniti aus Loredanos Domizil in den Palazzo Dandolos. Monica Miato: L'Accademia degli Incogniti di Giovan Francesco Loredan (1630–1661). Firenze 1998, 108 Anm. 274.

8 Giovan Francesco Loredan(o) (1606–1661), venezian. Patrizier, Schriftsteller und eigentlicher Gründer der Accademia degli Incogniti. Vgl. 440000 u. 460000A. Die Incogniti, die sich von 1630–1639 zunächst in Loredanos Hause versammelten, zählten 1647 über 106 Mitglieder. Deren Leben und Werke behandelt das Buch (wohl ihres Sekretärs Giovanni Battista Fusconi): LE GLORIE DE GLI INCOGNITI O vero GLI HVOMINI ILLVSTRI DELL' ACCADEMIA DE' SIGNORI INCOGNITI DI VENETIA (Venetia: Francesco Valuasense 1647). HAB: 58.20 Hist. — Zu Loredano und seiner Akademie s. *DBI* (2005), 761–770; *Maylender* III, 205–206; Donatella Riposio: Il laberinto della verità. Aspetti del romanzo libertino del Seicento. Alessandria 1995; Miato (s. Anm. 7).

9 S. 450919A. Auf das Beispiel italienischer Akademien, die Mitgliedschaft in mehreren Sozietäten erlaubten, hatte sich Harsdörffer hinsichtlich seiner Aufnahme in die Deutschgesinnete Genossenschaft in 450400 berufen. Während die Beziehungen F. Ludwigs zur Accademia della Crusca und zur Accademia Fiorentina historisch, strukturmäßig und ideell erforscht wurden (vgl. jüngst *Conermann: Akademie*, ders. *Hofmann*, ders. *Impresa*, ders. *TG* bzw. *Conermann/ Herz/ Schmidt-Glintzer*), trifft dies nur teilweise auf Hars-

dörffers Verhältnis zu den italienischen Akademien zu. S. *Conermann: Harsdörffers Plan*. Vgl. Rosmarie Zeller: Spiel und Konversation im Barock. Untersuchungen zu Harsdörffers „Gesprächspielen". Berlin u.a. 1974. Vfn. identifizierte italienische Vorlagen und Anregungen in den *Frauenzimmer-Gesprächspielen*. Italo Michele Battafarano stellte die Äußerungen Harsdörffers über die italienischen Gesellschaften vor allem in den *Frauenzimmer-Gesprächspielen* zusammen, ohne die Stellen zu nennen oder gar auf die Akademien und auf Harsdörffers Kontakte einzugehen: I. M. B.: Zwischen Bargagli und Loredano: Harsdörffers Vorstellung der accademie letterarie italiane. In: Res Publica Litteraria. Die Institutionen der Gelehrsamkeit in der Frühen Neuzeit. Hg. Sebastian Neumeister u. Conrad Wiedemann. Wiesbaden 1984, 35–43 (Wolfenbütteler Arbeiten zur Barockforschung 14). Wenige Ergänzungen in ders.: Harsdörffers Beitrag zur Entprovinzialisierung deutscher Kultur. In: Nürnberg und Italien. Begegnungen, Einflüsse und Ideen. Hg. Volker Kapp u. Frank-Rutger Hausmann. Tübingen 1991, 214–225; Vom Dolmetschen als Vermittlung und Auslegung. Der Nürnberger Georg Philipp Harsdörffer — ein Sohn Europas. In: der Franken Rom. Nürnbergs Blütezeit in der 2. Hälfte des 17. Jahrhunderts. Hg. John Roger Paas. Wiesbaden 1995, 196–212; Accademie letterarie und civil conversatione: Bargagli, Guazzo, Loredano, Harsdörffer. In I. M. B.: Glanz des Barock. Forschungen zur deutschen als europäischer Literatur. Bern usw. 1994, 75–84. Jürgensen faßt in *Utile,* 203f. den Forschungsstand zusammen: „Harsdörffer kannte aber auch aus eigener Anschauung gelehrte Sozietäten in oberitalienischen Städten, vornehmlich in Venedig und Florenz, und auch die französischen Dichterzirkel des 16. und frühen 17. Jahrhunderts wie die Académie des jeux floraux zu Toulouse waren ihm nicht verborgen geblieben, er selbst war Mitglied der Accademia degli Oziosi in Neapel und blieb nach seiner Italienreise in Briefkontakt mit Francesco Loredano, einem Mitglied der Accademia degli Incogniti zu Venedig. Von besonderer Bedeutung soll für Harsdörffer die Accademia degli Intronati in Siena gewesen sein, an deren Treffen er teilnehmen konnte, seine Gespräch-Spiele greifen auf Vorbilder von Girolamo und Scipione Bargagli zurück, die zu den Intronati zählten. Sicher gab es Übereinstimmungen zwischen diesen städtischen Gesellschaften, die sich der Pflege der Volkssprache widmeten, und dem Blumenorden [PBO], in dem sich Dichter zusammenfanden, die sich der Vervollkommnung der deutschen Verssprache widmen wollten und freundschaftlich miteinander verbunden waren, der Gedanke einer Hirtengesellschaft aber ist in der Tradition nicht vorgegeben. Während der Präsidentschaft Birkens gab es – soweit die Quellen ein Urteil erlauben – keine Beziehungen des Blumenordens zu einer Sozietät im Ausland, erst 1679 empfahl Helianthus, Johann Georg Volckamer [s. K II 3], seinem Kollegen Charles Patin in Venedig, Birken die Aufnahme in die Accademia de' Ricouperati zu ermöglichen, der er selbst angehörte." Vgl. auch *Herz: Harsdörffer und Sandrart*, Abschnitt IV: „Der Geist der Akademie". Im zweiten Band seiner *Frauenzimmer-Gesprächspiele* handelt Harsdörffer, in der FG der Spielende genannt, über Akademieimpresen in einem „Gespräch von Fremden Sinnbildern" (S. 4–18; Spiel LII), in welchem er „gewiese Genoß- oder Gesellschaften/ (Academie genannt) in Welschland" erwähnt, namentlich die Intronati von Siena, die Humoristi in Rom und die Intrepidi in Ferrara. In diesem Zusammenhang führt das Spiel auch die Imprese der Fruchtbringenden Gesellschaft (S. 11f) an. (In der Reihe der Akademien taucht auch „eine Geistliche Genoßschafft (der Jungfrauen Maria zu Ehren vermeint/)" auf; Augustin. Von der Stadt Gottes. B. 21. c. 4). Harsdörffer setzt hinzu: „Wann wir alle und jede bewuste Sinnbild/ welche zu Florentz die Furfurarij, zu Perugia die Insensati, zu Neapoli Los mitadore ociosi und die Ardenti: zu Meyland die Intenti, zu Ticino die Affidati, Incogniti und Invaghiti, zu Venedig die Academici della Notte, zu Paris La Conférence des beaux Esprits, und viel andere Gesellschaften erfunden haben/ anmelden sollten/

so würde uns der Tag viel zu kurtz werden." (S. 17). Im dritten Teil (1643) seiner *Frauenzimmer-Gesprächspiele* resultiert Harsdörffers Interesse an den italienischen Akademien eher beiläufig aus der Frage der Dialogteilnehmerin Julia, „warum sich niemand unterfangen wil/ die Gesprächspiele auß den Jtaliänischen Scribenten in unser Hochteutsches zu bringen." (S. 97). Der erfahrene alte Hofmann Vespasian erklärt, daß die „Senesischen von Adel" (S. 101) die Gesprächspiele erfunden hätten. Harsdörffer erwähnt Verfasser von Dialogen wie Castiglione und Doni, nennt unter seinen Vorbildern besonders den Bologneser Innocenzio Ringhieri und den ‚Intronato' Girolamo Bargagli: „Die Senesischen von Adel haben nachmals [nach Ringhieri] angefangen/ gewiese Zusammenkunften anzustellen/ zur Vbung der Gesprächspiele: unnd sind auch derselben meinste Erfindung dahin gerichtet/ wie solche dem Frauenzimmer gemäß seyn möchten: […]. und hat einer unter denselben von Adel* [„*Il Materiale in ihrer Geselschaft/ sonsten Girolamo Bargagli genant/ wie aus seinem Freudenspiel La Pellegrina überschrieben(n)/ zu ersehen"] ein besonder Büchlein darvon geschrieben/ und viel wolbedachte Erinnerung Gesprächsweiß beyfüret." (S. 132). Zu den Intronati s. auch 451101.

10 S. F. Ludwigs Schreiben 450529. Vgl. 450400 (Harsdörffers Ankündigung seiner „Hundert Andachtsgemählen"). Das Muster steht in Beil. I

11 In *Harsdörffer: Frauenzimmer-Gesprächspiele* I (²1644) erscheint auf der Rückseite des Drucktitelblatts im „Vbereigungsgedicht" an F. Ludwig in dem verzierten Großbuchstaben N („NEHRENDEN") eine Getreidegarbe (abgebildet auf S. 286; vgl. 440715 K 2), die der Fürst in 450611 als falsche Wiedergabe seiner Imprese monierte, welche im *GB 1629/30* (bzw. *GB 1646;* dazu 440130 K 3) ein Weizenbrot zeigt. Vgl. 450611 K 1 u. F. Ludwigs Antwort (450919A), in der er auf seiner Kritik beharrte. Die Garbe ziert auch im ersten der „HVNDERT SPJELREJMEN" auf den Nährenden in *Harsdörffer: Frauenzimmer-Gesprächspiele* III, 437 den Buchstaben N. Das Zitat im vorliegenden Brief ist ungenau. In Harsdörffers Buch heißt es:
Wie sich für Josefs Garb' die andern musten neigen/
So soll dem NEHRENDEN ein jeder Ehr' erzeigen.
Vgl. den Traum Josefs (1. Mo. 37, 7), von dem er seinen Brüdern erzählt: „Mich dauchte/ wir bunden Garben auff dem Felde/ vnd meine Garbe richtet sich auff vnd stund/ vnd ewre Garben vmbher neigeten sich gegen meine Garben." *Biblia (Luther 1545)*.

12 Zur Nachschrift: F. Ludwig wollte in der Debatte um die Regelung der deutschen Orthographie im Vertrauen auf den Sachverstand Christan Gueintz' (s. Anm. 14) eine Entscheidung herbeiführen. Harsdörffer, der befürchten mußte, aus der Diskussion ausgeschlossen zu bleiben, verständigte sich mit Schottelius und empfiehlt F. Ludwig hier die Einrichtung einer Schiedsgerichts, bestehend aus Augustus Buchner (FG 361. Der Genossene), Diederich v. dem Werder (FG 31. Der Vielgekörnte) und Johann Michael Moscherosch (FG 436. Der Träumende). F. Ludwig ging darauf in 450919A (K 14) nicht ein. Zu Harsdörffers fortwährendem Bedauern über die Uneinheitlichkeit der Rechtschreibung s. 440426 K 6.

13 Justus Georg Schottelius (FG 397. Der Suchende) verschob die Veröffentlichung der revidierten zweiten Auflage seiner *Sprachkunst (1641)* bis nach dem Tod F. Ludwigs: *Schottelius: Sprachkunst (1651).*

14 Der Ordnende, d. i. Christian Gueintz (FG 361), der unter Aufsicht F. Ludwigs und in Übereinstimmung mit dem Fürsten *Deutscher Sprachlehre Entwurf* (1641) und *Die deutsche Rechtschreibung* (1645) veröffentlichte.

15 Hans Philipp (v.) Geuder (FG 310. Der Ergänzende).

16 Martin Zeiller (1589–1661), Inspektor der Ulmer dt. Schulen und Publizist, welcher das Realienwissen seinen Zeitgenossen durch Gebrauchsschriften in deutscher Sprache

zugänglich machte, z. B. im Text von *Merian: Topographia.* Vgl. zu diesem Werk 450905 K 4.
17 Diederich v. dem Werder (FG 31. Der Vielgekörnte).
18 Augustus Buchner (FG 362. Der Genossene).
19 Johann Michael Moscherosch (FG 436. Der Träumende. 1645). Zum Ablauf seiner Aufnahme in die FG s. 450500 K 1. F. Ludwig erwartete vom Träumenden, wie er Harsdörffer in 451209 mitteilte, daß er seine Werke einschicke. Vgl. 451101.
20 Es handelt sich nicht um ein damals veröffentlichtes Buch dieser Akademie, sondern um einen schon 1611 erschienenen Sammelband oder einen Teil desselben: Delle commedie degl'Accademici Intronati, la seconda Parte. Appresso il Riaprimento dell'Accademia Intronat[a], &c. Siena, Appresso Matteo Florimi; ad instanza di Bartolomeo Franceschi 1611. Enthält *Gli Scambi, commedia del l'Aperto,* d. i. Belisario Bulgarini; *La Pellegrina, commedia del Materiale,* d. i. Girolamo Bargagli, Hg. Scipione Bargagli; *La Descrittione del nuouo riaprimento dell'Accadèmia Intronata L'Oratione in lode di quella,* von S. Bargagli; *Imprese di suoi Accademici.* 12°, 616 S. Auf S. 159–163 Scipione Bargaglis Widmung der *Pellegrina* an Großhz. Ferdinand II. v. Toskana. Harsdörffers Bezeichnung Gesellschaftsbuch würde am besten auf den hinteren Abschnitt des Bands passen: Zwischentitel: La descrittione del nuovo riaprimento dell'Accadèmia intronata l'oratione in lode di quella e l'imprese di suoi accademici nuovamente stampate, S. [409]; Text S. 411–451: Breve descrittione del nuovo risorgimento dell'Accadèmia degl'intronati di Siena; S. 452–553: Oratione in lode dell'Accademia degl'intronati dello Schietto intronato; Agostino Agazzari, S. 556–561: De origine salis Intronati Armonici intronati; S. 562–609 Imprese d'Accademici intronat[i]; S. 610–616 Index der Gesellschaftsnamen u. der Taufnamen.; 1. S. „correttioni", 1 S. „registro"[1], 2 S. „correzzioni". World Catalog. Nicht in Deutschland nachgewiesen. Das von Harsdörffer an Diederich v. dem Werder (s. Anm. 17) geschickte Gesellschaftsbuch (vgl. 451101, 451217 u. 460120) mag auf dem Wege verlorengegangen oder bei Werder hängen geblieben sein, da dieser sich auf diplomatischen Reisen befand. S. 451209 K 9 u. Beil. I. Bei dem Buch handelte es sich nicht um die erste, undatierte Auflage der *Fasti* der Akademie, von denen einige nur im Vorspann und Schluß im Umfang geringfügig abweichende Drucke existieren: Accademia degli Intronati: Fasti Senenses ... ab Academia Intronatorum editi. ([Senis]: Academia Intronatorum o. J.), [18], 279 S.; fol.; Università di Siena, Biblioteca di Area Giuridico-Politologica ‚Circolo Giuridico' (CIPE); Datenbank: WorldCat., OCLC-Nummer: 848506961. [8] leaves, 279 p, [1] leaf; 36 cm. (fo.) Da dieses Buch Papst Alexander VII. (reg. 1655–1667) gewidmet ist, kann es erst ab 1655 datiert werden. Die die weiteren Exemplare besitzenden Bibliotheken schätzen, daß das Buch um 1660 erschien (z. B. Biblioteca Nazionale Centrale, Florenz: „[16], 279, [3] p., [1] l. of plates: ill."; BL London) oder zwischen 1655 und 1662 (Biblioteca Berenson, Florenz; „[16], 279, [3] p., [1] l. of plates : ill."). Sommervogel schreibt den Text Sebastiano Conti u. Giovan Battista Ferrari zu. S. World Catalog.
21 Severinos Akademieschrift über die Konjunktion *Et.* S. unten Beil. IV.

K I Zu Harsdörffers geplanten 100 Andachtsgemählen oder geistl. Sinnbildern s. 450529 K 9. 12 Andachtsgemälde veröffentlichte Harsdörffer im 6. Teil der *Frauenzimmer-Gesprächspiele* (1646, Ndr. 1969), Ndr. 495–622, dort S. 562 f. zu Beginn der Anmerkungen eine Erklärung des Begriffs „Andachts Gemähl", und 152 in den zwei Teilen seiner *Hertzbeweglichen Sonntagsandachten* (Nürnberg 1649 u. 1652, Ndr. 2007).
1 Vgl. *Biblia (Luther 1545)*: Jk 5,11: „Sihe/ wir preisen selig/ die erduldet haben. Die gedult Hiob habt jr gehöret/ vnd das ende des HErrn habt jr gesehen/ Denn der HErr ist barmhertzig vnd ein Erbarmer."

2 Der Rebstock. Vgl. Rebe, m. u. f., *DW* VIII, 323; *Schmeller* II, 5 (Aussprache „Rebm, Re'n").
3 stümmelt, verstümmelt. *Stieler*, 2226.
4 Im übertragenen Sinne wie lat. pallidus, fahl, falsch. *Stieler*, 425.
5 Last, f., südl. des Mains damals oft m. *DW* VI, 243.
6 Jes. 7.23 f. und Hos. 2, 14 reden auch von Gottes Bestrafung Israels durch Verwüstung der Weinstöcke.

K II 1 Εὐφυία in einem Hippokrates zugeschriebenen Brief des Paetos an den pers. Großkönig Artaxerxes: „τῇ τῆς ψυχῆς εὐφυία", l'heureuse disposition de l'âme, die glückliche geistige Veranlagung (des Hippokrates). S. Œuvres complètes d'Hippocrate, traduction nouvelle avec le texte grec en regard ... Par É. Littré. 9 tomes. Paris 1839–1861, IX, 314 f. Concordantia in Corpus Hippocraticum. Editée par Gilles Maloney et Winnie Frohn. 5 tomes. Hildesheim usw. 1986, II, 1790.
2 G. B. Manso (s. Anm. 4) gründete am 3.5.1611 in Neapel die Accademia degli Oziosi, welche der span. Vizekönig Pedro Fernández de Castro conte di Lemos protegierte und kontrollierte. Daran nahmen teil Giovanni Andrea di Paolo, Francesco de' Pietri, Giovanni Battista della Porta, Giulio Cesare Capaccio und Giambattista Basile. Zu ihr gehörten u. a. auch Torquato Accetto, Antonio Basso, Giuseppe Battista, Tommaso Campanella, Angelo Grillo, Giovan Vincenzo Imperiali, Giambattista Marino, Francesco de Pietri (Sekretär), Francisco de Quevedo u. Marco Aurelio Severino (s. Anm. 4). Die Akademie traf sich im Kloster der Kirche Santa Maria a Caponapoli. Impresa war ein Adler, darüber eine Krone und ein Engel, die Devise lautete „Non pigra quies". Die Akademie überlebte den Tod Mansos (1645), erlosch aber am Anfang des 18. Jahrhunderts. S. *DBI* LXIX (2007), 148–152; Girolamo de Miranda: Una quiete operosa. Forme e pratiche dell'Accademia napoletana degli Oziosi, 1611–1645. Napoli 2000; Vittor Ivo Comparato: Società civile e società letteraria nel primo Seicento: L'Accademia degli Oziosi. In: Quaderni storici (1973), n. 23, S. 359–389; F. Fernandez Murga: La academia napolitano-española de los Ociosos. Roma 1951; *Maylender* IV, 183–190; Camillo Minieri Riccio: Cenno storico intorno all'Accademia degli Oziosi in Napoli. Napoli 1862 (Estratto dal Rendiconto dell'Accademia Pontaniana); ders.: Cenno storico delle accademie fiorite nella città di Napoli. Estratto dall'Archivio Storico per le Provincie Napolitane Anno III, Fasc. 4° e seg. Napoli 1879; Carlo Padiglione: Le leggi dell'Accademia degli Oziosi in Napoli ritrovate nella Biblioteca Brancacciana. Napoli 1879.
3 Johann Georg Volckamer (1616–1693), in Altdorf am 30.4.1643 zum medizin. Doktor promoviert. *Will* IV, 121–125. Mitglied des Nürnberger Collegium Medicum, privatisierte jedoch seit 1647 als Mittelpunkt eines gelehrten Zirkels von Ärzten, zu dem damals noch vier andere Mediziner gehörten: der Pegnitzschäfer Johann Helwig (1609–1674; PBO Montano 1645), Gregor Hilling (1614–1680), Heinrich Magnus Heigel (1613–1683/84) und der Altdorfer Professor Christoph Nicolai (1618–1662). S. Helwigs *Vita*, zit. in 451101 K 13. Der wohlhabende Volckamer, ein fruchtbarer wissenschaftlicher Autor, Lobredner, Herausgeber (u. a. von Werken Severinos) und nebenbei Gelegenheitsdichter, wurde 1646 (s. unten) von Harsdörffer unter dem Schäfernamen Helianthus in den PBO aufgenommen. Harsdörffer schrieb am 4.4.1646 an Sigmund Betulius (S. v. Birken; FG 681. 1658): „Accessit nuper ad nos Johannes Georgius Volkamerus Medicinae Doctor Vir ingeniosissimus et clarissimus per Jtaliam et Galliam, cum nomine Helianthi, eius Flos est Helianthimum ex solisequiorum genere (das kleine Sonnenblümelein). In limine partis VI[tae] Ludiloquiorum commoda occasio erit, huius negotii mentionem faciendi." Volckamer konnte sich aber erst 1647 durch eine kleine Prosaekloge in *Harsdörffer: Frauenzim-*

mer-Gesprächspiele VII (1647, Ndr. 1969), Bl.)( )(vij v ff. vorstellen. Er empfahl nach Harsdörffers Tod eine Auflösung des Blumenordens, trat 1676 jedoch auch unter seinem Hirtennamen Helianthus in die Leopoldina ein. Er stieg 1686 zu deren Präsidenten und zum ksl. Rat und Leibarzt auf. Erst unter ihm gewann diese Akademie große Bedeutung. *Jürgensen: Repertorium*, 156–167; *Jürgensen: Utile*, 23, 35, 38–40, 203 u. IX; Artur Kreiner: Nürnbergs und Altdorfs Anteil an der Kaiserl. Leopold.-Carolinischen Deutschen Akademie der Naturforscher. In: Mitteilungen d. Vereins f. Gesch. d. Stadt Nürnberg XXXVII (1940), 309–322. Über Volckamers Studien und Reisen geben die Matrikeln und sein Stammbuch (HAAB Weimar, Eintragungen 1638–1642, vereinzelt 1645, 1648, 1649; vgl. Beil. VI) Auskunft (aus Nürnberg, Altdorf, Padua, Florenz, Rom, Neapel, Genua, Paris, Montpellier, Bordeaux und wiederum Nürnberg, 1639–1642, 1645). Vgl. Karlheinz Goldmann: Nürnberger und Altdorfer Stammbücher aus vier Jahrhunderten. Ein Katalog. Register v. Regina Eusemann. Selbstverlag Stadtbibliothek Nürnberg 1981, Nr. 557, vgl. 556, 1638 u. ö. Er hatte sich in Jena (1. Sem. 1634) und Padua immatrikuliert (Stammbuch-Eintragungen Jan. 1639 – Mai 1640, Medizin), war am 26.6.1640 in Bozen, kehrte jedoch nach Padua zurück (Stammbuch v. 17.8.1640), studierte mindestens seit dem März 1641 in Altdorf, war im November 1641 jedoch wieder in Italien (Livorno 4.11., Florenz 9.11.) und verbrachte zwei Monate in Neapel (Dez. 1641 bis Jan./ Febr. 1642), wo er im Hause Severinos lebte. Vgl. unten Beil. VI u. *Herdegen,* 269–273 u. 851 f. Volckamer reiste sodann über Rom (Stammbuch 27.3.1642) und Genua (12.5.1642) nach Montpellier (1.8.1642) und Bordeaux (23.8.1642). Aus Neapel schrieb Severino an ihn in Rom (am 8., 15., 18. und 20.2.1642) und Volckamer an Severino aus Rom (am 21.2.1642) und vermutlich in einem undatierten Brief (UB Erlangen: Briefsammlung Trew, Nr. 8, 9, 10 u. 11; Nr. 229 u. 230). Volckamer unterzeichnete auch als Comes palatinus (fehlt bei *Flood*). Vgl. *Schnabel: Stbb.* I, Nr. 123/189 (22.10.1688). Der vorliegende Brief zeigt, daß Volckamer den Kontakt Harsdörffers zu Severino und damit zu den Oziosi vermittelte. Als Herausgeber der *Zootomia* Severinos publizierte Volckamer in dem Werk auch ein Porträt des Verfassers mit einem eigenen Epigramm, das er mit seinem pegnes. Schäfernamen zeichnete und damit auch seine Mitgliedschaft in dem Orden spätestens seit dem Erscheinen des Buches (früh im Jahre 1646) bewies. S. unten Anm. 6. Schon 1644 gab er heraus: CHOCOLATA INDA: OPUSCULUM De qualitate & naturâ CHOCALATÆ, Authore ANTONIO COLMENERO DE LEDESMA, Med. Fac. Professore in Ecisana urbe. Hispanico antehac idiomate editum: nunc verò curante Marco Aurelio Severino Tarsensi, Phil. Medico, & in Gymnasio Neapolitano Regio Anatomes & Chirurgiæ Prof. P. in Latinum translatum NORIMBERGÆ, Typis Wolfgangi Enderi, Anno 1644.; OPOBALSAMI ORIENTALIS In Theriaces Confectionem Romæ revocati EXAMEN, Doctoriorumque calculis approbati SINCERITAS, Reddita à JOHANNE GEORGIO VOLCAMERO, Med. Doctore, Typis Wolfgangi Enderi, Anno 1644. Norimbergæ. HAB: Me 108° (1) u. (2). Das erste Werk enthält das in Beil V. zitierte Werkeverzeichnis Severinos. Volckamer steuerte d.d. Nürnberg 1.5.1644 eine lat. Widmungsvorrede an Paulus Zacchia, „totius Ecclesiastici Status generali Archiatro", bei. Darauf folgt Bl. A 7rv ein Gedicht Harsdörffers:

Ad Tractatum
de INDA CHOCO-
LATA,
Quem Munere CL. V.
MARCI AURELII SEVERINI
publici juris facit
JOANNES GEORGIVS

> VOLCAMERVS:
> Anagramma:
> RES NOVAS MANV VELOCI OGGERIS:
> Phaleucium.
>
> PEr ventos celeres patere Neréo
> Orbem novimus: En Cubile Phœbi
> tentat Cymba volubilis, (stupendum!)
> Quasi Solis in æmulationem [A 7v]
> nec quosdam haud-habitabiles recessus
>> lignum sollicitat; sed universum
>> transcendit facinus, novasque merces
>> confert Africa, & usta Sole Tellus.
>> VOLCAMERE bonâ favente Hygeîâ,
>> hinc nobis quòque Tu MANV NOVAS RES
>> VELOCI OGGERIS. Vrget ÆsculapI
>> Gens & Natio multa Pharmacorum,
>> ut sumptu, studio, eruditione
>> Sic seclo benè consulas futuro!
>> Sic nobis benè consulas Tibique!
>>> jucundissimæ Amicitiæ testandæ studio adornabat
>>> Georg-Philippus Harsdörfferus.

Die Vorrede (Severinos) an den Leser erörtert die gesundheitliche Wirkung der Schokolade. Demgegenüber stellt der Verfasser den schon damals verbreiteten unbekümmerten Genuß des Getränks vor allem an Höfen in Italien, Spanien und den Niederlanden fest. In seiner Widmung berichtet Volckamer, er sei vor zwei Jahren in die Heimat zurückgekehrt. In Rom hätten ihn vor allem der berühmte Petrus Servius, der Arzt Nicolaus Larcaeus und der Botaniker Tobias Aldinus, Vorsteher des päpstlichen Viridarium, wohl empfangen. Über sein Verhältnis zu Severino und dessen Umgang mit dem Arzt Zacchia gibt Volckamer in den Worten Aufschluß: „opusculum nō proprii fructum laboris, sed Excellentissimi Severini benevolentiâ concessum, quod ob intimam, quam Tecum Vir iste Illustris sincerè colit, amicitiam, ad tuum deinceps favorem mihi quoque perennandum acceptissimum sisto pararium, observantiæ in Te meæ testem, quoad vixero, nullâ fortunæ injuriâ violandum; quem quippe quæstum laudum tuarum opulentiorem reddidit venerabilis ille noster Senex verus, severioris Chirurgiæ restaurator, & cultor, factâ toties Tui, dum hyberna apud eum agerem, illustriumque judicii tui κειμηλίων mentione honorificâ. Animus quidem erat, Te insignem Musarum Mecœnatum in luculentioris operis reservare editionem; quam tamen animi mei promtitudinem differe nullatenus potui, duplici ratus nomine Tibi gratiorem, cùm bis dare dicatur ille, qui citò det. Sunt etenim penes me pleraque Excell[mi] Severini manu[A 4v]scripta, quæ jam publicæ apparata sunt luci: inter cætera absolutissimum Chirurgiæ efficacioris opus, à commodiore elegantique ulcera, vulnera, aliosque corporis tàm internos quàm externos curandi morbos, qui ancipitem licet sanitatem reddant, pertractandi ratione ab Hippocr. Celso, Aëtio, cæterisque medicorum Principibus traditâ nobilitatum. Democritæa hanc excipit Zootomia, sagacissima Viri hoc seculo passim decantati indagatio, Anatomica scil. opificii animantium organici membrorumque suorum actionis & usus universi contemplatio, à primo Democrito diligentissimè exercitata, quo, promitto cum Experientissimo Romano, incurabilium medico, opere ad ἐνέργειαν Anatomicam nil videris optaverisve præstantius. Adsunt elabo[A 5r]ratissima In pleraque Hippoc. Celsique opera commentaria, aliaque quædam scripta cedro profectò digna, ob materiam Jassolini, Magni ejus Præceptoris reliquiis confinem adjungenda, quæ certè, si nō omnia, plurima tamen hactenus typis data fuissent, nisi temporum iniquitas remorata fuisset, unde Germaniæ haud sananda pestis, Italiæ refricatum ulcus, Gallis renovata lues, imò universus hoc contagio contaminatus orbis adoptato Bellonæ consortio Musas ubivis indignissimè sede protelat suâ. Hos autem aliosve, si qui obtigerint, Syrenios verè scopulos pro virili evitare conabor, nullum vel laborem aut molestiam subterfugiens, quin omnem moturus lapidem, ut prælo quam maturrimè illa subjiciantur." [Der Titel des erstgenannten Buchs erscheint in Severinos Werkeliste in *Chocolata*, 71 so: „Exegmatica Chirurgia, continens commentaria in Hippocratis librum de ulceribus & vulneribus capitis; in libros technicos ejusdem. In librum V. Cornelii Celsi. Paraphrasis prooemii generalis de re Medicâ Celsi."] Fast gleichzeitig war auch eine frz. Übersetzung von René Moreau erschienen: Antonio Colmenero de Ledesma: Du chocolate: discours curieux divisé en quatre parties par Antoine Colmenero de Ledesma ... trad. d'espagnol en françois sur l'impression faite à Madrid l'an 1631, & éclaircy de quelques annotations par René Moreau .... plus est ajouté un Dialogue touchant le même chocolate [par Barthélémy Marradon] (Paris: Sébastien Cramoisy 1643), (Du chocolate: dialogue entre un médecin, un indien, & un bourgeois).

4 Giovanni Battista Manso (1569–1645), dem Kg. Philipp IV. v. Spanien 1622 den Titel marchese di Villa Lago verlieh, war ein Diplomat, Schriftsteller, Militär und Freund Giambattista Marinos und Torquato Tassos. Er regte 1638 bei einem Besuch John Miltons denselben zur Beschäftigung mit Tasso und Marino an. Unter dem Gesellschaftsnamen *Il Tardo* fungierte Manso bis zu seinem Tode fast ununterbrochen als Principe der Accademia degli Oziosi. In seinem Testament wies er der Akademie einen Raum in seinem Palazzo zu und erlaubte ihr die Benutzung seiner Bibliothek. Da er die Aufsicht über eine wohltätige Stiftung (*Monte Manso* für die Unterrichtung junger mitteloser Adliger) den Jesuiten übertragen hatte, wollte er nach seinem Tode auch der Akademie die ‚Unterstützung' durch die Jesuiten sichern. Schon 1646 entstand deshalb Streit, und der Vizekönig untersagte die akademischen Versammlungen. S. *DBI* LXIX (2007), 148–152; Angelo Borzelli: Giovan Battista Manso Marchese Villa. Napoli 1916. Manso dichtete *Poesie nomiche ... divise in Rime amorose, sacre e morali* (Venezia 1635 u. 1640), die durch eine Anthologie von an ihn gerichteten Versen anderer aufgebläht sind, und schrieb vor allem das hier gemeinte dialogische Werk, eine Kompilation über Liebe und Schönheit, mit den *Argomenti* Marinos und dem angehängten Traktat, einer Erweiterung eines jugendlichen Dialogs Tassos: Erocallia Ouero Dell'Amore e della Bellezza Dialoghi XII. Di Gio. Battista Manso Marchese Della Villa, Con gli Argomenti à ciascun Dialogo del Caualier Marino. E nel fine vn Trattato del Dialogo dell'istesso Autore. Con tre tavole ... In Venetia Appresso Euang. Deuchino ... 1628. 16 Bl., 1032 S., 2 Bl., S. 1033–1065. (In Deutschland nur in SUB Göttingen: 8 PHIL. VI, 5184). Manso hinterließ eine unvollendete Enzyklopädie. Ihm verdanken wir die erste Biographie Tassos: VITA DI TORQUATO TASSO Scritta DA GIO. BATTISTA Manso Napolitano Sig. della Città di Bisaccio, e di Pianca. Al Sereniss. Sig. Duca d'Vrb. FRANCESCO MARIA Secondo, Duca Sesto. Con licenza, & Priuilegio. IN VENETIA, M DC XXI. Appresso Euangelista Deuchino. HAB: 598.33 Hist. Scipione Gentili (1563–1616), der sein späteres Leben als Jurist an der nürnberg. U. Altdorf verbrachte, hatte eine Teilübersetzung von Tassos *La Gerusalemme liberata* ins Lateinische veröffentlicht: SCIPII GENTILIS Solymeidos LIBRI DUO PRIORES DE TORQVATI TASSI Italicis expressi. LONDINI Apud Iohannem Wolfium, 1584. HAB: 35.2 Poet. (3).

5 Die Mitglieder der Fruchtbringenden Gesellschaft.

6 Der Text einer Aufnahmeurkunde Harsdörffers ist nicht im Erzschrein der FG erhalten. Dort fehlt auch das Original von Severinos Brief an Harsdörffer, da es der Spielende zurückzusenden bat. In seinen Briefen an Volckamer bestellt Severino immer wieder Grüße an Harsdörffer und macht diesem Hoffnung auf seine Aufnahme unter die Oziosi. In einem zerrissenen Brief vom 5.8.1645 n. St. heißt es: „dörffero Salutem ex animo, cui præter quæ ...tius significo, si nostrum Ociosorum Principe Vlysseo vin ... eant referre, non grauetur ad hunc quam officiosissimas ... cademicum eruditissimum sponsore me dare." (UB Erlangen: Briefsammlung Trew Nr.39, © Harald Fischer Verlag, Erlangen). Am 23.10.1645 (wie alle folgenden Schreiben Severinos wohl n. St.) wies Severino auf Schwierigkeiten beider Seiten hin: „Jam autem vbi expleui grauiora responsionis capita, commodum mox cum Generosiss.° Harsdorffero confabulor; cui felicitatem meis non tam verbis, quam animi sensis dicito cumulatiss.^{am}; deinde memora, quam sit arduum Fructiferos et Jndustrios conuenire cum Ociosis atque inertibus. quid enim tam dissitis, tam aduersis vitæ generibus, et institutis communem. Et nostro Ociosorum Principi tardigradi παρὼνομα, quod innixum est in delecto emblemate octavæ sphæræ saturnia et longa annorum vertigine percitæ cum accommodata, cuius in præsens non memini gnomem. Quibus aptum fit, quam cunctabundus hic γερόνδιον noster, licet operis consummatione non penitendus. Adde quod generosus hic heros (qui sortis huius est mos, autore Macrobio proprius) aura vertitur ætheria sibi cognata, idest, vt mihi videre videor, amica gloriæ; quas ob res, si nobis propositum et maria et montes insuper alios ab Academiarcho nostro extorquere, operæ precium erit, vt officiosis semel litteris Illustrissimum vix interpellent. sic ipsum omnino demerebimus, ac prope mancipabimus quam arcanam eius mentem vobis amicis intimis aperuisse, non mihi vitio sit. Cæterum de cohonestata per D. Harsdorfferum Zootomia, quas aut quot non ago gratias?" (A.a.O., Nr.40). Severino konnte „circa Idus" (13.12.) 1645 Harsdörffer aber durch Volckamer auf die freundliche Aufnahme des Antrags seitens des Principe hinweisen und ihm dessen Sendung der Aufnahmeurkunde in einer Briefbeilage verheißen: „Ampliss.^{i} D. Harsdörferi litteras exporrecta fronte legit D. Illustrissimus Villæ Academiæ Princeps nostræ, pollicitque cum auctario mittendum admiss.^{nis} diploma. Cætera rescribam maturius in posterum." (A.a.O., Nr.41). Der in diesem Brief auch angekündigte Porträtstich Severinos datiert das Erscheinen der vollständigen *Zootomia* auf 1646 (vgl. Anm.3). Der Neapolitaner schrieb an Volckamer am 13.1.1646: „Significasti de expressura faciem ærea tabella quæ ubi primum, mox et Ludtero nostro diligentissimo excusori cordi foret prospectui nostrarum editionem editionum solenni præfigere; quam ego studiosam uestram uoluntatem minime nolim adiuuare. Quo statuo, quantum in me erit, uel Neapoli, uel Romæ recudendam imaginem. quod si certissima esset conducendi commoditas eidem huic exemplari, quod tantopere uestris amicorumque oculis probatum est, mutuando non parcerem." (A.a.O., Nr.42). Da der Principe der Oziosi wohl schon Ende 1645 starb (Kodizill seines Testaments am 8.9.1645; *DBI* LXIX, 149), verzögerte sich Harsdörffers Aufnahme unter die Oziosi schon durch die Bestallung eines Nachfolgers. Im Februar 1646 schrieb er unter Verwendung eines falschen Rufnamens Harsdörffers, der neue, unergründliche Principe (Tiberio Caraffa) nehme sich seine Zeit, bereite aber die Aufnahmeurkunde vor: „Humanissim.^{i} pariter ac ampliss.^{i} Christophori Harsdörfferi meis p^{ma} salutati verbis opem et suffragia meis in rebus implora, cui nouus Academiæ Princeps &c responsorias litteras et diploma promissum parat. Hyperberatœi, doleo, sunt hi nostri Principes, verum quantum illi moræ tantumdem ego stimuli. interim Dominus iste meus imitetur Romanum, qui sedendo vicit." (A.a.O., Nr.43). Offenbar verwechselte Severino hier Harsdörffers Rufnamen — wohl auch ein Zeichen, daß er damals mit ihm nur durch Volckamer verkehrte. Am 15.3.1646 machte der Neapolitaner in einem neuen Brief an seinen Briefpartner Harsdörffer wieder Hoffnung auf eine schnelle Aufnahme: „Amplissimo Harsdörffero iam á nouo Academiarcha nostro expediuntur litteræ, quæ dilatæ tam diu sunt Superioris Principis interitu." (A. a. O., Nr. 44). Die bestätigt er nochmals und erwähnt neben seinem Briefverkehr mit dem Nürnberger Arzt Michael Rupert Besler offenbar nun auch direkte Korrespondenz mit Harsdörffer — am 19. 4. 1646: „Quas datas ad me significas, siue suas [Beslers Brief, K. C.], siue Harsdörfferianas expecto litteras, Beslinianas uero respondi protinus [...] Amplissimo Harsdörffero iam aduentat Academicum responsum." Am Schluß seines Schreibens wiederholt Severino das Versprechen und verbindet es mit einem Kompliment, das die Namen der beiden Akademien der Oziosi und der Fruchtbringer witzig zur Erklärung der zögerlichen Aufnahme Harsdörffers heranzieht: „Ampliss.° D. Harsdorffero iam iam maturant responsa Principis et Academiæ totius. Dispares aut si profitentur ociosi Fructiferis δὶς δαπασων." Im unvollständigen Brief Severinos an Volckamer vom 2. 5. 1646 (Nr. 46) ist keine Aussage über die leidige Angelegenhalt erhalten. In dem im Konvolut folgenden Schreiben des Neapolitaners vom 30. 10. 1646 mußte dieser dann schamrot gestehen, daß Harsdörffer noch nicht unter die Oziosi aufgenommen wurde, wobei Severino nicht den verstorbenen und den neuen Principe verantwortlich machte, sondern allgemein den Verfall der Wissenschaften in der Accademia degli Oziosi: „Ad Ampliss.^{um} uero D. Harsdörfferum subalacris eta uultuosus accedo salutandum, ut qui suffundar ingenuo rubore tandiu prorogatæ, quam meo pollicito festinatæ coaptationis eius in Academiam nostram. Verum intempestus abitus fortassis enim non obitus Jll.^{mi} nostri dictatoris inuidit conceptam omnem impetrationis meæ gloriam gratificationis complem.$^{ta.}$ Verum tamen æqui, boniqe faciat Principis successoris Epistolam, quam à tepescentis nisi et frigescentis, hoc est fatiscentis Academiæ reliquijs excepi fatale siquidem hoc opem [*recte:* opus] litterarum ubique locorum decrem.^{tum} ac detrectam." (A. a. O., Nr. 47). In den folgenden Stücken des in Erlangen erhaltenen Briefwechsels vom 21. 11. 1646, 1. 1. 1647, 20. 2. 1647 und 25. 3. 1647 kam Severino nicht mehr auf Harsdörffers Aufnahme zu sprechen. Er erwähnte ihn in diesen Schreiben auch nicht mehr außer durch einen kurzen Gruß (20. 2. 1647, Nr. 50). — Hatte die Ablehnung von Harsdörffers Vorhaben durch die FG (s. 450919A) eine positive Entscheidung der Oziosi verhindert? Wahrscheinlich hatte diese Weigerung — war sie von Harsdörffer überhaupt ausdrücklich mitgeteilt worden? — schlußendlich keine negative Auswirkung auf die Einstellung des Spielenden zu den Oziosi. Davon zeugt die Mitteilung Harsdörffers an F. Ludwig in *DA Köthen I. 8:* 470426, er habe gerade durch den neuen Principe der Oziosi einen Brief erhalten, in dem dieser durch den Empfänger die FG grüße und sich und seine Gesellschaft der Gewogenheit der FG befehle. Daß damit auch die Kooptation Harsdörffers durch die italienische Akademie verbunden war, bezeugt seine lat. Übersetzung aus dem Englischen des Juristen Richard Zouch (*1590, † frühestens 1660): The Sophister. A Comedy. London 1639. S. 440426 K I 0. Der Titel lautet: SOPHISTA, | sive | LOGICA ET PSEUDO- | POLITICA, | sub schemate | Comœdiæ repræsentata: | Studio | GEORGI PHILIPPI HARSDÖRFFERI, | Academici Otiosi. | 1647 | [Imprese mit dem Motto der Accademia degli Oziosi: Sonne, Landschaft, Schloß | QVIES NON PIGRA] | Ex Officina Endteriana. | Norimb. HAB: 160.3 Eth. u. Digitalisat, 71 Bll.; Variante mit dem Titelzusatz „repraesentata; scripta quondam Anglico idiomate nunc sermone Romano adornata", 72 Bll.: HAB: QuN 1090 (2). S. 440426 I. Das Buch enthält Harsdörffers Epigramm auf Principe Tiberio Caraffa und seinen Widmungsbrief an den Fürsten (s. *DA Köthen I. 8:* 470401), auch ein Gedicht auf die Mitglieder der Accademia degli Oziosi, alles in Latein. Harsdörffer hatte den Text unter Weglassung der Zugaben ins Deutsche schon zuvor in der Form eines langen Gesprächspiels übertragen: *Frauenzimmer-Gesprächspiele* V (1645), 85–280. Es gibt in dem erwähnten Erlanger Konvolut nur noch wenige Anzeichen des Kontakts zwischen Harsdörffer und Severino, vor allem den Passus in Severinos Schreiben an Volckamer vom

1. 8.1648 n. St.: „Ampliss.m D. Harsdorfferum reuerenter à me saluta, cuius ego litteras responsorias propter Ill. Principis absentiam propterque bellicos istos furores recuperare perdiligens et nequi. Ad eum Dominum et qui me in editione Zootomiæ perhumaniter ornauit singulatim nominatos communicationem eucharisticam rescripsi." Wahrscheinlich war ein Antwortbrief Harsdörffers, an Severino oder an Caraffa, auch Principe der Oziosi, gelangt und dort am 1.8.1648 für Severino unerreichbar, so daß dieser (einstweilen?) einen Dankesbrief an den nürnberg. Patrizier richtete, in dem er dessen Ehrengedichts in Severinos *Zootomia* gedachte (a. a. O., Nr.52). Ein Schreiben Severinos an Volckamer vom 25.12.1648 bittet denselben ohne weitere Angaben um Ausrichtung von Grüßen an Harsdörffer (a. a. O., Nr.53).

7 F. Ludwig.

8 Vgl. Werkeverzeichnis (Beil. V), Bl.325r Nr. „37. La Philosofia de gli Scacchi h. e. Ludus Scacchiorum per omnes eorum universales causas ad normam Philosophicam examinatus, eius origine planè inventa et ad Rythmomachiam Pythagoream revocata, problematisquè quam plurimis ad partem ludi tum materialem tum formalem et ad cunitas eiusdem minimas administrationes et ad momenta spectantibus accuratè resolutis." Kein Druck vor 1690 im Karlsruher Virtuellen Katalog nachgewiesen: La Filosofia Overo Il Perche Degli Scacchi Per Cui Chiaramante Si Mostra Prima l'artificio della fabrica universale, poscia la ragion particolare della ordinanza, & degli andamenti tutti degli Scacchi: Trattato Non tanto per lo gradevole scherzo, quanto per la riposta contezza delle cose pregiato Di M. Aurelio Severino Da Tarsia Su' Crathi, Medico, & Filosofo Napoletano (Napoli: Antonio Bulifon 1690). UB Mannheim. Vgl. Dell'Antica Pettia Overo Che Palamede non è stato l'inventor degli Scacchi. Trattato Di M. Aurelio Severino Di Tarsia Su' Crathi, Medico, & Filosofo Napoletano. Nel quale si dà piena contezza non solo de' Scacchi, ma di più Giuochi degli Antichi, non men dilettevoli, che necessarii all'intelligenza di molti luoghi di Greci, & Latini Scrittori (a. a, O. 1690), UB Mannheim.

9 Vielleicht ist der poln. Gesandte Reichsfürst Jerzy Ossoliński (1595–1650) gemeint, der 1633 und 1641 Reden vor Papst Urban VIII. und auch 1633 in Venedig eine Rede an die Republik hielt. S. Illustrißimi et Excellent.[mi] Domini D. GEORGII DVCIS IN OSSOLIN S. R. I. Principis, Comitis à Tenczyn Ossolinski, Supremi Regni Poloniae CANCELLARII ORATIONES ... DANTISCI, Sumpt. Georgii Försteri ... 1647. HAB: 19.8 Quod. (3). Vgl. auch *Opitz: BW* 340310 *ep* u. 380610 *ep*. S. HAB: Cod. Guelf. 8.7 Aug. 2°, Bl.207, Brief Johann Sauberts v. 23.10.1645.

10 In toskan. Sprache. Vgl. Anm. 8 u. Beil. IV.

11 Mehrere Darstellungen in *Digitaler Porträtindex*. Eines der Porträts erscheint vor Severinos *Zootomia Democritea* (Nürnberg 1645), s. K 4.

12 Sic. Präsenspartizip zu dem seltenen στομαζω, lat. stomachor, ärgerlich sein, sich ärgern. Thesaurus Graecae Linguae, ab Henrico Stepano constructus. Post editionem anglicam ... edd. Carolus Benedictus Hase et al. 8 v. Parisiis 1831–1865, VII, 811.

13 Michael Ruprecht Besler (1607–1661), nürnberg. Arzt und Gelehrter; studierte in Altdorf und Padua; Dr. med. 1631 U. Altdorf; sammelte und beschrieb sein Naturalienkabinett: GAZOPHYLACIUM RERUM NATURALIUM E REGNO VEGETABILI; ANIMALI ET MINERALI DEPROMPTARUM; NUNQUAM HACTENUS IN LUCEM EDITARUM; FIDELIS CUM FIGURIS ÆNEIS AD VIVUM INCISIS REPRÆSENTATIO OPERÂ MICHAELIS RUPERTI BESLERI MEDICI ET REIPUBLICÆ NORIB. PHYSICI ORDINARII ET OFFICINARUM PHARMACEUTICARUM p. t. VISITATORIS SENIORIS: ANNO MDCXLII; HAB: 6.2.3 Phys. 2° (auch Dig.). Er gab auch die im Brief erwähnte Arbeit Severinos heraus: Trimembris Chirurgia, in qua diætetico-chirurgica pharmaco-chirurgica & chymico-chirurgica traditio est auctore Marco Aurelio Severino ... ad clarissimum virum Michaelem Rupertum Beslerum (Francofurti: Ioannes Godefridus Schönwetterus 1653); UB Leipzig. *S. Jöcher* I; *Will* I; *DBA* I 94/ 184–187; *Jürgensen: Repertorium*, 28. Diese Arbeit erscheint in Severinos Werkeliste (Beil. V) offenbar unter Nr. 10. Die andere im Brief erwähnte Arbeit wird an 17. Stelle erwähnt: „De Lapide fungifero, deq̀; Tuberibus Soffilibus."

14 Dieses Emblem fehlt in *Zootomia*. Dafür steht dort Bl.)( )(3 v

VI.

COnscia fatorum quondam lustravit Haruspex
Inguina, fibrosis flexibus irrigua.
Scilicet adversas fortunas hostia signat;
prospera, vel latices cordis, heparque parant?
Hæc malefida Fides procul exulet, exulet, inquam,
    inter Christiadas vana superstitio.
Ecce SEVERINUS, venturi certus Haruspex,
    morborum causas, & nova signa refert.
Doctiùs ille secat, medicâ arte, Animalia bruta:
    morbifluos fontes elicita exta notant.
Gentili ritu, meruisset nunc Hecatomben,
    quòd primùm solers finxerit Artis opus.

Præmia sufficient laudum Democritus audit
    nobis: quod reliquum est, Posteritas referet.

honoris ergo lubens meritòque pos.
G. P. Harsdörffer

Das Gedicht wiederveröffentlicht von W. A. Kelly: Neugefundene Texte des deutschen Barock aus britischen Beständen. In: Daphnis 29 (2000), 699–708, hier 699f. Erwähnt in *Jürgensen: Repertorium*, 36.

15 Anagramm des lat. Namens Severinos.

K III Francesco Fontana (1580/90–1656; Tod durch Pest). Studierte die Rechte, sodann Mathematik in Neapel, widmete sich der Konstruktion von Fernrohren und Mikroskopen, wandte sich schließlich unter dem Einfluß des Freundes Giovan Camillo Glorioso auch stärker dem Studium der Astronomie zu. Er gewann jedoch nicht nur durch seine Fernrohre in Europa als Ingenieur Berühmtheit (Galileo Galilei, Athanasius Kircher, Marin Mersenne, Christoph Scheiner, Christian Huygens), sondern auch durch seine (noch der Erklärung bedürftigen) Beobachtungen, die er in dem in Q zitierten (einzigen gedruckten) Werk veröffentlichte. Fontana bestärkte die Annahme einer Drehung der Planeten um ihre Achse und die wechselnde Größe des Mars in Entsprechung zur Quadratur mit der Sonne, entdeckte unbekannte Saturn- und Jupitermonde, vor allem jedoch lieferte er in solcher Genauigkeit bisher unbekannte Ansichten des Monds. *DBI* IIL, 651–653. S. Abb. I u. II S. 627. Auch Manso, der Principe der Oziosi, war ein Kenner der Astronomie und der Optik. S. 451217. Wie die vorliegende Beilage zeigt, gelangten diese Entdeckungen vor ihrer Veröffentlichung durch Severino nicht nur zu Harsdörffer und nach Nürnberg, sondern auch an den Hof des Oberhaupts der FG.

K IV 1 Giovanni della Casa (1503–1558), päpstl. Nuntius (Venedig) und Sekretär, Dichter, Verfasser des *Galateo*. Der Vers erscheint in *Le rime. A cura di Roberto Fedi.* 2 t. Roma 1978 (I, Nr. XLVI v. 36–39):
Deh chi fia mai che scioglia
ver' la giudice mia sí dolci prighi,
ch'almen non mi toglia
dritta ragion, se pur pietà si nieghi?
Lt. *Chocolata* (s. K II 3), Titel XXXVI schrieb Severino „Rintrauiamenti delle Rime de Monsignor della Casa." Vgl. die von De Angelis (s. Beil. V Q u. K) angeführten Manuskripte Severinos: Lancisiana LXXIV – 2-3 Severino M. A., sopra i Sonetti di Mons. della Casa Cart. Sec. XVII C. 298; Lancisiana LXXIV – 2-18 Severino M. A., Vita di Mons. della Casa ed esposizione dei Sonetti Cart. Sec. XVII C. 214.

2 Imprese Marco Aurelio Severinos (s. K 4), die zu seinem Gesellschaftsnamen in der Accademia degli Oziosi (L'Assettatto, d. i. der Geordnete, Eingerichtete), zum Motto (dt.: Im Verhältnis zueinander überall gleich) und zur Res der Pictura (Würfel) paßt.

3 Thomas Bartholinus (1616–1680), berühmter dän. Anatom. Nach Studien u. a. in Leiden und Padua (Mitglied der Incogniti von Venedig) wurde er in Basel zum Dr. med. promoviert. Er schlug mehrere ihm angebotene Berufungen, u. a. nach Neapel, aus, wirkte aber seit 1648 als Prof. der Medizin in Kopenhagen. *Hirsch* V, 356–358. Vgl. den Zusatz zu Severinos Werkeverzeichnis in K V.

4 Onofrio Riccio, neapolitan. Arzt, Professor und Literat, starb wie Severino 1656 an der Pest. Mitglied der Infuriati (Il Bizarro). Vgl. *Jöcher* III, 2069; *ABI* I 846/ 103; Renata d'Agostino: Impegno intellettuale e pratico della poesia in Onofrio Riccio. Napoli 2000. Vgl. in De Angelis [s. Beil. V Q], 158 die Handschrift: „Lancisiana LXXVII – 3-18 Severino M. A. Il Medico a rovescio compilato da Onofrio Ricci Cart. XVII – C. 63".

5 Cassiano dal Pozzo (Puteanus, Turin 1588 – Rom 1657), D. utr. jur., Richter in Siena, im Stefansorden Komtur von Tropea und Cavour, Sekretär des Nipoten Papst Urbans VIII., Kd. Francesco Barberini (Linceo 1623), dessen Gesandtschaft nach Spanien und an den französ. Hof er in einem Tagebuch beschrieb. 1622 wurde er selbst in die Accademia dei Lincei aufgenommen. Giuseppe Gabrieli: Il Carteggio Linceo (Roma 1966), 766. Fruchtbarer Briefpartner, u. a. Galileos, aus dessen Hinterlassenschaft er Bücher und naturkundliche Gegenstände für seine große Wunderkammer kaufte. Er sammelte zwar auch Bücher, Antiken und (besonders franz.) Gemälde der Zeit, baute vor allem aber — wie z. B. vor ihm Jacopo Strada — zusammen mit seinem Bruder Carlo Andrea eine enzyklopädische graphische Dokumentation antiker Relikte auf, die später Johann Joachim Winckelmann als Bibliothekar Kd. Alessandro Albanos betreuen sollte. Pozzo wurde Mitglied der Accademia della Crusca (1626). *DBI* XXXII (1983); The Paper Museum of Cassiano dal Pozzo. A catalogue raisonné: drawings and prints in the Royal Library at Windsor Castle, the British Museum, the Institut de France and other collections (ed. by) Francis Haskell and Jennifer Montagu et al. London 1996; Anna Nicolò: Il carteggio di Cassiano dal Pozzo. Firenze 1991 (Quaderni di „Rinascimento", 11); Ingo Herklotz: Cassiano dal Pozzo und die Archäologie des 17. Jahrhunderts. München 1999; I segreti di un collezionista. Le straordinarie raccolte di Cassiano dal Pozzo 1588–1657. A cura di Francesco Solinas. Roma (2001, Museo del Territorio Biellese; Cassiano dal Pozzo: Il Diario del viaggio in Spagna del cardinale Francesco Barberini (a cura di Alessandra Anselmi). Aranjuez 2004; David Attenborough: Amazing Rare Things. The art of natural history in the age of discovery. 2., rev. ed. London 2007. Vgl. Gabriel Naudé: Epigrammata in virorum literatorum imagines, quas illustrissimus eques Cassianus a Puteo sua in bibliotheca dedicauit. Cum appendicula variorum carminum (Romae 1641: Ludovicus Grignanus); Il Camaleonte Esaminato Del Sig. Domenico Panarcio. Dedicato all'Illustriss. Sig. il Sig. Caualier Cassiano Dal Pozzo Commendatore dell'Ordine di San Stefano (Roma: Cavalli 1645), HAB: 294.2 Quod. (1). 3 S.

6 Motto der Accademia della Crusca, in die F. Ludwig im Jahre 1600 und Cassiano dal Pozzo im Jahre 1626 aufgenommen wurden. Das Lob der toskanischen Sprache Pozzos und die Anspielung auf seine Zugehörigkeit zur Sprachakademie verdient besondere Beachtung, weil Severino bzw. Harsdörffer damit wohl das Interesse F. Ludwigs erregte. Harsdörffers Plänen einer Vernetzung der FG mit italienischen Akademien hätte das nutzen können.

7 Cassiano dal Pozzo war im Hause seines Oheims Carlo Antonio dal Pozzo della Cisterna di Biella (1547–1607), des Erzbischofs von Pisa und großhzl. toskanischen Geheimrats in Kammersachen (1547–1607; *DBI* XXXII. 1986), auferzogen worden.

8 Kd. Ferdinando de' Medici, ab 1587 Großherzog der Toskana, der Carlo Antonio dal Pozzo 1582 die Würde des Erzbischofs v. Pisa verschafft hatte. Trotz seines ebfl. Amtes diente Carlo Antonio Großhz. Ferdinando — wie auch schon dessen Bruder und Vorgänger Francesco (*1587) — am florentin. Hof als Jurist und einflußreicher politischer Berater.

9 contezza, f., genaue Bekanntschaft, Vertrautheit.

10 compiete, d.i. compite, compiute, adj., vollendet.

11 Es handelt sich um eine scherzhafte, aber ernst gemeinte Anklage gegen sprachliche Verfehlungen. F. Ludwig, den Übersetzer von Petrarcas *Trionfi*, würde es z.B. interessiert haben zu lesen (Severino: *La Querela della & accorciata* [s. IV Q], 6–8, 55f.): „Così non approuano i Giudici buoni, che si toglia l'aspiratione al verbo hauere, dicēdo, Ai, Abbiamo, Abbiate, Anno; che leggiamo, & veggiamo non esser mica piaciuto à veruno de' primieri promouitori già nomati della lingua nostra; anzi questi vocaboli, & altri molti, che dal Latino, & dal Greco fonte caggiono, con la nota dell'aspiratione, vollero, che fossono sostentati. Io dissi sostētati, perciò che, si come saggiamēte auuertì Francesco Alunno da Ferrara; l'accento aspirato aggiugne pienezza, & da quasi polpa, & lena alla lettera vocale, à cui ella sta à canto à guisa di seruente. Per la qual cosa, sicome e' primi scrissero, così appūto io stimo, che si debba seguire; confermando ciò l'esempio; che nel trionfo secondo della fama ci propose il Petrarca, che disse;

Pithagora, che prima humilemente.

Philosphia chiamò con nome degno.

Dourassi, io dico con la (Phi) non altramente scriuere. Imperoche scriuendosi Filosofia, come si trarrà chi che sia ad inuestigare la dignità della Philosophia dal Petrarca accennata, se la verace di lei originanza non sa? & come questa saprà, se la luce del propio, & natiuo nome [Marginalnote „Necessità della Etimologia."; S.6] non haurà? ch'oscurato ritroua per la sua falsa descrittione? oltre che qual differenza fia per vostra fè, se si dirà Filosofo senza il vero intendimento, & senza la vera interpretatione del nome, o se si dirà Filosofo voce, che appresso Giouanni Boccaccio sciocamente si cacciò di bocca lo Idiota Mercatante. [...7] In tanto à me ritornando, io dico, che gli an-[8]tichi Maestri altra opinione non hebbero, ne altra costumanza tennero, se non di sempre intera scriuere questa particella di congiuntione, & così per li lor originali testi, & per gli altri fedelmente ripigliati si legge. [Marginalnote „Ripigliato ragionamento della Ortographia della (Et)"]. Per la qual cosa egli è gran marauiglia, come, & con qual baldanza il primo, che io non so veramente chi si fusse, ma ben Leonardo Saluiati, & quei, che costui seguirono buona parte di colpa ne hanno." Salviati war einer der Gründer der Accademia della Crusca! Am Schluß faßt Severino seine Meinung sehr differenziert zusammen, wobei er auch Schrift und Aussprache unterscheidet: Marginalnote: „Chi (&) indifferentemēnte vserà nel verso, non trasuierà egli", Haupttext: „Ma poi in somma direi, che CHI nel verso scriuerà ET con T, non farà errore alcuno, perche così han fatto il Petrarca & Dante, & perche il suono di quella voce si fa sentir forte, come s'è tante volte detto, & perche quella congiuntione è così di sua natura, & perche cosi si toglie via ogni confusione nell'intendimento della sentenza, tosto che le parole si veggono scritte, senza hauerui a pensar sopra, & aiutarsi con la discretione & col contesto di tutte l'altre voci che vanno seco. Et per questo si chiuderà all'incontro, che tanto più vitioso piu sconueneuole, & piu vano, & dannoso insieme sia l'vsar nelle prose E senza T, quando ella è congiuntione & che non si faccia per alcun modo da chi ha caro di saper render conto di se, & di mostrar di gouernarsi con ragione & con giudicio, & non a caso o mùouersi con ogni poco di ventarello, che gli ghiribizzi qualche debole tagionuzza in testa, come è quella che sola allega chi cosi senza T, la scriue, cioè, che nel pronuntiarsi non si sente in tutto & espressamente essa T. [... 56]. Et per finir ormai questo, dico [...] CHE nel verso quando non sia bisogno d'aiutarsi d'vna sillaba, & non voler che la E, s'incorpori con la vocale, che segue appresso (che allora si scriuerà ET intera) si scriua sempre E, & non ET, per lasciar'il verso libero nella vaghezza del corso suo. Nelle prose poi si scriua sempre intera, cioè con la sua T, fuor solamente quando per leggiadria, ò per priuilegio del numero si voglia tor via con l'articolo mascolino del primo & del secondo numero, l'amico, e'l fratello, il signore, e i vassalli, che ancor senza la I, ma con l'apostrofo si scriue & pronuntia vagamente, I miei, e' vostri. ED, per ET, che alcuni pur capricciosamente han voluta intromettere, non si riceua in modo alcuno, & non si vada in tante strane innouationi ogni giorno senza proposito, che non hauerebbon mai fine, & solamente si potria vsar quando le segue altra Et appresso per fuggir la replica, Bella ED Eterna." Vgl. damit *Vocabolario della Crusca 1623*, 304: „E. Copula. Latin et, atque, ac. [...] Talora, quando vogliam fuggir lo'ncontro delle vocali, gli aggiugniamo il D, ne mai il T, alla latina."

K V 1 Ohne Instrumente operierende Chirurgie. S. *Chocolata* (s. K II 3), Titel VI „undiquaque concinnatum atque locupletatum". Vgl. De Angelis, 152 (Lancisiana LXXIV – 2-10 u. 2-11 Severini M. A., Chirurgia inermis P. I u. II, Cart. Sec. XVII – C. 276 u. C. 286).

2 S. *Chocolata* (s. K II 3), Titel VIII. Vgl. De Angelis, 152 (Lancisiana LXXIV – 2-17 Severini M. A., Authentica Chirurgia Cart. Sec. XVII – C. 269).

3 S. K II 12 u. *Chocolata* (s. K II 3), Titel IX.

4 *Chocolata* (s. K II 3), Titel XIII. „Consultationum Medicarum centuria." Vgl. De Angelis, 158 (Lancisiana LXXV – 3-35 Severini M. A., Consultationes Medico–Chirurgica Cart. Sec. XVII – C. 565).

5 *Chocolata* (s. K II 3), Titel XV. Vgl. De Angelis, 153 (Lancisiana LXXIV – 3-4 Severini M. A., De respiratione piscium Cart. Sec. XVII – C. 321).

6 Über Blei- bzw. Silberglätte und pulverisiertes Spießglaserz als Medikament. S. *Chocolata* (s. K II 3), Titel XX.

7 *Chocolata* (s. K II 3), Titel XXI.

8 Die mit diesem Titel beginnende Seite (Bl. 325r) mit den restlichen Schriften Nr. 30–42, die unter der Überschrift „Philosophica" stehen, ist im Falz so tief eingebunden, daß mögliche Markierungen des Fürsten nicht erkennbar sind. Wir zitieren daher alle Titel. Zum ersten Titel s. *Chocolata* (s. K II 3), Titel XXXIII.

9 *Chocolata* (s. K II 3), Titel XXVIII. Begriff der aristotelischen Meteorologie bzw. sublunaren Physik. S. z.B. Augustino Nifo: AVGVSTINI NIPHI MEDICES PHILOSOPHI SVESSANI. IN LIBRIS ARISTOTELIS METEOROLOGICIS COMMENTARIA. Eiusdem generalia Commentaria in Libro de Mistis, qui a ueteribus Quartus Meteororum Liber inscribitur. Et a iunioribus Meteorologicon dicitur. (Venetiis: Hieronymus Schottus 1551).

10 *Chocolata* (s. K II 3), Titel XI. („ventis & animantibus apparet.").
11 *Chocolata* (s. K II 3), Titel XXX. („Philologicus").
12 *Chocolata* (s. K II 3), Titel XXXI. Vgl. De Angelis, 153 (Lancisiana LXXIV – 3-16 Severini M. A., Epistolae amoebaeae, et varia Miscellanea Cart. Sec. XVII – C. 338); ebd. (Lancisiana LXXIV – 3-17 Severini M. A., Quaestiones et Epistolae Medicae (figure) Cart. Sec. XVII – C. 646). Vgl. De Angelis, 152 (Lancisiana LXXIV – 2-8 Severini M. A., Lettere italiane Cart. Sec. XVII C. 245).
13 *Chocolata* (s. K II 3), Titel XXXIV. Vgl. De Angelis, 152 (Lancisiana LXXIV – 2-5 Severini M. A., Iuvenilia Carmina Cart. Sec. XVII C. –171).
14 *Chocolata* (s. K II 3), Titel XXIX. Vgl. De Angelis, 154 (Lancisiana LXXIV – 3-22 Severini M. A. Graecismus derivatus Cart. Sec. XVII – C. 114).
15 *Chocolata* (s. K II 3), S. 73 „Vernaculo sermone."
16 S. oben K II 8. Philipp Hainhofer versuchte 1644 das Buch für Hz. August d. J. v. Braunschweig-Wofenbüttel (FG 227), einen bekannten Schachschriftsteller, durch seinen Vetter in röm. Buchläden zu beschaffen. Da das nicht gelang, scheint sich der Vetter darauf nach Neapel gewandt zu haben. *Gobiet*, Nr. 1403.
17 *Chocolata* (s. K II 3), Titel XXXVII. „Topica di Giulio Camillo abbreviata." Es handelt sich um die Bearbeitung der (geplanten) Enzyklopädie des Humanisten Giulio Camillo (um 1480–1544), der in der Art eines Anatomen am menschlichen Körper alle Wissenschaften, Künste und Sprachen wie auch die Klassiker (einschließlich Petrarcas) darstellen wollte. Die Zusammensetzung seiner Topica bzw. des Kosmos zeigte er wiederum mittels des hölzernen Modells eines „teatro" und bezeichnete sie anhand einer figurativen Mnemotechnik. S. Giulio Camillo: L'Idea Del Theatro (Fiorenza: Torrentino 1550). HAB: QuN 139.2 (1). Zwei Titel Camillos beziehen sich ausdrücklich auf die *Topica*: IL SECONDO TOMO DELL'OPERE DI M. GIULIO CAMILLODELMINIO, CIOÈ, La Topica, overo dell'Elocutione (1560), SuStB Augsburg, und der Teildruck *Topica delle figurate locuzioni* (Venezia: Rampazetto 1560). *DBI* VII (1974), 218–230; Neuausgabe einschlägiger Texte Camillos in: Trattati di poetica e retorica del Cinquecento. A cura di Bernard Weinberg. Roma 1970, v. I; Giulio Camillo Delminio: L'idea del teatro e altri scritti di retorica. (Torino) 1990; Lina Bolzoni: Il teatro della memoria. Studi su Giulio Camillo. Padova 1984; Francesco Scaramuzza: Giulio Camillo Delminio. Un'avventura intellettuale nel '500 europeo. Udine (2004); Kate Robinson: A search for the source of the whirlpool of artifice. The cosmology of Giulio Camillo. Edinburgh 2006; Frances Amalia Yates: The Art of memory. London, Henley 1966, v. a. Kap. 6 u. 7: „Renaissance Memory: The Memory Theatre of Giulio Camillo" (S. 129–159) u. „Camillo's Theatre and the Venetian Renaissance" (160–172). Eine dt. Übersetzung des Buches erschien als „Gedächtnis und Erinnern" in 2. Aufl. in Weinheim 1991.
18 *Chocolata* (s. K II 3), Titel XXXIX. „Declamationi contra megliori Antichi, Phil. Oratori & Mosaici." Im benutzten Exemplar HAB: Me 108a ist „Mosaici" handschriftlich ersetzt durch „altri Saui."
19 S. K IV.
20 S. K IV 3.

450818   n. St.

Johann Michael Moscherosch an Georg Philipp Harsdörffer

Beantwortet in 450901. — Da Johann Michael Moscherosch (FG 436. 1645) sich am Pariser Hof in vornehmer französ. Gesellschaft aufhält, glaubt er, aus Höflichkeit sich auch der freimütigen und ungezwungenen frz. Sprache so bedienen zu sollen wie des besten Fleisches auf der Tafel. Denn die deutsche Sprache gilt den Deutschen wie gewöhnliches Brot, Latein wie Konfekt. Die anderen Sprachen schmeckten ihm zu salzig, wenngleich er sich auch von diesen gelegentlich einen Happen gönne, ohne Aufhebens davon zu machen. — Vor acht Tagen entstand an einer erlesenen Tafel eine nicht minder erlesene Konversation. Einer der Gäste vertrat energisch die Auffassung, daß Poeten für die Staatsgeschäfte und Auftritte in Gesellschaft ungeeignet seien. Die Debatte ging eine Weile hin und her, jedoch mochten nur zwei Teilnehmer, Gäste von Stand und Ansehen, der These widersprechen. Vielleicht hätten sich beide am Schluß sogar auch der Gegenmeinung angeschlossen. Bei den beiden Gegnern handelte es sich um den Residenten des englischen Parlaments (René Augier) und um (Johann Friedrich v.) Pawel(-Rammingen), einen Mann von großen Eigenschaften. Der wollte Moscherosch gern in die Kontroverse hineinziehen und ihm ein Lobeswort über Poesie und Poeten entlocken, doch hielt sich Moscherosch wegen der ihm obliegenden Geschäfte zurück und überließ sich der Steuerung Tilmanns v. Polhelm, des um das Wohl der Deutschen verdienten Residenten der Landgräfin (Amalia Elisabeth) v. Hessen(-Kassel). Freilich hätte er, Moscherosch, kraft seiner Vernunft die Vorteile der Autorität und des Geschicks überwinden können. Er habe später immer wieder ohne Erfolg über die unsinnige Behauptung nachgedacht, Poeten seien für Staat und Gesellschaft ungeeignet. Er zähle sich auch nicht zur illustren Schar der Poeten, deren hohe Fähigkeiten er seinem Geist nicht zumesse. Dafür brauche es mehr Lebhaftigkeit, Freizügigkeit, Reife, dichterische Gewandtheit, geistigen Schliff und auch Raffinesse. Moscheroschs Geist strebe eher nach Ernstem, Komprimiertem und möglichst Einfachem, er liebe über alles die Kürze, getreu dem Motto seines Lehrmeisters (Scaliger): „Mihi enim vehementer displicet loquacitas". Daher gefallen ihm die Epigramme seiner Freunde und scharfsinnige Entgegnungen großer Geister. Aus ellenlangen Verskolonnen ohne Maß und Pointe mache er sich hingegen nichts, verabscheue sie fast wie das Heilmittel Antimon, an dem er vor sieben Jahren beinahe gestorben wäre. Ihm gefielen kleine Verrücktheiten, er hasse langatmiges Gewäsch. Um auf jene übertriebene Vorstellung vom Dichter zurückzukommen: er kann sich darin nicht wiederfinden, nicht einmal als Idee kann er sie akzeptieren. Denn nichts wäre lächerlicher als ein äffischer Poet, der den lieben langen Tag nichts tue als wachen, träumen, trinken, essen, klagen und Verse herunterbeten. Die Natur gibt vor der Kunst den Ausschlag. Und poetisches Naturell ist bei Menschen aller Stände anzutreffen — wie kann man dann eine so widersinnige These vertreten? Die größten Staatsmänner und Monarchen waren oft von Natur aus größte Poeten. Wären Montaigne, dieser Sokrates der Franzosen, wären (Guillaume) du Vair, (Charles) Pascal, (Étienne) Pasquier und andere noch am Leben, sie würden solcher Unsinnigkeit entgegentreten. Wie würde Kardinal Richelieu, der klügste Staatsmann unter der Sonne, der falschen Auffassung begegnen? Hat er nicht Frankreich und fast der ganzen Welt zur Zufriedenheit seines Königs das Gesetz vorgeschrieben und dennoch die besten Gedichte in Frankreich geschrieben, woran selbst Vergil, Ovid und andere nicht zweifeln würden. Oder Grotius, das Wunder der Natur und Orakel der gesamten Gelehrsamkeit: wir finden bei ihm genau so viele Lehrsätze des Staatswesens wie beim größten Monarchen des Universums, und wer könne bezweifeln, in ihm den erlauchtesten Poeten unter allen Sterblichen zu erkennen? Karl der Große, die Sinnsprüche Ks. Karls V. oder Kg. Heinrichs d. Gr. von Frankreich — ihr exzellenter poetischer Geist hinderte sie nicht, in der Regierung ihrer Staaten und Reiche alle Könige und Kaiser zu übertreffen! Selbst mancher Bauer besiegt durch Schlagfertigkeit manchen Doktor, der nichts vollbringt als jeden Tag sich mit Gedichten abzugeben. Was jener von Natur aus besitzt, vermag dieser durch Kunst und Fleiß nicht zu erlangen. Daß Herr Klaus (Nikolaus v. der Flüe) für den Zustand seines Hauses oder seiner Scheune zu sorgen wußte, hat seinen Witz nicht beeinträchtigt. So kann die Kunst nicht völlig erreichen, was die Natur vermag. Ein von Natur zur Poesie, zu Gedanken, Erfindungen und geistigen Unternehmungen Befähigter kann jede Aufgabe meistern, sei es im Staat oder sonstwo. Wenn Kritiker überhaupt in ihrem Kopfe und in ihrem Tun Leben und Form verspüren, sollten sie neben Gott der Poesie dafür danken, auch wenn sie wegen mangelnder Geschicklichkeit und ohne menschliche Empfindung nicht dichten können. Der berufsmäßige Reimeschmied braucht Jahre dazu, an Versen zu feilen, der Staatsmann eine Stunde. Jenem ist die Poesie Lebenszweck, diesem Genuß, dem Ungebildeten Verdruß. Staatsgeschäfte zu führen und Poet zu sein, und als Poet staatsmännische Aufgaben zu erfüllen, beides geht durchaus zusammen! Schon Boethius dichtete über die hoffnungslosen Dichterlinge. — Harsdörffer möge Moscheroschs Abschweifung verzeihen. Was Nachrichten aus Paris anbetrifft, will Moscherosch sie alle den Zeitungsschreibern überlassen. Doch glücklicher als jenen Spanier, der nach Rom reiste und doch nicht Livius sprach, schätze er sich, denn er ist nach Paris gekommen und hat diese Stadt gesehen, diese Welt, dieses Universum, dieses Paradies, das seinesgleichen nicht im übrigen Europa findet. Seit seinen zwei früheren Besuchen hat sich Paris zu ganzer Größe, Schönheit, Pracht und Majestät entwickelt. Zudem hat Moscherosch den allerchristlichsten König Ludwig XIV. gesehen, der Frankreich die Hoffnung verleiht, zur vortrefflichsten Monarchie der Welt vor der Ankunft des Reiches Gottes zu werden. — Für Mängel in seinem Französisch bittet er um Nachsicht. — *Nachschrift:* Ein großmäuliger Schwätzer nenne Moscherosch einen „Mann schöner Projekte" wegen eines Gedichts, das Moscherosch zu Ehren der Republik Venedig für Harsdörffer geschrieben hatte. Der Schwätzer rede in einer gezwungenen Sprache, ganz im Gegensatz zur Rundheit, Natürlichkeit Moscheroschs, dessen Offenheit sich nicht mit Schmeichelei vertrage und ihn nicht befähige, sich den Lebensunterhalt mit Reimen zu verdienen. Er täte seinen Vorgesetzten ein Unrecht an, wenn er keine ehrenvollere Absicht verfolgte. Angesichts der Gefährdung der ganzen Christenheit durch eine fatale Nachlässigkeit, die dem Feind alle Handlungsspielräume läßt, setze er, Moscherosch, sich für die gemeinsame Sache ein und preise die erhabene Republik Venedig und verachte jeden Nachzügler, welcher den Ruin seiner Nachkommen befördert, indem er die Geschäfte und das Bedürfnis seines Nachbarn vernachlässigt, sei es wegen seiner Ehre, aus Geringschätzung, Verachtung oder aus Feigheit. Eine bedenkenswertere Maxime sollte der Christ befolgen, will er sich und die Seinen aus den Händen des Tyrannen retten: Es trifft Dich selbst, wenn das Haus Deines Nachbarn brennt!

Q Centuria | Epigrammatum | IOHANNIS-MICHAELIS | MOSCHEROSCH | Germani. | [Linie] | *Levant & Carmina curas.* | Olymp. Nomes. Eclog. 4. | [Signet: PMS] | ARGENTINÆ | *Typis & Sumptibus* | JOH. PHILIPPI MüLBII | ET JOSIÆ STÆDELII. | [Linie] | M. DC. XXXXVIIII, Bl. C 4r – [C 8]r. HAB: 230.8 Poet. (auch dig.). — BN: *Estermann,* 839 Nr. 1; *Bürger,* 1025 Nr. 12.
Die seltene Erstausgabe der Centuria prima der *Epigrammatum* (Straßburg 1630, ohne vorliegenden Brief) wurde von Walter Ernst Schäfer in den Blättern der Gesellschaft für Buchkultur und Geschichte 5 (Rudolstadt 2001), 75–118, als Faksimile veröffentlicht.

450818 n. St. Johann Michael Moscherosch

Nicht eingesehen werden konnte die vermutliche Titelauflage: Centuria II. | Epigrammatum | IOHANNIS-MICHAELIS | MOSCHEROSCH | Germani. | [Linie] | Levant & Carmina curas. | Olymp. Nomes. Eclog. 4. | [Signet] | ARGENTINÆ | *Typis & Sumptibus* | JOH. PHILIPPI MÜLBII | ET JOSIÆ STÆDELII. | [Linie] | M. DC. XXXXVIIII. UB Freiburg; s. *Dünnhaupt: Handbuch*, 2861.
Der gleiche Brief in: Centuria II. | Epigrammatum | JOHANNIS-MICHAELIS | MOSCHEROSCH. | *Levant & Carmina curas.* | Olymp. Nomes. Eclog. 4. | [Signet: SR] | FRANCOFVRTI, | Sumptibus SEBASTIANI ROHNERI, | Typis DANIELIS FIEVETI. | [Linie] | M. DC. LXV, S. 102–110. *Faber du Faur*, Nr. 436 (Mikrofilm). HAB: MF 1:92, Reel 92, Nr. 436. — Zit. als *1665*. Vgl. dazu *Kühlmann: Moscheroschs Korrespondenz*, 268.
Übers. aus dem Frz. in *Kühlmann/ Schäfer: Oberrhein*, 118–122; diese Übers. auszugsweise auch in *Schäfer: Moscherosch und Harsdörffer*, 157–162. — BN: *Estermann*, 839 Nr. 1; *Bürger*, 1024 Nr. 16 u. 1025 Nr. 12; *Kühlmann: Korrespondenz Moscheroschs*, 268 Nr. 12.

A   A Monsieur Monsieur de Harsdorff, Assesseur au Dicastere de la Republique de Nuremberg. &c.

Monsieur,

EStant icy en Cour[1] parmy tant d'honorables compagnies des François, ie croyrois les desobliger, si ie ne me servois aussy de leur franchise naturelle: ie veux dire, de la liberté[a] & franchise de leur langue: delaquelle la pluspart ie me traitte comme dela meilleure viande de ma table: Car pour l'Allemande, vous sçauez qu'elle nous sert de pain d'ordinaire: Et la Latine de confitures: Pour d'autres langues, elles sont trop salees á mon goust: combien que ie ne laisse pas á en aualler par fois quelque bon morceau, mais c'est sans faire grand bruit, & á la derobée. Nous fismes, arriuans en ceste ville, permettez moy de vous faire ce conpte, collation belle & bonne il y a huict iours. Le Discours n'estoit moins poly que la table paree de toutte sorte de viandes assaisonnees. Il y en auoit tel en la compagnie, qui entre propositions de consequence vouloit maintenir, sans aucune limitation dea, que les Poetes n'estoient pas propres aux affaires d'Estat & du Monde. Pourquoy? Ie vous en lais[se][b] deuiner là dessus. La these fut battue & de-[C 4v]battue quelque temps: il n'y en auoiet pourtant d'antagonistes que deux seulement: gens de condition & d'estime, qui ála fin ie ne sçay s'ils en tomberent d'accord tous deux; Moy petit homme pour de grandes parolles, ie me tenois coy là comme le souris qui sent le chat, faisant semblant n'auoir point de bec que pour manger. L'un d'eux, nommé Plau[c][2], car l'autre estoit Resident du Parlement d'Angleterre[3], homme de tres belles qualitez, m'ayant fort bien voulu tirer dans la meslee, me regardast parfois, pour á mon auis me leurrer á ceste chasse de cameleon, & pour me faire dire quelque bon mot á la louange des Poetes & dela Poesie; mais il n'y arriua point; Car ie faisois l'endormy de ce costé là; & laissois aller ma cabane où le gouuernail de mon Patron, (ce fut c'est Excellent homme, le Resident de Madame la Landgraue de Hesse, Polhelm[4], qui faisoit plus pour le bien de nostre nation que tout autre) me guidoit: sçauoir sur ce qui m'estoit plus necessaire pour les affaires dont ie me trouuois chargé par de plus grands que moy. Combien que si i'eusse voulu condescendre á ce sien desir, ie vous asseure, que bien facilement i'eusse peû obtenir par raison ce que luy peutestre eut peû emporter sur moy par authorité ou autre coup fauorable dela destinee. Qui sçayt tout, qu'il ne s'estonne point si son^d voysin ne sçayt rien. Qui veut estre ouys, qu'il parle á des gens qui sçauent escoutter. A un homme qui se veut faire voir sur les autres, il faut des voysins souples, & qui s'abbayssent quand Monsieur se leue. [C 5r] Toutefois ayant depuis songé & resongé sur le sens de ceste Proposition insensee; tant plus que ie sonde aprez la source, tant plus m'y perdie, & n'y peux trouuer que de la bouee. Aussy n'en tireray ie pas grand profit, que ie maintienne *Les Poetes sont propres aux affaires d'Estat & du Monde:* ou que ie conuienne *Les Poetes ne sont pas propres aux affaires d'Estat & du Monde.* Car á la verité ie ne m'y cognois pas, ny ne suis de ce beau nombre des Poetes: aussy ne pretend ie rien sur une qualité si haute & si releuee au dessus de la capacité de mon esprit. Et mesme ceux qui me croyront Poete, se fouruoyeront fort dans le labyrinthe de leur fantaisie. Car il me semble que pour meriter le nom du vray Poete, il faut un esprit plus gay, plus libre, plus meur, plus versifié, plus fin & rusé que le mien; qui ne s'attache qu'aux choses seurieuses, les plus pressees, les plus simples que possible. I'ayme sur tout la Briefueté, & si ie pourrois dire touttes les leçons de mon maistre en un seul mot, certes ie n'en voudrois pas employer deux. *Mihi enim vehementer displicet loquacitas.*[5] C'est ce qui me fait preferer les Epigrammes de mes amys, & les Reparties des Grands; Pour les poemes de cent lieues, sans mesure & sans poinctes, ie n'en fays point de cas, ie les abhorre plus quel'Antimoine[6], qui ne manquoit pourtant que de bien peu, á me faire mourir il y a sept ans. Ie me plais en de petites follies, ie hay les grandes, & qui surpassent l'espace d'une demye heure ou d'auantage. Et pour reuenir á ceste these si outree: á [C 5v] la maintenir il faut, si ie ne me trompe, estre bien mal auec soy mesme. Car ie ne puis m'imaginer, ny mesme dar Idee, la Definition qu'ils me voudroient presupposer du Poete. Il faut qu'elle soit bien ridicule, & tout autre que les Poetes mesmes n'ont sçeu iusques á ceste heure. Pour moy, ie n'appellerois iamais Poete celuy, qui eternellement singulier & singier en touttes ses conceptions, actions, contenances & grimaces, ne feroit autre chose que veiller-songer-boire-manger crier & prier des Vers. L'art n'y a iamais tant de pouuoir que la Nature; Et comme le naturel poetique se treuue en toutes les conditions d'hommes[7]; ie ne sçay comment l'on pourroit gloser une these si absurde pour la maintenir: veu mesme que les plus grands hommes d'Estat; les plus grands Monarques de la terre souuant ont esté les plus grands Poetes de leur naturel. Voire si cest grand personage Michel de Montaigne[8] Socrate des Gaulois, du Vair[9], Pascal[10], Pasquier[11] & autres estoient encore en vie, ils donneroient un rude choc á ceux qui se voudroient declarer pour la defence du contraire. Que leur en diroit ce semidieu de Richelieu?[12] Ce grand Cardinal. Le soleil en a il^e, durant son cours, veu icy bas^f un homme plus entendu aux affaires d'Estat que luy? N'est ce pas luy qui á donné la loy non pas seulement á la France, mais presque á toutte la terre jusques aux Indes? N'est ce pas luy, qui prudemmēt sçauoit commander & faire confus les^g plus fins & les plus rusez de toutte l'Europe: le tout neantmoins au contentement de son Roy, [C 6r] & au bien de sa Patriæ: Tellement que pour reformer l'univers, & le faire tout autre qu'il n'est, il ne seroit iamais besoing d'autre maistre que de luy seul, qui, accablé qu'il en estoit, ne laissoit pourtant d'emporter le priz du meilleur Poete que iamais la Gaule a porté, & tel, que ni Vergile ny Ovide ny tout autre en pourroient disconuenir qu'á leur grandissime honte: que l'on en demande l'Europe, elle me garandira de mon dire. Ie croy que ce grand Grotius[13], vray miracle de la Nature, & l'oracle de toutte la Doctrine, a autant de maximes d'Estat & d'aussy practicables s'il s'en veut preualoir, que le plus grand monarque de l'univers: Et qui est qui oseroit doutter qu'il ne soit le plus illustre Poete qui iamais parust en une personne de condition mortelle. Regardez s'il vous plaist un Charle Magne[14], les Apophthegmes d'un Charles Quint[15], d'un Henry le grand[16]: vous trouuerez en eux une ame toutte noble; & un esprit tout rassy, mais Poetique en excellence: lequel pourtant iamais ne les a empesché á bien gouuerner leurs Estats & Empires; au contraire les a fait surpasser le reste de tous les Empereurs & Roys de la Terre. Maint paysan pour descendre du plus haut au plus bas, est en Reparties si promt, si adroit, qu'il surpasse en beaucoup un Docteur de robbe longue, qui toutte sa vie n'a fait autre chose que lire & escrire des Poemes le beau long de l'annee: C'est que ce Paysan est de son naturel ce que l'autre s'efforce en vain par art & industrie: Et tout cela n'empesche point sire Colas[17], qu'il ne sçache tresbien [C 6v] manier l'Estat de sa maison ou de sa grange. Le Naturel va devant, & en peut bien plus; L'Art va aprez, & en peut beaucoup, non pas tant. Cela me fait dire hardiment, que comme le vray Poete est tres propre & tres necessaire au maniement des affaires d'Estat; ainsy celuy qui se mesle á ne sçauoir sa vie qu'aux vers & rymes, est hors du nombre de ceux, qui selon les maximes de mon jugement meritent le nom du vray Poete. Pour conclusion, Quiconque n'est Poete de son naturel, celuy manque de Conceptions, Inuentions & Expeditions d'esprit, & par consequent est incapable á tout ce où il doit estre employé, soit d'Estat ou autrement; Et tout ce que ces Censeurs mesmes ont de ioly & de poly dans leur teste, & en touttes leurs Expeditions, ie leur conseillerois, de n'en rendre iamais graces aprez Dieu, qu'á la seule Poesie, laquelle pourtant faute de dexterité ils ne sçauent, ny ne connoissent tant seulement faute de dexterité ils ne sçauent, ny ne connoissent tant seulement faute d'humanité, ny l'entendent. Le Poete de Profession employe des annees á rimer, l'homme d'Estat une heure: ce que sera de plus á la fois, est trop dur pour la digestion de son cerueau. tout á son temps. Estre homme d'Estat & faire le Poete, ce sont choses du tout compatibles; Estre Poete & faire l'homme d'Estat ce sont choses aucunement incompatibles: La Poesie á un homme d'Estat doit servir de confiture, á un professeur c'est sa vie, á un ignorant c'est de l'enuie.

 Eheu quam miseros tramite devio
  abducit ignorantia! [C 7r]

> Quid dignum stolidis mentibus imprecer?
> Opes, honores ambiant:
> Et cum falsa graui mole parauerint,
> Tum vera cognoscent bona. *Boeth. l. 3. metr. 8.*[18]

Mais, où vay-ie? passer aux Antipodes? ie m'esgare bien loing du chemin de vous trouuer, & á vous donner le contentement qu'auriez esperé peut estre de ma plume. Pardonnez moy ie vous prie, ceste mienne escapade longue & espineuse: Ie me suis mespris en marchant ainsy pensiv dans un pays estranger. Ie reuiens á vous, ou pour mieux dire á moy mesme, laissant les extrauagances, dans lesquelles une cause non pas mienne m'a poussé, dont les beaux effects de vostre patience & de vostre affection tout ensemble m'en promettent des Indulgences plenieres. Pour nouuelles, il y en a tant, que le choix me rend difficile l'election que ie desire en faire: ie les laisse touttes aux gazettiers; & vous dis ce qui vaut plus que le royaume de Chine: C'est que si iamais c'est Espagnol, qui du cabo Finisterræ[19] iadis est allé droit á Rome, pour nul autre subiect que d'y voir ce grand Historien Tite Live[20], ainsy qu'il fit, sans toute fois luy auoir parlé tant seulement, s'a peu vanter du contentement qu'il en auoit receu; Ie peux dire á son esgard, que ie me tiens de beaucoup plus hereux, qui aprez auoir mesuré deux cent lieues par Lyon, ay eu ceste felicité, de voir ceste ville de Paris, ce monde, cest univers, ce Paradis terrestre, où tout vient, où tout va, où tout est: Et ce que ny l'Allemagne, ny l'Espa-[C 7v]gne, ny l'Italie, ny l'Angleterre, ny les autres Royaumes pourront fournir ny faire voir, Paris seul vous le presentera. Et combien que cy deuant, i'y ay demeuré par deux diverses fois, si est ce qu'au regard de ce qu'elle á esté en ce temps là, elle est maintenant deuenue d'une partie un tout, un tout autre monde, aussy grande, aussy belle, aussy riche, aussy magnifique, aussy maiestueuse qu'elle á esté au parauant. Mais sur tout, ie me dois estimer heureux d'y auoir veu le Roy Louys XIIII.[21] Ce Roy tres Chrestien, ce grand Roy, ce Roy sans pareil en victoires: qui fait esperer á son peuple un Monde hors de son monde, & á son Royaume la Monarchie la plus accomplie & parfaitte que l'on sçauroit voir auant le Iugement du Monarque du Ciel & de la Terre. Monsieur en vous escriuant cecy, ie croy vous auoir tout dit, puis que ie vous ay dit ce sur quoy repose la felicité de toutte la France. Que si en des endroits ie n'ay[h] pas bien obserué les loix & proprietez du langage, vous me feréz encore pardon s'il vous plaist, qui comme Allemand de Nation, pour ne desobliger les honnestes compagnies françoises, ay bien voulu en leur complaisant m'exposer á la risee du Monde: Contre la rigeur dela quelle me seruira[i] Vostre belle affection, m'honnorant du tiltre

Monsieur

de vostre treshumble & tres obligé Seruiteur

Mouscheroche

de Paris ce 18. d'Aougst. 1645.

[C 8r] P. D.
Monsieur. Aprez auoir finy la precedente[22], *Voycy un bourdeur*[j] *á gros bec, qui, m'appellant homme de belles entreprinses, pour le poeme que te fis a'l'honneur de ceste Augustißime Republique de Venize*[23], *en dressa un verbal quarré, & tout contraire á la rondeur de mon genie, lequel est trop ouuert pour estre flatteur, & trop peu capable á me gaigner la vie en faisant de rimes. Ie ferois certes tort á mes Superieurs, si ie n'auois intention plus noble. Bien est il, que, considerant le danger où toutte la Chrestienté se va ietter par une non-chalance fatale, en laissant á cest grand ennemy le loisir & l'occasion á tout faire, ie prens interest á la cause commune, & me sens obligé á haultement loue[r] ceste Augustißime Republique, & á detester tout tard venant, qui, pour faciliter la ruine des ses propres enfans, neglige, soit par Reputation ou par mespris, ou par desdaing, ou par lascheté, les affaires & la neceßité de son Voysin, n'aduise point mon Chrestien, á une maxime plus considerable pour te sauuer & les tiens hors des mains du Tyran, que ceste-cy.*

Tunc tua res agitur paries cum proximus ardet.[24]

Adieu.

I

Moscheroschs Epigramme zum Lobe Venedigs

Q Centuria Epigrammatum IOHANNIS-MICHAELIS MOSCHEROSCH Germani ... ARGENTINÆ ... M. DC. XXXXVIIII (s. o. Q), S. 13 f. (Nr. 14 u. 15). HAB: 230.8 Poet. — Auch in der oben (s. Q) zit. Ausg. von 1665: Centuria II, S. 72 f. (Nr. 14 u. 15).

14.   Inscriptio
             Serenissimæ Reipublicæ
                     Venetum
                      dicata.

        Venetiæ.ἀνάγρ[a] Te ne viæ?
TE ne viæ Venetum suspensum pectore reddunt?
        Sunt Ratio Pontes, sunt pia Iura Viæ.
    Aquis regnandi natum est mirabile Nomen,
        Numen in invictis Hos comitetur Aquis!

15.   Protestatio
          Ad Christianæ Religionis Principes.
                     cum voto
            Pro Serenissima Republica Venetum.
                        S.

Illustrissimis atque Excellentissimis
Reipublicæ Legatis.

PRo causa Christi Venetum Respublica bello
Impetitur. Christi cætera Regna tacent? [14]
Vos! quibus Europæ commisit Regna Supremus.
Ite simul! Christi vos quoque causa vocat.
Quid vos, quid Fratrum juuat accelerare ruinam
Funeribus? fratres mittite! Turca venit!
Turca venit! fratres servate! Arma! imminet! Arma!
Arma! Arma! Ah fratres mittite! Creta perit.
Creta perit? pereunt tua propugnacula dulcis
Patria, Et Europæ cætera Regna patent.
O vos! ite simul Veneto cum Principe! munus
Qui negat hoc, Christum per sua membra necat.
At Tu, sacra Dei Respublica, vince Tyrannum!
Digna es ut Europæ cætera Regna regas.

T a *Aus* liberté — **b** *Von uns gebessert aus* en lais- | deviner *1665* en laisse deviner — **c** *1665* Pavvl — **d** *1665* sont — **e** *1665* ail *(d. i. aile, Schwinge, Flügel)* — **f** *1665* cas — **g** *les plus fins & fehlt in 1665*. — **h** *Druckfehler* n'nay — **i** *1665* servitra — **j** *1665* bourder

T I a *Abkürzung für* ἀνάγραμμα *o. Ä.*

K Zur Datierung: Obgleich wir in der Regel nach dem alten Stil unserer allermeisten Quellen datieren, wenn der neue nicht ausdrücklich angegeben wird, fragt es sich, ob Johann Michael Moscherosch (FG 436) in Paris nicht dem gregorian. Kalender gefolgt ist. Der Brief aus Paris könnte eher drei als (fast) zwei Wochen aus Paris nach Nürnberg gebraucht haben. Die Antwort Georg Philipp Harsdörffers (FG 368) 450901 aus Nürnberg dürfte im alten Stil datiert sein. Wir ziehen den 18.8.1645 auch deshalb gegenüber dem 8.8.1645 alten Stils vor, weil dieses Schreiben in der Forschung gewöhnlich unter dem 18. August zitiert wird.

1 Am 15. März 1645 zum „Fiskal" oder „Frevelvogt", d.h. Sekretär des „Policey-Gerichts" der Freien Reichsstadt Straßburg berufen, reiste Moscherosch im August im Auftrag der Stadtoberen nach Paris. (Einen zweiten Auftrag hatte ihm die verwitwete Hzn. Anna Sabina v. Württemberg-Weiltingen [TG 36] erteilt.) Die Stadt hatte Moscherosch an den kgl. Hof geschickt, um an der Seite der bereits dort weilenden Straßburger Abgesandten, des Residenten Tilmann v. Polhem (s. Anm. 4) u. des Sekretärs Johann Beck (†1695), Beschwerden über militär. Übergriffe vorzubringen u. im Vorfeld der Friedensverhandlungen in Münster u. Osnabrück die militär. u. polit. Absichten der Regierung unter Kd. Mazarin zu erkunden. Das vorwiegend ev. Straßburg wollte besonders die Absichten seines Bischofs am kgl. Hof erkunden. S. Kreditiv Straßburgs für Moscherosch an Polhem d.d. 9.7.1645, in: Johannes Beinert: Moscherosch im Dienst der Stadt Straßburg. In: Jahrb. f. Geschichte, Sprache u. Literatur Elsaß-Lothringens XXIII (1907), 138–146, hier S. 139f. Der im Mai 1643 als König inthronisierte Ludwig XIV. war, als Moscherosch über Lyon anreisend wohl Anfang August 1645 in Paris eintraf, erst 6 Jahre alt. In

450818 n. St. Johann Michael Moscherosch

Paris traf er außer mit Polhelm auch mit Philipp v. Zesen (FG 521. 1648) zusammen u. spielte ansonsten ein von allen Beteiligten einschließlich Polhelm rasch durchschautes Doppelspiel seiner beiden Aufträge, das für ihn heikle Züge (Verdacht der Untreue) annahm u. das Verhältnis zu Polhelm eintrüben sollte. Vgl. *Kühlmann/ Schäfer: Oberrhein*, 117f. u. 210; *Schäfer: Moscherosch und Harsdörffer*, 137 u. 156; *Schäfer: Moscherosch*, 137ff.; Kenneth Graham Knight: Johann Michael Moscherosch. Satiriker und Moralist des 17. Jahrhunderts. Stuttgart 2000, 24f. Eine genaue Schilderung der Parisreise Moscheroschs in Johannes Beinert, a. a. O.; Walter Ernst Schäfer: Moral und Satire. Konturen oberrheinischer Literatur des 17. Jahrhunderts. Tübingen 1992, 38–49. — Harsdörffer machte F. Ludwig in 451101 Mitteilung von Moscheroschs Reise u. dessen Reaktion auf die Aufnahme in die FG. Dazu F. Ludwigs Antwort 451209. Vgl. zur Aufnahme Moscheroschs in die FG auch 450500 K 1. — Hieronymus Imhof (1606–1668), nürnberg. Patrizier, Reisender, braunschweig. Hofrat, berichtete in einem undat. Brief wohl aus dem Jahre 1649 an Hz. August d.J. v. Braunschweig-Wolfenbüttel (FG 227), er habe ein Schreiben Harsdörffers über Moscherosch erhalten. Moscherosch gelte als arm, erwarte Geld für die Hz. August gesandten Epigramme. Nun finden sich in der *Epigrammata*-Sammlung von 1643 keine Epigramme auf Hz. August. Vgl. Epigrammatum | IOH: MICHAELIS | MOSCHEROSCH, | Germani. | Centuria prima. | [Linie] | [Griech. Zitat aus „Phocylid. v. 67. & 85."] | [Druckersignet J. P. Mülbe] | ARGENTINÆ | Iamnunc | Repetita | Typis & Sumptibus | IOH. PHILIP. MÜLBII. | M DC XXXXIII. HAB: 165. 11 Eth. (1). Die Ausgabe von 1649 (s.o., Q) — lt. *Dünnhaupt: Handbuch*, 2861f. ist zw. 1643 u. 1649 keine weitere *Epigrammata*-Ausgabe bekannt — ist dann sogar dem Herzog gewidmet (s. K I) unter Nennung seines Sohnes Anton Ulrich (FG 716. 1659), s. Bl. A3r–[A6]v, Epigramme Nr. 3, 5, 7, 9, 97 auf ihn u. seine Söhne (S. 19, 20, 21f., 47f.) Imhof schreibt: „[...] Mit dem letzten boten von Nürnberg bekam ich schreiben von Mons. Harsdörff. in welchen er mir zweyerley gedenckete. 1. eines so in Strasburg sich aufhelt **Michael Moscheroschius genandt**. und wohnhafft sein soll in dem haus, so e. F. Gnd. wegen der tractaten zu Münster eigen worden ist, soll einige Epigrammata vor disem F. E. F. gdn. dedicirt haben, vnd deßwegen einige liberalitet erwarten, es soll bey ihme sein res angusta domi, vnd gross armuth [...]." HAB: Cod. Guelf. 376 Nov., 186. (Die Rede ist vom Henneberger Hof. Moscherosch ersuchte lange in Wolfenbüttel um eine Verringerung der Miete.) — In der „Teutschen Zugabe" in der 2. Ausg. seiner *Gesichte* schreibt Moscherosch über Harsdörffer: „Es ist zeit/ vnd hohe zeit/ daß die zween fürtreffliche Trewe **Patrioten**: der Aedele Hochverständige Höfflichste Georg-Philips Harßdörffer von Nürnberg: Der Hochgelehrte Fleißeyffrichste Sinnreichste **Iustus-Georgius** Schottel von Einbeck/ herfür getretten/ vnd die vnartige Landsleut Jhres Ampts vnd natürlicher schuldgebühr gegen das Vatterland erinnert. warhafftig/ ohn Jhren Trewen Beystand wär ein grosser theil/ vnd der Haupstücke [sic] vnserer Teutschen Helden Sprach eines/ das beste/ zurück geblieben. Gott wolle jhre Arbeit dem lieben Vatterland zum besten segnen/ und Sie zu mehrerem behertzt machen." *VISIONES* DE DON QUEVEDO. Wunderliche vnd Warhafftige Gesichte Philanders von Sittewald. ... Zum andern mahl auffgelegt. von Philander selbsten/ vbersehen/ vermehret vnd gebessert (Straßburg 1642: Johann Philipp Mülbe), Zugabe S. 546–552, Zitat 551. HAB: 403.38 Quod. Die „Teütsche Zugab" auch in der von Moscherosch selbst besorgten u. illustrierten Ausgabe: Wunderliche und warhafftige Gesichte Philanders von Sittewald ... Hans Michael Moscherosch von Wilstädt ... Erster Theil. Von Jhme zum letztern mahl auffgelegt/ vermehret/ gebessert (Straßburg 1650: Johann Philipp Mülbe), S. 687–701, Zitat 699. HAB: Lo 5511. Moscherosch war 1642 bereits die Mitgliedschaft der beiden in der FG u. das Sprach-Engagement F. Ludwigs bekannt. Vgl. *Schäfer: Moscherosch und Harsdörffer*, 148ff., zu ihren gewechselten Briefen

450818 (dieses Dokument) u. 450901 s. S. 157 ff. Der Briefwechsel zw. Harsdörffer u. Moscherosch ist ansonsten verschollen.

2 Vermutlich Johann Friedrich Pawel v. Rammingen (Remmingen) (1608–1673, blieb unvermählt), manchmal auch nur mit dem Rufnamen Friedrich verzeichnet, aus der alten Braunschweiger Patrizierfamilie der Paul/ Pawel, die sich im 16. Jh. in einen Braunschweiger u. Halberstädter Ast verzweigte, welch letzterem Johann Friedrich entstammte. Um 1600 hatte sich sein reformierter Vater Carl (1568–1626) durch Heirat mit dem Geschlecht der württemberg. Adelsfamilie von Rammingen versippt. Johann Friedrich begegnet 1644/ 45 als kurpfälz. Geheimrat u. Resident in Paris u. ist dort 1656 auch als kurbrandenburg. Gesandter nachgewiesen. Er war ein gern gesehener Gast im Hause des schwed. Residenten in Paris, Hugo Grotius, an der Rue des Saints-Pères, der ihn bei der Wahrung der kurpfälz. Interessen unterstützte, während sich die franz. Regierung wahrnehmbar zurückhielt. Johann Friedrichs Bruder Carl Friedrich v. Pawel (1621–1693. FG 461. 1646) stand 1646 wohl schon ebenfalls in Diensten der Kurpfalz, 1676–80 dann in ksl. Dienst, dürfte hier aber ebenso wie sein Bruder Georg Friedrich (ca. 1610–1675/1680. FG 477. 1647; Hofmeister bei Pgf. Johann v. Zweibrücken) kaum in Frage kommen. Erst recht scheidet Andreas II. Pawel v. Rammingen (1574–1654. FG 625. 1654; aus dem Braunschweiger Zweig der Familie) aus. Vgl. *Acta Pacis Westphalicae* II B, Bd. 1, S. 557, 583, 592 u. 614; Otto Böcher: Die Pawels, eine Braunschweiger Patrizierfamilie von den Anfängen bis zur Gegenwart. In: Braunschweigisches Jahrbuch 62 (1981), 21–39, hier bes. 26–28, 33 u. 39; *Conermann III*, 557 u. 585 f.; *Grotius: Briefwisseling* XVI, S. XV, 5, 31, 57, 96, 117, 193, 224, 489, 490, 655, 656 u. ö.; *Kneschke* VII, 74 ff.; *Opitz: BW* II, S. 813 Anm. 3; Rudolf v. Pawel: Stammtafeln des aus Niedersachsen stammenden uradeligen und lehnssässigen Geschlechts der Pawel (Pawel-Rammingen). In: Familiengeschichtliche Blätter Bd. 2 (1906/07), 123 u. Tafel I, 152 f. (Tafel II) u. Bd. 3 (1908/09), 16 f. (Tafel IV); *Schäfer: Moscherosch und Harsdörffer*, S. 161 Anm. 55; Schäfer: Moral und Satire (s. Anm. 1), 45 f.; Urkunden und Actenstücke zur Geschichte des Kurfürsten Friedrich Wilhelm von Brandenburg. Politische Verhandlungen, Bd. 9. Hg. Reinhold Brode. Berlin 1890, 314.

3 René Augier (vor 1600 – 1658/59), franz. Hugenotte aus der Dauphiné. Seine diplomat. Karriere begann 1619 mit der Anstellung eines „Secretary for the French Tongue" unter dem engl. Gesandten in Frankreich, Sir Edward Herbert. In dieser Stellung verblieb er unter wechselnden ordentlichen u. außerordentlichen engl. Gesandten bis zum Ende der 20er Jahre. 1627 bis 1629 verbrachte er in England, 1628 begegnet sein Name in Irland, „when René Augier was made a denizen" (Lee, s. u., 105). Am 15.5.1629 kehrte er nach Frankreich zurück, im Februar 1630 wurde er der offizielle Agent Kg. Karls I. Kurz darauf kehrte er in seine Sekretärs-Funktion zurück. Aufgrund der Politik des seit 1635 amtierenden Gesandten John Viscount Scudamore, der der spanienfreundlichen Partei am Stuart-Hof angehörte, kam es bald zu Spannungen zwischen diesem u. Augier. Am 29.4.1640 entließ ihn Kg. Karl I. aus seinen Diensten. Zwischen Ende 1640 u. 1644 verliert sich seine Spur. Im Dezember 1644 ist er in Paris zurück, nun als akkreditierter Agent des engl. Parlaments, als welcher er aber erst 1647 von der franz. Regierung förmlich anerkannt wurde. Zur gleichen Zeit wirkte Richard Browne als offizieller Agent des Königs in Paris. 1650 gab das Parlament seine Hoffnung auf, die franz. Regierung für sich zu gewinnen u. zog Augier im März ab. Seine finanziellen Obligationen gegen Augier hatte es genauso vernachlässigt wie zuvor der König. Augier lebte fortan in prekären Verhältnissen, hochverschuldet u. in Prozesse verstrickt, was sich auch nicht nach seiner neuerlichen Demarche in Paris im Januar 1656 änderte. Im Mai erschien dann der erste offizielle Gesandte des Protektorats in Frankreich, Sir William Lockhart. Augier starb vermutlich zwischen August 1658 u. Februar 1659. Sein Sterbeort ist unbekannt. Vgl. Gary M. Bell: A

Handlist of British Diplomatic Representatives 1509–1688. London 1990, 110–113; Loic Bienassis: The Diplomatic Career of René Augier. In: Proceedings of the Huguenot Society of Great Britain and Ireland 28 (2004), 199–211; ferner Ian Atherton: Ambition and Failure in Stuart England. The Career of John, first Viscount Scudamore. Manchester 1999, 179, 181–183, 189, 200–203 u. 205; Robert Thomas Fallon: Milton in government. Pennsylvania State Univ. Press 1993, 2, 33, 70, 109 u. 247f.; Grace Lawless Lee: The Huguenot Settlements in Ireland. London [u.a.] 1936, 105.

4 Tilmann (Tilemann) v. Polhelm, Bruder Winands v. P. (FG 405), war am 27.5.1637 durch Lgf. Wilhelm V. v. Hessen-Kassel (FG 65) „en qualité de mon résident" am Hof des franz. Königs bestallt worden. Auch nach der bald darauf erfolgten Übernahme der vormundschaftl. Regierung für Lgf. Wilhelm VI. (FG 694. 1659) durch seine Mutter, Lgfn. Amalia Elisabeth, füllte er dieses Amt aus. Damit fungierte er als erster ständiger Resident u. Agent eines dt. Mittelstaates in Paris. Hans Philippi: Eine hessische Gesandtschaft in Paris im 17. Jahrhundert. Die Mission des Johann Caspar von Dörnberg 1646–1651. In: Hessisches Jahrbuch f. Landesgeschichte 30 (1980), 234–264, hier S.236f. Vgl. STA Marburg, Bestand 340: von Dörnberg, Nr.4233, 4234, 4235, 4237, 4329 u. 4331. Bereits zuvor, seit spätestens 1636, hatte er die Interessen der Reichsstadt Colmar in Paris vertreten. Seit 1639 vertrat er auch als „Chargé d'affaires" (*Acta Pacis Westphalicae* II.B 1.1, S.60 Anm.4) jene der Stadt Straßburg. S. Wolfgang Hans Stein: Protection Royale. Eine Untersuchung zu den Protektionsverhältnissen im Elsaß zur Zeit Richelieus (1622–1643). Münster 1978, 435f. Zugleich war er Geschäftsträger zahlreicher anderer Reichsfürsten, wie der Hz.e Eberhard III. v. Württemberg (1614–1674) u. Leopold Friedrich v. Württemberg-Mömpelgard (1624–1662). Unter den von ihm mit Vertretenen waren auch (damalige u. spätere) Fruchtbringer, so z.B. Mgf. Friedrich V. v. Baden-Durlach (FG 207) oder Gf. Friedrich Casimir v. Hanau-Lichtenberg (FG 695. 1659). S. Schäfer: Moral u. Satire (s. Anm.1), 44f.; *Schäfer: Moscherosch*, 142f.; *Schäfer: Moscherosch und Harsdörffer*, S.161 Anm.55. Vgl. GLA Karlsruhe: 46/5238 Nr.1: Relationes vndt Berichte von Monsr. Polhem Fl. Margg. Badisch., wie auch Heßen Caßellisch. Residenten am Kön. Frantzöß. Hoff, vberschickt. Ao 1640-47. Auch wurde er 1645 als hessen-kasselischer Rat u. Resident am kgl. franz. Hof zum Agenten der Gf.en Anthon Günther u. Christian IX. v. Oldenburg u. Delmenhorst (FG 351 bzw. 375) ernannt, um die Neutralität der Gft.en sowie eine Klärung hinsichtlich des Weserzolls u. der hess. Truppen in Ostfriesland zu erreichen. NSTA Oldenburg: Best. 20-38, Nr.46. Mit dem schwed. Botschafter in Paris seit 1634, Hugo Grotius (s. Anm.13), stand er in gutem Kontakt u. Einvernehmen. Vgl. *Acta Pacis Westphalicae* II B, Bd.1, S.60, 157, 385 u. 490; II B, Bd.2, S.211, 308f., 314, 339f., 599 u. 667; II B, Bd.3.1, S.195; *Grotius: Briefwisseling* XVI, S. XV, 626, 640 u. 697. Am 3.3.1646 berichtete Kd. Mazarin den franz. Gesandten bei den Westfäl. Friedensverhandlungen, dem Comte d'Avaux, Abel Servien u. dem Duc de Longueville, „de la mort du pauvre Polhem qui faisoit ses affaires en cette cour", also vom Tod des „bedauernswerten" hess. Gesandten. *Acta Pacis Westphalicae* II.B 3.1, 500–510, hier S.506. Tatsächlich war Tilmann v. P. in der 2. Hälfte des Februar 1646 in Paris verstorben. Philippi: Eine hessische Gesandtschaft in Paris (s.o.), 239. Vgl. Friedrich Wilhelm Strieder: Grundlage zu einer Hessischen Gelehrten und Schriftsteller Geschichte seit der Reformation bis auf gegenwärtige Zeiten. Bd.5, Kassel 1785, 42. Nach Tilmanns Tod reiste Winand v. P. (s. 440809A K 1) nach Paris zur Abwicklung der Hinterlassenschaft seines Bruders. Im Dezember 1646 kehrte er zurück. S. Familienbriefe der Landgräfin Amalie Elisabeth von Hessen-Kassel. Hrsg. Erwin Bettenhäuser. Marburg 1994, 90 u. 94f. Vgl. STA Marburg: Bestand 340: von Dörnberg, Nr.4527. Die Aufgaben Tilmanns v. P. als Agent in Paris übernahm 1646 für Hessen-Kassel Frh. Johann Caspar v. Dörnberg (1616–1680). Philippi: Eine hessische Gesandtschaft

in Paris (s.o.), 236–264. Neuer Resident für Württemberg u. Baden-Durlach wurde anfangs Jordan Guesont, ein Vetter des Verstorbenen, später (1650–1652) Johann v. Polhelm. Dieser war zugleich auch Agent Lübecks u. der Hanse. Bernd Wunder: Württembergs Eintritt in die Rheinische Allianz von 1658. Französisch-württembergische Bündnisverhandlungen 1650–1660. In: Zs. f. Württembergische Landesgeschichte 63 (2004), 67–117, hier S. 69. Vgl. HSTA Stuttgart: A 34 Bü 58 a; Daniel Tollet: Guerres et paix en Europe centrale aux époques moderne et contemporaine. Mélanges d'histoire des relations internationales offerts à Jean Bérenger. Paris 2003, 197. Die Interessen Straßburgs u. Colmars vertrat nach 1646 Tilmanns bisheriger Sekretär Beck (s. Anm. 1). Stein: Protection Royale (s.o.), 435.

5 „Mihi vehementer displicet loquacitas, atque adeo istos Asiaticos excursores aurium carnifices appellare solitus sum." Iulius Caesar Scaliger: Poetices libri septem. Sieben Bücher über die Dichtkunst. Unter Mitw. v. Manfred Furmann hg. v. Luc Deitz u. Gregor Vogt-Spira. Bd. 3, Stuttgart/ Bad Cannstatt 1995, 472 (Buch 4, Kap. 24, Abschn. 195b). Vgl. *Kühlmann/ Schäfer: Oberrhein*, S. 119 Fn. 91.

6 Antimon, Halbmetall (Stibium), kommt in der Natur vor allem als Grauspießglanz vor, das man für eine Art Blei hielt u. als Schminke sowie als Heilmittel zur Behandlung von Wunden u. Geschwüren einsetzte. Die von Paracelsus eingeführte innerliche Anwendung war im 16. u. 17. Jh. umstritten. „Die an sich hochgiftigen Antimon-Pharmaka wirken in entsprechend vorsichtiger Dosierung abführend, brechreizerregend und schweißtreibend"; sie galten den Iatrochemikern sogar als Universalheilmittel. In der Alchemie der Goldpurifizierung spielte Antimon eine große Rolle. Vgl. Claus Priesner, Karin Figala (Hgg.): Alchemie. Lexikon einer hermetischen Wissenschaft. München 1998, 49–51.

7 Mit dieser Auffassung der Poesie oder des poetischen Geistes als einer Naturanlage ist Moscherosch erneut Iulius Caesar Scaliger u. seinen *Poetices libri septem* (1561, s. Anm. 5) verpflichtet. Demnach standen nicht Gelehrte oder Philosophen am Anfang der Dichtung, sondern Hirten, Schäfer, eine frühe Menschheit im Naturzustand. Vgl. Volkhard Wels: Der Begriff der Dichtung in der Frühen Neuzeit. Berlin, New York 2009, 155 ff.

8 Michel Eyquem sieur de Montaigne (1533–1592), Richter, Kammerherr Heinrichs v. Navarra, des späteren Kgs. Heinrich IV. v. Frankreich, Bürgermeister von Bordeaux, der bekannte skeptisch-eklektische Philosoph u. Verfasser der berühmten *Essais* (erstmals Bordeaux 1580).

9 Guillaume du Vair (1556–1621) aus einer Amtsadelsfamilie der Auvergne; 1577–1582 Bediensteter des Thronfolgers, François-Hercule de Valois-Angoulême duc d'Anjou (1555–1584); Jurist u. Staatsmann (April 1584 Conseiller im Parlement von Paris, 1586 conseiller d'État, 1596 Präsident des Parlements in Aix-en-Provence), Diplomat, 1618 Bischof von Lisieux; befreundet u. a. mit François de Malherbe, Pierre Pithou u. Jacques-Auguste de Thou, neben Justus Lipsius u. Pierre Charron Haupvertreter des christlichen Neustoizismus. Er ergriff inmitten des Religions- u. Bürgerkrieges — wie fast alle Pariser Parlamentsjuristen — die Partei der Politiques, die gegen die Ligisten den Primat des Politischen vor der Religion u. die Unabhängigkeit der gallikan. Kirche gegenüber Rom verfochten. Er bewies 1589 Königstreue, als er Heinrich III. nach Tours folgte, trat dann zugunsten der Königswahl Heinrichs v. Navarra auf u. war bemüht, die Autorität des Königs u. den inneren Frieden wiederherzustellen. Er verfaßte eine Darstellung u. Erörterung der stoischen Moralphilosophie, der 1590 während der kgl. Belagerung von Paris sein *Traité de la Constance ès Calamitez publiques* folgte (Erstveröff. 1594, bezeichnenderweise erneut 1941 in Paris aufgelegt). Zu seinen Werken gehörten ferner die *Discours politiques* (1586), die *Méditation sur les sept pseaumes de la consolation* (1603), eine *Exhorta-*

tion à la paix (1592) u. eine Abhandlung *De l'éloquence françoise* (Paris 1590 u. ö., Ausg. Paris 1606 krit. ediert von René Radouant, Paris 1907; Ndr. Genève 1970) u. a. m. Briefe Du Vairs erschienen ebenfalls schon zu Lebzeiten im Druck; *Lettres inédites* wurden 1873 von Philippe Tamizey de Larroque in Paris herausgegeben. Vgl. ferner *Kühlmann/ Schäfer: Oberrhein*, S. 120 Fn. 92; *DBF* XII, 950 f.; Jochen Schmidt: Grundlagen, Kontinuität und geschichtlicher Wandel des Stoizismus. In: Stoizismus in der europäischen Philosophie, Literatur, Kunst und Politik. Eine Kulturgeschichte von der Antike bis zur Moderne. Hg. Barbara Neumeyr, J. S., Bernhard Zimmermann. 2 Bde. Berlin, New York 2008, I, 3–133, hier 68, 70, 73, 75 u. 99; Günter Abel: Stoizismus und frühe Neuzeit. Zur Entstehungsgeschichte modernen Denkens im Felde von Ethik und Politik. Berlin u. a. 1978, v. a. das Kap. V: „Neustoizismus als Denk- und Handlungsform (Guillaume Du Vair)", S. 114–152; Art. „Du Vair, Guillaume" in: Histoire et Dictionnaire des Guerres de Religion. Par Arlette Jouanna, Jacqueline Boucher, Dominique Biloghi, Guy Le Thiec. o. O. 1998, 866–868; Bruno Petey: Les méditations chrétiennes d'un parlementaire. Étude sur les priemières oeuvres de pieté de Guillaume Du Vair. Paris 2003; Bruno Petey-Girard: Une éthique de la parole. L'univers rhétorique de Guillaume Du Vair. In: Rhetorica 17 (1999), 289–312; René Radouant: Guillaume de Vair, l'homme et l'orateur jusqu'á la fin des troubles de la ligue (1556–1596). Paris 1907, Ndr. Genève 1970; Roman Schnur: Die französischen Juristen im konfessionellen Bürgerkrieg des 16. Jahrhunderts. Berlin 1962, 28, 29, 44 f. u. 50 ff.; Alexandre Tarrête: Un gallican sous la Ligue: Guillaume Du Vair (1556–1621). In: Revue de l'histoire des religions 226 (2009), 497–516; Guillaume Du Vair. Parlementaire et écrivain (1556–1621). Colloque d'Aix-en-Provence, 4.–6. octobre 2001. Actes réunis par Bruno Petey-Girard et Alexandre Tarrête. Genève 2005.

10 Charles Pascal (Paschal/ Carlo Pascale/ Pasquali, 1547–1625), vicomte de La Queute et Dargny, aus piemontes. Adel, ref., später kath., hatte in Paris die Humaniora u. die Rechte studiert u. sich dann dort niedergelassen. 1578 trug ihm ein Gesandtschaftsauftrag von Kg. Heinrich III. (1576 nach Polen) ein kgl. Adelspatent ein. Auch Kg. Heinrich IV. vertraute ihm diplomat. Aufträge an u. bediente sich seiner zur Befriedung des Languedoc, der Provence u. der Dauphiné. 1592 Conseiller u. Avocat Genéral am Parlement von Rouen, dem obersten Provinzialgericht der Normandie. Nach zehnjähriger Gesandtentätigkeit in der Schweiz (Graubünden) kehrte er 1614 nach Frankreich zurück u. diente als Conseiller d'État. Pascal veröffentlichte eine *Viti Fabricii Pibrachii Vita* (Paris 1584, HAB: Db 3533; in franz. Übers. Paris 1617) über seinen Förderer Guy Du Faur seigneur de Pibrac (1529–1584), einen *De Optimo genere elocutionis tractatus* (Rouen 1595, auch Paris 1601), ein Werk über den Gesandten: *Legatus* (Rouen 1598, HAB: Rq 442; erw. Paris 1613 u. Amsterdam 1643; moderne Ausg. *L'Ambassadeur* Limoges 2014), eine Sammlung *Gnomae seu Axiomata politica ex Tacito* (Paris 1600). Er gab zudem einen Kommentar zu den *Annalen* des Tacitus heraus (*C. Cornelii Taciti ... Excessv Divi Avgvsti Annalivm Libri Qvatvor Priores, Et In Hos Observationes Caroli Paschali Cvneatis*, Paris 1581), ferner zwei Bücher *Christianarum Precum* (Paris 1602; Ausg. Paris 1609 in HAB: Ti 370), schließlich verfaßte er einen Bericht über seine Gesandtschaft nach Graubünden (*Caroli Paschalii Regis In Sacro Consistorio Consilarii Legatio Rhaetica*. Paris 1620. HAB: Gq 122) sowie moralphilosoph. Abhandlungen. Vgl. *Kühlmann/ Schäfer: Oberrhein*, S. 120 Fn. 92; *ABF* I 811, 181–192; *Jöcher* III, 1278; Marc Fumaroli: La Prose de l'État: Charles Paschal, théoricien du style royal. Rhétorique et politique à la Cour sous Henri III. et Henri IV. In: ders.: La diplomatie de l'esprit. De Montaigne à La Fontaine. Paris 1994, 59–124; Art. „Paschal, Charles" in: Historisches Lexikon der Schweiz, http://www.hls-dhs-dss.ch/textes/d/D16902.php; Else-Lilly Etter: Tacitus in der Geistesgeschichte des 16. u. 17. Jhs. Basel, Stuttgart 1966, 37 ff.; Katherine M. MacDonald: Diplomacy and biography in the wars of religion: Charles Paschal's life of Guy du Faur de Pibrac (1584). In: Bruno Tribout and Ruth Whelan (eds.): Narrating the Self in Early Modern Europe. Bern 2007, 41–52.

11 Étienne Pasquier (Stephanus Paschasius, 1529–1615), gefeierter Jurist u. Historiker, gemäßigter gallikan. Katholik, der die überparteilichen u. überkonfessionellen Auffassungen der Politiques teilte u. auch mit Hugenotten sowie Dichtern der Pléiade u. Montaigne in freundschaftl. Verkehr stand. Als erbitterter Gegner der Jesuiten vertrat er z. B. 1565 in deren langem Streit mit der U. Paris die Interessen der letzteren. Seine antijesuit. Polemiken u. Satiren (u. a. *Le Catéchisme Des Iésuites: Ou Examen De Leur Doctrine.* [Paris] 1602) wurden auch ins Deutsche übersetzt, z. B.: Catechismus oder Gründlicher bericht von der Lehr unnd Leben der Jesuiten: Erstlich in Frantzösischer Sprach beschriben/ nun aber auß guthertziger Meinung/ meniglichen zur Nachrichtung verdeutschet. Freystatt (d. i. Mömpelgard) 1603; Von der Jesuiter Sect/ Das ist/ Kurtzer und Summarischer/ aber wahrhaftiger Bericht/ von der Jesuiter ersten ankunfft/ Stifftung/ Orden/ vermehrung desselben. Auch durch was für List und betrug/ sie in den Stand … Sonderlich in der Cron Franckreich gestigen seyen: Darinnen … dem Parlament zu Paris deutlich vor augen gestellet worden/ was für jammer … durch diese Sect/ der Cron Franckreich werde auffgestifftet und zugefüget/ Durch … Steffan Pasquier … Vor dem Königlichen Parlament öffentlich eyngebracht/ nachmaln beschriben … und in die Teutsche Sprach versetzt. Hanau 1611. — Pasquier entstammte einer amtsadligen Familie u. hatte die Rechte in Paris, Toulouse, Pavia u. Bologna studiert. Bereits 1549, aus Italien zurückgekehrt, erscheint er unter den Advokaten des Parlements von Paris. 1585 wurde er für zwei Jahrzehnte Generaladvokat am kgl. Rechnungshof (chambre des comptes). In seinen Mußestunden widmete er sich ausgiebig der Dichtung u. der Geschichtsschreibung. 1554 veröffentlichte er einen Dialog über die Liebe, *Le Monophile.* Ihm folgten zahlreiche Bücher Sonette, Epigramme, *Les Jeus poetiques* (1610, krit. Ausg. Paris 2001 von Jean Pierre Dupouy), Porträts berühmter Männer u. a. m. Sein geschichtliches Hauptwerk, die *Recherches de la France* in 10 Büchern (1. Teil 1560, 2. Tl. 1565) forschten den historisch-kulturellen Wurzeln Frankreichs nach, die er nicht in Troja oder dem antiken Rom, sondern in der genuin gallokeltischen Herkunft u. der davon ausgehenden franz. Nation suchte. Die *Recherches* enthalten auch eine Geschichte der franz. Poesie (1607). Harsdörffer zitierte die *Recherches* mehrfach in seiner „Schutzschrift für Die Teutsche Spracharbeit" (Anhang in *Frauenzimmer-Gesprächspiele* I ²1644, Ndr. 1968), Ndr. S. 357, 362 u. 374. Eine kritische Ausg. der *Recherches* wurde von Marie-Madeleine Fragonard u. François Roudaut besorgt (Paris 1996, 3 Bde). Harsdörffer zog nicht nur Montaignes *Essais* heran, um das Wort „Specimen" zu erklären, sondern auch die *Recherches* beim Wort „Disquisitiones". S. *Harsdörffer: Specimen (1646),* 304 f. Umfangreiche Ausgaben der literarischen *Lettres* Pasquiers erschienen seit 1586, darunter eine Ausg. in 5 Bdn. von 1619, u. moderne Editionen. Eine 2-bändige Ausgabe seiner *Oeuvres* erschien 1723 in Amsterdam (HAB: Lm 2° 23). Vgl. *Kühlmann/ Schäfer: Oberrhein,* S. 120 Fn. 92; *ABF* I 811, 226–253 u. III 355, 173 f.; *Jöcher* III, 1286 u. *Adelung* V, 1631; Art. „Pasquier, Étienne" in: Histoire et Dictionnaire des Guerres de Religion (s. Anm. 9), 1186–1188; Paul Bouteiller: Recherches sur la vie et la carrière d'Étienne Pasquier. Paris 1989; James H. Dahlinger: Etienne Pasquier on ethics and history. New York [u.a.] 2007; Roman Schnur: Die französischen Juristen (s. Anm. 9), 21, 23, 27, 30, 46, 48 u. ö.

12 Harsdörffer u. mit ihm Moscherosch war Kd. Richelieu auch als Sammler u. Förderer der Künste u. Literatur sowie als Gründer von Akademien wie der *Académie française* (1635) bekannt. In *Harsdörffer: Specimen (1646),* 95 f. heißt es, „Nec minorem apud Posteritatem laudem promeruit Cardinalis Richelius, qui in honorem & cultum Gallici idiomatis Collegium & Conventum, quot-Septimanis de quæstionibus variis habendum, Lutetiæ Parisiorum instituit". Er verweist dafür auf Théophraste Renaudots *Conférences au Bureau d'addresse*, Tom. 1. S. dazu *Conermann: Harsdörffers Plan*, 13 f. u. 38 ff. Darüber hinaus erwähnte Harsdörffer in 430920 seine Übersetzung eines auf Richelieu zurückgehenden Stückes. Es handelt sich um die im November 1642 uraufgeführte u. Anfang 1643 im Druck erschienene ‚comédie héroïque' *Europe*. Als Verfasser dieses politischen Dramas, das anfangs anonym erschien, wurde Jean Desmarets de Saint-Sorlin (1595–1676) bekannt, Günstling Richelieus, Dichter, Hofdramaturg u. Hofballettmeister, zuständig für die opulenten Inszenierungen der Ballets de cour Ludwigs XIII. Er schrieb in sechs Jahren neben den Balletten sieben Theaterstücke für Richelieu. Von letzterem stammte zumindest die Idee zu diesem Stück, dessen Ausführung u. Proben er verfolgte u. dessen Ausstattung er finanzierte. Die Uraufführung fand allerdings ohne den todkranken Richelieu statt, der am 4.12.1642 starb. Das Stück ist als eine Art europapolitisches Vermächtnis des Kardinals u. Ersten Ministers anzusehen. Vgl. Sylvie Taussig: Introduction. In: Europe, comédie héroïque. Attribuée à Armand du Plessis, Cardinal de Richelieu et Jean Desmarets, Sieur de Saint-Sorlin. Turnhout [2006], 9–172, hier 10 ff.; Roland Alexander Ißler: Der Dreißigjährige Krieg im allegorischen Gewand: Richelieus Europapolitik auf der Theaterbühne. In: Patrick Ramponi, Saskia Wiedner (Hgg.): Dichter und Lenker. Die Literatur der Staatsmänner, Päpste und Despoten von der Frühen Neuzeit bis in die Gegenwart. Tübingen 2014, 145–164, hier S.149f. Harsdörffer muß sofort nach der Erstveröffentlichung daran gegangen sein, das Stück ins Deutsche zu übertragen u. in Alexandrinerverse zu bringen: JAPETA. | Das ist | Ein Heldengedicht/ | gesungen | Jn dem Holsteinischen Parnasso | Durch | Die Musam Calliope. | 1643 [Nürnberg: Wolfgang Endter]. HAB: Textbuch 681, dig. Kürzlich erschien Georg Philipp Harsdörffer: Japeta. Édition, traduction, introd. et notes par Sylvie Taussig et Claus Zittel. Turnhout 2009. Vgl. 430920 K 8 u. 440324 K 22. — *Kühlmann/ Schäfer: Oberrhein*, 117 haben betont, wie sehr sich Moscheroschs Paris-Schilderung im vorliegenden Brief „von den etwa in den *Gesichten* benutzten Stereotypen der A-la-mode-Satire" unterscheidet. Vgl. Anm. 19.

13 Hugo Grotius (Huig de Groot), 1583–1645, der große politisch-philosophische u. juristische Schriftsteller, s. Anm. 2 u. 4. Seine dichterischen Arbeiten wie *Christus patiens* (1608) oder der von seinem Freund Martin Opitz (FG 200) übersetzte *Bewijs van den waaren godsdienst* (1622) stehen in einem Zusammenhang mit seiner Völkerrechtsschrift *De jure belli ac pacis* (1625) oder dem von Christophorus Colerus (auf Anraten von Opitz) übertragenen Werk *De veritate religionis Christianae* (1627). S. *Opitz: BW*. Moscheroschs Lehrer Matthias Bernegger stand mit Grotius in Korrespondenz. Vgl. hier Otto Kluge: Die Dichtung des Hugo Grotius im Rahmen der neulateinischen Kunstpoesie. Leiden 1940; Pieter Lodewyk Muller: Hugo Grotius als latijnsch Dichter beschouwd. Haarlem 1867.

14 Ks. Karl d. Gr. (ca. 747/48–814). Ihm wurde nachgesagt, deutsche Namen für die Monate u. Winde (Himmelsrichtungen) eingeführt, eine dt. Grammatik u. die Sammlung u. Rettung älterer dt. Dichtung in Auftrag gegeben zu haben. Vgl. 411200 K 5 u. 410706 K 14. In *Harsdörffer: Specimen (1646)*, Praefatio, Bl.)()()()(r teilt Harsdörffer mit: „*Karolus M.* rhythmicis carminibus delectatus, illa undique conquæsivit [...] et memoriæ mandavit. Inchoavit etiam Grammaticam patrii sermonis, procul dubio ad exemplum latinæ".

15 Ks. Karl V. (1500–1558), seit 1516 Kg. Karl I. v. Spanien, 1519 röm. König, 1530 bis zu seiner Abdankung 1556 Kaiser des Hl. Röm. Reichs. Moscheroschs 54. Epigramm im ersten Hundert seiner *Epigrammata*-Sammlung von 1649 (s. Q), S.36, bleibt ohne Bezug auf dessen literar. Leistung. Eine große Menge von Sinn- u. Denksprüchen sind von Ks. Karl V. überliefert. Viele davon hat Julius Wilhelm Zincgref (1591–1635) in den beiden

Teilen seiner Sammlung *Apophthegmata* herausgegeben. Julius Wilhelm Zincgref: Der Teutschen scharpfsinnige kluge Sprüch, Apophthegmata genant. 2 Bde., Straßburg 1628–1631, hier I, 89–105 bzw. II, 8–11. Diese Zincgrefsche Sammlung dürfte die unmittelbare Quelle Moscheroschs gewesen sein. Vgl. Julius Wilhelm Zincgref: Gesammelte Schriften IV: Apophthegmata teutsch. Hg. Theodor Verweyen, Dieter Mertens u. Werner Wilhelm Schnabel. 2 Tl.e, Tübingen 2011, hier I, 75–83 (Nr. 262–325), u. II, 314–332. Brieflicher Kontakt zw. Moscherosch u. Harsdörffer ist überliefert. Vgl. *Kühlmann: Korrespondenz Moscheroschs*, S. 274. Biographien zu Ks. Karl V. scheinen nicht auf dessen literar. Versuche einzugehen, vgl. etwa Alfred Kohler: Karl V. 3. Aufl. München 2001; Ferdinand Seibt: Karl V. München 1997 u. ö.

16 Kg. Heinrich IV. v. Frankreich (Henri le Grand) (1553–1610). Vgl. *Kühlmann/ Schäfer: Oberrhein*, S. 227. Zu den Sinnsprüchen Kg. Heinrichs IV. s. Zincgref: Der Teutschen scharpfsinnige kluge Sprüch (Anm. 15) II, 107–163. Vgl. Zincgref: Gesammelte Schriften IV (Anm. 15), I, 353–385 (Nr. 2027–2112), u. II, 714–757.

17 Herr Nikolaus/ Klaus. Moscherosch dürfte hier an den noch nicht selig- bzw. heiliggesprochenen, aber schon religiös verehrten Nikolaus von der Flüe (1417–1487) [frz. Nicolas de Flue] denken, den „Bruder Claus", der aus einem Bauerngeschlecht im Kanton Unterwalden stammte, zunächst als Kriegsmann, Landrat u. Richter ein weltliches Leben führte, aber im Alter von 50 Jahren zum Einsiedler wurde. Von vielen Leuten wegen seiner Frömmigkeit u. Weisheit aufgesucht, wurde er auch zum politischen Ratgeber u. Friedensstifter. Moscherosch scheint Nikolaus nicht als heiligmäßigen Mann, sondern als gewitzten Bauern, Familienvater u. Politiker anzusprechen. Vgl. David J. Collins: „Turning Swiss". In: Reforming Saints. Saints' Lives and Their Authors in Germany, 1470–1530. Oxford 2008, 99–122.

18 Anicius Manlius Severinus Boethius: De consolatione Philosophiae, III, 8, carmen 8, V. 1–2 u. 19–22 (die 2 ersten u. 4 letzten Verse des Gedichts): „Eheu, quae miseros tramite devios | abducit ignorantia! | […] Quid dignum stolidis mentibus imprecer? | opes honores ambiant, | et cum falsa gravi mole paraverint | tum vera cognoscant bona." Boethivs: De consolatione Philosophiae. Opvscvla theologica. Edidit Claudio Moreschini. München, Leipzig 2000, 75 f.

19 Cabo de Finisterre, Galizien/ Spanien. Vgl. Anm. 20.

20 Hieron. ep. 53, 1 (ad Paulinum): „Ad Titum Liuium lacteo eloquentiae fonte manantem de vltimis Hispaniae Galliarumque finibus quosdam venisse nobiles legimus. Et quos ad contemplationem sui Roma non traxerat, unius hominis fama perduxit."

21 Kg. Ludwig XIV. v. Frankreich. Schließen sich die hier geäußerten Auffassungen an die Hoffnungen u. Erwartungen an, die der junge Moscherosch mit Frankreich in den 20er Jahren des 17. Jhs. verband? Vgl. *Kühlmann/ Schäfer: Oberrhein*, 78 ff. Sie weisen auf S. 125 mit dem vorliegenden Brief nebst anderen Zeugnissen darauf hin, daß die einseitige Festlegung Moscheroschs auf einen reichsstädtisch-konservativen, altfränkischen A-la-mode-Kritiker zu kurz greift u. die europäischen Reform-Impulse, die er mittrug, zu berücksichtigen sind. Eine Übersicht über die kohärenten negativen Frankreich-Stereotype in den *Gesichten* u. *Epigrammata*, aber auch die positiveren Frankreich-Bezüge unter Heranziehung der *Gesichte* u. des vorliegenden Briefes in Jean Schillinger: Moscherosch, Frankreich und die Gallomanie der Deutschen. In: Simpliciana 22 (2000), 227–245. Vgl. auch 440616. Bedenkt der Leser allerdings, daß im Text Ludwig XIV. u. nicht dessen Vater Ludwig XIII., der König Richelieus, angesprochen ist, erscheint die Lobhudelei eher eine (ironische) Verbeugung vor der (Moscheroschs Korrespondenz sicher treffenden) kgl. Zensur als vor dem noch kindlichen Ludwig XIV. („ce Roy sans pareil en victoires") darzustellen — obgleich dem Siebenjährigen in der Sprache der Zeit durchaus auch die unter seinen Fahnen errungenen Siege zugesprochen werden konnten. Die Vermutung über die hier vermutete Lobhudelei erhärtet sich, wenn wir bedenken, daß der Brief an Harsdörffer ging, der noch 1645 das im selben Jahr erschienene Werk *Le Catechisme Royal* von Philippe Fortin sieur de la Hoguette verdeutschte. Moscherosch kann schon in Paris das frz. Buch gelesen oder es sogar Harsdörffer geschickt haben. Aus den Gesprächen (zwischen Ludwig XIV. u. seinem Hofmeister) gehen in diesem politischen Katechismus die Annexionspläne des Königs u. Kardinal Mazarins hinsichtlich deutscher Reichsgebiete (Elsaß, Lothringen, Freigft. Burgund) hervor. S. 451217 K 9.

22 *Kühlmann/ Schäfer: Oberrhein,* 126 f. halten diesen Text für einen Briefauszug von Harsdörffers Hand, der Moscheroschs „Gedichte auf Venedig" würdigt. Wir halten den Text für ein Postskript des vorliegenden Briefes, auch wenn er im Druck kursiv abgesetzt wurde. Moscherosch bezeichnet sich auch als Verfasser der beiden Epigramme auf Venedig aus der 2. Centurie der *Epigrammatum* (s. Beil. I). In Bezug darauf sagt Moscherosch: „le poeme que [e] te fis". Kühlmann/ Schäfer übersetzten den Nachtrag nicht. Seine Aussagen passen aber gut zur Selbsteinschätzung im Hauptbrief u. der Differenzierung des Poetenbegriffs angesichts der Frage, ob der Poet zum Gemeinwesen taugt. Moscherosch erwähnt im vorliegenden Brief, zuvor bereits zweimal in Paris gewesen zu sein. Eine weitere Reise Moscheroschs nach Paris zwischen seiner akadem. Peregrinatio 1624–1626 u. dieser Reise 1645 ist nicht nachgewiesen. Gemeint ist daher wohl sein zweimaliger Pariser Aufenthalt während der Studienreise: Moscherosch war im Juni 1625 u. dann erneut zwischen Ende 1625 u. Anfang 1626 in Paris. Vgl. *Schäfer: Moscherosch,* 68 ff.

23 S. Beil. I.

24 Horaz Epist. I 18, V. 84: „nam tua res agitur paries cum proximus ardet". Zit. nach Q. Horati Flacci Opera. Ed. D. R. Shackleton Bailey. Stuttgart 1985, 287.

K I Die Ausgabe der *Centuria Epigrammatum* von 1649 (s.o., Q) ist Hz. August d.J. v. Braunschweig-Wolfenbüttel (FG 227) u. dessen Sohn Anton Ulrich (FG 716. 1659) mit lat. Widmungsvorreden gewidmet (Bl. A r ff.), ebenso die Centuria II der Ausgabe von 1665 (s.o., Q; S. 57 ff.). Das 3. u. 97. Epigramm gelten Hz. August. Das 3. lobt die Brevitas als fürstengemäß. Auch das paßt zu 450818 (diesem Brief) u. zur Widmung des Epigrammbuchs an den Herzog. Epigramm 7 gilt Pz. Anton Ulrich. Ab S. 13 lat. Widmungsgedichte: Georg Philipp Harsdörffer (FG 368) für Johann Michael Moscherosch (FG 436. 1645), inc.: „EFfugium turbæ [...]"; Christian Gueintz (FG 361), inc.: „Dormio vel vigilo? [...]"; Melchior Erhardus, Augustanus D. J. U., inc.: „VIs, cur non laudem [...]"; Johann Matthias Schneuber (FG 498. 1648), inc.: „CEntum das Epigrammatum libellum [...]"; Robertus Königsmannus (1606–1663), inc.: „FElicioris pignus & spes seculi [...]"; Sebastianus König/ Past. & Superint. Palatinatus Luzel: „Ad Epigrammatum"; Samuel Gloner (1598–1642), inc.: „SCribere, quæ veterum sapiant epigrammata, morsus [...]"; S. 18–48 Moscheroschs 100 Epigramme. Diesen folgen (nichtpaginiert) lat. Briefe von Moscherosch an D. Polycarp Heyland, Hz. Augusts Bevollmächtigten beim Nürnberger Friedensexekutionskongreß, d.d. Straßburg 4.10.1649 (Epigrammata II. Centuria 1665, S. 96–101); der vorliegende Brief u. Harsdörffers Antwortschreiben 450901. — Das von uns gebrachte Gedicht ist ein beschwörender Aufruf zur Unterstützung Venedigs im Kampf um Kreta. *Kühlmann/ Schäfer: Oberrhein,* 95.

450900

Fürst Ludwigs Verzeichnis fruchtbringerischer Drucke bis 1645

F. Ludwig versendet an einen unbekannten Empfänger ein Verzeichnis fruchtbringerischer Drucke aus den Jahren 1619 bis 1645 und legt *Der Fruchtbringenden Gesellschafft Abgegangenes Schreiben An den Leimenden Vnd dessen Antwort An die gantze Gesellschaft. auch Des Grünen darauff erfolgter Send-brieff* ([Köthen] 1623) bei.

Q HM Köthen: V S 544, Bl. 107r, eigenh. — Bl. 107v: Adresse von unbekannter H.: „Der hochEdlen VielEhrentugentsamen Jungfer Anna Dorothea von Freiberger f. anhaltischen CammerJungfer […]". Zur Adressatin vgl. 461006 K 2. Ein dazugehöriger Brief fehlt im Lagenumfeld, so daß die Anschrift nicht ursächlich zur Liste gehört haben, sondern das Blatt von F. Ludwig zu Notizzwecken verwendet worden sein dürfte.
Lagenumfeld, Bl. 103r–106v: „Bernhardi lob und Jubelgesang" (s. 371124 I); Bl. 108r, v leer: „Verzeichnues der Bücher, so theils zu Cöthen gedruckt seind, und die Fruchtbringende Geselschafft in etwas angehen" (s. 430505 I).

A *Fehlt.*

Verzeichnüs der schriften aus der
Fruchtbringenden geselschaft
entsproßen.

Die verdeutschung **Giusto Bottajo.** aus dem Jtalianischen.[1]
Die zuschrift deßen an den Leimenden, mit seiner antwort, und des Grünen sendbriefe.[2]
Die **Circe** aus dem Jtalianischen verdeutschet[3]
Schatzkämmerlein heilsamer Zuneigungen aus dem Frantzösischen **Cabinet des saints affections** verdeutschet, durch den Bittern.[4]
Die andere woche des Herren von Bartas durch den Nutzbaren aus dem Frantzösischen[5]
Das Erlösete Jerusalem des Tasso aus dem Jtalianischen.[6]
Die erste woche des Herren von Bartas durch den Nutzbaren aus dem Frantzösischen.[7]
Der Christliche Fürst durch den Unverenderlichen aus dem Jtalianischen **il principe Cristiano.**[8]
Und andere kleine reimgedichte deren aber wenig mehr vorhanden, die neulichsten als den Verfolgten David[9], den weisen Alten[10], Christliche weltbeschreibung[11], und die Siegprachten des Petrarca[12] seind hernach heraus kommen.
Die zuschrift an den Leimenden, so aus dem **Canto di pazzia**, dem Jtalianischen meistentheils genommen wird hiermit uberschicket.[13]
Deutsche Sprachlehre[14], und Rechtschreibung[15]
Das Buch Hiob in Reime gebracht[16]
Der **Tamerlanes** verdeutschet aus dem Frantzösischen.[17]

K Vgl. eine ähnliche Liste von 1643: 430505 I. Zur Datierung des vorliegenden Dokuments: Die Liste nennt als zeitlich jüngstes Werk *Gueintz: Rechtschreibung (1645)*, die etwa im September 1645 erschien. Vgl. 440127 K 1. Die Anschrift gilt Anna Dorothea v. Freyberg (13.2.1613 – 15.1.1677), Tochter Ernsts v. Freyberg (FG 75) und seit 1652 2. Gemahlin Christian Ernsts (v.) Knoch (FG 265), 1645–1650 Geh. Rat F. Ludwigs, dann Direktor der Köthener Vormundschaftsregierung für den Sohn F. Ludwigs, Pz. Wilhelm Ludwig v. Anhalt-Köthen (FG 358). *Conermann III*, 297. — Die Liste dürfte an den Leipziger Handelsmann Georg Winckler gegangen sein, der einen Käufer zu finden suchte. S. 451019 (K 0).

1 JOHANNIS BAPTISTÆ GELLI Vornehmen Florentinischen Academici Anmutige Gespräch *Capricci del Bottaio* genandt (Köthen 1619), F. Ludwigs Übersetzung der *Capricci del bottaio* von Giovan Batista Gelli. S. *DA Köthen II. 1*, [173]–[474].

2 F. Ludwig (Hg.): Der Fruchtbringenden Gesellschafft Abgegangenes Schreiben An den Leimenden Vnd dessen Antwort An die gantze Gesellschaft. auch Des Grünen darauff erfolgter Send-brieff ([Köthen] 1623). S. 200125, 210401 u. 230430. Der Leimende war Jost Andreas v. Randow (FG 22. 1619), der Grüne Curt Dietrich aus dem Winckel (FG 35. 1621).

3 JOHANNIS BAPTISTÆ GELLI, Vornehmen Florentinischen ACADEMICI Anmütige Gespräch/ LA CIRCE genandt: Darinnen von allerhand lustigen vnd nützlichen Sachen gehandelt wird (Köthen 1620), F. Ludwigs Übersetzung von Giovan Batista Gellis *La Circe*. Vgl. 231210 K I 4 u. 5.

4 Schatzkämmerlein Heilsamer Zuneigungen/ Welches in dreissig Betrachtungen begriffen/ und mit etlichen hierzu gehörigen Reimen vermehret worden (Köthen 1623, ²1641), Hans Ernsts v. Börstel (FG 41. Der Bittere) Übersetzung des *Cabinet des saines affections* vermutlich der Madeleine de L'Aubespine, vermehrt um „stances" und 12 „discours" wohl aus der Feder von Marie Le Gendre Dame de Rivery. *Conermann: Vielsprachigkeit in der Frühzeit der FG*, 345 Anm. 29 (Hinweis v. Jean Balsamo). Die Verfasserangaben zur frz. Vorlage der Verdeutschung in 230809 K 21 u. 22 u. zuletzt in 410313 K 3 u. 421031A K 7 bedürfen also der Korrektur.

5 *Hübner: Andere Woche (1622)*, eine Übersetzung der *Sepmaine ou Création du Monde* des Guillaume de Saluste sieur Du Bartas. Tobias Hübner (FG 25) führte in der FG den Gesellschaftsnamen Der Nutzbare. Vgl. 310000 Q u. K 9. Zur Neubearbeitung von 1640 s. Anm.7.

6 Diederich v. dem Werder (FG 31): Gottfried von Bulljon, Oder Das Erlösete Jerusalem. Frankfurt a. M.: Daniel und David Aubry und Clemens Schleich 1626. Ndr. hg. Gerhard Dünnhaupt. Tübingen 1974 (Deutsche Neudrucke. Reihe: Barock, 14). Eine verbesserte Neuauflage war seit 1642 geplant, erschien aber erst 1651 in Frankfurt a. M.: Gottfried. | Oder | Erlösetes Je- | rusalem. | Deutsch. | Verbessert. | Zum zweyten mahl gedruckt. | [Vignetten] | Franckfurt am Mayn/ | Gedruckt bey Caspar Röteln/ | Jn Verlegung Johann Pressen. | [Linie] | Anno M. DC. LI. HAB: 14.3 Poet. (Dig.). Eine Übersetzung von Torquato Tassos *Il Goffredo. overo Gerusalemme liberata*. Vgl. 260617 K 3 u. 260831 K 4, zuletzt 420506 K 3; im vorliegenden Band auch 440310B K 2, 460125 K I 0 u. 460204 I.

7 *Hübner: Erste Woche (1631)*, vgl. Anm.5. Eine von F. Ludwig und Diederich v. dem Werder überarbeitete Neuausgabe beider *Wochen* erschien 1640: *Hübner, Fürst Ludwig, Werder: Die Erste und Andere Woche (1640)*. Sie erscheint wohl aus Bescheidenheit nicht in der Liste. Vgl. 310000, 400000 K 3 u. 420503 K 10.

8 F. Christians II. v. Anhalt-Bernburg (FG 51. Der Unveränderliche) *Vnterweisung Eines Christlichen Fürsten (1639)*, eine Übersetzung des *Libro llamado relox de principes*

von Antonio de Guevara nach der italien. Bearbeitung des Mambrino Roseo da Fabriano (d. i. Collenuccio Costo): *L'institutione del prencipe christiano*. Vgl. 231203 K 8, 390504 K 2 u. 430505 K I 3.

9 1643 war die von F. Ludwig und Diederich v. dem Werder gründlich überarbeitete Neufassung des *Verfolgten David* erschienen, eine Übersetzung des *Davide perseguitato* von Virgilio Malvezzi Marchese di Castel Guelfo, die Wilhelm v. Kalcheim gen. Lohausen (FG 172) 1638 erstmals vorgelegt hatte: Kalcheim: *David (1638)* und Kalcheim, Fürst Ludwig, Diederich v. dem Werder u. a.: *David (1643)*. Vgl. 410102 K 2, im vorliegenden Band auch 440130 K 2, 440426 K 7 u. 440525 K II 9. F. Ludwigs erst 1647 erschienene Übersetzungen von Malvezzis *Romulo* und *Tarquinio* fehlen in dieser Liste noch. S. 430505 K 1 u. 440426 K 7.

10 *Fürst Ludwig: Der weise Alte (1643)*, eine Übersetzung des *Sage Vieillard* von Simon Goulart de Senlis. Vgl. 430505 K I 12 u. 440824 K 8.

11 *Fürst Ludwig: Heilige Weltbeschreibung (1643)*, eine Übersetzung der *Saincte chorographie* des Paul Geslin de La Piltière. Vgl. 430505 K I 13; im vorliegenden Band 440130 K 2.

12 *Fürst Ludwig: Sechs Triumphi oder Siegesprachten (1643)*, eine Übersetzung der *Trionfi* Francesco Petrarcas. Vgl. 371027 K 2; 430624 K 2; im vorliegenden Band 440130 K 2, 441020 K 7 u. 16, 450817 K IV 11 u. 460825 K 19.

13 Der Hinweis auf einen „Canto di pazzia" als ital. Quelle des *Abgegangenen Schreibens*, welche dieses selbst aber mit keinem Hinweis preisgibt oder andeutet, ist in der Korrespondenz der FG durchaus neu; der ital. Text ist von uns aber schon in 210401 I entdeckt und veröffentlicht worden. Sandro Petris *Canto della Pazzia* von 1559 geht der menschlichen Verrücktheit durch alle Stände, Professionen und Affekte nach, worin ihm der Leimende in der FG in seiner Antwort folgt (s. 210401, Abschnitt 4). Daneben ist auch auf den 23. Gesang des *Orlando furioso* des Ludovico Ariosto zu verweisen, in dem sich Orlando in einen Eifersuchtswahn steigert und wie der Vogel in die Leim- oder Garnfalle verstrickt:

„come l'incauto augel che si ritrova
in ragna o in visco aver dato di petto,
quanto piú batte l'ale e piú si prova
di disbrigar, piú vi si lega stretto."

Ludovico Ariosto: Orlando Furioso e Cinque Canti. A cura di Remo Ceserani e Sergio Zatti. Vol. primo. Torinese 1997, 824 (Str. 105 Z. 3–6). Auch in Strophe 135 (a. a. O., 834) fungiert, wenngleich in andersgearteter Bedeutung, die Vogelstellerei als Bildspender. In Diederichs v. dem Werder nicht ganz vollständiger, aber dafür um andere Stoffe ergänzter Übersetzung des Epos, die in mehreren Stücken zwischen 1632 und 1636 erschien, lautet diese (hier leicht ergänzte) Stelle:

„Je mehr vom Elend er sich meinet zubefreyen/
Je mehr mus solches er vermehren und ernewen/
Dem albern Vogel gleich/ der in dem Garne hengt/
Ja oder eiffrig sich an der Leimruthe fängt.
Je mehr nun solcher schlägt mit Flügeln/ und sich windet/
Und fladdert/ je mehr er verwirrt sich befindet."

D. v. dem Werder: *Roland* III, 761. Vgl. auch S. 771.
Während die Imprese des Leimenden sich auf den aus dem Holz und den Beeren der Mispel gewonnenen Vogelleim bezieht und die schmarotzende Mistel aus dem auf dem Wirtsbaum abgesetzten Vogelkot („Von angehencktem schmeiß") hervorgehen sieht (vgl. dazu 450408 K 3), während das Reimgesetz das Fangen der Vögel mittels des Leims zur sozialen

Untugend, andere zu „leimen", d. h. zu betrügen oder zu hintergehen, verallgemeinerte und das Leimen des Leimenden just dagegen „Zum guten nur allein" verpflichtete, holte das *Abgegangene Schreiben* den Ariosto-Hintergrund ein wenig ein, indem es den Leimenden (Jost Andreas v. Randow) ermahnt — freilich unter Berufung auf seinen Namensvetter, den Böttcher Jost in den Zwiegesprächen mit seiner Seele in Gellis *Capricci* (s. Anm. 1) —, dem Geistig-Geistlichen vor dem Leiblichen, mithin der Vernunft vor dem Affekt die Oberstelle einzuräumen und „dem Guten alleine ankleben und anhangen" zu wollen. S. 200125, vgl. 210401; *Conermann II*, 82 ff.

14 *Gueintz: Sprachlehre (1641).* Vgl. 450504 K 9.

15 *Gueintz: Rechtschreibung (1645).* Vgl. 440127 K 1.

16 *Fürst Ludwig: Das Buch Hiob (1638).* Vgl. 381007 K 7, 390110 K 1 u. 421202 K 4.

17 *Fürst Ludwig: Tamerlan (1639),* eine Übersetzung der *Histoire du grand Empéreur Tamerlanes* von Jean Du Bec-Crespin, die Johann Joachim v. Wartensleben (FG 108) begonnen hatte. Vgl. 390901 K 4 u. 430505 K I 2.

450901

Georg Philipp Harsdörffer an Johann Michael Moscherosch

Antwort auf 450818 n. St. — Georg Philipp Harsdörffer (FG 368) fand Johann Michael Moscheroschs (FG 436. 1645) Schilderung eines Banketts der Poesie so anregend, daß er sich an der Diskussion der dabei erörterten Frage beteiligen möchte, ob Dichter sich zu Geschäften des Staats und der Welt eignen. — I. Verstehe man unter einem Poeten einen Pedanten, der nur ein schlechtes Sonett anzubieten hat, passe er trotz aller Schulgelehrsamkeit nicht in ansehnliche Gesellschaften. Verstehe man aber unter einem Poeten einen Mann von unverbildetem Geist, kenntnisreich in allen Disziplinen dieser Kunst und geübt in der Beredsamkeit, die man Poesie und sprechende Malerei nenne, so wird diesen Mann, wenn er auch die übrigen erforderlichen Eigenschaften besitze, die Fähigkeit zu dichten ehrenwert, nützlich und erfreulich machen. Warum könne die Rede neben der Vernunft nicht auch die Seele spiegeln? Die Alten wie Tyrtaios und die Germanen konnten mit Versen Soldaten zum Kampf anfeuern. Allein die Poesie verherrlicht die Tugend, denn allein die Musen machen als Töchter der Mnemosyne oder Memoria die Erinnerung an Heldentaten unsterblich. Moses, David und viele andere Propheten befanden nichts würdiger als die Poesie, um Gottes Lob zu singen. Musaeus, Orpheus und Linos, die Theologen des Heidentums, gossen die Gesetze in Oden, wie er, Harsdörffer, in seinem Versuch über die deutsche Philologie gezeigt habe. — Zu Anfang waren die Sprachen einfach notwendige Werkzeuge, ohne Kunstfertigkeit. Seither haben sie der Lauf der Geschichte und die Redekunst durch Regeln und Redeschmuck bereichert; schließlich hat die Poesie den Worten Zahl und Kadenz geschenkt, um über die Belehrung hinaus damit Erholung zu spenden, denn pure Wissenschaft schaffe Verdruß. Unsere Sprache ist das Gold in der Grube, mit Erde vermengt, geschliffen durch die Redekunst, die aus ihr einen von seinen Schlacken gereinigten Barren macht: Die Dichtung aber ist ein schönes goldenes Gefäß. Das Wort Dichter bezeichne einen Mann, der nicht einfach irgend etwas erfindet oder in Worten lebendig vorstellt, sondern der etwas hervorbringt: Er läßt Winde aufbrausen, Schiffe zerbersten, Waffengeklirr oder Kanonendonner hören, leichenübersäte Felder erblicken u. dergl. Um ein Meister dieser Kunst zu sein, müsse man durch umfassendes Wissen ebenso vor Tadel und Verachtung gefeit sein wie die Ärzte vor der Scharlatanerie. — II. „Geeignet für die Geschäfte des Staates und der Welt sein" — das sei die hier in

Frage stehende Eigenschaft. Die Staatsgeschäfte sind von vielerlei Art und die der mondänen Gesellschaft sind noch vielfältiger. Ein Dichter, der seines Namens würdig ist, kann die Existenz des Hofes und der Fürsten nicht ignorieren, um daraus Lobeshymnen oder Satiren abzuleiten; aber er besitzt auch andere Fähigkeiten für das öffentliche Leben. Plato und andere mehr verbannten die Poesie aus dem Staat, da die Dichter durch schamlose Berichte über die Sünden ihrer Götter die Bürger zur Nachahmung anspornten. Wenn aber die Dichter verbannt wurden, so auch Philosophen, Mediziner und Mathematiker, trotz ihres großen Nutzens für die menschliche Gesellschaft. Verfehlungen der Poeten können ja nicht der Poesie angelastet werden! Nur Ignoranten und eingeschworene Feinde wollen die Poesie aus dem Staate ausschließen, denn die Melodie liegt nicht nur in der Natur der Menschen, sondern in allen Dingen der Welt, die Gott nach Zahl und Maß geschaffen hat. Die Dichter sind ein Teil der Gerechtigkeit, denn sie belohnen die Tugend nach Verdienst und geißeln das Laster gemäß der Schuld. Die Theaterstücke dienen dem leseunkundigen Volk zum Unterricht. Tragödien erziehen die Fürsten und verschaffen der maskierten Wahrheit durch die Pforte des Vergnügens Zutritt. Ein Fürst, der inmitten seiner zahllosen Amtspflichten einen staatsklugen Zug vermittels der Poesie tun wollte, würde sich lächerlich machen. Wenn er sich aber mitunter der Poesie widmet, wie Augustus, Nero, Nerva, Antoninus Pius und Kg. Franz I. v. Frankreich, könnte er den Namen eines Herkules Musagetes davontragen und den Ruhm seines Namens unsterblich machen. — Übrigens müsse man als passenden Richter in diesem Streit einen Poeten anerkennen. Ein anderer werde nichts beurteilen können, was er nicht kennt, und so gehe der Prozeß an den Dichter als letzte Instanz. Harsdörffer bekennt, er spreche hier wie ein Unkundiger, doch nur Poeten könnten die Sprache vollkommen lehren. Dies sei ein kleiner Beitrag zu Moscheroschs Bankett — wenn die Diener die Fleischgerichte auftragen.

Q Centuria | Epigrammatum | IOHANNIS-MICHAELIS | MOSCHEROSCH | Germani. | [Linie] | *Levant & Carmina curas.* | Olymp. Nomes. Eclog. 4. | [Signet: PMS] | ARGENTINÆ | *Typis & Sumptibus* | JOH. PHILIPPI MüLBII | ET JOSIÆ STÆDELII. | [Linie] | M. DC. XXXXVIIII, Bl. [C 8]v – [C 11]r. HAB: 230.8 Poet., auch Dig. Vgl. 450818 Q. Die Kursivierung des Textes wurde von uns aufgehoben.
Nicht eingesehen werden konnte die vermutliche Titelauflage: Centuria II. | Epigrammatum | IOHANNIS-MICHAELIS | MOSCHEROSCH | Germani. | [Linie] | Levant & Carmina curas. | Olymp. Nomes. Eclog. 4. | [Signet] | ARGENTINÆ | *Typis & Sumptibus* | JOH. PHILIPPI MÜLBII | ET JOSIÆ STÆDELII. | [Linie] | M. DC. XXXXVIIII. UB Freiburg; s. *Dünnhaupt: Handbuch,* 2861.
Der gleiche Brief in: Centuria II. | Epigrammatum | JOHANNIS-MICHAELIS | MOSCHEROSCH. | *Levant & Carmina curas.* | Olymp. Nomes. Eclog. 4. | [Signet: SR] | FRANCOFVRTI, | Sumptibus SEBASTIANI ROHNERI, | Typis DANIELIS FIEVETI. | [Linie] | M. DC. LXV, S. 111–114. *Faber du Faur,* Nr. 436 (Mikrofilm). HAB: MF 1:92, Reel 92, Nr. 436. — Zit. als *1665.*
Übers. aus dem Französischen in *Kühlmann/ Schäfer: Oberrhein,* 126–128; diese Übers. auszugsweise auch in *Schäfer: Moscherosch und Harsdörffer,* 162f. – BN: Estermann, 597 Nr. 1; *Bürger,* 675 Nr. 54; *Kühlmann: Korrespondenz Moscheroschs,* 275 Nr. 11 u. 12.

A Monsieur de Harsdorff, Assesseur au Dicastere de la Republique de Nuremberg, & c.

Monsieur
IE trouve vostre banquet de la Poesie[1] d'un goust si savoureux, qu'il faut, que

i'en prēne part, bien qu'absent, & empesché aux affaires de plus difficile digestion. La Question est: Si les Poetes sont propres aux affaìres d'estat & du Monde? La distinction des termes mettra les plus scrupuleux d'accord.

I. Si par le nom d'un Poëte s'entend un Pedant crotté, qui vous presente un sonnet mal battu, remply des quelques antitheses cousues du fil blanc, & quelques Antinomasies[2] sauvages, jointes auec un rythme raboteux, qui est un homme tres sçavāt chez soy, mais fol en bonnes compagnies: (Veu q̀; la grande science & la sageße sont ordinairement detachées) un tel n'est pas capable a autres affaires d'Estat, que de l'eschole, où les verges luy serviront de sceptre. Mais si ce nom represente un homme d'un esprit naif, docte en toutes Disciplines requises pour l'accomplissement de cet art, pratique en ce genre d'Eloquence, que nous appellons Poesie & Peinture parlante[3], ie suis d'avis qu'apres les autres qualitez [C 9r] necessaires, celle d' un Poete luy soit honnorable utile & delectable: Car si l'homme sage doit estre reglé en toutes ses actions, pourquoy ne le sera-il en ses paroles, l'image de sa raison, comme la raison est l'image de son ame. La Poesie a tant de force sur les esprits, que Tirtee[4], & les anciens & Alemans au recit des vers animoient les soldats; la seule Poesie fournit de louange à la vertu. Et les Muses seules sont propres á immortaliser la memoire des actions Heroiques, estantes creues filles de Mnemosyne, ou Memoire.[5] Moyse, David & tant d'autres Prophetes n'ont rien trouvé de plus digne que la Poesie pour chanter les louanges de Dieu. Musée, Orphée & Linus[6] estoient les Theologiens du Paganisme, & les Loix des Legislateurs estoient des odes, comme i'ay monstré en mon Essay de la Philologie Allemandé.[7] Prennons l'affaire du poinct plus haut.

Au commencement les langues estoient seulement pour la neceßité, sans artifice. Depuis, l'Histoire & l'art Oratoire l'ont rendue plus riche, apres l'avoir ornée des preceptes & des fleurs: finalement la Poesie á adiousté á ces paroles le nombre & la cadence, á fin non seulement d'enseigner, comme les au-[C 9v]tres arts, mais de recreer par mesme moyen, pour empescher le degoust qu'apportent les disciplines en leurs rudiments. Nostre langage est l'or dans sa mine meslé de terre, poly par l'Oratoire y sort le lingot epuré de sa crasse: mais la Poesie est un beau vase d'or non moins riche de l'ouvrage que de la matiere.[8]

Le mot de Poete signifie un homme, non qui feint mais qui fait, ou qui represente par son Eloquence le suiet au vif, & realisé devant ses Auditeurs: il fait mutiner les vents, brizer les nauires, choquer des montagnes d'eau; il fait ouyr le cliquetis des armes, le tonnere des canons, voir la campagne iouchee des morts.[9] Tellement, que il faut tout sçauoir en perfection pour faire le maistre de cet art, si difficile & rare: car il y a force versificateurs, mais peu de Poetes, les quels ne prennet nō plus de part á leur blasme que les Medicins au mespris de charlatans; & comme plus un vin est delicat, plus son excez est nuisible au corps: ainsy la Poesie est d'autant plus excellente, que son abus est domageable.

II. Estre propre aux affaires d'Estat & du Monde est le predicat disputé en nostre question. Les affaires d'estat sont de plusieures sortes, c'elles du monde encore plus. [C 10r] Vn Poete, d'autant qu'il porte ce nom, ne peut ignorer le fait

des Princes & de la Cour, pour en tirer des Elogues ou des Satyres; mais[a] son autre employ se rapportera à ses autres qualitez civiles. Platon & plusieurs autres ont trouvé la Poesie dommagable à leurs Republiques imaginaires, & l'ont bannie en effigie; pour ce que les Poetes par leurs recits honteux Des vices de leurs Dieux induisoient les suiets à faire le semblable.[b10] Si les Poetes ont esté chassez des Estats, außi l'ont esté les Philosophes, Medicins, Mathematicins, recognus neantmoins tres utils à la societé humaine. S'il y a des vicieux d'entre eux, ce sont vices de Poetes non de la Po[e]sie: Mais il faut estre ennemy iuré des belles choses, que de vouloir bannir des Estats la Poèsie, laquelle n'est mesprise que des ignorants, & hayé de ceux qui ont les esprits dereglez: car la melodie n'est pas seulement naturelle à l'homme, mais á toutes les choses du monde, que Dieu à crees en nombre & mensure.[11] Les Poetes sont une partie de la Iustice; reconversants la vertu selon le merite, & chastiant le vice, selon le demerite. Leurs pieces Theatrales seruēt d'information au peuple, incapable de Lecture. [C 10v] Leurs Tragedies donnent des enseignements aux Princes, & font la verité masquée entrer par la porte du divertissement.[12] Vn Prince qui parmy la foule des occupations voudroit faire le coup d'Estat[13] par la Poesie, se feroit moquer: mais s'il poetise par fois, comme Auguste, Nero, Nerva, Antonin[14] & François le premier[15], il pourra emporter le nom d'Hercule Musagete[16], & immortaliser la gloire de son nom. Au reste faut il recognoistre un juge sortable en cette dispute. Qui sera-il? Vn Poete: il fera la partie. Vn autre qui n'est pas Poete: il ne sçaura estre juge en chose de la quelle il n'est pas informé, & il restera l'appel au dernier ressort. Ie confesse d'en parler comme ignorant; toute fois mes raisons, favorisent aux Poetes & á la Poesie, sans laquelle pas une langue se peut parfaitement apprendre & correctement prononcer.[17] Voila mon plat de ris, ou mon advis, en vostre banquet: s'il est aux valets d'apporter des viandes; voilà un mets de ma mal garnie Cuisine.
De Norimberg le 1. du Septembre 1645.

      Monsieur
      De Vostre tres humble & tresobligé Seruiteur
      George-Philippe Harsdorffer.

T a *1665* mais son autres qualitez civiles. — **b** *Druckfehler* sembable

K 1 In seinem als Sendbrief zu qualifizierenden Schreiben 450818 an Georg Philipp Harsdörffer (FG 368) hatte Johann Michael Moscherosch (FG 436. 1645) von einem Diplomatenbankett in Paris berichtet, auf dem die Frage diskutiert wurde, ob sich Poeten für Geschäfte des Staates und der Gesellschaft eignen. Moscherosch bejahte dies mit einer ähnlichen Argumentation wie Harsdörffer im vorliegenden Brief im Sinne eines modernen, antipedantischen, weltgewandten, lebensklugen und universal gebildeten, auch dichtenden Mannes.

    2 Antonomasie, rhetor. Stilfigur der Umschreibung eines bekannten Eigennamens durch charakterist. Beiwörter oder Eigenschaften bzw. einer Gattung durch den Eigennamen eines hervorragenden Vertreters (z. B. Aristoteles > der Stagirit; Verräter > Judas).

    3 Zur ästhetischen Engführung von Poesie als redender Malerei und Malerei als stummer Poesie bei Harsdörffer vgl. Andreas Herz: Der Hase des Zeuxis: Von Sandrart über Birken zu Harsdörffer. Harsdörffers unbekannter *Discurs Von der edlen Mahlerey*. In: Daphnis 25 (1996), 387–422, hier S. 396 f. u. 403 f.

4 Tyrtaios, griech. Elegiendichter im Sparta des 7. Jhs. v. Chr., berühmt durch seine Kampfaufrufe (Kampfparänese: ὑποθήκη), die das Heer zu höchstem Kampfgeist anspornen sollten. Seine Kampflieder (μέλη πολεμιστήρια) sind nicht erhalten. *N. Pauly* XII.1, 957 f.; Joachim Latacz: Kampfparänese, Kampfdarstellung und Kampfwirklichkeit in der Ilias, bei Kallinos und Tyrtaios. München 1977.

5 Die Musen, Töchter des Zeus/ Jupiters und der Mnemosyne/ Memoria. *Hederich*, 1654 f. u. 1669 f.

6 Zur Rolle des biblischen „Dichterkatalogs" und zum Rückbezug Harsdörffers auf die patristische und mittelalterliche Poetik vgl. Theodor Verweyen: Dichtungstheorie und Dichtungsverständnis bei den Nürnbergern. In: der Franken Rom. Nürnbergs Blütezeit in der zweiten Hälfte des 17. Jahrhunderts. Hg. John Roger Paas. Wiesbaden 1995, 178–195. — Orpheus, Musaios und Linos, drei sagenhafte Sänger/ Dichter der griech. Mythologie. Orpheus galt als Verfasser einer ganzen Reihe orphischer Texte, die ihn als Kultstifter und Begründer ritueller Handlungen und Mysterien erscheinen ließen. *N. Pauly* IX, 54–69. — Musaios erscheint in versch. Kontexten des archaisch-mythischen Zeitalters als Sproß der Musen, als Dichtungsarcheget und Schüler des Linos oder auch als Schüler oder Sohn des Orpheus. *N. Pauly* VIII, 501–504. — Linos, überliefert im Linos-Lied in Homers *Ilias*, war demnach Sohn des Apollon und einer Muse. Theben reklamierte ihn als einheim. Heros und machte ihn zum Musiklehrer des Herakles; anderen Zuschreibungen zufolge sollte er Orpheus in der Musik unterrichtet haben. Ihm wurde ein kosmolog. Gedicht zugeschrieben, das nur fragmentarisch überliefert ist. *N. Pauly* VII, 252 f. Alle drei mythisch-paganen Dichtertheologen führte, unter neuplaton. Einfluß, auch Martin Opitz (FG 200) in seinem *Buch von der Deutschen Poeterey (1624)*, 14 f. zur Illustration seiner These an, die Poesie sei „anfanges nichts anders gewesen als eine verborgene Theologie/ vnd vnterricht von Göttlichen sachen". Sie, wie auch Zoroaster, Homer, Hesiod und andere, seien die „ersten Väter der Weißheit/ wie sie Plato nennet/ vnd aller gutten ordnung" gewesen, die „die bäwrischen vnd fast viehischen Menschen zue einem höfflichen vnd bessern leben angewiesen."

7 Gemeint ist *Harsdörffer: Specimen (1646)*, das noch nicht im Druck vorlag. S. 460912, 461204A u. *DA Köthen I. 8*: 470119. Dort heißt es S. 176 ff., daß bei den Alten die Gesetze und Verfassungen in Liedform („genus carmen") abgefaßt worden seien, und noch heute werde die Strophe mit „Gesetz" verdeutscht (vgl. die „Reimgesetze" der FG-Gesellschaftsbücher). Diese Form stütze das Gedächtnis und finde sich eingegraben in Holz und Stein, auch bei den Ägyptern mit ihren hieroglyph. Steininschriften an den Pyramiden. „Sic apud Græcos quoque Cantilenæ vocantur Νόμοι ceu Leges; & apud Hebræos Decalogus cum duplici melodia canebatur […] dubio procul ex traditione Mosis, Davidis & Salomonis, de quorum Cantilenis mentio fit Devt. 31 vers. 30. 2 Sam. 22,1.1. Reg. 4,32." Diese Praxis habe sich auch bei den alten Deutschen, den Sachsen und anderen, gefunden, desgleichen bei den Galliern und ihren Druiden (179 f.).

8 Ähnlich wie Moscherosch (s. 450818 K 8) dürfte sich auch Harsdörffer hier auf den Gewährsmann Iulius Caesar Scaliger und seine *Poetices libri septem* (1561) stützen, der die Anfänge der Dichtung im Naturzustand der frühen Menschheit situierte. Demnach habe die Sprache anfänglich nur dem Notwendigen gedient, bevor sie ein natürliches Bedürfnis und natürliche Anlagen der Menschen ausgeschmückt und poetisch sublimiert hätten. Vgl. Volkhard Wels: Der Begriff der Dichtung in der Frühen Neuzeit. Berlin, New York 2009, 155. Die Poesie gab der Sprache Form und Anmut. Auch in der sinnlichen Welt, so griff

Martin Opitz das neuplaton. Erbe eines Marsilio Ficino auf, herrschen Maß, Harmonie und Ordnung, und diese bezeugen in Zusammenklang und Übereinstimmung das sittlich Gute. Vgl. Hans-Georg Kemper: Platonismus im Barock. Martin Opitz' Rede über die Dignität der Dichtkunst im *Buch von der Deutschen Poeterey* (Kap. I–IV). In: Olof Hildebrand, Thomas Pittrof (Hg.): „... auf klassischem Boden begeistert". Antike-Rezeptionen in der dt. Literatur. FS f. Jochen Schmidt zum 65. Geb. Freiburg i. Br. 2004, 37–66, hier S. 47 f. u. 52. Dieser Vervollkommnungstheorie kulturellen Fortschritts, hier: sprachlicher Verfeinerung, kontrastierte damals aber ein biblisch abgeleitetes Verfallskonzept, das sich auch bei Justus Georg Schottelius (FG 397) und Harsdörffer ausmachen läßt, wonach die adamitische Ur- und Natursprache mit dem Sündenfall und der Vertreibung aus dem Paradies, sodann mit der babylonischen Sprachverwirrung unheilbar verdorben und korrumpiert wurde und sich nur noch in Resten und angelegten Potenzen in den aus den Trümmern des babylonischen Turms hervorgegangenen Einzelsprachen, dabei besonders im Deutschen, erhalten habe. Zu Harsdörffers Theorie, die dt. Sprache könnte *vor* der babylon. *confusio linguarum* entstanden sein, vgl. 460915 K 11, ferner 440219 K 3. Immerhin erschien beiden Fruchtbringern ihre gegenwärtige Sprachepoche des Deutschen als eine der Verbesserung und des gelingenden Sprachausbaus nach Jahrhunderten der Verwahrlosung. Vgl. *Herz: Ratio und consuetudo*, 255 f. u. 275 f.

9 Die Wirklichkeiten evozierende mimetische Kraft, die Harsdörffer hier der Poesie zuspricht und die die laut- und klangmalerische Dichtung der Pegnitzschäfer prägt, zeichnete für ihn an anderer Stelle die deutsche Sprache generell aus, die in herausgehobener Weise im Zeichen das Bezeichnete, im Laut die Sache abbilde. Vgl. *Kühlmann/ Schäfer: Oberrhein*, 127 Fn. 114 u. 440826 K 11 u. 12.

10 Vgl. Plat. Pol. l. X: „EQVIDEM cogitanti mihi, inquam ego, de hac quam nuper uerbis condidimus ciuitate, cum alia permulta recte admodum statuisse uidemur, tum uel maxime quæ de poesi sunt lata. Quæ nam illa? inquit. Ne uidelicet ulla poesis pars, quæ in imitatione consistit, recipiatur." OMNIA DIVINI PLATONIS OPERA TRALATIONE MARSILII FICINI EMENDATIONE ET AD GRAECVM CODICEM COLLATIONE SIMONIS GRYNAEI, Nunc recens summa diligentia repurgata, quibus subiunctus est index uberrimus. BASILEAE IN OFFICINA FROBENIANA ANNO M D XXXIX. S. 958 OMNIA DIVINI PLATONIS OPERA TRALATIONE MARSILII FICINI EMENDATIONE ET AD GRAECVM CODICEM COLLATIONE SIMONIS GRYNAEI, Nunc recens summa diligentia repurgata, quibus subiunctus est index uberrimus. BASILEAE IN OFFICINA FROBENIANA ANNO M D XXXIX. S. 662 (übers. nach Plat. pol. 595, vgl. 598b, 607b). Dazu Ficino, a. a. O., 654: „imitationem inquam poeticam, qua ingeniosi poetæ dum perturbatos animos acrius exprimunt, interim audientium legentiumque animis perturbationes similes uehementius & profundius imprimunt. Proœmium uero eiusmodi finem noni congruene sequitur: ibi enim anima in rationem distribuitur, & in partes inferiores perturbationibus agitatas, quarum imperium in anima primum, deinde in ciuitate tyrannicum appellatur." Über die Darstellung der Laster der Götter heißt es dagegegen in Ficinos Übersetzung (Plat. pol. l. II): „Vincula autem Iunonis à filio iniecta, & Vulcanum cœlo à Patre proiectum, cum ille matri uerberatæ subuenire vellet, aut deorum pugnas, quotcunque Homerus scripsit, minime in ciuitate recipere debemus, siue per allegoriam dicta hæc dicta sint, siue sine allegoria. [...] O Adimante, poetæ quidem nos in præsentia, neque ego, neque tu sumus, sed ciuitatis institutores: hos autem nosse oportet figuras, in quibus fingere poetæ fabulas debeant: quas si excesserint, fabulæ huiusmodi admittendæ non snt. Neque tantum ad ciuitatis institutores pertinet fabulas fingere." (Plat. pol. 378f.).

11 „ABer du hast alles geordenet mit mas/ zal vnd gewicht." Buch der Weisheit (Weisheit Salomonis, apokr.) 11.21, n. *Biblia (Luther 1545)*. — Die zuvor angesprochene Dichterkritik und Verbannung der Dichter aus dem idealen Staat in Platons *Politeia*, 598b, 607b.

12 Harsdörffer schreibt hier klassische, moralisch-didaktische Topoi der Renaissancepoetik zur Rechtfertigung der Dichtkunst ab, wie sie bei Cicero, Quintilian, Horaz oder in der Herennius-Rhetorik vorgebildet waren und der Nobilitierung der Dichtung und des Dichters dienten. In seiner dreiteiligen Poetik des *Poetischen Trichters* (1650–1653, Ndr. Darmstadt 1969; der 1. Tl. ist Moscherosch zugeschrieben) wird Harsdörffer diese Argumente wiederholen, etwa in Tl. I, S. 3ff. oder in der Widmung des 3. Teils. Vgl. auch Joachim Dyck: Ticht-Kunst. Deutsche Barockpoetik und rhetorische Tradition. 3., erg. Aufl. Tübingen 1991, 113–134; Ludwig Fischer: Gebundene Rede. Dichtung und Rhetorik in der literarischen Theorie des Barock in Deutschland. Tübingen 1968, 92ff.; Hans Peter Herrmann: Naturnachahmung und Einbildungskraft. Zur Entwicklung der deutschen Poetik von 1670 bis 1740. Bad Homburg v. d. H. [u. a.] 1970, 48ff.; Boy Hinrichs: Rhetorik und Poetik. In: Die Literatur des 17. Jahrhunderts. Hg. Albert Meier. München 1999 (Hansers Sozialgeschichte der dt. Literatur, Bd. 2), 209–232, hier 229ff.

13 Nicht im heutigen Sinne von Putsch, Staatsstreich, staatlicher Umsturz, sondern als „ein staatskluger Streich". *Kühlmann/ Schäfer: Oberrhein*, 128 übersetzen *coup d'estat* falsch mit „Staatsstreich". Lt. *DW* X.2.1, 331 erst seit 1848 gebräuchlich, „umänderung der verfassung eines Staates: der Staatsstreich Napoleons III." Vgl. Trésor de Langue Française. Dictionnaire de la langue du XIXe et XXe siècle (1789–1960) VI (Paris 1978), 316 (zit. Jacques Bainville). In älterer Sprache bedeutet das Wort „stratagema politicum, artificium rationis status. vulgo Staats-Finte, Staats-List" lt. *Frisch dt.-lat.*, 313. Vgl. Grand Larousse de la langue française, t. 2 (Paris 1972), 1018 (zit. Corneille: „Sur ces grands coups d'État tout parle, et je me tais"). Nahezu im engeren Sinne von Staatstreich kommt das Wort im Frz. jedoch auch in Harsdörffers Zeit vor. S. *CONSIDERATIONS POLITIQVES SVR LES COVPS D'ESTAT* Par G. N. P. (Rome 1639), 71 f. Gabriel Naudé vergleicht hier Staatsstreiche mit ‚einfachen' Heilmitteln als Teil einer zusammengesetzten politischen Maßnahme. „Il y en a pareillement de simples qui se terminent par vn seul coup, comme la mort de Seianus, & de composez qui pour lors sont ou suiuis, ou precedez de quelques autres. Precedez comme la saint Barthelemy de la mort de Lignerolle, des nopces du Roy de Nauarre, & de la blessure de l'Admira; Suiuis, comme l'execution du Mareschal d'Ancre, de celle de Trauail, de sa femme la Marquis, & de l'exil de la Reine Mere."

14 Ks. Augustus (63 v. – 14 n. Chr.) widmete sich in seinen Nebenstunden nachweislich der Philosophie und Poesie, wie seine Regierungszeit eng verbunden war mit dem literar. Höhepunkt der „goldenen Latinität". Nur fragmentarisch erhalten sind seine Tragödie *Ajax*, Epigramme, ein Buch *Sicilia* in Hexametern, ebenso Prosa-Dichtungen und Reden. Erhalten sind Briefe und am bedeutendsten sein Tatenbericht, die *res gestae*. *N. Pauly* II, 302–314; Bernhard Kytzler: Reclams Lexikon der griechischen und römischen Autoren. Stuttgart 1997, 64–66. — Ks. Nero (37–68 n. Chr.), Schüler Senecas, widmete sich der Musik, dem Tanz und der Dichtung, und trat damit auch öffentlich auf, veranstaltete künstlerische Wettbewerbe. *N. Pauly* VIII, 850–855. — Ks. M. Cocceius Nerva (30–98 n. Chr., Ks. seit 96 als Nachfolger Domitians), zunächst protegiert von Nero, der ihm angesichts seiner literar. Versuche und Neigungen das Prädikat „Tibull seiner Zeit" attestierte. Von Nervas dichter. Übungen hat sich nichts erhalten. *N. Pauly* VIII, 856f.; *RE* 7. Halbbd., 133–154, bes. 152. — Ks. T. Aurelius Fulvus Boionius Arrius Antoninus (Antoninus Pius, 86–161 n. Chr., Ks. seit 138 als Nachfolger Hadrians). Briefe und Inschriften sind erhalten, poetische Werke nicht bekannt. *N. Pauly* I, 803–805; *RE* 4. Halbbd., 2493–2510.

15 Kg. Franz I. v. Frankreich (1494–1547) war ein bekannter Förderer der Künste u. galt als „Vater der französ. Renaissance". Auch wenn Franz I. nicht erkennbar durch eigene literarische Betätigung in Erscheinung trat, so machte er sich doch um Literatur u. Sprache verdient. So förderte er zum einen die klass. Sprachen, indem er unter Einraten des Humanisten u. Philologen Guillaume Budé (1468–1540) u. trotz Konflikten mit der mächtigen Pariser Sorbonne eigenständige Lehrstühle für Griechisch u. Latein (1530) sowie Hebräisch (1531) gründete. Mit diesen *lecteurs royaux*, die den Vorläufer des *Collège de France* bildeten, etablierte er eine universitätsunabhängige Sprachforschung. Zum anderen förderte Franz I. insbesondere die französ. Sprache, indem er Dichter u. Schriftsteller, wie Clément Marot (1496–1544), Mellin de Saint-Gelais († 1558) oder François Rabelais († 1553), an seinen Hof holte. In diesem Umfeld u. mit königl. Unterstützung entstanden z. B. die Dichtergruppe der „Pléiade" um Pierre de Ronsard (1524–1585) u. Joachim du Bellay (1522–1560), die sich durch Rückbesinnung auf antike Autoren u. nach Vorbild der griech.-latein. Literatur um die Schaffung einer frz. literar. Hochsprache bemühten. Nicht zuletzt dank der Sprachförderung, wie sie der königl. Hof bot, konnte sich die Sprechweise der Gegend um Paris u. Tour (Île-de-France, Touraine) gesamtfranzös. Geltung verschaffen. In diesem Sinne war Kg. Franz I. maßgeblich an der Entwicklung eines hochsprachl. Standards der französ. Sprache beteiligt. Zur Kunst- u. Sprachförderung unter Franz I. s. Alfred Kohler: Franz I. (1515–1547). In: Peter C. Hartmann (Hg.): Französische Könige und Kaiser der Neuzeit. Von Ludwig XII. bis Napoleon III. 1498–1870. 2. Aufl. München 2006, 52–70, bes. 54 u. 58; Robert J. Knecht: Renaissance warrior and patron. The reign of Francis I. Cambridge u. a. 1994, 425–477; Gerd Treffer: Franz I. von Frankreich (1494–1547). Herrscher und Mäzen. Regensburg 1993, 225–230. Zum literar. Umfeld am Hof Franz I. s. Jean-Eudes Girot: La poésie à la cour de François Ier. Paris 2012. — Zur Förderung der Literatur und Sprache durch Regenten vgl. auch bes. den europäischen Katalog in Opitz' Widmungsvorrede an F. Ludwig in der ersten eigenen Gedichtsammlung von 1625. S. 250700 u. *Opitz: BW* 251000 I. Vgl. Klaus Garber: Zur Konstitution der europäischen Nationalliteraturen. In: Nation und Literatur im Europa der Frühen Neuzeit. Hg. ders. Tübingen 1989, 1–55, hier 46 f. (Lit.).

16 Der Beiname Musagetes, Musenführer, wurde Apollon und Herkules gegeben, letzterem als Anzeige der Verbindung von physischer Stärke und Tapferkeit und ihrer Angewiesenheit auf die Verherrlichung und Verewigung in den Künsten bzw. deren Bedürftigkeit nach Förderung und Schutz der Starken. *Hederich*, 1675 f. Auch Sängerkriege und Turniere (Cartelle) verdeutlichen demnach das Bündnis von herrschaftlicher Kraft und Poesie. *Harsdörffer: Specimen (1646)*, Praefatio, Bl.)()()(2v: „Viri Principes & equestres, nonnumquam etiam Imperatores, Reges, certamina instituere poëtica, in quibus nobili familiâ Virgines offerebant præmium Cantus, non secus atque in hastiludiis &c." Ähnlich schon Harsdörffer in seiner „Schutzschrift für Die Teutsche Spracharbeit" (Anhang in *Frauenzimmer-Gesprächspiele* I ²1644, Ndr. 1968), Ndr. S. 386: „Bey den alten Teutschen hat die Poeterey nicht nach der Schul gestunken/ und ist des Adels gröster Ruhm gewesen die Lantzen und die Feder wol zu führen; in den Ritterspielen und derselben Beschreibungen der Jungfrauen Dank [...] darvon zu tragen". Es folgt ein Katalog mittelalterlicher „Spiel- und Gedichtschreiber", darunter Kaiser, Könige und Angehörige des Fürsten-, Grafen-, Freiherren- und Adelsstandes (S. 387 ff.). Johann Valentin Andreae (FG 464) pries in einem Brief an Johann Heinrich Boecklin Hz. August d. J. v. Braunschweig-Wolfenbüttel (FG 227) als „tantum Musagetam". S. 450722 K 2.

17 Harsdörffer betont, daß kein anderer als ein Poet letztinstanzlich den Streit über die Rolle des Dichters in Staat und Gesellschaft entscheiden kann, weil er allein vollkommen die Sprache zu lehren vermag. Er kokettiert mit der Aporie, daß nur er als Dichter, ein

Ignorant im Bereich von Staat, Gesellschaft und Recht, dieses Staatsproblem lösen muß: „il restera l'appel au dernier ressort." Denn „Les Poetes sont une partie de la Iustice".

450905

Matthäus Merian d. Ä. an Peter Knaudt

Antwort auf 450800. — Matthäus Merian d. Ä. bestätigt den Erhalt des Schreibens Peter Knaudts, dem die letzten Impresen-Visierungen des 3. und des gesamten 4. Hunderts beilagen. Man habe bereits 25 Impresen in Kupfer gestochen; er erwarte seinerseits keine Verzögerungen. Papier zum Drucken sei bereits gekauft, und sobald ein Anfang gemacht ist, werde er Druckproben schicken, was auch für die verfertigten neuen Kupferstiche gelte. Er hofft, zur nächsten Leipziger Ostermesse die versprochenen 300 Exemplare des *GB 1646* senden zu können. Bereits vor der Auslieferung bittet Merian Knaudt, einen Vorschuß über die schon gezahlten 200 Rth. hinaus durch Georg Winckler in Leipzig zu überweisen, da die Kosten für die neuen Kupferplatten, das Papier und den Druckprozeß hoch sind. Nach Auftragsbeendigung und dem Versand nach Köthen erwarte Merian den dann noch ausstehenden Betrag. Jedes Hundert Impresen werde, der Köthener Order zufolge, mit einem eigenen Titelblatt versehen. Falls es gegen Februar oder März nächsten Jahres wider Erwarten keine Transportgelegenheit für sämtliche 300 Exemplare gibt, werde Merian zumindest die bis zum Neuen Jahr gedruckten Exemplare nach Köthen und zu einem späteren Zeitpunkt die restlichen Exemplare überschicken, so daß er auf der Frankfurter Fastenmesse bereits Verkäufe tätigen könne. — Knaudt möge mitteilen, ob jeder Druckbogen in Köthen gesichtet werden soll und ob F. Ludwig dafür das Porto trage. — In der Anlage sendet Merian aktuelle Impresen-Kupferstiche samt seinem Stich der Schlacht von Alerheim. Fünf Teile seiner *Topographia* sind bereits veröffentlicht (1. die Schweiz, 2. Schwaben, 3. Bayern, 4. das Elsaß u. 5. die kurfürstl. Rheinpfalz). Im Augenblick arbeite Merian an folgenden Territorien: den drei (geistlichen) Kurfürstentümern Mainz, Köln und Trier und an Hessen, gefolgt von Franken, Thüringen/ Sachsen, Österreich usw.

Q HM Köthen: V S 546, Bl. 19rv [A: 19v]; eigenh., Adresse von Schreiberh.; rotes Lacksiegel. — D: Bircher: Merian, 702 f.; *Wüthrich: Merian Briefe*, 90–93. — BN: Bürger, 987 Nr. 9.

A Tt. Dem Ehrnvesten vnd GroßAchtparen herrn Petter Knaudt Fürst. Anhaltischen Cammermeistern *etc.* meinem großg. herrn *etc.*   Cöthen   Cito citò

Ehrenvester vnd GroßAchtparer Jnsonders gg. hochgeehrte Herrn *[sic]*

Berichte das mir die letzten, vnd das 4.te hundert abriß sampt des Herrn schreiben wol word*en*, mit der verfertigung der kupferplatten geht es nun schleunig fort, gestalt dan bei 25 Stuckh fertig sein, vnd noch täglich verfertiget^a werd*en*, also das meins theil keine hindernuß sein soll. Dise wegs^b kauffe Jch schreib pappir, worauff das werkh getrukt wirt, so baldt es angefang*en* will ich meinem gg.^{c} die ersten trukh zu sehen, vbersenden, auch von den verfertigten newen kupfern eine prob, Alßdan verhoffe ich gegen nechst künfftige Leipziger Ostermeß, die versprochenen 300 exemplar vollig zu vbersenden (so es Gott geliebet) vnd weiln mir mit verfertigung der newen kupferplatten, vnd verlag[,] pappir vnd truckens, vil auffgeht, Als habe meinen gg. herrn hiemit dienstlichen bitten wollen, Jnzwischen ehe die völlige liferung geschiht, mir mit ubermachung eines theils der bewilligten Summa noch[d] vber die allbereit empfangenen 200 Rthl. behülfflich zu sein, vnd solche mir an herrn Georg Wincklern[1] nach Leipzig, vbermachen welcher gutte gelegenheit hatt, mir solche schleünig zu verschaffen, Alß dan wan das werkh complet, vnd vbersendet sein wirt, will Jch des uberrests auch gewertig sein *etc.* Jch will iedes 100 wie gemelt, unter einem sonderbahren Tittul herauß geben, laut des herrn vbersendeten order.[2]

Wan wider verhoffen gegen dem Febr. oder künfftigen Mertzen, es keine fuhr oder gelegenheit gebe, die 300 gantze exemplar zu vbersende[n], wolte ich doch auffs wenigst gegen New Jahr, so viel als dan fertig sein wirt dieselben ubersenden, und dan den rest hernach, damit ich doch die künfftige hisige Fasten meß, davon verkauffen mochte, den sonst auß mangel fuhr veleicht *[sic]* Jch zu kurtz käme, wan ich warten solte mit verkauffen biß Jhr. fl. Gn. Jhre 300 exemplar zu vor haben solten, vnd also diser meß nicht genießen würde, so mir zu beschwerlich fallen möchte. Jch will aber mein Eüsserstes thun, damit nichts versaumpt werde,

Ob Jch solle von allen vnd jeden getruckten bogen ein exemplar send*en*, vnd ob Jhr. fl. Gn die postgelder darfür außlegen, oder mir wider erstatten wollen laßen, erwarte ich bericht. Sende hierbey ein prob etlicher newen kupfern, sampt der Jüngsten Schlacht zwischen den Beyrisch- vnd Frantzosen.[3] Von meinem vorhabend*en* deutschen Stett buch, sein Albereit 5 theil herauß, 1 Das Schweitzerlandt. 2 Der Schwäbsche Kreiß, 3 der Beyrsche kreiß. 4 das Elsaß. 5 Die untere pfaltz am Rhein,[e][4] Jetz bin ich im werck begriffen, die 3 Churfürsten am Rhein, Maintz. Coln. Trier, vnd das landt zu Hessen, herauß zu geben, und dan so fortan, Franken, Düringen Sachsen, Ostreich *etc.*[5]

Hiemit dem Allmächtig*en* wol befohlen.

Ffurt den 5. 7bris 1645.

Meines gg. Herrn Dienstwilligster

Mattheus Merian.

T a *Präfix* ver *eingefügt.* — b *Unsichere Lesung. Wohl im Sinne von* dieser Wegen, *d. i.* deswegen — c *Ergänze wohl* Herrn — d *Eingefügt.* — e *Folgt gestrichenes Wort.*

K 1 Der einflußreiche Leipziger Handelsherr Georg Winckler wickelte für F. Ludwig häufig den Finanzverkehr in der Messe- und Handelsmetropole Leipzig ab. S. 451019 K 0.
2 In 450922 erinnert Matthäus Merian d. Ä. an den Vorschuß, und in 450930 ist von einer konkreten Summe, nämlich erneut 200 Reichstalern, die Rede, die vor Projektabschluß gezahlt werden sollen. Zum Zahlungsverkehr und den Modalitäten s. 450127 K 1. Zum *GB 1646* allgemein 440130 K 3. Zur Einrichtung des *GB 1646* mit eigenen Titelblättern für jedes Hundert Impresen s. 450711 K 4.
3 Die außerordentlich verlustreiche Schlacht in Alerheim (Allerheim) bei Nördlingen, in der französ. Truppen unter Condé und Turenne, von weimarischen und hessischen Kontingenten verstärkt, nur mit Mühe das Feld gegen ein ksl.-bayer. Heer behaupteten.

450905 Matthäus Merian d. Ä.

Merian hielt sie im Kupferstich fest als „Haupt Treffen zwischē den Chur Bayrischen vnd Frantzösischen Armeen bey Allerheim geschehen den 3. Augusti A. 1645" und veröffentlichte das Stück im *Theatrum europaeum* V: 1642–1647 (Frankfurt a. M. 1647), [zwischen S. 822 u. 823]. S. Abb. S. 682 f. S. auch Lucas Heinrich Wüthrich: Das druckgraphische Werk von Matthaeus Merian d. Ae. Bd. 3: Die Merianbibel, Gottfrieds Chronik, Theatrum Europaeum, De Brys Reisen, Archontologia Cosmica, Basler Totentanz, Verlagskataloge (ohne die Topographien). Hamburg 1993, S. 190 Nr. 31. Armeeführer auf seiten Bayerns war der als Nachfolger Gf. Joachim Christians v. (der) Wahl (FG 109) am 31.5.1643 zum Generalfeldmarschall aufgestiegene Frh. Franz v. Mercy (FG 364), der in der Schlacht den Tod fand. Vgl. im vorliegenden Band die weiteren Erläuterungen in „Zu den Abbildungen", S. 139 f.; ferner *Bircher: Merian*, 703; *Conermann III*, 421–423.

4 Bereits erschienen sind zu diesem Zeitpunkt: *Merian: Topographia IV* (1 „Topographia Helvetiae, Rhaetiae, Et Valesiae" [1642]), *Merian: Topographia III, 2. Ausg.* (2 „Topographia Sueviae [1643]"), *Topographia VIII, 2. Ausg.* (3 „Topographia Bavariae" [1644]), *Merian: Topographia XIV* (4 „Topographia Alsatiae" 2. Ausg. [1644]), *Merian: Topographia XII, 2. Ausg.* (5 „Topographia Palatinatus Rheni" [1645]). Vgl. auch 450417 K 0, 450817 K 16, 450930 (K 6), 460303, 460324, 460519, 460620B, 460703, 460714 K 6, 460810, 461023 u. *DA Köthen I. 8:* 470223. Merian begann bereits 1642, eine allgemeine Topographie des Deutschen Reiches nach den Reichskreisen zu publizieren. Der Plan zur ganzen „Topographia Germaniae" lag bereits ein Jahr später vor. Die eigentliche Grundlage bildeten seit 1633 die ersten drei Bände des *Theatrum europaeum*. Als Textautor verpflichtete er den Ulmer Historiker Martin Zeiller (1589–1661). Die von diesem beschriebenen Orte wurden entweder alphabetisch oder nach ihrer polit. Einteilung lexikographisch erfaßt. Der besondere Wert der Topographiebände resultiert jedoch aus den ihnen beigegebenen Radierungen, die von Merian d. Ä. und später von seinem Sohn Caspar und ungenannten Mitarbeitern des Verlags ausgeführt worden sind. Was später dazukam, war in der Hauptsache das Werk von Caspar Merian, der in wenigen Fällen auch verlagsfremde Stecher heranzog. 1726 erschien der letzte Band, der mit der Verlagsbezeichnung von „Matthaei Merians Seel. Erben" publiziert wurde. Matthäus d. Ä. hatte 12 Bände veröffentlicht, seine Erben 19; insgesamt sind es somit 31 Bände (Deutschland 16, Frankreich 13, Italien und Rom) bzw. um 42 unter Einbeziehung der Nachträge und Zusätze. S. *Wüthrich: Merian Biographie*, 336–358, 392 u. passim; *Wüthrich: Merian Briefe*, 240–269, u. passim. Vgl. auch den Ausstellungskatalog: Unsterblich Ehren-Gedächnis zum 400. Geburtstag des hoch berühmten Delineatoris (Zeichners), Incisoris (Stechers) et Editoris (Verlegers) Matthaeus Merian des Aelteren worin eygentlich beschrieben und abgebildet wird sein gantzes Leben, seine Handzeichnungen, die Wercke zur Topographia, die Jcones Biblicae … Männglich zu Lust und Nutzen in die Teutsche Sprach gebracht Durch Wilhelm Bingsohn et al. Hg. Museum für Kunsthandwerk [Frankfurt a. M.] u. Historisches Museum [Basel]. Frankfurt 1993, 208.

5 In Arbeit befanden sich die folgenden Werke: *Merian: Topographia IX* („Topographia Archiepiscopatuvm Moguntinensis, Treuirensis et Coloniensis" [1646, erschienen 1675]), *Merian: Topographia I, 2. Ausg.* („Topographia Hassiæ" [1646]), *Merian: Topographia VII, 2. Ausg.* („Topographia Franconiae" [1648]), *Merian: Topographia XV* („Topographia Superioris Saxoniae, Thuringiae" [1650]), *Merian: Topographia XI* („Topographia provinciarum Austriacarum" [1650]). S. auch Anm. 4.

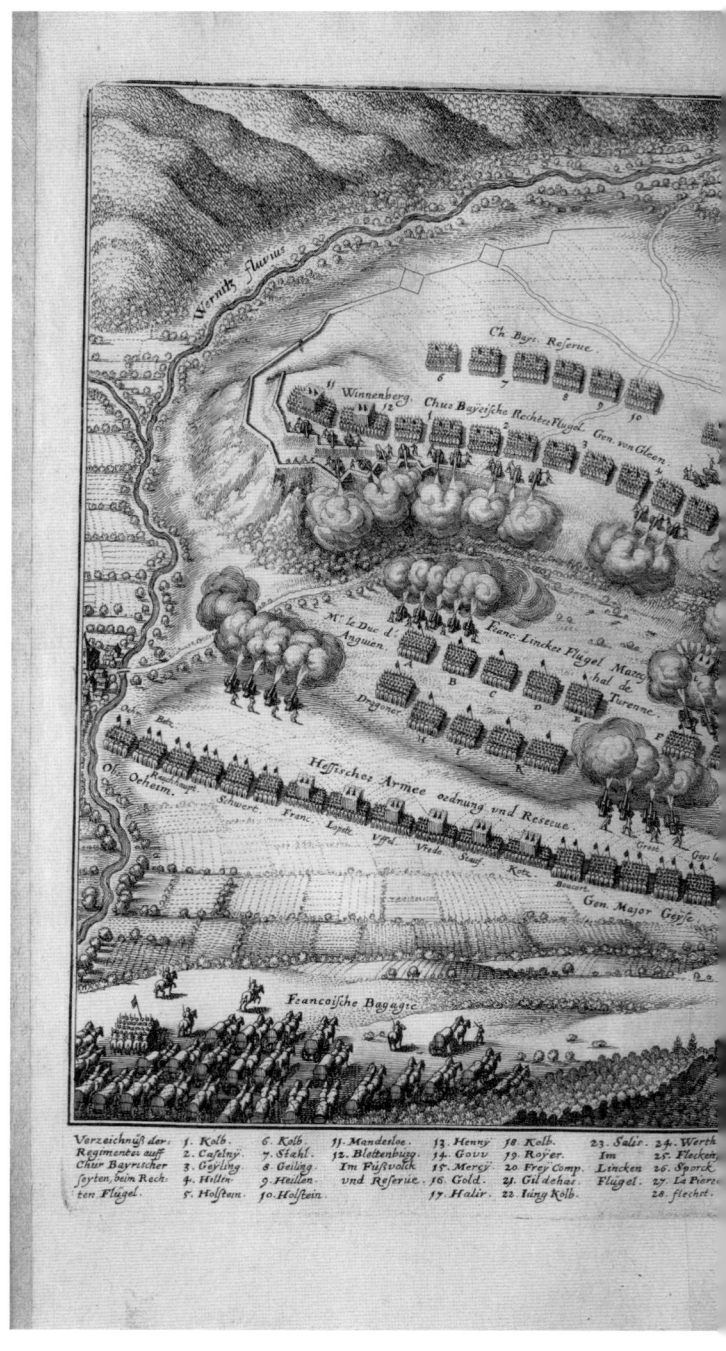

Schlacht von Alerheim am 3. August 1645. Zu 450905.

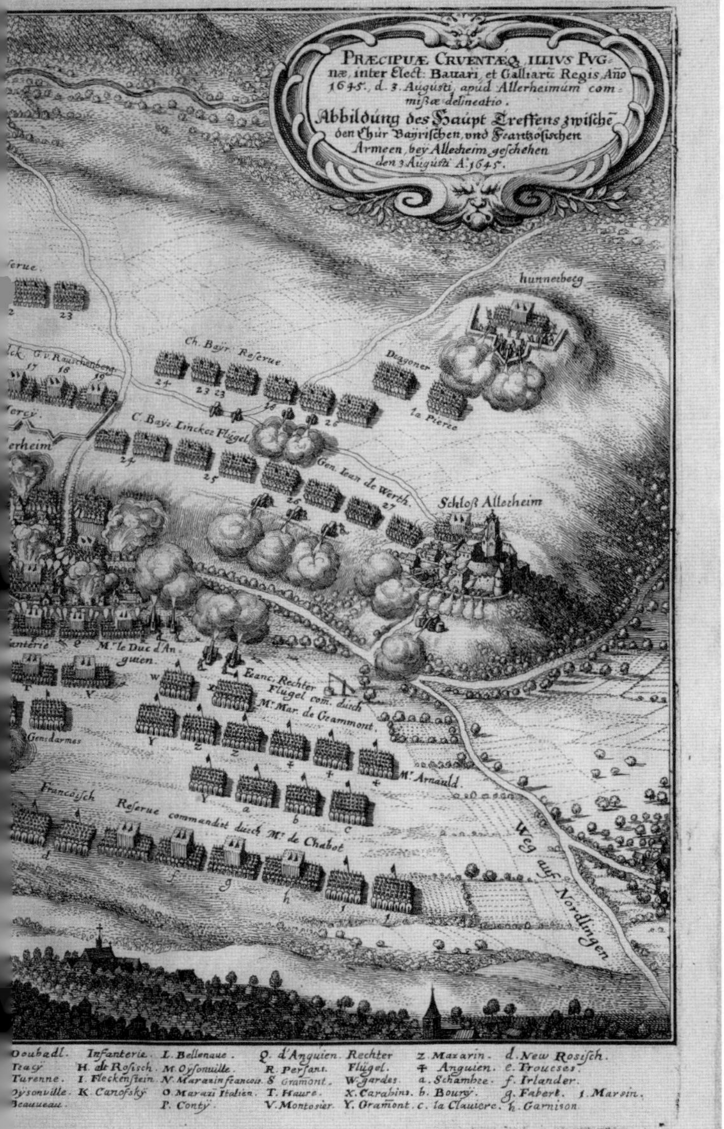
Præcipuæ Cruentæq. illius Pugnæ, inter Elect: Bavari et Galliarũ Regis Año 1645., d. 3. Augusti, apud Allerheimum commißæ delineatio.
Abbildung des Haupt Treffens zwischẽ den Chur Bayrischen, und Frantzösischen Armeen, bey Allerheim geschehen den 3 Augusti A°. 1645.
hunnerberg
Ch. Bayr. Reserue.
Dragoner
la Pierre
C. Bayr. Lincker Flügel.
Gen. Jean de Werth.
Schloß Allerheim
M.r le Duc d'Anguien.
Franc. Rechter Flügel com. durch M.r Mar. de Grammont
M.r Arnauld.
Frantzösisch Reserue commandirt durch M.r de Chabot
Weg auf Nordlingen
Doubadl. Tracy Turenne. Oysonville. Beauueau.
Infanterie. H. alt Rosisch. I. Fleckenstein. K. Canofsky.
L. Bellenaue. M. Oysonuille. N. Mazarin francois. O. Mazari Italien. P. Conty.
Q. d'Anguien. R. Persant. S. Gramont. T. Haure. V. Montosier.
Rechter Flügel. W. gardes. X. Carabins. Y. Gramont.
Z. Mazarin. 4 Anguien. a. Schambre. b. Boury. c. la Clauiere.
d. New Rosisch. e. Trouesses. f. Irlander. g. Fabert. h. Garnison
1. Marsin.

450919

Diederich von dem Werder an Fürst Ludwig

Beantwortet durch 450921. — Diederich v. dem Werder (FG 31. Der Vielgekörnte) sendet F. Ludwig (Der Nährende) einen für Georg Philipp Harsdörffer (FG 368. Der Spielende) bestimmten Posten Atlas-Stoff und einen eigenen Brief an Harsdörffer (zur Weiterleitung) zu. Die Antwort der FG an den Spielenden (450919A) findet Werders Zustimmung. — Falls ihn die hessen-kasselschen Auftraggeber (einer Gesandtschaft) nicht unaufschiebbar zur höchsten Eile drängen, will Werder noch F. Ludwig aufsuchen.

Q HM Köthen: V S 544, Bl. 465rv u. 467rv [A: 467v], 465v u. 467r leer; eigenh.; Sig. — Bl. 466rv eingelegter Zettel, Rückseite leer, s. 460705 III. — *D: KE*, 171 (ohne Jahresangabe; vgl. 178). — *BN: Bürger*, 1439 Nr. 6.

A *Dem Nehrenden   Cöthen   zuhanden*

Dem Nehrenden wird hiermit
1. das brief[1] v.[a] atlas bündlein, samt meinem an den Spielenden, überschickt[2]
2. Auch bericht gethan, das mir die andtwort an ihn wohlgefallen[3]
3. Wan mich die Hessen[4] nicht übereilen[5] wil ich mich einstellen
   Gott mit uns.
   Des Nehrenden dienstwilligster
   der Vielgekörnte.

Reinsdorff 19 Herbst Monats

T a v. atlas *eingefügt in das zusammengeschriebene* briefbündlein

K 1 Das Kompositum Briefbündlein legt nahe, hier an die (heute nur noch im Dimunitivum — ein Briefchen Nadeln usw. — gebräuchliche) Bedeutung von Brief als Papierumschlag, Tüte, kleines Päckchen zu denken. *Paul Wb.*, 189 (s. v. „Brief", unter Ziffer 3); *DW* II, 379 (dito, unter Ziffer 6). Hier ist wohl ein in Papier eingeschlagenes Päckchen Atlasstoff gemeint.

2 Diederich v. dem Werder (FG 31. Der Vielgekörnte) schickt F. Ludwig (Der Nährende) ein Paket, das neben seinem eigenen Begleitschreiben an Georg Philipp Harsdörffer (FG 361. Der Spielende) einen Posten Atlas — einen glatten, glänzenden Stoff ähnlich der Seide, heute meist Satin —, auf den Harsdörffers Wappen und Imprese (und wohl auch Johann Michael Moscheroschs, FG 436. 1645) zu sticken seien. In 451101 bedankt sich Harsdörffer bei F. Ludwig für den geschickten Stoff. Harsdörffer ließ am Ende seine Stikkereien in Leipzig ausführen und entrichtete dafür die vorgesehene Gebühr in Höhe von 10 Reichstalern. Die Einzelheiten dazu in 450504A K 5.

3 Werder scheint demnach auch der Entwurf von F. Ludwigs Antwort an Harsdörffer 450919A zugestellt worden zu sein, denn darauf dürfte sich seine hier geäußerte Zustimmung bezogen haben. Vgl. 450921 u. 450921A, in welch letzterem Schreiben sich Werder entschuldigt, F. Ludwigs Brief 450919A voreilig, also ohne Abwarten einer endgültigen Ausfertigung abgesandt zu haben.

4 Die Erwähnung der Hessen bezieht sich mit hoher Wahrscheinlichkeit auf eine bedeutsame diplomatische Mission, mit der Werder auch zu Beginn des Jahres 1646 beschäftigt war. S. 460125 Beil. u. K I. Werder sollte wohl noch im September nach Kassel oder auch schon nach Berlin reisen, um die Eheschließung zwischen dem jungen Lgf.en Wilhelm VI. v. Hessen-Kassel (FG 694. 1659) mit Pzn. Hedwig Sophia v. Brandenburg (1623–1683) zu sondieren.

5 Hier im Sinne von „zu allzu großer Eile drängen". Vgl. *DW* XI.2, 172 f.

450919A

Fürst Ludwig an Georg Philipp Harsdörffer

Antwort auf 450817. Beantwortet durch 451101. — F. Ludwig (Der Nährende) hat am 10. 9. 1645 Georg Philipp Harsdörffers (FG 368. Der Spielende) Brief mit einem lateinischen Schreiben (Marco Aurelio Severinos) und vielen Druckbögen empfangen, welche Ludwig teilweise zurücksendet. — Ablehnung von Harsdörffers Vorschlag, Beziehungen zur Accademia degli Oziosi aufzunehmen und deshalb unter dem Siegel der FG an (deren Oberhaupt) Giovanni Battista Manso Marchese di Villa Lago zu schreiben. Eine Beratung unter in der Nähe lebenden Mitgliedern der FG ergab, daß eine deutsche Gesellschaft in einer fremden Sprache schlecht mit einer ausländischen eine Korrespondenz eröffnen könne. Der Anstoß zum Vorschlag sei nicht von beiden Gesellschaften, sondern nur von jeweils einem ihrer Mitglieder gegeben worden, so daß es erst einmal bei deren Briefwechsel bleiben solle. Es sei auch ungeklärt, welche der beiden Vereinigungen älter sei, und von der müsse die jüngere zuerst gegrüßt werden — übrigens rühmten sich die Neapolitaner der Abkunft von den Deutschen. Auch hätten die Italiener nicht an die Deutschen in deren Sprache geschrieben, so daß diese aus Höflichkeit den Brief in Italienisch beantworten müßten. Schriebe die FG auf Florentinisch, riskiere sie durch die abgekürzte Konjunktion *e* (statt et) oder durch das *ed* Widerspruch. Auch sei man nach so vielen Jahren inzwischen des Toskanischen entwöhnt. Im übrigen schätze man Severinos gelehrte Schriften und bitte um Nachricht, wo man die von Harsdörffer mitgesandten Titel, besonders die in dem Verzeichnis markierten bekommen könne. — F. Ludwig bekräftigt seine Kritik an der Initiale eines Gedichts Harsdörffers in dessen *Frauenzimmer-Gesprächspielen*, welche den Buchstaben N (für Ludwigs Gesellschaftsnamen ‚Der Nährende') mit einer Weizengarbe (statt mit einem Weizenbrot) illustriert, was nicht zu seiner in Kupfer gestochenen Imprese im jetzt wieder aufgelegten Gesellschaftsbuch (*GB 1646*) passe. — F. Ludwig behält die von Harsdörffer überschickten beiden italienischen Sonette, den Anfang der Akademieschrift (Severinos) über die Konjunktion *e* und (Fontanas) beide Zeichnungen der Mondoberfläche (wenigstens einstweilen) zurück. — Der Fürst schickt Harsdörffer ein Exemplar der *Rechtschreibung* (Christian Gueintzens; FG 361. Der Ordnende), welche auf der eigenen Mundart beruhe. Wollen andere die Orthographie auf der Grundlage ihrer Mundart systematisch darstellen, mögen sie es tun, wie man es auch vom Suchenden (Justus Georg Schottelius; FG 397), dem ebenfalls ein Exemplar zugehe, erwarte, da er sich schon mehrfach dazu bereit erklärt habe. Einen gütlichen Austausch von Schottelius und Gueintz über die Sprachlehre würden der Nährende ebenso wie der Ordnende willkommen heißen. Da es vor allem um eine Sammlung und Abgleichung der Stammwörter gehe, hält F. Ludwig eine solche Vergleichung nicht für allzu umständlich, so daß Grammatik und Orthographie nach seiner Erwartung vervollkommnet werden können. — Der Fürst erkundigt sich nach Johann Michael Moscheroschs (FG 436. 1645) Reaktion auf den ihm zugeteilten Gesellschaftsnamen des Träumenden. Moscherosch möge doch, wenn es passe, der FG ein Exemplar der von ihm selbst herausgegebenen *Gesichte Philanders von Sittewalt* schicken, damit man sie von deren Nachdrucken unterscheiden könne. — Die Gesellschaft werde Harsdörffer auch für die künftige Übermittlung von erwähnten lateinischen, italienischen und deutschen Schriften schätzen.

Q Eigenh. Konzept: HM Köthen: V S 545, Bl. 326rv u. 329rv (329r Nachschrift, v leer). Abschrift: A. a. O., Bl. 327rv u. 328rv (328r Nachschrift, v leer); Schreiberh. mit Zusätzen und Korrekturen von F. Ludwigs H. In 450921A entschuldigte sich Diederich v. dem Werder (FG 31), weil er die Ausfertigung des Briefs aus Versehen direkt an Harsdörffer geschickt hat, anstatt sie nochmals an den Fürsten zu senden.

D: *KE*, 341–344 (nach der Abschrift); danach auszugsweise in *Schäfer: Moscherosch und Harsdörffer*, 172 f., Textauszug 173. — *BN: Bürger*, 950 Nr. 57.

Unsere Transkription folgt dem Konzept von F. Ludwigs Hand. Die wesentlichen Differenzen der Abschrift, das sind kleinere, evtl. vom Schreiber stammende Eingriffe (©) und Ergänzungen bzw. Verbesserungen von F. Ludwig (*Lw*), werden durch die Großbuchstaben ᴬ, ᴮ usw. bezeichnet und im Apparat **T Abschrift** vermerkt. Die im Konzept oft fehlenden, aber in der Abschrift vorhandenen Umlautzeichen tragen wir — wie es in unserer Veröffentlichung üblich ist — nicht nach. Auch vermerken wir die höchstwahrscheinlich vom Kopisten stammenden (Ad-hoc-)Korrekturen nur, wenn sie grammatikalischer Natur sind, zumal der Schreiber sich streng am Konzept F. Ludwigs orientierte. Trotz der marginalen Varianten der Abschrift im Vergleich zum Konzept könnten diese darauf hindeuten, daß der Abschrift eine leicht überarbeitete (verlorene) Zwischenversion zugrunde lag.

A *Fehlt.*

Des Spielendenᵃ antwortᵇ vom 17. abgewichenes Augustmonats ist dem Nehrenden den 10. dieses mit dem beygelegten lateinischen schreibenᶜ als den gedruckten unterschiedenen bogen, dieᵈ theilsᴬ hiermit wieder zurücke gefertiget werden, wol zu kommen;¹ Für welche mittheilung dem Spielenden gebührlicher danck gesaget wird.

Man hat auch daraus des Spielenden vorschlag vernommen, wie er vermeinet das unter des Ertzschreins Jnsiegel an h.ᴮ Marggraffen **Villa**² und seine geselschaft, Jtalianisch zu schreiben, und deren subtilen Geister kundschaft dadurch zu suchen, mit anfurung etzlicher ursachen, darzu dergleichen Briefwechselung dienen wurde.³

Nun ist denen alhierᵉ und in der nähe sich befindenden von der Fruchtbringenden geselschaft hiervon bericht geschehen, und seind darbey folgende bedencken fürgefallen, warum man in Nahmen der gantzen Fruchtbringenden als einer Deutschen geselschaft nicht wol an eine andere ausländische, und in fremder sprache noch zur zeit nicht schreiben könte.

1) Weil die veranlaßung dergleichen briefwechsels nur von einemᶠ gliede dieser Deutschenᵍ und einemʰ Jtalianischen jener geselschaftⁱ, nemlich des Spielenden, und des **Assettato**⁴, zu recht gesetzten, herrüret, das es darum sich nicht anders

geziemen^j wolle, weil der gantze leib nicht begrußet; es noch zur zeit bey der sonderbaren briefwechselung dieser beyden personen, bleiben zu laßen,

2) würde zuvor^k zu wißen vonnöten sein, welche geselschaft oder **Accademi** älter als die andere, were nun jene älter, solte es billich nach dem alten Deutsche^g C *[sic]* sprichworte gehen, daß der gruß von dem (ältesten) hoffe keme: Were aber diese älter so were auch zuerinnern, das doch die veranlaßung und ersuchung zum wenigsten von zweyen aus der geselschaft, oder dem haubte mitt aufgetragener volmacht geschehen sollen^l, und weil die Jtalianer, als insonderheit die **Napolitaner** guten theils sich^g der ankunft von den Deutschen^m wie^n bey zeiten der konige aus dem Schwäbischen geblute,^5 gar wol^o nach ausweisung der geschichte, geschehen können, rühmen und solche ihnen eine ehre zu sein erachten, man auch billich solcher ehre von dannen solle gewertig sein.

3) Solte es sich nicht gar wol fugen, das man aus dieser Deutschen geselschaft wolte an jene Jtalienisch schreiben, man hette dan vorerst aus jener an uns Deutsch geschrieben^p, auf das von beyden theilen die liebe und höfligkeit bey einer und der andern sprache gleich gultig in acht genommen wurde.

4) Solte man hiesiges ortes in Jtalianischer sprache etwas von hinnen in nahmen der gantzen Fruchtbringenden^g geselschaft^q in schriften^r gelangen laßen, und wurde sich der^s Florentinischen^t eingefurten art mit dem e,^u so das verkurtzte et genennet wird,^6 und des^g ed gebrauchen, so durfte es jenerseits wiedersprechung geben, zu geschweigen das man der rechten art in gut **Toscanisch** zu stellen, nach so viel verlauffenen Jharen entwohnet,^7 und^v leichte darinnen einen fehler begehn könte. [326v]

Aus^w obangezogenen ursachen nun wird dafur gehalten das es fur dismal bey den absonderlichen wechselbriefen zwischen dem Spielenden^x und h.^B **Marc Aurelio Severino** gar^y wol und fuglicher bleiben köne. Nichts desto minder aber werden dieses furnemen^D Mannes gelehrte schriften hochgehalten, und wan der Spielende kan anleitung geben wie und wo man dieselben^z und sonderlich die jenigen, so albereit gedruckt und^E mit einem schwartzen tiplein gezeichnet,^8 erlangen könne, sol es dem Nehrenden und vielen aus der Fruchtbringenden geselschaft sehr angenehm^F sein.^aa

Zu der erinnerung wegen des Nährenden^G gemählde hat die erklerung des buchstabens N hinden^ab an dem ersten wieder aufgelegten theile^ac des Spielenden^ad gesprächspiele ursache geben, darin die garbe im^ae buchstaben^g N. nicht anders genennet wird und das gemählde bey den nun wieder aufgelegten geselschaft gemählden in^af kupfer eben dieses zeigen wird.^9

Aus dem gemählde wird sich weitzenbrot wan es gemahlet fur dem Rocken brote wol erkennen laßen, und in dem^H kupfergestochenen, wan man sie mit Farben ausgestrichen, kan also darin kein fehler,^ag so wenig als bey andern dergleichen kupferstucken so^ah die farben nicht ausdrucken, angezogen werden, und wird insgemein von den gelehrten Naturkundigern insonderheit^ai in Jtalien dafur gehalten, das Weitzenbrot, beßer^g als Rocken oder ander brot^aj nehre.^10 Hiermit verbleibt

Des Spielenden gantzwilliger
Der Nehrende

Cöthen den 19 Herbstmonats^(ak I) 1645.

Die^(al J) beyden Jtalianischen Sonetti[,]^11 der eingang della querela della^(am) et und der abriß von den zweyen gestalten des Monden^12 am 31. Octob. oder Weinmonats 1629 und 20. Junij oder Brachmonats 1630^K seind zurucke alhier behalten worden; können aber auf begeren auch wieder von hinnen uberschicket^L werden. [329r]

N. S.
Dem Spielenden wird hiermit auch ubersendet die Rechtschreibung wie sie dieser örter Mundart nach^(an), eingerichtet, übersehen^g und^(ao) gedrucket;^13 wollen^(ap) nun andere ihre Mundarten auch durch ordentlich^M verfaßung an den tag geben, stehet es zu ihrem gefallen, diese sol verhoffentlich niemand ärgern können, weil sie mit genugsamen erheblichen ursachen ausgefuret; Ja der Suchende^14 wird sich zuversichtlich gerne darzu bequemen, inmaßen er sich schon^(aq) zum öftern anerboten,^(ar) auch dieses buchlein ihme an ietzo überfertiget wird.

Wil dan der Suchende mit dem Ordnenden ferner aus der Deutschen^A Sprachlehre schriftlich über eines und das ander^N in der gute handeln, wird es der Nehrende gerne sehen, auch dem Ordnenden nicht zu wieder sein, Und bedüncket dem Nehrenden die sache sey nicht weitlauftig^O, und beruhe vornemlich^P in samlung der Stamwörter, wan die verhanden, wird sich der ausschlag leichtlich finden; Und dan die Sprachlehre und Rechtschreibung volkömlicher konnen eingerichtet werden.

Ob und wie der Traumende seinen geselschaft nahmen angenommen möchte man bey dem Ertzschreine gerne nachricht haben. Und solte der geselschaft angenem sein, wan er derselben^Q seine gesichte so viel ihrer^(as) von ihme selbsten ausgegangen, bey^(at) guter gelegenheit überschickete, das man sie von den andern, so nachgedruckt worden, und herummer gehen, unterscheiden könte.^(au 15)

Jn mittheilung anderer angezogenen feinen sachen so in lateinischer, Jtalianischer, als Deutscher sprache ausgangen^A, wird der Fruchtbringenden geselschaft vom Spielenden, ein hoher angenemer gefallen geschehen, deren der Spielende allezeit in gutem gedechtnis^R befohlen ist. Es verbleibet auch
Des Spielenden gantzwilliger
Der Nehrend^S

Geben wie im brieffe.

T **a** *Statt* <Weitgeehrter Spielende.> *Unsichere Leseung, evtl. auch* <Weitgel[e]hrter Spielende.> — **b** *Anfang umgestellt aus* Dem Nehrenden ist <seine> antwort vom 17. abgewichenes Augustmonats — **c** lateinischen schreiben *eingefügt für* <schriften> — **d** *Eingefügt bis* gefertiget werden, — **e** alhier und *eingefügt*. — **f** *Folgt* <oder zwey> — **g** *Eingefügt*. — **h** einem Jtalianischen *eingefügt*. — **i** *Folgt* <herrüret> — **j** anders geziemen *eingefügt über* <schreiben> — **k** *Eingefügt über* <bedencken> — **l** *Eingefügt über* <muste> — **m** *Folgt Einfügung bis* geschehen können, — **n** *Eingefügt für* <wie es> — **o** *Folgt* <geschehen> — **p** geschrieben, auf das *eingefügt für* <das also> — **q** *Folgt* <etwas> — **r** in schriften *eingefügt*. — **s** *Folgt* <Toscani> — **t** *Folgt* <art> — **u** *Folgt* <und> — **v** *Folgt* <auch> — **w** Aus obangezogenen ursachen *zugleich Kustode*. — **x** *Wortanfang gebessert aus* Se — **y** *Eingefügt bis* fuglicher — **z** *Folgt* <und h> — **aa** *Folgt* <Wil aber der Spielende was er an dies [en] Mann ferner schreibet> *(Textverlust im Falz, Konjektur in eckigen Klammern)*. — **ab** hinden an *eingefügt für* <bey> — **ac** *Wortreihenfolge durch Ziffern umgestellt aus* theile wieder aufgelegten *Folgt* <des> — **ad** des Spielenden *eingefügt für* <der Sinn> <seinen> — **ae** *Gebessert aus unleserlichen Buchstaben*. — **af** in <den> kupfer *eingefügt*. — **ag** *Folgt* <ange> — **ah** *Bis* ausdrucken *eingefügt*. — **ai** *Eingefügt bis* Jtalien — **aj** *Folgt* <angezogen> — **ak** *Gebessert aus* <August>monats — **al** *Absatz auf der Seite am Rande quergeschrieben*. — **am** *Folgt* <&c &c> — **an** <und dieser> Mundart nach *eingefügt für* <ubersehen> — **ao** *Folgt* <nun> — **ap** *Eingefügt für* <Haben> — **aq** *Folgt* <den> — **ar** *Folgt* <Wollen> — **as** *Folgt* <aus> — **at** *Eingefügt bis* gelegenheit — **au** *Folgt* <Oder wie im lauffe>

T Abschrift — **A** *Einfügung Lw.* — **B** © herrn — **C** © Deutschen — **D** © fürnehmen — **E** *Einfügung Lw* albereit gedruckt und — **F** © angenem — **G** © Nehrenden — **H** © den — **I** *Lw gebessert aus* August — **J** *Lw Absatz auf der Seite am Rande quergeschrieben*. — **K** *Lw Zusatz*. — **L** *Lw* geschicket — **M** © ordentliche — **N** © andere — **O** © weitleuftig — **P** *Lw* furnemlich *gebessert aus* vornemlich — **Q** © aus <über> selben — **R** © gedächtnüs — **S** © Nehrende

K Zur Übermittlung der Ausfertigung dieses Schreibens an Georg Philipp Harsdörffer (FG 368. Der Spielende. 1642), das F. Ludwig Diederich v. dem Werder (FG 31) zur Durchsicht geschickt hatte, s. 450919, 450921 u. 450921A. In 450921A entschuldigt sich Werder, weil er den vorliegenden Brief aus Versehen direkt an Harsdörffer geschickt hat, ohne ihn zu seiner endgültigen Ausfertigung nochmals an den Fürsten zu senden.

1 S. 450817 mit den Beilagen. In 450923C erkundigt sich Harsdörffer bei F. Ludwig (der Nährende), ob die Beilagen aus Neapel in Köthen eingetroffen seien.

2 Giovanni Battista Manso Marchese di Villa Lago war der Principe der Accademia degli Oziosi (Neapel). S. 450817 K II 4, vgl. 451217 K 4.

3 Zu Harsdörffers Plan, die FG mit ital. Akademien zu vernetzen s. 450817, 451101 u. 451217. Vgl. *Conermann: Harsdörffers Plan*.

4 Marco Aurelio Severino hieß bei den Oziosi L'Assettato, von F. Ludwig hier als der „zu recht gesetzte" übersetzt. *Hille: Teutscher Palmbaum* (1647) übersetzte mit „L'Assettato" den Gesellschaftsnamen Der Bequeme, d.i. Cuno Ordomar v. Bodenhausen (FG 69). S. 450817 K 4 u. bes. IV Q (Severinos Gesellschaftsname u. Imprese).

5 Die Staufer, die durch die dynastische Verbindung mit den Normannen zu den Herrschern Süditaliens wurden.

6 S. Severinos Akademieschrift über die verkürzte toskan. Konjunktion *e* in 450817 IV.

7 F. Ludwig war 1600 in die Accademia della Crusca aufgenommen worden, hatte auch an deren erstem Wörterbuch mitgearbeitet und später Bücher seines Sprachlehrers und Crusca-Sekretärs Bastiano de' Rossi übersetzt und kommentiert herausgegeben (s. *DA Köthen II. 1*). Er hatte auch in toskanischer Sprache korrespondiert (s. z.B. 230819). Lud-

wigs Italienischkenntnisse hatte Barthold Nihusius in einem kritischen Epigramm zu seiner reformierten Konfession angesprochen: „*Illustrißimo D. LVDOVICO, Principi Anhaltino.* | Diligis Italiam, Princeps præclare, profanam. | Præclarum est, sacram diligere Italiam." BARTOLDI NIHVSII | DISTICHA. | LIBRI QVATVOR. | *Accedit ejusdem* | EPIGRAMMATVM | VARIORVM | LIBER SINGVLARIS. | [Zierstück] | COLONIÆ AGRIPPINÆ | Apud IOHANNEM KINCKIVM. | M DC XLII (HAB: Li 6685), 37.

8 S. die in Severinos Werkeliste so gekennzeichneten Schriften in 450817 V.

9 Vgl. 440715 K 2, 450611 u. 450817 K 11 zu der als Anspielung auf die Imprese des Nährenden verstandenen N-Initiale in Versen Harsdörffers. Die originale Imprese (‚Gemälde') F. Ludwigs, die schon im *GB 1629/30* abgebildet worden war, erschien erneut im *GB 1646*. Zu *GB 1629/30* s. Sachregister: Gesellschaftsbuch FG u. zum *GB 1646* 440130 K 3. S. Abb. S. 286.

10 Vgl. *Vocabolario della Crusca 1623*, 389: „GRANO. Quella biada, della qual communemente facciamo il pan per lo vitto, ned è, per la sua eccellenza, compreso sotto'l general nome dell'altre biade. Lat. *frumentum tritticum*. M. Aldobr. Grano è una biada temperata, conueneuole sopra tutte le biade alla natura dell'huomo." Die im *Vocabolario* zit. Quelle löst die „Tavola dell'abbreviatvre" so auf: „Volgarizzamento del trattato di Medicina di Maestro Aldobrandino. Testo a penna. Di Pier del Nero." Als Verfasser ist zweifelsohne der Arzt, Botaniker, Zoologe und Geologe Ulisse Aldrovandi (1522–1605) gemeint, der Sammler eines riesigen Herbariums und Begründer des Bologneser botan. Gartens. Ein Exemplar dieser Ausgabe des Wörterbuchs war auch in F. Ludwigs Besitz, s. 230802 (K 8). Vgl. auch das ital. Sprichwort „Grano pesto fa buon cesto".

11 Wohl der Gedichtwechsel zwischen Severino und Cassiano dal Pozzo, s. 450817 IV Q.

12 Vgl. die Beschreibung der in Köthen verbliebenen Teile von Severinos *La Qverela della (&) accorciata* in 450817 IV und die Darstellung der Mondansichten zu 450817 III. S. Abb. S. 627.

13 *Gueintz: Rechtschreibung (1645)*. S. allgemein dazu 440127 K 1. Der nachstehende Vorschlag, Sprecher anderer Mundarten sollten ihre Mundart in regulativer Weise beschreiben und dann die Ergebnisse untereinander vergleichen, ist die logische Konsequenz der phonographischen Auffassung, man solle schreiben, wie man spricht. Da es weder eine allgemein anerkannte Hochlautung/ Phonetik noch eine Leitvarietät der gesprochenen Sprache gab (vgl. *Conermann: Hochsprache und Umgangssprache*), und sich der Streit um die Normierungsparameter der dt. Rechtschreibung an genau diesem Problem entzündete — was denn überhaupt als beste und „reinste" Aussprache gelten könne —, war der Weg eines Ver- und Abgleichs der Mundarten naheliegend, wenngleich umständlich und wohl auch illusionär gegenüber der geschichtlich vorbereiteten Setzung des Omd. als sprachlandschaftliche Priorität. Die andere, von Schottelius (s. Anm. 14) und Harsdörffer vorgezogene Lösung bestand darin, die Rechtschreibungslehre auf der inneren morphologisch-grammatischen Gesetzmäßigkeit der Sprache zu errichten, d. h. im wesentlich morphematisch zu begründen. Zwischen diesen beiden Polen bewegten sich die fruchtbringerischen Argumentationen teils gegen-, teils miteinander. F. Ludwig wird die Anregung, die Mundarten lehrmäßig aufzuarbeiten und zu vergleichen, in 450923B (dem auch ein Ex. von *Gueintz: Rechtschreibung [1645]* für Schottelius beilag) u. in seiner Antwort auf Harsdörffers Brief 460131 (s. 460200 K 1) wiederholen und bekräftigen. Vgl. auch 460406; *Herz: Rechtschreibdebatte*.

14 Justus Georg Schottelius (FG 397. Der Suchende. 1642). F. Ludwig überließ es in seiner und Gueintz' Auseinandersetzung mit Schottelius diesem, eine Neubearbeitung des Sprachbuchs [*Schottelius: Sprachkunst (1641)*] herauszubringen, konterkarierte damit zwar

450921 Fürst Ludwig   691

den Vorschlag, die strittigen Punkte auf dem Wege der Korrespondenz abzuhandeln und sich durch ein Schiedsgericht zu einigen, befürwortete aber einen gütlichen Briefwechsel zwischen Schottelius und Gueintz über die strittigen Fragen. S. 450817, N. S. u. K 12, 450923B. Schottelius veröffentlichte die Überarbeitung seines Sprachbuchs erst nach F. Ludwigs und Gueintz' Tod: *Schottelius: Sprachkunst (1651)*. Im vorliegenden Brief wird die schiedliche Einigung in strittigen Sprachfragen als Grundlage eines gemeinschaftlichen Wörterbuchprojekts von F. Ludwig für möglich gehalten. Eine solche war schon im Hinblick auf die Lemmata-Ansetzung nötig angesichts der widerstreitenden Stammwort-Auffassungen. Eine Einigung wurde nicht erzielt.

15 Vgl. zu diesem Wunsch nach einer autorisierten Ausgabe von Johann Michael Moscheroschs (FG 436. Der Träumende. 1645) *Gesichten Philanders von Sittewald* auch 451209 u. 460406 K 8.

450921

Fürst Ludwig an Diederich von dem Werder

Antwort auf 450919. Beantwortet in 450921A. — F. Ludwig bittet Diederich v. dem Werder (FG 31) um ein bei ihm vermutetes Antwortschreiben, das Georg Philipp Harsdörffer (FG 362) direkt aus Köthen zugehen soll, und um den zweiten Teil des *Ibrahim*. Der Nährende wäre besonders froh, könnte diese Bitte noch vor der Abreise des Vielgekörnten erfüllt werden.

Q HM Köthen: V S 544, Bl. 489rv [A: 489v]; eigenh. — Der Empfänger schrieb den Text und die Anschrift seiner Antwort 450921A auf den von F. Ludwig geschickten Zettel. — Nicht in *KE*.

A Dem Vielgekörnten Ein zu hendigen.

Der Vielgekörnte hat jüngsten zu Reinsdorf behalten die antwort, so an den Spielenden von hinnen sollen abgehen,¹ die wird hiermit wieder begeret, als wol das zweite theil des Jbrahims geschichte², würden sie aber vor seinem abreisen³ mit hereingebracht, sollte es beyden Nehrenden⁴ desto lieber sein, welches bey zeigern mit wenigen sollen berichtet werden[.]
Cöthen den 21. Herbstmonats 1645

K 1 F. Ludwig glaubt, Diederich v. dem Werder (FG 31. Der Vielgekörnte) habe seine (Ludwigs) und der FG Antwort 450919A an Georg Philipp Harsdörffer (FG 368. Der Spielende) auf Reinsdorf zurückbehalten. Werder muß sich aber in 450921A entschuldigen, daß er den genannten Brief an Harsdörffer voreilig abgeschickt habe. Vgl. 450919.
  2 Madeleine de Scudéry: Ibrahim ou L'illustre Bassa, dt. v. Philipp v. Zesen (FG 521. Der Wohlsetzende. 1648): Jbrahims oder Des Durchleuchtigen Bassa/ und Der beständigen Jsabellen/ Wunder-Geschichte Anderer Teil (Amsterdam: Elzevier 1645). HAB: Lm 3375:1. — Zesen hatte dieses Werk bereits im Dezember 1644 der FG gewidmet. Zur Korrekturdurchsicht anhand seiner darin neu verwendeten Rechtschreibung spannte er verschiedene Mitglieder der DG ein, die 1643 von ihm (DG 1. Der Färtige) begründet wor-

den war, u.a. Johann Bellin (DG 38. Der Willige), Adolph Rosel (DG 6. Der Bemühete) u. im Februar 1645 Gf. Rüdiger Günther v. Starhemberg (DG 10. Der Fäste). Vgl. 441201.

3 Die geplante Abreise Werders stand sehr wahrscheinlich im Zusammenhang mit dem Auftrag Lgfn. Amalia Elisabeths v. Hessen-Kassel (1602–1651), die Eheschließung ihres Sohnes, Lgf. Wilhelms VI. (FG 694. 1659), mit Mgfn. Hedwig Sophia (1623–1683), einer Schwester Kf. Friedrich Wilhelms v. Brandenburg (FG 401), zu vermitteln. S. 450919 u. 451209 K 7. Mit dieser Mission war Werder vermutlich bereits im Juni 1645 von der Landgräfin persönlich betraut worden. S. 450613 (K 5). Seine Verbindungen zum Kasseler Hof waren seit seiner einstigen Pagen- und Hofmarschallzeit in enger Vertraulichkeit verblieben. S. etwa sein Kondolenzschreiben vom 6.1.1638 an Amalia Elisabeth zum Tode ihres Gatten, Lgf. Wilhelms V. (FG 65), zit. in 370422 K 7.

4 F. Ludwig (Der Nährende) und seine zweite Gemahlin, Fn. Sophia (AL 1629. TG 38), geb. Gfn. zur Lippe.

450921A

Diederich von dem Werder an Fürst Ludwig

Antwort auf 450921. — Diederich v. dem Werder (FG 31) übermittelt F. Ludwig (Der Nährende), daß ihm der erwähnte Brief an Georg Philipp Harsdörffer (FG 368. Der Spielende) nicht (mehr) vorliegt, sondern in das Paket hineingeraten sei, wie ihm dies häufig und in Eile passiere. Beim Auspacken des Pakets werde sich diese Vermutung bestätigen, denn das Schreiben befinde sich nicht in seinem Besitz. Werder habe die vorliegende Antwort, um Papier zu sparen, direkt auf F. Ludwigs Brief (450921) geschrieben.

Q HM Köthen: V S 544, Bl. 489rv [A: 489v]; eigenh. — Vorliegende Zeilen direkt im Anschluß an 450921. — Nicht in *KE*.

A Dem Nehrenden zuhanden. Cöthen

[D]ie antwort an den Spielenden ist hier nicht verblieben¹, sondern wird [i]n das paquet mit eingeschlagen worden sein, wie mir es bey vielen schreiben, vnd in der eyl zugehen pfleget, die eröffnung deßelben wird es ausweisen, dan hier ist es nicht verblieben. Wie oben[.]² [Um] pappier zusparen[,] hatt dis zue antwort hiehehr geschrieben werden müßen.

K 1 Diederich v. dem Werder (FG 31) weist F. Ludwigs (Der Nährende) Annahme in 450921 zurück, er habe seine (F. Ludwigs) und der FG Antwort, 450919A, an Georg Philipp Harsdörffer (FG 368. Der Spielende) auf Reinsdorf zurückbehalten.

2 Werder bezieht sich auf die identische Datierung (21.9.1645).

450922

Matthäus Merian d. Ä. an Peter Knaudt

Matthäus Merian d. Ä. sendet 25 Abrisse neuer Kupferstiche zum *GB 1646* und kündigt weitere an. Er wird alles tun, um den Auftrag rechtzeitig zu erfüllen und demnächst eine Schriftprobe vorlegen. — Er erinnert an die Anfang September geäußerte Bitte (450905), ihm einen Vorschuß auf die zugesagte Zahlung zu gewähren, welche ihm über den Leipziger Handelsherrn Georg Winckler zukommen könnte. Peter Knaudt wird zugesichert, daß Merian sich in der Folge mit besonderem Fleiß dem Abschluß der Arbeiten zuwenden würde.

Q   HM Köthen: V S 546, Bl. 18rv [A: 18v]; eigenh., Adresse von Schreiberh. — *D: Bircher: Merian*, 703f.; *Wüthrich: Briefe Merian*, 92f. — *BN: Bürger*, 987 Nr. 10.

A   Dem Ehrenvesten vnd GroßAchtparen herrn Petter Knaut Fürstl. Anhaltischen CammerMeistern *etc.* Jn Cöthen *etc.* meinem großg. hochgeehrten hern *etc.* Cöthen.

Ehrenvester vnd GroßAchtparer Jnsonders großg. h[ochgeehrter]ª herr *etc.*
   Hiemit sende meinem gg. herrn 25 A[briße]ª ᵇ von den new verfertigten kupfern zur Fruchtbringenden gesellschafft, mit nechstem sollen deren mehr folgen, vnd will an meinem ohrt nichts ermanglen lassen, das alles wol, und zu rechter zeit vollendet werde, so es Gott geliebt, vnd mit nechstem auch eine prob von den schrifften senden *etc.*
   Jn dessen gelangt mein dienstliche bitt an meinen gg. herrn, mir beförderlich zu sein damit mir noch etwas geldes, an der **veraccordirten Summ***a*, wie in meinem Jungsten gemeldt[1], auff rechnung möge vbermachet werden, welches am füglichsten durch herrn Winklern[2] in Leipzig allhero verschaffet werden kan, dan mir zum verlag dises werks vil auffgehn wirt.
   Jch wils vmb meinen gg. herrn dankbarlich wider verschuld*en*, vnd allen möglichsten fleiß an wenden, damit das gantze werkh zu rechter zeit fertig, vnd vbersendet werden könne, hiemit mein gg. dem Allmächtigen Schutz wohl befohl*en*.
   Ffurt den 22. 7bris 1645.
      Meines gg. Herrn Dienstwilligster
      Mattheus Merian.

T a *Textverlust durch Papierausriß; vgl. die Anrede in 450905 u. 450930.* — b *Merian gebraucht* abriß *in 450905 bzw.* abtrukh *in 450930.*

K 1 Einige Monate zuvor (450417) bat Matthäus Merian d. Ä. um 200 Reichstaler, um seine Arbeit am Druck des *GB 1646* fortsetzen zu können, und in 450905 um einen weiteren Vorschuß in ungenannter Höhe. Um diesen handelt es sich hier, bezieht man den Fortgang der Korrespondenz mit ein. So spricht Merian in 450930 davon, daß er darauf hoffe, daß ihm die (zugesagten) 200 Reichstaler von Georg Winckler (s. Anm. 2) übermittelt würden. Den Eingang der Abschlagszahlung erwähnt Merian in 451028B. Zum Zahlungsverkehr das *GB 1646* anlangend s. 450127 K 1. Zum *GB 1646* allgem. s. 450126 K 4.
   2 Der Leipziger Handelsherr Georg Winckler trat im Berichtszeitraum bereits im Juli 1644 als Vermittler zwischen Köthen und Frankfurt auf. So berichtete F. Ludwig Carl

Gustav (v.) Hille (FG 302) in 440723A, daß er sich erkundigt hätte, ob Hz. Augusts d.J. v. Braunschweig-Wolfenbüttel (FG 227) Beitrag zum *GB 1646* bei Winckler bereits eingegangen wäre. Da dies nicht der Fall war, bat F. Ludwig um Unterstützung bei der Beschaffung des zugesagten Verlagsbeitrags, was dann über den Braunschweiger Kaufmann Hans Beyer ermöglicht wurde. S. 450509 K 1. Zu Winckler s. 451019 K 0.

450923

Fürst Ludwig an Herzog Christian Ludwig von Braunschweig-Calenberg

F. Ludwig bezieht sich auf seinen Besuch in Hannover und die danach von Carl Gustav v. Hille (FG 302) bestätigte mehrfache Zusage Hz. Christian Ludwigs v. Braunschweig-Calenberg (FG 372), 200 Reichstaler für die Verlegung des *GB 1646* beizusteuern. Da Hz. Christian Ludwigs Betrag jedoch noch immer ausstehe, bittet F. Ludwig ihn erneut — um eine Verzögerung des Druckes zu vermeiden —, die Außenstände zu begleichen. Der Kupferstecher (und Kommissionsverleger) Matthäus Merian d. Ä. in Frankfurt a. M. habe mit Hilfe anderer Verlagszuschüsse seine Arbeit bereits aufgenommen, sei zur Fortsetzung der Arbeiten aber auf den hzl. Zuschuß dringend angewiesen. Bei der anstehenden Leipziger Herbstmesse möge die Auszahlung des Geldes gegen Quittung mit Georg Winckler in Leipzig abgewickelt werden. Von dort solle das Geld dann durch Wechsel an Merian überwiesen werden. — Merian habe angekündigt, alle 400 Kupfer bis zur nächsten Frankfurter Fastenmesse (1646) angefertigt zu haben. — Da Hz. Christian Ludwig das Anrecht auf 48 Exemplare (als Gegenleistung zu seiner Verlagsbeteiligung) habe, möge er mitteilen, ob er dieselben direkt in Frankfurt abholen lassen wolle. Die Entscheidung des Herzogs werde F. Ludwig an Merian weiterleiten.

Q   HM Köthen: V S 544, Bl. 61rv [A: 61r], 61v leer; eigenh. Konzept; Bl. 61r oben Konzept F. Ludwigs an Hz. August d.J. v. Braunschweig-Wolfenbüttel (FG 227), s. 450923A.

A   An hertzog Christian Ludwig zu Braunschweig und luneburg.

Hochgeborner furst, freundlicher vielgeliebter h. Vetter,
El. entbiete ich meine fr*eund*willige dienste, und werden sie sich sonder Zweiffel fr. erinnern, das sie sich gegen mir dahin freundlich[a] so[wol] bey meiner anwesenheit bey ihr zu Hannover, als hernacher durch Karl Gustaven von Hille unterschiedlich vernemen laßen, das sie *zur* wiederauflegung des geselschaftbuchs in kupfer zweyhundert thaler verlagsweise zuschießen wolten; darauf dan[b] die anordnung, bey dem Kupferstecher zu Franckfurt Mærian geschehen, das damit bisher[c] durch anderen wechsel ein anfang gemacht, es aber nun an El. versprochenen auszalung noch ermangelt;[1] Als ist an El. mein fr*eund*Vetterliches[d] ersuchen, damit[e] das werck [ni]cht gehemmet werde[,] sie wollen die verordnung aus ihrer kammer thun, das bey nechst[f] anstehendem leipzigschem[f] Michaelis Marckte dieses Jhares solche zweyhundert thaler George Wincklern[2] in leipzig auf quittung[g] mögen ausgezalet werden, sollen sie von dannen,[h] gleich auf Franckfurt durch

wechsel ubermacht werden; Mærian giebet vertröstung³ das^i [die]^j vierhundert gemählde auf die Fastenmesse aldar sollen alle fertig sein, und weil El. wegen dieses verlags 48^k stucke zu gewarten haben,⁴ als wollen sie sich freundlich^l erkleren, ob sie solche stucke wen^m sie fertig gleich auf Hannover^n von Franckfurt aus wollen abholen^o laßen, sol deshalben an vorgemeldeten Mærian auch von hinnen richtige verordnung geschehen. El. freundliche antwort bin ich hieruber bey Zeigern gewertig, und verbleibe
El.

Cöthen den 23 Herbstmonats 1645.

T **a** *Folgt* <fur> *Darüber eingefügt* so *im Sinne von „sowohl"*. — **b** *Folgt unleserlich gestrichenes Wort.* — **c** *Eingefügt bis* anderen wechsel — **d** *Folgt* <s> — **e** *Eingefügt bis* werde Bei [ni]cht *Buchstabenverlust im Falz, Konjektur in eckigen Klammern.* — **f** *Eingefügt.* — **g** auf quittung *eingefügt.* — **h** *Folgt* <auch zu> — **i** *Gebessert aus unleserlichem Wort.* — **j** *Unleserliche Streichung oder Besserung,* [die] *Hg.-Konjektur.* — **k** *Eingefügt für* <acht undvierzig> — **l** *Folgt* <ehest> — **m** *Eingefügt bis* fertig — **n** *Am Rand eingefügt* <oder Braunschweig oder wohin> — **o** abholen laßen *eingefügt für* <ubergebracht haben>

K 1 S. auch F. Ludwigs Brief 440723, in dem er seinen Besuch in Hannover (1642) erwähnt und bereits zu diesem Zeitpunkt um die Zahlung des Beitrags bittet. Neun Tage nach dem vorliegenden Brief, am 2.10.1645, erhält Hz. Christian Ludwig v. Braunschweig-Calenberg (FG 372) an seinem Geburts- und (zeitweiligen) Aufenthaltsort Herzberg im Harz von einem Boten F. Ludwigs ein Schreiben überbracht, das nach seiner Rückkehr „von Hannover auß der gepühr beantworttet werden soll". (HM Köthen: V S 546, Bl. 32r, Empfangsbestätigung der Fürstlich Braunschweigischen Kammerschreiberei). Eine erneute Zahlungserinnerung F. Ludwigs ergeht in 460218. Vgl. Anm. 2. Den Geburtsort bzw. Sitz Hz. Christian Ludwigs, Herzberg, erwähnen *Conermann III*, 433 u. *Bircher: Merian*, 707. Vgl. auch 460301, 460309 u. 460403.

2 Zum Leipziger Handelsmann Georg Winckler s. 451019 K 0. In 450905 (u. dann erneut in 450922 u. 450930) hatte Matthäus Merian d. Ä. gegenüber Peter Knaudt in Köthen um eine (weitere) Vorauszahlung in Höhe von 200 Rtl. gebeten, um seine Arbeitsunkosten abdecken zu helfen. F. Ludwig hoffte vielleicht, dieser Bitte mit dem Verlagszuschuß Hz. Christian Ludwigs entsprechen zu können, der mit 200 Reichstalern erstmals in 421031A genannt wird, s. auch 421129. F. Ludwigs Hoffnung zerschlug sich, da Christian Ludwig nicht reagierte, in 460301 seine Zahlungszusage sogar auf 100 Rtl. halbierte und in 460403 nur erneut seine Zahlungsabsicht bekundete. Erst mit *DA Köthen I.8*: 470223 liegt uns ein sicheres Zeugnis über die tatsächlich erfolgte Zahlung vor. Im Oktober quittierte Merian dennoch einen Geldzugang von 200 Reichstalern (s. 451028B). Sie dürften von Hz. August d. J. v. Braunschweig-Wolfenbüttel (FG 227) stammen, s. 451028. Zum *GB 1646* allgemein s. 440130 K 3. Zu den Briefdokumenten den Zahlungsverkehr des *GB 1646* anlangend s. 450127 K 1.

3 In der älteren, nicht mehr gebräuchlichen Bedeutung von *Versprechen, Trost, Vertrauen, Verläßlichkeit* (lat. *fiducia*), vgl. *DW* XII.1, 2008 f.

4 48 Exemplare des *GB 1646* waren die festgesetzte Gegenleistung gegen eine Verlagseinlage von 200 Reichstalern. Aufgrund des von Hz. Christian Ludwig auf 100 Rt. reduzierten Verlagszuschusses erhielt dieser nur 24 Exemplare. S. 450126 K 4 zu den fl. Verlagsbeiträgen.

450923A

Fürst Ludwig an Herzog August d. J. von Braunschweig-Wolfenbüttel

Beantwortet durch 451001. — Der Kupferstecher Matthäus Merian d. Ä. in Frankfurt ist stark beschäftigt mit dem Druck des Gesellschaftsbuchs der FG (*GB 1646*), will zur nächsten [Frühjahrs-]Messe in Frankfurt 1646 mit den 400 Impresenstichen fertig sein. Aufgrund des Verlagszuschusses Hz. Augusts d. J. v. Braunschweig-Wolfenbüttel (FG 227) in Höhe von 200 Reichstalern stehen ihm 48 Exemplare zu. Ob er sie, sobald das Werk fertiggedruckt vorliegt, in Frankfurt nach Braunschweig abholen lassen wolle? F. Ludwig werde Merian entsprechend instruieren.

Q HAB: Cod. Guelf. 3 Noviss. 2°, Bl. 69r–70v [A: 70v], 69v u. 70r leer; eigenh., A von Schreiberh. mit Zusatz von Schreiberh.; rotes Lacksiegel. — Eigenh. Konzept F. Ludwigs in HM Köthen: V S 544, Bl. 61r. Zit. als *K*. Auf dasselbe Blatt hat F. Ludwig auch den Brief 450923 (an Hz. Christian Ludwig v. Braunschweig-Calenberg [FG 372]) geschrieben. — Nicht in *KE*. — BN: Giermann, 3.

A *Dem Hochgebornen Fürsten Herrn Augusten, Hertzogen zu Braunschweig und Lüneburgk etc. Unserm freundlichen lieben Oheim und Schwagern etc.*
Wolfenbüttel.   Zu S. Ld. hand*en*.ᵃ
Neben der Adresse von der H. eines anderen Schreibers oder Kanzlisten: 48 Exemplaria des Kreuterbuches der Geselschafter.

Hochgeborner Furst, freundlicher vielgeliebter Herr Oheim und schwager.
E. L.ᵇ mag ich mit vermeldung meiner freundwilligen dienste nicht verhalten, dasᶜ der Kupferstecher Mærian zu Franckfurt an *[sic]* Main nun in vollem wercke die geselschaft gemählde zu verfertigen, verhoffet auch mit den vierhundertᵈ gemählden nechstkunftige Franckfurter Meße 1646 gantz fertig zu sein.¹ Wan danᵉ E. L., vermöge ihres darzuᶠ gethanen verlages der zweyhundert thaler² acht und viertzig stucke solches geselschaft-buchesᵍ haben mußen: Als stelle ich zu E. L. wolgefälligen erklerung, ob sie solche ihr zukommende achtʰ und viertzig stücke, wanⁱ sie fertig auf Braunschweig von Franckfurt aus abholen laßen wollen, sol deswegen von hinnen an obgemeldeten Mærian gebürende verordnung geschehen.³ EL. antwort erwarte ich hierauf, und verbleibe
E. L.

Dienstwilliger Oheim und Schwager
Ludwig fzu Anhalt

Cöthen den 23. Herbstmonats 1645

T a *K* An hertzog Aug. zu Br. und luneburg. — b *Satz in K:* E l. mag ich neben vermeldung meiner freundlichen bereitwilligen dienste nicht verhalten, *Satz gebessert aus:* E l. <mag ich seine> meine bereitwillige dienste <zuvorn> nicht verhalten, — c *Folgt in K* <nunmehr> — d *K hat hier und in den folgenden Worten:* vierhunderten gegen die

Franckfurter fasten Meße — **e** *Folgt in K* <nur> — **f** *In K eingefügt.* — **g** *Statt* solches geselschaft-buches *hat K* deroselben — **h** acht und viertzig *fehlt in K.* — **i** wan sie fertig *am Rand ergänzt. Nachfolgende Passage in K:* auf Braunschweig von Franckfurt aus so bald sie fertig wollen abholen laßen [abholen laßen *eingefügt für* <geliefert haben>]

K 1 Es handelt sich hierbei um das *GB 1646*, das im Frankfurter Verlagshaus Matthäus Merians d. Ä. in den Impresenstichen und im Druck hergestellt wurde. Der angesteuerte Abschluß des Drucks bis zur Leipziger Ostermesse bzw. Frankfurter Fastenmesse 1646 war in 450905 bzw. 450923 genannt worden. Vgl. 440130 K 3. Zum Zahlungsverkehr s. 450127 K 1. Zur Einrichtung des *GB 1646* s. 450711 K 4. Vgl. 421031A K 14.

2 Hz. August d. J. v. Braunschweig-Wolfenbüttel (FG 227) hatte schon vor längerer Zeit zugesagt, zum *GB 1646* 200 Reichstaler zuzuschießen s. 430121. S. 450126 K 4 allgemein zur Verteilung der fl. Verlagsbeiträge. Wie der Kaufmann Winckler F. Ludwigs Kammermeister Knaudt in 451019 mitteilte, war der Verlagszuschuß des Herzogs bis dahin noch nicht eingegangen. Die erfolgte Bezahlung konnte F. Ludwig aber schon in 451028 bestätigen.

3 In seinem Antwortschreiben 451001 bestätigt Hz. August die geplante Abholung der 48 Exemplare des *GB 1646* in Frankfurt.

450923B

Fürst Ludwig an Justus Georg Schottelius

Beantwortet in 451007. — F. Ludwig (Der Nährende) schickt Justus Georg Schottelius (FG 397. Der Suchende) ein Exemplar von *Gueintz: Rechtschreibung (1645)*, der die eigene (omd.) Mundart zugrunde liegt. Er schlägt Schottelius vor, mit Christian Gueintz (FG 361. Der Ordnende) und ihm zusammenzuarbeiten, um eine deutsche Grammatik zu verfassen und die deutschen Stammwörter für ein Wörterbuch der deutschen Sprache zu sammeln. Man habe sich in der dt. Sprachlehre an den Aufbau der lat. Sprachlehre gehalten, damit der deutsche Unterricht von deren (verdeutschten) Fachbegriffen und Ausdrücken ausgehen und sodann die Erklärung auf das Studium des Lateinischen übertragen kann. Schottelius möge hierzu seine Meinung äußern.

Q HM Köthen: V S 544, Bl. 62rv, 62v leer; eigenh. Konzept. — *D: KE*, 296; *KL* III, 247 (Auszug) u. 265. — *BN: Bürger*, 953 Nr. 111.

A *Fehlt.*

Dem Suchenden wird hiermit uberfertiget die Rechtschreibung[1], wie sie auf diese Mundart ubersehen[a] eingerichtet und gedrucket worden: der[b] zuversicht sie sol in vielen dingen ein gutes licht geben[.] Wegen der deutschen[c] Sprachlehre[2] sonderlich aber des Wortverzeichnußes[3] wird es dahin stehen das man solches nun nach[d] den Stamwörtern zusammen trage, und stellet[e] es zu des Suchenden gefallen, ob er mit dem Ordnenden auch wol Nehrenden hieruber gutliche schriftwechselung[f] anstellen wil, sol solche[g] wol aufgenommen werden[.][4] Die gewönliche lateinische ordnung ist in der deutschen[c] Sprachlehre darum gehalten worden, das die jugend wan sie im deutschen von[c] den kunstwortern und redarten erst wol unterrichtet und darinnen^c gewonet, dan durch den verstand zu der lateinischen sprache bey ihrer auslegung desto fuglicher gelangen könne. Es^h wird aber^c des Suchenden urtheil auch hieruber gerne vernommen werden.

Cöthen den 23. Herbstmonats 1645.

T a *Folgt* <und> — b *Eingefügt bis* licht geben — c *Eingefügt.* — d *Eingefügt bis* Stamwörtern — e *Gebessert aus* stehet — f *Folgt* <halten wil> — g *Eingefügt bis* werden — h *Eingefügt für* <Und>

K 1 Gemeint ist *Gueintz: Rechtschreibung (1645)*, die im September 1645 im Druck erschien und an deren Be- und Überarbeitung auch F. Ludwig (Der Nährende) beteiligt war. Vgl. 440127 K 1. Auch Georg Philipp Harsdörffer (FG 368) gegenüber hatte F. Ludwig betont, daß die *Rechtschreibung* von Christian Gueintz (FG 361) auf der hiesigen (omd.) Mundart beruhe, und daß andere, insbesondere auch Schottelius, aufgerufen seien, eine deutsche Orthographie nach ihrer jeweiligen Mundart aufzusetzen. S. 450919A.

2 In *Gueintz: Sprachlehre (1641)* und in *Gueintz: Rechtschreibung (1645)* wird zwar der Aufbau der lat. Grammatik zugrundegelegt, jedoch werden deren Fachbegriffe („Technica" bzw. „Kunstwörter") verdeutscht. F. Ludwig redet an dieser Briefstelle aber nicht von der *Sprachlehre* des Christian Gueintz (FG 361. Der Ordnende), sondern von einer künftig noch zu verfassenden (verbesserten) deutschen Grammatik der FG im Zusammenhang mit einem umfassenden deutschen Wörterbuch. F. Ludwig hat an dieser Stelle also nicht *Schottelius: Sprachkunst (1641)* übergangen. Das hätte sicherlich die hier von ihm angeregte Zusammenarbeit von Gueintz, Schottelius und ihm nicht gefördert. Dafür spricht auch F. Ludwigs Nachschrift in 450919A. Der folgende Satz ist gut ratichianisch gemeint, ein Sprachlernkonzept, das F. Ludwig auch in 460902 Harsdörffer gegenüber vertreten wird. Dafür hätte Ludwig auch auf die Köthener Drucke der *Grammatica Universalis Pro Didactica Ratichii* (1619) bzw. *Allgemeine Sprach-Lehr: Nach der Lehr-Art Ratichii* (1619) verweisen können, deren Restauflagen noch 1641 verkauft wurden. S. 410313.

3 Schottelius ergriff die Gelegenheit, um gleich Hz. August d. J. v. Braunschweig-Wolfenbüttel (FG 227) seine Mitarbeit am Wörterbuch anzuzeigen und um dessen Erlaubnis und Unterstützung zu erbitten. S. 450929, dem Schottelius den vorliegenden Brief augenscheinlich beigab. F. Ludwig scheint in der Reinschrift des vorliegenden Briefs noch einen Hinweis auf ein (nicht genau bezeichnetes) Buch zu geben. Schottelius bezieht ihn in 450929 auf *Henisch*. Zum Wörterbuchprojekt der FG vgl. ebd. u. 451219 K 8.

4 In herabgestimmter Form griff F. Ludwig hier wohl auch Georg Philipp Harsdörffers (FG 368) Hinweis auf Justus Georg Schottelius' (FG 397) Anerbieten auf, strittige Punkte in seiner schon damals überarbeiteten *Sprachkunst* (erst 1651 erschienen) vor deren Veröffentlichung mit Christian Gueintz (FG 361) oder anderen Kennern schriftlich zu beraten und sich gegebenenfalls dem besseren Argument zu fügen. Harsdörffer selbst regte an, über die zwischen Gueintz und Schottelius strittigen Punkte einen aus Diederich v. dem Werder (FG 31), Augustus Buchner (FG 362) und Johann Michael Moscherosch (FG 436. 1645) bestehenden Ausschuß befinden zu lassen und dann F. Ludwig die Entscheidung anheimzustellen. S. 450817. In 450919A hatte F. Ludwig einen gütlichen Briefwechsel von Schottelius und Gueintz über die Sprachlehre befürwortet. Schottelius' auf den 5.12.1645 datiertes Papier zu einigen Fragen der deutschen Sprachlehre (demnächst in *DA Köthen I.* 9) ist in diesem Zusammenhang entstanden und F. Ludwig zugeleitet worden. S. 451219.

450923C

Georg Philipp Harsdörffer an Fürst Ludwig

Beantwortet durch 451209. — Georg Philipp Harsdörffer (FG 368. Der Spielende) erkundigt sich nach F. Ludwigs (Der Nährende) Antwort auf seinen Brief 450817 samt den Beilagen aus Neapel. Er schickt den diesjährigen, nämlich 5. Teil seiner *Frauenzimmer-Gesprächspiele*, obwohl dieser viele Druckfehler enthält. Vor der Abfassung des 6. Teils will Harsdörffer sich an ein *Specimen Philologiae Germanicae* betiteltes Buch machen. Es vergleiche das Deutsche mit dem Hebräischen und sei in Lateinisch verfaßt, damit Harsdörffer so dem Vorwurf begegne, er verleite die Jugend zum Deutschen und lenke sie vom Latein und gelehrten Studien ab.

Q HM Köthen: V S 545, Bl. 330r–331v [A: 331v], 330v u. 331r leer; eigenh.; 3 rote Lacksiegel mit Bandresten. — *D: KE*, 344. — BN: *Bürger*, S. 674 Nr. 33.

A Dem Durchleuchtigen, Hochgebornen Fürsten, und Herrn, Herrn *LUDWIGEN Fürsten* zu Anhalt, Grafen zu Ascanien, und Ballenstat *etc*. Meinem gnädigen Fürsten und Herrn.   Cöthen
Eigenh. Empfangsvermerk F. Ludwigs: 25. Weinmonats 1645.

Höchstgeehrter Nehrender

Ob ich zwar nicht zweiffle, es werde mein jüngstes, vom [a]17ten Augustmonats gegeben, samt den Beylagen von Neapoli,[1] zu recht geliefert worden seyn, hab ich doch noch der Zeit keine Antwort darauf erhalten; und daher ursach genommen deswegen nachmals Erinnerung zu thun; benebens auch die heurige Frucht meiner geringen Gespräch-arbeit[2], dem Höchstgeehrten Nehrenden, aus schuldigem obliegen, gebührlich zu überreichen. Es ist in der Druckerey vielmals versehen, und gantze wörter ausgelassen worden, weil ich, wegen anderer Beschäfftigung, dem werk selbst nich [sic] hab abwarten können.[3]

Bevor ich den 6ten Theil dieser Spiele anfange, bin ich gesinnet in[b] lateinischer Sprache Speciemen [sic] Philologiæ Germanicæ zu verabfassen, in welchem von alterthum, und vergleichung der Teutschen und Ebreischen Sprache, in gebundener, und ungebundener Rede, zulesen seyn wird;[4] etlichen Mißgünstigen zubegegnen, welche mich beschuldigen, daß ich die Jugend von dem Latein und Studiren abführe, und zu den Teutschen allein verleite &c.

Hiermit verbleibet, nechst empfehlung des Allmächtigen obschutzes,

> *Des Höchstgeehrten Nehrenden*
>
> die zeit seines Lebens dienstverbundner knecht
>
> *Der Spielende.*

Nürnberg den 23 Herbstmonats 1645.

T a *Aus* 16 *gebessert.* — b *Aus* im

K 1 Der von Marco Aurelio Severino an Georg Philipp Harsdörffer (FG 368. Der Spielende) gesandte Brief samt Beilagen, die der Spielende an F. Ludwig weitergereicht hatte. S. 450817 II–V. F. Ludwig beantwortete Harsdörffers Brief (450817) noch ohne Kenntnis des vorliegenden Schreibens in 450919A. Beide Briefe haben sich also überschnitten.

2 Der 5. Teil von Harsdörffers *Frauenzimmer-Gesprächspielen* (1645; Ndr. 1969). Nach dem Verbleib dieses in zwei Exemplaren gesandten Buchs, für das sich F. Ludwig erst in 451209 bedankte, erkundigte sich der Spielende in 451101. Eins der beiden Exemplare war wohl für Diederich v. dem Werder (FG 231) bestimmt, s. 451101.

3 Dieser Hinweis ist wichtig, da Harsdörffer F. Ludwig versprochen hatte, sich an dessen frühere grammatisch-orthographische Hinweise zu halten, zugleich aber auch Klärungsbedarf reklamiert hatte. Vgl. 450400, ferner 430419, 430624, 430724, 430920, 431124 u. 440426. Verstöße gegen diese Richtlinien waren auch schon früher zum Teil auf die eigenmächtig nach ihren eigenen Schriftkonventionen setzenden Drucker zurückzuführen. Vgl. Harsdörffers „Kurtze Entschuldigung, Die begangene Fehler in den Hundert Spielreimen betreffend". HM Köthen: V S 545, Bl. 290rv u. 289rv (demnächst in *DA Köthen I. 9*).

4 *Harsdörffer: Specimen Philologiae Germanicae (1646)*, s. 451217 K 10, vgl. zur Integration von *Harsdörffer: Porticus Virtutis* (1646) in dieses Werk 450927 u. 461204A.

450927

Georg Philipp Harsdörffer an Herzog August d. J. von Braunschweig-Wolfenbüttel

Begleitschreiben Georg Philipp Harsdörffers (FG 368. Der Spielende) zu seinem Entwurf der *Porticus*, gesandt an Hz. August d. J. v. Braunschweig-Wolfenbüttel (FG 227. Der Befreiende). — Die Jesuiten begannen vor Jahren damit, die Feinheiten der Poesie und Prosa mit gelehrten Bildern zu schmücken, damit die Schönheit der Aussage durch das Gesicht den Geist berühre und so in der Übereinstimmung zweier Künste sich dem Gedächtnis umso fester einpräge. Harsdörffer sei in seinen *Frauenzimmer-Gesprächspielen* den Jesuiten mit der genauen Verbindung der Dicht- und Bildkunst gefolgt. Er hätte sich gescheut, dieses daraus entstandene Büchlein Hz. August zu unterbreiten, würde nicht Justus Georg Schottelius (FG 397. Der Suchende) es als Bürge einer gnädigen Aufnahme vorgelegt haben. Er habe sich daher nicht gescheut, trotz mangelnden Vertrauens auf seine eigene Erfindungskraft, die edelste Schreibart zu wählen und eine Säulenhalle der Tugend gewissermaßen als Vorstellung einer rühmenden Besinnung zu errichten, nicht eigentlich als Ausdruck der unaussprechlichen Tugenden des durchläuchtigsten Fürsten, jedoch als Zeugnis seiner Verehrung derselben. Es handelt sich um einen ersten handschriftlichen Entwurf, alles nur obenhin geschildert, damit er, Harsdörffer, durch sein Warten auf den Drucker sich bei dem Fürsten nicht unbeliebt mache. Wenn das Werk in den Druck gehe, müsse er vielleicht eine wortgeschichtliche Erinnerung über die (antike) Säulenhalle hinzufügen und den Text nochmals verbessern.

Q Eigenh. Brief, Bl. 1v–3r, in einem eigenh. Entwurf „PORTICUS VIRTUTIS, Serenissimo atque Celsissimo Principi, Domino, Domino AVGVSTO, Bruswicensium atque Lüneburgensium Duci etc. in Posteritatis documentum, aperta." (21 Bl.), gebunden vor dem Druck von: *Harsdörffer: Frauenzimmer-Gesprächspiele* V (1645), d.i.: GESPRECHSPJELE | Fünfter Theil; | Jn welchem | Vnterschiedliche/ in Teutscher Sprache niebekante/ Erfindungen/ | Tugendliebenden Gesellschaften aus zuüben/ | Vorgestellet worden: | Benebens einer Zugabe/ überschrieben | Die Reutkunst/ | Durch | Einen Mitgenossen der hochlöblichen | FRVCHTBRJNGENDEN GESELLSCHAFT. | Nürnberg/ | Gedrukkt und verlegt bey Wolffgang Endter. | Jm Jahre 1645. HAB: 166.11 Eth. — *D: Blume: Porticus,* S. 90. — Harsdörffers *Porticus Virtutis* wurde 1646 seinem *Specimen Philologiae Germanicae* [HAB: QuN 1090 (1)] eingefügt (460912, vgl. 461204A) und erschien Anfang 1647 auch selbständig (*DA Köthen I. 8*: 470119): PORTICUS Serenissimo ... AUGUSTO, Brunsvicensium ... M. DC. XXXXVI. HAB: 10.6 Pol.; Druck auch: Gn 4460. — *BN: Bürger,* 673 Nr. 9.

A *Fehlt.*

Alloquium
Serenissime atque Celsissime Princeps.
Jesuitæ, Monopolæ omnium Scientiarum, ab aliquot annis prosæ atque ligatæ Orationis elegantias, eruditis Picturis venustare coepere;[1] ut dicendorum amoenitas, per visum, sensuum excellentissimum, animos intimius adficeret, miraque Artium sympathiâ, res ipsæ, in memoria firmiorem invenirent locum.

Hos ego veluti vaga umbra secutus, amussitata Pöeticæ et Pictoriæ con-[2r]sortia, passim in ludiloquiis meis, imitari constitui: et huius etiam instituti est præsens libellus, quem, per tenuitatis meæ conscientiam, apud Serenit.^{em} et Celsitud.^{em} V.^{ram} deponere verecundatus fuissem, nisi Vir Clarissimus, Dn. Schottelius, amantissimus mei, vltrò se gratiosæ acceptionis sponsorem obtulisset.

Nihil igitur sum veritus, nobilissimum scriptionis argumentum eligere, cuius, non ingenii mei fiduciâ fretus, ad frontispicium huius opusculi Porticum Virtutum, sive Meditationem [2v] Panegyricam Serenit. atque Celsitud. V.^{ræ} submissè nuncupo. Respice Serenissime Princeps, et patere hanc qualemcunque structuram, si non in laudum tuarum (quæ mihi omnem satisfaciendi spem præripiunt,) præconium, saltem in cultus mei perenne testimonium extare. Prima manus est, & defunctoriè omnia (Tertulliani verbo vtor[2]) expicta,[3] ne fortè sub mora operis, à Typographo nuper absoluti, aliqua meæ ingratudinis species subesse videretur. Quod si verò typis hæc com-[3r]mittenda forent, id quod non præsumo, Philologica de Porticu præmonitio,[4] et secunda cura accedat oportet. Vale, Serenissime, atque Celsissime Princeps, Domine Clementissime et Fortunâ Virtute tua dignâ, prolixè fruere.
Norimb. die 27. Septemb. 1645.[5]
Serenitatis atque Celsitudinis Vestræ
omnibus studiis mancipatus.
Georg-Philippus Harsdorff.

I

Aus Harsdörffers *Porticus Virtutis* zum Ruhme Herzog Augusts

Q Harsdörffers eigenh. Brief, s. oben, gefolgt von diesem eigenh. Prosimetrum, Bl. 3v–21r, hier zit. Bl. 3v–7r = *Pms.* — Textvarianten aus HAB: QuN 1090 (1). Bl.)( )(r –)()(4r [Druck der in *Harsdörffer: Specimen (1646)* eingefügten *Porticus Virtutis* = *P. I*] u. HAB: 10.6 Pol., S. 1–3 = *P. II* [*Harsdörffer: Porticus (1647)*]. — S. 460912 II.

PORTICUS VIRTUTIS. in Posteritatis documentum aperta. Principis AVGVSTI, augustæ Virtutis Jmago Præbeat Exemplum: Posteritas stupeat!ᵃ [4r]

> Præludium Poëtæᵇ
> Æstus erat, Phoebus tenues contraxerat vmbras
>   tempore, quo Messisᶜ rura beare solet.
> Protinus argutos cantusᵈ Philomela sonabat,
>   tot plausus referens,ᵉ Stramina quot segetes.
>   [...; 4v]
> **Fructiferum tempus** modulantur fluminis vndæ,
>   cum mulcent placidâ, litora curva, fugâ.
> **Fructiferum tempus** resonat crepitantibus auris,
>   cumᶠ mitis Zephyrus lenia flabra movet.
> **Fructiferum tempus** decantat Teutona Lingua;
>   Fructiferi etᵍ Socii, ceu Philomela melos.

Sic Pöeta sub vmbrosæ Quercus tegmineʰ recubans, ludicris numeris lyram sollicitabat, cum nescio quid thyrsici furoris, velⁱ vertiginis passus, (quo morbo hoc genus [5r] hominum solemniter laborat,) videbatur sibiʲ in alium delatus Orbem. Narratio.ʲ

Mercuriusᵏ ille alipes, ex nitratis nubibus se proripiens, tanquam rerum novarum Præses et Præco, tale pronunciabatˡ effatum.

> Ocyus gressum celerate Vates!
> Nuncius cœli, facilis volatu,
> Filius Maja generatus adsum.
>   cernite Sceptrum.
> Vosque nunc linguis populi favete;
> vosqueᵐ mansuete animis adeste [5v]
> ipse quos Titan meliore finxit,
>   credite,ᴹ limo.
> Leuis hic auræ tepor, in relictis
> vallibus, rerum melior renascens
> Orbis: hic plenis agitata manant.
>   gaudia ripis.

Dumⁿ hæc edixerat, confluxereᵒ subitò Doctorum populiᵖ & Musarum alumniᑫ, quos rerum novarum sitis^Q adduxerat.

Georg Philipp Harsdörffers (FG 368) Porticus Virtutis (1645) *zum Ruhme Herzog Augusts d. J. von Braunschweig-Wolfenbüttel* (FG 227). Zu 450927.

Area.[r]

Erat area amplissima, cuius[s] centrum **Statua Equestris** occupabat, (vt postea rescitum,)[1] ambiente Porticu[t], vel ambulacro, ubi in [6r] vmbra Solis ardor vel imbres declinabātur, forma cycli, conclusa:
Porta Porticus.[u]

ad huius[U] introitum spectabantur columnæ[v] quatuor, binæ ad dextrum, ad normam operis Corinthii[w] elaboratæ, quarum inter columnium tenebat **Germania**, tum ex Romano-germana Aquila, & luctuosa[x] facie, tum ex **Inventione Typographiæ**, atque[y] Tormentorum bellicorum,[z] quorum figuræ ad eius pedes cernebantur, nobilis: eius manus cœlum versus sub latas hoc lemma adumbrabat: In quæ modò funera damnor?[aa] [6v] Ad sinistrum[bb] Intercolumnii Spatium videre erat Lingua Germanica, instar[cc] formosæ Nymphæ, squalido ex parte amictu[dd], de Cimbricis characteribus intexto, circumdata, cum Lauro[ee] insuper et Barbito conspicua. Epigraphe talis[ff] erat: — — —in quæ modo gaudia ducor?[aa]

(Inter has bipartitas Columnas patebat Porta[gg] ornamentis eiusdem ordinis condecorata, quibus imminebat Pallas admiranda pulchritudinis Diva, Insignia Serenissimi atque celsissimi[hh] Domini, Domini — [7r] **AVGVSTI** Brunsvvicens. et Lüneburgens. Ducis &c. manutenens[ii], quæ afflictam **Germaniam** melius sperare, **Linguam Germanicam** non nimium[jj] spirare jubens, duplex demittebat Lemma. Dextram versus

   — erit mensura malorum.[aa]

versus[kk] Sinistram:

   — non cunctis formosa places.[aa]

[...]

II

Zuschriften Georg Philipp Harsdörffers an Herzogin Sophia Elisabeth von Braunschweig-Wolfenbüttel

Q *Harsdörffer: Frauenzimmer-Gesprächspiele* V (1645, Ndr. 1969), 7–14 (Ndr.)

Dank und Denkseüle
Der Hochfürstlichen
Fruchtbringenden
Gesellschaft
Christlöblichen mit-
genossinn
Der
BEFREYENDENN[1].
aufgerichtet
von dem
Spielenden

[9] DJe[a] eitelschnelle Zeit vernicht der Menschen Werke/
Durchmottet das Gemähl/ verlescht die Kunstgemerke[2]/
 zerschleiffet die Paläst/ erschüttert Holtz und Stein/
 daß/ was bestehend heist/ verlieret Schein und Seyn:
Das reifbedachte Wort zerstiebet und verhauchet/
Wann es nicht durch die Schrift wird gleichsam eingedauchet

Von dergleichen Flüssen/ welche alles in Stein verwädelen/ ist zu lesen Plinius, Solinus, Mela und andere.[4]

 in Aganippe Fluß/[3] wie hier die Seule weist/
 die vormals nur Papier/ jetzt harter Marmol heist/
und in dem Palmenland so Wurtzelfest bestehet/
bis aller Zeiten Zeit zu Grund und Boden gehet/
 Hier fleust der schöne Brun/ der/ nechst der Musen Sitz/
 mit vollem Strudel qwillt aus einem Federritz/
erhärtend Felsendicht was darmit wird benetzet/
und diß zu Stein gemacht: Die Schrift hat eingeetzet [10]
 die tiefste Dankbarkeit/ für hocherwiesne Gnad.
Nicht daß die Sache selbst verhoffte solchen Grad/
aus aller Zeiten Ziel: Nein weil hierbey zu schauen
der Tugend Ebenbild dem Marmol eingehauen.
Wann man das Teutsche Volk von Altersher betracht/
 wie alle Wissenschaft von ihnen nicht geacht:
Der düsterwilde Wald/ die halbverwildten Leute/
verhülten sich zumal in Ochs- und Bärenhäute;

Hievon handelt Cluverius in Germ. Antiq.[5]

 der starke Jägerspieß bracht ihnen rauhe Kost/
 das schwache Rebenholtz den ungebauten Most.
Jhr höchster Schutz und Schatz war ein bewärter Degen/
das Recht/ mit kühner Faust/ in freyem Stand zu hegen:
 die höchstbeliebte Kunst/ aus Bidermanns Gemüht/
 bey ihrer Heldengrab das Lob- und Trauerlied. [11]

Germanis olim ingenium[b] in manu positum; nunc Græcie decoquenti & Italiæ dormitanti omnium artium gloriam præripuere, Euphorm. Icon. Anim.[6]

Sie haben dazumal von ihnen nichts geschrieben.
Doch ist die Tapferkeit im Werk bemerkt geblieben/
 bey Kindes Kindes Kind/ die nechst des Vaters Schild/
 und seiner Waffen Ruhm/ den Adel ausgebildt.
Jetzt/ kem' Artyrus[7] her (der vor zweytausend Jahren
Zu Alexanders Zeit bei Rügen angefahren/

Lazius l. 12. de Migr. Gēt. Henning. p. 2. Geneal. f. 287 Münster. Cosmograp. l. 3. c. 459. Limin. l[.] 5. c. 12 n. 3.[8]

 und/ nechst dem Steuermann/ das Greiffenthier geführt/
 so der BEFREYENDJNN Geburtes Wapen ziert)
Das freche Zimbervolk/ die Königlichen Ahnen
der Hürlen/ die das Haubt des Büffels in den Fahnen
 erhaben in dem Streit/ sie solten diese Sag'
 erheben/ ob dem Land der Guelphen/ heut zu Tag:

Besihe dē Anfangsbuchstaben dieser Zuschrift.[9]

Stammt diese her von uns/ die auf der Laute schläget?[10]
die mit der Wunderkunst der Himmels Gunst erreget? [12]
 es tönt das leere Holtz/ der stumme Faden singt/

Von den Barden hat der Spielende viel geschriebē/ zu der Lobrede der Teutschē Poeterey.[11]

die Seide lebt und bebt/ und unsern Geist bezwingt.
Was sol der Helden Ton/ den unsre Barden brummen?
    das grobe Reimgeplerr muß blötzlich hier verstummen.
Wir all erstaunen fast und sagen sonder Scheu/
    daß dieser Fürstinn Stimm/ und sie vergöttert sey.
Der Griech (wer' ihm erlaubt sich hierbey einzustellen/)
solt' aus dem Wahrheitsgrund ein solches Vrtheil fällen:
    Was Wunder ist es doch/ wann/ aus der Tugendtrieb/
    üm diese Pallas stralt des Phöbus Flammenlieb'
Jhr kluggeübter Sinn' ergeistert die Poeten/
und weist/ wo im Gedicht gefehlet/ mit erröten/
    des Meisters und der Kunst. Jn ihrem Mund entbricht/
    was sonst der Frantzman rühmt und was der Welsche spricht. [13]

Die Göttin der Gedechtniß der Musen Mutter.

Hört auch den Römer an: Mnemosine Beginnen/
der klugen MVSEN Freud/ und aller Charitinnen
    Sinn- Hand- und Meisterwerk erhellet Wolken weit/
    im Tempel/ der benamt/ der Tugend Ewigkeit.

Sophia/ zu teutsch Weissheit. Elisabeth/ die Ruhe Gottes von *El, DEVS* & *Sabbathū, quies*.[12]

der WEJSSHEJT HJMMELSRVH ist an die Pfort geschrieben.
mit guldnem Dintenglantz. Ein jeder wird getrieben
    zu schmükken den Altar. Jst meine Gab ein Stein/
    so muß er ob dem Bild der Tugend Edel seyn.
Es ist zu diesem Buch ihr Gnadenblikk gewendet/
der jenen Klügelmann mit strengen Stralen blendet:
    und/ wie des Himmelsliecht die Gärten trächtig macht;
    so grünt der Spiele Frucht durch dieser Sonnen Pracht.
    E. F. G. Zu unterthäniger Ehrbezeugung gewidmet von dem
SPJELENDEN. [14]

Sonnet de L'Auteur.
Sur le Pourtrait de son Altesse.

Superbe Ceres va! va t'enfler des verdures!
    Va Juno te parer des Astres des Cieux!
Va Nymphe des eaux, qui traine des murmures!
    Va Venus lie-cœurs des myrtes gracieux!
Deesses sans beautez! allez! vaines Peintures
    au pris de la VERTU plus charmante en nos yeux.
Ces traits-cy sont esclairs, des dards, des graces pures:
    Il faut pro^c les louer le languague des Dieux.
Or, ce Marbre pourtant me semble peu parfait:
    bienque L'Artiste main y monstra son effet,
        s'arrestant neüement à chose incorporelle;

450927 Georg Philipp Harsdörffer

> Mais ses divins appas, ses non-pareils attraits,
> rendent dedans nos cœurs si vivement pourt[r]aits,
> Ceste Ame, sans flatter, des Ames sa plus belle.

T I *Lesarten P.I u. P.II werden meistens ohne Berücksichtigung der Orthographie und Zeichensetzung wiedergegeben*: **a** *P.I* PORTICUS VIRTUTIS. *P.II* PORTICUS AUGUSTI. — **b** *Marginalnote in P.I u. P.II* Præludium scriptionis. — **c** *P.II* Messis spicea regna beat. — **d** *P.II* cantus geminabat Aëdon, — **e** *P.II* referens, quot nova grana seges. — **f** *P. II* cum mollis Zephyrus mitia flabra movet. — **g** *P.I u. P.II* & — **h** *Aus* <tegminæ> — **i** *P. I u. P.II ohne* vel vertiginis *bis* laborat,) — **j** *P.I u. P.II* sibi in — **J** *P.I. Dafür P.II* Mercurii convocatio — **k** *P.I u. P.II Beginn eines neuen Absatzes.* — **l** *P.I* proferebat *P.II* sic sermocinabatur — **m** *P.I* Vosque Mansuetis *P.II* vos quieturis *Pms* animis <favete> — **M** *P.II* viscera — **n** *P.I u. P.II* Cum — **o** *P.I u.P.II* confluxêre volentes & frequētes — **p** *P.I u. P. II* catervi — **q** *P.I u. P.II* amasii — **Q** *P.II* sitis illicò — **r** *P.I* Porta Porticus *P.II* Porta Porticus, quæ in frontispicio Operis videnda est. — **s** *P.I u. P.II* (cujus centrum occupabat statua Equestris) ambiente — **t** *P.I u. P.II* Porticu formâ Cycli — **u** *Vgl. Anm. r. P.I u. P. II anstelle Pms.* Area. — **U** *P.II* cujus — **v** *P.I u. P.II* Columnæ IV. operis — **w** *P.I* Corinthii, cujus anticolumnium tenebat *Germaniæ* statua, tum ex inventione *P.II Corinthii, quarum inter- vel antecolumnium tenebat* Germaniæ Statua: *luctuosa* — **x** *P.I* luctuosa veloque obnubilata facie *P.II* luctuosa facie, veloque obnubilata, ex inventione — **y** *P.I u. P.II* & — **z** *P.I* bellicorum, nobilis, quam tale adumbrabat: In quæ *P.II* bellicorum, *Romano Germanicâ insignitorum facile nobilis. Eam tale adumbrabat lemma:* — **aa** *Pms. durch rote Tinte hervorgehoben. P.I kursiv* — **bb** *P.I* Sinistram anticolumnii areolam tenebat Lingua *P.II* capiebat Lingua — **cc** *P.I* instar Nymphæ venustæ, quæ squalido *P.II venustioris instar Nymphæ, quæ squalido* — **dd** *P.I u. P.II* amictu circūdata — **ee** *P.I u. P. II* lauru, & testudine insignita erat. Epigraphe — **ff** *P.I* talis oculos legentium erudivit: In quæ *P.II* talis legentium oculos erudiebat: in quæ — **gg** *P.I* portæ aditus, eiusdē Ordinis Ornamentis affabrè decorus. Imminebat *Vrania* cœlestis pulchritudinis Genauso *P.II außer:* Imminebat Genius Guelphicus *cum face & totius structuræ titulo, aureis literis Præscripto:* PORTICUS AUGUSTI, Serenissimi atque — **hh** *In P.I u. P.II folgt:* Principis, DOMINI DOMINI AVGVSTI Brunsvvicensiū ac Muneburgensiū [*Druckfehler*] Ducis &c. — **ii** *P.I* manutenens: afflictam *Germaniam:* melius sperare, & Linguam *P.II* Genius hic afflictam Germaniam *melius sperare,* & Linguam — **jj** *P.I* nimium sibis sapere jubēs, duplici hoc Elogio: Dextram Genauso *P.II außer: Elogio, dextrorsum:* erit mensura malorum, & *sinistrorsum:* non cunctis — **kk** *P.I* & versus

T II **a** *In der Initiale D ein quadrierter, mit einem Herzschild belegter mecklenburg. Wappenschild. S. Anm. 9.* — **b** *Druckfehler* ingeninium — **c** *Lies:* pour [?]

K Zu *Harsdörffer: Porticus Virtutis* vgl. 450923C (K 4), 460112 (K 2), 460406 K 2, 460700, 460912 II (Fassungen der *Porticus*), 461204A, *DA Köthen I.* 8: 470119, 470215 u. 470507. S. Abb. auf S.703. Der in Q beschriebene Text erschien in zwei überarbeiteten Druckfassungen, einer längeren in *Harsdörffer: Specimen* (s. 460912) und der längsten in einem Separatdruck, den Georg Philipp Harsdörffer (FG 368. Der Spielende) an Hz. August d.J. v. Braunschweig-Wolfenbüttel (FG 227. Der Befreiende) zusammen mit dem Brief 470119 schickte. Zu einem frühen separaten Druck des *Specimen* noch ohne *Porticus* s. 460406.
  1 Als ein Beispiel hierfür konnte Georg Philipp Harsdörffer (FG 368. Der Spielende) an ein von dem Jesuiten Géronimo Nadal illustriertes Werk denken, das den Herzog

wegen der Bebilderung seiner *Evangelischen Kirchen-Harmonie* (s. 411214) interessierte. Es ist in seiner Bibliothek in mehreren Auflagen vorhanden: [Kupfertitel] EVANGELICAE HISTORIAE IMAGINES Ex ordine Euangeliorum, quæ toto anno in Missæ sacrificio recitantur, In ordinem temporis vitæ Christi digestæ. Auctore Hieronymo Natali Societatis IESV Theologo Antuerpiæ Anno Di M.D.XCI. SVPERIORVM PERMISSV.; [Drucktitel] MEDITATIONI SOPRA LI EVANGELII CHE TVTTO L'ANNO SI LEGGONO NELLA MESSA, & principali misterij della vita, & passione di Nostro Signore. COMPOSTE DAL R. P. AGOSTINO VIVALDI della Compagnia di GIESV. RESPONDENTI ALLE IMAGINI DEL PADRE Girolamo Natale della medesima Compagnia. IN ROMA, Appresso Luigi Zannetti. M. D. XCIX. CON LICENZA DE SVPERIORI. HAB: Th. 4° 36. S. 460804 K 1.

2 Ulpianus in Dig. lib. 38, 17 (Ad Senatus Consultum Tertullianum et Orphitianum), 31–33 „Quid si furioso tutorem vel curatorem non petiit? magis est, ut incidat. Non solum autem quae non petiit coercetur, sed et quae defunctorie petiit. ut rescripto declaratur, vel privilegio munitum vel oneratum tribus puta tutelis, sed ita demum, si data opera hoc fecit."

3 Lat. expicta, von expingere, ausmalen/ bildlich darstellen, ist hier nicht wörtlich zu nehmen, da Harsdörffer offenbar keine zeichnerischen Entwürfe mitgesandt hatte. Das bestätigt Harsdörffers Text zu K I 1. Entwürfe Harsdörffers werden in 460700 erwähnt. Sie sollte (u. a.) der Wolfenbütteler Hofmaler Albert Freyse ausführen.

4 Die erweiterte, separat erschienene Lobschrift *Harsdörffer: Porticus (1647)* enthält dennoch eine bedeutungsgeschichtliche PRÆMONITIO AD CORDATUM LECTOREM (B 3v), in der Harsdörffer das Wort (porticus) erklärt, antike Beispiele der Säulenhalle oder gemalten Halle (poecile) anhäuft und dahinter noch einen Fassadenaufriß und Grundriß der Porticus Augusti liefert. Als antike Quelle zitiert Harsdörffer in 461204A Plin. n. h. 16, 40.

5 Hz. Augusts Nürnberger Agent Georg Forstenheuser (421120 K 3) bestätigt das Datum des Briefs in seiner Mitteilung vom 4.10.1645 an den Fürsten. *Blume: Porticus*, 95 Anm. 14. Vgl. 460112 (Harsdörffer erhält ein Kleinod-Porträt Hz. Augusts zum Dank).

K I 1 Die folgende Beschreibung Harsdörffers gab der Zeichner (Albert Freyse) nicht in allen Einzelheiten wieder. Vgl. 460700 u. oben K 4. S. die Abb. des Kupferstichs mit dem Blick durch das halb geöffnete Tor auf die Reiterstatue Hz. Augusts d.J. im Innenhof der Porticus. Dieses Bild findet sich noch nicht in *Pms* oder *P.I*, sondern erst in *P.II*. Man erblickt die vier Säulen mit korinthischen Kapitellen, links unter der Inschrift „Erit mensura malorum." auf einem Sockel (Aufschrift IN QUÆ MODO FUNERA DAMNOR:) die trauernde Germania mit Szepter, begleitet von einer adlergeschmückten Kanone, einer Kaiserkrone, einem Buch mit der Aufschrift „typograph:", rechts unter der Inschrift „Non cunctis formosa" eine lautenspielende, singende und bekränzte Personifikation der Lingua Germanica auf einem Sockel mit Inschrift (IN QUÆ MODO GAUDIA DUCOR!). Über dem halbgeöffneten Tor (mit Durchblick zur Reiterstatue Hz. Augusts) eine Inschrift („COR. MAGIS.TIBI.MUSA.PANDIT."), über der ein Genius mit Fackel einen Schild mit der Inschrift „PORTICUS AUGUSTI" hält. Harsdörffers Hinweis auf die kimbrischen Buchstaben bzw. Runen (s. Abb. in *Harsdörffer: Specimen*, 109f.) griff der Zeichner nicht auf.

K II Der 5. Teil der *Frauenzimmer-Gesprächspiele* Georg Philipp Harsdörffers (FG 368. Der Spielende) kann nicht vor Mai 1645 erschienen sein, weil die Ehrengedichte vom 10. Dezember 1644 bis 16. Mai 1645 datieren. Daraus folgt die Datierung des Gedichts auf

450927 Georg Philipp Harsdörffer

450500. — In *Harsdörffer: Frauenzimmer-Gesprächspiele* V (1645), nach dem Drucktitel und der Abbildung einer „Dank und Denkseüle Der Hochfürstlichen Fruchtbringenden Gesellschaft Christlöblichen mitgenossinn Der BEFREYENDINN. aufgerichtet von dem Spielenden" folgt auf der Rückseite der Säule dasselbe Porträt der Gattin des Befreienden, Hzn. Sophia Elisabeth v. Braunschweig-Wolfenbüttel, geb. Pzn. v. Mecklenburg-Güstrow (AL 1629, TG 42b) wie zu 441200 I abgebildet, jedoch als Brustbild in einem ovalen Rahmen. Wir verzichten daher auf eine Abbildung und zitieren nur die neue „Zuschrift" des Spielenden in Versen. Es folgt ein frz. „Sonnet de L'Auteur. Sur le Pourtrait de son Altesse,". S. Beil. II./ Abb. Die Bezeichnung der Gemahlinnen oder Töchter durch die weibliche Form des Gesellschaftsnamens ihres Gemahls bzw. Vaters war in der FG gang und gäbe. Allerdings erhielten Damen „keine besondere Zahl/ Gemahl [Gemälde/ Pictura der Imprese] oder Spruch", also keinen eigenen Mitgliedsstatus. Dennoch ebnete Harsdörffers Huldigung an die „Mitgenossin" Sophia Elisabeth schon den Weg zur Anerkennung der eigenen künstlerischen Leistung der Befreienden und anderer Damen durch die FG (s. *Hille: Teutscher Palmbaum*, 189; *Neumark: Palmbaum*, 179f.). Vgl. auch *Ball: Sophia Elisabeth*.

1 Als Gattin Hz. Augusts d.J. v. Braunschweig-Wolfenbüttel (FG 227. Der Befreiende) und eng mit der FG verbundene Dame wird Hzn. Sophia Elisabeth, *Mecklenburg-Güstrow (AL 1629. TG 42b), durch die feminine Form des hzl. Gesellschaftsnamens benannt, so auch in der FG-Korrespondenz. Unter dem Gesellschafsnamen „Die Befreyende" ist Sophia Elisabeth als Autorin und Widmungsempfängerin in die Musik- und Literaturgeschichte eingegangen. S. *Geck*. Zu der Herzogin, ihrer Biographie, ihren Mitgliedschaften in Damengesellschaften u. der FG-Verbindung s. *Ball: Sophia Elisabeth*. Zur Bedeutung von Frauen in der FG 440209 K 5.

2 „Kunstgemerke", hier wohl eine Wortschöpfung im Sinne von: die Merkmale, die ein Kunstwerk als solches auszeichnen. Neben der juridischen Bedeutung ‚Grenzzeichen, Mark' und der gelegentlichen Verwendung als grammatischer Terminus (für Artikel) sind im Fnhd. auch die Bedeutungsschichten ‚(An-)Zeichen, Merkmal' und ‚Erinnerung, Gedächtnisfähigkeit' mit *Gemerk* verbunden. Vgl. *Stieler*, 1270 u. *DW* IV.1.2, 3276–3281. In ebd. Abschnitt 2) e) δ) wird darauf hingewiesen, daß Fischart Embleme als ‚Kunstgemärke' bezeichnet habe. Bei Fischart heißt es: „Hierum̃ dañ etliche hocherleuchte personen vervrsacht worden/ neben jren Anherrlichen Erbzeychen/ nach Exempel der alten Römischē Keyser besondere vergriffene Kunstgemärck vñ Fundzeychē/ samt darzu dienlichen kurtzen Sprüchen/ Reimen/ Divisen vñ buchstaben/ so die Deitung begreiffen vñ einhalten/ zuerfinden: vnd dieselbige jnen selbs/ oder andern zugleich neben jnen zu fruchtbarlicher Erinnerung offentlich fürzumalen." (Johann Fischart: Kurtzer vnd Woldienlicher Vorbericht/ von Vrsprung/ Namen vnd Gebrauch der Emblematen/ oder Eingeblömeten Zierwercken. In: Matthäus Holtzwart: EMBLEMATVM Tyrocinia: Sive PICTA POESIS LATINOGERMANICA. Das ist. Eingeblümete Zierwerck/ oder Gemälpoesy (Straßburg 1581), HAB: T 355.8° Helmst. (2), Bl. aiij r – b4 v, hier b2 r.)

3 Aganippe, eine den Musen geweihte Quelle und die ihr zugehörige Nymphe am Fuß des Helikons. *RE* I, 731.

4 In Pomponius Melas (1. Jh. n.Chr.) *De Chorographia* wird Aganippe nicht genannt. Gaius Julius Solinus (Mitte 4. Jh.) erwähnt sie in *De mirabilibus mundi*, VII.22, C. Plinius Secundus (gest. 79) in *Naturalis historia*, IV.25. Letzterer berichtet ebd. XXXI.25ff. von merkwürdigen Gewässern, deren Wirkung mitunter gar tödlich sei: Der Nonacris soll an seinem Ausfluß direkt zu Stein erstarren (XXXI.27), das Wasser anderer Quellen sei in der Lage, bei Kontakt das Erdreich und andere Gegenstände zu versteinern (XXXI.29f.).

5 Philipp Clüvers (1580–1622) 1616 erstmals in Leiden bei Elzevier erschienene deut-

sche Altertumskunde *Germania antiqua. NDB* III, 295 f. Vgl. 441000 (K 1) u. 450000 (K 1).

6 IOANNIS BARCLAII Icon Animorum (Francofurti: Daniel & David Aubrius & Clemens Schleichius 1625). John Barclay (1582–1621). Dig. SB München. Harsdörffer meint dieses gewöhnlich auch als 4. Teil des folgenden satirischen Romans veröffentlichte Werk Barclays: Euphormionis Lusinini Satyricon: Pars ... Nunc denuo recognita, emendata & variis in locis aucta (Francofurti: Schmidlinus, 1616–1623), HAB: Xb 2831. Vgl. Icon, Cap. II. „Secula pene suum genium habere, diversumque à caeteris. Esse praeterea cuilibet regioni proprium spiritum, qui animos indigenarum, in certa studia & mores quodammodo adigat. Hos spiritus inuestigari opera precium esse." Barclay bespricht in den folgenden Kapiteln die Begabung der einzelnen Völker, darunter der Deutschen und Niederländer (Cap. 5), sodann der einzelnen Berufe und Bildungsgruppen. In *Harsdörffer: Specimen (1646)*, disquisitio VIII, § 4, S. 157 findet sich Harsdörffers Marginalie erneut, dieses Mal mit deutlichem Verweis auf Cap. 5 von Barclays Text: „Certe si hodiernam Græciam cum nostra Germania conferamus, *nos* profectò *Græciæ decoquenti, & Italiæ dormitanti omnium artium gloriam præripuisse, nemo negabit, sunt verba Euphorm. in Icon. anim. cap. 5.*" Dieses Kapitel entbehrt eines solchen Zitats, es handelt sich dabei nur um eine Zusammenfassung der Bewunderung Barclays, die andere treffende, auch kritische Aussagen ausläßt.

7 Recte: Antyrius, ein sagenhafter Hauptmann skythischer Herkunft unter Alexander dem Großen, der an der Odermündung gelandet sein soll; fabelhafter Gründervater des Hauses Mecklenburg. Vgl. Anm. 8.

8 Die Landung von Antyrius (s. Anm. 7) an der Oder wird beschrieben im 12. Buch von Wolfgang Lazius' (1514–1565) DE GENTIVM ALIquot migrationibus, sedibus fixis, reliquijs, linguarúm*que* initijs & immutationibus ac dialectis, Libri XII (Basel 1557; zuerst ebd. 1555), 809f. — In Hieronymus Henninges (gest. 1597): SECVNDI ET TERTII REGNI IN QVARTA MONARCHIA PARS ALTERA, CONTINENS GENEALOGICIS TABELLIS (Uelzen 1587), 287 [HAB: T 126.2° Helmst. (2)] findet sich ein Stammbaum der Werlen (Herulen), beginnend mit „Anthyrius" (wobei explizit auf Wolfgang Lazius Bezug genommen wird). — Von Sebastian Münsters (1488–1552) *Cosmographia* (zuerst Basel 1544), einer umfangreichen Kartierung und Beschreibung der bekannten Welt, in der empirisch gewonnene und tradierte Wissensbestände miteinander verwoben sind, existieren zahlreiche Auflagen. Sie datieren vornehmlich auf das 16. Jahrhundert, VD 17 verzeichnet derzeit nur zwei: Basel 1614 u. 1628. Die frühen Drucke (gesichtet: Basel 1545 [dt.], 1548 [dt.], 1552 [lat.], 1554 [lat.], 1559 [lat.], 1567 [dt.], Köln 1575 [it.]) haben keine Kapitelzählung, werden von Harsdörffer mithin nicht benutzt worden sein. Darüber hinaus fehlt in den Ausgaben Basel 1545 u. 1548 das Kap. zu Antyrius, selbst das Kap. zu Mecklenburg ist dort noch rudimentär. Die Ausgabe Basel 1572 (dt.) hat zwar Numerierungen, das Kap. „Antyrius Künig der Werlen vnd Wenden" hat jedoch die Nr. 456 und nicht 459. Erst in den Ausgaben Basel 1578 und 1588 (beide dt.) hat „Antyrius König der Werlen vnd Wenden" im 3. Buch die Kap.-Nr. 459. Eine dieser Auflagen könnte Harsdörffer demnach verwendet haben. Die Ausgabe Basel 1598 (dt.) weist eine andere Kapiteleinteilung auf: Kap. 459 gibt eine sächsische Turnierordnung wieder, das Antyrius-Kap. hat die Nr. 474. Die Ausgaben aus dem 17. Jahrhundert scheiden allein deswegen aus, weil die Einteilung des gesamten Werks modifiziert wurde. — Johannes Limnäus (1592–1663) erwähnt Antyrius (auf das 459. Kap. in Münsters *Cosmographia* verweisend) in Buch 5, Kap. 12, Abschnitt 3, S. 272 des 2. Bandes seines Hauptwerks: TOMUS SECUNDUS IVRIS PVBLICI IMPERII ROMANOGERMANICI, Quo tractatur DE ORIGINE DIGNITATUM ILLUstrium, de juribus atque oneribus Principum aliorumque Imperii

Statuum ... (Straßburg 1631). HAB: 36.37 Jur. — Vgl. zu Lazius *NDB* XIV, 14f.; zu Henninges *ADB* XI, 778; zu Münster *NDB* XVIII, 539–541; zu Limnäus *NDB* XIV, 567–569.

9 Hzn. Sophia Elisabeth stammte aus dem Hause Mecklenburg-Güstrow, s. Anm. 1. In der Initiale am Anfang des Widmungsgedichts ist das gevierte Wappen der Mecklenburger Herzöge abgebildet. Unter dem Herzschild in Feld 1 ein Ochsenkopf mit Krone in Frontalansicht, in 2 ein Greif, in 3 ein nackter mit einer Binde umwundener Arm mit einem Ring in der Hand, in 4 ein Ochsenkopf mit Krone im Profil. *Siebmacher* I.1.2, 103 f., Tafel 103–106. Abbildungen des Wappens auch in *GB Kö.* I, Bl. Rr [j] v (Hz. Johann Albrecht II. v. Mecklenburg-Güstrow, FG 158; ihr Vater) u. Bl. Xx ij v (Hz. Adolph Friedrich I. v. Mecklenburg-Schwerin, FG 175).

10 Zu ihrem Lauten- oder Mandoraspiel s. 340107 K 21, auch *Geck*.

11 Auf dem Titelblatt von Johann Klajs *Lobrede der Teutschen Poeterey* (Nürnberg 1645) ist ein „Witdod" abgebildet, dessen wundersames Aussehen Harsdörffer in einem vorangestellten Lobgedicht mit Anmerkungen (Bl. [A iv] v) sowie einem mehrseitigen Anhang (Bl. E ij v – [E iv] v) erläutert. ‚Alt- und urdeutsche' Barden werden hier zwar als Sänger und Dichter erwähnt, Harsdörffer richtet den Text gleichwohl auf den Witdoden. Dieser ist auf dem Titelkupfer durch die ihm zu Füßen liegende Geige und ein aufgeschlagenes Notenbuch als Dichter-Sänger, durch die Weisheit symbolisierende Lilie in der Hand als Philosoph markiert. Tatsächlich schlägt *Harsdörffer: Specimen (1646)*, disquisitio I, § 5 f., S. 7–10 vor, „Witdod" als Verdeutschung des griech. Fremdworts *Philosoph* zu gebrauchen. Auf S. 181 des *Specimen* findet sich der gleiche Stich wie auf dem Titelblatt von Klajs Schrift noch einmal. Von einem Witdoden ist hier allerdings nicht die Rede, die Bildüberschrift lautet vielmehr: „L'habit anti*que* d'un Poëte Provançal, dit Troubadour." Dies ist nicht unbedingt eine widersprüchliche Auslegung des Bildes, denn in Klajs *Lobrede* formuliert Harsdörffer bereits, der Witdod trage „Fränkische Tracht". Es folgt die Anmerkung: „Die Teutschen und Franken oder Gallier sind vor Alters ein Volk gewesen." In seiner *Schutzschrift für Die Teutsche Spracharbeit* (in: *Harsdörffer: Frauenzimmer-Gesprächspiele* I [²1644], 351–395) bestimmt Harsdörffer die Witdoden als „Teutsche Sprach- und Kunstlehrer" (368), die vor 600 Jahren an deutschen Schulen die Muttersprache unterrichtet hätten. In der „Vorrede" des 5. Teils der *Gesprächspiele* dient das Adjektiv wiederum zur Übersetzung von *philosophisch*: „Witdodische (**Philosoph**ische) Händel" (*Harsdörffer: Frauenzimmer-Gesprächspiele* V, 107). Einen Poeten als „Barden" zu bezeichnen wird Christian Gueintz in einem Gutachten zu Harsdörffers *Specimen* übrigens als veralteten Wortgebrauch brandmarken, ebenso dessen Exhumierung des längst aus dem Gebrauch verschwundenen „Witdod". S. *DA Köthen* I. 9, zu 460720, auch die Zusammenfassung des Gutachtens in 460720 K 3. Vgl. 460915 K 3 u. 4; Conrad Wiedemann: Druiden, Barden, Witdoden: Zu einem Identifikationsmodell barocken Dichtertums. In: *Bircher/ van Ingen*, 131–150. Auch Philipp v. Zesen (FG 521. 1648) bzw. sein Umkreis in der DG äußerte Zweifel an dieser aus dem alten Niederdeutschen hervorgesuchten Wortprägung. S. *Habichthorst*, 77.

12 Hebr. אֵל (El) kurz für אֱלֹהִים (Elohim), ‚Gott'. Hebr. שַׁבָּת (Schabat), bedeutet auch ‚die Ruhe'.

450929

Justus Georg Schottelius an Herzog August d. J. von Braunschweig-Wolfenbüttel

Wie aus dem beiliegenden Brief hervorgehe, schreibt Justus Georg Schottelius (FG 397) an Hz. August d. J. v. Braunschweig-Wolfenbüttel (FG 227), will F. Ludwig die Arbeit an einem vollkommenen dt. Wörterbuch, das schon von vielen versprochen worden sei, unter Gelehrte der FG verteilen und hat dies schon getan, wie der Herzog aus beiliegendem Brief entnehme. Eine solche Grundlage zu schaffen, erscheine gewiß allen Mitarbeitern als schwierig. Da ein von F. Ludwig erwähntes Werk (Henischs Wörterbuch) sich zweifellos in Hz. Augusts Bibliothek finde, bittet Schottelius, es kurz ausleihen zu dürfen. Er werde eine große Menge bereits gesammelter Wörter zu dem geplanten Wörterbuch beisteuern. — Schottelius will eine genauere, ergänzte zweite Auflage seiner deutschen Grammatik ausarbeiten. Buchhändler zu Hamburg und Lübeck hätten sich dafür interessiert und schon angeboten, das Werk auf ihre Kosten zu verlegen. Sogar F. Ludwig scheine das Werk in Köthen drucken zu wollen. Da das kleine Buch Hz. August gewidmet sei und viel Neues und bisher unbekanntes Nützliches enthalten werde, auch viel Griechisches, Lateinisches, Französisches und sonstiges Fremdes genau verbessert werden müsse, wolle er, Schottelius, dem Herzog seine Absicht ankündigen, zumal ein Druck an einem anderen Ort nur mit dessen Erlaubnis oder die Veröffentlichung in dessen Stadt nur auf Hz. Augusts Befehl und mit einem Zuschuß geschehen könne. Der örtliche Drucker besitze allerdings nicht den benötigten Vorrat und Reichtum an Schriften, so daß nur Hz. August durch die Gebrüder Stern Abhilfe schaffen könne. Er möge Schottelius darüber informieren.

Q Hs. unbekannt. — *D:* Eduard Bodemann: Zwei Briefe von Leibniz betr. eine „Teutsche Gesellschaft" zu Wolfenbüttel nebst zwei Briefen von J. G. Schottelius an Herzog August von Braunschweig-Wolfenbüttel. In: Zs. des Histor. Vereins f. Niedersachsen (1899), 299–307, hier 306 f. — *BN: Bürger*, 1262 Nr. 2.

A *Fehlt.*

[a]Serenissime illustrissimeque Princeps Domine clementissime

De conficiendo Lexico perfecto linguae Germanicae viri eruditi dudum solliciti fuere, multique operam et subsidium promittunt, illustris etiam Princeps Anhaltinus[1] laborem hunc inter doctos ex societate dividendum arbitratur, ipseque eum dividet, sicuti Vestra Serenitas ex literis adjunctis clementissime[b] animadvertet: Difficultas autem rei vel imprimis in ponendo fundamento, quod omnes collaborantes approbare eique insistere [307] non dubiant, consistit: Quandoquidem autem liber iste, cujus mentionem Princeps Anhaltinus in literis facit, in Bibliotheca Vestrae Serenitatis procul dubio reperitur, egoque pro humillima tenuitate quid sentiam pluribus perscripturus, magnumque collectorum vocabulorum numerum huic operi collaturus, usum istius libri (ni fallor D. Henischii) ad aliquot dies humillime expeto.

Porro multas habeo causas, alteram editionem Grammaticae Germanicae[2] maturare, prodibit enim longe exactiori et auctiori facie; etiam bibliopola aut

450929 Justus Georg Schottelius

Hamburgi aut Lubecae suis sumptibus denuo edendam dudum expetit, Illustr. etiam Princeps Anhaltinus Cötheniis typis libellum istum exscribendam (sic!)[c] videtur velle: Cum autem opusculum Augustissimo Vestrae Serenitatis nomini sit dicatum,[3] quam plurima etiam nova et utilia hactenus taliter nondum collecta et ostensa (quod res ipsa volente Deo probabit) continebit, etiam Graeca, Latina, Gallica et alia exotica saepissime intercurrentia exactiorem correctionem merito requirant, indicium obedientissime facere debui, fierine possit clementi cum consensu Vestrae Serenitatis, ut alio in loco liber imprimatur, aut potius jussu et subsidio aliquo difficultatem clementissime sublevare et editionem in hoc celebri Vestrae Serenitatis loco fieri posse consentire: Typographus hic nec necessariam varietatem nec copiam typorum habet: an Stellae[4] autem lucem huic dare possint aut debeant, Vestrae Serenitatis est jubere, et me hac in re dubium aliquo clementissimi adsensus verbulo informare, qui illud obedientiae meae debitum putavi, indicium hujus propositi prius ad Vestram Serenitatem deferre, meque ut in hisce ita et in omnibus mearum virium aliis praestare
                    Vestrae Serenitati
                addictissimus obedientissimusque.

T a *Bodemann verweist auf die von Leibniz' H. stammende Anmerkung* Schottelii *in der linken oberen Ecke der Hs.* — b *Bodemann verweist darauf, daß Leibniz ein* non nihil *einfügt.* — c *In der Vorlage derart hervorgehoben.*

K Der undatierte Brief von Justus Georg Schottelius (FG 397) an seinen Dienstherren Hz. August d.J. v. Braunschweig-Wolfenbüttel (FG 227) dürfte nach dem Empfang des Schreibens F. Ludwigs an ihn (450923B) verfaßt worden sein, vielleicht an einem späten Septembertag wie dem 29.9.1645, vielleicht auch Anfang Oktober wie 451007, da Schottelius F. Ludwig seine Kooperationsbereitschaft am geplanten dt. Wörterbuch erklärt. Am 23.9. hatte F. Ludwig auch an Hz. August und Hz. Christian Ludwig v. Braunschweig-Calenberg (FG 372) geschrieben (s. 450923A u. 450923). Hz. August antwortete dem Anhaltiner mit 451001, Schottelius, wie gesagt, mit 451007. Diese beiden Briefe liefern uns daher auf jeden Fall auch den terminus ante quem für das Empfangsdatum des Ludwig-Briefs 450923B durch Schottelius, den dieser seinem vorliegenden Schreiben an Hz. August beilegte. Obgleich der Briefwechsel der Fürsten das Wörterbuchprojekt nicht erwähnt, dürfte Schottelius gleich die Gelegenheit ergriffen haben, um Hz. August von seinen Wörterbuch- und Grammatikplänen zu unterrichten. Zur Datierung vgl. auch Anm. 1 (Erwähnung Henischs).
  1 F. Ludwig teilte die Arbeit an dem geplanten vollkommenen Wörterbuch der deutschen Sprache in seinem Brief 450923B unter Christian Gueintz (FG 361), Schottelius und sich selbst auf. Dieser Brief ist uns nur als Konzept bekannt, dessen Text durch die Erwähnung eines Buchs als Grundlage oder Ausgangsbasis für die Zusammenarbeit dienen sollte. Titel oder Verfasser sind im Konzept nicht genannt; Schottelius vermutet aber richtig, daß der Fürst das unvollendete Wörterbuch von *Henisch* gemeint haben dürfte. Georg Henisch: Teütsche Sprach vnd Weißheit. THESAVRVS LINGVAE ET SAPIENTIAE GERMANICAE. In quo vocabula omnia Germanica, ... continentur, & Latinè ex optimis qvibusq; autoribus redduntur ... PARS PRIMA studio Georgij Henischij B. Medicinæ Doctoris, & Mathematici Augustani. Augustæ Vindelicorum, Typis Davidis Franci. M. D.

C. XVI. HAB: 16 Gram. 2°; Nachdr. Hildesheim usw. 1973. In 451028A schlägt F. Ludwig Schottelius gegenüber (erneut) vor, Henischs Wörterbuch zur Grundlage der gemeinsamen lexikograph. Arbeiten zu machen. In der Folgezeit lieh Schottelius dieses Werk aus Hz. Augusts Bibliothek aus: 460000, vgl. 451219 K 8.

2 Die erste Auflage war *Schottelius: Sprachkunst (1641)*. Obwohl in der Folgezeit gelegentlich von Schottelius' Arbeit an einer 2., erweiterten Auflage die Rede ist (vgl. 451007 u. 460100), erschien sie in Braunschweig erst nach F. Ludwigs Tod, *Schottelius: Sprachkunst (1651)*. In 451007 erklärte Schottelius aber noch, eine grundlegende und allgemein anerkannte dt. Grammatik sei die Voraussetzung für ein umfassendes (und in der Lemmata-Ansetzung stimmiges) Wörterbuch. Er sei bereit, eine solche überarbeitete dt. Grammatik, zu der er schon einiges Neues zusammengetragen habe, in Köthen drucken zu lassen, damit sie dort von F. Ludwig und der FG in der Rechtschreibung angepaßt und vereinheitlicht werden könne. Ein Grundsatzpapier zur Klärung strittiger Fragen setzte er am 5. 12. 1645 auf. S. 451219 K 1.

3 Da schon *Schottelius: Sprachkunst (1641)* Hz. August gewidmet wurde, will der Autor auch die veränderte Neuauflage seinem Herrn dedizieren. Das tat er auch in den beiden tatsächlich erschienenen Ausgaben von 1651 und 1663.

4 Die Verleger Hans und Heinrich Stern in Lüneburg.

450930

Matthäus Merian d. Ä. an Peter Knaudt

Matthäus Merian d. Ä. bestätigt den Eingang des (nicht erhalten gebliebenen) Briefes vom 17. 9., nach dessen Anweisungen er sich richten und künftig genau über alles Notwendige Nachricht geben werde. — Demnächst werde er den ersten Bogen (des *GB 1646*) senden und gegen kommende Fastnacht das Werk nach Möglichkeit beenden, indem er die Arbeit an den Kupferplatten fortsetze, und die nun folgenden Impresenstiche in der Ansicht den Visierungen analog (und nicht spiegelverkehrt) verfertigen werde, auch wenn dies einige Mühe mache. — Er hofft, daß Peter Knaudt die 25 Abdrucke, die vor 10 Tagen der Leipziger Buchhändler Andreas Kühne versandt hat, mittlerweile erhalten habe. — Bei Georg Winckler habe er wegen der (gewünschten Vorauszahlung der) 200 Reichstaler nachgefragt in der Hoffnung, daß dieser das Geld überweisen werde. Die restlichen 300 Reichstaler erwartet Merian erst nach der endgültigen Lieferung der kontrollierten Exemplare. — Des Zwiebelgewächses Yucca konnte er noch nicht habhaft werden, möchte jedoch sein Bestes tun, dieses noch zu erlangen. Falls es ihm nicht gelinge, werde er Knaudt benachrichtigen, allerdings empfiehlt Merian, Knaudt möge sich auch in seiner Gegend darum bemühen. — Fünf Bände der *Topographia* sind bereits erschienen: 1. Helvetia, 2. Suevia, 3. Alsatia, 4. Bavaria, 5. Palatinatus Rheni. Zusammen kosten sie 11 Reichstaler, was in der hiesigen Währung umgerechnet 16 Gulden und 10 Schilling ausmacht. Die Bände Hassia, wie auch Mainz, Köln und Trier sollen bis zur nächsten Ostermesse vorliegen, der Preis stehe noch nicht fest. F. Ludwig werde dann von jedem Band ein Exemplar erhalten. Die übrigen Provinzen: Franken, Österreich, Böhmen, Mähren, Schlesien, Thüringen, Sachsen, Meißen, Westfalen, Brandenburg und Pommern werden zu gegebener Zeit folgen, ein Teil nach dem anderen, die Beschreibungen (der jeweiligen Orte) wie auch ein Großteil der Kupferplatten sind bereits fertig, dennoch warten noch einige Jahre Arbeit auf ihn, ehe er ganz Deutschland erfaßt habe.

450930 Matthäus Merian d. Ä.

Q HM Köthen: V S 546, Bl. 14rv [A: 14v]; eigenh.; rotes Lacksiegel. — *D: Bircher: Merian*, 704 f.; *Wüthrich: Merian Briefe*, 94 f. — *BN: Bürger*, 987 Nr. 11.

A Tt. Dem Ehrnvesten und GroßAchtparen Herrn Petter Knaudt Fürst. Anhaltischen Cammermeister *etc.*, meinem Großg. hochGeehrten herrn *etc.* Cöthen

Ehrnvester GroßAchtparer Jnsonders gg. hochgeehrter herr,

Deßelben geliebts vom 17. diß habe ich wol empfangen und ableßendt alles verstanden, will solches zu recht in Acht nehmen, und fortan die Noturfft von Allem berichten, Auch mit nechstem den ersten bogen senden, und geliebt[s] Gott, gegen künfftigen Faßnacht, das werkh völlig darstellen, gestalt dan mit der Arbeit an den kupfer platten ich fleißig fortsetze, vnd die ietz volgende Alle den Abrißen gleich unumbgekehrt komen werden, welches zwar nicht geringe muhe machet. Verhoffe mein gg. herr werde, die vor 10 tagen durch H. Andreas Künne buchhendlern von Leipzig gesanten 25 abtrukh nunmehr empfangen haben.[1]

Jch habe hiemit auch an den herrn Winklern[2] wegen der 200 Rthl. geschrieben, verhoffe er mir solche allhero verordnen werde. Die ubrigen 300 Rthl. sollen verbleiben biß ich völlige liferung der verglichenen exemplarien gethan habe, Alsdann selbige auch volgen können.[3]

Das Zwiebel gewächß Giuoca habe ich noch nicht erfahren können, will aber nochmaln mein bestes thun ob ichs erlangen könne, wo nicht, solches berichten, wehre gutt wan auch Jhrer öhrtern darumb geworben würde.[4]

Deren[a] Stettbüchern sein albereit 5[b] theil herauß, 1 Heluetia, 2 Sueuia, 3 Alsatia, 4 Bauaria, 5 Palatinatus Rhenj: dise zusamen kosten 11 Rthl. thun hiesigen gelts f 16 ß 10.[5] Hassia, Jtem Maintz, Coln vnd Trier, werden künfftige Ostermeß, wils Gott auch fertig sein, deren preiß ich noch nicht wissen kan, Alsdan Jch ein exemplar von allen Jhr. f. G. vber senden, die vbrigen Prouintzen Als Francken, Ostreich, Böhmen, Mähren, Schlesien, Duringen Saxen Meißen Westphalen, die Markh Pommern werden auch zu seiner zeit volgen,[6] eines nach dem Andern, deren beschreibungen albereit fertig, Auch viel kupfer platten, werde noch etlich Jahr, vieleicht zu thun haben, ehe ich durch das gantze Große Teutschlandt hindurch kome,

Der Allmächtig Gott woll leben Gesundheit vnd Segen Darzu geben, damit es wol vollendet werden möge *etc.*

Dißmalen mehr nicht alß dem Allmechtigen zu Gnaden wol befohlen.

Ffurt den 30. 7bris 1645.

    Meines Großg Herrn Dienstwilligster
    Mattheus Merian.

T a *Senkrechter Markierungsstrich am Rand bis zur Datierungszeile.* — **b** *Gebessert aus* 4

K 1 Matthäus Merian d. Ä. verpflichtet sich, die Impresenstiche spiegelverkehrt zu deren Zeichnungen (Visierungen) anzufertigen, damit sie im Druck seitengetreu wiedergegeben werden. S. *Conermann II*, 100 u. Anm. 119. S. auch 451015. — Zum Leipziger Verleger Andreas Kühne s. 450124 K 2.

2 Der Leipziger Handelsherr Georg Winckler. S. 451019 K 0.

3 In 450905 hatte Merian zuzüglich der bereits erhaltenen 200 Reichstaler einen weiteren Vorschuß in derselben Höhe erbeten, um die laufenden Herstellungskosten abzudecken, und diese Bitte in 450922 wiederholt. Den Eingang der Zahlung konnte Merian in 451028B quittieren. Der Restbetrag von 300 Reichstalern wäre dann bei Lieferung der Gesamtauflage zu zahlen. S. zum Zahlungsverkehr in puncto *GB 1646* 450127 K 1. Zum *GB 1646* allgem. 440130 K 3 u. zur Einrichtung desselben s. 450711 K 4.

4 Eine für die Visierung der Imprese Jobst Heimarts v. Lenthe (FG 384) notwendige Ansicht der Yucca lag in Köthen nicht vor, deshalb wurde Merian gebeten, eine solche zu beschaffen. Am Ende konnte sich Merian einer Vorlage bedienen. S. dazu 450800 (K 4), 451015 u. 451119.

5 Die Geldeinheit Floren (Florenus), abgekürzt f, fl, ist seit dem Mittelalter durch die Wiederaufnahme des Goldmünzenprägens in Florenz bekannt. In Deutschland verbreitete sie sich bald unter dem Namen „Gulden". Die Trennung Deutschlands in Talerländer (Nord- und Ostdeutschland) und Guldenländer (Süd- und Westdeutschland) — hier repräsentiert durch Köthen auf der einen, Frankfurt a. M. auf der anderen Seite — entwickelte sich seit den Augsburger Reichsmünzordnungen im 16. Jahrhundert und festigte sich gegen 1700. Die Abkürzung ß für Schilling findet man bereits seit dem 15. Jahrhundert. S. Wolfgang Trapp: Kleines Handbuch der Münzkunde und des Geldwesens in Deutschland. Stuttgart 1999, 75–86. — Neben dem gebräuchlichen Reichstaler (Rtl.) zu 90 Kreuzern gab es seit der Reichsmünzordnung von 1559 einen Rechnungsgulden (fl.), der 60 Kreuzer wert war (d. h. 2/3 Rtl.) und als sog. Reichsguldiner als Silbergroßmünze ausgeprägt wurde. Die hier angegebene Summe der 11 Reichstaler entsprach demnach 990 Kreuzern und somit 16½ Gulden (Reichsguldinern). Da ein (Reichs-)Taler im Münzfuß zu 24 Groschen bzw. 32 Schillingen ausgeprägt wurde, entsprach ein Schilling einem ¾ Groschen. Ein Reichsguldiner ließ sich wiederum auf 16 Groschen berechnen, was demnach 21⅓ Schillingen entsprach. Die berechneten 16½ Reichsguldiner waren somit eigentlich 16 Reichsguldiner und 10⅙ Schillinge. S. dazu Wörterbuch der Münzkunde. Hg. Friedrich Frhr. v. Schrötter. Berlin, Leipzig 1930, 245 u. 556ff.; Heinz Fengler, Gerhard Gierow u. Willy Unger: Transpress-Lexikon Numismatik. 4. bearb. Aufl. Berlin 1988, 398ff.

6 Matthäus Merian d. Ä. thematisiert erneut seine Großunternehmung der *Topographia* und ergänzt die in 450905 (K 4 u. 5) zitierten um die folgenden: 1) Topographia Bohemiae, Moraviae et Silesiae. Frankfurt 1650 (HAB: Cd 4° 75 [2]); 2) Topographia Westphalicae. Frankfurt 1647 (HAB: Cd 4° 82); 3) Topographia Electorat Brandenburgici et Ducatus Pomeraniae. Frankfurt 1652 (HAB: Cd 4° 79 [2–4]). Vgl. 450417 K 0.

451000

Justus Georg Schottelius an Herzog August d. J. von Braunschweig-Wolfenbüttel

Der Drucker Johann Ritmar, an den im Auftrag Hz. Augusts d.J. v. Braunschweig-Wolfenbüttel (FG 227) geschrieben worden war, sei erfahren und habe einen guten Ruf. Ritmar habe, schreibt Justus Georg Schottelius (FG 397), in der Universitätsstadt Helmstedt einige Jahre nahezu allein eine Druckerei betrieben und sei in Hamburg und Braunschweig mehr als 10 Jahre lang als Drucker tätig gewesen. Am Montag komme er zurück, um Hz. August seine bereits vorhandenen Drucktypen vorzuzeigen. Er biete sich an, die Druckerei (in Wolfenbüttel) auf eigene Kosten einzurichten, jedoch mit Unterstützung, besonders hinsichtlich des Gebäudes und der Einrichtung. — Vor über fünf Jahren habe er, Schottelius, vom Herzog die Expektanz eines Kanonikats erlangt, die Pfründe aber im vorigen Jahr wegen eines Konkurrenten nicht bekommen. Es sei unsicher, ob der Herzog über die jüngst freigewordene Stelle im Braunschweiger Stift verfügen kann. Es sei wegen dieses Kanonikats an den Sekretär Berckelmann geschrieben worden, jedoch habe er, Schottelius, noch keine Zusicherung erlangt.

Q   NSTA Wolfenbüttel: 2 Alt Nr. 3520, Bl. 48r; eigenh.

A   *Fehlt.*

Serenissime Illustrissimeq̀ue Princeps Domine

Typographus, ad quem Vestræ Serenitatis iussu, scriptum fuit, vocatur Johan Ritmar,[1] *est* bonæ Famæ et notæ peritiæ homo: In Vestræ Serenitatis Academiâ Julia per aliquot annos typographiæ ferè solus præfuit; Hamburgi etiam, et in Vestræ Serenitatis urbe Brunsvico vel ultra 10 annos typographum egit. Reversurus *est* ad diem Lunæ, Vestræ Serenitati exhibiturus typorum suorum formas: eos enim in parato iam habet; expectaturus clementissimos Serenitatis Vestræ iussûs. Offert se typographiam proprio sumptu instituere, modò adjutamine aliquo, inprimis etiam accipiendis typographicorum ruderum reliquis, sublevarj possit. Vestræ Serenitati humillimè id indicare debuj.

   Ultra qvinquennium ferè *est*, quod expectantiam canonicatûs à Vestra Serenitate humillimè cu*m* gra*tiaru*m actione impetravj: Casus etiam ante annum se obtulit, sed tam̀ temporis alius mihi prælatus fuit: Mortuus nuperis diebus est Canonicus quidam Brunsvigæ:[2] in cuius locum vacantem præsentandi ius an ad Vestram Serenitatem pertineat, ambigimus: Scriptu*m* est eius rei causâ ad Secretarium Berckelmannu*m*,[3] cuius responsionis remissæ quia meâ maximopere interest, certior factus non dum sum: Subiectissimè ig*itu*r peto, indicium responsionis, manibus clementissimis Vestræ Serenitatis hodie oblatæ, mihi clementissimè concedi, quò acqvisito iure meo et impetratæ Principali concessioni, incumbere queam.

Vestræ Serenitati
humillimâ devotione obediens
Justus-Georgius Schottelius.

K Zum vermutlichen Datum (September/ Oktober 1645) dieses kurz vor dem Beginn des Drucks der Oktavausgabe der *Evangelischen Kirchen-Harmonie* Hz. Augusts d. J. v. Braunschweig-Wolfenbüttel (FG 227) geschriebenen Briefs vgl. auch 451001, 451100 und in Anm. 2 das Datum der Verleihung des Kanonikats an Justus Georg Schottelius (FG 397). Zur *Kirchen-Harmonie* selbst s. 411214. Es ist nicht ganz auszuschließen, daß Schottelius Ritmar auch für den Druck der für 1646 geplanten 2. Auflage seiner *Sprachkunst* (erschien erst 1651) in Betracht zog. S. dazu 450929.

1 Unbekannt, auch nicht in Leichenpredigten, VD17, *Benzing: Buchdrucker*, *Reske*, *Gobiet*, *Sammler Fürst Gelehrter*, *Reinitzer: Biblia* oder *Dumrese: Sterne* erwähnt. Auch nicht genannt in Carl Ludwig Grotefend: Geschichte der Buchdruckereien in den Hannoverschen und Braunschweigischen Landen. Hannover 1840; Linus Irmisch: Kurze Geschichte der Buchdruckereien im Herzogthume Braunschweig. Braunschweig 1890; Wilhelm Eule: Helmstedter Universitäts-Buchdrucker. Helmstedt 1921; Max Joseph Husung: Georg Calixtus zu Helmstedt, ein gelehrter Drucker des 17. Jahrhunderts. In: Gutenberg-Jahrbuch 1939, 283–290; Joachim Lehrmann: Die Frühgeschichte des Buchhandels und Verlagswesens in der alten Universitätstadt Helmstedt sowie die Geschichte der in diesem Zusammenhang von Helmstedter Patriziern gegründeten ehemals bedeutenden Papiermühlen zu Räbke am Elm und Salzdahlum. Hämelerwald 1994; 450 Jahre Braunschweiger Druckgewerbe. Ausstellung im Städtischen Museum Braunschweig, Februar 1958. [Kataloggestaltung: Heinz Bergmann] Braunschweig 1958. In Helmstedt wirkte Ritmar vielleicht in der Druckerei Georg Calixts oder in der Unternehmung Henning Müllers (Erben Jacobus Lucius) oder gar noch der Erben des Jacob Lucius d. J. Vgl. Eule, a. a. O., 21; Grotefend, a. a. O., o. S. Hier werden als Inspektor der Druckerei der Gebr. Stern in Wolfenbüttel Christian Voigt († Wolfenbüttel Jan. 1658) und als zeitgleicher Drucker Johann Bismarck († Wolfenbüttel 15. 8. 1666) erwähnt. Vgl. CHRONICON Der Stadt und Vestung Wolffenbüttel, in sich haltend des ... CHRISTOPH WOLTERECK Begräbniß-Buch der Kirchen B. M. V. zu Wolffenbüttel ... von RVD. AVGVST. NOLTENIO (Blankenburg bzw. Helmstädt 1747), 385 bzw. 417. Bismarck scheint aber nicht am Druck der *Evangelischen Kirchen-Harmonie* (1646) beteiligt gewesen zu sein. Hz. Augusts *Evangelische Kirchen-Harmonie* wurde durch eine Dependance der Gebrüder Stern in Wolfenbüttel hergestellt. Schottelius empfahl Johann Ritmar vielleicht, weil er ihn schon als Drucker seiner *Vers- oder ReimKunst* (1645) eingesetzt hatte. Vgl. 441011 K 4.

2 Am 7. 10. 1641 hatte Schottelius ein Kanonikat der Stiftskirche St. Alexander in Einbeck erlangt, das er jedoch wegen der Expektanz anderer nicht antreten konnte, so daß ihm am 10. 3. 1645 dort eine andere Anwartschaft zugesprochen wurde. Am 12. 11. 1645 wurde Schottelius dann zum Kanonikus im Braunschweiger Domstift St. Blasius ernannt. NSTA Wolfenbüttel: 1 Alt 30 Nr. 504; *Bei der Wieden: Schottelius*, 140; *Schottelius*, 24.

3 Der hzl. Lehnssekretär Julius Berckelmann († 1. oder 2. 5. 1659). S. Woltereck: Chronicon (Anm. 1), 64 u. 118.

451001

Herzog August d. J. von Braunschweig-Wolfenbüttel an Fürst Ludwig

Antwort auf 450923A. — Hz. August v. Braunschweig-Wolfenbüttel (FG 227) wird die ihm zustehenden 48 Exemplare des *GB 1646* über Verbindungsleute (in Frankfurt a. M.) abholen lassen. Davon möge F. Ludwig (den Verleger) Matthäus Merian d. Ä. in Kenntnis setzen, damit die Aushändigung der 48 Exemplare unbeschwert erfolgen möge. — Hz. Augusts Evangelienharmonie werde jetzt zu drucken begonnen. Er will das erste Exemplar F. Ludwig senden.

Q   HM Köthen: V S 544, Bl. 63r–64v [A: 64v], 63v–64r leer; eigenh., A von Schreiberh. — D: *KE*, 50; danach zit. in *Begemann: FG und Andreae*, 51. — BN: *Bürger*, 70 Nr. 555.

A   Dem *Hochgebornen Fürsten, Herrn Ludwigen*, Fürsten zu Anhaldt, Graffen zu Ascanien, Herrn zu Zerbst, und Berenburgk, Unserm freundl. Lieben Oheimb und Schwagern etc. — *Eigenh. Empfangsvermerk F. Ludwigs:* Pres. 14. Octob. 1645.

Hochgeborner Furst, fr. vielgeliebter Her Oheimb und Schwager, nächst anerbietung meiner freundwilligsten diensten unterhalte ich e. l., daß mir dero angenehmes handbrieflein[1] wol eingeheimschet[2] worden: Will auch deswegen an bekante Leute schreiben lassen, und die bewuste 48 Geselschaft- oder Kreuter Bucher[3] abfordern lassen: Und werden e. l. unbeschweret dem Merian[4] andeuten lassen, daß Er mir solche, auf mein begehren, ungeweigert abfolgen lassen müsse:[a] Meine einstimmige Evangelische Texte, werden izzo angefangen von dem Drukker alhie[5]: so bald der erste Teyhl wird fertig seyn: So wil ihn e. l. ich schikken:[b] Ich verbleibe e. l.

 stets dienstw. Oheimb und Schwager
 Augustushzbul mp

[Wolfe]nbüttel[, den 1. Octbr. 1645.][c]

T a *Folgt weiterer Doppelpunkt.* — b *Folgt Zierschnörkel.* — c *Textverlust im Falz. Datierung nach KE.*

K   Der vorliegende Brief ist der einzige im Köthener Erzschrein erhaltene Brief Hz. Augusts d. J. v. Braunschweig-Wolfenbüttel (FG 227) der Korrespondenzjahrgänge 1644–1646.
 1 D. i. 450923A. Darin hatte F. Ludwig Hz. August d. J. v. Braunschweig-Wolfenbüttel (FG 227) angekündigt, das *GB 1646* werde für die Frühjahrsmesse 1646 im Druck erwartet. Aufgrund seiner Zuschuß-Zahlung stünden Hz. August 48 Exemplare zu. Ob der Herzog sie aus Frankfurt abzuholen gedenke? Zum *GB 1646* allgemein vgl. 440130 K 3; zu den Verlagsbeiträgern vgl. 450126 K 4.
 2 D. h. eingekommen ist. *Stieler*, 820: „Heimen/ & Heimtschen/ messem facere, fruges succidere. *In specie autem* fructum reponere, condere, fruges in horrea convehere. *Dicitur & Einheimsen/* colligere, percipere fruges."

3 Zur Verlagsbeitragszusage Hz. Augusts über einen Zuschuß von 200 Reichstalern s. 430121; vgl. auch Anm. 1 u. 450923A K 2.

4 Der Kupferstecher und Verleger Matthäus Merian d. Ä., in dessen Verlag das illustrierte *GB 1646* erschien. S. auch Anm. 1.

5 Zu Hz. Augusts d.J. spätestens seit 1635 vorbereitetem Projekt einer Revision der Bibelübersetzung Martin Luthers s. 391217 nebst Beilagen sowie 411214. Das Vorhaben schlug sich zunächst in der von Johann Valentin Andreae (FG 464. 1646) unterstützten Ausgabe der revidierten Perikopentexte des Gottesdiensts nieder *(Evangelische Kirchen-Harmonie*. 1646 u.ö.), s. v.a. 411214. Zur Ablehnung durch lutherische Theologen s. 380320 u. I, 380417, 391217, 410406 K 1 u. 461204. Zu dem Werk allgemein s. 450100 u. I, 450200, 450219, 450410 K 19, 450722 K, 450927 K 1, 451000 K, 460127, 460131 K 2, 460200A, 460317 K, 460613, 460700, 460715, 460804, 460819 K 1, 461204. Im hohen Alter begann August nochmals, die Bibel vollständig mit Hilfe Johann Sauberts d.J. von Grund auf aus den Ursprachen zu verdeutschen, verstarb aber nach den ersten Probedrucken aus dem Alten Testament. — Seit spätestens 1641 befaßte sich Hz. August mit dem Plan einer Evangelienharmonie zur Beschreibung des Lebens und Wirkens Christi, zu dem seine erstmals 1640 in Lüneburg erschienene Passionsharmonie als Vorläuferin diente: Die Geschichte Von des HErrn JEsu des * Gesalbten Leyden/ Sterben und Begräbnisse: (* Joh. 1.41. Act. 4, 27.) Auß der Evangelisten Schrifften/ von newen ördentlich zusammen getragen. Lüneburg/ bey Hansen und Heinrichen den Sternen. Jm 1640. Jahre. HAB (4 Ex.): Th 2980; 698. 27 Theol. (1); Ys 1. 8° Helmst. (Kupfertitel u. -tafeln fehlen); 1023.5 Theol. (Pergamentdruck, in schwarzen Samt gebunden; 2 Kupfertafeln fehlen). Eine stark überarbeitete 2. Ausgabe erschien 1641 ebenfalls im Lüneburger Verlag der Sterne. S. *DA Köthen I. 5:* 401111 I Q (S. 589ff.). Sein Vorhaben machte Hz. August 1645 wahr, als seine in enger Zusammenarbeit mit Andreae entstandene zweiteilige Evangelien- oder Kirchen-Harmonie, die alle Sonn- und Festtagsevangelien und Episteln sowie sonstigen Lesungen des Kirchenjahres enthält und somit das Leben der Jünger einbezog, erstmals erschien: Evangelische KIrchen-Harmonie/ Das ist: Der hoch-heiligen göttlichen Skrift unterschiedene Texte/ und Worte: Welche Von unsern gottseligen Vorfahren/ aus den Geschicht-Büchern der Evangelisten/ und den Briefen der Apostel: So wol auch den Skriften des alten/ und ersten Bundes/ oder Testamentes/ vor vielen hundert Jahren/ herausgezogen/ und an gewissen Tagen des HErren/ und der Festen/ in öffentlichen Zusammen-Künften/ und Versammelungen/ den Gemeinen der Christen/ jährlich vorzulesen/ und zu erklären ... verordnet (Wolfenbüttel 1645). HAB: 508.16 Theol. 4°, s. *Sammler Fürst Gelehrter,* S. 203 Nr. 410 (seltener Probedruck). Die aufwendiger gestaltete und mit Illustrationen versehene 2. oder 1. offizielle Ausgabe (im Oktavformat) erschien ebd. Anfang Juni 1646 (HAB: 548.8 Theol. 4°). S. 460317 K 3, vgl. *Sammler Fürst Gelehrter,* S. 203 Nr. 411–413 u. 460613. Der Ausgabe von 1648 (HAB: 148.1 Theol. 4°) ist jener Erlaß des Herzogs an die General- und Spezialsuperintendenten vom 4.6.1646 beigefügt, in dem August anordnete, seine Kirchen-Harmonie offiziell in den Gottesdiensten der Landeskirche zu verwenden. Als Motiv wird angegeben, daß die lat. und dt. Übersetzungen der Bibel die „heiligen Grund-Sprachen in allem nicht recht treffen/ oder deren eigentlichen Verstand/ und Nachdruck erreichen". Um nun die „unordentliche gestümlete Texte" deutlicher und verständlicher zu machen, habe August selbst Hand angelegt, etliche Jahre die evangelischen und apostolischen Texte „nach dem Grunde der heiligen Sprachen/ und der gleich-lautenden Sprüchen/ und Texten des alten/ und neuen Testaments" eingerichtet, um „den Grund-Text so viel müglich/ klar/ und verständlich/ in unsere Mutter-Sprache" zu übertragen. Zugleich habe er „jede Evangelische Historie/ aus allen Evangelisten/ so derselben gedänken/ also zusammen gefüget/ daß verhoffentlich kein Umbstand vergessen ist" und

Titelblattentwurf von 1645 für den Oktavdruck der Evangelischen Kirchen-Harmonie (1646) Herzog Augusts d. J. von Braunschweig-Wolfenbüttel (FG 227). Zu 451001.

mit Sacherklärungen dem Verstehen der „Einfältigen" aufgeholfen. S. 411214 I; vgl. *Sammler Fürst Gelehrter,* S. 203 Nr. 414; Inge Mager: Die Beziehungen Herzog Augusts von Braunschweig-Wolfenbüttel zu den Theologen Georg Calixt und Johann Valentin Andreae. In: Pietismus und Neuzeit 6 (1980), 76–98, hier 86 f. u. 95. Der Widerstand der Landesgeistlichkeit gegen die verbindliche Einführung des Lektionars in den sonntäglichen Gottesdiensten war erheblich. Der erste Teil der *Evangelischen Kirchen-Harmonie* wurde in seiner Bearbeitung im Juni 1645 abgeschlossen, s. 411124 K III F 1 (*DA Köthen I. 6,* 386 f.). S. Abb. Titelblattentwurf S. 721.

451007

Justus Georg Schottelius an Fürst Ludwig

Antwort auf 450923B. Beantwortet in 451028A. — Justus Georg Schottelius (FG 397. Der Suchende) dankt F. Ludwig (Der Nährende) für die Übersendung von *Gueintz: Rechtschreibung (1645)* und verspricht, seine Pflichten durch die Mitarbeit an dem geplanten vollständigen dt. Wörterbuch zu erfüllen. Eine Grammatik, die auf das Fundament der Sprache gegründet ist und auf der damit übereinstimmenden Gewohnheit beruht, muß dem Wörterbuch voraufgehen und allgemeine Zustimmung erfahren. Viele Argumente sprechen dafür, eine solche Sprachkunst in Köthen zu verlegen. Er, Schottelius, habe nach seinen bisherigen Werken dazu schon Neues erarbeitet und einen nicht unbedeutenden Vorrat (an Wörtern) gesammelt. Obgleich er schon zwischen Verlagen in Hamburg, Lübeck, Lüneburg oder Braunschweig wählen könne, sei er bereit, seine Arbeit nach Köthen zu schicken, damit sie, namentlich in der Rechtschreibung, dort durch F. Ludwig und die FG vereinheitlicht und angepaßt werde. Den Umfang seiner Sprachkunst schätzt Schottelius im Druck auf etwa 60 Bogen. Er glaubt auch, daß das Buch schnell Absatz findet und in einer beträchtlichen Anzahl von Exemplaren nach Hamburg, Lübeck und Leipzig versandt werden kann.

Q   HM Köthen: V S 545, Bl. 254r–255v [A: 255v], rotes Lacksiegel, eigenh. Auf Bl. 255r eigenh. Antwortkonzept F. Ludwigs 451028A. — *D: KE,* 296 f.; *KL* III, 265 f.; *Barthold,* 313. — *BN: Bürger,* 1262 Nr. 15 u. 16.

A   Dem höchstgeehrten Nährenden zu Gnädigen hand*en*.
Eigenh. Empfangsvermerk F. Ludwigs: 14. Octob. 1645.

Höchstgeehrter Nährender

Wegen übersendung bewustes Büchleins,[1] wie auch angedeuteter gnädig-gewogener nachrichtung, bedanket sich der Suchende in Schuldiger demuht, wird sich auch wegen gegebener veranlaßung seiner hierbei befindenden obligenheit desto kühner erinneren, und mit seinen ubrigen gedanken ehester gelegenheit etwas weitleuftiger einkommen. Es wurde[a] die gantze Teutsche Welt dem 𝔑ährenden mit immerwehrender dankbarkeit auch daher desto mehr verbunden sein, wan durch deßen wolmögende vnd hochbeliebte anordnung ein Volles oder Volstendiges 𝔚örterbuch Teutscher Sprache verfertiget und[b] dero behuf unter etzliche gelahrte sothane arbeit ausgetheilet werden künte: Eine allerseits gantze, aus den gründen der Sprache und nach grundrichtiger gewonheit eingerichte, und mit[c] algemeiner beliebung angenommene *SprachKunst* wurde[a] müßen, zweiffels ohn, vorhergehn und zur durchgehenden Leitung angenommen werden[2]: Stünde Zu gnädiger beliebiger guhtbefindung, ob etwa, vieler hochwichtiger uhrsachen halber, derogleichen Sprachkunst Zu Cöthen aufzulegen were: Der Suchende hat an seinem gar geringen orte nicht wenig arbeit [254v] hierin aufs neu unternommen und einen zimlichen nicht so gar gemein-bekanten vorraht beihändig; wurde[a] auch viel lieber (unangesehen Er dan Verlage Jn Hamburg, Lubeck, Luneburg oder Braunschwig nach belieben haben kan) solche arbeit naher Cöthen senden, damit in einem und andrē auch sonderlich was die Rechtschreibung belanget, nach des hochstverständigen Nährenden und der LLöblichen *[sic]* geselschafft befindung und enderung verfahren, und eine desto durchgehendere gleichmeßige meinung erhalten oder zuwege gebracht werden künte[3]: Etwa 60 bogen würde das werklein wol haben[4]; hette der Verleger am abgange nicht zuzweiffelen, dan er sich versicherē kan, daß eine zimliche anzahl alsbald naher Hamburg Lubeck, Nurnberg und Leipzig verschiket werden künten. Es ist des Suchenden wolmeinender Vorschlag, stellet alles gleichfals zu wolgefelliger beliebung, und entpfelet hiemit den höchstgeehrten Nährenden der algütigen obhut und selbsterwünschten Segen des Almechtigen Gottes, aus getreuem demutigen vnd ergebenē hertzen

Der Suchende.

Wolfenbuttel den
7 Octobr. anno 1645

T a *Lies:* würde — **b** *Ergänze:* zu — **c** *Folgt* <aller>

K 1 F. Ludwig (Der Nährende) hatte Justus Georg Schottelius (FG 397. Der Suchende) *Gueintz: Rechschreibung (1645)* mit 450923B zugesandt.
2 Eine verbindliche grammatische Basis war für das geplante deutsche Wörterbuch der FG schon aufgrund der Lemma-Ansetzung zwingend erforderlich. Da diese nach Stammwörtern erfolgen sollte, stellte sich bereits hier ein grundlegender Konflikt, indem Schottelius (und Georg Philipp Harsdörffer, FG 368) die Stammform des Verbs im einsilbigen Imperativ erkannten, F. Ludwig, Christian Gueintz (FG 361), Philipp v. Zesen (FG 521. 1648) u. andere die durchgängige Einsilbigkeit des Imperativs aber bestritten. Differenzen in der Orthographie — schon bei der Schreibung teutsch vs. deutsch — kamen hinzu. Diese strittigen Fragen dürften die gemeinsame Wörterbucharbeit der FG belastet, am Ende einen Abschluß vereitelt haben. Vgl. etwa 450410 K 3, 441223 K 23, 451219 u. 451220.
3 Diesen Vorschlag greift F. Ludwig in 451028A bereitwillig auf, beklagte in 460902 das Ausbleiben des versprochenen Schottelius-Manuskripts. Tatsächlich sollte es zu keinem Ausgleich der Positionen in einer gemeinsamen deutschen Grammatik der FG mehr kommen. S. Anm. 4.
4 *Schottelius: Sprachkunst (1641)* zählt 42 Bogen und 2 Blätter im Oktavformat. Deren Überarbeitung, die Schottelius offenbar in den fortgeschrittenen 40er Jahren auf sich

nahm, ist aber in keiner Textüberlieferung greifbar; sie muß gleichwohl damals schon fast um ein Drittel umfangreicher gewesen sein. Die dann nach F. Ludwigs Tod in Braunschweig erschienene zweite Fassung *Schottelius: Sprachkunst (1651)* im selben Format scheint mit 63 Bogen und 4 Blättern nur unwesentlich erweitert zu sein. Dem Umfang nach gerechnet hätte die 2. geplante Auflage also schon 1646 erscheinen können. Zur Kürzung des ursprünglichen Manuskripts der 2. Ausgabe vgl. 460100. Zur Arbeit an dieser zweiten Auflage vgl. 450929 u. 460100.

451008

Carl Gustav von Hille an Fürst Ludwig

Beantwortet in 451028. — Carl Gustav v. Hille (FG 302. Der Unverdrossene) vermißt seit über einem Jahr eine briefliche Gnadenbezeugung F. Ludwigs (Der Nährende). Dies habe ihn in Sorge versetzt, ob er bei dem Nährenden unverdientermaßen in Ungnade gefallen sei. Um zu erfahren, was es damit auf sich habe, lege Hille dem Fürsten dieses Schreiben zu Füßen, mit der Bitte, ihm weiterhin gnädig gesinnt zu sein. Er erinnert sich an die Gnade seiner Aufnahme in die Gesellschaft, die vor nicht allzu langer Zeit zu der Bitte nach einer Übersetzung ins Deutsche geführt habe. Da es ihm jedoch bisher an einem nützlichen fremdsprachigen Werk mangele, habe er sich jetzt, mit dem Beistand und der Erlaubnis des Nährenden dazu entschlossen, ein eigenes Werk zu verfassen, dessen Titel lauten könnte „Der Teutsche Palmenbaum, das ist Lobrede, von der hochlöblichen Fruchtbringenden Geselschaft, Anfang, Satzungen, Vorhaben, Namen, Sprüchen, Gemählen, Schriften, Gesellschaftern und unverwelcklichem TugendRuhm *etc.*" (i. e. *Hille: Teutscher Palmbaum*). Sollte dieses Vorhaben die Billigung des Nährenden finden, wolle er das Werk im Verlauf des Winters verfassen und danach zur Korrektur dem Nährenden übersenden. Hille werde sich der diesbezüglichen Meinung des Nährenden unterwerfen. — Im Augenblick sei er im Begriff, mit der sächs. Herzoginwitwe auf seine Güter nach Mecklenburg zu verreisen, wo er ungefähr acht Wochen zu bleiben gedenke. — Hz. August d. J. v. Braunschweig-Wolfenbüttel (FG 227. Der Befreiende) habe, wie Hille vernehme, seinem Versprechen Genüge getan. Hille möchte sehr gerne das Gesellschaftsbuch des Nährenden sehen.

Q HM Köthen: V S 545, Bl. 37r–38v [A: 37v], Brief beginnt mit 38r; eigenh.; rotes Lacksiegel. Bl. 37r: Konzept F. Ludwigs an Hille 451028. — D: *KE,* 203 f.; *KL* III, 223 f. — BN: *Bürger,* 722 Nr. 9.

A Dem Durchleuchtigen, Hochgebornen Fürsten und Herrn, Herrn Ludewigen, Fürsten zu Anhalt, Grafen zu Aßcanien, Herrn zu Bernburg und Zerbst *etc.* meinem gnädigen Fürsten und Herrn, underth. *etc.*
Eigenh. Empfangsvermerk F. Ludwigs: Pres. 14. Octob 1645.

HöchstgeEhrter H. Nehrender,
Demselben seind meine gehorsame und Stetsgeflisse *[sic]* treue dienste ie und alleine bevor.

Demnach ich die vielzuschätzende gnade, ein Jhar und länger nicht gehabt, ein gnaden-brifflein von demselben zu erhalten[1], aß bin ich in den sorgfältigen[2] gedancken gestanden, der höchstgeEhrte h. Nehrende, hette etwan unverhoft eine doch unverdiente ungnade auf meine wenigkeit geworfen. Damit ich nun dessen eigendliche beschaffenheit erhalten möchte, habe ich alß der geringste diener der Fruchtbringenden Gesellschaft, diese gehorsamste Zeilen zu deroselben füse legen müssen:ª gehorsambst bittend, mein hochstgeEhrter g. Nehrender zu geruhen³. Jch erinnere mich, nach dem ich die gnade vom anfang meiner hochschätzenden *[sic]* einnemung gehabt, daß ich alß^b ein fruchtbringendeß-Mitglid *[sic]*, der hochlöb. fruchtb. Geselschaft, unlängsten ein danckbareß Kennzeichen zu fortsetzung der Teutschen Sprache ablegen sollen,⁴ weilen eß aber bis heer mir an einem Nützlichen in frembder Sprache beschrieben büchlein gemangelt, habe ich mich nunmehro vermittelst beystand und zulassung meineß höchstgeEhrten Nehrenden entschlossen, ein eigneß^c anß licht zu kommen lassen, dessen **Titul** seyn könte **Der Teutsche Palmenbaum**, das ist **Lobrede**, von der hochlöblichen Fruchtbringenden Gesellschaft, Anfang, Satzungen, Vorhaben, Namen, Sprüchen, Gemählen, Schriften, Gesellschaftern und unverwelcklichem TugendRuhm *etc.*⁵ Da ferne nun meinem hochgeEhrten Nehrenden [38v] dieß mein wolgemeinteß Vorhaben gnädig gefallen möchte, wolte ich das werk diesen Winter über verfertigen, und nachgehendß zur verbesser- und enderung meinem höchstgehrten *[sic]* Nehrenden gehorsambst uberschicken.

Waß nun meineß höchstgeEhrten Nehrenden hochschätzende^d gedankenßmeinung sein möchte, dem wolte ich mich auf erhaltener g. antwort underth. unterwerfen. Jtzo bin ich ihm begriff ersteß mit J. F. G. der verwitbeten hertzoginnen zu Sachsen⁶ *etc.* naher Mecklenburg meinen geringen güttern etzlich[er] massen^e vorzustehen, zu verreisen, welcheß sich dan auf ein 8 Wochen wol verstrecken möchte. Der höchstgehrte Befreyende, hatt wie ich verneme, seinem Versprechen ein genügen gethan.⁷ Trage hertzliches verlangen deß höchstgeEhrn. Nehrenden Gesellschaftßbu[ch]^e zu sehen.⁸ Womit nebenst Anwunschung allem Fürstlichen aufnemen und gewunschter Gesundheit, ich dieselben der obhutt Gotteß gehorsambst empfehlen thue, und lebet allezeit

    Meineß hochgeEhrten Nehrenden treugehorsambster Knecht,
    Der Unverdrossene

Wolfenbüttel den 8. th. WeinMonatß. 1645.

T a *Folgt* <underth.> — **b** *Eingefügt.* — **c** *Folgt unleserliche Streichung.* — **d** *Gebessert aus* hochz[u] — **e** *Buchstabenverlust im Falz. Konjektur in eckigen Klammern.*

K 1 Hille übertreibt etwas: Der letzte uns vorliegende Brief F. Ludwigs (Der Nährende) an Carl Gustav v. Hille (FG 302. Der Unverdrossene) ist 450221. F. Ludwig weist diese Klage in seiner Antwort 451028 zurück.
  2 Hier im Sinne von besorgt. *Stieler* kennt die Ansetzung „sorgfältig" nicht; das Wort ist aber im Mhd. und Fnhd. (md.), etwa bei Luther, in der angegebenen Bedeutung belegt. Erst später übernimmt es die heute übliche zweite Bedeutung von „Sorge": Hilfe, Unterstützung. *Paul Wb.*, 927; *Götze*, 203.

3 Durch Anschluß an „ruhen" Bedeutungswandel vom Mhd. zu „sich herbeilassen, belieben, urspr. von Hochgestellten oder Verehrten". *Paul Wb.*, 400. *Stieler*, 1633, bringt die hier zutreffende Bedeutung: „Geruhen/ […] consistere in re aliquâ".

4 Hille zeigte sich bereits mehr als eineinhalb Jahre zuvor willens, eine Übersetzung aus dem Französischen zu verfertigen. S. 440209A u. 440310.

5 Zwei Jahre später erscheint das Werk *Hille: Teutscher Palmbaum* mit leicht verändertem Titel und zugeeignet „Allen Liebhabern der Teutschen Sprache": Der teutsche Palmbaum: Das ist/ Lobschrift Von der Hochlöblichen/ Fruchtbringenden Gesellschaft Anfang/ Satzungen/ Vorhaben/ Namen/ Sprüchen/ Gemählen/ Schriften und unverwelklichem Tugendruhm. Allen Liebhabern der Teutschen Sprache zu dienlicher Nachrichtung verfasset/ durch den Unverdrossenen Diener derselben. Nürnberg 1647 (Ndr. 1970). Der *Teutsche Palmbaum* blieb das einzige selbständige Werk des Wolfenbütteler Frauenhofmeisters, der bereits im September 1647 verstarb. Die Drucklegung ohne vorherige Einreichung bei F. Ludwig lief über Georg Philipp Harsdörffer (FG 368). Vgl. *DA Köthen I. 8*: 470206. Der spätere Erzschreinhalter Georg Neumark (FG 605. 1653) wird seine FG-Geschichte (*Neumark: Palmbaum*) auf dieser von F. Ludwig nicht autorisierten aufbauen. S. zu *Hille: Teutscher Palmbaum* 440616 K III 0, 440715A K 9, 450126 K 11, 450504A K 2, 450725 K 5, 450927 K II 0, 451028, 460406 K 4, 460718, 460915A, 461029 u. 461106, *DA Köthen I. 8*: 470100, 470112, 470206, 470309, 470426 u. 470625.

6 Hzn. Elisabeth v. Sachsen-Altenburg, *Braunschweig-Wolfenbüttel (TG 13. 1593–1650), in 2. Ehe mit Hz. Johann Philipp v. Sachsen-Altenburg (FG 183; †1639) verheiratet. S. *Bepler: Hille*, 257, die erwähnt, daß der Vater Hilles, James Hill, erstmals 1619 als Besitzer verschiedener Güter im Mecklenburgischen auftaucht. Carl Gustav v. Hille war außerdem u. a. in Mecklenburg am Güstrower Hof tätig, zuletzt als Kammerjunker Hzn. Eleonora Marias (AL 1617. TG 17), Witwe Johann Albrechts v. Mecklenburg-Güstrow (FG 158). Im März 1637 wurde Hille — wie auch der Regierungsrat Hans Zacharias v. Rochow (FG 303) — von ihrem Schwager, Hz. Adolph Friedrich v. Mecklenburg-Schwerin (FG 178), im Rahmen der Regentschafts- und Vormundschaftsstreitigkeiten entlassen. Vgl. 371009 K 0 und *Ball: Tugendliche Gesellschaft*, 350–361. Möglicherweise geht die Reise als Begleitung Hzn. Elisabeths, Tochter Hz. Heinrich Julius' v. Braunschweig-Wolfenbüttel und Schwester Hz. Friedrich Ulrichs v. Braunschweig-Wolfenbüttel (FG 38), auf eine Bitte seines Dienstherrn Hz. Augusts (s. Anm. 7) zurück. Ob sich Hzn. Elisabeth in Wolfenbüttel aufhält oder Hille diese in Altenburg abholen soll, was einen Zwischenstopp in Köthen erlauben würde, läßt der Briefwechsel offen. Auch die LP der Herzogin und das *Christian: Tageb.* erwähnen diese Unternehmung nicht. S. Christ-Fürstlicher Lebens-Lauff, Bl. F [iv] v – J [ii] v (HAB: LP Stolberg 5905). — Zu Hilles Reise mit Hzn. Sophia Elisabeth v. Braunschweig-Wolfenbüttel (AL 1629. TG 42b) nach Mecklenburg im darauf folgenden Jahre 1646 vgl. 460718 und zu Hilles Kauf des Guts Lalendorf vgl. *Bepler: Hille*, 257 Anm. 15.

7 Hz. August d. J. v. Braunschweig-Wolfenbüttel (FG 227) hatte inzwischen seinen Verlagsanteil am *GB 1646* beglichen (450923A). Er hatte ihn bereits im Jahr zuvor, vor der Ostermesse 1644, zu zahlen beabsichtigt. Der Anteil wurde in der Korrespondenz bereits seit 1642 thematisiert, so z. B. in 421031A u. 440323. Zu fl. Verlagsbeiträgen allgemein s. 450126 K 4.

8 Hier bezieht sich Hille wahrscheinlich nicht auf das zukünftige *GB 1646* (dazu 440130 K 3), sondern auf das in Köthen geführte *GB Kö*.

451015

Matthäus Merian d. Ä. an Peter Knaudt

Matthäus Merian d. Ä. sendet den ersten Probebogen des *GB 1646* nach Köthen in der Hoffnung auf wohlwollende Aufnahme. Er läßt an dem Druck dieses Werkes intensiv arbeiten, um den vorgesehenen Erscheinungstermin zu halten. Titel und Vorwort („Kurzer Bericht") machen separat einen vorgebundenen Bogen aus. Ein Probedruck dieses Bogens folge mit nächster Post. — Wegen der Yucca-Pflanze hat er sich an verschiedene Bekannte gewandt, jedoch noch keine Antwort erhalten. Sollte sie in Augsburg vorhanden sein, werde die Pflanze ihm nicht versagt bleiben. — Die vorhergehenden Schreiben mitsamt den Kupferstichproben seien hoffentlich richtig angekommen. — Im weiteren Fortgang der Arbeit lasse er alle Embleme nach dem Vorbild der Visierungen und nicht seitenverkehrt stechen. — Im Postskriptum erläutert Merian, daß der tatsächliche Druck, den (mitgesandten) Teil einschließend, im Schrift- und Kupferstichbild viel klarer als die Probe sein wird, da die Druckerpresse beim ‚Andruck' noch nicht ordnungsgemäß gelaufen sei.

Q HM Köthen: V S 546, Bl. 17rv [A: 17v]; eigenh.; rotes Lacksiegel. — D: *Bircher: Merian*, 708f.; *Wüthrich: Merian Briefe*, 96. — BN: *Bürger*, 987 Nr. 12.

A Tt. Dem Ehrenvesten vnd GroßAchtparen Herren Peter Knaudt Fürst. Anhaltischen Raht vnd Cammer Meistern *etc.* zu Cöthen, meinem Großg. hochgeehrten herrn *etc.* Cöthen

Ehrnvester vnd HochAchtparer Jnsonders Großg. hochgeehrter Herr,
dem sein mein willige dienst jeder Zeit Anvor[1] *etc.*
 Vnd sende hiebei ein probe von dem ersten bogen der zweiten vnd ietzigen Edition der Fruchtbringenden Gesellschafft[2], verhoffe er werde Recht sein, Jch lasse Jetzunder starkh darinnen fortfahren, damit das werkh zu bestimpter Zeit möge fertig sein. Der Tittul vnd Præfation kompt auff einen besondern bogen vor dißem hin,[3] davon nechste post auch ein prob folgen soll. Jch habe an vnterschiedliche bekandte vmb das Zwibel Gewächse Giuoca[4] geschriben aber noch kein Antwort erhalten, so es imer in Augspurg ist, wirt es mir nicht versagt werden.
 Meine vorige schreiben sampt den kupfer proben verhoffe Jch werden zu recht komen sein, Jetz laße ich fortan alle Stuckh zu kupfer bringen das sie den visirungen gleich, und nicht vmbgewent sein,[5] diß maln mehrers nicht als dem Allmächtigen wol befohlen.
Ffurt den 15. 8bris 1645.

    Meines Großg. Herren Dienstwilligster
    Mattheus Merian

P. S. Jn dem gantzen trukh auch in disem bogen wirt die Schrifft und das kupfer viel säuberer komen, als dise probe ist, dan diß der erste trukh, und noch nicht recht im gang were.

K 1 Bevor, vorab. S. 450417 K 1.

2 Der erste Bogen nach dem Vorwerk (s. Anm.3), nämlich Bl. A r – A [iv] v des *GB 1646* bringt die ersten vier Impresen, i. e. Caspar v. Teutleben (FG 1. Der Mehlreiche), F. Ludwig (FG 2. Der Nährende), Hz. Johann Ernst d.J. v. Sachsen-Weimar (FG 3. Der Käumling) u. Hz. Friedrich v. Sachsen-Weimar (FG 4. Der Hoffende). Zur Einrichtung des *GB 1646* vgl. auch Anm.3, 5 u. 450711 K 4. Matthäus Merian d. Ä. spricht hier von der 2. Ausgabe des GB der FG, weil von den bisherigen GBB (1622, 1624, 1628, 1629/30 u. 1641/44) nur die Ausg. 1629/30 mit Impresenstichen (FG 1–200) aus der Merian-Werkstatt versehen und das *GB 1646* somit die 2. illustrierte Ausg. des GB war. Vgl. *Conermann II*, 45 ff.

3 Als Erscheinungstermin des *GB 1646* hatte Merian in 450905 die Leipziger Ostermesse 1646 vorgesehen. — Der erwähnte und den Impresen vorausgehende Bogen umfaßt neben dem Drucktitel das dreiseitige ‚Vorwort' *Kurtzer Bericht Von der Fruchtbringenden Geselschaft Zwecke und Vorhaben*, in dem knapp auf den Namen, das Wort u. das Emblem der FG u. die sozietären Ziele (Tugend- und Sprachförderung) eingegangen wird, ferner das Sonett „Auf die Fruchtbringende Gesellschaft" und die Palmen-Imprese der FG (Bl. [¶]r – [¶iiij]v). Zwei Probedrucke dieses Bogens wird Merian mit 451028B an Knaudt senden. Zum *GB 1646* allgem. s. 440130 K 3.

4 Zum Yucca-Kontext und der schließlich verfügbaren Abbildungsvorlage Merians in Johann Theodor de Brys „Florilegium Renovatum Et Auctum" von 1641 vgl. besonders 450800 (K 4) sowie 450930 u. 451119.

5 Hier betont Merian erneut, wie schon in 450930, daß er fortan seitengetreue Kupferstichabzüge (von den gezeichneten Impresen, d. h. den Visierungen) senden wird.

451019

Georg Winckler an Peter Knaudt

Georg Winckler hat die (nicht mehr nachweisbaren) Briefe vom 3. und 8.10.1645 erhalten und teilt Peter Knaudt mit, daß sowohl der Kasten als auch das Bücherfaß gut bei ihm angekommen seien. Sobald der Breslauer Buchführer Christoph Jacob dafür 125 Rth. biete und anweise, was bisher ausgeblieben sei, werde er ihm die Sendung überlassen, doch solle sowohl der leere Kasten als auch das leere Faß wieder an ihn, Winckler, zurückgehen. — Von Hz. Christian Ludwig v. Braunschweig-Calenberg (FG 372) hat Winckler bisher kein Geld erhalten; wenn hier etwas erfolgt, werde Winckler den Betrag entgegennehmen und quittieren. — Den Diener Samuel Schaf(f)s habe Winckler wegen der 50 Rth. gesprochen, die an seinen Breslauer Patron wegen der dortigen Kammer ausgezahlt worden sein sollen. Dem Diener sei der Sachverhalt nicht bekannt, er werde den Betrag vor Ort in Leipzig erst begleichen, sollte er darüber in ankommenden Briefen informiert werden. — Winckler habe sich bei ihm bekannten Händlern aus Bremen erkundigt, ob einer von ihnen wegen dorthin gesandter Bücher Order für einen Kredit erhalten habe. Es habe sich jedoch niemand dazu bereit erklärt. Winckler zufolge entschuldigt sich der Jude Samuel dafür, daß er kein Geld eintreiben konnte. Wie der Jude nun wegen der Bücher verhandelt oder tauscht, könne Winckler nicht sagen. Da der (oder Winckler) keine Barsendungen erhalten habe, bleiben auch die Anweisungen an Jobst Bant und den Avisenschreiber unerledigt. Alles was der Jude sonst an Waren laut beiliegender Aufstellung für Knaudt gewollt habe, mitsamt der seit langem hier lagernden Seide und Schnüre, habe Winckler ausgehändigt.

— Wie befohlen wird Winckler, falls ihn eine Zahlung erreichen sollte, Matthäus Merian d. Ä. davon einen Betrag in Höhe von 200 Rth. nach Frankfurt senden. — Das für (Georg) Philipp Harsdörffer (FG 368) bestimmte Paket ist nach Nürnberg weitergesandt worden. — Postskriptum: Da der Jude Samuel versäumte, dieses Schreiben mit (nach Köthen) zu nehmen, muß es per Boten überbracht werden. Mittlerweile habe Winckler den (verschollenen) Brief vom 11.10.1645 erhalten, zu dem es wenig zu sagen gäbe. Dem Juden wurde die Briefbeilage (Wechsel) über die insgesamt geliehenen 200 Rth. ausgehändigt. Diese Summe soll morgen nach Frankfurt an Merian überwiesen werden. Was Wincklers Anteil und die 12 Rth. für den Avisenschreiber angeht, hat Winckler das Geld noch nicht erhalten. Da der Jude bereits abgereist war, wird schwerlich noch etwas zu erwarten sein. Ein Brief wurde nach Wittenberg geschickt.

Q HM Köthen: V S 546, Bl. 30r–31v [A: 31v]; 31r leer; eigenh.; rotes Lacksiegel. — *D: Bircher: Merian*, 707f. (unvollst.). — *BN: Bürger*, 1455 Nr. 1 (dat. 14.10.1645).

A Dem Ehrnuesten GroßAchtbahren vnnd wohl fürnehmen herrn Peter Knaut. Fürstl. Anhalt. wohluerordneten Camermeister. Meinem Jnsonders hochgeehr*ten* herrn. Cöthen

Ehrnuester Groß Achtbarer vnnd wohlfürnehmer groß günstiger hochgeehrter herr: meine hinwiederum ganz willige dienste, negst freundtlicher **Salutation**.

Habe E. E. angenehme vonn 3. vnnd 8. dieß zue recht erhaltenn. Darauß ablesendt aufgetragene **Comission** verstandten. Jn antwort, wiederum berichte daß vbersandten Casten, vnnd Vaß büecher,[a] mier woh[l][b] zue kommen, wan nun der benandte buechführer von breßlau Christoff Jacob[1] gegen erlegung R. 125 darumb ansuechung thuet (so bieß hero nicht beschehen) erlaße ich ihme sollichte, doch daß der Ledige Casten v. vaß wiederum an mich komme.

Von dem Herzog zue Lüneburg, vnd Braunschweig ist mier auß Hannouer[2] bieß dato nichtes von geldte zue komme*n*[;] was eruolgt empfahe vnnd quitiere darüber.

Mitt Herrn Samuel Schaffens[3] diener habe der 50 rd. halben, so etwan an seinen Patron in Breßlau, wegen der Camer aldar vergnügt solten sein, gesprochen [.] Der will von nichtes wißen, es were dan daß mit negsten kommendten briefen, waß einkäme, wolte er die bezahlung alhier thuen. — Bey wellichen von Bremen habe mich erkundigt ob keiner **order** wegen dahin gesandter bücher, etwaß geldt zue erlegen. Hatt sich bieß dato auch niemandt fundten, der Jude wie wohl vernehme der wolle abkommen entschuldigt sich, kein geldt einbekommen, wie er nun sollichte verhandelt oder ver**baratiert**[4], kan nicht wißen, vnd weilen von con**tanten**[5] nirgendt waß erlanget[,] bleiben die anweisungen an Jost Bandten[6] vnd dem *[sic]* **avisoschreiber** auch vn**Effectuiert**; waß der Jude sonst für E. E. an wahren erfordert habe[c] laut Jnligendt*en* AußZügen nebenst der lengst hier gelegenen seiden und schnüre verwahrlichen eingehändigt.

Gegebenem **order** nach woferne annoch von geldt waß einkommen möchte, übermache dauon herrn **Merian** Rth. 200 nacher ffurt.[7] [30v]

Daß übersandte Paquet an herrn Philip Harsdorffen ist mit fleiß auf Nürnb.

besteldt,[8] dieses wohl meinendt zuer freundtlichen nachricht, melden sollen; negst schließ*licher* Göttlicher Protæction E E ganz trewlich empfehle
E. E. GAchtp. dienstgeflißn*er*

Georg Winckhler

Leibzig den 14. 8b. 1645

PS. Demnach der Jude Samuel verlaßen dieß schreiben abzufordern v*nd* mit sich zue nehmen alleine nicht eruolgt dahero durch den Poten senden müsen. Jnmitelst empfahe E. E. geliebtes vom 11. dieß, darüb*er* wenig zu meldten. dem Juden ist Jnschlueß alsobaldt eingehänd*igt* wordt*en*, welcher nach der Handt[9] Rth. 200 Paar hergeb*en* auf franckf. Merian zu v̈b*er*mach[en][d], welches mit morgender Post beschehen soll,[10] waß meinen rest belanget wie auch die 12 rd. für den auisenschreib*er* habe nichtes erhalten, vnd weil der Jude abgereiset, wirdt schwer waß volgen ferner daß Brief*lein* ist auf witenb. bestelt.
d. 19. 8b. 1645

T a *Folgt* <so> — **b** *Buchstabenverlust am zerknickten Seitenrand. Konjektur in eckigen Klammern.* — **c** *Eingefügt.* — **d** *Buchstabenverlust im Falz. Konjektur in eckigen Klammern.*

K Georg (v.) Winckler (1582–1654), Bürger und Handelsmann in Leipzig, Erbherr auf Dölitz und Stünz. Aus Salzwedel stammend wurde er 1596 nach Leipzig entsandt, um bei dem dortigen Handelsmann Christian Schell d. Ä. in den Dienst zu treten, bevor er Handelsdiener bei Hans Müller d. Ä. wurde. 1604 eröffnete Winckler seine eigene Handlung, aus der er sich 1642 zugunsten seiner beiden ältesten lebenden Söhne Benedikt und Andreas Winckler, Handelsmänner in Nürnberg bzw. Leipzig, zurückzog. 1650 wurde er in den Reichsadel erhoben. S. *LP Roth*, R 6280; *LP Stolberg*, Nr. 23149; Kneschke IX, 580. In den Dokumenten des vorliegenden Bandes erscheint Winckler häufiger als Bankier in der Abwicklung finanzieller Transaktionen, die auch das *GB 1646* betreffen. Vgl. 440130 K 3, 440310, 440723A, 450127, 450721, 450905, 450922, 450923, 450930, 451028, 451028B K 3, 451119, 460218, 460301 K 2, 460303, 460309, 460324, 460403, 460423, 460519, 460703, 461031 K 6 u. 461031A K 7. Vgl. auch 371208 (K 1) u. 430407 K 4. Zum Zahlungsverkehr im Kontext des *GB 1646* allgemein s. 450127 K 1. Zum *GB 1646* s. 440130 K 3. Zum Inhalt des in sehr verknapptem alten Kaufmannsdeutsch geschriebenen Briefs s. die vorausgeschickte Inhaltsangabe.
1 Christoph Jacob, um 1635/46 Verleger in Breslau. S. *Benzing: Verleger*, 1179. Die offenbar aus Köthen stammenden Bücher enthielten vermutlich überschüssige Exemplare Köthener Drucke, die F. Ludwig für 125 Rth. dem Breslauer Verleger verkaufen wollte.
2 Der in der Bezahlung seines Verlagsanteils am *GB 1646* säumige Hz. Christian Ludwig v. Braunschweig-Calenberg (FG 372). S. zuletzt F. Ludwigs Mahnung 450923. Zu den fl. Verlagsbeiträgen s. 450126 K 4.
3 Samuel Schaf(f) v. Weistritz, Reichskrämer und Ratsherr in Breslau (1589–1652). Aus Liegnitz stammend, siedelte er nach Breslau über und wurde Mitglied der Reichskrämerzunft, wo er zum Ältesten erwählt wurde. 1636 wurde er auf einem der vier Zunftplätze Mitglied des Rates zu Breslau, welchem er bis zu seinem Tod abwechselnd als Schöffe

oder Ratsherr angehörte. 1649 wurde er geadelt unter dem Namen „Schaf v. Weistritz" (1676 Bestätigung des böhm. Adelsstandes für seinen Sohn Hans Adam Samuel Schaf v. Weistritz und Genehmigung der Bezeichnung „v. Schaf"). S. *Kneschke* VIII, 81; August v. Doerr: Der Adel der Böhmischen Kronländer. Ein Verzeichnis derjenigen Wappenbriefe und Adelsdiplome, welche in den Böhmischen Saalbüchern des Adelsarchives im k.k. Ministerium des Innern in Wien eingetragen sind. Prag 1900; Rudolf Stein: Der Rat und die Ratsgeschlechter des alten Breslau. Würzburg 1963, 252. — Da Winckler Knaudt über sein Geschäft mit Schaf informiert, steht zu vermuten, daß es im Zusammenhang mit Jacob und dem geplanten Verkauf Köthener Drucke stand.

4 *Barratieren*, Tauschhandel treiben. *Barrat, m.* Tauschgeschäft (auch ‚Wechsel, Tausch' in nichtkaufmännischen Zusammenhängen). S. Wörterbuch der deutschen Kaufmannssprache auf geschichtlichen Grundlagen mit einer systematischen Einleitung v. Alfred Schirmer. Straßburg 1911, 28f.

5 Barsendungen, Barzahlungen. Abgeleitet von *kontant* für bar, *per contant* gegen Barzahlung. Im 17. Jh. aus dem Ital. u. Franz. übernommen. S. Wörterbuch der deutschen Kaufmannssprache (Anm. 4), 107.

6 Wahrscheinlich der Hamburger Kaufmann Jobst Bant (1609–1679), seit 1667 Mitglied des Gremiums der Oberalten (wichtiges Hamburger Bürgergremium mit weitreichenden politischen und sozialen Aufgaben). Zur Biographie s. LP-Titelblatt: Hertzliche Leich-Tränen Welche Bey hochansehnlicher Bestattung Des Wolehrenvesten/ GroßAchtbaren und Wolfürnehmen H. Jobst Banten/ Welcher Anno 1609 in Eißburg in Westphalen gebohren/ Anno 1645. am 21. Julii/ mit der HochEhr- und Tugend-Reichen/ ... Fr. Gerdrut Schweland/ in Hamburg verehligt/ mit welcher Er 34. Jahr/ 2. Monat und 15. Tage vergnüglich gelebet ... Anno 1650. den 28. April. zum Kirch-Geschworenen bey S. Jacob/ Anno. 1667 den 8. Julii zum Ober-Alten/ und in selbigem Jahr und Monat/ am 21. Tage/ zum Leichnams-Geschworenen bey S. Jacob erwehlet: Anno 1679. den 6. Octobr. des Morgens umb halb Fünff durch einen sanft-sehligen Tod abgefodert/ und am 13. dito. in St. Jacobi Kirch ... begraben worden/ Als ein schuldiges Dank-Opffer ... geopffert Georg Haccius, L. Pastor bey St. Mar-Magd. [St. Marien-Magdalenenkirche] in Hamburg./ Gedruckt im Jahr 1679. HAB: Db 749 (2). — Offensichtlich handelt es sich um von F. Ludwig bis dahin unbeglichene Rechnungen für von Bant gelieferte Waren wie Seide und Schnüre und für den geschuldeten Lohn eines Avisenschreibers, der den Fürsten mit Nachrichten versorgte.

7 Hier u. weiter unten (s. Anm. 10) bezieht sich Georg Winckler auf den von Matthäus Merian d. Ä. in 450905 geäußerten Wunsch nach einem Vorschuß, um die Arbeit am *GB 1646* fortsetzen zu können. In 450930 berichtet Merian dem Köthener Kammermeister Knaudt, daß er den Leipziger Kaufmann Winckler wegen des Vorschusses angeschrieben habe. S. auch 450922. In 451028B bestätigt Merian den Erhalt der Vorschuß-Summe.

8 Wie Georg Philipp Harsdörffer (FG 368. Der Spielende) F. Ludwig in 451101 bestätigte, hatte er am 22.10.1645 zusammen mit F. Ludwigs Brief (450919A) Christian Gueintz' (FG 361. Der Ordnende) *Rechtschreibung (1645)* empfangen, dazu Stoff für das Sticken seines Wappens und seiner darauf schon vorgezeichneten Imprese.

9 In Bausch und Bogen (alles in allem genommen), nach Schätzung. S. Wörterbuch der deutschen Kaufmannssprache (Anm. 4), 79.

10 S. Anm. 7. Der Vorschuß von insgesamt 200 Reichstalern kann nun an Merian weitergeleitet werden, was mit dem folgenden Tag, dem 20.10.1645, geschehen soll.

451028

Fürst Ludwig an Carl Gustav von Hille

Antwort auf 451008. — Carl Gustav v. Hilles (FG 302. Der Unverdrossene) Vorwurf, F. Ludwig (Der Nährende) habe ihm vielleicht aus Unwillen so lange nicht geschrieben, ist gegenstandslos, weil Hille nach eigenen Angaben nicht in Wolfenbüttel erreichbar war, sondern sich vielmehr in Diensten Hz. Christian Ludwigs v. Braunschweig-Calenberg (FG 372. Der Reinherzige) auf dem Lande aufhalten wollte. — Hz. August d. J. v. Braunschweig-Wolfenbüttel (FG 227. Der Befreiende) hat die zugesagten 200 Taler zum *GB 1646* gezahlt. Der Reinherzige ist vor kurzem wegen seines Versprechens erneut um das Gleiche gebeten worden. Leider sei außer einem Einlieferungsbeleg dieser Mahnung nichts weiter angekommen. Man hoffe deshalb auf Hilles Hilfe. Matthäus Merian d. Ä. erwarte, gegen Fastnacht 1646 seine Arbeit zu vollenden, werde das Buch *(GB 1646)* jedoch nicht ausliefern, solange die 200 Rth. nicht bezahlt seien, wodurch die anderen Verlagsbeiträger wiederum Nachteile hinnehmen müßten. Hille möge mithelfen, daß Hz. Christian Ludwig die 200 Taler bis zum Leipziger Neujahrsmarkt an Georg Winckler überweise. — Was die von Hille angebotene Arbeit *(Hille: Teutscher Palmbaum)* angehe, stehe es ihm frei, was er verfassen und dem Erzschrein zur Durchsicht überlassen wolle. Dies solle dann nicht nur wohl aufgenommen, sondern auch fleißig geprüft werden. — Falls er das in diesem Jahr gedruckte Werk *Gueintz: Rechtschreibung (1645)* noch nicht erhalten habe, würde dies nachgeholt. – Schließlich bittet der Nährende Hille, Grüße an Hzn. Eleonora Maria v. Mecklenburg-Güstrow (AL 1617. TG 17; Die Vollkommene in der FG) und Christina Margaretha v. Sachsen-Lauenburg (Die Weiße in der FG) auszurichten, sobald er in Mecklenburg angekommen ist.

Q HM Köthen: V S 545, Bl. 37r; eigenh. Konzept (auf demselben Bogen wie 451008). — Fehlt in *KE* u. *KL*.

A *Fehlt.*

Des Unverdroßenen brief vom 8. dieses ist[a] dem Nehrenden[b] gar annemlich gewesen, unangesehen er darinnen beschuldiget werden wollen, als wan etwa unwillen gegen ihme Unverdroßenen[c] bey dem Nehrenden sein solte, das aber jungsten der Nehrende an Unverdroßenen nicht geschrieben[,] ruhret daher, das er selbsten von sich zu verstehen gegeben, er wurde zu Wolffenbuttel nicht anzutreffen, auch bey dem Reinhertzigen alleine auf dem lande gelegenheit bekommen haben, wie er sich dan, da[d] gewisheit[e] verhanden gewesen, er sich ferner bey dem Reinhertzigen hette wollen gebrauchen:[f] [1] der Befreyende hat seine zweyhundert thaler zu dem Franckfurtischen geselschaftbuche richtig erleget;

Bey dem Reinhertzigen ist wegen gleichmeßigen verspruchs eben neuchlichst[2] mit eigener botschaft abermal[g] handschriftlich angehalten worden, aber nur ein bloßer schein der einlieferung wegen, und nichts mehr erfolget; Wan von dem Unverdroßenen beliebete[,] deswegen notwendige anregung zu thun[,] gereichete es dem Nehrenden zu gefallen, und der gantzen geselschaft zu gutem:[3] Es wird gehoffet[,] der Unverdroßene werde darbey noch etwas ausrichten können; Es vermeinet Merian gegen faßnacht 1646[4] gewis fertig zu[h] sein, wird aber nichts abfolgen laßen, die zweyhundert thaler seyn dan auch geliefert, darbey kemen die andern verleger in schaden[.] der Unverdroßene wolle seines theils und[i] dem vormahlig*en* seinem erbieten zufolge helffen befodern, des nechstkunftigen neuen Jharesmarkt in leibzig George Winklern[5] solche zweyhundert thaler vom Reinhertzigen mogen erleget, und also richtig inne gehoben werden.

Was die vom Unverdroßenen angebotene arbeit betrifft, stehet es zu seinem eigenen wolbelieben, was er hierunter aufsetzen, und dem Ertzschreine zu ubersehen zuschicken wil,[6] Es soll nicht alleine wol aufgenommen, sondern auch kein fleis dabei gesparet werden. Wan er die deutsche[j] Rechtschreibung[7] dieses Jhar gedruckt noch nicht uberkommen, soll sie ihme auch zu gefertiget werden,

Der Nehrende bitte[t][k] die [V]olkommene und Weiße,[8] da er doch derer orten ist, dienstlichen zu grußen und verbleibet

des Unverdroßenen gantzwilliger

[Cö]then[l] den 28. Wein[m]onats 1645.

T **a** *Eingefügt für* <ist dem> <hat> — **b** *Folgt* <mit> <ohne unmut, wie er ihme> — **c** *Folgt* <vom Nehrenden> — **d** *Folgt* <er> — **e** *Folgt ein gestrichenes Wort.* — **f** *Folgt* <laß> — **g** *abermal handschriftlich eingefügt.* — **h** *Gebessert aus* sein — **i** *Eingefügt bis* zufolge — **j** *Eingefügt.* — **k** *Wahrscheinlich Verschreibung.* — **l** *Buchstabenverlust im Falz. Konjektur in eckigen Klammern.*

K Der vorliegende Brief lag F. Ludwigs Schreiben 451028A an Justus Georg Schottelius (FG 397) bei.

1 Vgl. die ungerechtfertigte Klage Carl Gustavs v. Hille (FG 302. Der Unverdrossene) in 451008. In 450126 hatte Hille F. Ludwig (Der Nährende) von seinem geplanten (nicht eingetretenen) Wechsel aus wolfenbüttelschen in hannöversche Dienste informiert.

2 Wohl Verschreibung für: neulichst, Adv. *Stieler*, 1351: novissime, noviter, nuperè.

3 Während Hz. August d. J. v. Braunschweig-Wolfenbüttel (FG 227) nach wiederholter Ermahnung endlich den von ihm zugesagten Zuschuß zum Verlag des *GB 1646* überwies, ignorierte Hz. Christian Ludwig v. Braunschweig-Calenberg (FG 372. Der Reinherzige) die Aufforderungen F. Ludwigs noch bis ins Jahr 1646. Vgl. 460403. Zu den Verlagszuschüssen s. 450126 K 4.

4 D. h. Anfang Februar 1646, da in diesem Jahr Aschermittwoch als Beginn der vorösterlichen Fastenzeit auf den 11. Februar fiel. S. *Grotefend*, 158.

5 Georg Winckler (1582–1654), Leipziger Kaufmann, der für F. Ludwig Finanzabwicklungen aller Art, u. a. das *GB 1646* angehend, tätigte S. 451019 K 0. Zum Zahlungsverkehr das *GB 1646* betreffend s. 450127 K 1.

6 In 451008 kündigte Carl Gustav v. Hille (FG 302) seine FG-Geschichte (*Hille: Teutscher Palmbaum*) an. Später kam er auf die wohlwollende Reaktion F. Ludwigs wegen des genannten Werkes zurück, ließ das Buch aber in Nürnberg drucken, vermied eine Werkkorrektur durch die FG und übermittelte das Buch an den FG-Leiter erst nach dem Druck. S. 451008 K 5.

7 *Gueintz: Rechtschreibung (1645)*. Im Druck erschien dieses Werk wahrscheinlich im September 1645. S. 440127 K 1.

8 Herzoginwitwe Eleonora Maria v. Mecklenburg-Güstrow (AL 1617. TG 17) und ihre Stieftochter Herzoginwitwe Christina Margaretha v. Sachsen-Lauenburg. — Hzn. Eleo-

nora Maria (1600–1657), geb. Fn. v. Anhalt-Bernburg, war seit dem 23.4.1636 Witwe Hz. Johann Albrechts II. v. Mecklenburg-Güstrow (FG 194. Der Vollkommene) und lebte zu diesem Zeitpunkt auf ihrem Witwensitz in Strelitz. Vorausgegangen war ein aufsehenerregender Rechtsstreit um die Vormundschaft ihres Sohnes Hz. Gustav Adolph v. Mecklenburg-Güstrow (FG 511. 1648), den sie nach mehrjährigem Kampf verloren geben mußte. Zu ihrer Person, der Anwesenheit bei der Hänselung ihres Sohnes mit ausdrücklicher Erlaubnis F. Ludwigs und den Vormundschaftsstreitigkeiten s. *Ball: Tugendliche Gesellschaft*, 350–356 u. besonders zum Vormund- und Regentschaftsstreit 371009 K 0. — Ihre Stieftochter Christina Margaretha (1615–1666), die Schwester Hzn. Sophia Elisabeths v. Braunschweig-Wolfenbüttel (1613–1676; AL 1629. TG 42b), verlor ihren (ersten) Gatten Hz. Franz Albrecht v. Sachsen-Lauenburg (FG 194. Der Weiße) nach nur zweijähriger Ehe, als dieser am 10.6.1642 (n. St.) als ksl. Generalleutnant starb, und lebte auf ihrem Witwensitz (Amt Stintenburg) im Mecklenburgischen bis zu ihrer erneuten Eheschließung mit Hz. Christian Ludwig I. v. Mecklenburg-Schwerin (1623–1692) im Jahr 1650. Zu ihrer Biographie s. Jill Bepler: Christine Margarete, Herzogin von Mecklenburg-Schwerin, geb. von Mecklenburg-Güstrow. In: *Braunschweig. Biograph. Lexikon (Jarck)*, 143 f. Möglicherweise war F. Ludwig bekannt, daß sie sich zu diesem Zeitpunkt bei ihrer Stiefmutter in Strelitz aufhielt. Zur Reise Hilles s. 451008 (K 6). — Es gehörte zu den Gepflogenheiten der FG, die Ehegattinnen der Mitglieder mit den Gesellschaftsnamen zu belegen. Vgl. 440209 K 5.

451028A

Fürst Ludwig an Justus Georg Schottelius

Antwort auf 451007. — F. Ludwig (Der Nährende) dankt Justus Georg Schottelius (FG 397. Der Suchende) für seinen Brief und bietet an, Schottelius' (überarbeitete) *Sprachkunst* kritisch durchzusehen und bei der Drucklegung zu helfen. Der Briefverkehr soll über Eberhard Heitfeld in Quedlinburg erfolgen, über den auch der vorliegende Brief Schottelius zugeht. F. Ludwig legt einen Brief an Carl Gustav v. Hille (FG 302. Der Unverdrossene) bei (451028), den Schottelius bei Gelegenheit übergeben möge. — Im Hinblick auf das gemeinsame Wörterbuchprojekt sollte die Arbeit auf mehrere Bearbeiter aufgeteilt werden. Die Orientierung für ein solches deutsches Wörterbuch der FG könnte das vorlängst in Augsburg erschienene, unvollständig gebliebene Wörterbuch (von Georg Henisch) sein, das ihm, F. Ludwig, leider abhanden gekommen sei. F. Ludwig fragt Schottelius, ob er dieses kennt und ob dessen lexikalisches Verfahren zu übernehmen oder abzuändern sei. Ludwig schlägt vor, daß Schottelius und andere zur Probe jeweils einen Buchstaben bearbeiten. Danach wäre die Arbeit umso besser zu verteilen. — Georg Philipp Harsdörffers (FG 368. Der Spielende) Äußerungen im gerade erschienenen fünften Teil der *Gesprächspiele* über die Rechtschreibung und Silbentrennung findet der Fürst bedenklich.

Q HM Köthen: V S 545, Bl. 255r; eigenh.; Konzept in Schottelius' Brief 451007. — D: *KE*, 297 f.; *KL* III, 266 f.; *Barthold*, 313 f. — BN: *Bürger*, 953 Nr. 113 u. 114.

A *Fehlt.*

451028A Fürst Ludwig

Des Suchenden antwort vom siebenden dieses monats hat der Nehrende den 14. wol empfangen. Er wird die mittheilung seiner spracharbeit wen[a] sie angelanget gerne mit[b] fleiße ubersehen,[1] das[c] seinige darbey thun und wegen des druckens helffen mit[d] einrahten, die Brieffe können an Eberhard Heitfelden[2] in Quedlenburg, durch den dieses ankommet, mit dem werklein ubermachet werden. Es wird auch beygefuget ein brieflein an den Unverdroßenen uberschicket,[3] so vom[e] Suchenden mit gelegenheit zu rechte zu schicken begeret wird. Wegen des deutschen[d] wörterbuches[4] were wol nötig die arbeit auszutheilen, es hat schon fur etzlichen Jharen einer in Folio oder[f] in bogenlage zu Augpurg[g] einen anfang zu einem solchen deutschen[d] Wörterbuche gemacht, so auf etzliche Buchstaben ausgegangen war,[h][5] ich damals gehabt gehabt[i], mir aber von handen kommen, welche[j] entwurf[k] mir nicht uneben gedeucht, ob sie der Suchende etwa[d] gesehen hette, stunde es dahin, ob derselben art nachzugehen oder eine beßere art zu finden: Es kan[l] auch der Suchende[m] wo es ihme gefellig, einen kleinen versuch entwerfen, nur bey einem buchstaben, dergleichen sol anderer örter auch geschehen, ob man dardurch desto eher zu der austheilung gelangen könte. Jn des Spielenden funften theil seiner[n] gesprechspiele seind zwar allerhand feine sachen hin und[d] wieder, mit der rechtschreibung aber und der Schlußerinnerung hinten[o] an gefuget[6], sonderlich der rechten Sillabirung wegen, wird er befahrlich[7] nicht bestehen können.

Der Suchende wolle dieses im besten vermercken, darbey[p] verbleibet des Suchenden.
     gantzwilliger
        der Nehrende

Cöthen 28. Weinmonats 1645

T **a** *Am Rand eingefügt bis* angelanget — **b** mit fleiße *eingefügt.* — **c** *Wörterreihenfolge durch hochgestellte Ziffern geändert aus* und wegen des druckens <darauf> helffen einrahten, <und> das seinige darbey thun, <wan sie der Suchende überschicken wird> — **d** *Eingefügt.* — **e** *Eingefügt für* <der> — **f** oder in bogenlage *am Rand ergänzt. Dabei* bogen *eingefügt für* <blates> — **g** *Wohl Verschreibung für* Augpurg — **h** *Folgt fälschlich gestrichen* <und> — **i** *Eingefügt für* <aber> — **j** *Lies:* welcher — **k** *Eingefügt für* <ent> — **l** kan auch *eingefügt für* <wolle> — **m** *Folgt* <etwan> — **n** *Eingefügt für* <der> — **o** hinten an *eingefügt für* <darbey an> — **p** *Folgt* <dem>

K **1** Gemeint ist die von Justus Georg Schottelius (FG 397. Der Suchende) neu überarbeitete eigene Grammatik (*Sprachkunst [1641]*), die aber entgegen der Zusicherung des Suchenden der FG nicht zur gesellschaftlichen Diskussion und Korrektur eingereicht wurde, sondern erst nach F. Ludwigs Tod in Braunschweig erschien: *Schottelius: Sprachkunst (1651)*. Vgl. 450923B, 450929 u. 451007.
2 Eberhard Heidfeld war vermutlich Mitglied des Quedlinburger Ratsgeschlechts dem auch mehrere Tuchhändler, Goldschmiede, Advokaten etc. angehörten. Vgl. J. H. Mitgau: Alt-Quedlinburger Honoratiorentum. Genealogisch-soziologische Studie über einen Gesellschaftsaufbau des 17./18. Jahrhunderts. Leipzig 1934, 123 f. Vgl. schon 290510 K 6.

Ein Eberhard Heitfeld wird als Spender des Taufsteins der Marktkirche St. Benedikt in Quedlinburg 1648 erwähnt. S. Evangel. Kirchspiel Quedlinburg (Hg.): Quedlinburg. Marktkirche St. Benedikti, Passau 2005, 13 sowie Adolf Brinkmann: Beschreibende Darstellung der älteren Bau- und Kunstdenkmäler des Kreises Stadt Quedlinburg. 2. Tl. Magdeburg 1923 (Beschreibende Darstellung der Kunstdenkmäler der Provinz Sachsen Heft 33), 43. Ebenso wird ein D. Eberhardus Heidfeld, Quedlinburg als Widmungsempfänger einer Dissertation von 1626 genannt. HAB: 43.6 Jur. (2).

3 D. i. 451028. Über Carl Gustav v. Hille (FG 302. Der Unverdrossene) lief ein Großteil der fruchtbringerischen Korrespondenz F. Ludwigs mit dem Wolfenbütteler Hof unter Hz. August d. J. v. Braunschweig-Wolfenbüttel (FG 227).

4 Wie in 450923B, 451007 u. 451219 ist die Rede von einem vollständigen deutschen Wörterbuch, das nach dem Abschluß von *Gueintz: Rechtschreibung* (1645) (s. 440127 K 1) im Vordergrund der Spracharbeit der FG stehen sollte. Ähnlich wie bei dem Wörterbuch der *Accademia della Crusca*, an dem F. Ludwig als Cruscante mitgearbeitet hatte, war vorgesehen, die Arbeit an dem gemeinsamen Wörterbuch unter geeigneten FG-Mitgliedern aufzuteilen. Das Wörterbuchprojekt der FG wurde jedoch nie durch Zusammenarbeit vieler realisiert. Caspar v. Stielers Wörterbuch (*Stieler*) von 1691 (Ndr. München 1968) als spätes Ergebnis fruchtbringerischer lexikographischer Bemühungen blieb das beeindruckende Werk eines Einzelnen. Vgl. auch 440826 K 4 u. 451219 K 7 u. 8; ferner Antje Bielfeld: Methoden der Belegsammlung für das ‚Vocabolario della Crusca'. Exemplarisch vorgestellt am lexikographischen Werk Francesco Redis. Tübingen 1996, 2 ff.

5 Das von *Henisch* 1616 veröffentlichte Lexikon endet nach dem Buchstaben G. Es war Schottelius bekannt (s. 450923B u. 450929) und wurde von F. Ludwig auch Christian Gueintz (FG 361) gegenüber als mögliches Vorbild empfohlen. S. 451219, vgl. dort K 7.

6 Georg Philipp Harsdörffer (FG 368. Der Spielende) hatte den fünften Teil seiner *Frauenzimmer-Gesprächspiele* (1645) mit 450923C an F. Ludwig gesandt. Dabei machte Harsdörffer F. Ludwig schon auf die vielen Druckfehler aufmerksam. In seiner „Schlußerinnerung" in *Harsdörffer: Frauenzimmer-Gesprächspiele* V (1645, Ndr. 1969), Ndr. 739–744, entschuldigte sich Harsdörffer ebenfalls für zahlreiche Druckfehler, hinsichtlich seiner „Schreib-art" aber bat er darum, vom Usus abweichende Schreibweisen zunächst einmal in ihrer Begründung in acht zu nehmen. Zwei Aspekte stehen dabei im Vordergrund: 1. seine Eliminierung des -c- in der Buchstabenverbindung mit -k- zugunsten dessen Verdoppelung (kk statt ck). Als Hauptgrund dafür gibt er die unterschiedliche Lautung an: ein -c- werde niemals wie ein -k- ausgesprochen (S. 740 ff.), was die Verwendung des -c- im Deutschen überhaupt einschränke. In seiner „Schutzschrift für Die Teutsche Spracharbeit" (Anhang in *Frauenzimmer-Gesprächspiele* I ²1644, Ndr. 1968), Ndr. S. 378, hatte er zurückhaltend unter „die zweiffelhafte Schreibung" gerechnet, „daß etliche das kk für das ck" schreiben. Harsdörffer wird in 460131 gegenüber Gueintz und im *Specimen (1646)*, 213 ff. seine neue Auffassung bekräftigen. Gueintz wird sie in seinem Gutachten zum *Specimen* vom Juli 1646 erneut zurückweisen (s. 460720 K 3). Vgl. dazu auch 440129 K 5, 450420 (K 6), 451219, 460131 (K 9 u. 18), 460720 K 3, 460812 K 2 u. 460915. 2. Hinsichtlich der Silbentrennung plädiert Harsdörffer in seiner „Schlußerinnerung" für das morphologische Prinzip: Trennung nach (einsilbiger) Stammform und Derivations- bzw. Flexionsendungen, etwa lieb-en, lieb-et, lieb-es usw. In diese „durchgehende Richtigkeit" habe sich eine Zerrüttung eingeschlichen, wenn etwa grundlos lie-ben, lie-be usw. getrennt werde. Ohne einen Glaubensstreit entfachen zu wollen, lehnt er die Silbentrennung nach Sprechsilben ab (S. 742 f.). Auch Schottelius trennte in seiner *Sprachkunst (1641)*, S. 192, nach Wortmorphologie/ Grammatik, während Gueintz in seiner *Rechtschreibung (1645)*, S. 19, etwa schrei-ben, sin-gen trennte. F. Ludwig kritisierte auch in 451219 diese beiden

Positionen in Harsdörffers „Schlußerinnerung"; Harsdörffer verteidigte sie in 460131 gegenüber Gueintz und im *Specimen (1646)*: „*Omnes litteræ radicales* sive consonantes, quæ pertinent ad radicem thematis, *sunt inseparabiles*" (ebd. S. 150). Darum trenne man auch „Schänd-er/ non Schän-der/ herr-isch/ non her-risch" (ebd. S. 149). F. Ludwig zweifelte erneut in 460200, Gueintz in seinem Gutachten zum *Specimen* vom Juli 1646 (vgl. 460720 K 3), Harsdörffer konterte in 460915. Die Diskussion verlief sehr widersprüchlich, weil die Veränderlichkeit des Silbenschnitts noch nicht erkannt wurde. Vgl. zur Silbentrennung ferner 440129, 460816 K I 3, *Herz: Rechtschreibdebatte*, 28. — F. Ludwig bedankte sich für den Erhalt der Exemplare des 5. Teils der *Frauenzimmer-Gesprächspiele* erst auf Nachfrage von Seiten Harsdörffers im Dezember 1645. Vgl. 450923C K 2, 451101 u. 451209. F. Ludwig hatte schon zum dritten Teil von Harsdörffers *Frauenzimmer-Gesprächspielen* (1643) kritische Anmerkungen zu Fragen der Rechtschreibung u. ä. gemacht. Vgl. 430724.

7 Befahr, im Sinne von Besorgnis, Sorge, s. *DW* I, 1246. Vgl. 440310A K 3.

451028B

Matthäus Merian d. Ä. an Peter Knaudt

Matthäus Merian d. Ä. hofft, seine früheren Sendungen mit dem ersten gesetzten Bogen des *GB 1646* seien eingetroffen. Hiermit gehen Peter Knaudt nun der Titel und die Vorrede zu. Auf dem Titelblatt zieht er ein kleineres (Titel-)Kupfer als das ursprüngliche vor. Beide habe er probehalber auf je einen Bogen gedruckt und falls hier Änderungswünsche bestünden, bittet Merian umgehend um Nachricht, so daß er korrigierend eingreifen könne. Die erbetenen 200 Reichstaler habe Merian von Georg Winckler genau wie die vorigen empfangen, so daß nunmehr insgesamt 400 Reichstaler Vorschuß eingegangen seien.

Q HM Köthen: V S 546, Bl. 16rv [A: 16v; in der Mitte zerschnitten]; eigenh.; rotes Lacksiegel. — *D: Bircher: Merian*, 709f.; *Wüthrich: Merian Briefe*, 96–99. — BN: *Bürger*, 987 Nr. 13.

A Tt. Dem Ehrenves[ten vnd Groß]Achtparen H[erren Peter] Knaudt F[ürst. Anhaltischen Raht vnd] Cammer M[eistern etc. meinem] Großg. h[ochgeehrten herrn etc.] Jn [Cöthen][a]

Ehrnvester vnd GroßAchtparer, Jnsonders Hochgeehrter Herr,
 meine vorigen Schreiben sampt dem ersten bogen der Fruchtbringenden gesellschafft, verhoffe ich werden zu recht ein kommen sein, diß mals sende hiemit den Tittul und Præfatio,[1]
 Auff den Tittul werde ich ein ander kupferlein machen so kleiner ist, als das so ietz darauff getruckt ist, welchs nur zue prob auff 2 bogen getrukt worden, vnd so vielleicht Jhr. Fl. Gn. etwas daran zu ändern gedächten, bitte ich solches Cito mich zu berichten, damit ichs verbessern möge.[2]
 Die vbermachten Rth. 200 von H. Georg Wincklern habe ich wohl empfangen, sampt den vorigen, habe ich zu sammen nunmehr empfangen Rthl. 400 — vnd

also in Conto geschrieben.³ Dißmaln mehr nicht Alß dem Allmächtigen wol befohlen.
Ffurt den 28. 8bris 1645.

T a *Textverlust in der Adresse, da unmittelbar unterhalb der Datumszeile das Blatt zerschnitten wurde. Konjekturen nach der Anschrift in 451015.*

K 1 Matthäus Merian d. Ä. bezieht sich auf seinen Brief 451015, dem er einen probeweisen Druckbogen mit den ersten vier Mitglieder-Impresen beigelegt hatte, und in dem er ankündigte, mit nächster Post den Druckbogen mit Titel und Vorwort an Peter Knaudt abzusenden.
2 Ein Probedruck des Titelblatts des *GB 1646* mit einem bildlichen Schmuckelement ist im Erzschrein HM Köthen: V S 546 nicht überliefert. Vgl. auch 450711 u. 450800, in denen ein (hsl.) Titelblatt-Vorschlag thematisiert wird. S. Abb. S.574f. Das Titelblatt des *GB 1646* weist keinen Kupferstich auf. Aus 451119 wissen wir, daß Merian dort eine verkleinerte Abbildung des Palmen-Sinnbilds der FG vorgesehen hatte. Wahrscheinlich war eine kleine Palmenimprese geplant, wie sie in *Fürst Ludwig: Kurtze Anleitung zur Deutschen Poesi (1640)* überliefert ist. In 460206 gab Merian diese Absicht wegen Platzmangels auf. Zur Einrichtung des *GB 1646* s. 450711 K 4.
3 Merians Wunsch nach einer zweiten Abschlagszahlung von 200 Reichstalern zur Deckung der laufenden Kosten wird erstmals in 450905 und weiterhin in 450922 u. 451019 zur Sprache gebracht. Der von Georg Winckler höchstwahrscheinlich am 20.10.1645 (s. 451019 Postskriptum) auf den Weg gebrachte Beitrag in Höhe von 200 Reichstalern erreichte Merian demnach (spätestens) am 28.10.1645. Vgl. dazu 450923 K 2; zum Zahlungsverkehr das *GB 1646* betreffend s. 450127 K 1. Zum *GB 1646* allgemein s. 450126 K 4.

451030

Gaspar Corneille de Mortaigne dit de Potteles an Fürst Ludwig

Gaspar Corneille de Mortaigne dit de Potelles (FG 419) bittet F. Ludwig, ihm seinen Prediger Gottfried Limmer auch weiterhin abzustellen, um in der schwed. Armee reformierten dt. Gottesdienst abhalten zu lassen. F. Ludwig habe Limmer vor einem Jahr dafür freigestellt. Limmer habe nun zwar gewünscht, wieder in seine Pfarre in Mönchenienburg zurückzukehren, jedoch haben Mortaigne und die reformierte Gemeinde in der Armee großen Gefallen an ihm gefunden und zum Verweilen überreden können, sofern F. Ludwig zustimme. Mortaigne bittet daher den Fürsten, ihm Limmer noch eine Weile zu überlassen und ihm seine heimische Pfarre weiterhin solange freizuhalten.

Q HAB: Cod. Guelf. 170 Noviss. 2°, Bl.1r-2v [A: 2v], 2r leer; Schreiberh. mit eigenh. Schlußkurialie; rotes Lacksiegel. — Von der HAB im Okt. 2011 aus dem Antiquariatshandel erworben.

A Dem Durchlauchtigen Hochgebornen Fürsten vnd hern hern Ludwig, Fürsten zu Anhalt, Graven zu Ascanien, hern zu Bernburg vndt Zerbst, Meinem gnedigen Fürsten vnd hern.
Darunter Empfangsvermerk von F. Ludwigs H.: Pres. 14. Novemb. 1645

451030 Gaspar Corneille de Mortaigne dit de Potteles

Durchlauchtiger Hochgeborner gnediger Fürst vnd Her.

E FGn. werden sich gn. erinnern, welcher gestalt sie ohngefehr vor einem iahr, den **Pastor** zu MüncheNeuburg H. Gottfridt Limmern[1], gn. erlaubtt bey mir zu sein, der reformirten gemeine bey der **armée** vorzustehen, vnd vnderdeßen seine Pfarre zu Neuburg vor ihn vffzuhalten ihm gn. versprochen. Nu hatt zwar derselbe bey mir ümb seine erlaßung anhalten laßen ümb wider seine Pfarre daselbst zubedienen. Weill aber ich vnd die gantze reformirte gemeine alhir, an seiner person so ein gutes genügen haben, daß wir ihn nit gern mißen wolten, deswegen ich ihn dan wider dahin vermocht, daß er noch ein zeitlang bey mir zu bleiben sich erkleret, wan ich ihm Eflgn. fernern gn. **consens** vnd **suspendirung** seiner Pfarre daselbst erhalten würde; Gelanget derwegen himit an Eflgn. mein vntertheniges ersuchen, sie wollen gnedig geruhen drin zu willigen, daß gedachter Her Gottfridt Limmer, noch [1v] ein zeitlang möge bey mir bleiben, vnd ihm vnderdeßen die Pfarre zu Neuburg möge vffgehalten werden: Eflgn. werden sich dadurch vnsere gantze gemeine höchlich **obligirt** machen, vnd ich vor meine person werde mich befleißen Eflgn. hinwiderumb vnterthenige gefällige dienste zuerweisen. Eflgn. himitt der starcken bewahrung des Allerhöchsten vnterthenig empfelend.

Geben im haubtquartir **Jaromitz**[2] den 30. 8br. ao 1645.

Eu. f. g.

vnterthenig vndt gehorsambster Knecht

CCMortaigne *mp*.

K Der aus reformiertem fläm. Adel stammende Gaspard Corneille de Mortaigne dit de Potteles (auch Caspar Corneille de Mortaigne) (FG 419) stand seit 1629 im Dienst der schwed. Armee unter Kg. Gustav II. Adolf v. Schweden. Nach Johan Banérs (FG 222) Tod am 10.5.1641 in Halberstadt setzte er sich an die Spitze der unzufriedenen Offiziere, deren Protest gegen den allgegenwärtigen Zerfall der Ordnung im schwed. Heerwesen erst der neue Oberbefehlshaber Lennart Torstensson stillen konnte, der am 15.11.1641 bei der schwed. Hauptarmee bei Winsen a. d. Aller eintraf. Torstensson beförderte Mortaigne gleich im Frühjahr 1642 zum Generalmajor der Infanterie und lobte ihn als „een valliant cavallier, hafver stoort anhang i armeen, och altidh sigh väll i alla occasioner förhallet". S. 410621 K 3. Von Beginn an war Mortaigne bestrebt — vielleicht schon aus konfessionellen Gründen —, ein gutes Verhältnis zum Haus Anhalt zu pflegen. Er verhinderte seit 1639 mehrfach Schlimmeres bei Ein-, Durch- und Abzügen der Schweden, trat bei Kontributionsforderungen gemäßigt und kompromißbereit auf und galt als höflicher, diskreter Kavalier. Vgl. 390504 K 4. Banér bat Mortaigne in einem Brief vom 6. März 1639, „Es wolle der Herr Obrist mit deme, was er albereits aus dem Fürstenthumb Anhalt erhoben, Zufrieden sein". Mortaigne entsprach dem Gesuch und distanzierte sich von Übergriffen schwed. Soldaten, wie ein Auszug aus einem Brief vom 8. März 1639 an F. August v. Anhalt-Plötzkau (FG 46) veranschaulicht: Er entgegnet auf die Beschwerden des Fürsten, er habe daraus „mit nicht wenig befremdung vernommen, wie von dem in Bernburg liegenden Officieren alle Insolentien mit abnahme Viehes und Andern verübet werden. Wann aber dieser von mir gantz keinen befelsch hatt, […] So habe ich an ihn, sich dieses Zu enthalten […] ergehen laßen, bitte aber Efgn. vnterthenig, Dieselbe mich dießfals entschuldigt halten wollen." *KU* IV.1, 445 f. Vermutlich im Zusammenhang der geschilderten

Zuspitzung der Kriegslage in und um Bernburg 1644 wurden im Spätherbst dieses Jahres einige schwed. Militärs und Funktionsträger in die FG aufgenommen: Mortaigne (FG 419) als der „Gewidmede", Greve Robert Douglas (FG 420) und Friherre Alexander Erskein (FG 421). Sie alle haben sich eigenh. in das *GB Kö.* eingetragen, waren also vermutlich persönlich in Köthen anwesend. Mortaigne trug sich mit dem Wahlspruch „Wornach ich Trachte darauf hoffe ich" ein. Seine Gesellschaftspflanze war der Weihrauchbaum und sein Harz. Das seine FG-Imprese auslegende Reimgesetz hebt auf Andacht, Frömmigkeit und Gottergebenheit ab: „[...] Gewidmet heiß' ich nun und ruff' in andacht an | Gott der die wahre frucht mir reichlich geben kan." *GB Kö.* III (HM Köthen: V S 677b). Im 3. Band des Köthener Erzschreins (HM Köthen: V S 546), Bl. 51v Unterschrift und Devise von Mortaigne: „1644. J'espere ou J'aspire, GCMortaigne*emp*". Eine Überlieferung seiner Imprese und seines Reimgesetzes ebenfalls dort, Bl. 74r. Das gute, durch die Mitgliedschaft in der FG bekräftigte Verhältnis Mortaignes zum anhalt. Fürstenhaus dürfte dazu beigetragen haben, daß Torstensson das geplagte Fürstentum im Januar 1645 für ein Jahr von allen Kontributionen und Kriegslasten befreite. Vgl. 440927 K 1 u. 450721 K 3; *Conermann III*, 501. — Der Brief illustriert recht anschaulich jenen ersten Zweck der FG, wie er im *Kurtzen Bericht der Fruchtbringenden Gesellschaft Zweck und Vorhaben* (Köthen 1622, s. *DA Köthen II. 1*, S. [7]ff.) erstmals öffentlich gemacht wurde: die Pflege eines vertrauensvollen, höflichen und schicklichen Umgangs als Grundbedingung sicherer und verläßlicher gesellschaftlicher Verhältnisse und kulturellen Lebens. Der Brief dokumentiert so das fruchtbringerische Netzwerk, das sich auf den verschiedensten Gebieten zu bewähren hatte und das zweite Ziel, die Sprach- und Literaturarbeit, absicherte. Vgl. *Herz: Palmenbaum und Mühle*; ders.: „Edle Ritter dieser Zunft". Beobachtungen zur sozietären Performanz der Fruchtbringenden Gesellschaft (im Druck). Zu Mortaigne vgl. auch 390504A K; *KU* IV.1, 446ff.; *Christian: Tageb.* XV, Bl. 128r; *ADB* XXII, 339f.; LP von Sebastian Curtius: Christliche Leichpredigt Auß dem CXVI. Psalm. v. 15. Von dem Seelig-werthen Tod der Heyligen Gottes ..., Kassel 1647. HAB: Db 3276 (18) (VD17 39:110282R).

1 Ambrosius Gottfried Limmer (1605–1680), aus Kirchenthumbach (Oberpfalz), Archidiakon zu Köthen und Klepzig. Zu ihm s. die LP von Johann Sachse: Christliche Leichpredigt Bey Christlicher und Volkreicher Leich-Bestattung ..., Köthen 1681. VD17 39:108751X. *Graf: Anh. Pfarrerbuch*, 172, nennt einen Pfarrer „Limmer" an St. Johannis, das ist die Stadtkirche (im Ggs. zur Kloster- oder Schloßkirche) in Nienburg (auch Mönchenienburg genannt nach seinem ehemaligen Benediktinerkloster), der sein Amt von 1639–1660 versehen haben soll. *Beckmann* III, 454 nennt „Ambrosius Gottfried Limmer", Prediger an St. Johannis von 1640–1660. Das ehemalige Kloster wurde im Verlauf der Reformation aufgehoben und in ein fl. Schloß nebst Schloßkirche verwandelt. Das Amt Nienburg a. d. S. war, obwohl in der Nähe Bernburgs gelegen, bei der Landesteilung 1606 dem Teilft. Köthen zugesprochen worden. Die Stadtkirche ist, so *Beckmann* III, 453f., im 30jährigen Krieg so stark zerstört worden, daß sie bis zu ihrem Wiederaufbau 1687–93 kaum noch genutzt werden konnte und auf die Schloßkirche ausgewichen werden mußte. Auch das Städtchen und Amt wurde schwer in Mitleidenschaft gezogen, als sich im Sommer/ Herbst 1644 die beiden feindlichen Hauptarmeen des Kaisers und der Schweden bei Bernburg wochenlang gegenüberlagen. Nienburg wurde dabei zu großen Teilen zerstört. S. 440927 K 1. Die zeitweise Abordnung Limmers dürfte F. Ludwig daher leichtgefallen sein. Wann Limmer in seine Pfarre zurückkehrte, ist uns unbekannt, jedoch soll er sein Amt dort bis 1660 versehen haben.

2 Jaromeritz/ Jaroměřice nad Rokytnou in Mähren, westlich von Brünn. Dort befand sich im Oktober/ November 1645 das Hauptquartier der schwed. Armee unter Generalfeldmarschall Lennart Torstensson. S. *AOSB* SA VIII, 450 ff. — Die schwed. Armee unter Torstensson hatte, nachdem sie im Frühjahr 1645 in Böhmen einmarschiert war, dem ksl. Heer unter dem neuen Generalleutnant Gf. Melchior v. Hatzfeld — Gallas war dieser Position enthoben worden (s. 440927 K 1) — in der Schlacht bei Jankau/ Jankov (60 km südöstlich von Prag) am 24.2.1645 eine vernichtende Niederlage beigebracht. Obwohl die Schweden daraufhin in Niederösterreich einfielen, u. a. Korneuburg und Krems a. d. Donau eroberten und bis vor Wien vordrangen, vermochten sie — nicht zuletzt aufgrund des Ausbleibens der versprochenen militär. Unterstützung des Fürsten von Siebenbürgen, Georg Rákóczy (1593–1648) — nicht die Donau zu überschreiten oder gar Wien anzugreifen, zudem bissen sich die Schweden an der seit April 1645 belagerten mähr. Hauptfestung Brünn die Zähne aus, bis sie am 20. August die Belagerung aufgaben. Die Anfälligkeit der schwed. Verbindungs- und Nachschublinien veranlaßten Torstensson, sich allmählich wieder nach Norden zu wenden. Im März 1645 hatte er noch sein Hauptquartier in der Umgebung Wiens (Krems, bei Wien, Stammersdorf) im Juni (bis August) bereits wieder vor Brünn, ab Oktober dann in Jaromeritz. S. *AOSB* SA VIII, 450 ff. Im anbrechenden Winter verließ die schwed. Hauptarmee Böhmen und ließ die verbliebenen Besatzungen in Niederösterreich ohne Verbindung. Im Frühjahr 1646 erfolgte dann in einer gemeinsamen Aktion mit dem frz. Heer unter Maréchal Henri de La Tour d'Auvergne, Vicomte de Turenne (1611–1675) der Einfall in Bayern, wo das schwed. Heer u. a. Augsburg belagerte. Den folgenden Herbst und Winter verbrachten die frz.-schwed. Truppen in Südwestdeutschland. Vgl. *Englund*, 419 ff.; *Wilson*, 692 ff.; Mark Hengerer: Kaiser Ferdinand III. (1608–1657). Eine Biographie. Wien, Köln, Weimar 2012, 230 ff.; Der Schwed' ist im Land! Das Ende des 30jährigen Krieges in Niederösterreich. Ausst. der Stadt Horn im Höbarthmuseum, 22.6. – 2.11.1995. Horn 1995, 49 ff.; Beda Dudík: Schweden in Böhmen und Mähren 1640–1650. Nach kaiserl. österreichischen u. Königl. schwedischen Quellen dargestellt, und mit Unterstützung der Kais. Akad. der Wissenschaften hrsg. Wien 1879, 118–125 u. 208; Paul Gantzer: Torstensons Einfall und Feldzug in Böhmen 1645 bis zur Schlacht bei Jankau. Prag 1905 [auch abgedruckt in: Mitteilungen des Vereins für Geschichte der Deutschen in Böhmen 42 (1904), 421–442, und 43 (1905), 1–26 u. 168–185]. — Ausweislich seines Briefes hielt sich Mortaigne im Herbst 1645 bei der schwed. Hauptarmee auf. Dieser, nicht etwa einem separat von dem Generalmajor geführten Armeekorps, wird sein Angebot reformierter Gottesdienste gegolten haben. Bereits früher gab es im Umfeld Mortaignes gesonderte kirchliche Amtshandlungen für die reformierten Offiziere bei der schwed. Hauptarmee. So waren z. B. im Dezember 1642, kurz vor deren Abmarsch vom kursächs. Leipzig, im Haus des damaligen Prorektors der Universität, Dr. Georg Ernst Mosbach (1602–1660), insgesamt vier calvinistische Predigten abgehalten und die Kommunion nach reformiertem Ritus gereicht worden. Oberst Robert Douglas (FG 420), der bei Mosbach einquartiert war, hatte gegenüber dem protestierenden orthodoxlutherischen Leipziger Konsistorium erklärt, dass der Generalmajor Mortaigne neben anderen Offizieren reformierten Glaubens vor ihrem Abmarsch die Kommunion einnehmen wollte. Zur Durchführung der Predigten und der Kommunion, an der neben dem Generalmajor auch Oberstleutnant John Nairn of Mukkersy (FG 526. 1649) und weitere Offiziere teilnahmen, wurde der Superintendent aus Dessau, Johann Hofmeister (1596–1646), nach Leipzig geholt. Da der Leipziger Superintendent, Dr. Johann Höppner (1582–1645), dies nicht verhindern konnte, entsandte er als Beobachter zu den fraglichen Predigten zwei theologische Bakkalaureaten. Den vom als schwed. Unterkommandant in Leipzig verbliebenen Oberstleutnant Nairn geplanten Druck dieser vier Predigten konnte Höppner hingegen später untersagen. Universitätsarchiv Leipzig: Rektor B 17, Bl. 15v–19v (Konsistorium zu Leipzig an Kf. Johann Georg I., Leipzig 15. Juni 1643). S. Alexander

Zirr: Die Schweden in Kursachsen. Eine Untersuchung zur Besetzung Leipzigs im Spannungsfeld zwischen Dreißigjährigem Krieg und Westfälischem Frieden (1642–1650). Diss. (MS) Univ. Leipzig 2015, 498. Er erschien dann 1644 bei Johann Press in Frankfurt a. M. Vgl. 440310B K 4.

451100

Justus Georg Schottelius an Herzog August d. J. von Braunschweig-Wolfenbüttel

Die Prinzen Anton Ulrich (FG 716. 1659) und Ferdinand Albrecht (FG 842. Der Wunderliche. 1673) bäten wiederholt darum — wie ihr Präzeptor Justus Georg Schottelius (FG 397. Der Suchende) an deren Vater Hz. August d. J. v. Braunschweig-Wolfenbüttel (FG 227) schreibt —, in einer Rede auf den Advent sich hören lassen zu dürfen, um sich Hoffnung auf reichere Geschenke zu machen. Da er sich dem Wunsch nicht versage, habe man in den Nebenstunden schon mit der Vorbereitung des Stücks angefangen. Das Projekt hänge wie alles übrige von der Zustimmung des Fürsten ab, so daß Schottelius den Stoff und die Abfolge beschreiben möchte. — Am Anfang ertönt aus dem Hintergrund Musik und Verse kündigen die Gnadenzeit an. Es folgen die Rede des Simeon (Page Bernstorff) über die baldige Ankunft des Messias, ein Hymnus über die Geburt Christi und nach der Geburt eine Freudenharmonie. Der Himmel öffnet sich nun und der Engel (Pz. Anton Ulrich) verkündigt allen Menschen und auch den Hirten die frohe Botschaft, wobei am Schluß Musik ertönt. Nach einem Echo mit den Beiworten Gottes und den Antworten über Christus hält der Hirt (Pz. Ferdinand Albrecht) seine kleine Ansprache und führt schließlich alle zum Ort der Geburt Jesu. — Da die Reden und Gesänge nur Frommes und Nützliches beinhalten, erscheinen sie Schottelius für die Prinzen in ihrem jugendlichen Alter als angemessen, zumal diese danach so sehr verlangen und sich darauf freuen. Auch hält Schottelius diese Spiele für dienlich zur Stimmbildung, zur Erinnerung an Namen und Ereignisse in der Geschichte Jesu, auch zur sittlichen Erziehung und Erbauung durch gute Reden.

Q   NSTA Wolfenbüttel: 2 Alt Nr. 3520, Bl. 32rv, eigenh.

A   *Fehlt.*

Serenissime Princeps, D*omi*ne Clementissime
   Jnstabant subinde V*estræ* Serenitatis illust*rissi*mi Filij Dn. Dn. Anthon. Ulric*us* et Ferd. Albertus, oratiuncul*am* quandam,[1] more solito, poscentes, quâ adventum Salvatoris paululum explicarunt, et perorantes audirentur, spesq*ue*, ut putant, ditiores de futuris sibj donis formarent. Cupient*ibus* Principib*us* deesse non debuj, et horis sucsicivis[a] non nihil incepimus: Quandoquidem autem à consensu V*estræ* Serenitatis *omn*ia *nos*tra pendent, materiam et actionis seriem subjectissimè indicare debui.
   Initium faciet Musica[2] è longinquo ad aures allabens, sonus autem subinde increscet et in fine repetetur bis aut ter versiculus, quo iudicatur, venisse iam tempus Gratiæ etc.[3]

Exibit Simeon (Nobilis puer à Bernstorff) et oratione Propheticâ instantem Messiah adventum venisse etc. declarabit: quem Hymnus de Christo, et momento hoc natό, subsequetur lætabundâ harmoniâ.[4]

Sub cuius finem cælum se se aperiet et Angelus ex alto veniens pastoribus apparebit, annuncians hominibus omnibus et tandem Pastoribus nuncium lætum etc. Celsissimus Princeps Anth Ulr. orationem Angeli habebit.[5] Ultima verba angeli excipiat Musica cœlestis, debito ad hoc cantum et verborum tenore. Subsequetur Echo [32v] Epitheta Salvatoris continens, et de Christo respondens.[6] quâ evanescente Pastor (Celss. Princeps Ferdinandus Albertus) oratiunculam recitat et tandem simul omnes ad locum nativitatis ducit.[7]

Quia nihil orationibus et Cantilenis inest, nisi quod pium, sacrum et utile sit, arbitratus sum non dedecore et hæc talia puerili ætate Principes: Tum quod ipsi magnopere urgeant et exercitio eo valde lætentur,[8] tum quod non una evidens utilitas adesset, formari decenter vocem, iuvari delectamine memoriam, audiri et addisci omnia fere nomina et insignia, quæ de Christo in S.S. habentur, assumi decentes affectus et mores, recrearj animos laude bene perorantis et similia.[9] Vestræ autem Serenitatj, cuius iussum et dispositionem et in hisce et omnibus aliis obedientibus[b] exspectamus, hæc priùs indicandæ fuisse, ex debito id putavit eiusdem

Obœdientissimus Servus
JGSchottelius

I

Schottelius' Widmung und Sonett an Herzog Anton Ulrich von Braunschweig-Wolfenbüttel

Q *Schottelius: Fruchtbringender Lustgarte (1647)*, 89–91 (andere Abtheilung).

Dem Durchleuchtigen Hochgebornen Fürsten und Herrn/
Herrn Anthonio Vlrico/
Herzogen zu Brunswiegk und Lüneb. *etc.*
Meinem gnädigen Fürsten und Herrn.

WAn der Königliche Prophet David/ der Mann nach dem Herzen des HErrn/ auf das lieblichste und herrlichste seinen GOtt loben/ und dessen grossen Wunder-Namen preisen und erheben wolte/ alsdan richtete derselbe seine Lieder und Psalmen nach Poetischer Kunst und Zier/ und mit freudigem hohem Geiste also ein/ daß auch keine höhere treflichere Reden mehr zuersinnen/ noch mehr Musicalische Jnstrumenta zuerfinden/ als womit und worin der Prophet den gütigen/ und auch zornigen GOtt/ auf das andächtigste vorgebildet/ geehret und erhoben hat.

Wir Christen sind nicht weniger schuldig/ Gnädiger Herr/ Unseren allerliebsten Heyland Christum JEsum/ auf allerhand liebliche und bewegliche Art/ so unsere Teutsche Sprache an die hand zu geben vermögen wird/ zu ehren/ zu rühmen und zu preisen; Derowegen dan kein [90] Christliebendes Gemüht mit Misfallen aufnehmen wird/ daß auf gnädiges Befehl/ die Wunder-Gebuhrt unseres HERREN und Heylandes/ nach Poetischer Zier und Erlaubniß/ und mit aller Zuschauer sonderbahrer Vergnügung/ Wir also vorgestellet haben: Weiln Euer Fürstl. Gn. hierbey auch selbst die Englische Reden/ fast lieblich und wol getahn und abgelegt haben; als ist die ganze Vorstellung/ zu etwa einer wiederholender Andacht und Erlustigung/ deroselben hiermit in untertähniger Wolmeinung zugeeignet und überreichet worden/ Von Eur. Fürstl. Gn. getreuem Diener

Justo-Georgio Schottelio D. [91]

Sonnet
An seinen Gnädigen Herzhochgeliebten Herrn/
Herrn Anthon Ulrichen/
Herzogen zu Brunswiegk und Luneburg/ *etc.*

EJn Spiegel/ wan er ist sehr köstlich auspoliret/
    Mit Deamanten Bliz/ uñ Helfenbein ümsezt/
    Mit Flammengold bewirkt/ mit Smelzglaß ausgeezt/
An Kunst und Köstlichkeit aufs höchst' heraus gezieret/
Wan der lebhaftiglich das Gegenbild vorführet
    So dargestellet wird/ dan ist er hoch gesezt/
    Ein Wunder der Natur/ die sich in sich ergezt:
So/ hochbegabter Herr/ seid jhr wol ausstaffiret
    Mit reicher Himelsgunst des Herren Vaters Tugend/
    Daß mañ ein Alter siht schon izt in eurer Jugend.
Man siehet/ wie da helt/ eur Vater-voller Sinn/
Jn Tugend embsig seyn/ für Lust und für Gewin.
    An Euch hat die Natur gethā ein Meisterstükk/
    Nun Gott thu auch hinzu des Vaters Ruhm und Glükk.

T a *Lies* subsicivis — **b** *Davor* <sub>

K 1 Die ungefähre Datierung des Briefs geht aus einem Krippen- oder Weihnachtsschauspiel mit Musik hervor. Das Libretto stammt von Justus Georg Schottelius (FG 397), die Vertonung von Hzn. Sophia Elisabeth v. Braunschweig-Wolfenbüttel (AL 1629, TG 42b): „Die Gebuhrt unsers Heylandes: auf gnädiges Begehren/ Und in Gegenwart Fürstlicher/ und anderer vornehmen Personen/ vorgestellet im Fürstlichen Schloß zu Wolfenbüttel/ auf den Christabend Anno 1645." Vgl. *Geck*, 313–316. Komposition verschollen, Erstveröffentlichung des Texts in *Schottelius: Fruchtbringender Lustgarte (1647)*, 88–126. Das Spiel erscheint in der 2. Abteilung des Buchs und ist Pz. Anton Ulrich v. Braunschweig-Wolfenbüttel (*1633; FG 716. 1659) gewidmet. S. Beil. I. Die 4. Abteilung enthält „Eine neue ergetzliche Vorstellung Des WaldGott Pans/ Samt seinen Verrichtungen Benebenst Anderen Poetischen neuen Erfindungen" und ist Pz. Ferdinand Albrecht (*1636; FG 842. 1673) dediziert.

2 Vgl. *Schottelius: Fruchtbringender Lustgarte (1647)*, 92: „(Die Music war so wol oben in dem zubereiteten Himmel/ als hinter und im Theatro/ von allerhand Musicalischen Jnstrumenten. Die Melodeyen der folgenden Geistlichen Lieder/ welche hierzu eine HochFürstliche Person selbst/ sehr lieblich/ gesezet/ haben dismahl nicht künnen hierbey getrükket werden: Es werden aber dieselbe/ nebenst anderer/ derogleichen rühmlichen Kunst-Arbeit/ absonderlich in kurzen heraus gegeben werden.)"
3 Vgl. a. a. O., 93: „Der Schauplaz/ so im Fürstlichen Gemache angerichtet/ war anfangs ganz dunkel die Nacht gleichsam vorstellend: daß also nichts/ als die weitblickenden Sternen und Mondschein zu sehen waren: und wurde anfangs angehöret Folgendes:
   JZund weil ein jeder släft/ und der Sternlein Schaar aufblikt/
   Die swarzbraune Nacht hereylt/ stille Ruh der Welt zuschikt;
   Trit heran die Gnadenzeit die sich wunderbar eintringt: [...]"
4 Vgl. a. a. O., 93: „Hierauf trat der König David/ als Prophetischer Vorreder aus dem Tunkelen hervor/ mit folgender Rede." Nach dieser Rede S. 97: „(Hierauf ward als von fern und in stiller Nacht eine Lauten-Music angehört/ nach dero Endung aus dem annoch dunkelem Himmel gesungen ward Folgendes.
   1.
   WEil sich nun die Ewigkeit
   Wil umsliessen in die Zeit;
   Und das Gnadenjahr ohn End/
   Numehr sich zu uns gewendet: [...]"
5 Nach einer Rede Josephs heißt es a. a. O., 101: „(Joseph leget sich zur Ruhe/ da dan eine hellglenzende Wolke herunter komt/ und der Engel Gabriel daraus sich hervor tuht und also im slafe den Joseph anredet.)" Es folgt die Rede Gabriels, gehalten von Pz. Anton Ulrich, a. a. O., 102 f. Nach Josephs Antwort schließen sich im Spiel Szenen zwischen diesem und Maria an. Gabriel kommt noch mehrfach zu Wort.
6 Das Echo mit Lobpreisungen Gottes entspricht im Schauspiel wohl nicht den Wiederholungen im Gesang der himmlischen Heerscharen (a. a. O., 116 f.), da sie sich nicht auf den Heiland, sondern auf den Herrn „Zebaoht" beziehen. Nach dem Libretto folgen auf S. 127 f. nur „Endschallende Reime (So bey einer gehaltenen Theatralischen Music/ von den heiligen Engelen gesungen. Diese Theatralische neue Vorstellung von der Maria Magdalena/ hat der weitberühmte Herr Schuze zu Wolfenbüttel mit grossem Lob præsentiret" D. i. Heinrich Schütz.
7 Die kleine Rede Pz. Ferdinand Albrechts (Menalcas) eröffnet im Weihnachtsspiel einen Dialog zwischen den Hirten (a. a. O., 117–126).
8 Vgl. aber die Einschätzung, die Schottelius' Erziehung durch Theaterspiel in der Erinnerung des kapriziösen Ferdinand Albrecht (Der Wunderliche) erfuhr: „Bey seiner Erziehung/ gieng es auch offt sehr wunderlich und seltzam/ daß er sich wunderlichen Köpffen/ so Er zu Lehrmeistern bekomen/ auß kindlichem Gehohrsam unterwerffen muste/ absonderlich dem Suchenden/ welcher Jhn allerhand Lustspiele zu spielen zwang/ ehe Er kaum das ABC kunte/ und wann Er mehr Lust was Fürstliches und rechtschaffenes als solche Possen lernen/ biß endlich der Edle Erwachsene Jhn zu nützlichern Christlichern Sachen unterrichtete/ die lateinische Sprach wohl lehrete/ und in der Dichtekunst rühmlich unterwieß." [Hz. Ferdinand Albrecht I. v. Braunschweig-Wolfenbüttel-Bevern]: Wunderliche Begebnüssen und wunderlicher Zustand In dieser wunderlichen verkehrten Welt (Bevern 1678: Druckts Johann Heitmüller), S. 5. Der Erwachsene war der FG-Gesellschaftsname von Sigmund Betulius (v. Birken; FG 681. 1658; PBO 1645). S. Anm. 9.
9 Zur welf. Prinzenerziehung vgl. Jörg Jochen Müller: Fürstenerziehung im 17. Jahrhundert. Am Beispiel Herzog Anton Ulrichs von Braunschweig und Lüneburg. In: Stadt

– Schule – Universität – Buchwesen und die deutsche Literatur im 17. Jahrhundert. Hg. Albrecht Schöne. München 1976, 243–260, bes. 258f.: Schottelius' Gesuch an Hz. August, während seiner Abwesenheit Sigmund Betulius den Unterricht zu übertragen. S. HAB: Cod. Guelf 56 Extrav., Bl. 245r–247r. Beiliegend Entwurf eines Stundenplans. Betulius reiste am 7.12.1645 von Nürnberg nach Wolfenbüttel und wurde dort am 21.12.1645 als Schottelius' Mitarbeiter bei der Erziehung der Prinzen Anton Ulrich und Ferdinand Albrecht und der zugehörigen Pagen angestellt. In undatierten Briefen an Hz. August meldete Schottelius seine herannahende juristische Promotion an der U. Helmstedt („Appropinquat solemnis Promotionis Doctorum Juris tempus in illustrissima Vestræ Serenitatis Iuliâ 22. Febr.") und empfahl Betulius als fähigen Prinzen-Informator („Betulius enim est datus sedulus et probus adolescens, et informationi erit paulatim sufficiens solus"). HAB: Cod. Guelf. 56 Extrav., Bl. 245r–247v. Vgl. 440100 K 5. Am 9.10.1646 wurde Betulius aus seinem Dienstverhältnis entlassen, womit er — wie es in seinem Zeugnis heißt — „seine Studia noch fürters zucontinuiren und dadurch seine fernere Beförderung zusuchen gemeynt". Der hzl. Leibarzt und lat. Dichter Martin Gosky krönte ihn zum Abschied noch zum Poeten. Am 19. Oktober, am Tage der Ankunft des Großen Kurfürsten Friedrich Wilhelm v. Brandenburg (FG 401), scheint er Wolfenbüttel verlassen zu haben. *Birken: Werke u. Korrespondenz* XIV (Prosapia/ Biographia. hgg. Dietrich Jöns u. Hartmut Laufhütte), 31–38; vgl. Hartmut Laufhütte: Harsdörffer als Organisator des Zusammenspiels der Künste. In: Doris Gerstl (Hg.): Georg Philipp Harsdörffer und die Künste. Nürnberg 2005, 104–126 (mit wichtigen Informationen zu Birkens Wolfenbütteler Zeit als Prinzen-Präzeptor).

451101

Georg Philipp Harsdörffer an Fürst Ludwig

Antwort auf 450919A. Beantwortet durch 451209. — Zusammen mit F. Ludwigs (Der Nährende) Brief empfing Georg Philipp Harsdörffer (FG 368. Der Spielende) am 22.10.1645 Christian Gueintz' (FG 361. Der Ordnende) *Rechtschreibung (1645)*, dazu Zeichnungen (Visierungen) seiner Mitgliedsimprese und seines Wappens, die er in der vorgeschriebenen Weise (auf Atlas) aussticken lassen werde. — Der Spielende will (privat) ein Schreiben Marco Aurelio Severinos beantworten, in dem dieses Mitglied der Accademia degli Oziosi (Neapel) eine frühere Antwort (Harsdörffers, auf den Brief 450817 II) als Replik der FG auf diesen Brief aufgefaßt hat. Der Spielende möchte in seiner Antwort an Severino um Werke der Oziosi für die FG und sich bitten. Einige eigene Schriften Severinos seien in Deutschland erschienen und in Leipzig zu bekommen, andere müßten über Venedig bezogen werden. — Vermutlich haben Exemplare des 5. Teils der *Frauenzimmer-Gesprächspiele* Harsdörffers inzwischen F. Ludwig und Diederich v. dem Werder (FG 31. Der Vielgekörnte) erreicht, ebenso werde das Gesellschaftsbuch der Accademia degli Intronati bei der FG angelangt sein. Anderenfalls könne eine Auskunft bei dem Leipziger (Kaufmann) Gottfried Stahl eingeholt werden. — Harsdörffer hat Johann Michael Moscherosch (FG 436. Der Träumende. 1645), der sich auf eine Dienstreise nach Paris begeben mußte, von der Aufnahme in die FG informiert und erwartet stündlich dessen Reaktion. Moscherosch habe die Zulassung zu der Gesellschaft schon lange gewünscht; er werde den ihm vom Nährenden erteilten Gesellschaftsnamen, das Motto

451101 Georg Philipp Harsdörffer

und die Pictura der Imprese (Gemäl) sowie die Subscriptio (Reimgesetz) annehmen. Der Spielende ist sich sicher, daß der Träumende auch einen Dankesbrief verfassen, die letzte Vision seiner *Wunderlichen und Wahrhafftigen Gesichte Philanders von Sittewalt* (Ludwig) widmen und nach gehöriger Ermahnung (durch Harsdörffer) seine Werke an den Fürsten schicken werde. — Harsdörffer empfiehlt Georg Conrad Osthof (DG, PBO), der unter dem Titel *Der Weibliche Tugend-Schatz* (feministische) Schriften von Marie Le Jars de Gournay, Lucrezia Marinella und Anna Maria van Schurman kompiliert und übersetzt habe, für die Aufnahme in die FG, damit Osthof das fertige Werk unter einem Gesellschaftsnamen veröffentlichen und der Akademie widmen kann. Zwar stehe die Entscheidung bei F. Ludwig, doch schlage er diesem den Namen *Der Schätzbare*, die Pflanze *Frauenmünze* und die Devise *Die Tugend* vor, weil zumindest in italienischen Akademien der die Kandidaten Anmeldende solcherlei Vorschlagsrecht habe. — Der Nürnberger Patrizier Friedrich Wilhelm Böheim (recte wohl Georg Friedrich Behaim) übersetze Joseph Halls geistliche Werke (vermutlich James Howells satirische und allegorische Bücher über den englischen Bürgerkrieg). Der Nürnberger Arzt Johann Helwig (PBO. Montano. 1645) verdeutschte Boethius' *De consolatione philosophiae*. Die FG habe auch andere zu vorher nie gekannter Arbeit an der deutschen Sprache ermuntert, so daß sich etliche bei den Westfälischen Friedensverhandlungen nach Anleitung von Christian Gueintz stark um die Reinheit des Deutschen bemühten. — Harsdörffer verspricht, sich nach der (erhofften) Übereinkunft zwischen Gueintz und Justus Georg Schottelius (FG 397. Der Suchende) — besonders über die wesentlichen Buchstaben und die Veränderungsmöglichkeit der Stammwörter durch Vor- und Nachsilben — zu richten, zumal Schottelius in allen anderen Dingen Gueintz folgen wolle. — Harsdörffer hofft darauf, in dem (leider nicht verläßlichen) Johann David Zunner zu Frankfurt a. M. einen Verleger für eine neue Ausgabe von Werders *Rasendem Roland* zu finden.

Q   HM Köthen: V S 545, Bl. 332r–333v [A: 333v]; eigenh., rotes Lacksiegel. — D: *Barthold*, 314–316; *KE*, 345–347; *Schäfer: Moscherosch und Harsdörffer*, S. 157 Anm. 49 u. S. 173 (Auszüge). Falsch datiert auf 1.12.1645 in *Kühlmann/ Schäfer: Oberrhein*, 124 Anm. 104. — *BN: Bürger*, 674 Nr. 34 u. 35.

A   *Dem Durchleuchtigen, Hochgebornen Fürsten und Herrn, Herrn LUDWIGEN, Fürsten zu Anhalt, Grafen zu Ascanien und Ballenstat Herrn zu Zerbst &c:* Meinem gnädigen Herrn. Cöthen. — *Postvermerk:* Franco bis Leipzig da dieser Brief bei H. Stahlen abzugeben. — *Eigenh. Empfangsvermerk von F. Ludwig:* Pres. 9. Novemb. 1645.

Des Höchstgeehrten *Nehrenden* gnädig Beliebtes vom 19ten des Herbstmonats ist dem *Spielenden* den 22ten des Weinmonats hernach eingehändiget worden: er bedanket sich so wol wegen mitkommender Beylage, des Ordnenden Rechtschreibung als des aufgerissenen GesellschaftsGemählde, und Wapen, welches mit der zeit, beschriebner massen ausgestücket[a], zu rücke kommen wird.[1]

Der *Spielende* ist gewillet an H. Severinum wiederüm zu schreiben, und zu versichern, daß der Hochlöblichen *Fruchtbringenden Gesellschaft* nicht unangenem, wann die Academici Ociosi geruhen möchten, und von ihren Büchern zu[b] übersenden; welche der Spielende auch für sich begeret hat, und H. Severinus das begeren, als ob es im Namen der *Fruchtbringenden* beschehen, aufgenommen.[2]

Seine Schriften sind zum Theil hier gedruckt, und zu Leipzig zu bekommen, theils aber werden aus Welschland über Venedig gebracht werden müssen.[3]

Jnzwischen wird sonders zweiffel der fünfte Theil der Gesprächspiele bey dem Ertzschrein, und dem *Vielgekörnten* benebens dem Gesellschaftbuch de gl'Academici Jntronati angelanget seyn; wie wol dem Spielenden noch keine Nachricht deswegen ertheilet worden:[4] Jm fall es nicht geschehen, könte bey *H. Gottfried Stahl*[5] zu Leipzig deswegen die[b] Nachfrage befohlen[c] werden.

Der Träumende ist nach Paris verschicket worden, bevor ihm die erfreuliche Zeitung von seiner einnehmung in die Fruchtbringende Gesellschaft zukommen: ob er wieder zu rucke gelanget ist dem Spielenden verborgen[d]; erwartet aber deswegen alle stunde Nachrichtung, mit ankommenden Strasbürger Botten. Sonsten [332v] ist ihm wissend, daß er solche Ehrenstelle in der Fruchtbringenden Gesellschaft lang verlanget, und so wol den Name[n] als das Gemähl und beywort mit des *Nehrenden* Erklärung nicht ausschlagen, sondern sich ehest mit einem Dankbrie[f] und Zuschreibung seines letzten Traumgesichts einstellen wird. Wegen seiner Werklein sol behörige Erinnerung geschehen.[6]

Es sol auch der Spielende dem Höchstgeehrten Nehrenden nicht verhalten, das H. Georg Conrad Osthofen,[7] ein gelehrter, und in fremden Sprachen wolerfahrner Mann, zu Z[ell] ein Werklein unterhanden, betitelt: *Der Weibliche Tugend-Schatz*, in welchem er der Maria de Gornac,[8] Lucrezia Marinella,[9] Anna Römers[10], Anna Maria Schurmans[11] &c. und also der Frantzösin, Jtalianerin und Niederländerin Schriften mit grossem Fleiß zusammengezogen[e] druckfertig hat, und ist gewillet solche seine Arbeit der Hochlöblichen Fruchtbringend[en] Gesellschafft zuzuschreiben; erwünschet aber zuvor die Gnade unter dieselbe aufgenommen zu werden, damit er sich, zu ansehen und behuf seines Werkleins, des Gesellschaftnam[ens] bedienen könte. Die verordnung stehet bey dem *Nehrenden*, solte aber in H. Osthofens unterthäniges bitten gnädigst gewillig[t] werden, beschiht von dem *Spielenden* folgender vorschlag: d[aß] er könte heissen der *Schetzbare*, und zu seiner Frucht haben *Frauenmüntz*, mit dem beywort, *die Tugend*. Ob man nun wol des *Spielenden* Einrahten zu dergleichen nicht von nöhten, so steht er doch in dem Wahn, daß in diesem, wie auch ande[rn] Stücken, den Jtaliänischen Academien nachgeahmet werde, in welchen die Namen von dem jedesmals erstlich vorgeschlagen [333r] werden, der einen neuen Gesellschafter anmeldet: die angenemhaltung und bestattigung, oder auch die aberkantniß bestehet bey den Herren Oberen.

Es werden auch H. Josephs Hale Geistliche werklein, aus dem Englischen übersetzet, durch Friederich Wilhelm Böheim,[12] einen von denen Adelichen Geschlechten dieser Stadt. Ein anderer Joh. Helwig Doctor der Artzney, hat den Böethium gedolmetschet.[13] Etliche fragen was sie doch rühmliches und nützliches unternemen sollen; dergestalt, daß die Gesellschaft der Fruchtbringenden, viel aufmuntert zu der Teutschen Spracharbeit, und zu unserer zeit dieser sache mehr als niemals getrieben wird. Zu Münster und Ossnabruck haben etliche[14] angefangen Rein Deutsch und fast nach[f] des Ordnenden Anweisung zu schreiben, daraus

451101 Georg Philipp Harsdörffer

zu schliessen, was von fernerer Hochbringung unserer Sprache zu hoffen seyn möchte.

Was zwischen dem *Ordnenden* und *Suchenden*[15] verglichen werden wird, dem sol von dem Spielend*en* schuldige folge geleistet werd*en*. Der grösste Streit wird seyn, wegen der Stammwörter wesentlich*en* Buchstaben, ob solche durch die vor- oder nachsylben können vermindert, oder verändert werd*en*? Jn allen anderen Stücken wird der Suchende gerne weichen. Hiermit verbleibet, nechst empfehlung Göttliches Gnadenschutzes

Des Höchstgeehrten *Nehrenden* in underthänigkeit dienstergebener Knecht
Der Spielende.

N. S.

[J]ch hoffe zu des *Vielgekörnten* [R]asenden Roland einen Verleger [z]ufinden; Johann David Zunnern,[g] zu Frankfurt,[16] wann er nur [n]icht wendig gemacht wird; wie [m]ehr mals geschehen. Berichte hiervon [m]it nechstem, wann ich[h] von des *Vielgekörnten* wiederkunft nachricht [e]rlang*en* werde: Bitte deswegen, förderlichste Antwort.
Nürnberg den 1. Wintermonats 1645.

T *Text in eckigen [Klammern] ist im Falz des Bandes verborgen.* — **a** *Lies:* ausgestickt — **b** *Eingefügt.* — **c** *Eingefügt für* <gehalten> — **d** *Eingefügt für* <nicht wissend> — **e** *Folgt* <und> — **f** *Aus nach fast umgestellt.* — **g** *Folgt 1 gestrichenes unleserliches Wort.* — **h** *Folgt* <nur>

K 1 S. 450919A zu Christian Gueintz (FG 361. Der Ordnende) u. seiner an Georg Philipp Harsdörffer (FG 368. Der Spielende) überschickten *Rechtschreibung (1645)*. Für das Stikken von Wappen und Impresen war Harsdörffer durch Diederich v. dem Werder (FG 31. Der Vielgekörnte) ein Posten Atlas-Stoff gesandt worden. S. 450919 u. 450921. Vgl. 450504A K 5 u. 450613. Der Leipziger Bankier Georg Winckler bestätigte in 451019 K 8 wohl die Weiterleitung dieser Sendung nach Nürnberg.
2 Zu Marco Aurelio Severino, einem neapolitan. Mediziner und Mitglied der Accademia degli Oziosi, s. 450817. Harsdörffer und Severino planten, offizielle Beziehungen zwischen der FG und den Oziosi zu knüpfen. Dies stieß seitens F. Ludwigs und einiger befragter Mitglieder der deutschen Akademie auf Bedenken (450919A), so daß Harsdörffer seinen Plan privat, jedoch mit Wissen des Fürsten, weiter verfolgte. Vgl. *Conermann: Harsdörffers Plan* u. 451217.
3 Vgl. die Liste von Werken Severinos, an denen F. Ludwig sein Interesse bekundete, 450817 V.
4 *Harsdörffer: Frauenzimmer-Gesprächspiele* V (Nürnberg: Wolfgang Endter 1645; Ndr. 1969). Harsdörffer hatte das Buch an F. Ludwig (zusammen mit dem Brief 450923C) und an D. v. dem Werder geschickt. Der Fürst bedankte sich erst in 451209. — Zu dem 1611 erschienenen Gesellschaftsbuch der Accademia degli Intronati in Siena s. 450817 K 20. Harsdörffer erkundigte sich nach dem Verbleib des GB der Intronati erneut in 451217. Vgl. 460120.
5 Zu dem Leipziger Handels- und Verbindungsmann Gottfried Stahl d. Ä. s. 430920 K 1 u. 440426 K 1.

6 F. Ludwig reagierte auf diese Nachrichten Harsdörffers über Johann Michael Moscherosch (FG 436. Der Träumende. 1645) mit der Erinnerung, dieser solle seine Werke dem Erzschrein einsenden. Vgl. 430103 II Q (Ausgaben von Moscheroschs *Wunderliche und Wahrhaffte Gesichte Philanders von Sittewalt*), ferner 460406 K 8. Zur Aufnahme Moscheroschs in die FG und die Hindernisse der diesbezüglichen Verständigung vgl. 450500 K 1. Über seinen Aufenthalt in Paris (s. ebd.) hatte Moscherosch Harsdörffer in 450818 (8.8.1645 a. St.) berichtet. Vgl. Harsdörffers Antwort 450901.

7 Georg Conrad Osthof aus Celle. Zu Harsdörffers Empfehlung Osthofs s. schon 450400 K 6. Osthof, der sich an der U. Helmstedt am 12.10.1640 (*Mat. Helmstedt*, S. 21 Nr. 29) und am 23.10.1642 an der U. Altdorf (*Mat. Altdorf*, S. 252, 8242) immatrikuliert hatte, wurde Jurist. Mitglied der Deutschgesinnten Genossenschaft (DG 8. Der Sammlende. 8.10.1644) und des PBO (Amyntas). Er war Ende 1645 oder Anfang 1646 in den PBO aufgenommen worden, wie Harsdörffer am 7.2.1646 Sigmund Betulius (v. Birken; FG 681. 1658) berichtete. S. *Birken: Werke u. Korrespondenz* IX.1, 9; vgl. 441223 K 2, 450504A K 4, 451217 u. 461104 K 2. F. Ludwig behandelte Harsdörffers Vorschlag dilatorisch. S. 451209. — Osthof kehrte Ende 1644 aus Nürnberg nach Celle zurück, von wo er Harsdörffer von dessen Aufnahme in die DG berichtete. Vgl. 441223 („der Sammlende"). *Dissel*, 59; *Zesen SW* XI, 452. Der gerade aus seinem Hilfslehreramt in Wolfenbüttel ausgeschiedene Sigmund Betulius (v. Birken) besuchte ihn Ende Oktober 1646 auf seiner Reise zu Johann Rist (FG 467. 1647) nach Wedel (Holstein) und freundete sich mit ihm an. Birken notierte in *Werke u. Korrespondenz* XIV. Prosapia/ Biographia. Hg. Dietrich Jöns/ Hartmut Laufhütte, 39: „[…] sensi amicitiam Georgii Conradi Osthofen, quem nuper Sodalitium nostrum, me auspice, invento AMYNTAE vocabulo, quod prae ceteris ipsi arriserat, numero Pastorum suorum adscribserat." Über die zwischen Osthof, Rist, Birken und Harsdörffer gewechselten Ehrengedichte s. *Jürgensen: Repertorium*, 181f., darunter Rists nachstehend aufgeführtes Poem. Jürgensen kennt außer einem Brief O.s an Harsdörffer (31.1.1648) und seinen Gelegenheitsversen auf Zesen, Harsdörffer und Birken nur zwei Lobgedichte für ihn. Sie stammen von Betulius und Rist. Das Gedicht Rists führt auf die Spur des Werks, das Harsdörffer veranlaßt haben dürfte, Osthof F. Ludwig auch zur Aufnahme in die FG zu empfehlen: „An Herren Georg Kuhnraht Osthofen/ der Rechte Gewürdigten/ Als Er sein neü geschriebenes Buch von der herrligkeit und Fürtrefflligkeit des weiblichen Geschlechtes herauß zu geben bedacht war." In Johann Rist: Neuer Teutscher Parnass. Nachdr. der Ausg. Lüneburg: Gebr. Stern 1652, Hildesheim usw. 1978, 709f. Osthofs Werk ist wohl nie erschienen. Es handelt sich um eine Übersetzung aus dem Nl.: Ioh. van Bevervviick Van de wtnementheyt des vrouweliken geslachts. Verçiert met historyen, ende kopere platen; als oock Latijnsche, ende Nederlantsche verssen van Mr. Corn[elius]. Bo[e]y (Dordrecht: Jasper Gorisszoon 1642, Druck. Hendrick Esch), 2. verm. Ausgabe. SB Berlin — PK. S. 451209 K 4. Auf diese Vorlage wies Osthof Johann Rist hin: Der Adeliche Hausvatter/ Vor vielen Jahren/ von dem hochgelarten Jtaliäner Torquato Tasso in welscher Sprache beschrieben/ Hernach auß derselben/ durch J. Baudoin in die Französische übergesetzet (Lüneburg: Johann u. Heinrich Stern 1650), 117f.: „Jch wil hie nicht sagen/ wie die Schönheit der Weiber von so grosser und unglaublicher Krafft ist/ daß Sie die Augen und Hertzen der Männer vielmahls augenblicklich zu sich ziehet […]. Ein mehreres hievon ist in des hochgelehrten Herren Johan von Beverwik gahr schönem und geschichtreichem Buche/ welches Er **van de Uitnementheit des vrouweliken Geschlachtes** hat benamset/ zu finden/ welches Buch/ daß es Seiner Würdigkeit halber/ in dem es von der übertrefflligkeit des Weiblichen Geschlechtes so herlich/ zierlich und außführlich handelt/ daß seines gleichen schwehrlich zu finden/ entweder in unsere Hochteütsche Sprache solte übergesetzet/ oder auch ein anderes auff eben diesen schlag

von der Weiber Vortreffligkeit heraus gegeben werden/ Mir schon längst von Meinem wehrten und gelehrten Freunde Herren Konrad Osthofen guhte Hoffnung ist gemachet worden." Vgl. zu dieser unveröff. Übersetzung und dem Original 451209 K 4.

8 Marie Le Jars de Gournay (1565–1645), Philosophin, Feministin, Freundin des Michel de Montaigne und Herausgeberin seiner *Essais*, Übersetzerin, Dichterin und Verfasserin eines Romans (*Le Proumenoir de Monsieur de Montaigne*).

9 Lucrezia Marinella (1571–1653), venezianische feministische Schriftstellerin, Autorin des „Discorso" *La nobiltà et l'eccellenza delle donne co' diffetti et mancamenti de gli uomini* und der gegenteiligen *Essortationi alle donne et a gli altri se a loro saranno a grado*; geistliche Dichterin (*Vita del serafico et glorioso San Francesco; La vita di Maria vergine imperatrice dell'universo: Rime sacre; Vite de' dodici heroi di Christo, et Quatro Evangelisti* u. a.), Heldenepikerin (*L'Enrico ovvero Bisanzio acquistato*) und Verfasserin eines Schäferromans (*L'Arcadia felice*).

10 Anna Roemers Visscher (1583–1651), niederländ. Dichterin, Malerin und Glasgraviererin, Herausgeberin von Roemer Visschers *Zinn-poppen Alle verciert met rijmen, en sommige met proze* (1620); Übersetzerin von Georgette de Montenay: *Honderd Christelijke Zinnebeelden* (Hs. hg. 1854). Biografisch Archief van de Benelux I 704, 312–330; 705, 66–68; II, 276, 363; J. G. Frederiks en F. Jos. van den Branden: Biographisch woordenboek der Noord- en Zuidnederlandsche letterkunde. Amsterdam 1888–1891 (dig.).

11 Anna Maria van Schurman (auch: v. Schürmann), niederländ.-dt. Gelehrte, 1607–1678, auch Künstlerin, Labadistin. *ADB* 33, 90–94; *Biographisch-Bibliographisches Kirchenlexikon* IX, 1139–1141; Michael Spang: Wenn sie ein Mann wäre. Leben und Werk der Anna Maria van Schurmann. Darmstadt 2009; Pieta van Beek: The first female university student: A. M. van Schurman. Utrecht 2010.

12 Friedrich Wilhelm Böheim, d. i. F. W. Behaim (v. Schwartzbach)? Wahrscheinlich aus einem der ältesten Stadtadelsgeschlechter Nürnbergs (1322 Mitglieder im Kleinen Rat), seit 1681 Reichsfrh.-Stand. Genealogisches Handbuch des in Bayern immatrikulierten Adels XXII (1998), 69. Ein Friedrich Wilhelm B. wird nicht erwähnt bei Johann Gottfried Biedermann: Geschlechtsregister des Hochadelichen Patriciats zu Nürnberg. Bayreuth 1748, Ndr. Neustadt a. d. Aisch 1988. Auch wird er nicht unter den Mitgliedern der FG, DG, PBO und ESO genannt. Eine Übersetzung erbaulicher Werke des engl. Bf.s Joseph Hall (1574–1656) ist zweifelhaft. Sind Harsdörffers Namensangaben falsch? Als Gelehrten erwähnt Biedermann, a. a. O., Tab. X Georg Friedrich Behaim v. Schwarzbach (Nürnberg. 5. 3. 1616 – 4. 12. 1681), vgl. *DBA* I, 74, 339–341; *Will* I, 88 f. u. V, 78; *Jürgensen: Repertorium*, 107 u. ö. Nach *Jöcher* I, 912 f. studierte er in Altdorf, reiste nach Holland u. England, wo er zwei Jahre weilte. Harsdörffer könnte den Namen James Howells (1594–1666) wegen der ungewohnten, ähnlich klingenden Aussprache auf den bekannten Bf. Joseph Hall und damit auf vermutete erbauliche Werke bezogen haben. Jacobi Howels, Englischen Geschichtschreibers/ Historische und Politische Discoursen über den unlängst entstandenen innerlichen Krieg in denen Königreichen Engelland/ Schottland und Jrrland/ mit Anzeigung dessen Ursachen/ und alles daher entstandenen verderblichen Unheils. Nechst Beyfügung des damaligen Parlaments Declaration, sowol der wider den König geführten Beschuldigungen/ als auch der Ursachen/ um welcher willen es alle fernere Handlung mit dem König verboten. Endlich ist Engellands Magna Charta mit dessen Notis zu mehrer Erläuterung/ samt einem Teutschen und lateinischen Register/ mit angehängt worden. Gedruckt im Jahr/ 1665; HAB: QuN 1022 (1). Es handelt sich um eine Sammlung verschiedener Arbeiten Howells. Dessen *Familiar Letters* hatte Behaim bald nach dem Erscheinen des ersten Bands (1645) zu übersetzen begonnen. Erst allmählich wird er die Übertragung fortgeführt haben, vielleicht unter Verwendung der Folgebände.

Vgl. Epistolæ Ho-Elianæ ... Familiar Letters domestic and forren. Divided into six sections ... partly historicall, politicall, philosophicall, upon emergent occasions (London: H. Moseley 1645). In der nichtsignierten Vorrede der Ausgabe *Historische und Politische Discoursen*, „An den Geschichtliebenden Leser", heißt es nämlich: „Also sind auch diese Discours, von dem Autore, nach Beschaffenheit der dazumal nach und nach sich ereigneten Umstände/ aller sowol auf des Königs als des Parlaments Seiten geführten Actionen/ zu unterschiedlichen Zeiten/ auch in unterschiedlicher Form/ beschrieben/ und wegen der Gefahr/ welche derselben warhaffter Jnhalt auf sich gehabt/ bis auf diese Zeit verborgen geblieben/ und sich in offentlichen Druck nicht sehen lassen dürffen." Das Buch Behaims enthält S. 1–184 „Unterredung/ zwischen einem Landsmann/ und einem Fremdling; betreffend den zerrütteten Zustand in Engelland/ und wem die Ursach desselben zuzuschreiben." — S. 185–222 „Apologia Fabulosa, oder Eigentliche Vorstellung der Ursachen/ welche Engelland in Aufruhr gebracht; in Geheimen Abbildungen/ nemlich: I. Der grossen Conjunction oder Zusammfügung der Sterne. II. Des grossen rahts der Vögel. III. Der Zusammsetzung der Blumen. IV. Der Versammlung der Baumeister und Werkleut. V. Des Aufstands der Winde." — S. 223–264 „Mercurius Hibernicus, oder Gründliche Anzeig der Ursachen/ welche das Königreich Jrrland in dem jüngst-entstandenen/ grausamen Krieg gesetzt/ und alles daher entstandene Unheil erreget haben. Zu Vertheidigung der Königlichen Majestät/ welcher derselben Ursprung will beygemessen werden." — S. 265–302 „Das Königliche Schwerd oder/ Ein Discours von der Militia und Kriegs-Macht des Königreichs Engelland/ daß solche niemand/ dann dem König oder Landsfürsten zusteht." — S. 303–368 „Ein Jtaliänisches Fernglas/ durch welches Groß-Britannien ohne Vergrösserung seine gegenwärtige Gefahr sehen; auch dessen künftigen Untergang/ wofern nicht zeitlich vorgebawet wird/ vorsehen kann." — S. 369–414 „Nachwandlung durch die meinste Länder der Christenheit/ in einer Nacht/ vermittelst starker Einbildung/ vollbracht: Welche sich in den Nord-Westischen Jnsulen endet/ und anzeiget die leidige Zerrüttung/ in welche dieselbe zur selben Zeit eingeflochten." — S. 415–446 „Ein Blick in die Jnsul Wight; wie es mit Seiner Majestät Handlung daselbst dahergangen." — S. 447–465 „Rahtschlag eines vornehmen Staatisten in Florentz an einen seiner vertrauten Correspondenten in Engelland/ durch Schreiben wolmeinend eröffnet; wie Engelland/ vermittelst Widereinführung des Königs/ in vorigen Wolstand zu setzen." Inc: „Hochgeehrter/ werther Patron. Es ist eine nicht geringe Schmälerung meiner vorigen Glückseeligkeit/ daß ich innerhalb zweyer Monaten keinen Befehl von ihme empfangen/ welches verursachet/ daß ich die Beysorg trage/ es möchte ihm ein Unglücksfall bey diesem zerrütteten Wesen troffen haben; [...]". — S. 466–523 „Declaratio Senatus Populiq; Regni, in Parlamento Anglicano congregati ... 11. Feb.r. 1648". — S. 524 Kurze lat. Zurückweisung, o. D. „CAROLUS I. Magnae Brit. Franc. & Hib. Rex in Apophthegmat." — S. 525–641 Magna Charta. — S. 642 ff. Dt. u. lat. Register. — Einige der hier genannten Themen hatte Howell auch in anderen Publikationen behandelt, bes. in der allegorischen Satire: Δενδρολογια Dodona's Grove, or the vocall forrest (London: H. Moseley 1640), mit dem Anhang: or The Great Conjunction or Parliament of Stars; Ornilogia, or The Great Consult of Birds; Anthologia, or Parliament of Flowers; The Assembly of Architects; The Insurrection of the Winds. Vgl. auch Angliae suspiria et lachrymae ob horrendos hosce tumultus et bellum plusquam civile. Londoni 1646; SLUB Dresden: Hist. brit. B 995. Hinter das HAB-Exemplar von Behaims Übersetzung gebunden ist ein Werk wohl des Verlags, das auch Behaims Arbeit als Nürnberger Veröffentlichung enthüllt: NEU Politischer Tugendt-Spiegel DER Hof-bedienten/ Worinnen zusehen Wie sich ein Hofmeister u. Hofmeisterin Pfleger und Castner Secretarius ... gegen jhre Principalen/ Verhalten sollen. Gegeben/ durch den WOLMEJNENDEN. Nürnberg Drucks und Verlags/ Christoff

Lochnern/ 1665. Das Pseudonym ist kein deutscher Gesellschaftsname. Vgl. auch Bohemus in 450726 K. Zu Behaims Empfehlung s. schon 450400 K 6.

13 Johann Helwig (1609–1674) verdeutschte Anicius Manitius Severinus Boethius: De consolatione philosophiae: SEVERINI BOETHII Christlich vernünftiges Bedenken/ Wie man sich bey vordringendem Gewalt und Wohlergehen der Gottlosen/ auch unrechtmässigem Leiden und Ubelgehen der Frommen zu trösten habe/ Jn fünf Bucher verfasset/ Dem Liebhaber der Teutschen Sprache zu Nutzen aus dem Latein übergesetzt; benebenst richtiger Beschreibung des Boethii Lebenslaufes (Nürnberg: Johann Tauber 1660: Christoff Gerhard), Übersetzer zeichnet „J. H. Dr.", HAB: Lh 114. — Nach *Jürgensen: Repertorium*, 145–156 stud. Helwig in Altdorf (imm. 1627) und 2 Jahre in Montpellier und Padua. Jürgensen erwähnt wohl nach seiner Vita (s. u.) auch Straßburg als Studienort, jedoch nennen die *Alten Matrikeln der Universität Strassburg 1621 bis 1793. Bearb. v. Gustav Knodt* (Straßburg 1897) II, 230 am 9.1.1632 als Studenten der Medizin nur „Johann-Helwig Sinolt genandt Schütz. Giessensis" und am 13.3.1632 „Georgius Christophorus Volcamer, Patric. Norimb.", wohl ein Verwandter Johann Georg Volckamers, der wie unser Johann Helwig später Mitglied im Nürnberger Collegium medicum und Mitschäfer (s. 450817 K II 3) im PBO wurde: Montano (1645) bzw. Helianthus (1645). *Herdegen*, 242–245 bzw. 269–273. Nach der *Vita Hellwigiana* reiste H. über Tübingen, Straßburg (1 Semester), Basel, Genf, Lyon nach Montpellier (2 Jahre, bis 1633) und Marseille, von wo er in Gesellschaft Athanasius Kirchers nach Genua segelte. Über Piacenza, Mantua und Verona gelangte er zum Studium nach Padua. Hier wurde er Bibliothekar der dt. Nation, böhm. Rat und D. med. (1634). Im September 1649 folgte H. einem Ruf als Senior Physicorum und als Leibarzt Kd. Franz Wilhelms v. Wartenberg nach Regensburg. H. galt seiner *Vita* zufolge als „Antiquitatum curiosus spectator, rariorum sedulus collector, & naturalium impiger inquisitor." Volckamer gab eine Sammlung unveröffentlichter Schriften H.s heraus: JOHANNIS HELLWIGII ... OBSERVATIONES PHYSICO-MEDICÆ, postumæ, in lucem editæ, Scholiisque adauctæ à LUCA SCHRÖCKIO (Augusta Vindelicorum: Theophilus Goebelius 1680: Koppmayer), mit H.s Vita, Bl. b v ff.; HAB: Xb 398 (dig.). Abgesehen von früher erschienenen medizin. Publikationen veröffentlichte er Gelegenheitsgedichte, jedoch auch größere literar. Arbeiten, darunter namentlich: Francesco Pona: L'Ormondo, dt.: ORMVND Das ist: Lieb- und Helden-Gedicht/ in welchem des Hoflebens Sitten/ Gefahren und seltene begebenheiten eigentlich ab- und ausgebildet werden/ verfasset von dem weitberühmten Jtaliäner Francesco Pona; und durch einen Liebhaber der Teutschen Muttersprache in das Teuts[c]he ümgesetzet (Franckfurt: Joh. David Zunner 1648), eine Hz. Anton Ulrich v. Braunschweig-Wolfenbüttel [FG 716. 1659] gewidmete Satire; HAB: 136.13 (2); Die Nymphe NORJS JN Zweyen Tagzeiten vorgestellet; DArbey mancherley schöne Gedichte/ und warhafte Geschichte/ nebenst unterschiedlichen lustigen Rätzeln/ Sinn- und Reimenbildern/ auch artigen Gebänden mitangebracht DURCH einen Mitgenossen der PegnitzSchäfer &c. (Nürnberg: Jeremia Dümler 1650), eine Prosaekloge mit vielen Beiträgen von Pegnitzschäfern, HAB: 116.3 Quod. (2). In andere Sprachakademien (FG, DG und ESO) wurde H. nicht aufgenommen. S. 451209. Zu Helwigs Empfehlung s. schon 450400 K 6.

14 Die Diplomaten des Westfälischen Friedenskongresses. Vgl. z.B. den anhalt. Gesandten Martinus Milagius (FG 315. 1637), den erzbfl. magdeburg. Legaten Curt v. Einsiedel (FG 417. 1644) und den erzbfl. magdeburg. Sekretär und Protokollanten bei Verhandlungen des Fürstenrats, Christian Werner. Werner schrieb schon auf *Gueintz: Sprachlehre (1641)* Lobgedichte. S. 410324 I u. K I und 441223 K 20. Zu Harsdörffers allegorischer Behandlung des Orthographiestreits in seinem *Nathan und Jotham* (Nürnberg 1659, Ndr. 1991), Bd. II, S. 320, Nr. 80 s. *Schäfer: Moscherosch und Harsdörffer*, 174.

15 Justus Georg Schottelius (FG 397. Der Suchende) hatte nach Harsdörffers Bericht an F. Ludwig (450817) angeboten, strittige Punkte in seiner schon damals überarbeiteten *Sprachkunst (1651)* vor deren Veröffentlichung mit Christian Gueintz oder anderen Kennern schriftlich zu beraten und sich gegebenenfalls den besseren Argumenten zu fügen.

16 *D. v. dem Werder: Rasender Roland*, zuerst in Leipzig von 1632 bis 1636 in wenigen Gesängen erschienen, fand keinen neuen Verleger, der das vermutlich ergänzte und überarbeitete Werk herausbringen wollte. Vgl. 450725 K 5.

451119

Matthäus Merian d. Ä. an Peter Knaudt

Matthäus Merian d. Ä. bedankt sich für die beiden (verschollenen) Schreiben Peter Knaudts vom 22. u. 30.10., die ihn samt dem Probe-Titelblattdruck (zum *GB 1646*) am 6.11. erreicht haben. Die fehlenden Ziffern in den Impresen habe er einfügen lassen und angeordnet, daß in Zukunft die Stiche nach den Visierungen seitengetreu angefertigt werden. Zwar können Buchstaben und Fehler in den Kupferplatten verändert und ausgeschabt werden, dies jedoch nur mit viel Mühe. Die ersten 30 Impresen sind aber bereits gedruckt und können nicht mehr verändert werden. Wenn es in den übrigen (älteren) Kupferplatten (des *GB 1629/30*) Schreibfehler gibt, bittet Merian um rasche Mitteilung, um sie noch korrigieren zu können. Die 200 neuen Impresenstiche jedoch sollen mit besonderer Sorgfalt nach den Visierungen und den Überschriften darin vollendet werden. Merian werde darüber wachen, daß alle rechtzeitig fertig werden. — Den ersten Titelbogen wird Merian nur schwarz mit einem verkleinerten Stich (des FG-Sinnbilds) der Kokospalme gestalten und die angemerkten Fehler verbessern lassen. Er hofft, den Text bis zum 25. Dezember abzuschließen, für die Kupfer wird er jedoch mehr Zeit benötigen, wahrscheinlich noch bis zum nächsten Februar. — Die Anzahl der aus Köthen übersendeten Impresen-Sinnsprüche und -Gemälde beträgt 418. Da jeweils 100 ein eigenes Titelblatt erhalten, stellt Merian die Frage, ob die letzten 18 an das vierte Hundert angefügt oder für das fünfte Hundert aufgespart werden sollen. Da ihm nur 400 Visierungen vorliegen, vermutet er, daß die 18 auf die Warteliste gesetzt werden. — Hz. August d. J. v. Braunschweig-Wolfenbüttel (FG 227) ließ Merian wissen, daß ihm nach Fertigstellung des Werks umgehend 48 Exemplare auf seine Kosten nach Wolfenbüttel gesandt werden sollen. Ob die 48 nun von der Gesamtauflage von 300 abgezogen werden sollen, oder wie sonst hier zu verfahren sei, möchte Merian gerne wissen. — Merian sagt die schnelle Zusendung der 48 nach Vollendung des Werks zu und bittet um Benachrichtigung, wohin die übrigen geschafft werden sollen. — Aus Augsburg wurde Merian berichtet, daß in diesem Jahr die Yucca-Pflanze nicht geblüht habe, jedoch wollen die dortigen Bekannten zusehen, ihm von der Zwiebel eine Zeichnung anfertigen zu lassen. Es ist gut, daß Knaudt aus Berlin eine gute Zeichnung erwarte, um deren Zusendung Merian bittet. — Im Postskriptum berichtet Merian, daß ihm soeben die beiliegende Darstellung der Pflanze aus Augsburg zugeschickt worden sei. Ob es sich dabei um die richtige Yucca handelt, entzieht sich Merians Kenntnis. Es sei aber sein eigener Kupferstich der Yucca, den er nach einer aus Basel kommenden Visierung vor einem Jahr machen ließ. Knaudt könne den Abdruck behalten. Falls der Stich die Yucca richtig abbildet, bedürfe man der Zeichnung aus Berlin nicht mehr.

451119 Matthäus Merian d. Ä.

Q HM Köthen: V S 546, Bl. 15rv [A: 15v]; eigenh.; rotes Lacksiegel. — *D: Bircher: Merian*, 710f.; *Wüthrich: Merian Briefe*, 98f. u. 102f. — *BN: Bürger*, 987 Nr. 14.

A Tt. Dem Ehrnvesten vnd GroßAchtparen Herrn Petter Knaudt Fürst. Anhaltischen Cammermeistern *etc.* zu Cöthen, meinem großgvnstigen hochgeehrten herrn *etc.* Cöthen. herrn Georg Wincklern[1] Recommendirt zu Leipzig.

Ehrnvester GroßAchtparer vnd wohlfürnehmer Jnsonders Großg. Hochge[Ehrter Herr *etc.*][a]

Dem sein mein willige Dienste vnd was vermag Jederzeit Anvor[2], und brichte *[sic]* das mir des hern geliebte schreiben vom 22. vnd[b] 30. 8ctob. *[sic]* 6. diß sampt dem getrukten Tittul wohl worden vnd ablesendt verstanden,

Die Ziffern in die kupfer wo sie gemangelt habe ich ersetzen laßen, wie auch verordnet das forthin, die vbrigen gemälde alle nach den abrißen vnverendert ins kupfer gebracht werden sollen.[3]

Die Buchstaben und **Errata** so in den kupfern sich finden, können zwar verendert vnd außgekratzt werden, aber mit viel mühe, dise erste biß auff N°. 30 sein albreit getrukt vnd nun nicht mehr zu verendern, was aber in den vbrigen alten kupfern an fehlern in der schrifft sich fündet, bitte ich mir solches mit ehestem zu[c] brichten, so will ich sie laßen verbessern. Die 200 Neuwe aber sollen[d] mit sonderm fleiß nach den Abrißen vnd selbiger ober Schrifften gemacht werden[4], gestalt dan ich gar fleißig dorüber halte, das alle zu rechter Zeit mögen wohl verfertigt werden.

Den 1. **Tittul** bogen[e] will ich begerter maßen mit Schwartz allein, und mit dem veriüngten Jndianischen Nußbaum vornen darauff verfertigen[f] auch die angedeuteten fehler verbessern laßen, biß Christtag verhoffe Jch werde der gantze druckh, so viel die Schrifft betrifft, fertig se[in][g], die kupfer zu trucken aber will ein mehrer Zeit haben, und sich etwan biß in den nechstkünfftigen **Hornung** erstrecken mögen.

Die Anzahl der worter vnd gemählde in deme Zu Cöthen getrucken *[sic]* **exemplar** erstreckt sich auff 418[5] ist jetz die frag, weilen jedes 100 absonderlich unter[h] sonderem **Tittul** kompt, ob die vbrigen 18 stuckh hinten an das vierte hundert sollen angehengt, oder[i] ob selbige 18 stuckh sollen zu dem fünfften 100[j] verspart werden. Jch finde gleich wohl in den Abrißen nur 400 stuckh,[6] vermuthe die 18 mußen anstehen bleiben.

Es[k] haben Jhr Fürst. Gnad. herr Augustus der Elter[7] Hertzog zu Brunschweig und Lüneburg an mich schreiben laßen, und begehren, so baldt dises werkh vollendet das Jch Jhr. F. G. auff dero vnkosten also baldig 48 **exemplaria**[8] nacher Wolffenbüttel senden solle. ob nun dise 48 **exemplaria** an denen 300 verglichen, abgehen solle, oder wie es damit beschaffen, möchte ich gern bricht haben,

Alsdan will ich so baldt ich gelegenheit haben werdt, und das werkh vollendet solche senden, vnd sonsten wo ich die vbrigen hin verschaffen solle, brichts erwarten,

Von Augspurg habe ich Bricht das diß Jahr das Gewechse Giuoca nicht gebluet habe, sie wollen mir aber sehen, ein abriß von dem zwiebel⁹ zu machen laßen. Darumb ist mir sehr lieb das mein gg. herr ein gutten Abriß von Berlin bekommen wirt, dessen Jch zu seiner zeit gewertig bin, damit alles wol von statten gehen müge. Hiemit dem Allmechtigen woh[l] befohlen.

F[ran]kfurt den 19. 9bris 1645.

    Des herrn Dinstwilligster
    Mattheus Merian.

P. S. Beikomendes gewechße ist mir in diser stundt auß Augspurg zu komen, ob dises nun die Rechte Giuoca¹⁰ seie davon der herr geschriben weiß ich nicht. Dan dises kupfer ist mein und habe es vorm Jahr Machen laßen, von einem Abriß so mir auß Basel zu komen ist, vnd kan der herr solchen truckh nur behalten. wan es das Rechte ist, so darff man dessen von Berlin nicht.

T **a** *Textverluste am lädierten Seitenrand. Konjektur in eckigen Klammern.* — **b** *vnd 30 eingefügt.* — **c** *Eingefügt.* — **d** *Eingefügt für* <solchen> — **e** *Folgt gestrichener Buchstabe.* — **f** *Folgt* <laßen> — **g** *Unleserlich aufgrund des durchschlagenden Siegels der rückseitigen Anschrift.* — **h** *Irrtümlich im Zeilenwechsel geschrieben* unter-sonderm — **i** *Folgt überflüssiges* s *vielleicht für* selbige *oder* sollen — **j** *Folgt überflüssiges* sollen — **k** *Am Rand eine senkrechte Linie bis* zwiebel zu machen laßen.

K **1** Der Leipziger Handelsherr Georg Winckler, der die Post nach Köthen weiterleitete. S. 451019 K 0. Zum Zahlungsverkehr das *GB 1646* betreffend s. auch 450127 K 1.
   2 Bevor, vorab. S. 450417 K 1.
   3 Die Mitgliedsnummern in jeder Imprese, die die Reihenfolge der Aufnahme in die FG bezeichnen und somit die Anordnung dieser Sinnbilder im *GB 1646*; vgl. Anm. 4. F. Ludwig hatte verlangt, daß die Visierungen der Impresen auf der Kupferplatte seitenverkehrt gestochen werden, um die Abzüge seitengetreu zu erhalten. S. 450930.
   4 Die Kupferstiche der Impresen enthalten oben das Wort und unten die Mitgliedsnummer und den Gesellschaftsnamen des jeweiligen Mitglieds. Sie verstießen in den ersten 200 Impresen, deren Kupfer vom *GB 1629/30* übernommen werden konnten, aber auch in den letzten (neu angefertigten) 200 auch noch im *GB 1646* gelegentlich gegen den erreichten Rechtschreibstandard, etwa im V- statt korrektem U-Anlaut. Vgl. etwa FG 6, 75, 113, 212, 236, 239, 317 u. ö. Unter die Impresenstiche wurden dann die Reimgesetze im gewöhnlichen Letternsatz gedruckt. Zur Einrichtung des *GB 1646* s. 450711 K 4 u. Abb. ebd.
   5 *GB 1641/44*. Umfaßt nur Texte: Impresenangaben (Gesellschaftsname, „Wort", Angaben zum Pflanzen-Sinnbild), Reimgesetz, Namensinitiale und Eintrittsjahr der Mitglieder Nr. 1–417. Der Text auf das 1644 aufgenommene 418. Mitglied (Zacharias Prüschenk v. Lindenhofen. Der Fördernde), das sich im gleichen Jahr ins *GB Kö.* eintrug, dürfte handschriftlich gewesen sein. *Conermann III*, 499.
   6 Das *GB 1646* endet tatsächlich mit der 400. Imprese. Die durchaus bereits in Köthen vorliegenden folgenden Visierungen für Kupferstiche (FG 401 ff.) (s. *Weimarer Impresen*,

vgl. *Conermann II*: „Die Weimarer Gemälde der Fruchtbringenden Kräuter") waren Merian nicht zugesandt worden. Zum *GB 1646* s. 440130 K 3.

7 Es handelt sich um den „Befreienden" Hz. August d. J. v. Braunschweig-Wolfenbüttel (FG 227), nicht um Hz. August d. Ä. (1568–1636).

8 S. 450331 I. Darin verpflichtet sich F. Ludwig (Der Nährende), Hz. August d. J. 48 Exemplare nach Begleichung des Verlagsbeitrags von 200 Rth. zu liefern. S. auch 450923A, 451001 u. 460206 I u. II.

9 Merian wählt hier die maskuline Form, die in der Frühen Neuzeit, neben der sich später durchsetzenden femininen, noch ganz üblich war. S. *DW* XVI, 1129f. „m. u. f. [...] das geschlecht schwankt seit alters zwischen masc. und fem., sogar beim gleichen verfasser". Zur Giuoca s. Anm. 10.

10 Zum Yucca-Kontext und Merians Versuchen, die Pflanze zu erlangen s. besonders 450800 (K 4) u. auch 450930 u. 451015.

451209

Fürst Ludwig an Georg Philipp Harsdörffer

Antwort auf 450923C und 451101. Beantwortet durch 451217. — F. Ludwig (Der Nährende) dankt Georg Philipp Harsdörffer (FG 368. Der Spielende) für die Übersendung des 5. Teils der *Frauenzimmer-Gesprächspiele*. — Er erwartet von Johann Michael Moscherosch (FG 436. Der Träumende. 1645) nach dessen Rückkunft aus Frankreich die Übersendung eigener Werke. — Über zwei von Harsdörffer vorgeschlagene Aufnahmekandidaten der FG, Georg Conrad Osthof und Johann Helwig, ist mit anderen Mitgliedern der Gesellschaft gesprochen worden. Man sei ihrer Aufnahme nicht abgeneigt, jedoch will man vor einer Entschließung erst den Druck ihrer unter dem Verfassernamen oder einem Pseudonym geschriebenen deutschen oder verdeutschten Arbeiten abwarten. Auch Harsdörffer und Moscherosch seien so zum Zweck ihrer Qualifizierung verfahren. Über die Zuteilung von Gesellschaftspflanzen, Devisen und Impresengemälden an die neuen Kandidaten könne die FG danach befinden. Die von Harsdörffer (in 451101) als Pflanze vorgeschlagene Frauenminze sei schon in der FG vertreten. — Fürst Ludwig fügt ein Schreiben Diederichs v. dem Werder (FG 31. Der Vielgekörnte) bei, in dem dieser wohl auf einen Brief Harsdörffers geantwortet habe.

Q HM Köthen: V S 545, Bl. 334rv, v leer; eigenh. Konzept. — *D: KE*, 347 gekürzt. — *BN: Bürger*, 950 Nr. 58.

A *Fehlt.*

Dem Spielenden wird hiermit auf zwey seiner schreiben kurtzlich[a] geantwortet, das erste war[b] vom drey und zwantzigsten herbstmonats[c]: Und das zweyte vom ersten Wintermonats.[1] Bey dem ersten war des Spielenden funfter theil seiner[d] gesprechspile, fur welche ubersendung der Nehrende hohen und fleißigen danck saget:[2] Und wird, so viel des zweiten schreibens inhalt ehestens[e] betrift, gerne sehen wan von dem Treumenden, nach seiner wiederkunft aus Franckreich[f] seine[g] wercklein zum ertzschreine einkommen.[3]

Die zwey vorgeschlagenene personen zu der fruchtbringenden geselschaft, als

George Conrad Osthofen,[4] und Johan Helwigen[5] betreffende, ist mit andern mitgliedern der geselschaft darvon geredet worden, die ihnen[h] zwar die einnemung gefallen[i] laßen[j], alleine dafur halten wollen, es möchten zuvor[k] vorgemeldete personen ihre deutsche oder verdeutschte buchlein nur[l] laßen in den Druck kommen[m], es were unter ihren eigenen, oder andern erfundenen und verwechselten Nahmen, und[n] sich dadurch, zu[a] der geselschaft desto geschickter machen, inmaßen vom Spielenden und Treumenden auch erstlich geschehen, so wurde man sich dan ihrer einnemung wegen desto fuglicher mit alle[r] zubehörung der geselschaft[a] Nahmen, wörter und gemählde erkleren können. Die Frauenmuntze ist albereit in der geselschaft;[6] es sollen sich aber noch wol gewächse oder kreuter, die zu[o] beiden bequem seind finden.

Der Vielgekornete[7] der[p] in einer ziemlichen weiten reise begriffen, wird dem Spielenden beygefugt[8] auch wieder geantwortet haben, Es[q] verbleibet

des Spielenden gantzwilliger

Cöthen den 9.[r] Christmonats 1645.

T **a** *Eingefügt.* — **b** *Eingefügt über* <zwar> — **c** *Folgt* <darbey das funfte theil seiner gesprächspiele, welches der Nehrende mit dancknemigem gefallen empfangen> — **d** *Eingefügt für* <der> — **e** *Eingefügt. Unsichere Lesung.* — **f** *Folgt* <etwas> — **g** *seine wercklein eingefügt.* — **h** *Eingefügt für* <sich> *Lies:* sich — **i** *Eingefügt. Davor* <noch> — **j** *Folgt* <zu wieder sein> — **k** *Eingefügt für* <nur> — **l** *Eingefügt für* <nur> — **m** *Gebessert aus* gekommen — **n** *Eingefügt für* <so wurden und [?]> — **o** *Eingefügt für* <hierzu> *Lesung* beiden *unsicher (vielleicht auch* jedem*)* — **p** *Bis* begriffen, *eingefügt.* — **q** *Eingefügt für* <worbey> — **r** *Gebessert aus* 7 [?]

K 1 Vgl. die Schreiben Georg Philipp Harsdörffers (FG 368. Der Spielende) an F. Ludwig (Der Nährende): 450923C u. 451101.

2 Mit 450923C hatte Harsdörffer den 5. Teil seiner *Frauenzimmer-Gesprächspiele* (1645, Ndr. 1969) zugesandt.

3 Harsdörffer, der mit Johann Michael Moscherosch (FG 436. Der Träumende. 1645) auch während dessen Frankreichreise in brieflichem Kontakt stand, hatte davon und über die Reaktion des Träumenden auf seine Aufnahme in die FG F. Ludwig in 451101 berichtet. F. Ludwig hatte mehrmals um die Einschickung einer von Moscherosch autorisierten Ausgabe seiner *Gesichte Philanders von Sittewald* bzw. seiner Werke gebeten. S. 450919A.

4 Georg Conrad Osthof (DG 8; PBO Amyntas) aus Celle, fand keine Aufnahme in der FG. Vgl. 451101 K 7. Er übersetzte auch nach Hinweis von *Goedeke*, 121 ein Werk von Johan van Beverwijk (1594–1647), vgl. *NNBW* I, 327–332. Das Buch war nach *Graesse* zuerst 1636 lat. erschienen: De excellentia foeminei sexus. Dordr. Es handle sich um eine „apologie du sexe féminin, écrite en faveur de madem. Schurmann" (Anna Maria v. Schurman). Nl. erschien das Buch nach *Graesse* zuerst u. d. T.: Van de Uitnementheyt des Vroulyken Geslachts. Verciert met kopere platen ende versen van Mr. Corn. Boy. Dordrecht: Jasper v. Gorissz. 1639. Nur die nächste Aufl. von 1643 scheint erhalten zu sein: Joh. van Bevervviick Van de wtnementheyt des vrouwelicken geslachts. Verçiert met historyen, ende kopere platen; als oock Latijnsche, ende Nederlantsche versssen van mr.

Corn. Bo[e]y. In diesen tweeden druck op verscheyde plaetschen vermeerdert. Te Dordrecht gedruckt by Hendrick van Esch, voor Jasper Gorissz Esch. S. 451101 K 7. Philipp v. Zesen (FG 521. 1648) übersetzte Gedichte dieses niederländ. Autors und das Werk *Schat der Gesontheydt* (1636): Schatz der Gesundheit/ das ist Kurtzer Begrif der algemeinen Bewahrkunst: Dadurch der gantze Mensch vor Ungesundheit und Seuchen kan bewahret/ und in beständiger Gesundheit erhalten werden ... durch Johan von Beverwik/ fürtreflichen Artzt der Stadt Dordrecht; Und mit allerhand Kupferstükken/ wie auch ahrtigen Reimen des Edlen Ritters Jakob Katsens/ gezieret; ... 2 Tle. (Amsterdam: Johan Bla[e]u 1671), HAB: 31 Med. 2° (dig.), erweitert in 3 Tln. Franckfurt am Mayn: Daniel Fievets sel. Wittib. *Dünnhaupt: Handbuch*, 4306f.; s. *Zesen SW* III.2 (2003); *DBA* I 6, 375.

5 Zu dem Nürnberger Arzt, Dichter, medizin. Schriftsteller und seit 1645 PBO-Mitglied Johann Helwig, gen. Montano, s. 451101 K 13. Er wurde nicht in die FG aufgenommen. Den in 451101 (K 12) auch empfohlenen Nürnberger Übersetzer Friedrich Wilhelm Böheim (wohl Georg Friedrich Behaim) erwähnt der Fürst nicht einmal.

6 Hans Albrecht v. Halck (FG 323. Der Wohlschmeckende. 1638) hatte Frauenminze [Marienblatt, Chrysanthemum majus (Desf.) Aschers.] als Gesellschaftspflanze. *Conermann III*, 369. Vgl. 460125 K 1.

7 Diederich v. dem Werder (FG 31. Der Vielgekörnte) plante eine Gesandtschaftsreise wegen einer Fürstenhochzeit, die ihn im Januar 1646 nach Königsberg i. Pr. führte. S. 450919 K 4, 450921 u. 460125 u. K I. Diese Reise erwähnt F. Ludwig wiederum in seinem Brief 460120 an Harsdörffer. Der Gesandtschaft war eine Reise an den Hof nach Kassel vorhergegangen, wohl um entsprechende Instruktionen bei der Regentin, Lgfn. Amalia Elisabeth (1602–1651), einzuholen. Vgl. 450613.

8 Der erwähnte, von Werder für Harsdörffer hinterlassene Brief ist Teil der nicht erhaltenen Korrespondenz zwischen den beiden Fruchtbringern. Erwähnungen wie die vorliegende oder die erneute Sendung dieser abschriftlichen Werder-Beilage in 460120 und die dortige Erwähnung des (von Harsdörffer an Werder geschickten) Gesellschaftsbuchs der Intronati zeugen von einem dichten Briefwechsel. Vgl. auch 450921A. Nur die Widmungen und Gedichte in Harsdörffers Werken, besonders den *Frauenzimmer-Gesprächspielen*, bleiben uns als Zeugnisse eines sicherlich umfangreichen Konvoluts von Briefen und überschickten Gedichten und Büchern erhalten.

451217

Georg Philipp Harsdörffer an Fürst Ludwig

Antwort auf 451209. Beantwortet durch 460120. — Georg Philipp Harsdörffer (FG 368. Der Spielende) schickt F. Ludwig (Der Nährende) zur Messe Visierungen seiner FG-Imprese und seines Wappens und überweist 10 Reichstaler zur Begleichung der Stickkosten an den Kaufmann Gottfried Stahl. Er habe die Stickarbeit („Stückwerk") eigentlich selbst in Nürnberg anfertigen lassen wollen, jedoch sei der von ihm ausersehene Nürnberger Sticker gestorben und er habe keinen Ersatz gefunden. — Da Harsdörffer noch keine Antwort auf seine beiden Schreiben vom 23.9. und 1.11.1645 erhalten habe, bittet er F. Ludwig um Nachricht, ob die Briefe, Bücher und das Mitgesandte (Stickkosten u. das Gesellschaftsbuch der Accademia degli Intronati) den Fürsten überhaupt erreicht haben. — Der Spielende hat privat einen Dankesbrief an Giovanni Battista Manso Marchese di Villa Lago geschrieben und einen Gruß der FG beigefügt. Nach Mitteilung von Marco Aurelio Severino treibe Manso Astronomie und habe durch seine Fernrohre mehr als

Galilei erreicht. — Harsdörffer sendet — zusätzlich zu seinen (schon in 450923C geschickten) *Frauenzimmer-Gesprächspielen* von 1645 (= 5. Teil) — die Ausgabe der von ihm in den Liedern verbesserten und um einen 3. Teil ergänzten verdeutschten *Diana* (dt. v. Hans Ludwig v. Kuefstein). Zur Beschaffung des (vermuteten) spanischen 4. Teils habe er nach Sevilla geschrieben. Da der Roman die FG nichts angehe, habe er in seiner Übersetzung die Gesellschaft auch nicht erwähnt. — Harsdörffer schickt nur den Anfang des von ihm übertragenen *Catechisme Royal* (des Philippe Fortin sieur de la Hoguette), da seine Arbeit noch im Druck sei. — Sein *Specimen Philologiae Germanicae* sei druckfertig, der 6. Teil seiner *Frauenzimmer-Gesprächspiele* (1646) in Arbeit. — An die Imprese Hans Michael Moscheroschs (FG 436. 1645) werde Diederich v. dem Werder (FG 31. Der Vielgekörnte) wohl (nach Harsdörffers Brief) erinnert haben. Moscherosch werde seine Werke übersenden. — Wie es um die Möglichkeit einer Aufnahme Georg Conrad Osthofs in die FG stehe?

Q HM Köthen: V S 545, Bl. 335rv u. 337rv [A: 337v], 335v im Falz einige verdeckte Buchstaben, 337r leer; Sig. — D: *KE*, 348f. — BN: *Bürger*, 674 Nr. 37.

A *Dem Nehrenden Der Höchlöblichen Fruchtbringenden Gesellschaft Christ*ᵃ*lichen Urheber.* Bey Herrn G. Stahl[1] zu Leipzig, abzugeben — *Eigenh. Empfangsvermerk F. Ludwigs:* Pres. 21 Jan. 1646.

Höchstgeehrter Nehrender.

Es hat der Spielende nicht unterlassen sollen, bey bevorstehender Messe, sein Gesellschaft Gemähl, und Stammwapen bey dem Ertzschrein einzuschicken, und benebens zu ausfertigung desselben *Zehen Reichsthaler*, an H. Gottfried Stahlen[b] nach Leipzig, zu übersenden:[1] dann ob er wol solches Stückwerk zu Nürnberg machen zu lassen vermeinet, ist doch die person, so er darzu gebrauchen wollen, inzwischen Todes verblichen; sich auch niemand zu solcher Langweilliger Arbeit Verstehen wollen, diesem nach geruhe der Höchstgeehrte *Nehrende* die Verfertigung dieses werks in gnaden zu befehlen.

Weilen ferners des Spielenden jüngsten beeden, vom 23ᵗᵉⁿ des Herbst- und ersten des Wintermonats noch keine antwort wiederfahren; stehet er in sorgen, daß solche, wie auch das Gesellschaftbuch de gl'Intronati, vieleicht nicht zu recht überkommen:[2] bittet deswegen umb förderlichste Nachrichtung.

Es hat auch der Spielende an Herren Marggrafen Villa ein Danckbrieflein, in Lateinischer Sprache, für sich, abgegeben, und von der Hochlöblichen Fruchtbringenden Gesellschaft einen Grus angefüget.[3] Herr **Severinus** meldet, daß dieser Herr der Sternkundigung gantz ergeben, und mit den ferngläsern weiter kommen, als **Galilæus Galilæi**.[4] Wasᶜ ferners von dar erfolgt, verbleibet dem *Nehrenden* unverhalten. [335v]

Beygeschlossne Werklein hat der Spielende als eine Sch[alt]arbeit[5], benebens den Gesprächspielen dieses Jahrs[6] [der] presse untergeben; in der Dianæ ersten Theilen alle d[ie] Gedicht, den dritten Theil aber gantz gedolmetschet, und b[e]reit ümb den Vierten nach **Sevilla** geschrieben.[7] Weil aber solche Arbeit nicht für Fruchtbringend gehalten werden möch[te,] ist der Gesellschaft darinnen nicht gedacht worden. Jn de[n] Hirten Gedichten[8] seind seine liedlein, unter den Namen Strephons eingebracht. Jn dem Catechisme Royale ist ei[n] mehrers noch nicht gedruckt: die übersetzung ist des Spielen[den],[9] welcher auch ein lateinisches werklein Specimen Philologiæ Germanicæ betitelt[10] druckfertig[d], und an den VI[ten] Theil der Gesprechspiele[11] bereit einen guten Anfang gemacht hat. Wegen des Traumenden Gesellschafts Gemähl wird der *Vielgekörnte* sonders zweiffel erinnerung gethan haben, un[d] wird er nicht unterlassen seine Schriften mit guter Gelegenh[eit] zu übersenden.[12] Hiermit verbleibt, nechst empfehlung des höchste[n] Gnadenschutz,

Des Höchstgeehrten Nehrenden
DienstVerbundener Knecht
Der Spielende
Nürnberg den 17 Christmonats 1645.

N. S.
Ob das Gelt und die Bücher richtig geliefert worden, erwartet der Spielende schleunigste Nachrichtigung, bittet auch umb Antwort, wegen H. Osthofens.[13]

T **a** *Folgt eine von F. Ludwig gestrichene Silbe Harsdörffers.* — **b** *Folgt* <zu> — **c** *Folgt* <er> — **d** *Folgt* <hat>

K 1 Der Leipziger Kaufmann Gottfried Stahl d. Ä. (s. 440426 K 1) hat eine Überweisung Georg Philipp Harsdörffers (FG 368. Der Spielende) empfangen, die F. Ludwig (Der Nährende) zum Sticken von Harsdörffers mitgesandtem Geschlechtswappen und seiner FG-Imprese verwenden möge. Vgl. 450504A K 5, 450921A u. ö.

2 F. Ludwig hatte Harsdörffers Briefe 450923C und 451101 in seinem Schreiben 451209 beantwortet, jedoch hatte der Spielende diesen Brief zur Abfassungszeit seines vorliegenden Schreibens noch nicht empfangen. Zum Gesellschaftsbuch der Accademia degli Intronati zu Siena s. 450817 K 20, außerdem 451101 u. 460120. Das Exemplar, das ein Sammelwerk von 1611 repräsentiert, scheint verlorengegangen zu sein und F. Ludwig nie erreicht zu haben.

3 Harsdörffer informierte F. Ludwig in 450817 von seiner Idee einer Vernetzung der FG mit italien. Akademien und überschickte neben einem Brief auch andere Materialien seines Korrespondenzpartners Marco Aurelio Severino. Obgleich F. Ludwig und andere FG-Mitglieder die Aufnahme von offiziellen Beziehungen durch die FG bedenklich fanden (s. 450919A), führte Harsdörffer seine Korrespondenz mit Severino weiter (vgl. 451101) und trat auch selbst den Oziosi bei. Vgl. 450817 K II 6 u. *Conermann: Harsdörffers Plan.*

4 Der Akademiegründer, Dichter, Tasso-Biograph und Principe der neapolitan. Accademia degli Oziosi, Giovanni Battista Manso Marchese di Villa Lago, plante zwar die Abfassung einer Enzyklopädie, ist aber offenbar nicht als kreativer Astronom bekannt geworden (s. Lit. in 450817 K III). Er erfuhr aber von Paolo Beni als einer der ersten von Galileo Galileis Arbeiten und bereitete dessen Erkenntnissen den Weg in Neapel. S. *DBI* (2007), 148. Harsdörffers Briefpartner Marco Aurelio Severino hatte übrigens an Harsdörffer und durch diesen an F. Ludwig Ansichten von der Mondoberfläche geschickt

(450817 III), in denen der neapolitanische Optiker und Astronom Francesco Fontana die Arbeit Galileos ergänzte.

5 „Schalten etiam est intercalare, unde Schalttag/ dies intercalaris. Schaltjahr/ annus bisextilis, & die Schaltzeit/ intercalarium." *Stieler*, 1726f. S.430920 K 6.

6 *Harsdörffer: Frauenzimmer-Gesprächspiele* V (Nürnberg: Wolfgang Endter 1645), schon mit 450923C an F. Ludwig überschickt.

7 Jorge de Montemayor, Los siete libros de la Diana (1558 oder Anfang 1559), Tl. 1, fortgesetzt von Alonso Pérez: Segunda parte de la Diana (1564); beides übersetzt von Hans Ludwig v. Kuefstein, zuerst u. d. T.: Die schöne verliebte Diana/ Auß Hispanischer Sprach verteutscht/ Durch Herrn Hans Ludwigen/ Herrn Khueffsteinern Freyherrn/ &c. Gedruckt zu Lintz in Oesterreich ob der Ennß durch Johann Blancken. ANNO M. DC. XIX. Harsdörffer muß eine der 1619, 1624, 1628 u. 1629 erschienenen ergänzten Auflagen vorgelegen haben, z. B.: Erster vnnd anderer Theil Der newen verteutschten Schäfferey/ von der schönen verliebten Diana/ vnd dem vergessenen Syreno ... Auß Spanischer Spraach in Hochteutsch gebracht Durch ... Hans Ludwigen/ Herrn/ Khueffsteinern/ Freyherrn (Lintz 1619: Johan Blanck). S. *Dünnhaupt: Handbuch*, 2430f. Vgl. 430118 K 21; *Conermann: Lope de Vega*, S. 71f. Anm. 15 u. S. 78 Anm. 25; Gerhart Hoffmeister: Spanien und Deutschland. Geschichte und Dokumentation der literarischen Beziehungen. Berlin 1976, 58f.; Adam Schneider: Spaniens Anteil an der Deutschen Litteratur des 16. und 17. Jahrhunderts. Straßburg 1898, 233–245; Eugenia Fosalba: La *Diana* en Europa. Ediciones, traducciones e influencias. Barcelona 1994, 327–334 („La revisión de Harsdörffer"); Manuel Cerezo Magán: El mito clásico en la novela pastoril: Jorge de Montemayor y Gaspar Gil Polo. In: Faventia. Publicacions de la Universidad Autónoma de Barcelona 27 (2005), 101–119; Johann Georg Schönherr: Jorge de Montemayor. Sein Leben und sein Schäferroman die „Siete Libros de la Diana" nebst einer Übersicht der Ausgaben dieser Dichtung und bibliographischen Anmerkungen. Halle 1886, 19, 76 u. 83–88; Gerhart Hoffmeister: Die spanische Diana in Deutschland. Vergleichende Untersuchungen zu Stilwandel und Weltbild des Schäferromans im 17. Jahrhundert. Berlin 1972, 41ff. — Harsdörffer schrieb die Gedichte um, überarbeitete allgemein die Sprache, fügte auch seine Übersetzung von Gaspar Gil Polos *Los cinco libros de la Diana enamorada* (Valencia 1564) als 3. Tl. seines Gesamtwerks hinzu: DIANA, | Von | H. J. De Monte-Major, | in zweyen Theilen Spanisch be- | schrieben/ und aus denselben | geteutschet | Durch | Weiland | Den wolgebornen Herrn/ | Herrn Johann Ludwigen | Freyherrn von Kueff- | stein/ etc. | An jetzo aber | Mit deß Herrn C. G. Polo zu- | vor nie-gedolmetschten | dritten Theil | vermehret/ | und | Mit reinteutschen Red- wie auch | neu-üblichen Reim-arten | ausgezieret. | Durch | G. P. H. | [Linie] | Gedruckt zu Nürnberg/ Jn Verle-| gung Michael Endters. | Jm Jahr 1646. HAB: 137.19 Eth.; Ndr. Darmstadt 1970. Im Anhang zum 3. Teil weist Harsdörffer auf frz. und ital. Übersetzungen der *Diana* Montemayors und auf Caspar v. Barths lat. Bearbeitung *Erotodidascalus, Sive Nemoralium Libri V: Ad Hispanicum Gasperis Gilli, Poli* (Hanau 1625. HAB: QuN 472 [3]) der Gil Polo-Fortsetzung hin. Übrigens soll Martin Opitz (FG 200) bereits von Barth ins Lateinische übersetzte Gedichte des 3. Teils ins Deutsche gebracht und Harsdörffer soll sie „fast unverändert" übernommen haben. Hermann Tiemann: Das Spanische Schrifttum in Deutschland von der Renaissance bis zur Romantik. Hildesheim, New York 1971, 78f., vgl. 63. — Die *Diana* Harsdörffers erfuhr ihrerseits keine weitere Fortsetzung. Daß Johann Klaj an dem Nürnberger Werk mitgearbeitet hat, ist unbestreitbar, jedoch ist Art und Weise nicht bestimmbar. *Birken: Werke u. Korrespondenz* XIV, 79. Harsdörffer bemerkt, daß im Unterschied zum Spanischen „andere Sprachen die Reimarten nicht so glücklich nachkünsteln wie wir Teutsche." (S.233). Er weist daher auf die Behandlung des Vers- und Strophenbaus in seinen *Frauen-*

zimmer-Gesprächspielen V (1645), Nr. CCIV („Die Dichtkunst") und in *Schottelius: Teutsche Vers- oder ReimKunst (1645)* hin (Justus Georg Schottelius, FG 397) und entschuldigt sich für seine Sprache mit Kuefsteins Übersetzung: „Die Rechtschreibung hat in diesem Buch nicht können beobachtet werden/ weil es auß dem alten Exemplar gesetzet worden/ und der dritte Theil den zweyen ersten gleich kommen müssen" (a. a. O. III, 234). In seiner „Schlußerinnerung" hinter dem 2. Teil seiner *Diana*-Bearbeitung sagt Harsdörffer über Kuefsteins Deutsch: „Wolermelder Herr Dolmetscher hat das Teutsche/ mit allerhand frembden Wörtern durchmenget/ nach dem bösen Gebrauch bey Hof/ der noch heut zu Tag bey vielen für ein gutes Gesetz gelten will. Weil aber die erste Vbersetzung der Arcadia und Ariana ob solcher Menglingssprach verächtlich/ ja mit des Verlägers grossen Schaden/ unverkäufflich worden: Jst auch bey dieser schönen Diana zweyten Auflegung/ wie bey erstgedachten Schäfergedichten [im 1. u. 2. Teil]/ die Reinlichkeit unserer geehrten Muttersprache beobachtet und von den unnöhtigen fremden Wörterthand absondert/ zu bemerken." Auch die verdeutschten Lieder lassen bei Kuefstein zu wünschen übrig, „da man nemlich die Zahl der Sylben/ und nicht ihr Kunstreiches Zeitmaas (numerum syllabarum non quantitatem,) in acht genommen [...]." (Bl. P ij v f.). Harsdörffer betrachtete trotz seiner Bemühungen um Sprachreinheit und Poesie seine Arbeit nicht als eine Leistung, die den Roman für eine Widmung an die FG qualifizierte. Unter seinem bukolischen Gesellschaftsnamen Strephon (PBO) richtet er sich in der „Zuschrifft" des Gesamtwerks daher nur an „Löbliche Hirten/ geehrte Freunde" und versteht unter deren „Genoßschaft" [I, Bl.)(ij v] wohl auch den frühen Nürnberger PBO. Der Zusatz zum Gesamtwerk, *Mantissa Poetica*, enthält lateinische Gedichte, die von Mitgliedern des kleinen Schäferordens stammen (Johann Helwig, Johann Klaj und Sigmund Betulius, s. Anm. 8). Vgl. zu Harsdörffers *Diana* 441020 K 12, 450400 K 6, 460000A K 0 u. 460120.

8 Sigmund Betulius (d. i. S. v. Birken; FG 681. 1658; PBO Floridan): Fortsetzung | Der Pegnitz-Schäferey/ | behandelnd/ | unter vielen andern rein-neuen freymuhtigen | Lust-Gedichten und Reimarten/ | derer | von Anfang des Teutschen Krieges | verstorbenen | Tugend-berümtesten | Helden Lob-gedächtnisse; | abgefasset und besungen durch | Floridan/ | den Pegnitz-Schäfer. | mit Beystimmung seiner andern Weidgenossen. | [Holzschn.-Vignette mit Pansflöte] | Nürnberg/ Jn Verlegung Wolffgang Endters. | Jm Jahr M. DC. XXXXV. HAB: Lo 400 (2), auch Lo 397; Abweichungen („durch Floridan und Klajus/ Die Pegnitz-Schäfer. mit Beystimmung ihrer andern Weidgenossen", Johann Klaj) in VD17 12:634595W (Bayer. SB München u. a.). Vgl. 460120, wo sich F. Ludwig für das von Harsdörffer übersandte Exemplar bedankt.

9 Philippe Fortin sieur de la Hoguette: Le Catechisme Royal (1645), dt. v. Georg Philipp Harsdörffer: CATECHISME ROYAL. | Der | Königliche Catechismus/ | Das ist: | Ein Christliches Gespräch/ | Zwischen | Königlicher Majestät in Franckreich/ | und | Deroselben Hofmeister/ | behandelnd: | I. Deß minderjährigen Königs Anführung zu löblicher | Regierung. | II. Den jetzigen Zustand deß gantzen Königreichs. | III. Welcher gestalt die Christenheit in sichere Beruhigung gesetzet werden könnte. | Dem gemeinen Wesen zum besten/ aus dem | Frantzösischen getreulich übersetzet/ | durch | Einen Liebhaber der Teutschen Sprache. | Erstlich gedruckt zu | Pariß. | [Linie] | M DC XXXXV. HAB: QuN 200 (16). Es handelt sich um fiktive Dialoge des minderjährigen, offiziell seit 1643 regierenden Königs Ludwig XIV. v. Frankreich mit seinem Hofmeister, aus denen die Annexionspläne des Königs und Kardinal Mazarins hinsichtlich von Gebieten des Hl. Römischen Reichs Deutscher Nation (Elsaß, Lothringen, Freigft. Burgund) hervorgehen: *Dünnhaupt: Handbuch*, 1997. Mit seinem Brief vom 7.2.1646 an Sigmund Betulius (v. Birken) wird Harsdörffer ein Exemplar seiner inzwischen erschienenen Übersetzung mit der Bitte senden, es Franz Julius v. dem Knesebeck (FG 396) oder Carl Gustav v. Hille

(FG 302) vorzulegen und diese entscheiden zu lassen, ob es wert sei, Hz. August d.J. v. Braunschweig-Wolfenbüttel (FG 227) überreicht zu werden. Harsdörffer kommentiert gegenüber Betulius, daß nach Ausweis des *Catechisme* die Franzosen offenbar ganz andere Überlegungen zu ihrer Politik als früher anstellten, und er vermutet Mazarin als Autor des Originals. S. *Birken: Werke u. Korrespondenz* IX, 8f. u. 577ff., außerdem 450818 K 21 u. 460112 K 3. Mit der Politik Frankreichs hatte sich Harsdörffer schon früher in literarischen (Übersetzungs-)Arbeiten beschäftigt, vgl. 411126 K 6, 430920 K 8 u. 440324 (K 22). — F. Ludwig bedankte sich in 460120 für „den gedruckten anfang an dem Catechismi Royal". Obwohl in 460406 nicht ausdrücklich vom *Catechisme Royal* die Rede ist, muß Harsdörffer seine ganze Übersetzung diesem Brief an F. Ludwig beigelegt haben, denn der bestätigt in seiner Antwort 460426 dankend den Empfang eines mit 460406 erhaltenen Exemplars des *Königlichen Catechismus'*. — Zu Fortin de la Hoguette vgl. Giuliano Ferretti: Un ,soldat-philosophe', Philippe Fortin de la Hoguette. Genua 1988; ders.: The *Testament* of La Hoguette and its sources. In: French history 15 (2001), 123–138 (über la Hoguettes häufig aufgelegtes *Testament ou Conseils fidelles d'un bon père à ses enfans*, zuerst Paris 1648). — Die hier angeführten Belege sprechen für 1646 als Erscheinungsjahr, nicht wie bei *Dünnhaupt*, a. a. O., erst für 1648. Nach *Dünnhaupt: Handbuch*, 1997 verweist das angegebene Erscheinungsjahr auf die Zeit der Publikation des frz. Buchs. Harsdörffer sandte F. Ludwig jedoch den gedruckten Anfang des *Catechisme Royal* zusammen mit dem vorliegenden Brief, nicht erst mit 460120, wie Dünnhaupt angibt. In 460426 bekundete F. Ludwig, daß er gerade mit dem Brief des Spielenden (460406) die Fortin-Übertragung empfangen habe. Dünnhaupt behauptet irrtümlich, daß der Spielende (!) am 20.4.1646 dem Nährenden die Vollendung seines Manuskripts gemeldet habe. Die Jahresangabe 1645 im Druck bezieht sich also auf das dt. Buch, wenngleich es erst im Frühjahr 1646 fertiggestellt wurde. Zur Bezeichnung „liebhaber der Teutschen Sprache" vgl. 450400 K 6. Richtig, wenn auch noch ohne Auseinandersetzung mit Dünnhaupts Angabe, verstand W. E. Schäfer diese Umstände. Ders.: Die Lyrik Johann Michael Moscheroschs. In: Daphnis XIV (1985), 277–302, hier S.280. Schäfer hält das auch in der Bibliothek Johann Michael Moscheroschs (FG 437. Der Träumende. 1645) nachgewiesene frz. Buch, welches er Pierre Fortin de la Hoguette zuschreibt, für ein Mitbringsel des Träumenden von seiner Gesandtschaft nach Paris, so daß Moscherosch Harsdörffer den schleunigen Transfer brisanter politischer Inhalte ermöglichte. In den Gesprächen des jungen Königs Ludwig XIV. von Frankreich werden nämlich schon die französ. Annexionen von europäischen Grenzgebieten behandelt. Vgl. CATECHISME | ROYALE. | A PARIS. | [Linie] | M. DC. XLV. S.46: „Si V. M. sans aller plus loin veut jetter les yeux seulement sur le Regne du feu Roy son Pere, & sur le sein, elle verra que les Flandres qui faisoient il y douze ou quinze ans les limites de son Estat de ce costé-la, en font maintenant vne partie; Que ses conquestes vont au delà du Rhin; Que l'Alsace, la Lorraine, & vne partie de la Comté font à elle; Que les Alpes, ny les Pyrenées ne sont plus les frontieres de l'Italie, ny de l'Espagne; & que le sang le plus pure de sa Noblesse qui fume encore, est le prix de cette nouuelle estenduë de son Royaume." (SB München: Pol. gen. 44 m; dig.). Vgl. Harsdörffer, a. a. O., 21: „Wann E. M. betrachten die Regierung ihres jüngstverstorbenen Herrn Vatern/ so werden sie befinden/ daß Flandern/ welches vor zwölff oder fünffzehen Jahren an Franckreich gegränzt/ jetzund desselben ein theil sind: E. Majest. Gebiet erstrecket sich über den Rhein: Elsaß/ Lothringen/ und ein theil von der Grafschaft Burgund/ sind Frantzösisch worden. Die Alpen und Pyrener-berge marcken nicht mehr Jtalien und Spanien von Franckreich ab. Das Blut welches E. majest. Adel hin und wider vergossen/ bemerket die neuen Gräntze dieses Königreichs." Man muß diese Worte zwar als Information über die französ. Ansprüche auf die eroberten Gebiete lesen, nicht aber als mittelbare Anstachelung der Deutschen zur Revanche, denn Harsdörffer erkennt in seiner Vorbemerkung „Friedliebender Leser" (S. [2]) auch die guten Ratschläge des Kardinals Mazarin, auf die ihn der vom französ. Hof zurückgekehrte Moscherosch hingewiesen haben dürfte. Er verfolgt mit der Übersetzung auch das Sprachprogramm der FG (wenn er sie auch nicht mit ihrem Namen nennt): „ES haben sich etliche der Teutschen Sprache beflissene verglichen/ alle/ in fremden Zungen beschriebene Schriften/ welche wegen jhres Nutzens/ oder Ergetzligkeit/ leswürdig erachtet werden/ mit gesamter Hülffe zu übersetzen. Weil nun dieses Büchlein/ le Catechisme Royal betitelt/ in gantz Franckreich sehr hoch gehalten wird/ und viel gute und friedliche Rahtschläge/ (deren Urheber C. M. einer von den vornemsten Herren an dem Frantzösischen Hofe seyn sol) an die Hand gibet; ist solches der gestalt gedolmetschet/ daß viel mehr die Teutsche Mund- und Redart/ benebens der Grundsprache wolvernemlicher Meinung/ als nicht die eigentlichen Wort/ von Wort/ beobachtet worden." Daß Harsdörffer mit dieser Schrift nicht kriegerische Pläne unterstützt, sondern wohl unter dem Einfluß Moscheroschs Mazarin Friedenswillen zubilligt, dürfte sein Fingerzeig am Ende der Vorbemerkung andeuten, „daß zu ende deß zweyten Gesprächs so wichtige Gedancken befindlich/ daß/ wann selbe durchgehend beliebet werden sollten/ an einem allgemeinen redlichen Friede nicht zu zweiffeln." Das verweist ohne Zweiffel auf S. 32, wo der Verfasser dem Hofmeister — wohl C. M. zitierend — rät: „Zu Kriegszeiten kann man nicht verhüten/ daß es nicht einer mit diesem/ ein anderer mit dem andern Theil halte: niemand kann solche Meinungen vergleichen/ als der **Friede/ welcher ein ‚Geschenck ist/ das von Gott allein herkommet**. Ob zwar E. Maj. einer von den vornemsten Scheidmännern dieser Kriegszeiten ist/ sind doch ander vnterschiedliche Fügungen [Randnotiz: *conjonctures] zu diesem grossen Werk von nöhten/ **daß auch allen Menschen/ ohne sondere Gnade Gottes/ unmöglich were/ etwas auszurichten.'** Deßwegen nun solte*n* alle Unterthanen mit deren Elend ich E. Maj. nicht betrüben will/ **dieses Königreiches/ Augen/ Hände und Hertzen zu Gott auffheben/ den Frieden zu erbitten; welchen E. Maj. hierinnen folgen sollte/ zu erlangen die allgemeine Beruhigung/ so grosse und kleine/ hohe und niedrige Standspersonen gleicher weise von thun haben**. Daß diesem also sey/ bezeugen unter vielen andern die Strittigkeiten der höchsten Häuser in der Christenheit: Dan ob **gleich E. M. durch so beharrliche Siege die Oberhand hat/ sollen sie doch in betrachtung ziehen/ daß solche von dem HErrn der Heerscharen herkommen/ dessen Gnade man nicht mißbrauchen soll.**" Der König erklärt sich dazu (ungeachtet seines Grolls wider das Haus Habsburg) bereit, „ob wol mein HerrVater höchstseeligster Gedächtniß/ die Waffen ergriffen/ seine Bundsverwandte zu schirmen/ und zu hintertreiben/ die Macht eines hohen Hauses/ welches die gantze Welt willkürig zu bezwingen vermeinet [...]." Er fragt den Hofmeister: „Was würden wir dann thun?" Der empfiehlt nicht etwa Friedensverhandlungen, sondern Geduld und Unterwerfung unter den Willen Gottes, „Also halte ich nochmals darvor/ daß man auch von dieser bösen und verwirrten Zeit nicht übel reden sol/ und Gott danken/ daß er unser Volk erwehlet/ zu solcher Verrichtungen/ welche unserer Neigung/ und unserm Gemüt gantz zu wider ist." (S. 33). — Bemerkenswert erscheint auch, daß Wilhelm Heinrich v. Freyberg (FG 439) als Reisehofmeister Pz. Johann Georgs II. v. Anhalt-Dessau (FG 322) am 3.1.1646 aus Paris wohl an F. Ludwig berichtete, der Bibliothekar Mazarins, Gabriel Naudé, solle nach seiner Rückkehr aus Italien ihm Auskunft in der von F. Ludwig gewünschten Buchfrage geben. S. 460103.

10 GEORGI PHILIPPI | HARSDORFFERI | SPECIMEN | PHILOLOGIÆ | GERMANICÆ | Continens | Disquisitiones XII. | De Linguæ nostræ vernaculæ | Historia, Methodo, & Dignitate. | Præmissa est | PORTICVS VIRTUTIS, | Serenißimo atque Celsißimo Principi, | ac Domino, Domino | AUGUSTO, | Brunsvvicensium atq Lü- | næburgensium Duci | potentissimo &c. |

SACRA. | Norimbergæ | Impensis Wolfgangi Endteri. | M. DC. XLVI. — [Kupfertitel:] G. P. HARSDÖRFFERI Specimen Philologiæ Germanicæ. M D CXLVI. Sic labor assiduus linguæ fundamina nostræ firmabit junctis solicitè manibus. [Nürnberg: Wolfgang Endter 1646] HAB: QuN 1090 (1). Die Abfassung dieser Abhandlung kündigte Harsdörffer in 450923C an; in 460131 kann er mitteilen, daß sie dem Druck übergeben sei. Er schickte drei Exemplare des Buchs als Beilage zu 460406 an F. Ludwig, der den Empfang in 460426 bestätigte und versprach, die beiden zusätzlichen Exemplare an Diederich v. dem Werder (FG 31) und Christian Gueintz (FG 361) weiterzugeben. In 460609 erklärte F. Ludwig, daß er das Werk gelesen habe und im Allgemeinen für gut halte. Wegen der strittigen Fragen erwarte er noch das Urteil der „Gelehrten". Das *Specimen* wurde im Umkreis der FG kontrovers diskutiert und zog im Sommer 1646 Kritik von Marcus Fridericus Wendelin(us) und Christian Gueintz, später auch von Joachim Mechovius (FG 483. 1647) auf sich. Zum *Specimen* und kritischen Einwänden dazu s. 460609 K 3. Vgl. 450927 u. I, 451028A K 6, 460705, 460720, 460816, 460902, 460915, 460916 u. 461031A; vgl. ferner zum *Specimen* 441223 K 18 u. 23, 450410 K, 450818 K, 450901 (K 7), 450923C, 450927 u. I, 451028A K 6, 451219 K 8, 460112 K 3, 460131, 460200 K 2, 460406, 460410, 460426, 460609, 460610, 460620, 460700 K 4, 460705, 460720, 460816 u. I, 460902, 460915, 460916 u. 461031 K 1. — Den Kupfertitel, der Männer beim Einrammen eines Pfähle-Fundaments in unsicheren Grund zeigt, erläutert *Harsdörffer: Specimen* in einem auf Bl.)(v folgenden Gedicht „Trochæus Frontispicii interpres". Unter dem Bild liest man die Aufschrift:
Sic labor assiduus linguæ fundamina nostræ
    firmabit junctis solicitè manibus.
Das Bildmotiv folgt Harsdörffers und Schottelius' Sprachauffassung, die sich bei der Regulierung des Deutschen nicht auf den variantenreichen Sprachgebrauch, sondern auf die immanente Sprachgesetzmäßigkeit („Ratio") verlassen wollten: „EIn jedes standfestes Gebäu beruhet auf seinen unbeweglichen wolbepfälten Gründen", so auch „einer jeglichen Sprache Kunstgebäu". *Schottelius: Ausführliche Arbeit (1663)*, 50. — Zu dem in dieses Werk integrierten Panegyricus *Harsdörffer: Porticus Virtutis (1646)* s. 450923C, 450927, 461204A, *DA Köthen I. 8*: 470119, 470215 u. 470507.

11 *Harsdörffer: Frauenzimmer-Gesprächspiele* VI (Nürnberg: Wolfgang Endter 1645), an Christian Gueintz (FG 361. Der Ordnende. 1641) u. F. Ludwig mit Harsdörffers Schreiben 460916 (dem 460915 beilag) übersandt. — Im April 1646 war dieser Teil schon unter der Presse (s. 460406). Die Widmungsgedichte stammen von Juni und Juli 1646. F. Ludwig schickte seine eigenen Verse (s. 460705 u. Beilagen).

12 In seinem Schreiben 450919A hatte der Fürst über Harsdörffer an Moscherosch die Frage gerichtet, ob der Träumende seinen Gesellschaftsnamen annehme, und darum ersucht, daß Moscherosch der FG ein Exemplar der von ihm selbst herausgegebenen *Wahrhafftigen Gesichte Philanders von Sittewalt* schicken möge, um sie von den Nachdrucken unterscheiden zu können. Vgl. 451209 K 3. In 451101 hatte der Spielende versichert, Moscherosch werde den ihm vom Nährenden erteilten Gesellschaftsnamen, das Motto und die Imprese sowie das Reimgesetz annehmen. Harsdörffer drückt dort auch aus, daß der Träumende ein Dankschreiben verfassen, die letzte Ausgabe seiner *Gesichte* dem Fürsten widmen und nach gehöriger Ermahnung (durch Harsdörffer) sein Werk an Ludwig schicken werde. S. 450500 K 1. Die von Moscherosch besorgte und mit vielen Gelegenheitsgedichten der Freunde bereicherte Neuausgabe erschien erst 1650: Wunderliche und warhafftige | Gesichte | Philanders von Sittewald/ | Das ist | Straff-Schrifften | Hanß-Michael Moscherosch | von Wilstädt. | Jn welchen | Aller Weltwesen/ Aller Mänschen | Händel/ mit jhren Natürlichen Farben der | Eitelkeit/ Gewalts/ Heucheley/ Thorheit bekleidet/ of- | fentlich auff die Schau geführet/ als in einem | dargestellet und gesehen | werden. | Erster Theil. | Von Jhme zum letztern mahl auffgelegt/ ver- | mehret/ gebessert/ mit Bildnussen gezieret/ und | Männiglichen unvergreifflich zulesen | in Truck gegeben. | [Signet] | Straßburg/ | Bey Johan-Philipp. Mülben | und Josias Städeln. | [Linie] | M. DC. L. HAB: Lo 5511: 1 u. 2. Vgl. 460406 K 8.

13 Harsdörffer hatte sich für die Aufnahme Georg Conrad Osthofs verwandt (451101), die FG hatte sie zum damaligen Zeitpunkt jedoch abgelehnt (451209).

451219

Fürst Ludwig an Christian Gueintz

F. Ludwig (Der Nährende) bittet Christian Gueintz (FG 361. Der Ordnende) um sein Gutachten zur abschriftlichen Beilage (einem Grundsatzpapier zur Sprache von Justus Georg Schottelius, FG 397, Der Suchende) und um Rückgabe von Schottelius' *Teutscher Vers- oder ReimKunst (1645)*, die Gueintz vor einem Jahr empfangen habe. — (Zu Schottelius:) Die These, alle deutschen Stammwörter seien einsilbig, sei durch die Erfahrung widerlegt: Vater, Mutter, Apfel, Nagel, Regen usw. Auch daß die Stammform der Verben immer der angeblich einsilbige Imperativ („gebi[e]tungsweise") sei, erscheint F. Ludwig zweifelhaft, wie die Formen weise, reiche, trachte usw. zeigten. Die Basis einer korrekten Rechtschreibung liegt im Sprachusus und in der Aussprache, wie dies *Gueintz: Deutsche Rechtschreibung (1645)* erweist. — Hinsichtlich des (angestrebten vollständigen deutschen) Wörterbuchs biete Georg Henischs 1616 erschienenes Wörterbuch ein gutes Modell. Auf solche Weise ließen sich alle deutschen Stammwörter alphabetisch aufführen, wie sie in den Nomina („Nenwörter") und Pronomina („Vornenwörter"), den Verben („Zeitwörter"), den Adverbien („beywörter"), den Präpositionen, Konjunktionen und Interjektionen („vorwörter", „fügewörter", „Bewegewörter") begegnen. Ausgenommen sind die Partizipien („theilwörter"), da sie von Nomina und Verben abgeleitet werden. Im dt. Wörterbuch sollten bei den Nomina, wie in Gueintz' *Rechtschreibung* bereits angelegt, Geschlecht und Deklination („abweichung oder verwandelung") angegeben werden. — Zum (heute verlorenen) Schreiben Georg Philipp Harsdörffers (FG 368. Der Spielende) an Gueintz äußert F. Ludwig Kritik: die Schreibweise „herrisch" sei aussprachekonform und daher korrekt, nicht aber die Schreibweise „herrlich" [im Brief versehentlich „herrisch"]. Um göttlich, herrlich usw. aussprechen zu können, müßte ein -e- eingeschoben werden: „Göttelich", „Herrelich", oder der Doppelkonsonant müßte reduziert werden (götlich, herlich). Harsdörffer gebe doch vor, schreiben zu wollen, wie man spreche. — Die Ausmusterung des -ck- oder sein Ersatz durch -kk- überzeuge nicht, zumal er -ch- und -sch- beibehalte. Hier ist der hergebrachte Gebrauch einer Neuerung vorzuziehen. Harsdörffers Silbentrennung, wie im 5. Teil seiner *Frauenzimmer-Gesprächspiele* (1645) durchgeführt, ist auch nicht plausibel: es muß sin-gen, nicht sing-en usw. syllabiert werden. Andernfalls verfälsche man das Silbenmaß, als würden die Endungen -en, -er, -es lang gesprochen werden, wo sie doch kurz seien. Diese Endungen bedeuten außerdem nichts ohne den vorangehenden Konsonanten, also sin-gen. Darauf sollte Gueintz in seiner Antwort an Harsdörffer noch einmal hinweisen, denn die bisherigen Mahnungen (seitens F. Ludwigs) hätten nicht verfangen. Für das von Harsdörffer häufig gebrauchte „schicklich" sei „geschickt" oder „geschicklich" vorzuziehen. Harsdörffer führe auch sonst unnötig neue Wörter ein, die passender und anmutiger wiedergegeben werden könnten. Es ist zwar erlaubt, neue Wörter zu bilden, aber sie müßten zur deutschen Sprache passen.

Wenn auch „billich" so ausgesprochen und geschrieben werde, sei im Substantiv doch „Billigkeit" vorzuziehen, weil sich das -ch- vor dem -k- nicht gut aussprechen lasse. Gueintz habe dies schon in der *Rechtschreibung* angeführt, doch begegne dergleichen häufiger in Harsdörffers Schriften. Auch darin sollte er korrigiert werden.

Q HM Köthen: V S 545, Bl. 256v u. 259rv, 259v leer; eigenh. Konzept; Konjekturen in [Klammern]. Es beginnt auf der Rückseite einer Stellungnahme Justus Georg Schottelius' (FG 397) zu Fragen der Sprachlehre: 451205 (Bl. 256rv Abschrift; Schottelius' Original Bl. 257r–258rv, v leer. Zur Veröff. vorgesehen in *DA Köthen I. 9; Zusammenfassung hier in K 1*). — D: *KE*, 300f. (stark und willkürlich gekürzt); *KL* III, 267f. (dito). — Nicht in *Bürger*.

A *Fehlt*.

Der Ordenende wolle hieruber[1] sein bedencken[2] geben un[d][a] des Suchenden Reimkunst, so er fur einem Jhare empfang[en][a][3] wieder anhero schicken.

Es zeigt gleichwol die erfarung, das alle deutsche Stamwörter nicht einsilbig sein können. Als neben vielen andern, Vater, mutter, bruder, schwester, meßer, waßer, feder, apfel, nage[l,][a] nabel, regen, donner, hagel, kummer, finger, gesund, leb[er][b], ader, flugel, hammer, fenster, haspel, zucker, mantel, mand[el][a], teller, offen, thure, und dergleichen.[4]

Ob dan auch der radix oder Stamm der Zeitwörter in der g[e]bietungsweise[c] ist,[5] solches[d] ist auch sehr zweiffelhaftig, ja das die andere person drinnen allezeit einsilbig sein solte, als man saget weise mir deine wege, und nicht weis mir, reiche mir deine hand, und nicht reich mir, trachte darnach, und nicht tracht, welches das nenwort eine tracht ist[d] und also bey mehrern.

Bey und in der Rechtschreibung seind[e] die ursachen auch angefuret, die da bestehen im gebrauche, und der aussprach[e.][a][6]

[259r] Belangende das wortverzeichnus oder Lexicon, und was für eine ordnung darbey zu halten, giebet des Henischij seines im Jhare 1616 ausgegangen[7] eine feine anleitung, da sich dan in iedem buchstaben die Stamwörter finden werden, und werden solche sein Nenwörter, Vornenwörter, Zeitwörter, beywörter, vorwörter, fügewörter, und Bewegewörter: Die theilwörter alleine ausgenommen, die von andern als[f] Nenn- und Zeitwörtern herruren. Nur[g] wie[h] in der rechtschreibung angefangen, wird[i] bey den Nenwörtern das geschlecht und die abweichung oder verwandelung mußen darzu gesetzet werden.[8]

Des Spielenden schreiben an den Ordnenden[9] betreffende, so ist Herrisch darinnen wol und recht geschrieben, worum schreibet man aber auch herrisch[j] nicht mit zwey **rr**, so doch von Herr herkömmet. Wan allezeit die verduppelung[k] der mitlautenden in der mitte bey andern mitlautenden muste behalten werden, so muste man es auszusprechen[l] schreiben Göttelich, Herrelich, Allemächtig, Allegewaltig, Allewißend, Höffelich, Schließelich, weil dan das **e** nicht ausgesprochen wird, so[m] muß der eine mitlautender ausbleiben, das man schreibe wie man redet, welche regel der Spielende sonst[n] gar gerne wil[o] gehalten haben:[p][10] Das er auch[d] das **ck**[q] ausmustern wil, und[r] doch das **ch** und **sch** leßet, darbey findet sich keine erhelligkeit, und kann ein duppel[t]^s **kk** an deßen stat[,] weil es gantz neu[,] nicht zugelaßen^t werden, hier muß der gebrauch vorgehen, und behalten werden.[11] Also stehet auch die Sillabirung die er einfüren wil wie^u in seinem funften theil der gesprechspiele zu sehen nicht wol, als da er setzet wegen der Stambuchstaben: Sing-en, kling-en, Ring-en, Sondern es^v muß heißen Sin-gen — klin-gen, Rin-gen sol^w es recht sein. Ja es wolte dergleichen schrift das Maß der silben auch in^x eine richtigkeit bringen, als wan das **en er es**, wan es alleine an^y den mitlautenden gesetzet wird, lang were, so doch allezeit kurtz ist, ja^z es bedeuten diese endungen nichts, wan der mitlautende nicht darbey ist.[12] Dieses^{aa} solte billich bey dem Spielenden, sich darbey beßer in acht zu nemen, erinnert werden. wie^{ab} zwar von hinnen zeitlich geschehen, aber noch wenig fruchten wollen. Und stehet es^d zu des^{ac} Ordnenden^{ad} gefallen, ob er es nicht^d bey seiner antwort an ihme[13] ietzunder^d gedencken wolle, wie^{ae} es also vor nötig gehalten wird. Das wort schicklich so bey ihme sehr gewönlich, stünde auch beßer geschickt, oder geschicklich[14], als so bloß: Wie auch viel andere neue wörter^d die füglicher und anmutiger zu geben, wan er sich darinnen wolte beßern, oder erinnern laßen. Neue wörter kan man zwar machen, sie wollen aber auch ihre rechte art und weise haben. Man saget und schreibet wol billich und nit billig, Also wol billigkeit, und nicht billichkeit, weil das **ch** fur dem **k** sich nicht wol aussprechen leßet, das auch schon in der Rechtschreibung gemeldet[15]: dergleichen sol sich auch viel mehr in seinen schriften finden, das wie vorgemeldet, zu erinnern were.

T **a** *Buchstabenverlust im Falz.* — **b** *Buchstabenverlust im Falz. Mögliche Lesart auch* leben — **c** *Buchstabenverlust des 1. e im Falz. Folgt* <stehet und> — **d** *Eingefügt.* — **e** *Folgt* <gleichwol> — **f** *Im Sinne von* nämlich — **g** *Eingefügt für* <Alleine> — **h** *Folgt* <der> — **i** *Folgt* <man> — **j** *Verschrieben, wohl* her(r)lich *gemeint. Vgl. Anm. K 10.* — **k** *Folgt* <in> — **l** *Gebessert aus* auszu<sprechen> *[sic]. Lies:* um es aussprechen zu können — **m** *Folgt* <ka> — **n** *Wörterreihenfolge durch hochgestellte Ziffern geändert aus* gar gerne sonst *Unsichere Lesung:* gerne — **o** *Folgt* <hal[ten]> — **p** *Folgt* <Und> — **q** *Folgt* <weitter> — **r** *Eingefügt für* <da er> *Hier und im Folgenden Hervorhebung durch den Herausgeber.* — **s** *Lesebeeinträchtigung am Blattrand.* — **t** *Eingefügt für* <gesetzet> — **u** *Bis zu* sehen *am Rand ergänzt.* — **v** es muß heißen *eingefügt.* — **w** sol es *eingefügt für* <ist> — **x** *Bis* bringen *eingefügt für* <verendern> — **y** *Verschriebenes/ verbessertes Wort. Lesart an* erschlossen. — **z** *Bis* darbey ist *am Rand ergänzt.* — **aa** *Eingefügt für* <Dergleichen> — **ab** *Am Rand ergänzt bis* fruchten wollen. — **ac** *Folgt* <vorged> — **ad** *Folgt* <gutdüncken und> — **ae** *Bis* gehalten wird *am Rand ergänzt.*

K 1 Die auf Wolfenbüttel, 5.12.1645 datierte Stellungnahme Justus Georg Schottelius' (FG 397. Der Suchende) zu einigen (tw. strittigen) Grundsatzfragen der deutschen Sprachlehre. Das Original in HM Köthen: V S 545, Bl. 257r–258v, 258v leer. Eine Abschrift desselben (Bl. 256rv) sandte F. Ludwig (Der Nährende) mit dem vorliegenden Brief an Christian Gueintz (FG 361. Der Ordnende). Schottelius' Stellungnahme ist zur Veröffentlichung in *DA Köthen I. 9* vorgesehen. Sie ist im Zusammenhang der angestrebten Verständigung zwischen Schottelius und Gueintz über grammatische Streitfragen und einer auf dieser gemeinsamen Grundlage zu beginnenden Gemeinschaftsarbeit an einem dt. Wörterbuch entstanden. S. 451220 K 1. Wie diese Stellungnahme an F. Ludwig gelangte, bleibt unklar, da ein zu erwartender Begleitbrief nicht überliefert zu sein scheint.

Zu Schottelius' Papier: Es gebe zwei unfehlbare Grundlagen der dt. Sprache: den bis jetzt angenommenen Gebrauch („receptus hactenus usus") und die aus der Sprache selbst abgeleitete Analogie oder ihre innere „ratio" (als Regeltransfer und -generalisierung) („ipsa analogica linguae natura"). Diese erhebe sich vor allem aus jenem wunderbaren einsilbigen System, auf das sich die ganze Struktur der dt. Sprache stützt. Jedwede Sprache habe ihre sicheren Grundlagen, auch die deutsche habe solche festen Grundlagen von bewunderungswürdiger Kürze: die durchgängige, bündige Einsilbigkeit („nimirum Generalis illa et acutissima monosyllabitas"). Alle Stammwörter („radices") seien einsilbig, ebenso die Ableitungs- und Flexionsmorpheme. Die ganze Sprache werde somit von diesen einsilbigen Gründen oder Säulen getragen („tota denique lingua innititur fundaminibus seu columnis monosyllabicis"), und aus der unendlichen Kombination dieser einsilbigen Grundbestandteile gehen die vielen tausend Wörter hervor. Kein menschlicher Fleiß könnte dieses unvergleichliche einsilbige Meisterwerk, dieses natürliche, feste Fundament erfinden, seine Geburt falle gleichursprünglich mit der der Sprache selbst zusammen („ortum est unâ cum ortâ lingua"). Unter dem angenommenen und bewährten Gebrauch („receptus hactenus et probatus usus") aber versteht Schottelius jene Wörter, Redensarten und Schreibweisen, wie sie übereinstimmend bei den bewährten Autoren erscheinen („uti communiter occurrunt in probatis authoribus"). Für die Zweifelsfälle, die die Sprach-Ratio nicht klären kann, könne im Konsens des angenommenen und bewährten Gebrauchs Sicherheit gestiftet werden. Wenn ein jeder aber nicht nach dem aufmerksam beachteten Grund der Sprache, auch nicht nach dem angenommenen Gebrauch, sondern nach dem Maße seines Gehörs, etwa anhand der Richtschnur dieser oder jener Mundart, schreibe, Wörter bilde, Regeln zusammenschichte usw., werde nichts dabei herauskommen als, schnell und immer größer anschwellend, Unsicherheit. Wie viele Köpfe, so viele Sinne, und was in Meißen gefalle, müsse andernorts keineswegs Zustimmung finden. — Ein vollständiges Wörterbuch und eine Grammatik der dt. Sprache vorzulegen, wäre nicht nur ein lebensnotwendiges Werk des Jahrhunderts, sondern ein Heilmittel der irrigen Freiheit, und ein Mittel voranzuschreiten und dorthin zu gelangen, wo Griechen und Römer ruhen. — Zunächst bedürfe es aber der angeeigneten und aufgerichteten Grundlagen. Bis heute habe Schottelius angespannt darauf gewartet, ob nicht irgend jemand einige jener Grundlagen widerlegen oder erneuern könne oder wolle, die in seiner bereits veröffentlichten *Sprachkunst (1641)* und der nachfolgenden *Der Teutschen Sprache Einleitung (1643)* festgehalten sind. Nichts habe Schottelius in dieser Sache seitdem gesehen, ausgenommen weniges im Dissens hierauf Herbeigeschafftes, aber keine hinzugewonnene vernünftige Regularität. — Die dt. Sprache habe eine gewisse Anzahl an Stammwörtern, eine gewisse Anzahl an Ableitungsmorphemen, eine gewisse Kunst der Zusammenfügung. Wenn man sich darauf festlege und alles danach ausrichte, könne kein Zweifel an der glücklichen Lösung der Aufgaben des Sprachausbaus bestehen. Zu dem unter verschiedene Bearbeiter auszuteilenden Wörterbuch könne er eine nicht unbeträchtliche Anzahl von Wörtern beitragen. Man sollte mit eiliger Feder und zunächst unbesorgt um kritische Einwände skizzieren und sich hinterher mit den anderen Beteiligten am Wörterbuchprojekt verständigen. Wenn unterschiedliche Meinungen zusammenflössen, würden Irrtümer umso leichter erkannt, denn nichts sei annehmlicher, als belehrt und unterrichtet zu werden, um die bestmögliche Vollkommenheit der Sprache voranzutreiben. Soweit das Grundsatzpapier von Schottelius, vgl. auch Anm. 4.

2 Für Ende 1645/ Anfang 1646 wissen wir nur von einem Schreiben von Gueintz an Georg Philipp Harsdörffer (FG 368. Der Spielende) vom 11.1.1646, und dies auch nur aus

dem Antwortbrief Harsdörffers 460131. Zu diesem Brief hatte sich F. Ludwig in einer Stellungnahme kritisch geäußert (vgl. 460200 K 1) und dies Gueintz in 460200 auch zur Kenntnis gebracht. Für das ganze Frühjahr 1646 bleibt die Überlieferungslage hinsichtlich von Gueintz stumm, auch sein mögliches Gutachten zu Schottelius' Grundsatzpapier (Anm. 1) vom 5.12.1645 scheint nicht erhalten zu sein.

3 *Schottelius: Teutsche Vers- oder ReimKunst (1645)*. Mit 450204 übersandte Schottelius F. Ludwig ein Exemplar, in 450221 konnte dieser den Erhalt der *ReimKunst* bestätigen. Die Zuleitung der Schottelschen Poetik an Gueintz konnte also frühestens um diese Zeit erfolgt sein. Die uns vorliegende Korrespondenz läßt nichts darüber vernehmen; ein Antwortschreiben Gueintz' auf den vorliegenden Brief fehlt. Zu den kritischen Einwänden F. Ludwigs an der *ReimKunst* vgl. 450221 u. 450317A. Vgl. insgesamt 440900 K 2.

4 In seinem Grundsatzpapier vom 5.12.1645 (s. Anm. 1) hatte Schottelius die dt. Sprache auf ein System durchgängig einsilbiger Stammwörter und Ableitungs- bzw. Flexionsmorpheme gegründet: „[...] Illa analogica natura, seu potius fundamentalis linguæ ratio exsurgit vel imprimis ex mirabili illo monosyllabico artificio, cui tota linguæ structura innitit*ur*. [...] Jam autem sunt prorsus solida, firma et admirandæ brevitatis fundamenta in lingua Germanica, nimirum Generalis illa et acutissima monosyllabitas: Sunt enim omnes radices monosyllabæ, itidem omnes derivandi terminationes, omnes itidem casuum, gener*um*, numerorum, modor*um*, comparationum *etc*. formationes, tota denique lingua innitit*ur* fundamin*ibus* seu columnis monosyllabicis". Ganz ähnlich ein anderes, undatiertes Papier von Schottelius, das die Einsilbigkeit der Stammwörter aber nicht explizit herausstreicht. NSTA Wolfenbüttel: 2 Alt Nr. 40, Bl. 4r–5v (zur Veröff. in *DA Köthen I. 9* vorgesehen). Im Ansatz hatte Schottelius seine von Harsdörffer geteilte Theorie grundsätzlicher Einsilbigkeit der deutschen Stammwörter bereits in seiner *Sprachkunst (1641)*, 87f., vertreten, denn es seien „die ersten Würtzelen oder die Staṁwörter der Teutschen Sprache gleichfalls einsilbig/ [...] Also nun hat die mildreiche allgemeine Mutter/ die gütige Natur/ auch dieses allein den Teutschen verliehen/ daß sie [...] unendlich-viele einsilbige Wörter können außreden/ darunter auch alle Stammwörter". Vgl. auch a. a. O., 413 u. 444. In *Der Teutschen Sprache Einleitung (1643)*, 68 erklärte Schottelius, die einsilbigen Stammwörter seien „der unzerruttelende Grund" wie „ein harter Fels der festeste und unbeweglichste Grund" der dt. Sprache. — In seinem früheren Gutachten zu Gueintz' Sprachlehre hatte Schottelius noch formuliert, „die Teutsche Sprache ruhet fest und unbeweglich in ihren, von Gott eingepflantzten haubtgründen, welche lautere, reine, deutliche, meist-einsilbige Stam*m*wörter sind". 400528 I, S. 508. F. Ludwig und Gueintz, auch Philipp v. Zesen (FG 521. 1648), waren anderer Auffassung. Dazu Gueintz in seiner damaligen Gegenstellungnahme: „Daß alle stamwörter müßen einsylbig sein, ist so vi[el] nach dieses meinung gesagt, daß sie nicht alle Deu[tsch] sein, denn daß wortt Adam selber nicht einsyl[big] ist, vnndt derer viel tausendt." 400528 II (*DA Köthen I. 5*, S. 513). Vgl. F. Ludwigs Kritik an Schottelius' Grundsatzpapier vom 5.12.1645 in 460100 (HM Köthen: V S 545, Bl. 263r–264v, zur Veröff. vorgesehen in *DA Köthen I. 9*). Vgl. zur Stammwortdiskussion 450410 K 3.

5 Vgl. zum Imperativ Sg. als Stammform der Verben bei Harsdörffer und Schottelius 450410 K 3. *Schottelius: Sprachkunst (1641)*, 89: „Worbey anfangs zu wissen/ daß in Teutscher Sprache in den Verbis der Modus Imperativus das Staṁwort oder die Wurtzel sey/ denn darinn die Wesentlichen StammLettern bestehen/ die folgendes in den derivatis und compositis, exceptis anomalis, richtig verbleiben". Ebd., S. 413 wird der Imperativ mit „Gebietungsweise" übersetzt. Sie ist „bey den Teutschen die erste und das rechte Staṁwort/ welches alleine die Staṁletteren in sich begreifft [...]. Es ist wunderlich/ daß die Zeitstammwörter oder Gebietungsweisen einsilbig sind/ anzuzeigen jhre natürliche/ lautere/ reinliche ankunfft/ jhre schöneste Stammwürtzelen/ die so schön/ kürtz/ safftig und

rein sind". Hier liege der „Anfang der natürlichen Rede", wie in der ersten Kindersprache; aus diesen einfachen „wesentlichen Lauten" erwachse das ganze Sprachgebäude und „solches ist kein zufälliges barbarisches Wesen/ sondern eine von den höchsten Künsten der Sprachnatur". Ähnlich *Schottelius: Sprachkunst (1651),* 708f. Dagegen Gueintz in seiner Gegenstellungnahme zu Schottelius' Kritik an seiner Sprachlehre: „Daß ist noch zu erinnern, daß gesezt wirdt der Imperativus sey das stamwortt, aber ich kan e[s] nicht gleuben, weil darvon auch keine vrsache" usw. 400528 II, S. 517.

6 F. Ludwig läßt in seiner Aufzählung ein weiteres, wichtiges Normierungskriterium vermissen: die Etymologie (verstanden als „Wortforschung"), d.h. die Wortbildung oder -morphologie, welche aber weiter unten Anwendung findet, s. Anm. 10. Er verweist auf *Gueintz: Rechtschreibung (1645).* Zur Gueintzschen Rechtschreibung s. 440127 K 1. Tatsächlich führte Gueintz sowohl bereits in der Köthener Handschrift „Die Rechtschreibung angeordnet und der fruchtbringenden hochlöblichen Geselschaft übergeben von Dem Ordnenden" (HM Köthen: V S 670, S.5/ Bl.9r) als auch im Druck der *Deutschen Rechtschreibung (1645),* 6f. drei Gesichtspunkte für die Gewinnung einer deutschen Rechtschreibnorm an: 1. Der „ursprung und Stamm des Wortes/ woher dasselbe der vermutung nach entstanden", also die Etymologie, basierend auf der Morphologie/ Grammatik; 2. „die Aussprechung desselben", also die Phonetik; 3. „die Gewonheit", also hier der schriftsprachliche Usus, sofern darin „sich nicht gegen jene beyde wiedrigkeit/ oder etwas ungereimtes findet. Und weil nach diesen dreyen (dan die gewonheit/ wo sie vernünftig/ nicht auszulassen;) auch alle andere sprachen gerichtet werden: deswegen so kann und sol die Deutsche sich nit absondern". Vgl. *Herz: Rechtschreibdebatte,* 133f.; ders. *Ratio und consuetudo,* 271f.

7 Von Georg Henischs (1549–1618) Wörterbuch *Teutsche Sprach vnd Weißheit* (*Henisch*) ist nur der erste Teil (A–G) 1616 erschienen. S. 450410 K 3, 450923B K 3, 450929, 451028A K 5, 460000 u. I u. II, 460406 u. 461104. F. Ludwig hatte es auch schon in 451028A gegenüber Schottelius als mögliches Modell für ein vollständiges dt. Wörterbuch empfohlen. Henisch erhob den Anspruch, mit seinem „Thesaurus" ein völlig neues Wörterbuch zu schaffen, da es nicht nur den Wortschatz von den allgemein gebräuchlichen bis zu den höchst seltenen Wörtern, sondern durch genaue Bedeutungsangaben, Hinweise zur Verwendung der Wörter und Angabe von Redensarten und Sprichwörtern auch den im Wortschatz niedergelegten Erfahrungs- und Wissensfundus (sapientia/ Weisheit) wiedergeben sollte. Letzteres stellte eine — nach Schottelius eigener Aussage sogar die einzige — Unterstützung für sein Vorhaben dar, neben dem Stammwörter-Lexikon (s. Anm.8) auch ein weiteres zu dt. Redensarten und Sprichwörtern (Phraseologie) zusammenzustellen, s. 460000 II. Mit Nachdruck und von Anfang an betonte Schottelius die Notwendigkeit, sich in den wesentlichen grammatischen Fragen zu vereinheitlichen, bevor an ein gemeinsam zu erarbeitendes dt. Wörterbuch gegangen werden könnte. So war bereits lt. *Schottelius: Sprachkunst (1641),* 9f., ihres Verfassers ursprüngliches Ziel, ein vollständiges Wörterbuch aufzusetzen, für welches er bereits „einen ziemlichen Vorraht vieler tausend vocabulorum, phrasium, und sententiarum auß mancherley Authoren" zusammengetragen habe. Um aber dieses Vorhaben in die Tat umzusetzen, hätte es zuvor einer grammatischen Grundlegung bedurft, so sei die *Sprachkunst* entstanden. — Auch Harsdörffer kannte natürlich *Henisch* und benutzte ihn für seine eigenen lexikograph. Studien. S. seinen Brief an Sigmund Betulius (v. Birken; FG 681. 1658) vom 4.4.1646 in: *Birken: Werke u. Korrespondenz* IX.1, 9f. Zur Anlage und Ordnungsidee seines Wörterbuchs erklärte Henisch in dessen Vorrede: „Nam singula verba seu vocabula sua adjecta habet synonyma, deriuata, epitheta, phrases, proverbia, elegantesq̀; tum priscorum tum hodiernorum sapientū Germanorum sententias, quæ omnes vel ad pietatis cultum vel ad Remp[ublicam] gubernandam; vel formandos mores, uel rem domesticam administrandam apprimè facere possint." [Bl.):(4r]. Das Wörterbuch geht vom Hochdeutschen als Leitvarietät aus, bringt aber auch nd. Lemmata. Es setzt alle Wortarten bis hin zu Partikeln und Morphemen (Be, ent, er) an, dabei auch Eigennamen (Albrecht, Ammersee, Braband, Darius usw.) und Fremdwörter (wie allegiren, Ceremonien). Die Lemmata werden nach Stammwörtern angesetzt, ihre Bedeutung(en) durch Synonyme eingehend erklärt, Redensarten und Sprichwörter vertiefen die idiomat. u. pragmat. Verwendung. Lat., engl., nl., böhm. (tschech.), frz., griech., ungar., ital. und poln. Übersetzungen machen das Werk zu einem polyglotten Nachschlagewerk. Danach werden Ableitungen und Komposita zusammengetragen, die aber auch unter ihren Anfangsbuchstaben zu finden sind, wie das Wörterbuch überhaupt in vielerlei Hinsicht Inkonsequenzen, Wiederholungen, fehlerhafte Zuordnungen u. a. Mängel in der Durchführung der Systematik aufweist. Den Abschluß bildet ein alphabetisches Register (von A–Z!). Die Vorrede ruft die germanisch-deutschen Tugenden auf und bringt eine Lobeshymne auf die dt. Sprache aus. Interessant: schon Henisch feiert die Fülle der deutschen Sprache in der Kürze ihrer meist einsilbigen Stammwörter, und die brevitas der Wörter in ihrer Fülle rühmlich eindeutiger Denomination (wenige doppel- oder mehrdeutige Wörter): „copiam in breuitate, & breuitatem in copia" (Bl.):(4r). Schottelius wird ihm darin folgen, s. Anm. 1 u. 4, vgl. hier auch Anm. 8, 451028A K 5 u. Heidrun Kämper: Einführung und Bibliographie zu Georg Henisch, Teütsche Sprach vnd Weißheit. Thesavrvs lingvae et sapientiae Germanicae (1616). Mit einer dt. Übers. der Vorrede von Claudia u. Peter Barthold. In: Deutsche Wörterbücher des 17. und 18. Jahrhunderts. Einführung und Bibliographie. Hg. Helmut Henne. 2., erw. Aufl. Hildesheim u. a. 2001, 39–74, zur Anlage der Lemmata S. 53 f.

8 *Gueintz: Rechtschreibung (1645)* besteht nach der knappen Einführung allgemeiner und besonderer orthographischer Regeln aus einer jene Einführung im Umfang deutlich übertreffenden Homophonenliste. Diese ist also keine Stammwörterliste, sondern eine Liste gleichlautender Wörter unterschiedlicher Wortart und Bedeutung, die in unterschiedlicher Schreibung differenziert werden müssen. Bei den Substantiven werden immer das Geschlecht, gelegentlich auch weitere Deklinationsformen angegeben, z. B. „Aas unbenantes geschlechtes [= genus neutrum] das aas/ des aases/ und mit dem gedoppelten aa"; (S. 31), oder „Brot unbenantes geschlechts das brot/ mit dem t und langen o/ dan man sagt in der geburts- oder geschlechtsendung [Genitiv] des brotes [...] Und in der übereintzigen zahl [= Plural] [...] brote" (44). Diese Liste ist von Harsdörffer in der 2. Ausg. seines *Teutschen SECRETARIUS* (Nürnberg 1655. HAB: Xb 3479), 621–722, wörtlich übernommen worden und stellt, obwohl orthographisch motiviert, ein wichtiges Zeugnis fruchtbringerischer Lexikographie dar. Sie bettet sich in einen langen Prozeß fruchtbringerischer Wörterbuchdiskussion und -projektierung ein, an dessen Ende, keineswegs so singulär wie meist angenommen, Caspar Stielers erstes umfassendes deutsches Wörterbuch steht, *Der Teutschen Sprache Stammbaum und Fortwachs/ Oder Teutscher Sprachschatz* (Nürnberg 1691). Schon in 400301 hielt es Gueintz für „gut, daß ein wörterbuch (Lexicon) wie auch phrases oder Redensartbuch mit ehesten aus den besten Schrifften man verfertigget, ans tageliecht keme." Das Wörterbuchprojekt rückte dann ab etwa 1645 in den Vordergrund der fruchtbringerischen Spracharbeit. Harsdörffer schnitt es in seinem *Specimen Philologiae Germanicae* (Nürnberg 1646), etwa S. 251 ff. u. 272 f., an und trug die Diskussion um deutsche Lexikologie und Lexikographie durch eine Stammwörterliste im 2. Teil seines *Poetischen Trichters* (Nürnberg 1648) als Nucleus eines künftigen deutschen Wörterbuchs sowie durch ein handschriftliches „Bedencken, wie ein Teutsches Dictionarum oder wortbuch zuverabfassen", maßgeblich mit. S. „Anhang: bestehend Jn kurtzer Verfassung/ wo nicht aller/ jedoch der meisten Stamm- und Grund-Wörter unsrer Teutschen Sprach"

(1648). In: *Harsdörffer: Poetischer Trichter* II (Des Poetischen Trichters zweyter Theil [...] Samt einem Anhang von der Teutschen Sprache: durch ein Mitglied Der Hochlöblichen Fruchtbringenden Gesellschafft. Nürnberg 1648. Ndr. Hildesheim u. a. 1971), 113–186; das genannte „Bedencken" in HM Köthen: V S 545, Bl. 405r–408v, veröffentlicht in *KE*, 387–392. Vollends ist auch die alphabetisch gegliederte Wörterliste mit den jeweiligen semantischen Worterklärungen und den poetisch-bildlichen Umschreibungen im 3. Teil des *Poetischen Trichters* ein zeitgenössischer Beitrag zur Lexikographie: Prob und Lob der Teutschen Wolredenheit. Nürnberg 1653. Ndr. Hildesheim u. a. 1971, 112–504. Vgl. *Herz: Harsdörffers Teutscher Secretarius*, 59f. — Schottelius hatte in seinem Sprachwerk *Der Teutschen Sprache Einleitung (1643)* Klage über ein fehlendes „völliges vollkommenes Lexicon der Teutschen Sprache" geführt (S. 109). Georg Henischs Wörterbuch *Teutsche Sprach vnd Weißheit* von 1616 war zwar unvollständig geblieben (s. Anm. 7), galt Schottelius aber als ein trefflicher Versuch, wenngleich „die positio thematum, wie auch derivatio und compositio oftmals übergangen und misgesetzet" worden seien, also die Ansetzung der Stammwörter, ihrer Ableitungen und Kompositionen öfters nicht überzeugte (S. 110). Daß er mit Henischs Wörterbuch intensiv arbeitete, zeigt 460000. Schottelius' Konzept eines vollkommenen dt. Wörterbuchs sah vor: 1. Liste der Stammwörter; 2. zu jedem Stammwort Angabe von genus, casus genitivus und numerus pluralis; 3. Ableitungen (mit ihren „Haubtendungen"); 4. Komposita, geordnet nach ihrem Grundwort; 5. Richtige Kenntnis der Vorwörter (Präfixe); 6. Stammverben (Verba primitiva) mit Angabe, ob gleich- oder ungleichfließend (regular/ regelmäßig, irregular/ unregelmäßig), mit Angabe der 1. und 2. Pers. Präsens, Imperfekt u. Partizip Perfekt: „Brich/ ich breche/ du brichst. ich brach. gebrochen" usw.; 7. Erklärung der Bedeutung, Maßgabe dabei: „der Teutsche rechte Gebrauch". Ein solches Wörterbuch wäre wohl nur als Gemeinschaftsleistung „gelahrter Teutschliebender Männer" zu leisten (S. 112–114). Seine eigene Stammwörterliste in der *Ausführlichen Arbeit (1663)*, 1277–1450, gibt indes bei Substantiven nur das Geschlecht, das latein. Lexem und die Bedeutung, bei Verben nur den Imperativ (als Stammform), den Infinitiv, lat. Entsprechung(en) und die Bedeutung an. In einem undatierten Brief an Hz. August d. J. v. Braunschweig-Wolfenbüttel (FG 227) bekräftigte er den Wunsch nach einem dt. Wörterbuch: „Radices seu Primitiva Linguæ Teutonicæ erant colligenda et explicanda, quod non exiguo stetit labore, nemo enim hactenus præivit, et ob dialectorum varietatem res non adeò plana: Stevini interim et Henischij manus auxiliatrix subinde erat et per tot intervalla inter alios investiganda quàm ductricem etiam sæpissimè sum expertus, moræ ergò huic ultra annuæ veniam precor." S. 460000. — Zum Wörterbuchprojekt der FG vgl. ferner 400301; 440429, 440826 (K 4), 450000, 450308A, 450919A K 7, 450923B, 450929, 451007, 451028A, 460000 u. I u. II, 460217 u. 460406 K 4.

9 Unbekannter Brief Harsdörffers an Gueintz.

10 F. Ludwig kommt hier auf das Problem der Konsonantengemination zu sprechen: Es zeigt sich, wie stark sich an diesem Punkt die Herkunft des Deutschen aus der ahd. Silbensprechsprache, die sich seit dem Mhd. zu einer Wortsprache entwickelte, geltend machte. Obgleich er das Stammwort „Herr" ansetzte, plädierte er gegenüber Harsdörffer für die Schreibung „beherschet", „herlich", ähnlich „götlich" oder „beharlich". Für diese Schreibweise mit einfachem Konsonanten bei Folge eines anderen Konsonanten formulierte er eine klar gefaßte Regel, die durch Einführung eines Sproßvokals am phonographischen Prinzip festhielt — auf Kosten des Schreibusus und zu Lasten des morphematischen Wortstammprofils. Er ließ die Konsonantengemination nur zu, wenn ein nachfolgendes -e- (oder ein anderer Vokal) eine zusätzliche Silbe generiert und die Aussprache des verdoppelten Konsonanten gestattet. „Es kan verhoft und verhoffet, aber nicht verhofft fuglich geschrieben werden, also Hofnung, und Hoffenung nit aber Hoffnung, in beyden ist das eine F zu viel." F. Ludwig: „Etzliche erinnerungen, bey dem dritten theile der gesprächspiele am meisten die wortschreibung betreffende, auf begeren, vorgestellet." HM Köthen: V S 545, Bl. 419r–424v u. 426r (zur Veröff. in *DA Köthen I. 9* vorgesehen), hier Bl. 419r, vgl. 423v. Deshalb ist „Eigenschaften" mit einem (ebd., 421v), „Harffe" (ebd.) aber billig mit zwei -f- zu schreiben, wiederum „Die Luft[,] weibliches geschlechtes mit einem F", nicht wie bei Harsdörffer mit zweien (420r); ebenso „Schiflein, oder Schiffelein" (420v); „Treflichen ein F. oder treffentlichen" mit deren zwei statt „trefflichen" (422v) usw. Diese Regelung auch in Fürst Ludwigs Gutachten zu Gueintz' Rechtschreibung vom März 1644: „Erinnerungen bey der aufgesetzten deutschen Wort oder Rechtschreibung" (HM Köthen: V S 545, Bl. 227r–236v u. 217r–218v; zur Veröff. in *DA Köthen I. 9* vorgesehen), hier Bl. 227r. Gueintz gegenüber hatte Fürst Ludwig im Frühjahr 1644 erklärt: „Also das die Stambuchstaben geduppelt in der mitten sollen ausgelaßen werden, hat eine beßere erhellgkeit, als sie drinnen zu laß[en,] den sie seind mußig und uberflußig[,] man weis doch wol woher sie kommen". Fürst Ludwig: „Erinnerungen von der Rechtschreibung" (HM Köthen: V S 545, Bl. 219r–220v; zur Veröff. in *DA Köthen I. 9* vorgesehen), hier Bl. 219v. Ders.: „Erinnerungen bey der aufgesetzten deutschen Wort oder Rechtschreibung" (s.o.), Bl. 231r: „Helfft ist nicht so gut als helffet, und kan das Stamwort doch wol erkant und behalten werden, wen man schon hilft und helft mit einem f nur schreibet." F. Ludwigs Versuch, den geminierten Konsonanten phonologisch zu retten, setzte sich nicht durch. Zwar kannte das Ahd. noch den phonetisch langen Konsonanten, doch begann der Abbau dieser Geminaten schon im späten Ahd. Die weitere Entwicklung zum Nhd. führte dann dazu, den konsonant. Digraphen zur Anzeige der Kürze des voraufgehenden Vokals zu nutzen, unabhängig ob darauf ein Vokal (herrisch) oder ein weiterer Konsonant (herrlich) folgt. Vgl. *Herz: Rechtschreibdebatte*, 93 ff.; *Nübling*, 23 f. u. 35 f.

11 Das Bezugsschreiben Harsdörffers an Gueintz fehlt, jedoch läßt sich der Zusammenhang rekonstruieren. F. Ludwig hatte mit 450923C ein Ex. von *Harsdörffer: Frauenzimmer-Gesprächspiele* V (1645, Ndr. 1969) erhalten und sich gegenüber Schottelius in 451028A an verschiedenen Auffassungen gestoßen, die Harsdörffer in der „Schlußerinnerung" zu jenem Teil der *Frauenzimmer-Gesprächspiele* vertreten hatte. Dazu gehörte namentlich die Eliminierung des -c- aus der Verbindung -ck- zugunsten der Gemination -kk-. Diese Position muß Harsdörffer also auch im unbekannten Brief an Gueintz vertreten haben. Vgl. dazu 451028A K 6.

12 Dasselbe gilt für die Worttrennung. Auch hier hatte Harsdörffer in der „Schlußerinnerung" zum 5. Teil seiner *Frauenzimmer-Gesprächspiele* (1645) für eine strikt morphematische und gegen eine Trennung nach Sprechsilben plädiert, d.h. für eine Trennung nach Wortstamm und Derivationsmorphemen bzw. Flexionsendungen: Sing-en, und nicht Sin-gen, wie es F. Ludwig fordert. Vgl. dazu 451028A K 6.

13 Auch dieser Brief von Gueintz an Harsdörffer scheint sich nicht erhalten zu haben, jedoch gibt 460131 als Antwort auf ein verlorenes Schreiben von Gueintz an Harsdörffer vom 11.1.1646 den wohl entscheidenden Hinweis auf den Korrespondenzzusammenhang.

14 Diese Kritik an einer von F. Ludwig als unpassend empfundenen Wortwahl hatte der Fürst auch schon in seinen Verbesserungen zu Harsdörffers Schreibweisen im 3. Teil von dessen *Frauenzimmer-Gesprächspielen* (1643) geäußert: statt „schiklicher" passe an einer Stelle besser „geschickter". F. Ludwig: „Etzliche erinnerungen, bey dem dritten theile der gesprächspiele am meisten die wortschreibung betreffende, auf begeren, vorgestellet." HM Köthen: V S 545, Bl. 419r–424v u. 426r (zur Veröff. in *DA Köthen I. 9* vorgesehen), hier 424r. Hier scheinen sich auch im Bereich des Wortschatzes jene Ausgleichs- und Standardisierungsprozesse anzudeuten, die die im 15. und 16. Jahrhundert bestehenden tw. althergebrachten sprachlandschaftlichen Wortschatzprägungen in der Schriftsprache vereinheitlichten und sowohl die Integration semantischer Differenz als auch das Ausscheiden von Varianzen und Konkurrenzformen beinhalteten. *Herz: Rechtschreibdebatte,* 129.

15 Auch hier überlagert das phonographische Argument das morphematische Prinzip der durchgängigen Konstanz des Wortstamms und der Stammbuchstaben (vgl. Anm. 10). 450420 bezeugte bereits, daß bei einem jüngsthin abgehaltenen Gesellschaftertreffen die Frage diskutiert worden sei, ob Substantive, deren Adjektive/ Adverbien auf –g enden, das -g- beibehalten müssen, etwa im Falle von „barmhertzig" > „barmhertzigkeit". Werder vertrat in 450420 im Gegensatz zur Mehrheit der versammelten Gesellschafter die gegenteilige Ansicht und plädierte für den Wegfall des -g-: Schuld > schuldig > Schuldikeit usw. F. Ludwig argumentiert hier abweichend, das -ch- lasse sich vor dem -k- „nicht wol aussprechen", deshalb „billich", aber „Billigkeit". Die von Werder geforderte Schreibung zurückweisend und seine Ansetzung von billich > Billigkeit vertretend schon F. Ludwigs Stellungnahme zu einem Entwurf der deutschen Rechtschreibung von Gueintz vom Frühjahr 1644 (als Dokument „440200" zur Veröff. vorgesehen in *DA Köthen I. 9*). Ausführlich dazu 450420 K 7. *Gueintz: Rechtschreibung (1645)* scheint sich dem angepaßt zu haben, etwa in den Formen „lieblichen" (S. 21, 25), aber „liebligkeit" (S. 9, 14, 18), „billich" (S. 4, 15, 24) und „zierliche (n)" (S.7, 21), aber „zierligkeit" (S. 7) und „redligkeit" (Bl. [)(vi]r). Eine phonetisch abgeleitete Regel dieser Schreibung läßt sich in der *Rechtschreibung* aber nicht ausmachen.

451220

Marcus Fridericus Wendelinus an Fürst Ludwig

Marcus Fridericus Wendelinus antwortet auf F. Ludwigs Auftrag, ein Gutachten zu einem Grundsatzpapier Justus Georg Schottelius' (FG 397) über sprachtheoretisch-grammatische Grundfragen aufzusetzen. Sein Gutachten legt Wendelinus bei. Er lobt Schottelius' Fleiß und Sprachkompetenz, moniert aber Sprachdiktion und gewisse neologistische Wortbildungen (Komposita) bei Schottelius, die ihm gezwungen erscheinen und den Sprachusus hintansetzen. — Zwei ihm vom Fürsten ausgeliehene Bücher von Schottelius werde er demnächst zurücksenden. — Da er neulich gegenüber F. Ludwig Georg Crucigers *Harmonia Linguarum Quatuor Cardinalium* (1616) erwähnt habe, der auch die Abstammung vieler deutscher Wörter aus dem Hebräischen beschreibe, sendet er ihm das Buch. Er kenne Andreas Helwigs Werk *Etymologiae, Sive Origines Dictionum Germanicarum* (1611) nicht, habe aber vom (Zerbster) Superintendenten Christian Beckmann erfahren, es sei keine gründlich ausgearbeitete Untersuchung.

Q HM Köthen: V S 545, Bl. 472r–473v [A: 473v], 473r leer; Sig.

A Dem Durchlauchtigen Hochgebornen Fürsten und Herren, Herren *Ludwigen*, Fürsten zu Anhalt, Graven zu Ascanien, Herren zu Zerbst und Bernburg, meinem genedig*en* Fursten und Herren. — *Eigenh. Empfangsvermerk F. Ludwigs:* Pres. 24. Decemb. 1645.

Durchläuchtiger Hochgeborner Furst:

Eweren Furstlichen Genaden sein meine unterthänige gehorsame dienste, nebenst andechtigem gebett für o[a] deroselben langes leben, gute bestandige gesundheit, auch Christliche friedliche Regirung, ieder zeit zuuor, Genediger Furst und Herr
    Daß schreiben,[1] So E.F.G. durch Zeigern mir zuuerlesen, und mein untertha-

niges gutachten darüber zueroffnen mir uberschickt, hab ich empfangen, geleßen und deßen inhalt vernommen. Habe demnach zu unterthaniger folge meine meinung, so viel die enge der Zeit leiden wollen, schrifftlich zuverfaßen und in der beylag zuubersenden mich schuldig erachtet, unterthanig bittende, es wollen EFG. die freyheit zuurtheilen in genaden vernemen.[2]

Jch sehe daß von H Schottelio in dießem Werck[3] allbereit großer fleiß angewandt, laß mich auch bedüncken, daß Lateinische schreiben komme von Jhm her. Das lobliche Vorhaben halte und rühme ich hoch, weil es zu außübung und verbeßerung unßerer Teutschen sprach gereicht: Welche weil sie anderen heutiges tages üblichen sprachen nichts nachgibt, ia viel mehr einen guten Vorsprung für ihnen hatt, so wehre es fast unverantwortlich[b], wan sie minder alß andere in acht genommen werden solte. Vnterdeßen gleich wie in andern neuen und ungewöhnlichen sachen allezeit etwas bedencken fürfallet; also kan es in dießem werck auch nicht außenbleiben.

Der art Zureden, deren sich HSchottelius in seinen lobreden[4] gebraucht, komt mir fast etwas gezwungen und allzu Lateinisch fur: wie auch gar viel neue composita darinnen vorlauffen, worauf ich in meinem bedencken gesehen.[5] Wier müßten solcher gestalt fast gar eine neue art zu reden annehmen, welche weder bey den Alten gefunden, noch heutiges tages von denen, welche fur gute Teutschen wollen gehalten sein, gebraucht wirdt. Weichet also dießer neue Stylus von der gewohnheit ganz ab, da doch sonsten dieselbe fur ein fundament dießes werckes will gehalten werden, inmaßen auß dem Lateinischen schreiben[6] zusehen. Doch wolte ich HSchottelium dießes falles nicht gern zum wiederpart haben. [472v]

Die 2 bücher HSchottelij will EFG. Jch mit anderer ersten gelegenheit nebenst unterthanigem danck wiederumb uberschicken. Jch wolte mich noch gern etwas darinnen ersehen.[7]

Ewren Furstlichen Genaden uberschick ich hiermit Harmoniam linguarum quatuor Cardinalium, Hebraicæ, Græcæ, Latinæ & Germanicæ.[8] Deren gegen dieselbe Jch in neuligkeit erwehnet. Ob EFG. belieben wolte, darinnen sich zuersehen, und zuuernemen, welcher gestalt ein großes Theil der Teutschen sprach auß der Hebraischen herfur gebracht wirdt.

Andream Helwig betreffende, der origines Germanicæ Linguæ soll geschrieben haben,[9] hab ich derselben niemals gesehen. Es bericht mich aber unser Superintenden[t][c] Becmannus[10], daß er sie[d] vor diesem gesehen, wehre aber kein volkommenes und gründtlich außgearbeites werck.

Dießes habe EFG. Jch in unterthanigkeit nicht verhalten sollen, die ich auch in den Schuz des Allerhochsten treulich empfehle, und mein genediger Furst und Herr auch hinfuro zuuerbleiben unterthanig bitte.
Zerbst den 20 Decembris, 1645.

EFG
Vnterthäniger, gehorsamer Diener
Marcus Frideric[us][c] Wendelinus mp.

T a *Vermutlich Verschreibung. Lies:* für — **b** *Gebessert aus* unverantwortlichen — **c** *Textverlust im Falz. Konjektur in eckigen Klammern.* — **d** *Gebessert aus* es

K Marcus Fridericus Wendelinus (1584–1652) stammte aus Sandhausen bei Heidelberg, wo sein Vater den Pfarrdienst versah. Als kurpfälz. Stipendiat studierte er in Heidelberg, wo er 1607 den Magistergrad erwarb. 1609 als Informator zweier junger Adliger nach Genf gereist, lernte er Peter v. Sebottendorf (FG 57), den Hofmeister der Prinzen Johann Casimir (FG 10) u. Friedrich Moritz v. Anhalt-Dessau (1600–1610) und Christian II. v. Anhalt-Bernburg (FG 51) bei ihrem Studienaufenthalt in Genf 1608/09 kennen. Sebottendorf zog Wendelinus bei der Prinzenbildung heran und ließ ihn an der Kavalierstour durch Frankreich teilnehmen. Nach Pz. Friedrich Moritz' Tod in Lyon (1610) erhielt Wendelinus den Auftrag, den Leichnam nach Dessau zu überführen. Dort wurde er von F. Johann Georg I. (FG 9) zum Präzeptor seiner verbliebenen Söhne bestimmt, jedoch bereits 1611 als Nachfolger des verstorbenen Gregor Bersmann (1538–1611) zum Rektor des gesamtanhalt. Gymnasiums in Zerbst bestimmt, welches Amt Wendelinus bis zu seinem Tod versah. Vgl. *ADB* XL, 714–716; *Beckmann* VII, 366–368; *Jöcher* IV, 1887f.; *Zedler* LIV, 1997f.

1 Der Brief, in dem F. Ludwig Wendelinus damit beauftragte, ein Gutachten zu einem Grundsatzpapier von Justus Georg Schottelius (FG 397) (s. Anm. 3) zu erstellen, ist uns unbekannt. Er scheint dieses Papier ohne Angabe des Verfassers seinem Brief beigelegt zu haben, denn Wendelinus vermutet im vorliegenden Brief, „daß Lateinische schreiben komme von Jhm her", d.h. von Schottelius. Die Datierung mit Ortsangabe Wolfenbüttel (s.u.) dürfte die textimmanenten Referenzen auf den Verfasser Schottelius ausreichend erhärten. Schottelius' Expertise hat sich im Köthener Erzschrein erhalten: HM Köthen: V S 545, Bl. 257rv–258v, Bl. 258v leer, eigenh. Sie ist auf Wolfenbüttel, 5.12.1645 datiert. Wie sie an F. Ludwig gelangte, ist uns nicht bekannt. Ein Begleitbrief von Schottelius liegt uns nicht vor. Auch Harsdörffer legte mit 460131 ein Grundsatzpapier vor, das im gleichen Zusammenhang einer als zwingend erachteten Vereinheitlichung der Grundsätze entstanden ist. F. Ludwig reagierte darauf in 460200 (demnächst in *DA Köthen I. 9*) mit einer eigenen Stellungnahme. Von Schottelius' Papier ließ F. Ludwig zudem eine Abschrift nehmen (a. a. O., Bl. 256rv), die er mit 451219 an Christian Gueintz (FG 361) zur Begutachtung sandte. Dessen Gegengutachten scheint im Gegensatz zu Wendelinus' Stellungnahme (s. Anm. 2) nicht erhalten zu sein. S. 451219 K 1, 2 u. 4; in K 1 auch eine Zusammenfassung von Schottelius' Grundsatzpapier. Vgl. zu diesem Komplex außerdem 450919A, 450923B, 450929, 451007, 451028A, 451101 u. 460406 K 4.

2 Wendelinus' Stellungnahme ist sein undatiert im Köthener Erzschrein erhaltenes eigenhändiges Dokument HM Köthen: V S 545, Bl. 488r–489v (489v leer). Es ist zur Veröffentlichung in *DA Köthen I. 9* vorgesehen. Wendelinus vertritt in dieser Stellungnahme zusammengefaßt folgende Positionen:
Er plädiert für den Ausbau der dt. Sprache, die gegenüber den Nachbarsprachen vernachlässigt wurde, was nicht wenige für ein Zeichen des Verfalls der deutschen Freiheit, Tapferkeit und Beständigkeit halten. Bis heute übernehmen die Deutschen mit Ekel vor dem Eigenen nur zu gern fremde Sprachen, Sitten und Kleidungen. Es sei hohe Zeit und verspreche viel, die Reinheit und den Glanz der dt. Sprache der Dunkelheit so vieler Jahrhunderte zu entreißen und so „quasi de novo Germanam condere gentem". Dabei stimmt er (Schottelius') zwei sprachtheoretischen und -normierenden Grundsätzen zu, auch wenn sich daraus mancherlei Schwierigkeiten ergäben: dem noch heute gültigen Gebrauch der Sprache und ihrer natürlichen inneren Gesetzmäßigkeit („usus huc usq*ue* receptus, & Natura linguæ analogica"). Vgl. dazu Anm. 6. Letztere („Analogicam linguæ naturam & rationem funda-

mentalem") ist in den Stammwörtern („radices") aufzusuchen. Sie sind die Grundlage oder „materia prima" der Sprache, aus der alle Ableitungen, Komposita und Flexionsformen hervorgehen. Hier ist das Feld der Grammatik, „quæ quasi formam simplici inducit materiæ, eamque in varias diducit species". Allerdings kann er sich nicht selbst überreden, auch wenn die einsilbigen Stammwörter im Deutschen dominieren, daß alle dt. Stammwörter einsilbig seien oder sein müßten. Die nicht geringe Zahl zweisilbiger Stammwörter und die Unmöglichkeit, sie ohne Lächerlichkeit auf Einsilbigkeit zurückzuführen, klärt hinreichend darüber auf, z.B. „Vater, mutter, meßer, waßer, feder, himmel, eisen, kupfer, sielber, sattel, messing, haber, apfel, nagel, nabel, regen, donner, kummer, finger, gesund, leber, ader, flügel, schwester, bruder, hammer fenster, hagel, hassel, zuber, mandel, teller &c.". Ob sich die Einsilbigkeit so vieler Stammwörter nun auf menschlichen Fleiß oder höhere Prinzipien des Sprachursprungs gründen, vermag Wendelinus nicht zu entscheiden: „Tot vocabula monosyllaba utrum ab industriâ humanâ, an à sublimiore principio ortum trahant non disputo." (Schottelius hatte dazu in seinem Papier mitgeteilt: „Et ex harum monosyllabarum infinitâ consociatione proveniunt tot vocabulorum millia, omnia virili sono constantia et inter se discreta: Sanè humana industria incomparabile hoc monosyllabitatum artificium non invenit, nec invenire potuit, sed ortum est unà cum ortâ lingua". A. a. O. [s. Anm. 1], Bl. 257r.) Ursprünglich ist die hebräische Sprache, die erste und älteste. Die übrigen Zungen gehen aus der babylonischen Sprachverwirrung hervor. In den Schulen herrscht der Grundsatz, „verba valere usu, non naturâ. Sed ad rem præsentem hoc non facit" — zur gegenwärtigen Sach(frag)e trage dies allerdings nichts bei. Sicher verlief die Sprachentwicklung im Deutschen wie in den anderen Sprachen auch: von rauhen Anfängen beginnend und sich in verschiedene Dialekte aufteilend. Weil jedem seine Mundart am besten gefalle, ist hier ein einfaches Urteil kaum möglich, zumal alte wie neue Autoren Fehler und Verderbnisse in die Sprache gebracht haben. Auf diesem schwierigen Terrain sind daher Scharfsinn und Urteilskraft gefragt; wie in der Medizin kann durch angestrengte Arbeit das Heilmittel gegen die Übel gefunden, d. h. hier eine vollkommene dt. Grammatik und ein vollständiges dt. Wörterbuch aufgesetzt werden, Werke, die die Jahrhunderte überdauern und die grassierenden willkürlichen Fehler ausräumen. Die Anfänge sind gemacht. (Schottelius beipflichtend:) Für gewiß können die Zahl der Stammwörter, der Endungen und Ableitungen und die kunstvollen Verfahren der Zusammensetzung gelten. Gestützt auf sichere Regeln kann der allgemeine Konsens nicht ausbleiben. Deutsche Fachwörter können die lateinischen ersetzen oder doch wenigstens mit diesen verbunden werden, auch wenn etliche Gelehrte die dt. Fachtermini wie „abwandelung" usw. noch scheuen. Wendelinus lobt zwar die neuere Poesie und poetische Ausdrucksweise, jedoch erscheint sie ihm in manchem auch gezwungen und dem lateinischen Vorbild zu sehr verpflichtet zu sein. Angesichts der „elegantias suas nativas" besitzenden dt. Sprache hat diese das Fremde nicht nötig. Auch bei gewaltsamen neuen Wortzusammensetzungen empfehle sich Zurückhaltung. Geriere sich hier jeder nach freiem Dafürhalten, werde eine Vollkommenheit der Sprache nicht erreichbar sein. Was sich an neuen Wortbildungen bewährt, wird sich durchsetzen und die Sprache bereichern. Daß die dt. Sprache in ihrem Ursprung völlig allein gewesen und vom Austausch mit anderen Sprachen ausgenommen gewesen sein solle, dazu kann sich Wendelinus nicht verstehen. In der Rechtschreibung sollte man sich nicht auf etymologische Streitereien einlassen, sondern im Sprachenvergleich die Verwandtschaft der Stammwörter ausfindig machen und daraus, nicht allein aus der Aussprache oder der Übereinstimmung der Schriftsteller, orthographische Normen ableiten, da sowohl diese wie jene Ausnahmen zulassen. So schreibt sich das Wort „Thränen" mit -th-, „quia affinis Græca radix θρῆνος citra omnem controversiam per θ scribitur"; ähnlich ist „deutsch" mit -d- und nicht mit -t- zu schreiben, „quia affinis Hebraica radix est דָּרַשׁ &c.".

3 Zwar mag man bei „dießem Werck" zunächst an Schottelius' jüngste Veröffentlichung, *Schottelius: Teutsche Vers- oder ReimKunst (1645),* denken. Angesichts des Nachstehenden und der Ausrichtung seines Gutachtens (s. Anm. 2) dürfte Wendelinus aber die intensive Spracharbeit der FG im allgemeinen und die von Schottelius im besonderen im Blick gehabt haben.

4 In *Schottelius: Sprachkunst (1641)* ist die eigentliche Grammatik in 9 „Lobreden" — und in der nur angekündigten 10. Lobrede, die er in der 2. Ausg. 1651 ausarbeitete — eingeleitet. Diese Lobreden machen das erste Buch der *Sprachkunst (1641)* aus (S. 1–172).

5 S. Anm. 2. Wendelinus dürfte hier von Schottelius neu aufgebrachte Komposita wie „grundrichtig", „gleichständige Gründe", „Hauptgründen und künstlichsten Wunderstücken", „allerwortreicheste Sprache", „Welträumig" (S. 8, 11, 13, 58) usw. im Auge gehabt haben. Interessanterweise entspricht diese Kritik Augustus Buchners (FG 362) Reserve gegenüber Georg Philipp Harsdörffers (FG 368) übertrieben schmückenden Neologismen in seinem Wörterbuch-Entwurf (1648; *KE,* 387 ff.). S. *Buchner (1720),* 298 f.

6 In Schottelius Grundsatzpapier hatte Schottelius zwei Normierungsprinzipien zugrundegelegt: „Jn asserendis recipiendisq*ue* fundaminibus linguæ Germanicæ duo occurrunt, nimirum receptus hactenus usus, et ipsa analogica linguæ natura." Zum Usus schränkte er ein: „Accedit secunda receptus hactenus et probatus usus, qui non rarò fluctuanti indagatori succurrere poterit: Voco autem usum receptum, vocabula, phrases, harumq*ue* scriptiones uti communiter occurrunt in probatis authorib*us*: quædam q*uae* ut dubia, remanebunt, non magnopere regulis obstabunt, sed certitudinem suam à communi consensu tandem exspectare possunt." A. a. O. (s. Anm. 1), Bl. 257r u. 257v.

7 Vermutlich *Schottelius: Sprachkunst (1641)* und *Schottelius: Der Teutschen Sprache Einleitung (1643).* Nicht auszuschließen ist *Schottelius: Teutsche Vers- oder ReimKunst (1645).*

8 Georg Cruciger: Harmonia Linguarum Quatuor Cardinalium, Hebraicae Graecae Latinae & Germanicae: In Qua Praeter Summum Earum Consensum, acceptionumque propriarum ab impropriis distinctionem, perpetua unius ab altera, origo perspicue deducitur ... / Authore M. Georgio Crucigero Profess. Acad. Marpurgensis (Frankfurt a. M. 1616); HAB: 23 Gram. 2°. — Das Werk ist Lgf. Moritz v. Hessen-Kassel (FG 80) d. d. Marburg 1.3.1616 gewidmet. In der Widmungsrede liefert Cruciger 55 Beispiele für die Gleichheit der Wortstämme in 4 Sprachen (Hebräisch, Griechisch, Latein, Deutsch). Das Werk befand sich auch in der Bibliothek F. Ludwigs, *IP,* 339r. Am Schluß seines Gutachtens zum Schottelius-Papier greift Wendelinus diesen Ansatz auf (s. Anm. 2). — Georg Cruciger (1575–1637) war Informator von Pz. Moritz v. Hessen-Kassel (FG 80) gewesen und wurde nach dessen Regierungsübernahme zum Professor an der U. Marburg berufen, wo er Logik u. Metaphysik, die hebräische Sprache u. schließlich Theologie lehrte und zeitweise das Rektorat führte. Zu ihm s. *Jöcher* I, 2226; *Zedler* VI, 1755f. Vgl. *NDB* III, 428 (Eintrag zu seinem Vater Caspar Cruciger d. J.).

9 Andreas Helvigius: Etymologiae, Sive Origines Dictionum Germanicarum: Ex Tribus Illis Nobilibus Antiquitatis Eruditae Linguis, Latina, Graeca, Hebraea, Derivatarum / Auctore M. Andrea Helvigio P.L.C. (Frankfurt a. M. 1611); HAB: Kb 321. – Der Dichter u. Sprachforscher M. Andreas Helwig (Helvigius, 1573–1643) stammte aus dem mecklenburg. Friedland und war Konrektor an den Schulen in Salzwedel, Friedland u. Greifswald, bevor er als Rektor nach Berlin ging. Von 1614 bis 1616 übernahm er die Professur der Poesie an der U. Rostock, trat jedoch bald das Rektorat am Gymnasium in Stralsund an, welches Amt er bis zu seinem Tod bekleidete. Vgl. *ADB* XI, 715; *Zedler* XII, 1327f.; Ernst Heinrich Zober: Urkundliche Geschichte des Stralsunder Gymnasiums von seiner Stiftung 1560 bis 1860. In sechs Beiträgen. Stralsund 1860, III, 19–23.

10 M. Christian Beckmann/ Becmanus (1580–1648), seit 1625 Superintendent in Zerbst u. Theologie-Professor am dortigen Gymnasium illustre. Vgl. 440119 K 0; dort auch zu seinen sprachwissenschaftlichen Studien.

460000

Justus Georg Schottelius an Herzog August d. J. von Braunschweig-Wolfenbüttel

Justus Georg Schottelius (FG 397) gibt (nach über einjähriger Entleihung) Bücher von Simon Stevin und Georg Henisch an Hz. August d. J. v. Braunschweig-Wolfenbüttel (FG 227) zurück. Er hat sie für die neuartige und wegen der Mundarten schwierige Ermittlung und Erklärung von deutschen Stammwörtern benötigt. — Eisengruben müssen im gleichen Zustand, in dem sie verpachtet wurden, zurückgegeben werden, da sonst ein finanzieller Schaden entsteht. Schottelius habe dies häufiger bei eigenen Nachforschungen am Ort oder bei der Prüfung der Kammer bemerkt. Er werde zu Unterrichtungszwecken hierzu gewisse Punkte zusammenstellen.

Q   NSTA Wolfenbüttel: 2 Alt Nr. 3520, Bl. 33rv [A: 33v]; eigenh. — Vgl. *Bei der Wieden: Schottelius*, 142 f.

A   Serenissimo humillimè.

Serenissime Princeps ac Domine, Domine clementissime,

Stevinum[1] et Henischium[2] cum gratiarum actione humillima remitto, imprimis ob diuturniorem mihi clementer concessum usum: Radices seu Primitiva Linguæ Teutonicæ erant colligenda et explicanda, quod non exiguo stetit labore, nemo enim hactenus præivit, et ob dialectorum varietatem res non adeò plana: Stevini interim et Henischij manus auxiliatrix subinde erat et per tot intervalla inter alios investiganda quàm ductricem etiam sæpissimè sum expertus, moræ ergò huic ultra annuæ veniam precor.

Negotium fodinarum ferrariarum[3] quod attinet, omninò caput et summa rei erit, ut finito locationis tempore, tota res ferraria[a] in eodem conservato statu et bonitate, quâ tradita fuit, restituatur; subrepit aliàs damnum, non, nisi multis expensis, postea reparabile, et latent abstrusæ lucrandi et fallendj artes: Sæpius inquisitione et examinibus, tàm in locis ipsis quàm in Camera interfui, et inde non pauca notavj: Loco instructionis igitur, si visum clementer fuerit, puncta quædam ex fundamentis rei ipsius petita congeram, quorum norma servata et Ser[tis.] Vræ. nomine omnibus collaborantibus et interessatis severè injuncta, ea, quæ conversanda erunt, procul dubio conservabit, nostraque expeditio ad regulam ipsam fructuosior, ut puto, exsistet.

      Vestræ Serenitati
      humillimè, fidelissimeque obediens
      Justus-Georgius Schottelius D.

I

Justus Georg Schottelius an Herzog August d. J. von Braunschweig-Wolfenbüttel

Nach Vollendung seines kleinen Werks über die vaterländische Sprache schickt Justus Georg Schottelius (FG 397) Hz. August d. J. v. Braunschweig-Wolfenbüttel (FG 227) die aus dessen Bibliothek entliehenen Bücher mit Dank zurück. Schottelius werde dem Herzog am Tage des Erscheinens sein Büchlein überreichen.

Q NSTA Wolfenbüttel: 2 Alt Nr. 40, Bl. 8rv [A: 8v]; eigenh. — *BN: Schottelius* Nr. 58a.

A Serenissimo &c. humillimè.

Serenissime Princeps ac Domine, Domine clementissime,

Libros, quorum usum Serenitas Vestra hactenus mihi concessit, absoluto demum opusculo de Linguâ patriâ,[1] cum humillimâ gratiarum actione remitto; libellum ipsum, cui Gustavus Selenus[2] toties auxiliatricem manum præbuit, primo die subiectissimè oblaturus,

      Vestræ Serenitati
      humillimè, fidelissimeque obediens
      Justus-Georgius Schottelius.

II

Justus Georg Schottelius an Herzog August d. J. von Braunschweig-Wolfenbüttel

Justus Georg Schottelius (FG 397) möchte die aus der Bibliothek Hz. Augusts d. J. v. Braunschweig-Wolfenbüttel (FG 227) entliehenen Bücher von Stevinus und Henisch gern noch einige Monate behalten, da seine *Ausführliche Arbeit* (1663) noch im Druck sei. Er will die Werke im 5. Buch für die Erklärung der zuerst von ihm gesammelten Wurzelwörter benutzen. Stevins Zusammenstellung von über 2000 niederländischen Einsilblern helfe ihm, eine vollständig erscheinende Liste deutscher Stammwörter zusammenzubringen, denn er könne daraus Wörter unter seine Buchstaben stopfen. Das sei wegen anderer Pflichten nur in freien Stunden erlaubt. — Im 5. Buch will Schottelius auch in einem eigenen Abschnitt von deutschen Sprichwörtern und Redensarten handeln, wobei nur der Henisch ihm noch Unterstützung biete. Er werde Hz. August die Bücher sauber zurückgeben.

Q NSTA Wolfenbüttel: 2 Alt Nr. 3520, Bl. 50rv [A: 50v]; eigenh.

A Serenissimo, humillimè.

460000 Justus Georg Schottelius

Serenissime Princeps ac Domine, Domine clementissime

Stevinum[1] et Lexicon Henischij[2] commodatarius adhuc habeo, quorum gratiosam concessionem per unum atq*ue* alterum mensem ideò humillimè sollicitare adhuc[a] cogor, quia in libro quinto operis, quod sub prælo iam madet,[3] omnes Linguæ Germanicæ radices, à nemine hactenus plenè collectas, cum explicatione proponere est animus, et quia Stevinus ultra duo millia belgicarum radicum monosyllabicarum collegit, unde subinde manus auxiliatrix mihi porrigitur,[4] subsidio ergò hoc labor meus, si aliquo numero absolutus apparere vult[b], carere non poterit: nam litera unâ absolutâ, ex Stevino non pauca infercio, quod non nisi horis succisivis, ob alia officij debita est concessum.

Jn dicto libro quinto etiam peculiarem tractatum de adagiis seu proverbis Germanicis editurus,[5] ideo adhuc ex Henischio auxilium porrò precor, quia multa ad hanc rem facientia in eo inveni, alibi non exstantia, plenè autem non dum collegi: immaculatos restituam libros, Vestra Serenitas diuturnum ob dictas rationes usum inclementer non habeat, est quod humillimus oro[c].

Vestræ Serenitatj fidelissimè subiectissimeque inserviens
Justus-Georgius Schotteli*us* D

T a *Schottelius* ferrearia

T II a *Ersetzt* <quo> — b *Eingefügt.* — c *Ersetzt* <precor>

K Zur Schwierigkeit der zeitlichen Einordnung von undatierten Schottelius-Briefen s. 450000 K 0. Der dort behandelte erste Brief erwähnt schon eine Rückgabe des Werks von Simon Stevinus. S. dort K 2. Justus Georg Schottelius (FG 397) wird es im Laufe der Zeit mehrfach und auch sehr lange aus der Bibliothek Hz. Augusts d.J. v. Braunschweig-Wolfenbüttel (FG 227) entliehen haben. Vgl. Beil. I. Der vorliegende Brief erlaubt nur die Datierung der Ausleihe auf die Zeit nach Schottelius' Promotion (U. Helmstedt, 26.2.1646, s. 460414). Da Schottelius am Ende des Briefs von häufiger Inspektion von Gruben redet, dürfte der Brief auch bei späterer Arbeit an seiner *Sprachkunst* von 1651 oder seiner *Ausführlichen Arbeit* (1663) entstanden sein. Wir veröffentlichen jedoch schon hier, weil er die Kontinuität der Stammwortarbeit widerspiegelt.

1 Einen immer wieder entliehenen Sammelband mit Werken des niederländ. Mathematikers, Ingenieurs und Sprachforschers Simon Stevin (1548–1620), HAB: 8 Geom. (1)–(3). S. 450000 u. K 2. Vgl. unten K II.

2 Das unvollendete Wörterbuch von *Henisch* (1616). S. 450923B, 450929, 451219 K 7 u.ö.

3 Eisengruben im Harz. Schottelius wurde nach seiner Ernennung zum Hofrat im Mai 1646 auch wiederholt zur Inspektion im Salz- und Erzabbau eingesetzt. Diese amtliche Tätigkeit kam seinem philologischen Interesse an deutschen Fachbegriffen entgegen. Vgl. schon 450000 K 3 u. 4 und außerdem: Beschreibung Der Sulten oder Des Saltzwesens in Lünaburg Darin enthalten. Alle Heüser in der Sulten, und eine richtige Specification aller Pfannen- und Chorusgüter, so zu einem Jeden Hause gehören ... wie auch vom anfang, altem und Itzigen Zustande der Sulten, ... sambt den rechten Arcanis Salinaribus ... Nicht weniger von den Salingütern undt Gerechtsamen des Klosters Scharnbeck ... Anno 1665. [2. Titel]: OPUS MANUSCRIPTUM de RE SALINARIA LUNEBURGICA ut et de

bonis et jure Monasterii Scarnebecensis in salinis Luneburgicis, jussu ... PRINCIPIS AC DOMINI DN. AUGUSTI Ducis Brunsvicensis ac Lúneburgensis &c. ex variis antiquioribus et recentioribus Documentis, Recessibus, contractibus, annotatis et ipsa vera Praxi collectum & adornatum à Serenitatis suae consiliario Iusto Georgio Schottelio D. additus est in fine Index Generalis, qui ordinem et contenta horum collectorum monstrat: ANNO 1665. HAB: Cod. Guelf. 7.12 Aug. 2°; De Singularibus quibusdam & antiquis In Germania Juribus & Observatis. Kurtzer Tractat Von Vnterschiedlichen Rechten in Teutschland ... Ausgefertigt von JUSTO GEORGIO SCHOTTELIO D. (Wolfenbüttel: Conradus Buno 1671; Dr. Braunschweig: Johan Heinrich Duncker). HAB: 130.4 Jus. Zur zeitgenöss. Diskussion um Fachsprachen und deren Lexikographie s. 440826 K 4.

K I 1 Das Schreiben ist nicht auf das Jahr genau zu datieren. Zu Justus Georg Schottelius' (FG 397) Spracharbeit vgl. auch 450000 K 0. Es ist wahrscheinlich, daß der Brief sich auf die Rückgabe von Büchern bezieht, die Schottelius für eines der 1641 und 1643 erschienen Sprachwerke benutzte, da er seinen Namen ohne seinen (im Februar 1646 erworbenen) Doktortitel unterzeichnete. Zum Wort *Opusculum*, das sich auf *Schottelius: Der Teutschen Sprache Einleitung (1643)* beziehen mag, s. 450000 K 0.
 2 Kryptonym Hz. Augusts d.J. v. Braunschweig-Wolfenbüttel (FG 227). Vgl. 410706 K I 2.

K II Die Datierung des Briefs in die Zeit der dritten Fassung der Grammatik Justus Georg Schottelius' (FG 397), nach *Schottelius: Sprachkunst (1641)* u. *Schottelius: Sprachkunst (1651)*, d.i. *Schottelius: Ausführliche Arbeit (1663)*, ergibt sich aus der Erwähnung eines fünften Buchs und des bereits begonnenen Herstellungsprozesses des Werks. S. Anm. 4 bzw. 3. Die vorhergehenden Ausgaben weisen nur drei Bücher auf. Vgl. 450000 K 0. Trotz seiner späten Abfassung veröffentlichen wir den unbekannten Brief an dieser Stelle, da er die weitere Beschäftigung mit Henischs Wörterbuch und Stevins Stammwortsammlungen demonstriert.
 1 Zu Simon Stevin s. oben K 1.
 2 Das unvollendete deutsche Wörterbuch von Georg Henisch (1616), s. oben K 2.
 3 *Schottelius: Ausführliche Arbeit (1663)* schwitzte wohl noch im Januar und Februar 1663 unter der Druckerpresse, da Schottelius sie am 1.3.1663 Hz. August d.J. v. Braunschweig-Wolfenbüttel (FG 227) widmete.
 4 Über Stevins Listen europäischer Stammwörter s. 450000 K 2 u. 450410 K 3. In *Schottelius: Sprachkunst (1641)* wurde in einer Lobrede von den stets einsilbigen Stammwörtern gehandelt: „Die Vierdte Lobrede Von der Uhralten Hauptsprache der Teutschen/ begreifft Den Natürlichen Uhrsprung und vortreffliche Eigenschafften der Teutschen Letteren und Stammwörter ingemein." (S.74–95). In *Schottelius: Sprachkunst (1651)* ist in der 4. Lobrede (9–134) auch wieder die Rede „von Ankunft und Eigenschaft der Teutschen Letteren", die in der sog. Keltischen Sprache mit „eigenen Letteren" geschrieben worden seien, sowie „von der Einsilbigkeit der Teutschen StammWörter" (Bl. C 7). Vgl. bes. auch die „Kurtze Erklärung" in *Schottelius: Der Teutschen Sprache Einleitung (1643)*, 70–73 zu Henisch und Stevinus über Stammwörter und S.109ff. zum deutschen Wörterbuch. Erst *Schottelius: Ausführliche Arbeit (1663)* enthält ein 5. Buch, dessen 6. Traktat „Die Stammwörter Der Teutschen Sprache Samt dererselben Erklärung/ und andere die Stammwörter betreffende Anmerkungen" (S.1271–1450) behandelt und endlich S.1277–1450 die angekündigte Sammlung der deutschen Wurzeln oder Stammwörter vorführt. Zum in der FG kontroversen Begriff des Stammworts und seiner Theorie vgl. 450410 K 3.
 5 *Schottelius: Ausführliche Arbeit (1663)*, 1099–1147: „LIBRI QVINTI TRACTATUS

460000A Giovanni Francesco Loredano

TERTIUS De PROVERBIIS, Proverbialibusque locutionibus Germanicis; Addita sunt non nulla de Hieroglyphicis, Emblematibus, Symbolis, aliisq́.", d. i. „Des Fünften Buches Dritter Tractat Von den Teutschen Sprichwörteren Und anderen Teutschen Sprichwortlichen Redarten: Samt beygefügter erwehnung von den Sinnbildern/ DenkSprüchen/ Bildereien Gemählten und derogleichen." Vgl. zu Henischs Wörterbuch (*Henisch*) und dessen Berücksichtigung von Redensarten u. Sprichwörtern 451219 K 7.

460000A
Giovanni Francesco Loredano an Georg Philipp Harsdörffer

Loredano freut sich über den Erfolg, daß nun eines seiner Werke in einem deutschen Kleid auftrete. Er beginnt Deutsch zu lernen, um seine Dankesschuld zu erkennen. Zweifellos habe Harsdörffers Beredsamkeit seinem Werk einen Geist eingehaucht, den es zuvor nicht besaß. Dank.

Q LETTERE | DEL SIG. | GIO: FRANCESCO | LOREDANO: | Nobile Veneto. | Diuise in cinquantadue Capi, | e Raccolte. | DA | HENRICO GIBLET | CAVALIER: | [10 Zierstücke] | VENETIA; M. D.C. LIII. | Appresso li Guerigli. | Con Licenza de' Superiori, e Priuilegio. S. 353. HAB: Lk 477:6; vgl. LETTERE | DEL SIGNOR | GIO: FRANCESCO | LOREDANO | Nobile Veneto. | Diuise in cinquantadue Capi, e Raccolte | DA | HENRICO GIBLET | CAVALIER: | Parte Prima. | Decimasettima Impressione. | IN GENEVA, | Appresso. Gio. Herm. Widerhold. | [Linie] | M. DC. LXIX. S. 331 f. HAB: Lk 485. Zit. als *1669*. Das von uns benutzte Exemplar dieser Ausgabe trägt auf dem Frontispiz die eigenh. Besitzerangabe Hz. Ferdinand Albrechts v. Braunschweig-Wolfenbüttel-Bevern (FG 842. 1673) mit dem Zusatz „Cassel 1669". Brieffassung *1669* wiederveröffentlicht in *Narciss: Studien* 1928, 188. — BN: Estermann II, 596.

A Al Signor Giorgio Filippo Harsdorf. Norimberga.

NOn posso esprimere la mia consolatione nel vedere le mie Opere vestite alla Tedesca[a].

Io non credeua, che ne' Paesi esteri trouassero tanta fortuna, e nella virtù di Vostra Sig. tanta benignità. Niente intendo la lingua, ma comincio ad apprenderne i principij, per poter leggere le mie obligationi. Son sicuro, che dall'eloquenza di V. Sig. haueranno le mie Compositioni riceuuto quello spirito, che non le ha potuto communicar la mia penna. Ma chi benefica senza merito aspira sempre a gli eccessi. Resta, che V. Sig.[b] disponga d'vno, che ha[c] fatto suo con le proue della virtù, e con gli atti della gentilezza. Ringratiandola in tanto di sì cortese espressione, le bacio con tutto l'affetto le mani.
Venetia.

T a *1669* Todescha — b *1669* S. — c *1669* hà

K Der venezianische Patrizier Giovanni Francesco Loredano (s. 450817) hatte offenbar von der Verdeutschung seines Romans *La Dianea* (1644) erfahren, unter einem Pseudonym jedoch nicht Diederich v. dem Werder (FG 31) als Übersetzer entdecken können. S. 440000 K 2. [Giovanni Francesco Loredano: *La Dianea*, zuerst Venedig 1635, ins Deutsche übers. von Diederich v. dem Werder (FG 31):] DJANEA | Oder | Rähtselgedicht/ | in welchem/ | Vnter vielen anmuhtigen Fügnussen/ | Hochwichtige Staatsachen/ | Denklöbliche Geschichte/ und | klugsinnige Rahtschläge/ | vermittelst | Der Majestätischen Deutschen Sprache/ | Kunstzierlich | verborgen. | [Vignette: Purpurmuschel mt Schriftband, „Vol Königlicher Farb:"] | Nürnberg/ | Jn Verlegung Wolfgang Endters/ | [Linie] | M. DC. XXXXIV. — Faksimiledr. der Ausgabe von 1644. Hg. u. eingel. v. Gerhard Dünnhaupt. Bern usw. 1984. (Nachdrucke deutscher Literatur des 17. Jahrhunderts, Bd. 22.) Vgl. 440000. Zur Übersetzerfrage vgl. auch Gerhard Dünnhaupt: Giovanni Francesco Loredano's Novel La Dianea — Its Structure and Didactic Aims. In: Studi secenteschi 16 (1975), 43–52; Diederich von dem Werder oder Georg Philipp Harsdörffer? Zur Klärung der umstrittenen Autorschaft der Dianea von 1644. In: GRM 23 (1973), 115–118. — Loredano hielt Georg Philipp Harsdörffer (FG 368) irrtümlich für den Übersetzer seines Romans. Die Verwechslung resultierte offenbar aus der Namensähnlichkeit der Titelperson Loredanos mit der Diana in Harsdörffers Übersetzung des span. Romans: DIANA, | Von | H. J. De Monte-Major, | in zweyen Theilen Spanisch be- | schrieben/ und aus denselben | geteutscht | Durch | Weiland | Den wolgebornen Herrn/ | Herrn Johann Ludwigen | Freyherrn von Kueffstein/ etc. | An jetzo aber | Mit deß Herrn C. G. Polo zu- | vor nie- gedolmetschten | dritten Theil | vermehret/ | und | Mit reinteutschten Red- wie auch | neu- üblichen Reim-arten | ausgezieret. | Durch | G. P. H. | [Linie] | Gedruckt zu Nürnberg/ Jn Verle- | gung Michael Endters. | Jm Jahr 1646. Auch 1661 u. 1663 erschienen. Reprogr. Nachdr. Darmstadt 1970. Das Erstveröffentlichungsdatum dieser Übertragung (1646) muß allerdings nicht den Grund liefern, um den undatierten Brief Loredanos in das Jahr 1646 zu setzen. Denkbar ist, daß Harsdörffer bereits eher an Loredano geschrieben hatte. Er suchte, wie wir aus seinem Schreiben an F. Ludwig wissen (450817), schon zuvor, einen Austausch auch der FG mit Loredanos *Accademia degli Incogniti* und mit anderen italienischen Akademien einzufädeln. Harsdörffer könnte schon 1645 selbst an Loredano im Zusammenhang mit seinem Plan geschrieben haben, die FG und die Incogniti in eine Beziehung zueinander zu bringen. Zwar lehnte der Fürst es ab, an diese Akademien offiziell unter dem Siegel der FG zu schreiben, jedoch hatte Harsdörffer unter seinem Gesellschaftsnamen „Der Spielende" schon zuvor und auch danach privat Kontakte zu solchen Gesellschaften gepflegt, so daß Loredanos vorliegende Antwort in den Zeitraum 1644 bis 1646 gefallen sein könnte. Wir setzen seinen Brief nur deshalb in das Jahr 1646, weil Loredano durch einen Dritten von Harsdörffers *Diana*-Übersetzung erfahren haben mag, die in ihm die Vermutung entstehen ließ, der ihm wohl inzwischen bekannte Harsdörffer habe seine *Dianea* übertragen. Harsdörffer könnte Loredano erst danach Werders Buch als Zeugnis der fruchtbringerischen Arbeit geschickt haben, denn der Venezianer hätte trotz seiner Unkenntnis des Deutschen bemerkt, daß Harsdörffers *Diana*-Übersetzung nicht auf der *Dianea* beruhte. Mit seinem Brief vom 28.2.1647 (*Birken: Werke u. Korrespondenz* 9/I, 50 f.) sandte Johann Rist (FG 464. 1647) Sigismund Betulius/ v. Birken (FG 681. 1658), der ihn im November 1646 im holstein. Wedel besucht hatte, „die Dianeam" nach. Damit könnte aus zeitlichen Gründen auch schon die von Betulius mitgebrachte *Diana*-Übersetzung Harsdörffers gemeint gewesen sein, jedoch gibt es keinen zwingenden Grund zu der Annahme, Betulius habe diese und nicht Werders Übersetzung mit sich geführt und wohl aus praktischen Gründen einstweilen zurückgelassen. In *Birken: Werke u. Korrespondenz* 9/II, 670 f. ist Werders Übersetzerschaft der *Dianea* nicht erwähnt. Harsdörffer hatte seine Kuefstein-Bearbeitung, an der wohl auch Johann Klaj beteiligt war (*Birken: Werke u. Korrespondenz* 9/II, 598), Betulius allerdings schon am 1.8.1646 nach Wolfenbüttel geschickt (*Birken: Werke u. Korrespondenz* 9/I, 13). — Zeugnis einer weiteren Kontaktaufnahme mit einer italienischen Akademie ist die Übersendung von Publikationen des neapolitanischen Ozioso-Mitglieds Marco Aurelio Severino. S. 450817. Da dessen *Zootomia* vielleicht auch mit Rücksicht auf die Inquisition in Nürnberg gedruckt wurde, dürfte Harsdörffer sich der Kontakte von Nürnbergern, besonders Johann Georg Volckamers, bedient haben. Er schrieb auch ein Ehrengedicht für dieses Werk. S. 450817. — Im ersten Teil von Loredanos *Lettere* (1653, S. 352) findet sich ein undatiertes Schreiben Loredanos „Al Signor Cristiano Husmano. Vratislauia", dessen Adresse 1669 (S. 330 f.) aus „Christiano Horfmano. Vratislauia" entstellt ist. Der „RACCONTO DE'NOMI Di coloro a' quali sono state scritte le Lettere" der Ausgabe von 1669 enthüllt eine dritte Namensform: „Al Sig. Christiano Hosmano". Der Empfänger des Briefs dürfte Christian Hoffmann v. Hoffmannswaldau aus Breslau gewesen sein. Loredano bedankt sich für das ihm durch Hoffmann gespendete Lob. „Alle cortesi espressioni di Vostra Signoria, corrisponderó con l'opere, quando si risouerà di moderare gli encomi, e di operare I comandi. I Libri vsciti da tre anni in quà da gl'ingegni Italiani sono molti, onde la prego a concedermi qualche termine per sodisfare alla sua curiosità. I Poeti più celebri di quest'età sono nel Lirico Fuluio Test, e nell' Eroico Girolami Gratiani."

460103

Wilhelm Heinrich von Freyberg an einen Fürsten [F. Ludwig?]

Französischer Brief Wilhelm Heinrichs v. Freyberg (FG 439) aus Paris, auf der Reise Freybergs als Hofmeister Pz. Johann Georgs II. v. Anhalt-Dessau (FG 322). Freyberg habe dem Fürsten weder aus dem Haag noch bisher aus Paris über das Gewünschte unterrichten können. Er habe im Haag wegen der ihm aufgetragenen Sache mit Streso, Rivet und anderen gesprochen, mit denen der verstorbene Dr. Rumpf sehr vertraulich verkehrte, jedoch wollte keiner davon etwas wissen. Hier in Paris habe er mit Drelincourt und einigen gelehrten Katholiken gesprochen, jedoch habe keiner vernommen, daß die gesuchten Bücher hier gewesen seien; und wenn jemand das sagte, würden sie es für eine falsche Behauptung halten. Freyberg warte noch auf die Rückkehr von Nauderus (Gabriel Naudé), des Bibliothekars des Kd. Mazarin, aus Italien. — Neujahrswünsche.

Q   SB Berlin — PK: 141/11: FrbrGes, 1 Bl., v leer; eigenh. — Bibliothekseintrag aus dem 19. Jh.: Freiberg Wilh. Heinrich v. Mitglied d. fruchtbring. Gesells. d. „Reingefärbte."

A   *Fehlt.*

Monseigneur,

Vostre Altesse trouvera aggreable que la presente Luy fasse mes excuses pour avoir tant tardè de m'acquitter de mon debvoir envers Elle; l'unique raison en est, que j'ay esté si malhereux, que ny à la Haÿe, ny icy je n'ay rien trouvé qui eust peu contenter en quelq*ue* façon la curiosité de V*ostre* A*ltesse*, laquelle je n'ay voulu entretenir vainement, non plus que de Luy oster entierement toute esperance, auparavant d'avoir [Bl. 1v] essayè tous les moyens qui me pourroyent estre favorables au desir que j'aurray tout le temps de ma vie de satisfaire aux commendemens dont V*ostre* A*ltesse* me daignera d'honorer.[1] J'en ay parlè à la Haye à

Monsieur Streso², à Monsieur Rivet³, et à quelquesuns que le feu Docteur Rumpf⁴, homme tres-curieux a le plus familierement hanté, mais personne n'en a rien voulu sçavoir. Jcy je m'en sois enquis aupres de Monsieur Drelincourt⁵ ministre, et quelques autres sçavans hommes de l'eglise Romaine, mais d'un commun consentement, je n'ay eu pour toute responce, qu'ils n'ont jamais entendu dire que tels livres avoyent estez icy, et si quelquun le disoit, ils les estimeroyent supposez.

J'attend encore [Bl. 2r] le retour de Monsieur Nauderus⁶ [sic], bibliothecaire de Monseigneur le Cardinal Mazarini, à present en Jtalie; Sil me dira quelque chose qui puisse donner de la satisfaction à Votre Altesse, je Luy temoigneray que je n'ay rien de plus cher au monde que l'honneur de Ses commandemens, priant Dieu pour la conservation de Vostre Altesse et de toute Son Jllustre maison tant pour cette annee icy, qu'une infinité d'autres qui la soivront seon qu'est obligé.

Monseigneur
à Vostre Altesse un tres humble et tresobligeant serviteur
GH de Freyberg

Paris ce 3 Janv. l'an 1646

K Wilhelm Heinrich v. Freyberg (FG 439), der in der Garde F. Friedrich Heinrichs v. Oranien und im brit. Bürgerkrieg auf kgl. Seite gedient hatte, führte 1645–1647 Pz. Johann Georg II. v. Anhalt-Dessau (FG 322) in die Niederlande und nach Frankreich und Italien. Anschließend in Köthen tätig, trat er bald darauf in Dessau eine lange und steile Hofkarriere an, die ihn auf die Posten eines Geheimen Rats und Landeshauptmanns Johann Georgs beförderte. Er widmete sich auch der Glasmanufaktur, ließ auf seinem Gut Möhlau einen Saal mit Wappen und Impresen der FG ausmalen, war nach F. Ludwigs Tod 1651 an der Übertragung der Oberstelle der FG auf Hz. Wilhelm IV. v. Sachsen-Weimar beteiligt und übertrug und bereicherte Joseph Henshaws moralische und religiöse Überlegungen *Horae succisivae; or, Spare-houres of meditations* (London 1640, 5. Aufl.) in seinen *Horae SVCCISIVAE, Oder Spar-stunden Etlicher Betrachtungen/ Gerichtet auf unsere schuldigkeit Gegen GOTT/ Unsern nähesten/ Uns selbsten* (¹Köthen 1652). S. *Conermann III*, 529f. u. *Conermann: Anhalt*, 14f.

1 F. Ludwig suchte wohl nach der Papstsatire Pallavicinos (s. Anm. 6), bemühte sich jedoch auch weiterhin, im Haag für die Bestellung der großen, inzwischen dreibändigen Predigtharmonie seines Hofpredigers und Köthener Superintendenten Daniel Sachse zu werben. *Sachse: Einhelligkeit* I–III. Schon 1641 hatte er dort durch einen Reisenden (Christian Friedrich v. Einsiedel, FG 357) und den oranischen Hofmann Johann v. Mario (FG 100) die Finanzierung des Werkes durch Subskription zu verbessern versucht. S. 420120. Vgl. 420712 (K 1), 441205 (K 3), 450721 (K 1), 460119 u. ö.

2 Caspar Streso (1603–1664), ein wohl mit dem anhalt. Theologen Adam Streso eng verwandter Kontraremonstrant (Gegner von Passchier de Fijne), der in einen Streit mit Constantijn Huygens über den Gebrauch der Orgel im Gottesdienst geriet. Prediger in 's-Gravenhage. *NNBW* X, 984f. Vgl. 420120 K 11 u. 420630 K 4.

3 André Rivet (Saint-Maixent, Dépt. Deux-Serres 1572 – Breda 1651), aus hugenott. Kaufmannsfamilie, Hofprediger des Claude de la Trémoille duc de Thouars, 1617 Vorsitzender der Synode von Vitré, seit 1620/21 trotz des Widerstands seiner Kirche Prof. der

Theologie an der U. Leiden, seit 1632 Lehrer/ 1636 Hofmeister Pz. Wilhelms (II.) v. Oranien, 1646 Aufsicht über die neue „Doorluchtige School" zu Breda. *NNBW* VII, 1051. Vgl. 300725 K 8, 330603 K 1 (S. 473) u. 390822 K 19. Unter seinen vielen Schriften (s. *Haag* VIII, 444–449) fällt uns auf *Instruction Chrestienne Touchant les spectacles publics Des Comœdies & Tragœdies* (1639), mit der er sich gegen die Aufführung von Corneilles *Cid* bei der Hochzeit Johan Wolferts Heer van Brederode im Haag wandte. S. 380310 K I 1.

4 Christian Rumpf (Rumph, 1582 – 24.6.1645), ein aus Laasphe (Gft. Wittgenstein) stammender Mediziner (stud. U. Leiden), Leibarzt Kf. Friedrichs V. v. d. Pfalz (Kg. Friedrich I. v. Böhmen), sodann der Fürsten Moritz u. Friedrich Heinrich v. Oranien. Freund von Constantijn Huygens. *NNBW* VII, 1074f. Vgl. 420120 K 22.

5 Charles Drelincourt d. Ä. (1595–1669), ref. Prediger am Tempel zu Charenton. S. 191124 K 1, 380110 K 9, 400311 K 1, 400312 (K 1), 410101 u. I u. II, 430505 I u. ö. F. Christian II. v. Anhalt-Bernburg (FG 51) übersetzte sein Erbauungsbuch: *De la Persévérance des Saincts, ou de la fermeté de l'amour de Dieu* (Charenton 1625): Von der Beharligkeit der | Außerwehlten. | Oder | Von Besten- | digkeit der Liebe Gottes. | Anfangs im Jahre | 1625. | Durch Carlen Drelincourt, Pre- | diger und diener am worte Gottes/ in | der Reformirten Kirche zu Pariß Fran- | tzösisch geschrieben: | Nachgehendes aber ihme selbst/ und den | Seinigen/ auch andern frommen Chri- | sten zu nützlicher erbaulligkeit/ | Zusamt den letzten Stunden des Herren von | Plessis Mornay, verdeutschet | Durch ein Mitglied der Frucht- | bringenden Gesellschaft. | [Linie] | Gedruckt zu Cöthen im Fürstenthume | Anhalt/ | Jm Jahre unsers HErren/ | 1641. | Wer beharret biß ans ende/ der wird selig. HAB: 1293.11 Theol. (1); Lm 1133 (1). Freyberg mag Drelincourt ein Exemplar dieser Übersetzung überreicht haben. Vor allem könnte er eine Botschaft F. Ludwigs über religionspolitische Dinge überbracht haben, die wohl auch die Verhandlungen über die Stellung der deutschen Reformierten im Westfälischen Frieden betrafen. Sollte der weithin einflußreiche Drelincourt auch die Werbung für Sachses Werk in europ. Gemeinden unterstützen? Vgl. 411128: Vorschlag der St. Jakobsgemeinde in Köthen, F. Ludwig möge eine Verlagsbeteiligung bei der Stadt Basel einwerben.

6 Gabriel Naudé (1600–1653). In Padua hatte Naudé Medizin studiert, wurde auch 1633 zum Leibarzt Kg. Ludwigs XIII. gewählt, doch kehrte er nach Padua zurück, um im selben Jahr das Doktorat zu erlangen. Er wirkte jedoch vor allem als Bibliothekar im Dienst von Henri II. de Mesmes (Präsident des Pariser Parlaments, dem Naudé 1627 seinen *ADVIS POVR DRESSER VNE BIBLIOTHEQVE* widmete) und dreier Kardinäle: in Rom Giovanni Francesco di Bagni (G. F. Guido del Bagno, seit 1631) und Antonio Barberini (bis 1642), in Paris Jules Mazarin (Giulio Mazarini), der Nachfolger Richelieus (1642–1661). Naudé gehörte zur sog. Académie putéane, wurde auch Mitglied verschiedener italienischer Akademien. Als Freigeist galt er u. a. wegen seiner Abhandlung *CONSIDERATIONS POLITIQVES SVR LES COVPS D'ESTAT* (Rome 1639), die Christian v. Ryssel (FG 775. Der Beschirmete. 1661) verdeutschte: Gabriel Naudaeus Politisches Bedencken über die Staats-streiche Aus dem Frantzösischen übergesetzt durch den Beschirmeten (Leipzig 1668 u. 1678). Als universal gebildeter Gelehrter, schrieb er sich u. a. mit den Brüdern Dupuy, Nicolas-Claude Fabri de Peiresc, dem Reformierten Elia Diodati, Pierre Gassendi, La Mothe Le Vayer und dem Orientalisten Jacques Gaffarel, dem er seine einflußreiche *Bibliographia politica* (1633) widmete. Augustus Buchner (FG 362) schickte F. Ludwig eine Abschrift des Werks, bevor seine eigene Ausgabe erscheinen konnte, von der der Fürst zwei Exemplare erwarb (s. 391119 K 10, vgl. 391216, 400113, 400214). GABRIELIS NAUDÆI | Parisiens. | BIBLIOGRAPHIA | POLITICA. | In qua plerique omnes ad Civilem | Prudentiam Scriptores quà recensentur, | quà dijudicantur. | Opusculum elegans:

nunc primùm in Ger- | maniâ editum | Cum Accessorio non dissimilis | argumenti. | ê Muséo | Augusti Buchneri. | [Zierleiste] | WITTEBERGÆ | Impensis Balthasar Mevii Bibliopol. | Typis Röhneri Acad. Typogr. | Anno M DC XLI. Im Katalog von F. Ludwigs Bibliothek (darüber *Conermann: Nachlaßinventar*) ist der Wittenberger Druck mit zwei Exemplaren aus dem Jahre 1640 verzeichnet, wahrscheinlich ein Abschreibfehler (Bl. 309v). Dieses Werk dürfte F. Ludwig veranlaßt haben, Freyberg wohl mit der Bitte um Auskünfte zu ital. oder frz. Büchern zu schicken, die in Deutschland schwer zu ermitteln und zu kaufen waren. Dazu könnten nicht nur Publikationen von Virgilio Malvezzi marchese di Castel Guelfo gehört haben (außer den von ihm herausgegebenen und übersetzten, s. Personenregister), sondern auch die gesuchte Fortsetzung von Ferrante Pallavicinos Papstsatire *Il divorzio celeste*. S. bes. 431021 K 1–2, 431022 K 2 u. 450526 K 3. Vgl. Gabriel Naudé: Bibliografia politica, a cura di Domenico Bosco. Roma 1997; Estelle Bœuf: La bibliothèque parisienne de Gabriel Naudé en 1630. Les lectures d'un libertin érudit. Genève 2007 (mit Lit.); Jack A. Clarke: Gabriel Naudé 1600–1653. Hamden, CT 1970; weitere Literatur in 391119 K 10.

460104

Extrakt eines Briefs Pfalzgraf Ludwig Philipps von Simmern an Fürst Johann Casimir von Anhalt-Dessau

Pgf. Ludwig Philipp v. Simmern (FG 97. Der Gefährliche) bittet F. Johann Casimir v. Anhalt-Dessau (FG 10. Der Durchdringende) um Vermittlung bei F. Ludwig (Der Nährende), um von diesem die Erlaubnis zu erhalten, einige fürstliche und adlige Personen auf deren Wunsch in die FG aufzunehmen. Pgf. Ludwig Philipp bittet zugleich um Details über die zur Aufnahme notwendigen Zeremonien sowie mögliche Gesellschaftsnamen und -pflanzen, um in F. Ludwigs Auftrag die Hänselung mit gutem Fruchtwein vorzunehmen.

Q HM Köthen: V S 544, Bl. 65rv, v leer; Kopie v. Schreiberh. Das Stück erscheint isoliert im Lagenumfeld der Handschrift. — Nicht in *KE*.

A *Fehlt*.

Extract

Schreibens von Pfaltzgraff Ludwig Philips Fürstl. Gnad*en*. An Fürst Johann Casimirn zu Anhalt fürstl. Gnd. **De dato d***en* **4/14 Januarij 1646.**

Sonsten bitte Jch EL. reden, wann es gelegenheit giebet mit Fürst Ludwig von Anhalt, Ob ich macht habe, etzliche Fürstliche und Adeliche persohnen¹ in die Fruchtbringende Gesellschafft zu nehmen, mihr auch die **Ceremonien**, deren ich etliche noch wohl weiß, zu wißen zu thun, und waß vor nahme frucht ihnen zu geben dan so ein hauffen hier zu Lande sein, so gern die ehre hetten darinn zu sein, es were vnser gesellschafft auch gutt; Jch habe die freyheit nicht dörffen nehmen Fürst*en* Ludtwig selber zu schreiben, E. L. können es wohl thun vnd mihr Antwortt zu schreiben, Auch wer sieder² Martin Opitzen[,] so der 200. ist, eingenommen worden,³ Jch werde **Commission** von Fürst Ludwigen erwartten,

460104 Pfalzgraf Ludwig Philipp von Simmern

dem ich nach kommen werde. E. L. vergeßen nicht mihr Anttwortt zu schreiben, Jch wolte gern etzliche mit dem gutten beerwein hänßeln[4] *etc.*

K Als jüngerer Bruder Kf. Friedrichs V. v. d. Pfalz war Pgf. Ludwig Philipp v. Simmern (FG 97), obwohl nicht maßgeblich am glücklosen Unternehmen des „Winterkönigs" in Böhmen beteiligt, von span. Truppen aus seinen Besitzungen, die ihm gemäß väterlichem Testament 1610 zugewiesen worden waren (jüngere Linie Pfalz-Simmern bzw. Ft. Pfalz-Simmern-Lautern), nach 1621 vertrieben worden. Mithilfe des 1631 in den Dreißigjährigen Krieg eingreifenden schwed. Kg.s Gustav II. Adolf konnte er jedoch zurückkehren und übernahm nach dem Tod des Bruders 1632 die Administration für die Kurpfalz und die Vormundschaft für seinen Neffen Karl Ludwig, den späteren Kurfürsten. Als abhängig Verbündeter der Krone Schweden (Vertrag v. Heilbronn 4./14.4.1633) und Mitglied des Heilbronner Bundes mußte Ludwig Philipp aufgrund der infolge der Niederlage in der Schlacht bei Nördlingen 1634 zusammenbrechenden schwed. Stellung jedoch abermals weichen und sich von Heidelberg auf die Festung Frankenthal und später nach Sedan zurückziehen. Nach jahrelangen rastlosen Bemühungen um Restitution der pfälz. Territorien durfte Ludwig Philipp 1642 mit ksl. Genehmigung in einen Teil seiner Besitzungen zurückkehren, wo er sich in (Bad) Kreuznach niederließ. Von dort abermals durch span. Truppen vertrieben, schlug er schließlich 1644 in (Kaisers-)Lautern, wo franz. Truppen die ksl. Besatzung vertrieben hatten, seine Residenz auf. Nach längeren Verhandlungen wurde auf dem Westfälischen Friedenskongreß 1647 ein Kompromiß in der Pfalzfrage gefunden: Die Oberpfalz und die 5. Kur verblieben bei Bayern, für Karl Ludwig und seine Nachkommen wurde eine 8. Kur geschaffen. Pgf. Ludwig Philipp erhielt Lautern u. Simmern als eigenständiges Fürstentum zurück. Nach dem Friedensschluß von 1648 nahm er im Namen seines Neffen, der damals in London weilte, die restituierte Kurpfalz in Besitz. Zu ihm s. *Conermann III*, 100 f.; *ADB* XIX, 580 f.; *NDB* XV, 415 f. Zum Verlust und der Restitution der Pfalz während des Dreißigjährigen Krieges sowie zur reichspolitischen Bedeutung der Pfälzer um die Mitte des 17. Jahrhunderts s. allgemein *Croxton/ Tischer*, 219 f.; Anton Schindling: Die reformierten Kurfürsten aus der Linie Pfalz-Simmern und das Heilige Römische Reich (1559 bis 1685). In: Wilhelm Kreutz, Wilhelm Kühlmann u. Hermann Wiegand (Hgg.): Die Wittelsbacher und die Kurpfalz in der Neuzeit – Zwischen Reformation und Revolution. Regensburg 2013, 13–43; Karl-Heinz Rothenberger u.a. (Hgg.): Pfälzische Geschichte. 3. erw. u. erg. Aufl. 2 Bde. Kaiserslautern 2011, I, 262 f.; Meinrad Schaab: Geschichte der Kurpfalz, 2 Bde., Stuttgart u.a. 1992, II: Neuzeit, 109–123 u. 124–128; Volker Press: Bayerns wittelsbachische Gegenspieler – Die Heidelberger Kurfürsten 1505–1685. In: Hubert Glaser (Hg.): Um Glauben und Reich. Kurfürst Maximilian I. 2 Bde., München, Zürich 1980, I: Beiträge zur Bayerischen Geschichte und Kunst 1573–1657, 24–39; Ludwig Häusser: Geschichte der Rheinischen Pfalz nach ihren politischen, kirchlichen und literarischen Verhältnissen. Pirmasens 1970 (Ndr. d. Ausg. Heidelberg 1856), 519–580.

1 Pgf. Ludwig Philipp v. Simmern trat mit 460321 auch persönlich an F. Ludwig heran, um ihn an sein Anliegen zu erinnern. Der Fürst gewährte es lt. 460423 und setzte dazu 14 Impresenvorschläge auf (460423 I). F. Johann Casimir hatte das an ihn als Vermittler gerichtete pgfl. Ersuchen erst mit 460422 an F. Ludwig übersandt. 13 Personen sah der Pfalzgraf ursprünglich zur Aufnahme in die FG vor, zeichnete aber nur für sieben Kandidaten die vollen Personennamen auf, s. 460423 u. 460424A I. Die Originalliste des Pfalzgrafen scheint verlorengegangen zu sein, jedoch sind die Namen von F. Ludwig (460424A I) sowie die vorgeschlagenen Impresen in einer von F. Ludwig auf 14 potentielle Kandida-

ten verlängerten Liste überliefert. S. 460423 I u. 460424A u. I. Seine in 460424A erteilte Vollmacht nebst den Anweisungen und Impresen (460423 u. I) ließ F. Ludwig durch F. Johann Casimir an den Pfalzgrafen übermitteln (460424 u. 460424A). Am Ende wurden nach einem offenbar komplizierten Verständigungsprozeß 14 Neumitglieder bis zum Frühjahr 1647 aufgenommen, darunter aber nur acht aus der ursprünglichen dreizehnköpfigen Liste (vgl. 460424A K I). Nachdem Pgf. Ludwig Philipp die Vollmacht F. Ludwigs erst Mitte Oktober 1646 empfangen hatte, erklärte er seine Bereitschaft, die Neuaufnahmen in der gebotenen Weise zu vollziehen (461026). Bis Ende des Monats Oktober nahm der Pgf. die ersten vier Personen (FG 460–463) auf (s. 461031A I). Weitere vier Personen (FG 469–472) folgten bis Ende des Jahres 1646. Die übrigen sechs Neumitglieder (FG 473–478) wurden zwischen Mitte Januar und Ende Februar 1647 aufgenommen. S. die Namenlisten in den Beilagen zu 461031A. Die Benachrichtigung über die ersten vier, bis Ende Oktober 1646 erfolgten Aufnahmen erreichte Köthen erst im Dezember, wo F. Ludwig die Einträge in das *GB Kö.* III vornahm. Vgl. 461206. Seine verspätete Antwort *DA Köthen I. 8:* 470403A auf das pgfl. Schreiben 461031A lief ebenfalls über F. Johann Casimir (s. *DA Köthen I. 8:* 470403). Diesen Briefen lagen eine aktualisierte Mitgliederliste und die Reimgesetze für die ersten vier Neumitglieder bei. — Mit diesem Aufnahmevorgang tritt der in der FG durchaus repräsentierte Südwesten des Reiches in Erscheinung. Er hat aber nur vergleichsweise spärliche Spuren in der Erzschrein-Überlieferung hinterlassen.

2 D. h. „sieder" im Sinne von seit (temporal). Vgl. *DW* X.1, 370, 757 ff. u. 882.

3 Der bekannte Dichter Martin Opitz v. Boberfeld (FG 200. Der Gekrönte) war 1629 aufgenommen worden und hatte die ehrenvolle Mitgliedsnummer 200 erhalten. Zu Opitz s. die Personenregister unserer Ausgabe; *Conermann III*, 203–206; *Opitz: BW*; *Conermann: Opitz — Patria*. Mit ihm endet das *GB 1629/30*. Pgf. Ludwig Philipp war also über den Mitgliederstand nur bis zu diesem Zeitpunkt und vermutlich auf der Grundlage des *GB 1629/30* informiert. Seine Bitte um ein auf den aktuellen Stand gebrachtes Mitgliederverzeichnis bekräftigte Ludwig Philipp in 461031A. F. Ludwig kam dieser Bitte in *DA Köthen I. 8:* 470403A nach. Vgl. 460424 K 7.

4 Zum fruchtbringerischen Aufnahmeritual der Hänselung, in dem das Leeren des dazu eigens verwendeten Pokals „Ölberger" eine Rolle spielte, vgl. 171224, 460718 K 8 u. ö.

460112

Georg Philipp Harsdörffer an Herzog August d. J. von Braunschweig-Wolfenbüttel

Georg Philipp Harsdörffer (FG 368) vergleicht die Strahlkraft der Sonne mit dem Bild einer goldenen Münze, das ihren Spender, Hz. August d. J. v. Braunschweig-Wolfenbüttel (FG 227), darstellt. Dies sei ein Abbild der Tugend, die mit ihrem Glanz die Edelsteine des Kleinods übertreffe. Harsdörffer erklärt, sich nicht genug mit Worten bedanken zu können, und bekennt, dem Herzog für das Geschenk ewig verbunden zu bleiben. — Wenn der Text diesen Hinweisen gemäß ausfällt und die Stiche, so schnell wie sie vom Handwerker gemacht werden können, folgen, möge der Herzog gnädig befehlen, was vor dem Druck zu verbessern ist.

Q   HAB: Cod. Guelf. 376 Novi 2°, Bl. 152r–153v [A: 153v], 152v leer; eigenh.; Sig. — D: *Narciss*, 181 f. Vgl. Zitat in *Blume: Porticus*, 95 f. — BN: *Bürger*, 673 Nr. 10.

460112 Georg Philipp Harsdörffer

A + Serenissimo atque Celsissimo Principi ac Domino, Domino Augusto, Brunsvicensium atque Lunæburgensium Duci &c. Domino meo clementissimo. Wolffenbüttel.

Serenissime atque Celsissime Princeps, Domine Clementissime.

Feliter annare & perennare.
canescas: seclis innumerabilibus.

Hebescit oculorum nostrorum acies, quoties aureum Solis jubar intuetur: hebescit ingenii mei imbecillitas, cum Serenit.^{is} atque Celsitud.^{is} Vest.^{ræ} Imaginem, aureo nummo expressam, tanquam vnicum Musarum Phœbum, venerabundus contueor.[1] Enimverò in coruscis gemmarum stellutis vivus scintillat splendor; sed longè pulchrior radius, ex ipsius Virtutis Effigie, refulget, qui intuentium animos tentat, concitat, percellit.

Intelligo mihi verba tanto beneficio paria non suppetere: æternas verò gratias pro gratiosissime repono munere, dum me adamantino vinculo Serenit.^{i} atque Celsitud.^{i} Vest.^{ræ} perpetuum devinctum, ingenuè profiteor.

Ut autem aliqualem gratitudinis præstandæ significationem cogitare videar Umbram submitto, Picturam inquam, quibus Serenit.^{is} atque Celsitud.^{is} Vest.^{ræ} gloria, quantum quidem in hanc Genii mei tenuitatem cadere poterit, eximius illustrabitur. Si hæc delineata ad nutum Scripturam his indiciis adæquatam, et sculpturas, quàm citißimè ab Artifice fieri poterit, subsequentur: si quæ v. [152v] emendanda, aut demutanda Serenit.^{as} atque Celsitud.^{o} Vest.^{ra}, ante operas, velle jubere non dedignetur.[2]

His ego Serenit.^{em} et Celsitud.^{em} V. Deo immortali animitus commendo, summumque Numen submissè veneror, vt Vos, potentiæque Vestræ Imperium, non modò ad ingressum huius anni, sed sine fine benedictione suâ perfundat, propitius.

Serenit.^{is} atque Celsitud.^{is} Vest.^{ræ}

                               æternum devotus cliens.
                               Georg-Philippus Harsdorf.
                               Dicast. Noric. Adsessor.

Norimbergæ die 12/22 Januarii.
       A.° 1646.[3]

K 1 Georg Forstenheuser teilte Hz. August d.J. v. Braunschweig-Wolfenbüttel (FG 227) am 4.10.1645 mit, Georg Philipp Harsdörffer (FG 397) wünsche sich zum Dank (für die Widmung v. *Harsdörffer: Frauenzimmer-Gesprächspiele*, Teil V [1645] an den Fürsten) das Bild des Fürsten. *Blume: Porticus*, 95. Johann Valentin Andreae (FG 464. 1646) hatte 1643/44 die Anfertigung einer Reihe von Medaillen auf August durch den Straßburger Friedrich Fecher vermittelt. S. Annelise Stemper: Nachrichten über den Straßburger Medailleur Friedrich Fecher und seine Medaillen auf den Herzog August von Wolfenbüttel u. den Herzog Eberhard III. von Württemberg in der Korrespondenz des Johann Valentin Andreae. In: Blätter f. Münzfreunde und Münzforschung 78 (1954), 72–78.

2 Harsdörffer hatte auf den Herzog einen illustrierten *Panegyricus Porticus virtutis* ent-

worfen (s. 450927), der auch zusammen mit seinem *Specimen Philologiae Germanicae* (1646) veröffentlicht wurde (460912) und verändert 1647 auch separat erschien (s. 470114).

3 Um diese Zeit, am 7.2.1646, schrieb Harsdörffer an Sigmund Betulius (v. Birken; FG 681. 1658), den er nach Wolfenbüttel als Hilfslehrer der jüngeren braunschweig. Prinzen Anton Ulrich (FG 716. 1659) und Ferdinand Albrecht (FG 842. 1673) empfohlen hatte, er solle dort den Präzeptor Justus Georg Schottelius (FG 397) und (den Frauenhofmeister) Carl Gustav v. Hille (FG 302) grüßen und deren Gunst wie auch die des Hofmarschalls Franz Julius v. dem Knesebeck (FG 396) zu gewinnen suchen. *Birken: Werke u. Korrespondenz* IX.1, 8f. Er empfahl Betulius, Hille ein Exemplar seiner *Fortsetzung Der Pegnitz-Schäferey* (1645) zu schenken. Er, Harsdörffer, habe ihm Betulius empfohlen und werde dies auch in einem Schreiben an Knesebeck tun. Harsdörffer legte Betulius ans Herz, die hzl. Familie wie auch alle Mitglieder des Hofs ehrerbietig, aufmerksam und mit Zuneigung, Höflichkeit und Bescheidenheit zu behandeln. Besonders Herrn Schottelius solle er als Vorbild der Gewandtheit im Geist, in der Rede und im Verhalten nachahmen. Betulius, der ihm, Harsdörffer, vom Lob des Hofs über seine Dichtungen Mitteilung gemacht hatte, möge ihm schreiben, was der Herzog und die Herzogin darin schätzen und wie diese, Hzn. Sophia Elisabeth (AL 1629; TG 42b), sich für die Widmung des 6. Teils seiner *Frauenzimmer-Gesprächspiele* erkenntlich zeigen werde. Habe Schottelius seinen Brief noch nicht erhalten, dem ein Gratulationsgedicht und Schreiben an Betulius und dessen Bruder Christian beilägen? Harsdörffer werde sein Sprachbuch, *Specimen Philologiae Germanicae* (1646), mit dem *Porticus Virtutis* in ein oder zwei Monaten schicken. Den an Betulius mitgesandten *Königlichen Catechismus* (1645/46), Harsdörffers Übersetzung des *Catechisme Royal* (1645) des Philippe Fortin sieur de la Hoguette, solle Betulius Hille oder Knesebeck geben, die das Buch an den Herzog weiterreichen können, wenn sie das Werk dazu als würdig erachteten. Vgl. 451217 K 9. Den 6. Teil der *Frauenzimmer-Gesprächspiele* werde Harsdörffer erst nach Abschluß des *Specimen* in den Druck geben. So eröffnete sich Harsdörffer durch den Briefwechsel mit dem von ihm empfohlenen Betulius zusätzlich zur Korrespondenz mit Hz. August, Schottelius u.a. einen weiteren Kanal des Austauschs und der Information.

460119

Fürst Ludwig an Carl Gustav von Hille

F. Ludwig (Der Nährende) wünscht Carl Gustav v. Hille (FG 302. Der Unverdrossene) ein glückliches und friedliches neues Jahr und überschickt ihm den dritten Teil des Werks *Sachse: Einhelligkeit.* — An Hz. August d.J. v. Braunschweig-Wolfenbüttel (FG 227. Der Befreiende) möge Hille Grüße und Glückwünsche bestellen und ihm mitteilen, daß ihm in Kürze ein gebundenes Exemplar zugehe. Es mangelte wegen der Kriegsläufte bisher an der Gelegenheit, den Druck einbinden zu lassen. — F. Ludwig bittet um Nachricht, was Hille bei der Zahlung der Verlagsbeiträge Hz. Augusts u. Hz. Christian Ludwigs v. Braunschweig-Calenberg (FG 372. Der Reinherzige) ausrichten konnte. Die Arbeit an den Kupferstichen (zum *GB 1646*) kann nicht angeordnet werden, solange die vereinbarten Beträge nicht eingegangen sind. — Franz Julius v. dem Knesebeck (FG 396. Der Geheime) u. Justus Georg Schottelius (FG 397. Der Suchende) wolle Hille auch grüßen und über ihr Befinden berichten. In Köthen sei die Situation schlecht und man habe Unterstützung in der Landwirtschaft nötig.

460119 Fürst Ludwig

Q HM Köthen: V S 545, Bl. 39rv, v leer, eigenh. Konzept. — Nicht in *KE* u. *KL*.

A *Fehlt*.

Dem Unverdroßenen[1] wuntschet der Nehrende ein gluckliches und friedliches neues Jhar mit vielen folgenden, und uberschicket ihme angefüget das dritte theil der Einhelligkeit der Evangelisten, verhoffende es ihme gleich die zwey ersten theile gefallen sol.[2]

Dem Befreyenden wolle er des Nehrenden grus und gluckwuntschung auch vermelden, und darneben anzeigen, das in kurtzem fur ihme dergleichen auch folgen sol, mangelt nur am bande[3] darzu man wegen stetter unruhe nicht gelangen konnen. Was nun der Unverdroßene bey dem Befreyenden[4] und Reinhertzigen[5], wegen ihres vertrösteten verlags zu den geselschaf[t] gemählden ausgerichtet, davon begehret er nachricht: Sie können in kupfer zu stechen nicht angeordnet werden, bis dieses geld, als vorgeschrieben worden, bey handen. Jn deßen wolle er den Geheimen[6] und Suchenden[7] grußen, und von allen ihren zustand berichten[.] Alhier ist es in einem schlechten zustande, das man guter hulffe zu anbau hoch vonnöten, Hiermit verbleibt des Unverdroßenen

gantzwilliger der Nehrende

Cöthen den 19. des Jenners 1646.

K 1 Carl Gustav v. Hille (FG 302. Der Unverdrossene).

2 Die ungebundene Ausgabe *Sachse: Einhelligkeit* III (1644). S. 440323 K 6 u. 441205 K 3. Zur Übersendung dieses Bands an den Wolfenbütteler Hof s. Anm. 3.

3 *Sachse: Einhelligkeit* III (1644). Mehr als zwei Jahre zuvor erhielt Hz. August d. J. v. Braunschweig-Wolfenbüttel (FG 227. Der Befreiende) (als Beilage zum Brief 431201) das Werk *Sachse: Einhelligkeit* II und das Inhaltsverzeichnis von *Sachse: Einhelligkeit* III (1644). Im Frühjahr 1645 (450126) drückte Hille bereits die Erwartung Hz. Augusts aus, den dritten Teil zu empfangen, was sich mit 450721 erfüllte. Damals schickte F. Ludwig schon ein gebundenes Druckexemplar, während er ein Buch im Köthener Einband wegen der Kriegsläufte und der Abwesenheit des Buchbinders immer noch nicht übersenden konnte. Für ausgewählte Gesellschaftsmitglieder und aus besonderen Anlässen wurden Köthener Drucke in spezifischer Weise vor Ort gebunden. Das persönliche Ex. des *GB 1629/30* für Martin Opitz (FG 200) ist ein besonders auffälliges Beispiel, s. die Abb. des Vorderdeckels in *DA Köthen I. 3*, 505. Da der Fürst mit 431209 zwei Exemplare des 2. Teils des Werks überschickt hatte, wird er sich auch bemüht haben, mehr als ein Stück des 3. Teils an Hz. August bzw. an dessen Gemahlin Sophia Elisabeth (AL 1629; TG 42b) gelangen zu lassen. Vgl. auch 371120 u. F. Ludwigs Vorschlag an seinen Neffen F. Christian II. v. Anhalt-Bernburg (FG 51), das *GB 1629/30* vom Köthener Buchbinder einbinden zu lassen.

4 Hz. August hatte seinen Beitrag zum Verlag des *GB 1646* bis dahin noch immer nicht bezahlt. Da die Zahlung in zwei Raten zu je 100 Rth. vorgesehen war, wissen wir nicht, ob im Januar 1646 nur noch die zweite Tranche ausstand. Zu den fl. Verlagsbeiträgen s. 450126 K 4 und 450721. Zum *GB 1646* allgemein s. 440130 K 3.

5 Hz. Christian Ludwig v. Braunschweig-Calenberg (FG 372. Der Reinherzige). Vgl. 460301 u. 460309. Der wird seinen zugesagten Zuschuß in 460301 um die Hälfte auf 100

Rtl. kürzen und in 460403 die umgehende Überweisung ankündigen. Eine sichere Zahlungsbestätigung liegt uns aber erst mit *DA Köthen I. 8*: 470223 vor. Zu den fl. Verlagsbeiträgen s. 450126 K 4.

6 Der Wolfenbütteler Hofmarschall Franz Julius v. dem Knesebeck (FG 396. Der Geheime).

7 Der Wolfenbütteler Prinzenerzieher, Hof-, Kammer- und Konsistorialrat Justus Georg Schottelius (FG 397. Der Suchende).

460120

Fürst Ludwig an Georg Philipp Harsdörffer

Antwort auf 451217. Beantwortet durch 460406. — F. Ludwig (Der Nährende) dankt für Georg Philipp Harsdörffers (FG 368. Der Spielende) *Diana*-Ausgabe und für den gedruckten Anfang seiner Übersetzung des *Catechisme Royale* (von Philippe Fortin sieur de la Hoguette), außerdem für die *Fortsetzung der Pegnitz-Schäferey* (von Sigmund Betulius, d. i. v. Birken; FG 681. 1658; PBO Floridan) und für die Visierungen von Harsdörffers Imprese und Wappen. Diese sollen für das überwiesene Geld gestickt und (im Köthener Schloß) zum Gedächtnis aufbewahrt werden. Für den Fall, daß F. Ludwigs Brief 451209 Harsdörffer nicht erreicht hat, sendet der Nährende eine Abschrift. Er schickt auch eine Kopie eines Schreibens Diederichs v. dem Werder (FG 31. Der Vielgekörnte) mit. Ludwig informiert Harsdörffer, daß das Gesellschaftsbuch der Accademia degli Intronati nicht dessen Schreiben 450923C bzw. 451101 beilag. Auch habe der Vielgekörnte vor seiner Abreise keine Nachricht hinterlassen, daß er das Buch bekommen und zurückgehalten habe. — F. Ludwig sind Harsdörffers Sendungen willkommen. Er möge damit fortfahren. — Hans Michael Moscherosch (FG 436. Der Träumende) soll sein farbiges Wappen schicken und mitteilen, ob er eine Zeichnung seiner Imprese für eine Gesellschaftsmedaille haben will. Wenn der Maler wieder nach Köthen kommt, könne der Medaillen-Entwurf überschickt werden. Der Träumende möge auch wissen lassen, wie es mit dem Sticken (seines Wappens und seiner Imprese) gehalten werden solle (d. h., ob das an seinem Wohnort oder in Köthen geschehen solle).

Q HM Köthen: V S 545, Bl. 336rv, v leer; eigenh. Konzept. — *D: KE*, 349. — *BN: Bürger*, 950 Nr. 59.

A *Fehlt.*

Es empfahet vom Spielenden der Nehrende untenbenanten tages ein schreiben vom 17. Christmonats abgewichenen Jhares, mit angefugten dreyen theilen der Diana[1], der Pegnitschen schäferey fortsetzung,[2] den gedruckten[a] anfang an dem Catechismi Royal,[3] und dan den[b] abriß des Spielenden zum[c] ertzschreine wieder zurück geschickten gemähldes und wappens, welche[d], wie es der Spielende begeret, um das mit[e] anher[f] geschickte geld wol sollen[g] verfertiget, und zu[h] gutem gedechtnusse an gehorigen ort bey dem selben aufgehoben werden.[4]

Woferne der Spielende des Nehrenden schreiben im[i] Christmonate abgewichenes Jhares[5] gegeben[f], noch nicht empfangen hette, ist darvon[j] abschrift neben[k] des Vielgekornten seines[6] beygeleget, bey den angezogenen schreiben aber vom 23.

Der Träumende.

Johann Michael Moscherosch
in die Gesellschaft kommen 1645.

Porträt Johann Michael Moscheroschs (FG 436. Der Träumende). Zu 460120.

des Herbsts[-] und ersten des Wintermonats⁷ ist das geselschaftbuch de gli Intronati⁸ nicht gewesen, es muste es dan der Vielgekörnete überkommen¹ und bey sich behalten haben, davon er aber fur seinem abreisen nichts gemeldet.⁹

Es wird dem Spielenden fur alle solche überfertigung und bezeigung gebührender^m danck gesaget und gebeten mit fernerer zuschickung, seiner gelegenheit nach, fort zu faren, wie^n dan das uberschickete gerne sol durchlesen, aufgehalten^f und dan^f mit dem^o was nachfolget ebenmeßig gelehret werden.

Wan der Treumende sein gemählde zum pfennige¹⁰ abgerißen haben wil, kan es, sobald der Mahler¹¹ wieder^f bey^p handen verfertiget und übermachet werden, in^q deßen^r hette er^f sein^s wappen mit farben gemahlet zum Ertzschreine ein zuschicken und sich zu bedencken wie er es mit dem stecken¹² wolte gehalten haben.

Hiermit dem Spielenden alle gedeyliche wolfart wuntschend *etc.*
    Verbleibet des Spielenden gantzwilliger
              Der Nehrende

Cöthen den 20. Jenners 1646.

T a *Eingefügt. Fehlt in KE.* — **b** den abriß *fehlt in KE.* — **c** zum ertzschreine *eingefügt.* — **d** *Gebessert aus* welche<s> — **e** *Fehlt in KE.* — **f** *Eingefügt.* — **g** *Gebessert aus* sol — **h** *Gebessert aus* zu<m stetswehrenden> gedechtnusse — **i** *Statt* <vom> — **j** *Gebessert aus* <hier>von — **k** *Bis* seines *eingefügt. In KE ausgelassen.* — **l** überkommen und *eingefügt.* — **m** *Gebessert aus* <großter> — **n** *Bis* gelehret werden *in KE ausgelassen.* — **o** *Gebessert aus* deme — **p** *KE* zu handen — **q** *Bis* gehalten haben *fehlt in KE.* — **r** *Folgt* <er> — **s** *Bis* zuschicken und *am Rand ergänzt.*

K 1 Georg Philipp Harsdörffers (FG 368. Der Spielende) und Johann Klajs Übersetzung von Montemayors, Pérez' und Polos *Diana* (Nürnberg: Michael Endter 1646), s. 451217 K 7, vgl. 450400 K 6. Das Buch wurde mit der Übersetzung der *Dianea* Giovanni Francesco Loredanos durch Diederich v. dem Werder (FG 31. Der Vielgekörnte) verwechselt. S. 440000 K 1 u. 460000A K.

2 Sigmund Betulius (v. Birken; FG 681. 1658; PBO Floridan): *Fortsetzung Der Pegnitz-Schäferey* (1645), s. 451217 K 8.

3 Harsdörffers Übersetzung von Philippe Fortins sieur de la Hoguette *Catechisme Royal*: CATECHISME ROYAL. Der Königliche Catechismus/ Das ist: Ein Christliches Gespräch/ Zwischen Königlicher Majestät in Franckreich/ und Deroselben Hofmeister (Nürnberg 1645, recte 1646). S. 451217 K 9.

4 Harsdörffer hatte F. Ludwig (Der Nährende) zur Leipziger Messe Visierungen seiner FG-Imprese und seines Wappens geschickt und 10 Rth. zur Begleichung der Stickkosten an den dortigen Kaufmann Gottfried Stahl (s. zuletzt 451101) überwiesen. S. 451217. Die auf Atlas gestickten Abbildungen der Imprese und des Wappens wurden zu Wandteppichen zusammengenäht und in einem Saal des Köthener Schlosses aufgehängt. S. *Conermann: Nachlaßinventar,* 74 f.

5 451209. Die Abschrift ist verschollen.

6 Unbekanntes Schreiben Diederichs v. dem Werder.

7 450923C bzw. 451101.

8 Zum Gesellschaftsbuch der italien. *Accademia degli Intronati* s. 450817 (K 20). Vgl. 451217.

9 Diederich v. dem Werder war als Gesandter der Lgfn. Amalia Elisabeth v. Hessen-Kassel zu Heiratsverhandlungen an den Hof Kf. Friedrich Wilhelms v. Brandenburg (FG 401) nach Königsberg gereist. S. 460125 u. I (bes. K 3).

10 Johann Michael Moscheroschs (FG 436. Der Träumende) goldenes, farbig emailliertes Kleinod, der sog. Gesellschaftspfennig, ist selbst nicht nachgewiesen, jedoch auf seinen Kupferstichporträts häufig, aber nie genau dargestellt. S. Abb. auf S. 797. F. Ludwig hatte eine Übersendung des Impresengemäldes zur Vorlage für Moscheroschs Gesellschaftspfennig angekündigt, jedoch verzögerte sich dieselbe, s. 460426. Laut 460726 teilte Harsdörffer Moscherosch am 19.6.1646 das Gemälde der Imprese für seinen Pfennig mit. Zu dem an einem sittichgrünen Band um den Hals getragenen Gesellschaftskleinod vgl. 441223 K 9.

11 Aus dieser Zeit ist als Maler der Impresenvisierungen Christoph Steger bekannt. S. 460315, vgl. *Conermann II*, 114 ff. Die Wappenmalerei und Moscheroschs Sinnbild sind in *Conermann II*, Nr. 436, schwarzweiß wiedergegeben. Beschreibung und Kommentar in *Conermann III*, 525.

12 D. i. Sticken (des Wappens auf Atlas). Moscheroschs Wappen ist schließlich in den Erzschrein gelangt, s. 460620 u. 460705. Vgl. zu F. Ludwigs wiederholter Nachfrage nach Moscheroschs Wappen 450504A K 5.

460120A

Burggraf und Herr Achaz zu Dohna an Fürst Ludwig

Beantwortet in 460217. — Achaz (Achatius) zu Dohna dankt dem Fürsten aus seinem ostpreußischen ‚Winkel' heraus dafür, daß dieser sich seines alten, seit fast 50 Jahren treuen Dieners erinnert und ihm einen ganz ungewöhnlichen Druck in gewöhnlicher deutscher Sprache geschenkt habe. Er lobt Gott, weil er inmitten der Tumulte des Kriegs einen Fürsten von unermüdlicher Geisteskraft, Gelehrsamkeit und Beständigkeit über alle kriegerische Raserei und Grausamkeit triumphieren läßt. Dohna bittet um Verzeihung für sein ohne Hilfe der Accademia della Crusca mangelhaftes Toskanisch.

Q LHA Sa.-Anh./ Dessau: Z 70 Abt. Köthen A 9a Nr. 33[III], Bl. 141r–142v [A: 141v], 142rv leer; eigenh. — Der Brief wurde zusammen mit der Antwort 460217 an Diederich v. dem Werder (FG 31) geschickt.

A a V. A.
Eigenh. Empfangsvermerk F. Ludwigs: Pres. a' 16. di Febbrajo 1636[a].

Sereniss'. Principe

Degnando V. A di benignità sua singolarissima ricordarsi d'antico suo seruitore[1] qual io le sono divotissimamente da presso cinquant'anni in quà e darne anco fede sin'in quest'angolo sarmatico,[2] in queste lontananze, in questa mia vecchiaia anzi con saggio segnalato di stampa, non volgare, bench'in lingua volgare:[3] Resto stupito certo, di tanta grazia: ed a V. A. ne rendo grazie umilissime ed infinite: Lodando Jddio di vedere frà tanti fracassi della turbatissima Mag[ag]na nostra, conseruato pur'ancora in mezzo di essa un Principe Vigoroso, trionfante con esercizii infatigabili d'ingegno vivacissimo, d'erudizione sottilissima, et di pietà constante sopr'ogni furore e crudeltà guerresca. Piaccia alla [141v] bontà Diuina multiplicare a V. A. cotesto ben'e contento sourano in perpetuo: Ed jo domandandole perdono di queste scorretture[4], non avendo più la CRUSCA meco, mele raccommando in grazia favore volissima ed inviolata per sempre.

Di Prussia a' 20. del Gennaio 1646.
Di V. A fedeliss.° ed umillimo seruitore
Acasio Visconte di Dona il vecchio[1].

T a *Schreibfehler für* 1646

K 1 Burggf. u. Herr Achaz zu Dohna (1581–1647), Sohn Achaz' d. Ä. (1533–1601) und Bruder Christophs (FG 20). Vgl. 291013 K 10, 300725 K 10 u. 360600 K II. Ein anderer Bruder Achaz' und Christophs war der kurbrandenburg. Geh. Rat und Oberst Abraham (1579–1631). Wie Christoph (s. 360630 u. 400728) verfaßte er ein (postum veröffentlichtes) Erbauungsbuch, das auf dem Alten Testament basiert: Die Plagen Ægypti Bey der Außführung des Volcks Gottes/ Erkläret und hinterlassen Von dem ... hochseligen Herren Herren Abraham Burggrafen zu Dona ... Gedruckt zu Franckfurt an der Oder/ bey Johann Eichorns S. Witbe ANNO 1645. HAB: 512. 1 Theol. (2); Variante: Christliche Gedancken Vber die wunderbarliche Außführung des Volcks Jßrael auß Egypten Des ... Herren Abrahams Burggraffens zu Dohna ... Gedruckt zu Franckfurt an der Oder/ bey Johann Eichorns S. Witbe ANNO 1647. FB Gotha: H 8° 02296; Titelauflage: Wunderliche Auszführung der Jsraeliten ausz Egypten ... Verfertiget von dem ... Herrn Abraham/ Burggraffen zu Dona ... Franckfurt an der Oder Jn verlegung Melchior Klosemanns gedruckt Bey Erasmus Rösnern/ 1657. HAB: B 121. 4° Helmst.; Dig. — Achaz und Christoph zu Dohna reisten 1599 oder 1600 nach Italien, hielten sich kurz in Venedig auf, verbrachten um 1600, als F. Ludwig noch in Florenz weilte (1598–1600), ein Jahr in der Stadt, besichtigten sodann bis 1601 weitere Orte Italiens, neben Neapel besonders Rom. Der Aufenthalt in Florenz und die Zugehörigkeit zu einem Zirkel dort das Toskanische studierender deutscher Fürsten erklärt, warum Achaz in einem ital. Schreiben an die gemeinsame Zeit in Florenz anknüpfte. S. Frédéric de Spanheim: COMMENTAIRE HISTORIQUE DE la VJE et de la MORT de Messire CHRISTOFLE Vicomte de DHONA. Chez Iaques Chouet M. DC. XXXIX. S. 45 (ZB Zürich: Ochsner 93$_2$; UB Göttingen: H. Germ. IV 367): „La Cour du Grand Duc leur decouvrit vn temperament rare de magnificence & de mesnage, la nature ses beautés, l'art ses embellisemens & ses inuentions, & la conversation ordinaire, la pureté de la langue Toscane, & vn raffinage d'esprits. Ils y trouuerent d'abord vne Academie de Princes Allemans. *Auguste* Comte Palatin, Christian *Marquis* de Brandenburg, *Jean Frideric* Duc de Wirtemberg, & *Rodolphe* & *Louys* Princes d'Anhalt y vaquoyent à la culture de la langue Jtalienne, & aux exercises de Noblesse, sous le Sieur *Lorenzo* fameux Escuyer du Grand Duc. Le Vicomte [46] Christofle s'y joignit, & s'insinua en la cognoissance & en le faueur de ces Princes, desquels sa vertu fut recognuë, & sa conversation cherie. Vne annee estant escoulee pendant leur seiour à Florence, les Vicomtes Achatius & Christofle se resolurent de passer outre, & de voir le reste de l'Italie." Außer F. Ludwig und Christoph zu Dohna traten später nur noch F. Rudolph v. Anhalt-Zerbst (FG 12) und Mgf. Christain v. Brandenburg-Bayreuth (FG 145) der FG bei. F. Ludwig war von seinem Hofmeister Christoph v. Lehndorf (FG 32) begleitet worden.

460120A Burggraf und Herr Achaz zu Dohna

Wie Achaz zu Dohna kehrte er nach Preußen zurück (1613), nachdem er Ludwig in Köthen noch als Geh. Rat gedient hatte. Er starb Ende Juni 1625. *Conermann III*, 36. — Aus dem Fürstl. Hausarchiv Dohna-Schlobitten im GSTA Berlin (Rep. 92) gewinnen wir interessante Mitteilungen über Achaz' zu Dohna Biographie: 1) Karten 11a: Nr. 3 Reise von Sedan nach Paris (Tagebuch); Nr. 6 Bitte um Entlassung aus dem Amt eines Hofmeister des pfälz. Kurprinzen, des späteren Winterkönigs Friedrich I., o. D.; Nr. 18 u. 26 Berichte aus London, u. a. an den kurpfälz. Statthalter in Heidelberg, Pgf. Johann v. Zweibrücken, 1620/21; Nr. 38 u. 39 D. in England. 2) Karton 11b: Nr. 49 Exzerpte; 3.11.1643 D. entleiht von Amos Comenius ein Werk von Edward Herbert Baron Herbert of Cherbury: DE VERITATE. Prout distinguitur Á Reuelatione, Á Verisimili, á Possibili, et á falso. Hoc prout condidit. Edoardus Baro Herbert de Chirburg in Anglia et Castri Jnsulæ de Kerry in Hibernia. Et PAR utriusque Regni. Et Lectori cujuis, integri et illibuti Judici dicauit. Exc. Lutetiæ Parisor. 1625. Tum demo sed auctius et emendatius recud. Londini per Augustinum Mathæum. 1633; D. notiert hierzu: „N. Rivetus [André Rivet] helt nichts von diesem buch. Sagt Tribuj hoc virib. Huiusque ingenii nimium." Beiliegend eine Abschrift „Aus der Schweiz 10. Decemb. 1644. [...]" mit einer Mitteilung über Comenius: „Gegen bewusten vornehmen Man hab ich gedacht, was ihr mihr geschrieben, das ihr mit ihme gerne de magnis Periodis Universi conferiren möchtet. Daruff er geantwortet, man halte dafür das izo des Caroli Magni Periodus vorhanden sey, undt wolle man zwar vf solche ordenung viel geben, wer wisse aber ob etwas gewisses dran seye. Seyne meinung seye, nachdem Gott der herr das liecht des h. Euangelii so klar wieder herfür gebracht, so werde er nicht zugeben, das solches wiedrumb vertunckele oder verleße. So halte er auch, das Gott der herr im vergangnen Seculo die sententiam gegen den bapst habe lassen promulgiren, vndt werde nunmehr in diesem Seculo zur Execution sollen kommen, worin ich dergestalt mit ihm einig bin, das ich auch hoffe des Babstes vntergang zuerleben. Multum. &c. &c. &c."; Nr. 52 enthält einen lat. Einblattdruck mit dt. Übersetzung: PRECATIO PICI MIRANDVLANI. (Gedruckt zu Elbing/ bey Wendel Bodenhausen/ Jm Jahr 1636): „Præmia qui ut meritis longè majora rependit | [...] | Non Dominum, sed Te sentiat esse Patrem." Mit Dohnas eigenh. Verbesserung beginnt die Übersetzung: „O Herr/ in deiner güt gibstu vns viel mehr gaben | Nach deiner Mildigkeit/ als wir verdienet haben"; Nr. 57 Auszüge aus Pierre Du Moulins reformiertem Erbauungsbuch *Du Combat Chrestien* (Sedan 1622); Nr. 65 Reisebeschreibungen D.s an seinen Oheim Fabian zu Dohna, 1597–1600.

2 Dieser sarmatische Winkel bezeichnet das im damals poln. Hzt. Preußen gelegene Gut Karwinden (Kr. Preuss. Eylau).

3 F. Ludwig hatte Dohna *Gueintz: Rechtschreibung (1645)* und anderes in dt. Sprache Gedrucktes (aus der FG) zukommen lassen, vgl. 460217.

4 Dohna entschuldigt sein fehlerhaftes Toskanisch. Das Wort scorrettura fehlt in der damals gültigen (2.) Ausgabe *Vocabolario della Crusca 1623*, die Dohna hier vielleicht mit „CRUSCA" meint, wenn er nicht an den Beutelkasten (frullone) als Symbol der sprachkritischen Arbeit der Accademia della Crusca gedacht hat. Das Wörterbuch führt stattdessen „SCORREZIONE. Propriamente error di scrittura." (S. 764) auf. Anders als F. Ludwig, der 1600 unter dem Namen L'Acceso in die Accademia della Crusca aufgenommen wurde, finden sich die Dohnas, Mgf. Christian, F. Rudolph und Lehndorf nicht unter den Mitgliedern. Vgl. F. Ludwigs sehr bescheidene (oder kokette?) Erklärung über sein Toskanisch in 450919A.

5 Nach dem Tode seines gleichnamigen Vaters Achaz nannte sich der Briefschreiber mit Blick auf Achaz (1605–1651) nun selbst Achaz (Achatius, Acasio) d. Ä.

460125

Kurfürst Friedrich Wilhelm von Brandenburg an die Fürsten von Anhalt

Kf. Friedrich Wilhelm v. Brandenburg (FG 401) teilt den Fürsten August (FG 46), Christian II. (FG 51) und Ludwig (FG 2) v. Anhalt die Bestallung Diederichs v. dem Werder (FG 31) zum brandenburgischen Geheimen Rat und Kriegsobristen mit und bittet um ihr Einverständnis.

Q GSTA—PK Berlin: I. HA GR Rep. 9, A 3 Fasz. 5, Bl. 76r–77v [A: 77r], 77v leer; Konzept v. Schreiberh.

A An Fürst Augustus
     Fürst Christian   } zu Anhalt gefatter gefatter
     Furst Ludewig

Vnser freundtlich Dienst, vndt waß Wier mehr liebes vndt gutes Vermögen allezeith zuvor, Hochgebohrner Fürst[,] freundtlicher lieber Vetter,

wan sich Ew. Ld. bey diesen, immerzue leider Continuirenden bösen Zeiten, vndt zerüttetem Zuestande des Hey. Röm. Reichß, annoch in gedeylichen wollstande vndt guter gesundtheit befinden, würde Vns solches sehr hochlichᵃ erfrewen, maßen Wier dan derselben von dem Allerhögsten, alle hohe Fürstliche prosperitet, vndt selbst begehrendeßᵇ wollergehen von hertzen Wünschen.

Neben diesem, geben Wir Ew. Ld. hiermit freundtlich zuvernehmen, daß, nachdem Vns die hohe qvaliteten vndt geschickligkeit des Obristen Dieterichs von dem Werder, welcher von Vnserer fr. Lieben Muhmen der verwittibten Frawᶜ Landtgräffin¹ vndtᵈ ihres geliebten Sohnß H. Landtgraffᶜ Wilhelmßᵉ² zu Heßen Ld. Ld.ᶜ in angelegenen Verrichtungen³ [76v] an Vnß geschicket, nicht allein von andern Vnterschiedtlich hochgerühmet worden, besondern Wir dieselbe auch theilß in der that selbst erfahren, vndt Vns dabey erinnert, daß dergleichen von Gott begabte leuthe fürstlichen höffen wollanstendig, Wier dannenhero bewogen worden, die seinige Persohn in Vnsern Dienst zuebestellen, vndt zue Vnsern geheimbten Rhatt vndt Kriges Obristen in gnaden auf vndt anzunehmen, nicht zweifflende, gleichwie Ew. Ld. ermelten Obristen dem von Werder vor diesem allewege mit fürstlichen hulden vndt gnaden zugethan gewesen dieselbe auch solches immerzuehin zu Continuiren, ihr freundtVetterlich beliben laßen werden. Solches wie es Vnß zue sonderbahrn dancknehmenden gefallen gereichen wirdᶠ [,] Also seindt Wiers ümb Ew. Ld. mitt [77r] angenehmen freundtVetterlichen diensten, zuerwidern stetß willig vnd bereit.

Gegeben Konigsperg in Preußen den 25 Jan. Ao. 1646 etc.⁴

Die Imprese Kurfürst Friedrich Wilhelms von Brandenburg (FG 401. Der Untadeliche. 1641). Zu 460125.

I

Gesandtschaftsreisen Diederichs von dem Werder

Bericht aus der gedruckten Leichenpredigt auf Diederich v. dem Werder (FG 31) über dessen Auftrag zur Vermittlung einer Eheschließung zwischen Hessen-Kassel und Kurbrandenburg und seine in diesem Rahmen erfolgte Aufnahme zum Geheimen Rat und Kriegsobristen in kurbrandenburgische Dienste 1646.

Q Gottfried Colerus: Der | Vom Vater gegebene/ | Vom Sohne ausgeführete/ | Und vom H. Geiste versiegelte | Raht des Heils | Bey Hochansehnlicher Leichbestattung | ... Dieterichs von dem Wer- | der ... Welcher am 18. Decembris des 1657sten Jahres ... entschlaffen/ | Und im jahre 1658 den 13. maj/ ... daselbst ... beygesetzet worden (Cöthen: Jacob Brand in der Fürstlichen Druckerei, 1658), Bl. L ij v Liij v. HAB: Xa 1: 47 [10].

Anno 1646. ist von J. HochFürstl. Gnad. der Frau LandGräfin zu Cassel als damahlige Regentin Jhme eine ansehnliche Gesandschafft nacher Brandenburg ümb die Heyraht zwischen itzo zu Cassel regierender Durchleuchtigen Hochgebornen Fürsten und Herren/ Herrn Wilhelm Landgrafen in Hessen [e]tc. als dero Herren Sohn/ und dan S. ChurFürstl. Durchl. zu Brandenburg Fräulein Schwester zu **tractiren** und zu vollziehen/ in Gnaden auffgetragen worden/ Und ob Er nun wohl sein bereit angehendes hohes Alter/ insonderheit des reisens halber/ so weit als naher Preussen fürgewendet/ hat Er doch nicht können darvon erlassen werden/ Und weil von itzt höchstermelter Frau Landgräfin ferner darumb instendig und gnädig angehalten worden/ hat Er sich endlich der grossen Gnade/ so Jhme von Jugend auff von dem Fürstl. Hause Cassel erzeiget worden/ erinnern/ und also solches gnädige begehren weiter nichts abschlagen können. Welche **expedition** die Göttliche Allmacht auch also gesegnet/ daß beyderseits so wohl ChurFürstl. als Fürstl. Principalen ein gantz gnädigst und gnädiges Wohlgefallen [Liij r] drob geschöpffet/ und dannenhero der selige Herr Obriste nicht allein einen hohen Ruhm und gnädigsten Danck davon getragen/ besondern auch dazu in ansehung seiner damahls verspürten tapffern Qualitäten von mehr höchst benanter S. ChurFürstl. Durchl. zu Brandenburg in Diensten begehret/ auch endlichen/ unbeobachtet des Herrn Obristen dazumahl anführenden Entschuldigungen und **tenuität** zu dero geheimten Raht und KriegsObristen/ wie auch ferner zu dero Haubtman über das im Fürstenthum Halberstadt gelegne Ambt Alten Gaderßleben in Gnaden **constituiret** und angenommen/ Wie dan S. hohe Churfürstl. Durchl. es auch alsobalde/ laut eines Schreibens/ an hiesige unsere gnädige Herrschafft/ des Inhalts also: Nebens diesem geben Wir E. Liebden auch freundlich zuvernehmen/ daß nach dem uns die hohe Qualitäten und Geschickligkeit des Obristen Diderichs von dem Werder/ welcher von unser Freundlichen lieben Muhmen der verwittibten Frau Landgräfin zu Hessen und Jhres geliebten Sohns/ Herrn Landgraff Wilhelms Liebden in angelegner Verrichtung an uns

460125 Kurfürst Friedrich Wilhelm von Brandenburg

geschicket/ nicht allein von andern unterschiedlich hoch gerühmet worden/ besondern Wir dieselbe in der that auch selbsten erfahren/ und uns dabey erinnert/ daß dergleichen von GOtt begabte stattliche Leute Fürstl. Höfen wohl anstendig/ Wir dannenhero bewogen worden/ seine Person in unsere Dienste mit zubestellen/ und zu unsern geheimten Rath und KriegsObristen in Gnaden auff und anzunehmen/ Nicht zweifflende/ gleichwie E. Liebden [(Liij v)] ermelten Obristen den von Werder vor diesem alle weg mit Fürstl. Hulden und Gnaden zugethan gewesen/ dieselbe auch ferner gegen Jhn zu continuiren/ Jhr Freund Vetterlich belieben lassen. Solches wie es uns zu sondern dancknehmenden gefallen gereichen wird/ Also seynd wirs ümb E. Liebden mit Freund Vetterlichen Diensten zuerwiedern stets willig und bereit/ Also gleichsam in Gnaden selbsten publiciren und kündig machen lassen. Jn welchem sothanem Dienst Er auch bis an sein Ende verharret/ und sich verhalten/ daß seyn verlust/ wie man sattsame nachricht numehro wohl betrauret worden.

II

460100

Bestallung Diederichs von dem Werder in kurbrandenburgische Dienste

Kf. Friedrich Wilhelm v. Brandenburg (FG 401) bestallt Diederich v. dem Werder (FG 31) zu seinem Geheimen Rat und Kriegsobristen mit einem jährlichen Gehalt von 500 Reichstalern.

Q GSTA—PK Berlin: I. HA GR Rep. 9, A 3 Fasz. 5, Bl. 72r–74v; eigenh. (?) Konzept mit einer Ergänzung von Schreiberh. — Teilabdruck bei *Beckmann* VII, 287.

Von Gottes gnaden, Wir Friederich Wilhelm, Marggraff zu Brandenburg (titul) vhrkunden vndt bekenen hiemit,

Nachdem vns des Edlen, vnsers lieben besondern, Diterichs von dem Werder,[a] vornehme qvalitäten vndt geschickligkeitt geruhmet[b], vns selbst auch dieselbige nicht vnbekandt, welcher gestallt wir dannenhero bewogen worden, ihn aus dem, zu ihm habenden gnedigsten vertrawen, auch in vnsere bestallung zunehmen, vndt ihm beides, zu vnserm geheimbten Rhatt, vndt Kriegsobristen, in gnaden zu bestellen, thun auch [72v] solches hiemit vndt inn krafft dieses, der gestalt, vndt also, das er vns getrew vndt gewertig sein, vnsern nutzen vndt bestes Schaffen vndt befordern, Schaden vndt nachtheill aber verhüten vndt besten seines vermugens abwenden, insonderheitt aber, wann er von uns wirdt erfordertt werden (angesehen es seine[c] gelegenheitt[,] angetrettenen alters halber, nicht gibtt[d], stedts bey vnserm hoff, würcklich auffzuwarten) oder Wir seine einrähtige gedancken, in einem vndt dem andern begehren werden, Sich bei vns gehorsambst gestellen, vndt [73r] vns mit seinen vnvorgreifflichen vernunfftigen guttachten[e] zur handt gehen, Nicht weniger auch, wenn wir vns seiner in verschickungen sonderlich[f] an^g Sachsisch*en*, Hessisch*en*, Mecklenburgisch*en*, Braunschweigisch*en*, Lüneburgisch*en* vndt Anhaltisch*en*^h Chur^i- vndt Fürstlichen höffen wie^j auch inngleich*en* an die König*lich* Schwedische Generalitet¹ wan sie in der nähe ist oder sonsten zugebrauchen haben, Sich dabey vnverdrossen erzeigen, vndt willig befinden lassen^k, auch was er von vnsern geheimbten vndt angelegenen Sachen expediret, oder in erfahrung bringett, in hochster Geheim vndt verschwigenheitt behalten, vndt niemandten, dem es nicht zu wissen, [73v] gebuhrett, zu unserm Schaden vndt nachtheill offenbahren oder entdecken, sondern alle wege, bis in seine grube, wan er auch gleich nicht mehr in vnsern Diensten wehre, bey sich bleiben lassen, vndt in Summa alles das iehnige, was einen getrewen geheimbten Churfurstlichen Rhatt vndt tapfern Kriegsobristen, woll anstehett, eigentt^l vnd gebuhrett, vns in vntertheningsten gehorsamb leisten vndt verrichten solle, gestallt er vns dann, solches zu thun, vermittelst abgelegter eydtlicher pflichtt, festiglich versprochen vndt zugesagt hatt,

[74r] Vor Solche seine dienste vndt auffwartung, haben wir ihm iährlich, zu seiner ergotzligkeitt, Fünffhundert Reichsthaler, dieselbige qvartaliter aus vnser Cammer zu Cölln an der Spree, an Einhundert Fünff vndt zwantzig Rthalern zuentpfangen, vndt mit dero hebung, auff ehist^m kunftigen Ostern, dieses itztlauffenden iahrs den anfang zumachen, in gnaden verwilligtt vndt verheischen²,

Wann vndt so offtt wir aber ihn in verschickungen gebrauchen^n, oder ihn an vns erfordern werden, oder^o er auch^g sonsten seiner gelegenheit nach, etwan alle iahr einmahll zu vns kommen wirdtt, So wollen wir ihm iedesmahll mit notturftiger zehrung providiren vndt mit^p dem freyen tisch an vnserm hoff versehen [74v] auch^q auff Furst*en* diener das gewohnliche Kostgeldt, vndt auff achtt pferde das behorige^r futter geben vndt reichen lassen³,

Vndt Wir Friderich Wilhelm, Marggraff vndt Churfurst zu Brandenburg, nehmen also hiemit vndt in krafftt dieses, vorerwehnten Diterich von dem Werder, zu vnserm geheimbten Rhatt vndt Kriegsobristen, auff vndt an, verheischen vndt versprechen ihm auch das was obstehet, getrewlich vndt sonder gefehrde⁴.

Das zu vhrkunde haben Wir diese bestallung eingehändtlich vnterschrieben, vndt mit vnserm Cammer-Secret zubekrefftigen wollwissendt anbefohlen,

So gegeben vndt geschehen zu Künigsberg den^s ... januar. des 1646ten iahrs.

T a *Folgt* <Contentiren vnd> — **b** *Eingefügt für* <erwünschtes> — **c** *Eingefügt.* — **d** *Am Rand ergänzt bis* Wilhelmß — **e** *Folgt in der Randergänzung* <zu heßen> — **f** *Gebessert aus* würde

T II a *Folgt* <Fürstlichen Hessen-Casselschen Rhatts> — **b** *Folgt* <worden> — **c** *Durch hochgestellte Ziffern geänderte Wortreihenfolge aus* seine, angetrettenen alters halber, gelegenheit *Kommasetzung von uns angepaßt.* — **d** *Lies:* nicht zuläßt — **e** *Eingefügt für* <gedancken [?]> — **f** *Davor* <Chur> Von hier bis vndt Anhaltischen *am Rand ergänzt.* — **g** *Eingefügt in der Randergänzung.* — **h** *Folgt ein versehentlich stehengebliebenes* an *das durch die Randergänzung obsolet geworden ist.* — **i** Chur- vndt *eingefügt.* — **j** *Von Schreiberh. am Rand ergänzt bis* in der nähe ist *Der Zusatz müßte laut Einschaltzeichen bereits*

460125 Kurfürst Friedrich Wilhelm von Brandenburg

vor höffen eingefügt werden, was aber eine erhebliche syntaktische Störung bedeuten würde. — **k** *Folgt* <vndt in Summa alles das ienige, was einem getrewen geheimbten Rhatt, vndt tapfern Kriegsobristen, woll anstehet, eigenett vndt gebührett> — **l** *Lies:* eignet — **m** *Unsichere Lesung.* — **n** *Eingefügt.* — **o** *Am Rand ergänzt bis* wirdt — **p** *Am Rand ergänzt bis* hoff — **q** *Am Rand ergänzt bis* reichen — **r** *Lies:* behörige *[zugehörige].* — **s** *Folgt eine unleserlich gestrichene Zahl* <22 [?]> *als Tagesdatum, darunter ein dem Zahlzeichen 1 ähnliches Zeichen.*

K Obwohl der Brief und die Beilagen nicht als genuin fruchtbringerisch aufgefaßt werden können, haben wir uns aufgrund der Beziehungen Diederichs v. dem Werder (FG 31) und vieler anderer bedeutender Fruchtbringer zum Großen Kurfürsten entschlossen, Werders Bestallung in kfl.-brandenburgischen Diensten, bislang nie aus den verfügbaren Quellen veröffentlicht, hier zu dokumentieren. Werder widmete seine *Dianea* dem Günstling des Kurfürsten, Conrad v. Burgsdorff (FG 404), und Gustav v. Hille (FG 302) dedizierte seinen *Teutschen Palmbaum* (1647), die erste Geschichte der FG, dem Untadelichen (Kf. Friedrich Wilhelm v. Brandenburg. FG 401), s. dessen Imprese auf S. 803.

1 Lgfn. Amalia Elisabeth v. Hessen-Kassel (1602–1651), die als Witwe des vom Kaiser geächteten, am 21.9.1637 in Leer/ Ostfriesland gestorbenen Lgf.en Wilhelm V. (FG 65) die Lgft. Hessen-Kassel vormundschaftlich für ihren unmündigen Sohn Wilhelm (s. Anm. 2) regierte und auf der Basis von Allianzen mit Schweden und Frankreich sehr erfolgreich durch die Unwetter des Dreißigjährigen Krieges und die Westfälischen Friedensverhandlungen steuerte. Amalia Elisabeth war es auch, die die Teilnahme Diederichs v. dem Werder an der hessen-kasselschen Gesandtschaft bei den Heiratsverhandlungen wünschte. Vgl. 370422 K 1 u. 371028 K 9. Am 20.6.1646 lehnte Lgfn. Amalia Elisabeth übrigens den Major und anhalt-bernburg. Kammerjunker Hans Albrecht v. Halck (FG 323) ab, den F. Christian II. v. Anhalt-Bernburg (FG 51) und sein Vetter F. Joh. Casimir v. Anhalt-Dessau (FG 10) für eine Stellung in ihrem Dienst empfohlen hatten. LHA Sa.-Anh.: Abt. Bernburg A 10 Nr. 5^(a-1), Bl. 185r. Im folgenden Jahr wurde Halck dann dauerhaft Stallmeister der Witwe Kf. Georg Wilhelms v. Brandenburg (FG 307), geb. Pgfn. Elisabeth Charlotte. *Conermann III*, 368. Zu den im übrigen guten Beziehungen des Hauses Anhalt zur Witwe und zum Eintritt F. Friedrichs v. Anhalt-Harzgerode (FG 62) in hessen-kasselsche Kriegsdienste im März 1637 vgl. 370715, 371028 u. 380616; Werders hochinteressanter Kondolenzbrief an die Landgräfin vom 6.1.1638 zit. in 370422 K 7. Übrigens unterhielt F. Friedrich 1645 seinerseits gute Verbindungen zur kurbrandenburg. Regierung. In einem Brief vom 12.6.1645 fragte er beim kfl. Oberkammerherrn, Geheimen Rat, Obristen und Befehlshaber der märk. Festungen Conrad v. Burgsdorff (s. o.) nach, ob er „nicht zu wircklicher eintrettung in Seinen des h. Churf. dienst, mich qualificiren vndt einen anfang machen möge" (GSTA–PK Berlin: I HA GR Rep. 11 Nr. 2, Bl. 103r–104v). Vgl. neben der in den genannten Dokumenten unserer Edition angegebenen Literatur auch Tryntje Helfferich: The iron Princess: Amalia Elisabeth and the Thirty Years War. Cambridge/ Mass. 2013; Pauline Puppel: Die Regentin. Vormundschaftliche Herrschaft in Hessen 1500–1700. Frankfurt a. M. (u. a.) 2004, 190–227; Angelika Menne-Haritz: Familienpolitik und Verhandlungen im Vorfeld des Westfälischen Friedens um die Heirat zwischen Hedwig Sophia von Brandenburg und Wilhelm VI. von Hessen. In: Berlin in Geschichte und Gegenwart. Jahrbuch des Landesarchivs Berlin. Berlin 1982, 21–48, hier S. 22.

2 Lgf. Wilhelm VI. v. Hessen-Kassel (1629–1663. FG 694. 1659) übernahm im September 1650 die Regierung des Fürstentums. Zuvor hatte er 1646/47 eine Kavalierstour durch die Niederlande und Frankreich absolviert; am 9./ 19.7.1649 hatte er sich mit Mgfn. Hed-

wig Sophia v. Brandenburg (1623–1683), Schwester Kf. Friedrich Wilhelms, vermählt. S. Anm. 3. Vgl. *ADB* XLIII, 54–60; Eva Bender: Die Reise des Landgrafen Wilhelm VI. von Hessen-Kassel nach Paris im Jahre 1647. In: Formen internationaler Beziehungen in der Frühen Neuzeit. Frankreich und das Alte Reich im europ. Staatensystem. Festschr. f. Klaus Malettke. Hg. Sven Exterbrink u. Jörg Ulbert. Berlin 2001, 245–258, 246; Hans Philippi: Die Landgrafschaft Hessen-Kassel 1648–1806. Marburg 2007, 1–11. Über Mgfn. Hedwig Sophia v. Brandenburg existiert bisher noch keine Biographie. Ausführlichere Erwähnung in: Pauline Puppel: Die Regentin. Vormundschaftliche Herrschaft in Hessen 1500–1700. Frankfurt a. M. (u. a.) 2004, 236–279 sowie in Sophie Ruppel: Verbündete Rivalen. Geschwisterbeziehungen im Hochadel des 17. Jahrhunderts. Köln (u. a.) 2006.

3 Dabei handelte es sich um die Heiratsverhandlungen am kfl.-brandenburg. Hof, mit denen u.a. Diederich v. dem Werder durch Lgfn. Amalia Elisabeth v. Hessen-Kassel (s. Anm. 1) beauftragt worden war, um ihren Sohn, Lgf. Wilhelm VI. v. Hessen-Kassel (s. Anm. 2) mit der Schwester des Großen Kurfürsten zu vermählen. S. Beil. I u. K I. — Der Kontakt Werders zum Hause Hessen-Kassel bestand seit der Zeit Lgf. Moritz' (FG 80), in dessen Diensten er als Page, Kammerjunker, Geheimer Rat und Oberhofmarschall, Prinzenerzieher und Aufseher der Hofschule bis 1622 tätig war. Seine Position als fl.-anhaltin. Lehensmann und Vertreter der anhalt. Landstände im Engeren Ständeausschuß sowie Unterdirektor (letzteres seit 1641), mag erklären, warum Kf. Friedrich Wilhelm v. Brandenburg die anhalt. Fürsten über die Bestallung informierte und um ihr Einverständnis ersuchte. Vgl. 410117 K 6; insgesamt *Krause: Werder*, 53 f.; Angelika Menne-Haritz: Familienpolitik und Verhandlungen im Vorfeld des Westfälischen Friedens (s. Anm. 1), insbesondere S. 22; Tryntje Helfferich: The iron Princess (s. Anm. 1), 192, 210 u. 240.

4 Werder hat seinen Eid „abgeleget zu Königsbergh in Preußen den 25 Jan. A[nn]o 1646. in anwesenheit S. Churf. Mtt. Vndt des H. Ober Cammerherren." Letzterer ist Conrad v. Burgsdorff (s. Anm. 0). Das Dokument in: GSTA—PK Berlin: I. HA GR Rep. 9, Bl. 75rv, v leer. Vgl. 440000 u. I.

K I Diederich v. dem Werder (FG 31) reiste zu Beginn des Jahres 1646 im Auftrag der Regentin Hessen-Kassels, Lgfn. Amalia Elisabeths (s. K 1), zu Kf. Friedrich Wilhelm v. Brandenburg (FG 401) an dessen Hof nach Königsberg, um für die Eheschließung ihres Sohnes, Lgf. Wilhelms VI. v. Hessen-Kassel (FG 694. 1659), mit der Schwester Friedrich Wilhelms, Pzn. Hedwig Sophia v. Brandenburg (s. K 2), zu werben. Vermutlich bereits im Juni 1645 war Diederich v. dem Werder bei einer Reise zu Lgfn. Amalia Elisabeth von dieser beauftragt worden, die Eheschließung ihres Sohnes mit der kurbrandenburg. Pzn. zu vermitteln. S. 450613 (K 5). Die Wahl fiel aus verschiedenen Gründen auf Werder, zu jener Zeit in Diensten Anhalts als Unterdirektor der Landschaft. 1645 u. 1646 empfahl Lgfn. Amalia Elisabeth Werder mehrfach für diesen Auftrag. Vgl. neben Beil. I auch Kreditive u. sonstige Wechselschreiben in der Akte GSTA–PK Berlin: BHP Rep. 34 Nr. 114: „Werbung, Verhandlungen wegen verschiedener Eheverträgen und Copien derselben aus den Jahren 1645–1648". Zum einen war er an beiden Höfen — jenem Hessen-Kassels und jenem Kurbrandenburgs — bekannt und insgesamt gut vernetzt. Seine Jugend verbrachte Werder am Hof in Kassel, wo er als Kammerpage bei Lgf. Moritz (FG 80) diente. Zugleich erhielt er an der dortigen Hofschule, dem späteren Collegium Mauritianum, seine Ausbildung. Nach seiner Rückkehr von Universitätsaufenthalten in Leipzig, Jena und Marburg sowie einer Peregrinatio durch Frankreich und Italien wurde er von Lgf. Moritz zum Stallmeister und Kammerjunker ernannt. Später stieg er bis zum Oberhofmarschall und Geheimen Rat auf. Gleichzeitig wurde er als Ephorus Leiter des Collegium Mauritianum und Erzieher der lgfl. Kinder. Zum anderen war er ein erfahrener Diplomat. Bis zu seiner

460125 Kurfürst Friedrich Wilhelm von Brandenburg

Resignation aller seiner hess. Ämter im Jahre 1622 hatte Werder im Auftrag Hessen-Kassels wiederholt diplomatische Aufgaben wahrgenommen. Auch in seinen späteren Dienstbestallungen für Anhalt und als schwed. Obrist wurde er für diplomatische Missionen eingesetzt, u. a. auch in Kurbrandenburg. *Conermann III*, 34–36; Colerus: Raht des Heils (1658) (s. Beil. I), Bl. J iij v – N ij v. — Spätestens in der zweiten Septemberhälfte 1645 plante Werder seine Abreise aus Anhalt. S. 450919 u. 450921. Jedoch konnte er seine Reise wohl nicht vor dem Jahreswechsel 1645/46 antreten, wie sich anhand der erhaltenen Originalschreiben Werders zeigt. So befand er sich noch am 29.9.1645 in Reinsdorf, am 1.10. in Köthen und am 9. bzw. 24.10.1645 erneut in Reinsdorf. Letztere beide Daten ergeben sich aus zwei Briefen an Lgfn. Amalia Elisabeth. Am 6.12.1645 schrieb Werder, nach wie vor in Reinsdorf, an Lgf. Wilhelm VI. v. Hessen-Kassel. S. dazu die Auflistung der Schreiben Werders in: Diederich von dem Werder: Gottfried von Bulljon, oder das erlösete Jerusalem. 1626. Hg. Gerhard Dünnhaupt. Tübingen 1974 (Nachdr. Frankfurt am Main 1626), 47f. Die Gründe für die verzögerte Abreise lagen vermutlich in anderen wichtigen Geschäften Werders begründet, die er als Unterdirektor der anhalt. Landschaft zu versehen hatte. So erwähnt F. Christian II. v. Anhalt-Bernburg (FG 51) in seinem Tagebuch u. a. Mitte November 1645 Verhandlungen mit Vertretern der anhalt. Stände, an denen auch Werder beteiligt war. *Christian: Tageb.* XVIII, Eintrag vom 19.11.1645. Wahrscheinlich noch im Dezember 1645 muß die Abreise nach Königsberg erfolgt sein, wo Werder spätestens Mitte Januar 1646 eintraf. Im Rahmen seiner Gesandtschaft wurde er, wie erwähnt, dort von Kf. Friedrich Wilhelm zum Geheimen Rat und Kriegsobristen ernannt. Vgl. *Conermann III*, 34. Im obigen Brief teilte der Kurfürst diese Bestallung den anhaltin. Fürsten August (FG 46), Christian II. und Ludwig (FG 2) mit und bat um deren Zustimmung. Bereits Ende Januar 1646 war Werder wieder auf der Rückreise von Königsberg über Küstrin nach Cölln (Berlin), wo er Anfang Februar 1646 eintraf. S. 460204. Zur Gesandtschaft Werders u. seiner Bestallung s. auch 440000 (K 1), 451209 u. 460120 (K 9). — Aufgrund der erfolgreichen Gespräche in Königsberg wurde eine Eheschließung zwischen Lgf. Wilhelm VI. und Pzn. Hedwig Sophia vereinbart (s. „HeyratsPacta" vom 21.1.1646 in der Akte GSTA–PK Berlin: BHP Rep. 34 Nr.114), die drei Jahre später, am 19.7.1649, in Berlin vollzogen wurde. S. *ADB* XLIII, 54–60. Vgl. auch weitere diesbezügliche Schriftstücke und den endgültigen, von Werder mit unterschriebenen Ehevertrag in BHP, Rep. 34 Nr.115. Auch nach seiner Abreise vom kurbrandenburg. Hof ließ sich Werder über den weiteren Verlauf der Verhandlungen ausführlich informieren. So wurden u. a. noch Einzelheiten hinsichtlich der Morgengabe der Prinzessin bzw. ihres Leibgedinges u. hinsichtlich ihrer Ausstattung mit Bargeld u. Kleidung geklärt, wofür ihr schließlich 7.000 Reichstaler jährlich aus Einkünften der Herzogtümer Preußen u. Pommern zugedacht wurden. S. GSTA–PK Berlin: BPH Rep. 34, Nr.114, unfol. (Schreiben von Unbekannt an Diederich v. dem Werder, o. O. 4. Juli 1646). — Neben Werder waren noch andere Personen an der Gesandtschaft nach Königsberg beteiligt, z. B. der Jurist Dr. Rütger Clemens Deichmann (1613–1663). Als Vermittlerin wurde u. a. die Mutter Friedrich Wilhelms, Kfn. Elisabeth Charlotte v. Brandenburg (1597–1660), bemüht. Im Brief Deichmanns an diese vom 10.1.1646 heißt es z. B.: „der Allerhöchste, als welcher dies gutte werck angefangen, wölle ferner zu diesem Christlöblichenn propos seine gnade vndt Lob, Ehr vndt preys, Seiner Kirchen ausbreitung vndt erhaltung, zu Ew. Chrfr. Drl. vndt aller hohen Jnteressenten zeittlicher vndt Ewiger wolfahrt vndt volkommem selpsterwunschten contentement, Auch zu beider vornehmer Chur vndt Furstl. häuser mehrem aufnehmen vndt conservation, ergehen vndt gereichen möge" (GSTA–PK Berlin: BPH Rep. 34 Nr.114, unfol. 1r–2v [2v leer]). — Rütger Clemens Deichmann stammte aus Marburg, wo er als Sohn Christoph Deichmanns (FG 288), damals Professor der Jurisprudenz an der dortigen

Universität, geboren worden war. Der Vater wurde später gfl.-lippischer Kanzler und Vizehofrichter in Detmold, dann kgl.-schwed. Legat im Westfälischen Kreis und Resident in Osnabrück, darauf hzl.-mecklenburg.-güstrow. Kanzler und schließlich kfl.-brandenburg. wie auch fl.-hessen-kassel. Geheimer Rat und Resident zu Hamburg. S. *Conermann III*, 324f. — Rütger Clemens besuchte die Schulen von Schlüchtern und Herborn bevor er an der U. Marburg immatrikuliert wurde. 1642 promovierte er dort *De Legitimâ* zum Dr. jur. Durch die o. g. Gesandtschaft nach Königsberg mit Kf. Friedrich Wilhelm bekannt, wurde er von diesem als Rat in Dienst genommen, in welcher Funktion er u. a. im Hzt. Kleve tätig war. 1649 wurde er Regierungs- und Konsistorialrat im nunmehr kurbrandenburg. Ft. Minden, bevor er 1659 nach dem Tod des Kanzlers Matthaeus v. Wesenbeck (FG 433) Direktor der dortigen kfl.-brandenburg. Regierungskanzlei wurde, in welcher Funktion Deichmann bis zu seinem Tod wirkte. Er wurde in Petershagen bestattet. Aus seiner Ehe mit Johanna, der Tochter des fl.-hessen-kassel. Kriegskommissars Bernhard Becker, gingen zwei Söhne und vier Töchter hervor. Zu ihm s. Julius Schmidt: Sieg und Triumph der Kinder Gottes ... [LP auf Rütger Clemens Deichmann]. Rinteln 1663 (VD17 1:035103S). — Kfn. Elisabeth Charlotte, geborene Pgfn. bei Rhein, war die Tochter Kf. Friedrichs V. v. d. Pfalz, des geächteten „Winterkönigs". Seit 1616 war sie mit Kf. Georg Wilhelm v. Brandenburg (FG 307) verheiratet. Seit 1640 verwitwet, übersiedelte Elisabeth Charlotte in ihren letzten Lebensjahren nach Crossen a. d. Oder, wo sie auch verstarb. S. *ADB* VI, 15 f.

K II 1 Diederich v. dem Werder (FG 31) kommandierte von 1631 bis 1635 als Obrist ein Regiment in schwed. Diensten. Seine daraus resultierenden guten Beziehungen zu den militär. Spitzen der schwed. Armee, v. a. zum schwed. Generalissimus Johan Banér (FG 222), nutzten auch die Anhaltiner durch regelmäßige Abschickungen Werders zur schwed. Generalität, wenn Durchzüge, Einquartierungen, Kontributionen oder Kriegshandlungen das Fürstentum bedrohten, oftmals mit Erfolg bei der Abwendung oder Reduzierung der Kriegslasten. Vgl. besonders 320313 K 0, S. 432 f.; ebenso 371014 K 7, 380724, 380728, 390504 K 4, 390903, 401212 K 4 u. K I 2 u. 410621 K 3; vgl. auch 390807A K 3 u. 5.

2 D. i. verheißen; synonym mit versprechen, geloben. S. *Lexer: Taschenwb.*, 271; *Paul Wb.*, 1088; *Stieler*, 826.

3 Im Januar 1652 reduzierte Kf. Friedrich Wilhelm v. Brandenburg (FG 401) mit Bedauern und unter Hinweis auf die „vnümbgenkliche nohtt" die Entgeltung von Werders Diensten auf 500 Taler „alles vor allen". GSTA—PK Berlin: I. HA GR Rep. 9 A 3 Fasz. 5, Bl. 81rv; vgl. BPH, Rep. 35, B 6: Hofstaat 1641. 1647/48. 1651/52 etc., Bl. 120–122.

4 *Stieler*, 402: „Färde/ Gefärde/ die/ *periculum, qvasi casus dubius,* fraus, dolus." usw.; *Wachter*, 541: „GEFÆRde, fraus, dolus, insidiæ. V. faren insidiare."

460127

Herzog August d. J. von Braunschweig-Wolfenbüttel an Johann Valentin Andreae

Hz. August d. J. von Braunschweig-Wolfenbüttel (FG 227) bestätigt, Johann Valentin Andreaes (FG 464. 1646) Brief vom 7.1.1646 empfangen zu haben. Er bedauert ihn wegen einer Erkrankung und wünscht ihm Genesung und beständige Gesundheit. — Der Fürst sendet Andreae drei Bogen seiner *Evangelischen Kirchen-Harmonie*. In acht Tagen erwartet er die Durchsicht des (darein gehörigen) Schlusses der Leidensgeschichte Jesu. Die mei-

460127 Herzog August d. J. von Braunschweig-Wolfenbüttel

sten Neuerer der Orthographie halten Hz. Augusts Reform der im Deutschen lange vernachlässigten Schreibweise nahezu für vorbildlich. Im übrigen möge Andreae ihm beim Durchlesen entdeckte Fehler mitteilen, bevor die Quartausgabe der *Evangelischen Kirchen-Harmonie* in den Druck geht. — Andreaes Krankheit sei wohl noch dadurch verschlimmert worden, daß seine Amtskollegen ihn in den Weihnachtsfeiertagen nicht unterstützen konnten. Wie schon der Prediger sage, kommt ein Übel selten allein.

Q HAB: Cod. Guelf. 236.3 Extrav., Bl. 4rv [A: 4v]; eigenh. — Von Hz. August links oben als 4. Brief notiert. Von Andreaes H. als 4. Schreiben (1646) und insgesamt als 46. Brief notiert.

A Dem Ehrwurdigen und Hochgelahrten unserm Lieben Besonderen H. Johan-Valentino Andreæ SS Th.D. und F. Wurtembergischen Ober HofPredigern, und geistlichen Consistorial-Rahte, zu behandigen Stutgarten. — *Andreaes Vermerk:* Præs. 7 Feb. 46.

Ehrwürdiger Hochgelahrter lieber besond*er* und getreuer, sein skreib*en* vom 7 Jan. hab*en* wir wol erhalt*en* aber ungern vernom̄en, daß die beswerlicheit*en* des Leibes noch immer anhalt*en*:¹ Gott endere alles und beschere bestandige gesundheit: Hiemit folg*en* wied*er* 3 bogen Harmoniæ.² Uber 8 Tage, erwarte ich die lezte Censuram des Finals an d*er* PassionsHistorien.³ Anlangend die Orthographia haltens die meisten Neoterici⁴ dafur, daß es nahe Zum Ziehle geschossen, und das in einem rechten standt gebracht. was die lange gewohnheit et negligentia scribentium, eingeführet etc. Sonst*en* repetiere ich mein voriges suchen; Er wolle, was Er etwa im Durchlesen Dieses drukkes in malib*us* et formalib*us* befinden möchte, uns vor d*em* anfange des 4ᵗ· drukkes, Zum ende und v*er*bessern communicieren! Daß ihm seine Collegæ, das v*er*gangene Fest über, nicht haben helffen können; hat seinen morbū ohne Zweifel augiret:⁵ Ecclesiastes was d*er* vom vielen Predigen andeutet, findet sich in v. 12. seines lezten Capitis:·⁶ Es hat wol geheissen: Nulla calamitas sola. Gott stehe ihm, und uns allen mit seiner kraft Väterlich beÿ. Eyligst Wulfenb.⁷ den 27. Jan. ♂ 1646.
    Sein beständig affectionirter Freundt,
        AugustushzbulMS

K Hz. August d. J. v. Braunschweig-Wolfenbüttel (FG 227) hat seine Rechtschreibung während der Abfassung der *Evangelischen Kirchen-Harmonie* geändert bzw. entwickelt, aber keine Richtlinien dazu definiert. Der vorliegende Brief zeigt allerdings, wie sehr er sich seiner orthographischen Neuerungen bewußt war. Wir versuchen deshalb in diesem für die orthographischen Absichten des Herzogs wichtigen Brief, einmal über die in unseren „editorischen Richtlinien" beschriebenen Grenzen hinauszugehen und die Schreibweise des Herzogs so diplomatisch genau wiederzugeben, wie dies mit unserer Schrift möglich ist, also auch bei der Groß- und Kleinschreibung, der Zeichensetzung und der Markierung eigentlich eindeutiger Abkürzungen.
    1 Am 7.1.1645 hatte Johann Valentin Andreae (FG 464. 1646) dem Herzog geschrieben: „Meine Leibs indisposition helt abermahl hart an. habe gleichwoln dise weinacht feirtag vber 8 Predigten bei hof gehalten. Vnd iedoch alle nachmittag an terminibus zu Bett gelegen, welche ordinariè post prandium et cænam. secundum magis et minus sich einstel-

len. Hæc mihi uita semi-mortua est. Spiro tamen. et spero ad Serenit. Vestram meum aduentum". HAB: Cod. Guelf. 65.1 Extrav., Bl. 263r.

2 Andreae pflegte Hz. Augusts *Evangelische Kirchen-Harmonie* durchzusehen, die 1646 in Oktav-, Quart- und Duodezausgaben erscheinen sollte. S. 411214.

3 Der Schluß der Leidensgeschichte Jesu war noch in den Text der *Evangelischen Kirchen-Harmonie* des Herzogs zu integrieren. Vgl. 450219 (K 4) u. 450722 (K 4).

4 An Hz. Augusts Hof zu Wolfenbüttel war Justus Georg Schottelius (FG 397) ein solcher Neotericus. Viele der übrigen Neuerer gehörten zu seinem Freundeskreis, s. 441020 K 1.

5 Andreae berichtete am 4.2.1646 über seine kurz nach Weihnachten eingetretene Erkrankung: „Es hat mich aber der getrewe Gott. seit dem 26. d. passato zu bett gelegt, da ich mit der cardialgia, cachexia, vnd Colica zu conflictieren habe, zu mahlen auch ein fluß sich in locum sinistrj pedis malè afflictum gesezet [...]." HAB: Cod. Guelf. 65.1 Extrav., Bl. 267r. Am 11.2.1645 teilt Andreae hierzu mit: „Mit meiner leibes indisposition. hat es seine jntervalla. Verhoffe iedoch von dem lieben Gott beßerung. Meine beide Collegæ ligen noch ebenmäßig zu haus. vnd kan keiner zum anderen. Allein herr Zeller ist noch aufrecht, vnd hat alle arbeit auf ihme ligen." A. a. O., Bl. 268r. Zum Hofkaplan Christoph Zeller s. 450219.

6 Eccl. epilog., 12: „Faciendi plures libros nullus est finis; Frequensque meditatio, carnis afflictio est."

7 Wolfenbüttel.

460131

Georg Philipp Harsdörffer an Christian Gueintz

Antwort auf ein (nicht erhaltenes) Schreiben von Christian Gueintz (FG 361. Der Ordnende) an Georg Philipp Harsdörffer (FG 368. Der Spielende) vom 11.1.1646. — Harsdörffer faßt noch einmal seine wesentlichen Sprachauffassungen zusammen: Eine (orthographische) Regulierung des Deutschen kann nicht aus der Aussprache abgeleitet werden, da die Mundarten zu sehr voneinander abweichen. Auch Luthers Sprache und Schreibweise folge zu sehr dem damaligen Sprachgebrauch und wurde zudem durch eine Kette von Fehlern und Eigenmächtigkeiten der Drucker entstellt. Zudem sei er ein Redner wie Cicero, aber kein Grammatiker wie Varro gewesen. Allerdings würde Luther heute der Meinung des Justus Georg Schottelius (FG 397. Der Suchende) beistimmen, denn er beherrschte das Hebräische, dem die deutsche Sprache in vielem gleichkomme. — In der Grammatik kann nicht die Sprachgewohnheit den Ausschlag geben, sondern die Elemente und Strukturen der dt. Sprache selbst. Gewißheit könne erst die genaue Beachtung der Stammwörter, der Affixe, Endungen und Partikeln verschaffen. Die deutschen Stammwörter sind einsilbig, die vergleichsweise wenigen Ausnahmen bestätigen diese Regel. Die Anfügung eines Endungs-e an den Imperativ Singular (als Stammform der Verben) ist ein überflüssiger Zusatz und gehört zur Konjugationsform der 1. Person Sg. Indik. Aktiv. Das -c- in Fremdwörtern darf beibehalten werden. — Die gewünschte Sprachregulierung darf sich nicht nach dem richten, was ist (Sprachgewohnheit), sondern muß sich an das halten, was sein soll (Sprachnorm). Die Schreibweise -kk- (anstelle des -ck-) wird durch Hinweis auf Paulus Melissus Schede und heutige Autoren gerechtfertigt. Der Widerspruch Augustus Buchners (FG 362. Der Genossene) war voreilig und undifferenziert. „Silbe" ist ein zulässiges, weil eingebürgertes Fremdwort, kann auch durch „Wortglied" wiedergegeben werden. — Die Silbentrennung soll sich weder nach der Aussprache noch nach anderen Sprachen richten, sondern nach der eigenen Grammatik. Sie trennt die morphologischen Wortelemente als solche. Im Hebräischen ist der Imperativ das Stammwort, wie er, Harsdörffer, es im demnächst erscheinenden *Specimen Philologiae Germanicae (1646)* ausführlicher zeigen werde. — Gueintz möge dies reiflich und unvoreingenommen prüfen und seine Gegenargumente Schottelius und Harsdörffer zusenden. Der Sprachausbau des Deutschen bedürfe gesicherter Grundlagen, die in der Debatte gewonnen werden sollen. Schottelius' jüngste Antwort sei Harsdörffer bekannt. — Glückwünsche zum Neuen Jahr.

Q   HM Köthen: V S 545, Bl. 338rv; Köthener Abschrift von Schreiberh., mit einzelnen, wohl von F. Ludwig verbesserten Buchstaben. — *D: KE*, 349–352; *KL* III, 268–270. — BN: *Bürger*, 674 Nr. 17.

A   *Fehlt.*

Hochgeehrter herr *Ordenender.*
Deßelben, an mich abgelaßenes vom 11. Jenner, dieses Jüngst angetretenen Jhars[1], hab ich soviel erfreulicher erhalten, als ich des h. geselschafters treu offenes gemüt, und wol gemeinte erinnerung, ablesend verstanden. Wan man aber von kunstgründiger verfaßung unserer sprache handelen wil, mus man sich erstlich vergleichen, woher? wie? und mit was absehen die lehrsätze, oder regeln, sollen gestellet werden? Wan wir zu einen grund setzen die ausrede, so können wir der sachen nimmermehr eines werden; maßen eine iede mund art etwas besonders füret. D. Luthers S. schriften können gleichsfals fur keinen grund der rechtschreibung stehen, den er dem gebrauch derselben zeiten nachgehen müßen, und es bey seiner urschrift (dem Original) nicht geblieben, sondern durch die Drucksetzer (Mecænates jgnorantiæ) nach und nach geendert worden.[2] Zu dem ist D. Luther der Teutschen Sprache Cicero, aber nicht Varro gewesen. Ein Redner, aber kein Sprachlehrer.[3] Seine wort sind unwiedersprechlich für angenem zu halten, aber derselben schreibung ist deswegen nicht richtig. Wolte Gott dieser teure Man solte des Suchenden Sprachlehre[4] beurtheilen, er solte seiner meinung gewislich nicht ablegen: maßen er, die hebräische Sprache wol verstanden, nach welcher sich unsere teutsche durchgehend artet.[5] Also kan auch der böse gebrauch kein gutes gesetz geben, und nicht anders für angenem gehalten werden, als wo solcher den eigenschaften, unserer haubtsprache beystimmet. Woher sol man dan eine gewisheit in verfaßung der Sprachlehre ergründen?

[a] Principia Constitutiva et Linguarum sunt I. Radices. II. [p]ræfixa et suffixa [III.] [...]ni particulæ.[5,1]
NB
[O]mnes Regulæ fiunt [p]er inductionem exempl. [v]el per Jnstantias. quid [ind]aginè Catholica esse [o]ptima videtur.

[a] [Al]s Ausnahm pertinent [a]d exceptionem et [n]on ad regulam.
NB.
Die Francken, Schwa[b]en, Osterreicher und [S]chweitzer setzen das [e] nicht ad secundam imperativi.

Aus anfürung deroselben Stam- oder wurtzelwörter, der Vor- und nachsilben, benebens den bey[-] und fugwörtlein, durch richtige anführung dieser haubtstücke, werden die lehrsätze gemachet, und ist der beste unter denselben, welche am meinsten unter sich begreift. Der herr Ordenende bedencke, ob wir hier unrecht daran sind.

Wan also der h.[b] Nehrende[6] die andere Person der gebietungs weise, nicht wil für ein stamwort gelten laßen[7], ist die antwort; das Zweyerley Stamwörter[c], deren etliche nach heutiger aussprache sich in el, er und es enden, und sind derselben eine gewiße anzahl, die zu den abtritt[d] von der Regel gehören, welche unter sich mehr als tausend der andern Stamwörter begreift, das e, so etliche anfügen in folge, gehe[,] stehe, ist ein überflüßiger beysatz, so die hebräer ה paragogicum[8] nennen, dieses e aber gehöret eigentlich zu der ersten[b] person der gegenwertigen Zeit, in der Weise anzuzeigen. Jch folge, sequor, gehe eo das C in Mexico, Music, Courbettes[9] etc. wird billig behalten, weil es fremde wörter und zum theil eigene Nahmen[e] sind, [338v] welche in allen sprachen ihre an kunfts buchstaben mitbringen.[10] Die gewonh[eit][f] welche der h. Ordnende mit sondern schein vorschützet, sagt zwar [was][f] zugeschehen pfleget, darvon die frage nicht ist, sondern was geschehen [sol.][f] Niemand wird eines fehlers beschuldiget, der unwißend der gew[on]heit[f] folget, das man aber deswegen nichts beßers forschen sol, ist [dar]aus[f] nicht erweislich, Paulus Melissus[11] hat das kk. vor 74 Jhar[en][f] gebrauchet, ihm haben etliche gefolget, und sonderlich Zesien[,][12] Flemmi[ng][f] [13] und die Lübecker Druckerey[14]: unter uns der befreyende[g] (hertz[og][f] Augustus Von Brunschweig)[15], der unverdroßene[16], der Suchende[h] [17][,] aber der Genoßene (Augustus Buchnerus)[18] nennet sie narren, die das [kk][f] gebrauchen; er hat ihre ursachen nicht angehöret, sie aber haben se[ine][f] unbescheidenheit, mit verachtung gesehen.[19] Die wort[-]sylbe hat [das][f] Deutsche burgerrecht, kan aber wol genennet werden, das wo[rt]glied[f].[20]

Was zum zweyten der h. Ordnende Von de[r][f] sylben abtheilung meldet, ist gleichsfals also beschaffen, das de[r][f] Spielende seine meinung dadurch nicht geendert. Dan 1. die ausrede wieder die eigenschaft der sprache nicht gelten mag. 2. können andere sprachen, und sonderlich die lateinische, der u[n]sern^f nicht gesetz und ordnung geben. 3. in dem wort klingen^j, ist da[s]^f stamwort kling (sona) und die nachsylben en, liebst-en hab-en und in dem hebreischen ist nach der letzten sprachlehrer einstimiger meinung, die befehlsweise das stamwort. hiervon wird umstendig[e]^f ausführung zu lesen sein in **Specimine Philologiæ Germanicæ** das bereit dem Drucke untergeben.[21]

Diesem nach beliebe dem h. *Ordnenden* die sache vernünftig zu übe[r]legen^f, und seine fernere zweiffel und einreden an den Suchenden, und Spielenden, nach gelegenheit, zu überschreiben^j: des ungezweiffelten Versehens, das nach befindung^k der sachen gerne w[ei]chen^f, und beßern bericht gewonnen geben, werden. Es ist die fr[a]ge^f: Wie man das Deutsche Sprachwesen^l, in eine kunstrichtige, gleichgründige, und allen eigenschaften gemäße verfaßung setzen könne? Hierbey fallen nun allerhand bedencken, die kein Vorurthe[il]^{f m} nach der gewonheit, nach ansehen der person leiden wollen, sonder[n]^f aus gründlicher warheit zubeantworten sein. Was der Suchend[e]^f Jüngst geantwortet[22], ist dem Spielenden nicht unwißend.

Schlieslich erwüntschet dem *Ordenenden* bey anfang dieses neue[n] Jhars, alles was seelig und glücklich, friedlich und erfreulich, erspriesslich und dienlich.

Nürnberg den 31. Jenner 1646.

Der Spielende.

P. S.
Jnferior reliquis teneo subsellia, votis
haud absensurus, si meliora dabis
Dissentire licet, modo sit, Concordia salva
et maneat vere judiciosus Amor
Sic reputes animo Queinzi: in vernacula nostra.
An Consuetudo sit ratione prior?

Marginalien:
quod est Ratio Conjungendarum syllabarum, eadem est ratio disjungendarum.

Ex. de. catholica regularitate vernacula

T *Verstreut über den Text finden sich wiederholt interlineare Verbesserungen mit breiter Feder, wie sie F. Ludwig führte. Diese Korrekturen lassen deshalb nicht erkennen, welche Buchstaben überschrieben wurden. Wir ersparen uns Hinweise.* — **a** *Textverlust im Falz, unsere Konjekturen in eckigen Klammern.* — **b** *Eingefügt.* — **c** *Gebessert aus* Stamwörtter — **d** *Folgt ein Pluszeichen, das wohl auf die nebenstehende Marginalie verweist.* — **e** *Gebessert aus* Namen — **f** *Textverlust im Falz, Konjektur nach KE in eckigen Klammern.*

— g *Folgt* <Ertz> — h *Gebessert aus* <Ju> *Jüchtende [?]* — i *Gebessert aus* Kling — j *Gebessert aus* u[nt?]erschreiben — k *Folgt ein gestrichenes Komma* <,> — l *Durch Einfügung gebessert aus* wesen — m *Durch Einfügung gebessert aus* urthe[il]

K Christian Gueintz (FG 361. Der Ordnende) hatte im Herbst des Vorjahres *Die Deutsche Rechtschreibung*, die vor allem aus seiner und F. Ludwigs Feder hervorging, veröffentlicht. Der vorliegende Brief rekapituliert grundsätzliche Sprachauffassungen Georg Philipp Harsdörffers (FG 368. Der Spielende). Diese gehören in den Zusammenhang verschiedener Anläufe zu einer konkreten Verständigung zwischen F. Ludwig (der Nährende), Gueintz, Harsdörffer und Justus Georg Schottelius (FG 397. Der Suchende), die einen grammatischen Konsens heraufführen sollte, ohne die das geplante Projekt eines gemeinschaftlich zu erstellenden dt. Wörterbuchs aussichtslos erschien. Vgl. 451219 u. 451220. F. Ludwig hat eine eigene Stellungnahme zum vorliegenden Brief mit 460200 an Gueintz geschickt. S. dort K 1.

1 Das erwähnte Schreiben (vom 11.1.1646) von Gueintz an Harsdörffer ist ebenso wenig überliefert wie ein von Gueintz angefertigtes Antwortschreiben an Harsdörffer. Vgl. jedoch die Stellungnahme F. Ludwigs zu diesem Schreiben, die er an Gueintz sandte. S. 460200.

2 Martin Luther galt zwar einerseits als Gewährsmann und unbestrittene Autorität in Sachen Sprachausgleich und Normierung der deutschen Sprache. So hat er z.B. nach Philipp v. Zesen (FG 521. 1648) „die Hochdeutsche Spraache zu erst wieder ausgearbeitet und zu ihrem glantze gebracht". Philipp v. Zesen: Hooch-Deutsche Spraach-übung (1643). In: *Zesen SW* XI, 1–77, hier 24f. Immer wieder beriefen sich auch andere Sprachgelehrte der FG auf Luthers Sprachausgleich, dabei durchaus auch des historischen Abstands kritisch bewußt. S. z.B. 440219 K 2, 440313, 441223 K 23, 450410 K 3, 460200 K 1, 460720 K 3, 460902 K 3 u. 460915. Vgl. *Herz: Rechtschreibdebatte*, 85f., 116f. u. 130f. Andererseits wurden Luthers im 17. Jh. als veraltet empfundenes Idiom und seine offensichtlich hohe Variantentoleranz, die das Fnhd. des 16. Jh.s generell auszeichnet, kritisiert. Viele orthographische Unstimmigkeiten der Luther-Bibel wurden dabei jedoch auf Druckfehler bzw. Eigenmächtigkeiten der Drucker geschoben, so auch Harsdörffers Invektive im vorliegenden Brief. *Gueintz: Rechtschreibung (1645)*, 5: „Lutherus ist billich der Deutschen sprache in KirchenSachen Urheber/ die ReichsAbschiede in Weltlichen dingen die Hauptbücher/ Wie wol bey beyden/ weil sie von eintzelen Personen aufgesetzet/ auch zu der Zeit/ so wol als ietzo/ die Schreiber und Drucker oftmals gefehlet/ noch viel erinnerungen/ was die Rechtschreibung betrifft/ zu thun seind." Auch hatte z.B. Hz. August d.J. v. Braunschweig-Wolfenbüttel (s. Anm. 15) Anfang der 1640er Jahre eine sprachliche Revision der Luther-Bibel angestrebt, aber aufgrund des Widerstandes der luther. Geistlichkeit einstweilen aufgegeben und durch eine Modernisierung und Regulierung der Bibelsprache in seiner *Evangelischen Kirchen-Harmonie* (1646ff.) ersetzt. Vgl. 391217 I, 411214, 430515, 451001, 461204 u.ö. — Zur Rolle des Reformators bei der Standardisierung der deutschen Sprache allgemein vgl. Rolf Bergmann: Der rechte Teutsche Cicero oder Varro. Luther als Vorbild in den Grammatiken des 16. bis 18. Jahrhunderts. In: Sprachwissenschaft 8 (1983), 265–276; Werner Besch: Luther und die deutsche Sprache. 500 Jahre deutsche Sprachgeschichte im Lichte der neueren Forschung. Berlin 2014; Rolf Bergmann/ Claudine Moulin: Luther als Gewährsmann der Rechtschreibnorm? Zu Johann Girberts „Teutscher Orthographie". In: Manfred Lemmer (Hg.): Beiträge zur Sprachwirkung Martin Luthers im 17./ 18. Jahrhundert. Halle a. d. Saale 1987, 62–82; Dirk Josten: Sprachvorbild und Sprachnorm im Urteil des 16. und 17. Jahrhunderts. Sprachlandschaftliche Prioritäten, Sprachautoritäten, sprachimmanente Argumentation. Frankfurt a. M., Bern 1976, 48–55 u. 104–126;

Herbert Wolf (Hg.): Luthers Deutsch. Sprachliche Leistung und Wirkung. Frankfurt a. M. (u. a.) 1996.

3 Der Orator und Rhetoriker Marcus Tullius Cicero (106 v. Chr. – 43 v. Chr.) wird hier dem Grammatiker Marcus Terentius Varro (116 v. Chr. – 27 v. Chr.) gegenübergestellt, der als Sprachsystematiker bekannt war. Vgl. *Herz: Ratio und consuetudo,* 272 ff. Luthers Sprachleistung wird hier historisch und fachlich relativiert.

4 Justus Georg Schottelius hatte 1641 eine *Teutsche Sprachkunst* herausgegeben. Diese war im Grundsatz ein Gegenentwurf zu dem von Gueintz kurz zuvor im selben Jahr publizierten *Deutscher Sprachlehre Entwurf,* der trotz eines im Vorfeld bei Schottelius eingeholten, durchweg kritischen Gutachtens nahezu unverändert veröffentlicht worden war. S. 400528 nebst beiden Beilagen.

5 In der sprachwissenschaftl. Diskussion des 17. Jh.s wurde immer wieder eine nahe Verwandtschaft des Deutschen mit dem Hebräischen bzw. die direkte Abstammung des ersteren aus dem letzteren betont. So sah z. B. Schottelius im Deutschen eine der „Hauptsprachen", die im Zuge der Babylonischen Sprachverwirrung direkt aus der bibl. „Ursprache", dem Hebräischen, entstanden sei, ohne sich erst aus den klass. Sprachen Griechisch bzw. Lateinisch entwickelt zu haben. Somit wies er dem Deutschen eine herausragende Stellung unter den europäischen Sprachen zu, im Gegensatz z. B. zum Französischen oder Italienischen, die erst aus dem Lateinischen hervorgegangen waren. Harsdörffer stellte die enge Verwandtschaft des Deutschen mit dem Hebräischen v. a. in seinem *Specimen Philologiae Germanicae (1646)* heraus, Philipp v. Zesen z. B. in seinem undat. Brief an Adolph Rosel, vermutlich von 1644. In: *Bellin: Sendeschreiben (1647),* Nr. 10, Bl. [Dviij] v – G[i] v, hier Bl. Eii r. In einem wohl auf Januar 1645 zu datierenden Brief an Rosel behauptet Zesen die enge Verwandtschaft des Deutschen mit dem Hebräischen nicht nur, weil die alten Deutschen eher mit hebr. als lat. Buchstaben geschrieben hätten, vielmehr sonderlich auch wegen „der herstammung der wörter/ da die grosse zeuge-mutter sonderlich spielet/ und die wörter nach dem eigentlichen wäsen der dinge zu bilden weis". *Bellin: Sendeschreiben (1647),* Nr. 5, Bl. [B6]v – C[i]v, hier Bl. C[i]r. Von anderen Sprachforschern wurde diese proklamierte Vorrangstellung des Deutschen nicht explizit betont; Gueintz und Augustus Buchner etwa hielten sich hier zurück. S. dazu v. a. 440826 K 6, 450410, 450808 K 8, 460406 K 4 u. 451220; vgl. auch *Schäfer: Moscherosch und Harsdörffer,* 169 f.

5.1 *Harsdörffer: Specimen (1646),* Praefatio, Bl.)()()()(3v: „Sic in Lingua nostra teneamus. I. Radices, II. Præfixa & suffixa, III. Particulas". Vgl. schon 450410 K 4.

6 F. Ludwig nahm aktiv an diesen Diskussionen Anteil und vertrat wie Gueintz die Meinung, daß dem Sprachgebrauch vor analogistischen Hyperkorrekturen der Vorzug zu geben sei. S. u. a. seine Stellungnahme zu dem vorliegenden Brief, die er mit seinem Schreiben Gueintz zuleitete. S. 460200.

7 Der (einsilbige) Imperativ Singular als Stammform der Verben bei Schottelius und Harsdörffer, also folg, nicht folge, geh, nicht gehe, steh, nicht stehe (s. o. im Brief). Gueintz, F. Ludwig u. Zesen (s. v. a. 450308A u. 450808) widersprachen der Einsilbigkeitsdoktrin. Ausführlich dazu 450410 K 3.

8 Als „Paragoge" (griech. παραγωγή) bezeichnet man in der Sprachwissenschaft das Anhängen eines oder mehrerer Buchstaben am Ende eines Wortes. Dies geschieht oftmals im Zuge der Übernahme eines Lehnwortes, sofern dieses eine für die aufnehmende Sprache untypische Wortendung aufweist. Vgl. dazu *Zedler* XXVI, 786; *Diefenbach: Glossarium,* 411; Max Hermann Jellinek: Ein Kapitel aus der Geschichte der deutschen Grammatik. In: Abhandlungen zur Germanischen Philologie. Festgabe für Richard Heinzel. Halle 1898 (Ndr. Tübingen 1984), 31–110, hier S. 44 u. 56. Es kann als Barbarismus gelten, *Lausberg,* § 484. Vgl. *Dasypodius,* Bl. 164v: „Ein zuführung/ so am ende des worts ein buchstab/

oder gantze sylbe herzu wirt geworffen. ut potestur pro potest, admittier pro admitti. Aliàs Paralempsis uel Prosparalempsis dicitur."

9 Die aus der frz. Sprache stammenden „Courbettes" bezeichneten im höf. Zeremoniell eine tiefe Verbeugung („Bückling"). — In der unter den deutschen Sprachforschern des 17. Jhs. hitzig geführten Debatte um die korrekte Schreibung der deutschen Sprache war einer der Streitpunkte die Verwendung des -c-, v. a. in der Verbindung mit -k-. Wie Harsdörffer in seinen *Gesprächspielen* erklärte, zog er die Buchstabenfolge -kk- dem -ck- vor, weil das -k- im Gegensatz zum -c- ein originärer Buchstabe der deutschen Sprache sei. Im Falle eines fremdsprachigen Wortstammes sei hingegen die Verwendung des -c- gestattet. Vgl. Anm. 11. Gueintz kritisierte hingegen die Verwendung von -kk- statt -ck-, da es weder üblich sei, noch sich aussprechen lasse. Vgl. Anm. 12 u. 18, 450420 K 6, 451028A K 6, 451219, 460915 K 20 u. ö.

10 Die in der FG diskutierte Frage, wie Fremdwörter zu schreiben und zu behandeln seien — wie in der Herkunftssprache oder angeglichen an deutsche Schreibung und Grammatik? — verlief widersprüchlich. *Gueintz: Rechtschreibung (1645)*, 11 f.: „Wie dan auch im schreiben der fremden wörter/ nach der sprachen art daraus sie genommen zu gehen/ als *Philosophia* und nicht *Filosofia*: Dan die fremden wörter/ aus einer andern sprache entlehnet/ ihrer ankunft gemäß müssen gestellet werden. Jnsonderheit in den Griechischen und Lateinischen Menschen Nahmen/ das man sie nicht immerdar in der Nennendung [Nominativ] stehen lasse/ sondern nach ihrer grundsprache/ in ihre verwandelunge [Deklination] setze/ Als der *Plato*, des *Platonis*, dem *Platoni*, den *Platonem* [...] und dergleichen." Er läßt aber auch deutsche Deklinationsformen zu: „des Platons Sohn/ des grossen Alexanders Volck". Harsdörffer hatte das auch schon anders gesehen: Im 3. Teil seiner *Frauenzimmer-Gesprächspiele* (1643) hatte er statt des (griech.) -ph- die einfache, nach ital. Vorbild regulierte Schreibweise mit -f- vorgezogen, etwa „Profeten" und „Profeceyung", denn er war der Meinung: „Für das ph kann durch und durch ein f geschrieben werden/ wie bey den Jtaliänern". A. a. O., 315/ Ndr. S. 335. F. Ludwig korrigierte in seiner Stellungnahme zur Orthographie Harsdörffers im 3. Teil der *Frauenzimmer-Gesprächspiele* wieder zugunsten des -ph- und berichtigte beispielsweise „Josef" zu „Joseph" und „Delfin" zu „Delphin". F. Ludwig: „Etzliche erinnerungen, bey dem dritten theile der gesprächspiele am meisten die wortschreibung betreffende, auf begeren, vorgestellet." HM Köthen: V S 545, Bl. 419r–424v u. 426r, hier Bl. 421r, 423r u. 422v. (Die „Etzlichen erinnerungen" sind für die Veröffentlichung in *DA Köthen I. 9* vorgesehen.) Im Rechtschreibungs-Anhang zum 1. Teil des *Poetischen Trichters* (1650) wird sich Harsdörffer aber F. Ludwigs Meinung anschließen, „daß die fremden Wörter mit ihren eigentlichen fremden Buchstaben behalten werden/ als Prophet/ Nymphe/ Phöbus/ und nicht Profet/ Nymfe/ Febus: dann ich sonst auch in andern Wörtern das f für ein ph setzen müsste/ als Farao/ Filip/ Fenix/ welches sehr fremd". Harsdörffer: Poetischer Trichter, 1. Teil (zuerst 1647, 2. erw. Aufl. Nürnberg 1650, Ndr. 1969), 129. Zur Fremdwörter-Lexik vgl. v. a. 440525 K II 13.

11 Paulus Melissus (eigentl. Schede) (1539–1602), humanist. Dichter u. Übersetzer des Genfer Psalters ins Deutsche (zuerst Heidelberg 1572). Zu ihm s. *ADB XXI*, 293–297; *NDB XVII*, 15 f. Harsdörffer berief sich in seiner Verwendung des -kk- anstelle des -ck- auf Melissus, s. *Harsdörffer: Specimen (1646)*, 212, u. in der langen Ausführung zum Buchstaben -c- S. 213–217. Dort zitiert Harsdörffer einige Beispiele aus Schedes Psalterübersetzung („stükken", „schikken", „lokken", „hartnekkige" usw.). Melissus, so Harsdörffer, folge hier antiken Regeln, denn „apud latinos littera duplicanda duplicatur cum homogenea & non heterogenea", was die Schreibung mit ck folglich ausschließt. Von der Verwendung des ck nimmt Harsdörffer auch deswegen Abstand, weil es dann Wörter gäbe, die

anders geschrieben als gelesen würden. Mit dem -c- hätte man einen stummen Buchstaben eingeführt. Dem widerspricht eine Regel in *Gueintz: Rechtschreibung (1645)*, 18: „K wird niemals am ende ohne C gebrauchet/ auch niemals gedoppelt. Um der ursache willen/ weil es etwas zu schwer im aussprechen; und doch nichts anders als ein C im Lateinischen ist/ wie aus dem Griechischen zusehen. Es ist auch das K niemals mit unter die doppelbuchstaben gerechnet worden/ gibt auch keine richtige aussprache". — In 460915 bekräftigt Harsdörffer noch einmal seine Haltung und verweist auf die argumentativ ausholende „Admonitio" im 6. Teil seiner *Frauenzimmer-Gesprächspiele* (1646, Ndr. 1969), Ndr. S. 714–716. Sie lautet: „NOn ignoro, mi Lector, displicere plurimis **kk**/ loco **ck**/ à modernis Criticis, qvos seqvimur, introductum, Rationem audiamus philosophicam: *Quaelibet res habet formam suam quidditativam & propriam, per quam talis, vel talis est.* E. G. Homo habet formam hominis; Leo Leonis: quòd si verò Homo haberet formam Leonis, non poterit habere qualitates Hominis, sed Leonis, aut sub nomine monstri simul foret Homo & Leo. Sic *singulae litterae habent singulas formas, &, propter illas formas, potestates proprias, minimè confundendas.* **c** non est **k**/ et **k** non est **c**. Si linguae nostrae Elementa ritè constituenda sunt, nullum à Graecis, qui litteram c neq; à Latinis, qui litteram k non habent, admittimus praejudicium, sed ut in aliis, ita etiam in his summam intendimus perfectionem. Quibus autem Elenchus comparatorum, & consuetudo ex Latino perperam introducta, pro lege retinenda videtur, suo abundent sensu, nos nitamur ratione. Interim tamen in peregrinis vocibus litteras genuinas non adversamur, & scribimus **Capitel/ Centner/ Cicero/ Constantin Curiren/** &c. Moniti meliora sequemur. Vale [...]". F. Ludwigs Ablehnung des von Schede (angeblich) eingeführten -kk- und seine Zweifel an den sprachlichen Fähigkeiten des Übersetzers in seiner Stellungnahme zum vorliegenden Brief, s. 460200 K 1. Vgl. auch Anm. 9, 12 u. 18.

12 Philipp v. Zesen lehnte das -c- im dt. Alphabet ab, da es die Deutschen von den Lateinern „wider ihrer sprache eigenschaft" übernommen hätten. Im Deutschen stehe das -k- zur Verfügung und mache -c- wie auch -q- überflüßig. In der Verbindung mit -h- sei dem g vor dem -c- der Vorzug zu geben: möghte statt möchte, Toghter statt Tochter usw., in der Verbindung mit -k- sei das -c- überflüßig und auch die Niederländer begännen, das -c- vorm -k- und -h- wegzuwerfen oder in kk bzw. gh zu ändern. *Bellin: Sendeschreiben (1647)*, Nr. 10, Bl. [Dviij] v – G[i] v, hier Bl. Eii v ff. Daran übte Augustus Buchner (FG 362) in 460812 Kritik.

13 Wohl der aus Amberg stammende Dietrich Flemming (†1664). Zu ihm s. 450219 K 15.

14 Nicht ermittelt.

15 Hz. August d. J. v. Braunschweig-Wolfenbüttel (FG 227. Der Befreiende).

16 Carl Gustav v. Hille (FG 302. Der Unverdrossene).

17 Justus Georg Schottelius (s. o.).

18 Augustus Buchner (s. o.) hat in 460812 der Eliminierung des -c- aus dem deutschen Alphabet energisch (an die Adresse Zesens) widersprochen: erstens sei es bereits „in den ältesten schrifften zu finden" und könne im Deutschen daher nicht schlicht fremd sein, sondern trage zu einer differenzierten und angenehmen Lautung bei; zweitens ginge es nicht an, daß man „den bißhero eingeführten und numehr längst verjährten brauch fast gäntzlich aufheben wollte" usw.

19 Zur Harsdörfferschen Bedeutung von Unbeschiedenheit — im Sinne von mangelnder Unterscheidung, Differenzierung oder vernünftiger Überlegung (s. unten „die sache vernünftig zu überlegen"), auch Gegensatz zu Bescheidenheit im Sinne von εὐκρίνεια, s. 441020 K 14.

20 *Gueintz: Rechtschreibung (1645)*, 19, wählte den Terminus „sylbe oder buchstaben-

begrif"; ebd., Bl.)(ivr: „Buchstaben/ und deren begrif"; ebd., 13: „Sylben oder Buchstabbegriffs", ebenso S. 85.

21 Zum Dissens über eine Silbentrennung nach Sprechsilben (F. Ludwig und Gueintz) oder grammaticé (Schottelius und Harsdörffer) vgl. schon 451028A K 6. Dort auch der Hinweis auf Harsdörffers *Specimen Philologiae Germanicae* (1646), 149f., wo erneut das morphematische Prinzip der Syllabierung vertreten wird.

22 Es dürfte sich um jenes Gutachten des Schottelius handeln, das eine Art Grundsatzpapier darstellt und aus Wolfenbüttel auf den 5.12.1645 datiert ist. Es ist in eigenh. Ausfertigung und in einer Abschrift im Köthener Erzschrein erhalten: HM Köthen: V S 545, Bl. 257rv–258v u. Bl. 256rv (Abschrift). Das Papier ist zur Veröffentlichung in *DA Köthen I. 9* vorgesehen; Hinweise dazu und eine Paraphrase seines Inhalts in 451219 K 1.

460200

Fürst Ludwig an Christian Gueintz

F. Ludwig sendet Christian Gueintz (FG 361. Der Ordnende) seine Stellungnahme zu Georg Philipp Harsdörffers (FG 368. Der Spielende) Brief 460131 und bittet ihn, ggf. eigene Kritikpunkte aufzusetzen und selbige sowie ein Konzept, wie dies dem Spielenden hinterbracht werden soll, Ludwig zuzusenden. Auch bittet er Gueintz um Mitteilung, was er zuvor in dieser Sache an Harsdörffer abgehen ließ. — Die wohl entscheidende Frage sei, wie Harsdörffer die behauptete enge Strukturgleichheit des Deutschen mit dem Hebräischen beweisen wolle. Ferner, inwiefern die dt. Endungen -e, -el, -en, -er, -ern und -eln den hebr. Prä- und Suffixen gleich seien und was diese Endungen ohne einen vorangehenden Konsonanten bedeuten sollen.

Q HM Köthen: V S 545, Bl. 341r, v leer; undat. eigenh. Konzept im Anschluß an F. Ludwigs ebenfalls undatierte Stellungnahme zu Harsdörffers Brief 460131: „Bey des Spielenden schreiben vom 31. Jenners 1646 zuerinnern." A. a. O., Bl. 340r–341r (wird als „Zu 460200" veröffentlicht in *DA Köthen I. 9*). — D: *KE*, S. 354 Anm.

A *Fehlt*.

Wan der Ordenende bey diesem aufsatze[1] noch etwas zuerinnern, so wolle er[a] es thun und sein bedencken darbey[a] geben mit einem entwurffe wie er es an den Spielenden dan bringen wolle, auch mittheilung desjenigen, was er deswegen zuvor an ihme geschrieben.[2]

Das meiste wird ietzunder darauf beruhen wie man jenerseits[b] beweisen wolle, das sich die Deutsche Sprache, wie angezogen, in allem nach der Hebraischen arte.[3] und das die endungen e, el, en, er[,] ern[,] eln und dergleichen den Hebraischen **affixis**,[c] **suffixis** oder anhängen gleich seyen,[4] und dan was sie bedeuten, wan kein **consonans** oder mitlaut darbey ist.[5]

T a *Eingefügt*. — b jenerseits *eingefügt für* <ietzt> — c *Folgt* <oder>

K Zur Datierung: Der Brief 460131 von Georg Philipp Harsdörffer (FG 368. Der Spielende) an Christian Gueintz (FG 361. Der Ordnende) wurde offensichtlich über Köthen versandt oder von Gueintz F. Ludwig eingereicht, was die Abschrift von Schreiberhand im Erzschrein erklärt. F. Ludwig schrieb eine Erwiderung zu 460131 (s. Anm. 1), die er dem vorliegenden Brief an Gueintz beilegte. Die Laufzeiten der Briefe zwischen Nürnberg und Köthen betrugen — wie es die Präsentationsvermerke F. Ludwigs belegen — mindestens acht Tage (wie z. B. im Falle von 451101 u. 460620), nicht selten über einen Monat. Sie konnten sich wegen der Unwägbarkeiten des Kriegsgeschehens jedoch noch erheblich erhöhen (der Empfang von Harsdörffers Brief 440426 wird von F. Ludwig erst mit 450124 bestätigt). Brief und Gutachten F. Ludwigs sind somit frühesten auf die zweite Februarwoche 1646 zu datieren.

1 F. Ludwig legte dem vorliegenden Brief seine kritische Stellungnahme „Bey des Spielenden schreiben vom 31. Jenners 1646 zuerinnern" bei. Sie hat sich in einem eigenh. Konzept und in einer von F. Ludwig korrigierten und ergänzten Abschrift von Schreiberhand erhalten. HM Köthen: V S 545, Bl. 339rv (Konzept) u. 340r–341v; *KE*, 352–354. In vollem Wortlaut wird sie im Band *DA Köthen I. 9* veröffentlicht. An dieser Stelle sei sie wegen des Kommunikationszusammenhangs zusammengefaßt (der Vergleich mit 460131 zeigt die Bezugnahmen):
In eigenmächtiger Weise neue Regeln in die Sprache einführen zu wollen, wie dies Justus Georg Schottelius (FG 397. Der Suchende) in seiner *Sprachkunst (1641)* insinuiere, gehe nicht an. Die Regeln können nicht aus der Vorstellung eines oder zweier Menschen gewonnen werden, sondern müssen durch Sprachtradition und -gewohnheit eingeführt und legitimiert sein. Die Aussprache ist durchaus ein wichtiges Kriterium (für die Sprach-, insbes. Rechtschreibregulierung). Luthers Sprache in seiner Bibelübersetzung sei „reiner" als je ein Franke, Schwabe, Österreicher, Rheinländer oder Niedersachse gesprochen hat oder sprechen wird. Harsdörffers Schelte der fehlerhaften und entstellenden Druckersprachen findet zwar F. Ludwigs Zustimmung, jedoch haben es die Drucker damals nicht besser gekonnt. Daß Luther der *Sprachkunst* von Schottelius zustimmen würde, bezweifelt F. Ludwig, v. a. hinsichtlich der dort grundsätzlich auf nur eine Silbe verkürzten Stammwörter. Aber auch hinsichtlich Harsdörffers ungewöhnlicher Silbentrennung (grammaticé), die nun den Druckern aufgedrungen werde, obwohl sie gegen „den Accent, den thon, und die aussprache" verstoße, wäre kaum auf Luthers Zuspruch zu rechnen gewesen. F. Ludwig stellt die strukturelle Gleichheit der hebräischen und der dt. Sprache in Frage, und nicht einmal in ersterer seien alle Stammwörter einsilbig. Auch die Vor- und Nachsilben unterschieden sich in beiden Sprachen; zudem sei das Hebräische kürzer, während das Deutsche umfangreicher, klarer und bedeutungsreicher in seinem Wortschatz sei. Die angebliche Paragoge des -e-Zusatzes in Imperativen und bei einigen Nomen sei keineswegs ein überflüssiger Zusatz, sondern ein notwendiges Wortelement. Dies komme mit der Aussprache wie auch der Grammatik des Deutschen sehr wohl überein. Sodann erhebt sich die Frage, ob Stammwörter nicht in allen Wortarten (das Partizip ausgenommen [vgl. dazu 451219]) vorkommen. Die Imperativ-Form „gehe!" wird ebenso verteidigt, wie die Silbentrennung „ge-he" — ja sei nicht sogar statt des Imperativs die 1. Person Sg. Indik. Aktiv „(ich) gehe" als die Stammform des Verbs anzusehen? Der Streit darüber sei schon über 30 Jahre alt und und dauert unter den Fruchtbringern fort. Das -kk- bei Paulus Melissus Schede ist genauso roh wie seine dt. Poesie. Noch wunderlichere Sprachgrillen habe Philipp v. Zesen (FG 521. 1648) unter dem Einfluß der Niederländer und Franzosen in Umlauf gebracht. Ihn und andere heranzuziehen, bringe eine Klärung der Streitfragen schwerlich voran. Überhaupt sollte auf namentliche Parteibildungen verzichtet werden, da es doch allein um „warheit und einigkeit" ohne „ansehen der person" gehe. Übertrieben und künstlich seien auch etliche Wörterneubildungen, wie etwa „kunstrichtig", „gleichgründig", „hertztraurig" usw. „Rationem nostræ lingvæ müßen wir ex hodierna nostra

Consuetudine et pronunciatione nemen[,] wie sie heute zu tage ins gemein geschrieben, und am besten ausgesprochen wird". Sollte man diese aus der Sprachrealität abgeleiteten Regeln einmal aussetzen müssen, sollte dies gut begründet werden. „Das haben Varro und andere Grammatici auch gethan, und ist es den alten und neuen sprachlehrern die auf keinen andern grund gehen können, nicht zuwieder". Jeder Mundartsprecher sollte seine Mundart „zurechte bringen", dann könne man sich vergleichen [s. dazu 450919A]. Anscheinend aber habe man in Nürnberg Schottelius' *Sprachkunst* voreilig angenommen. — Soweit zusammengefaßt F. Ludwigs Reaktion auf Harsdörffers Brief 460131.

2 In 460720 wird sich Gueintz für den „langen Verzug" seiner Antwort entschuldigen und die gewünschten „anmerckungen" übersenden. Dabei handelte es sich nicht um eine Reaktion auf Harsdörffers Brief 460131, wie von F. Ludwig angeregt, sondern um eine Stellungnahme zu Harsdörffers *Specimen Philologiae Germanicae (1646)*, von welchem F. Ludwig irgendwann zw. dem 26.4. und dem 9.6.1646 Gueintz ein Ex. zugesandt hatte. Vgl. auch 460915.

3 In 460131 hatte Harsdörffer von der deutschen Sprache behauptet, daß sie sich „durchgehend" nach der hebräischen Sprache „artet". Vgl. ebd. K 5 und die dort aufgeführten Briefe zur postulierten Sprachenverwandtschaft zwischen Hebräisch und Deutsch.

4 F. Ludwig bezweifelt also, daß die Kasusendungen -e, -el, -en, -er, -ern, -eln den hebr. Suffixen entsprechen. Diese Stelle wird auch im Kontext nicht ganz verständlich: Stellten diese vermeintlichen Endungen für F. Ludwig Bestandteile des Stammworts dar, wie in Liebe oder Himmel? Harsdörffer hatte in 460131 laviert: Stammwörter, die nach heutiger Aussprache auf -el, -er und -es auslauten, seien Ausnahmen gegenüber der überwältigenden Mehrzahl an Stammwörtern, die diesen Auslaut und d. h. Zweisilbigkeit nicht aufwiesen.

5 Hier ist von Harsdörffers grammatisch orientierter Silbentrennung die Rede: kling-en (Stammwort - Infinitivendung), während F. Ludwig und Gueintz nach der Aussprache, also nach Sprechsilben trennten (klin-gen). In 451219 hatte F. Ludwig dafür u. a. das Argument an-, aber nicht ausgeführt, „es bedeuten diese endungen nichts, wan der mitlautende nicht darbey ist", daher sin-gen. Vgl. zur Silbentrennung 451028A K 6.

460200A

Justus Georg Schottelius an Herzog August d. J. von Braunschweig-Wolfenbüttel

Justus Georg Schottelius (FG 397) schickt Hz. August v. Braunschweig-Wolfenbüttel (FG 227) einige Zeilen und deutsche Verse nicht, weil diese lesenswürdig wären, sondern weil sie aus seiner Freude und Liebe wegen eines mit der süßen und großen Frucht der Frömmigkeit gefüllten Werks (Hz. Augusts *Evangelische Kirchen-Harmonie*) entspringen, das dem Stil und der Verehrung der vaterländischen Sprache sehr dient. — Im zweitletzten Vers könnte das Adjektiv in „übung frommer worte" — einer Formulierung von Martin Opitz (FG 200) — durch „frömder" oder „guter" ersetzt werden, jedoch passe „frommer" gut zum geistlichen Inhalt.

Q NSTA Wolfenbüttel: 2 Alt Nr. 3520, Bl. 3r; eigenh., undat.; mit einer eigenh. Bemerkung des Herzogs.

A *Fehlt.*

Jllustrissime Celsissime*que Princeps, Domine clementissime,*

V*estræ* Serenitati versiculos aliquot, germanico metro inclusos humillimè offero,[1] non quidem, quod digni sint. Tanti Principis inspectu aut perlectione, ne*que* etjam, quod aliorum oculos mereantur, sed tantum ut eo ipso erga V*estram* Serenitatem devotissime mentis lætitiam et amorem ob hanc operam tam dulci et largo pietatis fructu refertam, quam amabili Linguæ Patriæ puritate et cultu gratissimam, subiectissimè contester
        eiusdem[a] Servus obedientiss.
        Justus-Georgius Schottelius.

Posset quidem frömder vel potius guter,[b] aut simile, substitui, sed epitheton fromm non incongruè videtur hoc loci[c] indicare cultum seu culturam verbor*um* sacror*um,* seu verbor*um,* pietati fovendæ inservientium,[d] poterit tamen pro lubitu mutarj. quamvis hæc tria verba ex Opitio sint desumpta, qvi in simili iis utitur pag. 624.[2]

Antepenultimus[e] versus in fin [sic] habet, übung frommer[f] worte

T a *Danach folgen Hz. Augusts eigenh. Notiz (s. e) und Schottelius' Postskriptum.* — **b** *Darüber* unsrer — **c** *Folgt Verschreibung* <id> — **d** *Folgen eine gestrichene, unlesbare Zeile u. nach Punkt wohl 1 abgeschnittenes Wort.* — **e** *Zeile von Hz. Augusts H.* — **f** *Darunter forsan* frömbder

K 1 Auf die *Evangelische Kirchen-Harmonie* Hz. Augusts d. J. v. Braunschweig-Wolfenbüttel (FG 227) bezogener Brief, der wegen des fehlenden Doktortitels Justus Georg Schottelius' (FG 397) — die Promotion erfolgte in Helmstedt am 26.2.1646 (s. 460414) — zuvor datiert werden muß. Da nach einem Probedruck von 1645 (451001) die erste öffentliche Auflage des hzl. Buchs, die sog. Oktavausgabe (411214, S. 340) im 2. Viertel 1646 bis Anfang Juni gedruckt wurde (vgl. 460317 K 3), muß Schottelius das Gedicht und die Zeilen dem Herzog zuvor eingereicht haben, wenn er auf die Veröffentlichung in dem Buch hoffte. (Versiculi bezeichnen auch Prosazeilen, etwa ein Anagramm, das Schottelius vielleicht dem zuvor eingereichten Gedicht hinterherschickte. Vgl. das Anagramm in 440400.) Da Schottelius das Werk aber schon aus hsl. Fassungen und dem Probedruck des ersten Teils (1645) kannte, mochte er sein Gedicht schon vorher und nicht für die Oktavausgabe geschrieben haben. Die durch Hz. August notierten Wörter bzw. die von Schottelius vorgeschlagenen Adjektive fehlen in allen drei Gedichten, die Schottelius der Oktavausgabe (1) bzw. dem Handbüchlein (2) von 1646 beisteuerte. S. 411214, S. 344f., 374 u. 390. Sie müssen also auch nicht dem im vorliegenden Brief erwähnten Schottelius-Gedicht entstammen.
    2 Der Zusatz des Herzogs bezieht sich nicht auf eine der bis dahin erschienenen Sammelausgaben der Dichtungen von Martin Opitz v. Boberfeld (FG 200). Vgl. *Dünnhaupt: Handbuch,* Opitz.

460204

Diederich von dem Werder an Conrad von Burgsdorff

Diederich v. dem Werder (FG 31) bestätigt in Berlin den Empfang eines Briefes Conrads v. Burgsdorff (FG 404) vom 31. Januar, den er bei seiner Rückreise (von Königsberg) in Küstrin vorgefunden habe. Er bedankt sich für die damalige gute und ehrenvolle Aufnahme. Den Inhalt der von Burgsdorff mitgeteilten zwei vertraulichen Angelegenheiten haben Werders beide (ungenannte) Mitgesandten verschlüsselt notiert, um ihn in Kassel Lgfn. Amalia Elisabeth v. Hessen-Kassel vortragen zu können. Er selbst werde der Fürstin ebenfalls berichten. Diese werde zweifellos bald dazu Stellung nehmen, obgleich die Angelegenheit [Hochzeit Lgf. Wilhelms VI. v. Hessen-Kassel (FG 694. 1659) mit Mgfn. Hedwig Sophia v. Brandenburg] von Kf. Friedrich Wilhelm v. Brandenburg (FG 402) in die Wege geleitet werden muß. — Den Bericht des verstorbenen Levin v. dem Knesebeck (FG 107) über die pommersche Frage hat sich Werder zum genauen Studium in Berlin vorlegen lassen. Der Erbanspruch Kurbrandenburgs auf das Hzt. Pommern wird auch vom Kgr. Schweden anerkannt, wovon es hoffentlich nicht abrücken werde, es sei denn aus einem bestimmten, gegenüber Burgsdorff erwähnten Grunde. Schwedens faktische Besitzergreifung Pommerns und dessen Restitution müssen an höherer Stelle erforscht werden. Gottseidank sei die Erbberechtigung als solche unstrittig. Werder rät zur Besonnenheit und vertraut auf den unfehlbaren Wandel der Lage. Mit den Umständen werden sich auch Ratschläge und Überlegungen ändern. — Die Rückreise von Küstrin nach Berlin verlief bis auf übliche Unpäßlichkeiten ganz gut, auch wenn den N. N. Diede zum Fürstenstein sein Steinleiden quälte. Jetzt nach Berlin zurückgekehrt, sei Erholung eingekehrt, und man habe die Ehrerweisungen und gute Bewirtung genossen. Am Vortage hat man Patenschaften bei Isaak Ludwig v. der Groeben angetreten und mit vielen schönen Frauen gefeiert. Die poln. Geiger fehlten allerdings beim Tanz. — Ein seltsames Begebnis war das Zusammentreffen mit Gf. Zdenko v. Hoditz (Hodický) in Berlin, den alle Welt längst für tot hielt. Er spielte auf zwei Musikinstrumenten, der Diskantgeige (violino piccolo) und dem Zinken, was er zu der Zeit, da er und Werder in der schwed. Armee dienten, in keiner Weise konnte. — Werder bittet Burgsdorff, ihn Kf. Friedrich Wilhelm zu empfehlen. — Simon Dach habe er einen Auftrag erteilt und ihn gebeten, mit Burgsdorff darüber zu reden. Werder bittet Burgsdorff, Dachs beiliegenden Brief durch einen Diener aushändigen zu lassen.

Q GSTA–PK Berlin: BPH Rep. 34 Nr. 114; unfol., 2 Bl. [A: 2v]; eigenh., mit schwarzem Lacksiegel.

A A Monsieur Monsieur Curt de Burgstorff Conseillier d'Estat grand Chambellan, et Colonell general de forteresses pour son Altesse Electorale de Brandenbourg.
  aux mains   Königsberg
Enth. eine flüchtige Notiz[a] *u. Namenliste*[b] *von anderer H.*

HochEdelgeborner herr OberCammerherr insonders hochgeehrter vnd allerwerthester herr vnd freund.

Desselben geliebtes vom 31. januarij[1] habe ich, in meiner Zurückunft auf Cüstrin, für mir funden, Bedancke mich nochmals für alle erwiesene ehre vnd hohe freundschaft, deren ich ewig, als ein danckbarer aufrichtiger Knecht, vnvergessen bleiben werde.

Den inhalt beyder vertrauter geheimen sachen seines schreibens habe ich wohl eingenommen, Meine beyde herren Mitgesanten², so sich meinem hochgeehrten herren brudern auch zum besten hiermit nochmals empfehlen, haben aus obgedachtem seinem schreiben, in bewustem geheimnüs, einen auszug in versetzten buchstaben gemacht, damit dasselbe j. f. g. zu Cassel³ desto füglicher vor vnd beygebracht werden könte, So auch mit allem fleis geschehn wird, jnmassen ich dan auch, in meinem absonderlichem an j. f. g. abgehendem berichte, mich in gemein auf diese vertrauliche sache beziehen thue, Zweiffel nicht j. f. g. werden sich bald drauf erklären; Wiewohl der gantze anfang dieses vorhabens von jhrer Chrf. Durchl. meinem gnädigsten herren⁴ angefädemet⁵ vnd eingerichtet werden müssen wird.

Des Seligen herren Knesebecks⁶ ausführlichen bericht in der Pommerischen sache, habe ich mir alhier reichen lassen, So ich auch fleissig belesen wil. Dieses Meines gnädigsten herren recht⁷, ist nicht allein für sich, sondern auch bey den Schwedischen selber, unstreitig, werden es auch wohl, was Recht anlanget, nicht streitig machen, Es sey dan, aus dem grunde, wie ich einst gegen meinen hochgeehrten herren brudern gedacht habe, Wiewohl ich auch das nicht hoffen will. Wie aber ihre gewaltthätikeit, jhr itziger besitz, vnd das sie es ihnen für sehr gelegen halten, wiederlegt vnd benommen werden kan, Solches ist altioris indaginis. Gott lob aber, das das erste für sich richtig[.] Gott wird diesem letzterem, zu seiner Zeit auch rahten. Man übereile sich, bey itzigem Zustande, nicht, man neme sein recht in acht vnd sehe mehr aufs künftige, als gegenwertige. Der itzige status kan [1v] nicht ewig also bleiben, Vnd dan endern sich mit der verenderung der ümbstände, auch die sachen selbsten, Vnd also auch die rahtschläge vnd gedancken zugleich mit.

Jch werde erwarten was von meinem gnädigsten herren mir deswegen ferner zukommen wird, mein geringfügigstes bedencken drüber abzugeben.

Vnsere reise ist gott lob, gar wohl, wiewohl nicht ohne mancherley vnlust, an gewöhnlichen husten, wunden hälsen, Zahn vnd rückenweh, wie auch der von Dieden⁸ am Steine, abgelauffen, vnd hiehehr zum Berlin angelanget, alda wir vns auch guten theils wieder besser befinden, vnd über das, mit überflüssiger vnd gar zu hoher ehre, bewürtet vnd gehalten werden, Alda wir dan auch gestern ahnsehnliche Gevatterschaften beym herren Schloshaubtman dem von der Gräben⁹ verrichten müssen, darbey auch viel schönes FrauenZimmer (Seine liebste samt der tochter aber nicht) erschienen, Es gab auch wieder ein däntzgen, Es ermangelten aber die Polnische Violisten.

Sonst mus meinem hochgeehrten herren brudern ich hierbey noch etwas wunderlichs andeuten: Den Graven von Hoditz¹⁰, den iederman schon längst für todt gehalten, habe ich alhier zum Berlin angetroffen, Jch habe mich über ihn verwundert als ich ihn sahe, bevoraus, da ich ihn so wohl horte die discantgeige streichen vnd auf dem Zincken blasen. Bey der Zeit, da wir noch Cammeraden in der Schwedischen armée waren¹¹ da verstund der gute herr Nischt von den sachen, mich wundert wo er vnter dessen die Music gelernet haben mus.

[2r] Hiermit empfehle ich meinen hochgeehrten herren brudern dem allerhöchsten zu langwüriger beständiger gesundheit, vnd er^c verbleibe mein werther patron, Wie ich dan schwehre, das ich leben vnd sterben wil
        Meines vielwerthen vnd hochgeehrten herren brudern
        Sonsten juncker Curtens genant
        gantzeigener mit haut vnd haar.
           Diederich von dem Werder *mp*

Wan mir so viel gebüren wil, bitte ich, an jhre Cuhrfürstliche Durchl. mich vnterthänigst zurecommendiren. Meiner gemahlin berühre ich auch den Saum ihres hochfürstlichen Kleides, deren Gesundheit ich gestern allen FrauenZimmer, bey dem abendbanquet, ingesamt zutranck, vnd war recht Stoltz drauf. Herren Simon Dachen[12] habe ich etwas aufgetragen vnd ihn gebeten, mit meinem herren brudern daraus zureden, Bitte es nicht übel zuvermercken dessen inligendes brieflein durch einen diener einhändigen zulassen, habe ich dienstlichst zubitten.

Berlin 4/14 hornungs in grosser eyl 1646.

I

Simon Dachs *Lob-Spruch dem HochEdlen Gestrengen und Mann-Vesten Herrn Dietrich von dem Werder*

Q [Drucktitel]: **Lob-Spruch** | Dem | HochEdlen Gestrengen und MannVesten | **Herrn Dietrich von dem Werder/** | **Obristen/** etc. | **Fürstl: Anhaltischen geheimbten Rahte/** *etc.* | vnd Vnter **Directori** *etc.* Erbsassen vff Reinsdorff/ | Werders Hausen etc. | Jetzo | Seiner Fürstlichen Durchl. | **Hn. Wilhelmen Landgraffen zu Hessen/ etc. etc.** | **Abgesandten** | An dem Churfl. Brandenb. Hofe zu Königsberg/ | Vnterdienstlichst | geschrieben | Von | Simon Dachen/ | 1646. 26. Jenner. | [Linie] | Königsberg/ gedruckt durch Johann Reusnern. 4 Bl., Bl.1r: Titel, Bl.1v: leer. STB Berlin — PK: Yi 851-1, Dig. — Ein weiteres Exemplar in der *BU* Wrocław: 354313 (StB Breslau: 4 E 225 Nr.38, aus der Sammlung des Caspar Arletius).
Simon Dach: Gedichte. Bd.1: Weltliche Lieder, Hochzeitsgedichte. Hg. v. Walther Ziesemer. Halle 1936, 151–154 (Sigle Z). Ziesemer waren beide Exemplare bekannt (vgl. ebd. S.344). — BN: *Dünnhaupt Handbuch,* 1079 Nr.435; Hermann Oesterley (Hg.): Simon Dach. Stuttgart 1876, 998 Nr.783. Vgl. Klaus Garber: Martin Opitz — Paul Fleming — Simon Dach. Drei Dichter des 17. Jahrhunderts in Bibliotheken Mittel- und Osteuropas. Köln, Weimar, Wien (2013), 610.

[Bl. 2r] VNd ich sol also mich in meinem Glücke seumen/
O Werder wehrter Held/ sol schläffrig seyn vnd träumen/
Jn dessen^a hast Du hie das grosse Werck vollbracht/
Gedenckest heim/ vnd giebst vns wieder gute Nacht?
Sol ich nicht seyn bemüht jetzt auch bekant zu werden
Dir/ der Du bist bekant da/ wo der Kreiß der Erden

Der Tugend Käntnis hat/ weñ nur mein schlechter schein
Nicht vnwehrt were Dir in etwas kund zu seyn?
So niedrig ist mein Stand/ so hoch bist Du erhaben
Nicht durch das Glück so wol als deine schöne Gaben/
Hoch-Edlen Stammes seyn ist das geringst an Dir.
Wer nichts sonst darthun kan als seiner Ahnen Zier
Rühmt frembder Tugend sich. Man muß durch eigne Sachen
Sein Lob der Welt bekant vnd selbst sich Edel machen/
Gut daß der Vorfahrt Fleiß nach Ehren nur gestrebt/
Jhr aber keines hat auff vnsern Rhum gelebt.
Jn diesem allen/ Herr/ bist Du recht außerkohren/
Es thut Dir wenig noht Hochedel seyn gebohren/ [2v]
Denn was auch einem Schild vnd Fahnen geben kan
Diß hast Du reichlich lang von Jugend auff gethan.
Es sey ein Ritter-Spiel/ die strenge Zucht der Helden/
Die Mutter edler Schlacht/ wer kan jhr eines melden
Jn welchem Du nicht warst den andern vorzuziehn?
Diß zeugt noch jetzt von Dir das Käyserliche Wien.[1]
Es sey den Sitten nach in frembde Länder reisen/
Welch Ort/ da Tugend wohnt/ hat mit gelehrten Speisen
Nicht deinen Sinn erfüllt/ für deine grosse Lust
Hat weder Franckreich noch Jtalien mehr gewust.[2]
Woselbst du jeden Platz begierig durch-bist-gangen/
Vnd hast/ was merckens wehrt/ gantz sorglich auffgefangen/
Vnd fleissig beygelegt/ wie eine Biene thut/
Die aus dem Stocke fleugt/ vnd nirgends leichtlich ruht/
Ohn wo sie Hoffnung hat es sey da was zu holen/
Sie zieht die süsse Krafft den Rosen vnd Violen
Vnd tausent Blumen aus besackt sich vmb vnd an/
Daß sie sich für der Last kaum fort begeben kan.
Es sah' auch Niederland/ das seinen Rhum den Sternen
Lang eingetragen hat/ dich alle Künste lernen
Der Kriegs-vnd[b] Friedens-Zeit/ so kamst Du durch Verstand
Vnd Sprachen außgeübt heim in dein Vaterland.
Hat hie dich faule Rhue/ als sonst geschieht/ vmbgeben?
Durch Vnlust-volle Lust Dir abgenützt das Leben/
Vnd etwa einen Trunck von Circe beygebracht?
Mit nichten. Mars hat bald gereitzet deine Macht. [3r]
Du mustest Dich nun auch im Felde lassen schawen/
Jn dem Gustavus[3] Dir ein Kriegs-Heer zu vertrawen
Gantz kein Bedencken trug/ da hat der Feind erkant
Jetzt Deinen klugen Muht jetzt Deine strenge Hand.
Der Friedens-Zeug die Kunst kan mercklich sich erhöhen

Durch Deiner Mannheit Lob/ Du gibest zu verstehen/
Dem Krieg' vnd Büchern hold/ wie brüderlich vnd fein
Jn Friedens-Bündnis gehn gelehrt vnd streitbar seyn.
Doch hast Du jederzeit den Künsten mehr verhänget/
Vnd durch Apollos Huld Gradivus angestrenget/
So viel der Friede mehr als Krieg behäglich ist
So wird auch Glimpff vnd Kunst für wilde Schlacht erkiest.
Daher die Wissenschafft/ vnd was man je zu lesen
Von Sachen würdig hält/ Dir ist gemein gewesen/
Die Lehre selbst von GOtt vnd beydes Recht darzu/
Der Reich' Erweiterung der Städt' vnd Völcker Rhue/
Hast Du so gründlich Dir gesucht bekant zu machen
Als einer/ welcher blos sein Brod von solchen Sachen
Mit Müh erwerben wil. Liv/ Tacitus/ Tranquill
Vnd dieser Gattung mehr seyn Dir ein Kinderspiel.
Vnd hiedurch fället nichts sehr schwer Dir zu ergründen/
Du kanst in allen Lauff der Zeit Dich leichtlich finden.
Jn dem[c] sich Deutschland jetzt fast auffgezehret hat
Durch diesen Krieges-Brandt/ so findest Du noch Raht.
Du hast nicht nöhtig was von aussen zu begehren/
Weil Dein standhaffter Muht Dir alles kan gewehren/ [3v]
Was tröstlich heissen mag/ fiel auch der Himmel ein/
So wird Dein grosses Hertz doch vnbeweget seyn.
Sol die Beredsamkeit ich auch an Dir erheben?
Du hast/ wird mir gesagt/ gnug zu verstehn gegeben/
Als Du das schöne Werck der Eh' hie angebracht/
Daß Lieb vnd Freundlicheit vnd aller Redner Pracht
Aus Deinem Munde quillt. Was sol ich davon sagen/
Daß alt seyn vnd belebt sich so bey Dir vertragen?
Die Jugend gienge nicht mit Dir gern in den Streit/
Vnd dieses zeuget gnug von deiner Mässigkeit.
Wie soltest Du/ O Held/ mit diesen thewren Dingen
Der Hohen Häupter Gunst nicht leichtlich an Dich bringen?
Dieß einig ist/ warumb der Hessen freye Heldt
Auff dich die Zuversicht in Gnaden hat gestellt/
Daß Er sein Liebes-werck durch dich hie stifften lassen/
Es mus auch Glück vnd Heyl solch dein Gewerb vmbfassen/
Des Himmels Gunst zwar trägt des Handels allen Preis/
So kriegt doch einen Danck auch deiner Gaben fleiß.
Wie hochgewünscht wirst du nach Cassel wieder komen/
Mit was Verlangen wirst du werden auffgenommen
Von Jhm dem Fürsten[4] da von der Fraw Mutter[5] hie/
Der thewren Heldinn so wie jetzt nicht also nie

Fast Jhres gleichen hat! Du wirst Sie erstlich grüssen/
Vnd bald von allem Thun Bericht ertheilen müssen/ [4r]
Wirst sagen: dieses war die Liebe mannigfalt
Die vns vmbfangen hat/ so wahr die Braut gestalt/
Das wehrte Fürsten-Kind/ daß auch für einen Käyser
Gnug schön vnd prächtig ist. So ist die Stadt/ die Häuser
Darinnen so gebawt. Hie geht der PregelFluß/
Der Mawren-festes Eyß anjetzund tragen mus/
Vnd gutte Schlittbahn macht. So ist des Hofes wesen/
Der grosse Churfürst führt daselbst so auserlesen
Vnd herrlich seinen Standt/ dieß ist sein schöner Pracht/
Den Curt[6] Sein' Hand vnd Hertz voraus beliebet macht.
Ach daß du von vns eilst/ vnd ich daher mus schweigen
Von deiner Poësie[d]/ der ich auff meiner Geigen
Für allen willens wahr zu geben Preiß vnd Rhum!
Mit einem Wort: Sie ist vnd bleibt dein Eigenthum/
O daß wir doch von dir die Kriegs-vnd[e] Siegs-Sonnetten[7]/
Vnd dein erlösetes Jerusalem[8] noch hätten/
Das arbeitsame Werck/ das dein Gerücht' erhebt
Aus dieser finstern Klufft wo Mond vnd Sonne schwebt.
Der Kriegs-vnd[b] Sieges-Held hat deinen Fleiß empfunden/
Vnd in dem Himmel längst den Siegs-Krantz dir gewunden/
Wie Christi Krieg vnd[e] Sieg hoch über alles geht/
So hoch ist auch dein Kriegs-vnd Siegs-Geticht erhöht.
Vergebens bistu nicht in den Gesellschafft-Orden[9]/
Der reiche Früchte trägt/ mit angenommen worden/
Fürst Ludwig stehet selbs im Zweifel/ was er wol/
Sinn oder Arbeit mehr/ an dir erheben soll. [4v]
Du aber eilest fort/ machst daß ich mich mus zähmen.
Der Himmel wolle dich in sein Geleite nehmen/
Fahr in des Höchsten Hut vnd Auffsicht aus vnd ein/
Daß weder Wind noch Frost dir mög entgegen seyn.
Vnd kan ich etwa Platz in deiner Liebe finden.
So nimm/ O HERR/ mich an/ du wirst mich dir verbinden
Jn ewig-trewer Pflicht/ wofern[f] Du dieses Mir
Hie hinterlassen wirst/ so hab Jch gnug von Dir.

T a *Notiz, teils gestrichen, unsichere Lesung u. Bedeutung.* — **b** *Namenliste, teils gestrichen, unsichere Lesung u. Bedeutung.* — **c** *Eingefügt.*

T I *Z modernisiert die Interpunktion, gibt z. B. Virgel durch Kommata wieder. In Z aufgelöste Abkürzungen werden von uns ebenfalls nicht abgekürzt wiedergegeben. Wir berücksichtigen nur orthographische und lautliche Varianten.* — **a** Z Jndessen — **b** Z Kriegs- vnd — **c** Z Jndem — **d** Z Poesie — **e** Z Krieg-vnd — **f** Z sofern

K Der im Brief genannte „inhalt beyder vertrauter geheimen sachen" bezieht sich auf die Werbung für die Eheschließung Lgf. Wilhelms VI. v. Hessen-Kassel (FG 694. 1659), Sohn der Regentin Hessen-Kassels, Lgfn. Amalia Elisabeths (1602–1651), mit Mgfn. Hedwig Sophia (1623–1683), der Schwester Kf. Friedrich Wilhelms v. Brandenburg (FG 401). S. 460125 K 1–3, Beil. I u. II.

1 Dieser Brief Conrads v. Burgsdorff (FG 404) an Diederich v. dem Werder liegt uns nicht vor. Vgl. zu Burgsdorff K I 6.

2 Einer der beiden (vermutlich) lgfl. hessen-kasselschen Emissäre wird unten genannt: ein Mitglied der Familie Diede zum Fürstenstein. S. Anm. 8.

3 Lgfn. Amalia Elisabeth v. Hessen-Kassel (1602–1651), geb. Gfn. v. Hanau-Münzenberg, die in Vormundschaft ihres Sohnes Wilhelm VI. regierte. *NDB* I, 237.

4 Kf. Friedrich Wilhelm v. Brandenburg (FG 401).

5 Fädemen, d. i. mundartlich für einfädeln. *Mittelelb. Wb.* I, 919.

6 Wohl der kurbrandenburg. Rat bei der neumärk. Kammer zu Küstrin, Levin v. dem Knesebeck (FG 107), der 1638 unter mysteriösen Umständen gestorben war. *Conermann III*, 111 f.

7 Gemäß alten Vereinbarungen (Vertrag von Pyritz 1493, Vertrag von Grimnitz 1529) war Kurbrandenburg die Erbfolge im Hzt. Pommern zugesichert worden für den Fall des Aussterbens des dortigen Herrscherhauses der Greifen, der mit dem Tod von Hz. Bogislaw XIV. v. Pommern 1637 eintrat. Die Rechtmäßigkeit der Erbansprüche der brandenburg. Kurfürsten auf Pommern wurde auch von der Krone Schweden, die vor allem mit diesem Herzogtum auf dem Westfälischen Friedenskongreß die Erstattung für ihre Kriegsaufwendungen durchzusetzen hoffte, nicht grundsätzlich in Frage gestellt. Aus diesem Grund zielten ihre Verhandlungsbemühungen auch stets darauf, Kurbrandenburg eine territoriale bzw. finanzielle Entschädigung für den Verzicht auf Pommern zu verschaffen. Vgl. dazu 450326 K 4; Dirk Schleinert: Pommerns Herzöge. Die Greifen im Porträt. Rostock 2012, 97–100; Herbert Langer: Die Entwicklung der Pommernfrage bis zum Friedensschluß in Münster und Osnabrück 1648. In: Horst Wernicke, Hans-Joachim Hacker (Hg.): Der Westfälische Frieden von 1648. Wende in der Geschichte des Ostseeraums. Hamburg 2001, 121–134; Klaus Conrad: Herzogliche Schwäche und städtische Macht in der zweiten Hälfte des 14. und im 15. Jahrhundert. In: Werner Buchholz (Hg.): Deutsche Geschichte im Osten Europas: Pommern. Berlin 1999, 127–202, hier 180–192; Roderich Schmidt: Pommern von der Einigung bis zum Ende des Dreißigjährigen Krieges. Ebd., 203–236; Hans Branig: Geschichte Pommerns. Bearb. von Werner Buchholz. Bd. 1: Vom Werden des neuzeitlichen Staates bis zum Verlust der staatlichen Selbständigkeit 1300–1648. Köln 1997, 193–201.

8 Wohl ein Angehöriger der hess. Adelsfamilie Diede zum Fürstenstein (Wappen: von Schwarz u. Silber geviert), kaum schon der junge Hans Eitel Diede zum Fürstenstein (16.10.1624 – 12.2.1685) (FG 632. 1654), Burggf. zu Friedberg, hessen-darmstädt. Hofmeister, Kriegsrat, Geh. Rat, Hofrichter, Oberamtmann und Gesandter. Zeitlich paßt Georg Christoph Diede zum Fürstenstein (6.5.1586 – 3.11.1653), Sohn des Georg D. z. F. und der Anna v. Berlepsch.

9 Isaak Ludwig v. der Groeben († 1656), auf Kotzeband, Schloßhauptmann zu Berlin. Zwei seiner Söhne wurden später Mitglieder der FG: Ernst (FG 627. 1654) u. Levin Ludwig v. der Groeben (FG 701. 1659). S. Hermann Brockhaus (Hg.): Allgemeine Encyklopädie der Wissenschaften und Künste, Tl. 92, Leipzig 1872, 15.

10 Wohl Gf. Zdenko v. Hoditz (Hodický), ein mähr. Exulant, der seit spätestens 1633 als Oberst bei der schwed. Armee diente u. 1641 an den bei Wolfenbüttel erlittenen Verletzungen gestorben sein sollte. Vgl. *Pufendorf: Kriegs-Geschichte* I, 602; *Theatrum euro-*

paeum IV (1692), 594. — Dessen im Brief erwähnte „Wiederauferstehung" könnte auf einer Verwechslung beruhen, worauf auch die Ungereimtheit hinsichtlich der musikalischen Fähigkeiten des Grafen hinweist.

11 Werder diente von 1631 bis 1635 als Obrist in der schwed. Armee. Vgl. K I 3, 320313 K u. *Conermann III*, 34.

12 Simon Dach (1605–1659), seit 1639 Professor der Dichtkunst an der U. Königsberg. — Der erwähnte Auftrag betraf vielleicht das von Werder aus Anlaß der Königsberger Gesandtschaft bestellte Lobgedicht. S. Beil. I.

K I Den Anlaß für Simon Dachs (s. K 12) Gedicht lieferte die Reise Diederichs v. dem Werder (FG 31) von Anhalt über Kassel nach Königsberg als Hessen-Kasseler Gesandter an den Hof Kf. Friedrich Wilhelms v. Brandenburg (FG 401). Dort sollte er über die Vermählung Lgf. Wilhelms VI. v. Hessen-Kassel (1629–1663. FG 694. 1659) mit der Schwester des Kurfürsten, Pzn. Hedwig Sophie v. Brandenburg (1623–1683), verhandeln. S. 460125 u. I u. II.

1 Eine Anspielung auf Werders Aufenthalt in Frankfurt a. M. 1612, wo er der Wahl Ehz. Matthias' zum Kaiser beiwohnte und einen Preis bei einem Turnier davontrug. S. *D. v. dem Werder (LP 1658)*, Bl. [K iiij]v f. (Titel in 460125 I Q), „Massen dan sonderlich denckwürdig ist/ daß in dem Schleidano continuato, wegen dessen ruhmwürdigen bezeigens auff dem Keyserlichen Ringelrennen/ bey der Crönung des Weyland AllerDurchleuchtigsten/ Grosmächtigsten &c. Römischen Keysers Matthiæ/ Glorwürdigsten andenckens/ im Jahre Christi 1612. zu Franckfurt am Meyn gehalten/ unsers seligen Herrn Obristen gar honorificè mit folgenden formalien gedacht wird: Das vierte Gewinn hat gewonnen Landgraff Mauritij von Hessen Stallmeister/ Werder/ genant/ so ein gar sehr grosser Becher/ in form einer Weintrauben/ so ein Riese auf der Achsel getragen/ gewesen.) tapffer herfür gethan [...]." (Der Landgraf logierte im Gasthof zum Rebstock, a. a. O., Sp.19. Colerus korrigierte den im Druck angegebenen Namen des Landgrafen von Ludwig zu Mauritius) D. i. SLEIDANI CONTINVATI Pars Quarta: Das ist/ Vierdter Theil der Historischen Continuation Joh. Seidani (Straßburg: Christoff von der Heyden 1625), Sp.33. Dach verwechselt hier nicht den Wahlort mit dem Residenzort des Kaisers (um 1646), sondern betont, daß man am ksl. Hof in Wien noch später des Turniers von 1612 gedachte.

2 Werder absolvierte seine *Peregrinatio academica* u. a. in Frankreich und Italien, wo er 1609/10 die Universitäten Siena und Padua besuchte. *Conermann III*, 34 ff.

3 Kg. Gustav II. Adolf v. Schweden (1594–1632), hatte Werder nach der Schlacht bei Breitenfeld (7./17. September 1631) die Führung eines Infanterieregiments geworbener Söldner angetragen, welches dieser nach einigem Zögern und unter Zureden von General Johan Banér (FG 222) annahm und als Obrist in den Dienst der Krone Schweden trat. Nach dem Prager Frieden von 1635 legte Werder wie viele andere deutschstämmige Offiziere aufgrund der ksl. und kursächs. Patente, die diese bei ernster Strafe zum Verlassen der schwed. Dienste aufforderten (mandata avocatoria), dieses Militäramt nieder. Vgl. *D. v. dem Werder (LP 1658)*, Bl. L ij (s. 460125 I Q).

4 Hier kann nur Kf. Friedrich Wilhelm v. Brandenburg gemeint sein.

5 Lgfn. Amalia Elisabeth (1602–1651, s. oben K 3).

6 „Juncker Curt" nannte auch Werder selbst in der Schlußkurialie seines vorliegenden Briefes den kurbrandenburg. Geheimen Rat Conrad v. Burgsdorff (FG 404), einen Favoriten Kf. Friedrich Wilhelms, den dieser auch zum Befehlshaber der märk. Festungen und zum höchsten Hofbeamten („Oberkammerherr") gemacht hatte, bis er 1651 in Ungnade fallen sollte. Vgl. zu diesem 460125 K 0 u. *Conermann III*, 480 f.

7 *D. v. dem Werder: Krieg vnd Sieg (1631)*. Ex. FB Gotha: Poes. 8° 02949/04; UB Göttingen: 8 P. Germ. II, 6301. Eine 2. Auflage erschien 1633 bei Melchior Oelschlegel in Halle a. d. S. 1633. HAB: 65.6 Poet. (33). Vgl. 310800 K 2; *Merzbacher: Werder*, 53 f.
8 *D. v. dem Werder: Jerusalem (1626)*. Stark veränderte 2. Aufl. *D. v. dem Werder: Jerusalem (1651)*. HAB: 9 Poet. (Franckfurt a. M.: Aubry) bzw. 14, 3 Poet. u. Mikrofilm 1: 43 (Franckfurt a. M.: Rötel; Presse). Vgl. 420506 K 3 u. 450900 K 6.
9 FG.

460206

Matthäus Merian d. Ä. an Peter Knaudt

Matthäus Merian d. Ä. sendet die restlichen Titelbögen des *GB 1646* an Peter Knaudt. Auf dem ersten konnte der Palmbaum nicht abgedruckt werden, da der dafür vorgesehene Raum nicht reichte; deshalb habe er auf die Abbildung verzichtet. Das Werk selbst werde Merian in 14 Tagen ganz beendet haben. Er erwarte Anweisung, wohin dann die Exemplare zu liefern sind und ob er die Köthener Bücher über die Leipziger Meßtransporte oder bei anderer Gelegenheit schicken soll. — Merian habe im (Gesellschafts-)Wort „in seiner würtze" „würtzel" eingefügt. Der Kupferstich war noch nicht abgedruckt.

Q HM Köthen: V S 546, Bl. 42rv [A: 42v]; eigenh., Adresse von Schreiberh.; zwei rote Lacksiegel. Bl. 42r auch F. Ludwigs eigenh. Anweisung für Knaudt (Beil. I) und dessen eigenh. Nachricht an F. Ludwig (Beil. II). — D: *Bircher: Merian*, 711 f.; *Wüthrich: Merian Briefe*, 104 f. — BN: *Bürger*, 987 Nr. 15.

A Dem Ehrnvesten vnd GroßAchtparen Herren Peter Knaudt Fürstl. Anhaltischen Cammermeistern *etc.* meinem g.g. hochgeehrten herrn   Cöthen

Ehrnvester vnd GroßAchtparer Jnsonders Großg. hochgeehrter herr *etc.*
Dem selben sein mein willige dienst vnd was Jch vermag Jederzeit Anvor[1] *etc.*
    Vnd sende hiebey die vbrigen Tittul bögen, Auff den ersten hatt sich der Palmenbaum nicht fügen wollen, weilen das **Spacium** zu nider[2] ist, habe es dahero vnterlassen.[3]
    Das werkh geht zu Endt, werde in 14 tagen alles fertig haben, da ich dan erwarte wohin ich die bewußte Anzahl **exemplaria** hinlifern solle, vnd wie es mit dem versenden nach Cöthen solle gehalten werden, ob ich der leipziger fuhr auff die meß erwahrten, oder ob sonsten andrer gutte gelegenheit, sich finden möchte, dessen Jch bericht erwarte. Das wort in seiner würtze[4], habe ich **Corrigirt**, vnd würtzel darauß gemacht, es war noch nicht getrukt, nun ist es fertig. Hiemit dem Allmechtig*en* wohl befohl*en*.

Ffurt den 6. Februari 1646.

    Des herrn Dienstwilligster
    Mattheus Merian.

I

460222

Fürst Ludwigs Anweisung für Knaudts Antwort an Merian

Antwort auf 460206.

Q HM Köthen: V S 546, Bl. 42r; eigenh. Konzept, s. oben Q. — *D: Bircher: Merian*, 711 f., *Wüthrich: Merian Briefe*, 106 f.

A *Fehlt.*

Es mögen mit erster sicherer gelegenheit ein zwolf exemplar auf leipzig wan es schon erst auf den markt, oder von der Frankfurter Meße geschehen solte, gesendet werden,[1] die andern sol er so lange zu rucke halten bis auf weiteres zuschreiben, doch ausgenommen die, so an hertzog Augustum zu Braunschweig fur die zweyhundert thaler abzuliefern, die er wan sie gefodert werden, folgen zu laßen.[2]
22. Febr. 1646

II

Peter Knaudts Nachricht an Fürst Ludwig

Q HM Köthen: V S 546, Bl. 42r; eigenh., s. oben Q.

Dieses ist dem Merian also zugeschrieben, das er herzog Augusten zu Braunschweig 48 Exemplar soll folgen laßen.[1]

K 1 Bevor, vorab. S. 450417 K 1.
    2 *DW* VII, 745 (1b) „von geringer höhe [...] niedrig, kurz, klein".
    3 Kein Entwurf erhalten. Wir kennen nur den gedruckten Gesamttitel des *GB 1646*. Vgl. 451028B K 2. Zur Einrichtung des *GB 1646* s. auch 450711 K 4 (mit Abb.).
    4 Im *GB 1629/30* Hanns (von) Ruess (FG 199. Der Adeliche) mit seinem Gesellschaftswort: „An der Würtze". *Conermann III*, 202. Im *GB 1646* heißt das Wort korrigiert: „An der Würtzel". Zum *GB 1646* allgem. s. 440130 K 3. Zum Transport des *GB 1646* s. 450127 K 1.

K I 1 F. Ludwigs Anweisung, ihm 12 Exemplare des *GB 1646* (falls es bereits zum Verkauf steht) direkt nach Leipzig zu senden oder im anderen Fall von der Frankfurter Ostermesse (Beginn 19. 4. 1646, s. 460303 K 3) zu schicken, lag Matthäus Merian d. Ä. 10 Tage später (460303) noch nicht vor. Zur Ankunft der Sendung s. 460519. Zum *GB 1646* allgemein s. 440130 K 3. Zum Transport des *GB 1646* s. 460317 K 9. Zu den Verlagsbeiträgern s. 450126 K 4.
    2 Merian berichtet im Brief 460303, daß er der ihm von Peter Knaudt mitgeteilten Anweisung F. Ludwigs Folge geleistet habe, Hz. August d. J. v. Braunschweig-Wolfenbüttel (FG 227) 48 Exemplare des *GB 1646* zu schicken.

K II 1 S. K I 2.

460217

Fürst Ludwig an den Burggrafen und Herrn Achaz zu Dohna

Antwort auf 460120A. — F. Ludwig bedankt sich für ein Schreiben des Burggf. u. Herren Achaz zu Dohna und freut sich, daß ihm die Köthener Drucke in dt. Sprache, die der Zerbster Gymnasiumsdirektor (Marcus Fridericus Wendelinus) übermittelte, gefallen haben. Der letzte der Drucke (*Gueintz: Rechtschreibung [1645]*) enthalte ein Wörterbuch, das freilich ergänzt und vervollkommnet werden müsse. Der F. Ludwig und Dohna gut bekannte Inferigno (Bastiano de' Rossi, Sekretär der Accademia della Crusca) pflegte diese Aufgabe angesichts der Vielfalt der Mundarten und der Problematik der Rechtschreibung als eine mühselige und anrüchige Sache zu bezeichnen. Ohne die Orthographie, die in ihrem jetzigen Gebrauch und an vielen Stellen oft überflüssig oder unterschiedlos sei und in der sich ein großer Teil der Autoren verirre, könne man in der Sprache keine Gewißheit erlangen. Dohna werde auch (Philipp v. Zesens, FG 520. 1648) deutsche, in Amsterdam gedruckte Übersetzungen gesehen haben, deren Stil zwar überlegt sei, deren Rechtschreibung jedoch so geschmacklos und ungebräuchlich sei, daß sie die gebotene Richtigkeit und Reinheit unserer Sprache verletze. Es sei dringend geboten gewesen, in Kürze und geordneter Form einmal Vernunft und Gewohnheit gegen die mancherorts eingerissenen Mißbräuche zu demonstrieren. Wenn in Zukunft darüber hinaus etwas Ähnliches veröffentlicht werde, solle Dohna dessen teilhaftig werden. Einstweilen wisse er damit bzw. werde er wissen, daß die Fruchtbringende Gesellschaft Nutzen gestiftet habe. — In deutscher Sprache bittet der Fürst Diederich v. dem Werder (FG 31), Dohnas Brief und die Antwort nochmals durchzusehen und ihm seine Gedanken mitzuteilen. Falls er Zeit habe, könne Werder von F. Ludwig mehr Deutsches dazu geschickt werden.

Q LHA Sa.-Anh./ Dessau: Z 70 Abt. Köthen A 9a Nr. 33[III], Bl. 143rv, v leer; unsichere Abschrift einer unbek. H., die mit Korrekturen von Ludwigs H. an Diederich v. dem Werder zur Durchsicht und Ergänzung geschickt wurde. Grundlage unserer Veröffentlichung (*A*). — Der von uns in T nur an aussagekräftigen Stellen berücksichtigte Text *B* auf Bl. 144r ist ein früheres, eigenh. Konzept F. Ludwigs, das nach der Abschrift jedoch vom Fürsten offenbar nachkorrigiert wurde und das dieser außerdem auf dem Blattrand für einige nicht dazugehörige, daher von uns übergangene Rechnungen benutzte; Bl. 144v leer. — Der endgültige Text des Briefs an Dohna oder gar die Ausfertigung sind uns unbekannt.

A All'Jllustrissimo signor[a] Don Achasio Visconte di Dona Jn man. propria

      Jllustrißimo Signor

Mi rallegro della lettera di V. S. Jll[ma b] da' 20 del mese passato, che gli libretti[c] stampati in questi contorni[d] novamente nella nostra[e] Alamanna volgare, e mandatile da parte mia pel Rettore del Gimnasio di[f] Servesta,[1] le Sieno stati tanto aggradevoli. La materia ricercava una dichiarazione piu[g] ampia, ma mirando L'ultimo di questi trattati ad un Vocabulario intero della nostra favella piu ricca e copiosa delle[h] altre, non é da dubitare ch'n quello si troverrá[i] piu perfezione e gusto.[2] Cosa però laboriosa ed aromatica, come solea[j] dire il nostro Inferigno[k 3] per conto della grande diversita[l] di tanti Dialetti, e della[m] difficoltà che si truova nella vera Ortografia, La quale sin qui non ha avuta[n] certezza, e per ancora in molti[o] Luoghi[p] é o superflua o smorricata^{q r} nelle lettere, atteso^s che^s La piu gran parte de' nostri scrittori vi si smarrisce. Oltre di ció V. S. Jll^m. avrá^t veduto^u certi libri tradotti^v e stampati'n Ollanda a Amsterdam pure^w nella nostra lingua^x Todesca,[4] ancora che^y con uno stile assai^s ragionevole tuttavia'n una Ortografia si scipida^z ed incongrua convenevole,^s che confonderebbe affatto La nostra pulitezza e schiettezza^{aa}, alla quale ci doviamo con ogni nostro potere ingegnarsi. Egli era^{ab} piu che tempo di mostrare^{ac} una volta ben che con brevitá e L'ordine'l modo^{ad} piu ragionevole^{ae} e ricevuto^{ae} contro gli abusi introdotti'n^{af} diverse^{ae} parti. Se nell'avvenire^{ae} qualche^{ae} cosa di piu o simile sará pubblicata^{ae} in questa materia, V. S. Jll^m. ne sará fatta partecipe. Intanto ispero^{ae}, che si come V. S. Jll^m. ora^{ae} cognosce, cosi — cognoscerá ancora per L'avvenire^{ag} che la nostra Accademia fruttifiante, non sia stata senza qualche utile.

E con cio la raccommando nella protezione si, cura del Sommo Dio, Da Cotogna a' 17. di Febbrajo^{ah} 1646.^{ai}

Es wird der Vielgekörnte[5] gebeten, diesen entwurf neben des von Dona schreiben noch einmal zu übersehen und zu durchlesen, und mir seine gedancken mit wenigem druber zu forlegen. Wan er mussig kan ihme ein mehreres im deutschen zugefertiget werden.

T **a** *Folgt* <Barone> — **b** *In A u. B aus* Jll^{m<o>} — **c** *In A u. B aus* libr<o> — **d** *stampati über Rasur; die 3 folgenden Wörter mit Bezeichnung der Reihenfolge 2 3 4; B in questi contorni eingefügt.* — **e** *Folgt* <Lingua> — **f** *Aus* da — **g** *Aus* pi<o> — **h** *Aus* dell<a> — **i** *A u. B aus* troverá — **j** *In A folgt* <a>; *B* <dissi> giá — **k** *In A aus* <i>nferigno; *B* Inferigno — **l** *Aus* diversita grande *umgestellt; B* grande diversita — **m** *B del eingefügt.* — **n** *A aus* av<...>ta *B folgt* <ni ordine> — **o** *Aus* m<u>lti — **p** *Eingefügt.* — **q** *A eingefügt für bereits eingefügtes* <smorrica ...> *über* <troppo raccorciata> — **r** *B* <troppo raccorciata nelle lettere finali> *gebessert zu* smorricata in certe lettere — **s** *Eingefügt (in A u. B).* — **t** *A* avrá *gebessert; B* richtig. — **u** *A* veduto *gebessert; B* richtig. — **v** *A gebessert; B* tradotti <in> e — **w** *B bis* ancora che *eingefügt.* — **x** *A gebessert.* — **y** *A über gestrichenem Wort; B* che — **z** *A gebessert.* — **aa** *B für* <dolcezza> — **ab** *B* Egli era *für* <Tal che> *eingefügt.* — **ac** *A u. B aus* mostrar<i> — **ad** *A durch Ziffern aus* L'ordine e'l ben che con brevitá modo *umgestellte Reihenfolge; B* <il> modo — **ae** *A gebessert.* — **af** *A* introt<t>odotti <ne> — **ag** per L'avventre *v. F. Ludwig eingefügt. Schon in B für* <d'ora innanzi, come ella cognosce> — **ah** *Lesefehler in der Datierung A?* á 17. di Febbraje *für B* a' 14. di Febbrajo — **ai** *In A nichtabgeschriebene Zusätze in B* Affezionatissimo amico *und* per larazia di Dio di *[folgt 1 unleserliches korrigiertes Wort]* 04.

K **1** Marcus Fridericus Wendelin(us) (1584–1652), Rektor des anhalt. Gymasium illustre in Zerbst, bedeutender ref. Theologe. Er wurde von F. Ludwig auch zu gelehrten Arbeiten über die deutsche Sprache herangezogen. Vgl. 451220. Wendelin sah Christan Gueintz' (FG 361) *Rechtschreibung* durch, die er im vorliegenden Fall im Auftrag des Fürsten auch an Achaz zu Dohna (1581–1647) sandte. Zu Burggf. u. Herr Achaz zu Dohna s. 460120A K 1.

2 Gueintz: *Rechtschreibung (1645)* enthält am Schluß (S. 26–176) eine Homophonenliste, die aber wie ein Wörterbuch neben kurzen grammatischen und orthographischen auch semantische Erklärungen zu den jeweiligen deutschen Wörtern enthält und an der F. Ludwig intensiv mitgearbeitet hatte. Vgl. dazu auch 451219 K 8, 460825 K I 4 u. die in *DA*

Köthen I. 9 veröffentlichten Dokumente. Wie der Plural *libretti* (Büchlein) andeutet, wird Ludwig seinem alten Freund Dohna auch andere dt. Werke (auch aus der FG) geschickt haben. Der Tod Dohnas schon im Folgejahr könnte seine Aufnahme in die FG verhindert haben. Der Zusammenbruch der kurpfälz. Stellung 1620, die Wirren des schwed.-poln. Kriegs in Polen wie auch Dohnas eigene Verwicklung in die preuß.-poln. Politik dürften neben dem mühseligen Postverkehr im kriegsgeplagten Reich die Verbindungen F. Ludwigs zu (Abraham und) Achaz zu Dohna erschwert haben, so daß diese Brüder Christophs zu Dohna (FG 20) als geradezu natürliche Kandidaten keine Aufnahme in der FG erlangten. Zu dem schon verstorbenen Abraham zu Dohna s. 460120A K 1.

3 Bastiano de' Rossi (L'Inferigno), Sekretär der Accademia della Crusca und Toskanischlehrer F. Ludwigs in Florenz. Vgl. Roberto Paolo Ciardi, Lucia Tongiorgi Tomasi: Le Pale della Crusca. Cultura e Simbologia. Firenze 1983 (IV Centenario dell'Accademia della Crusca), 188 f. u. ö.

4 F. Ludwig spielt auf folgende Übersetzungen Philipp (v.) Zesens (FG 521. 1648) an, der erst nach herber Kritik und begleitet von Ermahnungen, sich von seinen unablässigen Schreibreformen zu trennen, Aufnahme in der FG fand:
[Vital d'Audiguier: *Histoire des amours de Lysandre et de Caliste*, dt.]: Liebes-beschreibung Lysanders und Kalisten (Amsterdam: Ludwig Elzevier 1644); [Madeleine de Scudéry: *Ibrahim ou l'illustre Bassa*, dt.]: Ibrahims Oder Des Durchleuchtigen Bassa Und Der Beständigen Isabellen Wunder-Geschichte: Durch Fil. Zesien von Fürstenau (Amsteldam: Ludwig Elzevier 1645). Obwohl keine Übersetzung, ist in diese Kritik F. Ludwigs vielleicht einbezogen Zesens Roman *Ritterholds von Blauen. Adriatische Rosemund* (Amsteldam: Ludwich Elzewihr 1645).

5 Diederich v. dem Werder (FG 31. Der Vielgekörnte). Als Tasso- und Ariost-Übersetzer konnte der F. Ludwig vertraute Werder auch Veränderungen im Italienischen und dt. Zusätze vorschlagen.

460218

Fürst Ludwig an Herzog Christian Ludwig von Braunschweig-Calenberg

Beantwortet durch 460301. — F. Ludwig erinnert Hz. Christian Ludwig v. Braunschweig-Calenberg (FG 372) an seine wiederholten Mahnungen, die vom Herzog zugesagten 200 Reichstaler zur Mitfinanzierung des mittlerweile im Druck befindlichen *GB 1646* anzuweisen. Da das Geld bisher nicht eingegangen sei und F. Ludwigs Bote in Hannover nur mit einer Empfangsbestätigung über F. Ludwigs (früheren Mahn-)Brief abgefertigt worden sei und darüber hinaus das Werk im Verlauf der Frankfurter Fastenmesse fertig gedruckt würde, würde F. Ludwigs Kredit, sollte die Zahlung ausbleiben, ernsthaft leiden. F. Ludwig bittet deshalb Hz. Christian Ludwig erneut, die Zahlung an Georg Winckler in Leipzig zu veranlassen und von demselben quittieren zu lassen, damit keine weiteren Verzögerungen oder Unannehmlichkeiten entstehen. Die Verlagsbeiträge aus Holstein, Wolfenbüttel und von F. Ludwig selbst seien bereits korrekt erfolgt. Als Gegenleistung zu Christian Ludwigs Verlagszuschuß werde er die einst bezifferte Anzahl von 48 Exemplaren des *GB 1646* aus Frankfurt erhalten. — F. Ludwig erwartet über den Boten die Erklärung des Herzogs.

Q HM Köthen: V S 544, Bl. 66r; Konzept von Schreiberh. mit eigenh. Korrekturen F. Ludwigs.

460218 Fürst Ludwig

A An herzog Christian Ludwigen Zu[a]

ELd. werden sich fr. erinnern, wie das von Uns unterschiedenen mahlen bei deroselben angehalten worden[b], das die Vorlengst zu dem Geselschaftbuche, welches anniezo in Ffurt gedruckt wirdt, von ihr bewilligte 200 Rth. in Leiptzig möchten erlegt werden.[1]

Weilen es aber bis daher darahn erwunden, und Unser bot jüngsten von Hannover nur mit einem bloßen schein wegen[c] der einantwortung unsers briefes[d], abgefertigt worden, Und aber das ganze buch wie es verdinget diese Mitfaste in Ffurt mit dem drucke wird zuend gebracht werden,[2] Darunter dan Unser credit, wan diese zahlung zurucke bleiben solte[,] ein ernstes leiden wolte.

Als ersuchen wier EL. hiermit nachmals fr. vetterlich, Sie bei den ihrigen die Verordnung thun wollen, weil[e] aus Holstein[,] von Wulffenbuttel wie[f] auch von uns und[g] sonsten richtigkeit erfolget solche[h] zwohundert Reichsthaler ehest George Wincklern[3] in Leiptzig möge ubermachet und[i] auf seine quittung [au]sgezahlet[j] werden, damit uns hierinn von EL seite auch nicht ermangeln und hinderung dem[k] wercke oder Uns Ungelegenheit daraus entstehen moge.

Wie dan ELd. dargegen die vormals angedeutete Zahl der bücher als 48 Exemplaren dargegen aus Ffurt werden zugewarten haben.[4]

Wier erwarten EL. fr. erclerung bei Zeigern hierauf und seind dero fr. dienste zuerzeigen[l]
Gegeben Cothen 18 Febr. 1646.
Auszf[m]
f.[n]

T a *Adreßort fehlt.* — **b** *Eingefügt.* — **c** *Durch Bezifferung Wörterreihenfolge umgestellt aus* der einantwortung wegen — **d** unsers briefes *am Rand ergänzt.* — **e** *Folgt* ⟨sonsten⟩ — **f** wie auch *von F. Ludwig eingefügt für* ⟨als⟩ — **g** und sonsten *von F. Ludwig eingefügt.* — **h** *Am Rand von F. Ludwig ergänzt bis* damit — **i** *Bis* [au]sgezahlet *Einfügung in F. Ludwigs Einfügung.* — **j** *Buchstabenverlust im Falz. Konjektur in eckigen Klammern.* — **k** dem wercke *von F. Ludwig eingefügt.* — **l** *Ergänze:* erbietig *oder* gantz willig — **m** *Von F. Ludwigs H., d. h.:* Auszufertigen — **n** *Wohl Ausfertigungsvermerk:* fecit *(ausgeführt). Vgl. auch* 450224 T l.

K 1 Vgl. 460119. Dort befragt F. Ludwig Carl Gustav v. Hille (FG 302) über die Zahlungswilligkeit Hz. Christian Ludwigs v. Braunschweig-Calenberg (FG 372). Dieses Thema ist schon im Juli 1644 virulent. Bereits in 440723 bat F. Ludwig um Begleichung des zugesagten Betrages über 200 Reichstaler. Im Verlauf der Korrespondenz wird deutlich, daß Hz. Christian Ludwig nur die Hälfte zu zahlen bereit (oder in der Lage) war. S. zu diesen Verhandlungen 450923, 460403 u. ö. Zu fl. Verlagsbeiträgen s. 450126 K 4. Zum *GB 1646* allgem. s. 440130 K 3. Zum Zahlungsverkehr das *GB 1646* betreffend s. 450127 K 1.

2 Zur Frankfurter Fastenmesse vgl. 460303 K 3. In 460206 verheißt Matthäus Merian d. Ä. (als Kommissionsverleger): „Das werkh geht zu Endt, werde in 14 tagen alles fertig haben". Gelistet ist das *GB 1646* bereits im Katalog der Ostermesse 1646: Catalogus universalis, hoc est designatio omnium librorum, qui hisce nundinis ... Francofurtensibus & Lipsiensibus anno ... vel novi vel emendatiores & auctiores prodierunt (Leipzig 1646), Bl. D 2r. Das *GB 1646* erschien tatsächlich noch im Februar, spätestens Anfang März 1646. S. 460303 u. 460324. Lt. 460303 händigte Merian die für Hz. August v. Braunschweig-Wolfenbüttel (FG 227) vorgesehenen 48 Exemplare am 2. 3. 1646 einem Kaufmann aus, der dieselben nach Wolfenbüttel übermitteln sollte. Bestätigung des Sachverhalts in 460324. — Ermöglicht wurde die Publikation v. a. durch Zuschüsse von F. Ludwig (400 Rtl.), Hz. August (200 Rtl.), Hz. Friedrich III. v. Schleswig-Holstein-Gottorf (FG 388. 200 Rtl.) und Anthon v. Wietersheim (FG 273. 100 Rtl.). Hz. Christian Ludwig reduzierte seinen Beitrag um die Hälfte auf 100 Rtl. S. Anm. 1.

3 Der Leipziger Handelsherr Georg Winckler, für F. Ludwigs finanzielle Transaktionen in Leipzig tätig, hier im Zusammenhang mit dem *GB 1646*. S. 451019 K 0.

4 Pro eingelegter 100 Rtl. waren als Gegenleistung 24 Exemplare des *GB 1646* vorgesehen. Vgl. 450126 K 4.

460301

Herzog Christian Ludwig von Braunschweig-Calenberg an Fürst Ludwig

Antwort auf 460218. Beantwortet durch 460309. — Hz. Christian Ludwig v. Braunschweig-Calenberg (FG 372) dankt für F. Ludwigs Brief 460218 und die darin mitgeteilten Informationen, auf die er wegen Arbeitsüberlastung bisher nicht habe eingehen können. Er erinnert sich nun auch an die Zusage, den Druck des *GB 1646* finanziell zu unterstützen und sei gewillt, 100 Reichstaler nach Braunschweig anzuweisen, da diese von dort aus leicht per Wechsel nach Frankfurt a. M. übermittelt werden könnten. Sobald der Betrag beglichen sei, würde Hz. Christian Ludwig F. Ludwig darüber in Kenntnis setzen. Da im Augenblick hohe Ausgaben anstünden, hoffe er, daß F. Ludwig mit der reduzierten Beitragssumme von 100 Reichstalern einverstanden sei.

Q HM Köthen: V S 544, Bl. 67r–68v [A: 68v], 67v u. 68r leer; Schreiberh.; Sig. — *D: KE*, 51f. — *BN: Bürger*, 238 Nr. 2.

A *Dem Hochgebornen Fürsten, Hern Ludwigen*, Fursten zue Anhaldt, Graffen zue *Ascanien*, hern zue Bernburgk vnd Zerbst, vnserm freundtlichen lieben Oheimb, *Eigenh. Empfangsvermerk F. Ludwigs:* Pst. 6. Martij 1646.

Unser freundtlich Dienst, vndt was wir vielmehr liebes vndt gutes vermögen zuvor,

Hochgeborner Furst, freundtlicher lieber Oheimb,

Ew. Ld abermahliges schreiben vom 18t*en* dieses, haben wir zu recht empfangen, daneben uns dan auch aus dero Vorigen schreiben Vnterthäniger bericht geschehen, welches wegen vieler überheuffer *[sic]* geschäffte bishero nicht beobachtet worden,

Nun erinnern wir uns, das wir zu befoderung des newen drucks des Gesellschafftbuchs etwas zuzuschießen uns anheisig gemacht, dabey wirs auch nachmahls bewenden laßen,

Seint auch gemeinet, Zwischen Ostern vnndt Pfingsten der behueff hundert

460303 Matthäus Merian d. Ä.

thaler naher Vnser Stadt Braunschweig übermachen zulaßen, von dannen sie leicht vff Franckfurth durch wechsell können gebracht werden,[1]

Wollen auch sopalt die Zahlung geschehen, solches Ew. Ld freundtöhmlich zuwißen machen, weill wir anietzo der außgaben sehr viell, werden Ew. Ld mit den hundert thalern friedtlich sein,[2]

Dero wir freundtliche dienste zuerweisen, allezeit gantz willig vnndt befließen, Geben Zelle den 1ten des Mertzens im Jahr 1646,

Von Gottes gnaden Christian Ludowig
Hertzog zu Braunschweig vndt Lüneburgk,
    E. Ldt.
        Dienstwilliger Vetter
        Christian Ludwig *mp.*

K 1 Im Jahre 1646 fiel Ostersonntag auf den 29. März, Pfingsten auf den 17. Mai 1646. Vgl. *Grotefend*, 158. S. Anm. 2.

2 F. Ludwig äußert in 460309 sein Mißfallen über den um die Hälfte reduzierten Betrag von 100 Reichstalern. Hz. Christian Ludwig v. Braunschweig-Calenberg (FG 372) hatte vier Jahre zuvor 200 Reichstaler zur Unterstützung des *GB 1646* zugesagt. Vgl. 421031A. Den reduzierten Betrag ist Hz. Christian Ludwig gewillt, zügig zu zahlen. S. 460403. Zu den fl. Verlagsbeiträgen im Detail s. 450126 K 4. Zum *GB 1646* allgem. s. 440130 K 3. Zum Zahlungsprozedere das *GB 1646* anlangend, in das der Leipziger Handelsmann Georg Winckler involviert ist, s. 450127 K 1. Zur Person Winckler s. 451019 K 0.

460303

Matthäus Merian d. Ä. an Peter Knaudt

Matthäus Merian d. Ä. hegt keinen Zweifel daran, daß sein kürzlich über Herrn (Georg) Winckler versandter Brief mit den beiden letzten Titelbogen zum *GB 1646* gut angekommen ist. Darin habe er mitgeteilt, daß das *GB 1646* mitsamt den 400 Kupfern gedruckt vorliege, auch habe er um Information gebeten, wohin die 305 Exemplare gesandt werden sollen. Er habe zur Zeit und bis zur nächsten Messe keine Transportmöglichkeit. Die 48 Exemplare für Hz. August d. J. v. Braunschweig-Wolfenbüttel (FG 227) habe er jedoch gestern bereits einem Kaufmann ausgehändigt, der sie zügig nach Wolfenbüttel bringen werde. Merian werde die verbleibenden 252 Exemplare des *GB 1646*, 5 weitere Exemplare für Knaudt sowie die *Topographia*-Bände zusammenstellen und abwarten, bis er Nachricht über den Bestimmungsort erhalte. Da die hiesigen (Handels-)Herren de Famars in regen Handelsbeziehungen zu Georg Winckler in Leipzig stehen, dürften sie wohl die besten Möglichkeiten haben, die Büchersendung rasch dorthin zu bringen. Durch Winckler und Famars könnten auch die ausstehenden 300 Reichstaler an Merian übermittelt werden und im Gegenzug die Exemplare des *GB 1646* samt den Topographiebänden zugestellt werden. — Die Kosten der *Topographia* belaufen sich pro Band auf 3 1/2 Gulden (*Helvetia, Suevia, Alsatia, Bavaria, Palatinatus Rheni*). Die Topographie der drei Kurfürstentümer Mainz, Trier und Köln werde in acht Tagen abgeschlossen. Falls dieser Teil (der *Topographia*) ebenso geschickt werden solle, koste das nochmals 3 1/2 Gulden.

Q HM Köthen: V S 546, Bl. 41rv [A: 41v]; eigenh., Sig. — *D: Bircher: Merian*, 712–716; *Wüthrich: Merian Briefe*, 106–109. — *BN: Bürger*, 987 Nr. 16.

A Tt. Dem Ehrenvesten vnd HochAchtparen hern Petter Knaudt Furst. Anhaltischen CammerMeister zu gg. handen. Cito Cito Citissime.
hern Georg Wincklern Jn Leipzig Recomendirt. Köthen

Ehrenvester hochAchtparer Jnsonders Großg. Hochgeehrter Herr *etc.*
Dem sein mein willige dienst und was ich vermag Jederzeit Anvor[1],
   Mir zweifelt nicht, das mein gg. herr mein Jüngstes vor 14 Tagen sampt den 2 letzten Tittulbogen zur Fruchtbringenden geselschaft, welches ich an herrn Wincklern gesandt, nun mehr wol empfangen haben wirt, worin Jch vermeldet, das die besagte Fruchbringende geselschafft im truckh gantz fertig[2] mit sampt den 400 kupfern, und begehrt, das man mich berichten[a], und order schreiben wolle, wie die 305 exemplaria zu versenden, und wohin ich solche allhie solle zustellen, dan ich ietzunder keine fuhr[b] weiß so dorthin abfahren wirt, biß in die bevorstehende Meß,[3] so es Aber dem herrn geliebt, will Jch solche exemplaria deren nur 252 sein (den Jhr Fürst. Gnaden hertzog Augusto zu Braunschweig vnd Luneburg habe[c] Jch 48 exemplaria gestrigs tags allhie auff befehl, einem kauffman[4] gelifert, welcher solche ehest dahin nach Wolffenbüttel verschaffen wirt)[5] die vbrigen 252 vnd dan die 5 für den Herrn neben der Toppographia,[6] will ich zusamen setzen, biß Jch befehl bekome wohin sie gelifert werden sollen. Weilen die Herrn De Famars[7] allhie viel mit Herrn Wincklern zu Leipzig handln, werden sie vermutlich die beste gelegenheit haben mit ehestem solche dahin zu verschaffen, vnd könen auch die Restirenden Rth. 300[8] durch gemelte Herren Wincklern vnd De Famars mir ubermacht, vnd ihme dahingegen, die gemelten exemplarien zugestelt werden, sampt den Toppographiis

1 Toppographia	Heluetiæ folio	f.	3 ½
1	Sueuiæ fol.........	f.	3 ½
1	Alsatiæ f	f.	2 ½
1	Bauariæ f	f.	3 ½
1	Palatinatus Rheni f	f.	3 ½
thut Rthaler 11[9]	Summa	f.	16 ½

Diese werde ich laut befehles mit senden. Die Beschreibung der 3 Churfürstenthumb Maintz, Trier vnd Cöln, wirt in 8 tagen auch fertig sein. Alßdann Jch solches auch sende wirt kosten f. 3 ½ — welches meinem gg. hern Jch hiemit habe berichten[a] sollen. Dem Allmächtigen hiemit zu gnaden wohl befohlen.
   Ffurt den 3 Mertz 1646.
         D. Herrn
         Dinstwilligster
         Mattheus Merian.

460303 Matthäus Merian d. Ä. 841

T a *Wohl Verschreibung:* brichten — b *Folgt* <habe> — c *Eingefügt.*

K Matthäus Merian d. Ä. drückt eingangs die Annahme aus, daß sein (verschollener) Brief mit den dort gemachten Mitteilungen und gestellten Fragen bei F. Ludwigs Kammermeister Knaudt eingetroffen ist. Er hat also noch keine Antwort Knaudts empfangen. Schon in 460206 hatte Merian die Vollendung des *GB 1646* angekündigt und nach dem Bestimmungsort der Exemplare und den Transportwegen gefragt. Wie aus 460206 I u. II hervorgeht, beantwortete Knaudt dieses Schreiben am 22.2.1646 oder kurz danach.

1 Bevor, vorab. S. 450417 K 1 u. die weiteren Merian-Briefe.

2 Merian meldete in seinem (verschollenen) Brief von Mitte Febuar den langerwarteten Abschluß des seit 1639 den Briefwechsel durchziehenden Vorhabens eines erweiterten illustrierten GB in der Nachfolge des *GB 1629/30*. Die beiden „letzten Tittulbogen" gingen wohl den 2 letzten Hundert der Impresen vorher (FG 201–300 u. FG 301–400). Auch diese positive Nachricht erwähnt den für das Gesamtunternehmen wichtigen Leipziger Handelsherrn Georg Winckler als Vermittler. S. zu ihm 451019 K 0. Zum Zahlungsverkehr das *GB 1646* betreffend s. 450127 K 1. Zur Einrichtung des *GB 1646* s. 450711 K 4.

3 Der Beginn der Ostermesse in Leipzig war für Jubilate, den 3. Sonntag nach Ostern, angesetzt. Der Ostersonntag fiel lt. *Grotefend*, 158 im Jahre 1646 auf den 29. März und der Beginn der Messe somit auf den 19. April 1646. Nach zwei Wochen endete die Leipziger Ostermesse traditionell am Sonntag Rogate (5. Sonntag nach Ostern). Im Jahr 1646 war dies der 3. Mai. Wenn die Fastenmesse zu Frankfurt a. M. 1646, wie seit dem 15. Jahrhundert üblich, auf die drei Wochen zwischen den Sonntagen Oculi und Palmarum (4. bis 1. Sonntag vor Ostern) fiel, so endete sie am 22.3. Das heißt für den vorliegenden Brief, daß die Fuhre Frankfurt nach Ostern (29.3.1646) verließ. S. 460324 (K 1).

4 Der hier ungenannte Kaufmann entpuppt sich in 460620B (K 5) als der Frankfurter Kaufmann Heinrich Bengerath (auch Bingenroth, Pengerode).

5 Merian reagiert hier auf das in 460206 II erwähnte Schreiben Knaudts an ihn. Die Sendung der 48 Exemplare des *GB 1646*, die Hz. August d.J. v. Braunschweig-Wolfenbüttel (FG 227) für seinen Verlagsbeitrag von 200 Rtl. zustanden (vgl. zuletzt in 460206 I u. II), wird durch den Brief 460324 bestätigt. S. außer 460703 auch 460620B, wo von dem Braunschweiger Mittelsmann (Kaufmann oder Postmeister?) Johann Gärtner in Braunschweig die Rede ist. S. auch 460317 K 9. Dort und in 460620B heißt es, daß zwei Exemplare (aus Hz. Augusts 48) für Johann Valentin Andreae (FG 464. 1646) bestimmt waren. Vgl. 460708. Zu den fl. Verlagsbeiträgen s. auch 450126 K 4. Zum *GB 1646* allgemein s. 440130 K 3.

6 S. zu *Merian: Topographia* 450905 K 4. S. auch die Exemplare der *Topographia* in der Bibliothek F. Ludwigs (Der Nährende). *IP*, 328v: „VII Topographia, Helvetiæ, Rhetiæ, Valesiæ, Sveviæ, Alsatiæ per Matt. Meran. 1642 1643 et 44. IIX Topographia Bavariæ et Palatinatus Rheni 1645 Franckfort IX Topographia Hassiæ". Letztgenannter Band ohne Veröffentlichungszeitpunkt wurde noch im gleichen Jahr 1646 publiziert.

7 Einflußreiche und wohlhabende Tuchhändlerfamilie aus Nordfrankreich (Valenciennes), die seit etwa 1560 in Frankfurt ansässig war. Die Familie kam durch einen Vetter des Noë du Fay, namentlich den Tuchhändler Johann Jouvenaeau, welcher die Witwe des Stefan de Famars geheiratet hatte, nach Frankfurt. Ein Sohn erster Ehe, Johann de Famars der Ältere, wurde 1580 nach dem Tode seines Schwiegervaters Johann Flammin an dessen Stelle Teilhaber der du Fayschen Handlung in belgischer Rohwolle. Johann de Famars starb 1631, und sein Sohn aus zweiter Ehe, Jakob, führte die Seidenhandlung zuerst mit Jakob Pergesen, dann mit seinem Sohn Jakob 40 Jahre lang weiter, ehe Jakob d.J. de Famars († 1703) trotz großer Erfolge wegen Spekulationsgeschäften den Bankrott erklären

mußte. S. Alexander Dietz: Frankfurter Handelsgeschichte. Glashütten im Taunus 1970 (Nachdr. der Ausgabe Frankfurt a. M. 1921), II, 281 f.

8 Bereits fünf Monate zuvor (450930) erwähnte Merian in einem Brief an Peter Knaudt, daß der Restbetrag von 300 Reichstalern nach Lieferung fällig sei. In 460309 gibt F. Ludwig die Leipziger Ostermesse als Zahlungstermin der noch ausstehenden Gelder an. In 460519 kann Merian dann den Eingang der Zahlung bestätigen.

9 16 1/2 Gulden (dies sind 16 Gulden und 10 1/6 Schilling) entsprechen 11 Reichstaler. S. die Ausführungen zu den verschiedenen Währungen und die Unterscheidung zwischen sog. „Talerländern" und „Guldenländern" in 450930 K 5.

460309

Fürst Ludwig an Herzog Christian Ludwig von Braunschweig-Calenberg

Antwort auf 460301. Beantwortet durch 460403. — F. Ludwig bestätigt den Erhalt des Briefes, in dem die Bereitschaft Hz. Christian Ludwigs v. Braunschweig-Calenberg (FG 372), 100 Taler zwischen Ostern und Pfingsten nach Braunschweig anweisen zu lassen, bekundet wird. F. Ludwig bedauert, daß die zugesagten 200 Reichstaler nicht in Gänze bezahlt werden, zumal er dafür mit seinem Namen gehaftet habe und dafür gerade stehen müsse, was ihm in der augenblicklich denkbar schlechten Situation und dem in so vieler Hinsicht erlittenen Schaden übel ankomme. Da der Druck jedoch bereits vor Ostern vorliegen werde und die ausstehenden Gelder beim Leipziger Ostermarkt abzurechnen seien, bittet F. Ludwig darum, die 100 Reichstaler entweder direkt nach Leipzig an Georg Winckler zu übermitteln oder den Braunschweiger Kaufmann zu nennen, durch den die Auszahlung erfolgen soll. In diesem Falle müsse der Betrag noch vor Jubilate in Braunschweig eintreffen.

Q HM Köthen: V S 544, Bl. 69r; unbekannte (Schreiber-)H. mit Ergänzungen und Korrekturen F. Ludwigs. — *D: KE*, 52. — *BN: Bürger*, 948 Nr. 24.

A An Herzog Christian Ludwig Zu Braunschweig *etc.*

Aus E Ld antwort Vom 1. dieses Monats hab*en* wir Vern*ommen*, wie das Sie zu dem Neuen Drucke des geselschaftbuchs 100 Rth. zwischen Negstkunftige Ostern und Pfingsten naher Braunschweig Uberzumachen sich ercleret.[1]

Nun solte Uns zwar lieb gewesen sein wan die vertröstete 200 Rth. vollig erlegt werden können, sintemal Unser treu und glauben darin haftet, und wir[a] das übrige werden gelten[2] müßen, so Uns bey Unserm großen Ungemach und erlitenen Vielfältig*en* schaden sehr übel kömmet, Weil aber der druck nunmehr und noch[b] fur Ostern wird fertig sein[c] die versprochene gelder noch[d] auf dem Leipziger Ostermarckt[e] zuerlegen seind, Als ersuchen wir ELd freundlich Sie wollen entweder diese 100 Rth vollend bis[d] in Leipzig an Georg Winklern[3] übermach*en*, oder doch Uns den kaufman in Braunschweig benennen, bei welchem die auszahlung erfolgen soll, Und das solche 100[f] Rth noch vor dem Sontag Jubilate[4] in Braunschweig sein mögen.

Hierüber erwarten wir, wie es die noturft erheischet Eld. förderlichen[d] fr. erclerung, und seindt *etc.*

Geben Cothen 9 Martij 1646.

Auszf[g]
f.[h]

T a *Eingefügt für* <fur> — b *Durch Bezifferung Wörterreihenfolge von F. Ludwig umgestellt aus* fur Ostern noch — c *Folgt* <Und> — d *Eingefügt von F. Ludwig.* — e *Folgt* <werden> — f 100 Rth *eingefügt.* — g *Von F. Ludwigs H., d. h.:* Auszufertigen — h *Wohl Ausfertigungsvermerk:* fecit *(ausgeführt). Vgl. auch 460218 T n.*

K 1 Hz. Christian Ludwig v. Braunschweig-Calenberg (FG 372) beabsichtigte, seinen eigenmächtig auf 100 Reichstaler halbierten Zuschuß zum Verlag des *GB 1646* zwischen dem 29. März und dem 17. Mai 1646 zu entrichten. S. bereits 460301. F. Ludwig erklärt sich im vorliegenden Brief nur unter Protest mit der Reduzierung der zugesagten Verlagseinlage einverstanden. Zu den Verlagsbeiträgern allgem. s. 450126 K 4. Zum *GB 1646* s. 440130 K 3.

2 Im Sinne von *entgelten, bezahlen*. S. *DW* IV.1, 3068 f.

3 Georg Winckler, Leipziger Handelsmann und wichtigste Kontaktperson F. Ludwigs in der Messestadt Leipzig hinsichtlich des Zahlungsverkehrs im Kontext *GB 1646*. S. zu seiner Person 451019 K 0; zum Zahlungsverkehr das *GB 1646* betreffend 450127 K 1.

4 F. Ludwig besteht darauf, daß die reduzierte Summe, sollte die Zahlung den Umweg über Braunschweig nehmen, wenigstens im April, noch vor Jubilate, dem Beginn der Leipziger Ostermesse, dort eintreffen müsse. Der Sonntag Jubilate fiel 1646 auf den 19. April. Vgl. *Grotefend*, 158.

460315

Christoph Steger an Christian Clepius

Der (Gesellschafts-)Maler Christoph Steger bestätigt den Erhalt des Briefes des anhaltischen Küchenmeisters in Köthen, Christian Clepius, und läßt wissen, daß er die Impresenvisierungen bis zur Nr. 468 „Der Vergnügte" (Johann Georg Reinhard) fortgesetzt habe. Es fehle noch an der orientalischen Wurzel „Hyazinthe", der „stechenden Winde", die in (Leonhart) Fuchs' Kräuterbuch zu finden sei, und dem „heiligen Holz", von dem er eine Pflanze erhalten habe. Der hiesige Gärtner berichtet, daß dieses Gewächs einem Kirschbaum gleich traubenförmige Früchte trage und auch nicht hoch wachse. Wenn es Seiner Fürstlichen Gnaden (F. Ludwig) beliebe, könnte Steger die Pflanze auch so in die Landschaft zeichnen. Was im Auftrag F. Ludwigs noch erledigt werden solle, möge Clepius mit (nächster Post) nach Halle senden.

Q HM Köthen: V S 546, Bl. 33r–34v [A: 34v], 33v u. 34r leer; Sig. — D: *Bircher: Merian*, 727 (falsche Datierung: 15. 3. 1648). — *BN: Bürger*, 1337 Nr. 1 (übernimmt falsche Datierung).

A Dem Ehrenvesten Grosachtbaren undt wohlgelehrten herrn Christian Clepio Fürstl. Anhaltischen wohlbestalten KüchenMeister Meinem insonders großgunstigen Herrn sehr werthen Freunde shd[a] Cöthen

Ehrenvester Grosachtbarer und Wohlgelehrter, insonder großgunstiger Her, und werther Freundt.

Desselben Brieflein habe ich wohl entpfangen vnd vernehme das S. F. G. gnedigst wißen wolten, wie weit ich die impresen an der zahl habe,[1] als berichte ich dem Herrn das derselben bis auf 468 als des vergnügte[2] sein, an den kräutern wird noch mangeln die Orientalische wurtzel hiacint[3] die grose stechende winde[4] welche aber in des Fuchsij Kreuterbuch zu finden und das heiligs holz[5], wovon ich aber alhier das kraut bekommen, der Gertner alhier berichtet er wachse wie der kirschbaum so traublich were auch nicht gar groser höhe und wen S. F. G. gnedigß vermeinten, so könte man den baum auf die selbe art in die landschaft mahlen, was nun S F G. noch werden zu verfertigen haben, werden sie schon mit anhero senden, Ergebe den Herrn in Gottes schuz, und ich verbleibe deßelben

[Ha]ll[b] am 15 Martij
1646.

AlZeitt
Dienstwilliger
Christoph Steger Mahler

T a seines herrn diener? — b *Buchstabenverlust im Falz. Konjektur in eckigen Klammern.*

K 1 Durch den vorliegenden Brief, der von *Bircher: Merian*, 727 fälschlicherweise auf das Jahr 1648 (exakt zwei Jahre später) datiert wurde, wissen wir um den vollen Namen des Gesellschaftsmalers Christoph Steger. S. *Conermann II*, 114. Es darf angenommen werden, daß er die bis zu diesem Zeitpunkt angefertigten Impresen gestaltet hat: Nr. FG 401 – FG 458, FG 460 – FG 462, wahrscheinlich auch FG 463 (s. Anm. 4), FG 464 – FG 466, Auslassung von FG 467 (S. Anm. 5). S. *Conermann III*, 570 unter Beachtung des verifizierten Briefdatums u. FG 468 (S. Anm. 2). Vgl. 430410 K 4; *Conermann III*, 574, *Wüthrich: Merian Biographie*, 275 f. S. zu Clepius auch *DA Köthen I. 8*: 470923.

2 Johann Georg Reinhard (FG 468. Der Vergnügte. 1647). S. *Conermann III*, 573–575 u. *Ball: Altmark-FG*, 93. Ihm wurde die Gesellschaftspflanze „Beerenklau" zugedacht.

3 Hz. Franz Erdmann v. Sachsen-Lauenburg (FG 459. Der Fortwuchernde. 1646), *Conermann III*, 553 f., erhält die gen. Wurzel „hiacint" als Gesellschaftspflanze.

4 Eberhard v. Sickingen (FG 463. Der Nachstellende. 1646). Ihm wurden die Gesellschaftspflanze „Smilax aspera L., Stechwinde" und das Gesellschaftswort „Allerley gift" zugeordnet. S. *Conermann III*, 559 f.

5 Johann Rist (FG 467. Der Rüstige. 1647). Das ihm zugehörige Impresengemälde in einem Entwurf ohne seine Gesellschaftspflanze „Das heilige Holz" oder auch „Guajacum officinale L., Gaiac" in den *Weimarer Impresen*, sein Reimgesetz im *GB Kö.* III, 68r. Vgl. *Conermann III*, 567–572 unter Zitation *Bircher: Merian*, s. Q. Vgl. auch *Conermann: Rist*, 49–51 (S. 50: Abb. des Entwurfs des Rist-Sinnbilds).

460317

Herzog August d. J. von Braunschweig-Wolfenbüttel an Johann Valentin Andreae

Antwort Hz. Augusts d. J. v. Braunschweig-Wolfenbüttel (FG 227) auf den Brief Johann Valentin Andreaes (FG 463. 1646) vom 25.2.1646. — Hz. August dankt, auch im Namen seiner Erben, für Andreaes Glückwünsche zur anstehenden Vollendung der Oktavausgabe seiner *Evangelischen Kirchen-Harmonie* (1646). Andreaes Gedicht *Templum virtutis* mit den Wünschen zu seinem Geburtstag werde er an den Schluß des Buchs stellen, so daß es Andreaes Vorrede gegenüberstehe. Hz. August schickt Andreae zur Durchsicht nochmals vier Bögen der Oktavausgabe. Es hätten fünf sein können, wäre der Setzer nicht krank geworden. In der Osterwoche solle der Satz des zweiten Teils des Werks vollendet werden. Dann müsse man die Hand an die Quartausgabe der *Kirchen-Harmonie* legen, zu der schon die Vorbereitungen getroffen worden seien. — Andreae werde wissen, daß er oft an (Johannes) Faulhaber [richtig: Josef Furttenbach d. Ä.] denke, den er zuvor um ein Porträt der 13. Sibylle (Pzn. Sibylla v. Württemberg) gebeten, aber in Andreaes Antwortbriefen nichts mehr darüber gelesen und „Faulhaber" es wohl vergessen habe. Ein Bildnis diene in Abwesenheit einem Zweck (der Vergegenwärtigung der Braut Sibylla vor dem geplanten Bräutigam), wie das biblische *Buch der Weisheit Salomonis* lehre. — August erwartet, daß Friedrich Greiff seine Dichtung (*Der vier Evangelisten ubereinstimmende Geschicht Beschreibung Christi*) vollenden werde, die vorhandenen abgeflachten Kupferplatten jedoch nicht mehr für die benötigten Abzüge ausreichen würden. — Der Herzog hofft, Andreae habe seine zugedachten beiden Exemplare des fertiggestellten *GB 1646* durch Matthäus Merian empfangen. Dieser habe ihm, Herzog August, geantwortet und die Lieferung versprochen. — Der Fürst dankt Andreae für das Angebot der illustrierten Augsburger *Teuerdank*-Ausgabe (1519) von Kaiser Maximilian und Melchior Pfinzing. Er besitze das Buch jedoch bereits, dazu eine Ausgabe in Klein-Folio und die von Burkhard Waldis erweiterte Oktav-Edition. In Wien sei ihm 1629 eine Pergament-Ausgabe angeboten worden, die er aber nicht erworben habe, weil sie nur im Anfang illuminiert gewesen sei. — Gott möge Andreaes oft geäußerten Wunsch erfüllen, die herzogliche Familie in Wolfenbüttel zu besuchen.

Q HAB: Cod. Guelf. 236.3 Extrav., Bl. 12rv; 11. eigenh. Schreiben Hz. Augusts, mit Andreaes Empfangsvermerk auf Bl. 12v „Pres. 8. April. 46". — Anschrift auf einem dem Brief vorgeklebten Zettel. — Teilw. zit. in *Begemann: FG und Andreae*, 34.

A Dem Ehrwürdigen und Hochgelarten, Unserm lieben besondern, Herren JohanValentin Andreæ SS. Th. D. F. Wurtemb. OberHofpredigern und geistlichenConsistorial Rahte etc. zu behandigen. Stutgardt. Abzugeben zu Nurnberg beym H. Forstenhäusern. 4. Apr. 46. — *Postal. Vermerk:* f. 57.

Ehrwürdiger Hochgelahrter lieber besonder und getreuer,

sein schreiben vom 25 Febr.[1] mit denen so geistreichen wolgemeinten Votis, aus einem redlichen Christlichen herzen herfliessenden habe ich wol empfangen, und werde ich das eine, Templum inscribieret, hinter das ganze werk cum pace suâ ordnen, damit Ers ende, wie Ers mit seiner Præfation ins feld führet, und vorhergehet: Gott bestätige alle herzliche Votas:[2]

Und ich tuhe mich billig gegen ihm bedanken; und meine hinterlassende werden es gegen Ihm, und die Seinen, hinwieder zu erkennen, uns bemühen:ª Izzo sckikke ich 4 bogen, hätten wol 5 seyn können, wann nicht des Sezzers krankheit einen Tag verhindert hätte: In der Oster-Woche vermeine Ich, werde 2da sine altera pars absolvieret werden.³ Dan müssen wir gedenken auf das quart format: darzu die Instrumentos et Subjecta, das mehrer Teihl zusammen gebracht, und täglich mehr ankommen &c.⁴ Des Faulhaberi, wird oft gedacht: Von wehm wird Er leicht zu errahten haben.ᵇ ⁵ Meines behaltens, habe ich vor, diesem, umb ein ritratto sive divæ cujusdam, e numero Sibyllarum terdecimæ erwehnung getahn:⁶ Dieweil ich aber in den responsoriis darvon nichts wahrgenommen, als muß Ichs etwa vergessen haben: Ich halte es nicht undienlich, dieweil noch zur zeit præsens facies illa divina nicht zu sehen ist: und mann also, nach dem 17. v. des 14 cap. Sap. dieses mittels sich vor diesmahl nuhr gebrauchen kan:⁷ [12v]

Des Fr. Greyff Teutsche Vers werden wol kommen, Aber die kupfer werden es swerlich aushalten; wie Er selber ohne daß erwehnet hat. Es seynd ohne das etliche nicht tief genug gesnitten, etc.⁸ Das geselschafft Buch ist fertig. Ich verhoffe, Er werde vor ankunft dieses 2 Exemplaria vom Merian empfangen haben:⁹ dan ich ihm solches zugeskrieben und Er hat auch albereit geantwortet und verheißen meinem begehren ein genüge zu tuhn. Die beskreibungen des Pfintzings vitæ Maximiliani 1. zu Augspurg Ao. 1519 mit 118 Figuren gedrukket, ist in meiner Bibliothec, nebest andern in kl. fol. und in 8.ᵛ durch Burkhard Wallis vermehret vorhanden. Zu Wien Anno 1629ᶜ ward mir eines zum kauf præsentieret, das war auf Pergamen geskrieben, und gar sauber die Figuren angefangen mit farben zu mahlen: dieweyl es aber nicht hinausgeführet, sondern ein imperfectum Opus war, so verblieb der kauff.¹⁰ Ich bedanke mich gleichwol, daß Ers mir uberskikken wollen. Der Allmächtige wolle sliesslich den so oft von ihm wiederholten wunsch, und vorhaben, zu uns anhero zu kommen; bestätigen und personaliter erfüllen lassen. Gott gebe es bald. Verbleibe sein alzeit beständig affectionierter Freundt,

Augustus HZBuL MP

WulfenBüttel, den 17. Martii, Gertrud. 1646 ♂

I

Justus Georg Schottelius an Herzog August d. J. von Braunschweig-Wolfenbüttel

Q HAB: Cod. Guelf. 11.12. Aug. 2°, Bl. 226rv [A: 226v], undat., eigenh.; dig. — Bl. 226r Datumsvermerk „4. Apr. 46" von Johann Valentin Andreaes H., d. i. Präsentationsvermerk. — Auf dieses Dokument war in 411214 K II B 11 irrtümlich als 450000A verwiesen worden.

A SERENissimo, humillè

460317 Herzog August d.J. von Braunschweig-Wolfenbüttel

Serenissime illustrissimeque Princeps
Domine clementissime,

Fr. Gr.i.[a]

Carmina[b] hæc germanica[1] rythmo et metro suo quædam constant, exactè autem examinaturo hinc inde desideranda obvenient quædam: Genius huius poetæ est mediocris, nec multum ultra vulgares Musas ascendit, illud, salvo cujusvis iudicio, candidè sentio.

À Celebrissimo Domino Dilhero transmissum nuperis diebus libellum[2] Vestræ serenitati humillimus ego tradidj, quem Vestram serenitatem accepisse spero: paginâ 289 passionale Guelphicum imitatus est, sed non, ut videtur, ad doctrinam et observationem Vestræ serenitatis ita exactè.[3] Est alias ille Author, Vir apud Norimbergenses et Germanis Academias magni nominis, et ob insignem orientalium linguarum peritiam et raræ eloquentis famam admodum celebris[4]

Serenitati Vestræ
humill. obediens
JGSChottelius.

T **a** *Folgt ein unleserliches Wort über* <werden den> — **b** *Randglosse J. V. Andreaes*: Furtenbachs vid. 198. — **c** Anno 1629 *eingefügt.*

T I **a** *Im C-Bogen des Worts* Carmina *steht in dt. Kurrentschrift* Fr. Gr. i. *D. h. Friderici Greifi.* — **b** *Folgt* <sed>

K **1** Johann Valentin Andreae (FG 464. 1646) hatte am 25.2.1646 zum herannahenden Geburtstag Hz. Augusts d.J. v. Braunschweig-Wolfenbüttel (FG 227) am 10.4.1646 seinen Beifall bzw. Glückwünsche gesandt: „Weilen nu auch E. F. G. natalis auspicatissimus widerumb herzu naht. habe zu Bezeugung meiner Vnd. herzlichen freuden. ich meinen geringen Plausum gehorsambst vbersenden, vnd darumb anticipieren wollen." HAB: Cod. Guelf. 65.1 Extrav., Bl.270r.

2 Es handelt sich um den bevorstehenden Abschluß der Oktavausgabe der *Evangelischen Kirchen-Harmonie* Hz. Augusts von 1646 (411214, S.355). Vgl. 451001 K 5. Andreaes „Vota" (Glückwünsche) kommen in seiner lat. Vorrede (wie in der folgenden Quartausgabe; beide d. d. 18.10.1644) und seiner lat. Dichtung zum Ausdruck „TEMPLUM VIRTUTIS, DN. AUGUSTO TEMPLUM VIRTUTIS, DN. AUGUSTO [...] In Natalem Ejus LXVIII. 10. Aprilis C. 1646" (S.574–581; in der Quartausgabe S.16–24). Dieser Ausgabe war ein Probedruck des ersten Teils vorausgegangen, der im Juni 1645 vollendet worden war und in dem die Passionsgeschichte und die Vorrede noch fehlten (411214, S.355).

3 Tl. 2 der Oktavausgabe der *Evangelischen Kirchen-Harmonie* Hz. Augusts (1646), s. 411214 u. 451001. Am 22.4.1646 schrieb Andreae: „Die beede Exemplar, hette ich nu mehr, das eine ganz, ohne den Titul, oder ersten Bogen, das andere aber, biß an secundæ partis Hh. Ii. Kk. Ll. und Nn. sambt dem Titul. Vnd verlanget mich, das Jch eines möge können binden Laßen, mich haben desto fuglicher darinnen zuersehen. Dem anderen gedenkhe ich mit sauberm bund vnd vergültem beschläg in rej illustris memoriam eine Ehr anzuthon. vnd der figuren alle illuminiren zu laßen. vnd verhoffe von E. F. G. vndst.

zuerbitten. daß sie etwa auf ein blätli Perquament in größe des formats. dero Nahmens vnd jnscription mich gnedigst werdigen wolten. welches des Buchs Coronis [eine] wehre." HAB: Cod. Guelf. 65.1 Extrav., Bl. 279r. Am 26.5.1646 teilte Andreae Hz. August mit: „Des Perquament blätlins, vnd Gesellschaft Buch will ich verlangentlich erwarten." A. a. O., Bl. 288r. Der Herzog sandte zur Illuminierung der *Evangelischen Kirchen-Harmonie* auch sein Bildnis. Er notierte auf einem Schreiben Andreaes vom 6.5.1646: „Den 2. Jun. haben wir dieses beantwortet, und das blätlein mit unserm gemahlten ritratto, mit gesandt." A. a. O., Bl. 282r. Am 3.6.1646 schrieb Andreae dem Herzog: „Mein eines Exemplar auch Illustris ist guten Nutzen darauß gebunden. Vnd wurt vnseren eruditis communiciert, Vnd in wahrheit hoch admiriert. Gemeine Leut aber die dergleichen Arbeit niemahlen gesehen, vnd die schöne information auch guten Nutzen darauß verspuren wunschen sie zu kauffen. Bin derowegen ersucht worden Nach Exemplarien zu fragen. Vnd den währt zuerkundigen. Darumben Jch vndertenigst gebetten haben will." A. a. O., Bl. 289r. Am 10.6.1646 heißt es dann in Andreaes Schreiben an den Herzog: „Das Octav exemplar ist nu mehr schön gebunden. vnd mit vergültenn silber beschlagen Ornamentum Bibliothecæ meæ præcipuum. vnd erwarte E. F. g. gnädiger Leutseliger jnscription auf ein Perquament blatlin. ich mit Vnd. verlangen. selbiger haben zu inserieren." A. a. O., Bl. 290r. Am 17.6.1646 konnte Andreae sich dann für die Eintragung und das Bild zugleich bedanken. A. a. O., Bl. 291r. Das endgültige Erscheinen der Erstauflage der Oktavausgabe hatte der Herzog ihm am 2.6.1646 gemeldet: „200 Exemplaria seynd vom 8. Trukke fertig, werden nuhn Apli. werden, und in die welt ausgehen: der Kupferdrukker hat sich in etwas versaumet: Nuhn wird Er weiter 100 Expl. austrukken: dan abermahl hundt., und also ferner bis die Lacunæ der Exemplaren impliret." HAB: Cod. Guelf. 236.3 Extrav., Bl. 24r.

4 Zusammenstellung der Quartausgabe der *Evangelischen Kirchen-Harmonie*. Vgl. 411214 S. 389f. In seinem Antwortbrief vom 24.3.1646 auf Andreas Schreiben vom 4. März schickte Hz. August seinem Geistlichen Rat und Mitarbeiter Andreae den Rest des ersten Teils und den vierten Bogen des zweiten Teils der Oktavausgabe (dessen Rest er in acht Tagen ergänzen wollte) und wiederholte seine Absicht, dann zur Quartausgabe zu schreiten. „Auch noch zu einem andern Druk kl. ohne Kupfer." HAB: Cod. Guelf. 236.3 Extrav., Bl. 13r. Dieser Duodezdruck, das *Hand-Büchlein aus der Evangelischen Kirchen-Harmonie*, erschien auch noch 1646. 411214 S. 357.

5 Johannes Faulhaber (1580–1635), Ulmer Astronom, Rechenmeister, Festungsingenieur, Kabbalist und Anhänger der Rosenkreuzer. Vgl. Johann Faulhabers Ulmensis Miracula Arithmetica. Zu der Continuatio seines Arithmetischen Wegweisers gehörig (Augspurg: Franck 1622); HAB: 5.1 Arith. (5). Dazu die Mitteilung Philipp Hainhofers an Hz. August, 21./31.3.1622, daß der Augsburger Arzt David Verbezius hierzu eine Vorrede geschrieben und das Werk Hz. August gewidmet habe. In einem undatierten Verzeichnis Hainhofers offerierte oder schickte Hainhofer dem Herzog einen von Faulhaber erfundenen Zirkel zum Zeichnen von Perspektiven. *Gobiet*, S. 356 bzw. 841. Vgl. Kurt Hawlitschek: Johann Faulhaber 1580–1635 und René Descartes 1596–1650. Ulm 2006; ders.: Johann Faulhaber 1580–1635. Eine Blütezeit der mathematischen Wissenschaften in Ulm. Ulm 1994; Ivo Schneider: Johannes Faulhaber (1580). Rechenmeister in einer Welt des Umbruchs. Basel 1993; Carlos Gilly: Adam Haslmayr. Der erste Verkünder der Manifeste der Rosenkreuzer. Amsterdam 1994, 139; *Brecht: Andreae Biographie*, 82. — Andreae antwortete auf die Bemerkung des Herzogs am 15.4.1646: „Warumber des Faulhabers gedacht werde, kan ich nicht errathen, Ob etwa der Furtenbach vnd deßen Reißladen damit gemeint welche nu mehr auf dem weg, stehet Vndt. zuerwarten." HAB: Cod. Guelf. 65.1 Extrav., Bl. 278r. Am 5.5.1646 korrigierte der Herzog seine Namensangabe:

„An stat Faulhabern, ist Furtenbach zu verstehen." HAB: Cod. Guelf. 236.3 Extrav., Bl. 20r. Vgl. Mechanische Reißladen/ Das ist/ Ein gar geschmeidige/ bey sich verborgen tragende Laden/ die aber solcher gestalt außgerüstet worden/ daß/ wofern in der eil nicht bessere/ oder grössere Jnstrumenten in Bereitschafft stünden/ dannoch alle fünffzehen Recreationen … der … Ingenieurkunst … können exercirt werden … Durch Iosephum Furttenbach (Augspurg 1644: Johann Schultes). HAB: 39.8 Geom. (2). S. Anm. 6.

6 Handelte es sich um ein Gemälde oder Kupferstich-Bildnis Pzn. Sibyllas v. Württemberg (1620–1707)? Joseph Furttenbach d. Ä. (1591–1667) malte auch gelegentlich und konnte als Architekt und Ingenieur sicher auch anderes als Gebäude und Maschinen zeichnen. *Thieme/ Becker* XII, 604–606. Oder hat sich der Herzog nicht doch getäuscht und aus Versehen Furttenbachs Namen mit dem Auftrag eines Porträts Sibyllas verknüpft? Hz. August d. J. v. Braunschweig-Wolfenbüttel wollte die Prinzessin mit seinem Verwandten, Graf Christian IX. v. Oldenburg-Delmenhorst (FG 375), vermählen. Das Projekt scheiterte wohl auch, weil Christian eine andere Dame im Sinne hatte. Andreae teilte dem Herzog auf einem undatierten Zettel bei dem Brief 450806 mit: „Es würt von etlichen orten alhero geschrieben. Ob solte C. C. O. [Comes Christianus Oldeburgensis] Delmenhorst. in einem Anderen F. [Fürstlichen? Fräuleins?] heurath stehen. vnd selbiger nu mehr seine Richtigkeit haben. quod autem nostram valde turbat." HAB: Cod. Guelf. 65.1 Extrav., Bl. 238r. Hz. August beabsichtigte jedoch, sie malen, zeichnen oder in Kupfer stechen zu lassen. Ein solches Werk können wir nicht nachweisen. Die Übersendung von Furttenbachs Mechanischem Reißladen, an die Andreae erinnerte, dürfte von dem Porträtauftrag zu unterscheiden sein. Für das Verständnis der wirren, um nicht zu sagen sibyllinischen Angaben des Herzogs über die 13. Sibylle liefert vielleicht dessen Brief an Andreae vom 12.5.1646 einen Hinweis: „sein Skreiben vom. Apr. 22. B habe ich wol erhalten und des FurtenBachs KupferStiche, unter meine Söhne ausgeteihlet". HAB: Cod. Guelf. 236.3 Extrav., Bl. 21r. Diese Kupferstiche könnten Furttenbachs Reißladen bezeichnen. — Sibylla widerstrebte der Verbindung mit ihrem Vetter Hz. Leopold Friedrich v. Württemberg-Mömpelgard, den sie am 22.11.1647 doch heiraten mußte. HAB: Cod. Guelf. 65.1 Extrav., Bl. 283r, 289r u. ö. Sie zeigte ihre Verbindung am 13.10.1646 auch Hz. August an (a. a. O., Bl. 310r). Andreae bezog sich auf die sibyllinische Anspielung Hz. Augusts und schrieb am 20.5.1656 an ihn: „Meine Vermutung gehet dahin. es werde sich Cumana ihres Cognatj de Monte-pelicardi schwerlich erwehren können." A. a. O., Bl. 283r. Sibylla wurde im Briefwechsel Andreaes und Herzog Augusts zusammen mit ihren Schwestern Antonia (TG 56) und Anna Johanna wiederholt als eine der drei Divae oder Grazien bezeichnet. Sibylla komponierte auch und sandte ihre dilettantische Arbeit an Hz. Augusts Gemahlin Sophia Elisabeth (AL 1629. TG 42b). A. a. O., Bl. 62r, 68r u. 76r. Andreae antwortete auf Hz. Augusts vorliegenden Brief am 22.4.1646 und bezweifelte die Wirkung des Bildnisses auf den Oldenburger: „Was das ritratto werde operieren. stehet in consilio Deorum, Vnß aber geduldig zuerwarten. Es ist aber Gott Lob bei dem archetypo ein mehrers vnd höhers vorhanden. Als sich Mahlen oder beschreiben Laßen. Welches der augenschein vnd Prob geben werde. bei deren ich mich wol getrawte (atque utinam) Persönlich finden zu Laßen." A. a. O., Bl. 279r. Am 7.7.1646 schrieb der Herzog an Andreae: „Cumana et Horstius utinam tandem conjungerent?" HAB: Cod. Guelf. 236.3 Extrav., Bl. 30. Damals beabsichtigte Hz. August, Sibylla nicht von Furttenbach, sondern von dem flämischen Zeichner und Maler Nikolaus van der Horst (1587/1598–1646) abbilden zu lassen. Kein Nachweis bei *Gobiet*, im Digitalen Portraitindex oder im Virtuellen Kupferstichkabinett der HAB und des Herzog Anton Ulrich Museums in Braunschweig.

7 *Biblia (Cramer 1634)*, Weish. Sal. 14, 17: „Desselbigen gleichen/ welche die Leute nicht kundten vnter Augen ehren/ darū das sie zuferne wohneten/ liessen sie aus fernen

Landen das Angesicht abmahlen/ vnd machten ein löblich Bilde des herrlichen Königes/ Auff daß sie mit fleiß heucheln möchten dem Abwesenden/ als dem Gegenwertigen."

8 Zu Greiffs geplanter Evangelienharmonie in Versen und ihrer Illustrierung s. Beil. I K. Der Tübinger Apotheker, Erfinder, Mediziner, Übersetzer und Dichter Friedrich Greiff (1691–1668) hatte Hz. August schon eine für die Rezeption der FG interessante Sammlung *Geistlicher Gedichte Vortrab* gewidmet. S. 431123. Dazu bemerkte Andreae in einem Schreiben an den Herzog am 28.8.1644: „Gryphius württ hocherfrewet werden. wann er vermerkhen solle daß E. f. g. seine arbeit zu g. angenommen. Jch vermeinet in Vnd. mit 10 oder meist 12 Rd. siue 1g8 f. würde er wol zu Contentieren sein. Vnd es fur eine hohe gnad halten [...]. Daß daß Calendarium mobile E. f. g. gebrauchsam. erfrewet mich sehr." HAB: Cod. Guelf. 65.1 Extrav., Bl. 181r.

9 Auf Hz. Augusts vorliegendes Schreiben vom 17.3.1646 konnte Andreae erst am 15.4.1646 antworten und Hz. August mitteilen: „Der Kreuter gesellschaft Buch habe vom H. Merian ich noch nicht empfangen. werde ihme destowegen hierumben zu zuschreiben haben." HAB: Cod. Guelf. 65.1, Bl. 278r. Am 12.5.1646 schrieb der Herzog: „Von der fruchtTragenden Geselschaft Buche, seynd meine Exemplaria, dafür ich das geldt vorlängstten voraus hergegeben, auch noch nicht angelanget." HAB: Cod. Guelf. 236.3 Extrav., Bl. 21r. Einen Tag später klagte Andreae: „Das Kreuter Geselschaft Buch will sich noch nicht sehen Laßen." HAB: Cod. Guelf. 65.1 Extrav., Bl. 281r. Andreae schrieb an den Fürsten jedoch am 10.6.1646: „Mit des Kreutergesellschaft Buch hat es kein eil. vnd wurt sich nochwol finden." A.a.O., Bl. 290r. Der Herzog meldete Andreae am 16.6.1646, er habe deswegen an Merian geschrieben. HAB: Cod. Guelf. 236.3 Extrav., Bl. 26r. Am 17.6.1646 schrieb er: „Die 400 Emblemata der Fruchtbringenden geselschaft hat Merian mir noch nicht zugeschaffet: Erachte Aber. daß Es der vnsicherheit der Straßen verursachet." A.a.O., Bl. 291r. Diesen Grund für das Ausbleiben des Werks nennt auch Andreaes Brief vom 24.6.1646. A.a.O., Bl. 292r. Noch am 26.5.1646 hatte auch Hz. August seinem Rat mitteilen müssen: „An Merian will ich erinnerung tuhn lassen, wegen des Buches der Fruchtbringenden Geselschafft; Ich habe selber noch kein einiges Exemplar, unangesehen ich etliche 100 Rth. zum verlage mit zugeschossen; Ob vielleicht die filii *[Martis]*, des *[Mercurii]* Arbeith zu rükke halten; dan einmahl daß buch ganz complet." HAB: Cod. Guelf. 236.3 Extrav., Bl. 23r. Die Soldaten des Mars mögen den Posttransport Merkurs aufhalten. Entschlossenheit verrät am 1.7.1646 Andreaes Brief an den Herzog: „Das Kreuterbuch ist noch nicht ankommen. habe also deßwegen eine Anmahnung an H. Merian Thon Laßen. Verhoffe dabej es werde an ihme nicht ermangeln Sondern er auf Sicherheit sehen. Es sein aber den hieländischen Kaufleuten etliche Schif mit wahren von FF. [Frankfurt a. M.] auß in arrest genommen worden. Der sie bißhero nicht Ledig können. Ob etwa dise Bucher auch darunter. stehet zu erwarten." HAB: Cod. Guelf. 65.1 Extrav., Bl. 294r. Zu den unangenehmen Folgen der Beschwerde Andreaes s. 460708. Hz. August hatte jedoch schon am 2.6.1646 die Ankunft des *GB 1646* in Wolfenbüttel gemeldet (vgl. 460620B), mit folgender Erklärung: „Die 400 Emblemata der Fruchtbringenden Geselschaft hoffe ich werden ihm geliefert sein: Merian hat uns die unsern gesandt, dafür ich zum Verlage ihm 200 Rth. zu hülffe übermachet." HAB: Cod. Guelf. 236.3 Extrav., Bl. 24r. Am 9.6.1646 heißt es in Augusts Brief: „Das Buch der Fruchtbringenden Geselschaft, wird Er nuhnmehr empfangen haben; Meine Exemplaria habe ich empfangen; woranne die beeden, ihm destienireten mangeln." A.a.O., Bl. 25r (Merian versuchte die beiden Exemplare in 460620B F. Ludwig in Rechnung zu stellen. S. Ludwigs Antwort 460708 u. K 1.) Andreae konnte den Erhalt des *GB 1646* dann doch am 15.7.1646 bestätigen. S. 460715 K 8. — Aus Merians Schreiben 460303 geht hervor, daß das *GB 1646* Mitte Februar 1646 samt aller Kupfer ausgedruckt war. Zugleich bat Merian F. Ludwigs Kam-

460317 Herzog August d. J. von Braunschweig-Wolfenbüttel

mermeister Peter Knaudt um Auskunft, wie er die 252 Exemplare dem Fürsten zustellen könne. An Hz. August habe er auf dessen Befehl bereits am 2.3.1646 die diesem zustehenden 48 Exemplare einem Kaufmann zum Transport anvertraut. Der Herzog mußte also rund drei Monate auf seine Exemplare warten, bis er zwei Exemplare aus diesem Kontingent an Andreae senden konnte. S. zum Transport des *GB 1646* auch 460620B. Zu fl. Verlagsbeiträgen s. 450126 K 4. Zum *GB 1646* allgem. s. 440130 K 3 u. zur Korrespondenz Merians betreffs Zahlungsverkehr in puncto *GB 1646* s. 450127 K 1.

10 Ks. Maximilian I., Bearb. Melchior Pfinzing: Die geuerlicheiten vnd eins teils der geschichten des lobliche streitbaren vnd hochherümbten helds vnd Ritters Tewrdannckhs (Augspurg: Schönsperger 1519). 4°, 289 Bl., 118 Illustrationen v. Hans Leonhard Schäufelein. Fürstl. Bibl. Corvey u. Lipp. Landesbibl. Detmold; nicht mehr in der HAB. Hz. August erwähnt sonst wohl noch eine Ausgabe in Klein-Folio und eine durch Burkhard Waldis erweiterte: 1. Thewerdanck Des Edlen/ Streitbaren Helden vnd Ritters/ Ehr vnd mannliche Thaten/ Geschichten vnd Gefehrlicheiten: Zu Ehren dem Hochlöblichen Hause zu Osterreich/ ... Mit schönen Figuren vnd lustigen Reimen auffs new zugericht. Getruckt zu Franckfurt am Meyn/ Bey Christian Egenolffs Erben. 1563. 2° (6), [4], CX Bl., Ill. HAB: 24 Bell. 2°. — 2. Gedenckwürdige Historia Deß Edlen vñ Streytbaren, und sieghafften Ritters Theurdancks mannliche Thaten, vnd außgestandene Gefährlichkeiten (Franckfurt am Mayn: Egenolff 1589), 8°, 197 Bll., Ill. Mitarb. Burcardus Wallis. HAB: 577 Hist. (1). — Am 25.2.1646 hatte Andreae dem Herzog mitgeteilt: „Jch habe eine edition des Teurdankhs Maximilianj 1. durch den Eltern Hansen Schönbergern, 1519. getrukht, bekommen, deroglechen wenig mehr zu sehen. vnd ich nur einen bei H. Forstenheusern zu Nurnb. auf Perquament, gefunden, So von einer herrlichen Schrift. wo nu E. f. g. ein solches Exemplar in dero Bibliotekh nicht hetten. oder dero H. Princen einem damit könte vnd. gedienet werde. stehet es zu vnd. diensten. vnd g. befehle." HAB: Cod. Guelf. 65.1 Extrav., Bl. 270r.

K I Die Datierung von der Hand Johann Valentin Andreaes (FG 464. 1646) „4. Apr. 46" (s. Q) verrät, daß Hz. August d. J. v. Braunschweig-Wolfenbüttel (FG 227) Justus Georg Schottelius' (FG 397) kleinen Brief an seinen Rat Andreae schickte. Das Schreiben kam nach Andreaes Tod durch dessen Sohn Gottlieb zusammen mit dem restlichen Briefwechsel zwischen dem Herzog und Andreae nach Wolfenbüttel zurück. In 460414 schrieb Schottelius dann selbst an Andreae. Er hatte schon in einem früheren Brief (440429) Kontakt zu dem Theologen aufzunehmen versucht. Andreae teilte dem Herzog am 22.4.1646 mit: „Herr D. Schottelius (cujus ingenium valde æstimo) hab ein hupsch Maisterstuhlein von einem Letterwechsel angehenkht. Die Teutsche sprache wurt anfangen den andern nichzit bevor zu geben. Jch kan aber zu dem Kreuter geselschaft buch. so ich von Frankhfurt zu gewarten. Noch nicht kommen welches zu sehen mich sehr verlanget." HAB: Cod. Guelf. 65.1 Extrav, Bl. 279r. — In dem genannten Schreiben hält Schottelius die in ihrem Rhythmus und Maß durchaus fest gegründeten deutschen Verse Friedrich Greiffs bei näherer Untersuchung nur für den Ausdruck eines mittelmäßigen Geistes, der sich kaum über das Gewöhnliche erhebe. Schottelius hofft, Hz. August habe das Buch des berühmten (Johann Michael) Dilherr bekommen, das er ihm neulich zugestellt habe. Dilherr habe auf Seite 289 das welfische Passionsbuch (des Herzogs) nachgeahmt, wenn auch nicht in Gehorsam vor dem Herzog und dessen Lehre. Dilherr habe in Nürnberg und an den Schulen Deutschlands einen großen Ruf und sei auch wegen seiner Kenntnis der orientalischen Sprachen und ob seiner Beredsamkeit berühmt. — Zu Schottelius' Anregung, Dilherr Hz. Augusts *Evangelische Kirchen-Harmonie* zu schicken, s. 460700.

1 Andreae schrieb am 8.4.1646 an den Herzog: „Herrn Schottelij ingenuo et accurato

judicio de Gryphianis rithmis, gebe ich gar gern beifall. Dan sie e nicht ultra mediocritatem sein, Vnd Thon E. F. g. sehr wol. daß sie solche muscas abigieren. Der E. f. g. zu importunieren, mich Vnaufhorlich anlaufen. Vnd gleichwolen nur ihren. Jch aber mich ihrer mit fugen nicht erwehren kan." HAB: Cod. Guelf. 65.1 Extrav., Bl. 277r. Von einer neuen Versdichtung Greiffs über die Evangelien hatte Andreae Hz. August am 14.1.1645 Mitteilung gemacht: „Es will vnser Jo. Frid. Greif sich vnderstehen die Euangelien nach E. F. g. Harmonj in Alexandrinische Vers. summarisch zu bringen. Vnd solle nach meinem wenigen Rhat an dem Paßion den Anfang machen. Wie sie nu gerathen werden. Werden E f. g. gnedig zu ersehen vnd judicieren haben." A.a.O., Bl. 264r. Am 25.2.1646 konnte Andreae dann dem Herzog eine Probe aus dem noch ungedruckten Hauptwerk Greiffs, *Der vier Evangelisten ubereinstimmende Geschicht Beschreibung Christi* (1647) (s. 431123 K 2), überschicken: „Hiebei ein Muster, des vorhabens Jo. [sic] Friderich Greifen. Der vermeinet die Harmoniam Vitæ Christi in Alexandrinische Vers zu bringen, vnd hierinnen Nach E. F. G. sich zu regulieren. Ob etwa die figuren nicht dabej getrukhen sein. Wie etwa bej des Merians Biblischen Historien absonderlich geschehen. Wiewol ich besorge es werden sich die Kupfer in den beeden 8 vnd 4 editionen Harmoniæ Euangelicæ also abtrukhen. Daß Jhnen Nit vil mehr daruber zuzumuthen." A.a.O., Bl. 270r. — Die abschätzige Beurteilung der Dichtung Greiffs war wohl auch von dessen mangelnder Bereitschaft beeinflußt, Kupferplatten zur Illustrierung seines Hauptwerks *Der vier Evangelisten ubereinstimmende Geschicht Beschreibung Christi* (1647) an den Herzog abzutreten. S. 460804 K 1. Das Werk erhielt zwar Kupfertitel, aber keine fortlaufenden Illustrationen zum Text. Solche finden sich jedoch in: Sieben Geistliche Andachten | vber die Hoh- | Fest als | Auff die Seeligmachende Geburth vnsers Heylandes Jesus Christus/ | Die Einsatzung deß Heyligen Hochwürdigen | Abendmahls/ | Das Bitter Leyden vnd Sterben/ | Die Siegreiche Aufferstehung/ | Die Triumphiere[n]de Himmelfahrt Christus/ | Die Sendung deß Heyligen Geistes/ | Vnd auff die Hochheylige Dreyeinigkeit. | Jn lange Alexandrinische Verß gesetzt | Neben etlichen Geistlichen Liedern auff eben solche Fest/ vnd jedes insonderheit gerichtet. | Auffgesetzet vnnd verfertiget | Durch | Friderich Greiffen/ | Tübingen/ | Bey Philibert Brunnen. | [Linie] | Jm Jahr 1647. 4°; HAB: 501.7 Theol. (2) und Th 1056. Mit sieben Illustrationen, also zu jeder Andacht eine.

2 Johann Michael Dilherrns/ Hertzens-Gespräch/ oder Betrachtungen/ vnd Seufftzer eines Christenmenschens. Nürnberg/ Jn Verlegung Wolffgang Endters. M.DC.X.V. HAB: Th 554. 12°, [13] Bl., 555 S., [4] Bl. Gemäß dem „Bericht an den Christlichen Leser" wurde das Buch schon vor acht Jahren aus einem lat. Werk des Johann-Gerhard-Schülers Dilherr mit Wissen Dilherrs übersetzt von Johann Matthaeus Meyfart (1590–1642). Dieser habe „dabey nicht sowol einen Dolmetscher/ als Erklärer gegeben. Dannenhero es offt im Teutschen fast anderst/ als im Lateinischen/ zu lauten scheinet." Da Meyfart starb, sei etwas von seiner Verdeutschung verlorengegangen, so daß ein zweiter Übersetzer zur Feder greifen mußte. Vgl. [Kupfertitel] CONTEMPLATIONES Et suspiria hominis Christiani Io Mich. Dilherri P.P.Imp. Johan Reifenbergeri JEN MDCXXXIII. HAB: 1302.14 Theol. (1). — Vgl. den vermutlich 1646 geschriebenen Schottelius-Brief über Dilherr: 460700.

3 In dem Erbauungsbuch Dilherrs handelt die 29. andächtige Betrachtung davon, „Wie der Mensch denen Dingen/ welche jhm das Wort Gottes nicht geoffenbaret/ nicht nachforschen soll." (S. 286 ff.). *Contemplationes* 1634, 215ff.: „De vitanda in rebus nobis non revelatis scrupolositate." In *Hertzens-Gespräch* heißt es S. 288 f.: „Wann wir nach der Haubtquellen vnd dem Vrsprung der Göttlichen Geheimnisse vns wenden/ so entfernen wir vns von dem Menschlichen Jrrthumb: vnd wenn wir die Beschaffenheit der himlischen Sacrament recht beschawen/ erhellet alles/ vermittelst dem Liecht der Warheit/ wz etwa vnter den düsteren Wolcken tunckeler Weise verborgen gewesen. [...; S. 289:] Dieses müs-

460321 Pfalzgraf Ludwig Philipp von Simmern

sen wir auch thun/ vnd solcher Massen Gottes Gebot halten: auch wenn es bey einem oder dem andern Stuck scheinet/ ob die Warheit wancke vnd aussenbleibe/ so bald zu dem Anfang vnd Vrsprung der Göttlichen/ Apostolischen vnd Evangelischen Schrifften vmbkehren/ vnd daselbst wider suchen/ wo all vnser Verständniß herquillet vnd fliesset. Etliche erdichte scheinbarliche Dinge betriegen mit jhrer Scharffsinnigkeit die Warheit. Das geschicht/ weil solche Heuchler nicht nach dem Vrsprung der Warheit gehen/ den Anfang der Weißheit nit suchen/ vnd die himmlische Lehre nit anhören: welche/ wenn sie betrach-[S. 290]tet vnd probiret wird/ nicht viel Beweiß oder Behandlung von nöthen hat. Der Grund des Glaubens ist leicht zu fassen/ vermittelst der Warheit." Die Übersetzung der *Contemplationes* weicht oft vom lateinischen Wortlaut, nicht jedoch vom Grundsinn Dilherrs ab. Vgl. die von Schottelius wohl besonders angegriffene Stelle (S. 216 ff.): „Non ideò falsum quid est, quòd ego non capiam aut intelligam: non est ratio rerum mensura, sed ad res illa sese tenetur applicare. Angusta est ratio, & rerum Cœlestium immensitatem si capere non potest, cur miraris? [...; S. 217] Hoc & nunc nos facere oportet, præcepta divina servantes: ut in aliquo si nutaverit & vacillaverit veritas, ad originem Dominicam & Evangelicam, & Apostolicam traditionem revertamur, & inde surgat actus nostri ratio, unde & ordo & origo surrexit. [S. 218] Dum alii verisimilia mentiuntur; veritatem subtilitate frustrantur. Quod eò sit: quia ad veritatis originem non reditur, nec caput quæritur, nec magistri cœlestis doctrina servatur." Vgl. Erich Trunz: Johann Matthäus Meyfart. Theologe und Schriftsteller in der Zeit des Dreißigjährigen Krieges. München 1987, 269–271.

4 Johann Michael Dilherr war in Jena Professor der Redekunst, auch der Poesie und Geschichte gewesen. Ein besonders umfängliches Werk der biblischen Philologie war: ECLOGÆ SACRÆ Novi Testamenti, SYRIACÆ, GRÆCÆ, LATINÆ. Cum notis & observationibus ita explicatæ, ut, præter rerum non inutilem cognitionem, adhihitis GRAMMATICÆ RUDIMENTIS, antehac excusis, Attentus Lector lingvam Syriacam proprio Marte possit addiscere. Adduntur indices locupletissimi, Et Manuale Lexici Syriaci Operâ JOHAN: MICH: DILHERRI Fr. JENÆ, Apud JOH. REIFFENBERGERUM Bibliop. Litteris BLASII LOBENSTEINII. Anno M. DC XXXIIX. 12°, [18] Bl., 623 [recte 624] S., [66], [16] Bl., 256 S. VD 17 39:144171Y.

460321

Pfalzgraf Ludwig Philipp von Simmern an Fürst Ludwig

Beantwortet durch 460424A. — Pgf. Ludwig Philipp v. Simmern (FG 97) erinnert F. Ludwig daran, unter Vermittlung von F. Johann Casimir v. Anhalt-Dessau (FG 10) um die Erlaubnis zur Aufnahme weiterer Mitglieder in die FG gebeten zu haben, da er aufgrund des Kriegsverlaufs nicht persönlich darum ansuchen konnte.

Q HM Köthen: V S 544, Bl. 70rv [A: 70v]; eigenh.; Sig. — *D: KE*, 52f. — *BN: Bürger*, 956 Nr. 2.

A A Monsieur mon cousin Monsieur Le Prince Louys danhalt *[sic]*.
Eigenh. Empfangsvermerk F. Ludwigs: 22. April 1646.

Hochgeborner Furst freundtlicher vielgeliebter herr vetter[.]
Jch habe die freyheit genohmen JL furst **casemir**[1] zu schreyben wegen der frucht-

bringende [sic] geselschaft[.] hoffe EL werden nicht vbel nehmen daß ich EL da mitt bemuhe [.] habe alß gehoft die ehr zu haben EL zu sehen vndt selber vhm erlaubtnuß ahnzuhaltten[,] weil ich aber furchte, die kriegslauften² mochte mich drahn verhindern alß habe ich JL furst casemir Die nahmen geschrieben vndt dero begehrenª nach wie sie gesinnet berichtet[.]³ werde EL befehl erwarten[.] thue EL hiemitt sambt den Lieben ihrichen in Gottes schutz entpfelen vndt verbleyb
　　EL
　　　Dienstwilliger Geborner Vetter vndt diener
　　　　Ludwig PhilipPfaltzgrave

den 21/31 martij

T a *Gebessert aus unleserlichem Wort.*

K Nachdem Pgf. Ludwig Philipp v. Simmern (FG 97) F. Johann Casimir v. Anhalt-Dessau (FG 10) um Vermittlung seines Anliegens, etliche Personen in die FG aufnehmen zu dürfen, gebeten hatte (vgl. den Extrakt 460104), wandte er sich nun direkt an F. Ludwig. Möglicherweise war eine Reaktion auf sein erstes Gesuch zu lange unbeantwortet geblieben. S. dazu 460424A. Am Ende wurden 14 Neumitglieder aufgenommen, s. 460104 K 1.
　1 F. Johann Casimir v. Anhalt-Dessau (FG 10).
　2 Seit dem Winter 1645/46 war das hauptsächliche Kriegsgeschehen aus den ksl. Erblanden wieder stärker in die Mitte des Reiches gerückt. Die schwed. Hauptarmee war unter der Leitung des neuen Oberkommandierenden, Generalfeldzeugmeister (Greve) Carl Gustav Wrangel (af Salmis) (FG 523. 1649), aus Böhmen kommend ins thüring.-sächs. Gebiet einmarschiert. Dort sollte sie u. a. für den notwendigen militär. Druck auf Kf. Johann Georg I. v. Sachsen sorgen, um eine Verlängerung des schwed.-kursächs. Waffenstillstandes zu erreichen, die tatsächlich im Vertrag von Eilenburg (31. März 1646 a. St.) vereinbart wurde. Der schwed. Hauptarmee war ein ksl.-kurbayr. Heer gefolgt, welches in Franken Stellung bezog, um deren Vordringen nach Oberdeutschland zu verhindern. *Chemnitz* IV.6, 71–74; *Pufendorf: Kriegs-Geschichte* II, 205f. u. 208. Zugleich operierten in der linksrhein. Gegend franz. Truppen. *Chemnitz* IV.6, 88f. u. 177f. Dies beeinträchtigte auch die Kommunikationslinien zwischen der (Unter-)Pfalz und Anhalt.
　3 Hinsichtlich der ursprünglich zur Aufnahme vorgeschlagenen 13 Personen s. 460423 u. 460424A. Vgl. dazu die Liste der tatsächlich aufgenommenen in 461031A I. Vgl. zu diesem Aufnahmevorgang insges. 460104 K 1.

460324

Matthäus Merian d. Ä. an Peter Knaudt

Matthäus Merian d. Ä. berichtet Peter Knaudt, daß ihm bisher die Gelegenheit fehlte, die 12 gewünschten Exemplare (des *GB 1646*) zu überschicken, jedoch werde er sie zur Ostermesse mit der nächsten Fuhre nach Leipzig senden, die in der Woche nach Ostern von Frankfurt a. M. abfahren werde. Wohin solle Merian die übrigen Exemplare schicken? Er habe danach schon in seinem letzten Schreiben gefragt. Allerdings habe er vor drei

460324 Matthäus Merian d. Ä.

Wochen an Hz. August d.J. v. Braunschweig-Wolfenbüttel (FG 227) schon 48 Exemplare versandt, welche zweifellos inzwischen den Empfänger erreicht haben sollen. — Weiterhin bittet Merian darum, die ausstehenden 300 Reichstaler an Georg Winckler zu überweisen, der diesmal gute Gelegenheit habe, sie (an Merian) weiterzusenden. Für diesen Freundschaftsdienst wäre Merian Knaudt sehr verbunden, und er werde ihm dies auf anderem Wege wieder vergelten. — Mit den genannten 12 Exemplaren sollen auch die bewußten fünf Exemplare (des *GB 1646* für Knaudt) sowie die (sechs) Bände von Merians *Topographia*, die zusammen 19 Gulden kosten, übersandt werden. Darauf könne sich Knaudt verlassen. Merian erwartet bald eine Antwort.

Q HM Köthen: V S 546, Bl. 38rv [A: 38v]; eigenh.; rotes Lacksiegel. — D: Bircher: *Merian*, 715; Wüthrich: *Merian Briefe*, 108f. — BN: *Bürger*, 987 Nr. 17.

A Tt. Dem Ehrenvesten und GroßAchtparen Herrn Peter Knaudt Fürst. Anhaltischen Cammer Meistern *etc.* meinen gg. Hochgeehrten Herrn *etc.* Cöthen

Ehrenvester und Großachtparer Jnsonders Großg. hochgeehrter Herr *etc.*
Berichte demselben, auff sein Jüngstes, das Jch noch keine gelegenheit gehabt, die begerten 12 **exemplar** zu ubersen*den*, wirt aber dise meß mit der nechsten fuhr geschehen, welche die wochen nach ostern von hir abfahren wirt,[1] aber Jch habe vor 3 wochen an Jhr. Fürstl. G. herrn herztog*en* **Augusto** zu Braunschweig *etc.* die 48 **exemplar** versandt, welche ohn Zweifel nun lang zurecht komen sein werd*en*, und erwarte nur, was ich mit den ubrigen thun soll, und wohin solche zu adresiren, bescheids: Wie ihn[a] meinem Jüngsten vermeldet habe *etc.*[2]
Gelangt dem nach mein dienstliche bitte, die ubrigen Restirenden Rthl. 300[3] herrn Wincklern[4] zu erlegen, welcher dißmalen gutte gelegenheit hat mir solche zu ubermachen, und geshciht mir hieran ein sonderliche freündschafft, so ich[b] ander weg wider verschulden will. Die bewußten 5 **exemplaria** sollen auch mit den obgedachten 12 neben den **Toppographien** (welche zusammen f. 19 betragen) ubersenden, worauff mein gg. herr sich zu verlassen, und erwarte ehestes wider antwort, dem Allmächtig*en* hiemit zu gnaden wohl befohlen.[5]
Ffurt den 24. Mertz 1646.
 Meines gg. herrn
 Dienstwilligster
 Mattheus Merian*mp*

T a *Lies:* sich — b *Folgt überflüssige Wiederholung* ich

K 1 Die Woche nach dem 29.3.1646. Vgl. 460303 K 3. Zu den von F. Ludwig gewünschten 12 Exemplaren als der ersten Lieferung der ihm zustehenden Exemplare des *GB 1646* s. 460206 I u. II und 460519.
  2 Vgl. 460303. Die Frage nach F. Ludwigs Anweisungen zur Lieferung des *GB 1646* hatte Merian schon in 460206 gestellt. Die Sendung von 48 Exemplaren des *GB 1646* an Hz. August d.J. v. Braunschweig-Wolfenbüttel (FG 227) wurde in 460206 I u. II, 460303, 460519, 460620B u. 460703 zur Sprache gebracht. Zu fl. Verlagsbeiträgen s. Anm. 3 u. 450126 K 4. Zum *GB 1646* allgem. 440130 K 3.

3 S. Anm. 2, auch 460303 u. 460519. Matthäus Merian d. Ä. bezieht sich wohl auf die beiden fl. Beiträger, Hz. August u. Hz. Christian Ludwig von Braunschweig-Calenberg (FG 372), die gemeinsam 300 Reichstaler, 200 Hz. August, 100 Hz. Christian Ludwig, zum *GB 1646* beitragen. In 460519 kann Merian den Eingang von 300 Rtln. bestätigen: „und ist diß malen nun alles Richtig, und bezalt."

4 Der Leipziger Handelsherr Georg Winckler. S. 451019 K 0. Über den Zahlungsverkehr zum *GB 1646* s. 450127 K 1.

5 Neben den 48 Exemplaren an F. Ludwig finden in 460303 auch die fünf Knaudt zugedachten Exemplare des *GB 1646* Erwähnung, sowie fünf Bände von Merians *Topographia*. Deren Preis erhöht sich durch einen weiteren, inzwischen gedruckten Band (Hassiæ) um 3½ auf 19 Gulden. Vgl. 460303 K 6. Merian verzichtete jedoch auf die Bezahlung. S. 460519. Vgl. auch die Auflistung in 450905 K 4. Zu den fünf Exemplaren des *GB 1646* für Knaudt vgl. auch *DA Köthen I. 8*: 470223.

460403

Herzog Christian Ludwig von Braunschweig-Calenberg an Fürst Ludwig

Antwort auf 460309. — Hz. Christian Ludwig v. Braunschweig-Calenberg (FG 372) bestätigt den Eingang des Briefes vom 9. März und teilt mit, daß in der Zahlwoche der bevorstehenden Leipziger Ostermesse die zugesagten 100 Taler an den von F. Ludwig benannten Kaufmann Georg Winckler anstandslos beglichen und bezahlt werden sollen.

Q   HM Köthen: V S 544, Bl. 71rv, v leer; Schreiberh.

A   *Fehlt.*

Unser freundtlich Dienst undt was wir vielmehr liebes undt gutes vermögen zuvor,
Hochgeborner Furst, freundtlicher lieber Oheimb,
   Ew. Ld. freundt Ohmbliches andtwordtschreiben vom 9ten dieses ist Vns zurecht eingelieffert worden, laßen deroselben daruff freundtlich Vnverhalten sein, das wir albereits die Verordnung gemacht, das beuorstehende Ostermeße in der Zahlwochen, die von Vns Versprochene Hundert thaler[1] an den von Ew. Ld. benandten Kauffman Georg Wincklern[2] gewiß vnndt ohne einigen mangell erlegt vnd bezahlet werden sollen, laßen Ew. Ld. sich freundtohmlich zuversichern, dero wir freundtliche Dienste zuerweisen allezeit gantz willig undt geflißen verpleiben,
   Geben in Vnser *ResidentzStadt* Hannouer den 3ten *Aprilis Anno* 1646.
   Von Gottes gnaden Christian Ludowig Hertzog zu Braunschweig vndt Lüneburgk
   Eᵃ Ld dienstwilliger Vetter
   Christian Ludwig *mp*

T a *Grußformel u. Unterschrift von Hz. Christian Ludwigs H.*

460406 Georg Philipp Harsdörffer

K 1 Die Leipziger Ostermesse begann traditionell am Sonntag Jubilate, d. h. 3. Sonntag nach Ostern, der im Jahr 1646 auf den 19. April fiel. *Grotefend*, 158. Die Messe dauerte in der Regel zwei Wochen, wobei die zweite Woche die sog. Zahlwoche war, in der die Rechnungen für die abgeschlossenen Verträge beglichen werden mußten. Diese endete am Sonntag Rogate (5. Sonntag nach Ostern), d. h. am 3. Mai 1646. Der Beitrag Hz. Christian Ludwigs v. Braunschweig-Wolfenbüttel (FG 372) von 100 Reichstalern zum *GB 1646* sollte demnach bis spätestens 3. Mai an den Leipziger Georg Winckler (s. Anm. 2) übermittelt werden. Ob bzw. wann dies genau geschah, ist unbekannt, jedoch dokumentiert erst *DA Köthen I. 8:* 470223 die erfolgte Zahlung. Zum *GB 1646* s. 440130 K 3. Zu den fl. Verlagsbeiträgen s. 450126 K 4.

2 Georg Winckler (1582–1654), Bürger und Handelsmann in Leipzig und wichtiger Vermittler in Leipzig in Sachen „Finanzmanagement" des *GB 1646*. S. zu ihm 451019 K 0. Zum Zahlungsverkehr das *GB 1646* anlangend s. 450127 K 1.

460406

Georg Philipp Harsdörffer an Fürst Ludwig

Antwort auf 460120. Beantwortet durch 460426 u. 460609. — Georg Philipp Harsdörffer (FG 368. Der Spielende) übersendet F. Ludwig (Der Nährende) sein *Specimen Philologiae Germanicae* (1646), das deswegen auf Latein geschrieben sei, weil die darin angesprochenen strittigen Punkte auch andere Sprachen betreffen und von den Gelehrten diskutiert werden müssen. Anlaß für das Buch war F. Ludwigs Aufforderung bei der Übersendung der *Deutschen Rechtschreibung* (1645) von Christian Gueintz (FG 361. Der Ordnende), daß Sprecher aus anderen Sprachlandschaften (als der „meißnischen") Sprachregulative nach ihrer jeweiligen eigenen Mundart aufsetzen sollten. Wenn die Gelehrten erst einmal ihre Auffassungen auf der Basis gesicherter Grundsätze vereinheitlicht haben, was durchaus leicht geschehen könnte, werde die übrige Sprachgemeinschaft ihnen bald folgen. Es bedarf verständiger Überlegungen vieler Gelehrter, wie diese Verständigung genau zu bewerkstelligen sei, doch wäre allein F. Ludwig ein geeigneter Richter. Ihm legt Harsdörffer auch sein *Specimen* zur gefälligen Beurteilung vor. Die zwei weiteren Exemplare des Buchs könnten anderen Sprachinteressierten, wie Diederich v. dem Werder (FG 31. Der Vielgekörnte) oder Christian Gueintz (FG 361. Der Ordnende) zugeleitet werden, um deren Urteil besonders zu den Kapiteln 7 und 10 Harsdörffer bittet. Er plane jährlich einen weiteren Teil dieses Werkes herauszubringen, wodurch er Schottelius' Lehren gegen alle Gegner zu stützen hoffe. — Der sechste Teil der *Frauenzimmer-Gesprächspiele* (1646) befindet sich im Druck und wird auch jährlich fortgeführt. — Johann Michael Moscheroschs (FG 436) *Gesichte Philanders von Sittewald* sollen in Straßburg noch einmal zusammen gedruckt und dann ebenfalls überschickt werden. Dessen Wappen lege Harsdörffer dem Schreiben bei. Sobald Moscherosch das erwartete Impresengemälde für seinen Gesellschaftspfennig erhalte, werde er 10 Rth. entrichten. An die FG wolle Moscherosch erst nach dem Druck der von der FG begehrten Schriften schreiben.

Q HM Köthen: V S 545, Bl. 345r–346v [A: 346v], 346r leer; eigenh.; zwei rote Lacksiegel mit teilw. erhaltenen Bändchen. — D: *KE*, 354f. — BN: *Bürger*, 674 Nr. 38.

A *Dem Durchleuchtigen, Hochgebornen Fürsten, und Herrn Herrn LUDWIGEN Fürsten zu Anhalt, Grafen zu Ascanien und Ballensta[t]t, Herrn zu Zerbst etc.*[a] Meinem Gn[ä]digen Fürsten und Herrn.　　Cöthen.　　Zu Leiptzig bey H. Gottfried Stahlen[1] abzugeben.[b]

Eigenh. Empfangsvermerk F. Ludwigs: 26. April. 1646.

Höchstgeehrter Nerender.

Mitkommendes[c] Werklein,[2] die Teutsche Sprache betreffend, hat der Spielende deswegen Lateinisch verabfasset, weil die darinnen angerechte Strittigkeiten in andere Haubtsprachen einlauffen, und nothwendig von den Gelehrten verglichen werden müssen. Zu solches fertigung ist er unterm andern veranlasst worden, durch des höchstgeehrten *Nerenden* Erinnerung, welcher bey übersendung des *Ordnenden* rechtschreibung vermeldet; es mögen andere ihre meinung, nach ihrer Mundart, auch zu papier setzen *etc.*[3] Wann sich die Gelehrten in der Schreibrichtigkeit, nach denen allgemeinen durchgehenden Sprachgründen vergleichen solten, wie leichtlich geschehen könte, würden gewisslich alle andere[d] nachfolgen, und nicht ein geringes geleistet werden: Welcher gestalt aber solches auszuwürken stehet bey mehr verständigen nachdenken aller Gelehrter, und unsrer Sprache Liebhaber bedenken hierüber einzuholen, und die vorfallende Zweiffel auf zu heben, geziemet niemand, als dem höchstlöblichen Stiffter der[e] Fruchtbringenden Gesellschaft, welches beurtheilung der Spielende dieses sein werklein, mit schuldigster Ehrerbietung untergiebet: nechst dienstlichen ersuchen, beede beykommende Stücke andern dieser sachen Erfahrnen als[f] etwan dem Vielgekörnten, und Ordnenden mitzutheilen, und derselben vernünftige Gedanken, absonderlich aber über das [345v] VII und X capitel zu erkundigen,[4] und dem Spielenden nachrichtlich zu eröffnen: massen er gewillet dieses werklein [auf][g] gut befinden, fortzusetzen, und jährlich, benebenß einem th[eil][g] der Gesprächspiele, von[h] welchen der[i] VI Theil der presse untergeben ist,[5] an das liecht zu bringen: damit alles so wider des Suchenden[j] lehrsätze aufgebracht werden solte, verhoffentlich mit Grund abgeleinet[6], und die Sache zu endlicher gewiss[heit][g] gebracht werden möchte.[7]

Des *Traumenden* Gesichte werden zu Strasburg zusammen, gedruckt, und sollen mit nechsten folgen:[8] er erwartet inzwischen das Gemähl zu seinen Gesellschafspfenning [sic], nach welches emp[fang][g] er die 10 Reichsthl. zu übermachen nicht unterlassen wird;[9] sendet hierbey sein Wappen[10], und wolte sich nicht gerne ohne seine [be]gehrete[g] Schriften, bey der hochlöb. Fruchtbringenden Gesellschaft mit[k] Zuschreiben, einfinden.

Hiermit verbleibet, nechst empfehlung des höchsten Gnadenschutz

Des höchstgeehrten Nehrenden dienstverbundener Knecht
Der *Spielende*

Nürnberg den 6 April. 1646.

T a *Vgl. 450400 T a.* — **b** *Einige Buchstaben durch Bandreste verdeckt, Konjekturen in eckigen Klammern.* — **c** *Folgt* ‹lateinisches› — **d** *Folgt* ‹leichtlich› — **e** *Folgt* ‹F› — **f**

460406 Georg Philipp Harsdörffer

Bis und *Ordnen*den *am Rand ergänzt.* — **g** *Textverlust im Falz. Konjektur in eckigen Klammern.* — **h** *von welchen eingefügt.* — **i** *Gebessert aus* der<er> *oder* der<en> — **j** *Folgt* <mein> — **k** *mit Zuschreiben, am Rand ergänzt.*

K 1 Der Leipziger Kaufmann Gottfried Stahl, über den der Briefverkehr zwischen F. Ludwig (Der Nährende) und Georg Philipp Harsdörffer (FG 368. Der Spielende) abgewickelt wurde. Vgl. 440426 K 1.

2 Harsdörffer schickt sein (in 450923C angekündigtes) *Specimen Philologiae Germanicae* (1646) an F. Ludwig. S. dazu 451217 (K 10). Sigmund Betulius (v. Birken; FG 681. 1658. Vgl. 460112 K 3) hatte wohl schon am 4.4.1646 ein Exemplar in seinem Besitz. Unter diesem Datum schrieb Harsdörffer nämlich an ihn und nahm dabei an, Betulius habe seine Meinung über das Sammeln von Stammwörtern bereits gelesen: „De radicum collectione sententiam meam in Specimine Philologico dubio procul legisti." *Birken: Werke u. Korrespondenz* IX.1, 9; vgl. 460410. Die drei Exemplare, von denen im Brief die Rede ist, können neben dem *Specimen* noch nicht Harsdörffers Lobschrift auf Hz. August d.J. v. Braunschweig-Wolfenbüttel (FG 227), die *Porticus Virtutis* (1646), enthalten haben, die dem *Specimen* noch beigedruckt wurde. S. dazu 460912. Vgl. 450927 und 451217. Wie aus 460426 hervorgeht, dürfte das mit dem vorliegenden Brief geschickte Paket Harsdörffers auch seine Übersetzung CATECHISME ROYAL. *Der Königliche Catechismus* (1645, recte 1646) enthalten haben. Der Nürnberger hatte sie schon in einem Teildruck F. Ludwig gesendet (s. 451217 K 9). An Betulius schickte er die Übersetzung schon am 7.2.1646 (s. 460112 K 3).

3 Mit 450919A ließ F. Ludwig Harsdörffer die *Deutsche Rechtschreibung* (1645) von Christian Gueintz (FG 361. Der Ordnende; s. 440127 K 1) zukommen. In diesem Zusammenhang bemerkte er, daß sich Gueintz nach der omd. (,meißnischen') Mundart gerichtet habe, und konzedierte: „Wollen nur andere ihre Mundarten auch durch ordentlich verfassung an den tag geben, stehet es zu ihrem gefallen". Vgl. dazu 450919A K 13.

4 Die „Disquisitio VII" des *Specimen* beschäftigt sich mit den strukturellen Entsprechungen und verwandtschaftlichen Beziehungen des Deutschen und des Hebräischen, „Disquisitio X" mit der deutschen Rechtschreibung und der Frage ihrer Normierung. Eine Inhaltsübersicht zum *Specimen* bietet *Banneck*, 33–36. — In dem in Anm. 2 zitierten Brief Harsdörffers an Birken (Betulius) vom 4.4.1646 eröffnete Harsdörffer seinen Plan, Stammwörter für ein geplantes umfassendes Wörterbuch des Deutschen nach dem Alphabet und unter Zuhilfenahme von Lexika wie *Henisch* zu sammeln. *Birken: Werke u. Korrespondenz* IX, 9f. Vgl. auch z.B. 450410 K 3 u. 4 u. 451219 K 7 u. 8. Zu dem hart von Fruchtbringern wie F. Ludwig, Christian Gueintz, Justus Georg Schottelius und dem späteren Mitglied Philipp v. Zesen (FG 521. 1648) umkämpften Streitpunkt der Anzahl von Silben in Stammwörtern schrieb Harsdörffer an Birken: „Radices sunt vel monosyllabicae, vel dissyllabicae, sive origine peregrinae, sive purè germanicae sint, nihil interest." A.a.O., 10. Birken möge Carl Gustav v. Hille (FG 302) bei dessen Rückkehr nach Wolfenbüttel ein für das Buch über die FG (*Hille: Teutscher Palmbaum*, 1647, 34*–45*, 49*f, 73*) bestimmtes „carmen" Harsdörffers überreichen. Harsdörffer (PBO Strephon) zeigte sich außerdem angetan durch den von Betulius (PBO Floridan) ausgeheckten oder doch übermittelten Vorschlag, den (poetisch talentierten, 1633 geborenen) Prinzen Anton Ulrich v. Braunschweig-Wolfenbüttel (FG 716. Der Siegprangende. 1659) zum Präses des jungen PBO zu machen und in Wolfenbüttel eine Kolonie dieser Schäferakademie zu etablieren: „Sein Fürstlich Braunschweigischer Schäferstab wird gewißlich von einem Fruchtbringenden Holze seyn". Strephon machte gleich Vorschläge für Schäfernamen und Gewächse des Prinzen, erwog die Zuschreibung des 7. Teils seiner *Frauenzimmer-Gesprächspiele* an

ihn und meldete die Aufnahme des für sein europäisches Akademieprojekt wichtigen Johann Georg Volckamer in den Schäferorden (s. 450817). Zu diesem Vorhaben und zur Struktur europäischer Akademien im allgemeinen (unter Einschluß der FG und des PBO) s. jetzt *Conermann: Harsdörffers Plan.*

5 Der 6. Teil der *Frauenzimmer-Gesprächspiele* erscheint im Frühherbst 1646. Mit 460915 schickt Harsdörffer einen fertigen Druck an Gueintz.

6 Zu mhd. „leinen", lehnen, auch in der Bedeutung ablehnen, widerlegen, zurückweisen, verwerfen, konnte aber auch gütlich beilegen, schlichten meinen. *Lexer Handwb.,* 1868; *DW* I, 72; *Fnhd. Wb.* I, 231 f.; *Götze,* 3.

7 Zwar hatte Harsdörffer zum Zeitpunkt seiner Einnahme in die FG noch versprochen, sich künftig nach *Gueintz: Sprachlehre (1641)* richten zu wollen (s. 411126), jedoch teilte er rasch die analogistische Sprachposition Justus Georg Schottelius' (FG 397. Der Suchende), die dieser erstmals in seiner *Teutschen Sprachkunst (1641)* gründlich niedergelegt hatte. Schon in 420608 berichtete Harsdörffer der Gesellschaft, daß Schottelius' *Teutsche Sprachkunst (1641)* in Nürnberg auf äußerst positive Resonanz gestoßen sei, eine Bewertung, die Harsdörffer in 430920 noch einmal unterstrich. „Weil nicht jederman sich nach guten Gesetzen richtet/ soll man deßwegen der Gerechtigkeit abhold seyn/ oder nicht schreiben/ was recht oder unrecht ist?", läßt Harsdörffer im 145. Gesprächspiel die Figur Raymund sagen. Den „vernünfftigen Vrsachen" sei in Fragen der richtigen Schreibung entschieden der Vorzug vor dem Usus zu geben. *Harsdörffer: Frauenzimmer-Gesprächspiele* III (1643/ Ndr. 1968), Ndr. S.340. Wie mit einer so entschiedenen Parteinahme für Schottelius' Position die im vorliegenden Brief doch akzeptierte und angeblich „leichtlich" herbeizuführende Verständigung in Sachen Orthographie zu vereinbaren ist, bleibt schleierhaft, wenn „ableinen" hier nicht in der Nebenbedeutung von „gütlich beilegen, schlichten" (s. Anm.6) gemeint ist. F. Ludwigs Antwort 460426 bleibt kurz und schneidet das Thema nicht an. In 460609 reagiert F. Ludwig dann wieder konziliant. Harsdörffer bleibt in 460915 bei seiner Auffassung.

8 F. Ludwig hatte in 450919A im Namen der FG um eine vom Verfasser autorisierte Druckausgabe von Moscheroschs *Gesichten* gebeten, die daraufhin immer wieder angekündigt wurde (451101, 451217 u.ö.). Die von Johann Michael Moscherosch (FG 436. 1645) besorgte, erweiterte, bei Johann Philipp Mülbe und Josias Staedle gedruckte Straßburger Ausgabe der *Gesichte Philanders von Sittewald* sollte aber erst 1650, nach F. Ludwigs Tod, erscheinen. S. *Schäfer: Moscherosch und Harsdörffer,* S.157 Anm.49; *Dünnhaupt: Handbuch,* 2852f. Nr.1.I.4–5. Zuvor erschien noch Adrian Wyngaerdens Leidener Ausgabe der *Gesichte.* S. *Dünnhaupt: Handbuch,* 2858f. Nr.7 I–VII. S. 451217 K 12, vgl. 440525 K II, 440616 K II 3, 450500 K 5, 450526 K 4, 450818 K 1, 450919A, 451101, 451209, 451727 K 12, 460620, 461031 u. 461104 K 1.

9 In 460120 (K 10) hatte F. Ludwig Moscherosch (über Harsdörffer) angeboten, ihm ein Gemälde seiner, Moscheroschs, Mitgliedsimprese zukommen zu lassen, als Vorlage für die Prägung seiner Gesellschaftsmedaille. 10 Rth. kostet das Sticken der Imprese und des Wappens des jeweiligen Mitglieds auf Atlas für die Impresen- und Wappengobelins im Köthener Schloßsaal. Vgl. dazu 450504A K 5.

10 Harsdörffer vergaß, eine farbige Zeichnung von Moscheroschs Wappen tatsächlich beizulegen; dies holte er mit 460620 unter Entschuldigungen nach. Vgl. auch 460426 (K 3).

460410

Georg Philipp Harsdörffer an Georg Sigmund Fürer von Haimendorf

Georg Philipp Harsdörffer (FG 368) widmet sein gerade erschienenes *Specimen Philologiae Germanicae* (1646) seinem Schwager Georg Sigmund Fürer v. Haimendorf.

Q BJ Kraków: acc. ms. 1913.21/9, 1 Bl.; eigenh.

A *Fehlt.*

Viro Nobilissimo, Amplissimo atque Prudentissimo,
DN. GEORGJO SJGJSMUNDO FÜRERO AB Haymendorf,
Senatori Norimberg.
Spectatissimo, Patrono, et cognatio[1] suo colendo,
hoc quale cunque Lingua Germanica specimen, offert
AUTOR

Norimb. 10 April. A°. 1646.

K Um diese Zeit, nämlich am 6.4.1646, sandte Georg Philipp Harsdörffer (FG 368) sein *Specimen Philologiae germanicae* (1646) auch an F. Ludwig mit zusätzlichen Exemplaren für Diederich v. dem Werder (FG 31) und Christian Gueintz (FG 361), s. 460406 u. 460426. Auch Sigmund Betulius (v. Birken; FG 681. 1658), damals gerade hilfsweise Prinzenerzieher unter Hz. August d.J. v. Braunschweig-Wolfenbüttel (FG 227), erhielt ein Exemplar. Am 7.2.1646 vertröstete ihn Harsdörffer noch: „Specimen Philologiae meae Germanicae post unum et alterum mensem videbis", zwei Monate später glaubte Harsdörffer, Birken werde seine Meinung zum Sammeln von Stammwörtern in seinem *Specimen* „dubio procul" gelesen haben (4.4.1646). S. *Birken: Werke u. Korrespondenz* IX, 8 u. 9; vgl. 460406 K 2.

1 Harsdörffer war seit 1634 mit Susanna Fürer v. Haimendorf (1616–1646) verheiratet, der Schwester des Widmungsempfängers Georg Sigmund Fürer v. Haimendorf (1612–1677). Sie starb am 27.12.1646 nach langer schwerer Krankheit. Acht Kinder gingen aus dieser Ehe hervor, die beiden Söhne Karl Gottlieb und Johann Sigismund überlebten den Vater. Vgl. *Birken: Werke und Korrespondenz* IX, 613; *Herdegen*, 66 u. Johann Michael Dilherrs Leichenpredigt auf Harsdörffer: Der Menschen Stand in Gottes Hand (Nürnberg 1658). — Nach Studium und ausgedehnten Reisen in der Zeit zwischen 1629 und 1636 machte Georg Sigmund in Nürnberg in zahlreichen Ämtern eine typisch patrizische Karriere: vom Ratsmitglied bis zum Bürgermeister, vom Gerichtsrat bis zum obersten Scholarchen und Kirchenpfleger, als der er das auch für den PBO relevante Zensoramt innehatte. 1671 wurde er schließlich Majoratsherr in seinem Stammsitz Haimendorf. Sein Tod wurde von Birken für den 14.1.1677 verzeichnet. Biographische Angaben in: Justus Jacob Leibnitz: Gewißheit der Seeligkeit ... Bey Hochansehlicher Leichbegängnuß/ Des Wol-Edlen ... Herrn Georg Sigmund Fürers/ von und zu Haymendorf/ &c. (Nürnberg 1677). SB München: 4° 38/1190 (Dig.); Johann Gottfried Biedermann: Geschlechtsregister des Hochadelichen Patriciats zu Nürnberg ... Nürnberg 1748, Tabula CCCLXXXV; Hart-

mut Laufhütte: Sigmund von Birken. Leben, Werk und Nachleben. Gesammelte Studien. Mit e. Vorw. v. Klaus Garber. Passau 2007, S. 395 f. Anm. 33.

460414

Justus Georg Schottelius an Johann Valentin Andreae

Ihr brieflicher Verkehr ruhe schon seit längerem, jedoch habe er, schreibt Justus Georg Schottelius (FG 397) an Johann Valentin Andreae (FG 464. 1646), im Geiste nie davon abgelassen, Andreae Wohlfahrt und für so viele Jahre wie möglich körperliche Kraft zu wünschen. Er erbittet von Andreae, den er noch nie von Angesicht zu Angesicht gesehen hat, ein kleines gestochenes Bildnis, um es seiner Porträtsammlung gelehrter Männer hinzuzufügen. So wolle er sich nicht nur in Büchern, sondern auch durch den Anblick der Verdienste berühmter Männer erinnern. Er erfreue sich an einer langen Reihe solcher Bildnisse, der einzigen Schönheit seines Studierzimmers. — Wenngleich er sich nicht würdig erachte, daß Andreae ihn betrachte, schickt Schottelius ihm sein Bild, weil viele aus der Fruchtbringenden Gesellschaft, die ihn mit dem Namen des Suchenden als Mitglied aufgenommen haben, Abwesende in einem solchen kleinen Kranz anzusehen pflegen. — Mit Wissen seines durchläuchtigsten Fürsten wurde Schottelius jüngst feierlich zusammen mit Freunden so zum Doktor der Rechte promoviert, wie es Andreae aus dem mitgesandten Programm ersehe. — Wegen seiner privaten, mitgesandten Schuldforderung bittet Schottelius Andreae, durch einen Boten den Johann Jacob Andler zu einer Antwort zu veranlassen und dessen Erklärung ihm zuzuschicken.

Q HAB: Cod. Guelf. 11.12 Aug. 2°; Bl. 227rv [A: 227v], eigenh. mit Eingangsvermerk von unbekannter H.: Maij. 46. — *BN: Merzbacher: Schottelius*, Nr. 16.

A Viro admodum-reverendo, Excellentissimo celeberrimoque Dño IOHANNI-VALENTINO ANDREÆ S. S. Theol. Doct. Ducis Wirtembergici Ecclesiasti Aulico & Consistorij Ejusdem CONsiliario &c. Fautorj & Amico meo honorando &c.

Vir admodum-Reverende, Excellentissime, celeberrimeque, Fautor & amice honorande

Abiit non exiguum temporis, quo per scripta colloquendj commercium inter nos quievit,[1] non autem meus animus veneratione Tui plenus, atque in tuam prosperitatem et firmum corporis robur, quàmplurimos adhuc annos intimâ prece concumulans.

Cum Venerandam T. Excellentiæ canitiem præsentj obsequio colere, & cupidis meis oulis viva Germanæ Virtutis Tuæ facies hactenus[a] denegetur, quæso succurre impetuj huic meo & desiderio, & devince munusculo Imaginis Tuæ sculptæ, quam semel hîc in forma minorj licuit adspicere. Musæoli mej unicam pulcritudinem arbitror, utj librorum, ita etiam imaginum celebrium virorum seriem, quam longam possideo, & adspectu eorum, non sine meritorum recordatione memet subinde exhilare. Submitto aliqualem meam, ut ut oculis Tuis indignam, quod non nullis ex Societate Fructifera, qui nomen **Der Suchende** mihi

Vir admodum-Reverende, Excellentissime, celeberrime,
Fautor et Amice honorande.

Abiit non exiguum temporis, quo per scripta colloquendi commercium inter nos quievit, non autem meus animus Veneratione Tui plenus, atq[ue] in tuam prosperitatem et firmum corporis robur, quam plurimos adhuc annos intima prece concumulans. Cum venerandam T. Excellentiæ canitiem præsenti obsequio colere, et cupidis meis oculis viva Germanæ Virtutis Tuæ facies hactenus denegetur, quæso succurre impetuj huic meo et desiderio et devinci munusculo Imaginis Tuæ sculptæ, quam semel hic in forma minori licuit aspicere. Musæoli mej unicam pulchritudinem arbitror, ut[ri] librorum, ita etiam imaginum Celebrium virorum seriem, quam longam possideo, et adspectu eorum, non sine meritorum recordatione menté subinde exhilaro. Submitto aliqualem meam ut[ri] oculis Tuis indignam, quod nonnullis ex Societate Palmifera, qui Nomen Leer Brifende mihi dedere, ita placuit, recepto inter Socios meos, absentes se nivium in parvula tali corona intueor. Convenit SERENISSIMo N[ost]ro nupero altj solemnj unà cum alijs amicis in Doctorem Juris promotus fuj, ut in adjuncto programmate Tua Excellentia nomina promotorum adspiciet. Repeto superius Vitam et valetudinem illam ipsi longam, dari perpetuò bonam Tuæ Excellentiæ à Numine omnis opto, qu[æ] Eidem omni honore cultu[que] et ad devotissimus

Justus-Georgius Schottelius

Wolfert. 14 April A[nn]o 1646

Brief von Justus Georg Schottelius (FG 397) an Johann Valentin Andreae (FG 464). Zu 460414.

dedere, ita placuit, recepto inter Socios more, absentes se invicem in parvula talj corona² intuerj.

Consensu SERENISSIMI Nri. nupero astu solemnj unà cum aliis amicis in Doctorem Iuris promotus fvi, uti in adjuncto programmate Tua Excellentia nomina promotorum adspiciet.³

Repeto superius Vitam & valetudinem, illam porrò longam, hanc perpetuò bonam Tuæ Excellentiæ à Numine ammi[t]tj opto, qvi Eidem omni honoris cultu sum et ero addictissimus

Justus-Georgius Schottelius
Welfenb. 14 april. a. 1646.

es ist vor weniger zeit an h. Johan Jacob Andlern⁴ geistlich^b Verwalter in Studgard geschrieben worden, wegen angelegener schuldfoderungs Sachen, weil ich dabei interessiret, bitte dienstfreundlich, bei demselben durch einen dienstboten etwa umb antwort anhalten zulaßen, und dieselbe mit muglichster ehester gelegenheit mit zuubersenden, mir auch wegen diser gelaßner muhenehmung grosgunstiglich zuverzeihen.

T a *Folgt* <mihj> — **b** *Bis* Studgard *eingefügt.*

K 1 Aus der früheren Korrespondenz zwischen Justus Georg Schottelius (FG 397) und Johann Valentin Andreae (FG 464. 1646) ist nur 440429 bekannt. Vgl. jedoch auch 460317 I, einen von Hz. August d. J. v. Braunschweig-Wolfenbüttel (FG 227) an Andreae mitgesandten, an ihn selbst gerichteten Brief. Darauf antwortete Andreae am 22.4.1646 indirekt in einem Brief an Hz. August. S. 460317 K I 1. S. Abb. der Handschriftenprobe S. 863.
2 Schottelius dürfte das Kupferstich-Porträt geschickt haben, das sein Brustbild in einem Pflanzenkranz (seine Gesellschaftspflanze Gämswurz?) mit der Unterschrift „Der Suchende." zeigt. S. *DA Köthen I. 6*, S. 522 (Abb.) u. 118 f. (Beschreibung) sowie die korrigierende Abbildungsbeschreibung im vorliegenden Bd. S. 143.
3 VOTA ET CARMINA quibus summum in utroq; jure gradum VIRO Amplißimo Consultißimoque DN. IVSTO GEORGIO SCHOTTELIO, Illustrissimi & Celsissimi Principis ac Domini, Dn. AVGVSTI Brunsv. & Luneb. Ducis Consiliario Consistoriali, & judicii provinc. Assessori Ordinario, Collatum 26. Februar. in illustri IVLIA, felicem apprecantur PRINCIPES, Fautores & Amici (Helmaestadii 1646: Henning Muller). SUB Göttingen; mit lat. Gedichten und Prosa u. a. von Schottelius' Schülern Pz. Anton Ulrich und Pz. Ferdinand Albrecht v. Braunschweig-Wolfenbüttel (FG 716. 1659 bzw. FG 842. 1673) sowie von Carl Gustav v. Hille (FG 302), Georg Philipp Harsdörffer (FG 368; d. d. postrid. Kal. Februarij 1646; PBO, DG), Sigmund Betulius (S. v. Birken; FG 681. 1658; PBO) und dessen Bruder M. Christianus Betulius Egr. (PBO). — Schottelius war als Lizentiat der Rechte am 5.6.1642 zum Assessor des Hofgerichts ernannt worden. Am 23.8.1643 bat er Hz. August d. J. um Erlaubnis, seine Studien fortsetzen und abschließen zu dürfen (NSTA Wolfenbüttel: 2 Alt Nr. 40, Bl. 20r–21v). Er rief dazu dem Herzog seinen Studiengang ins Gedächtnis: „Undecim annorum tempus iam præterlabitur, ex quo primúm Lugdunum Batavorum, exhinc Lipsiam et tandem Witebergam studij juridici causa me contulerim, eidem, quantum sumptus, tempus et ingenium non denegavit, invigilarem; in Patriam autem Witebergâ tendens, à Ser.te V.ra ad labores præsentis officij clementer vocatus fuj." Die Absicht und die Umstände der juristischen Prüfung beschrieb er

so: „Cum igitur ratione meæ ætatis et officij, aliisq*ue* me urgentibus causis summopere admonear, examinj iusto, publicæq*ue* disputationj cuiquum legalis mei studij subjicere (quod ante annum et biennium [20v] jam meditabar) et per debita testimonia personæ legitimationem adipisci: Animusq*ue* sit, in illustri Vestræ Serenitatis Juliei inauguralem, hebdomade, quæ septimanam S. Michaelis præcedit, durante ob causas graves Decanatu D. Lotichij, habere. [...] Duodecim dierum veniam, non ulteriorem, expeto: Præmittetur enim Disputatio (qvia est quodammodo prolixæ et difficilis materiej, continens Quomodo Delicti meritum iustè æstimarj debeat) qvo Dn. Professorum disqvisitioni et Typographo etiam iusto tempore veniat:" Schottelius disputierte pro gradu am 21.9.1643: DISPVTATIO INAVGVRALIS INAVGVRALIS IVRIDICA DE POENIS; IVXTA CVIVSCVNQVE DERELICTI MERITVM IVSTE ÆSTIMANDIS. QVAM ... IN ILLVSTRI IVLIA ... SVB PRÆSIDIO ... IOHANNIS LOTICHII IC, Professoris Ordinarii, Facultatis Iuridicæ p. t. Decani ... PRO SVMMIS IN VTROQVE IVRE PRIVILEGIIS ET HONORIBVS DOCTORALIBVS CONSEQVENDIS, Publico examini subiicit IVSTVS-GEORGIVS SCHOTTELIVS, Einbecensis, Dicasterii Guelphici Assessor (Helmestadii 1643: Henning Müller). HAB: 107.13 Jur. (4).

4 Johann Jacob Andler, seit 1633 der junge Calwer Untervogt, geriet offenbar in der Calwer Zeit in ein gespanntes Verhältnis zu Andreae als Vertreter der Sittenzucht. *Brecht: Andreae Biographie*, 271; *Andreae: Schriften* I.1, 261 u. 391.

460422

Fürst Johann Casimir von Anhalt-Dessau an Fürst Ludwig

Beantwortet durch 460424. — F. Johann Casimir v. Anhalt-Dessau (FG 10) übersendet F. Ludwig das Gesuch von Pgf. Ludwig Philipp v. Simmern (FG 97) zur Aufnahme etlicher Kandidaten in die FG und bittet um diesbezügliche Anweisungen. — Weiterhin übermittelt er Neuigkeiten über den in Wittenberg befindlichen Oberst (August Adolf v.) Drandorf (Trandorff), die F. Johann Casimir tags zuvor von seinem Kanzler (Dr. Gottfried Müller. FG 353) von dort empfangen hatte. Dabei erwähnt er die kostspieligen, doch letztlich erfolglosen Verrichtungen seines Kanzlers in Wittenberg. Schließlich verweist er auf die enormen Kosten, die Dessau durch den kürzlich erfolgten Truppendurchmarsch nach Wittenberg aufgebürdet wurden. Die Beschlüsse innerhalb der Gesamtung des Fürstentums seien falsch gefaßt, nämlich die alle betreffenden „publica" seien hintangesetzt worden. Das Teilft. Dessau bedürfe angesichts der aktuellen Belastungen dringend einer Unterstützung, anstatt solche anderen zu leisten.

Q HM Köthen: V S 544, Bl. 74r–75v [A: 75v], 75r leer; eigenh.; rotes Lacksiegel. — *D: KE*, 53. — *BN: Bürger*, 813 Nr. 1.

A A Monsieur mon treshonore Oncle Monsieur le Prince Louis d'Anhalt.
Eigenh. Empfangsvermerk Fürst Ludwigs: Pres. 22 April 1646

Hochgeborner Fürst, Freundtlicher Hochgeehrter Herr Vetter vndt gefatter, hierbei empfangen EG waß JL. Pfaltzgraff Ludewig[1] so wohl an Sie, alß mich, wegen einnehmung vieler vornehmer geselschaffter in die Fruchtbringende geselschaft, schreibet[2], Stelle demnach zu E L freundtlichen gefallen, was Sie in disfals verordenen wollen.

Wie es dem Obersten Drandorff³, itzo zu wittenberg gehet werden EL auf beiliegendem Zettel, so mein Cantzler⁴ mihr gestern auß Wittenberg geschicket, ersehen, Gott helffe nuhr das Jch von diesen bösen buben, nuhr nicht auch Vngelegenheit habe. Zu Wittenberg gehet viel gelt auff, vndt wirdt wenig auß-[74v]gerichtet, Jch habe vor zwei tagen, vberᵃ erste 200 thl. so der landtrentmeister mitgenommen, 100 thl. auß hiesigen steuren, hinnüber vermacht, vndt sehe Jch nicht woher die zehrung weiter zu nehmen, möchte wünschen mann hette die publica erst vorgenommen, vndt die pferde nicht hinter den wagen gespannet, durch die wittenbergische Marche⁵ welche diesen Antheil betroffen, vndt viel tausent thl. gekostet, ist hiesiege Stadt, in welcher 2 tage und eine nacht vber 1500 Pferde gelegen, so zugerichtet, das sie mehr beitrages benötiget, als muglich anderen beizutragen, wann anderst eine gesambtung sein soll.

Empfele hiermitt EL Göttlichem schutz vndt verbleibe
EL
treuer Vetter
Johann Casimir FzuAnhalt.

Dessaw den 22. Ap 1646

T a *Bis* mitgenommen *eingefügt*.

K 1 Pgf. Ludwig Philipp v. Simmern (FG 97) hatte durch die Vermittlung von F. Johann Casimir v. Anhalt-Dessau (FG 10) bei F. Ludwig um die Vollmacht zur Aufnahme von 13 Personen in die FG gebeten, bevor er sich aus gleichem Grunde direkt an letzteren wandte. Vgl. 460104 K 1.
2 Diese Beilage liegt dem Brief nicht mehr bei. Vgl. aber den Auszug 460104.
3 Frh. August Adolf v. Drandorf (Trandorff) (†1656), kursächs. Obrist und von 1640 bis 1646 Kommandant der Festung Magdeburg. 1649/50 war er, mittlerweile Generalwachtmeister, Kursachsens Gesandter auf dem Nürnberger Exekutionstag. Zu ihm s. Gothaisches Genealogisches Taschenbuch der Uradeligen Hauser. Der in Deutschland eingeborene Adel (Uradel) 18 (1917), 269. — Immer wieder hatte Oberst Drandorff Kontributions- und Proviantforderungen für die ksl.-kursächs. Garnison in der Stadt Magdeburg auch an die Fürsten zu Anhalt gestellt. Vgl. Anm. 4; *KU* IV.2, 176–183, 321 f., V.1, 207 ff. S. auch 410111 K 4, 410708 K 9 und die Stellennachweise im Personenregister dieser Edition.
4 Beilage fehlt. Dr. jur. Gottfried Müller (FG 353), seit 1616 Kanzler im Ft. Anhalt-Dessau, anfangs unter F. Johann Georg I. (FG 9), ab 1618 unter dessen Sohn u. Nachfolger, F. Johann Casimir. In dieser Funktion erscheint Müller u. a. in einer der Leichenpredigt auf den Dessauer Superintendenten Justus Albinus (†1635) angehängten Danksagungsschrift Sebastian Reinhardts (1586–1653) aus Anlaß seiner Vokation nach Wörlitz. Gustav Früh (Bearb.): Die Leichenpredigten des Stadtarchivs Braunschweig. 10 Bde. Hannover 1976–1990, I (1976), Nr. 46. Zu seiner Wirksamkeit Mitte der 1640er Jahre vgl. z. B. *KU* V.1, 249 ff. Müllers Nachfolger als fl. anhalt-dessau. Kanzler wurde 1654 der Gesamtrat und Kanzler zu Zerbst, Martin Milagius (FG 315). S. Georg Raumer: Idea. Boni Consiliarii. Das ist: Wahre Abbildung eines guten Rahts … (LP auf Martin Milagius). Köthen 1657 (VD17 1:048868Y); *LP Stolberg*, Nr. 15921. Zu Gottfried Müller s. *Conermann III*,

405. — Die mit einer ksl.-kursächs. Besatzung bedeckte Stadt Magdeburg war seit Herbst 1644 durch schwed. Truppen blockiert worden. Jahrelang mußte das Ft. Anhalt für die magdeburg. Garnison Unterhaltsmittel aufbringen. Im Rahmen der schwed.-kursächs. Verhandlungen zum Waffenstillstand von Kötzschenbroda (27. August 1645 a. St.) war nun ein Abzug dieser Truppen vereinbart, jedoch von Kf. Johann Georg I. v. Sachsen verzögert worden. „Magdeburgk soll neutral, vndt dem Ertzbischof [Hz. August v. Sachsen-Weißenfels. FG 402] die garnison zu schwehren, vndtergeben werden, hingegen Oberster Trandorf abdangken", hielt F. Christian II. v. Anhalt-Bernburg (FG 51) die Entwicklung hoffnungsfroh am 20.10.1645 fest, bestätigt am Folgetag, jedoch zeichnete sich ab: „Der Oberste Trandorf dringet gewaltig auf die resta [ausstehende Kontributionen], mit bedrowung der execution", also der gewaltsamen Eintreibung der ausstehenden Unterhaltsmittel. *Christian: Tageb.* XVII, (hier unfol.) Einträge vom 20. u. 21.10.1645. Am 30.10. wiederholte F. Christian die Gefahr, daß Trandorff „drowet, mit der execution auf Bernburgk", ebenso am 8. und 10.11.1645 (a. a. O.). Er nennt die Forderungen sarkastisch Trandorffs „praesent, semel pro semper zum abzuge" (9.11., unfol., a. a. O.). Nachdem am 13. Februar 1646 (a. St.) mit ksl., kursächs. u. schwed. Zustimmung ein Vertrag zwischen der Stadt Magdeburg und dem Administrator des Erzstiftes Magdeburg, Hz. August v. Sachsen-Weißenfels (FG 402) geschlossen worden war, welcher dem Magdeburger Magistrat erlaubte, die Stadt durch eine 250 Mann starke eigene Schutztruppe zu besetzen, war die schwed. Blockade Magdeburgs aufgehoben worden. Anfang April 1646 erfolgte schließlich der Abzug Oberst Drandorfs. S. dazu *Chemnitz* IV.6, 82–85; *Pufendorf: Kriegs-Geschichte* II, 206. Dessen Abmarsch mit der ksl.-kursächs. Besatzung aus Magdeburg die Elbe hinauf, der u. a. über anhalt. Gebiete erfolgte, verursachte die erwähnten hohen Kosten für die Stadt Dessau. Vermutlich war Kanzler Müller in Begleitung des Landrentmeisters nach Wittenberg gereist, um den Abmarsch der Magdeburger Besatzung zu überwachen und eventuell über deren rückständige Verpflegungsforderungen an das Ft. Anhalt zu verhandeln.

5 D. h. den Abmarsch der ksl.-kursächs. Besatzung aus der Stadt Magdeburg nach Wittenberg, s. Anm. 4. F. Johann Casimirs Kritik wird durch F. Ludwigs Schreiben 460424 etwas deutlicher, denn er scheint seinem Neffen zuzustimmen: „Jch habe fur diesem allezeit gerahten, das man bruder f. Augusti formundschaft sache solte von der gemeinen sache sondern, darum auch unsere abgeordnete, so lange bis solche furgenommen were worden, hetten können zurücke bleiben, und dan erst auf zuwißen fügung mit der gesamten Instruction können nachher ziehen, weil aber EL. Cantzler jüngsten außen blieben, und ich keinen beystand gehabt, so hat es so müßen gehen, wie es das Directorium darauf an gestellet."

460423

Fürst Ludwig an Pfalzgraf Ludwig Philipp von Simmern

F. Ludwig genehmigt die durch Vermittlung F. Johann Casimirs v. Anhalt-Dessau (FG 10) von Pgf. Ludwig Philipp v. Simmern (FG 97. Der Gefährliche) erbetene Aufnahme der vorgeschlagenen 13 Personen, von denen aber nur sieben namentlich genannt worden seien, in die FG. Dieser Bitte entsprechend übersendet F. Ludwig beiliegend sogar 14 Impresen-Entwürfe für die neuen Kandidaten. Für deren Aufnahme stellt er gewisse Bedingungen: 1.) Die übersandten Impresen sollen nach Pgf. Ludwig Philipps Gutbefinden und mit Einwilligung durch die Neumitglieder ausgeteilt werden; 2.) sollen die üblichen und nach Wunsch auszuweitenden Aufnahmezeremonien abgehalten werden; 3.) soll ein genaues Verzeichnis über Art und Zeitpunkt der Aufnahme übersendet werden, welches für jedes Neumitglied den vollständigen Namen, den Rang und das in Farbe ausgeführte Wappen enthalten soll. Damit sollen auch die noch fehlenden genauen Personennamen von 6 Kandidaten nachgeliefert werden; 4.) soll jedes Mitglied zwei Reichstaler per Wechsel an Georg Winckler nach Leipzig zur dortigen Michaelismesse einzahlen, um die Impresen für künftige Kupferstiche malen und zeichnen lassen zu können. Vorher soll aber noch der besagte genaue Bericht über die Aufnahme übersendet werden.

Q HM Köthen: V S 544, Bl. 76rv; v leer; eigenh. Konzept mit Streichungen u. Ergänzungen. Bl. 77rv: Beilage I. — *D: KE*, 53 f.; *KL* III, 21 f. — *BN: Bürger*, 952 Nr. 86.

A *Fehlt.*

Demnach durch[a] den Gefährlichen[1] sich unterschiedene personen in der Zahl dreizehen[2] angeben lassen, deren aber nur sieben[3] mit ihren taufnahmen genennet[b], das sie in die fruchtbringende geselschaft aufgenommen zu werden begereten, die gemählde, geselschaft Nahmen und wörter aber aus dem Erzschreine zu übersenden gesuchet worden: Als ist in solches suchen auf nachfolgende bedingungen gewilliget: Und werden erstlich auf dieselbe personen dreitzehen[c] und noch einer mehr beyligend übersendet die[d] gesuchten gemählde, geselschaft Nahmen und wörter, welche[e] dan der Gefährliche am besten nach seinem gutbefinden, und mit einwilligung deren, die iedes annehmen wollen auszuteilen. Furs andere seind[f] die gewönlich*en* Feyerligkeiten die[g] nach beliebung könten vermehret werden bey iedes einnemung in acht zu[h] haben.[4] Drittens ist[i] die ordnung und zeit wan ieder eingetretten richtig[j] aufzuzeichnen, und zum Ertzschreine, nechst iedes geselschafters tauf[j] standes und geschlechts nahmen auch[k] iedes wappen in farben einzuschicken, und seind[i] also die ermangelnde Taufnahmen zuersetzen. Viertens, wen iedes dieser[l] neu eintrettenden geselschafter gemählde, zum kunftigen kupferstechen sol gemahlet und abgerißen werden, inmassen[m] solches eingefuret und herkommen[,] wird hierzu zwey thaler von ieder person zu[n] entrichten und naher Leipzig an George Wincklern[5] durch[o] wechsel nechstkunftigen Michaelis Marck[t][6] dieses[p] Jhars zu übermachen sein[i]: Jedoch also[,] das inzwischen der bericht wen allen obigen zur nachricht und notwendiger ordentlicher[i] einschreibung erfolge, und[q] der fruchtbringenden geselschaft verfaßung hierdurch ein gebuhrliches genugen geschehe.

Deßen zu uhrkund ist dieses mit der geselschaft Jnsiegel bekraftiget, so geschehen an[r] dem bekanten orte des Ertzschreines den drey und zwantzigsten Aprilis im Jhare 1646.

460423 Fürst Ludwig 869

I

Fürst Ludwigs Vorschlag von 14 Impresen für durch Pfalzgraf Ludwig Philipp von Simmern neu aufzunehmende FG-Mitglieder

Q HM Köthen: V S 544, Bl. 77rv, v leer; eigenh. Konzept mit Streichungen u. Ergänzungen. Nicht in KE.

Vorschlag auf die neu angegebene geselschafter

Der Artige[a]	der Astichte blaue Hyacint	Wan er blühet.
Der Lustige	das Fingerhutkraut mit brauner[b] bluhet[c]	Anzusehen und in sich.
Der Andere	Spanischer Kerbel	Jn wirckung stärcker.
Der Beßere	die weiße hindleuft oder wegewart	Als sonst gemein.
Der Niedliche	die Haberwurtzel oder Bocksbart	Wol zugerichtet
Der Jnhaltende	Teschelkraut	Heftiges bluten
Der Leichte	Korck oder Pantoffelholtz	Jst dichte und schwimmet
Der Dünne	Gartenkreße	Voller saft und Kraft.
Der Kleine	der kleine Ungarische Mandelbaum	Gibt solche frucht.
Der Diensame	die Blühende Reinweiden	zum Mundwaßer
Der Honighafte	der Gelbe honigklee	dient zu Hälspflastern.
Der Wegtreibende	die blaue Scabiose oder grindkraut	den grind und Kretze.
Der Nachstellende	Die große Stechende winde	Allerley gift
Der Umbringende	Wandleusekraut	Die Wandleuse oder Wantzen[d]

T **a** durch den *eingefügt für* <vom> — **b** *Folgt* <worden> — **c** *Bis* noch einer mehr *am Rand ergänzt mit unleserlichen Streichungen.* — **d** die gesuchten *eingefügt für* <obgemeldete> — **e** *Gebessert aus* die — **f** *Eingefügt und gebessert aus* ist — **g** *Bis* vermehret werden *am Rand ergänzt.* — **h** *Eingefügt für* <zunemen> — **i** *Eingefügt.* — **j** *Bis* geschlechts *eingefügt statt* <nahmen> — **k** *Bis* farben *am Rand ergänzt, wobei* auch *aus* <und> *gebessert wurde.* — **l** dieser neu antrettenden *eingefügt statt* <solches> — **m** *Bis* herkommen[,] wird *am Rand ergänzt.* — **n** zu entrichten und *eingefügt.* — **o** durch wechsel *am Rand ergänzt.* — **p** dieses Jhars *eingefügt.* — **q** *Folgt* <also> — **r** *Bis* Ertzschreines *am Rand ergänzt.*

T I **a** *Verbessert aus unleserlichem Wort.* — **b** *Verbessert aus* blau [?]. *Unsichere Lesung.* — **c** *Verschreibung für* bluhte [?]. — **d** *Eingefügt für* <Schaben>

K 1 Anfang des Jahres 1646 wandte sich Pgf. Ludwig Philipp v. Simmern (FG 97. Der Gefährliche) an F. Johann Casimir v. Anhalt-Dessau (FG 10), um durch seine Vermittlung bei F. Ludwig (FG 2) die Aufnahme etlicher Kandidaten in die FG gestattet zu bekommen (vgl. den Auszug 460104). Dabei schlug er 13 Personen zur Aufnahme in die FG vor (s. die Namenliste in 460424A I). Diese Bitte um Aufnahme wiederholte Pgf. Ludwig Philipp im März desselben Jahres direkt bei F. Ludwig (460321). Mit dem hier vorliegenden Schriftstück genehmigte F. Ludwig die Aufnahme neuer Mitglieder durch Pgf. Ludwig Philipp und erhöhte deren Zahl auf 14, für welche F. Ludwig die Impresen aufsetzte und als Beilage übersandte. Möglicherweise hatte F. Ludwig die Unglückszahl 13 nicht zugesagt. Der Charakter des vorliegenden Schriftstücks (keine Adresse, keine Anrede, kein Schlußgruß) ist der einer Erzschrein-Urkunde, ähnlich (aber keineswegs identisch mit) der Vollmacht zur Aufnahme Gf. Anthon Günthers v. Oldenburg (FG 351) für Christian Ernst Knoch (FG 268) in 401107 oder der Instruktion für Hans Ludwig Knoch (FG 252) in FG-Angelegenheiten gegenüber Hz. Wilhelm IV. v. Sachsen-Weimar (FG 5) in 430410. Der Schluß des Konzepts zeigt, daß dieses Schriftstück als mit dem FG-Siegel beglaubigte Urkunde Köthen an den Pfalzgrafen verlassen haben muß, jedenfalls keine bloße Aktennotiz für den Erzschrein gewesen sein kann. (Eine Abb. des FG-Papiersiegels in *DA Köthen I. 5*, S. 581.) Höchstwahrscheinlich hat F. Ludwig das Schriftstück mitsamt seiner Beilage der 14 Impresen mit 460424 F. Johann Casimir zugeleitet, von dem es mit 460424A (F. Ludwig an den Pfalzgrafen) Ludwig Philipp zugesandt wurde. Tatsächlich spricht F. Ludwig in 460424 von „deme so aus dem Ertzschreine beygefugt". In 460424A schreibt er Pgf. Ludwig Philipp, er habe dessen Gesuch „stat gegeben, und EL. aus dem ertzscheine die notturft deswegen hierbey empfangen". Mit den genauen Erklärungen über die Gebotenheiten der Aufnahme kämen das vorliegende Schriftstück und die beiliegende Liste der 14 Impresenentwürfe dafür ganz plausibel in Frage. S. auch Anm. 3 und zu diesem Aufnahmevorgang insgesamt 460104 K 1.

2 Zu den vorgeschlagenen 13 Personen s. 460424A u. I.

3 Die Originalliste Pgf. Ludwig Philipps ist nicht erhalten, vgl. aber 460424A I, die die sechs unzureichend genannten Kandidaten der vorgeschlagenen 13 eigens markiert. Die Auflösung der Namen dort im Kommentar.

4 Zum fruchtbringerischen Aufnahmeritual der Hänselung vgl. 460718 K 8.

5 Georg Winckler (1582–1654), Bürger und Handelsmann in Leipzig, wurde wiederholt zur Abwicklung von finanziellen Angelegenheiten von F. Ludwig herangezogen. Zu ihm s. 451019 K 0. — Ein Beschluß der FG, für das Malen der für die Kupferstiche nötigen Impresenvisierungen eine Gebühr von zwei Reichstalern zu erheben, begegnet in 430410.

6 Der Michaelismarkt war eine der drei großen Leipziger Messen und fand beginnend am Sonntag nach dem Michaelistag (29. September) für 14 Tage statt, d. h. im Jahr 1646 vom 4. bis 18. Oktober. Zu den Leipziger Messen allgemein s. Manfred Straube: Die Leipziger Messen im Dreißigjährigen Krieg. In: Uwe John, Josef Matzerath (Hgg.): Landesgeschichte als Herausforderung und Programm. Festschrift für Karlheinz Blaschke zum 70. Geburtstag. Stuttgart 1997, 421–441.

K I Impresenvorschläge F. Ludwigs für die 13 von Pgf. Ludwig Philipp v. Simmern (FG 97) vorgeschlagenen Neumitglieder der FG, ergänzt um einen 14. Impresenvorschlag Ludwigs. Die Liste dürfte dem Mittelsmann F. Johann Casimir v. Anhalt-Dessau (FG 10) mit 460424 zur Weiterleitung übersandt worden sein, vgl. hier K 1 u. 3. Vgl. zu diesem Aufnahmevorgang insgesamt 460104 K 1. Zur Identifizierung der Kandidaten s. 460424A K I.

460424 Fürst Ludwig

Fürst Ludwig an Fürst Johann Casimir von Anhalt-Dessau

Antwort auf 460422. — F. Ludwig dankt für das Schreiben F. Johann Casimirs v. Anhalt-Dessau (FG 10) vom 22. des Monats samt beigelegter Schreiben Pgf. Ludwig Philipps v. Simmern (FG 97). Die Sendung habe er noch am selben Tage erhalten. Seine Beantwortung der pgfl. Schreiben läßt er über F. Johann Casimir bestellen, in der Zuversicht, daß dem Anliegen des Pfalzgrafen mit den Informationen aus dem Erzschrein Genüge geleistet werde. Ludwigs Antwort an den Pfalzgrafen könne während der angehenden (Leipziger Oster-)Messe nebst demjenigen, was dem Dessauer Amtmann zu Köthen mehrfach zugestellt worden war, über Leipzig nach Frankfurt am Main bestellt werden. Auf Begehren Pgf. Ludwig Philipps könne dann das fortgesetzte Verzeichnis der FG-Mitglieder, welches noch nicht gedruckt ist, abschriftlich übermittelt werden. — Hinsichtlich der Vormundschaftsangelegenheiten F. Augusts v. Anhalt-Plötzkau (FG 46) habe F. Ludwig von jeher zu einer Abtrennung von den allgemeinen Verhandlungsgegenständen geraten. Aufgrund des jüngsten Ausbleibens des anhalt.-dessau. Kanzlers (Dr. Gottfried Müller. FG 353) sowie des Fehlens sonstiger Unterstützung habe F. Ludwig die Verknüpfung entsprechend den Wünschen des anhalt. Gesamtdirektoriums zulassen müssen. Die Unkosten hierfür werde aber größtenteils derjenige zu tragen haben, für den die meiste Zeit aufgebracht wurde. Schließlich hofft F. Ludwig auf eine schnelle Erledigung der Angelegenheit und Rückkehr der Gesandten, da weder er noch F. Johann Casimir länger auf diese verzichten könnten. — Nur ungern erfuhr F. Ludwig vom Aufstand der kursächs. Truppen, doch vermute er, daß dieser bald befriedet werden könne. Unklar sei, inwieweit die schwed. Truppen, die nach Torgau marschiert waren, tatsächlich wieder zurückkehren sollten, wie Gerüchte aus Leipzig vom Vortag besagten. Dabei beklagt F. Ludwig die überall großen Kriegsbeschwerungen, die dennoch nicht zu innerfamiliären Entzweiungen führen dürfen, da diese am Ende doch niemandem nützten. — Der schwed. Generalleutnant Hans Christoph v. Königsmarck (FG 515. 1648) sei noch in Leipzig. Unterdessen erwarte F. Ludwig die Rückkehr seiner Abgesandten, die jedoch nicht vor künftigem Montag eintreffen dürften. — F. Ludwig bittet um Überlassung einer Pflanze des gerade blühenden kleinen blauen Baldrians aus F. Johann Casimirs Forsten in Mosigkau, um sie abmalen zu lassen.

Q LHA Sa.-Anh./ Dessau: Z 44 Abt. Dessau A 10 Nr. 44, Bl. 91r–92v [A: 92v]; eigenh.; Sig. — D: *KL* III, 22.

A A Monsieur mon treshonnoré Nepveu Monsieur Le prince Jean Casimir d'Anhalt. A Dessa.
 Les mains propres.

Hochgeborner Fürst, freundlicher vielgeliebter herr Vetter,
 E.L. handschreiben vom 22. dieses[1] ist mir neben denen von Pfaltzgraf Ludwigen[2] deßelben tages wol uberreichet worden. S. L. habe ich wieder^a geantwortet, wie sie beyliegend sehen und dan es zumachen können.[3] Verhoffe auch es sol dero sachen mit deme so aus dem Ertzschreine beygefugt[4], ein genügen geschehen sein: So El. dan mit gelegenheit dieses marcktes[5] wie auch das jenige, so ich mehrmals El. amtman[6] alhier zu gestellet in Leipzig nach Franckfurt am Mayn bestellen laßen können: Würden S. L. dan den verfolg der geselschaft begeren, so

kan das jenige so nit gedruckt dan mit nechster bequemigkeit abgeschrieben zugeschicket werden.[7]

Jch habe fur diesem allezeit gerahten, das man bruder f. Augusti formundschaft sache solte von der gemeinen sache sondern[8], darum auch unsere abgeordnete, so lange bis solche furgenommen were worden, hetten können zurücke bleiben, und dan erst auf zuwißen fügung mit der gesamten Instruction können nachher[b] ziehen, weil aber EL. Cantzler[9] jüngsten außen blieben, und ich keinen beystand gehabt, so hat es so müßen gehen, wie es das Directorium[c] darauf[d] an gestellt. Die unkosten aber werden den am meisten treffen, fur deme die zeit auch am meisten zugebracht worden[10], wan nur die abfertigung oder erledigung bald folgete, dan es so wol mir als El. beschwerlich fellet, das ich meine Leute so[e] lange nicht beysammen.

Den aufstand der Chur Sächsischen völcker[11] verneme ich ungerne, vermute aber es werde noch können gestillet werden; Ob aber der Schwedische zug auf Torgau[12] wieder zurücke gehen sol, wie gestern von Leipzig her ein geschrey auskommen, da weis ich nicht was ich darvon halten sol; die beschwerung ist uberal groß, man muß aber derhalben nicht von einander aussetzen, dan doch an keinem ort vortheil darbey sein wird.

Königsmarck[13] ist noch zu Leipzig, und wartet man der unserigen, die aber fur Montages hier nun nicht können auf sein. El. befehle ich hiermit in den schutz götlicher Almacht, und verbleibe

EL. getreuer Vetter
Ludwig fzu Anhalt

Cöthen den 24 Aprilis 1646.

Nachschrift oder Zusatz ohne Einschaltzeichen am Rande:
Die blume des blauen kleinen Baldrians[14] möchte ich gerne alhier zum abmalen haben, wan El. ihrem holtzförster zu Mußkau befelen möchten, weil sie meines behaltens, ietzunder blühet, das sie mit dem krauten und der blüht meinem unterläuffer[15] in Branicke möchte zugestellet, und durch ihn frisch herein gebracht werden.

T a *Folgt* <an> — b nach *eingefügt.* — c *Folgt* <dan> — d *Eingefügt.* — e so lange *eingefügt.*

K 1 S. 460422.
2 Pgf. Ludwig Philipp v. Simmern (FG 97). Er hatte sein Anliegen, 13 neue Mitglieder in die FG aufnehmen zu dürfen (s. 460104 u. dort K 1) über F. Johann Casimir v. Anhalt-Dessau (FG 10) vermitteln lassen, sich mit 460321 aber auch direkt an F. Ludwig gewandt.
3 Dem vorliegenden Brief lag also auch F. Ludwigs Antwort an Pgf. Ludwig Philipp 460424A (vielleicht auch die dortige Beil. I) zur Weiterleitung bei, höchstwahrscheinlich auch 460423 u. I (vgl. Anm. 4).
4 Dies dürften die Schriftstücke 460423 u. 460423 I (14 Impresenentwürfe mit Gesellschaftsnamen, -wörter u. -pflanzen) gewesen sein. Vgl. 460423 K 1.

460424 Fürst Ludwig

5 Gemeint war die Leipziger Ostermesse, die am 19. April 1646 (Sonntag Jubilate) eingeläutet wurde. S. 460303 K 3.
6 Nicht ermittelt.
7 Vgl. 460104, in dem Pgf. Ludwig Philipp zu verstehen gegeben hatte, daß seine Kenntnis des FG-Mitgliederstandes nur bis Martin Opitz (FG 200) reiche, also auf dem Stand des *GB 1629/30* verblieben war. In 461031A wird Ludwig Philipp seine Bitte um eine aktuelle Mitgliederliste wiederholen. Mit *DA Köthen I.* 8: 470403A kam F. Ludwig dieser Bitte nach u. sandte „ein verzeichnus aller geselschafter tauf und geselschaft nahmen, gemählde und worte bis auf gegenwertige Zeit, so El. als der älteste und das haubt dero orten fur sich behalten, und andern abschriftlich können mittheilen".
8 F. Ludwig bezieht sich hier auf die Klage seines Neffen Johann Casimir in 460422, wonach die „publica" zuerst u. gesondert hätten behandelt werden sollen. F. August v. Anhalt-Plötzkau (FG 46), der ältere Bruder F. Ludwigs, hatte bei der 1589 beschlossenen u. 1603 vollzogenen Teilung des Ft.s Anhalt gegen eine Geldzahlung auf eine eigenständige Herrschaft verzichtet. 1611 hatte August jedoch aus dem Bernburger Teil Schloß u. Amt Plötzkau übertragen bekommen, welches er fortan regierte. Seit 1621 führte er die Vormundschaft für seinen Neffen, F. Johann v. Anhalt-Zerbst (FG 398). Zugleich oblag ihm seit 1630 als Senior u. Oberdirektor der „Landschaftssachen" die Leitung des Gesamthauses Anhalt. *Conermann III*, 49f. Vermutlich gab es Klärungsbedarf über die Kosten der langjährigen Vormundschaftsregierung im Zerbster Teil.
9 Dr. jur. Gottfried Müller (FG 353), Kanzler des Ft.s Anhalt-Dessau. Vgl. 460422 K 4.
10 Damit dürfte wohl F. August (s. Anm. 8) gemeint sein.
11 Die Anfang April 1646 von Magdeburg abgezogene ksl.-kursächs. Besatzung forderte vermutlich ausstehende Verpflegungsgelder, Lebensmittel u. Fourage, für die auch die Fürsten von Anhalt aufkommen sollten. Vgl. 460422 K 4 u. *AOSB* SA VIII, 483 f.
12 Torgau war gemäß dem schwed.-kursächs. Waffenstillstand von Kötzschenbroda (27.8./ 6.9.1645) durch eine beiderseitige Schutzbesatzung (Salvaguardia) neutralisiert worden u. war als einziger Elbübergang für die schwed. Truppen in Kursachsen bestimmt worden. Diese Bestimmung war im Waffenstillstand von Eilenburg (31.3./ 10.4.1646) bestätigt worden. Bei dem erwähnten Marsch auf Torgau könnte es sich um schwed. Truppen handeln, die die aus Magdeburg abziehende ksl.-kursächs. Garnison nach Kursachsen hinein geleitet hatten. *Croxton/ Tischer*, 149f.; Heinz Duchhardt: Kötzschenbroda 1645 — ein historisches Ereignis im Kontext des Krieges und im Urteil der Nachwelt. In: Sächsische Heimatblätter 41 (1995), 323–329; Karl Gustav Helbig: Die sächsisch-schwedischen Verhandlungen zu Kötzschenbroda und Eilenburg 1645 und 1646. In: Archiv für die sächsische Geschichte 5 (1867), 264–288.
13 Der schwed. Generalleutnant (Greve) Hans Christoph v. Königsmarck (FG 515. 1648) befand sich im April 1646 offenbar kurzzeitig in Leipzig, wohl um mit dem dort anwesenden schwed. Generalfeldmarschall Lennart Torstensson das künftige militär. Vorgehen zu beraten. Insbesondere galt es, die Etablierung des schwed. Kriegsestats im Erzstift Bremen u. Hochstift Verden, in welchen Königsmarck als schwed. Gouverneur eingesetzt worden war, voranzutreiben. Zu ihm s. *Conermann III*, 653 ff.; *NDB* XII, 360 f.; *Croxton/ Tischer*, 148; *Findeisen*, 462 f.; vgl. auch *AOSB* SA VIII, 486.
14 Der „kleine blaue Baldrian" war die Gesellschaftspflanze Albrechts v. Zerbst (FG 408. Der Ballernde), der 1644 in die FG aufgenommen worden war u. wohl in Diensten F. Augusts (s. Anm. 8) stand. *Conermann III*, 486f. Sein schön ausgeführtes farbiges Impresengemälde in den *Weimarer Impresen*, Bl. 9, zeigt die Nummer „408.", den „kleinen blauen Baldrian" (nickende Kuhschelle) mit dem Namen „Der Ballernde" u. dem Wort „Blühend genoßen". Das *GB Kö.* III führt sein Reimgesetz auf sowie die farbige Wappen-

zeichnung mit Aufnahmejahr „1.6.44." u. eigenh. Eintrag Zerbsts. Zu Werders Verbesserungen am Reimgesetz s. 440816.

15 Forstgehilfe, -knecht. *DW* XI.3, 1660f.

460424A

Fürst Ludwig an Pfalzgraf Ludwig Philipp von Simmern

Antwort auf 460321. Beantwortet durch 461026 u. 461031A. — F. Ludwig bestätigt dankend den Erhalt von 460321 sowie der ihm von F. Johann Casimir v. Anhalt-Dessau (FG 10) zugestellten Schreiben Pgf. Ludwig Philipps v. Simmern (FG 97). Er genehmigt Ludwig Philipp die Durchführung der von ihm erbetenen Aufnahme etlicher vornehmer Personen in die FG und übersendet ihm das für die Aufnahme Notwendige aus dem Erzschrein der FG. Die Aufnahmefeier solle nach dem hergebrachten Usus, aber maßvoll verlaufen, wie ein solches Maßhalten der Imprese und dem Reimgesetz Heinrichs v. Sandersleben (FG 34. Der Erfreuende) zu entnehmen sei. Wenn der Bericht des Pfalzgrafen über die erfolgten Aufnahmen in Köthen eingegangen ist, sollen auch die Reimgesetze aufgesetzt werden.

Q HM Köthen: V S 544, Bl. 78rv [A: 78r]; 78v: Verzeichnus der personen, so durch Pfaltzgraf Ludwig in die fruchtbringende geselschaf[t] sich zu begeben begeren (Beil. I); eigenh. Konzept. — *D: KE*, 54f. (nur Brief). — *BN: Bürger*, 952 Nr. 87.

A A Monsieur mon treshonnoré Cousin Monsieur Le Duc Louys Philippe Conte Palatin du Rhin. An Pfalzgraf Ludwigen.[a]

Hochgeborner furst, freundlicher vielgeliebter herr Vetter,
gegen El. bedancke ich mich freunddienstlich, das sie mich mit dero handbrieflein[b] vom[c] 21/ 31. des Mertzen zu besuchen wurdigen wollen. Von Vetter f. Johan Casimirn[1] ist mir ihr schreiben auch[d] zugeschicket worden[2], darin sie wegen etlicher fornemer personen, in die fruchtbringende geselschat *[sic]* einzunemen ansuchung gethan,[e] Welchem den stat gegeben, und EL. aus dem ertzschreine die notturft deswegen hierbey[f] empfangen,[g][3] auch nicht zu zweiffeln sie in begehung der hergebrachten feyerligkeit[4] nichts verschmelern werden, wiewol auch[h] in allem das rechte maß nach dem gemählde des Erfreuenden und seinem achtzeiligen reim[i] gesetze zu halten.[5] Wan El. bericht von dieser einnemung wieder zu rucke gelanget, sol dan hand an[j] der neuen geselschafter achtzeilige Reimgesetze auch geleget werden. El. hab ich dieses zu freundlicher antwort nicht verhelen mugen, ergeben sie in den schutz götlicher macht zu allem furstlichen und friedlichen aufnemen, und verbleibe
    EL.
bereitwilliger freund und diener.

Cöthen den 24. April 1646.

EL.[k] wollen die neu eingehende geselschafter meinetwegen freundlich und geburlich grußen.

460424A Fürst Ludwig

I

Liste der von Fürst Ludwig notierten, von Pfalzgraf Ludwig Philipp von Simmern zur Aufnahme vorgesehenen FG-Mitglieder

Q HM Köthen: V S 544, Bl. 78v; eigenh. von F. Ludwig. — Nicht in *KE*.

Verzeichnus der personen, so durch[a] Pfaltzgraf Ludwig in die fruchtbringende geselschaf[t][b] sich zu begeben begeren

Hertzog Friderich von Zweybruck,   pfaltzgraf.
Hertzog Johan Ludwig   pfaltzgraf
Eberhard Zickingen
      Steinkallenfels.
Friederich Casimir Kundteroht.
Wolf Bernhard von Geispitz
      Botsheim.
     Pawel.
Loppus de Villanova.
    der bruder Pawels.
    Ob. leutenant Junge
Graf Friederich Eimerich von leiningen
Johan Casimir Kolbe

Verzeichnus der personen, tauf[c] und geschlechts Nahmen so uberschrieben[d] worden.

Friederich[e] Hertzog zu[f] Zweybruck. } Pfaltzgrafe.
Johan[g] Ludwig Hertzog
[h]Friederich[i] Eimerich Graf von leiningen
Eberhard Zickingen
Friederich Casimir Kunderoht
Wolf Bernhard von Geispitz.
Johan Casimir Kolbe.
     Folgende taufnahmen mangeln.
      Steinkallenfels.
      Botsheim.
      Pawel.
      de Villanova
      der bruder Pawels.
      Obriste leutenant Junge.

T a *Deutsche Adresse am Rand der ersten Briefzeile eingefügt.* — **b** *Gebessert aus* handsch[reiben] — **c** *vom 21./ 31. des Mertzen eingefügt. des gebessert aus* Mer — **d** *Eingefügt bis* worden — **e** *Folgt* <davor> — **f** *Am Rand ergänzt.* — **g** *Folgt* <werden> — **h** *Wörterreihenfolge durch hochgestellte Ziffern verändert aus* in allem auch — **i** *Eingefügt.* — **j** *Folgt* <ihre> — **k** *Schlußgruß am Rande eingefügt.*

T I a *Eingefügt.* — **b** *Buchstabenverlust im Falz. Konjektur in eckigen Klammern.* — **c** *Eingefügt bis* geschlechts — **d** *Eingefügt für* <eingeschicket> — **e** *Reihenfolge durch hochgestellte Ziffern umgestellt aus* Hertzog Friederich — **f** *Gebessert aus* von — **g** *Reihenfolge durch hochgestellte Ziffern umgestellt aus* Hertzog Johan Ludwig — **h** *Reihenfolge in der Namen-Aufzählung durch hochgestellte Ziffern verändert, so daß dieser Eintrag von der ursprünglich sechsten auf die dritte Position hochgerückt wurde.* — **i** *Reihenfolge durch hochgestellte Ziffern umgestellt aus* Graf Friederich Eimerich.

K 1 F. Johann Casimir v. Anhalt-Dessau (FG 10) war von Pgf. Ludwig Philipp v. Simmern (FG 97) als Vermittler für die gewünschte Aufnahmevollmacht erbeten worden. Seine Vermittlungsrolle blieb bei dem gesamten Aufnahmevorgang bestehen. S. Anm. 2 u. 460104 K 1.

2 F. Johann Casimir trat in Angelegenheit des pgfl. Ersuchens mit 460422 an F. Ludwig heran, nachdem der Pfalzgraf mit 460321 sein Anliegen auch persönlich F. Ludwig vorgebracht hatte.

3 Hier dürfte das Schriftstück 460423 nebst Beilage der 14 Impresenentwürfe F. Ludwigs für die vorgeschlagenen Neumitglieder gemeint sein. S. ebd. K 1.

4 Im fruchtbringerischen Aufnahmeritual der Hänselung spielte das Leeren des eigens dazu verwendeten Pokals „Ölberger" eine entscheidende Rolle. Vgl. dazu 460718 K 8.

5 Imprese und Reimgesetz des 1620 in die FG aufgenommenen Heinrichs v. Sandersleben (FG 34. Der Erfreuende). Sein Sinnbild in der FG war der rote Wein unter der Weinpresse, sein Wort: „Jn rechtem Gebrauch" (*GB Kö.* I, Bl. J ijr). Das Reimgesetz hielt dazu fest: „EJn roter Wein der pflegt den Menschen zu erfrewen/ | Zu trincken mässig jhn darff er sich gantz nicht schewen/ | [...] | Wer so das Trinckrecht helt/ daß er bey Zeit auffhört/ | Der wird vom Rebensafft wol nimmermehr bethört."

K I Die vorliegende Liste von F. Ludwig dürfte keine mitgesandte Beilage zum vorliegenden Brief gewesen sein, sondern wohl eine Aktennotiz zum eigenen Gebrauch und für den Erzschrein. Aus der im Original nicht erhaltenen Vorschlagsliste Pgf. Ludwig Philipps v. Simmern (FG 97) wurden unter den sieben mit Vor- und Familiennamen genannten Personen aufgenommen:

– Pgf. Friedrich v. Zweibrücken: FG 476. 1647. Der Artige. Wan er blühet. Ästig art vom blauen Hiacint. Die Imprese entspricht F. Ludwigs Vorschlag in 460423 I. Vgl. *Conermann III*, 584 f.

– Eberhard v. Sickingen, im Saarland beheimatet und wahrscheinlich zum Hofe Pgf. Ludwig Philipps gehörend: FG 463. 1646. Der Nachstellende. Allerley gift. Die große Stechende Winde. Die Imprese entspricht F. Ludwigs Vorschlag in 460423 I. Vgl. *Conermann III*, 559 f.

– Friedrich Casimir v. Günderode, pfalz-zweibrück. Amtmann von Lichtenberg: FG 478. 1647. Der Leichte. Jst dichte und schwimmet. Pantoffelholtz. Die Imprese entspricht F. Ludwigs Vorschlag in 460423 I. Vgl. *Conermann III*, 587 f.

– Wolf Bernhard v. Geispitzheim, seit 1638 in pfälz. Diensten, 1650 als pfalz-simmernscher Rat u. Amtmann bezeugt: FG 473. 1647. Der Umbringende. Die Wandleuse oder

460426 Fürst Ludwig

Wantzen. Wandlauskraut. Die Imprese entspricht F. Ludwigs Vorschlag in 460423 I. Vgl. *Conermann III*, 580 f.
– Johann Casimir Kolb v. Wartenberg, hoher Ämterträger der Kurpfalz, Geheimer Rat Pgf. Ludwig Philipps: FG 460. 1646. Der Bessere. Alles sonst gemein. Die Hindleuft mit weisser blüht. Die Imprese entspricht F. Ludwigs Vorschlag in 460423 I. Vgl. *Conermann III*, 554 ff.
Die in der Liste nicht mit Taufnamen genannten Aufgenommen waren:
– Carl Friedrich v. Pawel(-Rammingen), zur Zeit der Aufnahme vermutlich in Diensten Pgf. Ludwig Philipps: FG 461. 1646. Der Diensame. Zum Mundwasser. Die blühende Reinweiden. Die Imprese entspricht F. Ludwigs Vorschlag in 460423 I. Vgl. *Conermann III*, 557 f.; vgl. zu seiner Familie 450818 K 2.
– Dessen Bruder, Georg Friedrich v. Pawel(-Rammingen), in pfalz-zweibrück. Diensten: FG 477. 1647. Der Lustige. Anzusehen und in sich. Fingerkaut. Die Imprese entspricht F. Ludwigs Vorschlag in 460423 I. Vgl. *Conermann III*, 585 f.; vgl. zu seiner Familie 450818 K 2.
– Fridericus Justus Lopez de Villa Nova, aus urspr. span. Adelsgeschlecht, zur Zeit seiner Aufnahme vermutlich in Diensten Pgf. Ludwig Philipps v. Simmern: FG 462. 1646. Der Honighafte. Dient zum halßpflaster. Der gelbe Honigklee. Die Imprese entspricht F. Ludwigs Vorschlag in 460423 I. Vgl. *Conermann III*, 558 f.
Fünf der vorgeschlagenen Personen wurden nicht aufgenommen: der schwed. Obrist Pgf. Johann Ludwig v. Sulzbach (1625–1649), Gf. Friedrich Emich v. Leiningen-Dagsburg-Hartenburg (1621–1698), ein nicht näher genannter und identifizierbarer Oberstleutnant Junge sowie zwei ebenfalls nicht genau bestimmte Personen, eine aus der adligen Familie von Steinkallenfels, die andere mit dem Familiennamen Botsheim, d. i. Botzheim (vgl. Hans Bernd v. Botzheim FG 28). Der Grund der Nichtaufnahme ist nicht bekannt. Unter den bis Februar 1647 von Pgf. Ludwig Philipp aufgenommenen Neumitgliedern befinden sich auch sechs, die ursprünglich nicht vom Pfalzgrafen zur Aufnahme vorgesehen waren. Vgl. die zwei Listen in 461031A I.

460426

Fürst Ludwig an Georg Philipp Harsdörffer

Antwort auf 460406. Beantwortet durch 460620. — F. Ludwig (Der Nährende) bestätigt den Empfang von 460406 und dankt für die Übersendung von Georg Philipp Harsdörffers (FG 368. Der Spielende) *Specimen Philologiae Germanicae* (1646) und seiner Übersetzung des *Catechisme Royal* (1645) von Philippe Fortin sieur de la Hoguette. Das (angeblich beigelegte) Wappen Johann Michael Moscheroschs (FG 436. Der Träumende. 1645) fehle aber in Harsdörffers Sendung. — Das Impresengemälde (zur Vorlage) für Moscheroschs Gesellschaftspfennig konnte mangels eines Künstlers vor Ort noch nicht gefertigt werden. — Die beiden zusätzlichen Exemplare des *Specimen* sollen an die von Harsdörffer angegebenen Adressaten (Diederich v. dem Werder, FG 31, und Christian Gueintz, FG 361) weitergereicht werden.

Q HM Köthen: V S 545, Bl. 353rv, v leer; eigenh. Konzept (auf der unteren Hälfte von 353r das Konzept von 460609). — D: *KE*, 355. — BN: *Bürger*, 950 Nr. 60.

A An Georg Philip Harsdorffern.[a]

Vom Spielenden ist untenbenanten tages an den Nehrenden ein schreiben den sechsten Aprilmonats gegeben, nechst dreyen stucken eines lateinischen buchleins mit[b] dem tittel Philologia[c] Germanica,[1] und ein verdeutschtes der königliche Catechismus genant,[2] wol eingeliefert, des Traumenden wappen aber nicht darbey gefunden worden[3]: deßen gemählde zum geselschaft pfennige hat so bald in entstehung eines Mahlers dieses orts nicht können gefertiget werden, sol aber mit ehestem folgen,[4] und die zwey stucke der Philologia an uberschriebene ort zu rahte gebracht werden.[5] Uhrkundlich ist dieses unter der bekanten schrift[d] an bewustem ort ausgefertiget. So geschehen den 26. Aprilmonats im Jhare 1646.

T a *Die Anschrift steht am Rand zwischen den Konzepten der beiden an Harsdörffer gerichteten Briefe (460609 u. dem vorliegenden), ist mithin beiden zugehörig.* — b *Bis* tittel *eingefügt.* — c *Gebessert aus* Philologica — d *Folgt* <ausgefertiget>

K 1 Georg Philipp Harsdörffer (FG 368. Der Spielende) schickte F. Ludwig (Der Nährende) mit seinem Brief 460406 drei Exemplare seines gerade erschienenen *Specimen Philologiae Germanicae* (Ankündigung des Buchs in 450923C). Die beiden übrigen Exemplare dachte Harsdörffer Diederich v. dem Werder (FG 31) u. Christian Gueintz (FG 361) zu. Vgl. 451217 K 10. Er hatte um Rückmeldung besonders in Hinsicht auf Kap. VII (Verwandtschaft des Deutschen mit dem Hebräischen) und Kap. X (über die deutsche Rechtschreibung) gebeten.
2 Wie wir erst aus dieser Bemerkung erfahren, legte Harsdörffer 460406 auch eine (nun offenbar vollständig gedruckte) Übersetzung von Philippe Fortin sieur de la Hoguettes *Le Catechisme Royal* (1645) bei. Die ersten Druckbögen hatte er Ludwig bereits Ende des vorherigen Jahres geschickt. S. 451217 (K 9).
3 Harsdörffer schrieb in 460406, er lege dem Brief das Wappen Johann Michael Moscheroschs (FG 436. 1645) bei, was aber vergessen wurde. Harsdörffer holte das Versäumte mit 460620 nach, wobei er sich zugleich für seine Nachlässigkeit entschuldigte. Vgl. zu diesem ganzen Vorgang 450504A K 5.
4 In 460120 hatte F. Ludwig Moscherosch (über Harsdörffer) angeboten, ihm ein Gemälde seiner, Moscheroschs, Mitgliedsimprese zukommen zu lassen, als Vorlage für die Prägung seiner Gesellschaftsmedaille. Vgl. zuletzt 460406 (K 9). Als Impresenmaler begegnet in dieser Zeit Christoph Steger, der sich zumindest im März in Halle a. d. S. aufhielt. Vgl. 460315. Das Impresengemälde wurde angefertigt, denn mit 460609 sandte es F. Ludwig an Harsdörffer zur Weiterleitung an Moscherosch. S. Abb. S. 879. Vgl. 450504A K 5.
5 In 460406 hatte Harsdörffer den Nährenden gebeten, je ein Exemplar an Diederich v. dem Werder u. Christian Gueintz weiterzuleiten. S. Anm. 1.

460519

Matthäus Merian d. Ä. an Peter Knaudt

Matthäus Merian d. Ä. dankt Peter Knaudt für den letzten (nicht erhaltenen) Brief. Er hat daraus entnommen, daß die Exemplare des *GB 1646* und der *Topographia* gut (in Köthen) angekommen sind. Merian verzichtet auf die Bezahlung der *Topographia*, erhofft sich jedoch von Peter Knaudt Unterstützung mit Zeichnungen und Beschreibungen, falls Me-

Christoph Stegers Visierung der Imprese Johann Michael Moscheroschs (FG 436. Der Träumende). Zu 460426.

rian solche von Ortschaften und Schlössern in Sachsen und Meißen fehlen, damit der entsprechende *Topographia*-Band (*Topographia Superioris Saxoniae, Thuringiae* usw.) vervollkommnet werden kann. — Die fehlenden 300 Reichstaler (für das *GB 1646*) habe Georg Winckler an Merian überwiesen.

Q HM Köthen: V S 546, Bl. 35rv [A: 35v]; eigenh.; rotes Lacksiegel. — *D: Bircher: Merian,* 716; *Wüthrich: Merian Briefe,* 110f. — BN: *Bürger,* 987 Nr. 18.

A Tt. Dem Ehrenvesten und GroßAchtparen Herrn Petter Knaudt Fürst. Anhaltischen CammerMeistern *etc.* zu Cöthen meinem gg. herrn Cöthen

Ehrnvester und wohl fürnehmer Jnsonders gg. Herr *etc.*

Dem sein mein willige dienst und was Jch vermag Jederzeit Anvor[1], und berichte hiemit das mir des Herrn Jungstes wohl worden, darauß verstanden, das die gesandten Exemplarien von der frucht bringenden Geselschafft, wie auch die Toppographia, dem herrn Recht zukommen so mir lieb zu vernehmen, die Toppographia mögen im Nahmen Gottes in den Kauff gehen, Jedoch hoffe Jch da mir etwas von selbigen landen an abriß, und beschreibung der Stetten oder Schlößer mangelen würde, mit solchen mir gg. behülfflich sein werden, damit der theil so Sachsen und Meissen begriffen wirt, desto volkomener werden möge *etc.*[2]

Sonsten habe ich von Hern Georg Wincklern[3] die Rthl. 300 wohl empfangen und ist diß malen nun alles Richtig, und bezalt.[4] Hiemit dem Allmechtigen wohl befohlen.

Ffurt den 19. Maij 1646.
Des Herrn
Dienstwilliger
Mattheus Merian.

K 1 Bevor, vorab. S. 450417 K 1.

2 F. Ludwig hatte durch seinen Kammermeister Peter Knaudt 12 Vorausexemplare des *GB 1646* angefordert. S. 460206 I u. II, 460324. Merian verzichtete kulant auf die Bezahlung der bestellten 6 Bände seiner Topographien. Vgl. 460324 K 5. Der geplante Band *Merian: Topographia* Superioris Saxoniae usw. wurde vier Jahre später (1650) publiziert. Übersicht der Bände in 450905 K 4. Vgl. zum Thema auch 460303 (Merian an Knaudt). Auch Fruchtbringer, wie Justus Georg Schottelius (FG 397) im Falle der braunschweiglüneburgischen Topographie, und selbst F. Ludwig (s. 460810) halfen Merian bei der Fertigstellung seiner *Topographia*-Bände mit Zeichnungen, Texten und Textredaktionen aus. NSTA Wolfenbüttel: 8 Alt: Wolfb.; nach *Bei der Wieden: Schottelius,* 150 f.; vgl. *DA Köthen I. 2,* S. 90 f. u. *Conermann: Anhalt,* 12.

3 Der Leipziger Handelsherr Georg Winckler, über den F. Ludwig die Verlagsfinanzierung des *GB 1646* abwickelte. S. 451019 K 0.

4 Matthäus Merian d. Ä. bestätigt den Eingang der Verlagsbeiträge Hz. Augusts d. J. v. Braunschweig-Wolfenbüttel (FG 227) und Hz. Christian Ludwigs v. Braunschweig-Calenberg (FG 372) zum *GB 1646* in Höhe von 200 bzw. 100 Rth. S. 460303 u. 460324.

460609

Fürst Ludwig an Georg Philipp Harsdörffer

Antwort auf 460406. Beantwortet durch 460620. — F. Ludwig (Der Nährende) schickt Georg Philipp Harsdörffer (FG 368. Der Spielende) das mittlerweile fertiggestellte (Impresen-)Gemälde zu Johann Michael Moscheroschs (FG 436. Der Träumende) Gesellschaftspfennig. Auf die Zusendung des Wappens von Moscherosch warte man noch immer. Harsdörffers *Specimen Philologiae Germanicae* (1646) habe er nun gelesen und halte es im Allgemeinen für gelungen. Man müsse aber noch auf Antwort der Gelehrten warten, denen man Exemplare zugeschickt hat.

Q   HM Köthen: V S 545, Bl. 353rv, v leer; eigenh. Konzept (auf der oberen Hälfte von 353r ist das Konzept von 460426). — *D: KE*, 355f. — *BN: Bürger*, 950 Nr. 61.

A   An Georg Philip Harsdorffer.[a]

Dem Spielenden wird inliegend hiemit zugeschicket das begehrte neu[b] verfertigete gemälde des Traumenden zum geselschaft pfennige, und[c] dargegen zum Ertzschreine sein jungstes[d] ausgebliebenes wappen erwartet.[1]

Es hat der Nehrende des Spielenden **Philologiam Germanicam**[2] durchlesen, und findet viel gutes und richtiges[e] dinges drinnen, worinnen aber man noch nicht einig, wird er der Gelehrten bedencken, denen sie zugeschicket, auch[f] erwarten,[3] und dan auf weiteres ersuchen, alles in gute gleichstimmige richtigkeit helffen zu bringen, gerne so[g] viel an ihme das seinige thun.[h] verbleibet darneben des Spielenden

   gantzwilliger

Geben am bekanten orte den 9. tag des Brachmonats 1646.

T a *Die Anschrift steht am Rand zwischen den Konzepten der beiden an Harsdörffer gerichteten Briefe (460426 u. dem vorliegenden), ist mithin beiden zugehörig.* — b neu verfertigete *eingefügt für* <geselschaft> — c *Folgt* <erwartet man> (erwartet *aus einem unleserlichen Wort interlinear gebessert*). — d *Gebessert aus* jungsten — e *Gebessert aus* richtigen — f *Eingefügt.* — g *Bis* thun *eingefügt für* <gefließen sein> — h *Folgt* <und>

K 1 S. zum Wappen Johann Michael Moscheroschs (FG 436), das F. Ludwig schließlich mit 460620 erreichte, und zum Gemälde seiner Mitgliedsimprese als Vorlage für die Anfertigung seines Gesellschaftspfennigs 450504A K 5.

2 Drei Exemplare von Georg Philipp Harsdörffers (FG 368. Der Spielende) *Specimen Philologiae Germanicae* (1646) hatte F. Ludwig zusammen mit 460406 empfangen. Die beiden überzähligen Exemplare dachte Harsdörffer Diederich v. dem Werder (FG 31) u. Christian Gueintz (FG 361) zu. S. dort; vgl. 451217 K 10. Seine Absicht, ein Sprachbuch zu schreiben, hatte der Spielende dem Fürsten in 450923C kundgetan und dasselbe 451217 als druckfertig angekündigt.

3 Als Georg Philipp Harsdörffer (FG 368. Der Spielende) F. Ludwig (Der Nährende) mit 460406 den fertigen Druck seines *Specimen Philologiae Germanicae* schickte, legte er zwei weitere Exemplare bei mit der Bitte, diese Christian Gueintz (FG 361) und Diederich

v. dem Werder (FG 31) zukommen zu lassen. Deren Meinung wünschte er besonders hinsichtlich der Kapitel zum Verwandtschaftsverhältnis zwischen Deutschem und Hebräischem und zur deutschen Rechtschreibung zu erfahren. Vgl. 460406 (K 4). Kurze Zeit nach Abfassung des vorliegenden Briefes, am 15.6.1645 setzte Marcus Fridericus Wendelin(us) (1584–1652), Rektor des Zerbster Gymnasiums, im Auftrag F. Ludwigs ein erstes latein. Gutachten zum *Specimen* auf (HM Köthen: V S 545, Bl. 474r–480v); ein zweites, ebenfalls latein. folgte am 6.8.1646 (ebd., Bl. 481r–489v). Christian Gueintz verfaßte eine weitere Stellungnahme zum *Specimen*, die er seinem Brief 460720 an F. Ludwig beilegte (*KE*, 363–372), der sie mit 460816 an Harsdörffer weiterleitete. Wohl 1648 oder 1649 steuerte auch Joachim Mechovius (FG 483. 1647), ein Gutachten zum *Specimen* und zum 2. Teil des *Poetischen Trichters* (1648) bei (HM Köthen: V S 545, 504r–505v) (alle genannten Gutachten demnächst in *DA Köthen I. 9*). Möglicherweise beteiligten sich auch weitere Fruchtbringer an dieser kritischen Diskussion. Vgl. zum *Specimen* insgesamt 451217 K 10.

460610

Andreas Tscherning an Matthaeus Apelles von Löwenstern

Andreas Tscherning entschuldigt die Dürftigkeit seiner Mitteilungen an (seinen väterlichen Gönner) Matthaeus Apelles v. Löwenstern damit, daß auf der Universität (Rostock) Promotionen abzuwickeln waren, wobei es auch nicht ohne ihn als Dichter abging. Von öffentlichen und privaten Geschäften abgesehen, traten ungewöhnliche Männer von auswärts hinzu, die die Arbeit der Musen verlangten. Augustus Buchner (FG 362) fordert nach der Hochzeit seiner Tochter auch ein deutsches Gedicht Tschernings auf diesen Anlaß. Georg Philipp Harsdörffer (FG 368), den Apelles kenne, fordere von Tscherning Verse auf sein ihm gesandtes *Specimen Philologiae Germanicae*, das Tscherning allerdings noch genau zu lesen habe. Auch Johann Rist (FG 467. 1647) habe wiederum wegen eines Gedichts angeklopft, da er den Poetenlorbeer und wohl vor zwei Jahren vom Kaiser ein Wappen empfangen habe, das er in Kupfer stechen lassen wolle. Rist hat wieder deutsche Gedichte (unter dem Titel *Poetischer Schauplatz*) herausgebracht. — Der von Apelles Tscherning anvertraute Grundmann lebt in Kopenhagen als Hofmeister der Söhne des dortigen Dr. med. und Professors Simon Paulli, eines besonderen Freundes Tschernings. — Philipp v. Zesen (FG 521. 1648) ist aus Holland nach Hamburg zurückgekehrt und wird möglichst viel neuen Kram einführen. Buchner werde jedoch dafür sorgen, daß der eitle Zesen endlich Frucht zu bringen beginnt, wenn bei ihm lächerliche Einbildungen noch nicht jegliche Vernunft beseitigt haben. Der Breslauer Grutner schreibt aus Holland, Zesen nenne sich jetzt den blauen Ritter und habe wegen seines Namens aus eigener Machtvollkommenheit einen Orden gründen wollen. Grutner hat Tscherning mitgeteilt, Zesen müsse zu viel Prügel bekommen haben, weil er in seinen Anmerkungen den Namen Henrich bzw. französisch Henri von Hahnrei abgeleitet habe. Tscherning teilte einem Freund in Leiden Buchners Urteil über Zesens Recht- bzw. Linksschreibung mit. Der Freund habe es gegen sein gegebenes Wort öffentlich verbreitet. Buchner hat, wie sich Apelles erinnere, von Tscherning verlangt, die Jugend in einer Schrift zur Vermeidung solcher Eitelkeiten aufzufordern. Man sagt Tscherning nach, etwas gegen Zesen im Schilde zu führen. — Harsdörffer wisse auch davon. Wie er ihm schrieb, habe Elzevier Zesen schon Wege zu unablässiger Neuerung versperrt. Zesen rühme sich, schon 30 Bücher über die deutsche Sprache verfaßt zu haben und eine Grammatik aus eigener Erfindung zu schreiben. Er weise die Ermahnungen der Freunde zurück und wolle alles selbst nach eigenen Einfällen hervorbringen. — Tscherning übermittelt seine eigenen Grüße und die seiner Frau an das Ehepaar Apelles. Dem edlen (Daniel v.) Tarnau wünscht Tscherning alles Gute. Apelles möge Tscherning wissen lassen, ob in der Sache Schaevinius ein Hoffnungsfunke aufblitze, damit er den Mut der Witwe wieder aufrichten könne.

Q STB Berlin — PK: Dep. Breslau 17 (ehem. StB Breslau: Ms. Rehd. 402), S. 670–672 (Nr. 312), Abschrift von Matthias Machner. Zu dieser Quelle s. 440826 Q u. K 1, zu Machner s. 440324 K I 1. — Spätere Abschrift: BU Wrocław: Ms. Akc. 1949/ 713 (ehem. StB Breslau: Hs. Klose 175), Bl. 178rv (Brief Nr. 312), vollständige Abschrift der Machner-Abschrift durch den Breslauer Schulrektor Samuel Benjamin Klose (1730–1798) in zeitgemäß modernisierter Schreibweise (s. 440826 Q u. K 2). Zit. mit der Sigle *B*. — Ehemals auch StB Breslau: R. 3109, S. 63 (Abschrift Christian Ezechiels, verschollen), s. *Borcherdt: Tscherning*, 159. — D: *Borcherdt: Tscherning*, 159f. u. 311 Anm. 33 f. (kurze Auszüge). — BN: *Borcherdt: Tscherning*, S. 336 Nr. 103; *Bürger*, 1365 Nr. 25.

A *Fehlt.*

IDEM AD EUNDEM.
Maximis occupationibus impedior, Strenue ac nobilissime Dn. Parens; aliàs prolixiores ad te venirent. Creandi sunt in Academiâ n*ostrâ*[1] Doctores, creandi Magistri. Poscuntur carmina ad ravim us*que*. Sine vate nec Magister fit nec Doctor. Accedunt exteri. Lassant Camoenas n*ostras* viri οὐ τῶν τυχόντων. Ex his familiam ducit Buchnerus ὁ πάνυ,[2] qvi etiam post nuptias Filiæ Epithalamium Germanicum flagitat.[3] Est deinde ex illustrissimo Carpophororum sodalitio, qvem benè nosti, nobiliss. **Harsdorferus**,[4] qui qvantum ex Literis ejus conjicere habeo, judicium meum, sed versibus expressum haut obscurè reqvirit. Misit *enim* mihi specimen suum Philologiæ Germanicæ, cui pellegendo nondum vacare licet. Et qvod non putassem, **Ristius** etiam fores n*ostras* denuo putat. Lauream impetravit, et Insignia ab Imp. n*ostro* ante biennium, ni fallor. Poscit me itàq*ue* Carmen[5] et in Lauream et Insignia, qvæ in aes incidi curabit. Edidit iterum Pöemata Germanica, qvæ inscripsit Pöetischer Schauplaz.[6] Taceo negotia publica et privata alia.

Grundmannus[7] ille, qvem fidei meæ jure commendaveras, Hafniæ iam hæret. Præfectus est literis ac moribus filiorum **Simonis Pauli**, Med. D. et Prof. ibidem,[8] amici mei non è multis.

[671] Cæsius[9] ex Hollandiâ Hamburgi esse nunciatur: qvi domum reversus qvantam novorum struem dabit?[a] Videbit tamen CL. Buchnerus[10] noster, atq*ue* navabit operam, ut frugi esse incipiat. Sed si ridicularum opinionum vanitas nondum omnem in eo rationis usum obliteravit. Grutnerus ille Vratislaviensis ex Hollandia ad me perscripsit: Cæsius nenne sich den blauen Ritter, und habe aus eigener macht einen Orden stifften wollen: inductus ratione nominis sui.[11] Addit miserabiliter aliqvoties verberibus cæsum esse Cæsium, qvod alicubi in Notis scripsisset: henrich were eben so viel als hörnerträger oder hanrey: deceptus Gallico Henry. Judicium Buchneri de novâ Cæsii orthographiâ, *seu* potius σκαιογραφία communicavi amico cuidam, qvi agit Lugduni Bat*avorum* id contra datam fidem eliminavit. Buch-

nerus, uti forte adhuc meministi, auctor mihi erat, ut publico aliqvo scripto monerem adolescentes, ne vanitates istas, sapientias meras existiment. Ex hoc ubique fabula sum, me moliri aliqvid contra Cæsium. Ecce tibi, quæ nobiliss. **Harsdorferus** ad me. Sic ille: Ne*qu*e me latet, qvid contra Cæsii proterviam moliaris, cui jam ab Elzeviro via plura indies novandi occlusa est, qvod talia apud omnes vapulent. Jactat se XXX. Libb. de Lingvâ Germanicâ scripsisse, et jam parare Grammaticam ex suo ingenio. næ monentibus amicis ad rationem et bonam mentem redire recusat, et ex suo cerebro omnia pro lubitu effingere sibi integrum esse existimat. Hæc ille. Vale decus meam, et favere mihi numqvam desiste, qvi Te de-[672]morior. Cajæ tuæ, foeminæ rari exempli, etiamsi olim fuisset, meo et uxoris meæ nomine plurimam nunciabis salutem. Salveat et nobiliss. **Tarnow**, salveant, qvi mihi bene cupiunt. Roztoki a'd. 10 Junii A. 1646.

Quæ spes in negotio **Schæviniano** affulgeat, nisi grave est, me doce, ut habeam, q*uibus* viduæ a*ni*m*u*m fermè jam fractum rurs*us* erigam.[12]

T a *B setzt hier einfachen Punkt statt Fragezeichen.*

K 1 Die U. Rostock, an der Andreas Tscherning seit dem 16.5.1644 die Professur für Poesie innehatte. S. 440324 K 1. Zu seinem Förderer Matthaeus Apelles v. Löwenstern vgl. ebd.

2 Zu Augustus Buchner (FG 362) s. bes. Anm. 3 u. 10 sowie 440324 K 2, K 14 u. K I 1.

3 Tschernings Epithalamium auf eine Tochter Augustus Buchners. Für Tschernings Gedicht bedankte sich Buchner in einem auszugsweise erhaltenen Brief vom „d. V. Iduum Jan. anno M DC XLVI" (vermutlich richtig: Jun.) in: Vortrab | Des | Sommers | Deutscher Ge- | tichte | von | Andreas Tscher- | ningen/ ausgesen- | det und verlegt | in Rostock. | [Vignette] | Gedruckt/ durch sehl. Nicolaus | Keyln/ Acad. Buchd. Erb. 1655. Bl.)(3v. STB Berlin — PK, digit.: „ODe, qua Nominalia Sponsæ celebrasti, mirificè me cepit. Est enim morata egregie: cæterum delicata illa quidem, non fracta tamen: molliculaque magis quam dissolutua. Quo factum, ut cætera tua, quorum mentionem facis, eo impensius videre cupiam. &c." Vgl. die Nachricht in *W. Buchner*, 36: In einem 1863 im Besitz des Nachfahren Wilhelm Buchner befindlichen Brief des Vorfahren an F. Ludwig lud Augustus Buchner am 19.1.1646 den Fürsten zur Vermählung seiner ältesten Tochter Elisabeth ein. Diese heiratete Heinrich Cosel. Vgl. Fröliche Gedancken vnd Wünsche. Bey H. HEJNRJCH COSELS. von Petzlinowetz/ Beyder rechten Doct. Mit J. ELJSABETH BVCHNERJN. Am 3. des Hornungs/ des 1646sten Jahres in Wittenberg gehaltenen Verehligung Auffgesetzet vnd abgeleget Von Etlichen des H. Bräutigams gewesenen Tischgesellen. Gedruckt zu Wittenberg. Anno 1646. Ratsschulbibl. Zwickau: 6.5.18.b (1). Cosel, Wittenberger Hofgerichtsassessor und späterer Jura-Professor (vgl. *Buchner (1720)*, P. I, Nr. CX), war bei Augustus Buchners Tod (12.11.1661) schon verstorben. S. Abraham Calovius: I. N. J. ARTIFICII ORATORII MAGISTERIUM. Oder Sonderbahre Kunst und Meisterstück der göttlichen Beredsamkeit ... Bey ... Leich-Begängnüß Des ... Hn. AUGUSTI BUCHNERI (Wittenberg o. J.: Johann Röhner), Widmung.

4 Georg Philipp Harsdörffer (FG 368) hatte Tscherning schon in seinen Schriften erwähnt, als er im Winter 1643 über Matthaeus Apelles v. Löwenstern und Johann Rist (FG 467. 1647) den Kontakt mit Tscherning suchte. Vgl. 450726 K 0. Am 17.12.1643 schrieb Tscherning: „Harsdörfferi scripta nondum vidi: Quisquis vero ille sit, amo ejus ingenium studia et humanitatem, quia inductus mentionem nominis nostri dignatus est facere. Nihil antehac de ipso citius inaudivi, quam ejus nomine salutem mihi nunciaret Ristius et de Poetice mea aurem mihi velleret. Effigiem ejus exosculor." STB Berlin — PK: Dep. Breslau 17 (alte StB Breslau: Ms. Rhed. R. 402), S. 661. Vgl. bes. 440324. Ein Gedicht Tschernings über Harsdörffers Werk scheint unbekannt zu sein. Vgl. jedoch *Rist: Schauplatz (1646*; HAB: Lo 6467), Bl. a r – a v: Harsdörffers dt. und lat. Epigramm (emblemat. Subscriptio) unter Avers u. Revers einer Münze (Emblem): „Sinnebild-Pfenning Jn Des weitberühmten Herrn J. Risten Poetischen Schauplatz geworffen."/ „Nummus Emblematicus In [...] Johannis Ristii Theatrum Poeticum." Auch Tscherning war im *Poetischen Schauplatz* mit zwei Beiträgen vertreten, s. 440324 K I 3.

5 Zu Tschernings Gedicht auf Rists Schwan-Wappen in Rists *Allerunterthänigster Lobrede An die Allerduchlaüchtigste [...] Römische Kaiserliche Maiestätt/ Herren Ferdinand den Dritten* (Hamburg [1647]), Rückseite des Titelblatts. HAB: 43.6 Pol. (7), auch Dig., aus Anlaß der Verleihung des Adelsdiploms und des Poetenlorbeers, zu Tschernings weiterem Gedicht darin und dem Ndr. des ersteren in seinem *Vortrab des Sommers Deutscher Gedichte* (Rostock 1655) s. 440324 K I 3. Das Gedicht, das Harsdörffer an F. Ludwig sandte, im Wortlaut in *DA Köthen I. 8:* 470206 I.

6 *Rist: Schauplatz (1646)*, Bl. aiij r f.: Tschernings „Sonett Auff den Schauplatz der Freud- und Traurgedichte/ Des WollEhrwürdigen/ Ehrenfesten/ Großachtbahren und hochgelahrten Herrn Johann Risten/ ... Seines grossen Freundes". Dazu Bl. a iij v – a 5 r, Tschernings „Antwohrt An eben denselben/ auff seine mier neulich übergeschickte Ode." — Inc.: „SOlt' Jch deiner ie vergessen wehrter Freund/ o Licht der Zeit [...]". S. 440324 K I 3.

7 Wohl Christoph Grundmann, seit 1667 Ratsherr in Breslau im Wechsel als Schöffe und Konsul, starb als Ratsmitglied und Vorsteher des Almosenwesens und des Hospitals zu Allerheiligen in Breslau. Vgl. die Leichenpredigt von Gottfried Assig: Der Allerbeste Grund (o. O. u. J.: [Breslau:] Gottfried Gründer, vor 1680), BU Wrocław: 559001. Vgl. ferner Johann Glaubitz: Schuldiges Glueck zu! Dem ... Christoff Grundmann/ als selbiger dieses 1667. Jahr den 23. Februarii ein Mitglied des Raths der ... Stadt Breßlau ... erwehlet worden (Wittenberg: Berger 1667). Ratsschulbibl. Zwickau: 49.6.4 (56); ferner *Pusch* II, 14 u. V, 107.

8 Simon Paulli (Rostock 1603 – Kopenhagen 1680), Sohn des Rostocker Medizinprofessors Heinrich P., mit dem er 1604 nach Dänemark ging, als dieser zum Leibarzt der Königinwitwe Sophia in Nyköbing/ Falster ernannt wurde. Nach dem Tod des Vaters 1610 nach Rostock zurückgekehrt, studierte er dort seit 1617; Studienreisen führten ihn nach Holland und Frankreich. 1626–1629 Erzieher junger Adeliger in Sorø, 1630 in Wittenberg Promotion zum Dr. der Medizin, praktizierte danach einige Jahre in Lübeck; 1634 Prof. med. in Rostock, 1639 Prof. f. Botanik, Anatomie u. Chirurgie in Kopenhagen, 1650 Hof-, 1656 kgl. dän. Leibarzt. Seine erstmals 1648 erschienene *Flora Danica*, seine bis ins hohe Alter durchgeführten botan. Exkursionen u. sein hinterlassenes Herbarium erlangten große Bekanntheit. Vgl. *DBL* XVIII, 39–43 u. *Hirsch* IV, 531.

9 Philipp v. Zesen (FG 521. 1648), der sich von 1642–1648, von verschiedenen Reisen unterbrochen, in den Niederlanden (Amsterdam, Leiden, Utrecht) aufgehalten hat. S. *Ingen*, 23; *Ingen: Zesen*, 3.

10 Augustus Buchner (FG 362), Prof. der Poesie und Rhetorik in Wittenberg, Lehrer Zesens. Buchner gehörte wie Tscherning zum Kreis um Martin Opitz (FG 200) und ließ nach dessen Tod (1639) nicht den Kontakt zu Opitzens schles. Freunden abreißen. Am 21.3.1643 schrieb z.B. Bernhard Wilhelm Nüßler an Andreas Senftleben (1602–1643; *Cunrad: Silesia togata*, 256): „Quid Tscherningio nostro fiat, aut qvod vitae genus meditetur, scire pervelim. Buchnerus noster nuper admodum de eo accuratè ad me iterum scrip-

sit: neq*ue* difficile est conjicere, qvo ille collimet: Si vel tribus verbis de mente Tscherningii erudiri me contigerit, statim CL.^mum Virum absoluam." STB Berlin — PK: Dep. Breslau 17 (ehem. StB Breslau: Ms. Rhed. R 402), S. 654. In der Zwischenzeit hatte sich Tscherning schon bei Buchner gemeldet. *Borcherdt: Tscherning*, 70. Vgl. auch schon Tschernings Brief an Buchner in *Opitz: BW 401122 rel*. Tscherning hoffte von dem einflußreichen Buchner als Bewahrer von Opitz' poetischem Erbe anerkannt zu werden. Buchner tat ihm diesen Gefallen offenbar gern. Vgl. seinen (gekürzten) Brief vom 26.2.1642: „Macte itaque virtute tua, TSCHERNINGI, atque ostende seculo, multum quidem exstincto OPITIO amisisse Germanicas nostras Musas; non pauciora tamen expectanda esse abs te, per quæ jam semel in illo partum decus tueantur &c." S. Tscherning: Vortrab des Sommers Deutscher Gedichte (1655, s. Anm. 3), Bl.)(3v. Ein Gratulationsgedicht Buchners auf Tschernings Gedichtsammlung *Früling* (1642) findet sich u. d. T. „In ANDREÆ TSCHERNINGII Poëmata Germanica Ann. 1642" in *Buchner: Poemata (1720)*, 492 f. (HAB: P 1612b.8° Helmst., auch dig.). Wie wichtig Tscherning Buchners Hochschätzung war, zeigt sein Epigramm in: ANDREÆ TSCHERNINGII | SCHEDI- | ASMATUM | LIBER UNUS | [Zierleiste] | RostochI. | ANNO M. DC. XLIV, Nr. 80. *Faber du Faur* Nr. 264 = HAB: MF 1:59.
    De seipso
NOnnihil ergò sumus, BUCHNERO carmina Vati
    Nostra probantur.
Majoris facio, quàm si, quae scripsero, cantet
    Ultima Thule.
Buchner schickte F. Ludwig Gedichte unterschiedlicher Autoren, von denen diesem ausdrücklich Tschernings Verse am besten gefielen (s. 440324 K 0). In die FG fand Tscherning (1611–1659) dennoch keine Aufnahme, sicher auch wegen des mangelnden sozialen Status des bitterarmen Studenten, der es später (1644) nur zum karg besoldeten Professor der Dichtkunst brachte. Am 17.8.1640 hatte Buchner in einem Brief an Opitz' Freund Christophorus Colerus um Tscherning geworben, da gute Latein- und Griechisch-Studenten in Wittenberg zur Mangelware geworden seien. *Borcherdt: Tscherning*, 69 u. Anm. 28: Zitat des Briefs aus *Buchner (1720)*, 758. *Borcherdt: Tscherning*, 69 ff. nebst Anm. dazu S. 277 ff. geht, auf ausführliche Zitate gestützt, die brieflichen Zeugnisse des Werbens Buchners um Tscherning und dessen Antworten durch.

11 In seinem Brief vom 7.1.1646 an Apelles hatte Tscherning Zesens Pseudonym nach Johann Rists Information mitgeteilt, s. 440324 K 23. Zesen nannte sich „Ritterhold von Blauen" auf dem Titelblatt seines Romans *Adriatische Rosemund* (1645). Eigener Aussage im *Hochdeutschen Helikonischen Rosentahl* (1669) nach ist Zesens Deutschgesinnete Genossenschaft bereits am 1.5.1643 in Hamburg gegründet worden. *Zesen SW* XII, 192, 218 u. 225. Vgl. *Ingen*, 18.

12 In 450726 war bereits der dort eher als „Schrevinius" zu lesende Name gefallen. Dabei ging es um Logis-Kosten, die einer (Rostocker?) Witwe schuldig geblieben worden seien.

460613

Herzog Rudolf August von Braunschweig-Wolfenbüttel an Fürst Christian II. von Anhalt-Bernburg

Hz. Rudolf August v. Braunschweig-Wolfenbüttel (FG 754. 1660) bedankt sich für ein Schreiben F. Christians II. v. Anhalt-Bernburg (FG 51) und die darin zum Ausdruck kommende Sorge um das Wohl seiner Eltern (Hz. August d.J. [FG 227] u. Hzn. Sophia Elisabeth v. Braunschweig-Wolfenbüttel [AL 1629. TG 42b]) und Geschwister (Pz. Anton Ulrich [FG 716. 1659], Pz. Ferdinand Albrecht [FG 842. 1673], Pzn. Sibylla Ursula, Pzn. Clara Augusta u. Pzn. Maria Elisabeth) und erwidert die Grüße und guten Wünsche. — Zugleich übersendet er das Wappen des pommerschen Gesandten Joachim v. Glasenapp (FG 451. Der Erwachsende. 1646), das dieser ihm auf seine Nachfrage hin hat zukommen lassen. Die versprochene Quartausgabe der *Evangelischen Kirchen-Harmonie* seines Vaters Hz. August dagegen kann noch nicht übermittelt werden, da diese noch nicht abgeschlossen sei. Mit der Zusage, die Bibelbearbeitung baldmöglichst nachzusenden, bittet er diesbezüglich um etwas Geduld. — Die von F. Christian II. erwähnten Bücher, die er an Hz. August zu überschicken versprochen hatte, seien, so Rudolf Augusts Informationen, bereits im Bestand der väterlichen Büchersammlung. Das von F. Christian II. erwähnte Gesellschaftsbuch (*GB 1646*) habe Hz. Rudolf August noch nicht erhalten, er wisse auch nichts über dessen Verbleib, bedankt sich für die (aus der Zusendung) wahrnehmbare Gewogenheit und die damit verbundene Mühe und hofft auf die Ankunft des Buches. — Obwohl die mehrfache Hänselung Glasenapps wohl gegen die Statuten der FG verstoße, sei sie doch im Sinne des besagten Gesellschafters. Er sei davon überzeugt, daß es F. Ludwig nur recht sei, daß den Gesellschaftern des Öfteren „solche nahrung" vorgesetzt würde, die für sie annehmlich und stärkend sei. — Schließlich drückt Hz. Rudolf August seinen Wunsch aus, F. Christian II. und seine Verwandten an ihrem Ort (Bernburg) zu besuchen, auch um dabei seine Eignung für die FG unter Beweis stellen zu können und den „Ernährenden" (F. Ludwig. Der Nährende) zu seiner Aufnahme in die Gesellschaft zu veranlassen. Jedoch befürchtet er, aufgrund der Kriegsläufte vorerst an diesem Vergnügen gehindert zu werden.

Q LHA Sa.-Anh./ Dessau: Z 18 Abt. Bernburg A 10 Nr. 6, unfol., 2 Bl. [A: 2v]; Schreiberh. mit eigenh. Unterschrift; Sig.; Adresse mit eigenh. Anmerkung des Empfängers.

A *Dem Hochgebornen Fürsten* Herrn *Christian* Fürsten züe Anhalt, Graffen zu Ascanienn herrn Zu Zerbst vndt Bernburgk *etc.* Meinem frl. Lieben Vetternn *etc.*
Daneben von der Hand F. Christians II. v. Anhalt-Bernburg (FG 51): Nota Auß dieser antworth, ist bey nahe der gruß, zu errahten *etc.*

Hochgebohrner Fürst, vielgeehrter frl. Lieber Vetter,

Daß E. Ld. mitt dero angenehmen handtschreiben mich besuchen und ehren, und dadurch unsers sämptlichen zustandes freundtVetterlich sich erkündigen wollen, dafür bin E. Ld. nicht allein ich höchlich verbunden, sondern bedancken sich auch wegen der guten nachfrage so wohl Jhr J. G. Gd. mein herr Vater und Fraw-Mutter als mein hhl. Brüdere und Schwestern, und grüßen E. Ld. hinwieder gantz fr. und ehren gebührlich, und wie sie Gott bißhero im erträglichen wohl-wesen hatt leben laßen, also wündtschen sie allerseits, das E. Ld. gleichergestalt bey allen begehrender wohlstande mügen erhalten werden,

Bey dem Pommerischen Abgesandten Jochim *[sic]* von Glasennap¹ habe ich deß begehrten wapen halber erinnerung gethan und selbiges von Jhm, wie hierbey zufinden², erhalten, müchte wündtschen, daß Jch zugleich auch die gesuchte von Jhr Gd meinem hl Vatern außgegebene Harmony kündte überschicken, weil aber selbige und zware die edition in 4to noch nicht gantz verfertiget³, also bitten hochged. Jhr Gd. E. Ld. wollen mitt derselbigen überschickung noch etwas in gedult stehen, und sich gewiß versichern, daß sie ins künfftige erfolgen soll,

Die erwehnten Bücher, so E. Ld. [1v] J. Gd zu schicken sich erboten, habe ich verstanden, daß J. Gd. sie bereit in dero Bibliotheca⁴ hätten, sonsten wäre mihr zum höchsten lieb, daß ich das buch von der geselschafft⁵, davon E. Ld erwehnung thun müchte überkommen haben, es ist aber selbiges zu meinen händen noch nicht gelanget, wo es hingeblieben kan ich nicht wißen, daß E. Ld. aber mich damit ansehen wollen darauß erkenne ich deroselbigen wolgewogenheit, und bedancke mich genommener mühe halber, verhoffend derselbigen in diensten noch zugenießen.

Daß der erwachsende zu unterschiedtlichen mahlen allhier gehänseltt⁶ worden, halte ich wohl daß solches wieder die satz- und ordnungen der Fruchtbringenden geselschafft, aber dennoch nicht wieder den willen und vermügen deß gesagtenᵃ geselschaffters lauffen und halte ich, der Ernährende⁷ werdᵇ nichtᶜ ungerne sehen, wenn man den Geselschafftern solche nahrung offte vorsetze, die ihnen angenehme und so beschaffen seyn, daß sie dadurch zunehmen und wachsen können,

Ob mir zware nichts liebers wäre, als mir die ehre zu geben, und E. Ld, so wol auch dero hhl Vettern Ld an ihrem orte sämptlich einmahl zubesuchen, und durch dero annemblichen geselschafft mich so geschickt und würdig zumachen, daß Jch von dem Ernährenden in die Fruchtbringende geselschafft auffgenommen werden könte, so zweiffele ich doch sehr, daß ietzige böse zeit solche hohe vergnügung mihr zulaßen werde, unterdeßen so bleibe ich [2r] doch nichts destoweniger E. Ld zu dienen allezeit gefließen, und wündtsche nichts mehres, als das glück und die gelegenheit zuhaben E. Ld in der that zubezeigen, daß ich bin

    Deroselben
    Getrewer dienstwilliger Vetter
    Rudolph Augustus *mp*.
Wolffenb. d 13. Jul. ao 1646.

Ihr Ld. Fürst Ludwigen bitte ich unbeschwert bey gelegenheit dienstfr. zu grüßen.

T **a** *Gebessert aus unleserlichem Wort; unsichere Lesung.* — **b** *Gebessert aus* werde — **c** *Eingefügt.*

K Mit diesem Schreiben, das auf ein unbekanntes eigenh. Schreiben F. Christians II. v. Anhalt-Bernburg (FG 51) antwortete, bewarb sich der gerade 19-jährige Hz. Rudolf

460613 Herzog Rudolf August von Braunschweig-Wolfenbüttel

August v. Braunschweig-Wolfenbüttel (FG 754. 1660) um die Aufnahme in die FG, in der sein Vater, Hz. August d.J. v. Braunschweig-Wolfenbüttel (FG 227), bereits seit 1634 Mitglied war. Ein Brief F. Ludwigs an seinen Neffen Christian einen Monat später macht deutlich, daß F. Ludwig keine Einwände gegen eine Mitgliedschaft Hz. Rudolf Augusts in der FG äußert. S. 460714. Da die Aufnahme Rudolf Augusts aber erst 1660 unter dem Gesellschaftsoberhaupt Hz. Wilhelm IV. v. Sachsen-Weimar (FG 5) und sogar noch nach seinem jüngeren Bruder Anton Ulrich (FG 716. 1659) erfolgte, scheint dessen FG-Aufnahme nicht mit Nachdruck verfolgt worden zu sein. F. Christian hielt sich übrigens vom 23. bis 25. Mai 1646 in Wolfenbüttel auf, bevor er nach Hannover weiterreiste. In Wolfenbüttel traf er mit Hz. August, dessen drei Prinzen (Rudolf August, Anton Ulrich und Ferdinand Albrecht [FG 842. 1673]), mit dem Marschall Franz Julius v. dem Knesebeck (FG 396), dem pommerschen Gesandten Joachim v. Glasenapp (s. Anm. 1) u.a. zusammen. Am Sonntag Trinitatis (24.5.) wohnte er einem Gottesdienst bei, in dem „die Episteln vndt Text gelesen, nach des hertzogs newen Biblischen [ver]sion, vndt Harmonia des Lebens Christj, so er außgehen laßen" (*Christian: Tageb.* XVIII, 322r). Vgl. Anm. 3. Auch fiel ihm das Festhalten an etlichen „alten ceremonien" auf: „es gienge alhier nicht Helmstädtisch, zu" (322v). Beim Mittagsmahl war auch der von F. Christian geschätzte „weittberühmbte Doctor [Cali]xtus" zugegen, der sich über den erfolglosen Ausgang des Thorner Religionsgesprächs beklagte (323r). Vgl. zu Christians Wertschätzung des Helmstedter Theologen ausgiebig *Christian: Tageb.* XVIII, Eintrag vom 27.10.1645, wo Calixt unter vielem anderen schon deshalb Anerkennung findet, weil er „das horrendum Dogma Ubiquitatis, (wie fast alle Helmstädter thun) billich verwirft, vndt mit andern Flaccianern nicht einstim*m*et". Er werde daher „vor einen Calvinisten ausgeruffen [...], welches er doch nicht leyden will, gleichwol aber, seine Meynung, aus Gottes wortt, constanter behauptet, vndt sich nicht von der warheit abschregken leßet. Gott gebe einigkeit, vndt friede, in Geistlichen vndt weltlichen dingen, damit ein Hirte, vndt eine herde, baldt werden möge, nach Gottes gnedigem willen, vndt wolgefallen." (Tageb. hier unfol.) Bei seinem Wolfenbüttel-Aufenthalt Ende Mai 1646 erschien ihm Hz. August als „sehr moderat in geistl. vndt weltlichen vorfallenheiten" (a. a. O., Bl. 323r). In Hannover hielt sich Christian einige Tage auf. Am 29.5. brach er zur Rückreise auf und erreichte über Peine am 30.5. erneut Wolfenbüttel. Wieder traf er mit Pz. Rudolf August, Knesebeck u. anderen „Junckern" zusammen. Rudolf August zeigte ihm in einem Rundgang die Festung Wolfenbüttel; mit Hz. August, „un Prince fort accomply et vertieux" (Bl. 332r), spielte Christian Schach. Am 1. Juni zeigte ihm Hz. August die hzl. Bibliothek und das Zeughaus. In der Bibliothek „sollen in die 80000 bücher, von allerley scientiis, vndt faculteten sein, wie wir dann eine große Menge in guter ordnung, darinnen gesehen vndt dergleichen Bibliotheca in Deutschlandt itziger zeitt schwehrlich zu finden." (*Christian: Tageb.* XVIII, Bl. 332v). Die Heimreise führte über Schöppenstedt, Schöningen, Oschersleben und Staßfurt nach Bernburg, wo Christian am 3. Juni eintraf. Vgl. Anm. 1 u. 6.

1 Joachim v. Glasenapp (FG 451. Der Erwachsende. 1646) war damals Hofmeister und Rat der in Neustettin residierenden Hzn. Hedwig, geb. Hzn. v. Braunschweig-Wolfenbüttel (1599–1650), Schwester Hz. Friedrich Ulrichs (FG 38) und Witwe Hz. Ulrichs v. Pommern (1589–1622), mit dem sie sich 1619 vermählt hatte. Die Ehe war kinderlos geblieben. 1637 war mit Hz. Ulrichs Bruder, Bogislaw XIV., das pommersche Herzoghaus der Greifen ausgestorben (vgl. 450326 K 4); die Erbansprüche Kurbrandenburgs konnten gegen die schwed. Besatzungsmacht nicht durchgesetzt werden. Der Westfäl. Frieden teilte das Land und sprach Vorpommern Schweden, Hinterpommern Kurbrandenburg zu. Glasenapp wurde 1646 auf Vorschlag und Zuraten Hz. Augusts sowie des Wolfenbütteler Frauenhofmeisters Carl Gustav v. Hille (FG 302) und unter Vermittlung F. Christians II.

in die FG aufgenommen. S. auch Anm. 6; vgl. *Conermann III*, 544–546. Zu Glasenapp s. auch 460620A u. 460714.

2 Die erwähnte Beilage fehlt. Das Wappen ist unter der Nr. 451 im *GB Kö.* (III), wie üblich dem Reimgesetz gegenüber, eingemalt. Christian II. hatte somit das dem Brief hinzugefügte Wappen erhalten und an seinen Onkel, F. Ludwig, weitergeleitet. Dies muß alsbald geschehen sein, denn F. Ludwig bedankt sich bei Christian mit 460714 für die Weiterleitung des vorliegenden Briefes mitsamt dem Glasenapp-Wappen.

3 Hz. August d. J. v. Braunschweig-Wolfenbüttel arbeitete seit spätestens 1641 an der zweiteiligen *Evangelischen Kirchen-Harmonie*, um diese anstelle und neben den bisher üblichen Evangelien- und Epistelperikopen im Gottesdienst zu verwenden. Die *Kirchen-Harmonie* griff Texte der zuvor von Hz. August veröffentlichten *Passionsharmonie* (zuerst Lüneburg 1640, s. 401111 I) auf. S. 401111 K 15, 410406 K 3, 411214 u. im vorliegenden Band 451001, 460317 K 3 u. ö. In einer hzl. Handschrift (i. e. HAB: Cod. Guelf. 43 Noviss. 8°; s. 411214 IV) findet sich auch ein dt. Gedicht Glasenapps auf Hz. Augusts *Kirchen-Harmonie* von 1648 mit einem lat. Gedicht vom selben Autor. Letzteres wurde in die genannte 5. Druckauflage der *Kirchen-Harmonie* aufgenommen (s. 411214 III [K]). Während die Oktavausgabe der *Kirchen-Harmonie* bereits Anfang Juni 1646 gedruckt vorlag und ihre Verwendung mit Verordnung vom 6. des gleichen Monats von Hz. August in den Kirchen seines Landes festgelegt wurde, war die hier erwähnte Ausgabe im Quartformat (²1646) Mitte Juni 1646 offensichtlich noch nicht abgeschlossen. Sie erschien jedoch, genau wie die nicht illustrierte, duodezformatige Ausgabe, noch im gleichen Jahr (s. 411214 III [I], S. 357 u. K III I 1, S. 390). Vgl. 460804 (K 1). Im Zusammenhang mit der Bibelarbeit Hz. Augusts u. der Vermittlertätigkeit des ältesten Sohnes u. Briefverfassers, Hz. Rudolf August, erscheint das Geschenk der Antwerpener Bibel Johann Valentin Andreaes (FG 464. 1646) an Hz. August (mit hsl. Widmung Kf. Augusts v. Sachsen an Andreaes Großvater) fünf Jahre zuvor erwähnenswert. Hz. August kündigte nach der Geschenkübergabe an, daß er sein ‚Privatexemplar', das er von seiner ersten Gemahlin, Hzn. Clara v. Pommern, bereits zum Neujahr 1609 erhalten hatte, dem gemeinsamen Sohn Rudolf August übergeben werde. S. 410406 K 1.

4 Der in Dannenberg/ Hzt. Lüneburg geborene Hz. August d. J. begann bereits in Hitzacker, wo er 30 Jahre seines Lebens (seit 1604) verbrachte, Bücher zu sammeln. Mit der Regierungsübernahme im Ft. Wolfenbüttel 1635 und der 1643 in Folge des Goslarer Friedens erfolgten Übernahme von Residenz und Festung Wolfenbüttel intensivierte er seine Sammelaktivitäten. Er engagierte eine Reihe von Agenten zur Beschaffung von Büchern und nutzte auch seine Kontakte zu befreundeten Höfen, um seine Sammlung stetig zu erweitern. S. *Conermann III*, 243–245. Zur Herzog August Bibliothek vgl. Werner Arnold: Die Entstehung der Bibliothek aus dem Netzwerk. In: Geschichte, Öffentlichkeit, Kommunikation. FS Bernd Sösemann zum 65. Geburtstag. Hg. Patrick Merziger. Stuttgart 2010, 9–24; Petra Feuerstein: Dasein als verzaubertes Chaos: 20 Jahre Sammlung Deutscher Drucke 1601–1700 auf den Spuren von Herzog August d. J. (1579–1666). Wiesbaden 2009; Maria von Katte: Die Bibliotheca Augusta — Gestalt und Ursprung. In: Herzog August Bibliothek Wolfenbüttel. Braunschweig 1989, 50–57; Hans Ulrich Schneider: Bücher und Bewegung in der Bibliothek von Herzog August. In: Sammeln, Ordnen, Veranschaulichen. Zur Wissenskompilatorik in der Frühen Neuzeit. Hg. Frank Büttner. Münster 2003, 111–127.

5 Bereits 1643 hatte F. Ludwig entschieden, das illustrierte *GB 1629/30*, welches die Impresen der ersten 200 Mitglieder enthielt, um die bis Ende 1642 aufgenommenen weiteren 200 Mitglieder zu ergänzen. S. 430214 u. 421031A K 14. Erst nach langen Verhandlungen, insbesondere die Finanzierung desselben anlangend, und mit einiger Verspätung wurde ein neues Mitgliederbuch (*GB 1646*) mit den in Kupfer gestochenen Impresen der FG-Mitglieder bis zur FG Nr. 400 bei Matthäus Merian d. Ä. in Frankfurt a. M. gedruckt und publiziert. S. 440130 K 3, 450126 K 4 u. zur Finanzierung 450127 K 1.

6 Mit der als „Hänselung" bezeichneten Zeremonie wurde ein neues Mitglied feierlich in die FG aufgenommen. Dabei spielten u. a. das Trinkgefäß des „Ölbergers" und eine große Menge „stärkenden" Weins eine wichtige Rolle. S. dazu u. a. 401107 K 4, 410621 K 5 u. 460718 K 8. Glasenapps mehrfache Hänselung kommt mit den Beobachtungen F. Christians II. v. Anhalt-Bernburg bei seinen Wolfenbüttelbesuchen im Mai und Juni 1646 (s. Anm. 0) überein. Glasenapp erschien als „copioß von reden, hatte wol studiret, wuste viel dinges vndt war doch zu kennen, das er ein Pommer wahr": Es wurde nämlich „sehr stargk getrungken, vornehmlich umb deß Pomerenicken willen". Während sich Christian u. Hz. August mit „gesotten waßer" behalfen, mußten Glasenapp „vndt seine mittringker [...] heftig daran". (A. a. O., Bl. 323r). Auch während des Wolfenbüttel-Aufenthalts bei seiner Rückreise sei so „erschrecklich gesoffen worden, daß es mir ein grewel ist". Christian selbst wich auf Wasser aus, mußte aber „Meine Jungkern sich baldt todt sauffen sehen" (Bl. 332r). Am folgenden 1. Juni hielt man sich bei der Mittagsmahlzeit zurück, „vielleicht darumb, weil mein [Kammerjunker Abraham v.] Rindtorff [FG 352], heutte das fieber bekommen, [vndt] ich gewaltig wieder das tringken, protestiret". Auf den Abend aber wurde „desto beßer poculiret, vndt den [pomme]rischen Gesandten, in hofnung der einnehmung in die [Fru]chtbringende gesellschafft, gehänselt. Er der gesandte [ist] sehr trewhertzig darüber, vndt mein großer Freundt worden." (Bl. 333r).

7 F. Ludwigs eigentlicher Gesellschaftsname „Der Nährende" wird hier, ob bewußt oder in Unkenntnis des richtigen Namens, leicht verändert und als „Der Ernährende" wiedergegeben.

460620

Georg Philipp Harsdörffer an Fürst Ludwig

Antwort auf 460426 u. 460609. Beantwortet durch 460705. — Georg Philipp Harsdörffer (FG 368. Der Spielende) bestätigt den Empfang von F. Ludwigs (der Nährende) Briefen 460426 u. 460609 und schickt ihm das begehrte Wappen Johann Michael Moscheroschs (FG 436. Der Träumende). Er verspricht in dessen Namen, daß die (für den Erzschrein erbetenen) Schriften bald zugesandt werden. Seinerzeit seien keine Fuhren nach Leipzig abgegangen, der Student aber, dem er das *Specimen Philologiae Germanicae* (in drei Exemplaren) mitgegeben habe, sei so plötzlich und des Nachts aufgebrochen, daß Harsdörffer vergessen habe, der Sendung (460406) das besagte Wappen beizulegen. Ein Trauerfall habe ebenfalls zu diesem Versäumnis beigetragen. — Sein *Specimen* (1646) habe er nicht aus eitlem Kitzel aufgesetzt, sondern um den Kreis der einzubeziehenden urteilsfähigen Sprachgelehrten zu erweitern, damit die Regulierung der dt. Sprache hin zu einer durchgängigen Richtigkeit voranschreite und man dem letzten Ziel ihrer Vollkommenheit näher komme. Harsdörffer erwartet daher gespannt die Urteile der Gelehrten und versichert, sich willig dem Richterspruch F. Ludwigs zu unterwerfen. Bis dahin wolle er die Arbeit an einem projektierten zweiten Teil des *Specimen* ruhen lassen. — Für den sechsten Teil der *Frauenzimmer-Gesprächspiele* (1646), der wohl in sechs bis sieben Wochen erscheinen werde und zur Leipziger Herbstmesse mit anderen neuen Büchern dem Erzschrein eingeschickt werden soll, bittet Harsdörffer F. Ludwig um ein Widmungsgedicht. Der 6. Teil könnte der letzte sein, da Harsdörffer des Geizes seines Verlegers (Wolfgang Endter d. Ä.) überdrüssig und sein eigener Zeit- und Kostenaufwand sehr hoch seien.

Q HM Köthen: V S 545, Bl. 347r–348v [A: 348v], 348r leer; zwei rote Lacksiegel. Portoangaben mit roter Kreide unter der Adresse. — *D: KE*, 356f. — *BN: Bürger*, 675 Nr. 39.

A t. *Dem Durchleuchtigen Hochgebornen Fürsten und Herrn Herrn* Ludwigen *Fürsten zu Anhalt, Grafen zu Ascanien und Ballenstatt Herrn zu Zerbst und Berenburg etc.* Meinem g. Fürsten und Herrn. *Cöthen.* Zu Leipzig, bey H. Gottfr. Stahlen[1] *abzulegen.*
Eigenh. Empfangsvermerk F. Ludwigs: 28. Brachmonats 1646.

t.

Des höchstgeehrten *Nerenden* beede letzere, vom 26. April, und 6. des Brachmonats[2], sind dem Spielenden wol eingehändiget worden. Er übersendet hingegen mitkommend des *Traumenden* Wappen, und versichert benebens, daß seine Schriften mit ehster Gelegenheit folgen sollen.[3] Jüngsthin sind von hier keine fuhren nach Leipzig abgereiset, und hat der Student, welchem Specimen Philologiæ Germanicæ mitgegeben worden sich so eiligst auf den Weg gemacht, und solches bey Nacht abgeholet, das besagtes wappen und die Tagsbenamung vergessen worden:[4] theils aus eil, theils aus bestürtzung, und einem trauerfall[5], mit welchem dazumal Gott den Spielenden heimgesuchet hatte: bittet deswegen ümb gnädige Verzeihung.

Das Specimen Philolog. Germ. belanged, ist solches aus keinem wahnsüchtigen Kunstkützel, sondern zu steuer der Wahrheit[6] dergestalt zu papier gebracht worden, damit man mehr gelehrter, und verständiger urtheil darvon hören, und die Sp[r]ache zu <u>durchgehendern Gleichheit</u>, <u>Kunstrichtiger Verfassung</u>, und so viel thunlich zu <u>endlicher vollkommenheit</u> befördern möchte. Erwartet also der Spielende mit grossen verlangen der Sprachverständigen gründliche widerleg- oder gutsprechung[a]; sich des hochstgeehrten *Nerenden* richterlichen Ausspruch, vorbehaltlich seiner gegenantwort, willig unterwerffend.[7]

Der Gesprächspiele VI[ter] Theil, wird in 6 oder 7 Wochen zuende gebracht, und mit der künftigen Leipziger messe, benebens andern neuen Büchern zu den Ertzschrein überschicket werden; in fortsetzung aber der Winterarbeit, oder Speciminis II Philolog. German. [347v] kan[b] befehlter massen, ohne fernere Nachrichtung, nicht verfahren werden, wie wol künftige Forschungen oder Disquisitiones in andern seltnen Händlen[8] bestehen sollen.

Der Spielende erkühnet sich den hochstgeehrten *Nerenden* in unterthänigkeit zu ersuchen, ob [er] selber gnädig geruhen wolte zu berührten 6ten Theile seiner Gesprächspiele, etliche verslein zu übersenden; weil vielleicht dieser der letzte seyn möchte, so wol wegen des Verlegers Geitz, als der Unkosten die der Spielende, über seine mühe und Arbeit, aufwenden muß. Solche hohe Gnade verbleibet der Spielende auf alle Begebenheit eussersten vermögens zu bedienen schuldig, und erbietig.⁹

Der Allwaltige Gott erhalte den hochstgeehrten *Nerenden* in seinem beharrlichen Gnadenschutz, und allem Fürstlichen wolergehen.

Geben Nürnberg den 20ᵗᵉⁿ des Brachmonats 1646.

Des Höchstgeehrten *Nehrenden* Unterthänigster Diener
Der *Spielende*.

T a *Das* s *in* gutsprechung *gebessert aus* h *(Harsdörffer setzte wohl zunächst an, „gutheißen" zu schreiben).* — **b** *Gebessert aus* sol

K 1 Der Leipziger Kaufmann Gottfried Stahl, über den der Briefverkehr zw. F. Ludwig (Der Nährende) und Georg Philipp Harsdörffer (FG 368. Der Spielende) lief. Vgl. 440426 K 1.

2 Irrtümliche Datumsangabe bei letzterem Brief. Es kann nur 460609 gemeint sein.

3 In 450919A hatte F. Ludwig (der Nährende) bei Harsdörffer darum angehalten, daß der auf dessen Vermittlung jüngsthin aufgenommene Johann Michael Moscherosch (FG 436. Der Träumende) eine von ihm selbst besorgte Ausgabe seiner *Gesichte Philanders von Sittewalt* einsenden möge, damit man sie von unautorisierten Nach- und Raubdrukken unterscheiden könne. Diese Nachfrage blieb wiederholt Gegenstand in der Korrespondenz zwischen F. Ludwig und Harsdörffer. Vgl. 451101 u. 451209. In 460406 mußte Harsdörffer F. Ludwig vertrösten: Moscherosch lasse seine *Gesichte Philanders von Sittewald* gerade in Straßburg neu drucken. Die sich viele Jahre hinziehende Vorbereitung einer neuen Ausgabe seiner *Gesichte* durch Moscherosch fand mit der Straßburger Ausgabe von 1650 erst nach F. Ludwigs Tod ihren Abschluß. Vgl. 460406 K 8.

4 Harsdörffer wollte Moscheroschs Wappen bereits seinem Brief 460406 beilegen, hatte dies aber offensichtlich vergessen, so daß F. Ludwig in 460426 erstaunt bekannte, in der Sendung kein Wappen vorgefunden zu haben. In 460609 mahnte er erneut die Zusendung an. Unklar ist, was Harsdörffer mit der vergessenen „Tagsbenamung" meinte. Eventuell befürchtete er, den in aller Eile abgeschickten Brief nicht datiert zu haben. Tatsächlich ist 460406 mit einem vollständigen Datum versehen. Vgl. zur Korrespondenz um Moscheroschs Wappen 450504A K 5.

5 Ein Todesfall, der Harsdörffer in den ersten Apriltagen oder schon im März 1646 besonders schwer getroffen haben könnte (er muß um die Zeit von Brief 460406 liegen), ließ sich nicht ermitteln. Zu vermuten ist, daß ein Mitglied aus seinem engeren familiären Umfeld verstorben ist. Seine Frau Susanna (1616–1646), geb. Fürer v. Haimendorf, starb zwar im selben Jahr, allerdings erst am 27. Dezember. Aus einem nicht exakt datierbaren Brief von Harsdörffer an Birken, der im Dezember 1646, kurz vor ihrem Tod verfaßt sein muß, geht hervor, daß auch eine der drei Töchter Harsdörffers dem Tode nahe war (*Birken: Werke u. Korrespondenz* IX, 17f. u. 612–614). Aus dem „Lebens-Lauff" in der Leichenpredigt Harsdörffers von 1658 kennen wir zwar die Geburts-, aber nicht die Todesdaten seiner acht Kinder. S. Johann Michael Dilherr: Der Menschen Stand in GOTTES Hand. ... Volckreicher und Trübseeliger Leichbegängnis Deß Wohl-Edlen/ Gestrengen/ Fürsichtigen und Hochweisen Herrn Georg Philipp Harsdörffers ... Nürnberg [1658], 14–22 (Personalia), hier S. 18. Biedermann nennt von den Frühverstorbenen ebenfalls allein die Geburtsjahre; überlebt haben ihren Vater Carl Gottlieb (1637–1708) und Johann Siegmund (1639–1699), zuvor verstarben Philipp Sigmund (*1635), Georg Sigmund

(*1636), Susanne (*1642), Georg Philipp (*1643) und Susanne Maria (*1645). Vgl. Johann Gottfried Biedermann: Geschlechtsregister des Hochadelichen Patriciats zu Nürnberg ... Nürnberg 1748, T. CLIV B. Seine jüngste Tochter Susanne Helene (*1646) ist wohl erst im Juni od. Juli geboren, was aus Harsdörffers Brief an Birken vom 4.4.1646 hervorgeht, in dem er seinen Bekannten auf die Geburt eines weiteren Kindes in ca. drei Monaten hinweist (*Birken: Werke u. Korrespondenz* IX, 9–11, 580–588). Von einem Todesfall oder auch nur gedrückter Stimmung Harsdörffers ist zumindest in diesem Dokument noch nichts zu spüren. Im Brief von 1.8.1646 bittet er Birken dann um Gottvertrauen, obwohl der Herr alle — ihn eingeschlossen — durch Unglücksfälle prüfe, und am 17.10.1646 klagt Harsdörffer, er könne das ihn derzeit bedrängende Unglück nicht in Worte fassen (ebd., 13f., 596–603 bzw. 16f., 607–612). Die Vermutung, hinter dem im vorliegenden Brief genannten Trauerfall verberge sich der Tod eines seiner Kinder ist zumindest naheliegend. Vgl. auch *Bischoff*, 7–28; zur Biographie auch *DBA* I 186/ 390, 476/ 163–195, 938/ 92f., 990/ 294; *DBA* II 525/ 424–437; *DBA* III 352/ 194–220.

6 Im Sinne von ‚als Beitrag zur Wahrheit'. Die „Zusteuer" od. „Beisteuer" (Verben zusteuern bzw. beisteuern) definiert *Stieler*, 2153 als Hilfs- oder Unterstützungsmittel: „Zuesteuer/ subsidium, juvamen, & collecta in specie". Vgl. auch *DW* XVI, 853.

7 Das ihm hier von Harsdörffer angetragene intellektuelle Richteramt wird F. Ludwig in seiner Antwort 460705 bescheiden abweisen.

8 Lies: ‚in anderen, unregelmäßig erscheinenden, nicht sonderlich zahlreichen Abhandlungen'. „Selten" (in geringer Zahl, besonders) steht „seltsam" (unerwartet, verwunderlich) im Fnhd. semantisch näher als heute: *Stieler*, 2006: „Seltenheit/ & Seltsamkeit/ die/ raritas, infreqventia, insolitum, insperatum qvid, *it.* portentum, prodigium." *DW* X.1, 542–545 sieht in der Tendenz zur Bezeichnung des ‚Eigenartigen' eher eine Verschärfung der Grundbedeutung ‚rar'. „Händel" ist eine nicht mehr gebräuchliche Pluralform von Handel, die sich im heutigen Deutsch weitgehend verselbständigt hat (mit der Bedeutung ‚Streit, Zank'). Harsdörffer benutzt sie hier aber eher als ein (in dieser Form bisher nicht nachgewiesenes) Diminutiv von Handlung, Verhandlung, dabei jedoch Ab- oder Behandlung meinend. Vgl. *Stieler*, 753–756; *DW* IV.2, 368–373; Ernst Martin, Hans Lienhart: Wörterbuch der elsässischen Mundart. 2 Bde. Straßburg 1899, Bd.1, 348a–b, s.v. „Händel". — Ein zweiter Teil des *Specimen Philologiae Germanicae* ist jedenfalls nicht mehr erschienen.

9 Der sechste Teil der *Frauenzimmer-Gesprächspiele* erschien im Frühherbst 1646. Harsdörffer hatte ihn schon Ende März/ Anfang April dem Druck übergeben (vgl. 460406; ferner 451217); bis 1649 werden die letzten beiden Teile folgen. Mit 460705 sandte F. Ludwig das erbetene Widmungsgedicht an den Nürnberger, mit 460915 wird Harsdörffer ein fertiges Exemplar des 6. Teils an Christian Gueintz versenden, mit 460916 deren zwei an F. Ludwig. Der Band ist wie im Brief angekündigt im Katalog der Leipziger Michaelismesse von 1646 verzeichnet: Catalogus universalis, hoc est designatio omnium librorum, qui hisce nundinis ... Francofurtensibus & Lipsiensibus anno ... vel novi vel emendatiores & auctiores prodierunt (Leipzig 1646), D2v, http://www.olmsonline.de/purl?PPN525616772_1646_Michaelis. Vgl. zum 6. Teil der *Gesprächspiele* auch 441216 K I 0, 450400 K 11, 450529 K 9, 460112 K 3, 460131 K 11, 460803 u. 461031. — Über seinen steinreichen Verleger Wolfgang Endter d. Ä. (1593–1659) beschwerte sich Harsdörffer nicht nur hier, sondern z.B. auch in einem Brief an Birken vom 7.2.1646: „Nosti sordidum Enderi ingenium" (*Birken: Werke u. Korrespondenz* IX, 8). In einem nicht datierten Brief an Birken (zwischen August u. Oktober 1646) schimpfte Harsdörffer erneut über den geizigen Endter, der sich nicht einmal schäme, zwei Gulden für ein Exemplar des 6. Teils der *Gesprächspiele* zu verlangen. Ebd., 16. Aus 460916 geht allerdings hervor, daß

Endter wegen der kriegerischen Unruhen die Büchermessen nicht bedienen konnte, weswegen er wohl fürchtete, die Drucke nicht absetzen zu können. In seiner „Erinnerung deß Buchführers an den günstigen Leser" am Ende des 3. Teils der *Frauenzimmer-Gesprächspiele* (1643, Ndr. 1968) hatte Endter — in werbender Absicht — auf die hohen Kosten der Illustrationen aufmerksam gemacht: „die darzu erforderte starke Vnkosten/ wegen der Kupfer/ und sonderlichen Holtzarbeit" (d.h. Holzschnitte) hätten ihn dennoch nicht von der Verlegung des Werkes abbringen können. *Harsdörffer: Frauenzimmer-Gesprächspiele* III, 537. Die großen Druckkosten der aufwendig gestalteten Bände sprach Harsdörffer schon in 431124 gegenüber F. Ludwig selbst an: Allein für die Herstellung der Kupferstiche und Holzschnitte für den 4. Teil seien 100 Gulden aufzubringen. Vgl. zur Person Endters *Reske*, 718–721.

460620A

Joachim von Glasenapp an Fürst Ludwig

Joachim v. Glasenapp (FG 451. Der Erwachsende. 1646) bedankt sich bei F. Ludwig für die Aufnahme in die FG und erkennt auch dabei den Anteil seiner Förderer Hz. August d.J. v. Braunschweig-Wolfenbüttel (FG 227. Der Befreiende) und Hz. Christian II. v. Anhalt-Bernburg (FG 51. Der Unveränderliche). Glasenapp wünscht sich, F. Ludwig selbst die Hand küssen und ihm persönlich danken zu können. Leider kann dies aus Zeitmangel nicht geschehen. Der Aufgenommene verspricht, die Statuten der FG stets zu befolgen.

Q   HM Köthen: V S 545, Bl. 470r–471v [A: 471v], 471r leer; eigenh. — D: *KE*, 50. — *BN: Bürger*, 467 Nr. 2.

A   DEm DurchLeuchtigen hohgebornen Fürsten vndt herren, herrn *Ludewigen*, Fursten zu Anhalt, Grafen zu Ascanien, herren zu Zerbst vndt Berenburgk, Meinem gnadig*en* Fursten v*n*dt herren Vnterthangst ges*andt*
Eigenh. Empfangsvermerk Fürst Ludwigs: Pres. 25 Brachmonats 1640

DurchLeuchtiger Hochgeborner Furst,

E f g. sein meine vnterthanige gehorsame dienste in stetswerender bereitschafft.
    Gnadiger herr, daß E f g. mir die gnadige gewogenheit erzeigen v*n*dt alß ein Stiffter v*n*dt Vrheber der nie zum begnugen gelobten *Fruchtbringenden* geselschafft mich als[a] ein geringes gelit[1] derselben zuwürdigen vndt anzunemen[b2] sich gnediglich gefallen lassen, dafur sage E f G. sowoll auch meinen gnadigen Befoderenn dem Befreyenden[3] v*n*dt Unverenderlichen[4], als meine*n* allerseits gnadig*en* Fursten vndt herren, Jch vnterthanigst*en* danck[.] V*n*dt mochte von herzen wunschen, die ehre zu haben kegen wertig dafur E fg. die hande zu kussen v*n*dt meine [470v] schuldigkeit also gebüre*n*der maßen persohnlich*en* ab[zu]legen[c]! Weil aber dasselbe[a] die Zeit mir itz[o][c] misgönnet[d], so soll doch solches in meinem Vn[ter]thanig[c] danckbaren gemute E f g. nachstend[ig][c] [5] verpleiben! Wie ich mich dan

auch eußerst befleißigen werden *[sic]* der ordnung der hohs[t]ᶜ Loblichen geselschafft gebursambst nach zu Le[ben]ᶜ vndt Zeit meines Lebens zuverpleiben

    E F G.
    Vnterthanigster G[e]horsambsterᶜ diener
    Jochim v G[la]senapp*mp*

Geben aus Wolffenbutel den 20. Brachmonats 1646.

I

Impresenzettel des Erwachsenden mit Reimgesetz

Q HM Köthen: V S 545, Bl. 467rv, v leer; Schreiberh. mit Korrekturen v. F. Ludwigs H. — In leicht abgewandelter Orthographie gleichlautend im *GB Kö.* III, Bl. 52 u. *D: Conermann III*, 545.

[Joa]chim von Glasenap. *Der Erwachsende. Gemeine Hirse. Jm Feuchten Erdreiche*

    *Gemeine Hirs*ᵃ *Erwächst Jn Feuchter Erde gern,*
    Gedört und aufgelegt benimt des Leibes grimmen,
    Erwachsend' ist mein Nahm' ich werde nie sein fern',
    Noch von der tugend weit, viel mehr wil ich zustimmen,
    Damit *Erwachse* recht der Deütschen sprache kern,
    Des Vaterlandes lieb' in mir auch fort sol glimmen,
    Dasᵇ keine Feuchtigkeit sie nienicht dempfen kan,
    Weilᶜ sie zu guter frucht mich nützlich reitzet an.
    J v. G.   1646.

T a *Gebessert aus unleserlichem Wort.* — **b** *Gebessert aus* <annemen> — **c** *Textverlust im Falz. Konjektur in eckigen Klammern.* — **d** *Gebessert aus* <misköñet>

T I a *Gebessert aus* Hirse — **b** *Zeile gebessert aus* Von keiner Feuchtigkeit gedempft sie werden kan — **c** *Eingefügt für* <Dan>

K 1 Glied, mhd. gelit. S. *Paul Wb.*, 422.
    2 Joachim v. Glasenapp (FG 451. Der Erwachsende. 1646) gehörte zum Kreis der Gelehrten und Literaten um Hz. August d. J. v. Braunschweig-Wolfenbüttel (FG 227. Der Befreiende) und wurde auf dessen Betreiben hin aufgenommen. S. *Conermann III*, 544–546; vgl. *DA Köthen I. 8*: 470100 u. ö.
    3 Hz. August. S. Anm. 2.
    4 F. Christian II. v. Anhalt-Bernburg (FG 51. Der Unveränderliche). Er lernte Glasenapp auf seiner Besuchsreise in Wolfenbüttel Ende Mai 1646 persönlich kennen und wirkte ebenfalls vermittelnd bei seiner Aufnahme in die FG. S. 460613 K 0 u. 1. Der Brief 460613 dokumentiert, daß F. Christian II. das Wappen Glasenapps aus den Händen Hz. Rudolf Augusts v. Braunschweig-Wolfenbüttel (FG 754. 1660), Sohn Hz. Augusts, erhalten, 460714, daß es Christian an F. Ludwig weitergeleitet hatte.

5 Hier nicht im Sinne von rückständig (etwa bei Zahlungen) — s. *Diefenbach*, 775 (s. v. „nachstand"); *Lexer: Taschenwb.*, 147 („nachstendic") —, sondern im Sinne von nachhaltig, dauerhaft. Vgl. *Diefenbach*, a. a. O. („nachständig"); auch *DW* VII, 135.

460620B

Matthäus Merian d. Ä. an Peter Knaudt

Matthäus Merian d. Ä. bedankt sich für den (nicht überlieferten) Brief vom 10.6.1646 und die mitgeteilten Adressen der Herren und Interessenten, die das *GB 1646* geliefert haben möchten. Merian veranlasse die Sendung. Während der Leipziger Ostermesse 1646 hat Merian Johann Valentin Andreae (FG 464. 1646) zwei *GB 1646*-Exemplare über Heilbronn nach Stuttgart geschickt. Da diese Lieferung jedoch wie die Ulmer und andere Waren in Mainz und Heidelberg lange beschlagnahmt lagen und die Orte teilweise noch nicht verlassen haben, hofft er, daß die Sendung, falls sie noch nicht bei ihm angekommen wäre, Andreae bald erreichen werde. Die beiden Exemplare müßten von der für F. Ludwig (Der Nährende) bestimmten Anzahl abgezogen werden. — Die Zeichnung des Köthener Schlosses erwartet Merian; sie könne mit einem anderen Brief zusammen gesandt werden. Wegen der übrigen (Abrisse) möchte er noch Erkundigungen einziehen. Ansichten von Zerbst, Dessau, Bernburg und Köthen seien bereits in seinem Besitz, da es jedoch noch weitere Orte gäbe, wäre es ihm lieb, auch diese zu erhalten. — Den Transport der 48 Exemplare Hz. Augusts d. J. v. Braunschweig-Wolfenbüttel (FG 227. Der Befreiende) nach Wolfenbüttel habe er einem Frankfurter Kaufmann namens Heinrich Bengerath schon Anfang März aufgetragen. Ihr Ausbleiben verwundert Merian. — Gerade berichte ihm Bengerath, daß er Nachrichten von der Ankunft der Bücher vor 8 Tagen bei Hans Gärtner in Braunschweig erhalten habe. — Der Verkauf des *GB 1646* in Frankfurt a. M. für fünf Gulden, so Merian, gehe eher schleppend voran. Die Buchhändler wiederum, die es von ihm kaufen, bieten es teurer an, zu sechseinhalb bis sieben Gulden. Privaten Käufern überlasse Merian das Gesellschaftsbuch für sechs, dies zu Knaudts Kenntnis. — Postskriptum per 20.7.1646: Eben erhält Merian auch schriftlich Nachricht, daß die 48 für Wolfenbüttel bestimmten Exemplare samt der übrigen Waren angekommen sind und Hz. August daran sein Vergnügen habe.

Q HM Köthen: V S 546, Bl. 39r–40v [A: 39v]; eigenh.; Sig. Bl. 40r Postskriptum, 40v nicht erschließbare Zahlenkolumnen, die vielleicht schon für Peter Knaudt bestimmt waren oder später hinzugefügt wurden. Auf Bl. 39v auch F. Ludwigs Konzept 460708. — D: *Bircher: Merian*, 719f.; *Wüthrich: Merian Briefe*, 110–113. — BN: *Bürger*, 987 Nr. 19 (dat. 19.6.).

A Tt. Dem Ehrenvesten und GroßAchtparen Herrn Petter Knaudt *etc.* Fürstl. Anhaltischen Cam̄er Meistern *etc.* zu gg. henden   Cöthen

Ehrenvester und GroßAchtparer Jnsonders gg. Herr *etc.*

Dem sein mein willige dienst Jederzeit Anvor[1], und b[e]richte das mir des herrn geliebtes vom 10. diß wol worden, und wie die bey mir stehende **exemplar** sollen abgefolgt werden, ersehen[,] hieran soll nichts mangeln, wan gemelte Herren und Jnteressenten solche werden begehren, Alsdan ihnen lieferung geschehen soll. 2 **exemplar** habe ich dise Ostermeß an H. Doct. Joh. Valentin Andre uber

Heylbron nach Stutgart gesendt², es sein Aber selbige wie auch die Ulmer und andre gutter zu Maintz, und Heydelberg lang in Arrest³ gelegen, und theils noch nicht verlassen, verhoffe so ers nicht empfang*en* es doch baldt geschehen müsse oder werde. Die 2 exemplar werden an Jhr Fürstl. G. von Anhalt Anzahl müssen abkürtzt werden. Den Abriß des Fürst. Residentz Schloß, will Jch erwarten, kan durch einschlag gesendt werden.⁴ Wegen der ubrig*en*, will ich mich erkündigen. Die Abriß von Zerbst Dessaw, Bernburg und Cöthen habe ich, da aber andre mehr vorhanden wehren, wehre mir lieb solche zu bekommen.

Die 48 exemplaria der Fruchtbringenden geselschaft, habe ich auf befehl Jhr. F. G. Herrn hertzog Augusten zu Braunschweig, an einen hiesigen kauffman, nahmens Heinrich Pengerode,[a] ⁵ geliefert in ein packet versigelt, welcher befehl gehabt, solche neben andern wahren Jhr. F. Gn. nacher Wolfenbüttel zu versenden, ist gleich anfang des Mertzens gewesen, nimpt mich sehr wunder wo den dise sachen müssen bleiben.⁶

Jetz brichtet mich gemelter kauffman das er Auisen habe, das vor 8 tagen gemelte sachen zu Braunschweig an H. Hans Gärtner[b] ⁷ wol ankomen.

Die Fruchtbringende geselschaft verkauffe ich allhier umb bargelt das stukh à f. 5 — geht aber langsam Ab, die Buchhendler aber so es von mir[c] kauffen, gebens thewrer, zu f. 6 ½ oder f. 7. Andern aber so keine Buchhendler sein verkauffe ichs umb f. 6, — zur nachricht. Hiemit dem Allmechtig*en* wohl befohlen.

Ffurt den 19. Junij 1646.
    Dh.
    Dienstwilligster
    M. Merian

[40r] P. S. Großg. hochgeehrter Herr *etc.*
Jn diser Stunde bekome Jch schreiben von Wolffenbüttel vom 13. diß das die 48 exemplaria der Fruchtbringenden geselschaft, sampt den vbrigen wahren, alda wohl angelangt, und Jhr. fl. Gn. damit ein gnädiges vernugen⁸ haben, Jst also dises nun auch Richtig.⁹ Gott mit unß.

Ffurt den 20. Junij 1646
    Meines gg. Herrn
    D*iens*twilligster
    M. Merian[d]

T a *Folgt* <ges> — **b** *Gebessert aus* Gärtnen — **c** *Folgt* <so> — **d** *Auf Bl. 40v folgen Zahlenkolumnen, die an eine Rechnungslegung denken lassen. Darunter:* Herrn Petter Knaud g. g. zu hand*en* etc.   Cöthen

K 1 Bevor, vorab. S. 450417 K 1.
 2 Am 1.7.1646 meldete Johann Valentin Andreae (FG 464. 1646) Hz. August d.J. v. Braunschweig-Wolfenbüttel (FG 227), daß er sich bei Matthäus Merian d. Ä. darüber beschwert habe, daß seine beiden Exemplare des *GB 1646* noch immer nicht angekommen seien. HAB: Cod. Guelf. 65.1 Extrav., Bl. 294rv. Von diesen Exemplaren ist auch in

460703 u. 460708 die Rede, und in 460715 bedankt sich Andreae schließlich bei Hz. August allgemein für die Zusendung des *GB 1646.* Er erwähnt das 2. Exemplar nicht explizit. Die Sendung war demnach wegen ihrer Beschlagnahme gut dreieinhalb Monate unterwegs, da die Frankfurter Fuhre zur Leipziger Ostermesse nach dem 29.3.1646 Frankfurt a. M. verlassen hatte. S. 460324 K 1. Eigentlich hätten Andreaes zwei Exemplare von Hz. Augusts Deputat abgezogen werden müssen, der sie Andreae schließlich versprochen hatte, doch da Hz. Augusts 48 Exemplare schon ausgeliefert waren, wollte sich Merian anscheinend an F. Ludwig schadlos halten. Der wies das in 460708 zurück. Seltsamerweise vermeldete Hz. August am 9.6.1646 Andreae: „Das Buch der Fruchtbringenden Geselschaft, wird Er nuhnmehr empfangen haben; Meine Exemplaria habe ich empfangen; woranne die beeden, ihm destienierreten mangeln." Demnach hätte er nur 46 Exemplare erhalten. HAB: Cod. Guelf. 236.3 Extrav., Bl.25r. Vgl. 460317 K 9.

3 Lat. arrestum, das Beschlagnahmte, Beschlagnahme, rechts- und amtsspr. noch im 18. Jh. auch auf Sachen bezogen, dann meist auf Personen beschränkt. S. *Paul Wb.,* 92.

4 Den Erhalt der Darstellung von Residenzschloß und Garten Köthen bestätigt Matthäus Merian d. Ä. in *DA Köthen I. 8:* 470223. S. auch 460519 K 2, 460703, 460714 u. 460810; *DA Köthen I. 2,* 260f. Zur *Topographia* Merians s. 450905 K 4 u.ö.

5 Wir finden einen in Frage kommenden Rauchwarenhändler Heinrich Bengerath (Bingenroth) mit Ersterwähnung 1588 bzw. letzter Erwähnung 1605 in Alexander Dietz: Frankfurter Handelsgeschichte. Bd.2, Glashütten 1970, 56. Es dürfte sich bei dem im Brief gen. Heinrich „Pengerode" auch um ein Mitglied der wohlhabenden belgischen Kürschnerfamilie Bengerath handeln: Nachgewiesen werden konnten Johann Friedrich Bengerath (ebd., 344) u. Peter Bengerath (a. a. O., Bd.3, Glashütten 1972, 284f.). Daß es sich um die kath. Verlagsbuchhändlerfamilie Bencard handelt, aus welcher Agenten nachweisbar sind, ist aufgrund des doch deutlicher abweichenden Namens eher unwahrscheinlich (s. ebd., 132, 142 u. Bd.4, T. 1, Glashütten 1973, 43, T. 2, Glashütten 1974, 49). Dies gilt auch für die Weinhändlerfamilie Benckert, ebd., 67f. (hier Johann Friedrich Benckert in der Stelzengasse).

6 Diese Zusendung wird in 460206 I u. II sowie 460324 erwähnt. Merian erklärt in 460303, daß er die 48 Exemplare für Hz. August am Tag zuvor, am 2.3.1646, einem Kaufmann, offensichtlich jenem im Brief erwähnten Heinrich Bengerath (s. Anm.5), ausgehändigt habe. Vgl. das Postskriptum.

7 Johann Gärtner, Kaufmann oder Postmeister in Braunschweig. S. 460303 K 5.

8 *DW* XII.1, 926 weist darauf hin, daß das Wort *vernugen/ vernügen* im Hd. selten, jedoch im Nd. häufig belegt ist. Besonders dort, wo sich *Vergnügen* nicht entwickelt hat, hat es die Bedeutung von *vergnugen/ vergnügen* übernommen. — Bedenkt man die Herkunft Merians aus Basel, wäre auch eine Verschreibung denkbar.

9 Demnach sind die 48 Exemplare spätestens am 13.6.1646 in Wolfenbüttel angekommen. S. Anm.2.

460700

Justus Georg Schottelius an Herzog August d.J. von Braunschweig-Wolfenbüttel

Justus Georg Schottelius (FG 397) schickt Hz. August d.J. v. Braunschweig-Wolfenbüttel (FG 227) einen eigenhändigen Brief des Theologen Johann Michael Dilherr, den dieser an einen Freund gerichtet habe. Der Fürst könne daraus entnehmen, was dieser vielseitige

Mann über Hz. Augusts *Evangelische Kirchen-Harmonie* denke und äußere. — Hz. August möge entscheiden, ob die ihm jüngst übermittelten schönen Holzschnitt-Initialen für den Druck eines zu seinem Ruhm von den Nürnberger Gelehrten geplanten Buchs in Wolfenbüttel oder Nürnberg zum Einsatz kommen sollen. — Schottelius bittet um Hz. Augusts Zustimmung zu seiner Absicht, ein Exemplar der *Evangelischen Kirchen-Harmonie* an Dilherr nach Nürnberg und ein anderes an (Justus) Gesenius nach Hannover zu schicken.

Q NSTA Wolfenbüttel: 2 Alt Nr. 40, Bl. 9rv, v leer; eigenh. mit einer Randbemerkung von Hz. August.

A *Fehlt.*

Serenissime Illustrissimeque Princeps Domine clementissime

Quidnam de Harmonia[1] Celebris Theologus, nec minus multijugâ eruditione clarissimus Vir D. Dilherrus[2] sentiat, et in quem seorsum ad Amicum quendam[3] scripserit, VESTRA SERENITAS ex ipso, hisce incluso autographo clementissimè percipere poterit. Multorum aliorum iudicia, non absimilia, non semel ad manus habuj, quæ quidem omni voto laudatissimum pietatis opus concumulant.

Vna atque altera adjuncta litera, artificiosè ligno incisa, unà cum eiusmodj aliis, in opusculo, quod in SERENITATIS VESTRÆ duraturam memoriam,[4] Viri Eruditi Noribergæ parant, legentibus apparebit: Expectatur autem clementissimum à VEstrâ Serenitate indicium, an Noribergæ vel Wolferbyti libellus iste, typis (ad modum et formam per nuperas VESTRÆ SERENITATI transmissas literas indicatam) sit exscribendus:

Exemplar Harmoniæ, unum D. Dilherro Noribergam; alterum D. Giessenio[a][5] Hannoveram transmitterem lubentissimè, modò VESTRA SERENITAS, quod expeto, clementissimè adnuere velit.

                Vræ. Serenitati hu*milli*mè obediens
                Just*us* Georgius Schotteli[us]

T a *Hz. August notierte am Rand:* Gessenus hat von Sternen, ein Exemplar bekommen. *Zu Giessenius (d. i. Gesenius) s. Anm. 5.*

K Zur Begründung der Datierung s. Anm. 3 u. 4.

1 Hz. Augusts d. J. v. Braunschweig-Wolfenbüttel (FG 227) *Evangelische Kirchen-Harmonie.* S. 411214.

2 Johann Michael Dilherr, Pfarrer von St. Sebald und Leiter des nürnbergischen Schulwesens, Gründer des Auditorium Egidianum. Bedeutender geistlicher Schriftsteller und lutheranischer Theologe. Vgl. 460317 K I 2–4.

3 1646 hätte Dilherr schon auf die Oktav- oder Quartausgabe der *Evangelischen Kirchen-Harmonie* in einem Brief reagieren können. Auch das *Handbüchlein aus der Evangelischen Kirchen-Harmonie* in Duodez erschien noch 1646 (s. 411214, S. 357). Der Vorschlag von Justus Georg Schottelius (FG 397; PBO Fontano I.), Exemplare zu verschenken, legt nahe, daß der vorliegende Brief noch im Jahre 1646 geschrieben worden ist. Da Schottelius dem Herzog ein 1645 erschienenes Erbauungsbuch Dilherrs wohl bald danach überreichte (460317 I), könnte er Dilherr die zuerst erschienene Oktavausgabe der *Kirchen-Harmonie* (frühestens) im Juni 1646 gesandt haben. S. Anm. 4 u. 460317 K 3.

4 Geplante Initialen für den Druck von Georg Philipp Harsdörffers (FG 368) *Porticus Virtutis (1647)*, einem Panegyrikus auf Hz. August d. J. Neben Harsdörffers handschriftlichem Entwurf der *Porticus Virtutis* (s. 450927) existieren zwei Druckfassungen. Vgl. die Kupferstiche, Initialen und Texte zur *Porticus* der ersten Fassung (als Teil von *Harsdörffer: Specimen [1646]*) mit denen des Separatdrucks (1647) in 460912 II. S. auch 461204 sog. Flandrische Bilder von Kupferstichen. — In *Harsdörffer: Porticus Virtutis (1646)*, HAB: QuN 1090 (1), erschienen die Holzschnitt-Initialen der Buchstaben I (mit Palme; PROGRAMMA ad HEROES FRVCTIFERI SODALITII, Bl.](2]r) und A (Emblem in Harsdörffers Widmungsbrief an Hz. August, PARITAS EX IMPARI, Bl.)(4v). Das *Specimen* hatte Harsdörffer F. Ludwig schon mit seinem Brief 460406 übersandt. Wie aus 460912 hervorgeht, dürfte Schottelius den vorliegenden Brief schon im Sommer, vermutlich im Juli 1646 geschrieben haben.

5 Justus Gesenius (1601–1673), damals hannöver. Oberhofprediger Hz. Christian Ludwigs v. Braunschweig-Calenberg bzw. -Celle (FG 372), Generalsuperintendent im Fst. Calenberg. Eifriger Prediger, Katechetiker und Gesangbuchautor (Sammler u. Umdichter, zus. mit David Denicke). Als Calixt-Schüler gerieten er wie auch Calixtus und Hornejus in einen langen Katechismus-Streit durch den Vorwurf Statius Buschers (CRYPTO-PAPISMUS NOVÆ THEOLOGIÆ HELMSTADIENSIS. Das heimliche Papsthum [o. O. u. J.] u. Hamburg: Gundermann 1638), dem Calixtus widersprach: Gründliche Widerlegung Eines vnwarhafften Gedichts vnterm Titul. CRYPTO-PAPISMUS NOVÆ Theologiae Helmstadiensis (Lüneburg: Sterne 1641). Vgl. *Henke: Calixtus* II, 110ff. Im Vergleich mit Hz. Augusts *Evangelischer Kirchen-Harmonie* interessieren Gesenius: Biblische Historien Alten und Neues Testaments (Braunschweig: Christoff-Friedrich Zilliger 1656) u. ö. Gesenius schildert hierin als Vorläufer von Johann Hübner in eigenen Worten und abgeteilt in zweimal 54 Lektionen die biblische Geschichte. Gesenius und Denicke wurden irrtümlich als Mitglieder der FG bezeichnet. Vgl. Carl Bertheau: Art. „Gesenius, Ludwig". In: *RETHK (1896)*, Bd. 6 (1899), 624–626.

460703

Matthäus Merian d. Ä. an Peter Knaudt

Matthäus Merian d. Ä. dankt Peter Knaudt für den (verschollenen) Brief vom 17.6.1646. Er berichtet, daß er bereits Ansichten der Städte Köthen, Zerbst, Dessau und Bernburg habe, die das jeweilige Stadtbild vor 30 Jahren wiedergeben. Deshalb solle sich Knaudt keine weiteren Umstände machen. Wenn ihm der Entwurf des Köthener Schlosses und Gartens zukommt, wird dieser seinen Platz in der *Topographia* finden. — Aus Wolfenbüttel hat Merian Nachricht von der Ankunft der 48 Exemplare des *GB 1646* (für Hz. August d. J. v. Braunschweig-Wolfenbüttel [FG 227]) erhalten. Sobald nun die übrigen, sich noch in seinem Besitz befindlichen Gesellschaftsbücher gewünscht werden, wird er sie übersenden. — Knaudt habe ihm, Merian, von der Fertigstellung von 50 Visierungen des fünften Hunderts der FG-Impresen berichtet, er lehne die Bezahlung der Zeichnungen und deren kostspieligen Verlag jedoch solange ab, bis der Absatz der 400 veröffentlichten Sinnbilder (*GB 1646*) auf der kommenden Messe ihm eine Entscheidung darüber erlaube. — Merian bedankt sich für den Abriß des Köthener Schlosses etc. im voraus und teilt mit, daß er es zu gegebener Zeit in Kupfer stechen und dann einige Abzüge übermitteln werde.

Q HM Köthen: V S 546, Bl. 37rv [A: 37v]; eigenh.; Sig.; Anstreichungen am Rande. — *D: Bircher: Merian*, 722 f.; *Wüthrich: Merian Briefe*, 116 f. — *BN: Bürger*, 987 Nr. 20.

A Tt. Dem Ehrenvesten vnd GroßAchtparen Herrn Petter Knaudt Fürstl. Anhaltischen CammerMeistern zu Cöthen *etc.* Meinem gg. H.   Cöthen
Herrn Georg Winklern Recommendirt Jn Leipzig.

Ehrenvester vnd GroßAchtparer Jnsonders gg. herr,
Dem sein mein willige dienst jederzeit Anvor[1],
vnd b[e]richte das mir sein geliebtes vom 17. passato wol worden, Jn Antwort dessen, b[e]richte Jch dem Herrn, das Jch albereit, dise volgende Abriß von[a] Stetten habe, Cöthen, Zerbst, Dessaw, vnd Bernburg, wie solche vor 30 Jahren anzusehen gewesen, im prospect, wirt also nicht nötig sein Mehrere vnkosten[2] daran zu wenden, wan mir der Angedeutete Abriß des Fürst. Schloß vnd gartens zukomen wirt, soll derselbige der Toppographie einverleibt werden.[3] Von Wolffenbüttel habe ich schreiben, das die bewußten 48 exemplaria allda wohl eingelifert worden, wan die vbrigen bei mir stehenden, angedeuter massen, werden abgefordert, will ichs also volgen lassen.[4]
Das nunmehr widrumb 50 Newe abriß zu dem 5.ten hundert der Fruchtbringenden geselschaft fertig, vnd Jhr. F. G. begehren Jch solche auff mein Costen verlegen, auch die abriß bezalhen *etc.* hierauff kan ich mich noch nicht Resoluiren, biß ich sehen werde wie dise albereit getruckten 400, abgehen werden, Alsdann will Jch mich erklären, so ich spüren werde, das sie begehrt sein, welchs in künfftiger vnd volgender Meß, Abzunehmen sein wirt, Alßdan will ich mich gern bequemen, dafern aber sie nicht wohl abgehen solten, würde ich mich noch bedenken,[5] dan der verlag bey disen Zeiten köstlich ist, darzu habe ich vil ander wohl abgengige werken vnter henden, darzu mir vil auffgeht.
Wegen deß Abrißes des obgedachten Fürst. Schloßes *etc.* thue ich mich vnterthänig vnd demütig bedankhen, wils zu seiner Zeit (gliebts Gott) also ins Kupfer bringen, vnd alßdan etliche Abtrukh davon vbersenden. Hiemit dem Allmächtigen wohl befohlen.
Ffurt den 3. Julij 1646.
    Des herrn
    Dienstwilligster
    Mattheus Merian.

T a *Eingefügt für* <der>

K 1 Bevor, vorab. S. 450417 K 1.
2 *DW* XI.3, 1103: „mühe, last, opfer, schwierigkeit, unannehmlichkeit, umstände u. dgl.".
3 Vgl. die Übersicht zu den Topographiebänden Merians in 450905 K 4 und auf den gemeinten Band „Sachsen und Meissen" in 460519 K 2, 460620 B, 460714 u. *DA Köthen I.* 8: 470223. Im letztgenannten Brief wird deutlich, daß der Kupferstich des Köthener Schlosses und Gartens in der *Topographia Superioris Saxoniae* publiziert werden soll, was

tatsächlich geschehen ist. S. *Merian: Topographia* Superioris Saxoniae (1650), 38 (Faltblatt „Das Fürstl. Residenz-Schloß zu Cöthen."). Abgebildet in *DA Köthen I.* 2, 260f. (Beschreibung dort S. 90 f.)

4 Die 48 Exemplare kamen gut zwei Wochen zuvor in Braunschweig an. S. 460620B, vgl. auch 460303 u. 460324.

5 Das *GB 1646* blieb das letzte gedruckte Gesellschaftsbuch der FG. Der Gesellschaftsmaler Christoph Steger arbeitete 1646 aber an der Vervollständigung der Visierungen FG 401–500 und setzte seine Arbeit zumindest bis 1649 (FG 524) fort. Die Impresengemälde haben sich (mit Lücken) in den *Weimarer Impresen* erhalten. S. 460315 u. *Conermann II* u. *III*.

460705

Fürst Ludwig an Georg Philipp Harsdörffer

Antwort auf 460620. Beantwortet durch Harsdörffers Brief vom 17.7.1646 (in *DA Köthen I*. 9). — F. Ludwig (der Nährende) bestätigt den Empfang von Georg Philipp Harsdörffers (FG 368. Der Spielende) Brief 460620, dem auch das (mehrfach erbetene) Wappen Johann Michael Moscheroschs (FG 436. Der Träumende) beilag. — F. Ludwig sendet nun Harsdörffer das von ihm erbetene Widmungsgedicht für den sechsten Teil der *Frauenzimmer-Gesprächspiele*, das Harsdörffer nach seinem Dafürhalten aufnehmen oder verwerfen könne. — Darüber hinaus geht Harsdörffer hiermit ein Gutachten (von Marcus Fridericus Wendelinus) zu seinem *Specimen Philologiae Germanicae* (1646) zu. Falls später weitere Gutachten derjenigen, denen das *Specimen* auf Wunsch Harsdörffers zugeleitet wurde (Diederich v. dem Werder, FG 31, Christian Gueintz, FG 361), eintreffen, werde Harsdörffer diese ebenfalls erhalten. Ludwig selbst möchte das Werk nicht beurteilen oder sich gar zum Richter (über widerstreitende Meinungen dazu) aufwerfen. Dazu müßten alle Beteiligten einwilligen, die doch aber sicher bei ihrer Meinung blieben. Unterschiedliche Meinungen würden nämlich auch bei Gelehrten auf ihre jeweilige Mundart und persönlichen sprachlichen Auffassungen und Vorlieben zurückgehen, die niemand gern aufgebe. F. Ludwig werde daher den weiteren Verlauf (der Debatte) abwarten.

Q HM Köthen: V S 545, Bl. 349rv, v leer; Abschrift von Schreiberh. mit eigenh. Korrekturen F. Ludwigs.
Bl. 352rv, v leer; eigenh. Konzept F. Ludwigs, datiert auf 460702, zit. als *K*. — D: *KE*, 357 f.; *KL III*, 272 f. — BN: *Bürger*, 950 Nr. 62.
Bl. 350rv: Beilage II, Reinschrift *Y*.
Bl. 351rv: Beilage II, Reinschrift *X*.

A *Fehlt*.

Des *Spielenden* schreiben von 20. des Brachmonats ist den 28. deßelben mit einfertigung des Träumenden[a] wapen[b] zum ertzschreine wol einkommen,[1] und weil vom *Spielenden* gesuchet worden, auf das sechste theil seiner gesprächspiele etzliche[c] Reimlein auszulaßen, als werden solche von hinnen, so[d] gut sie in eil gefallen, mit überschicket, zu seinem gefallen stellende, ob er sie demselben anfügen wolle.[2] Es kommet hierbey auch über ein bedencken eines sprachkündigen[e]

gelehrten in diesem Fürstenthume, über das jüngst ausgegangene Specimen Philologiæ Germanicæ: Kömmet von andern^f, denen dieses büchlein auf^g begeren des Spielenden überschicket worden,^h noch ein mehrers^i ein, soll^j es ebener maßen überfertiget werden.³ Des Richterlichen ausspruchs über solches wercklein,⁴ wird sich der 𝔑ehrende nicht unterfangen können, es haben dan diejenigen, so hierinnen unterschiedener meinung seind, in denselben mit eingewilliget, welches dan daher unter andern schwer fallen^k dörfte, weil der Menschen^l, ja auch gelehrter^m Leute gedancken und mundarten unterschieden^n und mancherley, und da ieder seiner art^o und weise gewohnet, ja^p dieselbe für die schöneste^q und beste helt, darvon nicht gerne wird abweichen wollen. Des Verfolgs wird^r der Nehrende ferner erwarten und verbleibet
Des Spielenden

Auszuschreiben.^s ⁵

Cöthen den 5.^t Heumonats 1646.

I

Lobverse Fürst Ludwigs für den sechsten Teil der *Frauenzimmer-Gesprächspiele* (1646) von Georg Philipp Harsdörffer (Der Spielende)

Q *Harsdörffer: Frauenzimmer-Gesprächspiele* VI (1646, Ndr. 1969), Ndr. S. 17–19.

IN^a diesem sechsten Theil hat weiter fortgespielt
   Gesprächspiel aus der Kunst/ der SPJELEND' angetrieben
   Von seinem hohen Geist: Er ist auch nicht geblieben'
Bey schlechten¹ Fragen nur/ womit man sonsten fült

Mit schreiben das Pappier: Das nicht viel Nutzen bringet:
   Viel gutes habt ihr hier durch Antwort wol bedacht/
   Woraus erscheinet uns; dann seiner Feder Macht/
Die eins Theils weislich redt/ zum Theile lieblich singet.

Zu stellen manchmals für viel Umschweiff/ ist nicht not
   Jn kürtze liegt der Kern/ darin man balde sihet/
   Wie ein Geistreicher Sinn mit Willen ist bemühet
Zu dienen jederman/ und GOTT bis in den Tod. [18]

Aus^b Büchern weiser Leut/ die fremde Sprachen üben/
   Zeucht man den besten Saft/ und stellet ihm das für/
   Wormit zur Wissenschaft geöfnet wird die Thür
Und wir die freyen Künst in allem sollen lieben.

Ja sie in unsrer Sprach auch nützlich wenden an/
  Auf deren Eigenschaft gar lieblich seyn gefliessen/
  Weil in der Klarheit nur besteht das rechte Wissen/
Was ungezwungen geht ist wol und recht gethan.

Es mus auch jede Sach erst reiflich seyn erwogen/
  Die man bringt auf die Bühn/ auf daß sie halt die Prob/
  Und desto grösser sey auch des Verfassers Lob/
Das aus der Weisheit Grund er alles recht gesogen. [19]

Wir[b] müssen alle stets fort lernen in der Welt/
  Und zur Volkommenheit hin unsre Sinne richten/
  Dahin sol seyn gewand all unser Thun und Dichten:
Jn dieser Schwachheit Joch/ oft mancher Grosser fehlt.

Der SPJELEND dieses wol/ als es gemeint/ vermerk'/
  Und fahr im Schreiben fort/ die Sprache recht ausübe
  Nach ihrer Eigenschaft: Des Vaterlandes Liebe
Erfordert solches Werk/ die ihn grosmütig sterk!

Cöthen/ den 5. Heumonats 1646.

>>>>Von deme nach der Eintrettung noch lebenden Aeltesten der Fruchtbringenden Gesellschaft.
>>>>Dem Nehrenden.

II

Konzept der Lobverse Fürst Ludwigs

Q HM Köthen: V S 545, Bl. 418rv, v leer (älteste Textstufe), eigenh., im Folgenden zit. mit der Sigle *K*. S. Abb auf S. 907.
Reinschrift *X:* V S 545, 351rv, v leer (mittlere Textstufe), Schreiberhand mit eigenh. Verbesserungen F. Ludwigs.
Reinschrift *Y:* V S 545, 350rv, v leer (jüngste Textstufe), andere Schreiberhand mit eigenh. Verbesserungen F. Ludwigs. *Y* folgt im Wesentlichen *X* einschließlich der dort vorgenommenen Besserungen.

Auf des Spielenden Sechsten theil seiner Gesprächspiele.

<1.>

Jn diesem Sechsten theil'[a] hat weiter fortgespielt
  Gesprächspiel' aus der kunst[b] der Spielend' angetrieben[c]
  Von seinem hohen Geist, und ist er[d] nicht geblieben
Bey schlechten fragen nur, wormit[e] man sonsten fult[f]

<2.>
Mit schreiben das pappier: das nicht viel nutzen bringet^g
    Viel gutes habt ihr hier, antworten^h wol bedacht
    Woraus erscheinet uns dan seiner feder macht,
Die eins theils weislich redt^i, zum theile lieblich singet[.]^j

<3.>
Zu stellen manchmals fur^k viel' umschweiff' ist nicht not
    Jn kurtze^l ligt der kern, darin man balde siehet^g
    Wie ein geistreicher Sinn mit willen ist bemühet
Zu dienen iederman, und treulich^m seinem Gott'[.]

<4.>
Aus buchern^n weiser leut, die fremde sprachen üben,
    Man zeucht^o den besten saft, und den^p uns stellet fur^k,
    Wormit zur wißenschaft geöfnet wird die thur^q
Und wir die freyen kunst^r in allem^s sollen lieben.

<5.>
Ja sie in unsrer sprach' auch nutzlich^t wenden an,
    Auf deren eigenschaft gar lieblich sein gefließen,
    Weil in der Klarheit^u nur besteht das rechte wißen^g
Was ungezwungen geht, ist wol und recht gethan.

<6.>
Es muß'^v auch iede sach' erst reiflich sein erwogen^g
    Die man bringt auf die buhn'^w, auf das sie halt die prob'^g
    Und desto größer sey auch des verfaßers lob,
Das aus der weisheit er hab' alles recht gesogen.

<7.>
Wir mußen^x alle stets fort lernen in der welt,
    Und zur volkommenheit hin unsre sinne richten,^y
    Dahin sol sein^z gewand all' unser thun und tichten,^aa
Jn dieser schwachheit doch oft mancher großer fehlt.

<8.>
Die weisheit^ab drin^ac besteht, das man sich laße weisen^1
    Wo man auf abweg' ist, den^ad unterricht nehm' an,
    Und deme sey geneigt, so man begreiffen kan,
Dergleichen lehrsamkeit der weisen^ae freunde preisen.

F. Ludwigs eigenhändiges Konzept seines Widmungsgedichts zum 6. Teil von Georg Philipp Harsdörffers (FG 368) *Frauenzimmer-Gesprächspielen (1646). Zu 460705 II.*

<9.>
Der Spielend dieses wol, als es gemeint, vermerck'[g]
Jm[af] schreiben fahre fort, die sprache recht ausübe
Nach ihrer eigenschaft: des Vaterlandes liebe
Erfodert[ag] solches, drin er sich grosmutig sterck'.[ah]

Von dem noch[ai] lebenden ältesten der Fruchtbringend*en* geselschaft nach der eintrettung.[aj]

III

Korrekturen Diederichs von dem Werder zu Fürst Ludwigs Lobversen

Q HM Köthen: V S 544, Bl. 466rv, v leer (eingelegter Zettel in Bl. 465r–467v, d. i. 450919).

1. Gesprächspiel' aus der Kunst hat weiter fortgespielt
2. jn diesem Sechsten theil der Spielend' angetrieben
3. — — — — Er ist auch nicht geblieben
5.[a] — — — — durch antwort wohl bedacht
14. Zeucht man den besten saft, vnd stellet ihm das für
29. Die Weisheit steckt hierinn
30. — — — — — nem' unterrichtung an
34. vnd fahr' im schreiben fort

Von dem (nach Zeit der eintretung in die Fruchtbringende Geselschaft) noch lebendem Ältesten.
Oder
Von dem (nach[b] der eintretung) noch lebendem Ältesten der Fruchtbringenden Geselschaft.

T a *Von F. Ludwig gebessert aus* Traumenden *K ebenfalls ohne Markierung des Umlauts.* — b *Von F. Ludwig gebessert aus* wappen *K* wappen — c *In K folgt* <von> — d *In K eingefügt bis* gefallen — e *K* Sprachkundigen — f *Von F. Ludwig gebessert aus* anderen — g *Von F. Ludwig eingefügt bis* Spielenden *In K ebenfalls eingefügt, dort folgt* <ubermachet worden> — h *In K folgt* <auch> — i *In K folgt* <alhier> — j *K* sol — k *In K folgt* <wird> — l *In K bis* gelehrter *eingefügt.* — m *Gebessert aus* gelährter — n *In K unterschieden und eingefügt.* — o *art und weise in K eingefügt.* — p *In K eingefügt für* <und> — q *Von F. Ludwig gebessert aus* schönste *K* schönste — r *Eingefügt für* <sol> *K* sol — s *Eingefügt von F. Ludwig, fehlt in K.* — t *Von F. Ludwig gebessert aus* 2 *(unsichere Lesung), in K* Cöthen den 2. Heumonats 1646.

T I *Über dem ersten Vers steht* „Lobgedichte.", *womit jedoch nicht nur dieser, sondern auch die folgenden 16 Widmungstexte bezeichnet werden.* — a *Vegetabile vierzeilige I-*

460705 Fürst Ludwig

Initiale (Holzschnitt): Palmbaum mit Früchten, das I liegt über dem Stamm der Palme. — **b** *Zugleich Kustode.*

T II *Die durchgestrichene Numerierung der Strophen in K fehlt in X u. Y, wo darüber hinaus die Zeichensetzung am Versende häufig abweicht (Ergänzungen von Kommata bzw. Punkten oder Doppelpunkten). Jenseits der ergänzten bzw. gestrichenen Apostrophe wird die abweichende Verwendung von Zierschriften in X u. Y im Folgenden nicht aufgeführt.* — **a** *Y* theil — **b** *X hat Kommata nach* kunst *und* Spielend' — **c** *In Y sind die ersten beiden Verse umgestellt:* Gesprächspiel aus der kunst hat weiter fort gespielt | Jn diesem Sechsten theil, der *Spielend'* angetrieben *Durch Beziefferung wurde diese Abweichung in der Reihenfolge zu K und X in Y wieder rückgängig gemacht.* — **d** und ist er *in X durch Umstellung mit Ziffern, Streichung und Einfügung gebessert zu* er ist auch *Y* Er ist auch — **e** *Y* womit — **f** *X, Y* fült — **g** *Folgt Komma in Y.* — **h** *X gebessert durch Streichung und Einfügung zu* durch antwort *Y* durch antwort — **i** *X, Y* red — **j** *Zeichensetzung in X u. Y.* — **k** *X,Y* für — **l** *X, Y* kürtze liegt — **m** *K über dem letzten Halbvers* Gott bis in den tod *Dieser in X eingefügt für* ‹treulich seinem Gott'› *Y* Gott bis in den tod — **n** *X, Y* büchern — **o** *Reihenfolge in X* Man zeucht *durch Beziefferung umgestellt zu* zeucht Man *Darum in Y mit angepaßter Orthographie* Zeucht man — **p** den uns stellet *in X durch Umstellung übernommen. In Y mit Ziffern, Streichung und Einfügung gebessert zu* stellet ihm das — **q** *X* thür' *Y* thür', — **r** *X, Y* künst' — **s** *X* allen *Y* allem — **t** *X, Y* nützlich — **u** *X u. Y gebessert aus* Klugheit — **v** *X, Y* mus — **w** *X, Y* bühn' — **x** *X, Y* müßen — **y** *Zeichensetzung in Y.* — **z** *X gebessert aus* seind — **aa** *Doppelpunkt in Y.* — **ab** *X* weißheit — **ac** *X* steckt hierin *eingefügt für* ‹drin besteht› *Übernommen in Y.* — **ad** den unterricht nehm' *in X durch Umstellung mit Ziffern, Streichung und Einfügung gebessert zu* nehm' unterrichtung *Übernommen in Y.* — **ae** *In K darüber eingefügt* heit [weisheit] *In X verbessert* wei‹sen›sheit *Y* weisheit — **af** Jm schreiben fahre *in X durch Umstellung mit Ziffern, Streichung und Einfügung gebessert zu* Und fahr Jm schreiben *In Y mit angepaßter Orthographie* Und fahr' im schreiben — **ag** *X, Y* Erfordert — **ah** *X, Y* grosmütig sterck. — **ai** *In K* noch lebenden *eingefügt.* — **aj** *In X anstelle dieser Zeile eingefügt von F. Ludwigs Hand:* Von deme nach ‹Zeit› der ‹eintrettu› *(ad hoc gebessert aus* ‹eintreten›*)* eintrettung noch lebenden ältesten der Fruchtbringenden geselschaft *Y folgt dieser Einfügung, schreibt allerdings* eintretung *mit einem* t *(die Schreibung mit* tt *in K und bes. in X ist eine unsichere Lesung). In X davor die gestrichene Version der Schlußzeile von Schreiberh., die K folgt:* ‹Von dem ‹ältesten› *(vermutlich bereits vom Schreiber gestrichen)* noch lebenden ältesten der Fruchtbringenden geselschaft nach der eintretung.›

T III a *Recte 6.* — **b** *Folgt* ‹Zeit›

K 1 Seit Mai 1645 hatte F. Ludwig (der Nährende) wiederholt um die Einsendung des Wappens von Johann Michael Moscherosch (FG 436) durch den dessen Aufnahme in die FG vermittelnden Georg Philipp Harsdörffer (FG 368. Der Spielende) gebeten. Vgl. dazu 450504A K 5 u. zuletzt 460620.

2 In 460620 hatte Harsdörffer F. Ludwig um ein Gedicht für den schon im Druck befindlichen sechsten Teil der *Gesprächspiele* gebeten. Harsdörffer begründete seine Bitte mit der Aussicht, der sechste könne der letzte Teil der *Gesprächspiele* sein. Zu F. Ludwigs Gedicht s. die Beilagen I–III. In seinem Antwortschreiben 460717 (in *DA Köthen I. 9*) bestätigte Harsdörffer dankend den Empfang des „carmen gratulatorium".

3 Zu Harsdörffers *Specimen* sind zwei ausführliche latein. Stellungnahmen des Zerbster Gymnasialrektors Marcus Fridericus Wendelin(us) (1584–1652) im Köthener Erzschrein erhalten. Die erste ist datiert Zerbst 15.6.1646, die zweite auf den 6.8.1646. Letztere ist eine Replik auf Harsdörffers Schreiben vom 17.7.1646, mit dem er auf Wendelins erstes Gutachten ebenfalls in latein. Sprache reagierte. F. Ludwig sandte Harsdörffer Wendelins Duplik mit 460902 zu und brachte darin auch einige eigene Anmerkungen zu Wendelins Papier an. Auch wenn der Name des Gutachters aus dem Text nicht ersichtlich ist und in keinem Brief von F. Ludwig genannt wird, weiß Harsdörffer später, daß es sich um Wendelin handelt, wie aus der Nachschrift zu 460916 hervorgeht, möglicherweise aus den Initialen „MW" am jew. Schluß der beiden Gutachten und auf F. Ludwigs Andeutung („eines sprachkündigen gelehrten in diesem Fürstenthume") erschlossen. In seinem Antwortschreiben vom 17.7.1646 bezog er sich noch auf die „Anonymi censuram". Mit 460720 erreichte F. Ludwig aus Halle das Gutachten von Christian Gueintz (FG 361), das er mit 460816 an Harsdörffer weitersandte. Harsdörffer hatte in 460406 um Stellungnahmen Diederichs v. dem Werder (FG 31) und Gueintz' gebeten. Alle hier genannten Quellen demnächst in *DA Köthen I. 9*. Vgl. 460609 K 3 u. 460902.

4 Ein solches Richteramt über die strittigen Meinungen im und zum *Specimen* hatte Harsdörffer F. Ludwig in 460620 angetragen.

5 Anweisung F. Ludwigs an den Kanzlisten/ Schreiber, die Schlußkurialie in der Ausfertigung vollständig auszuführen.

K I 1 D. h. schlicht, einfach. S. 290131 K 3.

K II Obwohl die achte Strophe in allen Konzepten vorhanden ist und Diederich v. dem Werder (FG 31) sie bei seinen Verskorrekturen berücksichtigte (vgl. Beilage III), wurde sie in den Druck des 6. Teils der *Frauenzimmer-Gesprächspiele* (1646, Ndr. 1969) nicht aufgenommen. Platzgründe dürften hierfür nicht ausschlaggebend gewesen sein. Viele der insgesamt 16 Widmungstexte nehmen mehr Raum ein als das dreiseitige Gedicht F. Ludwigs; darüber hinaus müssen auf dem letzten Bogen mit Widmungstexten noch fünf Blatt frei gewesen sein. Er endet mit Bl. [)()()()()()(iij] (Ndr. S. 97f.). Vielleicht hat Georg Philipp Harsdörffer (FG 368. Der Spielende) die in Strophe 8 deutlich ausgesprochene Mahnung des Fürsten, sich unterweisen zu lassen und in den irrigen sprachtheoretischen Positionen („abweg'") nachzugeben, als unangemessen empfunden und sie fortgelassen.

1 In einem unveröffentlichten, vielleicht von F. Ludwig selbst stammenden Widmungsgedicht auf seine Übersetzung *Der weise Alte* (1643; s. 440130 K 5) — „Auf den weisen Alten, und | den Spruch, | Wer weise ist der leßet sich weisen" — heißt es: „Das ist ein weiser Man, der sich gar gerne weisen | Jn seinen fehlern leßt, die leichtlich er begeht …". Damals ging es hauptsächlich um die zwischen Harsdörffer und F. Ludwig strittige Frage des Daktylus. S. 431206 II.

K III Diederichs v. dem Werder (FG 31) Korrekturen müssen in den letzten Juni- oder ersten Julitagen entstanden sein: Georg Philipp Harsdörffers (FG 368. Der Spielende) Bitte um die Verse in 460620 ging bei F. Ludwig am 28.6.1646 ein, F. Ludwig hat die Korrekturen Werders in Konzept *X* (mittlere Textstufe) eigenhändig übertragen, eine Druckvorlage schickte er Harsdörffer mit dem vorliegenden Brief. Der Fürst hat alle Korrekturen Werders übernommen bis auf die Umstellung der ersten beiden Verse, die auch im Druck nicht zu finden ist. In Konzept *X* wurden die Umstellungen nicht eingetragen, für Konzept *Y* (jüngste Textstufe) hat sie der Schreiber zwar übernommen, die Reihenfolge wurde dann jedoch durch Bezifferung wieder rekorrigiert (vgl. T II c).

460708

Fürst Ludwig an Peter Knaudt

Konzept der Antwort auf den Brief Merians an Knaudt (460620B). — Über den Versand der beiden Gesellschaftsbücher nach Stuttgart an Johann Valentin Andreae sei in Köthen nichts bekannt, so daß Matthäus Merian d. Ä. sich von anderen diese Sendung bezahlen lassen und die Köthen zustehenden Exemplare wieder um die zwei Exemplare vermehren möge, die Andreaes wegen von F. Ludwigs Deputat abgezogen worden seien. Sollte jedoch bei Merian jemand ohne Order aus Köthen Exemplare bestellen, so soll Merian sie aus seinem eigenen Bestand verkaufen und ansonsten die für Köthen bestimmten Exemplare, wie vereinbart, dorthin übersenden. Die Bücher für Braunschweig sind wohl gut angekommen. Falls Merian dort (zusätzliche) Exemplare abverlangt werden, soll Merian die Bücher ihm (Hz. August d.J. v. Braunschweig-Wolfenbüttel [FG 227]) in Rechnung stellen. — Im dritten Hundert wurde die Imprese „Der Stete" (FG 253. Ernst Dietrich v. Starschedel) mit dem Gesellschaftswort „Jm grünen" ausgelassen und nur sein Reimgesetz gedruckt. Stattdessen wurde die pictura des „Verjüngernden" (FG 254. Torsten Stålhandske) zweimal hintereinander abgezogen. Da „Der Stete" jedoch einen Tannen- und nicht wie „Der Verjüngernde" einen Fichtenbaum erhalten soll, muß das Gemälde des „Steten" nachgedruckt werden, um ihn in den (bereits gedruckten) Gesellschaftsbüchern einzukleben. Die entsprechende Tannenvisierung sei Merian vormals gesandt worden.

Q HM Köthen: V S 546, Bl. 39v; Konzept auf der Rückseite von 460620B; eigenh. — D: Bircher: Merian, 720f. (unvollst.)

A Fehlt.

8.ᵃ Julij 1646. Die antwort hierauf kan sein, das von den zwey Geselschaft buchern, die auf Stuckgard an Doctor JohanValentin Andre abgefolget seind,[1] man alhier nichts weiß, und Merian sich dieselbe wol kann zahlen laßen, undᵇ die hieher gehörende exemplaria erge[ntzen.]ᶜ Solte sich aber iemand dort exemplaria zu haben, ohne verordnungᵈ von hinnen angeben, so möchte er ihme d[ie]selben vonᵉ den seinigen geben, auch zahlen laßen, sonsten die hieher gehende Exe[m]plaria also wie ihme vormals geschrieben, sicherlich uberschi[cken.] Die Braunschweigischen seind wol zu rechte gekomen. Wan aber von hinnen ihme zu geschrieben wurdt umᶠ ihm[e um]ᶜ geld etwas von diesen abfolgen zu laßen, als dan solte er es ihm dan anrechnen

Weiter ist zu mercken.

Das im durchlauffen der geselschaft gemälde, im dritten hundert das 253. nemlich der Stette im grünen gantz ausgelaßen worden, ob schon die Reime drunder gesetzt zu finden, und also der Verjungernde zwei mahl in kupfer nacheinander gedruckt worden, muß also der Stette, so derᵍ 253. ein Tannenbaumʰ und k[ein]ᶜ Fichtenbaum wie der Verjungernde ist, absonderlich nach[ge]druckt werden, das man ihn könte in den Buchern einkleben.[2] Das gemählde ist damals mit uberschicktt worden.

T a *Datum am Rand eingefügt.* — b *Fehlt bei Bircher: Merian bis* anrechnen — c *Unsicher. Wortende im Falz.* — d *Präfix eingefügt.* — e *Eingefügt bis* geben — f *Folgt gestrichenes Wort.* — g *der 253. am Rand ergänzt.* — h *Folgt* <auch [?]>

K 1 Vgl. 460303 K 5. Hz. August d. J. v. Braunschweig-Wolfenbüttel (FG 227) hatte zwei Exemplare des *GB 1646* Johann Valentin Andreae (FG 464. 1646) versprochen. Andreae bedankte sich in 460715 bei dem Herzog für die Ankunft des Geschenks. Zur Ostermesse hatte Matthäus Merian d. Ä. im Auftrag Hz. Augusts die zwei Exemplare für Andreae nach Stuttgart aufgegeben und verlangt, die beiden Exemplare „werden an Jhr Fürstl. G. von Anhalt Anzahl müssen abkürtzt werden." S. 460620B. F. Ludwig weist dieses Ansinnen im vorliegenden Brief zurück und fordert, daß Merian sich die Exemplare durch Hz. August bezahlen lassen solle. Irritierenderweise benachrichtigte Hz. August im Juni 1646 Andreae, daß dessen zwei Exemplare von seinem Deputat (48 Ex.) abgezogen worden seien. S. 460317 K 9, 460620B K 2 u. 460703.

2 Im *GB 1646* findet sich unter FG 254, Torsten Stålhandske (Der Verjüngernde), eine der Tanne ähnliche sehr vereinfachende Darstellung der Fichte (Bl. TTT ij r). Die im Gegensatz zur Tanne nach unten hängenden Nadeln der Fichte sind in Stålhandskes Impresenstich zwar recht uneindeutig ausgeführt, jedoch weisen die im Stich deutlich markierten, für die Fichte typischen endständigen Knospen, aus denen die Blütenzapfen entstehen, auf die Fichte hin: „DIe Spitzen von der Ficht' erjüngern/ was im leib' [...]". Von einer Identität der beiden Impresenstiche kann im (endgültigen) Druck keine Rede sein. Vgl. *Herz, Tölkki: Stålhandske.*

460714

Fürst Ludwig an Fürst Christian II. von Anhalt-Bernburg

F. Ludwig (Der Nährende) bedankt sich für die Zusendung des Wappens Joachim v. Glasenapps (FG 451), das ihn zusammen mit einem Handschreiben des Sohnes Hz. Augusts d. J. v. Braunschweig-Wolfenbüttel (FG 227. Der Befreiende) erreicht hat. Pz. Rudolf Augusts (FG 754. 1660) Brief wird er F. Christian II. v. Anhalt-Bernburg (FG 51. Der Unveränderliche) zurücksenden, jenen an die kursächs. Witwe weiterleiten. Was das (von Rudolf August gewünschte Exemplar des) *GB 1646* angeht, sei wohl sein Vater Hz. August am besten geeignet, ihn damit auszustatten, da er die ihm zustehenden Exemplare wohlbehalten erhalten hat, wogegen die Kriegsläufte die Sendung an den Köthener Hof bislang aufgehalten haben. — F. Ludwig bittet Christian, Pz. Rudolf August seinen Gruß und die Information zu übermitteln, daß seiner Aufnahme in die FG nichts entgegenstehe. Hz. August und Rudolf Augusts ehemaliger Hofmeister Justus Georg Schottelius (FG 397) könnten die Aufnahme und (Impresen-)Vorschläge in die eigene Hand nehmen. F. Ludwig werde bestimmt keine Vorbehalte äußern. — Er bittet zugleich um die Rücksendung der beiden Zeichnungen des Köthener Schlosses und Gartens. — F. Ludwig sagt die baldige Rückgabe des Buches *La vie du Cardinal Richelieu* zu und lobt die darin behandelten politischen Maximen.

Q LHA Sa.-Anh./ Dessau: Z 18 Abt. Bernburg A 10 Nr. 5^{a-2}, Bl. 208r–209v [A: 209v], 208v u. 209r leer; eigenh.; Papiersiegel.

A Dem Unveränderlichen zuhanden Bernburg.

460714 Fürst Ludwig

Das der Unverenderliche des von Glasenapen¹ wappen mit einem handbriflein von des Befreyenden Sohne² dem Nehrenden freundlichen mittheilen wollen, deßen thut sich der Nehrende gehöriger maßen freundlich bedancken, auch den gemeldeten brief hinwieder mit zu rucke senden, der an die kursächsische witwe ist auch bestellet.

Zu dem geselschaftbuche kan der Befreyende seinem sohne, weil er die seinigen alle wol überkommen am besten helffen, wegen der vnsicherheit seind die hiesigen noch zu rucke:³

El. wollen hertzog Rudolph Augusten meinen gruß mit gelegenheit wieder vermelden, und konnen S. l. in die fruchtbringende geselschaft gar leichtlich kommen, auch durch ihren herren vater und gewesenen Lehrmeister Schotelium⁴ die besten vorschläge thun laßen. Hier wird es kein bedencken geben.⁵ Wan ich die zwey abriße vom hiesigen hause und gärten wieder nun haben könte, were es mir lieb und angenehm.⁶

La vie du Cardinal Richelieu⁷ sol El. auch bald wieder zuhanden kommen, es seind hubsche Politische Regeln drinne,

ich befehle El. in den schutz gotlicher Almacht und verbleibet

Des Unverenderlichen
    dienstw. geselschafter
        der Nehrende

Cöthen 14 Heumonats 1646

K 1 Joachim v. Glasenapp (FG 451. Der Erwachsende), Rat u. Hofmeister der verwitweten Hzn. Hedwig v. Pommern (1595–1650), einer geb. Pzn. v. Braunschweig-Wolfenbüttel, wurde u. a. auf Anraten ihres Verwandten, Hz. Augusts d. J. v. Braunschweig-Wolfenbüttel (FG 227. Der Befreiende), und F. Ludwigs Neffen, F. Christians II. v. Anhalt-Bernburg (FG 51), 1646 Mitglied der FG. Vgl. 460613 K 1.

2 Hz. Rudolf August v. Braunschweig-Wolfenbüttel (FG 754. 1660; 1627–1704), ältester Sohn und designierter Nachfolger Hz. Augusts d.J. Er war im Mai/ Juni 1646 bei F. Christians Wolfenbüttelbesuch in engere Verbindung zu diesem getreten. S. 460613. Zu ihm jüngst Dieter Merzbacher: Herzog Rudolf August zu Braunschweig-Lüneburg und das Wolfenbütteler Pietisten-Edikt. In: Wirkungen des Pietismus im Fürstentum Wolfenbüttel. Studien und Quellen. Hg. D.M. u. Wolfgang Miersemann. Wiesbaden 2015, 155–223 u. im Sammelband passim.

3 Aus 460613 ergibt sich das Interesse Hz. Rudolf Augusts für ein Exemplar des *GB 1646*. Hz. August ist bereits seit (spätestens) Anfang Juli im Besitz seines Verlagsanteils von 48 Exemplaren. S. 460703. F. Ludwig dagegen, so erfahren wir aus einem zwischen Matthäus Merian d. Ä. und Peter Knaudt gewechselten Brief vom Oktober 1646, erhielt seine Exemplare frühestens Ende Oktober 1646. S. 461023.

4 Der Dichter u. Sprachgelehrte Justus Georg Schottelius (FG 397) war seit 1638 Präzeptor u. Informator etlicher Kinder Hz. Augusts d.J. zu Braunschweig-Wolfenbüttel, zuerst des Pz.en Anton Ulrich (FG 716. 1659), 1641 ausgedehnt auf Pz. Ferdinand Albrecht (FG 842. 1673) u. die Fürstentöchter. Nachfolger Schottelius' als Prinzenerzieher wurde Sigmund Betulius (v. Birken, FG 681. 1658). Von einer Bestallung des Schottelius als Erzieher Pz. Rudolf Augusts ist nichts bekannt. Der aus Mömpelgart stammende

Abraham Marconnet gilt zumindest bis 1644 als eigentlicher Lehrer Rudolf Augusts. S. 440100 K 4. Zu Marconnet vgl. schon 431028A K 3. Vgl. *Bei der Wieden: Schottelius*, 146; *Conermann III*, 466–468; *NDB* XXIII, 498–500. Vgl. zu Schottelius: Die vielen Gesichter des Justus Georg Schottelius (= WBN 39 [2012]).

5 Hz. Rudolf August hatte sich um eine Mitgliedschaft in der FG beworben. S. 460613. Er erlangte sie jedoch erst im Jahre 1660, zehn Jahre nach dem Tode F. Ludwigs. Möglicherweise unterstützte sein Vater, Hz. August, hier nicht ausdrücklich die Interessen des ältesten Sohnes. Die Vater-Sohn-Beziehung scheint angespannt gewesen zu sein. Rudolf August litt offensichtlich unter dem strengen Vater, der den in der Nähe des Schlosses gelegenen Prinzenhof als Wohnstatt für seinen Ältesten vorgesehen hatte. S. Friedrich Wagnitz: Herzog Rudolf August von Braunschweig-Wolfenbüttel (1627–1704). ‚Der Pietist auf dem Welfenthron'. Wolfenbüttel 1991 (masch.), 23–28. Rudolf August schrieb Hz. August am 31.10.1646: „Ich muß aber wohl bekennen, E. Gd. werden es auch selbst gut wißen, daß mihr als einem Jungen menschen, der eines adolescentis Jahre erreichet, nicht müglich sey, so sehr eingeschloß[en] ohne alle ergetzligkeit und nützliche gesellschafft zu leb[en,] sondern daß dadurch in mihr alle beliebung zum studiren und anderen nützlichen actionen Vergehet" (HAB: Cod. Guelf. 14 Noviss. 2°, Bl. 1rv, hier r). Rudolf August war später von zurückgezogener, meditativer Frömmigkeit, ein „Montaigne im Turm", ein Prospero auf seiner Insel. In seine persönliche Bibel (Lüneburg 1653. HAB: Bibel-S. 60) klebte er ein Zettelchen mit seiner FG-Imprese: „Der Nachsinnende Äschwurz vergifte Glieder zuhelfen. Weymar den 19.ten Aug. Anno 1660." Alles nach Dieter Merzbacher (s. Anm. 2), 162 f. u. 165 f.

6 Offensichtlich möchte F. Ludwig die Ansichten, die zu diesem Zeitpunkt im Besitz des Neffen sind, über Peter Knaudt an Matthäus Merian d. Ä. übermitteln. Wenn es sich dabei nicht um zwei verschiedene gemeinsame Darstellungen von Schloß und Garten handelte, mußte Merian aus den beiden Zeichnungen des Schlosses und der Gartenanlage eine gemeinsame Ansicht komponieren, so wie sie in *Merian: Topographia* Superioris Saxoniae (1650), Faltbl. nach S. 38 (beschrieben in *DA Köthen I. 2*, 90 f. u. Abb. S. 260 f.) erscheint. Wahrscheinlich wurden die Zeichnungen auch schon in Köthen (bzw. in Halle a. d. S. vom Gesellschaftsmaler Christoph Steger) zusammengezeichnet, denn in *DA Köthen I. 8*: 470223 bedankte sich Merian bei Peter Knaudt: „Des Fürst. Residentz Schloß und Gartens Cöthen, Abriß habe ich wol empfangen". Vgl. 460810 K 2. Ob F. Christian über die Verwendung der Zeichnungen vom Köthener Schloß und Garten, die in *Merian: Topographia* zum Abdruck gebracht werden sollten, informiert war, läßt der Briefwechsel offen. S. 460620B, 460703 u. 460810. Zu *Merian: Topographia* s. 450905 K 4.

7 Dabei handelte es sich mit großer Wahrscheinlichkeit um das anonym erschienene Werk *Observations sur la vie et les services de M. le Cardinal Duc de Richelieu*, das 1643 in La Haye (Den Haag) erschienen war. F. Ludwig scheint das Werk aus der Bibliothek seines Neffen Christian ausgeliehen zu haben. In dessen Bibliothek bzw. den einschlägigen Bibliothekskatalogen (*Catalogus primus*, *Catalogus secundus*, *Kat. Dessau BB*) läßt es sich nicht (mehr) nachweisen. Falls die Rückgabe von seiten F. Ludwigs nicht erfolgte, wäre es zumindest im fl. Inventar (*IP*) nachweisbar, was nicht der Fall ist. An der HAB findet sich eine Ausgabe im nichtaugusteischen Bestand: Gk 2192 (7).

460715

Johann Valentin Andreae an Herzog August d.J. von Braunschweig-Wolfenbüttel

Beantwortet in 460804. — Johann Valentin Andreae (FG 464. 1646) möchte gern die sich noch immer vergrößernde Bibliothek Hz. Augusts d.J. v. Braunschweig-Wolfenbüttel (FG 227) und noch lieber den Herzog selbst sehen. Er hätte ihn lieber als das Heilbad aufsuchen wollen. Die Ärzte haben ihm zum Bad geraten, jedoch habe die Kur sein Leiden nur verschlimmert. — Andreae offeriert dem Herzog viele seiner Bücher, die dieser auch für seine Söhne bekommen könne. Sein eigener Sohn Gottlieb sei anders als er veranlagt und interessiere sich nicht für fremde Sprachen, mathematische Studien und das andere, welches ihn umtreibe. Außerdem habe Gottlieb schon die für ihn passenden Bücher und werde einen großen Teil der Bibliothek seines Schwiegervaters Johann Saubert erben. Andreae sei demnach bereit, Hz. August eigene Bücher zu überlassen. — Württemberg erhoffe Frieden, sei aber die Scheidewand zwischen den Bayern und Franzosen und werde die Bühne für die abschließende Tragödie abgeben. Das Treffen zwischen (Hans Christoph v.) Königsmarck (FG 515. 1648) und Johann v. Werth werde kleingeredet. Warum die Kuttenträger im eigenen Land sich solche Dreistigkeiten erlauben, wisse er nicht. — Andreae wünscht der *Evangelischen Kirchen-Harmonie* des Herzogs eine gute Vollendung. — Andreae dankt dem Herzog, weil das *GB 1646* eingetroffen ist. Er habe darin gleich (Hz. Augusts Imprese mit dem) Gamander gefunden.

Q   HAB: Cod. Guelf. 65.1 Extrav., Bl. 296rv [A: 296v], eigenh., Sig. 28. Brief Andreaes in Antwort auf Hz. Augusts 26. Schreiben. — Kurzes Zitat in *Begemann: FG und Andreae*, 36.

A   Dem Durchleuchtigst. Hochgebohrnen Fursten vnd Herren, Herren Augusto, Hertzogen zu Brunschwig; vnd Lüneb. Meinem gnedigsten Fursten vnd Herren &c. Wolfenbüttel (.28.) 18. Julij.

Durchleuchtigster Hochgebohrner, Gnädigster Furst vnd Herr, E. F. g. 26. de 30. Junij[1] ist sambt 6 4tbogen[2] wol eingeliefert, woraußen ich vndst. vernommen, daß E. F. g. Bibliotheca noch immer zu Legen, daher ich intolerabile desiderium habe, selbige vide[re], mehr aber Bibliothecarium ipsum, sive verius vivam bibliothecam zu sehen, vnd vndst. aufzuwarten,[3] wünschet auch von herzen daß ich fur meine Saurbronnen. vnd Bader Cur, die liebe zeit vnd Müh auf die Wolfenb. rais verwendet hette. Es haben mich aber die hohe vertröstungen der Medicorum restituendæ in integrum valetudinis, hinderfuhrt, da es doch an iezo Laider ärger als zuvor ist. In meiner geringen Bibliotheca möchten vileicht noch stukh sein, die bei E. F. g. raum finden mochten, vnd werden E. F. g. mir große gnad Thun, wan E. f. g. dieselbige etwa vor sich, oder fur dero Herren Princen abfordern Thäten,[4] dan weil sie fur meinen einigen Sohn Gottlieb, der mit exoticis Linguis, mathematicis studijs, vnd anderem damit ich Mich oblectiert gar nichts zu Thun hat, vnd diuersissimo a me ingenio est, zu mahlen Nach seinem humor Mit zimblicher Bibliotheca versehen ist, vnd noch ein groß stukh von seinem Schwähr vatter, Herren Sauberto zu gewarten hat,[5] Als bin ich genzlich resolviert, ihme eines guthen theils Meiner Bibliothec, die ihme hinrerd her zu fuhren nur oneros sein wurde, zu entledigen, warinnen dan E. F. g. gnedigster disposition ich mich gern vnd*erthänig*st vndergeben, vnd mich fur glukhseelig achten wolte, wo hiedurch E. f. g. Herren Söhnen könte in etwa vnd. gedienet werden.

Des lieben fridens erwarten wir noch mit großem verlangen, ohne welchen wir besorglich novæ et exuente tragædiæ die scenam werden hergeben müßen, weilen zwischen Gallis et Bavaris wir die Schidmauer⁶ sein. Die Königsmarkhische rencontre⁷ würt alhier sehr extenuirt. Cuculliones nostrj verò, nescio qua fiducia, sunt insolentissimj.

Befehle E. F. G. dem Schuz des Almechtigen zu Leibes vnd Sehlen wolfart, auch glukhlicher vollendung des Harmonischen werkhs, darneben deroselben mich zu beharrenden gnaden, verbleibend biß in den Todt
E. F. G. vndertänigst gehorsamest. verpflichter Rhat, vnd getrewester diener
Jo. Valent. Andreæ D.

Das desiderierte Kreuterbuch⁸ ist Endlich angekommen, dafur ich mich undst. zu bedankhen habe. Das Gamanderle⁹ fig. 227 habe ich alsbalden gefunden, Deus omem impleat.

15. Julij 1646.

I

460715

Andreae an Philipp Hainhofer

Q HAB: Cod. Guelf. 74/ 75 Noviss. 2°, Bl. 251rv, eigenh.; Auszug hier Bl. 251r.

Von H. Augustissimo nostro habe ich ein schön Kreutergesellschaft buch¹ empfangen, darinnen 400. emblemata von Merians guter hand vnd inuention. Wo ich nicht zu alt vnd müde wehre, hette ich wol mögen auch der gesellen einen geben. Es sein aber nu mehr alle blumen vnd andere gewechs herauß, vnd wüste ich nichts mehr fur mich vbrig, als an einem alten abgestanden Baum, daß anwachsend mösch, mit dem Motto, Hernach, vnd dem Nahmen Der Müde.²

II

460723

Philipp Hainhofers Zitat aus einem Brief Andreaes und seine eigenen Bemerkungen darüber. An Herzog August

Q HAB: Cod. Guelf. 97 Novi 2°, Bl. 219r–226v [A: 226v]; eigenh., Sig. Zit. Bl. 220v-221r. — D: Auszug in *Gobiet*, Nr. 1481 (stark gekürzt); *Gobiet: Auszüge*, Nr. 203 (gekürzt).

460715 Johann Valentin Andreae

A Dem Durchleuchtigsten, hochgebornen Fürsten und herrn, herrn Augusto, hertzogen zu Braunschweig und Lunenburg, meinem gnädigsten Fürsten und herrn Vnderthänigst Wolfenbüttel — *Eigenh. Erinnerung Hz. Augusts:* Mösch! Hernach, Müede.

„Vom H. Augustissimo nro. habe Jch ain schönes Kräutter gesellschafft buch empfangen, darinnen 400 emblemata von Merians gueter hand und invention. Wan Jch nit zu alt und muede were, hette Jch wol mügen auch der gesellen einen geben. Es sein aber nun mehr alle blumen und andern gewechß herauß und wuste Jch nichts mehr für mich überig, alß an ainem alten abgestandenen baum daß anwachsende mösch, mit dem motto: hernach, und dem namen der Müede. Befehle hiemit Eh mich zu beharlichen grosen gunsten, unß samenlich aber cum obligatione gegen der löbl. societet fautorum dem schuz deß Allmechtigen, verbleibend biß in den tod &c."[1]
Dises Kreutter gesellen buch habe Jch noch nie gesehen. Dieweilen es aber sapientissimus Princips Augustus com̅endiret, so würdt es gewiß Augustis.^{mi} opus sein,[2] in dem es sonderlich von so vilen herrlichen, mancherley farbigen wolruchenden bluemen vnd gesunden Kräuttern, (die der allmächtige Gott dem menschen zur augen ergözlichkait, vnd menschen und vihe zur speiß, und heylung aller leibes gebrechen, auß der swarzen erden, zu deren wir alle mussen werden, iuxta illud Flos fænj vermis, pulvis cinis unde superbis? wachsen lasset) tractieret, et præsentem referat quælibet herba DEUM. warüber Joh. *Baptista* Helmund einen ganzen tractat geschriben haben solle.[3] [221r] Der löblichste Fürst herzog Philips in Pom̅ern, Christs. gedechtnus auf einem gnaden pfennig pro Sy̅mbolo: daß wörtlin philosophia, warinnen Philippj vnd Seiner fraw Gemahline Sophiæ namen begriffen, vnd pro emblemate: Chamæpitijm oder Ivam ehe länger ehe lieber bluemlin gefuert hatte.[4] Von herbarijs habe Jch ettliche authores: Vnd habe daß Florilegium Eystetense ad vivum illuminiert,[5] hochged. Fr. Gn. von Pom̅ern a.° 17 in Jhre bibliothecam verehrt, waist Gott, weil laider der ganze uhralte Pom̅erische stam̅e, wie aine blueme abgefallen, vnd wie ain graß verdorret ist, wer dieselbe bibliothecam geerbet hatt. Jn den bluemen und Kräuttern ist sonsten wol zu philosophiern, vnd hatt die natur so gar den gethieren etlicher Krautter erkhantnus eingebildet, und dem menschen durch die thiere zu erkhennen geben. quandoquidem Cervij dictamnum herbam,[6] quod vulneratis eius pastu telum venatorium eiecissent, sagittarum vulneribus mederj ostenderunt, ubi ferrum corporj inhæserit. Jtem cervæ secli herbam demonstrarunt: Testudines cunilam: mustelæ rutam: Accipitres Licracium: columbæ verbenacam: Hirundines chelidonium: Ciconiæ origanum, et alia denique animalia, alis innumeras herbas invenêre et monstravêre.

K 1 Hz. August d.J. v. Braunschweig-Wolfenbüttel (FG 227) beantwortet am 30.6.1646 Johann Valentin Andreaes (FG 464. 1646) 26. Schreiben vom 10.6.1646 „aus dem Ziller-Bade". Hz. August schreibt als Empfangsort „Zeller Baden". HAB: Cod. Guelf. 236.3 Extrav., Bl. 29rv.
2 Hz. August sandte regelmäßig Bögen der Quartausgabe seiner *Evangelischen Kirchen-Harmonie* (1646) — s. 411214 — seinem Rat Johann Valentin Andreae zur Durch-

sicht. Am 30.6.1646 hatte der Herzog „6 4tBogen der Harmonie" geschickt. A. a. O. (s. Anm. 1), Bl. 29r. Am 22.7.1646 schrieb Andreae an Philipp Hainhofer: „Die Euangelische Harmonia gehet mit macht auf tanquam Sol oriens, et terras illustrans. Vtinam etiam inter Germaniæ status Harmonia Pacis redux, concinnarj possit." HAB: Cod. Guelf. 74/75 Noviss. 2°, Bl. 253r. Der Druck der ersten Ausgabe der *Evangelischen Kirchen-Harmonie* (8° 1646) war schon im April 1646 abgeschlossen worden. Vgl. Philipp Hainhofer an Hz. August am 16./ 26.4.1646: „Das der 8.° trukh Harmoniæ Evangelicæ zu ende gehet, erfrewet für E. Fr. Gn. mich höchlich". HAB: Cod. Guelf. 97 Nov., Bl. 83v.

3 Andreae sollte nie nach Wolfenbüttel gelangen, um Hz. August und die riesige und berühmte Bibliothek zu sehen.

4 Der Herzog hatte Andreae am 30.6.1646 geschrieben: „Und berichte ihm daß ich meinen Catalogum zu pertexieren, izzo wieder angefangen habe, vermeine den 3. Tomum bald zu implieren, so hebet der 4tus Tomus darauf mit der 3601 pag. wieder an; dan der 2dus Tomus, mit 1201, der dritte Tomus, mit 2401 anfänget. Das papier ist fol. reg. oder Median Papier. Gott gebe daß Er selber in denselbigen Blädern und sie perlustrieren möge: Er möchte vielleicht noch Büchlein in denselbigen verzeichnet finden, daranne er ein gefallen haben möchte." HAB: Cod. Guelf. 236.3 Extrav., Bl. 29r. Diese Mitteilung benutzt Andreae in dem vorliegenden Brief, um dem Herzog einen Großteil seiner eigenen Büchersammlungen anzubieten. S. 460804, 460819 u. 460908. Auf die Katalogisierung und den Verkauf dieser Bücher weist summarisch hin *Brecht: Andreae und Hz. August*, 251.

5 Andreaes Sohn Gottlieb (1622–1683), Diakon in Cannstatt, hatte Johann Sauberts Tochter Barbara (*1623) am 1.6.1644 geehelicht. *Andreae: Schriften* I,2, 221. Zu Gottliebs Talent und wissenschaftlichen Interessen s. 460819.

6 Scheidemauer.

7 Der schwed. General (Greve) Hans Christoph v. Königsmarck (FG 515. 1648) hatte erst nach langen Operationen in Norddeutschland, Westfalen und am Rhein seine Reiter ins Hessische zu den Truppen seines kommandierenden Feldmarschalls (Greve) Carl Gustav Wrangel (FG 523. 1649) geführt. *Englund*, 463f. Vor dem Anzug der ksl.-kurbayer. Armee räumte Wrangel das eroberte Amöneburg, verschanzte sich bei Kirchhayn und verstärkte sich mit 5000 Franzosen aus dem Kasselischen. Schließlich standen sich die beiden Heere Ende Juni 1646 gegenüber, ohne daß es zur Schlacht kam. Die Kaiserlichen eroberten „das Haus Homburg an der Ohm, und das Schloß Schweinsberg, damit sie den General Wrangel aus seinen Schantzen bey Kirchhayn zu einem Haupt-Treffen hervorlocken mögten. Dieser hatte nach Cassel 500. Proviant-Wagen gesandt, welche der Oberste Dannenberg mit 2000. Pferden bedeckte. Weil man aber erfuhr, daß 6000. Kayserliche auf diese Convoy ausgerücket wären, verstärckte man solche bis auf 8000. Mann, und der General Königsmarck zog derselben mit einer gleichen Anzahl entgegen. Der General Johann von Wert kam also unverrichteter Sachen wieder zurück, die Kayserliche Armee brach aus ihrem Lager auf, und setzte sich zwischen Laubach, Lich und Hungen. Nach diesem Abzug machte sich der Hessische General Geiß an Homburg, welches die Kayserlichen dem Landgrafen Georg eingeräumet hatten, und eroberte den Ort auf Discretion […]." *Gottfried II*, 920 u. 922. Der kurbayer. General war Johann von/ Jan van Werth (1600–1652). Andreae hatte wohl in gewissem Sinne recht, als er vom Kleinreden des Treffens sprach. Der Herzog kannte jedoch eine dramatischere Version, als er Andreae am 30.6.1646 mitteilte: „Man sagt Jean de Werth und Konigsmarck haben stark auf einander getroffen. Solche velitationes seynd gemeiniglich præambula vor ein Haupttreffen: Man sagt, daß kaumt der vierte teihl, von 2000 Pferdten, auf der Swedischen Seiten, darvon entritten seye. Die Particularia werden folgen; und seynd viele verwundte in Cassel gebracht. Der Fried ist noch sehr slipferich anzugreiffen, uti angvilla." HAB: Cod. Guelf. 236.3

460715 Johann Valentin Andreae

Extrav., Bl. 29r. Zum weiteren Verlauf des Kriegs (französ.-schwed. Einfälle) s. 460804 u. 460909.

8 *GB 1646*. Hz. August hatte Andreae am 2.6.1646 geschrieben: „Die 400 Emblemata der fruchtbringenden Geselschaft hoffe ich werden ihm geliefert seyn. Merian hat uns die unsern gesandt, dafur ich zum verlage ihm 200 Rth. zu hulffe ubermachet; 200 Exemplaria seynd vom 8. Trukke fertig, werden nuhn *Amplissimi* werden, und in die welt ausgehen; der Kupferdrukker hat sich in etwas versaumet; Nuhn wird Er weiter 100 Expl. austrukken; dan abermahl hundert, und alsoferner bis die lacunæ der Exemplarum impliret." HAB: Cod. Guelf. 236.3 Extrav., Bl. 24r. Der zuletzt erwähnte Oktav-Druck bezieht sich nicht mehr auf das *GB 1646*, sondern auf die erste Ausgabe der *Evangelischen Kirchen-Harmonie* des Herzogs. S. 411214 S. 340. — Nachdem ihm der Herzog am 15.4.1646 ein Exemplar des *GB 1646* versprochen hatte, erkundigte sich Andreae immer wieder nach dem Verbleib des Buches. Vgl. die Übersicht solcher Anfragen bei *Begemann: FG und Andreae*, 33–36. S. 460317 K 9.

9 Im *GB 1646* fand Andreae Hz. Augusts (FG 227) Imprese mit dem Edelgamander. Andreae wußte schon seit langem von der Wahl dieser Pflanze. Am 30.4.1645 schrieb er an den Herzog: „Wegen gnediger information der hochlöb. gesellschaft, habe ich mich und. zu bedankhen, vnd will des Erwähnten buchs verlangenlich erwarten; Gamanderlej würt für ein antidotum gehalten, cuj benedicat Christus contra infernale, ciuile, et naturale venenum." HAB: Cod. Guelf. 65.1 Extrav. 2°, Bl. 221rv. Das Reimgesetz nennt Gegengift nicht als pharmazeutische Anwendung. S. *Conermann III*, 563.

K I 1 *GB 1646*. Daraufhin äußert sich Hz. August d. J. v. Braunschweig-Wolfenbüttel (FG 227) in 460804 darüber befriedigt, daß das lange von Johann Valentin Andreae (FG 464. 1646) ersehnte und immer wieder angemahnte Werk endlich in den Händen seines Geistlichen Rats angelangt war. Wie der Herzog Andreaes Wunsch aufnahm, einer der Gesellen der FG zu werden, zeigt 460915A I. Hz. August schickte Andreae F. Ludwigs Antwort in 461117, und dieser verpflichtete sich auf die Einhaltung der Gesellschaftsregeln in 461216 u. I.

2 Zur späteren Veränderung der Imprese vgl. bes. 461106 I, 461117 u. *Conermann III*, 563. Vgl. Beil. II.

K II 1 Von Johann Valentin Andreae (FG 464. 1646) selbst in 460715 I unterbreiteter Vorschlag für seine Gesellschaftspflanze, sein Wort und seinen Gesellschaftsnamen.

2 Es war ein Werk F. Ludwigs, der jedoch Einfälle und gelegentlich Dichtungen der Mitglieder beachtete, auch die Hilfe Diederichs v. dem Werder (FG 31) akzeptierte.

3 Jan Baptista van Helmont (1577–1644), brabant. Naturforscher und Mediziner, der in seinen Abhandlungen die Wirkung jatrochemischer Kräfte (Gas, „blas") und den Einfluß naturphilosophischer (paracelsischer) ‚archei' auf physiologische Prozesse untersuchte. Seine Schriften erschienen gesammelt u. d. T. Joannis Baptistæ Van Helmont, Toparchæ in Royenborch, Pellines, &c. Opuscula Medica Inaudita I. De Lithiasi. II. De Febribus. III. De Humoribus Galeni. IV. De Peste (Coloniae Agrippinae: Jost Kalcoven 1644). Von der HAB kürzlich nacherworbenes Ex.: Xb 5509. Im Altbestand der HAB erst die 2. Ausgabe Amsterdam: Elzevirius 1648 (28.5 Med.).

4 Hz. Philipp II. und Hzn. Sophia v. Pommern-Stettin. Werke der von Philipp II. gegründeten Greifenbibliothek sind noch in Stettin in der Ksianiza Pomorska im. Stanisawa Staszica erhalten. S. Handbuch der historischen Buchbestände in Deutschland, Österreich und Europa. Hg. Bernhard Fabian. Digitalisiert in https://fabian.sub.uni-goettingen.de/fabian. Vgl. auch 450326 K 4. — Die erwähnte Medaille des Augsburger Künst-

lers (Daniel Sailer?) aus dem Dresdner Münzkabinett beschreibt Tassilo Hoffmann: Die Gnadenpfennige und Schaugroschen des pommerschen Herzoghauses. Stettin 1933, 63 f. u. Abb. Taf. VI Nr. 34: Oval, Gold, 7,9 g; Avers mit Brustbild des Herzogs, Umschrift PHILIPPVS DVX POMERANORVM 1606; Revers ein wildes Stiefmütterchen (Viola tricolor L.) mit der Umschrift PHILOSOPHIA.

5 Hortvs Eystettensis, Sive Diligens Et Accvrata Omnivm Plantarvm, Florvm, Stirpivm, Ex Variis Terræ Partibvs, Singvlari Stvdio Collectarvm, Qvæ In Celeberrimis Viridariis Arcem Episcopalem Ibidem Cingentibvs, Hoc Tempore Conspicivntvr Delineatio Et Ad Vivvm Repræsentatio Operâ Basilii Besleri Philiatri Et Pharmacopoei. M.DC.XIII. HAB: 1 Med. 2°.

6 S. die Verse Burggf. u. Herr Christophs zu Dohna (FG 20) auf seine Gesellschaftspflanze Diptam in 280412 I. Vgl. *Conermann I* (20) und *III*, 22 f.

460718

Carl Gustav von Hille an Fürst Ludwig

Beantwortet durch 461106. — Carl Gustav v. Hille (FG 302) teilt F. Ludwig (Der Nährende) mit, daß er nicht alleine wegen eigener Angelegenheiten, sondern zusammen mit Hzn. Sophia Elisabeth v. Braunschweig-Wolfenbüttel (AL 1629. TG 42b) nach Mecklenburg gereist sei und dort ein halbes Jahr zugebracht habe. Mit seiner Rückkehr möchte er den Nährenden mit diesen Zeilen bedenken und seiner Freude darüber Ausdruck verleihen, daß das *GB 1646* mit den Kupferstichen jetzt veröffentlicht worden ist. Hz. August d. J. v. Braunschweig-Wolfenbüttel (FG 227. Der Befreiende) sei die seinem Verlagsbeitrag gemäße Stückzahl der Exemplare zugegangen. Da Hille selbst das Buch nicht gesehen habe und es käuflich nicht zu erwerben sei, bittet er den Nährenden, ihm nicht nur das *GB 1646*, sondern auch *Gueintz: Rechtschreibung (1645)* und andere Köthener Drucke auf eigene Rechnung zuzuschicken. Er würde dies als große Gnade zu schätzen wissen, zumal er nun schon seit langer Zeit nicht mit fürstlichen Briefen beehrt worden sei. — Krankheit und Reisetätigkeit hätten es bisher verhindert, sein Werk (*Hille: Teutscher Palmbaum*) zu beenden. Sobald es ihm jedoch etwas besser gehe, werde er sich nach Möglichkeit befleißigen, das von vielen gewünschte Buch zu vollenden, zumal sowohl Georg Philipp Harsdörffer (FG 362. Der Spielende) als auch Johann Michael Moscherosch (FG 436. Der Träumende) darauf aufmerksam machen. — Falls der Nährende einen Beitrag, besonders die Hänselung betreffend, aufsetzen und diesen überschicken wolle, würde es das Vorhaben sehr befördern.

Q HM Köthen: V S 545, Bl. 33r–34v [A: 34v], 34r leer; eigenh.; schwarzes Lacksiegel. — D: *KE*, 204 f.; *KL* III, 224 f. — BN: *Bürger*, 722 Nr. 10.

A Dem durchleuchtigen hochgebornen Fürsten und Herrn, herrn Ludwig Fürsten zu Anhalt, Grafen zu Ascanien, Herren zu Bernburg und Zerbst, meinen gnädigen Fürsten und herrn; underth. Cöthen *etc.*
Eigenh. Empfangsvermerk von F. Ludwig: Eingeben 7 Herbstmonat 1646.

HöchstgeEhrter Herr Nehrender *etc.*

Demselben verhalte ich hiermit gehorsambst nicht, daß ich nicht allein wegen meiner eignen sachen; sondern auch mit meiner gn. Frauen der Befreyendinn[1] nacher Mecklenburg verreiset gewesen; womit ich dann ein gantz halbeß Jahr zugebracht. Weilen nun zu meiner rückkunft ich mich gehorsambst verbunden befinde, meinen allergnädigsten Nehrenden mit diesen wenigen Zeihlen gehorsamst aufzuwarten; alß erfreue ich mich, daß der Gesellschafter Buch mit schönen Kupfermäsigen stücken[a] nunmehro herausser gekommen. Massen denn dem Befreyenden, so viel stükke, alß daß vorgeschoßene geld anbelanget vberschikket worden. Weilen ich aber selbigeß nicht habe können zusehen bekommen; viel weniger vmb daß gelt zu erhalten stehet, alß ersuche[b] meinen höchstgeEhrten Nehrenden ich[c] gehorsambst, sie wollen sich belieben lassen, nicht allein obgedachteß Gesellschafter Buch; sondern Eines von der Rechtschreibung[2] als andern deß Ortß außgegangenen herrlichen[c] Bücher[3] mir gn. auf meine bezahlung zu Uberschikken; so werde ichß[,] waß *[sic]* eine grosse gnade[,] zu schätzen haben; massen ich nun mit deroselben gn. handbrieffe, in langer Zeit nicht bin begnadiget [33v] worden.

Meine Krankheitten und verrichtete Reisen, haben mir daß gluck bis dahero nicht gönnen wollen; daß ich, meinem gehorsambsten versprechen nach, daß buch von der Fruchtbringenden Gesellschaft, hochlöblichen Vorhaben Etc. nicht habe vollenführen können; so bald ich aber gliebtß Gott ein wenig genesen; will ich mich nach mügligkeit befleisigen, daß von vielen gewünschete Werck zu volbringen, massen der h. Spilende[4], alß auch der h. Träumende[5] bey allen posten[6] dessen erinnerung thun.[7] Da mein höchstgeEhrter H. Nehrender etwaß auß sonderbahren gn. aufsetzen und mir eß uberschikken wolten, würde eß zu vol-[zihung][d] deß löblichen Vorhabendß, grosse beforderung thun; insonderheit, wie eß mit der Henselung ordendlich gehalten wird;[8] Bitte gehorsambst umb Verzeihung, und mich in dero hochschützenden gnade ie und allewege zuerhalten[,] alß der ich zeit meineß lebenß,

Meines höchstgeEhrten H. Nehrenden
gehorsambster und pflichtschuldig[ster][e] Knecht *etc.*
Der Unverdrossene *etc.*

Wolfenbüttel, den 18. HeuMonatß. 1646.

T **a** *Von Hille hier versehentlich zusammengeschriebenes Wort* Kupfermäsigenstücken — **b** *Folgt* <ich> — **c** *Eingefügt.* — **d** *Eingefügt für unleserliche Streichung. Buchstabenverlust im Falz. Konjektur in eckigen Klammern.* — **e** *Buchstabenverlust im Falz. Konjektur in eckigen Klammern.*

K 1 Hzn. Sophia Elisabeth v. Braunschweig-Wolfenbüttel (AL 1629. TG 42b) wurde in der FG, gemäß dem Gesellschaftsnamen ihres Gatten Hz. August d.J. v. Braunschweig-Wolfenbüttel (FG 227), „Die Befreiende" genannt. Zum Usus, den Gemahlinnen der FG-Mitglieder den jeweiligen Gesellschaftsnamen zu verleihen s. 440209 K 5. Es ist denkbar, daß Hzn. Sophia Elisabeth ihre Stiefmutter Hzn. Eleonora Maria v. Mecklenburg-Güstrow (AL 1617. TG 17), geb. Fn. v. Anhalt-Bernburg, auf ihrem Witwensitz in Strelitz besuchte. S. auch 450304, ein von Hzn. Eleonora Maria in Strelitz verfaßter Brief an F.

Christian II. v. Anhalt-Bernburg (FG 51). Ein knappes Jahr vorher begleitete Hille Hzn. Elisabeth v. Sachsen-Altenburg, geb. Hzn. v. Braunschweig-Wolfenbüttel, nach Mecklenburg. S. 451008 K 6. Hilles Reise dürfte auch dem Kauf eines Guts in Mecklenburg (Lalendorf b. Güstrow) gegolten haben. Vgl. *Conermann III*, 339 f. u. 450126 K 6.

2 *Gueintz: Rechtschreibung (1645)*. S. 440127 K 1.

3 Carl Gustav v. Hille (FG 302) bezieht sich höchstwahrscheinlich auf aktuelle Köthener Drucke. Das in Köthen gedruckte Werk *Sachse: Einhelligkeit* III ließ F. Ludwig Hille schon mit 460119 zustellen, Hilles damaliger Dienstherr Hz. August erhielt das Buch mit 450721. Vgl. zur *Einhelligkeit* im allgemeinen 441205 (K 3). Mit 440130 bekam Hille von F. Ludwig eine umfangreiche Buchsendung und die Zusage weiterer Lieferungen.

4 Georg Philipp Harsdörffer (FG 368. Der Spielende).

5 Johann Michael Moscherosch (FG 436. Der Träumende).

6 Standorte, Stellen, Ämter. S. *Paul Wb.*, 759 „¹Posten [...] Übertr. *angewiesener Standort*, ferner *Stelle, Amt*".

7 Harsdörffer war genau wie Moscherosch am Werk des „Unverdrossenen" (Hille: *Teutscher Palmbaum*. 1647) beteiligt. Wir finden beispielsweise von ersterem das *Lobgedicht Zu Erklärung des Kupfertitels beygefüget von Dem Spielenden*, *34 – [*46], i. e. Bl.)()()(v – [)()()(vii] v, ein frz. Sonett mit direkt folgender dt. Übertragung „Klingreimen fast nach dem Frantzösischen.", Bl. *49 f., i. e.)()()()(rv unterzeichnet mit „Le Iouant" resp. „gesetzet von Dem Spielenden", ferner ein Gedicht Carl Gottlieb Harsdörffers, „des Spielenden Söhnchen", S. 73*, i. e. [)()()()()(v] *[sic]* r und ein Gedicht unterzeichnet von Hans Michael Moscherosch „Uber des Unverdrossenen Teutschen Palmenbaum", S. 57*– 59*, i. e. Bl.)()()(*[sic]* rv, das mit folgenden Versen den inneren Adel der „Tugendhaftigkeit" und die Sprachfertigkeit und Ausdrucksfähigkeit (Hilles) dem äußeren Adelstitel an die Seite stellt:

„Jage fort den falschen Wahn/
Ob Sanftmut/ Kunst/ freye Sinnen
Stünden nicht dem Adel an/
Der von Hill schreibt ohne Tadel.
Desto mehr ist er von Adel."

S. auch *Hille: Teutscher Palmbaum* allgemein 451008 K 2.

8 In 461029 wiederholt Hille seine Bereitschaft und auch die Bitte um Information. Eine Darstellung des Aufnahmerituals der Hänselung, in dem das Trinkgefäß des „Ölbergers" eine entscheidende Rolle spielte, unterblieb, weil F. Ludwig offenbar Bedenken trug, Einzelheiten dieser leicht zu verhöhnenden Praxis an die Öffentlichkeit gelangen zu lassen. Wir kennen sie aber vornehmlich aus einem Aufsatz, den Hans v. Dieskau (FG 212) nach dem Tode F. Ludwigs im Zusammenhang mit der Überführung des Erzschreins nach Weimar (1651) schrieb oder zumindest erst dann weiterreichte. HAAB Weimar: Ms. Fol. 219b, Bl. 303–305. Vgl. 461106 K 6. Der Text wurde bereits in *Herz: Wältz recht*, 374 f. veröffentlicht. Zum fruchtbringerischen Aufnahmeritual der Hänselung u. zum Ölberger vgl. 171224 K 5, 410621 (K 5); 450500 K 7, 450508A, 450725, 460104, 460423, 460424A K 4, 460613, 460915A, 461029, 461031A, 461106; ferner *Herz: Wältz recht*, 368–376.

460720

Christian Gueintz an Fürst Ludwig

Sich für die lange Verzögerung entschuldigend, schickt Christian Gueintz (FG 361. Der Ordnende) F. Ludwig (Der Nährende) das erbetene Gutachten (zu Georg Philipp Harsdörffers [FG 368] *Specimen Philologiae Germanicae*, 1646). Es gehe ihm besonders darum, daß man unnötige Sprachneuerungen vermeide, sich dafür zugunsten ungefährdeter Verständigung am tradierten Gebrauch orientiere. Der einmal gebahnte Weg sei doch der beste.

Q HM Köthen: V S 545, Bl. 190r–191v [A: 191v], Bl. 190v u. 191r leer; Schreiberh.; Empfangsvermerk F. Ludwigs auf Bl. 190r. — Nicht in *KE*.

A tt. *Dem Nährenden etc.*   Halle   Cöthen *etc.*

Durchläuchtiger[a], Hochgebohrner Fürst, gnädiger Herr, E. Fürstl. Gn. ist meine unterthanige Schuldigkeit dargestellet, Bittende Sie wolten meinen langen Verzug in ungnaden nicht vermercken,[1] die Amtsgeschäfte und wiedrige Zeiten werden mich in etwas entschuldigen. Jetziger Ernden feyertage frist[2] hat mir muße gelaßen, daß Jch beygefügte anmerckungen[3] entworffen, welche E. Fürstl. Gn. hohem verstande und beobachtung hiermit untergeben werden; Vornehmlich aber[b] hat man dahin gezielet, wie man unnötige neuerung vermeiden und beliebete gewohnheit erhalten möchte, Jn dem die gebahnten wege doch die besten, Verbleibe sonst neben empfehlung göttlichem obhalt[4].

Des *Nährenden*
Unterthäniger Ordnender *etc.*

Hall den 20 HeuMonats 1646.

Darunter eigenh. Empfangsvermerk F. Ludwigs: Eingeben 24. Heumonats 1646.

T a *Achtzeilige D-Initiale, neben dem Text.* — b *Eingefügt.*

K 1 Für das Jahr 1646 ist die überlieferte Korrespondenz zwischen F. Ludwig (Der Nährende) und Christian Gueintz (FG 361. Der Ordnende) äußerst spärlich. So liegen uns auch keine Nachrichten vor, ob Georg Philipp Harsdörffers (FG 368) Brief 460131 nicht nur von F. Ludwig, sondern wie von diesem gewünscht auch von Gueintz beantwortet worden ist. S. 460200. Wenn Gueintz nun um Entschuldigung für das lange Ausbleiben seiner Antwort bittet, wird er sich auf einen nicht überlieferten Brief beziehen, der nach dem 26.4. und vor dem 9.6.1646 von Ludwig an Gueintz abging und ein Exemplar von Harsdörffers *Specimen Philologiae Germanicae* (1646) begleitete. Harsdörffer hatte F. Ludwig mit 460406 (empfangen am 26.4.) einen frischen Druck seines jüngsten Werks geschickt und ihn gebeten, zwei weitere Exemplare an Diederich v. dem Werder (FG 31) und Gueintz auszuhändigen, um sie von diesen begutachten zu lassen (Weiterleitung von F. Ludwig bestätigt in 460609. Zu Gueintz' Gutachten „Erinnerungen Bey des Spielenden Wercklein die deutsche Sprache betreffend" s. Anm. 3, vgl. 460705 K 3.

2 Ein allgemeiner Erntefeiertag vor Michaelis (29.9., Erntedankfest) konnte nicht

ermittelt werden. Gueintz ist seit 1627 Gymnasialrektor in Halle. Vermutlich bekamen seine Schüler um den 20. Juli herum frei, um bei der Ernte zu helfen, so daß er Zeit hatte, an dem Gutachten zu arbeiten.

3 Dem Schreiben liegt im Köthener Erzschrein Gueintz' Gutachten „Erinnerungen Bey des Spielenden Wercklein die deutsche Sprache betreffend" bei (HM Köthen: V S 545, Bl. 192r–200v; *KE*, 363–372; Auszug in *Jones: Sprachverderber*, 197 f. [zit. *KE*, 369 f.]; das Gutachten demnächst in *DA Köthen I. 9*, zu 460720), in dem sich Gueintz mit Harsdörffers *Specimen* auseinandersetzt und dabei hin und wieder auf seine *Rechtschreibung (1645)* rekurriert. Harsdörffer hatte in 460406 selbst um eine Stellungnahme von seiten Gueintz' gebeten. S. Anm. 1. F. Ludwig wird Gueintz' Gutachten mit 460816 an Harsdörffer weiterleiten. Dieser wird es mit 460915 beantworten, vgl. auch 460916. Es führt 15 Monita auf, die i. w. auf eine Berücksichtigung des Sprachusus hinauslaufen. 1.) Der Begriff des Philologen wird tiefer erfaßt als bei Harsdörffer. 2.) Harsdörffers Übersetzung „witdod" für Philosoph wird zurückgewiesen, auch wenn das Wort einstmals in Umlauf war: seine urspr. Bedeutung ist ungewiß; es wird nicht mehr verstanden, im Gegensatz zu „Weltweiser". Das gilt auch für andere herbeigesuchte alte Wortformen: sie sind unnötig, weil unverständlich, weil ungebräuchlich. 3.) „Deutsch" sei mit -D- und nicht mit -T- zu schreiben. 4.) Die Gewohnheit als eine verbindliche „Richtschnur" aller Sprachen. 5.) Keine Einzelsprachen (ausgenommen Hebräisch), auch nicht das Deutsche, bestanden vor der babylon. Sprachverwirrung. 6.) Mundarten und Schreibweisen (nicht aber die Stammwörter als solche) sind modern, d. h. sie weichen von der Sprache der alten Deutschen ab. Auch im Latein. gab es versch. Sprachstufen. 7.) Vor Karl d. Großen hatten die Deutschen keine Schrift, dann übernahmen sie die griech. und latein. Buchstaben. Die Etymologie „Buch(stabe)" von „Buche" ist zweifelhaft. „Letter" stammt von „Literas" her. 8.) Im Hebräischen und Deutschen gibt es mancherlei Entsprechungen, die aber nicht dazu berechtigen, von einer durchgängigen „Gleichheit" beider Sprachen zu sprechen. Auch verfügten das Griechische und Lateinische über weit ältere Grammatiken als das Hebräische, für das erst im Hochmittelalter die frühesten Grammatiken überliefert sind. Auch das Deutsche war einst noch nicht reguliert. 9.) Nicht der (einsilbige) Imperativ, sondern der Infinitiv sei beim Verb das Stammwort, wie im Hebräischen. Nicht alle Verben bilden einen Imperativ, nicht alle Nomen lassen sich von Verben (Verbstammformen) ableiten. Die Kürze (Einsilbigkeit) ist überhaupt kein Kriterium für die Natürlichkeit einer Sprache (vgl. dazu 450410). 10.) Silbentrennung nach Sprechsilben, nicht grammaticè. Anders zu reden als zu schreiben, widerspreche der ‚deutschen Aufrichtigkeit', Tradiertes abzulehnen und Neues einzuführen ihrer ‚Standhaftigkeit'. 11.) Mag sein, daß die dt. Sprache älter als das Griechische und Lateinische sei; aber die Sprache der alten Deutschen dürfte sich im neueren Deutsch verloren haben. Fremdwörter, für die es keine dt. Wörter gebe, sollen bleiben statt krampfhaft übersetzt zu werden. 12.) Die Poesie (Reimkunst) muß sich nach den Mundarten richten, je nachdem, an wen sie adressiert ist. 13.) Das „Geld", nicht „Gelt". 14.) Ob Luthers Schriften für die deutsche Orthographie maßgeblich sind, lasse sich durch einen Vergleich unterschiedlicher Schreibweisen ermitteln. Auch wenn manches geändert/ verbessert werden kann, dürfe man nicht so vermessen sein, sich für klüger als die Vorfahren zu halten und immer alles ändern zu wollen. 15.) Die von Harsdörffer propagierte Wortschreibung -kk- für -ck- lehnt Gueintz ab — sie sei nicht üblich. Solange keine vernünftigen Gegengründe vorlägen, sollte die Gewohnheit als Richtschnur dienen. „Wir lieben und loben was üblich, was vernünftig und dürfen in keiner Sprache nach vnsern Gefallen etwas ändern." Nicht einmal Kaiser hätten diese Regel außer Kraft setzen können. — Soweit in Kürze Gueintz' Gutachten.

4 Obhalt, d. h. ‚Schutz'. S. 431020 K 4.

460721

Herzog Georg Rudolph in Schlesien zu Liegnitz und Wohlau an Fürst Ludwig

Hz. Georg Rudolph (FG 58) erklärt die Auszahlung der ausstehenden 48 Reichstaler. Diese habe er vorlängst als 60 schlesische Zahltaler, die 48 Reichstalern entsprechen, an den Breslauer Handelsmann Samuel Schaf(f) v. Weistritz ausbezahlt. Da dieser in Leipzig an die Bevollmächtigten F. Ludwigs (Der Nährende) jedoch 60 Reichstaler beglichen habe, habe der Herzog die restlichen 12 Reichstaler nachschießen lassen. Nun hoffe er, daß die gesamte Summe F. Ludwig erreicht habe.

Q HM Köthen: V S 544, Bl. 81r–82v [A: 82v], 81v–82r leer; Schreiberh. mit eigenh. Unterschrift.

A Dem Hochgebohrnen Fürsten, Herren *Ludwigen* Fürsten zu Anhalt, Graven zu Ascanien, Herren zu Zerbst, vnd Berenburg; Vnserm freundlichen geliebten herren Vetter, Schwager, vnd Gevatter   Cöthen
Eigenh. Empfangsvermerk F. Ludwigs: Präs. ☉ IX post Trinitatis 21[1] Julij. Cöthen. An. 1646.

Unsere freundVetterliche dienste, vnd was Wier mehr liebes vnd guttes vermögen zuvor; Hochgebohrner Fürst, freundlicher geliebter Herr Vetter, Schwager vndt Gevatter,

Wier haben aus E. Ld. iüngst erhaltenem Handbrieflen verstanden, was massen deroselben, wegen Vnserer durch Samuel Schaffes[2] Handelsmannes allhier beförderung, die bewusten AchtvndVierzig ReichsThaler, welche Schlesischen werthes Sechzig Zahlthaler betragen[3], seindt gutgemachet worden, die Wier auch schon vor etlichen Wochen bemeltem Schaff allhier richtig auszahlen lassen;[4]

Nachdeme Vns Er aber vber dieses zuerkennen gegeben, das E. Ld. Leuten zu Leibzig Er Sechzig Reichsthaler[5] gutgethan, haben Wier die rückstendigen 12 Reichsthaler auch alsobalden erstatten lassen, vnd zweifeln nicht es werden E. Ld. entzwischen solches residuum empfangen haben:

solte es vber verhoffen nicht geschehen sein, wolten es E. Ld. ohnbeschweret nur ferner erinnern;

Sonst haben Wier deswegen keine Quittung von nöten, welches E. Ld. Wier zu freundVetterlicher nachricht nicht verhalten mögen; empfehlen dieselbe dabey Göttlicher gnaden obacht trewlichen.

Breßlaw den 21igsten Julij Anno 1646.

Von Gottes gnaden George Rudolff Hertzog in Schlesien zur Liegniz, Brieg, vnd Goldberg, Kayser- vnd Königl. Ober-AmbtsVerwalter in Ober vnd Nieder-Schlesien

    E.[a] L
        dienstwilliger Vetter
        Rudolph*mp.*

T a *Folgt eigenh. Schlußkuralie mit Unterschrift.*

K 1 Fälschlich aufgelöst? Der 9. Sonntag nach Trinitatis fiel im Jahr 1646 auf den 29. Juli. S. *Grotefend,* 158.
2 Samuel Schaf(f) v. Weistritz (1589–1652), Reichskrämer und Ratsherr in Breslau. S. 451019 K 3. Er hatte bereits zuvor für Hz. Georg Rudolph in Schlesien zu Liegnitz und Wohlau (FG 58) Zahlungen abgewickelt.
3 Während man in Kursachsen für einen (Reichs-)Taler seit spätestens 1580 24 (Silber-)Groschen bzw. 90 Kreuzer berechnete, behielt man in Schlesien die durch die Reichsmünzordnungen von 1551 u. 1566 für einen Taler festgelegten 72 Kreuzer bei. Dieser Schlesische Taler war Mitte des 17. Jahrhunderts nur noch eine Rechnungseinheit und wurde in der Folgezeit gegenüber dem Reichstaler weiter abgewertet, so daß er Mitte des 18. Jahrhunderts schließlich nur noch 2/3 Reichstaler (60 Kreuzer) galt. S. allgemein dazu Friedrich Frhr. v. Schrötter (Hg.): Wörterbuch der Münzkunde. Berlin/Leipzig 1930, 556 ff., 604 u. 676 f.; Heinz Fengler, Gerhard Gierow u. Willy Unger: Transpress-Lexikon Numismatik. 4. bearb. Aufl. Berlin 1988, 398 ff.; Wolfgang Trapp: Kleines Handbuch der Münzkunde und des Geldwesens in Deutschland. Stuttgart 1999, 80 u. 84 f.
4 In welchem Zusammenhang dieser Betrag fällig war, ja auch die widersprüchliche Rechnung selbst (s. Anm. 5) bleiben unerfindlich. Da der Brief aber im Erzschrein der FG archiviert wurde, liegt eine Kauffinanzierung etlicher Exemplare des *GB 1646* im Bereich des Möglichen. Schwerlich denkbar ist eine Beisteuer/ Verlagsteilhabe zum *GB 1646*, da Hz. Georg Rudolph nicht zum quellenmäßig belegten Kreis der Beiträger gehörte und auf einem Auslieferungszettel im Erzschrein (HM Köthen: V S 546, Bl. 178r) nur die bereits bekannten Verlagsbeiträger genannt werden: „Die 48 bücher nach Holstein [Hz. Friedrich III. v. Schleswig-Holstein-Gottorf (FG 388. Der Hochgeachte)], auß frankfurt bis nach Cothen zu bringen kosten Fuhrlohn, Confriergeld und andere costen ... th 6. Die 24 Exemplar nach Hannover [Hz. Christian Ludwig v. Braunschweig-Calenberg (FG 372. Der Reinherzige)] aus frankfurt bis Cothen zubringen costen fuhrlohn, Confriergeld und andere uncosten ... th 3. Als auch die dem von Wietersheim [Anthon v. Wietersheim (FG 273)] zukommen. ... 3". Vgl. ebd. Bl. 185r. Zu ergänzen ist Hz. August d. J. v. Braunschweig-Wolfenbüttel (FG 227), der für seine Verlagseinlage von 200 Reichstalern 48 Exemplare erhielt. S. auch 421031A K 15–18 u. 450126 K 4.
5 Diese Rechnung setzt voraus, daß ursprünglich eine Gesamtsumme von 60 Reichstalern ausstand, von der die „bewusten AchtvndVierzig ReichsThaler" bereits beglichen wurden, indem 60 *schlesische* Taler F. Ludwigs Bevollmächtigten ausgezahlt wurden. Die dann noch fehlenden 12 Reichstaler seien „alsobalden" auch erstattet worden.

460726

Johann Michael Moscherosch an Fürst Ludwig

Johann Michael Moscherosch (FG 436) bedankt sich für die Gnadenbezeigungen F. Ludwigs, von denen ihm Georg Philipp Harsdörffer (FG 368. Der Spielende) bereits vor einem Jahr nach Paris und seitdem durch mehrere weitere Schreiben berichtet habe. Moscherosch erfahre nun durch ein (nicht überliefertes) Schreiben (Harsdörffers) vom

19.6.1646 von seiner Aufnahme in die FG und erhalte das Impresenbild als Vorlage für den (zu bemalenden) Gesellschaftspfennig nebst Gesellschaftsname und -wort. — Moscherosch verspricht, zum Nutzen des Vaterlandes und zum Wohlergehen der FG beizutragen, deren Rat und Urteil er sich und seine Schriften künftig unterstellen wolle. Unter Verweis auf die Begrenztheit des vorliegenden Papiers verspricht er, sich künftig ausführlicher zu bedanken.

Q HM Köthen: V S 544, Bl. 79r–80v [A: 80v], 80r leer; eigenh.; Sig. — *D: Begemann: Andreae u. FG*, 48; *KE*, 60f.; *KL* III, 216f. — *BN: Kühlmann: Korrespondenz Moscheroschs*, 268; *Kühlmann/ Schäfer: Oberrhein*, 124. Nicht in *Bürger*.

A Dem Durchläuchtigen Hochgebornen Fürsten und Herren, Herren *Ludwigen* Fürsten zu Anhalt, Graven zue Ascanien und Bellerstat [sic], Herrn zu Zerbst undt Bernburg *etc.* Meinem Genädigsten Fürsten und Herren. *Cöthen.* — *Postalischer Vermerk:* Zu Leipzig bey H. Gottfried Stahlen[1] abzugeben. — *Eigenh. Empfangsvermerk F. Ludwigs:* Eingeben 30. Aug 1636 [sic].[2] — *Am Rand:* 14

Durchläuchtiger Hochgeborner Fürst *etc.*

Ew. Fürstl. Gdn. sindt meine Underthanigstgehorsamiste [sic] dienste in beständigster Trew iederzeit bevor,
Genädigster Fürst undt Herr.

E. Fürstl. Gd. undt dero Hochlöblichsten Gesellschafft genädigsten Willen undt Gewogenheit hab von dem Edelen *Spielenden* ich nicht allein vor schon einem Jahr, in Pariß,[3] undt seithero in Schreiben zu verschiedenen mahlen wohl vernommen; sondern auch auß deme vom 19. BrachMonats an mich abgeloffenen hocherfreuet ersehen, daß in die Hochlöbliche Fruchtbringende Gesellschafft, mit gdst. Vbersendung deß Gemählds zum Gesellschafft Pfenning, neben beygefügtem Wort vndt Namen, gdst. auffgenommen worden.[4]

Wie nun so hohe Gd. ich mir auß selbstbewusten meiner Unwürdigkeit niehmahlen einbilden dörffen; also wirdt mir die-[79v]selbe[a] umb so desto mehr anlaß undt Ursach geben, die eusserste schuldigkeit dergestalt in obacht zu nehmen, daß, wo Gott in künfftigen etwas Mueß undt Zeit bescheren soltte, solche zu deß Hochwertheten Vatterlands Nutzen, Undt, welches deme anhanget, der Hochlöblichsten Gesellschafft Auffnehmen, von mir eyfferigsten fleisses angewendet, mit faust undt feder erkennet werden möge.

Dero Genaden[b] Rühmlich und Weisestem Urtheil und Befehl, ich mich und meine wenige schrifften von iezt vnd fortan, in allem, zu beharrlichen Gd. demütigst anheim und undergebe.

Wan aber dieses wenige Pappier iezt so viel raum nicht gibt, meines wesens und wandels völlige beschaffenheit, alß ich zuthun verpflichtet were, zu überschreiben, so wird es iedoch mit füglichster gelegenheit künfftig in undertheniger schuldigkeit verrichtet werden.

E. Fürstl. Gd. hab ich nur dieses iezmahlen nicht perg*en*, den Allmächtigen aber für dero vndt deren Hochfürstlichen Hauses bestandigste Wolfart demütigst bitten: Auch dero Hochfürstlicher Gd. undt Hulden mich gehorsamist einbefehlen sollen.

Geben Straßburg den 26. HeuMonats 1646.

E. Fürstl. Gd.
Underthänigst gehorsamister Diener
Hanß-Michel Moscherosch.

T a selbe *auch Kustode.* — **b** *Folgt ein heute als Anführungsstriche zu lesendes Zeichen, hier auch als andernorts ähnlich verwendeter Bindestrich unverständlich.*

K 1 Der Leipziger Kaufmann Gottfried Stahl (d. Ä.) (1600–1670) wurde von F. Ludwig wiederholt für finanzielle Transaktionen, Einkäufe sowie zur Informationsweitergabe und Abwicklung der Korrespondenz herangezogen. Vgl. 440426 K 1.
2 Muß richtig heißen: 1646.
3 Georg Philipp Harsdörffer (FG 368. Der Spielende) hatte Johann Michael Moscheroschs (FG 436) Aufnahme in die FG vermittelt und zu ihm Verbindung gehalten, als Moscherosch im Rahmen einer diplomatischen Mission des Straßburger Rates vom August 1645 bis in den Sommer 1646 in Paris weilte. Die damit verbundenen Schwierigkeiten der Kommunikation erschwerten seine Aufnahme und erklären die Verzögerung des vorliegenden Dankesbriefes. S. 450500 K 1 u. 451101. Zeugnis dieses Paris-Aufenthalts sind v. a. die zwei literar. Briefe 450818 u. 450901.
4 Am 19.6. muß Harsdörffer Moscherosch eine Sendung geschickt haben, die das Impresengemälde (Visierung) für Moscherosch als Vorlage für seinen zu prägenden FG-Gesellschaftspfennig enthalten hatte. Dieses Gemälde war Harsdörffer von F. Ludwig mit 460609 zur Weiterleitung an Moscherosch zugesandt worden. Moscherosch wurden der Gesellschaftsname „Der Träumende" und das Gesellschaftswort „Hohe Sachen" nebst dem Schwarzen Nachtschatten als Gesellschaftspflanze erteilt. Vgl. 450504A K 2. Vgl. auch die zwei Abbildungen (Porträt u. Imprese) S. 797 und 879 sowie ihre Beschreibungen in „Zu den Abbildungen", S. 141–145.

460803

Justus Georg Schottelius an Georg Philipp Harsdörffer

Justus Georg Schottelius (FG 397. Der Suchende) ermutigt Georg Philipp Harsdörffer (FG 368. Der Spielende), seine *Frauenzimmer-Gesprächspiele* über den vorliegenden 6. Teil (1646) hinaus wie geplant zu Ende zu führen. Die Fortsetzung sei schon allein deswegen wünschenswert, weil in den bisherigen Bänden fast alle Wissenschaften und Künste mal mehr, mal weniger umfassend in guter deutscher Sprache behandelt worden seien; hier dürfe kein wichtiger Inhalt übergangen werden. Kein Ort sei für die Durchführung eines solchen Vorhabens in gleichem Maße geeignet wie Nürnberg (wo Harsdörffer ansässig ist). Denn nirgends sonst könne man über die ansässige Kaufmannschaft leichter die neuesten und besten Bücher aus dem europäischen Ausland beziehen, die aufgrund seiner Sprachenkenntnis von Harsdörffer auch fernerhin kompetent verwendet und ausgewertet werden mögen. Von spöttischen Verächtern derartiger Werke, die meinen, niemand werde durch sie zum Besseren geführt, der sich nicht bereits aus eigenem Antrieb in dieselbe

Richtung bewege, dürfe man sich nicht beeindrucken lassen. Auch wenn die Herstellung kostspielig sei — andernorts würde sie noch teurer werden —, sollten die verbleibenden Bände auf jeden Fall in Angriff genommen werden. Der Verleger werde aufgrund der positiven Aufnahme durch das Publikum gewiß auf seine Kosten kommen.

Q *Harsdörffer: Frauenzimmer-Gesprächspiele* VI (1646, Ndr. 1969), 667–670. — Nicht in *Estermann*.

Spatuberschikktes Sendschreiben
Des Suchenden an den Spielenden/
die Fortsetzung der Gesprächspiele betreffend.
Edler Spielender/ hochwehrter Hertzen-Freund.

ES hat mich ein sonderliches Verlangen belustiget/ als ich aus seinem nechsten an mich abgegebenen vernommē/ daß er nun den VI. Theil seiner Kunstgeziertē Gesprächspiele/ an das Liecht zu geben geruhet: Hinwiderüm aber betrübet/ als ich mitkommend verstanden/ aus was Ursachen er die Feder niederlegen/ und das dritte hundert solcher Fruchtbringenden Kunstspiele unvollendet erliegen zu lassen/ gesinnet.

Der Spielende hat sich üm unsre edle Muttersprache/ also verdient gemacht/ daß er sein beliebtes Gedächtniß/ und wolgehaltenen Nachruhm nicht [668] auf ein vergängliches Papier/ sondern dem gunstgeneigten Angedenken vieler hohen/ und gelehrten Personen unausbleiblich eingeschrieben hat.

Man befindet in denen bishero ausgefertigten Theilen der Gesprächspiele/ daß fast nichts von löblichen Künsten und Wissenschaften verhanden/ so nicht zum Theil wolberühret/ zum Theil grundmässig/ mit leichtvernemlicher Art/ und in guter Teutscher Rede ausgeführet worden/ daß derselben Fortsetzung billich zu erwünschen/ wann solche ohne Verabsaumung wichtiger Angelegenheiten beschehen könte.

Es ist sich aber nicht zu verwundern/ daß etwan ein und anderer Spötter sich bey solchen Werk verächtlich hören lässet: Massen diese Anführung zur Tugend und Künsten niemand/ als welche solchen folgen wollen/ gefallen kan/ und nichts so gut in der Welt ist/ das man nicht bößlich solte ausdeuten könen. Der Spielende hat auf verständiger/ und gelehrter Leute gründliche Beurtheilung mehr zu sehen/ als auf solcher Eselwitzigen Anschreyen.[1]

Die Statt Nürnberg ist sonderlich im Teutschen Reiche/ bewuster vieler [669] hohen Ursachen halber sehr berühmt/ beliebet und eines gantzen herrlichen Namens. Jn selber hat der Spielende mehr Mittel/ als vielleicht kein anderer/ (Wer und wo er auch sich aufhalte/) aus Spania/ Jtalia/ Frankreich/ und Niederland/ die neusten und schönsten Bücher/ vermittelst der Kaufmannschaft zu erhalten/ Er besitzt die Wissenschaft der Sprachen/ solche nach Befindung ihrer Würdigkeit den Gesprächspielen einzuverleiben/ und aus eigenen Nachsinnen mit vielen seltenen Erfindungen auszuschmükken; wie er bishero gethan/ und noch ferner zu thun/ von allen Tugend- und Sprachliebenden bittlich angelanget wird.

Solte aber der Spielende diesem Ansinnen nicht stat geben/ sehe ich nicht/ wer die zween hinterstellige Theile/ mit gleichen kunstfüglicher Hand/ und dazu gehörige Mitteln vollenden solte. Gewisslich es würde ausser Nürnberg/ die Arbeit kostbarer/ ja wegen der schönen Holtzschniede unthunlich fallen/ und ist nicht zu zweiffeln/ der Verleger werde seiner aufgewandten Unkosten mit der Zeit wol wieder vergnüget werden. Massen dieses Werk je mehr und mehr bey [670] allen Fürsten-Höfen/ da man sonst nicht gerne über Büchern sitzet/ gelesen/ und vielen Hohenschulen bekannt/ täglich grössern Abgang/ und Nachfrage gewinnet.

Diesem nach wiederhole ich mein dienstfreundliches/ doch ohnmaßgebliches Bitten/ der Spielende wolle ihm[a] gefallen lassen/ so wolangefangene Arbeit/ mit der Zahl/ des geliebt es Gott folgenden 1647. Jahrs/ zu des Spielenden Ruhm/ unserer Teutschen HeldenSprache Aufnemē/ und aller Tugendliebenden Wolgefallen/ großgünstig fortzustellē. Befehle hiermit den Spielenden Göttlicher Bewahrung/ und verbleibe

Sein Dienstergebener

Wollenbüttel[b] den 3. des Augustmonats 1646.

Der Suchende.

T a *Lies:* sich — **b** *Druckfehler, lies:* Wolfenbüttel

K Georg Philipp Harsdörffer (FG 368. Der Spielende) bat F. Ludwig in 460620 darum, für den 6. Teil der *Gesprächspiele* ein Lobgedicht zu verfassen, weil der gerade im Druck befindliche Band evtl. der letzte sein werde. Auch in 460916 zweifelt er noch daran, daß dem 6. Teil ein weiterer folgen könnte. Die Kosten, die die Produktion der *Gesprächspiele* verursachten, seien ihm zu hoch und sein Verleger Wolfgang Endter d. Ä. geizig und unsicher, ob er in der gegenwärtigen Kriegslage seine Drucke zu den Messen transportieren könne. Trotz dieser akuten Probleme wird Harsdörffer die anvisierten 300 *Gesprächspiele* zu Ende bringen und den 7. und 8. Teil (1647 bzw. 1649) wie geplant bei Endter in Nürnberg publizieren. S. zu den hohen Druckkosten 460620 K 9. — Das Projekt war vom ersten Band an auf mehrere Teile angelegt. So kündigt Harsdörffer in der 1. Aufl. des 1. Teils der *Gesprächspiele* (1641) in seiner Nachrede „An den Sprach- vnd Gesprächliebenden Leser" (hier Bl. P[j] v) bereits an, daß bei guter Aufnahme des Werks eine Fortsetzung mit weiteren 50 Gesprächspielen folgen werde, „vnnd mit der Zeit auch der dritte Theil völlig erstatten/ was in diesen beeden gleichsam entworffen vnd angewiesen ist." Als die 2. Aufl. des 1. Teils (1644) dem Druck übergeben wird, ist der projektierte Umfang bereits auf (mindestens) 7 Bände angewachsen. Harsdörffer spricht in seiner (im Vergleich zur Erstauflage stark überarbeiteten) Vorrede davon, daß er den neu aufgelegten 1. Teil durch insgesamt sechs weitere vermehren wolle, um den „gar kurtze[n] Entwurf", den der erste Band biete, zu vollenden (*Harsdörffer: Frauenzimmer-Gesprächspiele* I, ²1644, Ndr. 1968, 19). In der erstmals in der 2. Auflage des 1. Teils erschienenen *Harsdörffer: Schutzschrift (1644)*, 51 heißt es allerdings: „Es ist aber dieser erster Theil ein kurtzer Entwurff dessen/ was in Fortsetzung der Gesprächspiele bereit ümständig ausgeführet/ und/ beliebts Gott/ in nachfolgenden vier Theilen/ mit mehreren behandelt werden sol." Da ein fertiges

Exemplar des 4. Teils der *Gesprächspiele* (1644) bereits mit 440426 an die FG gesandt, die überarbeitete 2. Auflage des 1. Teils aber frühestens im Juli od. August 1644 dem Druck übergeben wurde (das Lobgedicht F. Ludwigs datiert auf den 15. Juli; in 440824 informiert Harsdörffer ihn, daß der Band sich im Druck befinde) und entgegen dem Titelblatt, das 1644 als Erscheinungsjahr angibt, erst im Frühjahr 1645 erschien (s. 450400), müßte Harsdörffer in der *Schutzschrift* von bereits vier vorliegenden Teilen ausgehen, demnach schon zu diesem Zeitpunkt an einen Gesamtumfang von acht Teilen gedacht haben. Wahrscheinlich scheint, daß die Überarbeitung der (nichtdatierten) Vorrede länger zurückliegt, die am Ende des Bandes befindliche *Schutzschrift* aber erst im Sommer 1644 oder gar noch später, während der Drucklegung der ersten Bögen abgeschlossen wurde. (Das unmittelbar vor dem Beginn der *Schutzschrift* eingerückte Lobgedicht von Wenzel Scherffer v. Scherffenstein datiert auf den 19.12.1644, also vier Monate nach dem angekündigten Beginn des Drucks! S. zum Erscheinen der 2. Auflage des 1. Teils 440824 K 4.) Zu diesem Zeitpunkt war die Vorbereitung des 5. Teils der *Gesprächspiele*, der spätestens im April 1645 dem Drucker übergeben wurde, nahezu abgeschlossen, es wird sich somit schon abgezeichnet haben, daß der verbleibende Stoff zu umfangreich war, um ihn auf nur zwei Bände zu verteilen (s. zum Erscheinen des 5. Teils 440824 K 5). Dies würde die widersprüchlichen Angaben zum geplanten Gesamtumfang erklären, kann bisher aber nicht verifiziert werden, weil uns über die Entstehungszeit der *Schutzschrift* keine gesicherten Informationen vorliegen. Fest steht jedenfalls, daß der Plan spätestens mit der Veröffentlichung des 5. Teils revidiert werden mußte, weil der Band zu voluminös geraten war: „Ob nun wol dieser Theil L. Spiele/ wie die vier ersten/ hätte begreiffen sollen/ so ist doch das Werk unter den Händen so sehr gewachsen/ daß es nicht mehr als XXV. derselben/ ohne unformliche Dikke/ leiden mögen. Die vollige Ersetzung dieses dritten hunderts [d.h. die Vollendung bis einschließlich des 300. Gesprächspiels] sol/ mit der Hülffe des Höchsten/ in noch drey unterschiedlichen Theilen erfolgen" (*Harsdörffer: Frauenzimmer-Gesprächspiele* V, 109). Bei den hier angekündigten acht Teilen wird es schließlich bleiben.

1 In *Harsdörffer: Schutzschrift (1644)*, 47f. wird — ohne Namen zu nennen — jenen geantwortet, denen die *Gesprächspiele* „mißfallen [...]/ weil das Frauenzimmer darbey eingeführet/ welche dergleichen Kurtzweil nach ihrem Wahn nicht fähig geachtet werden." Ihnen hält Harsdörffer entgegen, daß jeder Mensch, unabhängig von seinem Geschlecht, eine „natürliche Begierde zur Wissenschaft" habe, und fragt rhetorisch: „Hat dann das Teutsche Frauenzimmer der Tugend- und Sittenlehre nicht von thun *[sic]*/ oder können sie allein nichts aus den Gesprächen erlernen?" Vgl. zur Rolle der Frau in der FG die Einleitung „Zum vorliegenden Bande", S. 12f.

460804

Herzog August d. J. von Braunschweig-Wolfenbüttel an Johann Valentin Andreae

Beantwortet durch 460819. — Hz. August v. Braunschweig-Wolfenbüttel (FG 227) dankt für die illustrierten Texte zu seiner *Evangelischen Kirchen-Harmonie*. Der Ordner hat auf die Texte nicht sonderlich viel Sorgfalt verwandt und überläßt die Zusammenstellung den jeweilig Vortragenden. Der Herzog wird sie rechtzeitig zurückschicken. Er überläßt den Stechern die Umsetzung der mitgeschickten Figuren in Illustrationen der *Kirchenharmonie*. — Johann Valentin Andreae (FG 464. 1646) möge die für Hz. Augusts Bibliothek zu erwerbenden Bücher selbst taxieren, einpacken lassen und nach der Einigung über den Kaufpreis nach Augsburg oder Nürnberg senden, wo sie der Herzog bei Gelegenheit abholen lasse. Hz. August wünscht sich von Andreae auch eine Liste, damit er Dubletten ermitteln und sie seinen Söhnen überlassen könne. — Die Ankunft des *GB 1646* bei Andreae erfreut den Herzog. Die von Andreae an Philipp Hainhofer gesandte Erfindung seiner Imprese (Baummoos, Name „Der Müede", Motto „Hernach") findet der Herzog gut. — Nach der Arbeit an seiner *Evangelischen Kirchen-Harmonie* ist Hz. August jetzt wieder dazu gekommen, Büchertitel in seinen Katalog einzutragen. Dabei stoße er auf den ersten von zwei Bänden mit Kollektaneen, die vermutlich Andreaes Großvater Jakob Andreae aus den Schriften Luthers gezogen habe, so daß ihm jetzt nur noch der zweite Band aus den vier letzten Bänden Luthers fehle. Es wurde ihm angeblich auch ein Band mit Auszügen aus Johann Wolf, Andreas Hondorf und mit einer Beschreibung des niederländisch-spanischen Kriegs gesandt. Sollte Andreae Hz. August die beiden erwarteten Bände nicht geschickt haben, werde dieser sich an Hainhofer wenden, um den Absender zu ermitteln.

Q   HAB: Cod. Guelf. 236.3 Extrav., Bl. 34rv [A: 34v]; eigenh. — 31. Brief Hz. Augusts an Andreae im Jahr 1646, zusammen mit dem 32. Brief (Bl. 35) v. 11.8.1646 gesandt. — Teilw. zit. in *Keller: Akademien der Renaissance*, 106 u. *Begemann: FG und Andreae*, 36.

A   Dem Ehrwurdigen und Hochgelarten unserm lieben besondern, Herren Johan-Valentin-Andreæ, SS Th. D. F. Wurtenbergischen Ober HofPredigern. und geistlichen Consistorial Rahte Zu behandigen. Stutgart — *Andreaes Empfangsdatum, eigenh.:* 4. Octob. 46.

Ehrwürdiger Hochgelarter lieber besonder, und getreuer, an übersendung der zusamengesezten Evangelischen Texten[1] ist uns zu gefallen geschehen: Ich verhoffe ich will sie noch, innerhalb der gesezten zeit, wieder zu rükke senden. Der sie also geordnet hat keinen besondern fleis oder gedanken anwenden wollen[a]: Sondern stellet es deñ Lectoribus frey, wie es ein Jeder zusammen fügen, oder vergleichen könne. Sonsten geben die Figuren ferner[b] deñ Sculptoribus nachdenken:[2] Anreichend die Bibliothek, damit meine Musæ, konten locupletieret werden: Stelle ichs seinem belieben anheimb, wie er dieselbige Taxieren, und einslagen lassen wolle: Könten nach dem getroffenen vergleich; auf Augsp. oder Nürnberg in Kasten eingeslagen, gesandt werden; von dannen ich sie gelegenlich könte abholen lassen:[3] Solte es ihm auch belieben, eine listam darüber aufsezzen zu lassen, so hätte ich mich darinnen zu ersehen; und was[c] in meiner Bibliothec verhanden, meinen Söhnen zu überlassen:[4] Daß sich das Kreuter Buch endlich eingestellet[5] ist mir lieb zu vernehmen: Das er, an unsern Haynhofern gedenket,[6] wegen des mösches an einem alten baum, mit dem nahmen Der Müede, und dem motto Hernach, ist eine artige an Invention: Ich werde dem werke nachdenken, und es an unsere Commilitones gelangen lassen insonderheit an den Nehrenden[d]: So bald ich seine meynung ferner erfahren werde, obs ihm noch[e] gefellig seyn mochte, es auf die Ahrt gehen zu machen, so wil ichs incaminieren.[7] Ich habe diese Tage wieder angefangen, die Bücher in meinen Catalogum[8] zu Skreiben:

daranne mich bishero die Harmoney gehindert; und unter den Mss. in fol. eines gefunden, so auswendig mit N ° IX ge- [34v] zeichnet, und nî fallor sein Avus D. Jac. Andr. p. m. ex Lutheri Scriptis colligieret, und zwar den 1. Tomum: Wan nuhn alter Tomus, ex 4. Lutheri ultimis Tomis auch verhanden, so möchte ich es wol complet haben:⁹ Es ist noch ein Tomus gesandt, darauf N ° VIII. gezeichnet: welcher excerpt hat, aus dem Wolfio: Hondorffio: und eine Beskreibung des Niederländischen Krieges.¹⁰ Solten diese beeden Tomi, von ihm, mir nicht geschikket seyn; so werde ich beym Hainhofer zu fragen [haben]: dan ich dubitiere, wer mirs gesandt. Verbleibe ihm mit guter gewogenheit stets zugetahn als   Sein beständig affectionirter Freundt,   AugustushZBuL   (MH)ᶠ W.¹¹ den 4. Aug. 1646. ♂.

T a *Über einem gestrichenen Wort.* — b *Die beiden nächsten Wörter eingefügt.* — c *Danach bis* verhanden, *eingefügt über* <ich nicht hätte> — d *Am Rande ist* F. L. Z. A. *mit senkrechter Ergänzung der Majuskeln zu* Furst Ludwig Zu Anhalt: — e *Eingefügt.* — f *Lies:* Augustus hertzog zu Braunschweig und Lüneburg (Meine Hand)

K 1 Die *Evangelische Kirchen-Harmonie* Hz. Augusts v. Braunschweig-Wolfenbüttel (FG 227), die ab 1646 in verschiedenen Auflagen erschien und an deren vom Herzog übersandten Stücken Johann Valentin Andreae (FG 464. 1646) jahrelang mitarbeitete. S. 411214, 451001 u.ö. Bei den „zusamengesezten Evangelischen Texten" handelt es sich um eine „Combination der Evangelischen texten sambt denen Figuren" (460819). Andreae hatte dem Herzog Kupferplatten (HAB: Cod. Guelf. 65.1 Extrav., Bl. 300r), die oder deren Visierungen aus Italien stammten, für die Illustrierung der geplanten Duodezausgabe der *Evangelischen Kirchen-Harmonie* (1646) versprochen. Vgl. 411214 (S. 357). Am 3.6.1646 hatte Andreae dem Herzog den Grund genannt, warum er die Figuren nicht erwerben konnte: „Die Jtalienische 160 figuren Harmoniæ vitæ Chri. hette fur E. F. g. ich selbsten gern erhandelt, sein aber nicht zu zuerhalten, weilen sie nicht allein hoch geachtet werden, sondern auch der Greif zu vorhabenden seinem Harmonischen Reimenwerkh, selbiges zu zieren, vnd dem Patrono desto angenähmer zu machen gebrauchen will, von deme sie ob spem Lucrj nicht zu kauffen sein. Wan nur der titul, oder des Trukhens Nahm vnd Jahrzal vorhanden wehre, wolte ich mich bemuhen daß Buch durch h. Geizigkoflern (.qui nondum rediit, nec fortasse ad nos rediturus est.) zu vberkommen, der noch von Vlm auß mit mir corresp." (HAB: Cod. Guelf. 65.1 Extrav., Bl. 298r). Zu dem württemberg. Statthalter Ferdinand Geizkofler († 1653), der auch Beziehungen nach Italien unterhielt und durch Andreae Hz. August italien. Drucke zukommen ließ. S. 431123 K 1; vgl. 421225 K 9. Die Figuren, d.h. die Kupferplatten, gehörten also dem Tübinger Dichter und Apotheker Friedrich Greiff (s. 431123 K 3), der damit sein Hauptwerk illustrieren wollte: Der vier Evangelisten | ubereinstimmende | Geschicht Beschreibung CHristi | Von seiner Heylsamen Geburt/ biß zu seiner | Siegreichen Himmelfahrt. | Jn vier Theil oder Bücher/ nach den | Osterfesten/ unnd deren jedes gewisse Ge | schichten abgetheilt/ deren jeder Jnhalt kurtz in zwey baar | Versen verfaßt/ die Son- vnnd Feyrtägliche Evangelien | aber in Gesang/ oder Lieder gebracht/ vnd | mit einem kurtzen Gebettlin | beschlossen. | Alles in Reimen verfasset | durch Friderich Greiffen. | Sampt zweyen Vorreden | Eine von ... D. Melchior Nicolai Fürstl. Würt. | Rhat/ der heyligen Schrifft Doctorn vnd Profes- | sorn, wie auch ProCancellario bey hiesigen | Vniversität Tübingen. | Die ander von ... D. Valentin Andreæ | F. W. Rath/ vnd Hoffprediger zu Stutgarten. | Getruckt zu Tübingen/ | Bey

Philibert Brunnen. | [Linie] | Jm Jahr 1647. HAB: 501.7 Theol. Zur Vorrede Andreaes für dieses Werk s. 460819 I. Die Spannungen zwischen Greiff und Hz. August bzw. Andreae scheinen sich auch auf die abschätzige Beurteilung der Dichtung Greiffs ausgewirkt zu haben (s. 460317 K I 1). Am 15.4.1646 schrieb Andreae an den Herzog: „Fr. Greif ist mit seinem iniquo postulato billich abzuweisen, die kupfer werden ohne das Noth genug Leiden, wegen des 4. trucks. Jch wolte aber nur vmb 1 exemplar. aller kupfer sauber ohne schrift auf blettlin getrukht. Vndst. gebetten haben." HAB: Cod. Guelf. 65.1 Extrav., Bl. 278r. Am 1.7.1646 teilte Andreae dem Fürsten mit: „Daß duodec. büchlein gefället auch männiglich wol vnd wehre zu wünschen daß man die figuren haben könte, auf die Lehre blätlin aufzupappen. Ich habe vertröstung der Italienische figuren cum Harmonia vitæ Christi Lehnungs weis zuerhalten, die sollen E. F. g. furderlichst in Vnd. zugesandt werden." (Bl. 294r). Diese kleine Ausgabe wurde jedoch im Unterschied zur Oktav- und Quartausgabe nicht illustriert. Der Herzog hielt Andreaes Interesse an fremden Kupfern jedoch wach. Dabei ging es nun um die Quartausgabe der *Evangelischen Kirchen-Harmonie* (1646). August schrieb am 23.6.1646 an seinen Rat: „vernehme ungern daß die Harmonia vitæ Xhristi so wol auch die Französische und andere Bücher, derer Liste ich lezthin übersandt habe, nicht zu erlangen seyn. Er wolle mir zu gefallen, eines lassen abreissen, so will ichs mit meinem Exemplar conferieren, so in 4t gedrukket, und ni fallor, ein Jesuita, Nutius genandt, hervorgegeben hat:" HAB: Cod. Guelf. 236.3 Extrav., Bl. 28r. Andreae schrieb am 29.7.1646 an Hz. August: „Jch erwarte mit verlangen, ob die wälsche Figuren E. F. g. annämlich, vnd zu volfürung Harmoniae vitæ Christi furständig sein möchten." (HAB: Cod. Guelf. 65.1 Extrav., Bl. 298r). Am 8.7.1646 meldete Andreae dem Herzog: „Der figuren der Italienischen Harmoni sollen verhoffentlich erfolgen, weßen ich deßen vertröstet bin. Solte es aber fehlen, sollen wenigst'etliche figuren, selbsten, oder deren Copien E. F. g. Vnd. Communiciret werden, selbige haben mit des Nutij zu Conferiren. Sie sein von vngleicher hand, invention, vnd stich, Etliche sehr gut, etliche schlecht, würden gleichwolen zu complieren vitae Christi wol dienlich sein, inventis enim facile additur, vnd sein E. f. g. mit guten Maistern versehen, darunter der Alb. Freyse wol paßiret." (Bl. 295r). — Martinus Nutius war ein Drucker in Antwerpen, der Werke von Jesuiten herausbrachte. Hier gemeint sein dürfte: [Kupfertitel] EVANGELICAE HISTORIAE IMAGINES Ex ordine Euangeliorum, quæ toto anno in Missæ sacrificio recitantur, In ordinem temporis vitæ Christi digestæ. Auctore Hieronymo Natali Societatis IESV Theologo Antuerpiæ Anno Di M.D.XCI. SVPERIORVM PERMISSV.; [Drucktitel] MEDITATIONI SOPRA LI EVANGELII CHE TVTTO L'ANNO SI LEGGONO NELLA MESSA, & principali misterij della vita, & passione di Nostro Signore. COMPOSTE DAL R. P. AGOSTINO VIVALDI della Compagnia di GIESV. RESPONDENTI ALLE IMAGINI DEL PADRE Girolamo Natale della medesima Compagnia. IN ROMA, Appresso Luigi Zannetti. M. D. XCIX. CON LICENZA DE SVPERIORI. HAB: Th. 4° 36. Neuauflage Gerónimo Nadal: Adnotationes et Meditationes in Evangelia Qvae in Sacrosancto Missae Sacrificio Toto Anno Legvntur ... Auctore Hieronymo Natali Societatis Iesu theologo ... Secunda editio (Antuerpiae: Martinus Nutius 1595). HAB: Th 4° 35. Editio ultima Antverpiae: Moretus 1607: 143. HAB: Theol. 2°; Td 2° 4. Natalis figurenreiche Bilder nehmen jeweils eine Seite in Anspruch, einschließlich der Überschrift (Fest- bzw. Sonntagsname) und einer Legende darunter, die die Personen oder Gegenstände durch Majuskeln erklärt. Auf der Verso-Seite der Kommentar Vivaldis. Die Illustrationen der *Evangelischen Kirchen-Harmonie* nehmen selbst in der zweispaltig gesetzten Quartausgabe nur einen Teil der jeweiligen Seite ein und kommen ohne Titel und Legende aus. Stichproben ergaben keine übernommenen oder nachgeahmten Illustrationen. Nicht gemeint sein dürfte das Emblembuch: Antoni Svcqvet E Societate Iesu Via vitae aeternae iconibvs illvstrata per Boetium a Boiswert (Antuerpiae 1620: Martinus Nutius), HAB: Wt 315. Die Figuren sollten durch Hz. August zu einem bestimmten, jedoch wegen der unsicheren Straßen immer wieder verschobenen Termin zurückgegeben werden. Greiff wollte zunächst die in Hz. Augusts *Evangelischer Kirchen-Harmonie* benutzten Kupfer auch in seiner *Geschicht Beschreibung CHristi* verwenden. Andreae schickte dem Herzog ein Muster von Greiffs Dichtung mit dem Wunsch des Verfassers am 25.2.1646: „Hiebei ein Muster, des vorhabens Jo. Friederich Greifen, der vermeinet die Harmoniam Vitæ Christi in Alexandrinische Vers zu bringen, vnd hierinnen nach E. F. G. sich zu regulieren. Ob etwa dise figuren möchte dabej getrukken sein, wie bej des Merians Biblischen Historien absonderlich geschehen, wiewol ich besorge es werden sich die kupfer in den beeden 8 vnd 4 editionen Harmoniæ Euangeliæ also abtrukken, daß Jhnen nit vil mehr daruber zuzumuthen." (Bl. 270r) Der Herzog akzeptierte diesen Einwand in seiner Antwort vom 17.3.1646: „Des Fr. Greyff Teutsche Vers werden wol kommen, Aber die kupfer werden es swerlich aushalten, wie Er selber ohne daß erwehnet hat. Es seynd etliche nicht tief genug gesnitten, etc." (HAB: Cod. Guelf. 236.3 Extrav., Bl. 12v). Greiff wußte sich stattdessen die erwähnten italienischen Kupfer zu beschaffen und weigerte sich, sie dem Herzog zu verkaufen, lieh sie ihm jedoch auf Bitten Andreaes endlich doch. Am 13.9.1646 schrieb Hz. August über die Verwendung an Andreae: „Die Italiänische kupfer habe ich meinem M. Alberto [Freyse] non Dürero hingegeben; daß Er das Jehnige daraus klaube, was ins kunftige dienlich seyn möchte. Sie sollen sich, gönnets Gott, sicher bald wieder einstellen." (A. a. O., Bl. 38r). Sie stellten sich vielleicht nie wieder ein, und Greiffs Evangelienharmonie in Versen wurde nie aus der italien. Quelle illustriert. Das Werk enthält nur Kupfertitel vor den einzelnen Teilen und ein Porträt des Widmungsempfängers Conrad Widerholdt, Obrist u. Kommandant der Festung Hohentwiel: „Con. Meyer inv. et fecit." In dem Hz. August geschickten, reichlich mit Gold verzierten Band (HAB: 501.7 Theol.), dem eine gereimte, zierlich geschriebene und eigenhändig gezeichnete Widmung an den Herzog vorgebunden ist, finden sich außer dem Porträt und einem Titelkupfer, beide von der Hand Conrad Meyers, allerdings 5 Tafeln (ohne Erfinder- oder Stecheradresse) mit Andachtsbildern aus dem Leben Jesu (z.B. Taufe Jesu), eingefügt unter einer Überschrift (z.B. „Einfaltige vnd Andächtige Betrachtung Der Hoch-Heiligen Drey-Einigkeit.") und über 4 Versen. Sie ähneln 5 der 8 kleinen Szenen, die den Kupfertitel umrahmen, sind aber nicht mit Gewißheit dem Zürcher Künstler Conrad Meyer (1618–1689) zuzuschreiben. (*Thieme/ Becker* XXIV, 467 verzeichnet auch einen gleichnamigen Zeitgenossen aus Ulm, leider ohne nähere dienliche Angaben.) Der Titel dieses Andachtwerks Greiffs in Versen lautet: Sieben Geistliche Andachten vber die Hohe-Fest als Auff die Seeligmachende Geburth vnsers Heylands Jesus Christus/ Die Einsatzung deß Heyligen Hochwürdigen Abendmahls/ Das Bitter Leyden vnd Sterben/ Die Siegreiche Aufferstehung/ Die Triumphierēde Himmelfahrt Christus/ Die Sendung deß Heyligen Geistes/ Vnd auff die Hochheylige Dreyeinigkeit. Jn lange Alexandrinische Verß gesetzt Neben etlichen Geistlichen Liedern auff eben solche Fest/ vnd jedes insonderheit gerichtet; Auffgesetzt vnnd verfertiget Durch Friderich Greiffen/ Tübingen/ Bey Philibert Brunnen. Jm Jahr 1647. HAB: 501.7 Theol. (2).

2 Biblische Figuren, die die Kupferstecher (Conrad Bunos) noch für die Illustrationen der zweiten, in Quart gedruckten Auflage der *Evangelischen Kirchen-Harmonie* von 1646 umsetzen mußten. S. 411214.

3 Hz. August kaufte die ihm von Philipp Hainhofer in Augsburg, Georg Forstenheuser in Nürnberg und durch andere avisierten Bibliotheken zur Ergänzung seiner eigenen Büchersammlung. In seinem Schreiben 460715 bot Augusts Rat Andreae dem Herzog einen großen Teil seiner eigenen Bibliothek an. Vgl. 460908 u. ö.

4 Die Prinzen Rudolf August (FG 754. Der Nachsinnende. 1660), Anton Ulrich (FG 716. Der Siegprangende. 1659) und Ferdinand Albrecht (FG 842. Der Wunderliche. 1673). Tatsächlich dachte der Herzog hier an seine beiden jüngeren Söhne.

5 *GB 1646*. Andreae hatte am 15.7.1646 an den Herzog geschrieben, er habe das Werk empfangen und darin gleich die Imprese des Herzogs gefunden. S. 460715.

6 Andreae schrieb von seinem Wunsch, in die FG aufgenommen zu werden, zunächst an Hz. Augusts Augsburger Agenten Philipp Hainhofer (460715 I). Dem Herzog teilte er sein Verlangen erst in 460819 mit, nach Erhalt des vorliegenden, zustimmenden Briefs. Als er das Zitat aus Andreaes Brief durch Hainhofer (s. 460715 II) erhalten hatte, schrieb der Herzog es ab und beauftragte Carl Gustav v. Hille (FG 302) damit, die Abschrift an F. Ludwig (Der Nährende) zu schicken. So erfuhr der Nährende von Andreaes Verlangen und von Augusts Empfehlung des Kandidaten. Vgl. zur Aufnahme Andreaes 461117 K 1.

7 F. Ludwig billigte die Aufnahme Andreaes in 461106 u. I, nachdem er Mitglieder der FG (Commilitones) konsultiert hatte. Der Herzog informierte Andreae darüber im Brief 461117, den Andreae am 13.12.1646 empfing. Die Imprese Andreaes war durch F. Ludwig geändert worden. Vgl. außerdem 461206, *DA Köthen I. 8*: 470112 u. 470122.

8 Der in der HAB bewahrte, auf den Brettern eines Bücherrads liegende, eigenhändig geschriebene Katalog Hz. Augusts.

9 Möglicherweise bezog Hz. August die vermuteten Luther-Auszüge von Andreaes Großvater Jacob Andreae (1528–1590), den Tübinger Kanzler und Professor, Verfechter der Konkordienformel, auf die folgende Ausgabe: Der Fünffte [- Achte] Teil aller Bücher vnd Schrifften ... Doct. Mart. Lutheri vom XXX. [XXXXII.] jar an ... Zum dritten mal gedruckt/ aller ding dem Ersten vnd Andern druck gleich/ etc (Jhena: Richtzenhayn; Rebart 1566–1568); HAB: Li 4° 263.1:5–8. Daß solche Luther-Auszüge Jacob Andreaes heute in der HAB nicht aufzufinden sind, erklärt sich aus der Verwechslung des Großvaters mit seinem gleichnamigen ersten Sohn. S. 460819. *Brecht: Andreae u. Hz. August*, überlegt S. 249 f., ob Jacob Andreae (1549–1630), ein württemberg. Pfarrer (in Hagelloch, Dusslingen, Metzingen, Musberg und Kirchentellinsfurt) und Handschriftensammler, teilweise an der achtbändigen handschriftlichen „Historia Wirtembergica" gearbeitet hatte, deren Reste J. V. Andreae nach ihrer teilweisen Zerstörung dem Herzog überließ (s. 421206 K 10 u. 430215/25 K 12). Seinem Schreiben 430215/25 hängte Andreae eine „Vngefährliche Summarische Verzaichnus meiner gewesener Wurtemb. hystory" (HAB: Cod. Guelf. 65.1 Extrav., Bl. 35rv) an, die jedoch keinen Hinweis auf Luther oder Jacob Andreae enthält. HAB: Cod. Guelf 44.10 Aug. 2° enthält eine Liste von der H. des Großvaters Jacob Andreae (Vorderdeckel), darauf von anderer H. „Beschreibung der Jahr, von Erschaffung der Welt biß auff das Jahr Christi 1568 auß der H. Schrifft genommen, sampt etlichen außlegungen" (11 Bl.). Sonst finden sich nur Texte zur württemberg. Geschichte. Die von Brecht ermittelten Handschriftensignaturen schließen nicht ein: HAB: Cod. Guelf. 48.14 Aug. 4° aus dem Besitz eines angeblich Memminger Pfarrers Jacob Andreae, ein Band mit Drucken und Kollektaneen, welcher jedoch auch nur „Würtembergica varia ad historiam saeculorum XVI et XIII spectantia" enthält.

10 HAB: Cod. Guelf. 44.12 Aug. 2° enthält u. a.

1. Bl. 1–139 Beschreibung allerlay Zeichen, wunderbahrlichen vnd erschrockenlichen Geschichten, die sich in allen Landen zugetragen von A. 1501 biss auff A. 1621 aus dem Johanne Wolffio [Lectiones memorabiles et reconditae. Lauingae 1600] in die Teudtsche Sprach gebracht. Johan Wolf (1521–1571).

2. Bl. 139–275 Allerlay erschrockenliche wunderbahrliche Historien aus dem Promptuario exemplorum Andreae Hondorffers [erschien zuerst Frankfurt 1574. 2°].

3. Bl. 288–311 Geschichte des spanisch-niederländischen Krieges nach Sleidanus. Register

der fürnempsten Geschichten des Niderländischen Kriegs vnd andern mehr denckwürdigen Historien.
So auch verzeichnet in Otto v. Heinemann: Die Augusteischen Handschriften 3. Frankfurt/M. 1898, 261.
Andreas Hondorff, Pfarrer zu Drossig, †1572, Verfasser u. a. von: PROMPTVARIVM EXEMPLORVM, Historienn vnd Exempelbuch. Aus heiliger Schrifft vnd vielen andern ... Geistlichen vnd Weltlichen Historien ... Vnd zum dritten mahl vbersehen/ vnd ... gemehret (Leipzig 1572).
11 Wolfenbüttel.

460808

Herzog Franz Carl von Sachsen-Lauenburg an Herzog August d. J. von Braunschweig-Wolfenbüttel

Hz. Franz Carl v. Sachsen-Lauenburg (FG 269) bedankt sich für die Willkommensgrüße bei seiner Rückkehr und freut sich über das Wohlergehen Hz. Augusts d.J. v. Braunschweig-Wolfenbüttel (FG 227). — Was das von Hz. August angesprochene Pflanzenbuch angeht, verschweigt Hz. Franz Carl nicht, er habe sich des Buchs zunächst nicht erinnern können, zumal seine Kammerdiener, denen er es anvertraut hatte, nicht anwesend waren. Deshalb wurde der Bote des vorliegenden Briefes ein wenig aufgehalten. Jetzt aber, nachdem die Diener zurückgekommen seien, erfuhr er, daß es im Schloß Neuhaus in jenen Kästen bei den Sachen liegengeblieben sei, die er an den Kurfürsten (Kf. Friedrich Wilhelm v. Brandenburg. FG 401) habe senden wollen. Durch seine überstürzte Reise nach Italien wie auch durch den unvorhersehbaren Aufbruch des Kurfürsten in Preußen wurde er daran gehindert, die Sendung aufzugeben. Nun jedoch sei es Hz. August möglich, das Buch, auch in Franz Carls Abwesenheit, jederzeit in dem Schloß abfordern zu lassen. — Zwar hätte er das Buch auch dem Briefboten mitgeben können, da jedoch Hz. August diese Möglichkeit brieflich nicht erwähnt habe und das in Rede stehende Buch auch groß und schwer sei, so schien ihm dies nicht ratsam gewesen zu sein.

Q HAB: BA (Bibliotheks-Archiv) II, 3 Nr.265; 1 Bl.; Schreiberh. mit eigenh. Unterschrift.

A *Fehlt.*

Vnsere freundtVetterliche dienst, auch waß wir sonsten vielmehr liebes vndt guttes vermögen zuvor.
Hochgeborner Fürst, freundtlicher Vielgeliebter Herr Oheimb,
daß E. Ld. wegen vnserer glücklichen wiederkunfft, vnß **beneventiren** wollen, erkennen wir mitt schuldigem danck, erfrewen Vnß darneben zum höchsten, daß dieselbe gleichermaßen, annoch bey fürstl. **prosperität** sich befinden.
Anlangendt daß Kräuterbuch[1], wovon E. Ld. nachricht zu haben begehren, bleibet deroselben vnverhalten, daß Wir anfangs zwar Vnß deßen soeben nicht entsinnen können, weiln Vnsere Cammerdiener, denen wir eß anvertrawet, verschicket gewesen, dahero wiederbringer dieses, in etwaß auffgehalten worden;

Nunmehr aber, bey deren wiederkunfft erfahren wir, daß eß zum Newenhause², bey denen sachen, so wir hiebevor in etzlichen Kasten Jhr Churfl. Durchl.³ vbersenden wollen, aber durch vnsere schleunige reise nach Jtalien daran verhindert worden, maßen denn auch hochermelt Jhr Churfl. Durchl. vnverhoffter damahliger auffbruch in Preußen, eß removiret. Jetz aber können [Bl. 1v] E. Ld. obgedachtes Kreuterbuch, dero belieben nach, zum Newenhause stündlich abfordern laßen, gestalt denn Vnsere bedienten befehlicht, auff E. Ld. begehren, auch in Vnserer abwesenheit, eß außzuantworten,

Hetten eß zwar zeigern mittgeben laßen, weiln E. Ld. aber in Jhrem schreiben davon nichts melden, sothanes buch auch groß vndt schwer zu tragen, vber dieses auch vnterwegens leicht schaden nehmen, oder gantz von abhanden kommen könte, Alß haben wir eß nicht rahtsam befunden, Jnmittelst aber, dieses E. Ld. antwortlich melden wollen, dieselbe beschließlich Göttlicher gnädigem Tutell⁴, zu allem fürstlichen selbstbegehrenden hochergehen gantz trewlich empfehlende. Dat. Frantzhagen⁵ den 8. Augusti Anno 1646

Von Gottes gnaden Frantz Carll Hertzog zu Sachsen Engern vndt Westphalen
    EL
    stetß dienstwilliger
    Frantz Carl herzog zu Sachsen

K 1 Zu Hz. Franz Carl v. Sachsen-Lauenburg (FG 269), 1637 zum Katholizismus konvertiert und ksl. Generalwachtmeister, s. *Conermann III*, 298–300. — Unklar ist, um welches Kräuterbuch es sich handelt. Hz. August d.J. v. Braunschweig-Wolfenbüttel (FG 227) war für seine Bücherleidenschaft bekannt und nutzte seine Kontakte zu den dt. Fürstenhöfen zum Sammeln bibliophiler Kostbarkeiten. Daher könnte es sich bei dem bei Hz. Franz Carl v. Sachsen-Lauenburg (FG 269) erfragten Buch um eines der meist reich illustrierten botanischen Werke handeln, die sich noch heute auch im Bestand der HAB befinden, wie etwa Levin Fischers *D. Methodus Nova Herbaria, cum Iconibus aeneis. Neuw KräuterBuch/ Auß- und Einländischer Gewechs ... In sieben Theilen* (Brunopoli 1646; HAB: Me 130 [2]); Giovanni Battista Ferraris *Flora, seu De Florum Cvltvra Lib. IV* (Amstelodami: Janssonius 1646; HAB: 14.1 Phys.); Johann Popps *Kräuter Buch: Darinnen die Kräuter des Teutschen Landes* (Leipzig: Schürer, Götze 1625; HAB: 134.5 Phys.); Martin Pegies *Groß Kräutterbuch/ Deß Edelen und hochgelehrten Herren Bartholomaei Carrichters/ Weylandt der Röm: Kay: May: ... Leib Medici/ und HoffDoctoris: Darinn die Kräuter deß Teutschlands/ auß dem Liecht der Natur/ nach rechter art der Him[m]elischen einfliessung beschrieben* (Straßburg: Bertram 1619; HAB: 14.7 Phys. 2°); das *Florilegium, Das ist: Ein BlumenBuch: darinnen allerhand Blümlein gantz Artig mit Lebhafften Farben/ sampt iher Wirckung und Eygenschafften vorgemahlet und beschrieben sindt* (Franckfurt am Mayn: Weixner 1616; HAB: 34.2 Phys. 2°); Johannes Olorinus' *Centuria Herbarum Mirabilium Das ist: Hundert Wunderkräuter/ so da theils in der Newen Welt/ theils in Teutschland Wachsen* (Magdeburgk: Braunß 1616; HAB: 523.1 Quod. [9]) u. dgl. mehr. — Undenkbar ist, daß damit das *GB 1646* oder das schon frühere illustrierte *GB 1629/30* gemeint ist, welche die Impresen und Reimgesetze der FG-Mitglieder bis Nr. 400 bzw. Nr. 200 beinhalten. S. dazu 440130 (K 3). Dagegen spricht nämlich, daß Hz. Franz

460810 Matthias Götze

Carl das Buch als „groß vndt schwer zu tragen" bezeichnete, die fruchtbringerischen Gesellschaftsbücher jedoch als nicht sonderlich umfangreiche Quartbände dieser Beschreibung kaum entsprechen. Zu welchem Zweck der Kurfürst das schwere Buch Hz. Franz Carls benutzen wollte, entzieht sich unserer Kenntnis. Er könnte es durchaus auch für Auskünfte über seltene fruchtbringerische ‚Kräuter' wie seinen eigenen Mirabolanenbaum (s. *Conermann III*, 475 f.) benutzt haben, der auch in den Visierungen zu der Fortsetzung des *GB 1646* (s. Abb. zu 460125) in *Hille: Teutscher Palmbaum* (1647) (vor dem Wolfenbütteler Schloß) abgebildet wurde. — Illustrierte Kräuterbücher, die in jener Zeit im Umlauf waren, dienten jedenfalls auch als Grundlage für andere Pflanzendarstellungen in den Impresen der FG-Mitglieder. S. dazu u. a. 450408.

2 Schloß Neuhaus (1698 abgerissen) am rechtsseitigen Elbufer im sachsen-lauenburg. Amt Darzing (Dersingen) war eine der Hauptresidenzen der Herzöge v. Sachsen-Lauenburg. In das Schloß, welches nach dem Tod Hz. Franz' II. (1547–1619) von dessen Witwe Maria, geb. Hzn. v. Braunschweig-Wolfenbüttel (1566–1626), bewohnt worden war, zog nach deren Tod ihr Stiefsohn, Hz. August v. Sachsen-Lauenburg (FG 294), ein. In dem sich daraufhin um das zugehörige Amt entbrennenden Streit mit seinen Halbbrüdern — Julius Heinrich (FG 311), Franz Carl, Rudolf Maximilian (FG 283) und Franz Heinrich (FG 234) — wurde 1635 ein Vergleich geschlossen, der Franz Carl Schloß und Amt Neuhaus als Apanage zusprach. Jedoch konnte dieser erst 1646 das mittlerweile durch Kriegseinwirkungen stark zerstörte Schloß tatsächlich in Besitz nehmen. Er bewohnte es bis zu seinem Tod am 30.11.1660. Da Hz. Franz Carl ohne Nachkommen starb, fiel das Schloß an seinen Neffen Hz. Franz Erdmann v. Sachsen-Lauenburg (FG 459. 1646). S. dazu *Lexikon Geographie*, 907; W. Sparkuhle: Der Darzing mit dem Neuen Hause im Besitz der Herzöge von Sachsen-Lauenburg. In: Archiv des Vereins für die Geschichte des Herzogthums Lauenburg (1908), 99–124.

3 Kf. Friedrich Wilhelm v. Brandenburg (FG 401).

4 Schutz, Schirm, Obhut. Vom lat. (it., span.) tutela. *Diefenbach: Glossarium*, 603.

5 Franzhagen, ein 1608 unter Hz. Franz II. v. Sachsen-Lauenburg (1547–1619), dem Vater Franz Carls, erbautes Schloß mit großen Gartenanlagen westlich von Geesthacht. Nach dem Tod von Hz. Franz II. kam es an die Herzöge v. Schleswig-Holstein-Sonderburg. Vgl. *Lexikon Geographie*, 508.

460810

Matthias Götze an Peter Knaudt

Der Leipziger Verleger Matthias Götze bestätigt den Empfang eines (nicht erhaltenen) Briefes, dem die Ansicht des Köthener Schlosses und Gartens beilag. Götze habe sie wohl verwahrt und (an Matthäus Merian d. Ä.) weitergeleitet.

Q HM Köthen: V S 546, Bl. 44rv [A: 44v]; eigenh. — D: *Bircher: Merian*, 723 f. — BN: *Bürger*, 469 Nr. 3.

A Dem WohlEhrenwerten Hochachtbarn vndt Wohlgelahrten Herrn Peter Knaudten, Fürstl. Anhaltinischen Cammermeistern etc. Meinen Jnsonders großgünstigen Herrn vndt Hochgeehrten wehrten Freunde Jn Cöthen

tt
WohlEhrenvester Hochachtbar, vndt wohlgelahrter, Jnsonders großgünstiger Hochgeehrter Herr, Sehr wehrter undt vornehmer Freundt,

Nechst erbietung meiner bereitwilligsten Dienste, ist mir E. W. E. H. A.[1] schreiben benebenst den abris Jhres Fürstlichen Schloß vndt garten, zurecht vberantwordtet,[2] vndt habe auch solchen wohl verwahret alsobalden mit hinauß geschicket, verhoffe es werde auch wohl zurecht sein mit hinauß kommen, welches ich dem Herrn hinwiederumb in Antwordt zuuermelden nicht vnterlaßen sollen noch wollen, vnterdeßen thue ich E. W. E. H. A. in Gottes gnädigen schutz zum Trewlichsten befehlen. **Raptim** Leipzigk den 10 Aug. A. 1646

E. W. E. H. A.
iederzeit Dienstw.
Matthias Götze mppa

K 1 Wohl aufzulösen mit Euer WohlEhrenwerter HochAchtbarer. S. auch Adresse A.
2 Die Zeichnung und Veröffentlichung einer Ansicht des Köthener Schlosses und Gartens in Matthäus Merians d. Ä. *Topographia* wird in den Briefen 460620B, 460703 u. 460714 behandelt. In *DA Köthen I. 8*: 470223 bestätigt Merian den Empfang der Vorlage. Die Antwort ist nicht an den Vermittler und Leipziger Verleger Matthias Götze, sondern direkt an Peter Knaudt gerichtet: „P. S. Des Fürst. Residentz Schloß und Gartens Cöthen, Abriß habe ich wol empfangen, Bedancke mich gantz unterthänig, und werde solches in die **Topographia** Saxoniæ ein bringen". S. auch die Abbildung des Köthener Gartens und Schlosses in *DA Köthen I. 2*, 260 f. Zum Großunternehmen *Merian: Topographia* 450905 K 4.

460812

Augustus Buchner an Fürst Ludwig

Augustus Buchner (FG 362. Der Genossene) teilt F. Ludwig (Der Nährende) Philipp v. Zesens (FG 521. 1648) Wunsch mit, dem Fürsten aufzuwarten. Er setze sich hiermit für Zesen ein, obgleich er selbst in dieser Hinsicht eine Fürbitte brauche. Er verlasse sich jedoch auf die heldenmütige Leutseligkeit des Fürsten. F. Ludwig wisse, was Zesen in Sachen des Deutschen verrichtet habe und könne selbst am besten beurteilen, was von ihm künftig zu erwarten sei. Die Sonne des Fürsten könne Zesens unreife Früchte am stärksten reifen lassen. — *Nachschrift*: Zesen habe mit ihm, Buchner, geredet und sich dafür ausgesprochen, im Deutschen das C durch das K zu ersetzen, weil es kein genuin deutscher oder doch zumindest ein überflüssiger Buchstabe sei. Bescheiden habe er sich von Buchner belehren lassen, daß das C schon in den ältesten deutschen Manuskripten vorkomme und es die sonst rauhe Aussprache verfeinere. Zwar wird jeden Tag vielfach gegen die richtige Schreibweise des Deutschen verstoßen und Berichtigung sei hier nötig, dennoch sollte man die eingeführte und längst gültige Schreibgewohnheit nicht durch allzu subtile Nachforschungen umstoßen. Auch die gelehrten Lateiner und Griechen hätten sich dem herge-

460812 Augustus Buchner   941

brachten Gebrauch unterworfen, solange dieser nicht offenkundig ungereimt war. Auch Zesen werde dies künftig hoffentlich beachten und seinen kecken Jugendmut, der ihn nach Ruhm habe streben lassen, durch gütliche Belehrung kühlen. Niemand sei besser dazu imstande als F. Ludwig.

Q *Bellin: Sendeschreiben (1647),* Nr. 18, Bl. Jijrv, Nachschrift Bl. Jij v – Jiij v. — Aus der Nachschrift zitiert Gottfried Wilhelm Sacer: Nützliche Erinnerungen Wegen der deutschen Poeterey […] (Alten Stettin 1661), 62. Abgedr. in Marian Szyrocki (Hg.): Poetik des Barock. Stuttgart 1977 (Reclam UB 9854), 163. Nicht im Köthener Erzschrein, nicht in *KE.* — *BN: Estermann,* 222 Nr. 247.
Bei diesem Brief muß mit Eingriffen des Herausgebers Johann Bellin oder sogar von Philipp v. Zesen (FG 521. 1648) selbst gerechnet werden.

A *Fehlt.*

An den Nährenden

Durchleuchtiger Hochgeborner Fürst/ Gnädiger Herr/

WJE bey E. F. Gn. durch dieses ich meine unterthänige schuldigkeit abzulegen gesucht/ als wüntschet H. Zesius solches durch persönliche unterthänige aufwartung zuverrichten: Wird es auch billich für eine hohe [Jij v] Glückseeligkeit achten/ im fall ihm die jenige hand zu küssen erlaubet/ die er nun eine geraume zeit unterthänig geehret hat.[1] Jch darf mich kaum unterwinden/ seinet wegen bey E. F. Gn. in unterthänigkeit einzukommen/ weil ich der Vorbitt selbst benötiget/ und ist zu dem E. F. Gn. von solcher heroischen Leutseeligkeit/ daß sie für sich einem ieden den zutrit selbst leicht eröfnet/ der ihn durch tugend suchen wollen: Was bis anhero H. Zesius in unserer sprache gethan/ ist E. F. Gn. nicht unbekant/ was künftig von ihme zu hoffen/ kan niemand besser als eben Dieselbe urtheilē. Daß diese früchte nun zu ihrem volkomēnen reiftume gelangen möchten wird E. F. Gn. Gütiger Sonnenschein zum kräftigsten würken/ und daß Sie denselben mir wie bishero in gnaden auch ferner gönnen wollen/ bitte ich unterthänig/ der ich stets bin und verbleibe

   Gnädiger Herr E. F. Gn. Unterthäniger gehorsamer Diener
   Der Genoßene.
   A. B.

Wittenberg den 12. Augusti 1646.

Nach-Schrift.

ES hat auch/ Gnädiger Fürst und Herr gedachter H. Zesius seiner bishero geführten Schreib-ahrt halben mit mir geredet/ sonderlich aber des C halben/ darfür jhm sonsten [Jiij r] das K zusetzen beliebet/ in meinung daß es kein deutscher oder doch überflüßiger buchstabe were.[2] Als ich ihm aber beybracht/ daß es auch in den ältesten schrifften zu finden/ und dannenhero nicht also frembde/ als man gemeinet/ dan auch die aussprache desto genehmer zu machen/ und sie von der alten und rauen art abzuleiten sehr dienlich/ und solcher ursachen halben von unsern Vorfahren in mehrern schwang gebracht; hat er so wol in diesen als anderen sich dermaßen erkläret/ daß seine bescheidenheit ich billich rühmen muß. Ohne ists nicht/ daß in dem schreiben täglich viel fehler begangen werden/ die einer richtigkeit von nöhten haben/ daß man aber hierin alles so gar genau untersuchen und den bißhero eingeführten und numehr längst verjährten brauch fast gäntzlich aufheben wollte/ läßet sich nicht thun. Die Lateiner so wol als die Griechen seind in diesem Punct ebener maßen nicht allezeit auff den eußersten grund gangen/ haben sich dem hergebrachten brauch und gewohnheit/ wan sie nicht kundbar ungereumet/ unterworffen/ und dafür gehalten/ daß man zwar die gelehrten hören/ doch der gemeinen Art nach schreiben solte.[3] Und wird verhoffentlich H. Zesius künftig dieses auch in acht nehmen/ nicht aber die Jugend alleine hören/ die ihn bishero auf ein anders geleitet. Dan selbige so kützlich als mutig ist/ und sucht derohalben ger-[Jiij v]ne was neues/ ihr[a] einen nahmen zu machen/[4] darinnen sie allzeit zwar nicht zu straffen/ doch mit bescheidenheit und glimpf unterrichts von nöhten hat: den besten ausschlag wird E. F. Gn. geben.

T a *Lies:* sich

K Augustus Buchner (FG 362), Professor der Poesie und Rhetorik an der U. Wittenberg, setzte sich in diesem Empfehlungsschreiben für seinen ehemaligen Studenten Philipp v. Zesen (FG 521. 1648) ein. Dabei zeigt schon die ausweichende Formulierung — F. Ludwig (Der Nährende) wisse selbst, was „Zesius in unserer sprache gethan" habe und er, der Fürst, besitze genug „heroische Leutseeligkeit", um Zesen (dennoch) zu empfangen —, daß er sich der Vorbehalte gegen Zesens Neuerungssucht und Aufdringlichkeit bewußt war. Die (vorsichtig nachgeordnete) Nachschrift wirkt so, als ob Buchner Zesen den allgemeinen Empfehlungsbrief gezeigt bzw. mitgeteilt, das Postskript jedoch nachträglich hinzugefügt hat.
1 Zesen hatte bereits mehrere Versuche zu einer Annäherung an die FG unternommen. Seine Widmungszuschrift 441201 an die Gesellschaft in seiner Romanübersetzung *Jbrahims oder Des Durchleuchtigen Bassa Und Der Beständigen Jsabellen Wunder-Geschichte* (1645) war ein solcher Versuch, der aber aufgrund seiner in der „Schuz-räde" verteidigten Orthographie einschließlich seiner Ablehnung der in der dt. Sprache angeblich fremden und überflüssigen Buchstaben ph, c und q auf Widerstand stieß. Vgl. etwa F. Ludwigs Brief 450504, in dem er Zesens Schreibweise alarmiert zurückwies. Auch Georg Philipp Harsdörffer (FG 368) gegenüber monierte F. Ludwig in 450529 Zesens Schreibweise im *Ibrahim Bassa*. Darum sei zunächst auf die Mittel „zugedencken, Wie vorgedachter Cæsius [...] vollend zur rechtmeßigen gleichförmigkeit möge gebracht werden", ehe eine Aufnahme in die FG in Betracht zu ziehen sei. Vgl. 441201 K 0. Daß Harsdörffer mit Zesen in Verbindung stand, im Dezember 1644 in Zesens DG aufgenommen wurde und dabei die Fruchtbringende Gesellschaft ins Spiel gebracht wurde, zeigt 441223. Die Dokumente 450410 und 450808 erweisen Übereinstimmungen, aber auch deutliche Unterschiede in den Sprachauffassungen und lassen den Keim künftigen Zerwürfnisses zwischen Harsdörffer und Zesen sichtbar werden. Ein ähnliches Bild anfänglicher Wertschätzung,

dann aber bis zur Gehässigkeit gesteigerter Ablehnung begegnet im Verhältnis zwischen Johann Rist (FG 467. 1647) und Zesen. Vgl. etwa 440724. Auch Zesens Widmungszuschrift 450000A an Justus Georg Schottelius (FG 397) in seiner Venus-Dichtung *Lustinne/ Das ist/ Gebundene Lust-Rede von Kraft und Würkung der Liebe* (1645) kann als ein Annäherungsversuch an die FG und ihre führenden Köpfe gewertet werden. Doch erst um den 22.1.1647 herum kam es schließlich zu der angestrebten persönlichen Begegnung Zesens mit F. Ludwig in Köthen (vgl. *DA Köthen I. 8:* 470122A), noch ohne den von Zesen gewünschten Durchbruch, bis es in Folge eines weiteren Besuches in Köthen im Oktober 1648 dann zur Aufnahme Zesens in die FG als des letzten Mitglieds des Jahres 1648 kam. Im Mai 1649 brachen die Widersprüche erneut auf: der Bruch mit F. Ludwig war danach nicht mehr heilbar, zumal der Fürst Anfang Januar 1650 verstarb. Die Quellen dazu demnächst in *DA Köthen I. 8*; vgl. schon 440724 K 13.

2 Schon in der „Schuz-räde" seiner *Ibrahim*-Übersetzung (1645, s. Anm. 1) hatte Zesen das -c- als im Deutschen fremden und überflüssigen Buchstaben eliminieren wollen. In einem undatierten Brief Zesens an Adolph Rosel (DG 6, Aufnahme im Juli 1644) heißt es: Die deutschen Vorfahren haben „das c und q als zeuchen ihrer knechtschaft/ von den Römern/ wie auch eben von ihnen das griechische κ zugleich [...] sondern auch ihr ganzes abece" entlehnt. „Da doch das c, wie gleichfals auch das q nuhr lateinische neu erfundene buchstaben/ und aus dem ebräischen ümgekehrte schrift-zeuchen/ sein/ derer stelle in der unsrigen/ wie auch in allen deutschen neben-sprachen/ das k/ [...] gahr wohl und ganz [E iij r] aleine verwalten kan/ weil das c und q nuhr überflüssige buchstaben sein/ und uns nichts mehr nüzzen/ als daß sie unserer sprache schreib-ahrt nuhr verwürren und die wörter unverständlich und unkantlich machen." In der Rangfolge der Buchstaben des Alphabets solle auch das g das c ersetzen, „wan das c ein h neben sich hat/ als in **macht/ möchte/ gemächte/** gar wohl und besser als das c/ verwalten kan: dan aus dem uhrsprung' und der wurzel dieser wörter/ welche **mag** ist/ erhället es klährlich/ daß in **maght/ möghte (mögen) gemähgte** das **gh** und nicht das ch stehen sol. Das g würd von den Meisnern schohn als der Ebräer ג Ghimel aus-gesprochen/ also daß es dässelben plaz gahr wohl verträten kan." *Bellin: Sendeschreiben (1647)*, Nr. 10, Bl. [Dviij]v — G[i] v, hier Bl. E ij v f. Daher begegnet uns in einem weiteren Brief Zesens an Rosel, wohl um den September 1644 verfaßt, auch die Schreibweise „hartnäkkigen köpfen" — *Bellin: Sendeschreiben (1647)*, Nr. 6, Bl. C[i] v — Cij r, hier Bl. Cij r — oder in einem Brief an B. Knipping vom 6.2.1647 der Komparativ „kristlicher". Ebd., Nr. 20, Bl. Jiiij v — [Jvj] v, hier Bl. Jv v. In Zesens *Hooch-Deutscher Spraach-übung* (1643) hieß es bereits: „c. ist kein Deutscher sondern ursprünglich ein Lateinischer buuchstabe/ wird auch in andern Heupt-Spraachen nicht gefunden/ noch angenommen." Ganz falsch sei es vor allem, wenn sogar „die lautern uhrsprünglich-Deutschen wörter mit dem C/ alß/ Clagen/ crantz" geschrieben werden, wo sie doch „mit dem k. oder z" geschrieben werden sollten, also „krantz/ klagen/ krohne/ kreutz/ kammer [...] Zizero/ Zaesar/ Tapezerey [...] Zitrone/ Zepter/ etc.". *Zesen SW* XI, 44 f. Ähnlich der *Rosen-mând* (1651): „Diese Lateinische buchstaben haben mit ihrer ordnung die Deutschen zwar gantz und gar bis auf heutigen tag behalten/ aber nach der zeit was anders gebildet. Daher kommt es/ daß sie das c, q, y haben/ welche zu ihrer sprache sich gantz nichts schikken und nuhr überflüßig/ ja der Lateiner eignen erfündung zuzuschreiben". Ebd., 127. Vgl. zu dieser Diskussion in der FG um c/k 451028A K 6.

3 Buchner, ein gebürtiger ‚Meißner', scheint hier mit F. Ludwig und Christian Gueintz (FG 361) das Normierungskriterium des Sprachusus vor dem von Justus Georg Schottelius (FG 397), Harsdörffer, Zesen u.a. vertretenen Prinzip der durchgängigen Regelhaftigkeit anzuerkennen. Die Differenz zwischen der Strenge der Sprachsystematik und den Freiheiten des Sprachgebrauchs, zwischen dem Wissen, was richtig ist, und der prakti-

schen Verwendung dessen, was gefällig ist, hatte z. B. Cicero erkannt und die Lizenzen des letzteren gegen die Maßregelungen eines strikten Analogismus verteidigt: „Quid verum sit intellego; sed alias ita loquor, ut concessum est". Marcus Tullius Cicero: Orator. Lateinisch - deutsch. Hg. Bernhard Kytzler. München 1975, 136 (§ 156). Daher vermochte er, ratio und consuetudo getrennt zu ihrem Recht kommen zu lassen, die eine als theoretisches Wissen, die andere als legitime Praxis: „usum loquendi populo concessi, scientiam mihi reservari." A.a.O., 142f. (§ 160). Buchner hatte schon in seinem Gutachten zu *Gueintz: Sprachlehre (1641)* diese Differenzierung ähnlich vertreten: „Es wird alles mit der zeit außgearbeitet; und hatt nichts zugleich seinen anfang, und ist volkommen. Darumb muß mann nicht nach den ältesten exempeln regeln machen, Sondern nach denen, die am besten geredet, und solches nun in schwanck gebracht. Bey denen alten Lateinern, so wol Poëten allß Redenern, ist viel zu finden, waß nach der zeit alles uffgehoben, weill mann waß beßers haben können. Vnd eben auß diesem sindt nachmals regeln gemacht, ienes aber alleine nur angemerckt wor*den*, zur wißenschafft, doch nicht zur folge." 400122 I, S. 423. Vgl. *Herz: Ratio und consuetudo*, 275 f.

4 Vgl. die Warnung gegen Ruhmsucht in Buchners Stammbuchversen für Zesen in *Buchner (1720)*, 298 f. Demnächst in *DA Köthen I. 8:* 481023.

460816

Fürst Ludwig an Georg Philipp Harsdörffer

Antwort auf Harsdörffers Brief vom 17.7.1646 (in *DA Köthen I. 9*). Beantwortet durch 460916. — F. Ludwig leitet Christian Gueintz' (FG 361. Der Ordnende) Gutachten zu Georg Philipp Harsdörffers (FG 368. Der Spielende) *Specimen Philologiae Germanicae* (1646) zusammen mit einigen Anmerkungen dazu (die vermutlich von Marcus Fridericus Wendelin[us] stammen [Beilage I]) weiter. Harsdörffers lateinische Replik (auf Wendelins erstes Gutachten) habe er dem Verfasser zukommen lassen, der sich in dieser Sache noch einmal äußern werde.

Q HM Köthen: V S 544, Bl. 42r (42v: Anmerkungen zu Gueintz' Gutachten, s. Beilage I), eigenh. Konzept. — Nicht in *KE*.

A *Fehlt*.

Hiermit wird dem Spielenden des Ordnenden bedencken über die ausgegangene **Philologiam Germanicam** zugefertiget[a] so diese tage eingekommen worzu[b] etliche wenige anmerckun*gen* gesetzet.[1] Der Lateinische brief an den Nehrenden vom 12. Heumonats ist deme zugeschickt[c], so das erste bedencken[d] daruber gegeben, und wird[e] darauf anderweite antwort im kurtzen erfolgen.[2] Jn deßen dem Spielenden dieses angefuget werden sollen. Geben an dem bewusten[f] orte unter[g] bekanter schrift, und[h] Siegel den 16[i] Augustmonats im Jhare 1646.

460816 Fürst Ludwig

I

Anmerkungen zu Christian Gueintz' Gutachten über Harsdörffers *Specimen Philologiae Germanicae* (1646)

Q HM Köthen: V S 544, Bl. 42v, F. Ludwigs H.

Wenige erklerung und erinnerung bey des Ordnenden gutachten.

1. Cöthen wird in alten schriften Cathon geschrieben gefunden, wen man es nun von dem Hebraischen herziehen wolte, so muste sie heißen, H'accathon, die Kleine: Man vermeinet aber sie komme von Codan[a], so ein Schlavonisch wort sein[b], und einen Keßel bedeuten sol, weil das Städlein so tief als in einem Keßel[c] und[d] in gutem und[e] wen es regnet in tieffem lande lieg[et.][f 1]

2. Keuterling ist das bier so in dem kleinen Stätlein im Stifte Magdeburg dem Sahlkreiße nahe bey Halle[g] gebrauen und in Halle von den furnemesten am meisten getrunken wird.[2]

3. Dis wort Lerner ist[h] neu, auch[i] noch nicht angenommen, und solte beßer ein lernender[j] lehrschuler oder lehrbegieriger heißen, sonsten der unterscheid des lehren und lernen im Deutschen billich in acht zu nemen.[3]

Hoc scriptum est Marci Friderici Wendelini, Gymnas[ii][f] Anhaltini quod est Servestæ, pro tempore Rectoris.

T **a** *Folgt* <was sich> *Ab des Ordnenden* urprüngliche Reihenfolge *zugefertiget des Ordnenden bedencken über die ausgegangene* Philologiam Germanicam *durch Bezifferung geändert.* — **b** *Bis* gesetzet *eingefügt.* — **c** *Gebessert aus* zuge<fertiget> — **d** *Eingefügt.* — **e** *Folgt eingefügt* <auch> — **f** *Gebessert aus* be<kanten> — **g** *Reihenfolge der Wörter durch Bezifferung umgestellt aus* den 16 Augustmonats im Jhare 1646 unter bekanter schrift, und Siegel — **h** *Folgt* <siegelpetschaft> — **i** *Unsichere Lesung. Zuerst wohl* 19 *dann wurde die letzte Ziffer gebessert zu* 6 *oder* 8

T I **a** *Gebessert aus* Cödan — **b** *Folgt* <sol> — **c** *Folgt* <lieget> — **d** *Folgt eingefügt* <wen es reg[n]et tieffen> — **e** *Eingefügt bis* tieffem — **f** *Textverlust im Falz, Konjektur in eckigen Klammern.* — **g** *Folgt eingefügt* <in Sachsen> — **h** *Folgt* <nicht> — **i** *Bis* angenommen, *eingefügt.* — **j** *Eingefügt.*

K 1 Georg Philipp Harsdörffer (FG 361. Der Spielende) bat F. Ludwig in 460406, um ein Gutachten zu seinem *Specimen Philologiae Germanicae* (1646) bei Christian Gueintz (FG 361. Der Ordnende) nachzusuchen. Auch Diederich v. dem Werder (FG 31) kam für Harsdörffer für ein solches in Betracht. Gueintz' Gutachten erhielt F. Ludwig mit 460720 (das Gutachten demnächst in *DA Köthen I. 9*; Kurzbeschreibung in 460720 K 3); ob auch Werder eine Stellungnahme aufsetzte, ist fraglich, da im Köthener Erzschrein nichts dergleichen und auch keine Reaktion Harsdörffers darauf vorliegt. Die „wenige anmerckungen" zu Gueintz' Gutachten stammen von Marcus Fridericus Wendelin(us), s. Beil. I.

2 Bei der Datierung unterlief F. Ludwig ein kleiner Lapsus: Der Brief Harsdörffers datiert auf den 17.7.1646. Neben Gueintz' Gutachten zu Harsdörffers *Specimen Philolo-*

giae Germanicae (1646) schrieb damals auch der Zerbster Gymnasialrektor Marcus Fridericus Wendelin(us) zwei Gutachten, das erste ist auf den 15.6.1646 datiert und wurde Harsdörffer von F. Ludwig mit 460705 überschickt. Ein zweites ‚Bedenken' setzte Wendelin(us) am 6.8.1646 auf; es stellt seine Reaktion auf den genannten Harsdörffer-Brief vom 17.7.1646 dar, in dem Harsdörffer seinerseits ausführlich auf Wendelins erstes Gutachten reagierte. Alle drei Dokumente demnächst in *DA Köthen I. 9.* S. dazu im Detail 460705 K 3.

K I Die lateinische Notiz, mit der die Anmerkungen schließen, steht mit großem Abstand zum Text am Ende der Seite. Der in ihr genannte Marcus Fridericus Wendelin(us) schrieb zwei Gutachten zu Georg Philipp Harsdörffers (FG 368) *Specimen Philologiae Germanicae* (1646) (s. K 2). Ob die „wenige erklerung" in der abschriftlichen Form durch F. Ludwig, d.h. mit Verweis auf die Autorschaft Wendelins, auch an Harsdörffer ging, ist ungewiß, da er die „erklerung" Wendelins sicher im Original erhielt. Darauf weist zumindest die Bemerkung im Brief, das Gutachten von Christian Gueintz (FG 361) käme zusammen mit „etliche[n] wenige[n] anmerckung*en*", hin. Die Passagen, auf die sich die Anmerkungen Wendelins beziehen, wurden in dem Gutachten von Gueintz, das im Erzschrein erhalten ist (*DA Köthen I. 9*, zu 460720; *KE*, 363–372), durch Marginalien gekennzeichnet.

1 In Gueintz' Gutachten findet sich die etymologische Reflexion zur Herkunft der Wörter „Cöthen" und „Keuterling" im Zusammenhang mit der Frage nach der Schreibung des Wortes „Deutsch" (vs. Teutsch; vgl. 441223 K 23), die auch in Harsdörffers *Specimen* seine etymolog. Versuche grundierte (S.19f.) und wo der Ortsname Köthen aus dem Hebr. כהר (Kœhē) abgeleitet wurde (S.30). Gueintz schreibt dagegen: „Ist auch leichter zu beweisen als das Cöthen von dem Hebreischen Cohen komme, Nach des Orthes Beschaffenheit ist es beßer vom Koth, daher man es auch Lutetiam Anhaltinorum genennet vnd gemahnet mich gleich als Jener der das bier Keuterling von Griechischen καθαρὸς herfuhren wil da doch weder die Hebräer noch die Griechen in diesen Landen einigem Dinge den nahmen gegeben." HM Köthen: V S 545, Bl.192r–200v, hier Bl.194r. Auf welch „Jenen" sich Gueintz bei der Herleitung des „Keuterlings" aus dem Griechischen bezog, wissen wir nicht; in Harsdörffers *Specimen* taucht dies nicht auf. Wendelin(us) hatte für Köthen also eine bessere Etymologie als die von Gueintz präsentierte anzubieten, auch wenn sie mit den topograph. Verhältnissen der flachen Gegend wenig übereinzukommen scheint. Noch bei *Beckmann* III, 412 ist die Frage nicht geklärt. Da in der Gegend einst Wenden lebten, könne der Name aus dem Wendischen stammen und „seinen Ursprung von dem Worte Codan haben/ so eine Anfuhrt oder Hafen heissen soll". Melanchthon und andere Gelehrte meinten, „daß das Wort auf Wendisch oder Slavonisch so viel als einen Kessel bedeute". Gueintz' Vorschlag, den Namen von „Kot" abzuleiten, könnte auf den ebenfalls von Beckmann erwähnten Christian Brombei zurückgehen, der die Herkunft des Namens in seiner *Antiquitas Cothoniae* (1617) vom „fette[n] Erdreich/ so in diesem Fürstl. Antheile sich befindet/ welches man im Deutschen Koht oder Kaht hiesse", herleitete. Heute wird einer Ableitung aus dem Altsorbischen zugeneigt: Kot-n, von *kot*, d.i. Stall; auch ahd. *kot*, d.i. Abteilung, Kate; mnd. u. nd. *Kote*, d.i. Schuppen, Hütte, Stall, werden erwogen. Inge Bily: Ortsnamenbuch des Mittelelbegebietes. Berlin 1996, 227f.

2 Zu Gueintz' Erwähnung des „Keuterling" s. das Zitat in Anm.1. Keuterling (auch Keiterling, s. *DW* V, 504) war im 17. Jahrhundert ein in der Tat sehr bekanntes Wettiner Bier. Vgl. Ambrosius Stegmann: Genaue Untersuchung Des Keuterlings/ Wie derselbe Durch versetzte Buchstaben sich als Ein gut Kerl Wegen seiner Qualitäten bey Gesunden und Krancken … recommendiret mache (Leipzig 1694). In seiner Monographie preist

460819 Johann Valentin Andreae

Stegmann nicht nur den hervorragenden Geschmack des Bieres, sondern auch seine Heilkräfte. Zur Etymologie des Wortes schreibt er (S. 37–40): Auf den Namen des ersten Brauers sei das Wort „Keuterling" wohl nicht zurückzuführen, vielleicht aber auf „Keute oder Kiete d. i. von einem Orte/ wo die Alten vordiesen das Wasser zum Keuterlingsbrauen gesamlet". (S. 39) Möglich sei auch, daß sein „süßlieblicher und angenemer Geschmack" ihm den Namen „Euterling" eingetragen habe (wegen seiner Ähnlichkeit mit der Milch); das K sei eine spätere Ergänzung. (Ebd.) Die Herleitung aus dem Griechischen, die Gueintz ironisiert, erwähnt Stegmann nicht. Gueintz nennt die Biersorte wohl deswegen, weil es in Halle, wo er Gymnasialrektor war, sehr viel getrunken wurde. Wendelin(us) scheint hier eine Erklärung für nötig befunden zu haben.

3 Das Wort „Lerner" wird in Gueintz' Gutachten nicht eigens thematisiert. Es taucht in einer Passage auf, in der Gueintz fordert, die Worttrennung nicht morphologisch nach Stamm und Affixen, sondern nach der Aussprache, nach Sprechsilben, vorzunehmen, um dem „Lerner" das Deutschlernen nicht schwerer als nötig zu machen. HM Köthen: V S 545, Bl. 192r–200v, hier Bl. 197v. Zur Streitfrage der Silbentrennung vgl. 451028A K 6. Wendelin(us) lehnte das ungebräuchliche Wort „Lerner" ab, ohne das gebräuchliche des „Schülers" anzuführen.

460819

Johann Valentin Andreae an Herzog August d. J. von Braunschweig-Wolfenbüttel

Antwort auf 460804. Beantwortet durch 460908. — Johann Valentin Andreae (FG 464. 1646) bestätigt Hz. August d. J. v. Braunschweig-Wolfenbüttel (FG 227) den Empfang von sieben Bögen der hzl. *Evangelischen Kirchen-Harmonie*. — Andreae will sich bemühen, daß Hz. August die (von Friedrich Greiff) entliehenen italienischen Abbildungen biblischer Figuren länger als vorgesehen (für die Illustrierung des Handbüchleins der *Evangelischen Kirchen-Harmonie*) behalten kann. — Andreae bedankt sich, daß der Herzog die ihm angebotenen Bücher Andreaes übernehmen, auch seinen Söhnen überlassen und dadurch seine Bibliothek vor Zerstreuung schützen will. Dafür lieferten andere Gelehrte Vorbilder. Sein Sohn (Gottlieb Andreae) werde besser mit einer kleinen Summe als mit diesen Büchern geholfen sein, da sie nicht seinen Interessen und seinem wissenschaftlichen Bedürfnis entsprechen. Andreae schätzt die Sammlung auf 600 Bücher, 100 in Folio, 200 in Quarto und 300 in kleineren Formaten. Eine Liste soll folgen. — Sollte Andreae mit seinem Sinnbild in der Fruchtbringenden Gesellschaft auch Aufnahme finden, würde er das als hohe Gnade und Ehre empfinden. — Aus den Sammlungen seines Oheims Jacob Andreae — und nicht seines gleichnamigen Großvaters — habe Andreae die restlichen erhaltenen Handschriften in einem Paket Philipp Hainhofer zur Weitersendung an den Herzog geschickt. — Die Lage im Südwesten ist sehr unruhig, weil die Schweden und Franzosen Heilbronn belagern, die Kaiserlichen und Bayern jedoch die Stadt entsetzen wollen, so daß die Württemberger zwischen den Gegnern in die Bredouille geraten.

Q HAB: Cod. Guelf. 65.1 Extrav., Bl. 301rv [A: 301v]; eigenh.; Sig. — Andreaes 31. Brief als Antwort auf Hz. Augusts 33.

A Dem Durchleüchtist. Hochgebohrnen Fursten vnnd Herrn. Herren Augusto, Herzogen zu Braunschweig vnnd Luneburg. &c. Meinem gnedigsten Fursten vnd Herren. &c. Wolfenbuttel. (33.) 19. Aug.

Durchleuchtigst. Hochgebohrner, Gnedigster Furst vnd Herr, E. F. G. 31. auf mein 28. de 4. Aug.[1], ist mir sampt abernachmahligen 7 Bögen Harmoniæ wol angeliefert worden.[2] Gott gebe daß die Vollendung der Andern theile auch mit gutem glükh erfolge.

Wo die Combination der Evangelischen texten sambt denen Figuren, E. F. G. vnd dero sculptoribus in etwas dienlich, will ich mich Befleißen, das der terminus restitutionis, prorogiert werden möchte.[3] Daß E. F. G. mein Vndst. Vorschlag, Meine bucher So ich mit zimblichen Vncosten, vnd nicht, geringer muh, colligiert, vor besorgender Vnwärthin[4] vnd dissipation, in salvum zu bringen, vnd dero Princen zu mancipieren, in gnaden nicht zuwider, habe ich mich Vndst. zu erfrewen, vnd hohen danckh zusagen,[5] Exempla non desunt huius rej, Hieronimj Wolfij, D. Ludovicij Grempij, Jo. Pappi, Martinj Crusij, Andreæ Laubmarij,[6] et aliorum nostrorum. Vnd wurt also auch meinem Sohn mit etwas geringer ergözlichkeit, vil beßer, alß disen Buchern, so nicht seines humors vnd wißenschaft geholfen sein.[7] Meines bedunkhens vnd vngefalichen Vberschlags, möchten der Stuckh auf 600 werden, darunter der Folien, 100, der Quart 200, der octaven aber, 12 vnd[a] 16 bei 300, davon aber die Lista erfolgen, vnd aller E. F. G. Gehorsambst vndergeben werden solle.[8]

Wo bei der Hochlöbl. Kreutergeselschaft[9] ich meinem geringfugen Simbolo[b] auch solte einen Platz noch finden mugen, wolte ich ein solches für eine hohe gnade vnd sonderbahre Ehr halten.

Von den Mss. so nicht mein Avus,[10] sondern patruus, auch Jacobus Andreæ, Filiorum primogenitus. (.deßen nepotem ich an iezo bei mir in dienste habe.) colligieret, ist nichts weiter vorhanden; dan die vberige Tomos deren[c] noch etlich gewesen, die Soldaten verbrent vnd verderbet. Diese aber bloß erhalten worden, welche ich h. Hainhofern in einem einschlag zugesandt.[11]

Wir stekhen in großer Vnruw vnd gefarligkeit, weil Sueco-Galli die Stadt Heilbronn zu belagern, die Cæsareo-Bavarij aber zuentsehen gewillet, derentwegen wir interclusj beeden Theilen daß haar darbieten müßen[12]. Deus sit tutor, et auxiliator.

Befehle E. F. g. dem Schuz des Allerhöchsten, zu Leben vnd Segen. Auch deroselben mich zu beharrenden großen gnaden, verbleibend biß in den Todt

E. F. G. Vndertänigst. gehorsambe Verpflichtigter Rhat vnd getrewester diener

Jo. Valentin Andreæ D.

Sebaldi 19. Aug. ☿ [4]6.

I

Andreae sendet Herzog August einen von ihm kompilierten Index über das Gesellschaftsbuch von 1646

Q HAB: Cod. Guelf. 65.1 Extrav., Bl. 285r, Rücks. leer; eigenh. — *Begemann: FG u. Andreae*, 39; *Keller: Akademien der Renaissance*, 105.

Jch habe einen Indicem vber die hochlob. Kraütergesellschaft gemacht,[1] welchen E. f. g. ich hiebej vndst. Communiciere, Vnd solle der Index vber die Kreuter selbsten auch erfolgen, Ob etwa eine Arbeit dadurch erspatet werden möchte. An den Nahmens Buchstaben, habe von Furst. Heusern, Sachsen, Weimar, Altenburg, Lawenburg, Brandenburg, Brunschwig, Anhalt &c. ich Meines Vermeinens Vil Errathen. Die geringere aber vnd Priuati sein mir Nicht bekandt. Wo Es keine Heimbligkeit, vnd sich eröfnen Laßet[,] wolle E. f. g ich vndst. gebetten haben, etwa mit gelegenheit durch h. Schottelium mir elucidationem g*nedigst* laßen zuzukommen.

II

460725

Andreaes Vorrede auf Friedrich Greiffs Evangelienharmonie in Versen

Q Der vier Evangelisten | ubereinstimmende | Geschicht Beschreibung CHristi | Von seiner Heylsamen Geburt/ biß zu seiner | Siegreichen Himmelfahrt. | Jn vier Theil oder Bücher/ nach den | Osterfesten/ unnd deren jedes gewisse Ge | schichten abgetheilt/ deren jeder Jnhalt kurtz in zwey baar | Versen verfaßt/ die Son- vnnd Feyrtägliche Evangelien | aber in Gesang/ oder Lieder gebracht/ vnd | mit einem kurtzen Gebettlin | beschlossen. | Alles in Reimen verfasset | durch Friderich Greiffen. | Sampt zweyen Vorreden | Eine von ... D. Melchior Nicolai Fürstl. Würt. | Rhat/ der heyligen Schrifft Doctorn vnd Profes- | sorn, wie auch ProCancellario bey hiesigen | Vniversität Tübingen. | Die ander von ... D. Valentin Andreæ | F. W. Rath/ vnd Hoffprediger zu Stutgarten. | Getruckt zu Tübingen/ | Bey Philibert Brunnen. | [Linie] | Jm Jahr 1647. HAB: 501.7 Theol. Bl. [*3v]–**v.

Vorred
An den wolmeinenden Leser

NAch dem der Getreue Barmhertzige GOtt/ das Liecht seines H. Evangelii nach lāger Verdunckelung/ zu den letsten Zeiten der Welt widerumb erscheinen/ vnd durch den Dienst seines getrewen Werckzeugs Dct. Martini Lutheri herfür bringen/ zumalen sein H. Wort in der Bibel verfasset/ in vnser Teutsche Mutter Sprach so klar vnd deutlich/ daß es für eine Außlegung vnd Erklärung zuhalten/ versetzen lassen/ haben sich getrewe Lehrer vnd Seelen Hirten hoch beflissen/

daß nicht allein durch die Predig vnd Verkündigung desselben/ auch einfältigen Vnderricht der Jugend/ solches der Herd Christi beygebracht/ vnnd eingepflantzet/ sondern auch in den Häusern reichlich wohnen möchte/ vnnd von den Haußvätter vnd Müttern mit jhren Kindern vnd Gesind geübet/ vnd fortgetrieben werde/ vnnd zu solchem Ende die vornembste Stück Christlicher Lehr in angeneme Reimen/ auff liebliche Melodien oder Weisen [*4r] zusingen verfasset/ waran wolgedachter Herr D. Luther selbsten den Anfang gemacht/ vnd das beste gethon. Nachmalen aber viel andere gottselige Männer gefolget/ vornemblich aber der Leuthseelige Theologus Mathesius Pfarrer in dem Jochams Thal/ durch seinen Cantorem Niclas Herman nicht allein alle gewonliche Sonn vnd Feyrtägliche Evangelien/ sondern auch die vornembste Biblische Historien/ mit angehenckten Lehren vnd Erklärungen in gute Reimen bringen/ vnd der Christlichen Jugend bekand vnd gemein machen lassen. Welches Wercklin dann zu vnderschiedlichen malen auffgelegt/ vnnd von mäniglich sehr anmütig vnd erbawlich geachtet worden. Jnsonderheit aber haben gelehrte Leut in zimblicher Anzahl als Martinus Opitius[1], Johan Vogelius[2], Georg Rudolff Weckerlin[3]/ Adam Weinheimer[4]/ Paulus Flemming[5], Cornelius Becker[6], vnd viel andere mehr/ Jhr Geschickligkeit nicht allein an absonderlichen Biblischē Stücken vnd Historien/ sondern vornämblich den gantzen Psalter Davids/ als der kleinen Bibel/ jhne in gute Reimen zu bringen/ hochrümlich erwisen/ warunder gewißlich nicht der [*4v] wenigste ware/ Weylund H. David Hitzler[7]/ geweßner Probst allhie zu Stuttgarten/ so Herrn Lutheri Teutscher Version mit vngläu[b]lichem Fleiß so nahend kommen/ daß es bey so mancherley Reimen arten fast einer prosa gleich gelautet/ vnd wol schad were/ wann es solte verstecket bleiben/ oder gar zu grund gehen. Zu dessen Verhütung/ wo etwan das Wercklin noch zufinden were/ ich diese Andeutung thun wollen. Jn gleichem die fürnembste Articul Christlicher Religion/ neben Erklärung der hohen Fest/ und Gedächtnussen vnsers Ewigen Heyls/ in schöne vnnd lehrreiche Gesang gebracht/ daß hierinnen für den gemeinen Mann/ ein reicher Schatz vnnd guter Vorrath zufinden. Vornemblich aber das Böhmische Kirchen Gesang Buch in Anno 1566. Kayser Maximiliano 2. Lobseligst. Gedächtnuß/ aller vnderthönigst dedicirt/[8] zubeobachten ist. Was auch andere teutsche Poeten von Biblischen vnd Geistlichen Gedichten verfertigt/ vnd sonderbahren Nutzen bey einfältigen Leuten damit geschaffet/ ist weltkündig; gleich wol meines Wissens sich noch keiner gefunden/ der entweder die gesambte Geschichten der H. [**r] Schrifft/ oder doch das gantze Leben vnd Lehr vnsers Heylands JEsu CHristi/ in Reimen verfasset/ vnnd solcher gestalten eine völlige leyen Bibel außgelassen hette. Wann dann zu vnser Zeit vnser Teutsche Mutter Sprach durch besondern Eyffer vñ Fleiß gelehrter Leut/ darunder Martinus Opitius nicht gering Vorzug hat/ an Zierd vnd Reinigkeit sich sehr bereichet/ vnnd numehr anfahet mit den Außländischen Sprachen/ so wol mit aller Hand Arten der Reimen/ als gewisser Regul verfassung/ darunder H. D. Justus Georgius Schottelius fürbindig[9]/ vmb die Ehr vnd gewinnet zustreitten/ welche durch zuthun deren hochlöbl. Fruchtbringenden KreüterGesellschafft vnzweiffelig zuerlangen seyn werden: Als hat auch Herr Friderich Greiff/ mein sonders günstiger Herr vnd Freund/ hierunder der wenigste nicht seyn/ sondern seine hierin habende gute Gaben/ nicht allein in hie bevor außgelaßnē hübschen Wercklin vnnd Prodomo[10] erscheinen lassen wollen; Sondern auch jhme ein solche Materiam erlesen/ damit GOtt vnd der Christlichen Kirchen ein angenehmer Dienst vnnd Wohlgefallen beschehen möchte. Welches dann ich nach meiner [**v] Wenigkeit so wohl gern gesehen/ als rathsam befunden/ vnnd bester Müglichkeit befürdert/ angesehen hierinnen nicht eben hochtrabende Wort gebraucht/ vnnd vngewohnliche Art zu reden gesuchet/ vilmehr aber die einschleichende Haydnische Abgöttische Poeterey gäntzlichen außgeschlossen/ vnd hingegen dem reinen Text vnd lauterm Verstand nachgegangen/ vnd alles auff das einfaltigest/ dem gemeinem Mann zum besten/ angerichtet worden.

Gelebe demnach der getrösten Hoffnung/ es solle dieses Christ: vnnd Löbliche Vorhaben/ zu seinem wolmeinenden Zweck geraichen/ vnnd so wol den Authorn/ als den ohne zweiffelig von GOTT hierzu bescherten Patronen vnnd Verlegern/ bey dessen Heroischen Tugenden/ der Eyffer vnnd Freygebigkeit gegen Göttlichem Wort/ vnnd dessen Erbreittung den Vorzug hat/ bey allen Liebhabern Geistlicher/ reiner Poesi bester massen bekandt/ berümbt vnd recommendirt machen. Darzu der getrewe GOtt sein mildes Gedeyen geben/ vnd alles Gute schutzen/ vnd belohnen wölle. Stuttgart am Tag Jacobi den 25. Julii. Anno 1646.

      Joh. Valent. Andreæ D.
     Fürstl. Württ.ª Consistorials Rhat
       vnd Hoffprediger.

T **a** vnd *versehentlich doppelt.* — **b** *Folgt überflüssiges* Ich — **c** *Eingefügt bis* gewesen, <von>

T II **a** *Druckfehler* Würst

K 1 Die Antwort Hz. Augusts d. J. v. Braunschweig-Wolfenbüttel (FG 227) auf Johann Valentin Andreaes (FG 464. 1646) 28. Brief (des Jahres 1646) datiert vom 4.8.1646, s. 460804.

2 Die 2. oder Quartausgabe der *Evangelischen Kirchen-Harmonie* (1646) Hz. Augusts, an deren ihm vom Herzog regelmäßig übersandten Teilen Andreae jahrelang mitarbeitete. S. 411214. Die Ankunft eines früheren Teildrucks von 7 Bögen bestätigte Andreae in seinem Brief v. 12.8.1646 an den Herzog (HAB: Cod. Guelf. 65.1 Extrav., Bl. 300r). Hier teilte August ihm auch den Verkaufspreis der ersten oder Oktavausgabe von 1646 mit: 2 Rth.

3 In 460804 drückte der Herzog die Hoffnung aus, er werde die geliehenen Bilder (Friedrich Greiffs, s. 460804 K 1) zur Illustration der Duodezausgabe der *Evangelischen Kirchen-Harmonie* (1646) rechtzeitig zurückgeben können. Zu diesem *Handbüchlein* s. 411214 III I.

4 Genitiv Pl. zu Unwerte, f., contemptus, vilitas. *Aler*, 2110; *DW* XI.3, 2192.

5 Dubletten der Bücher Andreaes wollte der Herzog seinen Söhnen schenken. Vgl. 460804 K 4. Zum Verkauf eines großen Teils der Bibliothek Andreaes s. 460715 u. 460908.

6 Hieronymus Wolf (1516–1580), Philologe, Übersetzer aus dem Griechischen, Byzantinist, Bibliothekar Anton Fuggers u. Rektor des St.-Anna Gymnasiums in Augsburg. *Zedler* LVIII, 690–693. — Ludwig Gremp v. Freudenstein (1509–1583), Jurist, Syndikus der Stadt Straßburg und ihr politischer Unterhändler, anfangs zusammen mit Jakob Sturm. *NDB* V, 44f. online. — Johann Pappus (1549–1610), Straßburger Theologe. — Martin Crusius (1526–1607), Tübinger Homer-Philologe, schwäbischer Historiker (Annales Suevici; Paraleipomenos rerum Suevicarum), Förderer des Philhellenismus u. eines Projekts einer protestantisch- u. griech.-orthodoxen Ökumene. *NDB* III, 433 f. online. — Andreas Laubmair (1538–1604), schwäb. Jurist u. Prof., U. Tübingen. *Adelung* III, 1358.

7 Zur mangelnden Begabung seines Sohnes Gottlieb für die Studien seines Vaters s. 460715.

8 Zum Angebot seiner Bücher an Hz. August am 23.9.1646 schrieb Andreae an den Herzog (HAB: Cod. Guelf. 65.1 Extrav., Bl. 307r): „Jch habe mein **bibliothecam recensiert**, Befinde daß ich 600 Stukh ermanglen kan, darunter **in folio** 100, **in quarto** 200, **in octavo** 200, vnd **decima sexta forma** 100, welche zu æstimieren Mühsam fallen, vnd eine zimliche Summen geldes machen werde, so ich aber gar nicht begere. Habe demnach in Vndertänigkeit darfur gehalten, wann ein stukh in daß Ander, (.darunter gleichmalen nicht wenig kostbar.) vber haupt gerechnet, angeschlagen werde,

Folia 100 zu 40 x. ...... 66 f. — 40 x
Quarto 200 - 20 x. ..... 66 f — 40 x
Octavo 200 - 15 x ...... 50 f — 0 x
Dec. sext. 100 - 10 x .. 16 f — 40 x
----
          600 Stukh — Pro — 200 f

solle es der billigkeit nicht vngemäß sein, vnd könten dise 200 f auf 3 Zil, Circumcisionis, Paschalis, vnd Michaelis, iedes mahle 66f. 40 x, zerleget werden, iedoch alles E. F. g. gnedigstem Beliben gehorsamst Heimgesezt." D. i. anheimgestellt. Am 3.11.1646 schickte Andreae dem Herzog einen Katalog seiner damaligen Bibliothek (sehr viele Bücher waren 1634 in Calw verbrannt): S. HAB: BA (Bibliotheks-Archiv) II, 11.5, Bl. 32r–36v Bücherverzeichnis J. V. Andreaes. Er wolle nur wenige Stücke davon behalten. Andreae sandte in diesem Brief nochmals die zitierte Aufstellung mit dem Kostenanschlag vom 23.9.1646. Vgl. 461103 u. I–II. Beilage II bezieht sich auf den Katalog Andreaes. Andreae verhieß Hz. August nach Johann Sauberts Tod auch den Erwerb der Bücher, die Saubert an Gottlieb Andreae vererben werde. S. 460715. Saubert starb am 2.11.1647.

9 Hier gesteht Andreae dem Herzog erstmalig seinen Wunsch, in die FG aufgenommen zu werden, nachdem August ihm dazu schon seine Unterstützung mitgeteilt hatte. S. 460804 K 6 und allgemein zur Aufnahme 461117 K 1. Die Ankunft seines Exemplars des *GB 1646* hatte Andreae am 15.7.1646 dem Herzog gemeldet. Seinen Wunsch, selbst in die FG aufgenommen zu werden, offenbarte Andreae zuerst Philipp Hainhofer am 15./ 25.7.1646. Vgl. 460915A I (Hz. August empfiehlt F. Ludwig die Aufnahme Andreaes).

10 Andreaes Großvater war der württemberg. Reformator Jacob Andreae. Zu den Sammlungen seines gleichnamigen Oheims (1549–1630) zur württemberg. Geschichte s. 460804 K 9.

11 Paket Andreaes an Philipp Hainhofer, das nach Hz. Augusts Erwartung (s. 460804) den zweiten Band mit Luther-Auszügen Jacob Andreaes enthalten haben könnte.

12 Zur mißlichen Lage Württembergs zwischen den ksl.-bayer. Kräften und den schwed.-franz. vgl. 460715 u. K 7 u. 460909. Zur Lage Heilbronns s. *Gottfried II*, 903:

460819 Johann Valentin Andreae

„Die Französisch-Weimarische Armee belagerte um den 6. September die Stadt Hailbronn, daher die Chur-Bayerischen von der Donau zum Entsatz anrückten, und ob ihnen gleich das Regenwetter anfänglich sehr hinderlich fiel, die Belagerer dahin brachten, daß sie sich in den Weinbergen verschantzen und endlich gar aufbrechen mußten. Sie zogen sich gegen Dünckelsbühl, nachdem sie aus Mergentheim vielen Proviant abholen lassen; die Bayerischen aber giengen auf Heidenheim, und legten den Bayerischen Ausschuß, nebst etlichen Kayserlichen Regimentern zu Pferd, auf den Schellenberg, um Donauwert zu versichern." Vgl. *Merian: Topographia Sueviae*, 89: „Anno 1645. ward Hailbronn/ durch die Frantzosen/ vnnd Weymarischen/ von fernen geängstigt. So versuchten Anno 1546[recte: 1646]. die Schwedischen auch nicht mit Ernst etwas auff die Statt. Folgends ward sie/ vermög deß zu Vlm getroffenen Armistitii, von Chur-Bäyern/ den Frantzosen/ vnnd dann auff getroffenen GeneralReichs-Frieden/ ChurPfaltz/ anstatt Franckenthal/ zubesetzen vberlassen." Kf. Maximilian I. v. Bayern hatte am 14.3.1647 n. St. in Ulm auch für Kurköln einen Waffenstillstand mit Schweden, Frankreich und Hessen-Kassel abgeschlossen, den er jedoch zugunsten seines alten ksl. Alliierten aufgab (Passauer Vertrag v. 13.9.1647 n. St.).

K I Ein Zettel Andreaes, der im Bestand vor dem Brief Johann Valentin Andreaes (FG 1646. 1646) an Hz. August d. J. v. Braunschweig-Wolfenbüttel (FG 227) v. 26.5.1646 liegt. Da Andreae den Empfang eines Exemplars des *GB 1646* in 460715 meldete, kann er frühestens kurz darauf den (verschollenen) Index kompiliert haben. Es handelte sich offenbar um ein Verzeichnis von Initialen bzw. erratenen Mitgliedernamen, vielleicht in der Reihenfolge des Eintritts in die Gesellschaft. Ob die Gesellschaftsnamen, Eintrittsjahre und Motti (sog. Wörter) dabeistanden, ist ungewiß. Ein Verzeichnis der Kräuter der Impresen fehlte noch. *Begemann: FG und Andreae*, 105 datiert den Zettel auf die Zeit zw. 15.7. u. 19.8.1646.

1 Eine vielleicht von Justus Georg Schottelius (FG 397) abgeschriebene Mitgliederliste F. Ludwigs. In 460909 bedankt sich Andreae beim Herzog für „die Communication dern HochLob. Fruchtbringenden gesellschaft".

K II 1 Martin Opitz (1597–1640), FG 200. Der Gekrönte. Der bekannte Dichter und Reformer der deutschen Verssprache.

2 Johan Vogel(ius) (1589–1663), Anhänger Opitz', Schulmann, Lyriker, Dichter von Psalmen und Kirchenliedern. Vgl. *Literatur-Lexikon*[2] XII, 4f.

3 Georg Rodolf Weckherlin (1584–1653), engl. Beamter u. Diplomat, höf. Dichter und Lyriker. Vgl. *Literatur-Lexikon*[2] XII, 179–182.

4 Adam Weinheimer (1614–1666), Superintendent. Vgl. *DBA* I 1343/ 237–240.

5 Paul Fleming (1609–1640), Lyriker, Psalmendichter, Arzt; Rußland- und Persienreisen. Vgl. *Literatur-Lexikon*[2] III, 474–477.

6 Vermutlich Cornelius Becker d. Ä. (1561–1604), Leipzig, luther. Theologe in kursächs. Diensten, Liederdichter u. Verfasser einer Psalmendichtung in dt. Liedern: *Psalter Davids Gesangsweise*, Leipzig 1602 u.ö. Die Ausg. Leipzig 1603 in der HAB: Tl 17 u. weitere Ausgaben. Vgl. *ADB* 221; *DBA* I 70, 312–331; II 196f.; III 394–400; *Literatur-Lexikon*[2] I, 395f. — Sein gleichnamiger Sohn (†1632), luther. Pastor in Meuselwitz bei Leipzig, trat mit einer Handvoll Kirchenliedern hervor. *DBA* I 70, 332f.

7 Daniel Hi(t)zler (1576–1635), Musiktheoretiker und Kirchenlieddichter. S. 420627 K I 20. — Newe MUSICA Oder Singkunst M. DANIELIS HIZLERI Heydenheimii Wirtembergici. Zu fürderlichem vnd doch gründlichem Vnterricht Der Jugend. EDITIO SECUNDA & Auctior. Getruckt zu Tübingen/ bey Dieterich Werlin/ im Jahr Christi. M.

DC.XXIIX. SB Berlin—PK. — Christliche Kirchen-Gesäng/ Psalmen vnd Geistliche Lieder: Wie dieselbige Bey offentlichem Gottesdienst der Gemeinden Augspurgischer Confession gebräuchig seind. An Text vnd Melodien mit sonderm Fleiß durchsehen: Auch Auß berühmbten Authoribus Musicis mit vier Musicalischen Stimmen ordenlich zusammen getragen Durch M. DANIEL Hitzler/ damahlen Predigern in dem Landhauß zu Lintz in Oesterreich ob der Enß. Straßburg/ Getruckt bey Caspar Dietzeln. Jm Jahr/ M.DC.XXXIV. 208 Bl., 12° HAB: Tl 139. Vgl. Musicalisch Figurierte Melodien aller vnnd jeder gebräuchigen Kirchen-Gesäng/ Psalmen vnd Geistlichen Lieder/ Mit vier Musicalischen Stimmen von berühmbten Autoribus Musicis ... Mehrertheils von newem componirt Vnd Jn solcher Art zusammen getragen/ daß der Discant in allem das Choral führt. ... mit sonderm fleiß durchsehen ... Durch M. Daniel Hitzler ... Straßburg/ Gedruckt bey Caspar Dietzeln. Jm Jahr/ M.DC.XXXIV. 270 Bl. mit Noten, 12°. FB Gotha. (Mit Kompositionen von Hans Leo Haßler, Michael Praetorius, Melchior Vulpius, Johannes Jeep, Johannes Alexander Brassicanus u. Johann Ulrich Steigleder). Hi(t)zler verschaffte durch seine Kompositionen auch J. V. Andreae Melodien zu seinen vierstimmigen Liedern, welche aber 1634 zu Calw verbrannten.

8 Michael Tham, Johannes Geletzky (Jan Jelecký) u. Petrus Herbertus Fulnecensis (Petr Herbert): Kirchengeseng darinnen die Heubtartickel des Christlichen glaubens kurtz gefasst vnd ausgeleget sind: jtzt vom newen durchsehen/ gemehret/ vnd Der Rö. Kei. Maiestat/ in vnterthenigster demut zugeschrieben. ([Ivančice, bei Brünn]: Druckerei der Böhmischen Brüder] 1566. HAB: 49.3 Tl; Ks. Maximilian II. gewidmet. HAB: 49.3 Tl. Im Anhang: GEistliche Lieder/ dere etliche von alters her in der Kirchen eintrechtiglich gebraucht/ und etliche zu vnser zeit/ von erleuchteten/ fromen Christen vnd Gottseligen Lerern new zugericht sind/ nach ordnung der jarzeit. Umfang: [8], 291, LXXVIII, [4] Bl., mit Noten u. einem Holzschnitt-Porträt (Martin Luther); 8°.

9 Justus Georg Schottelius (FG 397), der bekannte Philologe und Dichter am Hof zu Wolfenbüttel. „Fürbindig" wie „ausbündig" im Sinne von hervor-, herausragend. *Stieler*, 156: „Fürbündig/ idem, qvod ausbündig/ praestans, egregius."

10 Zu Friedrich Greiff (1601–1668), Tübinger (Bibel-)Dichter, Übersetzer, Apotheker, Erfinder und Mediziner, vgl. 431123 u. Beilagen.

460825

Martinus Milagius an den Leser seines *Singenden Jesaia*

Die alle ordentlichen Geschäftsabläufe vereitelnden Kriegsläufte haben Martinus Milagius (FG 315) die Zeit eingeräumt, sich mit der poetischen Bibelparaphrase des Buchs Jesaja zu befassen. Den Jesaja wählte er nicht allein aus thematischen Gründen („Schwerter zu Pflugscharen"), sondern auch weil sich der sprachgewaltige Prophet selbst als Lieddichter betätigt habe. Das vorliegende Buch soll sowohl der eigenen Erbauung als auch der des Lesers dienen und nicht zuletzt als Beitrag zur deutschen Spracharbeit der Fruchtbringenden Gesellschaft gelesen werden, eine Arbeit, die er lange schuldig geblieben sei. — Als Vorlage für die Dichtung diente die Bibelübertragung Luthers, dessen Deutsch als besonders rein und zierlich einzuschätzen sei und dessen Wortwahl wie auch Kapitelgliederung Milagius beizubehalten suchte. Zur Ausräumung sprachlicher und inhaltlicher Unklarheiten habe er allerdings auch die lateinische Bibel von Immanuel Tremellius und Franciscus Junius d. Ä. herangezogen sowie die niederl. (Staaten-)Bibel und die (mit Erläuterungen und Neuübersetzungen schwer verständlicher oder falsch wiedergegebener Stellen versehene) Ausgabe der Luther-Bibel von Paulus Tossanus. Jeder Bibelvers wurde in eine Strophe umgedichtet, von einigen wenigen Ausnahmen abgesehen, wo die Korrespondenz von Vers und Strophe auseinandertritt. Die Melodien folgen nach dem Prinzip der Ähnlichkeit der Inhalte den Lobwasserschen Psalmen-Melodien. Dabei hat Milagius tunlichst darauf geachtet, ein allgemeinverständliches Werk zu verfassen, das sich der reinen deutschen Sprache befleißige, und deshalb ungewöhnliche neue Regeln der Sprachgelehrten außer acht gelassen. — Da er von seinen Amtsgeschäften zu stark eingenommen war, um eigene Nachforschungen anzustellen, habe er sich auf die Spracharbeit seiner Mitgesellschafter und der anderer Gelehrter gestützt, die auf Veranlassung F. Ludwigs durchgeführt worden sei. Durch diese Arbeit sei der Wunsch vieler Gelehrter wie auch der seines einstigen Bremer Lehrers Matthias Martinius erfüllt worden, sowohl die Muttersprache als auch das Vaterland zu fördern. Milagius nennt als Vorbilder Tobias Hübner (FG. 25. Der Nutzbare), Diederich v. dem Werder (FG 31. Der Vielgekörnte), Martin Opitz (FG 200. Der Gekrönte), Christian Gueintz (FG 361. Der Ordnende), Georg Philipp Harsdörffer (FG 368. Der Spielende), Justus Georg Schottelius (FG 397. Der Suchende), Augustus Buchner (FG 362), Philipp v. Zesen (FG 521. 1648), Johann Rist (FG 467. 1647) und Christian Brehme. Besonders Rists *Himmlische Lieder* (von 1641/42), deren zweiten Teil er erst unlängst in einem Osnabrücker Buchladen fand, haben ihn sehr angeregt. — Milagius schließt seine Vorrede mit der Aufzählung einiger sprachlicher und metrischer Regeln, die ihm als Richtschnur für seine Dichtung dienten. *Zur Metrik und Syntax:* Hinsichtlich der syntaktischen Gliederung der Verse postuliert Milagius eine Orientierung an der natürlichen Wortreihenfolge, wie sie in der ungebundenen Rede üblich sei. Vor Änderungen der regulären Wortfolge müsse man sich hüten: Besonders die Nachstellung von Adverbien sei zu vermeiden wie auch die Unart das Präfix von trennbaren Verben zu separieren und in eine irreguläre Wortfolge zu zwingen (**Er ist gelanget an*). Das Lateinische genieße in der gebundenen Rede mehr Freiheiten als das Deutsche, das eine gleichmäßige Wortfolge erfordere. Die Eigenheit der deutschen Sprache müsse gewahrt bleiben. — *Zur Reimfindung:* Rührende Reime (bei denen nicht nur der letzte Vokal, sondern auch der vorhergehende Konsonant der betonten Reimsilbe übereinstimmen) sollen vermieden werden. Ihm sei selbst der Fehler unterlaufen *bist* auf *gebüßt* zu reimen, ein Lapsus, für den Milagius eine Korrektur anbietet. Mitunter sei dergleichen jedoch nicht zu vermeiden gewesen wie im Falle von *Hiskia* und *Hilkia*. In diesem Zusammenhang sollte das Augenmerk auch auf die unterschiedlichen Qualitäten der Vokale gelenkt werden. Zu unterscheiden seien namentlich die offenen und geschlossenen („weiten und engen") Vokale, wie sie sich bspw. in *Fuß* und *Fluß* fänden. Doch Vorsicht vor einer allzu rigiden Regelhörigkeit! Aus stofflichen Gründen sei es gerade bei Übersetzungen kaum zu vermeiden, gelegentlich gegen derartige Regeln zu verstoßen. Der deutschen Dichtung sollte überhaupt kein allzu „enger zwang" auferlegt werden, drohe sie doch ansonsten „unfähig/ undeutsch/ unvernemlich" zu werden, was freilich keine Lizenz zu prosodischem Wildwuchs sei. Der Dichter solle der flüssigen, kräftigen Natur der deutschen Sprache folgen, die Worte sollten zwanglos aus der Feder strömen. — *Zu Synkope und Apokope:* Weil das (daktylische) Wort *Heiliger* häufig verwendet werden mußte, sich dem alternierenden Versschema aber nicht fügt, habe Milagius sich derselben Freiheit bedient wie Opitz und es zu *Heilger* synkopiert. Hierbei handelt es sich um den legitimen Ausnahmefall, ein dreisilbiges Wort für Verse aus Jamben und Trochäen passend zu machen. In Sachen e-Apokope hielt sich Milagius an die folgenden Regeln: Vor einem Wort mit vokalischem oder h-Anlaut muß bzw. kann es elidiert werden. Darüber hinaus sei die Elision zulässig, wenn dadurch zwei gleichlautende Konsonanten aufeinandertreffen. Als gleichlautend, spezifiziert Milagius, seien (neben identischen Konsonanten) die Konsonantenpaare d/t, b/p, g/k und die Trias tz/ts/s zu betrachten. Schließlich dürfe auch das auslautende E am Ende einer Strophe in jedem Fall apokopiert werden, auch wenn durch das erste Wort der folgenden Strophe keine der bisherigen Regeln greife. — *Zu sprachlichen Stil- und grammatischen Fragen:* Nicht nur im Ausdruck, sondern auch in der Rechtschreibung habe Milagius sich an seinen Vorbildern, nicht zuletzt an Luther orientiert. Er teile ferner die Auffassung der Grammatiker, daß sowohl im Dativ als auch im Ablativ (d. h. in Präpositionalgefügen, die den Dativ regieren) das auslautende E nicht entfallen dürfe, wie dies in der gesprochenen Sprache häufig zu geschehen pflege. Er habe sich darum in seinen Versen bemüht, in solchen Fällen Wörter mit vokalischem oder gleichlautendem konsonantischen Anlaut folgen zu lassen (um eine reguläre Elision zu ermöglichen und sich so der gesprochenen Sprache anzunähern). Zu guter Letzt erinnert er daran, daß Umschreibungen einfacher Verben mit *tun* (*er tat das sagen*) nicht dem reinen Deutsch entsprächen und darum zu vermeiden seien.

Q *Milagius: Singender Jesaia (1646)*, Bl.)(v r – [)(xi] v. HAB: Lo 5456. — Dig. UB Göttingen: 8 P GERM II, 5661.

A *Fehlt.*

Vorrede.
Christlicher lieber Leser/
WAs für ursachen mich zur übersetzung dieses Propheten auf solche masse und weise veranlasset/ davō könte ich viel melden. Allein gleich wie es unnöhtig ist/ dieselben alle zuerzehlen: Also wil ich gleichwol etliche auf das kürtzeste berühr̄e.

Vnd zwar es mag der Prophete **Jesaia** seinen Vrsprung aus Königs **Davids** Nachkommen haben oder nicht: wie jhn dan etliche der gelährten mit den Jäden für des Königs **Amaziæ** Enckel halten/ und zu den ende unter andern das erste sprüchlein des 5. Cap. anziehen; So ist doch dieses aus der H. Schrift bekand/ das er im volcke Gottes/ auch bey den königen ein ansehnlicher und fürtrefflicher Lehrer gewesen. Jn der art zureden wird jhn ein jeder hoch und gewaltig; in dem Geiste aber/ der kraft und dem nachdrücke noch viel höher und gewaltiger befinden. Was desselben fleissige betrachtung wircken kan/ ist ob dem exempel des Kämmerers der Königin Candaces aus dem Morenlande [)(v v] abzunemen.[1] Wie helle und deutlich er von zukünftigen dingen/ Jnsonderheit von des Messiæ empfängnüsse/ Geburt/ Tauffe/ dreifachen Amte/ Predigten/ Wunderwercken/ Zustande/ leiden/ sterben/ aufferstehung und himmelfart/ und von denen hiedurch erworbenen Wolthaten/ von der Christlichen Kirche/ dem jungsten gericht/ ewigen Leben und der verdamnüs rede/ davon lesset man alle Gottsfürchtige/ fürnemlich die jenige urtheilen/ die in geistlichen sachen vor anderen geschärfte und hoch begabte sinne haben/ und jhnen deswegen für einen Evangelisten des alten Testaments halten.

Mir kam der prophet gleich wieder an die hand/ als das land mit zweyen mächtigen krieges heeren überschwemmet/ zwar mit angst/ jammer und gefahr angefüllet/ sonsten aber an allen zeitlichen nothwendigkeiten entblösset ward.[2]

Vnd weil Gott aus gerechten heiligen ursachen abermals eine solche beschwerliche feyer ausgeruffen/ uñ alle ordentliche verrichtung nied*er* geleget waren/ so konte ich die zeit desto freyer an diesen prophetē anwendē. Jch that es auch gerne/ weil aus demselbē die ware ursachen des verhengten übels/ dabenebest aber auch die rechte unfeilbare ret-[)(vi r]tungs mittel konten erlernet werden. Vber dis hatte ich bey der wehrten hochlöblichen fruchtbringenden geselschaft/ als ein unwürdiges/ doch verbundenes Mitglied derselben/ meine lengst- hinterstellige schuldigkeit einmahl abzulegen und darauf billich zu gedencken/ daß nicht nur das recht der Deutschen sprache/ sondern auch die erbauung meiner selbst und anderer hierdurch möchte befordert werden.

Schließlich war auch auß der Bibel ein solcher Göttlicher lehrer zu erwehlen/ der zu der Poesie lust gehabt/ und besage seines eigenen buchs im singen sich geübet;[3] meines wissens aber auf diese art noch zur zeit nie gesungen hat: Ausser was auß demselben/ und benantlich dem 26 und 38. cap. Herr Johann Ristius für dieser zeit wol gefertiget/ so ich aber nur vor wenig wochen/ nach lenst *[sic]* beschlossener arbeit unter seinen Biblischen geistreichen liedern in dē zweyten zehen zur hand bekomen und gesehen habe[.][4] Wie die arbeit gerahten sein mag/ davon lasse ich billig andere urtheilen. Gleichwol liegt mir ob/ mit wenigem zu bedeuten/ was ich darunter bey der sache selbst/ und der deutschen sprache halber in acht genommen habe. [)(vi v]

Was die sache selbst betrift/ habe ich mich an Herrn Lutheri verdolmetschung am meisten gehalten und bin bey seiner eintheilung der Capiteln allerdinges verblieben/ weil beydes am besten bekandt/ und desto angenemer ist. Wan aber die grundsprache/ aufn bericht der sprachkündigen/ ein anders erfordert/ od*er* auch an dunckeln orten der rechte verstand herbey zu bringē gewesen/ habe ich mich nach anderen Bibeln und deroselben merckungen insonderheit auch des Tremellii und Junii Lateinischer/ des Tossani aber und der Niederländer deutschen Bibel geachtet.[5] Die worte selbst habe ich/ so viel nur müglich/ behaltē/ und bedencken gehabt/ den heiligen Propheten mit einigem götzennamen zu beschmitzen/ derowegen keiner heidnischen götzen über die jenige/ so der Prophete selbst einführet/ gedencken wollen.

Aus jedem Sprüchlein ist ein Gesetze gemacht: Jedoch hat es wegen enge der reime und weitläuftigkeit der sprüchlein dabey nit allezeit verbleiben können: Wie dan die neun örter/ da es anders sein müssen/ unter den gesängen benennet zufinden seind.[6] [)(vij r]

Bey eintheilung der Gesänge ist so viel müglich auf den unterschiedenen inhalt jedes Capitels/ und bey erwehlung der melodeyen mehrern theils auf einige gleichförmigkeit der materie zwischen den Psalmen und unserm Propheten gesehen worden: Gleichwol alles nach der gemeinen art; und nit/ wie es der gelehrten sinnreiche erwegung erfordert: Dan ich habe auf gemeine leute auch zu sehen gehabt. Daß aber ein jedes Capitel in den abgetheilten gesängen/ nicht eine durchgehende gleichstimmende melodey/ sondern jeder gesang/ seine absonderliche bekommen/ dasselbe wird verhoffentlich keiner verantwortung bedürffen.

Den inhalt jedes gesanges habe nicht ich/ sondern es hat jhn ein wolgeübter Diener am worte Gottes in einer fürnemen Reichsstatt/ einer von meinen guten freunden/ auf mein bitten aufgesetzet/ deme der guthertzige Leser davor nicht weniger/ als ich gethan habe/ gerne dancken wird.[7]

Was dan die sprache anreichet/ bezeuge ich hiemit offentlich/ daß ich mich lieber nach anderen hierunter zu richten begehre/ als daß ich gemeinet sein solte/ hiedurch den baßverständigen etwas für zu schreiben. Dan ob ich [)(vij v] gleich zu der reinen deutschen sprache mit anderen gleichmessige liebe trage/ so haben mir doch meine wichtige geschäfte die zeit nicht gegönnet/ so zu einer rechten nachforschung nöhtig ist. Es haben sich nun auf des **Nehrenden**[8] veranlassung viel fürneme Geselschafter hierinnen bemühet/ und üm jhre angeborene Muttersprache und das liebe vaterland/ mit jhrem eigenen ruhme und des gemeinen nutzens beforderung wol verdient gemacht/ und dasselbe bißhero geleistet/ was hie bevorn viel hohe personen und fürnehme hochgelährte Männer/ und darunter auch mein in Gott ruhender hochgeehrter lieber Lehrgebieter Herr **Matthias Martinius**[9]/ weiland Regente und Lehrer der heiligen Schrift in der hohen Schule zu Bremen/ ein hochbegabter und erfahrener Mann/ wie in allen/ also auch in der Deutschen sprache und deroselben liebhaber/ gewünschet. Vnter denselben wird billich **des Nutzbaren**[10]/ **Vielgekrönten**[11] *[sic]*/ **Gekrönten**[12]/ **Ordenden**[13]/ **Spielenden**[14] und **Suchenden**[15] auch an diesem orte/ mit sonderbarem dancke vor jhre sorgfalt und mühe/ gedacht. Vnd wer wil zweiflen/ daß nicht der zweite und die drey letztere: (dan der erste und dritte haben die [)(viij r] zeitligkeit verlassen) jhres wolvermögens und sonderbaren fleisses halber noch ein grosses bey den sachen thun können und werden/ bevorab/ weil es jhnen eines theils an der löblichen begierde/ anderer theils aber an sonderbarer gnad und anmanung hoher Fürstl. Personen nicht ermangelt? Auch ausser solchen fruchtbringenden geselschaft hat herr Buchner[16]/ herr Cæsius[17]/ herr Rist/ herr Bremer[18] nebst anderen die deutsche sprache wol befördert/ und habe ich mich insonderheit über den himlischen liedern des herrn Ristens/ so ich für wenig tagen in den buchladē zu Oßnabrügge gefunden/ recht erfreut/ Es wird aber derselbe üm der gemeinen begierde willen zu der reinē Deutschen sprache mir verzeihn/ daß ich für triumph-lieder lieber Sieges-lieder setzen würde/ dan jenes ist nicht Deutsch/ und wird durch das wort Siegs-pracht recht erstattet.[19] Jrre ich darinnen/ wil ich mich gerne auf freundliche weisung enderen.

Dieses muß ich dannoch vor mich und meist zu meiner entschuldigung berichten/ daß ich mich nach besser *[sic]* müglichkeit befliessen habe/ so wol in der sprache selbst/ als deroselben rechtschreibung den jenigen nach zu ge-[)(viij v]hen/ die sie am rein- und zierlichsten reden/ und am besten schreiben: Dahin dan des Herren Lutheri verdolmetschung mit allem fuge gerechnet werden sol und kan.

Das wort **Heiliger** kommet in diesem propheten ofte für/ ist auch üm des dabey befindlichen nachdrücks willen nicht wol durch ein ander wort zuerstatten gewesen; weil es aber in dē Jambischen und Trochaischen bey uns deutschen ohne einen übelklang nicht stehen kan/ sintemal alle **Dactyli,** wie man in dē schulen redet/ so wol in den Jambischen als Trochaischē (die namē ausgeschlossen) zuvermeiden seind/[20] So habe ich mich mit andern/ sonderlich auch dem **Gekrönten** d*er* freyheit gebraucht/ und dafür **Heilger** gesetzet.[21] Man hat aber diese freyheit/ oder viel mehr diese nothwendigkeit nicht alsbald auf eine nachfolge mit anderen wörtern zuziehen.

Vnd ob wol die deutsche Reimkunst dessen vor diesem/ und insonderheit bey den alten/ nicht gewohnet/ auch die Lateinische und Griechische art einen leichtlich irre machen kan; So habe ich mir doch lassen angelegen sein/ daß die gebundene rede mit der ungebundenen in der ordnung und dem lauffe der wörter übereinstimmen/ und die unartige/ übelklingende [)(ix r] versteck- und verrückung der wörter vermitten werden möchte. Aber ich bekenne gerne dabey/ daß die tief-eingesessene gewohnheit bey uns Deutschen auch einen wachenden beschleichen und einschläffern kan. Jnsonderheit in den beywörtern (**adverbiis**) welche ofte heimlich nachtreten/ da sie doch vorher gehen solten. Dan wiederum in den zusammen-setzungen (**compositionibus**) da offtmahls das vorwort (**propositio**) zur ungebühr nachschleicht: als/ **er ist gelanget an/** für. **er ist angelanget.** Jngleichen: **Daß Gott dir wohnet bey**: für/ **Daß Gott dir beywohnet**. Vnd das wird vermutlich/ auch mir unvermerckt widerfahren sein/ ob ich mich wol dafür hüten wollen.[22]

Bey den endungen ist es an jhme selbst richtig/ daß die gäntzliche gleichheit keine stat findet: als/ **Gerechtigkeit/ Barmhertzigkeit. Bracht'/ Pracht. elenden/ lenden. tücke/ dicke. deuten/ teuten. hält/ held. Mach'/ gemach:** und in dergleichen mehren. Aber in den namen habe ich es an zweenen orten/ meines behalts/ nicht vermeiden können/ als **Hißkia/ Hilkia/** *etc*.[23] Vnd ist endlich/ nach dem mir ein gut theil des gefertigten Druckes zur hand gekommen/ von [)(ix v] mir da erst wargenommen worden/ daß in des 14. cap. 1. gesange v. 8. Jch gesetzet habe in dem 2. reime/ bist/ und in dem letzten gebüßt/ welches sich mit meinen vorher gesetzten gedancken nicht vergleichen lesset/ dahero es dann also zu enderen ist:

Es wird nicht mehr gethan/ was dir gelüst.[24] Sonsten ist ein grosser unterscheid in der ausrede zwischen den weiten und engen selb lautendē (**Vocalibus**), Als: **sprache/ sache. Lassen/ faßen. schweben/ heben. pflegē Legen. jhn/ sinn. gebiet'/ trit. noht/ Gott. tod/ spot. fus/ flus. grus/ gus.**[25] Doch seind solche selb lautende bishero ohne bedencken vermenget/ und in den endungen gegen einander gebrauchet worden. Jch habe mich dafür/ so viel ich immer thun können/ gehütet; Es hat aber nicht allemal verhütet werden mügen. Dan wie der unterscheid an jhme selbst richtig/ und endlich in dem meistē gehalten werden kan/ zumal/ wan einer etwas von neuem macht/ und die enderung allzeit seiner freyen wilkühr unterworfen bleibet/ oder wan man es auch mit wenigen endungen zuthun hat: Also scheinet es alsdan fast unmüglich zu sein/ wan etwas übergesetzet wird/ und man an eines andern mei[)(x r]nung gebunden ist/ oder wan man auch mehr/ als zwo/ endungen/ und zwar ofte nach ein ander zusamen bringen mus:[26] Da dan das eintzige wort **Herr** einē jeden dessen leichtlich überzeugen kan. Jch mus auch bey mir anstehn/ ob darüm viel wolklingende nachdrückliche reime sollen auf die seite gesetzet/ und so gar ein enger zwang/ ohne einige bedingung/ der deutschen Poesie aufgeburdet werden. Meine meinung ist jederzeit die gewesen/ und sie ist es auch noch/ daß wir deutschen uns fürzusehen haben/ damit die deutsche sprache durch einen solchen und anderē gar zu genauen zwang und übermessige scharffe grübelung der poesie nicht unfähig/ undeutsch/ unvernemlich/ und ins gemein widrig gemacht werde. Dan diese sprache ist insonderheit flüssig/ und nit eingeschrencket; Sie hat jhre eigene freye/ doch rechtmessige/ wolklingende und vielgeltende art/ und kan sich zur dienstbarkeit der übermessigen gesetze nicht wol verstehen/ sondern sie wird dadurch von jhrer angestamten kraft und wichtigkeit fast verdrungen. Dahero sie dan bey dem übersetzen mercklich verstellet/ und jhr selbst gantz unähnlich wird/ wan man sich mehr nach der sprache/ aus welcher [)(x v] die übersetzung geschicht/ als nach der art und eigenschaft der deutschen sprache achten wolte. Es wird auch in einiger sprache so bald nicht/ als in der deutschen/ zumal bey der Poesie abzumercken sein/ wan ein wort einen nicht freywillig an die hand und in die feder gegangē/ sondern dazu genötiget worden ist. Jedoch ist sie auch so unbändig nicht/ daß sie nicht jhre gesetze und schrancken leiden solte. Vnd gehet sie in dem zwange der lateinischē weit vor/ dz sie nemlich in gebunder rede eine gleichmessige ordnung der wörter habē wil/ und keine verruckung duldet: da hingegen die Lateinischen Poeten in diesem fall viel mehr freyheit bekommen: eines mehren für dismal zugeschweigen.[27] Dan hierüber können andere baßverstendige/ und insonderheit die wehrte Mitgeselschafter/ derer ich zuvor albereits mit obligender gebühr und gehörigen ruhme gedacht/ zu rahte gezogen werden.

Dieses hab ich noch/ sonderlich wegen der unerfahrenen/ zuvermelden/ daß bey abschneid- oder verbeissung des selblautenden E- in der deutschen Poesie noch etwas in acht zunemen sein wolle.[28] Bekand ist es/ daß in der deutschen sprache das E. allein bisweilen mus/ bisweilen mag verbissen oder ausge-[a][)(xi r] laßen werden. Es mus solches geschehen/ wan auf das E. ein anderer selblautender (**vocalis**) folgt. Es mag dasselbe E. ausgelassen werden oder nicht/ wan ein H. oder ein gleichstimmender mitlautender (**consonans**) hernach folgt: welches dan auch zwischen D. und T. ingleichen tz/ als ts/ zwischen b. und p. g. und k. tz. als ts und. s. nachgegeben wird. So ist auch erlaubet im ende des gesetzes das E. abzuschneiden/ wan schon kein selblautender oder auch kein gleichstimmender mitlautender im anfange des anderen gesetzes folget. Allein wir deutschen habē viel wörter/ und ist bey vielen eingeführet/ daß wir das E. auch in der ungebundenen rede gar nicht/ oder doch wenig aussprechen/ Als: **im zorn/ dem Gott/ dem heil/ dem theil[/] im fürstenthum/ dem ruhm/** und in anderen mehren: da es doch sonsten nach der sprach-lehre/ und nach der Nem-endung/ (dem **casu ablativo**) und der geb-endung (dem **casu dativo**) besser stunde: **im zorne/ dem Gotte/ dem heile/ dem theile/ im fürstenthüme/ dem ruhme/** und dergleichen. Mich wil hierbey bedüncken/ daß man diese letztere meinung insonderheit in den reimen zubehalten habe/ und derowegen habe [)(xi v] ich nach solchen und dergleichen wörtern allzeit einen selblautendē oder gleichstim̄enden mitlautenden gesetzet:[29] und schlieslich mich fur der art zureden/ **er that das sagen[/] er that sich zu uns nahen** *etc.* mit fleisse gehütet: dan sie hat in der reinen Deutschen sprache keinen grund.[30]

Mein meister und fürnemster wunsch ist dieser/ dz der hochlöblichen fruchtbringenden Geselschaft und anderen rühmlichen liebhabern der Deutschen sprache diese abgelegte schuldigkeit gefallen/ zuforderst aber der allerhöchste durch den Deutsch-singendē Esaiam hertzlich gepriesen/ ein jedes frommes hertz mit mir hierdurch zu mehrer andacht erwecket/ und andre löbliche gemüter zur nachfolge in dergleichen erbaulichen Biblischen materien veranlasset werden mügen. Der Christliche leser gehabe sich wol! gegeben am 25. tage des Augustmonats Jm jahre 1646.

I

Erinnerungen Martinus Milagius' zur Orthographie

Q *Milagius: Singender Jesaia (1646)*, Bl. [)()(7–8]. HAB: Lo 5456. — Dig. UB Göttingen: 8 P GERM II, 5661.

Nothwendige Erinnerung

I. Für ein U soll kein V. im anfange/ mittel oder ende des worts geschrieben werden/ dan ein deutscher schreibet/ wie er redet: als **Usia/ Und/ Ursach** *etc.* nicht aber/ **Vsia/ Vnd/ Vrsach**.[1]

II. Au und Eu wird in **trauen/ euer/ neue/ treue/** besser geschrieben/ auch vernemlicher und lieblicher ausgesprochen/ als Aw und Ew.[2]

III. **Must du/ bist du/ hast du** *etc.* seind zwey wörter/ und derowegen billig auch also zu schreiben: Nicht aber **mustu/ bistu/ hastu**.[3]

IV. Ein gedoppelter mitlautender (consonans) wird nicht geschrieben/ er werde dan 1. auch außgesprochen: oder wan er 2. zwar in dem ersten falle (casu) nicht/ doch aber in den folgenden außgeredet wird: oder wan er 3. einen unterscheid unter den wörtern machet.[4]

Erstes Exempel.
Es muß geschrieben werden.

Auf/ fremde/ haus/ kraft/ brot/ tod/ todes/ preis/ gold/ goldschmied/ heidenschaft/ künftig/ wil/ sol/ und also ferner. [)()([7] v]

Zweytes Exempel.

Tritt trittes/ spott spottes/ mann mannes/ Zimmermann/ jedermann/ fuß/ grimm/ schlimm/ matt/ satt/ riß/ gewiß/ loß loses/ fluß/ naß/ gebott/ todt die todte.

Drittes Exempel.

Muß/ müssen/ zum unterscheide zwischē **mus**/ des muses: **Laßt** vom lassen und **last**/ die bürde: **haßt** vom haßen/ und **hast** vom haben: **Reißt** vom reißen/ und **reist** vom reisen: **Hallt** vom hallen/ und **halt** vom halten: **schafft** vom schaffen/ und **schaft** des schaftes: **schallt** vom schallen/ und **schalt** vom schelten: **frißt** vom fressen/ und **frist** vom fristen: **mißt** vom missen/ entpehren/ oder auch vom messen/ und **mist**/ des mistes. *etc.* Und wolte ich fast denen beystimmen/ welche den doppelten mitlautendē/ ob er zwar nicht außgesprochen wird/ dannoch im schreiben behalten/ so oft ein wort zusammen gezogen wird/ damit solches desto besser angemercket werden könne/ als: **fellt/** fellet/ **stellt/** stellet/ **rafft/** raffet/ **findt/** findet/ **bindt/** bindet.

Fehler

So den Leser irre machen/ nnd[a] den verstand verhindern können. [)()(8 r]

Gemeine.

I. An unterschiedenen orten seind die strich- und pünctlein/ so entweder die rede unterscheidē/ (/;:.) oder aus zweyē wörtern eins machen/ (-) Jngleichen die doppelten strichlein/ oder auch das e. über a. o. u. ohne noht gesetzet/ oder außgelassen/ welches der Leser unbeschwert in acht nemen wolle. Jnsonderheit ist am 66. bl. am ende des 1. gesetzes das pünctlein abzuthun/ und ein strichlein zusetzen/ weil die letztere reime mit dem 2. ges[e]tze verbunden seind.[5]

II. Das gewöhnliche/ jedoch eben nicht nötige zeichen/ wan das e verbissen wird/ (') ist nicht allzeit zu finden/ bißweilen aber auch ohne ursach gesetzet: Gleichwol kan es/ zumahl die anfahende[6]/ leichtlich verleiten.

III. Die merckzeichen/ wan **säen/ see/ seen/ knien/ knie/** eine oder zwo sylben machen/ (˜) seind mehrentheils außgelassen/ welches aber das maß des reimes baldt zeigen wird.[7] Hiebey ist dieses noch zu berichten/ daß der name **Eliakim** am 148. bl. 20. v. 3. reim/ am 238. bl. 3. v. 2. r. und 244. bl. 12. v. 2. r./ nach der art bey den Lateinischen/ nur zwo sylben hat/ weil das i. wie ein j. außgesprochen werden muß.[8] [)()(8 v]

Besondere Fehler.

1. Wo in den Noten geirret ist/ als 16.1.2. it. 20.1.8. it. 73.1.2./ dasselbe wolle ein jeder auß den melodeyen des Lobwassers endern.[9]

2. An unterschiedenen orten stehet/ **jetz/ Vatter/ tretten/ zertretten/ quael/** oder **quaal** *etc.* so aber **jezt/ Vater/ treten/ zertreten/ quahl** heissen soll.

3. Was weiter folget/ bestehet mehrentheils auf einer geringen enderung/ hinzusetzung/ oder abnehmung eines eintzigen buchstabens/ und wird es sich bey überlesung des reimes bald geben/ an welchem orte die enderung geschehen sol/ ist auch in den Druckfehlern[10] mehrentheils erinnert.

II

Milagius' Vorrede zum Anhang seines *Singenden Jesaja*

Q *Milagius: Singender Jesaia (1646)*, 465f. HAB: Lo 5456. — Dig. UB Göttingen: 8 P GERM II, 5661.

Vorrede.
Christlicher lieber Leser/

JCh habe für gut angesehen/ dem singenden Jesaiæ etliche Geist- und trostreiche Lieder beyzufügen/ und hiedurch meiner und anderer frommen Christen andacht zu dienē. Die neue seind von fürnemen personen geist- und weltlichen standes gemacht/ und ist daran fast nichts/ oder doch gar ein geringes geendert/ was nemlich der deutschen Reimkunst entgegen geschienen. Die alten meistentheils hat eine hohe person verbessert/ Vnd gleich wie derselben beste lust ist/ mit und bey Jhren schweren Regierungs-sachen sich in Geistlichen reimen und in übersetzung nützlicher und [466] erbaulicher schrifften auß dem Lateinischen/ Frantzösischen und Jtalianischen zu üben/ und hiedurch die reine deutsche sprache/ wie sie fast alleine das löbliche werck angefangen/ je lenger je mehr außzuschmücken: Also hat hochgemelte person alle gesänge nach jetziger art gestaltet/ und dero verbesserung albereits zu wercke gerichtet. Jch habe daraus nur etliche genom̄en/ und kömmet mir daran gar wenig zu. Zu allen gehöret ein eigen buch/ wie ich dan verneme/ dz man auch an einem andern hohen orte damit ümgehet. Diese wenige können einem jeden entwerffen/ wie leichtlich der sprache zu helffen sey: Gleichwol kan es ohne zwang nicht wol abgehen/ weil das alte/ wo nicht gantz/ doch mehrem theils billich zu behalten ist. Die melodeyen seind darüm dabey gedruckt/ weil die Lieder an allen orthen entweder gar nicht/ oder doch nicht auf solche weise gesungen werdē. Jn der Litaney/ **Gott Vater Herr im himmelreich/** solte zwar auff das wort (himmelreich/) ein selblautender folgen/ dan es heisset eigentlich: **im himmelreiche;**[1] Aber es ist üm gewisser ursachen willen also gelassen worden. Der Christliche Leser wolle alles im besten vermercken/ und gehabe sich durch Gottes gnade wol!

III

Widmung Martinus Milagius' an die Landgräfin Amalia Elisabeth von Hessen-Kassel

Q *Milagius: Singender Jesaia (1646)*, Bl.)(ij r –)(iij v. HAB: Lo 5456. — Dig. UB Göttingen: 8 P GERM II, 5661.

An
Die Durchleuchtige/ Hochgeborne
Fürstin und Frau/
Frau Amalie Elisabeth/
Landgräfin zu Hessen/ Geborne
Gräfin zu Catzenelnbogen/ Dietz/
Zigenhain und Nidda. *etc.*
Wittib/ Vormundin und Re-
gentin. *etc.*
Seine gnädige Fürstin und Frau.

EDle **Fürstin** vom geblüte/
Eures Standes grosser **ruhm**/
Fromme **Fürstin** vom gemüte/
Jn der **Hessen** Fürstenthum'
Eine treue **Pflegerinn**/
Hochbegabet an dem Sinn':
Nun Jhr weiset unsern zeiten/
Wie man sol die **Noth** bestreiten.)(ij v]

Als das Schiff ward ümgetrieben/
Durch der **Wellen** wüste flut/
Als der *STEUER-HERR* geblieben/
Vnd mit Jhm fast aller muth/
Kontet Jhr durch *GOTT* allein
Eine deutsche **Heldin** sein/
Vnd beweisen unsern zeiten/
Daß man **Wasser** kan bestreiten.

Wie das **donnern/ blitzē/ breñen**
Sich mit gleicher macht verbandt/
Auf *EVCH* grimmig loß zu rennen/
Vnd sich mancher abgewandt/
Habet Jhr beständigkeit
Spüren lassen in dem leid'/
Vnd bewiesen unsern zeiten
Wie man **Feuer** kan bestreiten.

Wan die **Sorgen** Euch beschweret/
Wie der **Erden** bürde drückt/
Ward erquickung Euch bescheret/
Vnd es hat Euch so geglückt/

460825 Martinus Milagius

    Daß Jhr durch des *HERREN* macht [)(iij r]
    Euren fürsatz fort gebracht:
    Jhr bewieset unsern zeiten/
    Daß die *ERDE* zu bestreiten.

    Ja Jhr habet auch erfahren/
    Was das wol für tage sind/
    Als die Menschen fertig waren/
    So zu brausen/ wie der *WIND*/
    Als es zu dem ween kam/
    Vnd die kraft den abschied nam:
    Jhr bewießt doch unsern zeiten/
    Daß der *WIND* sey zu bestreiten.

    Dan jhr hattet vom **Propheten**/
    Von dem *HERREN* selbst gefaßt/
    Daß in allen solchen nöhten/
    Da der stärckste Held erblaßt/
    Gott der HErr die mittel findt/
    Wasser/ Feuer/ Erde/ Wind/
    Noch zu diesen unsern zeiten
    Durch ein Wörtlein zu bestreiten. [)(iij v]

    Dies' und andre schöne lehren
    Fürgebracht durch **Amos Sohn**/[a]
    Könnet Jhr jetzt singen hören
    Jn bekandter Psalme thon'.
    Jhr/ so Euch dies Buch behagt/
    (Wie ich bitt') und waß es sagt/
    Werdet mehr und mehr bestreiten
    Alle widerwertigkeiten.

          Das singet und wünschet in
          unterthänigkeit
              Der Mindernde.

IV

Fürst Ludwig an Martinus Milagius

Q HM Köthen: V S 544, Bl. 73rv, v leer; eigenh.

A *Fehlt.*

An den Mindernden
Uber den in reine Reimgesänge gesetzten
Jesaiam.

Sehr nützlich fallen uns die Lehren der Propheten,
Wie Jesaias giebt ein helles klares Liecht
    Von Christi reich und amt, ja einen unterricht
Das zu ihm in der not wir künlich mögen tretten,
Und ihn als unser heil anflehen mit gebeten
    Dan will' er wenden nicht von uns sein angesicht,
    Viel mehr wan sunde, fleisch, tod, teuffel an uns ficht,
Will' er aus solcher angst durch seinen geist uns retten.
    Da Jesaias nun ist künstlich mit gemacht,
    Der Christenheit zu trost in Reime rein gebracht.
Der Mindernd' hats gethan, und hat dadurch vermehret
    Der deutschen sprache Ruhm, er hat ihn wol gesetzt,
    Die ungezwungen' art den leser hoch ergetzt.
Dafür er billig wird mit Lobe stets geehret

        Von dem ältesten der fruchtbringenden Geselschaft.

V

460421

Fürst Ludwig an Martinus Milagius

Q *Milagius: Singender Jesaia (1646)*, Bl.)(iij v –)(iv r. HAB: Lo 5456. — Dig. UB Göttingen: 8 P GERM II, 5661. — Hsl. Überlieferung (zit. als *SL*) von Schreiberh.: HM Köthen: V S 544, Bl. 72rv, v leer; Schreiberh.; Datierung von F. Ludwigs H.

A *Fehlt.*

An
Den Mindernden
Vber den in reine Reimgesänge gesetzten
Jesaiam.

SEhr nützlich fallen uns die lehren der Propheten/
    Dan **Jesaias** gibt[a] ein helles klares liecht
    Von Christi Reich' und amt'/ und[b] einen unterricht/
Daß wir zu Jhm[c] in not gantz künlich mögen treten[d]/ [)(iv r]
Vnd Jhn als unser Heil anflehē mit gebetē
    So wend'[e] er dan auch[f] nit[g] von uns sein angesicht:
    Vnd[h] wan je[i] wider uns fleisch/ tod/ und sünde ficht/

Woll'ʲ er der Retter sein in allē solchen nöten.
Was Jesaias nun vō Gott uns zugebracht/
Das spielt derᵏ **Mindernd'** uns durch seiner harfenˡ macht
Jnᵐ reiner Reime kunst und hat dadurch vermehret
    Der Deutschē sprache ruhm/ hat alles wol gesetzt/
    Dzⁿ dessen klarheit uns üm so vielmehrᵒ ergetzt/
Drüm man Jhn billigᵖ auch mit Lorberkräntzenᵠ ehret.

    Auß dem Ertzschreine der
    fruchtbringenden Gesel-
    schaft/

Denʳ 21. des April-Monatsˢ/
Jm Jahreᵗ 1646.

VI

Widmung Georg Philipp Harsdörffers an Martinus Milagius

Q *Milagius: Singender Jesaia (1646)*, Bl.)(iv rv. HAB: Lo 5456. — Dig. UB Göttingen: 8 P GERM II, 5661.

Friedens-Freude Hoffnung.
Deutschland redet.

MEine Söhne/ meine liebe/ höret eurer Mutter stimm':
Hasset alle meuchel-liste/ den vergallten eifergrimm. [)(iv v]
Laßt die späte friedens-freud' Euch mit Brüderliebe bindē
Vnd die deutsch gerühmte treu' endlich huld und gunst entzündē.
    Wie bißher die mörder-waffen blut vergossē fort und fort:
So sol auß der feder trieffen dientenᵃ und des Friedens wort.
Wie durch jedes land getönt die Cartaunen und Musqueten:
So viel uñ mehr kunstgedicht' höre man von den Poeten[.]
    Wie man bißher volck geworbē/ und gerichtet manches heer:
So viel bücher sol man schreiben zu des höchsten lob' und ehr':
Vnd so manche leut' und land' in sich mit verderben ringen
So viel reich und reife frucht sol der frommen arbeit bringen.
    Jesaias führt den reyen uñ **vermindert** alles leid.
Er vermehret durch das singen trost und ware hertzens-freud'.
Vberselig ist die hand/ welche dieses lied geschrieben/
Vnd der angefeurte sinn durch den hohen Geist getrieben.

    Dieses setzte eiligst zu dienstl.
      Ehrbezeigung
      Der Spielende.

T *Wortenden auf -der werden mehrfach durch ein Zeichen gekürzt, das einem Apostroph ähnelt (-d'). Diese Kürzung wurde durch Kursivierung aufgelöst, auch in den Beilagen.* — **a** *Folgt Kustode* lassen

T I a *Lies:* und

T III a *Senkrecht am rechten Textspiegel:* Esa. 43.v.2 und 37.v.3.4.

T V a *SL* giebt — **b** *SL* ja — **c** *SL* ihm' — **d** *SL* tretten — **d** *SL* wende<-et> *eingefügt* ' *(Apostroph).* — **f** *SL eingefügt.* — **g** *SL* nicht — **h** *SL* Ja, — **i** *SL* ie — **j** *Vers in SL:* Woll' er aus solcher angst durch seinen Geist uns retten. — **k** *SL* der — **l** *SL* harffen — **m** Jn reiner Reime kunst *in SL* Jn reine reime her, — **n** *SL* Das — **o** *SL* viel mehr — **p** *SL* billich — **q** *SL* lorbeer Kräntzen — **r** *SL ab hier F. Ludwigs H.* — **s** *SL* AprilMonats *ersetzt* <Mertzen> — **t** *SL* Jhare

T VI *Die Einteilung des Gedichts in vier Strophen ist im Druck typographisch nicht unmittelbar ersichtlich, weil die Einrückung des ersten Verses von Strophe 2 (Wie bißher die mörder-waffen usw.) offenbar vergessen wurde. Da der erste Vers sowohl der dritten als auch der vierten Strophe leicht eingerückt sind und die Verse durchgehend dem Reimschema aabb folgen, liegt eindeutig ein vierstrophiges Gedicht vor. Die fehlende Einrückung wurde ergänzt.* — **a** *Lies:* dinten *(Tinte).*

K 1646 erschien in Bremen *Der Singende Jesaia*, das Hauptwerk von Martinus Milagius (FG 315. Der Mindernde), als eine Sammlung von 114 geistlichen Kirchenliedern in deutscher Sprache. Ganz im Sinne der sprachfördernden Zielsetzung der FG bot das Werk eine allgemeinverständliche poetische Bibelparaphrase. Diesem Werk wurde im Anhang eine Sammlung vorbildhafter geistlicher Lieder durch Milagius beigegeben, die zu seiner und „anderer frommen Christen andacht" (*Milagius: Singender Jesaia [1646]*, 465) dienen sollten. Dies waren 33 teils revidierte alte Lieder, die aus dem Latein., Französ. oder Italien. übersetzt, teils neue Lieder, die „von fürnemen personen geist- und weltlichen standes" aufgesetzt worden waren. Bei einigen zeichnete der Autor als M[artinus] M[ilagius] C[ancellarius] selbst verantwortlich (ebd., 479 ff., 481 ff.). Andere wurden z.B. von H[errn] D[iederich] v[on] d[em] W[erder] O[brist] (FG 31) (473 ff., 549 ff., 551 ff., 565 ff.) bzw. H[errn] M[artin] O[pitz] (FG 200) (483 ff.) verfaßt. Ein Lied wurde vom Hallenser Organisten Samuel Scheidt (1587–1654) vertont (552 ff.). Eingriffe in die Liedtexte gestattete sich der Herausgeber Milagius nur im geringen Maße dort, wo etwas „der deutschen Reimkunst entgegen geschienen" habe (465). — Martinus Milagius (1598–1657) stammte aus dem kursächs. Triestewitz (b. Torgau). Nach dem Schulbesuch in Torgau, Colditz (ab 1608), Freiberg (1610/12), Zerbst (1612/13), Stettin (1613/15) u. Bremen (1615/19) immatrikulierte er sich 1619 an der U. Frankfurt a. d. Oder, wo er 1622 das jurist. Lizentiat erwarb. Seit 1623 Advokat in Zerbst wurde er 1626 Amtmann F. Christians I. v. Anhalt-Bernburg (FG 26). Von 1632 bis 1634 war er Rat unter dem kgl.-schwed. Statthalter in den Stiftern Magdeburg und Halberstadt, F. Ludwig v. Anhalt-Köthen (FG 2), in Halberstadt, danach Rat F. Ludwigs u. F. Augusts von Anhalt-Plötzkau (FG 46) u. schließlich seit 1635 anhalt. Gesamtrat, welches Amt er bis zu seinem Tod bekleidete. Daneben war Milagius zeitweilig auch Rat der Hzn.-Witwe Eleonora Maria v. Mecklenburg-Güstrow (AL 1617. TG 17) u. seit 1637 Kanzler des Ft.s Anhalt-Zerbst (bis 1654), seit 1650 Vormundschaftsrat Pz. Wilhelm Ludwigs v. Anhalt-Köthen (FG 358) und ab 1654 als Nachfolger des verstorbenen Gottfried Müller (FG 353) Kanzler für Anhalt-Dessau unter F.

Johann Casimir (FG 10). Auf unzähligen diplomat. Missionen u. Gesandtschaften vertrat er das Gesamthaus Anhalt, u. a. auf dem Frankfurter Konvent (1634), dem Reichstag zu Regensburg (1640/41), bei den Friedensverhandlungen in Osnabrück (ab 1645) u. dem Reichstag in Regensburg (1652/53). Zugleich übernahm Milagius wiederholt auch diplomat. Aufträge für andere Reichsfürsten, wie Kurbrandenburg, Hessen-Kassel, Mecklenburg-Güstrow, Pfalz-Simmern u. -Zweibrücken. S. Georg Raumer: Idea. Boni Consiliarii. Das ist: Wahre Abbildung eines guten Rahts ... (LP auf Martinus Milagius). Köthen 1657 (VD17 1:048868Y); *LP Stolberg*, Nr. 15921; *Conermann III*, 357–359. — Milagius war maßgeblich für die im Rahmen der Westfäl. Friedensverhandlungen angestellten Bemühungen zur Rückgewinnung der 1315 an das Hochstift Halberstadt verlorengegangenen alten Gft. Ascanien (Aschersleben) tätig, am Ende allerdings vergeblich. Vgl. 450326 K 4. — Trotz seiner vielfältigen administrativen Verpflichtungen u. diplomatischen Aufgaben fand Milagius die Zeit, sich an der in der FG geführten orthographisch-grammatischen Diskussion zu beteiligen, Reimgesetze für FG-Neumitglieder zu verfassen, z. B. für Gebhard v. Alvensleben (FG 479. Der Ausjagende. 1647), Friedrich Asche v. Hardenberg (FG 512. Der Grünrote. 1648) u. Thomas v. dem Knesebeck d. Ä. (FG 524. Der Emsige. 1649), sowie Werke anderer Autoren zu begutachten (u. a. F. Ludwigs Beschreibung der ital. Reise). *Conermann III*, 358.

1 „Jäden", die Nachfahren des Jada, eines Sohns von Onam, der seinerseits Nachfahre Judas gewesen ist; vgl. 1 Chr. 2,28. — Amazja, König von Juda; vgl. 2 Kön. 15. — Jes. 5,1, der auf eine Abstammung Jesajas von David hinweisen soll, lautet: „WOlan / Jch wil meinem Lieben ein Lied meines Vettern singen / von seinem Weinberge." — Kandake ist der Titel der Königinnen des nubischen Meroë. Bei dem „Kämmerer" handelt es sich um den sog. Eunuchen der Kandake, der durch den Diakon Philippus zum Christentum bekehrt worden sein soll und daraufhin selbst das Evangelium predigte. In Apg. 8,27–39 ist nicht nur von seiner Taufe die Rede, sondern auch davon, daß er im Buch Jesaja gelesen habe. *RE* Halbbd. XXII, 1858 f.

2 Milagius bezieht sich auf die Kriegssituation in Anhalt im Herbst und Winter 1644, als sich die ksl. und die schwed. Hauptarmee monatelang bei Bernburg gegenüberlagen und das Territorium ruinierten. S. 440927 K 1. Damals war Milagius anhaltin. Gesamtrat, seit 1637 zugleich Kanzler im Ft. Anhalt-Zerbst, und damit direkt betroffener Zeuge der Geschehnisse. Gesandtschaften nahm er erst wieder ab Februar 1645 wahr, im Laufe desselben Jahres wurde er zum Abgesandten des Gesamtft.s Anhalt bei den Osnabrücker Friedensverhandlungen. Vgl. 450220 K 1 u. 450721 K 3.

3 Milagius spielt wohl auf Jes. 38,20 an: „HERR hilff mir / So wollen wir meine Lieder singen / so lange wir leben / Jn dem Hause des HERRN."

4 Johann Rist (FG 467. Der Rüstige. 1647). Milagius nimmt auf Rists fünfteilige, je Teil 10 Lieder enthaltende Sammlung der *Himmlischen Lieder* Bezug, die im Laufe der Jahre 1641/42 gedruckt wurde. Der Gesamttitel auf dem (nachträglichen) Titelkupfer von 1643 lautet: Johann: Risten | Holst: Predigers | Himlische Lieder | mit sehr anmuhtigen von den weitberühm- | ten H: Johan Schopen | gesetzten Melodeyen (Lüneburg: Stern 1643), HAB: 1067.2 Theol. Die Zwischentitel der hier zit. Ausgabe sind alle auf 1642 datiert, weswegen zumindest das 1. „Zehn" nicht der Erstdruck sein kann; dieser erschien schon 1641. Vgl. die kritische u. kommentierte Neuedition v. Johann Anselm Steiger, Berlin 2012. Im 2. Teil („Das Ander Zehn"), den Milagius jüngst erworben hatte (vgl. Anm. 19), gibt Rist mit dem 4. Lied „Ein Danck-Lied der wahren Christen" (S. 21–26), bei dem es sich um eine Nachdichtung von Jes. 26 handelt, und mit dem 5. Lied „Ein Lob-Gesang des gottseligen Königs Hißkia" (S. 27–31), das sich inhaltlich aus Jes. 38 speist. Anders als Milagius dichtet Rist nicht zu jedem Bibelvers eigens eine Strophe; er behandelt den Stoff

freier. — 1651 erschienen Rists ebenfalls fünfteilige *Neue Himmlische Lieder*; vgl. hierzu die kritische u. kommentierte Neuedition von Johann Anselm Steiger, Berlin 2013.

5 Immanuel Tremellius (1510–1580), ital. Gelehrter aus jüd. Familie, konvertierte zum Protestantismus und ging ins Exil, wo er u. a. in Straßburg, Cambridge, Heidelberg und Sedan lehrte. Tremellius war Verfasser einer Grammatik für die chaldäische u. syrisch-aramäische Sprache (*Grammatica Chaldaea Et Syra* [Genf 1569]) und fertigte in Zusammenarbeit mit seinem Schwiegersohn, Franciscus Junius d. Ä. (François du Jon) (1545–1602), eine (lat.) Übersetzung des Alten Testaments aus dem Hebräischen bzw. Aramäischen an, die seit dem Ende der 70er-Jahre des 16. Jh. in zahlreichen Auflagen erschien. Vgl. *ADB* XXXVIII, 563–565. — Paulus Tossanus (1572–1634), Theologe, seit 1608 Pastor der Klosterkirche und Mitglied des Kirchenrats zu Heidelberg, seit 1613 an der dortigen U. Prof. für Dogmatik. Tossanus zeichnet für die Herausgabe einer Luther-Bibel verantwortlich, in der laut Titelblatt der Erstausgabe 1617 (VD17: 23:674326L) „der Text/ wo er etwas tunckel vnd schwer/ auß den besten Außlegungen/ die heutigs tags zu finden/ am rande kürtzlich vnd deutlich erklärt" wurde. Milagius könnte auch die Ausgabe von 1644 (VD17: 1:709754N) vorgelegen haben. Vgl. *ADB* XXXVIII, 474f. — Mit „der Niederländer deutschen Bibel" ist wohl die 1619 von den niederländ. Generalstaaten in Auftrag gegebene neue nl. Bibelübersetzung, die sog. „Statenbijpel" von 1637 gemeint. Es handelt sich um eines der einflußreichsten Dokumente für die Formung einer einheitlichen nl. Hochsprache, das in beträchtlicher Auflagenhöhe erschienen ist. Vgl. N. N.: Die „Staatenbibel" — die Bibelübersetzung von 1637, http://neon.niederlandistik.fu-berlin.de/de/nedling/taalgeschiedenis/statenbijpel/, 29. 10. 2015.

6 Milagius dichtet aus jedem Bibelvers („Sprüchlein") eine Strophe („Gesetz"). Die Strophen werden auf Gesänge verteilt, wobei die einzelnen Bibelkapitel in der Nachdichtung häufig aus mehreren Gesängen bestehen, deren Strophennumerierung sich gesangübergreifend nach der Numerierung der Bibelverse richtet. Aus diesem Grund beginnt bspw. Gesang 2 in Kap. 5 (a. a. O., 40) nicht mit Strophe 1, sondern mit Strophe 8, weil Gesang 1 mit Strophe 7 schloß. Zu den von Milagius erwähnten Abweichungen von dieser Regel gehört bspw. Kap. 30, in dem „allezeit aus jedem sprüchlein zwey gesetze gemachet sind." (A. a. O., 197.) — Zur Eindeutschung von *Strophe* als *Gesetz* vgl. 371222 K 3. Den dortigen Anmerkungen sei hinzugefügt, daß auch *Harsdörffer: Specimen (1646)*, 171 (disquisitio IX) die Übersetzung der Meistersänger von „strophæ" als „Gesetze" anführt. Das *Specimen* ist Anfang April 1646 im Druck erschienen (vgl. 460406), nur wenige Monate vor der Niederschrift von Milagius' *Vorrede*. Man denke ferner an die fruchtbringerische Adaption im Kompositum „Reimgesetze" (s. bspw. 440816, 441010). — Das Synonym *Sprüchlein* für Bibelvers findet sich nicht nur bei Milagius. Wilhelm v. Kalcheim gen. Lohausen (FG 172) verweist in 381028 III auf eine Passage aus Pred. 12,12, indem er schreibt: „Prediger Salomon in seinem letzten Capitel am zwölften Sprüchlein". Es ist in derselben Bedeutung schon bei Luther zu finden (s. *DW* X.II.I, 178, s. v. „Sprüchlein"). Denkbar ist, daß hier die Ableitung einer bereits gängigen Bedeutungsschicht von *Spruch* im Sinne von (nicht auf einen Vers beschränkte) ,Textstelle' vorliegt (vgl. *Paul Wb.*, 948 s. v. ,Spruch'). *Stieler*, 2103 kennt das „Dimin[utivum] […] Sprüchlein", ohne einen direkten Bezug zur Bibel herzustellen, doch folgt kurz darauf die Definition „Biblische Sprüche/ dicta biblica, loca S. Scripturæ". — Im Druck des *Singenden Jesaia* hat man sich freilich nicht durchgehend des Synonyms *Sprüchlein* für *Vers* bedient. So ist die erste Strophe eines Gesangs zwar häufig mit „Vers" (z. B. a. a. O., 5), „vs." (z. B. a. a. O., 59) oder „V." (z. B. a. a. O., 103) überschrieben, aber niemals mit ,Sprüchlein'.

7 Unter der Überschrift „Desselben Jnhalt" ist jedem Gesang eine kurze Inhaltsparaphrase vorangestellt, die demnach nicht von Milagius stammt. Als Autor darf Felix Haustedt (Steckby 1598 – Bremen 1652) vermutet werden, der bis 1644 Erster Prediger von St. Bartholomäi in Zerbst war. Der reformierte Pfarrer wurde 1644 durch F. Johann v. Anhalt-Zerbst (FG 398) entlassen, der mit seinem Regierungsantritt begann, das ursprünglich reformierte Teilft. lutherisch zu konfessionalisieren. Noch im selben Jahr berief man Haustedt zum Pfarrer der Ansgarikirche im reichsunmittelbaren Bremen. *Graf: Anh. Pfarrerbuch,* 276; Hermann Graf: Die Zerbster Geistlichen seit der Reformation. Ein Beitrag zur Anhaltischen Pfarrchronik. In: Zerbster Jahrbücher 14 (1929), 47–82, hier S. 60; *DBA* I 488/ 43–44, 488/ 46. — Zusätzlich zu den Inhaltsparaphrasen verfaßte Haustedt eines der dem *Singenden Jesaja* vorangestellten Lobgedichte (a. a. O., Bl.)()(6 rv). Milagius wird ihn spätestens in seiner Funktion als Zerbster Kanzler (seit 1637) kennengelernt haben. Ludwig Crocius (Laasphe 1586 – Bremen 1655), Prof. für Theologie und Philosophie am Bremer Gymnasium Illustre, erwähnt am Anfang seiner Widmungsepistel (a. a. O., Bl. [)(xij] r –)()([i] v), daß Haustedt ihm Milagius' Jesaja-Dichtung „gezeigt und zum offenem *[sic]* Druck zu bringen begehret hat" (Bl. [)(xij] v), womit man Crocius wohl als Vermittler bei der Drucklegung ausmachen darf. Denn gedruckt wurde der Band in der Offizin des Gymnasialbuchdruckers Berthold de Villiers in Bremen, bei dem auch der Gymnasialprofessor Crocius (laut VD17) seine Schriften in aller Regel publizierte. Ferner ist zu bedenken, daß Crocius mit Matthias Martinius (s. Anm. 9), Milagius' einstigem Lehrer, bekannt war (Crocius u. Martinius waren 1618/19 Bremer Abgesandte auf der Synode zu Dordrecht). Vgl. zu Crocius *NDB* III, 418; zu de Villiers *Reske,* 125. — Die Widmung des *Singenden Jesaja* an Lgfn. Amalia Elisabeth v. Hessen-Kassel (Beil. III) könnte sich aus dieser konfessionellen Verflechtung heraus erklären: Hessen-Kassel war nach dem Verlust der polit. Führungsrolle der Kurpfalz nach der Schlacht am Weißen Berg die letzte bedeutende militärisch-politische Vormacht der Reformierten in Deutschland im Kräftespiel des Dreißigjährigen Krieges und der Westfälischen Friedensverhandlungen. Diese Rolle wird im Widmungsgedicht direkt angesprochen.

8 F. Ludwig hat über Jahre die fruchtbringerische Sprachdebatte angestoßen und moderiert. Nicht nur bezeugen Christian Gueintz' *Sprachlehre (1641)* und *Rechtschreibung (1645)* F. Ludwigs enge Mitarbeit an diesen Initialwerken, sondern er hat eine Fülle von Stellungnahmen und Gutachten zu Sprachfragen beauftragt oder sogar selbst aufgesetzt. Sie sind in den bisherigen Bänden *DA Köthen I. 5* u. *I. 6* dokumentiert, fortgesetzt im vorliegenden Band sowie in den Folgebänden *DA Köthen I. 8* und v. a. *I. 9.*

9 Matthias Martinius (1572–1630), reform. Theologe, Pädagoge u. Philologe. Nach seinem Studium an der nassau. Hohen Schule Herborn (ab 1586/87) wurde er 1592 Präzeptor zweier Grafensöhne v. Sayn-Wittgenstein u. 1595 Hofprediger der Grafen von Nassau in Dillenburg. 1596 erhielt er eine Philosophie-Professur an der Hohen Schule, die zeitweilig von Herborn nach Siegen verlegt worden war. 1601 wurde er ebendort Rektor, 1607 wechselte Martinius als Pfarrer nach Emden u. wurde schließlich 1610 Rektor des Gymnasiums Illustre in Bremen. *NDB* XVI, 305–307.

10 Tobias Hübner (FG 25).

11 Der fehlerhaft wiedergegebene Gesellschaftsname von Diederich v. dem Werder (FG 31. Der Vielgekörnte).

12 Martin Opitz v. Boberfeld (FG 200).

13 Christian Gueintz (FG 361. Der Ordnende). Gueintz hat in den Vierzigerjahren auch an einer Poetik gearbeitet, die allerdings nie erschienen ist. Vgl. 400314 (K 3), in diesem Bd. 440313 u. 441231.

14 Georg Philipp Harsdörffer (FG 368).

15 Justus Georg Schottelius (FG 397).

16 Augustus Buchner (FG 362. Der Genossene), der der FG allerdings schon seit 1641 angehörte. Seit 1616 hatte Buchner zu Wittenberg die Poetikprofessur inne. Mitschriften seiner Poetik-Vorlesungen kursierten schon lange vor der postumen Erstveröffentlichung und waren auch in den Kreisen der FG bekannt, möglicherweise auch Milagius. Vgl. 420311 K 5. 1663, zwei Jahre nach Buchners Tod, veröffentlichte Georg Göze einen von Buchners Erben nicht autorisierten Druck der Poetik, 1665 erschien dort die gelungenere und heute maßgebliche Ausg. von Buchners Schwiegersohn Otto Prätorius *Anleitung Zur Deutschen Poeterey* (Wittenberg 1665) und im selben Jahr vom selben Herausgeber ebd. *Poet*, in dem die ersten drei Kapitel der *Anleitung* separat veröffentlicht wurden; die letzteren beiden im Ndr. hg. v. Marian Szyrocki (Tübingen 1966). Vgl. den Herausgeberkommentar S. 4* ff.

17 Philipp Caesius (v. Zesen; FG 521. 1648), damals noch nicht geadelt und noch kein Mitglied der FG.

18 Christian Brehme (1613–1667), 1640–1654 kfl.-sächs. Bibliothekar, ab 1657 mehrfach Dresdner Bürgermeister (im Amt verstorben). Brehme studierte Anfang der 1630er zwei Jahre lang in Wittenberg, wo er Buchners (s. Anm. 16) berühmte Vorlesungen besuchte. Er verfaßte den Briefsteller *Art vnd Weise Kurtze Brieflein zu schreiben* (Dresden 1640), eine Prosaschäferei *Die Vier Tage Einer Newen und Lustigen SChäfferey* (Dresden 1647), Konversationsliteratur à la Harsdörffer: *Erster Theil [– Dritter Theil] Christlicher Unterredungen Bestehendt Jn Zwölff Geistlichen Gesprächen* (Dresden 1659) und eine Vielzahl an Gelegenheitsdichtungen (vgl. die in 450808 K I 0 u. 461104 K 2 erwähnten Texte). Der 1637 erschienene Sammelband des jungen Brehme ist im wesentlichen eine Zusammenstellung solcher Gelegenheitsdichtungen: *C. Brehmens allerhandt Lustige/ Trawrige/ vnd nach gelegenheit der Zeit vorgekommene GEDJCHTE. Zu Passierung der Weyle mit dero Melodeyen mehrentheils auffgesatzt* (Leipzig: Lanckisch Erben 1637). — Vgl. *Dünnhaupt: Handbuch*, 787–794; *ADB* III, 284; *LP Stolberg*, Nr. 5013; *LP Roth*, R 5130.

19 Milagius stößt sich am zweiten Zwischentitel, der in Anm. 4 zitierten, fünfteiligen *Himmlischen Lieder* von Rist. Auf ihm findet sich die Wendung „Himlischer Triumph-Lieder", wo sonst nur von „Himlischer Lieder" die Rede ist. F. Ludwig hatte seine Übersetzung der *Trionfi* Petrarcas unter dem Titel *Sechs Triumphi oder Siegesprachten* 1643 herausgebracht. Vgl. 430624 K 2.

20 Zur Bevorzugung alternierender Versmaße s. den vielfach herbeizitierten *Opitz: Buch von der Deutschen Poeterey (1624)*, 52: „Nachmals ist auch ein jeder verß entweder ein iambicus oder trochaicus". Opitz schloß den Daktylus aber nicht schlechtweg aus der Poetik aus. Hieran orientierte sich auch *Fürst Ludwig: Kurtze Anleitung zur Deutschen Poesi (1640)*, der die dreihebigen Versfüße Daktylus und Anapäst zwar nicht verdammt wissen wollte, aber auf ihre Behandlung vorerst verzichtete, „weil sie noch so üblich nicht" seien und im Gegensatz zum Gesang „im lesen nicht allzu wol lauten" (Bl. a ij v; s. Details zu F. Ludwigs Haltung in 391028 K 3). *Buchner: Poeterey (1665)*, Kap. 7, „Vom masse der Verse und ihren Arten", 113–155 bes. ab S. 138 erkennt den Daktylus hingegen als unverzichtbaren Versfuß an, müßte man ohne ihn doch auf allzu viele Wörter in der gebundenen Rede verzichten. Dem schloß sich *Zesen SW* IX, 56–58 im *Deutschen Helicon* (erstmals 1641) an. S. 450124 K 6 und das Lemma „Daktylus" im kumulierten Sachregister des vorliegenden Bandes.

21 Eine Synkope gesteht im konkreten Fall auch F. Ludwig in seiner *Kurtzen Anleitung*, Bl. a ij r zu: „Der selblautende Buchstabe i kan auch zu zeiten in etzlichen worten füglich eingeschlungen oder außgelassen werden/ Als in den worten heilgen für heiligen". Opitz (Der Gekrönte) äußert sich hinsichtlich der Elision im Wortinnern im *Buch von der Deutschen Poeterey*, 48 freilich skeptisch, „weil durch die zuesammenziehung der sylben die verse wiederwertig vnd vnangeneme zue lesen sein." Die erwähnte Synkope findet sich aber bspw. in seinem *Hohen Liedt*, wo man gleich im ersten Lied die Wendung „heilges Schlaffgemach" findet (*Opitz* IV.1, 19). *Zesen SW* IX (*Deutscher Helicon* [1641], 50f.) ist gegenüber der Synkope des <i> zwar skeptisch, gesteht sie aber in Diminutiven zu und erwähnt „wie Opitz [...] *heilges* vor *heiliges* setzt; welchs nicht unrecht/ weils in ungebundner rede auch also gebraucht wird". Ferner verweist Zesen ebd. auf *Buchner: Poeterey (1665)*, der sich auf S. 69–83 allg. zur Synkope äußert und auf S. 75 im Zusammenhang mit der i-Synkope ebenfalls Opitz anführt, der „Heilger gesetzt an unterschiedenen Orten".

22 Die Vorstellung, daß Prosaschriften in syntaktischer Hinsicht als Vorbild für Texte in gebundener Sprache dienen sollten, könnte sich Milagius bei der Lektüre von *Fürst Ludwig: Kurtze Anleitung zur Deutschen Poesi (1640)*, 5 zu eigen gemacht haben. Dort heißt es: „Jn ungebundner red'/ als sie [die deutsche Sprache] dann auch geschrieben/ | Gebunden werden sol/ in wolgemeßnem band." Milagius könnte sich freilich ebenso aus *Buchner: Poeterey (1665)*, 22–26 bedient habe, wo „die natürliche Ordnung und der gemeine Brauch" der Wortfolge als Maßstab für die Schönheit des Verses und die Kunstfertigkeit des Dichters postuliert wird. Denn „je näher sie [die Ordnung und Zusammensetzung der Wörter] der Natur kömt / je gereimter und füglicher auch wird die Rede." Unter den Beispielen Buchners finden sich auch unzulässige Nachstellungen des Präfixes von trennbaren Verben. So korrigiert er den Vers: „Belieben lasset euch/ zu nehmen von mir an" zu „Last euch belieben doch/ dieß von mir anzunehmen" (S. 25). *Zesen SW* IX (*Deutscher Helicon* [1641]), 50 zieht zwar im Zusammenhang mit der Synkope wie Milagius oder F. Ludwig die ungebundene Rede als Maßstab für die gebundene heran, hält die von Milagius und Buchner inkriminierte Inversion bei trennbaren Verben allerdings für zulässig: „Also kann ich auch bißweilen die wörter trennen/ und sagen: *Du solt nun mercken auff/* vor/ *Du solt auffmercken.*" Ebd. dehnt er die Regel auf substantivische Komposita aus. Es sei erlaubt zu schreiben: „*der König auff dem Zaune*" für „*Zaunkönig*" (S. 56).

23 Die Passage ist als eine Absage an die Verwendung rührender Reime in gebundener Rede zu lesen. In den betonten Reimsilben der von Milagius genannten Beispiele liegt durchgehend eine lautliche Übereinstimmung sowohl des betonten Vokals als auch des vorhergehenden Konsonanten vor. Dazu muß ergänzend angemerkt werden, daß (1.) aufgrund der sächsischen Lenisierung für Milagius [p] > [b] wird, weswegen aus seiner Sicht „**Bracht**" und „**Pracht**" gleich lauten (vgl. Anm. 28), daß (2.) die biblischen Personen *Hiskia* und *Hilkia* nicht initial-, sondern endbetont werden (darum der rührende Reim in Kap. 36, Strophe 3, a. a. O., 237f.: „Auf sein begehren schickt' Hiskia | Eljakim/ einen Sohn Hilkia/") und daß (3.) die lautliche Übereinstimmung gewisser Umlaute und Vokale in den zeitgenössischen Poetiken systematisch konzediert wird, weswegen „**hält/ held**" (zusätzlich wegen der dt. Auslautverhärtung) ebenso als lautlich identisch zu betrachten sind wie „**tücke/ dicke**", wo darüber hinaus erneut die sächsische Lenisierung [t] > [d] greift. Quellen in Bezug auf Punkt 3. dürften sowohl *Buchner: Poeterey (1665)* (kursierte in der Form von Vorlesungsmitschriften bereits vor dem postumen Erstdruck) als auch *Schottelius: Teutsche Vers- oder ReimKunst (1645)*, 110 sein, der feststellt: „Wenn der Laut gleich ist/ ob schon die Buchstaben nicht gentzlich überein stimmen/ So mögen sie doch ohn alles Bedencken gereimet werden sagt Herr Buchner recht/ als: Blühen-ziehen: Lebetgräbet: Gethön-stehn &c." Die Umlaute („Kleinlaute") ließen sich hier problemlos mit den Vokalen in Einklang bringen, was ebd. 111 durch weitere Beispiele belegt wird; vgl. die Passage in *Buchner: Poeterey (1665)*, 157 u. in Zesens *Deutschem Helicon* von 1641 (*Zesen SW* IX, 43f.). Die Reimart, in der Vokale und „Kleinlaute" miteinander reimen, bezeichnet *Schottelius: Teutsche Vers- oder ReimKunst (1645)*, 112 als „Rührende", womit

sich seine nicht mit der heutigen Definition deckt. Wird in dieser die absolute Homophonie der betonten Reimsilbe festgestellt, spricht Schottelius in Bezug auf die gegebenen Beispiele von einer Reimart, in der „die Reimwörter nicht so gar rein und gleichlautend eintreffen/ sonderen sich nur Reimstimmig rühren", was als „eine zulässige Reimung" zu betrachten sei (ebd., 112). *Opitz: Buch von der Deutschen Poeterey (1624)*, 51 (auch *Buchner: Poeterey (1665)*, 162 f.) weicht von dieser Linie allerdings ab, wenn er die Endreime *gefunden* und *sünden* (Schottelius: Teutsche Vers- oder ReimKunst [1645], 112 führt als zulässige Reimung z. B. „Lust-küst" auf) oder *weidet* und *leitet* verwirft (letzteres wäre wegen der phonetischen d/t-Äquivalenz für Milagius kein Problem). Die heutige Reimforschung würde die näherungsweise Gleichlautung von „Drücken-blicken", „Treu-sey" oder „Kömt-nimt" (ebd., 111) ausschließlich der Kategorie des unreinen Reims, nicht aber der des rührenden zuschlagen. Für Schottelius handelt es sich in solchen Fällen sowohl um rührende als auch um unreine Reime. Denn die Kategorie des unreinen Reims wird seiner Definition nach gefüllt durch (1.) Reime mit lautlicher Konvergenz bei gleichzeitiger orthographischer Divergenz und (2.) Reime mit lautlicher Divergenz bei gleichzeitiger orthographischer Konvergenz: „Ein unreiner Reim oder eine unreine Reimung ist/ wan [1.] der Reimlaut oder die Reimletteren nach der Schreibung nicht behalten werden/ und doch dem Gehör gemäß kommen: oder aber/ [2.] wan die Schreibung zwar gleich ist/ die Ausrede aber ungleich eintrifft/ und etwas mislautet" (ebd., 117). Das von Milagius beschriebene Phänomen der absoluten Homophonie der Reimsilbe kennt Schottelius gleichwohl auch und wendet sich gegen die in der frz. Dichtung häufig anzutreffende Reimung: „Wörter/ die an Buchstaben und Endungen gantz gleich/ doch aber unterschiedlicher Bedeutung seyn" (ebd., 112), sollten in keinem Fall als Reimwörter dienen. Als Beispiel nennt er u. a. die Homophone *wagen* und *Wagen*. Dasselbe gelte für die End- und Derivationsmorpheme „Lein/ lich/ keit/ heit" (ebd., 113; vgl. hierzu Milagius' Bsp. **„Gerechtigkeit/ Barmhertzigkeit"**). Dieselbe Stoßrichtung mit Ablehnung der frz. Dichtungsart findet sich in *Buchner: Poeterey (1665)*, 158–162 und in *Zesen SW IX*, 47–49 (*Deutscher Helicon* [1641]).

24 Der von Milagius kritisierte Vers findet sich in Kap. 14, Strophe 8 (a. a. O., 99):
   Es lassen auch die Tannen frey erklingen
   Jhr freuden lied/ daß du gefallen bist:
   Die Cedern/ so bis an den himmel dringen
   Jm Libanon/ die sagen zu der frist:
   Weil du nun ligst/ so bleiben wir verschonet/
   Es wird nicht mehr die lust an uns gebüßt.

25 In den Poetiken des Barock wird der Umstand, daß ein und derselbe Vokal eine je verschiedene lautliche Quantität bzw. Qualität aufweisen kann, weswegen er sich nicht in jedem Fall zu einem Reim eignet, wiederholt formuliert. *Opitz: Buch von der Deutschen Poeterey (1624)*, 46 schließt zu Beginn von Kap. 7, in dem Reimlehre und Metrik verhandelt werden, aus, daß Wörter einen Reim bilden können, in denen die Vokale von unterschiedlicher lautlicher Qualität seien. Er nennt das Beispiel „ehren" und „nehren", in denen das betonte <e> der Aussprache eines griech. ε [ɛ:] bzw. η [e:] folge (in der heutigen Standardlautung verhält es sich freilich genau andersherum). *Buchner: Poeterey (1665)*, 156 bedient sich einer identischen Erläuterung im Hinblick auf die Verben „ehren" und „beschehren", wohingegen *Zesen SW IX* (*Deutscher Helicon* [1641]), 45 die von Opitz festgestellte Lautdifferenz von „ehren" und „nehren" auf dessen schlesische Aussprache schiebt, will er selbst doch keinen solchen Unterschied erkennen. Er rührt damit an ein Problem, das in *Schottelius: Teutsche Vers- oder ReimKunst (1645)*, 107–109 die Gestalt einer Aporie annimmt. Wegen der abweichenden Aussprache in den Mundarten lasse sich kaum eine einheitliche Regel formulieren: „Gewiß was dieser Per Eta/ wird jener E außsprechen/ und dz dieser ä ein ander hinwieder ee". Darüber hinaus ist zu bedenken, daß der Unterschied zwischen Vokalquantität und -qualität noch nicht klar erkannt wurde. Denn das Problem mit dem Reim stellt sich auch bei Milagius nicht durchwegs als Unterschied zwischen offenen und geschlossenen Vokalen („weiten und engen selb lautendē") dar, zumal sich in seinem Beispiel **„fus/ flus"**, in dem fälschlicherweise der Vokal [u:] mit [ʊ] gleichgesetzt werde, sowohl eine unterschiedliche Vokalqualität als auch -quantität konstatieren läßt, und in „Mach'/ **gemach**" gerade nicht die Qualität, sondern nur die Quantität der Vokale variiert: [a] vs. [a:]. Auf eine solche noch unvollkommene Differenzierung stößt man denn auch bei *Schottelius: Teutsche Vers- oder ReimKunst (1645)*, 107, wo er, auf die bereits zitierte Passage bei Opitz verweisend, auf die unterschiedliche Qualität abhebt, die Vokale annehmen können, was einen Reim unmöglich mache: „*der Scherfe/ Gelinde/ oder Gethöne nach*". *Zesen SW IX (Deutscher Helicon, 1641)*, 43 bedient sich eines ähnlichen deskriptiven Vokabulars, um die Differenz von „*glaß und vaß/ nach und bach*" zu erläutern: Man solle darauf achten, „daß der laut in einem Verse nicht scharff/ im andern gelinder ausgesprochen werde". Und *Buchner: Poeterey (1665)*, 156 erläutert den Lautunterschied zwischen „Glas und naß" dadurch, daß dort „das a gleich als gedoppelt und ausgedehnet: Hier einfach/ geschwind/ und scharf ausgesprochen" werde. Weiter unten verknüpft Schottelius seine Beobachtung mit einem orthographischen Argument, wenn er **„rasen-hassen/ lassen-blasen"** usw. als unzulässige Reime qualifiziert. Die lautliche Differenz sei darauf zurückzuführen, daß „der eine Reimlaut zu mitten mehr mittlautende Buchstabē/ als der ander habe" (a. a. O., 116), womit er erneut Opitz (a. a. O., 51) folgt, der in solchen Fällen ebenfalls auf die unterschiedliche Anzahl an Konsonanten im Wortinnern abhebt und nicht auf einen Unterschied der Länge des betonten Vokals (wie in seinem Beispiel „harren" und „verwahren") oder der lautlichen Qualität der Konsonanten (wie in seinem Beispiel „rasen" und „gleicher massen", wo [z] und [s] einen reinen Reim verhindern). Dieselbe Argumentationsweise findet sich ebenfalls bei Zesen (a. a. O., 46).

26 In ähnlicher Weise hat schon *Buchner: Poeterey (1665)*, 85 den Verstoß gegen einige poetologische Regeln eingeräumt, wenn es sich bei der Dichtung nicht um eine Originalschöpfung, sondern nur um eine Übersetzung handle: „Man soll aber wissen/ daß dieses Dolmetschungen seyn/ da ein Poet alles so genau nicht in acht nimmt/ als er in seinen eigenen Wercken thut."

27 Die Anastrophe, die im Lateinischen wegen der zumeist eindeutigen Flexionsendungen und der daraus resultierenden klaren Kongruenzen keine gravierenden Verständigungsprobleme hervorruft, wird in *Opitz: Buch von der Deutschen Poeterey (1624)*, 40 in Bezug auf die deutsche Dichtung als schlechter Stil moniert und als Zeichen dafür genommen, „das die worte in den verß gezwungen vnd gedrungen sein." Vgl. oben Milagius' Rede vom „gar zu genauen zwang", dem man die deutsche Sprache nicht unterwerfen dürfe, um sie nicht unverständlich und „undeutsch" zu machen.

28 Die wichtigsten der im folgenden genannten Regeln für die Elision des vokalischen Auslauts im Vers gehen auf Bestimmungen in *Opitz: Buch von der Deutschen Poeterey (1624)*, 46–49 zurück. Die Ergänzungen expliziert Milagius v.a., um die von den zeitgenössischen Grammatikern geforderte Flexionsendung im Dativ (vgl. *Takada*, 169–170) regelkonform elidieren zu können. — Zu den Regeln im einzelen: (1.) Wie bei Opitz (a. a. O., 46f.), *Buchner: Poeterey (1665)*, 83f., *Zesen SW IX (Deutscher Helicon* [1641]), 52 und *Fürst Ludwig: Kurtze Anleitung zur Deutschen Poesi (1640)*, 7 wird die Elision des Schluß-e gefordert, wenn ein Wort mit vokalischem Anlaut folgt. Im Text des *Singenden Jesaja* wird das J ebenfalls als vokalischer Buchstabe behandelt: vgl. z. B. Kap. 1, Strophe 5:

„schlag' je" (a. a. O., 3) od. Kap. 1, St. 28: „hatt' jhr" (a. a. O., 13). — (2.) Bei Elisionen vor Wörtern mit anlautendem H stimmt Milagius ebenfalls mit Opitz (a. a. O., 49f.), Zesen (a. a. O., 54) und Buchner (a. a. O., 86) überein. — (3.) Die Konzession einer Elision des Schwa, wenn dadurch Konsonanten aufeinandertreffen, die „gleichstimmend" sind, findet sich bei Opitz zwar nicht, aber bei Buchner (a. a. O., 87f.) und F. Ludwig (a. a. O., 7), der formuliert: „Wann die mitlautre [am Rand: Consonans] sich gleichförmig treffen an/ | Der Selblaut e als dan zu rück' und aussen bleibet/ | Er wird geschlucket ein/ und gleichsam auf sich reibet". (Allerdings formuliert F. Ludwig in Gutachten zu Gueintz' *Sprachlehre* und zu Harsdörffers *Frauenzimmer-Gesprächspielen* ein absolutes Verbot, das E zwischen Konsonanten zu apokopieren. Gegenüber Gueintz heißt es in 400214 I, S. 454: „Wan ein selblautt folgett kann das e. ausgelassen werden […] das Oberhäcklein, Apostrophe, kan nie zwischen zwey Mittlautenden gesetzet werden." Und unter seinen Korrekturen zu den *Hundert Spielreimen* aus dem 3. Teil der *Frauenzimmer-Gesprächspiele* heißt es ebenso unmißverständlich: „zwischen zwey mitlautenden kan nie ein Apostrophe oder häcklein stehen". Harsdörffer hatte das auslautende E aus *deine Red'* zu *dein Red'* apokopiert. S. das Gutachten in *DA Köthen I. 9*, zu 430802; HM Köthen: V S 545, Bl. 426v–428v u. Bl. 425rv, hier Bl. 427v.) Die folgenden Textbefunde aus dem *Singenden Jesaja* zeigen, daß Milagius diese Elisionsregel nicht nur auf die in seiner Vorrede explizit genannten Konsonantenpaare (dazu unten), sondern auf alle identischen Konsonanten übertrug. Denn im Text wird, Buchner und F. Ludwig folgend, das Schluß-e auch dann elidiert, wenn dadurch zwei identische Konsonanten aufeinandertreffen (die Regel findet auch über Vers- und Strophengrenzen hinweg Anwendung):
- b/b: „in meiner lieb' besteht" (a. a. O., 62; Kap. 8, St. 12) od. „Jch aber bleib' bestendig" (a. a. O., 64; ebd., St. 17);
- d/d: „Des ochsen weid'/ der schaffe plan und bahn." (a. a. O., 58; Kap. 7, St. 25);
- g/g: „am Sabbatthag' geschicht" (a. a. O., 7; Kap. 1, St. 13; „Sabbatthag'" im Anhang korrigiert zu „Sabbattag", ebd. Bl. [Aa xij] r);
- n/n: „an dem kinn'/ | Noch mehr" (a. a. O., 26; Kap. 3, St. 4);
- s/s: „Zum zeugnüß'/ Sieh' es ist in dieser stund' | Die missethat" (a. a. O., 48; Kap. 6, St. 7).

Daß in den meisten hier gegebenen Beispielen das dativische Flexionsmorphem elidiert wird, ist nicht der Auswahl geschuldet, sondern repräsentiert das Gros der Fälle: Die Regel diente Milagius offenkundig dazu, den Text der „ungebundenen rede" anzunähern, in der das Schluß-e im Dativ und Ablativ (gemeint sind Präpositionalgefüge, die den Dativ erfordern, vgl. *Gueintz: Sprachlehre (1641)*, 45) normalerweise nicht verwendet werde, wie er unten selbst feststellt. (Vgl. auch Zesen a. a. O., 50, der Elisionen auch im Wortinneren zuläßt, wenn „es in ungebundener rede breuchlich" sei.) Darum habe er in solchen Fällen bewußt „einen selblautendē oder gleichstimēnden mitlautenden" folgen lassen (s. auch Anm. 29). Die behauptete lautliche Übereinstimmung der Buchstabenpaare <d> und <t>, <b> und <p>, <g> und <k> basiert auf Milagius' dialektaler Aussprache. Die Lenisierung der Plosive [t] > [d], [p] > [b] und [k] > [g] ist ein typisches Merkmal des sächsischen Dialektraums, aus dem er stammt. Man kann hier mithin von einer Spezifizierung sprechen, welche Konsonanten als gleichlautend einzustufen seien. Fruchtbar wird diese Regel im *Singenden Jesaja* wohl ausschließlich im Falle von [t] > [d]. Beispiele wie „Mit solchē blut'/ das aus den froṁen quillt" (a. a. O., 8; Kap. 1, St. 15) sind außerordentlich häufig anzutreffen. Die Regel, daß eine Elision des Schlußvokals beim Aufeinandertreffen von b/p und g/k (und umgekehrt) ebenso zulässig sei, scheint eher die Frucht theoretischer Überlegungen zu sein. Im Gegensatz zur Regel <t> = <d> wurde bei einer Durchsicht der ersten 250 Seiten keine einzige Stelle gefunden, in der die Elision der anderen Plosive nach dem Muster *Im Grab' pennt die Leiche* oder *Im Gang' kriecht die Schlange* vorgenommen wurde (zumal es schwerfällt, alternierende Bsp. zu ersinnen). Elisionen, die auf die behauptete Lautidentität von „tz. als ts und. s" (eigtl. [ts] u. [z]) zurückgehen, ließen sich nicht finden. Die Elision „nach dem bleymaß' stehen" (a. a. O., 183; Kap. 28, St. 17) scheint eher den oben zitierten Prinzipien zu folgen ([s] = [s], wobei hier eigentl. [s] = [ʃt] gilt). Opitz hätte gegen diese Regeln von Milagius Einspruch erhoben, denn: „Wann auf das e ein Consonans oder mitlautender Buchstabe folget / soll es nicht aussen gelassen werden" (a. a. O., 48), außerdem gelte, daß „*t* harte vnd *d* gelinde außgesprochen wird." (a. a. O., 51; ebenso mit demselben Bsp. auch Zesen a. a. O., 46f.) — (4.) Am Ende des letzten Verses einer Strophe darf das Schluß-e in jedem Fall elidiert werden, egal ob die Elision anderen Regeln folgt oder nicht. Dieser Regel bedient Milagius sich im *Singenden Jesaja* häufig: So schließt der letzte Vers von Kap. 5, St. 6 mit „daß er keinen regen spür'", obwohl die 7. Strophe mit „Der berg ist" beginnt (a. a. O., 40); ebenso in Kap. 8, St. 2, wo im letzten Vers die Elision „vor der welt noch wol zu trauen stund'" zu finden ist, während die 3. Strophe mit „Mein Ehweib" beginnt (a. a. O., 60). Buchner (a. a. O., 87) nennt explizit eine Stelle bei Opitz, an der er am Ende eines Gedichts das Schluß-e apokopiert habe. Evtl. rührt Milagius' Bestimmung von dieser Bemerkung her.

29 *Schottelius: Sprachkunst (1641)*, 410 betont ausdrücklich, daß aus morphologischen Gründen das E im Auslaut in keinem Fall apokopiert werden dürfe (bei seinen Bsp. handelt es sich um Dative). Den Endsilbenverfall in der nominalen Flexion konnte das freilich nicht aufhalten. Unter dem im Deutschen nicht vorhandenen Ablativ (der „Nehmendung") verstand Schottelius Präpositionalgefüge, die den Dativ erfordern. Ebd., 285f. gibt er die Bsp. „von dem Menschen" (Sg.) bzw. „von denen Menschen" (Pl.). Da Dativ und Ablativ laut Schottlius „überall in beyden Zahlen gleich" seien, nennt auch Milagius sie in einem Atemzug (vgl. Schottelius' Begriffsdefinitionen ebd., 24, wo die „Gebendung" durch „Dativus casus" und „Nehmendung" durch „Ablativus casus" erläutert wird). *Gueintz: Sprachlehre (1641)* bedient sich derselben Terminologie; vgl. Kap. 9 u. 10, S. 43–47. S. auch *Fürst Ludwig: Kurtze Anleitung zur Deutschen Poesi (1640)*, 5, der auf die unbedingte Einhaltung korrekter Kasus in dichterischen Texten pocht.

30 Verbgefüge mit *tun*, wie sie noch im 17. Jahrhundert in Kanzleitexten anzutreffen sind, finden sich zwar auch bei Rist und Opitz, sie sind im Fnhd. jedoch im Schwinden begriffen und halten sich am Ende nur noch in volkstüml. Textsorten im Oberdt. Vgl. *Polenz*, 286. Neben Milagius lehnt sie Zesen im ersten Teil seines *Deutschen Helicons* ab (Ausgabe 1641: *Zesen SW* IX, 49; Ausgabe 1649: Bl. P[vi] r; Ausgabe 1656: *Zesen SW* X.1, 142). Auch Samuel v. Butschky (1612–1678) meint, daß „das flik-wort Tuhn/ welches von vielen/ wider die Natur/ der reinen Spraache/ eingeflikt wird/ und übel stehet/ alß wenn Sie setzen: Tuht demnach hiermit beschlüßen", nicht zu gebrauchen sei (vgl. *Zesen SW* IX, 49, der *tun* das „vornehmste" „aller flick-wörter" nennt). — Samuel v. Butschky: Perfertischer Muusen Schlüssel/ Zur Schreibrichtigkeit/ der Hooch-deutschen Haupt-Spraache/ Das ist/ Kurtzer/ iedoch wohl-gegründeter Unterricht/ wie man die Wörter/ in der Hooch-deutschen Haupt-spraache/ rein und unverfälscht zuschreiben/ erlernen sol (Leipzig 1645), hier zit. S. 37; SUB Göttingen: LING. VII 4306, Dig. Vgl. *Takada*, 234f.

K I 1 Die notwendige Beachtung der unterschiedlichen Lautung des vokalischen u/U und des konsonant. v/V (ebenso des i/I und j/J) auch in einer entsprechend distinkten Schreibung ist durchgängiger Konsens bei den Fruchtbringern, der sich auch für die in den dt. Frakturschriften fehlende U-Majuskel durchsetzte. S. *DA Köthen I. 5*, S. 420f., 429ff., 450f., 456 u. 465f.; *Herz: Rechtschreibdebatte*, 87f.

2 Das phonographische Argument ließ auch die Schreibung von /aw/ oder /ew/ für

/au/ bzw. /eu/ den Fruchtbringern als fehlerhaft und strikt zu meiden erscheinen. Vgl. *DA Köthen I. 5*, 431 f., 450 u. 456; *Schottelius: Sprachkunst (1641)*, 185; *Gueintz: Rechtschreibung (1645)*, 17.

3 Solche, bei Luther häufig auftretenden und auch noch im 17. Jh. verbreiteten Enklisen wurden von F. Ludwig konsequent abgelehnt. Vgl. *Herz: Rechtschreibdebatte,* 107. Im vorliegenden Bd. verwendet sie gleichwohl z. B. Moscherosch in seinem Briefgedicht 440525: „Mein Freund/ warumb wiltu dann | Daß dein Nahm verschwigen bleibe?"

4 Daß überflüssige, d. h. bei der Aussprache nicht hörbare Konsonanten nicht geschrieben werden sollten, war v. a. von F. Ludwig energisch vertreten worden. Dabei geriet er notwendig in Konflikt mit morphologischen Normierungsgrundsätzen, die die Stammform eines Wortes durch das ganze Wortparadigma hindurch behalten wollten. Schottelius und Harsdörffer v. a. vertraten den Standpunkt unbedingter Unveränderbarkeit der Stammbuchstaben (abgesehen von Ausnahmen der irregulären Verben). F. Ludwig traf also auf Widerstand, wenn er von Gott götlich oder von Herr herlich ableiten wollte, oder den Wolf im Genitiv des Wolffes ansetzte, da er eine Konsonantengemination nur zulassen wollte, wenn ein nachfolgender Vokal den 2. Konsonanten auszusprechen erlaubte. Vgl. 450420 K 6; *Herz: Rechtschreibdebatte,* 93 ff.; dazu auch *Gueintz: Rechtschreibung (1645),* 6f. Ebd., S. 11 wird ein nicht hörbarer Doppelbuchstabe allerdings zugestanden, wenn er zur Unterscheidung homophoner Wörter dient, was auch F. Ludwig zugestand. Gueintz nennt, wie Milagius, das Beispiel „Reisst" vs. „Reist". *Gueintz: Rechtschreibung (1645)* besteht zum größten Teil aus einer Homophonenliste, der Milagius in seinem nachstehenden „Dritten Exempel" weitere Beispiele hinzufügt.

5 Diese und die folgende Kritik zielt also auf die Setzer/ Drucker. Kap. 9, Strophe 1 endet mit einem unvollständigen Satz ohne Prädikat, aber trotzdem mit Punkt (a. a. O., S. 66):

    Doch am meeres-wege
    Jn der Jordans-pflege/
    Die viel volcks ernehrt.
    2. Dasselbe volck/ so da gewandelt
    An solchem ort' im finstern leid'/
    Dasselbe volck/ so sich verhandelt/
    Mit aberglauben seine zeit
        Hinzubringen/ siehet/
    Wan das heil nur blühet/
    Ein liecht/ so nicht klein; [...].

6 Die Anfänger in der dt. Sprach- und Rechtschreiblehre können durch diese Inkonsequenz im Buchsatz verwirrt werden, so Milagius. ‚Anfangend, beginnend'. *Stieler,* 393: „Anfahen/ *incipere, inchoare*". In *Adelung Wb.* I, 286 beschrieben als „veraltete Oberdeutsche Form des Verbi anfangen, welche im Hochdeutschen fast gar nicht mehr gehöret wird". S. auch *DW* I, 321 f.

7 Bei dem Akzentzeichen ̈ handelt es sich um eine altgriech. Dialytika Varia (auch Trema Gravis). Dialytika sind die beiden Trennpunkte (das Trema), die auf eine diphthongische Aussprache hinweisen. Auch wenn der Akzent laut Milagius nur „mehrentheils" ausgelassen wurde, ließ sich keine Textstelle mit einer derartigen Markierung finden. Dabei wären Beispiele durchaus denkbar, schwankt die Silbenzahl der von Milagius angegebenen Wörter doch mitunter:

– In Kap. 35, Strophe 3 ist der Vers: „Die knie/ so da sind" (a. a. O., 233), nur korrekt geformt, wenn *Knie* zweisilbig gelesen wird: [kniːə]. Ebenso muß *knien* in Kap. 46, St. 4 (vierhebige Jamben) zweisilbig sein ([kniːən]): „Sie knien/ wie vor einen thron'." (A.

a. O., 324) In Kap. 45, St. 23 (vierhebige Trochäen) wird *Knie* allerdings apokopiert und einsilbig gelesen ([kniː]): „Mir doch alle knie' allzeit" (a. a. O., 322).
- In Kap. 32, St. 20 (dreihebige Jamben, hier weiblich) ist *gesäet* zweisilbig zu lesen ([gəzɛːət]): „Die jhr die frucht geseet | An wassern/ wo man gehet" (a. a. O., 217). Ebenso in Kap. 37, St. 30 ([zɛːən]; hier ein vierhebiger Jambus): „Jm dritten/ was das säen bringt" (a. a. O., 258).

8 An den genannten Stellen (a. a. O., 148, 238, 244) weicht die Schreibung entsprechend ab: „Eljakim".

9 Die Stellengaben sind wie folgt zu lesen: „[Bl.] 16. [Gesang] 1. [Vers] 2.". In diesem Fall ist im *Düsseldorfer Gesangbuch*, 178 die Notenfolge: g d d c d e f e e d; im *Singenden Jesaja* jedoch: g d d c d d d e e d. Die Notenlängen sind korrekt wiedergegeben. — Ambrosius Lobwasser: Psalmen Dauids | Jn Teusche Reymen | verständlich vnd deutlich gebracht (Düsseldorf: Buyß 1621, Reprint Köln/ Bonn 1983).

10 Auf Bl. [Aa 12] rv folgt ein Verzeichnis von „Druck-Fehler[n]" mit Korrekturen zu Einzelwörtern.

K II Bei der „hohe[n] person", von der hier die Rede ist, handelt es sich um F. Ludwig, aus dessen *Etzliche Schöne Gesänge* (1642) einige der 33 Lieder im Anhang übernommen wurden. Ein ausführlicher Kommentar zu diesem Komplex findet sich bereits in 380504 K 14 (*DA Köthen I. 4*, S. 557–559), wo auch eine Liste der vermutlich von F. Ludwig revidierten Lieder gegeben wird. Zu den Liedtexten, deren Autoren durch Initialen angezeigt wurden, gehören die 14 Gesänge der folgenden Personen:
- H. R. S. (nicht ermittelt): „DAs walt' der liebe Gott!" (a. a. O., 469–473), „WEil nun der abend ist gekommen" (570–574);
- Diederich v. dem Werder (H[err] D[iederich] V[on] D[em] W[erder] O[brister]; FG 31): „So bald/ O! frommer Christ" (473f.), „JCh glaub' und weis dis Fürwar und gewis" (549–551), „WOlan! so kommet her jhr frommen" (551–559; Text und Korrekturen finden sich auch im Erzschrein, von uns wiedergegeben in 371222 K I u. II, S. 367–372), „WEil dir/ O! Gottes freund" (565–570);
- Martinus Milagius (M[artinus] M[ilagius] C[antzler]; FG 315): „Komm der Heiden heil geschwind" (479–481), „HERR Jesu Christ ein Schöpfer aller sternen" (481–483);
- Martin Opitz (H[err] M[artin] O[pitz]; FG 200): „VOm morgen/ da die Sonn' anfeht" (483–485);
- Martin Luther (H[err] D[octor] M[artin] L[uther]): „GElobet seist du/ Jesu Christ" (485f.), „CHRistus lag im todes-band'" (506–508), „NVn bitten wir den heilgen Geist" (515–517), „ERhalt' uns/ HERR/ bey deinem wort" (525f.);
- Philipp Nicolai (D[octor] P[hilipp] N[icolai]): „WJe schöne leucht mein Morgenstern" (543–546, der im *Jesaja* gegebene Text von Nicolais „WJe schön leuchtet der Morgenstern" wurde stark überarbeitet).

1 *Singender Jesaja*, 528: „GOtt Vater HErr im Himmelreich'/ | Gott Sohn/ Gott heilger Geist zugleich". Die hier durch ein Apostroph angezeigte Elision des Dativ-e im ersten Vers der ersten Strophe des Lieds folgt nicht den von Milagius formulierten Regeln. S. K 28.

K III Lgfn. Amalia Elisabeth v. Hessen-Kassel (1602–1651), geb. Gfn. v. Hanau, wurde nach dem Tod ihres Gatten Lgf. Wilhelms V. v. Hessen-Kassel (FG 65) im Jahr 1637 Regentin von Hessen-Kassel (bis 1650). S. zu ihr 460125 K 1. Sie war Anhängerin des reformierten Bekenntnisses, das sie vehement zu verteidigen verstand. Gibt es einen Zusammenhang mit den reformierten Theologen Martinius (s. K 9), Haustedt und Crocius

(s. K 7), die in Milagius' *Vorrede* explizit bzw. implizit erwähnt werden? S. oben, K 7. Für 1637 ist zumindest ein Aufenthalt Amalia Elisabeths in Bremen bezeugt; s. *DA Köthen I.* 4 370422 K 1, S. 138.

460829

Johann Michael Moscherosch an Johann Rist

Beantwortet in 461020. — Johann Michael Moscherosch (FG 436) las gern das Lob Johann Rists (FG 467. 1647) in dessen *POetischem Schauplatz* (1646) und in einem Brief Jesaias Romplers v. Löwenhalt (AGT), jedoch möge Rist, so wendet Moscherosch ein, sein literarisches Vermögen nicht überbewerten, da das Lob eines Freundes immer für voreingenommen gehalten werde.

Q *Moscherosch: Gesichte* II (1650): Gesichte | Philanders von Sittewald/ | Das ist | Straff-Schrifften | Hanß-Michael Moscheroschen | von Wilstädt. | Ander Theil. | [Vignette] | Straßburg/ | Bey Johan-Philipp. Mülben. | und Josias Städeln. | [Linie] | M. DC. L., 901 f. Nr. V. – Aus Straßburg ohne Abs. u. Anschrift. HAB: Lo 5511: 2. — *BN: Kühlmann: Korrespondenz Moscheroschs,* 268. „Nimmt Bezug auf Rists Erwähnungen Moscheroschs in *Poetischer Schauplatz,* 1646, abgedruckt ibid. S. 902, Nr. VI." — Nicht bei *Estermann.*

A *Fehlt.*

V.

Desselben in seinem Weltbeliebten Schauplatz/[1] wie nicht weniger in dem 12. Aprillen an Herrn Rumplern abgeloffenen schreiben/[2] von mir widerholtes hohes Lob/ hab ich ablesend zwar von hertzen gern vernommen/ weil ich weiß/ es seye kein besser Lob alß von vortrefflichen Leuten gelobet werden. Wan aber hierauß unschwer zu ersehen daß M. H. Herr mich sonders gönstig liebe/ hiergegen auch wahr/ daß das Lob eines Freundes von vilen für zweifelig gehalten werde/ alß bitte ich allein M. H. Herren/ so gar hohe sachen mir vñ meiner Geschicklichkeit nit zuschreiben wolle/ der ich in meiner flüchtigen Nichtigkeit mir selbsten am besten bewußt bin/ und wünsche nichts mehr alß Jhme all angenehmes ge-[902]fallen und dienst zuerweisen/ und dannenhero in solcher Hoffnung zuverbleiben alß lang ich lebe. Straßburg den 29 Augstmonat 1646.

I

Johann Rists Urteil über Moscheroschs *Gesichte Philanders von Sittewald*

Q *Rist: Schauplatz* (1646), Bl. ciij rv. HAB: Lo 6467.

Die trefflichsten Köpffe und allerklügeste Geister pflegen der Welt ihre Mängel in Satirischen Bücheren und Gedichten dergestalt bescheidentlich vor zumahlen/ daß ein Vernünftiger/ der sich getroffen befindet/ sich gahr nicht über den Schreiber/ aber wol über sich selber und seine ihme theils angebohrne/ theils angewehnete Laster kan erzürnen/ so gahr muß die Wahrheit wie das öl aller öhrter oben schweben. Und dieses erhellet nicht allein aus den Schrifften der Alten […], sonderen es bezeugens auch die neue […] und ist unter denen itzlebenden teutschen der treflich erfahrner und gelahrter Mann Herr Hans Michael Moscherosch/ (dessen Weltbekante Satirische Gesichter unter dem Nahmen Philanders von Sittwalt vor weinig Jahren an das Licht kommen) billig sehr hoch zu rühmen/ in deme er als ein redlicher Teutscher auch auffrichtig und Teutsch einem ieden die Meinung dergestalt unter die Augen saget/ daß sich [ciij v] keiner mit der Wahrheit kan entschuldigen/ noch auch ihn den **Herrn Moscherosch** im allergeringsten deßwegen schelten oder beschüldigen.

VI.

Es ist unter den jetzigen Satyrischen Poeten ein trefflich-erfahrner und gelehrter Mann (dessen Weltbekante Gesichte/ unter dem Namen Philanders von Sittewald vor wenig Jahren an das Liecht gekomen) billig hochzurühmen/ in dem er/ als ein redlicher Teutscher/ auch aufrichtig uñ Teutsch einem jeden die Meynung dergestalt unter die augen saget/ daß sich keiner mit der warheit entschuldigen kan/ noch ihn deßwegen schelten/ oder beschuldigen. Schauplatz Joh. Risten.

K 1 S. Beil. I.
2 Sonst unbekanntes Schreiben Johann Rists (FG 467. 1647) an Jesaias Rompler v. Löwenhalt (AGT). Zu demselben s. 390800 K 1, 450308A, 450806 u. ö. Vgl. *Kühlmann: Korrespondenz Moscheroschs*, 268, Brief vom 3.7.1648 (Mosch. an A. C.), lat. Ausz. aus Straßburg, ohne Absender und Anschrift in *Moscherosch: Gesichte* II (1650), 910, Nr. XXI: Johann Michael Moscherosch (FG 436. Der Träumende) verwahrt sich dort gegen den ihm von Rist zugesprochenen Titel eines „Syndicus Reipublicae". Vgl. zum Kontext 430103 (Justus Georg Schottelius, FG 397, an Moscherosch), verzeichnet in *Kühlmann: Korrespondenz Moscheroschs*, 275. Vgl. Rists Gedichte im Vorwerk des ersten Teils der *Gesichte* von 1650: „An die Europeische Völcker | Von denen Sinnreichen und Hochnützlichen Gesichtern des übertrefflichen Herrn Philanders von Sittewald | Kling-gedicht" (Bl. [†† vij] r); „An den viel- und weltsehenden Traumenden" (Bl. [†† vij] v); „An die mißgünstige Neider" (Bl. [†† viij] rv) und „Überschrifft An eben denselben […] Traumenden" (Bl. ††† r) letzteres d. d. 3.8.1648, alle gezeichnet mit Rists Gesellschaftsnamen ‚Der Rüstige'. Vgl. ferner 461020 und *DA Köthen I.* 8: 470801 (Rist an Moscherosch) sowie die undatierte Widmung Moscheroschs an Rist, vor *Gesicht I 6* [S. 332]: „S Johani Ristio S. | SVfficiat dixisse nudum id hoc Optimi Viri Nonem *[sic]* cui uni omnia consummat virtutis ornamenta nupsisse persuasum nobis". Rists *Poetischer Schauplatz* und das darin enthaltene Ehrengedicht auf Andreas Tscherning bot übrigens auch diesem einen Anlaß, um das übertriebene Lob zurückzuweisen. S. 440324 K I 3.

460902

Fürst Ludwig an Georg Philipp Harsdörffer

Antwort auf Georg Philipp Harsdörffers Brief (FG 368. Der Spielende) vom 17.7.1646 (in *DA Köthen I. 9*). Zur Beantwortung vgl. 460916. — F. Ludwig (der Nährende) legt dem Brief ein weiteres Schriftstück (von Marcus Fridericus Wendelin[us] zu Harsdörffers *Specimen Philologiae Germanicae* [1646]) bei und merkt zu diesem drei Dinge an: (1.) Den Unterricht der Freien Künste in deutscher Sprache einzuführen und das lateinische Fachvokabular ins Deutsche zu übersetzen, hält er für ein mögliches Vorhaben. Bei fleißigem Nachdenken können sowohl die Fachbegriffe wie die behandelten Gegenstände verständlich und ungezwungen so ins Deutsche übersetzt werden, daß diese Übersetzungen auch allgemeine Anerkennung finden. Junge Leute, die der alten Sprachen kundig und der dt. Sprache gegenüber aufgeschlossen sind, könnten dieser Aufgabe einer durch Beispiele illustrierten Verdeutschung sehr wohl gewachsen sein. Dazu müßten aber deutsche Schulen eingerichtet werden, in denen die Schüler das Lesen und Schreiben sowie die Grammatik des Deutschen lernten. Auf solcher Grundlage ließe sich das Lateinische dann umso leichter erwerben. Die latein. Lehrwerke zu den versch. Fächern („kunstlehren") müssen aber kurzgefaßt sein, und die deutschen Leitfäden mit jenen konform sein, um das Gedächtnis nicht zu überfordern. Die alten Lehrmeister hingegen, bisher nur gewohnt, die alten Sprachen zu unterrichten, sollte man nicht dazu zwingen, ihren Unterricht fortan auf Deutsch zu halten. Sie hätten nur Verdruß davon, die Schüler aber keinen Nutzen. — (2.) F. Ludwig plädiert dafür, die 1. Pers. Sg. Indikativ Präsens mit auslautendem -e zu schreiben („ich liebe" und nicht „ich lieb" etc.). — (3.) Desgleichen erscheine die 2. Pers. im Imperativ oft zweisilbig („liebe"! statt „lieb"!), zumal Nomina wie „Liebe" auf eben diese Form zurückgingen. Dies seien zumindest nach der hiesigen (omd.) Mundart die besseren und richtigeren Formen, und sie seien nicht verzwickt oder „abgebißen". — Justus Georg Schottelius (FG 397. Der Suchende) plane wohl, eine überarbeitete Auflage seiner *Sprachkunst* (1641) zu veröffentlichen. Es wäre besser, wenn er sein Manuskript vor der Drucklegung nach Köthen schickte, da man gewiß nützliche Verbesserungsvorschläge anbringen könne. Obwohl Schottelius sich in diesem Jahr dazu bereit erklärt habe, sei noch nichts eingetroffen. Harsdörffer möge ihn noch einmal erinnern.

Q HM Köthen: V S 545, Bl. 354rv, eigenh. Konzept. — *D:* KE, 361f.; KL III, 273f. — BN: *Bürger*, 950 Nr. 63.

A *Fehlt.*

Jüngster geschehenen vertröstung zufolge, wird dem Spielenden hiemit zugefertiget, was auf sein[a] lateinisches schreiben vom[b] 17 Heumonates fur eine anderweite schrift eingekommen.[1] Darbey dan mehr nicht als folgende wenige erinnerungen zu vermelden furgefallen.

Erstlich so viel darinnen von dem unterrichte der freyen Kunste in Deutscher sprache und[c] derer verdolmetschung angezogen, das man solche nicht fur unmuglich halte, sondern ein nachsinlicher fleiß so wol die Kunstwörter, als die sachen an sich selbst verständlich und ungezwungen zu geben, samt einem guten beyfalle der meisten, müße angewendet werden, und beyhanden sein. Darzu dan junge leute, die der Sprachen darinnen[d] sie geschrieben und verfaßet mächtig, auch ihrer kundig, und der Deutschen sprache sonderliche liebhaber seinde zu gebrauchen: Also das sie geubet seyen, erstlich die freyen künste den schulen in Deutsch recht furzulegen und durch beyspiele zu erkleren, worzu dan wolte[f] von nöten sein gantze Deutsche Schulen anzulegen, und wan dieg schüler mit dem deutschen lesen[,] schreiben, und der Sprachlehre angefangen jah solche wol gefaßet, dan siee zu dem lateinischen desto leichter, wan der verstand dar,[i] gelangen können[j]. Doch werden[k] die kunstlehren im lateinischen auch also mußen in[l] möglichster kürtze gefaßet sein, das siee so wol in der einen als der andern sprache eine gleichförmigkeit haben[m], und desto beßer im gedächtnüs behalten werden können. Alten lehrmeistern aber dergleichen, die der Lateinischen und Griechischen Sprache im lehren gewonet,[n] aufzudringen, würde ihnen nicht alleine wiedrig sein, sondern auch nicht viel nutzen schaffen, und sie billich darmit zu verschonen sein.[2]

Furs andere, wird an einem orte in Zweiffel gestellet, welches beßer und eigentlicher geredet, und geschrieben sey,

Jn gegenwertiger Zeit die anzeigungs weise erster[o] person; Jch liebe,[p] ich[e] lauffe, ich schreibe,[q] —

oder Jch lieb[r], ich lauf[,] ich schreib etc. —

Da dan das erste[s] dieser Mund- und[t] redeart nach[e] fur das beste und richtigste gehalten wird. Also

zum Dritten, in der gebietungs weise liebe[u] du, lauffe[u] du[,] schreibe[v] du —

oder lieb[w] du, lauff[w] du, oder schreib[w] du

Da auch das erste[x] fur richtiger und unverzwickter gehalten wird, Und[y] also sag, lieb[,] geh, steh, abgebißen ist, und sage, liebe, rede[z], gehe, stehe heißen sol, ja[aa] die Nenwörter, die sage, die liebe, die rede, der gang, und der verstand, von ihren[ab] Zeit- oder[ac] sprechwörtern entstehen.[3] [354v]

Schlieslichen als man vernimmt, das der Suchende seine Sprachlehre oder[ad] Sprachkunst anderweit ubersehen zusammengefaßet und in kurtzem wieder wil druck[en][ae] laßen, so were wol gut, das er sie fur dem Drucke zuvor möchte einschicken,[af] da dan sonder zweiffe[l][ae] allerhand nutzliche erinnerungen darbey kunten gethan werden. Er hat sich zwar noch in diesem Jhare dah[in][ag] erboten, es ist aber dieses ortes darvon[e] noch nichts eingelange[t.][ae] dem[ah] Spielenden wird anheim gestellet, ob er hi[e]runter[ae] etwas erwenung bey ihme Suchende[e] thun wolle[ai] [4] Wormi[t][ae] verbleibet

Des Spielenden gantzwilliger
der Nehrende

Geben am bewusten[aj] orte den 2. Herbstmonats 1646.

T **a** *Folgt* <jungstes> — **b** *Bis* Heumonates *eingefügt.* — **c** *Bis* verdolmetschung *eingefügt.* — **d** *Bis* auch ihrer *eingefügt.* — **e** *Eingefügt.* — **f** *Urspr. Reihenfolge der Wörter bis* anzulegen *durch Bezifferung geändert aus* gantz deutsche Schulen anzulegen wolte vonnöten sein — **g** die schüler *gebessert aus* die<selben> — **h** ja solche *eingefügt für* <und> — **i**

Folgt <wird zu> — **j** *Eingefügt für* <sein> — **k** *Gebessert aus* <wurden> — **l** *in möglichster kürtze eingefügt.* — **m** *Eingefügt für* <haben *oder* hetten> *(unsichere Lesung, mehrfach interlinear gebessert).* — **n** *Folgt* <dergleichen> — **o** *erster person eingefügt.* — **p** *Folgt* <nich> *(unsichere Lesung).* — **q** *Folgt* <underg [?]> — **r** *Gebessert aus* lieb<e> — **s** *Eingefügt für* <letzere> — **t** *und rede eingefügt.* — **u** *Schluß-e nachträglich ergänzt.* — **v** *Versehentlich zwei Schluß-e nachträglich ergänzt:* schreibee — **w** *Gebessert aus* lieb<e> *bzw.* lauff<e> *bzw.* schreib<e> — **x** *Eingefügt für* <letztere> — **y** *Eingefügt für* <das> — **z** *Versehentlich mit doppeltem e im Auslaut geschrieben:* redee — **aa** *Eingefügt für* <und darvon> — **ab** *Folgt* <sprach> — **ac** *Zeit- oder unterstrichen, vielleicht als Streichungsmarkierung.* — **ad** *Eingefügt für* <und> — **ae** *Textverlust im Falz. Konjektur in eckigen Klammern.* — **af** *Folgt* <vielleicht> — **ag** *Textverlust im Falz, Konjektur nach KE in eckigen Klammern.* — **ah** *Urspr. Reihenfolge der Wörter durch Bezifferung umgestellt aus* <Es> wird dem Spielenden — **ai** *Gebessert aus* wolle<n> — **aj** *Gebessert aus* bekanten

K 1 F. Ludwig (Der Nährende) schickt Georg Philipp Harsdörffer (FG 368. Der Spielende) Marcus Fridericus Wendelins Duplik vom 6. 8. 1646 (HM Köthen: V S 545, Bl. 481r–487v). Damit hatte er auf Harsdörffers Brief vom 17. 7. 1646 geantwortet, der seinerseits eine Replik auf Wendelins erstes Gutachten zum *Specimen Philologiae Germanicae* (1646) vom 15. 6. 1646 darstellte. Alle drei Dokumente demnächst in *DA Köthen I. 9.* F. Ludwig hatte den Schriftverkehr zwischen Harsdörffer und Wendelin(us) übermittelt und in 460816 Harsdörffer bereits angekündigt, daß eine weitere Einlassung Wendelins folgen werde. Vgl. zu den Gutachten Wendelins auch 460609 K 3 u. 460705 K 3.

2 Wendelinus sprach sich in seiner Duplik zu Harsdörffers *Specimen* (s. Anm. 1) zwar dafür aus, das Deutsche in seiner Reinheit und Unvermischtheit so zu pflegen, wie dies die Griechen und Römer mit ihren Sprachen getan hätten, und es auf keinen Fall sklavisch anderen Sprachen wie dem Latein zu unterwerfen; jedoch zögerte er, fremdsprachige Fachtermini unbedingt einzudeutschen. Es klinge doch lächerlich, wenn man „supinum" mit „das auf dem rück liegende" übersetze. Hier sei auch mit Widerstand der hohen Schulen zu rechnen. Man müsse bedachtsam und mit langem Atem an die Verdeutschung klassischer Schriften wie dem aristotelischen *Organon* gehen: „Etsi non nego technica vocabula Artisq*ue* terminos, qui hactenus non nisi Latini & græci fuerunt, in vernaculam nostram translatos quasi peregrinum quiddam & insolens sonare: ut, si verbi supinum reddamus, das auf dem rück liegende: quod sine risu vix audiretur. Quæ causa, quod sæpe mecum dubitem, an technica vocabula terminiq*ue* Artium germanice quoq*ue* sint reddendi & in institutione adhibendi. Vix enim futurum crediderim, ut publicæ scholæ græcis & latinis adsuetæ terminis passim recepturæ sint germanicos. Discendum hâc foret non discipulis tantum, sed & præceptioribus: qui si in novos illos & hactenus inauditos terminos inciderent, in plurimis non minus, quàm discipuli, hæsitaturi essent: quod de Organo Aristotelis germanico nuperrimè quoq*ue* monui. Nullius tamen labores & conatus carpo: si linguæ nostræ amplificandæ eiusdemq*ue* majestati asserendæ serviant" usw. Wendelins Duplik, a. a. O., Bl. 482r. Harsdörffer hatte hingegen schon in seiner *Schutzschrift/ für Die Teutsche Spracharbeit* (Anhang in der 2. Ausg. des 1. Teils seiner *Frauenzimmer-Gesprächspiele*, 1644, Ndr. 1968), 367, eine muttersprachliche Reform des Unterrichts angeregt: „Die Jtaliäner/ Frantzosen und Spanier haben ihre Sprache sehr hoch erhaben. Wir Teutsche könten es auch dahin bringen/ damit wir so viel Zeit in Erlernung des Lateins nicht verlieren dörfften/ sondern so bald mit den zarten Jahren die Wissenschaften selbsten angehen könten." Im *Specimen*, 225 ff. (Disq. X, § 11–14.) unterschied Harsdörffer zwischen jenen eingebürgerten Fremdwörtern, „quae absque scandalo Ecclesiae mutari non poterunt", wie Prophet, Apostel, Evangelium usw. (S. 229), sowie anderen Fremdwörtern, „quae in usum alterius linguae, per interpretationem transire non possunt" (231), und jenen, die sich sehr wohl sinnvoll ins Deutsche übertragen lassen, Kunstwörter im doppelten Sinne etwa wie die „Sinn-Bildkunst" (Ars Emblematica), „Schau-Spielkünste" (artes theatrales) usw. (233). Vgl. dazu auch 440525 K II 13. F. Ludwig geht hier ebenfalls auf Distanz zur Position Wendelins und knüpft mit seiner Umwertung der sprachlichen Priorität vom Latein zur Muttersprache an das ratichianische Reformprojekt in Köthen und Weimar um 1620 an, dessen Lehrbücher sich um die Verdeutschung latein. Fachbegriffe, etwa der Metaphysik, der Logik, der Rhetorik und natürlich der Grammatik bemühten. Vgl. 440525 K II 9 u. 450923B. Sogar analog aufgebaute Lehrwerke, wie er sie im vorliegenden Brief befürwortet, sollten damals die Vergleichbarkeit der Sprachen und somit das leichtere Erlernen derselben und der jeweiligen Unterrichtsgegenstände befördern. Vgl. 410208 K 8.

3 Es handelt sich um die in der FG seit längerem geführte Stammwort-Kontroverse, ob, wie vom Hebräischen angenommen, die Nomina von den Verben herrühren, und die Stammwörter der Verben stets mit dem vermeintlich einsilbigen Imperativ der 2. Person Sg. identisch seien. Justus Georg Schottelius (FG 397. Der Suchende) und Harsdörffer vertraten diese Auffassung, Christian Gueintz (FG 361), Philipp v. Zesen (FG 521. 1648) und auch Wendelin(us) in seiner Duplik (s. Anm. 1), Bl. 483v ff., widersprachen. Vgl. 450410 K 3. Harsdörffer plädierte in seinem *Specimen (1646)*, 146f. (disquisitio VII, § 11) dafür, die 1. Pers. Sg. Ind. Präs. Aktiv (bei regelmäßigen Verben) durch Anhängen eines -e zu bilden, wobei er diese Form als eine Zusammensetzung betrachtet, gebildet aus dem einsilbigen Stammwort (= der einsilbige Imperativ) und dem ‚Hilfsbuchstaben' -e- (‚littera servilis'). Darin folgt er *Schottelius: Sprachkunst (1641)*, 430f., der auf S. 444 explizit feststellt: „Es ist zu wissen/ daß die anzeigungsweise müsse allezeit in Teutscher Sprache zwosilbig seyn/ als ich lauffe[/] ich gebe/ ich bete. Es ist zwar zuweilen befindlich/ daß sie ohn ihr letztes E geschrieben werden; aber solches gibt in dem/ da es unrecht ist/ keine regulam." Harsdörffer neigte in seiner Schreibpraxis aber regelmäßig dazu, das e-Suffix zu apokopieren, wie es für das Obd., aber auch für das Luther-Deutsch typisch war. Vgl. schon 450124 K I 4 und *Herz: Rechtschreibdebatte*, 107f. u. 110. — Was den Imperativ (‚die Gebietungsweise') betrifft, richtete sich Harsdörffer ebenfalls nach *Schottelius: Sprachkunst (1641)*, 413, wo die „weise zu gebieten" als „das rechte Stam̃wort/ welches alleine die Stam̃letteren in sich begrifft" bestimmt wird. Diese „Zeitstammwörter oder Gebietungsweisen" seien grundsätzlich „einsilbig", eine These, der sich Harsdörffer anschloß. Obgleich F. Ludwig den Imperativ ohne Schwa im Auslaut als eine irreguläre Verkürzung kritisierte, bleibt Schottelius bei seiner Definition, s. *Schottelius: Sprachkunst (1651)*, 708f. In der Neuauflage verweist er sogar auf die entsprechende Passage in *Harsdörffer: Specimen (1646)*, 140–145 (disquisitio VII, § 9). Das überflüssige -e- am Ende eines Imperativs reiht *Schottelius: Sprachkunst (1641)*, 547–551 darüber hinaus unter die sieben fehlerhaften Verwendungsweisen ein, die im Deutschen bei diesem Buchstaben häufig zu beobachten seien. — Im Gegensatz zu F. Ludwig gingen Harsdörffer und Schottelius nicht davon aus, daß Nomina (‚Nennwörter') wie die hier genannten („die sage, die liebe" usw.) aus den „Schlieslichen sprechwörtern", also finiten Verbformen, hervorgingen. Die Basis der Wortbildung ist aus ihrer Sicht immer das mit dem Imperativ identische Stammwort. In *Harsdörffer: Specimen (1646)*, 138f. (disquisitio VII, § 8) heißt es explizit: Alle Nomina gehen auf Verba zurück. Darum bringe das Stammwort „sag" auch das Nomen „die Sage" hervor. Es gebe zwar Substantive wie „das Brod", aus denen sich keine Verben bilden ließen, denn „Broden" sage man nicht. Gäbe es jedoch ein solches Verb, müßte dessen Imperativ (und Stammwort!) zweifellos „Brod" lauten. Stammwörter ohne gebräuchliche Verben bezeichnet Harsdörffer als „Radices Nominales, Nenn-Stammwörter". Auch wenn er

den Bildungsweg nicht expliziert, geht aus seinem Argumentationsgang deutlich hervor, daß für ihn „Sage" eine Zusammensetzung aus Stammwort und ‚Hilfsbuchstabe' -e- sein muß. In 460915 bezeichnet er das den Imperativen angehängte -e- als eine „nachsylbe", die in vielen Mundarten nicht gebräuchlich sei.

4 Eine überarbeitete Auflage von *Schottelius: Sprachkunst (1641)* wird erst 1651, nach dem Tode F. Ludwigs im Januar 1650, erscheinen. Entgegen seiner Zusage in 451007 legte Schottelius die Neubearbeitung seiner Grammatik nicht der FG zur Prüfung vor — kein Wunder, denn in ihr sollte Schottelius die analogistische Position, gemessen an seinen anderen Spracharbeiten, am konsequentesten vertreten. Harsdörffer richtete sich seit seiner Aufnahme in die FG nach den Spracharbeiten von Schottelius. S. dazu 460406 K 7.

460908

Herzog August d. J. von Braunschweig-Wolfenbüttel an Johann Valentin Andreae

Antwort auf 460819. — Hz. August d. J. v. Braunschweig-Wolfenbüttel (FG 227) bestätigt den Empfang von Johann Valentin Andreaes (FG 464. 1646) Brief 460819, in dem dieser den richtigen Erhalt mehrerer Pakete mitgeteilt hatte. Mit dem vorliegenden Schreiben sendet Hz. August den letzten Druckbogen der Quart-Ausgabe seiner *Evangelischen Kirchen-Harmonie* (1646). — Der Herzog verspricht Andreae, an dessen gewünschte Aufnahme in die FG unter der beschriebenen Imprese zu denken. – Heute heirate Justus Georg Schottelius (FG 397) die hübsche Braunschweiger Jungfrau Margaretha Cleve. — Hz. August erwartet das Verzeichnis der ihm von Andreae angebotenen seltenen Bücher und die Angabe des Preises. — Seine Schüler, die Prinzen Anton Ulrich und Ferdinand Albrecht v. Braunschweig-Wolfenbüttel (FG 716. 1659 bzw. FG 842. 1673), werden Schottelius zur Trauung in die Kirche geleiten.

Q HAB: Cod. Guelf. 236.3 Extrav., Bl. 39rv [A: 39v], eigenh.; 36. Brief Hz. Augusts aus dem Jahr 1646. — *D:* Ernst Ludwig Henke: Georg Calixtus und seine Zeit. 2 Bde. Halle 1853–1860, II, 1, 63; auszugsweises Zitat in *Begemann: FG u. Andreae*, 41 u. 43; *Merzbacher: Schottelius*, 163.

A Dem Ehrwurdigen und Hochgelahrten, unserm lieben besondern, Herrn *Johan Valentino Andreæ*, der H. Schrift D. Furstl. Wurtembergischen OberHofpredigern, und geistlichem ConsistorialRahte, cito zu behandigen etc.   Stutgarten.
Darunter Empfangsvermerk: Ps. [...]ᵃ. Nov. 46.

ᵇEhrwürdiger und Hochgelahrter, lieber besonder und getreuer, sein Skreiben vom 19 Aug.ᶜ habe ich wol erhalten, und gern daraus verstanden, daß er bey dieser unsicheren zeit, die pacquetlein richtig empfangen. Hiemit schikke ich, den lezten bogen, der ziemblich viel mühe veruhrsachet im corrigieren,¹ bey den, deutzsch mehr gewohnten Sezzeren. Gott sey dank, daß es so weit gerahten: der es als seine Arbeit, wol wird erhalten, und frucht tragen lassen: Wegen vermehrung unserer Kreuter geselschaftᵈ dem *Müeden Hernach*, und *Mösch*, (laut

schreibens vom 15/ 25. Jul. ad Hainhoferum) werde ich eingedenk verbleiben:[2] Heute ist D. Schöttelij Ehrentag, mit einem hupschen Jungfräulein aus Braunschweig Magareta Cleven genandt.[3] Anlangendt die raren bücher, werde ich nicht allein die verzeichnis darvon erwarten, sondern auch den nähesten Tax, mich wegen übermachung des wexels, darnach habend zu richten.[4] Obgemeldter D. Schöttelius ist von seinen discipulis A. U. und F. A. zur Kirchen geführt worden:[5] daß Jehnem eine Ehre, diesen eine besondere freude gewesen: Verbleibe ihm mit guter gewogenheit ferner beygetahn und gewogen; als
    sein alzeit beständig wol affectionierter Freundt,
    AugustushzBuLmh[e]
Wulfenb. den 8. Sept. 1646 ♂[f]

I

Beigelegte Notiz Andreaes über den Katalog seiner zu verkaufenden Bücher

Q HAB: Cod. Guelf. 65.1 Extrav., Bl.314r, Rücks. leer, eigenh., undat. Zettel.

Jch bin beredt gewesen, es habe mein amanuensus den Catalogum meiner Bibliotheca ganz verfertiget, so befinde ich im Außzeichnen deren bucher so ich fur mich behalten wolte, daß kaum daß tritte theil aufgeschrieben. habe gleichwolen disen imperfecten catalogum wullen vnd. vbersenden, vmb etwas darauß g. zuersehen ob sie der Translation[1] währt sein möchte. Es sollen aber der stukh 600 völlig vberlifert werden.

II

461103

Andreae sendet Herzog August d.J. von Braunschweig-Wolfenbüttel einen Überschlag über seine zu verkaufende Büchersammlung

Q HAB: Cod. Guelf. 65.1 Extrav., Bl.315rv [A: 315v]; eigenh.; Sig. Andreaes 44. Brief in Antwort auf Hz. Augusts 36. Erst am 11.11. zusammen mit dem 45. Brief Andreaes v. 11.11.1646 (a. a. O., 317rv) abgesandt. — Hier ein Auszug aus Bl.315r.

Meiner geringen Bibliotekh catalogum[1], wie sie noch an ietzo beisamen, habe ich beigefugt. E. F. g. sich haben darinnen g. zu ersehen. Jch begehre Nur etliche wenige stukh davon fur mich zu behalten. Die vberige von 600 stukhen sollen zu E. f. g. befehl gehorsamlich gestellet sein, vnd habe ich einen vnvorgreiflichen vberschlag gemacht, daß wo

100 Folia eines Pro 40 x.	ästimiret......	66 f. — 40 x	
200 Quarto - â - 20 x.	würde	66 f — 40 x	
200 Octavo - â - 15 x	thete es.	50 f — 0 x	
100 Decima sext. - â - 10 x ..		16 f — 40	

	Summa	200 f	

welche zu 3. Zilen NewJahr, Ostern, vnd Michaelis iedes Mahls 66 f. - 40 x könten entrichtet werden. Solle iedoch Lieber zu E. F. G. gnedigst. arbitrio gesezet sein.

III

Anderer Überschlag der Herzog August angebotenen Bücher Andreaes

Q HAB: BA (Bibliotheks-Archiv) II, 11 Nr. 5, Bl. 32r–36v. Beidseitig, in einer oder zwei Kolumnen beschriebene Folio-Blätter. Wohl die Hand von Andreaes Helfer („amanuensis"). Auf jeder Seite Summe der dort aufgelisteten Bücher. Einteilung A, B, C. Am Schluß jedes Buchstabens Zählung der Bücher nach Formaten. — Hier ein Auszug.

	A	B	C	
Folio 35	42	26	= 103	
Quart. 96	24	82	= 202	
Octav. 63	139	83	= 285	
Duodez 88	4	18	= 110	

			700	

T a *Tagesdatum unleserlich.* — b *Über der Zeile von Andreaes H. mittig die Ziffer 36.* — c *Dazu am Rand von Andreaes H. die Briefzählung 33.* — d *Danach eingefügt bis* Hainhoferum) — e *Lies:* Augustus hertzog zu Braunschweig und Lüneburg (meine hand) — f *Darunter eingeklebter Zettel (Druck) mit Chronogramm für 1646:* EnCONCorDIsEVangeLIIDVXGVeLpherbItVs, | ConsCrIptIsLIbrIs, nobILefIuItopVs. | Vel | SICVtAqVILaportaVItPVLLusSVos, | SIC JehoVa ECCLesIaM tVetVr. | De. 32. V. 11.12.

K 1 Ende der Korrektur Hz. Augusts d. J. v. Braunschweig-Wolfenbüttel (FG 227) für die Quartausgabe seiner *Evangelischen Kirchen-Harmonie* (1646). S. 411214 u. 460909. Der Herzog hatte sie Stück für Stück Johann Valentin Andreae (FG 464. 1646) zur Durchsicht zugeschickt. Am 25.8.1646 verkündete der Herzog Andreae den bevorstehenden Abschluß der Arbeiten an der Quartausgabe: „schikke ihm 6 Bogen, und den lezten darzu, der über 8 Tage complet folgen wird, dan dieser noch nicht corrigieret, alsdan sollen auch die vorhergehende Bogen folgen." (HAB: Cod. Guelf. 236.3 Extrav., Bl. 37r). Hz. August konnte Andreae den erwarteten Rest aber wegen der angegebenen Schwierigkeiten erst am 8.9.1646 senden.

2 Hz. August versuchte durch seine Empfehlung an F. Ludwig (460915 I), Andreae den Weg in die FG zu bahnen. Andreae hatte sein Verlangen zuerst Philipp Hainhofer geoffenbart (460715). Unter dem 3.11.1646 schrieb Andreae an Hz. August: „Der reception zu der Hochlob. Fruchtbringenden geselschaft, etsi iam effectus et sterilis, will ich vnd. erwarten, vnd den Legibus mich gehorsamlich accomodieren." HAB: Cod. Guelf. 65.1 Extrav., Bl. 315r. Zit. v. *Keller: Akademien der Renaissance*, 107 u. *Begemann: FG und Andreä*, 43.

3 Justus Georg Schottelius (FG 397) heiratete an diesem Tag Margaretha, Tochter v. Johann Cleve, Kanonikus und Vitztum des Stifts St. Blasius zu Braunschweig. Sie starb bereits am 6.9.1647. Am 12.6.1649 vermählte er sich zum zweiten Mal, mit Anna Maria, geb. Sobbe. *Bei der Wieden: Schottelius*, 138; *Conermann III*, 466.

4 Zu Andreaes Plan, eine große Zahl seiner Bücher an den Herzog zu verkaufen, s. 460715, 460804 u. 460819. Zu Andreaes endgültiger Antwort auf Hz. Augusts Verlangen s. Beil. I–III.

5 Die Prinzen Anton Ulrich und Ferdinand Albrecht v. Braunschweig-Wolfenbüttel (FG 716. 1659 bzw. FG 842. 1673), die Schottelius seit 1638 bzw. 1641 bis 1646 unterrichtet hatte. Zur Ehrung des Präzeptors vgl. Andreaes Äußerung in seinem Brief an Hz. August v. 3.11.1646: „Daß H. D. Schottelio an seinem HochZeitlichen fest, durch F. Comitat, so große Ehr widerfahren, ist Hochrumlich zu vernemmen, vnd Benuget getrewe diener Vbi fidej et solertiae aliqua est aestimatio, Hingegen sagt Guevara in Menosprecio de Corte, Non ay en el mundo tan cruel imigo, como es el criado que anda descontento." HAB: Cod. Guelf. 65.1 Extrav. 315r. Der Hilfslehrer der Prinzen, Sigmund Betulius (S. v. Birken. FG 681. 1658), stellte vielleicht selbst eine Gratulationsschrift für Schottelius zusammen, welche neben seiner (anonymen) Prosaekloge „Götterschenkungen zu dem Freud-feyerlichen Myrten- und EhrenFeste des Lobwürdigen FONTANO und Seiner Viel-Tugendbegabten MARGARJS Verehret/ und mit einem Hertzmeinenden Wunschgedichte beygeschikkt" auch je ein von den beiden Prinzen gezeichnetes, aber von Betulius stammendes deutsches Gedicht enthält. Diese Gratulationen erschienen u. d. T. FESTO NUPTIALI Viri amplißimi, Consultißimi et excellentißimi DNI. IUSTI GEORGII SCHOTTELII J. V. Doctoris, Consiliarij & assessoris Guelphici, SPONSI: & ... Virginis MARGARITÆ ... CLEVEN ... SPONSÆ VIII. die Septemb. anni 1646. VVelferbyti Celebrato à Principibus, Fautoribus, Amicis dicata & dedicata Carmina Gratulatoria. Zu den Beiträgern gehörten u. a. auch der als pommer. Gesandter in Wolfenbüttel weilende Joachim v. Glasenapp (FG 451. 1646), der Arzt Martin Gosky und Abraham Marconnet, der Erzieher des ältesten Prinzen (Rudolf August; FG 754. 1660). — Die drei Beiträge Birkens wurden ediert und kommentiert von Hartmut Laufhütte und Ralf Schuster in *Birken: Werke und Korrespondenz*, Bd. 9/ I –II Schottelius, Nr. 2a–c.

K I 1 Überbringung, Transport.

K II 1 Dieser Überschlag weicht von dem Verzeichnis in Beil. III ab, dürfte sich aber auf dieselbe Sammlung beziehen. Offenbar entstand der Überschlag früher als der Katalog. Vgl. den Überschlag Andreaes in seinem Brief v. 23.9.1646 an den Herzog. S. 460819 K 8.

K III Ohne Gliederung nach Alphabet, Sachgruppen oder Formaten. Enthält 698 Titel. Zwei Titel gestrichen. Vgl. die geringeren Zahlenschätzungen der kleinen Formate im Überschlag vom 23.9.1646 (s. 460819 K 8).

460909

Johann Valentin Andreae an Herzog August d. J. von Braunschweig-Wolfenbüttel

Johann Valentin Andreae (FG 464. 1646) teilt wegen der verspäteten Ankunft eines Briefs Hz. Augusts d. J. v. Braunschweig-Wolfenbüttel (FG 227) seine Sorgen darüber mit, ob das Schreiben von Soldaten abgefangen worden wäre. Nun aber freue er sich über den Empfang der abschließenden Sendung der herzoglichen *Evangelischen Kirchen-Harmonie* (1646. 4°). — Andreae bedankt sich, vielleicht dafür, daß der Herzog ihm eine Mitgliederliste zum *GB 1646* übersandt hat. Er wiederholt seine Bitte, Hz. August möge sich für ihn einsetzen, damit er mit einer vorgeschlagenen Imprese in die FG aufgenommen werde. Er sei in seiner Jugend auch unter die Pritschmeister gegangen und habe ohne Kenntnis der opitzianischen Regeln über den Alexandriner den *Triumph desz Glaubens* aus dem Saluste Du Bartas übersetzt. — Kriegsbesatzung liege in Cannstatt, Schorndorf, (Hohen)Asberg und Heilbronn. — Wenn der Herzog (wirklich) nichts gegen Andreaes Veröffentlichung seines Briefwechsels mit Augusts Kindern habe, werde er dies mit Diskretion unternehmen, damit sich die Kinder öffentlich auszeichnen könnten. — Andreae gratuliert zum Jahrestag der Befreiung Wolfenbüttels (September 1643).

Q HAB: Cod. Guelf. 65.1 Extrav., Bl. 304rv [A: 304v]; eigenh.; Sig. — 34. Brief Andreaes als Antwort auf Augusts 36. Schreiben v. 26.8.1646. — Teilw. und unsicher zit. in *Begemann: FG und Andreae*, 41 u. 43.

A Dem Durchleüchtigst. Hochgebohrnen Fursten vnd Herren, Herren Augusto, hertzogen zu Brunschwig: vnd Luneburg &c. Seinem gnedigsten fursten vnd herren &c. Wolfenbüttel. (36.) 9. Septemb. — *Hz. Augusts Empfangsvermerk:* empfangen den 17 8br. 1646

Durchleüchtigst. Hochgebohrner, Gnedigster Furst vnd Herr, E. F. g. 34. auf mein 31. den 26. Aug. ist erst den 7. huius angekommen, vnd bin ich in großen Sorgen gestanden, Es möchten etwa die inciviles Martis filij dieselbe intercipiert haben, habe aber Gott Lob mit frewden daß End der Harmoniæ[1] gesehen, vnd E. f. g. vnd*erthänig*st. zu gratulieren, daß von deren sehr Muhsamen Correctur, sie nu mehr respirieren vnd deren verhoffentlich großen Nuzens so Ecclesia Christj zu genußen haben wurt, mit dero vnsterblichem Ruhm erfrewen mögen. Cuj Deus benedicat.

Fur die Communication dern HochLob. Fruchtbringenden gesellschaft,[2] thue ich mich vnder*thänig*st vnd zum höchsten Bedankhen. Wolle nu E. F. g. mir ferner die hohe Gnad Thun, vnd mich, der ich gleichwol eine vnzeitige geburt bin, auch als ein alten Calefactorem, anhenkhen Laßen, per simbolum, Der Mösische, cum lemmate, hernach, Als den Matten,[3] solle es mich wiewol vnwurdigen, hoch erfrewen. Jch bin zwar in Meiner Jugendt auch vnder den Pritschen Meistern gewesen, vnd mit den Alexandrinischen Versen, einen Versuch in Versione triumphi fidej ex Bartasio einen Versuch gethan.[4] Weil ich aber damahlen Nichts von den Opitianischen regeln gewußt, habe ich mich mehr der heilosen arbeit zu schämen, als beruhmen, stehet also alles zu E. F. g. gnedigster dispensation, vnd disposition.

Die algemeine tempestas diser Orten Machet pro diversitate affectuum, vil spej et metus, nos interim miserè patimur, vnd ist ein gut theil Länder jämmerlich verderbet. Zu Candstadt, ein stund von hier, Ligen 1500 Reuter, Gallo-germanj. Schorndorf ist besezt mit 600 Man hingegen hat Cæsar noch Asperg, vnd hohen Vrach Baiern aber, heilbronn besezet, vnd sizen wir vbrige in freier[a] theil Contribution.[5]

Wo die publicatio epistularum Principum juventutis[6], nur E. F. g. nicht entgegen, wil ich verhofentlich es also disponieren, daß sepositis privatis, et invidiosis, sie deßen Ruhm, vnd ander Junge herschaft ein jncitamem ad faria præstanda haben solle. Jnterest enim rej literariæ, in tanta paucitate illustrium exemplorum, hoc sanè illustrissimum, in publico Prostare.

De anniversario exaltatæ †, qua Serenitas V. post tot nubila, restituto Guelpherbuto,[7] caput in Germania extulit, fructusque Christianæ patientiæ ovans carpsit, ex animo gratulor, et ut sæpius ei salvus redeat, posterisque sit perpetuus. Deum ardentissimi precor.

Befehle E. F. g. dem Schuz des Almechtigen, Auch derselben mich zu beharrenden großen gnaden, verbleibend biß in den Todt.

 E. F. g. Vndertänigste, gehorsame verpflichter Rhat, vnd getreweste Diener
  Jo. Val. Andreæ D.

Pridie anniversarij Cladis Calvensis.[8] 9. Sept. ☿ 46

I

460805

Andreae plant seine *Seleniana Augustalia* (1649)

Q HAB: Cod. Guelf. 65.1 Extrav., Bl. 284rv, Rückseite leer; eigenh. — Undat. Zettel, wohl Mai/ Juni 1646.

Jch habe von E. F. g. geliebten Herren Princen, Meinen g. Fursten vnd Herren, nu mehr 78 Eruditas epistolas, vnd neben denselben noch Andere Princen das es fast auf eine Centuriam kommen solte. Wo nu E. f. g. mir g. wurden erLauben, oder nach dero hohem judicio es auch gut finden, wolte neben den Meinigen geringfügigen, ich ein Libellum in 12°, darauß formieren, vnd sepositis seponendis, in publicum zu ediren, welches hochgedachten h. Princen Nicht indecorum sein werde. Jedoch alles zu E. F. g. g. disposition vnd wilkur gehorsamst gesezet &c.

T **a** *Statt* <beeder>

K 1 Bevorstehendes Ende der Korrektur Hz. Augusts v. Braunschweig-Wolfenbüttel (FG 227) für die Quartausgabe seiner *Evangelischen Kirchen-Harmonie* (1646). S. 411214. Der Herzog pflegte sie Stück für Stück Johann Valentin Andreae (FG 464. 1646) zur Durchsicht zuzuschicken. Am 26.8.1646 hatte August sechs Bögen geschickt und ihm die Sendung des letzten ausstehenden Bogens in acht Tagen angekündigt. Am 1.9.1646 mußte er Andreae wegen der Langsamkeit des Setzers um weitere acht Tage vertrösten. HAB: Cod. Guelf. 236.3 Extrav., Bl. 36r bzw. 38r.

2 Den Empfang des *GB 1646* hatte Andreae bereits am 15.7.1646 bestätigt. Vgl. 460804. Vielleicht hatte Andreae inzwischen die in 460819 I von Justus Georg Schottelius (FG 397) erbetene Mitgliederliste der FG als Schlüssel zum GB erhalten.

3 Die von Andreae gewünschten Impresenangaben unterlagen mehrfach der Änderung. S. 460915A I, 461106 I u. *Conermann III*, 563.

4 Zu Andreaes Saluste-Du-Bartas-Übersetzung s. 270429 (in *DA Köthen I.2*). Dort auch über Andreae u. Opitz. S. unten Anm. 7.

5 Zur Lage Württembergs und Bayerns zwischen den französ.-schwed. und bayer.-ksl. Heeren vgl. 460715 u. 460819. „Jm Gegentheil rückte die Schwedische Armee vor Schorndorf [Rems-Murr-Kr.], nahm den Ort nach einigem Wiederstand ein, besetzte Nördlingen, und richtete darauf ihren Zug gegen Donauert, von da man derselben die Schlüssel der Stadt entgegen brachte. […] Jndem nun die Schwedisch-Französische Armee über die Donau theils gegen Rain [am Lech], theils gegen Augspurg, im Anzuge war, setzte der General Königsmarck mit 2000. Mann den Bayrischen, so bey Jngolstad über die Donau gegangen, auf dem Fuß nach […] Dieser Einfall setzte gantz Bayern in solche Furcht, daß die Einwohner mit Weib und Kind sich zu retten suchten, und alle Land-Strassen mit Wagen und Pferden angefüllet waren." *Gottfried II*, 926. Königsmarck ist (Greve) Hans Christoph v. K. (FG 515. 1648). Vgl. die Andreae-Zitate (ohne Erklärungen u. Belege) in *Brecht: Andreae u. Hz. August*, 117f. Cannstatt, heute Bad Cannstatt in Stuttgart, war von der weimar. Armee in französ. Diensten besetzt. Hohenurach (in Urach, Lkr. Reutlingen) besaß eine Burg, die im 16. Jh. zum württemberg. Staatsgefängnis geworden war. Asperg, heute (Hohen)asberg im Lkr. Tübingen, eine württemberg. Landesfestung. Vgl. *Merian: Topographia* Germaniae. Schwaben, 8: „Nach der Nördlinger Schlacht/ haben sich die Käyserischen der obernanten Vestung Hohen Asperg bemächtiget: Die aber An. 1649. nach dem GeneralFriedenSchluß/ Herren Eberharden/ Hertzogen von Würtemberg/ &c. restituirt worden ist." Zur Entsetzung Heilbronns durch Kurbayern s. 460819 K 12.

6 [Kupfertitel]: SELENIANA AUGUSTALIA IOHANNIS VALENTINI ANDREÆ, S.T.D. Una cum opusculis alijs. ULMÆ SUEVORUM. Typ. et Impens: BALTHAS. Kuhnen [1649]; HAB: 143.4 Rhet. u. Li 85. Das Buch enthält hauptsächlich den Briefwechsel Andreaes (1643–1649) mit den Prinzen Rudolf August (FG 754. 1660), Anton Ulrich (FG 716. 1659) und Ferdinand Albrecht (FG 842. 1673) v. Braunschweig-Wolfenbüttel. Am Schluß folgen drei Briefe Korrespondenz Andreaes mit der Prinzessin Sibylla Ursula v. Braunschweig-Wolfenbüttel und S. 543–578 einige Stücke des Briefwechsels Andreaes mit württemberg. Prinzen. Andreae hat das 422 Schreiben umfassende und mit vier Porträts der welf. Geschwister geschmückte Duodezwerk den Prinzen und Hz. August d. J. gewidmet. Am Schluß Ehrengedichte an Andreae von Martin Gosky (Arzt, Comes Palatinus), M. Jacobus Honold (Ulmer Dompfarrer und Gymn.prof.), M. Johann Mair (Ulmer Gymn.conrector), M. Rudolph Roth („Pastor Oelling. & Byssing."), M. Joh. Heinricus Faber (Pfarrer zu St. Ulrich in Augsburg), Marcus Dolmetsch („Consiliarius Wurber. annorum 77"), Joh. Joachim Schüele (Collega & Compater), Christophorus Zellerus („Collega Cogn. & & Comp."), Johannes Schmidt (Pastor zu St. Leonhard), Johannes Schübel („filio spirituali & compatre"), Tobias Pfisterus (Diakon) u. Petrus Meuderlinus (Ephorus am Gymn. St. Annae in Augsburg). Spätere Ausgabe 1654.

7 Fest Exaltatio Crucis am 14. September. Vgl. Anm. 8. Am 16.9.1646 schrieb Andreae an den Herzog: „hiebey ein plausum auf den 3. Anniversarium exaltatæ †. Gott geb Continuationem felicissimam. Poetis Guelphicis multum debeo, sum enim vix poetaster, ne dum Poeta poetaster, ne dum Poeta." HAB: Cod. Guelf. 65.1 Extrav., Bl. 305r.

8 Andreae erinnerte sich häufig der Einäscherung Calws und der Zerstörung seines Hauses. Vgl. etwa 401111. Am 16.9.1646 schrieb Andreae an den Herzog: „1. Sept. 1634, alß E. f. g. zu Br. [d.h. zu Braunschweig und nicht in Wolfenbüttel residierte, bin ich] von fewergefahr wundersam errettet worden, hat vnser publicum incendium Würtemb. angefangen, vnd ist 10. sequente Calw in die Aschen gelegt worden." HAB: Cod. Guelf. 65.1 Extrav., Bl. 305r. Hz. August hatte in seinem Brief vom 1.9.1646 (s. oben Anm. 1) die eigene Erinnerung Andreaes durch seine Bemerkung angeregt: „Wulfenbüttel, den 1. Sept. an welchem Tage Ao. 1634 hor. 4.30. a. m. zu Brunswig, Gott mich scheinbahrlich fur feuers gefahr bewahrete, das albereit daß bette, darinne ich ruhete, hatte angegriffen. Ipsi semper laus & Gloria, 1646. F Cras 2. 7br. Ao. 1641 verliessen die Alliierte Armeen, diese vestung und huben die belägerung auf, an diesem Ohrte, und liessen mich unter den Leuen und rebellen etc. in Vico Brunonis."

K 1 Der Zettel liegt im Bestand vor Andreaes Brief v. 26.5.1646, wurde von ihm aber als Beilage zu seinem Brief v. 5.8.1646 versandt (Ankunft bei Andreae am 7.9.1646). Darauf antwortete der Herzog nämlich am 25.8.1646: „Wie und ob die wolgemeinte brieflein meiner Söhne zu divulgieren, stelle ich seiner disposition anheim." HAB: Cod. Guelf. 236.3 Extrav., Bl. 37r.

460912

Georg Philipp Harsdörffer an Herzog August d. J. von Braunschweig-Wolfenbüttel

Georg Philipp Harsdörffer (FG 368. Der Spielende) kommt bei der Übersendung seines literarischen Geschenks an Hz. August d. J. v. Braunschweig-Wolfenbüttel (FG 227) das Beispiel eines jüdischen Lehrers in den Sinn, der auf die Frage des Königs Ptolemaios, wie er sein Reich regieren solle, antwortete, indem Du in allen Taten Gott nacheiferst. Gottes Gunst richte sich nach der Absicht des Schenkenden und nicht nach dem geringen Wert des Geschenks. In diesem Sinne möge auch der Herzog die Gaben seines Dieners wohlwollend annehmen. — Der Stecher hat die Druckplatten für die *Porticus Virtutis* noch nicht vollendet und fordert die Zeichnung des letzten Bildes mit den drei Grazien und den Musen, die er, Harsdörffer, vor über einem Monat an Justus Georg Schottelius (FG 397) geschickt habe.

Q HAB: BA (Bibliotheks-Archiv) II, 4 Nr. 313, 2 Bl. [A: 2v], 1v u. 2r leer; eigenh., Sig. — D: Blume: *Porticus*, 90f. Vgl. Dieter Merzbacher: Objektbeschreibungen. In: Pegasus und die Künste. Hgg. Claudia Brink u. Wilhelm Hornbostel. Katalogbuch zur Ausstellung im Museum für Kunst und Gewerbe, Hamburg, 8. April - 31. Mai 1993. München 1993, 161f., 178, 181, 191f. u. 220–226, zu 430526, 450927, 460912 (dieses Dokument), *DA Köthen I. 8*: 470119 u. 470507.

A Serenißimo atque Celsissimo Principi ac Domino DN. AUGUSTO Brunswicensium ac Lunæburgensium Duci potentissimo &ce.: Domino meo clementissimo. Wolffenbüttel.

Serenissime atque Celsissime Princeps, Domine clementiss.
Dum Serenit.[i] atque Celsitud.[i] Vestræ literarium hoc munus offero, in mentem venit illud Hebræi cuiusdam Doctoris,[1] qui Regi Ptolomæo interroganti, quo modo regnum suum benè administrare deberet? respondit: Si in omnibus tuis actionibus DEUM imitaberis. Optimum illud et maximum Numen, vt alia omittam, non oblationis vilitatem, sed devotum offerentis animum respicit propitius. Hoc mecum reputans labores hosce, licet exiguos, ad Serenit.[is] atque Celsitud.[is] Vestræ pedes humilimè deponere, nil dubito, divinámque bonitatem, vt gratiosè imitetur obnixè rogo, vel ut ex formula loquar: accipiat lubens dona clientis. Sculptor typos ad Porticum Virtutis, Seren.[ti] atque Cels.[i] V.[ræ] sacram, nondum absolvit, delineationem vltimi, quam ante mensem, et amplius per D.[um] Schottelium[a] submisi, efflagitans, trium Gratiarum & Musarum icones præ se ferentem.[2] Vale Sereniss.[e] atque Celsiss.[e] Princeps et conatibus meis, ut hactenus, ita etiam in posterum fave clementissime.
Serenitati atque Celsitudini V.[ræ]
   humilimus Cliens
   Georg-Philippus Harsdörffer *mpia*.
Norimbergæ die 12 Septemb. 1646.

I

Harsdörffers Gedicht auf die Helden der Fruchtbringenden Gesellschaft

Q *Harsdörffer: Specimen (1646)*, Bl.)(2r –)(4r. Das Gedicht fehlt im ersten, hsl. Entwurf der *Porticus* (450927) und auch im Separatdruck dieses Panegyrikus (s. 461204A, *DA Köthen I. 8:* 470119 u. 470215).

PROGRAMMA
ad
HEROES
FRVCTIFERI SODALITI

ILlustres[a] animæ, *quorum sub numine blando*
Victrix fructiferæ, *vernat vernacula* Palmæ,
quæ modò Teutonicas tutatur tegmine Musas.
Summæ molis erat Germanam condere gentem,
audacem & validam: priscâ de stirpe Japhethi,
nomine Celtarum, quæ dilatata per Orbem [)(2v]
Hispanos domuit, prædurâ et lege subegit;
pugnaces pariter contrivit robore Gallos;

Italiamàue simul prostratam clade Getharum,
frenavit. Nec enim hoc potuisset dextera Sueci,
ni Germanorum generoso è sanguine tradux,
immemor in veterem sævisset crudus amicum.

Quàm latè dominata, quibusàue potentia Celtæ,
testantur passim priscæ vestigia Linguæ,
mixtæ Europæis, varioàue Idiomate scriptis:
Hinc juvat, antiquos verborum inquirere ramos, [)(3r]
quo solido & solers adnixus germine sermo,
indagare atavûm mores, solemnia, ritus.

Respicite, ô Patriæ sublimia lumina, quorum
nisu, fructifero radiat Germanus amore.
Respicite & facilem scripto huic concedite vultum.
Vos quoque Doctorum semper-veneranda corona,
advoco: si vestrûm, quisquam heîc suffragia confert,
aut dubius renuit; Genium non turbet amici,
sincerumàue animum. Volupe esto, indagine veri,
innocuum lusum, circa incunabula Linguæ [)(3v]
ludere[1], *Teutonicæ versetur rectiùs illa*
in vestris manibus, studiis suffulta secundis.
Mî satis est, specimen tenui monstrâsse labore,
mentisàue affectum gratâ signâsse Camœnâ.
Ast, adeunda prius VIRTVTIS PORTICVS alta,
augusti AVGVSTI. Statuam stupeamus Equestrem,
quam statuit vindex Todiscæ Gloria Linguæ.[2]
Pegasus Heroem, subducit remige pennâ
Mercurii volucris sceptro, lauruàue decorum;
circumquaàue patent spatia extensissima eundi, [)(4r]
desuper æque[b] *tholis arguta Emblemata pendent,*[3]
quæ referunt variâ Picturâ illustria facta
Principis, exemplo, quo postera disceret ætas:
quæque figurâ suâ, celebrata est temporis æra.

Tandem summe Deus concedas aurea Pacis
tempora, quæ ferro riguêre, ærugine tincta
Armorum & sceleris! poliatur Lingua, scholæàue,
queîs segetes florent Templorum, & culmine surgant
frugifero; ut Virtus passim rediviva per orbem
consimilis Palmæ, præpes florescat in ævum.

II

Übersicht der Texte und Kupferstiche in den Fassungen von Harsdörffers *Porticus Virtutis*

Q HAB: QuN 1090 (1). 12°. Druck der in *Harsdörffer: Specimen (1646)* eingefügten *Porticus Virtutis* = *P.I*. Vgl. *P.I* mit der hsl. *Porticus* (s. 450927 I; HAB: 166.11 Eth.), abgekürzt als *Pms*, und der separat erschienenen *Porticus* = *P.II* (s. 461204A, *DA Köthen I. 8:* 470119 u. 470215; HAB: 10.6 Pol.). Zu den Initialen in *P.I* s. 460700 K 4.

P.I
(Faltbl.) Emblematischer Kupfertitel zu *Harsdörffer: Specimen (1646)*. Vgl. zu diesem Kupfertitel schon 451217 K 10. — Fehlt in *Pms* u. *P.II*.
Rücks. leer.
Drucktitel: GEORGI PHILIPPI HARSDORFFERI SPECIMEN PHILOLOGIÆ GERMANICÆ, Continens Disquisitiones XII. De Linguæ nostræ vernaculæ Historia, Methodo, & Dignitate. Præmissa est PORTICVS VIRTVTIS, Serenissimo atque Celsißimo Principi, ac Domino, Domino AUGUSTO, Brunsvvicensium atq Lünæburgensium Duci potentissimo &c. SACRA. Norimbergæ Impensis Wolfgangi Endteri. M. DC. XL VI.

P.II 2 leere Bll., gefolgt von Schmutztitel: PORTICUS AUGUSTI.
— Rücks. leer.

Bl. [)( ]r Frontispiz *Porticus Virtutis* (Titel auf geschlossenem Tor) — Fehlt in *Pms*.

P.II Kupferstich *Porticus:* halboffenes Tor, darüber Kurztitel PORTICUS AUGUSTI, Hz. August auf Pegasus zur Hälfte sichtbar. S. hierzu 450927 K I 0. — Rücks. leer.

P.II Titelbl.: PORTICUS Serenissimo atque Celsissimo Principi, ac Domino, Domino AUGUSTO, Brunsvvicensium atque Lunæburgensium Duci potentissimo, Principum eruditissimo, Domino Clementissimo &c. SACRA: Cultu GeorgI Philippi Harsdörfferi, Patricii Noric. & ejusdem Dicasterii Adsessoris. M. DC. XXX VI.
Rücks. leer.

Bl. [)( ]v Gedicht auf den emblematischen Kupfertitel (1.): „Trochæus *Frontispicii interpres*" — Fehlt in *Pms* u. *P.II*.

Bl. [)(2]v –)(4]v PROGRAMMA ad HEROES FRVCTIFERI SODALITII.
Bl.)(2r-)(4r. Initiale I (Palme). S. oben Beil. I. Inc. ILlustres animæ, quorum sub numine blando — Fehlt in *Pms* u. *P.II*.

P.II Bl. A 3rv Gedicht: PROGRAMMA, inc. HAud perstant, hominum. Initiale H (Wappen).

Bl.)(4v -)(6v Harsdörffers Widmungsbrief an Hz. August, undat. Initiale A (Emblem mit Inscriptio: PARITAS IMPARI). — Fehlt in *Pms* (dort Alloquium v. 27.9.1645, Text in 450927).
P.II Bl. B r – [B 3]r Neufassung des Widmungsbriefs Harsdörffers vom 4.12.1646 (s. 461204A). Initiale A (*Porticus* mit geschlossenem Tor).

P.II Bl. [B 3]v PRÆMONITIO AD CORDATUM LECTOREM. Initiale S (Harsdörffers FG-Pflanze „Bunte Bönelein").

P.II [B 4]r Kupferstich: Innenhof-Façade und Grundriß (Ichnographia Porticús AUGUSTI.) der *Porticus*
[B 4]v Rücks. leer.

Bl. [)(7]r Titelbl.: PORTICUS VIRTUTIS Serenissimo atque Celsissimo Principi, ac Domino, Domino AUGUSTO, Brunsvvicensium atque Lünæburgensium Duci potentissimo &c. SACRA cultu GEORGII PHILIPPI HARSDORFFERI.
Bl. [)(7]v leer.

Bl.)( )(r –)( )( )(8v Lat. Prosimetrum: PORTICUS VIRTUTIS. Inc. ÆStus erat, Phœbus tenues.
Auch in *Pms,* Bl. 3v–21v PORTICUS VIRTUTIS, in Posteritatis documentum aperta Principis AVGVSTI, augustæ Virtutis Jmago Præbeat Exemplum: Posteritas stupeat! — In *P.I* überarbeitet.
P.II. Bl. C r (S. [1])/ Initiale Æ (Getreideernte im Sommer) – Bl. F 2r (S.21) überarbeiteter Text. Gefolgt von einem lat. Gedicht:
Bl. F 2rv (S.21) – [F 4]r ACCESSORIVM. Palma Indica, Sive Illustrissimi Carpophororum Sodalitii EMBLEMA, ab Autore explicatum & in supplementum hujus operis admissum. — Inc.: CUr te FRUCTIFERÛM cœtus, colit INDICA PALMA? — Kolophon: Norimbergæ, ex officina Endteriana. M.DC.XLVI. Initiale C. — Rücks. leer. 1 leeres Bl.

Weitere Kupferstiche:

Bl. [)( )(5]r: Hz. August von vorn auf dem Pegasus, im Innenhof der Porticus.
P.II. Bl. C 3r Neuer Stich dieses Motivs, mit verschiedener Inschrift auf dem Denkmalssockel.

Bl. [)( )(5]v: Hz. August von hinten auf dem Pegasus, im Innenhof die Porticus.
P.II. Bl. C 3v Neuer Stich dieses Motivs, mit verschiedener Inschrift auf dem Denkmalsockel.

P.II. Bl. [E]r, zwischen S. 14 u. 15, Blick durch das halbgeöffnete Tor in den Innenhof der Porticus. Hz. Augustus von hinten, auf dem Pegasus. — Rücks. vacat.

P.II. Bl. [E 3]r, zwischen S. 16 u. 17 Stich Albert Freyses: Fama, Pegasus, Grazien, Musen, Apollo, Hirte u. a. — Rücks. leer.

Bl. [())( )(9]r Schlußkupfer *Porticus* mit Inschrift auf geschlossenem Tor. — Rücks. leer.

T a *Von uns aus D.^{ium} oder D.^{iu} korrigiert. In Blume: Porticus, a. a. O., fehlt per vor* Dominum

T I a *Bild-Initiale I mit Palmbaum. Vgl. 460700 K 4.* — **b** éque *wohl Lesefehler des Setzers.*

K Hiermit überreicht Georg Philipp Harsdörffer (FG 368) Hz. August d. J. v. Braunschweig-Wolfenbüttel (FG 227) das um seine Lobschrift *Porticus Virtutis* erweiterte *Specimen Philologiae Germanicae (1646).* Im Brief *DA Köthen I. 8:* 470119 wird er sodann Hz. August die erweiterte, separat gedruckte *Porticus* (s. Beil. II: P.II) schicken. Vgl. schon die Sendung des hsl. Entwurfs in 450927. Mit *DA Köthen I. 8:* 470215 reicht Harsdörffer noch 25 von ihm verbesserte Exemplare und andere Bücher an Schottelius nach. *Harsdörffer: Specimen (1646)* war schon vorher ohne die *Porticus* erschienen. Vgl. zum *Specimen* 451217 K 10. Zum Zeitpunkt des vorliegenden Briefs hat der Zeichner seine Arbeit noch nicht abgeschlossen, Harsdörffer hat dem Herzog nur Entwürfe geschickt. Die gezeichneten Vorlagen der Kupferstiche schickte Schottelius Hz. August offenbar mit 460700. Harsdörffer erwähnt im vorliegenden Brief das Kupfer mit den drei Grazien und dem Tanz der Musen, zu dem er die Zeichnung (Entwurf) vor einem Monat an Justus Georg Schottelius (FG 397) gesandt hatte. Der Künstler (Pictor) Albert Freyse zeichnet/ visiert dieses Bild. *Thieme/ Becker* XII, 446; *Braunschweig. Biograph. Lexikon (Jarck),* 231 f.; Karl Steinacker: Die graphischen Künste in Braunschweig und Wolfenbüttel während der letzten drei Jahrhunderte. In: Jahrb. d. Geschichtsvereins f. d. Hzt. Braunschweig 5 (1906), 62–128. S. *Köthen I.6,* 113 f., vgl. 460700 K 4. Der Separatdruck *Porticus* zeigt das danach gestochene Kupfer (nach S. 16). Es fehlt in der im *Specimen Philologiae Germanicae* integrierten Porticus.

1 Angeblich der Jude Aristobulos, aus priesterlichem Stamm und Lehrer des Königs Ptolemaios (Ptolemaios VI. Philometor), nach 2 Ma 1,10. Historisch ist der jüdisch-hellenistische Philosoph dieses Namens, dessen Werke (darunter wohl ein Dialog zwischen Aristobulos und Ptolemaios) nur in Zitaten anderer Autoren fortleben. Fragments from Helenistic Jewish Authors. Vol. 3. Aristobulos. Atlanta/ Ga. 1995; Paul Rießler: Altjüdisches Schrifttum außerhalb der Bibel. Augsburg 1928 (Nr. 12, S. 179–185). Jewish Encyclopedia. New York 1901–1906. Euseb. hist. ecc. 7,32 nennt A. unter den Autoren der Septuaginta, die die sog. 70 für Ptolemaios II. Philadelphos und dessen Vater ins Griechische übertrugen.

2 Daß Schottelius durch seinen Briefverkehr mit Harsdörffer auch eine Vermittlerrolle bei der Illuminierung von Harsdörffers *Porticus Virtutis* zufiel, zeigt sein Schreiben 460700 an den Herzog.

K I 1 Harsdörffer weist hier auf seinen Gesellschaftsnamen in der FG hin: Der Spielende.

2 Harsdörffers Einfall des auf dem Pegasus reitenden Herzogs (s. Beil. II, *P.I* Bl. [)( )(5]r Ansicht von vorn, s. Abb. auf S.703; *P.I* Bl. [)( )(5]v Ansicht von hinten) gilt also dem Befreienden als Retter der deutschen Sprache. Hierbei denkt der Spielende an die reformierte Sprache in der *Evangelischen Kirchen-Harmonie* (s. 411214) des Herzogs.

3 Das gibt die Darstellung in *P.I* (und *P.II*) nicht wieder, da sich der Himmel statt einer Kuppel über dem Gebäude wölbt. Allerdings erblickt der Betrachter eine Rotunde mit Reliefs (aus dem Leben des Herzogs), darüber Embleme und Wappen. Die von Harsdörffer entworfene Portikus ahmt das entsprechende Gebäude des römischen Kaisers Augustus nach, das auch eine Bibliothek enthielt. S. 461204A K 1.

460915

Georg Philipp Harsdörffer an Christian Gueintz

Georg Philipp Harsdörffer (FG 368. Der Spielende) schickt Christian Gueintz (FG 361. Der Ordnende) den 6. Teil seiner *Frauenzimmer-Gesprächspiele* (1646) aus Dank für das darin eingebrachte Lobgedicht von Gueintz. Er nimmt im folgenden Stellung zu Gueintz' ausführlichem Gutachten über sein *Specimen Philologiae Germanicae* (1646), das F. Ludwig (Der Nährende) ihm gesandt hatte, und schickt voraus, daß er wenig Gegenargumente darin gefunden habe, die sich nicht anfechten ließen. Zunächst verteidigt Harsdörffer seine Eindeutschungen der Wörter „Philosophus" und „Philologus" („Witdod" bzw. „Wortdod"). Die alten Deutschen hätten sich kaum in den beiden Wissenschaften geübt, kein Wunder, daß man hier nicht auf althergebrachte Wörter zurückgreifen kann. Das (von Gueintz für „Philosoph" vorgeschlagene) Wort „Weltweiser" komme nicht in Frage, weil es bereits zur Bezeichnung der „Politici" verwendet werde. In solchen Fällen sei es angezeigt, alte (vergessene) Wörter wieder in Gebrauch zu bringen; das alte Verb „thüren" für (das längst eingeführte) „dürfen" falle aber nicht darunter. — Über die alten deutschen Schriften und keltischen Gedichte gebe Olaus Wormius Auskunft. — Harsdörffer bleibt auch bei seiner im *Specimen* dargelegten Meinung, „Deutsch" könne man sowohl mit D als auch mit T im Anlaut schreiben. — Darüber hinaus hält er es (im Gegensatz zu Gueintz) nicht für glaubwürdig, daß Noah und Sem beim Turmbau zu Babel dabei gewesen seien. Sie hätten Ham sonst gewiß von seiner Hybris abgehalten. Harsdörffers Auffassung wisse sich einig mit der einiger Gelehrter, auch widerstreite sie nicht der Hl. Schrift. — Die einzelnen Mundarten würden sich mit der Zeit durchaus verändern (taugen also schwerlich als Normierungskriterium). Auch beharrt Harsdörffer darauf, daß sich „Buchstabe" etymologisch von der „Buche" herleite. Die hzl.-gottorf. Bibliothek verwahre noch alte, mit keltischen Schriftzeichen beschriftete Buchenstäbe. — Daß hebr. Grammatiken erst lange Zeit nach griechischen und lateinischen entstanden seien, räumt er ein. Dieser Umstand spreche jedoch nicht gegen viele Gemeinsamkeiten zwischen dem Deutschen und dem Hebräischen. — Ferner bleibt Harsdörffer bei seiner Stammworttheorie: Das Stammwort bleibt übrig, wenn alle Vor-, Nach- und Flexionssilben abgestrichen sind. Ein solches letztes Grundwort liegt nur in der singularen Imperativform vor. Werde dort ein -e- angefügt, ist es eine Nachsilbe und zudem in vielen Mundarten ungebräuchlich, auch bei Martin Luther. Jede Sprache besitze Anomalien und Ausnahmen, dennoch muß die Grammatik die Regelmäßigkeiten bestimmen, und erst hernach die Ausnahmen etwa bei den unregelmäßigen Verben anführen. Die Silbentrennung erfolgt wie die Wortbildung: nach morphologischen Einheiten. Die variantenreiche Aussprache könne hier kein Maßstab sein. Überhaupt räume Gueintz dem Sprachgebrauch viel zu große Rechte ein: Folge man in allem den sprachlichen Gewohnheiten, müßte immer alles so bleiben, wie es einmal war, und die Streitfragen wären erledigt. Aber *welche* Schreibgewohnheit, *welche* Mundart seien nun die richtige? Zur Verwendung des -kk- (statt des -ck-) verweist Harsdörffer auf das Ende (wohl des 6. Teils) der *Gesprächspiele* (1646). — Harsdörffer würde ein einigendes mündliches Gespräch mit Gueintz einer Fortsetzung der schriftlichen Kontroverse vorziehen.

Q   HM Köthen: V S 545, Bl. 355rv; Abschrift von Schreiberh. Gelegentlich Bleistiftmarkierungen von unbek. H. (Christian Gueintz?). — D: *KE*, 372–374. — BN: *Bürger*, 674 Nr. 18.

A   *Fehlt.*

Geehrter Ordnender

Derselbe hat beygeschloßen zuerhalten den Sechsten theil meiner Gesprächspiele, welche er mit einem schönen, aber meiner wenigkeit nicht gemäßen lobgedichte geehret, dafür ich dieses mal anderen danck zu leisten nicht vermag, und auf alle Begebenheit ihm und seinen angehörigen zu dienen verbunden bleibe.[1]

Der höchstgeehrte Nehrende hat mir zugefertigt, was der Ordnende wegen des **Speciminis Philologiæ Germanicæ** bey dem Ertzschreine eingeschickt, in welchen bedencken wenig wieder mich ist, das nicht mit guten grunde könte verfochten werden.[2]

Wie[a] man die wörter **Philologus** und **Philosophus** teutschen könne, habe ich dem Wortverstande nach gnugsam verhoffentlich erwiesen, iedoch an dem 7. blat vermeldet: multis voci*bus* & appellationibus non deesse robur significandj sed ratihabitio publica.[3]

Die alten Teutschen haben sich in **Philologicis** gar nicht, in **Philosophicis** wenig geübet, und ist also nicht zuverwunderen, wan wir hierzu neue wörter ersinnen müßen. Das Hebräische דוד[4] hat so viel als ein nechster Freund und taufvater geheißen. Weltweise[b] nennet man bey uns einen **Politicum**. Die alten wörter, so wir von nöten haben, muß man wieder in den gebrauch bringen, darunter das thüren[b] für dürfen[b] nicht kan gezehlet werden.[5] Der Ordnende lese des **Ronsards** seine meinung hierüber **Specimin**. fol. 37.[6] Wer solche sachen nicht verstehet, der mag es seiner unwißenheit zumeßen, darnach sich der Poet nicht zu richten hat. Was die alten Teutschen geschrieben, und wie **Celtischen** gedichte gereimet gewesen, lange vor **Taciti** Zeiten, ist zu lesen bey **Olao Wormio de literatura Runica**[.][7] Es folgt nicht, das was ich nicht weiß, kein mensch in der welt wiße. Wer ist so gelehrt, das er nicht solte mehr lernen können? Ob man Teutsch oder Deutsch schreiben soll ist genugsam beygebracht Speciminis disquisit. II. 8. vs⁸. Es kan beides stehen und bleibet man billich bey der Cantzleyen gebrauch, wan man deßelben ursach geben kan.⁹

Ob unsere vorfahren bey dem *Babelbau* gewesen, laße ich dahin gestellet seyn. Das Noa und Sem, die dazumal und noch lange hernach gelebet, den jüngsten Sohn Cham nicht darvon solten abgehalten haben, wan sie darbey gewesen, ist fast nicht zu glauben: Man lese Becanum und Salviani Annales vet. Testam. so wird man zu zweiflen ursach gnug find*en*. Was der Ordnende darwieder aufgebracht, läßet sich alles aus besagten sehr gelehrten Scribenten beantworten. Es ist nicht wieder die Heil. Schrift, wan man die Sache recht betrachtet, und die grundsprache zu hülffe nimt, wie zu anderer gelegenheit erwiesen werden soll.¹¹

Das sich die Mundart in vielen mit der Zeit geändert, ist aus dem Guyon am 36. blate angezogen.¹²

Von dem Worte Buchstab von Buchbaum hergenommen[,] ist bey dem gottdorfischen bücherschatz (Bibliotheca) zu sehen, da noch solche stäbe von Buchen mit Celtischen Characteren verwaret werden.¹³

Das die Griechen und Lateiner vor den Hebreern Grammaticas geschrieben ist außer Zweifel, das aber deswegen, die Eigenschaft der Teutschen Sprache mit der Hebräischen in vielen nicht solte können verglichen [355v] werden, das folget nicht: ich sage in Vielen, sonst weren es nicht zwo sprachen, wan sie in allen durchgehend gleich sein solten.¹⁴

Das Stamwort wird sein welches alle Stambuchstaben hat, und keine vor oder nachsylb[en.]ᵈ Dergleichen wird keines außer der gebietungsweise gefunden werden. Das e welches etzliche derselben anfügen ist eine nachsylbe, und nicht gebreuchlich nach vielen Mundarten. D. Luther schreibet, laß, komm, iß, sitz, gr[eif]ᶜ, nim *etc.* Sirach. 31. und hin und wieder an anderen orten meh[r.]ᶜ ¹⁵ Es ist aber fast wunderlich zu hören, das man erstlich exceptiones und hernach regulas machen will; man muß auf die durchgehende gleichheit sehen, und sich der ungle[ich]ᶜ flüßende Wörtlein nicht hinderen laßen: Es ist keine sp[ra]cheᶜ die nicht anomalias habe, solten darümb keine regeln können gemacht werden?

Die Sylben werden getheilet, wie sie zusammengesetzt werden, und nicht nach der Lateinischen Schreibart die uns nichts hierinnen vorschreiben kan. Solcher gestalt kan man sie kindern und fremden leichter lehren[,]¹⁶ wie H. Hager zu Ham-

---

Distinguendum inter divisionem orbis terrarum Gen. 9. & dispersionem Chamitarum Gen. 11. Jlla signum Grati*dem* per Prophetam ex inspiratione divina: hoc sign*um* poenam ob Chamitarum superbiam & impietatem. Vixit autem Noa cum Heber annos 253. cum Phaleg 219. videatur Torniell*us* Annal. Sacrar*um* AM. 2026. f. 551.¹⁰

burg und andere viel schulhalter deßen proben gethan, und solche Lehrart nicht gnugsam loben können.[17] Aber hiervon wird der Suchende als Urheber dieser sachen noch mehr ursach geben. Die Stambuchstaben müßen beysammen bleiben, oder wir werden keinen grund setzen in der gantzen sprache, also theilet man recht auf– bring– lich, schänd–en, herrisch. Dan lich, en, isch seind nachsylben, die an das Stamwort gefüget, und darvon gesondert werden, die ungegründete aussprache kan nicht richter sein.[18]

Schließlich will der Ordnende die Gewonheit allen richtigen Ursachen vorziehen: Wan man das wil behaubten, so müßen wir alles, wie es vor 100 und mehr Jahren gewesen, behalten, und hat der Streit ein end[e.]c Es ist aber eben die Frage: Ob die Gewohnheit so oder so zu schreiben richtig sey? Ein ieder schreibet nach seiner mundart, und darbey wird es bleiben. Man lese Quintil. lib. I. c. 12.[19] Von dem kk. ist zu ende der Gesprächspiele zu lesen.[20]

Der Spielende wüntschet nicht mehr als mündlich mit dem Ordnenden zu sprechen, des Vertrauens sich durch Antwort und gegenantwort also vernehmen zu laßen, das diese Streitfragen beßer als Schriftlich solte abgeholffen werden, welche[s]d sich dan mit der Zeit wol schicken könte.

Hiermit verbleibet negst empfehlung des Höchst[en]d Obschutz

Des *Ordnenden* Dienstgefließener
Der Spielende

Nürnberg den 15. HerbstMonats 1646.

T a *Anstreichung am Rande bis* taufvater geheißen. *Vermutlich von Gueintz.* — **b** *Unterstreichungen stammen vermutlich von Gueintz.* — **c** *Textverlust im Falz, Konjektur nach KE in eckigen Klammern.* — **d** *Textverlust im Falz, unsere Konjektur in eckigen Klammern.*

K Wie aus 461031 hervorgeht, lag der vorliegende Brief dem Schreiben 460916 (Harsdörffer an F. Ludwig) bei, fraglich ist nur, ob in dieser Reinschrift von Schreiberh. oder in einem anderen Original. Der Schriftverkehr der Gutachten zu Georg Philipp Harsdörffers (FG 368. Der Spielende) *Specimen Philologiae Germanicae* (1646) lief sämtlich über F. Ludwig; s. dazu 460902 K 1. Dabei nimmt der vorliegende Brief Harsdörffers direkt Bezug auf Christian Gueintz' (FG 361. Der Ordnende) Gutachten zum *Specimen*, das Harsdörffer in 460406 erbeten hatte. Gueintz sandte sein Gutachten mit 460720 an F. Ludwig, dieser mit 460816 an Harsdörffer: „Erinnerungen Bey des Spielenden Wercklein die deutsche Sprache betreffend" (HM Köthen: V S 545, Bl. 192r–200v. Demnächst in *DA Köthen I. 9*). Vgl. die Zusammenfassung des Gutachtens in 460720 K 3.

1 Gueintz' Lobgedicht, d. d. „Halle den 20. May 1646", incip.: „GOtt selber in sich selbst ohn End' und ohne Zielen" in *Harsdörffer: Frauenzimmer-Gesprächspiele* VI (1646, Ndr. 1969), Ndr. S. 24 f. Vgl. zum 6. Teil der *Gesprächspiele* 460620 K 9.

2 Gueintz' Gutachten zu Harsdörffers *Specimen Philologiae Germanicae* (1646), vgl. Anm. 0.

3 In *Harsdörffer: Specimen (1646)*, 7 ff. schlug Harsdörffer für den Philosophen die Übersetzung „Witdod", für den Philologen den „Wortdoden" vor, woran sich Gueintz in seinem Gutachten (s. Anm. 1), Bl. 192r ff., stieß: Die Verdeutschung „Witdod" sei, auch wenn sie dereinst existiert hätte, nunmehr ungebräuchlich. Die Wortwahl sei nicht glücklich, weil sowohl „wit" (,weiß, weise') als auch „dod" (,Freund, Pate, tot') polysem seien. Insgesamt solle man gebräuchliche Wörter bevorzugen. Darum schlägt Gueintz vor, „die Philosophos weltweisen" zu nennen, „welches den auch iederman stracks, wer damit gemeinet verstehen kan". In *Harsdörffer: Schutzschrift (1644)*, 366 wird das Wort „Weltweiser" ebenfalls in einer Weise benutzt, die nahelegt, daß es einen Philosophen und keinen „Politicum" bezeichnen soll: „Die Griechen haben ihre Sprache in der Weltweisen/ Redner und Poeten/ Schulen von Jugend auf studieret". — Im *Specimen* räumte Harsdörffer im Zusammenhang der Verdeutschung fremdsprachlicher Fachbegriffe ein: „non deest significandi robur, sed usus & publica ratihabitio." (S. 6 f.) — Es fehlt nicht an der Kraft zu bezeichnen, sondern am Gebrauch und der öffentlichen Akzeptanz.

4 Die Ableitung des Wortes „Witdod" vom hebr. „dod" hatte Gueintz in seinem Gutachten (s. Anm. 0), Bl. 192v f., in Zweifel gezogen: „Der Spielende nimmet es von dem Hebräischen dod. Wo kömmet aber das Wit her? mich deuchte, wie das wit alt Sächßisch ist, also sey das dod von dem Alten worte Täde, welches bey den Griechen[,] Lateinern vnd alten Deutsche[n] so viel als Vater bedeutet. Und ist also ein Taufdode so viel als TaufPathe oder Taufvater". Vgl. schon 450927 II (K 11). Interessant ist die Kritik des Johann Amos Comenius. Harsdörffers verunglückte Ableitung und Anwendung des alten deutschen Wortes „witdod" als Übersetzung für Philosoph sei ein Beleg, wie wichtig es sei, „eosdem esse polyglottos", daß also die Grammatiker und Sprachbeflissenen mehrere Fremdsprachen beherrschen. Den Polen müsse Harsdörffers Etymologie lächerlich vorkommen, da sie das Wort „Woiwode" bis heute in ihrem Wortschatz haben, ähnlich die Tschechen. „Woi-" aber heiße im Polnischen Krieg, „Wodze" Führer; der polnische Woiwode entspreche daher dem dt. Heer-zog, d. h. Heerführer. Johann Amos Comenius: NOVISSIMA LINGVARUM METHODUS ... Anno 1648. In: JOANNES AMOS COMENIUS OPERA DIDACTICA OMNIA. Editio anni 1657 lucis ope expressa. [3 Bde.] Tomus I, Pars I, II. Prag 1957. Der *METHODUS* hat eine eigene Paginierung, hier S. 278.

5 Gueintz hielt es grundsätzlich für „unnöthig ungebräuchliches wieder vorsuchen: Vnd wer wolte aniezo das wort thüren pro dürfen, so doch in der Wittenbergischen lezten Bibel Joh. 18 v. 32 gefunden wird, gebrauchen?" (Gutachten a. a. O., Bl. 193r). *Biblia (Luther 1545)*: Joh. 18. 31: „Da sprach Pilatus zu jnen/ So nemet jr jn hin/ vnd richtet jn nach ewrem Gesetz. Da sprachen die Jüden zu jm/ Wir thüren niemand tödten". Vgl. auch die „Worterklärungen zur Lutherbibel von 1545" in der von uns benutzten, von Hans Volz besorgten Ausgabe *Biblia (Luther 1545)*, Anhang S. 299*–397*, hier 377*: „türen wagen, dürfen, sich anmaßen, können". *Götze*, 58: „türren", d. i. wagen, sich getrauen, dürfen; ebenso *Stieler*, 2364: „Türen/ audere, nobis Dürfen" (s. v. Türk/ & Türke!) u. *Diefenbach*, 878: „Turren audere". Vgl. auch 400528 K II 29.

6 Zur Legitimation, ungebräuchliche alte Wörter wieder hervorzuziehen, hatte Harsdörffer in seinem *Specimen*, 36 f. u. a. Ronsards Vorrede zu seinem Fragment gebliebenen Epos *La Franciade* angeführt: „Nos hodie infinita vocabula Teutonica ignoramus, quae inter Anglos, Suecos, Danos, Belgas &c. ex primis Germanicæ Linguæ elementis, permansere, & à Poëtis in usum reducenda erunt, ut *Petrarcha* ex Latinitate; & *Ronsardus* ex antiquis Picardiæ, & Walliæ triviali sermone haud pauca carminibus suis inseruit, de quibus *in præfat. Franciadæ f. 27* ita ad Poetam suum scribit: *Ie t'advertis de ne faire conscience de remettre en usage les antiquis vocables, & principalement ceux du Langage VVallon & Picard lequel nous reste, per tant de siecles, L'exemple naif de la langue franzoise; j'entends de celle qui eut cours apres que la Latine n'eut plus d'usage en nostre Gaule, & choisir les mots les plus pregnans & significatifs &c.*"

7 Olaus Wormius/ Ole Worm (1588–1654): Runir Seu Danica Literatura Antiqvissima, Vulgo Gothica dicta (Kopenhagen 1636), bes. 175–241. HAB: 202.85 Quod. (2). Der in Dänemark geborene und wirkende Wormius war neben Olaus Magnus (1490–1557), Arngrimur Jonsson (1568–1648) und Johan Bure (1568–1652) einer der frühen skandinav. Altertumsforscher, der Runeninschriften sammelte und erforschte. Ihm galten die Runen als eigene germanische oder gotische Schrift. Vgl. schon 440317 K 3; Art. „Worm, Ole" in *DBL* XIX (1905), 186–195; *Herz: Aufrichtigkeit, Vertrauen, Frieden,* S. 350 Anm. 122. Harsdörffers *Specimen* beruft sich in der 6. und der 9. Disquisitio „De Litteris Germanorum" bzw. „De re Poëtica apud Germanos" auf Wormius. Von ihm (u. a.) erführe man, „qualis enim olim fuerit [nostra poësin]" (a. a. O., 189). Vgl. auch Anm. 13.

8 *Harsdörffer: Specimen (1646)*, Disquisitio II, § 8.

9 In seinem Gutachten (s. Anm. 0) in Abschnitt 3 plädierte Gueintz für eine Schreibung mit Anlaut D, wobei er für Details auf seine *Rechtschreibung (1645)* verwies; s. dazu 460816 K I 1. Anders *Harsdörffer: Specimen (1646),* disquisitio II, § 8–13, 28–33. Schon 1644 hatte Harsdörffer beide Schreibweisen zugelassen; Justus Georg Schottelius (FG 97. Der Suchende) forderte „Teutsch", Philipp v. Zesen (FG 521. 1648) verteidigte „Deutsch". Vgl. 441223 K 23.

10 *Biblia (Luther 1545)*, 1. Mo. 9,1: „VND Gott segenet Noah vnd seine Söne/ vnd sprach/ Seid fruchtbar vnd mehret euch/ vnd erfüllet die Erde." Ebd. 1. Mo. 11,8 f.: „Also zerstrewet sie der HERR von dannen in alle Lender/ das sie musten auffhören die Stad zu bawen/ Da her heisst jr name Babel/ das der HERR daselbs verwirret hatte aller Lender sprache/ vnd sie zerstrewet von dannen in alle Lender." — „AM", d. i. ‚Annus Mundi' (in Torniellis Werk erscheinen die Jahreszahlen neben der Paginierung im Kolumnentitel, um die Orientierung zu erleichtern). Harsdörffer oder seinem Drucker ist ein Zahlendreher unterlaufen: Die entsprechende Passage befindet sich auf S. 155, nicht auf 551 in: Agostino Tornielli: Annales Sacri & Profani, Ab Orbe Condito, Ad Evndem Christi passione redemptum (Frankfurt a. M. 1611). HAB: 13 Hist. 2°.

11 Eine wichtige Streitfrage im zeitgenöss. Sprachdiskurs war, ob das Geschlecht Japhets (mit Sem und Ham einer der drei Söhne Noahs), die Vorfahren der Deutschen, beim Turmbau zu Babel zugegen waren oder bereits vorher, nach der Sintflut, ins nördliche Europa ausgewandert waren. Anders als Schottelius stimmt Harsdörffer letzterer Auffassung im *Specimen,* Disq. 3, § 6 zu. Der Turmbau sei erst in der 4. Generation der Nachkommen Noahs erfolgt, als sich Japhets Nachkommen längst im nördl. Europa ausgebreitet hätten. Auf diese Weise kann Harsdörffer das bes. hohe Alter, die Unberührtheit des Deutschen von der *confusio linguarum* und die vorzügliche Nähe des Deutschen zur hl. hebr. Ursprache behaupten. Gueintz hingegen postuliert in seinem Gutachten im 5. Abschnitt die Ansicht, alle Nachkommen der drei Söhne Noahs (die Jafetiten, die Hamiten und die Semiten) hätten dem Turmbau zu Babel beigewohnt. Demzufolge hätten nicht nur alle eine gemeinsame Ursprache besessen, sondern auch die deutsche Sprache sei erst in Folge des babylon. Turmbaus nach Europa gebracht worden. Andernfalls wäre sie früher entstanden und die vorbabylon. *lingua prima* Hebräisch hätte ihr sakrosanktes Privileg verloren. Daher weist Gueintz jene These als nicht bibelkonform und „neue meinung" zurück. Vgl. auch schon 440219 (K 3). In *Harsdörffer: Specimen (1646)* werden die biblischen Erzählungen von der Aufteilung der Erde unter Noahs Söhnen, vom Turmbau zu Babel und der Verwirrung der Sprache(n) in Disquisitio III, §§ 6–15 ausführlich diskutiert. Vgl. *Banneck*, 136 ff. u. 253 ff. — Welches Werk des Kirchenvaters Salvianus Massiliensis (400 – nach 480) Harsdörffer genau meint, ließ sich nicht ermitteln. Überliefert sind sein Hauptwerk *De Gubernatione Dei*, ferner *Ad Ecclesiam* und eine geringe Anzahl an Briefen. Vgl. *BACh* 334/ 227–232. Harsdörffer könnte die Werkausgabe von 1623 gekannt haben: Salviani Massiliensis Opera: Ad Lvdovicvm XIII. Franc. et Navarren. Regem Christanissimum. Curante Cunrado Rittershusio, 2 Bde. (Nürnberg 1623; in den Kommentaren ergänzte Aufl. der Ausgabe Altdorf 1611). Daneben verweist Harsdörffer hier wohl auf ein Werk des ndl. Humanisten Joannes Becanus Goropius (1518–1572): Origines Antwerpianae, sive Cimmeriorvm Becceselana (Antwerpen 1569), 4. Buch („Cronia"), 372 ff. HAB: T 989.2° Helmst.

12 Wie Gueintz im 6. Abschnitt seines Gutachtens (s. Anm. 0) ging auch *Harsdörffer: Specimen (1646)*, 36 davon aus, daß die deutschen Mundarten nicht unveränderlich seien. Mundart meint hier die gesprochene Sprache, während die morphologische Basis der Sprache über die Jahrhunderte relativ stabil geblieben sei: „Ratio hujus differentiæ pronunciatio est, quæ ex diversitate temperamentorum & climatum psiciscitur". Harsdörffers zitierender Verweis auf Louis Guyon (1527–1633), einen frz. Mediziner, findet sich ebenfalls auf S. 36. Bei dessen Erfolgsbuch *Diverses Leçons* (zuerst Lyon 1604) handelt es sich um ein voluminöses polyhistorisches Werk, das thematisch ein weites Feld von der historischen Anekdote bis hin zu etymologischen Reflexionen abdeckt. Harsdörffer bediente sich einer zweibändigen Ausgabe und verweist a. a. O. auf Bd. 1, Buch 2, Kap. 2, das allerdings die Kunst, sich gefahrlos selbst zu loben, abhandelt. Gemeint ist wohl eher Buch 2, Kap. 3, 211–218 mit dem Titel: „Que la plus grande partie des peuples ne parlent plus de langue qui leur fut donnee, par le vouloir de Dieu, apres la destruction de Babel, ains l'ont changee." Hier heißt es u. a.: „en fin, de toutes ces langues, les Gaulois, à present François, se sont bastis vne langue particuliere, toute telle que l'auons auiourd'huy: tellement que tous les susdits nous ont fait changer en moins de quinze cens ans, à peu pres, trois fois de langue: car auiourd'huy, & d'icy en auant il sera impossibile d'entendre la langue qu'on parloit il y a quatre cens ans en France." (213) Einen solchen Sprachwandel habe einst schon Cicero für das Lateinische festgestellt, heißt es weiter. Im Gegenzug zu Gueintz betont Harsdörffer, und hier folgt er ganz Schottelius, daß das heutige Deutsch noch „im Grunde" das alte Deutsch der Altvorderen sei; der Sprachwandel beträfe die Sprechsprache und die Schreibung. Vgl. *Specimen*, Disq. 3, §§ 11–12; *Banneck*, 127 f., 261 u. 330 f.

13 Weder die Kelten, noch die Germanen kannten ursprünglich eine Verschriftlichung ihrer Sprache. Dennoch war in der ganzen Sprachargumentation Harsdörffers wichtig, daß das Deutsche und seine (vermeintliche) europäische Vorform des Keltischen eigene Buchstaben besessen hätten. Die 6. Disquisitio seines *Specimen* handelte daher „De Litteris Germanorum". Die alten Vorfahren der Deutschen hätten demnach noch vor den griech. und latein. Alphabeten eine eigene Runenschrift mit 16 Buchstaben entwickelt, aus der jene später geflossen seien. Und er führt als Beleg u. a. an: „In Bibliotheca Florentina & Gottorpiensi asservantur Alphabeta Cimbrica, Gothica, Danica aliaque numero sexaginta sex, ubi hæ literæ, pro diversitate tractûs Septentrionalis, nonnihil variant. […] Verisimile est Græcorum & Latinorum scribendi rationem […] ex his Cimbrorum vel Celtarum notis primordia duxisse", wie es älteste Monumente, Münzen, Bilder usw. bezeugen. *Specimen*, 110 f. Und weiter: „Antiquissima igitur Celtarum Lingua & scriptio fuit Runnica seu Cimbrica", danach habe man sich der griech. Buchstaben bedient, „post tempore

Caroli Mag. in Latinam, & ex hac hodiernam formam demutata". Im Anschluß werden gegenwärtige gebräuchliche deutsche (Druck-)Schriften abgebildet. Ebd., 115 ff.; vgl. *Banneck*, 145 ff. Im 7. Abschnitt seines Gutachtens (s. Anm. 0) bezweifelte Gueintz, „das die Alten Deutschen buchstaben oder Lettern gehabt", ihre Schriftlichkeit begann „allererst zur Zeit Caroli Magni [...] mit lateinischen oder vielmehr mit Griechischen Buchstaben". A.a.O., Bl. 196r. Den etymologischen Konnex zwischen Buche und Buchstabe stellte Gueintz ebenfalls in Frage. Er erwog eine Herleitung vom Verbum „bügen" (d.h. beugen), „in dem es sich zusammen schleust, daher den auch ein bogenpapier vnd dergleichen seinen nahmen hat." (Ebd.) Harsdörffers Etymologie des „Buchstabens" im *Specimen*, 121 ff. Auch in der modernen Etymologie ist die Herkunft des Wortstamms *Buch* nicht gesichert; die Ableitung von *Buche* wird mitunter wieder bezweifelt. Vgl. *Paul Wb.*, 193; *Kluge*, 106 (Buch) u. 107 (Buchstabe). — Im Inventar der Gottorfer Kunstkammer von 1743 wurde tatsächlich ein Stab mit alten Schriftzeichen verzeichnet, der allerdings auf das 17. Jhr. datiert wird: „1. breiter, aber halb abgebrochener Wurmstichiger Stock, mit Caracteren, vermuthl: Rhunischen." Daneben findet sich noch „1. Bündgen von 6. kleinen theils etwas beschädigten Brettern mit Rhunischer Schrifft, als Calender", das aus dem Jahr 1604 stammt. S. Gottorf im Glanz des Barock: Kunst und Kultur am Schleswiger Hof 1544–1713. Hg. v. Heinz Spielmann u. Jan Drees. Bd. 2: Die Gottorfer Kunstkammer. Schleswig 1997, 335 bzw. 343.

14 Gueintz machte in Punkt 8 seines Gutachtens (s. Anm. 0) darauf aufmerksam, daß hebräische Grammatiken erst nach griechischen und lateinischen geschrieben wurden, „das die Griechen vnd Lateiner eher den die Hebräer die spr[a]chen in Gewiße Regeln vnd Ordnung gebrach[t.]." A.a.O., Bl. 196v. Er bezog sich auf *Harsdörffer: Specimen (1646)*, Disquisitio VII, wo die (vermeintlichen) Übereinstimmungen („Conformitas") zwischen der hebr. und der dt. Sprache abgehandelt werden.

15 Wie eine Spirale windet sich diese Streitfrage durch die fruchtbringerische Sprachdebatte. Schottelius und Harsdörffer hielten die einsilbigen Singular-Imperative ohne -e- im Auslaut für die Stammform der Verben. Vgl. Anm. 18 u. detailliert dazu 460902 K 3. Dagegen hielt Gueintz weder den Imperativ noch das Stammwort für notwendig einsilbig. In Abschnitt 9 seines Gutachtens (s. Anm. 0) und in *Gueintz: Rechtschreibung (1645)*, 20 f. plädierte er bei Verben für „die unendige Weise", den Infinitiv, als Wortstamm.

16 Gueintz merkte unter Punkt 10 seines Gutachtens (s. Anm. 0) an, daß sich die Silbentrennung an der Aussprache orientieren solle und nicht an der Wortbildungs-Grammatik. So sei die Silbentrennung — nach Sprechsilben — für Schüler leichter zu erlernen, außerdem würden andere Sprachen (wie das Hebräische) ebenso verfahren. Auf diese Weise wird bereits in *Gueintz: Rechtschreibung (1645)*, 18 f. argumentiert. Harsdörffer hatte seine morphologisch-grammatische Trennweise (die sich im Nhd. nicht durchsetzen wird) schon in der „Schlußerinnerung" zum 5. Teil seiner *Frauenzimmer-Gesprächspiele* (1645) und dann im *Specimen* (1646), 149 f. vertreten, wie auch Schottelius bereits in seiner *Sprachkunst* von 1641. Vgl. Anm. 17 u. 18 sowie 451028A K 6.

17 Christoph Achatius Hager (Frankenberg i. Meißen 1584 – Hamburg 1657), seit etwa 1614 in Hamburg ansässig, wirkte dort als Lehrer der Mathematik und Buchhaltung, wobei er sowohl deutsche als auch ausländische Schüler unterrichtete. Aus seiner Lehrtätigkeit rührte auch sein Interesse für die deutsche Grammatik, die er den fremdsprachigen Schülern seiner Rechenschule notgedrungen vermitteln mußte. Hager weist in seiner *Teütschen Orthographia oder Schreibekunst* (Hamburg 1639; zuerst 1634 in erweiterter Form mit Übungstexten) darauf hin, daß die Worttrennung im Lateinischen und Deutschen voneinander abweiche, weil „die teütsche Sprache/ [...] ein andere Division und zerteihlung naturgemaßer Syllben/ als eine An- vnd vor sich selbsten vollkommene Haubtsprache/ erfoddert/ als etwan die Lateinische" (Bl. [D vij] r; die Formulierung ist eine wörtliche Entnahme aus der *Teutschen Grammatic* [1620] von Jakob Brücker, so U. Götz in ebd., S. LVIII Anm. 80. In seiner Vorrede macht Hager das Deutsche als eine der vier „Haubtsprachen" aus, womit er es gleichrangig neben das Hebräische, Griechische und Lateinische stellte, Bl. A iij r). Darum gibt er ebenso Regeln zur korrekten Trennung von lateinischen Wörtern (Bl. [D vij] v – [D viij] r) wie von deutschen (Bl. [C iv] r – [C v] v) an. Hagers knappe Definition dessen, was unter einer Silbe zu verstehen sei, rückt zwar die Aussprache in den Vordergrund: „EJne teutsche Syllbe ist ein begrieff etlicher Buchstaben/ welche auff einmahl können deütlich außgesprochen werden" (Bl. B ij r). Die von ihm gegebenen Regeln lassen jedoch eine klare Orientierung am Stammwortprinzip erkennen — auch in Bezug auf die Worttrennung. Erhellend sind hier u. a. Hagers Erläuterungen zur Funktion des Trennstrichs („Divisio"). Dieser diene dazu, die Wörter „inn ohnwandelbahre/ und der teütschen Sprache naturgemäße Syllben" zu zerteilen (von „ohnwandelbahre[n] Syllben", Bl. B[j] r, ist passim die Rede, z. B. auch auf Bl. Bij r: „ohnwandelbahre- oder ohnveränderliche Syllben"). Aus den darauffolgenden Beispielen wird deutlich, daß eine ‚naturgemäße' Trennung sich nicht an der Aussprache, sondern primär an der Wortbildung und ihren grammatisch-morphologischen Bestandteilen zu orientieren habe: „All-macht. Ew-ig. Herr-lich. All-mächt-ig. Ew-ig-lich. Herr-lich-er. All-mächt-ig-keit. Viel-fält-ig-keit." (Bl. [D vj] r) Derselbe Schluß kann aus der Liste der „Nänn-Wörter" gezogen werden, die Hager an den Anfang seines Werks setzt (Bl. [A vij] v – [A viij] v), um den Unterschied zwischen Primitiva, Derivativa und Composita zu verdeutlichen: Die von ihm identifizierten Silben werden in der Liste durch einen Trennstrich voneinander geschieden: „Himm-el" (Primitivum), „Bäum-e" (Derivatum), „Nacht-eül-e" (Compositum) usw. Schon hier ist ersichtlich, daß die Konzeption des Stammworts bei Hager von der Harsdörffers und Schottelius' in einem wesentlichen Punkt abweicht: Ein Stammwort muß aus seiner Sicht nicht notwendigerweise einsilbig sein. Darum kann er „Himm-el" auch zu den Primitiva, zählen, denn: „Ein jeder [sic] Vhrsprüngliches Nänn-Tuhn oder -Leidens Wort/ ist entweder Ein- Zwey- oder mehrsyllbig." (Bl. [C iiij] r). Ebd. bestimmt Hager, daß die zweite Silbe immer mit einem Vokal beginne. Das *-el* in „Himm-el" wäre demnach die zweite Stammsilbe des Wortes, das *-e* in „Bäum-e" jedoch Flexionsmorphem. S. Heino Lambeck: Düedsche Orthographia (1633) – Christoph Achatius Hager: Teütsche Orthographia (1639). Hg. Rolf Bergmann u. Ursula Götz. Hildesheim, Zürich, New York 2007; zu Hager vgl. *Moulin-Fankhänel: Bibliographie* II, 96–103.

18 *Schottelius: Sprachkunst (1641),* 192 reguliert: „Es ist ein fester Grund in Teutscher Sprache/ daß die zufälligen/ wesentlichen und die Stammbuchstaben unter sich nicht zertrennet/ sonderen in schreibung zusammengelassen werden müssen: [...] Müssen derowegen die Silben und Wörterleine/ welche wesentlich zusammen gehören/ auch zusammen unzertrennt geschrieben werden". Vgl. auch 440129 K 6, 451028A K 6 u. 451219.

19 In Abschnitt 4 seines Gutachtens (s. Anm. 0) konstatiert Gueintz, dass die „Gewonheit [...] aller Sprachen Richtschnur sey." — Harsdörffer benutzte offenkundig eine Quintilian-Ausgabe, die nicht der heute üblichen Kapitelzählung folgt. Ebenso wie in 460916, wo er aus Kap. 7 zitiert, aber Kap. 12 angibt, ist auch hier gewiß *Quintilian: Institutio oratoria,* Buch 1, Kap. 7 über die Rechtschreibung gemeint. In Satz 11 ist zu lesen: „Verum orthographia quoque consuetudini servit ideoque saepe mutata est" (indessen dient die Orthographie auch der Sprachgewohnheit und hat sich deshalb oft geändert). Im folgenden stellt Quintilian den sprachlichen Wandel des Lateins an zahlreichen Beispielen dar. Vgl. 460916 (K 4). Der Verweis auf Quintilian dient hier nicht einer Apologie der von der Gewohnheit in vielen Varianten disponierten Schreibweisen, sondern Harsdörffers Plädoyer, die Rechtschreibung an den unverbrüchlichen grammatischen Axiomen auszurichten. Vgl. zur Grundkontroverse zwischen Sprach-Ratio und -Consuetudo als Normierungsparameter: *Conermann: Purismus* und *Herz: Ratio und consuetudo*.

20 *Harsdörffer: Frauenzimmer-Gesprächspiele* V (1645, Ndr. 1969), Anhang der „Schlußerinnerung" (Ndr. S. 739–744, hier 740–742; vgl. 451028A K 6); dass. VI (1646, Ndr. 1969), Anhang der „Admonitio" (Ndr. S. 714–716). Hier begründet Harsdörffer seine Bevorzugung des -kk- statt des -ck- ‚philosophisch', genauer naturphilosophisch: das -k- sei anders als das -c- ein der dt. Sprache eigentümlicher Buchstabe. Da alles in der Welt seine eigene wesensgemäße Gestalt habe, „Sic singulæ litteræ habent formas, &, propter illas formas, potestates proprias, minimè confundendas." (Ebd., 714). Bei Wörtern mit einem fremdsprachigen Wortstamm aber sei es zulässig, das -c- zu verwenden. Darum „scribemus Capital/ Centner/ Cicero" (ebd. 715). — Gueintz moniert im 15. Abschnitt seines Gutachtens (s. Anm. 0) die Verwendung des -kk- anstelle von -ck-, „weil es 1. nich[t] üblich[,] in 2. aussprachen einerley, 3. das c au[ch] diese aussprache mit sich bringet, wie in dene[n] wörtern da ein a. o. u. drauf folget zu hör[en] und auch das k wan mans recht bedencke[t] auß zweyen c in eine Figur zusammen gezogen" sei. Vgl. schon 460131.

460915A

Carl Gustav von Hille an Fürst Ludwig

Beantwortet durch 461106. — Carl Gustav v. Hille (FG 302. Der Unverdrossene) hofft noch immer auf eine Antwort auf zwei F. Ludwig (Der Nährende) geschickte Briefe. — Hz. August d. J. v. Braunschweig-Wolfenbüttel (FG 227. Der Befreiende) habe keines der vierzig erhaltenen Exemplare des *GB 1646* für ihn erübrigt. Hille bittet daher F. Ludwig darum, ihm eines über Leipzig zuzusenden. — Da Johann Valentin Andreae (FG 464. 1646) gern in die FG eintreten würde, bitte der Herzog den Fürsten, ihm die Gunst zu erweisen und Andreae aufzunehmen, der zwar ein Geistlicher, aber doch ein Hofmann und Adliger sei. Ein Zettel von der Hand des Befreienden werde deshalb beigelegt. — Hille benötigt für sein fast vollendetes Buch über die FG (*Hille: Teutscher Palmbaum*) noch Auskunft über die Aufnahmezeremonie (,Hänselung') und die Namen, Devisen (,Wörter') und Impresen (,Gemälde') der neuen FG-Mitglieder vom 432. Gesellschafter an. Außerdem möge F. Ludwig mitteilen, wer Gottfried Müller (FG 353) sei und wo er lebe, da man darüber (bei Hofe) rätsele und streite. — Sobald sein Buch beendet sei, werde Hille es F. Ludwig zur Verbesserung überschicken. Er will die dabei anfallenden Transportkosten gern überweisen.

Q HM Köthen: V S 545, Bl. 35r–36v [A: 36v], 36r leer; rotes Lacksiegel. — *D: KE*, 205–207; *KL* III, 225 f. — *BN: Bürger*, 722 Nr. 11. Vgl. *Begemann: FG und Andreae*, 43 u. Ludwig Keller: Comenius und die Akademien der Naturphilosophen des 17. Jahrhunderts. Berlin 1895, 106.

A Dem dürchläuchtigen, hochgebornen Fürsten und Herrn, Herrn Ludwigen, Fürsten zu Anhalt, Grafen zu Ascanien, Herren zu Zerbst und Bernburg *&c.*, meinem gnädigen Fürsten und Herrn; underth.   Cöthen   Franco bis Magdebu*rg*
Eigenh. Empfangsvermerk F. Ludwigs: 7. Octobr 1646

HöchstgeEhrter H. Nehrender *&c.*
demselben seind meine gehorsame dienste, in und allewegen bevor.

Jch habe zu zweien unterschiedenen mahlen an meinen hochstg. Nehrenden geschrieben, ob dieselbe uberbracht worden, davon habe ich biß anietzo die geringste nachrichtung nicht erhalten können;[a] [1] lebe gleichwoll der gehorsamen hoffnung, ich werde in vorigen gnaden annoch erhalten; deßwegen ich nochmalen undert. bitte. Jch hette zwar der Hoffnung gelebet, eß würde der höchstgeEhrte Befreyende, von den 40 Uberschicketen Gesellschaftß Büchern, mir auch einß verEhret haben:[2] Wie ich aber verstehe so bin ich zu späte gekommen; dan dieselbigen, zum theil verschenket; zum theil aber an andere Örter verschikket worden. Weilen ich nun dessen auch gerne einß fhähig seyn möchte, Alß bitte gehorsambst, auß sonderbaren gnaden mir einß zuschenken; und bey der Ersten glegenheit [sic] uber Leipzig heruberschikken; verdiene eß gehorsambst wiederumb.

Alß auch der Befreyende mir gn. angezeiget, daß der H. Valentinus Andreae hertzlichen geneigt were, sich in die Fruchtbringende Gesellschaft einzulassen, und dan vernommen, daß er nicht allein von Adelichem heerkommen, sondern auch ein rechter Höfling seyn solle, alß ersucht der Befreyende den Nehrenden gantz geneigt, daß ob Zwar der H. V. Andreae ein Geistlicher, dennoch auß sonderbahren gunsten, und auf Vorbitte deß Befreyenden, in die Gesellschaft müge genommen werden; massen[b] dann deß Befreyenden Hand hiemit uberschikket wird; erwarte deßwegen günstige antwort.[3] [35v]

Mein angefangenes und fast zu Ende gebrachteß büchlein, von der Fruchtb. Gesel. vorhaben[4], ist nunmero bald verfertiget: Zu dessen ausfuhrung mir annoch mangeln thut Ein ausführliche bericht, 1. Wie eß mit der[c] henselung und einfhührung pfleget in acht genommen zu werden; auch gleicher gestald, mit der Uberlieferung deß Oelbergerß; und andern gebreuchen; und waß sonsten mehr etwan zu Außubung des[sen][d], mir möchte von nöthen seyn.[5] Zum 2. werden mir auch nötig seyn, der ubrigen Gesellschafterß namen, wörter, und Gemälde. Alß von dem 432. biß auf diese Zeit.[6]

Weilen auch allerhand Streittigkeitten wegen deß Gottfrid Müllerß, so der Aufwekkend genand wird, und in der Zahl der 353. ist, vorfallen[e], Alß bitte[b] gehorsambst zu berichten, wer er sey, und wo er sich aufhalte?[7]

Sobald diß mein büchlein zu Ende gebracht, wil ichß meinem höchstgeEhrten Nehrenden zue ender- und verbesserung gehorsambst[en][d] Uberschikken; damit eß mit derselben Zulasung[f] müge deß tageß Licht anschauen; hoffe eß soll ein Werk seyn, damit ich Ehre werde einlegen.[8]

Waß wegen uberbringung einß und andern auß zu geben sein wird, soll von mir dieseß orteß danckbar erleget werden. Gehorsambst bittend mit neuer forderlichen antwort mich[e] zu würdigen; Thue hiemit meinen höchstgeEhrten Nehrenden Gotteß obacht, mich aber in Dero beharliche gnade gehorsambst empfehlen, und verbleibet deroselben gehorsamen diener

Der Unverdrossene &c.

Wolfenbüttel, den 15. Herbst Monatß 1646.

I

Hille sendet Fürst Ludwig Abschriften Herzog Augusts d. J. von Braunschweig-Wolfenbüttel aus zwei Briefen Johann Valentin Andreaes

Q HM Köthen: V S 545, Bl. 465rv, v leer, Abschriften v. d. H. Hz. Augusts d. J. v. Braunschweig-Wolfenbüttel. — *D: KE*, 206 Anm. 1 und 2. Vgl. die Vorlage der ersten Abschrift in Philipp Hainhofers Mitteilung an Hz. August (460715 II) nach Andreaes Brief an Hainhofer 460715 I. Das 2. Zitat entstammt Andreaes Schreiben an den Herzog 460819. — Beide Zitate auch bei *Begemann: FG und Andreae*, 36 f.; die erste Notiz des Herzogs auch zit. bei *Keller: Akademien der Renaissance*, 105 f. (falsch datiert auf den 15./25. 7. 1645).

Carl Gustav von Hille schickt eine von Herzog August d. J. von Braunschweig-Wolfenbüttel erhaltene Information Johann Valentin Andreaes an Philipp Hainhofer (vom 15. Juli 1646) mit.

Vom H. Augustissimo habe[a] ich (Schreibet D. Joh. Valentinus Andreae, Wurtembergischer OberHofprediger)[b] ein schönes Kreuter[c] Gesellschaft buch empfangen, darinnen 400 Emblemata, von Merians guter Hand und Invention.[1] Wo ich nicht zu Alt und müede wäre, hätte ich wol mügen auch der gesellen einen geben. Es seyn aber nuhnmehr alle Blumen und andere gewäx heraus, und wuste ich nichtes mehr für mich überig, als an einem alten abgestandenen Baum, das anwaxende <u>Mösch</u>, mit dem Motto <u>Hernach</u>, und dem Nahmen, <u>der Müede</u>,[2] Ad Phil. Hainhoferum vom dato 15/25 Jul. 1646.

Carl Gustav von Hille teilt eine von Herzog August d. J. von Braunschweig-Wolfenbüttel erhaltene Information aus Andreaes Brief vom 19. August 1646 mit.

An uns schreibet Er von 19. Aug. 1646:
Wo bey der Hochlöblichen Kreutergeselschaft ich meinem geringfügigen Simbolo, auch solte einen Platz noch finden mögen, wolte ich ein solches, für eine hohe gnade und sonderbare Ehre achten.[3]

T a *Folgt ein Fragezeichen, das Hille wohl auf den indirekten* ob-*Fragesatz bezieht.* — **b** *Folgt ein gestrichenes Wort.* — **c** *Eingefügt ein gestrichenes Einschaltzeichen, dazu nach* henselung *ein anderes Einschaltzeichen zu der durch Bezifferung umgestellten Ergänzung am Rand:* einführung *und* — **d** *Buchstabenverlust im Falz. Konjektur in eckigen Klammern.* — **e** *Eingefügt.* — **f** *Lies:* Zulassung *(also mit F. Ludwigs Genehmigung).*

T I a habe ich *eingefügt.* — **b** *Folgt* <habe ich> — **c** *Folgt ohne Abstand* <Buch>

K 1 460718 und ein offenbar verschollener anderer Brief Carl Gustavs v. Hille (FG 302. Der Unverdrossene). Auch auf das vorliegende Schreiben hatte Hille keine Antwort erhalten, als er seinen Brief 461029 an den Fürsten richtete. F. Ludwig (Der Nährende) schrieb erst wieder in 461106 an Hille.

2 Hz. August d. J. v. Braunschweig-Wolfenbüttel (FG 227. Der Befreiende) hatte sich an der Verlagsumlage des *GB 1646* mit 200 Rtl. beteiligt und war deswegen mit 48 Exemplaren des kostbaren Buchs entschädigt worden. Spricht Hille hier von 40 Exemplaren, ist dies wohl nur ein Versehen. Vgl. 440323 K I 1 u. den vorhergehenden Briefwechsel Hilles und Hz. Augusts mit F. Ludwig. Hille, der für den Herzog den fruchtbringerischen Briefwechsel mit F. Ludwig führte, war nicht durch den Befreienden mit einem Geschenkexemplar bedacht worden. Er hatte dies schon in 460718 erwähnt und F. Ludwig um das Buch gebeten.

3 Johann Valentin Andreae, Angehöriger eines „ehrbaren" Geschlechts und Enkel des württemberg. Reformators Jakob Andreae, war als Oberhofprediger in Stuttgart nicht nur ein hoher luther. Geistlicher, sondern in gewissem Sinne auch ein Hofmann. Als geistlicher Rat Hz. Augusts, Mitarbeiter an dessen *Evangelischer Kirchen-Harmonie* (1646 u.ö.; s. 411214) und als sein Vertrauter konnte Andreae auch in seinem ungewöhnlichen Verlangen auf die Empfehlung des Befreienden zählen. S. Beil. I.

4 *Hille: Teutscher Palmbaum*. S. 451008 K 2.

5 F. Ludwig zögerte noch in 461106, Auskunft über das fruchtbringerische Aufnahmeritual der Hänselung und den Gebrauch des Trinkgefäßes „Ölberger" zu geben. Vgl. 460718 K 8.

6 F. Ludwig legte seinem Antwortbrief 461106 ein solches Verzeichnis bei.

7 S. 450126 K 11 u. F. Ludwigs Auskunft über den dessauischen Kanzler D. Gottfried Müller (FG 353) in 461106.

8 Zu einer Kritik oder Erweiterung des Werks durch F. Ludwig kam es nicht, da Hille es erst nach dem Druck an das Oberhaupt der FG gelangen ließ. Der Nährende hatte dem Unverdrossenen die vorherige Einsendung des Manuskripts zum Zwecke der Durchsicht angeboten, höflicherweise aber auch freigestellt (451028). Vgl. 460718 u. 461029.

K I 1 *GB 1646*.

2 F. Ludwig änderte zwar nicht die Pflanze (Moos), wohl aber das ‚Wort' und den Gesellschaftsnamen Johann Valentin Andreaes (FG 464. 1646) in *Bleibet doch frisch* bzw. *Der Mürbe*. Zu den Änderungen vgl. 461106 I u. *Conermann III*, 563.

3 Vgl. 460819.

460916

Georg Philipp Harsdörffer an Fürst Ludwig

Antwort auf 460816. Beantwortet durch 461031. — Das Gutachten von Christian Gueintz (FG 361. Der Ordnende) zu seinem *Specimen Philologiae Germanicae* (1646) hat Georg Philipp Harsdörffer (FG 368. Der Spielende) von F. Ludwig (Der Nährende) erhalten. Gueintz' Kriterium des Sprachusus bleibe die Antwort auf die Frage schuldig, ob eine gebräuchliche Form richtig oder falsch sei. Bliebe es dabei, so fahre man nur im alten fehlerhaften Trott fort und erspare sich den (wissenschaftlichen) Streit. Die Frage sei doch aber gerade, *welcher* Sprachgebrauch nun in Aussprache und Rechtschreibung der mustergültige sei. Manche verwerfen die meißnische Mundart als zu weich und „weibisch" in betracht der „männlichen" dt. „Heldensprache" und ziehen die schlesische oder fränkische vor. Wenn sich die mundartl. Unterschiede in der gesprochenen Sprache nicht ausgleichen lassen, so auch nicht die jeweiligen (auf den Mundarten basierenden) Schreibweisen. Harsdörffer zitiert Quintilian, der diese Normierungsaporie auch schon gesehen hat. — Harsdörffer überschickt den diesjährigen, sechsten Teil seiner *Frauenzimmer-Gesprächspiele* (1646). Ob die projektierten zwei weiteren Fortsetzungsbände zustande kämen, könne er noch nicht sagen, weil sein Verleger (Wolfgang Endter d. Ä.) wegen des Krieges nicht mehr mit Büchern handeln wolle. Er werde sich jedoch eines Besseren besinnen, wenn er auf Büchermessen wieder Geld verdienen könne. — Harsdörffer bittet um eine Liste der FG-Mitglieder vom 433. Gesellschafter (Matthaeus v. Wesenbeck) an und erinnert den Nährenden daran, den Brief (460726) Johann Michael Moscheroschs (FG 436. Der Träumende) zu beantworten. — Das gerade erschienene *GB 1646* sei nun auch in Nürnberg käuflich zu erwerben; er hätte es gern, jedoch sei ihm das zum Preis von 10 Reichstalern verkaufte Buch schlicht zu teuer. Ob es eine andere Möglichkeit gebe, es zu erwerben? — *Nachschrift*: Das zweite Gutachten von Marcus Fridericus Wendelin(us) (zu Harsdörffers *Specimen*) habe er gerade erhalten; eine Antwort darauf werde erfolgen.

Q HM Köthen: V S 545, Bl. 356r–357v [A: 357v], 357r leer; eigenh.; ein rotes Lacksiegel mit Resten von zwei Bändchen. — *D: KE*, 374 f. — *BN: Bürger*, 675 Nr. 41.

A *Dem Durchleuchtigen, Hochgebornen Fürsten, und Herrn, Herrn Ludwigen* Fürsten zu Anhalt, Grafen zu Ascanien, und Ballenstatt, Herrn zu Zerbst und Bernburg *etc.* Meinem gnädi[gen][a] Für*s*t*e*n und Herrn *Cöthen*
Postvermerk: Zu Leipzig bey H. Gottfried Stahlen[1] abzugeben.
Darunter eigenh. Empfangsvermerk F. Ludwigs: 29. October 1646.

Höchstgeehrter Nehrender.

Was bey des Spielenden Specimine Philologiæ Germanicæ von dem Ordnenden ist erinnert worden hat er aus neulich zugefertigtem Einschluß mit mehrerem nachrichtlich verstand*en*, und verbleibet deswegen zu würklicher Dank-erwiederung schuldigst v*e*rbund*en*.[2] Der Ordnende wil die Gewonheit zu einer Richtschnur setzen, sie sey gleich gut oder böß, richtig oder nicht: Wann dieses gelten solte, so hat aller Streit ein ende, und muß man in dem alt*en* Trab fort fehlen.[3] Es ist aber die Frage: Welche Gewonheit in dem Reden und Schreiben für gültig anzunehmen? Viel steh*en* in dem Wahn die Meisnische art zu reden sey als weibisch, und v*e*rzärtelt, der Männischen Deutschen Held*en*sprache gantz entgegen, und loben hingegen die Schlesische[b], andere halten es mit uns Franken. Wie sich nun in der Mundart nicht zu v*e*rgleichen, also wird sich auch die Rechtschreibung schwerlich lassen ausfündig machen. Quintilianus[c] sagt hiervon also: Sic scribendum cuiq*ue* judico, quomodo sonat: hic enim est usus literarum, ut custodiant vocem, et velut depositum reddant legentib*us*; itaq*ue* id exprimere d*e*b*en*t quod dicturi sumus.[4]

Der höchstgeehrte Nehrende geruhe mitkom*m*ende heurige[5] frucht der Gesprächspiele in Gnad*en* zu empfahen,[6] und die Gnädige[d] verordnung zu thun, daß dem Spielenden die fortsetzung der Fruchtbringend*en* Gesellschafter von 433 an, mitgetheilet [356v] werden möchte;[7] nicht zweifflend es werde dem

460916 Georg Philipp Harsdörffer

*Traumend[en]*ᵃ auf sein jüngst gegebenes, von dem Ertzschrein aus förderlichste Antwort wiederfahren.⁸

Der Fruchtbringend*en* Gesellschaft buch mit des Merians Kup[fern]ᵉ ist hieher gebracht word*en*, aber gringer nicht, als umb 10 Rth[l.]ᵉ zu v*er*kauffen: ob es zwar der Spielende gerne hette, so is[t]ᵉ es ihm doch zu teuer; wann erᶠ solches nicht andrer g[e]stalt*e*, als umb baar Gelt, haben solte.⁹

Wegen fortsetzung der noch hinterstelligen zween Theile der Gesprächspiele kan der Spielende nichts v*er*sprechen weil sein v*er*leger¹⁰ die Bücherhandlung bey diesen Kri[egs]zeitenᵉ eingezog*en* und die unkost*en* darzu nicht ferner v*er*schaff*en* wil: doch möchte er sich bald eines andern besin[nen]ᵉ wann die Messen wieder mit nutzen könten geba[uet]ᵉ werd*en*.

Hier mit befihlet den Höchstgeehrt*en* Nehr[enden]ᵉ des Höchst*en* Gottes Gnad*en*schutz, sich aber zu desselben beharrlichen Gewog*en*heit. Geben eiligst Nürnberg d*en* 16 des Herbstmonats 1646.

Des Höchstgeehrt*en* Nehrend*en*

Dienstverbundner Knecht
Der Spielende.

N. S. Eben diese Stunde wird mir H. Wendelins fernere Beantwortung eingehändiget, die v*er*fügung darauf sol zu andrer Zeit erfolg*en*.¹¹

T a *Anschrift zum Teil durch den Rest eines Bändchens verdeckt, Konjektur in eckigen Klammern.* — **b** *Wort getrennt und nachträglich gebessert:* Schle<s>-sische — **c** *Am Rand* L. 1. c. 12. — **d** *Folgt* <Verhe> — **e** *Textverlust im Falz. Konjekturen nach KE in eckigen Klammern.* — **f** *Folgt* <sol>

K 1 Der Leipziger Kaufmann Gottfried Stahl (d. Ä.) (1600–1670) wurde von F. Ludwig (Der Nährende) wiederholt für finanzielle Transaktionen, Einkäufe sowie zur Informationsweitergabe und Abwicklung der Korrespondenz herangezogen. Vgl. 440426 K 1.

2 Georg Philipp Harsdörffer (FG 368. Der Spielende) erhielt das Gutachten Christian Gueintz' (FG 361. Der Ordnende) zu seinem *Specimen Philologiae Germanicae* (1646) durch F. Ludwig mit 460816: „Erinnerungen Bey des Spielenden Wercklein die deutsche Sprache betreffend" (HM Köthen: V S 545, Bl. 192r–200v. Demnächst in *DA Köthen I. 9*). Vgl. die Zusammenfassung des Gutachtens in 460720 K 3. — Wie aus 461031 hervorgeht, lag diesem Brief auch Harsdörffers Brief 460915 an Gueintz bei, in dem Harsdörffer auf dessen Gutachten reagiert. Der Brief war wahrscheinlich offen, so daß man eine Kopie für den Erzschrein hat anfertigen können, bevor er an Gueintz weitergeleitet wurde. S. zu den verschiedenen Gutachten für das *Specimen* 460705 K 3.

3 Vgl. dazu 460915 K 19.

4 *Quintilian: Institutio oratoria*, Buch I Kap. 7 (!), Satz 30f. Die heutigen Editionen weichen nur minimal von Harsdörffers Zitat ab: „Iudicium autem suum grammaticus interponat his omnibus: nam hoc valere plurimum debet. ego, nisi quod consuetudo optinuerit, sic scribendum quidque iudico, quomodo sonat. hic enim est usus litterarum, ut custodiant voces et velut depositum reddant legentibus. itaque id exprimere debent quod dicturi sumus." Die ersten beiden Bücher der *Institutio* beschäftigen sich mit der Früherziehung des Redners, Kap. 7 von Buch I mit der Rechtschreibung. Vgl. 460915 K 19.

5 *Heurig,* hier ‚in diesem Jahr; diesjährig'; vgl. 440426 K 3. — Zwischen 1641 und 1649 erschien jährlich (ausgenommen 1648) ein neuer Teil der am Ende acht Bände umfassenden *Frauenzimmer-Gesprächspiele* Harsdörffers. Vgl. zu Harsdörffers zwischenzeitlich gefährdeter Gesamtplanung der *Gesprächspiele* 460803 K 0.

6 Es handelt sich um den sechsten Teil der *Frauenzimmer-Gesprächspiele*, dem F. Ludwig auf Bitten Harsdörffers ein Lobgedicht beigesteuert hatte. Vgl. 460705 u. Beil. I–III. Dem vorliegenden Brief hatte Harsdörffer zwei Exemplare des 6. Teils beigelegt, eins für F. Ludwig und eins für Gueintz, was aus F. Ludwigs Antwort 461031 hervorgeht.

7 Fruchtbringer wie Harsdörffer baten F. Ludwig immer wieder um Mitteilung der Gesellschafts- und Taufnamen der jüngst aufgenommenen Mitglieder, da letztere in den Gesellschaftsbüchern nicht veröffentlicht wurden, ausgenommen das gedruckte Verzeichnis der Mitglieder 1–353 im *GB 1641* u. *GB 1641/44*. Vgl. 450529 K 10. Der Fürst schickt Harsdörffer das gewünschte, aber anscheinend nicht in Kopie erhaltene Verzeichnis zusammen mit seinem Antwortschreiben 461031.

8 Gemeint ist wohl der Brief 460726 an F. Ludwig, mit dem sich Johann Michael Moscherosch (FG 436. Der Träumende) für seine Aufnahme in die FG bedankte. Harsdörffer hakt hier vielleicht nach, weil jener noch keine Antwort erhalten hat. F. Ludwig bestätigt Harsdörffer in 461031, das Dankschreiben Moscheroschs („ein hofliches brieflein von dem Traumenden") erhalten zu haben. Ein Antwortschreiben des Fürsten an Moscherosch ist nicht überliefert, die Korrespondenz zwischen dem Fürsten und Moscherosch lief ja auch regelmäßig über Harsdörffer. Moscheroschs Aufnahme in die FG war vom Spielenden und Diederich v. dem Werder (FG 31) angeregt worden. Vgl. 450500 (K 1).

9 Die Rede ist vom *GB 1646* mit den neuen Impresenkupfern für die FG-Mitglieder 201 bis 400, die Matthäus Merian d. Ä. mit seiner Werkstatt schuf. F. Ludwig erfüllte Harsdörffers indirekte Bitte, ihm ein Exemplar zu schenken, mit Brief 461213, nachdem er ihn in 461031 noch auf die kommende Leipziger Neujahrsmesse vertröstete. Es ist wahrscheinlich, daß durch die obigen kritischen Äußerungen Harsdörffers der bereits ein Vierteljahr zuvor (460620B) festgelegte Preis von 5 Gulden (bzw. 6½ bis 7 Gulden für Buchhändler) für die Leipziger Neujahrsmesse 1647 auch für Buchhändler auf 5 Reichstaler reduziert wurde. Der Bürgermeister Rotenburgs o. d. T., Johann Georg Styrzel schrieb am 26.10.1646: „Societatem Frugiferam, per-illustre et venustum, ut audio, opus, nondum vidi; qvm̀, propter ingens, et meae crumenae minime conveniens, quo venit, pretium, videre tantum — non despero. Neque enim res angusta domi tam sumtuosos comparare permittit libros, aere nostro vix ac ne vix contributionibus et exactionibus, quîs hactenus exhaurimur et emedullamur, sufficiente." HAB: Cod. Guelf. 11.12 Aug. 2°, Bl. 546v. — Es ist auch eine Nachricht (unbekannter H.) im Köthener Erzschrein erhalten, in der es heißt: „Zur nachricht, das in künftiger Leipziger Neujahrsmeße 1647, bey Friedrich Werdern am Neuen Marckt, die Geselschaftbücher, wie Sie zu Franckfurt am Meyen mit Vierhundert kupferstucken gedruckt, iedes um Fünf ReichsThaler zubekommen sein werden" (HM Köthen: V S 546, Bl. 447–449). Dieses Schreiben könnte im Oktober 1646 als Reaktion auf das vorliegende Dokument und nach der Michaelismesse, die 1646 auf den 18. 10. verschoben wurde und bis 25. 10 andauerte, mit Blick auf die kommende Leipziger Neujahrsmesse verfaßt worden sein.

10 Wolfgang Endter d. Ä., den Harsdörffer für einen Geizhals hielt. Vgl. 460620 (K 9).

11 Zu seinem *Specimen Philologiae Germanicae* (1646) erbat Harsdörffer in 460406 Gutachten von Christian Gueintz (s. o. Anm. 2) und Diederich v. dem Werder (FG 31).

Der Zerbster Gymnasialrektor Marcus Fridericus Wendelin(us) (1584–1652) schrieb ebenfalls zwei Gutachten (beide demnächst in *DA Köthen I. 9*), die über F. Ludwig mit 460705 und 460902 in Harsdörffers Hände gelangten. Auf das erste reagierte Harsdörffer mit seiner (für Wendelin bestimmten) latein. Erwiderung vom 17. 7. 1646 (ebenfalls demnächst in *DA Köthen I. 9*). Hier ist die Rede von Wendelins 2. Gutachten, nämlich der Duplik vom 6. 8. 1646 auf eben diesen Harsdörffer-Brief. Vgl. 460705 K 3. Werder scheint i. ü. keine Stellungnahme abgegeben zu haben.

461006

Johann Dietrich von Brincken an Christian Ernst von Knoch

Johann Dietrich v. Brincken (FG 403. Der Tötende) bedankt sich für ein Schreiben Christian Ernst (v.) Knochs (FG 268. Der Weichende) und berichtet in gesellenhafter Weise unter Benutzung der Gesellschaftsnamen über die nach dem Tod seiner Mutter zwischen ihm und seinen Brüdern einerseits und seinen Schwestern andererseits ausgebrochenen Erbstreitigkeiten. Nachdem die bei verschiedenen Universitäten eingeholten Gutachten den Streit nicht entscheiden konnten, haben sich die Geschwister nach sächsischem Recht, also zum Nachteil der männlichen Erben geeinigt. Er glaube, daß man sich im Braunschweiger Land wohl nach der juristischen Meinung Benedikt Carpzovs richte.

Q STB Berlin – PK: 141/11: FrbrGes; 1 Bl. [A: Rücks.]; eigenh.¹, mit Unterschr. u. Sig.

A A Monsieur Monsieur CE. Knochen Lieutenant Colonel. *etc.* Conseiller de son Altesse le Princ[!] Loys d'Anhalt *etc.* mon tres honnoré frere *etc.* presentement à Keuten.
Von ders. Hand folgt auf der Außenseite des Briefs: Bitte die Schwester Annen dortleinᵃ von Freyberg² gahr fr. zu grüesen. wie auch zuuoderst seine liebsten³.

HochEdel Gestrenger vielgeehrtester Herr Bruder *etc.*

Der Tödtender nebenst Seiner liebsten⁴ thut dem weichenden für aus dessen beliebtem schreiben, ersehenem grües hochfleisigen danck wissen, von hertzen wiederwünschendt, das der allerhogster des weiche[n]denᵇ wünsch bestattigen vndt an dessen seiten doppelt erstatten woll[e].ᵇ Diesem negst weiln in Eydt vndt pflichten, als müste billich mit der fr[a]geᵇ ⁵ verschonet worden sein, kan aber dieswohl schreiben, daß wir bruder mitt vnsern Schwestern in grose misverstende, nach absterben vnserer Sehl. Mutter, der frage halber gerieten, es auf vnterschie[d]licheᵇ Uniuersitäten schickten, die allemahl nicht eins wahren, wie auch in iure viel dispütirens hin vndt wieder darvberᶜ geschicht; da nün keine gewisse **statuta** alhie im lande, als vermeinten viel, daß das Saxische recht⁶ vns scheiden müste, da hero wir vns darnach vertrügen vndt wir brüder also den Kürtze[s]ten züegen⁷; Jm landt zu braunschweich weis eigentlich nicht wie es da gehalten, gleube aber auch daß Sie nach **Carpzovij meinünge**⁸ richten; weis also nicht mehr davon zü schreiben

Bitte dem Nehrenden geschlegte⁹ meine vnderthänig gehorsambe dienste zuvermelden vndt der Tödtende nebenst seiner liebsten Verbleibet negst Gottlicher Empfehlunge

des weichenden Alzeit dienstwilliger Knecht
J Dt vom¹⁰ Br. alias der Tödtende.
NB.

NB. Ein Quentin¹¹ Güehte wirdt mehr wehgen¹², als 1000 pfundt dispüten, et prius q*uam* incipias consulto¹³. NB.

Schauwenb¹⁴ den 6 8bris Ao. 1646.ᶜ

T a *Verschrieben* dorthein — **b** *Textverlust am Rande. Konjektur in eckigen Klammern.* — **c** darvber geschicht *eingefügt für* <geschigt> — **d** *Folgt die Notiz eines Sammlers oder Archivars:* „Brinck. Joh. Dietr. v. dem. Mitglied d. fruchtbringenden Gesellsch. der Tödtende genan*n*t."

K Das vorliegende Schreiben ist kein genuin fruchtbringerischer Brief, bedient sich aber der Gesellschaftsnamen der Sozietät zwischen einfachen Fruchtbringern in einer Privatangelegenheit und mag als Beispiel dienen, wie das FG-Netzwerk auch unterhalb eigentlicher Gesellschaftsthemen kommunikativ genutzt, also sozusagen privatisiert wurde. Noch wichtiger und für die Aufnahme des Briefs letztlich ausschlaggebend ist, daß hier der Sprach- und Bildungsstand eines eher typischen Adligen aus der FG dokumentiert wird, der in der Hinsicht sicher so manch anderen seiner Art vertreten kann. — Die Anrede „Bruder/ Schwester" u. die persönlichen Grüße zeigen ein hohes Maß an Vertrautheit, eventuell gar Verwandtschaft (vgl. FG 140), zwischen dem gfl.-schaumburg. Rat und Drosten zu Schaumburg Johann Dietrich v. Brincken (FG 403. Der Tötende) u. Christian Ernst (v.) Knoch (FG 268. Der Weichende). Knoch, obgleich Köthener Geheimrat, wird nicht um seine jurist. Expertise gefragt. Knoch war im Auftrag F. Ludwigs wiederholt in Belangen der FG tätig. So nahm er u. a. bei seiner Reise nach Schlesien im Sommer 1648 mehrere Mitglieder auf (FG 508–510) und war an der Verbesserung von Reimgesetzen beteiligt, z. B. bei Casimir Dietrich (v.) Krage (FG 465. 1647). S. *Conermann III*, 297f. Nach dem Tod F. Ludwigs wurde Knoch damit beauftragt, „die Uberlieferung der Hochlöbl. Fruchtbr. Gesellschaft" (*Neumark: Palmbaum*, 296) nach Weimar an das neue Oberhaupt der FG, Hz. Wilhelm IV. v. Sachsen-Weimar (FG 5), zu überbringen. Knoch konnte jedoch aufgrund der Erkrankung seiner Frau, die kurz darauf starb, dieser Verrichtung nicht nachkommen, sondern mußte von Wilhelm Heinrich v. Freyberg (FG 439) vertreten werden, der am 8.5.1651 die Urkunden und Siegel an Hz. Wilhelm überbrachte. *Harsdörffer: Fortpflantzung der FG*, 13–18. Vgl. *Neumark: Palmbaum*, 296f.; *Conermann III*, 297f. u. 529f.

1 Außergewöhnliche, an Schreiberh. erinnernde Handschrift. Vgl. auch Brinckens eigenh. Eintrag im *GB Kö.* III.

2 Anna Dorothea v. Freyberg (1613–1677), eine Tochter Ernsts v. Freyberg (FG 75) und Schwester Hans Ernsts und Wilhelm Heinrichs von Freyberg (FG 140 bzw. FG 439). Nach dem frühen Tod ihrer Eltern (1624 bzw. 1626) wurde sie aufgrund der Verdienste des Vaters nebst ihrer jüngeren Schwester Salome Elisabeth an den Hof von F. Ludwig nach Köthen geholt, wo sie im Frauenzimmer von dessen Ehefrau Fn. Sophia v. Anhalt-Köthen, geb. Gfn. zur Lippe (AL 1629. TG 38), Aufnahme fand, welcher sie alsbald als Kammerjungfer diente. In dieser Zeit wird sie vermutl. Christian Ernst Knoch kennengelernt haben, der sie später, am 26.2.1652, in seiner zweiten Ehe heiratete. S. Johann Sachse: Christ-Adeliches Ehren-Gedächtniß Der HochEdelgebohrnen/ HochEhr- und Tugendsa-

461006 Johann Dietrich von Brincken

men Frauen Annen Dorotheen/ Gebohrnen von Freyberg/ ... (Cöthen: Fürstl. Druckerey, 1677). HAB: Xa 4° 1:12 (16). S. auch *Conermann III*, 80f., 139f., 297f. u. 529f.
3 Christian Ernst Knoch war damals vermählt mit Anne Amelie v. Börstel (1610–1651). Ebd., 297f.
4 Johann Dietrich v. Brincken war seit 1643 mit Catharina Hedwig, der Tochter von Moritz v. Oeynhausen, verheiratet. Ebd., 479.
5 Eine nicht näher spezifizierte Rechtsfrage in einer Erbauseinandersetzung der Familie von Brincken hinsichtlich des Nachlasses von Lucia Maria, Tochter von Johann v. Steding auf (Borg-)Holzhausen (Gft. Ravensberg), zweite Ehefrau u. Witwe von Dietrich v. Brincken (1565–1626) auf Brincke, Iggenhausen, Bückeburg u. Riepen, gfl. schaumburg-holstein. Geheimer Rat u. Statthalter zu Stadthagen u. Bückeburg. Wahrscheinlich betraf dies einen von den Töchtern als Gerade beanspruchten Erbteil. Möglicherweise hatte die Erblasserin aber auch eigenen Besitz oder gar ein Frauenlehen in der nach 1640 zwischen den Häusern Braunschweig u. Lüneburg, Hessen-Kassel u. Lippe aufgeteilten Gft. Schaumburg zu vererben, wo ihr verstorbener Mann als Statthalter gedient hatte. Erbberechtigt waren Lucia Marias in der Ehe gezeugte 4 Söhne u. 3 Töchter: Johann Dietrich (1606–1661; s. Anm. 0), Hilmar Erich († 1660), Domherr des Hochstifts zu Minden, Eustachius (1615–1687; FG 529. 1651) u. Christoph Eberhard v. Brincken (1616–1647), Präzeptor u. Kammerjunker Georg Wilhelms u. Johann Friedrichs, der Söhne von Hz. Georg v. Braunschweig-Calenberg (FG 231); sowie Anna Margaretha (1608–1672), verheiratet mit Franz v. Ditfurth (FG 275), Maria Catharina (1610 – nach 1647), verheiratet mit dem Drosten Kurt v. Münchhausen bzw. dem kurköln. Oberstleutnant Hermann v. Westerholt auf Lembeck, u. Elisabeth (1613–1674), verheiratet mit dem generalstaatl.-niederländ. Obristwachtmeister Johann v. Münnich auf Ellerburg u. Lübbecke. Vgl. *Conermann III*, 306f. u. 479; Johann Franz Buddeus: Allgemeines historisches Lexicon. 3. Aufl., Bd. 1, Leipzig 1730, 672f.; Johann Prange: Christliche Leichpredigt/ Bey Volckreicher Begräbnüß des ... Dieterichen vom Brinck ... (Rintheln: Lucius 1626). VD17 7:660548D; Friedrich Winekker: Kurtze und einfältige Erörterung Der Frage ... [LP auf Christoph Eberhard v. dem Brincken] (Hannover: Glaser 1647). VD17 1:036653F; Ernst Wilhelm Prange: Seelen-Confect Wieder Noth und Todt ... [LP auf Anna Margaretha v. Ditfurth] (Minden an der Weser: Piler 1672). HAB: Da 602 (11); Christoph Schlichthaber: Unbeweglicher Glaubens-Grund/ Worauf Ihr festes Vertrauen gebauet ... [LP auf Elisabeth v. Münnich] (Minden: Piler 1674). HAB: Da 602 (15); Leopold Nedopil (Hg.): Deutsche Adelsproben aus dem Deutschen Ordens-Central-Archiv. Bd. 1, Wien 1868, 123f., Nr. 860; Rudolf Fhr. v. Buttlar-Elberberg: Stammtafel der Familie von dem Brinck. In: Der deutsche Herold 23 (1892), 80–82; Antje Stannek: Telemachs Brüder. Die höfische Bildungsreise des 17. Jahrhunderts. Frankfurt a. M. 2001, 130; Anke Hufschmidt: Adlige Frauen im Weserraum zwischen 1570 und 1700. Status, Rollen, Lebenspraxis. Münster 2001, 156.
6 Bereits 1625 hatte Hz. Friedrich Ulrich v. Braunschweig-Wolfenbüttel (FG 38) in einem Erlaß festgelegt, hinsichtlich der in einem Erbfall gemäß altem sächsischen Recht den weiblichen Verwandten zustehenden Gerade „durch lange vnd alte eingeführte Gewonheit/ vnd nicht nach Sachsen Rechte/ welches in vnsern Gerichten/ auffgehoben" sei, „Hergewette, Frawen Gerade vnd Mußtheil gentzlich aus den Grund/ daß die Sachsischen Rechte in den Fürstenthumben nicht gehalten/ sondern abgeschaffet" worden seien, auch in den zu seinem Herrschaftsbereich gehörenden Fürstentümern (Wolfenbüttel, Calenberg-Göttingen) u. Grafschaften (Blankenburg-Regenstein, Hohnstein, Obergrafschaft Hoya) abzuschaffen. Begründet wurde dieser Schritt damit, daß sonst unter dem Vorwand der Gerade den Söhnen bzw. Kreditoren gute Stücke vorenthalten, auch Häuser, Vorwerke u. Güter geschwächt u. sogar ganze Familien ins Verderben gestürzt würden.

Hertzogen Friederichen Ulrichs zu Braunschweig/ etc. Constitutio Wie es hinfüro in S. Fürstl. Gn. Fürstenthumben/ Graff: und Herrschafften/ mit ziehung des Heergewette/ Gerade und Mußtheil gehalten werden sol: Sub dato 8. Iulii, Anno 1625. Wolfenbüttel 1625 (VD17 1:016862K). 1657 wurde dieses von Hz. Friedrich Ulrichs Nachfolger, Hz. August d. J. v. Braunschweig-Wolfenbüttel (FG 227), erneuert. Von Gottes Gnaden/ Wyr Augustus/ Herzog zu BrunsWyk und LunäBurg/ Fügen ... allen Unsern Untertanen ... himit gnädiglich zu wissen/ Demnach albereit am 8. Julii/ Anno 1625 ... wegen Zihung des Heergewettes/ der Frauen Geräde und des Mustheyls ... sonderbare Sazzung gemachet ... : ... gäben in Unser Vestung Wulffen-Büttel/ den 12. May des 1657ten Jaars. [o. O.] 1657 (VD17 23:678696Q). Vgl. allgemein dazu *Zedler* X, 1043–1051; Wilfrid Bungenstock: Heergewäte und Gerade. Zur Geschichte des bäuerlichen Erbrechts in Nordwestdeutschland, [Bamberg] 1966.

7 Lies „den Kürzesten zögen". Vermutl. westfäl. Dialektfärbung. Vgl. nün, meinünge, zü et al.

8 Dr. jur. Benedikt Carpzov d. J. (1595–1666), Assessor am Oberhofgericht zu Leipzig sowie Professor an der dortigen Universität, tat sich insbesondere durch seine Arbeiten über das Strafrecht in der sächsischen Rechtstradition hervor, verfaßte jedoch auch Werke zu zivil- u. kirchenrechtl. Fragen. *NDB* III, 156f.

9 Die Familie von F. Ludwig (FG 2. Der Nährende).

10 In den alten Quellen, darunter auch in eigenh. Niederschriften, lautet der Familienname durchaus unterschiedlich: Von Brincken, von dem Brin(c)k(e), vom Brincken usw. S. z. B. *GB Kö* III. Vgl. *Conermann III*, 479: Johann Dietrich von Brincken.

11 Quentin, d. h. Quäntchen, leitet sich von Quent (mittellatein. *quentinus*) her, einem alten dt. Handelsgewicht (1,67 g). *Zedler* XXX, 359: Quintlein, Quent, Quentin, etc. Es bezeichnet daher im übertragenen Sinne eine kleine Menge.

12 Lies „wiegen". Vermutl. westfäl. Dialektfärbung.

13 Erster Teil eines berühmten Zitats aus Sallusts *De coniuratione Catilinae*.

14 Brincken war Drost zu Schaumburg.

461020

Johann Rist an Johann Michael Moscherosch

Antwort auf 460829. — Die von Johann Michael Moscherosch (FG 436) in seinem letzten Schreiben erbetenen Auskünfte wegen eines Feldpredigers der schwedischen Armee hat Johann Rist (FG 467. 1647) bereits beantwortet. Da er jedoch an der ordnungsgemäßen Zustellung seines Schreibens an Moscherosch zweifelt, berichtet er nochmals, daß besagter Feldgeistliche von dänischen Truppen bei der Einnahme der Festung Riberhus getötet worden sei. Dieser sei ein ungestümer Mann gewesen mit ähnlich lasterhaftem Verhalten, wie der Kommandant desselben Ortes, mit dem Rist mehrmals habe speisen müssen. Der Prediger sei ihm ein Greuel gewesen. Rist fragt sich, wie dergleichen Geistliche gottesfürchtige Soldaten machen können. Insgesamt plädiert er für eine Stärkung des Friedenswillens.

Q *Moscherosch: Gesichte* II (1650): Gesichte | Philanders von Sittewald/ | Das ist | Straff-Schrifften | Hanß-Michael Moscheroschen | von Wilstädt. | Ander Theil. | [Vignette] | Straßburg/ | Bey Johan-Philipp. Mülben. | und Josias Städeln. | [Linie] | M. DC. L.,

902f. Nr. VII. HAB: Lo 5511: 2. — *BN: Kühlmann: Korrespondenz Moscheroschs*, 275. Nicht bei *Estermann*. Vgl. 460829.

Mein Herr hat in seinem letzten wegen eines Feld-predigers von der Schwedischen **Armee** sich erkündiget/ worauff ich nähermahls geantwortet.[1] Dieweil ich aber an überbringung desselben zweiffele/ berichte ich nochmahlen/ daß derselbe von den Dänischen Völckern bei eroberung des Schlosses Rypen[2] ist erschlagen und jämmerlich umgekommen: er war sonst ein wilder wühster Mänsch/ tag und nacht toll und voll/ hurete und bubete ja so wohl als sein **Commendant**[3], mit welchem ich etliche mahl habe es-[903]sen müssen/ aber der Prediger war mir ein greuel: sind mir das nicht schöne Prediger? wie solten die können Gotsförchtige Soldaten machen? O Redlicher **Philander**,[4] nur immer eine neue Feder angesetzt/ aber sie muß entweder in Essig vn̄ Galle seyn genetzet/ von Diamanten und Stahl geschmiedet: dan wer kan das Teuflische leben zur genüge schelten? Gott stärcke **Philandern** und alle redlichen Christen/ daß sie den Krieges-Belial von gantzem hertzen hassen.

Sonsten zweiffle ich nicht (ich rede ohn alle Heucheley als die meiner offenhertzigen natur gantz zuwider) wan mein Herr solche gelegenheit/ zeit und weile/ vornemlich aber solche treffliche **Patronen** und Förderer hätte/ wie sie der berühmte **Ovvenus** zu seiner zeit gehabt hat/[5] er wirde es demselben vielleicht in vilem zuvor thun/ welche meine meynung auch neulich ein grosser Herr in meiner Gegenwarth bestätigte. Gott erhalte jhn lange/ den lieben seinigen/ vnd dem wehrten Vatterlande zu nutze und trost; dan wir doch leider bei dieser falsch-politischen Welt wenig Leute mehr haben/ welche die Teutsche warheit dörffen herauß reden. Daß mein Herr seine Gesichter[6] wider aufs neue lässet trukken/ solches vernehme ich/ und nebenst mir vile grosse Leute diser örter über die massen gerne.

Zu Wedel in Holstein 20. Weinmonat im 1646.

K 1 Unbekanntes Schreiben Johann Rists (FG 467. 1647) an Johann Michael Moscherosch (FG 436). Der Brief Moscheroschs vom 29.8.1646 enthält in dem uns bekannten Zitat (460829) auch nicht den hier angesprochenen Passus.

2 Das Schloss Riberhus in der dän. Stadt Ribe (dt. Ripen) in Jütland, welches im 12. Jh. als kgl.-dän. Grenzfestung errichtet, in der 2. Hälfte des 17. Jh.s jedoch zerstört u. schließlich abgetragen wurde. 1645 hatten sich während des schwed.-dän. Krieges schwed. Einheiten auf Riberhus verschanzt, wo sie von dän. Truppen beschossen wurden. Hans Klüche: Dänemark. Nordseeküste (DuMont Reise-Taschenbuch). Ostfildern 2015, 115 bzw. 122.

3 Weder der schwed. Feldprediger noch der Kommandant der Festung Riberhus konnten identifiziert werden.

4 Philander von Sittewald, Pseudonym Moscheroschs in seiner oben angeführten menippeischen Satire. S. Q.

5 John Owen (Johannes Audoenus/ Ovenus) († ca. 1622/28), walis.-engl. Schriftsteller u. Epigrammatiker. Seine Tätigkeit wurde nicht nur durch seine Familie, etwa seinen Bruder Charles Owen, befördert. Die Widmungen seiner Werke weisen vielmehr auch auf die

Unterstützung seiner Tätigkeit durch kgl. u. höchste Adelskreise, etwa durch Lady Arabella Stuart (1575–1615), Nichte der schott. Kgn. Maria Stuart u. Thronprätendentin auf den engl. Thron, sowie durch Henry Frederick Stuart, Prince of Wales (1594–1612). Als seine Mäzene nannte Audoenus zudem Sir Edward Noel, Sir William Sidley u. Sir Roger Owen. Seine letzten Lebensjahre verbrachte er unter der Gönnerschaft von John Williams (1582–1650), dem Bischof von Lincoln, Großsiegelbewahrer u. Lordkanzler sowie späterem Erzbischof von York, der auch dessen Begräbnis in der Londoner St. Pauls-Kathedrale organisierte. Vgl. Titika Aslanidou: Johannes Audoenus († 1622): Die Bücher VIII–X. Diss. (MS), Univ. Heidelberg 2007, o. S. (Online-Publikation: http://www.ub.uni-heidelberg.de/archiv/7612); Edward Bensly: Robert Burton, John Barclay and John Owen. In: Adolphus William Ward, Alfred R. Waller (Ed.): The Cambridge History of the Literature, Vol. 4: Prose and Poetry. Sir Thomas North to Michael Drayton. Cambridge 1966 (Neudr. d. Ausg. 1932), 242–267, hier 265.

6 Die oben angeführte Ausgabe der *Gesichte Philanders von Sittewald* (1650).

461023

Matthäus Merian d. Ä. an Peter Knaudt

Matthäus Merian d. Ä. berichtet auf der Grundlage des kürzlich ihm zugegangenen (nicht erhaltenen) Schreibens, daß mit der vor wenigen Tagen abgegangenen Fuhre die Hälfte der (F. Ludwig zustehenden) Exemplare des *GB 1646*, nämlich 74 Drucke, an Matthias Götze in Leipzig abgeschickt worden seien. Diese möge Peter Knaudt bei Götze unter Begleichung der Frachtgebühren abfordern. Für F. Ludwig mitgesandt habe Merian die *Topographia Hassiæ*, welche zur (Leipziger) Michaelismesse neu erschienen sei.

Q HM Köthen: V S 546, Bl. 36rv [A: 36v]; eigenh.; Sig. — D: *Bircher: Merian*, 724; *Wüthrich: Merian Briefe*, 118f. — BN: *Bürger*, 987 Nr. 21.

A Dem Ehrnvesten und HochAchtparen Herren Petter Knaudt Fürstl. Anhaltischen Cammer Meistern *etc.* zu gg. Henden Jn Cöthen

Ehrenvester und GroßAchtparer Jnsonders großg. hochgeehrter herr, dem sein mein willige dienst und was ich vermag Anvor[1] *etc.* Demnach berichte dem Herrn das auff sein ordern des jüngsten schreibens, mit der vor wenig tagen nach leipzig abgefahren fuhren durch einschlag herrn Matthias Götzen Jch dem herrn gesandt habe die helfft der allhie gelegenen Fruchtbringenden Geselschaft als Nemlich 74 **exemplaria**,[2] die wirt mein gg. herr Alda bei ihme abzufordern, und wegen der fracht abzufinden wissen. Jch habe auch dabej gethan 1 **Topographia Hassiæ**[3] so dise meß new ist,[4] für Jhr. Fürst. G. verhoffe es alles zurecht komen werde. hiemit dem Allmächtigen wol befohlen.
Ffurt den 23. 8bris 1646.
   Meines gg. herrn
   Dienstwiligster
   Mattheus Merian.

K 1 Bevor, vorab. S. 450417 K 1.

2 S. auch das Dokument *DA Köthen I. 8*: 470223, in dem der Abtransport der 74 Exemplare des *GB 1646* nach Leipzig z. Zt. der dortigen Michaelismesse 1646 bestätigt wird. Zugleich wird in 470223 der Versand weiterer 161 Stücke des *GB 1646* am 1.2.1647 nach Leipzig vermeldet. Es blieben mangels Platz damals erneut 5 Stücke bei Matthäus Merian zurück.

3 S. zu *Merian: Topographia* 450905 K 4. Die Vorbereitungen zur *Topographia Hassiæ* (Frankfurt a. M. 1646) werden explizit in 450905 u. 450930 erwähnt. HAB: 176.4 Hist. 2° (4). Die 2. Auflage erschien im Jahre 1655.

4 Üblicherweise dauerte die Leipziger Messe ab dem Sonntag nach Michaelis (29. September), im Jahre 1646 der 3.10., acht Tage lang, sie wäre also bereits vorüber. S. auch 461031 K 6. Sie wurde zwar tatsächlich am besagten 3.10. eingeläutet, jedoch mangels Nachfrage — zu wenige Kaufleute hatte sich eingefunden — auf den 18.10. verschoben und war noch in vollem Gange. Es bestanden somit gute Chancen, daß die *Topographia Hassiæ* noch pünktlich nach Leipzig geliefert wurde.

461026

Pfalzgraf Ludwig Philipp von Simmern an Fürst Ludwig

Antwort auf 460424A. — Pgf. Ludwig Philipp v. Simmern (FG 97) bestätigt den reichlich verspäteten Empfang des Briefes F. Ludwigs samt dessen Vollmacht, eine Reihe von Kandidaten in die FG aufnehmen zu dürfen. Deren Namen habe der Pfalzgraf in einem zweiten pgfl. Schreiben festgehalten. Ludwig Philipp entschuldigt sich für seine verspätete Antwort und drückt seinen Wunsch aus, F. Ludwig auch persönlich zu danken, in der Hoffnung, dazu alsbald die Gelegenheit zu erhalten. Auch die Neumitglieder verlangt es, F. Ludwig einmal persönlich aufzuwarten. Überdies bedankt er sich für dessen eigenhändige Antwort und versichert seine besten Bemühungen um die FG. — Grüße auch von Gattin zu Gattin.

Q HM Köthen: V S 544, Bl. 83rv, v leer; eigenh. — D: *KE*, 55. — BN: Nicht in *Bürger*.

A *Fehlt*.

Hochgeborner Furst Freundtlicher vielgeliebter Herrvetter

Jch hab zimlich langsam EL brief sambt derselben vol macht entpfangen[1] sonst hette ich nicht gelaßen EL eher dienstlich deßwegen danckzusagen[,] woltte wuntschen so glucklich zu sein es muntlich zu thun hoffe es mochte baldt gelegenheit darzu geben[.][2] EL werden auß mein ander schreyben sehen der[a] Jenichen nahmen so sich in die fruchtbringende geselschaft begeben[3][,] wuntschen nicht[s] mehr als die gnade zu haben EL.[b] einmahl aufzuwartten[.] bin EL hochlich verbunden daß sie mir mitt eygener handt haben antwortten wollen[.] EL seyen gewiß daß ich alles wohl in acht nehmen wil so zu der fruchtbringende *[sic]* geselschaft dienlich[.] thue EL hiemitt in Gottes des Almachtig[en] schutz entpfelen undt verbleyb

EL
Dienstwilliger Getrewer vetter vndt diener
Ludwig Philips Pfaltzgrave.
[L]autern^c [de]n^c 26 octobris

[M]itt^d EL permission mein gemahlin EL gemahlin [dien]stlich^c grußen.⁴

T a *Gebessert aus* die — b *Eingefügt.* — c *Textverlust im Falz. Konjektur in eckigen Klammern.* — d *Als Postskriptum bis* grußen *am Rand ergänzt. Textverlust im Falz. Konjektur in eckigen Klammern.*

K 1 Das Schreiben F. Ludwigs 460424A hatte Pgf. Ludwig Philipp v. Simmern (FG 97) erst am 20. Oktober 1646 empfangen. S. den Hinweis in 461031A.
2 Ob es später eine solche Gelegenheit gab, ist ungewiß. In das *GB Kö.* I, Bl. [Aa iv]v hatte sich Pgf. Ludwig Philipp schon 1632 eigenh. eingetragen. Für die von ihm aufgenommenen 14 Mitglieder (s. 461031A I B) fehlen solche persönlichen Einträge in *GB Kö.* III.
3 Bei diesem zweiten Schreiben handelte es sich wohl um 461031A, welchem eine Liste der bis dahin aufgenommenen vier Neumitglieder beilag. S. 461031A I A. Zu den am Ende aufgenommenen 14 Personen s. 461031A I B.
4 Pgfn. Maria Eleonora v. Simmern (1607–1675), Tochter Kf. Joachim Friedrichs v. Brandenburg, die Pgf. Ludwig Philipp am 4.12.1631 geheiratet hatte. — Fn. Sophia v. Anhalt-Köthen, geb. Gfn. zur Lippe (1599–1654. AL 1629. TG 38), seit 1626 mit F. Ludwig in dessen zweiter Ehe vermählt.

461029

Carl Gustav von Hille an Fürst Ludwig

Carl Gustav v. Hille (FG 302. Der Unverdrossene) informiert F. Ludwig (Der Nährende) darüber, daß der vorliegende Brief bereits der dritte, unbeantwortet gebliebene sei und vermutet, daß seine Briefe F. Ludwig nicht erreicht haben. Deshalb unternimmt er noch einen Versuch, einer Antwort glücklich habhaft zu werden. Er wolle F. Ludwig davon unterrichten, daß er der FG zu Ehren und Gedächtnis ein Büchlein mit folgendem Titel zu veröffentlichen beabsichtige: *Der Teutsche Palmbaum, das ist Lobrede von der hochl. Fruchtb. Gesell. Anfang, Satzungen, Vorhaben, Namen, Gemählen Wörtern Schriften, Gesellschaften und unverwelcklichen Tugend-Ruhm* (i. e. *Hille: Teutscher Palmbaum*). Deshalb benötige Hille eine Gesellschaftsmitgliederliste ab Mitglied Nr. 432 und zugleich Auskunft darüber, wie die Hänselung bzw. der Gebrauch des Ölbergers vonstatten gehe und was sonst in dieser *Lobrede* beachtet werden solle. Des weiteren bittet er F. Ludwig um die Gnade, ein Widmungsgedicht zu diesem Werk beizusteuern und auch den Obristen Diederich v. dem Werder (FG 31) und den Obristleutnant Christian Ernst (v.) Knoch (FG 268), seine hochgeschätzten Mitgesellschafter, deren in seiner *Lobrede* rühmlich gedacht werden wird, um gewünschte Gedichtbeigaben förderlich anzusprechen. Er hofft, daß das Werk Anfang 1647 überschickt werden könne. — Überdies sähe es sein Dienst- und Landesherr, Hz. August d. J. v. Braunschweig-Wolfenbüttel (FG 227) gerne, wenn

461029 Carl Gustav von Hille

Johann Valentin Andreae (FG 464) seiner Tugenden wegen in die FG aufgenommen werden könne, falls seine geistliche Profession dem nicht entgegenstehe. — Da Hille noch nicht in den Besitz des neuen GB gelangt sei, bittet er den Fürsten um schenkungsweise Überlassung eines Exemplars bei nächster sicherer Gelegenheit der Zusendung.

Q HM Köthen: V S 545, Bl. 40r–41v [A: 41v], 41r leer; eigenh.; schwarzes Lacksiegel. — Nicht in *KE*.

A Dem durchleuchtigen, hochgebornen, Fürsten und herrn, herrn Ludwigen, Fürsten zu Anhalt, Grafen zu Ascanien, herrn zu Zerbst und Bernburg *etc*. meinem gnädigen Fürsten und herrn. *etc*. — *Mit anderer Hand hinzugefügt:* Franco bis[a] Magdeburg
Eigenh. Empfangsvermerk F. Ludwigs: 14. Wintermonats 1646.

Durchleuchtiger hochgeborner Fürst, E. f. Gn. seind meine underth. und gehorsame dienste ie und allewege bevor gn. herr.
    Dieß ist daß dritte schreiben, so an E. f. Gn. ich in underth. abgefertiget, aber bißdahero mit keiner gn. antwort gewürdiget worden.[1] Weiln ich dan in den gedancken geruhe, daß obgedachte schreiben zu E. f. Gn. händen nicht möchten gelanget seyn, Alß werde auß angelegenheiten ich veruhrsacht, nochmah[l][b] einen underth. versuch zu thun, ob ich nicht so gelückselig werden möchte, nur ein zielige[2] antwort zuerhalten: den inhalt mit wenigem nochmahlen zu bemühen; so ist mein underth. suchen gewesen, weiln ich zu underth. und schüldigsten thun ein Gedechniß *[sic]* der hochl. Fruchtb. Gesellschaft zusetzen entschlossen, Und[c] ihm werde ein Büchlein außzugehen lassen: dessen Titul seyn solle: Der Teutsche Palmenbaum, daß ist *Lobrede* von der hochl. Fruchtb. Gesell. Anfang, Satzungen, Vorhaben, Namen, Schriften[d], Gemählen Wörtern, Geselschaftern und[e] unverwelklichem Tugend-Ruhm Und[f] dan hiezu bedürftich, der ubrigen Gesellschaftern Namen, von dem 432 an zurechnen, auch wie es mit der henselung und Oelbergerß gebrauchung[3] pfleget in acht genomen zu werden, auch was sonsten gedenckwurdigeß bey dieser *Lobrede* müste beobachtet[g] werden; Als gelanget an E. f. Gn. mein underth. ersuchen, Die[h] geruhen gnädig mir hierinnen zu wilfahren, Alß auch nicht weniger, mit einem [40v] unverdienten Lobgedichte anzusehen,[4] auch zu selbiger folge den H. Ob. Werder, und Ob. Leuht. Knochen, meine hochwerthe Mitgeselschafter[5], deren Tugenden unter anderm auch in der Lobrede erwehnet werden, gnädigst anzumahnen: Jch hoffe es solle daß werck gedrucket E f Gn. gegen daß Neue Jahr wolgefällig[i] uberschikket werden[6]: Alß auch mein gn. Fürst und herr hertzogk Augustus,[7] gerne sehen möchte, daß der h. Jacobus Andreæ[8] auch in E. f. Gn. Fruchtbring. Gesellschaft, seinen beywohnenden Tugenden nach, möchte eingenommen werden: Alß gelanget an E. f Gn. mein gleichmäßiges bitten[,] da eß möglich[,] daß ein Geistlicher sich dieser Fruchtb. Gesellschaft könte theilhaftich machen, denselbtigen auf und anzunehmen:[9]
    Alß ich auch noch zur Zeit deß Neuen außgegangenen Gesellschaftß buchß nicht[e] habe können mächtig werden, als gelange[t][j] an E f. Gn. mein underth. bit-

ten, selbigeß auß gn. mir zu schenken, und bey erster sichern gelegenheit zu Uberschi[kken.]^{j 10} Verdiene^{11} eß underth. und verbleibe

E. f. Gn.
underth. und gehorsamer Diener
Carl Gustav von Hille *mp*

Wolfenb. den 29th. 8bris 1646.

Bitte nochmalen underth. obgedachte sachen dem negsten mit f. gnaden mir zuzufertigen *etc.*

T a *Aufgelöstes Sonderzeichen.* — **b** *Wahrscheinlich versehentlich vergessenes* l — **c** *Gebessert aus <höchstwillich>?* — **d** *Ursprüngliche Folge* Wörtern Gemählen Schriften, *mittels hochgestellter Ziffern umgestellt.* — **e** *Folgt unleserliche Streichung.* — **f** *Gebessert aus unleserlicher Streichung.* — **g** *Ersetzt* <in acht genomen> — **h** *Verschreibung für* Sie [?] — **i** *Eingefügt.* — **j** *Textverlust im Falz. Konjektur in eckigen Klammern.*

K 1 Bereits ein Jahr zuvor, in 451008, u. in 460915A klagte Carl Gustav v. Hille (FG 302) darüber, daß er auf frühere Schreiben keine Antwort von F. Ludwig erhalten habe. In 461106 entschuldigt sich F. Ludwig für die Verzögerung seiner Antwort.
2 D. h. knappe, auf das jeweilige Thema gerichtete Antwort: „zielig", adj., d. h. beschränkt/ begrenzt; aber auch klein, mittelmäßig. S. *DW* XV, 1092f. So auch *Stieler*, 2618: zielicht, dahin zielende Sachen.
3 Darauf kommt F. Ludwig (Der Nährende) in seinem Antwortschreiben 461106 zurück. Er bemerkt dort ausweichend und Mißbrauch, Ärger und Spott fürchtend, daß eine knapp gehaltene Beschreibung der Hänselung noch nach dem Abschluß des Manuskripts hinzugefügt werden könne. Es ist dazu aber nicht gekommen. Zur Hänselung s. 460718 K 8.
4 Ein solches Ehrengedicht F. Ludwigs fehlt in *Hille: Teutscher Palmbaum*. Der Fürst machte Hille auch in 461106 keine Hoffnungen auf ein solches. Ausschlaggebend für das Ausbleiben einer Gedichtbeigabe war aber vermutlich der Umstand, daß Hilles FG-Beschreibung dem Fürsten nicht vor dem Druck zur Approbation eingereicht worden ist. S. Anm. 6.
5 Diederich v. dem Werder (FG 31) u. Christian Ernst (v.) Knoch (FG 268). Auch von diesen beiden findet sich kein Ehrengedicht in Hilles *Teutschem Palmbaum*.
6 Hille unterließ es, sein Werk vor der Drucklegung dem Fürsten zur Durchsicht und Genehmigung vorzulegen. F. Ludwig erfuhr von der bereits laufenden Drucklegung in Nürnberg (durch Wolfgang Endter d. Ä.) erst durch Georg Philipp Harsdörffers (FG 368) Schreiben 470100 (*KE*, 376–378, hier 377). Auf eine wohl erfolgte Benachrichtigung durch Harsdörffer verweist ein anscheinend von Krankheit geschwächter und schuldbewußter Hille in *DA Köthen I.* 8: 470112 (*KE*, 210f.). F. Ludwig reagiert darauf kritisch in 470625.
7 Hz. August d. J. v. Braunschweig-Wolfenbüttel (FG 227), der den Wunsch Andreaes (s. Anm. 8) nach einer Aufnahme in die FG unterstützt hatte. Vgl. schon 460908 u. 460915A u. I.
8 D. i. Johann Valentin Andreae (FG 464. 1646). Dessen Großvater war der lutherische Theologe Jacob Andreae (1528–1590), Tübinger Kanzler und Professor, Verfechter der

461031 Fürst Ludwig

Konkordienformel, dessen gleichnamiger erster Sohn, Jacob Andreae (1549–1630), ein württemberg. Pfarrer, Sammlungen zur württemberg. Geschichte anlegte. Vgl. 460804 K 9 u. 460819.

9 Zur Aufnahme Andreaes s. 461117 K 1.

10 In 460915A bemerkte Hille, daß er von Hz. August kein Exemplar des *GB 1646* aus dessen Deputat erhalten habe. F. Ludwig sagt ihm zwei Wochen später in 461106 ein Exemplar zu.

11 Im Sinne von ‚vergelten'. S. *DW* XII. 1, 223: „2) transitiv, dienste behufs einer sache thun (die sache im accusativ), die sache ist entweder etwas empfangenes oder etwas zu erwerbendes, in ersterem falle vergelten, gegendienste leisten."

461031

Fürst Ludwig an Georg Philipp Harsdörffer

Antwort auf 460916. Beantwortet durch 470100. — F. Ludwig (Der Nährende) hat die beiden Exemplare des 6. Teils der *Frauenzimmer-Gesprächspiele* (1646) mit dem Schreiben 460916 Georg Philipp Harsdörffers (FG 368. Der Spielende) und eines weiteren Schreibens (460915) von Harsdörffer an Christian Gueintz (FG 361. Der Ordnende) am 29. 10. 1646 dankend erhalten. Den Brief an Gueintz und das für ihn vorgesehene Exemplar des 6. Teils der *Gesprächspiele* werde der Fürst schnellstmöglich weiterleiten. Dank für das andere, dem Erzschrein zugedachte Exemplar. — Erfreut zeigt sich F. Ludwig über einen höflichen Brief (460726), in dem sich Johann Michael Moscherosch (FG 436. Der Träumende) für seine Aufnahme in die FG bedankte. F. Ludwig erinnert noch einmal an sein Ersuchen, Moscherosch möge die versprochene Neuausgabe seiner *Gesichte Philanders von Sittewald* der FG einsenden. Harsdörffer möge dies Moscherosch bei nächster Gelegenheit ausrichten, welcher ansonsten ordnungsgemäß in das Köthener Gesellschaftsbuch eingetragen wurde. — Ob die Meißnische Mundart, wie von Harsdörffer behauptet, als „weibisch und verzärtelt" der männlichen dt. Heldensprache entgegen und das Schlesische oder Fränkische ihr vorzuziehen sei, läßt F. Ludwig auf sich beruhen. Es sei nun einmal einem jeden die eigene Mundart die liebste. Die Fruchtbringende Gesellschaft orientiere sich bei ihrer Spracharbeit nicht an der gewöhnlichen Umgangssprache der eigenen (omd.) Sprachlandschaft, die durchaus wie bei anderen Mundarten auch Mängel aufweise, sondern an der deutschen Hochsprache, wie dies auch *Gueintz: Rechtschreibung (1645)* zu entnehmen sei. Was sprachlich als ‚weibisch und verzärtelt' anzusehen sei, werde von der FG vermieden. F. Ludwig verzichtet auf Beispiele und überläßt die Verständigung darüber einer möglichen späteren Unterredung. — Harsdörffer soll beim künftigen Leipziger Neujahrsmarkt ein gesellschaftsmäßig eingebundenes Exemplar des jüngst erschienenen *GB 1646* als Geschenk erhalten. Daß das Buch zu Nürnberg vom Kupferstecher (Matthäus Merian d. Ä.) oder seinen Buchhändlern nur zu einem überhöhten Preis angeboten werde, stimmt F. Ludwig keineswegs glücklich. — Die von Harsdörffer erbetene Fortsetzung der Mitgliederliste vom 433. Gesellschafter an liege dem Schreiben bei.

Q HM Köthen: V S 545, Bl. 358r; eigenh. Konzept (358v Konzept von 461213). — *D: KE*, 375 f. — *BN: Bürger*, 950 Nr. 64.

A *Fehlt.*

Des Spielenden schreiben vom 16. des Herbstmonats ist dem Nehrenden den 29 dieses beneben zweyen stucken des sechsten theils seiner ausgegangenen gesprächspiele, und einer schrift an den Ordnenden wol zukommen.¹ Die schrift mit dem stucke der gesprächspiele sol ehestes tages dem Ordnenden uberfertiget werden. Fur die übersendung zum Ertzschreine thuet sich der Nehrende auch bedancken: Der hat ein hoflichesᵃ brieflein von dem Traumenden jüngsten, worin erᵇ wegen einnemung in die Fruchtbringende geselschaft fleißigen danck saget[,] wol empfangen, weil aber zugleich ein erbieten geschehenᵃ, als solte von seinen sachen ins kunftige zum ertzschreine auch ein mehreres überkommen, als wird man deßen erwarten, in deßen wolle mit geburender begrußung dieses dem Traumenden der Spielendeᶜ bey ehester gelegenheit anfugen,² und istᵈ er sonsten in seine gehörige stelleᵉ eingeschrieben.³

Was wegen der Meisnischen art zu reden, als weibisch und verzärtelt der Mannischen,ᶠ alhier beßerᵃ würde Mänlichen heißenᵍ, deutschen heldensprache gantz entgegen erweget, und dargegen die Schlesische und Fränkische art, gelobet, und es mit ihr gehalten wird. Das leßet man alles an seinen ort gestellet sein; Man wird hierunter keinem zu nahe sein, weil doch einem ieden seine weise am besten gefellet. Alleine ist dieses gleichwol darbey zu wißen, wie es auch in derʰ rechtschreibung⁴ zu finden, das manⁱ bey der Fruchtbringenden geselschaft sich nicht auf die gemeine landes art, die viel mangels hatᵃ, als an andern orten auch ist, gegrundet, und dasjenige so fur weibisch undʲ zärtlich gehal[t]en wirdᵃ, oder andern deuchten kan, nicht gut geheißenᵏ, sondern viel mehr geflohen wird. Die beyspiel könen leichtlich furgeschrieben werden, man wil sich aber dismals damit nicht aufhalten, sondern es bis etwa einmal zu einer unterrede, darinnen es fuglicher erkleret werden kan, gesparet haben.⁵

Von dem zu Franckfurt am Meyn gedruckten geselschaftbuche sol der Spielende ein stuck geselschaftsweise eingebunden, gönnets Gott gegen nechstkunftigen leipzigischen neuen Jhares markt haben. Das sie vom Kupferstecher oder seinen buchführern uberteuret werden, höret man nicht gerne,⁶ und alsoˡ wird auch die fortsetzung der fruchtbringenden geselschaft von 433 an bis ietzo gegenwertig, eingeschloßenᵐ gebetener maßenⁿ überschicket.ⁿ ⁷ hat dieses dem Spielendenᵒ, fur dismal zur antwort werden sollen, darbeyᵖ verbleibet

des Spielenden gantzwilliger

Geben am bekanten orte⁸ den 31. Weinmonats 1646.

T **a** *Eingefügt.* — **b** *Folgt* <sich> — **c** *Erster Buchstabe gebessert aus* s — **d** *Folgt* <s> — **e** *Folgt* <nach der> — **f** *Folgt unleserliche Streichung.* — **g** *Eingefügt, davor eingefügt* <beßer> — **h** *Folgt* <Fruchtbringen> — **i** *Folgt* <sich> — **j** *Folgt* <so> — **k** *Folgt* <wird> — **l** *Bis* überschicket *eingefügt.* — **m** *Eingefügt für* <wird jedoch> (*unsichere Lesung*). — **n** *Folgt eingefügt* <eingeschloßen> — **o** *Reihenfolge durch hochgestellte Ziffern umgestellt aus* dem Spielenden hat dieses — **p** *Eingefügt für* <und>

K 1 S. 460916 und dort den Empfangsvermerk F. Ludwigs vom 29.10.1646. Georg Philipp Harsdörffer (FG 368. Der Spielende) hatte mit diesem Schreiben (460916) zwei Exemplare des jüngst erschienenen 6. Teils der *Frauenzimmer-Gesprächspiele* (1646) an F. Ludwig (Der Nährende) geschickt, eins für den Erzschrein und eins für Christian Gueintz (FG 361. Der Ordnende), für den er außerdem eine Replik (460915) auf dessen Gutachten zum *Specimen Philologiae Germanicae* (1646) beilegte. Gueintz' Gutachten „Erinnerungen Bey des Spielenden Wercklein die deutsche Sprache betreffend" (HM Köthen: V S 545, Bl. 192r–200v; *KE*, 363–372) demnächst in *DA Köthen I. 9.* Vgl. die Zusammenfassung des Gutachtens in 460720 K 3. F. Ludwig hatte Harsdörffer Gueintz' Gutachten mit 460816 zugeschickt. Vgl. insges. zum *Specimen* 451217 K 10.

2 Die Kommunikation zwischen F. Ludwig und dem 1645 in die FG aufgenommenen Johann Michael Moscherosch (FG 436. Der Träumende) lief über Harsdörffer. Vgl. 450500 K 1, auch 450504A K 2 u. 5. Mit 460726 übersandte Moscherosch dann ein außerordentlich höflich gehaltenes Dankschreiben für die Aufnahme in die FG direkt an F. Ludwig. Die vom Nährenden erwartete Ausgabe der *Gesichte Philanders von Sittewald* (an die er hier noch einmal erinnert), lag diesem Brief jedoch nicht bei. Schon in 450919A erbat F. Ludwig eine vom Verfasser autorisierte Ausgabe seines Werks, wurde aber mit 460406 von Harsdörffer auf die Fertigstellung der Neuauflage vertröstet. Diese erschien erst nach F. Ludwigs Tod 1650. S. 460406 K 8.

3 Moscheroschs Aufnahme in die FG erfolgte noch im Jahre 1645, irgendwann nach dem 19. Mai. Seine Eintragung als Nr. 436 im 3. Bd. des *GB Kö.*, Bl. 36vf. Vgl. 450500 K 1 u. 450504A K 2.

4 *Gueintz: Rechtschreibung (1645)*. S. dazu 440127 K 1.

5 F. Ludwig bezieht sich in diesem Absatz auf eine Äußerung Harsdörffers aus dessen vorhergehendem Brief 460916. Dort äußerte sich der Spielende zu Gueintz' Gutachten (s. Anm. 1) und lehnte die grundsätzliche Orientierung des Ordnenden am Sprachusus als Normierungsmaßstab ab. Die von vielen als Leitvarietät anerkannte omd. Mundart relativierte Harsdörffer mit dem Hinweis, sie werde von etlichen als „weibisch, und verzärtelt" abgelehnt. Dies widerstreite nämlich der „Männischen Deutschen Heldensprache", die manch einer eher im Schlesischen oder Fränkischen wiederfinde. Damit stellte Harsdörffer die Richtschnur der Sprachgewohnheit, sei es in Aussprache oder Schreibweise, grundsätzlich in Frage zugunsten der immanenten Ratio des Sprachsystems, die allein zwischen richtiger oder falscher, guter oder „böser" Gewohnheit unterscheiden lehre. Die Relativierung der Mundarten als Normierungsparameter durch F. Ludwig orientiert sich ebenfalls an einer noch auszubauenden überlandschaftlich-hochsprachlichen Standardsprache, in welcher dem Sprachgebrauch in Zweifelsfällen aber durchaus eine entscheidende Autorität zugesprochen wird. Diese Haltung begegnet auch in der „übereignungsschrift" in *Gueintz: Rechtschreibung (1645)*, Bl.)([iv] v –)(v r, die sich in Bescheidenheit übt: „Nicht als wan sie allen andern mundarten/ an orten und enden/ da man deren verhandenen und wolgefasseten grund/ noch nicht allerdings innen ist/ solte und müste eine Richtschnure sein/ sondern männiglich dahin zuveranlassen und zuerinnern/ das man sich billich einerley art recht zuschreiben vergleichen solte".

6 Im vorhergehenden Schreiben an F. Ludwig (460916) klagte Harsdörffer über den außerordentlich hohen Preis von 10 Reichstalern, zu dem das jüngst fertiggestellte *GB 1646* in Nürnberg angeboten werde. Dabei ließ er durchblicken, daß er es gern geschenkt bekäme. F. Ludwig verspricht ihm ein Exemplar zum Leipziger Neujahrsmarkt 1647. Seit Mitte des 15. Jahrhunderts fanden in Leipzig dreimal jährlich Messen statt. Die rechtliche Grundlage hierfür bildete das Meßprivileg Maximilians I. von 1497. In dieser den Aufschwung Leipzigs als bedeutende Messestadt einleitenden und sichernden Urkunde wurden die drei Jahrmärkte bestätigt und unter den Schutz des Reiches gestellt. Auch Zeitpunkt und Dauer wurden darin geregelt: Der Beginn der Ostermesse war für Jubilate (3. Sonntag nach Ostern) angesetzt und endete an Cantate (4. Sonntag nach Ostern), während die Herbstmesse ab dem Sonntag nach Michaelis (29. September) acht Tage dauern sollte, und der dritte Markt, der Neujahrsmarkt, vom Neujahrstag für acht Tage (bis 8. Januar) genehmigt wurde. Die tatsächlichen Meßtermine konnten freilich von der Norm abweichen: Aus 450124 erfahren wir z.B., daß 1645 in Leipzig ein Jahrmarkt zu Lichtmeß (2. Februar) stattfand. Solche Änderungen scheinen allerdings selbst während des Dreißigjährigen Kriegs die Ausnahme gewesen zu sein. Das regelmäßige Abhalten der Märkte kann durch die gedruckten Kataloge der Leipziger Büchermesse, von denen alljährlich zwei (je einer für die Oster- und die Herbstmesse) erschienen, belegt werden (s. http://www.olmsonline.de/dms/toc/?IDDOC=13594). Allein für die Jahre 1637 und 1644 sind ausnahmsweise Kataloge erschienen, die in einem Band beide Messen abdecken, was vermuten läßt, daß in diesen Jahren einer der Märkte ausgefallen ist. (Der unter den Digitalisaten fehlende Katalog für die Ostermesse 1643 scheint nicht auf einen Ausfall der Messe hinzudeuten, weil er bei Spirgatis [s.u., S.61 Anm.4] zitiert wird.) Gelistet ist das *GB 1646* bereits im Katalog der Ostermesse 1646: Catalogus universalis, hoc est designatio omnium librorum, qui hisce nundinis ... Francofurtensibus & Lipsiensibus anno ... vel novi vel emendationes & auctiores prodierunt (Leipzig 1646), http://www.olmsonline.de/purl?PPN525616772_1646_Oster, Bl. D2r. S. 440130 K 3. Für den kostspieligen Druck des neuen Gesellschaftsbuchs wurden mitunter Jahre im voraus Zuschüsse von Mitgliedern der FG akquiriert. Für die Verwaltung der Gelder war der Leipziger Kaufmann Georg Winckler verantwortlich (vgl. z.B. 440310, 451028, 460309, aber bes. 450930 u. 451028B, wo Merian sich direkt dazu äußert; vgl. zur Person Wincklers 451019 K 0). Winckler fungierte offenbar als Dreh- und Angelpunkt der Kommunikation mit Matthäus Merian in Frankfurt: Wie Harsdörffer seine Korrespondenz mit Köthen über den Leipziger Handelsmann Gottfried Stahl abwickelte (s. etwa 440426 [K 1]), so lief Merians Korrespondenz mit dem Köthener Kammerschreiber Peter Knaudt über Winckler (s. bes. die Anschrift in 460703). Winckler hat — das kann hier zumindest vermutet werden — auch Verteilung und Verkauf des fertigen Drucks in der Region besorgt. F. Ludwig könnte ihn demnach beauftragt haben, von der für den Neujahrsmarkt gedachten Charge ein Buch an Harsdörffer nach Nürnberg zu schicken. Für die im vorliegenden Brief genannte „gesellschaftsmäßige" Einbindung dieses Exemplars gibt das Ex. des *GB 1629/30* für Martin Opitz das Modell ab, abgebildet in *DA Köthen I. 3*, S.505. Vgl. hier ferner: Manfred Straube: „Wir Maximilian von Gottes Gnaden ...". Über die Bedeutung des Messprivilegs Maximilians I. von 1497. In: Leipzig: Stadt der wa(h)ren Wunder: 500 Jahre Reichsmesseprivileg. Leipzig 1997, 17–21; Nils Brübach: Die Reichsmessen von Frankfurt am Main, Leipzig und Braunschweig: 14. – 18. Jahrhundert. Stuttgart 1994; Max Spirgatis: Die litterarische Produktion Deutschlands im 17. Jahrhundert und die Leipziger Messkataloge. In: Sammlung bibliothekswissenschaftlicher Arbeiten 14 (1901), 24–61.

7 Harsdörffer bat in 460916 um die Fortsetzung der ihm vorliegenden Mitgliederliste ab Nummer 433, d.i. Matthaeus v. Wesenbeck, der wohl am 19.5.1645 in die FG aufgenommen worden war. Die Fortsetzungs-Liste ist nicht überliefert. S. ausführlich dazu 450529 K 10.

8 Die in F. Ludwigs Schreiben an Harsdörffer vielfach übliche Absenderadresse, oft auch „an dem bewusten orte des ertzschreines" (450124) oder „an dem bekanten orte der Fruchtbringenden Gesellschaft Ertzschreins" (450611) usw., d.i. F. Ludwigs Residenz in Köthen.

461031A

Pfalzgraf Ludwig Philipp von Simmern an Fürst Ludwig

Antwort auf 460424A. Beantwortet durch *DA Köthen I. 8:* 470403A. — Pgf. Ludwig Philipp v. Simmern (FG 97. Der Gefährliche) bestätigt den Erhalt von F. Ludwigs Brief 460424A, den er aber erst am 10. (a. St.) dieses Monats (Oktober) erhalten habe. Er erklärt seine ungeschmälerte Bereitschaft, die von F. Ludwig akzeptierten Kandidaten in die FG aufzunehmen, und versichert, daß diese willig danach verlangen und die Aufnahme für eine besondere Ehre erachten. Gleichwohl habe sich bisher noch nicht bei allen die Gelegenheit zur Einnehmung ergeben, was aber weiterhin verfolgt werde. Einige Kandidaten, wie die beiliegende Namensliste ausweise, seien aber von ihm bereits gehänselt und aufgenommen worden. Sobald ihre Wappenzeichnungen vorliegen, soll die feierliche Aufnahme abgeschlossen werden. Die Aufnahme der Übrigen werde er bei nächster Gelegenheit nachholen und auch deren Namen und Wappen dem Erzschrein einsenden. Auch sie sind sich der hohen Ehre bewußt und wünschen, F. Ludwig einmal persönlich aufzuwarten. Ludwig Philipp erbittet in ihrem Namen auch ein (auf den aktuellen Stand fortgeführtes) FG-Mitgliederverzeichnis, sofern dies F. Ludwig recht sei. Die Bezahlung der notwendigen Gelder habe wegen des verspäteten Empfangs des Briefes nicht wie gefordert über Leipzig erfolgen können, soll aber auf der künftigen Ostermesse zu Frankfurt am Main nachgeholt werden.

Q HM Köthen: V S 544, Bl. 84rv u. 86rv [A: 86v], Bl. 86r leer; Schreiberh. mit eigenh. Schlußkurialie und Unterschrift; Sig. — *D: KE,* 56. — *BN: Bürger,* 956 Nr. 34. Bl. 85rv Mitgliederliste (nicht die im Brief erwähnte Namensliste = Beil. I A), s. Beil. I B; andere Schreiberh. beginnend mit 85v. — *D: KE,* 57f.

A Dem hochgebohrnen Fürsten, vnserm freundtlichen lieben Oheimb, vnndt Schwagern, herrn Ludtwigen, fürsten zu Anhalt, Grauen zu Ascanien, herrn zu Bernburg, vndt zerbst *etc.*
Eigenh. Empfangsvermerk F. Ludwigs: ps. d. 6. Xbr. 1646.

Hochgebohrner Fürst, freundtlicher vielgeliebter Vetter.

Ob wir wohl vermög vndt in Crafft Eld. angenehmen handtbrieffleinß vom 24. t*en* Aprill jüngsthin, so vnß allererst den 10./ 20.t*en* dieß zukommen,[1] die darinnen vberschriebene Personen[2] mehr alß gerne in die fruchtbringende Geßellschafft mit einleiben helffen wollen[,] Gestalten Sie sich dan darzu nicht allein willig vndt ganz geneigt erzeugen, sondern auch ihnen solches vor eine sonderbare Ehre erachten, So hat sich iedoch bißhero darzu keine fügliche gelegenheit ereugnen wollen, wir werden aber daran sein, Sie nochmahlß mit nechster fürfallen- oder begebenheit deßwegen zuerinnern, Jnmittelst aber, vnndt damit Eld. in etwas genügen geschehen möge, So hat der gefährliche nicht außer weeg[3] zu sein ermeßen, die in gegenwerttiger verzeuchnüß geßezte Personen vor dießmahl zu henßeln[4], Eld. freundtlich versichernd, daß sobalden beruhrter Personen wapen erfolgen werden, das vbrige vnndt was noch weiter vor feyerligkeiten nöthig, diß orths auch in acht genommen werden[a] soll, sodan der Vbrigen Nahmen vndt wapen zum Erzschreun vberschickt werden sollen[5], vnndt Gleich wie es sonsten von denen bereits dießmahlß in die geßellschafft mit eingetrettenen ßehr wohl vnndt erfrewlichen vfgenomen worden, dießer Ehren theilhafft zu werden, Also erkennen Sie sich auch hingegen sambt vnndt sonders schuldig vndt verpflichtet, Eld. alß Stifftern, vnndt anfängern deßelben hinwider in vnderthänigkeit vfzuwartten, vndt wünschen ein ieder auß dem Erzschreun die verzeichnüß der Geßellschafft, wan es mit Eld. guttem belieben [84v] zugeschehen, zu haben,[6] Vnndt ob Sie auch wohl ganz willig geweßen weren, das beschriebene geldt vor dießmahl na[ch][b] Leipzig zuschicken,[7] So hat es doch, weilen Eld. schreiben vber verhoffen später, alß obgemelt, vnß zukommen, vor dießmahl nicht sein können, soll aber doch künfft[ig bey][b] Franckfurter ostermeß ohnfehlbar in obacht genommen werden, vnndt wir verbleiben Eld. alle angenehme wohl behegliche dienstgefalligkeiten zu erzeugen iederzeit geneiget. Gegeben zu Lauter[n][b] den lezten Weinmonat im Jahr <u>1646</u>.

    E.L
    Dienstwilliger[c] Getr[e]wer[b] vetter vndt Diener
    Ludwig Philip Pfal[tz]grave[b].

I

A. Liste der von Pfalzgraf Ludwig Philipp von Simmern bis Ende Oktober 1646 aufgenommenen FG-Mitglieder

Q HM Köthen: V S 546, Bl. 160rv, v leer; dieselbe Schreiberh. wie im vorliegenden Brief, also die einst dem Brief beiliegende Originalliste aus Kaiserslautern. Mitgliedernummern nachgetragen von F. Ludwig.

Verzeuchnüß der Jenig*en* so in die fruchtbringende Geßelschafft eingetretten, vndt gehenßelt worden.

460.[a] 1. Johan Casimir Colb von Warttenberg, ist eingetretten den 24.t*en* Weinmonath 1646 vndt hat den Nahmen bekomen der *Bessere*, gemählde, *Die Weiße hündtleufft*, wortt, *alß sonst gemein.*[1]

461. 2. *Carl Friederich Pawel.* ist eingetretten den 24. Weinmonath 1646 vnndt hat den Nahmen bekomen, der *diensame*, das gemählde *Die blüende Reinweide*, das Wortt *zum WundtWaßer.*[2]

462. 3. *Friederich* Justus Lopes de Villa Nova, hat den Nahmen bekomen *honighaffte*, daß gemählde, *der gelbe honigklee*, das wortt *dienet zum halßflaster*, den 24.t*en* Weinmonat <u>1646</u>.[3]

463. 4. Eberhardt von Sickingen ist den 26.t*en* Weinmonat <u>1646</u> eingetretten, vnndt hatt den Nahmen bekomen der Nachstellende, daß Gemählde, die große stechende Wunde,[4] daß wortt, allerlei gifft.

B. Liste aller von Pfalzgraf Ludwig Philipp von Simmern aufgenommenen FG-Mitglieder (frühestens 28. Februar 1647)

Q HM Köthen: V S 544, Bl. 85rv, beginnend mit Bl. 85v; andere Schreiberh. als im Brief und in Beil. I A. — *D: KE,* 57 f.

Verzeichnüß der Personen tauff vnndt Geschlechtnahmen.

Johan Caßimir Colb von Warttenberg ist eingetretten den 24.ten Octob. 1646 vnndt hatt den Nahmen bekommen der beßere gemahlde die weiße hindtläufft daß wort alß sonst gemein.[1]

Carl Friederich von[b] Pawel ist eingetretten den 24.ten Octob. 1646 vnndt hatt den nahmen bekommen der dhinsame daß gemahlde die blühende Rheinweide daß wort wundtwasser[2]

Fridericus Justus Lopes de Vilanoua Jst eingetretten den 24. Octob. 1646 vnndt hat den nahmen bekommen honighafft daß gemahlde der gelbe honigkle, daß wort dhinet zum halßpflaster[3]

Ebert von Sickingen ist den 26. Octob. 1646 eingetretten vnndt hatt Nahmen bekommen der Nachstelende, daß gemahlde, die gros[e] stechende Winde, daß wort allerlej gifft.[4]

Graue Philipß von *Leiningen* Westerberg [sic] ist eingetretten den 26. Nouemb. 1646 vnndt hatt den nahmen bekommen der Jnhaltende daß Gemahlde Teschell Kraut daß wort hefftig blute[5]

Hartmuth von vnndt zue Cronenberg ist eingetretten den 25. Decemb. 1646 vnndt hatt den Nahmen bekommen der Kleine daß gemahlde der kleine Vngarische Mandellbaum, daß wort giebet solche frucht.[6]

Johan Daniel von vnndt zue Cronenberg ist eingetretten den 25. Decemb. vnndt hat den Nahmen bekommen der wegtre[i]bende[c] daß gemahlde scabiose Kraut daß wort der grindt vnndt Kratz.[7]

Graue Christian von hohenlohe ist eingetretten den 19. Decemb. 1646 vnndt hatt den nahmen bekommen der Niedliche, daß Gemahlde die haber wurtzel oder bocksbart, daß wort wohl zugerichtet.[8] [85r]

Wolff Bernhardt von Geißpitzheimb ist eingetretten den 17.ten Januarij 1647 vnndt hatt den nahmen bekommen der[d] vmbringende daß gemahl Wanthläuß Kraut, daß wort die wanthläuß oder Wantzen.[9]

Hertzog Wilhelm von Birckenfeldt ist eingetretten den 20. Jan. 1647 vnndt hatt den Nahmen bekommen der andere, daß gemahlde, Körbel, daß wort in wirckung starck.[10]

Graue Ludtwig von Naßau Sarbrücken ist eingetretten den 20. Januarij 1647 vnndt hatt den nahmen bekommen der dinne daß Gemahlde Gartenkreß, daß wort voller safft vnndt Krafft,[11] dieße 3 seindt gehenselt worden in beysein 22 Fürstl. Personen So wohl Fürsten alß Fürstlich FrawenZimmer.

Pfaltgraue [sic] Friederich hertzog von Zweybrücken ist eingetretten den 28.

Februarij 1647 vnndt hat den Nahmen bekommen der artige, daß gemahlde, der Astiche blawe hyacint daß wort wan er blühet.[12]

Georgius F. von Pawel ist eingetretten den 28.ten Feb. 1647 vnndt hatt den nahmen bekommen der lustige, daß gemahlde daß fingerhut[e]Kraut, mitt[f] blaher bluht, daß wort anzusehen vnndt in sich.[13]

Friderich Caßimir von Günteroth ist eingetretten den 28 Feb. 1647 vnndt hat den nahmen bekommen der leichte, daß gemahlde, Pantoffellholtz, daß wort Jst dicht vnndt schwimmet.[14]

T a *Die Punktierung unter* werden soll *könnte auf eine Streichung hindeuten, zumal die Verbklammer weiter unten mit* vberschickt werden sollen *schließt.* — **b** *Textverlust im Falz. Konjektur in eckigen Klammern.* — **c** *Schlußkurialie und Unterschrift eigenh. von Pgf. Ludwig Philipp.*

T I a *Die Numerierung 460 bis 463 ist von F. Ludwig eigenh. ergänzt.* — **b** *von* gebessert *aus* Pa — **c** *Gebessert aus* wegschebende — **d** *Gebessert aus* die — **e** *Gebessert aus* fingerhabKraut — **f** *Eingefügt für* <vnndt>

K 1 F. Ludwigs Brief an Pgf. Ludwig Philipp v. Simmern (FG 97. Der Gefährliche) 460424A, den er über seinen Neffen F. Johann Casimir v. Anhalt-Dessau (FG 10) bestellen ließ. Vgl. 460424. Höchstwahrscheinlich hatte die kriegsbedingte Unsicherheit der Verkehrswege und Postverbindungen die Übersendung des erwähnten Schreibens so verzögert, daß es fast ein halbes Jahr unterwegs war, bis es der Pfalzgraf am 10.10.1646 a. St. empfangen konnte.
2 Pgf. Philipp Ludwig hatte ursprünglich 13 Personen in die FG aufnehmen wollen. S. 460423 u. 460424A I. Am Ende waren es 14 Neumitglieder, von denen nur acht der ursprünglichen Liste entstammten. S. hier Beil. I B. Vgl. zu diesem Aufnahmevorgang insgesamt 460104 K 1.
3 „außer weeg" vermutlich in der Bedeutung abwegig. Vgl. *DW* I, 149 („aus dem weg liegend"). Auch Georg Philipp Harsdörffer (FG 368) benutzte in 450817 diese Redensart.
4 Wie schon in 461026 angekündigt, hatte Pgf. Ludwig Philipp bereits einige Kandidaten, nämlich vier Personen der ursprünglichen Vorschlagsliste (s. Anm. 1) aufgenommen. Dabei handelte es sich um Johann Casimir Kolb v. Wartenberg (FG 460), Carl Friedrich v. Pawel (FG 461), Fridericus Justus Lopez de Villa Nova (FG 462) und Eberhard v. Sickingen (FG 463), von denen er die ersten drei am 24., den letzten am 26. Oktober 1646 in seiner Residenz Kaiserslautern aufgenommen hatte. S. die als Beilage I A angeführte Liste, die zwar dem vorliegenden Brief nicht mehr beiliegt, aber vom selben Schreiber stammt und daher als die im Brief erwähnte Beilage anzusehen ist. Die im Köthener Erzschrein, Band I, dem Brief angehängte Liste, die als Beilage I B abgedruckt ist, kann nicht die Originalbeilage zu diesem Schreiben gewesen sein, da sie frühestens Ende Februar 1647 erstellt worden war, nachdem das letzte der 14 Neumitglieder in die FG aufgenommen worden war. Wenngleich von anderer Schreiberh. dürfte sie nach Maßgabe der im Vergleich zu F. Ludwigs Kanzlei unregulierteren Schreibweise aber auch aus Kaiserslautern stammen (vgl. auch K I 2). Da F. Ludwig in seinem Schreiben an Pgf. Ludwig Philipp *DA Köthen I. 8:* 470403A noch immer nur von 4 Neuaufnahmen weiß, dürfte die Liste jünger als dieses Schreiben sein. Die übrigen zehn Mitglieder wurden zwischen dem 26. Novem-

461031A Pfalzgraf Ludwig Philipp von Simmern

ber 1646 und dem 28. Februar 1647 aufgenommen, s. Beilage I B. — Zum fruchtbringerischen Aufnahmeritual der Hänselung vgl. allgemein 460718 K 8, vgl. hier v. a. 460424A.

5 Ob die Wappen der 14 Neumitglieder (FG 460–463 u. 469–478) tatsächlich übersandt wurden, ist unklar, da sie im *GB Kö.* III sämtlich fehlen wie auch persönliche Eintragungen. Desgleichen haben sich auch im Köthener Erzschrein keine Wappenzeichnungen dieser 14 FG-Genossen erhalten.

6 Pgf. Ludwig Philipps Bitte um ein auf den aktuellen Stand gebrachtes FG-Mitgliederverzeichnis kam schon in 460104 zum Ausdruck. F. Ludwig entsprach diesem Wunsch dann in *DA Köthen I.* 8: 470403, s. 460424 K 7.

7 F. Ludwig hatte in seiner Genehmigung der Aufnahme die Auflage erteilt, daß jedes Neumitglied zwei Reichstaler zur kommenden Leipziger Michaelismesse 1646 per Wechsel an den dortigen Kaufmann Georg Winckler entrichten sollte. Von diesem Geld sollten die jeweiligen Impresen gezeichnet und in Kupfer gestochen werden. S. 460423 (K 5). Zu dem Leipziger Handelsherrn Winckler s. 451019 K 0.

K I 1 Johann Casimir Kolb v. Wartenberg (FG 460), s. 460424A K I.

2 Carl Friedrich v. Pawel(-Rammingen) (FG 461), s. 460424A K I. Sein Wort war „Zum Mundwasser". Die Fehlschreibung „wundtwasser" auch in der Liste I B — ein weiteres Indiz, daß auch diese Liste aus Kaiserslautern stammen dürfte.

3 Fridericus Justus Lopez de Villa Nova (FG 462), s. 460424A K I.

4 Eberhard v. Sickingen (FG 463). Seine Gesellschaftspflanze war „Die große Stechende Winde", richtig angesetzt in Liste I B. S. 460424A K I.

5 Gf. Philipp II. v. Leiningen-Westerburg zu Rixingen: FG 469. Der Inhaltende. Heftigeß bluten. Teschelkraut. Die Imprese entspricht einem Impresenvorschlag F. Ludwigs in 460423 I, Gf. Philipp II. war aber ursprünglich nicht von Pgf. Ludwig Philipp zur Aufnahme vorgesehen, vgl. 460424A I. Vgl. *Conermann III*, 575 f.

6 Frh. Hartmut v. Cronberg: FG 470. Der Kleine. Giebt solche frucht. Der kleine Ungarische mandelbaum. Die Imprese entspricht einem Impresenvorschlag F. Ludwigs in 460423 I, Cronberg war aber ursprünglich nicht von Pgf. Ludwig Philipp zur Aufnahme vorgesehen, vgl. 460424A I. Vgl. *Conermann III*, 577.

7 Frh. Johann Daniel v. Cronberg: FG 471. Der Wegtreibende. Den grind und Kretze. Die blaue Scabiose oder grindkraut (Schebekraut). Die Imprese entspricht einem Impresenvorschlag F. Ludwigs in 460423 I, Cronberg war aber ursprünglich nicht von Pgf. Ludwig Philipp zur Aufnahme vorgesehen, vgl. 460424A I. Vgl. *Conermann III*, 578.

8 Gf. Christian v. Hohenlohe-Waldenburg-Bartenstein: FG 472. Der Niedliche. Wol zugerichtet. Die Haberwurtzel oder Bocksbart. Die Imprese entspricht einem Impresenvorschlag F. Ludwigs in 460423 I, Gf. Christian war aber ursprünglich nicht von Pgf. Ludwig Philipp zur Aufnahme vorgesehen, vgl. 460424A I. Vgl. *Conermann III*, 579 f.

9 Wolf Bernhard v. Geispitzheim (FG 473), s. 460424A K I.

10 Pgf. Georg Wilhelm v. Birkenfeld, Bruder Pgf. Christians I. v. Bischweiler (FG 205): FG 474. Der Andere. Jn wirckung stärker. Spanischer Kerbel. Die Imprese entspricht einem Impresenvorschlag F. Ludwigs in 460423 I, Pgf. Georg Wilhelm war aber ursprünglich nicht von Pgf. Ludwig Philipp zur Aufnahme vorgesehen, vgl. 460424A I. Pgf. Georg Wilhelm wird hier unter dem Titel „Herzog" aufgeführt. Als Mitglied der pfälz. Wittelsbacher stand ihm u. a. der Titel eines Herzogs in Bayern (Dux Bavariae) zu. Aus diesem Grund wurde das Teilft. (Zweibrücken-)Birkenfeld wiederholt als Hzt. bezeichnet. Vgl. *Conermann III*, 581 f.

11 Gf. Johann Ludwig v. Nassau-Saarbrücken-Ottweiler: FG 475. Der Dünne. Voller Saft und kraft. Gartenkreße. Die Imprese entspricht einem Impresenvorschlag F. Ludwigs

in 460423 I, Gf. Johann Ludwig war aber ursprünglich nicht von Pgf. Ludwig Philipp zur Aufnahme vorgesehen, vgl. 460424A I. Vgl. *Conermann III*, 583f.
    12 Pgf. Friedrich v. Zweibrücken (FG 476), s. 460424A K I.
    13 Georg Friedrich v. Pawel(-Rammingen) (FG 477), s. 460424A K I.
    14 Friedrich Casimir v. Günderode (FG 478), s. 460424A K I.

461104

Johann Rist an Johann Heinrich Boeckler

Johann Rist (FG 467. 1647) bedankt sich für ein von Johann Michael Moscherosch (FG 436) überschicktes lateinisches Glückwunschgedicht Johann Heinrich Boecklers. Er habe dessen Freundschaft durch nichts verdient, verspricht dies jedoch nachzuholen. Rist lobt eine Rede, die Boeckler vor einiger Zeit in Straßburg gehalten hat, und bittet Boeckler, Johann Matthias Schneuber (FG 498. 1648) zu grüßen. Dieser habe (Johann Georg) Styrzel versprochen, ihm etwas zu übersenden, woran Boeckler ihn erinnern möge.

Q SUB Hamburg: Sup. ep. 24, Bl. 423r–424v [A: 424v]; eigenh.; schwarzes Siegel; die Anschrift ist größtenteils herausgeschnitten (Konjekturen und Markierung des Textverlusts in eckigen Klammern). — D: *Reifferscheid*, 613f. — BN: *Krüger* II, 850. Erwähnt in *Kühlmann: Korrespondenz Moscheroschs*, 275.

A Dem Edlen, Vesten und hoch[gelahrten ... herrn] Johann Hin[rich Boekler[1] ...] der hohen [...] berühmten [... meine]m sonders Hoch[geehrten ...] und groswehrten[a] [... Fre]unde. [...] *Strasburg*

Edler, Vester und hochgelahrter, sonders grosgünstiger hochgeehrter herr groswehrter[a] lieber freund,

Demselben verhalte Jch hiermit nicht welcher gestalt mein hochgeliebter herr und freund herr Moscherosch[1] mir vor weiniger Zeit ein Briefelein und unter anderm in demselben Ein lateinisches Glükwünschungs-gedichte von meinem hochgeehrten herren Boeklern meiner weinigkeit zu Ehren und gefallen gesetzet, hat übersendet.[2] Nun weis Jch nicht, wie Jch solche hohe freundschafft gegen demienigen, welchen Jch durch keine Dienste mir hiezu verpflichtet habe, einiger mahssen solle[b] erwiederen, Jch will aber, inmittelst Jch darauff bedacht bin, demselben mein getreues hertz zu pfande setzen, welches meinen grosgeehrten herren versichert, das Jch nicht ablassen werde alle guhte mittel meinem hochgeliebtem herren behägliche Dienste zu erweißen, hervor zu suchen, damit Jch den namen möge haben ein freund und Diener zu sein von dem berühmten herren Boekler, welchen [423v] Jch von der Zeit an, als Jch eine Rede, welche Er mit sehr schönen und zierlichen[c] wohrten zu Strasburg gehalten mit höhester belüstigung durchgelesen[3], iederzeit hoch geliebet und in meinem hertzen verehret, erfreue mich demnach über die mahssen sehr, das Jch die kundschafft eines so grossen freundes habe erlanget mit dienstlicher bitte, da Jch meinem herren einige angeneme Dienste könte erweisen, Er mich solches nur mit weinigen wolle wissen lassen, sol meine wilfährigkeit dergestalt spühren, das Jhn der angefangenen freundschafft verhoffentlich nicht wird gereuen. Bitte dienstlich dafern etwan die gelegenheit dazu vorfället, es auch meinem herren nicht gahr zu beschwehrlich ist, Er wolle dem herrn Schnäuber[4], einem Manne, der sich üm das allgemeine Vatterland nicht weinig verdient gemacht hat, meinen grus und stets geflissne Dienste vermelden. Jch erwahrte das, was Er in einem [424r] Briefelein mir ehister gelegenheit zuzusenden meinem hochwehrten lieben freunde dem herren Stirtzelio[5] unlängst hat versprochen, an welches übersendung Jch mit nichten zweifle. Befehle Jhn inmittelst der gnädigen obhut des höhesten verbleibend

Wedel in Holstein   Meines hochgeehrten herren
4 Novemb. 1646   Joh. Rist.

I

Johann Heinrich Boeckler auf Rists kaiserliche Dichterkrönung und Adelsverleihung

Q Johann: Risten | Allerunterthänigste Lobrede | An die | Allerdurchlaüchtigste Unüberwindlichste Römische | Kaiserliche Maiestätt/ | [Zierleiste] | Herren Ferdinand den Dritten | Als Allerhöchstgedachte Kaiserl. Maiest. | Jhn Durch den Hochwolgebohrnen Grafen und | Herren | Herren Herman Tschernin/ | Des Heiligen Römischen Reiches Graffen von | Chudenitz/ Herren auff Petersburg/ Gissibel/ Neüdek/ | Kost/ Mildschowes/ Sedschitz/ Schmidberg/ Römischer Kaiser- | licher Maiestätt Raht/ würklichen Kämmerer/ Landrechts Beisitzer | im Königreich Böheim/ Obristen und Oratorem an die Otto- | mannische Porten & cæt. | Mit Adelichen Freiheiten/ Schild/ Helm und Wapen | auch der Poetischen Lorberkrohn von dero Kaiserlichen | Hofe aus allergnädigst hatte verehren | lassen/ | Nebenst beigefügten nützlichen Anmerkungen und wolgemein- | ten Glükwünschungen vornemer Herren und vertrauter | Freünde. | [Linie] | Hamburg/ | Gedruckt bey Jacob Rebenlein [1647], S. 102 f.; HAB: 43.6 Pol. (7); dig.

Ad
Reverendum Clarissimumque Virum
Dn: JOHANNEM RISTIUM,
Cum is
â Sacra Cæsarea Maiestate
Laurea pariter Apollinari & Nobilitatis Insignibus
spontaneâ munificentiâ donatus esset.

EXiit & nostras etiam rumoribus aures
Implevit, duplicis laudatrix fama favoris [103]
Ac decoris, quo nempe tuas Augusta coronat
Maiestas ultro, RISTI *clarissime, dotes.*
   Quem pridem titulum doctus tibi debuit orbis,

Cæsare nunc dici mavis autore POETA.
Accedit decori decus, & ne Laurea, Tantum
Non satis Auctorem referat, nova pignora vatem
Addunt Nobilibus, generisque insignibus augent.
  Fallor, an optatæ præsagia pacis honores
Designant gemini. Nam reddita præmia doctis,
Ac iterum admissis in summa palatia Musis
Antiquus servatur honos, non Martia nobis
Tempora, sed studium pacis fructusque minantur.
  Det Deus, ut magnum tibi carminis argumentum
Pax nova, pax bona, sit; pax docto carmine digna:
Quæ titulis permissa sacris præfulgeat, atque
Jnter Cæsareas celebretur maxima laudes.
              Honoris & Officii causa
                    fecit
          JOH. HENRICUS BOECLERUS *Jn Aca-*
          demiâ Argentoratensi Professor
                  publicus.

II

Johann Michael Moscherosch auf Rists kaiserliche Dichterkrönung und Adelsverleihung

Q Johann: Risten Allerunterthänigste Lobrede, a. a. O. (s. I Q), 99 (erste 2 lat. Gedichte = 1a u. 1b), 99–101 (1. dt. Gedicht = 2) u. 101 (2. dt. Gedicht = 3); Veränderte Wiederveröffentlichung der lat. Gedichte: Centuria | Epigrammatum | IOHANNIS-MICHAELIS | MOSCHEROSCH | Germani. | [Linie] | Levant & Carmania curas. | Olymp. Nomes. Eclog. 4. | [Signet] ARGENTINÆ | Typis & Sumptibus | JOH. PHILIPPI MÜLBII | Et JOSIÆ STÆDELII. | [Linie] | M. DC. XXXXVIIII. S. 35f. HAB: 230.8 Poet. (= *CE*) — Mit dieser zweiten Veröffentlichung sinn- und lautgleich: Centuria II. | Epigrammatum | JOHANNIS-MICHAELIS | MOSCHEROSCH. | Levant & Carmina curas. | Olymp. Nomes. Eclog. 4. | [Signet] | FRANCOFVRTI, | Sumptibus SEBASTIANI ROHNERI, | Typis DANIELIS FIEVETI. | [Linie] | M. DC. LXV. S. 82f.

               1ᵃ
    Herren Risten Selber Dem Rüstigen.
             Nobili Viro
            JOHANNI RISTIO,
  Philosopho, Theologo, Mathematico, Chymico,
        Poetæ, Oratori Excellentissimo.
              ἀνάγραμμα
          JOHANNES RISTIUS.ᵇ
          ESTO VIR HIS ANNIS.

Annorum mores & Morum tempora, RISTI,
   hæc sunt: Osores Vir bonus omnis habet:
Osores quoq*ue* Cæsar habet, Caput Orbis, ab isto[c]
   intacto[d] nemo fulmine vivus abit.
Vis artem? RISTI, Certum vel Recipe contrá?
   Sursum oculis tendas, Artem Anagramma dabit.
Te, RISTI, Te Cæsar amat, fovet æstimat; hoc cui
   Contigit, Osores despicit ille suos.

Aliud.[e]
JOHANNES RISTIUS.
ἀνάγρ.
IN ARTES JUS SINO
TErsa dabas Patriæ: Cæsar tibi serta Deorum,
   Insigni Gentis Nobilitate tuæ.
Vox audita simul: RISTI! tibi Regis in Artes
   Jus SINO. Vox cujus? Cæsaris illa fuit.

2[a]
Seinen Feinden.
Wider den kunst- und gunstlosen Fratzen/
Neidharten Ristenfeind.

Nun was hilfft itz dein gezänk'
   Und vermeinte kluge ränk/
Dein mit hohn gespikte lügen?
   ligt doch alle lästerung
   Und dein selbst vergiffte zung
Spraachlos in den letsten zügen. [100]

Neidhard/ alles ist ümsunst/
   Und hast weder Ehr noch Gunst
Du zu hoffen noch zu sehen/
   Den nur/ das durch deinen Neid
   Du mit höchstem Hertzeleid
Must geneidet untergehen.

Bist du nicht ein thummes thier/
   Ein unsinnig grober stier
Das du nach den Sachen gehest/
   Und auf selbst geschöpftem wahn
   Dich des thörich nemest an
Das du selbst nicht verstehest?

Lobest was ein Biederman
Ohne schand nicht loben kan/
Und mit ungestühmen toben
Schmähst und tadelst guhte ding;
Achtest das für pfifferling
Waß König' und Kaiser loben?

Aber so bist du gemuht/
kein werk ist so fein und guht
Du kanst allem wiedersprechen.
Deine balken weist du nit/
Schläppst sie doch als Bäume mit/
Und siehst andrer Leut gebrechen.

Neidhart hirn- und Sinnen-toll/
lügen-gifft-und gallen voll/
Nun zieh' ab mit deiner Nasen.
Geh' und zörne bis in todt/
Den **Herr Rist** ist ausser noht/
Und lacht über deinem rasen. [101]

Dein verwürrter Neid und Haß/
dein verirrtes Diß und Daß/
dein ohn wehr gemachte Wunden
Hat **Herr Rist**/ doch ohne Schuld/
Ohne schwehrt-streich mit gedult/
Tugend-vest längst überwunden.

Drum sind alle deine pfeil'
und vermeinte Donnerkeil
Dir nur selbst-gemachte striemen/
kurtz: waß hier der Kaiser lobt/
Wen schon **Neidhart** zürnt und tobt/
Das sol billig ieder rühmen.

3ª
Seiner Feder.
Johannes Rist
versetzet
Er ist Jason
An seine Edle Feder.
Edle Feder sey gegrüsset!
deines Herren feste Hand
Sichert dich durch stätt' und land

Ob es Neidhart schon verdriesset.
Er ist Jason! Jst Er nicht?
Nein: Er ist der Musen licht/
Des das Vatterland geniesset.
Er ist Ja des Phæbus **Sohn**:
Trohn und Krohn hat Er zu lohn
Ob es Neidhart schon verdriesset.
Er Jst Ja des Pindus **Sonn!**
drum du unsre lust und wonn'/
Edle Feder sey gegrüsset.

Aus Strasburg übersendet dieses seinem Hochgeehrten Freunde
J. Michael Moscherosch
Reipublicæ Argentoratensis Syndicus.´

III

Georg Philipp Harsdörffer auf Rists kaiserliche Dichterkrönung und Adelsverleihung

Q Johann: Risten Allerunterthänigste Lobrede, a. a. O. (s. I Q), 90–92.

Der Musen
Erfreüliches Reyen Lied
über Des WolEhrwürdigen/ Edlen und hochgelahrten
Herren Johann: Risten
Jn der hochlöblichen Fruchtbringenden Geselschafft der Rüstige genant/
längstverdienten Lorberkrantz.

1
JHr Schwestern dichtet kunstklingende Lieder!
Es lige nun alle betrübniß danieder: [91]
   des krieges Gotts waffen
   Beginnen zu schlaffen.
    wir Musen von neüen
    Am Reyen uns freüen.
  Wir arme geplagte
  Jns elend veriagte
Verbinden und finden uns sämtlichen wieder.

2
Wir haben die Edelen Geister getrieben
So weiland weltrühmliche thaten beschrieben.

Die helden erliegen
Jm prächtigsten siegen/
  die palmen verwelken/
  Gleich buntlichen nelken:
der trauer Cipressen
wird leichtlich vergessen/
Die nirgend von unsern Poeten beschrieben.

3

*Helden sind vor alters Degen geneñet worden. Goldast Paræn. f. 365.

Wir pflegen von tapferen *degen[1] zu singen/
Die saiten von streiten behertzter zu zwingen.
  Die Musen erhalten
  die namen der alten/
    die ritterlich kämpfen/
    die wiedrigen dämpfen/
weil niemahls verwesen
die werden gelesen
Und stätig berühmet in ohren erklingen.

4

Eüch Teütschen sind unsere künste bescheret/
Als welche der **Löblichster Kaiser** verehret/
  der unserem Sohne
  Geschenket die Krohne/ [92]
    Von lorbernen zweigen/
    die gnade zu zeigen
So wissen verdienet
Und stetig begrünet/
die milde der Helikon mehret und nehret.

5

Wir wollen mit güldenen titeln schreiben/
Fernandus sol Ewig verewiget bleiben/
  Der Tugend Exempel
  Jn unserem Tempel.
    Wir wollen Jhn loben
    Mit zierlichsten proben/
Schaut unsere quellen
Mit lisplender hellen
Nun wallen von seiner Genade getrieben.

    Zu dienstfreündlicher Ehrbezeigung gesetzet
                    von
        Georg Philip Harsdörffer

461104 Johann Rist

IV

Johann Matthias Schneuber auf Rists kaiserliche Dichterkrönung und Adelsverleihung

Q Neüer Teütscher | [Zierleiste] | Parnass/ | Auff welchem befindlich | Ehr' und Lehr | Schertz und Schmertz | Leid- und Freüden- | Gewächse/ | Welche zu unterschiedlichen | Zeiten gepflantzet/ nunmehr aber Allen/ | der Teütschen Helden-Sprache und dero- | selben edlen Dichtkunst vernünfftigen Liebhaberen/ | zu sonderbarem Gefallen zu hauffe gesamlet und | in die offenbahre Welt außgestreüet/ | Von | Johann Risten. | [Signet] | Lüneburg/ | Gedruckt und verlegt durch Johann und Heinrich/ | denen Sternen/ Gebrüdern. | [Linie] | M DC LII., 874. HAB: Xb 3246. Auch Ndr. Hildesheim [u. a.] 1978. — Erneut mit Änderungen abgedruckt in: Joh. Matthias Schneübers | Teütscher gedichten | Anderer Theyl | [Signet] | Straßburg/ | Getrukt bej Josias Städel | [Linie] | Jm Jahr M. DC. LVJ., 283 f. (= TG)

An
Herren Johan Rist/
Alß derselbe neben andern Kaiserl. Freiheiten zu einem Poeten gekrönet worden.ᵃ

ES ist ein Wunderwerk/ das bei so bösen Zeiten/
Da unser Teütsches Land von der Verwildungs-Nacht
Und dunklem Krieges-rauch stok-finster ward ᵇ gemacht/
Ja da der grimme Mars mit mörden/ brennen ᶜ/ beüten/
Die Häuser guter Lehr und Künsten außzureüten
So hefftig ᵈ hat getobt/ daß alles hat gekracht. ᵉ
Jedoch die teütsche Zung mit wunderschönem Pracht
Und Glantz würd ᶠ außgerüst! die müh gelehrter Leüten/
Jn welchen ᵍ Gottes trieb daß Werk so weit geführt/
Daß solche Helden Sprach jetzt ʰ über alle pranget/
Wird billich mit der Ehr und Freiheit hoch geziert
Vom Haupt/ an dem daß Reich deß grossen Teütschlands hanget
Wir ruffen dir glük zu/ daß ⁱ auch du/ werther Rist/
Hierumb ʲ von Jhm gekrönt und recht geadelt bist. ᵏ

Auf Strasburg.   Jn Ehren und Freundschafft geschrieben
          Von
        Joh. Matthias Schneüber/
         Profess. pub.

T *Reifferscheid (Sigle R) normalisiert die Schreibung in seiner Transkription durchgehend, was zu vielen kleineren Abweichungen führt (Groß- und Kleinschreibung, vergessene Buchstaben), die im Folgenden nicht nachgewiesen werden.* — **a** R grosverehrter — **b** R solte — **c** R herrlichen

T II a *Die römischen Ziffern des Originals über den Gedichten der 2. Beilage wurden von uns durch arabische ersetzt.* — **b** *CE* Ad Reverendum atque Excellentissimum D. Iohannem Ristium. Theologum, Mathematicum, Oratorem, Poetam nobilem Cæsareum, singula optimum, & amicum maximum. Johannes Ristius. ἀνάγραμ. — **c** *CE* isthoc — **d** *CE* Intactus — **e** *CE* Ad Eundem.

T IV a *TG* An Herrn Joh. Risten/ als derselbe zu eynem Poeten gekrönet worden. — **b** *TG* wurd — **c** *TG* brännen — **d** *TG* häfftig — **e** *Folgt Klammerzeichen:*) — **f** *TG* wurd — **g** *TG* welchem — **h** *TG* ietz — **i** *Im Original:* dz — **j** *TG* hierum̄ — **k** *TG endet hier.*

K 1 Johann Heinrich Boeckler (1611–1672), Prof. der Rhetorik und Geschichte zu Straßburg. Zu Biographie u. Schaffen s. 440616 K II 0. Johann Michael Moscherosch (FG 436), von dessen Neuausgabe seiner menippeischen Satiren (*Gesichte Philanders von Sittewald.* 1650) auch Johann Rist (FG 467. 1647) erfahren hatte (vgl. 461020), wird die Verbindung Boecklers zu Rist geknüpft u. ihn zu dem in Beil. I. zitierten Gratulationsgedicht angeregt haben.

 2 S. I Q. Vgl. einen Kupferstich des Rist-Wappens in Rists *Lobrede* (S. I Q) u. in einem anderen Exemplar mit Andreas Tschernings Gedicht auf das Wappen, überschickt zusammen mit Georg Philipp Harsdörffers (FG 368) Schreiben an F. Ludwig (*DA Köthen I. 8*: 470206; *KE*, 380f., jedoch ohne die Beilagen). Abgedruckt auch in *Conermann: Rist*, 52; vgl. zu Rists Krönung S. 51–61. Rist wird sich auch bei den Bekannten u. Freunden für die Gratulationsgedichte zur Verleihung von Adel, Wappen u. Poetenlorbeer durch den Kaiser bedankt haben. Wir veröffentlichen die meisten Gedichte von Mitgliedern der FG in den Beilagen II u. III sowie das ebenfalls aus diesem Anlaß entstandene, aber erst später erschienene Gedicht in Beilage IV anstatt der uns nicht überlieferten einschlägigen Briefe Rists an diese Fruchtbringer. In der *Lobrede* Rists auf den Kaiser (s. Beil. I Q) finden sich die Ehrengedichte auf Rist, die in seinem Bekannten- u. Freundeskreis entstanden, unter dem Titel: „Folgen Unterschiedliche Lob- und Glükwünschungs gedichte Vornehmer Herren und vertrauter Freünde." (S. 86 ff.) Aus der FG bzw. dem PBO schickten lat. u. dt. Gedichte (der PBO-Stifter) Georg Philipp Harsdörffer (FG 368; S. 88–92) u. Johann Michael Moscherosch (FG 436), 1 lat. u. 2 dt. Gedichte, S. 99–101. Hinzu trat der junge, zum Poeten gekrönte Pegnitzschäfer Sigismund Betulius (Sigmund v. Birken, PBO, FG 681. 1658, S. 129–131). Als herausragende Beiträger neben Boeckler u. Styrzel (s. u. Anm. 5) sind noch die Pegnitzschäferin Diana (S. 88, dt., Sophia v. der Lippe, verh. Nicolai v. Greiffencrantz), der Dresdner Dichter u. kursächs. Sekretär Christian Brehme (S. 101, dt.), der Opitz-Nachfolger u. Rostocker Professor Andreas Tscherning (S. 103 f., lat.), der Rintelner Professor u. Romancier Andreas Heinrich Buchholtz (S. 104, dt.), der FG-Kritiker Jesaias Rompler v. Löwenhalt (AGT; S. 106–109, dt.), der dän. Dichter Søren Terkelsen (dän., S. 120–122) u. weitere Dichter des Nürnberger Hirtenordens zu nennen: Johann Klaj (PBO; dt., S. 123–125), Samuel Hund (PBO, dt., S. 126–128) u. Georg Konrad Osthof (PBO; dt., S. 128 f.). Diese wollten wohl ebenso wie Diana, Strephon (Harsdörffer) u. Floridan (Betulius) ihrem Ordensgenossen Rist (PBO 1645, Daphnis aus Cimbrien) ein ‚Ständchen' bringen. Wie aus dem Brief hervorgeht, erwartete Rist auch einen Text des 1648 in die FG aufgenommenen Johann Matthias Schneuber, der aber wohl zu spät für die Drucklegung der *Lobrede* eintraf (s. Beilage IV u. Anm. 4).

 3 Bei den zahlreichen kleineren Schriften Boecklers, die vor 1646 in Straßburg erschienen, handelt es sich in vielen Fällen um Gelegenheitsdichtungen zu Hochzeiten oder Begräbnissen in lateinischer Sprache. Rist bezieht sich hier wohl auf den einzigen (?) deutschen Text Boecklers aus dieser Zeit: sein Gratulationsgedicht *Herren Johann Küeffers*

Doctorat (Straßburg 1640, VD17 12:635632U), das er — laut Titelblatt des Drucks — am 9. April 1640 in Straßburg vorgetragen hat. Das fünfseitige Gedicht thematisiert spielerisch, daß Boeckler nahezu ausschließlich auf Latein publizierte. Es beginnt mit den Versen: „Auff der Teutschen Lyr zuspielen | ist mein hand schon lang entwohnt", u. schließt mit der Strophe: „Aber/ wie ich vor gedachte/ | meine Reimen sind zuschlecht/ auff deß alten Saxen [i. e. Hans Sachs] recht. | Den ich gleichwol nit verachte: | Schlechte [*d. h. schlichte*] wort vnd gut gemüth | Jst das rechte Teutsche Lied." Vorgetragen wurde das Gedicht anläßlich der Promotion (Disputatio Medica Inauguralis De Erysipelate, Straßburg 1640, VD17 23:277740D) Johann Küffers (1614–1674), eines weithin bekannten Mediziners. 1661 erwarb Küffer, durch ein Erbe u. die Ausübung seines Metiers zu Reichtum gelangt, die Ullenburg vom Haus Württemberg als Pfandlehen, wo ihm Grimmelshausen zwischen 1662 u. 1665 als Schaffner u. Burgvogt diente. Grimmelshausen verewigte seinen Dienstherren später u. a. im vierten Buch des *Simplicissimus* in der Figur des Monseigneur Canard. Vgl. Walter Ernst Schäfer: Dr. Johann Küffer (1614–1674), Prototyp der sozial aufsteigenden Akademikerschicht des 17. Jahrhunderts. In: Wilhelm Kühlmann, Walter Ernst Schäfer: Literatur im Elsaß von Fischart bis Moscherosch. Gesammelte Studien, Tübingen 2001, 135–146. Küffer stand der Straßburger Tannengesellschaft nah, deren Spiritus rector der mit Rist bekannte Jesaias Rompler v. Löwenhalt war (s. 440724 K 4).

4 Johann Matthias Schneuber (FG 498. 1648) studierte an der U. Straßburg (imm. 14. 8. 1634), an der er von 1642 an den Lehrstuhl für Poesie innehatte. Schneuber spielte eine führende Rolle in der Straßburger AGT. Rist erwartete auch von ihm ein Glückwunschgedicht für seine *Lobrede* (s. Anm. 2 u. I Q), das offenbar nicht rechtzeitig eintraf u. darum erstmals in Rists *Neüem Teütschen Parnass* (1652) unter die dortigen Lobgedichte eingerückt wurde (s. Beilage IV). Vgl. zu Schneuber auch *Bopp: Tannengesellschaft*, 39–53.

5 Vielleicht doch nicht Johann Valentin Andreaes Geschenk eines Exemplars des *GB 1646* an den Rotenburger Bügermeister Johann Georg Styrzel, vgl. den Brief von Johann Georg Styrzel an Johann Valentin Andreae, HAB: Cod. Guelf 11.12 Aug. 2°, Bl. 546rv, Dig. Johann Georg Styrzel (1591–1668), 1609 Philosophiestudium an der U. Jena, ab 1611 Jura, zunächst an der U. Tübingen, 1613 bis 1616 an der U. Altdorf. Zu den Lehrern des aus Augsburg stammenden Styrzel gehörte Georg Henisch(ius) (1549–1618), Bibliothekar u. Rektor des Gymnasiums St. Anna, Verfasser des großen, aber unvollendeten deutschen Wörterbuchs *Teutsche Sprach vnd Weißheit. Thesaurus linguae et sapientiae Germanicae* (Augsburg 1616; Ndr. Hildesheim [u. a.] 1973). Styrzel versuchte vergeblich, sich in seiner Vaterstadt beruflich zu etablieren. Nach dem Erwerb des Bürgerrechts in Rothenburg ob der Tauber, wo er 1624 eine reiche Witwe ehelichte, machte er allerdings rasch Karriere. Schon 1635 wurde Styrzel zum ersten von insgesamt fünfzehnmal zum regierenden Amtsbürgermeister von Rothenburg gewählt. Der literarisch interessierte Jurist pflegte eine umfangreiche Korrespondenz mit zahlreichen Gelehrten u. Schriftstellern wie den Straßburgern Boeckler u. Samuel Gloner. Besonders an den literarischen Entwicklungen der Zeit interessiert, tauschte Styrzel sich nicht zuletzt mit bedeutenden Mitgliedern zeitgenössischer Sprachgesellschaften aus: u. a. mit dem Straßburger Johann Matthias Schneuber (s. Anm. 4), Augustus Buchner (FG 362), Johann Michael Moscherosch (FG 436) u. Johann Rist (ESO, FG), den er in der *Lobrede* auf den Kaiser mit zwei lat. Gedichten ehrte (s. I Q, S. 96 f. u. 98). Dazu zählen auch die Nürnberger Blumenhirten Georg Philipp Harsdörffer (FG 368) u. Sigmund v. Birken (FG 681. 1658). Styrzel verfaßte zahlreiche, v. a. lat. Gedichte. Vgl. Ludwig Schnurrer: Johann Georg Styrzel (1591–1668), in: Fränkische Lebensbilder, N. F. 13 (1990), 62–74.

K I Zur Verleihung des Adels, des Wappens u. des Poetenlorbeers durch den ksl. Hofpfalzgrafen Gf. Hermann Czernin v. Chudenitz im Jahre 1646 gratuliert der Straßburger Professor der Geschichte u. Redekunst, Johann Heinrich Boeckler (s. 440616 u. ö.) Johann Rist (FG 467. 1647). Zur Ehrung des Wedeler Pastors, die diesem trotz seines geistlichen Stands wohl auch zur Aufnahme in die FG verhalf, s. *Conermann: Rist*, 51 ff. Als Politicus, aber auch als Patriot u. Förderer der deutschen Sprache (s. 440616 K I 0 zu Keck; *DA Köthen I. 8:* 480218 I) wünscht sich Boeckler, dem frühere Friedensdichtungen Rists (Irenaromachia, 1630; *Kriegs- vnd Friedens Spiegel*, 1640; *HOLSTEJNS Erbärmliches Klag- und Jammer-Lied*, 1644; *FRiedens-POsaune*, 1646) u. auch dessen Satiren gegen die Alamodesprache in etwa bekannt gewesen sein dürften, in dem Epigramm von Rist eine große gelehrte Dichtung, die (nach dem Prager Frieden) eines neuen u. wahren Friedens würdig sei.

K III Diesem dt. Lied gehen unter den Ehrengedichten zu Rists *Lobrede* zwei lat. Gedichte Harsdörffers voran: 1. IN INSIGNIA NOBILITATIS RISTIANÆ (inc.: QVid sibi vigineâ Laurea), auf Rists Wappen; 2. LAUDES LAUREÆ, cum Admodùm Reverendo, Clarissimo atque Excellentissimo Viro Dn. JOHANNI RISTIO, Wedeliensium Pastori vigilantissimo, Oratori, Poëtæ & Philologo eximio Ex ipsâ Cæsaris aulâ Laurea Poëtica ultrò mitteretur (inc.: FUisse Nymphas, credimus, arbores), auf Rist Poetenkrönung. — Das zweite lat. Gedicht ist vom 1.5.1646 datiert.
    1 Melchior Goldast v. Haiminsfeld: PARAENETICORVM VETERVM Pars I. In qua producuntur Scriptores VIII. ... Cum Notis MELCHIORIS HAIMINSFELDI GOLDASTI (Insulae 1604: Ioannes Ludovici), 365: „Dixi; *Degin* esse seruum an ministrum. ira gladius nuncupatus, quòd eius ministerio in defensione vtimur. Et quemadmodum *Degin* de homine bellicoso & heroico vsurpari cœpit, [...]."

461106

Fürst Ludwig an Carl Gustav von Hille

Antwort auf 460718 u. 460915A. Beantwortet durch *DA Köthen I.8:* 470112. — F. Ludwig (Der Nährende) bestätigt die Ankunft eines reichlich verspäteten Schreibens Carl Gustav v. Hilles (FG 302. Der Unverdrossene) vom 18. Juli und eines anderen zügig überbrachten Briefs Hilles vom 15. September 1646. Seinerseits entschuldigt sich der Fürst mit Verhinderungen und Unpäßlichkeit für die verzögerte Beantwortung dieser Schreiben. — F. Ludwig verspricht Hille, ihm ein Exemplar des in Frankfurt a. M. gedruckten *GB 1646* zu schicken, sobald ihm Hille den Postempfänger in Leipzig oder Wolfenbüttel nenne, desgleichen auch ein Exemplar von *Gueintz: Rechtschreibung (1645)*. — F. Ludwig legt seine Erklärung über die Aufnahme Johann Valentin Andreaes (FG 464) bei (Beil. I). — Er würde gern den Entwurf des Buchs Hilles über die FG (*Hille: Teutscher Palmbaum*) sehen. Die von Hille erbetene Beschreibung des FG-Aufnahmerituals könne nach Vollendung des Manuskripts leicht hinzugesetzt werden. Eine Beschreibung solle knapp ausfallen, um dem fremden Leser keinen Anlaß zu Mißbrauch, Ärger oder Spott zu geben. — Der Ausführende (Hans Ernst v. Freyberg, FG 140) habe Hille vor Jahren eine farbige Visierung seiner Imprese geschickt und ihm mitgeteilt, wie sowohl dieses Sinnbild als auch Hilles Wappen gestickt werden sollten. Falls Hille dies noch nicht veranlaßt habe, möge er die Visierung an den Ausführenden zurückschicken und zwar über Quedlinburg an

Andreas Heidfeld. — Der Aufweckende ist der dessauische Kanzler Gottfried Müller (FG 353). — F. Ludwig legt ein Verzeichnis vom 432. Gesellschafter an bei.

Q HM Köthen: V S 545, Bl. 42rv [A: 42v], Schreiberh. mit Zusätzen und Verbesserungen von F. Ludwigs H. — *D: KE*, 207f.; *KL* III, 226–228. Zitate in *Keller: Akademien der Renaissance*, 107 u. *Begemann: FG u. Andreä*, 44. — *BN: Bürger*, 951 Nr. 75. — Bl. 43r: 2 Beilagen, 43 v leer (s. hier Beil. I u. II).

A An[a] Carl Gustaffen von Hille furstlichen Braunschweigischen hofmeister zu Wulffenbutel

Vom Unverdrossenen[1] seind abgewichener Zeit zwey schreiben eines vom 18. des Heumonats das andere vom 15. des Herbstmonats dem *Nehrenden* zugekommen[b].[2] Das erste kam spat, das andere aber doch ziemlich zu rechte. Und das die antwort so schleunig nicht folgen wollen, seind unterschiedene verhinderungen, bisweilen auch etwas unpasligkeit, mit untergelaufen, derwegen es der *Unverdroßene* zum besten deuten und nicht etwa einer Vergeßenheit zuschreiben wolle.

Von denen, dem *Nehrenden* zugekommenen Geselschaftbüchern zu Franckfurt am Main, in[c] diesem jahre gedruckt, wiewol sie noch nicht alle angelanget, sol dem *Unverdroßenen* ein stück zugeschicket werden,[3] wan er nur berichten wird, wohin, oder weme es in Leipzig oder Wulffenbüttel sol überliefert werden.

Wegen[d] Johannis Valentins Andreae einnemung[e] in die Fruchtbringende Geselschaft ist[f] die erklerung hierbey.[4]

Anreichende die vom *Unverdrossenen* fürhabende erzehlung der geschichte des aufkommens der Fruchtbringenden geselschaft, so wird der *Nehrende* den entwurf gerne sehen, und nechstkünftig gewertig sein,[5] Was aber die, so genante, Henselung, bei der einnemung betrift, darin wolle sich der [42v] *Unverdroßene* viel aufzusetzen nicht bemühen, auf das nicht etwas entweder zu viel oder zu wenig geschehe, sondern wenn das andere fertig und fein gestellet, kann dieses stück gar leichtlich und füglich, doch ohne weitleuftigkeit hieneingerucket werden, also das es bey frembden keinen misbrauch und ärgernüs, oder gespötte gebe.[6]

Die Rechtschreibung[7] sol mit dem Geselschaftbuche überschicket werden und were zu wüntschen[g] man fürete anderer örter so viel neuerung im drucken und diese[h] materie nicht ein, darüber ihrer viel sich ärgern, solche neuerungen weniger grund haben, und lange nicht werden[h] bestehen können.

Demnach auch dem *Unverdroßenen* vor jahren, vom *Ausführenden* sein gemählde in Farben, wie es etwa könte, wie auch das wapen gesticket werden, zugestellet worden,[8] als wil man deßelben zu dem Erzschreine wieder gewertig sein, wo es nicht gemacht, dieser orten noch zu verfertigen, und kan es nur über Quedlinburg durch Andream Heidfelden auf Hätzgerode an den Ausführenden überschicket werden[.][9]

Der *Aufweckende* ist ieziger Cantzler zu Deßau, ein alter gelehrter mann und doctor, oder gelehrter in den Rechten.[10]

Die Geselschafter von der zahl 432 an bis hieher,[11] werden inliegend überschicket, und wird hiermit der *Unverdroßene* in den schutz Götlicher obacht befolen, es verbleibet des

Unverdroßenen

Cöthen am 6. Wintermonats[i] im jahre 1646

I

Fürst Ludwigs Erklärung über die Aufnahme Johann Valentin Andreaes in die Fruchtbringende Gesellschaft

Q HM Köthen: V S 545, Bl. 43r; eigenh. Konzept F. Ludwigs. — D: *KE*, 207f., Anm. 2. Vgl. *Keller: Akademien der Renaissance*, 107 u. *Begemann: FG und Andreä*, 44.

Der Zettel so absonderlich zu schreiben und mit einzulegen[1]

Herr Johannes Valentinus Andreæ, kann, wiewol dergleichen geistlichen[a] noch nicht in die Fruchtbringende geselschaft gekommen, auf geschehenes ansuchen gar wol eingenommen werden: Weil aus seinen erbaulichen schriften, die er bisher ausgelaßen, so viel zu sehen und zu spuren, das er sonder zweiffel einen verträglichen geselschafter in bruderlicher Christlicher liebe geben wird Und wie er sich bisher des streitens zu seinem großen nachruhme enthoben, so zweiffelt man nicht er auch ferner die Christliche gemeine furters zu ihrer seligkeit erbauen werde.

Das gemählde kann bleiben das Moß am baume[,] der Nahme der Mürbe, weil sich Müde auf kein Kraut schicket, das wort, bleibet doch Frisch,

Dieses wird auf gutachten etlicher erfarener geselschafter uberschrieben, und ist man hieruber fernerer nachricht gewertig.

II

Fürst Ludwig informiert Carl Gustav von Hille über den Ausführenden, Hans Ernst von Freyberg

Q HM Köthen: VS 545, Bl. 43r; eigenh. Konzept F. Ludwigs. — D: *KE*, 207f., Anm. 2. Vgl. *Begemann: FG und Andreä*, 44.

Der ander Zettel[1] ist kurtz also zu machen.
Der Ausfurende ist Hans Ernst von Freiberg[2] an ietzo Fürstlicher Anhaltischer hofmeister zu Hatzgeroda.

T **a** *Adressenangabe von F. Ludwigs H.* — **b** *Gebessert aus* zukommen — **c** *Gebessert aus* dieses iahres — **d** *Ersetzt* <die Einnehmung des> — **e** *Von F. Ludwigs H. eingefügt; es*

461106 Fürst Ludwig 1047

folgt <in die> — f *Eingefügt bis* hierbey. *Direkt daran anschließend die Streichung:* <betreffende, wiewol bisher dergleichen geistliche nicht hinein kommen, so wird es doch dahin gestellet, woferne seine erklerung also sein wird, das er sich als ein verträglicher geselschafter, in brüderlicher Christlicher liebe, gegen alle Geselschafter bezeigen, und nichts in schmäh- oder streit schriften wieder dieselbe sondern vielmehr nur was zum Christenthume erbaulich **inmaßen aus seinen bisherigen ausgelegten schriften und auch mit billichem aufnehmen vermercket worden, ferner wirt** schreiben und ausgehen laßen wolle, das er dan gar <wolle> wol könne eingenommen werden, das gemählde kan bleiben, <das> der Moß am baume, der Nahme **sol**<te> **seyn der Mürbe weil Müde sich uf kein kraut schicke** <oder Weiche>, das wort, bleibet doch frisch, <oder helt an>. Und ist man hierüber fernerer nachricht gewertig, <welcher nahme oder welches wort beliebet worden.> *F. Ludwigs Verbesserungen hier fett ausgezeichnet.* — g *Von F. Ludwig gebessert aus* wüntschung — h *Von F. Ludwig gebessert aus* wird — i *Gebessert aus* Weinmonats

T I a *Folgt* <bisher>

K 1 Der braunschweig.-wolfenbüttel. Frauenhofmeister Carl Gustav v. Hille (FG 302. Der Unverdrossene) führte den fruchtbringerischen Briefwechsel Hz. Augusts d. J. v. Braunschweig-Wolfenbüttel (FG 227) mit F. Ludwig (Der Nährende) in Köthen.
2 S. Hilles Briefe 460718 u. 460915A an F. Ludwig. Ein weiterer Brief, den Hille in 460915A u. 461029 erwähnt, scheint den Fürsten nicht erreicht zu haben. Hilles Schreiben 461029 erwähnt F. Ludwig im vorliegenden Brief nicht.
3 *GB 1646.* F. Ludwig schickt Hille mit *DA Köthen I. 8:* 470122 ein Exemplar des Gesellschaftsbuchs. Zu den Köthener Drucken, die im Besitz Hilles nachweisbar sind, vgl. 440130 K 2.
4 F. Ludwigs Erklärung über die Aufnahme Johann Valentin Andreaes (FG 464. Der Mürbe. 1646) in die FG in Beil. I. Diese Erklärung hatte F. Ludwig zunächst in den vorliegenden Brief aufgenommen, dann aber gestrichen (s. T f) und auf einem gesonderten Zettel in Reinschrift festhalten lassen, vermutlich, um die Weiterleitung des Textes an Andreae zu erleichtern. Tatsächlich erscheint ein aufgeklebter Zettel mit dieser Erklärung in Hz. Augusts Brief 461117 an Andreae. Vgl. K I 1. Vgl. zur Aufnahme Andreaes 461117 K 1 u. K I 1.
5 *Hille: Teutscher Palmbaum* (1647). S. 451008 K 2. Hille sandte dem Fürsten das Manuskript nicht zur Beratung, Ergänzung oder Korrektur. Vgl. 461029 K 6.
6 F. Ludwig scheute sich, Einzelheiten des burlesken Aufnahmerituals der Hänselung und der Rolle des „Ölbergers" dabei an die Öffentlichkeit dringen zu lassen. S. zur Hänselung in der FG 460718 K 8.
7 *Gueintz: Rechtschreibung (1645).*
8 Hans Ernst v. Freyberg (FG 140. Der Ausführende), Hofmeister F. Friedrichs v. Anhalt-Harzgerode (FG 62) sandte Hille eine farbige Visierung seiner FG-Imprese, die schwarz-weiß in *Conermann II* (Die Weimarer Gemälde der Fruchtbringenden Kräuter, d. i. *Weimarer Impresen*, Nr. 464) zur Abbildung gelangte. Hilles in Kupfer gestochene Imprese im *GB 1646.* S. *Conermann III*, 340.
9 In Harzgerode wurden also damals Impresen u. Wappen auf Atlas gestickt. Wahrscheinlich stickte F. Friedrichs Gattin Johanna Elisabeth (7.1.1619 – 2.3.1647), die Tochter F. Johann Ludwigs v. Nassau-Hadamar (FG 170), damals zusammen mit Hofdamen Impresen u. Wappen der FG. Zu den daraus zusammengehefteten Gobelins als Wandschmuck des Köthener Schlosses s. *Conermann: Nachlaßinventar,* 74f. Andreas Heidfeld

in Quedlinburg wird also ein Amtmann oder Kaufmann u. kein Seidensticker gewesen sein. Das Wappen Hilles ist abgebildet im *GB Kö.* II (Abb. *in Conermann II*, Wappen Nr. 302). S. *Conermann III*, 340.

    10 Gottfried Müller (FG 353. Der Aufweckende). Dieser Name fiel in Wolfenbüttel wohl deshalb auf, weil die dem *GB 1641* beigedruckte Mitgliederliste (mit Klarnamen!) mit Gottfried Müller als 353. Mitglied endet. Vgl. 450126 K 11. Zu den „Streitigkeiten" über die Identität Müllers am Wolfenbütteler Hof s. 460915 A.

    11 Das Konzept oder die Kopie einer Mitgliederliste liegt nicht im Köthener Erzschrein. Der 432. Gesellschafter war Pz. Friedrich v. Sachsen-Weimar (Der Friedenreiche. 1645). Die Liste dürfte den Gesellschafter Eberhard v. Sickingen (FG 463. Der Nachstellende) nicht mehr verzeichnet haben, der am 24.10.1646 zusammen mit den Hofleuten FG 460 bis FG 462 von Pgf. Ludwig Philipp v. Simmern (FG 97) in die Gesellschaft aufgenommen worden war. Der Bericht des Pfalzgrafen über die Aufnahme dieser vier Kandidaten ging zwar mit 461031 A an F. Ludwig, hat diesen aber höchstwahrscheinlich nicht mehr bis zum 6.11.1646 erreicht. Somit ging die Liste kaum weiter als bis zur FG-Nr. 456 (Johann v. Haxthausen. 1646), da die beiden Folgenden FG 457 (Hans v. Wallwitz) u. FG 458 (dessen Bruder Bastian) laut deren Eintragung im *GB Kö.* (am 11.11.1646) nach dem 6.11.1646 in die FG eingetreten sind.

K I 1 F. Ludwig überließ dieses Konzept einem Schreiber, dessen Abschrift dem Brief an Hille beigegeben u. in 461117 aufgeklebt als Brief Hz. Augusts v. Braunschweig-Wolfenbüttel (FG 227) an Andreae weitergeschickt wurde. Zu den Änderungen der Impresenvorschläge Andreaes s. 460909 u. 460915 A I. Vgl. auch *Conermann III*, 563; zur Aufnahme Andreaes in die FG 461117 K 1.

K II 1 Anweisung F. Ludwigs an den Schreiber. Vgl. K I 1.
    2 Zu Hans Ernst v. Freyberg (FG 140. Der Ausführende) s. K 8.

461117

Herzog August d. J. von Braunschweig-Wolfenbüttel schickt Johann Valentin Andreae Fürst Ludwigs Aufnahmebrief

Hz. August d. J. v. Braunschweig-Wolfenbüttel (FG 227) schickt Johann Valentin Andreae einen Zettel F. Ludwigs, auf dem dieser auf Ersuchen Hz. Augusts und gemäß dem Gutachten erfahrener Gesellschafter der Aufnahme Andreaes (FG 464. 1646) in die FG zustimmt. Obgleich Geistliche wie Andreae bisher nicht zugelassen wurden, sei dies im vorliegenden Fall unbedenklich, weil Andreae nach Ausweis seiner erbaulichen Schriften erwarten lasse, sich in der FG in christlicher Liebe verträglich und friedfertig zu bezeigen. Wie er bisher keine Streitlust an den Tag gelegt habe, werde er auch künftig dazu beitragen, die christliche Gemeinde zu einen. — Seine von ihm vorgeschlagene Impresenpflanze kann ohne Änderung das Moos am Baum bleiben, das Wort soll „bleibet doch frisch" sein. Der Gesellschaftsname müsse von *Der Müde* zu *Der Mürbe* geändert werden, da *Der Müde* auf keine Pflanze passe. — F. Ludwig erbittet eine Antwort.

Q HAB: Cod. Guelf. 236.3 Extrav., Bl. 47rv [A: 47v]; H. v. F. Ludwigs Schreiber, eigenh. Zusatz u. Adresse v. Hz. August. Andreaes eigenh. Briefdatierung und -numerierung. Zit. in *Keller: Akademien der Renaissance*, 107 u. *Begemann: FG und Andreae*, 44. —

461117 Herzog August d. J. von Braunschweig-Wolfenbüttel

F. Ludwig sandte sein Erklärung an Carl Gustav v. Hille (FG 302) als Beilage zu seinem Brief 461106: Vgl. dort als Beil. I. — Die Beilage F. Ludwigs aus dem Brief an Hille schickte Hz. August mit seiner Notiz als Beilage zu seinem Brief v. 17.11.1646 an Andreae (HAB: Cod. Guelf. 236.3 Extrav., Bl. 45rv). „Was unser Director von dem Mürben anhero gesandt, wird er empfangen und zu beantworten ihm gefallen lassen." — Andreae vermerkte auf F. Ludwigs Erklärung sein Empfangsdatum vom 13.12.1646 und setzte über den Text des Fürsten eine Überschrift. Der Brief Hz. Augusts und F. Ludwigs Erklärung wurden also zusammen versandt, die Erklärung ist aber nicht, wie Begemann (S. 44) behauptet, bloß irgendeine aufgeklebte Abschrift, sondern stellt Ludwigs Ausfertigung dar, auf die Hz. August seine Bemerkung über die Herkunft und Übermittlung des Köthener Dokuments und rückseitig die Anschrift an Andreae setzte.

A Dem Ehrwurdigen und Hochgelahrten unserm lieben besondern, Herrn Johan-Valentin Andreæ, der H. Schrift Doctori, und F. Wurtemb. Ober HofPredigern, und Geistlichem Consistorial-Rahte, zu behandigen. Stutgart: 9. Jan. 47.[a]

13. Dec. 46. Ludwig Fürst zu Anhalt[b]
Herr Johannes Valentinus Andreæ, kan, wiewol dergleichen Geistlichen noch nicht in die Fruchtbringende Geselschaft gekomen, auf geschehenes ansuchen[1] gar wol eingenomen werden: Weil aus seinen erbaulichen schriften, die er bisher ausgelaßen, so viel zu sehen und zu spüren, das er sonder zweifel einen verträglichen Geselschafter in brüderlicher Christlicher liebe geben werde, Und wie er sich bisher des streitens, zu seinem großen nachruhme, enthalten, so zweifelt man nicht er auch ferner die Christliche gemeine, zu ihrer seligkeit erbauen werde.

Das Gemählde kan bleiben das Moß am baume, der Nahme, der Mürbe, weil sich Müde auf kein Kraut schicket, das Wort, bleibet doch frisch[2]

Dieses wird auf gutachten etzlicher erfarner geselschafter überschrieben, und ist man hierüber fernerer nachricht gewertig.[3]

Vom[c] 6. 9bris 1646. aus Cöthen, Es ist uns, den 17 ejusd. geliefert; und von uns eod. volgr. gesandt &c.

31. 211[d]
36. 216.
46. 222.

T a *Empfangsdatum v. Andreaes H.* — b *Andreaes Empfangsdatum und Überschrift.* — c *Von hier an Zusatz Hz. Augusts.* — d *Andreaes Statistik zur Kontrolle seines Briefwechsels mit dem Herzog (Briefnummern im laufenden Jahr und Anzahl der bis zu dem jeweiligen Brief insgesamt gewechselten Schreiben).*

K 1 Hz. August d. J. v. Braunschweig-Wolfenbüttel (FG 227) hatte sich für die Aufnahme seines Geistlichen Rats, des Stuttgarter Oberhofpredigers Johann Valentin Andreae (1586–1654), in die FG verwandt (vgl. 460915A), obgleich wegen der gefürchteten Streit- und Herrschlust der Geistlichen die FG, die sich zwar als christliche, aber nichtkonfessionelle Gesellschaft verstand, bisher nur in dem Fall des Breslauer Domherren und kath. Priesters Nicolaus (v.) Troilo (FG 142), eines Freundes des ref. Hz.s Georg Rudolph in Schlesien zu Liegnitz und Wohlau (FG 58), eine Ausnahme gemacht hatte. Andreae, der sich in jugendlichem Alter im geheimen Zirkel der Rosenkreuzer mit vielen Schriften für eine Erneuerung und Fortsetzung der Reformation eingesetzt hatte und auch weiterhin für eine Frömmigkeitsreform (auch mittels Gesellschaftsgründungen: Societas Christiana, Unio Christiana, s. 420601 u. 420627) eingetreten war, war gewiß ein irenisch gesinnter Theologe, der deshalb auch die unter Lutheranern höchst verdächtige sprachliche Revision der Lutherbibel durch die *Evangelische Kirchen-Harmonie* (1646 ff.) Hz. Augusts unermüdlich durch Ratschläge, Gedichte und Vorreden förderte. S. 411214 u. ö. Kurz nach Andreae wurde auch der bedeutende Dichter und lutherische Pfarrer Johann Rist (FG 467. 1647) in die FG aufgenommen. Vgl. zur Aufnahme Andreaes 460804, 460819, 460908, 460915A u. I, 461029, 461106 u. I, 461216 u. I u. II; *DA Köthen I. 8:* 470112 u. 470122.

2 Andreae hatte in 460715 I Philipp Hainhofer seine Vorstellung von einer Imprese mitgeteilt, die Hz. August d. J. v. Braunschweig-Wolfenbüttel Carl Gustav v. Hille (FG 302) und dieser F. Ludwig schickte. Danach sollte das Gemälde ein an einem morschen Baum wachsendes Moos darstellen, das Wort „Hernach" und der Gesellschaftsname „der Müde" lauten. Vgl. auch 460915A u. *KE,* 206 Anm. 1. Zur Abfassung und zum Text des Reimgesetzes s. *Conermann III,* 563. Abb. der Visierung von Andreaes Imprese in *Conermann II,* s. 461106 K 9.

3 Andreae bedankte sich am 16.12. und 17.12.1646 auf Deutsch bzw. auf Lateinisch. S. 461216. Diese Erklärungen erreichten F. Ludwig als Beilagen zu Hilles Brief *DA Köthen I. 8:* 470112.

461124

Fürst Ludwig an Fürst Johann Casimir von Anhalt-Dessau

F. Ludwig übersendet den Brief mit jemandem, der etliche zusammengebundene, vor Jahren erschienene frz. Abhandlungen von (Pierre) Du Moulin (d. Ä.), die Oberst (Diederich v. dem) Werder (FG 31) bei F. Johann Casimirs (FG 10) Gemahlin (Agnes) hinterlassen hatte, abholen soll. Wie er Johann Casimir kürzlich bei dessen Besuch in Köthen mitgeteilt habe, brauche er sie, weil etliche Sachen daraus ins Deutsche übersetzt jetzt gedruckt werden sollen. Da bisher keine Reaktion auf diese erfolgt sei, erbittet F. Ludwig nochmals diese Traktate zurück, um den Druck zu beschleunigen, bietet zugleich aber an, sie nach Benutzung wieder nach Dessau zurückzuschicken. Die Herzöge v. Sachsen-Lauenburg waren bei F. Ludwig und bei Johann Casimir, es seien ganz passable Burschen. Der Regen hat verhindert, daß Ludwig an Johann Casimirs Jagd teilnahm, vielleicht kann es morgen oder später nachgeholt werden. F. Ludwig will erfahren, ob der Kf. (Johann Georg I.) v. Sachsen noch in Wittenberg sei. Man sei mit ihm bei der schwed. Generalität sehr unzufrieden wegen ausstehender bewilligter Zahlungen.

Q LHA Sa.-Anh./ Dessau: Z 44 Abt. Dessau A 10 Nr. 44, Bl. 93r–94v; eigenh.

A *Fehlt.*

Hochgeborner Fürst, freundlicher vielgeliebter herr Vetter und gevatter,
  EL. erinnern sich freundvetterlich, das ich jüngsten bey Dero anwesenheit

alhier, etlicher frantzösischen büchlein, die **Monsieur de Moulins**[1] fur Jharen ausgehen laßen, und der Obriste Werder[2] El. gemahlin[3] zugestellet, erwehnet, das ich deren, zwar zusammen gebunden, darum benötiget, weil etliche sachen daraus verdeutschet[a] ietzo gedrucket werden[4], das solcher druck desto geschwinder und gebürlicher fortgehe. Weilen ich dan von EL. deswegen noch keine antwort erlanget, als ersuche ich sie freundvetterlichen, sie es nochmals nechst freundlicher begrüßung meiner seits bey El. gemahlin dahin richten wollen; das ich vorgemeldete zusammen gebundene frantzösische tractätlein bey zeigern, zu vorgemeldetem ende wieder anher bekommen möge. Jch bin des freundlichen erbietens El. gemahlin, auf begeren daßelbe so[b] bald man es nicht mehr bedarf und ein mehrers, auf wiedersendung, gerne wieder abfolgen zu laßen.

Wan die hertzoge zu Sachsen lauenburg[5] mit meiner wenigen bewirtung alhier zufrieden gewesen, werde [93v] ich gerne vernemen, wie auch das EL. mit ihnen lustig gewesen. Es ist mit ihnen noch durchzukommen. Jch habe heute El. hasen hetzen und[c] jagd, so sie in dem meinigen vorgeschlagen, besehen wollen, es hat mich aber der regen abgehalten, ich wil es morgen, wan es wetter, oder mit ehesten thun, und dan mich gegen El. zu erkleren nicht unterlaßen.

Ob der Churfürst zu Sachsen[6] in der nähe bey Wittenberg[,] werden mir El. berichten können. Bey der Schwedischen **Generalität** ist man sehr übel mit ihme zufrieden, das er von dem gewilligeten dieses Jhares noch nichts gezalet[7], so ich El. vertraulich nicht verhalten sollen, es dürfte ein mal wieder böse nachbarn geben. Jch befele El.in den schutz götlicher Almacht, und verbleibe

El. getreuer Vetter
Ludwig fzu Anhalt
Cöthen den 24 Wintermonats 1646.

T a *Folgt* <an> — b *Bis* bedarf *am Rand ergänzt.* — c und jagd *eingefügt.*

K 1 Pierre Du Moulin d. Ä. (Petrus Molinaeus) (1568–1658), französ. hugenott. Theologe u. Professor, stammte aus Buhy im Vexin, studierte an der calvinist. Académie de Sedan, später in London u. Cambridge u. schließlich 1592 in Leiden, wo er auch einige Jahre lehrte. Nach dem Edikt von Nantes (1598) nach Frankreich zurückgekehrt, übernahm Du Moulin ein Kirchenamt der hugenott. Kirche in Paris u. später in Charenton-le-Pont. Auf Einladung Kg. Jakobs I. reiste er 1615 nach England zurück, wo er eine Präbende an der Kathedrale zu Canterbury erhielt. Während die Situation in Frankreich für Hugenotten immer schwieriger wurde, die sich gegen Kg. Ludwig XIII. erhoben, floh er 1621 nach der Zerstörung des „Tempels" von Charenton abermals nach Sedan, wo er als Professor bis zu seinem Tod lehrte. S. Lucien Rimbault: Pierre du Moulin 1568–1658, un pasteur classique à l'âge classique, étude de théologie pastorale sur des documents inédits. Paris 1966.

2 Diederich v. dem Werder (FG 31), schwed. u. kurbrandenburg. Obrist.

3 Lgfn. Agnes v. Hessen-Kassel (1606–1650), die Tochter von Lgf. Moritz (FG 80) u. Halbschwester von Lgf. Wilhelm V. (FG 65), war seit 1623 mit F. Johann Casimir v. Anhalt-Dessau (FG 10) verheiratet.

4 1646 wurden im Verlag von Andreas Betzel († 1655) in Zerbst die Übersetzung dreier Traktate Du Moulins gedruckt: Pierre du Moulin: Drey Erbauliche Büchlein Herren Petri

von Moulins Fürnehmen Predigers und Professoris in der Theologi zu Sedan 1. Wieder die Barbarey oder von unbekanter Sprache in den gebeten und bey dem Gottesdienste. 2. Gegensatz der Heiligen Schrift wieder die Lehre der Römischen Kirche. 3. Neuer Vorrath oder Zusatz zu dem Babylonischen gebeude ... Aus dem Frantzösischen ins Deutsche übergesetzet (Zerbst: Betzel 1646). HAB: 817.65 Theol. (3).

5 Im Rahmen eines Besuches von Hz. Franz Carl (FG 269) u. Hz. Julius Heinrich v. Sachsen-Lauenburg (FG 311) bei F. Ludwig in Köthen im November 1646 wurde des letzteren Sohn, der 17-jährige Hz. Franz Erdmann, unter Nr. 459 in die FG aufgenommen. Drei weitere Onkel des Neuaufgenommenen waren ebenfalls aktuelle FG-Mitglieder: der regierende Hz. August v. Sachsen-Lauenburg (FG 294), Hz. Rudolf Maximilian (FG 283) u. Hz. Franz Heinrich (FG 234). Ein weiterer Onkel u. ebenfalls FG-Mitglied, Hz. Franz Albrecht v. Sachsen-Lauenburg (FG 194), war bereits 1642 als ksl. Generalleutnant gefallen. S. *Conermann III*, 196–198, 255 f., 298–300, 318, 330 f., 352 f. u. 553 f.

6 Kf. Johann Georg I. v. Sachsen (1585–1656).

7 Gemäß dem schwed.-kursächs. Waffenstillstand von Eilenburg vom 31. März 1646 hatte sich der Kurfürst von Sachsen verpflichtet, bis zum Kriegsende oder dem Abschluß eines allgemeinen Waffenstillstandes monatlich 8.000 Reichstaler an die schwed. Kriegskasse zu Leipzig, dazu jährlich 5.000 Scheffel Getreide Leipziger Maß an das dortige Kriegsmagazin sowie ein monatliches Deputat an Heu, Hafer u. Stroh auf die in Leipzig stationierten schwed. Reiter zu zahlen. S. Karl Gustav Helbig: Die sächsisch-schwedischen Verhandlungen zu Kötzschenbroda und Eilenburg 1645 und 1646. In: Archiv für die sächsische Geschichte 5 (1867), 264–288. Dort (S. 283–288) auch ein Abdruck des Vertragstextes von Eilenburg. Trotz einer nachverhandelten Ermäßigung, die für das erste Jahr die Zahlung auf 7.000 Reichstaler senkte u. den Zahlungsbeginn auf den Mai verlegte, war die Zahlungsfähigkeit Kursachsens genauso wie dessen Zahlungsmoral jedoch alles andere als gut. So waren z. B. Mitte Oktober 1646 von den ab Mai des Jahres eigentlich zu zahlenden 42.000 Reichstalern noch über 29.000 Reichstaler, d. h. mehr als zwei Drittel, unbezahlt. S. dazu Alexander Zirr: Die Schweden in Kursachsen. Eine Untersuchung zur Besetzung Leipzigs im Spannungsfeld zwischen Dreißigjährigem Krieg und Westfälischem Frieden (1642–1650). Diss. (MS) Univ. Leipzig 2015, 650–653 u. 702–708.

461204

Herzog August d. J. von Braunschweig-Wolfenbüttel schickt Johann Valentin Andreae einen Auszug aus Jacob Wellers Kritik an seiner *Evangelischen Kirchen-Harmonie*

Jacob Weller will Hz. August d. J. v. Braunschweig-Wolfenbüttel (FG 227) vertraulich seinen Eindruck von dessen *Hand-Büchlein aus Der Evangelischen KirchenHarmonie* (1646. 12°) offenbaren, obgleich er das Buch nach dessen Einbindung nur soeben erhalten und darin bisher bloß geblättert habe. Er erdreiste sich darum nicht, darüber ausführlich zu urteilen. Es bestehe die Gefahr, auch ohne böse Absicht das Buch mißzuverstehen. — Weller lobt den gutgemeinten Fleiß, den der Herzog dem Wort Gottes angedeihen ließ und wünscht ihm und Hzn. Sophia Elisabeth (AL 1629, TG 42b) ein glückliches neues Jahr. — Gottes Wort in dieser Form zu predigen und im Gottesdienst statt der Predigt vorlesen zu lassen, rufe aber die Gegner auf den Plan und sei für den einfältigen Gläubigen schwer zu verstehen und zu behalten. Einhundert Jahre habe es gebraucht, um diesem die

Perikopentexte in etwa beizubringen; genausolang werde es dauern, um sie ihm wieder abzugewöhnen. — Weller versucht, durch Vergleiche des biblischen Texts mit Hz. Augusts Bibelharmonie beispielhaft zu erweisen, wie sehr dessen (schlicht-gegenständliche) Redeweise dogmatisch die notwendig figürliche Deutung gefährde und theologische Neuerungen einführe. August vermische unterschiedliche biblische Erzählungen, unterscheide dabei für die meisten Gläubigen nur undeutlich zwischen Gesetz und Evangelium oder schwäche Hinweise auf Christi Allmacht. Auch gelte es, in der Theologie unnötige Neuerung zu meiden. Der Herzog schaffe Verwirrung in der Wiedergabe der biblischen Erzählung und rede ungewohntes, aus dem Griechischen entlehntes Deutsch, er weiche ungewissen Glaubenssachen und dunklen Bibelstellen nicht aus. Man müsse mit dem Volk verständlich reden, aber wie ein Gelehrter denken. Anstatt Biblisches auszuschmücken und sich über Bibelworte ungewisse eigene Gedanken zu machen, solle der Herzog das Bibelwort einfach vorlesen lassen bzw. Theologen dazu befragen. Lasse er seine Kirchenharmonie mit Gewalt von der Kanzel verbreiten, könne er Zweifler animieren und seinen Namen in Verruf bringen.

Q HAB: Cod. Guelf. 236.3 Extrav., Bl. 102r–103v, 103v leer. Eigenh. Abschrift Hz. Augusts, die dieser z.B. wie 461106 an Johann Valentin Andreae (FG 464. 1647) schickte und die dieser gemäß seiner eigenen Notiz am 4.2.1647 erhielt. Abschrift v. Schreiberh. NSTA Wolfenbüttel: 2 Alt Nr. 14956, Bl. 23. In T I werden unter der Sigle *STA* nur inhaltliche Abweichungen vermerkt. — Kurzes Zitat in Ernst L. Th. Henke: Georg Calixtus und seine Zeit. Bd. 2, Abt. 2. Halle 1860, 54 Anm. 2 nach den „Consistorial Acten", inc. „Laudo conatum". — BN: Wolf-Dieter Otte: Die neueren Handschriften der Gruppe Extravagantes. 3 Bde. Frankfurt a. M. 1986–1989, Bd. 3, S. 46.

A *Fehlt.*

Extract eines Skreibens[1] aus Dresden vom 4. Xbr. 1646, D. J. W. ad **.[a]

Was Illustrissimi Harmoniam anlanget, wil ich zwar auf begehren, dem Herren mein gedanken in geheim offenbaren, dan weil ich es erst gebunden bekommen, und hin und her etwas geblättert, und also nicht mit fleis alles betrachtet, wäre es eine Temeritz[2] davon viele ullam partem, zu judicieren, kunte man auch leicht, welches dann à qvovis geschehen kan, da auch keine malitia animi verhanden, ein und das andere anders deuten als es zu verstehen. Laudo conatum, et in verbo Dei diligentiam Sereniss.[i] Jesus conservet[aa] eum, Ecclesiæ quam diutissimè adhuc et concedat Ipsi ac Soboli Illustrissimæ felicissimum et benedictissimum novum Annum per Jesum Christum, impleat omnes cordis ejus pias cogitationes; wird auch gewis das Lob nicht sterben: Allein es pro concione und in der Kirchen offentlich ablesen zu lassen, ist gewis (1) gefährlich, (2) der Evangelischen Kirchen præjudicierlich (3) denen Adversariis zu ärgern und lästern beqväm (4) so gar bey dem gemeinen man, solcher gestalt (loqvor de imperitis planè, periti non domi non sine egregio fructu eam legent) nicht erbaulich, daß es ihn vielmehr (a) turbiren wird im gedechtnus (b) swer seyn wird zu verstehen, und wol (c) fast zu behalten unmüglich. Man hat nuhn über 100 Jahr, ein wenig imperitæ plebi die pericopas Evangelii eingebläuet, länger als 100 Jahr, wird man haben müssen, ehe sie diese auslerneten. Ich wil dem herren nuhr ein und das ander Exempel anziehen, daraus vernünftig zu ermessen seyn wird, daß pro concione und offentlich in der Kirchen solches einzuführen, wol nicht so guth getahn sey. Dan (1) Dom. 18. Trin. wird in eine Harmoniam gebracht, Matth. Marc. Lucas: da doch circumstantia Temporis et rei bezeugt, bevoraus auch der Persohnen beschaffenheit, daß es distinctæ Historiæ.[bb] Zum andern lese der Herr v. 28 kaumpts[b] wird er die Harmoniam vernehmen, daß nicht Legis et Evangelii confusio daraus solte erwaxen, welches doch ein fundamental Artikel ist. Novi Sereniss. id non intendere: At qvi legit, nisi optimè hic sit versatus, et cautè [102v] informatus, Evangelii et Legis confusionem vix evitabit. Dan das Sezze es nuhr ins werk,[3] aliò commodè referri non poterit, qvàm ad id quid de amore in Deum et proximum ex lege erat dictum. Undè Christus non cognoscitur, qvum Lex et iram operatur et cognitionem peti saltem largeatur. (2) Im nächsten[4] Evangelio, sezzet ihre Durchl. Jedoch will Er sie bald[c] wieder anhero zu rukke senden;[5] Ziehet also das ἀποστελεῖ auf Christum, und sezzet hierinne persuadendi vim, damit sie die Eselin liessen hinführen. Allein wie (a) solches das argumentum, so pro omnipotentiâ Christi daher formieret wird, fast enerviret, also ist (b) der erste, so viel ich ex antiqvitate observieret, der diese glosse gemachet, ein Arrianizans, wie denen Criticis samptlichen woll bekandt: dan ob gleich das argumentum, welches pro omnipotentia Christi, in summo exinanitionis statu dahero von frommen formieret wird, weil Er die herzen der menschen,[d] die sonsten auf das ihrige so erpichtet, daß sie das leben wol darüber lassen, gelenket, nicht more humano persvasorio, sed virtute divina in verbis se exerenti vilibus, nicht eben ist apodicticum, et in acie contra adversarios collocandum, so ist doch einem Christen herzen lieb und angenehm, wan er etwa vestigia der Gotheit und Allmacht Jesu Christi, auch in dem stande der erniedrigung antrieffe: dan hiedurch wird er gewaltig getröstet. Und es heisset ohne das, terminos antiqvos nè facilè moveas: und soll man ja alle neuerung, wo nicht es summa necessitz urgieret, bevoraus in Theologicis meyden. (3) Eben in diesem Evangelio stehet: Er ritte aber auf derselben etc.[e][6] scheinet eine widerwertige rede zu seyn. Dan ist er schon über den Oelberg[7] (was olivenberg, wasserkumme etc. sey, werden viele deutsche Nationes nicht verstehen, und es wird lange mühe bedürffen, bis man dem gemeinen Manne so viele neue Arten[cc] kan beybringen). In Philosophia heisset es, Loqvendum est cum vulgo, sentiendum cum Eruditis. Wie vielmehr soll es wegen erbauung des gemeinen Mannes also heissen, in Theologia practicâ,[f] (da zu wünschen, daß wir alle nuhr einerley wort führeten) bis ans Stad Tohr darauf geritten, wie hat er sich dan erst vor demselben darauf gesezzet: (4) Kein recht Deutscher hat Jehmahls also geredet, wie in dem handbüchlein p. 288 geredet wird, in dem viele Junger zu Christo führen:[g][8] Græci sic loqvuntur, non Germani. Item nuhn ist des menschen Sohn herlich geworden:[9] dergleichen part 2. [103r] Harmoniæ. p. 258, O ihr grobe und unverstandige Narren, und eines solchen herzens, welches so längsam und träg ist den allen zu glauben:[10] Was von der badstuben,[11] p. 127 von dem fassen, zukken und rütteln des todten mägdleins (qvæ verbo, majestatico Christi mandato non adeo convenire vidente)[12] von der gefahr und noht des sterbens am Sabbath,[13] und derer dinge mehr, da nuhr im Evang. 2. Dom. Adventus[14] unterschiedlich zu erinnern: Item da man ungewisse sachen, als gar gewisse, der ich schon ein und das ander gemerket, herein gesezzet: Als daß <u>das weib Jairi, vor die tühr auf die gassen, Christo sol seyn entgegen gegangen</u>, da doch aus Marco das contrarium fast wol zu erhärten, (der herr lese unbesweret c. 5 Marci, da gedacht wird, Christus habe ihm niemand lassen nachfolgen, als Pet. Jac. und Joh. darnach da er in das haus schon kommen, alle ausgetrieben habe er[h] umb sich in das gemach, da das mägdlein lag, genommen die mutter die also in dem hause seiner gewartet, der auch dem lauffen auf die gassen, bey solcher mänge nicht wol wurde angestanden haben) daß Christus in die nächste bey ihm stehende Sallath Schussel getunket, darin auch Judas getunket *etc.* mag ich izzo nicht berühren, es konte leicht übel gedeutet werden. Und ist hie wol zu merken, daß in ablesung des Textes, Gottes wort sol gelesen werden, nicht aber dieses oder Jehnes gedanken: darumb es sich mit den Zweifelsworten Etwa, in ablesung des Textes so wol nicht reymen wil, welches gleichwol unterschiedlich stehet: daß ich wol wünschen möchte, Jhr fl. Durchl. hätte zuvor verständigen Theologen die Sache communicieret, oder aber führete es nicht auf die Canzel ein.[15] Dan solte es also mit gewalt getrieben werden, dörfte sich etwa auch wol ein scepticü[i] ingenium finden, oder ja ein anderer, der viele desiderieren dörfte; dadurch gewis der vortrefliche nahme et reliquæ virtutes, nicht wenig durften besmuzzet werden. Ich skreibe es dem herren auf sein begehren in vertrauen. Kan er etwa helfen, daß in die Kirche solches nicht introducieret werde, tuht er ein guten dienst. Dan sonsten möchte ein ärgernis daraus entstehen. Sed hæc in sinum amici. Thu hiemit sliessen.

T a *Lies:* Doctor Jacob Weller ad [an Hz. August bzw. an ihn als Verfasser des in K 3 zit. *Hand-Büchleins*, das bei den Gebrüdern Stern erschienen war] — **b** *Lies:* kaum — **c** *Folgt* <anhero> — **d** *Folgt Wortanfang* <ge> — **e** *Marginalnote* Non perlegit Errata et Gram., die Palmarum describtam. Sic. — **f** *Eingefügt von* practicâ *bis* führeten) — **g** *Randnotiz* Andreaes 137. — **h** *Folgt* <auch> — **i** *Statt fehlerhaftem* scopticü

T I aa *STA* conservat — **bb** *STA Marginalnote* NB *von unbekannter H.* — **cc** *STA Marginalnote* Non perlegit Errata et Harmoniam, die Palmarum describta. Sic.

K 1 Zu Andreaes Zurückweisung einer reformatorischen und lutherkritischen Absicht des Herzogs s. 461216 K 3. — Jacob Weller (1602–1664), ehemaliger Theologe in Wittenberg und 1641–1646 Superintendent in Braunschweig, trat 1646 als Dresdner Oberhofprediger an die Stelle Höes v. Höenegg. In diesem angesehensten und einflußreichsten Amt des deutschen Luthertums vertrat er zusammen mit Johann Hülsemann und Abraham Calovius die Position der luther. Orthodoxie im Synkretismus-Streit gegen die Calixtianer an der braunschweig.-lüneburg. Universität Helmstedt. Veranlaßt durch Konrad Hornejus' Schrift *de summa fidei quae per caritatem operatur necessitate ad salutem* vereinbarten Weller und die kursächsischen und jenaischen Theologen am 29.12.1646, also in der Zeit des vorliegenden Briefs, mit Johann Hülsemann eine *Admonitio*, die Calixtus und seinen Anhängern die Verletzung der Konkordienformel vorwarf. — Vgl. außerdem Georg Calixtus' Briefwechsel. In einer Auswahl aus Wolfenbüttelschen Handschriften herausgegeben von Dr. Ernst Ludw. Th. Henke. Halle 1833, 108f. u. bes. E. L. Th. Henke: Georg Calixtus und seine Zeit. Bd.2, Abt. 1–2. Halle 1856–1860. Dort auch Bd. II.2, 50ff. über die Rezeption der *Evangelischen Kirchen-Harmonie* Hz. Augusts. Burckhard: *Bibliotheca Augusta* I, 75–98; Rehtmeier: *Braunschweig-Lüneburgische Chronica* III, 531, 543, 584–586. Zu Weller vgl. im übrigen Johann Andreas Gleich: Leben der sächs. Oberhofprediger. In ders.: Annales ecclesiastici, oder, Gründliche Nachrichten der Reformations-Historie chur-sächs. albertinischer Linie: wobey zugleich von der churfl. sächs. Schloss-Kirche zu Dressden, und dem darinnen angeordneten Gottes-Dienste gehandelt wird (Dresden, Leipzig 1730), Tl. 2, 207–312; August Tholuck: Der Geist der lutherischen Theologen Wittenbergs im Verlaufe des 17. Jahrhunderts. Hamburg 1852, 171–185. — Die *Evangelische Kirchen-Harmonie* Hz. Augusts d.J. v. Braunschweig-Wolfenbüttel (FG 227) war von Anfang an auf die Kritik orthodoxer, aber auch frömmigkeitsreformerischer oder irenischer Lutheraner wie Johann Saubert d. Ä. und Georg Calixtus gestoßen. S. 380000, 411214, 451001 u. Burckhard: *Bibliotheca Augusta* I, 75 (Brief Sauberts 1640). Über die 2. Ausg. der *Passionsharmonie* (1641) Hz. Augusts schrieb Calixt an den Herzog am 11.10.1641 „[...] non putaveram, priorem editionem toties et tantopere à Sere*nit*ate Tuâ mutatam esse, quemadmodum video factum. Metuo ne calumnia, ut in suam rem attenta et solers esse consueuit, occasionem hinc sumat, Ser.^tem Tuam arrodendi, et inconstantiae alicuius arguendi. [...] Ceterùm in concinnandâ Evangelistarum Harmoniâ multa incertæ sunt locationis: et permitti in talibus potest, ut quisque abundet suo sensu: nempe unum vel alterum versiculum aliter ponat, quàm posuerunt alij; vel præponat, quos alij malint postponi." NSTA Wolfenbüttel: 14 Alt Nr. 133, Bl. 23r. Sogar die theologische Fakultät zu Helmstedt kritisierte die hzl. Neuerung in einem Gutachten vom 30.6.1646 als „contra praxin universae ecclesiae". A. a. O., Bl. 68r–79v u. 87r–97r (CONSIDERATIO ACCURATIOR CENSURÆ DOMINORUM LIPSIENSIUM SUPER HARMONIÂ EUANGELIORUM; Et EPISTOLARUM AUGUSTÂ; mit Hz. Augusts Bemerkung „remittatur"). *Rehtmeier: Braunschweig-Lüneburgische Chronica* III, 1447. Auf Betreiben von Augusts Schwägerin, der verwitweten Hzn. Sibylla v. Braunschweig-Dannenberg (1584–1652), die die Evangelienharmonie nicht in ihrem Wittum einführen wollte, kritisierte die Leipziger theologische Fakultät am 24.11.1646 im Werk Augusts den Versuch, das biblische Wort aus dem Gottesdienst zu verbannen, die Vermischung von göttlicher und menschlicher Rede und die Verschlechterung der Sprache Luthers. Das Volk werde verwirrt und in die Papstkirche zurückgetrieben. Vgl. *Henke: Calixtus* II.2, 52f. u. Anm. 1f. Vgl. Sammlung von alten und neuen theologischen Sachen 1729, 546–570. Die braunschweigischen Kirchen sollten dem Edikt Hz. Augusts nicht gehorchen, da es nicht durch sein Jus episcopale und die Facultas legislativa gedeckt sei. Der Herzog berief Joachim Lütkemann, einen Schüler des Straßburger Theologen Johannes Schmidt, 1649 nach Braunschweig. Der lieferte schon am 20.11.1649 ein Gutachten zur Verteidigung des Herzogs ab. S. Zitat in *Henke: Calixtus* II.2, 55 Anm. 55. Nach Henkes Meinung soll die Kirchenharmonie bis zum Jahre 1709 im Gottesdienst vorgetragen worden sein. A. a. O., 56. — Im Unterschied zu Hz. Augusts Schwägerin scheint die durchaus treue Lutheranerin Gfn. Anna Sophia v. Schwarzburg-Rudolstadt (1584–1652; TG 1), die Schwester F. Ludwigs, ebenso wie der Gothaer Theologe Salomon Glass (1593–1653), einer der Hauptarbeiter am Weimarischen Bibelwerk Hz. Ernsts I. v. Sachsen-Gotha (FG 19), keinen Anlaß zur Sorge verspürt oder geäußert zu haben. Glass schrieb am 27.2.1647 an den braunschweig-wolfenbüttelschen Generalsuperintendenten Heinrich Wideburg (1587–1648): „Aliquot modò pagellas operis huius (in octava qvod primùm forma prodiit) ante biennium, nisi fallor, hic vidi, ad Principem Anhaltino-Schwarzburgicam, Cranichfeldi qvae habitat, transmissas, et mihi ostensas; qvae adeò placuêre in veri Scripturarum S. Sensus literalis enucleatione, ut non potuerim non ὁμοψηφίαν ejus mihi vendicare et allegare, in explicatione Evangelii Dom. 2. Adventus; uti propediem in luce publicâ fiet manifestum. Imposterum igitur totum systema praestantissimum licebit mihi perlegere, qvod et summo animi prolubio fiet." NSTA Wolfenbüttel: 2 Alt 14956, Bl. (ungezählt). An einen ungenannten Welfen schrieb Hz. August am 29.1.1647: „Anreichend die weitläuffige anführung gegen die Harmonie, haben wir ausser Gotten, niemand darüber rechnung zu geben: lassen solches so dawider hat wollen angeführet werden, dahin gestellet seyn, und weiß es Gott der herzenkundiger am besten, wohin wir unsere intention, bey diesem Adiaphoro und indifferent Sache, gerichtet, und haben aus der freien Andacht, mit bedacht, diese nuzliche ablesung in dem unsrigen angeordnet." Vermutlich Hz. Friedrich IV. v. Braunschweig-Lüneburg (1574–1648) habe sogar den Adel mit Hilfe seiner Schwester (Sibylla) aufgewiegelt. „Was die Leipziger auf unrechten bericht, etwa herausgeben, wird sich auf anderen rechtern bericht, schon anders ins kunftige finden; [...] Bey nächster Zusammenkunft sollen die unseren, mit eil abgeordneten, sich darüber berufener besprechen: Sonsten haben wir aus fr. vetterlichen willen, nachgeben, daß die Lectio vor dem Altare (wiewol wir in OberSaxischen KirchenOrdnung so vor 100 Jahren angestellet, befinden, daß auch in haltung des gedechtnis mahles unsrs herren Jesu das Vatter unser, mit einer weitläuftigen paraphrasis soll gelesen, werden: wie dan dasselbige deutlich hinein gerukket ist: da wirt doch ausser derselbigen Handlung diese nuhr lesen lassen:) eingestellet werden, In der früe oder Catechismus Predigt aber (die mit grossem schaden der gemeine etliche Jahr, eingestellet und abgeschaffet gewesen, und noch ist) nach geendigtem gebete gelesen werden solle. [...]." A. a. O., Bl. 46r–47r.

2 Lat. temeritas, Verwegenheit, Unverfrorenheit.

3 S. Hand-Büchlein: | aus | Der Evangelischen Kir- | chenHarmonie: Von des HEr- | ren Jesu Ewigen Geburt: Menschwerdung: | Empfängnüs zu Nazareth: Geburt zu Bethlehem: Besneidung: Darstellung in dem | Tempel zu JeruSalem: Beschenkung von | deñ Morgen-Ländischē: Flucht in Aegypten: | Zwelften Jahre: Taufe in dem Jordan: Versuchung in der Wüsten: Einzuge in Jeru- | Salem: Leiden/ Sterben/ und Begräbnüs: | Wieder-Erstehen: Hinauf-Fahrt: und | Sendung des H. Geistes. | [Signet] | Wulfen-Büttel/ Im Jahre | 1646. | In Verlegung der Gebrüder/ | Hans und Heinrichen/ der Sternen. HAB: 1218.3 Theol. (1). Vgl. 411214 III I. — Die von Weller zitierte Stelle gibt die Formulierung des Herzogs in seiner Perikope auf den „XVIII. Tag des HErren" wieder, welche sich auf Mt 22, Mk 12 u. Lk 20 stützt. *Hand-Büchlein*, 684. Nachdem Jesu im Gespräch mit den Schriftgelehrten die beiden obersten Gebote gelehrt und einer der Gelehrten ihm zugestimmt hatte, antwortete Jesus V. 28 (nach Mk 12, 34): „Siehe/ **du bist** auf dem rechten Wege/ und **nicht ferne von dem Reiche Gottes**/ von der Erkandtnis des Evangelii/ dieweil du begehrest nachzufragen/ und etwas zu lernen. Sezze es nuhr ins Werk/ lerne den Messiah daraus recht erkennen/ und folge ihm in der Taht." Die fettgedruckten Wörter stehen bei Mk 12, 34 im Zusammenhang des Kapitels, das auch das Gleichnis vom Weinberg und die Versuchung Jesu durch die Pharisäer enthält. Als die Schriftgelehrten Jesu nach dem obersten göttlichen Gebot fragen, lehrt Jesus sie, Gott zu lieben, aber auch den Nächsten. Wellers Kritik, es handle sich um verschiedene Geschichten, trifft auf den verschiedenen Anfang des 22. Kapitels Matthaei zu. Allerdings enthalten Mt 22 und Mk 12 die gleiche Antwort auf die Frage des Pharisäers, also die gleiche Lehre von den zwei Geboten. Nur Markus berichtet vom Lob des Pharisäers. Offenbar teilt der Herzog nicht Wellers Besorgnis, die in der Frage des Pharisäers nach dem obersten Gebot implizierte Lehre vom Gesetz könne den einfältigen Hörer dazu verleiten, nicht zwischen Altem und Neuem Bund zu unterscheiden. Auch im folgenden Punkt übersteigt Wellers Kritik wohl das Verständnis des einfältigen Lesers, zu dessen Verteidiger er sich aufschwingt.

4 D. i. das vorhergehende, in diesem Sinne auch nächste Evangelium Mt 21 bzw. Mk 11 und Lk 19.

5 Hz. August erklärt, daß die Jünger eine Eselin zum Reiten (Einzug Jesu in Jerusalem) mit den Worten borgten, die Jesus ihnen zuvor gesagt hatte. *Hand-Büchlein*, HAB: 1218.3 Theol. (1), S.2 (Mt. 21): „**Der HErr** Jesus **hat ihrer**/ zu einer gewissen Verrichtung/ izzo **vonnöthen**/ iedoch wil er sie bald wieder anhero zurükke senden: **Darauf wird derselbige sie euch** willig (e) **alsbald überlassen.** (e) Mr. 11. v. 3." Vgl. „Vnd so euch jemand etwas wird sagen/ so sprechet/ Der HERR bedarff jr/ so bald wird er sie euch lassen." Mt 21, 3; vgl. Mk 11,3 ähnlich: „so wird ers bald hersenden." Vgl. Lk 19, 31. 34. Die Bibel wird hier von uns nach der auch von Hz. August benutzen Ausgabe zitiert: BIBLIA. Das ist Die gantze heilige Schrifft Deutsch/ D. Mart. Luth. … sampt den Summarien D. Danielis Crameri … Mit Churfürstl. Sächs. Privilegio (Lüneburg: Sterne 1634). HAB: Bibel-S. 4° 46.

6 *Hand-Büchlein*, HAB: 1218.3 Theol. (1), S.263 nach Jh 12, 14.15: Jesu „[…] **ritte** also ferner **auf dem jungen Eselein**/ (y) den Berg hinunter/ über das Tahl/ nach dem Stadt-Tohre zu." Hinweis y: Jd. [Richter] 10, 4 u. 12, 14. Vgl. Cramer-Bibel „JEsus aber vberkam ein Eselin/ vnd reit drauff: Fürchte dich nicht/ du Tochter Zion/ Sihe/ dein König kömpt reitende auff einem EselsFüllen."

7 Vgl. Mt 21, 1 „DA sie nu nahe bey Jerusalem kamen gen Bethphage an den Oelberg/", gebot er seinen Jüngern, in diesem „Flecken" die Eselin zu borgen, auf der er in Jerusalem einritt (V. 11). Vgl. Mk 11, 1 u. 7. S. *Hand-Büchlein*, HAB: 1218.3 Theol. (1), S.256f., Palmarum: Als Jesus und seine Jünger „**sich nuhn** der Stadt **JeruSalem näherten**/ **und bey** […] **Bethphage** […] **an den Oliven-Berg ankamen**" (S.256f.), befahl Jesu zweien seiner Jünger, ihm aus dem Ort eine Eselin mit dem Füllen zuzuführen. Sie setzten ihn darauf und zogen mit ihm nach Jerusalem: „**so bald sie** die Höhe und Spizze des Oliven-Berges erreicheten/ und **der Stadt** JeruSalem **ansichtig würden**/ **und den Oliven-Berg hinunter zogen**/ fieng an/ Gott mit Freuden zu loben […]." (S.261). „**Nachdem nuhn der HERR Jesus**/ den Berg (vv) also hinunter zog/ und **die Stadt** JeruSalem **ansahe**/ **da vergoß er über dieselbige seine Trähnen** mitleidentlich/ und mildiglich/ **und beklagete** sehr eiferig/ **ihre** so hartnäckige **Verstokkung**/ (x) **und ritte** also ferner auf dem jungen Eselein" (S.263; s.o. Anm.6). (x) S. U. Dn.10. p. Tr. v. 41. b. 44. Nach Lk 19,41. 44; Mt 21, 10; Mk 11, 11; Jh. 12, 14f. Vgl. ähnlich 1. Advent, *Hand-Büchlein*, HAB: 1218.3 Theol. (1), S.1ff.

8 *Hand-Büchlein*, HAB: 1218.3 Theol. (2), S.288. In Wellers Text bzw. in dessen Abschrift ist Führen klein geschrieben, so daß Herzog Augusts ungewohnte, aber aus der lat. (und z. Tl. griech.) Grammatik bekannte Fügung (in-dem-Jünger-zu-Christo-Führen) in der Wiedergabe noch schwerer verständlich wird: „NAchdem der HErr Jesus seinen Jüngern/ und Aposteln/ welche von Ihm erwählet/ und abgesondert waren/ einen Befehl/ und Unterricht/ wie sie in ihrem ApostelAmpte/ in dem Predigen/ in dem Taufen/ und in dem viele Jünger zu Christo Führen/ sich ins künftige zu verhalten hätten/ ertheilet/ und sich selbst ihnen durch vielerley/ und gewisse KenneZeichen/ und Beweisungen seines Lebens […] lebendig gezeiget […] Siehe/ da erschien Er ihnen das lezte Mahl zu JeruSalem […]." Bibelzitat und Zusatz sind in dieser Ausgabe des *Hand-Büchleins* nicht durch Fettdruck und unterschiedlichen Schriftgrad gekennzeichnet.

9 Wohl nachträglich noch im endgültigen Drucktext Hz. Augusts geändert, so daß Wellers Kritik ins Leere läuft. S. *Hand-Büchlein*, HAB: 1218.3 Theol. (2), S.294: „Und der HErr Jesus/ nach dem Er verherlichet war/ wirkete mit ihnen/ und beförderte ihre Verrichtungen/ durch seinen heiligen Geist […]."

10 Auch hier verwirrt Weller bzw. sein nichtkorrigierter Text den Leser. Richtig, wenn

Innenansicht der Wolfenbütteler Kirche Beatae Mariae Virginis nach Westen. Zu 461204.

auch mit ungewohntem Genitiv straft der auferstandene Jesus die ungläubigen Jünger, die von seinem leeren Grab zurückkehren, *Hand-Büchlein*, HAB: 1218.3 Theol. (2), S. 258: „O ihr grobe/ und unverständige Narren/ und eines solchen Herzens/ welches so langsam/ und träg ist/ dem[!] allen zu glauben/ was die Propheten/ von dieser Geschichte mit JEsu/ dem Messiah/ so deutlich vorher geredet/ und geskrieben haben: [...]."

11 Weller meint die Waschung der Füße der Jünger (*Hand-Büchlein*, HAB: 1218.3 Theol. (1), S. 271–274), als Petrus nach anfänglichem Sträuben Jesu auffordert, nicht nur seine Füße, sondern seinen ganzen Leib zu waschen. S. 274 „**JEsus sprach zu ihm: Es bedarf einer/ der** in einer Bade-Stuben an seinem ganze[n] Leibe **gewasschen ist/ nichtes mehr wasschen/ dann** nuhr **die Füsse**/ auf welche alles Unsaubere/ von dem Leibe herunter geflossen ist: Oder die er/ als er heimm gegangen/ wieder besudelt hat/ **sondern er ist** alsdann **ganz rein: Und ihr seyd**/ (geistlich zu verstehen/) **auch rein/ (y) wiewohl nicht Alle.**" (Jh 15, 3). (y) U. 15, 3. Die Seitenangabe Wellers „p. 127" bezieht sich auf die Kurzversion *Hand-Büchlein*, HAB: 1218.3 Theol. (2): „Jesu sprach zu ihm: Es bedarf einer/ der in einer Bade-Stuben an seinem ganze Leibe gewasschen ist/ nichtes mehr wasschen/ dann nuhr die Füsse/ auf welche alles Unsaubere/ von dem Leibe herunter geflossen ist: Oder die er/ als er heimb gegangen/ wieder besudelt hat/ sondern er ist alsdann ganz rein: Und ihr seyd/ (geistlich zu verstehen/) auch rein/ wiewohl nicht alle."

12 *Hand-Büchlein*, HAB: 1218.3 Theol. (1), S. 743 (24 Sonntag n. Trin.): „**Und ergrief das Kind**/ das Mägdelein/ **fassete**/ zukkete/ oder rüttelte **es bey der Hand/ rief** ihm zu/ wie man einem tiefslafenden Menschen zurufet/ befahl/ **und sagte ihm** auf syrisch/ Talitha Kumi, **auf deutsch/ Kind/ oder Mägdlein/ Ich sage dir/ stehe auf.**" (Mk 5,41; Mt 9,25; Lk 8,54).

13 Vielleicht meint Weller Hz. Augusts Wiedergabe von Bibelversen über das nach Jesu Lehre erlaubte Heilen am Sabbat, z. B. Mk 3, 2: „Vnd die gaben acht auff jhn/ ob er auch am Sabbathe jhn heilen würde/ auff daß sie ihn beschuldigen möchten." (Mt 12,10, Lk 6, 7, Lk 14,3). Vgl. *Hand-Büchlein*, HAB: 1218.3 Theol. (1), S. 667 zu Lk 14 (17. Sonntag n. Trin.): „3. **Und Jesus**/ als er diesen Wassersüchtigen ansichtig ward: **fieng an diese Gesez-Lehrer/ und Pharisäer anzureden**/ bereitete ihm aber dadurch den Weg zu der folgenden Heilung des Wassersüchtigen/ auf daß sie ohne Aergernus/ geschehen möchte/ und sprach also zu ihnen: ich wil euch eine Frage aufgeben/ höret Mir zu: **Ist es auch** in dem Gesezze **zugelassen**/ einen Bresthaften/ **an einem Sabbath/ gesund zu machen**/ oder wird der selbige dadurch verunheiliget? 4) **Sie aber swiegen** hierauf **stille** [...] **da rührete er diesen** Wassersüchtigen/ mit seiner Hand **an/ und heilete ihn** [...]."

14 Wellers Aussage über Augusts Evangelienharmonie auf den 2. Adventssonntag bezieht sich nicht auf eine Geschichte von der Heilung am Sabbath (z. B. Mk 5), sondern nach Mt 24, Mk 13 und Lk 21 auf das Ende der Welt *Hand-Büchlein*, HAB: 1218.3 Theol. (1), S. 14f. (Mt. 24, 39): „Allso und **auf diese Weise**/ sage Ich nochmahl/ wie es zu denen Zeiten des Noah/ und des Loths geschehen ist/ wird es auch an dem Tage der Rache/ und des Gerichtes/ **zugehen**/ wann des Menschen Sohn bey seiner Ankunft/ **wird geoffenbaret werden.**"

15 Nach Hz. Augusts gottesdienstlicher Ordnung (1648) sollten die Perikopen der *Evangelischen Kirchen-Harmonie* vor dem Altar, Luthers Texte dagegen von der Kanzel verlesen werden. S. 411214 I A S. 334, 335, 336, 339, 366 u. ö. S. Abb. S. 1059. Vgl. „Zu den Abbildungen". Zur Kritik selbst der Theologischen Fakultät der Landesuniversität Helmstedt an der Lesung der Kirchenharmonie in der Kirche vor dem Altar statt in der privaten Andacht s. 411214 S. 370.

461204A

Georg Philipp Harsdörffer an Herzog August d. J. von Braunschweig-Wolfenbüttel

Berichtet werde, daß der römische Kaiser Augustus nach griechischem Vorbild eine marmorne Säulenhalle mit einer griechischen und lateinischen Bibliothek gebaut und sie mit Schlachtenbildern, Statuen und Darstellungen von großen Taten geschmückt habe, um den Geist der Betrachter zu stärken und zu bessern. Hz. August d.J. v. Braunschweig-Wolfenbüttel (FG 227) habe dagegen nicht durch Steine, sondern durch Tugend und Bücher eine Halle errichtet, die nicht der des Stoikers Zenon gleiche, weil sie durch salomonische Weisheit und durch das Gedächtnis seiner eigenen Frömmigkeit und Bildung ewig dauern werde. — Das Glück des Staats beruht auf der Bildung seines Fürsten. Wie wir durch Platon wissen, gilt dies für die Staaten, in denen Philosophen die Herrschaft ausüben oder die Könige Philosophen sind. Platons Kommentator Marsilius Ficino fügt hinzu, daß der Fürst ebenso der durch Studien erworbenen Weisheit bedarf wie der Körper der Seele. Auch geziemt es vor allen dem Fürsten mehr und Besseres zu wissen, weil, wie Vegetius sich ausdrückt, seine Bildung allen Untertanen zu nützen vermag. Bacon führte zur Bestätigung Träume und Weissagungen römischer Kaiser an. Es ist keine Schmeichelei, fügt Harsdörffer hinzu, denn die Bildung und das Heldentum Eurer Durchlaucht zeugen schon von höchster Tugend. Während das Bild der Vorstellungskraft ohne Sprache stumm bleibt, erzeugt unser Denken in der vom Rhythmus belebten Rede Gefühl und willkommene Kraft. — Als zur Zeit Alexanders d. Gr. aus einer Orpheus-Statue Schweiß floß, weissagte dies, daß sich Poeten und Geschichtsschreiber abmühen würden, um heldenhafte Taten zu besingen und zu beschreiben. Harsdörffer will demnach denen, die sich um das Lob Hz. Augusts mühten, in Bescheidenheit nachfolgen, wenngleich in neuem Ausdruck und unübertroffener Verehrung. — Seine Durchlaucht möge daher ein Auge auf Harsdörffers Tugendrund (Porticus) werfen, wenngleich dessen Muse sich vor dem Anblick des Herzogs scheue und Harsdörffer, der seine Mängel kenne, dabei nicht erröte, da er sein Geschenk zum Ausdruck seiner Dankbarkeit anbiete.

Q *Harsdörffer: Porticus Virtutis (1647)*. HAB: 10.6 Pol., Bl. Br – B 3v. Seitentitel „DEDICATIO". Neuer, überarbeiteter, ergänzter und datierter Widmungsbrief in der Fassung der separat gedruckten *Porticus*. In T mit der kürzeren, früheren und undatierten Fassung des Schreibens in HAB: QuN 1090 (1), Bl.)(4v–[ )(7v verglichen, die als integrierter Vorspann der *Porticus* (durchlaufende Bogenzahlen) vor *Harsdörffer: Specimen (1646)* gedruckt wurde. Zit. *P.I* bzw. *P.II*. S. 460912 u. II, vgl. 450927.

A *Fehlt.*

SERENISSIME ATQUE CELSISSIME PRINCEPS, DOMINE CLEMENTISSIME.

AUgustum[a] Romanorum Imperatorem legimus[1] PORTICUM, cum BIBLIOTHECA græcâ & latinâ, è Numidico marmore, ædificasse; in quâ inter alia Belidum[b] Imagines fuêre cōspicuæ: procul dubio Græcorum imitatione, qui primi ambulacra, columnis suffulta erexêre, ubi in umbra Solis ardores, imbresve commodè declinarent. Accesserat pòst, successu temporum Picturarum elegantia; ne publico emolumento decus suum deesset: sicque circumvestiebāt parietes certamina, Statuæ, rerumque gestarum historiæ: quarum repræsentatione intuentium animi, cum lubentiâ, ad fortitudinem, & Bonam Mentem erudirentur. [B v]

SERENITAS ATQUE CELSITUDO VESTRA Porticum sibi exstruit, non caristiis saxis, sed propriâ virtute, & Bibliothecâ, æternitatis officina, illustrem. Porticum, inquam, non stoici Zenonis, sed summi Salomonis dogmatibus, sed ipsius Pietatis & eruditionis monumentis, perennem.[c]

Enimverò Reipub. felicitas nititur Principum eruditione; hinc Platonem affirmasse legimus: Tum demum respublicas fore felices, cùm aut Philosophi regnant, aut Reges philosophentur. Ubi commētator Marsilius addit; Sapientia (quæ absque studiis haud potest consequi) Principi nō aliter necessaria est, quàm corpori anima:[2] Nec quenque decet vel meliora scire, vel plura, quàm Principem, cujus doctrina omnibus potest [B 2r] prodesse subjectis, ut Vegetii verbis utar.[3] Hoc Domitiano in somnis præmonstratum erat, qui videre visus est Caput aureum sibi pone cervicē enatum esse: quod sanè vaticinium in Nerva, Adriano, Antonino, Trajano & succedentibus doctissimis Imperatoribus adimpletum notavit, Franciscus Bacon Baro de Verulamio.[4]

Absint blandimenta. SERENIT.[is] ATQUE CELSITUD.[is] V.[æ] summam eruditionem & heroicam Virtutē tot publica monumenta loquuntur: hanc ego, dum poëtico penicillo effigiare gestio, submissè veneror. Quemadmodū enim cogitatio nostra, antequā verbis circumscripta prodit, Imago est; (unde facultatis imaginativæ notatio invaluit) sic pictura per se muta & elinguis delineatio, fatisci; oratione verò, & [B 2v] ingenioso animata numèro, intimam sympathiam, & gratum robur commonstrat.

Orphei statua, Alexandri M. temporibus, continuis sudoribus fluxisse fertur, quo portento significari creditum, illius ævi Poëtas, & Historicos, in tanti Herois rebus gestis decantandis, describendisque magnopere laboraturos.[5] Video pariter & nostris temporibus eruditissimos Viros, in SERENITATIS atque CELSITUDINIS VESTRÆ laudibus celebrādis occupatissimos, quos ergo ego, veluti obscura umbra, novo ductu, novoque tractu sequor, non adsequor; humilimo autem cultu omnes, omnes anteverto.

Respice igitur, SERENISSIME ATQUE CELSISSIME PRINCEPS,[d] eximium isthuc Virtutis Circum, quem devotâ manu[e] [B 3r] adornare, Posterumque studio, ad vivum imitationis exemplum expingere volui, debui.[f] Verecundatur quidem hæc Musa, ad SERENITATIS, atque CELSITUDINIS V.[æ] intuitum;[g] dum autem SEREN.[is] atque CELSITUD.[is] V.[æ] gratiosum munus meditatur, quo nuper immerentem clementissimè affecit: hoc qualecunque[h] significandæ gratitudinis argumentum[i] offerre, & defectum suū, hoc affectu interpretari, haud erubescit. Vale SERENISSIME atque CELSISSIME PRINCEPS, &

FORTVNA HEROICIS VIRTVTIBVS TVIS
DIGNA, FRVERE PERPETVVM.[6]

Bildnis Georg Philipp Harsdörffers (FG 368). Zu 461204A.

ita vovet SERENITATI, atque CELSITUDINI V.ᵃᵉ devoto cultu
Norimb. prid. Non. Decemb.
M. DC. XXXXVI.
mancipatus
AVTOR.

T *Nur Wiedergabe inhaltlicher Unterschiede in P.I, ohne Berücksichtigung unterschiedlicher Interpunktion und Orthographie.* — **a** *P.II mit Initiale A in der Außenansicht der Porticus. P.I Emblem in einem Kreis: Auf der Spitze der Initiale A ein waagerechter Balken, an dessen kürzerer Seite ein größerer Würfel hängt, der auf der längeren Seite durch einen kleineren Würfel in der Schwebe gehalten wird. Umschrift:* PARITAS EX IMPARI. — **b** *Lies* Bellidum *zu* bellis, Gänseblume. — **c** *Folgendes bis* omnes anteverto *fehlt in P.I.* — **d** *P.I* respice eximium virtutis — **e** *P.I* manu, ad ingressum hujus operis deducere, & stud[i]o Posteritatis, ad vivum *usw.* — **f** *P.I folgt* Par erat, ut novum in lingua nostra conatum novo scribendi genere initiarer, & ratione nobilissimi argumenti pulcherrimo hoc exordio, publici favoris viam aperirem, & præmunirem. Verecundatur quidam — **g** *P.I folgt* tenuitatis suæ conscientiâ perculsa; dum autem — **h** *P.I* specimen — **i** *P.I fehlt.*

K Georg Philipp Harsdörffer (FG 368, s. sein Porträt auf S. 1063) hatte sein *Specimen Philologiæ Germanicæ* (1646) mit dem darin gedruckten Widmungsbrief schon vor der separat gedruckten, erweiterten Lobschrift *Porticus Virtutis* an Hz. August d. J. v. Braunschweig-Wolfenbüttel (FG 227) gesandt. Diese Fassung liegt im Exemplar HAB: QuN 1090 (1) vor, das dann in den Besitz Hz. Ferdinand Albrechts v. Braunschweig-Wolfenbüttel-Bevern (FG 842. 1673) überging u. im 18. Jh. (nach dem Tode Hz. Ludwig Rudolfs) in die HAB zurückkehrte. Die längere, separat gedruckte *Porticus* wurde von Harsdörffer mit seinem Brief DA Köthen I. 8: 470119 an den Herzog u. sodann in 25 Exemplaren an Justus Georg Schottelius (FG 397) geschickt: DA Köthen I. 8: 470215. Der vorliegende Widmungsbrief (im *Porticus*-Abschnitt) ist im *Specimen* nicht datiert, jedoch in der erweiterten, mit o. g. 470119 überreichten Fassung der *Porticus*. Die Annahme erscheint also plausibel, daß die kürzere, im *Specimen* integrierte *Porticus* in 460912 dem Herzog von Harsdörffer gesandt wurde. Anlaß dafür war die Unfähigkeit des Nürnberger Stechers, mit dem undat. gedruckten Widmungsbrief (als Teil des *Specimen*) rechtzeitig das letzte Kupfer zu liefern. (Dazu bedurfte es der Vorzeichnung des wolfenbüttelischen Malers u. Zeichners Albert Freyse, s. 460912 K 0). Harsdörffer hat aber nicht nur auf den letzten Stich gewartet, sondern *Porticus Virtutis* einschließlich des Widmungsbriefs umgeschrieben u. diesen auf den 4.12.1646 datiert. Möglicherweise stammen die heute dem HAB-Exemplar 10.6 Pol. beiliegenden 6 Abzüge der Kupferstiche (1 Wachsbild, 5 flandrische Bilder) von Harsdörffer bzw. dem nürnbergischen Kupferstecher. Aus dem Leim der Fischblase (Hausen, Stör u. a.) gewann man ein Material, mit dem transparente Abzüge von Kupferplatten gemacht wurden, welche noch vor dem Abdruck eine Ansicht von Buchillustrationen (image de Flandres) vermitteln konnten. S. *Krünitz* XXII, 473 u. LVI, 539f.

1 Randnotiz „Plin. l.16.c.40." Gemeint ist jedoch Plin. nat. 16, 17 (c. III), wo die aus einer Stiftung des M. Vipsanius Agrippa an seine Schwester Vipsania Polla an der Via Laeta in Rom hervorgehende Porticus erwähnt ist, welche Augustus vollendete. 28 v. Chr. baute Augustus an den Apollotempel auf dem Palatin eine Bibliothek. C. Plinii Secundi Naturalis Historiae Libri XXXVII. Hg. u. übers. v. Roderich König. 42 Bde. u. Reg.bd. Heimeran u. a. 1973–2004.

2 Vgl. Plat. rep. 3, bes. Kap. 19–21 (412a–414a) über die Bildung, Erziehung u. Auswahl des Herrschers. Vgl. OMNIA DIVINI PLATONIS OPERA TRALATIONE MARSILII FICINI EMENDATIONE ET AD GRAECVM CODICEM COLLATIONE SIMONIS GRYNAEI, Nunc recens summa diligentia repurgata, quibus subiunctus est index uberrimus. BASILEAE IN OFFICINA FROBENIANA ANNO M D XXXIX. S. 958 (Ficino): „Plurimum uero in animum posse iudicat harmoniam. Siquidem harmonia quædam diuina sit animus, cœlestisq*ue* harmoniæ aliquando, ut Platonice dixerim, assuetus. Rursus harmonia quadam consistit corpus, cōstatur & spiritus. […] In omnibus animaduerte quod non ciuili solum, sed etiam religiosa admodum obseruantia Plato suam erudiat ciuitatem, semperq*ue* quod & præcipit in Politico, temperantiam cum fortitudine misceat. […] Plurima uero de Musica tractat atq*ue* gymnastica. […] Illa enim animum spiritumq*ue*, hæc corpus animi gratia mirifice format atq*ue* componit. Addit, non ex corpore bono bonum animum, sed ex animo bono corpus fieri bonum."

3 „Antiquia temporibus mos fuit bonarum artium studia mandare litteris atque in libros redacta offerre principibus, quia neque recte aliquid inchoatur, nisi post Deum fauerit imperatur, neque quemquam magis decet uel meliora scire uel plura Principem, cuius doctrina omnibus potest prodesse subiectis. Quod Octauianum Augustum ac bonos dehinc principes libenter habuisse frequentibus declaratur exemplis." Veg. mil. 1, 1.

4 Francis Bacon Lord Verulam, Viscount St. Alban: The Essays or Counsels, Civill, and Morall. Ed. with intro., notes, and comm. Oxford (2000), 113 (The Oxford Francis Bacon XV, in: Of Prophecies): „Domitian dreamed, the Night before he was slain, that a Golden Head was growing out of the Nape of his Necke: And indeed, the Succession that followed him, for many Years, made Golden Times." Bacon gibt hier nur die Mitteilung Suetons am Ende seiner Domitian-Vita wieder.

5 Arr. an. 1, 11 erzählt, daß Aristander von Telmissus, der Weissager Alexanders d. Gr., das Schwitzen einer Orpheus-Statue zu Pieria richtig dahin gedeutet habe, daß Odenschreiber, Epiker u. andere sich anstrengen müßten, um Alexanders erfolgreichen Feldzug zu besingen. Vgl. Pl. Alex. 14,5. Arrianos; Plutarchos.

6 Chronogramm für 1646.

461206

Fürst Johann Casimir von Anhalt-Dessau an Fürst Ludwig

F. Johann Casimir v. Anhalt-Dessau (FG 10) übersendet F. Ludwig ein Schreiben Pgf. Ludwig Philipps v. Simmern (FG 97. Der Gefährliche), welches er am Vortag erhalten hat und bittet um Rücksendung mit näheren Anweisungen, wie es zu beantworten sei. — Die Gründe für seine schnelle Abreise vom Kurfürsten (zu Sachsen) und was dort vorgegangen sei, werde Ludwig von den fl. Vettern ausführlich erfahren. Johann Casimir möchte ihn nicht mit seiner unschönen Handschrift belästigen.

Q HM Köthen: V S 544, Bl. 87r–88v [A: 88v], 87v–88r leer; eigenh.; Sig. — *D: KE*, 58. — Nicht in *Bürger*.

A A Monsieur mon treshonoré Oncle.   Monsieur le Prince Louis d'Anhalt.

Hochgeborner Furst freundtlicher vielgeliebter herr Vetter,

was Jch gestern von dem Gefehrlichen[1] vor ein schreiben bekommen, empfangen EL hierbei[2], vndt werden mihr solches nach Dero belieben, mitt befehl wie Jch es wieder beantworten soll, wieder zu schicken,

warumb Jch so geschwinde wieder vom Churfursten weg gezogen,[3] vndt was sonsten alles dar vorgangen, werden EL die Vettern mitt mehre[r]m berichten *etc.* mag Jhr deswegen mitt meiner heslichen handt, nicht beschwerlichen sein,

Befehle sie nebens Dero fl. Gemahlin vndt lieben printzen, an Die Jch mich bester massen anbefehle, Göttlichem schutz, vndt verbleibe
   EL
     treuer vetter
     Johann Casimir, FzuAnhalt.

Dessau den 6 Dec. 1646.

K 1 Pgf. Ludwig Philipp v. Simmern (FG 97. Der Gefährliche). Dieser Brief ist der letzte des Korrespondenzjahrganges 1646, der die Aufnahme von 14 FG-Neumitgliedern durch den Pfalzgrafen behandelt. F. Johann Casimir v. Anhalt-Dessau (FG 10) ist dabei von Beginn an als Vermittler von Ludwig Philipp eingeschaltet worden. Vgl. zu diesem Aufnahmevorgang 460104 K 1.

2 Aus *DA Köthen I. 8*: 470403 geht hervor, daß es sich bei diesem Schreiben Pgf. Ludwig Philipps vermutlich um 461031A gehandelt hat, da sich Ludwig in 470403 auf die in 461031A genannten vier bereits erfolgten Neuaufnahmen bezieht. F. Ludwig entschuldigt sich dort auch für die verspätete Antwort auf das pgfl. Schreiben „vom Weinmonat vergangenen Jhares", das ihm im „Christmonat"/ Dezember eingehändigt worden sei. Ein Antwortschreiben Ludwigs auf den vorliegenden Brief Johann Casimirs liegt uns nicht vor, wohl aber seine verspätete Reaktion auf das erwähnte Schreiben des Pfalzgrafen vom Oktober 1646 mit 470403.

3 F. Johann Casimir hatte sich Ende November 1646 zusammen mit den beiden jüngsten Söhnen F. Augusts v. Anhalt-Plötzkau (FG 46), Lebrecht (FG 321) u. Emanuel (FG 486. 1648), spätere Fürsten v. Anhalt-Köthen, nach Wittenberg begeben, um mit Kf. Johann Georg I. v. Sachsen zusammenzutreffen. Ebenfalls anwesend waren die Söhne des Kurfürsten, darunter Hz. August v. Sachsen-Weißenfels (FG 402), der Administrator des Magdeburger Erzstifts. Darüber hinaus kamen auch F. Johann v. Anhalt-Zerbst (FG 398) u. Hz. Georg Friedrich v. Holstein-Sonderburg (1611–1676) zu diesem Treffen. *Christian: Tageb.* XVIII, Einträge vom 29. 11. u. 8.12.1646. Der genaue Grund des Treffens ließ sich nicht ermitteln. Das Tagebuch F. Christians II. v. Anhalt-Bernburg berichtet jedoch davon, daß sie „mit iagen sich verlustiren" wollten. Ebd., Eintrag vom 8.12.1646. Sicherlich wurden bei dieser Gelegenheit jedoch auch politische Themen behandelt. Vgl. 460422 u. 460424. — Die Ursache der überstürzten Abreise aus Wittenberg lag wahrscheinlich im Ausbruch der Pest in der Stadt, da bereits wenige Tage später der Bericht von den ersten Wittenberger Pesttoten auch Bernburg erreichte. Ebd., Eintrag vom 12.12.1646.

461213 Fürst Ludwig

461213

Fürst Ludwig an Georg Philipp Harsdörffer

Beantwortet durch 470206. — Wie in 461031 versprochen schickt F. Ludwig (Der Nährende) ein Exemplar des *GB 1646* an Georg Philipp Harsdörffer (FG 368. Der Spielende). Im Reimgesetz von Pierre de Brossard (FG 226. Der Lösende) sei allerdings ein Fehler bei der Benennung der Pflanze unterlaufen, den Harsdörffer verbessern möge — bei jedem Exemplar, das ihm in die Hände komme.

Q   HM Köthen: V S 545, Bl. 358v (358r Konzept von 461031); eigenh. Konzept. — Nicht in *KE*.

A   *Fehlt.*

Dem Spielenden wird vermöge der vertrostung unte[r]ª dem 31. des Weinmonats dieses Jhares, das geselschaft buch in kupferᵇ zugeschicket,¹ mit der anzeige, da[s]ª bey dem achtzeiligen gesetze des zweyhundert und sechsund zwanzigsten geselschafters, die erste Zeile ha[t]ª mußen geendert werden, dan bey dem gemälde zwar nicht, sondern bey dem nahmen des krautes ein irthum furgegangen war.² Da der Spielende vonᶜ den stucken so[lche]ª antreffenᵈ solte, darinnen diese verbeßerung noch nicht geschehen, kan er diese erinnerung kunlich³ darbey thun. Wom[it]ª er dan in den schutze götlicher almacht ergeben wird, und verbleibetᵉ

des Spielenden gantzwilliger
Der Nehrende

Geben den 13. Christmonats im Jhare 1646.

T a *Textverlust im Falz. Konjektur in eckigen Klammern.* — b *Folgt* <zuh> [?] — c *von den eingefügt für* <die> — d *Eingefügt.* — e *Folgt* <des Spielenden>

K 1 Georg Philipp Harsdörffer (FG 368. Der Spielende) hatte in 460916 den ihm unerschwinglich hohen Preis des *GB 1646* beklagt u. F. Ludwig (Der Nährende) indirekt um ein Exemplar gebeten. In 461031 vertröstete F. Ludwig Harsdörffer noch auf die Leipziger Neujahrsmesse 1647. In *DA Köthen I. 8*: 470206 bestätigte Harsdörffer dankend den Erhalt der Briefe 461031 u. 461213 u. des Exemplars des *GB 1646*.
  2 Die erste Verszeile des Reimgesetzes von Pierre de Brossard (FG 226. Der Lösende. 1633) im *GB 1646* lautet: „DAs gülden günselkraut in Lenden lößt den gries/". Da von der Goldrute die Rede ist, müßte die Pflanze richtigerweise „Güldne Rute" u. nicht „gülden günselkraut" heißen. Ähnlich das Reimgesetz im 2. Bd. des *GB Kö.*, Bl. 28r: „Das Gülden Günselkraut den gries in lenden löset". Diederich v. dem Werder (FG 31) hat diese Verbesserungen bereits in den in der Stadtbibliothek Dessau erhaltenen Exemplaren des *GB 1641* vorgenommen, indem er Pflanze u. erste Verszeile mit handschriftlichen Zettelchen überklebte. Der gebesserte Vers lautet dort: „Die güldne Rute löst der Lenden Harten gries/". Vgl. *Conermann II*, 51–53 u. *Conermann III*, 242. In einer Mitgliederliste vom Dezember 1637 heißt es zu Brossard ebenfalls noch: „226. Peter von Brossart *Der*

Lösende Virga aurea Gülden Ginsel *Den gries.*" (LHA Sa.-Anh./ Dessau: Abt. Köthen A 9a Nr. 167, Bl. 101v; die Liste auszugsweise veröffentlicht als 371220 I).

3 „Künlich" (kühn, adj. u. adv.) damals nicht nur in der heute üblichen Bedeutung von tapfer, verwegen, wagemutig, sondern auch im Sinne von vertrauensvoll, zuversichtlich, einvernehmlich (lat. confidenter); entsprechend „Künheit" als confidentia und confisio. *Stieler*, 1047. In dieser Bedeutung erscheint das Wort auch in einem Widmungsgedicht F. Ludwigs. S. 460825 IV u. V.

461216

Johann Valentin Andreae an Herzog August d. J. von Braunschweig-Wolfenbüttel

Antwort auf die Schreiben Hz. Augusts d. J. v. Braunschweig-Wolfenbüttel (FG 227) vom 3. und 17.11.1646. Johann Valentin Andreae (FG 464. 1646) hofft, daß auch seine verspäteten Briefe Hz. August erreicht haben. — Andreae will trotz der erwarteten Einwände die vom Herzog befohlene deutsche Vorrede zur Duodez-Ausgabe der *Evangelischen Kirchen-Harmonie* hoffentlich in 8 Tagen schreiben. Hz. August möge sie vor dem Erscheinen jedoch der Zensur seiner Theologen und Räte unterbreiten. — Andreae trauert um seinen verstorbenen Freund Johann Saubert d. Ä. Er will ihm, wie unter ihm und Saubert für ihren Todesfall verabredet, eine Standrede halten, in der er auch Hz. Augusts Zuneigung zu Saubert und dessen Billigung von Sauberts Eifer für die Förderung der christlichen Sache gedenken werde. — Andreae bedankt sich bei Hz. August für seine Aufnahme in die Fruchtbringende Gesellschaft und verspricht, deren Gesetze zu befolgen und sich als friedliebend zu erweisen. Er habe, unter Wahrung des Augsburgischen Bekenntnisses, immer Ärger, Zank und Streitlust verabscheut und darauf geachtet, in der Bestellung des Ackers des Herrn und bei der Ausrottung des Unkrauts alle Schwerter in Pflugscharen zu verwandeln. (Der seelige Dr. Meyfart habe das Universitätsleben genug getadelt.) Was nun seine Imprese anbetrifft, so treffe sein geänderter Gesellschaftsname (von *Der Müde* zu *Der Mürbe*) auf einen alten Mann wie ihn besser zu. Den Sinnspruch „Bleibet doch frisch" verstehe er als Verheißung Gottes. Falls für die Aufnahme in die Gesellschaft noch ein weiteres Ansuchen verlangt werde, erwarte er Nachricht und hoffe dabei auch auf die Vertretung seines Interesses durch den Herzog. Inzwischen habe er schon einmal den (beigelegten lat.) Text zur Anerkennung (der Regeln der Akademie) verfaßt. — Wünsche zum bevorstehenden Jahreswechsel.

Q HAB: Cod. Guelf. 65.1 Extrav., Bl. 326rv [A: 326v], eigenh.; Sig. — Andreaes 50. Brief (im Jahre 1646) als Antwort auf Hz. Augusts Briefe 44 u. 45. — Daraus zitieren *Keller: Akademien der Renaissance*, 107f. (ohne lat. Marginalien zur Imprese) u. *Begemann: FG u. Andreä*, 45. Vgl. die Wolfenbütteler Abschrift der die Aufnahme Andreaes in die FG betreffenden Passage (durch Anstreichung für den Kopisten hervorgehoben) in *DA Köthen I. 8*: 470112 I.

A Dem Durchleuchtigst. Hochgebornen Fursten vnd Herren, Herren **Augusto**, Hertzogen zu Brunschwig: vnd Lüneb. &c. Meinem gnedigsten Fursten vnd Herren. Wolfenbüttel. 50 16. Dece*m*b.

Durchleuchtigst. Hochgebohrner Gnedigster Furst vnd Herr, E. F. g. 44 vnd 45. (nach Calculation aber das 45. vnd 46. habe den Sontag 3. Adventus, 13. huius, ich mit vndst. reverenz vnd höchsten frewden empfangen,[1] vnd hiemit Meine sorgfalt fur E. f. g. wolstand, (.welchen zu vernemmen mir die weil schon zu Lang werden wöllen.) mit dankhsagung gegen Gott abgelegt. Der gebe im ferner. gnad. vnd hochgewunschte Continuation. Entzwischen wurt verhoffentlich Mein 40. so[a] noch gemanglet vnd nachgehendte das 44.45.46. so sich auch eingefunden haben.[2]

Die von mir gst. begehrte Teutsche Præfation, habe ich nicht zu disputieren, quicquid etiam obiectionis in promtu essent, Noch diese blanda imperia abzuschlagen, cum plura obsequia et omnia debeam,[3] Allein wolte E. f. g. ich vndst. gebetten haben, selbige vor dero Theologen vnd Rhaten zu vor Laßen Censieren, damit nicht ein wort darinnen, so etwa bedenkhlich fallen, oder sich selbigen Orten nicht schikhen möchte. Vnd solle dieselbe verhoffentlich vber 8 tag gehorsambst erfolgen.

Herren Sauberti *Senioris* discessus, quem inseparabilem et incomparabilem amicum habuj, ist mir wol Herzlich Laid. Jch werde ihme mit Gottes Hulf parentieren.[4] Dan wir eines solchen vnß gegen einander schon Langsten verbunden, vnd werde E. F. g. gegen ihme getragene g. affectation, vnd approbation seines studij in emendationem rej Christianæ ich wol wißen ingedenkh zu sein, quantumvis ringatur invidiæ.

Der[b] G. acceptation in die Fruchtbringende hochl. gesellschaft[5] habe ich mich und. zu bedankhen, vnd dabej zu versprechen, daß dero Legibus von mir in allem Punkhtlich vnd gehorsamest nachgesezet, vnd insonderheit Mein fridliebend gemuth verspüret werden. Jch habe Salva thesj August. Confessionis iederzeit vitilitiginem, altercationem, vnd pugnacitatem abhorriert, und hette sehen mugen, ut omnes gladij in vomeres excolendo agro Domini et exscindendo infelici lolio conversi fuerint, wo mit wir dan zu thun genug haben würden, vnd hat allein H. D. Maifardus Sehliger den Vniversiteten genug furgeschrieben[c][6]. Das Wort Mude ist in Mürb[d], sehr wohl verendert vnd reimet sich beßer auf mich, qui non tam fessus, quam fracidus et putris sum. Das simbolum (.Bleibet doch frisch.[d])[e] Et tamen viget vel Attamen vigens [vel] Adhuc dum Vegetum Nondum effœtum etsi á favente judicio profectum, Nemme ich iedoch tanquam bonum omen, mit und. gehorsam an, vnd wunsche, daß Gott noch ferner in mir Schwachen kreftig seyn wölle Ps. 71, 18. Ob nu ferneres und. ansuchen von nöthen, oder E. f. g. mich gst. vertretten wullen, Dero pro conciliatione ich ohne das höchst obligiert, haben E. f. g. mir ferner g. anzudeuten, vnd habe in eventum ich gleichwol dieses wenige auf ratificatione aufgesezet.

Befahre hiemit E. f. g. dem Schuz des Allerhöchst., Mit herzlichem wunsch das dises alte Jahr vollend mit glukh ablauft, das kunftige aber noch mehr segens vnd wolstands an Leib vnd Sehl, Hof vnd hauß, Land vnd Leuten, hab vnd guth, Ehr vnd Ruhm hienach bringe. Hochg. F. g. inmich zu beharrenden großen gnaden, Mich vnd die meinigen vndergebend, verbleibe bis [in] den Todt

E. F. G. Vnderthänigst. gehorsams verpflichter Rhat vnd getrewest. diener
et JVAnd.
Ananiæ 16. Dec. ☿ 46

I

461217

Andreaes lateinische Selbstverpflichtung gegenüber der Fruchtbringenden Gesellschaft

Q HM Köthen: V S 545, Bl. 468rv, v leer; eigenh. in Zierschrift mit Andreaes rotem Wachssiegel (Rosenwappen); auf der Vorderseite Hz. Augusts eigenh. Anweisung an Hille: „Sr L. Furst Ludwigen zu Anhalt zuzuschikken nebst dem Extract."[1] S. Abb. S. 1071. — Das Blatt wurde Hz. August d. J. zusammen mit obenstehendem Brief geschickt, dann von Carl Gustav v. Hille (FG 302) zusammen mit seinem Brief *DA Köthen I. 8:* 470112 an F. Ludwig weitergesandt.

Laudatissimæ Societatis
FRUCTIFERÆ
ILUSTRISSIMO CAPITI,
Eiusque membris, summæ et cuiuscunque
dignationis.

Pro clementissima et benevola in Ordinem receptione, gratias humillimas et perofficiosas agit, seque ad normam Societatis, Legesque obsequenter obstringit, animumque indagandæ Veritatis Christianæ studiosum, morum emendatiorum appetentem; Ingenij culturæ avidum; literarum exornandarum intentum, Germanæ Vernaculæ Linguæ excolendæ et amplificandæ assiduum; cætera pacificum, officiosum, et ductilem allaturum atque servaturum, (.salva Religionis suæ professione.) sanctè pollicetur, Fracidj agnomen, quod senio suo optimè quadret, et Muscj emblema, cum simbolo Et tamen viget, acceptaturus, Id quod bene Capitj[2]*; bene Ordinj; benè sibi vertat, Deum Opt. Max. ex animo precatur*

Studtgardiæ 17. Decemb.
   Anno 1646.

                              Johann. Valentinus
                                Andreæ T. D.

Laudatissimæ Societatis
FRUCTIFERÆ
ILLUSTRISSIMO CAPITI,
eiusq3 membris, summæ & cuiuscunq3
dignationis,

Pro clementissima Benevola in Ordinem
receptione, gratias humillimas & perofficiosas agit, seq3
ad normam Societatis, legesq3 obsequenter obstringit,
animumq3 indagandæ Veritatis Christianæ studiosum,
morum emendatiorum appetentem; Ingenij culturæ
avidum; literarum exornandarum intentum; Germanæ vernaculæ linguæ excolendæ et amplificandæ assiduum; cætera pacificum, officiosum, & ductilem
allaturum atq3 servaturum, (salva Religionis
suæ professione,) sancte pollicetur, Fracidj nomen,
quod senio suo optime quadret, et Muscj emblema, cum simbolo et tamen viget, acceptaturus
Id quod bene Capiti; bene Ordini; bene sibi ver-
fat, Deum Opt: Max. ex animo precatur

Studtgardiæ 17. Decemb.
  Anno 1646.

                    Johann: Valentinus
                    Andreæ T.D.

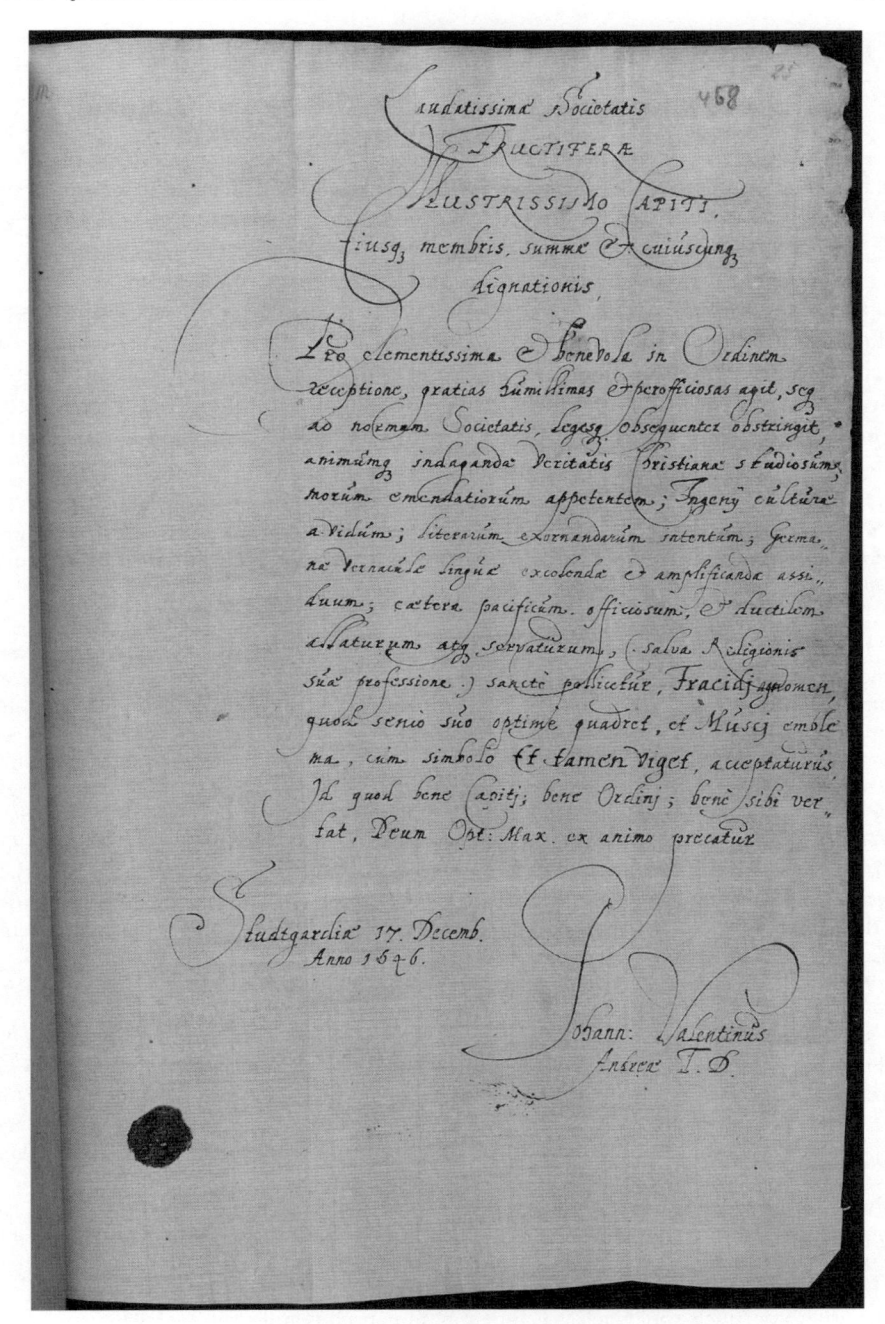

Johann Valentin Andreaes (FG 464. 1646) lateinische Selbstverpflichtung gegenüber der Fruchtbringenden Gesellschaft. Zu 461216 I.

II

Andreae über seine Aufnahme in die Fruchtbringende Gesellschaft

Q Johann Valentin Andreae: Autobiographie. Bücher 6 bis 8. ... Bearbeitet von Frank Böhling. Übersetzt von Beate Hintzen. Stuttgart-Bad Cannstatt 2012, 66 (*Andreae: Schriften*. Bd. I,2).

Supersunt quaedam privata, quorum veniam ab aequanimo lectore peto, nempe adlecus sum in ordinem Fructiferae Societatis, iam ab anno 1617. auspiciis Ludovici Principis Anhaltini Illustrissimi institutum, et ad numerum 433. sociorum successive auctum, 6. Novembris satagente Augusto Principe et Hero meo,[1] nomenque accepi Fracidi, senio meo et rudi conveniens, cum emblemate Musci effoetae arbori adhaerentis, et symbolo, Etiamnum viret.

T a *Eingefügt bis* gemangelt — b *Absatz angestrichen.* — c furgeschrieben *wohl von Andreae korrigiert.* — d *Wohl von Andreae rot unterstrichen.* — e Et tamen *bis* effœtum *eingefügt.*

K 1 Die Briefe Hz. Augusts d. J. v. Braunschweig-Wolfenbüttel (FG 227) an Johann Valentin Andreae (FG 464. 1646) v. 3.11.1646 u. 17.11.1646 (461117) in HAB: Cod. Guelf. 236.3 Extrav., Bl. 44 u. 45. Andreae setzte gewöhnlich seine Zählung (45 bzw. 46) mitten über die Briefe des Herzogs, welcher zuvor in seine Schreiben links oben als 44. bzw. 45. Brief notiert hatte. Die eigenen Briefnummern schrieb Andreae damals auch links oben an den Rand u. setzte die Nummern der in seinem Schreiben beantworteten Briefe des Herzogs mitten über seinen jeweiligen Brief. Der vorliegende Brief ist daher von Andreae als der 50. u. als Antwort auf Nr. 45 u. 46 gezählt. Auf der Anschriftseite (Bl. 326v) wiederholte Andreae „50." bzw. „Decemb." Wir verfolgen im laufenden Briefwechsel die Zählung durch die Briefpartner, geben aber nur die jeweilige Nummer des vorliegenden Briefs u. des beantworteten Briefs (oder dessen Datum) wieder, wenn keine Irregularitäten auftreten.
2 HAB: Cod. Guelf. 65.1 Extrav., Bl. 309 Nr. 40 (7.10.1646), Bl. 318 Nr. 44 (3.11.1646), Bl. 317 Nr. 45 (11.11.1646) u. Bl. 318 Nr. 46 (18.11.1646).
3 Die ersten beiden Ausgaben der *Evangelischen Kirchen-Harmonie* Hz. Augusts, die Oktav- u. Quartausgaben von 1646, enthalten nur lat. Vorreden Andreaes. Vor die Duodezausgabe des Werks (1647) setzte der Herzog die hier gemeinte dt. Vorrede, zit. in 411214 II B (S. 345–348). In Andreaes Worten ging es dem (nicht genannten) Herzog um Erläuterung des biblischen Textes „mit friedliebend und **fruchtbringender** Feder". Das Werk Hz. Augusts sollte also angesichts des fortwährenden Kriegs nicht nur als friedenstiftend, sondern auch als Arbeit der FG erkennbar sein, was Andreae diskret, jedoch für Eingeweihte deutlich hervorhob. Gegenüber luther. Eiferern u. Bedenkenträgern wie Johannes Müller, Nicolaus Hunnius (380320 K 7 u. I, S. 494f.) oder dem Dresdner Oberhofprediger Jacob Weller (s. 461204), die pastoral u. kirchenpolitisch argumentierten u. die Lutherbibel auch sprachlich gegen den grammatisch regulierten Text Augusts verteidigten, leugnete Andreae die reformerische oder lutherkritische Absicht des Herzogs: „Womit dañ von solchem hohen Gemühte/ nicht eigene Ehre/ (so vielleicht die Welt-Wei-

sen/ und Gewaltigen nicht begehren werden: Matth. II.V.25. I.Cor.I.V.26.) oder unnöhtige Reformation, der ruhm-würdigen Dolmetschung des teuren Gottes-Mannes/ D. Lutheri, viel weniger aber Aufhebung/ und Veränderung der gewöhnlichen Evangelien/ sondern allein/ mit dem fromen Könige David/ Ps. 84.V.11. * 119.V.24.27.46. die Ehre des Hauses Gottes/ und neben Unterricht der Einfältigen/ mit Beyfügung aller nohtwenigen Umbständ/ Andeutung eigentlichen Verstandes/ und Mitstimmung/ oder Gezeugnis anderer gleichlautender Stellen H. Schrift/ (wie solches Alles zu End jedes Textes zu befinden) gesuchet/ und zuversichtlich albereit erhalten worden." Zur vorsichtigen Distanzierung Johann Sauberts d. Ä. u. Georg Calixts vgl. 410119 K 4.

4 Johann Saubert d. Ä. (1592–1646), nürnberg. luther. Theologe, Prediger zu St. Sebald, Bibelherausgeber, Entwickler einer emblematischen Predigtkunst. *NDB* XXII (2005), 447 f.; *Bio-Bibliographisches Kirchenlexikon* XVI, Erg. III: Sauberts Tochter heiratete Andreaes Sohn Gottlieb. Saubert gehörte Andreaes Unio Christiana u. Societas Christiana an. S. 420627 u. I, vgl. 410119 K 4 u. ö. Auf den gegenüber Hz. Augusts Bibelprojekt nicht unkritischen Saubert († 2. 11. 1646) verfaßte Andreae: JOHANNIS SAUBERTI THEOLOGI. UMBRA Delineata à Johanne Valentino Andreae (Studtgardiae: Matthias Kauttius 1647), 4°; HAB: Da 581 (17). Dort heißt es zu der Verabredung zwischen Andreae u. Saubert: „ITa quidem inter JOHANNEM SAUBERTUM, & me, Amicos individuos jam abunde vicennio convenerat, ut alter alteri in hac ærumnarum palæstra superstes, supremum memoriæ & pietatis officium solveret, Testis integrior recti sensus, & innocentis instituti, contra omnem obtrectationem & invidiam, ad posteritatem futurus, sed cujus sors, utrique infelix, in me recidit." So steht es auch wortgleich in der Lüneburger 32°-Ausgabe gleichen Titels (LUNÆBURGI. Typis Sterniorum, M. DC. XLVII.)

5 Da Andreae seine dt. u. lat. Verpflichtung gegenüber der FG an Hz. August geschickt hatte, mußte dieser sie F. Ludwig zur Kenntnis bringen. Hz. August teilte Andreae am 12. 1. 1647 mit: „Seine Erklärung dem haupte unserer geselschaft geschehen, habe ich nach Cöthen albereit gesandt. Die fernere resolution hat man zu erwarten". HAB: Cod. Guelf. 236.3 Extrav., Bl. 53r. Carl Gustav v. Hille (FG 302) hatte vom Herzog den Auftrag erhalten, an das Oberhaupt der FG Andreaes lat. Erklärung u. abschriftlich das Zitat aus dem vorliegenden Brief zu schicken, was Hille in seinem Schreiben *DA Köthen I. 8:* 470112 tat. Der Fürst antwortete Hille in 470122 u. erklärte, der Mürbe (Andreae) werde unter der Mitgliedsnummer 464 noch für das Eintrittsjahr 1646 eingetragen, weil er sich zu seinem Gemälde, Namen u. Wort noch in diesem Jahr bekannt habe. Die Resolution F. Ludwigs vom 22. 1. 1647 erreichte Andreae erst am 11. 2. 1647. Vgl. zur Aufnahme Andreaes in die FG 461117 K 1.

6 Johann Matthaeus Meyfart (1592–1647), ehedem Rektor des Gymnasium Casimirianum in Coburg, veröffentlichte nach Antritt seines Lehr- u. Rektorenamts: Christliche vnd wolgemeinte/ auch demütige Erinnerung/ Von Erbawung vnd Fortsetzung Der Academischen Disciplin auff den Evangelischen Hohen Schulen in Deutschland; wo etwa dieselbige gefallen/ vnd Schaden verübet/ wie solcher in Richtigkeit zubringen vnd abzuwenden? ... An den Tag gegeben Durch Johann Matth. Meyfarten/ der heiligen Schrifft Doctorn/ anjetzo Professorn bey der vhralten vnd ernewerten Universitet zu Erffurdt (Schleusingen: Johann Birckner 1636). Zu den Titelvarianten s. *Dünnhaupt: Handbuch*, 2746f., zum Werk Erich Trunz: Johann Matthäus Meyfart. Theologe und Schriftsteller in der Zeit des Dreißigjährigen Krieges. München 1987, 245–255. Erfurt war damals von den Schweden besetzt, so daß die kleine Universität nicht mehr der Kontrolle des Kf. u. Ebf.s von Mainz unterstand. Hz. August trug Männern wie Georg Calixt Gutachten über Meyfarts Werk auf. Theologen wie Matthias Höe v. Höenegg u. Johann Gerhard kritisierten es sogar. Wegen der Absicht der Kirchenzucht schätze Hz. August d. J. das Werk jedoch, schrieb (der reservierte) Johann Saubert d. Ä. an den Straßburger Theologen Johannes Schmidt. A. a. O., 252 f.

K I 1 S. Hilles Brief *DA Köthen I. 8*: 470112 an F. Ludwig, dem die originale lat. u. die kopierte dt. Selbstverpflichtung Andreaes beilagen.
2 F. Ludwig schickte seine Zustimmung zur Aufnahme Andreaes in die FG zwar als Beilage zu seinem Brief 461106, jedoch erfolgte die Aufnahme tatsächlich erst in Ludwigs Brief *DA Köthen I. 8*: 470122, den Andreae am 11.2.1647 empfing. S. K 5, zur Aufnahme Andreaes allgemein 461117 K 1.

K II 1 Andreaes Eintragung in seiner Vita noch im Jahre 1646 zeugt von der Ungeduld, mit der er die langwierige Aufnahme in die Akademie erwartete.

Wörterverzeichnis

Erläuterte Wortformen und Bedeutungen. Schreibweise der Quellen. Einschließlich erklärter Namen.

abbittlich *adj.*   280412 K 10
Abendteu[r]er *n.*   391217 K 11
Abfluß *n.*   381028 K IV 3.6.37.47.63
abgeleinet *part.*   460406 K 6
abgeschreiben *part.*   270406 K 29
abito *n.*   381028 K IV 53
ablage *n.*   371123 K 13
ablanglich *adj.*   240118 K 2
abmeyen *v.*   250110 K I 19
abreit *adv.*   440927 K 7
abschewe/ schewe *n.*   350731 K I V. 289 f.
abschneiden *v.*   390807A K 4
abschnitt *n.*   400902 K I 1
absetzen *v.*   371222 K 8
absonderlicher *n.*   381028 K IV 34
abwechselung *n.*   280412 K 13
Academi/ Academie(n) *n. (pl.)*   DA Köthen I. 2, S. 18 f. 280411 K. 290310 K 3. 290614
Academia *n. (lat.)*   DA Köthen I. 2, S. 19. 280411 K 8. 290310 K 3
Academia/ Accademia *n. (ital.)*   230809. 280411 K 8. 290310 K 3
Academico *adj.*   280226 K 5. 280411 K 8
Academie/ Accademi(e)/ academien *n. (frz.)*   231203 K 11. 271201 K 2. 290310 K 3. 380810 K 4. 391113 K 6. 440525 K 1. 450919A
Academie gliedern *n.*   310108 K 5
Academique(s)/ Accademiques/ Accademiques fructifians *n. (pl.)*   280304 K 3. 280411 K 8. 290310. 371112A K 1. 390814 K 4. 410822. 411009
Accademie fructifiante   371028
accademiesteuer *n.*   320626 K 2
Accademiques (fructifians), s. Academique(s)
accomodirungk *n.*   390131 K 4

Achbar *adj.*   280122 I u. K I 7
Achspunct *n.*   381028 K IV 72
achten, sich *v.*   190322 K 1
äckel *adj.*   400122 K 6
acta *n. pl.*   380108 K 6
Adelspursch *n.*   360703 K 5
Adolger (Adelger) *Personenname*   260520 u. K 9. 260619 u. K 19
Adventurierer *n.*   391217 K 12
æquivocum/ Aequi vocare *n./ v.*   381028 K IV 70
affecti/ affectus/ Affetti *n (pl.)*   381028 K IV 47.61
affection *n.*   240717 T f
äher *n.*   380828 K I 44
ähnligkeit zu einander   381028 K IV 24
ahnnahmen *v.*   371031 K 9
Aiilocutii *n.*   190424 K 2
ἀκροαματικὸς *adj.*   381028 K IV 31
albereitt *adv.*   280412 K 7
Album *n.*   271001 K 5
Alchimisten *n. pl.*   381028 K VI 68
Alesifarmaco *n.*   381028 K IV 60
Alexipharmaca *n. pl.*   381028 K IV 60
aller ecken *adv.*   350731 K I V. 358
aller enden   281226 K 11
Allermanharnisch *Pflanzenname*   210626 K 1
Almanach *n.*   280122 I u. K I 9. 380423A
als *adv.*   240718 K 97
älte *n.*   370900 K 4. 401109 K 3
alter *n.*   390131 K 16
Alteratie *n.*   300410 K 38
Amber *n.*   350731 K I V. 175 f.
l'amor della prestezza *idiom.*   430418 K 7
amourettes *n. pl.*   281000 K 3
Analogia *n.*   381028 K IV 24
anbinden *v.*   270810 K 11

anbindung *n.*   431211 K I 5
andencken *n.*   371208A K 2
Andorf(f) *Ortsname*   300921 K 10
ἀνδρας δυνατούς   381028 K IV 7
anfahende *n. pl.*   460825 K I 6
anfengen *v.*   240718
Anflüsung/ Anflössung *n.*   440525 K II 2
anfristen *v.*   430103 K II 4
angedast *part.*   300410 K 11
angefädemet *part.*   460204 K 5
angeleibt *part., adj.*   380502 K 1
Angelstern *n.*   440000 Q
angeschnürt *part.*   350731 K I V. 336
Angesichts Deuteley   381028 K IV 21
angzen *v.*   250413 K I 9
anhalten *v.*   350731 K I V. 218
anhörlich *adj.*   381028 K IV 31
animati *part.*   381028 K IV 9
ankündigungsschreiben *n.*   290616 K 3
anlage *n.*   290510 K 7
anlenden *v.*   310411 K 11
Anliegen *n.*   381028 K IV 61; vgl. eigen Anliegen(heit)
anmassen *v.*   371123 K 5
anmerckung *n.*   371226 K 5
années Nestoriennes   280112 K 3
Anomalia *n.*   381028 K IV 24
Ansche Cchail, d. i. אַבְשֵׁי־הַיִל   381028 K IV 7
Anser Städte *n.*   221214 K 9
ansprengen *v.*   271215 K 4
anstehen *v.*   350312 K 5
Antorf(f), s. Andorf(f)
anvor *adv.*   450417 K 1
Aphorismi, s. Politici Aphorismi
αφορισμὸς *n.*   381028 K IV 3
arcana Imperii   381028 K IV 6
Arche *n.*   371110 K 11
Architectonicè *adv.*   381028 K II 12
Arequeira/ Arecca *Pflanzenname   DA Köthen I. 3*, S. 106 ff., 113, 116 f.
Arme Leute   280122 I u. K I 8
Armonia/ Arnonia *n.*   381028 K IV 22.28
Armut *n.*   390114 K 6
Arrest *n.*   460620B K 3
arrhe *n.*   280216 K 4
Artickelsbrief *n.*   390826 K 4
artzneylehre *n.*   381028 K II 10
Artztisch *adv.*   381028 K II 10

Ascalon *Ortsname*   300320 K II 23
Aspect *n.*   370421 K 14
Astrealische geselschaft   231206 K 9
Attione Morale   381028 K 14
au ich *interj.*   380000 K 5
aufbott *n.*   401214 K 8
auffsperrn *v.*   380828 K I 22
auffwesen *n.*   280412 K 1
Aufleger *n.*   381028 K III 3
aufsatz *n.*   450505 K 3
Auf-traags-schrift *n.*   441201 K 1
aufzüge *n. pl.*   450220 K 20
Aulicè *adv.*   381028 K II 7
auskleiden *v.*   240718 K 43 u. 73
auslesen *v.*   410727 K 3
ausmatten *v.*   250110 K I 28
ausrüsten *v.*   390131 K 18
Außbündige *n.*   410621 K II 15
Ausschweiffung *n.*   381028 K IV 17
außer weeg *adv.*   461031A K 3
Außführen *v.*   381028 K IV 38
außgetröget *part.*   250110 K II 3
außhecken *v.*   210401 K 16
außlegung *n.*   260520 K 7
außlehren *v.*   250413 K III 4
außlesen *v.*   371106 K 2
außthun *v.*   240718 K 72
außtragen *v.*   290501 K 5
Außtrit *n.*   381028 K IV 17
austheilung *n.*   381028 K IV 43
autheur *n.*   290310 K 3 u. K I 5
Autor *n.*   381028 K II 0

baden *v.*   250413 K IV 1
badzahr/ padzahr (Pazar) *n.*   381028 K IV 64
bahr *n.*   420630 K 48
Balckenstedt *Ortsname*   371116 K 4
Balordaggine *n.*   371009 K 10
Banck *n.*   280122 I u. K I 6
banda *n.*   230913 K 8
Bardus *n.*   381028 K II 26
Basilisck *Tiername*   350731 K I V. 9
baukunst *n.*   381028 K II 12
bauschauen *v.*   440324 K 8
Bawkünstlich *adv.*   381028 K II 12
Bayleõ *n.   DA Köthen I. 3*, S. 106
beansehnlichet *part.*   400311A K 3
bearten *v.*   310000 K I 2

bedutzt *part.* 250413 K III 3
befahren *v.* 270406 K 10. 340107 K 25.
 370422 K II 3
befahren, sich *v.* 440310A K 3
befahrlich *adv.* 451028A K 7
befindung *n.* 390125 K 9
befülen (bevilen) lassen, sich *v.* 270406
 K 4
Begängnus *n.* 440000 Q
begegen *v.* 290529 K 21
begleiben/ bekleiben *v.* DA Köthen I. 6,
 S. 124
begnügung *n.* 390125 K 7
beharren *v.* 250706 K I 6
beharrt *part.* 430920 K 7
behäusung *n.* 290529 K 6
behörligkeitt *n.* 290226 K 6
Beißfalcken *Tiername* 230430 K 7
beiten *v.* 281215 K 7
bekleiben *v.* 250413 K III 5
Bekümmernis/ bekümmernüs *n.* 381028
 K IV 61
belast *part.* 300410 K 52
bel esprit 281000 K 5
beliebte *n. pl.* 381028 K IV 15
benachrichtsammet *part.* 371123 K 7
benehren *v.* 371124 K I 9
bequemen *v.* 290529 K 18
bereit *adv.* 250110 K I 36
bericht *n.* 380402 K I 5
beriechen, sich *v.* 390125 K 3
beringen *v.* 280412 K II 6
Beringer/ Behringer/ Beringarius *Personenname* 260619. 280412 II
beschaffenheitten, eigentliche 240717 T b
bescheidenheit *n.* 380402 K I 3. 390723
 K 4
bescheidung *n.* 290529 K 28
beseelet *part.* 381028 K IV 9
besocht *part.* 290614 K 13
besondern *Konj.* 430118 K 9
besprochen *part.* 290529 K 16
bestürtzung *n.* 441231 K 4
besuchbriefflein *n.* 280726 K 2
besuchen *v.* 181207 K 1. 330920 K 1
betagen *v.* 271215 K 5
Bettela *Pflanzenname* DA Köthen I. 3,
 S. 106 ff., 118

Beutell, allgemeiner/ gemeiner 271209
 K 3. 280510 K 9
bewegen *n.* 350731 K I V. 485 (2)
Bewegung *n.*, s. brünstige Bewegung
Bewinthaber *n.* 310113 K 33
bewüst *adj.* 270406 K 7
beygaben *n. pl.* 381130
Beylage *n.* 401215 K II 2
Beysatz *n.* 381028 IV (8. 14)
beyverleibt *part. adj.* 380331 K 1
Bezoar/ bezoaro/ Bezoarstein *n.* 381028
 K IV 64
bieren *v.* 450529 K 4
Biesem *n.* 350731 K I V. 172
blanquet (blanchet) *n.* 390914 K 1
bleiben *v.* 240718 K 80
bode *n.* 300410 K 6
bögen *v.* 340716 K 3
Born Kreße *Pflanzenname* 250305 K 41
boße *n.* 250500 K 3
brast Kopf *Schimpfwort* 380503 K 17
brast *n.* 250413 K I 6
Bret *n.* 350731 K I V. 402
brewet *v.* (3. Pers. Sg.) 350731 K I V. 498
briefbündlein *n.* 450919 K 1
Brosam *n.* 410208 K I 16
brudel *n.* 300320 K II 22
brungen *n.* 290913 K 15
brünstige Bewegung 381028 K IV 47
brustlatz *n.* 290000 K I 2
bubones *n. pl.* 380417 K 7
Bucherschrein *n.* 410203 K 3
buchführer *n.* 411128 K 3
Buchgewarsam *n.* 180000 K 2
Buchstabe *n.* 460915 K 13
buttegel *n.* 410208 K I 13
Buttesell *n.* 370305 K 2

Caja *Personenname* 450726 K 15
Calendae/ Calende *n. pl.* 381028 K IV 58
Calw *Ortsname* 430215 K 2
Campagnie plato 420630 K 16
Campagnie raso 420630 K 16
Canarini *Personenname* DA Köthen I. 3,
 S. 107 f., 113 f.
Canterichen *n.* 271201 K I 6
Capel(le) *n.* 381028 K IV 68
Capitel schreiben 310224 K 17
Cappelletto *n.* 231008

Capriccij *n. pl.* 371009 K 10
Carmesin *n.* 280122 I u. K I 6
Carpentar *n.* 180714 K 1
Car(re)four de Mercure *Ortsname* 240109 K 11. 240301
cartel *n.* 380310 K I 13
Cartell *n.* 250500 K 1
Cataracta(e) (cœli)/ cataratte (del cielo) *n. pl.* 381028 K IV 33
Cavalleros *n.* 240718 K 68
Cavare *v.* 381028 K IV 38
Chapperon *n.* 381028 K II 0
characteres Salomonis 280128 K 3
chariot *n.* 280404 K 5
charten *v.* 391119 K I 2
Chasse *n.* 240718 K 75
Chauderin *n.* DA Köthen I. 3, S. 106
Chinge, wurtzel *Pflanzenname* 300921 K I 14
Chor/ Chorus *n.* 381028 K IV 56
cicalata *n.* DA Köthen I. 4, S. 10
Cimentar/ mettere a cimento *v.* 381028 K IV 37
Circulus Meridianus 381028 K IV 72
Circumscriptio *n.* 381028 K IV 16
Cisiarius *n.* 260617 K 4
Cisternen *n. pl.* 381028 K IV 5
Il Colio *n. (part.)* 410621 K II 14
Comedia *n.* 381028 K IV 59
Comet *n.* 381028 K IV 49
compagnia/ compagnie (compaignie) *n.* 250701 K 4. DA Köthen I. 2, S. 19. 280218 K 2. 280411 K 8
Compas verrucken 381107 K 16
Compendium *n.* 381028 K II 22
com'unque *conj.* 280106 K 12
compieto *adj.* 450817 K IV 10
confrairie *n.* 280218 K 2
consonanza *n.* 381028 K IV 29.31
contanten *n. pl.* 451019 K 5
contezza *n.* 450817 K IV 9
Contohr *n.* 290529 K 37
contramandiren *v.* 310311 K 3
copella *n.* 381028 K IV 68
Corallen tinctur *n.* 320715 K 7
Corbeillon *n.* 240718 K 87
Correlativo/ Correlativum *n.* 381028 K IV 32
Cose seconde 381028 K IV 19

Cottillon *n.* 240718 K 49
coup d'Estat *n.* 450901 K 13
credit *n.* 290510 K 4
creutztaffel *n.* 240717 K 10
Criticus *n.* 400528 K II 2. 410900 K 11. 450410 (vgl. Sprachrichter)
Culleola *n.* DA Köthen I. 3, S. 107 f.
Currant *n.* 420120 K 37
Currir *n.* 250218A K VII 16
Currirer *n.* 350731 K I V. 485 (1)

dacht *n.* 390828 K 3
Dacij *n. pl.* 231008 K 11
deinentwegen *praep.* 380828 K I 49
den danck verdienen 310000 K 13
Denckzeit *n.* 421110 K 1
deputat *n.* 260106 K 5
derivatio *n.* 381028 K IV 37.47.63
d'escrire *v.* 271201A K 9
desein *n.* 300410 K 12
Dessaw *Ortsname* 250305 K 48
Deuender *n.* 450400 K 15
deumlich *adj.* 350731 K I V. 37
Deuteley *n.*, s. Angesichts Deuteley
Deutligkeit *n.* 381028 K IV 15
deutsch *adj.* 301011 K 20
devis *n.* 380616 K 1
dey *art.* 371030 K I 5
Dialectica *n.* 381028 K IV 32.63
Dialecticè *adv.* 381028 K II 13 u. K IV 46
Dialecticus *adj.* 381028 K IV 34
dick *adv.* 260619 K 23
Dictionarij *n. pl.* 381028 K IV 31.32
Diederich *Personenname* 371031 K 8
Diener *n.*, s. Geheimbde *bzw.* vertrauete Diener
Dienerpietung *n.* 300216 T a
dienstverpflichtet *adv.* 280412 K 9
Digressione *n.* 381028 K IV 17
diporre *v.* 360630 K 5
Discordi *n. pl.* 381028 K IV 29
discorso/ discursus *n.* 381028 K IV 55
Disdeificare *v.* 381028 K IV 4
disner *v.* 210729 K 7
Dissonanza *n.* 381028 K IV 29
divertir *v.* 280216 K 8
do *adv., conj.* 310000 K 16. 371110 K 15. 401214 K I 7. 430724 K 8
doet *adj.* 300410 K 30

Don, s. thon
drie (drei) *num.* 270406 K 15
ducker *n.* 240717 K 17
Duello *n.* 381028 K IV 35.36
dülden *v.* 270406 K 7
Dünste *n. pl.* 381028 K IV 9
dur *praep.* 240718 K 30
dürch *praep.* 270406 K 7
Durchlaß *n.* 350731 K I V. 259
duytsch *adj. (nl.)* 430403 K 4

eben *adv.* 390125 K 13
Ebenmässigkeit *n.* 381028 K IV 22.43
Ebenredenheit *n.* 381028 K IV 22.43
Ebenstimmung *n.* 381028 K IV 31
ebuccinieren *v.* 450806 K 3
ebur *n.* 310703 K II 4
Ecstasis/ Estasi *n.* 381028 K IV 27
Effimera *n.* 381028 K IV 57
Ehehaf(f)t *n.* 240319 K 3. 300718 K 6. 400312 K 4
ehndung *n.* 350800 K 21
Ehrenlied *n.* 270810 K 4
Ehrnholde *n. pl.* 350731 K I V. 482
Ehrwürden *n.* 401214 K 10
eigen Anliegen(heit) 381028 K IV 54
Eigennutz *n.* 381028 K IV 54
eigenung *n.* 230819 K 6
eigen Vortheil 381028 K IV 54
ein *num.* 310224 K 41. 380110 K 6. 401214 K 6. 410706 K 5. 420630 K 6
ein hertz einsprechen *idiom.* 380120 K 4
Einbildung(en) *n. (pl.)* 381028 K IV 52, vgl. Vernünfftige Einbildung
einbrüche *n. pl.* 290501 K 2
eindacht *n.* 371014 K 6
eines *adv.* 250700 K 19
eingeheimschet *part.* 451001 K 2
eingejacht *part.* 301001 K 29
eingemachtt *part.* 280414 K 7
eingerühmt *adj.* 290529 K 5
eingeschnitten *part.* 350731 K I V. 35
einhelligkhlich *adj.* 301011 K 22
einschreiben *v.* 390131 K 19
eintzele person 381028 K IV 34
einwinden *v.* 250110 K II 4
Eisenstadt *Ortsname* 291104A I Q u. K I 3
Elend zu bauen *idiom.* 450126 K 7

eller *pron.* 281215 K 8
empfahen *v.* 371124 K I 4
empfelichen *v.* 300921 K 36
ἔμφασισ *n.* 381028 K II 15 u. K IV 6.16.54
ἐμφατικῶς *adv.* 381028 K II 19
Emphaticè *adv.* 381028 IV
emphaticus *adj.* 381028 K IV 6
Emplemanten *n. pl.* 310224 K 18; vgl. Emblema
L'Emply *n.* 410621 K II 91
ἐνάργεια *n.* 381028 K IV 15
enbrener *v.* 271201A K 8
encaparassoné *part.* 380310 K IV 2
endtbrechen *v.* 290510 K 10
enge *n.* 221214 K 11
Enthymema/ Entimemi *n. (pl.)* 381028 K IV 63
entlehnetes wortt 280411 K 7
entpfahen *v.* 280414
entzückung *n.* 381028 K IV 27
Ephimera *n.* 381028 K IV 57
Epitheton *n.* 381028 IV (8. 14)
equivocare *v.* 381028 K IV 70
erbärmbd *n.* 250110 K I 4
Erde *n.* 280122 I u. K I 6
Erheber *n.* 410101 K 4
ermeßigung *n.* 290510 K 12
Erregungen *n. pl.* 381028 K IV 47.61
ersättigung *n.* 381028 K IV 53
erschellen *v.* 380402 K I 4
ersetzen *v.* 240718 K 60
Erstaunung *n.* 381028 K IV 27
ertz *n.* 371124 K I 19
ErtzSchrein *n.* 371110 K 11
erwegen / erwegung *v./ n.* 381028 K IV 55
erweichen *v.* 250305 K 32
erweisen *part.* 270406 K 3
erwinden *v.* 181222 K 8
erzielen *v.* 310000 K I 5
L'Esmuovente *n. (part.)* 410621 K II 7
Espiegles courtisans 280106 K 7
Estafier *n.* 380310 K I 22
Estasi *n.*, s. Ecstasis
Ethicè *adv.* 381028 K II 4
etiandio *adv.* 230802 K 11
et quant et quant que *conj.* 340628 K 4
Etymologia *n.* 381028 K IV 41

eulich *adv.* 250218 K 13
expedition *n.* 240717 T a
expicta *part.* 450927 K 3
Eysenhütlein *Pflanzenname* 381028 K IV 51

façon *n.* 240718 K 55
falb *adj.* 450817 K I 4
Fantaseyen *n. pl.* 381028 K IV 52
fantasmi *n. pl.* 381028 K IV 52
fast *adv.* 300215 K I 4. 390904 K I 3
Fato/ Fatum *n.* 381028 K IV 41
favoriti *n. pl.* 381028 K IV 15.16
fendlen *n. pl.* 300921 K 20. 420630 K 19
Fenster (des Himmels) *n. pl.* 381028 K IV 33
Ferden (Verden) *Ortsname* 261010 K 10
ferire *v.* 381028 K IV 25
fertigkeit *n.* 381028 K IV 53
feüchtigkeit *n.*, s. Melancholische/ schwermütige
feuille morte *Farbe* 250500 K 12
Fichtelgebirge *Ortsname* 300320 II
Ficus Indiae *Pflanzenname* DA Köthen I. 3, S. 106 ff., 113, 117
Fieber *n.*, s. kurtztägig Fieber
figkiche *n.* 290410 K 6
firnen wein *n.* 250514 K 3
Fisionomia *n.* 381028 K IV 21
fisirlich *adj.* 240718 K 61
Flederwisch *n.* 210401 K 18
fließen *v.* 360800 K 2
florß Mantell *n.* 240718 K 29
folge *n.* 401214 K I 2
förderen *v.* 290529 K 4
formare *v.* 381028 III u. K IV 20
formiren *v.* 381028 K II 20
Il Forte *n.* 410621 K II 26
fortsatz *n.* 380331 K 7
Frage *n.*, s. vorgestellte Frage
FragsVorstellung *n.* 381028 K IV 40
france *adj.* 301011 K 17
freüd(en)spiel *n.* 381028 K IV 59
freunde *n. pl.* 280220 K 7
freundschafftt *n.* 260619 K 25
frömdgierigkeit *n.* 410706 K 4
fruchtbringen *v.* 230819
Fuchßschwentzen *v.* 350731 K I V. 275
fürbindig *adv.* 460819 K II 9

Fug *n.* 390911 K 4
fugung *n.* 450326 K 1
fundt *n.* 280208 K 15
Furchen (beziehen mit) *n. pl.* 381028 K IV 25

Gaben *n. pl.* 381028 K IV 69
gaigner *v.* 171224 K 3
Galee *n.* 321201 K 11
Galerus *n.* DA Köthen I. 3, S. 107 f.
Gallone *n.* 271201 K I 3
galouches *n.* 381028 K II 0
garçettes *n.* 381028 K II 0
garen *n.* 380828 K I 4
garmen *v.* 390112 K I 2
Garmänner *n. pl.* 430103 K II 1
gattung *n.* 371106 K 3
gebachen *part.* 301011 K 16
gebahret *part.* 371227 K 2
gebeert *part.* 380828 K I 9
gebleck *n.* 250305 K 47
Geburtsglück *n.* 381028 K IV 41
gefährung *n.* 350800 K 22
gefallen *adj.* 310108 K 3
gefehrde *n.* 460125 K II 4
gefehrt *v.* 440715 K 7
gefress *adj.* 350731 K I V. 41
gefreundte *n. pl.* 381123 K 3
Gedenckzeit, s. Denckzeit
gegenblick *n.* 381028 K IV 32
Gegenhalt *n.* 381028 K IV 32
gegenlage *n.* 381028 K IV 42
Gegenwurff *n.* 381028 K IV 42.52
geh *adj.* 300320 K II 11
geharter-Stern *n.* 381028 K IV 49
gehehlen *v.* 350731 K I V. 533
Geheimbte Diener 381028 K IV 16
gehling *adj.* 300509 K 1
gehöre *n.* 250110 K I 30
gehürnt *adj.* 310000 K I 4
geihte *n.* 240718 K 83
Geister *n. pl.* 381028 K IV 9
geißell *n.* 410208 K I 37
geit *v.* (zu geben) 250110 K I 20
gelacke *n.* 280412 K 8
gelänck *n.* 370900 K 7
gelefarbe *n.* 280122 I u. K I 12
gelit *n.* 460620A K 1
gelten *v.* 460309 K 2

gemahl *n.*   340716 K 8
gemählde/ gemälde *n.*   220824 K 3.
    240109 K 7. 380509 K 3
gemitten *part.*   310800 K 4
gemüschel *n.*   300320 K II 13
gemuthsam *adv.*   380331 K 6
Gemüths Bewegung(en) *n. (pl.)*   381028 K
    IV 61
Gemüths Entzückung *n.*   381028 K IV 27
Gemütsneigungen *n. pl.*   381028 K IV 47
geniegt *part.*   290120 K 5
genieß *n.*   290529 K 33
genießen *v.*   371124 K I 10
gentillesses *n. pl.*   281000 K 4
gepochet *part.*   350731 K I V. 35
gerichts *adv.*   380828 K I 40
German *Personenname*   230819 K 5
Germanen *n. pl.*   430103 K II 1
Germann *adj.*   230819
Germinare *v.*   230819
Gern-goldmacher *n. pl.*   381028 K IV 68
Gernriese *n.*   381028 K IV 39
geruhen *v.*   451008 K 3
Gesang *n.*, s. Zuhören angenehmer Gesang
    381028 K IV 29
gescheiden *part.*   350731 K I V. 98
Geschichten *n. pl.*   380108 K 6
Geschichtschreiber *n.*   381028 K II 5
Geschichtschrifftlich *adv.*   381028 K II 5
geschlacht *adj.*   *DA Köthen I. 6*, S. 124
geschlichtet *part.*   410206 K I 1
Geschnetter *n.*   350731 K I V. 354
geschoppet *part.*   370900 K 9
geschwistert *n.*   340107 K 6
gesein *v.*   371219 K 5
Geselschaft/ Gesellschaft/ gesellschafft *n.*
    240109 K 9. *DA Köthen I. 2*, S. 19.
    280411 K 8. 290310 K 3. 300426 K 7
gesellschafftt brieff *n.*   280414
gesetz *n.*   371222 K 3. 450901 K 7. 460825
    K 6
gesetzt *n.*   250500 K 21
Gesichtender *n.*   381028 K IV 72
Gesichtsstralen *n. pl.*   381028 K IV 72
gesocht *part.*   290529 K 14
gespannet *part.*   290510 K 3
gestalten *v.*   381028 III u. K II 20 u. K IV
    20

Gestirnkündigung *n.*   381028 K II 27
gestirnkunst *n.*   381028 K II 27
gesuchen *v.*   320729 K 3
gethraut *part.*   360703 K 8
getrecket *part.*   350731 K I V. 154
geuhte *n.*   240718 K 83
Gewahrsam *n.*   371123 K 3
gewehret *part.*   270919 K 7
gewierig *adv.*   440723 K 4
gewißen *part.*   450510 K 6
gewißkünstig *adv., adj.*   371014 K 2
Gewitter *n.*   370421 K I 1
Gewonheit/ gewohnheits-gestalt *n.*
    381028 K IV 53
gezaffell *n.*   240718 K 79
Giganteggi *n. pl./* Giganteggiare *v.*
    381028 K IV 39
glaubenspaffeisen, s. paffeisen
Gleeß *n.*   350731 K I V. 36
Gleichförmigkeit *n.*   381028 K IV 24
gleichmäßig *adv.*   390828 K 2
gleichmässige eintheilung   381028 K IV
    22
Gleichredenheit *n.*   381028 K IV 24
gleichsdeutend Wort   381028 K IV 28
gleich-stimmung *n.*   381028 K IV 29
gleich-wortig reden *v.*   381028 K IV 70
gleichwörtige reden *n. pl.*   381028 K IV 70
gloß *n.*   250500 K 23
Glück *n.*   381028 K IV 41
Gnomone *n.*   381028 K IV 65
gnügen *n.*   371124 K I 17
Gottbotts scheideweg *Ortsname*   240109
    K 11
Gottesdienst *n.*   381028 K IV 12
Gottes WortLehrer *n. pl.*   381028 K IV
    2.40
Grad *n.*   381028 K IV 62
grausam *adv.*   390727 K 7
greifen *v.*   240718 K 36
greißgrau *adj.*   350731 K I V. 487
Grewel *n.*   390727 K 7
Griefflein *n.*   371009 K III 4
griseln *v.*   250218A K V 5
grös(ses)te solcher Art   381028 K IV 34
grülle *n.*   180000 K 5
grund gesetz *n.*   380828 K I 56
Gunstzeichen *n.*   440000 Q

Haar *n.* 381028 K IV 10
haarbogen *n.* 240718 K 63
habitus *n.* 381028 K IV 53
haftieg *adj.* 250218 K 8
Hag(e), der *Ortsname* 190308 K 11
hahn/ han *v.* 280412 K II 3. 281021 K 2
haibeartig *adj.* 410406 K 8
halber himmelkreis 381028 K IV 72
halffter, Holfter *n.* 410208 K I 18
Hallon *n.* 370422 K 3
halten *v.* 390126B K 3
Hamen *n.* 350731 K I V. 35
Hammel *Tiername* 280122 I u. K I 6
han, s. hahn
Handveste *n.* 390826 K 5
Hansen *n. pl.* 360703 K 31
häringbussen *n. pl.* 300921 K 7
Harmonia *n.* 381028 K IV 21.28
harr, in die 250218A K VII 27
Hartmonat *Monatsname* 380221 K 8. 450221 K 1
Haspel sehen, auf den *idiom.* 300410 K 13
hassardiren *v.* 300410 K 53
hauffen *n.* 381028 K IV 56
Haupt-Vrsach/ Häuptwirckende Vrsach 381028 IV (72.2)/ K IV 19.41
Haußhältisch *adv.* 381028 K II 11
(gute) haushaltung *n.* 381028 K II 11
haut de chauces *n.* 380310 K I 37
Hedera *n. (lat.)* 421206 K 11
hefe *n.* 360600 K II 12
heidenthumb *n.* 250305 K 25
heil allwelt *Pflanzenname* 320715 K 5
heisch *adj.* 250413 K I 8. 350731 K I V. 80
Helikon *Ortsname* 360800
herauserfertigen *v.* 190322 K 5
herbst *n.* 401111 K 11
Herminianen *Personenname* 301011 K 20
hersingen *v.* 270810 K 5
hertzen kündiger *n.* 280721 K 12
Hertzensbewegungen *n. pl.* 381028 K IV 47
hertzensprast *n.* 250413 K I 6
Heumonat *Monatsname* 380803 K 3
heurig *adj.* 440426 K 3. 460916 K 5
Heyden *n. pl.* 381028 K IV 66
himmelkreis *n.*, s. halber himmelkreis

Himmelszeichen *n. pl.* 381028 K IV 44
hinbreiten *n.* 381028 K IV 27
hin dan setzen *v.* 240718 K 81
hinde *Tiername* 300320 K III 1
hindtbeere *Pflanzenname* 280327 K 3
hinlenden *v.* 371114 K I 13
Hippocratis vinc(u)lis 271010 K 17
Hippokrene *Quelle* 360800
Historice *adv.* 381028 K II 5
Höfflich *adv.* 381028 K II 7
högen *v.* 370900 K 10
hör *n.* 430215 K 23
hohe schule 280411 K 8. 290310 K 3
hollenstul *n.* 380000 K 10
Holtzschreyer *Tiername* 210401 K 13
hommelet *n.* 291013 K 4
honig treiff *n.* 380828 K I 11
hordt *n.* 200826 K 10
Horizon *n.* 381028 K IV 72
horn *n.* 300320 K II 18
Hulst *Pflanzenname* 230430 K 4
Humor melancolicus 381028 K IV 26
hündin *n.* 300320 K III 1
Hünnebrüden *n. pl.* 381028 K IV 27
Hüttlein *n.* 210401 K 19
hurd(e) *n.* 410208 K I 20
Huzeln *Pflanzenname* 280327 K 4

jach *adj.* 250305 K 24
jägermutzen *n.* 240718 K 57
jahrsatz *n.* 380619 K 6
Jarislaus *Personenname* 380302A K 5
ichs/ ichtwas *pron.* 320313 K 3
Jchtbas *pron.* 240116 K 5
idioten *n. pl.* 280128
Idiotismus *n.* 381028 K II 17.25
iegen *praep.* 290226A K 6
iegenwertig *adj.* 270306 K 1
iehe *adv.* 300718 K 5
Jehmer *adv.* 300426 K 14
ieman *pron.* 290913 K 9
imaginatio *n.* 381028 K IV 18
Imaginativa *n.* 381028 K IV 18.52
impatronirt *part.* 300410 K 28
in seltnen Händlen *idiom.* 460620 K 8
incontuite *adv., part.* 450508A K 1
L'Indirizzante *n. (part.)* 410621 K II 35
Individuatio/ Individuazione *n.* 381028 K IV 48

individui/ individuo/ Individuum *n.*, s. maggiori individui
inducas gehen *idiom.* 360428 K II 15
inducere *v.* 360428 K II 15
inful *n.* 380226 K 3
L'Innocente *n.* 410621 K II 6
Interesse *n.* 381028 K IV 54
jnterimsweyse *adv.*, s. mittlerweyle
inventionneux *adj.* 240718 K 86
jo/ jo ... jo 250110 K I 22
ist so jach *idiom.* 350731 K I V. 576
iter justum 291231 K 8
Iuridicè *adv.* 381028 K II 9
jus status *n.* 381028 K IV 6

Känster/ Kenster *Pflanzenname* 200125 K 2. 210401 K 3. 450408 K 3
Kalm *n.* 421101 K 4
Karch *n.* 250218A K V 8
kargen *v.* 360428 K III 4
karmen *v.* 380828 K I 27. 390112 K 3
karret(e) *n.* 410208 K I 24
Kesselstadt *Ortsname* 380328 K 8
kest(e) *n.* 410208 K I 20
Keuterling *n.* 460816 K I
Khinderbeth *n.* 310224 K 6
in der Klage gehen 310224 K 22
Klangtichter *n.* 371124 K 2
kluckerglaß *n.* 381107 K 26
Klügelschaum *n.* 440731 K I 7
Köthen *Ortsname* 460816 K I 1
Kolbe *n.* 371009 K III 3
Kolck *n.* 350731 K I V. 571
Körnung *n.* 350731 K I V. 34
kostbahr *adj.* 380126 K 5
köstung *n.* 290614 K 16
Krampff Fische *Tiername* 350731 K I V. 30 (2)
kraut *n.* 380602 K II 2
kriegen *v.* 240718 K 92. 260500 K 4
Kriegesläuffte *n.* 280517 K 2
krieges und streitkunst *n.* 381028 K II 8
Kriegsvnterrichtlich *adv.* 381028 K II 8
Kuh *n.* 350731 K I V. 35
kühr *n.* 401215 K II 3
kummer *n.* 391209 K 14
Kumpe, Kump *n.* 350731 K I V. 110
Künstler *n. pl.* 381028 K IV 71
kunlich *adv.* 461213 K 3

Kunstgemerke *n.* 450927 K II 2
Kunstwörter *n. pl.* **Technici**, Fachbegriffe 400301 K 2. 440525 K II 1. 440826 K 4
kürtzem, in *adv.* 290614 K 6
Kurtz(gefast)e Schlußreden 381028 K IV 63
kurtztägig Fieber 381028 K IV 57
kuschhaft *adj.* 240718 K 96

lahn *v.* 250305 K 17. 300330 K I 1
lahr *n.* 370715 K I 1
lamprehten *Tiername pl.* 371031 K I 2
langsam *adj.* 450711 K 5
Lanha/ Lanho *n.* DA *Köthen I. 3*, S. 106 f., 113 f.
lapis angulars *n.* 380320 K I 21
Lappe *n.* 250218A K V 2
las/ laß *adj.* 371124 K I 5. 391119 K II 4
Last *n.* (d. i. Auftrag) 300410 K 24
Last *n.* (d. i. Fracht) 420630 K 44. 450817 K I 5
latesten *adj.* 290614 K 18
lauffig *adj.* 310411 K 5
Il Leale *n.* 410621 K II 22
lefflen (löffeln) *v.* 300426 K 12
Leger *n.* 420630 K 23
Il Legorante *n. (part.)* 410621 K II 21
lehnen *v.* 350731 K I V. 425
Lehr-Sätze, s. Politische-Lehr-Sätze
leibeßaufnemung *n.* 450126 K 1
Leichnambsmessung *n.* 300215 K II 4
leicht *adj.* 450510 K 7
leichten *v.* 250110 K I 25
Leidselige *n.* 300426 K 7
Leim *n.* 230430 K 3
lenden *v.* 280600 K 3
lenge, die 250500 K 22
Lerner *n.* 460816 K I 3
Lethe *Flußname* 381028 K IV 13
Letterwechsel *n.* 411214 K II A 7
letzen, sich *v.* 250413 K II 3
letzte vntheilbarheit 381028 K IV 48
Leuffte *n. pl.* 280308 K 1
leunisch *adj.* 240718 K 76
leutselig *adj.* 300426 K 7
Leyden *n.* 381028 K IV 61
licentierungk *n.* 390131 K 4
liebhaberisch *adj.*, s. Weißheit liebhaberisch

Liecht der Natur/ Evangelij 280122 K II 6
Liechtes *n.* 290120 K 11
liechtlich *adv.* 290529 K 27
Lignon *Flußname* 250500 S. 406. 260000A. 291104A K 2
linckes und rechtes 250700 K 80
linkklingend *adj.* 300320 K II 3
Liquitation *n.* 321201 K 2
löffeln/ löfflen, s. lefflen
λογικός *adj.* 381028 K IV 6
Logres *Königreich* 230819 I
lösen, sich *v.* 401216 K 1
Loßzehlung *n.* 280216A K 2
lot *n.* 380602 K II 3
Lucriren *v.* 440927 K 2
lüstren *v.* 411214 K II A 8

maadggio *n.* 420124 K 14
maggiori individui 381028 K IV 34
Maintenator, s. Manitenator
maistres rimeurs *n.* 261010 K 13, vgl. Reimmeister
Malinconia *n.* 381028 K IV 26
malinconico *adj.*, s. umore malinconico
Mamluck/ Mammeluck *n.* 280122 I u. K I 10
mandar *n.* 340107 K 21
Manitenator *n.* 250218A K V 1. 391217 K 12
mänschreich *adv.* 370900 K 5
mantello nel cavallo *prov. ital.* 381028 K IV 10
marterwoche *n.* 190318 K 4
materÿ *n.* 240109 K 5
maulhenckolisch *adj.* 240718 K 26
meco *pron.* 280929 K 12
Medicè *adv.* 381028 K II 10
Meerbusen *n.* 440000 Q
mehlig *adv.* 411214 K II A 9
meilsch *n.* 240718 K 84
Mein *pron.* 410208 K I 46
meinentlich *adv.* 371126 K 6
meinst *adj.* 250218A K VII 10
Meisensprüe *n.* 210401 K 17
Melancholia *n.* 381028 K IV 26.27
melancolicus *adj.*, s. Humor melancolicus
Melancholische feüchtigkeit 381028 K IV 26

Melodia *n.* 381028 K IV 28
menassiren *v.* 440927 K 3
Mérovée *Personenname* 240112 K 9
Metaphora *n.* 381028 K IV 15.37.50
meteor *n.* 370422 K 2
Meto(po)scopia *n.* 381028 K IV 21
Mietze *Kosename* 371030 K I 13
Mild *Flußname* 250110 K II 1
Milte *n.* 430103 K II 5
Mine *n.* 240718 K 91
miserium (miserum?) schmelzen 381107 K 6
mishelligkeit *n.* 381028 K IV 29
Mispel *Pflanzenname* 200125 K 2. 210401 K 3. 450408 K 3
Mißstimmung *n.* 381028 K IV 29
Mistel *Pflanzenname* 450408 K 3
MittagsCirckel *n.* 381028 K IV 72
Mittelbild *n.* 300320 K II 24
Mittelursachen *n. pl.* 381028 K IV 19
Mittgelied *n.* 430526 K 4
mittlerweyle *adv.* 280327 K 6
Mitvnterseyn *n.* 381028 K IV 54
moderne *adj.* 281000 K 5
monstre du drap 370729 K 12
Morras *n.* 420630 K 17
Mörsel *n.* 350731 K I V. 501
Moß *Pflanzenname* 360800 K 2
muht *n.* 370715 K I 2
Mundart *n.* 431022 K 3
Muselmani *Personenname* 280122 I u. K I 11
Music *n.* 381028 K IV 30
Musica Acromatica 381028 K IV 31
muti *n. pl. (lat.)* 421206 K 4
mutung *n.* 410727 K 6
mutzen *v.* 300216 K 0

nach der Handt *idiom.* 451019 K 9
nachen 280412 K II 7
Nachkommen *part.* 371121 K 2
Nachrichtung *n.* 430121 K 9
nachrüchtiges *n.* 250700 K 49
nachsinnen *n.* 381028 K IV 55
nachsinnig *adv.* 381028 K II 23
nachsinnige Vmbsch[w]eiff 381028 K IV 55
Nachsinnung *n.* 381028 K IV 55
nachstendig *adv.* 460620A K 5

Nachtbar *n.* 380828 K I 6
nächten *n., dat. pl.* 240112 K 1
nachtheil, *n.* 380125 K 5
nachtmäntelgen *n.* 240718 K 64
Nachtruck *n.* 381028 K II 15 u. K IV 6
nachtrücklich *adj., adv.* 381028 K II 15.19 u. K IV 6.16.47
Nachtrückligkeit *n.* 381028 K IV 47.54
nahme *n.* 240109 K 7
Napello/ Napellus/ Napelles *Pflanzenname* 381028 K IV 51
Naturkündig *adv.* 381028 K II 3
Naturkündigung *n.* 381028 K II 26
natürkündisch *adj.* 381028 K II 26 u. K IV 19
nechst *adv.* 430403 K 2
nechstkünfftig *adj.* 291200 K 3
Neidthardt *Appellativname* 371123 K 14
Neruus bellj *idiom.* 360703 K 30
Netze *n. pl.* 410208 K I 25
neuchlichst *adv.* 451028 K 2
Neurikeit *n.* 440000 Q
Neustätter Rübelein *Pflanzenname* 250305 K 26
Newmonds Tage *n. pl.* 381028 K IV 58
neygungen *n. pl.* 381028 K IV 26.47
S. Nicola *Personenname* 171225
nider *adj.* 460206 K 2
nitt gar 281226 K 3
noch *adv.* 270919 K 9
Nöel *n.* 171224 K 2, 171225 K 3
nompair *n.* 280218 K 8
non chalamient *adv.* 240718 K 58
nuchtern *adj.* 240718 K 100
nurt/ nurtt/ nurten *adv.* 181023 K 4. 360428 K I 5. 371220 K 13
nutze *n.* 410208 K I 34
nütze *n.* 270406 K 23

Oberaufseher *n.* 380108 K 4
Obhaltt/ obhalt *n.* 190322 K 7. 431020 K 4. 460720 K 4
objectum *n.* 381028 K IV 42
oblage *n.* 380331 K 5
obschrift *n.* 450400 K 9
obsicht *n.* 280327 K 12
octroyrt *part.* 300410 K 47
Oeconomicè *adv.* 381028 K II 11
Ölberger *Gefäßname* 171224 K 5

Oggetto *n.* 381028 K IV 42
ohm *n.* 250514 K 2
ohne ein 300320 K V
ohne sich 370421 K 2
öhrlein *n.* 280510 K 8
ohrlog *n.* 420120 K 41. 420630 K 29
ohrtsprung *n.* 270827 K 8
Ola *n.* *DA Köthen I. 3*, S. 107 f., 114, 116
Olympos/ -us *Ortsname* 360800
operationes stellarum/ Operazioni delle stelle 381028 K IV 41
opinicht *adj.* 240718 K 70
orden *n.* 180000 K 7
Organi del intelletto 381028 K IV 23
Organum *n.* 381028 K IV 23
Originalia *n. pl.* 380108 K 5
Orizonte *n.* 381028 K IV 72
orlog *n.* 300921 K 5
orter *n.* 310113 K 51
osservandissimo *adj.* 290302 K 2
oweisig *adj.* 240718 K 82
Owitz *n.* 240718 K 65

paffeisen *n.* 280216A K 12
pagano/ Paganus/ Payen *n.* 381028 K IV 66
paggi *n.* 301011 K 19
palletto *n.* 240718 K 101
Panama *Pflanzenname* 320715 K 7
Paradoxum *n.* 381028 K II 1
Paragon/ paragone/ parangón *n.* 381028 K IV 67
Parenthesis *n.* 381028 IV (8.14)
Parnaß *Ortsname* 171224. 270429 K 19. 280411. 290129 K I
part *n.* 370422 K 4
particularien *n.* 240717 T b
pass *n.* (d. i. Schritt) 450420 K 4
paß *n.* (d. i. Passus) 221214 K 12
paßgang *n.* 381107 K 10
Passio(ne) *n.* 381028 K IV 61
patent *n.* 181207 K 7
Patrin *n.* 250218A K VII 1
Patrioten *n. pl.* 430103 K II 1
patron, prendre le 261010 K 15
Payen *n.*, s. pagano
Pazar *n.*, s. badzahr/ padzahr
Peeper *Pflanzenname* *DA Köthen I. 3*, S. 106 f.

Pelßreis *n.*   *DA Köthen I.* 6, S. 123
Pensel *n.*   430419 K I 1
Il Perdurevole *n. (part.)*   410621 K II 2
Peripetia *n.*   381028 K IV 59
periphen *n. pl.*   360703 K 33
Periphrasis *n.*   381028 K II 18
perschon *n.*   300410 K 17
person *n.*, s. eintzele person
perspecillia *n.*   291224 K 4
petardieren *v.*   360428 K II 2
Pfauenschwantz *n.*   381028 K IV 49
pfeiffer *n.*   450730 K 6
PfingstVogel *Tiername*   210401 K 12
pflichtschüldig *adj.*   290529 K 1
Pfreja tag *n.*   240109 K 12
Pfui dich *idiom.*   410208 K I 82
Pfund *n.*   381028 K IV 45.69. 390826 K 3
Pfund spannen, an sein *idiom.*   371123 K 10
Phantasia *n.*   381028 K IV 18.52
Philologicè *adv.*   381028 K II 21 u. K IV 44
Philologicus *adj., n.*   381028 K II 21 u. K IV 70
Philologus *n.*   460915 K 3
Philosophicè *adv.*   381028 K II 2
Philosophus *n.*   460915 K 3
Phisicè *adv.*   381028 K II 3
Phisiognomia *n.*   381028 K IV 21
pickes *n. pl.*   240910 K 13
picque geben, ein grosse *idiom.*   300410 K 45
Plakaat *n. (nl.)*   310113 K 32
plätzlein *n.*   380509 K 6
plönp *adj.*   240718 K 78
Poeterey *n.*   381028 K II 14
Poeticè *adv.*   381028 K II 14
polcy [policey] *n.*   250500 K 20
Polemicè *adv.*   381028 K II 8
Politicè *adv.*   381028 K II 6
Politici Aphorismi *n. pl.*   381028 K IV 3
πολιτικός / πολιτικώς *adj./ adv.*   381028 K IV 3
Politicus *n.*   460915 K 3
Politische-Lehr-Sätze *n. pl.*   381028 K IV 3
Polus *n.*   381028 K IV 72
post *n.*   250218 K 5
posten *n. pl.*   460718 K 6

Postiren *v.*   250218A K V 9
Potentat *n.*   381028 K II 0
pouppin *n.*   250500 K 16
Pracht *n.*   450220 K II 1
prædicatum *n.*   381028 IV (8.14)
Præservatif *n.*   381028 K IV 60
praesagiren *v.*   371009 K 5
Lo Precavente *n. (part.)*   410621 K II 20
Preludio *n.*   381028 K IV 36
Privado/ Privato *n.*   381028 K IV 16
Probierstein *n.*   381028 K IV 67
Probiertiegel *n.*   381028 K IV 68
Problema *n.*   381028 K IV 40
Professori *n. pl. (ital.)*   381028 K IV 71
Prophet *n.*   381028 K IV 12.56
Propositione *n.*   381028 K IV 11
Proportio *n.*   381028 K IV 24
Proportz *n.*   381028 K IV 22.43
Le Prouverdoyant *n. (part.)*   410621 K II 56
Proviant *n.*   381028 K II 0
Pudel *n.*   440324 K 11
Püffelshaut *n.*   250218A K V 6
pulvis *n.*   411214 K 9
puntila *n.*   371009 K 9
puoco *adv.*   230802 K 4

quant et   230809 K 6. 391113 K 5
quarti(e)r begehren *idiom.*   420630 K 20
quell *n.*   380828 K I 23
Quentin *n.*   461006 K 11
Quinte *n.*   371009 K 10

Rabatgen *n.*   240718 K 48
raccoustrer *v.*   280818 K 2
rack *adj.*   421108 K 3
Il Radicante *n.*   410621 K II 11
radii optici *n. pl.*   381028 K IV 72
Il Raffrictante (Raffreddante) *n.*   410621 K II 33
Ragione di stato   381028 K IV 6
Ragionevuole *adj.*   381028 K IV 6
ragioni *n. pl.*   381028 K IV 50
Raison d'Estat   381028 K IV 6
Raisonable *adj.*   381028 K IV 6
ranae *n. pl.*   380417 K 7
Rantion, Rantzon *n.*   300924 K 18. 300921 K 3
rantionirt *part.*   300921 K 3. 300924 K 18

Rantzion *n.*   420630 K 28
Ratio *n.*   381028 K IV 6
rationabile/ rationabilis *adj.*   381028
   K IV 6
rationalis *adj.*   381028 K IV 6
rationalita *n.*   381028 K IV 20
Ra(t)zenburg *Ortsname*   280620 K 1
Razonable *adj.*   381028 K IV 6
reassumption *n.*   440927 K 9
Rebarbara *Pflanzenname*   190424 K 5
Reben *n.*   450817 K I 2
rechnen *v.*   370422 K II 4
rechte vernunft   381028 K IV 20
rechtes, s. linckes und rechtes
rechtslehre *n.*   381028 K II 9
Rechtslerig *adv.*   381028 K II 9
recontrirt *part.*   300410 K 33
Reden von Staet/ Rede von Stat *n.*
   381028 K IV 6.12
redener lehre *n.*   381028 K II 13
Redengeb(ungs)künstig *adv.* (*adj.*)
   381028 K II 13 bzw. K IV 46
Redensart *n.*   381028 K II 25. 410909 K 3.
   431022 K 3
Redgeb(ig)kunst(s Wort/ Bedeutung) *n.*
   381028 K IV 32.34.63. 440525 K II 9
Redlich *adj.*   381028 K IV 6.7
Redligkeit *n.*   381028 K IV 20
Redner-Kunst *n.*   381028 K IV 63
Redoute *n.*   420630 K 18
Regel *n.*   381028 K IV 50
Regensärcken *n. pl.*   381028 K IV 5
reide *n.*   371030 K I 1
reige *n.*   240718 K 90
Reimdichterisch *adv.*   381028 K II 14
Reimmeister *n.*   260703 K 2. *DA Köthen
   I.* 2, S. 14, 15, 17. 280414 K 4. 280425
   K 4, vgl. maistres rimeurs
reiner treten   250706 K I 8
Religion *n.*   301011 K 22. 381028 K II 0 u.
   IV 12
reme *n.*   210626 K 2
Rengßpurg *Ortsname*   440824 K 9
rennlich *adv.*   290529 K 7
reservoir *n.*   371028 K 12
response *n.*   380310 K I 14
Rethorica *n.*   381028 K IV 63
retuyte, s. Redoute

Richtscheid *n.*   340912 K 1. 381028 K IV
   50.65
Richtschnur *n.*   381028 K IV 50.65
Riesengebirge *Ortsname*   300209 K 4.
   300320 II
Riesentzender *n.*   381028 K IV 39
rifarsi *v.*   230913 K 7
ring *adj.*   250110 K I 26
Il Rintuzzante *n.*   410621 K II 32
rohrdummel *Tiername*   380828 K I 52
rotomentado *n.*   301011 K 11
rucht *n.*   370421 K 3
rund *adv.*   371124 K I 12

Saale *Flußname*   300320 II. 340428 III
Saffran *Pflanzenname*   280122 I u. K I 12
sagon *n.*   240718 K 55
Sanfftmuth *n.*   270810 K 6
Sarsant *n.*   320313 K 6
Satz *n.*   380904 K 8
Satzung *n.*   390826 K 4
Sauerteig *n.*   240718 K 22
Sauerzäpfgen *Spitzname*   240718 K 12
Lo Scardassante *n.*   410621 K II 10
Lo Scavalcante *n.* (*part.*)   410621 K II 36
schaar *n.*   381028 K IV 56
schadelos/ schatelos/ schatloß *adv.*
   301011 K 4. 420630 K 34
Schaltarbeit *n.*   430920 K 6. 451217 K 5
Schaltreich *n.*   440525 II
schätt[en] *v.*   300426 K 13
Schatter *n.*   271201 K I 5
Schatzkasten *n.*   271215 K 3
schatzung *n.*   290529 K 9. 401214 K 7
Schatzungskasten *n.*   401214 K 7
Schaubühne *n.*   440000 Q
Schawspiel *n.*   381028 K IV 59
scheinen *v.*   240718 K 53
Scheitell *n.*   410208 I 26
schell *adj.*   250500 K 25
Schellhengst *n.*   190308 K 2
schellschaft *n.*   240718 K 99
schema *n.*   410208 K I 68
Scheps *n.*   280411 K 12
schetzken *n.*   290608 K 5
scheuchen *v.*   350731 K I V. 376
scheytel *n.*   380828 K I 3
schiell *adj.*   250500 K 25
Schierung *n.*   301001 K 30

SchiffAnhalter *Tiername* 350731 K I V.
  30 (1)
schlachten *v.* 310113 K 37
Schlaffkuntzen *Pflanzenname* 280327
  K 5
schlaverey *n.* 350800 K 16
schlecht *adv., adj.* 270810 K 7. 290131
  K 3. 371014 K 3. 410505 K 2. 460705
  K I 1
schleiffmüle *n.* 290529 K 29
schleüsen (des himmels) *n. pl.* 381028 K
  IV 33
schliefen *v.* 371124 K I 11
schloß *n.* 380828 K I 8
schloße *n.* 290616 K 7
schlumpfen *v.* 240718 K 52
Schlußreden *n. pl.*, s. Kurtz(gefast)e
  Schlußreden
schnecke *n.* 380828 K I 45
schnell *adj.* 350731 K I V. 474
Schnerre *Tiername* 210401 K 11
Schock *n. Mengeneinheit* 391119 K 5
schon *adv.* 250500 K 4
schond *adv.* 300320 K 11
schondt *adj.* 250514 K 7
Schöne *n.* 360800 K 3
Schöps, s. Scheps
schoß *n.* 380828 K I 7
Schoß Kinder *n. pl.* 381028 K IV 15
SchreibensArt *n.* 381028 K II 24
Schrein *n.* 371110 K 11
Schriben *n. pl.* 270827 K 5
Schrimpff *n.* 410221 K 3
Schu *n.* 210401 K 7
schwermütige feüchtigkeit 381028 K II
  26
Schwermütigkeit *n.* 381028 K IV 26
Scipiades *Personenname* 310703 K I 6
scorretture *n. pl.* 460120A K 4
sehen (sehgen) *v.* 210421 K 3
seiger *n.* 250305 K 21. 350731 K I V. 505
Seille *n. pl.* 420630 K 47
Seindt *praep.* 240718 K 13
selbschaft *n.* 450308A
Selbstand *n.* 450308A K 1
seufftz *n.* 250110 K I 35. 380828 K I 29
Seussiades *Personenname* 310703 K II 12
seyllen *v.* 300410 K 27. 420120 K 42.
  420630 K 37

sfera *n.* 381028 K IV 62
sie *pron. refl.* 300410 K 36
sieder *praep.* 280220 K 2. 450721 K 2.
  460104 K 2
Sieg(s)pracht *n.* 390723 K 3. 460825 K 19
Simmetria *n.* 381028 K IV 21.22.43
Sindicus (Syndicus) *n.* 380721 K 7
sinnen *v.* 400203 K 2
Sinnerregungen *n. pl.* 381028 K IV 47
Le Siringuant *n. (part.)* 410621 K II 64
Sittenlerisch *adv.* 381028 K II 4
sittenreich *adv.* 280412 K 12
Sittenthat, Christliche 381028 K IV 14
Sittig *adj.* 280122 I u. K I 7
Soggetto *n.* 381028 K IV 46
solæcismus *n.* 260617 K 7
solatium *n.* 390131 K 5
Il Sollazzante *n.* 410621 K II 16
sonder(n) *praep.* 301011 K 18
sönsten *adv.* 290529 K 3
Sonstet *adv.* 250514 K 6. 281105 K 6
Sorgfeltig/ sorgfältig *adj.* 180508 K 5.
  451008 K 2
sorgsam *adj.* 371123 K 11
Sors nascendi 381028 K IV 41
sorte del nascere 381028 K IV 41
sothan *adv.* 300215 K I 6
Le Souef *n.* 410621 K II 39
Spelt *n.* 450611 K 3
sperrn, s. auffsperrn
Spiegellfalcken des hoffs 280106 K 7
Spioni *n. pl.* 300209 K 7
spiriti/ Spiritus *n. pl.* 381028 K IV 9
Sprach- und Wortliebende *n. pl.* 381028
  K II 21
Sprachrichter (Criticus) *n.* 450410
Sprüchlein *n.* 460825 K 6
Staab *n.* 381028 IV (8.14)
Staat, s. stadt
stab *(militär.) n.* 280220 K 4
(le) Stable *Gesellschaftsname* 381028 K
  III
stacket *n.* 360600 K II 59
stadt [Staat] *n.* 280220 K 3
Stände *n. pl.* 410117 K 6
Staet *n.* 381028 IV; s. auch Rede(n) von
  Sta(e)t
stance *n.* 230809 K 25
stand *n.* 381028 K IV 62

Standhalter *n.*   391217 K 11
Stangen glas *n.*   250305 K 28
Statsrecht *n.*   381028 K IV 6.12
staube *n.*   290529 K 36
Steckgarn/ Stockgarn *n.*   350731 K I V. 35
Sternseherisch *n.*   381028 K II 27
stet *adv.*   250110 K I 27
steuer der Wahrheit *idiom.*   460620 K 6
Steẘer *n.*   280208 K 3
Steweranlage *n.*   271215 K 2
sticken *v.*   250413 K I 7
stickwerck *n.*   380828 K I 57
stimmeln *v.*   450817 K I 3
Lo Stimolante *n.*   410621 K II 3
Stimplen *n.*   440616 K III 2
Stirn-Betrachtung *n.*   381028 K IV 21
stirn- und gesichtskündigung *n.*   381028 K IV 21
Storea Pallanquinorum *n.*   *DA Köthen I.* 3, S. 107 f., 114
strack *adj.*   250413 K I 4
stracks *adv.*   250706 K I 7
Was Jch strauße sagen will *idiom.*   410208 K I 56
strich/ Strich *n.*   380828 K I 5/ 380602 K 6
strigell *n.*   410208 K I 15
Stul des Krieges *n.*   440504 K 1. 450124 K 8
stutz, auff einen *idiom.*   190318 K 10
Stylus *n.*   381028 K II 24
Subjectum *n.*   381028 K IV 46
süchen *v.*   290614 K 5
supernumeraire *adj.*   280304 K 2
surdisch *adj.*   300215 K II 6
syndikatsache *n.*   380721 K 7
Synonima *n. pl.*   381028 K IV 28
σύνοψις *n.*   381028 K II 22
Syzygia *n.*   431124 K 8

tabellio *n.*   190424 K 9
tagesatzung *n.*   380522A K 7
Tage verzeichnuß *n.*   380320 T I i
Talenti/ Talento/ Talentum *n.*   381028 K IV 45.69
Talionis Straffe   250413 K I 10
Tapezerey *n.*   271215 K 13
Tarantola *n.*   381028 K IV 31
taub *adj.*   300215 K II 6

täuffte/ teuffte *n.*   181207 K 14. 260619 K 7
taxt *n.*   410313 K 4
teidigen *v.*   250305 K 27
Temeritz *n.*   461204 K 2
temperiren *v.*   250218A K VII 20
Teologi *n. pl.*   381028 K IV 2.40
terrouër *n.*   240400 K 3
teuffe *n.*   380828 K I 48
teuffte, s. täuffte
Teutschheyt *n.*   440525 K I 2
Theilbarkeit *n.*, s. vnferner Theilbarkeit
theilhaftigmachung *n.*   390115 K 2
Theologicè *adv.*   381028 II u.III
Theonestus *Personenname*, s. Diederich
Thierkreis *n.*   381028 K IV 44
thon *n.*   270810 K 2
Thondichter *n.*   371124 K 2
thonkündigung *n.*   381028 K IV 30
thuchwammerst *n.*   240718 K 47
thüren *v.*   400528 K II 29. 460915 K 5
Tiegel *n.*   381028 K IV 68
tieren *v.*   250110 K I 32
Il Tignente *n.*   410621 K II 8
Toffet *n.*   271201 K I 4
Tragedien/ Tragödien *n. pl.*   381028 K IV 59
translatèe *part.*   280304 K 1
Trauerspiele *n. pl.*   381028 K IV 59
trawen *v.*   250218A K VII 26
trebes abent *n.*   250218 K 19
treuis (treves) *n.*   300410 K 35
treÿfues *n.*   300921 K 31
Trinckrecht *n.*   280407 K 4
trubsall *n.*   410208 K I 27
Trumpter *n.*   350731 K I V. 496
tuckmäuserisch *adv.*   371110 K 16
tügen *v.*   210401 K 23. 400122 K I 31
Tugendtbergk (Parnasso) *n.*   280411 K 5
Tutell *n.*   460808 K 4
Tyrann *n.*   381028 K IV 8
Tyraß *n.*   350731 K I V. 35

Vbelstimmung *n.*   381028 K IV 29
Vberdragung/ Vbertragung *n.*   381028 K IV 15.37.50
übereilen *v.*   450919 K 5
übereinstimmung *n.*   381028 K IV 22.29
überhuijet *part.*   371031 K 3

uberlegen *v.*   371106 K 4
vberrachsen *v.*   240718 K 5
überreime *n. pl.*   300320 K II 17
übersatz *n.*   411128 K 4
uberschlag *n.*   401228A K 2
überschlagen *v.*   410206 K I 2
vberteufeln *v.*   240718 K 46
L'Ubertoso *n.*   410621 K II 4
Vffboth *n.*   320313 K 10
uffgeschoßt *part.*   350731 K I V. 35
umbfahen *v.*   371124 K I 6
Umbrede *n.*   381028 K II 18 u. K IV 25
ümbsasse *n.*   390904 K I 1
umbschreibung *n.*   381028 K II 18
vmbschrifft *n.*   381028 K IV 16
Vmbsch[w]eiff *n.*, s. nachsinnige Vmbsch[w]eiff
Umfang *n.*   440000 Q
ummerlauffen *v.*   280510 K III 2
umore malinconico   381028 K IV 26
Vnadel *adj.*   350731 K I V. 231
unähnligkeit (zu einander)   381028 K IV 24
vnbelediget *adj.*   240421 T e
uneinigkeit *n.*   381028 K IV 29
vnferner-theilbarheit (letzte)/ vnferner-Theilbarkeit   381028 K IV 34.48
vngedültig *adj.*   270406 K 7
Vngefehrte *n.*   410621 K II 24
Vngefell *n.*   250110 K II 2
ungemach *n.*   401117 K I 2
Vngläubige *n. pl.*   381028 K IV 66
vnkosten *n.*   460703 K 2
vnmaßgebig *adv.*   280208 K 5
Vnruhe *n.*   381028 K IV 65
vnstatt *n.*   371224 K 7
unterdienstlich *adv., adj.*   371028A K 3
Vnterlage *n.*   381028 K IV 46
unterläuffer *n.*   460424 K 15
Vnterwurff *n.*   381028 K IV 46
vntheilbares *n.*   381028 K IV 34
vntheilbarheit *n.*, s. letzte vntheilbarheit/ letzte vnferner-theilbarheit
untractirten *adj.*   440927 K 5
untz *praep.*   430103 K II 8
unverfährt *adv.*   440204 K I 1
Vnwärthe *n.*   460819 K 4
ur-att *n.*   370900 K 3
vrbötig *adv.*   371110 K 4

vrgicht *n.*   380108 K 5
Vrheb *n.*   240109 K 3
vrheber *n.*   280411 K 6. 290310 K I 5. 310000 K 15
Vrsachen *v.*   250110 K I 33
Ursin(us) *Personenname*   260619

Veere, s. Wehr
Veränderung *n.*   381028 K IV 59
verbaratieren *v.*   451019 K 4
verbuttert *part., adj.*   380331 K 8
verdienen *v.*   391005 K 4. 461029 K 11
vergeben *adj.*   250110 K I 24
vergleichen *part.*   300203 K 3
verhandeln *v.*   370422 K III 2
verhandfestung *n.*   390826 K 5
verhandvesten *v.*   390826 K 5
verhängen *v.*   250700 K 93
verhartung *n.*   380417 K 6
verhegen *v.*   250110 K I 5
verheischen *v.*   460125 K II 2
verheissen *v.*   181023 K 15
verknüfft *part.*   280600 K 4
verkündigen *v. refl.*   340609 K 1
Verlag *n.*   371221 K 12. 390126A K 3
verlaß/ verlas *n.*   300209 K 1. 380321 K 7. 390807A K 2
verlassen *v.*   360428 K III 9
verlassen, sich *v.*   281226 K 6
verliehung *n.*   270406 K 21
verlogen *adj.*   440724 K 12
verlosen *v.*   410708 K 8
vermissen *v.*   441020 K 9
Vernennung *n.*   381028 K IV 15
vernügen *v.*   250110 K I 29
vernugen *n.*   460620B K 8
Vernünfftige Einbildung   381028 K IV 18
Verrichtung *n.*   240717 T a
verschienen *adj. part.*   430121 K 1
verschleuchen *v.*   360428 K III 7
verschorren *part.*   280716 K I 5
versehen, (sich) *part.*   300420 K 2
versehung *n.*   300420 K 2. 381028 K IV 41
Verselbsten *v.*   440000 Q
Verspruch *n.*   320313 K 5
Verstandt-Lehr *n.*   400122 T f u. K 5
verstandlehre *n.*   381028 K II 13
Verstandt(s)röhrlein *n. pl.*   381028 K IV 23

Wörterverzeichnis 1091

verstimmung n.   381028 K IV 29
verstockung n.   380417 K 6
verstokhet part.   430215 K 19
verstoßen, sich v.   371123 K 6
verstrecken v.   240718 K 71
verstricken v.   270406 K 16. 320313 K 4
verthunlich adj.   250110 K I 34
vertraglich adv.   320715 K 2
vertrauete Diener   381028 K IV 16
vertreugen v.   360428 K III 8
Vertröstung n.   450308 K 5. 450923 K 3
verungöttern v.   381028 K IV 4
verwogen part.   441231 K 10
verworffener Tag   380619 K 5
Verzeichniß n.   450400 K 14
vetter n.   450510 K 4
viellichtt adv.   290120 K 12
Vindigora Ortsname   240718 S. 279
Virginia Ortsname   190424 K 4
viscalgeneral n.   301001 K 8
Vocabolario n.   381028 K IV 1
volck n.   260619 K 26
VorbewahrungsArtzney n.   381028 K IV 60
vorbruch n.   371224 K 8
vorfalen, v.   440130 K 4
vorgang n.   310411 K 4
vorgestellte Frage   381028 K IV 40
vorhin adv.   450506A K 4
vorreisen v.   181207 K 2
vorschrifft n.   380128 K 13
vorsehen n.   371123 K 8
vor sein v.   300000 K 3
Vorspiel n.   381028 K IV 36
Vorstellung n.   381028 K IV 11
Vortheil n., s. eigen Vortheil
vorthetigen v.   270406 K 26
vorträglich adv.   380000 K 15
vortruck v.   181207 K 6
vorweiser n.   401107 K 2
Il Votante n.   410621 K II 19
Vous pron.   171224 K 1
vuhten, 3. Pl. Ind. Imp. zu vehten   390901 K 7
vulgaire adv.   281000 K 2

wachsposieren v.   271201A K 3
Wachsthumb, Jm   250305 K 42
wagenlade n.   440324 K 13

wahrerfolgt adj.   440731 K I 8
Wahrsam n.   371123 K 3
wahrsammen v.   371123 K 3
wämmeßer n. pl.   290314 K 3
Wärdigkeit n.   371009 K I 10
waser/ waserley pron.   410208 K I 48
Wecke n.   450611 K 2
wegen v. (wüge)   250500 K 26
wehgen v.   461006 K 12
Wehr (Veere) Ortsname   301011 K 9
Weidewerg n.   210401 K 10
weil(l) conj.   230819 K 1. 290510 K 11. 400301 K I 1
Weißheit liebhaberisch adv.   381028 K II 2 u. K IV 41
weittschüchtig adj.   401214 K 3
welcherer pron.   410208 K I 45
weltsch adj.   240718 K 77
Weltweiser n.   460915 K 3
Weltwitzig adv.   381028 K II 6
weltzrecht n.   271215 K 20
wenen pron. pl.   410208 K I 44
werbung n.   280208 K 4
Werckzeug n.   381028 K IV 23
Wesenkündigung n.   440525 K II 9
Wiedermeynungssatz n.   381028 K II 16
wiederschreiben n.   390125 K 4
willfheriglich adv.   240116 K 3
wincklicht adj.   380605 K 12
Wink n.   440000 Q
Wipstertz Tiername   210401 K 14
wirckungen des gestirns   381028 K IV 41
Witdod n.   460915 K
wittern, sich v.   250700 K 90
Wittich n.   350731 K I V. 35
Wo adv., conj.   340912 K 6
wolcken-gleisse n.   380828 K I 47
Wolff, Wölffin Beiname   240112 K 6, 9, 11
wolfhärigkeit n.   450126 K 2
Wolgefast Zusambstimmung, s. Zusambstimmung
Wolgemuth Pflanzenname   220824 K 4
Wolgeneygtheit n.   381028 K IV 47
wöllen v.   290614 K 1
Wort n., s. gleichsdeutend Wort
Wortbuch n.   381028 K IV 1
Wortdod n.   460915 K 3
wortenlich adj.   300921 K 30

Wort-liebhabig *adv.* 381028 K IV 44
Wortliebisch *adj.* 381028 K II 21 u. K IV 70
Wortnenner *n.* 381028 K IV 1.32.37
Wortsrechtdeutung *n.* 381028 K IV 41
wortt *n.* 240109 K 7
worttforschung *n.* 260619 K 18
wunder ding *n.* 390125 K 1
wunderbahr *adj.* 440724 K 10
wunderung *n.* 270810 K 10
wundre Bilder, die *idiom.* 350731 K I V. 506
wunzer *adj.* 401009 K 1
Wütterich *n.* 381028 K IV 8

zaffeln *v.* 240718 K 41
zauhen *v.* 300320 K II 33
zehendzahl *n.* 300215 K II 5
zeiger/ Zaiger *n.* (d. i. Bote) 180714 K 2. 260520 K 2. 380522A K 0
zeiger *n.* (d. i. Index) 440204 K 2
zeimlich *adv.* 290529 K 25
zeitig/ zeitlich *adj.* 260520A K 4. 360428 K I 5
ZeitRegister *n.* 350731 K I V. 487
Zendel *n.* 240718 K 50
zeter/ zetter/ zitter *n.* 401204 K 4
zeug *n.* 240109 K 3. 250305 K 31. 390800 K 4
zeuner *n.* 240718 K 28
Zhänwehtagerin *Spitzname* 240718 K 24
Zibete *n.* 350731 K I V. 173
zielig *adj.* 461029 K 2
Ziffer *n.* 280122 I u. K I 6

zigeusern *v.* 240718 K 89
Zirck *n.* 441231 K 1
zitter *n.* s. zeter
Zodiaco *n.* 381028 K IV 44
zoffel *n.* 240718 K 51
züegen *v.* 461006 K 7
zuentbietung *n.* 421230 K 1
zugeseyllet *part.* 420630 K 37
Zuhören angenehmer Gesang 381028 K IV 31
zum längsten *adv.* 300718 K 4
zuneigung *n.* 240717 T f
zuneigungen *n. pl.* 381028 K IV 47
zusamb ziehung *n.* 381028 K II 22
Zusamb-hängung *n.* 381028 K II 22
Zusambstimmung/ zusammenstimmung *n.* 381028 K IV 21.28
Zusamfassungen *n. pl.* 381028 K IV 29
Zusamklingung *n.* 381028 K IV 31
zuschlagen *v.* 250305 K 13
zuschneiden *v.* 380728 K 3
Zuschnitt *n.* 380728 K 3
zuwege bringen *v.* 381028 K IV 38
zwar *adv.* 250706 K I 4
zward/ zwarden/ zwardt/ zwart/ zwarten *adv.* 180000 K 3. 300320 K 8. 371027 K I 1
Zweig *n.* 410117 K 7
Zweykampff *n.* 381028 K IV 35.36
zwiebel *n.* 451119 K 9
zwier *adv.* 300320 K II 12
zwischensatz *n.* 381028 IV (8.14)
zwitzerlich *adv.* 300320 K II 19

Glossar der sprachwissenschaftlichen Terminologie („Technici"/ „Kunstwörter")

Es besteht kein Anspruch auf vollständige Mitteilung der Nachweisstellen oder gar auf Vollständigkeit der in der fruchtbringerischen Spracharbeit und deren publizierten Werken insgesamt verwendeten Terminologie.
Nachstehend die Kürzel für die Verwender der angegebenen Termini.

Bu   Augustus Buchner (FG 362)
EH   Elias Hutter
FCh   Fürst Christian II. v. Anhalt-Bernburg (FG 51)
FL   Fürst Ludwig (FG 2)
Fr   Abraham v. Franckenberg
Gu   Christian Gueintz (FG 361)
H   Hs. „Die Deutsche Sprach-lehr zur Lehr-art <verfertiget>", s. 400122 I Q
HA   Herzog August d. J. v. Braunschweig-Wolfenbüttel (FG 227)
Har   Georg Philipp Harsdörffer (FG 368)
Hag   Christoph Achatius Hager
HB   Heinrich Buscher
JVA   Johann Valentin Andreae (FG 464)
Kro   Johannes Kromayer
Mil   Martinus Milagius (FG 315)
Op   Martin Opitz (FG 200)
Ra   Wolfgang Ratke (Ratichius)
Ri   Johann Rist (FG 467. 1647)
Schi   Johann Heinrich Schill
Schn   Johann Matthias Schneuber (FG 498. 1648)
Scho   Justus Georg Schottelius (FG 397)
Wen   Marcus Fridericus Wendelinus
Wer   Diederich von dem Werder (FG 31)
Ze   Philipp v. Zesen (FG 521. 1648)

Abehäcklein (Gu), *Apostroph*   400301 I
Abfall (FL), *Ablativ*   410208 I
abfallende, s. Zahlendungen
abfließende, s. Fall, Fälle
Abfluß (Har), *Derivation/ Ableitung*   410909 K 3
abgebißen (FL), *apokopiert*   450410 K 3. 460902
Abgeleitete (Scho), *Derivativa*   440129 K 6

Ablativus, *Ablativ*
  (FL)   410208 I
  (Mil)   460825
  (Scho)   460825 K 29
Ableitung, *Derivation*
  (Har)   431124
  (Scho)   400528 I u. K I 17. 410900 K 6. 430329 K 3. 450420 K 7
Abschneidung, *Apokope*
  (Gu)   400301 I

(Mil) 460825
absönderliches, s. Vorwort
Abtheilung (Gu), *Silbentrennung* 440129
Ab- und zuleitung der zeit-wörter (Ze), *Konjugation* 450808
Abwandelung, *Flexion, meist Deklination*
  (Har) 431124
  (Scho) 450410 K 15
  (Wen) 451220 K 2
Abweichung (FL), *Deklination* 391217. 400214 I. 410208 I. 451219
Adiectivum, *Adjektiv/ beystendiges Nennwort*
  (Scho) 400528 I
  (Wer) 450124 I. 450420
Adverbium, Adverbia *pl.*, *Adverb/ Beywort/ Zuwort*
  (FL) 410208 I
  (Gu) 400528 II
  (Har) 450410 K 4
  (Scho) 400528 I
  (Wer) 450420
Als-zwe[i]lauter (Ze), *Umlaut* 450808 K 11
Analogia (Scho), *Analogie/ Grundrichtigkeit,* vgl. Ratio 430307
  Analogia linguae (Har) 450410
  ipsa analogica linguae natura (Scho), *innere Sprachsystematik* 451219 K 1. 451220 K 6
  Natura linguae analogica (Wen), *innere Sprachsystematik* 451220 K 2
Anzeigungsweise, *Indikativ*
  (FL) 460902
  (Gu) 400301 I
  (Scho) 400528 K I 22 u. K II 29. 460902 K 3
Apocope (Gu), *(Silben-/ Buchstaben-) Weglassung/ Abschneidung* 400301 I
Apostrophus, Apostrophe, *Apostroph*
  (FL) 400214 I
  (Gu) 400214 K I 23. 400301 I. 400528 K I 21
Ars compositionis (Scho), *Komposition/ Verdoppelung* 410900
Ars deriuandi (Scho), *Derivation/ Ableitung* 410900
Artickel (FL), *Artikel/ Gemerck/ Geschlecht(s)wort* 450124

Articul(us), Articulj *pl.*, *Artikel/ Gemerck/ Geschlecht(s)wort*
  (Bu) 400122 I
  (FL) 400214 I. 410208 I
  (Gu) 400528 K I 4
  (Scho) 400528 I
  (Wer) 450124 I
Ausrede (Wer), *Aussprache/ Pronuntiation* 450420

Barbarismus, *Barbarismus*
  (Bu) 400122 I
  (FL) 400214 I
Beschliessungsweise (Gu), *Infinitiv* 400528 K II 29. 410208 K I 92
Besitzendung, *Genitiv*
  (FL) 400214 I
  (Gu) 410208 K I 90
  (H) 400122 K I 43
Besitzfall, *Genitiv*
  (FL) 400214 I. 410208 I
  (H) 400122 K I 43
Beweg(e)wörter *pl.*, *Interjektionen*
  (Bu) 400122 I
  (FL) 410208 I. 451219
  (Gu) 400122 K I 35. 400301 I. 410208 K I 82
beyständiges, s. Nennwort
Beywörter *pl.*, *Adverbien*
  (FL) 410208 I. 451219
  (Gu) 400122 K I 33. 400528 K I 26. 410208 K I 40 u. 71
  (Mil) 460825
Bindewort (Bu), *Konjunktion* 391119 II
Buchstaben *pl.*, *Buchstaben/ Lettern*
  (Gu) 430329 K 3. 440129
  (FL) 440209
  (Scho) 430329 K 3
  (Wer) 450420
  wesentliche *pl.* (Scho), *Prä- u. Suffixe* 460915 K 18
  zufällige *pl.* (Scho), *Endungsmorpheme* 460915 K 18
Buchstaben begrieff (Hag), *Silbe* 460915 K 17
Buchstaben (Ze), *pl.*, *Buchstaben/ Lettern* 441201 K 0

Casus, *Kasus, Fall*
  (FL)   391119 I (*pl.*). 400214 I (*pl.*).
      410208 I. 440313 T ah
  (Gu)   400214 K I 16
  (Scho) 400528 I
  (Mil)   460825 I
Colon (HB), *Doppelpunkt*   400122 K I 46
Comma (HB), *Komma*   400122 K I 46
Composita *pl.*, *zusammengesetzte Wörter/ Verdoppelungen/ Komposita*
  (Bu)   400122 I
  (Har)   450410
  (Scho) 431124 K 6. 451219 K 5
  (Wen)   451220
Compositio(n), *Zusammensetzung/ Kompositum/ Verdoppelung*
  (Gu)   400528 II
  (Mil)   460825
  (Scho) 400528 I. 451219 K 8
Coniugatio(n), *Konjugation/ Verenderung*
  (Gu)   400528 II
  (Scho) 400528 I. 410900
  gleichfließende (Scho), *regelmäßige Konjugation*   400528 I
  ungleichfließende (Scho), *unregelmäßige Konjugation*   400528 I
Conjugiren (Gu), *konjugieren*   400528 II
Coniunctio (Scho), *Konjunktion/ Bindewort/ Fügewort*   400528 I
Consonans, *Konsonant/ Mitlaut*
  (FL)   391119 I. 400122 T I w
  (Mil)   460825 u. I
Consonanten (Wer) *pl.*, *Konsonanten/ Mitlauter/ Mitstimmer*   450420
Contracta (Bu) *pl.*, *zusammengefügte Wörter*   400122 I

Dativus, *Dativ*
  (Mil)   460825
  (Scho) 460825 K 29
Declinatio (Scho), *Deklination/ Verwand(e)lung*   410900
decliniren (Gu), *deklinieren*   400528 II
Derivata (Scho), *abgeleitete Wörter*
  431124 K 6. 451219 K 5
Derivatio(n) (Scho), *Ableitung*   400528 I
  u. K I 17. 451219 K 8
Deutschheit/ Teutschheyt, *Idiomatik des Deutschen (analog zum hellenismós und zur latinitas)*
  (Gu)   440504 K I 2
  (Schn) 440504 K I 2
Dialectus, *Dialekt/ Mundart*
  (Bu)   400122 I
  (FL)   430403. 431022
  (HA, JVA)   421206 u. K 2
  (JVA)   410406. 421225
  (Scho) 400528 K II 5
Dictionarium, *Wortbuch/ Wörterbuch*
  (FL)   410203
  (Har)   440826 K 4. 451219 K 8
Diphtongus (FL), *Diphthong/ Doppellaut*
  400122 T I w
Doctrina quantitatum (Scho), *Quantitätenlehre/ Maßforschung*   441000
Doppellaut(t)(end/-er), *Diphthong*
  (Bu)   400122 I
  (FL)   400214 I
  (Gu)   400122 K I 13. 400214 K I 23.
      400528 K I 4
  (H)   400528 K I 4
  (Scho) 400528 I
Doppelung/ dopplung, *Komposition/ Verdoppelung*
  (Har)   431124
  (Scho) 400528 K I 16. 410706 K I 5.
      410900 K 6
Duppellautt (FL), *Diphthong/ Doppellaut*
  400214 I
durchdringend, *transitiv*
  (FL)   400214 I
  (Gu)   400214 K I 24. 400301 I
durchgehend, *transitiv*
  (FL)   400214 I
  (Gu)   400214 K I 24. 400301 I

einfältige, s. Zahl
eingliederich/ eingliedrig (Ze), *einsilbig*
  450308A. 450410 K 3. 450808
einsilbig
  (FL)   450410 K 3
  (Scho) 450410 K 3
Einsilbigkeit (Scho), *Monosyllabitas*
  450410 K 3
einsylbig
  (Gu)   450410 K 3
  (Har)   450410

eintzel(n)e, s. Zahl
eintzige, s. Zahl
elidiert (Wer), *ausgelassen, entfernt* 450124 I
Endannemung (Gu), *Rektion (u. m.)* 400122 K I 35 u. 44. 400301 I. 410208 K I 82
Endsylben (Har), *pl. Suffixe* 430419 K I 2
Endung, Endungen *pl., Kasus/ Flexionsmorphem(e)/ -endung(en)*. Vgl. Hauptendung
  (FCh)   391028 I
  (FL)   391217. 400214 I. 410208 I. 440209. 440313
  (Gu)   400122 K I 28. 400214 K I 16. 400301 I. 400528 II. 410208 K I 28
  (H)   400528 K I 18
  (Scho)   400214 K I 16. 400528 I
zufällige (Scho), *Flexionsmorpheme/ -endungen* 400528 K I 17. 450124 K 6
Endung (Wer), *Suffix* 450420
Endung, *Terminatio/ Kadenz/ Versausgang*
  (FL)   400214 I
  (Mil)   460825
Endungsletteren, zufällige (Scho), *Flexionsmorpheme/ -endungen* 431124 K 6
Entspringliche, *Derivata/ abgeleitete Wörter*
  (FL)   410208 I
  (Gu)   410208 K I 4 u. 49. 410900 K 5
  (H)   410208 K I 49
Euphonia (Wer), *Wohlklang* 450420

Fall, Fälle *pl., Kasus/ Endung(en)*
  (FCh)   391028 I
  (FL)   391119 I. 391217. 400214 I. 410208 I. 440209
  (Gu)   400214 K I 16. 410208 K I 28
  (Mil)   460825 I
abfließende (Scho) *pl., Casus obliqui* 400528 I
fast vergangene, s. Zeit
Final buchstabe (Wer), *Endbuchstabe* 450420
Flexio (Scho), *Konjugation* 400528 I
Fohr-glieder (Ze) *pl., Vorsilben, Präfixe* 450808

folkommen-vergangene, s. Zeit
Formationes (casuum, generu*m*, numeroru*m*, modoru*m*, comparationum) (Scho), *Flexionsmorpheme/ -endungen* 451219 K 4
Fügewörter *pl., Konjunktionen*
  (FL)   410208 I. 451219
  (Gu)   410208 K I 80 u. 90
  (Scho)   400122 K I 34. 400528 K I 24
Fügwortlein (Har) *pl., Konjunktionen* 450410

Gebendung, *Dativ*
  (Bu)   400122 I
  (FL)   400214 I. 410208 I
  (Gu)   391028 K I 1. 400122 K I 27. 410208 K I 29 u. 88
  (Mil)   460825
  (Scho)   400122 K I 43. 460825 K 29
Gebfall (FL), *Dativ* 410208 I
Gebietungsweise, *Imperativ*
  (FL)   400214 I. 450410 K 3. 451219. 460902
  (Gu)   400214 K I 25. 400301 I. 400528 K II 29
  (Har)   460915
  (Scho)   400528 K II 29. 450410 K 3. 451219 K 5. 460902 K 3
Geburtsendung (Gu), *Genitiv* 451219 K 8
geendete, s. Weise
gegenwärtige/ gegenwertige, s. Zeit
Gemerck, Gemercke *pl., Artikel*
  (FCh)   391028 I
  (FL)   410208 I. 450124
Genitivus (Scho), *Genitiv* 400528 I
Genus, *Genus/ Geschlecht/ auch (Wort-) Gattung*
  (FL)   450124
  (Scho)   400528 I
  (Wer)   450124 I
masculinum, *männlich*
  (FL)   450124
  (Wer)   450124 I
Gerundium (FL) 410208 I
Geschlecht, *Genus*
  (FL)   450124
keinerley, *Genus neutrum*
  (FL)   410208 I

(H) 400528 K I 17. 410208 K I 7
mänliches (Gu), *Genus masculinum*
400528 K I 20
unbenamtes, *Genus neutrum*
  (FL) 410208 I. 440127 K 2
  (Gu) 400528 K I 17 u. 20. 410208
    K I 7
unbenanntes, *Genus neutrum*
  (Bu) 400122 I
  (Gu) 451219 K 8
weibliches, *Genus femininum*
  (Gu) 400122 K I 29. 400528 K I 20
  (Scho) 400122 K I 19
Geschlecht(ge)merck (FL, H), *Artikel*
  410208 K I 1
Geschlecht(s)endung, *Genitiv*
  (Bu) 400122 K I 43
  (FL) 400214 I. 410208 I
  (Gu) 400122 K I 27. 410208 K I 29 u.
    30. 451219 K 8
  (Scho) 400122 K I 43
Geschlecht(s)wort, -wörter *pl.*, *Artikel*
  (FCh) 391028 I
  (FL) 400214 I. 410208 I. 450124
  (Gu) 400528 II u. K I 4. 410208 K I 1
  (H) 400528 K I 4
  (Scho) 400528 I
Geschlechtwortlein (Har) *pl.*, *Artikel*
  450410
gewandelt (Har), *flektiert* 450410
Gleichbedeutendes (Schi), *Synonym*
  440525 II
Gleichbenahmte (Scho), *Homonyme*
  400528 K I 26
gleichfließend, s. Coniugatio(n), Zeitwandelung, Zeitwort
gleichförmig, s. Verenderung, Zeitwort
Grammatic/ Grammatica, *Grammatik/ Sprachlehre/ Sprachkunst*
  (Bu) 400122 I
  (Gu) 400528 II
  (Scho) 400528 I. 430307
Grammatica Germanica (Scho), *deutsche Grammatik* 410900
Grammaticalia, *zur Grammatik Gehöriges, die Grammatik betreffend*
  (HA) 410119 K 4
  (JVA) 410406

Grundrichtigkeit (Scho), *analogia fundamentalis* 400528 K 3
grundrichtich (Har), *systematisch nach der grammat. Analogie* 440426 K 6
grundrichtig (Ri), *systematisch nach der grammat. Analogie* 441216
Grund-stämme (der Wörter) (Ze) *pl.*, *Stammorpheme* 450808 K 11

Hauptendung (Scho), *Ableitungsmorphem/ -silbe/ pl. terminationes derivandi*
  391217 K III 2. 400214 K I 18. 400528 K I 17. 440129 K 6. 440209 K 3. 450420 K 7
herrürend (Gu), *abgeleitet* 430329 K 3
Hilfsbuchstabe, littera servilis (Har), *Endungsmorphem* 460902 K 3
Hinterstrich (Scho), *Apostroph* 400528 K I 21
Homonyme (Scho), *Gleichbenahmte* 400528 K I 26

Imperativus, *Imperativ/ Gebietungsweise/ Befehlsweise*
  (Gu) 400528 II u. K II 29. 450410 K 3. 451219 K 5
  (Scho) 400528 I

keinerley, s. Geschlecht
Kennletter (Scho), *Stammvokal/ Stammbuchstabe* 410900 K 7
Klagendung, *Akkusativ*
  (Bu) 400122 I
  (Gu) 400122 K I 43. 400528 K I 26. 410208 K I 29, 92 u. ö.
  (Scho) 400122 K I 43
Klagfall (FL), *Akkusativ* 410208 I
Kleinlaut (Scho), *Umlaut* 450410 K 15. 460825 K 23
kunstgründig (Har), *wissenschaftlich begründet* 450410
kunstmessige Fügung (Scho), *Syntax* 400122 K I 35
Kunstwort, Kunstwörter *pl.*, *Technicum/ Termini techn(olog)ici/ Fachbegriff(e)*
  (Bu) 400122 I
  (FL) 400214 I. 410208 I. 450124. 450923B. 460902
  (Fr) 440826

(Gu) 400301 u. I. 430329
(Har) 440826 K 4
(Scho) 400122 K I 47
Kurtzlaut (Har), *kurze Silbe/ kurzes Wort* 441020

Langlaut (Har), *lange Silbe/ langes Wort* 441020
Lauter (Ze), *Vokal/ Selbstlaut* 450808
leidender, s. Verstand
Letter(en *pl.*), *Buchstabe(n)/ Silbenglieder*
  (FL) 430403
  (Scho) 400528 K I 12 u. 21. 430329 K 3. 431124 K 6
Lexicon, *Wörterbuch*
  (FL) 410208 I. 451219
  (Gu) 400301. 400528 II. 410208 K 3 u. K I 57. 451219 K 8
  (Scho) 440429
Lit(t)erae
  accidentales (Scho), *Buchstaben der Flexionsmorpheme* 450100. 450410 K 4
  essentiales (Scho), *Buchstaben der Ableitungsmorpheme* 450100. 450410 K 4
  radicales, *Stammbuchstaben/ -lettern*
    (EH) 450410 K 4
    (Har) 450410 K 11. 451028A K 6
    (Scho) 450100. 450410 K 4
  serviles, *Hilfsbuchstaben*
    (EH) 450410 K 4
    (Har) 460902 K 3

Maasforschung, *Quantitätenlehre/ Doctrina quantitatum*
  (Har) 441020
  (Scho) 441000 K 6. 441020 K 1
Maißner-Art (Gu), *meißnische Mundart/ omd. Varietät* 430329
mehrere, s. Zahl
meischnische Sprache (Hag), *meißnische Mundart/ omd. Varietät* 450100 K 8
meisnische Mundart, s. Mundart
Merckzeichen (FL), *Artikel* 410208 I
Merckzeichen (Gu), *Apostroph* 400214 K I 23. 400528 K I 21
mittelste Stuffe [der Vergleichung], *Komparativ*

(FL) 400214 I
(Gu) 400214 K I 29
mittelster Grad [der Vergleichung] (H), *Komparativ* 400214 K I 29
Mittelwort, *Partizip*
  (FL) 410208 I
  (Gu) 410208 K I 67
Mit(t)laut(end/ -er), *Konsonant/ konsonantisch*
  (Bu) 391119 II. 400122 I
  (FL) 391119 I. 400214 I. 410208 I. 440209. 451219
  (Gu) 400214 K I 23. 400301 I. 400528 K I 13 u. 21. 410208 K I 53
  (H) 400528 K I 13
  (Har) 410909 K 3
  (Mil) 460825 u. I
  (Scho) 400122 K I 7. 400528 I u. K I 14
Mitstimmer (Har) *pl.*, *Konsonanten, Mitlauter* 450410
Modus, vgl. Weise
  modus imperativus (Scho), *Imperativ* 451219 K 5
monosyllaba vocabula, *einsilbige Wörter*
  (Scho) 451220 K 2
  (Wen) 451220 K 2
Monosyllabitas (Scho), *Einsilbigkeit* 451219 K 1 u. 4
Mundart, mund-ahrt *Dialekt*
  (FL) 431022
  (Gu) 440129. 440317 K 5
  (Har) 431124. 440426. 450410 K 3
  (Ze) 441223 K 3. 450808
  Meisnische oder Obersächsische M.
    (Ze) 441223. 450410 K 17. 450808

Nach-glieder (Ze) *pl.*, *Nachsilben/ Suffixe* 450808
Nachsylbe (Har), *Suffix* 441223. 450410. 460902 K 3. 460915
Nehmendung, *Ablativ*
  (FL) 410208 I
  (Gu) 391020 K I 1. 410208 K I 29
  (Mil) 460825
  (Scho) 460825 K 29
Nennendung, *Nominativ*
  (FCh) 391028 I. 391217 K 9

(FL)   440127 K 2. 440504 K II 13.
   450124
(Gu)   410208 K I 29
Nenn(e)fall, *Nominativ*
   (Bu)   391119 II
   (FCh)   391028 I
   (FL)   410208 I
Nenn-Stammwörter, *Radicales Nominales*
   (Har), *Nomen-Stammwörter (ohne
   Verbableitung)*   460902 K 3
Nenwort/ Nennwort, *Nomen/ Substantiv*
   (Bu)   391119 II
   (FCh)   391028 I
   (FL)   410727. 440209. 440313. 451219.
      460902
   (Gu)   400122 K I 18
   (H)   400528 K I 17
   (Hag), Nänn-Wörter *pl.*, *Nomen*
      460915 K 17
   (Har)   450410. 460902 K 3
   (Scho)   391217 K III 2. 400528 K I 11
      u. 20. 460902 K 3
   (Ze)   450410 K 3
Nennwort,
   beyständiges, *Adjektiv*
   (Scho)   391217 K III 4
   (FL)   400214 I. 410208 I. 450124
   (Gu)   400122 K I 39. 400301 I.
      400528 K I 20. 410208 K I 84
   (H)   400528 K I 18 u. 20
   (Scho)   400528 I
   eigenes, *Nomen/ Substantiv*
      (Bu)   400122 I
      (Gu)   400122 K I 9
   selbständiges, *Nomen/ Substantiv*
      (FL)   410208 I. 450124
      (Gu)   400122 K I 39. 400214 K I 25.
         410208 K I 42 u. 84
      (H)   400528 K I 18
      (Scho)   400528 I
Niederdeutsch/ Niederteutsch
   (FL)   410203 K 1
   (Scho)   410203 K 1
Niederländisch (FL)   410203 K 1
Niedersächsisch (Scho)   410203 K 1
Nomina/ Nomina substantiva *pl.*, *Nomina/
   selbständige Nennwörter/ Substantive*
   (Gu)   400528 II
   (Har)   450410

(Scho)   400528 I
(Wer)   450420
Nominativus, *Nominativ/ Nennendung/
   Nennfall*
   (FCh)   391028 I. 391217 K 9
   (FL)   450124
   (Wer)   450124 I. 450420
Nota Exclamationis (HB), *Ausrufungszei-
   chen*   400122 K I 46
Nota Interrogationis (HB), *Fragezeichen*
   400122 K I 46
Numerus, *Zahl*
   (Bu)   400122 I
   (FL)   450124
   (Gu)   400528 II
   (Scho)   400528 I
   (Wer)   450124 I
   Pluralis (numerus), *Plural*
      (FL)   410208 I. 450124
      (Gu)   400528 II
      (Scho)   400528 I
      (Wer)   450124 I
   Singularis (numerus), *Singular*
      (FL)   410208 I. 450124
      (Gu)   400528 II
      (Scho)   400528 I
      (Wer)   450124 I

Oberhäcklein, *Apostroph*
   (FL)   400214 I. 410208 I
   (Gu)   400214 K I 23
obersächsische Mundart, s. Mundart
oberste stuffe, *Superlativ*
   (FL)   410208 I
   (Gu)   410208 K I 91
ordentlich, s. Verenderung, Zeitwande-
   lung, Zeitwort
Orthographi (FL), *Rechtschreibung/ Wort-
   schreibung*   450529
Orthographia, *Rechtschreibung*
   (Hag)   450100 K 8
   (Scho)   450100

Parenthesis (HB), *Parenthese(zeichen)*
   400122 K I 46
Participium, *Partizip/ Mittelwort/ Teil-
   wort*
   (FL)   410208 I
   (Scho)   400528 I

Particul/ Particula/ -ae, *Partikel/ Praefix*
  (Bu)   400122 I
  (Scho) 400528 I
  (Har), *unflektierte Wortklassen*
    450410
Person (FL) 460902
Phrases (Gu) *pl., Redensarten* 451219 K 8
Pluralis, s. Numerus
Praefixa *pl., Vorsilben*
  (Har) 450410
  (Ze) 450808
Præpositio, *Präposition/ Verhältnis-/ Vorwort*
  (Gu)   400528 II
  (Scho) 400528 I
Praepositiones inseparabiles (Har) *pl., Vorsilben* 450410 K 4
Primitiva, *Primitiva/ Simplicia/ Stammwörter/ ursprüngliche Wörter*
  (Gu)   410900 K 5
  (Scho) 431124 K 6. 450410 K 4.
    451219 K 8
Pronomen/ Pronomina, *Vornennwort/ Vornennwörter*
  (FL)   431022
  (Har) 450410 K 4
  (Scho) 400528 I
Pronuntiation (Wer), *Ausrede/ Aussprache*
  450420
Prosodia (Scho), *Aussprache/ Betonung*
  400528 I
Punct, *Punkt (Satzzeichen)*
  (Bu)   400122 I
  (Gu)   400122 K I 9. 400301 I
Punctum (HB), *Punkt* 400122 K I 46

Radicales Nominales, Nenn-Stammwörter
  (Har), *Nomen-Stammwörter (ohne Verbableitung)* 460902 K 3
Radices *pl., Stammwörter/ Themata*
  (FL)   430403
  (Har) 450410. 460902 K 3
  (Scho) 400528 K I 1. 440429. 450410
    K 4. 451219 K 1 u. 9
  (Wen) 451220 K 2
Radix, *Wortstamm/ Wurzel*, vgl. Stammwort
  (FL)   450410 K 3. 451219
  (Wen) 451220 K 2

Radix thematis (Har), *Stammwort*
  451028A K 6
Ratio (Wer), *Regel* 450124 I
Ratio, vgl. Analogia
  fundamentalis linguae ratio (Scho), *innere Sprachsystematik/ Grundrichtigkeit* 451219 K 1
  linguae ratio fundamentalis (Wen), *innere Sprachsystematik* 451220 K 2
Rechtschreibung, *Orthographie*
  (FL)   440127. 450923B. 451028A.
    451219
  (Gu)   431206 K 2. 440317 K 5
  (Har) 430419 K I 2. 440426. 441223
    K 18. 450410
  (Mil) 460825
Redensart (FL), *Dialekt/ Mundart; auch Stil*, vgl. phrases 430403. 450504
Redensartbuch (Gu), *phraseolog. Wörterbuch* 451219 K 8
Reinigkeit/ reinligkeit/ reinlikeit, *Reinheit*
  (Bu)   400122 I
  (Hag) 450100 K 8
  (Har) 411200
  (Scho) 400528 I
  (Ze) 441223 K 3
Richtigkeit(t), *Richtigkeit*
  (Bu)   400122 I
  (FL)   390514. 400214
  (Har) 411200
Rufendung (Gu), *Vokativ* 410208 K I 29
Ruffall (FL), *Vokativ* 410208 I

Sachßen-Zunge (Gu), *niedersächs./ nd. Mundart* 430329
Schreiberichtigkeit (FL), *Rechtschreibung/ Orthographie* 441201 K 0
Schreibrichtigkeit/ Schreibe-rüchtigkeit
  (Ze), *Rechtschreibung* 440724 K 13.
    441201 K 0. 450308A
Selblaut(end/ -er), *Vokal/ vokalisch*
  (FL)   391119 I. 400214 I. 410208 I.
    440209
  (Bu)   391119 II. 400122 I
  (Gu)   400122 K I 29. 400214 K I 23.
    400301 I
  (Har) 410909 K 3
  (Mil) 460825
  (Op) 400528 K I 22

(Scho)   400122 K I 7. 400214 K I 2.
   450410 K 15
(Ze)   450308A. 450808
enger (Mil), *geschlossener Vokal*
   460825
weiter (Mil), *offener Vokal*   460825
selbliche eigenschaft (des Wortes) (Ze),
   proprietas   450808
selbständiges, s. Nennwort
selbsthaftend (Gu), *intransitiv*   400214 K
   I 24
Semicolon, *Semikolon/ Strichpunkt*
   (Bu)   400122 I
   (FL)   410208 I
   (Gu)   400122 K I 45
   (HB)   400122 K I 46
Semicomma, *Virgel*
   (FL)   410208 I
   (Gu, HB)   400122 K I 46
Silbe/ Sylbe
   (Gu)   400528 II u. K I 4. 410208 K I 50
   (H)   400528 K I 4
   (Kro)   410208 K I 69
   (Scho)   450410 K 3
Silbenglieder (FL), *Buchstaben/ Lettern*
   430403
sillabiren (FL), *Silben sprechen, schreiben, trennen*   440209
Sillabirung (FL), *Silbentrennung*
   451028A. 451219
Simplicia (Har) *pl.*, *einfache Wörter/ Simplicia/ Stammwort*   450410
Singularis, s. Numerus
Sprachkunst (Scho), *Grammatik/ Sprachlehre*   400528 K I 22. 410706
Sprachlehre, *Grammatik/ Sprachkunst*
   (Bu)   400122 u. I
   (FL)   391217. 400214 u. I. 410208.
      410727. 440313. 450923B
   (FCh)   391028 I
   (Gu)   400122 K I 1. 400301 u. I.
      400528 II. 410714
   (Mil)   460825
Sprechwörter, *Verba*
   (FL, H)   410208 I u. K I 3
   (FL)   460902
   (Har)   460902 K 3
   (Scho)   460902 K 3

schliesliche Sprechwörter, *finite Verbformen*
   (Har)   460902 K 3
   (Scho)   460902 K 3
Stamm, *radix/ Wurzel/ Stammorphem*
   (FL)   451219
   (Gu)   451219 K 6
Stam(m)buchstab(e/en) (*pl.*), *Buchstaben des Wortstamms/ Stammvokal/ Kennletter*
   (FL)   440209. 450410 K 3. 451219
   (Gu)   440129
   (Har)   450410 K 3. 460915
   (Scho)   400528 I u. K I 23. 410900 K 7.
      440129 K 6. 450420 K 7. 460915 K 18
   (Ze)   450308A
Stammletter, Stammlettern, *Stammbuchstaben*
   (Scho)   400122 K I 11. 400528 K I 23 u.
      K II 29. 431124 K 6. 450410 KI 3.
      451219 K 5. 460902 K 3
Stammverben (Scho), *verba primitiva*
   440209 K 3
Stam(m)wort, Stam(m)wörter *pl.*, *Radices/ Themata*
   (FL)   430403. 440209. 450923B. 451219
   (Gu)   400528 II. 450410 K 3. 451219
      K 4
   (Har)   431124. 441223. 450410. 451219
      K 8. 460902 K 3. 460915
   (Scho)   400528 K I 1. 400528 K II 5 u.
      29. 430329 K 3. 431124 K 6. 450410
      K 3. 451219 K 4 u. 5. 460902 K 3
   (Wer)   450420
   (Ze)   450308A. 450808
Stammwurtzlen (Har) *pl.*, *Stammorpheme, Wortstämme, Stammwörter*   450410
Stellen, das (FL), *Stylus/ Stil*   410208 I.
   440209
Stellung (FL), *Syntax/ Wortfügung/ Wortstellung*   410708 K 10. 410727. 410909
   K 3. 420503
Stimm-Buchstabe (Har), *Vokal*   410909
   K 3
Stimmer (Har) *pl.*, *Vokale*   450410
Strichpünctlein (Scho), *Semikolon*
   400122 K I 45
Substantivum, *Substantiv/ selbständiges Nennwort*

(FL)   450124
(Scho)   400528 I
(Wer)   450124 I. 450420
Suffixa *pl., Nachsilben*
   (Har)   450410
   (Ze)   450808
Supinum (FL)   410208 I
Sylbe, s. Silbe
Sylben theilung (Har), *Silbentrennung* 460915
Syllabe, *Silbe*
   (Gu)   400528 II
   (Wer)   440310A
Synonymum (Schi), *Synonym/ Gleichbedeutendes*   440525 II
Syntaxis/ Σύνταξίς, *Syntax/ Wortfügung/ Wortstellung*
   (Bu)   400122 I
   (Gu)   400122 K I 38
   (Scho)   400528 I. 410900

Technici (FL) *pl., Fachbegriffe/ Kunstwörter*   400214 I
Tempus (Scho), *Zeit*   400528 I
Terminatio(n), *Flexionsendung*
   (Gu)   400528 II
   (Scho)   400528 I
   (Wer)   450124 I
   Terminationes derivandi (Scho), *Ableitungsmorpheme*   451219 K 4
Termini technologici (Fr), *Fachbegriffe/ Kunstwörter*   440826
Teutschheyt, s. Deutschheit
theilbar (Gu), *zusammengesetzt (Kompositum)*   430329 K 3
Theilwort (FL), *Partizip*   410208 I. 451219
Thema/ Themata (Scho), *Stammwort, -wörter*   400122 K I 11. 400214 K I 20. 400528 I. 410900
Tohnzeichen (Ze), *Längenmarkierung bei Vokalen u. Silben*   400122 K I 7

überein(t)zige, s. Zahl
ubergehend, *transitiv*
   (FL)   400214 I
   (Gu)   400214 K I 24
unabsonderliches, s. Vorwort
unbenamtes, s. Geschlecht

unehnliche Zeitwörter, s. Zeitwort
unendige, s. Weise
unentspringliche, *Primitiva/ Unabgeleitete*
   (FL)   410208 I
   (Gu)   410208 K I 39
unfolkommen-vergangene, s. Zeit
ungleichfließend, s. Coniugatio(n), Zeitwandelung, Zeitwort
ungleich flüßende Wörtlein (Har) *pl., Anomalien*   460915
unordentlich, s. Zeitwandelung, Zeitwort
unwandelbare (Wörter) *pl., unflektierbare Wörter*
   (FL)   410208 I
   (Gu)   410208 K I 70
   (Har)   450410
   (Kro)   410208 K I 69
urspringliche Wörter, *Primitiva/ Simplicia*
   (Gu)   400122 K I 14. 410208 K I 49. 410900 K 5
   (H)   410208 K I 49
Usus, *Sprachgebrauch/ -gewohnheit*
   (Scho)   451219 K 1
   (Wen)   451220 K 2
   receptus hactenus usus (Scho), *überkommener Gebrauch*   451220 K 6
   probatus usus (Sch), *bewährter Gebrauch*   451220 K 6

vbereintzelne, s. Zahl
Verba *pl., Verben/ Zeitwörter*
   (Gu)   400528 II
   (Har)   450410
   (Scho)   451219 K 5
   Verba analoga (Scho), *regelmäßige/ schwache Verben*   400528 K I 23. 410900
   Verba anomala/ Anomalia *pl., unregelmäßige/ starke Verben*
      (Gu)   400528 II
      (Scho)   400528 I u. K I 23. 410900. 451219 K 5
   Verba irregularia (Har), *unregelmäßige/ starke Verben*   450410
   Verba regularia (Har), *regelmäßige/ schwache Verben*   450410
   Verba primitiva (Scho), *Stammverben*   440209 K 3
   Verba quadrata (Har) *pl., zweisilbige*

Stammwörter/ Radices dissyllabicae
  450410
Verbeissung (Mil), *Synkope* 460825
Verbum, Verba *pl.*, *Verb/ Verben/ Zeitwort/ Zeitwörter*
  (FL)   410208 I
  (Scho)   400528 I
verdoppelt, *zusammengesetzt (Kompositum)*
  (Har)   440426 I
  (Scho)   430329 K 3
Verdoppelung(e), *Komposition*
  (Fr)   440826
  (Gu)   400528 II. 440426 K I 2
  (Har)   440426 K I 2
  (Scho)   400528 I u. K I 17 u. 25. 410900 K 6. 440129 K 6. 440426 K I 2. 450420 K 7
Verenderung, *Flexion/ meist Konjugation*
  (FL)   440209
  (Gu)   400122 K I 31. 400301 I. 400528 II u. K I 23. 430329 K 3
  (H)   400528 K I 23
  (Scho)   400528 I
  gleichförmige (Gu), *regelmäßige Konjugation* 400528 II
  ordentliche (Gu), *regelmäßige Konjugation* 400528 K I 23
vergangene Zeit, s. Zeit
Vermindertes (Gu), *Diminutiv* 400301 I
Verstandt,
  leidender (Bu), *Passiv* 391119 II
  wirkender (Bu), *Aktiv* 391119 II
Verwand(e)lung, *Deklination*, vgl. Abweichung
  (FL)   391217. 400214 I. 410208 I. 440504 K II 13. 451219
  (Gu)   391028 K I 1. 400214 K I 20
verzwickt (FL), *apo-*, *synkopiert* 460902
vielfältige, s. Zahl
Vocal(is), *Vokal/ Selbstlaut*
  (FL)   391119 I. 400122 T I w
  (Gu)   400528 II
  (Mil)   460825
  (Scho)   400528 I
Vorne(n/nn)wort, *Pronomen*
  (Bu)   391119 II. 400122 I
  (FL)   400214 I. 410208 I. 431022. 440313. 451219

(Gu)   400122 K I 29. 400214 K I 20. 400301 I. 400528 K I 20. 410208 K I 39
(Scho)   400122 K I 7. 400214 K I 20
Zurücksehendes (FL), *Relativpronomen*
  410208 I
Vorsylbe (Har), *Präfix* 441223. 450410. 460915
Vorwort (Mil), *propositio/ Präfix* 460825
Vorwort, Vorwörter *pl.*, *Präposition(en)/ Verhältniswort/ -wörter*
  (FCh)   391028 I
  (FL)   451219
  (Gu)   400122 K I 42. 400528 K I 26
  (Har)   430419 K I 2
  (Scho)   400528 I u. K I 17 u. 24. 410208 K I 48. 410706 K I 6
abson(/sön)derliches, *Präposition*
  (FL)   410208 I
  (Har)   450410 K 4
  (Sch)   400528 K I 17
unabson(/sön)derliches, *Präfix/ praepositio inseparabilis*
  (Gu)   400528 K I 26
  (H)   400528 K I 17
  (Har)   450410 K 4
  (Scho), *praepositiones inseparabiles*
    400528 I u. K I 17
Vorwörtlein (Scho), *Präfix/ Partikel*
  400528 I
Vorwortlein (Har) *pl.*, *Präpositionen*
  450410

Wandlung (Scho), *Deklination* 400214 K I 20
Weise, vgl. Modus
  (Scho)   400528 K I 23 u. K II 29
  vgl. Anzeigungsweise, Gebietungsweise
  gebietende (Ze), *Imperativ* 450808
  geendete, *finite Verbform*
    (Bu)   400122 I
    (Gu)   400122 K I 42
    (Har)   450410
  unendige, *infinite Verbform*
    (Bu)   400122 I
    (Gu)   400122 K I 42. 450410 K 3. 460915 K 15
zu endigen (Har), *Infinitiv* 450410
zu gebieten, *Imperativ*

(Har) 450410
(Ze) 450808
wirkender, s. Verstandt
Wortbuch, *Wörterbuch*
  (FL) 410203
  (Har) 410203 K 3. 440826 K 4. 451219 K 8
Wortdopplung (Har), *Komposition* 430419 K I 2
Wortendungen (Har), *pl. Suffixe* 430419 K I 2
Wörterbuch
  (FL) 410208 I
  (Gu) 410208 K 3 u. K I 57. 451219 K 8
Wörterfügung (Gu), *Syntax* 400122 K I 38
Wortforschung, *Wort(bildungs)lehre/ Etymologie*
  (Gu) 440219 K 2
  (Ra) 440219 K 2
  (Scho), *Wortlehre* 410706 K 1
Wortfügung, *Syntax*
  (Bu) 400122 I
  (FL) 400214 I
  (Gu) 400122 K I 38. 400301 I. 400528 K I 27. 410208 K I 82
  (Scho) 400528 I u. K I 27. 410706 K 1 u. K I 7
Wortschreibung, *Rechtschreibung/ Orthographie*
  (FL) 430724. 431016. 431206. 440209. 440313. 450529. 451219 K 10
  (Gu) 431020. 431206 K 2. 440504. 440809. 441231
  (Har) 440426 K 6
  (Ra) 440219 K 2
Wortsprechung (Ra), *Lautsprache/ Phonetik/ Orthophonie* 440219 K 2
Wortstellung (Gu), *Syntax* 400122 K I 38. 400301 I
Wortt ordnung (FL), *Syntax* 400122 T I ay
Wortverzeichnus (FL), *Wörterbuch* 451219
Wortzeit, *Wort-/ Silbenlänge*
  (Har) 441020
  (Scho) 441000 K 6
Wortzusammenordnung (Bu), *Syntax* 400122 I

Wortzusammenstellung (Bu), *Syntax* 400122 I
Wurtzel (Scho) *Stammwort/ Radix* 431124 K 6. 450410 K 3. 451219 K 5
Wurzeln (Ze) *pl., Stammwörter/ Radices* 450308A. 450808
Würtzelen (Scho) *pl., Stammwörter/ Radices* 451219 K 4
Wurzel-wörter (Ze), *Stammwörter/ Radices*
  (Har) 450410
  (Ze) 450308A. 450808

Zahl, *Numerus*
  (Bu) 400122 I
  (Gu) 400214 K I 20. 400301 I
  (Scho) 400122 K I 39. 400528 K I 23. 450410 K 15
einfältige (FL), *Singular* 410208 I
eintzel(n)e, *Singular*
  (FL) 450124
  (Gu) 400214 K I 23. 400528 K I 21
  (Scho) 391217 K III 2. 450410 K 15
eintzige, *Singular*
  (FL) 410208 I. 440127 K 2
  (Gu) 400301 I
mehrere, *Plural*
  (FL) 450124
  (Gu) 400122 K I 29. 400528 K I 15. 410208 K I 38
  (Scho) 391217 K III 2 u. 3. 400528 K I 11. 450124 K 7. 450410 K 15
vbereinzeln(e) (Gu), *Plural* 400301 I
überein(t)zige, *Plural*
  (Bu) 391119 II
  (FL) 400214 I. 410208 I
  (Gu) 400122 K I 27. 400528 II u. K I 15. 451219 K 8
vielfältige, *Plural*
  (FL) 410208 I
  (H) 400528 K I 15
Zahlendungen, abfallende (Scho) *pl., Casus obliqui* 400214 K I 7. 400528 K I 14
Zeit, *Tempus*
  (Har) 450410
  (Scho) 400528 K I 14 u. 23
  (Ze) 450410 K 15. 450808
fast vergangene (Gu), *Imperfekt* 400122 K I 30

folkomne (Ze), *Perfekt* 450808
folkommen-vergangene (Ze), *Perfekt* 450308A. 450410 K 16
gegenwärtige/ gegenwertige, *Präsens*
  (FL) 460902
  (Gu) 400214 K I 25
  (Ze) 450308A
unfolkomne (Ze), *Imperfekt* 450808
unfolkommen-vergangene (Ze), *Imperfekt* 450308A
unvollkommene (Har), *Imperfekt* 450410
vergangene (Gu), *Perfekt* 400122 K I 30. 410208 K I 53
vollkommene (Har), *Perfekt* 450410
zu-künftige (Ze), *Futur* 450308A
Zeitstammwort/ -wörter (Scho), *Imperativ* 460902 K 3
Zeitwandelung, *Konjugation*
  (Har) 450410
  (Scho) 400528 K I 23. 430329 K 3
gleichfliessende (Scho), *regelmäßige/ conjugatio regularis* 400528 K I 23
ordentliche (Scho), *regelmäßige/ conjugatio regularis* 400528 K I 23
ungleichfliessende (Scho), *unregelmäßige/ conjugatio irregularis* 400528 K I 23
unordentliche (Scho), *unregelmäßige/ conjugatio irregularis* 400528 K I 23
Zeitwort, Zeitwörter *pl.*, *Verbum/ Verba*
  (Bu) 391119 II. 400122 I
  (FL) 410208 I. 440313. 451219. 460902
  (Gu) 400122 K I 42. 400214 K I 23. 400301 I. 400528 K I 21. 410208 K I 42, 50 u. ö.
  (Har) 450410
  (Scho) 400528 I, K I 14 u. K II 29. 410900 K 7
  (Ze) 450308A
gleichfließende, *regelmäßige/ schwache Verben/ Verba analoga*
  (Har) 450410
  (Scho) 400528 I u. K I 23. 440209 K 3

gleichförmige (Gu), *regelmäßige/ schwache Verben* 400528 II
ordentliche, *regelmäßige/ schwache Verben*
  (Gu) 400528 II
  (Scho) 400528 I
unehnliche (H), *unregelmäßige/ starke Verben* 400528 K I 23
ungleichfließende, *unregelmäßige/ starke Verben/ Verba anomala*
  (Har) 450410
  (Scho) 400528 I u. K I 23. 410900 K. 440209 K 3
unordentliche (Scho), *unregelmäßige/ starke Verben* 400528 I
Zhall, s. Zahl
zu-künftige, s. Zeit
zusammengefügte Wörter (Bu) *pl.*, *Contracta* 400122 I
zusammengesetzte Wörter (Bu) *pl.*, *Composita* 400122 I. 400301 I
Zusammen-setzungen (Mil) *pl.*, *compositiones/ Komposita* 460825
Zuwort, Zuwörter *pl.*, *Adverb(ien)*
  (FL) 410208 I
  (Gu) 400122 K I 33. 400214 K I 22. 400301 I. 400528 K I 26. 410208 K I 40 u. 71
  (Scho) 400528 K I 24
zweigliedrig (Ze), *zweisilbig* 450808
Zwe[i]lauter/ zweifachlauter (Ze), *Diphthong* 450808 u. K 11
Zwerchstrichlein (H), *Virgel* 400122 K I 45
Zwergstrichlein (Gu), *Virgel* 400122 K I 45
zweydeutige wörter (Har), *Homonyme* 440209 K 4
zweyfälig (Gu), *doppeldeutig/ homonym* 400301 I
zweysylbig (Har) 450410
Zwischenworte (Scho) *pl.*, *Interjektionen* 400122 K I 34
Σύνταξις (Bu), *Syntax* 400122 I

Sachregister

Aberglaube, s. Magie
Achtzeiler/ Huitain/ Ottaverime/ Stanze 231203 K 2. 250110. 260617 K 9. 270925 u. I–IV. 310000. 310411 K 13. *DA Köthen I. 4,* S. 14. 370113 K 2. 371112A K 4. 381218. *DA Köthen I. 5,* S. 10, 17, 100, 104. 391119 I. 400619. 400620. 400622 K 1. 401009 K 2. 401025 K 2. 401116 K 1. 401223 K 6. 401228A K 1. 401229 K 1. *DA Köthen I. 6,* S. 120. 410323 K 6. 410731. 421027 K 4. 421031A. 421105. 421200 K 1. 440130 K 3. 441223 K 17. 441226A K 5. 450900
Agenten 180000 K 9. 190322 K 3. 191229 K 1. 200318 K 7. 230802 K 10. 230809. 230913 K 1. 231006. 231101. 240319 K I 2. 271201A K 10. 280106 K 6. 280724. 281000 K 14. 290129. 290528. 290708. *DA Köthen I. 3,* S. 12, 16. 300410. 300921. 300924. 301001. 301011. 310113. 310119 K 2. 310224. 310311. 310725 K. 320416 K 2. 340628 K 0. 351112. 360703. *DA Köthen I. 4,* S. 9. 370517 K 6. 371009 K 0. 371027 K 8. 371112 K I 4. 371224 K 3. 380608 K 1. 380609 K 8. 391217 K 11. 401111 K. *DA Köthen I. 6,* S. 8. 410119 K. 410914 K 2. 411214 K 1. 421120 K 3. 421206 K 8. 430215 K 17. 430418 K 6. 430419 K 7. 430425 K 5. 430430 K 11. 430826 K 9. 450400 K 13. 450529 K 10. 450927 K 5. 460613 K 4
Alchemie/ Chemie 180714 K 3. 240116 K I. 240125. 280616A K 1. 280620 K 2. 290609. *DA Köthen I. 3,* S. 8, 20, 125 ff. 301102 K 1. *DA Köthen I. 4,* S. 9, 12 f., 94. 371009 I–III u. K 3. 371027 K III 1. 380128. 380310 III. 381028 IV. *DA Köthen I. 6,* S. 15. 430509 K 1. 430826. 431123 K 2. 450818 K 6. 460715 K II 3

Alexandrinervers 231203 K 2. 250110. 250218A K III 3. 260617 K 9. 270810 u. I. 270925 K II 1. 271001 K 9. 280818 II Q. 281021 K 3. 290510 K 11. 290629 K 12. 300320 II u. V. 300509 I. 310000. 360600 II. 360800 K 1. 371027 K 2. 371110 K. 380207 K 3. 380210 K 4. 380402 K I 2. 380828 K 3. 381007 K 6. 381218 K 9. *DA Köthen I. 5,* S. 17. 390114 K I 4. 390701 K 2. 390800 K 1. 391119 I. 400319 K 3. 400323. 400619. 400620. 400902. 401223 K 6. 420503 K 8. 420506 K 8. 421027 K 4. 421110 K 3. 421200 K 1. 421202 K 4. 430000A K 2. 430624 K 2 u. K I 1. 431014. 431021 K 1. 431123 II u. K 1. 431206 K 6. 440310A K 1 u. K I 1. 440816 K 1. 441200 u. I. 441223 K 17. 450124 K 6. 450220 K I 1. 450818 K 12. 460317 K I 1. 460804 K 1. 460909
Anapäst 380828 K 3. *DA Köthen I. 5,* S. 14. 391028 K 3. 391119 III. 400323. *DA Köthen I. 6,* S. 11 f. 431014. 431206 K 6. 440616 K 5. 440824. 441231A. 460825 K 20
Ars politica, s. Politische Wissenschaften
Astronomie, s. Physica

Ballet, s. Maskerade
Bankgeschäfte, s. Finanzwesen
Baukunst/ Festungsbau 300215 II u. K 1 u. K I 3. 300725 K 8. 300924. 301011 K 11. 310311. 320313 K 0. 371014 K 0. 380320A K 10. 381028 II u. III. *DA Köthen I. 6,* S. 114. 420630 K 22. 430000A K 1. *DA Köthen I. 7,* S. 8, 131, 140 f., 145. 440724 K 6. 441223 K 1. 450220 K 20. 450927 u. I u. II. 460317 K. 461204A
Bekenntnis/ Katechismus. Vgl. Frömmig-

Sachregister

keit, Religionsgemeinschaften, Religionsunterricht u. Theologie
371009 K. 371027 K III 1. 450420
Anglikanische Kirche 371223 K 9.
390822. 420120 K
Lutherische Kirchen 270406 K 13.
270429 K 10. 320313 K 0. 330920
K 0. 340604 K 2. 371028 K 11.
380000. 380320 u. I. *DA Köthen I. 5*,
S. 8 f. 390800. 390807 K 2. 391209.
401111 u. I. *DA Köthen I. 6*, S. 8, 13.
410119 K 4. 410323 I. 430826 K.
421123 K 1. 421230 K 4. 431211 I.
DA Köthen I. 7, S. 20. 440119 K 10.
450304 K. 450326 K. 450420 K 5.
450726 K. 450806 K 2. 460613 K 0.
460819 II. 460825 K 7. 461029 K 8.
461117 K 1. 461204. 461216
Orthodoxe Kirchen 291028. 300725
Reformierte Kirchen 190322 I. 270406.
291028 K 1. 300410 K 36. 300718 K.
300725. 330920 K 0. 350731 K I 0.
360600 II. 370305 K 16. 370422 K 7.
370517 K 6. 370715 K 12. 370902.
371028 K 11. 371219. 380000. 380110
K 9. 380128 K 12. 380320 K 4 u. K I 7.
381107 K. *DA Köthen I. 5*, S. 10, 17,
33. 390112. 390114. 390119 K.
391100. 391125 K 1. 391209. 400312
K 1. 400514 K 7. 401111 I. 401117
K 6. 401204 I. 401215 u. II. 401229
K 2. *DA Köthen I. 6*, S. 12 f. 410101 u.
I. u. II. 410106 K 5. 410111 I. 410706
K 6. 410731 I. 411009. 411126 K 6.
420120. 420124 I. 421031. 430118
K 15. 430505 K I. 430826 K 21.
431021 K 2. *DA Köthen I. 7*, S. 11.
440119 K u. 10. 440310B K 4.
440809A K 6. 450304. 450305 K 2 u.
K I 3. 450317 K. 450317A. 450400
K 13. 450420 K 5. 450506 K. 450526
K 1. 450726 K 17. 450818 K. 450919A
K 7. 451030. 460125 K I. 460613 K 0.
460825 K u. III. 461124 K
Röm.-katholische Kirche 380000.
380320 K u. K I 7. 401111 I. 401204
K 2. 440119 K 10. 440715A K 5.
450304 K 1. 450305 K 2 u. K I 3.
450317 K 1. 450317A. 450326 K 4.
450506 K. 450526 K 1. 450726 K.
450806 K 2. 450818 K
Bestechung/ Korruption *DA Köthen I. 2*,
S. 11. 280724. 290129 K 1 u. K I 3.
290528 K. 290708. 300725 K. 330311
K 2. 410111
Bibel, s. Religion u. Personenregister. Vgl.
Bibeldichtung, Bibelübersetzung
Bibeldichtung 191229 K 5. 191231.
210729. 220824. 230802. 230809.
230913. 231210 I. 250110. 250413.
251100. 260106. 260211. 260217.
260617. *DA Köthen I. 2*, S. 15. 270429
K. 280000 Q u. K 1. 280106. 280112.
280208. 280216A. 280218. 280716.
280821. 281000. 281021. 290302 K 4.
290304 K 2. 290310 K 11. 290629 K 11.
DA Köthen I. 3, S. 9, 10, 101 f., 130.
300320 II. 300426 I. 310000 u. I. 310703.
360630 u. I u. II. *DA Köthen I. 4*, S. 8,
11 f., 13 f. 371027. 371030. 371110.
371112. 371116 K 3. 371121 K 1. 371124
K I. 371126. 371127. 371208. 371222 I–
III. 371226 K 4. 371226A. 380120.
380122. 380125A. 380126. 380128.
380207 K 2. 380210. 380221. 380226.
380312. 380320. 380321. 380321A.
380402. 380405. 380411 u. I. 380423A K
I 1. 380504. 380522A. 380522B. 380602.
380606. 380608. 380608A. 380609.
380609A. 380616. 380619. 380625.
380720. 380721. 380724. 380828.
381006. 381007. 381105 K 4. 381114.
381116. 381116A. 381123. 381130 K 3.
381218. 381224. *DA Köthen I. 5*, S. 9 f.,
13, 35, 103 f. 390110. 390112. 390115
K 1. 390126B K 5. 390310. 390514.
390630. 390800A. 390807. 391000.
391100. 400000. 400218 K 5. 400619.
400620. 400714. 400810. 401111 K I.
401204. 401214. 401216. *DA Köthen I.
6*, S. 12-15. 410106. 410206. 410208 K 4.
420503 K 7. 421202. 430204. 430318.
430507. 430821. 431123 I u. K 2 u. K II
5. *DA Köthen I. 7*, S. 10. 440824 K 7.
441000 K 5. 450100 K 4. 450304.
450308. 450400 K 11. 450726. 450817 u.
I. 450900. 460317 u. K I 1. 460804 K 1.
460819 II. 460825 u. II

Bibelübersetzung/ Bibelbearbeitung als Aufgabe oder Kunst. Vgl. Personenregister: Bibel
380320 u. I. 380417. *DA Köthen I. 5*, S. 8 ff., 13. 391217 u. I u. II. 400104 u. I. 400218. 400301 K 8. 400313 K 3. 401111 u. I. *DA Köthen I. 6*, S. 8, 10, 12, 113 ff. 410106. 410119. 410406. 410714 K 2. 410914A K 1. 411214. 420114. 420601. 420712 K. 421011. 421031. 421101 u. III. 421120. 421206. 421225. 430118. 430121. 430208. 430215. 430418. 430425. 430430. 430515. 430826 K 9. 431123 I u. K 2. *DA Köthen I. 7*, S. 12, 16, 21, 141, 145 f. 440429 K. 441205. 450100 u. I. 450126. 450200. 450219. 450221. 450319. 450410. 450509 K 3. 450721. 450722. 450726 K 9. 450806. 450808 K 5. 450927 K 1. 451000 K. 451001. 451100. 460103 K 1. 460119. 460127. 460131 K 2, 460200 K 1. 460200A. 460317 u. I. 460613. 460700. 460715. 460718 K 3. 460804. 460819 u. II. 460825. 460908. 460909. 460915A K 3. 461117 K 1. 461204. 461216

Bibliotheken/ Buchbesitz
Agra (?)/ Indien: Bibliothek der Großmogulen 390909 K 3
Kd. Alessandro *Albano* 450817 K IV 5
Alexandria 400528 K 3
Gottlieb *Andreae* 460715
Jacob *Andreae d. J.* 460819
Johann Valentin *Andreae* 401111 K 4. 421225. 430118. 430215. 430425. 430515 K. 460715. 460804. 460819. 460908 u. I–III
F. Christian I. u. II. v. *Anhalt-Bernburg passim*, bes. 370828 K
F. Christian I. v. *Anhalt-Bernburg* 431021 K 2. 450305 K 5
F. Christian II. v. *Anhalt-Bernburg* 410106 K 7. 410914 K 8. 420712 K 2. 421009 K 8. 431021 K 2. 450305 K 5. 460714 K 7
Fn. Sibylla Elisabeth v. *Anhalt-Bernburg* 300330 K 3
Fn. Eva Catharina v. *Anhalt-Dessau* 400902 K 6
F. Johann Georg I. u. F. Johann Casimir v. *Anhalt-Dessau* 180714. 250413. 251100
F. Ludwig v. *Anhalt-Köthen passim*
F. August v. *Anhalt-Plötzkau* 180714 K 2
F. Rudolph v. *Anhalt-Zerbst* 250110 K 2
Athen 390828 K 5
Ks. Augustus 461204A
Giovanni Francesco di *Bagni* (G. F. Guido del *Bagno*) 460103 K 6
Antonio *Barberini* 460103 K 6
Johann Georg II. Fuchs v. Dornheim, Bf. v. *Bamberg* 310119 K 8
Berlin: kfl. Bibliothek 450726 K 6
Bernburg: Schloßbibliothek *DA Köthen I. 4*, S. 7
Beuthen: Gymnasialbibliothek 310119
Sigmund v. *Birken* 440000 K 2
Johan *Boreel* (Middelburg) 280128
Hz. Anton Ulrich v. *Braunschweig-Wolfenbüttel DA Köthen I. 5*, S. 101
Hz. August d. J. v. *Braunschweig-Wolfenbüttel* 231210 I. 240319 I. 300215. 300216. 310000 K 9. 330603 K. 370828 K 1. 381028 I. *DA Köthen I. 5*, S. 7. 390828. 391209 K 3. 400218 K 5. *DA Köthen I. 6*, S. 112 ff. 410625 K 0. 410706. 410900 K 1. 420114 K 1. 430118. 430215. 430418. 430425. 431209 K 5. 440000 Q. 441000. 450000. 450929. 460000 u. I u. II. 460613. 460715. 460804. 460808. 460819. 460908 u. I–III. 461204A
Hz. Ferdinand Albrecht v. *Braunschweig-Wolfenbüttel* 460000A Q. 461204A K 0
Hz. Rudolf August v. *Braunschweig-Wolfenbüttel* 460613 K 3
Bremen: STUB 280724 K 4. 310119
Breslau: Dombibliothek 330311 K 2
Breslau: Gymnas. Elisabethanum 440119 K 0
Breslau: Gymas. Maria Magdalena 440324 K 2. 450726 K 5
Breslau: Kirche Maria Magdalena 270429 K 1. 271001 K 4
Breslau: Neustadt 271001 K 4

Brieg: Gymnasialbibliothek 310000 K 9
Ernst *Brinck* (Harderwijk) 261010 K 16
Erasmus *Burkhardt* (Heidelberg) 310119 K 2
Georg *Busse (Bussius)* 430826 K 33
Corvina 250700 S. 434
Ernst Bogislaw v. *Croy* 450326 K 4
Frh. Daniel Ludolph v. *Danckelmann* 310800 K 1
Danzig: Ratsbibliothek 331223 I Q
Dessau: Schloßbibliothek *DA Köthen I. 4*, S. 7
Burggf. u. Herr Karl Hannibal zu *Dohna* 310119
Dresden: kfl.-sächs. Hofbibliothek 401116 K 3
Dupuy (Paris) 300725 K
F. Johann Ulrich v. *Eggenberg* (Graz) 280724 K. 290129 u. I. 290528. 290708
Johann Eberhard v. *Eltz* (?) 401204
Thomas *Erpenius* (Leiden) 280128
Bf. Johann *Fabri* v. Wien 310119
Michael *Flandrin* (Breslau) 390121A K 7
Georg *Frantzke* 290614 K 2
Marquard *Freher* (Heidelberg) 390800A
Heinrich v. *Friesen* d. J. 330918 K 4
Daniel *Fugmann* (Planitz) 280122
Matthias *Hafenreffer* 401111 K 16
Melchior *Goldast v. Haiminsfeld* 280724 K 4. *DA Köthen I. 3*, S. 18. 310119. 390121A. 390800A
Jacobus *Golius* (Leiden) 280128
Gotha: Hzl. Bibliothek 350312 K 3
Gottorf: Hzl. Bibliothek 460915
Ianus *Gruterus* (Heidelberg) 310119 K 2
Halle a. d. S.: ULB 310800
Hamburg: Stadtbibliothek 430826 K 33
Harderwijk: Veluwsche Kwartierschool 261010 K 16
Heidelberg: Palatina 310119. 390114 I
Heidelberg: U. 450726 K 3

Lgf. Georg II. v. *Hessen-Darmstadt* 310119 K 8
Lgf. Hermann IV. v. *Hessen-Rotenburg* 370421 K 1
Carl Gustav v. *Hille* 310000 K 10. 310411 I. 430208. *DA Köthen I. 7*, S. 132
Friedrich *Hortleder* (Weimar) 290614 K 2
Jena: UB 180000. 181207 K 10
Peter/ Friedrich/ Gottfried v. *Jena* 310800 K 1
Joachim *Jungius* 430509 K
Kassel: Hofbibliothek 370421 K 0
Kassel: Landesbibliothek 370421 K 1
Friedrich v. *Kospoth* (Jena) 350312 K 8
Köthen: Schloßbibliothek *DA Köthen I. 4*, S. 7. 410323 K 6
Leiden: UB 280128
Liegnitz: Rudolfina 310000 K 9
Gf. zur *Lippe* 280724 K 4 S. 339. 310119 K 8
Johann *Löw* (Wien) 280704. 290528. 290708
Kd. Jules (Giulio) *Mazarin* (Mazarini) 460103
Henri II. de *Mesmes* 460103 K 6
Joachim *Morsius* 430826 K 0
Johann Michael *Moscherosch* 451217 K 9
Nürnberg 430505 K 2
Martin *Opitz* *DA Köthen I. 3*, S. 18. 331223 I
Gaston *d'Orléans* 390701 K 2
Oxford: Bodleian Library 280128 K 20
Paris: Kgl. Bibliothek 300725 K
Hz. Philipp II. v. *Pommern-Stettin* 460715 II
Gf. Eberhard v. *Rappoltstein* 370900 K 2
Wolfgang *Ratke* 181023. 181207. 181225 K 9. 270406 K 18. 290529. 290614. *DA Köthen I. 3*, S. 18. 300203. 300406. 311205. 320729
Thomas *Reinesius* (Altenburg, Leipzig) 280122 K 10
Nicolaus *Rittershusius* 270429 K 8

Rom: Bibliotheca Apostolica Vaticana
310119. 390114 I
Rom: Ulpia   250700 S. 433
Sachsen, s. Dresden
Hzn. Elisabeth Sophia v. *Sachsen-Gotha*
431211 K I 3
Hz. Moritz v. *Sachsen-Zeitz*   280122
K 10
Johann *Saubert d. Ä.*   460715. 460819
K 8
Iosephus Iustus *Scaliger* (Leiden)
280128
Hz. Friedrich III. v. *Schleswig-Holstein-Gottorf*   421202 K 1
Herr Georg *Schönborner* v. u. zu Schönborn u. Ziesendorf   310119 K 4
Justus Georg *Schottelius*   440100
Peter v. *Sebottendorf* (Brieg)   220824 K 1. 310000 K 9
Suffridus *Sixtinus*   310119 K 2
Cyriacus *Spangenberg*   290528 K 2
Stockholm: Kgl. Hofbibliothek
400319 K 2. 450726 K 3
Straßburg: U.   450726 K 3
Jacques Auguste de *Thou* (Paris)
300725 K 1
Andreas *Tscherning*   440324
Herr Hans Georg v. *Wartenberg*
280122
Wien: Ksl. Bibliothek   450806 K 2
Wolfenbüttel: hzl. Bibliothek (vgl. oben: Hz. August d. J. v. *Braunschweig-Wolfenbüttel*)   420114 K 1. 460613 K 0
Veit *Wolfrum* (Zwickau)   280122 u. I
Bildungs-, Entdeckungs- und Pilgerreisen
DA Köthen I. 1, S. 14. *DA Köthen I. 3*, S. 19. 300330 K 1. 300921 K I 1. 310119 K 5. 331223 K 28. 371027 I–III. 371223 K 8. 400317 K 3. 430418. 430430. 430826 K 0
Afrika   280128. *DA Köthen I. 3*, S. 118. 371027 K III 3
Ägypten   371027 III. 380405 K I 1
Amerika, s. Westindien
Arabien   371027 III. 391100
Belgien   250218A K III 3. 300813
Böhmen   360630 I

Dänemark   371027 III
Deutschland:
allgemein   251100 K 1. 360630 I u. K 3. 371027 III
Amberg   360600 II
Ansbach   360600 II
Breslau   291005. 291013
Dresden   251100 K 1
Frankfurt a. M.   310119
Gotha   310119 K 1
Hamburg   360630 K 2 u. K I 5. 410731
Heidelberg   360600 II
Köthen   180102. 181023. 181207. 181222. 181225. 190220. 190424. 251100 K 1. *DA Köthen I. 2*, S. 11. 271107. 300330 K 7. 310113 K 3
Leipzig   310119 K 1
Ostfriesland   410731
Straßburg   271107 K 1. 400317 K 3
Wien   360630 K I 5. 460204 I
Wittenberg   251100 K 1
England   250218A K III 3. 260419 K 1. 271107 K 1. 280721 K 5. 290310 K 5. 300813. 300921 u. K I 1. 360600 II. 360630 I. 371027 III. 371030 I. 371112 K I 2. 381007 K 7. 390121A K 1. 420120 K 13. 430826 K 33. 440426 K I 0. 460120A K 1
Frankreich   190220 K 8. 250218A K III 3. 250627 K 1. 250702 K 2. 250705 K 3. 260106. 260211. 260217. 260419 K 1. 260520A K I 2. *DA Köthen I. 2*, S. 11. 270429 K 14. 271107 K 1. 271126 K 1. 271209 K I 16. 271215. 280216A. 280411 K 11. 280721 K 5. 280724 K 8. 280726 K 3. 290310 K 5. 290715 K 13. 290909 K 8. 291231. 300718 K 0. 300725 K 11. 300813 K 1. 300921 K 29. 301001. 310703. 330918. 331223 K I 2. 360428 K 1. 360600 II. 360630 I. 370305. 371009 K 0. 371027 III. 371030 K I 8. 371112 K I 2. 371209 K 3. 371226 K 2. 381007 K 7. 390121A K 1. 400728 K 1. 410621 K 1. 410731 I. 420120 K 13. 430826 K 33. 440724 K 4. 440826 K 3. 441205 K 3. 450817 K II 3. 451101

Sachregister 1111

K 13. 451220 K 0. 460103. 460120A
K 1. 460125 K 2. 460204 I. 460610
K 8
Griechenland 371027 I u. II
Indien, s. ‚Ostindien'
Irland 371027 I–III
Italien 200318 K 7. 230802. 230809.
230819. 231006. 250218A K III 3.
250705. 270429 K 11. 271209 K I.
280327 K 2. 280411. 280724 K 8.
280929. 290629. 291005 K 2. 291013.
360428 K 1. 360630 I. 370902 K 12.
371009 K 0. 371027 I–III. 381007
K 7. 390121A K 1. 400728. 410621
K 1. 410731 I. 420601 K 2. 420124 K
I 3. 430826 K 33. 450817 K II 3.
451101 K 13. 460103 K 0. 460120A
K 1. 460204 I
Niederlande 260619. 270115. 271107
K 1. 271126 K 1. 280404 K 12.
280716 K 4. 280721 K 5. 290310 K 5.
300921 u. I. 301001 K 21. 310113.
330918. 360428 K 1. 360600 II.
360630 I u. K 3. 371009 K 0. 371027
III. 371030 K I 8. 371112 K I 2.
371226 K 2. 381007 K 7. 390121A
K 1. 410731 u. I. 420120 K 13.
420219 K 4. 420630 K 21. 430826
K 33. 440724 K 6. 440826 K 3.
441205 K 3. 460103. 460125 K 2.
460204 I. 460610 K 8
Norwegen 371027 III
Orange 360630 u. K I 5
Osmanisches Reich/ Naher Osten
210421 K 10. 261010 K 16. 280122
K 10. 280128 u. K. *DA Köthen I. 3*,
S. 109. 371027 I–III
Osteuropa 371027 I u. II
‚Ostindien' *DA Köthen I. 1*, S. 79.
210421 K 10. 280128 K 4. *DA Köthen I. 3*, S. 105 ff. 300921 I. 310000
K I. 390909. 390929. 391100. 410914
K 6
Palästina 280128 K. 371027 III.
380405 K I 1
Jerusalem 360600 II
Paris 450818 K 22
Persien 210421 K 10. 360800 K 1.
391005 K 2

Polen 371027 III. 450326 K 4
Portugal 280724 K 8
Rußland 360800. 391005 K 2
Schottland 371027 III
Schweden 371027 I–III
Schweiz 190220 K 8. 250218A K III 3.
270429 K 14. 271107 K 1. 280411
K 11. 300718 K 0. 300813 K 1.
360600 II. 410731 I. 451101 K 13.
451220 K 0
Siebenbürgen 280128 K 21
Spanien 280724 K 8. 371027 III
Ungarn 371027 III
Westeuropa 450326 K 4
‚Westindien' *DA Köthen I. 3*, S. 104,
119. 310000 K I 1
Biographie, s. Geschichtsschreibung
Botanik, s. Pflanzen
Brief/ Gesellschaftsbrief (Form, Gattung,
Stil). Vgl. Gedichtwechsel u. Rede/ Redekunst
200125. 210401. 230430. 240109.
240301. 250228. 250305. 260000.
260000A. *DA Köthen I. 3*, S. 9. 300320.
310108 u. I. 310119 K 5. 320626. 330918
K 4. 350312 K 12. *DA Köthen I. 4*,
S. 10 f. 370113 K 0. 371110. 371231 K 1.
380000. 380108. 380125A. 380504.
380720. 381007. *DA Köthen I. 5*, S. 15.
390630. 390800 K 2. 390901. 390903.
400430 K 1. 400619. 400620. 401116
K 3. 401212 K 0. *DA Köthen I. 6*, S. 12.
410621 K I. 421105. 430403. 441020.
460825 K 18. 461006 K 0. 461031
Briefeausgabe/ Briefesammlung 450726
K 2. 450818 K. 460909 u. I
Bücherverkehr der FG (Buchleihe, Buchversand, Bücheraustausch etc.). Vgl.
Bibliotheken, Buchhandel u. Verlagswesen.
DA Köthen I. 1, S. 21. 180000. 180714.
181207. 190322 u. I. 191124. 191129.
191229. 191231. 210421. 210729.
211006. 220824. 220919. 230802.
230809. 230819. 230913. 231008.
231101. 231203. 231210 u. I. 240106.
240116. 240125. 240319. 240418.
240907. 250110. 250413. 250627.
250700. 250706. 251100. 260831.

270808. 271211. 271215. 271228.
280106. 280208. 280216A. 280218.
280226. 280401. 280404. 280411.
280412. 280414. 280425. 280510.
280616A. 280818. 280821. 280929.
281000. 281105. 281126. 290510.
291009. 291028. 291104A. 291222. *DA
Köthen I. 3*, S. 8. 300209. 300215 K 1.
300410. 301102. 340604. 340609.
340628. 340816. 350312. 350731.
360630. *DA Köthen I. 4*, S. 10, 11.
370828. 371106. 371112 u. I. 371112A.
371116. 371117. 371120. 371123.
371124. 371126. 371127. 371208.
371221A. 371224. 371226. 380000.
380108. 380120. 380122. 380125.
380125A. 380126. 380128. 380207.
380220. 380221. 380302. 380310.
380312. 380321. 380405. 380411.
380501. 380503. 380504. 380509.
380606. 380609. 380616. 380720.
380810. 381007. 381116A. 381123.
381218. 381224. *DA Köthen I. 5*, S. 9,
10, 14. 390110. 390112. 390114. 390115.
390119. 390121. 390126A. 390126B.
390310. 390504 K 2. 390514. 390630.
390701. 390800A K 1. 390807. 390814.
390828. 390903. 390909. 390911.
390921. 390929. 391005. 391100.
391125. 391200. 391203. 391209. 391217
K 11. 391223. 400127. 400209. 400214.
400218. 400301. 400311. 400319.
400430. 400506 u. I. 400509. 400514.
400605. 400619. 400620. 400728.
400810. 401029. 401116. 401216.
401223. 401228. 410101 K 0. 410102.
410106. 410117. 410203. 410708.
410914. 411126. 420120. 420311. 420503
K 10. 420630. 421031. 421031A. 421105.
421110 K 0. 421129. 421129A. 421200.
421202. 421207. 430101. 430307.
430312. 430318. 430328. 430403.
430407. 430419. 430505. 430526.
430724. 430801A. 430802. 430920.
431007. 431014. 431020. 431021.
431022. 431124. 431201. 431209.
440130. 440204. 440209A. 440310.
440313. 440724. 440824. 441205.
441226A. 441231. 450124. 450126 K 4.
450220. 450301 K 5. 450305. 450308.
450317. 450317A. 450319 K. 450326.
450400. 450507A. 450526. 450721.
450808. 450817 K 16. 450919A.
450923C. 451007. 451101. 451119.
451209. 451217. 451219. 460000 u. I u.
II. 460217. 460406. 460426. 460620.
460705. 460714. 460720 K 1. 460721
K 4. 460808. 460912. 460915. 460915A.
461031. 461106. 461213

Buchhandel. Vgl. Druckerei, Markt u. Verlagswesen
Amsterdam 441223 K 1
Danzig 371126. 371127. 390909 K 5
Frankfurt a. M. 210421 K 6. 290129
    K 3 u. K I. 291104 K 1. 310119 K 2.
    310703 K 7. 380606 K 3. 410313 K 2.
    420712 K 1. 430505 I. 430527.
    440130 K 3. 450124. 450126 K 4.
    450410. 450503K 0. 450509. 450711.
    450800 u. K I. 460620B
Halberstadt 430905 K 3
Hamburg 450929. 451007
Hanau 310703 K 7. 450417
Kassel 450305 I. 450506. 450507A
    K 3. 450526
Köthen 210421 K 6. 310000 Q. 311205
    K 1. 340628. 340816. 371116 K 2.
    371120. 380321 K 3. 380606. 390912.
    390921. 391113. 400619 K 4. 400620.
    411126 K 3. 450220 K 10. 450417
Leiden 450410
Leipzig 250609. 280716. 301102 K 4.
    310703 K. 370422 K I 2. 371112.
    371116. 380221. 380312. 380504.
    380606 K 3. 400104 K I 2. 410313
    K 2. 420506. 430505 I. 430527.
    430905. 440824 K 8. 450124. 450417.
    450507A K 3. 450509 K 3. 450930.
    451007. 451101. 460916
Lübeck 450929. 451007
Nürnberg 430505 K 2. 430624. 430724
    K 10. 450504 K 4. 450808. 451007.
    460803. 460916. 461031
Osnabrück 460825
Schmalkalden 291104A K I 3
Straßburg 270429. 310703. 421206 K 9
Venedig 451101
Wien 460317

Wittenberg 280716 u. K 18. 290715.
310703 K 7
Wolfenbüttel *DA Köthen I. 5*, S. 108

Canzonette, s. Kanzone
Chemie, s. Alchemie
Chiffren, s. Kryptographie

Daktylus 300320 K II 0. *DA Köthen I. 4*,
S. 8, 14. 380828 u. I. 381116. 381218. *DA Köthen I. 5*, S. 14, 15. 390126 K 4.
390800 K 1. 391028. 391119 u. I–III.
391216. 400317 I. 400323. *DA Köthen I. 6*, S. 11 f. 410203A. 410206 K 2. 420503.
420608. 421027 K 4. 421101 K IV.
421200 K 1. 430509 K 4. 431014.
431123. 431124. 431206. 440310A.
440426 K I 3. 440616. 440824. 441020.
441231A K 1. 450124. 450400 K 3.
450506A K 3. 450529 K 2. 460705 K II 1. 450808 I. 460825
Datierungsweise/ Kalender 200318 K 1.
230802 K 1. 230809 K 1. 231101 K 1.
250218 K 19. 250305. 250609 K 2.
260419 K 8. 280128 K 20. 280216 K 1.
280216A K 1. 280716 K 1. 281021 K.
290302 K 4. 290304 K 1. 290307 K 1.
290616 K 3. 310411 K 7. *DA Köthen I. 4*, S. 7 f. 370421 K 10. 371031 K 0.
371108. 371110. 371120 K 8. 371208A K 6. 371220 K 15. 371221. 371227 K 5.
380110 K 11. 380125A K 2. 380221 K 8.
380226 K 6. 380312 K 8. 380328 K 9.
380405 K 6. 380501 K 18. 380502.
380503 K 12. 380509 K 1. 380522A K.
380609A K 4. 380619. 380803 K 3.
381006. 381007 K 10. 381204. 390712A.
390800A K 1. 390807A. 390902. 401007.
401009. 401215 K. 401223 K 9. 401228 K 3. 410102 K 0. 410119. 411200 K 0.
411214 K II B 9. 420219 K 1. 421230 (K 6). 430103 K II 2. 430215 K 14. 450220.
450221. 450504. 450504A K 6. 460303 K 3. 460309 K 4. 460403 K 1. 460423 K 6. 460915 K 13. 461031 K 6
Dichterkrönung *DA Köthen I. 1*, S. 13.
250510 K 3. 250700 S. 434. 290715 K 29.
291013 K 7. 371027 K 2. 371208 I–IV.
430505 I. 430624 K 2. 440324 K I 3.
440724 K 4. 441223 K 16. 450806 K 2.
451100 K 9. 460610. 461104 I–IV
Drama. Vgl. Maskerade u. Ritterspiel
Aufführung/ Lektüre/ Kritik/ Beschaffung u. ä. 250700 S. 430 u. 432.
251100. 270429 K 1. 290410. 290608 K 3. 290629 K 20. 350312 K 3.
350731 K 4. 380310 I. 390114 I. *DA Köthen I. 6*, S .14. 420503. 421009.
430920. 431211 I. 440824 K 7.
450818 K 12. 450901. 451100. 460103 K 3
Werk/ Abfassung/ Adaptation/ Bearbeitung/ Übersetzung 181207.
190308. 190322 K I 2. 250510 K 12.
251100. 271001. 280128 K 24. 290410 K 5. 340107 K 20. 350731 K 4.
380310 K I 1. *DA Köthen I. 6*, S. 14.
411200 K 1. 420608. 421207. 430920.
431014. 431022. 440000 K I 1.
440209A. 440324 K 1. 440426 u. I.
450124. 450400 K 2. 450529. 450817 V u. K II 2. 450818 K 12

Druckerei
Amberg: Michael Forster 350731 K I 0
Amsterdam: Ludwig Elzevier 441223 K 1. 450410 K 2. 450504
Amsterdam: Menasseh ben Israel 450410 K 8
Antwerpen: Martinus Nutius 460804 K 1
Basel: Georg Decker 390800 K 3
Basel: Johann Jacob Genath *DA Köthen I. 3*, S. 130
Braunschweig: Balthasar Gruber 410706 I. 441000. 441011
Braunschweig: Johan Ritmar 451000
Braunschweig: Heinrich Werner 440724 K 12
Braunschweig: Christoph Friedrich Zilliger 441000 K 5
Bremen: de Villiers *DA Köthen I. 3*, S. 98. *DA Köthen I. 6*, S. 9. 460825 K 7
Breslau: Georg Baumann 440324 K 14 u. K I 1. 450726 K 2
Breslau: Peter Kirsten 280128

Breslau: Johann Richel (d. Ä. u. d. J.) 450726 K 8
Colmar: Georg Friedrich Spannseil 390800 K 6
Danzig 390909 K 5
Eisenstadt, s. Schmalkalden
Frankfurt a. M. 450217. 450800 u. I
Frankfurt a. M.: Daniel u. David Aubry/ Clemens Schleich 281126 K 5. 310703 K 7
Frankfurt a. M.: Thomas Matthias Götze 420712 K 1
Frankfurt a. M.: Matthäus Merian d. Ä. 450509
Frankfurt a. M.: Wechelsche Verlagsbuchhandlung u. Druckerei 281126 K 5
Genf 430505 K 2
Gotha 340604 K 2. 450217. 450224
Halle a. d. S.: Christoph Bißmarck 441231 K 6
Halle a. d. S.: Melchior Oelschlegel 380606 K 3. 410208 (K 4)
Halle a. d. S.: Christoph Salfeld d. Ä. 441231 K 6. 450504 K 9
Halle a. d. S.: Peter Schmied/ Petrus Faber 400314 K 4
Hamburg 440900
Hamburg: Tobias Gundermann 390904 I
Hamburg: Hans Gutwasser 390800 K 3
Hamburg: Jacob Rebenlein 440724 K
Hamburg: Johan Ritmar 451000
Hanau: Aubry/ de Marne/ Schleich 310703 K 7
Hanau: Johann Press 450417
Hanau: Clemens Schleich 410625 K 0
Hanau: de Villiers *DA Köthen I. 3*, S. 98
Helmstedt: Georg Calixt 451000 K 1
Helmstedt: Henning Müller (Erben Jacobus Lucius) 451000 K 1
Hersfeld: Wolfgang Ketzel 291104A K I 3
Hofgeismar: Salomon Schadewitz 440809A K 4
Kassel 450317 K 4. 450507A K 3. 450526

Kassel: Jakob Gentsch (Gentzsch) 440809A K 4. 450305 K 2. 450317 K 4. 450317A K 1. 450506 K 1
Kassel: Johann Saur 440809A K 4
Kassel: Johann (Hans) Schütz 450305 I. 450317 K 7
Kassel: Wilhelm/ Johannes Wessel 291104A K 2
Köthen 181023. 181207. 190308. 190318. 190324. 191229. 191231. 200826. 210421. 220919 K 3. 250700 K 91. 260211 K 4. 270406. 270827 K 10. 271025. 281105. 281126. 290410 K 5. 290501. *DA Köthen I. 3*, S. 120. 300203 K 1. 300509 K 4. 300718 K 13. 310000 Q u. K. 310411 u. I. 311205 K 1. 340604 K 2. 340609 K 2. 340628 K 6. 340816 K 5. *DA Köthen I. 4*, S. 7. 370902 K 11. 371027 K 1. 371106. 371112. 371124 K 5. 380100 K 8. 380110 K 9. 380128 K 6. 380221. 380321 K 3. 380606. *DA Köthen I. 5*, S. 8, 10, 12, 104. 390504 K 2. 390904 u. I. 390912. 390921. 391100. 391113. 391125 K. 391200. 400104 u. I. 400122 K I 6. 400127 K 2. 400209 K 1. 400312 K 1. 400619. 400620. 401216 K 2. *DA Köthen I. 6*, S. 7, 9. 410101 K 0. 410111 K I. 410117. 410208 K 4. 410313. 410714 K. 410727. 410914 K 1. 411009 K 5. 411126 K 2. 420219 K 3. 420601 K 2. 420712 K 1. 421031A. 421202. 430312. 430318. 430407. 430505 I. 430507 K 1. 430624 K I 1. 430724A. 430801A K. 430802. 430821. 431016. 431020 K 3. 431021 K 2. 431201 K 1. 431209. *DA Köthen I. 7*, S. 136 f. 440130. 440323. 441231. 450217. 450220 K 10. 450224. 450301 K 5. 450317. 450410. 450504. 450507A. 450529 K 10. 450900. 450929. 451019 K 1. 460119 K 3. 460217. 460718
Leiden: Elzevier 450410 K 2
Leiden: Thomas Erpenius 280128
Leiden: Franciscus Raphelengius 280128
Leipzig: Abraham Lambergs Erben 380606 K 3

Lübeck 380625. 441011. 460131
Lüneburg: Hans u. Heinrich Stern
 240106. 240116. 240125. 380320 K.
 401111 K 16. 410119. 420601.
 421206. 421225. 430118. 430204.
 430318. 430430. 450319 K 9. 460700
 T a
Nürnberg 440900. 441011
Nürnberg: Endter 340604 K 2. 371219
 K 5. 411126 K 6. 450504 K 4. 450808
Orange 300410 K 55
Paris: Imprimerie des langues orientales
 (François Savary [Comte] de Brèves)
 280128
Rom: Typographia Medicea linguarum
 externarum (Giovanni Battista Rai-
 mondi) 280128
Rom: Typographia Savariana 280128
Rostock: Johann Richel d. J. 440324
 K I 1
Rostock: Joachim Wilde d. Ä. 450324
 K I 1. 450726 K 6
Schleusingen 450217 K 1
Sedan: Jean Jacques de Turene 300725
 K 9
Schmalkalden: Wolfgang Ketzel
 291104A I u. K 2
Stuttgart: Rudolph Kautt 450319 K 9
Tübingen: Philibert Brunnen 410406
 K 6
Utrecht: Elzevier 450410 K 2
Venedig 430505 K 2
Weimar: 180508. 340604 K 2. 390904
 I. 390907. 390910. 450224
Wittenberg: Johann Röhner 381007
 K 7. *DA Köthen I. 6*, S. 9. 410208.
 421202 K 6
Wittenberg: U.-Buchdruckerei 380606
 K 3
Wolfenbüttel 440900. 450929
Wolfenbüttel: Johann Bismarck
 441011. 450100 K 11
Wolfenbüttel: Johan Ritmar 451000
Wolfenbüttel: Johann und Heinrich
 Stern 441011 K 4. 450100 K 2.
 451000 K 1
Zerbst: Andreas Betzel 380606 K 3.
 DA Köthen I. 6, S. 9. 430505 K 2
Druckprivileg, s. Verlagswesen

Ekloge *DA Köthen I. 2*, S. 18. 260217
 K 1. 280716 K 5. 290629 K 10. 291231
 K 3. *DA Köthen I. 3*, S. 8. 300209.
 300320 K II 2. 310703 II. 350312 K 4.
 350731 V. 406 f. *DA Köthen I. 4*, S. 12.
 370422 K 7 u. K III 3. 380221. *DA Köthen I. 5*, S. 8. 390112 K I 10. 400218
 K 5. 400314 K 4. 400502. 400506.
 400619. 410706 u. I. 440426 K 7. 440724
 K 11. 440824 K 7. 441020 K. 441216 I.
 450220 K II 0. 450400 K 6. 450504 K 4.
 450817 K II 3. 451101 K 13. 451217.
 460112 K 3. 460120. 460825 K 18.
 460908 K 5
Elegie *DA Köthen I. 2*, S. 18. 281021.
 300330 I. 310000. 310703 II. 360428 III.
 360600 u. II. 370715 I. 380828 K 3.
 441020 K
Emblem. Vgl. Imprese
 DA Köthen I. 2, S. 9 f., 90. 270700.
 280412 K II 1. *DA Köthen I. 3*, S. 8, 98,
 124 ff., 130. 350731 K I V. 30 (1). 370422
 K 7. 371124 I Q u. K I 0. 380331 K 9.
 401111 K 10. *DA Köthen I. 6*, S. 9 f.,
 118 f., 119, 121, 122 f., 123. 411126 K 6.
 421027 u. I. 421031A K 11. 421105 Q u.
 K 7. 421110 K 0. 421200. 430000.
 430101. 430121. 430204. 430208.
 430214. 430312. 430318. 430419 K I 2.
 430624 u. I. 430724. 431007 K 1.
 431124. 431206 K 4. *DA Köthen I. 7*,
 S. 132, 135. 440000 Q. 440400. 440616 K
 I 1 u. K III 3. 440715 Q u. K 4, 5, 9, 10.
 440731 II u. K I 2. 440900. 441020 K 1.
 441216 u. K I. 441223. 450100 K 13.
 450124 K 6 u. K I 4. 450219 K 6.
 450400. 450504A K 3. 450529. 450611
 K 1. 450817 u II u. K I u. IV Q. 450927
 u. K II 2. 460610 K 4. 460715 II. 460912
 I u. II
Endecasillabo 231203 K 2. 250500 K 1.
 401223 K 6. *DA Köthen I. 6*, S. 123 f.
 431124. 431206 I u. K 4. 440310A K I 1.
 450124 K 6
Engel 240319 I. 310108 K 12. 350731 I V.
 474 ff. 371226A I. 440204 I. 451100 u. I
Entdeckungsreisen, s. Bildungsreisen
Enzyklopädie 191231. 270919. 300320

K 9. 430509 K 4. 441000. 450817 K II 4
u. K V 17
Epigramm 181023 K 17. 250110 u. I.
250218A u. I u. III. 250510. *DA Köthen
I. 2*, S. 92 f., 94. 270429 K. 271001 K.
280000 K 1. 280716 u. II u. K I 1.
280818 I u. II. 310119. 310703 K 18 u. K
II. 330311 K 1. 360800 u. K II 4. *DA
Köthen I. 4*, S. 89, 90, 93, 97. 370422 K
III 1. 370715 K 12. 370900. 371226A
K 6. 380000 K 3. 381116. 381218. *DA
Köthen I. 5*, S. 98 f., 100. 390310.
390514. 390800 K 1. 390807. 400214.
410324 K I. 420627 K I 9. 421225.
430118. 430215. 430419 K I 2. *DA Köthen I. 7*, S. 11. 440324. 440616 K I 0 u.
K II. 441020 K 1. 450326 K 4. 450500
K 5. 450726 K 0. 450806 K 2. 450817 K
II 3. 450818 u. I. 450901 Q. 450919A
K 7. 460610 K. 461020. 461104 K I
Epos. Vgl. Roman
  Lektüre/ Kritik/ Beschaffung u. ä.
    171224 K 4. 250700 S. 430. 251100.
    260617. 260831. 270429. 271126 K 2.
    280000. 310703 I. 360800 I. 371117.
    380402. 400810
  Werk/ Abfassung/ Adaptation/ Bearbeitung/ Übersetzung 230802.
    230819 u. I. 250110. 250218A.
    250500 K 1. 250609. 270429. 270925
    K II 1. 280106. 280112. 280208.
    280218. 280411 K 2. 280412 I.
    280414 I. 280821. 281021. 281105
    K 5. 281126 K 5. 290510 K 11. *DA
    Köthen I. 3*, S. 10. 310000. 310411
    K 13. 310703 I u. K. 330311 K 9.
    350731 Q I. 371027 K 2. 371028A
    K 1. 371031 K 1. 371108. 371110.
    371112. 371112A. 371116 K 3.
    380226 K 1. 380608A. 380609A.
    380619 K 2. 380720. 380721. 381007.
    381105. *DA Köthen I. 5*, S. 10 f., 17,
    35, 103 f. 390115 K 1. 390125 K 8.
    390126B. 390701. 390800A. 391000.
    391200. 400000. 400619. 400620.
    400714. 400810. *DA Köthen I. 6*,
    S. 14. 410208 K 4. 420503 K 10.
    420506. 430121A. *DA Köthen I. 7*,
    S. 8. 440119 K. 440310B K 2. 441020

K. 450725 K 5. 450817 K II 4.
450900. 451101 K 16. 460204 I
Erbauung, s. Frömmigkeit/ Erbauung
Erzschrein *DA Köthen I. 4*, S. 7. 371110
K 11. 371120 T e. 371209. 371220.
371221. 371226. 380108. 380202.
380312. 380328. 380410 K 5. 380423.
381204. 390723. 400313 K 1. *DA Köthen
I. 6*, S. 31 f. 410323 K 8. 410621. 420311.
420503. 420608. 421123. 421207.
430407. 430410. 430505. 430724.
430801A K 6. 431028. *DA Köthen I. 7*,
S. 132. 440209. 440824. 450124. 450400
K 6. 450410. 450500 K 1. 450505.
450611. 450730 K 2. 450808. 450817.
450919A. 451028. 451101. 451209.
451217. 460423. 460424. 460424A.
460620. 460705. 460825 V. 460915.
461031. 461031A. 461106
Esel 380220. *DA Köthen I. 5*, S. 14.
390112. 390114 u. I. 390126A. 390126B.
421200 K 1. 461204
Etymologie/ Mundart. Vgl. Wortschatz
230819. 240112 K 9. 240718 K 84.
250305 K 48. 260617 K 7. 260619. *DA
Köthen I. 2*, S. 8. 270406. 270810 K 2.
280600. 280724 K 4. 281215. 290120.
290529. 290614. 290913. 300203 K 3.
300320 K II 15. 300406 K 1. 320416 K I
1. 350312 K 1. 371030 K 5. 371031 K 8.
371110 K 11. 371116 K 4. 380207 K 7.
380328. 380828 K I. 381007 K 9. 381028
II–IV. 390310. 390727. 390800A.
390901. 400214. 400319 K 3. 400528 I u.
II. *DA Köthen I. 6*, S. 11. 410406.
410909 K 3. 410900 K 5. 411126 K 3.
420506 K 5. 420608. 421206. 421225.
430118. 430329. 430403. 430509 K 4.
430515. 431016 K 1. 431021 K. 431022.
431124. *DA Köthen I. 7*, S. 10, 16, 18,
20 f., 22, 24. 440129. 440209. 440219
K 2. 440426. 441201 K 0. 441223 K.
450000A K 0. 450308A. 450410 K 16.
450420 K 6. 450504. 450808. 450817 IV.
450919A. 450923B. 451220. 460000.
460131. 460217. 460406. 460610. 460720
K 3. 460816 I. 460902. 460915. 460916.
461031
Exil 220919 K 1. 231210 K 2. 240717 K 4.

DA Köthen I. 2, S. 8, 10, 17. 270925 K 1.
271201A K 8. 271211 K 3. 280122 K 1.
280128 K 1. 280218 K 5. 280411.
280616A K 1. 280620 K 2. 280726.
281021 K. 281215. 290216 K 1 u. K I 12.
291005 K 1. 291009. 291222. *DA Köthen
I. 3*, S. 19. 300509 K. 300725 K 5. 300921
K 17. 301001 K 24. 310108 K II. 310224.
310311. 310703 II. 310800 K 3. 320416
K 6. 330603 K 7. 330918 K. 331223 K.
350800 K 7. 360428 K 1 u. K I 2 u. K II
21. 360703 K. *DA Köthen I. 4*, S. 9, 12,
93 f. 370422 K. 370517 K 6. 370722 K.
370828 K 1. 370902 K 12. 371009 K u.
K I 4. 371028 K. 371112 K I 0. 371223
K 8. 380616 K. 411009. 420120 K.
420124 K I. 420630 K 38. 421110 K 4.
430106 K 1. 430215 K 30. 430515 K 10.
431211 K I. *DA Köthen I. 7*, S. 14.
440525 K 0. 440731

Fabel, s. Mythos
Finanzwesen: Bankgeschäfte/ Schulden/
  Steuern/ Inflation u. ä. Vgl. Münzstätten
  u. Numismatik, auch Gesellschaftskasse/ -umlage.
  180000. 181207 K 4. 191229. 191231.
  230913 K 23. 250218. 260106. 260211.
  280620 K 2. 280724 K 4. 290129 K I.
  290216 u. I. 290302. 290510. 290616.
  290708 K 9. *DA Köthen I. 3*, S. 18.
  300209 K 4. 300410 K 54 u. K I 15.
  300718 K 13. 300921. 300924 K 17.
  301011. 301102 K 4. 310113. 310119
  K 2. 310311. 311205 K 2. 320313 K 0.
  321201. 340628. 340816. 360703. *DA
  Köthen I. 4*, S. 9. 370517 K 4. 370722 K.
  370729 K 11. 370828 K 1. 371009 K 0.
  371027 K 10. 371030 u. I. 371112 K I 2.
  371124. 371221. 371223. 380125.
  380207. 380303 K. 380320A K 8.
  380501. 380616. 380625 K 2. 380721
  K 6. 380724. 380728. 380904. 381004
  K 4. 381107 K 1. *DA Köthen I. 5*, S. 16,
  17. 390126B. 390131 K 7. 390504 K.
  390504A K 1. 390712A K 5. 390800A.
  390807A K 3. 390828. 390903 K 2.
  390909. 391005 u. I. 391125. 391223.
  400104. 400218. 400605 u. I. 400809
  K 1. 400810 K 10. 400902 Q u. K 0 u.
  III. 401204 K. 401212. 401214 u. I. *DA
  Köthen I. 6*, S. 8 f. 410102. 410106.
  410111. 410117. 410313 K 1. 410323.
  410621. 410731 u I. 410822 K 5. 411128.
  420120. 420124 K 1 u. I. 420219.
  420601. 420630. 420712. 421120. 430118
  K 7. 430214. 430215. 430306. 430418.
  430430. 430507. 430527. 430706.
  430801A. 430905 u. I. 431028A. 431208
  K 3. 431211. *DA Köthen I. 7*, S. 16, 25.
  440323 K I 3. 440324. 440900. 441011.
  450100. 450126. 450127. 450219.
  450308. 450331 u. I. 450417. 450419
  K 2. 450503. 450505A K 3. 450508.
  450509. 450510. 450721. 450726. 450800
  u. I. 450923. 450930. 451019. 460000.
  460103 K 1. 460125 K II 3. 460218.
  460301. 460303 K. 460309. 460324.
  460403. 460414. 460519. 460721. 460916
  K 1. 461124 K 7
Fische 240112 K 9. 240319. 350312.
  350731 I V. 30 ff. u. K I. 360703. *DA
  Köthen I. 4*, S. 12. 371009 II. 371031 I.
  380226. 380302A. 380303. 380312.
  380904
Friedensverhandlungen/ -schlüsse; Waffenstillstand
  211006 K 11. 231008 K 8. 240418 K 5.
  300410 u. I. 300725. 300921. 301001
  K 25. 301011 K 11. 310113. 310224.
  310311. 331223 K. *DA Köthen I. 4*, S. 9.
  370729 K 11. 371014 K 7. 371117.
  380125A. 380210. 380501 K 11. 380616.
  DA Köthen I. 5, S. 7 f. 390814. 391005 u.
  I. 410102 K 5. 401204 K 4
Friede von Alès (1629)   271201A K 8.
  411009 K 5
Augsburger Religionsfrieden (1555)
  330920 K 0. 371028 K 11. 380000
  K 14. 390800 K 1
Erfurter Waffenstillstand (Aug. 1637)
  380125A K 8
Friede von Brömsebro (1645)   440927
  K 8
Goslarer Frieden (1642)   410621 K 6.
  421011 K 7. 430418 K 11. 431123 I.
  431209 K 5. *DA Köthen I. 7*, S. 131.
  440100 K 3 u. K I 5

Hamburger Präliminarfriede (1641) 370715 K 16. 370729 K 11. 371117 K 8. 380810 K 7. 391005 I. *DA Köthen I. 6*, S. 7. 411009. 421009 K 10. 421202 K 3. *DA Köthen I. 7*, S. 7 f. 440927 K 9. 441223 K 20
Kaiserl.-schwed. Friedensverhandlungen 1635 ff. 370715 K 15. 380210 K 10. 380810 K 7. 390822. 390909 K 18
Kölner Kongreß (1636 ff.) 370715 K 16. 370729 K 11. 390800 K 2. 391005 I. 421009 K 6. 421202 K 3
Leitmeritzer Friedensverhandlungen (1634) 330918 K 7. 340912 K 0. 390504 K 5
Lübecker Friede (1629) 290302 K 7. 290715 K 25. 300410 K 35. 300725 K 1. 350800 K. 430826 K 16
Edikt von Nantes (1598) 271201A K 8. 301102 K 1. 411009 K 5. 461124 K 1
Friedensexekutionskongress Nürnberg 1649/50 410324 K I. 450818 K I
Passauer Vertrag (1552) 300924 K 32. 371028 K 11
Passauer Vertrag (1647) 460819 K 12
Pirnaer Friedenspräliminarien (1634) *DA Köthen I. 3*, S. 13, 16. 320313 K 0. 321201 K 1. 330920 K 0. 340912 K 0. 350800 K 19. 390504 K 5
Edikt von Poitiers (1577) 411009 K 6
Prager Friede (1635) *DA Köthen I. 2*, S. 12. 280616A K 1. *DA Köthen I. 3*, S. 7, 13, 15 f. 320313 K 0. 320416 K 1. 321201 K 1. 330920 K 0. 340912 K 0. 350800. 360703 K. *DA Köthen I. 4*, S. 9, 92. 370305 K. 370421 K 4. 370422 K 1 u. K III 3. 370517 K 6. 370729 K 11. 371014. 371124 K. 371226A. 380125A K 8. 380302A K 7. 380503 K 12. *DA Köthen I. 5*, S. 7. 390112 K I 1. 390131 K 15. 390504 K 5. 390800 K 2. 390807A K 1 u. K I 2. 390828 K 6. 390910 K 2. 391005 I. 400104 K I. 400810 K 11. 410706 K 16. 430215 K 30. *DA Köthen I. 7*, S. 7. 460204 K I 3. 461104 K I

Schwed.-kursächs. Waffenstillstand (Eilenburg, 31. 3. 1646) 460321 K 2. 460424 K 12. 461124 K 7
Schwed.-kursächs. Waffenstillstand (Kötzschenbroda, 27. 8. 1645) *DA Köthen I. 7*, S. 140. 450711 K 6. 460422 K 4. 460424 K 12
Schwed.-poln. Waffenstillstand (1629) 380616 K 9
Schwed.-poln. Friedensverhandlungen (1635) 370715 K
Frieden von Szőny (1642) 420124 K 7
Waffenstillstand von Stuhmsdorf (1635) 371030 K 5 u. K I 11. 390822
Westfälischer Friede (1648) *DA Köthen I. 3*, S. 12. 370422 K 1. 370715 K 16. 370729 K 11. 371009 K 13. 371117 K 8. 371124 K 8. 380000 K 14. 380125A K 8. 380310 K I 16. 380616 K 11. 390131 K 15. 390822 K. 400301 K 6. 401204 K 7. *DA Köthen I. 6*, S. 8. 410324 K I. 410731 K 0 u. I. 420120 K 32. 420124 K 14. 421009 K 6. 421202. 430103 K II 3. 430826 K 16. 431211 K 3. *DA Köthen I. 7*, S. 7 f., 18, 135. 440119. 440927. 441223. 450220 K 1. 450326 K 4. 450504A K 1. 450721 K 3. 450806 K 9. 450818 K. 451101. 460103 K 5. 460104 K 0. 460125 K 1. 460204 K 7. 460825 K
Frieden von Zsitvatorok (1606) 420124 K 7
Zwölfjähriger span.-ndl. Waffenstillstand (1609–1621) 300410 K 35
Frömmigkeit/ Erbauung. Vgl. Bekenntnis, Religionsgemeinschaften, Religionsunterricht u. Theologie
190322 K I 3. 191124 K 1. 231101. 231210 I. 250627 K 1. 250702. 260106. 260211. 260217. 270115 K 15. 270429 K. 271001. 271010. 280000. 280208. 280716. 280724 K 5. 281021. 290000 IV u. K I 1. 290909 K 3. *DA Köthen I. 3*, S. 127. 300921. 310000. 310108 I. 310411 u. I. 310703. 310800. 330311. 350731 I. 360428 I. 360600 II. 360630 u. I–II. *DA Köthen I. 4*, S. 8, 12, 14 f. 370305. 370421 u. I. 370422 I. 370900 K 1.

371009 u. II. 371030 K 4. 371121.
371124 I. 371209 I u. II. 371222 u. I–III.
371226A K I 2. 380110 K 9. 380321.
380405 K 5. 380504. 380609. 380625.
380828 I. 381007. 381116. *DA Köthen I.
5*, S. 10 f., 16 f., 33, 34. 390110 K 1.
390630 u. I. 390701 u. I. 390800 u. I.
390921. 391100. 391217 K 9. 400104 u.
I. 400218 K 5. 400310 u. I. 400311 K 1.
400311A. 400312. 400320. 400430 K 1.
400502. 400506 K u. I. 400509 K 1.
400514. 400619. 400620 K 3. 400902 u. I
u. II. 400917 u. I. 401025. 401111 K u. I.
401117 u. I. 401204. 401214. 401215 II.
401216. 401223. 401228. 401229 K 2.
DA Köthen I. 6, S. 8, 9, 10, 12 f., 15,
113–118. 410101. 410111 I. 410119 K 2.
410203 K 4. 410406. 410727. 410731 I.
410909 K 5. 411128. 411214. 420120.
420219. 420601. 420608 K 10. 420627.
420630. 420712. 421031. 421031A.
421105. 421207. 430118. 430121.
430204. 430208. 430312. 430318.
430407. 430418. 430430. 430505 K I.
430617 K 5. 430706. 430826. 431016
K 2. 431123 u. I. 431124. 431201.
431209. *DA Köthen I. 7*, S. 15, 16, 132.
440310A u. I u. II. 440310B. 440429.
440724. 440809A K 4. 440816 I u. II.
440824 K 8. 441010 K 0. 441205. 441223
K 11. 450304. 450317. 450400. 450529.
450806 K 9. 450817 u. K I. 450818 K.
450900. 460103 K. 460120A K 1.
460200A. 460317 K I. 460825 u. II, IV
u. V. 461106 I. 461117. 461124 K 4
Fürstenspiegel, s. Politische Wissenschaften

Garten, s. Pflanzen
Gedichtwechsel 250413 IV. 260500.
260520A. 270925 u. I–IV. 280600.
280616. 400312 I. 430000. 450817 IV
Gelegenheitsdichtung. Vgl. Gedichtwechsel, Maskerade u. Ritterspiel
DA Köthen I. 2, S. 15, 17. 270429 K 8.
271001 K 1. 271010 K 5. 271201 K I 1.
280412 K I 6. 280616. 280716. 300320 K
II 17. 300330 K 0. 310119. 330311 K 1.
370422 K III 3. 371112 K I 2. 380110

K 9. 380509A. 380522A. 390800 K 1.
390822 I. 400430 K 1. 401111 K 4.
410111. 410203A. 421120. 430000A.
430826 K. *DA Köthen I. 7*, S. 9, 11 f.,
132. 440324. 440724 K 7. 440731 I.
441223. 450325. 450400. 450722. 450726
u. I. 450806. 450817 I u K II 14. 450818.
460829 u. I
Ehe 440525 K I 3
Geburt 260500. 260520A u. I. 260619.
 290629 K 22
Geburtstag 270810 u. I. 300330 K I 0.
 411214 K III H 1. 430430 K 6.
 440400 u. I. 450220 I. 450301.
 450319. 460317
Heimführung 250218A VII
Hochzeit 240109. 250110 III. 270429
 K 8. 271001. 271010 K. 290715 K 23.
 DA Köthen I. 3, S. 9, 128 f. 300330 u.
 I. 300403 u. I–II. 360600 II. *DA Köthen I. 4*, S. 15. 371030 K I 3. 371208
 I u. II. 371226 K 4. 371226A. 380207
 K 3. 380310 K 1 u. I–V. 380402 I.
 380504. 380625 K 2. 380720. 390126.
 390131 K 20. 390921 K 6. 400317 I.
 410221. 430826 K 36. 440724 K 3.
 450726 K 6. 460610. 460908 K 5.
 461104 K 3
Namenstag 450506A K 3
Neujahr 400809 II. 440324. 441231A
Promotion 440324. 440525 K I 3.
 450726. 460414. 460610
Reise 400809 u. I. 460204 I
Taufe 250218A V–VI. 291009 K 6.
 291104A. 360600 II. *DA Köthen I. 5*,
 S. 103. 391217 K 11
Tod 250110 I–II. 250218A I–IV.
 250413 I–IV. 260217. *DA Köthen I.
 2*, S. 7. 270700. 270810 K 1. 270919.
 271001. 271010. 271025. 280000 K 1.
 280412 II. 280414 II. 280510 II.
 280716 u. I u. II. 290310 u. I. 290329.
 290510. 291104A K 1. *DA Köthen I.
 3*, S. 10, 19. 300509 I. 300725 K 1.
 310703 II. 310800. 330311 K 1.
 330918 K 1. 340107 K 16. 340912
 K 3. 360428 III u. K 1. 360600 u. I–
 II. 360800 u. K I 1. *DA Köthen I. 4*,
 S. 8, 15, 93, 95. 370305. 370422 K III

3. 370715 K 12 u. I u. II. 370900.
371027 u. I u. II. 371028. 371208 III
u. IV. 371222. 371226 K 4. 371226A
u. I. 380000 K 2. 380207 K 3. 380502
K 4. *DA Köthen I. 5*, S. 16, 35 f., 99 f.
390112 I. 390121A K 7. 390800 u. I.
390909 K 5. 390921. 391209 K 2.
400902 u. I u. II. 401029. 401116 K 5.
401117 u. I. 401215. 401216 K.
410106 K 4. 410221 K 3. 410500.
421225 K 12. 431211 K I 22. 440000
K I 1. 440324 K. 440525 K I 3.
450220 II. 450326 K 2. 450725 I.
461104 K 3

Trost   450817 I

Widmung   250700 I. 280000. 310000.
310411 u. I. 310703 I. 330311 K.
330918 K 5. 340912. 360800 I u. K II
5. *DA Köthen I. 4*, S. 15. 370900 K 2.
371009 I u. II. 371027 K. 371030 K I
5. 371031 K 5. 371106 K 1. 371121
K 1. 371126 K 4. 371209 u. I u. II.
371226 K 4. 371226A K 6. 380207
K 3. 380321. 380405 u. I. 380507.
380522A. 380522B. 380602 u. I u. II.
380606. 380608A. 380609. 381028
III. *DA Köthen I. 5*, S. 17. 400312.
401025. 401109 K 6. 401117. 401215
u. II. 401216 K. 410101 K. 410324 u.
I. 410505 u. I. 410510. 410625 K 0.
410714 K 3. 410727 K 1. 410900.
411214 II–III. 420506 K. 421101 II.
421110 K II 0. 421200 K 1. 430000
K 2. 430103 K 3 u. K II 3. 430307
K 1. 430329 K 2. 430624 I. 430801 u.
I. 430801A. 430802. 430821. 430920.
DA Köthen I. 7, S. 132, 133. 440130.
440204 u. I. 440324 u. K I 3. 440426
K 2. 440525 u. I. 440616 I u. III.
440715. 440724 K 13. 440824 K 7.
440900 K 2. 441020 K 1. 441200 u. I
u. II. 441216. 450400. 450500 K.
450504. 450611 K 1. 450726 K 6.
450808 u. I. 450817 K 11. 451100 I.
460406 K 4. 460610 K 10. 460620.
460705 u. I u. II. 460718 K 7. 460803
K 0. 460804 K 1. 460825 III, IV, V u.
VI. 460909 K 6. 460915. 460916 K 6.
461029

Wochenbett   270925 u. I–IV

Geleit   230809 K 2. 231101. 231210.
240106. 260211. *DA Köthen I. 3*, S. 15.
300410 K 55. 310311. 331223 K 10.
350800. 370113 K 1. 370517 K 4. 370715
K 7. 371009. 380728. 421202 K 3.
431201. 460908

Genealogie, s. Geschichtsschreibung

Geographie/ Reisebeschreibung. Vgl. Bildungs-, Entdeckungs- und Pilgerreisen
181225 K 6. 210421 K 10. 261010 K 16.
290715 K 3. *DA Köthen I. 3*, S. 104 ff.
300718. 360600 II. 360800 K. *DA Köthen I. 4*, S. 11. 370421 K 1. 370900 K 2.
371027 K III 3. 380302. 380427. 381007
K 7. 390909. 390929 K 1. 391005 K 2.
391100. 391125. *DA Köthen I. 6*, S. 9.
410900 (K 12). 430106. 430214. 430306.
430418A. 430513. 430826 K 20. 430905.
440426 K I 0. 440715. 450417 K 0.
450905. 450930. 460303. 460324.
460519. 460703. 460810 K 2. 460819
K 12. 461023

Geometrie, s. Mathematik

Geschichtsschreibung/ Biographie/ Genealogie   171225 K 1. 191124 K 1. 230819.
240109 K 12. 240112 K 9. 250110 K 2.
250700. 260000 K 4. 260217 K. 260619.
261010 K 16. 271201A K 11. 280122 K I
2. 280128 K 20. 280218 K 5. 280327
K 14. 280404 K 10. 280412 K I 6.
280724 K 4. 290129 I. 291009 K 4.
290129 I. 291013 K 0. 291222 K 2. *DA Köthen I. 3*, S. 97 f., 124. 300215 K 1 u.
K I 3. 300216. 300718. 300725 K.
301102 K 3. 310119. 330918. 350312
K 1. 350731 K I. 360600 II. 360630 II.
360703 K 38. *DA Köthen I. 4*, S. 11, 12.
370900. 370902. 371028. 371112A.
380000. 380100. 380110. 380120.
380122. 380126. 380221 K 5. 380302
K 2. 380321. 380328 K 6. 380405 I.
380427. 380509A K 4. 380602. 380608A.
380616. 381028 K 1 u. II–III. 381105.
DA Köthen I. 5, S. 10, 15, 33 f., 101.
390114 I. 390310. 390701 K 2. 390800A.
390814. 390822. 390901 K I 1. 390903.
390909. 390911 K 3. 390921. 390929 K.
391100. 391209 K 3. 400311 K 1. 400506

u. I. 400509. 400528 K. 400728. 401111
u. K 4. 410119 K 2. 410625 K 0. 410706.
410914A K 5. 421110. 421206. 421225.
430215. 430418 K 9. 430425 K 3.
430505. 430515 K 7. 430724. 430826
K 24. 431007. 431022. 431123 K 1.
431124. 440000 III. 440100 K 4. 440119
K. 440209. 440310. 440310A. 440313.
440317. 440426 K 7. 440616 K 0.
440715A K. 440809A K. 441000.
441226. 450000. 450219. 450319.
450326. 450817 K II 4. 450818 K.
450900. 450927 I u. II. 451000 K 1.
451100 K 8. 451101 K. 460120A K 1.
460714. 460804 K. 460819 K. 460915.
461029 K 8. 461204A

Gesellschaftsarchiv, s. Erzschrein
Gesellschaftsbrief, s. Brief
Gesellschaftsbuch
Accademia degli Intronati 450817 u.
II. 451101. 451209 K 8. 451217.
460120
AL *DA Köthen I. 3*, S. 18. 310108 II Q
DG 441223. 450308A
FG *DA Köthen I. 2*, S. 9, 17. 281215
K 7. *DA Köthen I. 3*, S. 8, 10 f., 18,
99, 110. 300320. 370113. 370722.
370805 K 4. 370900. 371028. 371031
K 5. 371106 K 6. 371116. 371120.
380501 K 4. 391100. 391203 u. I.
391209 K 3. 400323. 400605 u. I.
400619. 400620. 400622 K 1. 400810.
401007 K 1. 401009 K 2. 401025.
420124
GB 1622 *DA Köthen I. 1*, S. 16 f.
20. 230430 I. 240109. 240118 K 1.
DA Köthen I. 2, S. 9, 18 f. 270105
K 3. 270700 K 1. 280308 K 2.
280411. 280412 K I 3. 290310 K 3.
290715 K 20. *DA Köthen I. 3*, S. 7,
11, 96. 310000 Q u. K 2. 371028.
371106 K 6. 371116 K 2. 371120
K. 371123 K 7. 371220 K 5.
381028 K II 0. *DA Köthen I. 5*,
S. 15. 390121 K 8. 400203. 400218.
401116 K 1. 401216. 401229 K 1.
411200 K 7. 420503 K 14. S.
DA Köthen I. 7, S. 22. 441223 K.
451015 K 2. 451030 K 0

GB 1624 230430 II. 240109 K 7.
240717 I. 250627. 250701 K 4.
250702 K 3. 260520. 260619. *DA
Köthen I. 2*, S. 9. 270105 K.
270700 K 1. 280308 K 2. 280411
K 9. 280412 K I. 280425 K 3.
290310 K I 6. 290715 K 20. *DA
Köthen I. 3*, S. 11, 104. 371120 K.
451015 K 2
GB 1628 250305 K 26. 250627 K 4.
260419 K 1. *DA Köthen I. 2*, S. 9.
270105 K 4. 280106. 280112 K 10.
280216A K I. 280218. 280308 K 2.
280407 K 5. 280411 K 9. 280412 K
I 3. 290310 K 3 u. K I 6. 290715
K 20. *DA Köthen I. 3*, S. 11, 104,
110. 360428 K 1. 370900 K 11.
371120 K. 371123 K 7. 441223
K 9. 451015 K 2
GB 1629 u. *1629/30* 250627 K 4.
260419 K 1. *DA Köthen I. 2*, S. 9,
16, 94. 270700 K 1. 271126.
271201. 271209. 271211. 271215.
280112. 280208. 280216A. 280218.
280304 K 5. 280321 K 1. 280327
K 3. 280412. 280414 K 12. 280510.
280517. 281226 u. K 10. 290226.
290302. 290310. 290314. 290329.
290510. 290629. 290715. 290909
K 4. 291104. 291200 u. K 5. *DA
Köthen I. 3*, S. 11, 99, 103 f., 110,
129. 300203. 300410. 300420.
300420A. 310000 K I 1. 310224.
331223 I. 340628. 340816. 360703.
370900 K 11. 371116 K 2. 371120.
371211. 371220 u. K I 0. 380331.
380507 K 1. 380606 K 3. 380810.
381007. *DA Köthen I. 5*, S. 10, 17,
104, 106. 390514. 390630. 390712.
390723 K 3. 390807 K 3. 391203 I.
391217. 400203 K 3. 400218 K 4.
400620 K 1. 401216 K 6. 401223
K 6. 401228A K 2. 410323 K 6.
410731 K 2. 420311 K 7. 420808 K
I 1. 421031A K 7. 430214. 430306.
430312. 430418A K 1. 430513 K 1.
430527 K 4. 430706 K 10. 430905
K 2 u. K I 0. *DA Köthen I. 7*,
S. 137, 138. 440130 K 3. 440323

K 3. 440715 K 10. 441223 K 9.
441231 K 8. 450417. 450509 K 1.
450510 K 3. 450611 K 1. 450614
K 2. 450711. 450800 K 1. 450817
K 11. 450919A K 9. 451015 K 2.
451119. 460104 K 3. 460119 K 3.
460303 K 2. 460424 K 7. 460613
K 5. 460808 K 1
GB Kö. 260500 K 3. *DA Köthen I.
2*, S. 9, 86. 271201. 280216A K I.
281226 K 10. 290310 K 9. 291009
K. 291013 K 6. 291231 K 7. *DA
Köthen I. 3*, S. 97, 104 f. 300330
K 7. 300410 K 1. 300921. 310224
K 19. 310311 K 18. 331223 K 32
u. K I 2. 340628 K 2. 340716 K 1.
351112 K 9. *DA Köthen I. 4*, S. 10,
92, 93, 95, 96. 370722. 371031 K 5.
371110 K. 371116 K 4. 371120
K 2. 371123 K 1. 371209. 371220
K I 1. 371223 K 5. 371226 K 3.
380100 K. 380128 K 18. 380207
K 4. 380331 K 2. 380410 K 2.
380423 K 2. 380501 K 3. 380504
K 11. 380507 K 1. 380522 K 1.
380605 K 4. 380606 K 5. 380721 K
I. 381006 K I 1. *DA Köthen I. 5*,
S. 10, 104. 390712A K 6. 390723
K. 390807 K 8. 390826 K 2.
390901. 390902 K I. 390909 u. I.
391000 K 0. 400122 K I 6. 401107
I Q. *DA Köthen I. 6*, S. 118, 121 f.
410323 K 8. 410510 K 1. 410621 I
u. K 1 u. K II. 410727 K 2. 411126
K 4. 411200 K 0. 420124 K 10.
420503. 420808. 421027 K 4.
421031A K. 421108 Q u. K.
421110 K 5. 421123 K 3. 421129A
K 4. 421207 K 9. 421230 K 4.
430307 K 1. 430407 K 5. 430801A
K 6. 431206 K 6. *DA Köthen I. 7*,
S. 145, 146. 440000 K 1. 440809A
K 1. 440816 K u. K I u. K II.
441010 Q u. K 1. 441223 K 9.
441226 K 2. 450000A K 6. 450220
K. 450317 K 3. 450410 K 22.
450500 K 1. 450504A K. 450529
K 10. 450613 K 2. 450725 I Q u. T
I. 450730 K. 451008. 451030 K 0.

460104 K 1. 460315 K 5. 460424
K 14. 460613 K 2. 460620A I Q.
461026 K 2. 461031. 461031A.
461106 K 9. 461213 K 2
GB 1641 u. *1641/44* 280216A K I.
280327 K 5. *DA Köthen I. 3*, S. 11,
104. 310000 K I 1. 340628 K 2.
DA Köthen I. 4, S. 14. 370113 K 2.
371120 K 5. 371123 K 1. 371211
K 2. 371219 K 1. 371220 K I 1.
380128 K 18. 380721 K I. 381007
K 2. 381218 K 9. *DA Köthen I. 5*,
S. 16 f., 104. 390514 K 2. 390630
K 4. 390712A K 6. 390723 K 3.
390807 K 3. 390901. 390902 K I.
390909 K I. 391203 K I. 400203
K 6. 400218. 400323 K 6. 400620
K 1. 401116 K 1. 401215 K 2 u. I.
401223 K 6. 401228A. *DA Köthen
I. 6*, S. 9, 113. 410313 K 3. 410323.
410621 K I u. K II. 410731 K.
411126 K 4. 420124 K 10. 420808
K I. 421027 K 4. 421031A K 7.
421105. 421108 Q. 421129A.
430214 K 2. 430410. 430505 K I 6.
430505 K I 6. 430617 K 7. 430706
K 10. 440130 K 3. 440426 K 6.
440809A K 1. 440816 K u. K I u.
K II. 440824 K 10. 441223 K.
441226A. 441231. 450124. 450126.
450220 K 7 u. 15. 450301 K 5.
450317 K 9. 450319 K 3 u. 5.
450400. 450417. 450529 K 10.
450611 K 1. 450721. 451015 K 2.
451119. 460916 K 7. 461106 K 10.
461213 K 2
GB 1646 260419 K 1. 271201 K 4.
280216A K I. 280327 K 3. 280414
K 13. 280510 K 4. 290310 K 7.
DA Köthen I. 3, S. 11, 104, 110.
300410 K 2. 310000 K I 1. 310224
K 16. 320715 K. 340628 K 2. *DA
Köthen I. 4*, S. 97. 371028. 371031
K 7. 371120 K 5. 371123 K 1.
371211 K 2. 371219 K 1. 371220
K 8 u. K I 1. 380128 K 18. 380509
K 3. 380721 K I. 381218 K 9. *DA
Köthen I. 5*, S. 17, 104, 106.
390712A K 6. 390723 K 3. 390901.

Sachregister

390902 K I. 391203 K I. 391217.
400203 K 6. 400218 K 4. 401216
K 6. 401223 K 6. 401228A. *DA
Köthen I. 6*, S. 9, 14, 113, 120,
121 f. 410313. 410621 I Q, T I, K I
u. K II. 410919 K 3. 411126 K 4.
411200 K 0. 420311 K 7. 420311
K 7. 420808 K I. 421031A. 421105
K 9. 421108 Q. 421110 K 5.
421123 K. 421129 K 4. 421200
K 1. 421202. 421207 K 7. 430101
K II 14. 430103 K II 2. 430106.
430121. 430121A. 430204. 430208.
430214. 430214. 430306. 430312.
430318. 430407. 430410. 430418A.
430507. 430513. 430527 K 4.
430617 K 5. 430706 K 4. 430724A.
430801A K. 430821 K. 430905 K 2
u. I. 430920. 431014. 431209. *DA
Köthen I. 7*, S. *DA Köthen I. 7*,
S. 25, 133 f., 137, 138. 440130.
440209A. 440310. 440323 u. I.
440426. 440723. 440723A.
440809A K 1. 441020 K 3. 441223
K. 441226A K 5. 441231 K 8.
450126. 450127. 450220. 450221.
450301. 450308. 450317. 450319
K. 450319A. 450331 u. I. 450417.
450419 K 2. 450503 K 1. 450504A
K 3. 450509. 450510 K. 450529
K 10. 450611 K 1. 450614 K 2.
450711. 450721. 450722. 450800 u.
I. 450806. 450817 K 11. 450905.
450919A. 450922. 450923.
450923A. 450930. 451001. 451008
K. 451015. 451019 K. 451028.
451028B. 451119. 460119. 460206.
460218. 460301. 460303. 460309.
460317. 460324. 460403. 460519.
460613. 460620B. 460703. 460708.
460714. 460715 u. I u. II. 460718.
460721 K 4. 460804. 460808 K 1.
460819 I u. K 9. 460909. 460915A
u. I. 461023. 461029. 461031.
461104 K 5. 461106. 461213
TG 230000 (vgl. 300320 K 10) u. I.
DA Köthen I. 2, S. 9, 93 f. 280208.
280600 K 7. 290531. 290614. *DA Köthen I. 3*, S. 8, 12, 18, 98 ff. 300320 u.
II–V. *DA Köthen I. 5*, S. 16, 106.
400917 K u. K I
Gesellschaftsgründung FG *DA Köthen
I. 1*, S. 16 f., 20. *DA Köthen I. 2*, S. 13 f.
280414. 290307 K 2. 290310 K I 5.
310108 K 2. *DA Köthen I. 4*, S. 9 f.
371028 K 17. 411200. 440119 K 4
Gesellschaftskasse/ -umlage
AL 310108 u. I. 320626
FG *DA Köthen I. 2*, S. 9. 271126.
271201. 271209. 271211. 271215.
280112. 280208. 280216A. 280218.
280412. 280510. 280517. 281226.
290226. 290302. 290310. 290314.
290329. 290510. 291200. *DA Köthen
I. 3*, S. 9. 300420. 300420A. 300718.
310108 K I 2. 310224. 391203 u. I.
391223. 400000 K 3. 400203. 400218.
400323. 400605 u. I. 400810 K 13.
400902 K III. 401223. 401228A.
401229 K 1. *DA Köthen I. 6*, S. 8 f.
420219 K 3. 421031A. 421123.
421129. 421202 K 1. 430121. 430204.
430208. 430214. 430312. 430318.
430407. 430410. 430507. 430617.
430706. 430724A. 430801A. 430821.
431201 K 1. 431209. *DA Köthen I. 7*,
S. 25. 440130. 440209A. 440310.
440323 u. I. 440723A. 450126.
450220. 450221. 450301 K 3. 450308.
450317. 450721.4 450922. 450923.
450923A. 451001 K 1. 451008 K 7.
451028. 451119. 460119. 460218.
460301. 460309. 460403. 460718.
460721 K 4. 460915A K 2. 461031
K 6
Gesellschaftliche Kritik/ Korrektur von
Werken
DG 441201 K 0. 450921 K 2
FG 240109. 250701. 250705. 250706.
260703. *DA Köthen I. 2*, S. 17.
280226. 280304. 280411. 280412.
280414 u. I u. II. 280425. 280510 u. I
u. II. 280517. 280818. 280929.
281021. 290000 K I–IV. 290216 I.
290302. 290304. 290310. 290314.
290501. 290510. 290616. 291009.
291104A. *DA Köthen I. 3*, S. 9, 18,
104. 300209 K 4. 300330 u. I. 300403

I–II. 310411 u. I. *DA Köthen I. 4,*
S. 7 f., 10 f., 13. 370113. 371027 u. I.
371028A. 371031. 371106. 371108.
371110. 371112 K 10. 371112A K 9.
371124 K I 0. 371208 K II 1. 371209
u. I. 371222. 371226A. 380108.
380110 K 9. 380120 K 5. 380202.
380226. 380321. 380321A. 380402.
380405. 380411 u. I. 380423. 380427.
380502. 380504. 380522A. 380522B.
380602. 380606. 380608A. 380609.
380609A. 380619. 380625. 380721 u.
I. 380724. 380828 u. I. 381006 u. I.
381105 K 5. 381114. 381116 K 3.
381116A. 381123. 381130. 381218.
381224. *DA Köthen I. 5,* S. 10, 11, 14,
35. 390114 u. K I 4. 390115 K 1.
390125. 390126B. 390504 K 2.
390514. 390701 u. I. 390712A.
390723. 390727. 390807. 390814
K 10. 390828 K 1. 390901. 390902 u.
I. 390907 u. I. 390909 K I. 390911.
390914. 391028. 391100. 391119 u. I
u. II. 391125. 391200. 391203.
391216. 391217. 391223. 400000.
400104. 400113. 400122 u. I. 400214.
400218. 400301. 400310. 400311.
400312 u. I. 400313. 400314. 400320.
400323. 400502. 400506. 400509.
400528 u. I u. II. 400605. 400619.
400620. 400622. 400731. 400902 u. I
u. II. 401007. 401009. 401025.
401029. 401109. 401111 K 0. 401116.
401117. 401204. 401214 K 12. 401215
u. I. 401223. 401228A. *DA Köthen I.
6,* S. 10 f., 124. 410101. 410102.
410117. 410206 K 1. 410505 u. K I 1.
410510. 410900. 420311. 420503.
420608. 421031A. 421108. 430121.
430307 K 2. 430318. 430328. 430403.
430419. 430505. 430526 K. 430624 u.
K I 1. 430724. 430801. 430802.
430821. 430920. 431014. 431016.
431020. 431021. 431022. 431028.
431124. 431206 u. I u. II. 440127.
440209. 440219. 440310A. 440313.
440317 K 5. 440426 K. 440809.
440816. 441010 K 3. 441020. 441226.
441231. 450124 u. I. 450305. 450308.
450317A. 450400. 450420. 450500 K.
450504. 450505. 450506A. 450507 u.
I. 450529. 450613. 450730. 450806
K 2. 450817 K 11. 451008. 451028
K 6. 451028A. 451219. 460217 K 1.
460620. 460705 III. 460720. 460816
u. I. 460825 K 0. 460902. 460915.
460915A. 460916. 461029 K 6.
461106

PA 240718 K
TG 300320 II–V
Gesellschaftsnamen. Vgl. Gesellschaftsbuch, Mitgliederlisten u. Imprese
AL 310108 u. I–II
DG 440724 K 13. 441201 K 3. 441223.
450308A. 450400. 450410 K 24.
450808 K I 2
FG 260520. *DA Köthen I. 2,* S. 14, 16.
270700. 271201 K 10. 271209 u. I.
271215. 280106. 280112 K. 280226.
280414. 280425. 280928 K. 290131.
291009. 291028. 291222. *DA Köthen
I. 3,* S. 13. 300320 u. I. 300410 K 1.
300509 I u. K 1. 300921. 310224.
340628. 360428 K II 9. 360630 K.
DA Köthen I. 4, S. 7 f., 10 f., 13.
371028 K 16. 371031 K 6. 371108.
371110. 371112A. 371117. 371124
K 7. 371209 K 8. 371211. 371219 K 6.
371220 K 14. 371221. 371223 K 4.
371224 K 1. 380000. 380100. 380120
K 2. 380128. 380202. 380405. 380423.
380503. 380507. 380509. 380522B
K 6. 380602. 380605. 380616 K 1.
380803 K 2. *DA Köthen I. 5,* S. 15.
390131 K 17. 390630. 390814.
390901. 390909. 391125. 400619 K 8.
400809 II. 401107 u. I. 401204. *DA
Köthen I. 6,* S. 7, 118, 120, 121 f.
410101 K I. 410221 K 3. 410323.
410621 u. II. 410727 K 4. 410731.
410822. 410909. 410919 K 3. 411009.
411126. 420311 K 7. 420506 K 2.
420808 u. I. 421105. 421110.
421129A. 430403. 430617. 430706.
430724A. 430920. *DA Köthen I. 7,*
S. 12, 133. 440130. 440323 K 2.
440616 I u. III. 440826 K 0. 441216.
450126. 450319. 450325 K 2. 450410

K 24. 450500. 450504A K 2. 450505.
450505A. 450529. 450721. 450808 K
I 2. 450927 K II. 451101. 460104.
460414. 460718 K 1. 460915A u. I
- PBO *DA Köthen I. 7*, S. 14 f. 441216
K I
- TG 280600. 280616 K 3. 290913.
300000 K 10. 300320. 300426. 400917
u. I. 450301 K 8

Gesellschaftspfennig. Vgl. Imprese
- DG 441223
- FG *DA Köthen I. 1*, S. 7 f., 77 f.
240109. 240118. 250110 K I 7. *DA Köthen I. 2*, S. 7. 270306. *DA Köthen I. 3*, S. 17, 96 f. 300426 K 7. 300921 K I 4. 310113. *DA Köthen I. 4*, S. 97. 380501. 380509. 390429. 390902 K 2. *DA Köthen I. 6*, S. 118. 410727 K 2. 410914. 420311 K 6. 421123 K I. 421207. 430103 K II 2. 430419. *DA Köthen I. 7*, S. 142, 145, 146. 441223. 450100 K I 4. 450500 K 1. 450504A K 5. 460120. 460406. 460426. 460609. 460726

Gesellschaftssiegel FG 271201. 280106. 371110 K 11. *DA Köthen I. 5*, S. 106. 401107. 410909 K 10. 420503. 421207. 430410. 430505. 440209. 441223. 450410. 450817. 450919A. 460423. 460816. 461006 K 0

Gesellschaftstreffen
- AL 310108 I
- FG *DA Köthen I. 1*, S. 80–82, 86. 171224 K. 200125. 240109. 240717. 240910. 250305. 260211 K 10. 260419 K 1. 260619. *DA Köthen I. 2*, S. 86. 271201. 271215. 271228. 280112 K 14. 280407. 280412 K 5. 280620 K 5. 281021. 290131 I. 300330 K 1. *DA Köthen I. 4*, S. 10. 370517 K 6. 371120 K 2. 380423. 381006 u. K I 1. 381107. *DA Köthen I. 5*, S. 97. 390800 K 2. 390826 K 2. 401107. 410909. 411126 K 6. 411200 K 0. 420503 K 15. 420506 K 2. 421200. 421230. *DA Köthen I. 7*, S. 19 f. 441231. 450420. 450504 K 1. 450919A. 451219 K 15
- PA 240718. 250305. 250500

Glas. Vgl. Ölberger
171224. 171225. 381107. 420712 („Pokal"). 421011. 430000

Grammatik. Vgl. Sprachunterricht u. Personenregister: Gueintz, Christian; Ratke, Wolfgang; Schottelius, Justus Georg 371219 K 4. 391217. 410119 K 4. 430509 K 4. 450420. 450923B K 2
- aramäische 450410 K 5. 460825 K 5
- arabische 280128 K
- chaldäische 430509. 460825 K 5
- deutsche 180508. 181225 K 7. 190308 K 7. 190318. 190324. 260617. *DA Köthen I. 2*, S. 17. 270406 K 7. 280122 K II 6. 280616 K 4. *DA Köthen I. 3*, S. 9. 300410 K 1. 310411 u. I. *DA Köthen I. 4*, S. 11, 13 f., 97. 370305 K 3. 371027 K 5. 371226A. 380320 I. 380417. 380828 K I. 381105. 381116A. 381130 K 3. 381218. *DA Köthen I. 5*, S. 8 ff., 11 ff., 104 f. 390112 K I. 390114. 390115 K 1. 390514. 390800 K 1. 390807. 390814 K 10. 391028 u. I. 391119 u. II. 391216. 391217 u. K I u. K II. 400113. 400122 u. I. 400214. 400218. 400301 u. I. 400313. 400314 K 2. 400323. 400528 u. I. u. II. 400605. 400731. 400810. 401109. 401111 T u. K 0. *DA Köthen I. 6*, S. 10-13, 14 f. 410208 u. I. 410324 u. I. 410406. 410505 u. I. 410510. 410706 u. I. 410708 K 10. 410714. 410727. 410900. 410909. 410914A. 411126. 411200 K. 420503. 420608. 421031A. 421110 K 2 u. K II 0. 421207. 421225 K 5. 430103 u. K II 3. 430121 K 9. 430307. 430328. 430329. 430403 K 3. 430419 u. K I 2. 430505 I. 430509 K. 430526 K 2. 430920. 431016. 431020 K 1. 431028A. 431123 I. *DA Köthen I. 7*, S. 16 f., 18 ff. 440119 K 0. 440129 K. 440209. 440313. 440429. 440525 K I 2. 440715A K. 440824. 440826 K 11. 441223. 450100. 450124 u. I. 450308A. 450326 K 18. 450400 K 3. 450410. 450504. 450507 K 2. 450725 K 9. 450730. 450808. 450817. 450818 K 14. 450900. 450919A. 450923B.

450923C K 3. 450929. 451000 K 0.
451007. 451028A. 451101. 451219.
451220. 460000 u. II. 460131. 460200.
460406 K 7. 460610. 460720 K 3.
460812. 460816. 460825 u. I. 460902.
460915. 460916
französische 180102. 181225 K 7.
190220. 190308 K 7. 190318. 190324.
190424. 380321 K 3
griechische 180508 K 10. 190308 K 7.
380320 K 4. 391028 I. 430509 K 4.
431028A. 440209. 450217 K 1.
460720 K 3. 460915. 461204 K 8
hebräische 180508 K 10. 190308 K 7.
380320 K 4. *DA Köthen I. 5*, S. 13.
400528 K I 1. 430509 K 4. *DA Köthen I. 7*, S. 24. 450308A. 450410.
450808 K 8. 460200. 460720 K 3.
460915
italienische 190308 K 7. 230802.
340107 K 22. 410621 K 4 u. K II 0
lateinische 180508 K 10. 190220.
190308. 190318. 260617. 280616 K 4.
280716. 340107 K 22. *DA Köthen I.
5*, S. 11, 12 f. 390807A K 6. 391028 I.
400301 K I 5. 400528 K I 17. 421110
K 2. 431028A. 440119 K. 440209.
450217 K 1. 450808 K 12. 450923B.
460720 K 3. 460915. 461204 K 8
türkische 280128 K 15
Graphik/ Zeichnung/ Stechen. Vgl. Emblem, Gesellschaftsbuch, Imprese, Malerei, Schriftschneiden u. Wappen
DA Köthen I. 1, S. 80–82, 86, 199 f.
191229. 250218A K VII 3. *DA Köthen
I. 2*, S. 9, 85, 89, 92 f. 270105 K 4. 270306
K 4. 271001 K 4. 271209. 271211.
271215. 271228. *DA Köthen I. 3*, S. 97 f.,
98 ff., 104 ff., 112 ff., 120 ff., 127 f., 130.
300320 K II. 300410 K 26. 300921 K I 4.
300924 K 15. 310703 u. II. 340716. *DA
Köthen I. 4*, S. 89, 90, 93, 94, 97. 370805.
370900. 371028. 371126. 371221.
380226. 380302A. 380303. 380312. *DA
Köthen I. 5*, S. 97, 98 f., 100 f., 101, 102,
105, 108. 390121A K 2. 390514. 390800
K. 400203. 401111 K I 0. *DA Köthen
I. 6*, S. 8 ff., 112 f. 410406. 411214 K u. K
II–III. 420114 K 14. 420311 K 6. 420627

K I 16. 421011 Q u. K. 421027 u. I.
421031A. 421101 Q. 421105 u. Q.
421110 K 0. 421123 u. I. 421129. 421200
K 1. 421207. 421225. 430000A K 1.
430101 Q u. K. 430106. 430118. 430121.
430204. 430214. 430215. 430306.
430312. 430407. 430410. 430418 Q.
430418A. 430425 u. Q. 430507. 430513.
430527. 430724A. 430821 K 3. 430905 u.
I. 431124. *DA Köthen I. 7*, S. 8, 25, 131,
132–135, 137 f. 440130. 440310B K 2.
440323. 440324 K I 1 u. K I 2. 440715 Q
u. K 9. 440723. 440900. 441020 K 1.
441200 K I 0 u. II. 441231A K 1.
450100. 450127. 450219. 450220.
450317. 450319 K 9. 450331. 450400
K 3. 450417. 450504A K 5. 450505A.
450509. 450500 K 1. 450510 K 3.
450611. 450614 K 2. 450711. 450722
K 2. 450800 K 1 u. I. 450817 u. II–III u.
IV Q u. K IV 5. 450905. 450919A.
450922. 450923A. 450927 II. 450930.
451015. 451028B. 451101. 451119.
460119. 460206. 460303. 460317 u. K I
1. 460414. 460423. 460620B. 460700.
460703. 460714. 460804. 460810.
460819. 460909. 460912 u. II. 461204A
K 0
Greif (Vogel) 391200. 450927 II

Hänselung (Aufnahmezeremonie FG)
240910. 250305 S. 382 f. 260619. 280106.
280226 K 9. 280327. 280407. 280412.
290131 I. 291028 K 2. 330918 K 4.
371124 K 1. 371220. 380503. 381006 u.
K I 1. 390110 K 2. 390826 K 2. 401107.
410621 u. K 1. 421230. 441010. 441223
K 11. 450500. 450505 K. 450508A K 2.
450725 K 8. 450817 K 19 u. K II 6.
451028 K 8. 460104. 460423. 460424A.
460613. 460718. 460915A. 461029.
461031A u. I. 461106
Hendecasyllabi, s. Endecasillabo
Hexameter 310000 K 5. 310108 K II 15.
380828 K 3
Höfische Verhaltenslehre. Vgl. Politische
Wissenschaften
250700 S. 435. 270808. 280401. 280404
K 8. 290000 I. 301102. 310108 I. 310703

I. 350731 u. I. 360600 II. *DA Köthen I. 4*, S. 12. 370422 II. 371027 u. III. 380220 K 1. 380221 K 1. 381028 II u. III. *DA Köthen I. 5*, S. 16. 390112 I. 401212 K 4 u. K I 2. 410101 u. II. 410206 I u. II. 410300. 410625. 420124 I. 421108. *DA Köthen I. 7*, S. 12 f., 16. 440100 K 4. 441223 K 16. 450818. 450901. 451101 K 13. 460204 I

Huitain, s. Achtzeiler

Imprese. Vgl. Emblem, Gesellschaftsbuch, Gesellschaftsnamen, Gesellschaftspfennig, Graphik u. Malerei 430118. *DA Köthen I. 7*, S. 133. 441223 K 7. 450817 IV u. K u. K II

Accademia degli Oziosi *DA Köthen I. 7*, S. 132 ff.

Accademia della Crusca 460120A K 4

AL *DA Köthen I. 3*, S. 120 ff. 310108 u. I u. II

DG 440724 K 7. 441223. 450308A. 450400. 450529

FG *DA Köthen I. 1*, vor dem Titel, S. 20, 77, 80–82, 86, 199 f. 181023 K 16. 181207. 200125 I–II. 210401. 210626. 220824. 230000 (vgl. 300320 K 10). 230430 u. I–II. 240109. 240717. 250305 S. 382–384. 250627. 250701. 250702. *DA Köthen I. 2*, S. 8 f., 14, 86. 270105. 270129. 270700 K. 271126 K 3. 271201 u. I. 271209 u. I. 271211. 271215. 271228. 280106. 280112. 280208. 280216A. 280220. 280226 K 9. 280304. 280308 K 2. 280321. 280327. 280407. 280412. 280414. 280425. 280510. 280517 K 5. 280726. 280821. 280928. 280929. 281226. 290131 I. 290226. 290310. 290629. 290715. 290909 K 4. 291013. 291028. 291200. *DA Köthen I. 3*, S. 10 f., 18, 96 f., 99, 103 ff., 110 f., 123. 300320 K III. 300410 K 2. 300921. 301011. 310108 I. 310224. 320715 K. 331223 K I 2. 340628. 360428 K 1. *DA Köthen I. 4*, S. 10, 14. 370305 K 8. 370517 K 6. 370715. 370729. 370805. 370900 K 11. 370902 K 10. 371028 K 15. 371031 K 7.

371110 K 6. 371112 K I 3. 371120 K 2. 371123 K 1. 371209 K 6. 371219. 371220 u. I. 371221. 371223 K 5. 371226 K. 380100 K 3. 380128. 380207 K 4. 380320A. 380328. 380423. 380501. 380503. 380504 K 14. 380509. 380522A. 380605. 380606 K 3. 380616. 380721 u. I. 381006 u. I. *DA Köthen I. 5*, S. 10, 17, 104, 106. 390514. 390630. 390712. 390712A. 390723. 390807A I. 390826 K 2. 390901. 390902 u. I. 390903 K 1. 390906. 390907. 390909 K I. 390910. 391100. 391203 K I 3. 391217. 400000 Q. 400122 K 8. 400323. 400619. 401007 K 1. 401009 K 2. 401025. 401107 u. I u. II. 401111 K I 0. 401116. 401204. 401215 K 2 u. I. 401216. 401228A. 401229 K 1. *DA Köthen I. 6*, S. 7, 8 f., 111, 113, 118 f., 12 f., 121 f., 541, 577 f., 605 f. 410323. 410621 I. 410727. 410731. 410909. 410914 K 4. 411126. 411200. 420311. 420503. 420608. 420808 u. I. 421027 u. I. 421031A. 421105. 421108. 421110. 421123 u. I. 421129. 421200. 421207. 421230 K 4. 430101 K 1. 430103 K II 2. 430121. 430204. 430214. 430306. 430312 K 3. 430410. 430418A. 430419 u. K I 2. 430513. 430724A. 430905 u. I. *DA Köthen I. 7*, S. 18, 132 f., 137, 138. 440000 K 1. 440100 K I 3. 440130. 440323. 440525 K I 3. 440715. 440723. 440731 I. 440809A. 440816 u. I u. II. 440826 K 0. 441010. 441223. 441226A K 5. 441231. 450124. 450220 K. 450301 K 3. 450317 K 3. 450319. 450331. 450400. 450408 K 0 u. 3. 450410. 450417. 450500. 450504A. 450505. 450505A. 450529 K 10. 450611. 450613. 450711. 450721. 450725 u. I. 450730. 450800. 450817 u. II–III. 450905. 450919 K 2. 450919A. 450923A. 450930. 451015. 451019 K 8. 451028B K 1. 451030 K 0. 451101. 451119. 451209. 451217. 460103 K 0. 460104. 460120. 460206. 460315. 460406. 460423 u. I. 460424

K 4. 460424A u. K I. 460426. 460609.
460613 K. 460620A I. 460703.
460708. 460714. 460715 u. I u. II.
460726. 460804. 460808 K 1. 460819.
460825 K 0. 460908. 460909. 460912
II. 460915A u. I. 461006 K 0.
461031A I u. K 7. 461106 u. I.
461117. 461213. 461216
PBO *DA Köthen I. 7*, S. 15. 460406
K 4
TG *DA Köthen I. 2*, S. 8 f., 12, 93 f.
280208. 280216A. 280226 K 6.
280600. 280616 K 3. 281021.
290226A. 290614. 290913. *DA Köthen I. 3*, S. 98 ff. 300320 u. II–V.
300426. 300723. *DA Köthen I. 5*,
S. 16, 105 f. 400917 u. I
Inschrift
370422 K 1. 371126 K 7. 390121A K 2.
390800A
Altar *DA Köthen I. 6*, S. 112.
Brunnen 300509 K 5
Glas 430000
Grab 250110. 250218A u. I u. III u.
IV. 270919. 271025. 310800 K 3.
360600 u. I–II. 371014 K 7. 371222.
371226A K 7. 400122 K I 2
Plastik/ Sockel *DA Köthen I. 7*, S. 141.
450927 K I 1
Portal 430000A K 1. 450927 K I 1
Sarg 450326 K 10
Schild 450927 K I 1
Insekten 350312. 350731 I. 360630 K I 5

Jagd. Vgl. Vögel
240109. 240718. 250305 S. 380. 250609
K 17. 290000 II. 291104A. 350731 I.
371030 K 5. 380605. 390902 K 4.
401111. 430526 K 5. 450000. 461124.
461206 K 3
Jambus 350731 K I V. 602. 371124 K I 0.
380828 K 3. 381218 K 4. *DA Köthen I.
5*, S. 17. 401223 K 6. 420503. 430103 K
II 7. 431014. 431123. 431124. 431206.
440310A. 440426 K I 3. 440824. 441020.
441200. 450124. 450529 K 2. 450808 K I
1. 460825
Justizwesen, s. Rechtsprechung

Kalender, s. Datierungsweise
Kanzone/ Kanzonette *DA Köthen I. 2*,
S. 18. 291104A K 2. 340107 K 20
Kartell, s. Ritterspiel
Katechismus, s. Bekenntnis
Kleidung, s. Textilien
Korruption, s. Bestechung
Krankheit/ Medizin/ Heilkunde 181023
K 10. 210401 S. 145. 210729. 220824.
230430. 230802. 230819. 230913.
231006. 231008. 231101. 231203.
240319. 240907. 250110 I. 250218A u. K
VII 24. 250413. 250514. 260211. 260619.
261010. 270115. 270129. 270306.
271001. 271010 K. 271025 K 1. 280106.
280112. 280122 II u. K 10. 280128.
280216A. 280327. 280401. 280412 I.
280414 I. 280510 I. 281215 K. 290129 u.
K I 2. 290131 K I 4. 290529. 290629.
290715. 290909. 291028 K 5. 291231.
DA Köthen I. 3, S. 15, 107 ff., 115.
300000. 300209 K 4. 300330 K 3.
300403. 300410 K. 300921 u. K I 4.
301001. 301102 K 4. 310000 K I 1.
310224. 320626. 320715. 330918 K 4.
340107. 350731 u. I V. 38 ff. 360428 u.
I–II. 360600 II. 360703. *DA Köthen I. 4*,
S. 9, 12 f., 94. 370113 K 3. 370305.
370421 K 1. 370517 K 2. 370715 u. K I 0
u. K II 0. 370722. 370729. 371009 u. I–
III. 371027 III. 371123. 371223. 371224
K 4. 380000. 380128. 380310 III. 380417
K 5. 380423. 380522. 380904. 381028 II
u. III u. K IV. *DA Köthen I. 5*, S. 16.
390630. 390701 K 0. 390712 K.
390712A. 390800A K 1. 390814. 400809
I. 400902 K u. K III. 401029. 401117 I.
DA Köthen I. 6, S. 15. 410323. 410324 K
I. 410625. 410708. 410731 I. 420120.
420219. 420506 (K 10). 420630. 421108.
421202 K. 430106. 430509 K 1. 430826.
431123 K 2. 440816 I u. II. 450219.
450304. 450319. 450408. 450504A K 3.
450508A. 450722. 450726. 450806 K.
450817 II u. V u. K 4 u. K III u. K IV 3.
450818. 451209 K 4. 460127. 460204.
460715 u. II. 461206 K 3
Kriegslehre/ -kunst/ -übungen. Vgl. Baukunst

180102. 271201A K 8. 280726 K 3.
291009 K 4. 291222 K 2. 291224 K 2.
300215 K I 3. 300216. 300718. 360600
II. 370715 K 6. 380602 II. 381028 II u.
III. 390929 K 6. 410731 I. 420630 K 16.
430505 K I 2. 441223 K 16
Kryptographie/ Chiffren 220919. 231210.
240106. 240116 u. I. 240125. 240319 u. I.
240907. *DA Köthen I. 3*, S. 17. 300921 u.
I. 370828 K 3. 380226 K 3. 380302A.
380310 I u. IV. 380312. 380320 I.
401111 K 2. 430118 K 6. 430215.
430425. 430526. 460204

Leim 200125. 210401. 230430 u. I–II.
250706 I. 461204A K 0
Lexikographie, s. Wortschatz
Lied. Vgl. Ode
371121 K 1. 371227. 410203A. 410205.
410206 u. I u. II. 410208 K 4. 411200
K 5. 421207. 430312. *DA Köthen I. 7*,
S. 10. 450000 K 4. 450100 K 4. 451100 I.
451217. 460825 u. II
„ACh Bernhard liebster Bruder mein"
390800 I
„An Wasserflüssen Babylon" *DA Köthen I. 5*, S. 36, 100. 390800 K I 1
„A Solis ortus cardine" 381116 u. I.
390110 K 1. 390112. 390114
„Ach Gott vnd Herr/ Wie groß vnd
schwer" 380000 K 12
„auff den Namen der Goltgelbe"
300410 K 2
„CHrist vnser HErr zum Jordan kam"
381007 K 7
„Christum wir sollen loben schon"
381116 K 6 u. I Q
„DAs walt' der liebe Gott" 460825
K II 0
„Daß der weite baw der Welt" 380402
I. 380504
„Der Musen Erfreüliches Reyen-Lied"
461104 III
„Des Bernhardi lob und Jubelgesang"
371124 u. I
„Edle Ritter dieser Zunft" 410625 K 0
„Ein hüpsch new Lied/ Von der Belägerung vnnd Eroberung der Statt Breysach" 390800 K 6
„Ein Lämmlein geht und trägt die
Schuld" 390800 K I 1
„Ein Lied Hertzog Wilhelms zu Sachsen" *DA Köthen I. 5*, S. 35 f., 99 f.
390800 I
„Gott lob" *DA Köthen I. 4*, S. 95.
371222. 371226A u. I
„Guts Muts wöllen wir seyen" 250305
K 39
„JCh gläub vnd weiß diß Fürwar" *DA Köthen I. 4*, S. 95. 371222 u. III.
380122. 380125. 380125A. 380126.
380207 K 3. 380210
„Ich weiß, daß mein Erlöser lebt"
371222 K III 0
„JHr Christen freut euch ins gemein"
381007 K 7
„Jesu dulcis memoria" 371124 K I 0
„Le Roi boit" 171224
„Lied einer selig abgeschiedenen Seele"
450220 u. II
„Nun danket alle Gott" 371222 K I 0
„O Mensch beweine deine Sünd'"
380504
Passionslied *DA Köthen I. 4*, S. 14, 15.
380625. 380828. 381116
„Preiß der Liebe des HErrn Jesu"
421101 K I 1
„Sanct Reblinus" 250305 K 39
„Vespera iam venit" 431211 K I 12
„Von Morgen da die Sonn' entsteht"
381116 u. I. 381218
„Wem wöll' wir diesen Rebner bringen?" 250305 K 39
„Wohlan so kommet hehr ihr frommen" 371222 u. I–II. 371226A K I
1. 380122. 380125. 380125A. 380126.
380207 K 3. 380210
„Zwey schöne HochzeitLieder/ Vber
der Vestung Brysach" 390800 K 6
Löwe 220824. 300320 K II 14. 300723
K 3. 390727 K 7. 390904 I

Madrigal 340107 K 20. 371124 K 2.
371222 K III 0. 410625 K 0. 431123 K 1.
DA Köthen I. 7, S. 135. 441020 K 1.
441200 II
Magie/ Aberglauben. Vgl. Physica u. Prodigium

180714. 210729 K 1. 231006. 240116.
240125. 240418. 280412 K I 4. *DA Köthen I. 3*, S. 114, 126. 301001. 350731 I.
DA Köthen I. 4, S. 12. 370421 K 0.
370422. 380226. 380302A. 380303.
380502. 380522B K 7. 420120. 421101 I.
421120. 421202 K 4. 430215. 430826 K.
440826 K 6

Malerei. Vgl. Emblem, Gesellschaftsbuch, Graphik, Imprese u. Wappen
DA Köthen I. 1, vor dem Titel, S. 76 f., 78–80. 180000 K 5. 181023. 181207.
190220 K 12. 210626. 240718. *DA Köthen I. 2*, vor dem Titel, S. 9, 85–89, 95–97. 271001. 271010. 271201 u. K I 1.
271209 u. I. 271211. 271215. 280220.
280321. 280327. 280425. 280510. 280517 K 5. 280716. 281226. 290715. 290909.
291028. 291231 K 6. *DA Köthen I. 3*, vor dem Titel, S. 98, 111, 119 f. 300921 I.
300924 K. 310113. 310703 K 18. 340716.
DA Köthen I. 4, vor dem Titel, S. 7, 9, 88, 89, 90 ff. 370722 K 7. 370900 K 1.
371220. 371221. 380310 I. 380509. *DA Köthen I. 5*, vor dem Titel, 97 f., 98 f., 100 f., 102, 105 f., 107. 390909 K 3. *DA Köthen I. 6*, vor dem Titel, S. 13, 111, 118 f., 125, 541. 420114. 420311 K 6.
420503. 420601 K 1. 420608. 421105 K 7. 421123 K 2 u. I. 421207. 430000A K 1. 430121. 430204. 430208. 430312.
430410. 430419 I. 430425. *DA Köthen I. 7*, S. 131, 135 f. 450220. 450317. 450326.
450927 u. II. 451209. 460120. 460315.
460317 K 6. 460426 K 4. 460703 K 5.
461204A

Märchen, s. Mythos

Markt/ Messe u. ä.
490916
Frankfurt a. M. 190220. 190322.
200826. 210421 K. *DA Köthen I. 2*, S. 90. 270429. 271107 K 1. 280510.
280724. 281105. 281126. 290129 K I.
290629. 290708 K 5. 300725 K 2.
310000 Q. 310119 K 1. 310703 K.
380302 K 2. 380625. 391203 I.
410313. 420712 K 1. 430505 K I 8.
430624 K 2. 430920. 440426 K 2.
450419 K 3. 450507A. 450526 K 4.

450614. 450726 K 8. 450905. 450923.
450923A. 450930. 460206 u. I.
460218. 460303. 460324. 460703.
460803 K 0. 461031A
Hamburg 380616 (?)
Leipzig 191231. 210421. 230913.
250609. 270429 K 8. 270827 K 11.
280218. 280226. 280404. 280411 K 5.
280716 K 18. 280821. 281021 K 1.
281126. 281226. 290129 K I. 290226.
290310. 290510. 290629. 291104 K 4.
291231 K 1. 300725 K 1. 301102 K 4.
310000 Q u. K 9. 310703. 371028.
371123. 371124 K 5. 380128 K 6.
380312. 380321. 380321A. 380402.
380504. 381218 (?). 381224 K 3 (?).
400104 K I 2. 400502 K. 420506 K 4.
430624 K 2. 430905. 440130 K 3.
440323 I. 440426 K 2. 440824.
450124. 450305 K 5. 450419 K 3.
450509 K 2. 450726 K 8.
450905. 450923. 451001 K 1. 451015 K 3. 451028. 451217. 460206 u. I.
460218 K 2. 460303 K. 460309.
460403. 460423. 460424. 460620.
460620B. 460703. 460708 K 1.
460803 K 0. 460916 K 9. 461023.
461031. 461031A. 461213 K 1
Naumburg 360630 K 9. 430527
Querfurt 190318
Venedig (Fondaco dei Tedeschi) 230809 K 11

Maskerade/ Ballet. Vgl. Drama, Oper u. Ritterspiel
240717. 240718. 250500. 270406 K 5.
340107 K 20. 360600 II. 391119 u. III.
400218 K 5. 441020 K 4. 450220. 450818 K 12

Mathematik 240125 K 5. *DA Köthen I. 2*, S. 18. 271201A. 280122 II. 280128 K.
291009. 291222. 300215. 300718. 360600 II. *DA Köthen I. 4*, S. 12 f., 94. 370421 K 1. 371014 u. I. 371226A K I 2. 390114 I. *DA Köthen I. 6*, S. 15. 410119. 410406 K 6. 420601. 420627 K I 17. 420630 K 22. 421202 K 1. 430215 K 11. 430418.
430425 K 3. 430430 K 14. 430509 K 1.
430515 K 7. 430826. 431123 I. 450000

K 2. 450217 K 1. 450410 K 6. 450817 K
    III. 460317 K 5. 460715. 460915 K 17
Medaille, s. Gesellschaftspfennig, vgl. Numismatik
Medizin, s. Krankheit
Messe, s. Markt
Meteorologie, s. Physica
Metrik, s. Verskunst
Mitgliederlisten. Vgl. Gesellschaftsbuch u. Gesellschaftsnamen
  AL   310108 II
  DG   441223. 450308A K 2
  FG   260520. *DA Köthen I. 2*, S. 9.
    270105. 270129. 271209 u. I. 271215.
    280216A u. I. 280226. 280407.
    281215 K 7. 291028. 291200. *DA Köthen I. 3*, S. 8. 300410 K. 310224.
    360703 K 40. *DA Köthen I. 4*, S. 10.
    371028. 371112A. 371117. 371211.
    371220 u. I. 371221. 380100. 380128.
    380202. 380220 K 2. 380331 K 4.
    380423. 380605 K 4. 380616. 390514.
    390807. 390814. 390901. 390909 u. I.
    391100. 391125. 391217. 401107 II.
    410323. 410621 u. II. 410731. 410822.
    411009. 420311. 420503 K 3. 420808
    I. 421031A. 430617. 430706.
    430724A. 430801A. 440824. 441226A
    K 5. 441231. 450126. 450220. 450221.
    450317. 450319. 450400. 450500 K 2.
    450529. 450721. 450730. 460104 K 1.
    460321 K 3. 460423. 460424.
    460424A I. 460819 I. 460909.
    460915A. 460916. 461026 K 3.
    461029. 461031. 461031A u. I.
    461106
  TG   290226A. 290913 K 13. *DA Köthen I. 3*, S. 100 ff. 300320 I
Mittelalter (Geschichtsschreibung, Literatur, Philologie) *DA Köthen I. 5*,
    S. 10 f. 390121A. 390126. 390310.
    390514. 390630 u. I. 390701 u. I.
    390800A. 390807. 390822. 390901.
    400113. 400214. 400319. 400514. 400619
    K 6. 410406 K 5. 410706. 441020.
    450000. 450326 K 6. 450901 K 16.
    461104 K III 1
Mundart, s. Etymologie
Münzstätten

Anhalt-Köthen   *DA Köthen I. 1*, S. 21
Anhalt-Plötzkau *DA Köthen I. 3*, S. 124
Braunschweig-Wolfenbüttel   190220
Dänemark   280818 K II 3
Sachsen-Weimar   *DA Köthen I. 1*,
    S. 21. 180102 K 4. 181207. 181222.
    181225. 190220. 290614 K 2
Musik   240319 I. 250218A VII. 250305.
    270429 K 10. 271001. 280616 K 2.
    280716 K II 2. 280721. 281000. 290629
    K 20. *DA Köthen I. 3*, S. 19. 310108 I.
    310703 II. 340107. 350731 I u. K 4. *DA Köthen I. 4*, S. 8, 12, 15, 95. 370305.
    370421 K 0. 370900. 371124. 371219
    K 4. 371222 u. I–III. 371226A K 6 u. K
    I 1. 371227. 380122. 380125. 380125A.
    380126. 380210. 380221 K 2. 380310 I.
    380504. 380828 I Q. 381028 IV. *DA Köthen I. 5*, S. 15, 100. 390112. 390114 u. I.
    390800 I. 391028 K 3. 391119 u. III.
    391216. 400313. 400317 I. 401204 K 9.
    DA Köthen I. 6, S. 13. 410205. 410208 I.
    410625 K 0. 420114 K 12. 420120 K 11.
    420627 K I 20. 421202 K 1. 430215.
    430425 K 7. 430430. 430821. 431028A.
    431123 I u. K. *DA Köthen I. 7*, S. 8,
    135 f. 440324 K 1. 450000 K 4. 450217
    K 0. 450220 u. K II 0. 450726. 450927
    II. 451100 u. I. 460103 K 2. 460204.
    460317 K 6. 460819 K II 7
Mythos/ Fabel/ Märchen u. dgl., s. Personenregister u. Wörterverzeichnis

Numismatik. Vgl. Finanzwesen, Gesellschaftspfennig u. Münzstätten
    DA Köthen I. 1, S. 77 f. 181225. 190220.
    250110 K I 7. *DA Köthen I. 3*, S. 120,
    123 ff. 360703 K 12. *DA Köthen I. 4*,
    S. 7, 92 f. 370422 K 7. 370517 K 4.
    371124 K 9. *DA Köthen I. 5*, S. 100.
    390121A K 2. 390800 K 5. 400810 K 4.
    DA Köthen I. 6, S. 119. 430425 K 7.
    460112 K 1. 460610 K 4

Ode
    250510. 250700 I. 370517 K I. 440324
    K 1. 450400 K 11. 450506A K 3. 450901
    alkäische   440824

anakreontische 440824
pindarische 270429 K 11. *DA Köthen
I. 7*, S. 17, 132. 440100 u. I. 440400
K 1
Ringelode (Rondeau) 440100 u. II
sapphische *DA Köthen I. 6*, S. 14.
410203A K. 410205. 410206 u. I.
440824
Ölberger (zeremonielles Trinkgefäß der
FG) 171224. 171225. 190220 K 8.
240112. 250305 S. 382. 280112. 280226
K 9. 280327. 280407 K 1. 280412 K 5.
280620. 281215. 371110. 371220 K 9.
380503. 380602. 381107. *DA Köthen I.
5*, S. 105. 400312 u. I. 410621 K 1.
450500. 450508A. 450725. 460104 K 4.
460424A K 4. 460613 K 6. 460718 K 8.
460915A K 5. 461029. 461106 K 6
Oper 271001. 280112 K 17. 290629 K 20.
350731 K 4. 381030 K 9. 390126. 391119
u. III. 450726
Orakel, s. Prodigium
Orden. Vgl. Personenregister
DA Köthen I. 1, S. 18. 180000. 221214
K 1. 230802 K 15. 240109 K 1. 240717
K 19. 250218A K VII 4. 250514 K 12.
261010 K 8. *DA Köthen I. 2*, S. 10, 14,
19. 280112 K 15. 280216A K 4. 290310
K I 5. 380000 K 7. 380207. 380310.
380312. 380320A. 380501
Orthographie, s. Wortschatz
Ostern 190318. 190324. *DA Köthen I. 3*,
S. 123 ff.
Ottaverime, s. Achtzeiler

Pädagogik. Vgl. Personenregister: Ratke,
Wolfgang
180102. 181023 K. 200318 K 4. 231203
K 8. 250110 K 2. 280208 K 11. 280216A.
280821. 280929. 290501 K 1. 290510 K.
290616 K 4. 290629 K 12. 300215 K I 3.
300216 K 0. 300509 K 3. 300718.
301102. 310119. 310411. 340604.
340609. 350312 K. 360428 K 1. 370422
K 7. *DA Köthen I. 5*, S. 11 f. 390904 I.
DA Köthen I. 6, S. 15. 410208. 410625.
410706 u. I. 421129A. 430103 K II 0.
430418. 430509 K. 430826. 431211 I.
DA Köthen I. 7, S. 8, 16. 440204 I.

440715A. 441223 K 16. 450124 K 4.
450217 K. 450220. 450224. 450301.
450304. 450410 K 7. 450507A K 3.
450901. 451100. 460902. 461216 K 6
Papstwahl 230802. 250305 K 3
Pferde/ Reitkunst 190308. 240718.
250609 K 17. 271107. 271201A. 320313.
340107. 340421 K 1. 350731 I V. 153.
360630 K 3. 370517 K 4. 371030 u. I.
380310 I–II u. IV–V. 380504 K 11.
381107. 390114 K. 390904 I. 410621
K 1. 430118 K 19
Pflanzen/ Pflanzenkunde/ Garten
180000. 190424 K 4. 200125. 210401.
210626. 220824. 230430 u. I–II. 240717.
240910. 250110 K 2 u. K 17. 250305
S. 382 f. *DA Köthen I. 2*, S. 17, 90.
271126. 271215. 271228. 280128 K.
280304. 280308. 280412 I. 280414 I.
280510 I. 290131 K I 4. *DA Köthen I. 3*,
S. 8, 105–119. 300921 I. 301025. 310000
I. 310311. 310411 Q. 310703 I–II.
320715. 350731 I V. 624 f. 360630 K 6 u.
K I 5. *DA Köthen I. 4*, S. 97. 370517
K 5. 370900. 371009 I u. II. 371031.
371110 K 6. 371124 I. 371220 I.
380320A. 380328. 380331. 380423A.
380501. 380503. 380509. 380605.
380608A. 380828 I. 381028 K IV 51.
391113. 391125. 400104. *DA Köthen I.
6*, S. 122, 123 f., 606, 772. 410300. 410621
K I u. K II. 410727. 411126. 420808 K I.
421200 K 1. 430419 K I 2. 430826 K 33.
431206 I. *DA Köthen I. 7*, S. 133 f.,
137 f., 144. 440100 K I 3. 450100 K I 4.
450400. 450408. 450504A K 3. 450505.
450611. 450800 K. 450808 K I 1. 450817
I u. K 4 u. K II. 450900 K 13. 450919A
K 10. 450930. 451015. 451119. 460315.
460424. 460610 K 8. 460703. 460708
K 2. 460714. 460715 II. 460808. 460810
Phaleucus, s. Endecasillabo
Philologie, s. Sprachunterricht/ Sprachen-
kenntnis/ Sprachpflege/ Sprachkritik/
Philologie. Vgl. Etymologie, Grammatik, Wortschatz u. Personenregister,
z. B. Ratke, Wolfgang
Philosophie 190324. 190707. 191231.
200125. 200826. 210421. 211006.

230809. 231006. 231210 I. 240418.
250609 K 15. 251100. 260000. 270406
K 12. 270827 K 1. 280128 K. 280411
K 8. 280414 K 6. 280716 K 11. 290120
K 8. 300320. 310411. 310703 I. 330311
K 11. 340107 K 22. 350312. 350731 I.
360600 II. 370421 K 15. 370422 I.
371009 I. 371121. 371209 I u. II. 380000
K 3. 380122. 380126. 380128. 380221.
380321 K 1. 381028 II u. III u. K 1 u. K
IV. *DA Köthen I. 5*, S. 8, 12 f., 15.
390822. 390904 I. 391028 K 5. 391217
K 4. 400122. 400317 K 3. *DA Köthen
I. 6*, S. 120. 410300. 410324 K I. 410505
u. I. 410625. 410706 I. 410731 K I 1.
421101 I u. III u. IV. 430103. 430505 K
I 12. 430509 K. 430826. 431123 I.
431124. *DA Köthen I. 7*, S. 15. 440119
K 10. 440426 u. I. 440715A. 440816 I u.
II. 440826. 441020. 450124. 450400.
450529. 450817 V. 450818 K. 450901.
451101. 451220 K 8. 460103 K 0.
460120A K 1. 460912 K 1. 461204A
Phonetik/ Phonologie/ Prosodie
DA Köthen I. 7, S. 10, 23. 440129.
440209. 440324. 440826. 441000 K 6.
441020. 441231 K 9. 450100. 450124
K 6. 450204 K 1. 450308A. 450400 K 3.
450410 K 3. 450420. 450808. 450817 K
IV 11. 450919A K 13. 451219. 451220
K 2. 460131. 460200 K 1. 460812.
460825. 460915
Physica/ Astronomie/ Meteorologie. Vgl.
Magie
180714. 181023 K 10. 181207 K 12.
190324 K 8. 240116 I. *DA Köthen I. 2*,
S. 18. 280122 II. 280128 K. 291224.
330918 K 4. 350731 I V. 485 ff. u. K I V.
521. 360600 II. *DA Köthen I. 4*, S. 12,
89 f. 370421 u. I. 370422. 371009 II.
371226A I Q u. K I 2. 380509A.
380522A. 380522B. 380602. 380608A.
380609A K 5. 381028 II-IV. 390727. *DA
Köthen I. 6*, S. 15. 410119 K 7. 410406
K 6. 421202 K 1. 430509 K 1. 430826.
431123 I. *DA Köthen I. 7*, S. 139. 440715
K 5. 450410 K 6. 450817 K III u. V.
450919A. 451217. 460715 K II 3
Pilgerreisen, s. Bildungsreisen

Piraterie 230802. 230809. 300410 K.
300921. 301001. 301011. 360703
Plastik 300509 K 5. *DA Köthen I. 4*,
S. 91. 430526. 450927 K I 1. 461204A
Poetik. Vgl. Verskunst
250110 K 10. 250218A. 250413. 250609.
260617 K 9. *DA Köthen I. 2*, S. 15, 17 f.
270925 K II 1. 280000 K 1. 280208.
280616A K 3. 291013. 300320 K IV 3.
300403 K I–II. 310000 K. 310703.
350731 K 4. *DA Köthen I. 4*, S. 14.
371112 K 10. 380608A K 5. 381028 II u.
III. 381116A. 381123. 381130. 381204
K 2. *DA Köthen I. 5*, S. 10, 14, 101.
390115 K 1. 390126 K 4. 390902. 400122
K I 29. 400506. 400514. *DA Köthen I. 6*,
S. 11 f. 410706 K 4. 420311. 420503.
420506. 420608. 421105. 421110 K 2.
421120 K 7. 430000 K 2. 430307.
430328. 430407. 431016. 431020 K 1.
431028A. *DA Köthen I. 7*, S. 10, 15,
16 f., 21. 440119 K. 440324 K. 440715A.
440724. 440824 K 7. 441000. 441020
K 3. 450000A K 0. 450204. 450219.
450308. 450317A. 450504 K 6. 450726
K. 450818. 450901. 451100 K 8. 460609
K 3. 460825 K. 460909
Politische Streitschriften/ Publizistik
191124. 250627. *DA Köthen I. 2*, S. 12.
271201A. 271215 u. K 22. 271228.
280106. 280929. 290129 I. 290529 u.
K 17. 300410. 300725 K. 300924 K 3.
331223 K 11. 340912 K 0. 350800 K 15.
371009 K 0. 380423 K 9. *DA Köthen I.
5*, S. 7 f. 390131. 390800 K. 390807A K I
2. 390822. 410221 K 2. 410914 K 8.
420601 K 2. 421009. 430920. 431021
K 1. 431022. 431123 K 1. 431124 K 10.
450400 K 6. 450818 K 9. 451101.
451217. 460714
Politische Wissenschaften/ Ars politica/
Fürstenspiegel 220919. 231203.
231210 I. 240718 K 23. 271201A K 8.
271215 K 22. 280128 K 22. 280208.
280216A. 280716 K 18. 280818 K I 0.
280821. 280929. 290129 I. 290501.
290510. 290616. 300718 K 0. 300725.
300921 K 5. 301102. 320416 I u. K.
320715 K 8. 321201 K 8. 350312. 360428

K 1. 360703 K 12. *DA Köthen I. 4*, S. 11, 12. 370900. 371027. 371106. 371209 I u. II. 380110 K 9. 380120. 380122. 380126. 380128. 380405 u. I. 380502. 380522A. 380522B. 380602. 380606. 380608A. 380616. 381028 u. II–IV. *DA Köthen I. 5*, S. 33. 390110 K 3. 390921 u. K 4. 391028 K 7. 391100. 391119. 391209 K 3. 391216. 391217 K 9. 400113. 400214 K 2. 400312 K 1. *DA Köthen I. 6*, S. 120 f. 410101. 410102. 410111. 410117. 410208 K. 420124 I. 420601 K 2. 421202 K 6. 430103 K II 5. 430505 K I. 430826 K 4. 431211 K I 13. 440000. 440119 K 10. 440715 K 4. 450305 K 5. 450317A. 450726 K 3. 450818. 450900. 450901. 460103 K 6. 460112 K 3. 460120. 460406 K 2. 460426

Postverkehr. Vgl. Kryptographie 190308. 190322 I. 190707. 191129. 200318. 200826. 230809 K 12. 230913. 240106. 240112. 240400 K 1. 250218A. 250228. 260106. 260617 K. 260831. 260831A. 261010. 280226 K 4. 280821. 281105. 300320 K I 2. 300410 T g u. K. 300426. 300725. 300924. 301001. 310108. 310113. 310224. 310311. 340107. 340716. 360703. 370422. 370729. 370805. 371028. 371030. 371108 K 5. 371123 K 12. 371127. 371208. 371231. 380125A. 380202 K 3. 380210. 380402. 380405. 380410. 380411. 380417. 380502 K 0. 380522 K 1. 380522A K 0. 380602 K 1. 380606 K 5. 380609A. 380625. 380720. 380721 K 3. 380724 K 1. 380803 K 3. 380810. 381006. 381007. 381114. 381116A. 390126. 390310. 390514. 390701 K 2. 390807. 390814. 390909. 390910. 400209. 400311. 400619. 400620. 400810. 410914. 411126. 420120. 420219. 420311. 420608. 421009. 421011. 421129A. 421225. 430121A. 430215. 430419. 430425. 430430. 430527. 440324. 440824 Q u. A. 441205. 441226A K 2. 450124. 450317. 450419 K 3. 450921A. 451001. 451019. 451028A. 451119. 451217. 460218 K 2. 460303. 460317 K 9. 460324. 460406

K 1. 460620. 460620B. 460708. 460714. 460718. 460726. 460804. 460810. 460908. 460909. 461023. 461029. 461031A. 461106. 461206

Prodigium/ Prognostikation/ Orakel. Vgl. Magie 180714 K 4. 240112 K 9. 240319. 240418. 270115 K 5. 280128. 280620 K 2. 290616 K 9. 300320 K II. 300509 K 1. 300725 K 1. 310113. 310703. *DA Köthen I. 4*, S. 9, 12. 370421 u. I. 371112 K I 2. 380221 K 2. 380226. 380302A. 380303. 380312. 380320A. 380608A K 8. 380609A K 5. 390727. 400203. 410221 K 1. 421120. 421206. 421225. 430118. 430215. 430826. 440000 II. 440826 K 9. 460804 K 10. 461204A

Prosodie, s. Phonetik. Vgl. Verskunst

Psychologie 220919. 231210 I. 240718 K 23. 320715 K 12. 350731 I. 360600 II. *DA Köthen I. 6*, S. 112. 410625. 420124 I. 441020

Pyrrhichius 431206. 450124 K 6

Quatrains/ Quatrins, s. Vierzeiler

Rechtschreibung, s. Wortschatz

Rechtslehre/ -wissenschaft 190424. 210401. 210421. 270406 K 18. 270429 K. 271201A K 8. 280122 K I 3. 290129 K I. 290529 K 33. 300410 K 46. 300725 K 5. 310119 K. 320416 K I 3. 350800. 351112. 360600 II. 360703 K 12. 371209 I u. II. 380000 K 7. 380125. 380125A K 1. 380828 K I 56. 381028 II u. III. 390822. 390826 K. 400218 K 5. 401204. 410324 K I. 410706 K 7. 410731. 420124 I. 420627 K I. 430215 K 13. 430826 K. *DA Köthen I. 7*, S. 15, 135. 440426 K I 0. 440616 K 0. 440715A K. 441010 K 0. 450818 K 13. 461006 K

Rechtsprechung/ Justizwesen 410106 K 1. 410111. 410117. 410221 K 2. 410731 K 0. 410822. 411009. 411200. 411214 K I 1. 420124 I. 420219 K 8. 420630. 421009. 430215 K 13. 430826. 461006

Rede/ Redekunst/ Stil(istik) 270429 K. 280112. 280122 K II 6. 280716 u. K II 1.

281000 K 2. 290129 I. 290310 u. K I 2.
290715. 301102 K 2. 310411 K 1.
330311. 330918. 331223. 340421 K 3.
350312 K. 350731 u. I. 360600 II.
360800 K 6. *DA Köthen I. 4,* S. 10, 96.
370422 I u. III. 370900. 371226A.
380405 I. 380417 K 5. 381028 II u. III u.
K IV. *DA Köthen I. 5,* S. 7, 8, 11, 13, 36.
390112 I. 390727. 390822. 390904 u. I.
390907 u. I. 390910. 390912. 390921.
391119 I u. II. 400122 u. K I 1. 400218.
400301 K 6. 400502 K 4. 400514. 400528
K 3. 400605 K 3. *DA Köthen I. 6,* S. 10,
12. 410101 u. I u. II. 410102. 410106.
410117 K 1. 410206 I u. II. 410208 I.
410406 K 2. 410505 u. I. 410625 K 0.
411200. 420124 I. 421120 K 5. 430103.
430419 I. 430505 K. 430509 K 4.
430826. 431028A. 431123 I. *DA Köthen
I. 7,* S. 15, 19, 22. 440000. 440119 K 8.
440426 u. I. 440824 K 7. 440826 K 8.
441020. 441201 K. 441223 K. 450000A
K 0. 450124. 450305. 450317A. 450400
K 2. 450504. 450505. 450506A. 450529.
450722. 450726. 450806. 450808. 450817
u. VI–V u. K II 9. 450818. 450901.
451100 u. I. 460000A. 460131. 460204 I.
460217. 460317 I. 460705 I u. II. 460803.
460812 K 3. 460825. 461104. 461216
Geläufigkeit der Rede. Vgl. Brief/ Gesellschaftsbrief
   310411 S. 390/ 391 u. K 5. *DA Köthen I. 4,* S. 11. 371028. 371112A.
371209. 371224. 380000 K 0. 380100.
380110. 380125A. 380320 u. I.
380427. 381116A. *DA Köthen I. 5,*
S. 8 f. 390121. 400728. 431123 I.
441020. 450504. 450529
Reichsacht   230809. 230913 K 3. 231006
K 5. 231008 K 3. 231101. 240106.
240717. *DA Köthen I. 2,* S. 10. 280411.
280412 K I 1. 280616A K 1. 280620 K 2.
280724. 280726. 280929 K 10. 281021
K 5. 281215. 290216 K I 12. 291224 K 5.
300410 I u. K 10. 310113 K 41. 310224
K 33. 310311. 320416 K 1. 350800 K 10.
DA Köthen I. 4, S. 9. 370422 K. 371028
K. 390807A K 1. 401204 K 2. 430000A
K 1. 460125 K 1 u. K I

Reimgesetze, s. Gesellschaftsbuch FG u.
   Imprese
Reitkunst, s. Pferde
Religion, s. Bekenntnis, Frömmigkeit, Religionsgemeinschaften, Religionsunterricht u. Theologie. Vgl. auch die im
   Personenregister genannten Religionsgemeinschaften
Religionsgemeinschaften/ Kirchenwesen/
   Gottesdienst. Vgl. Bekenntnis, Frömmigkeit, Religionsunterricht u. Theologie. Vgl. auch die im Personenregister
   genannten Religionsgemeinschaften
   181023 K. 191124. 270115. 270406.
270429 K. 271201A. 280122 K I 4.
280128. 290129 I. 290629. *DA Köthen I.
3,* S. 126. 300410. 301001. 301011.
310108 I. 310411 K 7. 320313. 320416.
320715 K 9. 330603. 330920. 331223
K 20. *DA Köthen I. 4,* S. 9. 371030 K 4.
371223. 380207 K 5. 380320 K u. K I 7.
380423 K 9. 380608 K 1. 380904. 390904
I. *DA Köthen I. 6,* S. 15. 410101 K 2.
410406. 411214 u. I. 420114. 420120
K 20. 420601 u. I. 420627. 420712 K 2.
421101. 430215. 430312 K 6. 430318
K 7. 430418. 430430. 430505 I. 430802
K 1. 430826. 431016 (K 2). 431020 (K
3). 431211 I. 440310B K 4. 450000 K 5.
450219. 450420. 450818 K 9. 451001
K 5. 451030. 460613 K 0. 461117 K 1.
461204. 461216 K 6
Religionsunterricht. Vgl. Bekenntnis,
   Frömmigkeit, Religionsgemeinschaften
   u. Theologie
   191231 K 7. 270406 K 13. 300718.
340604 K 2. 340609 K 2. 350312 K.
421123 K 1. 421225. 430215 K 10.
450220
Rind   380320A
Ritterspiel/ Kartell. Vgl. Drama u. Maskerade
   DA Köthen I. 1, S. 12 f. 231006 K 10.
240718. 250218A u. V–VII. 250500.
250609. 270406 K. 291104A u. I Q u. K
I 3. *DA Köthen I. 3,* S. 10. 310000 K 13.
360600 II. *DA Köthen I. 4,* S. 9. 371121.
371124 K 5. 380226 K 4. 380310 u. I–V.

380312. 381105. *DA Köthen I. 5*, S. 103. 391217. 400728 K 4. 460204 I
Roman. Vgl. Epos
  DA Köthen I. 2, S. 18. 350308A Lektüre/ Kritik/ Beschaffung u. ä. *DA Köthen I. 1*, S. 19. 231206. 240109 K 11. 240112. 240301. 250228. 250500. 260000. 260000A. 260211. 260500 K 1. *DA Köthen I. 2*, S. 18. 270429. 270808. 280216 K 3. 280321 K 2. 281000. 290129 I. 290715. 291104 K 1. 291104A K 2 u. K I 3. 300320 K II 2. 360800 K I 2. 371124 K 5. 400514. 400619
  Werk/ Abfassung/ Adaptation/ Bearbeitung/ Übersetzung 240301 K 4. 240400 K 5. 240718 K. 250218A V–VII. 250228. 250305 K 39. 250500. 250700 S. 435. 260000. 260000A. 260217. *DA Köthen I. 2*, S. 18. 270429. 271001. 290629. 291104 K 1. 291104A u. I. 340107 K 20. *DA Köthen I. 4*, S. 9. 371112A. 371124 K 5. 371126. 371224. 380000 K 2. 380402. 380504. 380509A. 380625. *DA Köthen I. 5*, S. 10 f., 16. 400514. 400619. *DA Köthen I. 6*, S. 14. 410625. 420808 K I 1. *DA Köthen I. 7*, S. 8. 440000 u. I. 440209A K 4. 440724. 441020 K 12. 441201. 441223 K 1. 450308A K 1. 450400 K 7. 450504. 450506A K 1. 450529. 450725 K 6. 450726 K 6. 450808 u. I. 450817 K II 3. 450921. 450927 K II 6. 451101. 451217. 460000A K 0. 460120. 460217 K 4. 460317 K 10. 460610 K 11. 460812 K 1
Satire/ Parodie/ Groteske 250706. 280321 K 2. 280716 K 2. 280818 K 3. 290129 I. 370422 K I 1. 371009 K I 2. 371031 K I 0. 371110 K 12. 371124 K 5. 371224 K 6. 380000. 380110 K. 380220 K 1. *DA Köthen I. 5*, S. 14, 34. 390110 K 3. 390112. 390114 u. I. 390126A. 390126B. 390131. 400502 K 3. *DA Köthen I. 6*, S. 15 f. 420506 K 8. 430103 u. I u. II. 431021 K 1. 431022. *DA Köthen I. 7*, S. 11, 145. 440119 K 10. 440324. 440426 K I 0. 440525 K II 15. 440616 K II 3. 440715A

K 8. 450400 K 6. 450500 K. 450526 K. 450818 K. 450901. 450927 K II 6. 451101. 451209 K 3. 460103 K 6. 460406. 460620 K 3. 460829 I. 461020. 461031. 461104 K 1 u. K I
Schild, FG *DA Köthen I. 1*, vor dem Titel, S. 76–80. *DA Köthen I. 2*, vor dem Titel, S. 85. *DA Köthen I. 3*, vor dem Titel, S. 96, 104. *DA Köthen I. 4*, vor dem Titel, S. 88. *DA Köthen I. 5*, vor dem Titel, S. 97. *DA Köthen I. 6*, vor dem Titel, S. 111. *DA Köthen I. 7*, vor dem Titel, S. 131
Schmuck 190707. *DA Köthen I. 2*, S. 88 f. *DA Köthen I. 3*, S. 120. 340107. 350731 I. *DA Köthen I. 4*, S. 94. 370517 K 4. 371027 K III 1. 380310 I u. IV. *DA Köthen I. 5*, S. 97, 100. 421202 K 4. 430515. 431211 K I 6
Schrift/ Schriftschneiden 190308 K 10. 191229. 191231. 280128 K. 420601. *DA Köthen I. 7*, S. 136 f. 440900. 441000. 441011. 450217. 450224. 450722
Schulen
  450817
  Adelberg: Klosterschule 300426 K 4
  Allendorf: 391217 K 4
  Altenburg: Gymn. 400312 K 5
  Altdorf: U. 410324 K I. 420627 K 1 u. K I 15. 421120 K 10. 430826 K
  Amberg: Paedagogium 190220 K 12. 280929 K 10. 371223 K 8. 410106 K 5. 440119 K 0
  Amsterdam: Athenaeum 440119 K 8
  Angers: Akademie 300725 K 11
  Anhalt: Ritterakademie (geplant) 300718
  Augsburg: Gymnasium St. Anna 461104 K 5
  Aurich: Gymn. 450806 K 2
  Basel: U. 190220 K 12. 390119 K 2. 420627 K 1. 450410 K 5
    Ratkes Schule 191231 K 8
  Bernburg: Lateinschule 300509 K 3. 330603 K 6. 380122 K 7. 380126. 380128. 410106 K 5. 410708 K 5. 440119 K 0. 450304 K 5
  Beuthen: Akadem. Gymn. 270429 K 19. 310119

Sachregister

Blois: Akademie   271107 K 1
Bologna: U.   280122 K I 3. 390121A K 2
Braunschweig   *DA Köthen I. 5*, S. 102
Breda: Doorluchtige School   460103 K 3
Bremen: Domschule   450806 K 2
Bremen: Gymnasium Academicum   371030 K I 8. 460825
Brenz: Hofschule   300426
Breslau: 400312 K 5
Breslau: Elisabeth-Gymn.   270429 K 1. 390121A K 1. 440119 K 0. 440324 K 2
Brieg: Gymnasium   300718 K 3. 440324 K 1
Brieg: Hofschule   300718 K 0
Brieg: Ritterakademie (geplant)   300718 K 3
Cambridge: U.   380321 K 1
Coburg: Akadem. Gymn. (Gymnasium Casimirianum)   180102 K 1. 340421 K 3. 380417 K 5. 461216 K 6
Danzig: Akadem. Gymn.   390121A K 1. 440324 K 12
Dessau: Hofschule   300718 K 0
Dessau: Lateinschule   250110 K 2. 360600 K II 56
Detmold: Lateinschule   300813 K 3
Dordrecht: U.   440119 K 8
Dorpad: U.   430826
Durlach: Gymn.   420627 K I 12
Einbeck: Ratsschule   430509 K 2
Erfurt: U.   340421 K 3. 380417 K 5. 420627 K I 15
Franken, Hzt.   340604
Frankenhausen   391217 K 11
Frankfurt a. d. O.: U.   360600 II. 420120 K 12. 420124 K I 1. 440119 K 12. 450726 K 6. 460825 K 0
Freiberg: Gymn.   400312 K 5
Genf: U.   291028 K 1. 300718 K 0. 300813 K 1. 360600 K II 25. *DA Köthen I. 4*, S. 96 f. 380321 K 2. 390119 K 2
Gera: Hofschule   320416 K 9
Gießen: U.   270827 K 10. 391217 K 4. 420627 K I 10. 430509 K 1. 430826 K
Görlitz: Gymn.   400312 K 5

Gotha: Gymn. Vgl. Personenregister: Evenius, Sigismund; Reyher, Andreas   340604 K 2. 350312 K. 391217 K 4. 420311 K 4 [Schulwesen]. 431211 K I 17. 440119 K 1. 450217
Greifswald: U.   450326 K 4
Grimma: Fürstenschule   440119 K 0
Groningen: U.   430329 K 3. 430509 K 2
Güstrow: Knabenschule   370902 K 7. 371009 K 0. 450304 K 1
Halberstadt, Bst.   320416 K 7
Halle a. d. S.: Akadem. Gymn.   340604 K 2. 350312 K. *DA Köthen I. 4*, S. 97. 371226A K 6. 390112 K I 10. 400317 K 3. 430403 K 1. 441226A K 3. 450506A K 3
Halle a. d. S.: Elementarschule   360600 II. 440504 K 1
Hamburg: Gymn. Acad. Johanneum   430509. 430826 Q u. K 2. 440324 K 17
Harderwijk: U.   270115
Heidelberg: U.   330603 K 1. 360600 II. 390121A K 2. 410119 K 7. 410731 I. 420120 K 12. 430826 K. 440119 K 9
Heilbronn: Stadtschule   420627 K I 7
Helmstedt: U.   330603 K 1. 330920. 350312 K 4. 391209. 410914A K 1. 411214 K I 1. 420627 K 1. 421110 K 0. 430509 K. 430826 K. 451100 K 9. 460414 K 3. 461204 K 1
Herborn: Academia Nassauensis (akad. Gymnas.)   410731 I. 460825 K 9
Hildesheim: Gymn. Andreanum   430509 K 2
Hirsau   430418 K 12
Ingoldstadt: U.   420627 K I 14
Jena: U.   270827 K 10. 290120. 290614. 320416 K I 3. 340604 K 2. 370305 K 5. 391217 K 4. 400122 K 7. 400317 K 3. 420608. 430106 K 1. 430215 K 24. 430509 K 4. 430826 K. 431211 K I 13. 440119 K 0. 450410 K 7
Kassel: Hofschule/ Collegium publicum/ Collegium Mauritianum   260419 K 1. 300718 K. 371110 K 10. 371226A K 3. 460125 K 2
Kassel: Ritterakademie   300718 K

Kassel: U. 370422 K III 3
Kiel: U. 430826 K 18
Köln: Gymnas. (S.J.) 440119 K 10
Köslin: Stadtschule 321201 K 11
Köthen. Vgl. Personenregister: Ratke, Wolfgang
  DA Köthen I. 1, S. 16, 21. 180102. 181023. 181207. 181222 K 2. 181225. 190220. 190424 K 7. 191231. 200826. *DA Köthen I. 2*, S. 12 f. 270406. 270827 K 1. 290529 K. 290614. *DA Köthen I. 3*, S. 18. 340604 K 2. 371226A K 6. 390112 K I 10. 391028 K 5. 391217 K 4. 400122 K. 400301 K 4. *DA Köthen I. 6*, S. 12. 410208 K 8. 410313 K 3. 450217. 450410 K 7
Kranichfeld: Deutsche Schule. Vgl. Personenregister: Ratke, Wolfgang 290120
Leiden: U. 280128. 300410 K 55. 330603 K 1. 330918. 360630 K III 3. 390121A K. 390800A K 1. 420120 K. 430329 K 3. 430509 K 2. 430826 K. 440119 K
Leipzig: U. 320416 K I 3. 330918. 370305 K 5. 380417 K 3. 410106 K 5. 410324 K I. 411214 K I 1. 420627 K I 5. 430826 K 0. 461204 K 1
Liegnitz: Ritterakademie 270429 K 11
Linz: Gymn. 420627 K I 20
Löwen: U. 440119 K 10
Lübeck: Lateinschule 430826 K 2
Lüneburg: Gymn. Johanneum 391217 K 4
Lyon: U. 371027 K III 1
Magdeburg, Ebst. 320416 K 7
Magdeburg: Gymn. 350312 K 4
Marburg: Pädagogium 420627 K I 10
Marburg: U. 370422 K III 3. 410731 I. 420120 K 12. 420627 K I 10. 430826 K 25. 440119 K 12. 451220 K 2
Maulbronn 430418
Meißen: kursächs. Landesschule 420627 K I 5
Minden: Gymn. 450806 K 2
Molsheim: Akademie 270429 K 15. 420627 K I 13
Montauban: U. 380321 K 2
Naumburg: Stadtschule 410106

Neuhausen (Worms): Gymn. 250110 K 2
Nürnberg 450100 K 5
Nürnberg: Egidien-Gymn. 420608 K 9. 440824 K 7. 460700 K 2
Orange: Gymn. 300410 K 55
Orange: Ritterakademie 360630 K 1
Oxford: U. 280122 K I 3. 380321 K. 440119 K 8
Padua: U., Deutsche Nation 230809. 231008. 380000 K 3. 390119 K 2. 390121A K 2. 420124 K I 3. 430509 K 1. 430826 K 33. 451101 K 13. 460204 K I 2
Paris: Collège de France 450901 K 15
Paris: U. 280122 K I 3. 390121A K 2. 440119 K 9. 450818 K 11. 450901 K 15
Pernambuco (Missionsschule) 310113
Quedlinburg 350312 K 4
Regensburg: Gymn. 340604 K 2. 420627 K I 12
Reinsdorf 410203A K 1
Rostock: Gymn. 440324 K 17
Rostock: U. 321201 K 11. 340107 K 16. 370517 K I. 371014 K 7. 380417 K 3. 430509 K 1. 430826 K. 440324. 450726. 451220 K 9. 460610
Rudolstadt: Mädchenschule 290529 K 24
Sachsen-Gotha, Hzt. 340604 K 2
Sagan: U. 401204 K 2
Salamanca: U. 280122 K I 3
Saumur: Akademie 300718 K 0. 360600 K II 25
Schleusingen: Gymn. 340604 K 2. 391217 K 4
Schlüchtern: Gymn. 371028 K 11
Schwarzburg, Gft. 180508
Sedan: Akademie 330603 K 1. 390119 K 2. 461124 K 1
Siegen: Kriegsakademie 180102
Siena: U., Deutsche Nation 230809. 270429 K 11. 420124 K I 3. 430826 K 18. 460204 K I 2
Sorø: Ritterakademie 300718 K 12. 430826 K 15
Steinfurt: Akadem. Gymn. 260419 K 1

Steinfurt/ Gft. Bentheim: Gymn. Arnoldinum 430826 K 25
Stralsund: Gymn. 451220 K 9
Straßburg: Akademie 420627 K I 13
Straßburg: Gymn. 390800 K 1
Straßburg: U. 270429 K. 300813 K 1. 401111 K 3. 420627 K I 12. 430118 K 26. 430215 K 24. 430826 K 9. 450219 K 14. 451101 K 13. 461104 K
Stuttgart: Paedagogium 300426 K 4
Tübingen: Ritterakademie 300718 K
Tübingen: U. 270406. 270429 K. 380320 K I. 410119 K 7. 410406 K 6. 411214 K 2. 420601 K 2. 420627 K 1 u. K I. 421206 K 9. 430118 K 26. 430215 K. 430826 K. 431123 K I 3. 450219 K 14. 450410 K 6
Uelzen: Gymn. 450806 K 2
Ulm: Gymn. 420627 K I 10
Uppsala: U. 400319 K 3. 450726 K 3
Weimar. Vgl. Personenregister: Kromayer, Johannes u. Ratke, Wolfgang *DA Köthen I. 1*, S. 16, 21. 180508. *DA Köthen I. 2*, S. 12. 270827 K 1. 290120. 290410 K 5. 290529. 290614. *DA Köthen I. 3*, S. 14. 300203 K 4. 340604 K 2. 340609 K 2. 350312 K 3. 390112 K I 10. 400122 K. *DA Köthen I. 6*, S. 12. 410208 K 8. 410313 K 3. 450410 K 7
Wittenberg: U. 270429 K 14. 291028 K 1. 370305 K 5. 390911. 391028 K. 391217 K 4. 400122 K 3. 420627 K 1 u. K I 5. 430329 K 2. 430826 K. 440119 K 0. . 450726 K 19. 460812 K 0
Zerbst: Akadem. Gymn. 250110 K 2. 250218. 270406 K 11. 291028 K 1. 300718. 310800. 330603 K 6. 360600 II. 410106 K 5. 451220 K 0
Zerbst: Johannisschule 310800. 440119 K 0
Zwickau: Lateinschule 420506 K 7
Zwickau: Ratsgymn. 280122 I. 381116A K 3. *DA Köthen I. 6*, S. 14
Zwickau: Stadtschule 290529 K 29
Schweine 410206 I u. II
Sechszeiler/ Sixain *DA Köthen I. 5*, S. 102. 391119 I. 430103 II. 440400 I

Sixain, s. Sechszeiler
Skazon *DA Köthen I. 2*, S. 18. 271010 K 10
Sonett *DA Köthen I. 1*, S. 13, 78 f. 220824. 250110. 250413 II–III. 250700 II. 250705. 260500. 260520. 260520A u. I. *DA Köthen I. 2*, S. 94. 270429 K 9. 270810 K 1 u. I. 270919. 270925 II–IV. 271025. 280000 K 1. 280510 u. III. 280600. 290310 u. I. 290314. 290329. 290510 K 8. 291005 K 5. *DA Köthen I. 3*, S. 10, 19 f., 103 f., 110 f., 119, 122, 128 f. 300330 K I 0. 300509 I. 310000. 310411 u. I. 310800. 340912 K 3. 360800 u. I. *DA Köthen I. 4*, S. 12, 15. 370305. 370715 K II 0. 371027 u. I u. II. 371028. 371121 K 1. 371208 u. I–IV. 371209 u. I u. II. 371226A. 380207 K 3. 380321. 380405. 380522A K 2. 380522B. 380602 u. I u. II. 380606. 380608A. 380609. 390914. 391119 I. 400310 u. I. 400311. 400311A. 400312 K 1. 400320. 400502. 400506 u. I. 400509. 400902 u. I u. II. 410111 u. I. 401117 u. I. *DA Köthen I. 6*, S. 123 ff. 410111. 410203A. 410206 I. 410208 K 5. 410500. 410625 K 0. 420601 K 2. 430419 K I 2. 430624 I. 430724. 430801 u. I. 430802. 430821 K 5. 430920. 431007 K 1. 431124 K. 431206 u. I u. II. 431211. *DA Köthen I. 7*, S. 132, 137. 440130. 450220 I. 450711 K 4. 450725 I. 451100 K 8. 460204 I
Spiele. Vgl. auch Maskerade, Ritterspiel u. Tanz
370517 K 5. 410625 K 0. *DA Köthen I. 7*, S. 15. 440204 I
Abschlagspiel 280510 u. III. 280517
Anagramm 421101 III u. IV. 440400 u. I
Ballspiel 280304 K 9
Brettspiel 250305 S. 381. Vgl. Schach
Dreikönigsspiel 171224
Gesprächspiele 410300. 410909. 411126. 411200. 420311. 420503. 420506. 420608. 421207. 430000 K 2. 430419 u. I. 430526. 430724. 430801 u. I. 430802 K 3. 430920. 431014. 431124. *DA Köthen I. 7*, S. 13, 15, 133, 134, 145. 440204 u. I. 440426.

440616 u. I u. III. 440715. 440715A.
440724 K 4. 440824. 450124. 450220.
450317A. 450400. 450410. 450504
K 4. 450529. 450611. 450726 K 0.
450808 u. I. 450817 u. K I 0 u. K II.
460803
Kartenspiel   171224. 171225
Rätsel   260619. 430215 (K 26 u. 27)
Reimspiel   240718
Schach   231210. 240106. 240116.
240125. 240319. 240907 K 2. 370828.
401111 K 2. 430526. *DA Köthen I. 7*,
S. 135. 450817 II u. V
Spielreime   430419 K I 2. 430724 K.
430802. 430920 Q
St. Martinsfeier   *DA Köthen I. 6*, S. 14.
431208. 431211 u. I
Würfelspiel   240718. 250305 S. 381
Spondäus   420503 K 6. 431124 K. 431206
K 6. 441020 K 3. 450124 K 6. 450529
K 2
Sprachkritik, s. Sprachunterricht/ Sprachenkenntnis/ Sprachpflege/ Philologie.
Sprachunterricht/ Philologie, s. Sprachunterricht/ Sprachenkenntnis/ Sprachpflege/ Sprachkritik/ Philologie. Vgl.
Etymologie, Grammatik, Wortschatz u.
Personenregister, z. B. Ratke, Wolfgang
DA Köthen I. 1, S. 16, 18 f. *DA Köthen
I. 2*, S. 11. 290120. 300718. 310108 I.
310119 K 5. 330603 K 0. 340107 K.
340604 K 2. 350312 K 4. 360600 II.
371219 K 4. 371226A K I 2. 411200.
430509 K 4. 450200. 450202. 450220.
450308A
Arabisch   *DA Köthen I. 2*, S. 17 f.
280122 u. I–II. 280128. 370421 I.
371027. 390800A K 1. 430509 K 4.
450217 K 0. 450305 K 5. 450317A
K 4
Aramäisch   450410 K 5
Äthiopisch   280128
Chaldäisch   270115. 280122 I u. K II.
280128. 380320 K I 3
Dänisch   310000 K 5. 460915 K
Deutsch   *DA Köthen I. 1*, S. 16–19.
180508. 181023. 250110 K I. 270406
K 7. 270827. 280122 I u. K II. *DA
Köthen I. 3*, S. 17. 300718. 310000.

310411 u. I. 310703 I u. II. 350312
K 3. *DA Köthen I. 4*, S. 8, 13, 97.
370421 K 1. 370422 III. 370900.
371027 III. 380202. 380320 K I 1.
380417 K 3. 380828 K I 1. 381028 II
u. III. 381105. *DA Köthen I. 5*,
S. 8 ff., 11 ff., 16. 390115 K 1.
390121A. 390126. 390310. 390800A.
390807. 390822. 390901. 390911.
400122 u. I. 400218 K 5. 400301 u. I.
400314. 400323. 400430. 400528 u. I.
u. II. 400605. 401111 u. I. *DA Köthen
I. 6*, S. 9, 12, 123 f. 410102 K 2.
410111 K 8. 410117. 410119. 410208
I. 410300. 410324 u. I. 410406.
410505 u. I. 410706 u. I. 410909.
410914A. 411200. 411214. 420311.
420608. 421027 K 5. 421105. 421108
u. I u. II. 421200. 421206. 421225 K.
430000 K 2. 430103 u. II. 430121.
430204. 430208. 430307. 430312.
430318. 430329 K 3 (Niederdeutsch).
430403. 430419 u. K I 2. 430505 u. I.
430509. 430515. 430526. 430624.
430801 u. I. 430801A. 431007 K 3.
431016 (K 2). 431020 K 1. 431022.
431028A. 431123 I. 431124. 431206 I
u. K 4. *DA Köthen I. 7*, S. 10, 13, 15,
16 f., 18 ff. 440219 K. 440313. 440317.
440429. 440525 u. I u. II. 440616 u. II
u. III u. K I 0. 440715. 440715A.
440724 K 13. 440824. 440826.
441020. 441216. 441223. 441231A.
450000. 450000A. 450100 K 8.
450224 K 1. 450308A. 450319.
450400. 450410. 450420. 450504.
450526. 450726 K 0. 450808. 450818.
450901. 450923C. 450927 I. 451101.
451217. 451220. 460000 I. 460000A.
460120A. 460131. 460200. 460200A.
460217 K 1. 460317 u. K I. 460406.
460410. 460426. 460609. 460610.
460620. 460705 u. I u. II. 460720.
460803. 460812. 460816. 460819 II.
460825 u. II, IV u. V. 460902. 460912
u. I. 460915. 460916. 461104 IV u.
K I
Englisch   360630 I. 371027 III. 380321

K 1. 410706. 411214. 440209A K 2.
450305 K 5. 450526 K 3. 451101 K 12
Etruskisch   440209. 440313
Flämisch   380616. 460000 II
Französisch   *DA Köthen I. 1*, S. 19.
  180102. 181023. 181222. 181225.
  190220. 190308. 190318. 190324.
  190424. 250110 K I. 250413 II.
  250627 K 1. 250700 II. 270115.
  270406 K 13. 270429. 271107. 280122
  K II. *DA Köthen I. 3*, S. 17. 300426.
  300725 K 5. 310000 u. I. 310108 K I
  0. 310411 u. I. 311205 K 1. 340107
  K 16. 360600 II. 360630 I u. K 3. *DA
  Köthen I. 4*, S. 11 f., 13. 370422 I u.
  III. 371027 III. 371112A. 371117.
  371209 K 3. 380100. 380108. 380110.
  380120 K 3. 380202. 380321 K 3.
  380616. 381028 IV. 390909 u. I.
  400506. 400902 K 7. *DA Köthen I. 6*,
  S. 14. 410101. 410300. 410621 u. II.
  410625. 410706. 410731 I. 410822.
  410900. 430103 K 1. 430505 K I.
  430706 K 10. 431123 II. *DA Köthen
  I. 7*, S. 9. 440209. 440323. 441020.
  441226 K 2. 450305 K 5. 450317A.
  450420. 450504 K. 450818. 450900.
  450901 K 15. 450929. 451217 K 9.
  460131 K 5. 460915 K. 461124
Gotisch   390822. 460915 K 7 u. 13
Griechisch   190322 I. 280122 I u. II.
  280128. 291028 K 1. 300426. 310411.
  330918. 340604 K 2. 360600 II.
  360630 I. 371027 I–III. 371226A K 6.
  380320 K I. 380417 K 3. 381028 IV.
  381105 K 1. *DA Köthen I. 5*, S. 9, 12.
  390800A K 1. 391217. 400122 K 7 u.
  I. 400301 I. 400528 I u. II. 410324.
  410706. 410900. 411200. 430509 K 4.
  430515. 440209. 440313. 440317 K 3.
  441020. 450217 K. 450224. 450319.
  450410 K 7. 450808. 450929. 451220
  K 8. 460131 K. 460812. 460902.
  460915 K 13
Hebräisch   180508 K. 190324 K 1.
  191229. 191231 K 8. 250110 K I.
  250413 II. 250700 II. *DA Köthen I.
  2*, S. 18. 270115. 270406 K. 270827
  K 1. 280122 I u. K II. 280128. 290529

K 2. 291028 K 1. 300426. 310411.
  320416 K 3. 320715. 340604 K 2.
  350312 K 3. 371027 K III 1. 380320
  K I. 380417 K 3. *DA Köthen I. 5*,
  S. 12, 13. 391217. 400122 K 7. 400528
  I u. II. 410706 K 6. 410900 K 5.
  420608. 421202 K 1. 430103 K II 10.
  430515. *DA Köthen I. 7*, S. 24.
  440209. 450217 K. 450219 K 15.
  450224. 450308A. 450410. 450808.
  450923C. 451220. 460131. 460200.
  460406 K 4. 460426 K 1. 460609 K 3.
  460720 K 3. 460812 K 2. 460902 K 3
Indisch   280128
Italienisch (s. auch Toskanisch)   *DA
  Köthen I. 1*, S. 19. 230809. 230819.
  250110 K I. 250627 K 1. 270115.
  270406 K 13. 270919 K 1. 290310.
  300426. 310703 I. 340107. 360600 II.
  360630 I. *DA Köthen I. 4*, S. 12, 13.
  371027 I–III. 371209 K 3. 380108.
  380110. 380120 K 3. 381028 II–IV.
  DA Köthen I. 5, S. 11. 400809.
  400902 K 7. *DA Köthen I. 6*, S. 7, 9,
  15 f. 410300. 410621 u. II. 430505 u.
  K I. 430526 K 1. 430624. 430724.
  430801A. 430802. 431007. 431021.
  431022. 431028. 431123 K 1. *DA Köthen I. 7*, S. 9. 440209. 440323.
  440426 K 7. 440616 III. 441020.
  441226. 450305 K 5. 450420. 450504
  K 3. 450526. 450726 K 19. 450817 u.
  II u. IV. 450900. 450919A. 460120A
  K 1. 460131 K. 460217
Keltisch   280321 K 2. 371027 (?) I u. II.
  400528 I u. II. 450000 K II 4. 460000
  K II 4. 460912 I. 460915
Kimbrisch   460915 K 13
Langobardisch   390822 K 3
Lateinisch   *DA Köthen I. 1*, S. 19.
  180508 K. 191231 K 8. 250110 K I.
  270406 K. 271107. 280122 I u. II.
  280128. 290608. 291028 K 1. 300426.
  300718. 310411. 310703 K I 3 u. II.
  330918. 340604 K 2. 350312. 360600
  II. 360630 I. *DA Köthen I. 4*, S. 13.
  370421 I. 370900. 371027 III.
  371208A. 380221. 380302. 380320 K
  I. 380417 K 3. 380427. 381028 IV.

381105. *DA Köthen I. 5*, S. 12.
390807A K 6. 400122 I. 400317 K 3.
400528 K I 1 u. II. 400809 I u. II. *DA Köthen I. 6*, S. 12, 14. 410106 K 5.
410324. 410706 K 6. 410900 K.
411200. 421110. 430509 K 4. 430826.
431123 K II 2. 440119 K. 440209.
440313. 440317 K. 440525 K II 16.
440616 III. 440715A K 8. 450217
K 1. 450224. 450305 K 5. 450420.
450818. 450923C. 450929. 451100
K 8. 451101 K 13. 451220 K 8.
460131. 460406. 460720 K 3. 460812
K 2. 460902. 460915 K 13

Niederländisch 270115. 301011.
371027 III. 400528 K II 7. 400619
K 7. 400620. 401215 K II 0. 410203.
430329 K 3. 430403. 430407 K 7.
430505 K I 10. 430821 K 6. 451101
K 7. 460825 K 5

Orientalische Sprachen 430826 K 22.
460317 I

Persisch 280128. 390800A K 1. 450305 K 5

Polnisch 270115. 290608. 360630 I

Punisch, s. Arabisch

Sanskrit 450305 K 5

Schwedisch 371027 I u. II

Slawisch 371027 I–III

Spanisch 270115. 270406 K 13. 350731
K I 0. 360600 II. 360630 I. 371027
III. 371208A. 371209. 381028 IV.
410300. 440616 III. 441020. 441226
K 2. 450305 K 5. 450504 K 3. 451217
K 7

Syrisch 211006. *DA Köthen I. 2*, S. 18.
270115 K 5. 280122 K I 8 u. K II 1.
280128. 450217 K 0. 450224. 450305
K 5. 450726 K 19

Toskanisch *DA Köthen I. 7*, S. 9.
450817 IV

Türkisch 280122 II. 280128. 371027 I–III. 410706

Vandalisch 390822

Stanze, s. Achtzeiler/ Huitain

Stil(istik), s. Rede/ Redekunst/ Stil(istik)

Strambotto 270925 K II 1. 440310A u. K I 1

Tanz 240718. 250305. 280721. 290608.
360630 K 3. 380221 K 2. 380310 K 1.
380828 K 3. 390114 I. 400317 I. 431211
I. 460204

Technische Geräte u. Verfahren. Vgl.
Druckerei, Magie, Medizin, Münzstätten, Vogelstellerei, Waffen u. a.
190220. *DA Köthen I. 2*, S. 18. 271201A.
280128 K 24. 280620 K 4. 291224.
300330 K 3. 300924. 301011 K 11.
350731 I V. 505. 370421 K 0. 371009 I.
380310 I u. IV. *DA Köthen I. 5*, S. 102.
391203 I. 400605 I. *DA Köthen I. 6*,
S. 113. 420114. 420627 K I 16. 431123
K 2. 431211 I. 450817 K III. 460000 K 3.
460317 K. 461204A K 0

Textilien/ Kleidung. Vgl. Wandteppich (s. Impresen u. Wappen)
191229 K 2. 240718. 250218A K VII 19.
DA Köthen I. 2, S. 85 f., 88 f., 92, 95 f.
271201 I. *DA Köthen I. 3*, S. 98, 107 f.,
114, 120, 127. 300216 K 0. 350731 I V.
159 ff. *DA Köthen I. 4*, S. 7, 89, 90, 92,
97. 370729. 380310 I u. IV. 380501.
380503. 380509. *DA Köthen I. 5*, S. 97,
98, 100, 102. 400502. 400509. 401025.
DA Köthen I. 6, S. 111 f. 125. 431211 I.
DA Köthen I. 7, S. 135, 142. 450326 K 4.
450919. 451019. 451101 K 1

Theologie. Vgl. Bekenntnis, Frömmigkeit,
Religionsgemeinschaften u. Religionsunterricht
DA Köthen I. 1, S. 16 f. 181023 K 5.
190324. 191124. 260611 K. *DA Köthen I. 2*, S. 11–13. 270406. 270429 K 15.
270827. 271010 K. 271201A K 8. 271211
K 2. 271215 K 22. 280122 II u. K 5.
280128. 280216. 280721 K 12. 280929
K 10. 290120. 290129 K I. 290410 K 4.
290529. 290614. 290715. 290909.
291013. 291028. 291104A K I 3. *DA Köthen I. 3*, S. 16, 101, 124 ff. 300320 K u.
K II 24. 300330 K I 0. 300725. 301102
K 1. 310113. 310224. 310703 K 4.
320715 K 8. 330311 K. 330603. 330920.
340421 K 3. 350312 K. 350731 K I 0.
350800. 360428 K II 21. 360600 II.
360630 I u. II. 371009 II. 380320 u. I.
380321 K 1. 380417. 380608 K 1. 380828

Sachregister

K I 1. 381028 u. II–IV. *DA Köthen I. 5*,
S. 13, 36. 390119 K. 390121A. 390822.
390904 I. 391209. 400104 u. I. 400301
K 8. 400310 K I 1. 400312 K 1. 400714.
400902. 401111 u. I. *DA Köthen I. 6*,
S. 8, 10, 12 f. 410106 K 5. 410111 K I.
410119. 410406. 410914A K 1. 411214.
420114. 420120 K. 420601. 420627 I.
420712. 421101 u. I–IV. 421120. 421206.
421225 K 12. 430106. 430215 K. 430418.
430425. 430430. 430509 K 1. 430826.
431123 II. *DA Köthen I. 7*, S. 11.
440809A K 4. 440826. 441010. 450726.
450817 K 11 u. K I. 450818 K 13.
451220 K. 460700 K 5. 460915 K 11.
461204

Tiere/ Tierkunde/ Tierzucht, allgemein, s.
auch speziell Esel, Fische, Insekten,
Jagd, Löwe, Pferde, Rind, Schweine u.
Vögel
231210 I. *DA Köthen I. 3*, S. 112, 117 f.
320715. 350312. 350731 I. 360630 K 5.
DA Köthen I. 4, S. 89. 371009 II. 380310
I. 380331 K 9. 380608A. 380828 I. *DA
Köthen I. 5*, S. 106. 390904 I. 401029.
430526 K 5. 450325. 450504A. 450817 u.
K I 2 u. K II 13. 460715 II

Trinkgebräuche. Vgl. Ölberger
171224. 171225. 240109 K 1. 240112.
240718. 250305. 250514. 260520.
271201A. 280112. 280327. 280407.
280411. 280412. 280620. 291005 K 4.
300921 I. 310113 K 50. 310224 K 26.
320416. 320715 K 12. 340107. 400312 u.
I. 421230. 460204. 460613 K 6

Trochäus 380828 K 3. 391119 III. *DA
Köthen I. 6*, S. 12. 420503 K 6. 431123 I.
431124 K. 431206 I u. K 6. 440426 K I
3. 440824. 441020 K 3. 441231A. 450124
K 6. 450200. 450410 K 3. 450529 K 2.
450808 K I 1. 460825. 460912 II

Übersetzung als Aufgabe oder Kunst. Vgl.
Bibelübersetzung *DA Köthen I. 1*,
S. 15, 18. 180000. 191226 K 5. 211006.
220824. 230809. 230819. 231203. 250110
K I. 250705 u. I. 250706 K 4. 260211.
260617. 260703. 260831. 261010. *DA
Köthen I. 2*, S. 11 f., 15–18. 270115 K 6.
270429. 270919 K 1. 271001. 271010
K 15. (271211. 271215.) 280000 K 1.
280106. 280112. 280122 II u. K 5.
280208. 280226. 280304. 280411 K.
280412 u. I. 280414 u. I. 280510 u. I.
280818. 280821. 280929. 281021 K.
281126. 290304 K 2. 290501. 290510.
290616. 290629. 291009. 291104A u. I.
DA Köthen I. 3, S. 10. 300216 K. 300330
K 3. 300410. 301011 K 20. 301102.
310000 u. I. 310108 K I 0. 310411 u. I.
310703. 330311. 330918 K 6. 340107 K.
350731 K I 0. 360428 K 1. 360800 I u.
K 1. *DA Köthen I. 4*, S. 11 ff., 14. 370305
K 16. 370421 K 1. 370422 I–III. 370902
K 11. 371027 K. 371028. 371106 K 5.
371112 K 10. 371112A. 371117. 371124
K 5 u. K I 0. 371208A. 371209.
371221A. 380100. 380108 K 7. 380110.
380120. 380202. 380221. 380302.
380321. 380405. 380423. 380427.
380609A. 380616. 380721 K 1. 381028
II–IV. 381105. 381116. 381218. 381224.
DA Köthen I. 5, S. 8 ff. 390115 K 1.
390119. 390121. 390126B. 390310.
390504 K 2. 390630 K I 1. 390701 u. I.
390807. 390814. 390822. 390901. 390909
u. I. 390921. 391000 K 3. 391100.
391113. 391125. 391200. 391223.
400000. 400301. 400506. 400509 K 3.
400514 K 1. 400619. 400620. 401214.
DA Köthen I. 6, S. 7, 9, 13 f., 15 f.
410101 u. I u. II. 410102. 410111 u. I.
410203. 410208 I. 410300. 410323.
410621 u. II. 410625. 410727. 410731 K
I 1. 410909. 420506 K. 430103 K 1.
430121A K 2. 430505. 430526 K 1.
430624. 430724. 430801A. 430802.
430826. 431007. 431021. 431022. 431123
II. *DA Köthen I. 7*, S. 16. 440000 u. I.
440119 K. 440209A. 440310. 440323.
440426 K 7. 441226. 450305. 450317.
450317A. 450326 K 3. 450400. 450504.
450506A. 450526. 450529. 450725 K 5.
450808 K I 3. 450817 K 6. 450818 K 13.
451008. 451217 K 9. 460000A. 460317 K
I 3. 460426. 460825 u. II. 460902.
461124

Verlagswesen/ Verlagsbeitrag/ Druckprivileg/ Zensur. Vgl. Buchhandel u. Druckerei
220919 K 3. 231210 K I 9. 271001. 271010. 280128. 290614. 310000 Q u. K 9. 310703 K. 311205 K 1. 330311 K 11. 340604 K 2. 370422 K I 2. 371027. 371106. 371121 K 1. 371224 K 6. 380120. 380122. 380126. 380128. 380402 K 8. 380606. 380609. 380625. *DA Köthen I. 5*, S. 10, 16 f., 101, 108. 390904 K I 1. 390912. 390921. 391113. 391125. 391203 I. 391217. 391223. 400104 u. I. 400203. 400218. 400605 u. I. 400619. 400620. 400714. 401111 K 16. 401228A. *DA Köthen I. 6*, S. 9. 410117. 410119. 410208 K 4. 410300. 410313. 410323. 410505. 410510. 410625 K 0. 410706 I. 410714 K 1. 411128. 420506. 420630 K 5. 420712. 421031A. 421105 K 9. 421123 K 1. 421129. 421206. 430106. 430121A. 430204. 430208. 430214. 430306. 430312. 430318. 430407. 430410. 430418A. 430419. 430505 u. I. 430507. 430513. 430527. 430617. 430724A. 430801A. 430821. 430826. 430905 u. I. 431124. 431201 K 1. 431209. *DA Köthen I. 7*, S. 25. 440130. 440209A. 440310. 440310B. 440323 u. I. 440324. 440723. 440723A. 440809A K 4. 440824 K 8. 440900. 441000 K 5. 441011. 441201 K 0. 441205 K 3. 441231. 450126. 450127. 450217 K 1. 450220. 450221. 450301. 450305 u. I. 450308. 450317. 450317A. 450331 u. I. 450410. 450417. 450419 K 2. 450503. 450504 K 4. 450506. 450507A. 450509. 450510 K. 450526. 450711. 450721. 450725 K 5. 450726. 450800. 450808 K 5. 450905. 450922. 450923. 450923A. 450929. 450930. 451001 K. 451007. 451008. 451015. 451019. 451028. 451028B. 451101. 451119. 460119. 460206. 460218. 460301. 460309. 460324. 460403. 460519 K. 460620. 460620B. 460703. 460718. 460721 K 4. 460803. 460915A K 2. 460916. 461216

Vers commun   300320 K V. 391119 I. 400902 K I 1. 431123 II. 431206 K 6. 440824 K 7. 450124 K 6

Verskunst. Vgl. Poetik
DA Köthen I. 1, S. 13–16. 250110. 250218A. 250700 K 88. 250706. 260500. 260520A u. I. 260617. 261010. *DA Köthen I. 2*, S. 15, 18. 270429. 270810 K 3. 270925 K II 1. 280616 K 2. 281000. 281021. 290000 K I 1. 290310. 290629. 290715 K 8. 290909. *DA Köthen I. 3*, S. 9 f. 300320 II u. V. 300403 K I–II. 310000. 310411 u. I. 310703 K 10. 340107 K 20. 360600 II. 360800 II. *DA Köthen I. 4*, S. 13 f. 370900. 371028A. 371030 K 4. 371112A. 371116 K 3. 371126. 371222 K 7. 380310 K I 1. 380411 u. I. 380504. 380522B. 380609. 380828 u. I. 381105 K 4. 381116. 381218. *DA Köthen I. 5*, S. 14, 17, 101. 390114 I. 390800 K. 390911. 391028. 391119 u. I u. II. 391216. 400000. 400122 K I 6. 400218. 400310 K I 2. 400313. 400314. 400319. 400323. 400502. 400514 K 2. 400619. 400620. 400902 I. 401107 I. 401223. *DA Köthen I. 6*, S. 11, 14, 119. 410203A K 5. 410205. 410406 K 5. 410909 K 5. 420503. 420506 K 3. 420608 K 2. 421200. 421207. 430103 K II 3. 430121 K 9. 430204. 430318. 430328 K 1. 430329 K 2. 430624 K 2 u. K I 1. 431014. 431021 K 1. 431028A K 3. 431123 I. 431124. 431206. 431211. *DA Köthen I. 7*, S. 10, 17. 440100 u. K I 1 u. K II 1. 440119 K 5. 440310A u. I u. II. 440313. 440324. 440400 K I. 440616 K 5. 440715 K 5. 440824. 440900. 441000. 441011. 441020. 441200 K 1. 441216. 441231. 441231A. 450100. 450124. 450126. 450200. 450202. 450204. 450219. 450220 u. I u. II. 450221. 450308. 450308A. 450317A. 450529 K 2. 450808 K I 1. 450818. 451000 K 1. 451217 K 7. 451219. 460317 I. 460819 II. 460825 u. II

Vierzeiler/ Quatrains/ Quatrins   171225 K 1. 371112A K 4. 371124 K I 0. *DA Köthen I. 5*, S. 105. 391119 I. 400312 K 6 u. I. 400319 K 3

Sachregister

Vögel/ Vogelstellerei. Vgl. Greiff 200125. 210401. 230430. 250705 I. 350312. 350731 I. 380828 I. *DA Köthen I. 5*, S. 106. 400000 K 6. 400917 I. 431211 I

Wachsbossieren 271201A. 431211 I
Waffen 171224. 171225. 191229. 280721. 290129 K 3. 290708. 300924 K 4. 301011 K 11. 310703. 330311 K 2. 340421 K 1. 350731 I V. 501 u. K I V. 404 f. 360428 I u. II. 360630 K 9. *DA Köthen I. 4*, S. 90. 370517 K 4. 370722 K 9. 380310 I–II u. IV. 380608A K 7. *DA Köthen I. 5*, S. 97. 410731 K I 4
Waffenstillstand, s. Friedensverhandlungen
Wandteppich, s. Imprese u. Wappen
Wappen 260619. *DA Köthen I. 2*, S. 8 f., 90. 271201 u. I. 271209 u. I. 271211. 271215. 271228. 280106. 280112. 280208. 280220. 280327 K 2. 280412 u. K I 3. 280414. 280425. 280517 K 5. 280716 K 16. 280726. 280821 K 6. 280928. 280929. 281226 K 4. 290226. 291013. *DA Köthen I. 3*, S. 18, 119, 123 ff., 129. 300320 K II 14. 300410 K. 300509 K 2. 310113. 310224. 310703 II. 330918 K 4. 331223 I Q u. K I 2. 340716. 351112. 360703. *DA Köthen I. 4*, S. 10, 92, 93, 94 f., 96. 370517 K 4. 370722. 370729. 370805 K 4. 371009 K 3. 371014 K 7. 371028. 371110. 371112 K I 3. 371112A K 3. 371116 K 4. 371209. 371220. 371221. 371223. 371226. 371227. 380100. 380207. 380310 I. 380312. 380328. 380331. 380410 K 2. 380423. 380501. 380504. 380507. 380509. 380509A. 380522. 380522A. 380606 K 5. 380609 K 8. 380625. *DA Köthen I. 5*, S. 10, 107, 108. 390112 I. 390807. *DA Köthen I. 6*, S. 112, 114, 121. 410323. 410621 I Q. 410727. 410914. 410919. 411200 K 0. 420124 K 10. 420808. 421108 K 4. 421110 K 5. 421123 u. I. 421129A. 421200 K 1. 430101 Q u. K 2. 430106 K 1. 430407. 430507. 430801A. 430821. *DA Köthen I. 7*, S. 142, 146. 440715A T a. 440731 II. 441010 K 1. 450219 K 6. 450317.

450326. 450410 K 22. 450500 K 1. 450504A. 450505. 450505A. 450613. 450725. 450919 K 2. 450927 II. 451019 K 8. 451101. 451217. 460103 K 0. 460120. 460406. 460423. 460426. 460609. 460610. 460613. 460620. 460705. 460714. 460912 K I 3 u. II. 461031A. 461104 K 2, K I u. K III 0. 461106
Wappenbuch FG. Vgl. Gesellschaftsbuch FG: *GB Kö.*
WB Weimar 330918 K 4
Weihnachten 171224. 171225. 181222. 231203. 280112. 281215. 281226. 371221. 381116 u. I
Widmung, s. Gelegenheitsdichtung
Wortschatz/ Lexikographie/ Rechtschreibung. Vgl. Etymologie; s. auch Wörterverzeichnis
Arabisch 280122 I u. II. 280128 K 20. 381028 IV
Aramäisch 450410 K 5
Deutsch 171224 K 5. 180000. 200125 K 2. 210401 K 10. 220824 K 3. 240109. 240718. 250218 K 19. 260619 K 18. *DA Köthen I. 2*, S. 17. 270810 K 10. 270827 K. 271215 K 3. 280106. 280112. 280122 I u. II. 280411. *DA Köthen I. 3*, S. 9. 300216 K. 300410 K 1. 310000. 310411 u. I. *DA Köthen I. 4*, S. 12, 13. 370422 I u. K I 3. 370900 Q. 371014 K. 371027 K 5. 371030 K I 5. 371031 I. 371110 K 11. 380108 K 4. 380110 K 4. 380320 I. 380417. 380504 K 14. 380625. 380721. 380828 I. 381028 II–IV. 381105. 381114. 381116A. 381218 K 6. *DA Köthen I. 5*, S. 13, 104 f. 390114. 390800 K 1. 390800A. 390807. 390822. 390901. 391028 u. I. 391217 u. I. 400122 I. 400214. 400301 u. I. 400319. 400320. 400528 I u. II. 401111 T u. K 13 (Nd.). *DA Köthen I. 6*, S. 10 f., 12 f. 410208. 410406 K 2. 410706 u. K I 3. 410714 K 2. 410727 K. 410909. 410914A K 6. 411126 K 3. 411200 Q u. T u. K 5. 420311. 420503. 420506. 421031 K 4. 421101 I. 421200. 421225 K 5. 430103.

430328. 430403. 430419 u. K I 2.
430509 K 4. 430724. 430802 K 4.
430920. 431014. 431016. 431020.
431022. 431028 K 1. 431028A.
431124. 431206. 431227. *DA Köthen
I. 7*, S. 16, 18 ff. 440000 I Q. 440127.
440129. 440209. 440219. 440313.
440317. 440426. 440429. 440504.
440525 II. 440616 K I 0. 440715 K 5.
440715A K 4. 440724 K 4. 440809.
440826. 441201 K. 441223. 441226.
441226A. 441231. 450000. 450000A
K. 450100. 450124. 450308A.
450317A. 450326. 450400 K 2.
450410. 450420. 450504. 450505.
450506A. 450507 u. I. 450508 K.
450526 K 4. 450529. 450800. 450808
u. K I 2. 450817 K. 450900. 450919A.
450921 K 2. 450923B. 450923C.
450929. 451007. 451019 K 8. 451028.
451028A. 451101. 451219. 451220.
460000 u. II. 460127. 460131. 460200
K 1. 460217. 460406. 460426 K 1.
460609 K 3. 460610. 460718. 460720
K 3. 460812. 460816 I. 460825 u. I.
460902. 460915. 460916. 461031.
461104 K 5. 461106

Französisch 230809 K 25. 240417 T f.
240718. 250500 K 12. 260703 K 2.
261010 K 14. 280106. 280112.
310411. 370422 I. 371112A K.
380202. 380321 K 3. 381028 IV.
410621 II. *DA Köthen I. 7*, S. 22 f.
441223. 460915 K

Griechisch 380320 K 4. 381028 K II u.
III–IV. 410706 K 6. 430509 K 4

Hebräisch 380320 K 4. 381028 K IV 7.
400122 T I w. 450410 K

Italienisch 230802. 230819. 231203.
240718 K 68 u. 101. 270406 K 13.
270919 K 1. 310411. 381028 II–IV.
400122 T I w. *DA Köthen I. 6*, S. S. 7.
410621 II. 450817 u. V u. K IV 11.
450919A

Lateinisch 190424 K 5. 240109.
240417 T a u. b. 260520. 310411.
381028 II–IV. 381114. 430509 K 4.
DA Köthen I. 7, S. 22. 460915 K

Niederländisch *DA Köthen I. 3*, S. 17.
300410. 300921. 300924. 301001.
301011. 310113. 310224. 310311 K 3.
360703. 381028 II u. IV. 410203.
430403 K 4. 430509 K 4. 450000 K 2

Persisch 381028 IV
Slawisch 380328
Spanisch 240718 K 68. 381028 IV
Wendisch 380328 K 8

Zensur, s. Verlagswesen
Zoologie, s. Tiere

Personenregister

Das Register erfaßt historische Einzelpersonen, Personenverbände und Körperschaften, daneben auch literarische und mythische Gestalten, nichtentschlüsselte Gesellschaftsnamen (PA) und ausgewählte biblische Personen. Werke unbestimmter Verfasser und die Autoren der bis zum Jahre 1700 erschienenen Schriften sind hierin ebenfalls verzeichnet, auch wenn sie nur kurz im Kommentar erscheinen.

Abdallah Ibn Al Muqaffa   450305 K 5
Academia Naturae Curiosorum (seit 1677 *Sacri Romani Imperii Academia Caesareo-Leopoldina Naturae Curiosorum*) S. 138. 450817 K II 3
Académie française   S. 22 f. 450818 K12
Académie des jeux floraux (Toulouse) 450817 K9
Académie des Loyales (AL)   450304 K 1
Académie putéane (Paris)   460103 K 6
Accademia degli Affidati (Pavia)   450817 K 9
Accademia degli Ardenti (Neapel) 450817 K 9
Accademia degli Erranti (Neapel)   440000 K III 0
Accademia degli Humoristi (Rom) 441223 K 7. 450817 K 9
Accademia degli Incogniti (Venedig) 440000 K III 0. 450817. 460000A K 0
Accademia degl'Infuriati (Neapel) 450817 K IV 4
Accademia degli Insensati (Perugia) 450817 K 9
Accademia degli Intenti (Pavia)   450817 K 9
Accademia degli Intrepidi (Rom)   450817 K 9
Accademia degli Intronati (Siena)   441223 K 7. 450817. 451101. 451209 K 8. 451217. 460120
Accademia degli Invaghiti (Mantua) 450817 K 9
Accademia degli Oziosi (Neapel)   S. 139. 441223 K 7. 450817 u. II. 450919A. 451101. 451217 K 3. 460000A K 0
Accademia degli Ricouperati (Neapel) 450817 K 9
Accademia degli Unisoni (Venedig) 450817
Accademia dei Furfurrari (Florenz) 450817 K 9
Accademia dei Lincei (Rom)   450817 K 4 u. K IV 5
Accademia dei Ricovrati (Padua)   450817 K 9
Accademia della Crusca (Florenz)   S. 9, 15. 450611 K 1. 450817 IV u. K 9. 450919A K 7. 451028A K 4. 460120A. 460217
Accademia della Notte (Venedig)   450817 K 9
Accademia Fiorentina (Florenz)   450817 K 9
Accetto, Torquato   450817 K II 2
Adam   440826 K
Adam, Martha, s. Apelles von Löwenstern
Adami, Tobias   450319
Adjutus,
  Josephus   450726
  Blandina, *Cotten   450726 K 19
Aeneas   440313 K 6
Aëtius von Amida   450817 K II 3
Aganippe (Quellnymphe)   450927 II
Agazzari, Agostino   450817 K 20
Agricola, Georg   450000
Agrippa v. Nettesheim, Heinrich Cornelius   440826 K 6
Agrippa,
  Marcus Vipsanius   461204A K 1

Vipsania Polla   461204A K 1
Aihpos tebasile von Grublekem (Pseud.), s. Braunschweig-Wolfenbüttel, Hzn. Sophia Elisabeth v.
Aineias von Gaza   441010 K 0
Aix-en-Provence, Parlement   450817 K 9
Alamanni, Luigi   450725
Alba, Fernando Alvarez de Toledo, Hz. v.   441020 K 10
Albano, Kd. Alessandro   450817 K IV 5
Albert, Chr.   440324 K 2. 450726 K 16
Albertus, Laurentius   450410 K 3
Albinus, Justus   460422 K 4
Albrecht, Christof   450503. 450509 K 1
Aldenbrück gen. Velbrück, Frh. Conrad Gumprecht v.   440816 I u. II
Aldinus, Tobias   450817 K II 3
Aldringen, Gf. Johann v.   440000 K I 6
Aldrovandi, Ulisse   450919A K 10
Alewein, Frh. Johann Adolf v.   450808 K I 1
Alexander d. Gr., s. Makedonien
ʿAlī ibn Abī Ṭālib   440324 K I 1
Alighieri, s. Dante
Alischer, Sebastian   440324 K 2. 450726 K 16
Alkide, der, s. Herakles
Almogávar, Juan Boscán   441020
Alsted, Johann Heinrich   441000
Alvensleben, v.
   Cuno   450408 K 3
   Gebhard   460825 K 0
Amaziah, Kg. v. Juda   460825
Amor, s. Cupido
Amos (Prophet)   460825 III
Andler, Johann Jacob   460414
Andreae,
   Agnes Elisabeth, *Grüninger   450806 K 1
   Barbara, *Saubert   460715 K 5
   Gottlieb (Theophil)   460317 K I 0. 460715. 460819. 461216 K 4
   Jacob d. Ä.   460804. 460819. 460915A K 2. 461029 K 8
   Jacob d. J.   460819. 461029 K 8
   Johann Valentin (s. auch Societas Christiana)   S. 8, 11, 14, 16, 18, 21, 135. 440100 K 4. 440429. 440826 K. 440900 Q u. K 1. 441020 K 1. 450202 K 1. 450219. 450319. 450410 K 6. 450526 K 3. 450722. 450806. 450901 K 16. 451001 K 5. 460112 K 1. 460127. 460303 K 5. 460317 u. I Q. 460414. 460613 K 3. 460620B. 460708. 460715 u. I u. II. 460804. 460819 u. I u. II. 460908 u. I u. II u. III. 460909 u. I. 460915A u. I. 461029. 461104 K 5. 461106 u. I. 461117. 461204. 461216 u. I u. II
Anfriso   441020
Angelocrator, s. Engelhardt
Angelus, Andreas   450000 K 4
Anhalt, F./ Fn. v.
   Agnes, *Pommern, verw. Brandenburg   450326 K 8
   Anna Sophia, s. Schwarzburg-Rudolstadt
   Eleonora, s. Hessen-Darmstadt
   Ernst   450326
   Georg I.   450326
   Georg II.   450326 K 8
   Georg III.   450326 K 14
   Heinrich I.   450326
   Joachim Ernst   450326 K
   Margaretha, *Schwarzburg-Blankenburg   450326
   Margaretha, s. Sachsen
   Sigismund I.   450326
   Waldemar VI.   450326
   Wolfgang   450326
Anhalt, Ft.
   Landstände (mit Engerem u. Größerem Ausschuß)   450420 K 2. 460125 K 3 u. K I
Anhalt-Bernburg, F./ Fn. v.
   Christian I.   440000 II. 440119 K 0. 450305 K 5. 460825 K 0
   Christian II.   S. 7, 132. 440000 II. 440130 K 5. 440426 K 2. 440504 K 1. 440824 K 3. 440927. 441010 K 0. 450124. 450220 K 5 u. K II 0. 450304. 450305 K 5. 450326. 450420. 450504 K 2. 450529 T bw u. K 10. 450721 K 3. 450900. 451008 K 6. 451220 K 0. 460103 K 5. 460119 K 3. 460125 u. K I 0. 460422 K 4. 460613. 460620A. 460714. 460718 K 1. 461206 K 3

Eleonora Maria, s. Mecklenburg-Güstrow
Eleonora Sophia, *Schleswig-Holstein-Sonderburg   450304. 450326
  Ferdinand Christian   450326
  Friedrich, s. Anhalt-Harzgerode
  Maria   450304
  Sibylla Elisabeth   450304 K 3
Anhalt-Dessau, F./ Fn. v.
  Agnesa, *Hessen-Kassel   450508A. 461124
  Dorothea, *Pfalzgfn. v. Simmern   450220 K I 1
  Eleonora Dorothea, s. Sachsen-Weimar
  Friedrich Moritz   451220 K 0
  Johann Casimir   S. 7. 440525 K I 3. 450220 K 1. 450408. 450508A. 451220 K 0. 460104. 460125 K 1. 460321. 460422. 460423 u. I. 460424. 460424A. 460825 K 0. 461031A K 1. 461124. 461206
  Johann Georg I.   450220 K I 1. 451220 K 0. 460422 K 4
  Johann Georg II.   441205 K 3. 451217 K 9. 460103
  Kunigunde Juliana, s. Hessen-Rotenburg
  Louise, s. Schlesien zu Brieg
Anhalt-Harzgerode, F./ Fn. v.
  Friedrich   S. 7. 450220 K 1. 450529 T bw. 460125 K 1. 461106 K 9
  Johanna Elisabeth, *Nassau-Hadamar   461106 K 9
Anhalt-Köthen, F./ Fn. v.
  Emanuel   461206 K 3
  Lebrecht   461206 K 3
  Ludwig   *passim*
  Sophia, *Lippe   440209 K 5. 441205. 450220. 450301. 450325. 450326. 450921 K 4. 461006 K 2. 461026 K 4
  Wilhelm Ludwig   440826 K 3. 441010. 450220. 450301. 450325 (?). 450900. 460825 K 0
Anhalt-Plötzkau, F. v.
  August   S. 7. 440927. 441205 K 4. 441223 K 9. 450220 K 1. 450408 K 0. 451030 K 0. 460125. 460422 K 5. 460424. 460825 K 0. 461206 K 3
  Emanuel, s. Anhalt-Köthen
  Lebrecht, s. Anhalt-Köthen
Anhalt-Zerbst, F./ Fn. v.
  Dorothea, s. Braunschweig-Lüneburg-Dannenberg
  Johann   S. 7. 450529 T bw. 450721 K 3. 460424 K 8. 460825 K 7. 461206 K 3
  Rudolph   S. 9. 450319 K 9. 460120A K
Annius von Viterbo, s. Nanni, Giovanni
(Societas) Antilia   450319
Antyrius   450927 II
Apelles   440324 K 3
Apelles von Löwenstern (Apel/ Appelt),
  Barbara, *Tarnau u. Kühschmalz   440324 K 1. 450726
  Martha, *Adam   440324 K 1
  Matthaeus   440324. 440724 K 13. 450000A K 0. 450726. 460610
  Rosina   440324
Aphrodite, s. Venus
Apollo (Phoebus)   440324 K I 2. 440525. 441200 I. 450529 K 3. 450722 K 2. 450726 I. 450806 K 5. 450817 II. 450901 K 6. 450927 I u. II. 460112. 460204 I. 460912 II. 461104 II
Appelius, Johannes   450304 K 1
Appelt, s. Apelles von Löwenstern
Ares, s. Mars
Ariosto, Ludovico   S. 8. 440119 K 3. 450725. 450900 K 13
Aristander von Telmissus   461204A K 5
Aristippos von Kyrene   440715A K 8
Aristobulos   460912
Aristoteles   S. 19. 440826 K 3. 441020. 460902 K 2
Arminianer   440119 K 8
Arnim, Hans Georg v.   S. 8. 440000 K 1 u. K I 1
Arnisäus, Henning   450726 K 10
Arnold, Christoph   450808 K I 0
Arrianos   461204A K 5
Artyrus, s. Antyrius
Ascenas (Asch)   440209. 440313. 440317 K 4. 440715 K 6. 441200 I u. K 2. 450326 K 4
Athene, s. Pallas
Aubry, Peter   S. 142 f.
Audiguier, sieur de la Ménor, Vital d'   440724 K 6. 460217 K 4
Audoenus, Johannes, s. Owen, John

Aufrichtige Gesellschaft von der Tannen (AGT) S. 11, 13 f. 450525 u. I u. K II. 440616 K I 0 u. K III 0. 440724 K 4. 441223 K 12. 450308A K 0. 450410 K 12. 450726 K 3. 461104 K
Augier, René 450818
Austria, Don Fernando de, s. Spanien, Ferdinand, Kardinalinfant v.
Avaux, comte d', s. Mesmes, Claude de
Aventinus, Johannes Turmair gen. 440209 K. 440313. 440317. 440525 K II 0. 440715A

Bacchus 440119 K 11
Bach, Johann Michael 440324 K 1
Bacon of Verulam, Sir Francis 461204A
Baden-Durlach, Friedrich V., Mgf. v. S. 14. 440525 K 0. 450818 K 4
Bagni, Giovanni Francesco (Kd.) 460103 K 6
Balzac, Jean Louis Guez de 440119 K 11
Banér, Johan 451030 K 0. 460125 K II 1. 460204 K 3
Bant, Jobst 451019
Barberini,
    Antonio (Kd.) 460103 K 6
    Francesco (Kd.) 450817 K IV 5
    Maffeo, s. Papst Urban VIII.
Barby u. Mühlingen, August Ludwig, Gf. v. 440100 K 4
Barclay, John 450927 II
Bargagli,
    Girolamo 450817 K
    Scipione 450817 K
Baronio, Cesare 440715A K 5
Barth, Caspar v. 441010 K 0. 451217 K 7
Bartholinus,
    Caspar 450817 V
    Thomas 450817 IV Q u. V
Basel, Stadt 460103 K 6
Basile, Giambattista 450817 K II 2
Basso, Antonio 450817 K II 2
Battafarano, Italo Michele 450817 K 9
Battista, Giuseppe 450817 K II 2
Baumann, Georg 440324 u. K I 1. 450726
Bayern, Maximilian I., Kf. v. 460819 K 12
Beatus Rhenanus 440715A K 8. 450410 K 3

Bechius, Philippus 450000 K 3
Beck, Johann 450818 K 1
Becker, Bernhard 460125 K I 0
Becker,
    Cornelius d. Ä. 460819 II
    Cornelius d. J. 460819 K II 6
Becker, Henricus 440900. 441020 K 1
Beckmann (Becmanus), Christian 440119. 440525 K II 0. 440809A K 6. 450410 K 3. 451220
Beer, Johann 440426 K 1
Behaim v. Schwarzbach, Georg Friedrich S. 17. 450400 K 6. 450504A K 4. 451101. 451209 K 5
Beham (Behem/ Behaim), Simon 450219
Behme (Böhm/ Bohemus), David 440324 K 2. 450726 K
Belleforest, François de 441020
Belli, Francesco 450817 K 7
Bellin, Johann S. 44. 440129 K 5. 440724 K 12. 441201 K. 441223 K 21. 450308A Q u. K. 450410 K. 450808 Q u. K u. I Q. 450921 K 2. 460131 K 5. 460812 Q u. K 2
Bellona 450817 K II 3
Belsazar (Bel-šarru-uṣur) 440826
Bencard, Fa. 460620B K 5
Benckert, Johann Friedrich 460620B K 5
Bengerath,
    Heinrich 460303. 460620B
    Johann Friedrich 460620B K 5
    Peter 460620B K 5
Beni, Paolo 451217 K 4
Berckelmann, Julius 451000
Berg, Ernst v. 440130 K 3
Bergius, Johann 450726 K 17
Berlepsch, v.
    Anna v., s. Diede zum Fürstenstein
    Otto Wilhelm 440816 u. I u. II
Bernard, Samuel 440616 K I 0
Bernegger, Matthias S. 14. 440525 K II 0. 440616 K 0 u. K I 0. 450726. 450818 K 13
Bernhard v. Clairvaux (Hl.) 450900 Q
Bernstorff, N. N. v. (Page) 451100
Berosus (Berossos) 440209 K 10
Bersmann, Gregor 451220 K 0
Besler, Basilius 460715 K II 5
Besler, Michael Ruprecht 450817 II

Besold, Christoph   440525 K II 0. 450410 K 6
Betulius,
   Christian   460112 K 3. 460414 K 3
   Sigismund(us), s. Birken, Sigmund v.
Betzel, Andreas   461124 K 4
Beutnitz, Martin   440000 K 2
Beverwijk, Johan van   450400 K 6. 451101 K 7. 451209 K 4
Beyer, Hans/ Johannes   450503 K 1
Beyer, Hans   450127 K 1. 450331 u. I. 450417 K 2. 450419. 450503. 450509 K 1. 450510. 450721 K. 450922 K 2
Bianchi del Piano, Cambise   440826 K 0
Bibel
   440826 K. 450100 K I 4. 450219. 450304
   deutsche   S. 12, 18, 20, 22. 440313. 450410. 450504. 451001 K 5. 460131 K 2. 460200 K 1. 460819 II. 460825. 460915 K. 461117 K 1. 461204. 461216 K
   griechische   450319 K 8
   hebräische   450410 K 7
   lateinische   450100 K I 7. 450410 K 7. 450504 K 11. 460825 K 5
   niederländische   460613 K 3. 460825
Bidpai   450305 K 5. 450317A K 4
Bidpai, Fabeln des, s. Firenzuola, Agnolo
Biedersehe, Matthias v.   450220 K 7. 450500 K 2. 450504A K 2
Bingenroth, Heinrich, s. Bengerath
Birken, Sigmund v.   S. 12, 15, 17. 440000 K 2. 440100 K 5. 441223. 450808 K I 0. 450817 K 9 u. K II 3. 451100 K. 451101 K 7. 451217 K. 451219 K 7. 460000A K 0. 460112 K 3. 460120. 460406 K. 460410 K 0. 460414 K 3. 460620 K 5. 460714 K 4. 460908 K 5. 461104 K
Bisaccioni, Maiolino   450817 K 7
Bismarck, Johann (Hans)   441011 K 4. 450100. 451000 K 1
Bißmarck,
   Christoph   441231 K 6
   Ursula, s. Salfeld
Bittner, N. N.   440324 K 2
Boccaccio, Giovanni   450817 K IV 11
Bock, Hieronymus   450408 K 3
Bodenhausen, v.
   Bodo   440100 K I 3

Cuno Ordomar   440000 K 2. 450420. 450919A K 4
Ernst Lebrecht   440000 K 2
Bodin, Jean   450726 K 3
Boeckler, Johann Heinrich   S. 12, 14, 17. 440204 K I 0. 440525 K 1 u. K II 0. 440616 u. II u. III. 450219 K 6. 450319. 450722. 450806. 450901 K 16. 461104 u. I
Boethius, Anicius Manlius Severinus   450400 K 6. 450818. 451101
Bohemus, David, s. Behme, David
Böhm (Bohemus), David, s. Behme, David
Böhme, Jakob   440826 K
Böhmen, Kg./ Kgn. v.; s. Pgf./ Pgfn. bei Rhein bzw. (Hl.) Römisches Reich
   Friedrich I.   S. 14. 460103 K 4. 460104 K 0. 460120A K 1. 460125 K I 0
Böhmische Brüder   450726 K 17
Bohse, Johann Georg   450507
Boiardo, Matteo   450725 K 5
Börstel, v.
   Anne Amelie, s. Knoch, (v.)
   Christian Heinrich   440816 u. I u. II. 450408 K 1. 450508A
   Curt Christoph   450500 K 2
   Hans Ernst   450900
   Heinrich   450508A K 3
Borzelli, Angelo   450817 II K 4
Borzōy   450305 K 5
Bose (Bosse), Georg   S. 137
Botzheim, v.
   Hans Bernd   460424A I
   N. N.   460424A I
Bouillon, Henri de La Tour d'Auvergne, vicomte de Turenne, duc de   S. 140. 440616. 451030 K 2
Brandenburg, Mgf., Kf./ Mgfn., Kfn.
   Agnes, s. Anhalt
   Albrecht der Bär   450326 K 6
   Anna Sophia, s. Braunschweig-Wolfenbüttel
   Elisabeth Charlotta, Kfn., *Pfalz-Simmern   460125 K 1 u. K I 0
   Friedrich   450326 K 8
   Friedrich Wilhelm, Kf.   S. 8 f. 440000 K 1. 450326 K 4. 450504A K 1. 450613 K 5. 450725 K 5. 450800 K 3. 450818 K 2. 450921 K 3. 451100 K 9.

460120 K 9. 460125 u. I u. II. 460204 u. I. 460808
Georg Wilhelm, Kf.   440000 K 1. 460125 K 1 u. K I 0
Hedwig Sophia, s. Hessen-Kassel
Joachim Friedrich, Kf.   461026 K 4
Maria Eleonora, Mgfn., s. Pfalz-Simmern
Brandenburg-Bayreuth, Christian, Mgf. v. S. 9. 460120A K
Brassicanus, Johannes Alexander   460819 K II 7
Braunschweig u. Lüneburg, Hz./ Hzn., vgl. Einzellinien
   Otto das Kind   450319 K 9
Braunschweig-Calenberg, Hz./ Hzn. v.
   Christian Ludwig, s. Braunschweig-Celle
   Georg   S. 135. 440723. 461006 K 5
   Georg Wilhelm   461006 K 5
   Johann Friedrich   461006 K 5
   Sophia Amalia, s. Dänemark
Braunschweig-Celle,
   Christian Ludwig, Hz. v.   S. 135. 440130. 440310. 440323. 440715A. 440723. 440723A. 450126. 450127 K 3. 450221. 450308. 450317 K 2. 450319. 450410. 450721 K 7. 450923. 450923A Q. 450929 K 0. 451019. 451028. 460119. 460218. 460301. 460309. 460324 K 3. 460403. 460519 K 4. 460700 K 5. 460721 K 4
   Friedrich IV., s. Braunschweig-Lüneburg
Braunschweig-Lüneburg, Hz./ Hzn. v.
   Friedrich IV. v., zu Celle u. Harburg   461204 K 1
   Sibylla, s. Braunschweig-Lüneburg-Dannenberg
Braunschweig-Lüneburg-Dannenberg, Hz./ Hzn. v.
   August d. J., s. Braunschweig-Wolfenbüttel
   Dorothea, *Anhalt-Zerbst   450319 K 9
   Maria Catharina, s. Mecklenburg-Schwerin
   Sibylla, *Braunschweig-Lüneburg   461204 K 1

Sibylla Elisabeth, s. Oldenburg-Delmenhorst
Braunschweig-Lüneburg-Harburg, Hz. v. s. Braunschweig-Lüneburg, Hz. v., Friedrich IV.
Braunschweig-Wolfenbüttel, Hz./ Hzn. v.
   Anna Sophia, *Brandenburg   450304 K 2
   Anton Ulrich   S. 12, 15, 135 f. 440000 K 2. 440100. 440616 K I 0. 450219. 450319 K 9. 450818 K 1 u. K I. 451100 u. I. 451101 K 13. 460112 K 3. 460406 K 4. 460414 K 3. 460613. 460714 K 4. 460804. 460908. 460909 u. I
   August d. J. Administrator des Bst.s Ratzeburg   S. 8, 11 f., 14, 16, 20 f., 24, 131, 132, 134 ff. 440000 Q. 440100. 440130. 440209A. 440310. 440323 u. I. 440400 u. I. 440429 K 0. 440616 K I 0. 440723A. 440724 K 6. 440731 u. I u. K II 2. 440900. 441000. 441011. 441020 K 1. 441200. 441205 K. 441226A K 4. 441231A. 450000. 450100 u. I. 450124 K 6. 450126. 450127. 450200. 450202. 450219. 450221. 450308. 450317 K 2. 450319. 450331 u. I. 450410. 450417 K 2. 450419 K 2. 450503. 450507 K 2. 450509 K 1. 450510 K. 450526 K 3. 450529 K 10. 450614 K 2. 450711 K 2. 450721. 450722. 450726 u. I. 450800 K 3. 450806. 450817 K V 16. 450818 K 1 u. K I. 450901 K 16. 450922 K 2. 450923 Q u. K 2. 450923A. 450923B K 3. 450927 u. I u. K II 1. 450929. 451000. 451001. 451008. 451028. 451028A. 451100 u. I. 451119. 451217 K 9. 451219 K 8. 460000 u. I u. II. 460112. 460119. 460127. 460131 K 2. 460200A. 460206 I u. II. 460218 K 2. 460303. 460317 u. I. 460324. 460406 K 2. 460410 K 0. 460414 K 1. 460519 K 4. 460613. 460620A. 460620B. 460700. 460703. 460708. 460714. 460715 u. II u. K I 1. 460718. 460721 K 4. 460804. 460808. 460819 u. I. 460908 u. I u. II u. III. 460909 u. I. 460912 u. I u. II.

460915A u. I. 461006 K 6. 461029.
461106 K 1 u. K I 1. 461117. 461204.
461204A. 461216 u. II
Christina (zu Bevern), *Hessen-Eschwege 440715 Q
Clara, *Pommern 460613 K 3
Clara Augusta, s. Württemberg-Neuenstadt
Elisabeth, s. Sachsen-Altenburg
Ferdinand Albrecht I. (zu Bevern)
S. 12, 135 f. 440100. 440715 Q.
450219. 450319 K 9. 451100.
460000A Q. 460112 K 3. 460414 K 3.
460613. 460714 K 4. 460804. 460908.
460909 u. I. 461204A K 0
Friedrich Ulrich S. 135. 440100 K I 2.
440323 K I 3. 450304 K 2. 451008
K 6. 460613 K 1. 461006 K 6
Hedwig, s. Pommern
Heinrich Julius 451008 K 6
Ludwig Rudolf 461204A K 0
Maria, s. Sachsen-Lauenburg
Maria Elisabeth, s. Sachsen-Coburg
Rudolf August S. 136. 440100. 441020
K 1. 450219. 450319 K 9. 460613.
460620A K 4. 460714. 460804.
460908 K 5. 460909 u. I
Sibylla Ursula, s. Schleswig-Holstein-Glücksburg
Sophia Eleonora (zu Bevern) 440715 Q
Sophia Elisabeth, *Mecklenburg-Güstrow S. 134 ff. 440209 K 5. 440731
II. 441020 K 1. 441200 u. I u. II.
450100 K 13. 450126. 450202 K 2.
450219. 450308. 450721 K 2. 450927
u. II. 451008 K 6. 451028 K 8.
451100 K 1. 460112 K 3. 460119 K 3.
460317 K 6. 460613. 460718. 461204
Brederode, Johan (Joan/ Jan) Wolfert, heer van 460103 K 3
Brehme, Christian 450808 K I 0. 460825.
461104 K 2
Bremen, Ebf. v.
Friedrich III., s. Dänemark
Bremen, Stadt S. 7
Brennus 440209
Breslau, Stadt (Rat u. Bürgerschaft)
451019 K 3. 450726 K u. K 4 (Kanzlei)

Brinck in Harderwijk, Ernst (Friedrich v.)
440826 K 3
Brincken, v.
Anna Margaretha, s. Ditfurth
Catharina Hedwig, *Oeynhausen
461006
Christoph Eberhard 461006 K 5
Dietrich 461006 K 5
Elisabeth, s. Münnich
Eustachius 461006 K 5
Hilmar Erich 461006 K 5
Johann Dietrich 461006
Lucia Maria, *Steding 461006 K 5
Maria Catharina, s. Westerholt
Brombei, Christian 460816 K I 1
Brossard, Pierre de 461213
Brottuf, Ernst 450326 K 4
Browne, Richard 450818 K 3
Brücker, Jakob 460915 K 17
Brusoni, Girolamo 450817 K 7
Bry, Johann Theodor de S. 137. 450800
K 4. 451015 K 4
Buchner,
Augustus S. 10, 22. 440119 K 0.
440209 K 2. 440324 K u. K I 4.
440616 K 5. 440724 K 13. 441020
K 3. 441200 K 4. 450124 K 6. 450410.
450507 K 2. 450726 K 10. 450817.
450923B K 4. 451220 K 5. 460103
K 6. 460131. 460610. 460812. 460825.
461104 K 5
Elisabeth 460610
Bucholtz, Andreas Heinrich 440525 K II
0. 440724 K 13. 441216 K I 0. 450806
K 2. 461104 K 2
Budé, Guillaume 450901 K 15
Bugenhagen, Johannes Pomeranus
450326 K 4
Bulgarini, Belisario 450817 K 20
Buno, Conrad S. 134 f. 441231A K 1.
450100 K 13. 450219 K 5. 460804 K 2
Bureus (Bure), Johannes (Johan) 460915
K 7
Burgkmaier, Hans d. Ä. 440715A T a
Burgsdorff, Conrad v. S. 8 f. 440000.
460125 K 0. 460204 u. I
Buscher, Statius 460700
Butler, Walter 440000 K II
Butschky, Samuel v. 460825 K 30

Buxtorf, Johannes d. Ä.   440826 K 6. 450410

Cahlenus, Friedrich   440504 K 1
Calixt(us), Georg   441010 K 0. 450726 K 17. 451000 K 1. 460613. 460700 K 5. 461204 K 1. 461216 K 3
Callenberg, Otto Heinrich v.   450420 K 9
Calovius, Abraham   450726 K 17. 461204 K 1
Calvin, Jean   440826 K 3
Cambier, Leon   440826 K 3
Camillo, Giulio   450817 V
Cammin, Bf. v.
   Ulrich, s. Pommern
Camoenae, s. Musen
Campanella, Tommaso   450319 K 4. 450817 K II 2
Canaye, Philippe, Seigneur de Fresnes   441223 K 16
Capaccio, Giulio Cesare   450817 K II 2
Caraffa, Tiberio   450817 K II 6
Carmeni, Francesco   450817 K 7
Carpzov, Johann Benedikt d. J.   440616 K 0. 461006
Casa, Giovanni della   450817 K IV
Casaubon(us), Isaac   440119 K 9. 440616 K 0. 440715A
Castellio, Sebastian   440826 K 3. 450100 K I 7
Castiglione, Gf.
   Baldassare   S. 12. 440000 K III 0. 450817 K 9
   Francesco   440000 K III 0
   Valeriano   440000 III
Castro y Andrade, Pedro Fernández de   450817 K II
Catalogus universalis, hoc est designatio omnium librorum, qui hisce nundinis ... Francofurtensibus & Lipsiensibus anno 1644 ... vel novi vel emendatiores & auctiores prodierunt   450124 K 2
Catalogus universalis, hoc est designatio omnium librorum, qui hisce nundinis ... Francofurtensibus & Lipsiensibus anno 1645 ... vel novi vel emendatiores & auctiores prodierunt   450124 K 2
CATALOGUS UNIVERSALIS, Hoc est: DESIGNATIO omnium Librorum, qvi Nundinis Vernalibus FRANCOFURTENSIBUS & LIPSIENSIBUS Anno 1646 ... prodierunt. Das ist: Verzeichnüß aller Bücher/ so zu Franckfurt in der Fasten-Meß/ auch Leipzigischen OsterMarckte/ dieses jetzigen 1646. Jahrs ... zu befinden   450726 K 8. 460218 K 2. 460620 K 9. 461031 K 6
Cats, Jacob   451209 K 4
Celsus, Aulus Cornelius   450817 K II 3
Ceres   450927 II
Charites   441200 I. 450927 II
Charron, Pierre   450818 K 9
Châteillon, Sébastien, s. Castellio, Sebastian
Chemnitz, Bogislav Philipp v.   440616 K 0
Chigi, Fabio, s. Papst Alexander VII.
Chiron   450817 IV
Chorion, s. Schill, Johann Heinrich
Cicero, Marcus Tullius   440313 K 5. 441020. 450901 K 12. 460131. 460812 K 3. 460915 K 12
Civitas Solis   450319
Clajus, Johann, s. Klaj
Claudianus, Claudius   450806 K 5
Clepius, Christian   460315
Cleve,
   Johann   460908 K 3
   Margaretha, s. Schottelius
Clio   440525
Cluny, Abt v., s. Maiolus
Clüver (Cluverus), Philipp(us)   441000. 450000. 450927 II
Coccius, Huldrichus, s. Koch, Ulrich
Cocco, Tommaso   450817 K 7
Colerus, Christophorus (1602–1658)   S. 14, 17. 440119. 440324 K 2 u. K I 1. 450726 K. 450818 K 13. 460610 K 10
Colerus, Gottfried (Godofredus)   460125 I. 460204 K 1
Coligny, Gaspar II., Seigneur de Châtillon de   440310. 440310A
Collegium Medicum (Nürnberg)   450817 K II 3
Colmar, Stadt u. Bürgerschaft   450818 K 4
Colonna, Fabio   450817 K 4
Colletet, Guillaume   441020

Columna, Fabius, s. Colonna
Comenius, Johann Amos   440826 K 10.
   450217 K 3. 450726 K 17. 460120A K 1.
   460915 K 4
Condé, Pz. v.
   Henri II. de Bourbon, duc d'Enghien
      S. 139 f.
   Louis II. de Bourbon, duc d'Enghien
      440616 K 0. 450905 K 3
Conférence des beaux esprits (Paris)
   S. 15. 450817 K 9
Conring, Hermann   450817 K 4
Constantino Patiente, della buona Speranza (Pseud.), s. Hessen-Kassel, Lgf.
   Wilhelm V. v.
Conti, Sebastiano   450817 K 20
Cortese, Cortesi   450725 K 6
Cosel, Heinrich   460610 K 3
Costo, Collenuccio, s. Roseo da Fabriano, Mambrino
Cothmann, Johann   450304 K 4
Cotten, Blandina, s. Adjutus
Cramer, Daniel   450100 K I 7
Crasso, Lorenzo   450817 K 4
Crocius, Johann   440809A K 4
Crocius, Ludwig   460825 K 7 u. K III 0
Cromwell, Oliver   450410 K 8
Cronberg, Frh. v.
   Hartmut   460423 I. 461031A I
   Johann Daniel   460423 I. 461031A I
Croy, Hz./ Hzn.
   Anna, *Pommern   450326 K 4
   Ernst, Baron v. Fenestrage, F. zu Neugard u. Massau   450326 K 4
   Ernst Bogislaw   450326
Croyengreiff, Ernst v.   450326 K 4
Cruciger,
   Caspar d. J.   451220 K 8
   Georg   451220
Crusius, Martin   460819
Cupido/ Amor   441200 II. 450808 I
Czepko v. Reigersfeld, Daniel   440826
   K 0. 450726 K 0
Czernin v. Chudenitz, Gf. Hermann
   461104 I
Czi(e)renberg, s. Zierenberg
Czimmermann, Petrus, s. Zimmermann

Dach, Simon   S. 9. 460204 u. I

Dandolo,
   Antonio   450817 K 7
   Giovanni   450817 K 7
   Matteo   450817
Dänemark
   Christian IV., Kg. v.   440100. 440324.
      440927 K 8
   Friedrich III., (Kg.), Bf. v. Verden, Ebf.
      v. Bremen   S. 136
   Sophia, Kgn. v., *Mecklenburg   460610
      K 8
   Sophia Amalia, *Braunschweig-Calenberg   S. 136
Daniel (Prophet)   440826 K 9
Dannenberg (Tonneberg), Joachim Otto v.
   460715 K 7
Dante Alighieri   441020. 450817 K IV 11
David   440324 K I 3. 450901. 451100 K 4
   u. I. 460819 II. 460825
Deberol (ksl. Obrist), s. Deveroux, Walter
Dehn-Rotfelser, Moritz Adolph v.
   450529 K 10
Deichmann,
   Johanna   460125 K I 0
   Rütger Clemens   460125 K I 0
Delaporte, Jean   450400 K 15
Della Porta, Giambattista   450817 K 4
Demokritos v. Abdera   440715A K 8.
   450817 K 4 u. K II
Demosthenes   440715A
Denicke, David   460700 K 5
Desmarets de Saint-Sorlin, Jean   440324
   K 22. 450726 K 6. 450818 K 12
Deutsch, König, s. König Deutsch
Deutschgesinnete Genossenschaft (DG)
   S. 14 f. 440324 K 23. 440724 K. 441201
   K. 441223. 450000A K. 450308A.
   450400. 450410. 450500 K 1. 450504
   K 4. 450504A K 4. 450505 K 5. 450529.
   450808 u. K I. 450817 K 9. 450921 K 2.
   451101 K 7. 460610 K 11. 460812 K 1
Deveroux (Devereux), Walter   440000 K II
Diana/ Diane   450000A K 1
Diede zum Fürstenstein,
   Anna, *Berlepsch   460204 K 8
   Georg   460204 K 8
   Georg Christoph   460204 K 8
   Hans Eitel   460204 K 8
   N. N.   460204

Diepenbroick, Conrad Rötgers v. 440809A
Dierksen, Dirk, s. Diricks
Dieskau, Hans v. 441226. 441226A. 450504. 450507 u. I. 460718 K 8
Dietrich, Peter, (Petrus Theodoricus; Peter [Samuel] Thiederich) 440525 K 1
Dietrichsen, Dirk, s. Diricks
Dilherr, Johann Michael 440824 K 7. 441200 K 3. 450100. 450400 K. 450504A K 4. 450726 K 19. 460317 I. 460410 K 1. 460620 K 5. 460700
Diodati, Elia 460103 K 6
Diricks, Dirk 450100 K 13
Ditfurth, v.
    Anna Margaretha, *Brincken 461006 K 5
    Franz 461006 K 5
Dögen, Matthias 440724 K 6. 441223 K 1
Dohna, Burggf. u. Herr zu
    Abraham 460120A K 1. 460217 K 2
    Achatius d. Ä. 460120A K
    Achatius d. J. S. 9. 460120A. 460217
    Christoph S. 9. 450304. 460120A K 1. 460217. 460715 K II 6
    Fabian 460120A K 1
Dolmetsch, Marcus 460909 K 6
Domwald, Clara Maria 440204 K I 0
Donaloro, Gneo Falcidio (Pseud.), s. Loredano
Doni, Francesco 450305 K 5
Doni, Giovanni Battista 450817 K 9
Dordrecht, Synode v. 469825 K 7
Dörnberg, Frh. Johann Caspar v. 450818 K 4
Douglas, (Greve) Robert 440310B K 4. 451030 K
Drandorff (Trandorff), Frh. August Adolf v. 460422
Drelincourt, Charles d. Ä. 460103
Droschel, Peter, s. Troschel
Du Bartas, s. Saluste
Du Bec-Crespin, Jean 450900
Du Bellay, Joachim 450901 K 15
Du Faur, seigneur de Pibrac, Guy 450818 K 10
Du Faye, Noë 460303 K 7
Du Moulin, Pierre d. Ä. 460120A K 1. 461124

Du Vair, Guillaume, Bf. S. 11. 450818
Dupuy (Puteanus),
    Jacques 460103 K 6
    Pierre 460103 K 6
    vgl. Académie putéane
Duraeus, s. Durie
Dürer, Albrecht 460804 K 1
Durie, John 440119. 450410 K 8
Dürr, Salome, s. Schill
Dury, s. Durie
Duval, N. N. 440000 K I 3

Eckart, Anna Catharina, s. Kalcheim gen. Leuchtmar
Eggen,
    Blasius 440616 K I 0
    Carolus 440616 K I 0
Einsiedel, v.
    Christian Friedrich 460103 K 1
    Curt 440426 K 7. 441226. 441226A Q u. K 5. 441231. 450220 K 7. 450400 K 12. 450504. 450506A. 450507 K 1 u. K I 2. 450529 K 10. 451101 K 14
Elbschwanenorden (s. auch Rist, Johann) S. 14
Elloposcleron, Hultrich (Pseud.), s. Fischart, Johann
Elzevier,
    Fa. 450410
    Abraham 440310 K 4
    Bonaventure 440310 K 4
    Daniel 441223 K 1
    Ludwig (Lodewijk) 440724 K 6. 441201 K 0. 441223 A. 450410 K 2. 450808 K 3. 460610
Endter,
    Fa. S. 143 f. 450504 K 4
    Georg 450808 K 5
    Johann Andreas 450808 K 5
    Wolfgang d. Ä. S. 143. 440000 Q. 440426 K 2. 440715 Q. 441223 K 13. 450808. 460620. 460803 K 0. 460916. 461029 K 6
    Wolfgang d. J. 450808 K 5
Engelhardt (-hard, -hart),
    Andreas 450326 K 17
    Christoph 450326
    Matthias d. Ä. 450326. 450408
    Matthias d. J. 450326 K 17

Engelhardt, Michael (Angelocrator?) 450326 K 17
Enghien, Hz. v., s. Condé, Pz. Henri II.
England (u. Schottland)
    Jakob I., Kg. v. (Jakob VI. v. Schottland) 440715A K 5. 461124 K 1
    Karl I. (VI.), (Pz. v. Wales bzw.) Kg. v. 440119 K 9. 440426 K I 0. 450818 K 3. 451101 K 12
England, Parlament (House of Lords/ House of Commons) 450818. 451101 K 12
Enzmer, N. N.   450726
Epiktetos   440715A K 8
Erasmi, Georg Nicolaus   440324 K 3
Erasmus v. Rotterdam, Desiderius 440715A
Erfurt, Stadt   440616 K 0
Erhardus, Melchior   450818 K I
Eros, s. Cupido
Erskein, Friherre Alexander   451030 K 0
Este, Alberto Azzo II. d', Mgf.   450319 K 9
Euripides   441020
Evangelischer Ständetag, Frankfurt a. M. (1634)   460825 K 0
Exeter, Bf. v.
    Joseph, s. Hall
Ezechiel, Christian   460610 Q

Faber, Johann Heinricus   460909 K 6
Faber, Petrus, s. Schmidt, Peter
Fabri de Peiresc, Nicolas-Claude   460103 K 6
Fabritius, Adolph(us)   450305 I
Faesch, Remigius   450800 K 4
Fama   450806. 460912 II
Famar, de
    Fa.   460303
    Jakob d. Ä.   460303 K 7
    Jakob d. J.   460303 K 7
    Johann d. Ä.   460303 K 7
    Stefan   460303 K 7
Faulhaber, Johannes   460317
Fecher, Friedrich   460112
Felsecker, Ursula, s. Salfeld
Ferrari, Giovan Battista   450817 K 20. 460808 K 1
Fettlapp, Monsieur   440826

Ficino, Marsilio   450901 K 8. 461204A
Finsinger,
    Martha, s. Stahl
    Zacharias   440426 K 1
Firenzuola, Agnolo [d. i. Michelangelo Girolamo Giovannini]   450305 K 5. 450317A K 4
Fischart, Johann   440826 K 10. 450927 K II 2
Fischer, Levin   460808 K 1
Flacius Illyricus, Matthias   440525 K II 0
Flammin, Johann   460303 K 7
Fleming, Paul   460819 II
Flemming, Dietrich   450219. 450319. 460131
Flora   450000A K 1
Florilegium, Das ist: Ein BlumenBuch: darinnen allerhand Blümlein gantz Artig mit Lebhafften Farben/ sampt iher Wirckung und Eygenschafften vorgemahlet und beschrieben sindt   460808 K 1
Fludd (Fluctibus), Robert (Robertus de)   440826 K 6
Fontana, Francesco   S. 139. 450817 III. 450919A. 451217 K 4
Forbes, William   440927 K 1
Forstenheuser, Georg   450319 K 9. 450927 K 5. 460112 K 1. 460317 A. 460804 K 3
Forstnerus, Christophorus   450806 K 9
Förter, David   450100 K 7
Fortin sieur de la Hoguette, Philippe   S. 11. 450400 K 6. 450818 K 21. 451217. 460112 K 3. 460120. 460426
Franckenberg, Abraham v.   S. 17. 440324 K 2. 440826. 450000 K 3
Franke, N. N.   440324 K 2
Frankenberg-Ludwigsdorf, Ursula v., s. Hess und Stein
Frankreich, Kg. v.
    Franz I.   S. 11. 450901
    Heinrich III.   S. 11. 450818 K
    Heinrich IV., Kg. v.   S. 11. 440715A K 5. 441223 K 16. 450818
    Ludwig XIII.   S. 11, 15. 440000 K III 0. 450818. 451217 K 9. 460103 K 6. 461124 K 1
    Ludwig XIV.   440616 K 0. 450818. 451217 K 9

Frantz, Johann 441201 K 0
Frantzke, Georg 450220 K. 450504A K 2. 450725 I
Freher, Marquard 450507 K 2
Freig(ius), Johannes Thomas 440715A K 8
Freinshemius (Freinsheim), Ioannes (Johannes) S. 14. 440525 K 1 u. K II 0. 450726 K 3
Freitag, Christoph 440324 K 2
Frevol, Caspar 450509 K 1. 450614
Freyberg, v.
   Anna Dorothea, s. Knoch, (v.)
   Ernst S. 138. 450900 K 0. 461006 K 2
   Hans Ernst 461006 K 2. 461106 u. II
   Salome Elisabeth 461006 K 2
   Wilhelm Heinrich 441205 K 3. 450500 K 2. 450526 K 3. 451217 K 9. 460103. 461006 K 0
Freyse, Albert S. 131, 136. 450927 K 3 u. K I 1. 460804 K 1. 460912 II u. K 0. 461204A K 0
Freytag, Christoph 450726 K 16
Fruchtbringende Gesellschaft (FG) *passim*
Fuchs, Leonhart S. 134. 460315
Füetrer, Ulrich 440824 K 9
Fugger, Anton 460819 K 6
Fuhrmann, Philipp 440119 K 0
Fulnecensis, Petrus Herbertus 460819 II
Furck, Sebastian S. 131
Fürer v. Haimendorf,
   Georg Sigmund 460410
   Susanna, s. Harsdörffer
Furttenbach, Josef d. Ä. 460317
Fusconi, Giovanni Battista 450817 K 8

Gabriel (Erzengel) 451100 K 5
Gaffarel, Jacques 460103 K 6
Galilei, Galileo S. 139. 450817 K III u. K IV 5. 451217
Gallas, Matthias, Gf. v. Campo, Hz. v. Lucera 440000 K I. 440504 K 1. 440927. 441231 K 2. 450419 K 3
Gans, Friedrich Wilhelm (v.) 440130
Gargantua 440826 K 10
Gärtner, Johann (Hans) 460303 K 5. 460620B
Gassendi, Pierre 460103 K 6
Gaulmin, Gilbert 450305 K 5. 450317A K 4
Gebhard, Johannes 440826 K 1. 450726 K 20
Geispitzheim, Wolf Bernhard v. 460423 u. I. 460424A I. 461031A I
Geiß (hess. General; s. Geyso, Johann [v.]?) 460715 K 7
Geizkofler, Herr Zu Haunsheim
   Ferdinand 460804 K 1
   N. N. 440826 K 0
Geletzky (Jelecký), Johannes (Jan) 460819 II
Gelli, Giovan Batista 450900
Geneste, Sieur de la (Pseud.) 450500 K 5
Gentili, Scipione 450817 K II 4
Gentsch (Gentzsch), Jakob 440809A K 4. 450305 K 3. 450317A K 1. 450506 K 1
Geraldin, Robert 440000 K II
Gerarde, John 440800 K 4
Gerhard, Johann 461216 K 6
Gericcius (Gericke), Franciscus (Franz) 450304 K 5
Germersheim, s. Zang(e)
Gesenius, Justus 460700
Geslin La Piltière, Paul 450900
Gesner, Konrad 440525 K II 0
Geuder v. Heroldsberg, Hans Philipp (v.) 441223 K 3. 450400. 450529. 450817
Geyso, Johann (v.) S. 139
Giovannini, Michelangelo Girolamo, s. Firenzuola, Agnolo
Girone il cortese 450725 K 6
Gisenius, Johannes 441205 K 4
Glapthorne, Henry 440000 K I 1. 440209A
Glasenapp, Joachim v. S. 12. 450529 K 10. 460613. 460620A u. I. 460714. 460908 K 5
Glass (Glaß, Glassius), Salomon 450217 K 1. 461204 K 1
Gleichen, Gf. v., s. auch Hatzfeld
Gloner, Samuel 450818 K I. 461104 K 5
Glorioso, Giovanni Camillo 450817 K III
Goechhausen, Samuel v. 450220 K 16. 450725 I
Goehausen, Hermann 441205 K 4
Goeldel(ius), Christian(us) 450220 K II 0

Goldast v. Haiminsfeld, Melchior 440426 I. 440525 K II. 450507 K 2. 461104 III
Goltz, Georg v. der 450400 K 15
Gomer 440209 K 10. 440313. 440317. 440715 K 6
Gordon, John 440000 K II
Gorp van der Beken (Goropius Becanus), Jan (Ioannes) 440119. 440525 K II 0. 440715 K 6. 440826 K 12. 450308A. 450410 K. 460915
Gosky,
 Esaias 450726 K 10
 Gedeon 450726 K 10
 Martin S. 12, 131. 440100 I Q. 440400 Q I. 441223 K 16. 441231A K 1. 450200 K 2. 450319 K 9. 450726. 450806 K 2. 451100 K 9. 460908 K 5. 460909 K 6
Gotha, Stadt (Rat) 450217 K 3
Götze,
 Catharina, *Schürer 450509 K 3
 Margaretha, *Merian 450509 K 3
 Matthias 440130 K 3. 450127 K 1. 450417. 450509. 450510. 450614. 450711 K 2. 460810. 461023
 Thomas Matthias 450509 K 3
Goulart de Senlis, Simon S. 132. 440130. 440824 K 8. 450900. 460705 K II 1
Gournay, Marie Le Jars de 451101
Göze, Georg 460825 K 16
Gramont, duc Antoine III. S. 140
Granvelle, Antoine Perrenot de 440119 K 10
Gratia (personifizierte Grazie) 440525 II
Graziani, Girolamo 460000A K 0
Grazien, Die drei 441201 K 2. 450000A K 1. 450808 I. 460317 K 6. 460912 u. II
Greiff, Friedrich S. 17. 450219. 460317. 460804 K 1. 460819 u. II
Greiffenberg, Frh./ Frf.
 Johann Rudolf 440826 K 0
Greiffencrantz, v.
 Nicolai 461104 K 2
 Sophia, *Lippe, v. der 461104 K 2
Gremp v. Freudenstein, Ludwig 460819
Grillo, Angelo 450817 K II 2
Grimmelshausen, Johann Jakob Christoffel v. 461104 K 3

Grodnau, Carl Melchior Grotnitz v. 440616 K III 0
Groeben, v. der
 Ernst 460204 K 9
 Isaak Ludwig v. der 460204
 Levin Ludwig 460204 K 9
Groot, Huig de S. 11. 440616 K 0 u. K II 1. 450410 K 8. 450726 K 17. 450818
Großbritannien, s. England (u. Schottland)
Große,
 Gottfried 450124 K 2
 Henning d. Ä. 450124 K 2
Grotius, Hugo, s. Groot, Huig de
Gruber, Balthasar 441000. 441011
Grundmann, Christoph 460610
Grüninger, Agnes Elisabeth, s. Andreae
Grutner, N. N. 460610
Gryphius, Andreas 440119 K 9. 450726 K 6
Gualtherus, s. Walther, Balthasar
Guazzo, Stefano S. 12
Gueintz, Christian S. 13, 18 ff. 440127. 440129. 440209. 440219. 440313. 440317. 440426 K I 2. 440504. 440525 K 2 u. K II 13. 440724 K 9. 440809. 440824 K. 440826 K 4. 441200 K 4. 441201 K 0. 441223 K 20. 441226 Q u. K 2. 441226A. 441231. 450000 K 5. 450124. 450126 K 11. 450326. 450400 K 7. 450410 K. 450420 K. 450504. 450505. 450506A. 450507 u. I. 450508. 450529. 450808 K 8. 450817. 450818 K I. 450900. 450919A. 450923B. 450927 K II 11. 450929 K 1. 451007. 451019 K 8. 451028. 451028A K. 451101. 451217 K. 451219. 451220 K 1. 460120A K 3. 460131. 460200. 460217. 460406. 460410 K 0. 460426. 460609 K. 460705. 460718. 460720. 460812 K 3. 460816 u. I. 460825. 460902 K 3. 460915. 460916. 461031. 461106
Guesont, Jordan 450818 K 4
Guevara, Antonio de 450900 K 8
Guiron le courtois, s. *Girone il cortese*
Günderode, Friedrich Casimir v. 460423 u. I. 460424A I. 461031A I
Gustavus Selenus, s. Braunschweig-Wolfenbüttel, Hz. August d. J. v.
Guyon, Louis 460915

Guzmán Conde-Duque de Olivares, Don
    Gaspar de   440426 K 7

Haccius, Georg   451019 K 6
Hagedorn, Friedrich v.   440724 K 3
Hagedorn, Johann   440724
Hager, Christoph Achaz   450100. 460915
Hahn, Katharina (v.), s. Werder
Hainhofer, Philipp   450526 K 3. 450817 K
    V 16. 460317 K 5. 460715 I u. II u. K 2.
    460804. 460819. 460908. 460915A I.
    461117 K 2
Halberstadt, kgl.-schwed. Statthalter des
    Bst.s
    s. Anhalt-Köthen, F. Ludwig v.
Halck, Hans Albrecht v.   451209 K 6.
    460125 K 1
Hall, Joseph, Bf. v. Norwich   450526
    K 3. 451101
Hallervord, Johann   450726 K 6
Ham   460915
Hamburg, Stadt (Senat u. Bürgerschaft)
    451019 K 6
Hammer, Johann   440130 K 3. 450127
    K 1. 450419. 450503. 450509. 450510.
    450614
Hammerstein, Hans Adam v.   450325 (?)
Hanau-Lichtenberg, Friedrich Casimir,
    Gf. v.   450417 K 4. 450818 K 4
Hanau-Münzenberg, Amalia Elisabeth,
    Gfn. v., s. Hessen-Kassel
Hanmann, Enoch   440324 K 23
Hansebund   450818 K 4
Hardenberg, Friedrich Asche v.   450220
    K 7. 460825 K 0
Harsdörffer,
    Carl Gottlieb   460620 K 5. 460718 K 7
    Georg Philipp   S. 9 ff., 12 f., 14 f., 16 f.,
        18 ff., 132 ff., 138. 440000 Q u. K 2 u.
        K I 1. 440100 K 4. 440129 K 5.
        440130 K 5. 440204. 440209 K 4.
        440209A. 440219 K 3. 440324 u. K I
        3. 440426 u. I. 440525 II. 440616 u. I
        u. II u. III. 440715. 440715A. 440724
        K. 440731 u. I u. II. 440824. 440826.
        440900. 441020. 441200 II u. K I.
        441201 K 0. 441205 K 4. 441216 K I
        0. 441223. 441226 K 3. 450100.
        450124 u. I. 450219 K 11. 450220 u.
        K II 0. 450308A. 450317A. 450319.
        450326. 450400. 450410. 450420.
        450500. 450504. 450504A. 450505.
        450505A. 450506A K 6. 450507 K 2.
        450526 K. 450529. 450611. 450613.
        450725. 450726 K 0. 450730. 450808
        u. I. 450817 u. I–III u. V Q. 450818
        u. K I. 450901. 450919. 450919A.
        450921. 450921A. 450923B K.
        450923C. 450927 u. I u. II. 451007
        K 2. 451008 K 5. 451019. 451028A.
        451101. 451209. 451217. 451219.
        451220 K. 460000A. 460112. 460120.
        460131. 460200. 460406. 460410.
        460414 K 3. 460426. 460609. 460610.
        460620. 460700 K 4. 460705 u. I u. II
        u. III. 460718. 460720. 460726.
        460803. 460812 K. 460816 u. I.
        460825 u. VI. 460902. 460912 u. I u.
        II. 460915. 460916. 461029 K 6.
        461031. 461031A K 3. 461104 III u.
        K. 461204A. 461213
    Georg Philipp d. J.   460620 K 5
    Georg Sigmund   460620 K 5
    Hans Siegemund   440731 K 1
    Johann Siegmund   460410 K 1
    Karl Gottlieb   460410 K 1
    Philipp Sigmund   460620 K 5
    Sigismund   440731
    Susanna, *Fürer v. Haimendorf
        460410 K 1. 460620 K 5
    Susanna d. J.   460620 K 5
    Susanna Helene   460620 K 5
    Susanna Maria   460620 K 5
Hartman, Andreas   440127 K 2
Hartranfft, Balthasar   440100 K 4
Harvey, William   450817 K 4
Haßler, Hans Leo   460819 K II 7
Hatzfeld, Herr zu Wildenberg, Gf. v. Glei-
    chen u. Hatzfeld, Melchior   440927
    K 1. 450419 K 3. 451030 K 2
Haustedt, Felix   460825 K 7 u. K III 0
Haxthausen, v.
    Johann   461106 K 11
    Tönnies Wulf   440100 K I 3
Hecht, Andreas   440525 K 1
Hees, Willem van   450400 K 11
Hegenich, Ehrenfried   440826 K 0
Hegenitz, Gottfried   440724

Heidfeld, Andreas   461106
Heigel, Heinrich Magnus   450817 K II 3
Heilbronner Bund (Consilium formatum)
    460104 K 0
Hein, Heinrich   440826 K 0
Heinsius, Daniel   440119
Heitfeld, Eberhard   451028A
Heldenbuch   440525 K II 0
Helle(n), Balthasar   450726
Helwig, Johann   S. 17. 450808 K I 0.
    450817 K II 3. 451101. 451209. 451217
    K 7
Helmont,
    Franciscus Mercurius van   440826 K 6
    Jan Baptista van   460715 II
Helwig (Helvigius), Andreas   451220
Helwig, Christoph   440826 K 6
Helwig, Johann   450400 K 6. 450504A
    K 4
Hendreich,
    Christoph   450726 K 6
    Judith, s. Zierenberg
    Peter   450726 K 6
Henel (v. Hennenfeld), Nicolaus   440826
    K 1
Henisch, Georg   S. 23 f. 440525 K II 0.
    450410 K 3. 450923B K 3. 450929.
    451028A. 451219. 460000 u. II. 461104
    K 5
Henninges, Hieronymus   450927 II
Henshaw, Joseph   460103
Herakles/ Hercules   S. 11. 450726 I.
    450817 IV. 450901
Herbert, Sir Edward   450818 K 3
Herbert of Cherbury, Baron Edward Herbert   460120A K 1
Herbert, Petr   460819 II
Herbst,
    Anton   450726 (?)
    Georg   450726 (?)
    Nikolaus   450726
Herkules, s. Herakles/ Hercules
Hermann,
    Daniel d. Ä.   450726 K 20
    Daniel d. J.   450726
    Michael   450726
    Zacharias d. Ä.   450726 K 20
Hermann, Hans Caspar   440525 K II 13.
    440616 K I 0. 450500 K 5. 450526 K 4

Hermann, Nikolaus   460819 II
Hermes, s. Merkur
Herminianen, s. Arminianer
Hermogenes   441020 K 14
Herodes   440824 K 7. 441223
Herodianos   440616
Hersfeld, Administrator der Abtei, s. Hessen-Kassel, Lgf. Wilhelm V. v.
Hesiod   450901 K 6
Hesius, s. Hees
Hess und Stein, v.
    Heinrich Adolf   450726 (?)
    Ursula, *Frankenberg-Ludwigsdorf
        450726 K 13
Hessen-Darmstadt, Lgf./ Lgfn. v.
    Eleonora, *Württemberg-Stuttgart,
        verw. Anhalt   450220 K 15. 450326
        K 4
    Georg I.   450220 K 15
    Georg II.   450220 K 15. 460715 K 7
Hessen-Eschwege, Lgf./ Lgfn. v.
    Christina, s. Braunschweig-Wolfenbüttel
    Eleonora   440715 Q
    Friedrich   440809A K 1. 441205 K 5.
        450305 K 1
Hessen-Kassel, Lgf./ Lgfn. v.
    Agnesa, s. Anhalt-Dessau
    Amalia Elisabeth, *Hanau-Münzenberg
        440809A K 1. 441205 K 5. 450305
        K 1. 450613. 450818. 450921 K 3.
        451209 K 7. 460120 K 9. 460125 u. I.
        460204 u. I. 460825 III u. K 7
    Hedwig, s. Holstein-Schaumburg
    Hedwig Sophia, *Brandenburg
        450613 K 5. 450919 K 4. 450921 K 3.
        460125 I. 460204
    Hermann IV., s. Hessen-Rotenburg
    Juliana, *Nassau-Siegen   450305 K I 3
    Moritz   440809A K 4. 450305 K 3.
        451220 K 8. 460125 K 3 u. K I 0.
        460204 K I 1. 461124 K 3
    Wilhelm V., Administrator der Abtei
        Hersfeld   440323 K 1. 440809A K 1.
        450305 K 1. 450317 K 4. 450818 K 4.
        450921 K 3. 460125 K 1. 460825 III.
        461124 K 3
    Wilhelm VI.   450613 K 5. 450818 K 4.

450919 K 4. 450921 K 3. 460125 u. I.
460204
Hessen-Rheinfels, Lgf. Ernst v.   441205
K 5. 450305 K 1 u. K I 3
Hessen-Rheinfels-Rotenburg, Lgf. v.
Christian   440809A K 1
Ernst   440809A K 1
Hessen-Rotenburg, Lgf./ Lgfn. v.
Hermann IV.   440715 Q. 440809A
K 1. 441205. 450126 K 4. 450127 K 3.
450220 K 10. 450305 K 1. 450317.
450317A. 450506 Q. 450507A.
450526 K 4
Kunigunde Juliana, *Anhalt-Dessau
441205
Heubel, Michael   440525 K II 13
Heyden, Jacob van der   440324 K I 1
Heyland, Polycarp   450818 K I
Hieronymus (Kirchenvater)   450818 K 20
Hildebrand, Conrad   450808 K I 0
Hilkja (Hohepriester)   460825
Hille, v. (Hill),
Carl Gustav S. 12, 25, 132. 440000 K I 1.
440130. 440204 K I 0. 440209A.
440310. 440310A K 2. 440323 u. I.
440616 K III 0. 440715A. 440723.
440723A. 440826 K. 441020. 441205
K 3. 450126. 450220 K 10. 450221.
450308. 450319. 450326 K 4. 450331
K 1. 450417 K 2. 450504A K 2.
450529 K 10. 450721. 450725 K 5.
450808 K I 0. 450919A K 4. 450922
K 2. 450923. 451008. 451028.
451028A. 451217 K 9. 460112 K 3.
460119. 460125 K 0. 460131. 460218
K 1. 460406 K 4. 460414 K 3. 460613
K 1. 460718. 460804 K 6. 460915A u.
I. 461029. 461106 u. II. 461117 Q u.
K 2. 461216 Q u. K 5
Helena Catharina, *Oeynhausen, v.
440323 K 1
James   451008 K 6
Philip Carl   440323 K 1
Hilling, Gregor   450817 K II 3
Hiob   450817 I
Hippokrates   450817 K 4 u. II
Hippolytus a Lapide, s. Chemnitz, Bogislav Philipp v.

Hirschberg, Valentinus Theocritus v.
(Pseud.), s. Mögling, Daniel
Hiskja, Kg. v. Juda   460825
Hitzfeld, Ludwig v.   450808
Hi(t)zler, Daniel   460819 II
Hl. Römisches Reich deutscher Nation, s.
hinter Römisches Reich
Hochstad, Johann Wilhelm   450817 K 4
Hodenberg, Bodo v.   450126 K 4. 450308
Hodický v. Hodice (Hoditz), Gf. Zdeněk
(Zdenko)   460204
Höe v. Höenegg, Matthias   461204 K 1.
461216 K 6
Hofmann, Caspar   450817 K 4
Hoffmann (v. Hoffmannswaldau), Christian   460000A K 0
Hofmeister, Johannes   440310B. 451030
K 2
Hohberg, Frh. Wolf Helmhard v.   440000
K 2 (?). 440826 K 0
Hohenlohe-Waldenburg-Bartenstein, Gf.
Christian v.   460423 I. 461031A I
Holstein-Schaumburg, Gf./ Gfn. v.
Elisabeth, *Lippe   441205 K 4
Hedwig, *Hessen-Kassel   441205 K 4
Jobst Hermann   441205 K 4
Homburg, Ernst Christoph   450504A K 4
Homeros   440119 K. 440313. 450901 K 6.
460819 K 6
Hondorf, Andreas   460804
Honold, Jacobus   460909 K 6
Höppner, Johann   451030 K 2
Horatius Flaccus, Quintus   440426 K I 0.
441020. 450818. 450901 K 12
Hornejus, Konrad   460700 K 5. 461204
K 1
Hornschuch, Hieronymus   450217 K 4
Horst, Nikolaus van der   460317 K 6
Hortleder, Friedrich   441010 K 0. 450507
K 2
Howell, John   450400 K 6. 451101
Hübner, Johann   460700 K 5
Hübner, Tobias   440119. 450900. 460825
Hubrig, Johann   440324 K 2. 450726 K 16
Hugenotten   440310 K 4. 441223 K 16.
450305 K 2. 450818 K. 461124 K 1
Hugo, Hermann   441223
Hülsemann, Johann   461204 K 1

Hund, Samuel   441020 K 1. 441223.
    450100 K 13. 450808 K I 0. 461104 K 2
Hünefeld(t), Andreas   440324 K 14.
    440724 K 12
Hunibaldus   440525 K II 0
Hunnius,
    Aegidius   450220 K 15
    Nicolaus   461216
Huswedel(ius), Johann(es)   440324
Hutten, Ulrich v.   440715A K 8
Hutter, Elias   450410 K 4
Huygens,
    Christian   450817 K III
    Constantijn   460103 K
Huyn van Geleen, Gf. Gottfried   S. 139
Hynitzsch, Ursula, s. Salfeld

Jacob, Christoph   451019
Jada   460825 K 1
Jain   440209 K 10. 440313 K 5. 440317
    K 4
Janus   440209. 440313 K 5. 440317
Japhet   440219 K 3. 440313 K 4. 440317.
    440715 K 6. 460912 I. 460915 K 11
Jason   461104 II
Javan   440317
Jeep, Johannes   460819 K II 7
Jelecký, Jan, s. Geletzky, Johannes
Jesaia   S. 10. 460825 u. III–VI
Jessey, Henry   450410 K 8
Jesuiten   450400 K 11. 450529 K 9.
    450806 K 2. 450817 K II 4. 450818 K 11.
    450927
Illo(w), Frh. Christian v.   440000 K II 8
Imhof, Hieronymus   450818 K 1
Imperiali, Giovan Vincenzo   450817
    K II 2
Job, s. Hiob
Johann von Capua   450305 K 5
Johannes (Apostel/ Evangelist)   S. 141
Jon, François du, s. Junius d. Ä., Franciscus
Jonsson, Arngrimur   460915 K 7
Joseph (von Nazareth)   450817. 451100
    K 5
Jotham   S. 22
Jouvenaeau, Johann   460303 K 7
Irenicus, Franciscus   440313 K 6. 450410
    K 3
Israelita, Paulus, s. Ric(c)ius, Paulus

Juda   460825 K 1
Juden   450410 K 8
Judith   450726
Jülich, Kleve u. Berg, Hz. v.
    s. Brandenburg, Kf. Georg Wilhelm v.
Junius d. Ä., Franciscus   450100 K I 7.
    460825
Junius, Hadrianus   440525 K II 0
Iuno/ Hera   450000A K 1. 450901 K 10.
    450927 II
Iuppiter/ Zeus   440313 K 5. 440731 K I 3.
    450000A K 1. 450817 II. 450901 K 5

Kalau, s. Calovius
Kalcheim gen. Leuchtmar,
    Anna Catharina, *Eckart   440826 K 3
    Gerhard Romilian v.   S. 9. 440826 K 3
Kalcheim gen. Lohausen, Wilhelm v.
    440130 K 2. 440525 K II 9. 450900.
    460825 K 6
Kalila wa-Dimna, s. Firenzuola, Agnolo
Kalliope   441200 I
Kammin, Bst. (Domkapitel)   450326 K 4
Kandake, Kgn.   460825
Kappell, Frh. Detloff v.   440816 u. I u. II
Keck, Johann Christian   S. 14. 440525 K
    II 0. 440616 K 0
Khusrōy I. Anōshagruwan   450305 K 5
Kieseling, Christian   440127 K 2
Kilian, Wolfgang   450219 K 6. 450319 K 9
Kinsky v. Wchinitz u. Tettau,
    Radslav, Herr   441223 K 16
    Wilhelm, Gf. v.   440000 II
Kircher, Athanasius   440715 K 5. 450817
    K III. 451101 K 13
Kirchner,
    Caspar   450726 K 4
    Martha, *Queisser   450726 K 4
Kirke (Circe)   460204 I
Klaj, Johann   S. 14. 440824. 441020 K 12.
    441200 K 3. 441201 K 0. 441223.
    441231A K 1. 450400 K 6. 450504.
    450504A K 4. 450505. 450808 K I 0.
    450927 II. 451217 K. 460000A K 0.
    460120. 461104 K 2
Klumpaeus, Hermann   450304 K 1
Knaudt, Peter   440130 K 3. 440310 K 1.
    440310B. 440323 K I 2. 450126 K 4.
    450127. 450317 K 2. 450417. 450419.

450503 K 1. 450507A K 1. 450509 K 1.
450510. 450614. 450711. 450800 u. I.
450905. 450922. 450923 K 2. 450923A
K 2. 450930. 451015. 451019. 451028B.
451119. 460206 u. I u. II. 460303.
460317 K 9. 460324. 460519. 460620B.
460703. 460708. 460714 K. 460810.
461023. 461031 K 6
Knesebeck, v. dem
    Franz Julius S. 12. 440130. 440204 K I 0. 440310. 440400 K 1. 440826 K 12. 450126. 450319. 450808 K I 0. 451217 K 9. 460112 K 3. 460119. 460613 K 0
    Hempo S. 9
    Levin 460204
    Thomas d. Ä. 460825 K 0
Knigge, Frh. Jodok Hilmar (v.) 440816 I u. II
Knipping, B. 441201 K 2
Knoch, (v.)
    Anna Dorothea, *Freyberg 450900 Q u. K 0. 461006 A
    Anne Amelie, *Börstel 461006
    Caspar Ernst 450730 K 2
    Christian Ernst 440927 K 1. 441010. 44123 K 4. 450410 K 22. 450420. 450504A K 2. 450613. 450730. 450900 K 0. 460423 K 1. 461006. 461029
    Hans Ludwig 450417. 460423 K 1
Knorr v. Rosenroth, Christian 440826 K 6
Koch, Ulrich 440715A K 8
Kolb v. Wartenberg, Johann Casimir 460423 u. I. 460424A I. 461031A I
Köler, Christoph, s. Colerus, Christophorus
Kolhans, Johann Heinrich 450220 K II 0
König, Reinhardus 441205 K 4
König, Sebastianus 450818 K I
König Deutsch (Theut/ Thuisco/ Tuisco) 440209 K 10. 440313 K 4. 441200 K I 4
Königsberger Kürbishütte S. 9, 14
Königsmannus, Robertus 450818 K I
Königsmarck, (Greve) Hans Christoph v. 440504 K 1. 440927 K 1. 450126. 450219 K 1. 450711 K 6. 450721 K 3. 450730 K 7. 460424. 460715. 460909 K 5

Köppen, Johann 440209 K 1
Kornfeld, Theodor 450808 K 1
Kospoth, Wilhelm v. 440100 K 4
Krage, Casimir Dietrich (v.) 461006 K 0
Kromayer, Johannes 450220 K 15
Krosigk, Juliana Ursula v., s. Werder
Krüger, David 440127 K 2
Kuefstein, v.
    Georg Adams, Gf. 440826 K 0
    Hans Ludwig, Frh. 451217 K 7. 460000A K 0
Küffer, Johann S. 14. 440525 K II 0. 461104 K 3
Kühne, Andreas 440130 K 3. 440310B K 2. 440824 K 8. 450124. 450127 K 1. 450507A K 3. 450930

L'Aubespine, Madeleine de 450900 K 4
La Mesnadière, Hippolyte Jules Pilet de 441020
La Mothe le Vayer, François de 460103 K 6
La Noue, François de 441223
La Ramée, Pierre de 450410 K 5
La Tour d'Auvergne, s. Bouillon, Hz. v.
Labadisten 451101 K 11
Lampadius, Jacobus S. 135
Lancelot, Nicolas 450326
Lange, Christian 450419 K 4
Lange, Ernst 450324 K 2
Langer, Franz (Franciscus) 440324
Larcaeus, Nicolaus 450817 K II 3
Lastevin, Hz. v., s. Wallenstein
Laubmair, Andreas 460819
Lauremberg, Peter 440324 K 1. 450806 K 2
Lazius, Wolfgang 450927 II
Le Clerq, Johann (Clericus) 450507A K 4
Ledesma, Antonio Colmenero de 450817 K II 3
Le Gendre Dame de Rivery, Marie 450900
Legell, Christian 450220 K 16. 450725 I
Lehndorf, Christoph v. S. 9. 460120A K
Leib, Johann 450220 K II 0
Leibniz, Gottfried Wilhelm 440616 K 0. 450308A K 4. 450929 T
Leibnüz, Friedrich 450220 K II 0

Leiningen-Dagsburg, Friedrich Emich zu Hartenburg, Gf. v.   460423. 460424A I
Leiningen-Westerburg, Gf. Philipp II. v. 460423 I. 461031A I
Leipzig, Stadt   450419 K 4 (Rat). 450509 (Rat). 450510 (Rat). 451030 K 2 (Konsistorium)
Lenthe, Jobst Heimart v.   S. 137f. 450800. 450930 K 4
Leone Ebreo   440826 K 6
Leopoldina, s. Academia Naturae Curiosorum
Leppin, Nicolaus   450304 K 1
Leslie (of Balquhain), Walter   440000 K II
Levius,
    Dorothea   450326 K 4
    Ernst, s. Croyengreiff
Lewenhaupt, Axel, Gf. v. Raspurg u. Falckenstein   440616 K II 1
Liebenau, Hans Christoph v.   450000A K 2. 450308A K 5
Liebesgott, s. Cupido
Liga, Hl. (Frankreich)   450818 K 9
Liga, katholische   S. 8
Lillie, Axel   450711 K 6. 450721 K 3
Limmer, Ambrosius Gottfried   451030
Limnäus, Johannes   450927 II
Lincoln, Bf. v.
    John, s. Williams
Lingelsheim, Georg Michael   S. 14
Linos   450901
Lippe, Sophia, v. der, s. Greiffencrantz
Lippe, Gfn. zur
    Elisabeth, s. Holstein-Schaumburg
    Sophia, s. Anhalt-Köthen
Lippe-Detmold, Maria Magdalena, *Waldeck-Wildungen, Gfn. zur   441205 K 4
Lipsius, Justus   440119. 450308A K 4. 450726 K 3. 450818 K 9
Lisieux, Bf. v.,
    s. Du Vair, Guillaume
Livius, Titus   450818. 460204 I
Löbl, Obrist   440000 K II 0
Lobwasser, Ambrosius   460825 u. K I 9
Lockhart, Sir William   450818 K 3
Lohausen, s. Kalcheim gen. Lohausen, Wilhelm v.
Londorp, Michael Caspar   440324 K 18
Longueville, s. Orléans

Loredano, Giovanni Francesco   S. 8. 440000 u. I u. III. 440209A K 3. 450817. 460000A. 460120 K 1
Lotichius, Johann   440100 K 4. 441205 K 4. 460414 K 3
Löwenhaupt, s. Lewenhaupt
Lübeck, Stadt (Rat u. Bürgerschaft)   450818 K 4
Lucifer   450726 I
Lucius, Jacobus   451000 K 1
Lucius, Ludwig   440426 K I 0. 450124 K 4. 450400 K 2
Ludolf, Hiob   440724 K 7
Lukas (Evangelist)   S. 141
Lukianos v. Samosata   440715A
Lüninck, Niclas Henrich (v.)   440816 u. I u. II
Luther, Martin   S. 18, 20, 22. 440219. 440313. 440525 II. 440616 K 0. 450326 K. 450410 K 3. 450722 K 3. 450726 K 9. 450806 K 2. 451001 K 5. 451008 K 2. 460131. 460200 K 1. 460720 K 3. 460804. 460819 II. 460825 u. K I 3 u. K II 0. 460902 K 3. 460915. 461204 K. 461216 K 3
Lütke, Markus v. der   440816 I u. II
Lütkemann, Joachim   461204 K 1

Machiavelli, Niccolò   440616 K 0. 450726 K 3
Machner,
    Maria   440324 K I 1
    Matthias   S. 142. 440324 K u. I. 440826 K 1. 450726. 460610 Q
Macrobius, Ambrosius Theodosius   440313 K 5
Madai   440317 K 4
Maestlin (Mästlin, Moestlin), Michael   450410 K 6
Magdeburg, Ebf. v. u. Administrator des Ebst.s,
    s. Sachsen-Weißenfels, Hz. August v.
Magdeburg, Stadt   460422 K 4
Magnus, Olaus   440525 K II 0. 460915 K 7
Magog   440317 K 4
Maja (Nymphe)   440731 I. 450927 I
Majoli, Simone   440715A
Maiolus, Abt v. Cluny   440715A K 8

Major, Elias d. Ä.   440324 K 7
Mair, Johann   460909 K 6
Makedonien, Kg. v., Alexandros III. d. Gr.   450927 II. 461204A
Malherbe, François de   S. 22. 441020. 450818 K 9
Malvezzi marchese di Castel Guelfo, Virgilio   440426. 440525 K II 9. 440826 K 3. 441226. 450326 K 4. 450900. 460103 K 6
Mannus   441200 I
Manso, marchese di Villa Lago, Giovanni Battista   450817 u. II u. K III. 450919A. 451217
Manzini, N. N.   441020
Marcello, Lorenzo   450817 K 7
Marconnet, Abraham   440100. 441020 K 1. 460714 K 4. 460908 K 5
Maria (die Hl. Jungfrau)   451100 K 5
Maria Magdalena   451100 K 6
Marinella, Lucrezia   451101
Marino, Giambattista   450817 K II
Mario, Johann v. (zu Gammersleve/ Gammanotorn)   441205 K 3. 460103 K 1
Markus (Evangelist)   S. 141
Marot, Clément   450901 K 15
Marranen   450410 K 8
Mars/ Ares   440429. 461104 IV
Marsilius,
  Johann   440324 K 9
  Katharina, s. Tscherning
Martialis, Marcus Valerius   440426 K I 0. 441020 K 3
Martini, Jacob   440426 K I 0. 450124 K 4. 450400 K 2. 450507 K 2
Martinius, Matthias   460825 u. K III 0
Marzilly, sieur de (Pseud.), s. Sorel
Mathesius, Johannes   460819 II
Matthäus (Evangelist)   S. 141, 146
Mazarin (Mazarini), (Kd.) Jules (Giulio)   450818 K. 451217 K 9. 460103
Mechovius, Joachim   440209 K 1. 450326 K 2. 451217 K 10. 460609 K 3
Mecklenburg, Sophia, Hzn. v., s. Dänemark
Mecklenburg-Güstrow, Hz./ Hzn. v.
  Anna Sophia, s. Schlesien
  Christina Margaretha, s. Mecklenburg-Schwerin
  Eleonora Maria, *Anhalt-Bernburg   450304. 451008 K 6. 451028. 460718 K 1. 460825 K 0
  Gustav Adolph   450304 K 1. 451028 K 8
  Johann Albrecht II., Administrator des Bst.s Ratzeburg   450304 K. 450927 K II 9. 451008 K 6. 451028 K 8
  Sophia Elisabeth, s. Braunschweig-Wolfenbüttel
Mecklenburg-Schwerin, Hz./ Hzn. v.
  Adolph Friedrich I.   S. 136. 450304 K. 450927 K II 9. 451008 K 6
  Christian (Ludwig I.)   451028 K 8
  Christina Margaretha, *Mecklenburg-Güstrow, verw. Sachsen-Lauenburg   S. 136. 451028
  Maria Catharina, *Braunschweig-Lüneburg-Dannenberg   S. 136
Mela, Pomponius   450927 II
Melanchthon, Philipp   440715A K 8. 450326 K
Melissus, Paulus   460131. 460200 K 1
Menasseh ben Israel   450410
Mencelius, Johannes   450220 K 5
Merckel, Johannes   440826 K 3
Mercy, Frh. Franz v.   S. 139. 450905 K 3
Merian,
  Caspar   450905 K 4
  Margaretha, s. Götze
  Matthäus d. Ä. Vgl. *Theatrum europaeum*; Sachregister: Gesellschaftsbuch FG: GB 1629/30 u. GB 1646   S. 25, 134, 137 ff. 440130. 440310 K 1. 440310B K 2. 440323 K 3 u. K I 2. 440723 K 3. 440723A. 450126 K 4. 450127. 450301 K 3. 450317 K 3. 450331 K 2 u. K I 1. 450417. 450509. 450510 K 3. 450614. 450711. 450721. 450800. 450817 K 16. 450905. 450922. 450923. 450923A. 450930. 451001. 451015. 451019. 451028. 451028B. 451119. 460206 u. K I 1. 460218 K 2. 460303. 460317. 460324. 460519. 460613 K 5. 460620B. 460703. 460708. 460714 K. 460715 I u. II. 460810. 460909 K 5. 460915A I. 460916. 461023. 461031
Merkur/ Hermes   440426 I. 440731 K I.

441200 II. 441223. 450400 K 10. 450817
  II. 450927 I. 460912 I
Mersenne, Marin   450817 K III
Mesech   440317 K 4
Mesmes comte d'Avaux, Claude de
  450818 K 4
Mesmes, Henri II. de   460103 K 6
Meuderlinus, Petrus   460909 K 6
Meyer, Conrad   460804 K 1
Meyfart, Johann Matthaeus   440426 K I 3.
  460317 K I 2. 461216
Milagius, Martinus   S. 7, 10. 440209 K 1.
  440324 K 22. 440927 K 1. 441223 K 20.
  450124 I. 450220 K 1. 450326 K 4.
  450420. 450504A. 450505. 450721 K 3.
  451101 K 14. 460422 K 4. 460825 u. I u.
  II u. III u. IV u. V u. VI
Milchling von Schönstadt, Carl   440324
  K 23. 440724 K 13
Millenaristen   450410 K 8
Milton, John   440119 K 9. 450817 K II 4
Minerva, s. Pallas (Athene)
Mnemosyne   450901. 450927 II
Mochinger, Johannes   440324
Mockel, Friedrich Reichard   440616 II
Mögling, Daniel   450410 K 6
Molinaeus, Petrus, s. Du Moulin, Pierre
  d. Ä.
Moller,
  Eberhard   S. 138. 450504A K 4
  Vincent   S. 138. 450504A K 4
Molli, Clemente   450817 K 7
Momus   440204 I. 440426 I
Monseigneur Canard   461104 K 3
Montaigne, Michel Eyquem sieur de
  S. 11. 450818. 451101 K 8
Montalvan, Juan Perez de   441020
Montemayor, Jorge de   441020. 450400
  K 6. 451217. 460120
Montenay, Georgette de   451101 K 10
More, Thomas, s. Morus
Moreau, René   450817 K II 3
Moro, Vincenzo   450817 K 7
Morsius, Joachim   440724 K 6. 440826
  K 0
Mortaigne dit de Pottelles, Gaspard Corneille   440310B K 4. 451030
Morus, Thomas   440715A K 8
Mosbach, Georg Ernst   451030 K 2

Moscherosch,
  Johann Michael   S. 9 ff., 14 f., 16, 22.
    440204 K I 0. 440324 K 22. 440525 u.
    II. 440616 u. I u. II. 440715A K 0.
    440724 K 4. 440826 K 4. 440900.
    441020 K 1. 441223. 450000 K 3.
    450100. 450124 K 6. 450326 K 4.
    450500. 450504A. 450505. 450505A.
    450526. 450613. 450725. 450730.
    450808 K I 0. 450817. 450818 u. I.
    450901. 450919 K 2. 450919A.
    450923B K 4. 451101. 451209.
    451217. 460120. 460406. 460426.
    460609. 460620. 460705. 460718.
    460726. 460825 K 3. 460829 u. I.
    460916. 461020. 461031. 461104 u. II
  Quirinus   440616 K 0
Moser, N. N.   440324 K 2
Moses   450901
Mülbe, Johann Philipp   S. 145. 440616 K I
  0. 460406 K 8
Müller, Gottfried   440209 K 1. 440824
  K 10. 450126 K 11. 450529 K 10.
  460422. 460424. 460825 K 0. 460915A.
  461106
Müller, Hans d. Ä.   451019 K 0
Müller, Henning   440100 K 4. 451000 K 1
Müller, Johannes   461216 K 3
Münchhausen, v.
  Kurt   461006 K 5
  Maria Catharina, s. Westerholt
Münnich, v.
  Elisabeth, *Brincken   461006 K 5
  Johann   461006 K 5
Münster, Sebastian   450927 II
Münsterberg und Oels, Hz./ Hzn. v.
  Anna Elisabeth   440324 K 5
  Anna Magdalena, *Pfalz-Veldenz
    440324 K 5
  Anna Ursula, *Reibnitz   440324 K 5
  Heinrich Wenzel v.   440324 K. 450726
    A
  Karl Friedrich   440324 A u. K 1
Musaios (Musaeus)   450901
Musen, die   S. 13. 440204 I. 441200 u. I u.
  II. 441201 K 2. 441223 K 2. 450202.
  450400. 450529. 450817 K II 3. 450901.
  450927 I u. II. 460112. 460610. 460912
  u. I u. II. 461104 I–III

Mylius, Christoph   440100 K 4

Nadal, Géronimo   450927 K 1. 460804 K 1
Nairn of Mukkersy, John   451030 K 2
Nanni, Giovanni (Annius von Viterbo)
    440209 K 10. 440317 K 4
Nappelius, s. Appelius
Nassau-Dillenburg, s. auch Oranien
    Georg Ludwig, F. v.   450500 K 2
Nassau-Hadamar, F./ Fn. v.
    Johann Ludwig   461106 K 9
    Johanna Elisabeth, s. Anhalt-Harzgerode
Nassau-Saarbrücken-Ottweiler, Gf. Johann Ludwig v.   460423 I. 461031A I
Nassau-Siegen, Juliana, Gfn. v., s. Hessen-Kassel
Natalis, Hieronymus, s. Nadal, Géronimo
Nathan   S. 22
Nauclerus, Johannes   440209 K 10
Naudé (Naudaeus), Gabriel   450526 K 3.
    450817 K IV 5. 450901 K 13. 451217
    K 9. 460103
Neander,
    Paul d. Ä.   440324
    Paul d. J.   440324 K 7
Neidhart   440100 I. 461104 II
Nepos, Cornelius   440616
Nessel, Martin   S. 12. 450319 K 9. 450722.
    450806
Neu-Arianer   440715A K 5
Neuberger, Theophilus   440809A K 4.
    450317
Neuhausen, Barthold, s. Nihus(ius)
Neumark, Georg   440616 K 0. 451008 K 5
Nicolai, Christoph   450817 K II 3
Nicolai, Philipp   460825 K II 0
Nifo, Agostino   450817 K V 9
Nihus(ius), Barthold   450919A K 7
Nikolaus v. der Flüe   S. 11. 450818
Ninus   440209 K 10
Noah   440209. 440219 K 3. 440313.
    440317. 441200 K I 2. 460915
Noel, Sir Edward   461020 K 5
North, Sir Thomas   450305 K 5
Norwich, Bf. v.
    Joseph, s. Hall
Nürnberg, Stadt   460410 K 1

Nüßler, Bernhard Wilhelm   440119.
    460610 K 10
Nutius, Martinus   460804 K 1
Nymphen   440100 I. 450927 I

Observations sur la vie et les services de M. le Cardinal Duc de Richelieu   460714
Oeagrius, s. Orpheus
Oedipus   450000A K 1
Oels, s. Münsterberg und Oels
Oelschlegel, Melchior   460204 K 7
Oeynhausen, v.
    Catharina Hedwig, s. Brincken
    Helena Catharina, s. Hille
    Moritz   461006 K 4
Oldenburg, Gf. Anthon Günther v.
    450818 K 4. 460423 K 1
Oldenburg-Delmenhorst, Gf./ Gfn. v.
    Christian IX.   440323 K 3. 450126 K 4.
        450818 K 4. 460317 K 6
    Sibylla Elisabeth, *Braunschweig-Dannenberg   461204 K 1
Olearius, Gottfridus   440504 K 1
Olivares, Don Gaspar de Guzmán Conde-Duque de, s. Guzmán
Olorinus, Johannes   460808 K 1
Onam   460825 K 1
Opitz, Martin (v. Boberfeld)   S. 9, 11, 14,
    17. 440119. 440324 K u. I. 440400K I 0.
    440525 II. 440616 K 5. 440715A. 440724
    K 13. 440900 K 1. 441020 K 3. 441200
    K 3. 441216 u. K I 0. 450124 K 6.
    450507 K 2. 450726. 450806. 450818
    K 13. 450901 K. 451217 K 7. 460104.
    460119 K 3. 460200A. 460424 K 7.
    460610 K 10. 460819 II. 460825 u. K II
    0. 460909. 461031 K 6. 461104 K 2
Oranien, F. v.; Nassau-Dillenburg, Gf. v.
    Friedrich Heinrich, F., Statthalter Hollands etc.   460103
    Moritz, F., Statthalter Hollands etc.
        460103 K 4
    Wilhelm II., F., Statthalter Hollands etc.
        460103 K 3
Orléans, Henri II. d', duc de Longueville
    450818 K 4
Orpheus   450901. 461204A
Osiander,
    Lucas d. Ä.   450100 K I 7

Lucas d. J.   450410 K 6
Osnabrück, Bf. v.
    Franz Wilhelm, Kd., s. Wartenberg
Ossoliński, F. Jerzy (Georg)   450817 II
Österreich, Ehz. v. Vgl. (Hl.) Römisches Reich, Spanien, Böhmen
    Ferdinand (II.), s. (Hl.) Römisches Reich
    Ferdinand (III.), s. (Hl.) Römisches Reich
    Matthias, s. (Hl.) Römisches Reich
Osthof, Georg (Jürgen) Conrad   S. 17. 441223. 450400 K 6. 450504A K 4. 450808 K I 0. 451101. 451209. 451217. 461104 K 2
Otfrid v. Weißenburg   440525 K II 0
Otten,
    Rosina, s. Stahl
    Sebastian   440426 K 1
Ovidius Naso, Publius   440313 K 5. 440324 K 3. 450818
Owen (Ovenus),
    Charles   461020 K 5
    John   461020
    Roger, Sir   461020 K 5
Oxenstierna, Axel zu Kimito u. Nynäs, Friherre/ Greve (seit 1645 Greve Oxenstierna af Södermöre)   440000 K I 1. 440616 K II 1

Pachelbel, Johann   440000 K II 1
Page (Hund)   450325
Pallas (Athene)/ Minerva   441200 II. 441201 K 2. 450000A K 1. 450726 I. 450808 I. 450927 I u. II
Pallavicino, Ferrante   450526. 450817 K 7. 460103 K 6
Pan   451100 K 1
Pantagruel (Pseud.), s. Hessen-Kassel, Lgf. Wilhelm V. v.
Pantagruel (lit. Figur)   440826 K 10
Paolo, Giovanni Andrea di   450817 K II 2
Pappenheim, Gottfried Heinrich, Herr v. Treuchtlingen, Gf. u. Herr v., Reichserbmarschall   S. 131. 440100 K I 2
Pappus, Johann   460819
Papst
    Alexander VII.   450817 K 20
    Urban VIII.   450817 K II 9 u. K IV 5

Paracelsus (Philippus Aureolus Paracelsus, Theophrastus Bombastus v. Hohenheim)   440826 K 10. 450818 K 6
Paris, Parlement   450818 K
Pascal (Paschal/ Pascale/ Pasquali), vicomte de La Queute et Dargny, Charles (Carlo)   S. 11. 450818
Pasquier (Paschasius), Étienne (Stephanus)   S. 11. 450818
Patin, Charles   450817 K 9
Paulli,
    Heinrich   460610 K 8
    Simon   460610
Paulus (Apostel)   S. 141
Pawel(-Rammingen), v.
    Andreas II   450818 K 2
    Carl   450818 K 2
    Carl Friedrich   450818 K 2. 460423 u. I. 460424A u. I. 461031A I
    Georg Friedrich   450818 K 2. 460423 u. I. 460424A u. I. 461031A I
    Johann Friedrich   450818
Pax   440429
Peblis, v.
    Georg Hans   450526
    Juliana Ursula, s. Werder
Pegasus   S. 12. 450529 K 3. 460912 I u. II
Pegie, Martin   460808 K 1
Pegnesischer Blumenorden   S. 14 f. 440100 K I 3. 440824 K 7. 441216 K I 0. 441223 K. 450400 K 6. 450504 K 4. 450505 K 5. 450808 K I 0. 450817 K 9 u. K II 3. 450901 K 9. 451101 K. 451209 K 5. 451217 K. 460406 K 4. 460410 K 1. 461104 K 2
Peisker, Johann   440724 K 7
Pengerode, Heinrich, s. Bengerath
Pérez, Alonso   450400 K 6. 451217 K 7. 460120
Pergesen, Jakob   460303 K 7
Persien, Khusrōy I. Anōshagruwan, Kg. v.   450305 K 5
Peterson, Theodor   450000A K 2
Petrarca, Francesco   441020. 450817 K IV 11 u. K V 17. 450900. 460825 K 19. 460915 K 6
Petri, Sandro   450900
Petrus (Evangelist)   S. 141
Pfalz-Birkenfeld (u. Bischweiler)

Christian I.   461031A K I 10
Georg Wilhelm   460423 I. 461031A I
Pfalz-Simmern
  Dorothea, s. Anhalt-Dessau
  Elisabeth Charlotta, s. Brandenburg
  Friedrich V., Kf. der Pfalz, s. Böhmen, Kg. Friedrich I. v.
  Karl Ludwig, Kf. der Pfalz (1648)   460104 K 0
  Ludwig Philipp, Pgf.   S. 14. 441223 K 4. 450529 K 10. 460104. 460321. 460422. 460423 u. I. 460424. 460424A u. I. 461026. 461031A u. I. 461106 K 11. 461206
  Maria Eleonora, *Brandenburg, Pgfn.   461026
Pfalz-Sulzbach
  August   460120A K 1
  Johann Ludwig   460423. 460424A I
  Sabina, s. Wartenberg
Pfalz-Veldenz(-Lützelstein), Anna Magdalena, s. Münsterberg und Oels
Pfalz-Zweibrücken
  Friedrich   460423 u. I. 460424A I. 461031A I
  Johann II.   450818 K 2. 460120A K 1
  Karl Gustav (Z.-Kleeburg), s. Schweden, Kg. Karl X. Gustav v.
Pfann, Johann   S. 141
Pfau, Caspar   440816 u. I u. II. 440927 K 1
Pfinzing, Melchior   460317
Pfisterus, Tobias   460909 K 6
Pforr, Anton v.   450305 K 5
Philander von Sittewald (Pseud.), s. Moscherosch, Johann Michael
Philaretes Cosmopolita, Anastasius (Pseud.), s. Morsius, Joachim
Philippus (Diakon)   460825 K 1
Philomela   450927 I
Phoebus, s. Apollo
Piccolomini d'Aragona, Octavio (Duca d'Amalfi), F. v.   440000 K I u. K II 0
Pico della Mirandola, Giovanni   440826 K 6
Pierinnen, die. Vgl. Musen   441200 I. 441223 K 11
Pietri, Francesco de'   450817 K II 2
Pilpay, s. Bidpai

Pindaros   440525. 440715A K 1
Pirckheimer, Willibald   440715A K 8
Pisa, Ebf. v.
  Carlo Antonio, s. Pozzo
Piscator, Johannes   450410 K 5
Pithou (Pithaeus), Pierre (Petrus)   450818 K 9
Platon   S. 9, 19. 440324 K I 2. 440715A. 440826 K 11. 441020 K 10. 450901. 461204A
Pléiade, La   450818 K 11. 450901 K 15
Plinius, Gaius P. Secundus d. Ä.   440119 K 9. 440715A K 8. 450408 K 3. 450927 II. 461204A K 1
Plutarchos   441223 K 16. 461204A K 5
Polen, Wladislaus IV. Sigismund, Kg. v.   450726 K 17
Polhelm, v.
  Johann   450818 K 4
  Tilmann   450305 K 1. 450818
  Winand   440809A. 441205. 450305 u. I. 450317. 450317A. 450506. 450507A K 1. 450526. 450818 K 4
Politiques, Les   S. 11. 450818 K
Polo, Gaspar Gil   441020. 450400 K 6. 451217 K 7. 460120
Pommern, Hz./ Hzn. v.
  Agnes, s. Anhalt
  Anna, s. Croy
  Bogislaw XIV.   450326 K 4. 460204 K 7. 460613 K 1
  Clara, s. Braunschweig-Wolfenbüttel
  Hedwig, *Braunschweig-Wolfenbüttel   460613 K 1. 460714 K 1
  Ulrich, Bf. v. Cammin   460613 K 1
Pommern-Stettin, Hz./ Hzn. v.
  Philipp II.   460715 II
  Sophia, *Schleswig-Holstein-Sonderburg   460715 II
Pommern-Wolgast, Hz./ Hzn. v.
  Maria, *Sachsen   450326 K 4
  Philipp I. v.   450326 K 4
Pona, Francesco   451101 K 13
Popp, Johann   460808 K 1
Porta, Giovanni Battista della   450817 K 4 u. K II 2
Portugal, Kg. v. Vgl. Spanien
  Philipp I., s. Spanien, Kg. Philipp II.
  Philipp III., s. Spanien, Kg. Philipp IV.

Postel, Guillaume   440826 K 6
Pozzo, dal
    Andrea   450817 K IV 5
    Carlo Antonio, P. della Cisterna di Biella, Ebf.   450817 IV
    Cassiano   450817 IV. 450919A K 11
Praetorius, Michael   460819 K 7
Prasch, Johann Ludwig   440616 K 0
Prätorius, Otto   460825 K 16
Press(e), Johann   440310B. 450124 K 2. 450417. 450509 K 1. 451030 K 2
Priamos   440313 K 6
Prometheus   440426 I. 450817 IV
Prüschenk v. Lindenhofen, Zacharias   441010. 441226A K 5. 450220 K 7. 450400. 450529 K 10. 451119 K 5
Pseudo-Bernhard, s. Bernhard v. Clairvaux
Pseudo-Berosus, s. Nanni, Giovanni
Ptolemäer, Kg.
    Ptolemaios II. Philadelphos   460912 K 1
    Ptolemaios VI. Philometor   460912
Pufendorf, (Frh.) Samuel (v.)   440616 K 0
Puteanus, s. Dupuy

Quedlinburg, Stadt (Rat u. Bürgerschaft)   451028A K 2
Queisser,
    Marcus   450726 (?)
    Martha, s. Kirchner
    Zacharias   450726 (?)
Quevedo Villegas y Santibañez, Francisco Goméz de   S. 145. 450500 K 5. 450817 K II 2
Quintilianus, Marcus Fabius   440715A K 6. 450901 K 12. 460915. 460916
Quistorp,
    Johann d. Ä.   450726
    Johann d. J.   450726

Rabelais, François   450901 K 15
Radziwill, Boguslaw, F.   450326 K 4
Rahne (Rahnius), Heinrich   440324
Ramus, Petrus, s. La Ramée, Pierre de
Randow, Jost Andreas v.   450408 K 3. 450900
Rappoltstein, Eberhard, Gf. v.   S. 13. 440724 K 4
Rathgeb, Jakob   441223 K 16

Ratke (Ratichius), Wolfgang   S. 10, 16, 18. 440219 K 2. 440525 K II 9. 450217 K 3. 450410 K 5. 450420 K 7. 450507A K 3. 450923B K 2. 460902 K 2
Ratzeburg, Administrator des Bst.s
    s. Braunschweig-Wolfenbüttel, Hz. August d. J. v.
    s. Mecklenburg-Güstrow, Hz. Johann Albrecht II. v.
Rauch, Johann   450800 K 3
Raumer, Georg   460825 K 0
Rauschard,
    Felix   450220 K II 0
    Felix Hannibal   450220 K II 0
    Felix Ludwig   450220 K II 0
Rebenlein, Jakob   440724
Refuge, Eustache de   440100 K 4
Reibnitz, v., s. Münsterberg und Oels, Hz. v.
Reiche, Andreas   440323 I
Reinhard, Johann Georg   460315
Reinhardt, Sebastian   460422 K 4
Rembrandt, s. Rijn
Remonstranten, s. Arminianer
Renaudot, Théophraste   S. 15. 450818 K 12
Reuchlin, Johannes   440826 K 6. 450410 K
Reyher, Andreas   440119 K 1. 450217 K 1
Rhetorica ad Herennium   450901 K 12
Riccio, Onofrio   450817 IV Q u. K IV 4
Richel,
    Johann d. Ä.   450726 K 8
    Johann d. J.   450726 K 8
Richelieu, Kd. Armand Jean du Plessis (duc) de   S. 11, 15. 440000 K II 0. 440119 K 9. 440324 K 22. 450818. 460103 K 6
Richter, Christian (I.)   S. 143
Richter, Georg Andreas   450726 K 6
Ric(c)ius, Paulus (Paolo Riccio)   440826 K 6
Rijn, Rembrandt Harmenszoon van   450410 K 8
Ringhieri, Innocenzio   450817 K 9
Rist, Johann   S. 14 f., 17 f., 135. 440204 K I 0. 440324 u. I. 440525 II. 440724. 440900. 441020 K 1. 441200 K 3. 441201 K 4. 441216 u. I. 441223 K 16. 450100.

450410 K 12. 450504A K 4. 450726 K 0.
450806 K 9. 450808 K I 0. 451101 K 7.
460000A K 0. 460315. 460610. 460812
K 1. 460825. 460829 u. I. 461020.
461104 u. I–IV. 461117 K 1
Ritmar, Johann   441011 K 4. 451000
Ritz, Paul, s. Ric(c)ius, Paulus
Rivery, de, s. Le Gendre
Rivet, André   460103. 460120A K 1
Rivey, Pierre de la   450305 K 5. 450317A K 4
Rocco, Antonio   450817 K 7
Rochow, v.
  Hans   450400. 450529 K 10
  Hans Zacharias   451008 K 6
Roemers Visscher, Anna   451101
Rojas, Francisco de   441020
Römisches Reich, Ks.
  Antoninus Pius, Titus Aurelius Fulvus Boionis Arrius   S. 11. 450901
  Augustus   S. 11. 450901. 460912 K I 3. 461204A
  Domitianus, Titus Flavius   450901 K 14. 461204A K 4
  Hadrianus   450901 K 14. 461204A
  Marcus Aurelius Antoninus   461204A (?)
  Nero   S. 11. 450901
  Nerva, Marcus Cocceius   S. 11. 450901. 461204A
  Traianus   461204A
Hl. Römisches Reich,
  Ferdinand II., Kg., Ks.   440000 K I 3. 440100 K I 2. 440209A K 4. 440324 K 1
  Ferdinand III., Kg., Ks.   S. 7 f. 440100 K 3. 440130 K 2. 440324 A. 440324 K I 3. 440927. 441223 K 20. 450326 K 2. 450808 K 5. 461104 I–III u. K 2
  Karl der Große, Ks.   S. 16. 440525 K 16. 441231A. 450818. 460120A K 1. 460720 K 3. 460915 K 13
  Karl V. (Kg. Karl I. v. Spanien), Ks.   450818
  Leopold I., Kg., Ks.   440000 K II 0. 450806 K 2
  Margaretha Theresia, Ksn., *Spanien   450806 K 2

Matthias, Kg., Ks.   440000 K II 0. 460204 K I 1
Maximilian I., Ks.   460317. 461031 K 6
Maximilian II., Kg., Ks.   460819 II
Rudolf I., Ks.   440525 II
Hl. Römisches Reich, Reichsstände/ Reichstag
  Frankfurt a. M. (Reichstag 1612)   S. 18
  Frankfurt a. M. (Reichsdeputationstag 1643 ff.)   440927 K 8. 450504A K 1
  Regensburg (1640/41)   460825 K 0
  Regensburg (1652/53)   460825 K 0
Hl. Römisches Reich, Reichskreise/ Kreisstände/ Kreistage
  450905 K 4
  Fränkischer Kreis
    Fränkische Reichsritterschaft   450400 K 13
  Niedersächsischer Kreis   440927 K 8. 441223 K 20
  Obersächsischer Kreis   440927 K 8
Rompler v. Löwenhalt, Jesaias   S. 13 f. 440525 K 1 u. K II 15. 440616 K III 0. 440724. 441223. 450308A. 450410. 450806. 450808 K I 0. 460829. 461104 K
Romulus   441226
Ronsard, Pierre de   441020. 450901 K 15. 460915
Rosel(ius), Adolph   440129 K 5. 441201 K 0. 450308A K 7. 450410 K. 450808 K. 450921 K 2. 460131 K 5. 460812 K 2
Rosenkreuzer   440826 K. 461117 K 1
Roseo da Fabriano, Mambrino (Collenuccio Costo)   450900 K 8
Rossi, Bastiano de'   S. 9. 450919A K 7. 460217
Roth, Rudolph   460909 K 6
Rouen, Parlement   450818 K 10
Ruess, Hanns (v.)   460206
Rumpf (Rumph), Christian   460103
Ryssel, Christian v.   460103 K 6

Saavedra Fajardo, Diego de   440715
Sabatius, Kg.   440209 K 10
Sacer, Gottfried Wilhelm   460812 Q
Sachs, Hans   450000 K 5. 461104 K 3
Sachse,
  Daniel   S. 17. 440209 K 1. 440323 K 6. 440809A K 6. 441205. 450126.

450127 K 4. 450221. 450308 K 6.
450721. 460103 K 1. 460119. 460718
K 3
Elisabeth 450127 K 4
Sachsen, Hz./ Hzn., Kf./ Kfn. v.
August, Kf. 460613 K 3
Elisabeth, s. Sachsen-Altenburg
Johann, Kf., „der Beständige" 450326
Johann Georg I., Kf. 440927 K.
450711 K 6. 451030 K 2. 460321 K 2.
461124. 461206 K 3
Margaretha, *Anhalt 450326
Maria, s. Pommern-Wolgast
Sachsen-Altenburg, Hz./ Hzn. v.
Elisabeth, *Braunschweig-Wolfenbüttel, verw. Sachsen 451008. 460718 K 1
Johann Philipp 451008 K 6
Sachsen-Coburg, Hz./ Hzn. v.
Johann Adolf 440100 K 4
Maria Elisabeth, *Braunschweig-Wolfenbüttel, verw. Sachsen-Eisenach 440100 K 5. 460613
Sachsen-Eisenach, Hz./ Hzn. v.
Adolf Wilhelm 440100 K 5. 450220 u. I. 450301. 450725 I
Albrecht 450220 K II 0. 450725 I (?)
Johann Georg I. 450220 u. I. 450301. 450725 I
Maria Elisabeth, s. Sachsen-Coburg
Sachsen, Engern u. Westfalen, s. Sachsen-Lauenburg
Sachsen-Gotha, Ernst I. „der Fromme",
Hz. v. S. 137. 440127 K 1. 450126 K 4.
450217. 450220. 450224. 450301 K 3.
450504 K 10. 450725 K I 7. 450800 K 4.
450808 K 5. 461204 K 1
Sachsen-Jena, Bernhard, Hz. v. 450220 u.
I u. K II 0. 450301. 450725 I
Sachsen-Lauenburg, s. hinter Sachsen-Zeitz
Sachsen-Weimar, Hz./ Hzn. v.
Albrecht, s. Sachsen-Eisenach
Bernhard 450220 K II 0
Dorothea Maria, s. Sachsen-Zeitz
Eleonora Dorothea, *Anhalt-Dessau
S. 8. 450220 u. I. 450301
Ernst I., s. Sachsen-Gotha
Friedrich 450126 K 11. 450220 u. I.
450301. 450529 K 10. 451015 K 2.
461106
Johann Ernst (Sohn Hz. Wilhelms IV.)
450220 u. I. 450301
Johann Ernst d. J. (Bruder Hz. Wilhelms IV.) 451015 K 2
Wilhelm IV. S. 8, 27, 33. 440127 K 1.
440426 K 2. 440616 K 0. 440826 K 0.
440927. 441010 K. 441223 K 4.
450126 K. 450220 u. K I 1 u. K II 0.
450224 K 1. 450301. 450317 K 9.
450326. 450410 K 22. 450504 K 10.
450529 K 10. 460103 K 0. 460423
K 1. 461006 K 0
Wilhelmine Eleonora 450220 I
Sachsen-Weißenfels, August, Hz. v., Administrator des Ebst.s Magdeburg
S. 27, 33. 440130. 441226 Q u. K 0.
441226A Q u. K 0. 441231 K 7. 450504.
450506A K 5. 450507 K 1. 460422 K 4.
461206 K 3
Sachsen-Wittenberg, Hz. Bernhard III. v.
450326 K 6
Sachsen-Zeitz, Hz./ Hzn. v.
Dorothea Maria, *Sachsen-Weimar
450220 I
Moritz 450220 K I 2
Sachsen-Lauenburg, Hz./ Hzn. v.
August 460808 K 2. 461124 K 5
Christina Margaretha, s. Mecklenburg-Schwerin
Franz II. 460808 K 2
Franz Albrecht S. 136. 450800. 451028
K 8. 461124 K 5
Franz Carl 460808. 461124
Franz Erdmann 450529 K 10. 460315
K 3. 460808 K 2. 461124
Franz Heinrich 460808 K 2. 461124
K 5
Julius Heinrich 460808 K 2. 461124
Maria, *Braunschweig-Wolfenbüttel
460808 K 2
Rudolf Maximilian 460808 K 2.
461124 K 5
Sadeler, Johann 440715 K 4
Sailer, Daniel 460715 K II 4
Saint-Amant, Marc Antoine de Gérard de
441020
Saint-Gelais, Mellin de 450901 K 15

Salfeld,
   Christoph d. Ä. 440127 K 1. 441231 K 6. 450504 K 9
   Ursula, *Felsecker, verw. Hynitzsch, verw. Bißmarck 441231 K 6
Sallustius Crispus, Gaius 450726 K 3. 461006 K 13
Salmasius, Claudius, s. Saumaise, Claude de
Salomo 440715 K 9. 450304. 450901 K 7
Saluste sieur Du Bartas, Guillaume de 440119 K 2. 450400 K 11. 450900. 460909
Salvianus Massiliensis 460915
Salviati, Leonardo 450817 K IV 11
Salvius, Johan Adler S. 138
Samuel (Jude) 451019
Sanctius, Franciscus 450410 K 4
Sandersleben, Heinrich v. 460424A
Saturn 440313 K 5
Saubert,
   Barbara, s. Andreae
   Johann d. Ä. 440324 K 2. 450726 K 0. 450817 K II 9. 451001 K 5. 460715. 460819 K 8. 461204 K 1. 461216
Saumaise, Claude de 440119. 450410 K 8
Saur, Johann 440809A K 4
Savoyen, Hz./ Hzn. v.
   Carl Emanuel I. 440000 K III 0
   Katharina, *Spanien 440000 K III 0
   Victor Amadeus I., Pz. v. 440000 K III 0
Scaliger,
   Iosephus Iustus 440119 K 9. 450308A K 4
   Iulius Caesar 441000. 441020. 450818. 450901 K 8
Schadewitz, Salomon 440809A K 4
Schaf(f) v. Weistritz,
   Hans Adam Samuel 451019
   Samuel 451019. 460721
Schall, Johann Michael 450217 K 1
Schalter, Johann Rudolf 450219
Schamberger, Martha, s. Stahl
Schärtling,
   Ilse 440724 K 3
   Peter 440724 K 3
Schede, Paul, s. Melissus, Paulus
Scheffer, Wilhelm Ernst 450817 K 4

Scheidt, Samuel 460825 K 0
Scheiner, Christoph, S. J. 450817 K III
Schell, Christian d. Ä. 451019 K 0
Schenk v. Winterstedt, Friedrich 450126 K 4
Scherffer v. Scherffenstein, Wenzel 440324 K 1. 440715A K 0. 441223. 460803 K 0
Schernwebel, Heinrich 440324 K 14. 450726 K 6
Schickard, Wilhelm 450410
Schill,
   Johann Georg 440525 K 0. 440616 K I 0
   Johann Heinrich S. 14. 440525 u. I. 440616 K I 0
   Salome, *Dürr 440525 K u. K I 3
Schilling, Friedrich v. 450410 K 22
Schindler, Valentin 440525 K II 0
Schirmer, David 440127 K
Schlegel, Wolf (v.) 441010
Schleich, Clemens 450124 K 2
Schlesien, Hz./ Hzn. in
   Anna Sophia, zu Brieg u. Liegnitz, *Mecklenburg-Güstrow S. 136
   Georg Rudolph, zu Liegnitz u. Wohlau 440119 K 12. 460721. 461117 K 1
Schlesien zu Brieg, Wohlau und Liegnitz, Hz./ Hzn. in
   Christian 441223 K 11
   Louise, *Anhalt-Dessau 441223 K 11
Schleswig-Holstein-Glücksburg, Hz./ Hzn.
   Christian 440100 K 5
   Sibylla Ursula v., *Braunschweig-Wolfenbüttel S. 12, 136. 440100. 460613. 460909 u. I
Schleswig-Holstein-Gottorf, Friedrich III., Hz. v. 440130. 440323 K 3. 440723. 450126 K 4. 450221. 450317 K 2. 450721. 460218 K 2. 460721 K 4
Schleswig-Holstein-Sonderburg, Hz./ Hzn. v.
   Anna Sabina, s. Württemberg-Weiltingen
   Eleonora Sophia, s. Anhalt-Bernburg
   Georg Friedrich 461206 K 3
   Joachim Ernst, zu Plön 450126 K 4
   Sophia, s. Pommern-Stettin

Schlick, Heinrich Gf. v. Passaun u. Weiß-
  kirchen   440000 K II 0
Schmalkaldischer Bund   450326 K 11
Schmidt, Johann(es)   S. 14. 440616 K 0.
  460909 K 6. 461204 K 1. 461216 K 6
Schmidt, Julius   460125 K I 0
Schmidt (Schmid/ Schmied/ Schmidius),
  Peter   450217
Schneuber, Johann Matthias   S. 14. 440525
  K u. I u. II. 450219. 450319 K 9.
  450504A K 4. 450818 K I. 461104 u. IV
Schönborn, Johann Philipp v., Ebf. u. Kf.
  v. Mainz   440616 K 0
Schönhof, Georg   450726 K 17
Schop, Johann   460825 K 4
Schorer, Christoph   S. 14. 440525 K II 15.
  440525 K II
Schottelius,
  Anna Maria, *Sobbe   460908 K 3
  Justus Georg   S. 10, 12, 16 f., 18, 20 ff.,
    132, 134 ff. 440100. 440129 K.
    440130. 440204 K I 0. 440209 K.
    440219 K 2. 440313. 440324 u. K I 3.
    440400 u. I. 440426 K I 2. 440429.
    440525 K II. 440616 K I 0. 440715A.
    440724. 440824. 440826. 440900.
    441000. 441011. 441020. 441200 u. I.
    441201 K 0. 441216 u. I. 441223.
    441226A. 441231 K. 441231A.
    450000. 450000A. 450100 u. I.
    450124. 450126. 450200. 450202.
    450204. 450219. 450221. 450308.
    450308A K 3. 450317A. 450319.
    450326. 450410. 450420. 450504.
    450505. 450507 K 2. 450726 K 0.
    450808 K u. K I. 450817. 450818 K 1.
    450901 K 8. 450919A. 450923B.
    450927. 450929. 451000. 451007.
    451028 K 0. 451028A. 451100 u. I.
    451101. 451217 K. 451219. 451220.
    460000 u. I u. II. 460112 K 3. 460119.
    460127 K 4. 460131. 460200 K 1.
    460200A. 460317 I. 460406 K.
    460414. 460519 K 2. 460700. 460714.
    460803. 460812 K. 460819 I u. II.
    460825. 460902. 460908. 460909 K 2.
    460912. 460915 K. 461204A K 0
  Margaretha, *Cleve   460908
Schottland, vgl. England

Maria Stuart, Kgn.   461020 K 5
Schrevinius/ Schaevinius, N. N.   450726.
  460610
Schrieck, Adriaan van (Schrieckius Rodor-
  nius, Adrianus)   440209 K 8
Schröter, N. N.   450726
Schübel, Johannes   460909 K 6
Schüele, Joachim   460909 K 6
Schürer (Wittenberger Verlegerfamilie),
  440130 K 3
  Catharina, s. Götze
  Thomas   450509 K 3
  Zacharias d. J.   450509 K 3
Schulmann, Otto   450124 K 2
Schumacher, Heinrich   450730
Schupp, Johann Balthasar   440525 K II 0.
  450726 K 0
Schurman, Anna Maria van   451101.
  451209 K 4
Schütz, Heinrich   451100 K 6
Schütz, Johann (Hans)   440809A. 450305
  I. 450317. 450317A. 450506. 450507A.
  450526
Schwarzburg-Blankenburg zu Franken-
  hausen, Gf./ Gfn. v.
  Günther XX.   450326 K 9
  Margaretha, s. Anhalt
Schwarzburg-Rudolstadt, Anna Sophia,
  *Anhalt, Gfn. v.   440525 K II 18.
  450301. 450326. 461204 K 1
Schwarzenberg, Adam, Gf. v.   440000 K 1
Schwechhausen, Heinrich v.   440826 K 0.
  450526 K 3
Schweden, Kg./ Kgn., Pz./ Pzn. v.
  Christina   440119 K 9. 440324. 440616
    K 0. 450326 K 2
  Gustav II. Adolf   440616 K II 1.
    451030 K 0. 460104 K 0. 460204 I
  Karl IX.   440616 K II 1. 440724 K 7
  Karl X. Gustav   450500 K 1
Schweden, Reichsrat (Rijksrad)   S. 7.
  440324 K 18
Schwenckfelder   440715A K 5
Schwerin, Frh. Otto v.   450326 K 4
Scrieckius Rodornius, Adrianus, s.
  Schrieck
Scudamore, John, 1st Viscount   450818
  K 3
Scudéry,

Georges 441201 K 0. 450400 K 7
Madeleine de 441201. 450400 K 7.
  450504 K 6. 450529 K 6. 450921 K 2.
  460217 K 4
Scultetus, Gottfried 440324 K I 1
Sebottendorf, Peter v. 451220
Sechst, Johann 450808 K I 0
Seckendorff, Veit Ludwig v. 440119 K 1.
  440616 K 0
Seidel, Georg 440324 K 2. 450726 K 16
Sejan, s. Geizkofler, Ferdinand
Selenus, Gustavus (Pseud.), s. Braunschweig-Wolfenbüttel, Hz. August d. J. v.
Selmnitz, Ernst Friedemann v. 450220 K 16
Sem 460915
Seneca, Lucius Annaeus d. J. 440119 K 10. 441020. 450726 K 3. 450901 K 14
Senno, Giovanni Battista 440000 K II
Senftleben, Andreas 460610 K 10
Serres, Jean de 440310 K 4. 440310A K 2
Servien comte de la Roche-des-Aubiers, Abel 450818 K 4
Servius, Petrus 450817 K II 3
Servius Honoratius, Maurus 450806 K 5
Severino, Marco Aurelio S. 139. 450817 u. II–VI. 450919A. 450923C. 451101. 451217. 460000A K 0
Sibyllen, die 460317 K 6
Sickingen, Eberhard v. 460315. 460423 u. I. 460424A I. 461031A I. 461106 K 11
Sidley, Sir William 461020 K 5
Sidney, Sir Philip 440209A K 4
Siebenbürgen, F./ Fn. v.
  Georg I. (Gyoergy I.) Rákóczy 451030 K 2
Sigershoven, Maximilian v. 450800 K 3
Simeon 451100
Sittewalt, Philander v. (Pseud.), s. Moscherosch, Johann Michael
Sobbe, Anna Maria, s. Schottelius
Socinianer 440715A K 5
Societas Christiana (s. auch Andreae, J. V.) S. 18. 450319. 461117 K 1. 461216 K 4
Sokrates 440715A
Solinus, Gaius Julius 440119 K 9. 450927 II
Sonna 441200 K I 4

Sophokles 441020
Sorel, Charles S. 15
Spanheim (Spanhemius), Friedrich (Frédéric/ Fridericus) S. 9. 460120A K 1
Spanien
  Ferdinand, Kardinalinfant v., Ebf. v. Toledo, Statthalter der Niederlande 440426 K 7
  Karl I., Kg., s. (Hl.) Römisches Reich, Ks. Karl V.
  Katharina, Infantin v., s. Savoyen
  Margaretha Theresia, Infantin v., s. Hl. Römisches Reich
  Philipp II., Kg. 440715A K 8
  Philipp IV., Kg. S. 8. 440426 K 7. 440927 K 9. 450817 K II 4
Spener, Philipp Jakob 440616 K 0
Speranza, Francesco Paolo 450817 K 7
Sprenger, Johannes Theodorus 441205 K 4
Squilla, Settimontano (Pseud.), s. Campanella, Tommaso
Staden, Adam 440204 K I 0
Staedle, Josias 460406 K 8
Stahl,
  Gottfried d. Ä. 440426 A u. K. 440824. 450400 A. 451101. 451217. 460120 K 4. 460406 A. 460620 A. 460726 A. 460916 A u. K 1. 461031 K 6
  Gottfried d. J. 440426 K 1
  Martha, *Finsinger, verw. Schamberger 440426 K 1
  Rosina, *Otten 440426 K 1
Stålhandske, Torsten 460708
Stälin (Stählin),
  Christoph 450319 K 9
  Johann Christoph 450319 K 9
  Konrad 450319 K 9
Starhemberg, Gf. v.
  Rüdiger Günther 441201 K 0. 450400 K 8. 450921 K 2
Starschedel, Ernst Dietrich v. 460708
Steding,
  Johann 461006 K 5
  Lucia Maria, s. Brincken
Steger, Christoph S. 144. 460120 K 11. 460315. 460426. 460703 K 5. 460714 K 6
Stegmann, Ambrosius 460816 K I 2

Steigleder, Johann Ulrich 460819 K II 7
Steinkallenfels, N. N. v. 460424A I
Stellbogen, Ernst 440130 K 2. 440310. 440323 K I 1
Stern,
    Hans (Johann) 441011. 450100 K 2 u. K I 7. 450219 K 6. 450319 K 9. 450929. 451000 K 1. 451001 K 5. 460700 T a. 461204 T a
    Heinrich 441011. 450100 K 2 u. K I 7. 450219 K 6. 450319 K 9. 450929. 451000 K 1. 451001 K 5. 460700 T a. 461204 T a
Stevin(us), Simon S. 24. 450000. 450410 K 3. 460000 u. II
Stieler, Caspar (v.) S. 22 f. 440130 K 1. 440204 K 2 u. K I 1. 440426 K 3. 440525 K II. 440616 K III 2. 440715 K 7. 440724 K. 440731 K. 440927 K 7. 441020 K 9. 441201 K 1. 441231 K. 450220 K II 1. 450400 K. 450417 K 1. 450420 K 4. 450611 K 2. 450730 K 6. 450817 K I 3. 450927 K II 2. 451001 K 2. 451008 K. 451028 K 2. 451028A K 4. 451217 K 5. 451219 K 8. 460125 K II. 460620 K 8. 460825 K 6 u. K I 6. 460915 K 5. 461213 K 3
Strada, Jacobo 450817 K IV 5
Straßburg, Stadt (Rat u. Bürgerschaft) 450500 K 1. 450818 K
Strauch, Georg S. 146
Streso,
    Adam 460103 K 2
    Caspar 460103
Strozzi, Giulio 450817 K 7
St. Stephansorden (Florenz) 450817 K IV 5
Stuart,
    Arabella 461020 K 5
    Henry Frederick, Prince of Wales 461020 K 5
    Maria, s. Schottland
Sturm (Sturmius),
    Gottfried 440826
    Johann(es) 440826 K 3
Sturm, Jakob 460819 K 6
Sturm, Samuel 440000 K I 1
Styrzel, Johann Georg 440616 II. 460916 K 9. 461104

Suetonius Tranquillus, Gaius 440616 K I 0. 460204 I
Sveser, Johann Friedrich 440809A K 4

Tacitus, Publius (oder Gaius) Cornelius 440119 K 10. 440209 K 10. 440616 K 0. 441020 K 1. 450726 K 3. 450818 K 10. 460204 I. 460915
Tackius, Johann 441205 K 4
Tannengesellschaft, s. Aufrichtige Gesellschaft von der Tannen
Tarnau u. Kühschmalz, v.
    Daniel 440324. 460610
    Barbara, s. Apelles von Löwenstern
Tarquinius (Superbus, röm. Kg.) 441226
Tasso, Torquato S. 8. 440119. 440310B K 2. 450817 K II 4. 450900. 451217 K 4
Tattenbach, Gf. Wilhelm Leopold v. 440927 K 8
Taubmann, Friedrich 440119 K 0
Tauler, Johannes 440826 K 0
Terkelsen, Søren 461104 K 2
Tertullianus, Quintus Septimius Florens 450927
Testi, Fulvio 460000A K 0
Teut/ Teuto, s. König Deutsch
Teutleben, Caspar v. 450611 K 1. 451015 K 2
Tham, Michael 460819 K II
Theatrum europaeum S. 134. 440324 K 18. 440504 K 1. 440927 K. 450711 K 6. 450905 K
Theodoricus, Petrus, s. Dietrich, Peter
Thessaloniki, Nilus v., Ebf. 440119 K 9
Theut, s. König Deutsch
Thiederich, Peter (Samuel), s. Dietrich, Peter
Thiras 440317 K 4
Thossanus, s. Tossanus
Thou (Thuanus), Jacques Auguste de 450818 K 9
Thubal 440313 K 4. 440317 K 4
Thuisco, s. König Deutsch
Thurn, N. N. 440000 K I 3
Timokrates 440715A
Titan(en) 450927 I
Titz,
    Christoph 440324 K 2
    Johann Peter 440324 K 14. 440826 K 0

Toledo, Ebf. v., s. Ferdinand, s. Spanien, Kardinalinfant v.
Tonneberg, s. Dannenberg, Joachim Otto v.
Tornielli, Agostino   460915
Torretti, Giambattista   450817 K 7
Torstensson, Lennart   440324 K 18. 440504 K 1. 440616 K II 2. 440927. 450419 K 3. 450509 K 2. 450800 K 5. 451030 K
Toskana, (Groß)hz. v.
　　Ferdinando I., Kd.   450817 K IV 8
　　Ferdinando II.   450817 K 20
　　Francesco   450817 K IV 8
Tossanus (Toussain), Paulus   460825
Toxites, Michael   440826 K 10
Trandorff, s. Drandorff
Trauttmannsdorff, Gf. Maximilian v.   440000 K II 0
Trčka v. der Lipa, Gf. Adam Erdmann v.   440000 II
Tremellius, Immanuel   450100 K I 7. 460825
Trémoille duc de Thouars, Claude de la   460103 K 3
Trithemius, Johannes   440525 K II 0
Troilo, Nicolaus (v.)   461117 K 1
Troschel, Peter   S. 143
Tscherning,
　　Andreas   S. 14, 17. 440324 u. I. 440724 K. 441216 K I. 450000A K 0. 450726 u. I. 450806 K 2. 460610. 460829 K 2. 461104 K 2
　　David   440324 K I
　　Katharina, *Marsilius   440324 K 9. 450726
Tugendliche Gesellschaft (TG)   450304 K 1
Tuisco, s. König Deutsch
Tuisco/ Tuisto (Erdgott)   441200 K I 4
Turenne, vicomte de, s. Bouillon, Hz. v.
Turmair, s. Aventinus
Tyrtaios   450901

Ulpianus, Domitius   450927
Ungar (Unger), Stephan   450127. 450220. 450301
Unio Christiana   S. 18, 450319. 461117 K 1. 461216 K 4

Valentini, Michael Bernhard   S. 138
Valois-Angoulême, François-Hercule de, duc d'Anjou   450818 K 8
Varro, Marcus Terentius   441223. 460131
Vega Carpio, Félix Lope de   441020
Vega, Garcilasso de la   441020
Vegetius Renatus, Flavius   461204A
Velleius Paterculus   440616 K 0 u. K I 1
Venator, Balthasar   S. 14
Vendramin, Paolo   450817 K 7
Venedig, Republik   450817 K II 9. 450818 u. I
Venus   441201 K 2. 450000A. 450808 I. 450927 II. 460812 K 1
Vera Zuñiga y Figueroa, Juan Antonio   450326
Verbezius, David   460317 K 5
Verden, Bf. v., Friedrich III., s. Dänemark
Vergilius Maro, Publius   440313 K 5. 441020. 450806 K 5. 450818
Villa Nova, Fridericus Justus Lopez de   460423 u. I. 460424A I. 461031A I
Villani, Giovanni   440209 K 10
Villiers, Berthold de   460825 K 7
Villon, François   440731 K II 1
Vischer, Christoph   450000 K 5
Vivaldi, Agostino   460804 K 1
Vives, Juan Luis   440426 K I 0. 440715A
Vogel(ius), Johan   450100. 460819 II
Voigt, Christian   451000 K 1
Volckamer, Johann Georg   450817 u. II u. V Q u. VI. 451101 K 13. 460000A K 0. 460406 K 4
Vossius,
　　Gerardus Ioannes   440119
　　Isaak   450410 K 8
　　Johannes   440119
Vulcanus   450901 K 10
Vulpius, Melchior   460819 II 7
Vulson sieur de La Collet, Marc de   440809A. 450305 K 2 u. K I 2. 450317 K 1. 450317A K 2. 450506. 450526

Wahl, Frh./ Gf. Joachim Christian v. (der)   450905 K 3
Wahremund(us) ab Ehrenberg (Pseud.), s. Weyhe, Eberhard v.
Walbot, Peter   450000 K 5

Waldeck-Wildungen, Maria Magdalena, Gfn. v., s. Lippe-Detmold
Waldis, Burkard   460317
Waldstein, Gf. Maximilian v.   440000 I
Wales, s. England
Wallenstein, Hz. v. Friedland/ Sagan/ Mecklenburg, Albrecht Wenzel Eusebius v.   S. 8. 440000 I u. II u. III. 440209A
Wallwitz, v.
  Bastian   450529 K 10. 461106 K 11
  Hans   461106 K 11
Walther (Gualtherus), Balthasar   450410. 450507 K 2
Warnstedt, Bernd Heinrich   440504 K 1. 441010
Wartenberg, Gf. Franz Wilhelm v., Kd., Bf. v. Osnabrück   451101 K 13
Wartenberg, Herr/ Frau v.
  Hans Georg   440324 K 1
  Sabina, *Pfalz-Sulzbach   440324 K 1
Wartensleben, Johann Joachim v.   450900
Weckherlin, Georg Rodolf   440525 K II 0. 440724 K 4. 460819 II
Wegleiter, Christoph   440100 K I 3
Weinheimer, Adam   460819 II
Weinrich, Thomas   450726 K 4
Weise, Christoph   440127 K 2
Weise, Melchior   440119 K 0
Weitz, Johannes   440119
Weller, Jacob   461204. 461216 K 3
Welser, Markus   440525 K II 0 (?)
Wendelin(us), Marcus Fridericus   S. 17, 18. 440209 K 1. 440809A K 6. 451217 K 10. 451220. 460217. 460609 K 3. 460705. 460816 u. I. 460902. 460916
Wense, Wilhelm v. der   450319
Werdenhagen, Johann Angelius v.   440826 K 6
Werder, Friedrich   460916 K 9
Werder, v. dem
  Diederich   S. 8 f., 10, 20. 440000 u. I u. II. 440119. 440130 K 2. 440204. 440209A K 3. 440310 K 5. 440310A u. II. 440310B. 440426 K 2. 440715 K 5. 440816 u. II. 440824. 440927 K 1. 441200 K 3. 441223 K 17. 450124 u. I. 450220 K 17. 450325. 450326. 450420. 450500. 450504 K. 450504A. 450505. 450505A. 450507 K 2. 450613. 450725 u. I. 450730. 450817. 450900. 450919. 450919A Q u. K 0. 450921. 450921A. 450923B K 4. 450923C K 2. 451101. 451209. 451217. 460000A K 0. 460120. 460125 u. I u. II. 460204 u. I. 460217. 460406. 460410 K 0. 460426. 460609 K 2. 460705 u. III u. K II 0. 460715 K II 2. 460720 K 1. 460816 K 1. 460825 u. K II 0. 460916 K. 461029. 461124. 461213 K 2
  Gebhard   450725 K 7
  Hartwig   450613 K 4
  Juliana Ursula, *Peblis, verw. Krosigk   440209 K 5
  Katharina, *Hahn   450725
  Paris   440310 K 5. 440310A. 450808 K I 0
Werner, Christian   441223 K 20. 451101 K 14
Werner, Heinrich   440724 K 12
Werner, Johann   450420 K
Werth, Reichsfrh. (Reichsgf.) Jan (Johann) v.   S. 139 f. 460715
Werthern, Dietrich v.   450220 K 16
Wesenbeck, Matthaeus v.   S. 18. 450220 K 16. 450500 K 1. 450504A A. 450529 K 10. 460125 K I 0. 460916. 461031
Westerholt, v.
  Hermann   461006 K 5
  Maria Catharina, *Brincken, verw. Münchhausen   461006 K 5
Wettgerstein, Adrian v.   440204 K I 0
Weyhe, Eberhard v.   440525 K II 0
Wideburg, Heinrich   S. 131. 440100 K 6. 461204 K 1
Widerholdt, Conrad   460804 K 1
Wiedertäufer   440715A K 5. 450000 K 5
Wietersheim, v.
  Anthon   440130 K 3. 440323 K 3. 450126 K 4. 450317 K 2. 460218 K 2. 460721 K 4
  Ernst   440130 K 3
Wilde, Joachim d. Ä.   450726 K
Willershausen, Heinrich Julius   450100 K 1
Williams, John, Bf. v. Lincoln, Ebf. v. York   461020 K 5

Wimpfeling, Jakob   440313 K 6. 440525 K II 0
Winckel, Curt Dietrich aus dem   450900
Winckler,
    Andreas   451019 K 0
    Benedikt   451019 K 0
    Georg   440130 K 3. 440310. 440723A.
        450127 K 1. 450721. 450900 K 0.
        450905. 450922. 450923. 450923A
        K 2. 450930. 451019. 451028.
        451028B. 451101. 451119 A. 460218.
        460301 K 2. 460303. 460309. 460324.
        460403. 460423. 460519. 460703 A.
        461031 K 6. 461031A K 7
Winterkönig, s. Böhmen, Kg. Friedrich I. v.
Witte v. Lilienau, Nikolaus   440724.
    450400 K 9
Wittigau, Johann   440119 K 0
Witzleben, Georg Friedrich v.   450220
    K 16
Wohlfart, Caspar   440324 K 14
Wolf, Hieronymus   460819
Wolf, Johann   460804
Worm (Wormius), Ole (Olaus)   440317
    K 3. 460915
Wrangel,
    Carl Gustav, Friherre (Greve af Salmis)
        460321 K 2. 460715 K 7
    Helm(old Wilhelm)   440927 K 8
Wulff, Caspar   441000
Württemberg, Hzt.
    Landstände   450219
Württemberg-Mömpelgard, Hz./ Hzn. v.
    Georg II.   450806 K 9
    Leopold Friedrich   450818 K 4. 460317
        K 6
    Sibylla, *Württemberg-Stuttgart
        460317
Württemberg-Neuenstadt, Hz./ Hzn. v.
    Clara Augusta, *Braunschweig-Wolfenbüttel   S. 136. 440100. 460613
    Friedrich   440100 K 5
Württemberg-Stuttgart, Hz./ Hzn. v.
    Anna Johanna   460317 K 6
    Antonia   460317 K 6
    Eberhard III.   450722. 450818 K 4.
        460909 K 5
    Eleonora v., s. Hessen-Darmstadt
    Johann Friedrich   460120A K 1

Sibylla, s. Württemberg-Mömpelgard
Württemberg-Weiltingen, Hzn. v.
    Anna Sabina, *Schleswig-Holstein-Sonderburg   450818 K 1
Wyngaerden, Adrian   460406 K 8

York, Ebf. v.
    John, s. Williams

Zacchia, Paulus   450817 K II 3
Zang(e),
    Hans Georg   440324
    Johann   440324 K 3
    Ursula, *Germersheim   440324 K 3
Zeiller, Martin. Vgl. Merian, Matthäus
    d. Ä.
    440525 II. 450817. 450905 K 4
Zeller, Christoph   450219. 460127 K 5.
    460909 K 6
Zenon aus Kition   461204A
Zerbst, Albrecht v.   440816 u. I u. II.
    450800 K 3. 460424 K 14
Zesen, Philipp (v.)   S. 14, 16 f., 18, 21 f., 24.
    440129 K 5. 440209 K 2. 440324 u. K I
    3. 440400 K I 0. 440525 K II. 440616
    K 5. 440724. 440826 K. 441201. 441216
    K I. 441223. 441231 K 9. 450000A.
    450100 K 10. 450308A. 450400. 450410.
    450420 K. 450504. 450504A K 4.
    450505. 450506A. 450507 K 2. 450529.
    450806 K 9. 450808 u. I. 450818 K 1.
    450921 K 2. 450927 K II 11. 451007 K 2.
    451101 K 7. 451209 K 4. 451219 K 4.
    460131. 460200 K 1. 460217. 460406
    K 4. 460610. 460812. 460825. 460902
    K 3. 460915 K 9
Zeus, s. Iuppiter
Zierenberg,
    Daniel Ernst   450726 K 6
    Judith, *Hendreich   450726 K 6
Zilliger, Christoph Friedrich   441000 K 5
Zimmermann (Czimmermann), Petrus
    440324. 450726
Zincgref, Julius Wilhelm   440525 K II 0.
    450818 K
Zoroaster   450901 K 6
Zouch, Richard   440426 K I 0. 450817
    K II 6
Zunner, Johann David   450725 K 5.
    451101